joy of cooking

Irma S. Rombauer
Marion Rombauer Becker
Ethan Becker
John Becker
Megan Scott

Illustrations by John Norton
Papercuts by Anna Brones

SCRIBNER
New York London Toronto Sydney New Delhi

Scribner
An Imprint of Simon & Schuster, Inc.
1230 Avenue of the Americas
New York, NY 10020

This Scribner hardcover edition November 2019

Manufactured in China

1 3 5 7 9 10 8 6 4 2

Library of Congress Control Number: 2019943735

ISBN 978-1-5011-6971-7
ISBN 978-1-4391-3082-7 (ebook)

In memory of Irma and Marion,

and dedicated to our readers—

past, present, and future.

CONTENTS

ACKNOWLEDGMENTS

We often hear from readers that they are the second, third, or fourth generation of their family to cook from the *Joy of Cooking*. They might have multiple editions, older and newer, or maybe just a single passed-down copy. Regardless, we are always moved and a bit in awe of the community of home cooks that Irma and Marion inadvertently created. We owe everything to our readers, and we would like to thank you all and your parents, grandparents, and great-grandparents for the trust you have placed in our family's book over the years. We are truly honored to be given a place in your kitchens.

We also owe Irma, Marion, and Ethan a debt of gratitude for the years they spent revising and stewarding *Joy*. Irma was the visionary, and, frankly, there is no logical reason her "little book" should have made the impact that it did. To say that she saw possibility where others did not is putting it mildly, and readers have cherished her wit and off-the-cuff wisdom for generations. Marion was the steadfast researcher. She applied herself to *Joy*'s improvement in a measured, comprehensive way, and her additions to the book are some of our favorite things about it. Ethan has seen the book through some particularly rough times but has always tried to honor and protect his mother's and grandmother's legacy in his work for *Joy*. The last two editions would not have been possible without his unwavering determination and integrity.

Listening to family anecdotes and remembrances, perusing test notes (recorded on index cards!), holding treasured kitchen tools, smirking at saucy headnotes as we scoured previous editions . . . all of these gave us invaluable insight into who Marion and Irma were, but much of what we know of them we owe to *Joy*'s biographer, Anne Mendelson. Anne's tireless, painstaking research is priceless to us, and the Rombauer-Becker family is indebted to her for the care and detail she put into *Stand Facing the Stove*.

We want to thank the many people at Scribner who have placed their trust in us and have worked so hard to bring this book to fruition. First and foremost, Roz Lippel, who has spent many, many long hours shepherding us through the revision process and making sure we had the support we needed to make this edition possible. We have had several editors whose hands are on this project. Among them, Whitney Frick, Michelle Howry, and Cara Bedick. Marah Stets, who has worked on more than one edition of the book, provided crucial feedback at a pivotal moment in this revision, and we are immeasurably grateful to her for helping us make this book better. Our copy editor, Kate Slate, did a phenomenal job of keeping us honest and consistent—and her witty asides kept us chuckling when we needed it most. We owe a huge debt of gratitude to Carolyn Reidy, Susan Moldow, Nan Graham, Brian Belfiglio, Rebecca Strobel, Julia Lee McGill, Abigail Novak, and the incredible production team at Scribner, including Mia Crowley-Hald (congratulations on your well-deserved retirement!), Kathleen Rizzo, Erich Hobbing, and Hilda Koparanian. This book would have been impossible without their efforts and support. Carrie Bachman, our publicist, jumped right into the fray to champion *Joy*'s release, and we could not be more grateful.

Our support network in Portland has been phenomenal. So much love and gratitude to Kim Carlson, James Berry, Ivy Manning, Katherine Cole, Diane Morgan, Lane Selman, Jen Bryman, and Mollie Harris. Our good friends who have served as taste testers and have provided the moral support we so needed during the revision process include Shannon Larson, Jon Washington, JR Heard, Carissa Mylin, Rachel Ranch, David Browning, Kyle and Bryce Donovan, Sara Grimes, Dan Kumprey, Helena and Dave Root, Marisa Mitchell, Brian Hogan, Jared Goodman and family, Elizabeth Savage, Michael Schopf, Sarah and Dirk Marshall, Anika Toro, Doug Campbell, Avi and Alissa Askey, Adam Spannaus, Julia Smith, Kate McCracken, and Claire Oliphant.

We had so many incredible recipe testers working on this project. Nicole Kondra, also a dear friend, was there from the beginning and tested hundreds of recipes for this edition. The meticulous test notes and suggestions of Heather Arndt Anderson and Nora Mace have improved this book tremendously, and we could not have done it without them. Yeojin Park and Kusuma Rao, friends and incredible cooks, added so much to the book with their recipes, advice, and expertise. There was a bevy of volunteer recipe testers who worked on this project as well, and we are overwhelmed with gratitude for the time and effort they put into their work. Thank you all.

Others who contributed to this book and undoubtedly made it better include Katherine Cole, Maria Speck, and especially Hank Shaw, whose expertise on game, wildfowl, and fish was invaluable. Maggie Green is a force of nature who has worked for *Joy* in some capacity for nearly two decades, through thick and thin. She is one of the most pragmatic, down-to-earth people we know and is a true advocate for American home cooks. Anna Brones, the creative force behind the chapter-heading papercuts in this edition, brought our ideas to life. Her work is so full of care, and we are honored to have been able to work with her on this project. John Norton, our illustrator, is one of the most meticulous and patient people we have ever worked with. Thank you for translating our scribblings and half-articulated notes into illustrations that will be useful to our readers.

We approached revising this book in the same manner we imagine artisans would as they continue building a large cathedral: Since the *Joy* project spans multiple editions (and generations), we expand and improvise upon the work of those who have gone before us—all the while trying to keep the original design, or intention, faithfully intact. While this certainly includes Irma, Marion, and Ethan, we would also like to acknowledge and thank the large, talented group of contributors, testers, and editors who made the 1997 and 2006 editions such a huge success. I hope the direction we have taken *Joy* is worthy of your collective efforts.

We owe unending gratitude to Kat Kinsman, who listened (like really *listened*) to our story and used her platform to share it. Kat, you are a force for good in this world. Samin Nosrat let us into her life in the most generous way, sharing her experiences and ideas with us and showering us with kindness. Samin, thank you for being utterly and completely yourself.

Joan, I could not have done this without you: Your enthusiasm and curiosity for new ingredients, foods, and techniques have been an inspiration. If, in these pages, we motivate readers to be half as adventurous as you encouraged me to be, then we have done our job. Ethan, thank you for being so supportive as we have worked on this project. Though I may shrug when you tell us how proud you are, please know that it means everything to me, and that I am immeasurably grateful to have such a great dad.

Teresa, thank you for the thousands of meals you have cooked for me. You always made it look so effortless, but now I have a general idea of how much work cooking is and am overwhelmed by the love you put into those meals. Jeff, thank you for absolutely always being there for me, believing in me, and making sure I knew you were proud of me. There isn't enough space here to give you both the thanks and praise you deserve. Kelly and Erin, growing up with two younger sisters didn't always seem appealing, but the two of you have enriched my life immeasurably. To see you both grow into smart, strong, beautiful women has been one of the highlights of my life. And Erin, thank you especially for your taste-testing skills. Grandma and PawPaw Bryan and Nana and PawPaw Tom, your houses were my second and third homes growing up. You filled me with warm memories: The meals we shared, the hours I spent wandering around the fields behind your houses, the summer corn shuckings and bean shellings, the way the world was muffled and dark beneath the quilting frame as Grandma and her cousins hand stitched the afternoon away. You did everything to give me a beautiful childhood, and knowing I had your love and support made the rough patches easier.

INTRODUCTION TO THE 2019 EDITION

This edition—our family's ninth since Irma first published *Joy of Cooking* in 1931—is the result of more than nine years of recipe testing and nearly five years of outlining, researching, and writing by my wife, Megan, and me. We had help from several part-time recipe testers—all of us working in our own kitchens. As I sit at my kitchen table to write this introduction, I cannot believe this project is nearly complete. It is difficult to convey how much of our waking (and dreaming) lives we have dedicated to making sure this edition of *Joy* is the best we are capable of producing. Megan and I are both perfectionists—in our own idiosyncratic, obsessive, slightly unhealthy ways—and I hope our indulgence in this shared vice has paid off for you, our readers.

There are many different ways to revise a cookbook. Faced with the task of updating *Joy* in the mid-1990s, my father, Ethan, and his editor Maria Guarnaschelli took a modern approach: Food writers were hired on contract to lend a hand in their areas of expertise, a professional test kitchen was employed—"the works." Many trusted publications use this method, and we certainly see the allure of applying this winning formula to *Joy*. However, soon after the 1997 edition was released, my family began to have regrets. Longtime readers complained about absentee recipes—even whole chapters—sacrificed to make room for what was, essentially, a rewrite rather than a revision. Nine years later, Ethan, his then-wife Susan, a new editor, and a smaller set of contributors published the 2006 edition. They were intent on eliminating the perceived mistakes of the 1997 edition and turning back the clock by using my grandmother Marion's 1975 edition as its starting point. All the preservation chapters were restored, as were cocktails, ice creams, and retro touches from older editions like Shrimp Wiggle (sadly not reprised in these pages, R.I.P.).

When Megan and I started working for *Joy* in 2010, we began a long process of acquainting ourselves with the book. This involved recipe testing, recipe "genealogies" (tracing each recipe back to its original edition), organizing and studying family documents, answering fan emails, and generally immersing ourselves in the book's rich history. We came to know the book backward and forward and became intimately familiar with its strengths, as well as its shortcomings: recipes that weren't clear, techniques we felt were missing, information on ingredients that had not been updated since the 1970s, and so on. While none of these was utterly damning, we began to feel that we could make the book better suited to the way people cook and think about food today. We had a detailed knowledge of the book that no one else had. We had been steeping ourselves not only in current food media, but also in what our readers were saying, both good and bad. Above all, we both had a deep love of cooking that propelled us to keep learning and trying new dishes and techniques.

In 2013 we read through *Joy* together, line by line, and crafted a detailed outline: what we thought needed to be fact-checked, added, cut, expanded, rewritten, or just revised. After eight long months, we no longer *thought* we might be able to improve the book; we *knew* we could. We realized why the previous two editions left us feeling that something was wanting. In 1997, the emphasis was on modernizing and updating at all costs; in 2006, it was on looking back. We felt that, while both editions were sincere, they were missing the vital spark of the older books.

From my great-grandmother Irma's first, self-published edition through Marion's last, *Joy* was updated with a light hand: recipes added or improved, others cut—all with an eye toward making the book better, more complete, more comprehensive, more *useful*. This may sound like a simplistic approach—at least until you begin trying to decide *what* will be more useful, or identifying which areas and subjects *Joy* should cover more thoroughly. All of this was determined by the two of us "to taste"—albeit after long deliberations, with an eye to past editions, and a desire to acknowledge and celebrate ingredients new to *Joy* and dishes we are especially fond of. Though I am confident that we have not pleased everyone, I hope we have managed to meld past with present in a manner that readers will find elegant, informative, and perhaps even inspiring. This balance was difficult to find. In the end, we were guided by an overwhelming sense of obligation, love, and respect for Irma, Marion, and Ethan. Perhaps more important, throughout this revision, we were constantly trying to anticipate the needs of home cooks—especially those who find themselves in the kitchen for the first time. We have, as Marion counseled in her dedication to the 1963 edition, kept *Joy* "a family affair, as well as an enterprise in which the authors owe no obligation to anyone but themselves—and you."

I suppose it would behoove me to say that I always knew I would work on the book, that I learned to flip an omelet at my mother's knee, that I was a natural *saucier* by the age of five, or that I spent years coming up in a restaurant or culinary school to prepare for this project. In fact, reading Marion's dedication for the first time was what gave me the initial push that eventually resulted in this edition.

I grew up with *Joy* the way many readers have. It was always on my mother Joan's shelf in the dining room of our Portland condo, a talismanic presence stained with the drippy evidence of a life of cooking. My mother and father separated when I was quite young, so I have no memory of their falling-out, nor did I witness any enmity or resentment. To me, divorce was part of the natural lifecycle of a relationship; it simply meant you became friends, lived far away, and—in special, serendipitous moments—let your child get away with a bit more than their friends seemed to. I spent the school year with Mom in the drizzly Northwest, and summers with Dad in the humid Ohio River Valley, at the house Marion and her husband, John, built, which they called Cockaigne.

I had two homes, two sets of rules, and two very different notions of where I came from. My mother worked as an oncology nurse. She loves to cook and has an adventurous palate, but was always pressed for time, and certainly not averse to cutting culinary corners after picking me up from after-school care on the heels of a ten-hour shift. In contrast, my father, Ethan, is a gifted, professionally trained cook who had flexible hours and a small team of people working on *Joy*, as well as someone in the garage making knives. (A side project that has grown into a successful business.)

As supportive parents, Ethan and Joan always encouraged me to find what I liked doing and make a living out of it. No one ever expected me to take on the cookbook as my own project or even contribute to it in any way at all. And so I didn't: My passions led me in a wayward manner to aerospace engineering and, after a regrettable semester of calculus, to literature and philosophy. The 1997 edition was published the year I graduated from high school, and I took it to college with me. Consequently, I came to know the book in the same way many readers do: on my own for the first time, not really knowing what I was doing, frantically paging through recipes as I cooked.

While working at restaurants and going to culinary school undoubtably educate and enrich, my loping stumble through the culinary arts for most of my early adult life has been useful. My wanderings led me to work as an assistant researcher and editor on over a dozen books, an experience that I hope has contributed to the quality and depth of information contained in this edition. As nonprofessionals, Megan and I take little for granted, do our own dishes, pose questions that many amateurs will likely have, and perhaps have more insight into what recipe directives will seem onerous or confusing to the beginner. This is not to say that expertise is unimportant to us or that it has no place in *Joy*. Rather, as we researched and tested in preparation for this edition, the perspective of inexperienced home cooks was always foremost in our minds.

Thus, *Joy* is not a translation of professional practices for laypeople. We do not promise (and therefore do not expect) mastery, nor do we wish for our readers to aspire to perform every kitchen task "like a pro." Both ends are worth pursuing but seem less urgent to us than enabling readers to approach the act of cooking—of feeding oneself and others—with confidence and ease. We wish to be there for all cooks—absolute beginners, harried parents, dabblers/aspirers, and professionals alike. Regardless of your skill level or how much time and effort you are comfortable giving, learning to cook begins in the home kitchen, and *Joy* is written by and for home cooks. This may seem like a fine point, but we think it is central to what has made *Joy* different from other cookbooks, and why it has found its way into so many kitchens and hearts.

GETTING STARTED

Joy is different than most modern cookbooks. We do not mean to differentiate ourselves from our "competition," but rather to suggest to first-time readers that it is best to take a different approach when perusing our book. As its heft might betray, *Joy* is not just a cookbook to choose recipes from: Since the 1960s, we have endeavored to be an essential companion for cooks, many of whom are not only in need of trusted recipes, but also a wide-ranging, dependable source of culinary knowledge. Recipes and inspiration are indeed central to what we offer, but *Joy* is also intended as a supplement for when other, less comprehensive books fall silent. Cooking from recipes invariably leads to questions; we have attempted to anticipate these and offer reliable answers. (When we must defer on a subject for lack of space, we have provided the curious with directions to other sources in our bibliography, 1077.) We can promise you that you will have a much more rewarding relationship with *Joy* if you treat it as both a book of recipes and as a resource to consult when you need a firmer grasp of the ingredients and techniques at play.

For those who are used to the convenience of keyword searches, we encourage you to utilize our Index, 1081, which we have taken great pains to make as comprehensive as possible.

WATCH FOR THESE SYMBOLS

➤ Pointer to success
▲ High-Altitude
( ) Optional

INGREDIENTS

We love talking about ingredients so much that we have an entire (very lengthy) chapter devoted to them. See Know Your Ingredients, 950, for an alphabetical compendium of ingredients both common and less so. Throughout the book we make an effort to cross-reference Know Your Ingredients when we call for something that we think readers may wish to read more about. This is probably our favorite chapter in the book, so we would love for you to look into it every now and then. We promise it's interesting.

One of the most important ingredients in all cooking is **salt.** Our recipes are written to use standard table salt unless otherwise specified. Fine sea salt or Morton's kosher salt can be used without having to make any adjustments. If you wish to substitute Diamond kosher salt, use twice as much by volume as the recipe indicates.

When our recipes call for chopped or minced **herbs,** the assumption is that they are fresh. When dried herbs are called for, we specify dried.

We understand the convenience of buying preground **spices,** but we strongly recommend going to a little extra trouble by buying them whole and grinding them yourself. See Spices, 1020, for more information.

When we call for nuts to be toasted or bread crumbs to be ground, we often cross-reference Know Your Ingredients, as that is where the instructions for doing both those things lives. If, however, you are familiar with those processes, there is really no need to look them up. In many cases, the cross-references are there for the absolute beginner or the curious. They are not always integral to the recipe.

MEASURING

While we strongly believe that cooking is based just as much on experience and intuition as it is scientific accuracy, knowing how to properly measure ingredients is important. Please read Measuring Ingredients, 1042, for a thorough discussion of the topic. We have added gram weights to most of *Joy*'s baking chapters, not only because it is a more accurate way to measure than by volume, but also because it saves the baker from having to do so many dishes. We encourage you to embrace the scale!

Also see Measuring Temperatures, 1043, for information on using thermometers.

APPLIANCES

Many of us cook in kitchens with limited space and appliances not of our choosing. Generally, ovens and cooktops are a "given" to factor in when cooking. Get to know the particular quirks of your appliances and trust your gut. If a recipe says medium heat, but that seems to result in things cooking consistently faster than recipes indicate they should or things tend to overbrown or burn, then you should probably turn the heat down a bit.

See About Indoor Cooking Equipment, 1070, for information on different types of appliances and how to adjust your cooking according to which type you have.

KNIVES AND KNIFE CUTS

There are very few tools actually necessary for cooking, but a knife is one of them. Find a knife you like, and keep it sharp. For information on knife types, knife care, and sharpening, see About Knives, 1074.

For a description of basic knife cuts, see Knife Cuts, 1044, and Cutting Vegetables, 200.

SETTING UP YOUR KITCHEN

Beyond a knife and a heat source, probably the most important tool for cooking is space. Always keep this in mind as you ponder purchasing the latest gadget. If your countertops are so cluttered that there is no room for a cutting board, your cabinets so overstuffed that coherent organization is an impossibility, or your drawers so full that they constantly get stuck, the best thing you can do is clean out your kitchen to make room for actual cooking.

For starters, avoid single-use gadgets. We are not absolutists: If using a garlic press makes your life better, by all means have one around; if you make a mean cherry pie with fresh cherries, a cherry pitter is probably a worthwhile tool for you to have. The key is to keep it minimal and be honest with yourself about what you will use and what will just end up creating clutter.

Clean out your utensil drawer and put the things you use most often in crocks for easier access. If you can, hang pots and pans from a pan rack or peg board rather than keeping them in cabinets. If you lack counter space, do you have room to bring a work table into your kitchen? Do you have bare walls for shelving? Think about the best way to maximize your space. Making your kitchen more efficient does not have to mean an expensive remodel.

Our current kitchen—the one in which we tested and developed most of the recipes in this book—is nothing special. We have a fair-to-middling amount of cabinet and counter space, but we brought in a butcher's block (purchased at an estate sale by Megan's grandfather) and a restaurant kitchen-style work table with a lower shelf that holds some small appliances and mixing bowls. We also installed shelving along one wall and keep larger appliances that we use less often on shelves in the garage. It's not a perfect system, nor is it going to win any design awards, but it works.

SEASONING "TO TASTE"

No two words in cooking literature provoke as much head scratching. This is not because there is some secret meaning, but because learning how to taste is a skill that comes with time and practice. It is nearly impossible to teach someone how to taste. That said, we recommend taking these directives more or less literally: Taste everything you can, and often. In this book "to taste" is not some tricky recipe writer speak for "we were too lazy to give you an exact amount." Taste is subjective, and the idea that a recipe could relay the perfect level of seasoning for every person is preposterous.

Typically, the ingredients added "to taste" are salt and acid. However, in some cases it may be something spicy or sweet. Don't think too hard about it. For example, if you're making Whipped Cream, 791, which calls for a range of sugar, think about what you will be serving it with. If the whipped cream is being used to top an already sweet dessert like Pavlova, 826, the smaller amount of sugar will suffice. If it's going to be dolloped on some roasted rhubarb, however, the greater amount of sugar will likely be a better choice.

If, at the end of preparing a recipe, you find it lacking in flavor, think about what you can add to really make the flavors pop. Sometimes that is salt, and sometimes it is acidity (see Acidic Ingredients, 950, for a discussion of different types of acids), but it might also be umami (see Flavor Enhancers, 984, for a litany of umami-rich ingredients). Adding sugar rarely helps the flavor of a dish, but keep an open mind.

HOW TO READ OUR RECIPES

We use the "action method" of recipe writing, which was invented by John's great-grandmother Irma in the mid-1930s. The action method intertwines ingredients and instructions, giving recipes a natural flow. We continue to prefer it to other recipe writing styles because it does not require the reader to jump between an ingredient list and the recipe instructions. In our experience, this can cause the reader to lose their place in the recipe, leading to frustration and error if ingredients or steps are skipped over. (This is particularly true of recipes spanning multiple pages.) Moreover, we never have to specify "divided" for a particular ingredient that is used twice. There are several other advantages to the action method; find them discussed in the sample "recipe" that follows.

Because *Joy* is a very old book, there are naming conventions that give clues to the origins of some of the recipes. Marion Becker and her husband, John, called their Cincinnati home **Cockaigne,** a mythical land of plenty where the ills of human existence do not hold sway and food is so plentiful that it rains from the sky. Marion applied the name to recipes she had a special fondness for. Recipes with **Becker** in the title are from Ethan Becker.

RECIPE TITLE (FOREIGN NAME FIRST, TRANSLATION IN PARENTHESES)

The yield of the recipe, either in servings, volume, pieces, or weight

Our headnotes generally contain cross-references to sections About Important Subjects Pertinent to the Recipe, 000, but they also may suggest a **delicious additional or alternate ingredient,** or perhaps an **alternate name** for the dish.

Directions are given in a story-like format in that they proceed from beginning to end with ingredient quantities bolded, indented, and called for as they are used or added:

The most numerous ingredients are called for first
Followed by ingredients in smaller quantities
Unusual ingredients or ones that require a special process get explanatory cross-references, 000
(Optional ingredients are in parentheses)

This makes jotting down a grocery list slightly more complicated, but your eyes will not have to flit back and forth between directives and an ingredient list when it matters most: in the kitchen. Since this is a large book that has many basic recipes to draw from, we frequently call for other recipes to be made:

So be sure to read the recipe through and make any recipes we call for first, 000

We regret this state of affairs, but other cookbooks cover less ground and this allows us to use:

A basic recipe, 000

In many different dishes without wasting space (you may also notice that *Joy* is not laid out in a manner that prioritizes white space, for the same reason). Often times, we will give a brief list of possible accompaniments at the end, which you might also want to check out before commencing. These could be:

Simple garnishes
Starches or side dishes
Glazes, pan sauces, table sauces, or condiments

VARIATION RECIPES

These are based on **Recipe Title, xiv,** but written in a paragraph format where modifications are described and any **additional ingredients** bolded. They may not occur directly below their "parent" recipe, but they generally do.

FOLLOWING AND RIFFING ON RECIPES

Recipes are teaching tools, not sacred texts. We have lots of recipes in this book, not because we think that you should only cook by following recipes, but because recipes are the easiest way to transmit information on how to cook something and get predictable, desired results. Over time, you will become comfortable enough to alter recipes or even to go without them for the majority of your time in the kitchen.

While we cannot promise that you will always be successful when you modify a recipe, we can promise that you will probably learn more from experimentation than from always going by the book. That said, we recommend that beginners wait until they feel comfortable with cooking before they start to improvise. (Especially if you have never cooked the recipe as written!)

Even experienced cooks will tell you that you should never modify baking recipes. While it is certainly true that doing so is more complicated than tweaking, say, a beef stew recipe, it is certainly not impossible. The one caveat we will offer is that it takes a great deal more experience with baking (and a solid understanding of the principles and techniques behind it) to alter baking recipes successfully.

In other kinds of recipes, making substitutions based on what you have on hand can lead to wonderful new dishes. Let circumstance be your inspiration, not just a hindrance to overcome with another trip to the grocery store.

One of the hallmarks of a good cook is knowing how to read the room. Always keep your audience in mind. If you're feeding small children who are sensitive to spicy foods, it may not be the best time to try a dish known for piquancy (unless you are trying to train them to tolerate heat, in which case, Godspeed). Likewise, if a recipe gives a range for a spicy or challenging ingredient, go with the smaller amount first. You can always add more, but it is much harder to salvage a dish to which you have added too much of something.

NUTRITION AND FOOD SAFETY

We consider this book to be a refuge from dietary dogma, where cooks can learn about cooking or find their favorite recipes in an atmosphere free of judgment or pseudomoralistic talk of "wellness" or "clean eating." That said, determining what is healthy to eat can be confusing: Scan any number of websites or articles and you will encounter contradictory advice and headline-grabbing news items (often flimsily based on limited scientific studies) decrying fat, sugar, gluten, or specific ingredients like eggs. Some of these conclusions hold for decades; others are challenged and overturned rather quickly. One thing is clear: Nutrition is an evolving science, so as new discoveries are made, the prevailing wisdom of the day shifts. Thus, we feel compelled to touch upon the subject and provide some reasonable recommendations.

Luckily, good food safety practices have been relatively uncontroversial since the time of Louis Pasteur. For basic information on how to discourage the spread of pathogens and keep a clean kitchen, see About Food Safety, xx.

MAKING GOOD CHOICES

Eating a healthy diet means choosing delicious foods that satisfy the appetite while meeting the body's needs. Pursuing this goal does not necessarily require that we give up all of our favorite foods: No single food or meal will throw a healthy diet off track, and no single food is unhealthy in and of itself. Rather, we must balance out our choices. Restricting or eliminating foods from the table can be agonizing, which in turn makes it harder to maintain a healthy lifestyle. Nourishment is obviously important, but finding enjoyment in many foods—even those that should be eaten less often—is what often inspires us to cook. For us, this is the most important choice to make, since it enables us to take control of what we eat and serve to others.

While we understand that there are many barriers in place to cooking—time, money, proximity to a grocery store, desire, aptitude in the kitchen—we do ultimately think that cooking at home has the potential to positively impact your health. Doing so gives you the freedom to choose the quality and types of ingredients you use, and most of us tend to make healthier choices when given the opportunity.

Regardless of the current state of nutrition science, a single, general guideline has remained fairly constant over the last several decades: ➤ Choose whole foods—that is, unprocessed vegetables, fruits, grains, and proteins—over highly processed ones. Here are some other factors to consider as you balance out your plate.

CARBOHYDRATES

Carbohydrates, or carbs, are found in fruits, vegetables, legumes, and grains. Once eaten, carbohydrates are broken down into glucose (blood sugar), which is the primary source of energy for the cells throughout your body. As you'll see in the following sections, some carbohydrates are better for your body than others, so choose wholesome ones most of the time.

PROTEIN

Every cell in your body relies on protein for structural support, and it's a component of not just muscles, but also skin, hair, nails, and bones. While many diets emphasize protein, the truth is, few people in America eat insufficient amounts. Still, for those who want to eat more, most healthy people can certainly up their intake without any harm. You can get protein from meat and poultry, fish and shellfish, dairy, eggs, and plant-based sources, such as soy, beans, nuts and seeds, and to a lesser degree, whole grains.

Of course, meat is still the most convenient way to get protein—just prioritize leaner cuts for most meals. Lean pork and beef, fish, shellfish, and poultry are all good options. And remember, this isn't an all-or-nothing situation. Keeping the idea of balance in mind means that you can go for a juicy steak or fall-off-the-bone ribs when the mood strikes, but most of your meals should encompass leaner choices.

Cheeses, milk, yogurt, and other forms of dairy provide protein as well as many essential nutrients, and they can certainly be part of a healthy diet, as can nutritious plant-based alternatives. One side note here: Many dairy alternatives don't match the protein content of dairy itself, so if you're choosing a plant-based option and protein is a priority, look for those that contain a higher amount.

FATS

You could fill a whole chapter with the debate about fat. Here's what you need to know: Fats play in important role in our health, they taste good, and they keep you satisfied. Instead of getting caught up in the amount of fat in foods, it's better to consider the quality of the fats you eat. The healthiest fats are unsaturated fats, which include monounsaturated fats and polyunsaturated fats. Though it's been hotly contested, the science supports the health-protective benefits of these types of fats over saturated ones.

Monounsaturated fats are found in foods like olives, peanuts, and avocados as well as their oils. It's also found in canola oil. You can incorporate these healthy fats into your menu in a number of ways. Nuts are a perfect choice for snacking and they add a crunchy dimension to salads and stir-fries. Avocados—rich and creamy on their own—are a good match for both sweet and savory dishes. Try them in Avocado and Citrus Salad, 125.

Polyunsaturated fats are found in corn and soybean oil, seeds, nuts, whole grains, and fatty fish, such as salmon and tuna. The omega-3 fats that are abundant in fatty fish, walnuts, flax, and chia seeds are a particularly important type of polyunsaturated fat. They help with everything from normal brain and nerve development to healthy functioning of the immune system, heart, and blood vessels. Plus, they reduce inflammation levels that are thought to be at the root of many chronic diseases. To meet your body's needs for these fats, it's a good idea to choose seafood as a main dish twice a week. If you're reluctant to cook fish, we recommend starting off with Chinese Steamed Fish, 82, Fish Curry, 383, and Veracruz-Style Snapper, 380.

One quick note about seafood: Though two servings per week are recommended, it's a good idea to strictly limit high-mercury choices. See Fish Safety and Nutrition, 372, for more information.

Saturated fats are found in red meat, dairy products, and a few vegetable oils, like palm and coconut oils. This is where things get a little tricky and where much of the confusion surrounding fat lies. The basic gist is that while unsaturated fats are considered healthy and trans fats (covered below) are considered unhealthy, saturated fats are somewhere in between. So even though saturated fats might not be as harmful as once thought, they aren't beneficial, either. For that reason, most health professionals recommend getting most of your fats from sources with known benefits (such as monounsaturated fats) over saturated ones.

Trans fats found in processed food are doubly bad for the heart, and have therefore been largely phased out of our food supply. Though trans fats have been removed from more than 98 percent of packaged foods, you may still find these fats in foods like pie crusts and other pastries.

SODIUM

It's hard to argue over the merits of choosing more whole foods over highly processed ones. But in case you need more convincing, consider that about 70 percent of the sodium in our diet comes from processed foods and restaurant meals. Sodium is an essential mineral, but most of us exceed the upper limit of 2,300 mg per day, which can lead to high blood pressure and other health concerns. The easiest way to cut back on sodium is to cut back on heavily processed foods.

Cooking more helps you do that. Instead of relying solely on the salt shaker for flavor, turn to spices. (For more on spices, see the sections on individual spices in Know Your Ingredients, 950.)

VITAMINS, MINERALS, AND OTHER NUTRIENTS

With one or two exceptions, our bodies cannot make vitamins and minerals, so they must come from food or, if necessary, from supplements. Of course, supplements are not a fix for an unhealthy diet, nor are they a one-size-fits-all solution—a lot depends on your diet, medications you take, your medical concerns, and other factors. In short, check with your healthcare provider to determine which supplements will benefit you the most.

That said, the one supplement most people need is vitamin D. Though the sun provides plenty for those of us who go outdoors often (and without sunscreen), few of us get enough vitamin D during the short, cold days of winter. If you do decide to take supplements, always look for brands that have been certified by the US Pharmacopeia (USP), a third-party safety verification.

STRATEGIES FOR EATING HEALTHIER

While there are lots of approaches to a healthy diet, there are a few common threads: Eat plenty of vegetables; eat more whole foods and fewer processed foods; and reduce the amount of sugar and refined grains you consume. How you balance your choices is up to you.

EAT MORE PRODUCE

Fruits and vegetables provide a wide range of vitamins, minerals, and fiber. Eating a variety of produce is the best way to protect yourself from a number of health concerns. A simple rule of thumb is to make half your plate fruits or vegetables. It's much easier than it seems. Start your day with a Fruit Smoothie, 12; add fruit to Baked Oatmeal, 327, or Muesli, 327; or enjoy an omelet, 158–60, or Frittata, 159, filled with sautéed vegetables. Have a filling, main-dish salad for lunch like Quinoa Salad with Broccoli and Feta, 132, or a hearty bean soup like Garbure, 87, or Spicy Chickpea Soup, 87. (Beans are the best of two worlds, a prime source of vitamins and minerals as well as protein, see below.) For dinner, have one or two vegetable-based side dishes, such as Sichuan-Style Dry-Fried Beans, 211, Sautéed Mushrooms, 217, and Roasted Broccoli, 221, or choose a vegetable-based main dish like Chana Masala, 217, Vegetable Tagine, 205, or Ratatouille Provençale, 204. See the Vegetables chapter, 199, for more ideas.

There are obvious environmental and animal welfare advantages to eating **plant protein,** as well as nutritional benefits. Plant-based proteins, such as black beans and chickpeas, can be a significant source of important vitamins, minerals, and fiber, and studies show that eating them improves our health. Whether from nuts, seeds, or pulses, plant proteins have also been linked to better health and weight control. A plate of Caramelized Tamarind Tempeh, 288, or a bowl of Black Bean Soup, 89, can be delicious and filling. Or, another approach is to supplement meat with plant proteins by making dishes like Mapo Dofu, 286, Black-Eyed Peas and Greens, 216, or Red Beans and Rice, 216, which stretch the savory, satiating flavors of meat to delicious effect.

CHOOSE WHOLE GRAINS

Whole grains have all the germ, bran, and endosperm intact. (For a discussion of these parts, see Grains, 317.) By contrast, refined grains like white rice have had one or more of these parts removed during production. Like fruits and vegetables, eating whole grains promotes a healthier weight and reduces the risk of health conditions, including heart disease, cancer, and diabetes.

Whole grains have a clear edge over refined grains, but here's where balance comes into play: Current dietary guidelines advise us to make half the grains we consume whole grains. The other half may come from the refined breads, cereals, pastas, and grains we sometimes crave. So feel free to fill out your menu with recipes like Pasta alla Norma, 297, and Risotto, 336. Keep in mind that on a balanced plate, the grain portion takes up about one-quarter of the space, meaning that most often, grains should be a side dish rather than the main course. See the Grains chapter, 317, for more information on different types of grains.

STAY HYDRATED

The longstanding advice to drink eight 8-ounce glasses of water a day is a little simplistic since fluid needs differ from person to person. You can use this number to check if you're in the right ballpark, but the best advice is to drink when you are thirsty.

Water is the best choice because it doesn't contain any unneeded sugar or calories. Caffeinated drinks technically act as a diuretic, but the net result is still an increase in fluid intake. Water-rich foods, such as soups and fruits, also boost your fluid intake. These foods bring an added bonus: They supply nutrients and fill you up.

Milk, soda, and juice do help you stay hydrated, but their calories can add up. Use milk or an unsweetened dairy alternative in coffee or tea, or in smoothies, but skip the flavored varieties, which have a lot of added sugar. Other store-bought beverages also tend to contain lots of added sugar, including coffee and tea drinks, sports drinks, and juice drinks.

Alcohol can be part of a balanced diet if you stick to the limits of one drink a day for women and two for men. This amount can raise HDL (the good form of cholesterol) and protect against heart disease and stroke. On the other hand, regularly going above this limit can lead to a variety of health problems, and heavy drinking is a major cause of preventable death, so if you enjoy alcohol, don't overdo it. And if you're not a drinker, there's no reason to start. You'll get plenty of disease-protection with a healthy diet and active lifestyle.

SHOPPING FOR HEALTHFUL FOODS

One of the biggest myths around healthful eating is to only shop around the perimeter of the grocery store. Whole grain breads and pastas, beans, nuts and nut butters, and more are all shelved in the center aisles, not to mention frozen fruits and vegetables. Rather than relying on the location of a food in the grocery store to tell you whether it has a place in your diet, learn how to decode a food label. This is one of the best things you can do to ensure you're choosing the most nutritious packaged foods. Here are some pointers for reading a food label.

INGREDIENTS

The ingredients are usually off to the side in very fine print, which makes them seem like an afterthought. But the ingredient list contains the most critical information. Package claims (like low-fat, healthy, organic, or all natural) don't actually tell you what you're eating, and knowing the calories or grams of fiber doesn't provide a complete picture, either. To get clear on the quality of the food, zero in on the ingredient list.

Ingredients are listed in order of predominance, so look for whole-food ingredients, like nuts, seeds, whole grains, fruits, beans, and the like to be at the top of the list. Beyond that, be on the lookout for additives and artificial colors, flavors, and sweeteners. These signal that the food is highly processed, so you might want to find something else. (The FDA considers these ingredients safe, but as a general rule, it's better to eat foods that are closer to their whole form.)

Nutrition Facts	
8 servings per container	
Serving size	**2/3 cup (55g)**
Amount per serving	
Calories	**230**
	% Daily Value*
Total Fat 8g	**10%**
Saturated Fat 1g	**5%**
Trans Fat 0g	
Cholesterol 0mg	**0%**
Sodium 160mg	**7%**
Total Carbohydrate 37g	**13%**
Dietary Fiber 4g	**14%**
Total Sugars 12g	
Includes 10g Added Sugars	**20%**
Protein 3g	
Vitamin D 2mcg	10%
Calcium 260mg	20%
Iron 8mg	45%
Potassium 235mg	6%

* The % Daily Value (DV) tells you how much a nutrient in a serving of food contributes to a daily diet. 2,000 calories a day is used for general nutrition advice.

SERVING SIZE AND SERVINGS PER CONTAINER

The serving size is based on a standard reference amount, but you might eat more or less. Once you figure out which direction you're going in, do the math on calories, carbs, sugar, and fiber to get a better sense of what you're consuming.

Servings per container is just as it sounds; it can be useful for judging portion sizes.

CALORIES

This number tells you how many calories are in the standard serving size. It can be helpful to keep an eye on calories but it is better to factor in the quality of foods you're eating, which you can determine from the ingredient list.

➤ It's a good idea to have a general sense of your daily calorie needs, which you can determine using this online tool: https://www.niddk.nih.gov/bwp.

Your needs depend on your age, activity levels, sex, whether you're looking to lose weight, and a few other factors. Knowing your daily range will come in handy when you're reading labels at the grocery store and choosing products that support your needs.

% DAILY VALUE

This shows how much of each listed nutrient the food provides based on a 2,000-calorie-per-day diet. It's worth mentioning that while 2,000 calories per day is the reference amount, some people may need more, while others may need less. Overall, the daily value can help you determine if a food is high or low in a specific nutrient.

TOTAL FAT AND SATURATED FAT

The total fat isn't as important as the type of fats within foods. The best scientific evidence to date suggests favoring mono- and polyunsaturated fats, so use this information to steer your choices.

SODIUM

Since most of the sodium in our diet comes from packaged foods, it's a good idea to look for products lower in sodium. The daily target is 2,300 mg or less.

TOTAL CARBOHYDRATES, FIBER, AND ADDED SUGARS

Total carbohydrate figures are useful for people with diabetes and others managing their carb intake. Foods high in dietary fiber are unequivocally great, but keep in mind that some foods include processed ingredients to drive up fiber levels. Though these ingredients are considered beneficial to health, we recommend checking the ingredient list and choosing foods where the fiber comes from a whole-food source. Added sugars tell you how much sugar the manufacturer added, as opposed to the sugar found naturally in the ingredients.

PROTEIN

Foods with 5 grams of protein are considered a good source; those with 10 grams or more are considered excellent sources.

USDA Recommended Daily Amounts for Each Food Group

Recommended Calories per Day:	1,600 calories	1,800 calories	2,000 calories	2,200 calories	2,400 calories	2,600 calories
Vegetables						
1 cup-eq (equivalent) is equal to 1 cup raw or cooked vegetables or 2 cups leafy greens	2 cups-eq	2½ cups-eq	2½ cups-eq	3 cups-eq	3 cups-eq	3½ cups-eq
Fruits						
1 cup-eq (equivalent) is equal to 1 cup raw or cooked fruit or ½ cup dried fruit	1½ cups-eq	1½ cups-eq	2 cups-eq	2 cups-eq	2 cups-eq	2 cups-eq
Grains						
1 ounce-eq (equivalent) is equal to 1 ounce dried rice, pasta, or grains; ½ cup cooked rice, pasta, or grain; 1 medium slice of bread; or 1 cup cereal flakes	5 ounces-eq	6 ounces-eq	6 ounces-eq	7 ounces-eq	8 ounces-eq	9 ounces-eq
Dairy						
1 cup-eq (equivalent) is equal to 1 cup milk, yogurt, or fortified soy milk; 1½ ounces Cheddar or other natural cheese; or 2 ounces processed cheese	3 cups-eq	3 cups-eq	3 cups-eq	3 cups-eq	3 cups-eq	3 cups-eq
Protein Foods						
1 ounce-eq (equivalent) is equal to 1 ounce lean meat, poultry, or seafood; 1 egg; ¼ cup cooked beans or tofu; 1 tablespoon peanut butter; or ½ ounce nuts or seeds	5 ounces-eq	5 ounces-eq	5½ ounces-eq	6 ounces-eq	6½ ounces-eq	6½ ounces-eq

VITAMINS AND MINERALS

Most Americans get insufficient levels of the four vitamins and minerals listed on the food label. Foods that provide 20 percent of the daily value for these nutrients are good sources.

> **WHAT IS A SERVING?**
>
> Serving sizes vary depending on whether you're looking at packaged food, restaurant food, recipe servings, and so on. For the purposes of this book, the serving size given in the recipe yield is meant to be generous so you can count on dishing up satisfying portions to the number of people indicated without running out of food (and possibly having leftovers). Whether you want to serve larger or smaller portions is up to you and those being served, everyone's appetites, and common sense.
>
> Beyond appetite and common sense, serving sizes can be calculated based on your age, activity level, height, and weight. First, find your recommended daily caloric intake using the online tool here: https://www.niddk.nih.gov/bwp. On page xix, find the recommended daily servings for each food group for some common calorie levels.

ABOUT FOOD SAFETY

While there is nothing you can do about food safety practices used in food production, you can be vigilant about food safety in your own kitchen. Most food safety measure are fairly common sense: Don't let perishable foods sit out at room temperature for a long time; don't let juices from raw meats come into contact with other foods; make sure foods are properly cooked through. Even so, it is a good idea to brush up on these food safety guidelines. To keep up to date with food recalls, visit the USDA's Food Safety and Inspection Service website at www.fsis.usda.gov where you can sign up to receive regular updates regarding food safety.

CLEANING AND SANITIZING WORK SURFACES

Perhaps the most elemental first step when preparing foods is to thoroughly wash your hands before and after handling food. ➤ If handling or cutting up raw poultry, meats, and other items that must be cooked to be safely eaten, always wash your hands, utensils, and surfaces immediately after preparing them, even if other ingredients need to be dealt with. This will help avoid **cross-contamination,** or the spread of bacteria from meat (which will be rendered safe by cooking) to items that will be eaten raw, such as salad ingredients, garnishes, and condiments.

Though dish detergent is necessary for removing oils and dirt, areas exposed to raw poultry and meats should also be treated with a **sanitizing solution** of chlorine bleach and water before drying.

➤ ***To make a sanitizing solution,*** mix ¾ teaspoon household bleach with 1 quart of cool water. The best option is to keep a 32-ounce spray bottle under the sink for easy access and convenient use.

To clean and sanitize cutting boards, kitchen sinks, and other work surfaces, first remove any bits of food or dirt as best you can. Scrub exposed areas thoroughly with a sponge or kitchen towel moistened with water and dish detergent. Wring out the towel or sponge, moisten with water, and rinse the area (or rinse cutting boards with hot water in the sink). Again, wring out the towel or sponge, blot the area dry, and then spray with sanitizing solution. Give a final wipe with a clean, dry towel.

FOOD HANDLING, STORAGE, AND THE TEMPERATURE DANGER ZONE

The temperature danger zone—40° through 140°F—is the range at which bacteria thrive best. A simple, important rule should be followed for all perishable foods: ➤ Do not let cooked foods or raw foods that need to be refrigerated sit at temperatures between 40° and 140°F for more than 2 hours.

When shopping, select fresh and frozen items last, and schedule shopping trips at the end of your other errands to avoid keeping food in the cart or car where it may be subject to unsafe temperatures. Keep raw meat, poultry, and seafood separate—both in the cart and at home—to prevent any drips or leaks (which may be undetectable) from contaminating other foods.

Make sure your refrigerator is set at or below 40°F and your freezer is at or below 0°F. Most fresh food can be safely stored in the refrigerator for 2 to 5 days, and meats, seafood, and poultry can be stored in the freezer if you do not plan to cook them within that period. Frozen food should be thawed in the refrigerator—never on the counter—and raw meats and poultry should be placed on a rimmed baking sheet or baking dish (to catch any drips) on the lowest refrigerator shelf to avoid contact with other foods. If you have leftovers, make sure to refrigerate or freeze them as quickly as possible. For detailed information on proper food storage, see Keeping and Storing Food, 878.

SAFE INTERNAL TEMPERATURES

Cooking fish, meats, and poultry to the proper internal temperature is an important step in minimizing foodborne illness. Using an accurate digital probe thermometer is the best way to measure a food's internal temperature. For the minimum safe cooking temperature for meats, see Timing and Doneness, 452. For poultry and game, see individual entries in their respective chapters.

Among common foodborne bacteria, **Salmonellae** survive but remain inactive from freezing temperatures up to 39°F; ➤ they are destroyed when heated to 165°F. **Staphylococci** react to temperatures similarly, but the toxin they produce—also called staphylococcus—is destroyed only by long boiling at 240°F. **Clostridium botulinum** grow best between 70° and 110°F; the bacterial cell form is destroyed at 212°F, but ➤ the deadly spore form is not destroyed until held at 240°F or above. These spores are the usual form found on food, so care is needed to prevent them from becoming a problem in home-canned low-acid foods such as green beans, corn, beets, 901 temperatures, attained only by the use of a steam-pressure canner, are necessary for canning low-acid foods.

Note that there are some instances in this book when we recommend internal temperatures lower than those recommended by the USDA. For instance, even though all poultry is supposed to be cooked to an internal temperature of 165°F, duck breasts taste overcooked beyond about 140°F. In these cases, we usually defer to taste over absolute by-the-book safety. Also keep in mind that lots of foods are somewhat risky to eat: runny eggs, oysters on the half-shell, medium-rare hamburgers, and even sprouts carry some risk. We have weighed the likelihood of foodborne illness against the flavor of these foods and decide many are worth the risk. That said, if you are cooking for anyone with a compromised immune system, children, the elderly, or pregnant women, defer to safety and choose foods that still taste good when cooked to the USDA's recommended internal temperatures.

BE MINDFUL OF THE PLANET

There's a lot of overlap between eating for our own health and the health of the planet. You might consider reducing meat consumption, buying foods that were produced sustainably, and being mindful of food waste and packaging. Here are some ideas that help you eat both healthfully and sustainably.

VEGETARIAN AND VEGAN DIETS

Among the foods you eat, meat has the most dramatic impact on our environment. Plant-based proteins tend to be less draining on natural resources, so reducing meat consumption and opting for plant-based proteins instead—at least some of the time—can be a planet-friendly practice. Beyond that, eating less meat may also lead to a reduction in disease risk that helps you live a longer, healthier life. But for those who can't fathom giving up meat, you can be more flexible about it. Plan a meat-free day once a week, and on the days you do eat meat, stretch out your portions with recipes that include both meat and plant proteins. Mapo Dofu, 286, is a perfect example.

If you decide to exclude meat from your menu, there are a few extra things to consider on the nutrition front. Plan carefully to ensure you're getting adequate calcium, iron, and zinc. You can get these minerals through your diet if you're deliberate about selecting foods that supply them, but it's not possible to get the vitamin B_{12} you need. If you're following a strictly plant-based plan, consider supplementing.

WHAT DO ORGANIC AND NON-GMO MEAN?

The term "organic" refers to regulatory standards for food production based, in theory, on more planet-friendly methods. These standards address factors like soil quality and animal welfare (though they can tend toward the unspecific in the latter instance, meaning animals raised for organic meat may not be raised all that differently from their nonorganic counterparts). They also ensure that no synthetic pesticide GMOs (see below) are used in food production. These measures are intended to protect the environment, reduce antibiotic exposure, improve the conditions of animals, and protect farm workers and their families who are most vulnerable to pesticide exposure. Organic production methods also reduce synthetic pesticide residue on our fruits and vegetables. However, organic does not mean pesticide-free: An approved list of pesticides derived from natural substances, such as hydrogen peroxide, may be applied to organic crops.

"GMO" stands for genetically modified organisms, and most soy and corn currently grown in the United States was developed using this technology. One example of a GMO crop is "Bt corn." Bt is shorthand for *Bacillus thuringiensis*, a soil bacterium that produces toxins lethal to some insects, including some that are particularly problematic for corn growers. In fact, Bt has been widely used as a pesticide in organic gardening since the 1960s. However, once scientists modified the DNA of corn to produce some of the same toxins that *Bacillus thuringiensis* produces, there was public backlash. One concern is that the widespread growth of Bt corn will result in insects developing resistance to the toxins, which would likely have repercussions that we simply cannot predict. (This concern is not unfounded—pests of all kinds, including insects, can develop resistance to any pesticide over time.) That said, the technology results in higher yields and less need for pesticides, which is significant.

Though scientists consider genetic engineering safe, and farmers have been cross-breeding plant species for hundreds of years, the practice of biotechnology remains controversial. People want more transparency related to how their food is produced. Concerns about the future of our food supply, seed sovereignty, the unknown (and unknowable) environmental impact of altering crops, the effects of growing these crops in a monoculture, and potential long-term health consequences are among the reasons consumers are skeptical about GMOs. We encourage skepticism, but also believe that skepticism should be coupled with an understanding of facts supported by good data rather than knee-jerk emotional responses. It is reasonable to have concerns about biotechnology, but arm yourself with understanding.

A HEALTHY PANTRY

Having a well-stocked kitchen means you're always ready to cook up a nutritious meal. Here are some items to always have on hand at home.

Swap refined grains for whole grains

- Whole-grain breads, pasta, crackers, and low-sugar hot or cold cereals
- Whole-grain ingredients, like wheat or rye berries, wild rice, brown rice, millet, or quinoa

Favor healthy fats

- Extra-virgin olive oil, avocado oil, and canola oil
- A variety of nuts and seeds, such as peanuts, almonds, cashews, pumpkin seeds, chia seeds, and flaxseeds
- Avocados and olives

Use spices and acidic ingredients to reduce sodium

- Herbs and spices, including cardamom, cayenne pepper, cinnamon, cloves, coriander, cumin, ginger, nutmeg, oregano, pepper, smoked paprika, and turmeric
- A splash of citrus juice or vinegar can increase the perception of salt, meaning you do not need to add as much. Sumac, black lime, amchur powder, and other tangy spices can also have the same effect. (For more on these, consult the Know Your Ingredients chapter, 950.)

MANAGING FOOD WASTE

Though we spend plenty of time thinking about the food we eat, it is worth considering the food we do not eat. Wasted food squanders labor, energy, and water; contributes to pollution; and, oftentimes, could benefit the community if it were donated, rather than being thrown away. A conversation about sustainable habits must include measures to reduce food waste.

As of this writing, almost 40 percent of the food we produce is wasted. Some of this food is undistributed—it doesn't make it past the farm or dock. Other times, it is wasted at the grocery store, or goes uneaten in our own homes. Reducing food waste can benefit the environment, while also saving you money.

Sometimes "Use By" and "Sell By" dates prompt us to throw away food before it has truly spoiled. These dates often designate when the product will be at its peak quality, rather than when it is no longer safe to eat. Many foods, including milk and eggs, can be consumed after these dates, assuming they have been properly stored. Canned foods can usually be eaten well past their indicated dates, provided there are not visible signs of rust or bulging.

Properly storing foods can also help you reduce food waste. Meats, poultry, seafood, cooked grains, flours, soups and sauces, sturdy fruits and veggies, and leftovers can be stored in the freezer if you think you won't be able to eat them before they go bad. Another option is to take to social media to give away food that would otherwise be wasted. Many local groups (the most popular being Buy Nothing) exist that enable neighbors to post items, including food, that they wish to give away. We used one of these groups when testing recipes for this book to give away extra food.

Of course, strategic cooking is another opportunity to reduce waste. See Streamlined Cooking, xxxviii, for ideas on how to use "scraps" in cooking and how to cook more efficiently.

ENTERTAINING AND MENUS

Having people over for dinner must have been one of our first evolutionary milestones as social beings. We have no way of confirming this in the fossil record, but it sounds reasonable enough. Regardless of which civilizing acts came first, we find it comforting to recall the elemental simplicity of the act itself. All of this is to say: Relax! Try not to feel that something unusual or original is expected of you as a host. It isn't. Provide a space to gather, be yourself, and share what you have.

The best advice we can offer to anyone who wants to host a sizable get-together boils down to two things: First, set yourself up for success by preparing as much as you can ahead of time. Second, and perhaps most important, invite one or several friends to help. From shopping to chopping, having less on your plate will make everything else easier, calmer, and more enjoyable for you and your guests. As the number of guests swells, consider asking others to contribute side dishes or appetizers. There is no secret to why potluck-style gatherings are so popular: They tend to be as easy as lighting a grill and providing some beverages.

Guests can contribute other things as well. For instance, task a friend who has good taste in music with assembling a party playlist. If you know a cocktail enthusiast, ask them to put together a punch or batched cocktail. Some of the best parties we have thrown were those where everyone pitched in. Or perhaps we simply remember them more fondly because there was less stress involved.

Regardless of the menu or who helps, try to have everything in readiness 5 minutes before your guests are expected: appetizers, wine, and cocktails—which may be simple—on a convenient side table or kitchen countertop; plates warming in the oven, a warming drawer, or the dry cycle of the dishwasher; and the dining table completely set. If, at the last minute, something does happen to upset your well-laid plans, rise to the occasion. The mishap may be the making of your party. Remember the poet Horace's observation, "A host is like a general: It takes a mishap to reveal their genius."

THE MENU

We find that the most memorable gatherings are rarely the ones where the greatest culinary prowess is displayed through a parade of decadent courses or complex dishes. Rather, we think flavorful, nourishing foods lend themselves to a convivial, comfortable atmosphere. If you are cooking the meal yourself, choose foods that can be prepared ahead of time, so you can spend more time at the table and less hovering over the stove. This is especially important as parties grow in size: ➤ The larger the number of guests, the more your menu should favor advance preparation, so you can avoid last-minute fussing. Unless you feel especially confident or the recipe is very straightforward, avoid making dishes for company that you have never made before.

Let common sense prevail in your menu planning. For dinner-time get-togethers, ➤ consider serving just three courses: a small spread of appetizers (or a party platter, 45), a main dish with one or two sides, and perhaps a dessert (which may be as simple as a bowl of the season's best fruit with homemade whipped cream). If the occasion warrants more courses, offer enough to show that you've gone to some trouble, but not so many that you (or the guests) feel overwhelmed. Try to plot out a varied and well-balanced progression of dishes, considering the richness, textures, and flavors of each one and how they will fit together. Let the menu reflect the season, serving lighter dishes in hot weather and heartier ones when it's cold. For specific combinations, see Menus, xxviii.

Unless you know your guests' food preferences well, avoid serving "challenging" or overly spicy foods. If possible, ➤ inquire discreetly about food allergies or vegetarian preferences. Do not hesitate to serve guests what you like to eat yourself. Serving something you enjoy and are confident making is part of sharing yourself—even if that something is a roast chicken and mashed potatoes or spaghetti and meatballs.

It is also perfectly acceptable to serve at least some commercially prepared food. We often present appetizers from the local deli or market: pâté, bread, and cheeses, with an assortment of olives. And no guest has been known to turn down cake from a bakery, or store-bought ice cream and cookies. Maybe you didn't make these foods, but you certainly made them possible.

We like to keep the food for most of our gatherings homey and inviting, whether that means serving up a big pot of Red Posole, 324, and fresh garnishes; Cassoulet, 216, good bread, and a big green salad; or Spicy Sichuan Hot Pot, 97, with an ample array of ingredients for dipping. Pizzas are perhaps the surest crowd pleaser and need little more than a salad to accompany them. Pizzas like Chicago-Style Deep-Dish Pizza, 616, and Grandma-Style Pan Pizza, 616, can be made before guests arrive; for those who do not mind tending the oven (or grill), smaller thin-crust pizzas, 614, can be fun for everyone to help top and bake.

INFORMAL DINING

The vast majority of meals we serve and enjoy are "informal," but this does not mean they are formless. There are several basic strategies for serving food: (1) Platters or serving dishes of all the food are put in the middle of the table, and then passed "family-style"; (2) Foods are arrayed on a kitchen countertop, side table, or buffet and guests amble by each item with their plates in hand before sitting down; (3) The food is arranged on individual plates in the kitchen, with everyone given the same amount of the same food. This last strategy requires the most intervention on your part, so we recommend avoiding it unless an item you are serving is especially delicate, in need of careful portioning, or if you have a compelling "vision" for how the food should be plated.

For most informal dinner parties, a combination of serving styles may be appropriate. Appetizers might be plated in the kitchen, for instance, and platters of the roasted meat or other main course passed around the table. Certain courses might be arranged on a sideboard or in the kitchen for buffet service. This is particularly appropriate when serving a mixed appetizer course or assorted desserts. If you are an accomplished carver, consider practicing your art at the table, impressing your guests with your deftness and offering each one the cut they prefer. If, on the other hand, you don't want your guests to see you wrestle with a turkey or a leg of lamb, carve it safely out of sight and bring the platter to the table.

For setting the table, the basic arrangement of fork to the left of the plate and knife and spoon to the right is all you need to know. We are sometimes so informal as to place all utensils in canning jars so guests can help themselves at the beginning or end of a buffet.

Table setting for an informal meal

When dinner is finished, resist the urge to do any extensive cleaning up while your guests are still present; your job and your pleasure as host is to spend as much time with them as possible. Resist, as well, the kind of good-intentioned rush to help that often turns a dinner's aftermath into a volunteer free-for-all. On the other hand, two hosts can share preliminary cleanup duties, and there's nothing wrong with accepting an unobtrusive dependable assist from one good friend who knows their way around your kitchen. In general, though, the more people who remain at the table at meal's end the better—and that includes you.

Before serving dessert, clear all plates, serving dishes, and condiments from the table. Set the dessert plates if you are using them. Serve coffee or tea with dessert, or save it for afterward. Invite guests to have after-dinner beverages in the living room, if you wish; often, though, the conversation is at its best and most expansive during and after dessert, and guests would rather stay at the table. At this point in the evening, hostly duties taper off, limited to refilling guests' cups or liqueur glasses. For the host, these final moments can be some of the best of the evening.

BRUNCH

Brunch is an easy meal to prepare and a good way for beginners to practice their entertaining skills. Brunch may be served buffet-style or family-style. Choose your menu carefully, keeping things simple and avoiding complicated egg dishes that might be difficult to prepare for a crowd, such as individual omelets or eggs Benedict. ➤ Quiches, 162, frittatas, 159, and stratas, 164, are excellent savory brunch dishes that may be made or assembled in advance and served warm. Bagels with spreads, quick breads, coffee cake, and scones are other brunch favorites. It is customary to serve something alcoholic with brunch, but keep this simple, too: Mimosas, 42, Bellinis, 42, or a pitcher of Bloody Marys, 21, or Screwdrivers, 22, will usually suffice.

BUFFETS

Buffets are a good choice for large, casual get-togethers when dining table space is limited. Choose a colorful, varied array of foods and display them on a handsomely appointed table or countertop. Plan generously, for guests are apt to take larger portions at buffets. ➤ Everything offered on a buffet should be easy to eat with a fork or with fingers—only minimal knife cutting, if any, should be required. Label any food that isn't easily identifiable with a small card placed beside the dish. Drinks should be set up away from the buffet table so as not to disrupt traffic. If you're having more than a dozen guests, set up a two-sided buffet line if space allows so that guests can serve themselves quickly and still have the chance to sample everything—and make sure that there are cutlery and plates for both lines.

Restrict the number of hot foods to those you can serve quickly straight from the pot or a hot serving dish, or get chafing dishes from a party rental company. For dishes that must be kept cold, use ice packs instead of ice, which makes a mess as it melts, or pans specifically manufactured for keeping foods cold. Put the frozen packs on a rimmed tray or pan and arrange your platters on top.

Whether you are planning a picnic, holiday feast, or casual get-together, a **potluck,** where each guest brings a dish and all are presented buffet-style, is a resourceful way of creating a meal. Distribute assignments for prepared dishes evenly, depending on the occasion. We suggest category assignments, such as salads, hot side dishes (you may want to specify a vegetable or starchy side dish), main dishes, and desserts. If you know one guest makes a breathtaking coconut layer cake, request it. And don't forget to assign ice, beverages, and bread. Some hosts prefer to provide the main dish and ask guests to bring accompaniments only. Preheat the oven for guests who need to reheat their contributions before serving. A potluck is also a great place for a recipe exchange: Have guests bring enough copies of their recipes to distribute to all. For any buffet-style party, brush up on food safety guidelines, xx.

CHILDREN'S PARTIES

Entertaining is not just for adults. The best children's parties bring together a manageable number of children for food and games. For very young children, it is best to invite a parent of each as well. For older children, estimate that 1 adult will be needed for every 6 to 7 children. An afternoon event of 2 to 3 hours allows time for games, playtime, and food. See xxx for menu ideas. Keep children's parties simple, and perhaps let the guests help with food preparation. Decorating cupcakes with frosting, sprinkles, and colored sugar or putting toppings on homemade pizzas provides food as well as an activity to keep small hands busy.

COCKTAIL PARTIES AND OPEN HOUSES

The cocktail party is an estimable social institution. We steadfastly defend it as an American invention and an uncomplicated and pleasant means of entertaining. A good cocktail party begins with good liquor, wine, and beer (see Cocktails, Wine, and Beer, 17). Unless you plan to hire a professional bartender or the number of guests is so small that you or a guest volunteer can handle cocktail-mixing duties without missing the fun, it's best to serve just one type of cocktail, made up in batches—pitchers of martinis or margaritas, for example, or an alcoholic punch, 29–32. See Batching Cocktails, 19, for information on how to scale up cocktail recipes. We like to assemble the ingredients and equipment for a simple cocktail or two—say Manhattans, 23, or Old-Fashioneds, 23—and place recipe cards on the bar so guests can feel confident mixing their own drinks. Wine, both red and white, and beer or cider should also be part of the bar, and there should always be something nonalcoholic available (see About Thirst Quenchers, 13); sparkling mineral water is never out of place.

There must always be food at a cocktail party, of course, or the cocktails will quickly overwhelm the party. As a general rule, before dinner, 2 or 3 kinds of lighter party foods with cocktails will usually suffice. For a cocktail party without dinner, prepare 5 to 7 substantial hors d'oeuvre and finger foods. The food need not be complicated, nor even homemade. Store-bought pâtés and terrines or a platter of assorted, well-chosen cheeses, 45, served with crackers or sliced breads of good quality, are sufficient for informal gatherings. More sophisticated cocktail parties call for elegant hors d'oeuvre, such as an attractive service of thinly sliced smoked salmon with Buckwheat Blini, 641, sour cream, and lemon wedges. In general, cocktail parties shouldn't last more than 2 hours, and should be somewhere between 5 and 8 pm—never later, unless enough food is served to constitute a light dinner. A shorter cocktail period is appropriate if it is a prelude to another event—a dinner out with the same guests, for instance, or a concert or the theater. In that case, keep both drinks and food as simple as possible. Champagne and smoked salmon are perfect for this sort of gathering.

A variation on the cocktail party, usually specific to the year-end holidays, is the **open house.** The same basic rules apply, but the event may run for 3 to 4 hours or even more, with the expectation that guests will drop by at their convenience during a prescribed period of time and rarely stay more than an hour or so. This means of entertaining is particularly appropriate for busy holiday weekends for which guests may be expected to have several invitations; it also permits the host to invite a larger number of people than might fit comfortably in the available space at one time. Because of the inevitable ebb and flow of guests, passed finger foods are not appropriate for an open house of any size and duration, and the food tends to be rather more substantial than at a simple cocktail party. A modified buffet table is a better fit, preferably involving nothing that needs to be kept warm or cold. Baked ham, turkey, or a whole poached salmon make attractive and satisfying centerpieces for such occasions.

OUTDOOR ENTERTAINING

The backyard barbecue offers perhaps the easiest and most comfortable way of cooking for friends and family during warm weather. As with any form of entertaining, however, the host should consider the guests' comfort and anticipate potential problems. What's the weather likely to be? If rain is possible, there should be a place for guests to gather indoors. If it will be very hot, there should be plenty of shade and cold drinking water. Some protection should be offered against insects if they're likely to be a problem (screened porches, citronella candles, insect repellent). If the affair will go on after dark, there should be outdoor lights, hurricane candles, or other light sources. Plastic or compostable glasses and utensils and paper plates and napkins are perfectly acceptable, but if you'll be serving adults on a terrace or on a porch, real glassware, flatware, plates, and a cloth tablecloth and napkins add flair to the proceedings—even if the food is corn on the cob, hot dogs, and spareribs.

For small groups of people, an excursion to the park, beach, or mountains with coolers, bags, and baskets of food and drink in hand for a **picnic** is casual entertaining at its best. Leave highly perishable foods at home or carry them in well-chilled coolers (dishes made with mayonnaise must be kept cool). Again, if appropriate, real wineglasses, silverware, and cloth napkins can add elegance to a picnic. Because you're not at home, it's a good idea to bring along a strictly practical ➤ "picnic kit" containing a corkscrew, a small sharp knife, a small lightweight cutting board, a serving spoon, a can opener, a bottle opener, a small salt-and-pepper set and other dried seasonings, a package of napkins, a roll of paper towels, tablecloth clips, a small first aid kit, insect repellent, sun block, and a trash bag.

For **tailgating** as well as backyard barbecues, prepare a portable grill, either charcoal or gas, as well as a few key grilling accessories: long-handled tongs for turning the food, clean brushes to apply sauces, heavy-duty oven mitts, and matches or a lighter. Since you will probably tailgate in a parking lot or a field before a sporting event, this is not the time or place for dainty foods. Grilled beef, chicken, and sausages are favorites, served with potato chips and beer and wine.

SUPPER AND COOKING CLUBS

A popular practice that has sprung from the dinner party is the supper or cooking club. Members are usually friends who share a love of creating menus, cooking, and eating and gather for regularly scheduled dinner parties.

There are two ways to organize a successful supper or cooking club event. The more common is to establish a theme—regional cooking, recipes from the same cookbook, or a season's best ingredients—and assign each member a dish. Club members rotate serving as host or hostess for each dinner. Occasionally such clubs may hold a progressive dinner, where each course is served at a different location, usually the various members' homes. As with any dinner party, a good number of guests is about 8.

CANNING CLUBS

Canning clubs are not as popular as supper clubs or cooking clubs, but they are worth considering if several of your friends like to make pickles, jams, or other preserved foods. We are members of our local canning club, and it is an event that we look forward to each month. Our canning club usually meets in the early evening once a month, and each guest brings a snack and something to drink, whether that is a bottle of wine, a six-pack of beer, or a jug of lemonade. Everyone brings 5 jars of any homemade item to trade with the other attendees. Many people like to prepare a snack that features the preserve they made, such as a homemade jam spread over a block of cream cheese or baked into jam bars, or a homemade spice blend sprinkled over hummus.

You and your friends, of course, may determine the rules of your canning club, but the one we attend is fairly flexible about items brought for trading. While the traditional preserved goods like pickles and jams are the most common, we have also seen unprocessed items make an appearance. These include homemade salted caramel sauce, granola, candies, spice blends, hummus, and pesto. Each person labels their jars with the name of the item, the date it was made, and whether it is shelf stable or must be refrigerated. The jars are placed on a central table. After about an hour of snacking and mingling, trading commences. Everyone stands in a circle and, starting with the host, each person introduces themselves and describes what they brought and how it might be used. Then, again starting with the host, each person chooses one item from the table. To keep things fair, when the last person in the circle chooses their item, they choose a second one and then the direction is reversed. When it is once again the host's turn, they take 2 jars and the direction is reversed again. This continues until each person has selected 5 jars.

We like canning clubs not only because they are an informal way to host or participate in a gathering of close friends, but also because they allow you to share some of your home-canned bounty and receive in return a diverse selection of canned goods with which to fill out your pantry.

AFTERNOON TEA

The tea party might seem to some unsuited to the modern world—too time-consuming, too much of an air of the raised pinkie about it. The truth is, though, that offering guests a well-brewed pot of tea is almost as easy as pouring them mugs of coffee. A proper afternoon tea is served between 4 and 6 pm. Set a tea table as you would a buffet table, putting out cups on their saucers and teaspoons to one side, along with small cloth napkins and small plates for the edibles being served. No other silverware should be necessary unless you are serving jam, butter, or clotted cream to accompany scones or other baked goods. You'll want to provide an array of foods, such as small tea cakes, pastries, muffins, and the traditional scones, 634, as well as tea sandwiches, 66, cut into a variety of shapes. Arrange tea cakes and sandwiches on small plates or tiered stands, if you have them. At an informal tea party, the host pours the tea. For a more formal tea, the guest of honor "does the honors" and pours tea.

FORMAL DINING

Here lie the hallowed rituals and rites of formal entertaining, presented for those readers who wish to reenact the aristocratic table of a bygone age. In choosing your menu, the traditional order of courses is meant to guide, not rule: hors d'oeuvre, soup or other first course, seafood, meat or main course, salad, a cheese course or dessert (or both), and coffee, which may be accompanied by chocolates, small confections, and liqueurs. For some examples and ideas, see Formal Dinner Menus, xxx.

TABLE DECOR

Table decorations can be as natural or as whimsical as you like, but make sure they won't interfere with passing the serving dishes or with the guests' views of one another. Floral centerpieces or decorations should have no detectable scent, nor be tall enough to obstruct conversation across the table. If guests bring flowers, put them in a vase on the sideboard or in the living room. Candles are a pleasing touch for any dinner table, but use only dripless unscented candles. As with your flowers, make sure the candles are below or above eye level.

Although an attractive tablecloth adds to a formal party, it may not be strictly necessary. Cloth or rush place mats look good on a wooden table and can stand alone depending upon the occasion and decor. Cotton or linen napkins are essential for any smaller dinner party. Napkins should be folded into quarters and then in half into rectangles. The open corners should face the bottom left, making it easy for the seated diner to pick up the napkin by one corner, let it drop and unfold completely, and place it on their lap. A napkin folded into quarters and then in half to form a triangle is also simple and elegant. The napkin can be placed on top of the plate, open corners facing the guest, or to the left of the plate, top of the triangle pointing outward, underneath the fork or beside it. Salt and pepper sets should be placed on the table—at least 1 set for every 4 to 6 guests. Saltcellars (tiny shallow bowls filled with salt to pinch up with fingers or scoop with tiny spoons) may also be used.

TABLE SETTING

There are certain time-honored positions for tableware and equipment that result from the way food is eaten and served. Some of these implements (and their placement) may seem quaint—perhaps even antiquated—but we challenge you to find a better use for all of the specialized silver floating around. Without putting too fine a point on the subject, the basic principles at work are: ➤ Forks to the left, spoons and knives to the right (knife edges turned toward the plate); flatware that is to be used first is placed farthest from the plate.

GLASSWARE

A good-sized wineglass with a capacity of 8 or 9 ounces and a tulip-shaped bowl is fine for both red and white wines, but you may wish to arrange 2 glasses at each place setting for a more seamless transition if 2 wines are to be served. Clear long-stemmed or stemless glasses, uncut or etched, are best. Water glasses may be stemmed, but tumblers are perfectly adequate. Usually both wine and water glasses are set on the table before the diners arrive, but no more than 3 wineglasses per setting should be positioned at the same time, no matter how many wines are being served. The wineglass to be used during the main course should be placed about a half inch above the point of the main-course knife. All other wineglasses are then placed on a diagonal from this point, according to when they will be used, as shown below. The water glass goblet is placed above the wineglasses. If you are setting out a tall tumbler for iced tea, lemonade, or another beverage in place of wine, place it where the main-course wineglass would normally sit.

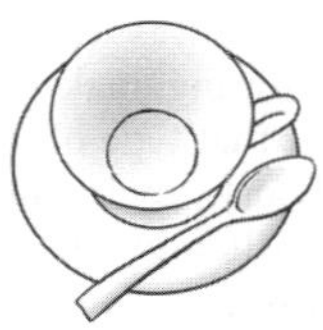

Beverage spoons are placed to the right of all other flatware, but small coffee spoons should rest on the saucer

SEATING

Experienced hosts swear that the key to a successful dinner is seating. Think about which friends may share similar hobbies or professions. Place cards are helpful at a dinner of more than 8 or 10. They go directly atop the napkin if it is centered on the plate, or just above the plate and in the center of the place setting if it is not. For a smaller party, simply indicate where each guest should sit (or, for the daring, let guests sit where they wish). Clear place cards with the first course so guests aren't wondering what to do with them, unless you're hosting a large party with guests unknown to one another—in which case they may be left on the table to ease mutual identification.

Wine and water glasses are placed on a diagonal, with the main-course glass about a half inch above the point of the main-course knife

SERVICE

When the guests come into the dining room, the table should be set. A charger or service plate—a decorative plate larger than the dinner plate—is at each place. ➤ To ensure that each guest has sufficient elbow room, there should be at least 30 inches from the center of one service plate to the center of the next. The appetizer plate and then the soup bowl are set on top of the service plate. The butter plate and its accompanying knife are to the left. The water glasses should be about two-thirds full; the empty wineglasses stand in place, see above. Water and wine are poured from the right. The glasses may stay in place throughout the meal, but it is preferable to remove each wineglass after use. If more than 3 wines are to be served, fresh glasses replace the used glasses as the latter are removed.

The host may prefer to pour the wines from a decanter or from a bottle. If the wine is chilled, it should be wrapped in a napkin, and a napkin should be held in the left hand to catch any drip from the bottle. Condiments may be passed from one guest to another or arranged at strategic places on the table.

Table setting for a meal that includes soup and dessert (the fork and spoon above the plate), with butter knives placed on each butter plate in a position identical to the main-course knife

As to the setting and using of flatware or silverware, the simple rule is to work from the outside in. As each course is finished, its accompanying utensils should be removed with the used plate or bowl. Thus, the guest may be confident in using the knife or fork now found at the outside.

For courses requiring guests to use their fingers, such as lobster in the shell, finger bowls are much appreciated. The finger bowl, partially filled with water, may have a scented geranium leaf, a fragrant herb or flower, or a thin slice of lemon floating in it. Finger bowls are often brought to the table on top of the dessert plates, with the dessert fork and spoon resting on the plate on either side of the bowl; the guest places the fork and spoon to either side of the plate and puts the finger bowl opposite the water glass, to the upper left.

If coffee is served at the table, a demitasse (espresso cup) or small coffee cups and saucers are placed at this time to the right of each diner. The demitasse spoons are on the saucers, parallel to the handle. Coffee is poured from the right and cream and sugar passed on a small tray from the left. Liqueurs may be served with the coffee at the table or passed on a tray should the host and guests choose to move to the living room for conversation and coffee.

When no knife is set, as for pie and coffee, the fork is placed on the right with the spoon

COOKING FOR LARGE PARTIES

To begin, ➤ cook dishes in several moderate-sized batches, rather than in one massive batch, because, mysterious as it sounds, quantity cooking is not always a matter of unlimited multiplication. While most of the recipes in this book make 4 to 6 servings and can be doubled for 8 to 12, do not assume that they can be tripled or quadrupled without other changes needing to be made. Strongly flavored ingredients like cayenne pepper and other spicy ingredients, vinegars and other acids, and very salty ingredients should not be doubled or tripled. Leave the amount as stated in the original, undoubled recipe, then add more to taste toward the end of cooking if needed.

Choose recipes that can be scaled up easily and that are more forgiving. Soups, stews, braises, and salads are easily scaled and hard to ruin. Then there are the large-format dishes practically designed to feed a small army. These include lasagne, 310–11, Braised Pulled Pork, 495, Brunswick Stew, 470, and Macleid's Rockcastle Chili, 502, as well as large roasts such as Roast Beef, 450, Classic Roast Turkey, 428, and Baked Ham, 500.

Take into account the longer time needed in preparation—not only for the peeling and washing of vegetables, but for heating up large quantities of food. Even more important, you will likely be confronted with a dearth of refrigerator space—discovering that the shelves are needed for properly chilling cold soups or cream pies just when they are also needed for keeping other sizable quantities of food at safe temperatures. Clean out your refrigerator in advance, organizing everything for the most efficient use of space. ➤ Have coolers and ice at the ready to take on food and beverages that will not fit in the refrigerator.

If the meal is a hot one, plan to use recipes that will involve both the oven and stovetop. Increase limited heating surfaces by supplementing them with slow cookers, hot plates, and the age-old chafing dish, to hold food in good serving condition—above 140°F.

Sit down with a paper and pen (or note-taking software, if you prefer) and mentally walk through the process of cooking, keeping food warm or cold, and serving, writing down all necessary equipment and utensils. Then, satisfied that the mechanical requirements are met, schedule the actual cooking of food so that enough can be done in advance to relieve the sink and work surfaces of last-minute crowding and mess.

If faced with a significant event where only a formal meal is appropriate, do not undertake this alone. Service help is a must. By service help we mean trained, experienced service and kitchen staff. Some turn to professional caterers at such a moment.

WORKING WITH A CATERER

Knowing how to work with a caterer to make an event a great success requires understanding your needs and the caterer's capabilities. Keep the kind of event and number of guests in mind. Do you need a bartender? Will you need to rent chairs, tables, glassware, silverware, and/or dishes? Do you need just food for a small group, or do you need servers as well to handle a crowd? Schedule a tasting of the proposed menu and make adjustments. Sometimes there is an additional fee for a tasting, but it is well worth the price. If you are hiring a caterer for formal dining, make sure they are skilled in the special service required for that type of entertaining. Get a written agreement that details all costs, including food, service, and rentals. Agree upon a date for when you will confirm the guest count. The caterer will usually assign a specific person to be in charge of the event—this is the person to whom you give a tip (usually 20 percent) at evening's end for the entire staff, from bartenders and servers to cooks.

MENUS

Good meals, whether simple or elaborate, or for family or friends, are built on balance and harmony. When planning a meal, consider the season, climate, time of day, and, of course, the preferences and restrictions of those you are serving. When entertaining a group of people whose preferences you do not know, serve familiar foods that everyone loves.

Your family can be the most important assembly you ever entertain. The success of family meals lies first in sharing the fun and responsibilities of planning the menu and shopping for ingredients.

A well-stocked pantry is the foundation for cooking, making grocery store and market trips necessary only for perishable items such as meat, poultry, seafood, produce, and dairy products. We like to keep the ingredients on hand for at least a couple dishes that can be made from pantry and freezer items alone. This provides a good backup plan for especially hectic days when the fridge is a bit bare but a trip to the supermarket is not feasible (or tolerable). To read more about strategies for efficient home cooking, see Streamlined Cooking, xxxviii.

Beyond cooking for family, these menus can be a guide to planning dinner parties or other get-togethers, whether formal or informal. Or they might provide inspiration when you have been asked to contribute a dish to a potluck. This section can also be used to navigate through some of the thousands of recipes in this book thematically. Remember that these menus are suggestions only. Your taste, budget, market, mood—and we hope, your imagination—can change them. Please read About Food Safety, xx, for a primer on the proper handling of food.

THANKSGIVING

Appetizers: Crisp Spicy Pecans, 46, or Brown Butter–Hazelnut Crackers, 50, with a soft cheese
First Course: Roasted Cauliflower Soup, 105, or Pumpkin or Butternut Squash Soup, 105
Main Course: Classic Roast Turkey, 428, with Basic Bread Stuffing or Dressing, 532, and Turkey Giblet Gravy, 545
Vegetarian Main Course: Savory Cabbage Strudel, 703, Roasted Mushroom Lasagne, 310, or Root Vegetable Braise, 203
Side Dishes: Creamy Mashed Cauliflower, 230, or Mashed Potatoes, 265; Sweet Potato Pudding, 279; Creamed Pearl Onions, 256; Green Bean Casserole, 210; Baked or Roasted Winter Squash, 275; Whole-Berry Cranberry Sauce, 179, or Uncooked Cranberry Relish, 180
Salad: Bitter Greens with Apples and Pecans, 117, or Becker House Salad I, 116
Bread: Parker House Rolls, 617
Dessert: Pumpkin, Squash, or Sweet Potato Pie, 681, Pumpkin or Squash Chess Pie, 678, Pecan Pie, 677, or Honey, Sorghum, or Maple Syrup Pie, 678
Beverage: Mulled Wine, 31, or Mulled Cider, 32

NEW YEAR'S EVE

Appetizers: Texas Caviar, 52, or salmon roe with Buckwheat Blini, 641, and sour cream, Broiled Stuffed Mushrooms Cockaigne, 58, Pickled Shrimp, 65, or Gougères, 70, Hungarian Mushroom Soup, 88
Main Course: Pan-Seared Duck Breasts, 432, with Fig and Red Wine Sauce, 552
Side Dishes: Megan's Beets with Goat Cheese, 219, or Melted Leeks, 247
Dessert: Baked Alaska, 854, or Individual Molten Chocolate Cakes, 743, with Hazelnut Gelato, 845
Beverage: Champagne Cocktail, 42, French 75, 42, or Champagne Punch, 29

NEW YEAR'S DAY

Main Course: Caldo Verde, 98, Treva's Chicken and Dumplings, 93, Caribbean Callaloo, 101, Pan-Roasted Pork Tenderloin, 489, with Sauerkraut, 940, or Braised Lentils with Sausage, 218
Side Dishes: Wilted Tender Greens, 243, Southern-Style Greens, 243, Hoppin' John, 331, or Red Beans and Rice, 216

ST. PATRICK'S DAY

First Course: Potato Leek Soup, 104
Main Course: Corned Beef, 472, Shepherd's Pie, 506, Irish Stew, 483, or Roasted Lamb Shoulder, 478
Side Dishes: Colcannon, 266, or Champ, 265 (see headnote to Additions to Mashed Potatoes)
Bread: Irish Soda Bread, 628, with salted Irish butter
Dessert: Ice Cream Float, 13, made with Irish stout

GAME DAY

Seven-Layer Dip, 52, or Beer Cheese Dip, 51
Buffalo Chicken Wings, 60, or Thai-Style Chicken Wings, 61
Crispy Potato Skins, 59
Nachos, 57
Texas Caviar, 52
Muffuletta, 137, or Sub or Hero Sandwich, 138
Chili con Carne, 468
Chocolate Sheet Cake, 734

MARDI GRAS

Appetizers: Pickled Shrimp, 65, or raw oysters on the half shell, 349
Main Course: Oyster Po'Boy, 141, Shrimp or Crawfish Étouffée, 366, Chicken Jambalaya, 331, Chicken Étouffée, 426, Becker Barbecued Shrimp, 364, Chicken Gumbo, 95, Seafood Gumbo, 101, Gumbo z'Herbes, 244, or Blackened Fish Steaks or Fillets, 389
Side Dishes: Red Beans and Rice, 216, Stewed Tomatoes or Tomatoes Creole, 281, Southern-Style Greens, 243, Okra and Tomato Stew, 253, or Fried Okra, 253
Dessert: New Orleans Beignets, 653, Calas, 653, New Orleans Bread Pudding, 830, Bananas Foster, 176, Coffee Ice Cream, 840, sprinkled with crushed French Praline, 873, New Orleans–Style Pecan Pralines, 873
Beverage: Sazerac, 23, Milk Punch, 24, Vieux Carré, 27, or Sweet Southern Iced Tea, 8

WEDDING BUFFET

Appetizers: Crudités, 45, with homemade Ranch Dressing, 577, Muhammara, 53, Marinated Cheese, 56, a cheese platter, 45, Brie Baked in Pastry, 57, Miniature Turnovers or Tartlets, 69, Spinach or Mushroom Phyllo Triangles, 68, and/or Gougères, 70
First Course: Gazpacho, 107, Cold Cucumber and Yogurt Soup, 108, Pumpkin or Butternut Squash Soup, 105, or Poached or "Boiled" Shrimp, 364, with Becker Cocktail Sauce, 569
Main Course: Chicken Breasts Baked on a Bed of Mushrooms, 409, Chicken Kebabs, 412, Pan-Roasted Beef, 456, or Seared Sea Scallops, 356, served over Fresh Corn Risotto, 336

Vegetarian Main Course: Vegetable Tian, 205, Vegetable Tagine, 205, or Millet Cakes with Parmesan and Sun-Dried Tomatoes, 326, served over mixed greens
Side Dishes: Asparagus with Orange and Hazelnuts, 209, Megan's Beets with Goat Cheese, 219, Garlic-Braised Broccoli Rabe, 221, or Glazed Carrots, 228
Salad: Asparagus Sesame Salad, 125, Becker House Salad, 116, Arugula and Heart of Palm Salad, 126, or Bitter Greens with Apples and Pecans, 117
Dessert: Mexican Wedding Cakes, 793, or Croquembouche, 698
Beverage: Champagne Punch, 29

OUTDOOR ENTERTAINING

Appetizers: Satay Skewers, 61, Texas Caviar, 52, Table Salsa, 573, with tortilla chips, Melon and Prosciutto, 58, or Lemon Rosemary Chicken on Skewers, 61
Main Course: Jamaican Jerk Chicken, 413, Broiled or Grilled Barbecued Chicken, 411, Barbecued Pork Ribs, 497, Smoked Pork Shoulder, 496, Carne Asada, 459, or Fish Kebabs with Vinaigrette, 385
Vegetarian Main Course: Grilled Pizza, 616, Grilled Leeks with Romesco Sauce, 248, or Grilled Fennel and Tomatoes with Olives and Basil, 240
Side Dishes: Elotes, 235, Corn on the Cob, 235, Grilled Mushrooms, 252, Macaroni and Cheese for a Crowd, 296, or Creamy Macaroni Salad for a Crowd, 132
Salad: Coconut-Cucumber Salad, 185, Classic Coleslaw, 119, or Dee's Corn and Tomato Salad, 126
Dessert: Grilled or Broiled Fruit Kebabs with Honey and Lime, 171, Grilled Peaches with Goat Cheese, 190, Macerated Fruit, 168, with Vanilla Ice Cream, 840, Banana Pudding, 817, Chocolate Sheet Cake, 734, or Mississippi Mud Cake, 735
Beverage: Planter's Punch, 29, Lemonade or Limeade, 13, Iced Tea, 8, or Sweet Southern Iced Tea, 8

PICNIC

Appetizers: Hummus, 52, White Bean Dip with Rosemary and Garlic, 52, Treva's Pimiento Cheese, 55, with crackers, or Deviled Eggs, 151
Main Course: Cold Skillet Fried Chicken, 417, Pan Bagnat, 138, or Muffuletta, 137
Salad: Creamy Potato Salad, 127, Spicy Watermelon Salad, 129, Panzanella, 128
Dessert: Brownies Cockaigne, 764, Chocolate Chip Cookies, 769, or Gooey Chocolate Oat Bars, 766
Beverage: Cold-Brewed Tea, 8, Agua Fresca, 14, or Spicy Ginger Ale, 14

TACO NIGHT

Appetizers: Guacamole, 51, Table Salsa, 573, and tortilla chips, or Queso Fundido, 51
Main Course: See the list of Fillings for Tacos and Burritos, 146; serve as for Tacos, 146
Side Dishes: Refried Beans, 215, Frijoles de la Olla, 213, Jalapeños en Escabeche, 930, Jicama Salad, 127, Roasted Cactus Pad Salad, 227, or Coconut-Cucumber Salad, 185
Dessert: Sopapillas, 654, or Flan with Condensed Milk, 814
Beverage: Margarita, 26, Paloma, 27, Michelada, 42, or Papaya-Mango Batido, 12

PIZZA PARTY

Appetizer: Bagna Cauda, 58, Vegetables à la Grecque, 204, Crudités, 45, with Tonnato Sauce, 564, Antipasto platter, 45, or Melon and Prosciutto, 58
Main Course: See About Pizza, 613
Salad: Caesar Salad, 117, or Becker House Salad II, 116
Dessert: Baked Figs with Ricotta, 186, Affogato, 851, or Anise-Almond Biscotti, 778, with Fior di Latte Gelato, 845
Beverage: Negroni, 21

CHILDREN'S PARTIES

Fruit Salad, 167
Quick Cheese Crackers, 70
Chicken Fingers, 415, with Honey Mustard Dipping Sauce, 556, or Pigs in a Blanket, 70
Tea Sandwiches, 67, filled with peanut butter and jelly, and cut into shapes with cookie cutters
Quesadillas, 57
Cupcakes (see Cupcake Suggestions chart, 748), or Confetti Cake, 724, with Vanilla Ice Cream, 840
Shirley Temples, 28, or Watermelon Punch, 15

BREAKFAST OR BRUNCH MENUS

Lemon–Poppy Seed Muffins, 633, or Herb and Roasted Garlic Muffins, 633
Artichoke Frittata for a Crowd, 160
Megan's Seeded Olive Oil Granola, 327, with yogurt
Broiled Grapefruit, 184
French 75, 42

Citrus Salad, 168
Socca, 650, topped with Wilted Tender Greens, 243, Fried Eggs, 155, and feta or crumbled soft goat cheese
Pimm's Cup, 21

Asparagus Strata, 164
Pecan and Cheddar "Sausage" Patties, 289
Megan's Kale Salad, 117
Bloody Mary, 21

Liège-Style Waffles, 644
Roasted Fruit, 171
Whipped Crème Fraîche, 791
Baked Bacon, 498
Mimosa, 42

FORMAL DINNER MENUS

Gravlax, 393, with Olive Oil Flatbread Crackers, 49, and Yogurt-Dill Sauce, 569
Roasted Cauliflower Soup, 105
Pan-Roasted Beef, 456, with Horseradish Sauce I, 566

Endive and Walnut Salad, 118
Vanilla Pots de Crème, 815, with Roasted Fruit, 171

Buckwheat Blini, 641, with sour cream and caviar or salmon roe
Chicken Kiev, 416
Crispy Smashed Potatoes, 268
Beet, Fennel, and Citrus Salad with Horseradish, 125
Phyllo Napoleons, 701, with Mocha Pastry Cream, 801

Crudités, 45, with Aïoli, 564
Seared Sea Scallops, 356, served over Fresh Corn Risotto, 336
Becker House Salad I, 116
Tomatoes Provençale, 282
Vanilla Soufflé, 818, with Fresh Berry Coulis, 805

Fried Halloumi with Honey and Walnuts, 56
Fesenjoon, 433
Chickpea and Roasted Cauliflower Salad, 130
Persian Rice, 333
Ambrosia II, 168, or Oranges in Syrup, 183, with Whipped Cream, 791

Summer Rolls, 70
Grilled Vietnamese-Style Pork, 493
Becker House Salad II, 116, with Crispy Fried Shallots, 256
Steamed Broccoli, 220, with Nuoc Cham, 571
Coconut Tapioca Pudding, 829

DINNER FOR FAMILY AND FRIENDS

Roast Chicken with Vegetables, 408
Saffron Millet, 326
Rachel's Kale and Lentil Salad, 130
Olive Oil Cake, 735

Baked or Slow-Roasted Fish, 378, with Zhug, 567
Roasted Cauliflower with Green Olives and Lemon, 229
Megan's Kale Salad, 117
Blueberry and Peach Buckle, 684

Pasta e Fagioli, 299
Sicilian Orange, Fennel, and Onion Salad, 129
Crusty bread
Fruit Galette or Crostata, 689

Guyanese Pepperpot, 468
Coconut Rice, 333
Roasted Plantains, 263, or Fried Plantains, 263
Rombauer Jam Cake, 732 or Fresh Ginger Cake, 737

Spicy Sichuan Hot Pot, 97
Tangerines or mandarin oranges

MENUS WITH GUEST PARTICIPATION

At the risk of suggesting this strategy too many times, we think it is worth repeating: The easiest and best way to have everyone feel like they have contributed to a meal is to make it a potluck and ask several guests to bring a side dish, dessert, salad, appetizer, or beverages. The level of planning and specificity involved should be minimal: only enough so that people do not bring the same thing. For those entertaining outdoors, another option that splits the difference between potluck and cookout is asking guests to bring their favorite foods to put on the grill for everyone to share. Of course, if guests are bringing main-dish proteins, it might be best to provide a few versatile sides and a salad.

Pizza, 614–16, is a classic way to keep guests involved in the process: Prepare the dough and grate, slice, or precook a wide variety of toppings. The crusts for Grilled Pizza I, 616, can be grilled ahead of time, topped, and then finished; Pizza Margherita, 614, and any pizza that is baked on a stone will require you to roll out dough for guests to top.

A taco bar is another good approach. Guests can bring their favorite taco toppings, while you provide tortillas and some other basics like cilantro, sour cream, and hot sauce. Or apply the principle to Banh Mi, 139, giving guests different assignments to flesh out the feast: One person brings a vegetarian sandwich filling, others bring pâté or cold cuts, someone is responsible for the pickled carrot and daikon, another brings the bread, and so on. As host, you can provide a more substantial topping, like Braised Pulled Pork, 495, seasoned with Vietnamese Caramel Sauce, 578. The fillings and toppings can be arranged buffet-style so everyone can build their own sandwich.

Another approach is to choose dishes that are intended to be prepared ahead, but cooked and eaten communally. Most require a hotplate, electric skillet, or fondue pot (and for everyone to be within arm's reach). These include appetizers like Cheese Fondue, 57, and Bagna Cauda, 58; main course meals like Spicy Sichuan Hot Pot, 97, and Sukiyaki, 462; or desserts like Chocolate Fondue, 833.

VEGETARIAN RECIPES

This is by no means a comprehensive list of the vegetarian recipes in this book. There are hundreds, and hundreds more can easily be made vegetarian with simple substitutions or omissions. We intentionally did not list most of the recipes in the Vegetables chapter here, as there are simply too many. Some of the recipes in this list also happen to be vegan.

APPETIZERS

White Bean Dip with Rosemary and Garlic, 52
Tangy Black Bean Dip, 53
Dolmas, 63 (see headnote for vegetarian version)
Muhammara, 53
Fried Halloumi with Honey and Walnuts, 56
Patatas or Papas Bravas, 59

STOCKS AND SOUPS

Parmesan Broth, 81
Pappa al Pomodoro, 91
Spicy Chickpea Soup, 87
Gazpacho, 107
One-Eyed Bouillabaisse, 88 (omit the bacon)

Kimchi Jjigae, 87 (vegetarian variation in headnote)
Hungarian Mushroom Soup, 88

MAIN COURSES

Savory Cabbage Strudel, 703
Roasted Mushroom Lasagne, 310
Root Vegetable Braise, 203
Vegetable Tian, 205
Millet Cakes with Parmesan and Sun-Dried Tomatoes, 326, served over mixed greens
Roasted Vegetable Lasagne, 311
Tagliatelle with Wilted Greens, 299
Tomato and Goat Cheese Quiche, 163
Vegetable Tagine, 205
Leek Tart, 163
Barley "Risotto" with Mushrooms, 320 (use vegetable broth instead of chicken broth)
Three Sisters Tamales, 325 (use shortening instead of lard in the masa mixture)
Freekeh with Greens, Chickpeas, and Halloumi, 338
Pasta Primavera, 297
Pasta alla Norma, 297
Baghali Ghatogh, 212
Broccoli Cakes, 221
Stuffed Cabbage Rolls II, 227
Tandoori Cauliflower, 230
Eggplant Parmigiana, 238
Rolled Stuffed Eggplant, 238
Palak Paneer, 245
Glamorgan Sausages, 248
Mushroom Ragout, 251
Stuffed Bell Peppers, 262
Chiles Rellenos, 263
Baked Stuffed Zucchini, 274
Squash Blossoms Stuffed with Cheese and Herbs, 277
Meatless Dinner Loaf, 288
Pecan and Cheddar "Sausage" Patties, 289
Banh Mi, 139 (made with Baked Marinated Tofu, 287)
Tempeh Reuben, 141 (see headnote)
Tortas, 143 (see headnote variation)
Roasted Mushroom Burgers, 145
Sabich, 145
Tostadas, 147
Any taco or burrito, 146–47 made with a vegetarian filling

SALADS

Taco Salad, 123 (using tempeh crumbles)
Asparagus Sesame Salad, 125
Avocado and Citrus Salad, 125
Shaved Carrot Salad, 126
Arugula and Heart of Palm Salad, 126
Chickpea and Roasted Cauliflower Salad, 130
Rachel's Kale and Lentil Salad, 130
Wheat Salad with Pesto and Zucchini, 131
Quinoa Salad with Broccoli and Feta, 132

OTHER

Any vegetarian sandwich idea in Cold Sandwich Combinations, 136, or Hot Sandwich Combinations, 139

VEGAN RECIPES

This is not an exhaustive list of every vegan recipe in the book. Many more can be found in the Vegetables chapter, 199, and some of the recipes in the vegetarian list above are vegan.

APPETIZERS

Crudités, 45, with Tahini Dressing, 576
Thai-Spiced Peanuts, 46
Kale Chips, 48
Spanish-Style Marinated Olives, 48
Guacamole, 51
Olive Oil Flatbread Crackers, 49
Texas Caviar, 52
Baba Ghanoush, 53

STOCKS AND SOUPS

Vegetable Stock, 78
Mushroom Stock, 79
Vegetable Soup, 85
Soupe au Pistou, 86
Spicy Chickpea Soup, 87
Mediterranean White Bean Soup, 89
Black Bean Soup, 89
Pappa al Pomodoro, 91

MAIN COURSES

Green Posole, 323 (see headnote variation)
Megan's Vegan Chili, 89
Mujadara, 330
Jamaican Rice and Peas, 331
Spaghetti Aglio e Olio, 296
One-Pan Pasta with Tomatoes and Herbs, 298 (omit the Parmesan)
Pasta e Fagioli, 299 (omit the Romano)
Sesame Noodles, 302
Shoyu Ramen, 304 (using mushroom stock)
Japchae, 304
Vegan "Egg" Salad, 124
Basic Vegetable Stir-Fry, 202
Vegetable Breakfast Hash, 202
Ratatouille Provençale, 204
Vegetable Tagine, 205
Falafel, 214
Chana Masala, 217
Dal, 218
Jeweled Quinoa, 328 (omit the feta)
Roasted Cauliflower Wedges, 229, served with Romesco Sauce, 570
Aloo Gobi, 230
Gobi Manchurian, 231
Spinach Pakoras, 245

Pumpkin Curry, 276 (omit the fish sauce and add salt to taste)
Sweet Potato Stew with Peanuts, 279
Mapo Dofu, 286
Tofu Scramble, 286
Crispy Pan-Fried Tofu, 286
Baked Marinated Tofu, 287
Sambal Goreng Tempeh, 287
Caramelized Tamarind Tempeh, 288
Kung Pao Seitan, 289
Beet Burgers, 144

SALADS

Becker House Salad, 116
Megan's Kale Salad, 117
Sesame Greens with Roasted Shiitakes, 118 (use vegetarian oyster sauce)
Becker Coleslaw, 119 (using vinaigrette)
Spicy Chinese-Style Slaw, 119
Avocado and Mango Salad, 125
Beet, Fennel, and Citrus Salad with Horseradish, 125
Dee's Corn and Tomato Salad, 126
Cucumber Salad I, 126
Panzanella, 128
Shaved Fennel and White Bean Salad, 129
Brown Rice Salad with Dates and Oranges, 131

OTHER

Megan's Seeded Olive Oil Granola, 327
Muesli, 327
Vegan Eggnog, 310
Mushroom Bacon, 252
Korean Green Onion Pancake, 257
Seasoned Tempeh Crumbles, 287
Seitan, 288
Soy Milk, 1019
Tofu, 285
Megan's Avocado Club Sandwich, 137
Mushroom Gravy, 547
Vegan White Sauce or Béchamel, 548

DESSERTS

Vegan Chocolate Cake, 735
Vegan Orange Cake, 736
Vegan Chocolate Frosting, 793
Making Vegan Molded Desserts, 820
Tembleque, 817
Coconut Sticky Rice with Mango, 828
Molasses Ice Cream, 843
Dairy-Free Vanilla Ice Cream, 843
Any sorbet, 847–48
Roasted Banana–Coconut Pops, 85

COOK FOR A DAY, EAT FOR A WEEK

Use these recipe suggestions to meal prep for the week ahead. See Streamlined Cooking, xxxviii, for more meal planning and kitchen efficiency tips.

BREAKFAST

Baked Oatmeal, 327
Sunrise Muffins, 633
Slow-Poached Eggs, 153
Baked Eggs, 154
Frittata, 159
Basic Strata, 164
Megan's Seeded Olive Oil Granola, 327
Four-Grain Flapjacks, 641

SOUPS

Garbure, 87
Sauerkraut Soup, 86
Black Bean Soup, 89
Asopao de Pollo, 93
Sopa de Lima, 94
Chicken Gumbo, 95
Pot-au-Feu, 96
Borscht with Meat, 98

MEAT AND FISH DISHES

Any dish from About Braising, Stewing, and Barbecuing Beef, 463
Any dish from About Braising, Stewing, and Barbecuing Pork, 494
Any chili recipe, 502–3
Spiced Ground Meat for Tacos, 503
Picadillo, 503
Meatloaf, 506
Any dish from About Poaching, Stewing, and Braising Chicken, 419
Roast Chicken, 407
Roasted Chicken Parts, 409
Italian Meatballs, 507
Bolognese Sauce, 558
Baked or Slow-Roasted Fish, 378
Poached Fish, 381
Butter- or Olive Oil–Poached Fish, 283

BAKED DISHES

Any enchiladas, 539–40
Baked Manicotti or Shells, 309
Any lasagne, 310–11
Any quiche, 162–63
Any strata, 164–65

SAUCES

Tomato Sauce, 556
Amatriciana Sauce, 557
Puttanesca Sauce, 557
Meaty Tomato Sauce, 557
Any vinaigrette or salad dressing, 575–78
Any flavored butter, 559–60
Corn and Tomato Relish, 568
Tomato-Olive Relish, 568
Jen's Basil Oil, 570

Romesco Sauce, 570
Peanut Dipping Sauce, 571

BREADS

Any yeast bread, 599–608
Any quick bread, 626–28
Corn Bread, Corn Muffins, or Corn Sticks, 630
Any muffin, 632–34
Quick Cream Biscuits or Shortcakes, 636

SALADS

Sesame Greens with Roasted Shiitakes, 118
Spicy Chinese-Style Slaw, 119
Larb, 122
Thai Beef Salad, 122
Chinese Chicken Salad, 122
Taco Salad, 123
Chicken or Turkey Salad, 123
Asparagus Sesame Salad, 125
Beet, Fennel, and Citrus Salad with Horseradish, 125
Carottes Râpées, 125
Dee's Corn and Tomato Salad, 126
Cucumber Salad I, 126
Jicama Salad, 127
Basic Bean Salad, 129
Shaved Fennel and White Bean Salad, 129
Edamame and Carrot Salad, 130
Rice Salad with Chicken and Olives, 130
Brown Rice Salad with Dates and Oranges, 131
Quinoa Salad with Broccoli and Feta, 132
Basic Pasta Salad, 132

QUICK RECIPES

When time is of the essence, these recipes will get food on the table in short order. For additional ideas, see Streamlined Cooking, xxxviii.

BREAKFAST

Shakshouka, 154
Breakfast Chilaquiles, 156
Tex-Mex Migas, 157
Frittata, 159
Kuku Sabzi, 159
Baked Eggs, 154
Overnight Steel-Cut Oats, 328

FISH

Tuna or Salmon Poke, 377
High-Heat Roasted Fish, 379
Fish en Papillote, 379
Oven-Fried Fish Fillets, 380
Poached Fish, 381
Chinese Steamed Fish, 382
Fish Curry, 383
Microwaved Fish Fillets, 383
Spice-Rubbed Grilled or Broiled Fish, 385
Pan-Fried Salmon Cakes, 389

GRAINS

Becker Rustic Polenta, 322
Saffron Millet, 326
Fried Rice, 332
Kimchi Fried Rice, 332
Coconut Rice, 333
Pressure-Cooker Risotto, 336

MEAT

Sautéed Steak, 461
Beef and Broccoli Stir-Fry, 462
Becker Mongolian Beef, 462
Becker Pork Hash, 491
Sautéed Pork Chops, 493
Spiced Ground Meat for Tacos, 503
Becker Burgers, 505
Becker Lamb Patties, 505
Keftedes, 62

PASTA

Spaghetti Carbonara, 295
Macaroni and Cheese I, 296
One-Pan Pasta with Tomatoes and Herbs, 298
Fettuccine with Salmon and Asparagus, 298
Pasta e Fagioli, 299
Orecchiette with Sausage and Broccoli Rabe, 299
Sesame Noodles, 302
Japchae, 304

POULTRY

Roast Cornish Hens, 409
Mediterranean Chicken Breast Packets, 410
Broiled Cornish Hens, 412
Pan-Fried or Sautéed Chicken II, 414
Pan-Fried Chicken Cutlets, 414
Chicken Piccata, 415
Shoyu Chicken, 419
Thai-Style Yellow Chicken Curry, 421
Turkey or Chicken Burgers, 430

SALADS

Greek Salad, 117
Megan's Kale Salad, 117
Wilted Spinach Salad, 118
Bistro Salad, 118
Chef's Salad, 120
Cobb Salad, 120
The Mallory's Shrimp Salad, 121
Larb, 122
Thai Beef Salad, 122
Chinese Chicken Salad, 122
Taco Salad, 123
Chicken or Turkey Salad, 123
Asparagus Sesame Salad, 125
Carottes Râpées, 125
Chinese Smacked Cucumber Salad, 126

Shirazi or Israeli Salad, 128
Basic Bean Salad, 129
Shaved Fennel and White Bean Salad, 129
Quinoa Salad with Broccoli and Feta, 132
Basic Pasta Salad, 132

SHELLFISH
Mixed Shellfish in Tomato Sauce, 347
Shellfish with Mushrooms and Greens, 348
Steamed Mussels, 351
Steamed Clams, 352
Stir-Fried Clams or Mussels with Oyster Sauce, 354
Thai Clam Pot, 354
Seared Sea Scallops, 356
Quick Skillet Shrimp, 363
Blackened Shrimp, 363
Becker Barbecued Shrimp, 363
Camarones a la Diabla, 364
Camarones al Mojo de Ajo, 365
Shrimp Scampi, 365
Grilled or Broiled Shrimp or Scallops, 365
Thai Shrimp Curry, 366

SOUPS
Egg Drop Soup, 84
Stracciatella, 84
Miso Soup, 84
Spicy Chickpea Soup, 87
Hungarian Mushroom Soup, 88
Black Bean Soup, 89 (see headnote)
Sopa de Ajo, 91
Pappa al Pomodoro, 91
Tom Kha Gai, 94
Salmon Chowder, 104
Pumpkin or Butternut Squash Soup, 105
Tomato Soup, 105
Broccoli-Cheddar Soup, 106
Mushroom-Scallion Soup, 106
Carrot-Ginger Soup, 106
Cold Avocado Soup, 107

VEGETABLES
Basic Vegetable Stir-Fry, 202
Root Vegetable Braise, 203
Vegetable Tagine, 205
Stir-Fried Asparagus, 208
Asparagus with Orange and Hazelnuts, 209
Baghali Ghatogh, 212
Ful Medames, 214
Broccoli Cakes, 221
Stir-Fried Bok Choy with Mushrooms, 224
Sauerkraut Fritters, 225
Okonomiyaki, 226
Creamy Mashed Cauliflower, 230
Aloo Gobi, 230
Utica Greens, 234
Spinach with Pine Nuts and Raisins, 244
Mushroom Ragout, 251
Pea and Ricotta Toasts, 259
Pumpkin Curry, 276

BAKED GOODS AND SWEETS
Quick Cream Biscuits or Shortcakes, 636
Quick Drop Biscuits, 636
Any quick bread, 626–28
Quick Coffee Cake, 629
Quick French Bread, 604
Quick or One-Bowl Cakes, 734–39
Quick Chocolate Fudge, 863
Quick PB&J Thumbprints, 785
Almond Macaroons I, 744
Any cornstarch pudding, 816–17

AUTHOR FAVORITES

APPETIZERS
Thai-Spiced Peanuts, 46
Olive Oil Flatbread Crackers, 49
Brown Butter–Hazelnut Crackers, 50
Muhammara, 53
Fromage Fort, 55
Fried Halloumi with Honey and Walnuts, 56
Thai-Style Chicken Wings, 61
Five-Spice Ribs, 61
Keftedes, 62
Pickled Shrimp, 65
Gougères, 70
Quick Cheese Crackers, 70

BEVERAGES
Cold-Brewed Coffee, 5
Cold-Brewed Tea, 8
Thai Iced Tea, 8
Champurrado, 10
Kai, 10
Kale-Ginger Lemonade, 12
Vietnamese Avocado Shake, 13
Agua Fresca, 14
Switchel, 15

COCKTAILS
Chan Chan, 20
Negroni, 21
Horseradish-infused vodka, 22
Hot Toddy, 24
Jungle Bird, 25
Spanish Coffee, 26
Paloma, 27
Fish House Punch, 29
Chatham Artillery Punch, 29
Becker Deluxe Eggnog, 30

Wassail, 32
Aperol Spritz, 42
Michelada, 42

SOUPS AND STOCKS

Pressure Cooker Stock, 79
Parmesan Broth, 81
Mushroom Stock, 79
Vegetable Bouillon Paste, 80
Sauerkraut Soup, 86
Kimchi Jjigae, 87
Spicy Chickpea Soup, 87
Megan's Vegan Chili, 89
Sopa de Ajo, 91
Treva's Chicken and Dumplings, 93
Asopao de Pollo, 93
Spicy Sichuan Hot Pot, 97
Borscht with Meat, 98
Caldo Verde, 98
Roasted Cauliflower Soup, 105
Cold Avocado Soup, 107
Cold Cucumber and Yogurt Soup, 108

SALADS

Becker House Salad, 116
Megan's Kale Salad, 117
Sesame Greens with Roasted Shiitakes, 118
Spicy Chinese-Style Slaw, 119
Brussels Sprout Slaw with Spiced Yogurt, 120
Salade Niçoise, 121
Larb, 122
Carottes Râpées, 125
Panzanella, 128
Green Papaya Salad, 129
Shaved Fennel and White Bean Salad, 129
Rachel's Kale and Lentil Salad, 130

MAIN DISHES

Veracruz-Style Snapper, 380
Chinese Steamed Fish, 382
Black Cod Misozuke, 387
Pla Raad Prik, 391
Guyanese Pepperpot, 468
Kalbi, 459
Beef Braciole, 470
Braised Lamb Shanks with Chickpeas, 482
Grilled Vietnamese-Style Pork, 493
Pork Adovada, 496
Chashu Pork, 496
Cincinnati Chili Cockaigne, 502
Adana-Style Lamb Kebabs, 504
Roast Chicken I, 407
Pan-Fried Chicken Cutlets III, 415
Shoyu Chicken, 419
Chicken Makhini Masala, 423
Chicken Chili Verde, 425
Fesenjoon, 433
Steamed Mussels, 351
Thai Clam Pot, 354
Becker Barbecued Shrimp, 364
Kimchi Fried Rice, 332

VEGETARIAN MAIN DISHES

Millet Cakes with Parmesan and Sun-Dried Tomatoes, 326
Pasta alla Norma, 297
Jamaican Rice and Peas, 331
Pasta e Fagioli, 299
Chana Masala, 217
Caramelized Tamarind Tempeh, 288
Roasted Mushroom Burgers, 145
Mapo Dofu, 286

SIDE DISHES

Saffron Millet, 326
Jeweled Quinoa, 328
Mujadara, 330
Coconut Rice, 333
Indian Lemon Rice, 333
Garlic-Braised Artichokes, 206
Sichuan-Style Dry-Fried Beans, 211
Frijoles de la Olla, 213
Ful Medames, 214
Megan's Beets with Goat Cheese, 219
Roasted Broccoli, 221
Sautéed Cabbage II, 224
Cabbage Gratin, 225
Sauerkraut Fritters, 225
Roasted Cauliflower with Green Olives and Lemon, 229
Miso-Glazed Eggplant, 238
Utica Greens, 234
Roasted Mushrooms, 252
Sautéed Shredded Collard Greens, 245
Spinach Pakoras, 245
Champignones al Ajillo, 251
Korean Green Onion Pancake, 257
Charred Shishito or Padrón Peppers, 262
Crispy Smashed Potatoes, 268

BREADS

Cracked-Wheat Bread, 601
Buttermilk Potato Bread, 602
Ciabatta, 604
Fougasse, 606
Molasses Bread, 607
Lefse, 611
English Muffins, 621
Banana Bread Cockaigne, 626
Lemon Brown Butter Loaf, 627
Megan's Southern Corn Bread, 631
Megan's Cheddar-Scallion Biscuits, 636

DESSERTS

Mimosa Pound Cake, 727
Coconut Milk Cake Cockaigne, 724

STREAMLINED COOKING

When Irma first wrote and published the *Joy of Cooking* in 1931, she was not known for her skills in the kitchen. Irma was a socialite, not a domestic goddess. She valued being the life of the party, not being stuck in the kitchen. After the stock market crash of 1929 and her husband's death in 1930, Irma found herself in reduced circumstances and with a sudden need to figure out a livelihood. When she chose cookbook author as profession, there were more than a few raised eyebrows.

But Irma had something her competitors did not: perspective. At the time, most popular cookbooks were written by experts, either veterans of home economics (at the time, one of the few careers women were encouraged to pursue) or women who simply excelled at domesticity. Irma was different. Cooking was not her passion, and so she related to the millions of women who were forced, by circumstance, to cook every day but who perhaps did not revel in it. Irma met her readers where they were. She never condescended to them. Their constraints—time, money, aptitude—were her own.

Nowhere is Irma's concern for these limitations more strongly felt than in "Brunch, Lunch, and Supper Dishes"—a chapter she included in early editions that was dedicated to casual, quick dishes and using leftovers. With apologies to Irma and longtime fans, we feel modern readers are better served by a discussion of what sustainable home cooking actually looks like. Here, we outline several strategies and habits that will help you maximize your time in the kitchen—and hopefully keep you out of it so often, if that's your preference.

A note on the chapter title: We decided to name this primer after Irma's small, little-known cookbook *Streamlined Cooking*, published in 1939. Though Irma's focus in *Streamlined* was how to take advantage of canned goods, frozen vegetables, and other convenience products—a sort of early precursor to the "quasi-homemade" strategies popularized by several food personalities—the name and the concept are closely aligned with our own here. Whereas slyly incorporating frozen and canned foods were the principle "hacks" covered in Irma's book, this chapter focuses on how to economize your efforts and utilize *all* of what you purchase. In this new context, "streamlined" is a word that captures the link between 30-minute recipes, slow-cooking, pressure-cooking, meal prep, repurposing leftovers, preventing food waste, and, in the end, saving time and money.

TWO APPROACHES

Irma wrote in the 1951 edition: "Any experimental cook can produce a good meal when her financial means and her sources of supply are unlimited, but it is an art to make delicious dishes with meager means." There are two common approaches to home cooking embedded in this statement. The first—where we create ideal conditions by procuring everything we need for a recipe and blocking off a sufficient amount of time to prepare it—is how most of us start off: We find a recipe, buy the ingredients it calls for, follow the recipe verbatim, and repeat this process over and over, making everything from scratch or nearly so.

While this approach is a fantastic way to learn technique and requires little creativity, it is an oppressive way to cook day in and day out. Even "quick" recipes are by their very nature specific and inflexible to what you may or may not have; grocery trips take time, and a list of ingredients for several recipes can get quickly out of control. If the recipe is scaled to the number you are serving and no more, you will be forced to go back to the store and start over again rather quickly. We are exaggerating a little bit for effect, but many readers are probably familiar with what this kind of cooking feels like—and the fatigue it causes.

The second approach—making dishes out of "meager means"—sounds sort of cheap, or otherwise impoverished. On the contrary, the artistry to which Irma refers is a seasoned cook's ability to economize *effort*—either by cooking more food than you need for one meal, utilizing what you have in the pantry, or repurposing foods that you have already cooked. The latter, in particular, can result in surprisingly intricate dishes and amazing results.

Put another way, the second approach is not of someone cooking *a* recipe, but of a cook who has internalized the practice. This cook knows how to budget their time wisely, how to use leftovers creatively, what to do with the aged produce in the crisper before it goes bad, and how to make sure the fruits of their labor are not wasted. They still try new things, but they tailor most of their day-to-day cooking to fit into their lifestyle and means, rather than the other way around.

BUDGETING TIME

While we suppose there are some home cooks out there who have unlimited time to make dinner, that is simply not the case for most people. While we wish it were otherwise, cooking is often crammed between other pressing tasks like work or taking the kids to swimming lessons or getting to an appointment on time. These time constraints make it impractical to always start from scratch. If at 5 p.m. every day you are in a position of having to decide what to make for dinner, make a shopping list, go to the store, and come home and cook the food, you will probably not like cooking very much. It will be a source of stress in your life and you will come to dread it.

It does not have to be this way! As tempting as it is to fly by the seat of your pants, it is probably the least efficient way to cook. We admit to finding discussions of **meal planning** quite boring, but planning is critical if you are short on time. On a relatively quiet weekend afternoon, or any day when you have an hour or so to spare, sit down with your calendar and a blank piece of paper. On the paper, make a list of ingredients you already have, prioritizing those that have the shortest shelf life. Also think about the contents of your pantry and freezer. Then note which evenings are busier and which are less so. On hectic days, you don't want to commit to making something complicated or time-consuming for dinner. On the other hand, a slow night can be a good opportunity to spend a little extra time cooking, with the idea that you can use leftovers from that night on an evening where time is short.

Keeping that list of ingredients you already have first and foremost in mind, sketch out a rough plan for the week's meals. You can start by filling in the easy stuff. Say, you always get takeout on Friday nights. Go ahead and fill in that gap. Maybe you always have soup and sandwiches on Wednesday; add that to the list. Perhaps you have salad greens in the fridge that need to be used. Make salad part of Monday night's dinner, or make the salad into a meal by choosing a protein and some toppings that will bulk it up. Planning a week of family dinners can be as simple or complex as you like. Just getting something on paper can make the prospect of having to prepare a week's worth of meals less intimidating.

Pull in a significant other to help you with this task. If you have kids, ask them what they would like to have for dinner (and how they might help) that week. Getting the whole household involved in the planning stages can make the task go more quickly, and everyone will feel a little more invested in dinner time.

Once you have a basic plan, think about what you need to pick up at the store for the week. Try to get everything you need in one run (with, of course, the exception of highly perishable items like fresh fish and poultry). Tacking a trip to the grocery store onto a long day at work can be demoralizing. Try to avoid that if at all possible. Half the battle when it comes to cooking is keeping morale high.

Maybe you have one day a week that you can devote to getting ready for the rest of the week. This is where **meal prep** comes in. If you have the time, it makes sense to do a bunch of cooking at once, then enjoy the results for the rest of the week. Meal prep has become popular not only because it is a way to manage time wisely, but also because it encourages healthier eating and helps save money. When you have a stockpile of ready-made food, ordering out or relying on convenience foods (both of which tend to be less healthy and more expensive than home-cooked food) becomes less appealing.

When we meal prep, we stick to foods that keep well over an extended period of time. We often take the "cook for a day, eat for a week" approach, cooking one or two dishes—say a roast pork shoulder or a big pot of beans—that take time on the weekend and then, after its first appearance as a meal, convert the leftovers into soups, sandwiches or burritos, casseroles, and pasta dishes throughout the week; see Cook for a Day, Eat for a Week, xli, for more on this. Or we might cook a big batch of some kind of grain, half a dozen hard-boiled eggs, a braise or stew, a couple sheet pans of roasted vegetables, and a big jar of homemade salad dressing. (If we're feeling ambitious, we might also make a dozen breakfast burritos and a pan of muffins to freeze for busy mornings.) Throughout the week we intersperse meals largely made from our weekend efforts with recipes that take less than 30 minutes from start to finish (see the list of quick recipes in the Entertaining and Menus chapter, xxiii), as well as with meals from the slow cooker, 1058, and, in the summer months, grilling.

Keep recipes simple when building a repertoire of family favorites, but try out a new dish every few weeks. Invite children into the kitchen to help with age-appropriate tasks so they can share in the experience of cooking—such as tearing lettuce, cutting soft fruit, or peeling hard-boiled eggs. When possible, cleanup duties should be shared among the family as well. This can mean each family member taking their plate to the kitchen and either washing it or placing it in the dishwasher, or family members may rotate cleaning responsibilities. Cooking can be a thankless, time-consuming job, and we like to honor the efforts of the cook by providing them relief after dinner.

While meal planning and meal prep can seem like busywork, in the end, they help free up more of your time and prevent cooking from feeling like a constant struggle. The effort of a little planning and prep work is offset, we believe, by the rewards of cooking regularly: eating what you want, knowing the ingredients in everything, saving money, and learning a skill.

MISE EN PLACE

The French term *mise en place* (meeze ahn plahce) simply means "putting in place." Much like a woodworker or an artist might organize their tools before beginning a project, a cook can benefit from laying out everything they need before beginning a recipe. (For more on this concept, see Prep Methods, 1044.)

For the beginning home cook, mise en place is an especially good strategy: The act of assembling and preparing the ingredients for a dish forces you to thoroughly read through a recipe. Then, since everything is prepped, the cooking itself can proceed smoothly, as you will not be scrambling to find ingredients or tools. All of this allows you to observe and learn from the actual cooking process and how different ingredients respond to heat. You can watch as onions turn translucent then start to brown in hot oil. You can observe the progression from a bare simmer to a brisk simmer to a rolling boil. Much of learning how to cook is really learning how to observe. It is difficult to observe much of anything if you are running from one end of the kitchen to the other.

That said, we also believe that mise en place has limitations. It can take a lot of time to do a proper mise en place, and that's time added to how long it actually takes to cook the dish. The more ingredients in the recipe, the longer mise en place takes. For the more experienced cook, it makes more sense to do a "partial" mise en place. To do this, prepare the ingredients and equipment you need to get started, then prep the remaining ingredients while the recipe is already underway. For instance, if a recipe starts by having you sauté onions, you might decide that the only mise en place you need to do is to chop the onions. Then, once the onions are cooking, you can use that time to prepare the ingredients you'll need next. This kind of multitasking is much more efficient since there is no downtime.

That said, even experienced cooks benefit from mise en place in some cases. In baking, for instance, having all the ingredients measured out and ready to be mixed makes the process much smoother. For most candy making, doing mise en place is absolutely essential to ensure that sugar syrups don't overcook while you are off trying to assemble the next ingredients you will need. Mise en place is also critical for very quick cooking methods like stir-frying, in which the total cooking time is so short that there is no time to prepare ingredients while the food is cooking.

As you gain experience in cooking, you will learn when mise en place is essential and when it is not. For the beginner, however, we recommend always doing mise en place. It is the cook's insurance against chaos.

SPEEDY COOKING

One way to save time when you cook is to choose recipes that are simple and cook quickly. Entire categories of dishes are quick by default. For example, most **egg dishes** cook quickly. We think of them as breakfast food, but there's nothing stopping you from preparing them for dinner. Similarly, many **pasta dishes** are quick and very satisfying. **Fish and shellfish** cook incredibly quickly, as do **slender boneless cuts** like chicken thighs and steaks or **pounded cutlets** of pork and chicken breasts. Many **vegetables** cook quickly, including asparagus, green beans, peas, greens, and mushrooms. Think of these foods when you are in a rush. They can all be prepared very simply, or dress them up by serving them with a simple sauce or condiment. (For relatively simple sauces that take little time to prepare, see About Table Sauces, Dipping Sauces, and Condiments, 565.)

For a list of specific recipes in this book that are quick to prepare, see Quick Recipes, xxxiv. As you cook more and get faster at prep work, recipes that might not have seemed quick at first may become weeknight staples. You are also likely to discover shortcuts and substitutions of your own that enable you to simplify more complex recipes into weeknight-friendly fare.

Another approach to fast cooking is to choose speedy methods or techniques. Stir-frying, 1052, is a classic example. In a stir-fry, the ingredients are all cut very small, then cooked over extremely high heat. Though stir-fries require more advance prep work, once the ingredients are ready, the cooking takes very little time. Other examples include sautéing and pan-frying, 1052, microwave cooking, 1060, and pressure-cooking, 1059.

Pressure-cooking deserves special attention here, thanks to the widespread adoption of countertop electric models (the most popular of them made by the brand Instant Pot). While we only provide a handful of recipes written specifically for pressure-cooking, there are dozens of recipes in this book that can be cooked in a pressure cooker, particularly meat stews and braises. See Pressure-Cooking, 1059, for a guide to adapting recipes for the pressure cooker. Any stew or braise makes a good candidate for pressure-cooking. In fact, the pressure cooker is a great tool for implementing one of the strategies we discussed in meal planning, above: namely, spending a little time on the weekend turning ingredients that ordinarily take a long time to cook into a good basis for or addition to a quick dinner. For instance, dried beans, long-cooking grains, dense vegetables like parsnips and artichokes, and homemade stocks will take a long time to make if you start from scratch, but if you cook them ahead of time in the pressure cooker, they can easily be part of a quick recipe. For pressure-cooking times for vegetables, see individual entries in the Vegetables chapter, 199. For pressure-cooking times for long-cooking grains, see the Grains Cooking Chart, 340; also see Pressure-Cooker Risotto, 336, and About Cooking Grains, 318, for other strategies for preparing long-cooking grains efficiently.

While slow-cooking and sous vide cooking may seem out of place in a discussion of "fast" cooking methods, we think of these techniques as integral to getting dinner on the table in an efficient way. **Slow cookers** (or a covered Dutch oven set in an oven at a low temperature) can cook stews and braises while you are at work, allowing you to come home to a fully cooked meal. Slow cookers also have the advantage of running in the background while you are doing other things. For example, you can cook a pork shoulder in the slow cooker on a Sunday while you are doing laundry, cleaning the house, or running errands. At the end of the day, not only is dinner practically ready with almost no effort, you will have leftovers that can be eaten the rest of the week or frozen for a future occasion. Almost any recipe for braises or stews can be tweaked for use in a slow cooker. To adapt standard recipes for the slow cooker, see 1058.

Sous vide cooking, 1054, which uses an appliance called an immersion circulator, operates on a similar principle of being a "set it and forget it" way to cook. The main difference between sous vide cooking and slow-cooking is that sous vide is used to cook foods to a precise level of doneness. Also, instead of cooking things like stews and braises, sous vide works for whole food items like chicken breasts, steaks, or whole or cut-up vegetables. Use the technique to help prepare a week's worth of lunches by cooking boneless chicken breasts, then slicing them for salads, pasta dishes, lettuce wraps, sandwiches, and so on. The same goes for vegetables like carrots and asparagus. For recommended cooking temperatures, see Low-Temperature and Sous Vide Cooking, 1054.

WORKING WITH PREPARED INGREDIENTS

As much as we wish we always had time to start from scratch, we often use prepared ingredients to help speed the cooking process.

Even though homemade food usually tastes better than store-bought, sometimes making a small tradeoff in flavor for a big payoff in convenience is worth it.

Of course, there are the trusted pantry ingredients that have become so common to our cooking that we don't even think of them as prepared ingredients anymore: canned beans of all kinds, canned tomatoes, canned tuna and salmon (and sardines!), and cartons of chicken or vegetable stock. Dozens of meals can be made with the help of these ingredients. Any of our bean soups, 89, made with dried beans can be tweaked to use canned beans, which dramatically shortens the cooking time. Canned tomatoes—whole, diced, or pureed—are essential for making quick pasta sauces like Tomato Sauce, 556, and Marinara Sauce, 556.

Canned tuna can be tossed with Spaghetti Aglio e Olio, 296, and steamed broccoli or Wilted Tender Greens, 243, for a quick, filling dinner. Use canned salmon to make Pan-Fried Salmon Cakes, 389, or substitute it for smoked or fresh salmon in Fettuccine with Salmon and Asparagus, 298. Canned sardines are fantastic in Pasta con le Sarde, 297.

Other prepared proteins like rotisserie chicken can be eaten as is, but they are also convenient for recipes that call for already cooked chicken, such as Chicken or Turkey Salad, 123, Pasta Salad with Chicken or Shrimp, 132, or Chicken Enchiladas, 539. Toss shredded rotisserie chicken with tomato sauce, stuff the mixture into cooked large pasta shells, and bake topped with cheese. Use the chicken to make a quick version of Becker Chicken Soup, 92, by simmering the vegetables in the chicken stock until tender, then stirring in the shredded chicken right before serving. Or just make any of the green salads, 112–14, and top with lightly dressed chicken to make it a meal.

Stock your freezer with frozen vegetables and fruits for those days when going to the supermarket for fresh produce just isn't an option. Most frozen fruits and vegetables are quite high in quality (especially when compared to out-of-season produce) and do an admirable job in stir-fries, fried rice, soups, pasta dishes, and casseroles. See Buying Vegetables, 199, for more information on frozen vegetables. Frozen fruits, while not quite as versatile as their vegetable counterparts, are great to have on hand for smoothies, baked goods, pies, cobblers, and crisps.

One thing to keep in mind when buying convenience foods like sauces and soups is that they often contain a lot of salt or sugar (or both) to make up for their "flat" flavor. While no single food is unhealthy on its own, and we think convenience foods can be part of a well-rounded diet, it is worth seeking out prepared foods that make an effort to reduce added sugars and excessive amounts of salt. Remember that you can and should doctor up prepared foods by adding acidity, complexity from spices and aromatics, and salt if needed. When buying prepared chicken stock, opt for low-sodium versions to avoid oversalting the dishes they are added to.

COOK FOR A DAY, EAT FOR A WEEK

"Leftovers" is a dirty word for some people, signifying cold, flabby meat, dried out rice, and forlorn vegetables. We actually prefer the term the French use—*les restes*, or "the rest"—as it seems less judgmental and not as evocative of warmed-over food. No matter what you call them, leftovers are the backbone of our weekly cooking strategy.

We think of leftovers not as the result of simply cooking too much food, but as a way of maximizing your efforts in the kitchen. No matter what anyone says, cooking takes a lot of time and effort. To cook something, you have to plan, make a shopping list, go to the grocery store, prepare and cook the food, then clean up afterward. If you're going to cook, we think it's a good idea to use the time wisely.

The best leftover dishes are soups, stews, and braises, which are essentially one-pot meals that can be accompanied by little more than a salad and bread. They tend to be flavorful, filling, and frugal as well and make just as much sense for a household of one as for a household of five. Not only do these types of dishes often taste better after a day or two, but they also retain their quality when frozen.

Below are several examples of how to repurpose, not just reheat, leftovers. Note that, depending on the size of your household, you may want to double the recipes to ensure you have enough for future meals.

MENU 1

Braised Pulled Pork, 495, or Braised Carnitas, 495
Frijoles de la Olla, 213
Cooked long-grain white rice, 343
Warmed corn tortillas, sliced avocado, salsa, and Cotija or queso fresco (or your favorite cheese for eating with tacos)

Leftovers option 1: For lunch, make a rice bowl topped with the pork, beans, and any leftover taco fixings. You could use all the leftovers this way and have lunch for the rest of the week, or save some leftovers for other uses.

Leftovers option 2: Crisp up the pork in a skillet and serve in Banh Mi, 139, with a side of shrimp chips.

Leftovers option 3: Use leftover rice and some of the pork to make Fried Rice, 332. For breakfast, top it with a Fried Egg, 155, or for dinner, serve it with a vegetable side like Steamed Broccoli, 220, or Basic Vegetable Stir-Fry, 202.

Leftovers option 4: Use leftover beans and pork in a modified Tortilla Soup, 92 (add them to the soup along with the stock or broth and beer).

Leftovers option 5: Use any leftover stale corn tortillas to make Tex-Mex Migas, 157.

MENU 2

Roast Chicken, 407
A medley of root vegetables cooked as for Roasted Carrots, 228
Saffron Millet, 326
A flavorful table sauce such as Salsa Verde, 567, or Chimichurri, 567

After dinner, pull all the meat from the bones, put the bones in a bag, and freeze them to start a stock bag, 73. Add any trimmings from nonstarchy root vegetables as well.

Leftovers option 1: Make hash with the leftover roasted vegetables (see Vegetable Breakfast Hash, 202, for inspiration) and top with Fried Eggs, 155, or mix them into a Frittata, 159.

Leftovers option 2: Dice some of the leftover chicken for chicken salad, 123.

Leftovers option 3: Add shredded chicken to Spicy Chickpea Soup, 87, and stir a spoonful of the leftover millet into each bowl.

Leftovers option 4: Prepare Thai-Style Green Chicken Curry, 421, using leftover chicken instead of the boneless thighs and stirring it in at the end of cooking to heat through.

MENU 3

Baked or Slow-Roasted Fish, 378, using salmon
Megan's Kale Salad, 117
Roasted Cauliflower with Green Olives and Lemon, 229
Yogurt-Dill Sauce, 569

Leftovers option 1: Use leftover salmon to make a half batch of Pan-Fried Salmon Cakes, 389, substituting the leftover cooked salmon for the canned salmon. Serve with leftover yogurt-dill sauce and leftover kale salad. If you make the salmon cakes a bit larger and flatter, they can be served like burgers on buns with the yogurt-dill sauce as a condiment and topped with the kale salad.

Leftovers option 2: Make Salade Niçoise, 121, using leftover salmon instead of tuna.

Leftovers option 3: Toss leftover salmon and roasted cauliflower with pasta, grated Parmesan, and enough pasta water to lightly coat the pasta and bring everything together.

Leftovers option 4: Eat cold leftover salmon on crisp flatbreads or crackers drizzled with leftover yogurt-dill sauce.

Leftovers option 5: Chop up the roasted cauliflower (along with any olives and lemon slices) and mix it with drained and rinsed canned chickpeas, lemon juice, olive oil, chopped parsley, and grated Parmesan for a hearty bean salad.

MENU 4

Crispy Pan-Fried Tofu, 286
Cucumber Salad I, 126, or Chinese Smacked Cucumber Salad, 126
Coconut Rice, 333

Leftovers option 1: Add cubed leftover tofu to Basic Vegetable Stir-Fry, 202.

Leftovers option 2: Toss the tofu and any leftover cucumber salad with Sesame Noodles, 302.

Leftovers option 3: Use leftover coconut rice to make Caribbean-inspired burritos. Stuff flour tortillas with the rice, black beans, cubes of roasted sweet potato, diced leftover tofu, and Fruit Salsa, 574, made with mango.

Leftovers option 4: Make lettuce wraps with any combination of leftover tofu, cucumber salad, and rice. If desired, serve with Ssamjang, 571, or Dipping Sauce for Dumplings, 572.

MENU 5

1 pound dried chickpeas, cooked until tender, 212, then used to prepare Chana Masala, 217
Rice Pilaf, 329
Sautéed Cabbage II, 224
Cilantro-Mint Chutney, 568

Leftovers option 1: Bake sweet potatoes, 279, cut them open, and pile them high with leftover chana masala.

Leftovers option 2: Use leftover chana masala in phyllo samosas (use the recipe for Quick Phyllo Samosas with Potatoes and Peas, 68, as a guide) and serve with leftover chutney.

Leftovers option 3: Use leftover cooked chickpeas to make Hummus, 52, Basic Bean Salad, 129, Spicy Chickpea Soup, 87, or Roasted Chickpeas, 47, for topping a green salad.

Leftovers option 4: Use leftover cabbage to make Okonomiyaki, 226 (to make it vegan, substitute vegetable broth for the dashi and omit the shrimp).

Leftovers option 5: Put any leftover rice in a saucepan, add vegetable broth, and simmer as for Congee, 333, until the rice forms a porridge. Serve topped with cubes of browned tofu, green onion, soy sauce, and sesame oil.

SAVING MONEY

Knowing how to cook creatively can help you stretch your budget. Cooking creatively means not being wedded to specific recipes or dishes on a given day, but rather allowing the prices at the supermarket to dictate what you make. For the beginning cook, it can be challenging to cook off-the-cuff, but the only remedy for that is to cook more often. Learning to cook is truly a journey, so embrace your own uncertainty and be excited about all the things you are going to learn.

We've already talked about the importance of versatility to streamlined cooking (see the menus above). This applies not only to the dishes you prepare but also to the ingredients you buy. Opt, for example, to buy plain yogurt instead of flavored, and buy it in tubs rather than individual portions. You can top the yogurt with fruit or jam for breakfast, use it in baked goods, and use it to make flavorful sauces like Tzatziki, 569, Raita, 569, and Yogurt-Dill Sauce, 569. It can also stand in for sour cream atop chili or borscht. Peanut butter is another good example. Spread it on toast, blend it into smoothies, eat it with apples or carrots as a snack, use it to make hearty stews like Sweet Potato Stew with Peanuts, 279, and use it in cookies, 771.

Buying some foods, usually produce, can be cheaper if you shop in season. Another benefit to buying produce in season is that it often tastes better. In particular, look for cheaper apples and pears in the fall, zucchini and tomatoes in the summer, and citrus fruits in winter. If you have a farmers' market near you, it might also be a good idea to strike up a conversation with some of the farmers to see if they sell leftover produce at a discount at the end of the market day. Some farmers may offer lightly bruised produce at a discount, and you can often get good deals on bulk fruits and vegetables at peak season, when supply outpaces demand.

Buying foods from bulk bins rather than in packages can be part of a budget-friendly approach to cooking. Most large supermarkets have bulk bins, and they can be a good place to find affordable staple foods like grains, seeds, beans, and flours. Some supermarkets have bulk spices as well, which can be a great way to save money, since jars of spices can be extremely expensive. It's also a good way to try out spices you've never had before without spending a lot of money on them.

Speaking of spices, you will get the best deals at Mexican, Indian, and pan-Asian supermarkets. This is where we buy almost all of our spices and dried chiles. These stores often carry both whole and ground spices. If you can afford it, buy a small, cheap coffee grinder and use it to grind whole spices at home, as whole spices are cheaper than ground and they stay fresher for much longer. Having a dedicated spice grinder will also allow you to make your own spice blends.

If you are on a tight budget, make the bulk of your food purchases on things like dried beans and lentils, grains, vegetables and fruits (fresh and frozen), eggs, chicken, tofu, peanut butter, plain yogurt, canned fish, and nuts and seeds. Remember that meat isn't the only good source of protein and that beans, eggs, yogurt (especially Greek yogurt), peanut butter, nuts and seeds, and grains such as quinoa can be used to supplement meat.

If meat is non-negotiable for you, choose more affordable proteins like whole chickens (chicken parts cost more per pound, and buying a whole chicken gives you plenty of bones for making stock), and tougher cuts of meat like pork shoulder or beef chuck or round (see About Braising, Stewing, and Barbecuing Beef, 463, and About Braising, Stewing, and Barbecuing Pork, 494, for recipes featuring these kinds of cuts). When it comes to seafood, just keep your eyes peeled for the best bargains. Usually, fish like tilapia, trout, catfish, flounder, red mullet, and mackerel are cheaper options. Of course, the best thing to do is head to the seafood counter and find something that aligns with your budget.

Another habit that helps save a bit of money is to start keeping a stock bag, 73. We have been doing this for years now and have completely stopped buying prepared stock. While the stock you make with a stock bag may not be as rich as that made by following a recipe for stock, we find the results are always better than store-bought (and it adds nothing to your grocery expenses). Having good stock on hand will make your food taste better, which will encourage you to cook more often, which will, in turn, save you even more money.

Unless you are on an absolutely inflexible shoestring budget, we recommend "splurging" on a few items from time to time. These are things that will make your food taste better, which, we think, will improve your quality of life. We like to spend a little extra money on things like extra-virgin olive oil, Parmesan, maple syrup, and fresh herbs. Of course, what you decide to splurge on will depend on what you like to cook. If you like to bake, you might deem the better flavor of high-quality cocoa powder well worth the expense. If you love to cook Japanese food, you will probably want to seek out premium soy sauce; if you find yourself cooking Sichuan dishes a lot, consider purchasing a high-quality chile bean paste, 970. Think about where your cooking values lie and proceed from there.

PREVENTING WASTE AND USING "SCRAPS"

Much has been made in recent years of food waste. An astonishing amount of food is wasted, and while most of that waste occurs before food is purchased by the consumer, there is something to be said for preventing food waste in your kitchen. It's part of any approach to smart cooking, whether or not you are on a tight budget.

The first step in preventing waste is keeping a keen eye on what you already have in your fridge, freezer, and pantry. You might even go so far as to stick a magnetic dry erase board on the side of the fridge to keep track of things you need to use before they go bad. If you have a stand-alone freezer, be especially vigilant. It can be easy to stuff something in the freezer and forget about it until it has lost quality or is so freezer burnt that it has to be thrown away.

Every so often we like to challenge ourselves to use up all the perishable ingredients in our refrigerator before we go grocery shopping. It's a little like being a competitor in your own private cooking show, but without the risk of being thrown out of the house. Even if you only have a carrot, half a bag of frozen peas, an egg, and a container of leftover rice, you can still make a perfectly good batch of fried rice.

But beyond using what you have, how do you maximize the food you buy and prevent waste? Below are common "scraps" and ideas for using them.

Green tops: Fresh beet and radish tops can be sautéed or added to soups; carrot tops can be made into pesto, 586, or used in Salsa Verde, 567; fennel tops can be used as a bed for grilling or roasting fish or in Pasta con le Sarde, 297, chop the fronds and add to salad, or add some to a stock bag, 73.

Vegetable scraps: Trimmings from carrots, onions, celery, mushrooms, parsnips, celery root, and tomatoes can all be compiled in a stock bag, 73.

Bones: Chicken, pork, and beef bones can be mixed together in a stock bag, 73; bones from nonoily fish can also be saved, but start a separate stock bag especially for fish stock.

Stale bread: Turn into crumbs, 957, or Croutons, 638, or use in Panzanella, 128, Pappa al Pomodoro, 91, Sopa de Ajo, 91, Ribollita, 91, Bread Pudding, 829, or strata, 164–65.

Parmesan rinds: Save in a bag in the freezer and use as a flavor booster for soups like Minestrone, 85, or to make Parmesan Broth, 81.

Corn cobs: Simmer in water to make a stock to use for Corn Chowder, 88, or Fresh Corn Risotto, 336.

Egg yolks: Use in Lemon Curd, 802, ice cream bases, 840–45, Pastry Cream, 801, and custards, 813–16.

Egg whites: Use for meringue, 793, Meringue Kisses, 775, Macarons, 782, Angel Food Cake, 719, or in cocktails like the Clover Club, 21, and the Whiskey Sour, 23.

Shrimp, lobster, crab, and crawfish shells: Use to make Shrimp or Shellfish Stock, 78, or Shrimp or Lobster Butter, 560.

Fruit pulp from jelly making: Add lemon juice and sugar to taste, spread in a very thin layer on a silicone baking mat, and bake at your oven's lowest temperature until dried into fruit leather.

Pickle brine: Use to marinate chicken that will be fried (see About Frying Chicken, 417); bring the leftover brine to a boil, pour over hard-cooked eggs, and let the eggs marinate, refrigerated, for a couple days; use for "picklebacks," which are shots of pickle brine served as chasers with whiskey or beer; add to salad dressings or bean dips for tang; use the brine in place of the lemon juice and salt in Mayonnaise, 563.

Beet stems: Chop and add to jars of pickles to add a bright pink color.

Cilantro stems: Chop and add to salsas, 573–74; use in Green Curry Paste, 585; blend with the tomatillos for Green Posole, 323.

Leftover cooked rice: Use in Beet Burgers, 144, Fried Rice, 332, or Congee, 333; add at the last minute to soups; season well, bind with egg and flour, and pan-fry to make rice cakes; simmer with milk, sugar, and spices to make an ad hoc rice pudding, 828.

Fresh herbs: Use them to stuff a whole chicken for roasting; use in Tabbouleh, 131, Kuku Sabzi, 159, Zhug, 567, Cilantro-Mint Chutney, 568, Salsa Verde, 567, or Chimichurri, 567; mince them and add olive oil, salt, and pepper for a dipping sauce for bread.

Leftover wine: Use for deglazing and to make a pan sauce, 545; use for Poached Fruit, 170; add sugar to taste and freeze as for granita, 849; use in Chicken Breasts Baked on a Bed of Mushrooms, 409, Chicken with 40 Cloves of Garlic, 420, Beef Stew, 465, or Hearty Beef Ragu, 466.

BEVERAGES

We drink first out of necessity, but this is only one of the reasons we seek refreshment. Throughout our history, we have concocted a seemingly endless variety of drinks to reinvigorate, calm, or simply savor. Offering a guest a drink is one of our most basic forms of hospitality, and countless elaborate social rituals have sprung from this simple kindness.

Aside from fresh water and milk, coffee and tea are the most popular beverages in the world. Hot or cold, strong or mild, sweetened or plain, what has made them valued for so long—more than a thousand years—is caffeine, nature's own stimulant. Six hundred years ago, all of our major, natural sources of caffeine—tea, coffee, cola, chocolate, and yerba mate—had been discovered. We have been enthusiastically consuming them ever since, creating increasingly specialized equipment to enhance their enjoyment and efficacy.

Other, less rousing brews are made from pressing or blending fruits and vegetables or infusing water with leaves, roots, bark, blossoms, and seeds. Fruit juices make some of the most refreshing beverages of all, along with carbonated, flavored waters and grain or nut-based beverages, such as Horchata, 14. Some blended beverages, like smoothies, may offer enough sustenance to replace an entire meal, and milk shakes, the smoothie's indulgent and irresponsible sibling, are a perfect stand-in for dessert.

The recipes in this chapter are nonalcoholic; see Cocktails, Wine, and Beer, 17, for serving these convivial refreshments.

ABOUT COFFEE

Coffee beans are the seeds of a flowering, evergreen shrub that bears red, cherry-like fruit. When the fruit is picked, the flesh is removed to reveal pale-green seeds; they do not acquire their familiar brown color and aroma until they are roasted. Nearly all commercial coffee beans belong to one of two species, **arabica** or **robusta.** Arabica beans produce the finest flavor; robusta beans contain considerably more caffeine, but they are also quite bitter, which often leads to them being roasted in a darker style. Higher-quality arabica varieties are valued for the peculiar and often unique flavors of the crop itself, as well as any idiosyncratic methods used to process it. Lighter to medium roasts preserve these flavors, which vary from citrus and blueberry to wine and flowers. Some beans are left in their fruit and laid out to dry and ferment in the sun, which lends them an earthy piquancy; another infamous (and expensive) type is collected after being fed to and excreted by civet cats. In general, most of these subtleties become lost the longer you roast the bean.

The darkest roasts are often called espresso, Italian, or French roasts; as they are roasted longer and at higher temperatures, they taste charred and bittersweet. Darker roasts also have less caffeine and less acidity than lighter roasts, so the pervasive idea that stronger-tasting coffee will make you jittery or give you more energy is largely false. Many roasters have moved to labeling their coffee with its country of origin rather than by a roast level or blend name. In some cases, a batch of specialty coffee is roasted with beans acquired from only one growing region, even one farm, estate, or plantation. These are often referred to as **single-origin coffees,** but the term is unregulated and can refer to beans sourced from a wide area.

In addition to origin and roast, coffees are often labeled with an array of certifications and jargon. As with other products, there are **organic coffees,** derived from crops that have not been sprayed with synthetic fertilizers or pesticides. **Shade-grown coffee** crops are grown under a canopy of trees, which significantly reduces a plantation's ecological impact by allowing the local flora and fauna to coexist with coffee farming. **Fair trade** is a certification standard that means farmers who grew the beans are paid a higher, "fair" price, which, in theory, promotes economic development. **Direct trade** signifies that the coffee roaster sources their beans directly from individual farmers rather than a middleman or cooperative, but this term is unregulated.

For **decaffeinated coffee,** we recommend those processed without the use of chemical solvents; caffeine can be leached out with pressurized carbon dioxide or water-based methods, such as the Swiss Water Process. It may also be helpful to remember that the caffeine content of coffees can vary: Robusta beans have almost twice the caffeine of arabica beans on average. Our other favorite source of caffeine, tea, has less caffeine than arabica coffee, depending on the strength of the brew and type of tea.

Flavored coffees are extremely popular, but those commonly available tend to rely on flavoring essences that leave much to be desired. In the kitchen, you have an array of natural flavorings for your coffee. Add 1 tablespoon ground chicory or cacao nibs to every 4 tablespoons ground coffee before brewing. Stir spices into the grounds—such as a cracked cinnamon stick or star anise, crushed cardamom pods, or a few whole cloves.

Instant coffee is brewed coffee that has been freeze- or spray-dried. Thanks to advances in extraction, drying, and packaging, instant coffee has made great strides in quality, and is now sold in a variety of strengths. Consult the package for how much hot water to add. We take the time to grind our own beans and brew fresh coffee daily, and recommend you do the same if time allows. However, ➤ do not underestimate the value of instant coffee when backpacking or hiking, as the weight and bulk of coffee and brewing equipment can be burdensome.

BREWING COFFEE

There are several ways of preparing coffee, and guidance for most of them follows. Whatever device you choose, ➤ follow the manufacturer's directions carefully, especially as to the grind recommended. We prefer grinding coffee beans, 3, the same morning they are brewed. To assure a full-bodied brew, ➤ use about 2 level tablespoons (⅜ ounce or 12 grams) of ground coffee for each ¾ cup (6 ounces) of water.

➤ Water heated to 200° to 205°F is ideal for extracting flavor from coffee without drawing out acids. Note that at sea level, water boils at 212°F, so if using a method that requires you to add hot water manually, let the water sit off the boil for 30 seconds or so before adding it to the ground coffee (for those who boil water for their coffee every day, temperature-controlled kettles are a luxury worth considering). If possible, use cold water that is freshly drawn from the tap—soft, not softened, and not hard, 1032. If your tap water is of questionable quality, use filtered water.

For drip brewing and some other methods, you will have the opportunity to choose what type of filter to use. ➤ The filter material will affect the flavor and consistency of your coffee: Paper filters absorb some of the flavorful oils extracted from the coffee beans and produce a cleaner-tasting cup; metal filters allow these oils to pass through, yielding a richer, lingering brew. One is not necessarily better than the other; we have enjoyed the results of both.

The most common method for brewing coffee in this country is the so-called **drip method,** where ground coffee is scooped into a filter and placed above a cup or coffee pot. Hot water is poured over the grounds and collects in a cup or pot below. Nearly all **electric coffeemakers** employ this simple principle, as do **"pour over" coffee brewers, Chemex pots,** and **Neapolitan "flip pots."** The coffee is ground just fine enough to slow down the water for a sufficient brewing time. The main difference between these brewers is that electric coffeemakers are automatic, dispensing heated water at a steady rate, whereas the coffee grounds in a Chemex or pour-over brewer must be kept saturated with hot water from a kettle throughout the brewing time. Pour-over brewers are made from metal, ceramic, or plastic and must be set on a carafe or cup to collect the coffee, while Chemex brewers are a one-piece glass carafe, with a cone-shaped top that holds a filter and coffee grounds.

Other devices, like **Vietnamese-style coffee filters,** also called phin filters, employ very finely ground coffee (and a correspondingly fine filter). This combination increases the brewing time and strength of the resulting coffee—which is comparable to espresso. **Percolators** extend the brewing time in another way: Water is brought to a boil and forced up a tube, which distributes it over coffee grounds. After dripping through the grounds, the coffee rejoins the rest of the boiling water and gets forced up through the tube again (and again) in a continuous brewing cycle. Given time, percolators are very thorough at extracting flavors from coffee—including bitter compounds that other methods do not. For this reason, percolators have fallen out of favor.

Perhaps the second most common brewing method is **steeping,** which involves grinding coffee to a coarser consistency and letting it sit in water for a prescribed amount of time before being filtered out. The simplest, most primitive example of this method is known as **camp, river, or cowboy coffee:** Water is heated, grounds are stirred in, and at the end of the brewing time the grounds are coerced to settle to the bottom—either by adding a splash of cold water or crushed eggshells. The coffee is then promptly poured into cups to keep it from overextracting. This procedure is rustic to say the least, and can result in a "chewy" cup if the grounds remain at the top of the pot. A much more civilized result can be achieved with a **French**

press, where the brewed grounds are forced to the bottom of the pot by a plunger fitted with a metal filter. We highly recommend French presses for their convenience and their ability to produce a richly flavored cup. **Vacuum brewers** or **siphons** also belong to this category, despite their chemistry-set appearance. They long required the use of the stovetop or a lab-style Bunsen burner, and their fragile bases were prone to breakage. Today's freestanding electric models make vacuum brewing far easier than it once was, and advocates praise the tea-like result produced by this method.

Another steeping method that has recently gained popularity is **cold brewing,** which involves mixing cold water into coffee grounds and leaving them for a long time before filtering them out. The result is a concentrate that can be diluted with water. The biggest advantage of cold brewing—aside from not having to heat water—is the smooth-flavored result: Cold water does not extract as many of the bitter and acidic compounds from coffee beans as hot water does.

Much quicker results can be achieved by using pressurized water to brew coffee. Pressure aids extraction, and is used in conjunction with a finer grind of coffee. Perhaps the most ubiquitous and affordable steam-pressure device made for home use is the **moka pot.** The bottom chamber of a moka pot is filled with water, a metal filter basket filled with finely ground coffee is placed over the chamber, and the top reservoir is screwed on. The water is brought to a boil on the stovetop. When the bottom chamber is pressurized by the buildup of steam, hot water passes through the puck of coffee grounds above and collects in the top chamber. The result is a strong, espresso-like cup of coffee. **Steam-based espresso machines** are very similar, except their pressurized tanks hold more water and they provide their own heat source. They release steam from the top of their tank through a milk steaming wand and hot water from the bottom of the tank through a detachable filter, called a portafilter, which is filled with finely ground coffee. In general, they are considered inferior to the bulkier and more expensive **pump espresso machines**, which are better at regulating the pressure of the liquid being forced through the grounds (and do not require their water tanks to be refilled and brought up to pressure after two or three drinks). Some of these are driven by a hand-operated piston and lever, which is fun to operate and adds an extra level of control to the brewing process.

Several new types of pump-based devices have appeared on the market in recent years. **Pod-based coffeemakers** are countertop appliances that heat a serving's worth of water and pump it through a sealed pod filled with preground coffee. Though they are convenient, mess-free, and produce decent, consistent results, the pods are very costly—at least four times as expensive as bulk coffee beans by weight—and generate an unacceptable amount of packaging waste. You can avoid some of these drawbacks by using refillable pods, but the convenience of the device is lost. On the other hand, there are several new, inexpensive, hand-powered pump options for making espresso-like coffee, best exemplified by the **Aeropress** coffeemaker. Here, a filter is fitted to the bottom of a cylinder, fine coffee grounds are added, hot water is stirred in, and a plunger is quickly fitted to the top of the cylinder and pressed downward, expelling an espresso-like beverage into the cup below. This is our preferred method for brewing one or two cups of coffee at a time, as it is quick, tastes great, and affords the easiest cleanup. When serving four people or more, we prefer to use a large French press, Chemex pot, or electric drip coffeemaker.

Pour-over brewer, French press, vacuum brewer

Coffee beans contain oil. This oil can accumulate on brewers and grinders, along with other residues, leading to off flavors and rancidity. Electric drip coffeemakers should be cleaned every few months. Run a combination of 1 part vinegar to 4 parts water through the machine, or use a cleaning powder especially for this purpose. Run several cycles of fresh water through the machine to rinse it after cleaning. French presses, moka pots, pour-over drippers, and other manual brewers should be washed well with dish soap and rinsed thoroughly after each use. ➤ Do not use abrasive cleaners. Espresso machines are often cleaned with a descaling solution (consult the manufacturer's directions). Be sure to empty coffee grounds out of the portafilter promptly and occasionally brush any stray grounds out of the gasket area above.

Vietnamese coffee brewer, moka pot, Aeropress

GRINDING AND STORING COFFEE BEANS

In general, ➤ the shorter the brewing time, the finer the grind must be. Espresso, which brews in less than 30 seconds, requires a fine grind, resembling superfine sugar. French press coffee requires a coarse grind, resembling coarsely ground cornmeal. Drip coffee, which falls between the two, requires a medium grind, resembling granulated sugar. You can grind your coffee using the grinder at the market, or you may choose instead to grind your coffee at home. Propeller-like **blade grinders** are the most popular. They are inexpensive and easy to use, but they produce an array of particle sizes, which can lead to sediment in French press coffee and mixed results. **Burr mill grinders** have two notched grinding plates whose positions can be set to change the fineness of the grind. They are noisier and slower than blade grinders, but you can grind larger amounts at a time and obtain consistent results. Old-fashioned hand-cranked grinders are burr mills.

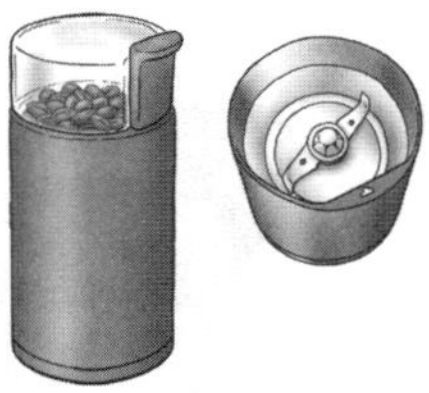

Blade grinder

Burr mill grinder

For blade grinders, you can increase the consistency of the grind by pulsing small quantities of coffee at a time. ➤ To clean blade grinders, grind 2 to 3 tablespoons of uncooked rice in them and repeat. Wipe out the grinder and lid with a dry paper towel. To clean burr-mill grinders, you will need to partially disassemble the grinder and remove the burrs (see the manufacturer's directions).

➤ The best way to store coffee is unground, in a closed, opaque container kept at room temperature. Do not store coffee in the freezer—it can pick up flavors from the surrounding foods.

DRIP COFFEE

This is the basic method for pour-over brewers, Chemex pots, and the like. If you have an electric drip coffeemaker, follow the manufacturer's directions, using the water-to-coffee proportions listed here.

Place in a drip filter:

About 2 tablespoons (3/8 ounce or 12 grams) medium- to fine-grind coffee for every 3/4 cup (6 ounces) water

Bring the water to a boil, then remove it from the heat and wait about 30 seconds for the water to cool to 200° to 205°F. Slowly pour just enough water over the ground coffee to moisten it thoroughly. Wait another 30 seconds or so, allowing the coffee to "bloom," and gradually pour in the water, making sure all of the grounds stay saturated throughout brewing. When the drip process is complete, serve coffee at once or keep warm in a thermal carafe.

STEEPED COFFEE

This method is for steeping in a French press or a camp coffeepot or kettle. If using a French press, prime it with hot water before brewing and wrap in a kitchen towel while it steeps to keep it warm.

Place in a French press or have ready:

About 2 tablespoons (3/8 ounce or 12 grams) coarse-grind coffee for every 3/4 cup (6 ounces) water

Bring the water to a boil, then remove it from the heat and wait about 30 seconds for the water to cool to 200° to 205°F. Pour the water over the coffee in the French press, or add the coffee to the camp coffeepot or kettle, and stir well. Cover and let steep for 5 minutes.

For a French press, slowly push the plunger all the way down after the brewing time has elapsed, forcing the coffee grounds to the bottom of the pot.

For camp, cowboy, or river coffee, open the kettle after the brewing time is up and add a splash of cold water to encourage the grounds to settle to the bottom. To be doubly sure that you are not serving excessive amounts of coffee grounds to yourself and your camping companions, pour the coffee through a metal strainer before doling it out.

VACUUM-METHOD COFFEE

Boiling water in the lower bowl of the vacuum coffeemaker is forced into the upper chamber, where it mixes with the coffee and then filters back into the lower bowl. If using an electric vacuum coffeemaker, follow the manufacturer's directions, using the water-to-coffee proportions listed here. Allow for every serving:

About 2 tablespoons (3/8 ounce or 12 grams) medium- to fine-grind coffee for every 3/4 cup (6 ounces) water

Measure water into the lower bowl. Place on the heat. Add the ground coffee to the upper bowl. (If your equipment has a vented stem—a small hole in the side of the tube above the hot water line—you can place the upper bowl on the coffeemaker and place the whole thing on the heat; if it does not have a vented stem, wait until the water is actively boiling before putting the upper bowl in place.) Insert the upper bowl into the lower one with a light twist to ensure a tight seal. When nearly all the water has risen into the upper bowl (some of it will always remain below), stir the water and coffee thoroughly. In 1 to 3 minutes (the finer the grind, the shorter the time), remove from the heat and allow the coffee to run back into the lower bowl.

PERCOLATED COFFEE

This is the method for stovetop percolators; if you have an electric machine, follow the manufacturer's directions, using the water-to-coffee proportions listed here. This method will extract bitter notes from the coffee if it is left on. Turn off or remove from the heat promptly after the brewing time has elapsed.

Fill the bottom of the percolator with water. Place in the percolator's basket:

About 2 tablespoons (3/8 ounce or 12 grams) medium-grind coffee for every 3/4 cup (6 ounces) water

Place the percolator over medium heat and bring the water to a boil. Allow the coffee to percolate slowly, 6 to 8 minutes. Remove from the heat and serve.

COFFEE IN QUANTITY

For large percolators, follow the manufacturer's directions. For large coffee urns, measure out:

3 cups coarse-grind coffee (about 10 ounces) for every 1 gallon water

Put the ground coffee in a jelly bag, nut milk bag, or cotton pillowcase large enough to allow for double expansion and securely tie it off. Bring the water to a low boil and take it off the heat. When the water has cooled to 200° to 205°F, pour into the coffee urn. Place the coffee-filled bag in it. Let stand, covered, for 5 minutes. Agitate the bag several times during this period. Remove the bag, cover the urn, and serve at once.

COLD-BREW COFFEE

About 14 servings

This overnight method for making coffee results in a highly concentrated but extremely smooth brew. You can buy all kinds of filters and gadgets to make cold brew, but all you really need is a jar, a lined sieve, and patience. We prefer to line the sieve with a thin cotton kitchen towel, but any thin, finely woven natural fabric will work (the cheesecloth sold at supermarkets is too gauzy to filter out coffee grounds).

Place in a 2-quart container:

2 cups coarse-grind coffee (about 7 ounces)

Stir in:

4 cups room-temperature water

Make sure all the coffee grounds are thoroughly wet. Cover and let stand at room temperature for at least 12 hours, but no more than 24. Strain the coffee through a sieve lined with a piece of clean, thin kitchen towel or other natural fabric. Transfer to a quart-sized jar and store in the refrigerator for up to 2 weeks. To serve, dilute to taste with hot water, or dilute with cold water and serve on ice. For an 8-ounce cup of hot coffee, we use 2 ounces cold-brew concentrate and 6 ounces hot water. For an iced 12-ounce beverage, we use 2 ounces cold-brew concentrate, 4 ounces cold water, and ice cubes to fill the glass.

ICED COFFEE

I. This quick method requires no special equipment. Prepare brewed coffee any way you wish, 4–5, using for each serving:

About 4 tablespoons coffee (3/4 ounce or 24 grams) for every 3/4 cup (6 ounces) water

Pour this double-strength coffee directly over ice in a metal pitcher or small pot and stir it for 15 seconds. Strain the cooled coffee into tall glasses filled with more ice.

You may sweeten it with:

(Sugar or Simple Syrup, 16, to taste)

If desired, stir in:

(Milk or cream to taste)

II. For each serving, pour over ice in a tall glass:

2 ounces espresso, below, or Cold-Brew Coffee, above

Top up the glass with:

4 ounces or more cold water

If desired, add sweetener and cream as in **I, above.**

BREWING ESPRESSO

This Italian specialty is famous for its strength. A properly brewed cup of espresso measures only 1½ to 2 ounces, but uses roughly the same amount of ground beans as a regular cup of coffee. In addition to its concentration, espresso is valued for its characteristic, full-bodied flavor; no matter how concentrated a cup of coffee you brew by steeping or dripping methods, it will lack pressurized espresso's distinctive richness, as well as the foamy layer of emulsified oils (called *crema*) that forms on the top.

There are several ways to make espresso at home. The moka pot, 3, yields coffee that is roughly halfway between drip coffee and true espresso in body and flavor. An Aeropress or other hand-powered pump-type brewer can be used as well, 3.

For those committed to making espresso regularly, steam-based and pump espresso machines, 3, are appliances to consider. Many of them are capable of producing enough pressure to achieve the syrupy consistency and pleasantly bittersweet flavor found in espresso from your favorite local coffee shop. Follow the manufacturer's directions for the particular machine, but in general it's a good idea to preheat the metal filter and its holder by running hot water through them and into the espresso cup. This also primes the pump. Be sure to use a sufficiently fine grind of coffee—preground coffee labeled "espresso" is a good choice if you do not have a burr grinder. Serve espresso after dinner, in demitasse cups or espresso glasses, and offer sugar alongside —we prefer deeply flavored, unrefined sugar such as demerara, 1025. Give the brew a tasty alcoholic kick with a dash of sambuca or Tia Maria. To turn a small cup of espresso into a delightful, regular-sized cup of coffee, dilute it with hot water to taste (you may then call it an **Americano**).

ESPRESSO DRINKS

Caffè macchiato is espresso "marked" with just a tablespoon or two of steamed milk foam. **Cappuccino,** named for the brown robes of Capuchin monks, whose color it is thought to resemble, is the glory of the Italian coffee bar. It is made of espresso, steamed milk, and foam in equal proportions. "Wet" and "dry" cappuccinos vary these proportions with slightly more milk or foam, respectively. **Caffè latte** is 1 part espresso diluted with 2 parts or more steamed milk and a little foam on top. Add a tablespoon or so of Cocoa Syrup, 9, and you have a **mocha** (replace the foam with Whipped Cream, 791, if desired).

To steam and foam milk for these drinks, first consult the manufacturer's directions for your espresso machine. Fill your steaming pitcher no more than two-thirds full; clip on an instant-read thermometer so that it will register the temperature of the milk. With the steam wand pointed in a safe direction, briefly turn it on to blow out any excess water. Completely submerge the nozzle in the milk, and turn it on again. To make foam, keep the nozzle of your steam wand close to the surface so that air starts to get incorporated in the vortex created by the steam. Aim for a small hiss rather than large slurps of air to keep the foam dense and silky. When the milk hits 100°F, raise the pitcher so that the wand is completely submerged and continue steaming until the milk reaches 140° to 160°F. ➤ Do not steam milk over 180°F; it will start to scorch and eventually bubble over. You can get rid of larger bubbles in your foam by gingerly tapping the bottom of the steaming pitcher on a countertop.

To make foam without the use of a steam wand, you may use a handheld milk frother or a French press. Pour milk that has been heated to 160°F into a clean French press and work the filter up and down near the surface of the milk. Do so gradually, as the hot milk will froth quickly and may start spitting out of the top if you are overzealous.

Finally, brew espresso into warmed serving cups, pour the milk in according to the type of drink you want, and spoon the foam over the top.

TURKISH OR MIDDLE EASTERN COFFEE

This simple method is thought to have originated in the coffeehouses of Cairo in the fifteenth century, but is now popular throughout the Mediterranean. Presweetened very finely ground coffee is lightly boiled several times in a long-handled brass or copper vessel called a *cezve* in Turkish and *ibrik* or *briki* in Greek. The average content of the pot is 10 ounces of liquid, and it should never be filled to more than two-thirds capacity. The coffee is not filtered, but the grounds stay in the bottom of the pot; some sediment always finds its way into each cup, where it sinks to the bottom and remains. This is sometimes dumped onto the saucer with one smart rap after the coffee is consumed and then used to tell fortunes.

To brew Turkish coffee, start with specially ground coffee—ground almost to a powder—available, along with the pots, at Greek or Middle Eastern markets. You can use regular coffee and grind it at home, but this can be tricky, as even grinders with a "Turkish" setting often don't grind the coffee fine enough. If you do not have an *ibrik*, you may use any small pot that is easily removed from the heat (again, do not fill more than two-thirds full).

For each serving, place in the pot:

½ cup water
2 teaspoons very finely ground coffee
Sugar to taste
(Pinch of ground cardamom)

Bring to a frothing simmer over medium heat. Just as the coffee puffs and is about to boil over, remove the pot from the stove and pour a bit of the foam into warmed cups. Return the pot to the heat for two or three brief boilings, removing it quickly each time as it is about to boil over. Divide the brewed coffee among the cups, distributing the remaining foam equally.

ABOUT COFFEE DRINKS

Coffee by itself or with nothing more than sugar and cream is probably the closest thing we have to a national beverage. The French **café au lait**—made with equal parts strong coffee and hot milk—is also popular in New Orleans, where the coffee is often brewed with chicory. Add sugar to taste. Coffee can be blended with alcohol and other flavorings to produce a variety of deliciously assertive and warming, or cooling, drinks. For coffee-chocolate combinations, see Brazilian Chocolate, 10, and Kai, 10.

VIETNAMESE COFFEE

1 serving

This is delicious hot or iced. If you do not have a Vietnamese coffee filter, or phin, 2, make **Café Bombón,** a similar drink popular in Spain, by pouring the condensed milk into a small tumbler and adding **2 ounces brewed espresso,** 5, on top. You can also make this in quantity with a French press. Prepare a small cup of strong coffee per person and pour over the condensed milk in individual cups.

Add to a glass tumbler:

2 tablespoons sweetened condensed milk

Place a Vietnamese coffee filter over the tumbler and add to the filter:

2 tablespoons fine-grind dark-roast coffee or coffee with chicory

Pour over the grounds to moisten:

2 tablespoons hot water

Place the top filter over them and press or screw down lightly. Fill the filter with hot, not boiling water (200° to 205°F) and cover with the metal lid. Allow the coffee to drip into the glass. This should take 3 to 5 minutes (if it is faster than 3 minutes, either the coffee is too coarse or the filter is not pressed tight enough; if it is slower than 5 minutes, either the coffee is too fine or the filter is pressed too tight). Serve hot with a small spoon for stirring the dark and white layers together. To serve cold, stir the condensed milk into the coffee and pour into a glass filled with ice.

CUBAN COFFEE

4 small but potent servings

Cuban coffee is very dark, very strong, and sweet. Its most notable feature is the layer of foam on top, which is created by frothing sugar with some of the brewed coffee. This is traditionally made with Cuban, preground coffee brewed with a moka pot, but feel free to make the espresso in any of the ways mentioned in Brewing Espresso, 5.

Prepare:

1 cup brewed espresso

Meanwhile, add to a small measuring cup or heatproof pitcher with a pouring spout:

3 tablespoons sugar

Add a teaspoon or so of the brewed coffee to the sugar in the pitcher. Stir the sugar vigorously with a spoon until it is very frothy and appears to foam. Pour in the remaining coffee and stir gently until the sugar is completely dissolved. Pour into cups. There should be a layer of dark brown foam, or *espuma*, on the top of each cup.

FROZEN COFFEE

2 servings

Place in a blender:

¼ cup double-strength coffee as for Iced Coffee, 5, cold-brew concentrate, or brewed espresso, 5
1 cup whole milk
2 tablespoons sugar or sweetened condensed milk
(2 ounces rum)

Add:

10 ice cubes

Blend thoroughly. Serve in chilled glasses.

ABOUT TEA

The tea plant, an evergreen shrub originally from southern China and northern India, is cultivated in a dozen or so countries in Asia and Africa. Considering how many very different kinds of tea there are in the world—white, green, oolong, Assam, black, gunpowder, jasmine, Earl Grey, and many more—it's astonishing to discover that they all come from just one type of plant. The processing, grading, and blending of these leaves creates considerable differences in the finished product, as do the additions of blossoms and flavorings. For teas brewed from other plants, see About Herbal Teas, 7.

There are five principal methods of processing tea leaves, resulting in white tea, green tea, black tea, oolong tea, and pu-erh tea. All start in more or less the same way. Tea leaves are brittle when fresh and must be "withered" to make them supple enough to handle. They are then rolled, twisted, and lightly broken, usually by machine. The essential oils that give tea its flavor come to the surface at this point. Tea picked and harvested before the leaves are fully open is called **white tea.** If development is stopped by "firing," or heating, the leaves, the tea is called **green,** even though its color varies widely. All Japanese tea and most Chinese tea is green.

Tea leaves turn **black** if their flavor-giving oils are exposed for a long period to air—usually very humid air—and allowed to oxidize. Oxidation darkens the color of the leaves and allows them to develop new flavor compounds—among them the astringent ones called polyphenols but commonly known as tannins. A sort of middle-ground process allows the leaves to oxidize only partially, so that some of the fresh flavors of green tea and some of the deeper flavors of black tea are combined. These types of tea, called **oolong tea** and **yellow tea,** are produced in China and Taiwan. Taiwan's former name, Formosa, is still used for the oolong produced there, which some connoisseurs consider to be the best.

Another type newer to most Americans—**pu-erh tea**—is inoculated with a type of *Aspergillus* mold while still green and left to "ripen." As the tea ferments, it gets darker and darker. When the desired stage is achieved, the blackened leaves are compressed into dense cakes and wrapped in cloth or paper. Young pu-erh can be grassy and tannic, while darker, aged pu-erh has an earthy complexity.

Almost all black tea sold commercially is blended, and there are often as many as twenty or more types in a blend—most of them black, sometimes from several countries, and often with a full-flavored tea such as Assam from India predominating. Much tea is flavored, and the most famous of these is **Earl Grey**, a blend of black tea flavored with oil of bergamot, a musky citrus fruit, 181. Tea may be tumbled with flower petals, as green or oolong teas are for **jasmine** tea, or smoked until dry over pinewood fires, as for **Lapsang souchong.**

Most tea bags are filled with "fannings" or "dust"—two sorting grades that describe size, not quality. Although most packers use lesser-quality teas for bags than for loose tea, sometimes the fannings or dust can be quite good. Some tea, such as the emerald-colored **matcha,** is intentionally ground very fine so that it may be whisked directly into hot water. Regardless of whether your tea is ground, in bags, or loose leaf, buy types whose packaging is well sealed. Store in airtight containers; tea leaves, especially finely chopped or pulverized leaves, grow stale quickly.

Don't overlook tea's usefulness on the dining table in places such as flavored vodka, 22, custard, 813, and Tea-Flavored Ice Cream, 840. Also read about Kombucha, 943, a fermented tea beverage.

ABOUT HERBAL TEAS

From time immemorial, various plants, less stimulating than tea or coffee, have been used the world over to soothe and refresh. These are not really teas but rather infusions (commonly called *tisanes*), made with herbs, roots, spices, flowers, and dried fruits rather than tea leaves. An old herbalist recommended them for "wamblings of the stomach," and they are especially welcome shortly after dinner.

They range all the way from commonplace chamomile and mint to South African **rooibos**, or redbush, and the South American, caffeine-packed **yerba mate.** You can purchase specialty teas at natural foods stores, specialty shops, and online.

For strong herbs and spices such as rooibos, yerba mate, hyssop, lemon verbena, mint, sage, basil, thyme, and fennel seeds, use ½ to 1 tablespoon fresh or 1 teaspoon dried per 1 cup water.

For mild herbs and blossoms such as chamomile, rose petals, rose hips, blackberry leaves, hibiscus, clover, linden, orange, lemon, wintergreen, and elderflower, use 1 to 2 tablespoons fresh or 1 to 2 teaspoons dried per 1 cup water.

For dried roots such as licorice and ginger, use up to 1 tablespoon per 1 cup water. ***For fresh ginger,*** use a 1-inch piece, thinly sliced, per 1 cup water (simmering the ginger slices for 5 minutes will extract more flavor).

BREWING TEA

All you need to brew tea well is the best tea you can afford and water—the water being almost as important as the tea. Use cold water that is freshly drawn from the tap—soft, not softened, and not hard. If your tap water is of questionable quality, use filtered water.

Preheat the teapot or mug with boiling water or very hot tap water. Different teas respond best to different brewing temperatures and times. In general, the darker the tea leaves, the hotter your water should be; find our recommendations below:

Type	Teaspoons per 8 ounces water	Water temperature	Brewing time in minutes
White	2	170° to 175°F	3
Green	2	170° to 175°F	2
Oolong and Yellow	1	195°F	2
Black	1	200°F	2
Pu-erh	1 for aged; 2 for fresh	200° to 210°F	2 to 4
Herbal	See About Herbal Teas, above	212°F	5 to 10

To brew the finely ground green tea called matcha, scoop ¾ teaspoon matcha powder into a warmed serving cup or small ceramic bowl and add enough 175°F water to wet the tea. Thoroughly whisk together into a uniform paste, then add another 4 to 6 ounces hot water, and whisk again until frothy and well combined. Serve immediately. It helps to have a specially designed bamboo whisk (called a *chasen*) for the task, but a small balloon whisk will do; you may also add the water and tea to a screw-top container and shake to combine. This is especially useful for making a cold matcha beverage; simply shake the matcha powder with cold tap water and ice and serve. We recommend brewing loose-leaf tea in a teapot that contains a wide, deep inset basket, which gives plenty of room for the leaves to expand and can be lifted out as soon as the tea is ready. The second-best option is to use a French press, well cleaned to remove any coffee residue, or a wire mesh tea ball that shuts with a clasp. Individual metal tea filters are also useful. Look for one with a cylinder that extends to the bottom of the cup, which offers the most water-tea contact. You may also brew loose tea in a separate pot or a covered saucepan and then pour it through a sieve into a warmed serving pot. In any case, ➤ stirring the brew just before serving is imperative, since it circulates through the liquid the essential oils that contribute so much to tea's characteristic flavor.

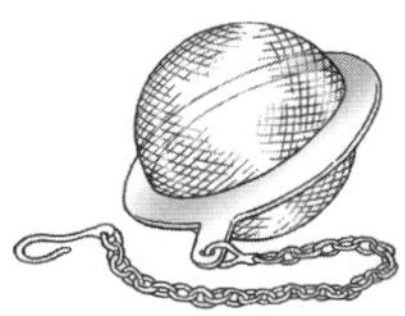

Tea ball

To keep tea warm both during and after brewing, you can wrap the teapot in a tea cozy or thick towel. Once you've removed the leaves, the tea can be transferred to a clean thermal carafe—less elegant than a teapot but a more practical way to serve it fresh and hot. To serve tea to a crowd, you may wish to brew it in advance in a pot using twice as much tea as usual, then fill each cup or pot with half of this tea essence and half hot water.

COLD-BREWED TEA

8 servings

This recipe works well with teas of all kinds, including herbal teas. The resulting tea will not have the bitterness that hot brewed teas have, and the flavor will not be as intense. Use the smaller amount of tea if it is fine, such as rooibos. Use the larger amount if the tea leaves are "fluffier" (like white tea).

Add to a glass container or pitcher:

2 to 3 tablespoons any loose-leaf tea

Fill the container with:

8 cups cold water

Refrigerate and let sit 8 hours or overnight. Strain out the leaves and serve the tea over ice.

MASALA CHAI

4 to 5 servings

This sweet and creamy Indian drink with an enticing combination of spices is popular the world over. Be sure to use a strong black tea, such as Assam—the flavor of lighter teas will be lost among the spices and milk.

Bring just to a boil in a medium saucepan:

3 cups water
1½ cups milk
½ cup sugar, or to taste
2 cinnamon sticks
16 green cardamom pods, crushed
1 teaspoon whole cloves
½-inch piece ginger, thinly sliced
½ teaspoon black peppercorns

Remove from the heat, cover, and let stand for 20 minutes. Return to a simmer, then remove from the heat and stir in:

2 tablespoons black tea leaves

Cover and let stand 2 minutes. Strain and serve at once. Or let cool and serve over ice.

ICED TEA

This beverage originated in our family's native town, St. Louis. The inventor was actually an Englishman who arrived at the concoction as an act of desperation, when the general public showed indifference to his hot tea offerings in the sweltering midwestern heat. Try adding mint, lemon zest strips, or dried hibiscus flowers to the tea as it brews. Flavored syrups, 15–16, and fruit juices can be added to taste. Or, mix half tea with half Lemonade, 13, to make an **Arnold Palmer.**

Prepare tea, using the chart on 7, doubling the quantity of leaves (but not the water). Stir, strain, and pour over ice. Serve with:

Lemon slices
(Sprigs of mint)
(Sugar or Simple Syrup, 16, to taste)

SWEET SOUTHERN ICED TEA

6 to 8 servings

In the South, iced tea is sweet and strong—too dark to read the newspaper through.

Brew tea, 7, using:

4 cups water
6 to 7 bags black tea (or 8 teaspoons black tea leaves)

Steep for 5 to 10 minutes. Remove the tea bags (or strain) and stir in while hot:

1 cup sugar, or to taste

Transfer to a large pitcher and add:

2 to 4 cups water, depending on the desired strength of the tea

Chill. Serve over ice. If desired, garnish with:

(Lemon slices)

THAI ICED TEA

4 servings

Thai iced tea is typically made only with black tea, but to achieve its characteristic (usually artificial) color, we add rooibos as well. For Thai iced tea that is closer to the restaurant version in sweetness, use the larger amount of sugar.

In a medium saucepan bring to a boil:

5 cups water
½ to ¾ cup packed brown sugar or palm sugar

Remove from the heat and add:

2 tablespoons rooibos tea
1 tablespoon black tea leaves

2 green cardamom pods, crushed
1 whole star anise
Seeds scraped from 1 vanilla bean or 1 teaspoon vanilla extract or vanilla bean paste

Steep for 20 minutes. Strain. Fill 4 tall glasses with ice and divide the tea among the glasses. Pour over the top of each:

2 tablespoons half-and-half or sweetened condensed milk (½ cup total)

ABOUT CHOCOLATE AND COCOA BEVERAGES

Chocolate as a beverage was first consumed by the ancient Mayans and later by the Aztecs, who introduced it to Spanish colonists. That original beverage has been elaborated upon countless times in its travels. In Spain and France, it is made with milk and cream. Viennese hot chocolate is known for its generous topping of whipped cream. In Brazil, coffee is added, and in Mexico, we find in it cinnamon, masa, and orange zest. In the United States, hot chocolate is sweet, creamy, and often topped with marshmallows.

Cocoa powder does not dissolve instantly in liquid but tends to form lumps that must be smoothed by vigorous stirring. It helps to first combine the cocoa with sugar in the saucepan. Don't confuse cocoa powder, which is unsweetened, with **instant cocoa,** which usually contains sugar and has emulsifiers added to make it dissolve readily in either a hot or cold liquid. Hot cocoa is much better when made with unsweetened cocoa powder and sweetened to taste. **Stone-ground chocolate** is available in tablets and is commonly used to make Mexican hot chocolate. It contains sugar and sometimes spices and may simply be chopped up finely and added to hot milk. ➤ For quick preparation of hot or cold chocolate drinks, keep on hand Cocoa Syrup or Ganache for Hot Chocolate, below. These concentrates also make great gifts when packaged with homemade marshmallows, 868. For more information on chocolate, see 970.

HOT COCOA

4 servings

The proportions here will produce a cocoa richer in flavor but much less sweet than you will get from most commercial mixes. You may substitute nondairy options for the milk, such as almond or soy milk.

Whisk together in a medium heavy saucepan:

¼ cup unsweetened cocoa powder
2 to 3 tablespoons sugar, to taste
¼ teaspoon salt

Whisk into the cocoa mixture in a slow, steady stream:

3 cups milk or half-and-half

Heat over medium heat, stirring frequently and scraping the bottom of the pan, just until bubbles appear around the sides. Remove from the heat. If desired, stir in:

(½ teaspoon vanilla or 1 tablespoon Kahlúa or Grand Marnier)

If desired, top each serving with:

(Ground nutmeg or cinnamon)
(Whipped Cream, 791, or marshmallows)

COCOA SYRUP

1½ cups; enough for 12 servings Quick Hot Cocoa

This syrup is quick and easy to prepare, and its flavor far exceeds anything you can buy. It can be used to make hot and cold cocoa drinks alike.

Whisk together in a medium saucepan:

1 cup unsweetened cocoa powder
¾ cup sugar

Add and stir to combine:

1 cup cold water
(½ cup malted milk powder)

Bring just to a boil over medium heat, stirring constantly. Remove from the heat and let cool. Store covered at room temperature for several days, or refrigerate for up to 3 weeks. To liquefy refrigerated syrup, heat on the stove or in the microwave.

QUICK HOT COCOA

1 serving

Stir together in a small saucepan or mug:

¾ cup milk
(2 tablespoons heavy cream)
2 tablespoons Cocoa Syrup, above

Heat over medium-low heat, or in a microwave on high for 30 to 45 seconds, until warm but not boiling.

GANACHE FOR HOT CHOCOLATE

About 1½ cups; enough for 6 servings Quick Hot Chocolate or Drinking Chocolate I

Ganache is often used for truffles or icing. Here we use it to make an extraordinary beverage, richer than hot cocoa.

Bring to a rolling boil in a medium heavy saucepan:

1 cup heavy cream

Immediately remove from the heat and add, whisking until smooth:

8 ounces dark, bittersweet, or semisweet chocolate (60 to 72% cacao), finely chopped

Use immediately or let cool, then refrigerate, covered, for up to 2 weeks.

QUICK HOT CHOCOLATE OR DRINKING CHOCOLATE

1 serving

I. Stir together in a small saucepan or mug:

¼ cup Ganache for Hot Chocolate, above
½ cup milk, water, or coffee

Heat over low heat, or in a microwave on high for 30 to 45 seconds, until warm but not boiling. If desired, stir in:

(⅛ teaspoon vanilla or ½ teaspoon Kahlúa or Grand Marnier)

Top with:

A dollop of Whipped Cream, 791
Ground nutmeg or cinnamon

II. Bring just to a boil in a small saucepan or microwave-safe bowl:

½ cup half-and-half

Remove from the heat and whisk in until melted:

1 ounce dark, bittersweet, or semisweet chocolate (60 to 72% cacao), finely chopped

SPICED HOT COCOA

4 servings

Stir together in a medium heavy saucepan:

6 tablespoons unsweetened cocoa powder
6 tablespoons sugar

Vigorously stir in, first by tablespoons and then in a slow, steady stream:

3 cups milk

Heat over medium heat, stirring constantly and scraping the bottom of the pan, just until bubbles appear around the sides. Remove from the heat and stir in:

2 cinnamon sticks, crushed
6 whole cloves, crushed
1½-inch piece ginger, peeled and sliced

Let stand, covered, for 30 minutes. Reheat until steaming, strain, and pour into mugs. If desired, top with:

(Whipped Cream, 791)

SPICED HOT CHOCOLATE

4 servings

Prepare **Spiced Hot Cocoa, above,** using ½ **recipe Ganache for Hot Chocolate, 9,** instead of the cocoa powder and sugar. Let stand, covered, for 30 minutes. Reheat until steaming, strain, and pour into mugs. If desired, top each serving with **(Whipped Cream, 791)**.

CHAMPURRADO (MASA-THICKENED HOT CHOCOLATE)

6 servings

Champurrado is typically made with Mexican chocolate, which is very sweet and sold in tablets. We prefer the flavor of bitter, dark chocolate, but you may use Mexican chocolate if desired. Simply leave out the sugar and then add sugar to taste after cooking. If you can't find *piloncillo*, which is Mexican brown sugar, use dark brown sugar.

Bring to a simmer in a medium saucepan:

4 cups whole milk
3 ounces dark, bittersweet, or semisweet chocolate (60 to 72% cacao), finely chopped
½ teaspoon ground cinnamon
⅓ cup chopped piloncillo or packed dark brown sugar
¼ teaspoon salt

Gradually whisk in:

½ cup masa harina

Reduce the heat to medium-low and cook, whisking frequently, until thickened, about 4 minutes. Remove from the heat and whisk in:

1 teaspoon vanilla

MAYAN HOT CHOCOLATE

4 servings

This spiced hot chocolate has a remarkably clean chocolate flavor because no dairy is added. Use a high-quality chocolate that you would be happy eating on its own.

Combine in a small saucepan:

2½ cups water
½ teaspoon ground cinnamon
⅛ teaspoon cayenne pepper
⅛ teaspoon salt

Bring to a brisk simmer, remove from the heat, and add, whisking until melted and completely combined:

4 ounces dark, bittersweet, or semisweet chocolate (60 to 72% cacao), finely chopped

BRAZILIAN CHOCOLATE

4 servings

Combine in a small heatproof bowl:

1 ounce dark, bittersweet, or semisweet chocolate (60 to 72% cacao), chopped
¼ cup sugar
⅛ teaspoon salt

Combine in a saucepan:

1½ cups strong coffee
1 cup water
1 cup half-and-half

Bring to a boil, then pour over the chocolate, whisking to dissolve the chocolate and sugar completely. Stir in:

1 teaspoon vanilla
Pinch of ground cinnamon

KAI

4 to 6 servings

"When out at sea, on look-out watch, / The hours pass slowly by, / But maybe someone brings to me / A mug of steaming kai." This rich and delicious drink was a longtime staple of the British Royal Navy, meant to keep men on night duty nourished as well as wide awake. For those of us with more modest agendas, our version is a superb sustainer on a cold winter's day.

Place in a medium saucepan:

4 ounces unsweetened chocolate or dark chocolate (72% cacao or above) finely chopped
1½ cups water

Heat, whisking frequently, until the chocolate is melted. Add:

One 14-ounce can sweetened condensed milk
(2 tablespoons malted milk powder or instant custard powder)

Whisk to combine and heat through. Remove from the heat. If desired, add:

(4 ounces rum or brewed coffee)

EGG CREAM

1 serving

This soda-fountain classic from Brooklyn contains no eggs or cream.

Pour into a tall glass:

1 cup very cold milk
2 tablespoons Cocoa Syrup, 9

Stir vigorously until mixed well and top off with:

⅓ cup sparkling water

ABOUT JUICES AND FRUIT BEVERAGES

Many of these beverages can be made with store-bought juices, while others require juicing or blending fresh fruits and vegetables. There are two main types of juicers: **masticating or cold-press juicers** and **centrifugal juicers.** Both effectively filter out fruit or vegetable solids, including insoluble dietary fibers, though centrifugal juicers are less efficient at extracting juice. If you do not have a juicer, you can puree fruit or vegetables in a blender, adding water as needed, and filter out the solids by pouring through a fine-mesh sieve or a few layers of cheesecloth. Gently press on the solids to extract all the juice. For coaxing the juice from citrus fruit, there are electric or manual reamers or lever-type crushers. We recommend one that is large enough to handle grapefruit as well as oranges. ➤ For how to best juice citrus fruits, see 182.

Of store-bought juices, the refrigerated, flash-pasteurized type are the best. Frozen concentrates are a convenient alternative. As for canned, bottled, or boxed juice, quality ranges so widely that the government has seen fit to identify several juice drink categories. These categories range from those in which genuine fruit juice predominates to those that are partially or almost entirely artificial. All products claiming to be juice must list a percentage of actual juice they contain, but that percentage may be a concentrate. **Fruit nectar,** which is made from fruit puree that has been enhanced with sweeteners and lemon juice or ascorbic acid, is much more viscous than fruit juice and has a concentrated flavor. If you wish to avoid "juice-like" products, scan the label for the following words: "concentrate," "reconstituted," "diluted," "drink," "beverage," "flavored," or "cocktail."

TOMATO-VEGETABLE JUICE

4 servings

I. FRESH TOMATOES

Combine in a large saucepan and simmer 30 minutes:

12 medium tomatoes, chopped
2 celery ribs, with leaves, chopped
1 slice onion
3 sprigs parsley
½ bay leaf
½ cup water

Strain into a pitcher. Season with:

1 teaspoon salt
¼ teaspoon paprika
¼ teaspoon sugar

Serve thoroughly chilled.

II. CANNED OR BOTTLED TOMATO JUICE

This juice is best the day it is made. Sprigs of bruised tarragon, basil, or other herbs may be steeped in the juice and then strained out before it is served.

Combine in a pitcher:

2½ cups canned or bottled tomato juice
1½ tablespoons lemon juice
1 teaspoon grated celery
½ teaspoon grated onion
½ teaspoon grated peeled horseradish root
¾ teaspoon salt
¼ teaspoon sugar
⅛ teaspoon paprika
A dash of Worcestershire or hot pepper sauce

Serve thoroughly chilled.

CITRUS JUICE MEDLEY

2 to 3 servings

Combine in a pitcher:

¾ cup grapefruit juice
¼ cup lemon or lime juice
½ cup orange juice
¼ cup sugar or Simple Syrup, 16

Serve chilled or over ice, garnished with:

Sprigs of mint

CRANBERRY JUICE

4 to 6 servings

Combine in a medium saucepan:

One 12-ounce bag cranberries
3 cups water

Cook over medium heat until the skins pop, about 5 minutes. Strain through a cheesecloth-lined sieve into a medium saucepan, squeezing to extract all the juice from the berries. Bring to a boil and add:

⅓ to ½ cup sugar, to taste
(6 whole cloves)

Cook for 2 minutes. Remove from the heat and cool (removing the cloves, if they were used). Add:

¼ cup orange juice or 1 tablespoon lemon juice

Chill thoroughly. Garnish with:

Lime slices

ABOUT JUICE BLENDS

Most fruits and vegetables can be turned into nourishing, delicious beverages by processing in a blender or juicer. The only trouble in making these is that the enthusiast often gets drunk with power and whirls up more and more odd and intricate combinations, some of them quite undrinkable. That said, we enjoy spiking our juices with fresh ginger, lemon, and herbs for more complexity. Below are some combinations we enjoy. If you do not have a juicer, blend and strain the ingredients as described in About Juices and Fruit Beverages, above.

TOMATO-CELERY-CARROT JUICE

2 to 4 servings

Process the following in a juicer or blender:

2 medium tomatoes, quartered (about 8 ounces)
2 large celery ribs, cut into chunks (about 4 ounces)
2 large carrots, cut into chunks (about 6 ounces)
4 sprigs parsley
(½-inch piece peeled horseradish root)

PINEAPPLE-MANGO JUICE

4 servings

Cut into cubes:

1 pineapple, peeled and cored, 191
2 large mangoes, pitted and peeled

Process in a blender or a juicer. Add:

Lime juice to taste

Garnish with:

Sprigs of mint

CARROT-BEET-GINGER JUICE

1 serving

Process the following in a juicer or a blender:

2 small beets, trimmed and cut into chunks (about 8 ounces)
1 large carrot, cut into chunks (about 3 ounces)
2-inch piece ginger, cut into chunks (peeled if using a blender)
1 small lemon, quartered (juiced if using a blender)

KALE-GINGER LEMONADE

1 serving

This is one of Megan's favorite midafternoon pick-me-ups: a tart, spicy green juice.

Process the following in a juicer or a blender:

1 cup packed shredded kale
1 medium tart-sweet apple, quartered (cored if using a blender)
1 small lemon, halved (juiced if using a blender)
2-inch piece ginger, cut into small chunks (peeled if using a blender)

ABOUT SMOOTHIES AND ICE CREAM DRINKS

A smoothie is like a milk shake, but made with fruit and sometimes milk, nondairy milk, or yogurt, and thickened with ice or frozen fruits. Frozen bananas are our favorite cooler and thickener for smoothies, as they result in less watery beverages with a creamy texture. When you find discounted ripe bananas at the grocery store, snap them up, then peel, halve, and freeze them for future use.

FRUIT SMOOTHIE

1 or 2 servings

The basic proportions in this recipe can be used to create a wide variety of smoothies tailored to ingredients you have on hand. Note that if using a dark fruit such as blueberries, adding spirulina will turn your smoothie a muddy color.

Combine in a blender:

1 cup frozen fruit (such as berries, cherries, or peach, mango, or pineapple chunks)
1 frozen ripe banana, cut into chunks
½ cup milk, nondairy milk, coconut water, water, or fruit juice (or ½ cup yogurt and 3 tablespoons water or milk)
(Up to 1 tablespoon sweetener, such as honey, maple syrup, or agave syrup, or 2 pitted dried dates)
(1 tablespoon nut or seed butter, such as peanut, cashew, or sunflower)
(1 teaspoon spirulina powder, 1016, chia seeds, or flaxseeds)

Blend until smooth. Pour into a glass and serve, or serve in a bowl and top with any of the following:

Bee pollen
Seeds or nuts, such as sunflower, pumpkin, flaked coconut, chia, or hemp
Granola
Cut-up fresh fruit

GREEN SMOOTHIE

1 or 2 servings

Some green smoothies tend to be a tad . . . vegetal. We think of this pleasant and milder version as an entry-level green smoothie.

Combine in a blender:

1 cup packed baby spinach or shredded deribbed, 243, kale
1 cup frozen mango, pineapple, or banana chunks
1 cup unsweetened almond milk, beverage-style coconut milk, coconut water, or water (or ½ cup plain yogurt plus ½ cup water)
(½ avocado, pitted, peeled, and chopped)
2 tablespoons lime juice
1 tablespoon maple syrup, honey, or agave syrup, or 2 pitted dried dates
(1 teaspoon spirulina powder, 1016)
Pinch of salt

Blend until smooth.

CHOCOLATE-CHERRY SMOOTHIE

1 or 2 servings

Combine in a blender:

1¼ cups milk or nondairy milk
1 cup frozen sweet cherries
1 cup ice cubes
3 tablespoons Cocoa Syrup, 9

Blend until smooth.

PEANUT BUTTER AND BANANA SMOOTHIE

2 servings

We also enjoy almond butter in this creamy, satisfying concoction.

Combine in a blender:

3 frozen ripe bananas, coarsely chopped
2 cups milk or nondairy milk
¼ cup peanut butter
(1 tablespoon unsweetened cocoa powder)

Blend until smooth.

PAPAYA-MANGO BATIDO

2 servings

Also known as *licuados*, *batidos* are often thinner than a smoothie and use milk as an ingredient.

Combine in a blender:

1 cup papaya nectar
1 cup frozen mango chunks

1 cup milk
3 tablespoons lime juice
Blend until smooth.

MANGO LASSI
3 or 4 servings

Alphonso or Kesar mango puree, available canned at Indian grocery stores, is especially good here (use 2 cups of the puree and add sugar to taste). For making this into a frozen yogurt dessert, see 846.

Combine in a blender:
2 cups plain yogurt
2 large mangoes (about 1½ pounds), pitted, peeled, and chopped
2 tablespoons sugar
10 ice cubes
Process until the ice is partially crushed. Pour into chilled glasses.

FRUIT KEFIR
4 to 6 servings

Kefir is a close relative of yogurt and is sold in liquid form. If you cannot find it, cultured buttermilk is a fine substitute.

Combine in a blender:
2 cups plain kefir
2 cups raspberries, blueberries, blackberries, chopped strawberries, or peeled, pitted, and chopped peaches, apricots, or mangoes
Process until smooth. Refrigerate for about 24 hours. Stir before serving.

ICE CREAM FLOAT
1 serving

For an adult version, use stout or porter.

Add to a glass:
1 scoop or more vanilla ice cream
Fill the glass with:
Root beer, cola, or other soft drink

MILK SHAKE
2 servings

For a **malted milk shake,** add **½ cup malted milk powder**.

Combine in a blender:
2 cups any flavor ice cream
2 cups milk
(¼ cup Cocoa Syrup, 9)
Process until smooth and frothy.

FRUIT MILK SHAKE
2 servings

Combine in a blender:
1 cup vanilla ice cream
1 cup milk
2 cups sliced ripe bananas, peeled peaches, or strawberries
Process until smooth.

VIETNAMESE AVOCADO SHAKE
Serves 2

While Americans tend to think of the avocado as a savory food, in many parts of the world it is used in sweet preparations. This rich shake is a strong argument in favor of the avocado as dessert. Play with the ratio of sweetened condensed milk to milk depending on the level of sweetness you prefer.

Combine in a blender:
1 large avocado, pitted and scooped from the peel
4 to 6 standard ice cubes or ¾ cup crushed ice
⅓ cup sweetened condensed milk
⅓ cup milk or coconut milk
Pinch of salt
Blend until smooth.

ABOUT THIRST QUENCHERS

While most beverages are hydrating, there are some that seem to quench thirst especially well. These are the drinks to prepare on hot summer days and serve over generous quantities of ice. Some of these drinks are sweet and tart, like lemonade, while others use flavored syrups and sparkling water to perk up the taste buds. In any case, thirst quenchers are our answer to too-sweet sodas and technicolor sports drinks. They are also welcome additions to parties as alternatives to alcoholic beverages. For more ideas, see About Virgin Cocktails, 28.

LEMONADE OR LIMEADE
8 servings

Orange, pineapple, raspberry, white grape juice, or other fruit juices may be combined with lemonade or limeade. To add a subtle twist, make the sugar syrup with **2 to 3 sprigs rosemary, a small bunch of mint or thyme,** or a **2-inch piece ginger, thinly sliced.** Let the syrup cool to room temperature and strain before proceeding. For **Pink Lemonade,** add **3 tablespoons grenadine.** To make an **Arnold Palmer,** mix equal parts lemonade and Iced Tea, 8. For a tarter beverage, use the smaller amount of sugar listed below.

Combine in a saucepan and boil for 2 minutes:
3 cups water
1½ to 2 cups sugar, to taste
Add:
5 cups cold water
1 cup lemon or lime juice
Pour over ice cubes in tall glasses or into a pitcher of ice.

FLAVORED OR ITALIAN SODAS
1 serving

This is an excellent way to use up jelly that didn't set properly. Or, gently melt an equal amount of any jelly and use it instead of the syrup. For a tangier drink, use **Fruit Shrub, 16,** instead of the syrup.

Add to a tall glass:
3 tablespoons any flavored syrup, store-bought or homemade, 15–16, or to taste
Fill the glass with crushed ice, then top up with:

Sparkling water

If desired, pour over the top:

(2 tablespoons heavy cream or half-and-half, or to taste)

FRUIT SODAS

1 serving

Fruit nectars, 11, are delicious served this way.

Pour over ice in a tall glass:

½ cup sparkling water
½ cup lemonade, limeade, orange, pineapple, cranberry, guava, apricot, or other juice or nectar
(Any flavored syrup, 15–16, to taste)
(Lemon or lime juice, to taste)

AGUA FRESCA

About 3 cups; 6 servings

Agua fresca, Spanish for "cool water," is a way of distilling the essence of ripe fruit into a refreshing summer drink. For a boozy version, frost the rim of each glass with **coarse salt.** Add several ice cubes to the glass and pour ½ cup agua fresca over them. Add **1 to 2 ounces vodka, rum, or tequila.** Serve with a **lime wedge** or a **piece of the fruit** the *agua fresca* was made with.

Place in a blender (using the larger amount of water for fruits that don't release enough liquid to blend easily):

4 cups cubed, seeded fruit such as cantaloupe, peach, mango, pineapple, watermelon, honeydew, or cucumber
¼ to ½ cup water

Depending on the fruit, you may need to add even more water than called for above. Blend until very smooth. Strain through a fine-mesh sieve, pressing the solids to extract all the juice. Whisk in:

1 to 3 tablespoons honey, warmed slightly, or to taste
2 tablespoons lemon or lime juice, or to taste

Chill thoroughly. To serve, stir together equal parts fruit juice and:

Sparkling water

HORCHATA

6 servings

Aside from a lime-garnished Mexican lager, this sweetened and spiced grain and nut milk is the best accompaniment to tacos we know. One of our testers turned her leftover horchata into popsicles, which we think is a fabulous idea!

I. Finely grind in a blender:

½ cup white rice

Add:

½ cup slivered almonds
½ cup sugar
1 stick canela, 972, or 1 teaspoon ground cinnamon
¼ teaspoon salt
(1-inch-wide strip lime zest)
(1 vanilla bean, split lengthwise)

Pour over the almond-rice mixture in the blender:

4 cups boiling water

Let sit overnight. Blend the mixture until smooth, about 3 minutes on high speed. Strain through a very fine-mesh sieve, a sieve lined with several layers of cheesecloth, or a nut milk bag. Stir in:

2 cups cold water
1 teaspoon vanilla if not using the vanilla bean

Serve over ice.

II. A less authentic version that is tasty, easy to prepare, and much quicker.

Combine in a blender:

3 cups unsweetened almond milk
3 cups unsweetened rice milk
½ cup sugar
1 teaspoon vanilla
1 teaspoon ground cinnamon

Blend until the sugar is dissolved. Serve over ice.

PANAKAM

1 serving

This cooling Indian beverage is typically made with jaggery, or palm sugar, 1025. If desired, you may substitute jaggery for white sugar in the simple syrup. Extracting the ginger juice is the hardest part of this recipe, so feel free to use store-bought ginger juice, if available. When happy hour rolls around, add **1 ounce dry gin** for a spicy, refreshing cocktail.

Mince in a food processor:

4 ounces ginger, peeled and thinly sliced crosswise
¼ cup water

The ginger should be in very, very fine pieces. Transfer the ginger pulp to a fine-mesh sieve or a sieve lined with a thin kitchen towel. Press as much of the juice from the ginger as possible. You should have about ⅓ cup of ginger juice, or enough for around 16 servings. The juice will keep refrigerated for up to 1 week.

To serve, add to each glass:

1 teaspoon ginger juice, above, or store-bought ginger juice
1 tablespoon lime juice or 1 teaspoon tamarind concentrate
1 to 2 teaspoons Simple Syrup, 16, or agave syrup, to taste
⅛ teaspoon ground cardamom
Pinch of salt
(Pinch of black pepper)

Stir to combine, then fill the glasses with ice. Top off each glass with:

About 4 ounces sparkling water

Serve with long spoons for stirring and garnish with:

Lime wedges

SPICY GINGER ALE

6 to 8 servings

This recipe makes a rich ginger syrup that you can keep on hand for making one glass of ginger ale at a time. To make ginger ale for a crowd, pour the strained ginger syrup into a pitcher, then add **½ to ¾ cup lime juice, to taste,** and top with **4½ cups sparkling water, or more to taste.**

Combine in a blender:

½ cup sugar
½ cup water
4 ounces ginger, peeled and thinly sliced crosswise

Blend until the ginger is completely pureed and there are no chunks left. Strain through a fine-mesh sieve set over a medium bowl, pressing on the solids with a rubber spatula to extract all the liquid. Or place the pureed ginger in the center of a thin kitchen towel, bring the ends together and twist tightly over the bowl, squeezing every last bit of juice from the ginger pulp. Ginger syrup can be refrigerated for up to 2 weeks. Shake well before using.

For each serving, add 1½ to 2 tablespoons ginger syrup, to taste, to a glass filled with ice, then add:

1½ to 2 tablespoons lime or lemon juice, to taste

Fill the glass with:

About 6 ounces sparkling water

Stir well.

SWITCHEL

4 servings

This lightly sweet and tart beverage is like a healthy sports drink, perfect for sipping while working or playing outside on a hot day.

Combine in a medium saucepan:

2 cups water
2-inch piece ginger, thinly sliced

Bring to a boil. Remove from the heat, cover, and let sit for 20 minutes. Strain into a pitcher or quart jar and stir in:

¼ cup honey or maple syrup
2 tablespoons cider vinegar
⅛ teaspoon salt

Stir until the honey or maple syrup and salt are dissolved. Stir in:

2 cups ice cubes

Chill completely.

ABOUT FRUIT PUNCHES

These punches are nonalcoholic and suitable for all ages; for alcoholic punches, see 29–32. Do not add carbonated ingredients until just before serving—to ensure plenty of fizz, you may wish to divide the punch base in half and serve in two batches, adding the sparkling ingredient as needed. For best results, chill all the ingredients before mixing. The classiest way to keep a punch cold is to fashion a Decorative Ice Mold, 29, but these will eventually water down the punch. ➤ To keep a punch chilled without diluting it, fill a zip-top bag with water, seal, freeze it solid, and add to the punch bowl. You may remove it before serving or leave it in (unsightly, perhaps, but effective). Using frozen fruit as your garnish—even freezing juice in an ice cube tray or the bottom third of a Bundt pan—are other, crafty ways to keep a punch cool and undiluted.

WATERMELON PUNCH

Twenty 6-ounce servings

Prepare:

Simple Syrup, 16, using 1 cup sugar and 1 cup water

Let cool. Trim the rind from:

4 pounds watermelon

Cut into cubes, removing any seeds (you should have 5 to 6 cups). Working in batches, puree in a blender with the simple syrup, then strain through a medium sieve into a punch bowl. Stir in:

1¼ cups lemon juice

Just before serving, stir in:

1 liter ginger ale, chilled
1 liter club soda or sparkling water, chilled
1 quart strawberries, hulled and sliced, or melon balls

CRANBERRY-MANGO PUNCH

Twenty 6-ounce servings

Combine in a large punch bowl:

2 quarts raspberry-cranberry juice or cranberry juice cocktail, chilled
1 quart mango nectar, chilled
1 liter club soda or sparkling water, chilled
One 750ml bottle sparkling apple cider, chilled

Float on top:

Lime wheels

PINEAPPLE PUNCH

Twenty 6-ounce servings

Combine in a large bowl and stir well:

2 cups cooled strong black tea
2 cups orange juice
¾ cup lemon juice
2 tablespoons lime juice
1 cup sugar
Leaves from 12 sprigs mint

Refrigerate for 2 hours. Shortly before serving, strain the punch and add:

10 slices fresh pineapple or one 20-ounce can sliced pineapple, including juice
2 liters ginger ale, chilled
1 liter club soda or sparkling water, chilled

Pour over ice in a punch bowl.

FRUIT PUNCH

Twenty 6-ounce servings

Prepare and pour into a large punch bowl:

Simple Syrup, 16, using 1¼ cups sugar and 1¼ cups water

Add:

2½ cups cooled strong black tea

Cool, then add:

2½ cups noncitrus juice, such as cherry, white grape, or strawberry
2 cups orange juice
1 cup lemon juice
1 cup canned crushed pineapple

Add enough water to make 4 quarts of liquid. Chill for 1 hour. Immediately before serving, add:

1 liter club soda or sparkling water, chilled

Add ice and serve.

ABOUT SYRUPS

A simple sugar syrup is a useful ingredient when sweetening cold beverages such as sparkling water, Iced Tea, 8, Lemonade or Limeade, 13, or Flavored Sodas, 13. Substituting flavored syrup for plain sugar syrup in a beverage adds complexity. A wide assortment of flavored syrups can be easily made at home. All syrups should be stored in glass or plastic containers.

SIMPLE SYRUP (SUGAR SYRUP)

2 cups

This can be made in different proportions, the most common being one part sugar to one part water. This recipe yields a richer simple syrup, which we prefer, since it keeps better and less is needed to sweeten a drink. Less syrup means less dilution of the other ingredients, which is especially important for cocktails.

Combine in a saucepan:

2 cups sugar
1 cup water

Cook over low heat, stirring occasionally, until the sugar has completely dissolved. Let cool, then chill until needed. Rich simple syrup will keep in the refrigerator for 6 months; a weaker one-to-one syrup will keep for 1 month.

FRUIT SYRUP

About 2½ cups

Proceed as for **Simple Syrup, above.** Once the sugar has dissolved, stir in **2 cups sliced or cubed peaches, plums, pineapple, or prickly pear, or 2 cups raspberries, blackberries, or blueberries, or 3 cups sliced strawberries.** Simmer, covered, for 10 minutes. Let cool. Strain and chill until needed. Store refrigerated for up to 1 month.

CITRUS SYRUP

About 3 cups

Proceed as for **Simple Syrup, above,** adding to the pan with the water and sugar **thin strips of zest from 2 lemons or limes, or from 1 large orange or grapefruit.** Simmer, covered, for 5 minutes. Once cool, you may add **(1 cup lemon, lime, orange, or grapefruit juice).** Strain and chill until needed. Store refrigerated for up to 1 month.

HERB SYRUP

About 2 cups

I. Proceed as for **Simple Syrup, above.** Once the sugar has dissolved, stir in **1 small bunch lavender, rosemary, or lemon verbena.** Simmer, covered, for 5 minutes. Let cool. Strain and chill until needed. Store refrigerated for up to 1 month.

II. Prepare **Simple Syrup, above.** Remove the hot syrup from the heat and add **1 bunch mint or ¾ cup mint leaves.** Cover and let stand 20 minutes. Strain and let cool. Chill until needed. Store refrigerated for up to 1 month.

SPICED SYRUP

About 2 cups

Prepare **Simple Syrup, above.** Remove the hot syrup from the heat and stir in one of the following: **1½ teaspoons whole cloves, 4 cinnamon sticks, 6 whole star anise, or one 3-inch piece ginger, thinly sliced.** Cover and let stand 30 minutes. Strain and let cool. Chill until needed. Store refrigerated for up to 1 month.

GRENADINE

About 1½ cups

Combine in a medium saucepan:

1 cup unsweetened pomegranate juice
1 cup sugar

Heat gently, stirring, just until the sugar is dissolved. Do not boil. Remove from the heat and stir in:

½ teaspoon orange flower water

Cool completely. Store refrigerated up to 3 weeks.

FRUIT SHRUB

About 2 cups

A concentrated, tangy syrup made by infusing equal parts fresh fruit, sugar, and vinegar. Use shrubs instead of syrups in Flavored Sodas, 13, and Fruit Sodas, 14, or as a topping for ice cream. You may use different kinds of mild-flavored vinegar depending on the fruit. For instance, pair champagne vinegar with raspberries or white balsamic vinegar with peaches. Cider vinegar is perfectly fine to use with any fruit.

Combine in a medium saucepan:

1 cup sugar
1 cup water

Bring to a simmer, stirring to dissolve the sugar. Place in a heatproof medium bowl or quart jar:

2 cups fresh fruit, such as any berry, chopped peaches, apricots, plums, or rhubarb

Pour the syrup over the fruit, let cool completely, then cover and refrigerate for 24 hours. Strain the syrup and measure it. Add half as much:

Vinegar

as you have syrup. Store refrigerated for up to 6 months.

COCKTAILS, WINE, AND BEER

In our experience, food is inseparable from alcohol. Or, at least, the latter should be cautiously consumed without the former. Conversely, sitting down to a roast with a glass of wine—or to a cheeseburger with a pint of beer—can greatly enhance our enjoyment of the meal. For ideas of what to serve with cocktails, see the introduction to the Appetizers chapter, 44; to pair wine with food, see 34; for beer pairings, see 41.

ABOUT COCKTAILS

We love cocktails because they taste good, but also because they have an incredible ability to set the mood. Whether it's a pitcher of Margaritas, 26, at a backyard barbecue, an icy and crisp Gin and Tonic, 20, on the first hot day of summer, or a Bloody Mary, 21, at a late Sunday brunch, cocktails are signifiers of the good life, a time when social mores are laxly enforced, events unfold at a leisurely pace, and engaging conversation and camaraderie are valued above all.

In 1931, Irma quipped: "Cocktails are made today with gin and ingenuity. In brief, take an ample supply of the former and use your imagination." Despite the passage of years (and repealing of laws), we think this advice still holds true: Do not let mixers completely overtake the booze and do not be afraid to experiment. Some of these recipes are often treated as sacred, but do not hesitate to bend them to your whim (or the current contents of your liquor cabinet).

When making drinks, it helps to understand a few key terms. **Proof** designates alcohol content: A 100-proof liquor contains 50 percent alcohol, 200-proof contains 100 percent, and so on. A drink served **neat** is served straight out of the bottle; a drink served **straight up** or **up** is shaken or stirred with ice before being strained into a glass with no ice; and a drink **on the rocks** is served over ice. For **punches**, see 29.

TOOLS FOR COCKTAIL-MAKING

A **zester** and a **channel knife** are designed to remove citrus rind for garnishing drinks. While there are many sleek corkscrews available, the **waiter's corkscrew or wine key** is a reliable bar companion. A **muddler** is used to bruise fresh herbs or smash soft fruits, often together with sugar, but the end of a wooden spoon handle or a French-style rolling pin may be substituted. A **two-sided jigger,** typically with the standard 1½-ounce jigger on one side and a 1-ounce pony on the other, is the standard way to measure out alcohol, but we prefer the **¼-cup liquid measuring cups** now available (as a bonus, these small measuring cups are excellent kitchen tools as well). As citrus juice plays a predominant role in most cocktails, a **citrus reamer** or **handheld citrus juicer** is another necessary bar companion. A **Boston-style cocktail shaker** produces well-chilled results (and makes an incredibly satisfying sound), although we have used a lidded mason jar in a pinch. For stirred drinks, a wide, tall **mixing glass** with a pouring lip, and a long **barspoon** are handy, but a large glass measuring cup can also be used. Finally, a **Hawthorne strainer** is the ideal tool for straining drinks made in a cocktail shaker. Not pictured here, but quite necessary, are a small knife and a cutting board for preparing citrus and garnishes.

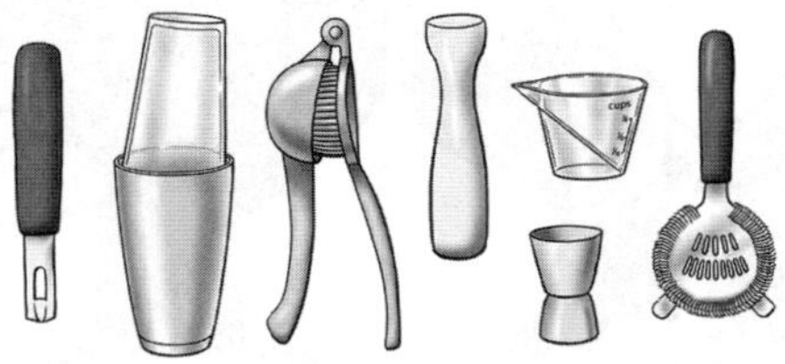

Channel zester, Boston-style shaker, citrus juicer, muddler, ¼-cup measuring cup, two-sided jigger, strainer

MIXERS, INGREDIENTS, AND GARNISHES

While we sometimes fantasize about having a well-stocked bar, it can be difficult (and expensive) to make the dream a reality. As a result, we take the approach of most home bartenders by keeping on hand the ingredients needed to make the drinks we consume the most. We suggest you do the same. However, it is worth having an understanding of the most common cocktail ingredients.

Simple Syrup, 16, is a frequent cocktail addition. However, unless you make cocktails often, it is best to make simple syrup on an as-needed basis. It must be refrigerated and eventually spoils, sometimes in as little as two weeks. Bitters, 956, are another key cocktail ingredient, with Angostura and Peychaud's being the most common. Grenadine, though not as commonly called for as it once was, is good to have, but we find the standard store-bought version insipid. Try making your own, 193.

Club soda, sparkling water, tonic water, ginger ale, cola, and tomato juice or Bloody Mary mix (store-bought or homemade, 21) are good to have on hand depending on your cocktail preferences. For any cocktail containing citrus, fresh lemons, oranges, limes, and grapefruits are necessary. ➤ We do not recommend substituting bottled citrus for fresh in any cocktail. You may also wish to keep a Fruit Shrub, 16, or two on hand to add acidity and sweetness to mixed drinks.

To garnish cocktails, olives, real maraschino cherries (not the suspiciously fire engine red variety), pickled cocktail onions, and coarse salt are all good, shelf-stable bar companions. Depending on the ingredients in a given cocktail, sprigs of fresh herbs, cucumber rounds, celery ribs, wedges of fruit, citrus wheels, or strips of citrus zest may make the best garnish. To make citrus twists, use a paring knife or vegetable peeler to remove roughly 1½-inch-long strips of citrus zest. Twist the zest over the drink, then drop it in. To flame an orange twist for cocktails like the Old Fashioned, 23, see Citrus Zest and Juice, 972.

Frosting—sometimes called **rimming**—a cocktail or other glass with sugar or salt is another way to add flavor, texture, and eye appeal to drinks.

To frost a glass, swab the outer edge of the rim with a wedge of lemon or lime. Hold the glass at an angle and roll the rim in granulated sugar or coarse salt. Avoid coating the inside of the glass. Lift the glass and tap it gently, upside down, to remove any excess sugar or salt.

GLASSWARE

While we usually drink our cocktails from a motley assortment of mason jars, repurposed sake containers, and miscellaneous thrifted glassware, a stock of basic glasses of varying sizes can be useful for the home bartender. Shown left to right are: a **coupe; cocktail** or **martini glass;** an **old-fashioned glass or rocks glass;** a **highball glass;** and a **collins glass.**

The other glassware pictured is more specialized. Narrow **Champagne flutes** preserve the bubbles in drinks made with sparkling wine, releasing them slowly. **Silver** or **pewter cups** are favored by some for such drinks as mint juleps. **Punch glasses** or **cups** are made of porcelain or glass. **Margarita glasses** have broad rims designed to hold lots of salt. **Hurricane glasses** are ideal for serving piña coladas and other festive drinks served blended or over ice.

Coupe, cocktail or martini, old-fashioned or rocks, highball, collins, Champagne, silver or pewter cup, punch cup, margarita

ABOUT ICE

The ice with which a drink is shaken, stirred, or served is an important ingredient. It not only chills the drink, but also dilutes it. While dilution may sound like a bad thing, all cocktails rely upon dilution to open up the flavors of the drink and provide an enjoyable experience rather than a purely inebriating one. In recent years, ice-making has become something of an art in itself at high-end bars, and for good reason. Beautiful, clear ice is visually stunning and doesn't shatter into tiny shards, clouding the drink. Clear ice is also free of impurities that can affect appearance and flavor.

To make crystal-clear ice cubes, start with hot filtered water and let the water sit for an hour before freezing. It may sound counterintuitive to use hot water to make ice, but hot water contains fewer dissolved gases than cold water, and these gases are part of what makes ice cloudy. When using ice cube trays, don't stack them on top of each other, as stacking will promote cloudy ice in the centermost trays.

Whenever drinks are served on the rocks, use larger ice cubes to avoid diluting the drinks too much. Some drinks, such as the Mint

Julep, 24, are designed to dilute quickly, and thus are made with crushed ice. Crushed ice can be made with a countertop ice crusher or by hand.

To crush ice by hand, place whole ice cubes in a sturdy zip-top plastic bag (or a **Lewis bag,** which is made specifically for crushing ice), wrap the bag in a kitchen towel, and give it several strong whacks with a rolling pin, hammer, or meat mallet. If you need a large quantity of cracked ice, make it in advance, and freeze. For Decorative Ice Molds, see 29.

MEASUREMENTS FOR DRINKS

1 dash	=	6 drops or 0.03 ounces
1 teaspoon	=	6 dashes or 0.18 ounces
1 tablespoon	=	½ ounce
2 tablespoons	=	1 ounce
¼ cup or 4 tablespoons	=	2 ounces
1 jigger (large cup)	=	1½ ounces
1 jigger (small cup)	=	¾ ounce
1 cup	=	8 ounces
750ml	=	25.4 ounces
1 quart	=	32 ounces or 4 cups
1 liter	=	33.8 ounces
1 lemon	=	2 to 3 tablespoons juice
1 lime	=	1½ to 2 tablespoons juice
1 medium orange	=	4 to 6 tablespoons juice
1 medium grapefruit	=	10 to 12 tablespoons juice

BATCHING COCKTAILS

Apart from the party drinks and punches, 29–32, the recipes in this chapter are all single-serving. However, there will likely be an occasion when you need to scale up a drink for a crowd (unless you prefer to hold court by the bar all evening). The easiest approach is to determine how many servings of a drink you need, then simply scale the recipe up. However, if you're trying to scale up a recipe to fit into a specific container—like a pitcher or a clean 750ml wine or liquor bottle to take to a party—you will need to use some basic math. Use the equivalents in Measurements for Drinks, above, to help you.

Select the cocktail you would like to batch. First, convert all the ingredients to the same unit of measure (i.e., ounces). For something like bitters, this will be a very small number. Add up the ingredients to determine the total volume of one cocktail. Then, determine the volume of the vessel you wish to fill, using the same unit of measurement (for instance, a 1-quart mason jar has a 4-cup capacity, which is equivalent to 32 ounces). Divide the volume of the container by the volume of the cocktail. Multiply each ingredient by the resulting number to get the amount of each ingredient needed to fill the vessel.

At this point, mix everything together. For inconvenient numbers, feel free to fudge them (within reason) to a quantity that is easier to measure and multiply. After mixing, taste the cocktail and add more sweetener, liquor, acid, or bitters to taste, keeping in mind that the cocktail will ultimately be diluted with ice.

ABOUT GIN

Much of gin's distinctive flavor comes from the juniper berry. Victorian novelists tended to assume that only the lower classes—footmen, scullery maids, and the like—had a taste for gin. The "bathtub" concoctions of the Roaring Twenties did nothing to enhance gin's reputation. Recent generations, however, have recognized the fact that this liquor, regardless of its shady past and its limited possibilities as a straight drink, is possibly the best mixing base ever invented. It is our favorite anyway.

Gin, or at least its precursor, was invented in Holland in the seventeenth century. Dutch gin, called **jenever** or **genever,** is sweet, malty, and has a pronounced flavor of juniper and other herbs and spices. It is usually drunk straight and chilled. The British reformulated and lightened gin, and it is the **London dry** style that is most popular today. **Old Tom** is a style somewhat in-between—less intense than genever but maltier and sweeter than dry gin. With the resurgence of small artisan distilleries, there has been a profusion of gins, and they tend to vary widely as distillers like to vary the aromatics they use. Some even favor locally harvested botanicals. Our favorite Oregon gin is flavored with hazelnuts, Oregon grape, hops, and local juniper. Before you mix cocktails with specialty gins, taste them on their own. An especially distinctive or unusual gin might not be the best choice for a classic martini, but it may make a superb gin and tonic.

MARTINI

1 serving

Vermouth is not the enemy of the martini, it is its defining element. Good gin is a potent spirit with real flavor of its own, but it needs more than a whisper of vermouth to turn it into a cocktail. A pitted green olive is the traditional garnish, but some prefer a lemon twist. Adding a dash of olive brine along with the olive makes a **Dirty Martini.** In our household, a dry martini (version I, below) with olive brine is affectionately called a **Dusty Martini.** With a small pickled onion in the glass, the martini becomes a **Gibson.** When vodka takes the place of gin, the cocktail is a **Vodka Martini.**

I. Fill a mixing glass three-quarters full with ice cubes. Add:

2½ ounces London dry gin
½ ounce dry vermouth

Stir until well chilled, about 30 seconds. Strain into a chilled martini or coupe glass. Add:

1 small pitted green olive or a lemon twist

II. A formula we prefer, perhaps closer to what the first martini tasted like. While serving martinis on the rocks is a bit dated, we think the approach has merit, especially for the summertime martini drinker.

Fill a chilled rocks glass three-quarters full with ice cubes. Add:

2½ ounces London dry gin
½ ounce dry vermouth
½ ounce sweet vermouth
(A dash of orange bitters)

Stir until well chilled, about 30 seconds. Add:

1 small pitted green olive

IRMA'S GIN AND JUICE
1 serving

Irma's signature gin cocktail, a Prohibition-era staple, has been in the book since 1931, where it appeared on the opening page. Called simply "gin cocktail," it was a solid formula for polishing the rough edges off of illicit bathtub spirits. We think it's even better with decent gin.

Fill a cocktail shaker with ice cubes. Add:

2 ounces gin
2 ounces grapefruit or orange juice
¾ ounce lemon juice
(1 teaspoon Simple Syrup, 16, Fruit Syrup, 16, or Citrus Syrup, 16)
A dash of orange bitters

Shake until well chilled, about 12 seconds. Strain into a chilled rocks glass.

GIN AND TONIC
1 serving

If you must, use vodka in place of the gin for a **Vodka Tonic,** but we prefer substituting reposado tequila. For a spicy, gingery alternative to a gin and tonic, see Panakam, 14.

Pour over ice cubes in a chilled highball glass:

2 ounces gin

Fill the glass with:

Tonic water

Garnish with:

A lime wedge

THE LAST WORD
1 serving

This cocktail is a bracing combination and one we heartily recommend to those who love the peculiar herbal twang of Chartreuse.

Fill a cocktail shaker with ice cubes. Add:

¾ ounce gin
¾ ounce green Chartreuse
¾ ounce lime juice
¾ ounce maraschino liqueur

Shake until well chilled, about 12 seconds. Strain into a chilled cocktail or coupe glass and garnish with:

A brandied cherry

BRONX
1 serving

Fill a cocktail shaker with ice cubes. Add:

1½ ounces gin
½ ounce orange juice
A dash of dry vermouth
A dash of sweet vermouth

Shake until well chilled, about 12 seconds. Strain into a chilled cocktail glass and garnish with:

An orange wheel

GIMLET
1 serving

Replace the gin with vodka for a **Vodka Gimlet.**

Fill a cocktail shaker with ice cubes. Add:

1½ ounces gin
¼ ounce lime juice

Shake until well chilled, about 12 seconds. Strain into a chilled coupe or martini glass. Garnish with:

A lime wedge

GIN FIZZ
1 serving

Fill a cocktail shaker with ice cubes. Add:

1½ ounces gin
1 ounce lime juice
½ ounce Simple Syrup, 16

Shake until well chilled, about 12 seconds. Strain into a chilled highball glass. Fill the glass with:

Club soda

Stir and serve.

TOM COLLINS
1 serving

Substituting vodka for gin produces a **Vodka Collins.**

Fill a cocktail shaker with ice cubes. Add:

1½ ounces gin
¾ ounce lemon juice
½ ounce Simple Syrup, 16

Shake until well chilled, about 12 seconds. Strain over crushed ice in a chilled collins or highball glass. Fill the glass with:

Club soda

Garnish with:

A lemon wheel

SINGAPORE SLING
1 serving

This was invented in the early 1900s at the legendary Long Bar at the Raffles Hotel in Singapore. There are countless versions, the only constants being gin and cherry brandy.

Fill a chilled, tall glass with ice cubes. Add:

1 ounce gin
1 ounce cherry brandy or Cherry Heering
1 ounce lime juice
1 ounce Bénédictine
A dash of Angostura bitters

Stir well. Top with:

2 ounces club soda

CHAN CHAN
1 serving

This summertime drink is the invention of two close friends, Rachel Ranch and David Browning. They named the drink after a Buena Vista Social Club song.

Muddle in a cocktail shaker:

½-inch slice cucumber
4 basil leaves
1 ounce lime juice
Pinch of salt

Fill the shaker with ice cubes. Add:

1½ ounces Old Tom gin
1 ounce St-Germain elderflower liqueur

Shake until well chilled, about 12 seconds, and strain into a chilled coupe glass. If desired, float on top:

(A paper-thin cucumber slice)

NEGRONI

1 serving

This is our favorite bitter cocktail. A lower-proof version, known as the **Americano,** omits the gin and adds a few ounces of club soda on top. For a **Negroni Sbagliato,** omit the gin, reduce the Campari and vermouth to 1 ounce each, and top off with 3 ounces Prosecco.

Fill a mixing glass three-quarters full of ice cubes. Add:

1½ ounces gin
1½ ounces Campari
1½ ounces sweet vermouth

Stir until well chilled, about 30 seconds. Strain into a chilled cocktail glass. Alternatively, fill an old-fashioned glass with ice, add the above ingredients, and stir. Garnish with:

An orange twist

CLOVER CLUB

1 serving

See About Egg Safety, 979. Combine in a cocktail shaker:

2 ounces London dry gin (1½ ounces if using vermouth)
1 ounce lemon juice
(½ ounce dry vermouth)
½ ounce Fruit Syrup, 16, made with raspberries
1 egg white

Shake without ice for 10 seconds. Fill the shaker with ice cubes and shake until well chilled, about 12 seconds. Strain into a chilled coupe or martini glass. Garnish, if desired, with:

(A skewer of raspberries)

PIMM'S CUP

1 serving

A gin-based liqueur enhanced with fruits and herbs, Pimm's No. 1 is especially suited to summertime outdoor parties.

Pour over ice in a chilled, tall glass:

2 ounces Pimm's No. 1
½ ounce lemon juice
(Several borage flowers or a small borage leaf, bruised and torn)

Fill the glass with:

Ginger ale

Garnish with:

A cucumber stick
A lemon or orange wheel
Sprig of mint

ABOUT VODKA AND AQUAVIT

Vodka may look deceptively like water (in fact, the word means "little water" in Russian), but it is actually a neutral spirit distilled from grain, usually barley or wheat, sometimes rye or corn, and occasionally potatoes, grapes, or even beets. Many consider vodka the perfect cocktail mixer because it doesn't impose much of its own flavor. However, there are differences between vodkas, and, to a certain degree, higher-quality vodkas are worth the extra expense. It can mean the difference between a balanced, smooth drink and a harsh, burning one.

Also available are an increasing number of flavored vodkas, enhanced with lemon, lime, orange, vanilla, or chile peppers, among other things. Infused vodkas are quite easy to make at home, and they often have a better flavor, see 22.

Aquavit is very similar to vodka (its name is derived from the latin *aqua vitae* or "water of life"), and is distilled from potatoes or grain. The primary difference is that aquavit is infused with herbs and spices (notably caraway and/or dill), and is sometimes aged in oak casks. As such, you may find clear, yellowish, or brownish aquavit. It is excellent on its own, served ice cold, but it may also be used in cocktails. One of the best Bloody Marys we know is made with aquavit and a healthy dose of grated fresh horseradish.

BLOODY MARY

1 serving

When tequila takes the place of vodka in a Bloody Mary, it becomes a **Bloody Maria**; made with gin, it is a **Ruddy Mary**. A Bloody Mary without any alcohol is, of course, a **Virgin Mary**.

Fill a cocktail shaker with ice cubes. Add:

1½ ounces vodka or aquavit
6 ounces tomato juice
(½ teaspoon prepared horseradish)
2 to 3 drops lemon juice, to taste
2 to 3 drops Worcestershire sauce, to taste
Hot pepper sauce to taste
Pinch of celery salt
Pinch of salt
Pinch of black pepper

Shake until well chilled, about 12 seconds. Strain over ice in a chilled highball glass. Garnish with:

A small celery stalk
(A skewer of mixed pickles, such as cocktail onions, cornichons, pickled okra, pickled beets, etc.)

BLOODY BULL SHOT

8 servings

Mix together in a pitcher:

32 ounces tomato or tomato-vegetable juice
One 10- to 11-ounce can condensed beef consommé

Pour over ice in each highball glass:

1½ ounces vodka (12 ounces total)
¾ teaspoon lime juice (2 tablespoons total)
A dash of hot sauce

Fill with the tomato-consommé mixture. Season to taste with:

Black pepper

SCREWDRIVER

1 serving

To make a **Greyhound,** substitute grapefruit juice for the orange juice. To make a **Salty Dog,** use grapefruit juice and rim the glass with coarse salt.

Fill a cocktail shaker with ice cubes. Add:

1½ ounces vodka
4 ounces orange juice

Shake until well chilled, about 12 seconds. Strain over ice in a chilled highball glass. Garnish with:

An orange wheel

COSMOPOLITAN

1 serving

Fill a cocktail shaker with ice cubes. Add:

1 ounce vodka
1 ounce cranberry juice
½ ounce triple sec
¼ ounce lime juice

Shake until well chilled, about 12 seconds. Strain into a chilled cocktail glass.

WHITE RUSSIAN

1 serving

To make a **Black Russian,** omit the heavy cream. For a vegan version, substitute **well-shaken, canned full-fat coconut milk or coconut cream** for the heavy cream.

Fill a cocktail shaker with ice cubes. Add:

1½ ounces vodka
1½ ounces heavy cream
1 ounce Kahlúa or other coffee liqueur

Shake until well chilled, about 12 seconds. Strain over ice in a chilled rocks glass.

MOSCOW MULE

1 serving

Pour over ice in a chilled mug or highball glass:

1½ ounces vodka
½ ounce lime juice

Fill the mug or glass with:

Ginger beer (5 to 7 ounces)

Stir well.

JOY TEA

1 serving

Fill a cocktail shaker with ice cubes. Add:

1½ ounces tea-infused vodka, below
1 ounce water
½ ounce Simple Syrup, 16

Shake until well chilled, about 12 seconds. Strain over ice in a chilled highball glass. Garnish with:

A lemon wheel

INFUSED VODKAS

Use the amounts in the chart below to infuse your own vodka. All amounts are for flavoring one 750ml bottle of vodka. ➤ Avoid over-steeping or the vodka can become bitter. Let vodka steep at room temperature. After straining, return the vodka to the bottle and store in the freezer indefinitely (we recommend serving it straight out of the freezer). Serve alone, or use in place of regular vodka in cocktails.

FLAVORING	AMOUNT	INFUSION TIME
Citrus	Zest of 1 medium lemon or orange, cut into strips	1 week
Tea	¼ cup black tea leaves	2 hours to 3 days
Pepper	½ cup black peppercorns	4 hours to 3 days
Horseradish	3 ounces horseradish root, peeled and cut into cubes	1 week
Vanilla	1 vanilla bean, split lengthwise	2 to 4 days
Herbs	2 large sprigs mint, basil, thyme, or rosemary	24 hours

ABOUT WHISKEY, WHISKY, AND SCOTCH

Whisky—or whiskey, as it is spelled in the United States and Ireland—is a distilled grain spirit made mainly from barley, corn, rye, or wheat and aged in oak barrels. **Scotch** gets its particular flavor from malted barley smoked over peat fires. Most Scotch is **blended;** that is, a percentage of malted barley liquor is mixed with a liquor made from another grain, often fairly neutral, which results in a milder drink. **Single-malt Scotch,** however, comes from a single distillery and is made exclusively from malted barley in old-fashioned pear-shaped copper stills, which result in strong and individualistic flavors, laden with overtones of smoke and malt. Scotch lovers sip single-malts in brandy snifters, neat or with a splash of water. **Blended malt whiskies** are a cheaper, intermediate category of Scotch, in which several single-malts are combined. Single-malts are generally preferred by connoisseurs, but blended Scotch can be superb as well, though they tend to be milder—which makes them especially useful for cocktails. Single-malts tend to overwhelm other ingredients in a mixed drink; that said, their smoky character can be appreciated when judiciously added to drinks like the Penicillin, 24.

Irish whiskey is somewhat similar to Scotch, but there are several important differences in the method of manufacture: The barley is dried with coal instead of peat fires, a percentage of raw grain is used in the mash, and it's distilled more than once, making it a milder, less smoky drink.

Bourbon whiskey is primarily distilled from corn, and its characteristic flavor comes from the charred oak barrels in which it is aged. Bourbon is somewhat sweeter and smoother than other whiskies. Most bourbon is made in Kentucky, but it is not a protected designation. Whiskey with a corn content greater than 80 percent is called **corn whiskey. Tennessee whiskey** is filtered through sugar maple charcoal, adding a layer of unique flavor. **Rye whiskey,** made predominantly from rye rather than corn or barley, has a limited but steady popularity. It is spicier and drier than bourbon.

Canadian whisky may be made from a combination of rye, corn, barley, or wheat, and is usually lighter than other whiskies. **Japanese whisky** is relatively new to the whisky family, and Japanese regulations on the process are much looser than those for Scottish, Irish, or American whiskies. However, many Japanese whiskies are exceptional and command a premium price.

Cask-strength whiskey is stronger than other whiskies, as it is not diluted with water and is bottled straight from the barrel. These whiskies can be overpowering, so it is best to add a small splash of water to mute their nose-burning bite and bring out their subtleties.

MANHATTAN

1 serving

My grandfather John, a prolific tender of the family bar, referred to these as "Manhappies," and with good reason: At the end of a long day, they never fail to raise our spirits. A **Perfect Manhattan** uses half dry and half sweet vermouth. Scotch may replace the bourbon or rye in the formula, in which case it's called a **Rob Roy.**

Pour over ice in a chilled rocks glass:

2 ounces bourbon, rye, or blended whiskey
1 ounce dry or sweet vermouth
A dash of Angostura bitters

Stir well. This cocktail may also be shaken with ice and strained into a chilled cocktail glass. Garnish with:

An orange twist or a small skewer of brandied cherries

OLD-FASHIONED

1 serving

Using Scotch instead of bourbon or rye also makes a tasty drink. You may also muddle a sugar cube with the bitters (and an orange wheel, if desired), then add the whiskey, stirring to dissolve the sugar, and strain over ice.

Fill a mixing glass halfway with ice cubes. Add:

1½ ounces bourbon or rye whiskey
½ teaspoon Simple Syrup, 16
2 dashes Angostura bitters

Stir until well chilled, about 30 seconds. Strain over a large ice cube in a chilled rocks glass. Garnish with:

A lemon or orange twist
(A maraschino cherry)

WHISKEY SOUR

1 serving

Try a gin, rum, brandy, or **Tequila Sour** (for tequila, substitute lime juice for the lemon juice, if desired). You may also add an egg white, shaking the white with the whiskey, citrus, and sugar or syrup for 10 seconds before adding ice, then shaking 12 seconds with ice before straining into a chilled glass. Please read About Egg Safety, 979.

Fill a cocktail shaker with ice cubes. Add:

2 ounces blended whiskey
1 ounce lemon juice
1 teaspoon Simple Syrup, 16, or sugar

Shake until well chilled, about 12 seconds. Strain into a chilled old-fashioned glass. Garnish with:

A lemon wheel or lemon twist and/or a maraschino cherry

HIGHBALL OR RICKEY

1 serving

Put 2 large ice cubes into a chilled highball glass. Add:

2 ounces whiskey, bourbon, Scotch, rye, or gin

Fill the glass with:

Club soda

Stir lightly and serve.

SAZERAC

1 serving

A classic New Orleans cocktail that has been getting Mardi Gras revelers in trouble since the late 1800s. If you have a small, clean atomizer, fill it with absinthe and spray the inside of the glass rather than rinsing it. This saves absinthe and is less messy.

Rinse the inside of a chilled rocks glass with:

Absinthe

Pour out any excess (if making multiple Sazeracs, pour excess into the next glass). Fill a mixing glass three-quarters full with ice cubes. Add:

2 ounces rye whiskey
1 teaspoon Simple Syrup, 16
2 dashes Peychaud's bitters
2 dashes Angostura bitters

Stir until well chilled, about 30 seconds. Strain into the absinthe-rinsed glass. Twist over the drink:

A wide strip of lemon zest

Discard the lemon peel.

BLOOD AND SAND

1 serving

This cocktail's namesake is a 1922 silent film about a matador whose career ends predictably. Making this cocktail is, fortunately, a pursuit less likely to end in tragedy.

Fill a cocktail shaker with ice cubes. Add:

1½ ounces blended Scotch whisky
¾ ounce sweet vermouth
½ ounce Cherry Heering
½ ounce orange juice

Shake until well chilled, about 12 seconds. Strain into a chilled coupe glass. If desired, garnish with:

(An orange twist or brandied cherry)

PENICILLIN

1 serving

This pseudo-medicinal cocktail has the flavors of a hot toddy, but in a more concentrated form and with an extra helping of smokiness from the single-malt Scotch. This drink is usually made with a honey-ginger syrup, but we have simplified the process for more immediate gratification. Omit the ginger and swap the whisky for gin, and you've got the Prohibition-era classic, the **Bee's Knees**.

Place in the bottom of a cocktail shaker:

3 thin slices ginger
¾ ounce lemon juice
1 teaspoon honey

Muddle the ginger until bruised and fragrant and add ice cubes to the shaker, along with:

2 ounces blended Scotch

Shake until well chilled, about 12 seconds. Strain into a chilled rocks glass filled with ice. Pour on top:

¼ ounce single-malt Islay Scotch

BOULEVARDIER

1 serving

Using dry vermouth instead of sweet makes an **Old Pal** cocktail.

Fill a mixing glass three-quarters full with ice cubes. Add:

1½ ounces bourbon or rye whiskey
1 ounce sweet vermouth
1 ounce Campari

Stir until well chilled, about 30 seconds. Strain over a large ice cube in a chilled cocktail glass. Garnish with:

An orange twist or a brandied cherry

MINT JULEP

1 serving

This drink is superlative. And it is well, at this point, to remember that, as Voltaire put it, "The good is the enemy of the best." Use the best bourbon you can afford, tender mint leaves for bruising, and very finely crushed ice. To make a **Whiskey Smash,** muddle **½ lemon, cut into quarters,** with the mint and simple syrup.

Muddle in a chilled highball glass or silver julep cup:

5 to 6 fresh mint leaves
1 teaspoon Simple Syrup, 16

Pour in:

2 ounces bourbon

Fill the glass with:

Crushed ice

Stir once, and garnish with:

A bushy mint sprig

MILK PUNCH

1 serving

Another New Orleans classic, from the French 75 bar in Arnaud's restaurant. It is often consumed at brunch, and we agree that this is a cocktail worth getting out of bed for.

Fill a cocktail shaker with ice cubes. Add:

2 ounces milk or half-and-half
1½ ounces bourbon
½ ounce dark rum
½ ounce Simple Syrup, 16
½ teaspoon vanilla

Shake until well chilled, about 12 seconds. Strain into a chilled cocktail glass and dust with:

Freshly grated nutmeg

HOT TODDY

1 serving

Though we do not make any health claims for this warm tipple, it is our cold remedy of choice and takes the chill off icy winter evenings.

Place in an 8-ounce ceramic or earthenware mug:

2-inch piece unpeeled ginger, cut lengthwise into thin slabs

Pour over the ginger:

4 ounces boiling water

Cover the cup with a saucer to keep warm and steep for 5 minutes.

Stir in:

2 ounces bourbon
1 to 2 tablespoons lemon juice, to taste
Up to 2 teaspoons honey, to taste

ABOUT RUM

Rum is distilled from the juice of sugarcane or from molasses made from sugarcane. As it is produced primarily in the Caribbean and South America, it is hardly surprising that rum is the traditional alcoholic component of tropical drinks. Heavier, more pungent rums (for instance, those of Jamaica) and some of the lighter ones from the islands of Guadeloupe and Martinique can achieve great subtlety and complexity when well aged and can be served like fine brandy in a snifter. Don't waste these fine rums in mixed drinks. In general, light rums (also called white or silver) should be used for cocktails, and medium-bodied (also called amber or gold) ones for punches and long drinks. The color of rum may or may not be indicative of age—many white rums are barrel-aged and then filtered to render them colorless; conversely, many dark rums are artificially colored. **Rhum agricole** is a product of Martinique, made with pure sugarcane juice and can be found unaged (*rhum blanc*), gold (*rhum paille*), or aged (*rhum vieux*). **Spiced rum** is infused with cinnamon, cloves, and other warm spices after distillation. The best spiced rums are made with gold rum, while cheaper spiced rum is made with white rum that is tinted with caramel color. **Jamaican rum** is made from molasses and as a result is nearly black in color. These rums are rich in flavor from barrel-aging and contribute a distinctive funkiness to many tiki cocktails. If you are a rum lover these are well suited to sipping by themselves.

Cachaça is a Brazilian liquor made from fresh sugarcane juice. It may be rested in stainless steel casks, resulting in a light, grassy product, or aged in wood barrels, resulting in a richer, more complex flavor.

CUBA LIBRE

1 serving

A Caribbean classic. Although any cola may be used, the drink was made originally with and is indelibly associated with Coca-Cola.

Pour over ice in a chilled highball glass:

6 ounces cola
1½ ounces light rum
½ ounce lime juice
Stir, and garnish with:
A lime wheel

DAIQUIRI

1 serving

With grenadine substituted for the simple syrup, this cocktail becomes a **Pink Daiquiri** or **Daiquiri Grenadine.**

Fill a cocktail shaker with ice cubes. Add:
2 ounces light rum
¾ ounce lime juice
2 teaspoons Simple Syrup, 16
Shake until well chilled, about 12 seconds. Strain into a chilled cocktail glass.

FROZEN DAIQUIRI

1 serving

This is a formula that can be interestingly varied. For a frozen fruit daiquiri, add 1 cup sliced fresh or frozen strawberries, sliced peaches or bananas, or cubed melon or substitute Fruit Syrup, 16, for the simple syrup.

Process in a blender until smooth:
2 ounces light rum
1 ounce grapefruit or orange juice
1 ounce lime juice
½ ounce Simple Syrup, 16
½ ounce maraschino liqueur or Curaçao
2 cups ice cubes
Pour into a chilled wineglass.

JUNGLE BIRD

1 serving

An excellent bittersweet tiki cocktail that contains accessible ingredients.

Fill a cocktail shaker three-quarters full with ice cubes. Add:
1½ ounces Jamaican or blackstrap rum
1½ ounces pineapple juice
¾ ounce Campari
½ ounce lime juice
¼ ounce Simple Syrup, 16
Shake until well chilled, about 12 seconds. Strain into a chilled cocktail glass filled with ice.

CAIPIRINHA

1 serving

The classic Brazilian cocktail. Using whole pieces of lime with the peel adds a bitter complexity to this simple drink. To make a **Caipiroska**, substitute vodka for the cachaça.

Halve crosswise:
1 lime
Reserve half of the lime for another use, cut the other half into quarters, and place the lime quarters in a chilled old-fashioned glass. Add:
2 teaspoons sugar or raw sugar
Muddle the lime pieces with the sugar just enough to extract the juice (bruising the lime peel too much will make the drink overly bitter). Add:
2 ounces cachaça
Stir to dissolve the sugar. Fill the chilled glass with roughly crushed ice and stir to chill.

PIÑA COLADA

1 serving

Process in a blender until smooth and frothy:
2 ounces light rum
2 ounces pineapple juice
2 ounces sweetened cream of coconut, such as Coco López
½ ounce lime juice
1 cup crushed ice or pebble ice
Pour into a chilled highball glass. Garnish with:
½ slice pineapple

MAI TAI

1 serving

Orgeat is an almond-flavored syrup scented with orange flower water. It is a staple ingredient in many tiki cocktails.

Fill a cocktail shaker with ice cubes. Add:
1 ounce dark rum
1 ounce light rum
¾ ounce lime juice
½ ounce Curaçao
½ ounce almond syrup or orgeat
(A dash of grenadine)
Shake until well chilled, about 12 seconds. Strain into a chilled old-fashioned glass, with or without ice. Garnish with:
A lime wedge and a mint sprig, or a skewer of fresh fruit

DARK ’N STORMY

1 serving

Though ginger beer is really the thing to use here, when we can find it we love to substitute Blenheim’s Old #3 Hot-Red Cap.

Fill a chilled highball glass with ice cubes. Add:
2 ounces dark rum, such as Goslings Black Seal
½ ounce lime juice
About 4 ounces ginger beer, to fill the glass
Stir with a long spoon. Garnish with:
A lime wheel

MOJITO

1 serving

A Cuban highball well known and loved for its refreshing combination of white rum, lime juice, and mint.

Add to a cocktail shaker:
6 mint leaves
1 teaspoon sugar
½ ounce lime juice
Muddle until the mint leaves are well crushed. Add:
2 ounces white rum

Fill the cocktail shaker with ice cubes and shake until well chilled, about 12 seconds. Strain the cocktail into a chilled highball glass filled with ice. Top off the cocktail with:

2 ounces club soda

Garnish with:

A bushy mint sprig

SPANISH COFFEE

1 serving

Every winter we make the pilgrimage to Huber's, the oldest restaurant in Portland, to have Spanish coffees. The bartenders make a show of lighting the booze on fire and pouring the liquors into the glass from above their heads. We could never perform these feats at home, but this formula is otherwise faithful to their time-tested recipe.

Run around the rim of a thick, squat wineglass with a stem:

1 lime wedge

Frost the rim of the glass, 18, with:

Sugar, preferably superfine

Add to the glass:

¾ ounce overproof rum
½ ounce triple sec

Tilt the glass slightly, and light the liquor with a match (if you have trouble lighting it, use two matches at once). Holding the glass by the stem, rotate it slowly so the flame caramelizes the sugar all the way around the rim. This will take a couple minutes and the glass will become very hot. To extinguish the flames, add:

1½ ounces Kahlúa
3 ounces hot brewed strong coffee

Garnish with:

Whipped cream, 791
Freshly grated nutmeg

Wait a minute or so before drinking, as the rim of the glass will be very hot.

GROG

1 serving

This cocktail is based on a mixture of water and rum rationed to British seamen to raise their spirits, make stagnant water more palatable, and prevent scurvy. Maple syrup, molasses, or honey may be substituted for the sugar.

Stir together in an 8-ounce mug:

1½ ounces dark rum
½ ounce lime juice
1 to 2 teaspoons raw sugar, to taste

Fill the mug with:

Very hot tea or water

Garnish with:

A lemon or orange twist
A pinch of ground nutmeg or cinnamon

HOT BUTTERED RUM

1 serving

An old-time New England favorite that is said to make one see double and feel single.

Place in a warmed 8-ounce mug:

2 ounces dark rum
1 tablespoon salted butter
1 to 2 teaspoons powdered sugar, to taste
Pinch of ground cinnamon
1 whole clove

Fill the mug with:

Boiling water

Stir well. Sprinkle on top:

Freshly grated nutmeg

ABOUT TEQUILA AND MEZCAL

Tequila is distilled from the fermented sap of the blue agave plant, usually mixed with neutral spirits of various kinds. Tequila's popularity in the United States follows a slow arc from obscurity until Prohibition, when those with means traveled south of the border to find legal alcohol, to the present day, when no fewer than a dozen brands of tequila are available on even the most scantily stocked liquor store shelves.

Blanco or silver tequila is unaged. **Reposado** tequila is aged for at least two months and up to less than twelve months. **Añejo** tequila is aged for at least a year in oak barrels. In **extra añejo** tequila, the youngest tequila in the blend is aged for at least 3 years in barrels. **Gold** tequila contains up to 49 percent sugars from sources other than agave, meaning it is not 100-percent agave tequila. To ensure that you are buying 100-percent agave tequila, look for "no sugars added" on the label.

Mezcal, made from many different types of agave, is notable for its production process, which results in a markedly different product from tequila. While tequila is made by roasting agave *piñas,* or hearts, in brick ovens or steaming them in autoclaves, then crushing and fermenting the sap, mezcal is made by slowly roasting the *piñas* in deep pits heated with wood fires for days or even weeks before they are crushed. The resulting mash is fermented with natural yeasts and bacteria, then distilled. The slow roasting process gives mezcal its distinctive smoky flavor.

Tequila is most commonly consumed in the United States by the shot, with salt and a lime wedge chaser, but it is worth seeking out tequilas that are smooth and delicious enough to sip on their own. Besides the tequila cocktails found here, substitute tequila for gin in a Gin and Tonic, 20, or try a Tequila Sunrise, 27.

MARGARITA

1 serving

Run around the rim of a chilled cocktail or margarita glass:

A lime wedge

Frost the rim of the glass, 18, with:

Coarse salt

Fill a cocktail shaker with ice cubes. Add:

2 ounces silver or reposado tequila
¾ ounce triple sec, Cointreau, or Grand Marnier
¾ ounce lime juice
1 teaspoon Simple Syrup, 16

Shake until well chilled, about 12 seconds. Strain into the prepared glass. Garnish with the lime wedge.

FROZEN MARGARITA

Place the ingredients for a **Margarita, 26,** in a blender, increasing the lime juice to 1 ounce and the simple syrup to ½ ounce. Add **1 cup roughly crushed ice** and blend until the ice has a slushy consistency. Pour into a chilled cocktail or margarita glass.

PALOMA

1 serving

We do not normally advocate for specific brands of ingredients, but we would be remiss not to tell you that Mexican Squirt is truly the best grapefruit soda to use here. It is widely available at Mexican grocery stores and markets. If you cannot find it, Jarritos grapefruit soda is a decent substitute. To avoid using a soft drink altogether, substitute **2 ounces grapefruit juice**, **2 ounces club soda or sparkling water**, and **1 teaspoon Simple Syrup, 16.**

Run around the rim of a chilled rocks or cocktail glass:

1 lime wedge

Frost the rim of the glass, 18, with:

Coarse salt

Add to the glass:

3 ounces Mexican grapefruit soda
2 ounces silver or reposado tequila or mezcal
½ ounce lime juice

Stir, then fill the glass with ice cubes. Garnish with:

A grapefruit wedge

TEQUILA SUNRISE

1 serving

This cocktail helped introduce tequila to wary Americans in the 1930s, but truly hit its stride in the 1970s, when it gained notoriety as the debaucherous beverage of choice for the Rolling Stones's 1972 American tour.

Pour over ice cubes in a chilled highball glass:

2 ounces silver or reposado tequila
4 ounces orange juice

Stir well. Pour over the top:

1 teaspoon grenadine

Do not stir. Garnish with:

An orange wheel

ABOUT BRANDY

Brandy is distilled from fruit, most commonly grapes. All wine-producing countries make brandy (the word comes from the Dutch *brandewijn,* meaning burnt wine). **Cognac**—the world's most famous brandy—is made only in the Cognac region of France, and prized for its lightness and finesse. VS (very special) or three-star Cognac has been barrel-aged for at least two years; VSOP (very superior old pale) Cognac is aged at least four years; and XO (extra old) Cognac is at least six years old—theoretically, the older the spirit, the smoother it will be. In general, VS is the best spirit for mixed drinks. While we adhere firmly to the belief that "the better the liquor, the better the drink," we recommend sipping brandies of VSOP and XO quality on their own. **Armagnac** is a close cousin, made in the Armagnac region of France and similarly labeled. As a general rule, Armagnac tends to be more full-bodied than Cognac.

Many other European countries produce high-quality brandies, such as German **Asbach.** There are several stellar brandies to be found stateside as well, especially from California and Oregon. **Pisco** is a Peruvian and Chilean brandy made from a single grape variety or a mixture of them.

While brandy is distilled from wine, **marc** (as the French call it) and **grappa** (the Italian name) are distilled from the mush of grape skins and stalks left after wine is made. Unlike brandy, marc and grappa are usually colorless. They are fiery spirits, often with a rough finish, although at their best they can be intensely aromatic and quite delicious.

Calvados, which comes from Normandy, France, is distilled from apple cider and barrel-aged for at least two years. At its best, it can rival Cognac and Armagnac. **Applejack** is an American-made apple brandy. Another class of nongrape brandies are generally known by their French name, **eaux-de-vie,** or "waters of life." Colorless and very agreeable in flavor and aroma, though never very complicated, eaux-de-vie are served in snifters. The most popular varieties are **poire** or **poire Williams** (pear), **framboise** (raspberry), **Mirabelle** or **slivovitz** (plum), and **kirsch** (cherry); but virtually any kind of fruit can be used.

BRANDY ALEXANDER

1 serving

Notoriously rich and sweet, making it a good after-dinner drink.

Fill a cocktail shaker with ice cubes. Add:

1½ ounces brandy
¾ ounce dark crème de cacao
¾ ounce heavy cream

Shake until well chilled, about 12 seconds. Strain into a chilled coupe or cocktail glass. Garnish with:

A dusting of freshly grated nutmeg

VIEUX CARRÉ

1 serving

One of the classic New Orleans cocktails, invented in the French Quarter's Hotel Monteleone.

Fill a mixing glass three-quarters full with ice. Add:

1 ounce rye whiskey
1 ounce Cognac
1 ounce sweet vermouth
1 teaspoon Bénédictine
2 dashes Angostura bitters
2 dashes Peychaud's bitters

Stir until well chilled, about 30 seconds. Strain into a chilled rocks glass filled with ice. Garnish with:

A lemon twist or brandied cherry

PISCO SOUR

1 serving

Both Peru and Chile claim this cocktail as their national drink. Pisco is simply a type of grape brandy. See About Egg Safety, 979.

Add to a cocktail shaker:

2 ounces pisco
¾ ounce lime juice

½ ounce Simple Syrup, 16
1 egg white

Shake for 10 seconds without ice, then add ice and shake until well chilled, about 12 seconds. Strain into a chilled cocktail glass. Garnish with:

A few drops of Angostura bitters

SIDECAR

1 serving

If desired, frost the rim of a cocktail glass, 18, with:

(Sugar)

Fill a cocktail shaker with ice cubes. Add:

1½ ounces VS Cognac
¾ ounce triple sec or Cointreau
¾ ounce lemon juice
1 teaspoon Simple Syrup, 16 (omit if frosting the rim with sugar)

Shake until well chilled, about 12 seconds. Strain into a chilled cocktail glass.

STINGER

1 serving

Fill a mixing glass three-quarters full with ice cubes. Add:

2 ounces brandy
½ ounce white crème de menthe

Stir until well chilled, about 30 seconds. Strain into a chilled cocktail or old-fashioned glass and garnish with:

A mint leaf

NIKOLASHKA

The peculiar drink of Grand Duke Nicholas's regiment, as recreated by our dear friend Sasha Vereschagin. *Vashe zdorovie!* To your health!

Slice as thinly as possible:

1 lemon

Dredge one side of each lemon slice in:

Freshly ground coffee

Place coffee side down on a platter and sprinkle with:

¼ teaspoon sugar

If desired, grate over the lemon slices until they appear peppered:

(Milk, semisweet, or dark chocolate)

Place a lemon slice in your mouth, chew for a few seconds, and quickly sip:

Cognac

ABOUT CORDIALS AND LIQUEURS

Cordials and liqueurs are made by infusing liquor, such as vodka, brandy, or whisky, with other flavors. There is a remarkable array of liqueurs, including Italian **amari,** herbal liqueurs such as Chartreuse, Jägermeister, and Bénédictine, and fruit-based liqueurs like crème de cassis. A common characteristic of almost all cordials and liqueurs is their sweetness. They may have one predominant flavor: caraway in kümmel, mint in crème de menthe, anise in anisette, cherry in maraschino liqueur; or they may have a very complex flavor profile, as evidenced by Chartreuse, Bénédictine, and Drambuie. Cordials and liqueurs are used in small doses in mixed cocktails, or they may be taken on their own, as a softer, sweeter alternative to brandy or a stomach-soothing digestif.

GRASSHOPPER

1 serving

Jeffrey Morgenthaler, bartender at Clyde Common and Pépé Le Moko in Portland, Oregon, turned this classic into a creamy, frothy **Grasshopper Shake**: Omit the half-and-half, add ½ **cup vanilla ice cream**, and process in a blender with **1 cup crushed ice.**

Fill a cocktail shaker with ice cubes. Add:

1 ounce green crème de menthe (or white crème de menthe and a drop of green food coloring, if desired)
1 ounce white crème de cacao
1 ounce half-and-half
(A dash of mint bitters or ½ teaspoon Fernet Branca Menta)

Shake until well chilled, about 12 seconds. Strain into a chilled cocktail glass.

ABOUT VIRGIN COCKTAILS

"Virgin," or nonalcoholic, drinks may be appreciated by adults and the underaged alike. In addition to those that follow here, see the nonalcoholic variations for Bloody Mary, 21, and Mulled Cider, 32. Also see the Beverages chapter, especially the Thirst Quenchers, 13–15, many of which are elegant alternatives to spiked drinks.

SHIRLEY TEMPLE

1 serving

For generations, this has been the first cocktail sampled by American children—named for the 1930s child movie star. Substituting cola for ginger ale produces a **Roy Rogers**.

Stir together with ice in a chilled old-fashioned glass:

1 dash grenadine
Ginger ale

Garnish with:

A maraschino cherry

CRANBERRY COLLINS

1 serving

Stir together with ice in a chilled highball glass:

4 ounces sweetened cranberry juice
¾ ounce lemon juice

Fill the glass with:

Club soda

Garnish with:

A lemon wheel

ROCK SHANDY

1 serving

Angostura bitters contain alcohol, but determining the amount held in a single dash brings to mind the similarly confounding question of how many angels can dance on the head of a pin.

Stir together with ice in a chilled highball glass:

4 ounces lemonade
2 ounces club soda
A dash of Angostura bitters

Garnish with:
A lemon wheel

ABOUT PUNCHES

The punch bowl tends to draw people together and animate social gatherings in ways that go beyond the effects of the alcohol it may contain. Punches and other party drinks can also be served in pitchers. To keep hot party drinks warm, serve in a slow cooker set to its lowest heat; ➤ this is not recommended, however, for egg-based drinks.

Ideally, punch mixes should be allowed to blend for an hour or so; if served cold, they should be chilled in the refrigerator before club soda, water, or ice is added. With cold punches, be on the alert for dilution. Ice only two-thirds of the liquid at the outset and add the remainder of the punch with more ice when it runs out (replenish with more club soda or Champagne).

As for the ice itself, avoid small pieces; even regular-sized cubes melt fairly quickly. Large ice blocks can be made by freezing water in mixing bowls or other containers; when ready to use, dip the bottom of the bowl into cold water and invert onto a plate. Slide into the punch bowl. Best yet, decorative ice molds, below, are unique and don't melt as quickly.

DECORATIVE ICE MOLD

1 ice ring

For an unclouded ice ring, let filtered tap water sit at room temperature for 1 hour before using.

Place in the bottom of a 4- to 6-cup ring mold, tube pan, or Bundt pan:

Fresh strawberries, cherries, raspberries, or cranberries, or thin slices of citrus fruit
Sprigs of fresh mint, thyme, or sweet woodruff

Cover with ice cubes or crushed ice, then add enough water to cover the fruit, herbs, and ice and freeze. When ready to serve, dip the bottom of the mold in cold water for a few moments, and invert onto a plate. Slide the ice ring into a punch bowl to float in the drink.

CHAMPAGNE PUNCH

Twenty-four 6-ounce servings

Combine in a large bowl:

6 ounces Fruit Syrup (made with raspberries or strawberries), 16, or to taste
6 ounces lemon juice
4 oranges, thinly sliced
4 cups fresh pineapple chunks

Stir and refrigerate for 4 hours. Just before serving, place in a chilled punch bowl. Stir and add:

Four 750ml bottles brut Champagne, chilled

SANGRÍA

8 to 12 servings

Combine in a large pitcher:

Two 750ml bottles dry red wine such as rioja, malbec, or shiraz
½ cup brandy
¼ cup Cointreau
6 tablespoons lemon juice
½ cup sugar, or to taste

Stir to dissolve the sugar. Add:

1 orange, cut into small chunks
1 lemon, cut into small chunks
1 tart apple, cored and cut into small chunks
(1 cup sliced pitted peaches or plums)

Cover with plastic wrap and refrigerate for 2 hours.

FISH HOUSE PUNCH

About twenty 4-ounce servings

This potent colonial punch was first formulated at Philadelphia's Schuylkill Fishing Company. Peach brandy can be very hard to find. Cocktail historian David Wondrich recommends substituting **3 ounces bonded applejack** and **1 ounce high-quality peach liqueur.** Do not substitute peach liqueur for the full amount of brandy or the drink will be far too sweet.

Chill the ingredients first, then mix in a chilled punch bowl:

3 cups water or brewed black tea
2 cups dark rum
1½ cups lemon juice
1¼ cups Simple Syrup, 16, or to taste
1½ cups brandy
½ cup peach brandy

Keep cold with large ice cubes or an ice mold, above.

PLANTER'S PUNCH

About twenty 4-ounce servings

Mix in a large pitcher or bowl:

3½ cups dark rum
2½ cups pineapple juice
¾ cup orange juice
¾ cup lime or lemon juice
¾ cup Simple Syrup, 16

Fill tall glasses three-quarters full with:

Crushed ice or pebble ice

Pour the punch mixture to within ¾ inch of the top of each. Decorate with:

Pineapple wedges or orange wheels

Serve with straws.

CHATHAM ARTILLERY PUNCH

About twenty 6-ounce servings

This is the original artillery punch, as relayed by David Wondrich in his exquisite book, *Punch: The Delights (and Dangers) of the Flowing Bowl.* This recipe calls for making what is referred to as an **oleo saccharum:** a mixture of lemon peels macerated with sugar until the peels release their oils.

Add to a large jar or bowl and chill in the refrigerator or freezer:

1¾ cups VSOP Cognac
1¾ cups bourbon
1¾ cups Jamaican rum

Meanwhile, using a Y-shaped vegetable peeler, pull off strips of zest (getting as little white pith as possible) from:

6 lemons

Place the strips in a large nonreactive bowl and add:

¾ cup sugar

¼ cup packed light brown or demerara sugar

Muddle the zest and sugar vigorously until the sugar looks like wet sand, then cover and let sit at warm room temperature until the oils in the zest have nearly liquefied the sugar, about 1 hour. Add:

1 cup lemon juice

Stir until the sugar is completely dissolved, then strain, discarding the lemon zest, and refrigerate until well chilled. Transfer the chilled lemon-sugar mixture to a large punch bowl. Fill the punch bowl half full with finely cracked ice and add the chilled mix of liquors, along with:

Two 750ml bottles brut Champagne, chilled

Serve immediately.

BOWLE

About twenty-five 6-ounce servings

A German favorite made with any of a variety of fruits. If desired, substitute 2 bottles sparkling white wine for 2 of the bottles of white wine.

Slice and place in a large bowl:

6 unpeeled peaches, 8 unpeeled apricots, 1 pineapple, or 1 quart strawberries

Sprinkle with:

1¼ cups powdered sugar

Pour in:

2 cups Madeira or cream sherry

Allow to chill for 4 hours. Stir, then pour into a chilled punch bowl. Add:

Four 750ml bottles dry white wine, chilled

MAITRANK (MAY WINE)

About twenty-five 5-ounce servings

Another German drink, dedicated to springtime and featuring fresh sweet woodruff, 1027, which, incidentally, may be grown in a shady corner of your backyard. Use the leaves before the plant's fragrant white flowers have bloomed.

Place in a bowl in the order listed:

12 sprigs young sweet woodruff

1¼ cups powdered sugar

One 750ml bottle riesling, chilled

(1 cup brandy)

Cover and let stand, refrigerated, for 30 minutes, no longer. Remove the woodruff. Stir thoroughly and pour into a chilled punch bowl. Add:

Three 750ml bottles riesling, chilled

1 liter club soda or one 750ml bottle Champagne, chilled

Thinly sliced oranges, sticks of pineapple, and, most appropriate of all, sprigs of woodruff may be used to decorate the bowl. Put a hulled strawberry in the bottom of each glass, to be eaten when the drink is finished.

BECKER DELUXE EGGNOG

About eighteen 6-ounce servings

This is our family's favorite eggnog, and it has graced our holiday table for many years. Be sure to let the egg yolks mingle with the liquor in your refrigerator for the full time. If you don't, your nog may taste more like a naughty omelet than holiday cheer. This eggnog will keep indefinitely in the refrigerator (in fact, some would argue that eggnog improves with time; we can at least vouch for it still being wonderfully tasty for up to a year). If desired, reserve the egg whites, beat them to stiff peaks with a couple tablespoons sugar, and fold them into the eggnog just before serving. See About Egg Safety, 979.

Beat in a large bowl until light in color:

12 egg yolks

Gradually beat in:

1 pound powdered sugar

Add very slowly, beating constantly:

2 cups light rum

Let stand, covered, in the refrigerator for 1 hour to dispel the eggy taste.

Add, beating constantly:

2 quarts heavy cream or half-and-half

2 cups Cognac or Asbach

1 cup Grand Marnier or Cointreau

Refrigerate, covered, for at least 3 hours. Serve sprinkled with:

Freshly grated nutmeg

COOKED EGGNOG

Please read About Egg Safety, 979. Assemble the ingredients for **Becker Deluxe Eggnog, above.** Whisk the egg yolks with the sugar in a large bowl. In a large saucepan, heat 1 quart of the heavy cream over medium-low heat until steaming. While whisking, slowly add about half of the hot cream to the egg yolks. Then slowly pour the cream and egg mixture back into the saucepan, stirring constantly. Cook, stirring, until the mixture thickens a little and reaches a temperature of 175°F. Do not overheat or the mixture will curdle. Remove from the heat and immediately stir in the remaining quart of heavy cream or half-and-half. Strain, cool completely, and chill until cold. Stir in the rum, Cognac, and Grand Marnier. Cover and refrigerate for at least 3 hours. Serve sprinkled with nutmeg.

VEGAN EGGNOG

About eight 6-ounce servings

This eggnog is quite boozy, which is how we like it, but feel free to scale back on the rum, if desired.

Soak overnight in water to cover:

1 cup raw cashews

Drain and transfer to a blender along with:

One 13½-ounce can coconut milk

1 cup water

½ cup sugar or maple syrup

1 tablespoon vanilla

Blend until completely smooth and creamy. Strain into a punch bowl or pitcher and stir in:

1 cup light rum
½ cup Grand Marnier or Cointreau

Serve garnished with:

Freshly grated nutmeg

If making ahead of time, the eggnog may separate when refrigerated. Simply let it sit for 20 minutes at room temperature, then whisk well or reblend before serving.

SYLLABUB

About 10 servings

The original syllabub was made by milking a cow directly into a basin of wine or cider. Today a syllabub is a cream-based concoction flavored with sherry or white wine and acidified with lemon juice. It remains a favorite Christmas "drink" in parts of the American South—though its texture is more reminiscent of a creamy, airy mousse.

Combine in a 2-quart glass jar or glass or metal bowl:

¾ cup sugar
¾ cup cream sherry
Finely grated zest of 2 lemons
¼ cup strained lemon juice
2 tablespoons brandy or Cognac
½ teaspoon freshly grated nutmeg

Shake or whisk thoroughly. Cover tightly and refrigerate for at least 4 hours and up to 24 hours. Shake or whisk again to mix in any undissolved sugar, then strain if desired. In a large bowl, beat on high speed until very soft peaks form:

2½ cups cold heavy cream

Reduce the speed to low and slowly add the sherry mixture. Ladle into cups and dust with:

Freshly grated nutmeg

Serve with spoons.

TOM AND JERRY

About 20 servings

See About Egg Safety, 979.

Beat in a large bowl until stiff but not dry:

3 egg whites

Set aside. Beat together in a medium bowl:

3 egg yolks
1 cup powdered sugar
1½ teaspoons vanilla
¼ teaspoon ground cinnamon
⅛ teaspoon ground allspice
Pinch of ground cloves

Fold the yolk mixture into the beaten whites. (The egg mixture will keep, refrigerated, for up to 2 days.) To serve, place 2 tablespoons of the egg mixture into each warmed 8-ounce mug and add to each:

1 ounce dark rum
1 ounce brandy or Cognac

Fill each mug with:

Very hot water, milk, or coffee

Stir vigorously until foamy. Dust the tops with:

Freshly grated nutmeg

GLÖGG

Sixteen 4-ounce servings

This traditional Scandinavian Christmas drink was originally mulled wine, but over the years it came to acquire a considerably stronger alcoholic kick. Some Swedes even make it with high-proof neutral alcohol—a personal antifreeze for icy Scandinavian winter nights—but brandy and aquavit or vodka give it a nicer flavor.

Combine in a large nonreactive pot:

One 750ml bottle red wine
One 750ml bottle tawny port
Zest of 1 orange, removed in wide strips with a vegetable peeler
1 cup raisins

Tie up in a small square of cheesecloth:

4 cinnamon sticks
10 whole cloves
10 cardamom pods, lightly crushed
(2 whole star anise)

Add to the pot, cover, and bring almost to a boil. Reduce the heat to low and simmer, covered, for 1 hour. Discard the spice packet and orange zest. Stir into the wine:

2 cups brandy
1 cup aquavit or vodka

Hold a lighted long match near the liquid until the alcohol fumes ignite. Let burn for about 5 seconds, then extinguish by covering the pot. Ladle into warmed cups (be sure to spoon a few raisins into each) and garnish each cup with:

A few slivered almonds

Serve with small spoons for the raisins and almonds. Alternatively, you may strain, transfer to bottles, and store the glögg at room temperature for several months before serving. To serve, gently reheat until warm and garnish each serving with raisins and almonds.

MULLED WINE

About sixteen 6-ounce servings

Combine in a saucepan:

Four 750ml bottles merlot or other dry, full-bodied red wine
6 cinnamon sticks
10 whole cloves
8 allspice berries
Zest of 2 oranges, removed in wide strips with a vegetable peeler
¾ to 1 cup sugar, to taste
(2 whole star anise)
(1 vanilla bean, split lengthwise)

Bring to a simmer, reduce the heat to low, and simmer, covered, for 30 minutes. Ladle into warmed mugs, placing a cinnamon stick or a strip of orange zest in each one. If desired, add to each serving:

(1 tablespoon brandy or Cognac)

To make **Vin Brûlé,** a French variation, bring the same ingredients to a boil, covered, over high heat. Remove from the heat, uncover, and carefully ignite with a long match. When the flames have died, ladle the wine into warmed mugs, garnishing them as above.

WASSAIL

About twenty 6-ounce servings

The best time to "come a-wassailing" is, of course, Christmas week. See About Egg Safety, 979.

Core and bake as for Baked Apples I, 174:

8 all-purpose apples such as Pink Lady, Winesap, Braeburn, or Granny Smith

Combine in a saucepan:

1½ cups sugar
1 cup water
2 teaspoons ground ginger
1 teaspoon ground nutmeg
½ teaspoon ground mace
6 whole cloves
6 allspice berries
1 cinnamon stick

Bring to a boil, cover, and cook for 5 minutes. Meanwhile, beat in a large bowl with an electric mixer until stiff but not dry:

12 egg whites

Beat in another large bowl until light in color:

12 egg yolks

Fold the whites into the yolks. Strain the hot sugar and spice syrup into a large pot. Add to the syrup in the pot and heat just until steaming:

6 cups dry hard cider
6 cups apple cider
2 cups brandy

Whisking briskly, gradually beat the hot brandy mixture into the egg mixture. Cut the baked apples into chunks and add to the wassail. Ladle into warmed mugs, placing a piece of baked apple in each mug.

MULLED CIDER

Twenty 6-ounce servings

Particularly good when the weather is cool and fresh apple cider abundant. A nonalcoholic version can be made by omitting the rum.

Combine in a saucepan:

1 gallon apple cider
5 cinnamon sticks
10 whole cloves or 5 lightly crushed cardamom pods
Zest of 4 oranges, removed in wide strips with a vegetable peeler, or 4 small oranges, thinly sliced
(2-inch piece ginger, thinly sliced)
(1 vanilla bean, split lengthwise)

Bring to a simmer, reduce the heat to low, cover, and simmer for 30 minutes. Stir in:

1¾ cups light or dark rum

Ladle into warmed mugs, placing a cinnamon stick, a piece of orange zest, or an orange slice in each one.

ABOUT WINE

Wine is simply fermented grape juice: Grapes are crushed, the juice ferments, and its sugar is converted into alcohol, resulting in wine. According to the latest findings, humans have been making and consuming wine since the Stone Age. To be sure, modern technology has improved upon this basic, eight-thousand-year-old method of making hooch. Even a hundred years ago, the winemaker would open the doors to the wine cellar and let in the cold night air of autumn to cool the wooden barrels. Today, the majority of wine is made in temperature-regulated steel tanks that precisely control fermentation and flavor development. This ensures modern wines are of a higher overall quality than those that came before them. That said, many winemakers and drinkers believe the most authentic, flavorful wines are those made from grapes farmed and vinified according to the most traditional methods (see natural wine, 32).

The color of wine comes from the grape skins. Pink wine, aka rosé, or even white wine (such as blanc de noirs Champagne) can be made from red grapes if the juice is separated from the skins soon after the grapes are crushed. Some major factors that affect quality are soil and climate (or **terroir**), the ripeness and quality of the grapes, and the handling of the grapes and the burgeoning wines. These latter factors—the grit and determination of winemakers—can win the day: Despite the climatological odds being stacked against them, intrepid vine tenders and oenologists produce delicious wines in places like the Nandi Hills near Bangalore, India, where monsoons are a constant concern, and the Spanish Canary Islands off Morocco, where fierce Saharan winds, a desert climate, and black sands all add up to improbable—but not impossible—growing conditions.

Aside from the name of the winemaker, wines are named in two ways: Many are sold under the name of their principal grape, or **varietal;** many also include their growing region, or **geographical indication.** Specificity of these place names vary; some are vast (California's North Coast growing region encompasses three million acres) while others denote a tiny area (like the Cole Ranch region, which spans less than two hundred acres). Taken alone, these place names can mean very little. On the other hand, many European wines must be grown to specific standards if they are to be known by a **controlled appellation.** The famed wines of Bordeaux, Burgundy, Chianti, Rioja, and Dão rely on hundreds of years of cultivation, history, and tradition for their identities. Of course, some appellations are more controlled than others; when shopping among these illustrious names, remember: Though they may suggest a certain style of winemaking or grape type, appellations do not guarantee a wine's quality.

Vintage dates tell you when the grapes were picked. The majority of wines sold today are not really made with extended bottle aging in mind (this includes nearly all wines that sell for a reasonable price). In fact, some types of wine do not age well at all, especially wines that have low acidity or sugar content. Even those wines that do age well—pinot noir, cabernet sauvignon, Barolo, and the like—have their ups and downs, even when they come from the best producers. A basic rule of thumb is the more expensive the wine is, the more likely the weather was at its best for that vintage.

Another important piece of information wine labels convey is **alcoholic strength.** Table wines come in at between 7 and 15 percent alcohol by volume (dessert wines may be as high as 24 percent). Alcohol in wine is increased when grapes are left to ripen on the vine for longer. Boldly flavored wines can balance a high amount of alcohol, but more often than not, a higher-alcohol wine will create an unpleasant burning sensation on the palate, akin to the feeling of heat that a sip of liquor leaves on your tongue. This is an indicator that the alcohol content is out of whack, which is a sure recipe for a headache later.

Some European labeling practices have been widely adopted across the world. Wine made from grapevines owned by and close to the winery are often labeled **estate wines;** others may be even more specific, indicating the wine was produced with grapes from a single vineyard. The term **reserve** is inconsistently used to describe special, small batches kept separate and aged longer than the regular bottlings.

Organic wines are certified to have been produced without the use of pesticides, herbicides, or synthetic fertilizers. **Biodynamic** wines are harder to explain. Suffice it to say that those who produce biodynamic wines follow organic farming practices and a quasi-mystical observance of lunar cycles and events in the astrological calendar (these govern when grapes are pruned, watered, and harvested). Biodynamic farmers also use special compost preparations, some involving cow horns and nettles. Ultimately, biodynamic wines do not necessarily taste any different from conventionally grown wines. Many gravitate toward them simply because of the care taken in producing them.

There is no official set of standards for **natural** wine, nor are these wines reliably labeled as such. Despite this, natural wine is a growing category. The term is applied to wines made from organic or biodynamically farmed grapes, which are manipulated as little as possible during processing and fermentation, with nothing added or removed. In some cases, the grape mash is spontaneously fermented by exposure to ambient, wild yeasts. Natural wines are unpredictable and inconsistent from vintage to vintage, which is exactly how their fans like them: as unsparing, unique expressions of *terroir*.

With regard to **wooden corks, synthetic corks, screw tops, cans,** and **wine boxes:** They are simply no longer a mark of quality or lack thereof. Since time immemorial, wines good and bad have been spoiled by infected corks, which give them a moldy stink. Respected winemakers are turning to screw tops and synthetic corks to preserve quality. Twisting a metal cap off may take away a bit of the glamour of popping a cork, but it increases the odds of getting a decent wine. We are also happy to report that boxed wine is no longer to be avoided outright; many of them are surprisingly good, and what you fail to finish will keep for at least a month or two without becoming stale (which also makes them especially efficient for cooking with, 952).

Finally, a word on taste: You should. When in doubt about a wine, the answers are on the tip of your tongue. Informal opportunities for comparisons abound, to say nothing of amazing, new smartphone apps that can take an image of a wine label and immediately provide novice and expert reviews. Other help may be just around the corner at your local wine shop: Discuss your preferences and budget with your neighborhood wine merchant, follow through by stopping in regularly to discuss what you've tasted, and you will be rewarded with new finds.

WINE-TASTING TERMS

In their efforts to account for the unaccountable, wine experts use a special vocabulary to describe how wines taste. References to fruit are common, as well as comparisons to flowers, vegetables, spices, herbs, minerals, and smoke. Personifications can creep in (one wine may be "muscular," another "voluptuous," and so on). No matter; a few simple ideas and key words are enough to aid us.

Acidity: Various acids (citric, tartaric, malic) occur in grapes and wine. Balanced acidity makes a wine refreshing and crisp. Too much, and it tastes sour or harsh. Too little, and it's known as *flabby*—limp and dull.

Aftertaste or finish: It may be harsh, mouth puckering, or nearly nonexistent in a low-acid or characterless wine. Ideally, though, it should be refreshing, and linger.

Body: The density, weight, and fullness of a wine in your mouth, coming from the alcohol and the components of the dissolved grape pulp, make the wine feel heavy or light as you drink.

Bouquet: The smell of a wine, which is composed of the scent of the grape itself and other smells resulting from aging and fermentation. Bouquet is a nebulous term that we find, frankly, a little silly, but there is something to smelling a fine wine before drinking it (aroma, after all, is a huge part of flavor), and wineglasses are shaped in certain ways to better showcase the fragrance of wines. You may also hear the term "nose" to indicate the smell of a wine.

Dry: Wines characterized as "dry" are not sweet. Grapes contain fructose and glucose. These sugars are turned into alcohol by fermentation, which can be stopped while there is still sweetness in the wine (ranging from predominant to a hint) or go on to total dryness.

Fruit: The aroma and flavor of the grapes used, depending on their grape variety and vinification technique, can evoke those of other fruits, such as apples, peaches, apricots, berries, or even tropical fruits. These flavors are often faint, but they add to a wine's complexity.

Oxidation: If overexposed to air, a wine's virtues can fade. White wines darken and taste and smell like bruised fruit or old apples; reds taste stale, flat, and dried out.

Tannins: These occur naturally in the seeds and skins of fruit, and have an astringent, mouth-puckering quality (think of the drying sensation from drinking strong tea or the sensation of chewing the skin of an apple or plum). Too much tannin can make a wine seem harsh or overly dry, which can be especially apparent in young red wines. Luckily, tannins mellow with aging, and help preserve wines as they age in the bottle.

Texture: Various winemaking techniques such as barrel-aging, controlled exposure to oxygen, and a secondary fermentation all contribute to a wine's texture, or mouthfeel. If a wine is quite tannic, it can create an astringent feeling in the mouth. A light and refreshing white or rosé is often said to have a "crisp" texture, while an aged pinot noir may have a texture described as "silky."

SERVING WINES

Serving temperature can enhance the enjoyment of wine. Room temperature (an average of about 70°F) is too warm to bring out the full flavor of any wine, and refrigerator temperatures are too cold to show white wines to good effect. All wines should be chilled a little; some more than others (effervescent wines like Champagne should be chilled more than any other type of wine). For those of us without a dedicated wine refrigerator, an excellent rule of thumb is to ➤ put red wines in the refrigerator 15 minutes before serving, and take chilled white wines out of the refrigerator 15 minutes before serving.

Using the freezer isn't recommended. It isn't really much quicker, and you may forget the wine, which can freeze and crack the bottle. ➤ A safer and more efficient method is to put the bottle in a bucket filled with a mixture of half ice and half water. This chills the wine more quickly than ice alone; it will go from room temperature to cold in about 15 minutes.

Many wines benefit from **decanting,** or pouring out of the bottle and into a vessel before pouring into glasses. This is an especially common practice with aged wines and ports, since they can have sediment in the bottle (as they are decanted, the dregs are left behind in the bottle). Another (disputed) reason for decanting is to let aged wines **breathe,** or become aerated by exposure to oxygen over the course of 15 minutes or longer. This is said to improve their bouquet. There are several inexpensive devices that can be used to accomplish these tasks. Perhaps the most convenient option is to simply pour yourself a glass.

Red wine glass, white wine glass, all-purpose wineglass, Champagne flute

WINE AND FOOD

Wine-and-food pairing is fraught subject matter. Much breath and ink have been expended in an attempt to clarify the issue, and yet we are still stuck with the old "red meat/red wine and fish/white wine" dichotomy. While this directive is largely true, there are so many exceptions to the "rule" that the rule hardly matters. For example, any Oregonian will tell you that grilled salmon goes splendidly with pinot noir. In the end, deciding which wine to drink with which food is not as complicated a matter as it's sometimes made out to be. The simple and very pleasant truth is that there are usually several wines that go well with almost any dish. Regardless of color or style, ➤ we prefer wines under 12 percent alcohol for pairing with food (dessert wines are a notable exception).

What's really most important is that you *like* the wine that you're serving. After you've established this to be true, then seek flavors that complement each other, so that the wine enhances the food and the food brings out the best in the wine served with it.

One easy way to ensure an amiable match is to think in terms of weight. Steak is heavy, and so are syrah and cabernet sauvignon. Ergo, these reds match red meat nicely. Chicken and pork are mid-weight, and pair best with light reds, heavier whites, and rosés. More delicate foods, like salads, ceviche, or spring vegetables, work with lighter whites.

Keep the cooking technique and seasoning in mind. Raw vegetables in a salad might call for light white wine, like a pinot blanc, but fire-roasted vegetables drizzled with olive oil and balsamic vinegar might taste better with a red, such as a Chianti. You can't go wrong serving sushi with Prosecco. For umami-rich dishes like Rumaki, 64, Black Cod Misozuke, 387, or Shoyu Chicken, 419, try a rich, savory red like a mourvèdre.

You may pair wines by region. For instance, an Italian red alongside pasta with Bolognese Sauce, 558, or a Spanish red or white with paella, 334. But it's also fun to try the "opposites attract" theory of wine matching. Just as sweet caramel tastes superb when offset by sea salt, so do many wines complement their comestible opposites. For example: Try smoky grilled octopus, 369, with a fruity red such as a sparkling lambrusco, or a red-chile-laden Pork Adovada, 496, with a firm white from France's Rhône Valley. Parallel pairings also work. For example: buttery chardonnay with buttered corn; or spicy, fruity zinfandel with piquant North Carolina–Style barbecue, 583.

If you've gotten the sense that the possibilities are endless, you are correct. In time, wine lovers develop a gut sense for matching. But if you're unsure of your abilities, simply confer with your trusted local wine merchant for guidance and inspiration. For more pairing ideas, see the individual sections on specific types of wines, below.

For information on cooking with wine, see Alcoholic Ingredients, 951.

WINE AND CHEESE

The long-standing partnership of wine and cheese is a natural—both are born of similar fermentations and often have similar types of acidity. More important, both offer endless variations of compatible flavors. With all the possibilities, it's fair to wonder about which wine with which cheese, but it's really an opportunity rather than a problem. Pair young, mild cheeses such as unaged goat cheese or nutty alpine cheese with medium-bodied white wine, such as light and fairly dry rieslings, pinot gris or pinot grigio, or pinot blanc.

In general, red wines are not terribly flexible with cheese because their tannins can sometimes taste bitter with pungent or salty cheeses and they overwhelm mild cheeses. Many sweet wines offer more elegant possibilities, from Sauternes with Roquefort to late-harvest riesling with ripe Taleggio, Camembert, or Brie. Fortified wines such as Marsala and aged tawny port are lovely with aged Parmesan and pecorino. In any case, you'll never go wrong by asking your cheesemonger or wine merchant for assistance. For more on cheese types, see The Cheese Course, 834, and Know Your Ingredients, 950.

WHITE WINES

Chardonnay is the most popular wine in America. Originally from the Burgundy region of France, the best chardonnays have the crispness of apples and peaches, often with hints of mild honey, and light touches of vanilla or butterscotch, acquired during aging in oak barrels. When all of these elements are balanced, they provide a delicious complexity all the way through to the wine's aftertaste. Though many of our most popular chardonnays of the last two decades have been high in alcohol and heavily oaked, many winemakers are starting to pull back to a leaner, drier style. Well-executed, oaky chardonnays are excellent with rich foods, like butter-dipped lobster or crab, seared scallops, roast or grilled salmon, herbed roast pork, and bouillabaisse and other rich fish stews. Leaner, unoaked chardonnays are a bit more versatile when it comes to pairing with food; they are "quiet" enough to let the delicate flavor of raw oysters shine, but acidic enough to stand up to full-flavored fish like tuna, barbecued chicken, grilled pork chops, Caesar salad, and Thai curries. This versatility makes them especially suited to mixed-food occasions such as buffets and potlucks.

Chenin blanc, originally from the Loire Valley, can be vinified sweet or dry, still or sparkling. It can be very aromatic, with notes of honey, flowers, and tropical fruit. Like chardonnay, it is excellent with seafood. It is also a good accompaniment to a salad course or steamed spring vegetables.

Sauvignon blanc is more distinctive, with spicy, penetrating aromas and a flavor that can be musky and tart. When balanced, sauvignon blanc is crisp, refreshing, and lively, with a scent of fresh-cut grass and a clear zing of acidity. The white wines of **Sancerre** and the **Pouilly-Fumé** wines of the Loire are famous appellations built on these grapes. The extra sunshine of California and Washington (where it is also known as **fumé blanc**) mellow it out somewhat. **Sémillon,** a close relative, has a subtle flavor comparable to figs or melons that, combined with a full-bodied aspect, makes it good company for a variety of foods. All of these are fine partners for fish, chicken, or pork cooked with herbs, or vegetables like asparagus and artichokes. They are also a good fit with dishes flavored with chiles, lemongrass, ginger, garlic, and cilantro.

Riesling is a German grape varietal that makes one of the lightest table wines, although it comes in a variety of guises that fall along a complicated scale of richness and sweetness. Rieslings range from bone-dry to sweet (which its high acidity balances well). At their best, drier rieslings are terrific with lobster salad, crab, chicken salad, and cold meats (or on their own as a low-alcohol refresher). Sweeter reislings work beautifully with piquant dishes laden with seasonings like chiles, ginger, cumin, or coriander. The bold rieslings of Alsace, Australia, and New Zealand are made in a bone-dry style, with lemon-lime tartness and an assertive zing of alcohol. These can complement heavily spiced and seasoned fish dishes or stir-fries, grilled shellfish, and barbecued pork. Riesling is also excellent with cheese.

Pinot grigio or **pinot gris** grapes make a wine that tends to be relatively low in acid, medium-bodied, and quite dry. Pinot grigio is usually unoaked, made in a zippier style, and has an appealing apricot aroma and flavor. Other wines made with this varietal—especially pinot gris from Alsace and Switzerland—are especially full-bodied and rich. **Pinot blanc,** a closely related varietal, tends to produce a more mild-mannered white wine. All are good companions to light fish dishes and pasta with pesto or cheese-based sauces.

Soave is grown on the rolling hillsides near Verona, made from a blend of garganega and other native Italian grapes. It was once Italy's most popular white wine. Look for soaves labeled "Classico," "Superiore," and "Riserva," which possess an appealing citrus aroma and refreshing, tart flavor. ➤ A perfect match for most fish preparations, soave is also a good accompaniment to heartier salads like Shaved Fennel and White Bean Salad, 129.

Albariño, from Spain and Portugal (where it is called **alvarinho**), is full-bodied and distinctively flavored, with a strong hint of peaches in its aroma and a crisp bite of acidity in every sip. Portuguese **vinho verde** blends this grape with several others. Its name ("green wine") refers not to its color but to its young age. It is light, fresh tasting, pleasantly acidic, and faintly effervescent with floral and fruity aromas. It is one of our favorite inexpensive, food-friendly summer wines and pairs well with anything from the grill.

Gewürztraminer grapes are pink, and make a golden wine with a pronounced aroma of mixed spices and roses, with a flavor likened to lychee fruit. They tend to be highly alcoholic and low-acid. Though grown in many regions, gewürztraminers from Alsace are prized for their complexity. They pair well with foods seasoned with elements like ginger and star anise, in large part because of this bouquet. Wines from the **viognier** grape are also prized for distinctive aromas and flavors of apricots, peaches, and mixed wildflowers. Like gewürztraminer, viognier tends to be a fairly full-bodied, rich white. Due to its relatively high alcohol content, it can coat the mouth, fending off the painful effects of hot chiles, while underscoring the complementary aromatics of spices like cumin or coriander.

Muscat grapes (also known as **moscato,** or **moscatel**) are one of the oldest cultivated species in the Mediterranean and produce wines that range from dry to golden-hued and sweet (most tend toward the latter). As their name implies, they are highly aromatic, almost musky. **Muscadet,** a dry French white wine, bears no relation to muscat. **Torrontés,** however, is a distant Argentinian relation that produces acidic, medium-bodied wines with aromas of stone fruit and elderflower. These wines are drunk when young and are best served with highly spiced foods such as satay skewers or tacos; or try an Argentinian pairing of torrontés with grilled beef and chimichurri. There is also a Spanish torrontés, although it is genetically distinct from the Argentinian grape.

Greek **retsina** mimics the taste of ancient wines traditionally made with seawater and fermented in resin-sealed amphorae. Pine resin and salt are added to the fermenting grapes, and the result is a floral, pine-infused white wine that is sweet and ever-so-slightly salty.

Another interesting category seeing a resurgence is **orange wine** or **skin-contact wine,** which is made with white grapes that have been left to ferment with their skins and seeds for much longer than is typical. These wines are golden to amber or orange in color and have more tannins than most white wines. Many Hungarian and Georgian wines are made in this style, though it is becoming more popular among natural wines, 33.

RED WINES

Red wines tend to be heavier and bolder, their flavors boosted by higher percentages of alcohol and a prolonged soaking of crushed skins, pulp, and seeds prior to or during fermentation, which gives them their dark color and high level of tannins, 33. Tannins, which can make a wine seem harsh or overly dry, soften with age and eventually contribute a bracing firmness to wine. For this reason, red wines usually require at least a few years of age to mellow into their most pleasant form. That said, many inexpensive red wines have softer tannins, and are thus ready to drink soon after purchase.

Cabernet sauvignon is the world's most-consumed red wine varietal, and enjoys a high status thanks to the top-ranked wines of Bordeaux, along with "cult" (collector's) wines from California, Washington, and Australia, and a few outliers from Italy. It is quite heavy in tannins, and therefore bottle-aged extensively to allow the tannins to soften. In its original home, Bordeaux, and most other places, cabernet sauvignon is blended with small amounts of other varieties (especially merlot and cabernet franc grapes) to add aroma, spice, or fruitiness. Even when blended, young cabernets can be rough, with mere hints of concentrated blackberry fruitiness, counterbalanced by more challenging flavors such as gravel, graphite, and coffee grounds, as well as astringent tannin, and vaguely herbal aromas. Cabernet may initially seem to be quite an unpromising wine, but after five years or so, it begins to soften, and the fruitiness comes to the fore. The best food partners for cabernet sauvignon are assertive in terms of flavor and texture: grilled lamb chops, char-grilled steak, venison, or squab.

Merlot is the other red grape of Bordeaux. It tends to make a wine that is fruitier, softer, and more velvety on the palate, and is usually blended with a little cabernet sauvignon for depth and structure. Merlot's relative smoothness means that it is ready to drink at an earlier age. Merlot can be a smooth and lively fine wine, a splendid partner for braised meat in reduced sauces, caramelized vegetables, and earthy moles, 553.

Zinfandel is the popular name for a thin-skinned grape also known as **primitivo,** which originally hails from Croatia and southern Italy. California is now the leading producer of zinfandel wines. Zinfandel is robust in every way, bursting with ripe blackberry jam flavor, vibrantly acidic, and fairly high in alcohol, with a bracing jolt of astringent tannin. Like merlot, zinfandels are ready to drink more quickly than cabernet sauvignon, but a well-made wine will be superb five years after the vintage date and can easily age for at least ten years. Its boldness and fruitiness makes zinfandel a good match for barbecued pork, pasta with spicy sausages, tomato-based chicken fricassees, or cheeseburgers.

For many, **pinot noir** is the ultimate wine, both for savoring and for the challenge it presents to winemakers: It is notoriously finicky to grow and produces highly variable wines. Good pinot noir is smooth and relatively light but with a persistent, lingering flavor. It can smell and taste of violets, raspberries, black cherries, and forest floor; is slightly earthy and tangy; and stands alone among all other red wines, distinctive and different. Originally from Burgundy, the grape has been transplanted all over the world. In terms of quality, **red Burgundy** *grand crus* are still rated highest; Oregon, California, and New Zealand pinots are a strong second (Oregon's tend to be more delicate and nuanced). The smooth texture and persistent yet delicate flavor of pinot noir makes it a good match for poultry, from duck or turkey to delicate squab or quail. Its earthiness makes it a good partner with dishes featuring mushrooms, such as chanterelles or morels, as well as oven-roasted vegetables, and lentils. Boeuf Bourguignon, 465, is traditionally both made and served with pinot noir; in Oregon, grilled salmon is the classic pairing.

Syrah most famously comes from the steep, terraced hillsides above the Rhône River. Syrah was transplanted to Australia and became that continent's most esteemed and popular red wine, renamed **shiraz.** These wines tend to be the weightiest and darkest examples of the variety, which is also vinified in California, Washington, South Africa, and even Italy, where lighter, more vibrant versions can often be found. Syrah is noted for its black-pepper aftertaste, which makes it a splendid partner for smoky grilled meat, Steak au Poivre, 461, and roast pork.

Syrah is also a blending partner with other red grapes, such as grenache, in the warmer southern part of the Rhône Valley, and is included to firm up softer, more voluptuous wines, resulting in smooth, rich, and refreshing blends. **Syrah blends,** sometimes labeled GSM (for grenache, syrah, and mourvèdre) have spread around the world, and most are a good value. The most famous from France are **Châteauneuf-du-Pape** and **Gigondas,** while **Côte-du-Rhône Villages** are the everyday renditions. They go nicely with a lot of different foods: grilled tuna, Cioppino, 102, any garlicky stew, Cassoulet, 216, and anything flavored with bacon.

Barolo and **Barbaresco** are arguably Italy's finest red wines, bearing up for more than a century under the cliché of "the king of wines, the wine of kings." The hype isn't far off the mark. Made in northwestern Italy from the nebbiolo grape, these reds can be unapproachable in youth but sensual and irresistible with a decade of bottle aging. Their complex aromas can evoke violets, tar, and dried rose petals and their flavors can hint at plum, cherry, and earth. These are wines for special occasions, and it's no accident that precious Italian black truffles pair beautifully with them. **Barbera** is from the same region, but is a more casual, weeknight wine. It can be quite robust and tangy, a good match for any meat-and-tomato dish, sausages, or mushroom-laden pizza.

Sangiovese, which literally means "Jove's blood," is an Italian grape variety known for its acidity and moderate tannins. Tuscan **Chianti** is an intriguing blend of sangiovese and cabernet sauvignon grapes. Chianti is medium-bodied and firmly dry, with a cherry-like fruitiness and a tangy aftertaste. Like Tuscan food, Chianti is known for a kind of rustic elegance, good with tomato-based pastas, balsamic vinegar, polenta with wild mushrooms, Osso Buco, 476, or ragus.

Montepulciano is a deep-red Italian grape variety that produces spicy, tannic, and full-bodied wines with overtones of dark berries. Serve it with rich foods that can stand up to its considerable character, such as braised beef, roast lamb, or meat ragus.

Rioja, Spain's leading red wine, is a blend of grapes: Tempranillo provides smoothness and firmness and a lovely aroma of violets, **grenache** (garnacha) grapes give it fruitiness, and a mixture of a few ancient varieties provides a touch of complexity. It's matured in barrels made of American oak, which gives it a pleasant hint of vanilla. Those labeled *crianza* and *reserva* are barrel aged for one year, and the latter must be bottle aged for another three years; *gran reserva* must be kept in barrels for at least two years and bottle aged for another four years. **Priorat,** a superlative red wine from the Catalonian region, carries similar aging distinctions. Keep in mind that even the youngest *crianza* wines can be smooth and enjoyable. These wines are a fine match for Moroccan couscous, or dishes that incorporate roasted red peppers or sun-dried tomatoes.

Beaujolais, from the region just south of Burgundy in France, is made from the **gamay** grape. It is dry, light-bodied, and very fruity; think of it as a fruitier, more rustic cousin of pinot noir. Those sold two months after harvest are known as **Beaujolais nouveau;** these wines are especially fruity and have almost no tannins to speak of. Their quality is variable. Wines labeled **Beaujolais-Villages** tend to be succulent and earthy, and are meant to be drunk within a year or two after the vintage date. The more prestigious and expensive Beaujolais wines carry the names of specific villages on the labels. These can be gamey, savory, and spicy, with floral aromatics, and just enough concentration to make a good match with rich, rustic food like charcuterie, baked ham, shepherd's pie, or grilled chicken. Both styles are best lightly chilled for about 30 minutes before pouring.

Another notable red is **malbec,** which can make a brutally tannic (yet still highly prized), inky-black wine in the Cahors region of its native France. It can be a pleasantly plush, licorice-scented, black-plum-flavored delight in Argentina, where it's the leading red. Malbec is very good with skirt steak and vegetables like grilled eggplant. Similarly, **carménère** is a French grape varietal that found a new home in Chile. It is medium-bodied, only lightly tannic, and has notes of cherry, bell pepper, and earth. Serve it with sturdy greens like kale or grilled or roasted meats with green, herb-based sauces like salsa verde, chimichurri, or mint sauce.

ROSÉS AND BLUSH WINES

Rosé wine is made from red grapes or pink-skinned white grapes. Some rosés acquire their color simply from pressing. Others are macerated with the skins for a brief period, then drained and fermented. The result is light to dark pink, depending on the grape variety and time spent in contact with the skins. **Blush** wine is simply white wine made with dark-skinned grapes: The juice is pressed and fermented without any contact with the skins. Known in France as **vin gris,** the most famous variety of blush wine now sold in the United States is **white zinfandel.** They are usually quite mild, and lightly sweet.

Rosés were once considered to be the finest wines of Europe, and a few historic regions, such as **Tavel** in France's Rhône Valley, cling to this tradition. With its festive deep watermelon hue and tart cranberry flavor, Tavel is a marvelous match for Thanksgiving dinner. Just south of the Rhône is the classic rosé-producing region of Provence, as well as the small autonomous wine town of **Bandol.** Southern French rosés tend to be dry and higher in alcohol than their peers due to the Mediterranean climate of the region; try them with highly spiced foods.

After suffering through a few decades of ignominy—perhaps spurred by the popularity of blush wines like white zinfandel—rosé has returned. A recent explosion in popularity has brought with it increasing variety and focus on quality.

In general, rosés labeled with a varietal name, such as pinot noir rosé or cabernet sauvignon rosé, are liable to be drier and at least echo the flavor of the parent grape. With European labels, you may need the assistance of your wine merchant just as you would with a red or white—it's not obvious to most shoppers, for example, that a rosé stamped with the name of the Loire Valley town of Chinon is made from cabernet franc.

Fine, dry rosés are easy to drink on their own and are excellent with almost anything you'd care to eat during summer, from grilled chicken to Caprese Salad, 127, to baked clams. Southern French foods, like Salade Niçoise, 121, Moules Frites, 351, or Cassoulet, 216, are particularly divine when matched with pink wine.

SPARKLING WINES

Sparkling wines are versatile, but particularly famed for setting off celebrations and creating occasions. **Champagne** is made from chardonnay, pinot noir, and pinot meunier grapes, which lend it considerable character and nuance under those cheerful bubbles. The types seen most often are the dry, **brut** style, which uses all three grapes; **blanc de noirs,** which are copper-tinged white wines made from dark-skinned grapes; **blanc de blancs,** which are made from chardonnay, and occasionally pinot blanc; and **rosé,** a pink style that's most commonly made by adding some red wine to a white sparkling wine for color and aromatics.

The term "Champagne" may only be used on wines using the "traditional method" and hailing from the Champagne region of France. This method is notable for a secondary fermentation inside the bottle. Yeasts and sugars are added to the bottle, and when the yeasts die off, the wine is clarified. The yeasts are allowed to collect in the neck of the bottle and the bottle necks are stuck in ice, which freezes the lees that are then disgorged. To finish the wines, the bottles are topped off with more wine and sugar before corking. Many fine sparkling wines not labeled Champagne are made by this classic method in other winegrowing regions. Look on the label for terms such as *méthode traditionnelle, méthode champenoise, méthode cap classique,* or *crémant* on French wines; or *metodo classico* or *franciacorta* on Italian wines. Domestic wines typically use the terms *méthode champenoise* or simply "traditional method."

Because Champagne carries a sought-after name, it doesn't come cheap, but any fine sparkling wine made by the traditional method can rival Champagne in flavor and certainly in price. **Blanquette** and **crémant** are appellations used for French sparkling wines produced in other areas (e.g., Crémant de Loire, Crémant de Bourgogne, or Blanquette de Limoux). **Cava** is a Spanish sparkling wine produced with the traditional method that ranges from very dry to sweet. Aged cavas can be exceptional and are much more affordable than Champagne.

Italy's light, lovely, and barely sweet **Prosecco** is made by the Charmat method, where secondary fermentation occurs in a tank rather than in the bottle. The sweet and faintly musky **Asti** is also made with this method; it is a popular after-dinner or dessert wine made from muscat grapes. **Lambrusco** is a sparkling red from Italy that has seen a resurgence in recent years and can be quite good.

Another category of sparkling wines is made with the *méthode ancestrale*, where wine is chilled for several weeks halfway through the fermentation process and bottled with no additional sugar. The wine finishes fermenting in the bottle, resulting in a lightly carbonated wine. A variation on this method termed **pétillant naturel** (or pét-nat, for short) has become popular of late among natural wine makers, and dispenses with the chilling step. Pét-nat wines are unpredictable but refreshing, with much less carbonation than Champagne, and a hazy appearance from the yeast sediment left in the bottle. As with natural wines, fans of pét-nat wines love them because they are a little bit funky. True Champagne lovers will probably not be converted, but these wines are a fun departure from the usual suspects of the sparkling wine world.

Any dry sparkling wine cuts through salty or smoked flavors well, which is why they work with caviar, smoked salmon or other smoked fish, and charcuterie. They are excellent with egg dishes such as omelets, making them superb brunch wines. Sparkling wines in general are always a winner with oysters on the half shell, and Champagne in particular is a revelation with sushi.

DESSERT WINES

Every vine-growing country in the world makes sweet wines, sometimes against long odds and with great ingenuity: Grapes are left on the vine till they shrivel into moldy raisins, dried or semi-dried in barns, or even baked, and then made into intensely sweet wines. Other versions are only slightly fermented and then fixed in place with a jolt of brandy (see Fortified Wine, below). Dessert wines can have as little as 5 or 6 percent alcohol, but some weigh in at a domineering 24 percent. Some are meant to accompany dessert, while some replace it—more a matter these days of personal preference than anything else.

Some basic limiting factors in matching wine and desserts are temperature (frozen desserts dull the palate) and texture (creamy puddings and soft custards can coat your tongue and block other flavors). The acidity of some fruits can throw off the flavor of a sweet wine. ➤ One good rule of thumb is to choose a dessert that's slightly less sweet than the wine. Another is to serve your most interesting bottle with neutral cookies, like Scotch Shortbread, 780, which will allow the wine to shine through.

Among the wide array of sweet wines, **port** is still the most popular (see Fortified Wines, below). The rarest and most expensive of all dessert wines is **Sauternes,** the golden, richly sweet wine of southern Bordeaux in France, which tastes of honey and apricots. It's the best-known example of "late-harvested" wines, which are made from grapes left on the vines long after all other grapes have been picked, well into late autumn, when a beneficial mold known as "noble rot" shrivels them into sweet raisins. Some sweet and very fine German rieslings and Hungarian **Tokay** (Tokaji) are also made this way. Simple fruit cakes and tarts are good partners. **Vin santo** is an Italian dessert wine produced by partially drying grapes before they are pressed and fermented for a long time. It is famously served with biscotti, 778.

Ice wine (or **eiswein**) is made in Switzerland, Germany, Canada, Michigan, and upstate New York from several different varieties of grapes left on the vine until they freeze in early winter. When the ice is removed, the remaining grape juice is concentrated nectar, and it ferments into a wine that tastes much like exotic marmalade—unique, delicious, and dessert all by itself. In New World regions where the winemaking regulations are less stringent, you will often see an "ice wine" made *à la Frigidaire*—that is, from grapes that have been chilling out in a freezer.

FORTIFIED WINE

There is plenty of overlap between dessert wines and fortified wines, as fortified wines are usually (but not always) sweet and certainly have a higher alcohol content, making them the perfect bookend to a meal. They may be served with, instead of, or after dessert.

Port is the best-known fortified wine. Named for the second-largest city in Portugal (Oporto), it is now made in California, South Africa, and Australia (any port-style wines from these regions may be labeled as port in the United States). Grapes are fermented for a short time, during which they are continuously macerated to extract as much flavor and color as possible. After they ferment for a day or two, grape brandy is added. This process yields a large family of robust, sweet wines of different intensity: **Ruby** is the cheapest variety and often very sweet and fruit-forward (**reserve** is a step up); **white** port is made with light-skinned grapes (including muscatel) and is generally sweet; **tawny** is amber-colored and sometimes barrel-aged; and **aged tawny** must be barrel-aged for at least six years. Good tawny ports are medium-dry and have a nutty character from the aging process. **Colheita** ports are made from a single vintage year and must be barrel aged for at least seven years; **vintage** ports are barrel aged for less time but use the finest grapes. They are intended to be bottle aged (other styles of port are generally drunk soon after purchase). Most vintage ports are unfiltered and need to be decanted, 34, to rid them of sediment. Redder ports go well with bittersweet chocolate, berry pies, and milder blue cheese like Gorgonzola dolce. Tawnies are good with dark chocolate, chocolate desserts, pecan pie, Parmesan, aged Cheddar, Manchego, Stilton, and other strong cheeses.

Sherry is a Spanish fortified wine that ranges from dry to very sweet. It is aged in oak casks with a technique called the solera system: When sherry is drawn off the barrels that have aged the longest, it is replenished from a barrel containing slightly younger sherry, which is replenished with a younger barrel, and so on. The youngest barrels are topped off with fresh wine. Thus, every bottle of sherry contains a blend of older and younger sherries, resulting in an incredibly complex final product. Legally, sherry must be an average of three years old before it is sold, but most sherries contain wine that is considerably older. Especially old bottles may be labelled with "VOS" (unofficially translated as very old sherry) if they are twenty years old, or "VORS" (very old rare sherry) for blends that average thirty years old or more.

When making **fino** and **manzanilla sherry,** airspace is left at the top of the barrels to promote the growth of *flor,* a film of yeast that adds to sherry's character but also protects the wine from coming into contact with the air. If the *flor* on a cask of fino dies and it begins to oxidize, it is called **amontillado sherry. Oloroso sherries** contain about 18 percent alcohol, which is too high to sustain the *flor*, thus they oxidize from the beginning, which contributes to their robust flavor and turns them dark brown. Amontillado and oloroso sherries can be very dry and complex; sweeter styles like **cream sherry** are made by adding juice from sun-dried grapes that has been fortified with alcohol. Nectarous, luxurious **Pedro Ximénez sherry,** the finest and most flavorful sweet style, is made by adding a late-harvest wine made from sun-dried grapes of the same name. It is a favorite.

Sherry is excellent with Marcona almonds, Spanish cured ham, prosciutto, or country ham, and hard cheeses such as Manchego. Sweeter sherries go well with chocolate and nut-based desserts. Once a bottle of sherry has been opened, it should be consumed within a few days.

Madeira is oxidized and heated—two things that are usually the kiss of death for a fine wine—to develop its characteristic nutty, slightly salty, caramel flavors. It may be dry to sweet. **Rainwater Madeira,** aged for at least three years, has aromatics of hazelnuts and molasses, but finishes dry, and can be paired with appetizers such as cheese or pâté. **Finest Madeira** is also aged for three years; **reserve** is aged for at least five years, with **special** and **extra reserve** denoting ten- and fifteen-year aging. Depending on whether the Madeira in question is dry or sweet, it may be paired with a wide variety of foods. Blends almost always announce their character—"dry," "medium sweet," etc.—on the label. Among the varietals, **sercial Madeira** is the driest and can be served as an aperitif or with light fish dishes, even sushi. **Verdelho** is richer and may be served with cream soups or bisques. **Bual** is sweet, very aromatic, and goes well with chocolate desserts or rich cheeses like Roquefort. **Malmsey** is the richest, sweetest Madeira and is quite adequate on its own as a dessert.

Marsala is a fortified Sicilian wine with flavors of apricot, vanilla, tamarind, and even tobacco. It is aged, like sherry, using the solera system. It is primarily known as a cooking wine, but finer varieties are excellent for sipping. Marsala is also often labeled by color—gold, amber, and ruby—but any of these may be dry, semi-dry, or sweet. Like other fortified wines, Marsala is barrel aged to varying degrees: **fine** is aged one year, **superiore** two years, **superiore reserve** four years, and **vergine** for five years or more. Dry Marsalas are delicious with goat and sheep cheeses. Sweet Marsalas go well with biscotti or other dry, crumbly cookies like shortbread. **Banyuls** is a French fortified wine made from grenache grapes and tastes of fig, cherries, and strawberries with notes of orange and herbs. It is excellent with chocolate.

Vermouth is a fortified wine that is also aromatized with herbs, bitter roots, and spices such as wormwood, citrus peel, angelica, and star anise, among many others. Unlike port and sherry, vermouth is notable for its bitterness and tends to be mixed rather than sipped on its own. It is best known for its role in cocktails like the Manhattan, 23, and the Martini, 19. **Lillet** is another aromatized fortified wine that is consumed on its own, over ice or with sparkling water as an aperitif.

ABOUT SAKE AND OTHER FERMENTED RICE BEVERAGES

Sake is the best-known fermented rice beverage, but it is rarely consumed by most people outside the setting of a sushi restaurant. A shame, since sake is incredibly complex, diverse, and delicious in its own right. Sake is made by washing, soaking, and steaming polished or semi-polished rice (polishing removes the outer layers of bran and germ to reveal the starchy endosperm), then inoculating it with **koji,** 997, a type of mold also known as *Aspergillus oryzae.* This mold helps convert the rice's starch into sugar, which is necessary for fermentation.

Sake may be light to medium bodied to rich and aged (sometimes called **koshu**). **Futsushu,** also known as table sake, is of the lowest quality and the most common to find; it has had distilled alcohol added to it and is usually served warm. **Honjozo** is made with polished rice and can be drunk warm or chilled. **Ginjo** is made with highly polished rice and can be very fragrant; **daiginjo,** the highest grade of sake, is aromatic and smooth. Both should be drunk chilled. **Junmai** denotes pure sakes that have had no distilled alcohol added, and is usually applied to ginjo and daiginjo sakes. **Namazake** is left unpasteurized, which makes it even more aromatic (and perishable). Unfiltered sake, or **nigori,** appears cloudy and has a creamy texture (always serve it chilled). Light- and medium-bodied sakes pair well with simply prepared green vegetables, raw or poached fish, and citrusy sauces. Richer sakes are excellent with rich foods like salmon, tempura, and black cod. Nigori sake is excellent with desserts, especially those containing coconut or mango. Almost no sake pairs well with red meat.

Chinese **Shaoxing** rice wine is made by steaming and fermenting sweet glutinous rice with herbs. The resulting wine is aged in clay jars; the longer it is aged, the better it gets. Shaoxing wine is yellow to amber in color, mildly sweet to semi-dry, and has a nutty, savory flavor with a hint of saltiness (this can be especially pronounced in cheaper wines). In addition to being enjoyed as a beverage, it is used often in Chinese cooking, 952. Serve these wines warmed to accompany rich, mildly spiced meat dishes.

Makgeolli is a low-proof Korean rice-based beverage, but it is made from other grains as well. It is opaque, milky in color, and usually unfiltered. It may taste barely to very sweet and can be somewhat tangy. In Korea it is easy to find unpasteurized makgeolli, but in the United States it is mostly available pasteurized. Makgeolli may be flavored with fruit, chestnuts, or even sweet potatoes, but plain makgeolli is a good place to start. It is commonly enjoyed with Korean pancakes, especially on a rainy day. **Soju,** on the other hand, is a distilled Korean beverage with a much higher alcohol content than makgeolli, around 20 to 24 percent (for comparison, vodka contains about 40 percent alcohol and makgeolli around 6 to 8 percent). It is commonly made from rice but may also be made from sweet potatoes, wheat, and tapioca, among other starches. It is mild, slightly sweet, and is consumed with food, specifically a range of small dishes that are collectively known as *anju*. Soju is a convivial beverage, and there are specific rules for drinking it. Usually, the older person pours a shot for a younger person, and the shot is to be taken graciously with both hands by the recipient. They then turn their head to take a drink. You should never pour yourself a glass of soju, although pouring for others is encouraged, especially if you are the youngest. All that said, these rules are not strictly enforced in the modern world, so the most important thing is that no one's glass should ever be empty.

ABOUT HARD CIDER

If you have ever purchased unpasteurized, fresh apple cider and let it sit a little too long you know how readily it ferments. For centuries, the fermentation of apple juice was a preservation method with inebriating side effects, but now we enjoy hard cider simply because it tastes good. It is also a reliable, low-alcohol tipple for those with gluten sensitivities who cannot drink most beer.

Cider was traditionally made with cider apples—apples that are astringent, sour, and not particularly delicious when eaten out of hand. These days, cider is mostly produced from standard apple varieties, and the resulting ciders tend to be one-dimensional and quite sweet. However, due to an increased interest in hard cider, some small producers are reviving more obscure apple varieties and producing exceptional ciders. You may also encounter **perry** (*poiré* in French), which is a cider-like drink made from astringent varieties of pear.

French cider may be found sweet (*doux*), dry (*brut*), and sparkling. It is largely produced in Normandy, but Basque cider is well worth seeking out and tends to be more astringent and funky due to oxidation. Some French ciders are mild and approachable, others are intensely barnyardy. We enjoy both kinds. French apple ciders are excellent with savory buckwheat crêpes (called *galettes* in France) and all kinds of mild cheeses.

British and American hard ciders have seen a resurgence in recent years. Interest in traditional methods, as well as palates made receptive by the creative boom in craft beer brewing, mean that there are an incredible number of ciders to choose from. Mass-produced ciders tend to be flat but pleasant, but small cider producers, many of whom grow their own apples, are turning out ciders that are a pleasure to drink. Pair ciders with foods that come to mind when you think of apples: sausages, butternut squash soup, and Thanksgiving dinner.

ABOUT BEER

Beer making starts with barley and sometimes wheat, which are soaked in water and allowed to sprout. The grain is then dried in a kiln, and sometimes roasted to a browned toastiness, which results in the darker color and fuller body and flavor of dark beers. This **malt** (which is usually a combination of lighter and darker malts) is then ground, combined with water, and heated at exact temperatures for a specific amount of time to bring out its soluble sugars and enzymes. Cooked barley is added with the malt—though wheat, rice, or corn are also commonly used—which produces a lighter, milder beer. The spent grains are strained out, and the sweet liquid, or **wort,** is combined with **hops** and boiled in a kettle. The resinous flower buds of a climbing vine, hops are a functional ingredient, since they act as a preservative, but they can have a profound influence on the brew. Their flavor ranges from bitter and piney to floral or fruity, even tropical. Once boiled, the wort is filtered and cooled. The majority of beers are then inoculated with special strains of yeasts to start fermentation; sour beers, 41, are exposed to natural yeasts from the surrounding environment. After this fermentation is complete, sugars may be added to promote further fermentation in a closed cask (if it is fermented further in the bottle, it is called **bottle-conditioned**). This second fermentation is how beers are traditionally carbonated, though many are now force-carbonated in the same way as soda, since it is more predictable (and leads to fewer exploding bottles).

Lagers are by far the most popular type of beer in the world. They are inoculated with lager yeast and fermented for a long time at refrigerator temperatures. They are then **lagered**, or stored at even colder temperatures, during which time they mature and the yeast settles to the bottom. This can result in an exceptionally clean-tasting pale-gold beer, such as a bitter, bready **pilsner,** a mild, medium-bodied **helles,** a malty, dark **dunkel** and **schwarzbier,** or a potent **bock** or **doppelbock. Rachbier** is unique for its use of smoked malt. At the other end of the spectrum, light, American-style lagers have dominated the shelves of our grocery stores for years and owe their mellow flavor to additions of rice and corn to the wort. **Mexican lagers** are restorative on a hot day, especially with a squeeze of lime.

Ales ferment faster than lagers and do so at higher temperatures with a different type of yeast. The vigor of this fermentation produces more complex flavors than those of lagers and results in an even wider variety of styles. On the bitter end is the **India pale ale,** or IPA, a popular style that relies on a light to copper malt and a heavy hand with the hops. Their herbal aroma and piney, bitter taste is not for everyone. **Pale ale** is less bracing, as are beers marked **bitter** and **extra special bitter** (but the latter two are still worthy of their names). **Kölsch,** a German style of light-bodied pale ale, has balanced hoppiness and is quite refreshing. **Brown** and **amber** or **red ales** tend to be much milder, sometimes maltier, and slightly sweet. Belgian Trappist monks are famous for their bottle-conditioned ales. **Belgian tripel ales** are golden in color, while **dubbel ales** are darker; both are usually fruity, malty, occasionally spiced, and run from dry to rich and sweet.

Belgium and Germany produce ales made with wheat. **Hefeweizen** is the most common and is usually pale and pleasantly yeasty (there is also a **dark hefeweizen,** made with toastier malts). Belgian **white beer,** or **witbier,** is unfiltered, has a cloudy, gold appearance, and is flavored with citrus peel and spices (it is often served garnished with an orange slice or lemon slice). For a similar citrus-beer combination, see Shandy, 43. **Saison,** sometimes called farmhouse ale, is a much drier Belgian style of bottle-conditioned beer; it is fruity, spicy, bready, tart, and occasionally spiced.

Stout and **porter**-style beers are very distinctive. They are made with roasted malts that give them a brown to black color and flavors of chocolate and coffee. The most-renowned type is the **Irish stout. Oatmeal stouts** have a fuller mouthfeel, and **milk stouts** tend to be sweeter and slightly creamy from the addition of lactose. **Imperial stouts** are especially high in alcohol (this term is often applied to other styles of high-percentage beer).

Sour beer is another distinctive style of ale that is becoming increasingly popular. These beers are traditionally made sour by the lactic, acetic, and formic acids produced by exposing the wort to a variety of wild yeast strains, especially *Brettanomyces*, and *Lactobacillus* bacteria. Typically thought of as contaminants in the industry, these ambient yeasts produce interesting, tart, funky notes in the finished product that reflect the unique microflora from where the beer was brewed (some have compared this variability with the subtle effects of *terroir* on winemaking, 32). Though some of these yeast strains are now commercially produced for reliable results, many breweries still rely on spontaneous fermentation, and relish the nuanced differences from batch to batch.

Belgian **lambic** is a style of sour wheat beer. **Gueuze** denotes a lambic made by combining an older lambic with a younger one, which is used to referment it. The older gueuze are very funky, even barnyardy, but younger lambics are quite approachable. The Belgians have a long tradition of boosting export sales by adding fruit to the beer as it ferments a second time in casks (sometimes a simpler, fruitier beer is made by adding fruit syrup). The classic addition is cherries, which results in **kriek,** but raspberry and peach lambics are common as well.

German **Berliner weisse** is another style of mildly sour wheat beer. **Oud bruin** is a brown, sour style from Flanders; like lambic, older batches are mixed with younger, sweeter ones to moderate their acidity. It has a nutty flavor and little of the funky barnyard aromas associated with older lambics. **Flanders red ales** are similar, but generally fruitier and with a pronounced sourness.

Some other terms are worth noting when making sense of beer at the store: **Session beers** are low in alcohol, no higher than 3 or 4 percent. By contrast, **barley wine** is beer with a very high alcohol content, up to about 12 percent. The term **high-gravity** refers to beer with a high alcohol content. **Barrel-aged beer** has been matured in oak barrels to take on different flavors. Sometimes, the barrels are simply charred and impart vanilla or caramel notes, and sometimes whiskey, Scotch, and sherry barrels are used to add their own characteristic flavors.

BEER AND FOOD

As with wine, beer has a definite place at the table with food. One need look no further than a pub menu or a backyard barbecue to discern a pattern: Cheeseburgers, fries, grilled bratwurst, and rich smoked brisket are all fatty and salty. Crisp lagers and bitter ales cut through the richness. One can imagine many rich foods that may benefit from this pairing, like pizza, carnitas, or duck confit. Tacos, enchiladas, tamales, and posole, as well as Tex-Mex specialties like chili con carne and nachos may be the best match of all for lagers.

The British "ploughman's lunch" reveals another pattern: Several kinds of strong cheese, bread, pickles, a pungent relish or chutney, and raw fruit or vegetables are natural partners to a fruity ale or dark beer. Porters and stouts are wonderful with roasted beef or grilled steaks, as well as lighter fare like oysters or pork chops. Wheat beers are delicate enough to pair well with fish, especially fattier fish like salmon, or fried fish of any type; they are also good to pair with spicy food. Pale ales also pair well with spicy dishes, such as Thai satay or Indian curry. ➤ Avoid serving heavily carbonated beers with spicy dishes (they may amplify the heat). Hoppy, bitter ales are especially good with spicy, citrusy dishes. Sweet, malty beers are also good with tart ingredients like sauerkraut, as well as rich duck, game, and pork dishes.

SERVING BEER

Beer is usually served directly out of the refrigerator, or at about 42°F, and this is what we recommend for hop-heavy beers and pale lagers. Though a colder temperature enhances a beer's crispness and ability to refresh, it will also dull some of a beer's characteristic flavors. To pick up a bit of these flavors, try leaving ales, stouts, and porters out at room temperature for 10 to 20 minutes; the fruity and roasted malt flavors will come to the fore.

If you have purchased a **growler** of beer, be sure to consume it fairly quickly to keep it from going flat (we purchase them only when we know several people will be interested in having a pint). There is much specialized glassware designed to serve specific types of beer (see the illustration below for a few of them). When pouring into glasses, ➤ tilt the glass so that the stream of beer runs down the side to keep foaming under control. This is especially important for highly carbonated, bottle-conditioned ales like lambics, which must be poured slowly to avoid serving a glass of foam. Unless serving a beer cocktail, garnishes are seldom used, aside from the obligatory lime wedge served with Mexican lagers or the orange or lemon slice commonly squeezed into hefeweizen or witbier. For those interested in a more dessert-like approach, we have seen chocolaty porters and stouts served like an Ice Cream Float, 13, or with a skewered, toasted marshmallow laid across the top of the glass to evoke the flavor of s'mores.

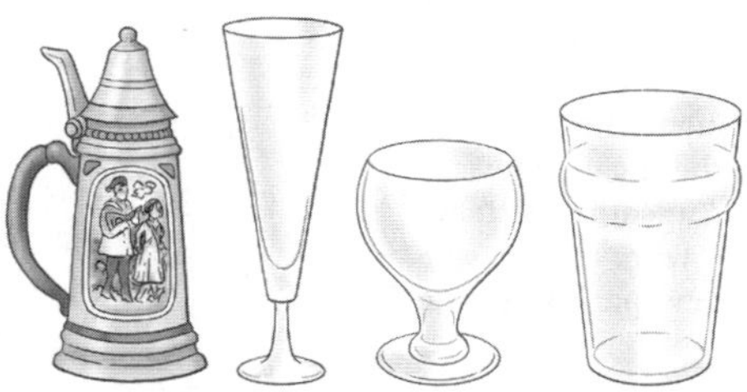

Beer stein, pilsner glass, beer goblet, nonic pint glass

WINE AND BEER COCKTAILS

Adulterating wine or beer with mixers can result in refreshing, festive beverages. They are ideal for parties where punch or cocktails might prove too inebriating. Do not waste expensive bottles on these concoctions, but be sure to select a wine or beer good enough to drink on its own.

KIR

1 serving

Canon Félix Kir was the mayor of the city of Dijon, in the Burgundy region of France, and a hero of the Resistance during World War II. His favorite drink was then called *vin blanc cassis,* based on Aligoté, the everyday white wine of the region, and another local product, black currant liqueur. Locals renamed the beverage in his honor. Today Kir is most often made with chardonnay. A **Kir Royale** replaces the white wine with Champagne.

Combine in a large wineglass and stir:

6 ounces chilled chardonnay
Dash of crème de cassis

MIMOSA

1 serving

For a **Ruby Duchess,** replace the orange juice with **pomegranate juice.**

Pour into a chilled Champagne flute:

2 ounces orange juice

Fill the glass with:

Chilled sparkling wine

BLACK VELVET

1 serving

Pour into a chilled Champagne flute or wineglass:

3 ounces chilled stout beer

Fill the glass with:

Chilled sparkling wine

CHAMPAGNE COCKTAIL

1 serving

I. Pour into a chilled Champagne flute:

½ teaspoon Simple Syrup, 16
¾ ounce chilled brandy

Fill the glass almost to the top with:

Chilled dry sparkling wine

Add:

2 dashes yellow Chartreuse
2 dashes orange bitters

II. Place in a chilled Champagne flute:

1 small sugar cube

Drop onto the sugar cube:

2 drops Angostura bitters

Fill the glass with:

Chilled dry sparkling wine

FRENCH 75

1 serving

You'll notice that this formula is similar to the Tom Collins, 20, but with Champagne instead of club soda. Oh, what a difference those French bubbles make!

Fill a cocktail shaker with ice cubes. Add:

1 ounce Cognac or gin
2 teaspoons lemon juice
1 teaspoon Simple Syrup, 16

Shake until well chilled, about 12 seconds. Strain into a chilled Champagne flute and add:

2½ to 3 ounces brut Champagne

Garnish with:

A lemon twist

WHITE WINE SPRITZER

1 serving

Combine over 1 or 2 ice cubes in a chilled wine- or highball glass:

6 ounces chilled riesling or other semidry white wine
4 ounces club soda

BELLINI

1 serving

Process in a blender until smooth:

½ peach, pitted

Push the pulp through a sieve to extract the juice. Pour the juice into a chilled Champagne flute, then fill with:

Chilled Prosecco or other dry sparkling wine

APEROL SPRITZ

1 serving

Aperol is an Italian liqueur made with bitter orange and various botanicals, such as gentian and cinchona. Combined with Prosecco and club soda it makes a pitch-perfect summer sipper.

Fill a chilled stemmed wineglass with ice cubes. Add:

2 ounces Aperol
1 ounce club soda

Top off the glass with:

3 to 4 ounces Prosecco

Garnish with:

An orange wheel

KALIMOTXO (CALIMOCHO)

1 serving

While this may sound like a sacrilegious combination, just think of the cola as a flavored light syrup. Dark cola has flavors of vanilla, tamarind, citrus, and cinnamon, all of which nicely complement cheap-ish red wine. We recommend seeking out Coca-Cola with real sugar instead of corn syrup.

Fill a chilled tall glass with ice cubes. Add:

4 ounces Coca-Cola
4 ounces dry Spanish red wine

MICHELADA

1 serving

For a **Chelada,** frost the glass with **coarse salt** and add only a couple pinches of salt, **2 ounces lime juice,** and ice cubes before pouring in the beer.

Run around the rim of a chilled pint glass:

1 lime wedge

Frost the rim, 18, with:

Prepared chili-lime salt, such as Tajín

Fill the glass with ice and add:

2 ounces tomato juice
2 ounces lime juice
1 teaspoon Mexican hot sauce
1 teaspoon Worcestershire or soy sauce

Have ready:

One 12-ounce can or bottle Mexican lager

Fill the glass with lager, stir once, and serve the michelada alongside the can or bottle of remaining beer. As the michelada is consumed it should be topped up with the rest of the beer.

SHANDY

1 serving

If you use sparkling lemonade, this drink is called a **Radler.**

Combine in a chilled large beer glass:

12 ounces lager
4 ounces lemon-lime soda, lemonade, orange juice, ginger ale, or ginger beer

Serve with:

A lime wedge

APPETIZERS AND HORS D'OEUVRE

The words "hors d'oeuvre" and "appetizer" are at most times interchangeable. The main difference is that hors d'oeuvre are served outside the meal and are typically finger foods, whereas appetizers can also be the first course of a meal. "Canapés" can be either, with the distinction that they are served on bread or a cracker (the word "canapé" means "sofa" or "couch," the bread being the couch that the food sits on). Call them what you will—all are eaten with drinks before the main meal. Of course, amass enough of them for sharing around the table and they can be a meal in themselves.

For cocktail parties, simple, salty foods will usually suffice: seasoned nuts and popcorn, dips, cheese spreads, raw or marinated vegetables, and olives. But when staging a special party, you may want to explore more complex, more substantial foods.

Many hors d'oeuvre are rich or highly flavored, in part to buffer the impact of alcohol on the system. However, when choosing which appetizers to serve, bear in mind the meal to follow. ➤ Before a dinner, two or three hors d'oeuvre are usually plenty—a bowl of nuts or olives, crudités with a dip, perhaps a canapé. ➤ For a cocktail party without dinner to follow, offer five or six different appetizers, including at least two that involve meat or seafood and at least two that are hot. ➤ Allow four to six pieces per person if a meal is to follow. If appetizers are the only food being served, allow for double that amount per person. In either case, aim for a selection that is balanced with respect to texture, flavor, and richness.

While we approve of imaginative combinations, it is important to remember that, unlike the opera overture, the hors d'oeuvre course should not forecast any of the joys that are to follow. For example, forget cheese balls if you are serving a cheesy potato gratin at dinner, and likewise skip popcorn shrimp if your entrée is fried chicken.

When considering food for a cocktail party, ➤ choose self-contained bite-sized canapés or hors d'oeuvre unless you are furnishing plates. A table of such tidbits often looks more appealing if there is variety in color and texture. Don't torture or obscure the food with fussy detailing, but small concessions to attractiveness go a long way. For instance, a healthy drizzle of olive oil, a dusting of smoked paprika, and a sprinkling of toasted pumpkin seeds can turn an otherwise plain-looking bean dip into an attractive appetizer. Similarly, a display of freshly cut crudités, 45, is much more likely to pique the interest of your guests than a plastic tray of precut vegetables. ➤ Keep in mind, too, what plated foods will look like as guests dig in and empty spaces appear. It is often more sensible to arrange several small plates that are easily replaced or replenished than one big one that may be difficult to restore to its pristine glory.

APPETIZERS AND FOOD SAFETY

When serving appetizers and hors d'oeuvre over a lengthy amount of time, keep in mind that, unless they are to be consumed within 1 hour, ➤ cold foods should be kept below 40°F and ➤ hot foods should be kept above 140°F. Any fried appetizers must be served hot and preferably immediately after being fried. However, you may also hold fried foods for a short time in a warm oven. Scatter the pieces of fried food in a single layer on a rack set on a rimmed baking sheet lined with paper towels and keep warm for up to 2 hours in a 200°F oven (the less time the better). ➤ Serve hot appetizers in small batches and replenish from the oven when they run low. Alternatively, use a chafing dish or warming tray. ➤ Remove cold foods from the refrigerator just before serving, or, if they need to be out for an extended time, set them on chilled platters over ice or replace platters frequently.

ABOUT PARTY PLATTERS

A party platter is often the most efficient way to serve a merry mob in short order. These trays usually consist of meat, cheese, fruit, and vegetables served with dressings, relishes, dips, or sauces that complement the foods you offer, as well as an assortment of crackers or breads. Arranging a tray can be a fun and creative pursuit. Rather than the typical rolled up slices of deli meats and baby carrots accompanied by a tub of ranch dressing, look to the various traditions of preprandial snacking across the globe, 45–46.

MEAT OR CHARCUTERIE PLATTERS

Cured meats, sausages, confits, and rillettes are perfect for pairing with cocktails, wines, and beer. Some of our favorites include thinly sliced country ham, prosciutto, bresaola, finocchiona, coppa, soppressata, pepperoni, salami, summer sausage, mortadella, and cured chorizo. Thick slices of pâtés and terrines are especially decadent; see 513 to make your own (it's easier than it might seem). Little pots of Chicken Liver Pâté, 62, and Pork Rillettes, 514, are also quite easy to whip up for company. Serve with tart pickles, such as cornichons and pickled pearl onions, whole-grain mustard, prepared horseradish, and sturdy crackers, sliced baguette, or Crostini, 49. ➤ For a cocktail party without dinner to follow, serve 2 to 4 ounces per person depending on how many other appetizers are present. For appetizers preceding a meal, 1 to 2 ounces per person should suffice.

CHEESE PLATTERS

Serve three or four cheeses, from mild and fresh to sharp and funky, or choose a couple crowd-pleasers as part of a larger appetizer spread. High-quality Cheddar is delicious and beloved by all. A wheel of Brie or, for the more adventurous, a round of Époisses can easily stand alone. For a more diverse cheese board, choose an unaged cheese such as chèvre, a mild aged cheese such as Comté, and a well-aged cheese such as Parmigiano-Reggiano, aged Gouda, or Romano. A blue cheese such as Gorgonzola, Roquefort, or Stilton can easily stand in for, or supplement, the aged cheese. Cheese is best accompanied by good bread and fresh or dried fruit or honey. Some cheeses have traditional accompaniments, such as Manchego with Membrillo (Quince Paste), 194, or Stilton with pears or port. ➤ Serve cheese at room temperature. ➤ For a cocktail party without dinner to follow, allow 1½ ounces of each cheese per person. If dinner is to follow, serve 1 ounce of each cheese per person. Also see The Cheese Course in the Desserts chapter, 834, and Cheese in Know Your Ingredients, 962.

VEGETABLES AND CRUDITÉS

At its simplest, a crudité platter is a selection of raw vegetables and a dip or dressing to accompany them. But there is still a measure of creativity to be had. Select beautiful vegetables—slender carrots, sugar snap peas, radishes, English or Persian cucumber rounds, purple or green cauliflower florets, and endive leaves. You may even create a platter of lightly cooked vegetables—blanched haricots verts and asparagus, boiled new potatoes, and crisp-tender broccoli. ➤ Plan on 6 to 8 ounces of vegetables per person, or 4 to 5 pounds for every 10 people (use the larger amount if you are not serving any other hors d'oeuvre alongside). Serve with a traditional dipping sauce such as homemade Ranch Dressing, 577, or Green Goddess Dressing, 577. For a less traditional approach, serve with Muhammara, 53, Hummus, 52, or Skordalia, 564. Almost any thick dressing, 576–78, would be excellent with crudités. For a warm take on crudités, see Bagna Cauda, 58. The sauces and dressings below are especially suited to the crudité platter.

Tahini Dressing, 576
Roasted Red Pepper Dressing, 576
Roasted Garlic Dressing, 576
Russian Dressing, 577
Creamy Blue Cheese Dressing, 577
Tonnato Sauce, 564
Aïoli, 564, or any flavored mayonnaise, 563

FRUIT

Fruit offers a light, refreshing counterpoint to savory hors d'oeuvre. Combine cut melons, pineapple, or other fruit on a platter with some whole fruit with stems, like strawberries, small clusters of seedless grapes, or cherries. Choose fruit that is ripe and in season.

For a spicy arrangement, prepare a platter of sliced peeled honeydew melon, watermelon, cantaloupe, mango, and green apple. Just before serving, sprinkle with lime juice and a mixture of salt and chili powder. Also consider skewered fruits served with a dip made from Greek yogurt and honey to taste. Grilled fruits, 171, such as pineapple, plums, or peaches, are another possibility—an especially convenient one if your savory hors d'oeuvre or entrées are to be grilled as well. Or serve Strawberries Cockaigne, 178, or Melon and Prosciutto, 58. Also see the Fruits chapter, 166, and About Fruit Appetizers, 58.

ANTIPASTO

Italian antipasto—or "before the meal"—is an assortment of salami, prosciutto, and other cured meats; fruit, such as melon or figs; fish, such as anchovies, sardines, and oil-packed tuna; pickled vegetables or pepperoncini; marinated artichokes, cauliflower, and/or mushrooms, 58; and roasted red peppers, olives, or Caponata, 54. It may also include fresh tomatoes and fennel, cheeses such as Fontina, Parmigiano-Reggiano, and Asiago, and crusty breads.

TAPAS

Derived from the Spanish for "cover," tapas were originally snacks served on small plates placed atop glasses of sherry. They were, from the beginning, meant to be served with alcohol. Of course, we need not always bow to the past; tapas are perfectly at home in an appetizer spread or even as a communal meal. Tapas range from simple fare like Spanish-Style Marinated Olives, 48, or thin slices of cured chorizo and *jamón* (prosciutto or thinly sliced country ham are good substitutes) to more elaborate preparations, like Salt Cod Croquettes, 655, cold slices of Tortilla Española, 160, with Aïoli, 564, Patatas Bravas, 59, with Romesco Sauce, 570, Champignones al Ajillo, 251, or Charred Shishito or Padrón Peppers, 262.

MEZZE

Derived from the Persian word for "snack," *mezze* are traditionally a prelude to more feasting. However, a *mezze* platter can be a satisfying communal meal in and of itself. Serve a combination of Baba Ghanoush, 53, Hummus, 52, Tahini Dressing, 576, Pita Bread, 610, Fried Halloumi, 56, Falafel, 214, Dolmas, 63, Muhammara, 53, Tabbouleh, 131, and spinach pies like Spanakopita, 706, or Fatayer bi Sabanekh, 702.

SMÖRGÅSBORD AND ZAKUSKI

Smörgåsbord in its home territory of Sweden is a square meal in itself, not the prelude to one. Its mainstays of meat and fish—and the aquavit that washes them down—are climatic imperatives when subarctic weather hovers for months outside the door. Smörgåsbord is an especially nice spread for Christmas parties (in which case it is called *julbord*). Traditionally, smörgåsbord has five parts and is done in a particular order; but for a more casual presentation (and one that is less stressful for the host), serve everything together. Smörgåsbord may include pickled herring, mild cheeses, cold boiled potatoes seasoned with dill, Gravlax, 393, served with Scandinavian Mustard-Dill Sauce, 566, as well as Swedish Meatballs, 508, Baked Ham, 500, Swedish Rye Bread, 600, with an abundance of salted butter, and plenty of aquavit or Glögg, 31.

Zakuski, the Russian cousin of the smörgåsbord, similarly celebrates the merits of consuming smoked, pickled, and sauced foods with strong drink. Serve smoked sprats, trout, or salmon on buttered rye bread or pumpernickel, caviar with Buckwheat Blini, 641, roasted beets or blanched spinach mixed with Garlic and Walnut Sauce, 570, or Piroshki, 703. If the company is game, don't forget to supply a healthy array of flavored vodkas, 22, alongside the *zakuski* tray.

ABOUT PARTY SNACKS

Here is a collection of simple, salty munchies that can be eaten with the fingers. These snacks are excellent for cocktail parties or informal gatherings and require little effort to put together and no utensils to consume. Keep chips and crackers at room temperature in airtight containers with a paper towel. This will keep them crisp for up to 1 week. Roasted nuts—aside from chestnuts, which are highly perishable—can keep for quite a while in airtight containers at room temperature, but we recommend making only as many as you will consume in 2 weeks.

ROASTED NUTS

4 cups

Preheat the oven to 400°F. Toss to coat:

1 pound raw, unsalted mixed nuts (cashews, pecans, almonds, hazelnuts, peanuts, walnuts)
1½ tablespoons butter, melted, or olive oil
Salt and black pepper to taste

Spread in an even layer on a rimmed baking sheet. Bake until lightly browned, 10 to 12 minutes. Let cool before serving.

CURRIED NUTS

Prepare **Roasted Nuts, above,** adding along with the butter or oil **1 tablespoon curry powder or Garam Masala, 588,** and **⅛ teaspoon cayenne pepper.**

ROSEMARY AND BROWN SUGAR NUTS

Prepare **Roasted Nuts, above,** adding, along with the butter or oil, **3 tablespoons finely chopped rosemary** and **2 tablespoons brown sugar.** After removing the nuts from the oven, stir them occasionally until the coating dries, about 5 minutes. Let cool completely before serving.

CRISP SPICY PECANS

3 cups

A mixture of almonds, walnuts, and pecans may also be used.
Preheat the oven to 325°F.
Combine in a small bowl:

3 tablespoons butter, melted
1 tablespoon sweet paprika
1½ teaspoons Worcestershire sauce
1 teaspoon cayenne pepper

Set aside to cool. Beat in a medium bowl with an electric mixer until very foamy:

1 egg white
1 teaspoon salt

Gradually add and beat until soft peaks form:

6 tablespoons sugar

Fold in along with the butter mixture until well coated:

3 cups pecan halves (12 ounces)

Spread in a single layer on a baking sheet. Bake, stirring twice, until crisp and browned, about 30 minutes. Remove from the oven and pour onto a large sheet of foil to cool, then break into clusters or individual nuts.

THAI-SPICED PEANUTS

About 3 cups

Have ready in a medium bowl:

1 pound roasted, salted Spanish peanuts

Heat in a small skillet over medium-high heat:

1½ tablespoons vegetable oil

Add:

8 fresh or frozen makrut lime leaves, slivered
2 to 3 teaspoons red pepper flakes
2 stalks lemongrass, tender parts only, minced

Sauté briefly, until the mixture is fragrant, about 1 minute. Pour the oil over the nuts and toss to coat. Taste and add salt if needed. Serve warm or cool. Store leftovers in an airtight container. Reheat leftover nuts in a 350°F oven for 5 to 8 minutes.

BOILED PEANUTS

About 15 servings

Boiled peanuts are a favorite convenience-store snack in the South, but they are also a popular street-food snack in China, where they are boiled with star anise and cinnamon.

Place in a large stockpot:

3 pounds fresh green or raw peanuts in the shell
1½ cups salt

Cover with water and bring to a boil. Reduce the heat to a simmer and cook until the peanuts are soft, at least 1 hour and up to 4 hours (dried peanuts will take considerably longer than fresh). Alternatively, pressure-cook at high pressure for 1 hour in a stovetop cooker or 1 hour 15 minutes in an electric model, letting the pressure release naturally, 1059. Alternatively, slow-cook on high for 6 to 8 hours. When cooked, drain and serve immediately.

ROASTED CHESTNUTS

Once purchased, roast fresh chestnuts as soon as possible, as they are prone to drying out. For more on chestnuts, see 232.

Preheat the oven to 425°F. Have ready:

Chestnuts

Cut an X on the flat side of each nut. Spread on a baking sheet and roast until fragrant and ready to pop out of the skins, 20 to 25 minutes. Let cool slightly, but peel while still warm.

TOASTED PUMPKIN OR SQUASH SEEDS

Delicious all by themselves or as a crunchy garnish for salads and soups. If desired, add a pinch of chili or curry powder with the salt. A medium butternut squash will yield approximately ¼ cup seeds, a medium pumpkin much more.

Preheat the oven to 350°F. Pick the fibers and pulp from:

Pumpkin or winter squash seeds

Pile the seeds on a baking sheet. For each ½ cup seeds, add, tossing to coat:

½ teaspoon olive or vegetable oil
¼ teaspoon salt

Spread the seeds out on the sheet so none overlap. Bake, stirring occasionally, until golden brown, about 20 minutes.

ROASTED CHICKPEAS

4 servings

Coated with olive oil and garlic and roasted until golden brown, these chickpeas are great as a snack, tossed into a salad, or sprinkled over rice pilaf.

Preheat the oven to 350°F. Toss together on a baking sheet:

One 15-ounce can chickpeas, drained and rinsed, or 1½ cups cooked chickpeas
2 tablespoons olive oil
2 garlic cloves, minced

Spread out the chickpeas and bake, stirring often, until they are golden, 30 to 40 minutes.

Sprinkle with:

½ teaspoon salt
(½ teaspoon Baharat, 589, curry powder, ground chipotle, or smoked paprika)

Serve warm.

EDAMAME

These can be eaten as an informal cold snack, in the Japanese manner, scraped from the pod with your teeth. Once cooked, shelled edamame can be roasted as for **Roasted Chickpeas, above.**

Boil or steam until tender, 4 to 5 minutes:

1 pound frozen edamame in the pod

Drain. Toss with:

1 teaspoon salt
(1 teaspoon shichimi togarashi, 1017)

Serve warm.

POPCORN

About 8 cups

Popped kernels of corn have been found in the remains of New Mexico settlements dating back three thousand years—a time-tested snack. The method below requires no special equipment. Wire poppers are also available, and are designed to be used over coals. They can usually pop about ¼ cup of kernels at a time and require no butter or oil. Another oil-free method is to use a microwave. ➤ To make popcorn in the microwave, add ¼ cup of kernels to a 2½-quart microwave-safe bowl, cover with a microwave-safe plate, and microwave on high until the popping slows to one pop every 5 seconds. For electric poppers, follow the manufacturer's directions.

Add to a lidded 3-quart heavy-bottomed pot:

2 tablespoons vegetable oil

Have ready:

½ cup popcorn kernels

Add 3 popcorn kernels to the oil and place over high heat. When the kernels start to pop, add the rest of the kernels and shake to coat. Cover and cook, shaking the pot, until the popping stops, about 2 minutes. Transfer to a large bowl. Sprinkle with:

Salt to taste
(Melted butter)

SAVORY ADDITIONS TO POPCORN

For the best distribution of flavorings, vigorously shake the popcorn and seasoning in the pot with the lid on (paper bags also work well). When seasoning, remember that finer ingredients—table salt rather than kosher salt, for example—will adhere better to a buttered or oiled surface. To turn popcorn into a delectable sweet, see Caramel Corn, 865.

Prepare **Popcorn, above,** and toss with one or more of the following:

3 tablespoons butter, melted, Brown Butter, 558, or olive oil

½ teaspoon cayenne pepper or 1 teaspoon ground chipotle or smoked paprika
Up to ½ cup finely grated Parmesan (2 ounces)
½ teaspoon garlic or onion powder
¼ cup nutritional yeast
1 tablespoon minced rosemary or thyme
2 tablespoons furikake, 1016, Za'atar, 590, curry powder, or chili powder
1 tablespoon Cajun seasoning or crab boil seasoning

KALE CHIPS

3 to 4 servings

You can flavor these with a variety of spices and seasonings, including nutritional yeast, garlic or onion powder, paprika, or curry powder.

Preheat the oven to 300°F. Derib, 243:

1 bunch kale (10 to 12 ounces)

Cut the kale into 3-inch pieces and toss in a bowl with:

2 tablespoons olive oil or butter, melted
¼ teaspoon salt

Spread out the leaves into a single layer on two baking sheets. Bake until crisp, turning halfway through, 20 to 25 minutes. Taste and sprinkle with more salt, if desired. Let cool completely before serving. These are best the day they are made.

PARTY MIX

About 12 cups

You can use your favorite spice blends in this versatile snack. Instead of garam masala, try Ras el Hanout, 590, Chili Powder, 588, or Baharat, 589. If adding a blend that contains salt, omit the added celery or seasoned salt.

Preheat the oven to 300°F. Combine in a large bowl:

7 cups crisp square cereals, rice, corn, or wheat-based
2 cups bite-sized pretzels
2 cups roasted, unsalted peanuts or mixed nuts
1 cup raw pumpkin seeds

Melt in a medium saucepan:

1 stick (4 ounces) unsalted butter

Add:

5 garlic cloves, smashed

Let sit over very low heat for 10 minutes. Fish out the garlic cloves (reserve for another use). Add to the butter:

¼ cup Worcestershire sauce
2 tablespoons Dijon mustard
1½ tablespoons curry powder or Garam Masala, 588
2 teaspoons paprika (preferably smoked)
1½ teaspoons salt, celery salt, or seasoned salt

Pour the butter over the cereal mixture and toss to coat evenly. Divide between two baking sheets and bake, swapping the position of the baking sheets and stirring every 15 minutes, until dry and toasted, about 1 hour. Let cool completely on the baking sheets and store in an airtight container.

SPANISH-STYLE MARINATED OLIVES

4 cups

For information on olive types, see 1008.

Combine in a bowl:

2 cups black or green olives, or a combination, pitted or unpitted
½ cup extra-virgin olive oil
3 garlic cloves, chopped
2 bay leaves
(3-inch sprig rosemary)
2 sprigs thyme
1 sprig oregano
(1 tablespoon red wine vinegar or sherry vinegar)
½ teaspoon smoked paprika
(One 3 × ½-inch strip orange zest)
Pinch of red pepper flakes

Use a spoon to bruise the herbs, which will help flavor the oil. Transfer the olives to a quart-sized jar, cover, and refrigerate for at least 2 days and up to 1 month. Serve at room temperature.

POTATO OR ROOT VEGETABLE CHIPS

6 servings

Using a lower frying temperature preserves the flavor and color of the root vegetables while delivering a satisfying crunch. Please read about Deep-Frying, 1051.

Peel, then slice as thinly as possible with a sharp knife, mandoline, vegetable peeler, or food processor slicing attachment any combination of the following:

1½ pounds russet potatoes, celery root, carrots, parsnips, rutabaga, sweet potatoes, red or golden beets, lotus root, sunchoke

Place the sliced vegetables in cold water to prevent discoloring. Heat to 300°F in a deep-fryer, deep heavy pot, or Dutch oven:

3 inches vegetable oil

Drain the vegetables and pat dry. Fry each type of vegetable separately in small batches (so as not to overcrowd and stir to prevent sticking) until golden, 2 to 3 minutes; the time will vary slightly for each vegetable. Transfer to a baking sheet lined with paper towels to drain. Season immediately with:

Salt

Serve while still hot, or let cool and store, covered, for up to 4 days.

TORTILLA CHIPS

48 to 72 chips

I. FRIED

Cut into quarters or sixths:

12 corn tortillas

Heat to 300°F in a medium skillet:

½ inch vegetable oil or lard

Add as many tortilla wedges as will fit in a single layer and fry, turning once, until the chips stop bubbling and are golden on both sides, 2 to 3 minutes. Transfer to a baking sheet lined with paper towels to drain. Repeat with the remaining tortillas. Sprinkle immediately with:

Salt

II. BAKED

Preheat the oven to 400°F. Lightly brush one side of:

12 corn tortillas

with:

Vegetable oil

Cut the tortillas into quarters or sixths. Place the pieces on a baking sheet, oiled side up, and lightly sprinkle with:

Salt

Bake until browned and crisp, 10 to 12 minutes. Let cool completely.

BAGEL OR PITA CHIPS

Preheat the oven to 400°F. Lie flat and cut into ⅛-inch-thick slices:

Bagels

or cut into 8 wedges:

Pitas

Lay out on a baking sheet and brush one side with:

Olive oil

Sprinkle with:

Kosher or coarse sea salt
(Cracked black pepper)

Bake until golden brown, 5 to 7 minutes. Transfer to a wire rack to cool. Break into smaller pieces, if desired. Store in an airtight container after completely cooled.

CROSTINI

42 to 64 pieces

Crostini are easy and quick to prepare and ideal for serving with dips and spreads. They can also be the base for canapés like Bruschetta with tomatoes and basil, 67. Use any leftovers to make Croutons, 638.

Preheat the oven to 400°F. Cut crosswise into ¼- to ½-inch-thick slices:

2 baguettes, about 3 inches in diameter and 16 inches long

Place the slices on baking sheets and lightly brush one side of each slice with:

Extra-virgin olive oil

Bake until lightly browned and toasted, 6 to 10 minutes. Rotate the pans front to back halfway through baking to ensure even toasting. Season to taste with:

Salt and black pepper

Serve warm or at room temperature. Leftovers can be stored in an airtight container at room temperature for several days.

SODA CRACKERS

About 100 crackers

Whisk together in a medium bowl:

1½ cups all-purpose flour
1 envelope (2¼ teaspoons) active dry yeast
¼ teaspoon salt
¼ teaspoon cream of tartar

Combine in a small bowl:

⅔ cup hot water
½ teaspoon honey
2 tablespoons vegetable shortening

Add the liquid to the dry ingredients and beat with a wooden spoon until smooth. If the dough is sticky, beat in a little more flour. Turn the dough out onto a floured surface and knead until smooth and elastic, about 5 minutes. (Or mix and knead the dough in a stand mixer fitted with a dough hook.) Place the dough in a greased bowl and turn once to coat. Cover and refrigerate for at least 1 hour, or overnight.

Preheat the oven to 425°F. Grease a large baking sheet. On a floured surface, roll the dough into a 18 × 6-inch rectangle. Fold into thirds, as if folding a business letter, and roll out again into a rectangle of the same size. Loosely roll the dough around the rolling pin and transfer to the baking sheet. Prick the dough all over with a fork and cut into 1-inch squares. Sprinkle with:

Salt
(Poppy, sesame, or caraway seeds)

Bake until crisp and browned, 10 to 20 minutes, depending on the thickness of the dough. Transfer to wire racks to cool.

OLIVE OIL FLATBREAD CRACKERS

4 large cracker sheets

Topping these crackers is a fine occasion to experiment. Our favorite spice blend to use here is Za'atar, 590, mixed with flaky sea salt; or use Everything Seasoning, 590; or a blend of sesame, sunflower, and pumpkin seeds for a seeded cracker.

Whisk together in a medium bowl:

1¾ cups all-purpose flour
1 teaspoon baking powder
¼ teaspoon salt

Make a well in the center and add:

½ cup lukewarm water
⅓ cup olive oil

Stir until a rough dough forms. Knead briefly on a work surface until it comes together in a smooth ball. Let rest for 10 minutes. Divide the dough into 4 pieces, and roll each piece into a ball. Let rest for another 10 minutes.

Meanwhile, preheat the oven to 450°F and place a heavy baking sheet, baking stone, or cast-iron pizza pan on the middle oven rack. Flatten out one piece of dough on a sheet of parchment paper, then top with a second parchment sheet. With a rolling pin, roll out the dough as thinly as possible into an irregular, organic shape. Because the parchment tends to get bunched up, after each time you roll, peel off the top parchment, reposition it, flip the whole arrangement, then peel off the back parchment, reposition it, and continue rolling. The dough should be very thin. Remove the top piece of parchment. Sprinkle on top any of the following, or a combination:

Up to ½ teaspoon dried herbs per piece of dough
Up to 3 tablespoons seeds per piece of dough
Up to 3 tablespoons finely grated Parmesan or Asiago per piece of dough
⅛ to ¼ teaspoon flaky salt per piece of dough

Press the toppings into the dough. Slide the dough (still on the bottom piece of parchment) onto the hot baking sheet, stone, or pizza pan and bake until the cracker is light to deep golden brown, 5 to

8 minutes. It will bubble in spots, and the color will be somewhat irregular. Repeat this with the remaining pieces of dough. Transfer to a wire rack to cool completely. Serve whole, for your guests to break apart, or break the crackers into pieces.

BROWN BUTTER–HAZELNUT CRACKERS

About 75 crackers

This recipe is adapted from a book called *Crackers & Dips*, by Ivy Manning. Ivy is a dear friend and recipe wizard, and these gluten-free crackers are our favorites for serving with blue or bloomy cheeses. They have a rich hazelnut flavor and a tender, delicate texture. This recipe may be made with almonds instead of hazelnuts, if desired.

Preheat the oven to 350°F. Place on a rimmed baking sheet:

2¼ cups raw hazelnuts

Toast until light brown and fragrant, 10 to 15 minutes. Set aside to cool completely. In a small skillet, melt over medium-low heat:

3 tablespoons unsalted butter

The butter will melt, then foam. After the foam dies down, swirl the skillet frequently until the butter is browned and fragrant. Pour the butter into a small bowl and let cool for 10 minutes. Transfer 2 tablespoons of the browned butter to a second small bowl and add:

2 large eggs

Beat with a fork to combine and set aside. In a clean kitchen towel, rub the hazelnuts together to remove the skins. Transfer the nuts to a food processor and add:

1 tablespoon sugar
¾ teaspoon salt

Pulse until the nuts are the consistency of fine cornmeal. Do not overprocess or the nuts will turn into nut butter. With the machine running, gradually add the egg mixture until the nuts come together in a moist ball (you may not need to use all of the egg mixture).

Divide the dough in half and place each half on a piece of parchment paper. Working with half the dough at a time, form into a 4 × 6-inch rectangle. Cover with a sheet of plastic wrap and roll out until the dough is 1/16 inch thick. Remove the plastic wrap and transfer the dough, on the parchment paper, to a baking sheet. With a pastry wheel or pizza cutter, cut the dough into 2-inch squares.

Bake the crackers until light brown and firm, 12 to 15 minutes, switching racks and rotating the baking sheets front to back halfway through baking. A layer of white foam may appear on the crackers as they bake. This is normal, and the foam will subside after baking. Be careful the last few minutes of baking—these crackers can burn quickly.

Cool the crackers completely on the baking sheets on wire racks. Store in an airtight container for up to 2 weeks.

RYE CRACKERS

Makes about 60 crackers

These tender, caraway-scented rye crackers were created by our friend and pastry mentor Helena Root. They are especially suited for serving with cheese or Gravlax, 393.

Combine in a food processor:

1 cup all-purpose flour
1 cup rye flour
2 tablespoons brown sugar
2 teaspoons baking powder
4 teaspoons caraway seeds
1 teaspoon salt

Pulse several times to combine. Add and pulse until the butter is in tiny pieces:

1 stick (4 ounces) cold butter, cut into small cubes

Add all at once and pulse until a dough forms:

⅓ cup plus 2 tablespoons milk

Form the dough into a disk, wrap in plastic wrap, and chill for at least 30 minutes and up to 2 days. Preheat the oven to 400°F. Divide the dough into 4 pieces. Working with one piece at a time (keep the other pieces refrigerated), roll the dough out between two sheets of parchment paper until very thin—just under ⅛ inch thick. Alternatively, use a pasta roller. Cut into 4 × 1½-inch strips. Place on a parchment-lined baking sheet, leaving ½ inch between the crackers. Poke each cracker three times with a fork. Bake until browned and crisp, 8 to 10 minutes. Cool the crackers completely on the baking sheets on wire racks. Store in an airtight container for up to 2 weeks.

ABOUT DIPS

Dips can be built on a variety of bases, including sour cream, yogurt, soft cheese, mayonnaise, avocado, and cooked beans or vegetables. Salsas, 573–74, Caponata, 54, thicker dipping sauces and salad dressings, 575–78, sandwich spreads, 135–36, and flavored mayonnaises, 563, also make great dips.

Prepare cold dips an hour or even a day in advance to allow the flavors to blend. Cover and refrigerate until ready to serve. In warm weather, place the dip container in a bowl filled with crushed ice to serve. The ingredients for hot dips can be assembled ahead, covered, and kept refrigerated until ready to cook. Spreads should be brought to room temperature for 30 minutes or so to make them spreadable. Accompany dips with an assortment of cut-up raw vegetables, crackers, breads, toast, or chips. Be sure any crackers or chips served with a dip are up to the task: If a dip is very thick, provide a spoon for applying it to thin crackers or simply serve with something sturdy, like Crostini, 49, or Bagel Chips, 49. ➤ One cup of dip serves about 4 people.

BECKER SOUR CREAM DIP

2 cups

For a richer dip, replace ½ cup of the sour cream with **½ cup mayonnaise**.

Mix well in a large bowl:

2 cups sour cream
1 tablespoon soy sauce or 2 teaspoons Worcestershire sauce
1 teaspoon black pepper
2 garlic cloves, minced
½ teaspoon salt
Finely grated zest of 1 lemon

If desired, add one or more of the following:

(3 to 4 green onions, thinly sliced, or 2 tablespoons minced chives)

(1 tablespoon minced parsley, dill, thyme, oregano, or other fresh herbs)
(1 tablespoon prepared horseradish)
(½ cup chopped Sautéed Onions, 255, or Caramelized Onions, 255)
(1 cup chopped cooked or drained canned clams)
(8 ounces cooked shrimp, chopped)
Chill for 1 hour before serving.

RED ONION DIP

About 2 cups

Melt in a large nonstick skillet over medium-high heat:
1 tablespoon butter
Add and cook, stirring, for 5 minutes, or until softened:
3 small red onions, finely chopped (about 2 cups)
Stir in:
2 teaspoons sugar
½ teaspoon salt
Cook, stirring, until the onions turn golden brown and are very soft. Add:
2 cups beef or vegetable broth
3 garlic cloves, minced
1 teaspoon fresh thyme leaves or ½ teaspoon dried thyme
Boil, stirring occasionally, until almost all the broth has evaporated, about 15 minutes; watch carefully so that it doesn't burn. Transfer to a bowl and stir in:
1 teaspoon balsamic vinegar
Let cool completely, then stir in:
1 cup sour cream
Salt and black pepper to taste
Chill for 1 hour before serving.

GUACAMOLE

About 2 cups

Serve guacamole with tortilla chips or cut-up raw vegetables, as a topping for tacos, or as an accompaniment to grilled fish. In place of Hass avocados, 1 very large or 2 medium smooth-skinned Florida avocados can be used, but the guacamole will be less flavorful. Guacamole is best the day it is made. To keep a bowl of guacamole from discoloring before guests arrive, level the surface with a spoon and cover with a thin layer of olive oil.
Peel and pit:
4 Hass avocados (about 2 pounds)
Place in a bowl and mash to a coarse consistency with a fork or potato masher. Stir in:
3 tablespoons lime juice, or more to taste
¼ cup finely chopped onion or thinly sliced green onions
¼ cup finely chopped cilantro
(1 to 2 jalapeño or serrano peppers, seeded and minced)
1 to 2 garlic cloves, minced
(½ teaspoon ground cumin)
Salt to taste
Taste and adjust seasoning; more lime juice and/or salt may be needed. Gently stir in, if desired:
(½ to 1 cup finely diced tomatoes)
Serve at room temperature.

SPINACH DIP

About 2 cups

For a richer dip, replace ½ cup of the yogurt or sour cream with **½ cup mayonnaise.**
Squeeze the moisture from:
One 10-ounce package frozen chopped spinach, thawed, or 1 pound fresh spinach, cooked, 243, and chopped
Mince in a food processor:
3 green onions, coarsely chopped
1 to 2 garlic cloves, coarsely chopped
Add the spinach along with:
2 cups plain Greek yogurt or sour cream
¼ cup grated Parmesan
¼ teaspoon black pepper
⅛ teaspoon cayenne pepper
Salt to taste
Pulse until smooth. If desired, stir in:
(One 4-ounce can water chestnuts, drained and chopped)
Refrigerate for 1 hour before serving.

BEER CHEESE DIP

About 2 cups

Melt in a medium saucepan:
2 tablespoons butter
Add and whisk in:
2 tablespoons all-purpose flour
When smooth, slowly whisk in:
1 cup beer (any kind except very hoppy IPAs)
½ cup evaporated milk
Bring to a simmer and cook, whisking, until thickened, about 2 minutes. Lower the heat and whisk in ½ cup at a time, allowing each addition to melt before adding the next:
2 cups grated sharp Cheddar (8 ounces)
2 ounces cream cheese, cut into pieces
(¼ cup crumbled blue cheese)
½ teaspoon Dijon mustard
½ teaspoon Worcestershire sauce
Pour the dip into a serving dish and serve hot with:
1-inch cubes dark rye bread

QUESO FUNDIDO (HOT CHORIZO AND CHEESE DIP)

6 to 8 servings

We recommend using a combination of a stringy, melty type like Oaxaca cheese, and a sharp cheese like Cheddar.
Preheat the oven to 400°F. Cook in a medium skillet over medium heat until browned, 4 to 6 minutes:
4 ounces fresh chorizo, crumbled
Transfer to a plate lined with paper towels to drain. Have ready:
3 green onions, thinly sliced
2 jalapeño peppers or ½ poblano, seeded and minced
1 garlic clove, minced
Place in a 9-inch pie dish or shallow baking dish:

3 cups grated Cheddar, Monterey Jack, Oaxaca, asadero, or Muenster cheese or a combination (12 ounces)

Top with the chorizo, green onions, jalapeños, and garlic and bake until bubbling and browned, about 10 minutes.

Serve warm with:

Tortilla chips or warmed small flour tortillas
Any salsa, 573–74

HOT CRAB DIP

About 2 cups

Preheat the oven to 325°F. Butter a 2-cup broilerproof bowl or small baking dish or skillet. Puree in a food processor or mix in a bowl until smooth:

8 ounces cream cheese, softened
½ cup grated Fontina (2 ounces)
1 teaspoon crab boil seasoning
1 teaspoon Worcestershire sauce

Fold in:

One 6-ounce can crabmeat, drained
2 tablespoons minced onion or chives

Transfer the mixture to the buttered dish. Sprinkle with:

½ cup grated Fontina (2 ounces)

Bake until heated through, about 25 minutes. If desired, turn the oven to broil to brown on top.

BAKED ARTICHOKE DIP

About 2½ cups

Preheat the oven to 400°F. Combine in a medium bowl:

One 14-ounce can artichoke hearts, drained and finely chopped
1 cup mayonnaise
1 cup grated Parmesan (4 ounces)
(¼ cup finely chopped onions or green onions)
1 tablespoon lemon juice or dry white wine
½ teaspoon black pepper

Taste and season with salt if needed. Scrape into a small baking dish or ovenproof crock. Sprinkle over the dip:

2 tablespoons grated Parmesan
(Paprika, preferably smoked)

Bake until browned, about 20 minutes.

SEVEN-LAYER DIP

20 servings

Spread evenly in a 13 × 9 × 2-inch glass dish:

One 16-ounce can refried beans or 2 cups Refried Beans, 215

Mash together and spread over the beans:

3 large Hass avocados, peeled and pitted
3 tablespoons fresh lime juice

Mix together and spread over the avocado layer:

2 cups sour cream
3 tablespoons chili powder
1 teaspoon garlic powder

Layer in the order listed:

One 7-ounce can chopped green chiles, drained
One 6½-ounce can sliced black olives, drained
8 Roma or plum tomatoes, chopped, or 3½ cups any tomato salsa, 573–74
2 cups grated sharp Cheddar (8 ounces)
(Chopped fresh cilantro or green onions)

Serve with:

Tortilla chips

TEXAS CAVIAR

About 8 cups

A great stand-in for salsa or bean salad, this can be eaten immediately or refrigerated overnight. The longer it sits, the better it gets.

Prepare in a large bowl:

Vinaigrette, 575

Add and toss with the vinaigrette:

Three 16-ounce cans black-eyed peas, drained and rinsed
One 6-ounce jar pimientos, chopped, with juice
(3 fresh or pickled jalapeño peppers, chopped)
1 large tomato, chopped
(1 green bell pepper, chopped)
½ cup sliced green onions
¼ cup chopped parsley or cilantro
3 garlic cloves, minced
(1 tablespoon chopped oregano)
(1 tablespoon Worcestershire sauce)
1 tablespoon hot pepper sauce
1 teaspoon black pepper

HUMMUS

About 2 cups

Hummus is the Arabic word for "chickpeas," so while dips made from other types of beans may be delicious, we reserve the term "hummus" for this particular preparation.

Combine in a food processor:

One 15-ounce can chickpeas, drained and rinsed, or 1½ cups cooked chickpeas, 213
⅓ cup tahini
3 tablespoons lemon juice, or more to taste
2 tablespoons extra-virgin olive oil
2 garlic cloves, chopped
(½ teaspoon ground cumin)
½ teaspoon salt, or to taste

Puree until smooth, gradually adding up to ¼ cup cold water as needed to achieve a soft, creamy consistency. Transfer to a shallow serving bowl and garnish with:

1 tablespoon extra-virgin olive oil
Sprinkling of paprika, sumac, Aleppo or Urfa chile powder, Baharat, 589, or Za'atar, 590
(Dollops of a spicy condiment such as Harissa, 584, or Zhug, 567)

WHITE BEAN DIP WITH ROSEMARY AND GARLIC

About 3 cups

Heat in a medium skillet over medium-low heat:

¼ cup extra-virgin olive oil

Add:

2 garlic cloves, minced
2 teaspoons minced rosemary
½ teaspoon black pepper

Cook, stirring, until fragrant, about 3 minutes. Stir in:

Two 14- to 16-ounce cans navy, Great Northern, or cannellini beans, drained and rinsed, or 3 cups cooked white beans, 213

Mash or process in a food processor until smooth. Serve warm or at room temperature. If desired, drizzle with:

(Extra-virgin olive oil)

TANGY BLACK BEAN DIP

About 1 cup

Combine in a food processor:

One 15-ounce can black beans, drained and rinsed, or 1½ cups cooked black beans, 213
2 tablespoons distilled white vinegar
1 jalapeño pepper, seeded, if desired, and chopped
1 tablespoon olive oil
2 teaspoons tomato paste
2 garlic cloves, chopped
½ teaspoon onion powder
½ teaspoon salt
¼ teaspoon ground cumin
¼ teaspoon ground chipotle

Process until very smooth, scraping down the sides of the bowl as needed. If desired, serve topped with:

(Chopped cilantro)

ANY BEAN DIP

1½ to 2 cups

Any bean can be turned into a delicious and easy appetizer or sandwich spread. Use the flexible recipe below to get creative. For instance, pair white beans with paprika, dill, and a cooked beet or chickpeas with cumin and chipotles in adobo.

Combine in a food processor:

One 15-ounce can beans, drained and rinsed, or 1½ cups cooked beans, 213
¼ cup olive oil
1 to 2 garlic cloves, if not using roasted garlic
½ teaspoon salt

Add one or more of the following, if desired:

(¼ cup pesto, for chickpeas or white beans)
(1 roasted red pepper, jarred or homemade, 262)
(1 medium beet, cooked, 218, peeled, and chopped)
(2 medium carrots, cooked, 228 and chopped)
(¾ cup chopped cooked winter squash)
(Cloves from 1 head Roasted Garlic I, 241)
(1 to 2 chipotle peppers in adobo sauce, seeded if desired)
(1 tablespoon minced herbs, such as dill, cilantro, thyme, chives, or parsley)
(1 teaspoon cumin, chili powder, curry powder, or paprika)

Process until smooth, scraping down the sides of the bowl as needed. Serve with:

Pita or tortilla chips
Crudités, 45

or use as a sandwich spread.

BABA GHANOUSH (ROASTED EGGPLANT DIP)

About 3½ cups

For a smoky flavor, broil the eggplants or grill on an open flame until collapsed and blackened all over. After having a particularly fine rendition at a local restaurant, we asked the proprietor for his secret. "Jarred, roasted eggplant," he replied, to our surprise. We've been stocking it in our pantry ever since. It is available at most Mediterranean and Eastern European grocery stores. Just drain it of any liquid and substitute 3 cups of it for the fresh eggplant in this recipe.

Preheat the oven to 400°F. With a paring knife, pierce in several places each:

3 large eggplants (about 4 pounds)

Place on a baking sheet and roast until they are dark mahogany in color and very soft, 45 to 60 minutes. Let stand until cool enough to handle. Split the eggplants, scoop the flesh into a colander, and allow to drain for 20 minutes. Transfer to a food processor and add:

¼ cup tahini
2 tablespoons lemon juice
1 to 2 garlic cloves, chopped
1 teaspoon salt
(½ teaspoon ground cumin)

Pulse until smooth. Taste and adjust the lemon juice and salt. Transfer to a shallow serving bowl and garnish with:

2 tablespoons extra-virgin olive oil
2 tablespoons finely chopped parsley
(A dusting of paprika)

Serve with:

Warm pita bread

MUHAMMARA (ROASTED RED PEPPER AND WALNUT DIP)

About 1 cup

This Syrian pepper spread is delicious as a dip or sandwich spread, but it may also be used as a sauce for grilled meats or fish. If you can find Aleppo pepper flakes, we encourage you to give them a try. They are lightly spicy and have a rich, raisin-y flavor.

Roast, 262:

2 large red bell peppers

Transfer to a paper bag and let cool. Peel off the charred skin and discard. Remove the stems and seeds. In a food processor, combine the peppers and:

¾ cup walnuts, toasted, 1005
¼ cup extra-virgin olive oil
¼ cup fresh bread crumbs, 957
1 tablespoon pomegranate molasses, or ½ tablespoon honey and ½ tablespoon balsamic vinegar
2 garlic cloves, chopped
½ teaspoon red or Aleppo pepper flakes, or to taste
½ teaspoon ground cumin
½ teaspoon salt, or to taste

Process until smooth. Serve in a wide, shallow bowl, topped with:

Extra-virgin olive oil
Chopped toasted, 1005, walnuts

Serve with:

Warm pita bread

CAPONATA (EGGPLANT RELISH)

About 4 cups

A hearty Italian accompaniment for fish, poultry, or meat, as well as a spread to be served with pita bread, crackers, or Crostini, 49.

Peel and cut into ½-inch cubes:

1 medium eggplant (about 1 pound)

Sprinkle generously with:

Salt

Place in a colander and let stand at least 30 minutes and up to 1 hour. Rinse and pat dry. Heat in a large heavy skillet over medium heat:

2 tablespoons olive oil

Add and cook, stirring often, until softened, about 6 minutes:

1 cup finely chopped celery
1 medium onion, finely chopped
1 garlic clove, minced

Transfer the vegetables to a bowl. Add to the skillet:

2 tablespoons olive oil

Add the eggplant cubes and cook, stirring frequently, until lightly browned, 5 to 7 minutes. Add the celery mixture along with:

One 14½-ounce can diced tomatoes, drained
12 pitted green olives, such as Castelvetrano, coarsely chopped
2 tablespoons red wine vinegar
1½ tablespoons drained capers
1 tablespoon tomato paste
2 teaspoons sugar
1 teaspoon minced fresh oregano or ¼ teaspoon dried oregano
1 teaspoon salt
Black pepper to taste

Bring to a boil, then reduce the heat to low and simmer, uncovered, until thickened, about 15 minutes. Taste and adjust the seasonings with additional salt, pepper, and vinegar if needed. Transfer to a serving bowl, let cool, and garnish with:

2 tablespoons minced parsley

Serve at room temperature.

TAPENADE (OLIVE-CAPER SPREAD)

About 2¾ cups

Capers are an essential ingredient in this olive spread. Tapenade made without capers or with only a hint of them is sometimes called **olivade.** Both are traditionally served with crusty bread or crudités, 45. For more on olive types, see 1008.

Combine in a food processor:

2 cups olives, such as Kalamata or Niçoise, pitted
(3 anchovy fillets, rinsed and patted dry)
3 tablespoons drained capers
3 tablespoons olive oil
2 tablespoons lemon juice or brandy
2 garlic cloves, coarsely chopped
2 teaspoons fresh thyme leaves or 1 teaspoon dried thyme
Salt and black pepper

Pulse the mixture to a coarse puree.

ANCHOÏADE (ANCHOVY DIP)

About ½ cup

A little goes a long way with this punchy dip. Serve with crusty bread and crudités, 45.

Combine in a food processor:

One 2-ounce can oil-packed anchovies, drained and rinsed (about 12 fillets)
2 garlic cloves, chopped
1 tablespoon red wine vinegar or lemon juice

With the machine running, add in a thin stream:

½ cup extra-virgin olive oil

Stir in:

Black pepper to taste

BRANDADE DE MORUE (CREAMY SALT COD DIP)

About 3½ cups

Soak in cold water to cover:

1 pound salt cod, preferably boneless

Refrigerate for 24 hours. Drain, rinse well, and remove any skin and bones. Set aside. Place in a medium saucepan:

1 small russet potato (8 ounces), peeled and quartered

Add cool water to cover and bring to a boil. Reduce the heat to a simmer and cook until the potato is tender, about 15 minutes. Transfer the potato to a food processor with a slotted spoon. Bring the water back to a boil, add the fish, and remove from the heat. Let stand for 15 minutes, then drain and pat dry. Add the fish to the food processor, along with:

2 to 4 garlic cloves, chopped

Pulse until the fish is finely chopped. With the machine running, add in a slow stream:

½ cup extra-virgin olive oil
½ cup heavy cream

Process until the mixture is the consistency of mashed potatoes. Season to taste with:

Lemon juice
Black pepper

The brandade may be made up to 2 days in advance. To serve, preheat the oven to 400°F. Spread the brandade into a shallow baking dish and bake until browned, about 15 minutes. Serve warm with:

Sliced baguette, Crostini, 49, or crackers

SMOKED SALMON OR TROUT SPREAD

About 1½ cups

Doubled, this makes an excellent cheese ball (see page 55).

Beat until smooth with a wooden spoon or in a stand mixer:

8 ounces cream cheese, softened

Add and gently stir in until combined:

4 ounces smoked salmon or trout, flaked

Chill.

ABOUT CHEESY APPETIZERS

Cheesemaking is an art whose fruits need no adornment. With that caveat, here are some recipes for transmuting cheese into crispy sticks, encrusted spheres, spreads, and other delicious morsels meant for sharing. For further ideas, see our section on serving cheeses, 45, and our recipes for Gougères, 70, Savory Stuffed Dates, 185, Puff Pastry Cheese Straws, 70, and Cheese Puff Canapés, 68.

ABOUT CHEESE BALLS

Cheese balls are classic party fare. Feel free to experiment with flavorings and coatings, using the basic proportions of cheese in the recipes below. Cheese balls made from cream cheese are great blank canvases for interesting additions such as smoked paprika or chipotles in adobo. If using cheeses that are very flavorful in their own right, such as blue cheese or Muenster, leave out other complex additions in favor of simplicity. Below are some combinations for inspiration:

Equal parts cream cheese and goat cheese blended with minced chives; rolled in toasted, 1005, chopped hazelnuts or chopped fresh herbs

Cream cheese and sharp Cheddar blended with chopped green onions and chipotles in adobo; rolled in toasted pumpkin seeds

Cream cheese and blue cheese blended with chopped dried figs; rolled in toasted, 1005, chopped walnuts

Cream cheese blended with cloves from 1 head Roasted Garlic, 241; rolled in Everything Seasoning, 590

CREAM CHEESE BALL

One 5-inch ball

Blend well in a large bowl:

Two 8-ounce packages cream cheese, softened
1/3 cup grated Parmesan
1/4 cup mayonnaise
1/4 cup finely chopped green onion
2 tablespoons finely chopped carrot
2 tablespoons finely chopped celery
(1 teaspoon drained prepared horseradish)
1/2 teaspoon salt

Place the mixture on a large piece of plastic wrap. Bring up the edges of the wrap and form the mixture into a ball. Place in a small deep bowl to help it hold its shape and refrigerate for at least 1 hour. When it is firm, roll the cheese ball in:

1 cup chopped toasted, 1005, walnuts or pecans

Press the nuts to make them adhere. The cheese ball can be stored in the refrigerator for up to 3 days.

ADDITIONS TO CHEESE BALLS

See About Cheese Balls, above, for several specific pairing suggestions. Add any of the following, alone or in combination, to the cheese mixture:

1 teaspoon smoked paprika
1 chipotle pepper in adobo sauce, finely chopped
1 head Roasted Garlic, 241
1/3 cup finely chopped dried figs or apricots
1/2 cup finely chopped Sautéed Onions, 255, or Caramelized Onions, 255
1/3 cup chopped roasted red peppers or green chiles, store-bought or homemade, 262
1/3 cup finely chopped water chestnuts
1/3 cup finely chopped, well-drained kimchi
4 to 6 ounces flaked smoked salmon

Form the cheese ball as directed and roll in one of the following:

1 cup chopped toasted, 1005, nuts
3/4 cup toasted seeds (sesame, sunflower, pumpkin), 1005
1/2 cup chopped herbs
1/2 cup Dukkah, 589, Za'atar, 590, or Everything Seasoning, 590

CHEDDAR CHEESE BALL

One 5-inch ball

Process in a food processor until smooth:

2 1/2 cups shredded sharp Cheddar (10 ounces)
3 ounces cream cheese, softened
6 slices bacon, cooked until crisp and crumbled
2 tablespoons milk
1 tablespoon drained prepared horseradish
1/8 teaspoon salt

Proceed as for **Cream Cheese Ball, above,** rolling the ball in:

1 cup chopped toasted, 1005, walnuts or pecans

TREVA'S PIMIENTO CHEESE

About 1 1/2 cups

Megan's great-grandmother, the matriarch of her close-knit North Carolina family, made enough pimiento cheese for everyone to take home with them after Sunday lunch (or, as they call it, dinner) every week until she was ninety-seven years old. Her recipe is one of the simplest we know—sharp Cheddar, just enough mayonnaise to hold everything together, jarred pimientos, and a pinch of sugar—but probably the best. We have added some optional ingredients for the adventuresome, but we prefer it done Treva's way.

Combine in a medium bowl:

2 cups grated sharp Cheddar (8 ounces)
1/4 cup chopped well-drained jarred pimientos
6 tablespoons mayonnaise
Pinch of sugar
(1 garlic clove, minced)
(1 1/2 teaspoons lemon juice)
(1/2 teaspoon dry mustard)
(1/8 teaspoon cayenne pepper)

Beat with a wooden spoon until combined. Serve with:

Crackers

or use as a sandwich spread.

FROMAGE FORT (STRONG CHEESE)

Yield varies

A transformative, French spread made from cheese scraps that might otherwise be thrown away or neglected—an especially useful recipe for the day after a party. If using blue cheese, do not let it exceed one-quarter of the total amount. Keep in mind that garlic (especially raw) or herbs will intensify the longer the spread sits, so use a light hand. Serve with crusty bread and crudités, 45.

Pulse in a food processor until finely ground:

Cheese scraps, rinds removed, any hard cheeses grated

Add, as desired:

(Garlic, raw or roasted, 241)
(Herbs, fresh or dried)
(Black pepper)
(Red pepper flakes)
(A splash of Cognac)

With the food processor running, gradually add enough:

Dry white wine

for the cheese mixture to become spreadable, but not runny, in texture. If the spread gets too firm as it sits, return it to the food processor and add more wine. Serve right away or cover and store refrigerated for up to 1 week.

BLUE CHEESE SPREAD WITH WALNUTS

About 1½ cups

This makes a fantastic cheese ball as well—just double the recipe to make a sizable ball and roll it in 1 cup chopped walnuts. Serve with sliced French bread, sliced apples or pears, and quartered fresh figs.

Puree in a food processor until smooth:

8 ounces cream cheese, softened
½ cup crumbled blue cheese (4 ounces)
(2 tablespoons port)

Scrape into a small bowl. Sprinkle with:

¼ cup chopped toasted, 1005, walnuts

ROASTED GARLIC AND PARMESAN SPREAD

About 1¼ cups

Preheat the oven to 400°F. Place in a baking dish:

4 heads garlic, top third cut off to expose the cloves
1 small yellow onion (6 to 8 ounces), left whole

Drizzle over the garlic and onion:

¼ cup olive oil

Cover the dish tightly with foil and roast until the garlic and onion are very soft, 1 hour to 1 hour 15 minutes. Cool slightly. Squeeze the garlic pulp from the skins into a food processor. Peel the onion and discard the skin and root end. Add to the food processor, along with any oil left in the baking dish. Pulse to combine. Add:

½ cup finely grated Parmesan (2 ounces)
1 tablespoon chopped thyme

Process briefly to blend. If desired, stir in:

(¼ cup pitted Kalamata olives, finely chopped)

Taste and season with:

Salt and black pepper

Serve with:

Sliced crusty bread or Crostini, 49

MARINATED CHEESE

8 servings

If making yogurt cheese to use here, salt it to taste after draining.

Warm in a medium skillet over medium heat until fragrant:

½ cup olive oil

Add:

2 garlic cloves, thinly sliced
12 black peppercorns
3 large sprigs rosemary or 6 sprigs thyme
¼ teaspoon salt
Pinch of red pepper flakes

Remove from the heat and let cool to room temperature. Remove and discard the rosemary or thyme sprigs. Place in a bowl or on a serving plate one of the following:

8 ounces fresh mozzarella, cut into 1-inch cubes, or small mozzarella balls (bocconcini)
8 ounces soft goat cheese
8 ounces feta, cut into ¾-inch cubes
8 ounces Yogurt Cheese, 1035, rolled into small balls

Pour the oil over the cheese and let stand at room temperature for several hours, or cover and refrigerate for up to 4 days. Bring to room temperature before serving.

FRIED MOZZARELLA STICKS

About 25 pieces

Please read about Deep-Frying, 1051.

Cut into 3½ × ½ × ½-inch sticks:

1-pound block mozzarella

Spread in a shallow dish:

½ cup all-purpose flour

Beat in a shallow bowl:

2 eggs

Spread on a plate:

½ cup seasoned dry bread crumbs

Dredge the mozzarella sticks lightly in the flour, shaking off the excess. One by one, dip in the egg, coating completely, then roll in the bread crumbs to coat. Put the sticks on a plate and freeze for 15 minutes. Meanwhile, heat to 365°F in a deep-fryer, deep heavy pot, or Dutch oven:

3 inches vegetable oil

Fry the mozzarella sticks in batches until golden brown, about 1 minute. Drain on paper towels. Serve hot with:

Marinara Sauce, 556

FRIED HALLOUMI WITH HONEY AND WALNUTS

4 servings

Halloumi is a firm, mild cheese with a high melting point, which makes it perfect for grilling or frying. If you cannot find Halloumi, paneer, queso blanco, or aged provolone are good substitutes, though paneer will benefit from a healthy sprinkle of salt after browning.

Heat in a heavy skillet over medium heat:

1 tablespoon vegetable oil

Add and brown well on all sides, about 2 minutes per side:

8 ounces Halloumi, cut into 4 rectangular slabs

Transfer to a serving platter and top with:

¼ cup chopped toasted, 1005, walnuts
1 tablespoon honey
Chopped mint

BRIE BAKED IN PASTRY

28 servings

Please read About Puff Pastry, 691.

Thaw:

One 17½-ounce package frozen puff pastry sheets

Unfold the two squares. On a lightly floured surface, roll out each into a 12-inch square. Center one sheet in a 9-inch pie pan. Top with:

One 2.2-pound wheel Brie (8 inches in diameter)

If desired, spread the top of the cheese with:

(3 to 4 tablespoons finely chopped fruit chutney, or sweet preserves)

Fold the edges of the pastry up and over the Brie, pleating the excess and trimming it to 1 inch over the top rim of the cheese. Cut the second pastry sheet into a round the diameter of the Brie, using the top of the cheese box as a template. Lay the pastry round on top of the Brie. Gently roll the top and bottom edges together and crimp to seal. Refrigerate for at least 30 minutes, and up to 24 hours. Preheat the oven to 400°F. Stir together in a small bowl:

1 large egg yolk
1 tablespoon milk

Gently brush the egg wash over the pastry. Bake for 10 minutes. Reduce the oven temperature to 350°F and bake until golden and puffy, 30 to 40 minutes. Let stand for 1 hour and transfer to a plate. Cut a small wedge and partially remove it, then set out the Brie with a knife, surrounded by:

Sliced fresh or dried fruit
Sliced French bread

CHEESE FONDUE

4 to 5 servings

The cheese or combination of cheeses used must be natural, not processed. Kirsch is traditional, but another nonsweet alcohol, such as Cognac or applejack, can be substituted. Measure all ingredients and have them ready to add, for the pot must be stirred constantly from the time the wine is hot enough for the cheese until the fondue is ready to eat, about 10 minutes of cooking. Never make fondue in advance. When ready to serve, the fondue will be on the thin side, but will thicken as the feast progresses.

Tear into bite-sized pieces:

1 loaf crusty white French or Italian bread

Rub the interior of a medium stainless steel pot or fondue pot with:

1 garlic clove, peeled and halved

Discard the garlic. Add to the pot:

1¼ cups Swiss Fendant or other dry white wine

Bring to a simmer over medium heat. Add gradually, stirring constantly:

1 pound Gruyère or Emmantaler, cubed
Pinch of freshly grated or ground nutmeg

Cook, stirring with a wooden spoon, until the cheese is melted (the cheese and wine will not yet be blended). Mix together thoroughly in a small bowl:

1 tablespoon cornstarch
2 tablespoons kirsch, Cognac, or applejack

Stir into the cheese mixture. Continue to stir and simmer until the mixture is smooth, about 5 minutes. Season to taste with:

Salt and black pepper

If the fondue is too thick, add up to:

¼ cup Swiss Fendant or other dry white wine

Quickly transfer to a fondue pot or chafing dish set over a low flame and serve with the bread cubes.

NACHOS

10 to 12 servings

Preheat the broiler. Spread on a baking sheet (they can be slightly overlapping):

4 ounces tortilla chips (about 4 cups)

Sprinkle with:

1½ cups grated Cheddar (6 ounces)
1½ cups grated Monterey Jack (6 ounces)
(One 4½-ounce can chopped green chiles, drained, or 1 poblano pepper, roasted, 262, seeded, and chopped)

Broil until the cheese is melted, 2 to 3 minutes. Top with your choice of:

Sour cream
Cooked pinto or black beans
4 ounces fresh chorizo, crumbled and browned
Chopped green onions
Pickled or fresh jalapeño slices
Chopped cilantro
Salsa, store-bought or homemade, 573–74
Guacamole, 51

Serve immediately.

QUESADILLAS

20 or 30 pieces

Lay out on a work surface:

Ten 6-inch flour tortillas

Divide among half of the tortillas:

2 cups shredded Monterey Jack or Cheddar (8 ounces)
(One 4½-ounce can chopped green chiles, drained)
(¾ cup chopped green onions)
(2 tablespoons minced cilantro)
Salt and black pepper to taste

Top with the remaining 5 tortillas. Preheat the oven to 200°F and place a baking sheet inside. Heat a medium skillet, preferably nonstick, over medium-high heat for 3 minutes. Brush lightly with:

Vegetable oil

Transfer 1 quesadilla to the skillet and cook until browned and crisp on the first side, about 2 minutes. Flip the quesadilla and cook until the second side is crisp, about 2 minutes longer. Transfer to the baking sheet in the oven and cook the remaining quesadillas in the same manner. Cut each quesadilla into 4 or 6 wedges and serve at once with one or more of the following:

Sour cream, Guacamole, 51, or any salsa, store-bought or homemade 573–74

ABOUT FRUIT APPETIZERS

Though fruit platters are lovely and simple to put together, 45, cut fruit and a little ingenuity can result in delectable, sweet-savory appetizers. In addition to these recipes, see Savory Stuffed Dates, 185, and Pickled Grapes, 928.

BACON-WRAPPED DATES

35 to 40 pieces

For larger pitted dates like the Medjool variety, use 12 ounces and cut each one crosswise into 2 or 3 bite-sized pieces.

Preheat the oven to 400°F. Have ready:

8 ounces small pitted dates, such as Deglet Noor or Halawi
1 pound sliced bacon, cut into 3-inch pieces

Tuck inside each date:

1 Marcona or roasted almond (35 to 40 total)

Wrap one length of bacon around each date. Place seam side down on a wire rack set on a rimmed baking sheet. Bake until the bacon is crisp and well browned, 15 to 18 minutes. Serve warm.

MELON AND PROSCIUTTO

4 to 6 servings

One of summer's most refreshing first courses. If desired, you may wrap **8 halved or quartered figs** or **4 peaches, pitted and cut into 8 wedges.**

I. Cut in half and scoop out the seeds from:

1 cantaloupe, honeydew, or Crenshaw melon

Slice each half into 6 wedges and remove the rind. Place 2 or 3 wedges on each plate. Cut into wide strips:

8 ounces thinly sliced prosciutto or Serrano ham

Drape the ham over the slices. Top with:

Parmesan shavings

Serve at once, and pass the pepper mill.

II. This is one of our favorites. To grill, prepare as above but cut the melon wedges into 2-inch chunks. Wrap each piece of melon with ham and secure with a toothpick. Grill 4 inches from the heat for 2 to 3 minutes per side.

WATERMELON AND GOAT CHEESE

4 servings

Prepare:

One 2-pound piece watermelon, rind and seeds removed, cut into bite-sized, ½-inch-thick squares

Arrange on a platter and top the melon squares with:

Slices of soft goat cheese (from a 4-ounce log)
Freshly ground black pepper
Flaky sea salt

Drizzle them with:

Extra-virgin olive oil

ABOUT VEGETABLE APPETIZERS

Cooked, marinated, and raw vegetables are some of the most colorful and appreciated foods for grazing. Some of these recipes, like Marinated Vegetables, below, contrast nicely with richer appetizers while others, such as Crispy Potato Skins, 59, are quite filling in their own right. For a vegetable-centric dish that walks the line between these extremes, see Summer Rolls, 71. For a discussion of crudités, see 45.

BAGNA CAUDA

About 1 cup

Traditionally, this dip is served with Steamed Artichokes, 206, or young cardoons, celery, and fennel. But, really, any tender vegetable is enhanced by a dip in this garlicky bath.

Have ready:

Your choice of crudités, 45

Place in a heavy fondue pot or other heavy pot:

1 stick (4 ounces) butter
½ cup olive oil
8 anchovy fillets, mashed
4 garlic cloves, minced
½ teaspoon salt
½ teaspoon black pepper

Simmer gently for 5 minutes, stirring occasionally. Using fondue forks or skewers, dip the vegetables in the warm sauce.

MARINATED VEGETABLES

2 cups

Have ready one of the following:

2 large red bell peppers, roasted, 262, and peeled
1 large English cucumber, cut into half-moons
One 14- to 16-ounce can hearts of palm, drained and sliced into 1-inch pieces
2 cups halved cherry tomatoes
One 9- to 12-ounce package frozen artichoke hearts, prepared according to package directions and halved

Or, steam one of the following over rapidly boiling water until crisp-tender, 2 to 4 minutes:

2 cups green beans
2 cups small whole mushrooms
2 cups cauliflower florets
1 pound asparagus

Toss with:

Vinaigrette, 575

Marinate in the refrigerator for at least 1 hour, preferably overnight. Serve chilled or at room temperature.

BROILED STUFFED MUSHROOMS COCKAIGNE

24 pieces

In place of the filling below, you may also stuff mushroom caps with goat cheese mixed with minced garlic and herbs, any flavored butter, 559–60, or Creamed Spinach, 244.

Preheat the oven to 375°F. Clean, then remove and reserve the stems from:

32 medium cremini or white button mushrooms (about 1½ pounds)

Count out 24 same-sized mushroom caps and toss with:

3 tablespoons olive oil or butter, melted

Slice the remaining caps. Chop the stems. Heat in a medium skillet over medium heat:

2 tablespoons butter or olive oil

Add the sliced mushrooms and stems along with:

1 large shallot, minced
(1 garlic clove, minced)
1 teaspoon minced fresh thyme or ½ teaspoon dried thyme

Cook, stirring occasionally, for 5 minutes. Stir in:

½ cup dry bread crumbs
¼ cup chopped pecans or other nuts
3 tablespoons minced chives or chopped basil
2 tablespoons heavy cream, broth, dry vermouth, or sherry

Transfer to a food processor and coarsely chop the mixture. Season with:

Salt and black pepper

Fill each mushroom cap with a heaping tablespoon of the filling. Place on a baking sheet. Sprinkle with:

2 to 3 tablespoons grated Parmesan

Bake until the tops are bubbling, about 15 minutes.

STUFFED RAW VEGETABLES

Hollowed-out vegetables make terrific cases for any number of fillings. When stuffing round vegetables, first cut a small slice off the bottom of each vegetable to keep them from rolling around the platter. Fill the vegetable cases using a small spoon or pastry bag.

Prepare one of the following:

Blue Cheese Spread with Walnuts, 56
Basic Cream Cheese Spread, 136
Treva's Pimiento Cheese, 55

Pipe or spoon this mixture into:

Celery ribs; Belgian endive leaves; small, sweet peppers, halved and seeded; scooped-out baby yellow squash or zucchini; hollowed out ½-inch cucumber rounds

POTATOES STUFFED WITH SOUR CREAM AND CAVIAR

24 pieces

For a less expensive variation, top the potato halves with **12 ounces flaked hot-smoked salmon** instead of caviar.

Place in a saucepan or pot:

Twelve 1½- to 2-inch red potatoes (1½ pounds)
1 tablespoon salt

Add enough water to the pot to cover by 1 inch.

Bring to a simmer over medium-high heat. Cook, uncovered, just until the potatoes are tender, about 20 minutes. Drain and let cool to room temperature. Cut each potato in half. Using a melon baller, scoop a small crater out of each half and reserve the scooped out potato flesh in a bowl. Cut a thin slice off the rounded side of each half so the potatoes will sit flat. Sprinkle the potatoes with:

Kosher or coarse sea salt

Add to the bowl of potato flesh and mix until smooth:

½ cup sour cream or crème fraîche

Spoon or pipe the sour cream mixture into the potatoes. Top with:

4 tablespoons caviar or other roe

Sprinkle generously with:

Sliced chives

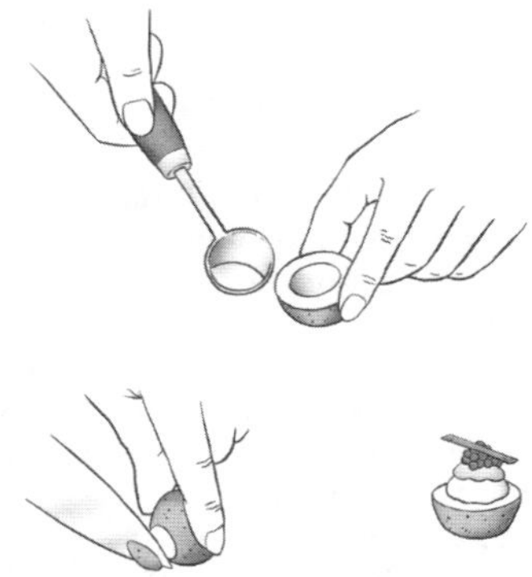

Scooping out the center of the potato with a melon baller; cutting a thin slice off the rounded side of a potato half; completed Potato Stuffed with Sour Cream and Caviar

CRISPY POTATO SKINS

16 pieces

Use the scooped-out potato flesh for Latkes, 269.

Bake, 267:

Four 8-ounce russet potatoes

Let cool completely. Cut each potato lengthwise into quarters. With a spoon, scoop out most of the pulp, leaving a ¼-inch shell. Arrange the potato skins on a baking sheet, cut side up. Combine:

6 tablespoons (¾ stick) butter, melted
1 tablespoon chili powder and/or 2 teaspoons finely minced garlic

Brush on the potato skins. Season generously with:

Salt

The potatoes can be covered loosely and refrigerated up to 12 hours. Shortly before serving, position a rack in the upper third of the oven and preheat the oven to 450°F. Bake the potato skins until very brown and crisp, about 30 minutes. Sprinkle with:

1 cup shredded Monterey Jack or Cheddar (4 ounces)
(8 slices bacon, cooked until crisp and crumbled)

Return to the oven until the cheese begins to brown, about 5 minutes. Serve at once, accompanied with:

Chopped green onions and/or cilantro
(Sour cream and/or any salsa, 573–74)

PATATAS OR PAPAS BRAVAS (SPANISH FRIED POTATOES)

4 servings

A classic tapa, prepared here with the easy, oil-saving cold-start frying method, 270. The sauce served with these fried potato cubes is known as *salsa brava,* and it is very good served atop Steamed Mussels, 351, or as a condiment for Tortilla Española, 160. If you wish to avoid frying altogether or want to double the recipe, consider roasting the potatoes instead, 267.

Heat in a medium saucepan over medium heat:

3 tablespoons olive oil

Add:

1 medium onion, chopped

Cook, stirring, until translucent and softened, about 5 minutes. Add:

2 garlic cloves, chopped
1 teaspoon Spanish smoked paprika
¼ teaspoon cayenne pepper

Cook until fragrant, about 1 minute. Stir in:

One 14½-ounce can diced tomatoes
¼ cup white wine vinegar or sherry vinegar
1 teaspoon sugar
½ teaspoon salt

Simmer until thick, about 15 minutes. Remove from the heat, puree in a blender or food processor, and taste for seasoning.

Scrub well and cut into 1-inch cubes:

2 pounds russet potatoes

Place in a deep, heavy skillet (preferably cast iron) and barely cover with:

Vegetable oil

Bring the potatoes and oil to a simmer over high heat, reduce the heat to medium, and simmer until the potatoes are soft in the center, well browned, and crispy, 15 to 20 minutes. Remove from the skillet and drain on paper towels. Dust immediately with:

½ teaspoon salt
½ teaspoon sweet or smoked paprika

Serve hot with the *salsa brava* and, if desired:

(Aïoli, 564)

JALAPEÑO POPPERS

About 50 pieces

A grapefruit spoon works perfectly for removing the seeds from the peppers. No matter how you choose to remove the seeds, wear gloves and wash your hands immediately afterward.

Preheat the oven to 425°F. Have ready:

25 jalapeño peppers, halved lengthwise and seeded

Combine in a medium bowl:

8 ounces cream cheese, softened
8 ounces Monterey Jack, grated
2 tablespoons chili powder
4 green onions, minced
(8 ounces bacon, cooked until crisp and crumbled)
Salt to taste

Divide the cream cheese mixture among the jalapeño halves. Set aside.

Whisk together in a small bowl:

1 egg
1 tablespoon water

In another bowl, have ready:

1 cup panko bread crumbs

Dip the cheesy side of each jalapeño in the egg wash, then in the panko. Place bread crumb side up on a baking sheet. Bake until the cheese is bubbling and the tops are nicely browned, about 15 minutes. If necessary, turn the oven to broil to brown the tops. Let cool briefly and serve warm.

ABOUT MEAT-BASED APPETIZERS

Aside from an antipasto spread, 45, or charcuterie platter, 45, meaty appetizers are generally served hot, and thus require a little extra planning. Wings, skewers, ribs, and meatballs are best kept warm in a 200°F oven, covered with foil. Transfer to serving dishes as they disappear. Grilled skewers can be kept warm on a cooler part of the grill, wrapped in foil. ➤ Do not hold meat appetizers at room temperature for more than 1 hour, though the recipes below are delicious enough that they should disappear long before then. For more ideas, see Piroshki, 703, Empanadas with Picadillo, 702, and Ham Biscuits, 68.

BUFFALO CHICKEN WINGS

About 24 pieces

These were invented at the Anchor Bar in Buffalo, New York, in 1964. The classic hot sauce for this recipe is Frank's RedHot, but other sauces can be substituted. If using hotter varieties such as Tabasco, start with 2 tablespoons hot sauce and add more as desired. The wing tips can be reserved for making stock, 73.

I. FRIED

Please read about Deep-Frying, 1051.

Preheat the oven to 200°F. Remove the wing tips from:

12 chicken wings (3 to 3½ pounds)

Cut each wing into 2 pieces at the joint. Season the wings all over with:

1 teaspoon salt
1 teaspoon black pepper

Heat to 375°F in a deep-fryer or deep heavy pot:

1 inch vegetable oil

A tip of a wing held in the oil should make a lively sizzle. Add as many wings as will fit in a single layer and fry, turning once, until golden brown and cooked through, 10 to 13 minutes. Drain on paper towels and keep warm on a wire rack set over a baking sheet in the oven. Repeat with the remaining wings. Melt in a small saucepan over medium-low heat until foaming:

4 tablespoons (½ stick) butter
(2 garlic cloves, minced)

Remove from the heat and stir in:

¼ cup Frank's RedHot sauce, or to taste
2 tablespoons cider vinegar
¼ teaspoon salt

Transfer the wings to a large bowl. Pour the sauce over them and toss until evenly coated. Taste and adjust the seasonings. Serve hot with:

Celery sticks
Creamy Blue Cheese Dressing, 577

II. ROASTED

Though not "traditional," roasting chicken wings is less of a hassle, especially if you are doubling the recipe for a large party of Super Bowl fans. If your wings need to be divided between two baking sheets, be sure to switch their position on the oven racks when it is time to turn the wings.

Preheat the oven to 425°F. Trim and cut the wings as in **version I, above.** Toss them in a large bowl with **2 tablespoons vegetable oil,** and season with the salt and black pepper. Place the wings on a broiler pan or a wire rack set over a rimmed baking sheet and roast for 20 minutes. Take the wings out, flip them with tongs, and roast until nicely browned and cooked through, about 20 minutes more. Meanwhile, make the butter-pepper sauce as in **version I.** When the wings are done, toss them in a bowl with the sauce and serve as above.

THAI-STYLE CHICKEN WINGS

24 pieces

These wings are loosely inspired by Andy Ricker's fish sauce wings, a popular staple in Portland, Oregon. If you opt for the garnish of Crispy Fried Shallots, 256, fry them before frying the chicken and transfer to a plate lined with paper towels. Please read about Deep-Frying, 1051.

Mix together in a large bowl:

½ cup fish sauce
½ cup packed brown sugar, coconut sugar, or palm sugar
4 garlic cloves, minced
1½ teaspoons ground white pepper
1 teaspoon ground coriander
1 teaspoon ground cumin

Remove the wing tips from:

12 chicken wings (3 to 3½ pounds)

Cut each wing into 2 pieces at the joint and pierce each muscle a few times with the tip of your knife (this allows the marinade to penetrate deeper). Toss the wings in the bowl with the marinade and refrigerate, covered, for at least 2 hours and up to 6 hours, stirring occasionally. When ready to cook, remove the wings from the marinade, scraping off any excess. Transfer the marinade to a small saucepan. Pour onto a plate:

1 cup cornstarch

Coat the wings with the cornstarch, shake off the excess, and set aside. Bring the reserved marinade to a simmer over medium heat and cook for 5 minutes. Remove from the heat and whisk in:

4 tablespoons (½ stick) butter
¼ cup rice vinegar
2 to 4 tablespoons chili garlic sauce, sambal oelek, 969, or sriracha
1 tablespoon hoisin sauce, red miso, or mashed fermented black beans
(½ teaspoon toasted sesame oil)

Preheat the oven to 200°F. Heat to 375°F in a deep-fryer, deep heavy pot, or Dutch oven:

2 inches vegetable oil

A tip of a wing held in the oil should sizzle briskly. Add as many wings as will fit in a single layer and fry, turning once, until golden brown and cooked through, 10 to 13 minutes. Drain on paper towels and keep warm on a wire rack set over a baking sheet in the oven. Repeat with the remaining wings. Transfer the wings to a large bowl, pour the sauce over them, and toss until evenly coated. Liberally sprinkle the wings with:

Toasted sesame seeds
¼ cup sliced green onions
¼ cup chopped cilantro
(Crispy Fried Shallots, 256)

Serve immediately with:

Lime wedges

LEMON ROSEMARY CHICKEN SKEWERS

14 to 16 pieces

If using wooden skewers, either soak them in water for 1 hour or cover the exposed ends with foil.

Stir together in a medium bowl:

3 tablespoons olive oil
Finely grated zest of 1 large lemon
2 tablespoons lemon juice
1 teaspoon chopped fresh rosemary or ½ teaspoon dried rosemary
1 garlic clove, minced
½ teaspoon salt
¼ teaspoon black pepper

Cut crosswise into 8 strips each:

2 boneless, skinless chicken breasts

Add the chicken to the marinade and stir to coat. Cover and refrigerate 1 to 2 hours. Prepare a medium-hot grill fire or preheat the broiler. Thread the chicken strips onto 16 skewers. Grill or broil just until cooked through, turning once, about 2 minutes per side. Serve hot or at room temperature.

FIVE-SPICE RIBS

6 to 8 servings

Cut off and discard the green tops, then thinly slice the tender pale parts of:

2 stalks lemongrass

Place in a blender or food processor along with:

3 tablespoons sugar
2 tablespoons chopped shallots or green onions
2 tablespoons minced garlic
2 tablespoons fish sauce
2 tablespoons soy sauce
2 tablespoons toasted sesame oil
2 tablespoons vegetable oil
2 tablespoons Five-Spice Powder, 590
1 teaspoon chili garlic paste or sambal oelek, 969, or ¼ teaspoon red pepper flakes

Process until pureed, then transfer to a large bowl. Rinse, pat dry, and add:

3 pounds pork back ribs or spareribs, cut into individual ribs

Turn to coat each rib thoroughly. Cover and refrigerate for at least 8 and up to 24 hours. Preheat the oven to 325°F. Lightly brush a large broiler pan or rimmed baking sheet with vegetable oil. Arrange the ribs meaty side down on the pan and bake 45 minutes. Turn the ribs and bake until completely tender, 45 minutes to 1 hour longer. If desired, sprinkle with:

(2 tablespoons toasted sesame seeds)

SATAY SKEWERS

6 to 8 servings

A variety of proteins work here. Tougher cuts of beef or pork such as flank steak or shoulder chops should be sliced across the grain.

Process in a blender or food processor until smooth:

½ cup canned coconut milk
1 large shallot, chopped
2 tablespoons brown sugar or coconut sugar
2 tablespoons fish sauce or soy sauce
2 garlic cloves, chopped

1 teaspoon ground cumin
1 teaspoon ground coriander

Place in a shallow dish:

1 pound large shrimp (16/20), deveined, 363, or beef steak, pork chops, or chicken breasts or boneless thighs, thinly sliced into 3 × 1-inch strips

Pour in the marinade and toss to coat. Cover and let stand for 1 hour at room temperature, or refrigerate for up to 24 hours. Prepare:

Peanut Dipping Sauce, 571

An hour before cooking, soak about twenty 6-inch-long bamboo skewers in water to cover. Prepare a medium-hot grill fire or preheat the broiler. Thread a skewer through each strip of meat or shrimp. Lightly brush on both sides with:

Vegetable oil

Grill or broil, turning once, until browned, 2 to 3 minutes. Serve immediately, passing the peanut sauce for dipping.

DEVILED HAM

About 1½ cups

We once received a letter from a hard-working scientist thanking us for the efficacy of our deviled ham recipe, specifically its ability to efficiently satisfy his nutritional needs. He made big, economical batches to have around as a quick protein source—a sort of hammy precursor to Soylent. Use as a sandwich spread or serve in a crock with crackers.

Combine in a food processor and process to a paste:

1½ cups diced deli ham (about 8 ounces)
5 tablespoons butter or mayonnaise
2 tablespoons chopped parsley
1 tablespoon Dijon or whole-grain mustard
1 teaspoon lemon juice or dill pickle brine, or to taste
½ teaspoon sweet paprika, smoked if desired
¼ teaspoon cayenne pepper
Salt and black or white pepper to taste

CHICKEN LIVER PÂTÉ

About 3 cups

Cut into small pieces and place in the freezer:

1 stick (4 ounces) butter

Melt in a large skillet over medium heat:

2 tablespoons butter

Add:

¾ cup finely chopped shallots (about 2 large)

Cook, stirring, until softened, 2 to 3 minutes. Add:

1 small Granny Smith apple, peeled, cored, and grated

Cook, stirring constantly, until softened, about 3 minutes. Transfer to a food processor. Rinse and pat dry:

1 pound chicken livers, trimmed and halved

Heat in the same skillet over medium-high heat until the foam subsides:

1 tablespoon butter

Add the chicken livers and season with:

½ teaspoon salt
½ teaspoon black pepper

Cook until browned on the outside but still pink in the center, about 2 minutes on each side. Remove the skillet from the heat. Pour in:

3 tablespoons Calvados or Cognac

Ignite with a long match or lighter. Return the skillet to the heat and swirl until the alcohol has burned off. Add to the food processor. If desired, also add:

(½ teaspoon Quatre Épices, 591)

Process until smooth. With the machine running, drop in the pieces of chilled butter one at a time. Taste and adjust the seasonings. Scrape into a small crock or bowl and smooth the top with a spatula. Press plastic wrap directly on the surface and refrigerate until firm, at least 2 hours. Serve cold or at room temperature.

COCKTAIL MEATBALLS

About 70 meatballs

Preheat the oven to 350°F. Combine:

2 pounds lean ground beef
1 cup crushed cornflakes
⅓ cup ketchup
2 large eggs, beaten
2 tablespoons soy sauce
¼ cup finely chopped parsley
3 tablespoons minced onion or 2 tablespoons dried onion
3 garlic cloves, minced
¼ teaspoon black pepper

Form into meatballs 1 inch in diameter. Arrange in a 13 × 9 × 2-inch baking pan. Combine in a medium saucepan:

16 ounces jellied cranberry sauce (1½ cups)
1 tablespoon lemon juice
One 12-ounce bottle mild, tomato-based chili sauce

Stir over medium heat until the cranberry sauce melts. Pour over the meatballs in the pan. Bake, uncovered, until cooked through, about 30 minutes.

KEFTEDES (GREEK MEATBALLS)

30 small meatballs

Broiling instead of frying these meatballs makes them easy to whip up with virtually no mess. The meat mixture can also be shaped into patties for lamb burgers.

Preheat the broiler. Lightly oil a large baking sheet. Combine in a large bowl:

1 pound ground lamb
½ medium red onion, grated or minced
¼ cup dry bread crumbs
2 tablespoons minced parsley
2 tablespoons minced mint
2 tablespoons red wine vinegar
1 large egg, beaten
2 garlic cloves, minced
½ teaspoon dried oregano
½ teaspoon salt
½ teaspoon black pepper

Mix with your hands just until combined. Do not overmix. Scoop out level tablespoons of the mixture and roll into balls. Place on the prepared baking sheet and broil until the internal temperature reaches 160°F and the meatballs are browned, 8 to 10 minutes. Serve with:

Tzatziki, 569

PORK AND MUSHROOM LETTUCE WRAPS

About 16 lettuce wraps

Heat in a large skillet over medium-high heat:

1 tablespoon vegetable oil

When the oil shimmers, add:

1½ pounds ground pork

Brown the pork thoroughly, then transfer to a plate and set aside. If there is no fat left in the skillet, add:

(2 teaspoons vegetable oil)

Add:

1 small onion, finely chopped
4 ounces shiitake or oyster mushrooms, chopped
4 garlic cloves, minced
1-inch piece ginger, peeled and minced

Sauté until the mushrooms have released their liquid, about 5 minutes, scraping any browned pork bits from the bottom as you go. Add:

½ cup Shaoxing rice wine or dry sherry

Cook until the liquid has almost evaporated. Return the pork to the skillet along with:

¼ cup hoisin sauce
2 tablespoons oyster sauce
1 tablespoon rice vinegar
1 tablespoon soy sauce
½ teaspoon chili oil or 1 Thai chile, minced
½ teaspoon toasted sesame oil

Stir to combine. Remove from the heat and stir in:

¼ cup roasted unsalted peanuts, chopped
¼ cup chopped cilantro

Let the mixture cool for a few minutes. Meanwhile, rinse:

16 leaves romaine lettuce, butter lettuce, or savoy cabbage

Shake the leaves dry and place about 2 tablespoons of the pork mixture in the center of each leaf. Serve with:

Sriracha, sambal oelek, 969, or chili garlic sauce
Lime wedges
Cilantro

DOLMAS (STUFFED GRAPE LEAVES)

About 30 pieces

For a vegetarian version, omit the lamb, double the amount of rice, and add ½ **cup dried currants** and **2 tablespoons toasted, 1012, pine nuts** to the filling mixture; pour an additional 1 cup water into the pan before cooking. To use fresh grape leaves, see 1057.

Drain:

Two 8-ounce jars grape leaves

Separate the leaves in water and rinse well. Gently pat dry. Combine in a medium bowl:

8 ounces ground lamb
1 large onion, finely chopped
¼ cup finely chopped parsley
¼ cup finely chopped dill
¼ cup finely chopped mint
½ cup uncooked long-grain white rice
2 garlic cloves, minced
½ teaspoon salt

Line a Dutch oven with several grape leaves, using the small or torn ones. To stuff the dolmas, one at a time, place each leaf vein side up on a plate. Put a heaping tablespoon of stuffing on the leaf near the stem end. Fold the stem end over the stuffing, then fold in the two sides and roll up the leaf like a small cigar, tucking in the edges to make a neat package. Place seam side down in the prepared pot. Pack the stuffed leaves in a single layer, then repeat with a second layer until all the stuffing is used. Drizzle over the top:

3 tablespoons olive oil

Pour in:

2 cups chicken, beef, or vegetable broth or water

Cover the top with a few grape leaves and weight with a heatproof plate. Cover the pot and simmer over low heat until the rice is cooked, 30 to 40 minutes. Serve hot or cold.

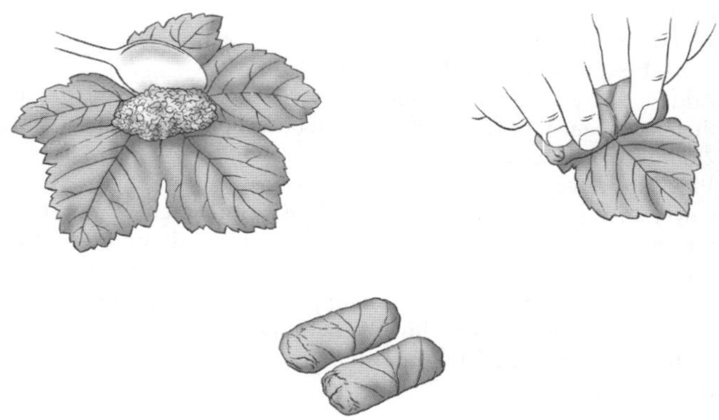

Folding stuffed grape leaves

POT STICKERS OR GYOZA

About 50 dumplings; 8 to 10 appetizer servings

Gyoza and wonton wrappers are often sold in packs of 50, so the filling amounts are written for that number. Only 20 to 25 dumplings will fit in an average skillet, so this is a "double batch." You can cook them in two skillets for serving at once, do a second batch once the first is devoured, or freeze the second batch on the baking sheet and transfer to a bag for later. Frozen gyoza will lose some of the moisture in their filling, but are otherwise delicious (cook them straight from the freezer).

Combine in a medium bowl:

2 cups packed shredded napa cabbage (about 8 ounces)
½ teaspoon salt

Let stand for 15 minutes to draw out the water, then transfer to a thin, clean kitchen towel and wring out as much moisture as possible. Rinse and dry the bowl the cabbage was salted in, and add the wrung-out cabbage along with:

1 pound ground pork
2 garlic cloves, minced
1-inch piece ginger, peeled and minced
½ cup finely chopped green onions or Chinese chives
1 tablespoon soy sauce
1 tablespoon toasted sesame oil
1 teaspoon sugar
¼ teaspoon salt
¼ teaspoon black pepper

Mix until combined. Have ready:

50 gyoza or round wonton wrappers

Working with 6 wrappers at a time, place a rounded teaspoon of filling in the center of each. Brush the edges of the wrappers with water and fold in half to make a half-moon shape, pressing out the air and sealing the edges. If desired, pleat the rounded edge. Place the sealed dumplings seam side up on a baking sheet lightly dusted with:

Cornstarch

gently pressing the dumplings down to flatten their bottoms. Allow to rest for 30 minutes. In the meantime, prepare:

Dipping Sauce for Dumplings, 572

Heat a large, preferably nonstick, skillet over medium-high heat. When hot, add:

2 tablespoons vegetable oil

Add 20 to 25 dumplings to the skillet in a circular pattern so that their sides touch. Let cook until golden brown on the bottom, about 2 minutes. Add to the skillet:

⅔ cup water

Cover and cook until the water has almost completely evaporated, 6 to 8 minutes. Carefully uncover and cook the dumplings until crisp, 1 to 2 minutes longer. Remove from the heat and let sit for 2 minutes. Sometimes, the dumplings will fuse together. If they have, you can invert the whole mess of dumplings onto a serving plate so the browned bottom side is facing up. Serve with the dipping sauce.

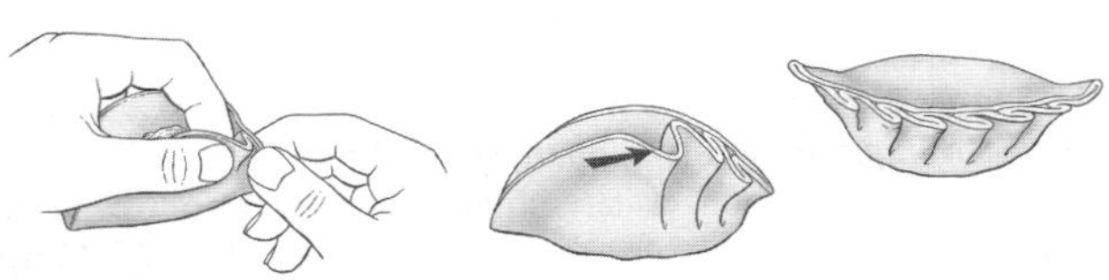

STEAK TARTARE

6 servings

The essential ingredient for this classic dish is top-quality lean beef, preferably tenderloin, although top round or sirloin may be substituted. Purchasing whole cuts of beef and keeping the meat cold helps the flavor and texture and decreases the risk of contamination. ➤ Do not substitute ground beef and be sure to mince the meat just before serving.

Trim well and chill thoroughly:

1½ pounds beef tenderloin

Mince the tenderloin by hand with a sharp knife. Alternatively, cut into ½-inch cubes and pulse in small batches in a food processor until the meat is chopped into ⅛-inch pieces, 7 to 10 seconds; do not overprocess. Transfer the meat to a chilled platter or individual plates and gently form into 6 individual mounds. If desired, make a spoon-shaped indentation into each mound and top with:

(6 egg yolks)

Divide and arrange in small mounds around each serving:

½ cup minced onions or shallots
½ cup minced parsley
¼ cup minced cornichons
¼ cup minced drained capers
(8 to 12 anchovy fillets, minced)

Serve immediately, passing separately:

Lemon juice
Worcestershire sauce
Dijon mustard
Hot pepper sauce
Flaky sea salt and freshly ground black pepper

Serve with:

Thin-sliced pumpernickel, toasted French bread, or potato chips

RUMAKI

36 pieces

Assemble ahead of time on the day you serve them and bake just before needed. You can also make these using whole water chestnuts in place of the liver.

Rinse, trim, and cut into quarters:

8 ounces chicken livers

Whisk together in a medium bowl:

2 tablespoons soy sauce
2 tablespoons sake or dry sherry
1-inch piece ginger, peeled and grated
2 teaspoons brown sugar

Add the livers and toss to coat. Cover and marinate in the refrigerator for 1 to 2 hours. Preheat the oven to 400°F. Have ready:

18 very thin slices bacon, halved crosswise
36 slices rinsed canned water chestnuts (from one 8-ounce can)

Lay 1 piece of chicken liver and 1 slice of water chestnut on each piece of bacon, roll up, and secure with a toothpick. Place on a rimmed baking sheet. Bake for 10 minutes. Turn the oven to broil and cook until the bacon is crisp and the livers are cooked through, about 2 minutes. Drain briefly on paper towels, then transfer to a platter and serve hot.

NEGIMAKI (BEEF AND SCALLION ROLLS)

About 30 pieces

To make slicing easier, freeze for 30 minutes to 1 hour:

1¼ pounds boneless beef sirloin, trimmed of fat

Meanwhile, trim and cut into 2-inch lengths, then divide into 15 bundles (2 or 3 pieces each):

8 to 10 green onions

Cut the beef into 15 very thin slices. Place each slice between 2 sheets of plastic wrap and pound lightly to an even thickness with a mallet or the bottom of a small skillet. Roll a piece of beef snugly around each green onion bundle, wrapping it 2 to 3 times, and secure with a toothpick.

Heat in a large skillet over high heat:

1½ tablespoons vegetable oil

Add the rolls seam side down and sear. Once the seams have sealed, turn to brown the rolls on all sides. After about 2 minutes, when the beef has changed color, whisk together and add:

2 tablespoons sake
2 tablespoons soy sauce
1 tablespoon sugar

Reduce the heat slightly and cook for 1 minute, shaking the skillet to keep the rolls from sticking. Transfer the rolls to a plate and let cool slightly, then remove the toothpicks. If there is a lot of sauce left in the skillet, reduce over high heat to 2 tablespoons. Just before serving, return the rolls to the skillet over high heat and shake to glaze them with the sauce. Slice each roll crosswise in half and serve warm.

ABOUT SEAFOOD APPETIZERS

Fish and shellfish hors d'oeuvre are easy to prepare, as most of the work can be done ahead of time, and à la minute preparations come together quickly. Besides the recipes in this section, see Serving Raw Shellfish, 347, Gravlax, 393 (serve with Rye Crackers, 50, and Scandinavian Mustard-Dill Sauce, 566), Grilled or Broiled Shrimp or Scallops, 365, Becker Barbecued Shrimp, 364, and Ceviche, 377. Oysters and clams for serving on the half-shell should be opened as close to serving time as possible. ➤ For the best flavor and quality, we do not recommend holding hot seafood appetizers for extended periods of time. Make sure you buy the freshest shellfish and store carefully before cooking. See Buying and Storing Fresh Shellfish, 346.

GRILLED OR BROILED SHRIMP COCKAIGNE

30 to 40 pieces

Peel, leaving the tails on, and devein, 363:

2 pounds large shrimp (16/20)

Combine in a large bowl:

½ cup olive oil
½ cup white wine
1 tablespoon lemon juice
3 tablespoons basil and parsley chopped together
2 garlic cloves, minced
1 teaspoon salt
¼ teaspoon black pepper

Add the shrimp, turning to coat. Cover and marinate in the refrigerator for several hours. Prepare a hot grill fire or preheat the broiler. Grill or broil the shrimp, turning once, until opaque throughout, 4 to 7 minutes. Serve at once with:

Melted butter or Lemon and Parsley Butter, 559

CAJUN POPCORN SHRIMP

8 to 10 servings

This recipe can also be made with clams, oysters, or, as is traditionally done in Louisiana, with crayfish. These will be scooped up and eaten as easily as a handful of popcorn, so make sure you have plenty. Please read about Deep-Frying, 1051.

Stir together in a medium bowl:

1 cup all-purpose flour
1 teaspoon sugar
1 teaspoon salt
1 teaspoon black pepper
½ teaspoon onion powder
½ teaspoon garlic powder
½ teaspoon cayenne pepper
½ teaspoon dried thyme

Make a well in the center of the mixture. Gradually pour in, whisking constantly:

1½ cups milk
2 large eggs, lightly beaten

Let stand for 30 minutes. Meanwhile, heat to 365°F in a deep-fryer, deep heavy pot, or Dutch oven:

4 inches vegetable oil

Stir into the batter:

2 pounds small shrimp (31/40), peeled, or larger shrimp, peeled, deveined, 363, and cut into ½-inch pieces

Remove with a slotted spoon and lightly toss with:

2 to 3 cups dry bread crumbs or fine cornmeal, as needed

Fry the shrimp in batches until crisp and lightly browned, 2 to 3 minutes. Transfer to paper towels to drain. Serve with:

Aïoli, 564, or Rémoulade Sauce, 564

PICKLED SHRIMP

8 servings

Despite admonitions to never mix seafood and cheese, we find these especially tasty when sitting atop a cracker mounded high with Treva's Pimiento Cheese, 55.

Prepare:

Poached or "Boiled" Shrimp, 364

Combine in a large bowl:

2 cups cider vinegar
1 cup flat beer
1 large lemon, very thinly sliced
½ red onion, sliced paper thin
5 garlic cloves, smashed
1 tablespoon cracked black peppercorns
1 tablespoon sugar
1½ teaspoons salt
Leaves from 1 bunch celery
(1 tablespoon celery seed)
1 to 2 teaspoons Tabasco, to taste

Add the shrimp to the pickling liquid. Weight the shrimp with a plate to keep them submerged beneath the brine and marinate in the refrigerator for 24 hours before serving. We like to serve these with:

Saltine crackers or Soda Crackers, 49

ANGELS ON HORSEBACK

24 pieces

No angels, no horses; a fanciful name for a time-tested combination.

Preheat the oven to 400°F. Shuck, 349, or drain if shucked:

24 medium oysters

Set aside. Spread:

8 slices firm white bread

with:

4 tablespoons (½ stick) butter, softened

Using a biscuit or cookie cutter, cut the slices into twenty-four 2-inch rounds. Place on a rimmed baking sheet and toast in the oven until lightly browned, about 5 minutes. Transfer the toasts to a platter. Cut in half:

12 very thin slices bacon, prosciutto, or ham

If desired, spread one side of each bacon slice lightly with:

(Anchovy paste)

Wrap a slice of bacon or ham (anchovy side in) around each oyster and place seam side down on a wire rack set in the rimmed baking sheet. Turn the oven to broil. Broil the oysters until the bacon is cooked or the ham is crisp, about 10 minutes. Place the oysters on the toasts and sprinkle with:

3 tablespoons minced parsley

OYSTERS ROCKEFELLER

24 pieces

Preheat the oven to 450°F. Shuck, 349, leaving on the half shell:

24 medium oysters

Process in a food processor just until minced:

One 10-ounce package frozen spinach, thawed and drained, or 1½ cups cooked spinach
⅓ cup fresh bread crumbs, 957
3 green onions, chopped
2 tablespoons chopped parsley
½ teaspoon salt
4 drops hot pepper sauce

Add:

4 tablespoons (½ stick) butter, softened
1 tablespoon Pernod or anisette, or to taste

Process for 10 seconds more. Cover a baking sheet with:

Kosher or coarse sea salt

Nestle the oysters in their half shells in the salt. Spoon 1 heaping teaspoon of the spinach mixture over each oyster. Bake until plumped, about 10 minutes. Turn the oven to broil to brown the tops, 2 minutes more.

CLAMS CASINO

24 pieces

This treatment is also quite tasty with oysters or mussels.

Preheat the broiler. Combine in a bowl and mix well:

4 tablespoons (½ stick) butter, softened
1 green onion, finely chopped
1½ tablespoons minced parsley
1 tablespoon lemon juice
¼ teaspoon salt

Shuck, 349, leaving on the half-shell:

24 small hard-shell clams, such as cherrystone or littleneck

Place the clams on a rimmed baking sheet. Divide the butter mixture among the clams. Top them with:

6 slices bacon, cooked until crisp and crumbled

Broil until the butter is bubbling, about 3 minutes.

CAVIAR AND ROE

Someone was once moved to ask plaintively why caviar is so expensive, to which a helpful maître d' replied, "After all, it is a year's work for a sturgeon." The best caviar is the cured roe of the sturgeon, and the most sought-after caviar, **Beluga** and **Osetra** (or *Oscietre*), originally came only from the Caspian Sea. A third type, **Sevruga,** is taken from a smaller Caspian sturgeon. At present, bans have gone into effect to protect the wild sturgeon, and trade of its caviar has been prohibited by several international organizations. Today sturgeon are farm-raised for caviar all over the world, from California to Israel. Even "no-kill" caviar is now available, which is extracted from the sturgeon with a nice massage.

Spoonbill or paddlefish roe comes from fish native to the Mississippi and Tennessee rivers. It is small, silvery, rich, and flavorful. There are other fish roe that, unlike spoonbill roe, look nothing like caviar but are nevertheless enjoyed in their own right, from the large, robustly flavored orange roe of salmon to the small, firm, and mild-tasting golden roe of whitefish.

Buy caviar only from a reputable source, and read labels carefully. The eggs should be shiny, translucent, and intact. If at all possible, taste before buying. No caviar should taste excessively salty or truly fishy. ➤ As fresh caviar spoils in a few hours in temperatures of 40°F or above, always serve it on ice. Caviar may be kept, unopened, at 35°F for a month. Once opened, it should be eaten within a day or two. To cure fresh roe, see 935.

To serve individual portions, heat the back of a metal spoon, press it into an ice cube, and fill the depression with caviar using a plastic spoon or a special caviar spoon. ➤ Never allow caviar to touch metal or to be served on it. If you spread it on canapés, or Buckwheat Blini, 641, be careful not to bruise the eggs. The classic accompaniments are lemon wedges and parsley, and black bread, pumpernickel, or toast. Minced hard-boiled eggs and onions are frequently used as a garnish. Other ways to serve caviar are with potatoes, 59, or mixed with butter or sour cream and spread on toasts. Caviar should be accompanied by either chilled dry white wines or, preferably, Champagne, vodka, or vodka flavored with black pepper, 22.

ABOUT CANAPÉS AND TEA SANDWICHES

Canapés are open-faced hors d'oeuvre with a bread, cracker, or pastry base. They are eaten in one or two bites. Canapés have four components: base, spread, main ingredient, and garnish. If using bread as the base, it may be cut into any number of shapes—squares, triangles, or rounds, or other decorative shapes—with cookie cutters. Small crackers, Beaten Biscuits, 637, miniature Buckwheat Blini, 641, tiny tartlet shells, 69, phyllo shells, small Gougères, 70, and puff pastry shells may be used for canapés. For more inspiration, see About Pastry Party Foods, 68.

Tea sandwiches are small, delicate sandwiches made with a variety of fillings. They may be cut into decorative shapes. Tea sandwiches require a bit of time and handiwork, but they can be made in advance and stored for up to 24 hours. Arrange the sandwiches

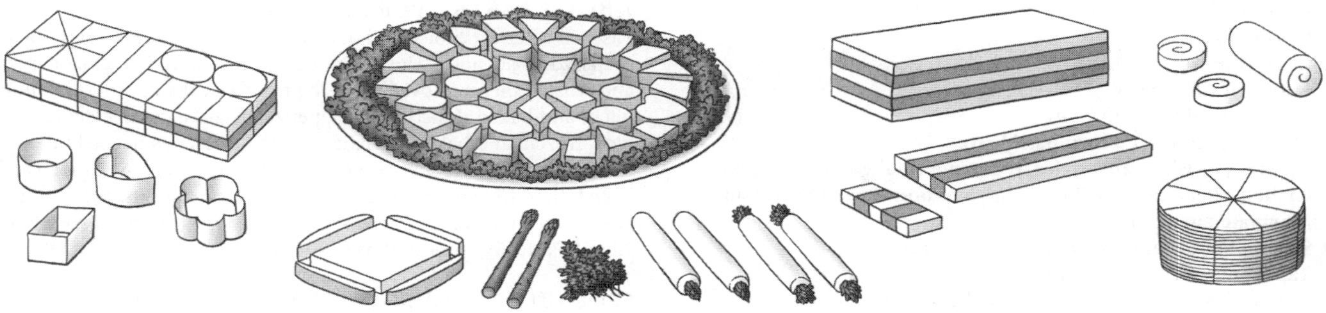

Shapes for tea sandwiches

on a tray, top with wax paper, then cover with a damp paper towel. Tightly wrap the tray in plastic wrap and refrigerate until ready to serve.

CANAPÉS

Using the suggested combinations below, have ready:

¼-inch-thick slices baguette, 2 × 2 × ½-inch crustless squares Challah, 602, Brioche, 603, or any white bread, or 2 × 2 × ¼-inch squares any dense dark bread (black bread, pumpernickel, etc.)

Cover with any one of the following (use about ½ teaspoon butter or 1 teaspoon spread for each piece of bread):

Thinly sliced strawberries and sour cream or crème fraîche (challah)
Brie, fig jam, and butter (dark bread)
Treva's Pimiento Cheese, 55, thin slices country ham, and bread-and-butter pickle slices (toasted white bread)
Sliced tomato, cooked bacon squares or sliced avocado, and Aïoli, 564 (brioche)
Apple slices, Caramelized Onions, 255, and melted sharp Cheddar (dark bread)
Blue cheese, thinly sliced pears, and butter (baguette)
Thinly sliced smoked salmon or Gravlax, 393, dill, capers, and Horseradish Sauce II, 566, or cream cheese (dark bread or Bagel Chips, 49)
Smoked trout or sablefish, cucumber, and sour cream mixed with horseradish to taste (pumpernickel)
Poached, 65, or Pickled Shrimp, 354, parsley or tarragon leaves, and mayonnaise (baguette or soda crackers)
Flaked crabmeat, thinly sliced avocado, and mayonnaise (baguette)
Caviar, minced onions, and butter (pumpernickel)
Sliced chicken or turkey breast, thinly sliced Granny Smith apples, and mayonnaise flavored with curry powder to taste (baguette or challah)
Sliced roast beef, Sautéed Onions, 255, or Caramelized Onions, 255, and Horseradish Sauce II, 566 (baguette)
Sliced roast pork or beef tenderloin, watercress, and Snail Butter, 560 (baguette)

TEA SANDWICHES

Tea sandwiches hold together better when filled with a thin layer of spreads and softer ingredients. To cut tea sandwiches into shapes, use the illustration above as a guide.

Prepare any of the fillings for **Canapés, above,** and have ready **½-inch-thick slices Challah, 602, Brioche, 603, any white bread, or ¼-inch-thick slices dense, dark bread (black bread, pumpernickel, etc.)**. If desired, whole loaves may be cut into long, lengthwise slices, as shown. Cut off the crusts and spread the bread thinly with the desired filling. Top with a second bread slice and cut into shapes as desired.

BENEDICTINE SANDWICHES

About 1½ cups

These sandwiches are traditionally served at festivities surrounding the Kentucky Derby. They are made even better by the addition of thinly shaved country ham (and accompanied by a Mint Julep, 24).

Grate on the large holes of a box grater:

1 medium cucumber, peeled and seeded
½ medium onion

Wrap in a kitchen towel and squeeze to remove excess moisture. Transfer to a medium bowl and add:

8 ounces cream cheese, softened
Pinch of cayenne pepper
¼ teaspoon salt
(Dab of green food coloring)

Mix together with a wooden spoon until fluffy. Have ready:

12 slices white bread, crusts removed

Spread the cream cheese mixture on half the bread slices and top with the remaining bread. Cut in half for rectangles, in quarters for small squares, or on the diagonal for triangles.

BRUSCHETTA

At its most basic, bruschetta is grilled or toasted bread rubbed with garlic cloves and brushed with olive oil. This simple preparation serves as a foundation for a wide variety of toppings.

Prepare a medium-hot grill fire or preheat the broiler. Grill or broil until golden brown on each side:

Thick slices crusty bread

Remove from the heat and rub one side of each slice with:

Garlic cloves

Drizzle with:

Extra-virgin olive oil

Top with one of the following:

Diced tomatoes and torn basil leaves
Sardines or white anchovies, red pepper flakes, and arugula
Grilled, sliced portobello mushrooms and shaved Parmesan
Marinated artichoke hearts
Shaved Fennel and White Bean Salad, 129
Tapenade, 54, or Caponata, 54
Burrata and jarred roasted red bell peppers
Ricotta mixed with minced thyme, parsley, and lemon zest; and prosciutto or speck

Sprinkle with:

Coarse sea salt and black pepper to taste

CHEESE PUFF CANAPÉS

12 to 16 pieces

Preheat the broiler. Beat in a medium bowl until very stiff:

3 egg whites

Fold in:

1½ cups shredded Gruyère or Swiss (6 ounces)
1½ teaspoons Worcestershire sauce
1½ teaspoons Dijon mustard
¾ teaspoon sweet paprika

Toast, then arrange on a baking sheet:

Four 4-inch square slices white bread, crusts removed, quartered

Spread with the cheese mixture and place under the broiler until the cheese is puffed and brown.

HAM BISCUITS

20 to 24 biscuits

In addition to this filling, try spreading the biscuits with a flavored butter, 559–60.

Preheat the oven to 425°F. Prepare the dough for:

Buttermilk Biscuits, 635

adding, if desired:

(¼ cup minced chives)

Roll out the dough to about ½ inch thick. Cut into 2-inch rounds with a biscuit or cookie cutter. Place 1 inch apart on ungreased baking sheets and brush the tops with:

Melted butter

Bake until golden on top, about 15 minutes. Prepare:

Honey Mustard Dipping Sauce, 566

Or have ready:

4 tablespoons (½ stick) butter, softened
(Pepper jelly, store-bought or homemade, 911)

When the biscuits are cool enough to handle, split them. Spread with the honey mustard sauce or butter (and pepper jelly if using) and top with:

12 ounces thinly sliced ham, country ham, or prosciutto

Serve warm or at room temperature.

ABOUT PASTRY PARTY FOODS

Pastry is a perfect choice for hors d'oeuvre that can be at least partially prepared in advance. The pastry dough can be rolled, cut, shaped, and frozen, then removed from the freezer at the appropriate time, filled, and baked. Most pastry appetizers can be completely assembled, frozen, and baked straight from the freezer as needed (allow a few extra minutes cooking time). Choux Paste, 697, can be piped and baked, then frozen, or piped onto lined baking sheets, frozen, then baked when needed. For details on specific types of pastry, see About Choux Paste, 697, About Phyllo, 700, and About Puff Pastry, 691.

SPINACH OR MUSHROOM PHYLLO TRIANGLES

32 triangles

Prepare one of the following:

1½ recipes Duxelles, 252, stirring in 2 ounces soft goat cheese
Filling for Spanakopita, 706, omitting the eggs

Preheat the oven to 375°F. Grease a baking sheet. Melt in a small saucepan:

4 tablespoons (½ stick) butter

Lay on a work surface and cover with a damp towel:

8 sheets phyllo dough, thawed if frozen

Remove 1 sheet of phyllo and lay it on the work surface, with a long side facing you. Brush lightly with melted butter, lay a second sheet on top, and brush it with melted butter. Cut the sheets vertically into 2½ -inch-wide strips. Cover the strips with a sheet of wax paper or plastic wrap and cover that with a damp towel. Working with 1 strip at a time, scoop up a rounded teaspoon of the filling and pat it over the bottom right-hand corner of the strip, so that it fills the entire corner. Fold the corner to the other side to make a triangle and continue folding to the end of the strip, as if folding a flag, shown on 69. Place on the baking sheet and brush the top with melted butter. Repeat with the remaining phyllo and filling. Bake until lightly browned, about 15 minutes. Serve hot.

QUICK PHYLLO SAMOSAS WITH POTATOES AND PEAS

About 60 samosas

Samosas are traditionally made with a soft pastry. Here they are conveniently made with phyllo. They freeze well when tightly wrapped in plastic, and they can be baked frozen—simply add 5 minutes to the baking time. For another delicious filling, substitute Keema Alu, 503, for the potato-pea mixture below.

Drop into boiling salted water to cover:

1½ pounds red potatoes (6 to 8 potatoes)

Cover and cook until tender, 15 to 20 minutes. Drain, peel, and mash in a medium bowl.

Heat in a small skillet over medium-high heat:

1 tablespoon vegetable oil

Add and heat until they pop:

1 teaspoon black or yellow mustard seeds

Add and cook for 20 seconds more:

3 garlic cloves, thinly sliced

Stir the garlic mixture into the mashed potatoes, along with:

1 cup frozen peas, thawed
1 small onion, finely chopped (about ½ cup)

¼ cup chopped cilantro
1 serrano or jalapeño pepper, seeded, if desired, and minced
2 tablespoons lemon juice
1¼ teaspoons salt

Preheat the oven to 375°F. Grease 2 baking sheets. Unroll on a dry work surface:

1 pound phyllo dough, thawed if frozen

Cover with a damp towel. Melt:

1 stick (4 ounces) butter

Remove 1 sheet of phyllo and lay it on the work surface, with a long side facing you. Brush lightly with melted butter, lay a second sheet on top, and brush it with melted butter. Cut the sheets vertically into 2½-inch-wide strips. Cover the strips with a sheet of wax paper or plastic wrap and cover that with a damp towel. Working with 1 strip at a time, scoop up a rounded teaspoon of the potato mixture and pat it over the bottom left-hand corner of the strip, so that it fills the entire corner. Fold the corner to the other side to make a triangle and continue folding to the end of the strip, as if folding a flag, shown below. Place on a baking sheet and brush the top with melted butter. Repeat with the remaining phyllo and filling. Bake until lightly browned, about 15 minutes. Serve immediately with:

Raita, 569
Cilantro-Mint Chutney, 568, or Tamarind Chutney, 566

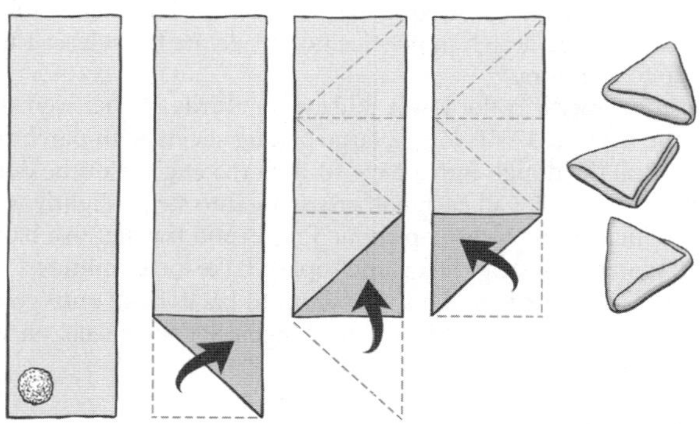

Folding phyllo triangles

MINIATURE TURNOVERS OR TARTLETS

24 shells or turnovers

I. TURNOVERS

Have ready about 1 cup of any of the following:

Melted Leeks, 247
Mushroom Ragout, 251, or Duxelles, 252
Picadillo, 503, garnished with cilantro leaves
Tapenade, 54
Sun-Dried Tomatoes Pesto, 586 (for a taste of the 90s)
Winter Squash Filling, 312, topped with grated Parmesan
Caramelized Onions, 255, with blue cheese
Creamed Mushrooms, 251
Creamed Spinach, 244

Prepare:

Cream Cheese Pastry Dough, 665

Divide the dough in half, flatten each half into a disk, wrap in plastic, and refrigerate for at least 1 hour and up to 24 hours. On a floured surface, roll one half of the dough ⅛ inch thick into a 12-inch round. Cut out 3-inch rounds of dough using a cookie or biscuit cutter. Transfer to a large baking sheet lined with parchment paper and refrigerate. Set the scraps aside. Roll and cut the other half of the dough in the same way. Gather the scraps from both batches into a ball, roll out, and cut into additional rounds, making 24 total.

Place 1 heaping teaspoon of filling in the center of each round. Generously moisten the edges of each round with cold water and fold in half. Firmly press the edges with your fingers, then press with the tines of a fork. Prick the top once with a fork. Arrange on the parchment-lined baking sheet. Refrigerate for at least 1 hour and up to 8 hours. Preheat the oven to 425°F. Combine in a small bowl and beat with a fork:

1 egg white
Pinch of salt

Lightly brush the top of each turnover with the egg wash. Bake until golden brown, 12 to 15 minutes.

II. TARTLETS

The easiest way to make tiny tartlets is to buy frozen phyllo cups and bake them according to the package directions. The following alternative is more labor-intensive but also more flavorful.

Have ready 1½ cups of any of the fillings listed in version I. Prepare:

Pat-in-the Pan Butter Dough, 666

Preheat the oven to 400°F. Press 1 tablespoon dough into each cup of a mini muffin tin, prick the dough all over with a fork, and chill until the dough is firm, about 15 minutes. Bake until golden brown, 12 to 15 minutes. Let cool in the pan, then remove the pastry shells to a wire rack. Fill each cooled pastry shell with 1 tablespoon warm or room temperature filling.

MINIATURE QUICHES

24 quiches

Bake on a baking sheet lined with parchment paper according to package directions:

24 store-bought phyllo cups

Remove the phyllo cups from the oven, but leave the oven on and increase the temperature to 425°F. Have ready:

¼ cup finely chopped ham, cooked broccoli, or roasted red peppers

Whisk in a medium bowl until thoroughly blended:

2 large eggs
½ cup heavy cream
⅓ cup grated Parmesan
1 tablespoon minced onion or shallot
¼ teaspoon salt
⅛ teaspoon black or white pepper

Place ½ teaspoon of the finely chopped ingredients in the bottom of each phyllo shell, then fill to the brim with the egg mixture. Bake until the filling is set and puffed, 12 to 15 minutes.

STUFFED CHOUX PUFFS

48 puffs

Please read About Choux Paste, 697.

Preheat the oven to 400°F. Prepare:

Choux Paste, 697

Scoop the paste into a pastry bag fitted with a ½-inch plain tip. Alternatively, scoop into a plastic bag and cut off the corner to form a ½-inch hole. Pipe the paste into forty-eight 1-inch puffs on two ungreased baking sheets. Bake for 15 minutes. Reduce the oven temperature to 350°F, rotate the baking sheets front to back, and bake until browned and firm, 10 to 15 minutes more. Have ready:

3 cups Treva's Pimiento Cheese, 55, Smoked Salmon or Trout Spread, 54, Basic Cream Cheese Spread, 136, Duxelles, 252, Egg Salad, 124, Lobster or Shrimp Salad, 123, Chicken or Turkey Salad with curry powder added, 62, Deviled Ham, 62, or Chicken Liver Pâté, 62

For the chunkier fillings, split the puffs, place 1 tablespoon filling on the bottom halves, and replace the tops. For smoother fillings, use the same method or pierce the unsplit puffs in the side and pipe filling into them using a pastry bag fitted with a large plain tip.

GOUGÈRES (CHEESE PUFFS)

About 48 puffs

Pass these on a tray and serve with Champagne. Please read About Choux Paste, 697.

Preheat the oven to 400°F. Prepare:

Choux Paste, 697

stirring in:

1 cup grated Gruyère (4 ounces)

Pipe the dough as for **Stuffed Choux Puffs, 69.** Sprinkle with:

½ cup grated Gruyère (2 ounces)

Bake for 15 minutes. Reduce the oven temperature to 350°F and bake until browned and firm, 10 to 15 minutes more. Fill as above, if desired, or serve as is.

PIGS IN A BLANKET

16 pieces

Kids love helping to roll this classic.

Preheat the oven to 375°F. Have ready:

One 8-ounce can refrigerated crescent roll dough or Cream Cheese Pastry Dough, 665

If using crescent roll dough, carefully unroll it. If using cream cheese dough, roll out into an 8 × 14-inch rectangle (about ¼ inch thick). For both, cut and separate into 4 equal rectangles. Cut each rectangle into four 3-inch-long strips. Brush each strip lightly with:

Dijon mustard

Top each strip with:

1 cocktail frank (16 franks total)

Roll the dough up around each frank, pushing together at the seam to seal. Place seam side down on an ungreased baking sheet about 2 inches apart. Bake until the dough is puffy and golden brown, about 15 minutes. Serve with:

Honey Mustard Dipping Sauce, 566, or mustard

PUFF PASTRY CHEESE STRAWS

About 100 pieces

Please read About Puff Pastry, 691.

Unbaked straws can be frozen in a covered container, the layers separated by sheets of wax paper, for up to 1 month. Bake (without thawing) as needed.

Have ready:

One 17½-ounce package frozen puff pastry sheets, thawed, or 1 pound Puff Pastry, 691

If using frozen puff pastry, unfold the two sheets and stack on top of each other. If using homemade pastry, roll the dough on a lightly floured work surface into a 16 × 10-inch rectangle. Turn the dough so a short side faces you. Lightly brush the bottom two-thirds of the rectangle with water, then sprinkle evenly with:

¾ cup grated Parmesan (3 ounces)
⅛ to ¼ teaspoon cayenne pepper, to taste

Lay a sheet of plastic wrap over the cheese and roll over lightly with the rolling pin to adhere the cheese to the dough. Remove the wrap and set aside. Fold the top third of the dough down and bring the bottom third up over the top third, like folding a business letter. Roll again into a 16 × 10-inch rectangle. Again brush the bottom two-thirds with water and sprinkle evenly with:

¾ cup grated Parmesan (3 ounces)
⅛ to ¼ teaspoon cayenne pepper, to taste

Roll over the cheese and give the dough a business letter fold as before. Wrap the dough in plastic and refrigerate for at least 1 hour and up to 24 hours.

Position racks in the lower and upper thirds of the oven. Preheat the oven to 375°F. Line 2 large baking sheets with parchment paper. Roll the dough into a 16 × 10-inch rectangle. Cut the dough lengthwise in half. Cut each half crosswise into strips slightly wider than ¼ inch. Twist each strip about 3 times and transfer to a baking sheet, spacing the strips just ½ inch apart. Bake for 15 minutes, then switch racks and rotate the sheets front to back. Bake until golden brown and crisp, 10 to 15 minutes longer. Set the sheets on wire racks to cool.

QUICK CHEESE CRACKERS

About eighty 1½ × 2-inch crackers or 250 one-inch square crackers

The dough keeps for up to 1 week in the refrigerator or 3 months in the freezer.

Place in a food processor:

1½ cups all-purpose flour
¼ teaspoon salt
¼ teaspoon cayenne pepper or ½ teaspoon black pepper

Pulse briefly to combine. Add:

1 stick (4 ounces) unsalted butter, softened
8 ounces sharp Cheddar or blue cheese, grated or crumbled
1 teaspoon Worcestershire sauce

Process until the mixture comes together. Wrap the dough in plastic wrap and refrigerate for 30 minutes. Preheat the oven to 350°F. Divide the dough into 4 equal pieces. Working with one piece at a time, roll the dough out between 2 sheets of parchment paper to ⅛ inch thick. Remove the top piece of parchment and cut the dough into 1-inch squares or 1½ × 2-inch rectangles. Slide the parchment onto a baking sheet and bake until crisp and lightly browned, 10 to 15 minutes. Repeat with the remaining pieces of dough. Let cool completely on the sheet on a wire rack.

SUMMER ROLLS

8 rolls or 16 pieces

To make a vegan version of these, substitute **Baked Marinated Tofu, 287,** for the shrimp.

Break in half and soak in warm water to cover for 30 minutes or until tender:

2½ ounces dried, thin rice noodles

Transfer the noodles to a colander and rinse under cold water. Bring a saucepan of water to a boil and add:

16 extra-large shell-on shrimp (about 1 pound)

Return the water to a simmer and cook until they turn pink, about 2 minutes. Drain in a colander and rinse under cold water. Peel, halve them lengthwise, and rinse under cold water to remove the veins. Drain on paper towels.

Have ready:

4 large leaves red-leaf or Boston lettuce, torn lengthwise in half and midribs removed
1 large carrot, shredded
1 cup bean sprouts, rinsed
½ cup mint leaves
½ cup cilantro leaves
3 green onions, thinly sliced
Eight 12-inch spring roll rice paper wrappers

Lay a damp kitchen towel in front of you and set out a large bowl of hot water (115° to 120°F). Dip 1 sheet of rice paper into the hot water, being sure to immerse it completely to make it pliable. Quickly remove it and place on the towel. Place a piece of lettuce along the bottom edge of the sheet, about 2 inches from the edge. Top the lettuce with one-eighth each of the cooked noodles, herbs, sprouts, green onions, and carrot. Top with 4 shrimp halves. Fold the sides of the rice paper over the filling, then roll up tightly into a neat cylinder. Set seam side down on a large platter and cover with a damp towel. Repeat with the remaining rice paper and filling ingredients. To serve, cut each roll in half on the diagonal. Serve immediately or the rice paper will toughen. Pass for dipping any of the following:

Peanut Dipping Sauce, 571, sriracha, chili garlic sauce, sambal oelek, 969, hoisin sauce, or Nam Prik, 571

EGG ROLLS

About 20 egg rolls

Please read about Deep-Frying, 1051. To make vegetarian egg rolls, simply substitute 8 ounces additional vegetables for the meat, or use 8 ounces crumbled, drained tofu or crumbled, browned tempeh.

Heat in a large skillet or wok over high heat:

1 tablespoon vegetable oil

When the oil is hot, add:

4 ounces small shrimp (26/30), peeled and finely chopped
4 ounces ground pork

Cook, stirring, until no longer pink, about 3 minutes. Transfer the meat to a large bowl. Have ready:

1 pound cabbage, finely shredded (about 3½ cups)
1 large carrot, shredded (about 1 cup)
2 celery ribs, finely chopped (about 1 cup)
One 8-ounce can water chestnuts, drained, rinsed, and chopped
8 ounces mung bean or soybean sprouts, rinsed
3 green onions, finely chopped
2 garlic cloves, minced
2-inch piece ginger, peeled and grated

Return the skillet to the heat and stir-fry in three batches in:

Vegetable oil (1 tablespoon per batch)

As each batch is cooked, add it to the bowl with the meat, stirring everything together at the end. Set aside to cool. As the filling sits, it may exude some liquid. If so, transfer to a sieve and drain thoroughly. Have ready:

About twenty 6-inch square egg roll wrappers

Arrange 1 wrapper on a work surface with a corner facing you. Spoon a scant ¼ cup of the filling one-third of the way up the wrapper, leaving a 1-inch border on the left and right sides. Fold the bottom point over the filling, then fold in the left and right sides so that they overlap slightly. Roll up to enclose the filling, moistening the last point with a little water to seal. Place on a tray and repeat with the remaining wrappers and filling. They may be wrapped in plastic wrap and refrigerated overnight or frozen for up to 1 month; thaw overnight in the refrigerator before proceeding.

Heat to 375°F in a deep-fryer, deep heavy pot, or Dutch oven:

2 inches vegetable or peanut oil

Fry the egg rolls in batches, turning once, until golden, 2 to 3 minutes. Remove and drain on paper towels. Serve hot with one or more of the following condiments for dipping:

Soy sauce or Dipping Sauce for Dumplings, 572
Chinese hot mustard
Sweet-and-Sour Sauce, 565

FRIED WONTONS

30 wontons

Please read about Deep-Frying, 1051.

Preheat the oven to 200°F. Prepare:

Wontons, 315, or Vegetable Wontons, 315

Heat to 350°F in a deep-fryer, deep heavy pot, or Dutch oven:

2 inches vegetable or peanut oil

Fry the wontons in batches, making sure they don't stick to the bottom, until the skins are golden and crisp, 2 to 3 minutes. Transfer to a baking sheet lined with paper towels to drain, and place in the oven to keep warm while you fry the remaining batches. Serve with:

Sweet-and-Sour Sauce, 565, or Dipping Sauce for Dumplings, 572

STOCKS AND SOUPS

A pot of soup simmering on the stove epitomizes home cooking. The wafting, soul-warming smell is grounding, a homespun form of aromatherapy that beckons us to rest; a cue that we have arrived at a place where we can be warmed, restored, and nurtured. In short, soup is a sign of care—for oneself and others.

In addition to the soups in this chapter, look for brothy dishes in About Asian Noodles, 300, as well as in our sections devoted to braising and stewing chicken, 419, beef, 463, lamb, 481, and pork, 494.

ABOUT STOCKS

Antique dealers may respond hopefully to dusty bits in attics, but true cooks palpitate over more curious odds and ends: mushroom stems, onion peelings, leek tops, turkey carcasses, chicken feet, celery leaves, fish heads, and tomato skins. Combining these "scraps" with a few extra herbs and water can yield something of immense culinary value.

In France, stocks are called *fonds,* or "foundations," which signals their importance. It is hard to overstate how instrumental stocks are for preparing many of the dishes we crave, from soups and stews to braises and sauces. Though making stock takes time, most of it is hands-off, and all of the dishes that utilize your homemade stock will simply taste better than if you use store-bought stock or broth.

Stocks are traditionally judged on three attributes: flavor, body, and clarity. Of the three, flavor is paramount, and is dependent upon the quality and quantity of your ingredients, as well as whether or not they are browned first. **Brown stocks,** which have some or all of their ingredients roasted, sautéed, or charred until they are brown, are especially flavorful and form the foundation for many richly flavored dishes. Recipes that forgo this initial step (often referred to as **white stocks**) can be flavorful in their own right—especially if there is a high proportion of ingredients to water—but they are less assertive, and thus more versatile. For heightening the flavor of stocks, see Seasoning Stock, 73.

The body of a stock depends completely on how much gelatin it contains. Gelatin is extracted by cooking bones and connective tissue rich with collagen. Shellfish and vegetables do not contain collagen, thus stocks made from them are light-bodied. The best meat, fish, and poultry stocks are made from collagen-rich bones and connective tissue. This translates to more gelatin, which results in a velvety texture. If reduced until most of their water has evaporated, meat, poultry, and some fish stocks will turn into a thick, almost sticky paste called a **glaze** or *glace*; if taken only partway to that extreme, the result is **demi-glace,** 75.

Clear stock is achieved by blanching any raw bones with boiling water prior to adding them to stock, by keeping the stock at a very low simmer, or by clarifying stock after it has been cooked, strained, and skimmed of any fat. Frankly, we are rarely in pursuit of this goal. The preparations where clarified stocks shine—aspics, terrines, and clear soups—are not quite as popular as they once were. Though some may value the appearance of a pristine, diaphanous stock, few of us mind clouded ones, especially since the stock will most likely be clouded by the dish it is ultimately destined for. For those who still wish to read newsprint through their stocks and broths, see Clarifying Stock, 74.

➤ We recommend meat stocks for long-cooking recipes, as vegetable and fish stocks tend to deteriorate in flavor. Purists may insist on using only fish stock in a fish soup or beef stock in a beef stew, but chicken and vegetable stocks are versatile enough to be used for both.

Of course, not everyone has the time to make a long-simmering preparation that is not, in the end, a meal in itself. Luckily, there are a wide variety of store-bought products to assist the casual (or hurried) cook. For more on store-bought stocks and how to improve them, see 79.

TOOLS FOR MAKING STOCK

The best **stockpots** are narrow, tall, and heavy-bottomed, which allows the stock to simmer gently without too much evaporation. Less surface area at the top also makes skimming easier. An 8- to 10-quart stockpot is ideal for making worthwhile batches of stock, but a small pot or large saucepan can be called into service for smaller quantities. Just be sure the pot is large enough to accommodate all the solids. Enameled Dutch ovens or wide soup pots also work, as long as you add more water whenever the level drops below the solids. ➤ Avoid aluminum pots, which may react with the ingredients and affect the flavor of the stock.

Pressure-cooking stock is significantly faster and more efficient than regular stovetop simmering. You may use an electric model, but most of these appliances only have a 6- or 8-quart capacity (which means they will only yield 4 or 5 quarts of stock). A larger, **10-quart stovetop pressure cooker** is ideal. Though it still does not have the capacity of our preferred size of stockpot, there is no evaporation during cooking, and the increased temperature is very efficient at extracting flavor with less water. Please see Pressure Cooker Stock, 79.

Slow cookers may be used to make stock, and they do offer a level of convenience. However, be aware that the resulting stock will be much weaker-bodied and less flavorful than any other method because the temperature never gets high enough to effectively extract flavor (or gelatin) from bones.

A **roasting pan** is useful for roasting the bones used in brown stocks. A **colander** and an **8-quart bowl** are absolutely essential for straining stocks. A **fine-mesh sieve** or **chinois** can be useful for those who wish to filter out smaller particles, but lining the colander with a double-layer of cheesecloth or a flour sack towel is just as effective. For fat removal, we prefer to leave the cooled stock in the refrigerator overnight and remove the solidified fat from the top, but a **gravy separator** is a boon to those in a hurry.

KEEPING A STOCK BAG

If stock making seems an implausible habit to form, keeping a stock bag may change your perspective. Bones from last week's roast, onion leavings, the outer ribs of a celery bunch, shiitake stems, tough leek tops, carrot peelings, thyme stems, or bones from a rack of lamb . . . any and all of these may fill a gallon-sized zip-top bag in our freezer at any given moment. When the bag is full, we make stock; this routine nicely balances our need for stock with our accumulation of kitchen "waste."

Though the formulas for stock given in this chapter are classic and guaranteed to work well, the stock bag strategy has yet to fail us, especially with a few tweaks before cooking. If your bag is light on onion scraps, carrots, or celery, add a few fresh ones. If you want a full-bodied stock but no collagen-rich cuts made it into the bag, add some chicken feet or wings. Results vary, which is the beauty of it.

Most everything is fair game for the stock bag, with some important exceptions. ➤ Do not add fatty trimmings that have no meat, connective tissue, or bone to contribute flavor or body. Avoid starchy vegetable scraps like those from potatoes. Cabbage and its many relatives—broccoli, mustard, kale, kohlrabi, etc.—can lend an undesirable sulfurous note. Turnip, beet, parsnip, asparagus, rutabaga, and pepper scraps may contribute too much of their own characteristic flavors to a stock, but they may be added in moderation. Eggplants add nothing of interest. Avoid dominating the bag with any single type of vegetable scrap; no one flavor should predominate (with the exception of meat and possibly onions). ➤ Wash vegetables thoroughly before peeling or trimming if you plan to add the scraps to your stock bag. A stock bag can be kept up to 3 months in the freezer before being used to make stock.

To make stock with the contents of a stock bag, empty the bag into a pot and add water to cover. Because the scraps are frozen, they will take up more space in the pot initially then reduce in size as they thaw, so resist the temptation to add more water than needed (water can always be added to cover once the ingredients thaw and shrink down). Cook according to the type of bones and vegetables in the stock bag. For instance, if the scraps are mostly chicken bones and vegetable scraps, cook for the same amount of time as Poultry Stock, 76. Then strain, skim off any fat, cool, and chill as directed in the sections below.

SEASONING STOCK

A classic stock should be perfumed with aromatic vegetables, herbs, and the umami-rich flavor of mushrooms, meats, fowl, and fish. Excessive seasoning can limit their versatility.

Bouquet garni—a bundle of parsley, thyme, and bay leaves tied together or bundled in a square of cheesecloth—is the classic herb combination, but we enjoy small additions of oregano, savory, or marjoram as well. A pinch of dried fenugreek leaves, available in Indian markets, is our all-time favorite addition to poultry stock. It adds a subtle flavor that we feel enhances and enriches the stock. Whole spices such as peppercorns, cloves, allspice, cinnamon, smashed black cardamom pods, and star anise are excellent accents to poultry and meat stocks when used in moderation. Fresh fennel fronds and stalks are a classic flavoring for seafood stocks.

When possible, ➤ tailor the ingredients to suit the recipes the stock will be used in. If a stock is destined for Southeast Asian dishes, cut back on the celery and carrots and add ginger, or a bruised stalk of lemongrass.

The toasty caramel flavors of browned meats and vegetables form the foundation of flavor in brown stocks, but there are other ways to achieve a similar end. Vietnamese cooks char onions and ginger to add an extra layer of savoriness to beef stock. Lightly fry tomato paste in a little oil until browned to add caramelized depth to a stock.

Japanese Dashi, 78—based entirely on savory bonito flakes and kombu (dried kelp, 1016)—is the quintessential example of what glutamate-rich ingredients, 984, can do to enhance the flavor of stock. Fresh or dried mushrooms, tomato paste, smoked ham hocks, bacon ends, dried shellfish, and Parmesan rinds are other excellent sources of umami, 984, that may find their way into stocks.

➤ Never salt stock. The considerable reduction involved both in the original cooking and in subsequent cooking—when the stock is used as an ingredient—makes it almost impossible to judge the amount you will need, and even a little extra salt can ruin your results.

STRAINING AND SKIMMING FAT FROM STOCK

Strain finished stock through a fine-mesh sieve, chinois, or a colander lined with a double layer of cheesecloth or flour sack towel into another pot or a large heatproof bowl, then discard the solids. You may strain the stock more than once, first through a colander, then through a fine-mesh sieve. Pressing heavily on the solids while straining may cloud the stock. Do not let stock sit out at room temperature for long, as it is a good breeding ground for bacteria.

To cool stock for storing, place the uncovered stockpot in the sink and partially immerse in ice water (smaller amounts of stock may be transferred to a bowl set in a larger bowl of ice water). Stir it a few times, and once it cools ➤ refrigerate. Any grease will conveniently rise in a solid mass and can be easily scraped off with a spoon.

Straining and cooling stock

To remove fat from stock for immediate use, ladle into a gravy separator until it is full. Let sit for a few minutes until the fat rises to the top, then pour the stock collected in the bottom of the separator into a measuring cup and discard the fat. Repeat until you have the amount of stock needed. If you do not have a separator, removing fat from the surface with a shallow spoon can be modestly effective, as can using a turkey baster.

STORING STOCK

Stocks keep 3 to 4 days refrigerated, but they can be frozen for up to 6 months. Transfer the stock to freezer-safe pint or quart containers or zip-top freezer bags. Be sure the bags are thoroughly sealed, lay them flat in a single layer on a rimmed baking sheet, and freeze. Once frozen, remove the pan and stack the bags. Small amounts of concentrated stock may be frozen in ice cube trays (once frozen, store the cubes in a zip-top bag). Concentrated stock cubes can be used whenever small amounts of stock are needed, such as pan sauces, 544–47, or vegetable braises. See Reducing Stocks or Glazes, below, for other storage possibilities. ➤ For shelf-stable storage, you may transfer the stock to mason jars and process in a pressure canner, 904.

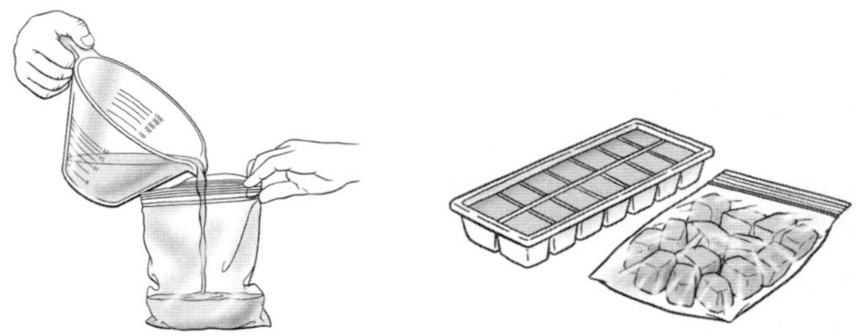

Storing stock in zip-top bags

CLARIFYING STOCK

For extra-sparkling clear stocks, you may wish to clarify them. It is best to start out on the path to a clear stock rather than trying to turn a cloudy stock into a clear one. When you make stock that you wish to be clear, use cold water to cover the solids. Bring the stock to a very low simmer, and periodically skim off any foam that rises to the surface for the first hour. Never let the stock boil.

To clarify stock, first be sure it is chilled and all of the fat has been removed. Transfer it back to a pot and ➤ stir in one beaten egg white and one crushed eggshell for every quart of stock. Bring the stock very, very slowly, without stirring, to a low simmer (around 180°F). As the stock heats, the eggs will bring a heavy, crusty foam to the top. Do not skim this, but push it very gently away from one side of the pot. Through this small opening, you can watch the movement of the simmering stock. ➤ Make sure it never boils. Continue simmering for 10 to 15 minutes. Remove the pot carefully from the heat and let it stand for 10 minutes to 1 hour.

Line a colander with dampened cheesecloth and place it over a bowl. Push the foamy crust to one side and ladle the stock carefully into the sieve, straining it through the cloth. Cool, skim any fat, and store as described in the sections above.

For another, more flavorful alternative to clarified stock, see Consommé, 83.

REDUCING STOCKS OR GLAZES

Once strained and skimmed of any fat, stocks can be added back to the stockpot and concentrated by simmering until a significant percentage of their volume has evaporated or "reduced." **Reductions** concentrate the stock's flavors, which makes it especially useful for creating savory sauces. Reducing stock has the added benefit of making large batches easier to store in the freezer (if you wish for "regular-strength" stock, simply dilute with water as needed).

Glazes are stocks that have been reduced until they are syrupy and thick, or 10 to 15 percent of the original amount of liquid. Any gelatin-rich stock can be used for a glaze, but brown beef and veal stocks are traditional. **Demi-glace,** or "half glaze," is thick enough to coat the back of a spoon when hot; a "full glaze" or **glace de viande,** is the consistency of honey. Both turn into a solid gel when cool, and last for months tightly covered in the refrigerator or freezer. Though time-consuming, these potent glazes are the culinary equivalent of a magic potion; all the deep, savory notes of browned and long-simmered meats can be added in an instant to a variety of dishes. Since it is mostly gelatin, a spoonful or two of glaze can thicken batches of sauce quite nicely, especially pan sauces, 544–47. For instructions, see Meat Glaze, 76; for utilizing in sauces, see About Glazes, 578, and About Brown Sauces, 550.

ABOUT MEAT AND POULTRY STOCKS

There is a strange irony to stock making: While much cooking revolves around what is young and tender, meat and bones from mature animals are highly prized for their fuller flavor. Remember, too, that instead of making every effort to keep juices within the materials you are cooking, you want to extract and trap every vestige of flavor from them. ➤ Bones should be disjointed or cracked and trimmed of excess fat.

As noted on page 72, gelatin gives stock body and a rich, smooth texture. ➤ Beef or veal bones such as neck, shoulder, and knuckle bones or oxtails contain a large amount of collagen, which turns into gelatin during the process of stock making. For poultry stock, ➤ backs, necks, and wings are good sources of collagen, as are feet. When roasting fatty bones for brown stock, pour off any grease that renders (this means less to skim off later).

Always start meat stocks in cold water and add just enough to cover the bones for maximum flavor. Starting with cold water allows albumin to be drawn out from the bones as the stockpot heats. This albumin and other impurities in the bones will rise to the surface and form a layer of frothy scum. Skim off any accumulated scum after the first hour of simmering. Another way to reduce this scum is to blanch the bones. Bring them to a boil in plain water, drain them, then proceed with the stock.

To retain maximum flavor ➤ keep stocks at a steady low simmer, partially covered, with the lid at an angle, until you are sure you have extracted all the goodness from the ingredients, at least 2 hours, and as long as 12 hours. For ways to quicken this process, see 79. Additional water is needed only if ingredients are exposed to the air as liquid evaporates. Follow the recipes for ideal ratios of liquids to solids, but the principle is more important: ➤ just keep the solids covered while cooking (some of them may float, which is fine).

Simmering stock past the recommended cooking time can produce an unpleasant bitter taste. Stocks should be strained when all the flavor and essence have been fully extracted from the meat, bones, and vegetables (bone broth is the exception to this; see below). If in doubt, retrieve a meaty bone from the simmering stock. If the meat still has some flavor, allow the stock to simmer longer. If the meat is tasteless and the bone joints are falling apart, it is time to strain the stock. ➤ If a stock tastes weak after straining, remove and discard the fat, then simmer the stock briskly to reduce it and concentrate the flavor (see Reducing Stocks and Glazes, 74).

Bone broth is much like stock in that it relies primarily upon bones rather than meat for its flavor and body. The main differences are simmering time and when the vegetables are added. Bone broth is simmered until the bones nearly fall apart. Because of this extra-long cooking time, we add any vegetables during the last hour or so (there is no advantage, either flavor- or nutrient-wise, to simmering vegetables for an eternity). To judge when bone broth is done, remove a bone from the pot and press it with a finger. It should crumble under relatively little pressure. We recommend roasting the bones before simmering for better flavor. A pressure cooker will significantly shorten this process, 79.

BROWN BEEF STOCK

About 8 cups

Please read About Meat and Poultry Stocks, above. For a **White Beef Stock,** follow the directions for White Veal Stock, 76, substituting beef bones for the veal. To make **Lamb Stock,** replace the beef bones in this recipe with **4 pounds lamb or mutton breast or neck, cut into thick slices, or shoulder chops** (do not use lamb stock in a recipe calling for poultry or other kinds of meat, as its distinctive flavor can overpower the dish).

Preheat the oven to 425°F. Place in a lightly oiled roasting pan and roast for 15 minutes:

5 pounds meaty beef bones

Add:

2 medium unpeeled onions, quartered
2 carrots, cut into 2-inch pieces
2 celery ribs, cut into 2-inch pieces

Roast, stirring occasionally to prevent the vegetables from burning, until the bones are well browned, about 40 minutes. Transfer to a stockpot. Carefully pour off the fat from the roasting pan and add:

2 cups water or 1 cup white wine

Scrape up any browned bits, then pour the deglazed liquid into the stockpot. Add:

1 leek, halved lengthwise, well cleaned, and cut into 2-inch pieces
3 or 4 sprigs parsley
2 or 3 sprigs thyme
1 bay leaf
¼ teaspoon white or black peppercorns
(2 whole cloves)

Add:

Cold water to cover

Bring to a boil over high heat, then reduce the heat and simmer, partially covered, for 6 to 8 hours. Skim off any impurities that rise to the surface during the first hour of cooking and add water as needed to keep the ingredients covered. Strain and cool uncovered, then refrigerate covered. Skim off any fat before storing or using. Use within 4 days or freeze for up to 6 months.

WHITE VEAL STOCK

About 8 cups

Please read About Meat and Poultry Stocks, 75. For **Brown Veal Stock,** begin by roasting the bones as for Brown Beef Stock, 75, substituting veal for the beef.

Combine in a stockpot:

4 to 5 pounds veal knuckles or meaty bones
Cold water to cover

Bring to a boil over high heat and blanch the veal bones for a few minutes to remove impurities. Drain the water off and rinse the bones by submerging in another change of cold water. Drain again and add:

1 unpeeled onion, coarsley chopped
3 celery ribs, coarsley chopped
1 carrot, coarsley chopped
3 or 4 sprigs parsley
2 or 3 sprigs thyme
1 bay leaf
8 white or black peppercorns
3 whole cloves

Once more, add:

Cold water to cover

Bring to a boil over high heat, then reduce the heat and simmer, partially covered, for 6 to 8 hours. Skim off any impurities that rise to the surface during the first hour of cooking and add water as needed to keep the ingredients covered. Strain and cool uncovered, then refrigerate covered. Skim off any fat before storing or using. Use within 4 days or freeze for up to 6 months.

PORK OR HAM STOCK

About 8 cups

So watery, and yet there's a smack of ham to it. Use this rich stock in place of the ham hock and water in Southern-Style Greens, 243, or Black-Eyed Peas and Greens, 216, or in any soup or stew made with pork. Please read About Meat and Poultry Stocks, 75.

Combine in a stockpot:

5 pounds pork neck bones, ham hocks, shanks, trotters, bacon ends, or a combination (up to 2 pounds may be smoked)
1 unpeeled onion, coarsely chopped
1 carrot, coarsely chopped
1 celery rib, coarsely chopped
4 sprigs parsley
3 sprigs thyme
1 bay leaf
¼ teaspoon white or black peppercorns

Add:

Cold water to cover

Bring to a boil over high heat, then reduce the heat and simmer, partially covered, for 5 hours. Skim off any impurities that rise to the surface during the first hour of cooking and add water as needed to keep the ingredients covered. Strain and cool uncovered, then refrigerate covered. Skim off any fat before storing or using. Use within 4 days or freeze for up to 6 months.

POULTRY STOCK

About 10 cups

Please read About Meat and Poultry Stocks, 75.

Combine in a stockpot:

4 to 5½ pounds poultry parts, preferably backs, necks, wings, and feet
1 unpeeled onion, coarsely chopped
1 carrot, coarsely chopped
1 celery rib, coarsely chopped
3 or 4 sprigs parsley
2 or 3 sprigs thyme
1 bay leaf
(1 teaspoon dried fenugreek leaves)
¼ teaspoon white or black peppercorns
(2 whole cloves)

Add:

Cold water to cover

Bring to a boil over high heat, then reduce the heat and simmer, partially covered, for 4 hours. Skim off any impurities that rise to the surface during the first hour of cooking and add water as needed to keep the ingredients covered. Strain and cool uncovered, then refrigerate covered. Skim off any fat before storing or using. Use within 4 days or freeze for up to 6 months.

BROWN POULTRY STOCK

About 10 cups

Preheat the oven to 425°F. Lightly grease a roasting pan. Have ready all the ingredients for **Poultry Stock, above,** but quarter the onion and leave the celery and carrot in 2-inch chunks so they are easier to turn. Add the poultry and vegetables to the pan and roast, stirring occasionally, until everything is well browned, about 1 hour. Transfer to a stockpot. Carefully pour off the fat from the roasting pan, keeping the caramelized cooking juices. Add **1 cup water or white wine** to the roasting pan and scrape up any browned bits. Add this liquid to the stockpot along with the herbs and spices called for in Poultry Stock and enough cold water to cover the contents. Simmer, strain, and cool as directed.

DEMI-GLACE AND MEAT GLAZE

About 1 cup demi-glace or ⅔ cup meat glaze

The reward for making stock and reducing it for hours is this potent source of umami that takes up very little space and keeps for months in the refrigerator or freezer. Use to add flavor and body to sauces, braises, and soups.

Prepare:

8 cups Brown Beef Stock, 75, White Veal Stock, above, or Brown Poultry Stock, above

Strain and skim any fat from the stock, 74. Transfer to a medium saucepan and set over medium-high heat. Allow the stock to simmer vigorously, skimming off any foam. When the stock begins to thicken, reduce the heat to avoid burning. For **demi-glace,** the reduction is complete when it is the consistency of a light syrup. For **glaze,** the mixture should coat the back of a spoon and be of a honey-like consistency. Depending on the amount of gelatin in the stock and the size of the pot, this can take anywhere from 2 to 4 hours for the given amount of stock. Once the desired consistency has been reached, remove from the heat, transfer to a bowl or other container, and let cool. Once solidified, demi-glace will jiggle a bit like an aspic or gelatin dessert (glaze will be stouter and feel rubbery to the touch). Cover and refrigerate or cut into small squares and freeze in a zip-top freezer bag.

HOUSEHOLD STOCK

6 to 8 cups

This recipe is intended to use whatever bones you have on hand—we recommend saving bones in a bag in the freezer until you have enough. Bones from pork chops, roast chicken, steaks, or even lamb chops are all good additions. The formula below will result in a well-flavored all-purpose stock for everyday cooking. You may roast the bones and vegetables if you like, following the guidelines in Brown Poultry Stock, 76. If using more than 4 pounds of bones, double the vegetables called for below. For an open-ended approach that uses kitchen scraps, see Keeping a Stock Bag, 73.

Combine in a stockpot:

1½ to 4 pounds bones
1 carrot, cut into 2-inch pieces
1 large unpeeled onion, quartered
1 celery rib, cut into 2-inch pieces, or ½ fennel bulb
(A few sprigs of thyme or parsley)
(Leek greens, well rinsed)
(½ teaspoon black peppercorns)
(1 tablespoon tomato paste)

Add:

Cold water to cover

Bring to a boil over high heat, then reduce the heat and simmer, partially covered, for 6 to 8 hours. Skim off any impurities that rise to the surface during the first hour of cooking and add water as needed to keep the ingredients covered. Alternatively, cook for up to 2 hours in a pressure cooker, 79. Strain and cool uncovered, then refrigerate covered. Skim off any fat before storing or using. Use within 4 days or freeze for up to 6 months.

GAME STOCK

About 8 cups

Before proceeding, ➤ check with state game and wildlife authorities for recommendations regarding bones harvested from local venison (in some areas, there is concern over the heat-resistant prions that cause chronic wasting disease in deer, elk, and moose populations and the potential effect on public health).

Proceed as for **Brown Beef Stock, 75,** substituting **5 pounds venison or other game bones** for the beef bones. Instead of water, deglaze the roasting pan with **1 cup dry red wine** and add **8 juniper berries** and **one 3-inch sprig rosemary** to the stockpot. Proceed as directed.

BONE BROTH

8 to 12 cups

A stock cooked for so long that it moonlights as a broth, 81. Gather the ingredients for **Brown Beef Stock, 75, White Veal Stock, 76, Pork or Ham Stock, 76, Poultry Stock, 76,** or **Brown Poultry Stock, 76.** At least half the bones should be rich in collagen (such as chicken feet, turkey wings, pork neck bones, veal knuckles, and oxtails). Set the vegetables and herbs aside, and roast or blanch the bones as directed. Place the bones in a stockpot and add **cold water to cover by 3 inches.** Bring to a low simmer and skim any scum that rises to the top for the first hour. Partially cover and simmer gently until the bones begin to disintegrate when prodded with a spoon, at least 10 hours for poultry and veal and up to 16 hours for beef and pork bones. Check the water level every 2 hours and add boiling water as needed to keep the bones submerged (for beef bones, you may have to add up to 12 cups water). Add the vegetables and herbs for the last hour of cooking. Strain, cool, skim off any fat, and store as directed.

ABOUT SEAFOOD STOCKS

Fish and shellfish stocks are much more convenient than meat and poultry stocks, as they require only a fraction of the simmering time. ➤ Onions, celery, and other aromatics should be thinly sliced, chopped, or shredded so they can impart flavor to the stock during the shorter simmer. The shells of shrimp, crab, and lobster are thin and have no collagen to extract, so there is little reason to simmer them longer than 30 minutes. Fish bones have plenty of collagen, but they are quite thin, so most of their goodness is extracted after only 30 minutes of simmering.

If you have not grilled, roasted, or braised enough whole fish to make a good quantity of stock, fish heads, collars, and bones can be obtained at some fish counters. They will likely not be on display, so you may have to ask for them or call ahead. Fish heads, collars, and bones must smell fresh. If they have gills or viscera attached, trim off and discard them. Rinse bones thoroughly and remove any blood. Fish heads are particularly flavorful, but for mild-tasting all-purpose stock, ➤ avoid heads or trimmings from oily, strong-flavored fish like herring, mackerel, or mullet. ➤ Use salmon only for stock to be used with salmon dishes, such as Salmon Chowder, 104. If bones are unavailable, use inexpensive whole fish such as porgies.

FISH STOCK OR FUMET

About 6 cups

Shells from crab, shrimp, and lobster are delicious additions to fish stock.

I. Combine in a stockpot:

2 pounds fish heads, collars, and bones from white fish such as halibut, cod, snapper, bass, or tilefish
1 small onion, thinly sliced
1 large leek, halved lengthwise, well cleaned, and sliced
(½ fennel bulb, thinly sliced, or a few fennel stalks, coarsely chopped)
(4 ounces cremini mushrooms, sliced)

(1 to 2 garlic cloves, smashed)
(1 cup dry white wine)
(4 thin slices lemon)
4 sprigs parsley
3 sprigs thyme
1 bay leaf

Add:

Cold water to cover

Bring to a boil, reduce the heat, and simmer gently, uncovered, for 30 minutes. Strain and cool uncovered, then refrigerate covered. Use within 4 days or freeze for up to 6 months.

II. Assemble the ingredients for **version I, 77.** Add **2 tablespoons butter or olive oil** to a stockpot over medium heat. Add the sliced onion, leek, fennel, and garlic to the pot and cook, stirring, until the onion has softened, about 5 minutes. Add the fish bones and white wine and cook for another 3 minutes, or until fragrant and the wine has cooked off a bit. Add the herbs and cold water to cover. Simmer, strain, and store as directed.

SHRIMP OR SHELLFISH STOCK

About 4 cups

Shrimp and lobster are the most flavorful shellfish to use here.

Have ready:

Shells from 2 pounds shrimp, or 2 picked crab or lobster carcasses, organs and gills removed

Rinse the shells or carcasses and drain well. Wrap larger crab and lobster shells in a kitchen towel and smash them into small pieces with a rolling pin or the spine of a large knife. Heat in a stockpot over medium-high heat:

2 tablespoons vegetable oil

Add the shells and cook, stirring occasionally, until their color brightens and they become aromatic, 3 to 5 minutes. Add:

1 small unpeeled onion, thinly sliced
1 small carrot, thinly sliced
1 celery rib, thinly sliced
1 bay leaf
1½ teaspoons lightly crushed black peppercorns
(Splash of Pernod or ¼ teaspoon fennel seeds)

Add:

Cold water to cover

Bring almost to a boil, reduce the heat, and simmer gently, partially covered, for 30 minutes. Strain well. Let cool uncovered, then refrigerate covered. Use within 4 days or freeze for up to 6 months.

DASHI

About 4 cups

A foundation of Japanese cuisine, this stock is made quickly from just three ingredients: water, kombu (dried kelp, 1016) and *katsuobushi* (dried bonito flakes, 956). Both of these ingredients can be found in Asian markets and at some well-stocked grocery stores. Dashi should never be boiled or cooked for too long, nor does it freeze well. Though we prefer scratch-made dashi, do not dismiss the instant kind known as **hon dashi**, which need only be dissolved in water (follow the directions on the package for specific amounts).

Combine in a saucepan over high heat:

One 5 × 4-inch piece kombu
4½ cups cold water

Bring almost to a boil. Immediately remove from the heat and stir in:

⅓ cup katsuobushi

Let stand until the flakes begin to sink, 2 to 3 minutes. Strain at once. Let cool uncovered, then refrigerate covered. Reheat dashi gently, and use within 4 days.

ABOUT VEGETABLE STOCKS

Beyond the standard vegetables and aromatics in the recipes below, corncobs, fresh herbs, ginger, garlic, and leeks are good additions to vegetable stocks. Vegetable stocks do not require more than 1 hour to cook. ➤ Because vegetable stocks are cooked for a short period of time, vegetables should be thinly sliced, grated, or chopped in a food processor. To heighten and enrich the flavor of vegetable stocks, brown the vegetables; alternatively, add a Parmesan rind, miso paste, dried mushrooms, or another umami-rich seasoning, 73.

To give a vegetable stock more body, you may add gelatin: For every quart of stock, sprinkle 1 envelope (2¼ teaspoons) unflavored gelatin over ¼ cup cold water in a small bowl. Let the gelatin bloom for 5 minutes, whisk in some of the strained, hot stock to dissolve the gelatin, then stir into the stock. The cooking liquid from a batch of beans also adds body, though it will cloud the stock.

VEGETABLE STOCK

About 8 cups

Heat in a stockpot over medium-high heat:

1 tablespoon vegetable oil or butter

Add and cook, stirring, until the onions have softened, 6 to 8 minutes:

1 large unpeeled onion, thinly sliced
2 celery ribs, including leaves, chopped
1 large carrot, chopped or shredded
(1 medium turnip or parsnip, chopped or shredded)

Add:

(2 cups shredded lettuce)
(1 ounce dried mushrooms or 4 ounces fresh mushrooms or mushroom trimmings)
(1 tablespoon tomato paste, or any tomato skins)
4 sprigs parsley
3 sprigs thyme
1 bay leaf
1 teaspoon white or black peppercorns

Add:

Cold water to cover

Bring to a boil, partially cover, and simmer until the vegetables are very tender, about 45 minutes. Strain well, cool uncovered, then refrigerate covered for up to 4 days or freeze for up to 6 months.

BROWN VEGETABLE STOCK

Preheat the oven to 425°F. Prepare the ingredients for **Vegetable Stock, above,** cutting the vegetables into 2-inch chunks and leaving any fresh mushrooms whole. Place in a lightly oiled roasting pan or on a rimmed baking sheet and roast, stirring occasionally, until everything is well browned, about 45 minutes. Transfer the vegetables to a large saucepan or pot and add **8 cups cold water** along with the parsley, thyme, bay leaf, peppercorns, and any dried mushrooms. Bring to a boil, partially cover, and simmer for 30 minutes. Strain well, cool uncovered, then refrigerate covered for up to 4 days or freeze for up to 6 months.

MUSHROOM STOCK

About 8 cups

I. This is the richer of the two versions. Use in place of beef stock. Heat in a Dutch oven over medium heat:

2 tablespoons olive oil

Add:

1 small onion or large shallot, chopped
1 small carrot, chopped

Sauté until starting to brown, about 7 minutes. Add:

8 ounces mushrooms or mushroom scraps (if possible, use some flavorful mushrooms such as shiitakes), chopped

Sauté until the mushrooms have softened and released their juices, about 5 minutes. Add:

1 tablespoon tomato paste

Stir and allow a dark brown fond (or crust) to develop on the bottom of the pot. Add:

¼ cup dry red wine

Scrape the browned bits off the bottom of the pot. Add:

12 cups water
(1 ounce dried mushrooms, such as shiitake or porcini)

Simmer, partially covered, for 45 minutes. Strain, pressing the vegetables with a spoon to extract as much liquid as possible. Cool uncovered, then refrigerate covered for up to 4 days or freeze for up to 6 months.

II. This version is better suited to replacing chicken or pork stock. Use in Hungarian Mushroom Soup, 88, ramen, 304, or Miso Soup, 84. Preheat a cast-iron skillet over medium-high heat. Place cut side down in the skillet:

1 large leek (about 12 ounces), trimmed (reserve the green tops), halved lengthwise, and well cleaned
3-inch piece ginger, halved lengthwise

Cook until the vegetables are well charred, about 5 minutes. Remove from the heat and set aside. Warm in a pot or large saucepan over medium-high heat:

1 tablespoon vegetable oil

When the oil shimmers, add and sauté until starting to brown:

1 carrot, diced
1 celery rib, diced

Add:

2 pounds chopped mushrooms (any kind, or a combination) and/or mushroom scraps

Sauté until the mushrooms start to release their juices, about 5 minutes. Add the charred leek, ginger, and leek tops along with:

12 cups cool water
2 garlic cloves, smashed
5 sprigs thyme
6 black peppercorns
1 bay leaf

Bring to a gentle simmer, partially cover, and cook for 45 minutes. Strain through a fine-mesh sieve, pressing on the solids with a ladle to extract all the liquid. Stir in:

1 tablespoon tamari

Cool uncovered, then refrigerate covered for up to 4 days or freeze for up to 6 months.

ABOUT QUICK AND STORE-BOUGHT STOCKS

For those who do not have the time or desire to endlessly simmer stock, there are several shortcuts that make the process faster, and more than a few alternatives to the whole endeavor.

One way to speed up the extraction of flavors is to start with smaller ingredients: Chop or thinly slice vegetables and thoroughly crack poultry (for raw bones, you need a cleaver; for cooked bones, layer them in a kitchen towel and strike with the spine of a large knife to shatter them). To speed the cooking of large, sturdy bones, ask your butcher to saw them into smaller pieces.

If you are short on time but still determined to make long-simmering meat or poultry stocks from scratch, a 10-quart stovetop pressure cooker is a good investment. Strong chicken stocks are done in 2 hours, beef stocks in 4 hours. Slow cookers, though best for braising and stewing, may be pressed into service for stock making as well. While they are indeed slow, they may be left unattended. Be aware that slow cooker stocks will not have the same body as those cooked in a pot or pressure cooker.

When there is not time enough to prepare stock from scratch, the best solution is store-bought stock, broth, consommé, or clam juice. These pantry staples can be used straight out of the package, or you can boost their flavor with the "quick" recipes on page 80. Reduced or low-sodium products are preferable because the lesser amount of sodium and MSG leaves the cook free to adjust the seasonings. Taste a variety of store-bought stocks and broths until you find one you like, and keep in mind that price is not necessarily indicative of flavor. Concentrated stock bases generally have the best flavor, though they tend to be very salty. However, most store-bought stocks and broths are not ideal for making classic French sauces, which depend on gelatin-rich, full-flavored stocks as their base. Some butcher shops make their own stocks, which are well worth seeking out, as they tend to taste richer and have better body than stocks found at most grocery stores.

PRESSURE COOKER STOCK

Using any stock recipe, 75–79, except for fish, shellfish, or vegetable stock, prepare the ingredients as directed, using 1½ times the amount of onions called for. Place the ingredients in a 10-quart pressure cooker and add just enough cold water to cover. Do not fill past the fill line or maximum capacity. Bring to full pressure over high heat, then reduce the heat to maintain high pressure. For beef or veal stock, cook for 4 hours. For poultry or lamb stock, cook for 2 hours. If making Bone Broth, 77, cook for 6 hours for beef or veal or 4 hours for poultry. Turn off the heat and allow the pressure cooker to depressurize naturally. Strain the stock, cool completely, and skim off the fat. Refrigerate for up to 4 days or freeze for up to 6 months.

To adapt a stock recipe to use a countertop electric pressure cooker, be aware that the capacity may be too small to fit all the ingredients for a full recipe of stock, and that it has a maximum cook time of 120 minutes. Caveats aside, these cookers are still an excellent tool for preparing smaller batches of stock, as they require no tending during the process. For electric pressure cookers, cook all stocks at high pressure for 2 hours and allow the cooker to depressurize naturally. For Bone Broth, 77, set the cooker for an additional 2 hours at high pressure.

QUICK CHICKEN OR BEEF STOCK

About 3½ cups

Thinly slice, or cut into chunks and pulse in a food processor until finely chopped:

1 small unpeeled onion
1 small carrot
1 small celery rib, with leaves
(1 leek, white part only, halved lengthwise and well cleaned)
(1 garlic clove, smashed)

Heat in a heavy saucepan over medium heat:

1 tablespoon olive oil or butter

Add the vegetables and cook, stirring, until softened, 6 to 8 minutes. If desired, add:

(½ cup dry white wine)

Cook until most of the wine has evaporated. Stir in:

4 cups store-bought chicken or beef stock or broth (preferably reduced sodium)
(Any meat trimmings or bones on hand)
(1 tablespoon soy sauce)
4 sprigs parsley
3 sprigs thyme
1 bay leaf

Bring almost to a boil over medium-high heat, then reduce the heat and simmer gently for about 30 minutes, skimming any scum. If added body is desired, 5 minutes before the stock is finished, stir together in a small bowl:

(1 envelope [2¼ teaspoons] unflavored gelatin)
(¼ cup cold water)

Let the gelatin bloom for 5 minutes. Strain the stock and whisk in the gelatin until dissolved. Use the stock immediately or let it cool, cover, and refrigerate for up to 4 days.

QUICK SEAFOOD STOCK

About 3 cups

A reliable stock for when fish bones and shrimp shells are in short supply.

Heat in a medium heavy skillet over medium-low heat:

2 teaspoons olive oil

Add and cook, stirring, until the onion is soft:

1 onion, thinly sliced, or 1 leek, trimmed, halved lengthwise, well rinsed, and thinly sliced
1 carrot, thinly sliced

Add:

½ cup dry vermouth or dry white wine

Stir for about 1 minute, then stir in:

Four 8-ounce bottles clam juice
(Any fish bones or shrimp shells on hand)
(¼ small lemon)
3 or 4 sprigs parsley
2 or 3 sprigs thyme
1 bay leaf

Simmer, partially covered, for 20 minutes, skimming and stirring occasionally. Strain and use immediately or let it cool, cover, and refrigerate for up to 4 days.

COURT BOUILLON

About 8 cups

Court bouillons are seasoned liquids that are cooked only a short time (*court* is French for "short"); they are not broths or stocks in themselves, but rather prototypes that may develop into them. Their composition varies, but most contain some kind of acid (lemon juice or vinegar) and plenty of aromatic herbs and vegetables. They are used as a cooking medium, especially for poaching fish, shellfish, vegetables, and offal. Afterward, they may either be discarded, strained and used as a light broth for making sauces, or served with the food poached in them, as in the case of Louisiana Court Bouillon, 102, or Vegetables à la Grecque, 204. You may freeze court bouillon after using it as a poaching liquid, then thaw and use again to poach another batch of fish; the resulting liquid will turn into a fuller-bodied broth with each use.

Bring to a boil in a large saucepan:

8 cups water
2 celery ribs, chopped
1 small onion, chopped
3 or 4 sprigs parsley
2 or 3 sprigs thyme
1 bay leaf

Reduce the heat to a simmer and cook uncovered for 20 minutes. Add:

¼ cup sherry vinegar or lemon juice or 1 cup dry white wine

Simmer for another 10 minutes. Strain and season to taste with:

Salt and black pepper

VEGETABLE BOUILLON PASTE

1 pint bouillon concentrate

This homemade vegetable bouillon is a quick, easy, and long-keeping substitute for vegetable stock or broth. We gave some to a friend who said she also enjoyed it stirred into cooked rice.

Place in a food processor:

1 leek, trimmed, well rinsed, and chopped
½ cup chopped peeled carrot
½ cup chopped celery
½ cup chopped peeled parsnip
½ cup finely chopped fennel or cabbage
½ cup chopped onion
½ cup packed chopped parsley leaves and stems

3 tablespoons salt (2 ounces)
1 tablespoon tomato paste
(1 tablespoon white or red miso)
(2 teaspoons mushroom powder, such as shiitake or porcini)

Pulse until ground to a paste. Pack the bouillon paste into a pint jar and store in the freezer. Scoop directly into any dish where a vegetarian flavor boost is needed (the mixture will be scoopable straight from the freezer). To use, start with 1½ teaspoons per cup of water and go from there—you may wish to add more. When you cook with this, be aware that it is salty, so adjust the salt in the recipe accordingly.

ABOUT BROTHS

What is broth and how is it different from stock? Traditionally, broth was made with meat and, sometimes, bones; stock was always made with bones, but not necessarily meat. Broth is simmered a short time; stock is simmered for much longer. Despite this simple, old-fashioned classification, confusion abounds with the common use of phrases like "vegetable stock"—and especially with the rise of newly popular terms like bone broth, 77. Perhaps it is best to think of stock as an ingredient and broth as more of a destination: a simple, clear soup made from meat, poultry, fish, shellfish, or vegetables that is often eaten (or sipped) as is. Broth is often used in soups, grain dishes, and other recipes where added flavor is welcome—and its light-bodied consistency is not an issue. Broth should have an eye-appealing golden or amber color, a balanced flavor, and a delicate aroma.

Because broths do not have the gelatin content of stocks, they are not good candidates for reducing into a glaze, 76. Choose flavorful cuts for making beef broths, such as chuck, shin, or brisket; in the case of poultry or chicken broth, stewing hens or mature game birds make the most flavorful broth, but any chicken will do. Broth lends itself to many additions such as ginger, lemongrass, garlic, shallots, or wild mushrooms.

CHICKEN BROTH

About 12 cups

Thinly slice, or cut into chunks, and pulse in a food processor until finely chopped:

1 unpeeled onion
1 carrot
1 celery rib

Combine in a stockpot with:

One 3½- to 4-pound chicken, cut into parts
Cold water to cover

Bring to a boil over medium heat, reduce the heat, partially cover, and cook gently for 1 hour and 15 minutes, skimming often. Strain and let cool uncovered, then refrigerate covered. Skim off any fat. Use immediately, store refrigerated for up to 4 days or freeze for up to 6 months.

BEEF BROTH

About 4 cups

Pulse in a food processor until coarsely chopped:

1½ pounds boneless beef chuck, cut into 1-inch cubes

Transfer to a stockpot and add:

5 cups cold water

Bring to a simmer over medium heat, then reduce the heat, partially cover, and cook gently for 30 minutes, skimming often. Add:

1 unpeeled onion, cut into 1-inch chunks
1 large leek, halved lengthwise, well rinsed, and chopped
1 carrot, coarsely chopped
1 tablespoon tomato paste
5 sprigs parsley
½ teaspoon dried thyme
3 black peppercorns, lightly crushed
1 whole clove

Simmer for 1 hour more. Strain and let cool uncovered, then refrigerate covered. Skim off any fat when ready to use. The broth will separate, so whisk before using. Store refrigerated for up to 4 days or freeze for up to 6 months.

VEGETABLE BROTH

About 4 cups

Melt in a large saucepan over medium heat:

3 tablespoons butter

Add and cook gently for 5 minutes:

1 onion, chopped, or 1 leek, well rinsed and chopped
1 carrot, parsnip, or turnip, chopped
1 celery rib, chopped
(½ cup chopped fennel)
(4 ounces fresh mushrooms, chopped, or 1 ounce dried mushrooms)

Do not let the vegetables brown. Add:

5 cups water

Bring to a boil, then reduce the heat and simmer gently, partially covered, for 40 minutes. Strain and let cool uncovered, then refrigerate covered. Season to taste with:

Salt and black pepper
(1 tablespoon soy sauce)

Store refrigerated for up to 4 days or freeze for up to 6 months.

PARMESAN BROTH

About 7 cups

Save Parmesan rinds in the freezer until you have enough to make this broth. Many grocery stores grate their own Parmesan and have rinds available for sale. Use this broth in risotto, beans, pasta dishes, soups, or even as a deglazing liquid.

Heat in a medium, dry cast-iron skillet over medium-high heat cut side down:

1 small unpeeled onion, halved

Cook until the onion is charred, about 5 minutes. Add the onion to a medium saucepan along with:

1 pound Parmesan rinds
2 garlic cloves, smashed
2 sprigs thyme
2 sprigs parsley
1 bay leaf
1 teaspoon cracked black peppercorns

Add:

8 cups water

Bring to a boil, reduce the heat, and simmer gently, partially covered, for 2 hours. Strain and cool, then refrigerate for up to 4 days or freeze for up to 6 months. After refrigeration, there will be a fat cap on top of the broth—do not discard the fat. It is flavorful and will enrich the dishes it is added to, so simply stir it back in.

ABOUT SOUPS

There is no doubt that homemade stocks and broths are the basis of some of the very best soups. However, for those who don't have the time or inclination to make homemade stock or broth, never hesitate to make soup with their store-bought counterparts. Some soups, such as Egg Drop Soup, 84, or Matzo Ball Soup, 84, contain little else to disguise the quality of the stock or broth used, so homemade is preferred. Other soups "make their own" stock, calling for nothing more than water as a cooking medium for savory ingredients, which, in turn, lend their essences to the broth.

Some soups are served hot, some cold, and some either way. To serve soup so that it stays warm at the table, use preheated bowls or cups. Cold soups should be well chilled and served in chilled bowls. ➤ Consider 1 cup of soup an appetizer, 1½ to 2 cups a main course, depending on how hearty it is. Do not serve thick, filling soups as the first course of a heavy meal; they are practically a meal in themselves, especially if balanced by a green salad, or fortified with a slice of buttered toast.

SEASONING SOUP

Many of the seasonings for stock, 73, are equally at home in soups. Since they are a final dish rather than an ingredient to be used in other recipes, soups can be flavored with more assertive ingredients.

A small quantity of salt pork, a ham hock, or a few slices of bacon will add flavor and depth. Judicious additions of soy sauce or tamari, miso, fish sauce, demi-glace (store-bought or homemade, 551), or mushroom seasoning, 984, can add savory depth to soups that seem weak or underseasoned.

Adding alcohol to the cooking liquid is another way to add character to soup. Beer adds a tang to bean, cabbage, and vegetable soups, as well as chili, 502–3. Beef soups are improved by the addition of dry red wine; dry white wine and vermouth add zest to a fish, crab, or lobster bisque or chowder. ➤ Add ¼ to ½ cup wine to 1 quart soup, and add it at least 15 minutes before the soup is done so the alcohol can evaporate a bit. Fortified wine, such as a medium-dry sherry or Madeira, blends well with veal or chicken soup, while ruby or tawny port may be added to robust game soups and stocks; fortified wines should be added just before serving.

Of course, it is always good to salt to taste near the end of cooking, or let diners add salt as desired. This is especially true if using store-bought stock.

➤ If using store-bought stock or broth in any of the recipes that follow, hold back on any added salt; wait until just before serving to add salt to taste.

Finally, soups nearly always benefit from a bit of acid—a dash of vinegar or a squeeze of lemon juice—to round out their flavors. Always add to taste, right before serving, or provide a lemon wedge or cruet of vinegar for diners to add themselves.

For adding flavor with garnishes, see below.

PUREEING AND THICKENING SOUPS

Vegetable soups are often pureed to make them smooth, others are partially pureed to give them a creamier texture. An **immersion blender** is exceptionally convenient, since using one does not involve shuttling hot liquids back and forth between the soup pot and a countertop appliance. ➤ Always place the blade of the immersion blender close to the bottom of the pot before turning it on; never bring it close to the surface. Start on low speed, then gradually increase the speed. Stir it around the bottom of the pot until you achieve the desired texture. Carefully rotate the wand so that the whirring blades are at a slight angle to avoid creating suction on the bottom of the pot, which can make it harder to move the blender.

All **countertop blenders** work well for pureeing thinner soups to a uniform texture—professional-style models will tackle thick soups handily. ➤ When blending hot soup in a traditional blender, do not fill the blender more than half full. Be sure the lid's vent is at least partially open to let steam escape; for added insurance, wrap a kitchen towel around the lid and start on a low speed, then gradually increase the speed.

A **food processor** may also be used to puree thick soups. ➤ Do not fill food processors past the top of the blade insert, as liquids may overflow through the blade shaft or leap out through the lid. Because the capacity of most food processors is smaller than that of most blenders, puree soups in batches. Alternatively, transfer chunky ingredients to the food processor with a slotted spoon, add just enough liquid to make a smooth puree, and stir it back into the soup.

A **food mill** purees and strains simultaneously. It is useful when a soup has been cooked until the ingredients are quite soft, and especially if some of the soup's ingredients are fibrous, like celery, leek, or ginger. Interchangeable disks help the cook control the final texture of the soup.

See About Thickeners for Sauces, 542, for more ways to thicken soups.

ABOUT GARNISHES AND ACCOMPANIMENTS FOR SOUP

Soups may be embellished with a complementary garnish. In general, rich or heavy soups are best enlivened with fresh herbs and citrus; lighter soups and broths benefit from heartier toppings. Crispy or crunchy toppings like croutons or toasted nuts are a nice contrast to the smooth texture of purees and cream soups.

FOR CLEAR SOUPS AND BROTHS

Filled dumplings, 313–15, or drop dumplings, 305–7, cooked separately or in the broth as directed

Meatballs, 507, formed into 1-inch balls and cooked separately or simmered in the broth as for Italian Wedding Soup, 98

Poached Eggs, 153

Croutons, 638

Cubes of tofu
Finely julienned vegetables, or sliced green onions
Thin lemon or lime slices
Thin avocado slices

FOR CREAM SOUPS, PUREES, AND THICK SOUPS

Croutons, 638
A dollop of Pesto and Pistou, 586, Zhug, 567, or another a spicy condiment like Harissa, 584, or Charmoula, 586
A drizzle of Jen's Basil Oil, 570, or another flavored oil, 1006–8
Grated or crumbled cheese
Toasted, 1005, and chopped almonds, walnuts, pistachios, hazelnuts, or cashews
Sour cream or crème fraîche

HERBS AND GREENS FOR SOUPS

Always use tender greens and leafy herbs for garnishing. We prefer arugula, watercress, escarole, basil, dill, parsley, and chives. But really, the best greens and herbs to use are those you have on hand, as long as they are compatible with the flavor of your soup. ➤ For every 2 cups of soup, allow **1 to 2 tablespoons chopped fresh herbs** or **½ cup thinly sliced greens.** For the best results, ➤ always add tender herbs and greens to individual bowls of soup (especially if you plan to store any leftovers).

BREADS TO SERVE WITH SOUPS

Rosemary-Olive Bread, 628, Dill Batter Loaf, 600, Focaccia, 613, or Herb and Roasted Garlic Muffins, 633
Beer Bread, 627, or Pimiento Cheese Bread, 599
Corn Bread, 630, or Megan's Southern Corn Bread, 631
Megan's Cheddar-Scallion Biscuits, 636
Garlic Bread, 638
Melba Toast, 638
Crackers, store-bought or homemade, 49–50

STORING SOUPS

Most soups keep very well tightly covered in the refrigerator, improving in flavor as they sit. Fish and shellfish soups do deteriorate; their delicate flavors are best appreciated as soon as they are cooked (chowders, which ripen somewhat overnight, are an important exception).

➤ If you plan to serve a soup over several days, it is best to cook any beaten eggs, pasta, or grains separately—in a portion of the soup, or in water or broth. Egg drops will disintegrate upon reheating and shorten the soup's storage time; cooked pasta and grains become mushier each time the soup is reheated. Poached eggs should be cooked in the broth as needed. Delicate greens and herbs like parsley and cilantro will deaden in both color and flavor as they sit in soup. As noted above, avoid this predicament by simply adding them (as well as any other garnishes) to each serving.

When completely cool, cover tightly and refrigerate soup. Fruit soups and soups made with meat, poultry, milk, cream, and eggs will keep for up to 4 days. Vegetable and legume soups will keep for up to 6 days. All soups can be frozen if they don't contain eggs, seafood, or cheese. Chunky vegetables will degrade in texture and flavor, especially starchy ones like potatoes.

To freeze soup, cool it completely and ladle into labeled, dated zip-top bags or containers with tight-fitting lids. ➤ Allow 1½ inches of headroom for expansion in plastic containers (we do not recommend freezing liquids in glass canning jars). Soups that contain chunks of vegetables that do not freeze well—root vegetables, for example—can be pureed after thawing, then diluted with stock or milk to the desired consistency. In busy households, it may be useful to freeze main-dish soups in individual portions.

Reheat soups gently on the stovetop or in the microwave. Stir thicker soups often to ensure even heating. They can be reheated directly from the freezer in a covered saucepan (add a little water or stock to the pot to start the steaming process). To thaw soups frozen in zip-top bags, run the bag under hot water to loosen it, then peel the bag off like a banana skin, allowing the frozen block of soup to fall into a saucepan. Soup frozen in a hard-shell container will need to sit in a bowl of warm water to loosen the container's grip. ➤ Do not let soups reach a boil or simmer any longer than is necessary to heat them through.

ABOUT CLEAR SOUPS

These brothy elixirs are best made with a full-bodied homemade stock or broth. You can intensify the flavor of a stock by reducing it, 74, or by simmering it with sautéed chopped vegetables—finely diced carrots, celery, and onions—and fresh herbs, then strain them out. For another, superlative clear soup, see Udon Noodles in Broth, 304.

CONSOMMÉ

About 6 cups; 4 servings

The most classic and pure example of a clear soup, consommé makes an elegant start to a formal dinner party. This consommé can be used in any recipe calling for clarified stock.

Thoroughly degrease and add to a soup pot:

8 cups Poultry Stock, 76, Household Stock (made with beef), 77, or Brown Beef Stock, 75

Pulse in a food processor until coarsely chopped:

1 small unpeeled onion, quartered
1 small carrot, cut into 2-inch pieces
1 small celery rib, cut into 2-inch pieces
2 tablespoons packed parsley leaves
½ teaspoon fresh thyme leaves

Add:

1 pound boneless, skinless chicken breasts, fat trimmed and cut into 2-inch pieces, or 1½ pounds beef round or rump steak, fat trimmed and cut into 1-inch pieces

Pulse until chopped. Add:

3 egg whites

Pulse until the mixture is well combined and whisk it into the stock. Very slowly bring to a simmer over medium heat, stirring occasionally and scraping the bottom of the pot, until the egg foam rises to the surface, about 30 minutes. (Do not stir after the broth reaches a simmer.) When the egg foam starts to solidify, make a small hole in the center with a wooden spoon. Continue to simmer very gently until the egg foam mixture is solid, about 30 minutes more. Remove the pot from the heat. Line a sieve with several layers of damp cheesecloth and place it over a large saucepan or pot. Gently move the foam to the side of the pot and ladle the consommé into the colander (discard the egg foam mixture). Warm once more and season before serving with, if desired:

(3 tablespoons Marsala)
(Lemon juice to taste)

EGG DROP SOUP

3 cups; 2 servings

Heat in a small saucepan until boiling vigorously:

3 cups Poultry Stock, 76, Brown Beef Stock, 75, or Chicken Broth, 81

Reduce the heat so the broth simmers. Break into a cup:

2 large eggs

Beat with a fork, just long enough to combine the yolks and whites. When the fork is lifted high, the egg should run off the tines in a watery stream. With the broth simmering, hold the cup in one hand, 5 inches above the rim of the saucepan. Pour the beaten egg in a thin stream into the broth. As you pour, stir wide circles on the surface of the broth with a fork, catching the egg as it strikes and drawing it out into long filmy threads. Season to taste with:

Salt and black pepper

Serve at once in warmed cups. If desired, add:

(A generous squeeze of lemon juice)

STRACCIATELLA

Prepare **Egg Drop Soup, above,** mixing in ¼ **cup finely grated Parmesan or Romano** with the eggs and simmering ½ **cup firmly packed, shredded spinach** in the stock until tender before adding the egg as directed in the recipe.

AVGOLEMONO (GREEK LEMON SOUP)

About 4 cups; 2 to 3 servings

For a more substantial soup, increase the stock or broth to 4 cups. Poach **1 boneless, skinless chicken breast** in the broth along with the rice until the internal temperature reaches 165°F in its thickest part, about 15 minutes. Shred the chicken with a fork and add the meat to the finished soup.

Bring to a rolling boil in a medium saucepan:

3 cups Poultry Stock, 76, or Chicken Broth, 81
½ cup long-grain white rice

Reduce the heat, cover, and simmer until the rice is tender, about 20 minutes. Whisk in a medium bowl just until combined and uniform in color:

2 large eggs
¼ cup lemon juice

Stir in 2 tablespoons of the hot stock. Gradually pour the eggs into the hot but not boiling soup, stirring constantly. Season to taste with:

(Lemon juice)
Salt and black pepper

Serve in hot cups, garnished with:

Chopped parsley or minced dill

MISO SOUP

About 4½ cups; 3 servings

To read more about miso, see 1002. There are many kinds available, especially in Japanese groceries. We often use a combination of red and white miso for this soup.

If desired, soak in cold water for 10 minutes:

(1½ teaspoons dried wakame seaweed flakes, 1016)

Meanwhile, heat in a medium saucepan over medium heat:

4 cups Dashi, 78, or 4 cups water and 2 teaspoons instant dashi granules

Once at a low simmer, add:

3 shiitake mushrooms, stems removed, caps thinly sliced

(Save the stems for stock or another use.) Cook over medium-low heat for a few minutes to cook the mushrooms. While they simmer, place in a small bowl:

4 tablespoons red or white miso paste, or a combination

Add about ¼ cup of the warm dashi and whisk to dissolve the miso. When the mushrooms are cooked, whisk this mixture back into the soup. If using the wakame, drain it and divide among 3 soup bowls, along with:

3 green onions, thinly sliced
(2 ounces soft or firm tofu, cut into small cubes [about ⅓ cup])

Ladle the broth and mushrooms into the bowls.

HEARTY DUMPLING SOUP

About 8 cups; 4 servings

This soup is for filled dumplings; for making soup with simple drop dumplings, use any of the broths suggested here and choose a dumpling mixture, 305–6. Cook as directed in About Dumplings, 305, and garnish with any of the suggestions below (or those in About Garnishes and Accompaniments for Soup, 82).

Bring to a simmer in a medium saucepan:

6 cups Poultry Stock, 76, Chicken Broth, 81, Beef Broth, 81, Vegetable Broth, 81, or Parmesan Broth, 81

Season the broth to taste and add:

16 to 20 Kreplach, 314, Pierogi, 314, Pelmeni, 315, Tortellini, 313, Ravioli, 313, Wontons, 315, or Vegetable Wontons, 315

Bring back to a bare simmer and cook until the dumplings float, 2 to 3 minutes. Pelmeni, which contain raw meat, should be cooked for an additional 4 minutes after they first float to the surface. Divide the dumplings among 4 soup bowls and ladle the broth over them. Garnish, if desired, with any of the following:

(Shredded carrot or radish)
(Tender greens such as arugula or watercress)
(Thinly sliced green onions)
(Finely chopped parsley, cilantro, or dill)

MATZO BALL SOUP

7½ cups; 4 servings

Beat in a medium bowl with a whisk until well combined:

4 large eggs
(2 tablespoons chicken fat)
1 teaspoon salt

Stir in:

2 tablespoons minced dill
(½ cup finely diced fennel)
(1 tablespoon minced chives or 2 tablespoons chopped parsley)
⅓ cup plus 1 tablespoon seltzer water or club soda

Fold in until well blended:

1 cup matzo meal
¼ teaspoon black pepper

Cover and refrigerate for at least 1 hour and for up to 4 hours. With wet hands, form the matzo mixture into 2-inch balls. Drop gently, one at a time, into a large pot of boiling salted water. Cover, reduce the heat, and simmer for 25 minutes. When the matzo balls are almost cooked, heat in a soup pot:

6 cups Poultry Stock, 76, Chicken Broth, 81, or Becker Chicken Soup, 92

Season to taste with:

Salt and black pepper

Add the matzo balls to the soup pot. Ladle the soup into warmed soup bowls, with 2 matzo balls in each bowl.

HOT-AND-SOUR SOUP

About 5 cups; 3 to 4 servings

Combine in a medium bowl:

8 dried shiitake mushrooms (4 if using wood ears)
(10 dried wood ear or cloud ear mushrooms)
(10 dried tiger lily buds)

Pour in:

1½ cups hot water

Let stand until the mushrooms and lily buds, if using, are softened, about 20 minutes. Meanwhile, stir together in a small bowl:

5 tablespoons rice vinegar
3 tablespoons soy sauce
1 tablespoon cornstarch

Add, turning to coat:

4 ounces boneless pork loin or boneless, skinless chicken, cut into ¼-inch-wide strips

Reserving the soaking liquid, scoop out the mushrooms and lily buds, if using. Slice the mushrooms into strips and cut the lily buds in half, discarding any tough pieces. Line a fine-mesh sieve with a dampened paper towel and strain the liquid through it into a soup pot and add:

4 cups Poultry Stock, 76, Brown Poultry Stock, 76, or Chicken Broth, 81

Bring to a boil. Add the mushrooms and lily buds, if using, reduce the heat, and simmer for 3 minutes. Meanwhile, stir together in a small bowl:

3 tablespoons cornstarch
3 tablespoons water

Add to the soup and simmer, whisking constantly, until slightly thickened. Add the meat along with:

4 ounces firm tofu, well drained and diced
¾ teaspoon black pepper

Bring back to a simmer, then stir in:

1 large egg, well beaten

Remove from the heat and stir in:

2 teaspoons toasted sesame oil

Serve garnished with:

Thinly sliced green onions

Season at the table with:

Rice vinegar
Chili oil

ABOUT VEGETABLE SOUPS

Though they may not have the simple sophistication of consommé or the popularity of chicken noodle, soups studded with chunky vegetables are some of the most fulfilling and wholesome we know. When making the soup, cut ingredients uniformly to ensure even cooking, and bear in mind that some vegetables, such as potatoes or carrots, take longer to cook than others. These should be added first, followed by vegetables such as celery, onions, and green beans. Leave quick-cooking greens, such as spinach and chard, for last. For pureed vegetable soups and those fortified with cream, see About Cream Soups and Purees, 104.

VEGETABLE SOUP

About 7 cups; 4 servings

Heat in a large saucepan over medium heat:

2 tablespoons olive oil or butter

Add and cook until slightly softened:

1 onion, diced
2 celery ribs, diced
1 carrot, diced

Add:

4 cups stock, broth, or water
2 medium tomatoes, chopped
(1 large red or gold potato, diced)
(1 turnip, peeled and diced)
1 teaspoon salt (only if using unsalted stock or broth)
¼ teaspoon black pepper

Cover and simmer until the vegetables are tender, about 35 minutes. If desired, add:

(1 cup chopped cabbage or spinach)

Cook 5 minutes more. Add:

2 tablespoons chopped parsley
Salt and black pepper to taste

MINESTRONE

About 12 cups; 6 servings

Heat in a large soup pot over medium heat until the bacon has rendered its fat, 2 to 3 minutes:

2 slices bacon (or 1 tablespoon olive oil and 1 ounce pancetta), chopped

Add:

1 large onion, chopped
1 carrot, chopped
1 celery rib, including leaves, chopped
½ small head green cabbage, chopped

Cook, stirring, until the cabbage begins to wilt, about 8 minutes. Stir in:

10 cups Poultry Stock, 76, Chicken Broth, 81, water, or a combination

One 15-ounce can cannellini or other white beans, drained and rinsed, or 1½ to 2 cups cooked white beans, 213, half of them mashed
One 14½-ounce can diced tomatoes
2 garlic cloves, minced
One 4-inch sprig fresh rosemary or 1 teaspoon dried rosemary
(1 Parmesan rind)

Bring to a boil, reduce the heat, and simmer, partially covered, for 30 minutes. Remove the rosemary sprig, and stir in:

1 cup elbow macaroni or orzo (4 or 6 ounces, respectively)
3 chard leaves, chopped

Simmer for 15 minutes or until the pasta is tender. Season to taste with:

Salt and black pepper

Top each serving with:

A drizzle of extra-virgin olive oil
2 tablespoons chopped parsley, basil, or a combination
(Grated Parmesan or Romano cheese)

SOUPE AU PISTOU (PROVENÇAL VEGETABLE SOUP)

About 12 cups; 6 servings

Heat in a large soup pot over medium heat:

2 tablespoons olive oil

Add and cook, stirring, until tender but not browned, about 8 minutes:

1 onion, chopped
1 small leek, halved lengthwise, well rinsed, and chopped
1 carrot, chopped
1 large celery rib, chopped

Stir in:

2 medium tomatoes, peeled, 281, seeded, and chopped
1 small red or gold potato, chopped
8 cups water
1 teaspoon salt
(Pinch of saffron threads)

Bring to a boil, reduce the heat, and simmer until the potatoes are tender, about 30 minutes. Stir in:

One 15-ounce can cannellini or other white beans, drained and rinsed, or 1½ to 2 cups cooked beans, 213
1 cup broken thin spaghetti or elbow macaroni (4 ounces)
1 small zucchini, halved lengthwise and sliced
1 cup 1-inch pieces green beans

Simmer just until the pasta is tender. Meanwhile, prepare without adding salt or pepper:

Pistou, 586

Stir the pistou into the soup along with:

1 teaspoon black pepper
Salt to taste

Serve hot, at room temperature, or cold.

WINTER MELON SOUP

About 8 cups; 4 to 5 servings

The subtly flavored, firm flesh of winter melon takes well to the savory notes in this broth. You may find winter melon at pan-Asian markets; otherwise, substitute peeled and seeded chayote squash, which is widely available at Latino markets.

Soak in warm water for 20 minutes:

4 dried shiitake mushrooms

Drain and chop, then add to a large saucepan with:

4 cups chicken stock or broth
1 pound peeled, seeded winter melon, cut into 1-inch cubes (about 3½ cups)
1 small leek, halved lengthwise, well rinsed, and chopped
One 5-ounce can sliced bamboo shoots, drained, rinsed, and diced
⅓ cup diced country ham or Canadian bacon
½-inch piece ginger, peeled and grated or minced
(4 small dried scallops, 1016)

Bring to a boil, then cover, reduce the heat, and simmer until the winter melon is very tender, 15 to 20 minutes.

GREEN PEA SOUP

About 5 cups; 3 servings

If using fresh green peas, they may need a longer simmering time to soften.

Have ready:

1 pound frozen petite peas or shelled fresh green peas

Melt in a soup pot over medium-low heat:

2 tablespoons butter

Add:

1 head butter lettuce, shredded
1 onion, diced
1 small celery rib, including leaves, diced

Cook, stirring, until the onion is tender, about 7 minutes. Add 2 cups of the peas along with:

4 cups chicken or vegetable stock or broth
8 ounces potatoes (2 small gold or 1 small russet), peeled and diced
(1 tablespoon minced tarragon or mint)

Simmer, covered, until the potatoes and peas are very soft, 25 to 30 minutes. Puree the soup with an immersion blender (or in batches in a food processor or regular blender) until very smooth. Add the remaining peas to the soup and heat through. Season to taste with:

Salt and black pepper

Serve with:

Butter Dumplings, 306, or Croutons, 638

Or top with:

Sour cream or crème fraîche
Chopped mint or tarragon

SAUERKRAUT SOUP

About 10 cups; 5 to 6 servings

This tangy soup is an excellent way to use an abundance of homemade sauerkraut, 940. For a vegetarian soup, simply omit the kielbasa.

Heat in a Dutch oven or soup pot over medium heat:

1 tablespoon vegetable oil

Add and brown on both sides, about 8 minutes:

8 ounces kielbasa, cut into ½-inch-thick rounds

Drain on paper towels. Add to the pot:

1 tablespoon vegetable oil

Add and sauté until softened, 6 to 8 minutes:

1 large onion, chopped

Add and sauté until fragrant, about 2 minutes:

4 garlic cloves, chopped
1 tablespoon smoked paprika
(2 teaspoons caraway seeds)

Add and cook, stirring, until wilted, about 8 minutes:

¼ head cabbage, shredded
½ teaspoon salt

Chop the kielbasa and add to the pot along with:

2 cups sauerkraut, drained
One 14½-ounce can diced tomatoes
5 cups chicken or vegetable stock or broth
1 large russet potato, cut into ½-inch cubes

Simmer until the potatoes are tender, about 30 minutes. Season to taste with:

Salt and black pepper

Serve with:

Sour cream or yogurt

KIMCHI JJIGAE (KIMCHI-TOFU STEW)

About 8 cups, or 4 servings

If you make your own kimchi, 941, this stew is a great way to use up the last of a batch. A combination of pork and tofu is traditional, but this is easily made vegetarian by simply omitting the pork, or replacing it with **4 ounces shiitake mushrooms, stemmed and sliced.**

Heat in a soup pot or Dutch oven over medium heat:

1 tablespoon vegetable oil

When the oil shimmers, add:

2 tablespoons gochujang, 970
3 garlic cloves, minced

Allow the *gochujang* to fry until the oil is bright red, about 1 minute. Stir in:

2 cups drained and chopped kimchi
½ pound pork shoulder, country ribs, or pork belly, trimmed and cut into ½-inch cubes
1 tablespoon gochugaru, 969, or ½ teaspoon red pepper flakes

Cook, stirring, until the *gochujang* starts to stick to the bottom of the pot, about 5 minutes. Stir in:

6 cups water, vegetable broth, or chicken stock
(Up to ½ cup kimchi brine)

Simmer, partially covered, for 30 minutes. Add:

12 ounces firm tofu, cut into 1-inch cubes, or crumbled soft or silken tofu
1 tablespoon toasted sesame oil

Cook 5 minutes more. Once the mixture has come back to a simmer, if desired, make four depressions in the soup and add:

(4 large eggs)

Cover and cook for 6 to 10 minutes more, depending on how done you want your eggs. Remove from the heat. If using eggs, transfer an egg to each of four serving bowls. Stir into the broth:

4 green onions, chopped
½ teaspoon black pepper
Soy sauce or fish sauce to taste

Ladle the soup into the bowls and serve piping hot with:

Cooked short-grain white rice, 343

GARBURE (BEAN SOUP WITH VEGETABLES)

About 9 cups; 5 servings

Soak overnight in water to cover:

1 cup dried flageolet, navy, or fava beans, rinsed and picked over

Drain the beans and add to a soup pot along with:

8 cups water
(1 ham hock)
2 tablespoons olive oil
3 sprigs thyme
2 garlic cloves, smashed

Bring to a boil, then reduce the heat, cover, and simmer for 30 minutes. Add:

1 pound cabbage, thinly sliced
2 medium red or gold potatoes, cut into ½-inch chunks
2 carrots, cut into ¼-inch-thick slices
1 large turnip, peeled and cut into ½-inch chunks
1 leek, white part only, well rinsed, and thinly sliced
½ onion, sliced
1 teaspoon salt
½ teaspoon black pepper

Simmer, covered, until the vegetables and beans are tender, about 30 minutes.

SPICY CHICKPEA SOUP

5½ cups; 3 to 4 servings

This is an extraordinarily easy and nourishing soup that gets much of its flavor from spicy harissa paste. If using store-bought harissa, keep in mind that the heat level can vary wildly. Sample a little bit of it and add to taste.

Heat in a soup pot or Dutch oven over medium heat:

2 tablespoons olive oil

When hot, add and cook, stirring, until softened, 6 to 8 minutes:

1 onion, chopped

Stir in and cook 1 minute more:

4 garlic cloves, thinly sliced
2 tablespoons Harissa I, 584, or store-bought harissa paste
1 teaspoon sweet paprika, plain or smoked
1 teaspoon ground cumin
¾ teaspoon salt (less if using salted stock)
(¼ teaspoon red pepper flakes or ½ teaspoon Urfa, Aleppo, or Marash chile flakes, 968)

Add:

4 cups vegetable or chicken stock or broth
One 15-ounce can chickpeas, drained and rinsed, or 1½ to 2 cups cooked chickpeas

Bring to a boil, then reduce the heat, partially cover, and simmer for 15 minutes. Stir in:

1 cup packed baby spinach

Simmer 2 minutes more. Place in each bowl:

2 tablespoons uncooked fine bulgur or couscous (6 to 8 tablespoons total)

Bring the soup to a rolling boil, then remove from the heat and ladle the soup over the bulgur or couscous and let sit 5 minutes before eating. If desired, garnish with:

(Chopped parsley or cilantro)

ONE-EYED BOUILLABAISSE

About 8 cups; 4 hearty servings

We first learned of this "poor man's bouillabaisse" from *Jane Grigson's Vegetable Book*. Instead of calling for several kinds of fish and shellfish, this humble potage relies on leeks, green peas, and poached eggs. We add bacon for a touch of luxury, but this can easily be omitted, if desired (cook the leek in 2 tablespoons olive oil). Add to a Dutch oven or soup pot over medium heat:

4 slices bacon, cut crosswise into ½-inch strips, or 4 ounces slab bacon cut into ½-inch cubes

Cook, stirring, until the fat is rendered and the bacon is crispy. Transfer the bacon to a small plate. Add to the bacon fat:

1 large leek, white and light-green parts only, halved crosswise, well rinsed, and thinly sliced

Cook until lightly browned, about 7 minutes. Add:

4 cups chicken stock or broth
1 cup dry white wine
2 large tomatoes, peeled, 281, and chopped, or one 14½-ounce can diced tomatoes
6 small red or gold potatoes, cut into ½-inch cubes
8 garlic cloves, smashed
(1 or 2 fennel fronds)
(One 3-inch strip orange zest)
1 teaspoon salt
¼ teaspoon saffron threads
¼ teaspoon black pepper

Bring to a rapid boil, then reduce the heat, cover, and simmer until the potatoes are tender, about 15 minutes. Add:

1½ cups shelled green peas, fresh or frozen

If the fresh peas taste a bit starchy, simmer for an additional 5 minutes; if using frozen peas, just bring the soup back to a simmer. Make four depressions in the soup with a spoon and carefully slide into the soup:

4 large eggs

Poach for 6 to 10 minutes or until cooked to the desired degree of doneness. As the eggs poach, divide among 4 serving bowls:

4 large slices stale or lightly toasted baguette

Scoop a poached egg into each bowl, divide the vegetables among them, and spoon broth over the vegetables. Garnish with the cooked bacon and:

Chopped parsley
Black pepper to taste

HUNGARIAN MUSHROOM SOUP

5 to 6 cups; 4 servings

This hearty soup is even more delicious when made with Mushroom Stock, 79.

Melt in a Dutch oven or large saucepan over medium heat:

2 tablespoons butter

Add and cook, stirring, until softened, 6 to 8 minutes:

1 large onion, chopped

Add:

1 pound assorted mushrooms, sliced

Sauté until the mushrooms release their liquid and wilt a bit, about 8 minutes. Add and stir until combined:

3 tablespoons all-purpose flour
1 tablespoon smoked paprika
(1½ teaspoons dried thyme)

Whisk in:

1 cup milk or half-and-half
3 cups vegetable stock or Mushroom Stock, 79

Bring to a simmer, cover, reduce the heat to low, and cook for 15 minutes. Remove from the heat and whisk in:

½ cup sour cream
2 tablespoons chopped dill

Taste and season to taste with:

Salt and black pepper

CORN CHOWDER

About 6 cups; 4 servings

Add to a soup pot and cook, stirring over medium heat, until beginning to crisp, about 10 minutes:

4 slices bacon, chopped

Leaving the bacon in the pan, spoon off all but 2 tablespoons of fat. Add and cook, stirring, until tender and slightly browned, about 10 minutes:

1 small onion, chopped
2 celery ribs, diced

Meanwhile remove the kernels from:

6 small ears corn

Set the kernels aside. Add the cobs to the pot, then add:

4½ cups milk
2 gold or red potatoes, diced

Push the corncobs down into the milk. Bring the milk almost to a boil, reduce the heat, cover, and simmer until the potatoes are tender, about 15 minutes. Remove the cobs. Stir in the reserved corn kernels along with:

1 teaspoon salt
½ teaspoon white or black pepper

Simmer gently until the corn is tender, about 5 minutes. Remove from the heat. With a slotted spoon, remove 1½ cups solids from the soup and puree until smooth. Return to the soup and add:

1 tablespoon butter

Let stand until the butter is melted, then stir and serve.

ABOUT HEARTY BEAN AND LEGUME SOUPS

Bean and legume soups are easy to prepare in large batches, require little attention while cooking, and freeze well. The ingredients are easily kept in the pantry. Soaking beans overnight is hardly necessary, but it will shorten the cooking time. For instructions on soak-

ing and cooking beans, see About Dried Beans and Legumes, 212.
➤ Canned beans may be substituted for dried in the recipes below. For every 1 cup of dried beans, substitute two 15-ounce cans beans, drained and rinsed. Reduce the liquid in the recipe by 1½ cups and skip the bean cooking step.

For other soups with beans, see Minestrone, 85, Garbure, 87, and Soupe au Pistou, 86.

US SENATE BEAN SOUP

About 6 cups; 4 servings

There's a reason this soup has been on the menu of the US Senate restaurant every day since 1901.

If desired, soak overnight in water to cover:

1¼ cups small dried white beans, such as navy or Great Northern, rinsed and picked over

Drain and place in a soup pot along with:

1 meaty ham hock
7 cups cold water

Bring to a boil, then reduce the heat, and simmer, partially covered, until the beans are tender, about 1 hour 15 minutes for soaked beans and 2 hours for unsoaked. Remove the ham hock (leave the soup at a gentle simmer). Discard the bone, skin, and fat. Dice the meat, return it to the pot, then add:

1 large onion, diced
3 celery ribs, with leaves, chopped
1 large potato, peeled and finely diced
2 garlic cloves, minced
1 teaspoon salt
½ teaspoon black pepper

Simmer until the potato pieces are quite soft, 20 to 30 minutes. Remove from the heat and mash with a potato masher until the soup is a bit creamy. Taste and add more salt if needed. Stir in:

2 tablespoons chopped parsley

MEDITERRANEAN WHITE BEAN SOUP

About 6 cups; 4 servings

If desired, soak overnight in water to cover:

1 cup dried white beans, such as Great Northern or cannellini, rinsed and picked over

Drain and place in a soup pot with:

1 sprig fresh rosemary or ¾ teaspoon dried rosemary
8 garlic cloves, chopped or sliced
7 cups Poultry Stock, 76, or Vegetable Broth, 81

Bring to a boil, then reduce the heat and simmer, covered, until the beans are tender, about 1 hour 15 minutes for soaked beans and 2 hours for unsoaked. Discard the rosemary sprig and stir in:

1 medium tomato, chopped
¼ cup chopped parsley
¼ cup olive oil
½ teaspoon black pepper or red pepper flakes

Heat the mixture through, seasoning with:

1 tablespoon red wine vinegar, or to taste
Salt to taste

Garnish with:

Chopped parsley, oregano, or a combination

BLACK BEAN SOUP

10 cups; 6 servings

This soup is a good candidate for pressure cooking. Use unsoaked beans and only 5 cups water. Cook at full pressure for 30 minutes, and allow the pressure to release naturally for 15 minutes.

If desired, soak overnight in water to cover:

1 pound dried black beans, rinsed and picked over

Heat in a soup pot over medium heat:

2 tablespoons vegetable oil

Add and cook, stirring, until softened, 6 to 8 minutes:

2 large onions, chopped

Add and cook for another minute:

6 garlic cloves, minced
2 serrano peppers, seeded if desired, and minced
1 tablespoon chili powder
2 teaspoons ground cumin
2 teaspoons dried oregano
1½ teaspoons salt

Drain the beans, if soaked, and add to the pot, along with:

10 cups Vegetable Stock, 78, Poultry Stock, 76, or water

Bring to a boil, then reduce the heat and simmer, partially covered, until the beans are completely tender, about 1 hour 15 minutes for soaked beans and 2 hours for unsoaked. Scoop 2 cups of beans into a small bowl or food processor and mash or process. Stir back into the soup and simmer for 5 minutes more to thicken. Taste the soup and season with more salt if needed. Serve in soup bowls with:

Sliced avocado
Chopped cilantro
Hot sauce
Lime wedges

MEGAN'S VEGAN CHILI

About 8 cups; 5 servings

We like to toast and grind dried chiles for better flavor, but you can substitute ¼ **cup chili powder** or your own combination of ground dried chiles for those called for in the recipe. If using prepared chili powder, reduce the cumin and coriander to 1 teaspoon each.

Toast in a dry skillet over medium-high heat until fragrant, about 3 minutes:

3 guajillo chiles, stemmed and seeded
2 chipotle chiles, stemmed and seeded
2 ancho chiles, stemmed and seeded

Cool and grind the toasted chiles to a powder in a spice grinder. Set aside. Coarsely crumble with your fingers:

8 ounces tempeh

Heat in a Dutch oven over medium heat:

2 tablespoons vegetable oil

Add the tempeh and cook, stirring occasionally, until browned and crisp, about 10 minutes. Add and sauté until tender and starting to brown:

1 onion, chopped
1 red bell pepper, chopped
2 jalapeño or serrano peppers, seeded and chopped

Add the ground chiles and:

8 garlic cloves, coarsely chopped
2 tablespoons tomato paste
2 teaspoons ground cumin
2 teaspoons ground coriander
1 teaspoon dried oregano

Cook until fragrant, 3 to 5 minutes. Allow the spices and tomato paste to form a dark brown crust on the bottom of the pot. Pulse in a food processor until chopped fine, or very finely chop:

8 ounces mushrooms

Add the mushrooms to the Dutch oven and allow them to cook until they have released their liquid, scraping the bottom of the pot to loosen the brown bits. Let the mushroom liquid boil off. Add and reduce to about ½ cup:

One 12-ounce beer (a dark beer or lager) or 1½ cups water or vegetable broth

Add:

One 14½-ounce can diced tomatoes
Two 15-ounce cans pinto or black beans or a combination, drained and rinsed
1 cup vegetable broth or water

Let the chili simmer, covered, for 30 to 45 minutes or until thick. Season to taste with:

Salt and black pepper

Serve with:

Chopped green onions
Chopped cilantro
Sour cream or a vegan sour cream substitute

LENTIL SOUP

About 9 cups; 5 servings

Heat in a large soup pot over medium-low heat:

1 tablespoon olive oil

Add and cook, stirring, until the vegetables are tender but not browned, 5 to 10 minutes:

1 large carrot, diced
1 celery rib, diced
1 large onion, diced
3 garlic cloves, minced
(4 ounces pancetta or Canadian bacon, diced)

Stir in:

1 cup dried green or brown lentils, rinsed and picked over
One 14½-ounce can diced tomatoes
1 teaspoon dried thyme
6 cups water
½ teaspoon salt

Bring to a boil, then reduce the heat, and simmer, covered, until the lentils are tender, 30 to 40 minutes. If desired, add for the last 5 minutes:

(1 bunch kale, deribbed and thinly sliced)

Stir in:

1½ teaspoons lemon juice, sherry vinegar, or balsamic vinegar
½ teaspoon black pepper
Salt to taste

LENTIL SOUP WITH SAUSAGE AND POTATO

Prepare **Lentil Soup, above,** omitting the optional pancetta or bacon. After the lentils have cooked for 30 minutes, add **1 large gold potato, peeled and diced,** and cook for 10 minutes. Add **4 ounces cured Spanish chorizo, diced, or 6 ounces kielbasa, sliced,** and **½ cup water.** Simmer until the potatoes are tender and the sausage is just heated through, about 5 minutes.

SPLIT PEA SOUP

About 6 cups; 4 servings

Combine in a soup pot:

A small ham hock or ham bone
2 cups green split peas, rinsed and picked over
8 cups cold water

Bring to a boil, reduce the heat, and simmer for 1 hour. Stir in:

1 large carrot, diced
1 large celery rib, diced
1 onion, diced
2 garlic cloves, chopped
1 bay leaf

Simmer until the ham hock and peas are tender, about 1 hour more. Remove from the heat, discard the bay leaf, and remove the ham hock or ham bone. Discard the bone, skin, and fat. Dice the meat and stir into the soup. For a thicker soup, simmer to the desired consistency. Season to taste with:

Salt and black pepper

Garnish with:

Croutons, 638

PEANUT SOUP

About 6 cups; 4 servings

This soup is claimed by both Virginia and Georgia, but its roots are undoubtedly in the peanut stews of Senegal and Gambia.

Melt in a soup pot over medium-low heat:

2 tablespoons butter

Add and cook, stirring, until tender but not browned, about 5 minutes:

1 onion, finely chopped
1 celery rib, finely chopped
1 garlic clove, minced

Stir in:

2 tablespoons all-purpose flour

Cook, stirring, for 5 minutes. Whisk in:

4 cups Poultry Stock, 76, or Chicken Broth, 81

Simmer, stirring often, until the soup begins to thicken, about 5 minutes. Ladle about 1 cup of the hot broth into a medium bowl and add:

1½ cups natural peanut butter

Stir together with a fork until the mixture is well combined and free of lumps. Stir back into the soup pot, then stir in:

1 cup heavy cream or half-and-half
1½ teaspoons salt
¼ teaspoon cayenne pepper
½ teaspoon hot pepper sauce, or to taste

Heat through, but do not boil. Serve garnished with:

3 tablespoons chopped dry-roasted peanuts
¼ cup chopped green onions
(Lime or lemon wedges)

ABOUT BREAD SOUPS

Bread is a wonderful companion to soup, whether torn from a fresh loaf or toasted for croutons. Many classic "peasant" soups take this pairing further and use bread as a primary ingredient. Fried or toasted bread adds a distinctive flavor and texture, and in some cases provides a buoyant vessel for cheeses to be melted on. Other soups are simmered with slices of bread, which thickens their broth and lends them body—an especially useful trick for anyone who has the stale remnants of a loaf lingering in their bread basket. Economy aside, the results are invariably tasty and nourishing.

SOPA DE AJO (GARLIC AND BREAD SOUP)

I. ***About 4 cups; 2 to 4 servings***

This makes a perfect light supper or lunch for two.

Heat in a medium saucepan over medium-low heat:

3 tablespoons olive oil

Add and cook, stirring, until very fragrant but not browned, 10 minutes:

1 head garlic, separated into cloves and peeled (about 16 cloves)

With a slotted spoon, transfer the garlic to a small bowl. Add to the pan:

2 or 4 slices French or country bread

Cook in the oil over medium-high heat, turning once, until golden, 1 to 2 minutes on each side. Remove from the pan and rub on both sides with:

1 garlic clove, peeled

Stir into the pan:

1 tablespoon sweet or hot paprika (preferably smoked)
¼ teaspoon cumin seeds

Stir in the cooked garlic along with:

4 cups Poultry Stock, 76, Chicken Broth, 81, or water
½ teaspoon salt
¼ teaspoon black pepper

Bring to a boil, then reduce the heat, partially cover, and simmer until the garlic is very tender, about 20 minutes. Meanwhile, preheat the oven to 400°F.

When the garlic is very tender, remove it from the pan with a slotted spoon and mash with a fork. Return it to the pan, then bring the soup to a low simmer. Set 2 or 4 ovenproof bowls or crocks on a baking sheet and fill with the soup. One at a time, crack into a small bowl, then slide into each bowl of soup:

2 or 4 large eggs

Bake just until the egg whites are set (the yolks should still be runny), 4 to 7 minutes. Top each serving with a garlic crouton, allowing the soup to soak into the bread.

II. ***6 cups; 4 servings***

This bread-thickened soup is a superlative way to utilize stale, half-eaten baguettes. The soup is even richer served in individual ovenproof bowls, topped with the cheese, and browned under the broiler.

Peel and thinly slice the cloves from:

2 heads garlic

Heat in a large saucepan over medium heat:

¼ cup olive oil

Add the garlic and fry until the garlic is just beginning to color, about 4 minutes. Add:

6 cups Poultry Stock, 76, Chicken Broth, 81, or water

Bring to a simmer and gradually stir in:

About 3 cups cubed stale, crusty white bread

Once the first addition of bread has dissolved a bit, gradually add more bread, stirring, until the soup has thickened. Season to taste with:

(Sweet or hot paprika, preferably smoked)
(Sherry vinegar)
Salt and black pepper

Serve topped with:

Grated Parmesan or Manchego cheese

PAPPA AL POMODORO (TUSCAN BREAD AND TOMATO SOUP)

About 4 cups; 3 servings

Have ready:

3 slices stale crusty white bread

(If your bread is fresh, preheat the oven to 200°F and dry the bread in the oven for 15 to 20 minutes.) Rub the bread on both sides with:

1 garlic clove, peeled

Heat in a large saucepan over medium heat:

3 tablespoons olive oil

Add:

1 red onion, chopped

Cook, stirring, until the onion is softened and beginning to brown, about 10 minutes. Add:

4 large garlic cloves, coarsely chopped

Reduce the heat to medium-low and cook until the garlic is fragrant, 2 to 3 minutes. Add:

1½ pounds tomatoes, peeled, 281, and coarsely chopped, or one 28-ounce can whole tomatoes, drained and chopped
Pinch of red pepper flakes

Cook, stirring, over medium-high heat until thick and fragrant, about 5 minutes. Stir in:

2 cups Poultry Stock, 76, or Vegetable Stock, 78

Bring to a boil and boil for 2 minutes. Season to taste with:

Salt and black pepper

Tear up the toasted bread and distribute among 3 soup bowls. Ladle in the hot soup and top each serving with:

1 tablespoon chopped basil
Drizzle of extra-virgin olive oil
Grated Parmesan

Serve hot or at room temperature.

RIBOLLITA

Prepare **Minestrone, 85,** substituting for the pasta **4 cups stale or toasted crusty bread, cut into cubes.** Proceed as directed.

FRENCH ONION SOUP

About 6 cups; 4 servings

Heat in a soup pot over medium heat until the butter is melted:

2 tablespoons butter
2 tablespoons olive oil

Add and stir to coat:

5 onions, thinly sliced

Cook, stirring occasionally and keeping an eye on the onions so they do not scorch. As soon as they start to brown, about 30 minutes, reduce the heat to medium-low and continue to cook, stirring frequently, until they are a rich brown, about 1 hour. Stir in:

2 tablespoons dry sherry or Cognac

Increase the heat to high and cook, stirring constantly, until the sherry has evaporated. Stir in:

4 cups Brown Beef Stock, 75, Beef Broth, 81, Brown Poultry Stock, 76, or Brown Vegetable Stock, 78
4 sprigs thyme
1 bay leaf

Bring to a boil, then reduce the heat, partially cover, and simmer for 20 minutes. Season with:

1 teaspoon salt, or to taste
¼ teaspoon black pepper, or to taste

Place 4 broilerproof soup bowls or crocks on a baking sheet. Ladle the hot soup into the bowls and top each with:

Two 1-inch-thick slices French bread, toasted (8 slices total)

Sprinkle each bowl with:

3 tablespoons grated Gruyère or Swiss (¾ cup or 3 ounces total)

Broil until the cheese is melted and browned.

TORTILLA SOUP

About 8 cups; 5 servings

For a more substantial soup, divide **2 cups shredded, cooked chicken** among the serving bowls before adding the hot broth, avocado, and garnishes.

Heat a medium cast-iron or other heavy skillet over medium heat. Place in the skillet:

1 or 2 jalapeño peppers
3 large unpeeled garlic cloves
1 onion, peeled and quartered through the root end

Roast in the skillet, turning occasionally, until the peppers are blistered and blackened on all sides, the onion quarters are charred, and the garlic is soft to the touch, 10 to 15 minutes. Once cool, seed and stem the peppers, peel the garlic, and transfer to a blender. Set the onions aside. Add to the blender:

One 14½-ounce can diced tomatoes

Blend to a smooth puree. Heat in a soup pot over medium-high heat:

1 tablespoon vegetable oil

Add the tomato puree to the pot and cook, stirring, until the mixture has darkened and slightly thickened, about 5 minutes. Dice the reserved onion and add to the pot, then add:

6 cups Poultry Stock, 76, Chicken Broth, 81, or other light stock or broth
1 teaspoon dried oregano, preferably Mexican, or ½ teaspoon dried epazote

Simmer, stirring occasionally, for 15 minutes. Meanwhile, have ready:

2 cups tortilla chips

Or heat to 365°F in a heavy skillet:

½ inch vegetable oil

Cut into ¼-inch-wide strips:

4 stale corn tortillas

and fry in the oil until crisp. Drain on paper towels and set aside. Season the broth to taste with:

Salt and black pepper

Divide half of the chips or fried tortilla strips among serving bowls and ladle the broth over them. Top with the remaining tortilla pieces and garnish with:

1 avocado, pitted, peeled, and diced
½ cup crumbled queso fresco or grated Monterey Jack (2 ounces)
Chopped cilantro
(Sour cream)
Lime wedges

ABOUT POULTRY SOUPS

In the recipes below, we call for bone-in chicken, but turkey can be easily substituted, as may stewing hens, which are very flavorful—keeping in mind that both will require a significantly longer simmer. Duck may be used as well, but substitute it for only half of the poultry called for in a recipe the first time you try it (duck is very rich). Duck will also need to be aggressively trimmed of its plentiful fat and skin (or refrigerate the resulting soup overnight to solidify the rendered fat for easy removal).

Skin may be left on chicken pieces for maximum flavor and body, but removing it means you will have less fat to skim off the finished soup. In general, we prefer soups made with bone-in dark meat for its flavor and ease of cooking. ➤ Poultry is done when it pulls away from the bone easily in tender chunks; overcooked poultry becomes stringy. Breasts become particularly unpleasant and dry when simmered too long, so remember to ➤ check bone-in white meat for doneness after 25 minutes of simmering (boneless pieces may need as little as 15 minutes). If using a mixture of white and dark meat in a soup, simply transfer the white meat to a plate when it is done, let the dark meat finish cooking, and add it back in to heat through before serving.

When reheating these soups—especially those with breast meat—do so gently, and just until hot. For other soup-like chicken dishes, try the noodle dish Khao Soi Gai, 303, or hominy-studded posole, 323–24. For thicker poultry stews, see About Poaching, Stewing, and Braising Chicken, 419.

BECKER CHICKEN SOUP

About 7 cups; 4 servings

The flavor of this soup can be enhanced by first browning the chicken pieces and vegetables in vegetable oil (discard any fat left in the pot before proceeding).

Place in a soup pot over medium heat:

8 cups Poultry Stock, 76, Chicken Broth, 81, or water
2 to 2½ pounds bone-in chicken parts, skin removed and trimmed of any fat
3 carrots, diced

3 celery ribs, diced
(2 small parsnips or turnips, peeled and diced)
3 to 4 garlic cloves, coarsely chopped
1 large onion, diced
3 or 4 sprigs parsley
2 or 3 sprigs thyme
1 bay leaf

Bring to a boil, then reduce the heat, partially cover, and simmer for 1 hour 15 minutes, skimming the foam occasionally. Remove from the heat. Transfer the chicken pieces to a platter to cool. Remove the herb sprigs and skim the fat from the broth. When cool enough to handle, pull the meat off the bones, dice or shred, and return to the soup. Gently reheat the soup and stir in, if desired:

(1/4 cup chopped parsley)
(1 1/2 teaspoons curry powder, or to taste)

Season to taste with:

Salt and black pepper

Serve in soup bowls garnished with:

Chopped parsley
Lemon wedges

CHICKEN NOODLE SOUP

Prepare **Becker Chicken Soup, 92.** Cook **4 ounces egg noodles or small pasta, such as orzo or ditalini** in a separate pot of boiling salted water until they are just tender. Divide the pasta among the soup bowls and ladle the soup over them. Garnish and serve as directed.

TREVA'S CHICKEN AND DUMPLINGS

About 14 cups; 6 to 8 servings

Based on Megan's great-grandmother's recipe. You can make this with store-bought chicken stock, a shredded rotisserie chicken, and premade dough, but we can't help but feel that the joy (and richness) of this recipe is in the doing. To use other types of dumplings in this recipe, omit the pie dough and use any recipe for drop dumplings, 305–7.

Place in a large soup pot or Dutch oven:

One 4- to 5-pound chicken, giblets and skin removed
1 carrot, cut into 2-inch pieces
1 celery rib, cut into 2-inch pieces
1 onion, quartered

Add:

Cold water to cover

Bring the water to a boil over high heat, then reduce the heat to low, cover, and simmer until the chicken is very tender and the meat is falling off the bone, about 1 hour. Meanwhile, prepare:

1/2 recipe All-Butter Pie or Pastry Dough, 664

Immediately after mixing the dough, lightly flour a work surface and roll the dough as thin as possible. Cut into 1 1/2 × 4-inch strips, place on a baking sheet, and refrigerate for 1 hour.

When the chicken is cooked, transfer it to a cutting board to cool slightly. Strain the chicken broth; you should have about 12 cups. If not, add additional water or chicken stock to make 12 cups. When the chicken is cool enough to handle, pick the meat off the bones. Skim off any fat.

When the dough strips have chilled, bring the broth to a low simmer and add:

1 1/2 teaspoons salt

Add the dough strips to the gently simmering broth and let them cook, covered, for 15 minutes. Meanwhile, mix together in a medium bowl until smooth:

4 tablespoons (1/2 stick) butter, softened
1/4 cup all-purpose flour

Add to the broth and cook, stirring frequently, until it thickens, about 15 minutes longer. Add the cooked chicken and heat it through, another 5 minutes. Season with:

Salt and black pepper to taste

ASOPAO DE POLLO (PUERTO RICAN CHICKEN AND RICE SOUP)

About 9 cups; 5 servings

Chicken soup may be our go-to when feeling ill, but this recipe is our favorite kind of comfort food: deeply savory chicken and rice with briny, spicy, and herbal accents. After Thanksgiving, we use this recipe as a template for repurposing leftover turkey. To use already cooked poultry, replace the water with **6 cups Poultry Stock, 76.** When the rice is cooked, add **3 to 4 cups cooked, shredded chicken or turkey** and heat through.

Heat in a soup pot over medium heat:

3 tablespoons vegetable oil

Add:

1 onion, diced
1 green bell pepper, diced
1/2 cup diced ham (about 3 ounces)
1 Scotch bonnet pepper or 2 jalapeño peppers, seeded and diced
3 garlic cloves, chopped

Cook, stirring, until the vegetables are tender but not browned, 6 to 8 minutes. Stir in:

2 to 2 1/2 pounds bone-in chicken parts, trimmed of visible fat (skin removed if desired)
6 cups water
1 1/2 cups diced tomatoes or one 14 1/2-ounce can diced tomatoes
(2 teaspoons ground annatto seeds, 953)
1 1/2 teaspoons dried oregano
1/2 teaspoon ground cumin
1/2 teaspoon salt
1/2 teaspoon black pepper

Bring to a boil, then reduce the heat, partially cover, and simmer for 25 minutes. Stir in:

1/2 cup long-grain white rice

Simmer until the chicken and rice are cooked, about 20 minutes. Remove from the heat, remove the chicken, and let cool slightly. Discard the skin and bones, and dice or shred the meat. Return it to the soup and stir in:

1 cup fresh or frozen peas
1/2 cup sliced pimiento-stuffed green olives
Salt to taste

Simmer gently to heat through, 2 to 3 minutes. Divide among soup bowls and garnish with:

Chopped cilantro

TOM KHA GAI (THAI CHICKEN AND GALANGAL SOUP)

About 6 cups; 4 servings

Kha is the Thai word for galangal, 989, a root that somewhat resembles ginger but has a distinctly different flavor.

Combine in a soup pot:

3 cups Poultry Stock, 76, Chicken Broth, 81, or other light stock or broth
One 13½-ounce can coconut milk
4 ounces oyster or shiitake mushrooms, sliced (stems removed if using shiitakes)
6 makrut lime leaves, 998, or 2 lemongrass stalks, cut into 2-inch lengths and lightly pounded with the heel of a knife handle until fragrant
4 fresh red Thai chiles, stemmed, or 3 dried red chiles, such as bird's-eye or árbol, stems and seeds removed
1 small shallot, thinly sliced
1-inch piece galangal or ginger, cut into thin slices

Bring to a low simmer, cover, and cook for 10 minutes. Stir in:

12 ounces boneless, skinless chicken breast or thigh meat, cut into ½-inch cubes
¼ cup lime juice
2 tablespoons fish sauce, or to taste
(1 teaspoon sugar)

Bring back to a simmer and cook, covered, until the chicken is done, 5 to 8 minutes. Remove the lime leaves, dried chiles, and galangal slices, if desired. Taste and add more salt or fish sauce if needed. Serve garnished with:

Chopped cilantro
Lime wedges

COCK-A-LEEKIE

About 8 cups; 5 to 6 servings

We modeled this after Tuppy Glossop's recipe, foolishly passed over by Slingsby Soups.

Split in half and clean thoroughly:

4 medium leeks (about 1½ pounds)

Cut off the tough green tops and reserve. Thinly slice the tender white and light-green parts and set aside. Add the leek tops to a large saucepan along with:

2 pounds bone-in chicken thighs, skin removed and fat trimmed
8 cups water or Brown Beef Stock, 75
¼ cup pearl barley
1 teaspoon salt

Bring to a boil, then reduce the heat, partially cover, and simmer until the chicken is cooked and the barley is tender, 30 to 35 minutes. Fish out and discard the leek greens, and transfer the chicken to a platter to cool slightly. Skim any excess fat from the broth. Add the reserved leek slices to the broth along with:

12 pitted prunes, chopped

Simmer for 10 minutes. Meanwhile, pull the chicken off the bones and shred it. When the leeks are tender, return the chicken to the pot and heat through. Season to taste with:

Salt and black pepper

SOPA DE LIMA (YUCATECAN CHICKEN-LIME SOUP)

11 cups; 5 to 6 servings

This soup is built on a bay- and cinnamon-scented broth, which is then enhanced with tomatoes, chiles, and lime slices. Like any chicken soup, it is restorative during the winter months, but its zingy broth and array of fresh and crunchy garnishes make it perfect for summer dining.

Place in a pot and bring to a simmer over high heat:

1½ pounds bone-in chicken breasts or thighs, skin removed and fat trimmed
8 cups water
1 small onion, thinly sliced
2 garlic cloves, smashed
One 2-inch cinnamon stick, preferably canela, 972
1 bay leaf

Reduce the heat to maintain a simmer and cook, partially covered, until the chicken is tender, about 25 minutes for breasts or 30 to 35 minutes for thighs. Skim off any scum that rises to the surface. While the chicken cooks, make tortilla strips as directed in Tortilla Soup, 92, or have ready:

2 cups tortilla chips

When the chicken has cooked through, transfer to a plate and let cool. Strain the liquid through a sieve into a bowl. Add to the pot over medium heat:

2 tablespoons vegetable oil
1 onion, finely chopped
½ large green bell pepper, finely chopped

Cook until the onions are translucent, about 10 minutes. Add the strained cooking liquid along with:

1 cup diced plum tomatoes or 1 cup canned diced tomatoes
2 garlic cloves, minced
(1 habanero chile, seeded and minced)
1 lime, scrubbed and thinly sliced, or the finely grated zest of 2 limes
1 teaspoon dried oregano, preferably Mexican
1 teaspoon salt
½ teaspoon ground cumin
(⅛ teaspoon ground cloves or allspice)

Bring to a simmer and cook for an additional 15 minutes. Meanwhile, shred or dice the chicken meat and discard the bones or save them for stock. Add the meat to the soup and warm through. Stir in:

Up to ¼ cup lime juice
Salt and black pepper to taste

Fish out the lime slices and ladle the soup into bowls. Top with the tortilla chips or fried tortilla strips, along with:

1 avocado, pitted, peeled, and diced
Chopped cilantro

CHICKEN GUMBO

About 11 cups; 6 servings

This recipe has gone through several incarnations since it first appeared in the original 1931 edition of *Joy*. Irma's version was very brothy and probably unrecognizable as a gumbo. This version walks the line between soup, stew, and fricassee. It is rich, spicy, and made for topping a steaming mound of rice.

Pat dry:

3 pounds bone-in chicken parts

Season with:

1 teaspoon salt
½ teaspoon black pepper

Set aside. Place a Dutch oven over medium heat and add:

8 ounces andouille, kielbasa, or other smoked sausage, cut into ½-inch slices

Cook, stirring until the sausage is well browned. With a slotted spoon, transfer the sausage to a plate lined with paper towels. In the rendered fat in the pot, fry the seasoned chicken pieces in batches until browned on all sides, about 10 minutes per batch (do not crowd the pot). Transfer the chicken pieces to the plate with the sausage and pour the fat into a measuring cup. Add:

Vegetable oil

to reach ½ cup. Pour the oil back into the pot, then whisk in bit by bit:

½ cup all-purpose flour

Cook, stirring frequently, with a wooden spoon over medium heat, until the roux turns dark mahogany brown, about 20 minutes. As the roux darkens, prepare:

1 large onion, chopped
1 large green bell pepper, chopped
2 celery ribs, chopped

Once the roux is ready, add the vegetables and cook, stirring, until softened, about 10 minutes. Whisk in:

8 cups Poultry Stock, 76, Chicken Broth, 81, or other light stock or broth

Bring to a boil, whisking. Reduce the heat and add the chicken along with:

4 garlic cloves, minced
½ teaspoon cayenne pepper

Simmer, uncovered, until the chicken is cooked through, about 25 minutes for breast pieces and 35 minutes for thighs. If desired, you may add for the last 10 minutes of cooking:

(1 cup sliced okra)

When the chicken is done, you can serve the pieces whole and provide knives to your guests, or remove them from the pot, let cool, and remove the bones and skin. Shred or coarsely chop the meat, and add it back to the pot, then add:

4 green onions, chopped

Skim excess fat from the top of the soup. Season to taste with:

Salt
Louisiana-style hot sauce

Serve over:

Cooked white rice, 343

Garnish with:

Sliced green onions

If desired, serve with a shaker of:

(Filé powder, 543)

MULLIGATAWNY SOUP

About 6 cups; 4 servings

A comforting, Anglo-Indian classic.

Heat in a soup pot over medium heat:

4 tablespoons (½ stick) butter or ¼ cup vegetable oil

Add and cook, stirring, until softened:

1 onion, diced
1 carrot, diced
1 celery rib, diced

Stir in:

1½ tablespoons all-purpose flour
1-inch piece ginger, peeled and minced
2 garlic cloves, minced
1 tablespoon curry powder

Cook for another 3 minutes. Add:

4 cups Poultry Stock, 76, Chicken Broth, 81, or other light stock or broth
8 ounces boneless, skinless chicken thighs, cut into ½-inch chunks
½ cup long-grain white rice
½ to 1 teaspoon salt, to taste
¼ teaspoon black pepper
¼ teaspoon dried thyme
1 bay leaf

Simmer, partially covered, until the rice is tender, about 20 minutes, then remove the bay leaf. Immediately before serving, stir in:

½ cup heavy cream or canned coconut milk
½ cup diced tart apples

Heat through, but do not boil. Top each soup bowl with:

(A spoonful of yogurt)
Chopped cilantro

Serve with:

Lemon wedges

ABOUT BEEF, PORK, AND LAMB SOUPS

With the exception of Spicy Sichuan Hot Pot, 97, the soups here require long simmering. Tougher cuts of meat have the most flavor and thus make the best soups, but they need time to become fully tender and surrender their gelatin to the broth. For thicker meat stews, see our sections on braising and stewing beef, 463, veal, 476, lamb, 481, goat, 484, pork, 494, and our recipes for chili, 502–3.

BEEF BARLEY SOUP

About 8 cups; 4 servings

For **Mushroom Barley Soup,** omit the beef. Begin by heating the butter or oil over medium heat. Add the mushrooms and shallot and proceed as directed.

Season:

1 pound beef chuck or brisket, cut into 1-inch cubes

with:

½ teaspoon salt
½ teaspoon black pepper

Heat in a soup pot or Dutch oven over medium-high heat:

1 tablespoon vegetable oil

Brown the beef on all sides in batches without crowding the pot. Transfer to a plate and set aside. Reduce the heat to medium, pour off any drippings, and add:

4 tablespoons (½ stick) butter or ¼ cup olive oil

Add:

1½ pounds mushrooms, sliced
1 large shallot, finely chopped

Cook, stirring often, until the mushrooms are wilted, about 10 minutes. Add:

¼ cup dry sherry, Madeira, stock, or water
1 tablespoon chopped fresh thyme or 1 teaspoon dried thyme

Reduce the heat to low and scrape any browned bits off the bottom of the pot. Return the beef to the pot, along with:

4 cups Brown Beef Stock, 75, Brown Vegetable Stock, 78, or Beef Broth, 81
¾ cup pearl barley
½ teaspoon salt
½ teaspoon black pepper

Bring to a boil, then reduce the heat, cover, and simmer until the barley is tender, about 1 hour. Taste and add salt if needed. Serve garnished with:

Chopped parsley or thyme leaves

POT-AU-FEU (FRENCH SIMMERED BEEF AND VEGETABLES)

10 to 15 servings

This is much more than a soup; think of it as a fancy New England Boiled Dinner, 472, or a subtly spiced hot pot where everything is cooked together. Prepared with chicken alone, it is called **Poule au Pot**.

Combine in a very large soup pot:

4 quarts water, Brown Beef Stock, 75, Poultry Stock, 76, or a combination
4 pounds beef chuck roast or brisket, rolled if necessary and tightly tied
(1½ pounds marrow bones, oxtails, or beef neck bones)
2 onions, each stuck with 2 whole cloves
2 carrots, chopped
2 celery ribs, chopped

Bring to a boil, then reduce the heat to low, partially cover, and simmer, skimming occasionally, for 1½ hours. Add:

4 chicken legs, separated at the joint into thighs and drumsticks, skin removed

Simmer, partially covered, skimming occasionally, for 30 minutes. Preheat the oven to 200°F. With a slotted spoon, transfer the beef, bones, and chicken to a rimmed baking sheet, tent with foil, and keep warm in the oven. Strain the broth and discard the vegetables. Return the broth to the pot, bring back to a simmer, and add:

(1 pound smoked sausages)
4 carrots, cut into 3-inch pieces
4 leeks, halved lengthwise and well cleaned
2 turnips, peeled and cut into 1-inch-thick wedges
3 celery ribs, cut into 3-inch pieces
1 small head cabbage, cut into 1-inch-thick wedges
4 sprigs parsley
3 sprigs thyme
1 bay leaf

Simmer, covered, until the vegetables are tender, 30 to 45 minutes. Discard the herbs and transfer the vegetables to a large platter. For a clearer broth, strain again. Slice the beef and sausages, if using, and arrange with the vegetables on the platter. Skim the fat from the broth and season to taste with:

Salt and black pepper

Ladle the broth into bowls. Pass the meat and vegetable platter after the broth, accompanied with:

Dijon mustard
Flaky sea salt
Cornichons
Toasted baguette slices

PHO BO (VIETNAMESE BEEF NOODLE SOUP)

4 or 5 servings

Asian markets often sell thinly sliced round steak for adding to hot pots and *pho*. If you cannot find it, buy a portion of eye-of-round roast and slice it yourself with a very sharp knife. The meat is easier to slice thinly if placed in the freezer for 20 minutes beforehand.

I. Place in a large soup pot:

2½ pounds meaty beef bones
2½ pounds oxtails, cut into 2-inch pieces

Add water to cover and bring just to a rolling boil, then drain the liquid from the pot into the sink. Rinse out any scum from the pot and rinse the bones. Return the bones to the pot, then add:

14 cups water
1 pound beef brisket, trimmed of excess fat
(¼ cup dried shrimp, 1016)
4 whole star anise
1 tablespoon salt
1 tablespoon sugar or one ½-inch piece Chinese rock sugar
1 cinnamon stick
(1 Chinese black cardamom pod, 962, crushed)

Bring to a boil over high heat. Meanwhile, in a dry skillet over medium-high heat, or with long metal tongs over an open flame, char:

One 3-inch piece ginger, unpeeled
1 large unpeeled onion, quartered through the stem, or 12 ounces unpeeled shallots, halved

When the pieces are blackened all over, transfer to a plate. Once cool, peel the charred skin off the ginger and onions or shallots, coarsely chop them, and add to the soup pot. When the water comes to a boil, reduce the heat, partially cover, and simmer for 3 hours, occasionally skimming off any scum for the first hour. If desired, halfway through cooking, add:

(12 ounces honeycomb tripe, prepared, 518, and sliced into shreds)

Thirty minutes before serving, soak in hot water to cover:

12 ounces dried rice stick noodles (banh pho)

Mound the following garnishes on a plate:

2 cups mung bean sprouts
5 bushy sprigs basil, preferably the purplish Thai variety
10 sprigs cilantro or culantro leaves
2 limes, quartered
3 serrano or 2 jalapeño peppers, thinly sliced

When ready to serve, strain the broth and discard the bones. Skim any excess fat from the broth and transfer to a stock pot or large saucepan. Thinly slice the brisket. Bring the broth to a boil over high heat. Divide the soaked noodles and brisket among 4 or 5 heated soup bowls. Divide among the bowls:

12 ounces raw eye-of-round steak, very thinly sliced
1 small onion, very thinly sliced, or 5 green onions, sliced on the diagonal

Fill each bowl with boiling broth and serve. Place the garnishes in the center of the table (tear the herb leaves before adding to the soup for the most fragrance). Each diner should season their own bowl to taste with:

Fish sauce
Hoisin sauce
Sriracha
(Thai fried chili paste, 969)

II. PRESSURE COOKER PHO

Before proceeding, be sure your pressure cooker has a 10-quart capacity. Prepare the soup as directed above, using the pressure cooker instead of a pot. After adding the charred ginger and onion to the pot, place the lid on the pressure cooker and bring up to high pressure. Cook for 1½ hours, then use the quick-release method to release the pressure, 1059. If using the optional tripe, after 45 minutes of cooking use the quick-release method to release the pressure, open the pressure cooker, and add the tripe. Place the lid back on the pressure cooker and bring back to high pressure to cook 45 minutes more. Proceed as directed.

SPICY SICHUAN HOT POT

6 to 8 servings

Hot pots are a wonderful, participatory form of eating and well suited to parties (the informal kind, with people you do not mind making a mess with). This broth is quite powerful, an example of *ma la*, or the numbing-hot sensation found in many Sichuan dishes. The heat comes from dried chiles and Sichuan chili bean paste, 970, and the numbing effect from Sichuan peppercorns. This broth is often served alongside a tamer counterpart, essentially a light pork and chicken stock. If desired, prepare Poultry Stock, 76, Pork or Ham Stock, 76, or use half chicken and half pork bones to make a stock to serve alongside the one below. To make slicing easier, place meats in the freezer for 20 minutes beforehand. Alternatively, thinly sliced meats for hot pot are often available in the freezer section of Asian grocery stores.

Puree in a food processor until smooth:

1 cup Sichuan chili bean paste, 970
¼ cup fermented black beans, 983
One 3-inch piece ginger, peeled and chopped
5 garlic cloves, coarsely chopped

Set the paste aside. Heat in a wok or large heavy-bottomed pot over medium heat:

1¼ cups combination of vegetable oil and lard or beef tallow

When the oil shimmers, add and allow to fry until fragrant, about 3 minutes:

8 dried Chinese or Thai red chiles or chiles de árbol, stemmed and seeded

Carefully add the paste to the oil along with:

1 tablespoon Sichuan peppercorns
2 whole star anise
One 3-inch cinnamon stick
(1 Chinese black cardamom pod, 962, crushed)
4 green cardamom pods, crushed

Allow to sizzle in the hot oil until very fragrant and the oil turns bright red, about 1 minute. Add slowly:

8 cups Brown Beef Stock, 75, or Beef Broth, 81, Poultry Stock, 76, or Chicken Broth, 81
½ cup Shaoxing wine, 952
1 tablespoon sugar

Simmer the broth for 15 minutes to allow the flavors to meld. Meanwhile, cook, 343:

2 cups short-grain white rice

Prepare an array of meats and vegetables to dip in the hot pot:

2 pounds mixed raw meats such as very thinly sliced pork, lamb, beef, and/or chicken; bite-sized pieces of Chinese sausages; meatballs or fish balls; large shrimp (16/20)
1 pound mixed vegetables such as quartered baby bok choy; enoki, shiitake, or button mushrooms; sliced daikon radish or kohlrabi; 1-inch cubes of potato or sweet potato; mature spinach leaves; 3-inch pieces of green onion
12 ounces firm tofu, cut into 1-inch cubes, and/or yuba (tofu skins)

Combine in a small measuring cup:

½ cup soy sauce
¼ cup toasted sesame oil
3 garlic cloves, minced

Pour the soy sauce mixture into a small cup or bowl for each guest. Give each guest a bowl of cooked rice. Place the pot of broth on a hot plate in the center of the dining table. Adjust the heat to maintain a low simmer.

To serve, have guests add ingredients of their choosing to the simmering broth in small batches. Allow the items to cook (things like potatoes will take a little while; others, like spinach leaves or very thinly sliced pork, will be done in seconds). When they are done, use a small spider or skimmer to fish them out. Have each guest transfer the cooked ingredients to their bowl of rice where they can dip the items in the dipping sauce and eat.

Since this is a communal meal, don't get too attached to specific items added to the hot pot. There should be enough of each ingredient to satisfy everyone. At the end of the meal, the bowls of rice will be highly seasoned from the broth and oil that dripped off the items cooked in the hot pot. Eat the rice as the final course of the meal. Because this hot pot is so richly flavored, we like to finish the meal by serving tangerines, or another sweet-tart fruit, although this is our own invention, and not traditional.

BORSCHT WITH MEAT

About 10 cups; 5 to 6 servings

This hearty but not heavy soup is a staple in our winter repertoire. We sometimes substitute **1 cup drained sauerkraut** for the shredded cabbage (season with the red wine vinegar to taste).

Sprinkle:

1 pound boneless beef chuck or lamb shoulder, cut into 1-inch cubes

with:

1 teaspoon salt
½ teaspoon black pepper

Heat in a soup pot or Dutch oven over medium-high heat:

2 tablespoons vegetable oil

Add the meat and brown on all sides. Transfer the meat to a plate and pour off all but 2 tablespoons of the fat. Add to the pot:

1 onion, chopped
2 carrots, sliced
2 celery ribs, sliced
2 garlic cloves, minced

Cook, stirring, until the vegetables are slightly softened, about 5 minutes. Return the meat to the pot along with:

4 cups beef, chicken, or vegetable stock or broth, or water, or a combination
One 28-ounce can whole tomatoes, drained and chopped
2 medium beets (12 to 16 ounces), peeled and cut into ½-inch pieces
(1 tablespoon sweet paprika, plain or smoked)
1½ teaspoons tomato paste

Bring to a boil, then reduce the heat, partially cover, and simmer until the vegetables and meat are tender, about 1 hour. Stir in:

2 cups shredded green or red cabbage
2 tablespoons red wine vinegar

Simmer, partially covered, for 15 minutes. Season to taste with:

Salt and black pepper

Garnish each serving with:

Sour cream
Chopped dill, minced chives, grated peeled horseradish, and/or grated lemon zest

SCOTCH BROTH

About 6 cups; 4 servings

Irma and Marion used *grünkern*, or freekeh, 337, in place of the barley called for here. To substitute freekeh, add whole grains 20 minutes after the vegetables are added; for cracked freekeh, simmer for the last 25 minutes of cooking.

Combine in a soup pot:

6 cups water
1½ pounds boneless lamb shoulder, trimmed of fat and cut into ½-inch pieces

Bring to a boil, then reduce the heat and simmer for 10 minutes, skimming to remove scum. Stir in:

½ cup pearl barley
3 medium leeks, white part only, well rinsed and chopped
1 large carrot, diced
1 large celery rib, diced
½ teaspoon salt

Bring to a boil, then reduce the heat, partially cover, and simmer until the meat is tender, about 1½ hours. Add water as needed. Spoon off the fat from the surface and season with:

2 tablespoons chopped parsley
Salt and black pepper to taste

CALDO VERDE (PORTUGUESE GREENS SOUP)

About 10 cups; 5 to 6 servings

A family favorite, and an inspiration to use greens in many of our soups. For a soup with even more character, swap in mustard greens for half of the milder ones listed below.

Heat in a large soup pot over medium heat:

2 tablespoons olive oil

Add and cook, stirring, until tender but not browned, 6 to 8 minutes:

1 onion, chopped
2 garlic cloves, minced

Stir in:

8 cups Poultry Stock, 76, Chicken Broth, 81, or other light stock or broth
1½ pounds gold or red potatoes, well scrubbed or peeled, thinly sliced
1½ teaspoons salt
½ teaspoon black pepper

Bring to a boil, then reduce the heat and simmer until the potatoes are soft, about 20 minutes. Remove the pot from the heat. Using a potato masher, lightly mash the potatoes in the pot. Heat in a medium skillet over medium-high heat:

1 tablespoon vegetable oil

Add and cook, stirring, until browned:

6 ounces Portuguese linguiça, kielbasa, or andouille, or 4 ounces cured chorizo, thinly sliced

Add to the pot. Discard any oil left in the skillet and pour 1 cup of the soup into the skillet. Scrape up the browned bits and return the liquid to the soup. Simmer for 5 minutes. Stir in:

8 ounces kale or collard greens, deribbed, or whole chard leaves, thinly sliced

Simmer 5 minutes more. Stir in:

2 tablespoons lemon juice

ITALIAN WEDDING SOUP

About 11 cups; 6 servings

Once the meatball mixture is assembled, this flavorful soup comes together quickly. If desired, prepare the meatballs a day ahead of time and refrigerate, covered, or freeze. The egg-Parmesan mixture adds richness and body, but if you prefer a clear Italian wedding soup, it may be omitted.

Prepare the mixture for:

Italian Meatballs, 507

Form into ½- to ¾-inch meatballs (a heaping ½ teaspoon of the meat mixture apiece) and set aside. Bring to a boil in a soup pot or Dutch oven:

8 cups Poultry Stock, 76, Chicken Broth, 81, or other light stock or broth

Season to taste with:

Salt and black pepper

Reduce the heat so it simmers gently. Carefully lower the meatballs into the simmering stock along with:

12 ounces escarole, chard, or curly endive, coarsely chopped

Simmer for 15 minutes. Whisk together in a small bowl until well combined:

2 eggs
1/4 cup grated Romano or Parmesan

With the broth simmering, hold the bowl in one hand, 5 inches above the rim of the pot. Pour a little of the beaten egg at a time in a thin stream into the broth. As you pour, stir wide circles on the surface of the broth with a fork, catching the egg as it strikes and drawing it out into long filmy threads. After ladling the soup into bowls, add to each bowl, if desired:

(2 tablespoons cooked acini de pepe, orzo, or other small pasta; 3/4 cup total)

PEPPER POT

About 9 cups; 5 servings

A Philadelphia specialty dating from the founding of our nation, this tripe soup was sold on the street with cries of "All hot! Pepper pot! Makes backs strong, makes lives long! Pepper pot!" Though delicious, this mild-mannered soup does not really live up to its name, and most likely originates from spicier recipes brought by slaves from the West Indies (like Guyanese Pepperpot, 468). This recipe first appeared in *Joy* in 1936.

Have ready:

12 ounces honeycomb tripe, prepared, 518

Cut the tripe into fine shreds and set aside. Cook in a soup pot or Dutch oven over medium heat:

4 slices bacon, chopped

Add and cook, stirring until softened, about 5 minutes:

1 large onion, chopped
2 celery ribs, chopped
2 green bell peppers, chopped

Add:

8 cups Brown Beef Stock, 75, White Veal Stock, 76, or Poultry Stock, 76
1 bay leaf

Bring to a boil and add the reserved tripe. Bring to a simmer, reduce the heat, cover, and cook until the tripe is tender, 1½ to 2 hours. Add:

1 cup diced peeled red or gold potatoes
(1 teaspoon dried marjoram or savory)
1/2 teaspoon black pepper

Gently simmer, uncovered, until the potatoes are tender, about 15 minutes more. Meanwhile, work together in a small bowl with your fingers until smooth:

2 tablespoons butter, softened
2 tablespoons all-purpose flour

When the potatoes are done, remove the bay leaf. Add the butter mixture gradually to the pot, stirring until dissolved. Simmer for 5 minutes, then stir in:

1/2 cup heavy cream

Heat through, but do not boil. Season to taste with:

Salt and black pepper

ABOUT FISH AND SHELLFISH SOUPS

Most seafood cooks very quickly, resulting in hearty, flavorful soups in comparatively little time. **Chowders** are cooked with diced potato, which lends them body, and are further enriched with milk or cream. **Bisques** have a smoother texture, punctuated with chunks of fish or shellfish. They are spiked with cream as well, and often another thickener, such as pureed cooked rice or eggs. **Fishermen's stews** like Bouillabaisse, 102, and Cioppino, 102, have particularly flavorful broths, and are often populated with several types of fish and shellfish. Though today this medley of sea creatures seems luxurious, it is a relic of quite the opposite: These stews were originally concocted to use the portion of the catch that would not fetch a good price at market—and to ensure that even those who came in empty-handed were still able to fill their bellies. In this same spirit of frugality, we encourage you to experiment with a combination of what is freshest in your area and within your budget. Results vary—often deliciously.

For advice on choosing fresh fish at the market, see 373; for shellfish, see 346. Fish and shrimp should be fresh or frozen, never canned. Canned clams and pasteurized oysters are fine to use in chowders and stews, but when available, choose fresh, live mussels, clams, and oysters for more flavorful results. ➤ When shucking oysters, 349, do not waste any of their precious liquor.

Fish and shellfish stocks can be made quickly, 77; if a large supply of bones, heads, or shells are not on hand, see Quick Seafood Stock, 80. For strongly seasoned soups like Tom Yum Goong, 101, a white chicken stock may be substituted for fish stock as well.

A potential downside to seafood soups being so quick to cook: ➤ They are easy to overcook. Remove fish from the pot—or the pot from the heat—as soon as it is cooked through. Oysters, clams, and mussels, need so little heat that the stock and vegetables are simmered first and the shellfish just heated through before serving.

Sometimes, cooked fish and shellfish are served on the side to ensure they do not overcook in the broth, but we find this presentation a little tedious. With the exception of most chowders, which tend to sit well overnight, seafood soups are best eaten as soon as they are cooked. If you need to reheat them, do so gently (a double boiler comes in handy for this task).

CHARLESTON SHE-CRAB SOUP

About 4 cups; 4 servings

"She-crab" alludes to the traditional use of female crabs in this soup, along with their ruby-red roe. To use fresh crabs (and, potentially, their roe) you will need approximately **6 pounds blue crabs or 4 pounds Dungeness crabs.** Poach or boil if necessary, 358, crack the shells and pick the meat out, 357, and proceed as directed, adding any roe along with the crabmeat.

Melt in a large saucepan over low heat:

2 tablespoons butter

Whisk in:

2 tablespoons all-purpose flour

Cook, whisking, until the flour smells toasted but is not browned, about 3 minutes. Remove the pan from the heat and slowly whisk in:

3 cups milk

Return to the heat, bring to a simmer, and cook over medium-low heat whisking constantly, until thickened and smooth. Reduce the heat to low and stir in:

1 pound lump crabmeat, picked over for shells and cartilage
1 to 2 tablespoons dry sherry
½ teaspoon salt
1 teaspoon Worcestershire sauce
(½ teaspoon hot pepper sauce, or to taste)
⅛ teaspoon ground mace

Adjust the seasonings. Heat gently just until the crab is warmed through. Garnish with:

Thinly sliced green onions

LOBSTER BISQUE

About 6 cups; 4 servings

Make no mistake: Lobster bisque is a laborious dish, but sometimes nothing else will do. Serve with a salad of butter lettuce and plenty of toasted bread.

Remove the meat and coral (roe), if any, from:

2 medium lobsters (about 3 pounds), steamed, 360

Shred the meat, leaving some pieces in large chunks. Place the shells between two kitchen towels and coarsely crush them using a cast-iron skillet or a rolling pin. Use the shells to make:

Shrimp or Shellfish Stock, 78, using 4 cups bottled clam juice and 2 cups water

Strain the stock through a fine-mesh sieve into a medium saucepan, pressing on the shells to extract as much liquid as possible. Add to the stock:

½ cup long-grain white rice
½ cup dry sherry
2 tablespoons tomato paste
½ teaspoon salt
¼ teaspoon black pepper

Bring to a simmer, cover, and cook until the rice is very tender, about 25 minutes. Transfer to a blender and blend until completely smooth. Transfer the mixture back to the saucepan, passing it through a fine-mesh sieve, if desired. Force the reserved roe, if any, through a fine-mesh sieve into the bisque. Bring to a bare simmer over medium heat. Whisk in:

1 cup heavy cream or crème fraîche
¼ teaspoon ground nutmeg
⅛ teaspoon cayenne pepper

Stir in the reserved lobster meat and heat through. Add more salt and black pepper to taste, if needed. Serve at once, garnished with:

Minced parsley and/or chives
Sweet paprika

BILLI-BI (CREAM OF MUSSEL SOUP)

About 4 cups; 3 servings

Place in a large soup pot:

3 pounds small mussels, scrubbed and debearded, 350
1½ cups dry white wine
⅓ cup chopped shallots
5 sprigs parsley
3 sprigs thyme

Cover and steam over medium heat until the mussels open; discard any that do not open. Remove the mussels and set aside. Strain the cooking liquid through a sieve lined with several layers of dampened cheesecloth or paper towels into a medium saucepan. Bring to a simmer. Remove the mussels from their shells. Whisk together in a small bowl:

½ cup heavy cream or half-and-half
1 egg yolk

Gradually whisk about 1 cup of the cooking liquid into the egg mixture, then whisk back into the saucepan. Heat through, but do not boil. Season with:

Salt and white or cayenne pepper to taste
(½ teaspoon curry powder)

Garnish with the reserved mussels and sprinkle with:

Minced chives

OYSTER STEW

About 4 cups; 3 servings

We recommend buying shucked oysters for this recipe: shucking dozens of oysters can get old (and expensive). To shuck live oysters, see 349.

Combine in a pot or large saucepan over medium-low heat:

4 tablespoons (½ stick) butter
1 celery rib, minced
½ small onion or white leek bottom, well cleaned and minced
1 garlic clove, minced

Cook, stirring, until the butter is melted and the onion and celery are tender but not browned, about 7 minutes. Remove from the heat and stir in:

1 to 1½ pints shucked oysters, coarsely chopped, with their liquor (20 to 30 large or extra-large oysters in the shell)
1½ cups milk
½ cup heavy cream
½ teaspoon salt
⅛ teaspoon white pepper or sweet paprika

Set over medium heat and stir frequently. When the milk is steaming and the oysters float, add:

2 tablespoons chopped parsley

OYSTER BISQUE

Prepare **Oyster Stew, above.** Before adding the parsley, remove the soup from the heat. Beat **2 egg yolks** in a small bowl and whisk in a small quantity of hot soup. Slowly stir this mixture into the hot soup. Heat over low heat for 1 minute; do not allow to boil. Add the parsley and serve at once.

TOM YUM GOONG (THAI HOT-AND-SOUR SHRIMP SOUP)

About 7 cups; 4 servings

This intensely aromatic, spicy, and sour soup is truly revivifying. Once you find the ingredients, it comes together remarkably quickly.

Rinse:

1¼ pounds large (16/20) shell-on shrimp (preferably head-on)

Peel and devein them, 363, collecting the shells, tails, and any heads in a soup pot. Transfer the shrimp to a bowl and set aside. Add to the pot:

5 cups water

Bring to a boil, then reduce the heat to a simmer, cover, and cook for 20 minutes. Strain the liquid into a bowl, pressing on the shells to extract all the juices. Discard the shells. Return the stock to the pot and add:

1 lemongrass stalk, trimmed and bruised, 998
1 small onion or shallot, thinly sliced
1-inch piece galangal or ginger, peeled and thinly sliced
4 ounces oyster mushrooms, sliced, or 6 ounces shiitake mushrooms, stems removed and caps sliced
5 makrut lime leaves, 998
½ teaspoon Thai fried chili paste, 969, or 4 to 6 dried bird's eye chiles, stemmed and lightly crushed
2 teaspoons sugar

Bring to a simmer and cook, covered, for 10 minutes. Add the peeled shrimp, return to a simmer, and just cook them through, about 5 minutes. Add:

¼ to ⅓ cup lime juice, to taste
2 to 3 tablespoons fish sauce, to taste

Serve garnished with:

Chopped cilantro
Lime wedges

SEAFOOD GUMBO

About 9 cups; 5 to 6 servings

Brown in a Dutch oven over medium heat:

8 ounces andouille sausage or tasso ham, cut into ½-inch-thick slices or chunks

Transfer to paper towels to drain. Drain the rendered fat from the pot and add:

4 tablespoons (½ stick) butter
¼ cup vegetable oil

Once the butter has melted, whisk in a little at a time:

½ cup all-purpose flour

Cook, stirring constantly with a wooden spoon or whisk until the roux turns dark mahogany brown, about 20 minutes. Add and cook, stirring, until softened, about 10 minutes:

2 onions, chopped
3 celery ribs, chopped
1 large green bell pepper, chopped

Add and cook, stirring, for another 3 minutes:

4 to 6 garlic cloves, minced
1 to 2 jalapeño or serrano peppers, seeded and minced
1 bay leaf
1 teaspoon salt
1 teaspoon black pepper
1 teaspoon dried thyme
1 teaspoon dried oregano
½ teaspoon cayenne pepper

Add:

5 cups Shrimp or Shellfish Stock, 78, Fish Stock, 77, Quick Seafood Stock, 80, Poultry Stock, 76, or Chicken Broth, 81

Bring to a boil, add the reserved browned sausage, and simmer for 20 minutes. Add:

8 ounces peeled shrimp
8 ounces lump crabmeat, picked over for shells and cartilage
(1½ cups sliced okra)

Return to a boil, then reduce the heat and simmer for another 10 minutes. Add:

16 medium to large live oysters, shucked, 349, with juices strained and added, or about 1 pint of pasteurized oysters, with their liquor

Heat just until the oysters are plump. Season with:

Salt and black pepper to taste

Serve over:

Cooked jasmine rice, 343

Sprinkle with:

Chopped parsley or celery leaves
Chopped green onion

Have on the table:

(Filé powder, 543)
Louisiana-style hot sauce

CARIBBEAN CALLALOO

About 11 cups; 6 servings

Callaloo is not only the name of this dish, which varies from country to country, but also refers to a number of different leafy greens throughout the Caribbean region, from taro and okra leaves to amaranth greens. Use any of these, or the chard and spinach suggested below. For more information, see About Greens for Cooking, 242.

Place in a soup pot and cook, stirring, over medium heat until almost crisp:

3 slices bacon, cut into 1-inch pieces

Leaving the bacon in the pot, pour off all but 2 tablespoons of the fat. Add and cook, stirring, until the onion is tender but not browned, 6 to 8 minutes:

1 onion, chopped
1 garlic clove, minced
3 green onions, thinly sliced

Stir in:

1 pound callaloo, mature spinach, kale, or chard, trimmed and coarsely chopped
4 cups Poultry Stock, 76, Chicken Broth, 81, or other light stock or broth
1 cup canned coconut milk

1 to 2 Scotch bonnet or habanero peppers, seeded and minced
1 teaspoon salt
¼ teaspoon dried thyme

Cover, bring to a boil, then reduce the heat and simmer for 5 minutes. Uncover and add:

8 ounces white fish fillets (tilefish, cod, grouper, orange roughy, or sea bass)
1 cup sliced okra or frozen sliced okra

Simmer until the okra and fish are cooked, about 10 minutes. Break up the fillets with a spoon and add:

8 ounces lump crabmeat, picked over for shells and cartilage, or small peeled raw shrimp

Let the shellfish heat through for about 3 minutes more. Season to taste with:

Salt and black pepper

Garnish with:

Chopped cilantro

LOUISIANA COURT BOUILLON

About 7 cups; 4 servings

Heat in a large skillet over medium heat:

3 tablespoons vegetable oil

Add and cook, stirring, until lightly browned, about 5 minutes:

3 tablespoons all-purpose flour

Add and cook, stirring, just until softened, 6 to 8 minutes:

½ small green bell pepper, diced
1 small celery rib, diced
½ small onion, diced
2 garlic cloves, minced
½ teaspoon dried thyme

Stir in:

One 28-ounce can whole tomatoes, drained and coarsely chopped
2 cups Fish Stock, 77, Shrimp or Shellfish Stock, 78, or Quick Seafood Stock, 80

Bring to a boil, reduce the heat to medium-low, and simmer for 10 minutes. Stir in:

1 pound white fish fillets (tilefish, cod, grouper, orange roughy, or sea bass), cut into 2-inch pieces
12 small shrimp, peeled and deveined, 363 (about 4 ounces)

Cover and cook until the fish is opaque throughout, 3 to 5 minutes. Season with:

2 teaspoons Worcestershire sauce or 1 teaspoon salt
Louisiana-style hot sauce to taste

Stir in:

¾ cup cooked long-grain white rice, 343

CIOPPINO

4 to 6 servings

A classic fisherman's stew from San Francisco. For the yield listed, choose clams or mussels, not both. If Dungeness crabs are not available, blue crabs or lobsters may be substituted. If the crabs are already cooked, clean them, crack open the claws and legs as directed, and add with the clams. You may also substitute **12 ounces lump crabmeat**, picked over for shells and cartilage (just add the crabmeat and heat it through before adding the herbs and lemon juice).

Kill, 356:

2 live Dungeness crabs (about 4 pounds)

Crack the claws once or twice to expose the meat. Remove and discard the top shell, gills, and viscera, and cut the body into 4 pieces. Set aside. Add to a soup pot or Dutch oven over medium heat:

3 tablespoons olive oil
(1 small fennel bulb, quartered, cored, and thinly sliced)
6 garlic cloves, chopped
2 dried red chiles or ½ teaspoon red pepper flakes

Cook until fragrant, about 2 minutes. Increase the heat to high and add the crab pieces along with:

One 28-ounce can whole tomatoes, chopped or crushed
3 cups Shrimp or Shellfish Stock, 76, Poultry Stock, 78, or 2 cups water and one 8-ounce bottle clam juice
1½ cups dry white wine
2 wide strips lemon zest

Bring to a simmer, reduce the heat to medium, cover, and cook for 5 minutes. Add to the pot if using:

(16 small hard-shell clams, scrubbed)

Cover and cook for 5 minutes. Add:

1 pound firm white fish fillets (halibut, rockfish, or cod), cut into 1-inch cubes
(16 mussels, scrubbed and debearded, 350)

Cover and cook until any shellfish have opened, about 5 minutes longer. Remove from the heat. If desired, you may pick the meat from the crab, or provide lobster or crab crackers (along with plenty of napkins) for diners at the table. Divide the seafood among soup bowls. Stir into the broth:

2 tablespoons chopped basil
2 tablespoons chopped parsley
Lemon juice to taste
Salt and black pepper to taste

Ladle the broth over the seafood. Serve with a bowl to collect shells and:

Hunks of warmed French bread or Crostini, 49

BOUILLABAISSE

About 10 cups; 5 to 6 servings

Many insist that the unique flavor of this dish depends on fish native to the Mediterranean alone. Regardless of how it compares to the original, we have enjoyed many bouillabaisse variations made with fresh fish from our shores.

Heat in a soup pot over medium heat until the butter is melted:

1 tablespoon olive oil
1 tablespoon butter

Add and cook, stirring occasionally, until the vegetables are tender but not browned, 6 to 8 minutes:

1 leek, halved lengthwise, well cleaned, and cut into ½-inch pieces
1 small fennel bulb, quartered, cored, and thinly sliced
1 celery rib, thinly sliced on the diagonal
1 bay leaf

(1 whole star anise or ¼ teaspoon anise seeds or fennel seeds)
(Zest of ½ orange, removed in large strips with a vegetable peeler)
½ teaspoon salt
¼ teaspoon saffron threads

Add and cook, stirring, for 3 minutes:

3 garlic cloves, minced
1 tablespoon tomato paste

Add:

4 cups Fish Stock, 77, Shrimp or Shellfish Stock, 78, or Quick Seafood Stock, 80
1½ cups canned crushed tomatoes
½ cup dry white wine
¾ teaspoon salt

Bring to a boil, then reduce the heat, cover, and simmer for 20 minutes. Increase the heat and bring to a boil. Add:

12 littleneck clams, scrubbed
2 tablespoons olive oil

Cook, covered, for 3 minutes. Stir in:

12 ounces monkfish, sea bass, red snapper, or halibut fillets, or a combination, cut into 1½-inch pieces

Cook, covered, for 1 minute. Stir in:

8 ounces sea scallops

Cook just until the seafood is done, 2 to 3 minutes more. Discard any clams that are not open. Remove the star anise, orange zest, and bay leaf. If desired, stir in:

(1 to 2 tablespoons anisette or Pernod)

Divide the seafood and broth among soup bowls. Top:

5 or 6 slices toasted French bread

with a small dollop of:

Rouille, 565

and place a slice on each serving. Pass the remaining rouille separately.

NEW ENGLAND CLAM CHOWDER

5 to 6 cups; 4 servings

I. If using the larger, tougher chowder-sized quahog clams, chop the meat finely before adding.

Scrub:

5 pounds or 2½ to 3 quarts littleneck, topneck, or other hard-shell clams

Place the clams in a large soup pot and add:

2 cups water
(Any scraps of onion, celery, thyme, or bay leaf)

Cover and steam over high heat until the clams open, 5 to 10 minutes. Transfer the clams to a bowl, discarding any that do not open (reserve the cooking liquid). Remove the clams from their shells, holding them over the bowl to catch any juices. Coarsely chop the clams and set aside. Line a fine-mesh sieve with several layers of cheesecloth and strain the cooking liquid from the pot and any juices from the bowl into a measuring cup. You should have about 4 cups; if there is less, add:

(Water or bottled clam juice as needed)

Add to a soup pot over medium heat:

2 ounces salt pork or bacon, diced

Cook, stirring occasionally, until browned and crisp. Using a slotted spoon, transfer the pork to paper towels to drain. Add to the pot:

1 tablespoon butter
1 onion, diced
½ teaspoon chopped thyme
1 bay leaf

Cook, stirring, until the onion is translucent, about 5 minutes. Add and stir until blended and lightly browned:

1 tablespoon all-purpose flour

Add the reserved cooking liquid and:

8 ounces red potatoes, cut into ½-inch pieces

Bring to a boil, reduce the heat, and simmer until the potatoes are tender, about 15 minutes. Remove the bay leaf. Stir in the chopped clams and reserved pork along with:

1 cup heavy cream

Simmer for 5 minutes; do not boil. Season with:

1 tablespoon chopped parsley
Black pepper to taste

Serve with:

Quick Cream Biscuits, 636, soda crackers, or oyster crackers

II. For a quicker (and more economical) preparation, use canned clams. Proceed as for **version I, above,** omitting the clams and beginning with cooking the pork. Proceed as directed, and add along with the potatoes:

4 cups Shrimp or Shellfish Stock, 78, Quick Seafood Stock, 80, or bottled clam juice

Stir in with the cream:

1½ cups drained canned or frozen chopped clams

Heat through, season as directed, and serve.

RHODE ISLAND CLAM CHOWDER

About 8 cups; 4 to 5 servings

If using larger, chowder-sized quahog clams, chop the meat finely.

Scrub:

5 pounds or 2½ to 3 quarts littleneck, topneck, or other hard-shell clams

Place the clams in a large soup pot and add:

2 cups water

Cover and steam over high heat until the clams open, 5 to 10 minutes. Transfer the clams to a bowl, discarding any that do not open (reserve the cooking liquid). Remove the clams from their shells, holding them over the bowl to catch any juices. Coarsely chop the clams and set aside. Line a fine-mesh sieve with several layers of cheesecloth and strain the cooking liquid from the pot and any juices from the bowl into a measuring cup. You should have about 4 cups; if there is less, add water, or more of the stock called for below.

Add to a soup pot over medium heat:

4 ounces salt pork or bacon, diced

Cook, stirring occasionally, until browned and crispy. Using a slotted spoon, transfer the pork to paper towels to drain. Add to the pot:

2 onions, chopped
1 large celery rib, diced

Cook, stirring, until tender but not browned, 6 to 8 minutes. If desired, stir in:

(2 tablespoons tomato paste)

Stir in the reserved cooking liquid along with:

3 cups Fish Stock, 77, Shrimp or Shellfish Stock, 78, or Quick Seafood Stock, 80

Bring to a boil. Stir in:

1 pound russet potatoes, cut into ½-inch pieces

Reduce the heat to a simmer and cook until the potatoes are tender, about 20 minutes. Stir in the chopped clams and reserved pork. Season with:

½ teaspoon black pepper
2 tablespoons chopped parsley

MANHATTAN CLAM CHOWDER

About 10 cups; 5 to 6 servings

Prepare **Rhode Island Clam Chowder, 103,** adding ½ **green bell pepper, diced,** with the onions and celery, and **one 28-ounce can whole tomatoes, drained and chopped,** with the stock and reserved cooking liquid.

SALMON CHOWDER

About 5 cups; 3 to 4 servings

Melt in a soup pot over medium heat:

1 tablespoon butter

Add and cook, stirring, until the leeks are tender but not browned, 6 to 8 minutes:

2 leeks, white part only, well rinsed and chopped
¼ cup dry vermouth
1 garlic clove, minced

Stir in:

3 cups Fish Stock, 77, Shrimp or Shellfish Stock, 78, or Quick Seafood Stock, 80
2 medium red or gold potatoes, diced
½ teaspoon salt

Bring to a boil, then reduce the heat and simmer until the potatoes are tender, about 15 minutes. Reduce the heat to low. Add:

12 ounces salmon fillets, skin removed
⅔ cup heavy cream
¼ teaspoon black or white pepper

Simmer just until the salmon is cooked, 8 to 10 minutes. Break apart the fillet with a spoon. Serve garnished with:

Small dill sprigs

FISH CHOWDER

12 to 14 cups; 6 to 8 servings

Add to a large soup pot and cook, stirring, over medium heat until beginning to crisp, 6 to 8 minutes:

4 ounces salt pork or bacon, diced

Add:

2 large onions, chopped
3 bay leaves
1 tablespoon chopped thyme

Cook, stirring, until the onions are tender but not browned, 8 to 10 minutes. Stir in:

3 medium red potatoes, peeled, halved lengthwise, and cut into ¼-inch slices
3 cups Fish Stock, 77, Shrimp or Shellfish Stock, 78, or Quick Seafood Stock, 80

Bring to a boil, reduce the heat, and simmer until the potatoes are tender, about 20 minutes. Remove the bay leaves and stir in:

3 pounds firm fish fillets (salmon, monkfish, cod, or wolffish), skin removed
1 cup heavy cream

Simmer (do not boil) until the fish is cooked through and beginning to flake, 8 to 10 minutes. The fish will come apart in large chunks. Season with:

Salt and black pepper to taste
2 tablespoons chopped parsley and/or chervil

ABOUT CREAM SOUPS AND PUREES

These rich, smooth soups can be served at lunch or as a first course at dinner. They may be strained for the finest texture, but we do not usually bother, unless the ingredients are especially fibrous. For everyday cream soups, cook the vegetables directly in the stock, puree with an immersion blender or in a food processor or blender, and then stir in milk or cream. For more on pureeing and other thickening methods, see 82.

➤ Do not puree seafood or poultry, which tend to be unpleasantly stringy; remove the meat from the soup once cooked and add back after it has been pureed (for another approach, see Lobster Bisque, 100).

➤ Do not boil soups once egg or cream has been added. Keep warm or heat through over low heat. Reheat these soups with the same caution, over gentle heat (a double boiler comes in handy here). Many cream soups are equally good hot or cold; when serving cold, adjust the seasoning before serving.

POTATO LEEK SOUP

About 8 cups; 4 to 5 servings

Melt in a soup pot over medium-low heat:

3 tablespoons butter

Add and cook, stirring, until very tender but not browned, about 20 minutes:

6 leeks, halved lengthwise, well cleaned, and chopped

Stir in:

1¼ pounds gold potatoes, peeled and thinly sliced
6 cups Poultry Stock, 76, Chicken Broth, 81, Vegetable Stock, 78, Vegetable Broth, 81, or water

Bring to a boil, then reduce the heat, partially cover, and simmer until the potatoes are soft, about 25 minutes. Puree the soup with an immersion blender (or in batches in a food processor or regular blender) until smooth. For a finer texture, you may push through a chinois or fine-mesh sieve. Return to the pot and warm through if necessary. Season to taste with:

Salt and white or black pepper

Thin, if necessary, with:

Additional stock or water

VICHYSSOISE

About 9 cups; 5 to 6 servings

This famous leek soup may be served hot or very cold. Yes, the last "s" is pronounced.

Prepare **Potato Leek Soup, 104.** Add **½ to 1 cup heavy cream or half-and-half** depending on the desired degree of richness. Reheat gently, or chill and serve cold. If desired, garnish with **(minced chives)**.

PUMPKIN OR BUTTERNUT SQUASH SOUP

About 8 cups; 5 servings

Almost any winter squash can be substituted. For a faster preparation, use three 10- to 12-ounce packages frozen cooked squash puree.

Prepare **Baked or Roasted Winter Squash II, 275,** using:

1 small pumpkin or a medium to large butternut squash (about 3½ pounds)

If desired, reserve and toast the seeds, 1005. Heat in a soup pot over medium heat:

3 tablespoons butter or vegetable oil

Add and cook, stirring, until the leeks are tender but not browned, about 5 minutes:

2 large leeks, halved lengthwise, well cleaned and thinly sliced

Scrape the cooked squash flesh from the skin and stir it in along with:

4 cups chicken or vegetable stock or broth
(Up to 1 tablespoon curry powder or Garam Masala, 588)
(1 tablespoon white miso)

Bring to a simmer and cook for 20 minutes to marry the flavors, stirring and breaking up the squash with a spoon. Puree the soup with an immersion blender (or in batches in a food processor or regular blender) until smooth. Return to the pot and stir in:

2 cups chicken or vegetable stock or broth, or enough to reach the desired consistency
1 teaspoon salt, or to taste

Heat through. Serve garnished with:

Croutons, 638
(Reserved toasted squash seeds)

TOMATO SOUP

About 6 cups; 4 servings

A classic lunch when served with a Grilled Cheese Sandwich, 141, for dunking. Fresh tomatoes may first be grilled for a smoky flavor, 556, or roasted to caramelize their sugars, 282.

Heat in a soup pot over medium-low heat:

2 tablespoons olive oil

Add and cook, stirring, until tender but not browned, about 10 minutes:

1 onion, coarsely chopped

Stir in:

3 pounds tomatoes, peeled, 281, seeded, and chopped, with their juices, or two 28-ounce cans whole tomatoes, chopped

Simmer until the tomatoes are covered in their own liquid, about 25 minutes. Puree the soup with an immersion blender (or in batches in a food processor or regular blender) until smooth. Return to the pot and stir in:

¾ teaspoon salt
¼ teaspoon black pepper
(¼ cup heavy cream)

Heat through.

ROASTED CAULIFLOWER SOUP

About 6 cups; 4 servings

The outstanding flavor of this soup belies how simple it is to prepare. It gets its creaminess and flavor from roasted cauliflower and tender, sweet leeks rather than dairy or flour.

Preheat the oven to 425°F. Toss together on a large rimmed baking sheet:

1 large head cauliflower (about 2 pounds), trimmed and cut into florets
2 tablespoons vegetable oil

Roast until the edges of the florets are quite browned, about 30 minutes. Heat in a soup pot or Dutch oven over medium heat:

2 tablespoons olive or vegetable oil

Add and sauté until softened, about 5 minutes:

1 large leek, halved lengthwise, well cleaned, and thinly sliced

Add the roasted cauliflower along with:

4 cups Vegetable Stock, 78
(Cloves from 1 or 2 heads Roasted Garlic, 241)

Simmer, covered, for 10 minutes. Puree the soup with an immersion blender (or in batches in a food processor or regular blender) until smooth. Return to the pot and season to taste with:

Salt

Add more vegetable broth or water if needed to thin the soup to the desired consistency.

Stir together in a small bowl:

3 tablespoons extra-virgin olive oil
2 teaspoons smoked paprika

Serve the soup drizzled with the paprika oil.

CREAM OF CAULIFLOWER OR BROCCOLI SOUP

About 8 cups; 5 servings

Melt in a soup pot over medium heat:

4 tablespoons (½ stick) butter

Add and cook, stirring, until tender but not browned, about 10 minutes:

1 large onion, chopped
2 celery ribs, chopped

Stir in and cook for an additional 2 minutes:

¼ cup all-purpose flour

Whisk in slowly:

4 cups Poultry Stock, 78, Chicken Broth, 81, or other light stock or broth

Add:

1½ pounds cauliflower or broccoli, trimmed and coarsely chopped

Bring to a boil over high heat, then reduce to a simmer, partially cover, and cook, stirring occasionally, until the cauliflower or broccoli is very tender, about 15 minutes. Puree the soup with an immersion blender (or in batches in a food processor or regular blender) until smooth. Return to the pot and stir in:

½ to 1 cup heavy cream or half-and-half

Heat through, but do not boil. Taste and add:

Salt and black pepper to taste

Serve garnished with:

Chopped parsley, chives, or arugula

BROCCOLI-CHEDDAR SOUP

Prepare **Cream of Broccoli Soup, 105**, adding **2 cups shredded Cheddar (8 ounces)** with the cream or half-and-half and heat through, stirring, until the cheese has melted.

CREAM OF MUSHROOM SOUP

Remove the stems from **1½ pounds mixed mushrooms, such as button, portabella, shiitake, chanterelle, and morel** and use the caps to prepare **Roasted Mushrooms, 252.** As the mushrooms roast, finely chop the stems and prepare **Cream of Cauliflower or Broccoli Soup, 105,** omitting the cauliflower or broccoli. Add the finely chopped mushroom stems with the onions and celery. Once softened, stir in the flour and add the stock. When the roasted mushrooms are finished, coarsely chop them and add to the pot. For added flavor, if desired, deglaze the roasting pan with **(½ cup dry sherry or white wine)** and scrape up any browned bits. Add the pan juices to the soup, bring to a simmer, and proceed as directed.

MUSHROOM-SCALLION SOUP

6½ cups; 4 servings

Melt in a medium saucepan over medium heat:

4 tablespoons (½ stick) butter

Finely chop:

3 bunches green onions (about 12 ounces)

Reserve ½ cup of the chopped green onions for garnish. Add the rest to the pan along with:

1 teaspoon salt
½ teaspoon black pepper

Cook, stirring occasionally, until the green onions are softened, about 6 minutes. Stir in:

12 ounces mushrooms, thinly sliced

Cook until the mushrooms release their juices, about 4 minutes. Add:

2 tablespoons all-purpose flour

Cook, stirring, for 1 minute. Slowly add while stirring:

4 cups Poultry Stock, 76, Chicken Broth, 81, or Mushroom Stock, 79

Bring to a boil, then reduce to a simmer, cover, and cook for 10 minutes. Transfer half of the soup to a blender and puree until silky smooth. Pour it back into the pan. Remove the pot from the heat and stir in:

½ cup heavy cream

Taste and add seasoning if needed. Ladle the soup into warmed bowls. Top each bowl with the reserved chopped green onions.

CARROT-GINGER SOUP

About 6 cups; 4 servings

Melt in a soup pot over medium heat:

4 tablespoons (½ stick) butter

Add and cook, stirring, until tender but not browned, about 6 minutes:

1 large onion, coarsely chopped

Stir in:

1½ pounds carrots, sliced
4 cups Vegetable Stock, 78, or Poultry Stock, 76
½ cup orange juice plus ½ cup water
1-inch piece ginger, peeled and minced
(Up to 2 tablespoons curry powder or Garam Masala, 588)

Bring to a boil, then reduce the heat, partially cover, and simmer until the carrots are tender, 15 to 20 minutes. Puree the soup with an immersion blender (or in batches in a food processor or regular blender) until smooth. Return to the pot and stir in:

¼ to ½ cup heavy cream or half-and-half, to taste
½ teaspoon salt

Heat through, but do not boil. Garnish with:

Croutons, 638

CREAM OF SPINACH SOUP

About 7 cups; 4 to 5 servings

Fresh spinach is best for this soup, but you can substitute **three 10-ounce packages frozen chopped spinach, thawed and drained.** Any cooking green can be cooked until tender and used here, such as chard, collards, or nettles, 246.

Stem and wash thoroughly:

2 pounds spinach

Place in a pot with:

¼ cup water

Cover, set the pot over medium heat, and cook until the spinach has wilted, about 5 minutes. Transfer to a colander to drain, then press out the excess water and coarsely chop. Set aside. Return the pot to medium-low heat and add:

2 tablespoons butter
1 small onion, chopped

Cook, stirring, until tender but not browned, about 5 minutes. Stir in:

2 tablespoons all-purpose flour

Increase the heat to medium and cook, stirring constantly, for another 2 minutes. Do not brown the flour. Gradually whisk in:

2 cups milk
2 cups Poultry Stock, 76, Vegetable Stock, 78, or Chicken Broth, 81

Simmer over low heat, stirring occasionally, until slightly thickened, about 10 minutes. Add the reserved spinach and puree the soup with an immersion blender (or in batches in a food processor or regular blender) until smooth. Return to the pot and stir in:

¾ to 1 cup heavy cream or half-and-half, to taste

Set over low heat until warmed through. Season with:

1 teaspoon salt, or to taste
¼ teaspoon black pepper
(¼ teaspoon freshly grated or ground nutmeg)

CREAM OF WATERCRESS SOUP

About 6 cups; 4 servings

Any flavorful green can be used here, like sorrel, orach, or arugula.

Bring to a boil in a soup pot:

5 cups Poultry Stock, 76, Chicken Broth, 81, or other light stock or broth
3 tablespoons white rice

Reduce the heat to a simmer, partially cover, and cook until the rice is very tender, about 20 minutes. Stir in:

1 medium bunch watercress or purslane (about 7 ounces), minced in a food processor
½ cup heavy cream, half-and-half, or milk

Simmer the soup about 5 minutes; do not boil. In small bowl, beat together:

3 egg yolks

Stir a small quantity of the hot soup into the egg yolks, then stir the yolk mixture into the rest of the soup. Heat the soup for 5 minutes; do not boil. Season to taste with:

Salt and black or white pepper

Serve at once.

BEER-CHEESE SOUP

About 6 cups; 4 servings

Melt in a soup pot over medium heat:

6 tablespoons (¾ stick) butter

Add and cook, stirring, until tender but not browned, 8 to 10 minutes:

1 onion, diced
1 celery rib, diced
1 carrot, diced

Sprinkle with:

¼ cup all-purpose flour

Cook, stirring, 3 to 4 minutes more. Slowly whisk in:

One 12-ounce beer (ale, lager, or pilsner)
2½ cups Poultry Stock, 76, Chicken Broth, 81, or other light stock or broth

Bring to a boil, whisking constantly. Reduce the heat to a simmer and cook until thickened, about 15 minutes. Puree the soup with an immersion blender (or in batches in a food processor or regular blender) until smooth. Return to the pot, bring back to a simmer, and stir in:

1 cup heavy cream or half-and-half
2 cups grated Cheddar (8 ounces)
1 teaspoon dry mustard

Reduce the heat to low and stir until the cheese is melted. Do not let the soup boil: If the soup is too hot, the oil will separate out of the cheese. Season to taste with:

(Hot pepper sauce)
(Worcestershire sauce)
Salt and black pepper

Garnish with any of the following:

Croutons, 638
Finely chopped smoked ham
Minced chives
Ground chipotle or smoked paprika

ABOUT COLD SOUPS

Cold vegetable soups make refreshing first courses or light main courses on the hottest summer days. If serving any of these to a crowd when it is particularly hot, place the serving bowl in a large bowl of ice to keep the soup cool. For other cold soups, see Vichyssoise, 105, and Cherry Soup, 108.

COLD AVOCADO SOUP

About 4 cups; 4 to 5 servings

This is our favorite cold soup. It is very rich.

Puree in a food processor until smooth:

2 Hass avocados (about 8 ounces each), pitted, peeled, and diced
1 small garlic clove, minced

Add and process to blend:

2 cups buttermilk
4 teaspoons lime juice
¼ teaspoon salt
Pinch of cayenne pepper

Transfer to a bowl and refrigerate until cold. Thin, if necessary, with:

(¼ to ½ cup buttermilk, cream, or milk)

Taste and adjust the seasonings. Ladle the soup into chilled bowls and garnish with any of the following:

Pico de Gallo, 573
Sour cream or plain yogurt
8 ounces lump crabmeat, picked over for shells and cartilage

GAZPACHO

About 6 cups; 4 servings

The stale bread gives this cooling soup a wonderful, rich texture.

Puree in a food processor:

1 medium red or green bell pepper, coarsely chopped

Add to the processor:

2½ pounds flavorful plum or Roma tomatoes, peeled, 281, and coarsely chopped
1 thick slice stale or toasted baguette, coarsely crumbled
1 medium cucumber, peeled, seeded, and diced
¼ cup extra-virgin olive oil
3 tablespoons sherry vinegar or red wine vinegar
2 garlic cloves, minced
½ teaspoon salt

Pulse until completely blended and smooth. Refrigerate for 2 hours. Taste and season with more salt or vinegar, if needed, and serve in chilled bowls. Top with:

Diced cucumber, minced sweet onion, or sliced green onion
A drizzle of extra-virgin olive oil
(Croutons, 638)

BECKER GAZPACHO

About 12 cups; 6 to 8 servings

This old favorite is what happens when a Spanish soup is invited to a midsummer house party in the Midwest. It is inauthentic, chunky, and delicious.

Combine in a large stainless steel bowl:

One 46-ounce can tomato or tomato-vegetable juice
One 10½-ounce can condensed beef consommé, undiluted
2 tablespoons lemon or lime juice or red wine vinegar, or to taste
2 tablespoons chopped basil
(2 tablespoons minced thyme)
(1 tablespoon soy sauce)
2 garlic cloves, minced
½ teaspoon hot pepper sauce

Add to a food processor:

1 cucumber, peeled, seeded, and coarsely chopped
3 large carrots, cut into chunks
½ small head red cabbage, cored and cut into chunks
2 celery ribs, cut into chunks, or 1 bunch watercress, tough stems trimmed and chopped
¼ cup chopped parsley (omit if using watercress)
1 bunch green onions or 1 medium onion, cut into 1-inch chunks
(½ red or green bell pepper, cut into chunks)

Process until finely chopped (do not puree) and add to the bowl with the tomato juice. Season to taste with:

Salt and black pepper

Cover and chill until very cold, 1 to 2 hours. Taste and adjust the seasonings as needed. Serve in chilled bowls, topped with:

(Croutons, 638)

COLD CUCUMBER AND YOGURT SOUP

About 3 cups; 4 servings

Combine in a medium bowl:

1½ cups finely diced, peeled, and seeded cucumbers
1¼ cups plain yogurt
½ cup chopped toasted, 1005, walnuts
2 tablespoons extra-virgin olive oil
1 tablespoon chopped dill
1 teaspoon salt
¼ teaspoon white pepper
1 garlic clove, minced

Refrigerate, covered, for at least 2 hours and up to 6 hours. The soup should have the consistency of heavy cream. If necessary, it can be thinned with a small amount of:

(Milk, cream, or water)

Garnish with:

Minced dill
A drizzle of extra-virgin olive oil

ABOUT FRUIT SOUPS

Fruit soups can be served as a dessert or chilled as a summertime prelude to the entrée. You can mix fresh and dried fruits, and use one variety or a combination, cooked until they can be pureed easily. Fruit soups are also refreshing when made with frozen fruits. ➤ If the soup is served at the beginning of the meal, go easy on the sugar.

DRIED FRUIT SOUP

About 6 cups; 6 to 8 servings

While this is technically a soup, it may also be used as a sort of fruit compote on oatmeal or atop yogurt and sprinkled with granola. Or serve for dessert with scoops of vanilla ice cream.

Combine in a large saucepan:

¾ cup dried apricots or peaches, quartered
¾ cup prunes, pitted and quartered
3 tablespoons raisins or golden raisins
2 tablespoons dried currants
2 cinnamon sticks
Finely grated zest of 1 orange
3 tablespoons quick-cooking tapioca
4 cups apple juice, cranberry juice, or water

Stir in:

Up to ¼ cup sugar

Bring to a boil, then reduce the heat to low and simmer, stirring occasionally, until the fruit is soft and the soup has thickened, about 30 minutes. Add:

2 tart apples, peeled, cored, and cut into ½-inch pieces

Cook until the apples are tender, about 8 minutes. Let cool slightly. Remove the cinnamon sticks and serve warm or cold, garnished with:

Sour cream or heavy cream
(Toasted, 1005, sliced almonds)

CHERRY SOUP

About 6 cups; 4 servings

Have ready:

2 pounds sour cherries, stemmed and pitted

Set aside half the cherries and place the other half in a soup pot with:

2 cups gewürztraminer or medium-dry white wine
2 cups water

Bring to a boil, then reduce to a simmer, partially cover, and cook until the cherries are soft, about 15 minutes. Puree the soup with an immersion blender (or in batches in a food processor or regular blender) until smooth. Return to the pot. Stir together in a small bowl:

¼ cup sugar
4 teaspoons cornstarch
3 tablespoons cold water

Pour the mixture into the pot and cook over high heat, stirring, until thickened, about 5 minutes. Reduce the heat and stir in the reserved cherries along with:

Finely grated zest of ½ orange
1 tablespoon orange juice

1 tablespoon lemon juice
(A splash of Cognac)
Heat until warmed through. Taste. If not sweet enough, add additional:
(Sugar)
If too sweet, add additional:
(Lemon juice)
Serve warm or cold, garnished with:
Sour cream or plain yogurt
Mint sprigs

ROSE HIP SOUP

About 4 cups; 3 to 4 servings

Be sure the bushes from which you gather the rose hips were not sprayed.
Wash, pat dry, and pulse in a food processor until coarsely chopped:
2 cups fresh or 1 cup dried rose hips
Add to a nonreactive pan, along with:
4 cups water
Bring to a boil, then reduce to a simmer, cover, and cook until the rose hips are very soft, about 45 minutes. Line a sieve with several layers of cheesecloth and strain the liquid into a large measuring cup, pressing on the solids to extract all the liquid, then discarding the solids. Add enough:
Raspberry juice, peach nectar, or orange juice
to make 4 cups liquid in all. Transfer to a medium saucepan. Mix in a small bowl:
1 tablespoon arrowroot
with a small quantity of the liquid and:
1/3 cup honey
Bring the liquid to a simmer, take off the heat, and thoroughly whisk in the arrowroot mixture. Let cool, then chill in the refrigerator until ready to serve. Garnish with:
Sour cream
(Almond Macaroons, 774, coarsely crumbled)

ABOUT QUICK AND CONDENSED SOUPS

Over the years, *Joy* has included a smattering of time-saving recipes that leverage canned, condensed soups—a novel, life-changing innovation in foodstuffs when Irma first turned her attention to their usefulness in the late 1930s. In recent times, supermarket shelves have continued to change with the addition of higher-quality prepared soups in an ever-widening array of flavors, processed with new methods of pasteurization and in new packaging materials. By contrast, we feel the condensed soups of yesteryear that Irma based many of her recipes on have declined precipitously in quality (and popularity).

So, in light of this turn of events, instead of providing specific formulas for the use of one range of products, we suggest here a general approach for achieving better results with any shelf-stable soup base.

The seasonings and textures of shelf-stable soups are often bland and challenged. Bolster (or camouflage) their flavor by adding herbs, seasonings, citrus juice or vinegar, and plenty of garnishes. Use fresh herbs lavishly, and dried herbs more discreetly. Improve their texture by dicing and briefly simmering any fresh vegetables you have on hand to give the soup a bit of interest. Or, if you have leftover bones or meat trimmings, dilute the soup's shortcomings with a quick stock, 80, and build on this new foundation. Leftover proteins—diced pork roast, steak, or flaked salmon fillet—can be heated through in the soup just before serving, as can leftover pasta, rice, and other cooked grains. Leftover cooked vegetables can be easily transformed into a quick cream soup—see Quick Cream of Broccoli or Cauliflower Soup, below.

For those who still wish to use condensed soups, a word of caution: ➤ The more concentrated the soup, the more likely it is oversalted. Taste, dilute, and correct accordingly.

QUICK BORSCHT

4 to 5 cups; 4 servings

Puree in a blender or food processor until smooth:
2 cups tomato juice, chilled
One 15-ounce can beets, with liquid, chilled, or 2 cups chopped cooked beets
3 cornichons (not sweet)
1 small shallot, minced
1 teaspoon Worcestershire sauce
1/4 teaspoon black pepper
1/4 teaspoon hot pepper sauce
1 garlic clove, minced
Chill. Serve garnished with any of the following:
4 Hard-Boiled Eggs, 151, thinly sliced or diced
Sour cream
Chopped dill or fennel fronds

QUICK CREAM OF BROCCOLI OR CAULIFLOWER SOUP

About 3½ cups; 2 servings

Melt in a large saucepan over medium heat:
2 tablespoons butter
Add and cook, stirring, until softened, 6 to 8 minutes:
1/4 cup chopped onion
2 small celery ribs, with leaves, minced
Add:
One 14½-ounce can chicken broth
1 cup finely chopped cauliflower or broccoli
Bring to a boil, then reduce to a simmer, cover, and cook until the cauliflower or broccoli is very tender, about 10 minutes. If desired, puree the soup with an immersion blender (or in batches in a food processor or regular blender) until smooth. Return to the pan and stir in:
1 cup half-and-half
Heat through, but do not boil. Season to taste with:
Salt and black pepper
Garnish with, if desired:
(A light grating of nutmeg or a pinch of ground coriander)

CHILLED FRESH TOMATO CREAM SOUP

About 2½ cups; 2 servings

An excellent way to use surplus garden tomatoes.

Peel, 281, and coarsely chop:

1 pound very ripe, flavorful tomatoes

Add to a blender or food processor, along with:

½ cup heavy cream
1 tablespoon chopped parsley
1 tablespoon chopped basil

Blend or pulse so the soup is not exactly chunky but still has some texture. Season to taste with:

Salt and black pepper

Chill. Serve with:

Lemon wedges

SALADS

The word "salad" denotes an incredibly broad category of dishes. Salads may be composed of leafy greens, cooked or raw vegetables, beans, grains, eggs, finely chopped meats, or various ingredients suspended in gelatin. Salads defy easy definition, the exceptions perhaps more notable than the rules. No matter how we define them, though, salads are invaluable at the table, serving as first courses, palate-cleansing interludes, accompaniments to a meal, or, in some hearty cases, as repasts all their own. Regardless of type, if your salad is to be one of several dishes on the table, balance its richness, acidity, and heartiness with the other foods being served. For **salad dressings,** see 574–78.

ABOUT SALAD GREENS

Buy the freshest greens with crisp leaves, free of brown spots or yellowing. Packaged cut lettuces and salad mixtures are appealing for their convenience, but they tend to be more expensive than lettuce or greens sold in heads or bunches. The containers also retain moisture—examine the contents carefully for signs of spoilage, and regardless of washing claims on the package, always wash packaged greens before serving.

As soon as possible after purchasing, discard any leaves that are wilted or show signs of decay such as yellowing, browning, or sliminess. Remove any rubber or metal bands holding the greens together, and ➤ dry them thoroughly—greens are often misted with preposterous amounts of water to keep them glistening and fresh, which makes them look appealing in the store but has the unfortunate side effect of promoting spoilage in plastic produce bags.

Store loose greens in the crisper bin of the refrigerator in a bag or container with a paper towel folded around them to absorb excess moisture. Small-leafed greens with their stems attached, like watercress, keep longer when stored refrigerated in a glass of water and loosely covered with a plastic bag. ➤ Slightly wilted salad greens can be revived by a soak in ice-cold water for 5 to 10 minutes; then dry well. ➤ Wash and prepare salad greens only just before using and see that they are well chilled, crisp, and—especially—dry. Use delicate greens like watercress as soon as possible; mature kale and other hearty greens can be kept for several days.

To clean greens, separate leaves, discard any that are discolored or wilted, and place in a large bowl or sink full of cold water. If you are especially concerned about ridding your greens of bacteria, place them in a solution of 1 part vinegar to 3 parts water and let them soak for 2 minutes. Swish around for 30 seconds or so, then lift them from the water so that the dirt and grit remain in the water. Repeat the process until the water is clear. Take care not to bruise tender leaves while cleaning.

➤ ***To lessen the bitterness of chicories and other strong greens,*** soak them in ice water for 30 minutes after cleaning.

To dry greens, you may simply drain them in a colander, shaking the colander several times, and lightly wrap them in an absorbent towel until dry. Salad spinners are a wonderful convenience. Overcrowding a salad spinner, however, will both bruise the greens and hinder the device's ability to dry them adequately. Fill the spinner only about half to two-thirds full. Alternatively, place the greens in a tea towel and swing the towel around to sling off the water—just be sure to do this outside.

To cook greens, see the Vegetables chapter, 199.

SELECTING AND SUBSTITUTING SALAD GREENS

When selecting greens, we highly recommend experimenting with different lettuce varieties, as well as the plethora of chicories, mustards, spinaches, and kales available at markets. Combine them at your whim and according to taste. **Mesclun,** also called **spring mix,** is a mixture of young greens, both mild and assertive (and sometimes herbs). A good salad mixture has a variety of flavors, textures, and colors. Combine mild spinaches and baby lettuces with spicy arugula or mizuna, bitter frisée or radicchio, sour purslane or sorrel, or pungent celery leaves and whole herbs. In the table below, greens in the same category may be substituted for one another. Mixed green combinations are best when they draw from several of these categories—as well as from our suggested Herbs and Edible Flowers, 114, or, if available, salty succulents like agretti or sea beans, 114. Regardless of the type of green, always taste a leaf or two. The flavor of greens may vary quite a bit depending on the time of year and the varietal, being more or less spicy, bitter, or tart.

Mild Greens	Bitter Greens	Spicy Greens	Sour Greens
Crisphead, butterhead, looseleaf, and romaine lettuces	Belgian endive	Arugula	Sorrel
Kale and young chard	Curly endive	Mizuna	Purslane
Mâche	Dandelion greens	Komatsuna	
Cabbages	Frisée	Young mustard greens	
Spinaches	Escarole	Watercress, garden cress, and upland cresses	
Tatsoi	Radicchio	Nasturtium leaves	
Pea shoots	Treviso		
	Puntarelle		

ARUGULA

Also called **rocket,** arugula has tender dark-green leaves, and a pungent peppery bite that gets spicier as it matures. Some varieties have smooth-edged leaves, others have serrated leaves. Arugula can stand alone or be used as a spicy accent in mixed green salads.

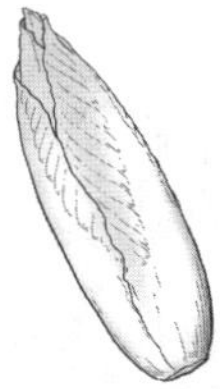

BELGIAN ENDIVE

This pale, bitter chicory heart looks rather like young unshucked ears of corn. The outer (larger) leaves may serve as receptacles for hors d'oeuvre. Belgian endive may be substituted for other bitter greens like radicchio; mix with a mild lettuce (like Bibb), tart sorrel, or peppery watercress or arugula.

CABBAGE

Though all types of cabbage are candidates for use in a green salad, **napa** and **Savoy cabbages** work best, as they have thin, delicate leaves. Tender **baby bok choy** is also a good option. All types of cabbage, including napa and Savoy cabbage and bok choy can be used for slaw, 119–20.

Red cabbage, napa cabbage, Savoy cabbage, bok choy

CRESS

These spicy, peppery greens belong to the same family as mustard and cabbage. **Watercress,** the most widely available type, is also the mildest, and sports small, rounded leaves and crisp stems. Do not confuse **garden cress** with watercress. Garden cress has very tiny leaves that can be lacy, like those of flat-leaf parsley; some varieties have ruffled or crinkled leaves, like curly parsley. Most garden cresses are quite spicy. **Upland cress,** also known as **creasy greens,** is similar to watercress; if grown in hot weather, it can become so strong as to be nearly inedible. **Nasturtium leaves,** a distant relative, are also very pleasant and peppery—their name is Latin for "nose twister." Their brightly colored blossoms are beautiful in salads as well, 114. **Winter cress** is, as its name implies, highly resistant to cold. It is spicy, but also bitter like wild dandelion. The rosettes of smooth, dark green leaves may be gathered as new growth either in early spring or late fall. ➤ Taste cresses—especially those that are foraged—before adding them to a salad to gauge their pungency.

Watercress

Curly endive

CURLY ENDIVE AND FRISÉE

These two types of chicory are sometimes confused for each other. **Curly endive** has coarse, spiky green leaves, pale at the bottom and darker on top. It adds a bitter flavor and a somewhat lacy texture to a tossed salad. **Frisée** has small, tender, lacy green leaves that are very pale at the center of the head, with a mild tartness and a more delicate taste than other chicories.

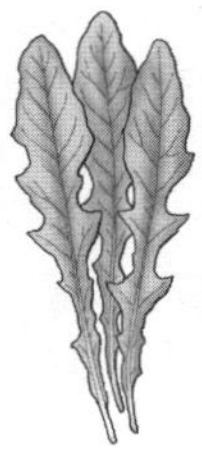

DANDELION GREENS
The cultivated dandelion greens sold in markets are actually a type of chicory. These bitter greens have serrated, arrow-shaped leaves. Both raw and cooked, they have a rich, bracing flavor that stands up well to pungent ingredients. For preparing the common weed, see About Foraging for Wild Greens, 115

ESCAROLE OR BROAD CHICORY
The leaves of this chicory are broader, paler, and less crimped than curly endive, 112. The taste is less bitter, though the sturdy leaves do have a pronounced tartness and a firm, chewy texture. Though perfectly acceptable in salads, we prefer to braise escarole, in recipes like Utica Greens, 234.

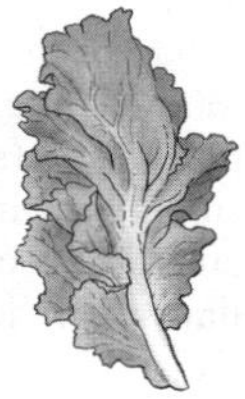

KALE
Traditionally thought of as a braising green, kale has become a well-known salad mainstay. The young, tender leaves of any kale variety may be added to salads (see Young Leafy Greens, 114), but **lacinato** (or **dinosoaur**) **kale** and thinner Russian varieties are best for using at maturity. Still, the texture of mature kale can be quite resilient, which is why the leaves are often massaged with dressing and/or left to macerate for a short period. Be sure to remove kale midribs before proceeding, 243.

LETTUCES
Looseleaf: Mild and mellow, these lettuces have sprawling crisp leaves with sweet and refined flavors; they may have ruffled edges and/or red tips. Varieties include **green leaf, red leaf,** and **oak leaf. Coral lettuces** have loosely packed, open heads as well, but a firmer leaf and frilled outer edge. **Batavian** or **summer crisp** varieties have large, open heads like other looseleaf types, but are crisper, juicier, and sweet.

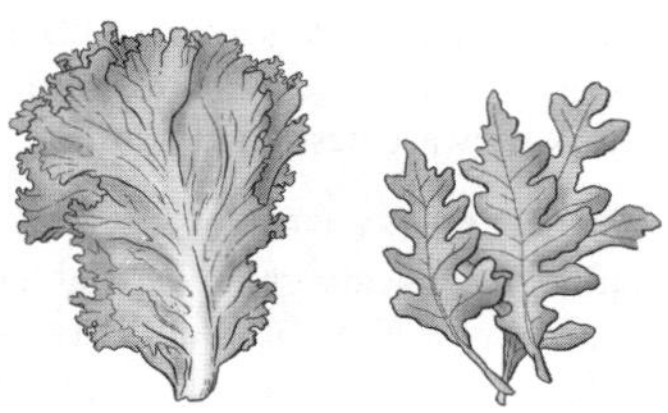

Looseleaf, oak leaf

Crisphead: The most famous of these varieties is the pale, juicy, and ubiquitous **iceberg,** friend to hamburgers and wedge salads alike. Crispheads are large, firm, brittle, and tightly packed. Outer leaves are medium green, inner ones pale green. Some varieties are tinged with red, and may have a more assertive flavor. The leaves can be torn or shredded like cabbage. They add a pleasant crunch and do not readily wilt.

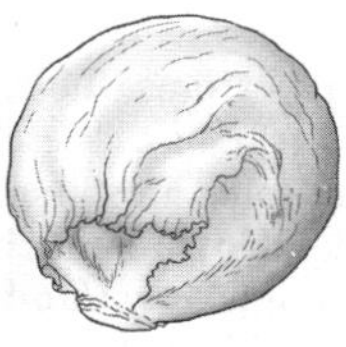

Iceberg

Butterhead: These lettuces have smaller, looser heads than iceberg, as well as a softer texture. The leaves are delicate—the outer ones dark green, the inner light green to yellowish—and have a mild, sweet taste. Familiar varieties include **Boston, buttercrunch,** and some red-hued types, but the aristocrat of the line is undoubtedly **Bibb** (also known as **limestone Bibb**). The subtly sweet, buttery flavor of these lettuces combines well with more strongly flavored greens.

Butterhead

Romaine: Also known as **cos**, the elongated heads are made up of long stiff leaves with crisp, juicy midribs, and a slightly bitter flavor. The dark-green outer leaves have a stronger flavor than the prized, pale center or "heart." The wide midribs may be torn up with the leaves as long as they are not overly fibrous. Occasionally, you may encounter romaine heads with purplish-red leaves, or a sweet, miniature romaine variety called **Little Gem**.

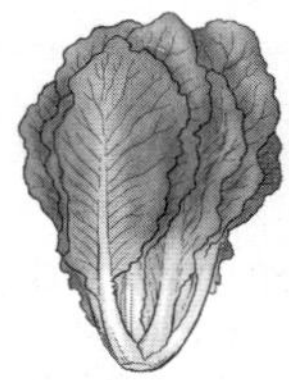

Romaine

MÂCHE
This delicate, sweet, and nutty green is also called **rapunzel, lamb's lettuce,** and **corn salad.** It grows in small clusters or rosettes, and has tender, smooth leaves.

MUSTARD GREENS
Though mustards are typically thought of as a braising green, some varieties are delicate enough to be included in salads, even when mature. Like tougher varieties of kale, stronger mustards can be added to salads when they are still young and tender, and are frequently mixed with milder greens.

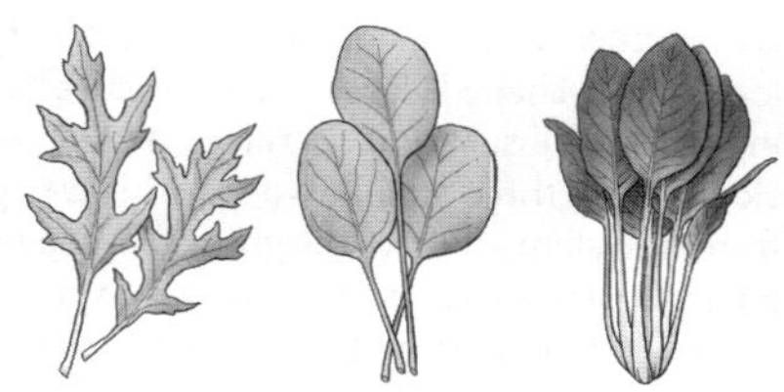

Mizuna, tatsoi, komatsuna

Mizuna is one of the most delicately flavored of the mustards. With feathery leaves that run from dark green to purple, mizuna is mild enough to be the star of a green salad, even at maturity. Related is **mibuna,** which is similar in flavor but slightly stronger, with a distinctive appearance of long, narrow, densely packed stems that explode into a spray of leaves. **Tatsoi,** also called **spoon mustard,** has rounded, thick leaves and stalks that add flavor and crunch to salads. **Komatsuna,** also known as **Japanese mustard spinach,** has thick, dark green leaves. Its flavor combines cabbage with the bite of mustard. The young stalks are delicious.

ORACH

Orach thrives in salt-rich soil, which causes its leaves to taste mildly salty. The arrow-shaped leaves of this green vary in color from deep burgundy to greenish-yellow. Orach has a mild spinach flavor, but the leaves are thinner and not as succulent.

PEA SHOOTS

The first 3 to 5 inches at the tip of a snow pea vine, including the tendrils, leaves, pods, and sometimes flowers, comprise the pea shoot. Freshly picked, they are crisp, with a light pea flavor. They are exquisite in salads and, though delicate, hold their own with stronger flavors.

Radicchio and treviso

RADICCHIO AND TREVISO

These chicories have a pleasantly bitter flavor and striking purple leaves with tender ivory midribs. **Radicchio** has a round head and tightly packed leaves; **treviso** is an oblong variety with thicker midribs. These "greens" really stand out in spring mix, 112, where they add character and color. As with any bitter green, soaking cleaned and cut leaves in ice water for 30 minutes will mellow them out a bit. Treated in this way, they are an excellent substitute for romaine in Caesar Salad, 117.

SORREL

Best in spring, when young, tender, and mild, sorrels are wonderful in salads. The cultivated type has long, arrow-shaped leaves; some varieties have striking red midribs. **Wood sorrel,** or **oxalis,** resembles clover, with three small, two-lobed leaves growing from thin stems close to the ground in shady forests. **Sheep sorrel,** or **red sorrel,** thrives in recently disturbed soil in full sun. Its leaves are similar in shape to cultivated sorrel, but much smaller. The leaves have a pleasantly sour taste and can be eaten raw or cooked. Use any of these sorrels discreetly, since their sour flavor can be overwhelming.

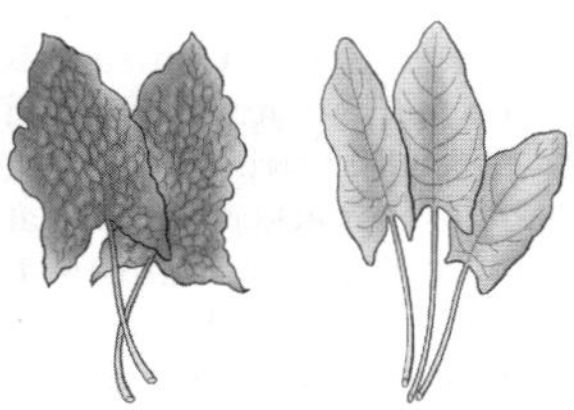

Curly and flat-leaf spinach

SPINACH

Spinach leaves are a versatile, valuable salad green. Curly or crinkly leaved spinach is best cooked or used for a wilted salad, 118. Flat-leafed types are the mildest and best for raw salads. Include chopped stems—and if the pink roots are still attached, drop them in, too, for their crunch. Spinach leaves are often sandy, so wash thoroughly, repeating a second or third time if necessary. Unrelated though similar in taste, the kite-shaped leaves of **New Zealand spinach** may be used in salads or cooked.

SUCCULENTS AND WILD SEASIDE GREENS

Purslane

There are quite a few edible succulents worth mentioning, as well as a few greens found in salty soils, often by the sea. **Purslane** is considered a weed in most of the United States, but it has been eaten for centuries in the eastern Mediterranean and Mexico. It grows in disturbed soil (such as tilled gardens), resembles a small creeping jade plant, and has juicy stalks and thick, oval-shaped leaves with a lemony flavor. The leaves of the cultivated **Goldgelber** variety are larger and golden green. Serve bite-sized pieces of the stem along with the leaves in salads.

Agretti has crisp, slender leaves and a soft stem; it looks like a flimsy cross between rosemary and chives. It has a spinach-like taste, but mildly salty and a little tart. It can be cooked as for tender greens, 243, but we like the crunch it adds to salads. **Sea beans** or **samphire** grow on the coastline and have thick, stubby leaves that resemble seaweed. They are quite salty, and very crisp. **Sea rocket** grows on sandy beaches near the high-tide line. A small shrub, it has slender, thick, succulent greens, and a pleasant peppery taste. We think of it as "beach arugula." **Oyster leaf,** a relative of borage, 956, is diminutive, with beautiful rounded, grayish-green leaves. It has a distinctive briny, mineral taste that indeed resembles oysters. **Sea kale** is exactly as its name suggests: a relative of kale that thrives by the sea. Use only young leaves (in salads, or cooked as for kale, 113) and shoots (cook them like asparagus, 208). **Iceplant,** also known by its French name **ficoïde glaciale,** has thick, succulent leaves that taste like a tart spinach. The most interesting thing about iceplant are the tiny, juicy sacs resembling tiny raindrops that cover the exterior of their leaves and stem. Though they may be cooked, we think they are best enjoyed raw.

YOUNG LEAFY GREENS

Fully grown leafy green vegetables such as **kale, broccoli rabe,** and **chard,** as well as **beet** and **turnip greens,** are commonly cooked before eating; but younger greens of the same varieties are more delicate in texture and flavor and can be eaten raw in salads. Young red- or green-leafed **amaranth** can be quite tender and has an intense spinach-like taste. For more on these, see About Greens for Cooking, 242.

HERBS AND EDIBLE FLOWERS

To add flavor and color to salads, add herb leaves or blossoms whole, tear them into bite-sized pieces, or cut them into ribbons. These herbs are mild enough to be added to salads as you would any other assertive salad green: **basil, celery leaves, chervil, cilantro, fennel fronds, mint, mitsuba, parsley, salad burnet, shungiku (garland chrysanthemum greens), sweet cicely,** and **tarragon.** The following herbs are more pungent and should be used as garnishes: **anise, anise hyssop, caraway, chives, dill, hyssop, lemon balm, lovage, marjoram, oregano, perilla (shiso),** and **savory.**

Try any of the following colorful flowers: **borage, clove pinks, elderflowers, lavender (sparingly), lemon, mustard, nasturtium, rose, rosemary, scented geranium, shungiku (garland chrysanthemum), sweet woodruff,** and **violets.** Use only unsprayed flowers. You may want to gently rinse and pat the blooms dry. If the blossoms are small, add them whole; separate larger blooms into petals. Also see Growing Herbs, 993.

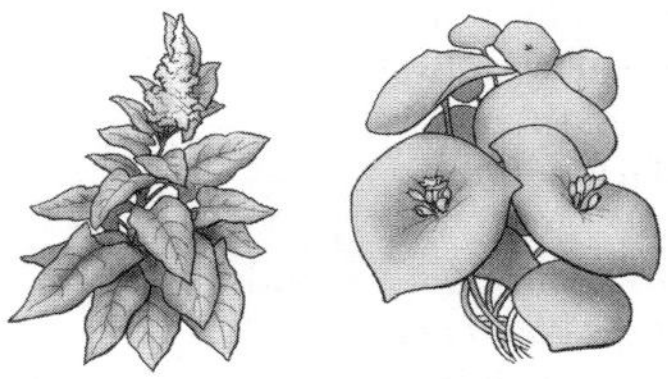

Good King Henry, miner's lettuce

ABOUT FORAGING FOR WILD GREENS

Some young, tender wild greens can be gathered and used raw in salads. On the mild side, **miner's lettuce** is a delectable, tender green that is abundant in the spring in the western United States. The plant is easy to identify by its tiny, star-shaped white or light pink flowers and the way it grows in rosettes. **Chickweed** grows in plentiful clumps all over North America. It is mild, tender, and excellent for salads. **Good King Henry** and **lamb's quarters** are goosefoot species that sport spade-shaped leaves. The greens pair nicely with tender red-leaf lettuces.

Spicier greens include **wild mustards,** which are widespread and plentiful (in the case of **garlic mustard,** plentiful to the point of being a noxious weed). Their leaves are more tender and less pungent in spring, becoming tough, bitter, and unpleasantly peppery as the season goes on. Related to mustards, **peppergrass** and **shepherd's purse** grow in every state in the continental United States. They should be used in combination with other milder greens in salads. **Wild cresses** are peppery and succulent; they are excellent salad greens in early spring, when they are still young and relatively mild.

Wild dandelion weed, bane of gardeners everywhere, is easy to identify and easy to handle if it is cut off at the root crown so that the leaf cluster holds together. Select young, tender plants. After the dandelion plant flowers, the mature leaves are tough and quite bitter. For the chicory relative available in stores and at farmers' markets, see 233. **Sorrels,** including sheep sorrel and garden sorrel, are extremely sour. Use them sparingly in salads to add tartness. For **purslane** and other succulents, see 114.

For use in salads, it is prudent to use all wild greens when they are young and tender, usually in the springtime before they flower. Add them in relatively small amounts to more conventional greens because many of them contain oxalates that may be dangerous to ingest in quantity (not to mention that many tend to be very strongly flavored—either sour, spicy, or bitter—and can easily overwhelm the palate). ➤ Always consult an identification guide or, preferably, a knowledgeable and experienced forager before gathering and consuming wild greens. Be doubly sure you can identify the greens you plan to use, and wash them with great care. Some of these greens are abundant in urban areas, along roadsides, or near highly trafficked trails. Be aware that these greens may be especially dirty, so either wash them especially well with a vinegar solution, 111, or let them be and confine your foraging to more remote areas. Also see Succulents and Wild Seaside Greens, 114.

ABOUT DRESSING AND SERVING SALADS

With a few simple guidelines in mind, recipes for green salads are nearly superfluous: Aside from a few classic combinations that we return to time and time again, the salad universe is large and for the most part free of consequence. Here follow the basics, a handful of suggested embellishments, and, finally, some favorite salad formulae.

For delicate, simply dressed greens, we recommend tearing leaves into bite-sized pieces. Sturdy, crisp greens like romaine and radicchio may be sliced, shredded, chopped, or torn. ➤ Allow 1½ to 2 cups loosely packed greens per serving, the larger amount being more appropriate for meal-sized salads. Use an ample bowl so that leaves do not stray. Unless dressing a sturdy, mature green such as kale or cabbage, ➤ add the dressing as close to serving time as possible, since oil and salt permeate delicate leaves in short order, causing them to release their juices and turn limp.

While we provide dressing recommendations in the recipes that follow, you are by no means limited to those. We prefer to make dressings from scratch, but we also understand that store-bought dressings can be a boon to the harried cook. Feel free to use your favorite prepared dressings with the recipes in this chapter, pairing their flavor with the other ingredients in the salad.

As a general rule, hearty or crisp greens like kale, romaine, iceberg, and cabbage stand up better to thick, creamy dressings. For a thorough discussion of vinaigrettes and other dressings, including specific recipes, see 574. If you wish to "wing it" by making a vinaigrette directly in the salad bowl with oil, vinegar, and intuition, just remember ➤ the classic oil-to-vinegar proportions are 3 parts oil to 1 part vinegar or citrus juice, although you may find you favor different proportions. Add seasonings incrementally and taste as you go by dipping a leaf into the dressing.

Remember, your dressing should enhance the salad by complementing its flavors and adding acidity or richness. ➤ Use just enough to lightly coat the greens. A rough guideline: Use 1 tablespoon of thin, vinaigrette-type dressings per cup of greens, or about 1½ tablespoons of creamy dressing per cup of greens. Put another way for easier scaling, figure on ½ cup vinaigrette or up to ¾ cup creamy dressing for an 8-cup, 4-serving salad.

You may plate salads before bringing them to the table or, for a more informal table setting, simply bring the salad bowl out with a pair of tongs. Chilled plates are the epitome of class, but are by no means necessary. ➤ To transport salads to potlucks and picnics, put washed and thoroughly dried salad greens in a bag or covered container, take the dressing along in a separate container, and combine right before serving. For mature kale, simply combine it with the dressing when you pack it (the sturdy leaves benefit from a bit of softening).

➤ To dress smaller, dense additions to salads such as beans, chopped vegetables, or fruits, lightly dress the greens first, distribute among salad plates or transfer to a serving bowl, then toss the dense ingredients with a bit more dressing and scatter them on top.

ABOUT ADDITIONS TO GREEN SALADS

The simplest way to enhance green salads is to add other ingredients that provide flavor and texture. With enough accoutrements, a salad can become the centerpiece of a meal (see About Combination Salads, 120).

Croutons, 638, or Browned or Buttered Bread Crumbs, 957, are valued as much for their crunchy texture as for their flavor. Toasted nuts and seeds or Roasted Chickpeas, 47, also add crunch. With a light coat of dressing on the greens, small accents like very thinly sliced green onions and finely shredded hard cheeses will cling to the salad greens and are less apt to fall to the bottom of the salad bowl. Larger items, like slices of grilled chicken, carrot ribbons or spiral-cut carrots, halved cherry tomatoes, and marinated artichoke hearts, are also fine to toss with the greens, as they are easily retrieved from the bowl with tongs.

The following salad additions should be sprinkled on top of the dressed salad rather than tossed with the greens: crumbled cooked bacon (or Mushroom Bacon, 252), diced ham, dried fruits, chopped hard-boiled eggs, beans, olives, chopped vegetables or fruit, flaked smoked fish, Crispy Fried Shallots, 256, avocado slices, or tomato wedges. Soft cheeses such as Stilton or Camembert may be smeared on small toasts and served alongside, or cut into chunks (or crumbled) and sprinkled on top. ➤ To evenly coat salads with a dusting of soft cheeses such as fresh goat cheese or Roquefort, freeze them solid and finely grate them with a rasp grater over the greens. This is an excellent way to add flavor to salads without bogging them down with chunks or globs of cheese.

FRICO (CHEESE CRISPS)

These shatteringly crisp Italian cheese wafers are a fantastic addition to life (and salads in particular). For an even more substantial salad topping, see Frico Eggs, 155.

I. ***Makes 1 large, unruly crisp***

Toss together in a small bowl:

½ cup grated Gruyère, Asiago, aged sharp Cheddar, or any aged cheese (2 ounces)
1 tablespoon grated Parmesan

Sprinkle in an even layer in a large nonstick skillet to form an 8-inch round. Cook over medium heat until lightly browned, about 4 minutes. Using a spatula, carefully lift the pancake onto a baking sheet lined with paper towels and blot dry.

II. ***Makes 8 crisps***

Preheat the oven to 300°F. Have ready a large nonstick baking sheet or line a large baking sheet with parchment and lightly brush with olive oil. Have ready:

½ cup grated Parmesan (2 ounces)

Using 1 tablespoon cheese per chip, sprinkle into 3½-inch rounds on the baking sheet. Bake until the chips are golden and have stopped bubbling, 10 to 15 minutes. Transfer to a baking sheet lined with paper towels to cool completely.

PAN-FRIED GOAT CHEESE MEDALLIONS

4 servings

Some may be satisfied with serving cheese-laden toasts to garnish a green salad. This treatment is for those who ask for more. After letting these cool slightly, we like to nest them on the top of a green salad, preferably dressed with a vinaigrette and garnished with fruit or pickled onions. You may substitute **finely chopped nuts** for half the bread crumbs (just be careful not to burn them).

Stir together in a shallow bowl:

⅓ cup fresh bread crumbs, 957
½ teaspoon dried thyme
½ teaspoon black pepper
¼ teaspoon salt

Cut crosswise into eight ½-inch rounds:

Two 4-ounce logs goat cheese

Gently press each round in the seasoned bread crumbs so that they are covered on both sides, transfer to a plate, and refrigerate for at least 30 minutes and up to 1 hour. Heat in a nonstick skillet over medium-high heat:

¼ cup olive oil

When hot, add the medallions and cook until browned on one side, about 2 minutes. Carefully flip the medallions and brown on the other side, about 2 minutes more. Transfer the medallions to a plate lined with paper towels and let them cool for a few minutes before placing 2 atop each plated salad.

BECKER HOUSE SALAD

4 servings

I. This is the green salad we make most often and never seem to tire of.

Prepare:

Megan's Lemon-Dijon Dressing, 575

Combine in a salad bowl:

1 head butter lettuce, washed, dried, and torn into bite-sized pieces
4 radishes, thinly sliced
¼ cup minced chives
¼ cup parsley leaves

Add the dressing to taste and toss. Divide the greens among serving plates. If desired, top with:

(Browned or Buttered Bread Crumbs, 957)

II. Because we can never decide which we like better—clean, crisp, mild greens or bitter, peppery ones—we rotate between version I and this lively blend.

Combine in a salad bowl:

1 bunch watercress, tough stems trimmed, or 1½ cups loosely packed arugula leaves
1 small head radicchio, torn into bite-sized pieces, or 2 Belgian endives, cored, leaves cut crosswise into 1-inch slices
2 cups torn and loosely packed Bibb or romaine lettuce
(⅓ cup loosely packed parsley, torn basil, or celery leaves)

Toss well to coat with:

About ½ cup Vinaigrette, 575, Feta or Goat Cheese Dressing, 577, or Miso Dressing, 576

Top, if desired, with any of the following:

(Crumbled bacon or diced Mushroom Bacon, 252)
(Crispy Fried Shallots, 256)
(Croutons, 638)

WEDGE SALAD

4 servings

A steakhouse favorite. Iceberg is classic, but romaine or butter lettuce may be substituted (cut them into serving-sized wedges).

Have ready:

Creamy Blue Cheese Dressing, 577, or Ranch Dressing, 577
4 slices bacon, cooked until crisp and crumbled
2 Hard-Boiled Eggs, 151, finely chopped

Cut into 4 wedges, leaving the core intact to help hold the leaves together:

1 head iceberg or butter lettuce

Place the wedges on serving plates and drizzle with dressing to taste. Sprinkle with the bacon, egg, and:

(1 medium tomato, diced)
¼ cup minced chives, red onion, or Quick-Pickled Onions, 930
(2 radishes, thinly sliced)
Freshly cracked black pepper

BITTER GREENS WITH APPLES AND PECANS

4 to 6 servings

Prepare:

Buttermilk-Honey Dressing, 577

Combine in a salad bowl:

4 cups loosely packed arugula leaves
1 small head radicchio, torn into bite-sized pieces
2 Belgian endives, cored, leaves sliced lengthwise into strips

Add just enough dressing to the greens to lightly moisten them and toss to coat. Divide the greens among salad plates. Add to the salad bowl:

1 Granny Smith or other tart apple, cored and very thinly sliced

Moisten the apple slices with more dressing, toss, and scatter over the salads, along with:

½ cup pecan halves, toasted, 1005, and chopped

CAESAR SALAD

6 servings

It is customary to prepare the dressing for this salad directly in the bowl. Top with slices of grilled chicken or shrimp for an entrée salad. If using egg, please read About Egg Safety, 979. For an eggless, anchovy-optional dressing, substitute ¾ cup Creamy Parmesan Dressing, 578, for the one provided here.

Mince and mash together with the flat side of a knife until a paste is formed:

2 garlic cloves, peeled
3 to 4 anchovy fillets
½ teaspoon salt

Transfer the paste to a large bowl and whisk in:

2 tablespoons lemon juice
1 large egg or 2 tablespoons mayonnaise
1 teaspoon Worcestershire sauce

Add in a slow, steady stream, whisking constantly:

½ cup extra-virgin olive oil

Season the dressing to taste with:

Salt and black pepper

Add to the bowl:

2 heads romaine lettuce, torn into bite-sized pieces
Croutons, 638

Toss together with the dressing and transfer to a serving bowl or individual plates. Sprinkle with:

Grated Parmesan to taste

GREEK SALAD

4 to 6 servings

Combine in a salad bowl:

2 large or 3 small heads Boston or romaine lettuce, torn into bite-sized pieces (about 8 cups loosely packed)
1 cup cherry tomatoes, halved, or 1 large tomato, cut into thin wedges
½ cup crumbled feta (2 ounces)
6 thin slices red onion, separated into rings, or 4 green onions, thinly sliced
½ cucumber, peeled, seeded, and sliced
½ cup Kalamata olives, pitted
(¾ cup sliced celery hearts)
6 radishes, sliced
(One 2-ounce can anchovy fillets, drained, rinsed, and halved lengthwise)

Toss well with:

½ cup Vinaigrette, 575, or Feta or Goat Cheese Dressing, 577, made with feta

MEGAN'S KALE SALAD

4 servings

This salad is our bid for kale's longevity as a salad green; smoky, toasted pumpkin seeds add richness and texture to the leaves, which soften slightly from being massaged in lemon juice and oil. Kale has logistical advantages as well: Since its leaves are sturdy, it may be dressed well ahead of time, making it perfect for picnics and potlucks.

Remove the midribs, 243, from:

1 bunch lacinato kale (about 12 ounces)

Shred the leaves crosswise into thin strips. In a salad bowl, combine:

2 tablespoons lemon juice
1 tablespoon extra-virgin olive oil
1 large garlic clove, minced or grated on a rasp grater
¼ teaspoon salt
⅛ teaspoon black pepper

Add the kale leaves, toss with the dressing, and massage until they soften, about 1 minute. Set aside. Warm in a small skillet over medium heat:

1 teaspoon vegetable oil

Add and stir frequently until toasted, about 5 minutes:

¼ cup pumpkin seeds

Remove the skillet from the heat and toss the pumpkin seeds with:

½ teaspoon smoked paprika

Top the salad with the pumpkin seeds and, if desired:

(Grated Parmesan)

SESAME GREENS WITH ROASTED SHIITAKES

4 servings

Toasted, soy-glazed sunflower seeds and roasted mushrooms make this salad especially satisfying. If desired, use vegetarian "oyster-flavored" sauce.

Stir together in a large bowl:

3 tablespoons white wine or rice vinegar
1 tablespoon oyster sauce
2 teaspoons toasted sesame oil
2 teaspoons soy sauce or tamari
1 garlic clove, grated or mashed to a paste

Add to the bowl:

1 bunch Swiss chard (about 12 ounces), finely shredded, ribs and all (4 packed cups)
¼ small head red cabbage, finely shredded (about 2 cups)

Toss well and allow to sit while you prepare the remaining ingredients.

Position a rack in the lower third of the oven and preheat the broiler. Toss together on a rimmed baking sheet:

4 ounces shiitake mushrooms, stems removed and caps thinly sliced
2 tablespoons vegetable oil
¼ teaspoon salt

Broil the mushrooms until well browned, 4 to 7 minutes. While the mushrooms cook, place a small skillet over medium heat. Add:

⅓ cup sunflower seeds or chopped cashews

Cook, stirring, until toasted. Remove from the heat and immediately add to the skillet:

2 teaspoons soy sauce

Stir to coat the seeds with the soy sauce until the liquid has evaporated.

Taste the greens for salt and acid and adjust the flavor accordingly. Add the mushrooms and toasted sunflower seeds and toss. Serve topped with:

Toasted sesame seeds

ENDIVE AND WALNUT SALAD

6 servings

Combine in a salad bowl:

4 Belgian endives, cored and leaves cut crosswise into ½-inch slices, or 1 head frisée, trimmed and cut into bite-sized pieces
2 large bunches watercress, tough stems trimmed

Toss until lightly coated with:

Vinaigrette, 575, made with half walnut oil, or Walnut Vinaigrette, 575

Divide the greens among serving plates. Add to the same bowl:

1 large Comice or Anjou pear, cored and thinly sliced
(6 fresh figs, halved)

Lightly coat with more vinaigrette. Top the greens with the fruit and sprinkle with:

½ cup walnuts, toasted, 1005, and chopped
1 cup crumbled Gorgonzola, Roquefort, or feta (4 ounces)
(Additional vinaigrette)

ABOUT WARM OR WILTED SALADS

"Wilted salad" may seem like a pejorative, but these recipes for salads with hot dressings are a testament to their appeal (and a reminder that there are exceptions to most rules with regard to taste). Serve warm salads immediately because they can become soggy. Also see Hot Slaw, 120.

WILTED SPINACH SALAD

4 servings

We think bacon fat is essential to the warm dressing, but you may discard it and use **2 tablespoons butter or vegetable oil** in its place. Baby spinach will work here, but we prefer the flavor and texture of mature spinach in this dish. Young mustard greens, dandelion greens, or kale may also be substituted.

Cook in a large skillet over medium heat until crisp:

5 slices bacon

Reduce the heat to low, drain the bacon slices on paper towels, and set aside. Pour all but 3 tablespoons of the bacon drippings out of the skillet and add:

⅓ cup cider vinegar
(2 teaspoons sugar)
(2 teaspoons yellow mustard seeds)
1 teaspoon minced or grated onion

Heat the dressing for about 5 minutes, or until it is fragrant and the mustard seeds have softened. Meanwhile, place in a salad bowl:

2 large bunches spinach, stems removed (about 8 cups packed)

Bring the vinegar mixture to a boil over high heat, then immediately pour it over the spinach and toss. Crumble the reserved bacon on top of the greens and serve at once, garnished with:

2 Hard-Boiled Eggs, 151, sliced or chopped

BISTRO SALAD

6 servings

Cook in a large skillet over medium heat until crisp:

8 ounces thick-cut bacon, cut crosswise into ½-inch-wide strips

Drain on paper towels. Pour the fat into a glass measuring cup and add:

Enough extra-virgin olive oil to make ½ cup total

Set aside. Add to the skillet and cook until softened, about 2 minutes:

2 shallots, thinly sliced

Add and cook until softened and fragrant, about 1 minute:

2 garlic cloves, minced

Add and cook 30 seconds, scraping up the browned bits in the skillet:

3 tablespoons red wine vinegar

Remove from the heat and whisk in the bacon fat/olive oil mixture. Stir in:

1 tablespoon minced parsley
1 teaspoon thyme leaves
Salt and black pepper to taste

Meanwhile, place in a salad bowl:

2 large heads frisée, trimmed and torn into bite-sized pieces (about 8 cups)

Toss with the bacon and add:

Croutons, 638

Toss with just enough of the hot dressing to coat. Divide among 6 salad plates and top with:

6 Poached Eggs, 153, well drained and trimmed
(Minced parsley)

ABOUT COLESLAW

Slaw is traditionally made with red or green cabbage, or a combination. We sometimes like to substitute napa cabbage or Brussels sprouts. When time is short, packaged shredded cabbage or broccoli stems can be pressed into service. ➤ One 16-ounce bag is roughly equivalent to 4 cups.

Once shredded, cabbage releases a lot of moisture as it sits in the dressing. If serving a small batch to be consumed with a sit-down meal at home, this is not as much of a concern. However, if you are preparing the slaw ahead of time for a buffet or cookout, we recommend briefly salting, rinsing, and draining the cabbage as described below to rid it of excess moisture. Further, wait to dress the slaw until just before serving.

To salt cabbage, carrots, and other shredded vegetables for slaw, cut as directed and toss in a large bowl with **1½ teaspoons salt** for every 1 pound of shredded vegetables (or every 4 cups packed). Leave to drain in a colander for 10 minutes and rinse well. Thoroughly drain or dry in a salad spinner and proceed with the recipe; any salt added should be to taste. Add dressing sparingly; you will need less than usual to coat the cabbage.

CLASSIC COLESLAW

6 to 8 servings

This creamy slaw is the American favorite. For a more flavorful creamy dressing, substitute **Alabama White Barbecue Sauce, 582.** For a lighter slaw with a vinegary bite, omit the mayonnaise and add more vinegar to taste, or toss it with **Vinaigrette, 575,** instead.

Remove the outer leaves and core from:

1 small head green or red cabbage (about 2 pounds)

Finely shred or chop by hand, on a mandoline, 201, or in a food processor (you should have 8 to 9 cups). Salt the cabbage, see above, if desired. Place in a deep bowl with one or more of the following:

1 large carrot, grated
(8 green onions or 1 small red onion, thinly sliced, or ½ cup Quick-Pickled Onions, 930)
3 or 4 slices bacon, cooked until crisp and crumbled
2 tablespoons chopped parsley, chives, or other herb
½ teaspoon dill, caraway, or celery seeds, or a combination

Mix together in a separate bowl:

¾ cup mayonnaise
¼ cup cider vinegar or rice vinegar

Add this dressing to the vegetables bit by bit, tossing, until it lightly coats the cabbage. Season to taste with:

Salt and black pepper

BECKER COLESLAW

4 to 6 servings

Remove the outer leaves and core from:

½ small head green or red cabbage (about 1 pound)

Cut the cabbage into ¼-inch dice (you should have 4 cups). Combine in a large bowl with:

1 large carrot, diced
10 radishes, diced
1 celery rib, diced
½ cup lightly packed, chopped parsley
2 to 3 dashes hot pepper sauce
Grated zest of 1 lemon

Combine, then toss until barely coated with:

Up to ¾ cup Vinaigrette, 575, or ½ cup Vinaigrette mixed with ½ cup mayonnaise

Cover and refrigerate until chilled.

SPICY CHINESE-STYLE SLAW

6 to 8 servings

This slaw is a garlicky favorite. For a superlative pickle that uses many of the same seasonings, see Quick Sichuan-Style Cucumber Pickles, 929.

Place one of the following in a large bowl:

2 pounds kohlrabi, daikon radish, or turnips, peeled and cut into matchsticks

Toss with:

1 tablespoon salt

Transfer the vegetables to a colander in the sink and let stand for 30 minutes. Meanwhile, add to the bowl:

½ cup rice vinegar
1 tablespoon vegetable oil
1 tablespoon toasted sesame oil
2 teaspoons sugar
½-inch piece ginger, peeled and minced
1 to 2 fresh red Thai chiles, seeded and minced, or ½ to 1 teaspoon red pepper flakes
1 garlic clove, minced
(½ teaspoon ground Sichuan pepper)

Rinse the vegetables in the colander well. Drain thoroughly, preferably with a salad spinner. Add them to the bowl and toss with the dressing. If possible, let the slaw sit 30 minutes before serving, stirring a few times. Add:

Salt to taste

Serve at room temperature or chilled.

HOT SLAW

4 to 6 servings

Have ready:

4 cups shredded red or green cabbage (about 1 pound)
(1 large tart apple, cored and grated)

Cook in a large skillet over medium heat until crisp:

6 slices thick-cut bacon

Drain the bacon on paper towels. Add to the hot fat in the skillet:

3 tablespoons cider vinegar
2 tablespoons water
1 tablespoon brown sugar
(½ teaspoon caraway or celery seeds)
½ teaspoon salt

Bring to a boil, then reduce the heat to a simmer and stir in the cabbage and apple. Simmer for 2 minutes. Crumble the bacon and sprinkle on top of the cabbage.

BRUSSELS SPROUT SLAW WITH SPICED YOGURT

6 servings

A warm, hearty slaw for wintertime; perfect for the Thanksgiving table.

Cook in a large skillet over medium heat until crisp:

4 slices bacon, diced

Drain the bacon on paper towels. Add to the hot fat in the skillet:

2 garlic cloves, smashed

Cook the garlic until it starts to brown, turning it to brown both sides, about 5 minutes. Remove the garlic, mince it, and set aside. Add to the skillet:

1 pound Brussels sprouts, trimmed and shredded
½ teaspoon salt

Cook, stirring occasionally, until the sprouts are tender and starting to brown, 10 to 12 minutes. Meanwhile, add the minced garlic to a medium bowl, along with:

½ cup plain Greek yogurt
Finely grated zest of 1 lemon
2 tablespoons lemon juice
½ teaspoon ground coriander
½ teaspoon ground cumin
¼ teaspoon black pepper

Add the softened Brussels sprouts to the bowl. If there are any browned bits, deglaze the skillet with a splash of water and add to the bowl as well. Crumble and stir in the reserved bacon. Add:

Salt to taste

If desired, garnish with:

(Pomegranate seeds)

ABOUT COMBINATION SALADS

Also known as **main-course salads,** and the antiquated-but-catchy name **salmagundi,** these are served as an entrée and typically contain generous quantities of meat, seafood, chicken, eggs, or cheese. Most of the various components can be prepared ahead, then chilled, and the salad assembled just before serving. Or, let leftover proteins and on-hand pantry items be your guide: Roasted chicken makes for a fine Niçoise (just don't tell the French), julienned salami can enhance a chef's salad, and any mixture is made better with a few pickled peppers in our opinion, but to each their own.

CHEF'S SALAD

4 to 6 servings

Place on a large platter:

About 10 cups bite-sized pieces Bibb lettuce

Prepare:

Vinaigrette, 575, Creamy Blue Cheese Dressing, 577, or Thousand Island Dressing, 576

Toss the lettuce with just enough dressing to lightly coat the leaves. Arrange on top:

1 cup thinly sliced cooked chicken or turkey breast
4 ounces ham, cut into thin strips, or thin slices of prosciutto, rolled into cigar shapes
5 ounces sharp Cheddar, Gouda, Swiss, or other firm cheese, cut into thin strips

Garnish with:

2 medium tomatoes, cut into wedges, or 1½ cups cherry tomatoes (8 ounces), halved
3 Hard-Boiled Eggs, 151, quartered
12 olives, pitted and sliced
1 cup chopped arugula or watercress
Salt and black pepper to taste

COBB SALAD

4 to 6 servings

When you do not have this formula close at hand, remember: **E**gg, **A**vocado, **T**omato, **C**hicken, green **O**nion, **B**acon, and **B**lue cheese spells "eat Cobb." The original recipe from Hollywood's swanky Brown Derby restaurant calls for a mix of mild, bitter, and peppery greens, but you can use a whole head of romaine or Bibb lettuce instead if desired.

Prepare:

Vinaigrette, 575

Wash, dry, and place in a large bowl:

1 bunch watercress, tough stems removed and coarsely chopped
½ head romaine or Bibb lettuce, coarsely chopped
1 small head radicchio, coarsely chopped

Toss with enough dressing to lightly coat the leaves and transfer to a platter or individual plates. Arrange in rows on top of the greens:

1 avocado, pitted, peeled, and diced
2 to 3 cups diced cooked chicken or turkey breast (from about 12 ounces raw chicken)
4 to 6 slices bacon, cooked until crisp and crumbled
3 Hard-Boiled Eggs, 151, diced
3 medium tomatoes, coarsely chopped, or 2 cups cherry tomatoes (about 10 ounces), halved
4 green onions, thinly sliced, or ¼ cup minced chives
½ cup crumbled blue cheese (2 ounces)

Lightly drizzle vinaigrette over the salad(s) and serve.

SALADE NIÇOISE

4 to 6 servings

A classic summer entrée. If authenticity is no obstacle, upgrade the canned tuna with Grilled Fish Steaks, 385. Just plate the dressed greens and vegetables, top each with a portion of sliced grilled tuna (or salmon), and garnish as directed.

Place in a large saucepan:

6 small red potatoes or 12 fingerling potatoes
1 tablespoon salt

Add cold water to cover, bring to a boil over high heat, then reduce the heat to a simmer until the potatoes are tender, about 20 minutes. As the potatoes cook, prepare:

½ cup Vinaigrette, 575, made with 2 teaspoons Dijon mustard

Set aside. Remove the potatoes from the boiling water with a slotted spoon and let cool. Meanwhile, add to the pan and boil until bright green but still crisp, 2 to 3 minutes:

1 pound green beans (preferably haricots verts), trimmed

Transfer to a bowl of ice water to stop the cooking. Let cool and drain well. Place in a medium bowl. Cut the cooled potatoes into ½-inch-thick slices and add to the beans.

Drizzle one-quarter of the dressing over the potatoes and beans and gently toss to coat. Arrange on a large platter:

1 head Boston lettuce, separated into leaves, or about 5 cups loosely packed mixed salad greens
2 large tomatoes, cut into 8 wedges each, or 1½ cups cherry tomatoes (8 ounces), halved

Drizzle another one-quarter of the dressing on top. Arrange the green beans and potatoes on the platter, along with:

5 Hard-Boiled Eggs, 151, halved
6 ounces canned tuna, preferably packed in olive oil, drained and flaked

Drizzle with the remaining dressing. Scatter over the top:

½ cup Niçoise or Kalamata olives, pitted
4 green onions, thinly sliced
¼ cup minced parsley or chiffonade of basil, 993
2 tablespoons drained capers
(Up to 6 anchovy fillets, rinsed and patted dry)

Sprinkle with:

Salt and black pepper to taste

LOBSTER SALAD VINAIGRETTE

4 servings

If lobster is too pricey or unavailable, feel free to substitute **crabmeat,** or **peeled cooked shrimp, 363,** cut into ½-inch chunks.

Prepare:

Vinaigrette, 575, made with minced basil

Combine in a salad bowl:

2 cups watercress, tough stems trimmed
2 cups mixed salad greens, baby romaine, or baby spinach leaves
1½ cups Belgian endive, cored and thinly sliced

Toss with just enough vinaigrette to coat. Divide the greens among salad plates. In the same bowl, toss together, adding just enough vinaigrette to coat:

12 ounces cooked lobster, cut into ½-inch chunks
1 avocado, pitted, peeled, and diced

Spoon the lobster and avocado over the greens. Garnish with:

⅔ cup cherry or grape tomatoes, halved (about 4 ounces)

CRAB LOUIS

4 servings

This classic recipe is also excellent atop shredded kale and radicchio instead of butter lettuce. Use a little of the vinaigrette used in the Sauce Louis to dress the greens before piling the crab on top.

Line a platter or a salad bowl with:

Boston or Bibb lettuce leaves

Place on top:

About 2 cups thin strips Boston, Bibb, or red-leaf lettuce

Heap on top of these:

2 cups lump crabmeat, picked over for shells and cartilage

Pour over the crab, to taste:

Sauce Louis, 564

Garnish with:

(2 Hard-Boiled Eggs, 151, sliced)
Minced chives

SEARED SCALLOP, GRAPEFRUIT, AND RADICCHIO SALAD

4 servings

We sometimes serve this salad topped with Pan-Fried Goat Cheese Medallions, 116.

Soak in ice water for 30 minutes:

1 small head radicchio, cored and coarsely chopped (about 3 cups)

Meanwhile, cut into suprêmes, 182:

1 large grapefruit

Prepare:

Vinaigrette, 575, made with sherry vinegar and 2 teaspoons honey

Dry the radicchio and place it in a large bowl along with:

3 cups lightly packed arugula

Prepare:

Seared Sea Scallops, 356

While the scallops cook, toss the greens with enough vinaigrette to lightly coat the leaves, and divide among plates, along with the grapefruit sections. Top with the hot scallops, lightly drizzle them with more vinaigrette, and garnish with:

(2 tablespoons minced chives)
1 tablespoon chiffonade of mint, shiso, or basil leaves, 993

THE MALLORY'S SHRIMP SALAD

4 servings

When my father, Ethan, came to visit during the holidays, he stayed at the now-defunct Mallory Hotel in Portland, Oregon. We would invariably find ourselves in the hotel's plush, 1940s-era restaurant for lunch (a frequent hometown haunt of James Beard, as it turns out). Dad never failed to order this salad.

Line 4 plates with:

Torn iceberg lettuce

Halve, pit, and peel, 209:

2 large avocados

Nestle an avocado half in the center of each plate, cut side up. Divide among the avocado cavities:

1 cup cooked bay shrimp

Dividing evenly, arrange around the avocado halves:

4 Hard-Boiled Eggs, 151, quartered
1 cucumber, peeled, halved lengthwise, seeded, and thinly sliced on the diagonal
½ cup pitted ripe black, oil-cured, kalamata, or niçoise olives, sliced

Drizzle the salads with:

Vinaigrette, 575, or Sauce Louis, 564, to taste

Garnish with:

Lemon wedges

LARB (THAI MINCED PORK SALAD)

4 servings

Thai *larb* or *laap* are fragrant, punchy salads seasoned with herbs, fish sauce, lime juice, and curry paste. If desired, you may substitute **ground duck** or **chicken** for the pork. **Toasted rice powder** is a common garnish for this salad; though not essential, it adds a nice roasted flavor and crunchy texture. It is available at Thai markets, or you can make it yourself: Add uncooked sticky rice grains to a dry skillet, place over medium heat, and cook, stirring, until the grains are lightly browned and fragrant, 10 to 15 minutes. Once cool, pound the rice into a coarse powder with a mortar and pestle.

Mix together thoroughly in a small bowl:

¼ cup red curry paste, store-bought or homemade, 585
1 teaspoon ground Sichuan pepper
½ teaspoon black pepper
¼ teaspoon grated or ground nutmeg

Divide among 4 plates:

4 cups thinly sliced cabbage (about 1 pound)
1 large cucumber, peeled, halved lengthwise, seeded, and sliced

Set aside. Heat in a large skillet over medium heat until hot:

3 tablespoons vegetable oil

Add the paste mixture and fry, stirring, until fragrant and lightly browned, about 2 minutes. Increase the heat to medium-high and add:

1½ pounds lean ground pork or minced pork loin

Quickly stir together with the paste until thoroughly mixed and flatten in the skillet with a spatula. Cook, undisturbed, until browned on the bottom, 5 to 7 minutes. Add to the skillet:

½ cup water

Stir, breaking up the pork and scraping any browned bits off the bottom. Simmer until the pork is cooked and the water has evaporated, about 4 minutes more. Remove from the heat and stir in:

4 green onions, thinly sliced
¼ cup chopped cilantro
¼ cup chopped mint
2 tablespoons lime juice
2 tablespoons fish sauce
(¼ teaspoon red pepper flakes)

Top the cabbage and cucumbers with the pork mixture, drizzling any remaining sauce over the top. Top each serving with:

Sprigs of cilantro and mint
(Crispy Fried Shallots, 256)
(Chopped pork rinds or cracklings)
(Toasted rice powder, see headnote)
(Additional red pepper flakes)
Lime wedges

THAI BEEF SALAD

6 servings

Have ready:

1½ pounds skirt, flank, or hanger steak

Sprinkle the steak all over with:

1 tablespoon fish sauce
1 tablespoon lime juice
1 tablespoon black pepper
½ teaspoon salt

Let sit while you prepare the remaining ingredients. Combine in a salad bowl:

8 cups lightly packed spicy greens, 112, or a combination of spicy greens and romaine lettuce
1¼ cups lightly packed mint leaves
1¼ cups lightly packed cilantro leaves
10 radishes, thinly sliced
2 medium shallots, thinly sliced

Stir together in a small bowl:

3 tablespoons lime juice
2 tablespoons fish sauce
1 tablespoon sugar
1 stalk lemongrass, tender part only, very thinly sliced
½ teaspoon red pepper flakes or 2 fresh Thai chiles, thinly sliced
1 garlic clove, minced

Prepare a medium-hot grill fire, 1063, or preheat the broiler. Grill or broil, 459, the steak to the desired degree of doneness. Slice the beef across the grain into ½-inch-wide strips. Add the beef and dressing to the greens. Toss to combine.

CHINESE CHICKEN SALAD

4 to 6 servings

A Chinese-American creation everyone can love. We like the mouthwatering combination of savory chicken, sweet mandarin oranges, crunchy peanuts and chow mein noodles, and refreshing napa cabbage.

Combine in a large bowl:

4 cups thin strips cooked chicken (about 1½ pounds)
One 11-ounce can mandarin oranges packed in juice, drained and juice reserved
6 green onions, thinly sliced

Whisk together well in a small bowl:

½ cup reserved mandarin orange juice
¼ cup vegetable oil
2 tablespoons lemon or lime juice
1 tablespoon soy sauce
2 teaspoons toasted sesame oil
1-inch piece ginger, peeled and minced
1 teaspoon dry mustard
(½ teaspoon red pepper flakes)
½ teaspoon salt, or to taste
(½ teaspoon ground Sichuan pepper or Five-Spice Powder, 590)

Toss enough dressing with the chicken mixture to moisten. Taste and adjust the seasonings. Serve over:

4 cups shredded napa cabbage (about 12 ounces)

Top with:

1 cup chow mein noodles
1 cup chopped roasted unsalted peanuts or ¾ cup sliced almonds, toasted, 1005
(1 tablespoon toasted sesame seeds)

TACO SALAD

4 to 6 servings

A salad in name, but not in spirit. Diners may eat this and say "I'm eating a salad," without failing a polygraph.

Layer in individual shallow bowls or on a serving platter in the order listed:

8 cups tortilla chips, broken into bite-sized pieces
½ recipe Picadillo, 503, 1 recipe Seasoned Tempeh Crumbles, 287, or 3 cups cooked chicken or turkey, shredded (about 1 pound)
1½ cups shredded Cheddar or Monterey Jack (6 ounces)
1 small head iceberg or romaine lettuce, thinly sliced
4 green onions, chopped, or 1 cup Quick-Pickled Onions, 930
1 large tomato, coarsely chopped, or 1 cup cherry tomatoes (6 ounces), halved
(4 radishes, sliced)
1 cup salsa, store-bought or homemade, 573–74

Serve with, if desired:

(Sour cream)
(Guacamole, 51)

ABOUT BOUND SALADS

Absurdities abound in the English language, and calling a meaty mixture dressed with mayonnaise a "salad" is most certainly one of these. Though we occasionally still serve these salads on a bed of greens in a nod to their name, these rich mixtures usually make their way into sandwiches—though they are good in cucumber and tomato cases or halved avocados as well.

A few preliminaries: Always fully cool cooked meats before combining with mayonnaise, or it may separate. Crisp vegetables like radishes, carrots, and celery add welcome texture as well as flavor (as do toasted nuts). If desired, you can marinate plainly seasoned cooked chicken in a flavorful vinaigrette or dressing before adding to the mayonnaise (drain off all the vinaigrette to avoid making the mayonnaise runny). The same applies to vegetables: Quick-Pickled Onions, 930, or carrots, 929, can add zest to a tuna or egg salad, as can store-bought pickles of all kinds. Though our minds jump to mayonnaise when we think of these salads, a wide variety of dressings and sauces may be used instead, such as Vinaigrette, 575, Mojo, 567, Sauce Gribiche, 568, Feta or Goat Cheese Dressing, 577, Tzatziki, 569, Tahini Dressing, 576, Pesto, 586, Japanese Steakhouse Ginger Dressing, 576, or the sauce for Bún bowls, 305, or Sesame Noodles, 302. Just be sure your choice of dressing complements the flavor of the ingredients in the salad.

CHICKEN OR TURKEY SALAD

4 servings

Include both dark and light meat for the best flavor. For the ultimate chicken or turkey salad, smoke or grill the poultry. Cool the meat completely before mixing everything together, and refrigerate the salad until serving.

To scale this recipe up for a crowd, remember: A 5-pound chicken will yield about 5 cups diced meat; a 3-pound boneless turkey breast will yield around 9 cups diced meat.

Combine in a medium bowl:

2 cups diced or shredded cooked chicken or turkey (about 8 ounces)
½ cup diced celery or cucumber
(½ cup halved seedless grapes or ¼ cup diced pickles)
(4 green onions, thinly sliced)
(¼ cup coarsely chopped toasted, 1005, almonds, walnuts, or pecans)

Mix in:

½ cup mayonnaise, store-bought or homemade, 563, or ⅓ cup Vinaigrette, 575
(1 tablespoon chopped parsley or tarragon)
(1 teaspoon Dijon mustard or curry powder)
Lemon juice to taste
Salt and black pepper to taste

CHICKEN SALAD COMBINATIONS

Follow the recipe for **Chicken or Turkey Salad, above.** Keep the proportions to twice as much meat as the other ingredients and add only enough dressing to moisten.

Mayonnaise, diced celery, diced apples, halved grapes or raisins, and walnuts
Green Goddess Dressing, 577, Quick-Pickled Onions, 930, and chopped Hard-Boiled Eggs, 151
Tzatziki, 569, sliced green onions, diced radishes, pitted Kalamata olives, and finely chopped oregano
Vinaigrette (made with tomato), 575, sliced green onions, diced cucumber, and crumbled bacon
Tahini Dressing, 576, crumbled feta, sliced green onions, chopped parsley, and Za'atar, 590

HAM SALAD

4 servings

Combine in a bowl:

2 cups diced cooked ham
¼ cup finely chopped pickles (dill or sweet) or pickle relish
¼ cup mayonnaise
(3 Hard-Boiled Eggs, 151, finely chopped)
2 tablespoons minced onion or green onion
(1 tablespoon lemon juice)
½ teaspoon Dijon mustard
⅛ teaspoon black pepper, or to taste

Cover and refrigerate until chilled.

EGG SALAD

4 servings

Egg salad is extremely versatile. Add herbs, olives, capers, anchovies, or pickled peppers. If desired, leave out the mayonnaise and add the Dijon mustard and lemon juice for a more piquant flavor.

Combine in a medium bowl:

6 Hard-Boiled Eggs, 151, finely chopped
¼ cup mayonnaise
3 tablespoons minced celery
3 tablespoons minced dill pickle or cornichons
1 tablespoon minced onion or 2 tablespoons minced green onion
(1 tablespoon minced herbs, such as dill or parsley)
(1 tablespoon Dijon or whole-grain mustard)
(1 tablespoon lemon juice)
(¼ teaspoon curry powder)
Salt and black pepper to taste

Cover and refrigerate.

VEGAN "EGG" SALAD

4 servings

This tofu-based salad is excellent on a sandwich or served atop Broiled Tomatoes, 282.

Place in a thin, clean kitchen towel:

14 to 16 ounces extra-firm tofu

Squeeze the tofu over the sink to remove excess moisture (it's okay if the tofu crumbles a bit). Crumble the tofu into a medium bowl and mix in:

⅓ cup vegan mayonnaise
¼ cup minced red onion or chives
¼ cup minced celery or fennel
(¼ cup minced carrot)
2 tablespoons chopped parsley or 1 tablespoon minced dill
(1 tablespoon minced cornichons or sweet pickle relish)
1 tablespoon Dijon mustard
½ teaspoon ground turmeric
1 teaspoon lemon juice
Salt and black pepper to taste
(Pinch of black salt, 1013)

Refrigerate until chilled, about 1 hour.

TUNA SALAD

4 servings

Combine in a medium bowl:

Two 5-ounce cans tuna, drained, or 8 ounces cooked tuna, flaked with a fork
1 celery rib, diced

Add:

2 tablespoons extra-virgin olive oil plus 2 tablespoons lemon juice, or ¼ cup mayonnaise
(2 tablespoons chopped pickles or 1 tablespoon capers, drained)
(2 tablespoons chopped herbs, such as chives and parsley)
Salt and black pepper to taste

Combine the mixture with a fork.

BECKER TUNA SALAD

4 servings

Our crunchy, go-to formula, especially if we remembered to grill an extra tuna steak the night before to have in this salad.

Combine in a large bowl:

Two 5-ounce cans tuna, drained, or 8 ounces cooked tuna, flaked with a fork
½ cup Vinaigrette, 575, made with lemon juice, or ¼ cup Vinaigrette and ¼ cup mayonnaise
½ cup chopped red or green cabbage
1 small carrot, diced
1 celery rib, diced
¼ cup chopped parsley
(2 radishes, diced)
(1 tablespoon capers, drained)
2 to 3 dashes hot pepper sauce
Finely grated zest of ½ lemon
½ teaspoon black pepper, or to taste

Cover and refrigerate until chilled.

LOBSTER OR SHRIMP SALAD

3 to 4 servings

Serve on crackers or in endive leaves as an appetizer, or on lightly dressed butter lettuce leaves as a salad.

Combine in a medium bowl:

2 cups coarsely chopped cooked lobster meat, 360, lump crabmeat, or peeled and cooked shrimp or whole bay shrimp (about 12 ounces)
½ medium cucumber, peeled, halved lengthwise, seeded, and diced
3 to 4 tablespoons sour cream or mayonnaise, to taste
1 celery rib, diced
(1 Hard-Boiled Egg, 151, chopped)

Stir in:

Up to 2 tablespoons minced herbs, such as parsley, chives, and/or tarragon
Finely grated zest of ½ lemon
1 to 2 teaspoons lemon juice, to taste
Salt and black pepper to taste

Garnish with:

Minced chives or tarragon

ABOUT VEGETABLE SALADS

Almost any vegetable can serve as the base for a salad, from thinly shaved or spiral-cut raw carrots to sliced cucumbers to blanched green beans to roasted beets. In addition to the recipes below, keep in mind that practically any vegetable—snap peas, fresh peas, blanched green beans, cooked artichokes, or asparagus—can be lightly tossed in Vinaigrette, 575, and served as a side dish. This is especially useful as a means of serving leftover steamed vegetables without turning them to mush with further cooking.

ASPARAGUS-SESAME SALAD

4 to 6 servings

Steam, 208, until just tender:

1½ pounds asparagus, trimmed and cut into 2-inch pieces

Meanwhile, whisk together in a small bowl:

2 tablespoons toasted sesame oil
4 teaspoons white wine vinegar or rice vinegar
4 teaspoons soy sauce
1 tablespoon toasted sesame seeds
1 tablespoon sugar

Toss the asparagus with the dressing while warm. Serve warm or chilled.

AVOCADO AND CITRUS SALAD

4 servings

Prepare:

Vinaigrette, 575, Miso Dressing, 576, or Poppy Seed–Honey Dressing, 575

Cut into suprêmes, 182:

1 large grapefruit
2 large oranges

Cut crosswise on a slight diagonal into ¼-inch-thick slices:

2 avocados, pitted and peeled

Marinate the avocado for 5 minutes in ½ cup of the prepared dressing. Place in a large bowl:

1 small head romaine lettuce, shredded, or about 6 cups baby spinach leaves

When ready to serve, toss in enough dressing to lightly coat the leaves. Plate the greens and alternate the avocado and citrus sections on top. Sprinkle, if desired, with:

(Toasted sesame seeds)

AVOCADO AND MANGO SALAD

4 servings

Prepare:

½ recipe Vinaigrette, 575, made with lime juice

Thinly slice lengthwise:

1 mango, seeded and peeled, 187
2 avocados, pitted and peeled

If the salad will sit for a time, gently coat the avocado slices with a bit of the vinaigrette to prevent browning. Toss with more dressing until lightly coated:

2 cups arugula or watercress, tough stems trimmed
½ small red onion, thinly sliced, or 4 green onions, thinly sliced on a diagonal

Divide among plates. Alternate the slices of avocado and mango around the arugula. Spoon dressing over the slices to taste. If desired, sprinkle with:

(Aleppo, Marash, Urfa, or piment d'Espelette pepper flakes, 968)
(Flaky sea salt)

BEET, FENNEL, AND CITRUS SALAD WITH HORSERADISH

4 servings

A vibrant winter salad. The sweetness of the beets and fennel is balanced by the citrus and the welcome bite of horseradish (if using a prepared type, opt for one that is not "creamy").

Prepare, 219, or have ready:

1 pound cooked and peeled beets, sliced or cut into wedges

Cut into suprêmes, 182:

2 oranges or 1 large grapefruit

Thinly slice crosswise:

1 large fennel bulb

Whisk together in a medium bowl:

¼ cup extra-virgin olive oil
2 tablespoons lemon juice
1 tablespoon finely grated fresh or prepared horseradish
½ teaspoon black pepper
¼ teaspoon salt

Add the beets, citrus, and fennel and toss to coat. Taste and adjust the seasoning, if necessary, and garnish with:

2 tablespoons minced chives or parsley

CARROT AND RAISIN SALAD

6 to 8 servings

Combine in a medium bowl:

4 large carrots, coarsely grated (about 2½ cups)
½ cup raisins
(½ cup coarsely chopped pecans or unsalted roasted peanuts)
Finely grated zest of 1 lemon
1 tablespoon lemon juice
¾ teaspoon salt
Black pepper to taste

Toss the salad with:

¼ cup sour cream or mayonnaise, or to taste

CAROTTES RÂPÉES (FRENCH GRATED CARROT SALAD)

4 to 6 servings

This salad is ubiquitous in France, perhaps to help balance out all the cheese and wine.

Combine in a medium bowl:

1 pound large carrots, grated
⅓ cup coarsely chopped flat-leaf parsley

Shake together in a small jar:

3 tablespoons extra-virgin olive oil
2 tablespoons lemon juice or white wine vinegar
1 teaspoon Dijon mustard
1 teaspoon sugar
¼ teaspoon salt

Pour the dressing over the carrots and toss.

SHAVED CARROT SALAD

4 to 6 servings

This salad is a beautiful tangle of carrots, sweet fennel, and crisp radishes, all tossed with a tangy, bright-green yogurt dressing. For even more color, use rainbow carrots. You will have carrot "cores" left over, which can be saved for stock making, reserved for use in soups or stir-fries, or eaten as a cook's snack.

Prepare:

Herbed Yogurt Dressing, 577

Using a vegetable peeler, cut into long, thin ribbons, rotating them with each stroke:

1 pound medium carrots

Transfer the carrot ribbons to a large bowl, along with:

4 radishes, thinly sliced
½ fennel bulb, thinly sliced

Toss with enough dressing to lightly coat everything and transfer to a serving dish. Sprinkle with:

(½ cup crumbled feta)
Minced chives or parsley or cilantro leaves

CELERY ROOT RÉMOULADE

4 to 6 servings

Peel and cut into ¼-inch-thick rounds:

2 medium celery roots

Cook in a pot of boiling salted water until tender, 3 to 4 minutes. Drain and let cool, then cut into very thin strips. Place in a shallow bowl and cover with:

Rémoulade Sauce, 564

allowing about ½ cup sauce for every 2 cups celery root. Cover and refrigerate until well chilled. Serve on a bed of:

Watercress, tough stems trimmed

DEE'S CORN AND TOMATO SALAD

4 servings

Few things symbolize summer as well as corn and tomatoes. This salad is perfect for celebrating both when they are at peak ripeness.

Cut from the cob:

3 cups corn kernels (about 6 ears)

Combine in a bowl with:

1 large tomato, diced
½ red onion, diced, or 4 green onions, thinly sliced
2 tablespoons chopped basil

Barely moisten with:

Vinaigrette, 575

Serve, chilled or at room temperature, within 2 to 3 hours, garnished with:

Basil leaves

CUCUMBER SALAD

4 servings

I. For a special treat, add crabmeat to make a seafood cocktail.

Combine in a medium bowl:

¼ cup rice vinegar or white wine vinegar
(4 teaspoons toasted sesame seeds)
2 teaspoons sugar
(1 garlic clove, minced)
(¼ teaspoon red pepper flakes)

Add and toss to coat:

1 large cucumber, peeled, halved lengthwise, seeded, and cut into thin strips or slices

Cover and refrigerate until chilled, about 1 hour.

II. CREAMY CUCUMBER SALAD

Make a double batch of **Raita, 569,** or **Tzatziki, 569** (use 2 cucumbers for the latter). Cut the peeled and seeded cucumbers into bite-sized chunks or slices.

CHINESE SMACKED CUCUMBER SALAD

4 to 6 servings

This recipe gives you permission to hit your vegetables, but know when to stop. The cucumbers should be cracked all over, not turned into mush.

Place on a cutting board:

2 English cucumbers or 6 Persian cucumbers

Smack the cucumbers with a rolling pin or the flat side of a cleaver several times until the cucumber cracks in places. Coarsely chop the cucumbers and toss in a bowl with:

1 tablespoon chili oil or Spicy Chinese Chile Crisp, 572
1 tablespoon soy sauce
1 tablespoon Chinese black vinegar or rice vinegar
1 garlic clove, minced
1 teaspoon sugar
(½ teaspoon ground Sichuan pepper)
¼ teaspoon salt

Allow to marinate for at least 10 minutes and up to 30 minutes.

ARUGULA AND HEART OF PALM SALAD

4 servings

This salad boasts peppery arugula, spicy jalapeño, and nutty pumpkin seeds to contrast with the almost creamy, lightly tart palm hearts.

Have ready:

Vinaigrette, 575, using lime juice, Roasted Garlic Dressing, 576, or Megan's Lemon-Dijon Dressing, 575

Place in a large bowl:

4 cups lightly packed arugula
2 celery ribs, thinly sliced

Toss with enough dressing to moisten and divide among plates or transfer to a serving dish. Add to the bowl:

One 14-ounce can hearts of palm, drained and cut crosswise into ½-inch lengths
(1 jalapeño pepper, very thinly sliced)

Add a little more dressing and toss to coat. Arrange the vegetables on top of the greens along with:

1 large avocado, pitted, peeled, and sliced

Sprinkle with:

¼ cup pumpkin seeds, toasted, 1005

JICAMA SALAD

6 to 8 servings

Peel and cut into matchsticks:

1 medium jicama (about 1 pound)

Cut crosswise into ¼-inch-thick slices:

2 small cucumbers, peeled, halved lengthwise, and seeded

Cut both ends off:

3 medium navel oranges

Stand the oranges on a cutting board and cut away the peel and all the white pith and outer membrane. Halve lengthwise, then cut crosswise into ¼-inch-thick slices. Toss the jicama, cucumbers, and oranges in a large bowl along with:

6 radishes, thinly sliced
1 small red onion, thinly sliced
⅓ cup lime juice

Let stand for 20 minutes, then season to taste with:

Salt

Spoon the salad and juices onto a platter. Top with:

2 teaspoons chili powder
⅓ cup chopped cilantro

THREE-PEA SALAD

6 servings

For a main-course salad, add sautéed shrimp.

Prepare the dressing for:

Asparagus Sesame Salad, 125

Cook in a large pot of boiling salted water for 2 minutes:

2 ounces sugar snap peas (about 1 cup)

Add and cook for 1 minute:

1 ounce snow peas (about ½ cup)
½ cup fresh or frozen green peas, thawed

Drain and rinse under cold water. Pat dry. Toss the peas in a bowl with the dressing and:

6 cups pea shoots or bean sprouts (about 8 ounces)

POTATO SALAD

4 servings

The vinaigrette used here is best for picnics, as it will not spoil.

Boil, 265, until just soft enough to pierce with a fork:

1 pound red or gold potatoes

Drain. When cool enough to handle, slice or cut into cubes. Marinate in:

⅓ cup Vinaigrette, 575

Serve warm or cold. Just before serving, fold in gently:

(½ cup chopped watercress or arugula)
1 tablespoon chopped parsley
1 tablespoon minced chives

CREAMY POTATO SALAD

6 to 8 servings

Boil, 265, until just soft enough to pierce with a fork:

2 pounds red or gold potatoes

Drain. Peel, if desired, and cut into bite-sized pieces. Let the potatoes cool completely in a medium bowl. Toss with:

¾ cup mayonnaise
1 to 2 celery ribs, diced
4 green onions, sliced, ⅓ cup chopped Quick-Pickled Onions, 930, or 2 tablespoons grated onion
(3 Hard-Boiled Eggs, 151, diced)
(¼ to ½ cup minced parsley, watercress, or arugula)
2 tablespoons lemon juice or red wine vinegar
(1 to 2 tablespoons capers, pickle relish, diced dill pickles, chopped olives, or chopped pickled peppers)
(1 tablespoon whole-grain or yellow mustard)
(2 teaspoons prepared horseradish)
Salt and black pepper to taste

Cover and refrigerate until chilled.

GERMAN POTATO SALAD

6 servings

Boil, 265, until just soft enough to pierce with a fork:

2 pounds red or gold potatoes

Drain, peel, and slice or cut into cubes. Cook in a skillet over medium heat until crisp:

4 slices bacon

Transfer to paper towels to drain and set aside. Pour off all but 2 tablespoons of fat from the skillet. Return the skillet to medium-high heat and add:

½ medium onion, chopped
1 celery rib, chopped

Cook until golden, about 7 minutes. Add and bring to a boil:

½ cup cider vinegar
¼ cup water or chicken broth
¼ cup chopped dill pickles
½ teaspoon sugar
½ teaspoon salt
(¼ to ½ teaspoon dry mustard)
⅛ teaspoon sweet paprika

Remove from the heat, crumble in the reserved bacon, and add the potatoes, stirring to coat. Serve warm, garnished with:

Chopped parsley or chives

TOMATO SALAD

6 to 8 servings

For those determined to make this out of season, please read About Tomatoes, 280, for tips on choosing and serving tomatoes in the winter. To make this a **Caprese Salad,** layer **12 ounces fresh mozzarella, cut into ¼-inch-thick slices,** between the tomatoes. Shower with **chopped basil,** drizzle with **extra-virgin olive oil** and **balsamic vinegar to taste,** and sprinkle with **salt and pepper.**

Arrange, overlapping, around a chilled platter:

6 large tomatoes, cut into ½-inch-thick slices or wedges

If desired, alternate with the tomato slices:

(1 red, Bermuda, or Vidalia onion, very thinly sliced)

Drizzle over the tomatoes:

½ cup extra-virgin olive oil and a splash of balsamic vinegar, or Vinaigrette, 575

Sprinkle with:

¼ to ½ cup chopped parsley, summer savory, tarragon, basil, or a combination
Salt and black pepper to taste

Do not chill; serve at room temperature.

SHIRAZI OR ISRAELI SALAD

4 servings

For a more texturally interesting salad, slice some of the cucumbers and chop the rest. Include different kinds of tomatoes—chopped large heirlooms of different colors as well as cherry tomatoes. We like to throw in diced radish as well.

Combine in a salad bowl:

1 pound very ripe tomatoes, chopped, or halved cherry tomatoes
5 Persian cucumbers or 1 large English cucumber (about 12 ounces), sliced or diced
½ red onion, thinly sliced or finely chopped, or 5 green onions, sliced
⅓ cup flat-leaf parsley leaves
⅓ cup mint leaves
(2 tablespoons chopped dill)
(1 teaspoon ground sumac)

Pour over the vegetables and toss to combine:

¼ cup extra-virgin olive oil
2 tablespoons lemon or lime juice, or red wine vinegar
¼ teaspoon salt
¼ teaspoon black pepper

PANZANELLA (TUSCAN BREAD AND TOMATO SALAD)

6 to 8 servings

Preheat the oven to 350°F. Place on a baking sheet:

5 cups 1-inch bread cubes (from a 1-pound loaf of rustic bread)

Toss the bread cubes with:

3 tablespoons olive oil

Spread the cubes out evenly and bake, shaking the pan once or twice, until browned, 10 to 15 minutes. Meanwhile, whisk together in a small bowl:

⅓ cup extra-virgin olive oil
⅓ cup red wine vinegar
3 tablespoons lemon juice
3 tablespoons minced parsley
1 garlic clove, minced
½ teaspoon salt
Black pepper to taste

Toss the croutons in a salad bowl with:

2 cucumbers, peeled, halved lengthwise, seeded, and cut into ½-inch cubes
2 large tomatoes, cut into ½-inch cubes
½ medium red onion or 5 green onions, thinly sliced
⅓ cup pitted and halved black olives
⅓ cup coarsely chopped basil, parsley, or a combination

Add the dressing and toss well. Sprinkle with, if desired:

(½ cup Parmesan shavings [about 2 ounces])

Serve at once.

FATTOUSH (LEBANESE PITA SALAD)

6 to 8 servings

Along with Panzanella, above, this bread salad is a summer darling; just the thing to make when tomatoes and cucumbers are abundant and appetites crave refreshment. For a simple, satisfying outdoor meal, prepare the vegetables and dressing and keep them separate, then proceed to grill any fish, chicken, or kebabs. With the grill still on, lightly oil and grill the pitas until they are toasted and crispy. Toss the salad and serve the grilled protein on top. Sumac is by no means essential, but we highly recommend you seek it out for its distinctively bright, tangy flavor and its beautiful brick-red color.

Prepare:

Pita Chips, 49, using two 7-inch pita breads

Break the chips into bite-sized pieces and set aside. Combine in a large bowl:

½ large head romaine lettuce, torn into bite-sized pieces
1 cup cherry tomatoes, halved, or 3 Roma or plum tomatoes, cut into thin wedges or half-moons
1 small cucumber, peeled, halved lengthwise, seeded, and sliced
6 radishes, thinly sliced
6 green onions, thinly sliced
⅔ cup loosely packed flat-leaf parsley leaves
¼ cup coarsely chopped mint

Toss well with:

½ to ⅔ cup Vinaigrette, 575, made with lemon juice
(1½ tablespoons ground sumac)

Add the pita toasts and toss again.

ABOUT SAVORY FRUIT SALADS

For sweeter fruit salads, see the Fruit chapter, 166. ➤ To keep cut fruits from browning, toss them with lemon juice. Make fruit salads as close to serving time as possible. Choose fruits with a hard, crisp texture when it is necessary to mix the salad in advance.

WALDORF SALAD

4 servings

Combine in a medium bowl:

1 cup diced celery
1 cup diced cored and peeled apples

½ cup coarsely chopped toasted, 1005, walnuts
½ cup halved seedless red grapes

Stir in:

⅓ to ½ cup mayonnaise or plain yogurt, to taste
¼ teaspoon salt
⅛ teaspoon black pepper

Serve at room temperature or chilled.

SPICY WATERMELON SALAD

4 to 6 servings

Toss together in a serving bowl:

6 cups ½-inch pieces seeded watermelon
½ small red onion, diced
1 small jalapeño pepper, seeded and diced
3 tablespoons lime juice, or to taste
2 tablespoons chopped cilantro or parsley
½ teaspoon chili powder
½ teaspoon salt, or to taste
⅛ teaspoon cayenne pepper, or to taste

Serve at room temperature.

GREEN PAPAYA SALAD

4 servings

Green papaya is not actually a unique type of papaya—it is simply underripe, with crisp flesh and a tart flavor. If you cannot find green papaya, an approximation of this salad may be made with kohlrabi or green mango (also underripe).

Mix together in a large bowl:

2 tablespoons fish sauce
2 tablespoons lime juice
(1 tablespoon dried shrimp, toasted, 1016, and very finely minced)
2 garlic cloves, minced
2 teaspoons packed brown sugar
1 teaspoon red pepper flakes or 1 to 2 fresh red Thai chiles, seeded and minced

Add:

2½ cups shredded peeled green papaya
2 ounces green beans, cut into bite-sized pieces (about 1 cup)
2 Roma or plum tomatoes, seeded and cut into strips, or 1 cup halved cherry tomatoes

Toss with the papaya mixture. Sprinkle with:

¼ cup finely chopped roasted salted peanuts

Serve with:

Lime wedges

SICILIAN ORANGE, FENNEL, AND ONION SALAD

4 to 6 servings

Cut both ends off:

4 medium navel oranges

Stand the oranges on a cutting board and cut away the peel and all the white pith and outer membrane. Cut crosswise into ¼-inch-thick slices. Toss together in a large bowl with:

1 large fennel bulb, halved through the core, and thinly sliced crosswise
1 small red onion, thinly sliced, or ½ cup drained Quick-Pickled Onions, 930
½ cup pitted black olives, halved
2 tablespoons thinly sliced mint leaves
2 tablespoons extra-virgin olive oil, or to taste
4 teaspoons lemon juice
Coarse salt and black pepper to taste

Arrange in the center of a platter. Garnish with:

1 tablespoon mint leaves

ABOUT BEAN SALADS

Bean-based salads are a favorite lunchtime go-to in our house. They are delicious, filling, healthy, and easy to prepare. Beans have the best flavor when they are cooked from their dried state, but we often use canned beans as well. To cook dried legumes, see 212. ➤ As a general rule, 1 cup dried beans yields 2 to 2½ cups cooked beans. ➤ One 15- or 16-ounce can of beans holds about 1½ cups drained beans. For another wonderful chilled bean dish that borders on salad territory, see Texas Caviar, 52.

BASIC BEAN SALAD

4 to 6 servings

We love to make this with chickpeas, lots of fresh herbs, and celery or fennel for crunch.

Mix together in a medium bowl:

2½ to 3 cups cooked beans, 213, or two 15-ounce cans, drained and rinsed
(½ cup diced red onion or sliced green onions)
(Up to 1 cup diced celery, cucumber, fennel, radish, or corn kernels)
(1 cup cherry tomatoes, halved, or chopped Slow-Roasted Tomatoes, 282)
(Up to ½ cup grated Parmesan or Romano or crumbled feta)
(2 tablespoons chopped parsley, cilantro, or mixed herbs)
2 tablespoons extra-virgin olive oil
2 tablespoons lemon juice
½ teaspoon salt
¼ teaspoon black pepper
(¼ teaspoon red pepper flakes)

Taste and add more salt, lemon juice, or pepper, if desired.

SHAVED FENNEL AND WHITE BEAN SALAD

4 servings

If you do not like fennel, you can also make this salad with celery, thinly sliced on the diagonal, or puntarelle, 233, if you can find it. Cannellini and Great Northern beans work well here, but large corona or gigante beans are even better. This is good served with canned, oil-packed tuna or sardines, as a side for grilled tuna steaks, 385, or topped with Grilled Marinated Octopus, 369.

Have ready:

1½ to 2 cups cooked white beans, 213, or one 15-ounce can, drained and rinsed

Trim the stalks and fronds from:

1 medium fennel bulb (8 to 10 ounces)

Very thinly slice the bulb crosswise (almost paper thin) with a mandoline, 201, or sharp knife. Heat in a small skillet over medium-low heat:

3 tablespoons extra-virgin olive oil

When the oil is warm, add:

2 garlic cloves, grated or minced
(2 teaspoons chopped fresh rosemary or sage)
¼ to ½ teaspoon red pepper flakes, to taste

Allow the garlic to sizzle for 30 seconds, then remove from the heat and leave the oil to infuse for a few minutes. Combine the beans, fennel, and infused oil in a bowl with:

2 tablespoons lemon juice, or to taste
2 tablespoons chopped parsley or fennel fronds
Salt and black pepper to taste

Serve at room temperature or chilled. If desired, shave on top:

(¼ cup Parmesan or Romano)

EDAMAME AND CARROT SALAD

8 servings

Combine in a medium bowl:

One 10-ounce bag frozen shelled edamame, cooked (about 2 cups)
3 large carrots, coarsely grated (about 2 cups)
½ cup thinly sliced green onion
(2 tablespoons chopped cilantro)

Whisk or shake together in a bowl or jar:

2 tablespoons rice vinegar
2 tablespoons lemon juice
1 tablespoon vegetable oil
1 garlic clove, minced
½ teaspoon salt
¼ teaspoon black pepper

Add to the salad, tossing to coat evenly. Serve at room temperature or chilled.

CHICKPEA AND ROASTED CAULIFLOWER SALAD

4 to 6 servings

Roast as for Roasted Broccoli, 221:

1 medium head cauliflower, cut into florets

Combine the cauliflower in a medium bowl with:

One 15-ounce can chickpeas, drained and rinsed
½ medium cucumber, peeled, seeded, and diced
⅓ to ½ cup Zhug, 567, Cilantro-Mint Chutney, 568, or Tahini Dressing, 576
½ cup crumbled feta (2 ounces)
(¼ cup minced red onion)
Salt and black pepper to taste

If desired, serve over:

(Arugula)

RACHEL'S KALE AND LENTIL SALAD

4 to 6 servings

One of our closest friends shared this salad with us. It quickly became a staple in our house and is truly greater than the sum of its parts.

Bring to a boil in a medium saucepan:

1½ cups water
½ cup brown or green lentils

Reduce the heat to simmer, cover, and cook until tender, 20 to 30 minutes. Meanwhile, prepare:

Vinaigrette, 575, made with balsamic vinegar

Drain the lentils and transfer to a large bowl. Add about ½ cup of the dressing and toss together with:

1 bunch lacinato (dinosaur) kale, deribbed, 243, and shredded
(½ head radicchio, shredded, or 8 ounces Brussels sprouts, trimmed and shredded)
½ to ¾ cup toasted, 1005, pecans or hazelnuts, or Crisp Spicy Pecans, 46, to taste
½ cup crumbled fresh goat cheese (2 ounces)

ABOUT GRAIN AND RICE SALADS

Grain salads are perfect for those who have trouble thinking of salad as a filling meal. With a hearty base of cooked grains, a flavorful dressing or vinaigrette to season them, and lots of add-ins like raw or cooked vegetables, dried fruit, toasted nuts, and protein, grain salads are just the thing to make when you crave the freshness of a salad but need something a little more substantial. When cooking grains destined for a salad, add salt as they cook so the end result is well seasoned. You may dress the grains while they are still warm or cook the grains ahead of time (or use leftover grains) and use them cold or at room temperature. As a general rule, use about ½ cup dressing for 3 cups cooked grains. For choosing and cooking grains, see 340.

RICE SALAD WITH CHICKEN AND OLIVES

6 to 8 servings

Cook, 343, or have ready:

1½ cups uncooked short-grain white or brown rice, or 3½ to 4 cups cooked

Place the rice in a medium bowl and toss with:

2 cups packed baby spinach or arugula, coarsely chopped
1½ cups diced cooked chicken (from about 8 ounces raw boneless chicken)
1 red, yellow, or orange bell pepper, diced
½ cup Vinaigrette, 575, made with preserved lemon, if desired (see Additions to Vinaigrette)
½ cup coarsely chopped pitted green olives, preferably Castelvetrano

Toss well. Serve warm, at room temperature, or chilled.

WILD RICE SALAD WITH SAUSAGE

4 to 6 servings

This is a superb grain salad for fall and winter, and it makes a perfect Thanksgiving side dish. For a crowd, double the recipe.

Cook, 343, or have ready:

1 cup uncooked wild rice or 3 cups cooked

Whisk together in a large bowl:

1 tablespoon white wine vinegar, red wine vinegar, or champagne vinegar
1½ teaspoons Dijon mustard
2 tablespoons extra-virgin olive oil
¼ teaspoon black pepper
Salt to taste

Toss the warm rice with the dressing.
Cook in a medium skillet over medium heat, breaking up clumps with a spoon:

8 ounces sweet Italian sausage, casings removed

When the sausage is fully cooked, stir in:

2 teaspoons minced fresh rosemary

Cook, stirring, until fragrant, 1 minute more. If the sausage is very greasy, drain on paper towels. Transfer to the bowl with the rice. Add to the bowl and mix well:

2 celery ribs with leaves, thinly sliced
1 cup seedless green or red grapes, halved

Taste and adjust the seasonings. Serve at room temperature.

BROWN RICE SALAD WITH DATES AND ORANGES

4 to 6 servings

Cook, 343, or have ready:

1 cup uncooked long-grain brown rice or 3 cups cooked

Transfer the rice to a large bowl and toss together with:

2 large navel oranges, peeled and separated into segments, then coarsely chopped
8 dates, pitted and diced
4 green onions, thinly sliced
(⅓ cup toasted, 1005, pistachios)
¼ cup minced parsley
¼ cup extra-virgin olive oil
2 tablespoons lemon juice
½ teaspoon salt
¼ teaspoon ground cinnamon
¼ teaspoon ground cumin
Pinch of red pepper flakes

Serve at room temperature.

TABBOULEH

6 to 8 servings

Tabbouleh is a popular Middle Eastern salad loaded with fresh herbs. While it is usually eaten as part of a *mezze* spread (see About Party Platters, 45), we also like to serve it as a tart, refreshing counterpoint to richly flavored meats like lamb.

Place in a small bowl:

¼ cup fine or medium bulgur

Pour ½ cup boiling water over it and let stand for 30 minutes. Meanwhile, combine in a large bowl:

3 medium tomatoes, diced, or 12 ounces cherry tomatoes, halved
Leaves from 2 bunches parsley (about 4 lightly packed cups), finely chopped
1 cup lightly packed mint leaves, finely chopped
(1 cup chopped purslane)
4 green onions or ½ medium onion, finely chopped

Stir in the plumped bulgur along with:

⅓ cup lemon juice
⅓ cup extra-virgin olive oil
½ teaspoon salt
(½ teaspoon ground allspice)
¼ teaspoon ground cinnamon
¼ teaspoon black pepper
(¼ teaspoon cayenne pepper)

Toss to combine and season to taste. Serve in a bowl. If desired, surround with:

(Romaine or little gem lettuce leaves)

If using, spoon the tabbouleh onto the lettuce leaves to eat.

WARM BARLEY, MUSHROOM, AND ASPARAGUS SALAD

4 to 6 servings

Cook, 340:

1 cup pearl barley

Meanwhile, add to a small skillet over medium heat:

3 tablespoons olive oil

Add to the skillet and cook, stirring, until softened, about 2 minutes:

2 shallots, minced

Add and cook, stirring, until the mushroom liquid is evaporated, 3 to 5 minutes:

3 ounces mushrooms, sliced (about 1 cup)

Stir in:

Finely grated zest of 1 lemon
1 tablespoon lemon juice
1 tablespoon minced parsley
Salt and black pepper to taste

Remove the skillet from the heat. When the barley is tender, drain off any excess liquid, transfer to a large bowl, and cover to keep warm. Return the skillet to medium-high heat and add:

6 ounces asparagus, trimmed and cut on the diagonal into 1-inch pieces (1½ cups)

Cook, stirring, until the asparagus is bright-green and tender, about 4 minutes. Toss the asparagus-mushroom mixture with the barley and season to taste. Serve warm.

WHEAT SALAD WITH PESTO AND ZUCCHINI

4 to 6 servings

This salad makes a good desk lunch or potluck dish. Add feta, goat cheese, or cubes of Fried Halloumi, 56, if desired.

Cook, 340:

1 cup wheat, rye, or spelt berries, or emmer, Kamut, or farro

Let cool completely. Prepare, using arugula instead of basil and walnuts instead of pine nuts:

Pesto, 586

Toss the cooked grains in a large bowl with the pesto. Add:

1 medium zucchini, shaved into ribbons with a vegetable peeler
⅓ cup toasted, 1005, almonds or Marcona almonds, chopped
1 tablespoon lemon juice
Salt to taste

Toss well to combine and serve chilled or at room temperature.

QUINOA SALAD WITH BROCCOLI AND FETA

4 to 6 servings

While the pomegranate seeds are optional here, we highly recommend adding them, as they impart just the right amount of sweetness and a beautiful pop of color.

Cook, 342:

1 cup quinoa

Transfer the quinoa to a bowl and while still warm, toss with:

⅓ to ½ cup Miso Dressing, 576, Tahini Dressing, 576, or Vinaigrette, 575

Steam, 220, until just tender:

1 pound broccoli, cut into bite-sized florets

Coarsely chop the broccoli and stir into the quinoa, along with:

½ cup crumbled feta (2 ounces)
(½ cup pomegranate seeds)
¼ cup sliced almonds, toasted, 1005

ABOUT PASTA SALADS

Though most any pasta shape will work in a salad, we prefer "grippy" ones that hold on to dressings and other ingredients, such as fusilli, rotini, radiatori, macaroni, penne, ziti, campanelle, gemelli, cavatelli, and farfalle. Small vegetable- or cheese-filled pastas such as tortellini or ravioli can also be the basis of a tasty pasta salad. When cooking pasta for a salad, cook it al dente—tender yet still firm to the bite. Rinse in cool water to rid the pasta of excess starch and to stop the cooking, then mix with the dressing. If adding vegetables or chopped fresh herbs, stir in just before serving to maintain texture and color.

In general, ➤ 8 ounces dried pasta will serve 4 to 6 people, depending on the other ingredients you add. Pasta salads can be made ahead and refrigerated but are best served at room temperature. Before serving, taste, adjust the seasoning, and add more dressing if needed. For those serving pasta salad at a buffet or potluck, ➤ never leave these salads at room temperature for more than 2 hours.

Treat the basic pasta salad recipe below as a template. Substitute different fresh herbs, mix in all kinds of vegetables—whether raw, steamed, grilled, or roasted—or add diced, shredded, or crumbled cheese, or diced cooked meat. ➤ If you prefer a creamy pasta salad, substitute ½ cup mayonnaise for the vinaigrette.

For salad-like noodle dishes, see Sesame Noodles, 302, and Bún, 305.

BASIC PASTA SALAD

4 to 6 servings

Cook in a large pot of well-salted boiling water:

8 ounces elbow macaroni, penne, orzo, rotelle, farfalle, or orecchiette

Drain, rinse, and place in a large bowl while still warm. Combine with:

½ cup Vinaigrette, 575, made with fresh herbs or grated tomato, Pesto, 586, Sun-Dried Tomato Pesto, 586, or Romesco Sauce, 570

Let cool to room temperature. Stir in any of the following:

1 cup cherry tomatoes, halved
½ medium red onion, finely diced, or 4 green onions, sliced
½ cup fresh or thawed frozen green peas
½ cup coarsely chopped arugula or watercress leaves
(¼ cup diced salami or ham, or sliced prosciutto)
¼ cup chopped pitted olives
¼ cup crumbled feta, fresh goat cheese, or grated Parmesan
¼ cup chopped parsley, basil, oregano, tarragon, or a combination
Finely grated zest of 1 lemon
Salt and black pepper to taste

Serve at room temperature.

PASTA SALAD WITH CHICKEN OR SHRIMP

About 10 servings

Prepare one of the following:

Broiled Chicken, 411, or Grilled Chicken, 411, made with 2 pounds bone-in chicken parts or 1 pound boneless
Grilled or Broiled Shrimp I, 365, or Blackened Shrimp, 363

Let your chosen protein rest until cool enough to handle. Peel and halve the shrimp, if using, or pull the chicken off the bone, discard any skin, and cut into bite-sized pieces. Cook in a large pot of well-salted water until al dente:

1 pound fusilli or penne

Drain, rinse, and place in a large serving bowl. Once cool, add the shrimp or chicken, along with:

3 medium tomatoes, seeded and chopped
(1 cup jarred roasted red peppers, cut into strips)
4 green onions, thinly sliced
2 garlic cloves, minced
½ cup pitted and chopped olives or ¼ cup drained capers
(¼ cup pine nuts or sliced almonds, toasted, 1005)
¼ cup finely chopped basil or parsley
¼ cup extra-virgin olive oil
2 tablespoons lemon juice, or to taste
½ teaspoon salt, or to taste
½ teaspoon black pepper

Toss together and serve at room temperature.

CREAMY MACARONI SALAD FOR A CROWD

16 to 20 servings

Cook in a large pot of well-salted water until al dente:

1 pound elbow macaroni

Drain, rinse, and place in a large bowl. Add:

1 red bell pepper, diced
1 green bell pepper, diced
(1½ cups thawed frozen green peas)
2 carrots, diced
¾ cup diced red onion or thinly sliced green onions
½ cup chopped parsley

Add and toss to coat with:

Dressing from Classic Coleslaw, 119, or 1 cup Alabama White Barbecue Sauce, 582

Taste and add more salt and black pepper if needed. Serve at room temperature.

ABOUT SALAD-STUFFED VEGETABLE AND FRUIT CUPS

In *Joy*'s third edition (published in 1943), the book reached "peak stuffed tomato," sporting twenty-two different formulas for filling the fruit, as well as a freeform list of possible ingredients with which to strike out into uncharted stuffed-tomato territory. Though our collective enthusiasm for the tomato as vessel has waned in the last seventy-odd years, vegetable cases are still a handsome presentation, as well as an ingenious way to serve individual portions as an hors d'oeuvre or part of a buffet. In addition to the venerable tomato, you may use lemon juice–slathered avocado halves (leave the flesh in the peel), hollowed-out cucumbers, Steamed Artichokes, 206, small, halved melons, or lettuce and cabbage leaves.

To prepare tomatoes for filling, slice off the round top of each tomato. Hollow them out with a paring knife and spoon, leaving a wall thick enough to support the filling. Lightly sprinkle the tomatoes with salt, invert, and drain for 20 minutes. Fill the hollows with one of the suggested fillings, below, and chill. Or cut tomatoes crosswise in half and fill the hollowed-out halves separately.

To prepare cucumbers for filling, peel if the skin is waxy or tough. For smaller cucumbers, halve lengthwise, scoop out the seeds and flesh with a spoon, to about ½-inch thickness, and fill the halves. For large cucumbers, peel and slice crosswise into 2- to 3-inch pieces and hollow the pieces from one end, leaving enough on the bottom to prevent the filling from falling out.

Practically any bound salad, 123–24, or grain salad, 131–32, can be used to fill avocados, cucumbers, or tomatoes. Cucumber salads are especially good in avocados and tomatoes. Our favorite combination is avocado halves filled with Lobster or Shrimp Salad, 124.

To add a finishing touch and a bit of texture and seasoning, garnish filled vegetables with fried sage leaves, 1013, Browned or Buttered Bread Crumbs, 957, Crispy Fried Shallots, 256, crumbled crisp bacon, Everything Seasoning, 590, Za'atar, 590, Dukkah, 589, or a sprinkle of smoked paprika and flaky salt.

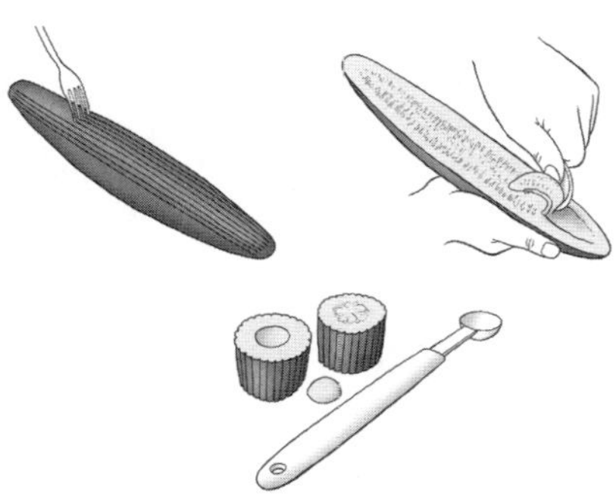

Scoring and seeding cucumbers and making cucumber cups

ABOUT ASPICS

Aspics and gelatin salads were a touchstone of mid-century American cuisine. Immobilizing meats, vegetables, and other odds and ends in gelatin is certainly in keeping with the tendency of our forebears to hide foods inside tomato cases and bake creamed vegetables in mysterious casseroles. While many of us are comfortable with gelatin-suspended fruit, 821, our relationship with savory gelatin dishes remains fraught. However, if you've ever made a rich stock that sets when chilled, you have essentially made aspic.

The most delicious aspics of all are made with reduced chicken or veal stock, 74, and we would argue that if you're going to the trouble of making an aspic, you may as well make the base from scratch. A batch of stock or broth that solidifies at refrigerator temperatures may be boiled down even further and the gelatin omitted altogether. Unfortunately, only experience will reveal whether or not your stock is sufficiently gelatinous to serve for long at room temperatures.

To test a stock's jelling strength, pour a small amount of stock into a glass or measuring cup. Let it set in the refrigerator for 2 hours or until completely chilled, and unmold it onto a plate. If the gel holds for 30 minutes at room temperature, proceed with the recipe (if not, reduce the stock further or add gelatin).

Strong meat, fish, and poultry stocks with added gelatin are second best; canned consommés are last in preference. For a nicer presentation, you may wish to clarify homemade stock, 74. ➤ One envelope (2½ teaspoons) gelatin will thicken 2 cups of thin stock or other liquid, with or without any added vegetables or meats. To set vegan molded salads with agar, see 820.

Regardless of the liquid you are using, ➤ sample the mixture before pouring it into the mold, and season to taste. Undersalt if it is to be held for 24 hours, as too much salt will loosen the gel.

Before adding ingredients to gelatin, drain them well. Certain ingredients naturally come to rest either at the top or bottom of a jelling salad, and you can achieve interesting layered effects by manipulating ingredients of different weights. To have more control over where your additions land, chill the stock mixture until it is the consistency of egg whites, then pour a little into the mold. Arrange the ingredients you want to show on top of the aspic, then pour in a little more stock. Continue arranging ingredients and adding stock until the mold is filled. ➤ Fresh or frozen pineapple, kiwi, papaya, honeydew, figs, and ginger—and their juices—cannot be added to a gelatin salad. They contain enzymes that inhibit jelling.

The recipes that follow can be made either in a large mold or individual ones. Use ring molds if you wish to fill the centers.

To unmold gelatins or aspics, have a chilled plate ready. Lightly moisten its surface, which will prevent the aspic from sticking and enable you to center it more easily. Run a thin knife along the edge of the mold to release the vacuum. Dip the mold in warm water for 5 to 10 seconds. Dry the outside of the mold, cover with the serving plate, and invert. Shake or tap to release the salad. If the mold does not release, shake the mold lightly, holding it tightly against the serving plate.

Molded salads can be prepared a day or so in advance and kept chilled in the refrigerator. ➤ Never freeze molded salads. For fruity gelatin desserts (some of which might be considered salads), see 820.

BASIC SAVORY ASPIC

6 to 8 servings

Please read About Aspics, 133, and Gelatin, 990. If using store-bought stock, be mindful of its salt level when seasoning the stock mixture.

Combine in a medium bowl and let stand for 5 minutes to soften the gelatin:

1 envelope (2½ teaspoons) unflavored gelatin
¼ cup cold water, stock, or broth

Bring to a boil in a small saucepan:

¼ cup stock, broth, or consommé, store-bought or homemade, 75–83

Whisk the hot liquid into the softened gelatin until completely dissolved, then stir in:

1½ cups cold stock, broth, or consommé, store-bought or homemade, 75–83
White wine vinegar or lemon juice to taste
Salt to taste

Refrigerate the stock mixture. When it is the consistency of raw egg whites, about 30 minutes, layer the stock mixture in a lightly oiled 4-cup mold, bowl, or 9 × 5-inch loaf pan with any of the following:

1½ cups chopped, cooked lobster or lump crabmeat, peeled shrimp, or other seafood, if using seafood or chicken stock; cooked diced chicken, duck, or turkey, if using poultry stock; cooked diced beef or lamb, if using meat stock
(½ cup chopped or julienned raw celery, radishes, cucumbers, or carrots)
(1 avocado, pitted, peeled, and diced)
(½ cup olives, pitted and halved or sliced)
(¼ cup drained capers or chopped, toasted, 1005, nuts)

Refrigerate until set, at least 3 hours, but preferably overnight. Unmold the aspic, 133, onto a platter and garnish with:

Lettuce leaves

Serve cold, with or without:

Mayonnaise, 563, or Horseradish Sauce I, 566

TOMATO ASPIC

8 to 10 servings

Please read Gelatin, 990.

Combine in a medium saucepan and simmer, covered, for 30 minutes:

4 cups tomato juice
½ cup tomato puree
½ medium onion, chopped
2 celery ribs, chopped
2 tablespoons lemon juice
(1 tablespoon balsamic vinegar)
2 teaspoons sugar
2 teaspoons dried basil, tarragon, thyme, and/or oregano or 2 tablespoons chopped fresh herbs
1 teaspoon black peppercorns
1 whole clove
1 bay leaf

Combine in a large bowl and let stand for 5 minutes to soften the gelatin:

2 envelopes (5 teaspoons) unflavored gelatin
½ cup cold water

Strain the hot tomato juice mixture, then taste and add salt if needed. Stir 3½ cups of it into the gelatin and refrigerate. When it is the consistency of raw egg whites, about 2 hours, layer it in a lightly oiled 6- to 8-cup mold or bowl with up to 3 cups of any combination of the following:

Diced avocado
Sliced or diced cucumber
Diced yellow bell pepper
Lump crabmeat, picked over for shells and cartilage, flaked
1 jalapeño pepper, seeded and minced
1 tablespoon chopped cilantro, basil, or tarragon

Refrigerate until set, at least 3 hours, but preferably overnight. Unmold the aspic, 133, onto a platter and garnish with:

Herb sprigs, or thinly sliced vegetables, such as bell peppers or green onions

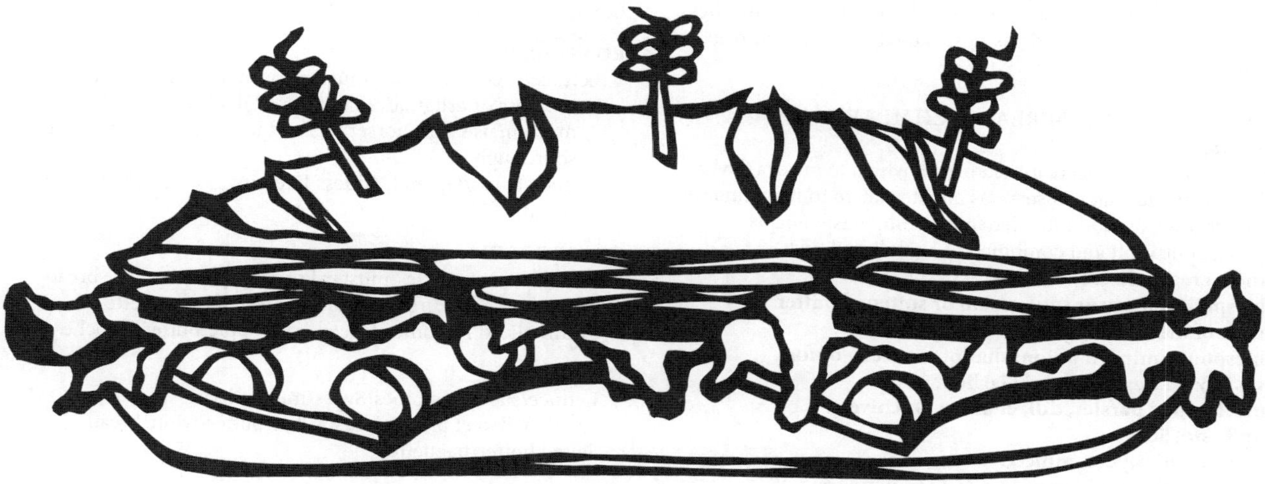

SANDWICHES, TACOS, AND BURRITOS

We would be remiss not to recount the legend of the Earl of Sandwich—gastronomy's most famous gambler—who could not be bothered to put down his cards for a knife and fork, thus demanding from his cook the convenient comestible that now bears his name.

Sandwiches range greatly in size and complexity, from the massive corned beef sandwiches of Jewish deli fame to diminutive tea sandwiches. Though the Earl was responsible for the name, he certainly didn't invent the concept, as almost every culture has assembled something similar, which is why we include tacos, burritos, and pitas here. The "sandwich umbrella" is more than large enough to accommodate them (just don't tell the Internet we said so).

For tea sandwiches, see About Canapés and Tea Sandwiches, 66.

ABOUT BREAD FOR SANDWICHES

Because sandwiches vary so much, almost any bread can be called into service as a sandwich base. The sandwich as we tend to think of it is made, unsurprisingly, with sandwich bread. ➤ A standard loaf weighing 1 to 1½ pounds should yield 18 to 20 slices. Whether you make your turkey sandwich on white or whole wheat is a matter of personal preference, but heartier fillings demand more robust bread. While soft sandwich breads are ideal for cold cuts, firm, dense rye bread, crusty sourdough loaves, ciabatta rolls, and baguettes are better suited to hot, messy, or substantial sandwich fillings.

Besides sandwich bread, there are numerous other breads available for making sandwiches and related portable foods. Flour tortillas, lavash, and other soft flatbreads work well for wraps. Pita, croissants, challah, brioche, bagels, and biscuits are also perfectly serviceable breads, depending on the filling. In many cases, tailor-made breads are available for specific sandwiches. *Telera* rolls, which are used specifically for Mexican *tortas* are soft and yielding, with a dense crumb. Vietnamese *banh mi* is a baguette-style loaf, often made light and crisp with the addition of rice flour. Of course, you do not have to prepare these sandwiches with their prescribed breads, but it is worth visiting a local *panaderia* or Vietnamese bakery to see what is available.

ABOUT SPREADS AND DRESSINGS FOR SANDWICHES

All sandwiches benefit from some kind of sauce, spread, or dressing. Not only do they add flavor, they also contribute moisture. The most common sandwich spread is mayonnaise, to which all sorts of flavorful ingredients may be added, 563. Then there is softened butter, which may also be flavored, 559, or left plain. Cream cheese or a flavored cream cheese spread, below, is an excellent choice for vegetable-based sandwiches. Tapenade, 54, Treva's Pimiento Cheese, 55, Hummus, 52, and Caponata, 54, may be used on sandwiches to good effect. Thick, creamy dressings, 576–78, can also enliven a sandwich.

BASIC CREAM CHEESE SPREAD (SCHMEAR)

1¼ to 1½ cups

Cream cheese is the perfect blank slate from which to make a flavorful sandwich spread that can serve as an alternative to mayonnaise or butter. Or use it as God intended: on a fresh, toasted bagel.

Mash or beat until soft and combined in a medium bowl:

8 ounces cream cheese, softened
2 tablespoons heavy or sour cream or softened butter

Beat in any of the following:

2 tablespoons minced onion, shallot, or green onion
Cloves from 1 head Roasted Garlic I, 241
¼ cup chopped parsley, dill, cilantro, or chives
¼ cup Pesto, 586
¼ cup drained capers, minced
⅓ cup finely chopped jarred roasted red peppers
⅓ cup pitted and chopped green or black olives
2 ounces smoked salmon, finely chopped
2 tablespoons drained prepared horseradish
2 tablespoons minced anchovies
½ cup finely chopped toasted, 1005, nuts
2 tablespoons chive blossoms or marigold petals

If desired, season with:

(Salt, black pepper, paprika, and/or cayenne pepper)

Use at once or cover and refrigerate for up to 1 week.

ABOUT COLD SANDWICHES

Cold sandwiches typically include cold cuts, lettuce, tomato, cheese, and mayonnaise but in an astonishing number of variations. A few preliminary steps help toward serving cold sandwiches in prime condition. Most sandwiches are best served within 4 hours of being made, especially if they contain greens, tomatoes, or other fresh vegetables. Some sandwiches, such as Pan Bagnat, 138, or subs and Muffulettas, 137, actually benefit from being allowed to sit: The bread soaks up flavor from the sandwich filling and the ingredients have a chance to meld.

For keeping sandwiches to be eaten later from getting soggy, especially those that include watery ingredients like tomatoes, spread butter or mayonnaise to the edges of the bread or, better yet, ➤ pack moist fillings like tomato, lettuce, and pickle slices in a separate bag or container and add to the sandwiches just before eating. Wrap or bag sandwiches immediately to prevent them from drying out. Of course, it helps to use fewer moist ingredients and less-perishable spreads and fillings, such as cheese, cold cuts, nut butters, jelly, honey butter, or cream cheese spreads.

COLD SANDWICH COMBINATIONS

The suggested sandwich combinations below pair fillings with the bread that we think best suits them, but, of course, follow your heart.

ROAST BEEF

Lettuce/sliced tomatoes/mustard or mayonnaise/white bread
Watercress or arugula/red onion or Quick-Pickled Onions, 930/mayonnaise with horseradish added/black pepper/toasted sourdough
Lettuce/Swiss/Green Goddess Dressing, 577/cracked wheat bread

ROAST PORK

Lettuce/sweet pickles/mustard or mayonnaise/white bread
Arugula or watercress/tomatoes/Aïoli, 564/baguette
Thinly sliced red onion/sliced crisp apple/butter/brioche

DELI HAM

Lettuce/sliced tomatoes/Swiss/mustard/rye
Cheddar/sweet pickles/mustard or butter/white bread
Salted butter/baguette

CHICKEN OR TURKEY

Brie/Whole Berry Cranberry Sauce, 179/walnut bread
Lettuce/bacon/Cheddar/mayonnaise or Thousand Island Dressing, 576/white bread
Shredded radicchio/prosciutto/Aïoli, 564/ciabatta roll
Radish sprouts/sliced avocado/Pesto, 586/whole wheat

FISH

Sardines/avocado/watercress/toasted sourdough

BOUND SALADS, 123 (TUNA SALAD, EGG SALAD, ETC.)

Bibb or Boston lettuce/bacon/white bread
Thinly sliced avocado/sliced tomatoes/pita
Watercress/thinly sliced red onion or Quick-Pickled Onions, 930/whole wheat

CHARCUTERIE

Prosciutto/sliced apple or figs/arugula/Vinaigrette, 575/ciabatta
Chicken Liver Pâté, 62/cornichons/Dijon mustard/mâche/baguette
Serrano ham/cold Tortilla Española, 160/Aïoli, 564/toasted baguette rubbed with tomato
Braunschweiger or other liverwurst/red onion/horseradish/cucumber/pumpernickel or rye

NUT BUTTERS

Peanut butter/jam or jelly/white bread
Peanut butter/bacon/apple butter/whole wheat
Peanut or almond butter/sliced bananas/cinnamon/white bread
Cashew or almond butter/sliced pear/cream cheese/sourdough

VEGETABLES

Mozzarella/sliced tomato/Vinaigrette, 575, with basil, or Pesto, 586/ciabatta

Sprouts/cucumber/mango chutney and/or cream cheese/whole wheat
Hummus, 52/cucumber/tomato/avocado/Bibb or Boston lettuce/wrap or multigrain bread

BLT

4 sandwiches

This was Irma's favorite sandwich. To make the inauspiciously named **BLAT**, add **1 large avocado, sliced.**

Lay out on a work surface:
8 slices white bread, lightly toasted
Spread lightly with:
Mayonnaise (about 3 tablespoons total)
Divide among 4 of the slices:
2 medium tomatoes, sliced
8 lettuce leaves
12 slices bacon, cooked until crisp (about 12 ounces)
Salt and black pepper to taste
Top with the remaining 4 slices bread, mayonnaise side down. Press together gently and cut in half, if desired.

CLUB SANDWICH

4 sandwiches

If you like your sandwiches with three pieces of bread, cut in half twice, and impaled with frilly toothpicks, then you are an honorary club member.

Lay out on a work surface:
12 slices white bread, lightly toasted
Spread lightly with:
Mayonnaise (about 4½ tablespoons total)
Divide among 4 of the slices:
8 lettuce leaves
8 ounces thinly sliced turkey breast or chicken
Top with another 4 slices bread, mayonnaise side down. Spread the tops with:
Mayonnaise (about 1½ tablespoons total)
Divide among the sandwiches:
8 lettuce leaves
1 medium tomato, thinly sliced
12 slices bacon, cooked until crisp (about 12 ounces)
(1 avocado, pitted, peeled, and sliced)
Top with the remaining 4 slices bread, mayonnaise side down. Stab 4 frilly toothpicks through each sandwich midway between the center and each side of the bread. Then, slice the sandwich in an X, from one corner to the opposite corner. Arrange the sandwich triangles in a circle on each plate, filling the void in the center with:
Potato chips or potato salad, 127

MEGAN'S AVOCADO CLUB SANDWICH

2 sandwiches

This vegetarian club gets an extra boost of flavor from miso mayonnaise and salty, chewy mushroom bacon. Eating one has no bearing on your membership in the club mentioned above.

Mash together with a fork in a small bowl until smooth:
½ cup mayonnaise or vegan mayonnaise
1 tablespoon white miso
Lay out on a countertop:
4 slices country white or multigrain bread, lightly toasted
Spread the mayonnaise mixture on the inside of all 4 slices of bread (you will have extra—reserve it for another use). Divide between 2 of the pieces of bread:
½ avocado, pitted, peeled, and thinly sliced
4 slices fresh tomato or 6 slices Slow-Roasted Tomatoes, 282
½ cup Mushroom Bacon, 252, or 4 slices of your favorite vegetarian bacon, cooked until crisp
4 lettuce leaves
Top with the remaining bread slices.

MUFFULETTA

6 servings

This New Orleans specialty is built on massive, round loaves. They are crusty, but have a soft, light crumb. Do not let their scarcity deter you from making this sandwich. Any large, crusty loaf will work (just choose a lighter, more yielding bread).

Combine well in a medium bowl:
1½ cups chopped pitted green olives
½ cup chopped pitted Kalamata olives
½ cup drained and chopped giardiniera pickles
¼ cup chopped jarred roasted red peppers
(¼ cup chopped pepperoncini or pickled jalapeños, stems and seeds removed)
¼ cup red wine vinegar
¼ cup extra-virgin olive oil
3 tablespoons drained small capers
2 garlic cloves, minced
2 tablespoons minced parsley
2 teaspoons minced fresh oregano or 1 teaspoon dried oregano
Let the mixture marinate at room temperature for at least 30 minutes before using, or store in the refrigerator for up to 2 weeks. Split horizontally:
1 large crusty round loaf (8 to 9 inches) Italian or French bread
Remove some of the soft inner bread, creating a cavity inside each half. Drain the olive mixture, reserving the marinade. Brush the insides of both halves of the loaf generously with the marinade, then spread half of the olive mixture in the bottom half. Add in layers:
4 ounces thinly sliced salami
4 ounces thinly sliced capicola or ham
4 ounces thinly sliced provolone
2 cups shredded lettuce
Top with the remaining olive salad. Cover with the top half of the loaf and wrap tightly in plastic. Place on a large plate, cover with another plate, and weight down with several pounds of canned goods. Refrigerate for at least 30 minutes, and up to 6 hours. To serve, cut into wedges.

PAN BAGNAT (PROVENÇAL PRESSED TUNA SANDWICH)

4 servings

This is like a Niçoise salad in sandwich form. Our take is a little unconventional with the addition of roasted eggplant, but you can leave it out, if desired, or substitute cooked artichoke hearts.

Preheat the oven to 400°F. Slice lengthwise into ¼-inch-thick slabs:

1 medium unpeeled eggplant

Flatten with the palm of your hand:

1 large red bell pepper, halved

Brush both sides of the eggplant slices and bell pepper with a little olive oil. Place them on a baking sheet and roast until tender, 15 to 20 minutes. Cool the peppers and eggplant slightly. When cool enough to handle, remove the skin from the pepper.

Meanwhile, combine in a medium bowl:

One 12-ounce can or two 5-ounce cans albacore tuna, drained
⅓ cup coarsely chopped pitted olives
¼ cup coarsely chopped parsley
3 tablespoons extra-virgin olive oil
2 tablespoons lemon juice
1 tablespoon Dijon mustard
Salt and black pepper to taste

Split horizontally:

1 baguette, 4 ciabatta rolls, or 1 large crusty round loaf (8 to 9 inches)

If using a round loaf, remove some of the soft inner bread, creating a cavity. Lightly toast the bread, then rub over the toasted surfaces:

1 garlic clove

Cover the bottom piece(s) of bread with:

12 to 15 basil leaves

Pile the tuna mixture on top of the basil. Top with the roasted eggplant, bell pepper, and:

1 large tomato, sliced
3 Hard-Boiled Eggs, 151, sliced
Cracked black pepper

Cover with the top piece(s) of bread, and wrap tightly in several layers of plastic wrap. Place on a rimmed baking sheet or cutting board and weight down with a cast-iron skillet or other heavy weight (or, if you'd like to follow M.F.K. Fisher's advice, have someone sit on it). Allow the sandwiches to marinate, refrigerated, for at least 1 hour and up to 24 hours.

BAGELS AND LOX

2 servings

A Jewish deli classic that pairs perfectly with a strong cup of black coffee and the Sunday paper.

Split horizontally and toast, if desired:

2 bagels, preferably "everything"

Spread the halves with:

4 ounces cream cheese or ½ cup Cream Cheese Spread, 136

Divide among the bagel halves:

4 ounces thinly sliced lox or other smoked salmon
4 thin slices tomato
4 thin slices sweet or red onion
2 tablespoons drained capers

Serve open-faced; enjoy life.

SUB OR HERO SANDWICH

4 sandwiches

The sub, short for submarine—also known as a hero, bomber, grinder, wedge, zep, or hoagie—is essentially a long, wide roll filled with deli meats and cheese. The bread used varies, and they may be served hot or cold. For a hot sub, see Sausage and Pepper Sub, 140.

Split in half lengthwise:

One 24-inch Italian or French bread loaf

If desired, spread the cut sides with a thin layer of:

(Mayonnaise)
(Spicy brown mustard)

Layer on half of the bread a combination of 3 or more sandwich meats:

About 1 pound thinly sliced salami, turkey, roast beef, prosciutto, mortadella, and/or capicola or ham

Stack on top of the meat:

6 ounces thinly sliced provolone, Swiss, or Cheddar
(1 cup sliced pickled hot peppers)
(1 onion, thinly sliced)
(1 tomato, thinly sliced)
2 cups finely shredded lettuce

Moisten the lettuce with a drizzle of:

Extra-virgin olive oil
Red or white wine vinegar

Season lightly with:

Salt and black pepper
(Dried oregano)

Cover with the top half of the bread. Serve immediately or, to let the flavors blend, wrap tightly in foil or plastic wrap and let stand for 30 minutes before serving. Cut into 4 sandwiches.

LOBSTER ROLL

4 sandwiches

The classic New England seashore sandwich. The ideal buns for lobster rolls are Martin's long potato rolls. In the absence of those, your best bet is fancy hot dog buns made with brioche dough.

Combine in a medium bowl:

2 cups cooked lobster meat (from 3 pounds lobster in the shell)
½ cup finely diced celery
(1 tablespoon finely chopped celery leaves)
(1 tablespoon finely chopped parsley)
1 tablespoon lemon juice, or to taste
¼ teaspoon salt, or to taste
Black pepper to taste

Stir in:

¼ cup mayonnaise or melted butter (or more to taste)

Split along the top (but not all the way through):

4 hot dog buns or brioche or challah rolls

Melt in a large skillet over medium-low heat:

3 tablespoons butter

Place the buns on their sides in the skillet (slit facing sideways) and move them around the pan to distribute the butter. Weight the buns down with another skillet and griddle them for 5 minutes on each side, or until golden brown.

While they are still warm, fill the buns with the lobster and serve with:

Lemon wedges

BANH MI (VIETNAMESE SANDWICHES)

4 sandwiches

Banh mi are made with an astonishing variety of fillings. Really, any leftover meat will work in a pinch (the more flavorful, the better), as will cold cuts, small meatballs, cooked pork belly, and pulled pork. Peel and cut into 2½ × ⅛-inch matchsticks:

4 ounces carrots
4 ounces daikon radish

Pack in a glass pint jar. Bring to a boil in a small saucepan:

½ cup distilled white vinegar
½ cup water
1½ teaspoons sugar
1 teaspoon salt

Pour the brine over the vegetables and let stand for 30 minutes. Lay out on a countertop:

Four 6-inch lengths Vietnamese baguette, French bread (not sourdough), or 4 large, crusty rolls

Divide across the bread:

½ cup mayonnaise
1 cup chicken liver pâté, store-bought or homemade, 62, 12 ounces sliced Grilled Vietnamese-Style Pork, 493, or 8 slices Baked Marinated Tofu, 287
12 sprigs cilantro
1 medium cucumber, peeled and cut into ¼-inch-thick matchsticks
12 thin slices jalapeño pepper, or to taste

Top the sandwiches with the carrot and daikon pickle, and serve with:

Maggi seasoning, Golden Mountain sauce, or soy sauce
Sriracha

ABOUT HOT SANDWICHES

Many of the dishes in this book may be given the hot sandwich treatment—including boneless fried chicken, meatballs, meatloaf, fried fish, among many others. Gently griddled slices of leftover meatloaf, barbecue, or roasted meat can anchor an inspired sandwich, especially when dressed with a sauce or topped with cheese.

HOT SANDWICH COMBINATIONS

BEEF AND LAMB

Sliced steak/crumbled blue cheese/sautéed onions/arugula/hero roll
Sliced steak/Horseradish Sauce, 566/Quick-Pickled Onions, 930/toasted bun
Meatloaf, 506/Green Goddess Dressing, 577, or mayonnaise/romaine or butter lettuce/white bread
Italian Meatballs, 507/Tomato Sauce, 556/sliced provolone/hero roll
Smoked Brisket, 469/Chipotle Barbecue Sauce, 582/pickle slices/onion slices or Quick-Pickled Onions, 930/toasted bun
Kentucky-Style Smoked Mutton Shoulder, 484/Kentucky-Style Mutton Dip, 583/lettuce/tomato/pickle slices/toasted bun

PORK

Braised Pulled Pork, 495, or Smoked Pork Shoulder, 496/Classic Coleslaw, 119/barbecue sauce, 582–83/toasted bun
Sliced pork roast/Garlic-Braised Broccoli Rabe, 221/provolone/hero roll
Bacon/cream cheese/raspberry jam/arugula/toasted poppy or "everything" bagel
Breaded Pork Chops or Cutlets, 493/Horseradish Sauce, 566/lettuce/lemon juice/ciabatta roll

CHICKEN

Pan-Fried Chicken Cutlets, 414, or boneless deep-fried chicken, 417–18 / honey/dill pickle chips/hot sauce or mustard/toasted bun
Chicken Parmigiana, 415/basil leaves/hero roll
Grilled Chicken, 411(using boneless pieces)/Green Goddess Dressing, 577/Quick-Pickled Onions, 930/sourdough
Smoked Chicken, 412, shredded off the bone/Alabama White Barbecue Sauce, 582/dill pickle chips/toasted bun

FISH AND SHELLFISH

Pan-Fried Fish Fillets, 387, or Southern-Style Deep-Fried Catfish, 390/lettuce/tomato/Classic Coleslaw, 119/mayonnaise or Tartar Sauce, 563/sesame bun or hoagie roll
Spice-Rubbed Grilled or Broiled Fish, 385/frisée or arugula/Aïoli, 564/ciabatta roll
Fried Fish I, 390/shredded cabbage/sliced radishes/Salsa Verde Cruda, 573/warmed corn or flour tortillas
Deep-Fried Shellfish, 348 (especially shrimp, clams, or oysters), Crab Cakes, 358, or Pan-Fried Salmon Cakes, 389/shredded lettuce or cabbage/Tartar Sauce, 563/hero roll or hamburger bun

VEGETABLES

Mushroom Ragout, 251/fresh goat cheese/arugula/toasted sourdough
Baked Marinated Tofu, 287/Roasted Broccoli, 221/Tahini Dressing, 576/hoagie roll
Baked or Roasted Beets, 219, peeled and sliced/herbed goat cheese/Quick-Pickled Onions, 930/arugula/multigrain
Roasted Eggplant slices, 237/Fried Halloumi, 56/Romesco Sauce, 570/pita
Eggplant Parmigiana, 238/basil leaves/hero roll

CHEESE AND EGGS

Cheddar/bread and butter pickles/white bread
Avocado/Pesto, 586/tomato/Fried Egg, 155/English muffin
Fried Egg, 155/Cheddar or Swiss/English muffin

HOT ROAST BEEF SANDWICH

4 sandwiches

To make an **Italian Beef Sandwich,** divide **½ cup drained Chicago-style giardiniera, store-bought or homemade, 942,** among the

sandwiches, top with **sautéed green bell peppers,** and use split, crusty **Italian sandwich rolls** for the bread (they should be sturdy enough to withstand being doused with the "gravy").
Slice:
1 pound cold roast beef
Prepare:
1½ to 2 cups Quick Brown Sauce, 550
Add:
1 tablespoon finely minced dill pickle or ½ cup pitted and chopped green olives
Lay out on a work surface:
8 slices white or dark bread
Blend in a small bowl until soft:
2 tablespoons butter
¼ teaspoon prepared mustard or 1 teaspoon prepared horseradish, drained
Spread the bread with this mixture. Dip the beef slices in the hot gravy. Place them between the slices of bread. Serve the sandwiches on a hot platter, covered with the remaining gravy.

FRIED SOFT-SHELL CRAB SANDWICH
4 sandwiches
Prepare:
Deep-Fried Soft-Shell Crabs, 358
Lay cut side up on a work surface:
4 hamburger buns, split and toasted
Combine:
⅓ cup mayonnaise
1 tablespoon lemon juice
Spread the mixture on both halves of the buns. Divide among the bottom halves:
1 medium tomato, thinly sliced
Place the crabs on the bottom halves of the buns. Top with:
Boston, Bibb, or any lettuce leaves
Cover with the top halves of the buns, press together gently, and serve.

SLOPPY JOE
6 servings
The Sloppy Joe—somewhat regrettably known as "loosemeat" in certain parts of the country—dates from the 1950s. We don't know who "Joe" was, but "sloppy" is obvious enough.
Heat in a large skillet over medium heat:
1 tablespoon vegetable oil
Add:
1 small onion, finely diced
1 small red or yellow bell pepper, finely diced
4 garlic cloves, minced
2 celery ribs, finely diced
(1 teaspoon fresh thyme leaves)
½ teaspoon salt
Black pepper to taste
Cook, stirring frequently, until the onion is softened but not browned, about 10 minutes. Transfer to a plate. Add to the skillet and increase the heat slightly:
1¼ pounds ground beef chuck or sirloin
Cook, breaking up any lumps with a wooden spoon, just until no longer pink, 3 to 4 minutes. Add the onion mixture, along with:
½ cup tomato-based chili sauce or ketchup
½ cup beer or water
3 tablespoons Worcestershire sauce
Hot pepper sauce
Partially cover and simmer, stirring occasionally, until the sauce is slightly thickened, about 15 minutes. Meanwhile, toast:
6 large rolls or six 6-inch lengths French bread, split
Sprinkle the Sloppy Joe mixture with:
3 tablespoons minced green onion
Spoon onto the bottom halves of the rolls and cover with the tops. Serve hot.

SAUSAGE AND PEPPER SUB
4 sandwiches
Cook slowly in a large skillet over medium heat until browned and cooked throughout:
4 sweet or hot Italian sausages, pricked several times with a fork or paring knife
Transfer the sausages to a plate. Pour off all but 2 tablespoons of fat from the skillet. Add:
2 tablespoons olive oil
1 large onion, thinly sliced
3 garlic cloves, minced
2 large bell peppers or 1 pound Italian frying peppers, 260, seeded and cut into thin strips
(1 teaspoon dried oregano)
Salt and black pepper to taste
Cook over medium-low heat, stirring often, until the peppers are very soft, about 25 minutes. If desired, stir in:
(1 tablespoon balsamic vinegar)
Return the sausages to the skillet and heat through, about 3 minutes. Place one sausage on each of:
Four 6-inch hero rolls, split and warmed
Top with the onions and peppers. Gently press the sandwiches together and serve.

PHILLY CHEESE STEAK
4 sandwiches
To make the meat easier to slice, place it in the freezer 30 minutes before slicing. For the authentic cheese-sauce experience (known as "whiz"), forgo the shredded provolone and pour ¼ cup processed cheese sauce over the filling of each sandwich (stock extra napkins).
Preheat the oven to 350°F. Wrap in foil and warm in the oven:
Four 6-inch hero rolls, split
Heat in a large nonstick skillet over medium heat until hot but not smoking:
3 tablespoons vegetable oil
Add and cook, stirring, until the vegetables are soft, about 10 minutes:
2 medium onions, thinly sliced
(1 small green bell pepper, cut into thin strips)

Add and cook, stirring, until the meat is no longer pink, about 5 minutes:

1 pound beef sirloin or rib eye, sliced into ⅛- to ¼-inch strips

Season to taste with:

Salt

Hot pepper sauce

Divide the beef mixture among the bottom halves of the rolls (set the tops aside). Top equally with:

1 cup shredded provolone (4 ounces) or 8 slices white American cheese

Place in the oven for 2 to 3 minutes to melt the cheese. Press the rolls together gently, and serve hot.

OYSTER PO'BOY

4 sandwiches

Originating in New Orleans, the po'boy is a large sandwich made with French bread. Popular fillings include hot Italian sausage, ham, fried shrimp, or, as here, deep-fried oysters.

Cook as for Deep-Fried Shellfish I, 348, using cornmeal and flour:

24 large oysters, shucked

Split lengthwise (but not all the way through):

Two 15-inch loaves soft-crusted French or Italian bread

Spread the cut sides generously with:

Mayonnaise, Tartar Sauce, 563, or Rémoulade Sauce, 564

Divide among the bottom sides of the loaves:

1 large tomato, thinly sliced

About 2 cups shredded iceberg lettuce

Top with the oysters, cover with the top halves of the bread, and press together gently. Cut each sandwich loaf in half and serve warm.

ABOUT GRIDDLED, PRESSED, AND BROILED SANDWICHES

Some hot sandwiches are simply warmed, or "toasted." Others, like panini and *tortas*, are pressed. Special sandwich presses are available, but the most practical approach is to cook pressed sandwiches in a heavy skillet and place a grill press, 1052—or just another skillet—on top of the sandwich to weight it down and compress it. Because heat is not applied from both sides with this method, the sandwich must be flipped halfway through cooking to brown both sides. Relatively thin sandwiches on soft bread may be cooked in a waffle iron. Lightly spread the outside of both slices of bread with soft butter or mayonnaise and cook in the waffle iron until golden brown.

Other sandwiches, like the grilled cheese, below, are cooked in a skillet or on a griddle. Then there is the aptly named **melt,** in which filling is placed on a slice of bread, then the sandwich is bedecked with cheese and warmed in a hot oven. Depending on your preference, you may bake it long enough to melt the cheese, or until the filling is warmed through (it may be broiled to brown the cheese at the end).

GRILLED CHEESE SANDWICH

1 sandwich

Tomato soup's best friend. We prefer to use grated sharp Cheddar, allowing some of the shreds to fall over the edge of the bread so they crisp in the skillet. Fancy people have been known to use several cheeses in one sandwich. Grilled cheeses fashioned with sturdier breads may be pressed to improve browning and encourage the cheese to ooze forth and beget "crusties," but keep in mind that airy, soft sandwich bread will flatten under the weight.

Make a sandwich of:

2 slices white sandwich bread or crusty sourdough

2 slices American or sharp Cheddar, or other melty cheese

Generously spread on both sides of the sandwich:

Softened butter or mayonnaise

Cook the sandwich slowly over medium-low heat in a skillet or on a griddle until golden brown on one side. Turn and brown the second side. Serve at once.

ADDITIONS TO GRILLED CHEESE SANDWICHES

Fresh basil leaves or Pesto, 586

Sliced pickled peppers, Quick-Pickled Onions, 930, or bread-and-butter pickles

Peeled cloves from a head of Roasted Garlic I, 241

Roasted Peppers, 262

Apple butter or thinly sliced apples

Thinly sliced tomatoes, Slow-Roasted Tomatoes, 282, or Smoky Tomato Jam, 914

Slices of bacon, bologna, or mortadella, fried until crisp and golden

REUBEN SANDWICH

4 sandwiches

While this sandwich conjures images of New York delis, it was actually invented by the son of a hotelier in Omaha, Nebraska. For a **Rachel,** substitute **turkey** for the corned beef. For a **Tempeh Reuben,** cut **1 pound steamed tempeh, 287,** into ½-inch-thick strips. Brown in a skillet over medium heat in **2 tablespoons butter or vegetable oil.** Proceed as directed, substituting the browned tempeh for the corned beef or pastrami.

Lay out on a work surface:

8 slices rye bread, toasted

Spread thinly with:

Russian Dressing, 576

Divide among 4 slices:

About 1¼ pounds sliced corned beef or pastrami

About 1½ cups well-drained sauerkraut

4 slices Swiss cheese

Cover with the remaining slices of bread. Spread both sides of each sandwich with:

Softened butter

Cook the sandwiches slowly over medium-low heat in a skillet or on a griddle until golden brown on one side, pressing down gently with a spatula. Turn and brown the second side. Serve at once with:

Dill or half-sour pickles

CROQUE-MONSIEUR

4 sandwiches

Preheat the broiler. Lay out on a work surface:

8 thick slices hearty white bread

Spread 4 slices with:

2 tablespoons softened butter
(Dijon mustard)

Top with:

4 thin slices ham (about 3 ounces)

Cover with the remaining slices of bread. Place the sandwiches under the broiler until golden. Turn the sandwiches over and cover with:

¾ cup grated Gruyère (3 ounces)

Broil until the cheese is bubbling and golden. Serve warm.

CROQUE-MADAME

Prepare **Croque-Monsieur, above.** When the sandwiches are almost golden, remove from the broiler and use a paring knife to cut a small round out of each top piece of the cheese-covered bread, exposing the ham. Reserve the rounds. Break 1 small egg into each hole and place under the broiler until the eggs are set, 2 to 3 minutes (you may need to move the sandwiches farther from the broiler so the eggs cook before the cheese burns). To serve, top the eggs with the cheese-covered rounds.

MONTE CRISTO

2 servings

This sandwich is sometimes pan-fried, sometimes deep-fried, and sometimes served as a double decker. Regardless of the preparation, it is always epic.

Whisk together in a shallow bowl:

¼ cup milk
2 eggs

Lay out on a work surface:

4 slices white bread

Spread all 4 slices with:

Softened butter
Dijon mustard

Top 2 of the slices with:

4 thin slices ham
4 slices Swiss cheese or a layer of grated Gruyère
4 thin slices turkey

Place the remaining 2 slices of bread on top, buttered side down. Melt in a large nonstick skillet over medium heat:

2 tablespoons butter

Dip the sandwiches in the egg mixture on both sides. Place in the skillet and fry until golden brown, about 2 minutes per side. Transfer to a cutting board and cut in half on the diagonal. Serve sprinkled with:

Powdered sugar

with a side of:

Red currant jelly

CUBAN SANDWICH

4 sandwiches

Traditionally made with a sandwich press, you can achieve the same effect with two heavy skillets. Crusty bread with a soft inside is best for this sandwich. *Telera*, hoagie, and *bolillo* rolls are good substitutes. French or Italian bread will also work, as long as it is not too chewy.

Split lengthwise in half:

One 24-inch-long loaf Cuban bread or 4 large crusty rolls

Spread the bottom half or halves lightly with:

Softened butter

Spread the other half or halves generously with:

Prepared mustard

Layer on the bottom half:

8 ounces thinly sliced ham
8 ounces thinly sliced Swiss cheese
8 ounces Pork Loin Roast, 488, or Latin Roasted Picnic Shoulder, 490, thinly sliced
(4 ounces thinly sliced Genoa salami)
Sliced dill pickles

Cover with the top half of the bread and slice crosswise into 4 sandwiches (leave whole if using rolls). Melt in a heavy skillet over medium heat:

1 tablespoon butter

Place the sandwiches, 2 at a time, in the skillet and place a grill press or heavy skillet on top to press them down. Grill the sandwiches, flipping once, until the cheese has melted, about 10 minutes. Add another:

1 tablespoon butter

to the skillet and repeat with the remaining 2 sandwiches. Serve hot.

PANINI

4 sandwiches

Panini means "little bread" in Italian, and in Italy a *panino* is simply a sandwich that may be served cold or hot and pressed. In this country panini are always pressed and heated until the bread is crisp. A countertop electric grill or panini press is ideal. Alternatively, place a skillet on the stovetop and weight down the sandwich with a grill press or second skillet.

Preheat a panini grill or heavy skillet to medium. Split:

Four 5 × 4-inch squares of focaccia, or 4 ciabatta rolls

Drizzle the inside of both halves lightly with:

Olive oil
(Balsamic vinegar)

Divide any of the following combinations evenly among the bottom halves:

8 ounces thinly sliced prosciutto/8 ounces thinly sliced mozzarella/16 basil leaves
1 large tomato, thinly sliced/8 ounces thinly sliced mozzarella/16 basil leaves
8 ounces thinly sliced bresaola/2 cups arugula/4 ounces Parmesan, shaved
8 ounces mortadella/8 ounces Fontina, grated

Sprinkle with:

Salt and black pepper to taste

Cover with the top halves. Grill the sandwiches in the panini press until the cheese melts and the bread is crisp, about 4 minutes. Alternatively, griddle and press them as for Cuban Sandwiches, 142 (they will need 8 minutes total).

TORTAS

4 tortas

For a **vegetarian torta,** omit the meat and bulk up the sandwich with more of the other ingredients or use Scrambled Eggs, 156, or a vegetarian meat replacement.

Have ready one of the following:

About 2 cups sliced or shredded cooked meat, especially Carne Asada, 459, Braised Carnitas, 495, Chicken Tinga, 425, or Crispy Pan-Fried Tongue with Onions and Jalapeños, 517

12 ounces sliced ham

1 pound Mexican chorizo, browned, drained, and crumbled

Place in a dry skillet over medium heat, if desired:

(4 large jalapeño peppers)

Cook, turning occasionally, until all the sides of the peppers are blistered and browned, about 10 minutes. Set aside. Alternatively, have ready:

(½ cup pickled jalapeños)

Lay out on a countertop:

4 bolillo or telera rolls, or large crusty rolls, split horizontally

Hollow out the rolls by removing some of the soft inner bread. Spread the inside of the top and bottom of the rolls with:

½ cup mayonnaise

Spread thinly on the bottom halves of the rolls:

¾ cup Refried Beans, 215

Divide your chosen filling among the sandwiches and top with:

1 large avocado, pitted, peeled, and thinly sliced

1 large tomato, thinly sliced

1 small onion, thinly sliced

2 cups shredded iceberg lettuce

If using fresh jalapeños, cut the stems off and cut the peppers into 4 lengthwise "chips" each, cutting just to the side of the center core of seeds. Discard the seeds. Divide the roasted or pickled jalapeños among the sandwiches and cover with the tops of the rolls. If desired, you may griddle and press the *tortas* as for Cuban Sandwiches, 142 (they will only need 6 to 8 minutes total).

TUNA MELT

4 sandwiches

This diner classic is usually filled with a simple tuna salad, but we love using a deluxe batch of Becker Tuna Salad, 124, for the added crunch.

Preheat the broiler. Lay out on a work surface:

8 slices rye or sourdough bread, toasted

Spread on 4 slices:

Tuna Salad, 124

Top with:

1 cup grated Cheddar, Monterey Jack, Fontina, or American (4 ounces)

Broil until the cheese is melted and golden, 1 to 2 minutes. If desired, top the melts with:

(Tomato slices)

(Arugula leaves, watercress, or shredded lettuce)

And spread on the top slices, if desired:

(Spicy brown mustard)

Slap together and garnish each sandwich with:

A dill pickle spear

HOT BROWN

4 servings

Developed at the Brown Hotel in Louisville, Kentucky, in 1923, this delight remains on the menu to this day.

Preheat the broiler. Divide among 4 small gratin dishes:

4 slices lightly toasted and buttered white bread, cut into quarters

Top with, dividing the ingredients evenly:

8 ounces thinly sliced turkey

8 slices tomato

Pour over the top:

1 to 1⅓ cups Sauce Mornay, 548, to taste

Broil until bubbling. Top with, dividing evenly:

8 slices bacon, cooked until crisp

Serve immediately.

ABOUT HOT DOGS

An American backyard grill classic, reminiscent of summertime and baseball games, hot dogs can be dressed with a huge variety of condiments. Many hot dogs are precooked, so all you have to do is heat them up; sausages such as bratwurst are usually sold raw. Even if they are precooked, we think dogs benefit from char and grill smoke, or a browned crust from a good griddling. Many different kinds of sausages can be treated as for hot dogs. See Cooking Sausage Links, 509, for more information.

HOT DOGS

4 hot dogs

Prepare as desired according to Cooking Sausage Links, 509:

4 hot dogs, precooked sausages, or fresh sausages

Meanwhile, toast:

4 hot dog buns (or hoagie rolls for larger sausages), split

If desired, spread each bun with:

(Softened butter)

Place the hot dogs in the prepared buns. Top with any of the following, to taste:

Mustard, ketchup, mayonnaise, or sriracha

Pickle relish, Tart Corn Relish, 925, Quick-Pickled Onions, 930, sliced pickled peppers, sauerkraut, or kimchi

Diced red or white onion or Sautéed Onions, 255

Shredded cheese, Treva's Pimiento Cheese, 55, or Sauce Mornay, 548

Any chili, 502–3
Classic Coleslaw, 119

HOT DOG COMBINATIONS

There are many special dogs out there. Here are a few of our favorites (add all toppings to taste):

Reuben dog: grated Swiss cheese/spicy brown mustard/drained sauerkraut/Russian Dressing, 576
Cincinnati-style cheese Coney: Cincinnati Chili Cockaigne, 502/diced onion/yellow mustard/grated Cheddar
Chicago dog: sliced tomato/pickled peppers/dill pickle spear/sweet pickle relish/diced onion/yellow mustard/a dash of celery salt/(preferably with a beef hot dog on a poppy seed bun)
Sonoran dog: crisp, bacon-wrapped hot dog/split *bolillo* rolls/any of the toppings listed for Tortas, 143
Carolina dog: meat-only chili/yellow mustard/diced onion/finely chopped Classic Coleslaw, 119

CORN DOGS

8 corn dogs

Please read about Deep-Frying, 1051. Whisk until smooth:

½ cup plus 2 tablespoons yellow cornmeal
¼ cup all-purpose flour
1 tablespoon sugar
½ teaspoon salt
¼ cup plus 3 tablespoons buttermilk
1 large egg
¼ teaspoon baking soda

Let the batter rest 10 minutes to thicken. Preheat the oven to 225°F. Heat to 375°F in a deep-fryer, deep heavy pot, or Dutch oven:

3 inches vegetable oil

Meanwhile, impale on wooden skewers:

8 hot dogs

Pour the batter into a tall, narrow glass and dip each skewered hot dog in the batter, turning to coat evenly. Fry the corn dogs, turning the skewers for even cooking, until browned, 3 to 4 minutes. Keep warm in the oven until all are fried. Serve with:

Ketchup and mustard

ABOUT BURGERS

Back in a simpler, sweeter time, the word "burger" signified a ground beef patty and nothing more (we will not delve too far into history; suffice it to say, people have been eating finely minced beef for a very long time under many different names). Now, however, the preparation has ballooned into an entire category of foods. "Burger" can now refer to sandwich patties made out of anything from ground lamb to mushrooms, shrimp, or even beets. The only unifying factor is their shape and the way they are served. Because veggie burgers are more fragile than their meaty counterparts, they benefit from griddling rather than grilling. ➤ For preparing venison burgers, see 528; for chicken or turkey burgers, see 430; for lamb burgers, see 505. For more information on buying, storing, and working with ground meat, see About Ground Meat, 501.

HAMBURGERS

4 burgers

Prepare:

Hamburger Patties, 504

Meanwhile, toast:

4 hamburger buns, split

Place the hamburger patties in the prepared buns. Top with any of the accoutrements listed below.

FRESH OR COOKED VEGETABLES

Thinly sliced tomato
Iceberg or Bibb lettuce leaves
Thinly sliced red or sweet onions, Sautéed Onions, 255, Caramelized Onions, 255, Melted Leeks, 247, Crispy Fried Shallots, 256, or Onion Rings, 256
Sautéed Mushrooms, 251
Sliced avocado

(MORE) PROTEINS

Crisp-cooked bacon strips
Fried Eggs, 155
Chili con Carne, 468
Thin slices of Cheddar, pepperjack, Gouda, or Swiss
Crumbled blue cheese

CONDIMENTS AND PICKLES

Mustard and/or ketchup
Mayonnaise, Aïoli, 564, or any flavored mayonnaise, 563–65
Treva's Pimiento Cheese, 55
Kansas City Barbecue Sauce, 582
Dill chips or bread-and-butter pickles
Chow Chow, 925

PATTY MELT

4 servings

Prepare, using red onions:

Sautéed Onions, 255

Prepare:

Hamburger Patties II, 504

While the burgers cook, toast:

8 slices rye bread

Place each burger on a slice of toast. Top the burgers with the onions and:

8 slices Swiss cheese

Top with the remaining toast. Return the sandwiches to the skillet or griddle and heat over medium-low heat, turning once, until the cheese melts. Serve immediately.

BEET BURGERS

4 servings

Using a food processor helps these burgers hold their shape without the use of a binder like beaten egg. However, you can make these without a food processor by mashing the beans well, adding the other ingredients, and kneading the mixture with your hands until it holds together. The patties will be a little more fragile, so handle them with care.

Heat in a medium skillet over medium heat:

1 tablespoon vegetable oil

Add and cook, stirring, until browned, about 8 minutes:

½ medium onion, finely chopped

Stir in and cook until fragrant, about 1 minute more:

3 garlic cloves, minced

Scrape the onion mixture into a food processor. Add:

One 15-ounce can white beans, drained and rinsed
1 cup cooked brown or white rice
1 medium beet (6 to 8 ounces), peeled and grated
¼ cup dry bread crumbs
3 tablespoons minced dill
¾ teaspoon salt
½ teaspoon black pepper

Pulse, scraping down the sides of the bowl several times, until the mixture is finely ground and holds together when squeezed (if there are some whole beans or grains of rice that is fine). Shape into 4 patties. Heat in a large skillet (preferably nonstick) over medium heat:

1 tablespoon vegetable oil

Place the burgers in the skillet and cook, flipping once, until well browned on both sides, about 5 minutes per side. You may need to add more oil to the skillet to brown the second side. Serve on:

4 hamburger buns, split and lightly toasted

With:

Tzatziki, 569
Lettuce leaves
Thinly sliced tomato
(Sliced avocado)

ROASTED MUSHROOM BURGERS

4 servings

These richly flavored burgers will fool no one but please many. Roasted mushrooms, toasted pecans, soy sauce, Parmesan, and porcini powder make for a flavor profile that is, if not meaty, supremely savory.

Preheat the oven to 425°F. Toss together on a large baking sheet:

1 pound shiitake or a blend of shiitake and cremini mushrooms, stems cut off, coarsely chopped
2 tablespoons vegetable oil

Save the stems for stock, 73. Roast the mushrooms until well browned and shriveled, 20 to 25 minutes. Meanwhile, heat in a medium skillet over medium heat:

1 tablespoon vegetable oil

Add and cook, stirring, until softened, about 5 minutes:

1 medium onion, finely chopped

Stir in and cook 2 minutes more:

2 garlic cloves, minced

In a large bowl, mash until no whole beans remain:

One 15-ounce can black beans, drained and rinsed

Stir in the mushroom/onion mixture, along with:

½ cup pecans, toasted, 1005, and finely chopped
(½ cup finely grated Parmesan [2 ounces])
¼ cup dry bread crumbs
2 tablespoons soy sauce
1 tablespoon chili powder
(1 teaspoon porcini powder)

Mix well with your hands until the mixture is combined and holds together when squeezed. Shape into 4 patties. Cook as for Beet Burgers, 144. Serve with any of the additions to hamburgers, 144.

ABOUT FLATBREAD SANDWICHES

Flatbreads designed specifically for wraps are sold in most supermarkets, but we will gladly pass them over for naan, paratha, lavash, chapati, pita, and flour tortillas. To roll wraps and flour tortillas in the standard burrito shape, fold the exposed edge of the bread closest to you over the filling, fold over the right and left sides, and then roll up. Place the wrap seam side down and, if desired, cut in half on the diagonal. For pita pocket sandwiches, cut off about one-fifth of each pita bread to make an opening to the pocket for stuffing. Pita bread is less likely to tear when stuffed if slightly warmed in a dry skillet or on a grill. Some pitas do not have pockets and should be warmed and folded around the filling.

Almost any of the combinations in Cold Sandwich Combinations, 136, will work in a wrap or flatbread situation. Combination salads, 120, also make good templates for filling a wrap.

FLATBREAD OR PITA SANDWICH

4 sandwiches

Prepare one of the following:

Falafel, 214
Lamb Shawarma, 480, Becker Lamb Patties, 505, Adana-Style Lamb Kebabs, 504, or Keftedes, 62
Beef Kebabs, 460
Pork Souvlaki, 492

Prepare one or more of the following:

Tahini Dressing, 576, Zhug, 567, Tzatziki, 569, Herbed Yogurt Dressing, 577

Warm until pliable:

4 pitas

Open the pitas on one side for pocket sandwiches. Divide the falafel, lamb patties, kebab meat, or souvlaki among them. Drizzle with the desired sauce(s), then top with:

1½ cups shredded lettuce
¾ cup diced tomatoes
¾ cup diced peeled cucumbers
(¼ cup diced red onion or sliced green onion)
(Crumbled feta)

Drizzle with more sauce.

SABICH (ISRAELI PITA SANDWICH)

4 sandwiches

Iraqi Jews brought this sandwich to Israel when they emigrated, fleeing religious persecution in their home country. It is now an extremely popular street food, eaten for breakfast or lunch. *Amba*, 953, is a salty, tangy condiment made from pickled mangoes. We highly recommend seeking it out.

Have ready:

1 cup Hummus, 52, or ½ cup Tahini Dressing, 576
8 slices Roasted Eggplant II, 238, or Fried Eggplant, 238
4 Hard-Boiled Eggs, 151, sliced
2 cups Shirazi or Israeli Salad, 128
(1 cup sliced dill pickles)
Zhug, 567, and/or puréed amba, 953

Warm until pliable:

4 pitas

Open the pitas on one side and spread with the hummus or tahini dressing. Stuff with the eggplant, eggs, salad, and pickles (if using). If using flatbread-style pitas that do not have a pocket, simply top with the ingredients and fold the pita around them. Drizzle with zhug and/or amba as desired.

ABOUT TACOS, TOSTADAS, AND BURRITOS

The foundation of any taco, tostada, or burrito is a corn or flour tortilla. To make homemade flour tortillas, see 612. Corn tortillas may also be made at home, either using masa harina or fresh masa dough, 612. If you live in an area with a substantial Mexican-American population, look for fresh masa dough at *tortillerias* or Mexican supermarkets. Or, even better, try to find freshly made tortillas. In the absence of either, tortillas made with masa harina can be excellent.

Tacos are Mexican street food. They are served on small griddled or steamed corn tortillas that are double stacked (two tortillas per taco). They are topped with a wide range of meats (chicken, beef, pork, fish, and offal are all very common), cilantro, and chopped onion. They may be served with radishes, lime wedges, Taqueria Pickles, 930, and a selection of hot sauces. American-style tacos are vastly different, made with hard, folded and fried taco shells and ground beef filling.

Burritos are thought to be a Mexican-American invention, probably originating in California. They consist of warmed flour tortillas filled with various meats or vegetables and cheeses. Burritos can be incredibly simple, consisting of a few ingredients, or they may veer closer to the "Mission style" burrito, which is enormous and filled with meat, beans, rice, guacamole, cheese, sour cream or *crema*, salsa, and iceberg lettuce. These larger burritos are usually buttressed by a foil wrapper, which is necessary to prevent them from bursting. Burritos can be filled with just about anything, from beef, chicken, and pork, to eggs, potatoes, and peppers, to rice, guacamole, and beans. They can be served as is or "smothered" in a red chile sauce (like New Mexico–Style Chile Sauce, 554) and sprinkled with cheese.

To warm store-bought tortillas on the stovetop, sprinkle each one with a little water and place on an ungreased griddle or skillet over medium heat until they bubble slightly. Turn and heat the other side. To heat in a microwave, wrap in a damp paper towel or kitchen towel and heat in 30-second bursts until warm. To warm in the oven, wrap tightly in foil and place in a preheated 350°F oven for 10 minutes.

To fry tortillas, heat ½ inch vegetable oil in a skillet. Fry one at a time, turning once, until crisp, and drain on paper towels. Fried tortillas are best served immediately, but they can be kept briefly in the oven. Place on a baking sheet and keep warm in a 200°F oven.

FILLINGS FOR TACOS AND BURRITOS

Any cooked, sliced or shredded meat or poultry reheated in Green Mole, 554, Mole Poblano, 553, New Mexico–Style Chile Sauce, 554, or the sauce for Chicken Enchiladas, 539

Beef: Spiced Ground Meat for Tacos, 503, Picadillo, 503, Carne Asada, 459, Crispy Pan-Fried Tongue with Onions and Jalapeños, 517

Goat: Goat Birria, 485

Pork: Braised Carnitas, 495, Pork Adovada, 496, Braised Pulled Pork, 495, shredded Smoked Pork Shoulder, 496, or cooked Mexican chorizo, store-bought or homemade, 511

Poultry: Chicken Chili Verde, 425, Chicken Tinga, 425, Turkey in Red Mole, 430

Fish and Shellfish: Fried Fish, 390, Spice-Rubbed Grilled or Broiled Fish, rubbed with chili powder, 385, Camarones al Mojo de Ajo, 365, Camarones a la Diabla, 364, Grilled or Broiled Shrimp I, 365

Vegetables: Fried potatoes, onions, and poblanos, Refried Beans, 215, drained Frijoles de la Olla, 213, Rajas con Crema, 262, Picadillo, 503, made with soy crumbles or Seasoned Tempeh Crumbles, 287

TACOS

12 tacos; about 4 servings

This recipe is written to work with a wide variety of fillings and toppings. To go the classic street food route, look for 4- to 6-inch corn tortillas and use 2 stacked tortillas per taco.

Prepare or have ready:

Any of the Fillings for Tacos and Burritos, above
Twelve 6-inch corn or flour tortillas, warmed, or 12 taco shells

Meanwhile, place in separate serving bowls:

Shredded lettuce
Chopped onion
Chopped cilantro
Sliced red radishes
Crumbled Cotija, or shredded Monterey Jack, Cheddar, or queso fresco
Pico de Gallo, 573, Table Salsa, 573, and/or Guacamole, 51
Sour cream or crema
Taqueria Pickles, 930

Transfer the filling to a serving bowl. Wrap the warm tortillas in foil or place the taco shells in a basket. Allow guests to assemble their own tacos.

TOSTADAS
4 tostadas
Ceviche, 377, is a common topping for tostadas. If using ceviche, do not spread the tostadas with beans.
Prepare:
Refried Beans, 215
Any of the Fillings for Tacos and Burritos, 146
When ready to serve, spread the beans onto:
4 corn tortillas, fried until crisp, 612, or 4 store-bought tostadas
Top with some of the filling, then top with:
Shredded lettuce
Diced tomato or Pico de Gallo, 573
Sliced avocado
(Sour cream or crema and/or crumbled Cotija)
(Chopped cilantro)

BURRITOS
4 burritos
I. Preheat the oven to 350°F. Wrap in foil and warm in the oven for 10 minutes:
Four 10-inch flour tortillas
Have ready:
2 cups any of the Fillings for Tacos and Burritos, 146
1½ cups shredded Monterey Jack, Oaxaca cheese, or queso fresco (6 ounces)
(½ cup finely chopped onion)
(¼ cup chopped seeded jalapeño peppers or drained canned sliced jalapeños)
Remove the tortillas from the oven and slip 1 tortilla out of the foil, leaving the rest wrapped. Place the tortilla on a work surface. In a wide strip parallel to you, place ½ cup filling just south of center on the tortilla. Sprinkle with about ⅓ cup cheese, and, if using, 2 tablespoons onions and 1 tablespoon jalapeños. Fold the sides of the tortilla in, then fold the edge closer to you over the filling and roll up tightly. Place seam side down on a baking sheet lined with foil. Make 3 more burritos in the same way and heat in the oven until warmed through, about 10 minutes. Serve with:
Shredded romaine or iceberg lettuce
Sour cream
Pico de Gallo, 573, or Table Salsa, 573
II. Smothered or "wet" burritos forgo their portability in favor of a warm blanket of sauce and melted cheese. They are best eaten with a fork and steak knife.
Prepare burritos as for **I, above.** Serve each burrito topped with:
⅓ cup warmed New Mexico–Style Chile Sauce, 554, or the sauce for Chicken Enchiladas, 539 (1⅓ cups total)
2 tablespoons shredded Monterey Jack, Oaxaca cheese, or queso fresco (½ cup total)

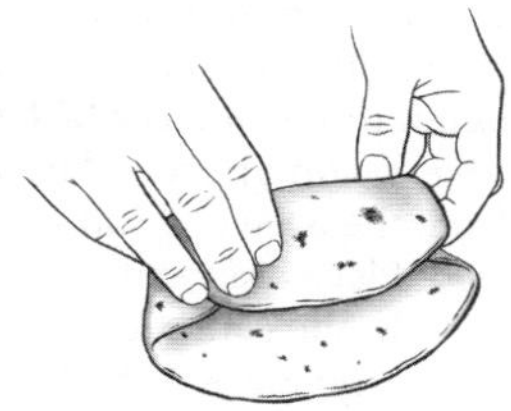
Folding a burrito

MISSION-STYLE BURRITOS
4 burritos
If you can find 14-inch tortillas, use them to make extra-large burritos, using slightly more rice, beans, and filling.
Preheat the oven to 350°F. Wrap in foil and warm in the oven for 10 minutes:
Four 12-inch flour tortillas
Have ready:
1 cup Guacamole, 51
1⅓ cups cooked rice or Spanish Rice, 330
One 15-ounce can pinto or black beans, drained and rinsed, or 1⅓ cups Frijoles de la Olla, 213
2 cups any of the Fillings for Tacos and Burritos, 146
1½ cups shredded Cheddar or Monterey Jack (6 ounces)
1 cup Pico de Gallo, 573, or any salsa
(½ cup sour cream or crema)
Remove the tortillas from the oven and slip 1 tortilla out of the foil, leaving the rest wrapped. Place the tortilla on a work surface. In a wide strip parallel to you in the center of the tortilla, spread ¼ cup guacamole. Top with ⅓ cup rice, ⅓ cup beans, and ½ cup filling of choice. Sprinkle with about ⅓ cup cheese, ¼ cup salsa, and 2 tablespoons sour cream (if using). Fold the sides of the tortilla in. Then fold the edge closer to you over the center and roll up tightly. Place seam side down on a baking sheet lined with foil. Make 3 more burritos in the same way and heat in the oven until warmed through, about 10 minutes. Or for a **burrito dorado,** heat in a large skillet over medium heat:
1 tablespoon vegetable oil
Fry the burritos 2 at a time, flipping once, until golden on both sides. Serve with:
Hot sauce
Chopped cilantro

BREAKFAST BURRITOS
4 burritos
These burritos may be wrapped in foil, frozen, and reheated when needed. To reheat, remove the burrito from the foil and microwave until warmed through, about 2 minutes.
Preheat the oven to 350°F. Wrap in foil and warm in the oven for 10 minutes:
Four 10-inch flour tortillas
Have ready:
Double recipe Scrambled Eggs, 156, or a single recipe Tofu Scramble, 286

Pan-Fried Potatoes, 268 (add the optional chili powder as directed in the headnote) or Roasted Potatoes, 267
1 cup shredded Cheddar or Monterey Jack (4 ounces)
(1 cup crumbled crisp bacon or cooked breakfast sausage)

Remove the tortillas from the oven and slip 1 tortilla out of the foil, leaving the rest wrapped. Place the tortilla on a work surface. In a wide strip parallel to you in the center of the tortilla, place ½ cup scrambled eggs and ½ cup potatoes. Sprinkle with ¼ cup cheese, and, if using, ¼ cup bacon or sausage. Fold the sides of the tortilla in. Then fold the edge closer to you over the center and roll up tightly. Place seam side down on a baking sheet lined with foil. Make 3 more burritos in the same way and heat in the oven until warmed through, about 10 minutes. Serve with:

Pico de Gallo, 573, or Table Salsa, 573

EGG DISHES

When we crack open a fresh egg, we are reminded of M.F.K. Fisher's observation that "one of the most private things in the world is an egg until it is broken." Indeed, the egg, in its elegant and delicate wrapping, seems to hold within it some of the secrets of the universe. But more prosaically, it also holds the secrets to a thousand different ways to breakfast, lunch, and dinner.

The egg's versatility knows no absolute rules. We once said that no egg dish really succeeds unless the eggs are very fresh. The exception to this case is hard-boiled eggs, which are easier to peel if the eggs are slightly older. We have also said that because eggs cook with a very low degree of heat, they should be treated gently; that they "like the consideration and will respond by being tender." While that may be a nice thought as you gently poach or coddle your eggs, what of hard fried eggs with their crisp, frilly edges? Or the Thai specialty, Son-in-Law Eggs, 152, which are hard-boiled, then fried until golden? The world is too large and the egg too versatile to make tidy generalizations—see the cooking methods throughout for useful particulars.

ABOUT EGGS

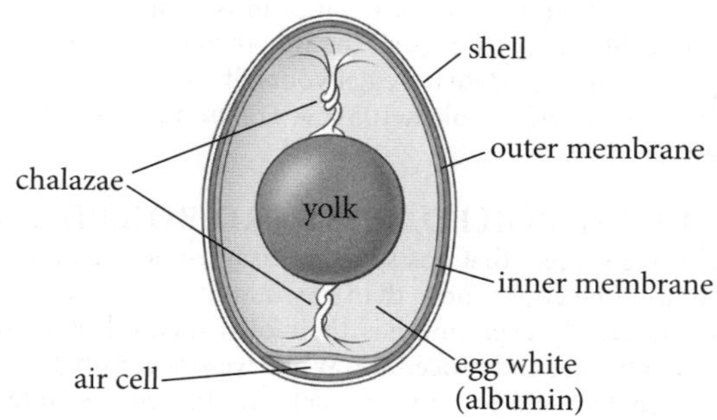

See the illustration above for the component parts of the egg. The **shell** is the egg's most obvious protective structure. Egg shells, however, are permeable, letting in air and moisture. Unwashed eggs are covered in a **bloom** or **cuticle,** which prevents bacteria from entering the egg. This is why you may find unrefrigerated eggs in countries where egg washing is not the default. The **inner and outer membranes** just beneath the shell are the second and third lines of defense against bacterial infection. The **air cell** is simply a small pocket of air that forms when the egg cools after being laid and grows slightly in size as the egg ages. The **egg white** or **albumin** is made mostly of water and several types of proteins, some of which help create and stabilize foams. The **yolk** contains more protein, along with fat and almost all the minerals found in the egg. The yolk also contains lecithin, a substance that attracts both water and fat, thus making it a superb emulsifier and thickener of sauces. The **chalazae** connect to the yolk on either side and hold it in place. You may have noticed these thin, white strands when separating eggs.

The eggs we use most often are chicken eggs, and if you buy eggs at a grocery store, they will be of a uniform size. However, if you buy eggs at farmers' markets, the eggs will vary in size, shape, and color. ➤ When we refer to **large eggs** in recipes we mean eggs that weigh about 2 ounces or 57 grams in their shell, or measure about 3 tablespoons cracked. To account for irregularly sized eggs, calculate how much egg you need by weight or volume for the recipe in question. If you do not have a scale, crack the eggs into a bowl, beat to combine the yolks and whites, and measure their volume. The same logic goes for duck, goose, and turkey eggs, which are all larger than chicken eggs and have a richer flavor. For more on egg sizes and grades, see 976.

Emu and ostrich eggs are rarities and weigh an average 1¼ pounds and 4¼ pounds respectively. Should you find one and work up the gumption to try it, we would recommend inviting a few friends over for an epic frittata. Quail eggs fall at the opposite end of the spectrum, clocking in at about 9 grams or just over ¼ ounce apiece. Though impractical for scrambling, they are a beautiful garnish when hard-boiled, fried, or pickled; and the raw yolks are lovely atop servings of Steak Tartare, 64.

In general, when cooking with eggs, use the same care you would with any perishable ingredient and no harm is likely to befall you. However, when cooking for the very young, the elderly, pregnant women, and those with compromised immune systems, use greater caution: Cook eggs all the way through or use pasteurized eggs. You may pasteurize eggs yourself using an immersion circulator or sous vide cooker, 1054. ➤ For more information on egg safety, see 979.

ABOUT SOFT-BOILED AND HARD-BOILED EGGS

If there is one subject that has sparked disagreement among food writers and home cooks more than any other, it is the best way to boil an egg. Nearly everyone has their own method, with slight variations in timing and procedure. While we sincerely believe that there is more than one path to a perfectly cooked egg, we offer our preferred methods on the pages that follow.

For starters, you never want to actually boil eggs, but rather, gently simmer them (unfortunately, "simmered eggs" just doesn't have quite the same ring to it). Some cooks like to start their eggs in a pan of cool water, while others bring the water to a boil and lower eggs into it. Both methods work, though there are pros and cons to each. The advantage of the **cold-water start** is that you do not have to drop eggs into a pan of boiling water, which can cause them to break. However, eggs cooked this way may be harder to peel, which is the chief advantage of the **boiling-water start**—an easier time peeling.

We have recently become devotees of the **steam method,** where eggs are placed in a steamer basket above rapidly boiling water. Eggs cooked this way are almost uniformly easy to peel—and it is much faster to bring an inch or two of water to a boil than a filled pan. Carefully inspect the eggs before steaming them—even a small crack will cause the egg white to burst through the shell during cooking. For slow-poached eggs, which are cooked in the shell but have the texture of a poached egg, see 153.

If your eggs are on the fresher side, use a boiling-water start or the steam method to ensure easier peeling. Older eggs will be easier to peel no matter what method you use.

➤ *To determine the age of eggs,* place them in a bowl of water. Very fresh eggs will lie on their sides on the bottom of the bowl; eggs that are the perfect age for hard-boiling will stand upright on the bottom; and eggs that float are too old and should be thrown away.

Hard-boiled eggs are at home on many dishes. We love halved eggs with barely set yolks on Bistro Salad, 118, or Salade Niçoise, 121. In dishes like Miso Ramen, 304, halved eggs with set whites and runny yolks add a sublime richness to the broth. Hard-boiled eggs with firmer yolks are a necessity for Egg Salad, 124, and Sauce Gribiche, 233.

SOFT-BOILED EGGS

Soft-boiled eggs require very precise timing. For that reason, we recommend using a boiling-water start or steaming them.

I. BOILING-WATER START

Fill a saucepan with enough water to cover the number of eggs you plan to cook. Bring the water to a boil, reduce to a simmer, and use a slotted spoon to gently place in the water:

Unshelled eggs, from the refrigerator

Time the eggs from the moment they go into the water and maintain a simmer throughout. Large eggs will take 5 minutes, and extra-large or jumbo eggs will take 5½ minutes (small and medium eggs will take 4½ minutes). ➤ For room temperature eggs, subtract 1 minute from these cooking times.

To serve a soft-boiled egg in an eggcup, place the egg in wide end down. Use a table knife or teaspoon to crack off the top third of the shell, season with salt and pepper, and serve with strips of toast, or "soldiers." Alternatively, spoon the egg out of the shell, using a napkin to protect your hand from the heat, and serve in a small bowl.

II. STEAM METHOD

Have ready:

Unshelled eggs, from the refrigerator

If using a steamer insert, gently place the eggs inside, bring 1½ inches of water to a rapid boil in a pot, and fit the insert onto the pot. If using a steamer basket, place it inside the pot, bring the water to a boil, and gently place the eggs in the basket with long-handled tongs. Cover immediately and steam the eggs 5 minutes on high heat for large eggs. Remove from the heat and serve as for I above.

HARD-BOILED EGGS

Hard-boiled eggs can have a wide range of textures, from a hard white and barely set yolk (which the French call **mollet**) to a chalky and green-tinged yolk. We encourage you to experiment with egg cooking times to find your favorite degree of doneness. Hard-boiled eggs can also be cooked with the boiling-water start method, but we prefer either the cold-water start or the steam method.

I. COLD-WATER START

Place in a pot in a single layer:

Unshelled eggs, from the refrigerator

Cover them by 1 inch with:

Cold water

Bring to a boil over high heat. Promptly remove the pot from the heat, cover, and let the eggs stand: 8 to 12 minutes for large eggs, or 11 to 15 minutes for extra-large and jumbo eggs (6 to 10 minutes for small and medium eggs). ➤ For room temperature eggs, subtract 1 minute from these cooking times. The lower amount of time will yield eggs that have set whites and barely set yolks, while the higher amount of time will yield eggs that are hard-cooked all the way through. When the eggs are done, run cold water over them to stop the cooking.

To peel hard-boiled eggs, crack the shell all over and roll the egg gently between the palms of your hands to free the thin tough skin from the egg and make shelling easier. Find the air cell and start peeling from there, peeling away the inner membrane along with the shell. Rinse the eggs after shelling to remove any shell fragments.

To slice eggs smoothly, dip a knife blade into water before slicing. ➤ Hard-boiled eggs are best stored in their shells in the refrigerator. A peeled hard-boiled egg should be used within a few days.

II. STEAM METHOD

Have ready:

Unshelled eggs, from the refrigerator

If using a steamer insert, gently place the eggs inside, bring 1½ inches of water to a rapid boil in a pot, and fit the insert onto the pot. If using a steamer basket, place it inside the pot, bring the water to a boil, and gently place the eggs in the basket with long-handled tongs. Cover immediately and steam the eggs on high heat for 8 minutes for large eggs with a set white and fudgy yolk, or 11 minutes for eggs that are firm all the way through. ➤ For room temperature eggs, subtract 1 minute from these cooking times. As the eggs cook, fill a bowl with ice water. Immediately transfer the eggs to the ice water and cool completely. Peel as directed in I, above.

DEVILED EGGS

24 stuffed eggs

Hard-boiled eggs are a blank slate for adventurous cooks. This is Marion's husband's formula, but you may moisten the egg yolks with a vinaigrette, sour cream, softened butter, or even pickle juice—you may also stuff Pickled Eggs, below. For other flavorful excursions see Additions to Deviled Eggs, below.

Prepare and peel:

12 Hard-Boiled Eggs, above, cooked until the yolks are set

Cool and peel as directed. Halve the eggs lengthwise. Remove the yolks carefully, so as not to damage the whites. Crush the yolks without packing them and mix them in a bowl with:

⅓ cup mayonnaise
(1 tablespoon mild, tomato-based chili sauce)
(1½ teaspoons curry or chili powder)
½ teaspoon black pepper
½ teaspoon salt or celery salt
½ teaspoon dry mustard

Put the filling in the whites using a small spoon or, for elaborate effects, a pastry bag fitted with a plain or star tip. Chill for 30 minutes before serving. Garnish with:

Sweet paprika or smoked paprika

ADDITIONS TO DEVILED EGGS

Supplement the filling above with any of the following, to taste:

Anchovy fillets, minced, or anchovy paste
Roasted Garlic, 241, mashed to a paste
Chutney, finely chopped
Smoked salmon, finely chopped
Green onions, thinly sliced
Celery or fennel, minced
Dill pickles, cornichons, pickled jalapeños, or Quick-Pickled Onions, 930, minced
Sriracha or sambal oelek, 969
Pesto, 586
Chives, tarragon, chervil, parsley, basil, or dill, minced

Garnish deviled eggs with any of the following:

Sliced olives or radishes, or shaved truffles
Crispy Fried Shallots, 256
Capers
Caviar or other fish roe
Fresh herbs
Bacon, cooked until crisp and crumbled

PICKLED EGGS

12 servings

Pickled eggs are highly underrated and, if you are a pickle connoisseur, an excellent way to use leftover brine from store-bought or homemade pickles. Simply substitute your brine of choice for the one in the recipe below, bringing the brine to a boil before pouring it over the cooked eggs. Pickled eggs make a superb appetizer and can be prepared as for Deviled Eggs, above, or used in Egg Salad, 124. If you are making pickled eggs for one of these dishes, do not neglect the pickled onions in the jar, which can serve as a garnish or be finely chopped and added to the salad or seasoned yolks.

Prepare:

12 Hard-Boiled Eggs, above, cooked until the yolks are not quite set (7 to 8 minutes for large eggs)

Cool and peel as directed. Place the eggs in a container or jar just large enough to hold them. Combine in a medium saucepan:

2½ cups cider vinegar
1½ cups water
⅔ cup sugar

1 small onion, thinly sliced
8 garlic cloves, smashed
2 tablespoons pickling spice, 923
1 tablespoon salt

Bring to a boil, then reduce the heat and simmer for 5 minutes. Pour the hot brine over the eggs and allow to cool completely. Transfer to the refrigerator and let sit for at least 24 hours. The flavor of the eggs will improve over time. Store the eggs in the refrigerator for up to 3 weeks.

BEET-PICKLED EGGS

Prepare **Pickled Eggs, 151.** Combine the vinegar, water, sugar, and **2 medium beets, peeled and grated on the large holes of a box grater** in a saucepan. Simmer, covered, for 5 minutes, then strain out the beets. Return the liquid to the pan and add the onion, garlic, pickling spice, and salt. Simmer 5 minutes more and pour over the eggs. Proceed as directed.

CURRY-PICKLED EGGS

Prepare **Pickled Eggs, 151,** adding to the pickling liquid **2 teaspoons curry powder, a 2-inch piece ginger, thinly sliced,** and **2 dried red chiles.**

SON-IN-LAW EGGS

4 to 6 servings

This sweet and salty Thai specialty has an intriguing name. The most interesting explanation is that this dish was served to new sons-in-law as a tongue-in-cheek warning of what might happen to them if they step out of line.

Prepare:

6 Hard-Boiled Eggs, 151, cooked until the yolks are not quite set (7 to 8 minutes for large eggs)

Cool and peel as directed. Meanwhile, pour into a deep saucepan, skillet, or wok:

1 inch vegetable oil

Heat to 350°F over medium-high, then reduce the heat to maintain that temperature. Add the peeled eggs to the oil and fry, turning occasionally, until golden brown all over, 5 to 8 minutes. Transfer the eggs to a cutting board. Use the same oil to make:

Crispy Fried Shallots, 256

When golden, transfer the shallots with a spider or slotted spoon to paper towels to drain, and sprinkle lightly with:

Salt

Add to the hot oil and fry very briefly, about 10 seconds, until crisp:

2 small, dried red chiles

Transfer the chiles to the plate with the shallots. Combine in a small saucepan:

¼ cup palm sugar or packed brown sugar
2 tablespoons fish sauce
2 tablespoons water
1 tablespoon seedless tamarind pulp or extract, 195

Bring to a simmer and cook briefly until thickened and syrupy. Halve the eggs lengthwise and pour the sauce over them. Chop the fried chiles and sprinkle over the eggs, then top with the fried shallots. Serve with:

Cilantro
Lime wedges
Sliced cucumber

SCOTCH EGGS

6 servings

If you can imagine it, early versions of this dish were served with gravy. We recommend boiling large eggs for only 7 minutes to avoid overcooking the yolks when the eggs are fried.

Please read about Deep-Frying, 1051. Have ready:

1 pound bulk sausage or ½ recipe Country Sausage, 510
6 Hard-Boiled Eggs, 151, cooked until the yolks are not quite set (7 to 8 minutes for large eggs)

Cool and peel as directed. Thoroughly mix the sausage in a bowl with:

1 large egg, beaten

Place on a plate:

¼ cup flour

Beat in a shallow bowl:

1 large egg

Spread on another plate:

1½ cups fresh or dry bread crumbs, 957

Wet your hands with cold water to prevent the sausage from sticking to your hands. Shape the sausage into 6 patties. Mold each patty around a hard-boiled egg. Roll each egg in the flour to coat and shake off the excess, dip in the beaten egg, and then roll in the bread crumbs to coat.

Pour into a deep heavy pot:

3 inches vegetable oil

Heat to 325°F over medium-high, then reduce the heat to maintain that temperature. Fry the eggs in two batches until the outside is golden brown and the sausage is cooked through, about 6 minutes. Let stand for 5 minutes, then cut into halves or quarters and serve hot or at room temperature with:

Whole-grain mustard

ABOUT CODDLED AND POACHED EGGS

Coddling simply refers to the gentle cooking of eggs. Technically, there is no real difference between a soft-boiled egg, a poached egg, and a coddled egg. In fact, you might say that poaching and soft-boiling are forms of coddling. For another form of in-shell poaching, see Slow-Poached Eggs, 153.

Poached eggs are cracked into simmering liquid and cooked until the whites are set and the yolks are thickened but still runny in the center. They can be poached in water, stock, sauce, milk, heavy cream, soup (as in Sopa de Ajo I, 91), or tomato sauce (as in Shakshouka, 154, or Eggs in Purgatory, 154). When the yolks are broken, they add richness and a silken texture to the surrounding soup or sauce.

Although various egg-poaching devices are available, all that is necessary to poach eggs are a saucepan and a slotted spoon. For best results, use very fresh eggs, which have thicker whites and hold their shape well. The thinner portion of the whites tends to spread into fine, white tendrils when added to the poaching liquid. You can avoid this by cracking eggs one by one into a fine mesh sieve over a sink, which allows the thinnest part of the white to drain away. Adding vinegar to the water also helps the white to set more quickly. Or take a cue from Julia Child, who simmered her eggs in the shell for 10 seconds before cracking and poaching them. Our preferred method is to not worry about this "problem" at all, and simply trim away any thin streamers of white after the eggs are poached.

POACHED EGGS

2 to 4 servings

An 8-inch skillet comfortably holds 4 eggs; you may add up to 6 eggs to a 10-inch skillet, or 10 eggs to a 12-inch skillet. For an especially large brunch crowd, poach the eggs in batches and keep warm, or prepare them the day before and reheat (see below). Or, for an extremely easy way to prepare large quantities, see Slow-Poached Eggs, below.

Bring to a brisk simmer in a nonstick skillet:

2 inches water

Have ready:

4 large eggs

One at a time, break an egg into a small bowl or cup, bring the edge of the bowl about 1 inch above the surface of the water, and allow the egg to gently drop into the water. When all the eggs are added, cover the skillet, remove from the heat, and let sit until the whites are set, 4 to 6 minutes. With practice, you will be able to judge the right degree of doneness. Remove the eggs with a large slotted spoon and drain well before serving, patting the eggs dry with a paper towel or kitchen towel.

To keep poached eggs warm, transfer to a wide shallow bowl of water warmed to 150°F, cover, and hold for up to 30 minutes.

To prepare poached eggs ahead of time, transfer the poached eggs to a bowl of cold water the moment they are done. Store in the water, refrigerated, for up to 24 hours. When ready to serve, transfer the eggs to a large pan of 150°F water, cover, and let stand for at least 5 minutes, or up to 20 minutes. Return the pan to very low heat if the temperature of the water drops below 145°F.

CODDLED EGGS

To coddle by boiling, lower unshelled eggs carefully into boiling water with a spoon. Cover the pan and remove from the heat. Allow 6 to 8 minutes for delicately coddled eggs. If you want the eggs to remain shapely when opened, turn them several times within the first few minutes of coddling so that the white of the egg solidifies evenly in the air space and the yolk is centered.

To use an egg coddler, place a rack or folded towel in a saucepan and fill with enough water to reach the rim of the egg coddler and bring to a boil over high heat. Butter the insides of the egg coddler and break an egg into it. Top with ½ **teaspoon butter, 2 teaspoons heavy cream,** and **salt and black pepper.** Screw the top on tightly. Set the coddler in the pan, cover, and immediately reduce the heat to a simmer. Simmer for 6 to 8 minutes for a medium-set egg.

SLOW-POACHED EGGS

Here, eggs are cooked in their shells for an hour or longer at a very low temperature with an immersion circulator. When cracked open, they are perfectly poached. The number of eggs you can cook at once is only limited by the size of the water bath, which makes this an excellent method to use for a large brunch crowd.

Please read Low-Temperature and Sous Vide Cooking, 1054.

Fill a pot with water. Place an immersion circulator in the pot and set to 147°F. When the water is preheated, gently lower into the pot:

Large eggs in their shells

Cook for 1 hour. Before serving, crack the eggs into a slotted spoon to allow any excess liquid to drain off.

To prepare slow-poached eggs ahead of time, transfer the eggs to a bowl filled with ice water and chill completely. Store in the water, refrigerated, for up to 24 hours. To reheat, place the eggs in a pot and set the immersion circulator to 147°F. Heat through for 15 minutes, then serve.

EGGS FLORENTINE

Prepare **Poached Eggs** or **Slow-Poached Eggs, above.** Cover the bottom of a shallow buttered baking dish with **Creamed Spinach, 244.** Arrange the poached eggs on the spinach, cover with **Sauce Mornay, 548,** sprinkle with **Au Gratin II or III, 958,** and brown quickly under a hot broiler.

EGGS BENEDICT

2 to 4 servings

For variations on a theme, place the eggs and ham on top of Fried Green Tomatoes, 282, Latkes, 269, Crab Cakes, 358, or any unsweetened biscuit, 635–37. For **Eggs Blackstone,** top the English muffin halves with **8 slices crisp bacon** and **Broiled or Slow-Roasted Tomatoes, 282,** before topping with the eggs and Hollandaise.

Prepare, drain well, and keep warm:

4 Poached Eggs, above, or Slow-Poached Eggs, above

Place on warmed plates or a warmed serving platter:

2 English muffins, split, toasted, and buttered

Cover with:

4 thick slices ham or Canadian bacon, warmed

Top with the eggs, then top the eggs with:

½ cup Hollandaise, 561, or more if desired

Serve immediately, passing extra sauce on the side.

LATKES BENEDICT

2 to 4 servings

What was once our decadent use for leftover latkes has now become one of our primary motivations for making them in the first place. In addition to smoked salmon, this dish is fantastic with **8 ounces salmon fillet, poached, 381, or slow-roasted, 378.**

Prepare or have ready:

4 Latkes, 269

Keep warm in a 200°F oven. Prepare, drain well, and keep warm:

4 Poached Eggs, above, or Slow-Poached Eggs, above

Place the latkes on warmed plates or a warmed serving platter. Cover the latkes with:

4 ounces lox or hot-smoked salmon, thinly sliced or flaked apart

Top with the eggs, then top the eggs with:

½ cup Hollandaise, 561

Garnish with:

Chopped parsley or minced chives

OEUFS EN MEURETTE (POACHED EGGS IN RED WINE SAUCE)

4 servings

This is a labor-intensive recipe, but the flavor is well worth the effort. If you happen to have leftover sauce from Coq au Vin, 420, or Boeuf Bourguignon, 465, simply use it instead of the sauce called for below.

Prepare, adding the optional mushrooms:

Sauce Meurette, 553

Keep the sauce warm. Prepare and drain well:

8 Poached Eggs, 153

Arrange on a serving platter:

8 slices toast, buttered

Top each slice with a poached egg. Pour the sauce over and around the eggs and garnish with:

Minced parsley

SHAKSHOUKA (EGGS POACHED IN TOMATO-PEPPER SAUCE)

4 to 6 servings

Shakshouka is a popular North African dish that made its way across the Middle East and gave rise to many variations. Depending on where you are, you may find *shakshouka* with potatoes, Merguez Sausage, 511, or diced Salt-Preserved Lemons, 942, but we are partial to the simple version below. If making this for a large group, you may double or triple the tomato sauce, pour it while warm into baking dishes so that it is at least 1 inch deep, add the eggs, and bake at 350°F for about 10 minutes or until the eggs are set.

Heat in a large skillet over medium heat:

2 tablespoons olive oil

When the oil is hot and shimmering, add:

1 large onion, halved and thinly sliced
1 red bell pepper, thinly sliced
2 to 3 jalapeño peppers, seeded and chopped

Cook, stirring, until softened, about 10 minutes. Add:

2 tablespoons tomato paste
3 garlic cloves, chopped
1 tablespoon sweet paprika
1 teaspoon ground cumin
½ teaspoon salt
(½ teaspoon ground caraway or fennel seeds)
(¼ teaspoon cayenne pepper)

Cook until fragrant, 1 to 2 minutes. Stir in:

Two 14-ounce cans diced tomatoes

Bring to a simmer and cook, stirring occasionally, until the sauce is slightly thickened, about 5 minutes. Add:

Salt to taste

Make 6 depressions in the sauce and drop into them:

6 large eggs

Cover the skillet and simmer until the eggs are cooked as desired, 6 to 10 minutes. Serve with:

Crusty bread
Chopped parsley or cilantro, or Zhug, 567
(Crumbled feta cheese)

EGGS IN PURGATORY

4 to 6 servings

This is a perfect hangover dish—you may start your morning feeling hellish, but this will put a spring in your step.

Prepare **Amatriciana Sauce, 557,** or add **1 teaspoon red pepper flakes** to **Marinara Sauce, 556,** or **Tomato Sauce, 556.** Make 6 depressions in the sauce and proceed as for **Shakshouka, above,** topping the eggs with **chopped parsley** and **(grated Parmesan or Romano)**. Serve with **crusty bread.**

ABOUT BAKED EGGS

Baked eggs served in individual ramekins, casseroles, or cocotte dishes always look beautiful on a brunch table. Four-ounce ramekins, which hold 1 egg, are appropriately sized for baked eggs, but you can also use 6-ounce custard cups, ovenproof coffee cups, small bowls, or muffin tins. For tender, evenly cooked eggs, we recommend baking them in a **water bath,** 812. The eggs should be cooked until the whites are just set but the yolks are still soft and runny. Keep in mind that the ramekins will retain heat and continue to cook the eggs after they are removed from the oven.

BAKED EGGS

1 serving

Use this recipe as a baseline, varying it with any of the Additions to Baked Eggs, below.

Preheat the oven to 350°F. Grease ramekins, other ovenproof dishes, or a muffin tin. For each serving, break into a ramekin or muffin cup:

1 large egg

Season lightly with:

Salt and black pepper

Drizzle over the top:

1 teaspoon heavy cream or melted butter

Bake in a water bath, 812, about 15 minutes. Garnish with:

(Chopped herbs)

ADDITIONS TO BAKED EGGS

I. Before baking, top the eggs with any of the following:

Sautéed Mushrooms, 251, or asparagus tips
Chopped tomatoes, or Slow-Roasted Tomatoes, 282
Creamed Spinach, 244, or Braised Greens with Garlic, 244
Finely chopped roasted vegetables
Crumbled cooked bacon, sausage, or diced ham
Flaked smoked salmon or picked crabmeat

Crumbled soft cheese, such as fresh goat cheese or feta, or grated hard cheese, such as Cheddar, Gruyère, or Parmesan
Chopped herbs or green onions

II. Place one of the following in the bottom of the baking dish or muffin tin before the egg:

A round of toast covered with Gruyère
Smoked Salmon Hash, 393, Corned Beef Hash, 473, or Vegetable Breakfast Hash, 202
Hash Brown Potatoes, 269
Ratatouille Provençal, 204

LOST EGGS

4 servings

Inspired by a dish from the Portland restaurant Broder Café, these eggs are baked beneath a blanket of cheese and bread crumbs, perched atop ham slices and creamed spinach.

Preheat the oven to 425°F. Prepare in a large ovenproof skillet:

Creamed Spinach, 244

Top the spinach with:

4 ounces thinly sliced ham, torn into large pieces

Sprinkle over the ham:

½ cup shredded mild cheese, such as Swiss, Gruyère, or Emmenthaler (2 ounces)

Make 4 divots in the cheese, ham, and spinach and crack into them:

4 large eggs

Sprinkle with:

½ cup shredded mild cheese, such as Swiss, Gruyère, or Emmenthaler (2 ounces)
½ cup panko bread crumbs

Bake until the eggs are set, the cheese has melted, and the bread crumbs are browned, about 15 minutes. Serve with:

Toast

ABOUT FRIED EGGS

Frying is the most convenient route to getting eggs on the table. When we are struck with the desire to "put an egg on it," our minds usually drift to this convenient preparation. If you choose to leave the yolks runny, they provide a wonderful sauce for anything lurking underneath, such as home fries, hash, salads, or steak. When frying eggs, there are two easy ways to promote success. First, use enough butter, olive oil, or other fat to generously coat the bottom of the pan. Second, use a nonstick skillet, which makes it easy to turn the eggs and slide them onto a plate.

FRIED EGGS

2 to 4 servings

For tender whites, use medium heat. For whites with lacy, brown edges, use medium-high heat.

Melt in a large nonstick skillet:

1 to 3 tablespoons butter or other fat

When the butter is sizzling but not browned, carefully crack into the skillet:

4 large eggs

Season with:

Salt and black pepper

Cook until the whites are completely set and the yolks are just barely beginning to thicken around the edges, 4 to 5 minutes. For **sunny-side up** eggs with runny yolks, simply cover the skillet during cooking. For whites that are done and yolks that are between syrupy and thickened—**over easy** or **over medium**—insert a spatula under the egg when the whites are firm, supporting the yolk area, and cautiously turn it in the skillet. Cooking the second side will take very little time, 15 to 30 seconds. Fried eggs **over hard** or **well** are cooked a bit longer on the second side, until the yolk is nearly set.

FRICO EGGS

Melting and lightly frying a small mound of grated, aged cheese and then adding the eggs will produce a delectable, crispy crust. Do not use part-skim or reduced-fat cheeses. Prepare **Fried Eggs, above,** using medium heat and only 1 tablespoon butter or fat. Before adding the eggs to the skillet, place **1 tablespoon grated hard cheese (such as sharp Cheddar, Parmesan, or Asiago)** in a separate round for each egg in the pan. Allow the cheese to melt and sizzle, then crack an egg on top of each round of cheese. If the eggs stubbornly slip off their cheesy thrones, gently corral them back with a spatula. Cook to the desired degree of doneness as directed above.

BREAD CRUMB–FRIED EGGS

Another way to add flavor and texture to eggs while they fry. Prepare **½ recipe Browned or Buttered Bread Crumbs, 957.** Once lightly browned, season as desired and scoot the crumbs into mounds (one per egg you plan to cook). If the skillet looks dry, add more butter or oil. Prepare **Fried Eggs, above,** cracking one egg over each mound of bread crumbs. Cook to the desired degree of doneness as directed above.

ADDITIONS TO FRIED EGGS

It is often the extras that give punch to eggs, especially for brunch and lunch dishes.

Serve the eggs on a small mound of:

Cooked rice, noodles, or toast, or on top of a green salad, 116–18

Top with any of the following:

Hot pepper sauce, sriracha, chili garlic sauce, or Harissa, 584
Chopped fresh herbs or Salsa Verde, 567
Cotija or feta cheese
Aleppo pepper, Dukkah, 589, or bread crumbs browned in butter, 955

EGG IN A BASKET

2 servings

Whether you call it Rocky Mountain toast, egg in a hole, or egg in a basket, kids get a big kick out of this dish, especially when they get to make the basket.

Using a 2½-inch biscuit cutter or small glass, cut a hole out of the center of:

2 slices sandwich bread

Melt in a large skillet over medium heat:

2 tablespoons butter, plus more as needed

Add the bread and cook for about 30 seconds. Crack into the holes:

2 large eggs

Don't worry if some of the white remains on top of the bread or runs out from underneath. When the eggs begin to set, 2 to 3 minutes, flip the bread and eggs, using a spatula. Add more butter as needed. Fry the other side until the eggs are done to your liking. Toast the cut-out rounds of bread in butter and serve them as well, perched slightly off-kilter over the egg yolk.

HUEVOS RANCHEROS

4 servings

This dish can be served with a variety of salsas, meats (chorizo in particular), and beans.

Preheat the oven to 200°F.

Prepare and keep warm:

Refried Beans, 215, or Frijoles de la Olla, 213

2 cups any salsa, store-bought or homemade, 573–74, or New Mexico–Style Chile Sauce, 554

Heat in a large nonstick skillet over medium-high heat until hot:

2 tablespoons vegetable oil

Add one at a time:

4 to 8 corn tortillas

Fry for 2 to 3 seconds per side, adding more oil if necessary. Transfer to paper towels, wrap in foil, and keep warm in the oven. Set the skillet over medium-low heat and add a bit more oil if needed. Prepare, in batches if necessary:

4 to 8 Fried Eggs, 155, cooked as desired

As the eggs cook, divide the tortillas among 4 warmed plates and top with a generous spoonful of beans. As they finish cooking, top each serving with 1 or 2 eggs, and ½ cup of the warm salsa or chile sauce. Serve immediately topped with:

Chopped cilantro

(Finely crumbled queso fresco or Cotija cheese)

(Sliced avocado)

BREAKFAST CHILAQUILES

2 servings

Chilaquiles is not always served with eggs, but the combination is one of our breakfast favorites. Some versions of chilaquiles are simmered until the chips are completely soft, even falling apart, but we love the contrast of soft tortilla chips with crunchy ones. If you keep chips and salsa in your pantry, this is an easy, quick breakfast dish.

Have ready:

1 cup any salsa, store-bought or homemade, 573–74, or New Mexico–Style Chile Sauce, 554

Prepare:

4 Fried Eggs, 155, cooked as desired

Transfer the eggs to a warm plate and tent with foil. Adjust the heat to medium if necessary and add:

2 large handfuls store-bought tortilla chips (about 4 ounces)

Toast the chips, stirring occasionally, until they have darkened slightly and become fragrant, about 3 minutes. Add the salsa or sauce to the skillet, stir to coat the chips, and simmer until they are softened slightly. If desired, stir in:

(½ cup grated queso fresco, Oaxaca cheese, or Monterey Jack [2 ounces])

Divide the chilaquiles between 2 plates. Top with the eggs and:

Chopped cilantro

(Sliced avocado)

ABOUT SCRAMBLED EGGS

Scrambled eggs are no exception to egg controversy: Some like them soft and almost custard-like, others prefer them dry and with large curds. Some eccentric souls "framble" their eggs by cracking them right into the skillet and scrambling them haphazardly with a spatula.

To prepare soft and creamy scrambled eggs, beat the eggs until the whites and yolks are completely blended and cook them over low heat. The addition of a small amount of milk, half-and-half, or yogurt will keep the eggs tender, as will salt or a little lemon juice. Infrequent stirring produces large curds; constant stirring results in smaller, creamier curds.

To prepare fluffy scrambled eggs, egg whites beaten to firm peaks, 977, may be added to whole eggs in the proportion of 1 additional white to each 3 whole eggs.

Contrary to popular belief, seasoning the eggs with salt before cooking does not toughen them. Soft cheeses like fresh goat cheese may be whisked in before cooking as well. Add Cheddar and other aged cheeses at the end of cooking, folding them into the warm eggs to melt; adding earlier may cause the oil to separate out of the cheese, making for a greasy scramble. Remove the eggs from the pan just before they reach the desired consistency, as the residual heat will continue to cook them briefly. For a vegetarian or vegan alternative, see Tofu Scramble, 286.

SCRAMBLED EGGS

1 to 2 servings

I. This method gives you tender eggs with large curds.

Beat with a fork or whisk until completely blended:

3 large eggs

¼ teaspoon salt

(2 tablespoons milk or heavy cream)

Melt in an 8-inch skillet, preferably nonstick, over medium-low heat:

1½ tablespoons butter

Pour in the eggs and, with a silicone spatula, stir slowly and constantly, pushing the eggs to the center of the skillet and scraping the bottom and sides. When the eggs begin to thicken, after about 2 minutes, continue stirring until not quite cooked to the desired consistency. Stir in, if desired:

(1 tablespoon softened butter or heavy cream)

Sprinkle with, if desired:

(Pinch of black pepper)

II. A slower but foolproof alternative is to use a double-boiler, 1058.

Melt in a double boiler over, not in, gently simmering water:

½ tablespoon butter

Have ready:

Seasoned egg mixture from I, above

When the butter has melted, pour in the egg mixture. Stir with a spatula until the eggs have thickened into soft creamy curds.

ADDITIONS TO SCRAMBLED EGGS

I. Cook or reheat up to ½ cup of one of the following in the pan before adding the eggs:

Sautéed asparagus pieces
Wilted Tender Greens, 243
Sautéed Mushrooms, 251
Sautéed Onions, 255, or Melted Leeks, 247

II. Whisk one of the following into the eggs before cooking:

Pinch of grated or ground nutmeg
¼ cup soft goat cheese, cottage cheese, farmer cheese, cubed cream cheese, or yogurt
Up to 2 tablespoons finely chopped green onion

III. Fold one of the following into the eggs toward the end of cooking:

¼ cup grated or crumbled Cheddar or other hard cheese
Up to 1 tablespoon chopped herbs
Crumbled cooked bacon, sausage, or diced ham
Small chunks of smoked salmon or picked crabmeat

TEX-MEX MIGAS

2 servings

Migas, or "crumbs," is a tortilla scramble. It's a brilliant way to use stale tortillas or the dregs from a bag of tortilla chips. If desired, brown **2 ounces crumbled, fresh chorizo** in the skillet before cooking the onions. Reserve the sausage, substitute the flavorful drippings for the oil, and fold the sausage back in with the eggs.

Heat in a medium skillet, preferably nonstick, over medium heat:

2 tablespoons vegetable oil, bacon fat, or lard

Add and cook, stirring, until softened, about 5 minutes:

½ medium onion, finely chopped

Add and cook 1 minute more:

2 garlic cloves, minced
1 jalapeño or serrano pepper, seeded and minced

Stir in and cook until starting to get toasty, about 5 minutes:

1 cup crushed tortilla chips or three stale 6-inch corn tortillas, crumbled

Meanwhile, whisk in a medium bowl:

4 large eggs
¼ teaspoon salt

Reduce the heat to medium-low, add the eggs, and cook, folding the eggs into the tortilla mixture. Continue to cook until the eggs are set. If desired, stir in:

(¼ to ½ cup grated queso fresco, Oaxaca cheese, or Monterey Jack)

Serve the eggs with:

Any salsa, store-bought or homemade, 573–74
Sliced avocado

MATZO BREI

1 serving

If making a large quantity for a crowd, use two pans and keep the cooked matzo brei warm in a 200°F oven.

For each serving, use:

2 unsalted matzos
1 large egg, well beaten in a medium bowl

Hold the matzos briefly under hot running water to wet both sides without making them soggy. Drain and tear into 2½- to 3-inch pieces and add to the beaten egg. Stir to coat the matzo. Season with:

Pinch of salt

Heat in a large skillet:

⅛ inch vegetable oil or chicken fat

Using a large spoon or spatula, spread the matzo mixture in the skillet in a very thin layer. Cook, turning the pieces as they brown, until medium-brown and crispy. Serve warm, passing the salt shaker or:

(Cinnamon Sugar, 1026)

EGG FOO YOUNG

4 servings

A classic Chinese-American staple, these egg-vegetable-meat pancakes are typically served with a brown sauce. To make a **St. Paul Sandwich** (which is, confusingly, a St. Louis specialty), place an egg foo young patty, dill pickle slices, sliced onion, lettuce, and sliced tomato between 2 slices of white bread spread with mayonnaise.

If desired, prepare and keep warm in a covered saucepan over very low heat:

(Quick Brown Sauce, 550)

Whisk together in a medium bowl:

6 large eggs
8 ounces shrimp, peeled, deveined, and finely chopped, or 6 ounces diced picked crabmeat, cooked chicken, or ham
½ cup mung bean sprouts
4 green onions, thinly sliced
1 medium carrot, shredded
2 tablespoons soy sauce
2 teaspoons toasted sesame oil

Heat in a large nonstick skillet over medium heat:

⅓ cup vegetable oil

When the oil is hot, add the egg mixture in ⅓-cup amounts. Cook until golden brown on the bottom, then flip and cook the second side. Repeat with the remaining batter. Serve the cakes hot with the brown sauce, if using, or any of the following:

(Oyster or hoisin sauce, black vinegar, Spicy Chinese Chile Crisp, 572, or Dipping Sauce for Dumplings, 572)
Chopped cilantro

ABOUT OMELETS

Andrew Carnegie once counseled: "Put all your eggs in one basket. Then watch that basket!" When the container is a skillet and the objective an omelet, his advice is especially apt. The name "omelet" is loosely applied to many kinds of egg dishes, but there are four basic types of omelets: French, firm, flat, and souffléed. All are made from beaten eggs cooked so that the exterior is firm and smooth while the inside remains custardy.

The classic omelet, the **French omelet,** is rolled or folded, typically around some sort of savory filling. The **firm omelet** is easier to make—perfect for the novice—as it is cooked into a fairly firm cake before being folded. A **flat omelet,** called a **frittata** in Italy, is thick compared to a French omelet, partially cooked on the stovetop, and generally finished under the broiler or covered with a lid to cook the top. A **souffléed omelet** is made puffy and light by beating the egg whites until airy.

Since omelet making is so rapid, see that you have ready everything you are going to serve the omelet with or on, and be sure you have your diners captive.

The success of all omelets demands that ➤ the pan and the fat be hot enough to bind the base of the egg at once so as to hold the softer egg above, but not so hot as to toughen the base before the rest of the egg cooks. Finding the optimum temperature for omelet making on your stovetop can take a little practice.

It was once believed that adding salt to eggs at the beginning of the cooking process caused them to become tough. This is simply not true. In fact, adding salt encourages the eggs to coagulate at a slightly lower temperature, which can make for tenderer scrambles and omelets. So we say, for omelets that are well seasoned, feel free to salt the eggs to your heart's content.

When making more than one omelet, beat the total number of eggs you will need, then use a ladle or measuring cup to pour 3½ ounces, or about ½ cup, for each 2-egg omelet. Keep the butter and filling ingredients by the stove and move quickly as you make the omelets one by one. Serve them as they are ready, or keep them warm in a 200°F oven and serve when all are finished. If you have more than four to feed, use a second pan, or even three to make several omelets at once. Attention to more than one pan at a time is a skill that needs to be developed, so practice before your debut. Stagger the cooking so the omelets are not all at the same stage at once. Or, to avoid feeling like a short-order cook, ➤ make things easier on yourself and prepare a large frittata, 160, or strata, 164–65, instead.

Filling omelets is not necessary, but we recommend it. For ideas see Fillings for Omelets, below, and Additions to Scrambled Eggs, 157.

To glaze an omelet, brush it lightly with softened butter.

FRENCH OMELET (ROLLED OR FOLDED)

1 serving

For French omelets, either rolled or folded, the eggs should be beaten only enough to thoroughly blend the whites and yolks, not enough to incorporate air or make them frothy. Using a fork rather than a whisk to beat the eggs helps ensure that you do not overbeat them.

Beat with a fork until the whites and yolks are blended:

2 or 3 large eggs
⅛ teaspoon salt
Pinch of black pepper

Have ready a hot serving plate. Heat in a 6- to 8-inch skillet, preferably nonstick, over medium-high heat:

2 tablespoons butter

Tilt the skillet to coat the sides and bottom thoroughly, until the butter has melted. Pour in the eggs. With one hand, agitate the skillet forward and backward, keeping the egg mass sliding as a whole over the bottom. At the same time, "scramble" the eggs by quickly swirling in a circular motion, as shown below. The rhythm of the skillet and the stirring is like a child's trick of patting the head while rubbing the stomach. At this point the heat in the skillet may be sufficient to cook the eggs, and you may want to lift the skillet from the heat as you gently swirl the eggs. If desired, once the egg is nearly set, spread it evenly in the skillet by pressing it with the spatula and sprinkle the top with:

(**⅓ cup any Fillings for Omelets, below, at room temperature**)

Tip the handle up to a 45-degree angle and flip the omelet over, away from the handle, as shown in the center. Fold it over once or twice, or roll it bit-by-bit for a more elegant presentation. If the omelet shows any tendency to stick, slip a spatula underneath it or give the skillet handle a sharp rap or two with the fist, as shown below. Slant the skillet to 90 degrees or more over the serving plate until the omelet slides out of the skillet with its ends folded under on the plate—ready to serve. If desired, for a shiny, glazed surface, rub the top with:

(Softened butter)

Serve at once.

Preparing a rolled French omelet

FILLINGS FOR OMELETS

Herbs or finely grated cheese may be added to the beaten eggs before cooking or more substantial fillings may be placed in the middle of the omelet just before it is rolled. Use ⅓ to ½ cup filling at room temperature for a 2-egg omelet; ½ to ¾ cup cooked filling is required for a 3-egg omelet.

Roasted Garlic, 241, and fresh goat cheese
Duxelles, 252, or Sautéed Mushrooms, 251
Pico de Gallo, 573, and sliced avocado
Ricotta or fresh goat cheese mixed with tomatoes and herbs
Chopped ham and grated cheese
Sautéed or Caramelized Onions, 255, and spinach
Sautéed zucchini, asparagus tips, or roasted red peppers

FIRM DINER-STYLE OMELET

French omelets require finesse, an appropriate pan, a deft hand, and are commonly enjoyed with no filling. Diner-style omelets are the opposite: They are always filled, easy to make, and breakfast joints across the country are whipping them up by the thousands on flat-top griddles as you read this. If you doubt your ability to flip the thin egg layer over the filling without tearing it, use the trifold method. To make them on a well-seasoned griddle, confine the spread of the beaten eggs by quickly corralling the egg into a rough, 6- to 8-inch square shape with a large spatula or turner (turn using the trifold method). To make an **egg white omelet,** substitute **4 egg whites** (about ½ cup).

Have ready:

⅓ to ½ cup any Fillings for Omelets, 158, at room temperature

Beat with a fork until the whites and yolks are blended:

2 or 3 large eggs
(1 teaspoon minced herbs such as thyme, parsley, tarragon, or chervil)
⅛ teaspoon salt
Pinch of black pepper

Melt in a 6- to 8-inch nonstick skillet over medium heat:

1 tablespoon butter

Tilt the skillet to coat the sides and bottom thoroughly. When the butter is hot and has reached the point of fragrance, but is not browned, pour in the eggs. Tilt the skillet to evenly distribute the eggs, going halfway up the buttered sides if the skillet is on the small side. ➤ For a fluffier texture and quicker cooking, lift the edges of the solidified egg layer up with a spatula and tilt the skillet so the uncooked egg mixture fills the gap (repeat on all sides). When the top of the egg layer is beginning to set, add the filling in a wide strip down the center for a **trifold** omelet or distribute on one side for a **half-moon.** For the former, flip the small, untopped sides over the filling; for the latter, fold the empty half over. If the filling needs to be melted or heated through (or if you want to ensure that the egg is completely firm), carefully flip the omelet over, remove the skillet from the heat, and let sit for an additional minute or two. Slide the omelet onto a warmed plate and serve immediately, garnished with, if desired:

(Chopped herbs)
(Melted butter)

FRITTATA

3 servings

Flat omelets and their Italian counterparts, frittatas, are made with vegetables, meats, or other savory ingredients mixed into the eggs. You may use any of the Fillings for Omelets, 158, except perhaps, sliced avocado, ➤ allowing about 1 cup of filling to 3 eggs. Frittatas are served hot or at room temperature cut into wedges. ➤ To avoid sticking, use a well-seasoned 10- to 12-inch cast-iron skillet or nonstick ovenproof skillet.

Have ready:

1½ to 2 cups any Fillings for Omelets, 158, preferably a combination of several

Beat with a fork until blended:

6 large eggs

Stir in the filling. If the filling has not been seasoned, add:

½ teaspoon salt
¼ teaspoon black pepper

Heat in a 10-inch skillet over medium heat:

1½ tablespoons olive oil

Swirl the oil around to coat the skillet well. Pour in the egg mixture. With one hand, agitate the skillet forward and backward, keeping the egg mass sliding as a whole over the skillet bottom. At the same time, "scramble" the eggs by swirling in a circular motion with a spatula until the bottom of the frittata is set and the top is still creamy. To finish cooking the top, place the frittata under a hot broiler until the top is firm. A traditional frittata is not browned, but we don't mind a slightly bronzed omelet. Transfer to a warm platter, cut into wedges, and serve.

KUKU SABZI (PERSIAN HERBED OMELET)

4 servings

This bright-green, herb-packed omelet is traditionally made during the Persian new year (Nowruz). You may use spinach or other greens in place of some of the herbs. Adding barberries, 181, is traditional.

Heat in a 10-inch skillet over medium heat:

1 tablespoon olive oil

Add and sauté until softened, about 5 minutes:

1 large leek, white and tender green parts only, halved lengthwise, well washed, and thinly sliced

Meanwhile, whisk together in a large bowl:

8 large eggs
1 cup finely chopped parsley
1 cup finely chopped cilantro
1 cup finely chopped dill
(¼ cup chopped toasted, 1005, walnuts)
(2 tablespoons dried barberries or chopped dried cranberries)
1 teaspoon baking powder
½ teaspoon salt
¼ teaspoon black pepper

Preheat the broiler. Reduce the heat on the stovetop to medium-low and add to the skillet:

2 tablespoons olive oil

Add the herb-egg mixture and stir to combine with the leek. Allow to cook, undisturbed, until set on the bottom, 8 to 10 minutes. Transfer the skillet to the oven and broil until the top is set, 1 to 2 minutes. Transfer to a warm platter, cut into wedges, and serve.

HANGTOWN FRY

4 servings

First whipped up for gold prospectors in Hangtown (now Placerville), California, in the 1850s. All of the ingredients were hard to come by, thus the perfect way for a lucky '49er to celebrate good fortune.

Have ready:

12 oysters, shucked, 349, or a generous ½-pint shucked oysters, drained

Stir to combine on a plate:

½ cup flour
½ teaspoon salt
¼ teaspoon black pepper

Dredge the oysters in the flour mixture and set aside. Cook in an 8- to 10-inch skillet, preferably nonstick, over medium heat until crisp:

4 slices bacon

Remove the bacon and drain on paper towels. Pour out the excess fat and set the skillet over medium-high heat. Add:

2 tablespoons butter

Add the dredged oysters and fry them until golden and crisp, about 2 minutes per side. Crumble the bacon into the skillet, then add:

5 large eggs, lightly beaten
¼ teaspoon salt
⅛ teaspoon black pepper

Reduce the heat to medium and let cook, undisturbed, for about 5 seconds, then use a spatula to slowly move the eggs toward the center, tilting the skillet to allow the uncooked eggs to run to the bottom of the skillet. Stop moving the eggs as they set. Flip the mixture and cook the other side for a few seconds, or brown under the broiler. The omelet should still be a bit soft in the center.

ARTICHOKE FRITTATA FOR A CROWD

8 servings

Perfect for a small brunch crowd.

Drain and cut in half lengthwise:

Two 14-ounce cans artichoke hearts

Drain and slice into ¼-inch-wide strips:

⅔ cup jarred roasted red peppers

Set the artichokes and roasted peppers aside. Whisk together in a bowl:

12 large eggs
1¼ cups half-and-half
1 cup grated Parmesan (4 ounces)
½ cup chopped parsley or basil
1 teaspoon salt
½ teaspoon black pepper

Set the egg mixture aside. Melt in a 12-inch ovenproof skillet over medium heat:

3 tablespoons butter

Add and cook, stirring, until softened and lightly browned, about 10 minutes:

2 medium leeks, halved lengthwise, well washed, and chopped
1 large garlic clove, finely chopped

Add the artichokes and roasted peppers along with:

2 tablespoons butter

Swirl to melt the butter and coat the skillet. Add the egg mixture and cook over medium-low heat until the center is almost set, about 18 minutes. Preheat the broiler. Broil the frittata 7 inches from the heating element until browned, about 5 minutes. Let cool slightly before serving.

TORTILLA ESPAÑOLA (SPANISH POTATO OMELET)

6 servings

This classic dish is often cut into wedges and served as one of several tapas, 46. We like to eat cold or room-temperature slices of this omelet on a baguette with cured ham and Aïoli, 564.

Heat in a 10- to 12-inch ovenproof skillet over medium heat:

2 tablespoons olive oil

Add:

1 large onion, cut into ⅛-inch slices
Salt and black pepper to taste

Cook, stirring, until the onion is soft and golden, about 10 minutes. Transfer to a large bowl. Heat in the same skillet over medium-high heat:

¼ cup olive oil

Add:

1 pound red potatoes, peeled and cut into ⅛-inch slices

Cook until golden brown, 10 to 12 minutes. Transfer the potatoes to paper towels to drain. Set the skillet aside with the oil in it. When the potatoes are cool, sprinkle them with:

Salt and black pepper to taste

Add the potatoes to the onions in the bowl and stir in:

6 large eggs, beaten
½ teaspoon salt

Toss to coat. Set a rack in the middle of the oven, preheat the broiler, and return the skillet to medium-high heat. When the oil shimmers, add the egg mixture and immediately reduce the heat to low. Let the omelet cook undisturbed for 3 to 4 minutes, until the bottom is golden and the egg is two-thirds to three-quarters set. Shake the skillet from time to time to make sure the omelet does not stick. If it does, slide a spatula under it to free it from the skillet. Transfer the skillet to the oven and broil until firm. Shake the omelet to loosen it from the skillet and slide onto a plate. Cut into wedges and serve hot or at room temperature with:

Aïoli, 564, or the sauce for Patatas Bravas, 59

SOUFFLÉED OMELET

4 servings

A properly executed souffléed omelet has a lovely brown, firm, dry exterior enveloping a soft, airy center.

I. SAVORY WITH CHEESE AND HERBS

Preheat the oven to 375°F. Whisk until thick and light:

4 large egg yolks
¼ teaspoon salt
¼ teaspoon black pepper

In a large bowl, beat until stiff but not dry, 978:

4 large egg whites
Pinch of salt

Fold the yolk mixture gently into the whites. Melt in a 10- to 12-inch ovenproof skillet over medium heat:

1½ tablespoons butter

When the foam has subsided, pour the egg mixture into the skillet, spread evenly, and smooth the top. Shake the skillet after a few seconds to discourage sticking, then cover with a lid whose underside has been buttered to prevent sticking. Reduce the heat and cook for about 5 minutes. Remove the lid and sprinkle on top of the omelet:

2 tablespoons minced chives, parsley, chervil, or a combination
¼ cup grated Parmesan

Place the skillet in the oven and cook until the top is set, 3 to 5 minutes. Fold the omelet in half, if desired, and slide it out onto a warmed plate.

II. SWEET JAM-FILLED

Prepare **Savory Souffléed Omelet, 160,** omitting the salt and pepper in the egg yolk mixture and adding instead **3 tablespoons sugar.** Omit the herbs and cheese. Before folding the omelet, fill it with **2 tablespoons warm jam mixed with 1 teaspoon rum, brandy, or lemon juice.**

ABOUT SOUFFLÉS

The air trapped inside a foam of well-beaten egg whites is responsible for the lightness of soufflés: The air expands in the oven as it warms, forcing the mixture to rise and puff up to a dramatic height. Though set by the heat, this foam is rather delicate, thus soufflés are rushed from oven to table for all to see before they begin to collapse. The short window of time during which soufflés hold on to their puff has given them an undeserved reputation for being the fussy prima donna of egg cookery. On the contrary: Soufflés are actually very easy to make if certain pointers are carefully heeded (and your expectations properly managed). For dessert soufflés, see 818.

Proper beating of the egg whites, 977, is crucial to the success of any soufflé. Once the whites have reached stiff but not dry peaks, immediately fold them into the soufflé base, 978. ➤ Soufflés can be made lighter by adding an extra egg white for every 2 whole eggs.

Soufflé dishes are nice, but any straight-sided deep baking dish will do. Eight-ounce ramekins are ideal for individual soufflés. To make one large, impressive soufflé, use a 6-cup soufflé dish for one made with 4 or 5 egg whites, enough for 4 servings, or an 8-cup dish for one made with 6 or 7 egg whites, enough for 6 servings. Grease the bottom and sides well with butter and then coat the buttered surface with a thorough dusting of flour, grated dry cheese such as Parmesan, bread crumbs, or fine cornmeal, depending on the flavor of your soufflé. Tilt the dish in all directions until the bottom and sides are well coated, then invert the dish and tap out any excess.

Fill the soufflé dish no more than three-quarters full. Before baking, run your thumb around the inside rim of the dish, making a 1-inch-deep groove (make a ½-inch groove for individual ramekins), or moat, in the soufflé mixture. This will promote an even rise and give the cooked soufflé a top-hat appearance. The fluffiest soufflés are baked as soon as they are assembled, but they can sit at room temperature, covered, for up to 1 hour before baking.

A soufflé is most fragile as it first rises, so keep the oven door closed during the first half of the baking time. ➤ Test for doneness when it has risen 3 to 4 inches above the rim of the dish and the crust is golden. When a skewer inserted in the center comes out clean, the soufflé is done. Or touch the top lightly with your hand. If it feels firm with a slight wobble in the middle, it is done. A soufflé can be served slightly moist and creamy inside, or firm and dry all the way through. If you prefer a drier soufflé, bake it a bit longer—but not too long, or it will begin to deflate.

Soufflés can also be baked in a water bath, 812, until risen and brown. This will take 5 to 10 minutes longer. They will not rise as high, and their texture will be more dense and custard-like, but they will hold their loft longer after baking.

Once baked, a soufflé should be served immediately. It will begin its inevitable fall within a minute or two of leaving the oven. Soufflés are sometimes accompanied by a sauce, which can be passed separately or spooned into a hole created in the center of the soufflé.

CHEESE SOUFFLÉ COCKAIGNE

4 to 6 servings

Please read About Soufflés, above. Preheat the oven to 350°F. Generously butter a 6-cup soufflé dish or four 8-ounce ramekins. Dust the insides with:

¼ to ½ cup dry bread crumbs or grated Parmesan

Shake out the excess. Bring to a simmer in a large saucepan:

1 cup White Sauce II, 548

Remove from the heat and let stand for 30 seconds. Add, stirring well:

¼ cup grated Parmesan
¼ cup shredded Gruyère
(¾ cup finely chopped smoked ham)

Add:

4 egg yolks, beaten

Mix in well. Beat until stiff but not dry, 978:

4 egg whites

Stir one-quarter of the whites into the cheese mixture to lighten it, then fold in the rest. Pour into the prepared soufflé dish or ramekins. Bake until risen and set, 25 to 30 minutes for a large soufflé, 20 to 25 minutes for individual soufflés. Serve immediately.

VEGETABLE SOUFFLÉ

6 servings

Please read About Soufflés, above. Preheat the oven to 350°F. Generously butter an 8-cup soufflé dish or six 8-ounce ramekins. Dust the insides with:

¼ to ½ cup dry bread crumbs or grated Parmesan

Shake out the excess. Combine in a large bowl:

1½ cups White Sauce II, 548, at room temperature or slightly warmed
(1½ teaspoons chopped marjoram, rosemary, thyme, or dill)
¾ teaspoon salt
⅛ teaspoon grated or ground nutmeg or cayenne pepper
Pinch of white pepper

Combine in a medium bowl:

6 large egg yolks
½ to 1 cup grated Parmesan, Swiss, Cheddar, or Gruyère, or crumbled fresh goat cheese (2 to 4 ounces)

Beat ½ cup of the sauce mixture into the egg yolks, then combine the egg yolk mixture with the rest of the sauce, beating vigorously to blend. Add one of the following:

1½ cups chopped Sautéed Mushrooms, 251, Sautéed Onions, 255, Roasted Asparagus, 208, or Steamed Broccoli, 220, or well-drained Wilted Tender Greens, 243
1½ cups pureed cooked carrots or sweet potato
1½ cups fresh corn kernels

Beat until stiff but not dry, 978:

6 large egg whites
Pinch of salt

Stir one-quarter of the whites into the soufflé base to lighten it, then fold in the rest. Pour into the prepared soufflé dish or ramekins. Bake until risen and golden brown on top, 40 to 45 minutes for a large soufflé, 20 to 25 minutes for individual soufflés. Serve immediately.

GOAT CHEESE AND WALNUT SOUFFLÉS

8 servings

These soufflés can be made up to 3 days ahead of time; they are resilient enough to be served turned out of their ramekins to show off their walnut crust.

Please read About Soufflés, 161. Preheat the oven to 350°F. Generously butter eight 6-ounce ramekins or custard cups. Combine in a small bowl:

3/4 cup walnuts, toasted, 1005, and finely chopped
1/4 cup fine cornmeal

Sprinkle the insides of the ramekins with the mixture, tilting them in all directions until completely coated. Scatter any nuts that do not adhere over the bottoms of the dishes. Melt in a saucepan over medium heat:

3 tablespoons butter

Add and stir until smooth:

1/4 cup all-purpose flour

Cook, stirring, for 1 minute. Remove from the heat and whisk in:

2/3 cup milk

Return to the heat and, stirring briskly, bring to a boil until the mixture is very thick. Scrape into a bowl. Add and mash until melted:

8 ounces fresh goat cheese

Beat in:

4 large egg yolks
2 garlic cloves, minced
1/2 teaspoon minced fresh thyme or 1/4 teaspoon dried thyme
1/4 teaspoon salt
1/4 teaspoon white or black pepper

Beat until stiff but not dry, 978:

5 large egg whites
1/4 teaspoon cream of tartar

Stir one-quarter of the whites into the soufflé base to lighten it, then fold in the rest. Pour into the prepared ramekins and smooth the tops. Place the ramekins in a water bath, 812. Bake until a knife inserted in the center comes out almost clean, about 30 minutes. Let stand for 15 minutes in the water bath, then invert the soufflés onto a greased baking sheet. The soufflés can be served immediately or cooled, covered tightly with plastic wrap, and refrigerated for up to 3 days. Before serving, heat the soufflés in a 425°F oven until warmed through, 5 to 7 minutes.

VEGETABLE TIMBALES

6 servings

"Timbale" is simply the name for a type of deep mold, thus many different dishes are encompassed by the term, whether they contain pasta, minced meats, or seafood. Many are eggless; some are even lined with a pastry or rice crust. Here, we use the term for firm, savory custards studded with vegetables and gently baked in a large dish or smaller ramekins.

Preheat the oven to 325°F. Butter six 6-ounce ramekins or one 8-cup soufflé dish.

Combine in a bowl and beat with a whisk:

1 1/2 cups warm heavy cream
4 large eggs, at room temperature
(1/2 cup grated Gruyère, Swiss, or white Cheddar [2 ounces])
(Cloves from 2 heads Roasted Garlic, 241)
3/4 teaspoon salt
1/2 teaspoon sweet paprika
(2 tablespoons minced herbs such as parsley, tarragon, or thyme)
(1 garlic clove, minced)

Add to the soufflé dish or divide among the ramekins:

1 1/2 cups chopped and well-drained Sautéed Mushrooms, 251, Sautéed Onions, 255, Roasted Asparagus, 208, Wilted Tender Greens, 243, or Steamed Broccoli, 220

Pour the egg mixture over the vegetable filling, place in a water bath, 812, and bake until a knife inserted in the center comes out clean, about 45 minutes for a large timbale, or 20 to 25 minutes for individual timbales. Invert onto a serving platter or individual plates. Garnish with:

(Crumbled crisp bacon)
Chopped parsley

ABOUT QUICHE

Quiche is certainly the most famous of savory custards, perhaps owing to the wonderful richness and contrast in texture offered by the pastry crust it is baked in. The basic proportions for quiche are ➤ 3 or 4 whole eggs for every 2 cups milk or half-and-half. Using cream in place of milk or replacing 1 whole egg with 2 yolks results in a richer, more custardy quiche. Though traditionally prepared in a blind-baked pie crust, quiche can also be baked in individual tart shells.

For a quick preparation, mix the custard filling and other ingredients the day before and refrigerate in covered containers. Then, when ready, all you need do is fill the prebaked shell and pop in the oven. Alternatively, you can assemble the uncooked quiche, wrap tightly, chill in the refrigerator, and freeze for up to a month. Frozen quiches can be baked straight out of the freezer. Simply add 15 to 20 minutes to the cooking time.

Cooked quiche can be refrigerated for up to 4 days or frozen, tightly wrapped, for up to 3 months. Reheat in a 350°F oven until heated through, about 10 minutes for refrigerated quiche or up to 25 minutes for frozen quiche.

QUICHE LORRAINE

6 servings

Traditional quiche Lorraine does not contain cheese; omit it, if you wish, for authenticity's sake.

Preheat the oven to 375°F. Roll out and line a 9-inch tart or pie pan with:

½ recipe Basic Pie or Pastry Dough, 664, or Pat-in-the-Pan Butter Dough, 666

Blind bake the crust, 664. While still warm, brush the baked crust with:

Beaten egg yolk

Cut into 1-inch lengths:

4 slices bacon

Cook in a heavy skillet over medium heat, turning often, until most of the fat is rendered but the bacon is not yet crisp. Drain on paper towels. Whisk together in a bowl:

2 cups milk, half-and-half, or heavy cream
3 large eggs
¼ teaspoon salt
⅛ teaspoon black pepper
Pinch of grated or ground nutmeg
Up to 1 tablespoon chopped chives

Sprinkle the bacon in the bottom of the pie shell. If desired, sprinkle in:

(½ cup diced Swiss cheese)

Pour the custard mixture over it. Bake until the top is golden brown, 35 to 40 minutes.

CHEESE QUICHE

6 servings

This is an excellent quiche template. Use the suggested Additions to Quiche, below, to riff on the basic recipe.

Preheat the oven to 375°F. Roll out and line a 9-inch tart or pie pan with:

½ recipe Basic Pie or Pastry Dough, 664, or Pat-in-the-Pan Butter Dough, 666

Blind bake the crust, 664. While still warm, brush the baked crust with:

Beaten egg yolk

Place the pan on a baking sheet. Sprinkle in the bottom of the pie shell:

1 to 1½ cups shredded Cheddar, Swiss, or Gruyère (4 to 6 ounces)

Whisk together thoroughly in a medium bowl until no streaks of egg white remain:

1 cup half-and-half or heavy cream
3 large eggs
½ small onion, grated or minced
(⅛ teaspoon grated or ground nutmeg)
½ teaspoon salt
¼ teaspoon white or black pepper

Pour the mixture over the cheese in the pie shell. Bake until the filling is puffed around the sides and a knife inserted in the center comes out clean, 30 to 40 minutes. Let stand 10 minutes before slicing.

ADDITIONS TO QUICHE

Quiche is perhaps the perfect excuse for cheese lovers to make a **Cheddar Pie or Pastry Dough, 665.** As for the filling, prevent it from becoming watery by cooking and thoroughly draining vegetables, meat, and seafood before adding to the egg mixture. Use 1½ cups total:

Sautéed, thinly sliced onions, shallots, or leeks
Cooked broccoli or asparagus, chopped
Sautéed Mushrooms, 251, chopped
Canned artichoke hearts, drained and roughly chopped
Slow-Roasted Tomatoes, 282
Cubed Roasted Winter Squash, 275
Sautéed spinach, Swiss chard, or kale, chopped
Ham, cooked bacon, prosciutto, or pancetta, chopped
Cooked shrimp, peeled and deveined, picked lobster or crabmeat, or smoked salmon
Chopped tarragon, chives, or basil

TOMATO AND GOAT CHEESE QUICHE

6 servings

Roll out and line a 9-inch tart or pie pan with:

½ recipe Basic Pie or Pastry Dough, 664, or Pat-in-the-Pan Butter Dough, 666

Blind bake the crust, 664. While still warm, brush the baked crust with:

Beaten egg yolk

Refrigerate. Place a rack in the lowest position in the oven. Preheat the oven to 400°F. Core, quarter, and seed:

1 pound tomatoes

Blend with the back of a wooden spoon in a large bowl until smooth:

6 ounces fresh goat cheese
1¼ cups half-and-half

Add and whisk until smooth:

3 large eggs
1 tablespoon chopped parsley
1½ teaspoons chopped thyme or 3 tablespoons chopped basil
¼ teaspoon salt
Black pepper to taste

Arrange most of the tomato quarters in the prepared pie shell like the spokes of a wheel. Fill in the center with the remaining tomato quarters. Pour the cheese mixture over the tomatoes. Bake until the top is golden brown, 40 to 45 minutes. Let rest for 10 minutes before slicing.

LEEK TART

6 servings

This quiche-like French tart is one of our favorite brunch dishes.

Prepare and fit into a 9-inch quiche, tart, or pie pan:

½ recipe Basic Pie or Pastry Dough, 664, or All-Butter Pie or Pastry Dough, 666

Brush the dough with:

Beaten egg yolk

Refrigerate. Melt in a medium skillet over medium heat:

2 tablespoons butter

Add:

2 pounds leeks, white and tender green parts only, halved lengthwise, well washed, and cut into ¼-inch slices

½ teaspoon salt
Black pepper to taste

Cover and cook, stirring occasionally and reducing the heat as the leeks cook, until they are very soft, about 20 minutes. Meanwhile, preheat the oven to 400°F. Beat together in a bowl until well combined:

2 large eggs
½ cup heavy cream or half-and-half
¼ teaspoon grated or ground nutmeg
Salt and black pepper to taste

When the leeks are done, add to the custard. Transfer to the prepared pie shell. Bake until the top is golden and the custard is set, 20 to 30 minutes. Let rest for 10 minutes before slicing.

ABOUT STRATA

This dish, also referred to as a **breakfast casserole** or **savory bread pudding,** is made by layering bread with cheese and meat or vegetables in a baking dish, pouring a savory custard base over them, and baking until the egg has set. Stratas can be assembled and refrigerated overnight, then baked the next day, leaving you with nothing to do but brew coffee (for a sweeter make-ahead alternative, see Baked French Toast, 645).

BASIC STRATA

6 to 8 servings

Strata is incredibly versatile. Use ingredients that you have on hand or put leftovers into service. Any vegetables or meat should be cooked before adding to a strata.

For any strata, whisk together in a bowl until blended:

2½ cups milk or a mixture of milk, half-and-half, heavy cream, and/or yogurt
5 large eggs
Up to 2 tablespoons chopped fresh herbs or 2 teaspoons dried herbs
¼ teaspoon salt
¼ teaspoon black pepper

Have ready:

About 6 cups cubed bread, such as French, Italian, sourdough, or sandwich bread
Up to 3 cups of any of the suggested ingredients in Strata Combinations, below
2 to 3 cups shredded white Cheddar, crumbled fresh goat cheese, or any of the suggested cheeses in Strata Combinations, below (8 to 12 ounces)

Or make up your own filling out of ingredients you have on hand. Generously grease a 13 × 9-inch baking dish. Scatter half of the bread cubes over the bottom of the dish. Cover with the filling of your choice and all but ½ cup of the cheese. Top with the remaining bread and sprinkle with the reserved cheese. Pour the egg mixture over the bread cubes. Press down with a spatula until the egg mixture rises to the top and the bread appears well soaked. Cover and refrigerate for at least 2 hours and up to 24 hours.

Preheat the oven to 350°F. Bake until the strata is puffed and a knife inserted into the center comes out clean, about 45 minutes.

STRATA COMBINATIONS

Use up to 3 cups of any of the following combinations of ingredients and 2 to 3 cups of the suggested cheese(s) here or in the Basic Strata recipe above.

Slow-Roasted Tomatoes, 282, fresh basil, and dried oregano with shredded mozzarella or provolone
Cooked and drained fresh chorizo (store-bought or homemade, 511), green onions, and roasted Anaheim or Hatch chiles, 262, with a combination of crumbled cotija and shredded queso fresco or Monterey Jack
Jarred roasted red peppers, Roasted Potatoes, 267, and dollops of Pesto, 586, with a combination of crumbled feta and shredded mozzarella
Cooked and drained breakfast sausage and sautéed kale with shredded sharp white Cheddar
Garlic-Braised Broccoli Rabe, 221, and jarred roasted red peppers with a combination of shredded mozzarella and Parmesan

SAUSAGE AND MUSHROOM STRATA

6 to 8 servings

Cook, stirring, in a large skillet over medium-high heat until no longer pink, about 10 minutes:

1½ pounds bulk sausage, Country Sausage, 510, or Italian Sausage, 511

Tilt the skillet and spoon out all but 2 tablespoons of fat. Add:

8 ounces mushrooms, sliced (about 2½ cups)
(4 to 6 shiitake mushroom caps, sliced)
½ cup chopped onion

Cook, stirring, until the onion is translucent and the juices released by the mushrooms have mostly evaporated, about 10 minutes. Set aside. Proceed as for:

Basic Strata, above

using the sausage-mushroom mixture for the filling and shredded Swiss or Cheddar for the cheese.

ASPARAGUS STRATA

6 to 8 servings

Heat in a large skillet over medium heat:

2 tablespoons olive oil

Add:

1 large onion, chopped

Cook, stirring frequently, until the onion is translucent, about 7 minutes. Stir in:

1 pound asparagus, trimmed and cut into 2-inch pieces

Cook, stirring frequently, until the asparagus is fork-tender, about 5 minutes. Remove from the heat. Proceed as for:

Basic Strata, above

Use the asparagus mixture for the filling and for the cheese, use:

4 ounces crumbled fresh goat cheese
4 ounces grated Gruyère or Swiss cheese

Add the goat cheese to the egg mixture and reserve the Gruyère or Swiss for sprinkling on top. Add to the egg mixture:

Up to ⅓ cup chopped herbs such as basil and parsley

Proceed as directed.

CRAB STRATA
6 servings
Generously grease an 8-inch square baking pan. Trim the crusts from enough:

½-inch-thick bread slices

to cover the bottom of the pan, trimming as necessary to make them fit. Cut any trimmings into small cubes and scatter over the top of the bread (discard the crusts). Scatter on top of the bread:

6 to 8 ounces canned or cooked crabmeat (1½ to 2 cups)
¾ cup shredded Swiss or Fontina cheese (3 ounces)

Whisk together in a bowl until thoroughly blended:

4 large eggs
2 cups half-and-half
½ cup milk
½ small onion, grated or minced
½ teaspoon salt
⅛ teaspoon cayenne pepper

Pour the egg mixture over the bread, moistening it evenly. Let stand for 15 minutes, or cover and refrigerate for up to 3 hours. Preheat the oven to 325°F. Sprinkle the top of the strata with:

¾ cup shredded Swiss or Fontina cheese (3 ounces)

Bake in a water bath, 812, until a knife inserted in the center comes out clean, about 1 hour. Let stand for 15 minutes, then cut into squares.

FRUITS

"It was not a watermelon that Eve took," observed Mark Twain. "We knew it because she repented." There is something about a piece of fruit—so tidy, shapely, self-contained, and full of promise as to appeal to the larcenous instincts in all of Eve's children. Ambitious hosts often take themselves too seriously, ending a rich meal with a disastrously heavy dessert, forgetting that fresh fruit would be a far happier conclusion to the meal for all concerned, especially when paired with cheese (see The Cheese Course, 834). Because many fruit recipes fit more neatly in other chapters in this book, also see About Fruit Appetizers, 58, fruit pies, 667, and fruit desserts, 834. Of course, fruit also makes a wonderful accent to grilled chicken, pork, or fish in salads and stuffings. For yet more possibilities, see Fruit Salsa, 574, sweet sauces, 805, and Jams, Jellies, and Preserves, 906.

ABOUT FRESH FRUITS AND SEASONALITY

Pomologists have long worked to hybridize fruits in order to extend the harvest, to produce plants more resistant to disease and adverse climate, to improve shipping and keeping characteristics, and to maximize yield. Unfortunately, much of this effort has been carried forward with little regard to flavor. In recent years, more small growers have been working to revive flavorful heirloom fruit varieties and breed new varieties for flavor above all else. We rejoice in this move away from single-minded efficiency at all costs, and spend our dollars accordingly at local farmers' markets when we can.

For many, the term "seasonal fruit" is known only as a distant, theoretical fact of agriculture, which has been conveniently erased from our lived reality in modern supermarkets. When strawberries can be bought January through December, what do growing seasons actually have to do with fruit as we buy and consume it? After all, it is, apparently, always strawberry season somewhere. There is certainly nothing wrong with buying fruit out of season, but we think it is worth knowing when fruits will likely be at their best, no matter where you shop.

The most foolproof way to determine what's ripest at the moment in your area is to visit your local farmers' market. Aside from this self-evident observation, it is hard to generalize about seasonality in a book meant to be read in several different climates. There are, however, some patterns worth noting: Citrus fruits are best in winter, berries in late spring and summer, and pome fruits like apples, pears, and quince in fall and winter. Some specialty and natural foods grocery stores do an admirable job of stocking local fruit in its season. For those who know of local orchards and farms that specialize in a particular fruit, inquire with them to see when their harvest will start, or when it is at its peak (this is especially good advice for anyone who wants to put up preserves, 906).

RIPENING AND STORING FRUIT

Fruit shipped considerable distances is usually picked unripe. This has become the norm to ensure the fruit is less susceptible to damage. The fruit ripens as it travels and sits on the shelf, a practice that has lessened the flavors of many varieties. **Climacteric** fruits continue to ripen after being picked. **Nonclimacteric** fruits ripen on the plant and should be picked or purchased at peak ripeness and eaten as soon as possible. See the chart below for specific examples of each.

➤ Underripe, climacteric fruits should be stored at room temperature out of the sun.

To ripen fruits, put each variety in its own partly closed paper bag. Adding an apple, pear, or avocado to the bag will help speed the process (they emit substantial amounts of ethylene gas, which enhances the ripening of many fruits). Examine fruit often and remove any fruit that shows signs of spoilage. Spoilage is contagious and will quickly ruin surrounding fruits.

Fruit Category	Will ripen after being picked?	Refrigerate?
Apples, pears, and quince	Yes	No, unless fruit is at peak ripeness
Berries, cherries, and grapes	No	Yes
Peaches, apricots, nectarines, persimmons, plums, and kiwis	Yes	No, unless fruit is at peak ripeness
Citrus fruits	No	No
Bananas	Yes	No
Mangoes, papayas, and pineapples	Yes	No
Melons	Yes	No

PREPARING FRUIT

Wash fruit quickly under cold running water just before serving or using in a recipe. Washing with soap or detergent will remove only the surface contaminants from fruits that have been waxed, such as apples. To remove fungicide or pesticide residues trapped in the skin, peel, then rinse. Organically grown fruits may also be coated with food-grade wax, such as carnauba or beeswax. The wax is harmless, but washing fresh fruit before eating is always a good idea.

Apricots, peaches, nectarines, and most varieties of plums can be peeled by **blanching,** or dipping in boiling water.

To peel fruits by blanching, drop them—no more than 3 or 4 at a time—into a large pot of boiling water. Leave the fruit in the water for 15 to 30 seconds, then transfer to a bowl of ice water. The skin should slip off easily. If not, repeat the blanching process or peel the fruit with a knife or vegetable peeler.

When fresh fruits such as apples, pears, bananas, and peaches are cut, they begin to oxidize and brown. To keep these fruits from browning in the short term (they will discolor eventually no matter what precautions you take), soak them in an antibrowning solution.

➤ *To prepare an antibrowning solution,* add 1 tablespoon lemon juice or distilled white vinegar for every 4 cups water. Or simply toss the cut fruit with a sprinkle of citrus juice. ➤ Apples respond best to a salt solution of 1 teaspoon salt for every 4 cups water.

➤ If fruit lacks flavor, toss the cut fruit with a little citrus juice and/or sugar to compensate for a lack of acidity or sweetness. You may also enliven sad fruit by steeping cut pieces in the juices of other fruits or in liqueur, or compensate for its blandness by blending it with other fruits in a puree. Poaching lackluster fruits in flavored syrup is another strategy for adding flavor, 170. Or, concentrate a fruit's flavor by preparing Roasted Fruit, 171.

ABOUT FRUIT SALADS AND MACERATED FRUIT

Fruit salad can mean a mixture of cut fruits tossed together in a simple dressing, or it can refer to gelatin-based fruit concoctions. In either case, commonsense rules apply: Use a mixture of tart, sweet, soft, firm, and crisp fruits, and combine fruits of different colors for a striking presentation and more visual and gustatory interest. If the fruits are on the sweet side, add lemon or lime juice. If they are tart, add a little sugar, honey, or maple syrup. You may use all fresh fruits or combine fresh, dried, and even candied fruits. Citrus zest, vanilla bean or vanilla extract, and spices (added with a light hand) all contribute complexity to a good fruit salad. See About Savory Fruit Salads, 128, for more ideas. **Macerated fruit** is simply fruit that has been tossed with sugar and allowed to sit until it exudes juices, which create a light syrup. This is perhaps the easiest way to a simple fruit sauce that we know of, and it shows off the flavor of ripe, seasonal fruit in an understated but luxurious way.

FRUIT SALAD

8 to 10 servings

Combine:

2 oranges, peeled, seeded, and cut into bite-sized chunks
2 large apples, cored and cut into bite-sized chunks
1 large pear, cored and cut into bite-sized chunks
1 large banana, peeled and sliced

Or combine 1½ cups each of 4 of the following fruits:

Apricots, pitted and cut into bite-sized chunks
Kiwis, peeled and sliced or chopped
Strawberries, hulled and halved or quartered
Raspberries, blueberries, or blackberries
Sweet cherries, pitted
Melon or watermelon balls or cubes
Peaches or nectarines, pitted and cut into bite-sized chunks
Plums, pitted and cut into bite-sized chunks
Seedless green or red grapes

Toss with:

¼ to ⅓ cup honey or sugar, to taste
1 tablespoon lemon juice, or to taste

AMBROSIA

I. CLASSIC

6 servings

Canned mandarin orange sections and pineapple chunks can be substituted for the fresh oranges and pineapple.

Peel and section, 182, into a bowl:

6 oranges

Add and gently combine:

3 bananas, sliced
½ pineapple, peeled, cored, and diced (2½ to 3 cups)
½ to 1 cup shredded sweetened coconut, to taste
(½ to 1 cup miniature marshmallows, to taste)
(¼ cup orange liqueur, sherry, or port)

If you have not used marshmallows, stir in:

(¼ to ⅓ cup sugar, to taste)

Cover and refrigerate for at least 3 hours and up to 12 hours to blend the flavors.

II. MEGAN'S MODERN AMBROSIA

4 to 6 servings

For a fantastic dessert, top this with Whipped Crème Fraîche, 791, and serve with Almond Macaroons II, 775.

Peel and section, 182, over a medium bowl to catch the juice:

4 oranges, blood oranges, or a combination

Add to the fruit and its juice:

¼ cup dry white wine, dry vermouth, or Lillet Blanc
5 dried dates, pitted and chopped
(1 tablespoon honey)
A few drops orange flower or rose water

Refrigerate for at least an hour to allow the flavors to meld. Just before serving, add:

⅓ cup flaked or shredded unsweetened coconut, toasted, 973
¼ cup pistachios, toasted, 1005, and chopped

MACERATED FRUIT

4 servings

If using the optional liquor, some good combinations include brandy with cherries, bourbon with peaches, dark rum with mango, and kirsch with strawberries.

Place one of the following in a medium bowl:

½ pound strawberries, hulled and quartered or sliced
½ pound raspberries, blackberries, or pitted cherries
½ pound peaches, apricots, plums, or mango, pitted and sliced or chopped

Sprinkle over the fruit:

1 to 2 tablespoons sugar, to taste
(1 to 2 tablespoons liquor, liqueur, or wine, to taste)
(Scraped seeds from a 1½-inch piece of vanilla bean)

Allow the fruit to sit at room temperature, stirring occasionally, until it softens slightly and a light syrup collects in the bottom of the bowl, 30 to 45 minutes. Store refrigerated.

CITRUS SALAD

6 servings

Grate 3 tablespoons of zest from:

4 navel oranges

Place the zest in a medium bowl. Section the oranges, 182, or peel and cut into bite-sized pieces. Add the oranges and their juices to the bowl with the zest. Section or peel and cut up, removing seeds:

2 grapefruits
2 tangelos or 3 mandarin oranges

Combine with the oranges. Gently stir in:

Sugar to taste
(2 tablespoons orange liqueur)

Cover and refrigerate until chilled and ready to serve. If desired, sprinkle with:

(Chopped mint)

SUMMER FRUIT SALAD

8 servings

Peel, 182, pit, and slice:

4 peaches (about 1½ pounds)

Place in a bowl and add:

2 cups blueberries, blackberries, or a combination
¼ cup sugar, or to taste
1 to 2 tablespoons lemon juice, or to taste

Stir gently and let sit, refrigerated, for at least 30 minutes. If desired, just before serving, stir in:

(2 tablespoons chopped mint, tarragon, or basil)

Serve with:

Whipped Cream, 791

ABOUT CANNED AND FROZEN FRUITS

A wide assortment of conventional canned fruits is available at virtually any supermarket, while other specialty canned fruits may require more of a search. Look for canned lychees, mango, jackfruit, and rambutan at Asian supermarkets, and canned guava, acerola, and papaya at Mexican markets. Most canned fruits are packed in light or heavy sugar syrups, but some are available in their own juices; check the label. We recommend purchasing fruits packed in light syrup or juice. Fruits for commercial canning are picked in a riper state than those sold fresh, which explains why canned apricots (not to mention canned tomatoes) often taste better than their fresh counterparts bought out of season.

Frozen fruits are available both sweetened and unsweetened and are referred to as dry-pack or individually quick frozen (IQF). Sweetened frozen fruits are particularly useful for quick dessert sauces. Thaw and, if desired, puree in a blender or food processor, straining through a sieve if seedy. ➤ Dry-pack frozen fruits may also be substituted for fresh fruit in any recipe where the fruit is cooked or baked, and they are perfect for smoothies. ➤ Measure before thawing, and add while still frozen. For information on pies made with frozen fruit, see 668.

ABOUT DRIED AND CANDIED FRUITS

The high caloric and nutritional values of dried fruits can be readily grasped once you realize that ➤ it takes 5½ pounds of fresh apricots to yield 1 pound dried. When fruits are dried without cooking, their subsequent contact with the air—as well as the enzymatic activity that takes place within them—tends to darken the pulp. A sulfur dioxide solution is often used to lessen darkening. Some people prefer to avoid this; if you are interested in drying your own fruits, see 944.

Apples, apricots, cherries, cranberries, currants, dates, figs, and grapes are among the fruits most often dried. They should all be stored in an airtight container in a cool, dark place. Under most household shelf conditions, they will keep for several months. All dried fruit must be watched for insect infestation. For dried plums, or prunes, see 192. For raisins, see, 186.

Tough dried fruits are improved by **plumping.**

To plump dried fruit, place it in a saucepan and cover with a liquid such as water, brewed tea, fruit juice, wine, or liquor. Bring to a simmer, cover, remove from the heat, and let sit for at least 15 minutes and up to 30 minutes. If using the plumped fruit in a baking recipe, drain it well before adding to the batter or dough. Otherwise, save or discard the soaking liquid as directed in the recipe.

Dried fruits are often messy to cut or chop. For a cleaner, easier cut, put dried fruit in the freezer for about 40 minutes. Or coat your knife, shears, or food processor blade with cooking spray. Dipping the knife or shears in hot water will also help. A food processor can be used to chop a quantity of dried fruit: Use quick pulses. Should the fruit begin to stick together, add up to 2 tablespoons sugar to help separate it. When baking with dried fruit, use a portion of the flour called for in the recipe to flour the fruit after chopping. This prevents the fruit from sinking to the bottom during baking.

Candied, or **glacéed, fruits** have been cooked in a sugar syrup, then drained and, to varying degrees, dried. The candied fruits most commonly found in stores are lemon, orange, and citron rind, cherries, ginger, and pineapple. To candy your own orange slices and citrus peels, see 876.

Freeze-dried fruits have become more widely available in recent years. Strawberries, raspberries, bananas, mango, pineapple, and even blueberries may be available. They are expensive, but they provide a crunchy burst of fruit flavor to homemade granola or chocolate bark and can be pulverized into a powder and sprinkled on desserts for extra flavor. Pastry chef and cookbook author Stella Parks pulverizes the fruit and uses it to flavor and color whipped cream.

DRIED FRUIT COMPOTE

3 cups; 8 servings

Eat this over oatmeal or yogurt at breakfast or serve as a dessert with cookies, cake, custard, or ice cream.

Combine in a medium heavy saucepan:

1 pound dried fruit, one kind or mixed
3 cups water
(Zest of 1 lemon or orange removed in strips with a vegetable peeler)
(1 cinnamon stick)

Bring to a gentle simmer, cover, and cook until the fruit is plumped, 25 to 35 minutes, adding more water if necessary to keep the fruit covered. Add:

½ to 1 cup sugar, to taste

Simmer, uncovered, 5 minutes longer, stirring to dissolve the sugar. Serve warm or chilled.

CHAROSET

Eaten during Passover as one of the symbolic foods of the Seder plate, *charoset* varies depending on where it is made. These two versions, however, are perhaps the most common. Sephardic *charoset* is a dried fruit paste. Ashkenazi *charoset* is more of a chunky, spiced apple relish.

I. SEPHARDIC

About 2 cups

Combine in a medium saucepan:

1 cup pitted dried dates, coarsely chopped
1 cup dried figs, coarsely chopped
1 cup dry or sweet red wine, apple juice, or grape juice

Bring just to a boil, then remove from the heat, cover, and let the fruit plump for 30 minutes. Meanwhile, toast, 1005:

1 cup almonds or walnuts

Coarsely chop the nuts and add them to a food processor. Strain the plumped fruit, reserving the wine, and add the fruit to the food processor along with:

½ teaspoon ground cinnamon
¼ teaspoon ground allspice
¼ teaspoon salt
(⅛ teaspoon ground cardamom)
(Finely grated zest of 1 orange)

Pulse until the mixture is finely ground into a sticky, slightly chunky paste, adding a little of the reserved wine if needed. The *charoset* may be served as is or rolled into balls. Store indefinitely in an airtight container at room temperature.

II. ASHKENAZI

About 4 cups

Combine in a medium bowl:

3 tart-sweet apples such as Honeycrisp or Pink Lady, peeled, cored, and finely chopped
3 tablespoons dry or sweet red wine
2 tablespoons honey
½ cup coarsely chopped toasted, 1005, walnuts or almonds
½ teaspoon ground cinnamon

Store, refrigerated, for up to 3 hours before serving.

PANFORTE DI SIENA (DRIED FRUIT CAKE)

20 servings

This is a very heavy, dense "cake" that keeps well for months. It can be served in tiny slivers on its own, but we love it served with a cheese plate.

Preheat the oven to 300°F. Butter the bottom and sides of a 10-inch round springform pan and line the bottom of the pan with:

1 sheet edible rice paper or parchment paper, cut to fit the pan

Toast, 1005:

1½ cups almonds
½ cup hazelnuts

Add to a food processor and pulse until the nuts are coarsely chopped. Transfer to a medium heatproof bowl and add:

¾ cup candied orange peel, finely chopped
½ cup candied lemon peel or citron, finely chopped

½ cup dried figs, apricots, or raisins or a combination, finely chopped
½ cup all-purpose flour
¼ cup unsweetened cocoa powder
1 teaspoon ground cinnamon
½ teaspoon ground coriander
¼ teaspoon ground cloves
¼ teaspoon grated or ground nutmeg
¼ teaspoon salt
⅛ teaspoon ground white pepper

Stir until well mixed. Combine in a small heavy saucepan:

¾ cup sugar
¾ cup honey
3 tablespoons butter

Stir over medium-low heat until the sugar is dissolved, about 5 minutes. Increase the heat to medium-high and bring the mixture to a boil. Cook until it reaches the firm-ball stage, 245° to 248°F (for details on this step, see 857). Quickly pour the syrup over the dry ingredients and stir with a wooden spoon until completely coated. Transfer the mixture to the prepared pan. Dampen your fingertips, then press evenly into the pan and smooth the top. Bake for 35 minutes. The panforte may not look set, but it will firm as it cools. Cool completely in the pan on a rack. Run a thin, sharp knife around the edge of the pan, then carefully remove the sides of the springform. Dust heavily with:

Powdered sugar

Cut into very thin slices or store, tightly wrapped, at room temperature, until ready to use.

NO-BAKE FRUIT AND NUT BARS

Twelve 2 × 2¾-inch bars

These "energy" bars are easy to make. Vary the flavor to your taste by substituting ½ cup dried cherries or raisins for an equal amount of the dates, using different kinds of nuts, adding spices, toasted coconut, or even chopped dark chocolate.

Line a 9-inch square baking pan with parchment paper so the parchment extends over 2 sides. Pulse in a food processor until very finely ground:

1½ cups raw or roasted almonds, cashews, walnuts, or hazelnuts

Add:

2 cups packed moist dried dates, pitted and coarsely chopped
¼ cup unsweetened cocoa powder
(½ cup cacao nibs)
¼ teaspoon salt

Process until the mixture comes together and everything is finely ground. The mixture should be pasty enough to hold together when pressed into a ball. If it is too dry, add a tablespoon of water at a time until it comes together. Press it evenly into the prepared pan. Cut into bars and store in an airtight container for up to 1 month. Alternatively, you may roll the mixture into balls.

ABOUT POACHED FRUIT

Poaching fruit is quite simple: Drop the fruit into a simmering liquid (usually syrup) and cook over low heat until it is barely tender. Remove the fruit from the syrup immediately so it will not continue to cook, reserve the cooking liquid, and set aside to cool. The fruit can be served drizzled with the cooking syrup, and any uneaten poached fruit can be stored in the syrup. Fruit may also be poached in the oven. Simply combine fruit and syrup in a baking dish and bake, covered, at 350°F until tender.

Soft, juicy fruits, such as peaches, stand up best when poached in a single layer in a skillet with a heavy syrup; apples and other hard fruits benefit from being poached in a thin syrup (see below for instructions). Store poached fruit up to 3 days in the refrigerator before serving. You can use the syrup again for a compatible fruit—it will keep refrigerated for up to 1 week. Serve poached fruits with Pound Cake, 726, biscotti, 778–79, macaroons, 774–75, shortcake, 834, Whipped Cream, 791, Panna Cotta, 821, or cheesecake, 752.

POACHING LIQUIDS FOR FRUITS

When making syrups for fruit, keep in mind that wine can be used instead of water, or mixed half and half with water. You may also use honey instead of sugar. For another flavorful adaptation, use fruit juices as the liquid in the syrup. For instance, use pomegranate juice in a syrup to poach pears. Leftover poaching syrup can be reduced to create a sauce for garnishing the poached fruit.

I. THIN SYRUP

For apples, Bosc pears, and quince. Combine in a saucepan and heat, stirring to dissolve the sugar:

1 cup sugar
3 cups water
Dash of salt

II. MEDIUM SYRUP

For apricots, cherries, pears, and prunes. Use:

2 cups sugar
3 cups water
Dash of salt

III. HEAVY SYRUP

For berries, figs, peaches, and plums. Use:

3 cups sugar
3 cups water
Dash of salt

POACHED FRUIT

6 to 8 servings

Please read About Poached Fruit, above. Prepare one of the following for poaching:

12 apricots, halved and pitted
4 to 5 cups sweet cherries, pitted
6 large peaches or nectarines, peeled, halved, and pitted
6 pears, peeled, halved, and cored
6 apples, peeled, cored, and quartered
1 large pineapple, peeled, cored, and cut into rings
12 plums, halved and pitted

Based on the fruit chosen, prepare one of the:

Poaching Liquids for Fruits, 170

In a pan large enough to accommodate the fruit (keep in mind that soft fruits like peaches are best poached in a single layer in a wide skillet). For pears or apples, make a double batch of the poaching liquid. If desired, add any of the following:

(2 cinnamon sticks, 2 whole star anise, and/or 10 lightly smashed cardamom pods)
(One 2-inch piece ginger, thinly sliced)
(½ vanilla bean, split lengthwise)
(Zest of 1 lemon, lime, or orange removed in strips with a vegetable peeler)

Set the pan over medium heat and bring to a simmer, then cover and cook for 5 minutes. Add the fruit, increase the heat to high and bring back to a simmer. Reduce the heat to simmer gently and cook, uncovered, stirring the fruit occasionally, until tender when pierced with a knife, 5 to 20 minutes depending on the fruit. Transfer the fruit to a serving dish or storage container. If the syrup is very thin, reduce it until thickened, then let cool completely and pour over the fruit. Serve warm, at room temperature, or chilled.

ABOUT BAKED OR ROASTED FRUIT

Roasting is an excellent strategy for improving lackluster fruit. Roasting not only concentrates the flavor of the fruit by cooking off much of the water contained within, but it also enhances flavor by promoting browning. The natural sugars of the fruit (and any sugar sprinkled on it) caramelize and create a super-concentrated, syrupy compote that is outstanding served just about any way you can imagine: over toasted and buttered bread as a sort of rustic jam, over yogurt or oatmeal, on creamy desserts such as baked custard, or between the layers of a cake.

The difference between roasting and baking is a matter of degrees. Baking is done at a lower temperature and is best for larger, dense fruits, such as whole apples or pears. The results can be much the same as roasting, though caramelization is slower and not as dramatic. See Baked Apples, 174, Baked Figs with Ricotta, 186, and Baked Stuffed Peaches, 190.

ROASTED FRUIT

About 4 servings

Use a combination of the fruits below for a roasted fruit "salad" that can be eaten on its own, over ice cream, or with a cheese plate.

Preheat the oven to 375°F. Prepare one of the following fruits for roasting:

1 pound cherries, pitted, hulled strawberries (halved if large), or halved figs
6 apricots or 3 peaches, nectarines, or large plums, halved, pitted, and sliced
3 ripe pears, quartered and cored
1 pound rhubarb, cut into 2-inch lengths
1 pound grapes

Toss the fruit in a baking dish with:

¼ cup sugar or honey
(Finely grated zest of 1 lemon or orange)
(Scraped seeds and pod from ½ vanilla bean, split lengthwise)
(A few herb sprigs such as thyme or rosemary)

Spread the fruit in an even layer and roast, stirring every 15 minutes, until tender, juicy, and caramelized, about 30 minutes for tender fruits like strawberries and apricots, and up to 40 minutes for firm fruits such as pears. If desired (and you did not use the vanilla bean), stir in:

(1 teaspoon vanilla or 1 tablespoon liqueur)

Serve warm, at room temperature, or chilled. If desired, top with:

(Chopped toasted, 1005, almonds, hazelnuts, or walnuts)

ABOUT GRILLED OR BROILED FRUIT

Grilling fruit caramelizes its sugars and adds a smoky flavor. Place cut fruit around whatever meat, poultry, or fish is on the fire for a barbecue-friendly dessert that goes well with vanilla ice cream. Thread smaller pieces of fruit onto skewers, putting soft fruits and firmer fruits on separate skewers as they will not finish cooking at the same time. When broiling, allow 3 to 6 inches between the fruit and the heat source, depending on the thickness of the fruit and its sugar content. Very sweet fruit may burn if broiled too close to the heat. For more on these cooking methods, see Grilling, 1062, and Broiling, 1050.

GRILLED OR BROILED FRUIT

4 to 6 servings

I. GRILLED

Prepare a medium-hot grill fire or preheat a gas grill to medium-high. Lightly brush one of the following with vegetable oil:

6 large apricots, halved and pitted
4 large or 6 small bananas, peeled
6 large figs, stemmed and halved lengthwise
4 peaches or nectarines, halved and pitted
6 large juicy plums, halved and pitted
6 pineapple rings (about ½ inch thick)

Grill the fruits directly over the flames, arranging the halved fruits cut side down. Cook until lightly charred, 2 to 3 minutes. Turn and cook 2 to 3 minutes longer. Serve at once.

II. BROILED

Preheat the broiler. Prepare the fruit as directed in version I and place, hollow side up, in a shallow, broilerproof baking pan. Sprinkle lightly with:

Sugar
Salt

Broil 6 inches from the heat until lightly browned and juicy.

GRILLED OR BROILED FRUIT KEBABS WITH HONEY AND LIME

4 to 6 servings

Combine in a large bowl:

½ cup grapefruit juice
Finely grated zest and juice of 1 lime
¼ cup honey
2 tablespoons orange liqueur or orange juice

Add, turning to coat, and marinate 30 minutes:

2 medium-firm peaches, pitted and cut into 1-inch pieces
1 cup peeled and cubed pineapple
1 cup strawberries, hulled
1 banana, cut into 1-inch pieces
1 mango, peeled, pitted, and cut into chunks

Prepare a medium-hot grill fire, preheat a gas grill to medium-high, or preheat the broiler. If using wooden skewers, soak them in water for 30 minutes before using. Thread the fruit onto skewers. Grill or broil until lightly browned, about 5 minutes total, turning once and basting with the marinade. Serve sprinkled with:

Chopped mint

FRUIT BRÛLÉ

4 to 6 servings

This is one of the stranger recipes in the book but also one of the most delicious. For brûléed citrus fruit, see Broiled Grapefruit, 184.

Spread in a 9-inch round broilerproof baking dish or pie plate:

3½ cups raspberries, blackberries, blueberries, small hulled strawberries, or pitted cherries

Mix together, then spread evenly over the fruit:

1½ cups sour cream
1 teaspoon vanilla

Cover and refrigerate until thoroughly chilled, or for up to 8 hours. Preheat the broiler. Dust the sour cream evenly with:

1 cup packed brown sugar

so that none of the sour cream shows through. Place the dish about 6 inches from the heat and broil until the sugar caramelizes, 1 to 2 minutes. Watch closely so that the sugar does not scorch. Alternatively, use a propane torch or kitchen torch to brûlé the sugar. Serve at once.

SAUTÉED FRUIT

4 to 6 servings

Melt in a wide skillet, preferably nonstick, over medium-high heat:

3 tablespoons butter

Sprinkle into the skillet in an even layer:

⅓ cup white or brown sugar

Cook until the mixture is combined and bubbling. Add any of the following, arranging halved fruits cut side down:

6 large apricots, halved and pitted
6 large or 8 to 12 small figs, stemmed and halved lengthwise
4 peaches, peeled, halved, and pitted
4 nectarines, peeled, halved or quartered, and pitted
6 large plums, halved and pitted
4 pineapple rings (about ½ inch thick), halved

Cook 2 minutes, periodically shaking the skillet to keep the fruit from sticking. Turn the fruit and cook, again shaking the skillet, just until it is warmed through and has begun to release its juices. Serve at once with the pan juices drizzled over. If desired, sprinkle with:

(Ground cinnamon)

ABOUT PUREED FRUIT

Unsweetened fruit purees can be served with savory dishes, especially roasted meat. Lightly sweetened, they are excellent desserts. They add body and flavor to sauces and dressings, or make good sauces in and of themselves; see About Fruit Sauces, 805. See the list of Garnishes for Pureed Fruits, below, for serving ideas.

Many fruits, such as ripe peaches and berries, are tender enough to be pureed raw. Remove the peel, pit, seeds, or core. Cut into small pieces before pureeing to ensure even results. Strain fruits with tiny seeds, or ones that are stringy, through a sieve. ➤ Firm fruit such as apples, rhubarb, quince, some pears, and dried fruits must be cooked until soft before pureeing. Combine peeled and sliced fruit with a small amount of water and cook in a covered pan over gentle heat until very tender when pierced with a knife. Sugar can help intensify the flavor of purees, and fruit purees can be reduced with sugar for a thicker, richer sauce. Fresh lemon juice preserves color and brightens the flavor of fruit purees. Add water or fruit juice as necessary to thin purees to the desired consistency.

COOKED FRUIT PUREE

About 1¼ cups

While this versatile puree is ideal for Fruit Fool, 173, it is almost like a quick fruit butter. Use it on toast with butter, swirled into yogurt or oatmeal, or anywhere else you might use jam. For Applesauce, see 174.

Place one of the following in a medium saucepan:

2 cups blueberries, raspberries, blackberries, or chopped hulled strawberries
2 cups chopped pitted plums, peaches, nectarines, or apricots

Add and bring to a simmer over medium heat, stirring to dissolve the sugar:

¼ cup sugar
1 tablespoon lemon juice

Simmer, stirring occasionally, until the fruit is very soft and starting to break down, about 10 minutes. Transfer to a blender and blend until completely smooth. If raspberries or blackberries were used, pass the puree through a fine-mesh sieve to remove the seeds, if desired (if a little texture doesn't bother you, feel free to leave them in). Taste and, if needed, add a little more lemon juice. Let cool completely and store refrigerated.

GARNISHES FOR PUREED FRUITS

Finely grated lemon zest, ground cinnamon, or nutmeg
Heavy cream or Whipped Cream, 791
Chopped toasted, 1005, walnuts or almonds
Crushed Almond Macaroons, 774, and Whipped Cream, 791
Sour cream, yogurt, or crème fraîche mixed with sugar and rum or vanilla
Bread or cake crumbs browned in butter
Chopped mint

FRUIT FOOL
4 to 6 servings

We are partial to old-fashioned recipes that combine fruit with whipped cream or rich custard. If using cream, serve within 2 hours; pastry cream adds stability, and can be made a day ahead of time. To make a fruit fool with Cooked Fruit Puree, 172, substitute 1¼ cups sweetened puree for the fresh fruit mixture.

I. WITH CREAM

Puree in a food processor or blender and set aside:

2 cups blackberries, blueberries, raspberries, or hulled strawberries
¼ to ⅓ cup powdered sugar, depending on the sweetness of the fruit
1 tablespoon lemon juice, or to taste

Whip in a large bowl until the mixture holds firm peaks:

1¼ cups cold heavy cream
1 tablespoon sugar
½ teaspoon vanilla

Gently fold the berry puree into the whipped cream, leaving streaks of the fruit mixture. Pour into a glass bowl or divide among cups or glasses and chill thoroughly. Alternatively, layer the fruit mixture with the whipped cream in glasses or cups.

II. WITH CUSTARD

Prepare:

Pastry Cream, 801

Let cool completely and chill until cold. Coarsely blend in a food processor or blender (leave some larger chunks of fruit) and set aside:

1½ cups blackberries, blueberries, raspberries, or hulled strawberries
¼ to ⅓ cup powdered sugar, depending on the sweetness of the fruit

In a medium bowl, stir the chilled pastry cream just until smooth, then fold in:

1 cup heavy cream, beaten until stiff, 791

Fold in the fruit. Do not fold in the fruit puree until perfectly incorporated. Leave some pockets of fruit and some pockets of pastry cream. Transfer to a serving bowl or divide among cups or glasses. Alternatively, layer the fruit with the pastry cream mixture in cups or glasses. Chill thoroughly. Before serving, sprinkle the top with:

Almond Macaroons, 774, crumbled

Or serve with:

Ladyfingers, 750

ABOUT APPLES

Apples are so familiar to us that we take them for granted, but in another era they might have been considered an exotic fruit. Apples come from Kazakhstan, where they still grow wild in some places. Apples do not grow true to seed, meaning: An apple seed from a store-bought apple could very well grow into a tree, but the resulting fruit would not resemble the apple the seed came from, and it might not be very good to eat at all. Apples are propagated by grafting, a process that essentially clones trees that produce good eating apples by inserting small stems of the desired apple-producing tree into cuts in another tree, which serves as the rootstock. There are more than seven thousand varieties of apples, though only a handful are common in grocery stores; below are the most plentiful and noteworthy, arranged by their best uses.

The following apple varieties are best eaten out of hand or in salads; none of these varieties holds their shape when cooked, but they do very well for applesauce. **Red Delicious,** the thick-skinned, flavorless scourge of our nation's produce departments, is undeserving of its name (though we must admit that it is indeed quite red). **McIntosh, Empire, Macoun,** and **Cortland apples** are all fine-grained and have a pleasant tartness to them; **Fujis, Galas,** and **Braeburns** are on the sweeter side. Gala apples can be crisp when fresh, but we do not recommend them for baking whole. ➤ Cortland, Empire, Fuji, and Gala apples do not brown quickly when cut, which makes them good for fruit salads or for slicing and presenting on a cheese board.

Firm, **all-purpose apples** are good for eating out of hand or using in baking recipes. The most versatile and widely available all-purpose variety is **Golden Delicious.** Sweet and aromatic when raw, it becomes even more so when cooked, holds its shape beautifully, and exudes little juice. **Rome Beauty,** another common all-purpose apple, has a rich texture when cooked, making it a particularly good choice for baking whole. **Granny Smiths,** the firmest and tartest variety in most supermarkets, give off a great deal of juice when cooked but are wonderful for applesauce, sautéed apple rings, and Tarte Tatin, 673. Other all-purpose apples worth seeking out include: **Newtown Pippin, Mutsu** (or **Crispin**), **Northern Spy, Spigold, Esopus Spitzenburg, Baldwin, Stayman Winesap, Black Twig, Gravenstein, Grimes Golden, Jazz, Pink Lady, Honeycrisp, Ida Red, Jonagold, Arkansas Black, Ashmead's Kernel,** and **Rhode Island Greening.**

Crab apples are generally not good eating apples; They tend to be tiny, incredibly tart, and astringent. However, if you have access to a crab apple tree they are worth a try for applesauce and apple butter. **Cider apples** are similar to crab apples in that they tend toward acidity, astringency, and mealiness. Their complex flavors can be overwhelming when eaten out of hand, but they produce excellent hard cider.

Some apples bear ripe fruit in late summer, but most varieties are at their peak in fall. Of course, apples store well under refrigeration, which allows supermarkets to stock them year-round. Unfortunately, most supermarkets have the same three or four types, so we encourage the curious to seek out more unusual heirloom varieties from small orchards and farmers' markets during autumn. Select apples with smooth skins; inspect carefully for dents, signs of bruising, and insect damage. Avoid any that are more than slightly soft when pressed.

Apples are often picked when they are underripe, which helps them survive long storage times; the best way to tell if they are ripe is to taste one. For fast ripening, keep apples at room temperature. If they are ripe, store apples in a cold, dry place; for longer storage, store them so they are not touching each other. If you receive a windfall from a friend's orchard and want to reserve some of it, let the fruit stand in a cool, dark place for 24 hours, then inspect for blemishes. Set aside any blemished apples to use as soon as possible. Wrap unblemished fruit in paper and store in slotted boxes in a cold, dark, airy place.

With long storage, apples tend to lose flavor and become mealy. Such apples can be improved somewhat in cooking by the addition of lemon juice, but nothing can really compensate for a lack of natural tartness. Applesauce is a forgiving thing to make with subpar apples. Flavor can be corrected with citrus juice, a sweetener, and spices.

Peel apples with a paring knife or vegetable peeler. To core apples for serving whole or cutting into rings, use an apple corer. For all other preparations, cut the fruit into quarters through the stem and cut away the core with a paring knife. Alternatively, cut the apple into 4 pieces around the core as shown below. Pair apples with sausage, pork, or ham. Apples are particularly complemented by cinnamon, cloves, nutmeg, mace, rosemary, sage, coriander, lemon and orange zest, vanilla, dark rum, brandy, bourbon, and almonds.

For other apple recipes see Apple Butter, 915, Apple Dumplings, 688, Apple Pie, 670, Sour Cream Apple Soufflé Cake Cockaigne, 819, Apple Cake, 736, Apple Strudel, 699, Apple-Walnut Muffins, 633, and Crêpes with Caramelized Apples, 647.

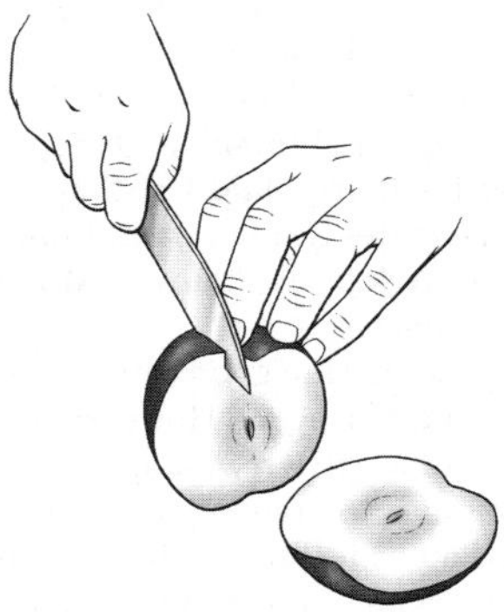

Cutting around the core

SAUTÉED APPLE RINGS

4 servings

Good as a topping for ice cream, on top of pancakes and waffles, or alongside roast pork.

Core and cut crosswise into ¼- to ½-inch slices:

2 large all-purpose apples, 173, such as Golden Delicious or Rome Beauty

Melt in a large skillet over medium heat:

2 tablespoons butter or bacon fat, or more if necessary

Add a single layer of apple rings to the skillet. Cook until the bottoms are golden and beginning to caramelize, about 3 minutes. Turn and cook the apples until just tender when pierced with a fork. Set aside on a platter. Cook the remaining rings in batches, adding more butter or bacon fat to the skillet as needed. When all are done, sprinkle with:

1 to 3 tablespoons brown sugar, to taste
(Calvados, apple brandy, or applejack)
Ground cinnamon

APPLESAUCE

4 to 6 servings

Peel, core, and chop:

3 pounds apples, such as McIntosh or Empire

Combine the apples in a heavy-bottomed saucepan or pot with:

½ cup water or apple juice
(2 tablespoons lemon juice, or to taste)
(One 3-inch cinnamon stick or ½ teaspoon ground cinnamon)

Cover and simmer, stirring occasionally, until the apples are soft and falling apart, 20 to 30 minutes. Stir in:

¼ to ½ cup white sugar, brown sugar, or maple syrup, to taste

Increase the heat to medium and cook uncovered, stirring frequently, until the applesauce thickens. For a smooth sauce, puree with an immersion blender or in a regular blender. If desired, stir in:

(2 tablespoons butter, softened)
(1 teaspoon vanilla)

Serve warm or cold. To serve as a dessert, pair it with:

Crème Anglaise, 806, or vanilla ice cream

BAKED APPLES

6 servings

Golden Delicious, Pippin, Granny Smith, and other firm all-purpose apples, 173, hold their shape when baked.

I. Preheat the oven to 350°F. Arrange in a deep baking dish or heavy pot:

6 large all-purpose apples, cored

Divide evenly among the hollows:

½ to ¾ cup white or brown sugar, to taste
2 tablespoons butter, cut into small pieces

If desired, sprinkle with:

(½ to 1 teaspoon ground cinnamon)

Pour into the dish:

⅔ cup water, apple juice, or cider

Cover tightly with foil or a lid and bake until the apples are nearly tender when pierced with a fork but not mushy, about 20 minutes. Uncover and bake the apples, basting frequently with the cooking juices, until soft but still firm enough to hold their shape, 20 minutes longer. If the juices are thin, transfer the apples to a serving dish and reduce the juices in the dish, then pour over the apples. Serve hot or chilled.

II. A richer dish than I above. This may be assembled up to 8 hours ahead, refrigerated, uncovered, then baked.

Preheat the oven to 300°F. Core and peel:

6 large all-purpose apples

Pour into a small bowl:

1¼ cups sugar

Place in another bowl:

1 cup heavy cream

Roll each apple in the cream, then roll in the sugar until coated. Reserve the leftover cream. Place the apples in a 13 × 9-inch baking dish. Combine in a bowl, then stuff into the hollows of the apples:

½ cup raisins, chopped figs, or chopped dates
½ cup walnuts or pecans, toasted, 1005, and chopped
(Finely grated zest of 1 lemon or ½ orange)

Mix together the leftover cream and sugar, then stir in:

1 teaspoon ground cinnamon
(½ teaspoon grated or ground nutmeg)
(¼ teaspoon ground cloves)

Spoon as much of this mixture into the hollows of the apples as they will hold, then pour the rest into the bottom of the pan, along with:

1 cup water, apple juice, or cider
(¼ cup dark rum or brandy)

Bake, uncovered, without basting, until the apples are tender when pierced with a fork but still hold their shape, about 1 hour. Serve warm with the pan syrup, accompanied with:

Heavy cream, sour cream, crème fraîche, or vanilla ice cream

BAKED APPLES STUFFED WITH SAUSAGE

6 servings

A homey, rustic winter dish.

Preheat the oven to 350°F. Wash:

6 large baking apples, such as Ida Red or Golden Delicious

Cut a slice from the tops. With a spoon or melon baller, scoop out the cores and pulp, leaving ¾-inch-thick shells. Cut the pulp away from the core and seeds, chop it, and combine in a bowl with:

8 ounces bulk sausage, store-bought or homemade, 510

Put the apple shells in a baking dish. If desired, sprinkle with:

(2 tablespoons brown sugar)

Fill the shells heaping full with the sausage mixture. Bake, uncovered, until the apples are tender when pierced with a fork but still hold their shape and the sausage is cooked, 30 to 40 minutes.

ABOUT APRICOTS

Originally from China, apricots have been cultivated by humans for more than four thousand years. They are commonly found fresh and dried, and their kernels are used to make almond extract and the Italian cookies called amaretti.

While there are many apricot varieties in the world, only a few are commonly available to purchase. **Blenheims** are the most sought-after apricots and can be hard to find as they are difficult to grow. They taste of honey and have a good balance of sweetness and acidity. **Moorpark apricots** are another good-tasting variety, although they are also scarce. **Patterson** and **Castlebrite apricots** are much more prolific than Blenheims (and what you see most often at the grocery store), but most of them are picked while still green and are bland and mealy. We find the vast majority of supermarket apricots to be insipid, so this is one fruit we highly recommend seeking out from a small farmer who picks the fruit when fully ripe.

Fresh, ripe apricots have a beautiful blush and should be firm in texture. Avoid if shriveled, tinged with green, or lacking aroma. Apricots should be stored at room temperature in a single layer. If they are very ripe and will not be eaten right away, they may be refrigerated for a couple days. Serve apricots at room temperature, as chilling dulls their flavor. Apricot skin is tender and generally left on whether the fruit will be eaten raw or cooked.

Firm-ripe apricots are delicious in Fruit Salad, 167. They can also be sautéed, baked, grilled, or pureed. Remove the apricot pits before cooking. Apricot pits can be cracked to extract the kernel inside, which has a bitter almond flavor (similar to almond extract), but use caution. Apricot kernels contain cyanide, and while consuming a small number is not harmful, fewer than 20 can provide a lethal dose for an adult, and much fewer for a child. Nonetheless, you may see recipes that call for apricot kernels in small amounts, to provide a rich almond flavor. We have used them sparingly in apricot preserves with no deleterious effects. As with any potentially harmful food, consume them at your own risk.

Dried apricots are excellent—tart, sweet, and chewy. Those with a brighter color have been treated with sulfur dioxide. To revive dry, tough dried apricots, follow the plumping instructions in About Dried and Candied Fruits, 168.

Apricots go well with orange zest, vanilla, pistachios, almonds, honey, black pepper, cardamom, saffron, sweet white wine, and yogurt or crème fraîche. For other recipes featuring apricots, see Apricot Preserves, 917, Apricot Butter, 916, Curried Apricot Chutney, 933, and Fresh Fruit Kuchen, 726.

BAKED HONEYED APRICOTS

4 servings

Serve these soft, buttery apricots with homemade ricotta, 965, ice cream, Greek yogurt, or crème fraîche.

Preheat the oven to 375°F. Butter a 9-inch square or round baking dish or pie plate. Place cut side up in the dish:

8 medium apricots (about 1 pound), halved and pitted

Drizzle the apricots with:

3 tablespoons honey

Scatter over the fruit:

2 tablespoons butter, cut into small pieces
Finely grated zest of 1 lemon
(2 teaspoons fresh thyme leaves)

Bake until the fruit is very soft and lightly caramelized, about 25 minutes. Sprinkle with:

¼ cup finely chopped roasted pistachios

ABOUT BANANAS

Delicious, nutritious, inexpensive, and always available, bananas are one of the most popular fruits in the world—and one with a troubled history of exploitation. While there are many varieties of bananas—some sweet, some tangy, some with dense, hard flesh like a potato—the commercial banana crop is almost exclusively composed of one variety called the **Cavendish.** The Cavendish replaced the **Gros Michel banana,** which succumbed to a fungal pathogen known as Panama disease. The United Fruit Company, an American behemoth, amassed land across Central America in order to propagate its monoculture of Gros Michel, then, after those bananas succumbed to Panama disease, Cavendish bananas. The company was notorious for doing its business at any cost, including bribing government officials, evading taxes, exploiting workers, and stealing land. Though now defunct, the corporation's legacy lingers in Central America in the form of depleted land, cleared forests and marshes, and political unrest.

Now the Cavendish banana is under threat by a relative of the pathogen that killed off the Gros Michel. It seems increasingly likely, barring developments in treating the pathogen, that the Cavendish will go extinct. It may be replaced by a new variety of banana, bred from other banana types that are resistant to the pathogen, but it is still too early to say.

Bananas are picked green and ripen off the tree. They appear at markets year-round in varying stages of ripeness. Though the Cavendish banana is the main banana you will find, there are some other varieties available at specialty markets. **Lady finger** or **dwarf bananas** are tiny and very sweet, good for desserts or eating out of hand. **Plantains, 263,** are not a specific type of banana, but rather a generic term used to describe any banana that is cooked rather than eaten raw. There are several varieties of **red banana**; though red-skinned, their flesh is creamy and pale. The ones you are likely to find will be sweet.

Depending on the ultimate use, purchase bananas that are underripe, at perfect ripeness, or overripe. For poaching, sautéing, grilling, and using in fruit salads, firm-ripe bananas are preferable because they will hold their shape. Many grocery stores sell overripe bananas at a discount, which are ideal for making banana bread, cake, muffins, or pancakes; or peel and freeze them for smoothies.

To ripen bananas, simply leave them on the counter, enclosed in a paper bag if you wish to hasten the process. Bananas that become overripe can be refrigerated; though the skins will blacken, their flesh remains palatable for up to 3 days.

In the United States, we think of bananas as a fruit for snacking or using in desserts and other sweet preparations. In much of the rest of the world, the banana is a workhorse crop that provides an affordable and plentiful source of starch. In India, bananas may be found in chutneys and potato dishes. In the Philippines, banana ketchup is a staple condiment. In Uganda, starchy bananas are cooked and mashed and are such a staple food that they might be compared to bread in Europe. In Thailand, banana blossoms, 955, are used in many dishes, including Pad Thai, 303, to which they contribute crunch and a tannic flavor.

Pair bananas with rum, cardamom, nutmeg, peanut butter, chocolate, brown butter, pecans, walnuts, and other tropical fruits such as mango, coconut, and lime. For other banana recipes, see Banana Pudding, 817, Banana Bread Cockaigne, 626, Banana Cake Cockaigne, 733, Banana Cream Pie, 680, Banana Muffins, 634, and Banana Split, 851. For using **banana leaves** and **banana blossoms,** see 955.

CHOCOLATE-DIPPED BANANAS

8 servings

Peel and halve crosswise:

4 ripe bananas

Firmly insert a wooden popsicle stick or chopstick into the cut end of each half. Freeze on a sheet of foil for at least 1 hour. Prepare:

Chocolate Shell, 808

Transfer the chocolate sauce to a tall, narrow container such as a tall glass for easier dipping. Remove the bananas from the freezer and dip them one by one into the chocolate, twirling to ensure complete coverage. If desired, sprinkle the chocolate-dipped bananas with one of the following before the chocolate sets:

(Chopped roasted, salted peanuts or other nut)
(Multicolored sprinkles)
(Toffee bits)

Serve at once, or let set on wax paper, then return to the freezer in a plastic bag for later. Keep any leftover chocolate shell in an airtight container or jar at room temperature.

BAKED BANANAS

4 servings

I. Bananas take on a surprisingly rich flavor when baked. This is also an excellent treatment for bananas to be used in Banana Bread Cockaigne, 626, especially if the bananas are not as ripe as you would like them to be.

Preheat the oven to 375°F, prepare a medium-hot grill fire, or preheat a gas grill to medium-high. Place in a shallow baking dish or on the grill:

4 bananas in their skins

Bake or grill over indirect heat, turning occasionally, until the skins are black and have begun to split, about 20 minutes. Serve hot, in their skins. If desired, on opening, sprinkle with:

(Lemon or lime juice)
(Salt or powdered sugar)

II. CANDIED

Preheat the oven to 375°F. Melt together in a small saucepan and boil for 5 minutes:

½ cup packed dark brown sugar
¼ cup water

Cool slightly, until just warm. Peel, halve crosswise and then once lengthwise, and place in a buttered shallow dish:

2 slightly underripe bananas

Sprinkle lightly with:

Salt

Add to the cooled syrup:

1½ tablespoons lemon or lime juice

Pour the syrup over the bananas and bake for 30 minutes, turning the fruit after 15 minutes. Serve sprinkled with:

Rum
(Chopped candied ginger)

BANANAS FOSTER

4 servings

A '50s-era tableside classic from Brennan's Restaurant in New Orleans. If you have an electric skillet or chafing dish, you may (cautiously) reenact the entire, pyrotechnic experience for your guests.

Peel and halve lengthwise:

4 firm-ripe bananas

Cut each half into 4 pieces. Melt in a large heavy skillet or chafing dish:

2 tablespoons butter

Place the bananas in the skillet cut side down. Cook over low heat, turning once, for about 5 minutes per side, just until fork-tender—do not overcook. Sprinkle with:

3 tablespoons light brown sugar
¼ teaspoon ground cinnamon
⅛ teaspoon grated or ground nutmeg

Transfer the bananas to a heatproof serving dish and arrange in a single layer. Add to the skillet:

½ cup dark rum
(1 tablespoon brandy)

Increase the heat to medium and use a spatula to loosen the caramelized bits while the spirits heat. When they are hot, carefully ignite with a long wooden match or lighter, then pour over the bananas. Spoon the bananas and sauce over:

Vanilla ice cream

CAMPFIRE BANANAS

1 or 2 servings

These can be cooked in the embers of a hot grill fire, but they are best enjoyed at the end of a long day of hiking, cooked in a campfire. Cut a slit lengthwise down:

1 ripe banana, peel intact

Do not cut all the way through the bottom of the peel. Spread inside the peel on the banana:

2 tablespoons peanut butter

Stuff into the cut part of the banana:

A few squares dark or bittersweet chocolate or 2 tablespoons chocolate chips
(2 tablespoons mini marshmallows)

Wrap the banana tightly in foil and place in hot coals. Allow to cook until the chocolate is melted and the banana is soft, 15 to 20 minutes. Eat with a spoon, scooping the soft banana from the peel.

ABOUT BERRIES

Botanically speaking, a berry is a fruit produced from the ovary of a single flower (a group that includes bananas, eggplants, and tomatoes). We, however, will be speaking of berries in a culinary or colloquial sense: blueberries, blackberries, strawberries, raspberries, and the like. Despite the botanical heresy, the fruits we call berries are stored and prepared in similar ways, and are (mostly) good substitutes for one another in recipes. For information on specific types, see the individual sections that follow. For wild berries and exotic berries, see 181.

Regardless of type, ➤ all berries should be picked at peak ripeness, as they do not ripen off the plant. This goes a long way to explaining why locally grown, in-season berries are always preferable to imports at the supermarket: In order to survive shipping and storage, these berries must be picked underripe. On the other hand, fruit packers harvest and freeze berries at peak ripeness, which results in sweeter berries with better flavor. For this reason, ➤ we recommend purchasing individually quick frozen (IQF) berries when possible rather than spending more on underripe or out-of-season fresh berries.

In general, wash berries just before using. ➤ The exception to this is using a **vinegar rinse.** Fragile fruits such as strawberries, blackberries, and raspberries benefit from a quick dip in a vinegar solution, which kills molds on the surface of the fruit and can extend shelf life significantly. In a large bowl, combine 4 cups cool water and 1 cup distilled white vinegar. Add fresh berries and swish them around gently with your hand. Drain the berries and lay them out in a single layer on kitchen towels to dry or line a salad spinner with paper towels and gently spin them dry.

To store fresh berries, keep them covered and unwashed in the refrigerator. Do not crowd or press them, and store more fragile berries, such as raspberries, in a single layer. Placing them on a paper towel is a good idea, as it absorbs excess moisture and cushions the berries. Ripe berries freeze well, 882, for use out of season. To dry berries, see 944.

BERRY CONES

Kids love this unusual and attractive way to serve berries. Marion and John Becker were first introduced to these in Puerto Rico, where they were greeted beside a waterfall by children with wild berries in leaf cones. We recommend using ice cream cones. Serve them nested in a tray made from a box top with holes. Glorify your tray with colored paper or foil.

Berry cones

ABOUT STRAWBERRIES

Strawberries are the first berries of the year. The best are deep red all the way through and should be very fragrant, although the kind we see most in grocery stores tend to be large, underripe, and odorless. Try to find locally grown berries that are allowed to ripen fully on the plant. They will likely be smaller and more fragile than their supermarket counterparts, but their flavor will be superb. Even peak-season local strawberries can sometimes taste waterlogged if there have been heavy rains. If you do purchase less than stellar strawberries, roasting, 171, is a good way to concentrate their flavor. To store strawberries, see the section on storage in About Berries, above.

To hull a strawberry, remove its leafy top and pale cone-shaped core by cutting around it with the point of a paring knife, or scoop it out with a strawberry huller, 178. ➤ Always hull after washing, not before.

Strawberries pair well with vanilla bean, orange zest and juice, balsamic vinegar, rosewater, Whipped Cream, 791, sour cream, crème fraîche, Camembert, basil, black pepper, chocolate, and almonds. Also see Red Red Strawberry Jam, 912, Strawberry Rosé Jam, 912, Strawberry Shortcake, 834, and Fresh Berry Coulis, 805.

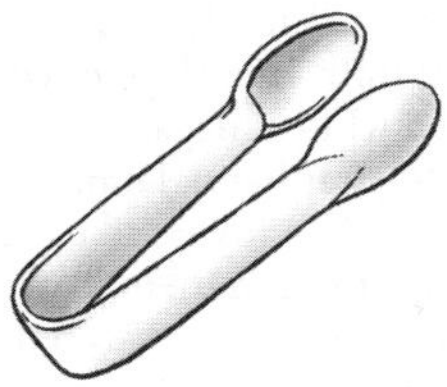

Strawberry huller

STRAWBERRIES COCKAIGNE

As delicious and elegant as it is simple to prepare. Marion was allergic to strawberries, but she could never pass up this treat.

Arrange:

Whole strawberries

on a plate around a mound of:

Brown sugar

Pass a dish of:

Sour cream

To eat, dip the berries in the sour cream, then in the brown sugar.

CHOCOLATE-DIPPED STRAWBERRIES

4 servings

Wash and dry thoroughly:

1 quart unhulled strawberries

Temper, 858:

1 pound semisweet or bittersweet chocolate

Hold the strawberries by their green tops, and dip into the chocolate. Place on a baking sheet lined with wax or parchment paper and refrigerate for 20 minutes to set the chocolate.

STRAWBERRIES ROMANOFF

6 to 8 servings

Hull and slice lengthwise into a shallow bowl:

1½ quarts strawberries (2 to 2½ pounds)

Sprinkle over them:

6 tablespoons Grand Marnier or strained orange juice

¼ cup powdered sugar

Stir gently to mix. Cover and refrigerate for 2 to 3 hours. Soften at room temperature for 10 minutes:

1 pint vanilla ice cream

Whip until soft peaks form:

½ cup cold heavy cream

Fold the ice cream and whipped cream together very lightly with a spatula. Serve at once topped with the strawberries and their juices.

ABOUT BLUEBERRIES AND HUCKLEBERRIES

Blueberries are plump, cheerful little berries with a whitish bloom on the skin. Look for blueberries with taut, smooth skin. They should not be wrinkled or dry. Many commercial varieties tend to be a bit insipid, as they lack tartness, but there are some with an excellent balance of sweet and tart. Taste your way around until you find a blueberry with a flavor you like. Commercial blueberries are also called highbush blueberries. **Wild blueberries,** sometimes called lowbush blueberries, are intensely flavored; they are abundant in late summer and early fall, but also available frozen. **Dried blueberries** have a rich flavor and are outstanding in baked goods or granola.

Huckleberries, the name given to several close relatives, tend to have larger seeds. Despite this mark against them, most huckleberries are highly prized—especially the red huckleberry, and the blue or Cascade huckleberry, which can have an intense, ultrablueberry flavor.

To store fresh blueberries and huckleberries, see 177. They may be paired successfully with lemon, cream, yogurt, cinnamon, and peaches. A lack of tartness in blueberries can be remedied with a little lemon juice, or, for something like preserves, combine fully ripe berries with some that are underripe and have a pinkish tinge. Also see Blueberry Muffins, 633, Blueberry and Peach Buckle, 684, and Blueberry Butter, 916.

BLUEBERRY COMPOTE

About 1¼ cups

Serve this richly flavored compote over pancakes or waffles, ice cream, or cheesecake.

Combine in a medium saucepan:

2 cups fresh or frozen blueberries, wild blueberries, or huckleberries

¼ cup sugar

Finely grated zest of 1 lemon

2 tablespoons lemon juice

(1 cinnamon stick or ¼ teaspoon ground cinnamon)

(½ vanilla bean, split lengthwise)

Bring to a boil over medium-high, then reduce the heat and simmer until the berries release their juices and the mixture looks soupy, about 5 minutes. Stir together in a small bowl:

1 teaspoon cornstarch

1 tablespoon cold water

Stir the cornstarch mixture into the blueberries and simmer until the sauce thickens, about 1 minute. Let cool and keep refrigerated. Serve cold or warmed.

ABOUT BLACKBERRIES, RASPBERRIES, AND OTHER CANE BERRIES

Raspberries, blackberries, and their tasty relatives (collectively known as **cane berries**) are among the most appealing of berries: plump and deeply colored, they almost explode in the mouth in a burst of sweet-tart juice. Raspberries, of which there are only a few species, come in four colors: red, amber, purple, and black. There are hundreds of species of blackberries, which are truly tart—whether wild or domestic—and often require sugar to make them palatable.

There are a host of hybrid cane berries that are every bit as succulent as their parents: **Marionberries, olallieberries,** and **logan-**

berries all look like blackberries, though loganberries are a deep red color rather than blackish purple, and Marionberries are particularly large and juicy. **Boysenberries** are exceptionally delicious, with a good balance of sweetness and acidity. **Tayberries** resemble raspberries and are sweet and large.

All cane berries are in season during the summer; they should be plump, firm, and deeply colored. Since these berries are very fragile, handle and wash them with great care. They are especially susceptible to spoiling from surface molds, so consider rinsing them with vinegar, 177. For more storage information, see About Berries, 177.

Raspberries are good partners to heavy cream, sour cream, and crème fraîche, vanilla, lime zest, apricots and peaches, and thyme. For other recipes, see Fresh Berry Coulis, 805, Fruit Brûlé, 172, Raspberry Sorbet, 847, and Raspberry Streusel Bars, 766.

BLACKBERRY OR RASPBERRY FLUMMERY

4 to 6 servings

This can be eaten for breakfast, with oatmeal and milk or yogurt, or as a dessert.

Combine in a large saucepan:

1 quart blackberries or raspberries
½ cup water
2 tablespoons to ⅓ cup sugar, to taste
¼ teaspoon ground cinnamon
Pinch of salt

Bring to a boil over medium-high heat, then reduce the heat and simmer, stirring gently, for 5 minutes. Stir together in a small bowl:

3 tablespoons water
2 tablespoons cornstarch

Stir the cornstarch mixture into the berry mixture and cook, stirring until thick, about 3 minutes. Cool, then refrigerate until chilled. If desired, serve drizzled with:

(Heavy cream)

ABOUT CRANBERRIES

Cranberries grow on low shrubs. To harvest the ripe berries, cranberry growers flood the beds in the fall. Cranberries are incredibly tart—too tart to eat on their own. However, they make delectable sauces or relishes and baked goods. Fresh cranberries are available in markets from October through early January. They should be bright red, plump, and firm. They keep exceptionally well and can be bought several weeks ahead and refrigerated in their original packaging. Or, spread them on a baking sheet and freeze, transfer to bags, and store frozen for up to 1 year.

To prepare for cooking or freezing, pick over the cranberries, removing any shriveled berries or twigs, then rinse. Frozen cranberries may be used straight from the freezer, no thawing necessary. **Dried cranberries** are usually sweetened, although you may find unsweetened ones at natural foods stores. Use them in baked goods or granola. To plump dried cranberries, see 169.

Cranberries' tartness makes them ideal for sweet-savory combinations; they are superb with pork, game birds, venison, and turkey. Pair cranberries with ginger, orange zest and juice, cinnamon, star anise, and fresh, soft cheeses.

CRANBERRY SAUCE

6 to 8 servings

I. Wash and pick over:

4 cups cranberries (1 pound)

Place in a saucepan and add:

2 cups water

Bring to a boil over medium-high heat, cover, reduce the heat, and simmer until the skins burst, 3 to 4 minutes. Put the berries through a food mill, or puree in a blender or food processor. Transfer the puree to a saucepan and stir in:

2 cups sugar
1½ tablespoons lemon juice

Bring to a rolling boil and immediately remove from the heat.

II. JELLIED CRANBERRY SAUCE

Proceed as for **I, above,** and boil the sauce for an additional 5 minutes. Skim any scum or foam from the surface of the sauce and strain through a medium-mesh sieve into a 4-cup mold coated with cooking spray. Cover and refrigerate until firmly set, at least 4 hours or overnight. To unmold, submerge the bottom of the mold in warm water just long enough to encourage the sauce to release. Invert onto a serving plate.

WHOLE-BERRY CRANBERRY SAUCE

6 to 8 servings

Bring to a boil in a medium saucepan, stirring until the sugar is dissolved:

2 cups sugar
2 cups water

Boil the syrup for 5 minutes, then add:

4 cups cranberries (1 pound), picked over

Simmer the berries in the syrup very gently, uncovered, without stirring, until the berries are translucent, about 5 minutes. Skim off any foam. If desired, add:

(Finely grated zest of 1 orange)

Pour the berries into a serving dish. Chill until firm.

ADDITIONS TO CRANBERRY SAUCE

Prepare Cranberry Sauce I, or Whole-Berry Cranberry Sauce, above, adding along with the sugar:

Up to ½ teaspoon coarsely ground black pepper, ground cinnamon, or Five-Spice Powder, 590
Up to ¼ teaspoon ground cloves
1 tablespoon minced peeled fresh ginger or ½ teaspoon ground ginger
Up to 1 tablespoon minced thyme or rosemary
3 tablespoons port, bourbon, dry red wine, cherry or pomegranate juice, or balsamic vinegar
½ cup dried cherries, currants, or raisins
1 cup diced apples
¼ cup minced shallots
½ cup pecans or walnuts, toasted, 1005, and chopped
1 tablespoon molasses or sorghum syrup, or to taste

Instead of 2 cups sugar, you may sweeten cranberry sauce with one of the following:

2 cups brown sugar or coconut sugar
1 to 1½ cups honey or maple syrup, to taste

UNCOOKED CRANBERRY RELISH

About 2½ cups

Pick over:

One 12-ounce package cranberries (3 cups)

Cut into eighths, removing any seeds:

1 unpeeled navel orange

Place half the cranberries and half the orange in a food processor and pulse until the mixture is finely chopped but not pureed. Transfer to a medium bowl. Repeat with the remaining cranberries and orange. Stir in:

1 cup sugar, or to taste

Cover and refrigerate for at least 1 day, or up to 2 weeks.

ABOUT GOOSEBERRIES

These translucent orbs are tart, sweet, and pop in your mouth like a grape. There is limited cultivation of gooseberries in this country; if you are to find them fresh at all, it will be from a farm stand, farmers' market, a friend or neighbor, or your own backyard. The common varieties are the size and shape of marbles and are pale green, yellow, amber, pink, or purplish when ripe. We occasionally encounter dark-purple **jostaberries,** a cross between two gooseberry types and black currants, below.

Early summer is prime gooseberry season. To store, see About Berries, 177. Gooseberries are generally harvested when underripe, sour, and green and used in recipes that cook them with sugar. When fully ripe, though, gooseberries are sweet enough to eat out of hand. To "top and tail" a gooseberry means to pinch off the stem at the top end and the blossom remnant at the other end.

Gooseberry fool is a classic English dessert. To make it, prepare Fruit Puree, 172, using gooseberries, cool the puree completely, and prepare Fruit Fool I or II, 173, using the gooseberry puree instead of the fresh fruit puree. Do not confuse gooseberries with Cape gooseberries, 196, which are an unrelated species and react differently in cooking. Gooseberries go well with strawberries, heavy cream or clotted cream, elderflowers or elderflower liqueur, and toasted almonds. See also Gooseberry or Currant Jelly, 910.

ABOUT CURRANTS

Currants are in peak season from mid-June through August, depending on climate. These tiny, round, shiny berries divide into two principal types, **red currants** and **black currants. White currants** are a less acidic variety of red. Black currants are much less common than red as they are difficult to harvest, but should you find them, snatch them up! They have an exquisite flavor. **Dried currants** are actually a type of dried grape. See About Grapes, 186, for more information.

Currants are very tart and seedy and are generally cooked. Red currants make one of the world's most beloved jellies, while black currants, sweeter and fuller in flavor, make delicious jams as well as the liqueur crème de cassis, a key ingredient in Kir, 42. Currants are generally sold in clusters still attached to their stems. They are beautiful as a garnish for chocolate cakes or fruit tarts, and they are stunning in fruit salad. Use a fork or your fingers to gently free them from their stems. Store refrigerated in a covered container with a paper towel inside. Currants pair with game, rich red meats, cream, and chocolate. Also see Gooseberry or Currant Jelly, 910, and Five-Fruit Jam Cockaigne, 913.

ABOUT MULBERRIES AND ELDERBERRIES

While not related, both of these fruits grow on trees and are primarily foraged, though they may show up at farm stands in the summer. **Mulberries,** which look somewhat like elongated blackberries, are very sweet, sometimes one-dimensionally so, and make delicious syrups, liqueurs, and preserves. White mulberries are very sweet, with little to no tartness. You may also find dried purple or white mulberries, which can be used as for other dried fruits. **Elderberries** are small, purplish berries that grow in sprays. Freeze the sprays on baking sheets, then shake them over a deep bowl or inside a paper grocery bag—the berries will drop off. Elderberries are used primarily to make wine, jelly, and jam, since they are often too tart to eat raw. You may use them to make Fruit Syrup, 16, which can then be used to flavor and color beverages and cocktails. Keep in mind that ➤ every part of the elderberry plant except for the berries and flowers is poisonous; underripe, green elderberries may also harbor toxins. While a stem here and there will not hurt, it is worth taking the time to remove as many stems and green berries as possible before using. Both mulberries and elderberries should be kept refrigerated in a covered container lined with a paper towel.

Elderflowers are intoxicatingly fragrant and traditionally used to infuse jams, custards, and cordials. We have used them to infuse the cream for Panna Cotta, 821, with excellent results. Elderflowers go well with other springtime delicacies such as strawberries, rhubarb, and gooseberries. Store elderflowers in a container lined with a paper towel in the refrigerator for up to 3 days.

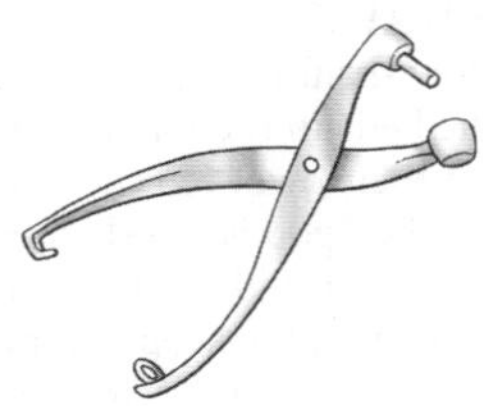

Cherry pitter

ABOUT CHERRIES

These are available in two sharply contrasting types: sweet cherries and sour, or tart cherries. The peak season for **sweet cherries** runs from late May through August. Two principal kinds of sweet cherries are found in markets: the familiar red **Bings** and the golden **Rainiers** or **Queen Annes.** In purchasing either type, select those that are plump, glossy, and firm. The darkest-red Bings are the ripest; Rainiers and Queen Annes should have a rose blush. Sweet cherries can be refrigerated in a covered container for up to 1 week. They are superb in Fruit Salad, 167.

Sour cherries, or "pie cherries," are available in some markets from June to August. Cooking and sugar mellow their tartness, but we also enjoy them eaten out of hand. They have an incredible flavor and are usually not too tart to enjoy on their own. The **Early Richmond cherry** is the first pie cherry of the season. Widely cultivated varieties derive from the **Morello.** The **Montmorency cherry** is the most commonly available sour cherry and is a stunning fire-engine red. Select and store sour cherries as for sweet cherries, keeping in mind that they tend to be more fragile than their sweet counterparts and consequently do not keep as long, 3 to 4 days. As their season is short, we often buy far more sour cherries than we can use right away and tray-freeze them for later use, 882. All cherries are most easily and neatly pitted with a cherry pitter, 180.

Dried cherries tend to be soft and sweet and are a good alternative to fresh cherries for some baked goods, as adding them will not contribute any moisture to doughs or batters. To plump dried cherries, see 946. All cherries have an affinity for spirits, especially kirsch and Maraschino liqueur, both made from the fruit, as well as dark rum, brandy, and amaretto. They are also exceptional with almonds, basil, tarragon, cinnamon, vanilla, and chocolate.

SOUR CHERRIES WITH RICOTTA, HONEY, AND ALMONDS

4 servings

The quality of the ricotta is crucial to the success of this recipe. We recommend making some from scratch, 965, but you may also find high-quality ricotta at specialty markets. Instead of the almonds, try crushing amaretti cookies and sprinkling them on top.

Combine in a small mixing bowl:

1⅓ cups whole-milk ricotta (12 ounces)
3 tablespoons honey

Divide the ricotta among 4 bowls. Use a spoon to make a depression in the center of the ricotta and fill each with:

¼ cup pitted sour cherries (1 cup total)

Pour over each:

1 tablespoon kirsch or Maraschino liqueur (¼ cup total)

Sprinkle over each:

2 tablespoons coarsely chopped Marcona almonds or toasted, 1005, almonds (½ cup total)

CHERRIES JUBILEE

About 1 cup

Heat in a small saucepan over medium heat:

½ pound Bing or other sweet cherries, pitted and halved
¼ cup sugar

Cook, stirring, until the sugar is dissolved and the cherries exude enough juice to create a sauce. Add:

¼ cup brandy, bourbon, or white rum

Heat until the liquor is warm, then carefully ignite it with a long wooden match or lighter. When the flames have died down, add:

2 tablespoons kirsch

Serve hot on or with:

Sweet Crêpes, 645, vanilla ice cream, or any cheesecake, 752–54

MACERATED CHERRIES WITH HERBS

4 servings

Serve as a side dish to grilled or roasted poultry or pork, or as a dessert with ice cream and pound cake.

Mix together in a medium bowl:

1 pound sweet cherries, pitted and halved
¼ cup sugar
3 to 4 tablespoons lemon juice or balsamic vinegar, to taste
¼ teaspoon black pepper

Let marinate for at least 15 minutes at room temperature, stirring once or twice, or up to 2 days in the refrigerator. Mix in just before serving:

2 tablespoons chopped basil, mint, or tarragon

Serve at room temperature.

ABOUT WILD AND UNCOMMON BERRIES

Many wild-growing berries can be foraged if you are lucky to live in a climate that supports them. **Dewberries** look like very small blackberries (and taste much like them as well), and they grow wild across much of the southeastern United States. **Thimbleberries** are a wild treat, pleasantly tart, deep red, and even more fragile than raspberries. **Salmonberries** have a pinkish color and can be a tasty trailside snack, although their flavor is muted. **Mayhaws** can be found in the deep South near rivers, streams, or marshland, and they are commonly used to make jelly. **Salal berries** are plentiful in the Pacific Northwest and, like many wild berries, were an important indigenous food. **Aronia** or **chokeberries** are almost black in color and are quite tart, though they are good when processed with sugar or other, sweeter berries.

Some berries are more commonly found dried or processed than fresh. **Barberries** are small, tart red berries frequently used in Persian cuisine in rice dishes, baked goods, and sweets. **Goji berries** have a dull red color and are elongated. They are more sweet than tart, but also have a savoriness that is sometimes likened to cherry tomatoes. **Açai berries,** deep-purple fruits from a type of palm, are readily available as a powder or a frozen puree for using in smoothies.

Rasp grater, citrus juicer, citrus reamer

ABOUT CITRUS FRUITS

Citrus represents another immense fruit family with thousands of members, though only a small fraction of those are commercially viable. All citrus varieties are hybrids of some combination of three citrus fruits: the pomelo, mandarin, and citron. Choose citrus fruits that feel firm in the hand but slightly yielding (rock-hard fruits tend to yield less juice) and heavy for their size. When they appear at the market, citrus fruits are usually covered with a thin coating of wax. The wax is harmless, but it is undesirable if you are grating the zest. Remove the wax by scrubbing with a brush under running water.

When grating or zesting, ➤ do not take off more than the highly colored outer layer of the peel as the white pith is bitter. The best tool for removing very thin strips of zest is a zester; a vegetable peeler or channel knife, 18, may be used to remove wider strips of zest. A rasp grater, 181, shaves off the zest in very fine shreds. Or you can use the smallest holes on a box grater.

To extract citrus juice, first roll the fruit beneath your palm over a hard surface, exerting pressure. Cut the fruit crosswise in half, and if juicing only one fruit, remove the juice with a citrus reamer, shown on 181—a pair of tongs in the closed position also works well in a pinch. When juicing several fruits, a standard citrus juicer with a bowl for collecing juice, shown on 181, is ideal, as is a hinged citrus juicer or an electric citrus juicer. ➤ Citrus juice, notably lemon and lime, is probably one of the most important ingredients in all cooking. We always have these two fruits in our kitchen. They brighten rich dishes (or can be used in sauces to complement rich dishes), are crucial in salads of all kinds, and provide much-needed acidity and complexity to baked goods. The peels of most thick-skinned citrus are prime for candying, 876.

Citrus fruits do not ripen off the tree, but they are usually picked ripe. Store them at room temperature for up to a week or refrigerated for 3 to 4 weeks.

To section citrus fruit, cut off the top and bottom of the fruit so it will sit flat on a cutting board. Use a sharp knife to carve off the peel and white pith, following the curve of the fruit with the knife and cutting away as little of the fruit pulp as possible. Hold the fruit over a bowl to catch all the juices, and loosen the sections by cutting on either side of the white membranes that separate the citrus segments. Lift out each section (sometimes called a **suprême**) in one piece and remove any seeds. After removing the citrus sections, squeeze all the juice from the membranes into the bowl.

Preparing citrus fruit sections (suprêmes)

ABOUT LEMONS AND LIMES

Both of these fruits are quite indispensable. ➤ A squirt of lemon or lime juice can enhance the natural flavor of any ingredient, just as a dash of salt does. For more information on zest, juice, and peels, see About Citrus Fruits, 181, and Citrus Zest and Juice, 972. The juiciest lemons are those with thin, smooth, yellow skins. **Meyer lemons,** a lemon-tangerine cross, are sweeter and less tart than common lemons, have a distinctive aroma and flavor, and may be added to tossed salads and fruit cups as well as desserts or marmalade, 920–21. They may also be used in any way that ordinary lemons are or they may be preserved as for Salt-Preserved Lemons, 942.

The most common limes are **Persian limes,** also known as **Bearss** or **Tahiti limes.** Tiny **Key limes** have a tart, complex flavor that some find indispensable for Key Lime Pie, 682, although we often irreverently substitute regular lime juice with no ill effects. The fragrant zest and leaves of the small, wrinkly **Makrut lime** (unfortunately long known by the South African racial slur *kaffir*) is often used in Southeast Asian dishes; for the use of its leaves as an herb, see 998. Makrut lime juice is fragrant as well, but incredibly bitter (it is generally not used). **Finger limes** are a bit of an oddity, even for the citrus family. They are 1 to 2 inches long and slender. Like all citrus fruits, their juice is contained in little vesicles or pouches, but those of the finger lime are durable enough and separate readily enough to be used as a garnish, providing an appealing pop of lime flavor. **Rangpur limes** are actually a cross between lemons and mandarin oranges; they are sometimes used as an aromatic in gin making, and we can attest that their juice is an excellent addition to a Gin and Tonic, 20. For dried **black limes,** or **loomi,** see 956.

In a pinch, lime juice can be substituted for lemon juice as a seasoning, and vice versa, although the flavor is different. For lemon- and lime-centric recipes, see Salt-Preserved Lemons, 942, Citrus Granita, 850, Lemon Curd, 802, Lemonade or Limeade, 13, Lemon Bars, 767, Lemon Meringue Pie, 681, Key Lime Pie, 682, Ohio Shaker Lemon Pie, 681, Avgolemono, 84, Sopa de Lima, 94, and Coconut-Cucumber Salad, 185.

ABOUT CITRONS

Though relatively scarce and little consumed, we owe many of our beloved citrus fruits to the existence of citron. Along with pomelo and mandarin oranges, citron is one of the oldest citrus types, and all citrus varieties—from lemons to bergamot to grapefruit and Key limes—are the hybridized grandchildren of these three ancestors.

Like bergamot oranges and Makrut limes, citrons are primarily grown for their fragrant peel rather than their juice. The zest and thick rind is candied and used in cakes and desserts. Traditionally, citrons were used as a table decoration (or put in linen closets). Their resinous fragrance can perfume an entire room. The yellow, octopus-tentacled **Buddha's hand citron** is almost entirely rind and zest, with no pulp or juice. **Etrog citron** looks like a large, elongated lemon and has a bumpy or ridged surface. Though its rind is still quite thick, this citron has a bit of juicy flesh in the center. Other citron types abound in groves around the Mediterranean: They range from green to yellow in color and have varying levels of acidity and juiciness. Some remain the size of a lemon, others may be as large as a cantaloupe.

Buddha's hand citron and rounded, Mediterranean varieties can occasionally be found in the fall and winter at specialty grocery stores or at farmers' markets in citrus-growing areas.

Candied citron is sold in strips or small pieces; it is often tasteless, which has given the fruit an ill-deserved reputation. Higher-quality candied citron can be found at Middle Eastern and Indian markets or online, where it is often sold in quarters or halves. To candy your own citron peel, see 876.

ABOUT ORANGES

The orange is a hybrid of the mandarin and the pomelo. It made its way from China to the Mediterranean to North America, where it now grows abundantly in Florida, Texas, and California.

Sweet oranges are often broken into several groups. Common or "white" oranges include the ever-popular **Valencia.** Known as "juicers," they make up the majority of the yearly crop. Though they are primarily grown for juice, Valencias are perfectly good to eat out of hand. **Navel oranges** are so named because they grow a small, second fruit opposite the stem end when left to mature on the tree (young navels may not show any sign of this). Navels are considered table oranges, or "eaters." The flesh of **Cara Cara navels** has a beautiful, reddened hue and is especially fine eating. **Blood oranges,** with their dark maroon flesh, are available from December through March. These fruits are absolutely striking to the eye and have a flavor to match. They are more tart than regular oranges and incredibly fragrant. **Moro** and **Tarocco** blood oranges are the most commonly available varieties, and they may have a reddish blush on their skins. The color of the skin is not indicative of the color of the pulp, which varies.

The **sour orange** (also known as **bitter orange** or **Seville orange**) is harder to find, but worth seeking out in late fall and winter. Sour oranges are best known for their use in classic English marmalades, 920, the intense flavor their rinds impart to liqueurs, and the fragrance their blossoms lend to orange flower water, 980. Sour orange juice is an essential ingredient in many Caribbean and Yucatecan sauces, such as Mojo, 567, and Habanero-Citrus Hot Sauce, 571. To approximate the taste when no sour oranges can be found, we suggest equal parts lime and orange juice for convenience, but adding grapefruit juice to the orange side of the equation is said to be more accurate. **Bergamot oranges** are best known for their role in flavoring Earl Grey tea. Their rind and juice are very aromatic. They are not very good for eating out of hand, but their fragrance can be harnessed in baked goods and is used in some liqueurs.

Mandarins are small and have loose, easily peeled rinds and juicy, sweet flesh. **Tangerines** and **clementines** are both mandarin hybrids that are likewise small, juicy, and sweet. **Satsumas** are a sweet, seedless variety that are very fragrant and have loose skin—their fruit is excellent, but their peel is also of culinary value. Dry it for using in stews and desserts. **Tangors,** mandarin-orange crosses, have the flattened look, loose skins, and juiciness of mandarins but taste like oranges. **Kishus** are another mandarin type but are very tiny and intensely flavorful. The **yuzu** is a satsuma hybrid rarely found in US markets, though bottled yuzu juice may be found at Japanese grocery stores. Yuzu juice is often mixed with soy sauce and served alongside grilled matsutake mushrooms. It is also an ingredient in ponzu sauce, 1020, which is sometimes used as a condiment for sashimi.

Tangelos are tangerine-pomelo crosses. **Minneolas** are a type of tangelo instantly recognizable by their fiery orange rind and prominent knobby neck. They are juicy, but also quite tart, and some prove seedy. **Ugli fruits** are large, bumpy-skinned, yellowish tangelo-types with a decided grapefruit flavor. However, they are much sweeter and juicier.

Kumquats are the size of robins' eggs. They are edible in their entirety, both rind and flesh, and unlike other citrus, the skin is very sweet and without bitterness, and the pulp is very sour. There are two principal types: an elongated oval variety called **Nagami,** and a slightly larger round variety called **Meiwa.** Both may be eaten raw, either out of hand or sliced in Fruit Salad, 167, though the oval variety is delicious when candied, 168, made into preserves, or served as a compote, 184. **Mandarinquats** are a cross between the mandarin and the kumquat. They are small, but a fair bit larger than kumquats and have an oval shape with a protruding stem end. They may be eaten peel and all, are bracingly tart, and have seeds. We hoard these when we find them.

All members of the orange family—excepting perfumed bergamot oranges, yuzus, and seedy sour oranges—are delicious in sweet fruit salads as well as savory preparations like Sicilian Orange, Fennel, and Onion Salad, 129. Orange juice provides a brightening effect in cakes, compotes, sauces both sweet and savory, marinades, and sherbets or granitas. Every citrus season we like to dehydrate, 944, the peels of the thinner-skinned varieties such as satsumas and tangerines for using in mulled cider or wine, stews, or desserts. Oranges pair well with vanilla, other citrus fruits, dried dates, pistachios, almonds, chocolate, and ginger. Also see About Making Marmalade, 920.

ORANGES IN SYRUP

About 5 cups

Serve these with ice cream; use any leftover syrup in cocktails.

Wash and dry, grate the zest from, and set aside:

1 large navel orange

Combine the zest in a small saucepan with:

1 cup sugar
½ cup orange marmalade
¼ cup water

Bring to a boil over medium-high heat, stirring constantly, then reduce the heat as low as possible and simmer for 10 minutes. Remove the syrup from the heat and let cool to tepid. If desired, stir in:

(2 tablespoons Cognac or other brandy or 1 teaspoon orange flower water)

Set aside. Slice off the peel as for sectioning, 182 (but do not separate the segments), from the zested orange as well as:

5 large navel oranges

Cut the oranges crosswise into ¼-inch-thick slices. Arrange them in slightly overlapping rows in a large shallow dish and pour the syrup over them. Cover and refrigerate for 12 to 24 hours. Serve with:

Lemony Butter Wafers, 774, Tuiles, 787, or Almond Macaroons, 774

KUMQUAT COMPOTE

6 servings

Spoon this bright and versatile compote over yogurt, ice cream, Panna Cotta, 821, or any custard.

Combine in a saucepan with water to cover:

2 cups kumquats

Bring to a boil, then drain. Slice the kumquats into rings and remove any seeds. Combine in a medium saucepan:

2 cups water
1 cup sugar
(½ vanilla bean, split lengthwise)

Bring to a boil over medium-high heat. Add the kumquats and simmer until tender and the sugar is dissolved, about 5 minutes. Scoop out the kumquats and transfer to a bowl. Boil to reduce the syrup by half. Strain the syrup over the kumquats, cover, and refrigerate until chilled.

ABOUT GRAPEFRUIT AND POMELO

Grapefruits are a hybrid of the pomelo and the orange. They are sweet and juicy and get their notable bitterness from a flavonoid called naringin. You are likely to find a few grapefruit varieties, including **Oroblanco,** which has pale pulp and is very sweet and juicy with no bitterness, **Star Ruby** and **Rio Red,** which have bright pink pulp, and the **White Marsh,** which is one of the most common grapefruit varieties grown today.

Pomelo, or **shaddock,** is an ancestor of today's grapefruit. This large citrus fruit is at least grapefruit-sized, often bigger. It can be round or vaguely pear-shaped, with firm white or pink flesh. The **Chandler,** the most common pomelo, has delicious sweet pink flesh, usually with few seeds. For both grapefruits and pomelos, look for heavy fruit with glossy skins. Blemishes are not necessarily an indicator of substandard fruit.

White, pink, and ruby red grapefruit have their peak season from January to June. Grapefruits and kin are enhanced by candied ginger, honey, and sparkling wine. Marvelous in tossed salads, with its tart, bracing flavor, grapefruit also makes an excellent companion for rich foods like avocados, fatty fish, and shellfish, especially scallops and shrimp. For all such purposes, section the fruit, 182, as the pith can be off-puttingly bitter. Grapefruit peel is a good candidate for candying, 168. Pomelos are used in the Thai salad called yam som-o, which is made with cooked shrimp, broken up pomelo segments, coconut, chiles, shallots, lime juice, and fish sauce. Also see Seared Scallop, Grapefruit, and Radicchio Salad, 121, Avocado and Citrus Salad, 125, Beet, Fennel, and Citrus Salad with Horseradish, 125, and Pink Grapefruit Sorbet, 848.

BROILED GRAPEFRUIT

4 servings

This dish can be served for dessert or breakfast. If you find it more convenient, you may use a blowtorch to brûlé the cut grapefruit instead of using the broiler.

Adjust an oven rack so the grapefruit will be about 4 inches below the heating element. Preheat the broiler. Halve horizontally:

2 grapefruits, preferably pink or red

Remove any large seeds. If desired, snip out the tough centers. Loosen each section by cutting along the membranes and pith with a grapefruit knife or small serrated knife. Place the halves on a small rimmed baking sheet. Sprinkle each half with:

1 tablespoon white sugar or brown sugar (¼ cup total)
(Pinches of ground ginger or minced candied ginger)

Broil the grapefruit until the tops begin to brown, about 5 minutes. Serve at once. If desired, garnish the centers of the grapefruit with:

(4 small raspberries or strawberries)

ABOUT COCONUT

Coconuts are a large nut from the *Cocos nucifera* palm tree. While not botanically a fruit, coconut deserves a place here because of how we tend to use it: Coconut is typically added to fruity dishes or as a way of imparting aroma and sweetness to savory dishes, baked goods, and beverages.

Coconuts are most commonly sold young and green, or mature and already stripped of their thick, fibrous outer husk. If the coconut is green, the top can be simply lopped off with a large, heavy knife or cleaver (use caution). Inside you will find coconut water and edible jelly-like pulp or very soft white coconut meat. Young white, Thai coconuts may be opened by turning the coconut on its side and cutting off the white fiber at the top of the nut with a cleaver to reveal the hard shell beneath. Then, with the coconut still on its side, carefully whack the hard shell with the cleaver, lodging the blade in the nut. Turn the coconut right side up and twist the cleaver to pop off the top of the shell and reveal the coconut water inside.

If you live in a place where coconuts grow abundantly, you may find mature ones still in the husk, which you will need to remove yourself. Lacking power tools, you can throw it repeatedly onto the sharp edge of a large rock. If it doesn't crack open enough so that the husk pulls away, you may escalate the situation and use an ax or cleaver. For the last two tools ➤ use caution in selecting your cutting surface so that it will not damage or be damaged by sharp blades, and take care not to maim yourself or others with a stray, glancing blow.

Assuming you are not deterred or too exhausted to proceed, remove the husk to reveal the fiber-covered nut. Shake it. A sloshing noise means that the nut is fresh and that you can count on some coconut water.

To open the hard dark brown shell of the mature coconut, hold it sideways over a large bowl. Find the three ridges that run from pole to pole on the coconut (sometimes these are easier to see if you look at the coconut from the top where the "eyes" are). Tap the nut briskly on these ridges with the spine of a cleaver or a hammer. The coconut should split in half, and the bowl underneath will catch the coconut water. Place the coconut halves cut side down on a cutting board and use the spine of the cleaver to break the coconut into smaller chunks. Pry the white coconut meat from the hard shell with a butter knife. Usually, a thin, brown, papery layer of shell will come away with the meat. This can be eaten or peeled off with a paring knife or vegetable peeler. The resulting coconut flesh can be grated on a box grater.

Coconut milk and **coconut cream** are made from the firm, mature white meat of the nut. For their use as an ingredient, see 973. For **coconut sugar,** see 1025.

To make coconut milk, use a vegetable peeler to remove the thin brown skin. Cut the meat into small chunks and chop in the blender, no more than ½ cup at a time. Return all the chopped coconut meat to the blender and add the coconut water and about 2 cups hot water per coconut. Blend until smooth. When the mixture has cooled, strain the coconut milk through several layers of cheesecloth or a thin kitchen towel. Squeeze the meat retained in the cloth until dry. Refrigerate the drained liquid; it will separate, and the coconut fat will rise to the top and solidify. It may be heated and stirred back into the coconut milk or removed and used as a cooking fat.

Pair coconut with other tropical ingredients such as lime juice, mango, pineapple, papaya, rum, banana, chocolate, lemongrass, Makrut lime, and chiles. Also see Coconut Milk Cake Cockaigne, 724, Coconut Macaroons, 775, Coconut Rice, 333, Coconut Cream Pie, 680, and Coconut Ice Cream, 842.

COCONUT-CUCUMBER SALAD

5 servings

Serve this salad with grilled fish or shrimp. Mango and papaya are great additions.

Combine in a large bowl:

2 cups grated fresh coconut meat
1 cup grated seeded cucumber
½ cup chopped cilantro
Finely grated zest and juice of 1 lime
1 jalapeño pepper, seeded and minced
¾ teaspoon salt
¼ teaspoon black pepper
2 tablespoons olive oil

Let stand for 15 minutes before serving.

ABOUT DATES

Date palms originated in Mesopotamia and were subsequently spread by nomads making their way across the desert regions of North Africa and the Middle East. They planted the palms at oases to serve as a staple food for their long journeys. Dates are now cultivated in Asia and North America as well.

There are well over one thousand date varieties, but the most common are **Medjool, Deglet Noor,** and **Khadrawy dates.** All were first cultivated in the Middle East. There are three overarching types of dates—soft, semi-dry, and dry. Medjool and Khadrawy dates are soft, and Deglet Noor dates are semi-dry. Dry varieties, such as **Thoory dates,** are chewy or almost crisp.

If you live in a date-growing area, such as California, you may find fresh dates in the fall. They have a mild flavor and delicate texture, and they are delicious when paired with creamy fresh cheeses or ripe Camembert. Look for soft, brown fruits. Immature dates are tinged with green, but even mature-looking dates can still be very hard; at both stages they can be astringent. If this is the case, ripen them at room temperature until they soften.

Dried dates are sold whole (pitted or unpitted) and chopped. To pit dried dates, cut a slit lengthwise in the date and extract the large pit. Dates are easier to slice or chop ➤ if first frozen for 1 hour, or use oiled kitchen shears to snip them into pieces. Because they are high in sugar, dried dates keep for about a month at room temperature, several months in the refrigerator, and up to 1 year in the freezer.

Dates are incredibly rich in sugar, which accounts for the grayish crystallization that shows up on both fresh and dried dates. This high sugar content makes them an excellent, high-energy snack for hiking and backpacking. They also make a lovely dessert. Serve them as is with tangerines or mandarins, or stuff them with cream cheese and nuts, marzipan, or fondant flavored with almond extract and rose water. Dates go well with oranges, almonds, walnuts, coconut, rosewater or orange flower water, and pistachios. See Brown Rice Salad with Dates and Oranges, 131, Date Nut Bread, 626, and Sticky Toffee Pudding, 831.

SAUTÉED DATES WITH ALMONDS

4 servings

These dates straddle the sweet-savory divide with grace. They can be the perfect end to an elegant dinner or part of breakfast.

Melt or heat in a medium skillet over medium heat:

2 tablespoons butter or olive oil

Add and sauté until the butter starts to brown and the dates are heated through, about 2 minutes:

12 large pitted dates
(1 teaspoon minced fresh rosemary)

Sprinkle with:

3 tablespoons Marcona almonds
Flaky sea salt such as Maldon

Serve warm.

SAVORY STUFFED DATES

30 pieces

To prepare these in advance, stuff the dates as directed, place in an airtight container, and refrigerate until ready to serve. Bake as directed, but increase the baking time to 15 minutes.

Preheat the oven to 350°F. Have ready:

30 large, moist pitted dates

Mix together in a medium bowl until smooth:

4 ounces fresh goat cheese
2 ounces cream cheese, softened
1 tablespoon minced thyme
½ teaspoon black pepper

Stuff the dates with the goat cheese mixture. Place on a baking sheet and bake until warmed through, 10 to 12 minutes. Serve warm.

ABOUT FIGS

A fig tree marked the founding of Rome, Siddhartha Gautama meditated his way toward enlightenment beneath one, and Adam and Eve used the leaves of the fig to hide their shame after the original sin. In brief, it is hard to overstate the importance of the fig in human history. For whatever reason—its soft, lobed leaves, sensual fruit, or broad canopy—the fig tree has captured our imagination for thousands of years.

There are hundreds of varieties of the fruit, in a multitude of shapes, sizes, and colors. There are four general categories of figs: **common figs, Smyrna figs, caprifigs,** and **San Pedro figs.** Common figs do not need to be pollinated to produce fruit, making them the most popular choice for backyard gardeners. The best known of the common figs are the **Brown Turkey,** which has purplish brown skin and is sweet and mild, and the **Black Mission,** which is dark purple and tastes rich and earthy. **Desert King** and **Kadota** are also common figs, both with green skin and deep red flesh. Smyrna figs must be pollinated by fig wasps, which breed inside the flowers of the caprifig. Caprifigs do not produce edible fruit, but they are needed because they are hosts to the wasps that will carry pollen to Smyrna figs. **Calimyrnas** are Smyrna figs that are grown in California, and they have a buttery, nutty flavor. San Pedro figs have two potential annual crops—the first does not require pollination, but the second does. **Fig leaves** are also of culinary value. They have a tropical flavor and aroma, somewhat like coconut. Use them to wrap fish for cooking on the grill or in coals, to infuse custards or ice cream bases, or to infuse spirits.

Fig season lasts for only a few weeks in late summer. They do not ripen off the tree, and once they are ripe they do not keep for very long. Thus, figs are one of the few fruits that cannot be found out of season in produce departments. Choose figs that are plump and with taut but yielding skins. Ripe figs can be stored covered and refrigerated for 3 or 4 days, but eat them as soon as possible. **Dried figs** will keep for much longer, about 8 months in the pantry or up to a year in the freezer.

Figs pair well with orange zest and juice, heavy cream or custard, honey, salty cured meats such as prosciutto or country ham, thyme and lavender, pistachios, mild fresh cheeses such as chèvre, Cognac and red wine, and gamy meats. Fresh figs are generally eaten raw but they are also delicious sautéed, baked, or deep-fried in batter, drizzled with honey, and sprinkled with sea salt. Follow the recipe for Fritter Batter for Fruit, 656, using 12 large figs. Grilled figs make an excellent accompaniment for grilled chicken, lamb, or pork, as well as a dessert, served with Crème Anglaise, 806, ripe Brie, or vanilla ice cream. Dried figs can be quite hard; plump as directed in About Dried and Candied Fruits, 168. Also see Fig Keplers, 784, Fig Jam, 913, and Fig and Pistachio Conserves, 919.

BAKED FIGS WITH RICOTTA

4 servings

Preheat the oven to 350°F. Combine in a small saucepan:

⅓ cup sugar
3 tablespoons water
Scraped seeds and pod from ½ vanilla bean, split lengthwise

Bring to a boil, stirring to dissolve the sugar. Remove the syrup from the heat and add:

¼ cup sweet or dry Marsala

Remove the stems and halve from top to bottom:

8 large fresh figs

Place cut side up in a shallow baking dish. Spoon the Marsala syrup over the figs and bake until the figs are tender, about 20 minutes. Meanwhile, stir together in a small bowl:

⅓ cup whole-milk ricotta
¼ cup heavy cream
1 teaspoon sugar

Place the figs in serving dishes, dab some of the cheese mixture into the center of each, and spoon the syrup around them. Serve warm or at room temperature. If desired, garnish with:

(Shaved or grated semisweet or bittersweet chocolate or chopped toasted, 1005, almonds)

FIG COMPOTE WITH LEMON AND GINGER

6 to 8 servings

Excellent with yogurt, as part of a cheese plate, or alongside roast duck.

Combine in a medium saucepan:

1 pound dried figs, stems removed
3 cups water
Zest of 1 lemon removed in wide strips with a vegetable peeler
One 2-inch piece ginger, peeled and thinly sliced

Bring to a simmer, cover, and cook until the figs are plumped, 25 to 35 minutes. Add more water if needed to keep the figs covered. Add:

¾ cup sugar
2 tablespoons lemon juice

Simmer, uncovered, 5 minutes longer. Remove from the heat. If desired, stir in:

(1 to 2 tablespoons Cognac, brandy, or ruby port, to taste)

Serve warm or chilled. Store covered and refrigerated for up to 1 month.

ABOUT GRAPES AND RAISINS

There are thousands of varieties of grapes, but only a small percentage are sweet enough to be eaten out of hand or used in cooking. The most common commercially grown grapes are known as *vinifera.* They include wine grapes such as **chardonnay, cabernet sauvignon,** and **pinot noir,** as well as many table grapes (for more information on wines and the grape varieties used to produce them, see About Wine, 32). Seedless table grapes include the pale-green **Thompson seedless** and **Perlette grapes** and red varieties such as **Red Flame** and **Ruby Seedless.** Seedless grapes are the best for cooking and for fruit salads, 167.

Labrusca grapes are native to America. They have thicker skins that slip easily from the pulp, so they are sometimes referred to as slip-skins. Fox grapes are the principal American species; they are sweet, with a musky (or "foxy") flavor and aroma. **Concords** are the most famous variety of fox grapes, followed by **Catawba grapes.** Concords provide the archetypal grape flavor to purple grape juice and jelly. Look for them, and many other hybrids ranging in color from palest green or yellow to red to darkest purple, from July through October.

The other native American species are the **Muscadines,** of the vine *rotundifolia.* Most are sweet, and some are even muskier and more richly aromatic than the foxes. **Scuppernongs** are the best-known muscadine; they are so sweet their jelly can taste like honey. At their peak in September and October, they are usually too fragile to ship but are often found in local markets.

When buying grapes, always taste before committing. They should be plump, not shriveled, and they usually have a whitish bloom on the skins that is a natural waxy barrier to protect the fruit. It is harmless and flavorless, but you should rinse grapes before eating regardless. Grapes can be stored refrigerated in a perforated plastic bag for up to 1 week.

Grapes have a natural affinity for highly seasoned meats such as sausage or herbed roast or grilled lamb, fennel, cinnamon, star anise, rosemary and sage, and honey. See Grapes and Sausages, 512, Pickled Grapes, 928, Concord Grape Pie, 671, and Grape Jelly, 910, for more grape-centric recipes.

Raisins, which of course are dried grapes, divide into **seedless,** those that grow without seeds, and **seeded,** which have had the seeds removed. As their flavors are quite different, it is wise to use the specific type called for in recipes. The common dark and golden raisins sold at supermarkets are both dried Thompson seedless grapes and are interchangeable in recipes. **Muscat raisins** are very aromatic and sweet; they can be found around the holiday season and are used for baking into rich cakes and confections. **Sultanas** are larger, paler, and more acidic. They are most often found in specialty stores, as are **Monukkas,** which are large, dark, and sweet. Both are delicious eaten plain. Raisins are used in both sweet and savory dishes, such as Pasta con le Sarde, 297, Vegetable Tagine, 205, and Spinach with Pine Nuts and Raisins, 244. **Dried currants** are actually small raisins—traditionally dried Zante or Black Corinth grapes. They are commonly used in British baked goods, including scones, Hot Cross Buns, 619, Mincemeat Pie, 692, and Steamed Plum Pudding, 833. To plump raisins or currants, see 169.

Grape leaves are another important ingredient. They are used to make Dolmas, 63. For this purpose, the leaves are preserved in brine and sold in jars. Adding fresh grape leaves to pickles is an old-fashioned practice that serves a utilitarian as well as aesthetic purpose: In addition to adding visual flair to the pickle jar, grape leaves contain tannins, which help vegetables such as cucumbers stay crisp, 923. Grape leaves can also be used to wrap food, 1056, for cooking over a fire or in coals.

ABOUT GUAVAS

Guavas vary widely in color and size. **Cattleya guavas** (also known as **Strawberry guavas**) are very small and can be reddish purple or white. These are superb landscape plants and produce sweet, if seedy, fruit. **Common** or **tropical guavas** (also called **apple guavas**) are the most common type and are almost exclusively the kind called for in recipes. They have green skin and beautiful rose to red flesh. For information on the "pineapple guava," see Feijoa, 197.

Guavas grown in warmer climates have an arresting fragrance and, generally, better flavor. Select guavas that are firm but yielding, somewhat like ripe avocados. There should be no bruising. They should have yellowish, as opposed to green, skin, and be fragrant. Underripe guavas will ripen if allowed to sit at room temperature. Place them in a paper bag to speed ripening. Ripe guavas should be refrigerated.

Guavas are delicious pureed, baked, poached, or served fresh, alone, or in combination with other tropical fruits like bananas, pineapple, mango, and coconut. Puree them for use in Agua Fresca, 14. The simplest way to enjoy guavas is to cut them in half and eat the flesh with a spoon. To add to a Fruit Salad, 167, peel with a vegetable peeler, slice crosswise, and scrape out the pulp and seeds. Chop the remaining flesh.

ABOUT KIWIS

Kiwis come from northern China, where they are called *yang tao*. They are commercially grown in California and New Zealand and are available year-round. The hairy, dull-brown exterior of the kiwi does not prepare one for the fruit's vivid green or golden translucency or the lovely pattern the seeds reveal when it is sliced. Also available are diminutive **kiwi berries** from the hardy kiwi vine. They are smooth skinned, bright green, and very sweet.

For either fruit, select firm, heavy specimens without wrinkles or bruises and store them at room temperature. Halve large kiwis lengthwise and serve with a spoon for scooping the flesh from the shell. Kiwi berries may be eaten whole, skin and all. Kiwi flesh never darkens, even if cut hours in advance, making it a good candidate for a cut fruit spread, brunch buffet, or dessert garnish. We do not recommend cooking kiwis, as their flavor and texture is best when the fruit is raw. Kiwis contain an enzyme called actinidin, which, like bromelain in pineapples and papain in papayas, cuts apart protein bonds. This makes kiwis a bad choice for gelatin-based desserts, as they will prevent the gelatin from setting.

ABOUT MANGOES

There are few fruits as ambrosial as the mango. They are rich and sweet but never cloying, and their almost creamy flesh has a delectable slippery quality to it. A perfectly ripe mango gives slightly when squeezed, much like a ripe avocado. The color of a mango's skin is not necessarily an indicator of ripeness, and so depending on the variety, green-skinned mangoes may be just as ripe as any mango with a reddish-orange blush. The mango's skin should be smooth and taut, though splotches and minor blemishes are fine. One exception is the **Champagne** or **Ataulfo mango,** whose skin is yellow and wrinkled when ripe. These fruits are incredibly succulent and sweet and should not be passed over because they are wrinkled, though avoid fruit with obvious bruises. The most common variety of mango found in the United States is the **Tommy Atkins,** which is a very large, almost round fruit. These are good, but they can be fibrous and are not as exceptionally delicious as the Ataulfo. **Alphonso mangoes,** an Indian variety considered by many to be one of the best, are nearly impossible to find fresh. Thankfully, they are readily available as a canned puree. Store mangoes at room temperature, especially if they are underripe. The fruit will ripen on the counter, faster if placed in a paper bag with a banana. For dried mango, or **amchur,** see 953.

The mango seed, which extends the length of the fruit, makes cutting up a mango a challenge.

To peel and dice a mango, start by cutting the mango on either side of the pit into two convex pieces, or "cheeks," as shown on page 188.

Score the mango flesh in a crosshatch pattern without piercing the skin, then push the cheek inside-out. The flesh may then be cut away from the skin. To remove the flesh from the cheeks in large, uncut pieces, force the lip of a thin but sturdy drinking glass, such as a pint glass, between the flesh and "scoop" the flesh out of the skin. The mango flesh will separate from the skin in one piece and fall into the glass. Finally, you may peel mangoes with a sharp vegetable peeler, then cut them into pieces, but the flesh is extremely slippery, so use caution.

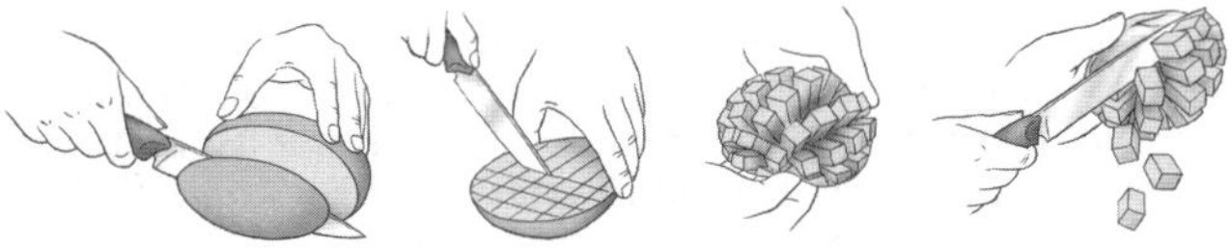

Dicing a mango

Pair mangoes with coconut milk, sticky rice, chiles (especially habaneros), lime juice and zest, dark or Jamaican rum, and other tropical fruits. Serve sliced mangoes sprinkled with chili powder, salt, and lime juice. They are also delicious in a Fruit Salad, 167, with other tropical fruits such as pineapple and kiwi, or served sliced on vanilla or coconut ice cream. Fruit Salsa, 574, made with mango is a natural with tortilla chips and as an accompaniment to white-fleshed fish or fish tacos. Use mangoes in chutneys or dice and freeze, 882, for use in smoothies. The fruit can also be pureed and used as a fruit coulis, 805, or frozen. You may also find canned, sweetened mango puree at Indian markets, which is excellent in Mango Lassi, 13, or for making an incredibly easy sorbet or frozen yogurt, 846. For other mango recipes, see Papaya-Mango Batido, 12, Agua Fresca, 14, Mango Sorbet, 847, Avocado and Mango Salad, 125, and Coconut Sticky Rice with Mango, 828.

ABOUT MEDLARS

Medlars are small, tannic fruits that resemble crab apples or very large, brown rose hips (in fact, like apples, they are a member of the rose family). Because they are so astringent, they must be "bletted," or allowed to sit until they become extremely soft, almost rotten, before they are palatable. In this way, they are somewhat like Hachiya persimmons, 191. In England, far north in their range, they are always overtaken by frost, which is actually beneficial, as it starts the bletting process. The fruits look shabby indeed by the time they are edible, but their flavor is desirable (it has been compared to a rich-tasting applesauce or apple butter), especially for jellies, purees, conserves, and preserves.

Perhaps because they are related to apples and quinces, they have affinities with some of the same flavors, including warm spices like cinnamon, nutmeg, cloves, and allspice, vanilla, honey, cider, and toasted almonds. The pureed fruit can be substituted for persimmon puree in Persimmon Buttermilk Pudding, 830, or run the mushy, ripe fruits through a food mill and cook with sugar and spices into an applesauce-like treat.

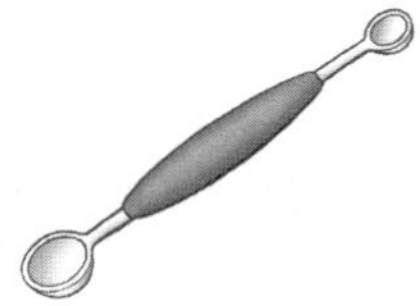

Melon baller

ABOUT MELONS

As part of the large *Cucurbitaceae* genus, melons are closely related to cucumbers and squash. A larger distinction is usually made between **winter,** or smooth-skinned, melons and **summer** melons, whose skin is netted, the patterns raised and of a light color. The flavor of melons varies widely, but almost all are musky, perfumed, and very sweet with little acidity. Summer melons come into season as their name implies; winter melons actually ripen in fall. Summer melons tend to be more fragrant and flavorful, while winter types are milder.

Fragrant **muskmelons** (*Cucurbita melo*) include **cantaloupe, green nutmeg, Charentais,** and **Persian melons,** which are all in the summer or netted group. **Honeydew, Santa Claus** or **Christmas, Canary, Crenshaw,** and **casaba melons** are winter melons. Some, like the honeydew, have very smooth skin, while others, like the casaba, have wrinkled skin. **Bitter melons** are long, like cucumbers, but have distinct, ribbed skin and a mouth-puckering astringency. **Winter melon** is quite a bit milder. Both are used in savory preparations such as stir-fries and soups. They are well loved in India and China. For more on these types, see About Squashes, 86.

Watermelons are literally a breed apart (*Citrullus lanatus* to be precise). The flesh may be red, pink, orange, or gold; it may have seeds or be seedless. There are too many varieties of watermelon to list them all, but some notable ones include **Crimson Sweet,** which has deep-red, sweet flesh, **Sugar Baby,** which is also called an **Icebox melon** as it is a good size to stick into the refrigerator whole, and **Desert King,** a golden-fleshed watermelon that is drought-resistant. Some are the size of a small cantaloupe and others a small child.

All muskmelons ripen slightly after picking, but for the best flavor they should be picked when mature. Keep these melons at room temperature to ripen, if needed. Watermelons do not ripen after being picked, so take care when choosing one. It is said that a ripe watermelon, when thumped with a finger, will make a hollow sound. We do not find the art of watermelon-thumping very enlightening, but some think it a useful metric. Regardless of type, pick melons with a dull sheen on the rind, and check underneath to make sure it is yellowish—a sign it ripened on the ground. If buying sliced melon, it should be fragrant through the plastic wrap, and the flesh should appear dense and firm.

Whole melons keep for several days between 50° and 70°F, away from sunlight. Chill lightly just before serving. ➤ Thoroughly wash the outside of any melon before cutting into it to avoid introducing any bacteria on the skin to the inside of the fruit. Cut fruit should be kept refrigerated in an airtight container for up to 5 days.

Melons are usually eaten raw, and they may be served singly or in combination. They can be served from one end of a meal to the other, from appetizers and salads to desserts. Melons can be cut into decorative shapes, and they respond favorably to lime or lemon juice or a sprinkling of chile powder, lime juice, and salt. Pair muskmelons with vanilla, honey, sweet white wine, mint, berries, ginger, and olive oil. Watermelons are excellent with salty cheeses such as feta, basil, tarragon, pepper, blueberries, and tequila. For other melon recipes see Watermelon and Goat Cheese, 58, Agua Fresca, 14, Watermelon Punch, 15, Honey-Melon Jam, 913, and Pickled Watermelon Rind, 928.

MELON BASKETS OR FRUIT CUPS

8 to 10 large servings

Have ready:

4 cantaloupes or 1 large watermelon

Cut a thin slice off both ends of the cantaloupes or the bottom of the watermelon to keep them from wobbling, then halve the cantaloupes or cut the watermelon into a basket, as shown below. Remove the seeds. Using a melon baller, remove and reserve 1 to 2 cups of the flesh for the baskets or cups. Store the leftovers in the refrigerator for another use. Scallop the edges of the baskets or cups and chill.

Melon baskets

Combine the following ingredients:

2 cups sliced peeled oranges, seeded or seedless
2 cups sliced peeled peaches or hulled strawberries
2 cups diced pineapple, fresh or canned
1 cup blueberries or sliced peeled kiwi
1 to 2 cups reserved melon balls
(Sugar to taste)

Chill thoroughly. Just before serving, fill the melons with the fruit. If desired, pour over each cantaloupe half (or pour the total amount over the watermelon):

(1 tablespoon orange liqueur or rum [½ cup total])

ABOUT PAPAYAS

Papayas grow up to 20 inches in length. Mexican papayas are much larger than Hawaiian ones, though their flesh is not as flavorful. Papayas do not really ripen after being picked, though they will soften. The most flavorful fruits are tree-ripened, which is unfortunate unless you live in Hawaii or Florida, because you are unlikely to encounter a papaya that was not picked green for ease of transport. When fully ripened, papaya flesh is bright reddish-orange or deep salmon colored, and the green rind turns soft and yellow. Ripe papaya is quite perishable and should be eaten within a few days (even uncut ripe papayas do not keep well refrigerated). Papaya juice, when chilled, makes a pleasant nectar-like drink, and peppery black papaya seeds are used for garnish, eaten raw, or dried and used for seasoning. Papaya contains the enzyme papain, which is used to tenderize meat. It will also keep gelatin from setting, so ➤ do not add raw papaya to gelatin desserts.

Underripe **green papaya** may be cooked as for summer squash or used raw in the Thai specialty Green Papaya Salad, 129. Green papaya may also be shredded and used in marinades to help tenderize meat.

To prepare papayas, peel with a vegetable peeler, then halve and scrape out the seeds and strings (if desired, reserve the seeds as a garnish for salads). The fruit may then be cut as desired. Papayas are delicate, sweet, and best paired with other tropical fruits like mango, pineapple, guava, and banana; tangy or spicy ingredients such as lime juice, ginger, and hot chiles; coconut milk, yogurt, cured meats like prosciutto, honey, and rum. Chill and sprinkle ripe papaya with lime or lemon juice, chili powder, and salt. Papaya is excellent in fruit salads, too, especially with other tropical fruits. See Green Papaya Salad, 129, Papaya-Mango Batido, 12, and Agua Fresca, 14. Papaya may also be used in a Frozen Daiquiri, 25.

ABOUT PASSION FRUIT

This fruit was named by sixteenth-century Jesuits, who found its flower emblematic of the Passion of Christ. Passion fruits grow on beautiful, sprawling vines, and even if you do not live in an area where the fruits will ripen, the vines alone are worth growing as an ornamental. The duck egg–sized fruit is at its best when overripe, purple, and wrinkled-looking. **Lilikoi** is a variety of passion fruit that is yellow when ripe and has slightly tarter pulp. **Maypops** are another variety of the fruit that tend to be yellow, orange, or even green when ripe. Passion fruit has an intoxicating fragrance and flavor: tropical and pleasantly tart, somewhat reminiscent of a very flavorful mango mixed with lime juice.

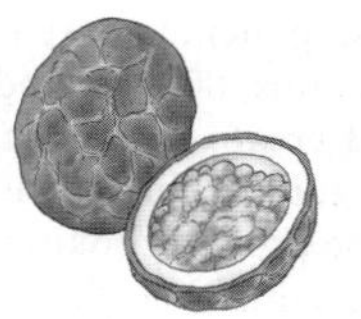

Passion fruits picked unripe will never ripen, but mature fruits will soften and sweeten off the vine. The fruit is available in many markets year-round but tends to be expensive. Passion fruit can be stored whole in the refrigerator for up to 2 weeks. The sweet, aromatic pulp surrounds small, black seeds, but the seeds are crunchy and may be eaten along with the pulp. To prepare, slice off the top of the fruit and spoon out the pulp. To remove the seeds, rub the pulp through a fine-mesh sieve or simmer the pulp with a little water and sugar to make a syrup, then strain out the seeds. To make a dessert sauce, puree the seeded pulp, dilute it slightly with water, and sweeten to taste, heating it gently to dissolve the sugar.

Passion fruit is a natural with other tropical fruits, lime juice and zest, milk chocolate, and coconut. Use unseeded passion fruit pulp to dress tropical fruit salads, to spoon over Pavlova, 826, or as a sauce for ice cream, especially Coconut Ice Cream, 842. Or cut off the top of the fruit and serve with spoons for eating straight out of the shell. Seeded pulp may be used in Fruit Fool, 173, instead of lemon juice for Lemon Curd, 802, or in cocktails such as a Daiquiri, 25, or Champagne Cocktail, 42.

ABOUT PAWPAWS

The pawpaw is the largest edible fruit native to America. When ripe, it has a custard-like creaminess and tastes like a cross between a mango, banana, and pineapple. The domestication process of this fruit is well under way in the United States, and some believe it will be as readily available one day as kiwis and mangoes are today. For now, frozen pawpaw pulp, jam, chutney, and sauce are available through some specialty online retailers. Of course, one can find them in the woods of the Eastern United States.

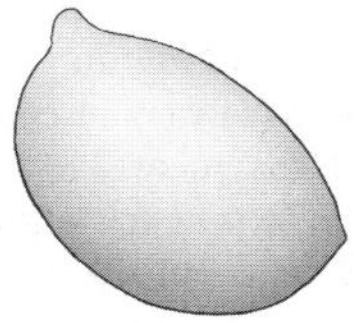

Many say that pawpaws should only be picked after the first heavy frost, or when they fall from the tree (good luck beating the wildlife to this fragrant fruit). Others say that mature pawpaws can be ripened at room temperature and will keep up to 3 weeks in the refrigerator if slightly underripe. We know from personal experience that pawpaws will not ripen if they are picked when green and hard; additionally, we know that ripe pawpaws have a very short shelf life. The fruits can be frozen whole, as can the pureed fruit. To make pawpaw puree, remove the skin and the two rows of inedible seeds and puree in a food processor or press through a sieve. Add a little lemon juice or a pinch of citric acid as the pulp will oxidize and discolor.

Since pawpaws are so dear, we recommend using them in preparations that do not require heating, such as a coulis, 805, layered with cake squares, tropical fruit, and whipped cream in a trifle, 827, or in sorbets (use Mango Sorbet, 847, as a guide, substituting ripe pawpaws for the mangoes). Pawpaws can be used in cooking, such as in quick breads or puddings, but heat can dull their flavor. If you are lucky enough to find a ripe pawpaw, you are probably better off just eating the pulp with a spoon. Should you find yourself with an abundance of the fruit, however, you may substitute pawpaw pulp for the persimmon pulp in Persimmon Buttermilk Pudding, 830. To show off the delicate flavor of the fruit, omit the cinnamon.

ABOUT PEACHES AND NECTARINES

There is nothing quite so good as a perfectly ripe summer peach eaten over the sink as its juices run down your chin and forearms. There are two varieties of peaches—freestone and clingstone—named for the ease or difficulty of removing the pit from the flesh. The mostly yellow-fleshed **freestone peaches** are favorites for eating fresh, out of hand. **Clingstones,** with white or yellow flesh that clings to the pit and a somewhat sharper flavor and firmer flesh, are excellent for cooking, canning, poaching, or sautéing with a little butter and sugar. **White peaches,** though not as visually appealing as their yellow-fleshed brethren, can be just as flavorful. Peaches may be found in markets as early as May, but the best ones usually appear in July and August.

Although their smooth skin and their flavor strongly suggest a cross between a peach and plum, **nectarines** are simply a fuzz-free variety of peach, resulting from what botanists call "bud variation," and they can be of the clingstone or freestone variety.

A good, ripe peach or nectarine will be fragrant and should not be green. Choose firm, but not hard, well-colored fruit without any flattened brownish bruises. Peaches and nectarines do not ripen once picked, but if you keep slightly hard fruits at room temperature for a day or two, preferably in a paper bag, they will soften a bit, but not sweeten any further. Once ripe, peaches are ephemeral and will only keep for 2 to 3 days at room temperature. They may be refrigerated, but that will not extend the shelf life by much. To efficiently peel peaches and nectarines, blanch them, 167.

Peaches have an affinity for blueberries, cured meats like prosciutto, toasted almonds, ginger, and goat cheese. Also see Peach Custard Pie Cockaigne, 671, Peach Pie, 671, Blueberry and Peach Buckle, 684, and Peach or Apricot Butter, 916.

GRILLED PEACHES WITH GOAT CHEESE

4 servings

A perfect summer dessert when the grill is fired up.

Prepare a hot grill fire or preheat a gas grill on high. Halve and pit:

2 large freestone peaches

Place the peach halves on the grill, cut side down, until warmed through and slightly charred. Transfer to a plate. Divide between the peach halves:

4 ounces fresh goat cheese, softened

Top with:

2 tablespoons honey
Chopped mint
Freshly ground black pepper
(Flaky sea salt)

BAKED STUFFED PEACHES

4 or 8 servings

An unassuming but astoundingly good dessert that can be assembled and refrigerated up to 3 hours before baking. We usually consider it a fool's errand to try to improve upon a perfectly ripe peach, but this is a notable exception to the rule.

Preheat the oven to 350°F. Peel, 167, halve, and pit:

4 large freestone peaches

Place the peaches in a baking dish large enough to hold them in one layer. Mix together to dissolve the sugar, then sprinkle over the peaches:

½ cup orange juice
¼ cup powdered sugar

Toss gently with your hands until the peaches are evenly coated. Turn the peach halves cut side up in the dish. Pulse in a food processor until the almonds are in very fine pieces:

⅓ cup slivered almonds, toasted, 1005
¼ cup packed dark brown sugar
Finely grated zest of ½ orange

Add and pulse until the mixture is crumbly:

1 tablespoon cold butter, cut into pieces

Divide the almond mixture evenly among the hollows of the peaches. Bake until the pan juices are bubbling, 15 to 20 minutes. Serve warm with:

Vanilla ice cream

ABOUT PEARS

While pears can be found year-round in supermarkets, they are a fall crop. As summer ends, we find red-skinned **Bartletts,** sweet and juicy but perishable. **Starkrimson pears,** another early variety, are fragrant and have stunning red skin that makes them ideal for fruit salads or other applications where their color can be shown to good effect. Apt to come next are the tiny, sugar-sweet **Seckels** and **Forelles,** ideal for canning. In November, a dazzling array of hardier fall varieties arrives, all of which can be bought far into the winter months. These include the squat teardrop-shaped green or red **Anjou,** firm in texture and mild in taste; the russet **Bosc,** which is crisp and apple-like when still flecked with green, soft and sweet when fully ripe; and the ruddy **Comice,** whose juicy flesh makes it the queen of dessert pears. In some markets you may also find **Winter Nellis,** a pear generally reserved for cooking, and green, long-necked **Concorde pears,** which are good for both eating and cooking. **Asian pears** are round with dull gold or russeted skins and might almost be mistaken for apples (though some are much larger and rounder than the typical apple). Choose fruits that are firm, without wrinkling or shriveling. Asian pears have very crisp flesh, and are best eaten raw and unpeeled. They are uncommonly juicy, provoking a friend of ours to call the experience of eating them "a waterfall in your mouth."

Most pears can be tested for ripeness by pressing the top of the neck near the stem; it should give slightly. Like bananas and avocados, pears are picked slightly green and will ripen at room temperature. If the pears in question are very hard, they may take a week or more to ripen. Do not rush the process—a perfectly ripe pear is a delicacy worth waiting for. To preserve a ripe pear for a short time, refrigerate it. ➤ If you plan to cook pears, do so when they are still firm. To prepare, peel if desired and halve lengthwise. Scoop out the core with a teaspoon or melon baller, and, if desired, cut out the fibrous string that runs from core to stem. The two halves may be quartered lengthwise, sliced, or diced. To prepare whole pears for poaching, see 834.

All types of pears are congenial company for cheese, and they are compatible with warm spices such as cinnamon, clove, allspice, ginger, and cardamom; lemon or orange zest; and vanilla bean. If serving them cut, toss with lemon juice to prevent discoloration. Pears are an excellent addition to a Fruit Salad, 167, or green salads. For cooking, choose Anjou, Bosc, or Winter Nellis. Pears can also be sautéed, 172, or used to make a fruit compote. See Poached Pears in Red Wine, 834, Pear Butter, 915, Apple or Pear Pandowdy, 686, and Apple or Pear Turnovers, 915

ABOUT PERSIMMONS

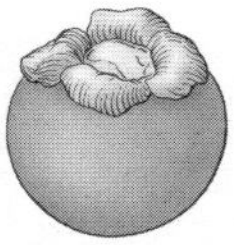

Fuyu persimmon

Brilliant-orange persimmons come to market in the fall and remain available through much of the winter. The common market type is Asian, called **Kaki,** which subdivides into two varieties, the large, acorn-shaped **Hachiya** and the smaller, pincushion-shaped **Fuyu.** Hachiyas are edible only when extremely ripe and almost as soft as jelly; otherwise, they are far too astringent. Fuyus may be eaten ripe and soft, but they are also pleasant when underripe, hard, and crisp. Neither Hachiyas nor Fuyus are likely to be fully ripe at the market, but both can be ripened at home sealed in a plastic bag with an apple. There is also a native **American persimmon,** generally gathered in the wild in the Midwest and South. Like Hachiyas, American persimmons are inedibly astringent unless very ripe and soft, usually after the first frost. Ripe, soft persimmons should be refrigerated or eaten right away. In Japan, Hachiya persimmons are peeled, hung, and massaged until dried. The result, called **hoshigaki,** appear to be dusted with a white bloom, which is actually the sugars in the fruit that have come to the surface. Enjoy *hoshigaki* on their own or with a cup of green tea.

Persimmons have no acidity to speak of, so they can be a bit cloying. We like to liven them up with lemon juice. To prepare, remove the core, then slice or cut the fruit into wedges. Firm Fuyu persimmons are excellent sliced and added to green salads or a Fruit Salad, 167, where they benefit from the acidity of citrus juice or vinegar. Ripe, soft persimmons may be turned into a puree. Remove and discard any seeds, then scrape the flesh from the skin with a spoon and force through a sieve or food mill, or puree in a food processor. The pulp can be frozen for later use or used in baked goods such as Persimmon Buttermilk Pudding, 830.

ABOUT PINEAPPLES

The pineapple, while common today, was a symbol of status and extravagance in the colonial era. Unless you lived in a place where pineapples grew, procuring one was an expensive feat. So beloved was this fruit that in many fine homes it was carved above the door as a symbol of hospitality. However, the pineapple also has a legacy of plantation-style farming, exploitative labor practices, and heavy pesticide use. For this reason, we recommend seeking out organically grown fruit.

A small, compact crown usually denotes the finest fruit. The spiny tops should be a healthy green color, never brown. As skin color does not indicate ripeness, look for very slightly yielding flesh and a delicious aroma as reliable tests for ripeness. Store at room temperature, away from sunlight. Once cut, keep refrigerated.

Pineapple lends itself magnificently to all kinds of combinations, but watch for one thing: ➤ Be sure to cook fresh pineapple before combining it with any gelatin mixture as it contains an enzyme, bromelain, that will prevent the gelatin from setting. This enzyme makes fresh pineapple juice an effective tenderizer in meat marinades, 450, but take care not to marinate the meat too long in the juice or it can become mushy. Also ➤ do not add uncooked pineapple to cottage cheese or yogurt until the last moment, for it quickly turns dairy products watery.

To prepare pineapple, cut off the crown of leaves along with ¼ inch or so of the top of the fruit, then trim ¼ inch off the bottom. Stand the pineapple on end and slice off the skin with wide downward strokes. If desired, the "eyes" may be individually cut out with the tip of a vegetable peeler, or use a knife to follow the eyes in diagonal stripes around the pineapple and cut them out. The fruit may then be sliced crosswise into rings or into wedges or flat slices from top to bottom. Trim out the core.

Pineapple pairs well with coconut, mango, banana, hot chiles, lime juice, avocado, and cilantro. Raw pineapple is excellent, whether eaten on its own or added to a fresh Fruit Salad, 167. Cooked pineapple is delicious, if less complex. See Sautéed Fruit, 172, Grilled or Broiled Fruit, 171, and Grilled or Broiled Fruit Kebabs with Honey and Lime, 171. Dried pineapple is generally processed with a great deal of sugar. For use in a Dried Fruit Compote, 169, try to find unsweetened dried pineapple. Don't forget one of our childhood favorites, Pineapple Upside-Down Cake, 738.

CARAMELIZED GRILLED PINEAPPLE

6 servings

The perfect dessert for a backyard barbecue or anytime you've got the grill fired up.

Prepare a medium-hot grill fire or preheat a gas grill to medium-high. Peel as directed in About Pineapples, 191, and cut lengthwise into 12 wedges:

1 large pineapple

Cut out the tough core. Combine in a small saucepan:

½ cup packed brown sugar
½ cup orange juice
4 tablespoons (½ stick) butter
(Finely grated zest of 1 lime)
1 tablespoon lime juice

Bring to a boil and cook, stirring frequently, until the mixture has thickened and looks syrupy, about 5 minutes. If desired, stir in:

(1 to 2 tablespoons dark rum, to taste)

Lightly brush the pineapple wedges with this mixture and place on the grill over direct heat. Grill, turning the wedges frequently and basting with the brown sugar mixture after each turn, until the wedges have grill marks and the sugar caramelizes, about 5 minutes total. Transfer to a platter and brush with more brown sugar mixture. Serve with:

Vanilla ice cream or Whipped Cream, 791

PINEAPPLE TIDBITS

8 servings

This must be made with very ripe pineapple.

Trim two-thirds from the leafy top of:

1 chilled ripe pineapple

Cut the fruit into 8 lengthwise wedges. Cut off the core and place each part so that it resembles a boat (illustration above). Run a knife between the peel and flesh, leaving the flesh in 1 piece and in place, then cut the flesh crosswise into 5 or 6 slices, retaining the boat shape. If desired, serve each boat on an individual plate, with a small mound of:

(Powdered sugar)

Garnish each plate with:

5 or 6 large unhulled strawberries

ABOUT PLUMS

Plums are another large and diverse group of fruit belonging to the genus *Prunus*, which encompasses peaches and nectarines, cherries, and almonds. Meaty Japanese plums, which peak in August, comprise the most common market types, including the dark purple **Friar,** green **Kelsey,** golden **Shiro,** and red-fleshed **Santa Rosa** and **Elephant Heart. Ume plums,** another Japanese variety, are not very good eating when fresh, but they are processed to make **umeboshi:** wrinkled, salty-sour pickled plums that are often a reddish color from being pickled with shiso, 1017. European plums, harvested in the fall, are generally smaller, oval rather than round, and more meaty than juicy. They include the small, oval **Italian plums, mirabelles,** and various **prune plums,** which are indeed dried for prunes but also make excellent cakes and tarts. The luscious, extremely flavorful **greengages, damsons,** and **sloes** are generally reserved for preserving, as are native **American plums,** also called **plum cherries.** There are many hybrid varieties of plum. **Pluots** have dappled reddish yellow or green skin and are three-quarters plum and one-quarter apricot; **plumcots** are amber-colored half plum and half apricot hybrids; and **apriums,** three-quarters apricot and one-quarter plum, resemble apricots but have a rosier tint to the skin.

Choose aromatic, soft plums. Hard plums will never ripen, and consequently their flavor will never be very good. Size is no indication of flavor—many small plums are more flavorful than their larger counterparts. A whitish bloom or film on the surface is natural. Plums can be stored at room temperature for 3 to 5 days, depending on how ripe they are. Expect the skins of plums to detach, wholly or partially, when the fruit is cooked. To peel plums, blanch them, 167.

Plums generally go well with allspice, black pepper, cardamom, brandy, crème fraîche, sour cream, yogurt, honey, orange, and port wine. They are our favorite fruit to use in Megan's Frangipane Fruit Tarts, 677, especially the red- or purple-skinned varieties. Also see Tart Plum Jelly, 911, Plum Jam, 914, Plum Butter, 916, and Jellied Damson Sauce, 916.

STEWED PRUNES

8 servings

Bergamot-flavored Earl Grey tea is especially nice here, providing a tannic contrast to the sweet prunes.

Cover with cold water in a saucepan:

1 pound pitted prunes

Bring to a boil, then reduce the heat and simmer gently for 20 minutes. Add:

¼ cup sugar, or more to taste
(2 bags Earl Grey tea)
(½ lemon, sliced)
(1 cinnamon stick)

Cook 10 minutes more. Serve warm or chilled.

ABOUT POMEGRANATES

By eating a single orb (or **aril**) of the pomegranate offered her by the wily Pluto, Persephone was obliged to return periodically to the infernal regions, leaving earth for six months in the cheerless embrace of each winter. We have always wondered, since our own first encounter with the crimson cells enclosing seed and luscious juice, how Persephone managed to eat only one.

When choosing pomegranates, avoid dry-looking fruits. Remember that skin color is not an accurate gauge of ripeness.

To remove the arils from a pomegranate, cut it lengthwise in quarters and submerge them in a bowl of cool water. Gently pry the arils from the pithy skin and thin white membranes, which will float to the top. Remove and discard the skin and pith from the water, then drain off the water, leaving the arils behind in the bowl. The arils may be stored, tightly covered, in the refrigerator for up to 5 days. Store whole pomegranates for 2 weeks or longer in the refrigerator (they dry out quickly at room temperature).

The jewel-like arils make a beautiful garnish for salads, including Fruit Salad, 167, and Brussels Sprout Slaw with Spiced Yogurt, 120; braised meat dishes, especially those featuring lamb, rice pilafs, and desserts. Pomegranates make a stunning jelly and can be used to make pomegranate molasses and Grenadine, below. However, for these applications you are better off purchasing pomegranate juice unless you live somewhere where pomegranates are abundant and cheap. But if you prefer juicing your own:

To juice pomegranates, seed the pomegranates as directed above, then process the arils in a blender or food processor and strain out the seeds. Alternatively, cut the fruit in half crosswise and ream it using a lever-style or electric citrus press.

GRENADINE

About 1½ cups

This pomegranate juice–based syrup is a common ingredient in cocktails.

Combine in a medium saucepan:

1 cup unsweetened pomegranate juice
1 cup sugar

Heat gently, stirring, just until the sugar is dissolved. Do not boil. Remove from the heat and stir in:

½ teaspoon orange flower water

Cool completely. Store refrigerated for up to 3 weeks.

POMEGRANATE MOLASSES

1 cup

This dark, tangy syrup can be used as a base for a cooling spritzer—just add club soda, or sparkling water or wine. Brush it over meats and poultry toward the end of cooking as a glaze. Stir a little into salad dressing, mix it into fruit salads, or use it in the Persian specialty Fesenjoon, 433. Extracting the juice is a nuisance, so feel free to start with store-bought pomegranate juice.

Roll on the counter to free the juices:

5 pounds pomegranates (or use 2 cups unsweetened pomegranate juice)

Extract the pomegranate juice as directed above. Ladle the clear pomegranate juice into a deep heavy saucepan and add:

½ cup sugar
⅓ cup strained lemon juice

Cook over medium-low heat, stirring until the sugar dissolves, then simmer, uncovered, until the liquid is reduced to 1 cup, about 2 hours. Cool and pour into a sterilized jar. Seal and store refrigerated for up to 3 months.

ABOUT PRICKLY PEARS

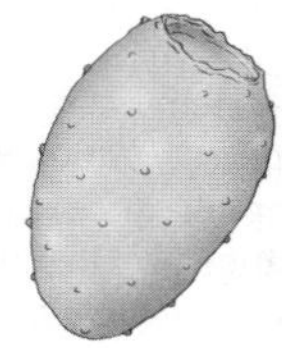

The cactus that bears the prickly pear, also known as the **cactus pear,** is native to northwest Mexico and what is now the American Southwest. Long ago it was transported to the shores of the Mediterranean, where it is as much at home as in its native habitat. Most varieties are shaped like truncated eggs, with thick purplish-red or green skins and magenta flesh. Purple-skinned fruits are said to be the sweetest. At their prime, they are juicy and taste faintly of melon, with no acidity. The hard seeds are edible.

In Hispanic markets, prickly pears are oftensold as *tunas*. Choose fruits that give slightly in the hand but be careful of the fruit's hair-like spines. Wear leather gloves when handling, or use kitchen tongs to keep the spiny fruits at arm's length. Often, most of the spines are removed before the fruit is placed on the store shelf, but there are usually some stragglers, and once embedded in your skin they are almost impossible to see and ferret out.

To peel a prickly pear, cut off the top and bottom, then slit the skin lengthwise and peel it off, either with gloved hands or by slipping the blade of a small knife under the skin and coaxing the fruit out. Prickly pear pulp is usually eaten raw in salsas, but the juice can be boiled into a paste or syrup. Use prickly pear–infused Fruit Syrup, 16, in your next Margarita, 26, or make Prickly Pear Jelly, 912. The fresh juice can be used to flavor mixed drinks, vinaigrettes, or fruit salads, or pureed and made into a dessert sauce. Because prickly pears are not acidic, they benefit from a generous squeeze of citrus juice. As with fruits like fresh pineapple, prickly pears contain an enzyme that will ruin a gelatin dish. For **nopales,** the paddles of the prickly pear cactus, see 227.

MELON WITH PRICKLY PEAR SAUCE

6 servings

Wearing gloves, peel as directed above:

1 pound ripe prickly pears (about 6)

Cut into 1-inch chunks and transfer to a food processor or blender along with:

3 tablespoons orange juice
2 tablespoons lime juice
2 tablespoons sugar

Puree until smooth. Taste and, if desired, add more lime or orange juice. Transfer to a bowl, cover, and chill at least 1 hour. Halve, seed, cut into wedges, and remove the rinds from:

3 pounds melon, such as cantaloupe, honeydew, or Crenshaw

Set a melon wedge on each plate and spoon a ribbon of sauce over it.

ABOUT QUINCES

An ancestor of apples, quinces belong to the rose family. According to Greek myth, Paris gave a golden quince to Aphrodite, thus causing the Trojan War. Regardless of the particulars, quince is a more ancient fruit than Eve's apple, and certainly seems like it has been through an ordeal: Mottled, lumpy, and misshapen on the outside, all but a few rare varieties have hard, dry, and astringent flesh that must be cooked to be eaten. Quince's bedraggled appearance and unyielding temperament is balanced by its intoxicating, tropical fragrance when ripe, which can perfume an entire room. When cooked, their flesh tastes of apples, pears, and rose, and turns beautiful shades of pink and red.

You will find quinces in the fall. Because they are a specialty fruit, look for them at farmers' markets. Quinces are knobby fruits, often bearing a layer of coarse fuzz on their skins, and they often have blemishes. Unless the blemishes are severe, or the fruits are bruised, don't worry about minor imperfections. Ripe quinces have a fuller flavor and can be selected by their incredible fragrance and golden color (underripe quinces are green). Like apples, the fruits are high in pectin; slightly underripe fruits are especially high in pectin and preferred by some for jelly, jam, and preserves. Ripe quinces can be stored for 3 weeks in the refrigerator or in a single layer in a cool, dark place for 3 months. If stored in a place that is too warm, quinces tend to rot from the core outward, which is an unpleasant surprise when cutting into one.

To prepare quinces for cooking, peel them and then cut the fruits lengthwise into quarters or eighths. This directive sounds easier than it is, as quinces are very hard fruits, so use caution to avoid cutting yourself. Cut out the core from each wedge with a paring knife. The flesh darkens quickly, so you can toss the cut fruit with lemon juice, but any discoloration will be negated by the cooking process, so don't stress too much. Quinces are compatible with honey, warm spices, other pome fruits like apples and pears, orange zest, vanilla, ginger, and almonds. Quinces are delicious poached, 170, in a medium to thick syrup, 170. If desired, substitute honey for the sugar and add spices like cinnamon, cloves, and allspice. The fruits may also be halved, cored, and poached in red wine until tender, then stuffed with a mixture of seasoned ground lamb and pine nuts and baked. Also see Apple, Crab Apple, or Quince Jelly, 910, and Quince Preserves, 918.

BAKED QUINCES

4 servings

Preheat the oven to 350°F. Wash, halve, and core:

4 quinces

Rub generously with:

Softened butter

Place in a baking dish, cover, and bake until just tender when pierced with a knife. Check after 1 hour and if the flesh is still very firm, continue baking and checking for up to 1 more hour. Remove from the oven (but leave the oven on). Scoop out most of the flesh, reserving the rinds for presentation. Mix the flesh with:

1 cup packed brown sugar
⅓ cup dry bread or cake crumbs
¼ cup chopped toasted, 1005, walnuts
Finely grated zest of 1 lemon
¼ teaspoon salt

Stuff the quince shells with the mixture. Return to the oven and bake until tender, about 15 minutes more. Serve hot or chilled.

MEMBRILLO (QUINCE PASTE)

About 2 pounds

Traditionally served with cheese, especially Manchego. If using a food mill, the pulp left in the mill may be boiled with sugar and water and used to make Quince Jelly, 910.

Combine in a large heavy saucepan and bring to a simmer over medium heat:

2 pounds quinces (2 to 4 medium), peeled, cored (if not using a food mill), and sliced
1 cup water

Cover, reduce the heat slightly, and simmer until the quinces are very soft, about 40 minutes. Puree the quinces in a food processor or food mill, then return to the pan. Stir in:

3 cups sugar

Simmer over medium-low heat, stirring occasionally, until the mixture is very thick and pulls away from the sides of the pan, about 2½ hours. Spread the paste in a ½-inch layer on a greased pan or rimmed baking sheet and let dry overnight at room temperature. Cut the paste into squares or other desired shapes with a biscuit or cookie cutter. Continue to dry, turning the pieces occasionally, until the surface dries out completely.

ABOUT RHUBARB

Only by the wildest stretch of botanical definitions can rhubarb, the stem of a plant, be included here, but its tart flavor and customary uses make it more at home in this chapter than any other. Field-grown rhubarb is in season only in spring, although depending on where you live it may be available for up to a few months. Whichever type, choose crisp, firm stalks, preferably no more than an inch wide. Rhubarb may be a vibrant pink, deep green, or somewhere on the spectrum between those two colors. The color comes from the variety of rhubarb in question; green rhubarb is no less "ripe" than red. If any leaves are attached, cut them off before storing and discard. ➤ Never eat the leaves; they contain poisonous oxalic acid.

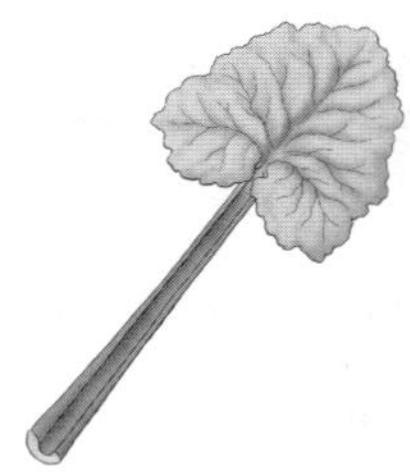

To prepare rhubarb for cooking, rinse well. Cut off and discard 1 inch from the base of the stalks, then cut the remainder of the stalks into ½- to 2-inch pieces or as directed in the recipe. Should the stalks be tough, peel them like celery to remove the strings before cooking. Rhubarb makes a delectable sweet or savory compote. It can be sautéed and served as a side dish, or used in baking. Baked rhubarb pairs well with lemon, apples, pears, strawberries, vanilla, orange, and ginger. See Strawberry Rhubarb Pie,

671, Strawberry and Rhubarb Preserves, 917, and Spiced Rhubarb Conserves, 919.

ROASTED RHUBARB
6 servings
Roasting preserves some of the texture of the rhubarb. Serve this over yogurt, custardy desserts, or ice cream.
Preheat the oven to 400°F. Prepare for cooking and cut into 2-inch lengths, 194:
1 pound rhubarb
Toss the rhubarb in a 13 × 9-inch baking dish with:
1/3 cup packed brown sugar
Finely grated zest and juice of 1 orange
1-inch piece ginger, peeled and grated
Scraped seeds and pod from 1 vanilla bean, halved lengthwise
Roast until tender when pierced with a knife, 15 to 20 minutes.

POACHED RHUBARB
3 servings
Versatile poached rhubarb is delicious with pork or duck, or spooned over vanilla ice cream. For dessert applications, use the larger amount of sugar. Try adding balsamic vinegar; cinnamon, cloves, or fresh or ground ginger; or sautéed shallots or onions to sharpen the flavor.
Combine in a medium heavy saucepan:
4 cups diced rhubarb (about 6 stalks)
1/4 to 1/2 cup sugar
Let stand at room temperature until the rhubarb exudes some juice, at least 15 minutes. Bring the mixture to a boil over medium-high heat, stirring constantly. Reduce the heat to low, cover, and simmer, stirring occasionally, until the rhubarb is tender and the liquid thickened, 10 to 12 minutes. Remove from the heat and let cool, without stirring. Refrigerate for at least 2 hours, or for up to 2 days. The mixture will thicken when chilled.

ABOUT ROSE HIPS

The fruit of the rose, rose hips are not found on many modern rose cultivars, which have been bred for their showy blooms. While rose hips do not have much flavor beyond a pervading tartness, they impart a beautiful color to dishes. Rose hips are used in Sweden to make a soup, 109. They also make a tart, pink jelly, 911, and can be used to flavor Simple Syrup, 16. Dehydrate rose hips, 944, to use them as an ingredient in tisanes. If using pureed rose hips, ➤ strain out the seeds, which can irritate the mouth and stomach.

ABOUT TAMARINDS

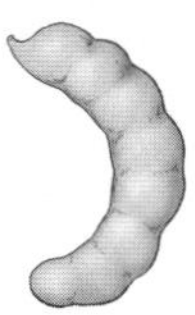

Tamarinds are beans, which makes them, technically, a fruit. The 2- to 6-inch brownish pods from the graceful tamarind tree can be found in Asian markets as well as some supermarkets. The fibrous brown pulp scraped from the pods is deeply flavorful: Tamarind flesh has both a caramel-like sweetness and a puckering sour twang, like a cross between a date and an apricot, with a hint of savoriness. This unique flavor is the result of high levels of tartaric acid (the same acid that makes apricots and grapes tart), as well as browning reactions that occur as the tamarind pods hang from the tree. Before tamarind pods are picked, they are left to bake in the sun. This concentrates their flavor and causes the fruits' sugars to caramelize and brown.

Some eat tamarind pulp as a sweet snack straight from the pod. Beware of the hard, inedible seeds and resilient strings that connect them along each side of the pod; have moist napkins handy to attend to sticky fingers.

Minimally processed **tamarind pulp** can be bought in plastic-wrapped bricks at Asian markets. Kept in a plastic bag, the pulp can be stored on a shelf for many months or in the refrigerator or freezer more or less forever. Much of it is marked as "seedless," which it most definitely is not.

To prepare tamarind pulp for cooking, combine 1/2 cup pulp with 1 1/4 cups hot water. Knead with your fingers until a viscous, brownish liquid forms, then strain to remove the seeds and fibers.

Tamarind extract or **tamarind concentrate** is sold as a paste and is a much more convenient way to add tamarind flavor to dishes. Some brands must be refrigerated; others can be kept tightly sealed in the pantry (check directives on the package to be sure). ➤ For a **tamarind paste substitute,** combine **1 tablespoon lime juice, 1 tablespoon molasses,** and **1 teaspoon Worcestershire sauce.**

Tamarind is a key ingredient in Worcestershire Sauce, 932, as well as other condiments like Tamarind Chutney, 566. Dishes like Pad Thai, 303, and Tom Yum Goong, 101, rely on tamarind for their tantalizing balance of sweet-sour-salty-spicy flavor. Tamarind's sweet-sour flavor also makes it ideal for candy making, or using in beverages as a flavoring syrup. For other tamarind-enhanced dishes, see Caramelized Tamarind Tempeh, 288, and Son-in-Law Eggs, 152.

ABOUT TROPICAL FRUITS

These fruits are becoming increasingly available, particularly at specialty markets and through online retailers.

ACEROLA

The habitat, size, and color of this fruit are indicated by its common aliases, **Barbados cherry** and **West Indian cherry,** although the fruit is botanically unrelated to the cherry and native to South and Central America. Shallow grooves in the bright red skin indicate the positions of the three pits, which should be removed before eating. The fruit has a raspberry or sour apple flavor when eaten raw. It contains more vitamin C than fresh citrus fruits.

ACKEE

Related to lychees and longans, ackee is the national fruit of Jamaica. It is a yellowish-orange color when ripe, has thick, hard skin and three bulbous lobes that split apart to reveal three shiny, black seeds that are attached to yellowish edible flesh. Ackee flesh is creamy and buttery with a mild flavor somewhat reminiscent of heart of palm. The unripe fruit is poisonous. Ripe ackee splits open on its own. While difficult to find fresh in the United States, it is available canned. Ackee is perhaps best known for its role in the Jamaican breakfast specialty, ackee and saltfish, which is made from salt cod, boiled ackee, tomatoes, spices, and Scotch bonnet peppers.

BREADFRUIT AND JACKFRUIT

Both relatives of the mulberry and fig, these fruits are structurally similar in that they contain segmented pulp that surrounds many seeds. Unlike mulberries and figs, breadfruit may weigh up to 9 pounds and jackfruit as much as 90 pounds. Breadfruit, a native of the Pacific Islands, has a high starch content, making it well suited to savory preparations in which the fruit functions much as potatoes or bread. When underripe it may be boiled, fried, or stewed. Breadfruit tostones are superb: Follow the recipe for Fried Plantains I, 263, substituting breadfruit for the plantains. Also see About Breadfruit, 220. Jackfruits are native to India and have, when ripe, a flavor that conjures pineapples, banana, and mango. Ripe jackfruits are often used in sweets, though they are excellent eaten on their own. Underripe jackfruit has a stringy texture and a mild flavor that makes it an excellent meat substitute. The seeds can be roasted and eaten as well. Jackfruit may be found at Asian markets in the United States, but breadfruit is much harder to come by as it is extremely perishable. Once cut, breadfruit quickly turns black and so must be used immediately.

Breadfruit

CAPE GOOSEBERRY OR GROUND CHERRY

These small yellow-green or orange berries, like their relative the tomatillo, grow inside papery husks. The flesh is sweet, with a gooseberry, melon, or pineapple flavor. Some varieties lean toward the savory, tasting more like cherry tomatoes. Before using, pull off the husks and rinse the fruit. Cape gooseberries can be added to a Fruit Salad, 167, dipped in chocolate, used as a pizza topping along with salty cured meats such as prosciutto, added to pie fillings, or just eaten out of hand.

CARAMBOLA OR STAR FRUIT

A member of the wood sorrel family, this semitropical fruit is native to Southeast Asia. It is readily identifiable by its translucent golden skin and five prominent ridges, which, when the fruit is sliced, form the points of a star. The flesh is crisp and sweet, although it tends toward blandness and is perhaps better as an attractive garnish than as the focal point of any dish. Ripe fruits can be refrigerated for up to 1 week. To serve, rinse, pat dry, and slice crosswise. Add to Fruit Salad, 167.

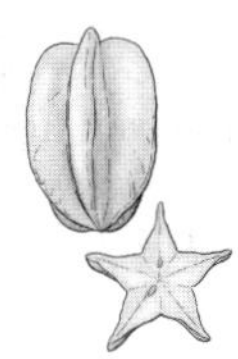

CERIMAN OR MONSTERA

Monstera is a split-leaf philodendron, a tropical houseplant with long, perforated leaves (which has earned it the nickname "Swiss cheese plant"). When grown in subtropical climates it produces 8- to 10-inch cylindrical pine cone–like fruits with a pineapple-banana flavor. The plant is also called **fruit salad plant.** A single fruit ripens over a 3- to 4-day period, and the lower sections, which break apart at the base of the stem, should be eaten only when fully ripe. The rind will turn yellow. To keep the top sections unbruised until ripened, place the fruit stem end up in a jar, and pluck off the segments as they ripen. Or wrap the fruit in plastic and set aside at room temperature until the entire rind is loose; peel, then pull the creamy flesh off the core with a fork. Be sure to remove and discard the sharp, black bits from between the segments. Serve plain or with vanilla ice cream.

CHERIMOYA OR CUSTARD APPLE

The nineteenth-century German naturalist Alexander von Humboldt, who traveled widely in Latin America, declared that this fruit—with its custard texture and flavor of tropical fruits—was worth a trip across the Atlantic. Cherimoyas somewhat resemble artichokes in size and shape, and they have a scale-like pattern on their skin. The fruit must be tree-ripened but still firm when picked. It bruises easily. When ripe, cherimoyas yield to gentle pressure in the hand, like a ripe peach. Refrigerate ripe fruits for no longer than a day or two.

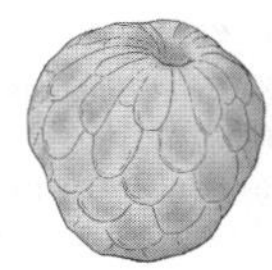

Cherimoyas are generally cut into wedges and scooped from the skin with a spoon (discard the large black seeds as they are poisonous) or blended into drinks, sherbets, and sorbet. You may also freeze the fruit and eat it like ice cream. Peeled and diced cherimoya may be added to Fruit Salad, 167. If the salad does not include a citrus fruit, toss the cherimoya with lemon juice to prevent discoloration and heighten the flavor. Or use cherimoyas to make a *batido,* 12. Other fruits of the *Annona* family are the **sweetsop** or **sugar apple** and the **soursop,** which is also called **guanabana.**

DRAGON FRUIT OR PITAYA

Like prickly pear, 193, this fruit is harvested from a type of cactus. The most common varieties have a vibrant red coloring, but yellow-skinned fruits can sometimes be found. The flesh is juicy and flecked with small, edible black seeds. Some varieties have white flesh, others are a striking shade of violet. Though some sour pitaya varieties can be found, most dragon fruit has a mild, sweet, melon-like flavor. Dragon fruits are especially satisfying when chilled, cut in half, and eaten with a spoon. They are a popular addition to beverages, especially smoothies. They make a stunning addition to Fruit Salad, 167.

DURIAN

Fruits of this famous tree, native to Southeast Asia, weigh up to 20 pounds. They tend to either provoke admiration or disgust, as they have a strong smell that is capable of clearing out a room (though it must be noted that different varieties of durian have different smells, some much more appealing than others). Much like many stinky cheeses, however, durian actually has a mild flavor and a custard-like texture. Durians resemble jackfruit, but they are spiky and not botanically related. Durian can be eaten raw or mixed into drinks or ice cream. The large seeds are roasted and eaten like nuts.

FEIJOA

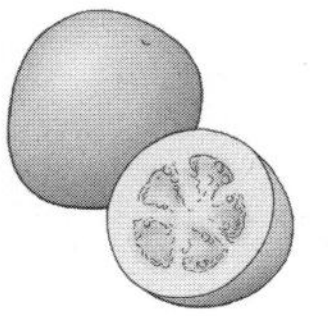

Often called **pineapple guava,** a sobriquet that aptly reflects the feijoa's delicious and complex flavor, this fruit is dark green and about 2 inches long, with a white interior. The flesh has the slightly granular texture of a ripe pear and tastes of pear and pineapple; the jelly-like center is filled with tiny edible seeds. Feijoas are used chiefly for jellies and preserves, and are also delicious split in half and eaten with a spoon. They may be added to Fruit Salad, 167. Remove the bitter skin with a vegetable peeler, then cut the fruit into cubes or quarters. Toss the flesh with lemon juice to prevent discoloration.

GENIP OR MAMONCILLO

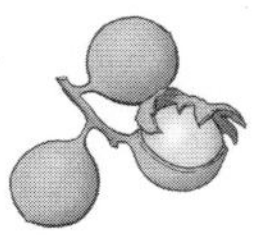

These grape-sized, lime-green Caribbean fruits grow in clusters and come to market in summer. They are mostly pit, but their orange-pink flesh is sweet and reminiscent of grapes. Peel off the tough skin with your fingers, then eat out of hand, spitting out the large pits.

JUJUBE OR CHINESE DATE

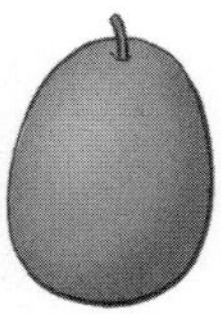

These fruits, long prized in China, resemble dates in size and taste and have a single pit in the center. They are available fresh in Asian markets in the fall. Look for orange-red fruits just beginning to spot with brown. The flesh starts out white, crisp, and dry, with hardly any acidity. Though most often served raw like dates, jujubes can be poached, 170, and combined with other poached fruits to make an intriguing compote. Puncture their tough skins in several places with a skewer before cooking so that the syrup can penetrate. **Dried jujubes** can be found in Asian markets.

KIWANO OR AFRICAN HORNED CUCUMBERS OR HORNED MELON

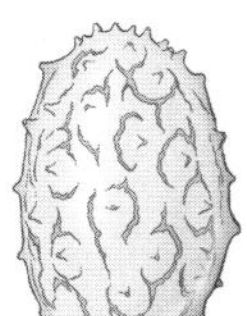

These small, spiky orange fruits suggest exotic sea creatures. Actually, they are relatives of melons and cucumbers, and their orange-green flesh is mucilaginous, seedy, and cucumber-like in taste. They are native to sub-Saharan Africa. The skin is hard and sturdy, and the fruits may be cut in half, the jelly-like pulp scooped out and mixed with other fruits, and the resulting fruit salad served in the emptied out kiwano shells.

LONGAN

A relative of lychee and ackee, longan fruits are small and round with dry, gold to brown skin that must be peeled off before eating. Inside, the fruit resembles lychee or a peeled grape, and the flesh clings to a shiny, black seed in the center. The Cantonese word for longan means "dragon eye" owing to the fruit's eyeball-like appearance. The flavor is similar to lychee, but is less sweet and not as fragrant.

LOQUAT

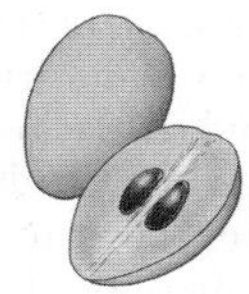

These olive-sized fruits, yellow and loosely clustered, mature in the springtime. They are hard to find in markets outside their growing areas, as they bruise easily. Depending on the variety, the orange flesh is somewhat sour but pleasant, and tastes of apricot, plum, and lychee. Loquats can be refrigerated for up to 3 days. To eat out of hand, simply slice or snap off the stem, if still attached, and enjoy, discarding the toxic brown seeds and the tough bit at the blossom end. To add to a Fruit Salad, 167, halve lengthwise and remove the seeds.

LYCHEES

The deep red to brownish shells of these walnut-sized fruits contain a highly perfumed flesh that is a bit like fragrant jelly or an especially luscious peeled grape. Select heavy, bright-red or brownish-red fruits without cracks. Pale fruits are underripe, very brown ones past their prime. Store the fruit at room temperature in a loosely closed plastic bag for a week or so. The flavor dulls over time, so plan to eat ripe lychees soon after you buy them.

Peel lychees with your fingers. Lychees are usually served unpitted because the flesh does not hold its shape well when cut away from the seed. Lychees are best eaten on their own, so as to enjoy their delicate flavor, but they are quite fine in a fruit salad made with kiwis and raspberries (for this use, remove the pit). They pair well with tropical fruits, ginger, vanilla, and sparkling wine. For a fragrant treat, drop a peeled and pitted lychee into a Champagne Cocktail, 42.

MANGOSTEEN

This 2- to 3-inch-diameter fruit has a most exquisite milky juice and a floral flavor akin to lychees. Its sections—5 to 6 in number—may be easily scooped out and eaten with a spoon, and it can also be made into preserves.

RAMBUTAN

These hairy fruits are native to Malaysia (in fact, their name is derived from the Malay word for hair, *rambut*). Rambutans are closely related to lychees and longans, and their white, jelly-like flesh may be used in similar ways. The best way to eat a rambutan, however, is out of hand, peeling away the skin and nibbling around the hard central seed.

SAPODILLA

Sapodilla is an evergreen tree whose sap produces chicle gum, from which chewing gum is sometimes made. The fruit, eaten only when ripe, has rather grainy but entirely edible flesh, with a texture somewhat like moist brown sugar. The seeds must be removed, after which the raw pulp may be eaten fresh or used in puddings and other desserts. A sprinkling of lemon juice helps. A close relative, the **sapote,** has similar traits and makes excellent sherbet.

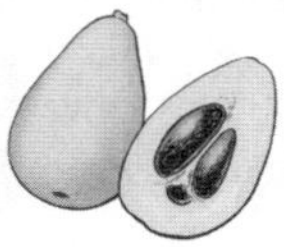

TAMARILLO OR TREE TOMATO

This ovoid fruit has smooth red-yellow skin, edible black seeds, and red-yellow flesh that tastes sweet and somewhat acidic. It is in the nightshade family and depending on the variety may taste like tropical fruit or tomato. The skin is bitter. Ripe tamarillos can be refrigerated, tightly wrapped, for up to 10 days. To prepare, remove the skin and the outer layer of flesh to get at the succulent flesh that holds the seed. Cut in half to scoop out the pulp and eat it plain, add it to sauces, or blend it with water and sugar to make a drink.

VEGETABLES

The most widespread advice regarding vegetable cookery is to buy the best produce you can find or afford and do very little to it. Perhaps this advice was the most effective way to nudge earlier generations of cooks—who had been directed by cookbooks and prevailing tastes to cook vegetables to smithereens—in a more nutritious and texturally interesting direction. Luckily, this corrective is now less urgent than it once was. Many diners now prefer simply cooked vegetables over limp, heavily sauced ones. While vegetables are delicious when "left alone"—that is, served crisp-tender with little more than a slick of olive oil and a dusting of sea salt—they can be equally appealing when enriched with spices, caramelized by prolonged roasting, or made supple and tender in a stew or braise. There is room for both approaches, and we have expanded this chapter accordingly.

BUYING VEGETABLES

Many produce markets offer both conventionally grown and **organic** vegetables. In order to be labeled organic, a crop must be grown without the use of certain synthetic pesticides and fertilizers, as specified by the USDA. Though produced with fewer synthetic compounds, organic vegetables are not necessarily tastier or more nutritious than their conventional counterparts. Also keep in mind that the certification process is often too expensive for small farms even though their practices may meet or exceed those set by the USDA. The smallest farms—those selling less than $5,000 worth of crops annually—may by law label their produce organic without being inspected or certified.

Rather than rely on labeling, we prefer, when possible, to buy locally grown vegetables in their season. They are more likely to be picked when ripe and bred for flavor rather than uniformity or their ability to survive long-distance shipping. Use the tests for ripeness we describe under individual vegetable listings and be ready to change your menu plan to adapt to what looks best; ➤ in other words, purchase whatever is in good condition rather than buying vegetables in decline just because they are on your shopping list. This advice stands whether you shop at a farmers' market or the supermarket.

Frozen vegetables are convenient, last a long time, and are picked and frozen at peak freshness. In some cases, they surpass fresh vegetables in their utility and economy. For instance, frozen spinach is a practical alternative in recipes that call for blanching and chopping fresh spinach. We are particularly fond of frozen pearl onions because they save the cook the onerous task of peeling. Green peas are perhaps the best example of a frozen vegetable that is often better than its fresh counterpart, and certainly easier to prepare. The sugars in fresh peas that make them so delicious turn to starch very quickly after being picked, so unless you are able to find fresh peas at a farmers' market (or in your garden), you are better off buying them frozen. To freeze fresh vegetables, see 884.

Although most vegetables retain quality better in frozen than in canned form, **canned vegetables** can be a boon to the home cook. They are easy to store, keep indefinitely, and do not take up precious freezer space. Canned beans, artichoke hearts, and tomatoes destined for sauces and braises are our favorites to keep in the pantry. Other canned vegetables, such as green beans, asparagus, and mushrooms, may taste stale and tend to be texturally challenged. For these, and other vegetables that are best when still slightly crisp, choose fresh or frozen over canned. If you plan to serve canned vegetables, cook them gently to retain whatever texture they still possess.

STORING VEGETABLES

See individual entries in this chapter for specific storing instructions. As a general rule ➤ most vegetables keep best if stored loosely wrapped in plastic bags in the vegetable crisper of a refrigerator. Most vegetables benefit from moderate humidity, which keeps them from drying out or going limp, but it may be necessary to wrap a paper towel around them to control condensation (which promotes mold growth). If there is any excess moisture on your produce, especially herbs and leafy greens, dry them off. Remove rubber bands and twist-ties from stems to keep them from molding prematurely. Cut the leaves from all root vegetables and store separately.

Now, some exceptions to the rule: ➤ Potatoes, winter squashes, mature onions, and cured garlic are best kept in a dry, cool place (once cut, however, they should be tightly wrapped and refrigerated). Dried peas and beans should be sealed in a plastic bag or airtight canister. To ripen tomatoes and avocados, store at room temperature in a paper bag (which will trap ethylene gas and hasten ripening). ➤ Do not wash vegetables until you are ready to use them, as the added moisture and the inevitable nicking of skin and/or leaves invites spoilage.

Certain vegetables and fruits should not be stored together. Apples give off ethylene gas, which can overripen vegetables, and onions cause potatoes to spoil quickly.

PREPARING VEGETABLES FOR COOKING

Prepare vegetables close to the time they will be cooked. Unless they are to be peeled, wash them thoroughly. Most thin-skinned vegetables can be cooked unpeeled. Some vegetables discolor once their flesh is exposed to air. Some, like potatoes, can be submerged in water to keep their color pristine. Others—like artichokes, burdock, and salsify—should be submerged in water that has been spiked with vinegar or lemon juice. See acidulated water, 951.

➤ Whether you cook vegetables whole or peeled and cut, see that the pieces are uniform in size so they will all cook through in the same length of time. Use vegetable scraps in stocks (see Keeping a Stock Bag, 73), unless they are starchy or belong to the *Brassica* family (broccoli, cauliflower, cabbage, etc.).

CUTTING VEGETABLES

Before we delve into specific cuts and techniques, let us impart a bit of general advice we have found to be invaluable: A sharp knife and a patient hand will make prepping vegetables safer and more enjoyable. Prepare your ingredients ahead of time, if possible (for more on this, see *mise en place*, 1044). If you need to be efficient because time is short, do not compensate by speeding up the motion of your hands. Instead, try achieving faster results by strategy. For example, before slicing several celery ribs, carrots, or green onions, cut them in half or thirds, gather them into a bundle, and thoughtfully slice through them together. If a sack of onions needs to be thinly sliced, work in the order of the task—trim all the onions first, then halve them all, peel them all, and slice them all—rather than working onion by onion. Other innovations will occur to you as you become more at ease in the kitchen; some may work better than others, but the pursuit of them, or, learning to accomplish more with less effort and fuss, is stimulating, empowering, and a process we enjoy for its own sake.

The shapes of different cuts affect how vegetables cook and what kind of texture they have. For instructions on preparing onions and shallots, see 254. **Chiffonade** means to thinly or finely shred—a frequent treatment for herbs and greens. Stack leaves on top of one another, roll into a cigar shape, and thinly slice crosswise into ribbons. For an example of this technique, see Sautéed Shredded Collard Greens, 245.

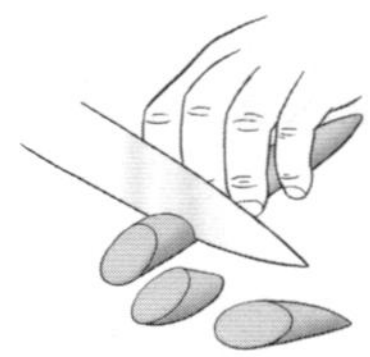

Diagonal cuts

Long, slender vegetables like celery, carrots, green onions, and cucumbers may be sliced **on the diagonal** or **on the bias,** by holding your knife at an angle to the vegetable. This creates longer slices than a simple crosswise cut (and can also add visual appeal). When slicing round vegetables like potatoes, first cut a thin slice off one side of the vegetable so that it rests flat on the cutting surface. Whatever the object to be sliced, hold it so that your fingers are out of harm's way.

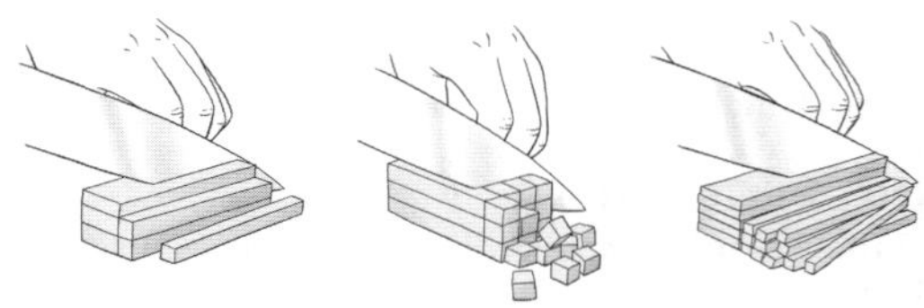

Batonnet, medium dice, fine julienne

Potatoes, carrots, and other root vegetables are often cut into cubes. **Brunoise, small dice, medium dice,** and **large dice** are, respectively, ⅛-, ¼-, ½-, and ¾-inch cubes—no need to get out your ruler. For **julienne,** or **allumette** (which means "matchstick" in French), vegetables are cut longer and thinner, 2 to 3 inches long and ⅛ inch thick. **Batonnet,** or **baton,** is a long rectangular cut, most often used for French fries. To make any of these, trim the vegetable into as squared a shape as possible, then cut into slices, stack the slices and cut into sticks. To make dice, cut the sticks crosswise into cubes.

Shingled julienne

We have come to prefer another, easier method for cutting julienne that involves fewer steps: Slice vegetables on the diagonal into planks of the desired length. Shingle them out to resemble a neat row of overlapping dominos that have fallen toward your dominant hand. Cut into matchsticks, starting on the side closest to your cutting hand and moving toward the first domino to fall. As you slice your way across the shingled vegetables, your helping hand can hold them in place by pressing on planks farther away from the blade, which reduces your chances of getting cut and speeds things up considerably.

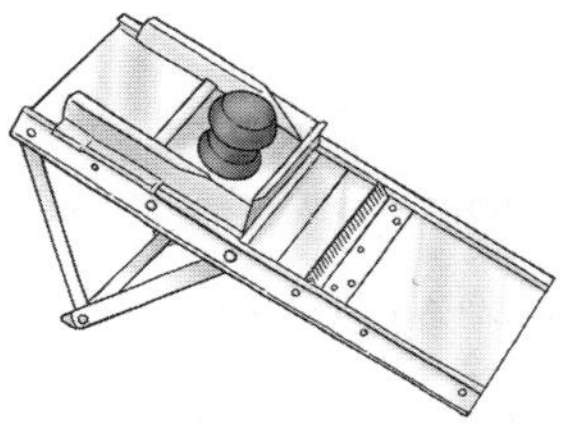

Mandoline slicer

Mandoline slicers can be incredibly useful for slicing (or shaving) vegetables uniformly thin. First, choose firm vegetables that will not compress when they make contact with the blade. Peel the vegetable, if desired, and grasp it so that your fingers will be out of harm's way. Slide it over the blade a few times, examine the thickness of the slices, and adjust the mandoline as needed. If your mandoline does not have a safety guard, ➤ always be aware of how close your fingers are getting to the blade. Though many mandolines come with sharp teeth to produce julienne cuts, ➤ we highly recommend using the device to make slices, and then stack them and make julienne cuts by hand with a sharp knife.

Firm vegetables to be served raw may also be turned into **ribbons** by shaving with a vegetable peeler. Carrots, large radishes like daikon, broccoli and cauliflower stalks, asparagus, cucumber, and zucchini and other summer squashes may be shaved in this way; vegetables with ribs such as celery and fennel must be sliced across the grain with a sharp knife or mandoline. **Spiral slicers** can be used to obtain long, fine ribbons. Or simply **shred** firm vegetables on the large holes of a box grater. You may also find Y-shaped **julienne peelers** that have sharp teeth for shredding vegetables.

Just in case you enjoy going to trivia nights, when vegetables are whittled with a paring knife into small, round shapes you may call them **pearls;** if they are elliptical, they are **olivette** at ⅜ inch, **noisette** at ½ inch, and **Parisienne** if about 1 inch at their widest diameter. These shapes are the province of classically trained chefs (most of whom never carve them after training).

ABOUT VEGETABLES FOR A ROAST

Cooking vegetables in the same roasting pan as a whole chicken or pork roast has two key advantages: Using one pan means less cleanup, and the vegetables are basted with savory drippings. Set whole small potatoes, or larger ones halved or quartered—or root vegetables of similar size—in the pan with the roast and turn occasionally to moisten with drippings. We are especially fond of celery root chunks and thick onion wedges.

Unfortunately, there are a few drawbacks to this approach: It is difficult to achieve crisp-tender vegetables and perfectly cooked meat at the same time; vegetables cooked under a roast are often very soft. If you crowd the pan with too many vegetables, they will keep the drippings from browning on the bottom, which makes it impossible to whip up gravy or a pan sauce after the roast is done. To us, the tasty benefits outweigh the risk of slightly overcooked vegetables. If you want to make a gravy or pan sauce—or if overdone vegetables are your kryptonite—it is better to cook them separately.

ABOUT STUFFED VEGETABLES

Tomatoes, peppers, squashes, cucumbers, onions, cabbage leaves, and mushrooms all make decorative and delicious vegetable cases. Some vegetable cases are blanched prior to stuffing; see recipes for individual vegetables for when this is necessary. Fill them with other prepared vegetables, contrasting in color or flavor, or enhance them with a highly seasoned meat, seafood, cheese, or grain stuffing. For other filling ideas, see Stuffings and Casseroles, 531, and About Stuffed Pasta, 311.

ABOUT MASHED AND PUREED VEGETABLES

Potatoes, the vegetable most commonly mashed or pureed, are handled in a special way, described on 265. ➤ Other vegetables may be coarsely mashed or finely pureed, as you prefer, with a food mill or potato ricer, 265. For a lumpier texture, mash with a potato masher, a fork, or a slotted spoon. For a fine puree, whirl the vegetables in a food processor or, in small batches, in a blender, adding liquids like milk, cream, or melted butter, if necessary. Carrots, sweet potatoes, parsnips, rutabaga, winter squash, and cauliflower all make excellent purees.

ABOUT COOKING FROZEN VEGETABLES

Frozen vegetables are a help to the busy household; there is virtually no preparation time involved, and they can be tastier than out-of-season produce. As a rule, ➤ cook frozen vegetables without thawing until just tender. They may be cooked in a covered pan with a bit of added liquid, in a steamer basket, in a covered bowl or plate in a microwave, or added to a soup or stew. Corn on the cob should be partially thawed before cooking, so that the cobs will be heated through by the time the corn is cooked. ➤ Most frozen vegetables will cook in one-third to one-half the time of their fresh equivalents. When using frozen vegetables in a recipe calling for fresh, shorten their cooking time—for example, add them to stews during the last minutes of cooking. For pureed vegetables, partially thaw by placing the container or bag under warm running water, then transfer to a dish and microwave until completely thawed.

Whatever method you use, break blocks of frozen vegetables into chunks and arrange in a shallow layer in a steamer, pan, or microwave-safe dish with a lid.

To cook frozen vegetables on the stovetop, use a pan that is large enough for the vegetables to lie flat, add a small amount of stock or water, bring to a simmer, cover, and cook until the vegetables are thawed and tender. Use about ½ cup of stock or water for every 2 cups of vegetables (for lima beans, use 1 cup liquid).

To microwave frozen vegetables, simply cover and cook until the vegetables are tender, checking after one-third of the fresh-vegetable cooking time has elapsed (or as directed on the package).

ABOUT REHEATING AND REPURPOSING COOKED VEGETABLES

Leftover vegetables can still be delicious and make versatile supporting players in a meal. To simply hit the replay button, heat the vegetables through in a steamer basket over boiling water or in a pan with a few teaspoons of water or stock. Sautéing and browning in a little butter or olive oil is an excellent treatment, or you may bind chopped leftovers with beaten egg and bread crumbs into small cakes and pan-fry until golden. Serve still-crisp leftover vegetables in a salad, tossed with vinaigrette. You can also work leftover vegetables into omelet fillings, 158, frittatas, 159, stratas, 164, a Vegetable Soufflé, 161, or you can add them to a soup for the last few minutes of simmering.

▲ COOKING VEGETABLES AT HIGH ALTITUDES

In baking or roasting vegetables at high altitudes, use approximately the same temperatures and timing given for sea-level cooking. When cooking vegetables at high altitudes by any process involving moisture, both more liquid and a longer cooking time are needed, as liquids boil at lower temperatures. The cooking time can be reduced if the vegetables are thinly sliced or cut into small pieces.

Use these adjustments as an approximate timing guide: For each 1,000 feet of elevation, add about 10 percent to the cooking time given in the recipes for whole beets, carrots, and potatoes and about 7 percent for green beans, squash, green cabbage, turnips, and parsnips. In cooking frozen vegetables at high altitudes, whole carrots and beans may require as much as 5 to 12 minutes additional cooking, while other frozen vegetables may need only 1 or 2 more minutes.

When pressure-cooking vegetables at altitudes over 2,000 feet, increase cooking times 5 percent for every 1,000 feet above 2,000 feet. For instance, increase cooking time by 10 percent at 4,000 feet. As always, we recommend you consult the manufacturer's instructions.

BASIC VEGETABLE STIR-FRY

4 servings

Please read about Stir-Frying, 1052. Use this method for most vegetables, from green beans to julienned carrots to asparagus. Or use a medley of vegetables, such as peas, carrots, broccoli, and water chestnuts. Cut all vegetables into pieces small enough to cook very quickly—broccoli into small florets, sugar snap peas on a diagonal, mushrooms sliced, and cabbage shredded.

Prepare:

Stir-Fry Sauce, 552

Trim and cut into thin, small pieces:

1 pound vegetables (broccoli, cabbage, bok choy, carrots, peas, mushrooms, snow peas, etc.)

Heat in a wok or a large skillet over high heat:

2 tablespoons vegetable oil

When the oil begins to shimmer, add:

2 garlic cloves, smashed
4 thin slices peeled ginger

Cook until the garlic begins to brown and is fragrant. Add the prepared vegetables and cook, stirring frequently, until crisp-tender, 5 to 8 minutes. Add longer-cooking vegetables to the pan first and quick-cooking vegetables later to ensure that everything is done at the same time. Give the sauce a good stir to disperse the cornstarch, then pour the sauce into the pan, stirring to coat the vegetables. Cover the pan, remove from the heat, and allow to sit for 3 minutes. Serve with:

Cooked white rice
Sesame seeds
Chopped green onions

VEGETABLE BREAKFAST HASH

4 servings

For a smoky, savory boost, fry **4 to 6 slices bacon** until crisp and use 2 tablespoons of the bacon fat for cooking the potatoes (chop or crumble the bacon and stir it in after the mushrooms have softened).

Steam until fork-tender, about 10 minutes:

2 medium beets (about 8 ounces), trimmed, peeled, and cut into ⅜- to ½-inch cubes

Heat in a large skillet over medium heat until hot:

2 tablespoons olive or vegetable oil

Add:

1 pound potatoes (any variety or a combination), peeled or scrubbed and cut into ½-inch cubes
1 medium onion, chopped
¾ teaspoon salt

Cover and cook for 8 minutes, then uncover and continue to cook until tender and nicely browned, 10 to 12 minutes more. Scrape the potatoes up off the bottom of the skillet occasionally with a metal spatula. If the browned bits on the bottom of the skillet start to get too dark, add a splash of water and scrape them up.

Stir in the beets along with:

1 cup sliced shiitake mushroom caps (about 3 ounces)
2 garlic cloves, minced

Cook until the mushrooms have softened, about 5 minutes. Add:

(1 cup packed shredded beet greens)
(½ teaspoon red pepper flakes)
¼ teaspoon black pepper

Stir to combine and cook, stirring occasionally, for 5 minutes more to allow the flavors to meld. Taste and, if needed, season with:

Salt and black pepper

Serve with:

4 Fried Eggs, 155, or Tofu Scramble, 286

GLAZED ROOT VEGETABLES

3 to 4 servings

A simple technique with attractive results.

Combine in a heavy saucepan:

1 pound root vegetables, such as carrots, turnips, parsnips, celery root, rutabaga, salsify, potatoes, or sweet potatoes, peeled and cut into ½-inch pieces
1½ cups stock or broth
4 tablespoons (½ stick) butter
(2 tablespoons white wine vinegar)
2 teaspoons sugar
½ teaspoon salt

Bring to a simmer, then cover, reduce the heat, and cook until the vegetables are just tender. Uncover and continue to cook, shaking the pan constantly over medium-high heat, until the liquid has reduced and the vegetables are coated with a golden glaze.

ROOT VEGETABLE PUREE

4 to 6 servings

The potatoes lend this puree a light texture and delicate flavor.

Place in a large saucepan:

1 pound carrots or parsnips, peeled and cut into thick slices, or 1½ pounds celery root, salsify, turnips, or rutabaga, peeled and diced
8 ounces all-purpose or russet potatoes, peeled and thickly sliced

Add cool water to cover generously, bring to a boil, reduce the heat, and simmer until the vegetables are completely tender, 20 to 25 minutes. Drain and return the vegetables to the pan. Over low heat, mash the vegetables with a potato masher or beat with a handheld electric mixer until smooth. Mix in:

½ cup milk or heavy cream
2 tablespoons butter, softened
½ teaspoon salt
¼ teaspoon black or white pepper

Taste and adjust the seasonings. If desired, top with:

(Brown Butter, 558, Chile Butter, 560, or the fried-spice mixture for Dal II, 218)

ROOT VEGETABLE BRAISE

4 servings

Serve this robust, savory stew with Garlic Bread, 638, or mashed potatoes. Substitute an equal amount of parsnips, salsify, carrots, red or gold potatoes, or Jerusalem artichokes for any of the vegetables in the recipe, if desired.

Heat in a pot or Dutch oven over medium heat:

1½ tablespoons olive oil
1 tablespoon butter
1 bay leaf
1 large sprig thyme

Add and cook, stirring occasionally, until they begin to brown, about 12 minutes:

2 medium onions, diced

Add and cook, stirring, for 3 minutes:

4 large mushrooms, thickly sliced (2 to 3 ounces)
2 garlic cloves, minced

Pour in:

½ cup dry white wine

Increase the heat and boil, scraping the bottom of the pot, until the liquid is reduced to a syrup, about 5 minutes. Add:

1 pound celery root, peeled and cut into 1-inch cubes
8 ounces turnips, peeled and cut into 1-inch cubes
8 ounces rutabaga, peeled and cut into 1-inch cubes
1 tablespoon all-purpose flour
½ teaspoon salt

Stir the vegetables, then pour in:

2½ cups chicken or vegetable stock or broth

Bring to a boil, then reduce the heat, cover, and simmer until the vegetables are tender, 20 to 25 minutes. Remove the bay leaf and thyme sprig. Mix together and pour into the stew:

3 tablespoons heavy cream
1 tablespoon Dijon mustard

Stir well and season to taste with:

Salt and black pepper
Chopped parsley

BATTERED AND DEEP-FRIED VEGETABLES

4 to 6 servings

Please read about Deep-Frying, 1051, and About Battering Fried Foods, 656. To fry larger pieces of very firm vegetables like sweet potatoes, parcook them to ensure they are tender by the time they finish frying. This may be accomplished by steaming or boiling until barely tender (for an example of this, see Jojos, 271).

I. PAKORAS

Chickpea flour, 985, adds a wonderful, nutty savoriness to batters. It can be found at natural food stores and Indian groceries. We love preparing an assortment of vegetables this way. For another superlative fritter, see Spinach Pakoras, 245.

Prepare in a large bowl:

Pakora Batter, 657

Preheat the oven to 200°F. Heat to 350°F in a deep-fryer, deep heavy pot, or Dutch oven:

3 inches vegetable oil

While the oil heats, prepare for frying:

2 pounds mixed vegetables, such as cauliflower, broccoli, zucchini, eggplant, onion, or peeled potatoes, sweet potatoes, or yams

Cut the broccoli or cauliflower into bite-sized florets; cut the zucchini and eggplant into ½-inch-thick rounds; cut the potatoes into ¼-inch-thick slices; cut the onions into ¼- to ½-inch-thick slices. Add the vegetables to the batter and toss to coat. Fry in batches until golden brown and crisp, 2 to 4 minutes depending on the vegetable. Do not crowd the pot. Remove from the oil with a spider or slotted spoon and drain on a baking sheet lined with paper towels. Keep the finished pakoras hot in the oven. Serve with any of the following:

Tomato Achar, 569, Raita, 569, Cilantro-Mint Chutney, 568, or Tamarind Chutney, 566

II. TEMPURA

Some of our fondest, early food memories involve tucking into a plate of freshly fried mixed vegetable tempura. Prepare the tempura batter last and use it promptly. For a crunchier texture, pour **2 cups panko bread crumbs** on a plate and dredge the battered vegetables in them before frying.

Preheat the oven and frying oil and prepare the vegetables as for **I, 203.** Just before frying, prepare:

Tempura Batter, 657

Promptly dip the vegetable pieces into the batter one at a time and transfer to the hot oil. Fry in batches until crisp and cooked through, 2 to 4 minutes depending on the vegetable. Remove from the oil with a spider or slotted spoon and drain on a baking sheet lined with paper towels. Keep the finished tempura hot in the oven. Serve with:

Tempura Dipping Sauce, 572
Lemon wedges

III. BEER-BATTERED

Asparagus, broccoli, and mushrooms are perfectly at home in this all-purpose batter.

Prepare:

Beer Batter, 657

Preheat the oven and frying oil and prepare the vegetables as for **I, above.**

Dip the vegetable pieces into the batter one at a time and transfer to the hot oil. Fry in batches until crisp and cooked through, 2 to 4 minutes depending on the vegetable. Remove from the oil with a spider or slotted spoon and drain on a baking sheet lined with paper towels. If desired, sprinkle with:

(Salt)

Keep hot in the oven. Serve with:

Aïoli, 564, Mayonnaise, 563, flavored with curry powder or chipotles in adobo, Tartar Sauce, 563, or Quick Ketchup, 565
Lemon wedges or malt vinegar

VEGETABLES À LA GRECQUE

4 servings

These mixed vegetables become aromatic by simmering in a seasoned marinade. They make excellent hors d'oeuvre or additions to salads or an antipasto tray.

Prepare:

2 pounds mixed vegetables

Suitable choices include artichoke hearts, julienned carrots, cauliflower florets, celery or fennel pieces, trimmed green beans, whole or halved mushrooms, pearl onions, strips of bell pepper, and whole olives. Eggplant slices or strips are delicious, but they should be salted first; see 237.

Squeeze over the cut vegetables to prevent browning:

Juice of 2 lemons

Reserve 2 of the lemon shells and place in a medium stainless steel or enameled saucepan along with:

4 cups water, or 3 cups water and 1 cup dry white wine
½ cup olive oil
(3 shallots, peeled and halved)
2 garlic cloves, smashed
2 teaspoons fresh thyme leaves or ½ teaspoon dried thyme
6 sprigs parsley
12 whole black peppercorns
(10 coriander seeds, crushed)
1 teaspoon salt
(1 teaspoon dried oregano)
(⅛ teaspoon fennel or celery seeds)

Bring to a boil over high heat, reduce the heat, cover, and simmer for 15 minutes. Add the vegetables and cook until tender. Remove the vegetables with a slotted spoon, and place in a bowl. Let the marinade cool, pour through a strainer, then cover the vegetables with the marinade to store in the refrigerator for up to 3 days. Bring to room temperature to serve. After the vegetables have been eaten, use the marinade for sauces or reuse to cook more vegetables.

RATATOUILLE PROVENÇALE

8 servings

Served on a platter that shows off its contrasting colors, this dish looks like a colorful Cubist still life.

Heat in a large skillet or Dutch oven over medium heat:

¼ cup olive oil

Add and cook, stirring, until golden and just tender, 10 to 12 minutes:

1 medium eggplant (about 1 pound), peeled and cut into 1-inch chunks
2 large zucchini (about 1 pound), cut into 1-inch chunks

Transfer the vegetables to a plate. Add to the pan and cook, stirring, until the onion is slightly softened:

2 tablespoons olive oil
1 large onion, sliced

Add and cook, stirring occasionally, until the vegetables are just tender but not browned, 8 to 12 minutes:

2 large red bell peppers, cut into 1-inch squares
3 garlic cloves, finely chopped

½ teaspoon salt
¼ teaspoon black pepper

Add:

1½ cups peeled, 281, seeded, chopped fresh tomatoes or one 14½-ounce can diced tomatoes
2 or 3 sprigs fresh thyme or ½ teaspoon dried thyme
1 bay leaf

Reduce the heat to low, cover, and cook for 5 minutes. Add the eggplant and zucchini and cook until everything is tender, about 20 minutes more. Taste and adjust the seasonings. Stir in:

¼ cup chopped basil
(Chopped pitted Niçoise or Kalamata olives to taste)

VEGETABLE TIAN

4 servings

Think of this Provençal dish as a more orderly version of ratatouille. We like to use a long Chinese eggplant rather than a stout Italian eggplant to get more slices. If you have a mandoline, 201, this is a good time to use it.

Preheat the oven to 375°F. Toss together in the bottom of a 13 × 9-inch baking dish:

1 large leek, trimmed, halved lengthwise, well cleaned, and thinly sliced
2 tablespoons olive oil
1 tablespoon fresh thyme leaves
½ teaspoon salt
¼ teaspoon black pepper

Cut into ¼-inch-thick slices:

1 medium eggplant (about 1 pound)
2 large zucchini (about 1 pound)
3 large slicing tomatoes (about 1¾ pounds)

Layer the vegetable slices—like dominos, or shingles—in the baking dish, alternating eggplant, zucchini, and tomato, overlapping the slices tightly. If desired, after every third slice, tuck in:

(1 basil leaf)

Drizzle the tian with:

¼ cup olive oil

Sprinkle with:

¼ teaspoon salt

Cover with foil and bake for 30 minutes. Remove the foil and bake until all the vegetables are very tender, about 30 minutes more.

VEGETABLE TAGINE

6 servings

Heat in a Dutch oven over medium heat:

2 tablespoons butter or olive oil

Add and cook, stirring, until softened, 6 to 8 minutes:

2 medium onions, chopped
5 garlic cloves, chopped

Stir in and cook until fragrant, about 1 minute:

1 teaspoon ground cumin
1 teaspoon salt
½ teaspoon red pepper flakes or 1 teaspoon Harissa, 584
½ teaspoon ground cinnamon
½ teaspoon grated or ground nutmeg
¼ teaspoon ground cardamom
¼ teaspoon black pepper
Pinch of ground cloves

Stir in:

2 cups chicken or vegetable stock or broth
1 small butternut squash (1½ pounds), peeled, halved, seeded, and cut into ½-inch cubes
1 large russet potato, peeled, halved lengthwise, and cut into ¾-inch-thick slices
3 medium carrots, cut into ¼-inch slices
2 medium zucchini, halved lengthwise and cut into ½-inch-thick slices
One 15-ounce can chickpeas, drained and rinsed
⅓ cup halved and pitted oil-cured black olives
¼ cup raisins

Bring to a simmer, then reduce the heat to medium-low, cover, and cook until the vegetables are completely tender, about 20 minutes. Stir in:

3 tablespoons lemon juice

Serve with:

Couscous, 325
Chopped parsley or cilantro

ABOUT ARTICHOKES

Artichokes are the immature flower buds of a thistle plant; the green "globe" variety is the most common, but you may also encounter purple-tinged ones. The edible parts of a full-grown artichoke are the base of the leaves, the saucer-shaped piece above the stem called the **heart,** and the peeled stem. Once trimmed, artichoke hearts are a delicious addition to salads and pizzas; they are available frozen, canned, and marinated. Large artichokes are most commonly steamed whole and untrimmed, and served one to a diner. To the uninitiated, an artichoke can be daunting to eat; for instructions, see Steamed Artichokes, 206.

For those who do not want to fuss with cleaning and peeling, **baby artichokes** are a dream come true: With the outer leaves removed and the stem trimmed, baby artichokes can be steamed, sautéed, or deep-fried and eaten whole. They can be hard to find, but may be ordered online. Regardless of size, ➤ select tightly closed artichokes that feel heavy for their size and make a squeaking sound when squeezed. Store in a plastic bag in the refrigerator crisper for up to 1 week.

Artichokes contain the acid cynarin, which causes wines and foods served with them to taste sweet. When serving a special wine, it is best to keep artichokes off the menu, but in general, white wines and rosés pair well with artichokes. In cooking, artichokes go well with citrus juice, vinegars, white wine, olives, capers, ham, bacon, onions, peas, garlic, shallots, thyme, tarragon, fennel, basil, and oregano.

To prepare artichokes for cooking, wash each one, holding the stem end and plunging rapidly and repeatedly in a bowl of water. Use stainless steel, not carbon steel, knives and cookware to prepare artichokes, as carbon steel will react with the vegetable and cause discoloration and off-flavors. ***For eating whole,*** cut off the top quarter of the artichokes and snip off the spiny tips of the leaves with kitchen shears. Use a paring knife to peel the stem; the prickly choke is easiest to remove after cooking. ***For any preparation where the artichokes are cut into pieces,*** trim as directed on 205, then remove tougher outer leaves. Be aggressive in trimming the leaves. It will feel a bit wasteful, but tough leaves will never become tender. Halve the artichokes through the stem and use a paring knife or spoon to dig out the fuzzy choke (a grapefruit knife or spoon or a melon baller is especially helpful). Then, depending on the size of the artichoke, you may leave it halved or cut further into quarters. Artichokes discolor when trimmed or cut; if trimming them ahead of time, place them in a bowl of acidulated water, 951.

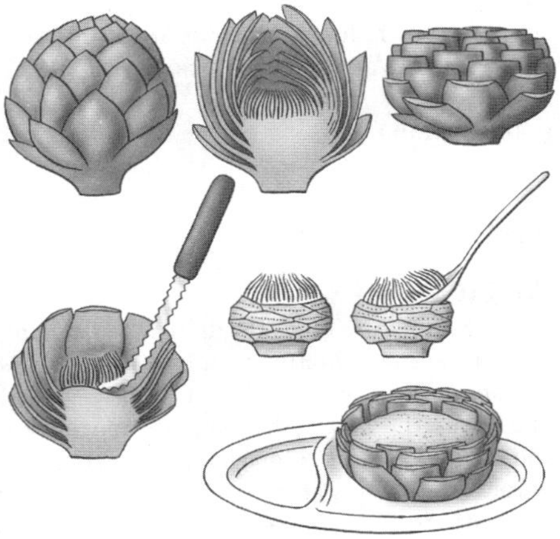

Trimming and serving artichokes

To grill, prepare Steamed Artichokes II, below. Brush lightly with vegetable oil and grill over direct heat until browned. Sprinkle with salt and lemon juice.

Pressure-cook whole, large artichokes with 1 inch of water at 15 psi for 10 minutes; use the quick release method, 1059. Medium artichokes will take about 8 minutes.

STEAMED ARTICHOKES

I. WHOLE

Prepare for eating whole, above:

1 medium to large artichoke per serving

If you wish to serve them filled with sauce or melted butter in the center, part the center leaves and pull out the prickly pinkish leaves in the center. Using the tip of a spoon or a melon baller, scrape out the fuzzy choke; be careful not to cut into the heart. To avoid discoloration, rub the cut surfaces with:

Lemon juice

Place in a steamer basket over 2 to 3 inches of boiling water, first adding to the water, if desired:

(1 onion, sliced, or 1 garlic clove, smashed)
(1½ tablespoons lemon juice or dry white wine)
(A bay leaf)

Cover and steam until the bottoms feel tender when pierced with a paring knife, about 30 minutes for medium artichokes and up to 45 minutes for especially large ones. Check the water level halfway through cooking and replenish with boiling water if necessary. Drain and serve hot or chilled with:

Melted butter, Brown Butter, 558, Mayonnaise, 563, Aïoli, 564, Hollandaise, 561, or a vinaigrette, 575

Provide a bowl for discarding spent leaves.

To eat whole artichokes, remove the leaves one by one and dip the thick, fleshy end into the butter or sauce. Bite down gently on the leaf and pull it through your teeth to scrape off the tender edible portion (discard the fibrous remains). When you reach the inner, light-colored cone of young leaves, pull it up with one movement. Then, with a spoon or knife, scrape away the fuzzy choke and discard it. Eat the heart and tender portion of the stem with a fork, dipping each piece into the butter or sauce.

II. HALVED OR QUARTERED

Wash:

1 medium to large artichoke per serving

Leave the stems attached. Snap off the toughest outer leaves and discard. Cut off the top one-third of the artichokes, and peel the stem with a paring knife. Lay each artichoke on its side and cut into halves or quarters through the stem. Using the tip of a spoon or a melon baller, scrape out the fuzzy choke. Place the artichokes in a steamer basket over 1 to 2 inches of rapidly boiling water, cover, and steam until they are easily pierced with a fork, about 15 minutes. Serve as for I, above.

GARLIC-BRAISED ARTICHOKES

4 servings

In this simple method, artichokes are braised in white wine until tender. When the wine evaporates, the artichokes brown in the garlicky olive oil.

I. HALVED

Wash:

4 medium to large artichokes

Trim off the tough, outermost leaves, and cut off the top one-third of the artichokes. Trim the stems to about 1 inch and peel them. Halve the artichokes through the stem and cut out the chokes. Rub all cut surfaces liberally with:

Lemon juice

Place the artichoke halves, cut side down, in a skillet or sauté pan large enough to hold them in a single layer, along with:

1 cup dry white wine, water, or chicken stock or broth
3 tablespoons olive oil
(¼ cup diced prosciutto or country ham)
2 garlic cloves, smashed
½ teaspoon salt
¼ teaspoon red pepper flakes or black pepper

Bring the liquid to a boil over high heat. Reduce the heat, cover, and simmer until the artichokes are easily pierced with a fork, about

15 minutes. Uncover, increase the heat to medium-high, and cook until the liquid has evaporated, about 3 minutes. Reduce the heat to medium-low and cook the artichokes until they are nicely browned, about 5 minutes more. Serve garnished with:

Lemon wedges
Minced herbs
Grated Parmesan or Romano

II. TRIMMED, STORE-BOUGHT ARTICHOKE HEARTS

Prepare **I, 206,** using **two 9-ounce packages frozen artichoke hearts, unthawed, or three 14-ounce cans artichoke hearts in water, well drained.** Cover and simmer the artichoke hearts for 5 minutes or until heated through. Uncover and proceed as directed.

STUFFED ARTICHOKES ALLA ROMANA

4 servings

Preheat the oven to 350°F. Clean, trim well as for whole artichokes, 206, and halve through the stem:

4 large artichokes

Scrape out the chokes, trim the stems to 1 inch, and peel them. Place the halved artichokes in a steamer basket over 1 to 2 inches of boiling water, cover, and cook until just tender, about 10 minutes.

Warm in a medium skillet over medium heat:

2 tablespoons olive oil

Add and sauté until tender, about 5 minutes:

1 small onion, diced
1 celery rib, diced

Add and sauté 1 minute more:

3 garlic cloves, minced
½ teaspoon red pepper flakes

Remove from the heat and stir in:

½ cup grated Parmesan (2 ounces)
¼ cup chopped parsley
¼ cup dry bread crumbs
(4 oil-packed anchovy fillets, rinsed and chopped)
½ teaspoon salt
¼ teaspoon black pepper

Lay the artichokes cut side up in a baking dish. Fill each one with the bread crumb mixture and drizzle with:

2 tablespoons olive oil

Pour into the baking dish:

1 cup water or chicken stock or broth

Cover with foil and bake until tender, about 45 minutes. Remove the foil and bake for 10 minutes more.

FRIED ARTICHOKES

4 servings

I. FOR ARTICHOKE HEARTS AND BABY ARTICHOKES

You may also prepare Steamed Artichokes II, 206, and use them here.

Rinse and cut in half:

24 walnut-sized baby artichokes, top third trimmed off; two 9-ounce packages frozen artichoke hearts, thawed and drained; or three 14-ounce cans artichoke hearts in water, drained

If using baby artichokes, pull off any tough outer leaves and trim the stems flush with the bottoms.

Heat to 325°F in a large skillet over medium-high heat:

1 cup olive oil

As the oil heats, mix in a shallow bowl:

½ cup flour
1 teaspoon salt
1 teaspoon black pepper

Lightly beat together in a second shallow bowl:

2 large eggs

Toss the artichokes in the seasoned flour, then dip them into the eggs, turning to coat, and toss again in the flour. Keeping the oil near 325°F, fry the artichokes in batches, turning often, until golden and tender, 5 to 6 minutes. Do not crowd the skillet. Drain briefly on paper towels, then pile them on a platter and season with:

Salt

Serve with:

Lemon wedges

II. ROMAN JEWISH-STYLE FRIED ARTICHOKES

Here, artichokes are trimmed and steamed until just tender, then the leaves are splayed outward and the artichokes are fried. This method results in beautiful, golden artichokes that look like flowers.

Wash:

4 large or 8 medium artichokes

Trim off the tough outer leaves. Be aggressive when trimming. Cut off the top half of the artichokes, leaving only about 1 inch from the base of the heart to the top of the trimmed leaves. Trim and peel the stem and scrape out the choke. Place the artichokes stem side up in a steamer basket over 1 to 2 inches of boiling water. Cover and steam until just barely tender, about 8 minutes for medium artichokes and 12 minutes for large artichokes. Let sit until cool enough to handle.

With the artichokes stem side up on a work surface, gently splay the leaves outward and press down on the artichokes. The heart of the artichoke may split. This is okay. Simply splay the leaves as best you can.

Heat to 325°F in a large, deep skillet or Dutch oven over medium-high heat:

½ inch olive oil

Add the artichokes to the skillet, stem side up. Fry, maintaining the temperature of the oil at 325°F, until golden brown, 5 to 7 minutes. Use tongs to grab the stems and lay the artichokes on their sides in the oil and continue to fry, turning every couple of minutes, until the artichoke hearts and stems are completely tender and browned, about 6 minutes more. Transfer to a plate lined with paper towels to drain and sprinkle immediately with:

Salt (preferably flaky sea salt)
(Lemon juice)

To eat, separate the leaves from the heart one by one. The inner leaves should be completely tender. Some of the outer leaves may need to be scraped with your teeth. Eat the heart and the stem whole.

BRAISED BABY ARTICHOKES AND PEAS

4 to 6 servings

Rinse, dry, and pull the tough outer leaves off:

24 baby artichokes, about 1 to 1½ inches in diameter

Peel the stems and trim the top quarter off each artichoke. Heat in a large, deep skillet or Dutch oven over medium heat:

2 tablespoons olive oil

Add and cook, stirring, until browned around the edges, 7 to 10 minutes:

1 small onion, chopped

Transfer the onion to a small bowl. Add the artichokes to the pan and cook, stirring occasionally, until they are browned all over, about 10 minutes. Add:

¼ cup white wine, chicken stock or broth, or water
2 tablespoons butter
2 large garlic cloves, minced

Bring to a simmer, cover, reduce the heat, and cook gently, stirring occasionally, until the artichokes are nearly tender, 20 to 25 minutes. Add more liquid if needed. Return the onion to the pan and stir in:

2 cups fresh or frozen green peas

Cook for another 5 minutes and season with:

Salt and black pepper to taste
Shredded basil leaves, thyme leaves, or chopped tarragon or parsley
2 teaspoons lemon juice

ABOUT ASPARAGUS

Spring to early summer is the peak season for asparagus, but it shows up in grocery stores throughout the year. Out-of-season asparagus is not as sweet or tender but it is perfectly serviceable. Choose taut, firm stalks with tightly grouped tips; avoid woody stalks or bunches with damaged, soft, or slimy tips. Asparagus varies in width from the size of a thumb to that of a pencil. Thickness is not a good indicator of tenderness or age. Thicker spears are more forgiving when broiled or grilled as they will not overcook so quickly. **White asparagus** is grown by mounding soil on top of the spears to prevent them from being exposed to the sun. You may find purple asparagus as well, which retains its color even after cooking, though it will dull somewhat (treat them as you would green).

Asparagus does not store well; wrap in moist paper towels, store in a plastic bag in the crisper, and use promptly. Extend the life of asparagus by standing bundles with their cut ends down in a bowl or cup with a couple inches of water. Loosely cover the bundle with a bag and store in the refrigerator.

To prepare asparagus for cooking, rinse well and cut off the tough, pale bottom portion of the stalk, or simply bend the stalk until it snaps. The latter method may waste a bit more of the tender stem, but it is quick (and much more satisfying). If desired, you may shave off the tougher outer layers near the bottom of the stalks with a vegetable peeler. White asparagus must be peeled before cooking—peel them from just below the tip.

Asparagus benefits from any quick-cooking method. Try roasting, broiling, or grilling whole spears or stir-frying cut pieces. They may also be battered, deep-fried, and served as an appetizer (see Battered and Deep-Fried Vegetables II, 204). Or serve asparagus raw in salads by slicing the stalks on the diagonal into thin pieces, or use a vegetable peeler to turn them into ribbons and dress as for Shaved Carrot Salad, 126. Asparagus ribbons can also be briefly stir-fried or sautéed, or lightly coated with olive oil and used as a pizza topping, 614.

STEAMED ASPARAGUS

3 to 4 servings

Trim, above:

1 pound asparagus

Leave the spears whole or cut into 2-inch sections. If leaving whole, tie the spears into bunches with a piece of twine. Bring 1 inch of water to a boil in a deep pot. Place pieces in a steamer basket or stand bunches upright in the pot. Cover and steam until tender, 3 to 5 minutes.

Transfer to a serving dish and serve with:

Hollandaise, 561, Béarnaise Sauce, 561, Sauce Gribiche, 568, or Miso Beurre Blanc, 559

Or toss with:

2 to 4 tablespoons melted butter, extra-virgin olive oil, Brown Butter, 558, or a vinaigrette, 575

If desired, sprinkle over the top:

(Buttered Bread Crumbs, 957, or Crispy Fried Shallots, 256)
(Chopped or riced Hard-Boiled Egg, 151, finely sliced prosciutto or country ham, or crisp, crumbled bacon)

ROASTED ASPARAGUS

3 to 4 servings

Position a rack in the top third of the oven and preheat it to 500°F.

Trim, above:

1 pound asparagus

Place the spears on a baking sheet and drizzle very lightly with:

Vegetable oil

Toss the spears to coat and arrange them in a single layer. Roast until just tender, 6 to 8 minutes. Serve with any of the accompaniments suggested for Steamed Asparagus, above, or simply sprinkle with:

(2 tablespoons minced parsley, tarragon, and/or chives)
(Grated Parmesan)
Salt and black pepper to taste

Serve hot or at room temperature, garnished with:

Lemon wedges

STIR-FRIED ASPARAGUS

4 to 6 servings

Please read about Stir-Frying, 1052.

Trim, above, and cut into 2-inch pieces:

2 pounds asparagus

Heat in a wok or skillet over high heat:

2 tablespoons vegetable oil

Swirl the oil in the pan, then add the asparagus along with:

1 tablespoon slivered peeled ginger

Stir-fry for 2 to 3 minutes, then add:

2 garlic cloves, slivered
¼ teaspoon salt

Stir-fry for 1 minute, then add:

¼ cup chicken stock or broth

Cover, reduce the heat slightly, and cook until the asparagus is tender, 3 to 5 minutes. If desired, serve sprinkled with:

(1½ tablespoons toasted, 1017, white or black sesame seeds)
(1 teaspoon toasted sesame oil)

ASPARAGUS WITH ORANGE AND HAZELNUTS
3 to 4 servings

Trim, 208, and steam, 208, until just tender:

1 pound asparagus

Set aside. Cook in a large skillet over medium heat until the butter is slightly browned:

2 tablespoons butter
¼ cup hazelnuts, toasted, 1005, and chopped

Stir in the asparagus along with:

Finely grated zest of 1 orange
3 tablespoons orange juice

Toss several times to heat through. Season to taste with:

Salt and black pepper

ABOUT AVOCADOS

Here we enter murky waters: Avocados are fruits, botanically speaking. Nonetheless, we tend to think of them as vegetables because they are mostly used in savory preparations. In short, with apologies to botanists everywhere, we discuss avocados in this chapter for this very reason. For avocado leaves, see 954.

Avocado trees are native to the Americas. **Hass avocados** are the most common in stores. They are grown in California as well as Central and South America. Their thick, dark-green skin darkens even further as they ripen. Once cut, they are quick to brown unless coated or mixed with an acidic ingredient like vinegar or citrus juice. They are available year-round. **Fuerte avocados** are much larger and have a thin, bright-green skin (it does not darken as it ripens). Though easier to bruise than Hass avocados, Fuertes do not turn brown as readily once cut. They are grown in Florida or farther south, and their season runs from late fall to early spring. For most purposes, including guacamole, choose Hass avocados, which have a deeper flavor and richer, smoother texture than Fuerte avocados, in part because they contain twice as much fat. Fuerte avocados do very nicely in salads and sandwiches, which benefit from their lighter flavor and moister texture. There are dozens of other varieties, some of which are positively gigantic. The **Sharwil avocado,** a hybrid of the Hass and Fuerte, is grown commercially in Hawaii, and has just been cleared by the USDA for importing to some states.

Smaller Hass avocados result when the growing season is especially poor, and they occasionally find their way to supermarkets as **baby avocados.** Though impractical for making guacamole, they are a perfect single-serving amount for mashing on toast, or slicing for use as a garnish. You may also stuff them with a spoonful of salsa and serve as an hors d'oeuvre. Miniature, seedless **cocktail avocados** are created by keeping the tree's blossoms from pollinating. About the size and shape of a small pickling cucumber, they are a rare treat.

To test an avocado for ripeness, hold it in your hand and apply even, gentle pressure. If it yields slightly, it is ready to eat. Never buy an avocado that feels soft or that has loose, puffy or indented skin; it is most likely bruised or overripe. If you cannot find a ripe avocado, simply pick harder specimens and ripen them at home. Even the hardest avocados will ripen within 2 to 4 days at room temperature, and often within just 1 day if placed in a paper bag. Once ripened, store avocados in the refrigerator and use within 2 days.

To cut an avocado, make a lengthwise cut into the center of the fruit with a large knife. Carefully rotate the fruit, cutting the flesh down to the pit all the way around. Twist the avocado open by rotating the two halves of the fruit in opposite directions. To remove the pit, place the half with the pit lodged in it on a cutting surface and firmly whack the blade of a knife into it, embedding the sharp edge in the pit. Take the half in your hand and carefully twist the pit out. Scoop the avocado cup from the peel with a large spoon. Or, for a carefree method of dicing or slicing, hold the pitted avocado half in your hand and gently score the pulp into cubes or slices before scooping.

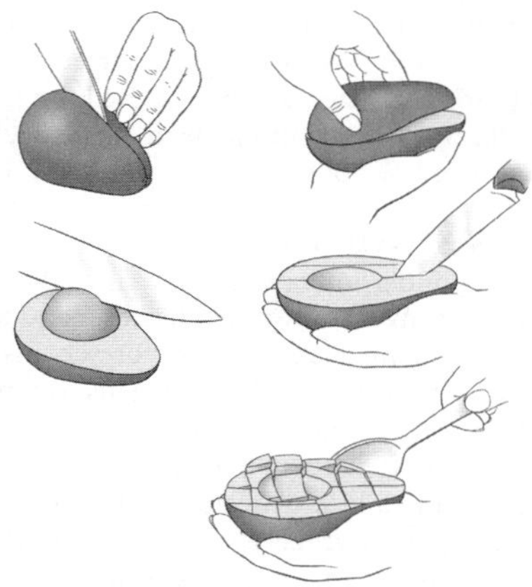

Cutting and dicing an avocado

The flesh of an avocado darkens when exposed to air, especially Hass avocadoes. Tossing or rubbing the cut fruit with lemon or other citrus juice slows the process but does not stop it, so it is best to slice avocados just before serving.

To store an avocado half, leave the pit in and use the other half. Sprinkle the exposed flesh with lemon juice, cover tightly with plastic wrap, and refrigerate.

➤ Avocados can become bitter when subjected to high heat, so add to soups and other hot foods only at the last minute as a garnish. For salad combinations, see Avocado and Citrus Salad, 125, and Avocado and Mango Salad, 125. For Guacamole, see 51. In many parts of the world, avocados are treated more like fruits and are used in sweet dishes. For an example, see Vietnamese Avocado Shake, 13.

ABOUT BAMBOO SHOOTS

These slightly acidic shoots are marvelous in stir-fries, Thai curries, and soups. Canned shoots are readily available; whole, vacuum-packed shoots can be found at Asian markets. Rinse and slice them before cooking. Fresh, young shoots are sometimes available in spring. Unpeeled, they will keep for several weeks wrapped in a paper bag in the refrigerator crisper.

To prepare fresh bamboo shoots, peel away the outer layers down to the pale inner core and cut off the base. Slice the core and cook in boiling water for a minimum of 20 minutes to dispel any hydrocyanic acid (the same bitter, heat-sensitive toxin found in cassava and apricot kernels). Sample a small piece. If it tastes bitter, boil in fresh water for 5 more minutes, sample again, and repeat until the bitterness is gone.

ABOUT BEANS

Beans are a large and diverse clan of vegetables, to which **lentils,** 217, and **peas,** 258, also belong. There are four stages at which we eat beans. **Bean sprouts,** below, are either eaten raw, briefly cooked in stir-fries and noodle dishes, or added at the last second to soups. Fresh **snap or green beans,** below, are young, with small or undeveloped beans and pods that are tender enough to eat raw or quickly cooked. **Shell beans,** 211, are mature, with plump beans that need to be freed from their tough, inedible pods. **Dried beans,** or **pulses,** 212, are perfect for pantry storage and require long simmering. See also Tofu, 285, Tempeh, 287, About Bean Salads, 129, and About Hearty Bean and Legume Soups, 88.

ABOUT BEAN SPROUTS

Sprouts have come under intense scrutiny since they are grown in an environment that invites unwanted bacteria and are often consumed raw. In fact, many large grocery store chains do not carry sprouts of any kind to avoid liability concerns. If you are cooking for anyone with a compromised immune system, we recommend avoiding sprouts or cooking them before serving.

Mung bean sprouts add a delicate crunch to stir-fried dishes. Asian markets and some groceries also carry **soybean sprouts,** which are thicker, longer, and have yellow heads. Unlike mung bean sprouts, which are often enjoyed raw, soybean sprouts should be cooked briefly—either stir-fried, steamed, or parboiled for at least 5 minutes—to rid them of off-flavors and neutralize trypsin inhibitors, which interfere with the digestion of protein. They remain pleasantly crunchy despite the cooking. Various **sprouted legumes** are also available—more bean than sprout in most cases—and are excellent in salads. Sprouts contribute texture and color to rice; add them, without stirring, for the last few minutes of cooking. Be sure sprouts are fresh when you buy them, with no wilting, browning, or sliminess. To store, line a produce bag with a paper towel and refrigerate in the crisper. Use within 2 days of purchase. Before using, rinse and spin dry in a salad spinner. To sprout beans, seeds, and grains yourself, see 1021.

ABOUT FRESH SNAP OR GREEN BEANS

Many of these were once called **string beans,** because their strings had to be removed, but today many have been bred to be stringless and need only have the stem ends snapped off. **Haricots verts** are a slimmer and more tender version of green beans. Other edible-pod beans are yellow or purple **wax beans** and the richly flavored broad **Romano beans.** Beautiful and meaty **yard-long** or **snake beans,** 211, are actually a relative of black-eyed peas and crowder peas. For snow peas and sugar snap peas, see About Peas, 258.

Edible-pod beans are available year-round. Choose plump, firm beans with a bright color, and store in a partially closed bag in the refrigerator crisper. Edible-pod beans have a great affinity with butter, bacon, and chopped toasted nuts, particularly almonds and hazelnuts. Especially good herbs for beans are dill, chives, parsley, and basil. In addition to the preparations below, tender green beans are excellent battered and fried, 203. See About Bean Salads, 129, for more options.

STEAMED OR BOILED GREEN BEANS

4 to 5 servings

Trim the stem ends of:

1 pound green beans

You may cut them crosswise or on the diagonal or leave them whole. Place the beans in a steamer basket over 1 inch of boiling water and cover. Alternatively, place them in a saucepan full of rapidly boiling water. Cook until barely tender, 6 to 10 minutes. Drain and toss with:

(2 tablespoons extra-virgin olive oil, butter, Brown Butter, 558, or up to ¼ cup vinaigrette, 575)
Salt and black pepper to taste

If desired, top with any of the following:

(¼ cup Buttered Bread Crumbs, 957)
(2 to 4 slices cooked bacon or pancetta, crumbled)
(2 tablespoons chopped parsley, basil, tarragon, chives, or a combination)
(Toasted, 1005, chopped almonds, hazelnuts, or peanuts)
(Crispy Fried Shallots, 256, Sautéed Mushrooms, 251, or Sautéed Onions, 255)

ROASTED GREEN BEANS

3 to 4 servings

Prepare **Roasted Asparagus, 208,** substituting **1 pound trimmed haricots verts or tender green beans** for the asparagus.

GREEN BEAN CASSEROLE

6 servings

A classic recipe first concocted by Dorcas Reilly in the 1950s to promote condensed cream of mushroom soup. We find that it works well with or without the help of this old convenience product.

Preheat the oven to 350°F.

Place in a buttered 13 × 9-inch baking dish:

1 pound green beans, trimmed

Mix in a medium bowl:

¾ cup milk
Creamed Mushrooms, 251, or one 10¾-ounce can condensed cream of mushroom soup
½ cup Crispy Fried Shallots, 256, or canned fried onions
Salt and black pepper to taste

Pour over the beans and bake, uncovered, for 30 minutes. Sprinkle with:

⅔ cup Crispy Fried Shallots, 256, or canned fried onions

Bake until browned, 5 to 10 minutes more.

BRAISED GREEN BEANS

4 to 8 servings

I. WITH PORK AND POTATOES

Place in a medium pot:

One smoked ham hock or 4 ounces country ham

Add water to cover, bring to a simmer, and simmer for 30 minutes. Add:

1 pound green beans, trimmed
1 pound red potatoes, quartered
(1 onion, chopped)

Simmer, covered, until the beans are very tender, 10 to 15 minutes. Drain and season to taste with:

Salt and black pepper

Chop or shred the pork and toss with the beans.

II. WITH ONIONS, TOMATOES, AND DILL

This treatment is especially tasty with Romano beans or any late-season beans beginning to toughen.

Heat in a large skillet or Dutch oven over medium heat:

2 tablespoons olive oil

Add and cook until softened, about 5 minutes:

1 medium onion, finely chopped, or 1 bunch green onions, white part only, finely chopped
1 large garlic clove, thinly sliced
(¼ teaspoon dill seeds)

Add:

1 pound green beans, trimmed
4 Roma or plum tomatoes, grated, or one 14½-ounce can diced tomatoes
¼ cup water, vegetable stock or broth, or tomato juice

Simmer, covered, until the beans are very tender, about 25 minutes. Season with:

1 tablespoon chopped dill
1 tablespoon chopped parsley
¼ teaspoon salt, or to taste

Serve hot or at room temperature.

SICHUAN-STYLE DRY-FRIED BEANS

4 servings

Dry-frying requires an extra step, but the results are worth it. For straightforward stir-frying see Basic Vegetable Stir-Fry, 202, and Stir-Fried Snow Peas, 259. We prefer yard-long beans, or snake beans as they are sometimes called. You can often find them in Asian supermarkets. For a vegetarian version, simply omit the pork or replace it with crumbled tempeh.

Heat in a wok or large skillet over medium heat until shimmering:

2 tablespoons vegetable oil

Add and fry, stirring occasionally, until tender and starting to wrinkle and blister, about 8 minutes:

12 ounces yard-long beans or green beans, trimmed and cut into 2-inch pieces

Transfer the beans to a plate. Increase the heat to medium-high and add:

4 ounces ground pork

Cook, breaking up the meat, until no longer pink and beginning to brown, about 5 minutes. Stir in:

1-inch piece ginger, peeled and cut into matchsticks
2 garlic cloves, thinly sliced
3 green onions, white parts only, finely chopped
1 teaspoon Sichuan peppercorns, lightly crushed
½ teaspoon red pepper flakes or 3 dried chiles de árbol, stemmed and seeded

Cook, stirring, until the spices are fragrant and the meat is cooked through, about 3 minutes. Return the green beans to the pan and stir in along with:

1 tablespoon soy sauce
Thinly sliced green onion tops
(½ teaspoon toasted sesame oil)
(Chopped roasted peanuts)

ABOUT FRESH SHELL BEANS

We prefer many types of beans when they mature and have tough pods, but are still plump and moist. The most popular include **cranberry** or **borlotti beans, runner beans, lima beans** and smaller **butter beans, flageolet** or **cannellini beans,** and **fava** or **broad beans.** Be aware that ➤ raw red kidney beans and lima beans are toxic; boil lima beans for at least 10 minutes and red kidney beans for at least 30 minutes. Some people are allergic to fava beans as well, but for those who are not, they are fine to eat raw.

To shell beans in the pod, pry open the pod along the inner edge. The beans will pop out easily. In the case of shelled favas, the individual beans are also encased by a thin membrane; though it is customary to peel this off, it is by no means necessary, especially for very young favas, and many think it diminishes their flavor.

To peel fava beans, bring a large saucepan of water to a boil, add the favas, and blanch for 30 seconds. Transfer to an ice water bath and cool completely. The skins should slip off easily. If you cannot find favas, you may substitute fresh or frozen lima beans for them in recipes.

Shell beans always taste richer when seasoned with something from the onion family, and they are delicious with tomatoes, peppers, ham, sausages, chiles, garlic, cumin, coriander, and herbs including summer savory, cilantro, epazote, sage, parsley, thyme, and bay. For that famous combination called Succotash, see 236. For bean salads, see 129. Cook fresh, immature soybeans, or **edamame,** in their pods, as described on 47.

Pressure-cook shell beans with twice as much water as beans. Cook at 15 psi for 8 minutes; cook larger beans at 15 psi for 15 minutes. Allow the pressure to release naturally, 1059.

BRAISED LIMA BEANS

6 servings

If desired, add a couple smashed garlic cloves, sprigs of thyme, and a few grated Roma tomatoes for more flavor.

Place in a large skillet and add water to barely cover:

4 cups shelled fresh (about 4 pounds in the pod) or frozen lima beans
2 tablespoons butter or olive oil
1 teaspoon salt

Bring to a boil, then cover, reduce the heat, and simmer until tender, 25 to 35 minutes depending on the age of the beans. Check the beans periodically and add a little water if needed. Stir in:

1 tablespoon lemon juice
1 tablespoon chopped parsley, chives, or dill

WANDA'S STEWED CRANBERRY BEANS

8 servings

Megan grew up eating these beans every Sunday; they were a staple crop in her grandparents' garden. Her family calls them October beans, and they are never served without corn bread and stewed greens.

Combine in a large saucepan and cover with water by 1 inch:

4 cups shelled fresh cranberry or borlotti beans (about 2½ pounds in the pod)
8 ounces ham or 4 ounces country ham, cut into small chunks

Bring to a boil, then reduce the heat, partially cover, and simmer slowly until the beans are very tender and creamy and the liquid has transformed into a thick bean "gravy." The time will vary depending on the beans, but start checking them at 30 minutes. Season to taste with:

Salt

Serve with:

Southern Corn Bread, 630
Southern-Style Greens, 243

BAGHALI GHATOGH (IRANIAN FAVA BEAN STEW WITH EGGS)

4 servings

Many Iranian dishes rely heavily on *sabzi*, or fresh herbs. This stew is no exception. Do not be tempted to scrimp on the amount of dill here. It seems like a lot, but it is tempered by simmering and adds a lovely, herbal note to the stew.

Shell and peel, 211, or have ready:

3 pounds fava bean pods or one 14-ounce package frozen fava or lima beans

You should have about 2 cups. Heat in a deep skillet or sauté pan over medium heat:

2 tablespoons olive oil

Add the beans and cook, stirring, until they turn bright green, about 4 minutes. Stir in:

3 garlic cloves, minced
½ teaspoon ground turmeric
½ teaspoon salt

Cook until the garlic is fragrant, about 1 minute. Stir in:

2 cups vegetable or chicken stock or broth or water
1 cup chopped dill

Bring to a boil, then reduce the heat to medium-low, cover, and simmer until the beans are tender, 10 to 15 minutes. Uncover and make 4 depressions in the stew. Working one at a time, crack into a small bowl or ramekin and slide into a depression:

4 large eggs

Cover the pan and cook the eggs until just set or to the desired degree of doneness, 4 to 6 minutes. Serve the stew with:

Cooked basmati rice, 343

Sprinkle with:

Chopped dill

ROMAN-STYLE FAVA BEANS

3 to 4 servings

Shell and peel, 211, or have ready:

3 pounds fava bean pods or one 14-ounce package frozen fava or lima beans

You should have about 2 cups. Heat in a large skillet over medium heat:

2 tablespoons olive oil

Add and cook, stirring, until softened, about 4 minutes:

½ small onion, finely chopped
(2 slices bacon or pancetta, diced)
(½ teaspoon red pepper flakes)

Add the beans along with:

¾ cup chicken stock or broth or water

Simmer uncovered, stirring occasionally, until the beans are tender, 10 to 20 minutes depending on the age and size of the beans. By the time the beans are done, the liquid should be reduced to just a little sauce to coat them. If necessary, reduce the liquid over high heat. Before serving, stir in:

1 tablespoon chopped parsley
1 tablespoon lemon juice
Salt and black pepper to taste

ABOUT DRIED BEANS AND LEGUMES

There are dozens of varieties of dried beans and peas available. They include **fava** or **broad, black** or **turtle, cranberry** or **borlotti, scarlet runner, red, kidney, black-eyed peas** (also known as **cowpeas** or **field peas**), **soybeans, pintos, chickpeas** or **garbanzos, flageolets, lentils, tepary beans, Great Northern, navy, cannellini,** and **adzuki** beans. Each variety has, for the connoisseur, its own charm.

Regardless of type, rinse dried beans thoroughly and pick them over, removing debris and any small, fractured, or discolored beans. If you are tempted to save yourself some time in front of the stove, you may soak beans before cooking; this will cut the cooking time nearly in half.

To soak dried beans, combine them in a bowl with three to four times as much water as beans and leave on the counter overnight. Remove any that float. If desired, drain the beans, then add fresh water to cover for cooking. This is not strictly necessary—the beans may be cooked in their soaking water.

There is also the so-called **quick-soak method,** in which beans are brought to a boil for 5 minutes, then taken off the heat and allowed to sit for 1 hour. The problem with this method is that, by the time the beans have soaked, you could be well on your way to a fully cooked pot of unsoaked dried beans. The quick-soak method only saves about 30 minutes of cooking time, so we think you're better off either soaking beans overnight or cooking beans from dried.

Many believe that adding salt to the cooking water will toughen beans. This is not quite true. Beans cooked in salted water may take slightly longer to become tender, but they will be evenly seasoned. We recommend simmering beans gently until almost tender, adding a healthy pinch of salt (about 1 teaspoon per pound of beans), and continuing to cook them until creamy and tender.

Acidic ingredients, on the other hand, will definitely slow down or prevent beans from becoming tender. Do not add tomatoes, citrus juice, vinegar, molasses, or any other acidic ingredients until near the end of cooking, after the beans are tender. This principle is conveniently applied in reverse for Boston baked beans: The precooked beans do not turn mushy when baked for hours in the oven because the added molasses and tomatoes keep the beans firm.

Canned beans can be substituted in recipes, though they may be softer and less flavorful. Rinsing canned beans improves the taste and removes excess salt, which is especially beneficial for bean salads. That said, we often include the liquid from the can to add body to chilis and stews.

Remember that ➤ 1 cup of dried beans, peas, or lentils will expand to 2 to 2½ cups after cooking. ➤ One 15- or 16-ounce can holds about 1½ cups of drained beans. The number of cups in a 1-pound package varies by variety, but ➤ in general, 1 pound of dried beans measures around 2½ cups.

In addition to these recipes, see About Hearty Bean and Legume Soups, 88, Macleid's Rockcastle Chili, 502, and bean dips, 52–53.

To cook dried beans, bring them just to a boil in water to generously cover. If desired, add a glug of olive oil, a bay leaf, half an onion, and a few garlic cloves to the cooking liquid. Reduce the heat, cover, and simmer gently until tender. The time it takes for beans to cook depends on where they were grown and on their age—usually two unknowns for the cook—and the type of water used in cooking them; see Water, 1032. Chickpeas are usually the toughest of the lot and may take up to 3 hours to cook. Dried limas, after soaking, and lentils, which don't require soaking, may cook in as little as 30 minutes.

▲ At high altitudes, dried beans take more time to rehydrate and cook. The difference starts to be noticeable above 3,500 feet; the cooking time may be as much as doubled.

Pressure-cooking is an excellent, time-saving way to cook dried beans and, we think, one of the finest uses for a pressure cooker. Dried beans may also be cooked in a slow cooker, but never slow-cook red kidney beans without boiling them first. ➤ Red kidney beans contain high levels of a toxin called *phytohaemagglutinin*, which can cause severe gastric distress. To eradicate this toxin, cook red kidney beans at a full, rolling boil for at least 10 minutes before proceeding, either by simmering or slow-cooking.

To pressure-cook dried beans, add unsoaked beans to the pressure cooker and add water to generously cover. Times for pressure-cooking vary according to the size and type of the bean, but for smaller beans like black beans or black-eyed peas, start with 20 minutes at 15 psi. For tougher beans like chickpeas, start with 35 minutes. Allow the pressure to release naturally for 10 minutes, then open the valve to release the pressure completely, 1059.

FRIJOLES DE LA OLLA

8 servings

Traditionally cooked in a clay pot, these beans will taste just as delicious cooked in whatever kind of pot you have available.

If desired, soak overnight, 212, in a pot:

1 pound dried beans, such as pintos or black beans, rinsed and picked over

Drain, return to the pot, and cover with water by 1 inch. Add to the beans in the pot:

1 medium onion, quartered
2 garlic cloves, smashed
3 sprigs epazote or oregano
(1 dried chile, such as New Mexico or guajillo)
(1 dried avocado leaf)

Bring to a boil, then reduce the heat, partially cover, and simmer until the beans are almost tender, 30 minutes to 1 hour. Add:

1 teaspoon salt

Continue to cook until the beans are completely tender and creamy, about 15 minutes more. Mash some of the beans with a potato masher or remove 1 cup of beans and puree in a food processor, then stir back into the pot. Serve with:

Warm corn tortillas
Crema or sour cream
Crumbled Cotija or shredded cheese, such as Cheddar, Monterey Jack, or Oaxaca cheese

TUSCAN BEANS

6 to 8 servings

Tuscans love beans so much that the rest of Italy calls them *mangia fagioli*, "the bean eaters." We feel as if we would fit right in.

If desired, soak overnight, 212:

1 pound dried cannellini, pinto, or cranberry beans, rinsed and picked over

Drain the beans and set aside. Heat in a large pot over medium heat until hot:

¼ cup olive oil

Add and fry until fragrant:

12 fresh sage leaves
3 garlic cloves, halved
¼ teaspoon red pepper flakes, or to taste

Add the beans to the pot along with water to cover by 2 inches. If available, add:

(1 Parmesan rind)

Bring to a boil, then reduce the heat, partially cover, and simmer gently for 30 minutes. Season to taste with:

Salt and black pepper

Continue to simmer until the beans are tender, 15 to 20 minutes more. Mash some of the beans with a potato masher or remove 1 cup of beans and puree in a food processor. Stir them back into the beans and simmer to thicken the broth slightly. Serve warm or at room temperature, drizzling over each portion:

About 1 teaspoon extra-virgin olive oil (2 to 3 tablespoons total)

FUL MEDAMES (SIMMERED FAVA BEANS)

2 servings

This simple Egyptian bean dish is commonly served for breakfast, lunch, or dinner. It is excellent served with Shirazi or Israeli Salad, 128. You can substitute **1 cup dried fava beans** for the canned ones. Simply simmer them in water to cover until very tender, peel if needed, and proceed with the recipe.

Combine in a medium saucepan and simmer for 10 minutes:

One 15- to 20-ounce can peeled fava beans and their liquid
2 tablespoons extra-virgin olive oil

Remove a big spoonful of the beans, mash them, then stir back in. Add:

4 garlic cloves, minced
1 tablespoon lemon juice

Simmer for 5 minutes. Taste and add salt and more lemon juice if needed. Serve garnished as desired with any of the following:

Extra-virgin olive oil
Ground cumin
Marash, Aleppo, or Urfa pepper, or red pepper flakes, 968
Yogurt or labneh
Crumbled feta cheese
Chopped parsley

FALAFEL

12 falafel

I. FRIED

Soak for at least 12 hours, or overnight, 212:

1¼ cups dried chickpeas, rinsed and picked over

Drain the beans thoroughly, transfer to a food processor, and finely chop. Add and process until coarsely pureed:

½ cup chopped onion
¼ cup packed parsley leaves
2 garlic cloves, chopped
2 teaspoons ground cumin
1½ teaspoons salt
½ teaspoon ground coriander
½ teaspoon baking soda
½ teaspoon ground turmeric
¼ teaspoon cayenne pepper

Transfer to a bowl and stir in:

2 tablespoons all-purpose flour or chickpea flour

With wet hands, form the mixture into 12 balls. Let stand for 15 minutes.

Heat in a deep skillet until hot:

½ inch vegetable oil

Fry the falafel in batches, turning occasionally, until golden, 6 to 8 minutes. Drain on paper towels.

II. BAKED

Prepare the mixture for **version I, above.** Preheat the oven to 375°F. Lightly oil a baking sheet. Form the falafel into balls as directed and place on the baking sheet; You may leave them round or flatten slightly into patties. Brush with olive oil and bake, flipping halfway through and brushing with more oil if shaped into patties, until browned and crisp, 15 to 20 minutes.

FEIJOADA (BRAZILIAN BLACK BEAN STEW)

8 servings

This long-simmered meat and bean stew can feature a wide variety of meaty odd bits. Any combination of pork ribs, pork tongue, *carne seca* (dried beef), or corned beef may be substituted for the meat in this recipe. Just be sure to use a combination of salted and fresh meat to avoid oversalting the stew. Feijoada may also be prepared in a slow cooker. Simply combine all the ingredients and cook on low for 8 to 10 hours or until the meat is extremely tender. Stir in the browned onions and garlic just before serving. *Farofa*, a mixture of toasted cassava flour and fried bacon and onions, is the traditional garnish. You may find this topping in South American grocery stores, but it is not absolutely necessary. If you find coarsely ground cassava flour (*not* tapioca starch), try making your own, 986.

Place in a pot or Dutch oven:

1 pound dried black beans, rinsed and picked over
1 pound pig's feet, split in half, or smoked ham hock
1 pound boneless pork shoulder, cut into 1-inch chunks
(½ pound pig's tails)
½ pound slab bacon, cut into ½-inch cubes
2 bay leaves

Add water to cover by 1 inch. Bring to a boil over medium-high heat, then reduce the heat to medium, partially cover, and simmer. Skim any scum off the top of the stew for the first 30 minutes. Continue to simmer until the meat is very tender and the beans are cooked, about 2 hours. If necessary, add hot water to keep the ingredients covered. While the stew cooks, prepare the Brazilian hot sauce. Combine in a blender and blend until smooth:

2 jalapeño peppers, seeded and chopped
½ red onion, chopped (reserve the other half)
2 garlic cloves
⅓ cup lime juice
½ teaspoon salt

Alternatively, for a coarser sauce, hand-mince the jalapeños, onion, and garlic and stir in the lime juice and salt. Let the hot sauce sit while the stew finishes cooking.

Skim any pooled fat from the top of the stew and reserve. Add to the stew:

½ pound fresh chorizo link sausages or kielbasa, cut into ½-inch slices

Simmer until the stew is very thick, about 1 hour more. Warm 2 tablespoons of the reserved fat in a medium skillet over medium heat. Thinly slice the reserved onion half from making the hot sauce, and add to the skillet, along with:

1 large onion, thinly sliced
¼ teaspoon salt

Cook, stirring, until golden brown, about 10 minutes. Add:

6 garlic cloves, minced

Cook until fragrant, about 2 minutes more. Stir the onions and garlic into the stew. Remove the ham hock or pig's feet (and pig's tails, if using), let cool slightly, and shred the meat from the bone. Stir the meat back into the stew. Serve with the hot sauce and:

Farofa, store-bought or homemade, 986
Orange slices

Sautéed Shredded Collard Greens, 245
Cooked white rice, 343

REFRIED BEANS

6 servings

A classic side dish with enchiladas, burritos, or chiles rellenos. The beans are easier to mash when they are warm.

Cook, 213:

2 cups dried pinto or black beans, rinsed and picked over

or have ready:

Three 15-ounce cans pinto or black beans

Drain the beans, reserving 1 cup of the liquid. Heat in a large skillet over medium-high heat:

2 tablespoons vegetable oil, bacon fat, or lard

Add and cook, stirring often, until golden brown, about 10 minutes:

1 medium onion, chopped

Add and cook, stirring, for 1 minute:

4 garlic cloves, minced

Add the beans 1 cup at a time, mashing each addition to a coarse puree with a potato masher or the back of a large spoon before adding the next. Stir in:

1 cup reserved bean cooking liquid

Cook, stirring often, over medium heat or slightly lower until the beans are a little soupier than you would like to serve them—they will thicken as they sit. The whole mashing and cooking process should take 10 to 15 minutes. Season to taste with:

Salt

Serve warm with:

Crumbled Cotija or queso fresco

JAMAICAN STEW PEAS

4 to 6 servings

You may also use **two 15-ounce cans kidney or red beans** instead of dried beans. If using canned beans, start the recipe at the meat-browning step. For a vegetarian dish that showcases many of the same flavors, see Jamaican Rice and Peas, 331.

Add to a pot along with 8 cups water:

1½ cups dried small red beans, or kidney or pinto beans, rinsed and picked over

Bring to a boil, then reduce the heat, cover, and simmer until the beans are tender, 1 to 1½ hours. Drain, reserving 4 cups of the bean cooking liquid.

Heat in a large saucepan over medium heat:

1 tablespoon vegetable oil

Add, in batches if necessary, and brown on all sides:

1 pound boneless pork shoulder, cut into 1-inch cubes

Add and cook, stirring, until softened, about 5 minutes:

1 large onion, chopped
3 garlic cloves, smashed
1 teaspoon salt

Add the cooked beans and the reserved cooking liquid (or, if using canned beans, 4 cups water) along with:

1 medium sweet potato, peeled and cubed
One 13½-ounce can coconut milk
1 Scotch bonnet or habanero pepper, minced
3 sprigs thyme
½ teaspoon black pepper
¼ teaspoon ground allspice

Reduce the heat and simmer, uncovered, until the pork is tender and the stew is thick, about 1½ hours. Serve with:

Cooked white rice, 343
Chopped cilantro

BAKED BEANS

6 to 8 servings

Baked beans are as traditional in Sweden as they are in Boston.

I. DRIED BEANS

If desired, soak overnight, 212:

1½ cups dried white beans or navy beans, rinsed and picked over

Drain and add to a pot, along with 8 cups water. Bring to a boil, then reduce the heat, cover, and simmer gently until tender, 45 minutes to 1 hour.

Preheat the oven to 250°F. Grease a 9-inch square baking dish.

Drain the beans, reserving the cooking liquid. Combine the beans in the baking dish with:

½ cup chicken stock or broth, beer, or water
¼ cup chopped onion
3 tablespoons molasses
3 tablespoons ketchup
1 tablespoon dry mustard
(1 tablespoon Worcestershire sauce)
(1 teaspoon curry powder)
1 teaspoon salt
(½ teaspoon cider vinegar)

Top with:

4 ounces sliced bacon or sliced salt pork

Cover and bake for 3 hours. Uncover and bake for 1 hour longer. The beans should be tender and silky, with a concentrated savoriness. Hold in the oven until serving; if the beans become dry, add a little:

Hot chicken stock or reserved bean cooking liquid

II. CANNED BEANS

Preheat the oven to 350°F. Grease a 9-inch square baking dish. Place in the dish:

Two 15-ounce cans white or pinto beans, drained and rinsed

Add and stir lightly to combine:

¼ cup ketchup or mild, tomato-based chili sauce
¼ cup minced onion
2 tablespoons molasses
2 tablespoons brown sugar
1 tablespoon cider vinegar
(1 tablespoon yellow mustard)
(3 dashes hot pepper sauce)
(2 tablespoons bacon fat)

Cover the top with:

6 slices bacon

Bake, covered, for 30 minutes. Uncover and bake 30 minutes more.

CASSOULET

8 to 10 servings

This bread crumb–topped bean casserole comes from the south of France, and may include a combination of pork, sausage, bacon, duck, wildfowl, or lamb. If you happen to have **Duck or Goose Confit, 433,** you may omit the duck legs here, shred the confit, and layer about 1½ cups of it in with the beans (halve the amount of salt and pepper for seasoning the pork). Tarbais beans are traditional, but Great Northern, flageolet, or cannellini beans are easier to find and work well here.

Combine in a pot:

1 pound dried Tarbais, Great Northern, or flageolet beans, rinsed and picked over
8 cups chicken stock or water
(1 ham hock, especially if using water instead of stock)
1 medium onion, peeled and stuck with 3 whole cloves
¼ cup tomato paste
6 garlic cloves, smashed
6 sprigs thyme
5 sprigs parsley
1 bay leaf

Bring to a boil over medium-high heat, skimming off any foam. Reduce the heat to maintain a simmer, cover, and cook until the beans are almost tender but still slightly chalky, about 1 hour. When the beans are nearly parcooked, add to the pot for the last 10 minutes of cooking:

12 ounces garlic sausages or bratwurst, pricked a few times with a fork

Meanwhile, cook in a Dutch oven over medium heat, stirring occasionally, until rendered and browned:

8 ounces pancetta or slab bacon, cut into ½-inch cubes

As the meat cooks, season:

1 pound boneless pork shoulder, cut into 1-inch chunks
1 pound duck legs

with:

1 teaspoon salt
1 teaspoon black pepper

Transfer the pancetta or bacon to a plate. Add the seasoned pork and duck pieces in batches to the pot and brown all over. Transfer to the plate with the pancetta or bacon. Pour off the fat into a bowl and set aside. Pour into the pot:

½ cup white wine, chicken stock, or water

Deglaze by scraping up any browned bits, then remove the pot from the heat.

Preheat the oven to 350°F. When the beans are parcooked, remove the sausages and ham hock from the pot and set aside. Discard the onion, thyme, parsley, and bay leaf. Drain the beans, reserving the cooking liquid. Shred the meat from the hock (discard the bone) and thickly slice the sausages. Place one-third of the beans in the bottom of the Dutch oven (or a wide 4-quart baking dish). Top the layer of beans with the duck legs and about one-third of the pork, pancetta or bacon, and sausage. Layer with another third of the beans, then distribute the rest of the meat on top, followed by the remaining beans. Pour enough bean cooking liquid into the pot to come to the surface of the beans. Mix 2 tablespoons of the reserved fat with:

1 cup dry bread crumbs

Sprinkle in an even layer over the top of the beans. Bake until the layer of bread crumbs is nicely browned, about 1½ hours. After 1 hour of cooking, you may "crack" the bread crumb layer all over with a spoon, then spread and pat down the crumbs in an even layer again (this helps brown the crumbs more thoroughly). Once browned to your liking, remove the cassoulet from the oven and let rest for 10 minutes before serving.

RED BEANS AND RICE

6 to 8 servings

Ham-simmered red beans spooned over rice is a signature dish of Louisiana Creole cooking. New Orleanian Louis Armstrong perfectly captured the local enthusiasm for the dish with his now-famous valediction, "Red beans and ricely yours."

If desired, soak overnight, 212, and then drain:

1 pound dried small red beans (kidney or pinto beans may be substituted), rinsed and picked over

Combine the beans in a large pot or Dutch oven with:

2 smoked ham hocks (about 1½ pounds)
3 celery ribs, chopped
1 large onion, chopped
1 green bell pepper, chopped
5 garlic cloves, chopped
5 sprigs fresh thyme or 1 teaspoon dried thyme
2 bay leaves
1 teaspoon dried oregano
1 teaspoon white or black pepper
½ teaspoon cayenne pepper

Add water to cover by 1 inch. Bring to a boil, then reduce the heat and simmer, covered, stirring occasionally, until the beans and ham hocks are tender, 1 to 1½ hours. Remove the ham hocks. When they are cool, trim and shred the meat from the hocks. Return the ham to the pot along with:

1 pound andouille or kielbasa sausage, cut on the diagonal into ½-inch-thick slices

Warm through. Remove the thyme sprigs, if used, and bay leaves. Season to taste with:

Salt

Serve over:

Cooked rice, 343

Top with:

Chopped green onions
Tabasco or other Louisiana-style hot sauce

BLACK-EYED PEAS AND GREENS

4 servings

This dish is inspired by two Southern specialties: collards cooked with salt pork and black-eyed peas cooked with a ham hock.

If desired, soak overnight, 212, and then drain:

1½ cups dried black-eyed peas, rinsed and picked over

Combine the peas in a large pot with:

6 cups water
1 smoked ham hock (about 12 ounces)
1 small onion
1 small carrot, peeled
1 leafy celery rib
1 garlic clove, peeled
1 bay leaf

Bring to a boil, then reduce the heat and simmer, covered, until the peas are tender, about 45 minutes. Drain, reserving about 1 cup of the cooking liquid. Discard the onion, celery, garlic, and bay leaf. Return the peas to the pot along with the reserved cooking liquid. Shred the meat from the ham hock and add it. Cut the carrot into small chunks and add it. Stir in:

1 bunch collard, mustard, or turnip greens, or kale, deribbed and coarsely chopped

Bring to a boil, then reduce the heat, cover, and simmer until the greens are tender, 10 to 15 minutes. Stir in:

1 tablespoon red wine vinegar or cider vinegar
½ teaspoon salt, or to taste
¼ teaspoon black pepper

CHANA MASALA (TOMATO-CHICKPEA CURRY)

4 servings

A satisfying vegetarian main dish seasoned with fried whole spices. For a tangier curry, add with the chickpeas **1 tablespoon tamarind paste, 1 tablespoon ground anardana, 953 (dried pomegranate seeds),** or **1 teaspoon ground amchur, 953 (dried mango).**

Heat in a deep skillet or pot over medium heat until hot:

3 tablespoons Clarified Butter, 960, or vegetable oil

Add and fry, stirring frequently, until fragrant and beginning to pop, 1 to 2 minutes:

2 tablespoons cumin seeds
1 tablespoon black mustard seeds
2 or more dried small red chiles, seeded and stemmed
(½ teaspoon ajwain seeds)

If desired, cautiously stir in (the leaves will sputter):

(8 fresh curry leaves)

Fry for another minute, then add:

2 medium onions, thinly sliced

Cook, stirring frequently, for 5 minutes. Stir in:

2-inch piece ginger, peeled and finely chopped
6 garlic cloves, chopped
1 to 3 serrano peppers, to taste, seeded and chopped

Cook for another 2 minutes. Add:

One 28-ounce can crushed tomatoes
3 cups cooked chickpeas, 213, or two 15-ounce cans chickpeas, drained
1 cup water
1 teaspoon salt
1 teaspoon ground coriander

Bring to a boil, then reduce the heat and simmer, partially covered, until the chickpeas are tender, 30 to 45 minutes (for canned chickpeas, 30 minutes will suffice). Serve with:

Cooked basmati rice, 343, Naan, 611, or other flatbread
Chopped cilantro
Lime wedges
(Yogurt or Raita, 569)

ABOUT LENTILS AND SPLIT PEAS

Thanks to their small size, lentils and split peas cook much faster than other legumes. **Split peas** are a green or yellow variety of field pea, which are grown specifically for drying. Though split peas are almost always associated with a ham-infused soup, 90, they can be cooked and added to salads and rice dishes, used in Dal, 218, or added to vegetarian chilis for body and flavor.

The olive-drab lentils sold everywhere are sometimes called green, other times brown, and are actually shades of both; they cook to a somewhat soft texture and mild taste. **French green lentils** (like **Le Puy**) are about half the size of common lentils, are a much darker green, and have a deeper flavor. The small, black **beluga lentils,** named for their resemblance to caviar, are very striking on a plate. **Red lentils,** which are actually a bright orange color, are usually sold split or with the seed coat removed. **Yellow lentils** do not have a seed coat either.

Yellow and red lentils have a silky texture once cooked, making them ideal for Dal, 218. Brown lentils also become very soft when cooked. The smaller plump green or black lentils hold their shape, making them perfect for salads. ➤ 1 cup of dried lentils will yield 2½ to 3 cups cooked (1 pound dried lentils equals 7½ cups cooked).

Regardless of color, all lentils are earthy and peppery, and adapt well to a variety of seasonings. Plainly cooked and simply seasoned lentils make a perfect side dish, or you can use them in salads or combine them with cooked vegetables or rice. For a celebrated rice dish that features lentils, see Mujadara, 330.

SIMMERED LENTILS

4 servings

To serve as a salad, season the cooked lentils with a vinaigrette, 575, and garnish with chopped fresh herbs.

Rinse and pick over:

1 cup brown or green lentils

Heat in a saucepan or skillet over medium heat:

¼ cup olive oil

Add and cook, stirring, until golden brown:

1 small onion, thinly sliced or chopped

Add the lentils along with:

3½ cups water
(2 sprigs parsley or celery leaves)
(1 bay leaf)

Bring to a boil, then reduce the heat and simmer, covered, until the lentils are tender, 20 to 30 minutes. Remove any herbs and season to taste with:

Salt and black pepper
(Lemon juice)
(Chopped herbs)

Serve hot or at room temperature.

DAL (INDIAN LENTIL STEW)

4 to 6 servings

Dal is the Hindi word for both an array of legumes used in Indian cooking and this preparation of legumes. Dal may be thick or thin, as the cook chooses.

I. Rinse, pick over, and place in a large saucepan:

1 cup yellow split peas or red lentils

Add:

3 cups water
1 small onion, sliced
2 serrano or jalapeño peppers, seeded and finely chopped
1 Roma or plum tomato, diced
2 garlic cloves, minced
1-inch piece ginger, peeled and minced or grated
½ teaspoon ground turmeric

Bring to a boil, then reduce the heat, cover, and simmer until the legumes are tender, 20 to 25 minutes. Stir in:

¾ teaspoon salt

Simmer, partially covered, until the dal is thickened to the consistency of split pea soup, about 20 minutes. Ladle into serving bowls and garnish with:

Chopped cilantro

Serve with:

Cooked basmati rice, 343, Naan, 611, or other flatbread

II. DAL TADKA (WITH FRIED SPICES)

Our favorite lentil dish by a long shot. Fried whole spices and spice-infused ghee or oil is the perfect seasoning for a bowl of dal.

Prepare all of the ingredients for:

Dal I, above

Set aside the peppers, garlic, and ginger. Bring the lentils and onions to a simmer and cook as directed. Meanwhile, heat in a small saucepan or skillet over medium heat:

3 tablespoons vegetable oil or Ghee, 960

Add the reserved peppers, garlic, and ginger along with:

1 teaspoon cumin seeds
1 teaspoon coriander seeds, crushed
1 teaspoon black or brown mustard seeds
(4 dried small red chiles, seeded if desired)
(¼ teaspoon ajwain seeds)

Allow to sizzle briskly in the oil until very fragrant, about 1 minute, but be careful not to burn the garlic. If desired, cautiously stir in (the curry leaves will sputter):

(15 fresh curry leaves)
(¼ teaspoon asafoetida, 954)

Remove from the heat and set aside. When the dal has finished simmering, top each bowl with a spoonful of the fried spice mixture. Garnish and serve as directed above.

BRAISED LENTILS WITH SAUSAGE

8 to 10 servings

A New Year's dish from northern Italy. The coin-shaped lentils and sausage slices are thought to bring good fortune.

Bring 3 quarts water to a gentle simmer in a pot large enough to hold the sausage. Add:

1½ to 2 pounds cotechino sausage or fresh Italian sausage links, pierced in several places with a fork

Adjust the heat so the water stays just below a simmer, cover, and cook until the internal temperature of the sausages reaches 160°F, about 45 minutes. Remove from the heat and keep the sausages warm in the water. Meanwhile, bring 10 cups water to a boil in a large saucepan. Add:

1 pound (about 2½ cups) brown or green lentils, rinsed and picked over
1 teaspoon salt

Reduce the heat, partially cover, and simmer until barely tender, about 20 minutes. While the lentils cook, heat in a large skillet over medium heat:

3 tablespoons extra-virgin olive oil

Add and cook, stirring, until golden brown, about 10 minutes:

1 medium red onion, minced
1 medium carrot, minced
1 small celery rib with leaves, minced
1 bay leaf

Stir in and cook for 30 seconds:

1 large garlic clove, minced
2 teaspoons chopped fresh marjoram or oregano or ½ teaspoon dried marjoram or oregano

Stir in and cook over medium-high heat until very thick, 10 to 15 minutes:

One 28-ounce can tomatoes, drained
1 cup sausage cooking liquid or chicken stock or broth

Stir, breaking up the tomatoes by crushing them against the side of the skillet with a spoon. Drain the lentils, stir into the tomato mixture, and cook for 10 minutes. Remove the bay leaf. Season to taste with:

Salt and black pepper

Mound the lentils on a serving platter. Cut the sausage into ¼-inch-thick slices and arrange the slices over the lentils.

ABOUT BEETS

Once, to paraphrase Gertrude Stein, "a beet was a beet was a beet," the crimson-staining menace, earthy and sweet. Markets now carry many hues of beet, from gold, orange, and white varieties to the candy-striped **Chioggia.** They can be perfectly round or long and slender, no bigger than a golf ball or as big as your fist. While it is tempting to say that the color and variety of beets is merely cosmetic, there are some slight differences. The earthy flavor beets are known for comes from a substance called geosmin. Chioggia and cylinder-shaped varieties have higher concentrations of geosmin than standard dark-red beets (see page 219 for ways to diminish its effect).

When selecting beets, choose bunches with leaves that are not yellowing, tattered, or wilted. The greens are an indication of the freshness of the beet roots; if they look moist and fresh, the beets will be too. If beets are sold without leaves, avoid any that look dry, cracked, or shriveled or that yield when pressed. Cut off the leaves, leaving 1 to 2 inches of stem on the beets, and store the beets and leaves separately in plastic bags in the refrigerator crisper. Beet roots will keep for several weeks. Like chard, their leafier relative, **beet greens** are tasty once sautéed; unfortunately, uncooked greens only keep for a few days. If the greens are in good shape, prepare them as quickly as you can, either with the beets, 220, or as for Braised Greens with Garlic, 224.

Scrub beets just before cooking. You do not need to remove the skin or trim off the rootlets, or tails. However, if you wish to reduce a beet's earthy flavor, remove the skin and outer flesh (it has six times the amount of geosmin as the rest of the root). Just remember: Red beet juice stains. Wear gloves and an apron when preparing them and work over a sink.

Beets are delicious hot or cold, sliced or whole if small, as a side dish or in a salad. You may peel and serve them raw, thinly sliced, grated, or julienned (simply toss in a vinaigrette, 575).

Because beets are so sweet, they benefit from being paired with acidic ingredients. Citrus juice or segments, vinegar, sour cream, tangy fresh goat cheese, or crumbled feta or blue cheese are all good options. Adding acids to beets also lessens their earthiness by turning their geosmin into a much milder substance. Of course, some beet enthusiasts love them for this earthy flavor, which is complemented by onions and meats (see Borscht with Meat, 98, and Red Flannel Hash, 473); smoked or cured ingredients like bacon and smoked salmon; or toasted, 1005, nuts—especially walnuts and pistachios. Beets take well to strong, pungent seasonings—ginger, horseradish, capers, caraway seeds, dill, tarragon, mustard, and peppery greens like arugula or watercress.

When sliced thin and fried, red beets make a striking crimson chip, 48. Julienned or shredded beets make a tasty veggie burger, 144, or a fine addition to Latkes, 269. To serve beets cold, see Quick-Pickled Beets, 930, and Beet, Fennel, and Citrus Salad with Horseradish, 123.

Pressure-cook whole, unpeeled 2½-inch beets with 1½ cups liquid at 15 psi for 15 minutes; small beets with 1 cup liquid for 12 minutes. Use the quick release method, 1059.

STEAMED OR SIMMERED BEETS

4 servings

Scrub and trim:

1 pound beets

leaving 2 inches of stem. If the tops are young, reserve. To steam, place the beets in a steamer basket over 3 inches of boiling water and cover. Alternatively, place them in a saucepan and cover with water. Bring to a boil, cover, and simmer until tender. Allow 30 to 40 minutes for young, small beets, 1 hour or more for large beets; add more boiling water to the pot if needed (pay special attention to the water level if steaming the beets).

When the beets are done, cool them slightly and slip off the skins. If small, serve whole. If large, slice or cut into wedges. Toss them in:

3 tablespoons butter, Brown Butter, 558, or a vinaigrette 575

or top the beets with:

Sour cream, Horseradish Sauce, 560, Garlic and Walnut Sauce, 570, Raita, 569, or Tzatziki, 569

and sprinkle with any of the following:

Chopped parsley, chives, or dill, Gremolata, 587, Dukkah, 589, or Browned Bread Crumbs, 957

Lemon juice to taste

Salt and black pepper to taste

BAKED OR ROASTED BEETS

4 servings

Preheat the oven to 350°F.

Place in an 8-inch square baking pan:

1 pound beets, stems trimmed to 1 inch

Add ½ cup water to the pan. Cover tightly with foil and bake until the beets are easily pierced with a thin skewer or knife tip, about 45 minutes for small beets, 1 hour for medium, and 1¼ hours for large beets.

Slip off the skins and leave the beets whole or slice into rounds or wedges. Season to taste with:

Salt and black pepper

Toss with:

2 tablespoons melted butter, olive oil, or walnut oil

Optionally, increase the oven temperature to 425°F, return the beet rounds or wedges to the oven, and roast until nicely browned around the edges, 10 to 15 minutes. Sprinkle with:

1 tablespoon minced parsley, chives, or dill

Lemon juice or red wine vinegar to taste

MEGAN'S BEETS WITH GOAT CHEESE

4 servings

This dish has been known to convert beet-haters. If your kitchen has poor ventilation, you may warm ¼ cup store-bought balsamic glaze over low heat rather than making your own.

Preheat the oven to 425°F. Toss together in a 13 × 9-inch baking dish:

1½ pounds red or golden beets, peeled and cut into ½-inch wedges

2 tablespoons olive oil

½ teaspoon salt

¼ teaspoon black pepper

Arrange the beets in a single layer and add ¼ cup water. Cover tightly with foil and bake until the beets are tender, about 30 minutes. Remove the foil and continue to bake until the water has evaporated and the beets are slightly caramelized, about 15 minutes more. While the beets cook, combine in a medium saucepan:

½ cup balsamic vinegar

¼ cup maple syrup

Turn on an exhaust fan or open a window. Bring the mixture to a boil and simmer, stirring, until reduced and syrupy, about 10 minutes. When the beets are done, drizzle them with the balsamic glaze and sprinkle with:

½ cup crumbled fresh goat cheese (2 ounces)

(¼ cup toasted, 1005, chopped walnuts or pistachios, or Dukkah, 589)

BEETS WITH THEIR GREENS

4 servings

Fresh and crisp beet greens are essential; if they look tired, throw them out. You may prepare this recipe with chard if you cannot find beets with robust greens.

Remove the tops from:

1 bunch beets (1 to 1½ pounds, or 3 to 4 medium beets)

Steam or simmer the beets, 219, until fork-tender. Meanwhile, dice the beet stems and shred the leaves. Heat in a medium skillet over medium heat:

1 tablespoon olive oil

Add the beet stems and cook until tender, about 5 minutes. Add:

3 garlic cloves, minced

Cook, stirring, for 1 minute. Add the greens along with:

¼ teaspoon salt

Cook until wilted and tender, 3 to 5 minutes. Pile the greens on a platter. Slip the skins off the beets, cut into rounds or wedges, and place atop the greens. Sprinkle with:

⅓ cup toasted, 1005, walnuts or hazelnuts, chopped

⅓ cup crumbled feta cheese

1 tablespoon lemon juice

ABOUT BREADFRUIT

Native to the South Pacific, breadfruit was introduced to the Caribbean, Africa, and India in the eighteenth and nineteenth centuries. Breadfruit can be small or quite large, round or oblong, and is scaled all over. The slightly fibrous meat is light yellow, high in starch, and has a potato-like flavor.

When moderately ripe, breadfruit are green with starchy, absorbent flesh; as they ripen, the skin yellows and the flesh turns sweet, much like a ripe plantain. Moderately ripe breadfruit is the most desirable for savory dishes. You may remove the center core with its seed, if it has one, before or after cooking. Breadfruit is very perishable once picked and is hard to find fresh. Use promptly; but if storing at all, submerge whole breadfruit in water to inhibit spoilage. Once breadfruit is cut open, it should be prepared immediately or the flesh will oxidize and turn black.

Like potatoes, starchy, moderately ripe breadfruit can be boiled until tender and mashed, or cut into chunks and roasted. Like plantains, they are wonderful when fried until tender, smashed flat, and fried again into Tostones, 263 (a Puerto Rican specialty). The resulting texture is reminiscent of flaky pastry with a flavor somewhere between yeasty bread and a French fry. Another classic preparation from Samoa is boiled or steamed breadfruit simmered in ample coconut milk with onions and salt. Breadfruit plays well with tropical and Caribbean flavors such as coconut, lime, and chiles. Serve promptly, as the flesh contains latex and tastes waxy if left to cool.

ABOUT BROCCOLI

All members of the brassica family of vegetables—cauliflower, cabbage, mustard, turnips, collards—will eventually bolt and produce flowering tops with florets of varying size and flavor. Essentially, they are all *broccoli* (from the Italian *brocco*, or "sprout," and the Latin *brocchus*, or "projecting"). The variety of brassica that produces our familiar, green-blue florets and thick, sweet stalks has been bred to be the largest and most tender.

There is also the leafier turnip "broccoli" known as **broccoli rabe,** or **rapini.** It has a mustardy bite and is somewhat bitter, though this can be lessened by blanching, 1047. Smaller, lesser-known types of "broccoli"—from flowering kale, collards, red cabbage, arugula, and mustard—can occasionally be found at farmers' markets, and are usually labeled with the type of plant and "rapini" or "rabe" at the end. **Spigarello** is a mild relative of broccoli rabe that does not grow florets.

The diminutive, asparagus-flavored **broccolini** and toothsome **purple sprouting broccoli,** an English heirloom variety, are especially good roasted. Thick-stemmed **Chinese broccoli,** or **gai lan,** has small florets hidden by large, tender leaves. It is very mild and best sautéed or stir-fried. To preserve the texture of the leaves, you may trim them off and cook the stems until tender before adding. Many broccoli-cauliflower hybrids have been bred, such as the fractal-shaped **Romanesco** and the creatively named **broccoflower.** For more on these, see About Cauliflower, 229.

For plain old green broccoli, choose heads that are dark green with a purple or blue haze. Yellowish heads are overly mature and should be avoided. Store in an open plastic bag in the refrigerator crisper for up to 3 days.

To trim broccoli, snap or cut the florets off the thick center stalk. If some florets are much larger than others, cut them to match the rest. If the skin of the stalks is fibrous, peel it down to the tender, sweet flesh. You may also leave the stalk and florets connected by splitting whole broccoli apart lengthwise into slender wedges or "bouquets"—an especially good way to roast them. If removing the florets from the stalk, remember: ➤ Do not discard broccoli stalks; they are delicious. Slice them on the diagonal into pieces ¼ to ½ inch thick—or julienne them—for stir-frying or using raw in slaws, 119.

Green broccoli is delicious seasoned with citrus juice, butter or extra-virgin olive oil, nut oils, garlic and shallots, ginger, fresh or dried chiles, soy sauce, oyster sauce, fish sauce, sweet peppers, cheeses, and warm seasonings like curry powder, or Garam Masala, 588.

For smaller "broccolis" like broccoli rabe, look for bunches with unwilted leaves and tender stems. Store in an open plastic bag in the refrigerator crisper for up to 5 days. When tender, flowering kale, collard, and arugula tops are excellent when cooked as for Garlic-Braised Broccoli Rabe, 221, roasted whole, or sliced on the diagonal and stir-fried (see Basic Vegetable Stir-Fry, 202). If their stems are tough or woody, peel them and blanch, 1047, for 2 minutes before cooking further.

STEAMED BROCCOLI

4 to 6 servings

Trim, above, and cut into florets:

2 pounds broccoli

Peel the stalks and cut into ½-inch slices. Place florets and stalk pieces in a steamer basket over 1 inch of boiling water. Cover and steam until barely tender, 4 to 6 minutes. Season to taste with:

Salt

Sprinkle with:

Buttered Bread Crumbs, 957

Or toss with:

Brown Butter, 558, or melted butter and lemon juice

Or serve with one of the following sauces:

Any vinaigrette, 575
Sun-Dried Tomato Pesto, 586, or Romesco Sauce, 570
Tahini Dressing, 576, Raita, 569, or Tzatziki, 569
Hollandaise, 561, or Sauce Mornay, 548
Miso Beurre Blanc, 559 or Nuoc Cham, 571

ROASTED BROCCOLI

4 servings

Broccoli develops a rich, concentrated flavor and crisp, lacy edges when roasted.

Preheat the oven to 425°F. Have ready:

1 large head broccoli or 1 to 1½ pounds purple sprouting broccoli, broccoli rabe, or other small variety

Leave tender, small broccolis whole; trim and peel any tough or woody stems. For large broccoli, peel the stem. Cut the head into wedges or separate the broccoli stem from the florets and cut the florets and stem into bite-sized pieces. Toss the broccoli in a large bowl with:

2 tablespoons olive or vegetable oil
½ teaspoon salt
(¼ to ½ teaspoon red pepper flakes, to taste)

Spread the broccoli out on a rimmed baking sheet in a single layer. Roast, stirring halfway through cooking, until the broccoli is tender and charred in spots, 15 to 20 minutes. Remove from the oven and sprinkle with:

Lemon juice
(¼ cup grated Parmesan)

Or, use any of the suggestions for Steamed Broccoli, 220.

BROCCOLI CAKES

4 servings

These bright-green fritters are a welcome change from the usual steamed broccoli side dish.

Steam, 220, until just tender, about 4 minutes:

1 medium head broccoli (about 1 pound), trimmed and cut into florets, or 12 ounces broccoli florets

Allow to cool briefly, until the steam stops rising, then transfer to a food processor and pulse until coarsely chopped. Or coarsely chop with a knife and transfer to a bowl. Add to the broccoli:

2 large eggs
½ cup dry bread crumbs
½ cup grated Parmesan, Gruyère, or sharp Cheddar (2 ounces)
¼ teaspoon salt
¼ teaspoon black pepper

Pulse or stir to combine. Shape the mixture into cakes, using a ⅓-cup measure to portion it. Heat in a large nonstick skillet over medium heat until hot:

2 tablespoons vegetable oil

Add 4 cakes to the skillet and cook undisturbed until browned on the bottom, about 4 minutes. Flip and cook the second side until browned, about 4 minutes more. Transfer to a plate and cook the remaining cakes. Serve with:

Lemon wedges
Sour cream, plain yogurt, or Horseradish Sauce, 566

BROCCOLI-CHEESE CASSEROLE

4 to 6 servings

In the 1963 edition of *Joy*, Marion recommends topping this casserole with a crust of crushed corn flakes and grated Romano cheese. We agree.

Preheat the oven to 425°F. Butter a 9-inch square baking dish. Prepare:

Steamed Broccoli, 220

Drain, finely chop, and set aside. Melt in a medium saucepan:

2 tablespoons butter

Add and sauté until softened:

1 small onion, minced

Stir in until blended:

2 tablespoons all-purpose flour

Add while whisking constantly:

1 cup milk
½ teaspoon salt

Bring to a simmer, whisking, until thickened. Remove from the heat and stir in:

1 cup grated Cheddar (4 ounces)

Add the broccoli and stir to combine. Pour into the baking dish and top with:

1 cup corn flakes, lightly crushed
½ cup grated Romano (2 ounces)

Bake until bubbling around the edges and browned, about 20 minutes.

GARLIC-BRAISED BROCCOLI RABE

4 servings

Bring 4 quarts water to a rolling boil in a large pot and add:

1½ tablespoons salt

Meanwhile, cut into 1-inch pieces:

1 bunch broccoli rabe (about 1 pound), stems peeled, if desired

Add to the boiling water and boil for 2 minutes, then drain and cool slightly. Squeeze the moisture out of the leaves. Heat in a large skillet over medium heat:

2 tablespoons olive oil

Add:

1 garlic clove, thinly sliced
(1 small dried red chile pepper)

Add the broccoli rabe and cook, stirring occasionally, until tender, about 4 minutes. Remove and discard the chile. Season to taste with:

Salt and black pepper

ABOUT BRUSSELS SPROUTS

These miniature green cabbages are in season during winter months. They are sweet, nutty, and have a nice crunch. You may also find a hybrid of Brussels sprouts and kale sold as **kale sprouts** or **kalettes.** They are much leafier than their relatives from Brussels and have an open structure, which makes them perfect for roasting whole or halved until crispy, as for broccoli, 221.

If you find Brussels sprouts still attached to their stalks, choose a small stalk—it will be younger and its sprouts sweetest. When sprouts are sold loose, select those that are heavy for their size and tightly closed, without any touch of yellow or signs of drying. Store Brussels sprouts in the refrigerator crisper in a closed plastic bag lined with a paper towel to control moisture.

Before cooking, pull off damaged or loose outer leaves and trim the stems. Rinse and drain. Small Brussels sprouts (1 inch in diameter) may be cooked whole. To cook larger sprouts quickly and evenly, slice them in half from top to bottom (through the stem end). Of course, you can also slice or shred Brussels sprouts and make a slaw, 120, or sauté them. We prefer high-heat methods for cooking Brussels sprouts, such as roasting and sautéing, which help them brown and take on flavor without getting soggy. Brussels sprouts pair well with almonds, bacon, butter, Parmesan, chestnuts, cream, garlic, and vinegar. For a classic, indulgent side dish, boil or steam Brussels sprouts and top them with Hollandaise, 561.

To boil or steam whole sprouts, cut an X in the base (stem end) of each and place in a steamer basket over 1 inch of boiling water and cover. Alternatively, place them in a saucepan full of rapidly boiling water. Cook until barely tender, 8 to 10 minutes.

ROASTED BRUSSELS SPROUTS

4 servings

Cooking Brussels sprouts with high heat encourages them to brown and crisp.

Preheat the oven to 425°F. For easier cleanup, line a rimmed baking sheet with parchment paper. Toss together on the sheet:

1½ pounds Brussels sprouts, trimmed and halved through the stem
(1 red onion, cut into ½-inch-thick wedges)
5 garlic cloves, smashed
3 tablespoons olive oil
½ teaspoon salt
¼ teaspoon black pepper

Arrange the Brussels sprouts in a single layer, cut sides down. Roast until golden brown and crisp, 20 to 25 minutes.

BRAISED BRUSSELS SPROUTS WITH CHESTNUTS

6 servings

If fresh chestnuts are not available, use **8 ounces vacuum-packed chestnuts.** For a crispier treatment, prepare Roasted Brussels Sprouts, above, using the smaller amount of sprouts, chestnuts, and halved shallots listed here.

Melt in a large skillet over medium heat:

2 tablespoons butter or bacon fat

Add:

4 small shallots, halved, or 12 pearl onions, peeled
1 pound fresh chestnuts, peeled, 232

Cook, gently shaking the pan occasionally, until both the shallots and chestnuts are lightly browned, about 10 minutes. Add and bring to a boil:

1 pound Brussels sprouts, trimmed and halved through the stem
1 cup chicken or vegetable stock or broth or water
(3 tablespoons dry vermouth or dry sherry)
3 sprigs parsley
1 sprig fresh thyme or ¼ teaspoon dried thyme
1 bay leaf
¼ teaspoon salt
⅛ teaspoon black pepper

Reduce the heat to medium, cover, and simmer until the Brussels sprouts are tender, about 15 minutes. Remove the parsley sprigs, thyme sprig, if used, and bay leaf before serving.

BECKER BRUSSELS SPROUTS

2 to 4 servings

This simple, garlicky side dish is a Thanksgiving favorite at our table.

Trim and halve through the stem:

12 Brussels sprouts

Heat in a medium skillet over medium-low heat:

3 tablespoons butter

Add and cook, stirring, until beginning to brown:

1 or 2 garlic cloves, to taste, smashed

Discard the garlic. Place the sprouts cut side down in the garlic butter, cover, and cook over low heat until tender, 15 to 20 minutes. Arrange the sprouts on a warm platter and drizzle any remaining butter on top. Serve with, if desired:

(Grated Parmesan)

BRUSSELS SPROUT GRATIN

6 servings

To make this vegan, use olive oil and substitute **canned coconut milk** for the cream. For a deluxe version, cook **4 slices bacon** in the skillet until crisp. Reserve the bacon, pour off all but 2 tablespoons of the fat, then proceed with the recipe, stirring the crumbled bacon back in right before topping with the bread crumbs.

Preheat the oven to 350°F. In a large ovenproof skillet, heat over medium heat:

2 tablespoons butter or olive oil

Add and sauté until softened and translucent, 5 to 7 minutes:

2 large shallots or 1 medium onion, chopped

Add and cook until wilted and bright green, about 5 minutes:

1 pound Brussels sprouts, trimmed and shredded

Stir in:

¾ teaspoon salt
Pinch of grated or ground nutmeg

Remove from the heat and stir in:

½ cup heavy cream

For the crumb topping, heat in a small skillet over medium heat:

2 tablespoons butter or olive oil

Add and stir frequently until deep golden brown and nutty smelling, 5 to 8 minutes:

1/3 cup dry bread crumbs or panko
1/3 cup chopped hazelnuts or almonds
1/4 teaspoon salt
1/4 teaspoon black pepper

Top the sprouts with the bread crumb mixture, place the skillet in the oven, and bake until heated through and bubbling, 15 to 20 minutes.

ABOUT BURDOCK

Burdock is the long, slender root of a plant in the lettuce family that has fibrous, mildly sweet, and earthy flesh. Though native to Europe, burdock is most popular in Japan, Korea, and China, where it is used in stir-fries, tempura, pickles, and stews. Although burdock root doesn't look like much, it has a subtle, nutty flavor.

Look for burdock in Asian groceries and at farmers' markets. Select firm, crisp roots with no soft spots. They will probably have dirt clinging to them. Wrap, unwashed, in moist paper towels, place in a plastic bag, and keep in the refrigerator crisper. When ready to cook, rinse and scrub gently with a stiff brush. Snip off any hairy roots. Because the flesh quickly discolors when cut, submerge pieces in a bowl of acidulated water, 951, and use promptly.

Burdock can be cooked any way carrots can, 228, so slice or cut accordingly. Julienned burdock is a welcome addition to vegetable tempura, 203. Like sunchokes, 277, burdock contains a compound called inulin, which may cause flatulence if consumed raw or undercooked.

KINPIRA GOBO (JAPANESE BRAISED BURDOCK AND CARROTS)

4 servings

This is a traditional Japanese preparation for burdock root (*gobo*). Normally, both the carrot and burdock are cut into matchsticks, but we prefer the texture of sliced burdock.

Trim and cut into matchsticks:

1 medium carrot

Scrub well, trim, and cut into very thin slices on the diagonal:

8 ounces burdock root (about 2 cups sliced)

Warm in a large skillet over medium-high heat until shimmering:

1 tablespoon vegetable oil

Add the carrot and burdock and sauté until just starting to brown, about 4 minutes. Add:

2 tablespoons mirin
2 tablespoons soy sauce
2 tablespoons water

Cook uncovered until the liquid is nearly evaporated and the vegetables are beginning to caramelize. If the burdock is not yet tender, add a little more water and continue to cook until tender. Remove from the heat and stir in:

1 tablespoon sesame seeds
2 teaspoons toasted sesame oil
(1/4 teaspoon shichimi togarashi, 1017)

ABOUT CABBAGE

Cabbages are the most recognized member of the brassicas, perhaps the most diverse extended family in the vegetable world. The old standbys are the **head cabbage,** including many firm green or reddish-purple varieties, as well as the soft-leaved, crinkly **Savoy.** Head cabbage is available year-round. Choose firm heads with unblemished leaves. Stored in the refrigerator, head cabbage will keep for several weeks; they can be stored for shorter periods at room temperature if they remain uncut. Savoy cabbage can be used in any recipe for head cabbage, though it is milder in taste and texture. It must be stored in a bag in the refrigerator crisper to keep its delicate leaves from wilting. If your cabbage looks a bit dry, soak it in ice water for 30 minutes after cutting or shredding.

Chinese head cabbages, such as **napa cabbage** and its close relative **Michihili,** have oblong heads with thin, juicy, full-flavored leaves. Shredded, they are perfectly at home in salads or as a raw garnish for grilled meats, and can retain some crunch if briefly stir-fried (do not overcook). Select and store as for Savoy cabbage. **Bok choy** is a mild-flavored Chinese cabbage with thick, hearty stems and thin, green leaves. They may be quite large, or as small as a spice jar (these are referred to as "baby bok choy"). Large bok choy are best sliced on the diagonal and stir-fried or added to soups (you may remove the leaves and add them after the stems are tender). We prefer to halve baby bok choy lengthwise and grill, pan-fry, or sear cut side down until lightly browned. Select brightly colored, firm bok choy and store as for Savoy cabbage.

To shred cabbage, cut the head into eighths through the core. Thinly slice crosswise, or shred on the large holes of a box grater. You may also shred in a food processor fitted with a shredding disk, first cutting out the core. Cabbage cores are quite sweet and pleasantly crisp when raw or cooked; julienne or shred them and add to the dish with the shredded cabbage or simply snack on them.

In the European tradition of cabbage cookery, cabbage is paired with rich meats, cured and smoked meats, game, and root vegetables. It goes well with red or white wine, beer, citrus juice, vinegar, caraway, dill, horseradish, apples, onions, chestnuts, juniper berries, and sour cream. Looking elsewhere, cabbage is often cooked with dried and fresh chiles, ginger, garlic, mustard seeds, cumin, coriander, turmeric, fish sauce, oyster sauce, fermented black beans, and Sichuan chili bean paste, 970.

Raw cabbage adds a satisfying crunch to salads and slaws and is good braised, fried, sautéed, simmered in soups, 87, or stir-fried. We are fans of slicing head cabbage into thin wedges, seasoning them, and grilling or roasting until they are slightly blackened and crispy along the edges. Most head cabbage leaves are sturdy enough to use as a wrapping: See about Leaf Wrappings, 1057. Also see Savory Cabbage Strudel, 703, and Egg Rolls, 71. When fermented into Sauerkraut, 940, and Kimchi, 941, cabbage takes on a second, delicious life as a pickle to serve with starches and meats, or as an ingredient for dishes like Sauerkraut Fritters, 225, Sauerkraut Soup, 86, Kimchi Fried Rice, 332, and Kimchi Jjigae, 87.

SAUTÉED CABBAGE

4 servings

I. WITH BACON AND HERBS

Shred:

One medium head cabbage (about 2 pounds), trimmed and cored

Cook in a large skillet over medium heat until crisp:

4 slices bacon

Tranfer the bacon to paper towels to drain. Increase the heat to medium-high. Add and sauté in the bacon fat until golden, about 5 minutes:

1 small onion, thinly sliced

Add the shredded cabbage along with:

½ teaspoon salt

Cook, stirring, until the cabbage is crisp-tender. Serve with the bacon crumbled over the top along with:

¼ cup chopped herbs such as parsley, thyme, tarragon, dill, or a combination

Lemon juice or cider vinegar to taste

II. WITH CHILES AND FRIED SPICES

Shred:

One small head cabbage (about 1½ pounds), trimmed and cored

Heat in a large skillet or wok over medium heat until shimmering:

3 tablespoons Clarified Butter, 960, or vegetable oil

Add and fry, stirring frequently, until fragrant and beginning to pop, 1 to 2 minutes:

1 teaspoon mustard seeds

½ teaspoon cumin seeds

½ teaspoon coriander seeds

(2 small dried red chiles, seeded and stemmed)

Add and fry for a minute or less (be careful, the leaves will sputter a bit):

2 garlic cloves, thinly sliced

(1 sprig curry leaves, stem discarded)

Promptly add the shredded cabbage and increase the heat to medium-high. Stir in:

¾ teaspoon salt

½ teaspoon ground turmeric

Cook, stirring, until the cabbage is crisp-tender, 5 to 8 minutes. Remove from the heat and stir in:

1 tablespoon lemon juice

(¼ cup chopped cilantro)

Serve immediately as a side dish or as a light meal with:

Dal, 218, and cooked basmati rice, 343

CABBAGE WITH POTATOES AND HAM

4 servings

For a sort of miniature New England Boiled Dinner, 472, substitute **8 ounces cooked corned beef or pastrami** for the ham.

Scrub well or peel:

1 pound small red potatoes

Quarter the potatoes and place them in a large saucepan. Add water to cover along with:

½ teaspoon salt

Bring to a boil and add:

One small head cabbage (about 1½ pounds), trimmed, cored, and quartered

Reduce the heat, cover, and simmer until the potatoes are tender, about 20 minutes.

Stir in:

8 ounces smoked ham, coarsely chopped

3 tablespoons chopped parsley, dill, or a combination

Salt and black pepper to taste

You may drain the vegetables and serve on a large platter, or serve in individual bowls with the cooking liquid. Serve with:

Lemon wedges or red wine vinegar

(Prepared horseradish or whole-grain mustard)

STIR-FRIED BOK CHOY WITH MUSHROOMS

4 to 6 servings

Place in a small heatproof bowl:

6 dried shiitake mushrooms

Pour over the mushrooms:

½ cup boiling water

Let soak for 20 minutes, stirring occasionally. Lift the mushrooms from the bowl, reserving the soaking liquid. Cut the mushrooms into ¼-inch-thick slices. Strain the soaking liquid and transfer 2 tablespoons to a small bowl. Stir in:

1 tablespoon Shaoxing wine, 952, or dry sherry

2 teaspoons cornstarch

¾ teaspoon white pepper

Combine in another small bowl:

1 cup chicken stock or broth

½ teaspoon salt

½ teaspoon sugar

Heat in a wok or a large skillet over high heat:

3 tablespoons peanut or vegetable oil

Add the sliced reconstituted mushrooms and:

1½ to 2 pounds bok choy, cut crosswise into 2-inch pieces

Stir-fry until the bok choy is starting to wilt, 3 to 4 minutes. Add the chicken broth mixture, cover, and steam until crisp-tender, 1 to 2 minutes. Stir the cornstarch mixture, add to the pan, and bring to a boil, stirring. Add:

2 teaspoons toasted sesame oil

Stir well and serve immediately.

ROASTED CABBAGE WEDGES WITH YOGURT SAUCE

4 Servings

High heat concentrates cabbage's flavor to good effect. While the dukkah is optional, we highly recommend including it. You may, like some of our recipe testers, find yourself making the yogurt sauce to go with all kinds of roasted vegetables.

Preheat the oven to 425°F. Cut into 1-inch-thick wedges, leaving the core intact to hold the wedges together:

½ large head of green or red cabbage

You should get about 8 wedges. Place the wedges on a baking sheet (lined with parchment, if desired) and brush with:

¼ cup olive oil
Sprinkle with:
½ teaspoon salt
¼ teaspoon black pepper
Roast until beginning to crisp, 20 to 25 minutes.
While the cabbage roasts, make the yogurt sauce. Combine in a small bowl:
½ cup plain Greek yogurt
(2 tablespoons Dukkah, 589, or toasted, 1005, and finely chopped walnuts)
1 tablespoon olive oil
Finely grated zest of 1 lemon
1 garlic clove, minced
Salt to taste
Serve the roasted cabbage wedges with the yogurt sauce, and sprinkle with extra dukkah or walnuts, if desired. Drizzle the wedges with:
(Balsamic vinegar)

CABBAGE GRATIN
4 to 6 servings
While the words "decadent" and "cabbage" are not often found together, we make an exception for this dish. It is excellent served as part of a winter meal or as a holiday side dish.
Preheat the oven to 375°F. Butter a 9-inch square or round baking dish. Dust the dish with:
¼ cup finely grated Parmesan
¼ cup dry bread crumbs
Heat in a large skillet over medium heat:
2 tablespoons olive oil or butter
Add and sauté until tender, 3 to 5 minutes:
1 leek, trimmed, halved lengthwise, well cleaned, and chopped
Add and sauté until tender and most of the liquid has cooked off:
6 cups shredded cabbage (about 1½ pounds)
Meanwhile, whisk together in a large bowl:
2 large eggs
1 cup heavy cream or whole milk
½ cup grated Swiss cheese, Comté, or Gruyère (2 ounces)
¼ cup all-purpose flour
1 teaspoon salt
¼ teaspoon black pepper
(½ teaspoon caraway seeds, toasted, 1005)
(Pinch of grated or ground nutmeg)
Add the cooked cabbage and stir to combine, pour into the baking dish, and cover the top with:
¼ cup grated Swiss cheese, Comté, or Gruyère
Bake until golden on top, 40 to 50 minutes.

BRAISED RED CABBAGE
4 servings
An old favorite with turkey, pork, or game.
Thinly shred:
1 medium head red cabbage (about 2 pounds), trimmed, quartered, and cored
Place the cabbage in a large bowl and cover with cold water. Place in a large heavy skillet or Dutch oven over medium heat:
2 slices bacon, diced, or 2 tablespoons butter or vegetable oil
If using bacon, cook until it has rendered most of its fat. Add and cook, stirring, until golden, about 10 minutes:
1 medium onion, chopped
(½ teaspoon mustard seeds or ¼ teaspoon caraway seeds)
Drain the cabbage well and add it to the skillet along with:
1 large green apple, peeled, cored, and thinly sliced
¼ cup red wine vinegar or cider vinegar
2 tablespoons honey or sugar
¾ teaspoon salt
Cover and cook over low heat, stirring occasionally, until the cabbage is very soft, 1 to 1½ hours, adding boiling water if the mixture becomes dry during cooking. Or, if liquid is left when the cabbage is done, uncover the pot and cook gently until it is absorbed. If desired, top with:
(⅓ cup chopped toasted, 1005, walnuts)

BRAISED SAUERKRAUT
6 servings
Once a necessary method of preservation, we now enjoy sauerkraut for the lactic tang and funkiness it adds to our plates. When braised for a lengthy time, these flavors are mellowed, and can be augmented with wine, spices, and other vegetables.
Heat in a large ovenproof skillet over medium heat:
2 tablespoons butter, bacon fat, or vegetable oil
Add and cook, stirring frequently, until translucent, 7 to 10 minutes:
1 medium onion or 4 shallots, sliced
Add and cook, stirring, for 5 minutes:
4 cups (2 pounds) drained sauerkraut, store-bought or homemade, 940
Add:
1 medium potato or cored tart apple, peeled and grated
1 teaspoon caraway seeds
Cover the sauerkraut with:
Vegetable stock or broth or water
¼ cup dry white wine
Cook, uncovered, at a low simmer for 30 minutes. Cover and gently simmer 30 minutes more. Season with, if desired:
(1 to 2 tablespoons brown sugar, to taste)

SAUERKRAUT FRITTERS
4 servings
One of our favorite uses for sauerkraut. For **Reuben Fritters,** substitute **4 ounces diced corned beef or pastrami** for the cooked bacon and serve with **Russian Dressing, 576.** If not using bacon, begin the recipe where everything is mixed together in a bowl.
Preheat the oven to 200°F. Line a baking sheet with paper towels.
If desired, cook until crisp in a medium skillet:
(4 slices bacon, cut into ¼-inch pieces)
Transfer the bacon to a large bowl. Pour the bacon fat into another bowl and deglaze any browned bits in the skillet with a little water,

scraping the bottom of the skillet with a spoon. Add the pan juices to the bowl with the bacon along with:

2 cups drained sauerkraut, store-bought or homemade, 940
4 ounces Swiss cheese, Emmenthaler, or Gruyère, cut into ¼-inch cubes
2 large eggs, beaten
½ cup dry bread crumbs or panko
(2 tablespoons minced dill)
(2 teaspoons caraway seeds)
½ teaspoon salt
¼ teaspoon black pepper

Add the bacon fat back to the skillet or add:

2 tablespoons vegetable oil

Set the skillet over medium heat. When hot, add the sauerkraut mixture in batches (using a ¼-cup measure) to the skillet. Flatten the cakes slightly with a spatula and pan-fry until golden on the bottom, about 4 minutes. Flip and cook the second side until well browned. Transfer to the baking sheet lined with paper towels and keep warm in the oven. Cook the remaining mixture. Serve with:

Sour cream or plain yogurt
Whole-grain mustard

OKONOMIYAKI (JAPANESE CABBAGE PANCAKES)

2 to 3 servings

Okonomiyaki means "how you like it," so play around with the vegetable and meat additions in this savory pancake. Mountain yam is not absolutely necessary for this recipe, but it is traditional. It has an extremely gluey texture when grated, which helps bind the batter together and makes it a little lighter and fluffier. Feel free to substitute instant dashi granules mixed with water for the dashi to save time. **Okonomiyaki sauce** is a sweet, savory brown sauce made with dates. Though readily available at stores that stock Japanese foods, you may substitute Katsu Sauce, 572. Japanese **Kewpie mayonnaise** is sweeter, thinner, and richer than American brands. If you cannot find it, thin out regular mayonnaise with rice vinegar until it has a sauce-like consistency and stir in a pinch of sugar.

Whisk together in a medium bowl:

¾ cup all-purpose flour
1 teaspoon sugar
½ teaspoon baking powder
¼ teaspoon salt

Whisk in gradually to make a thin batter:

¾ cup Dashi, 78

Stir in:

2 packed cups finely shredded green cabbage (about 8 ounces)
1 large carrot, shredded
3 green onions, finely chopped
(⅓ cup grated mountain yam, or nagaimo)
(¼ cup Beni Shōga, 930)

Heat in a nonstick skillet over medium heat:

1 tablespoon vegetable oil

Have ready:

½ cup chopped shrimp or cleaned squid cut into tentacles and rings, or 4 slices uncured pork belly, cut into 2-inch strips

When the oil is hot, add half the batter to the pan. Scatter half of the shrimp, squid, or pork on top of the pancake. Cook until the bottom of the pancake is set and golden brown, about 5 minutes, then flip the pancake, and cook the second side until brown, about 5 minutes more. Transfer to a plate and repeat with the remaining batter. Top the pancakes with:

Okonomiyaki sauce
Kewpie mayonnaise
Katsuobushi (dried bonito flakes), 956

STUFFED CABBAGE ROLLS

12 rolls; 6 servings

Stuffed cabbage makes a satisfying cold-weather dish—wonderful with potato pancakes or mashed potatoes. The rolls are even better when prepared 2 to 3 days in advance, and they can be frozen for up to 1 month. Because this dish is a bit involved, we recommend preparing the filling and sauce ahead of time and assembling and cooking the rolls the following day.

I. HEARTY MEAT-RICE FILLING

Combine in a large bowl:

1 pound ground beef, lamb, chicken, or turkey
1 large egg
½ cup dry bread crumbs
½ cup uncooked long-grain white rice
½ cup water
1 large carrot, grated
1 large onion, finely chopped
3 garlic cloves, minced
1 tablespoon minced parsley, oregano, thyme, or a combination
1 teaspoon salt
¼ teaspoon black pepper

Bring 4 quarts water to a rolling boil in a large pot. Add:

1½ tablespoons salt

Cut out the core with a small, sharp knife, then drop cored side down into the water:

1 head Savoy or green cabbage (about 2 pounds)

Boil for 5 minutes, then remove from the pot and carefully remove the softened outer leaves. Return the cabbage to the simmering water to continue to soften as you begin to fill the leaves. (Alternatively, freeze the whole cabbage for 24 hours, then thaw and separate the leaves.) Trim off enough of the midrib of each leaf to make the leaf supple enough to roll. Wrap the meat mixture in the leaves as shown, folding the sides first. Roll up the leaf loosely, as the rice will expand. Repeat with more leaves until all the filling is used. Place the rolls seam side down to cook.

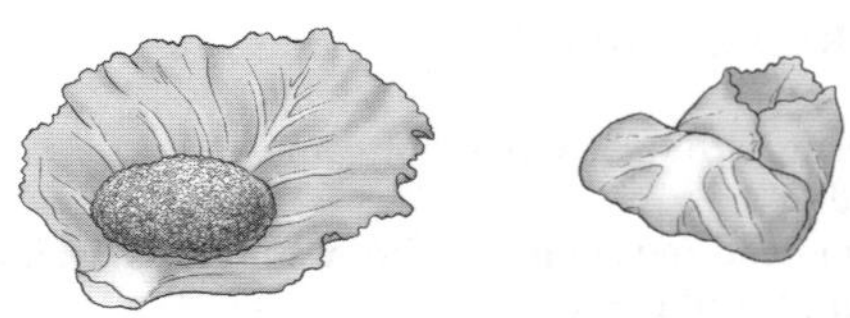

Making stuffed cabbage rolls

Chop enough of the remaining cabbage leaves to make 1 cup. Heat in a large heavy pot or Dutch oven over medium-high heat:

3 tablespoons vegetable oil

Add the chopped cabbage along with:

1 medium onion, chopped

Cook, stirring, until golden brown. Add:

½ cup dry white wine

Bring to a boil, then reduce the heat to low and simmer for 5 minutes. Add:

One 28-ounce can crushed tomatoes
1 cup water
¼ cup packed brown sugar
(8 small gingersnaps, crumbled)
3 tablespoons lemon juice
½ teaspoon salt

Bring to a boil. Place the cabbage rolls seam side down in the sauce; if the sauce does not cover the rolls, add a little water. Reduce the heat, cover, and simmer for 1½ hours, shaking the pot every 30 minutes to prevent sticking.

Taste the sauce and adjust the flavor with more lemon juice if necessary. Serve hot with:

Sour cream

II. VEGETARIAN FILLING

Made with leeks, mushrooms, kasha, and bulgur. An equal amount of almost any grain can be substituted here, so experiment with what you have on hand.

Heat a large skillet over medium-high heat. When hot, add:

1 cup whole kasha (roasted buckwheat)

Toast, stirring, until the kasha is fragrant and slightly darkened, about 3 minutes. Transfer to a large bowl. Reduce the heat to medium and heat in the skillet:

1 tablespoon olive oil

Add and cook, stirring, until the mushrooms are tender, about 10 minutes:

8 ounces mushrooms, chopped
1 large leek, trimmed, halved lengthwise, well cleaned, and chopped
½ red bell pepper, chopped

Mix into the kasha and let cool. Add to the bowl:

1 cup water or vegetable stock or broth
½ cup fine or medium bulgur
1 large egg, beaten
3 garlic cloves, minced
Finely grated zest of 1 lemon
1 tablespoon fresh thyme leaves or 1 teaspoon dried thyme
½ teaspoon salt
¼ teaspoon black pepper

Mix until thoroughly combined and proceed to soften the cabbage leaves, stuff, prepare the tomato sauce, and simmer as for **I, 226.**

ABOUT CACTUS PADS

Nopales, the oval green pads of the prickly pear cactus, are used fresh in salsas and salads and are also sold pickled and canned. (See 193 for preparing the prickly pear fruit.) They have a slightly tart flavor that reminds us of green bell pepper and green beans. Select thin pads that are about 4 inches wide, bright green, and somewhat stiff. Avoid pads that are fibrous, turning yellow, or limp. Some markets sell packages of cactus pads that have already been diced and rinsed. If you can only get them with spines, handle the pads with sturdy gloves or tongs and use a knife to shave off the spines. Refrigerate in a bag or container for up to 1 week.

To prepare cactus pads for cooking, trim the edges with a vegetable peeler and remove any eyes where spines were. Cut off the thick base and rinse the pads. Grill them whole (see below), or cut into pieces for roasting, simmering, or using raw. Once cut, cactus exudes a thick gel, much like okra. Rinse it off for raw preparations. Add to moles, 553–54, tacos, or bean dishes such as Frijoles de la Olla, 213.

To parboil, bring a saucepan of salted water to a boil, drop in diced cactus, and simmer until tender, about 10 minutes. Drain and rinse several times in cold water, until no longer sticky.

To grill whole, score each pad twice on both sides, lightly brush with vegetable oil, and cook over a medium-hot fire until tender and lightly charred on both sides, about 10 minutes.

ROASTED CACTUS PAD SALAD

4 cups; 8 servings

Preheat the oven to 375°F. Trim and remove the spines from:

1½ pounds cactus pads

Cut into ¾-inch squares. Place on a baking sheet and toss with:

1 tablespoon vegetable oil
½ teaspoon salt

Roast, stirring occasionally, until the cactus is tender, about 20 minutes. Let cool. Combine the cactus in a bowl with:

1½ cups any salsa, 575
Salt to taste
Lime juice to taste

Line a serving bowl with:

Romaine lettuce leaves

Add the salad. Sprinkle with:

¼ cup crumbled queso añejo or Cotija

ABOUT CARDOONS

Cardoons, like artichokes, are a plant in the thistle family. The thick, fleshy stalks look like very large, coarse, matte-gray celery with pronounced ribs. The tender inner stalks are eaten, rather than the immature flower. Select crisp, unbruised stalks—the smaller, the better. Wrap the base of the stalks in a moist paper towel and store in an open zip-top bag in the refrigerator crisper.

If cardoons are very young and tender, you may blanch the stalks with their greens attached for 2 minutes and serve with a dipping sauce, or as part of Bagna Cauda, 58. Once simmered, 228, cardoons are delicious simply sautéed with garlic in butter or olive oil and sprinkled with grated Parmesan, fresh herbs, and lemon juice. They are delectable when battered and deep-fried, 203, or breaded and pan-fried as for artichokes, 207. You may also treat parcooked cardoons as for Brussels Sprout Gratin, 222, or add to a frittata, 159.

Before cooking, discard the tough outer stalks, wash well, and trim off any leaves. Scrape off strings with a vegetable peeler. Cut the stalks into 2- to 3-inch pieces, stopping where the stalk becomes tough. Because cardoons tend to darken, cooking them promptly in simmering water with lemon juice is the preferred basic cooking method; ➤ steaming is not recommended.

SIMMERED CARDOONS

4 servings

Bring to a boil in a large saucepan:

8 cups water
2 tablespoons lemon juice
1 tablespoon salt

Prepare, 227:

1 pound cardoons

Add the cardoons to the boiling water, partially cover, and reduce the heat to maintain a gentle simmer. Younger cardoons can be tender in as little as 15 minutes while mature ones may take up to 1 hour. Add more boiling water to the pan if needed. Drain well. You may cook them further as suggested in About Cardoons, 227, or simply toss while warm with:

2 tablespoons butter or extra-virgin olive oil
(¼ cup grated Parmesan or Browned Bread Crumbs, 957)
1 tablespoon chopped parsley
Salt and black pepper to taste

ABOUT CARROTS

Cultivated carrots are descended from the wild Queen Anne's lace, and the sturdiness of that weed hints at the resilience of this vegetable, both in the refrigerator and in the pot. The great quantity of beta-carotene in carrots sometimes actually increases during storage, and the vegetable grows sweeter when cooked to softness, making it an indispensable flavoring agent in soups and stews and a good friend of cooks who are not too attentive to timing.

Carrots can be found in various colors—from white and yellow to orange, red, and purple—but the colors do not necessarily reflect a difference in flavor. Size, rather, is a better indicator of flavor. Larger carrots tend to be less sweet and can be bitter; small, young carrots are usually sweeter, milder, and have a nice, snappy texture. Small carrots are most plentiful in spring and fall, while large ones are available year-round. Young, immature roots may be sold as **baby carrots,** but the ubiquitous pill-shaped carrots sold by that name are not actually young. Rather, they are an ingenious use of larger, blemished or strangely shaped carrots that are trimmed, cut to size, and processed into a smooth uniform shape.

➤ Regardless of size or shape, avoid carrots that are limp, shriveled, cracked, or soft or moldy at the stem end. Before storing, cut off the green tops (for using these, see below). Store carrots in a closed plastic bag in the refrigerator crisper. They will keep for 2 to 3 weeks.

Young, sweet carrots are excellent scrubbed or peeled and left whole for simple side dishes, added to stews like Navarin Printanière, 482, or served raw for Bagna Cauda, 58, or crudités, 45. Large carrots should always be peeled and cut into rounds, dice, or julienne. You may shred them with a cheese grater or spiral cutter, or shave them with a peeler—these techniques are especially useful for serving them raw in salads, 126. Carrots may be prepped a few hours ahead of time; if cut carrots start to look dry, they may be refreshed by spending 15 minutes in a bowl of ice water.

Carrots are practically inseparable from onions and celery in most European cuisines; see Mirepoix, 1002. Other alliums—leeks, garlic, and shallots—are frequent companions. Carrots are also quite good with fennel, ginger, and other root vegetables like parsnip and celery root, or with fresh green chiles like serranos and jalapeños (for a superlative pickle along these lines, see Jalapeños en Escabeche, 930). Pair them with acidic ingredients like citrus juice, yogurt, or tangy cheeses to balance their sweetness. We prefer to season carrot-centered dishes with aromatics from the same family of plants, like cumin, coriander, caraway, parsley, chervil, or dill. Warm spice blends such as Five-Spice Powder, 590, and curry powder are welcome, as well as brighter herbs like thyme, mint, and oregano. In addition to the recipes here, you may combine them with potatoes or celery root in a Root Vegetable Puree, 203, or shred and add to Latkes, 269.

A bunch of carrots may have **carrot tops** attached, which can be used in several, delicious ways. We like to use them in Spicy Carrot Top Pesto, 586, or swap them for some of the parsley in Salsa Verde, 567. They can be substituted in part for spinach in a cream soup, 106, or chopped fine and used to garnish Carrot-Ginger Soup, 106. Use only the frond-like leaves, not the central stems, which are tough.

To steam or boil, place carrots in a steamer basket over boiling water or add to a saucepan with water to cover and bring to a boil. Cook, covered, until tender, 10 to 15 minutes for whole carrots under 1 inch thick, 5 to 10 minutes for thick slices.

GLAZED CARROTS

4 servings

Place in a medium saucepan:

1 pound carrots, sliced (leave whole if small)
½ cup water or stock
2 tablespoons butter
2 tablespoons sugar
¼ teaspoon salt
(1 teaspoon lemon juice)

Bring to a boil over high heat, then reduce the heat, cover, and simmer until tender, about 15 minutes. Uncover the pan, increase the heat, and boil off the liquid, about 5 minutes. Sprinkle with:

Chopped parsley, tarragon, dill, or chervil

Or top with:

Grated Gruyère or Parmesan

ROASTED CARROTS

4 servings

Preheat the oven to 425°F.

Toss together on a rimmed baking sheet:

1½ pounds slender whole carrots or medium carrots, halved lengthwise
1½ tablespoons vegetable oil
1 teaspoon salt
½ teaspoon black pepper

Spread the carrots into a single layer and roast until golden and tender, 30 to 45 minutes, depending on the thickness. Cut into chunks if desired and serve warm with:

Yogurt-Dill Sauce, 569, Harissa, 584, Cilantro-Mint Chutney, 568, or Pesto, 586 (made with carrot tops, if on hand)

Or simply toss the carrots with:

1 tablespoon lemon juice
2 tablespoons chopped herbs, or a seasoning blend like Za'atar, 590, Gremolata, 587, or Dukkah, 589

CHARRED CARROTS

4 servings

Prepare a hot grill fire, preheat the broiler and position a rack in the top third of the oven, or set a heavy skillet or grill pan over medium-high heat.

Trim and peel or scrub well:

1 pound small whole carrots, or medium carrots halved lengthwise

If you are using a skillet, cut them crosswise so that they will fit in the pan. Toss them on a baking sheet or in a bowl with:

2 tablespoons vegetable oil
½ teaspoon salt
¼ teaspoon black pepper or Cajun Blackening Spice, 587

If cooking on the grill, place the carrots over direct heat (use a grill basket or lay them perpendicular to the grates). If broiling, spread the carrots on the baking sheet and place it under the broiler. If pan-searing, place in the skillet in a single layer. Cook undisturbed until the carrots have deeply browned spots or edges, about 4 minutes. Turn the carrots and brown on the other side, about 3 minutes more. Remove from the heat, cover with foil, and let stand for 5 minutes (they will continue to cook). Serve while hot, tossed with:

Vinaigrette, 575

Or top with one of the following:

½ cup crumbled fresh goat cheese, and 2 tablespoons chopped parsley or tarragon
Tzatziki, 569

ABOUT CAULIFLOWER

This flowering cabbage, a pale, mild relative of broccoli, 220, has dense florets and a pleasantly nutty flavor. Purple and orange (or "cheddar") cauliflower may also be found at markets. The broccoli-cauliflower hybrids **broccoflower** and **Romanesco** are also increasingly common and have a similarly mild taste and firm texture. They are both chartreuse-colored, and Romanesco sports conical florets that grow in a fractal-like spiral pattern. No matter the color, select heads of cauliflower that feel firm and whose florets are tightly packed and without brown discoloration. Small brown blemishes may be pared off with only cosmetic damage. Store in a bag in the refrigerator crisper for up to 5 days.

You may cook cauliflower whole or in florets. Or cut cauliflower heads top to bottom into wedges for roasting, pan-frying, or grilling; or crosswise into several large, thick steaks (reserve any stray florets for another use).

To prepare as florets, cut the florets off the central stem, then cut any large florets into halves or quarters. Cut the stem into thick slices or bite-sized chunks. You may save them for another purpose, cook along with the florets, or munch on them as a kitchen snack. If your cauliflower had a significant number of leaves attached, with large, edible midribs, you may slice them and stir-fry as for bok choy, 224, add to a pot of Southern-Style Greens, 243, or leave them whole and roast as for broccoli, 221. Cauliflower may also be cut into florets, then pulsed in a food processor into fine pieces. The cauliflower, which resembles couscous or rice, can then be tossed with a vinaigrette, herbs, and sliced radishes for an unusual but delicious salad. Or briefly sauté the ground cauliflower with a little oil and salt and use as a substitute for rice.

Though milder, cauliflower can be prepared in the same ways as broccoli, 220. It is regularly served with butter sauces, 558, and especially Sauce Mornay, 548 (sharper cheeses are best). Cauliflower is good when enlivened with curry powder, or the cured, briny flavors of ham, capers, olives, or preserved lemons. Cauliflower may also be served raw as crudités, 45, or in salads.

To steam, place cauliflower in a steamer basket, stem side down if left whole. Bring the water to a boil, cover, and cook until barely tender, up to 15 minutes if whole, 5 to 7 minutes if in florets.

ROASTED CAULIFLOWER WEDGES

4 servings

Cutting cauliflower heads into wedges creates large, flat surfaces, allowing them to brown better than florets.

Preheat the oven to 425°F. For easier cleanup, line a rimmed baking sheet with parchment paper.

Cut lengthwise into 8 large wedges:

1 large head cauliflower (about 2 pounds)

Place them on the baking sheet. Any small florets that fall off can be roasted alongside the wedges. Drizzle them with:

2 tablespoons vegetable oil

Sprinkle on all sides:

½ teaspoon salt
¼ teaspoon black pepper

Roast, flipping once, until browned on both sides and tender, about 40 minutes. Serve with:

Salsa Verde, 567, Chimichurri, 567, Romesco Sauce, 570, a vinaigrette, 575, Nuoc Cham, 571, or Beurre Blanc using lemon juice instead of vinegar, 558

ROASTED CAULIFLOWER WITH GREEN OLIVES AND LEMON

4 servings

Roasting lemon slices with the cauliflower sweetens and browns them around the edges, which mellows out the rind. You may substitute the **rinsed and coarsely chopped rind of one Salt-Preserved Lemon, 942,** but do not add any salt until after tasting the roasted cauliflower.

Preheat the oven to 425°F. For easier cleanup, line a rimmed baking sheet with parchment paper. Cut into bite-sized florets:

1 large head cauliflower (about 2 pounds)

Toss the cauliflower on the baking sheet with:

1 lemon, very thinly sliced, ends and seeds discarded
½ cup pitted green olives, preferably Castelvetrano, halved
3 tablespoons olive oil
½ teaspoon salt
¼ teaspoon black pepper or red pepper flakes

Spread the cauliflower in an even layer and roast, stirring halfway through cooking, until browned and tender, about 30 minutes. Transfer to a serving dish and toss with:

Lemon juice to taste
(¼ cup toasted, 1005, pine nuts, chopped walnuts, or chopped hazelnuts)
(2 tablespoons chopped leafy green herbs, like parsley or cilantro)

TANDOORI CAULIFLOWER

4 servings

Though we usually associate tender chicken and lamb with this famous yogurt-based marinade, cauliflower is a wonderful vegetarian alternative.

Whisk together in a large bowl:

½ recipe Tandoori Marinade II, 580

Cut into florets and toss with the marinade in a bowl until well coated:

1 large head cauliflower (about 2 pounds)

Allow to sit for at least 15 minutes, or overnight.

Preheat the oven to 500°F. Line a rimmed baking sheet with foil, lightly grease the foil, and spread the cauliflower out in a single layer. Roast until tender and very well browned, about 20 minutes. Serve with:

Naan, 611
Cooked basmati rice, 343
Chopped cilantro

CAULIFLOWER WITH BROWN BUTTER BREAD CRUMBS

4 servings

This classic French treatment, also known as **Cauliflower Polonaise,** may be used for roasted cauliflower florets as well. We sometimes add **1 minced garlic clove** to the bread crumbs. Minced fresh tarragon, thyme, or rosemary can be substituted for half the parsley in the garnish.

Cut into florets or leave whole, cutting out the stem and core, and steam until tender, 229:

1 large head cauliflower (about 2 pounds)

Meanwhile, melt in a small skillet over medium heat:

4 tablespoons butter

When the butter has browned slightly and smells nutty, add:

¼ cup dry bread crumbs
½ teaspoon salt
¼ teaspoon black pepper

Gently fry the bread crumbs, stirring, until they are golden brown, about 2 minutes. Remove from the heat and add:

Juice of ½ lemon (about 1½ tablespoons)

Place the cooked cauliflower in a serving dish and toss with the bread crumb mixture. Sprinkle with:

2 tablespoons chopped parsley
(2 Hard-Boiled Eggs, 151, finely chopped)

CREAMY MASHED CAULIFLOWER

4 servings

This mashed potato alternative is much quicker and very tasty.

Cut into florets, cutting off the tough end of the stem of:

1 large head cauliflower (about 2 pounds)

Place in a large saucepan and add:

1 cup chicken or vegetable stock or broth or water
2 garlic cloves, chopped
½ teaspoon salt

Bring to a boil, cover, reduce the heat, and simmer until the cauliflower is tender, about 10 minutes. Mash or puree in the pan with an immersion blender or transfer to a food processor and puree, adding:

½ cup heavy cream, sour cream, or plain yogurt
1 tablespoon butter

Season with:

Black pepper to taste
(Minced chives)
(1 tablespoon chopped parsley or tarragon)

SCALLOPED CAULIFLOWER

4 servings

Preheat the oven to 350°F. Butter a shallow 2-quart baking dish.

Remove the stem, cut into florets, and steam until tender, 229:

1 large head cauliflower (about 2 pounds)

Spread the florets in the prepared dish. Spoon over them:

2 cups White Sauce I, 548, mixed with ¼ teaspoon grated or ground nutmeg or 1 tablespoon Dijon mustard

Sprinkle over the top:

½ cup plain or buttered fresh bread crumbs, 957
⅓ cup grated Parmesan, Gruyère, or aged Cheddar

Bake until bubbling and browned on the top, about 25 minutes. Serve sprinkled with:

Sweet paprika

ALOO GOBI (CURRIED CAULIFLOWER AND POTATOES)

4 to 6 servings

This dish is part of our comfort food repertoire. If desired, add **1 large tomato, diced** after frying the spices.

Remove the stem and cut into florets:

1 large head cauliflower (about 2 pounds)

Cook for 5 minutes in a saucepan of boiling salted water. Transfer with a slotted spoon to a bowl. Add to the boiling water and cook for 5 minutes:

1 pound red or gold potatoes, cut into ½-inch cubes

Drain and transfer to the bowl with the cauliflower. Heat in a Dutch oven over medium heat:

¼ cup vegetable oil or Ghee, 960

Add and cook until softened, about 5 minutes:

1 medium onion, chopped

Stir in and cook 1 minute more:

4 garlic cloves, minced
2-inch piece ginger, peeled and minced or grated
(2 serrano peppers, seeded and minced)

Add and cook, stirring, until the mustard seeds start to pop:

1 teaspoon yellow or black mustard seeds
1 teaspoon cumin seeds

If desired, cautiously stir in (the leaves will sputter):

(15 fresh curry leaves)

Cook until the leaves are fragrant, about 30 seconds. Stir in the cauliflower and potatoes, along with:

1 tablespoon curry powder or Garam Masala, 558

Cover and cook until the vegetables are tender, about 5 minutes. Season with:

Salt to taste

Serve with:

Cooked basmati rice, 343

GOBI MANCHURIAN (INDIAN-CHINESE FRIED CAULIFLOWER)

4 to 6 servings

This lesser-known, spicy cousin of General Tso's chicken was concocted by Chinese restaurateurs in India. Though not typical, we sometimes like to coat the cauliflower in ½ **batch Pakora Batter, 657.**

Please read about Deep-Frying, 1051.

In a small bowl, combine and set aside:

¼ cup ketchup, store-bought or homemade, 931
1 tablespoon soy sauce
1 tablespoon distilled white or rice vinegar
(2 teaspoons toasted sesame oil)

In a second small bowl, combine and set aside:

¼ cup cold water
1 tablespoon cornstarch

Trim and cut into bite-sized florets:

1 medium head cauliflower (about 1¼ pounds)

Prepare:

Cornstarch Batter, 657, adding 1 tablespoon curry powder or Garam Masala, 558

Heat to 375°F in a Dutch oven, wok, or large heavy saucepan:

2 inches vegetable oil

Preheat the oven to 200°F and line a baking sheet with paper towels. Coat the cauliflower in the batter and fry in batches until deep golden brown and crispy, about 4 minutes. Do not crowd the pot, and check the temperature of the oil frequently to make sure that it stays around 375°F. Transfer the florets using a spider or slotted spoon to the lined baking sheet and keep warm in the oven as you fry the remaining florets.

Heat in a large saucepan or wok over medium-high heat until hot:

2 tablespoons vegetable oil

Add and sauté until softened:

1 medium onion, finely chopped

Add and cook, stirring, until fragrant and just starting to brown:

3 to 6 serrano peppers, seeded, if desired, and chopped
4 garlic cloves, minced
1-inch piece ginger, peeled and minced or grated

Add the ketchup mixture and bring to a simmer. Give the cornstarch mixture a stir, add to the sauce, and stir. When the sauce thickens, add the cauliflower and toss with the sauce. Serve topped generously with:

Chopped cilantro
Chopped green onions

ABOUT CELERY

Celery, indispensable in so many recipes, always seems to get short shrift when considered by itself. Perhaps it's because many of us have ambivalent memories of "ants on a log," the ubiquitous, "healthy" children's snack of celery ribs filled with peanut butter and topped with raisins (we, for our part, love them). Or perhaps celery's year-round availability simply discourages us from taking notice. Celery is appreciated more for the part it plays in famous aromatic trios like mirepoix, 1002, or the Cajun "holy trinity" of celery, onions, and green bell pepper. Regardless of the cause, there is much to recommend celery, from its mild saltiness to its extraordinary crunch and pungent leaves.

The most common varieties of celery are grown to be pale, and bred to produce large stalks. Some varieties are bred to be leafier, and are called **cutting celery.** They include tall **Chinese celery,** as well as the lesser-known **French Dinant** and **Ventura.** All of them are quite slender, sport dark-green stalks or ribs, and have bushy leaves when left untrimmed. Their stalks are more flavorful than the pale, thick-stemmed varieties. For **celery root** or **celeriac,** see below. For **celery leaves, celery seeds,** and **celery salt,** see 962.

Regardless of variety, select compact bunches that are heavy for their size, with fresh-looking leaves. Keep in a plastic bag in the refrigerator crisper. To prepare, separate the stalks and rinse them well, giving a light scrub to the bases, where grit often gathers. Trim off the ends of the stalks (they can be saved for stock) and discard any thick outer stalks that are bitter or tough. For stir-frying and serving in salads, we prefer to slice celery on the diagonal—razor-thin for salads, ¼ to ½ inch thick for stir-fries. When chopped or thinly sliced, celery strings are imperceptible, but if the stalks are to be served whole or in large pieces, strip off the strings with a paring knife or vegetable peeler. If the stalks are limp after storage—or if you want them to be super crisp for serving raw—soak them in ice water until they firm up.

STIR-FRIED CELERY

4 servings

Heat in a large skillet over medium-high heat:

1 tablespoon vegetable oil

Add and cook, stirring, until fragrant, about 1 minute:

2 garlic cloves, smashed
1 dried red chile pepper (such as de árbol) or ¼ teaspoon red pepper flakes

Add and cook, stirring, until just crisp-tender, about 3 minutes:

3 large celery ribs, thinly sliced on the diagonal

Remove from the heat and stir in:

1 tablespoon soy sauce
(1 teaspoon toasted sesame oil)

ABOUT CELERY ROOT (CELERIAC)

This type of celery is grown for its knobby root, and is prized for its succulent, subtly sweet flavor. It can be tough and woody if too old;

peak season is autumn and winter. To prepare, scrub well with a stiff brush under cold running water. Cut off any roots. Because its skin is knobby and tough, peel the root with a sharp paring knife rather than a vegetable peeler (loosely follow the procedure for cutting away citrus peel, illustrated on 182). Select small to medium roots that feel heavy for their size. Any stalks on top should be crisp and fresh. Leave any stalks on and store in a plastic bag in the refrigerator crisper.

Celery root is delicious raw when thinly sliced, shaved into ribbons, or julienned and tossed with a vinaigrette, 575. Let sit several hours to tenderize and "mellow" the vegetable, or follow the procedure for Spicy Chinese-Style Slaw, 119. For a rich, piquant classic, see Celery Root Rémoulade, 126. The root may be cooked with and substituted for up to half of the potatoes called for in potato salads, 127, or Potatoes au Gratin, 266. Other options including cutting into wedges or chunks and roasting as for carrots, 228, or thinly slicing and frying into crispy chips (see Potato or Root Vegetable Chips, 48), or pureeing, 203. We especially like cutting a celery root into large chunks or wedges, mixing it with onion wedges in a roasting pan, and placing a chicken on top to roast, 407.

To steam or boil, peel celery root and cut it into ½-inch cubes. Place in a steaming basket or add to a pan of boiling water and cook until tender when pierced with a knife, 6 to 10 minutes.

Pressure-cook 2-inch chunks of celery root with 1 inch of water for 8 minutes at 15 psi. Use the quick release method, 1059.

BAKED CELERY ROOT

4 servings

Baking celery root whole results in a texture much like a baked potato, and can be served the same way, 267. They may also be twice-baked, 267. Surprisingly, the skin sometimes turns out tender enough to eat. For a crisper, browned result, peel the root, cut into wedges or chunks, and roast as for carrots, 228.

Preheat the oven to 350°F.

Trim, scrub, and pat dry:

2 medium celery roots (about 2 pounds)

Brush with:

2 tablespoons olive oil

Place in an 8-inch square baking pan and roast, uncovered, until tender all through when pierced with a thin skewer, about 1 hour. Turn with tongs after 30 minutes.

To serve, slice the roots in half and mash the centers just enough to absorb butter or a sauce, and drizzle with:

4 to 6 tablespoons (½ to ¾ stick) butter, melted, or Brown Butter, 558

Sprinkle with:

Salt and pepper to taste
Minced parsley

ABOUT CELTUCE

Also called **asparagus lettuce** or **stem lettuce,** this lettuce variety was bred to grow a thick stalk. Raw celtuce has the firm, succulent texture of a radish or cucumber and tastes like nutty celery or water chestnut. We enjoy peeled, thinly sliced celtuce in green salads, or julienned and dressed with Vinaigrette, 575. Diced, it adds a subtle, refreshing accent to cold soups, 107–8. Though delicious raw, celtuce can be used in stir-fries, 202. Peel off the outer layer of the stem before using and trim off the bottom and small leaves at the top. The leaves can be used in salads, or rolled up and thinly sliced for garnishing celtuce dishes.

ABOUT CHESTNUTS

Chestnuts are unique among nuts, as they store energy in the form of carbohydrates rather than fat. Thus, they tend to be used as a starch. They are commonly ground into meal or flour. In fact, chestnut meal was used in the precursor to Italian polenta, which became the dish we are familiar with only after the introduction of corn to Europe in the fifteenth century. For the botanically unrelated water chestnut, see 284.

Fresh chestnuts are available from fall to midwinter. Choose nuts that feel rigid and unyielding when squeezed. Refrigerate in a plastic bag and use promptly, as they have a tendency to dry out. Chestnuts are also available dried, canned, or vacuum-packed—the last is the best option if fresh ones are not available. When substituting vacuum-packed for fresh, remember that they are already cooked (but still firm enough that they need to be simmered further). ➤ One pound unpeeled chestnuts yields a little more than 8 ounces peeled, or 2 cups.

Chestnuts are equally delicious served as a vegetable, as an accompaniment to roasted meats, or as dessert (see Mont Blanc, 827). A handful of cooked whole chestnuts can be added to cabbage dishes—they are especially good with Brussels sprouts, 222—and they are a classic ingredient in stuffings, 532.

To peel and skin chestnuts, cut an X on the flat side or bottom of each nut. You may roast them on a rimmed baking sheet in a 425°F oven until fragrant and the skin curls back, 15 to 20 minutes. Or place them in a steaming basket or pot of boiling water and cook for 5 minutes. Remove a few nuts at a time and peel off the outer shell and the inner membrane or skin. If some resist peeling, return them to the pot or oven. Chestnuts are easiest to peel while still warm, so do not let them cool in the shell. After peeling, the chestnuts are ready to be used in a number of cooked dishes, or eaten out of hand.

BOILED CHESTNUTS

6 servings

To prepare as a vegetable, peel and skin, above:

1½ pounds fresh chestnuts (3 cups peeled)

or use:

12 ounces vacuum-packed chestnuts

Bring 8 cups water to a boil in a large saucepan. Add the chestnuts along with:

2 celery ribs, coarsely chopped
1 small onion, coarsely chopped
1 tablespoon salt

Simmer gently, uncovered, until the nuts can be pierced easily with the point of a paring knife, 30 to 40 minutes for fresh or about 15 minutes for vacuum-packed chestnuts. Drain well (discard the celery and onion).

Toss with:

2 to 3 tablespoons butter, to taste
Salt and black or white pepper to taste

CHESTNUT COMPOTE

About 2 cups

This compote is delicious with roasted poultry, game, or pork.
Peel and skin, 232:

1 pound fresh chestnuts (2 cups peeled)

Or use:

8 ounces vacuum-packed chestnuts

Place in a saucepan and add water to cover by 2 inches. Bring to a boil and reduce the heat to a simmer. Cook, covered, until the nuts can be pierced easily with the point of a paring knife, 30 to 40 minutes for fresh or about 15 minutes for vacuum-packed chestnuts. Drain, reserving ½ cup of the liquid, and coarsely chop the chestnuts. Combine the reserved liquid in a saucepan with:

½ cup sugar
(½ cup raisins)
(½ cup chopped hazelnuts)
Finely grated zest of 1 lemon
Finely grated zest of ½ orange
3 tablespoons lemon juice
3 tablespoons orange juice
2 whole cloves
1 cinnamon stick
¼ teaspoon ground ginger

Bring to a simmer and simmer gently, uncovered, until the syrup is slightly reduced, about 10 minutes. Add the chestnuts and cook at the barest simmer until reduced to a syrup, about 25 minutes. Allow to stand for 30 minutes. Discard the cloves and cinnamon stick before serving.

ABOUT CHICORIES AND ENDIVES

From **curly endive** or **frisée** to the rare, slender **puntarelle;** from purple **radicchio** and **Treviso** to their pale relative the **Belgian endive,** all members of the chicory family have a bracing touch of bitterness. Chicories and endives are actually lettuces, something not readily apparent unless you are looking at the green, romaine-like **sugarloaf chicory** (one of the mildest) or the sprawling **escarole,** which looks like gigantic leaf lettuce. The plant typically sold as **dandelion greens** is an Italian variety of chicory.

Though breeders and farmers work hard to grow pleasantly bitter greens, their flavor can be a bit overwhelming, especially if they are mature. ➤ Soaking chicories in ice water for 1 hour can tame their bitterness, making them an exceptional salad green. This is especially true with radicchio, Treviso, and the large-stemmed type of puntarelle, whose stalks must be halved and julienned lengthwise before soaking. Other varieties of puntarelle are long and slender with thin stems and dark green leaves; these are less bitter, and can be treated like any other tender green. ➤ Another method to counteract the bitterness of chicories is to blanch, 1047, them in a large pot of boiling water for 30 seconds, although this renders them unsuitable for salads.

All chicories can be torn into pieces or sliced into ribbons and sautéed like other greens, 245. Because Belgian endive and radicchio have compact heads, they can also be baked, roasted, or grilled. Radicchio adds gorgeous purple color to the plate.

The bitterness of chicories and endives makes them a natural for pairing with acidic ingredients, rich meats, and the pungent, cured flavors of aged ham, capers, olives, and anchovies. They also go well with fresh, pickled, or dried chiles, strong cheeses such as Roquefort, Parmesan, or feta, and hard- or soft-boiled eggs. To store, shake off any excess moisture and place the greens in closed bags with a paper towel in the refrigerator crisper.

BELGIAN ENDIVE AU GRATIN

4 servings

Position a rack in the center of the oven. Preheat the oven to 325°F. Lightly butter a broilerproof 8-inch square baking dish.
Melt in a large skillet over medium heat:

2 tablespoons butter

Place in the pan cut side down and cook until deeply browned:

8 medium Belgian endives, halved lengthwise

Place the endives in the baking dish (you may have to do two layers of endive) and pour in:

2 tablespoons water, stock or broth, or white wine
2 teaspoons lemon juice

Cover with foil and bake until tender, about 45 minutes. While the endives cook, prepare:

White Sauce I, 548

When the endives are tender, pour off any liquid in the baking dish. If desired, wrap each endive half in:

(1 thin slice ham [16 slices total])

Spoon the white sauce over the endives, and sprinkle with:

½ cup grated Gruyère or Emmenthaler (2 ounces)

Turn on the broiler, return the dish to the oven, and allow the cheese to melt and brown.

GRILLED TREVISO WITH SAUCE GRIBICHE

4 servings

For an indoor alternative that does not require a grill pan, you may cook the bacon in a heavy skillet and brown the Treviso in the bacon fat over medium-high heat.
Soak in cold water for 1 hour:

2 small heads Treviso, halved lengthwise, or 2 large heads radicchio, quartered through the stem

Have ready:

(4 slices bacon, cooked until crisp and crumbled)
Sauce Gribiche, 568

Drain the Treviso well and shake off as much water as possible. Prepare a hot grill fire or heat a grill pan over medium heat. Add the Treviso or radicchio to the grill or pan and grill briefly, just until charred on the cut sides and slightly wilted. Divide among plates and top generously with the sauce, bacon, if using, and:

4 red radishes, thinly sliced
(Capers, drained)

UTICA GREENS (SPICY BAKED ESCAROLE)

4 to 6 servings

A specialty of Upstate New York, this deeply satisfying dish can serve as a side, but it is hearty enough to carry a meal if accompanied by warm, crusty bread. If escarole is unavailable, any sturdy cooking green—curly endive, radicchio, kale, collards, chard—will be enlivened by this treatment.

Heat in a large broilerproof skillet over medium heat until hot:

2 tablespoons olive oil

Add and cook until softened, about 5 minutes:

1 small onion, diced

Add and cook until the meat is crispy, about 5 minutes:

2 ounces prosciutto, country ham, salami, or capicola, diced
4 garlic cloves, thinly sliced

Stir in:

1 large head escarole (about 1½ pounds), washed and cut into wide strips or torn into pieces
½ cup pickled cherry peppers or pepperoncini, seeded and coarsely chopped
½ teaspoon black pepper

Cover the skillet and steam the escarole, stirring once or twice, until wilted, about 5 minutes. Meanwhile, position a rack in the center of the oven, preheat the broiler, and mix together in a small bowl:

¾ cup dry bread crumbs
¾ cup grated Parmesan (3 ounces)
(½ teaspoon dried oregano)
(¼ teaspoon red pepper flakes)

Remove the skillet from the heat and mix two-thirds of the bread crumb mixture into the greens. Toss the remaining crumbs with:

1 tablespoon olive oil

and sprinkle evenly over the greens. Place the skillet under the broiler until the cheese and bread crumbs are golden brown, about 4 minutes. Serve immediately.

BRAISED RADICCHIO

4 to 6 servings

This is excellent served with fresh pasta. To lessen the bitterness, soak the radicchio wedges in ice water for 1 hour and drain well.

Cook in a large skillet over medium heat until crisp, about 5 minutes:

4 ounces pancetta or bacon, chopped
(1 tablespoon olive oil, if using pancetta)

Transfer the meat to a plate with a slotted spoon and, if necessary, pour off all but 2 tablespoons of the fat. Increase the heat to medium-high and add:

1 pound radicchio, cut into 4 to 6 wedges each

Cook until browned on both sides and transfer to the plate with the pancetta or bacon. If needed, add a bit more olive oil to the skillet and cook, stirring, until softened, about 5 minutes:

1 medium onion, finely chopped
(2 garlic cloves, smashed)

Return the pancetta or bacon and radicchio to the skillet and add:

½ cup dry white wine
(⅓ cup chopped pitted olives, such as Castelvetrano)

Simmer over medium heat until the wine is evaporated, turning the radicchio once or twice. Pour in:

½ cup chicken or vegetable stock or broth, heavy cream, or a combination

Simmer for about 3 minutes, scraping up any browned bits in the skillet. Serve sprinkled with:

Salt and black pepper to taste
Grated Parmesan
(Toasted, 1012, pine nuts)
(Balsamic vinegar)

ABOUT CHILES

For fresh and roasted chiles, see About Peppers, 260, for dried chiles and chile powders, see 967.

ABOUT CORN

Fresh corn brightens a meal and is one of the most loved of all vegetables (for popcorn and the types used as a cereal grain, see 47 and 321, respectively). Although corn has become ubiquitous in processed food as corn syrup and processed corn products, it is also a traditional food of Central and South America as well as the southern United States.

Sweet corn is at its peak in summer and, ideally, eaten soon after picking, since most heritage varieties of corn will begin converting their sugars into starch once picked. Thanks to a spontaneous mutation—caused by exposing corn to nuclear radiation during bomb tests in the 1940s—and diligent breeding, the sweetness and shelf life of newer corn hybrids has been dramatically increased. These sweet corn hybrids are twice as sweet as older varieties, and convert their sugar to starch at a much slower rate. Thus, whether the kernels are yellow, white, or "butter and sugar" (a combination of yellow and white), modern sweet corn remains sweet even if shipped long distances and stored for several weeks.

If corn is sold in the husks, the husks should be bright green and fresh looking, not dry. The kernels should appear plump and moist—the first to dry out are located at the tip, so a quick peek into the corn silk will suffice. If fresh corn is unavailable, purchase frozen corn before canned.

Store corn in the husk or, if shucked, in a closed plastic bag in the refrigerator crisper. Though sweet corn hybrids are bred to keep for several weeks after picking, it is still best to use corn, whether hybrid or heirloom, promptly after buying. Whole, shucked cobs freeze well, 885. Leftover cobs (and good-looking husks) may be used in vegetable stocks and add extra corn flavor if left to simmer in Corn Chowder, 88. Fresh or softened, dried husks may also be used as a leaf wrapping, 1056, and for tamales, 324–25.

Corn smut, or **huitlacoche,** is a fungus that swells the kernels of infected ears of corn. It is considered a blight by most American farmers. It is, however, completely safe to eat and considered a delicacy in Mexico, where the darkened, enlarged kernels are harvested soon after they are inoculated and sold for a high price. Once dubbed "the Mexican truffle" and frequently translated as "corn mushroom," *huitlacoche* tastes sweet, woodsy, and mushroom-like; it is often used to flavor sauces, tamales, and quesadillas, or sautéed with sweet corn kernels. It may be found frozen, canned, or, rarely, fresh.

In New Mexico and other Southwestern states, ears of young (or "green") field corn are left in their husks in adobe ovens overnight and then dried. Called **chicos,** the slightly shriveled, dry kernels are very sweet and mildly smoky. They are typically cooked with beans until soft, or they may be simmered in water until tender and added to dishes or served on their own.

To prepare corn, first remove the husks and silk. To remove the whole kernels from the cob, cut off the stem end to create a flat base. Place on a rimmed baking sheet to collect any stray kernels. Grasp the tip of the cob and cut downward, removing two or three rows at a time. Press along the rows with the dull side of a knife to retrieve the richly flavored juices and the heart of the kernels. Or, to remove the corn as a creamy pulp, run the tip of a knife down through the center of each row of kernels, opening the kernels. Then, with the back of the knife, scrape down the cob and press out all the pulp. ➤ One ear of corn yields about ½ cup kernels or 3 to 4 tablespoons creamy pulp.

Fresh sweet corn tastes delicious uncooked in salads and salsas; unless it has become starchy during storage, it only requires a few minutes of cooking. That said, caramelizing the corn's sugars—or charring the exterior over a grill—can be quite tasty. Corn goes well with butter, bacon, cream, cheese, chiles, tomatoes, chili powder, basil, parsley, cilantro, and lime. In the following recipes, corn can be fresh or frozen (or canned, as a last resort) except when otherwise noted.

CORN ON THE COB

Allow 1 to 3 ears per person, depending on appetites. Remember, with most sweet corn, all you need to do is heat the kernels, not cook them. If you are serving bread or rolls with your meal, suggest that diners liberally butter their bread, then rub the corn over the buttered surface.

Remove the husks and silk from:

Ears of corn

Drop them one at a time into a large pot of rapidly boiling water. If you have a steamer basket that can accommodate all of the ears, you may steam them for an equal amount of time. Cover and cook until hot and tender, 2 to 8 minutes, depending on maturity. Remove from the water with tongs. Serve hot with:

Butter or any Flavored Butter, 559–60
Salt and black pepper

GRILLED, ROASTED, OR BROILED CORN

I. Soak ears of corn in their husks in water for 2 hours before grilling. Do not worry about removing the silks; they will come off later with the husks. Lay the ears in the husks directly over a medium-hot grill fire, 1063. Cook, turning the ears with a pair of tongs so they roast evenly on all sides, about 20 minutes. Or roast the corn in their water-soaked husks in a 450°F oven for 8 to 15 minutes. Serve as for Corn on the Cob, above.

II. To concentrate their flavor and caramelize their natural sugars, shuck ears of corn and lay them on a grill rack over very hot coals or place them under a preheated broiler on the top rack. If grilling, you may pull the leaves back, tie them if desired, and use as a handle. Grill or broil, turning the ears to brown them evenly, for 5 to 7 minutes. Serve as above, or as for Elotes, below.

ELOTES (MEXICAN GRILLED CORN)

4 servings

This is one of our favorite corn dishes. For a less messy eating experience, simply cut the kernels off the grilled ears, toss in a bowl with the other ingredients, and sprinkle with chopped cilantro (you may call the dish **esquites**).

Prepare with 4 ears of corn:

Grilled, Roasted, or Broiled Corn II, above

When the corn is cooked, transfer to a platter. Spread on each ear of corn:

2 tablespoons mayonnaise or Mexican crema (½ cup total)

Roll the corn in:

Finely crumbled Cotija or feta cheese, or finely grated Parmesan

Season to taste with:

Chile powder
Lime juice
Salt

SAUTÉED CORN

4 servings

Cut the kernels from:

6 ears corn (about 3 cups)

Add to a skillet over medium heat:

2 tablespoons butter or olive oil or 2 slices bacon

Crisp the bacon, if using, and transfer to a plate. If desired, add any of the following to the skillet and cook until softened, about 5 minutes:

(2 jalapeño or serrano peppers or ½ poblano pepper, seeded and diced)
(2 garlic cloves, coarsely chopped)

Add the corn and cook, stirring often, until heated through, 3 to 4 minutes. Crumble and stir in the bacon, if using, along with any of the following:

1 ripe slicing tomato or 2 Roma or plum tomatoes, finely diced
2 tablespoons chopped parsley, cilantro, or basil
(Pinch of chili powder or curry powder)

Season to taste with:

Salt and black pepper
(Lemon or lime juice)

CREAMED CORN

4 servings

Cut and then scrape the creamy pulp, above, from the cobs of:

5 ears corn (about 2½ cups)

Melt in a medium nonstick skillet over low heat:

1 tablespoon butter

If desired, add and cook, stirring, until softened, 3 to 4 minutes:

(¼ cup thinly sliced green onions or chopped shallots)

Add the creamy corn pulp along with:

¼ cup heavy cream

Cook over low heat, stirring once or twice, until thickened, about 2 minutes. You may stir in:

(¼ cup grated Parmesan or crumbled feta cheese)

Season to taste with:

Salt and black or cayenne pepper

CORN PUDDING

6 servings

For a lighter, fluffier texture, you may separate the eggs and beat the whites until stiff but not dry, 978. Add the yolks to the pudding base and gently fold in the whites just before turning it into the baking dish. The addition of vanilla was inspired by our friend Maggie Green.

Preheat the oven to 350°F. Butter an 8-inch square baking pan or 1½-quart baking dish.

Mix together in a large bowl:

2 cups fresh, frozen, or drained canned corn kernels
¾ cup milk or half-and-half
2 large eggs, well beaten
2 tablespoons butter, melted
1 tablespoon all-purpose flour
1 teaspoon salt
(1 teaspoon vanilla)

Pour into the prepared baking dish. Bake until the center is set, about 1 hour.

ADDITIONS TO CORN PUDDING

2 poblano or New Mexico chile peppers or 2 red bell peppers, roasted, 262, and chopped
1 cup shredded Monterey Jack, Muenster, or sharp Cheddar (4 ounces)
2 garlic cloves, minced
1 small onion, diced and sauteéd, 255

CHEESE-CHILE CORN SQUARES

About 9 servings

Preheat the oven to 350°F. Generously butter a 9-inch square baking pan.

Combine in a large bowl:

3 cups shredded Monterey Jack (12 ounces)
1½ cups fresh, frozen, or drained canned corn kernels
1 cup fine yellow cornmeal or masa harina
6 large eggs, well beaten
3 jalapeños or 1 poblano or New Mexico chile pepper, roasted, 262, chopped
2 tablespoons chili powder
½ teaspoon salt

Scrape the mixture into the prepared pan. Bake until the top is nicely browned, about 30 minutes. Let cool until it firms sufficiently to be cut, then cut into 3-inch squares. Serve with:

Salsa, store-bought or homemade, 573–74
Frijoles de la Olla, 213

SUCCOTASH

4 servings

Succotash takes its name from the Narragansett word *msickquatash*, meaning "boiled kernels of corn." This is entirely acceptable made with canned or frozen vegetables.

Cook in a medium saucepan over medium heat, stirring occasionally, until heated through:

1 cup fresh, frozen, or drained canned corn kernels
1 cup cooked lima beans or finely chopped green beans
2 tablespoons butter
½ teaspoon salt
⅛ teaspoon sweet paprika
Chopped parsley or thyme to taste

FRESH CORN FRITTERS

4 servings

The author of the following account graciously permitted us to use it when we told him how much it pleased us.

"When I was a child, one of eight, my father frequently promised us a marvelous treat. He, being an amateur arboriculturist, would tell us of a fritter tree he was going to plant on the banks of a small lake filled with molasses, maple syrup, or honey, to be located in our backyard. When one of us children felt the urge for this most delectable repast, all we had to do was to shake the tree—the fritters would drop into the lake, and we could fish them out and eat fritters to our hearts' content. Mother was a good cook, and she duly developed this fabulous fritter." The following is, we hope, a faithful transcription of her recipe.

Scrape from the cobs into a bowl:

2½ cups fresh corn kernels (about 5 ears)

Stir in:

2 large egg yolks, well beaten
2 teaspoons all-purpose flour
½ teaspoon salt
¼ teaspoon black pepper

Whip in a medium bowl until stiff but not dry, 978:

2 large egg whites

Fold into the corn mixture. Heat in a large nonstick skillet over high heat:

1 tablespoon butter or vegetable oil

Drop in the batter a heaping tablespoon at a time, without crowding. Reduce the heat to medium and cook, turning once, until browned on both sides, 2 to 3 minutes per side. Wipe out the skillet between batches and add more butter or oil. Serve immediately with any of the following:

Maple syrup or honey, lemon wedges, any salsa, 573–74, Shirazi or Israeli Salad, 128, Chow Chow, 925, or Smoky Tomato Jam, 914

ABOUT CUCUMBERS

A relative of squashes and melons, cucumbers are easily the juiciest and most refreshing raw vegetable. The most common **slicing cucumber** (or "burpless") variety can have thick skin; **English** or **hothouse cucumbers** are long, thin-skinned, and virtually seedless.

Smaller **Persian** or **beit alpha cucumbers** (sometimes marked as **mini cucumbers** or **baby cucumbers**) have a fine texture, thin skin, and sweet flavor. **Japanese** and **Korean cucumbers** are exceptionally crisp. Long, pale **Armenian cucumbers** are actually a type of musk melon; they have thin skin and sweet, crisp flesh. Round, bright-yellow **lemon cucumbers** and oblong brownish-yellow **poona kheera cucumbers** are striking to look at, juicy, and high proportion pleasantly flavored (both contain a high proportion of seeds).

Pickling cucumbers are bred to keep their crispness and absorb brines. In general, ➤ varieties that have small bumps all over their skin are the best for pickling. On this side of the cucumber family is the classic American pickling cucumber, which often goes by the name **Kirby.** Diminutive **gherkins,** best known for their use in Cornichons, 924, are full-flavored and used exclusively for pickling. **Mexican sour gherkins** have thin, smooth skin and resemble tiny watermelons, hence their affectionate nickname "mouse melons."

Regardless of type, look for firm cucumbers with no soft spots, bruises, or cuts. They should have lustrous skin, but do not be misled by the heavy waxy finish that has been applied to those in many markets. Store uncut cucumbers at room temperature and use within a few days (refrigeration actually hastens their spoilage). Of course, to enjoy them "cool as a cucumber," chill them before serving.

If a cucumber's skin is waxed or especially thick, remove it with a vegetable peeler or paring knife. If the skin is thin enough to leave on, an attractive finish for slicing is made by running a fork down the length of the cucumber, scoring it all around; or peel off the skin in stripes. To remove their seeds, halve cucumbers lengthwise and use the tip of a spoon to scrape them out, 133.

The texture and flavor of cucumbers begins to disappear as they cook. While we have seen instances of cucumbers being cooked or grilled, we recommend enjoying them raw and at their crunchiest. For dishes that celebrate raw cucumber, see Cucumber Salad, 126, Fattoush, 128, Shirazi or Israeli Salad, 128, Panzanella, 128, Gazpacho, 107, Cold Cucumber and Yogurt Soup, 108, Tzatziki, 569, and Raita, 569. For making cucumber pickles, see 924; for fermenting them, see Half-Sour Pickles, 941.

ABOUT EGGPLANT

Eggplants are also known by their French name, *aubergine*, or the Italian *melanzana*, from its undeserved (but tantalizing) Latin name, which roughly translates as "apple of madness." The eggplants most commonly available are the **globe** varieties, such as **Black Beauty,** which are usually quite large, inky purple, and teardrop- or globe-shaped. However, there are also **white eggplants,** and it is from these varieties the vegetable gets its English name. Many eggplant varieties grown in the Mediterranean and throughout Asia are smaller than the globe-types, and range from purple to striped, or green. They may be diminutive and round, like many **Indian** types, or long and slender like **Japanese** and **Taiwanese** varieties. Most of the smaller varieties of eggplant are thin-skinned and perfect for quick-cooking methods. An exception is the tiny, round, thick-skinned **Thai green eggplant,** which contains many seeds and is primarily simmered in dishes like green curry, 421. Most any eggplant can be used in recipes calling for standard eggplant, except where their shape or low yield of flesh is problematic, such as Baba Ghanoush, 53, Eggplant Parmigiana, 238, or Rolled Stuffed Eggplant, 238.

Select eggplants that are heavy for their size. Their skin should be taut and glossy; dull skin usually means they have been stored for too long. Look for a fresh, green cap and intact stem; avoid any that have soft spots, cuts, or bruises. Eggplants should give only slightly when pressed and spring back when released. Unyielding flesh is not ripe; soft, dented flesh is overripe and potentially bitter. As a rule, slender Asian varieties and small to medium eggplants weighing 1 pound or less are the choicest for stir-frying, sautéing, or batter-frying, since they usually have the fewest seeds and the thinnest skins. They are much more perishable than globe-types, so use promptly. Store all eggplants in a cool, dry place and use as soon as possible. Eggplants deteriorate faster at refrigerator temperatures after several days.

Eggplant can have a blotter-like capacity for oil or butter. Salting and draining serves to compact the flesh, helping it absorb less oil when cooking and giving the cooked vegetable a firm, creamy texture.

To salt eggplant, trim off the stem and cap. Cut as directed in the recipe, and generously sprinkle the exposed flesh with salt. Place in a colander and let stand for at least 30 minutes and up to 60 minutes. Rinse and pat it dry.

Eggplant goes well with lamb, tomatoes, onions, peppers, cheese, oregano, marjoram, soy sauce, miso, and garlic. Microwaving and pressure-cooking are not recommended. In addition to the recipes here, see Baba Ghanoush, 53, and Caponata, 54.

ROASTED EGGPLANT

4 to 6 servings

I. WHOLE

Roasting whole eggplant produces a tender pulp that can be used for dips and purees. You can also roast whole eggplants on a hot grill—or, if you manage to think ahead, in the residual heat of the grill after you have cooked dinner—allowing them to char for a distinctive smoky flavor. You may also roast them over embers in the hearth, 1068. A 1-pound eggplant will yield about 1½ cups pulp.

Preheat the oven to 400°F. Make several slits with a knife tip in:

1 whole eggplant

If desired, fill the cuts with:

(Garlic slivers)

Set in a baking dish. Bake until the eggplant has collapsed, 30 minutes to 1 hour, depending on size. Transfer to a colander so that any juices can drain off, then cut in half and scoop out the pulp. Leave it coarse or mash it to a puree. Use for eggplant dips, such as Baba Ghanoush, 53, or season to taste with any of the following:

Extra-virgin olive oil, melted butter, or toasted sesame oil
Chopped herbs, such as marjoram or basil
Lemon juice or any vinaigrette, 575
Plain yogurt
Salt and black pepper

II. HALVES OR SLICES

Halved or sliced eggplant, brushed with oil, is delicious roasted and topped or seasoned with a variety of delicious ingredients. For a meaty main-course dish, you may top with Keftedes, 62, or Becker Lamb Patties, 505. For slices, see Pasta alla Norma, 297.

Preheat the oven to 400°F. Halve lengthwise or peel and cut crosswise into ½-inch-thick slices:

2 medium eggplants (about 2 pounds total), stem ends trimmed

If using eggplant halves, score the flesh in parallel diagonal lines, then make perpendicular slashes to create a diamond pattern (do not puncture the skin). Liberally brush the cut surfaces of the eggplant halves or slices with:

Olive oil

Dust evenly with:

½ teaspoon salt

¼ teaspoon black pepper or 1 teaspoon Baharat, 589

Place the eggplant halves or slices cut side up on a baking sheet and roast until very tender, 20 to 25 minutes for slices and about 30 minutes for halves. For a simple side, garnish with:

Chopped herbs such as parsley, mint, or basil

Lemon juice or dollops of plain Greek yogurt or labneh

Or top with any of the following:

Raita, 569, Tzatziki, 569, Tahini Dressing, 576, Zhug, 567, Tapenade, 54, or a tomato sauce, 556–58, and a grating of Parmesan

MISO-GLAZED EGGPLANT

4 servings

This Japanese preparation is one of our favorite ways to cook eggplant.

Position a rack in the center of the oven. Preheat the oven to 450°F. Lightly grease a baking sheet.

Halve lengthwise:

4 slender Japanese eggplants

Brush the cut sides liberally with:

2 tablespoons vegetable oil

Roast cut side down on the baking sheet until the eggplant is slightly softened and just beginning to brown around the edges, 15 to 20 minutes. Meanwhile, mix in a small bowl until smooth:

¼ cup red or white miso

2 tablespoons mirin or white wine

1 tablespoon sake or water

Remove the baking sheet from the oven, turn the eggplant halves over, and brush or spread the miso mixture onto the cut sides. Turn on the broiler, return the sheet to the oven, and cook until well browned and starting to char in spots, about 5 minutes.

FRIED EGGPLANT

4 servings

The bread crumb coating is essential for Eggplant Parmigiana, below. You may also peel and cut the eggplant as directed here and fry in a batter, 203 (we especially like them dipped in Pakora Batter, 657).

Peel and cut into ½-inch-thick slices or sticks:

1 medium eggplant, stem ends trimmed

If desired, salt the eggplant as instructed, 237. Whisk together in a shallow bowl:

3 large eggs

1 tablespoon water

Dredge the eggplant in:

⅓ cup flour

Shake off the excess, dip in the egg mixture, letting the excess drip off, and dredge in a mixture of:

1½ cups dry bread crumbs

(¼ to ½ cup grated Parmesan [2 to 4 ounces])

(1½ teaspoons dried rosemary, thyme, or oregano, crumbled)

1½ teaspoons salt

1 teaspoon black pepper

Arrange the eggplant slices on a wire rack and let dry for at least 30 minutes (or overnight in the refrigerator). Heat in a large skillet over medium-high heat:

¼ cup vegetable oil

Add as many eggplant slices as will fit without crowding and cook for 4 to 5 minutes on each side. Transfer to a plate. You may have to add more oil to fry the remaining batches.

EGGPLANT PARMIGIANA

4 to 6 servings

Prepare or have ready:

Fried Eggplant, above

3 cups tomato sauce, store-bought or homemade, 556–58

Position a rack in the upper third of the oven. Preheat the oven to 425°F.

Coat a 13 × 9-inch baking dish with half of the tomato sauce. Arrange the fried eggplant slices in a single layer, or slightly overlapping if necessary, in the dish. Top with the remaining tomato sauce and:

2 teaspoons dried oregano

¼ teaspoon black pepper

Combine and sprinkle over the eggplant:

1½ cups shredded mozzarella (6 ounces)

⅔ cup grated Parmesan (about 2½ ounces)

Sprinkle over the top:

2 teaspoons chopped parsley

Bake until the cheese is melted and bubbling, about 15 minutes. Serve at once.

ROLLED STUFFED EGGPLANT

4 servings

Also known as **involtini,** this dish is a good, quicker alternative to Eggplant Parmigiana since it has similar appeal and does not involve frying. To make things even quicker, substitute your favorite store-bought tomato sauce for the homemade sauce. No shame here.

Preheat the oven to 400°F. Lightly oil 2 rimmed baking sheets.

Cut lengthwise into ½-inch-thick slabs:

2 large eggplants (about 2½ pounds total), stem ends trimmed

Divide the eggplant slices between the baking sheets and brush with:

2 tablespoons olive oil

Sprinkle with:

½ teaspoon salt

Bake until just tender, about 20 minutes. Meanwhile, prepare:

Cheese Filling, 311

3 cups tomato sauce, store-bought or homemade, 556–58

When the eggplant is done, remove from the oven and let cool. Leave the oven on. Lightly oil a 13 × 9-inch baking dish. Spread a thin layer of tomato sauce over the bottom of the dish. Roll up about 2 tablespoons of the cheese filling in each eggplant slice and place seam side down in the baking dish. Top with remaining tomato sauce and sprinkle with:

1 cup shredded mozzarella (4 ounces)

Bake until the cheese is melted and the filling is heated through, about 25 minutes. Let stand for 5 minutes before serving. Sprinkle with:

Chopped parsley

MOUSSAKA

6 to 8 servings

We top this moussaka with a mixture of yogurt and eggs, which is lighter than the traditional béchamel, or white sauce.

Cut lengthwise into slabs about ⅓ inch thick:

2 large or 3 medium eggplants (2 to 2½ pounds), stem ends trimmed

Salt the slices generously and place on a baking sheet lined with paper towels. Let stand for 30 minutes to 1 hour.

Meanwhile, heat a large skillet over medium-high heat and add:

1 pound ground lamb or beef

Cook, stirring, until the meat has browned and rendered its fat, 3 to 5 minutes. Using a slotted spoon, transfer the meat to a bowl. Pour off all but 2 tablespoons fat from the skillet (if the meat has rendered less, add enough olive oil to make 2 tablespoons). Add and cook, stirring, until tender, about 5 minutes:

1 large onion, chopped

Scrape the bottom of the skillet with a wooden spatula as the onion cooks to scrape up any browned bits. Add and cook, stirring, until fragrant, about 30 seconds:

2 large garlic cloves, minced

Return the meat to the skillet and stir in:

One 14½-ounce can diced tomatoes
1 heaping tablespoon tomato paste
½ teaspoon sweet paprika
½ teaspoon sugar
Heaping ¼ teaspoon ground cinnamon
⅛ teaspoon ground allspice
1 bay leaf
½ cup water, or enough to just barely cover the meat
½ teaspoon salt
½ teaspoon black pepper

Bring to a simmer, then reduce the heat to low, cover, and simmer, stirring occasionally, until the mixture is thick and very fragrant, about 1 hour. Uncover and cook until the liquid in the skillet is just about gone, another 5 to 10 minutes. Remove from the heat and remove the bay leaf. Taste and adjust the seasonings. Let cool slightly, then stir in:

½ cup chopped parsley
1 large egg, well beaten

Preheat the oven to 350°F. Grease a 13 × 9-inch baking dish.

Rinse and pat the eggplant dry. Make an even layer of half the eggplant in the bottom of the dish, and spread all the sauce over the eggplant. Top with the remaining eggplant. Bake, covered with foil, for 30 minutes.

Meanwhile, beat together in a bowl:

1¼ cups plain Greek yogurt
4 large eggs
½ teaspoon salt
Pinch of sweet paprika
Black pepper to taste

Remove the foil and pour the yogurt/egg mixture over the eggplant. Sprinkle evenly over the top:

½ cup mixed grated kefalotyri and Parmesan, or Parmesan only (2 ounces)

Return to the oven and bake until the topping is golden, another 25 to 30 minutes. Serve warm.

ABOUT FENNEL

There are two types of fennel. One is bred for its crisp, sweet, licorice-scented bulb, and the other for its seeds. You may find fennel bulbs trimmed or with their long stalks and delicate fronds attached. Though it adds a complex sweetness to many dishes—especially one of our quick weeknight favorites, Pasta con le Sarde, 297—we appreciate fennel bulbs most when they are thinly sliced across the grain and served raw in salads, such as Shaved Fennel and White Bean Salad, 129, or simply dressed with a vinaigrette as a sort of "slaw" to accompany meats and fish. Fennel's crunchy texture also makes it well suited to quick-pickling, 929, or as a substitute for celery in bound salads, 123.

Like its relative, celery, fennel moonlights as a spice and an herb. Pungent seeds are harvested from a tall, spindly variety of the plant, and are indispensable in many cuisines (for more on **fennel seeds,** see 984). **Fennel fronds** may be stripped off the stalk and used as an herb for the dish you are using the fennel bulb in; used to garnish fish; added to Salsa Verde, 567, for a hint of sweetness and complexity; or sprinkled into a Mignonette Sauce, 570, for serving with oysters on the half shell. **Fennel pollen** is prized as a seasoning, but its complex, concentrated flavor should be used sparingly. For more on its use, see 983. All but the youngest fennel stalks are too tough to eat, but they have a few uses. In the south of France, fennel stalks are used to cook fish: The stalks are laid on the grates of a grill, then cleaned and seasoned fish are placed on top of them. The smoldering stalks keep the fish from sticking to the grill, and the fennel adds a subtle flavor. You may also use fennel fronds still attached to the stalks as a brush for basting meats, fish, or vegetables with sauce or butter as they cook on the grill.

Use fennel promptly after purchase. Cut off the stalks and fronds and store with the bulbs in a bag. Store in the refrigerator crisper for up to 5 days.

To prepare fennel, pull away any tough outer layers of the bulb. If serving raw, ➤ we recommend cutting fennel across the grain with a sharp knife or on a mandoline so that its celery-like fibers can be masticated with ease.

Steam, braise, or sauté sliced or chopped fennel alone or in combination with other vegetables. In small quantities, fennel is an excellent addition to homemade vegetable or chicken stock. Roasting tends to cause fennel to dry out and toughen, but it can be done with a bit of caution. Fennel is especially good with fish, and its sweetness is complemented by acidic tomatoes, citrus, vinegars, and tangy cheeses. Fennel also pairs well with apples, dill, toasted walnuts or hazelnuts, and oranges.

BRAISED FENNEL

4 servings

A hearty side dish. For a main course, you may chop up the fennel wedges and serve atop risotto or polenta, or toss with pasta and a bit of the pasta's cooking liquid.

Trim and quarter lengthwise so they are still held together at the core:

2 large fennel bulbs (about 1 pound)

Sprinkle over the cut surfaces:

½ teaspoon salt
¼ teaspoon black pepper

Heat in a skillet over medium-high heat:

2 tablespoons vegetable oil

Add the fennel cut side down and cook until browned, about 4 minutes. Turn and brown the other cut side, about 4 minutes more. Meanwhile, stir together until dissolved:

1 cup dry white wine, dry vermouth, or chicken or vegetable stock or broth
2 tablespoons tomato paste

When the fennel has browned, carefully add the wine mixture to the skillet along with:

4 garlic cloves, thinly sliced
6 sprigs thyme, parsley, oregano, or a combination
1 bay leaf
(One 2-inch strip of lemon or orange zest)

Cover the skillet and reduce the heat to maintain a simmer. Cook until the fennel is fork-tender, about 20 minutes. Uncover and discard the herbs and any zest. Serve as is, or increase the heat to medium-high and reduce the cooking liquid to a thick glaze. Serve sprinkled with any of the following:

Lemon or orange juice, or red or white wine vinegar
Chopped parsley or minced chives
Shredded Romano or Parmesan

GRILLED FENNEL AND TOMATOES WITH OLIVES AND BASIL

4 servings

Prepare a medium-hot grill fire, 1063. Cut lengthwise into ½-inch-thick wedges held together by the core:

2 large fennel bulbs (about 1 pound)

Halve lengthwise:

4 Roma or plum tomatoes

Rub the fennel and tomatoes with:

¼ cup olive oil
Salt and black pepper

Place on the grill and cook until the fennel is slightly soft and the tomatoes are nicely browned, 3 to 4 minutes per side. Remove from the grill and place in a large bowl along with:

½ cup coarsely chopped pitted black olives, such as Kalamata
⅓ cup coarsely chopped basil
¼ cup extra-virgin olive oil
2 tablespoons lemon juice
Salt and black pepper to taste

Toss lightly and serve at once.

ABOUT FIDDLEHEAD FERNS

The new shoots, or "fiddleheads," of the ostrich fern have a flavor reminiscent of asparagus, artichoke, and green beans. They are available at specialty produce stores and farmers' markets in the spring. Choose ferns that are bright green, tightly coiled, and firm. To prepare, trim the "tail" to the same thickness as the coil. Immerse the ferns in cold water, swirl and rub off any brown fuzz, then rinse well. If desired, soaking them in cool water for 1 hour will diminish any lingering bitterness. ➤ Do not serve fiddleheads raw or undercooked.

To cook fiddleheads, simply boil in salted water until tender and cooked through, 10 to 15 minutes. Or, cook them in the salted water for 5 minutes and finish by sautéing with butter and garlic until browned, about 5 minutes more. Serve with melted or Brown Butter, 558, and lemon juice or with Hollandaise, 561.

Caution: Some people are allergic to ferns. ➤ Do not pick fiddleheads in the wild, since, although many ferns send up the coils, only the ostrich fern is safe for eating.

ABOUT GARLIC

There is little that escapes our kitchen that does not involve garlic—usually in amounts more copious than we dare admit, let alone suggest to readers. Roasted, minced, mashed, or smashed, garlic just makes life better.

There are two broad categories of garlic: **hardneck** and **softneck garlic.** Softneck garlic is the type we find most often in supermarkets. Perhaps the most important difference has to do with the arrangement and size of garlic cloves in the bulb: Softneck bulbs have two rings of cloves, the inner one being smaller (and more frustrating to peel). Hardneck varieties tend to have larger cloves encircling the stem in one layer.

Garlic is useful at every stage of its cultivation. The bunches of **green garlic** you may find at the farmers' market in spring are harvested before the bulb has formed. It has a mild, fresh flavor and may be substituted for mature garlic in cooked dishes. As it matures, hardneck garlic plants send up curved, bud-topped green shoots, called **garlic scapes** or **whips.** These are often cut off in early summer to force the plant to put all its effort into growing larger bulbs. Scapes are another excellent, fresh-tasting substitute for garlic in cooked recipes. They are tender when young, but it's always a good idea to slice them crosswise before or after cooking (they can be fibrous). Mature garlic with fully formed cloves is usually cured (hung in a dry well-ventilated environment for a period of time to dry) for long-term storage. Moist, uncured bulbs can be found for sale at farmers' markets in spring and summer months. Use as you would regular, cured garlic.

Elephant garlic is not true garlic but a type of leek. Its cloves are the size of Brazil nuts or larger, and their flavor is very mild. Elephant garlic is pleasant when roasted and may be substituted for chopped or minced garlic in recipes if a milder flavor is desired.

Green garlic, garlic scapes, and fresh garlic bulbs should be firm, with no yellowed or withered spots. Cured garlic and elephant garlic bulbs should have firm heads with tight, papery skins, which may be white, purplish, or tinged with red. Avoid bulbs with soft cloves or ones that give noticeably when squeezed. Cloves with brown spots or protruding green sprouts are past their prime and should be discarded. Store cured garlic at room temperature, away from light. Store green garlic, garlic scapes, and uncured, fresh garlic in a bag in the refrigerator crisper for up to 1 week.

Like onions and chiles, garlic is one of the most important (and beloved) ingredients in our kitchen. ➤ For more on the instrumental role garlic plays as a seasoning, as well as information on **garlic powder** and **black garlic,** see 990.

To peel garlic for chopping, cut off the woody root end of each clove and place your knife blade flat over the cloves. Rap the knife with the bottom of your fist and lightly smash the cloves. The skin should slip off. Gather the fractured pieces of garlic together and chop them until they are the desired size.

To peel garlic cloves whole for mincing, grating, or slicing, lay the clove on a cutting board, with the part of the clove that would be facing outward in the bulb facing up. Press down gently but firmly with your thumb until you hear a "pop" and the skin has split a little (too much pressure will crack the clove). Peel from the root end with a fingernail; the skin should pull off easily. Cut off the root end.

To slice, cut one side of the clove so that it will lie flat, rotate the clove onto the flattened side, and slice lengthwise.

To mince, slice the clove horizontally, with your knife parallel to the cutting board, without cutting completely through the end, cut through the clove lengthwise several times with your knife perpendicular to the cutting board, then chop crosswise into very fine pieces. Or, ➤ grate whole, peeled cloves on a rasp-style grater (this is our favorite technique for adding garlic to salad dressings and sauces, as it allows the garlic to meld completely into the sauce).

To mash to a paste, hold the knife blade almost flat against minced garlic and crush the pieces while pulling the knife back and forth through the pulp until it becomes as smooth as you can make it. Sprinkling with a pinch of salt makes it easier to work the garlic into a paste.

Running garlic cloves through a **garlic press** is a convenient method of getting "minced" garlic. Some models are designed to work even with unpeeled garlic. However, this process leaves the garlic spicier and harsher than it would be otherwise. Rubbing garlic on the rough surface of toasted or grilled bread has a similar effect. Of course, this harsh, spicy bite is sometimes desirable (see Bruschetta, 67). ➤ When cooking pressed or minced garlic in oil over higher heat settings, be especially careful not to burn it, which makes it strong and acrid. The same goes for grilling or broiling items that have been marinated in a mixture containing minced garlic (we recommend grating the garlic to avoid this, or brushing off minced pieces before cooking).

Despite the sticky, often frustrating rigmarole of peeling and preparing garlic, it is, in our opinion, vastly superior to the store-bought minced and chopped garlic sold in jars in the produce section. Prepeeled garlic, sold in sealed bags or containers, is a good compromise (keep refrigerated and use promptly).

Garlic lovers should seek out our recipes for Sopa de Ajo, 91, Chicken with 40 Cloves of Garlic, 420, Garlic Bread, 638, Garlic and Walnut Sauce, 570, Aïoli, 564, and Pickled Garlic, 928.

ROASTED GARLIC

4 to 6 servings

I. WHOLE OVEN-ROASTED HEADS

To eat this as a first course, squeeze the pulp from each clove, spread on slices of buttered toasted French bread, and sprinkle with salt. Or use in Roasted Garlic and Parmesan Spread, 56.

Preheat the oven to 400°F. To expose the cloves, cut the top third from:

4 large heads garlic

Drizzle over the cut portions of the heads:

2 tablespoons olive oil

Wrap each head tightly in foil, place in a baking dish, and bake until the garlic is soft and tender, about 45 minutes. Serve hot or at room temperature.

II. QUICK PAN-ROASTED GARLIC CLOVES

This method produces a firmer result with a toasty flavor. Pan-roasting is ideal for mellowing out garlic before using in salsas, 573–74, or uncooked table sauces like Habanero-Citrus Hot Sauce, 571.

Place in a heavy skillet over medium heat:

Garlic cloves, unpeeled, excess skin removed

Let the skin of the cloves blacken, and then turn them. Repeat until the cloves have charred spots on all sides, about 15 minutes. Transfer to a cutting board and let cool.

GARLIC CONFIT

About 1½ cups

Think of this as a "twofer": You get meltingly tender cloves of garlic for garnishing, adding to sauces, or spreading on toast, as well as a richly flavored oil for drizzling on bread, tossing with pasta, or using in vinaigrettes and mayonnaise.

If using the oven, preheat it to 225°F. Peel and trim:

Cloves from 2 heads garlic

Place the cloves in a baking dish or small saucepan and add:

1 cup olive oil, or to cover

(3 sprigs thyme, 1 small sprig rosemary, or 1 bay leaf)

Place the baking dish in the oven, or bring the saucepan to the barest simmer (about 200°F) over medium heat and reduce the heat to gently poach the garlic (small bubbles may form, but they should not percolate on the surface of the oil). Cook for 1 hour, or until very tender. Use immediately, or let cool, transfer to a covered container (making sure the garlic stays submerged) and refrigerate for up to 1 month.

GARLIC CHIPS

About ½ cup

These crunchy chips are perfect for adding texture and garlic flavor to salads, cream soups, and braised meats or vegetables.

Very thinly slice crosswise:

Peeled cloves from 2 heads garlic

Add the garlic slices to a small saucepan along with:

1 inch vegetable oil

Place the pan over medium heat and allow to heat until the garlic begins to bubble and sizzle. Continue to cook until the garlic slices are light golden brown, about 10 minutes. To test for doneness, remove a few slices from the oil and let cool for 30 seconds. They should be crisp and break cleanly in half.

Place a fine-mesh sieve over a metal bowl and pour the oil into the strainer. Transfer the garlic slices to a plate lined with paper towels to drain. When cooled, transfer to an airtight container and store at room temperature for up to 2 weeks. Use the garlic-infused oil for stir-fries or sautés. (Refrigerate in a covered container for up to 1 month.)

ABOUT GREENS FOR COOKING

"Greens" are almost too numerous to talk about responsibly in brief. Entire books have been devoted to describing their intricacies. Nonetheless, how we treat greens varies only slightly from one variety to the next, and most of the recipes below that are written for one type of green can be used for others to good effect. For bitter greens like **chicory, escarole, radicchio,** and **endives,** see 233. Though many of the types covered here are close relatives, the varieties we refer to as **cabbage** are resilient, thick-leaved, and very juicy, thus demanding different treatment. For more, see About Cabbage, 223.

Spinach is perhaps the most popular cooking green. It is puréed into soups, 106, stuffed into pies (Fatayer bi Sabanekh, 702) and in between layers of crispy pastry (Spanakopita, 706), and eaten raw or lightly wilted in salads, 118. Dishes that are garnished with or served on gently cooked spinach are often given the appellation **Florentine.** A relative of beets, spinach has a mild but distinctive tartness and minerality, especially when the plants grow larger. Mature spinach has large, crinkly leaves and is preferred for cooking: It stands up to the heat better, is more toothsome, and has more flavor. Though it will work in many of the recipes listed below, we think baby spinach is best eaten raw. ➤ Ten ounces of frozen spinach is roughly equivalent to 1½ pounds fresh spinach, wilted.

Amaranth (used in Caribbean Callaloo, 101) and **New Zealand spinach** are botanically unrelated to spinach, but are similar in flavor and texture. **Water spinach,** or **ong choy,** has a long hollow stem, small leaves, and a crunchier texture. The stem is often shredded, cut into manageable lengths, blanched, and then soaked in ice water to make it curl. This tangled nest of crunchy stem ribbons can be dressed in a simple vinaigrette. There is a special tool for shredding the stems, available in some Asian markets, but they can be split with a paring knife or julienne peeler.

Chard, or **Swiss chard,** is another beet relative, which helps explain the colorful varieties at markets, with their reddish-pink, orange, and yellow veins and midribs. Chard has a mild yet slightly bitter flavor, and the leaves are thin and brittle. Chard ribs are broad, flat, and usually tender, so they do not need to be removed before cooking. If desired, remove the ribs, chop or thinly slice them, and add before the greens to a sauté or braise. See Sesame Greens with Roasted Shiitakes, 118, for a raw chard preparation.

Kale, a cabbage relative, is one of the more inspiring underdog stories in the vegetable world. Once maligned or ignored, kale is now enjoyed raw in salads, 117, smoothies, 12, or as chips, 48, as well as in more traditional sautés, braises, soups, and gratins. The dark blue-green **lacinato** (also known as **cavolo nero, Tuscan,** or **"dinosaur" kale)** and frilly pink-stemmed **Russian** varieties are the easiest to love. The curly-leafed varieties are, in our opinion, not ideal for salads, but excellent otherwise. **Baby kale** is excellent in salads. Kale is available year-round, but it is most flavorful and abundant during the winter. Select deeply colored bunches with small leaves. Unless the leaves are very young, kale's fibrous midribs should be removed before cooking, see the illustration, 243.

Collard greens, another leafy cabbage relative, are beloved all over the South, where their huge, leathery leaves are sold in generous bunches and stewed with ham, yielding a silky mess of greens and rich "potlikker." Collards are the most resilient of greens and can withstand long simmering. They may be blanched until pliable and used to wrap fillings as for Stuffed Cabbage Rolls, 226. Collard stems and midribs are very tough, and we recommend removing them before cooking (see 243)—especially if you intend to cook them for only a short time.

Mustard greens are one of our favorite cooking greens. Their thin, tender leaves vary in color from bright green to purplish-black. As you might expect, most varieties have a hot and pungent "mustardy" flavor. If you wish, cook them in combination with other greens to tone down their spiciness. Many varieties are tender enough to eat raw in salads when young, like the stunning **purple Osaka** type. Others are good raw even when they are mature, such as **mizuna;** curly-leafed varieties are best cooked, especially in dishes like Palak Paneer, 245. Any variety, regardless of pungency, can be used raw to add a kick to green sauces; we love their bite when substituted for or combined with parsley in Chimichurri, 567, or Salsa Verde, 567.

Beet greens are mild in flavor and invariably sold attached to the beets themselves, 218. They must be used promptly, as they are delicate and wilt quickly. **Radish greens** are even more prone to wilting, so much so that we cannot recommend them except when they are impeccably fresh (even then, we usually find them unappealing). Some radishes, such as daikon, have more substantial greens. They are pleasantly peppery when cooked. Young **turnip greens** are tender enough to be added to salads; they become tougher and spicier as they age, making them perfect for long-simmering dishes like Southern-Style Greens, 243. Though the tops that may accompany a bunch of salad turnips are of fine flavor, most of the turnip greens we eat are harvested from varieties bred specifically for their leaves.

Sorrel leaves are very tart when raw and are used more often as an herb than a vegetable. Sliced into thin strips, their tender leaves are a bright-tasting garnish for salads and soups. Cooking mellows their flavor. Use a nonreactive pan and knife when preparing sorrel. Thinly slice leaves and add off the heat to garnish fish and poultry dishes, simmer briefly in cream and puree to create a simple sauce, or add to Creamed Spinach, 244, or Cream of Spinach Soup, 106.

Home gardeners often find themselves with sudden surpluses of **lettuce** and wish they had rabbits instead of children—failing to realize that a crisp nibble is not the only approach to this vegetable. If your lettuce crop has bolted and turned bitter in the summer sun, cook as for chicories, 233. If the leaves are not bitter, you may cream or wilt them like spinach, 118, cook them with green peas, 259, stuff them like cabbage, 226, or use to wrap fish fillets for steaming.

For other greens not normally seen in markets, such as **nettles, lamb's quarters,** and **wood sorrel,** see Cooking Wild Greens, 246.

Store greens, unwashed, in a plastic bag in the refrigerator crisper. Use thin-leafed greens within a few days, as they are prone to wilting. Others, like collards and kale, will last a bit longer. ➤ Wilted greens may be refreshed by soaking in ice water for 15 minutes. Before cooking, all greens need to be washed thoroughly to remove grit and dirt. Fill a salad spinner or large bowl with water (for larger quantities, fill the sink). Submerge the greens in the water and swish the leaves around, then lift the greens out of the water and place in a colander. Drain, refill, and repeat until the water is clear and free of grit.

Young greens can be cooked whole or sliced crosswise with the midribs left in if they seem tender. Mature greens can have tough stems. These stems may be fibrous, or they may simply need longer cooking than the greens.

To trim the stems and midribs from greens, fold the leaves in half and cut along the midrib to remove it along with the stem. ➤ For greens that have tough stems and midribs but fairly tender leaves (like kale), grasp the leaves at the stem end with one hand and grasp the stem with the other. In one quick motion, yank the stem and leaves in opposite directions. The leafy part should come away from the midrib in one piece. Discard the midribs or, if they are not woody or fibrous, slice them thinly, on the diagonal, and add them to the pan or pot first along with a little oil and cook until tender before adding the greens.

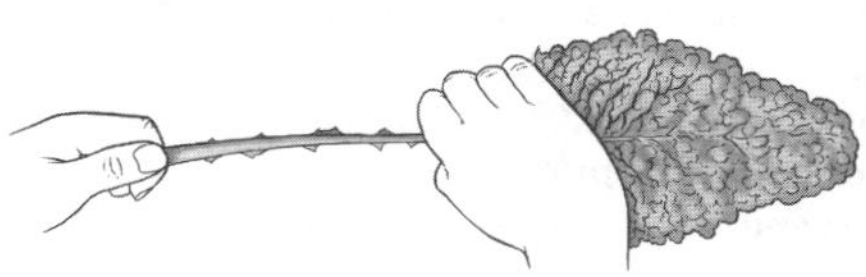

Deribbing kale

Mild greens like spinach, kale, and chard get along with lots of flavors. Though we customarily associate them with cured pork, cream, chiles, and citrus or vinegar, lightly dressing them in soy sauce and melted butter—or Brown Butter, 558—is a superb treatment.

To microwave, remove the stems and, if they are large and tough, the midribs from 1 pound greens. Place the leaves in a 3-quart microwave-safe baking dish with the water that clings to them from rinsing. Cover and microwave on high until tender, 5 to 10 minutes, stirring every 2 minutes. Let stand, covered, for 2 minutes.

SOUTHERN-STYLE GREENS

8 servings

A classic treatment for mature turnip and collard greens, though any green—tender or tough—is excellent cooked in a rich ham stock. In the South, some cooks like to add resilient greens with the cured pork and simmer for an hour or more. Here we recommend cooking the cured meat until tender first.

Combine in a large pot and bring to a boil:

6 cups water
5 ounces salt pork or bacon, diced, or 1 pound smoked ham hocks or pork neck bones
(1 small onion, chopped, or a few garlic cloves, smashed)

Reduce the heat slightly, partially cover, and simmer gently for 1 hour. Wash well:

3 pounds sturdy greens, especially collard and turnip greens, but also kale or mustard greens, or a combination

If necessary, remove the midribs, above, then tear or coarsely chop. Add to the pot along with, if desired:

(1 small dried red chile, seeds removed, or ½ teaspoon red pepper flakes)

Bring back to a boil, reduce the heat, partially cover, and simmer just until the greens are tender, 30 minutes to 1 hour, depending on the type, stirring occasionally. Transfer the greens to a bowl for serving; remove any ham hocks from the pot and shred the meat off the bone. Add the meat to the greens and ladle some of the pot liquor onto them. Serve with:

(Wanda's Stewed Cranberry Beans, 212)
(Southern Corn Bread, 630)
Vinegar or hot pepper sauce

WILTED TENDER GREENS

2 to 3 servings

The simplest treatment for young greens.

Wash thoroughly but do not dry:

12 cups tightly packed trimmed spinach, chard, baby kale, young mustard greens, or a combination (about 1 pound)

Coarsely chop, then place in a large skillet. Season with:

¼ teaspoon salt

Cook, stirring frequently, over medium heat until completely wilted but still bright green, about 5 minutes. Transfer to a serving dish and toss with:

Extra-virgin olive oil, melted butter, or Brown Butter, 558
Dash of lemon juice, vinegar, or hot sauce
Black pepper to taste

Or top with any of the following:

Garlic and Walnut Sauce, 570, or Hollandaise, 561
Sliced Hard-Boiled Egg, 151
Crumbled crisp bacon
Browned Bread Crumbs, 957

CREAMED SPINACH

4 servings

While we prefer the mature spinach sold in bunches for this recipe, baby spinach will work—as will kale, chard, or turnip greens.

Melt in a large skillet over medium heat:

2 tablespoons butter

Add and cook, stirring, until softened, about 5 minutes:

1 small onion, thinly sliced

Add and cook 1 minute more:

2 garlic cloves, minced

Stir in:

3 tablespoons all-purpose flour

Add to the skillet:

1 pound spinach (preferably mature), well washed, tough stems trimmed, coarsely chopped
½ cup heavy cream or half-and-half
½ teaspoon salt

Bring to a simmer, cover the skillet, and cook until the spinach is wilted. Uncover and continue to simmer, stirring, until the spinach is cooked and the liquid is thickened. If desired, serve topped with:

(Browned Bread Crumbs, 957)
(4 slices bacon, cooked until crisp and crumbled)
(2 Hard-Boiled Eggs, 151, chopped)

SPINACH WITH PINE NUTS AND RAISINS

4 servings

This dish is the perfect combination of sweet and savory, with a buttery, toasty flavor from the pine nuts.

Place in a heatproof bowl:

⅓ cup golden raisins

Bring to a boil in a small saucepan, stirring to dissolve the sugar:

⅓ cup white wine vinegar or cider vinegar
2 teaspoons sugar
1 teaspoon mustard seeds
½ teaspoon red pepper flakes

Pour the boiling vinegar mixture over the raisins, cover, and let plump while you finish the rest of the dish. Heat in a large skillet over medium heat:

2 tablespoons olive oil

Add and sauté until fragrant, about 1 minute:

2 garlic cloves, minced or grated

Add:

1 pound mature spinach, well washed and tough stems trimmed
¼ teaspoon salt

Sauté just until the spinach is wilted. Toss the spinach with as many of the raisins as desired and serve topped with:

2 tablespoons toasted, 1012, pine nuts or chopped toasted, 1005, almonds

BRAISED GREENS WITH GARLIC

4 to 6 servings

Wash well and separate the leaves from the stems and midribs of:

1½ pounds chard, spinach, kale, turnip greens, mustard greens, or beet greens

Cut the stems and midribs into ½-inch pieces. Coarsely chop the leaves. Rinse well, but do not dry.

Heat in a large skillet over medium-low heat:

2 tablespoons olive or vegetable oil

Add and cook until the oil is fragrant and the garlic is just beginning to color:

2 garlic cloves, thinly sliced
(1-inch piece ginger, peeled and thinly sliced, or 2 anchovy fillets, chopped)
(1 small dried red chile, crumbled, or ¼ to ½ teaspoon red pepper flakes, to taste)

Add the stem and rib pieces and cook, stirring occasionally, until nearly tender, about 2 minutes. Add the leaves and cook, partially covered, until both the leaves and stems are tender, 3 to 5 minutes more. Season to taste with:

Lemon juice or red wine vinegar
Salt

Or, if not using anchovies, dot with:

Soy sauce, Nuoc Cham, 571, or Nam Prik, 571

GUMBO Z'HERBES

6 servings

Gumbo z'herbes is often made during Lent, which happens to be a very good time of year to find a variety of greens. Authentic versions of this dish often contain upwards of ten different kinds of greens, but use what you have. For a slightly thicker, more deeply flavored stew, add **3 tablespoons all-purpose flour** to the oil and cook, stirring, until the roux is blondish-brown, 542. Add the onions, peppers, and celery, and proceed as directed.

Heat in a Dutch oven or soup pot over medium heat:

3 tablespoons vegetable oil

Add and cook, stirring, until softened, about 10 minutes:

1 large onion, chopped
1 green bell pepper, chopped
1 celery rib, chopped

Add and cook, stirring, for 2 minutes:

4 garlic cloves, minced
1 tablespoon minced fresh thyme or 1 teaspoon dried thyme
½ teaspoon salt
¼ teaspoon black pepper
¼ to ½ teaspoon cayenne pepper, to taste

Add and bring to a simmer over high heat:

4 cups chicken or vegetable stock or broth
(1 smoked ham hock)
1 bay leaf

Add a big handful at a time:

2 pounds mixed greens, such as collards, turnip greens, mustard greens, or kale, well washed and coarsely chopped

Wilt each handful into the simmering stock before adding the next. Reduce the heat, cover, and simmer slowly until very tender, about 1 hour. Season to taste with:

Salt and black pepper
Lemon juice

Remove the ham hock, if using, scrape off any meat with a fork, and stir the meat back into the soup. Discard the bay leaf. Serve over:

Cooked white rice, 343

with:

Hot pepper sauce
Filé powder, 543
Chopped green onions

SPINACH PAKORAS

4 servings

These fragrant fritters are hard to stop eating. Feel free to use almost any green in place of the spinach (we are especially fond of kale). Please read about Deep-Frying, 1051.

In a medium bowl, stir together:

1 cup chickpea flour
½ cup water
1 tablespoon Garam Masala, 558, or curry powder
½ teaspoon salt
(¼ teaspoon asafoetida, 954)

Fold in until coated in the batter:

2 cups packed spinach (about 4 ounces), well washed and coarsely chopped
½ cup finely chopped red onion
1 serrano pepper, seeded and minced

Heat to 350°F in a Dutch oven or heavy pot:

1½ inches vegetable oil

Preheat the oven to 200°F. Line a baking sheet with paper towels. Carefully drop spoonfuls (roughly 2 tablespoons each) of the mixture into the hot oil and fry until deep golden brown, 2 to 5 minutes. Be careful not to crowd the pot as it will cause the temperature of the oil to drop. Transfer the pakoras with a spider or slotted spoon to the paper towels to drain, and keep warm in the oven. Repeat with the remaining pakoras. Serve hot with one or more of the following:

Cilantro-Mint Chutney, 568, Tamarind Chutney, 566, or Raita, 569

SAUTÉED SHREDDED COLLARD GREENS

4 servings

This preparation treats tough collard greens with a light hand rather than the usual long simmering. Since they are sliced thinly, the greens take on a wonderful texture in the short cooking time. In Brazil, this is a traditional accompaniment to Feijoada, 214.

Have ready:

1 pound collard greens, well washed, tough stems and midribs removed

Stack the leaves, roll them into a tight cylinder, and shred as thinly as possible. Heat in a large skillet over medium heat:

1 tablespoon olive oil

Add and cook until fragrant, about 30 seconds:

2 garlic cloves, minced

Add the collards and cook very briefly, until tender but still bright green, about 2 minutes. Season to taste with:

Salt

PALAK PANEER (CURRIED SPINACH WITH FRESH CHEESE)

4 servings

Though this Indian classic is often made with spinach, the best renditions we have eaten use mustard greens instead, or in combination with spinach, kale, or turnip greens. Usually, the greens are pureed after they are cooked, but we prefer the rustic texture of chopped greens (and there are fewer items to clean). For a long-simmered curry, see Lamb Saag, 484. If desired, substitute 6 ounces store-bought paneer for homemade.

Bring to a boil in a medium heavy saucepan:

4 cups whole milk

Remove the pan from the heat and add:

3 tablespoons lemon juice

Stir until the milk curdles and separates into bits of solid curd floating in the liquid whey. Let stand for 5 minutes. Line a fine-mesh sieve with a double layer of cheesecloth and set over a bowl. Ladle the curds and whey into the sieve and let stand until cool enough to handle. Pull the edges of the cheesecloth together over the curd and squeeze out as much liquid as possible. Flatten the curd, still in the cheesecloth, to a thickness of ½ to 1 inch. Set it on a plate and top with another plate. Weight with a can and let stand for 20 minutes, then cut the paneer into ½-inch cubes.

Coarsely chop:

1½ pounds mature spinach, well washed and tough stems trimmed

Heat in a large nonstick skillet over medium-high heat:

¼ cup vegetable oil or Ghee, 960

Add the paneer cubes and cook, shaking the skillet every now and then to turn the cubes, until golden brown, 3 to 4 minutes. Transfer the paneer to a plate. Add to the oil remaining in the skillet:

1 teaspoon cumin seeds
1 teaspoon coriander seeds, crushed
½ teaspoon mustard seeds
3 dried red chiles (preferably Kashmiri chiles) or ½ teaspoon red pepper flakes

Cook, stirring, until the mustard seeds start to pop, about 1 minute. Add and cook until softened, about 5 minutes:

1 medium onion, thinly sliced
½ teaspoon salt

Add and cook 1 minute more:

4 garlic cloves, thinly sliced

Add as much spinach as will comfortably fit into the skillet, cover, and cook until wilted enough to add more spinach. Add a few more handfuls and repeat until all the spinach is wilted. Cook, uncovered, until all the water is evaporated. Fold in the paneer and serve immediately.

ABOUT WILD GREENS, SHOOTS, AND ROOTS

If you wish to forage for edible wild foods, ➤ try to find a local expert. Guided forays and workshops are the best way to learn what is safe to eat and ecologically responsible to harvest, when it is in season, and where you are likely to find it. If such a person or group is not available, the best advice comes from a reliable field guide to edible plants that focuses on your particular geographical region. Please see the bibliography for our recommendations, 1077.

➤ Do not eat any wild food unless you are 100 percent certain of its identity and that it is safe to eat. Bear in mind that plants look quite different at different stages of maturity (another reason why learning from experts in the field is ideal). All plants have seasons when they are succulent and periods when they are inedible or unpalatable, and they all need careful washing to remove grit. Finally, remember that not all parts of edible wild plants are safe to eat. Do plenty of research before eating any wild food. When you research, make note of rare or endangered wild edibles that should not be harvested simply because they are scarce. Further, never harvest wild foods with abandon (with the exception of invasive types). Leave more than you take so plant colonies may regenerate themselves.

Finally, we must mention that even when you know with certainty what you are harvesting, there are some attendant risks. Some wild edibles—like garlic mustard and pigweed—are invasive species, and frequently sprayed with herbicides. There is also the potential for exposure to herbicides by consuming native species that happen to be next to weeds. To mitigate this risk, ➤ only forage in areas where you know herbicides have not been used. Do not forage along roadsides; seek out locales far away from refuse, polluted areas, and manufacturing activity.

COOKING WILD GREENS

After these caveats and precautions, some words of encouragement: Foraging is fun and can yield unique flavors. Young, spring greens are best in salads, 115. When greens like **chickweed, pigweed (an amaranth), broad-leaved** and **curly dock, lamb's quarters,** tiny **plantains, evening primrose, bladder campion, purslane, dandelion greens, Japanese knotweed, wild chicories, wild mustards, peppergrass, upland cress** (known in some parts of the country as "creasy greens"), and **miner's lettuce** are past their salad stage and grow tougher, simply cook them as for other greens, 242. Before cooking any of these, sample them to see how bitter they are. If they are overly bitter, parboil them for a few minutes, discard the water, and continue with the recipe. Even after blanching and cooking, some greens may remain slightly bitter, which you can hedge against by cooking them with cultivated greens like spinach or kale. **Nettles,** regardless of age, must be cooked to get rid of their prickly defenses. They should be gathered with impervious gloves and handled in the kitchen with tongs before they are cooked.

Along coastlines, look for salty **sea beans** or **samphire,** which is a briny addition to potato salad and may be quick-pickled, 929, for an unusual but tasty garnish (do not add salt to the pickle brine as sea beans are salty enough on their own). **American searocket** is a fleshy coastal plant with peppery, arugula-like leaves. They are edible raw, but taste best when blanched for an instant and then dunked in ice water. (Their spicy buds may be quick-pickled as well, 929, and used in place of capers.) Among water plants, the young leaves of **pickerelweed** are the quickest to prepare. Treat them as you would any cooking green or chop the raw leaves and add to a salad of mixed greens. Older leaves must be parboiled. While **pokeweed** is a traditional spring purgative in some Southern kitchens, the entire plant is known to be toxic. The stems and leaves are only made palatable after several blanchings in fresh water. We advise against eating them, as the effort to make them edible far outweighs the resulting flavor and texture. Again, before foraging, consult a local expert on wild foods or a reliable field guide to wild edible plants.

COOKING WILD SHOOTS

There are certain wild shoots that bring rave reviews—**wild asparagus** comes first to mind. Also delicious (and abundant!) are the shoots of **cattails, fireweed, milkweed, knotweed, burdock,** and **common greenbrier.** All shoots are best when picked young, and well before the plant flowers. All may be cooked until tender as for asparagus, 208. Burdock shoots should be peeled prior to cooking.

COOKING WILD ROOTS

Gathering certain wild roots is for the hearty forager, or for those who like to feel the squish of mud between their toes. **Bulrushes** and **cattails** can be dug year-round. Trim away the hairy rootlets from the large rhizome and peel it. Parboil at least 10 minutes to remove some of the starch, then boil in fresh water or roast until tender. Or leave the skin on the roots and roast in coals until tender. **Arrowhead** tubers, or **wapato,** dug in the fall, are best fried or roasted as for potatoes, 264, or simmered in a stew. The long, spongy roots of the yellow **spatterdock** water lily may be boiled and eaten, but some roots may prove to be very bitter. However, as a consolation prize, spatterdock seeds can be collected and fried like popcorn.

Among land-based roots, **sunchokes,** also found in cultivated forms, 277, are favorites. Nutty, potato-like **apios** roots (also called **American groundnut** or **potato bean**), **burdock** roots, and—after their runners are removed—the small tubers of the **day lily** may be cooked as for sunchokes or potatoes. To prepare the buds and flowers, see 998.

ABOUT JICAMA

The uninspiring appearance of jicama—like a rough, brown-skinned turnip—belies its sweet, crisply juicy white flesh. It is a favorite for crudités, 45, or salad, 127, as well as a fine substitute for water chestnuts in dumpling fillings and stir-fries. Shreds or matchsticks of jicama are also good in Summer Rolls, 71, or quick-pickled, 929. For a quick snack, sprinkle jicama sticks with lime juice, salt, and chile powder—or cut the jicama into matchsticks and toss for a slaw-like taco topping.

Select small to medium tubers that are uniformly hard and heavy for their size, with no sign of shriveling or drying. Store at room temperature, unpeeled. Scrub well, then use a sharp paring knife to peel. Remove the thin, fibrous layer beneath the skin. Cut into slices, wedges, cubes, batons, or matchsticks.

ABOUT KOHLRABI

Kohlrabi—which means "cabbage turnip" in German—is aptly named: Its bulbous lower stem is crisp and turnip-like, but with a milder flavor. Kohlrabi greens may be cooked as for other sturdy greens, 242. Trim the tops well; the stems and midribs are usually too fibrous to eat. Store the bulbs unpeeled in a closed bag in the refrigerator crisper. Unless very small, peel the tough skin with a paring knife or vegetable peeler.

We try to stick with smaller (2- to 3-inch-diameter) kohlrabi for most raw preparations, but large ones can be surprisingly tender, and are especially good for making slaw, 119.

Kohlrabi can be substituted in any recipe for nonstarchy root vegetables; cook as for Braised Turnips with Leeks and Bacon, 283, quarter and roast as for carrots, 228, or cut into matchsticks for Spicy Chinese-Style Slaw, 119. Shredded kohlrabi makes an admirable substitute for green papaya in Green Papaya Salad, 129. Thinly sliced kohlrabi can be layered with potatoes in Potatoes au Gratin, 266. Or boil or steam whole kohlrabi until tender then stuff as for Louisiana-Style Chayote, 275.

Kohlrabi is mild and takes to a wide variety of flavorings. It pairs well with tart, citrusy dressings, most green herbs, mustard, chili powder, cumin, garlic, and red pepper flakes.

ABOUT LEEKS

Leeks are the mildest, sweetest members of the onion family. Like other onion types, leeks are often used as seasoning, but they can certainly stand alone. Leeks resemble gigantic green onions and are usually 1 to 2 inches thick, although younger, thinner ones can sometimes be found at farmers' markets. The green tops of leeks are tough and fibrous. The lower white portion is fibrous as well, and must be cut across the grain for sautéing, pureed in soups, or braised or simmered until meltingly tender.

Select leeks with bright green tops that are not dry. Since only the white and pale-green portions are used, choose leeks that have a higher proportion of those shades. Store in an open plastic bag in the refrigerator crisper. ➤ Leeks must be carefully washed to free grit from their tightly layered leaves.

To wash leeks, cut off the dark green tops (see below for some uses for leek tops) and trim off the roots, leaving the root pad attached. Starting at the leaf end, split the leek lengthwise in half. Hold each leek half under running water and spread apart the layers with your fingers, until all the grit is washed away. (Most dirt will be at the top of the light green portion of the leek, or where it emerged from the soil.)

Classic preparations like Leeks Vinaigrette, 248, call for cooking small leeks whole, but ➤ we recommend slicing larger leeks (over 1 inch thick) across the grain, as their fibers can be quite resilient, even after prolonged cooking. When serving leeks that are cooked whole or halved lengthwise, set the table with small, sharp knives and instruct diners to cut them across the grain for easier eating.

Leek tops are usually discarded, but we prefer to rinse them and reserve for the stock bag, 73. Or dry them in a dehydrator, 944, until brittle and grind into a mild seasoning powder. As with hard-neck varieties of garlic, **leek scapes** are routinely trimmed from the plant and can occasionally be found at farmers' markets. Slice across the grain and use in place of onions in any recipe.

Leeks are compatible with many foods, but especially so with lemon, butter, cheese, cream, mushrooms, potatoes, garlic, ham, bacon, thyme, parsley, and chives. See Leek Tart, 163, Potato Leek Soup, 104, and Cock-a-Leekie, 94, for some classic combinations.

BRAISED LEEKS

4 servings

Bring to a simmer in a large skillet or Dutch oven over medium-high heat:

¾ cup chicken stock or broth
2 tablespoons butter
(¼ teaspoon salt, if using unsalted stock)
¼ teaspoon black pepper

Add to the skillet, cut side down:

4 large leeks, trimmed, halved lengthwise, and well cleaned

Reserve the leek greens for stock or discard. Reduce the heat to medium-low, cover, and simmer until very tender when pierced with a knife, about 15 minutes. Uncover, increase the heat to medium, and cook the leeks until golden brown and the liquid is almost gone, about 5 minutes. Meanwhile, melt in a small skillet over medium heat:

1 tablespoon butter

Add and cook, stirring frequently, until golden brown:

½ cup coarse dry bread crumbs or panko

Transfer the leeks to a serving plate, cut side up, and top with the bread crumbs along with:

(Chopped toasted, 1005, hazelnuts)
A sprinkle of lemon juice

MELTED LEEKS

4 servings

A delectable side dish that also makes a fine topping for pizza or crostini, or use as you would Caramelized Onions, 255.

Melt in a large skillet over medium-low heat:

2½ tablespoons butter

Add and cook until starting to soften, 4 to 5 minutes:

3 large leeks, trimmed, halved lengthwise, well cleaned, and thinly sliced

Add:

1 cup chicken or vegetable stock or broth or 1 cup water
¼ teaspoon salt
1 sprig fresh thyme or ¼ teaspoon dried thyme

Cover and simmer until the leeks are tender, about 5 minutes. Uncover, increase the heat to medium-high, and add:

¼ cup dry white wine

Boil until the liquid is reduced by half, 10 to 15 minutes. Stir in:

2 tablespoons heavy cream
(½ teaspoon curry powder or a pinch of grated or ground nutmeg)

Cook until the cream is absorbed. Discard the thyme sprig, if using, and season to taste with:

Salt and black pepper

If desired, garnish with:

(Minced chives or chopped parsley)

LEEKS VINAIGRETTE

4 servings

If possible, use thin leeks for this classic French first course. The cooking liquid is turned into a mustard vinaigrette.

Trim and clean:

16 baby leeks (about ¾ inch thick), or 4 large leeks, trimmed, quartered lengthwise, and well cleaned

Heat in a large skillet over medium-high heat until hot but not smoking:

¼ cup olive oil

Add the leeks in batches and cook, turning, until golden brown, about 10 minutes. Return all the leeks to the skillet and add:

1 cup chicken stock or broth
¼ cup dry white wine

Cover and cook, turning occasionally, until the leeks are tender, about 8 minutes. Transfer to a serving platter. Add to the skillet:

¼ cup chicken stock or broth
2 teaspoons red wine vinegar, or to taste

Cook, stirring, for 3 minutes. Remove from the heat and stir in:

2 teaspoons minced parsley
1 teaspoon Dijon mustard
Salt and black pepper to taste

Pour the vinaigrette over the leeks and let cool. Serve at room temperature, garnished with:

Minced chives
(1 Hard-Boiled Egg, 151, pressed through a medium-mesh sieve)

LEEK GRATIN

4 servings

Preheat the oven to 375°F. Butter a 13 × 9-inch baking dish.

Have ready:

4 medium to large leeks, trimmed, halved lengthwise, and well cleaned

After washing, shake off as much water as possible and place cut side down in the baking dish. Sprinkle with:

½ teaspoon salt
¼ teaspoon black pepper

Pour over the leeks:

1 cup heavy cream

Cover the dish with foil and bake until the leeks are tender, about 30 minutes. Remove the foil and sprinkle with:

¼ cup finely grated Parmesan

Return to the oven and bake until browned, about 15 minutes more.

GRILLED LEEKS WITH ROMESCO SAUCE

4 servings

This is a Spanish dish traditionally made with **calçots,** 254, a type of green onion. Because calçots are hard to find in the United States, you may use large green onions, small leeks, or halved and blanched large leeks. In Spain, grilled calçots are served with roasted lamb, sausages, beans, and plenty of red wine.

Have ready:

12 baby leeks or calçots; 4 large leeks, trimmed, halved lengthwise, and well cleaned; or 4 bunches large green onions

If using halved leeks, trim the roots but leave the root pad intact and blanch, 1047, for 5 minutes. Prepare a hot grill fire, 1063. Lightly brush the leeks or green onions with:

Olive oil

Grill until charred on all sides, moving the leeks to a cooler part of the grill if necessary to finish cooking. Wrap in newspaper or a paper bag and let steam for 5 minutes. Serve with:

Romesco Sauce, 570

To eat, peel off and discard the charred outer layer and dip the leeks in the sauce.

GLAMORGAN SAUSAGES (VEGETARIAN LEEK AND CHEESE "SAUSAGES")

4 servings

This Welsh specialty is bound with egg and bread crumbs and formed into sausage-shaped cakes. They will fool no one, but they are quite tasty when dressed with mustard and flanked by an ale.

Melt in a large skillet over medium heat:

1 tablespoon butter

Add and cook, stirring occasionally, until softened, about 4 minutes:

1 large leek, trimmed, halved lengthwise, well cleaned, and thinly sliced

Meanwhile, combine in a medium bowl:

1½ cups grated Caerphilly or white Cheddar (6 ounces)
¾ cup fresh bread crumbs, 957
2 large eggs, beaten
1 tablespoon fresh thyme leaves or 1 teaspoon dried thyme
1 teaspoon dry mustard
½ teaspoon salt
¼ teaspoon black pepper

Add the leeks and stir the mixture until combined. Shape into 8 oblong sausage shapes about 1 inch thick and refrigerate for 30 minutes. Whisk well in a small bowl:

2 large eggs

Have ready on a shallow plate:

½ cup dry bread crumbs

Wipe out the skillet used for cooking the leeks and heat over medium heat:

3 tablespoons vegetable oil

When the oil is hot, roll the "sausages" in the egg, then in the bread crumbs, and place in the skillet. Cook for about 10 minutes, turning them frequently until golden brown all over. Serve with:

Whole-grain mustard

ABOUT LOTUS ROOT

The roots of the tropical lotus plant are plump, oblong, and jointed. They grow connected end-to-end, like sausage links, and their mild, crisp flesh is perforated with holes. Like water chestnuts, lotus root remains firm even after cooking.

Find fresh lotus roots in Asian markets year-round. Select firm, buff-colored pieces without soft spots, blemishes, or bruises. Size has no effect on texture or flavor. Store the roots in a cool, dark place, as you would potatoes. To prepare, cut apart at the joints, trim off the knobby connecting sections, peel, and thinly slice. The flesh darkens rapidly once cut, so have a bowl of acidulated water, 951, ready to drop the slices into.

Sliced lotus root may be added to stir-fries or deep-fried as for Potato or Root Vegetable Chips, 48. In China, they are sometimes cut open at one end, stuffed with sweet rice, and simmered or steamed whole until tender. Their resilient crispiness also makes them a welcome addition to soups, curries, braises, and quick pickles, 929.

ABOUT MUSHROOMS

Mushrooms have a special place in the produce department of our hearts, as they are meaty and add a satisfying savoriness to anything they are paired with. Many of the mushroom types listed below that are generally thought of as "wild" are also cultivated, with the notable exception of porcinis, chanterelles, and matsutakes. If you plan to forage for mushrooms, ➤ read Foraging for Wild Mushrooms, 250, and always consult an authority to properly identify the fungi you collect. For information on **truffles,** see 1028.

Common mushrooms, sometimes referred to as **button mushrooms,** are the most widely available in supermarkets. They may be **white** and brown (or **cremini**) and have mild flesh. If they are very small, use them whole. Brown **portobello mushrooms** are the same type, just grown larger (which is why small brown button mushrooms are occasionally marketed as **baby bellas**). These giants can be 6 inches wide and have a meaty, robust flavor. Their large, flat, and sturdy caps make them naturals for grilling and broiling (and their large, open gills readily soak up marinades, pastes, and seasoning). ➤ To stretch the flavor of more costly mushrooms like porcinis or morels, buy a few of them and combine with these mild-tasting mushrooms.

Beech, shimeji, or **clamshell mushrooms** are a small, cultivated species sold in white and brown varieties. They have button-like caps, slender stems, and grow in small clumps. Though sometimes bitter if raw or undercooked, they are mild and have a pleasant texture.

Cauliflower mushrooms are white or pale yellow and grow in irregular clumps. This is where the similarities between the mushroom and its namesake end. Cauliflower mushrooms are made up of a tightly packed tangle of wavy, lasagna noodle–like lobes. The crevices between these lobes are hard to clean. We recommend cutting these mushrooms into chunks and swishing them in cool water to dislodge dirt and pine needles. Cauliflower mushrooms may be roasted, broken into pieces and sautéed until golden, or added to soup.

Chanterelles, or **girolles,** resemble a curving trumpet. They are occasionally available in grocery stores and are a popular species to forage. Their golden or orange-brown caps and slender stems can have a delicate, apricot-like aroma or be mildly earthy. They have an affinity with cream, whether over toast, pasta, or polenta. The similarly shaped black mushrooms variously called **black trumpets, horns of plenty,** or **trumpets of death** are closely related and similar in taste but have thinner flesh. **Yellowfoot** chanterelles are a bit smaller, and **hedgehog mushrooms,** another chanterelle relative, are an excellent mushroom for beginner foragers, as they are easy to identify thanks to the spiny "teeth" under their caps.

Chicken of the woods are yellowish-orange shelf mushrooms that grow on tree trunks and logs. Unlike most other varieties, they actually taste somewhat of their namesake and have a meaty texture when young. Thinner parts of the mushroom may be sautéed or grilled, but thicker, tougher portions should be braised until tender.

Enoki mushrooms grow in dense clumps and are very slender, like bean sprouts with tiny caps. They are a pretty salad ingredient, adding a faint sweetness, but we prefer them heated through in Dashi, 78, or added to ramen, 304, or Miso Soup, 84. Trim off the spongy base and separate the strands.

Lion's mane mushrooms, also known as **bear's head** or **white pompom,** remind us of *Star Trek*'s "tribbles"—if only they were plentiful enough to be troublesome! Incredibly, these furry-looking mushrooms can grow to be fifty pounds or more. Their tightly packed clumps of thin, delicate spines have a unique texture. Larger specimens can have a tough, chewy stem that needs to be braised for a long time to become tender (we do not bother with them). Though rare to find in stores, lion's manes are cultivated. If you find them, snatch them up promptly, cut into bite-sized pieces, gently fry in butter until browned, and serve sprinkled with lemon juice.

Lobster mushrooms are notable for two reasons: their bright, reddish-orange "cooked lobster shell" color and the fact that they are composed of two organisms—a mushroom and a parasitic fungus. They can grow quite large and have firm flesh. Some think they taste of lobster, others think they are bland. We enjoy them in risottos, 335, and sautés.

Maitake or **hen-of-the-woods mushrooms** are widely cultivated and increasingly common in specialty and Asian markets. Some maitakes have a feathery appearance, with thin, overlapping caps, while others have thicker, sturdier, fan-shaped caps. All maitakes crisp up nicely when roasted at high heat. Or select beautiful clumps of maitakes, poach them whole in flavorful broth, and serve in bowls. The crevices in feathery maitakes hold on to sauces and marinades well, though they hardly need either with their rich, meaty flavor. These are a favorite in our kitchen.

Matsutake mushrooms are highly prized, especially in Japan. Though their caps can become very large, the round immature mushrooms are the most sought after (they require no cleaning). Matsutakes are especially aromatic, with notes of pine and cinnamon. Firm and occasionally chewy, they are often thinly sliced and cooked with rice—which becomes perfumed with their delicate flavor.

Morels are available in specialty grocery stores and by foraging. They have conical, honeycomb-like caps, and range in color from the common brown hue to golden and black. The caps are hollow on the inside, making larger specimens good for stuffing. The honeycombed surface allows morels to soak up sauces. Unfortunately, these nooks and crannies make morels especially prone to collecting dirt and debris. If they are in good shape and sturdy, we spray them inside and out with a can of compressed air (fragile morels may start to disintegrate). You may rinse especially dirty morels in a bowl of water, patting them dry thoroughly before using.

Nameko mushrooms are a cultivated Japanese variety that grow in dense clumps, like shimejis. The most common types have a mucilaginous coating on their caps, and are often served in Miso Soup, 84. The closely related **cinnamon cap**—often sold as nameko—has dry, button-mushroom-like caps and long, tasty stems. These are a favorite of ours, especially sautéed or roasted.

Oyster mushrooms grow in clusters of ear- or oyster-shaped caps and are widely cultivated (they are also found wild). Their flesh is cream-colored to grayish brown on the outside with a smooth, dense texture. You may also find pink or yellow varieties of oyster mushrooms, which are considerably thinner and more delicate. **King oysters** (also known as **king trumpets**) are quite large, with thick, long stems. The stems may be cut into slabs (or thick coins) and seared as for steak or scallops.

Porcini, also called **cèpes** or **boletes,** are considered by many to be the tastiest of all mushrooms. They look something like large common mushrooms with very thick, pale stems and reddish-brown caps. Unlike common mushrooms, they have sponge-like pores underneath their caps rather than gills. Use promptly after purchase or harvest. If possible, cut them open and inspect them before purchase for worms—fresh porcinis are often sold cut in half for this very reason. The worms are harmless, and if you do find some just cut them out—or keep the extra protein a kitchen secret. Porcinis are classic in soups and risottos, and are added to cream sauces, ragus, and simple sautés destined to be tossed with pasta. They may also be sliced, floured, and pan-fried as for baby artichokes, 207. Brush large ones with olive oil and lemon juice and broil or grill as you would meat. If you find an abundance of them, slice and dry them in a dehydrator, 944.

Shiitakes are brown and umbrella shaped with slender, fibrous stems. Used extensively in Chinese and Japanese cuisine, they are cultivated on logs and have a distinctive, earthy taste. We appreciate their firm texture and full flavor in stir-fries and soups. Younger, **baby shiitakes** are a special treat and are best used whole, stem and all. Trim off the chewy stems of large or medium-sized shiitakes and add to a stock bag, 73.

Wood ear or **cloud ear mushrooms** are one of the few types of jelly fungus we eat. Unlike other fresh mushrooms, these should look damp. They are dark brown to black on their top side, very thin, and crunchy when raw. Though rare to find fresh, dried wood ears are a common staple found in many Asian and specialty markets. They give Chinese dishes like Hot-and-Sour Soup, 85, a boost of umami.

In general, choose mushrooms that are heavy for their size, with dry, firm caps and stems—nothing damp or shriveled, no dark or soft spots. They should smell earthy, not ammoniated. Keep unwashed mushrooms in a loosely closed paper bag or wrap loosely in paper towels. Leave packaged mushrooms unopened. Store on a refrigerator shelf; do not place them in the crisper, or in a container that will collect condensation (moisture hastens spoilage).

Wipe mushrooms with a soft-bristled brush or damp cloth to clean. Though we hardly ever find this necessary, you may rinse mushrooms or briefly immerse especially dirty ones in cool water, agitate them, and repeat until the water is clear. Dry them thoroughly and cook promptly. If only caps are called for in a recipe, cut the stems off flush with the cap, but do not discard the flavorful stems. Chop them finely and add to the dish with the caps, save for stock (see Keeping a Stock Bag, 73) or use in Duxelles, 252. Mature shiitake stems are too tough for most everything except stock.

To extend the life of mushrooms for a short time, make Mushroom Confit, 252. Mushrooms can be stored for extended periods if pickled, 927, dried, or frozen. For information on freezing mushrooms, see 886. Add frozen mushrooms to simmering sauces, braises, and soups, or simply reheat in a covered skillet with a bit of water or stock. **Dried mushrooms** add intense mushroom flavor to sauces, soups, stews, and gravies. They may be ground up in a blender or spice grinder or reconstituted. For more information on using them, see 1003. For instructions on drying mushrooms, see 944.

Mushrooms shine on their own or as the focal point of a dish, especially the more distinctive "wild" types. We like enriching them with cream or seasoning them with lemon or a fruity vinegar, garlic, shallots, onions, grated hard cheese, tarragon, or thyme. Mushrooms are an indispensable ingredient in dishes that need a savory boost, especially those that do not contain meat. Most mushrooms are quite juicy and are best when cooked until they release their liquid and start browning. Juices released in the pan will deepen in flavor as they reduce, and any left will be reabsorbed by the mushrooms along with any other liquids added to the pan. We are especially fond of simmering "sweated" mushrooms with garlic and sherry or wine until they are plump again and the liquid in the pan is well reduced (see Champignones al Ajillo, 251). Thin or dense mushrooms like shiitakes and maitakes do not release as much liquid, making them well suited to quicker cooking methods like stir-frying, 202. Button mushroom caps and thin varieties like maitakes, cinnamon caps, and chanterelles can be battered and deep-fried, 203. We recommend using tempura batter to allow their character to shine through as much as possible. For other recipes featuring mushrooms, see Roasted Mushroom Burgers, 145, Roasted Mushroom Lasagne, 310, Broiled Stuffed Mushrooms Cockaigne, 58, and Hungarian Mushroom Soup, 88.

FORAGING FOR WILD MUSHROOMS

If you plan to forage for wild mushrooms, ➤ be aware that some poisonous mushroom types, during various stages of development, resemble edible forms. Members of the widely distributed and often innocent-looking *Amanita* genus of fungi include varieties so deadly that they are frequently assumed to have provided the murderous potions so useful to the princely houses of the early Renaissance. Although many mushrooms are poisonous, few are deadly; and many more simply don't taste very good. In sober truth, though, ➤ there is no simple way to identify most mushrooms and other related fungi. Even the experts often prefer to examine up to ten specimens of a single variety before announcing a verdict.

With a few exceptions (including truffles, 1028), wild mushrooms should not be eaten raw. ➤ Eat only those mushrooms you can identify with 100 percent certainty. The novice should remember that there are bold mushroom hunters and old mushroom hunters, but no bold, old mushroom hunters. Begin collecting with an experienced forager and consult a good field guide for your region, 1077.

SAUTÉED MUSHROOMS

4 servings

Quarter or thinly slice to uniform thickness:

1 pound mushrooms

Heat a very large skillet over medium-high until hot. Add:

3 tablespoons butter or vegetable oil

Add the mushrooms and shake the skillet to coat the mushrooms. If desired, add:

(1 garlic clove, thinly sliced)

Cook over medium-high heat, shaking the skillet frequently. At first the mushrooms will seem dry and will absorb the fat. Continue to shake the skillet until the mushrooms begin to color and release their juice, 3 to 4 minutes. Season to taste with:

Salt and black pepper

Use as a garnish for cooked meats, pasta, and grains, or simply serve on:

Toast rounds

CREAMED MUSHROOMS

4 servings

A very rich side dish or sauce, or an opulent first course when spooned over toast.

Heat in a large skillet over medium heat:

4 tablespoons butter or olive oil

Add and cook, stirring, until translucent, about 5 minutes:

½ medium onion, finely diced

Add:

1 pound mushrooms, thinly sliced

Increase the heat to medium-high and cook, stirring often, until the mushrooms release and then reabsorb their juices, about 5 minutes. Add:

1 cup heavy cream or crème fraîche
2 garlic cloves, minced
1½ teaspoons fresh thyme leaves or ½ teaspoon dried thyme
Salt and black pepper to taste

Reduce the heat to medium and simmer until the sauce is slightly thickened. Taste and adjust the seasonings, then stir in:

1 tablespoon chopped parsley

CHAMPIGNONES AL AJILLO (GARLICKY SPANISH-STYLE MUSHROOMS)

4 servings

This classic Spanish tapa, 46, is one of the tastiest mushroom preparations we know. Relish the pan juices by soaking them up with crusty bread.

Have ready:

1 pound mushrooms

Leave smaller mushrooms whole or slice larger ones in half or quarters if needed (they should be the size of a small, comfortable bite). Heat over medium-high heat in a large skillet until shimmering:

¼ cup olive oil

Add to the pan:

3 to 6 garlic cloves, to taste, coarsely chopped or sliced
(Pinch of red pepper flakes)

Cook until golden, about 30 seconds. Add the mushrooms and quickly toss with the garlic to keep it from burning. Cook, stirring occasionally, until the mushrooms exude juice, about 5 minutes. Add:

¼ cup dry sherry or dry white wine

Simmer until the liquid is reduced by half. Remove from the heat and stir into the mushrooms:

¼ cup chopped flat-leaf parsley
½ teaspoon salt
½ teaspoon black pepper

Transfer the mushrooms to shallow bowls, distributing any pan juices equally. If desired, into each bowl add a few drops of:

(Sherry vinegar or white wine vinegar)

or serve with:

(Lemon wedges)

Lightly sprinkle the mushrooms with:

Sweet paprika, preferably smoked

Serve with:

Fresh crusty bread, warmed or toasted

MUSHROOM RAGOUT

4 servings

Serve over pasta, polenta, rice, garlic-rubbed croutons, or in popovers. For more intense flavor, soak ½ ounce dried mushrooms, such as porcini, then chop and add with the fresh mushrooms; use the strained soaking water for part of the liquid.

Heat in a large saucepan over medium-high heat:

2 tablespoons olive oil or butter

Add and cook, stirring, until golden, about 8 minutes:

1 onion, finely chopped

Stir in:

1 pound mushrooms, thickly sliced

Cook until they begin to release their liquid, about 5 minutes. Add:

2 garlic cloves, finely chopped
1 tablespoon tomato paste
1 to 2 teaspoons chopped rosemary, thyme, oregano, marjoram, or a combination, to taste
Salt and black pepper to taste

Cook, stirring, until the mixture begins to brown, another 5 minutes. Add:

1½ cups chicken or vegetable stock

Bring to a boil, reduce the heat to medium-low, and simmer for 10 minutes. Gradually stir in:

2 tablespoons cold butter, cut into pieces

Add:

1½ teaspoons balsamic vinegar

Garnish with:

(Grated Parmesan)
Chopped parsley

ROASTED MUSHROOMS

4 servings

Practically any mushroom benefits from roasting, but our favorites are small shiitakes and maitakes, which become delightfully crispy around the edges and take on an especially meaty flavor. However, even plain old creminis are improved by this treatment.

Preheat the oven to 425°F. For easier cleanup, line a rimmed baking sheet with parchment paper.

Have ready:

1 pound mushrooms

For button-shaped mushrooms, remove the stems (discard tough shiitake stems or save for stock, 73) and leave whole or halve them. If they are larger, quarter or slice them. For maitakes, separate into clumps about the size of broccoli florets. Toss the mushrooms with:

2 tablespoons vegetable oil
½ teaspoon salt

Roast until the mushrooms are browned and crisp around the edges, 25 to 30 minutes.

MUSHROOM BACON

4 to 6 servings

Upon discovering that roasted mushrooms have an unmistakable meatiness, we decided to take it a step further, roasting mushrooms with the spices and seasonings often used on bacon. The result is good for snacking, piling on a vegetarian BLT, 137, or sprinkling on a salad.

Preheat the oven to 350°F. Line 2 rimmed baking sheets with parchment paper.

In a medium bowl, whisk together:

2 tablespoons olive oil
1 tablespoon maple syrup
2 teaspoons soy sauce
2 teaspoons smoked paprika
½ teaspoon salt or smoked salt
½ teaspoon black pepper
¼ teaspoon garlic powder

Toss in the bowl with the seasonings:

8 ounces shiitake mushrooms, stems discarded, thinly sliced

Spread the shiitakes out on the baking sheets in a single layer. Bake until browned and dry to the touch, 30 to 35 minutes. Cook time will depend on whether you prefer a chewy texture or a crisp texture. To test for doneness, remove one mushroom piece from the oven and let it cool, then taste it. Let the mushrooms cool completely.

GRILLED MUSHROOMS

6 servings

The best mushrooms for grilling directly on grill grates are portobellos, large maitakes, lobsters, chicken of the woods, and large shiitakes. For smaller mushrooms, use a grill basket, 1063, or grill pan, or roast them instead, above.

Prepare a medium-hot grill fire, 1063. Remove the stems from:

2 pounds mushrooms

Toss in a bowl with:

¼ cup olive oil
½ teaspoon salt
½ teaspoon black pepper

Place the mushrooms on the grate (or in a grill basket) and grill, turning once, until tender, 5 to 8 minutes a side. Place on a large platter and garnish with:

Chopped parsley

Serve on garlic-rubbed toast as for Bruschetta, 67, or as a side dish.

DUXELLES

About ½ cup

This concentrated mushroom-onion mixture is wonderful folded into scrambled eggs or omelets, stuffed under the skin of chicken, spooned onto mashed potatoes, or simply spread on toast. Squeezing all the moisture out of the chopped mushrooms is not essential, but it will help them brown more quickly in the pan. Mycologist and winemaker Michael Beug recommends using riesling with this recipe, especially with wild mushrooms like chanterelles.

Chop very fine or pulse in a food processor until they resemble oatmeal:

8 ounces mushrooms

Squeeze about ½ cup of the mushrooms at a time in a thin cotton towel, wringing them very hard to extract their juices. The mushrooms will be in a solid lump if you have squeezed hard enough.

Melt in a medium skillet over medium-high heat until the foam subsides:

2 tablespoons butter

Add and cook briefly, until softened:

¼ cup minced shallots, onions, or green onions (white part only)

Add the mushrooms and cook, stirring often, until they have begun to brown and there is very little liquid left, 5 to 6 minutes. Stir in:

2 tablespoons dry sherry, dry red or white wine, Madeira, or port

Cook until completely evaporated. Stir in:

(¼ cup heavy cream)
(Finely grated zest of ½ lemon)
Salt and black pepper to taste
Pinch of dried thyme or grated or ground nutmeg

Let cool. Refrigerate in a covered container for up to 10 days or freeze for up to 3 months.

MUSHROOM CONFIT

About 6 cups

We first encountered mushroom confit in a Thomas Keller cookbook, and we've been tweaking the recipe for years. In our opinion, this is the perfect way to preserve wild mushrooms from a successful foraging venture. Serve as part of an antipasto spread or cheese board, or toss with pasta, serve over polenta, or pile on thickly sliced toasted bread.

Toss together in a colander placed in the sink or over a bowl:

2 pounds mushrooms, larger ones quartered, any tough stems removed
1 tablespoon salt

Let sit for 1 hour. Gently press any excess moisture out of them (do not rinse). Set aside.

Preheat the oven to 200°F.

Combine in a large ovenproof saucepan or Dutch oven:

2 cups olive oil
(2 shallots, thinly sliced)
4 garlic cloves, smashed
4 sprigs thyme
1 small sprig rosemary
1 bay leaf
½ teaspoon black pepper

Set the heat to medium and wait for the garlic to start faintly bubbling. Reduce the heat to maintain a low simmer and cook for 4 minutes. Remove from the heat and let the mixture steep for at least 15 minutes.

Add the mushrooms, cover, transfer to the oven, and bake for 1 hour. Remove from the oven, uncover, and stir in:

¼ cup sherry vinegar or white wine vinegar
(1 teaspoon smoked paprika)

Cool completely before packing into a jar with a tight-fitting lid, making sure the mushrooms are completely submerged in the oil. Store refrigerated for up to 1 month.

ABOUT OKRA

Okra is the young seedpod of a prolific plant related to hollyhocks and hibiscus. Whole raw okra are wonderful to snack on: The pods are pleasantly crisp and have a fresh, green bean–type flavor. Okra pods retain their crispness when steamed, sautéed, or fried whole. Once cut, however, okra begins to soften and release a slimy liquid that many find off-putting. There are benefits to this goo: Cut okra acts as a natural thickener, which is why it plays such an instrumental role in many gumbos. For those who would rather have their okra pods sliced yet still crisp, there are ways of preparing it that do not end in gooey disappointment. One is to quickly "cauterize" cut surfaces by searing them, although this is a bit of a hassle. Instead, we like to use the goo to our advantage by making Bhindi Kurkuri, below, where freshly cut okra is tossed in a mixture of spices and flour and then fried. The sticky cut surfaces help the coating adhere and stop the pieces from releasing more liquid.

Though at its peak in mid to late summer, okra is often available in the market year-round—if not fresh, then frozen. If possible, choose pods no more than 4 inches long (smaller, younger pods are less fibrous). Pods should be heavy for their size, plump, and blemish free, with stems intact. Store up to 3 days in a closed plastic bag in the refrigerator crisper. Wash and dry okra before cooking.

Okra goes well with tomatoes, peppers, onions, garlic, ham, curry powder, and citrus juice or vinegar. To pickle okra, see 925.

OKRA AND TOMATO STEW

4 to 6 servings

Okra and tomatoes are a classic Southern pairing. For added flavor, add a little diced country ham to the pot, or cook a few slices of bacon in the pan and use the fat to cook the onions, sprinkling the crumbled bacon onto the dish before serving.

Heat in a large saucepan or Dutch oven over medium heat:

3 tablespoons olive or vegetable oil

Add and cook, stirring, until softened and starting to brown around the edges, about 10 minutes:

2 medium onions, chopped

Add and cook, stirring, 1 minute more:

2 garlic cloves, minced

Add:

1 pound fresh tomatoes, diced, or one 14½-ounce can diced tomatoes
1 teaspoon sugar
½ teaspoon salt

Cook over medium heat until thickened, about 10 minutes (fresh tomatoes may need longer than canned to thicken). Add:

1 pound okra, stems trimmed, cut into ½-inch-thick pieces

Cook until the okra is tender, about 10 minutes more. Taste and season with more salt, if needed, and:

Lemon juice to taste

Serve in bowls over:

Creamy Grits, 323, Creamy Polenta, 322, or Buttermilk Biscuits, 635

FRIED OKRA

4 to 6 servings

Heat to 365°F in a large skillet:

½ inch vegetable oil

While the oil heats, wash, dry, trim off the stems, and slice into ½-inch pieces:

1 pound okra

In a medium bowl, combine:

1 cup fine cornmeal
2 tablespoons all-purpose flour
1 teaspoon salt
1 teaspoon garlic powder or onion powder
¼ teaspoon cayenne pepper
¼ teaspoon black pepper

Set aside. Whisk together in a second medium bowl:

⅓ cup milk
1 large egg

Toss the okra in the milk mixture, then in the cornmeal mixture. Add the okra to the hot oil in batches and fry, stirring occasionally, until browned, 4 to 6 minutes. Do not crowd the skillet and keep an eye on the temperature of the oil, adjusting the heat of the burner as needed. Remove the okra with a slotted spoon and drain on paper towels. Serve immediately.

BHINDI KURKURI (CRISPY INDIAN-STYLE FRIED OKRA)

4 servings

The sticky surfaces of cut okra grab onto this spicy, sour mixture. The result is succulent and can be served as a snack or appetizer with condiments.

Combine in a large bowl:

1 teaspoon curry powder or Garam Masala, 558
¼ teaspoon Indian red chile powder or cayenne pepper

(½ teaspoon amchur powder, 953)
½ teaspoon salt
Wash, dry, and trim the stems off:
1 pound okra
Halve each pod lengthwise, transfer to the bowl with the spices, and toss well. Set aside. Preheat the oven to 200°F. Line a baking sheet with paper towels. Pour into a large skillet over medium-high heat:
½ inch vegetable oil
Heat the oil to 350°F, then reduce the heat to maintain the temperature and thoroughly toss the okra with:
¼ cup chickpea flour
Fry the okra in batches, without crowding the skillet, until golden brown, about 3 minutes. Transfer to the lined baking sheet and keep warm in the oven while you fry the rest of the okra. When all the okra has been cooked and drained, transfer to a serving plate and sprinkle with:
Lime juice to taste
(Chaat Masala, 589)
Serve hot. If desired, accompany with:
(Raita, 569, Cilantro-Mint Chutney, 568, or Tamarind Chutney, 566)

ABOUT ONIONS AND SHALLOTS

Onions find their way into nearly every savory dish we cook. They are, quite literally, ubiquitous in kitchens across the world. Raw, they add a spiciness to salads, salsas, and relishes. Cooked, they bring sweetness to acidic tomato sauces and, when browned, a welcome, caramel-like depth to dishes of all kinds. For further suggestions regarding their use as an ingredient, and for information on dried onion products, please read Onions as Seasoning, 1009. For **leeks,** see 247.

Fresh or **spring onions** were once harvested just in the spring but are now sold year-round as **green onions, scallions,** or **bunching onions.** Some, like **green shallots,** are still an exclusive, springtime treat. They are either picked when very young or are a variety of onion that does not form a bulb. Some form bulbs, others remain slender and of uniform thickness. They have soft flesh, long green tops, and a mild or sweet taste, which is why they are ➤ the best type of onion for eating raw in salsas and salads. The green tops as well as the white portion are edible. Though there are many red varieties available young, the most common is the mild, sweet **Tropea** or **torpedo onion,** which we almost always roast whole as for shallots, 257. All of these varieties can be used raw, stir-fried, or sautéed. Onion greens are as useful and desirable as the bulbs; slice or chop them to add at the end of cooking or as a vibrant garnish. Thick green onions are excellent left whole and grilled over direct heat or roasted in a dry skillet until they are tender and charred on the outside. Some are specially bred for this treatment: Spanish **calçots,** a thick, sweet, slender-bulbed variety, is half-buried in dirt while it grows to make the white section especially large and tender. They may be served whole with a sauce (Grilled Leeks with Romesco Sauce, 248) or coarsely chopped and added to tacos, burritos, beans, sauces, braises, or salsas. Fully grown onions may be harvested and sold while fresh, sometimes with their greens still attached. Otherwise they are cured for long-term storage.

Once cured, **storage** or **dry onions** have firm flesh, papery skins, and develop spicy, sulfurous flavors. They can be kept in a cool, dry environment for months and are available year-round. **Yellow onions** are the most flavorful and preferable for general cooking uses. Their flavor can be pungent and, generally, they are best cooked or pickled, 930. **White onions** are often thought of as milder than the yellow type, but are generally reserved for cooking as well. **Red onions** are purportedly sweet enough to eat raw, but we find them to be quite strong. **Sweet onions,** though actually lower in sugar content than regular storage onions, also have less of the pungent, sulfuric compounds in their flesh, which allows their sweetness to shine through. There are several different varieties, often named after the region in which they're grown: **Bermuda, Vidalia, Walla Walla, Texas 1015,** and **Maui** are but a few examples. Along with green onions, these are our favorites for serving raw: Thinly slice and add to salads, salsas, burgers, and sandwiches. Thicker slices may be skewered and grilled. White, red, and sweet onions tend to be moister than yellow onions, thus they do not store as well and should be used promptly.

Pearl onions are a type of tiny storage onion that are often cooked whole, pickled alone or with Cornichons, 924, added to stews and braises, creamed, or glazed. Pearl onions can be frustrating to peel, but they are temptingly sold already peeled in the frozen foods aisle.

To peel pearl onions, cut off the root end, place them in a bowl, and cover with cool water. Let them soak for 30 minutes. Drain the onions and peel off the papery skins with the help of a paring knife.

Boiling onions, rarely seen in produce markets, are slightly larger than pearls and used primarily in long-simmered stews and braises. **Cipollini,** an Italian variety, are also a bit larger than pearl onions, with a squat, bulgy shape. They are perfect for stews and braises as well as roasting as for shallots—or alongside a whole chicken or lamb leg, with other root vegetables.

Shallots are fairly small, varying from the size of a Brussels sprout to a lemon, with copper, gold, or gray-brown skin. If large, what often appears to be one round shallot will be two or more connected bulbs; simply pull them apart. To some, the flavor of a shallot is milder than that of onions though we find them quite pungent. Shallots are typically used as a component of other dishes, but they can also be roasted whole, 257, or very thinly sliced, floured, and fried into an irresistibly crispy tangle, 256.

Ramps are an especially potent species of wild onion with elongated leaves that taste and smell strongly of garlic and onion. Growing only for a short window in early to midspring, ramps are widely foraged by hand from the forested hillsides of Appalachia. Despite being notoriously difficult to cultivate, ramps are now distributed widely, largely in response to their growing popularity and the high price chefs and home cooks are willing to pay for them. Ramps may be judiciously substituted for garlic, green garlic, or green onions in most dishes, but they are traditionally served with fried potatoes, griddled ham, eggs, or small pan-fried fish. To experience their fullest flavor, we suggest lightly frying the bulbs (chopped or whole) in butter or bacon fat until tender and then cooking potatoes, eggs, or ham in the infused fat. Thinly slice the greens and add them toward the end of cooking. The bulbs may also be quick-pickled in hot brine, 930, or canned as for Pickled Asparagus, 926.

Green onions, ramps, and fresh mature onions will not store for long; try to use them within 1 week of purchase. Dry them well and keep refrigerated, wrapped in a towel in a bag to control moisture. Cured yellow onions may be stored for about 2 months in a well-ventilated area; white, sweet, and red onions begin to deteriorate after only 1 month. If possible, spread them out to increase airflow.

Green onions and ramps should be rinsed well; discard any limp outer layers or wilted greens. To save time slicing green onions, cut all of them into equal lengths 3 or 4 inches long, gather the sections together into a tight bundle, and slice crosswise to the desired thickness. ➤ You will have better results—cleaner cuts and vibrant green color—by using a sharp knife and sliding your blade through the greens rather than rocking it up and down. If you wish, cut them on the diagonal—if you do so thinly, the resulting slice resembles the silhouette of a horse ear, which is how Chinese cooks refer to the cut. If you wish to finely chop or mince the white portion of thicker green onions, first halve or quarter them lengthwise, leaving the onion intact toward the greens to hold it together, and then slice crosswise.

When it comes to cutting storage onions, ➤ a sharp knife is the best way to prevent tears—dull blades tend to spray more eye-watering vapors into the air.

To slice storage onions into rings, slice off the top and peel the papery skin off, as well as any layers that seem soft or show any discoloration or translucence. Slice it to the desired thickness, being careful to keep the onion from rolling.

To slice storage onions into crescents for stir-frying and other preparations, cut the stem and root ends off and halve the onion through the root, from top to bottom—the skin and outer layers are then easy to peel off. Slice each onion half to the desired thickness lengthwise or crosswise.

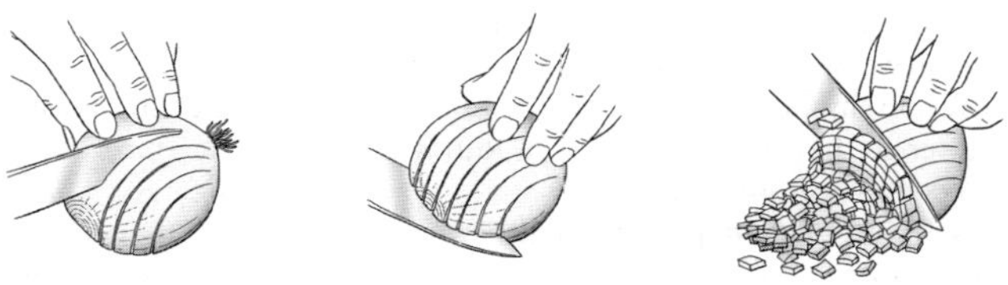

Dicing an onion

To chop, dice, or mince a storage onion, cut off the top, stand the onion on the cut side, and halve it through the root end; the root will prevent the onion from falling apart as you chop it. Peel off the papery skins and place the onion halves cut side down. Make ⅛- to ½-inch lengthwise parallel cuts without cutting through the root end. For fine dice, carefully slice the onion parallel to the cutting board without slicing through the root end. Make these slices at ⅛- to ¼-inch intervals. Finally, make ⅛- to ½-inch slices from the top perpendicular to the cuts you just made, working your way toward the root. The onion will fall into dice. Unless they are to be used in a long-simmering braise or stew, the pieces should be uniform in size so they cook at the same rate.

If you cook onions over low heat so that they wilt and turn translucent without browning, they are said to be **sweated.** At this stage, their taste is gentle but not sweet. **Browned** onions are cooked over moderate heat until golden, 10 to 15 minutes, depending on the amount. For a sublime method that combines these two approaches, see Caramelized Onions, 255. When browning or caramelizing, be careful not to burn the onions as this brings on an acrid flavor.

As noted before, onions are a universally loved ingredient; as such, they go well with practically everything. Along with celery and carrots they make up the famous French mixture known as mirepoix, 1002. They are also part of the Cajun "holy trinity" of onions, celery, and green bell pepper, and Sofrito, 1018. For other dishes and condiments that conspicuously celebrate onions, see French Onion Soup, 92, Red Onion Dip, 51, Sauce Soubise, 549, Red Onion Marmalade, 568, and Quick-Pickled Onions, 549.

SAUTÉED ONIONS

2 to 4 servings

Cooked quickly over high heat, onions emerge lightly browned—crisp on the outside and moist on the inside—perfect for filling omelets, garnishing braises, or topping mashed potatoes, grain dishes, Patty Melts, 144, burgers, and steaks or chops of all types.

Heat in a large skillet over medium-high heat:

2 tablespoons vegetable oil

Add and cook, stirring frequently, until lightly browned around the edges, 10 to 15 minutes:

1 pound yellow, red, white, or sweet onions, halved and thinly sliced or cut into ½-inch or larger dice

Season well with:

Salt and black pepper

CARAMELIZED ONIONS

About 4 cups

Whereas sautéed onions can still have some pungency and texture, caramelized onions are meltingly tender and savory-sweet with—as their name implies—caramel notes. They are a wonderful, flavor-packed garnish for all types of cooked dishes. These cook down to a fraction of their original volume and can be refrigerated for a few days or frozen for several months.

I. TRADITIONAL

The traditional method of slowly sweating the onions does not have to be burdensome. Think of it as a kitchen-bound lacuna in the story of your life, where contemplation and mindfulness can flourish as the onions slowly surrender their moisture and turn a deep bronze.

Heat in a very large skillet over medium-high heat until the butter is melted:

2 tablespoons butter

2 tablespoons olive oil

Add:

3 pounds yellow or white onions, thinly sliced

Sprinkle with:

1 teaspoon salt

Cook, stirring constantly, for 15 minutes. Reduce the heat to low to medium-low and continue cooking, stirring occasionally, until the onions are soft and brown, about 40 minutes. When the residue from the juices has built up in the skillet, add:

½ cup dry white wine or water

Stir and scrape the skillet to dissolve the browned bits. They will immediately mix into the onions, darkening them further. Remove from the heat and season with:

Salt and black pepper to taste

II. QUICK

If you do not need to make such a large quantity of onions or simply do not have an hour to spend properly caramelizing them, prepare **Sautéed Onions, 255,** adding **½ teaspoon sugar** halfway through cooking. When the onions are browned, deglaze the skillet with **¼ cup white wine,** scrape up any browned bits, and cook, stirring, until the liquid has evaporated.

CREAMED PEARL ONIONS

4 servings

This dish can be assembled 1 day ahead, covered, and refrigerated, then baked when ready to serve. If desired, substitute already peeled frozen pearl onions for the fresh onions and skip the blanching and peeling steps.

Preheat the oven to 350°F. Drop into a large saucepan half-filled with cold water:

1 pound pearl onions

Bring to a boil and blanch for 1 minute. Using a slotted spoon, remove the onions and peel, then return to the boiling water. Simmer until tender, about 10 minutes. Drain, reserving ⅓ cup of the cooking liquid. Butter a shallow, 8-inch square baking dish and, if desired, line the bottom with:

(4 slices buttered toast)

Transfer the onions to the baking dish and set aside.

Prepare:

White Sauce I, 548

Pour the mixture over the onions and sprinkle with:

1 cup shredded Cheddar or Swiss cheese (4 ounces)

Bake until bubbling, about 15 minutes. Sprinkle with any or all of the following:

Crumbled cooked bacon
Chopped parsley
Smoked paprika

ONION RINGS

4 servings

Try dusting the hot onions with paprika as well as salt, or dust with Chaat Masala, 589. Please read about Deep-Frying, 1051.

I. BATTERED

Peel, cut crosswise into ¼- to ½-inch slices, and separate into rings:

4 large yellow, red, white, or sweet onions (about 3 pounds)

Batter and fry as for:

Battered and Deep-Fried Vegetables, 203

Drain on a rack or on paper towels. Sprinkle to taste with:

Salt

II. BREADED

Prepare the onions as for **I, above,** and apply **Bound Bread Crumb or Cracker Coating, 658,** to the rings. Place on a rack to dry for at least 20 minutes before frying (refrigerating for 1 hour or overnight will produce better results). Heat to 350°F in a heavy 10-inch pot:

3 inches vegetable oil or shortening

Add the onion rings to the hot oil and fry in batches until golden brown, 3 to 5 minutes, turning once or twice. Do not crowd the pot. Drain and season to taste as directed above.

CRISPY FRIED SHALLOTS

About 3 cups

Use these crisp, sweet shallots atop noodle dishes, stir-fries, rice, and sautéed greens.

Heat to 325°F in a small heavy saucepan:

1 inch vegetable oil

Toss together in a bowl:

4 large shallots, peeled and sliced into thin rings
½ cup cornstarch or flour

Separate the shallot rings as you toss them. Fry the shallots in several batches until golden. Remove with a spider or slotted spoon to a plate lined with paper towels and immediately sprinkle to taste with:

Salt
(Curry powder)

Once cool, they will keep for a month at room temperature in a tightly covered container, although they are best when used immediately.

GRILLED SWEET ONIONS

4 servings

Large red onions can be used when sweet onions are unavailable. These are a great topping to grill alongside hamburgers, sausages, or steaks.

Prepare a medium-hot grill fire.

Peel and slice into 1-inch-thick rounds:

3 large sweet onions

Carefully impale each slice horizontally through the center with a skewer so they will not fall apart. Rub with:

¼ cup vegetable oil
Salt and black pepper to taste

Grill until tender and lightly charred, turning once, about 6 minutes per side. Remove the skewers to serve.

OVEN- OR FIRE-BAKED WHOLE ONIONS

I. OVEN-BAKED

Preheat the oven to 375°F. Line a rimmed baking sheet or broiler pan with foil. Place on the pan:

Medium to large unpeeled yellow, red, white, or sweet onions

Bake until very soft, 1 to 1½ hours. Cut a slice from the root end of each onion, then remove and discard the skins. Season to taste with:

Melted butter
Salt and black pepper
(Grated Parmesan)

II. FIRE-BAKED

Please read about Fireplace or Hearth Cooking, 1068. The outer layers of the unpeeled onions protect the inner portion and are discarded after cooking (you may wrap the onions in foil, if desired). Bury in a bed of embers for about 45 minutes:

Large unpeeled onions

When the onions are tender, puncture the skin to let the steam escape. Scoop out the tender onion flesh and season to taste with:

Salt and black pepper

Garnish with:

Sour cream or melted butter

ROASTED SHALLOTS

4 servings

A delectable accompaniment to simply cooked fish, poultry, or meat. Tropea and cipollini onions are a fine substitute, when available.

Preheat the oven to 425°F.

Peel:

1½ pounds small to medium shallots

Trim off the root ends, and halve any larger shallots so they all cook at the same rate. Toss in a baking dish that will hold the shallots in a single layer with:

2 tablespoons vegetable oil
½ teaspoon salt
Black pepper to taste
(A few sprigs thyme)

Roast until tender when pierced with a fork and browned around the edges, about 30 minutes. To glaze the shallots, if desired, brush with a mixture of:

(1 tablespoon maple syrup)
(1 tablespoon balsamic vinegar)

Return to the oven for 5 minutes more.

BAKED ONIONS STUFFED WITH SPINACH AND SAUSAGE

4 servings

Cut off the top quarter from:

4 medium yellow, red, white, or sweet onions

Trim off any roots, but leave the root end intact. Peel off the skin. Use a sharp paring knife to carefully cut out a cone-shaped section from the center of each onion and use a spoon to dig out all but ¼ to ½ inch of the onion. There should be 2 to 3 layers of onion left. Reserve the onion bits and coarsely chop half of them. Reserve the remaining onion for another use or save in a stock bag, 73. Set the onions in a steamer basket above a few inches of water. Steam until the onions are tender enough to be pierced by a skewer but still feel slightly resistant, about 15 minutes. Remove the onions and let stand until cool enough to handle.

Preheat the oven to 375°F. Butter a baking dish just large enough to hold the onions and arrange the onions in the dish.

Crumble into a medium skillet and brown well over medium heat:

4 ounces bulk pork sausage, Fresh Chorizo Sausage, 511, or Italian Sausage, 511

Without draining off the fat, add the chopped onion bits and cook, stirring, until golden and very soft, about 10 minutes. Meanwhile, squeeze dry and finely chop:

One 10-ounce package frozen spinach, thawed, or 1½ pounds fresh spinach, wilted, 243

Add the spinach to the sausage mixture, reduce the heat to medium-low, and cook for 5 minutes. Pour in:

⅔ cup heavy cream

Cook for about 1 minute more; the mixture should be quite thick. Remove from the heat. Stir in:

¼ cup fresh bread crumbs, 957, or enough to make the stuffing hold its shape
(⅛ teaspoon grated or ground nutmeg)
Salt and black pepper to taste

Pile the sausage stuffing into the onions. Sprinkle with:

2 tablespoons fresh bread crumbs, 957
1 tablespoon butter, cut into small pieces

Bake until lightly browned, 25 to 30 minutes. Let stand for a few minutes before serving.

KOREAN GREEN ONION PANCAKE

1 large pancake; 2 or 3 servings

This hearty pancake turns tender green onions into a substantial side dish or appetizer.

Whisk together in a medium bowl:

½ cup all-purpose flour
½ cup water
¼ teaspoon salt

Heat in a medium skillet (preferably nonstick) over medium heat:

2 tablespoons vegetable oil

Add to the skillet in a single layer:

4 green onions, trimmed and halved lengthwise

Cook until lightly browned, 4 to 6 minutes. Pour the batter over them and cook until golden brown on the bottom, about 5 minutes. Flip the pancake and brown the second side, about 4 minutes more.

Combine in a small bowl and serve with the pancake:

2 tablespoons soy sauce
1 tablespoon rice vinegar or distilled white vinegar
1 teaspoon toasted sesame oil

If desired, serve with:

(Kimchi, 941)

ABOUT HEARTS OF PALM

Like bamboo shoots, 209, palm hearts are the tender, innermost core of the tree's small, immature shoots. Though many (but not all) species have an edible heart, the **pejibaye** or **peach palm** is the most common to find fresh or canned, since it produces many shoots over its lifetime and does not discolor when cut. They are cultivated in Hawaii and Central and South America. Fresh peach palm hearts taste mildly astringent and sweet. Other, less common commercial varieties like the South American **juçara** and **açai** are said to have a stronger flavor, while Southeast Asian coconut palm hearts are said to be sweeter. All of them have a unique, crisp-yet-tender texture.

Canned hearts of palm have a softer texture, and taste somewhat like canned artichoke hearts.

A heart's size depends on how quickly the shoot is harvested; some whole hearts are quite young and thin, others resemble a large, off-white carrot. The hearts are composed of different layers, like an onion. Most fresh hearts are sent to market trimmed of their fibrous exterior layer. Select fresh hearts that are moist at both ends and have no signs of cracking or of the layers separating. Fresh hearts are very perishable, so store in a closed plastic bag in the refrigerator crisper and use promptly.

Palm hearts have a delicate flavor, so simple treatments are often best. Fresh, raw heart of palm slices add a nice crunch to salads, but the soft, delicate texture of canned and cooked hearts are also a welcome addition to greens (see Arugula and Heart of Palm Salad, 126). Fresh hearts of palm may also be sliced and stir-fried, sautéed, or roasted in any way you would bamboo shoots, asparagus, or artichoke hearts.

To prepare fresh hearts of palm, rinse well and, if necessary, peel away any fibrous material to reach the tender white core. To serve raw in salads, slice crosswise into rounds ¼ to ½ inch thick and soak in ice water for 1 hour. Drain and pat dry.

To steam, leave the hearts whole and cook covered over rapidly boiling water until tender when pierced with a knife, 5 to 10 minutes. Chill, or slice at once and serve warm with a squeeze of lemon, a drizzle of melted butter or extra-virgin olive oil, and a little chopped parsley.

ABOUT PARSNIPS AND PARSLEY ROOT

Parsnips resemble pale carrots and are prized for their nutty flavor and sweetness—which greatly increases after the first winter frost. Unlike carrots, they are starchy and have a creamy texture once cooked—perfect for mashing. Select unblemished small to medium roots. Large parsnips can have woody cores.

You may encounter **parsley root,** or **Hamburg parsley,** in some markets. They resemble small parsnips, but are less sweet, with the savory character of celery root. To fully take advantage of this root, choose examples that have healthy-looking greens still attached. Our friend, cookbook author Diane Morgan, recommends simmering the peeled, cubed root in chicken soup (see Becker Chicken Soup, 92) and garnishing bowls with the curly, herbal tops.

Store parsnips and parsley roots in a closed plastic bag in the refrigerator crisper for up to 3 weeks. Scrub well or peel with a vegetable peeler and trim the stem ends just before using (parsnips will discolor once exposed to air). To prepare larger parsnips, halve or quarter and cut out their fibrous cores.

Use both parsnips and parsley root as you would carrots. Smaller parsnips and most parsley roots may be kept whole or halved for glazing, 228, roasting, 228, and braising, 203; shaved into ribbons and added raw to salads (Shaved Carrot Salad, 126); or cut into cubes, slices, or matchsticks for use in sautés, soups, stir-fries, hashes, pickles, and slaws. Slices may also be fried into chips, 48. Mash cooked parsnips in equal proportion with potatoes, 265, to accompany roast beef or pork, or shred and use similarly in Latkes, 269.

To steam or boil, place parsnips in a steamer basket over boiling water or add to a saucepan with water to cover and bring to a boil. Cook, covered, until tender: 10 to 15 minutes for whole parsnips under 1 inch thick; 5 to 10 minutes for thick slices.

Pressure-cook whole parsnips with 1 inch of water at 15 psi for 10 minutes. Halve very large (1-inch diameter or more) parsnips lengthwise. Use the quick release method, 1059.

PARSNIP-CHEESE GRATIN

6 to 8 servings

This gratin is a rich, warming treat for the coldest winter evenings, with sweet parsnips enrobed in cream and tucked under a generous blanket of molten cheese.

Preheat the oven to 350°F. Butter a 13 × 9-inch baking dish. Peel and trim:

1¾ pounds parsnips

If the parsnips are thin, halve them lengthwise. If they are larger, cut them lengthwise so they are in roughly ½-inch-thick batons, 201. If the parsnips have a woody core, cut it out. Set aside. Have ready:

1 large onion or large leek, trimmed, halved, well cleaned, and thinly sliced
(4 ounces thinly sliced prosciutto, about 6 slices)
1¼ cups grated Swiss cheese (5 ounces)

Mix together in a medium bowl:

1½ cups heavy cream
1 tablespoon minced fresh thyme or marjoram or 1 teaspoon dried thyme or marjoram
1 teaspoon salt
½ teaspoon minced fresh sage or rosemary or ¼ teaspoon dried sage or rosemary
½ teaspoon black pepper

Scatter the onion over the bottom of the dish and place the parsnips on top. If using, top with the prosciutto, then sprinkle with the cheese. Pour the cream mixture over everything. Bake until the top is golden and the parsnips are tender, 45 to 55 minutes. If desired, sprinkle halfway through baking with:

(Au Gratin II, 958)

ABOUT PEAS

For many people, lilacs and robins are welcome, cheering signs that spring is here once again. Good enough, certainly, but best of all is the appearance of peas, bright green, lightly sweet, and thoroughly delicious. Some varieties, called **field peas,** are dried for storage—see About Dried Beans and Legumes, 212, for how to prepare them. Green peas are of two types: those that need to be shelled, or **garden peas,** and **edible pod peas.**

Garden peas, also known as **English peas,** or simply **green peas,** are perhaps the most common. Sweet and plump, garden peas are best in the springtime, especially if you ➤ cook or freeze them quickly after harvest; a pea's natural sugars start to convert into starch the longer they are stored. Luckily, shelled peas freeze quite well—we actually prefer frozen peas to fresh peas that have been stored for too long. Frozen peas may be substituted for fresh; ➤ do not thaw them before adding to cooked dishes. Though canned peas are also available, their texture is quite soft and their flavor less vibrant, which makes them a distant second choice. To freeze peas at home, see About Freezing Vegetables, 884.

Select medium pods that are bright green, firm, and filled end to end with fat peas. Avoid blemished or puffy peas, as well as those where the peas are not thick and pronounced. You may refrigerate garden peas in their pods, in a bag or container, but plan to use them as soon as possible. Peas go well with cream, mint, parsley, chervil, thyme, onions, and bacon or ham.

To shell green peas, rinse thoroughly and snap off the stem, pulling down with it the thick fiber or string, which will unzip the pod like a purse. Press the pod at the seam, opening it, and the peas will pop out. No need to rinse them. ➤ One pound of well-filled pea pods will yield 1¼ to 1½ cups hulled peas.

Of the edible pod varieties, the aptly named **sugar snap** is the sweetest, plumpest, and has the biggest peas. Like garden peas, they are best in the springtime, and can turn starchy if harvested late or stored for too long. ➤ Use promptly. We love to eat them raw, as a quick garden snack or as part of a crudité plate, 45. Look for plump, firm sugar snaps with no blemishes or dry spots. Flatter and wider, **snow peas** are much more forgiving, and need not be consumed immediately. Though associated with Chinese cooking, the variety actually originates from Holland. We prefer them cooked very quickly and find their meaty texture and fresh flavor indispensable in stir-fries. Avoid any that are dry-looking or limp.

Most sugar snap peas and snow peas must have their stem and strings removed. Snow peas may need just the string removed from the seam side, but sugar snaps will probably need strings from both sides removed. Sugar snaps and snow peas may be left whole, or cut into bite-sized chunks or thin slices for eating raw in salads or sautéing and stir-frying.

Pea shoots, the leafy tendrils of new growth trimmed off English, sugar snap, or snow pea vines, are commonly available in Asian groceries and at local farmers' markets when in season. Those with thin, tender stems are usually eaten raw as a garnish or in salad. They may also be added in the last minutes of a stir-fry, stirred into soup before serving, or cooked as for any delicate green (see About Greens for Cooking, 242). They are very perishable and best used promptly. To store, refrigerate in a bag wrapped with a paper towel.

To steam garden peas and edible pod peas, shell them or remove any fibrous strings, place in a steamer basket over boiling water and cook, covered, until tender, about 5 minutes. Mature garden peas that have become starchy will need longer, about 10 minutes.

BRAISED GARDEN PEAS

2 servings

If shelling fresh peas, you may add two or three pods to the pan for extra flavor. If fresh peas are unavailable, substitute **one 10-ounce package unthawed frozen peas.**

Wash, then shell:

2 pounds English or garden pea pods (about 2 cups shelled)

Bring ¼ inch water to a boil in a skillet over medium-high heat. Add, if the peas are starchy:

(A pinch of sugar)

Add the peas to the skillet, cover, reduce the heat, and simmer until tender, 5 to 15 minutes, depending on the maturity of the peas. Add more water if the skillet becomes dry. Discard the pods, if using, and drain any excess water. Season the peas to taste with:

Butter or cream
(Minced parsley or mint)
Salt and black pepper

STIR-FRIED SNOW PEAS

4 servings

On Marion's frequent visits to the downtown Cincinnati library to do research for *Joy*, she regularly lunched at a nearby Chinese restaurant. The chef ordered his snow peas, which were unavailable in local markets, by air freight, and Marion relished them several times a week prepared in this simple way. You may substitute sugar snaps, but they will need to cook a bit longer.

Remove the stems and strings from:

1 pound snow peas

Leave them whole or slice on the diagonal into bite-sized pieces. Heat in a wok or large skillet over high heat until almost smoking:

1 tablespoon vegetable oil

Add:

1 tablespoon minced peeled ginger

Stir-fry for 30 seconds, then add the peas and stir-fry vigorously until shiny and coated with oil. Sprinkle with:

½ teaspoon salt

Stir-fry until the peas are crisp-tender, another minute or two. Garnish with, if desired:

(A dash of soy sauce)

PEAS WITH PROSCIUTTO AND ONIONS

4 to 6 servings

Shell or have ready:

2 pounds English or garden pea pods (about 2 cups shelled, or one 10-ounce package frozen peas)

Heat in a large skillet over medium heat:

3 tablespoons olive oil

Add and brown lightly, shaking the skillet occasionally:

24 pearl onions, peeled, 254 (or use thawed frozen pearl onions)

Add:

3 tablespoons water

Cover and cook over medium-low heat until the onions are tender, about 5 minutes. Stir in the shelled or frozen peas along with:

4 ounces prosciutto or ham, finely diced
(1 to 2 teaspoons water, if using fresh peas)
Salt and black pepper to taste

Cover and cook until the peas are tender, 5 to 8 minutes for fresh peas, 3 to 5 minutes for frozen.

PEA AND RICOTTA TOASTS

2 to 4 servings

These toasts may be served as an appetizer or cut into smaller canapés, 67, but we enjoy making a light lunch of them. You may

substitute **1 cup thawed frozen peas** here, but this simple treatment is best when the peas are fresh.
Shell:

1 pound English or garden pea pods (about 1 cup shelled)

Steam, 259, until tender, about 5 minutes. Set aside. Combine in a medium bowl:

8 ounces whole-milk ricotta
Finely grated zest of 1 lemon
1 tablespoon extra-virgin olive oil
1 tablespoon lemon juice
1 teaspoon minced thyme
Salt and black pepper to taste

Divide the mixture among:

4 thick slices rustic or sourdough bread, well toasted

Top with the peas and drizzle with a little:

Extra-virgin olive oil

If desired, garnish with:

(Tender pea shoots, pea sprouts, microgreens, or arugula)

ABOUT PEPPERS

Peppers are the fruits of five domesticated species of shrub in the nightshade family, originally native to Bolivia. Since their spread across the Americas and subsequent introduction to Europe and Asia, peppers have grown incredibly diverse. Fleshy and mild varieties are popular as a vegetable; other types are very spicy and added sparingly to dishes, treated more like a spice than a vegetable. Though milder varieties have been a mainstream vegetable since *Joy*'s first edition in 1931, hot chiles are becoming more and more popular as our collective palate adjusts to their fiery temperament and becomes more enamored of their diverse flavors.

Before we go further, some may ponder: Is it a "pepper" or a "chile?" The words can be used interchangeably, but we choose to refer to most dried peppers and those associated with Latin American cuisines as "chiles"—a Spanish word borrowed from the Nahuatl *chilli*. For all other types, we tend to use "peppers"—a Spanish conflation with the other spicy ingredient Spaniards knew well, peppercorns. For information on different types of **dried chiles** and how to toast, soak, or grind them, see 969.

Peppers produce a number of compounds to deter hungry mammals, collectively called capsaicin or capsaicinoids. These substances are responsible for their spiciness. In most peppers, capsaicin is concentrated in the white, inner flesh to which the seeds are attached. This is why many cooks prefer to remove the seeds and white parts before cooking (in addition to their slightly bitter, "pith-y" flavor). However, scientists have recently discovered that so-called superhot peppers—such as ghost and scorpion, among others—store as much capsaicin on the inner wall of their flesh as they do around the seeds. This is good news, as we now have no reason to excavate the interior of these explosively hot peppers to rid them of excess capsaicin, which can severely irritate your skin and eyes. Remember, ➤ chiles are comparatively mild in their green, immature state and become hottest when they just begin to ripen and turn red, orange, or yellow.

The most common kind of sweet pepper, **bell peppers** can be green, red, orange, yellow, or dark purple. Roasting, 262, changes their flavor and softens their flesh. Large with thick flesh, they are perfect for stuffing, and are diced along with other aromatic vegetables for use in soups, stews, braises, and grain dishes, especially in Spanish and Cajun cuisines. Fleshy sweet-to-hot **pimientos** are usually available only in the red-ripe stage and commercially canned. Spanish **piquillo peppers** are very similar, though we have only encountered them roasted and jarred.

New Mexico chiles are all derived from a single cultivar that was bred in the 1950s to be mild and large. They are usually picked when still light to dark green. Most have thick to medium flesh and a mild flavor, though some varieties (such as "Barker's Hot" and "Lumbre") can be quite hot. Other New Mexico chiles include **Anaheims,** which are mild and pale green, **Hatch chiles,** which are grown in or around the city of Hatch, New Mexico, and **Big Jims,** an especially large and mild cultivar. The superlative native chile of northern New Mexico, often called the **Chimayo chile,** is not bred from the same cultivar as the rest, and is usually picked when red. Mild New Mexico varieties are almost certainly in the cans labeled **"green chiles"** on supermarket shelves. Roasted and peeled, they are our favorite pepper to use for Chiles Rellenos, 263, or they may be diced and added to stews, sauces, 554, corn breads, 630, tamales, 324, sopes, 612, or posole, 323–24.

Thin-fleshed and pale-green **cubanelle peppers,** as well as the smaller, red **Jimmy Nardellos,** are perfect for frying with onions and sausages (which is why they are often referred to as **Italian frying peppers).** Other types, such as those grown in Basque country, especially in the town of **Espelette,** are good for frying, though they are usually allowed to mature until ripe, dried, and ground into a powder. Pale yellow to orange-red crisp **banana peppers** are sweet to very piquant and perhaps best known in their sliced, pickled form. Peppers sold as **pepperoncini,** the generic Italian word for "hot pepper," are similar to banana peppers, as they are of medium heat and usually reach us pickled, albeit whole, with stem attached. They are mild-mannered, have thin flesh, and are perfect for serving with antipasto, 45.

Two other diminutive green peppers have recently skyrocketed in popularity: the **padrón** and the **shishito.** Both have thin flesh and are generally mild in flavor, though one will occasionally surprise you with a burst of short-lived heat. Padróns and shishitos are usually sautéed whole until blackened in spots, and served as an appetizer or side dish, 262.

Poblanos are dark green, rich tasting, and relatively mild. Fry them with onions and garlic for an enchilada filling, before simmering beans (Frijoles de la Olla, 213), or sautéing corn, 235. Though they may be roasted, peeled, and added to soups, sauces, and stews, or used whole for Chiles Rellenos, 263, we find removing their skin to be tedious, since their thin flesh tears easily. **Chilaca chiles** are slender cousins of the poblano. They have a bit more heat and, in our opinion, a superior flavor.

Cayenne peppers are long and slender. Though found fresh at farmers' markets, cayennes are more familiar to shoppers as a spice: They were one of the first peppers to become available in dried and ground form throughout Europe and North America. You may sauté fleshier cayennes as you would cubanelles or poblanos, but thinner-fleshed ones can be spicier, and should be treated with more caution. **Holland finger hots,** similar to cayenne, are long, fruity, and sold as both green and red peppers. They are used in Korea and Southeast Asia, and are perfect for making Sriracha, 572.

Named for their ping-pong ball–sized round fruits, **cherry peppers** are usually pickled whole in both their green and red stages. They range from mild to hot and have many seeds, a slightly sweet taste, and tough skin. The most common cherry pepper is native to Calabria, Italy, though other long, cayenne types from that region are slender and exceptionally spicy. These small, spicy specimens are available dried and crushed, or salted, pickled, and packed in oil, 935.

Fresh **jalapeños** are available virtually everywhere in their green state and vary from mild to very hot. We find those bigger than 1 inch in diameter can be substituted for bell peppers in Cajun dishes with only slightly spicier results. When ripe, red jalapeños are smoked and dried or simmered in Adobo Sauce, 585; they are known as **chipotles,** 968. Green jalapeños can be used in many dishes as seasoning, from salsas to soups and stews, and even stuffed and fried or baked, 60. They also make an excellent pickle; see Jalapeños en Escabeche, 930, and Pickled Peppers, 927.

Other peppers with similar heat levels to the jalapeño include **Hungarian hot wax peppers,** which are a very pale, greenish-yellow color when immature. They are good sautéed or pickled. **Fresno chiles** are similar in appearance and heat level to jalapeños, but are more triangular in shape, lightly floral, and always sold ripened to red. We enjoy them in Sriracha, 572. **Serrano chiles** are also similar to jalapeños in flavor, though they are small and slender—about the size of a pinky finger—and consistently spicier.

Lantern-shaped **habaneros** are very spicy, with a fruity, floral flavor that pairs perfectly with citrus juice (see Habanero-Citrus Hot Sauce, 571). They can be nearly ten times as hot as a jalapeño. Sold green and ripened to a yellowish to bright orange or red, habaneros are used in salsas, sauces, and condiments. One type bred from habaneros, amusingly called the **habanada,** has all the fruity, floral characteristics of habaneros with none of the heat (look for it at farmers' markets). The similarly shaped and colored **Scotch bonnet peppers** of Jamaica can be distinguished from the habanero—the two are often confused—by their pleated, crinkly shape and sweeter flavor. They are a defining element in several dishes, including Jamaican Jerk Paste, 584, and Jamaican Rice and Peas, 33 (habaneros make a fine substitute).

Manzano or **peron peppers** are originally from South America, but are now cultivated in Mexico. Manzanos have a rounded lantern shape and are about the size of a small lemon, with a color that runs from yellow to orange. It is the only type we regularly find that has black seeds. Like bell peppers, they have substantially thick flesh, but their tropical, floral flavor is much like a habanero's, albeit not quite as hot. Use in place of habaneros when slightly less heat is desired, or when the pepper's thick flesh will add welcome body; see salsas, 573–74, and Habanero-Citrus Hot Sauce, 571. Aside from manzanos, other South American peppers go by the name *ají*, the Taíno word for "pepper." The most common of these to find its way north is the **ají amarillo,** a slender yellow pepper with a fruity, mildly hot character.

There are several different types of peppers that go under the generic name of **"Thai chiles,"** the most common one being the small, fiery **bird's eye chile,** sold green or red. The pale green to yellow-orange to red **Tabasco pepper** is similar, and most often encountered packed in vinegar as a sort of condiment or in the ubiquitous Louisiana-style fermented hot sauce, 942. It is very spicy.

As spicy peppers have gained popularity, so has the compulsion to find or breed ever-spicier types. Once considered the hottest around, habaneros ceded their reputation to the **ghost pepper** (also known as *bhut jolokia*), which is more than fifteen times as hot as a jalapeño. This was followed by the **Trinidad Maruga scorpion** (which contains up to twenty-four times as much capsaicin as a jalapeño) and the **Carolina reaper** (up to thirty-two). Needless to say, these peppers are nearly useless from a cook's perspective and should be exclusively "self-inflicted." Handle with extreme caution. On the bright side, there is no need to seed them, as they carry as much capsaicin in their flesh as they do in their seeds and inner white membranes.

Regardless of heat level or size, look for plump, firm peppers with no soft, translucent, or dry spots and healthy-looking stems. Store them unwashed in the refrigerator for up to 2 weeks, wrapped in a paper towel and placed in a bag or container.

➤ Wear gloves when handling all but the mildest of peppers, and wash your hands in soapy water immediately afterward.

To seed bell peppers for stuffing, simply cut around the stem end along the top shoulder, remove the stem and seeds, and trim the white membranes from the inside.

To seed New Mexico, jalapeño, or poblano peppers for stuffing, roast and peel (see 262), if directed, then make a lengthwise incision on one side, and carefully remove the seeds and white membranes with a spoon.

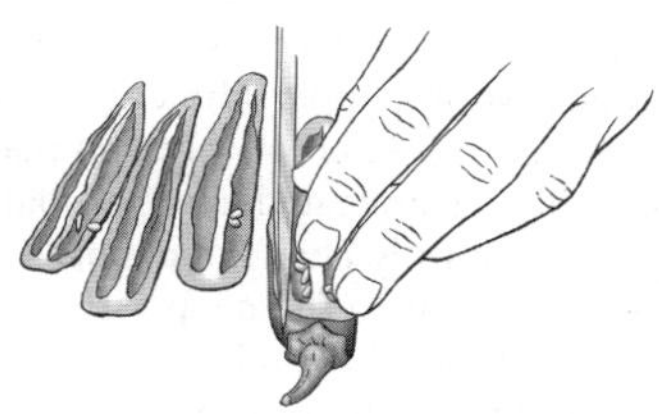

Removing the seeds from a hot pepper

To seed and slice, chop, or dice a pepper larger than a serrano, lay the pepper on its side and slice lengthwise down one side, just to the left or right of where the seeds are. Rotate the pepper onto the cut side and slice to the side of the seeds again. Repeat until you have cut all the flesh from the stem and seedy core. Discard the core, and slice the relatively flat pieces of pepper as thinly as desired. You may then rotate the resulting strips and cut into medium or fine dice.

To cut peppers into rings, slice them crosswise into the desired thickness and push out any seeds or white flesh individually.

ROASTED PEPPERS

"Roasting" peppers involves charring their skins with high heat, and usually peeling it off afterward. The process softens their flesh, rounds out their heat, and adds an enticing smoky flavor.

I. BROILED OR GRILLED

This is our preferred method for roasting large bell and New Mexico peppers in quantity. If you have a grill fire started, you may find it convenient to char the peppers directly over the coals instead.

Line a rimmed baking sheet or broiler pan with foil and place on it:

Whole peppers

Preheat the broiler and place an oven rack so that the peppers will be within 4 inches of the heating element. Broil the peppers, turning with tongs, until blistered or partially blackened all over. If the peppers have thick skins and need to be peeled, transfer them to a paper bag or a bowl. Fold or tie the bag shut (or place a lid or plate on top of the bowl) and let the peppers stand for 10 minutes. Peel the skin off (it should rub off easily), discard the seeds, and use as desired. To store, put the peppers in an airtight container and refrigerate for up to 1 week. Roasted peppers can also be frozen for up to 6 months, but leave them whole and unpeeled, add them to freezer bags while still warm, and peel and seed only when you thaw them for use. Frozen peppers will lose texture but are good in sauces, soups, and stews.

II. PAN-ROASTED

The best way to roast smaller, thin-skinned chiles for salsas and other dishes. Since the skin is paper-thin, we do not recommend peeling these types.

Place a dry skillet or griddle over medium heat. Arrange in one layer:

Whole jalapeños, serranos, habaneros, or other small chiles

Cook, turning the chiles, until they are lightly charred and softened, about 10 minutes. Remove from the heat, let cool somewhat, trim off the stem, and remove the seeds (if desired).

III. TORCHED

Though this is the least efficient method, it may be the most convenient if only one or two roasted peppers are needed. With a pair of long metal tongs, place whole peppers directly in the flames of a gas burner on its highest setting. Alternatively, you may set the pepper in a stainless steel skillet or uncoated, rimmed baking sheet, place on your stovetop, and carefully char the pepper's skin with a propane torch. In both cases, rotate the pepper frequently with metal tongs (and move the flame of the torch around) so that it is evenly charred. Cover and peel the peppers as described in version I.

STUFFED BELL PEPPERS

4 servings

An American classic. Create a vegetarian version by substituting ½ **pound firm tofu, drained and crumbled,** or **Seasoned Tempeh Crumbles, 287.** Or, simply increase the amount of cooked rice to 2 cups. If the peppers are huge, you may halve them lengthwise through the stem instead (do not completely remove the stem, as it helps hold in the stuffing).

Position a rack in the center of the oven and preheat it to 375°F. Grease a baking dish in which the peppers will fit snugly. Prepare for stuffing, 261:

4 medium bell peppers

If the peppers will not stand upright, level them by cutting a thin slice from the bottom trying not to create a hole. Steam the peppers on a rack or steamer basket over boiling water until tender, about 10 minutes. Set aside. Heat in a large skillet over medium heat:

2 tablespoons olive or vegetable oil

Add and cook, stirring and breaking the beef up with a spoon, until it is lightly browned, about 10 minutes:

8 ounces ground beef, lamb, or pork, or chorizo sausage (store-bought or homemade, 511)
1 small onion, finely chopped

Remove from the heat and stir in:

1 cup cooked rice or any cooked grain, 340–45
1 medium tomato, finely chopped, or ½ cup drained canned diced tomatoes
2 large eggs, well beaten
1 garlic clove, minced
1 teaspoon dried thyme or oregano, crumbled
(Worcestershire sauce to taste)
(Red pepper flakes to taste)
Salt and black pepper to taste

Fill the peppers with the meat mixture and set them in the baking dish. Sprinkle over the tops:

Au Gratin I or II, 957–58

Bake until the peppers are tender and the filling hot and firm, about 25 minutes. If desired, brown the tops under the broiler.

RAJAS CON CREMA (CREAMY ROASTED POBLANO STRIPS)

6 to 8 servings

A classic preparation that can be served on its own with tortilla chips and salsa, or used to fill tacos, burritos, enchiladas, or sopes.

Roast, above:

2 pounds poblano or chilaca chiles

Peel, seed, stem, and slice them into thick strips. Heat in a large skillet over medium-high heat until hot:

2 tablespoons vegetable oil

Add and cook until starting to brown, 5 to 8 minutes:

1 large onion, thinly sliced
(2 garlic cloves, smashed)

Add the pepper strips and:

½ cup Mexican crema
½ cup milk or water
2 teaspoons dried oregano
½ teaspoon salt

Let the mixture come to a simmer, reduce the heat to medium-low, and cook until the peppers and onions are tender, about 5 minutes. Remove from the heat and stir in:

½ cup shredded Oaxaca cheese or Monterey Jack (2 ounces)

CHARRED SHISHITO OR PADRÓN PEPPERS

4 servings

These flavorful peppers are often served as an appetizer, but we enjoy them as a summer side dish as well.

Heat in a large heavy skillet (such as cast iron) over medium-high heat:

1 tablespoon vegetable oil

When the oil is hot, add:

8 ounces shishito or padrón peppers

Cook, tossing the peppers in the skillet occasionally, until they are soft and unevenly charred, about 4 minutes. Season to taste with:

Salt
Lemon or lime juice

CHILES RELLENOS

6 servings

Typically, these chiles are stuffed simply with cheese, but the filling may be varied quite a bit depending on your tastes. Replace up to half the cheese with fresh corn kernels, Picadillo, 503, Braised Carnitas, 495, or Frijoles de la Olla, 213. If you're feeling indulgent, use these stuffed fried peppers as a burrito filling, 146. Our favorite chiles to use in this dish are Big Jims, a New Mexico variety, with Anaheims a close second. Poblanos may be substituted, but their flesh is thinner, which makes peeling off the outer skin difficult. Please read about Deep-Frying, 1051.

Roast, 262:

6 large green New Mexico or Anaheim chiles

Peel the charred skin from the chiles. Make a long slit in one side of each chile and remove the seeds. Pat dry. Preheat the oven to 200°F. Mix together in a medium bowl:

2 cups coarsely shredded Monterey Jack, mild Cheddar, or Oaxaca cheese (8 ounces)
2 green onions, minced

Stuff the chiles with the cheese mixture. Prepare using 3 eggs and folding in the optional whipped egg whites:

Beer Batter, 657

Heat to 350°F in a large, deep skillet or Dutch oven:

2 inches vegetable oil

Place one chile in the batter at a time and spoon the batter over the top. Lift it out of the batter, allow the excess to drip off, and place gently in the oil (a fish spatula is excellent for this task). Fry 3 chiles at a time until golden brown on both sides, about 4 minutes per side. If the batter runs off and leaves a chile looking bare, you may spoon more batter over that spot and turn to fry again. Transfer to a baking sheet lined with paper towels, cover loosely with foil, and keep warm in the oven while you fry the remaining chiles. Serve topped with:

New Mexico–Style Chile Sauce, 554, or store-bought green chile sauce
Mexican Adobo II, 585, made with additional liquid
Any salsa, 573–74

ABOUT PLANTAINS

Plantains, a collection of various banana cultivars, are distinguished by their large size and starchiness. ➤ They must be cooked before eating. Plantains are available year-round, and can be prepared in their green state as well as when semiripe or quite mature, when the skins turn black and mottled. When still green, plantains are firm and starchy, much like potatoes. Green plantains are best when sliced thin and fried as for Tostones, below, but can be simmered until tender and roasted as for potatoes, 267. Mottled yellow plantains are half-ripe, creamy, tender, and a bit sweet. They may be treated like green plantains, or baked whole. Ripe, black plantains are sweeter still, with a banana-like flavor; They are soft, but still firmer and a bit starchier than bananas. If you wish to ripen plantains, place them in a paper bag and keep at room temperature.

Ripe plantains peel easily, but green ones can put up a bit of resistance. Like all bananas, their flesh darkens quickly once peeled or cut, so remove their skin and fibrous strings just before cooking.

To peel green plantains, make a lengthwise incision just through the skin. Cut them crosswise into several pieces and peel the skins off, starting at the incision you just made. Yellow plantains and black, fully ripe plantains can be peeled like a banana.

To simmer green plantains, cut into 2-inch pieces, peel, and simmer in water to cover for about 30 minutes or until very tender. Drain and toss with butter and salt and pepper, or treat as for Mashed Potatoes, 265.

ROASTED PLANTAINS

Preheat the oven to 400°F. Grease a baking dish that will hold the plantains in a single layer.

Cut off the top and bottom, slit the skin lengthwise, and peel:

Brown-black ripe plantains

Arrange in a single layer in the prepared baking dish and bake until the flesh is fork-tender, about 40 minutes. Serve (as you would a baked potato) with:

Butter

If desired, sprinkle to taste with:

(Lime juice and hot sauce, or Habanero-Citrus Hot Sauce, 571

FRIED PLANTAINS

6 servings

Serve these alongside Asopao de Pollo, 93, Jamaican Rice and Peas, 331, Frijoles de la Olla, 213, or any type of roast chicken or pork. Don't forget the hot sauce.

I. TOSTONES

Starchy green plantains are perfect for this traditional, double-fried preparation. You may use yellow, half-ripe plantains for a creamier result. Serve these crispy chips as a side, as suggested above, or use them instead of corn tortillas as a base for tostadas, 146. Please read about Deep-Frying, 1051.

Peel and cut on the diagonal into 1-inch slices:

1½ pounds green plantains (about 6 medium)

Heat to 325°F in a deep-fryer, deep heavy pot, or Dutch oven:

2 inches vegetable oil

Deep-fry the plantain slices in batches until golden, about 3 minutes per side. Do not crowd the pot. Drain well on paper towels. Place the fried slices in a single layer on a baking sheet and flatten each slice with the bottom of a glass to an even ¼-inch thickness. Reheat the oil to 350°F, and refry the plantain slices a few at a time until golden and crisp, 2 to 3 minutes. Drain well on paper towels and serve immediately, sprinkled with:

Coarse salt to taste

II. PAN-FRIED

Ripe plantains are sweeter and creamier. We prefer to slice them thinly and pan-fry.

Cut off the ends, slit the skin lengthwise, and peel:

1½ pounds ripe plantains (about 6 medium)

Cut into ¼-inch slices. Heat in a large nonstick skillet over medium heat:

2 tablespoons butter or vegetable oil

Add only as many plantain slices as will fit in a single layer and cook, turning once, until golden on both sides, 8 to 10 minutes. Transfer to a plate and keep warm while you fry the remaining slices, adding more butter or oil as needed.

Sprinkle with, to taste:

Coarse salt
(Black pepper)
(Chopped cilantro)

ABOUT POTATOES

Potatoes, native to the Andes mountains, were regarded with suspicion by the Europeans who first encountered them in the sixteenth century. Since then, they have more than recovered in the popularity department, having risen in the commodity ranks to become the fourth-largest crop in the world. In the United States, they are our favorite vegetable to consume. For sweet potatoes, see 278.

The vines of full-sized potatoes are left to wither and their tubers are cured in the soil for several weeks. **New potatoes** are harvested when the plant's vine is still green and the tubers are small and thin-skinned. Though most potatoes labeled as "new" in grocery stores are red-skinned boiling (waxy) potatoes (see below), any potato can be harvested young, and many types are now available, especially at farmers' markets. Intermediate-size potatoes are sometimes sold as **petites, pearls,** or **creamers. Fingerling potatoes** are the mature tubers of varieties that grow to be slender and finger length.

Though most potatoes we find at grocery stores have red, yellow, or brown skins (and yellow to white flesh), some varieties have purple to black skins with blueish flesh to match. Others may look normal on the outside and have a rosy-hued interior. Some lose their unique cast once cooked, while others retain their color. Aside from size and color, potatoes fall into three groups based on how they respond to cooking.

Boiling or **waxy potatoes** are relatively high in moisture and sugar and lower in starch. Practically all **red potatoes** are waxy, as are many fingerling varieties, including **French, La Ratte,** and **Russian Banana.** All boiling potatoes hold their shape well when cubed or sliced, so they are best for potato salads and adding to soups or stews where you want them to remain firm and distinct. We enjoy smaller ones roasted whole, smashed, 268, and pan-fried, 268.

Baking potatoes are low in moisture and sugar and high in starch. When cooked, their flesh is dry and fluffy. The best-known baking variety is the **russet** or **Idaho potato,** identifiable by its rough (and very tasty) brown skin and elongated shape. They are perfect for baking whole, make the fluffiest mashed potatoes, and are excellent for frying, potato soufflés, and thickening soups like Vichyssoise, 105, or sauces like Skordalia, 564.

All-purpose potatoes are moderate in moisture and starch content, making them good for boiling, baking, and frying, and in stews, salads, and soups. The **Yukon Gold** has thin, smooth golden skin and yellow flesh. Other all-purpose potatoes include the fingerlings **Yellow Finn** and **Butterfinger,** as well as **Kennebec, Katahdin, Red Gold,** and **Purple Peruvian.**

Select potatoes that are firm and heavy for their size, with taut skin and no cuts, dark spots, cracks, mold, or other signs of spoilage. Avoid those that have sprouted; they will be soft and can have an off-taste. Don't use frostbitten potatoes, which are watery and have a black ring under the skin when cut. If there is a greenish cast to the potato or a green patch on it, avoid it—the green part was exposed to the sun and will be bitter (even mildly toxic). In fact, avoid all green parts of the potato: ➤ the vine and leaves of the plant are poisonous.

Store potatoes at room temperature, unwashed and loose, in a cool, well-ventilated spot away from sunlight. New potatoes should be used within a week of purchase; mature potatoes (including fingerlings) can keep for many weeks, even months, if stored properly. ➤ Keep away from onions, which cause them to spoil more quickly.

Potatoes pair well with butter, heavy or sour cream, cheese (really, dairy of any stripe), chives, dill, onions, garlic, rosemary, sage, and bacon. They are often combined and mashed with other cooked vegetables in varying proportions (see Root Vegetable Puree, 203).

To prepare potatoes for cooking, remove any **eyes,** or nascent sprouts, with a spoon or paring knife. Potato skins provide flavor and nutrients, but if peeling is called for, the most efficient method is to use a swivel peeler. Flesh exposed to air will turn brown, so drop peeled potatoes into a bowl of cold water.

A mandoline, 201, makes quick work of cutting raw potatoes uniformly, whether paper-thin slices for Pommes Anna, 268, or perfect shoestring potatoes for frying. A handheld electric mixer is no doubt the most used tool to mash a potato and does a fine job; a friend swears by his stand mixer. ➤ Do not puree cooked potatoes with a food processor, as the result has an unappetizing gluey texture.

We appreciate **potato mashers,** as they do not involve lugging out an appliance. The **potato ricer,** a levered press that extrudes cooked potatoes through a basket lined with small holes, is the best tool for achieving light, even-textured mashed potatoes. Look for a sturdy metal ricer with at least a 2-cup bowl. Some ricers come with two disks with different-sized perforations that can be inserted into the cup. One has smaller holes for finely riced potatoes. The other disk has larger holes that can be used to press out Spätzle, 308, or to remove excess moisture from cooked spinach or other vegetables.

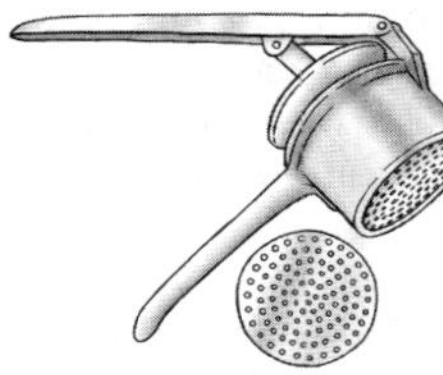

Potato ricer

In addition to the recipes here, see Corned Beef Hash, 473, Smoked Salmon Hash, 393, Vegetable Breakfast Hash, 202, Crispy Potato Skins, 59, Potato Leek Soup, 104, Potato Salad, 127, Potato Gnocchi, 306, Potato or Root Vegetable Chips, 48, and Buttermilk Potato Bread, 602.

To microwave, arrange 4 medium baking potatoes, peeled and quartered, in a 2-quart baking dish. Cover and cook on high in 3½-minute increments until tender, 7 to 9 minutes. Let stand, covered, for 3 minutes. Mash microwaved potatoes immediately if your goal is a fluffy texture.

Pressure-cook whole large (2½-inch-diameter) potatoes with 1 inch of water at 15 psi for 15 minutes; 1½-inch-diameter potatoes will be done in 10 minutes. Let the pressure release naturally for 10 minutes, then open the valve to release the pressure completely, 1059.

BOILED POTATOES

6 servings

Potatoes may also be steamed, 1056, but ➤ be sure there is ample water so the pan does not run dry before they are done.

Scrub clean or peel (if desired):

2 pounds potatoes

If in haste, you may cut large potatoes into quarters; if doing so with russet potatoes, their cut surfaces will start to disintegrate so keep a close watch on them. Transfer to a pot and add enough cool water to cover them by a few inches. For every quart of water, add:

½ teaspoon salt

Place over high heat and bring to a boil. Reduce the heat to maintain a simmer and cook until tender. Smaller red potatoes will be done in about 10 minutes; quartered large potatoes in about 15 minutes; large, whole potatoes may take up to 40 minutes. Drain well. If serving plain, cut larger potatoes into bite-sized pieces, if necessary, and toss to taste with:

2 to 3 tablespoons butter, melted
(3 to 4 tablespoons chopped parsley, chives, or dill, or a combination)
(Grated peeled horseradish)
Salt and black pepper

MASHED POTATOES

6 servings

Baking, or russet, potatoes make the best mashed potatoes, followed by gold potatoes. We have found that baking the potatoes, rather than boiling or microwaving them, yields the fluffiest texture. While baking takes longer than boiling or microwaving, as long as the oven temperature is at or below 400°F the potatoes can be baked alongside a roast, casserole, or other dish. (The timing will vary, so check for tenderness with a fork.) If desired, buttermilk, sour cream, or crème fraîche may be used instead of cream or milk, but do not heat these with the butter or they may curdle.

Boil, above, or bake, 267, until tender:

2 pounds potatoes (about 6 medium), peeled and cut into large chunks (left whole and unpeeled if baking)

Meanwhile, heat in a small saucepan over medium-low heat:

½ cup heavy cream, half-and-half, or milk
6 tablespoons butter
½ teaspoon salt
¼ teaspoon black or white pepper

Do not let the mixture boil. If using boiled potatoes, transfer them to a colander placed in the sink and briefly rinse off any excess starch. Return to the pot they were cooked in and shake over medium heat until mealy and dry. If using baked potatoes, wait until they are just cool enough to handle and carefully peel off the skin, or cut each potato in half and scoop out the flesh into a large bowl. Mash the hot potatoes or run them through a potato ricer (if using a ricer, you can rice large chunks of boiled potato with the skin intact—the skin will be left behind in the ricer). Fold the cream mixture into the potatoes, stirring just enough to incorporate (overworking the potatoes will turn them gummy). If the potatoes seem stiff, add more hot cream or milk. Taste and add more salt and pepper, if needed.

Transfer to a serving dish and serve at once. If desired, top with:

(2 tablespoons butter, softened)

Mashed potatoes can be kept hot for up to 30 minutes by covering the (heatproof) serving dish with foil and placing it in a warm oven.

ADDITIONS TO MASHED POTATOES

To make the Irish specialty called **Champ** add **4 finely chopped green onions, ¼ cup sliced chives, or 6 finely chopped ramps** to the hot butter and cream. Some add **4 ounces chopped stinging nettles, 246,** as well. Using gloves or tongs, add the nettles to the hot cream, cover, and let them cook for a few minutes before adding to the mashed potatoes. Make Champ with half potatoes and half rutabaga and you have a Scottish specialty called **Clapshot.**

Aside from these traditional combinations, mashed potatoes can be flavored with a vast number of ingredients. Here are some of our favorites:

Peeled cloves from 2 heads Roasted Garlic I, 241
2 pinches saffron threads, crushed and steeped in 2 tablespoons warm chicken stock or broth or water for 10 minutes
¼ cup finely chopped mild herbs, such as parsley and chives, or 2 tablespoons minced rosemary, sage, or thyme
Up to 1 cup Duxelles, 252
Up to 1 cup Sautéed Onions, 255, or Caramelized Onions, 255
Up to 1 cup grated Swiss, Gruyère, or Cheddar (4 ounces) or ½ cup soft goat cheese (2 ounces)

COLCANNON (MASHED POTATOES WITH KALE OR CABBAGE AND GREEN ONIONS)

6 to 8 servings

This is an Irish favorite. The British often form leftover colcannon—or leftover mashed potatoes and cabbage—into a cake, fry it, and call it **"bubble and squeak,"** after the noise it makes while cooking.

Place in a large saucepan or Dutch oven with cold water just to cover:

2 pounds Yukon Gold or other all-purpose potatoes, peeled and cut into 1½-inch chunks

Bring to a boil, then cover, reduce the heat to maintain a gentle boil, and cook for 10 minutes. Uncover and pile on top of the potatoes:

2 bunches green onions or 2 medium leeks, trimmed, halved lengthwise, well cleaned, and sliced

1 bunch kale, trimmed, or 1 small green cabbage (about 1 pound), cored and chopped into 1-inch pieces

Cover the pan again and cook until the potatoes are tender, about 5 minutes more. Drain and return the potatoes, green onions or leeks, and kale or cabbage to the pan. Mash the mixture over low heat, adding:

½ cup milk or half-and-half, warmed

½ to 1 stick (2 to 4 ounces) butter, to taste, softened

(¼ cup minced chives)

¾ teaspoon salt

¼ teaspoon black pepper

When the mixture is coarsely mashed, taste and adjust the seasonings.

MASHED POTATO CASSEROLE FOR A CROWD

18 to 20 servings

This is an excellent way of serving mashed potatoes to the masses that can be prepared up to 2 days in advance, sparing you the last-minute frustrations of a steamy kitchen covered in potato flotsam. For a modest 6 servings, scale this recipe back by a third and bake the potatoes in a 9-inch pie pan. If you make this with a triple recipe of Colcannon, above, and top with the shredded Cheddar only, you may call it **Rumbledethumps.**

Prepare:

Triple recipe Mashed Potatoes, 265

If desired, fold in:

(Any of the Additions to Mashed Potatoes, 265)

Preheat the oven to 375°F. Generously butter a 13 × 9 × 2-inch baking dish.

Fold into the mashed potatoes:

1½ cups grated Cheddar (6 ounces)

Spread the potatoes evenly in the prepared dish. Combine in a small bowl:

½ cup grated Cheddar (2 ounces)

½ cup dry bread crumbs

½ teaspoon salt

½ teaspoon black pepper

Sprinkle the cheese mixture over the potatoes. Dot the top with:

2 tablespoons butter, cut into small pieces

Bake until golden brown on top, about 30 minutes. Or, if desired, cover and refrigerate up to 2 days. To serve, preheat the oven to 350°F and cover the dish with foil. Bake for 45 minutes, then remove the foil and bake until browned on top, about 15 minutes more.

PAN-FRIED MASHED POTATO CAKES

4 servings

A superlative method for reheating leftover mashed potatoes.

Place in a bowl:

2 cups Mashed Potatoes, 265

Beat in:

2 large eggs

Add any of the following, if desired:

(½ cup sautéed onions or mushrooms)

(5 green onions, thinly sliced)

(2 tablespoons chopped thyme, parsley, or chives)

Heat in a large nonstick skillet over medium heat:

2 tablespoons butter, olive oil, or vegetable oil

Add big spoonfuls of the potato mixture, flatten them into cakes, and fry until nicely browned, about 5 minutes on each side. Drain on paper towels. Serve hot.

POTATOES AU GRATIN (SCALLOPED POTATOES)

6 to 8 servings

The classic French preparation, **Gratin Dauphinois,** is made with little more than raw potato slices and cream, which reduces, browns, and takes on a cheese-like flavor in the oven. This recipe includes plenty of cheese (simply omit if you prefer not to buck French tradition). For a bit more flavor, you may scatter over the inner layers of potatoes **1 thinly sliced medium onion, 4 ounces diced ham,** or both.

Preheat the oven to 350°F. Butter a 12-inch gratin dish or a shallow 3-quart baking dish.

Whisk together in a medium bowl:

2 cups half-and-half or heavy cream

(1 tablespoon fresh thyme leaves or 1 teaspoon minced fresh rosemary or sage)

(2 garlic cloves, minced)

1 teaspoon salt

¼ teaspoon black pepper

(Pinch of grated or ground nutmeg)

Have ready:

1 cup grated Swiss cheese, Gruyère, sharp Cheddar, or Parmesan (4 ounces)

Cut into ⅛-inch-thick slices with a knife or mandoline, 201:

2½ pounds russet or all-purpose potatoes, peeled if desired

Place a layer of potatoes in the prepared dish, pour one-quarter of the cream mixture over them, and sprinkle with one-quarter of the cheese. Repeat this layering 3 more times, ending with cheese. Bake until the top is golden and the potatoes are tender, 45 minutes to 1 hour.

If desired, sprinkle halfway through the baking time with:

(Au Gratin II, 958)

BAKED POTATOES

The best baked potatoes are flaky when served, so use starchy types like russets. Although boiling and all-purpose potatoes can be used—and will need only about half as much baking time—they will never be as flaky. Wrapping potatoes in foil inhibits flakiness, because too much moisture is retained. To make **loaded baked potatoes,** scoop out the flesh of the cooked potatoes and mix in a bowl with butter, salt, and pepper to taste, then place back in the potato skins and top with **shredded Cheddar, sour cream, chopped chives or green onion,** and **crumbled crisp bacon.**

Preheat the oven to 400°F. Scrub:

Russet potatoes

Pierce them in 6 or 8 places with a fork and place the potatoes directly on the oven rack. Bake until tender when pierced with a fork, 40 to 60 minutes, depending on size. If you wish to do so for your diners, cut a slit in each potato and fluff up the interior by squeezing on both sides and working with a fork. Serve at once topped with any of the following:

Butter, sour cream, or Sauce Mornay, 548
Chopped chives, thinly sliced green onion, Sautéed Onions, 255, or Crispy Fried Shallots, 256
Minced parsley or cilantro
Crisp bacon or browned Fresh Chorizo Sausage, 511, drained and crumbled

TWICE-BAKED POTATOES

4 servings

Loaded and baked a second time. Feel free to let your imagination run wild with the choice of cheese and seasonings.

Bake, above:

4 small or 2 large russet potatoes (2 to 2½ pounds)

Meanwhile, combine in a small bowl:

½ cup grated sharp Cheddar (2 ounces)
4 tablespoons butter, softened
¼ cup sour cream
(4 slices bacon, cooked until crisp and crumbled)
2 green onions, minced
¾ teaspoon salt
½ teaspoon black pepper

When the potatoes are tender, leave the oven on. Halve the potatoes lengthwise and scoop out the flesh, leaving a ¼-inch-thick shell. Mix the potato flesh with the cheese mixture to combine. Place the potato shells in a baking dish and fill with the cheesy potato filling. Bake until the cheese is melted and the potatoes are browned, 15 to 20 minutes. If desired, broil briefly to brown the tops.

DUCHESS POTATOES

8 servings

Preheat the oven to 400°F. Butter a baking sheet.

Boil, 265, until tender:

8 medium russet potatoes (about 3 pounds), peeled and quartered

Drain the potatoes, return to the hot pan, and shake to dry them out. Rice the potatoes into a large bowl. Add while the potatoes are still hot:

½ cup heavy cream
4 tablespoons butter, softened
2 large egg yolks, beaten
(A dash of dry mustard)
Salt and black pepper to taste

Transfer the mixture to a pastry bag fitted with a large fluted or star tip and pipe onto the baking sheet in eight 4-inch-wide mounds. Bake until golden, about 20 minutes. Serve at once.

ROASTED POTATOES

4 to 5 servings

Preheat the oven to 450°F. Position a rack in the upper third of the oven.

Place in a large saucepan or pot:

2½ pounds russet or gold potatoes, cut into 2-inch chunks
1 tablespoon salt

Fill the pot with cool water to cover the potatoes. Bring to a boil over high heat, then reduce the heat to medium-low, cover, and simmer until the potatoes are just tender, 15 to 20 minutes. Drain the potatoes well in a colander, then transfer to a large bowl. Add:

3 tablespoons olive or vegetable oil, chicken fat, duck fat, or bacon drippings
1 tablespoon minced fresh rosemary
1 teaspoon paprika or smoked paprika

Toss the potatoes well to coat with the oil and seasonings. The potatoes will start to disintegrate around the edges—this is okay. Transfer the potatoes to a large baking sheet and spread out in a single layer. Roast, undisturbed, for 20 minutes. Use a metal spatula to turn the potatoes, then return to the oven until deeply browned and crispy, about 20 minutes more.

HASSELBACK POTATOES

4 servings

Created in the 1940s at Stockholm's Restaurant Hasselbacken, these potatoes are as adorable on the plate as they are satisfying.

Preheat the oven to 400°F. Have ready:

4 medium gold potatoes or small russet potatoes (about 2 pounds)

Cut a thin slice lengthwise from one of the flatter sides of each potato to allow it to sit flat on a work surface. Working with one potato at a time, place a wooden skewer or flat wooden chopstick on either side of the long edges of the potato. Slice the potato very thinly crosswise, but not all the way through (the skewers will prevent the knife from cutting all the way through). Repeat with all the potatoes and place them in a baking dish.

If desired, slice as thinly as possible:

(4 garlic cloves)

Using 1 clove per potato, tuck the slices between the leaves of the potatoes. Sprinkle the potatoes with:

½ teaspoon salt
¼ teaspoon black pepper

Place on top of the potatoes:

4 sprigs thyme, 8 sage leaves, or 1 tablespoon minced rosemary

3 tablespoons butter, cut into small pieces
Alternatively, drizzle the potatoes with:
3 tablespoons olive oil
Roast until browned and tender, 50 to 60 minutes. To test for tenderness, stick a skewer through the potatoes.

CRISPY SMASHED POTATOES

4 servings

We think these potatoes are the perfect side for a steak (especially when French Fries, 270, seem like too much of a hassle). Use small potatoes—about 1½ inches in diameter or less. For even crispier results, fry the cooked and smashed potatoes in 2 inches of 375°F vegetable oil until golden.
Preheat the oven to 450°F. Add to a large saucepan or pot:
1½ pounds small red potatoes or fingerling potatoes
Add water to cover, bring to a boil, then reduce the heat and simmer until the potatoes are easily pierced with a knife, 10 to 15 minutes. Drain and allow to cool for 10 minutes. Lightly grease a baking sheet. Place the potatoes on the baking sheet and smash each one with the bottom of a drinking glass. Brush generously with:
Olive oil or melted butter
and sprinkle with:
Salt and black pepper
Roast the potatoes until starting to brown on the bottom, 15 to 20 minutes. Flip the potatoes with a spatula and roast another 15 minutes or until browned on the second side. If desired, serve with:
(Romesco Sauce, 570)

POMMES ANNA

6 to 8 servings

Even though we inherited Marion Becker's *pommes Anna* pan, a beautiful copper piece of cookware specifically made for this dish, we usually use a heavy-lidded ovenproof skillet instead. A mandoline, 201, makes slicing the potatoes a breeze.
Position a rack in the center of the oven and preheat the oven to 425°F. Have ready:
2 sticks (8 ounces) butter, clarified, 160, or 1½ sticks (6 ounces) butter, melted
Pour the butter into a medium ovenproof skillet or *pommes Anna* pan to a depth of ¼ inch. Set over medium-low to low heat and layer in:
2½ to 3 pounds russet potatoes, peeled and sliced ⅛ inch thick
Build the bottom layer carefully with overlapping, nicely shaped slices. As you assemble, sprinkle each layer with:
Salt and black pepper to taste
(Melted butter)
When all the potatoes are layered in the pan and the bottom has formed a light crust, lightly butter or oil a skillet slightly smaller than the pan and press it firmly on top of the potatoes to compress them. Cover the pan tightly with foil, or cap with the *pommes Anna* pan lid. Put the pan in the oven on a baking sheet to catch drips. Bake for 20 minutes, uncover, and press down firmly on the potatoes again. Bake, uncovered, until the sides are visibly browned and crisp, 20 to 25 minutes more. Holding the skillet or lid firmly against the potatoes, tilt the pan and pour off any melted butter that has not been absorbed. To serve, loosen the edges from the pan with a thin metal spatula, then invert the potatoes onto a plate and slice into wedges. Sometimes the bottom gets stuck in the skillet. Don't panic! Use the spatula to loosen the misbehaving potatoes from the bottom of the skillet and gingerly place it where it belongs, on top of the finished *pommes Anna*. No one will be the wiser.

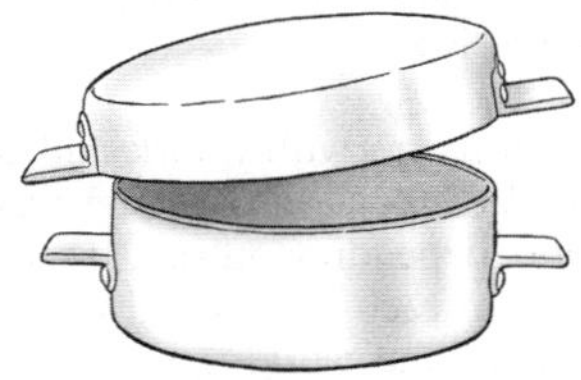

Pommes Anna pan

POTATO KUGEL

8 to 10 servings

A Jewish-American classic, this shredded potato casserole can be flavored with fresh herbs, sautéed onions, curry powder—practically any of the Additions to Mashed Potatoes, 265—but we adore the simplicity of the traditional version below.
Preheat the oven to 375°F. Generously grease a 13 × 9-inch baking dish with:
3 tablespoons melted schmaltz, 1015, duck fat, or vegetable oil
Using a food processor fitted with the grating disk, or on the large holes of a box grater, grate:
3 pounds russet potatoes, peeled (3 to 4 large)
Immediately transfer the potatoes to a bowl of cold water. Grate:
1 large onion
Drain the potatoes well and spread out between two kitchen towels to remove excess moisture. Dry the bowl used for soaking the potatoes and whisk in it:
4 large eggs
⅓ cup flour or potato starch
1 teaspoon salt
½ teaspoon black pepper
Add the potatoes and onions and stir to combine. Transfer to the baking dish and spread into an even layer. Drizzle over the top:
2 tablespoons schmaltz, 1015, duck fat, or vegetable oil
Bake until tender and golden brown, about 1 hour. Cool for 10 minutes before serving.

PAN-FRIED POTATOES

4 servings

When made with new potatoes, you may call these **Potatoes Lyonnaise.** When cut into cubes, seasoned with **1 teaspoon chili powder,** and served with breakfast, you may call them **Home Fries.** For making these in the oven, see Oven "French-Fried" Potatoes, 271.

Peel, if desired:

1½ pounds red potatoes or other waxy potatoes

Quarter small red potatoes or cut into ½-inch slices; cut larger potatoes into ½-inch cubes. Place in a medium saucepan and cover with cold water. Add to the pot:

2 teaspoons salt

Bring to a boil and cook for 5 minutes. Drain the potatoes well, then spread on a kitchen towel to dry. Melt in a large skillet over medium heat:

2 tablespoons butter, beef drippings, or duck fat

Add and cook, stirring, until browned:

1 small onion, thinly sliced

Transfer to a small bowl and set aside. In the same skillet, melt over medium heat:

¼ cup (½ stick) butter, beef drippings, or duck fat

Add the potatoes and cook without stirring until well browned on one side, about 10 minutes. Using a metal spatula, flip the potatoes and brown on the second side, about 10 minutes more, adjusting the heat as needed to prevent burning. Return the onions to the skillet along with:

2 tablespoons chopped parsley
½ teaspoon salt
½ teaspoon black pepper

Toss to combine. Serve hot.

HASH BROWN POTATOES

4 servings

A breakfast classic. For those who desire the texture of shredded potatoes, see Potatoes Rösti, below.

Combine in a medium bowl:

3 cups finely diced all-purpose potatoes
½ small onion, grated
1 tablespoon chopped parsley
½ teaspoon salt
¼ teaspoon black pepper

Heat in a nonstick skillet over medium heat:

3 tablespoons bacon drippings, oil, or other fat

Spread the potato mixture in the skillet and press it with a spatula into a cake. Cook the potatoes slowly, shaking them from time to time to keep them from sticking. When the bottom is browned, cut the potato cake in half and turn each half with 2 spatulas. If the potatoes fall apart, simply shape them into a cake again and compress them with a spatula. Drizzle evenly over the potatoes:

¼ cup heavy cream

Brown the second side. Serve the potatoes piping hot.

LATKES (POTATO PANCAKES)

About fourteen 3-inch cakes

The high starch content of russet potatoes helps hold the cakes together. Shredded celery root, parsnip, sweet potato, or carrot may be substituted for up to half the potatoes.

Wrap in a clean kitchen towel and wring to squeeze out as much moisture as possible:

1 pound russet potatoes (about 2 medium), peeled and shredded (about 2 cups)
1 medium onion, grated

Combine in a bowl with:

2 large eggs, well beaten
3 tablespoons all-purpose flour or matzo meal
1¼ teaspoons salt

Preheat the oven to 200°F. Heat in a large heavy skillet over medium-high heat until hot:

¼ inch or more vegetable oil or butter

Place spoonfuls of the potato mixture into the skillet, in batches, and form them into 3-inch patties about ¼ inch thick. Brown on the bottom for about 4 minutes, reducing the heat to medium if necessary to prevent scorching. Turn and brown the second side until crisp, about 4 minutes more. Transfer to a plate or rimmed baking sheet lined with paper towels and keep warm in the oven while frying the remaining latkes. Serve at once with:

Applesauce, 174
Sour cream or Greek yogurt
Minced chives

POTATOES RÖSTI

4 servings

Rösti is essentially a giant potato pancake. This recipe works with russet potatoes only, since their starch helps bind the shreds together. For diner-style **shredded hash browns,** you may break up or "scatter" the cake into several pieces after it has browned on the first side and stir them until browned to your liking.

Shred on the large holes of a box grater over a kitchen towel:

1 pound russet potatoes (about 2 potatoes), peeled if desired

Top with another towel and dry the potato shreds well. Transfer to a bowl and toss with:

(2 tablespoons grated onion)
¾ teaspoon salt
½ teaspoon black pepper

Heat in a large skillet (you'll get the best crust with cast iron) over medium heat:

3 tablespoons vegetable oil, duck, goose, or chicken fat, or bacon fat

When the oil shimmers, add the shredded potatoes, using a spatula to spread them out into an even layer covering the bottom of the skillet. Cook until the bottom of the pancake is a deep golden brown, 12 to 15 minutes. Loosen the cake from the skillet with a spatula. Carefully flip the pancake by sliding it onto a plate and carefully inverting the plate over the skillet. Cook until golden on the second side, 8 to 10 minutes more. Serve as for Latkes, above, or with:

Sour cream or Horseradish Sauce, 566
Hot-Smoked Salmon, 393, flaked
Chopped dill, parsley, tarragon, or a combination
Lemon wedges

SOUFFLÉED OR PUFFED POTATOES

6 servings

According to one of the origin stories for this dish, which we like to believe, Louis XIV, on campaign against the Dutch, had sent a courier ahead to his chef, detailing just what he desired for dinner. The roads were nearly impassable, the hour grew late, and the chef, who had managed to keep most of the elaborate menu in reasonably prime condition, found to his consternation as the king's party clattered into the courtyard that his *pommes frites* had gone utterly limp. In a frenzy, he immersed the potatoes in the hot fat a second time, madly agitated the pan, and behold!—the potatoes puffed dramatically, turning hollow and crisp.

In his relief at having something to serve, the chef evidently didn't mind throwing out a significant number of unpuffed slices: Even experts who make the dish daily expect a 10 percent failure rate. To improve upon this dismal statistic, restaurants famous for the dish age potatoes to lower their water content. It is said that potatoes with skin that can no longer be pierced or scraped off with a fingernail are ideal.

Please read about Deep-Frying, 1051.

Scrub and peel:

8 large russet potatoes

Square off the potatoes, then cut them lengthwise into ⅛-inch-thick slabs that are of uniform thickness (a mandoline, 201, is ideal). Once you have these long even slices, you can cut them into the classic rectangular shape with rounded corners, as shown, or into ovals. Soak the slices in ice water for at least 25 minutes. Drain and dry them thoroughly. Meanwhile, heat to 275°F in a deep saucepan or sauté pan:

3 inches rendered beef suet, lard, or vegetable oil

Preparing souffléed or puffed potatoes

Working in batches, drop in the potato slices one by one. Do not crowd the pan. The slices will sink. This next admonition is not without danger for the unskilled! When, after a few seconds, the slices rise, shake the pot back and forth continuously. This will create a wave-like action to keep the floating slices bathed in the fat. Continue to cook, turning at least once, until the slices begin to turn transparent toward the centers. Drain on paper towels. The potatoes may be refrigerated up to 4 hours before the second cooking, but bring them to room temperature before frying the second time. To proceed at once, let them cool and drain for about 5 minutes.

Just before you are ready to serve, heat the fat to 385°F. Drop the potato slices again one by one into the fat, again agitating the pan as described. The potatoes should puff at once. Cook to a golden brown. Drain on paper towels. Sprinkle to taste with:

Salt

Serve the puffed potatoes at once, preferably in a basket as shown, to keep them crisp. If they are not crisp enough, return them to the fat for a few seconds. Drain again.

FRENCH FRIES

4 to 6 servings

I. DOUBLE-FRIED

This is the tried-and-true method for creating large quantities of crispy fries. The first fry cooks the potatoes and drives out moisture; the second fry is done at a higher temperature to crisp and brown the exterior. To fry multiple batches, fry all the potatoes at the lower temperature first—fries may be held at that point for up to 2 hours and fried at the higher temperature just before serving. Please read about Deep-Frying, 1051.

Soak in a bowl of cold water to cover for 30 minutes:

4 large baking potatoes, peeled and cut into 2¼ × ⅜ × ⅜-inch batons, 201

Drain and dry on a kitchen towel to remove excess starch and moisture. Meanwhile, heat to 350°F in a deep-fryer, deep heavy pot, or Dutch oven:

3 inches vegetable oil

Drop in the potatoes in batches, about 1 cup at a time, and fry until all the sputtering ceases, about 2 minutes. Scoop out the potatoes (which will be rather limp) with a slotted spoon and drain on paper towels. Let cool for at least 5 minutes before the second frying; the potatoes can be held for up to 2 hours.

For the second frying, heat the oil to 365°F. Fry until the potatoes are golden brown and crisp, 2 to 3 minutes, then drain on paper towels. Never cover them, or they will get flabby. Sprinkle with:

Salt

Serve at once.

II. COLD-START

First popularized by the French chef Joël Robuchon, these small-batch, "cold-start" fries could not be easier—you do not need a thermometer, the fries require less fat to fry than standard French fries, which makes it more feasible to use duck fat, lard, or beef drippings. The only drawback is that it can only be done with one batch per pot of oil. If you do use a thermometer, you will see that the oil initially rises only to the temperature of boiling water. When all the moisture is simmered out of the potatoes, the oil temperature rises and the potatoes brown. Because this recipe does not get up to normal frying temperatures until the very end, you can even use moderate smoke-point fats like extra-virgin olive oil.

Cut **potatoes, preferably Yukon Gold, peeled if desired, into fries as above.** Make an even layer of them in the bottom of a saucepan or pot. Be sure the layer is on the thin side, no more than 2 inches thick (wider pans will be able to accommodate a larger batch). Add enough **oil or melted lard, beef drippings, or duck fat** to cover the fries by 1 inch. Bring the potatoes and oil to a simmer over high heat. Reduce the heat to medium. Cook, shaking the pan and gently stirring several times, until the potatoes turn crispy and golden brown, about 25 minutes. Remove the pan from the heat and fish out the fries with a spider or slotted spoon. Drain on paper towels and promptly sprinkle with **salt.**

III. SHOESTRING FRIES

Cut the potatoes into strips no more than 3/16 inch thick and cook as for **version I, 270.** A mandoline, 201, or other vegetable slicer makes perfect shoestrings, but you can also use a knife or a food processor to cut the potatoes. They should brown in 2 to 3 minutes during the second frying; do not let them brown faster, or they will end up limp.

ADDITIONS TO FRENCH FRIES

Malt vinegar is a time-honored favorite for seasoning fries. Or, drizzle a little **truffle oil** over fries while they are hot and toss to coat before you sprinkle with salt (or **grated Parmesan, black pepper,** and **minced herbs,** if you like).

For dipping, we find it hard to look beyond **Quick Ketchup, 565,** but **Aïoli, 564, Mayonnaise, 563,** flavored with chipotles in adobo, and **Ranch Dressing, 577,** are also quite tasty.

French fries serve admirably as a base or vehicle for a variety of toppings. For **Chili-Cheese Fries,** generously ladle **Chili con Carne, 468,** onto fries and top with **chopped green onions** and **shredded Cheddar.** For **Poutine,** an even-messier French-Canadian classic, top fries with **chopped cheese curds** and smother them with a healthy drizzle of **Sauce Velouté, 549.** For **disco fries**—a stateside interpretation of poutine found in diners throughout New Jersey and New York City—replace the curds with **shredded mozzarella or Cheddar.** Of course, our minds never stray far from planning our next bowl of **Moules Frites, 351.**

JOJOS (FRIED POTATO WEDGES)

4 servings

A food born of pressure-fried chicken joints, jojos, as they are affectionately known in the Pacific Northwest, are essentially chicken-fried potatoes, and typically fried alongside chicken. Please read about Deep-Frying, 1051.

Cut lengthwise into 8 wedges each:

2 pounds russet potatoes, unpeeled (about 3 medium)

Place in a steamer basket in layers so that all of the cut faces are exposed. Steam, 1056, for 5 minutes. Meanwhile, whisk together in a small bowl:

1½ teaspoons salt
1½ teaspoons onion powder
1½ teaspoons garlic powder
1½ teaspoons smoked paprika
½ teaspoon black pepper
½ teaspoon cayenne pepper
½ teaspoon dried thyme

Let the potato wedges cool slightly, then transfer to a large bowl. Gradually sprinkle the seasonings over the potatoes, gently tossing them by shaking the bowl back and forth. When the potatoes are coated, place them skin side down on a plate or baking sheet to dry and cool further. If possible, let them dry out like this for 1 hour, uncovered.

Preheat the oven to 200°F. Heat to 365°F in a deep-fryer, deep heavy pot, or Dutch oven:

2 inches vegetable oil

Add about one-third of the potato wedges and fry until golden, about 5 minutes. Transfer the fried potato wedges to a rack over a baking sheet and keep warm in the oven as you fry the remaining potatoes. Serve with:

Ranch Dressing, 577, Creamy Blue Cheese Dressing, 577, or ketchup

OVEN "FRENCH-FRIED" POTATOES

4 servings

Rutabagas, sweet potatoes, and turnips also can be cooked this way.

Preheat the oven to 450°F.

Peel and cut lengthwise into ½-inch-thick batons, 201:

4 medium baking potatoes (about 1 pound)

Soak in cold water for 10 minutes, then drain and dry well between towels. Toss the potatoes with:

2 tablespoons vegetable oil or bacon fat
½ teaspoon salt

Spread on a baking sheet and bake, turning several times, until golden, 30 to 40 minutes. If desired, sprinkle with:

(Paprika or black pepper)

ABOUT RADISHES

A spicy member of the prolific cabbage family, radishes are valued for their often-vibrant colors, crunchy texture, and peppery bite. Radishes were once so esteemed as a stimulant for the appetite that people used to start their day with a handful. In addition to the round, red, mild **cherry belles** typically found in grocery stores, try the carrot-shaped **icicles,** or red and white **French Breakfast** types. We like to serve all small radishes with softened butter (or perhaps a flavored butter, 559) and flaky sea salt. Or we serve them as part of a crudité platter, 45.

Daikon or **mooli radishes** are among the largest radishes. The Korean **mu radish**—often used in Kimchi, 941—is similar to daikon, though squatter and rounded, with white-to-green skin. A large specimen of either type can easily weigh a pound or, often, quite a bit more. Their large size makes them ideal for cutting into matchsticks. Excellent when tossed with salad, added to Banh Mi, 139, or scattered over bowls of Bún, 305, they are also suited to quick-pickling, 929, and slaws (especially Spicy Chinese-Style Slaw, 119). Peeled and grated, they add character to Raita, 569.

Watermelon radishes, also known as **beauty heart,** are an Asian variety with pale green to white skin and reddish-pink flesh. A bit firmer and drier than daikon, they are one of the more attractive root vegetables, and make for a colorful addition to salads or crudité platters, 45.

Black radishes tend to be consistently spicier than other types and have the firmest, driest flesh. Slender and tapered or perfectly round, they have dark, scaly skin and pure white flesh. They are a favorite for thinly slicing and adding to vegetable salads, though we like fermenting them as for Sauerkraut, 940, or serving on pumpernickel or dark rye toasts slathered with butter or sour cream.

Choose firm, flawless roots. If greens are attached and you wish to use them, they should be bright and crisp. Red radishes are often sold with wilted or undesirable leaves—simply trim them and discard. As long as the radishes themselves are firm and unblemished, the presence of lackluster greens should not be a deterrent. Trim the leaves from the roots and either discard or store separately in perforated plastic vegetable bags in the refrigerator crisper. If radishes are not thoroughly crisp, they can be revived once cut by soaking in ice water.

Aside from the recipes below, you may cook radishes as for turnips, 283. Drier types, such as black radishes, may be fried into chips, 48, or stand in for celery root, especially in Celery Root Rémoulade, 126.

RADISHES WITH GREEN ONION

4 servings

If the radish tops are in good shape, chop them up and add them when you uncover the pan. This treatment is also excellent for small, tender turnips.

Trim the leaves and any excessively long roots from:

2 bunches radishes, well scrubbed (about 1 pound)

Halve or quarter any especially large ones. Melt in a large skillet over medium heat:

2 tablespoons butter

Add and cook, stirring, until softened, about 4 minutes:

8 green onions, white part only, cut into ½-inch pieces (thinly slice the green tops and reserve)

Add the radishes along with:

½ cup chicken stock or broth

Cover the skillet and simmer for 4 minutes. Uncover, increase the heat to medium-high, and boil rapidly to reduce the pan juices while shaking the skillet back and forth a few times. Stir in the reserved green onion tops and season to taste with:

Salt
Lemon juice

PEAS AND RADISHES WITH MISO BUTTER

4 servings

Lightly sweet green peas and peppery, crisp radishes pair perfectly with white miso and butter.

Mash together in a small bowl with a fork:

2 tablespoons butter, softened
2 tablespoons white miso

Set aside. Cut the green tops and any long roots from:

1 or 2 bunches radishes, well scrubbed (about 10 ounces)

Quarter any large radishes, halve them if smaller. In a large skillet over medium heat melt the miso-butter mixture. Arrange the radishes in the skillet, cut side down. Reduce the heat to medium-low and cook the radishes until their cut sides start to brown, about 10 minutes.

Once the radishes are browned and the miso mixture smells heavenly, increase the heat to medium-high. Add to the skillet:

12 ounces frozen or fresh green peas
Several grinds of black pepper

Cook, stirring, until the peas turn bright green, about 2 minutes. For some fresh peas you may need to add a splash of water or dry white wine, cover, and simmer for a few minutes, or until the peas are tender and cooked through. Serve with:

Chopped parsley
Lemon juice

ABOUT RUTABAGA

Rutabagas have pale yellow to purple skin, creamy or yellow flesh, and can reach the size of grapefruits. From the Swedish word meaning "root bag," they are also called **swedes, neeps** (our favorite), **yellow turnips,** and **turnip-rooted cabbage.** Popular in colder countries, they become sweet after the first frost.

Rutabaga will keep for several weeks, unwrapped, in a cool, dry place or in the refrigerator. Sometimes, they are coated with food-grade wax to increase shelf life. The wax and tough skin can be stripped off with a vegetable peeler, though it may be necessary to go over the same spot several times to expose the flesh of the vegetable. Alternatively, the vegetable can be halved, placed cut side down on a work surface, and peeled with a knife.

➤ Cook rutabagas as for turnips, 283, though some may take longer to become tender. Their sweet, peppery flesh pairs well with butter, cream, bacon, lemon, sage, and thyme. When mashed with potatoes, the British affectionately call the result **Neeps and Tatties.** Rutabagas may be peeled, grated, and added to potatoes to make Latkes, 269. Or substitute rutabagas for half of the potatoes in Potato Leek Soup, 104, or cook and puree as for Cream of Cauliflower or Broccoli Soup, 109.

ABOUT SALSIFY AND SCORZONERA

There are two roots referred to as salsify. Both are in the lettuce family, and related to sunchokes, 277, and burdock, 223. **White salsify,** or **oyster plant,** resembles a large beige carrot covered with tiny rootlets; and **black salsify,** or **scorzonera,** is a long, thin, dark-skinned root that looks much like burdock. Both types are almost identical in texture and flavor, with white to cream-colored flesh that tastes subtly of artichokes and (supposedly) oysters, as their alternate name implies.

Select only firm, unblemished roots, and store in an open plastic bag in the refrigerator crisper. To avoid discoloration, put peeled or cut pieces in acidulated water, 951.

Peeled, cooked salsify can be mashed with butter, salt, pepper, and a pinch of mace or nutmeg (see Root Vegetable Puree, 203). Larger chunks may be roasted or glazed as for carrots, 228, scattered under roasting poultry with new potatoes and carrots, or cooked as below until crisp-tender and sautéed in butter until browned. Smaller chunks or cubes of salsify can be thrown into stews, chowders, and braises, or cooked through and pureed as for Cream of Cauliflower or Broccoli Soup, 109. Cooked salsify may also be used in a gratin (see Parsnip-Cheese Gratin, 258).

SALSIFY WITH HERBS

4 servings

Bring to a boil in a medium saucepan:

8 cups water
2 tablespoons lemon juice or distilled white vinegar
1 teaspoon salt

Peel and cut into 3-inch lengths:

2 pounds salsify

Add to the boiling water. Return the mixture to a boil, reduce the heat to maintain a brisk simmer, and cook, uncovered, until the salsify is tender when pierced with a knife, 10 to 20 minutes. Drain and toss immediately with:

¼ cup extra-virgin olive oil, melted butter, or Brown Butter, 558
¼ cup chopped parsley or 2 tablespoons chopped tarragon
(¼ cup chopped toasted, 1005, hazelnuts)
(1 tablespoon minced chives)
Lemon juice or white wine vinegar to taste

SHALLOTS

See About Onions and Shallots, 254.

SPINACH

See About Greens for Cooking, 242.

ABOUT SQUASHES

Squashes are members of the gourd family (*Cucurbitaceae*), along with melons and cucumbers. We distinguish them from other parts of this family for two reasons: They are less sweet than melons, and we typically prefer them cooked—though many are perfectly edible in their raw state (see Wheat Salad with Pesto and Zucchini, 131). Squashes are divided into two categories: summer squash and winter squash. Summer squash are best harvested young, when their flesh is juicy and tender; winter squash are best picked in autumn when their flesh is dense and fully matured (they store well all winter long, hence their name). We often call for specific varieties in the recipes that follow, but different types of summer squash are generally interchangeable, as are winter varieties, as long as they are of an equal size or cut into similar shapes.

Summer squash are usually very mild and have thin skin. As anyone who has cooked them can attest, they contain a lot of water. The **zucchini,** a year-round fixture in supermarkets, has many relatives, like the slender Italian **cocozelle,** and the Middle Eastern **cousa. Pattypan squash** are shaped like 2- to 5-inch diameter spinning tops with scalloped edges. **Yellow crooknecks** are bright yellow, with bumpy skin and slender curved necks. Zucchini and pattypan varieties are often available as **baby squash** at farmers' markets, and are delectable roasted, sautéed, or grilled whole.

All summer squashes should be firm to the touch and heavy for their size. Unless the squash is to be stuffed, always choose smaller specimens. If they are young, there is no need to peel them. Avoid any that have tough or wrinkled skin or black stems. Use within a few days of purchase.

Winter squash varieties are available in the market from fall to early spring, although due to their popularity, some varieties may be found year-round in supermarkets. The most common varieties are the dark green or orange **acorn;** the long, orange-fleshed **butternut;** and the **spaghetti squash,** with its yellow, noodle-like fibers. Most of the other available winter squash—**banana, kabocha, Hubbard, buttercup** or **turban, Cushaw,** and **delicata**—have soft, sweet, rich flesh suggestive of butternut squash or pumpkin. **Pumpkin** is the name given to winter squash with round shapes and orange flesh. Though many Americans think of this squash first as pie, 680, and next as soup, 105, it is as versatile a vegetable as any other winter squash.

Except for delicatas, winter squashes have very tough skins; any that do not feel firm should be avoided (watery spots indicate decay). Store whole squash unwrapped in a cool, dark, dry place for a month or longer (thin-skinned delicatas should be used within a few weeks of purchase). Winter squash may also be cooked, mashed, 276, and frozen in bags for many months.

There are a few unruly squashes that do not fit the summer-winter mold, in one way or another. The pear-shaped, pale to dark green **chayote squash,** also called **mirliton** and **christophene,** has a much firmer and finer texture than other summer squash, and requires slightly longer cooking. Most have smooth skin with deep, lengthwise ridges, though you may also find them covered in prickly spines. The chayote's single, large seed is unique among squashes; you may remove it or cook it with the squash (it is edible and delicious). Chayote can be stored successfully for a week or more in a plastic bag in the refrigerator crisper.

Another green, ridged contrarian—the **bitter melon**—has the texture of a summer squash but is harvested in late fall through winter. Depending on the variety, the ridges may be small and smooth or pronounced and jagged. Choose solid green specimens without a hint of yellowing. Bitter melon may be cooked in the same ways as other summer squash, though its characteristic bitterness should be complemented by other strong flavors. They are used in China, India, and Southeast Asia in stir-fries, curries, pickles, and stews. **Winter melon**—though it outwardly resembles winter squash with its thick, inedible green skin—is harvested in summer and has firm, cucumber-like flesh that is favored in soups, 86. Despite their "melon" names, these gourds are not sweet, nor served raw.

To prepare summer squash, wash and cut into pieces. If the squash is very tender or small, it may be left whole. To turn summer squash into a noodle-like dish, see Spaghetti Squash and Squash Noodles, 276.

To prepare chayote, remove the skin with a vegetable peeler (or a knife if the chayote is spiny)—unless you plan to stuff and bake them, 275. Halve them, remove the seed, and slice or cube as desired.

To prepare winter squash, scrub the squash. If baking whole or in pieces, leave the skin on. For all other cooking techniques, halve the squash, or cut into pieces if very large, before peeling it. Cutting into the thick hard skin and firm flesh of winter squash can be difficult. We prefer to use a strong, sharp knife; others prefer a serrated blade. Set the squash on a thick towel so it does not roll around and cut slowly and deliberately. If using a serrated knife, start sawing through the skin slowly and without exerting much downward pressure. Once your cut into the squash is 1 inch deep, you may proceed with a bit more pressure as you saw through the remaining flesh. If using a straight-edged knife, puncture the squash in the center with the tip of the blade and carefully push it in. Once there is no chance of the knife slipping out of your incision, push it in the rest of the way and try to pull the handle downward and split the flesh. If necessary, lift the knife out and start again from the other side. Remove the seeds and strings, and peel with a vegetable peeler or a paring knife. Cut the squash into chunks, cubes, or slices.

Because squash is subtly flavored, it benefits from imaginative treatment. They may be cut lengthwise, scooped out into "boats," and filled with well-seasoned cargo; or roasted or sautéed over high heat to add depth and texture. All squash are excellent with butter, cream, garlic, tangy and salty cheeses, thyme, sage, pork, and toasted nuts (or the seeds they contain). Winter squash are often baked, mashed, added to soups, stews, gratins, and savory tarts, or combined with other vegetables in purees. Chayotes may be stuffed and baked like winter squashes, cubed and cooked in soups and stews, or cubed, steamed, and seasoned. Summer squashes go well with summery flavors, especially tomatoes, onions, peppers, garlic, and fresh herbs such as oregano, parsley, and basil.

To roast winter squash seeds, see 47.

To turn squash into noodles, see 276.

To steam summer squash, slice or cube them and add to a steamer basket. Place the basket in a pot or saucepan with 1 inch of water in the bottom. Bring the water to a boil, cover the pan, and cook until tender, about 5 minutes for zucchini slices and 15 minutes for chayote slices.

To microwave a whole acorn squash, pierce in 4 or 5 places with a sharp knife. Place on a paper towel and cook on high until tender, 7 to 10 minutes, turning the squash after 4 minutes. Let stand for 5 minutes before cutting. To microwave spaghetti squash, see 276.

Pressure-cook 1-inch cubes or slices of winter squash with 1 inch water for 5 minutes at 15 psi. Quick release the pressure, 1059. Summer squash is too delicate for a pressure cooker.

SAUTÉED SUMMER SQUASH

4 servings

Cut into ½-inch pieces:

1½ pounds summer squash (about 3 medium)

Heat in a large skillet over medium-high heat until it shimmers:

2 tablespoons vegetable oil

Add the squash along with:

½ teaspoon salt

Sauté, stirring occasionally, until browned and tender, about 7 minutes. Stir in:

3 green onions, thinly sliced
½ teaspoon black pepper, or to taste

Cook for another minute or so and transfer to a serving bowl or plates, sprinkling with:

Lemon juice to taste

SUMMER SQUASH CASSEROLE

6 servings

Our biggest beef with casseroles is that they make lots of dirty dishes. We modified our old recipe so that now the squash is "steamed" in the skillet with the onion and garlic, meaning one less pan to clean. We've kept the seasonings simple here, but feel free to add chopped thyme and parsley or spice blends like curry powder to liven things up.

Preheat the oven to 350°F. Lightly butter a 2-quart baking dish.

Heat in a large skillet over medium-high heat:

2 tablespoons butter or olive oil

Add and cook, stirring, until softened and golden, about 7 minutes:

1 small onion, finely diced
(1 to 2 jalapeño peppers, to taste, seeded and diced)

Add:

1½ to 2 pounds summer squash, cut into ½-inch cubes
2 garlic cloves, minced
2 tablespoons stock, dry white wine, dry vermouth, or water

Cover the skillet and cook until the squash is crisp-tender, 7 to 9 minutes. Uncover and allow any excess liquid to cook off. Transfer to a medium bowl and let cool for 5 minutes. Stir in:

1 cup grated Cheddar, Monterey Jack, or Swiss cheese (4 ounces)
⅓ cup sour cream or heavy cream
2 large eggs, beaten
(2 tablespoons grated Parmesan)
(¼ teaspoon cayenne pepper)
½ teaspoon salt
Black or white pepper to taste

Spread the squash mixture into the prepared baking dish. Combine in a small bowl and sprinkle over the top:

½ cup dry bread crumbs, panko, or cracker crumbs
½ teaspoon paprika (sweet or smoked)

Dot with:

1 tablespoon butter, cut into small pieces

Bake until bubbling and golden, about 35 minutes.

BAKED STUFFED ZUCCHINI

2 to 4 servings

Preheat the oven to 400°F. Halve lengthwise:

4 medium zucchini (about 1½ pounds)

Scoop the pulp into a kitchen towel, leaving ½-inch-thick shells. Squeeze the moisture from the pulp and set aside.

Melt in a small skillet over medium-high heat:

2 tablespoons butter

Add and cook, stirring, until golden, about 7 minutes:

¼ cup finely chopped onion

Reduce the heat to medium and add the squash pulp along with:

2 garlic cloves, minced

Cook, stirring, for another 2 minutes. Transfer the mixture to a bowl and add:

½ cup dry or fresh bread crumbs, 957
½ cup grated Parmesan (2 ounces)
¼ cup finely chopped parsley, basil, tarragon, or a combination

1 large egg, beaten
½ teaspoon salt
¼ teaspoon black pepper

Mix the filling well and spoon it into the hollowed-out zucchini. Place in a baking dish and sprinkle the tops with:

Grated Parmesan

Bake until tender, 20 to 25 minutes, depending on their size.

LOUISIANA-STYLE CHAYOTE

6 servings

This piquant, ham-and-shrimp-studded filling will work with large zucchini as well. For zucchini, simply skip the boiling step and bake as described, 274. If desired, substitute **3 ounces cooked crabmeat or crawfish tails** for the shrimp.

Boil in salted water to cover until tender but firm, 6 to 10 minutes:

3 chayotes, halved and pitted

Drain and set upside down on a rack to cool. Scoop out the insides, leaving roughly ⅜-inch-thick shells. Pat the shells dry and place in a 13 × 9-inch baking dish. Chop the pulp.

Preheat the oven to 375°F.

Heat in a large nonstick skillet over medium-high heat:

1 tablespoon vegetable oil

Add and cook, turning once, until bright pink, about 2 minutes:

6 large shrimp (about 3 ounces), peeled and deveined

Remove the shrimp and let cool. Add the squash pulp to the skillet along with:

⅓ cup finely diced red bell pepper
⅓ cup chopped parsley
¼ cup finely diced ham
1 green onion, chopped
1 garlic clove, minced
1 teaspoon chopped fresh thyme or ¼ teaspoon dried thyme
Salt and black pepper to taste
Pinch of cayenne pepper

Cook, stirring, until the vegetables are softened, about 4 minutes. Meanwhile, finely chop the shrimp. Remove the filling from the heat and stir in the shrimp. Divide among the squash shells and sprinkle with:

¼ cup dry bread crumbs
2 tablespoons butter, cut into small pieces

Bake until heated through and browned on top, about 35 minutes.

ZUCCHINI FANS

4 servings

When Megan was little, her mother made these regularly, perhaps as an inducement for the children to eat their green vegetables. With their striking fan-shaped look and crunchy, cheesy topping, these zucchini are irresistible to children and adults.

Preheat the oven to 400°F. Oil a large baking sheet. Wash and dry:

1 pound baby zucchini or small zucchini (no longer than 6 inches)

Starting at the blossom end, make thin, lengthwise slices in the zucchini, being careful not to cut through the stem end, leaving it intact so the slices stay together. Gently fan the slices out; some of them may tear a bit at the stem end (no one will know but you). Lay the fanned zucchini on the baking sheet.

Combine in a bowl:

½ cup buttery cracker crumbs or panko
¼ cup grated Romano or Parmesan
½ teaspoon smoked paprika
¼ teaspoon black pepper
¼ teaspoon salt

Sprinkle the crumb mixture evenly over the zucchini. Scatter or drizzle over the top:

2 tablespoons butter, cut into small pieces, or olive oil

Bake until tender, 15 to 25 minutes, depending on the size of the zucchini.

BAKED OR ROASTED WINTER SQUASH

I. WHOLE

Preheat the oven to 375°F.

Scrub:

Acorn squash or other small winter squash

Deeply pierce each squash in 4 or 5 places with a knife. Set in a baking dish or on a rimmed baking sheet. Bake until the flesh is tender when pierced with a thin knife, 45 minutes to 1½ hours, depending on the size and type.

Halve through the stem end, scoop out the seeds and strings, and serve with:

Butter
Salt and black pepper
Finely chopped herbs such as chives, oregano, and thyme, or fried sage leaves, 1013

II. LARGE PIECES

Preheat the oven to 375°F.

Halve, quarter, or cut into slabs:

Large winter squash

Remove any seeds and strings. Arrange the squash cut side up in a baking pan. Add ¼ inch water to the pan and cover with foil. Bake until the squash is tender when pierced with a thin knife, 30 to 45 minutes. Halfway through baking, if desired, uncover the pan and brush the squash with:

(Butter or vegetable oil)

and sprinkle with one of the following:

(Brown sugar and nutmeg or another spice)
(Grated Parmesan and smoked paprika)

Serve in the shell, cut into chunks, or mashed.

III. SLICES AND SMALL CHUNKS

Preheat the oven to 400°F.

Peel (except for delicata squash), seed, and cut into ½-inch chunks or slices:

Any winter squash

Toss on a large baking sheet with:

Olive or vegetable oil
Salt and black pepper to taste

Roast until the squash is tender and golden brown, 25 to 30 minutes.

MASHED WINTER SQUASH

On average, 1 pound untrimmed squash yields a generous 13 ounces edible flesh or 1¾ cups cooked puree.
Prepare:

Baked or Roasted Winter Squash I or II, 275

Scrape the squash from the skin and mash the pulp with a fork or potato masher. For each 1 cup mashed squash, add:

1 tablespoon butter
¼ teaspoon salt

Mix in enough:

Warm heavy cream

to make a soft, smooth puree. Serve plain, or, for a sweeter dish, season as for Mashed Sweet Potatoes, 278. For savory embellishments, see Additions to Mashed Potatoes, 265.

BAKED BUTTERNUT SQUASH STUFFED WITH SAUSAGE AND APPLES

4 servings

Preheat the oven to 375°F. Grease a baking dish large enough to hold the squash comfortably. Halve lengthwise and remove the seeds and strings from:

2 butternut squash (about 1 pound each)

Arrange cut side up in the baking dish and brush with:

1 tablespoon vegetable oil

Cover with a lid or foil and bake until almost tender, 30 to 40 minutes. Remove from the oven and let the squash cool slightly. Keep the oven on.
Prepare:

½ recipe Basic Bread Stuffing or Dressing, 532, made with sausage and apples

When the squash has cooled, scoop out most of the flesh, leaving ⅜-inch-thick shells. Lightly mix the squash pulp into the stuffing mixture, breaking up the squash as little as possible.
Pile the stuffing into the squash halves. Dot each half with:

1 tablespoon butter, cut into small pieces
1 tablespoon dark brown sugar

Bake, uncovered, until piping hot and browned and crusty on top, 20 to 25 minutes. Let cool for several minutes before serving.

PUMPKIN CURRY

4 to 6 servings

Here the sweetness of winter squash is balanced with the pungent, spicy, and herbaceous flavors of Thai curry. For a hearty soup, simply puree after seasoning and thin with stock or water as needed.
Have ready:

1 small pumpkin or medium winter squash (about 1½ pounds), such as butternut, peeled and cut into 1-inch pieces

Heat in a large skillet over medium heat:

2 tablespoons vegetable oil

Add and cook, stirring, until tender, about 5 minutes:

1 small onion, thinly sliced
1 red bell pepper, thinly sliced

Add and cook, stirring, until fragrant:

4 garlic cloves, minced
2 tablespoons red or green Thai curry paste, store-bought or homemade, 585
1-inch piece ginger, peeled and minced
(2 Thai or serrano chiles, seeded and minced)
½ teaspoon salt

Add the pumpkin or squash along with:

One 13½-ounce can coconut milk

Bring to a simmer, cover, reduce the heat, and simmer until the pumpkin or squash is tender, about 20 minutes. Add:

1 to 2 tablespoons fish sauce to taste
1 tablespoon brown sugar or coconut sugar
1 tablespoon lime juice, or to taste

Serve over:

Hot cooked rice, 343

Garnish with:

Chopped cilantro or Thai basil
Thinly sliced shallots

ABOUT SPAGHETTI SQUASH AND SQUASH NOODLES

Before you begin the process of making squash noodles, keep your expectations realistic: Squash noodles will not be as hearty or toothsome as their starchy namesake. There are two ways to turn squash into noodles. First, you may use a **spiral slicer (spiralizer)** or a **julienne peeler** to efficiently turn squashes into thin strips. Many types of squash can be treated in this way, from whole zucchini, to peeled and seeded chunks of butternut and pumpkin-type squashes. You may even find squash noodles at your local grocery store. Raw summer squash noodles may be used in salad (Wheat Salad with Pesto and Zucchini, 131) and as a substitute in cold-noodle dishes like Sesame Noodles, 302. Or use them in pan-fried noodle dishes such as Pad Thai, 303, or Chow Mein, 301. Summer squash noodles need only the briefest cooking in a hot pan with a little oil. Add minced garlic, spices, or herbs to liven them up. Winter squash noodles are more resilient and have a firmer texture. ➤ Squash noodles may be tossed with salt (about ½ teaspoon per pound) in a colander and left to drain for 30 minutes to firm them up and help them keep their texture during cooking.

The second option is to buy **spaghetti squash.** The long fibers of this winter squash really do resemble spaghetti when cooked, and can be used as a stand-in for pasta. ➤ For the longest strands, cut open spaghetti squash crosswise.

To bake spaghetti squash, halve it crosswise, remove the seeds and strings, lightly rub the squash with oil, and bake, cut side down, in a 375°F oven until completely tender. Turn the cooked squash over and use a fork to tease apart the strands.

To microwave spaghetti squash, pierce with a knife tip in several places, place it on the turntable, and cook on high until tender when pressed with your fingers, about 15 minutes, turning every 5 minutes. Let cool for 10 minutes before cutting the squash. Halve the cooked squash crosswise and remove the seeds and strings, then scrape the strands into a bowl, separating them with a fork. We prefer to treat the resulting noodles as for Fettuccine with Butter and Cheese, 295, or Spaghetti Carbonara, 295.

ABOUT SQUASH BLOSSOMS

Female blossoms produce squash, but male flowers (which outnumber them) do not and so are ideal for eating. Squash blossoms have a wonderful, delicate flavor. They are available during the summer months at farmers' markets, and occasionally at specialty markets and Latino grocery stores. If picking yourself, be sure the flowers are unsprayed. Blossoms can be harvested after they close and drop, but it is preferable to pick them off the plant while still fresh.

Do not wash unless the blossoms are dusty. Remove the stem and calyx—the outer green cap where the flower connects to the stem—if they seem tough. Remove the pistils if stuffing and inspect for insects. Squash blossoms should be used promptly; they can be kept in a closed storage container in the refrigerator for a day if necessary.

Squash blossoms are often stuffed with soft cheese like ricotta or fresh goat cheese. They can be chopped or julienned and added to frittatas, tossed with pasta, or used as a garnish for Corn Chowder, 88. Briefly sauté in butter or olive oil with a little minced garlic and herbs and serve as a side dish, fold into Savory Crêpes, 646, or add to the filling for Quesadillas, 57.

SQUASH BLOSSOMS STUFFED WITH CHEESE AND HERBS

4 servings

Serve these with a light tomato sauce, 556–58, beneath them. ***To bake,*** leave the stuffed blossoms uncoated, lay them side by side in a greased baking dish, and place in a 350°F oven until heated through, about 20 minutes.

Remove the pistils, leaving the stems on:

12 large squash blossoms

Combine in a small bowl:

¾ cup fresh goat cheese, ricotta, or shredded mozzarella or Monterey Jack (3 ounces)
½ cup grated Parmesan (2 ounces)
1 tablespoon chopped parsley
1 tablespoon chopped basil or 2 teaspoons chopped thyme
1 garlic clove, minced
¼ teaspoon salt
Black pepper to taste

Carefully open the petals of each blossom and stuff with about 1 tablespoon of the mixture. Twist the tops of the petals together. Dip the blossoms one at a time into:

1 large egg, lightly beaten

Then coat with:

Flour

Shake off any excess. Heat in a medium skillet over medium heat:

½ inch olive oil

Fry the blossoms 3 or 4 at a time, turning occasionally, until golden, 2 to 4 minutes. Drain briefly on paper towels. Serve right away.

ABOUT SUNCHOKES (JERUSALEM ARTICHOKES)

"Jerusalem artichoke" should win a prize in the misnomer sweepstakes. It is not even a thistle, like the true artichoke, but the tuber of a sunflower; and "Jerusalem" is likely a corruption of the Italian *girasole*, or "turn-to-the-sun," as sunflowers are obliged to do.

When purchasing sunchokes, select tubers with tight-fitting skins of uniform color that are firm and free of discoloration or mold. Store in an open plastic bag in the refrigerator crisper. Sunchokes can be sliced very thin and eaten raw in a salad, but we do not recommend it; these tubers are rich in inulin, an indigestible fiber that—unless subjected to prolonged cooking—may give you gastrointestinal discomfort.

When cut, the flesh of sunchokes discolors quickly. Toss slices with an acidic dressing immediately if you plan to serve them in a salad, or keep in acidulated water, 951, for up to 30 minutes before cooking.

Like potatoes and other root vegetables, sunchokes are quite tasty when sliced thin and fried into chips, 48; roasted, below; mashed or pureed (Root Vegetable Puree, 203); or glazed like carrots, 228. They are especially good with lemon, butter, cream, garlic, and tarragon.

Pressure-cook peeled and halved sunchokes with 1 cup water at 15 psi for 10 minutes. Use the quick release method, 1059.

SUNCHOKES IN GARLIC BUTTER

6 servings

Wash, peel, and cut into 1-inch pieces:

1½ pounds sunchokes

Steam, 1056, or boil in well-salted water until tender. Test with a fork after 15 minutes. Drain.

Meanwhile, melt in a small skillet:

3 tablespoons butter

Add and cook until fragrant but not browned:

2 garlic cloves, minced

Add the drained sunchokes and stir to coat in the butter. Remove from the heat and stir in:

2 tablespoons chopped parsley
1 tablespoon lemon juice
Salt and black pepper to taste

CRISPY ROASTED SUNCHOKES

4 servings

We've enjoyed sunchokes prepared in just about every way imaginable—sliced paper thin and served raw, pureed into soup, braised—but our favorite way to serve them is roasted, and, taking a cue from the Brits, served with a few dashes of malt vinegar.

Preheat the oven to 400°F. Halve lengthwise:

1 pound sunchokes, well scrubbed

The large, nubby slices should be around ½ inch thick. If the sunchokes are very large, cut them accordingly. Toss the sunchokes on a large rimmed baking sheet with:

2 tablespoons olive oil
(1 tablespoon thyme leaves or minced rosemary)
½ teaspoon salt
½ teaspoon black pepper

Arrange the sunchokes in a single layer cut side down, and roast until golden brown and tender, about 45 minutes. Serve with:

Malt vinegar

ABOUT SWEET POTATOES AND YAMS

Potatoes are botanically unrelated to sweet potatoes. The confusion began long ago: "Potato" is derived from the Taíno word for "sweet potato." The Spanish (and other European diners) had been familiar with sweet potatoes by that name for many years, and, decades later, when they first encountered the tubers we now know as potatoes, they misapplied the old name, which has stuck to the less-sweet impostor ever since. To make matters more confusing, the sweeter, moister, orange-fleshed varieties of sweet potato are often sold as yams (see below), another vegetable with which the sweet potato shares no common ancestor. Regardless of these naming difficulties, sweet potatoes are easy to love: European colonizers and traders took this resilient and nutritious tuber with them to Africa and East Asia (sweet potatoes mysteriously made their way to Polynesia and New Zealand much earlier). They are now grown as a staple food crop wherever the climate permits.

There are two basic categories of sweet potato: those with soft, moist, sweet flesh and those with firm, starchy flesh. Starchy varieties of sweet potato are preferred in much of the world. The red-skinned, pale-fleshed **boniato** varieties are typically the driest and least sweet, and are best cooked as for French Fries, 270, or baked whole (see Baked Potatoes, 265). **Japanese** or **kotobuki sweet potatoes** have reddish-brown skin, firm flesh, and a mild sweetness. The white-fleshed **Hannah** variety turns yellow when cooked, and **Okinawan sweet potatoes** are a vibrant, bright purple inside; both are quite firm, but also very sweet.

Soft, moist sweet potato varieties are the holiday favorite, perfect for casseroles and pies. Orange-fleshed **Beauregard, Covington, Carolina Ruby, Jewel,** and **Garnet** varieties have brown to reddish-purple skin; other varieties, such as **O'Henry, Nancy Hall,** and **Jersey yellow** are tan and have yellow or pale, creamy flesh. Orange-fleshed types—especially the thin-skinned Jewels and Garnets—are often labeled as yams; canned sweet potatoes are also commonly sold as yams. Unlike the poisonous vines of the potato, **sweet potato greens** are perfectly edible; cook fresh-looking leaves and thinner stems as for other tender greens, 242.

Yams, as noted earlier, are an unrelated family of tubers with crisp, pale to purple flesh. Like potatoes and sweet potatoes, some yam varieties are starchier than others. Most yellow and white varieties can be treated like potatoes. Sweet and moist, **purple** or **ube yams** are often used in desserts and ice creams. Other starchy types are used to make noodles, such as those used for Japchae, 304. When shredded or pureed, some varieties can become very sticky. **Nagaimo,** or **Japanese mountain yam**—a long, slender variety with hairy, pale skin—is shredded and added as a binding agent to Okonomiyaki, 226. Aside from this mucilaginous variety, which can be eaten raw, ➤ all yams must be peeled and cooked, as many contain a skin irritant that dissipates once cooked.

Choose sweet potatoes and yams that are firm, heavy for their size, and free of soft spots, cracks, discoloration, or mold. Store in a cool, well-ventilated, dark, and dry place. Sweet potatoes keep their color once cut, but yams will begin to turn brown. Some sweet potatoes have thin, delectable skin worth saving. Other specimens have thick skin, and sometimes a fibrous layer underneath. We recommend peeling these before or after cooking, as well as all yams. When peeling or cutting yams, avoid possible skin irritation by wearing gloves.

Sweet potatoes, especially the drier, starchier ones, lend themselves to most of the cooking methods used for potatoes. Unlike potatoes, ➤ gentler heat and longer cooking times make sweet potatoes sweeter. Many love to pair the sweet, orange-fleshed varieties with other sweet or dessert-oriented ingredients like orange, pineapple, apple, pecans, cinnamon, nutmeg, brown sugar, or marshmallows. For our taste, sweet potatoes have enough sugar, and we prefer to balance their sweetness with chiles, cilantro, green onions, Parmesan, garlic, lemon, lime, white miso, and coconut milk. Yams tend to be much blander than most sweet potatoes and are therefore adaptable to most seasonings.

To microwave, pierce as many as 4 whole medium sweet potatoes in several places each. Place on a paper towel on the turntable in a spoke pattern. Cook on high until tender, 5 to 9 minutes for 2 sweet potatoes, 10 to 13 minutes for 4 sweet potatoes, turning them over and rearranging after 5 minutes. Cover with a towel and let stand for 5 minutes.

To boil sweet potatoes, scrub them and leave whole or cut into 1-inch-thick pieces for quicker cooking. Transfer to a pot, cover with water, and bring to a boil over high heat. Reduce the heat to maintain a brisk simmer, and cook until tender, about 10 minutes for pieces and 25 to 35 minutes for whole sweet potatoes.

To bake sweet potatoes, preheat the oven to 400°F. Pierce scrubbed and dried sweet potatoes several times with a knife. Bake directly on the oven rack, with a baking sheet on the rack below to catch drips, until very soft, 45 minutes to 1 hour.

Pressure-cook whole large sweet potatoes with 1 inch of water at 15 psi for 15 minutes. Use the quick release method, 951.

MASHED SWEET POTATOES

4 to 6 servings

Boil or bake, above, until thoroughly tender:

2 pounds sweet potatoes, scrubbed

Let stand until cool enough to handle. Remove the skins, then mash, rice, or put through a food mill into a bowl. Add:

4 tablespoons butter, softened, or to taste
Salt to taste

Thin with:

Warm heavy cream or orange juice

For a savory dish, see Additions to Mashed Potatoes, 265. For a sweeter dish, season with any of the following:

½ cup chopped pineapple, or to taste
½ cup chopped pecans or ¼ cup chopped black walnuts, toasted, 1005
3 tablespoons diced candied ginger or ½ teaspoon ground ginger
2 tablespoons brown sugar
1 tablespoon bourbon or dry sherry
1 teaspoon finely grated orange or lemon zest
Pinch of ground cloves or ½ teaspoon ground cinnamon

Beat the potatoes with a fork, whisk, or electric mixer until light. Serve immediately, or reheat at serving time at 375°F in a buttered baking dish.

SWEET POTATO PUDDING

12 to 15 servings

This decadent casserole is Megan's grandmother's recipe. It is served as a side dish on holidays, but could almost be considered dessert.

Preheat the oven to 350°F. Combine in a medium bowl:

4 cups mashed sweet potatoes (from about 3 pounds sweet potatoes)
½ cup packed brown sugar
½ cup half-and-half or heavy cream
4 tablespoons butter, melted
2 large eggs
1 teaspoon ground cinnamon
1 teaspoon vanilla
½ teaspoon salt

Spread the mixture in a 9-inch square baking dish. In another bowl, combine:

½ cup packed brown sugar
½ cup chopped pecans
½ cup shredded coconut
⅓ cup all-purpose flour
4 tablespoons butter, melted

Sprinkle this mixture on top of the sweet potatoes. Bake until browned on top, about 1 hour. Let cool slightly before serving.

TWICE-BAKED SWEET POTATOES

6 servings

For a different flavor profile, top these with lots of butter, some brown sugar, nutmeg, and pecans or black walnuts, and replace the sherry with bourbon or 1 teaspoon vanilla. Marshmallows may be substituted for the bread crumb and butter topping.

Bake until tender, 278:

3 large sweet potatoes, scrubbed

Reduce the oven temperature to 375°F. Halve the sweet potatoes lengthwise and scrape most of the pulp into a bowl, leaving ¼-inch shells. For a savory dish, season the pulp as for Twice-Baked Potatoes, 267. For a sweet dish, mix in any of the suggestions in Mashed Sweet Potatoes, 278, or add the following:

2 tablespoons butter, softened
¼ cup heavy cream, warmed
½ teaspoon salt
(2 tablespoons dry sherry)

Beat with a fork until fluffy. Fill the shells and place on a baking sheet. If desired, cover the tops with:

(Au Gratin II, 958)

Bake the sweet potatoes until browned, about 20 minutes.

CANDIED SWEET POTATOES

4 servings

Boil, 278, until nearly tender:

5 medium sweet potatoes

Meanwhile, preheat the oven to 375°F. Grease a 13 × 9-inch baking dish.

Drain the sweet potatoes, peel, and cut lengthwise into ½-inch-thick slabs. Place in the baking dish and season to taste with:

Salt

Sprinkle with:

¾ cup packed brown sugar
1½ tablespoons lemon juice
½ teaspoon ground ginger
(Finely grated zest of 1 lemon)

Dot with:

2 tablespoons butter

Bake, uncovered, until glazed, about 20 minutes.

SWEET POTATO FRIES

4 servings

Do not judge these fries by potato standards; sweet potatoes do not have as much starch, and will never be as crisp. Sweet, moist, orange varieties can be used here, as well as the starchier boniato sweet potatoes (which will yield crispier, fry-like results). To oven-fry, see Oven "French-Fried" Potatoes, 271. Please read about Deep-Frying, 1051.

Cut into long ⅜-inch-thick batons, 201:

4 large sweet potatoes, scrubbed and peeled, if desired

Heat to 365°F in a deep-fryer, deep heavy pot, or Dutch oven:

3 inches vegetable oil

Deep-fry the sweet potatoes in batches until golden brown. Drain on paper towels. Sprinkle to taste with:

Salt

To serve, see Additions to French Fries, 271.

SWEET POTATO STEW WITH PEANUTS

6 servings

Heat in a large heavy saucepan over medium heat:

¼ cup vegetable oil

Add and cook, stirring, until the vegetables are tender but not browned, 7 to 10 minutes:

1 large onion, chopped
1 red bell pepper, chopped
1 jalapeño or serrano pepper, seeded and chopped

Add and cook, stirring, 1 minute more:

4 garlic cloves, minced
1-inch piece ginger, peeled and minced
1 tablespoon chili powder
1 teaspoon ground cumin
½ teaspoon red pepper flakes

Add, along with enough water to barely cover the vegetables:

1½ pounds sweet potatoes (about 2 medium), peeled and cut into 1-inch pieces

Bring to a boil, then reduce the heat, cover, and simmer, stirring occasionally, until the sweet potatoes are just tender, 30 to 35 minutes. Add:

2 small zucchini (1 inch in diameter), sliced

Cook for another 15 minutes. Place in a small bowl:

½ cup peanut butter (chunky or smooth)
⅓ cup tomato paste

Add 1 cup of the stewing liquid, stir until smooth, and stir the mixture into the stew. Simmer for another 15 minutes. Season to taste with:

Salt

Serve with:

Cooked jasmine or basmati rice, 343
Chopped cilantro
Chopped green onion
Lime wedges

ABOUT TARO

"Taro" is the Polynesian name we use to refer to a number of starchy tropical roots; true taro, also known as **dasheen** or **eddo,** is one widely grown type, as is American taro, usually referred to as **malanga** or **yautia.** Both types have been introduced to tropical areas across the world, thus there are many varieties of taro, and perhaps as many names. Despite this diversity, all are generally potato-like: starchy, mild, a bit sweet, with nutty and earthy overtones. ➤ Taro must be cooked. The most commonly available varieties have hairy brown skin and pale or lavender flesh—which becomes grayish or violet when cooked. The roots are used as a vegetable or as the base for puddings and confections. **Taro leaves** can be stewed as for Southern-Style Greens, 243; ➤ do not eat raw or barely cooked leaves.

Select firm roots with no soft spots, shriveling, or blemishes. You may bake taro roots in their jackets and peel afterward or remove the skin with a vegetable peeler before cutting and cooking. If handling raw, ➤ exposed taro flesh may prove irritating to the skin, so wear gloves.

Like potatoes, starchy taro flesh holds together well, and may be peeled, shredded on a box grater, and used to make Latkes, 269. Taro can also be thinly sliced and fried into chips, 48, or cut into cubes, cooked until tender, and pan-fried (see Pan-Fried Potatoes, 268).

To bake taro, remove loose fibers and parboil for 15 minutes, then leave whole or peel and cut into chunks. Bake at 375°F until tender.

To boil taro, peel, cut into 1-inch chunks, and place in a pot. Cover with cool water, bring to a boil over high heat, then reduce the heat and simmer until tender, 20 to 25 minutes. Drain.

POI

About 5 cups

This native Hawaiian dish tastes a little like sauerkraut but with a pureed, slightly gluey texture.

Boil, above:

2½ pounds taro roots, peeled and cut into 1-inch cubes

Mash in a large bowl with a potato masher until a starchy paste forms. Work in gradually with your hands:

2½ cups water

To remove lumps and fibers, force the poi through a fine-mesh sieve. Serve, seasoned with salt to taste, or let stand, covered, 2 to 3 days in a cool place until it ferments and has a sour taste.

ABOUT TOMATILLOS

Tomatillos resemble small tomatoes but are encased in papery husks, much like the closely related ground cherry, 196. Ranging from yellow to bright green to dark purple, they have dry flesh and small seeds, which are more numerous and crunchier than those of a tomato. They are pleasantly tart, and lend sprightliness to salsas, sauces, soups, and braises.

Tomatillos are available at most supermarkets year-round. Select fruits that are firm and fill their husks. Store them, unwashed and unhusked, loose in the refrigerator crisper—they will keep for weeks. To prepare, peel off the papery husks and rinse (the surface of tomatillos is sticky—this will dissipate with cooking).

Cooking—especially roasting—tomatillos intensifies their unique flavor and brings out their natural sweetness. They are sometimes left raw and pureed into salsas, but keep in mind that their high pectin content will make the sauce very thick—we prefer a combination of roasted and raw tomatillos in salsas (see Salsa Verde Cruda, 573). Tomatillos are most often paired with other Mexican staples, such as avocados, chiles, cilantro, lime, cumin, coriander, and the like. Their tanginess balances rich meats like pork shoulder (especially when used for Green Mole, 554) and adds interest to white-fleshed fish. See Green Posole, 323, Roasted Tomatillo Spinach Sauce, 555, and Chicken Chili Verde, 425.

To roast tomatillos, you may use a hot dry skillet and brown on all sides in the manner of chiles, 262, but it is much more convenient to arrange larger quantities of peeled tomatillos on a rimmed baking sheet and place directly under a hot broiler until they blister, darken, and soften on one side, 6 to 10 minutes.

ABOUT TOMATOES

Summer tomatoes are our most treasured garden delight—and perhaps our most fetishized vegetable (or fruit, if you are a nitpicky botanist). **Slicing** or **beefsteak tomatoes** grow to be the biggest. Their variation in size, shape, and color is truly remarkable. Some are round, red, and hybridized to be emoji-perfect; other heritage or "heirloom" breeds may have pronounced lobes or pleats. They may be bright yellow, orange, striped and green (like the **Green Zebra**), or darker and greenish-purple—like the celebrated **Cherokee Purple** and **Black Krim.** While some people use them in cooked preparations, we think they are best sliced and served on their own in a puddle of good olive oil, tossed into salads, or layered in sandwiches. In season, they are rich and juicy; out of season, they can be dry, with mealy flesh (see our method for improving them, 281).

Plum tomatoes are valued for their thick, meaty flesh, high acidity, and full flavor. They are the best type to make tomato paste and sauce with, which is why some refer to them as **sauce** or **paste tomatoes.** These last names, however, do little justice to their versatility: Plum tomatoes contribute body and tangy-sweet flavor to soups, stews, and other cooked dishes, as well as salsas and salads. The slender **Roma** is the most common plum tomato variety (of which **San Marzano** is the most prized), but other types of varying shapes and colors can be found at farmers' markets, such as the rounder **Amish paste** variety and the ribbed **Costoluto Genovese.**

Cherry, grape, and **pear tomatoes** are often just as juicy as slicers, despite their diminutive size and year-round availability. Like slicers, we prefer to use them raw in salads and salsas, though they may be roasted whole or added to simmered sauces. Generally, they are sweeter and more acidic than other types, especially varieties like the superlative, yellowish-orange **Sun Gold.**

Locally grown or garden tomatoes tend to be superior to those that have been shipped from far away because they are more likely to be picked when ripe. Pick tomatoes when their color has turned and they have softened a bit and become fragrant. Fruit of mature size but still green in color may be ripened on a windowsill but will lack some of the flavor of its vine-ripened counterparts. Immature small-sized tomatoes will not ripen satisfactorily after harvesting. **Green tomatoes** are most famously fried, 282, though they may also be used along with apples in Apple Pie, 670, or as a substitute for cabbage in Chow Chow, 925.

➤ ***To improve out-of-season slicing tomatoes,*** slice and marinate them for 30 minutes in a splash of oil and vinegar, a sprinkle of salt, and other seasonings, as desired. The oil and salt will soften them and draw out moisture, which makes them seem juicier; the acidity will perk up their flavor and highlight whatever natural sugars they possess. Marinated like this, all but the saddest tomato slices will be rendered acceptable for sandwiches or salads that do not depend too heavily on them.

When shopping for tomatoes, select firm specimens that feel heavy for their size. Scarring around the stem end is harmless but attached stems and leaves should look fresh. As noted on 280, plum, cherry, and grape tomatoes are tastier out of season than slicing tomatoes. Though those grown in hothouses continue to improve, we recommend approaching all slicing tomatoes with skepticism in wintertime. Do not be confused by the tomatoes marketed as "vine-ripened" and sold still connected to a portion of the vine. The tomatoes were harvested by snipping the vine while the tomatoes were still green and offer little added value. Store ripe tomatoes at room temperature for as long as 5 or 6 days in a single layer out of sunlight with the stem side down. If you can't consume them quickly enough and they continue to ripen, place them in the refrigerator and use as soon as possible, bringing them to room temperature before eating.

Whether fresh, canned, cooked, or as paste or sauce, the tomato weaves its way into innumerable dishes. From the simple BLT, 137, to complex, rich ragus, the tomato's acidity provides a perfect counterpoint to butter, olive oil, and rich meats. Its tangy sweetness can be enhanced with vinegar, citrus juice, or salty, piquant capers and olives. Peppers and eggplants, both distant relatives, are good companions, as are cucumbers and summer squash. Cheeses, both soft and aged, onions, garlic, and most fresh herbs are at home in tomato-focused dishes. For tomato-centric recipes besides those below, see About Tomato Sauces, 555, salsas, 573–74, vegetable salads, 127–28, Pappa al Pomodoro, 91, Tomato Soup, 105, Gazpacho, 107, Chilled Fresh Tomato Cream Soup, 110, Tomato Cobbler, 706, and Tomato-Ricotta Tart, 706. To preserve tomatoes, see the Guide to Canning Tomatoes and Tomatillos, 900, Tomato Ketchup, 931, and Smoky Tomato Jam, 914. For more on tomatoes as seasoning, and instructions on making tomato paste, see 1027.

In decades past, most cooking authorities considered the tomato's skin, juices, and seeds an impediment to their flavor and texture. As with so many other subjects, history has made fools of us. According to the latest science, much of a tomato's savory flavor resides in the gelatinous substance surrounding the seeds. Though tomato peels tend to become tough during cooking, they have high concentrations of lycopene, an antioxidant. Regardless of the skin's alleged nutritive value, we still peel tomatoes for canning and to rid sauces and soups of unwanted, tooth-festooning bits.

To peel tomatoes one at a time, cut an X in the skin on the bottom of each tomato. Lower one by one into a pot of boiling water for about 15 seconds. Lift them out with a slotted spoon and drop into a bowl of ice water to stop the cooking. Pull off the skin with the tip of a knife. If the skin sticks, return the tomato to the boiling water for another 10 seconds and repeat.

To peel a large quantity of tomatoes, freeze them on a baking sheet then let them thaw (the peels will slip right off). Or, for a quicker procedure, place in a single layer in a roasting pan and cover with boiling water. Wait until the tomatoes are cool, slip the skins off, and cut out the stems and any blemishes or green areas.

To seed tomatoes, slice them across the equator and squeeze them gently to eject excess juice and seeds. If you finely dice peeled and seeded tomato flesh, you have earned the right to call the result **Tomato Concassé,** a classic French preparation that can be used as a simple sauce or garnish for chicken and fish.

To halve many cherry, grape, or pear tomatoes at once, place the shallow lid of a plastic, quart-sized yogurt container upside down on a countertop. Place one even layer of cherry tomatoes in the lid, then sandwich them with another lid on the top. Apply light pressure to the top lid with one hand. Using a sharp (or serrated) knife, carefully saw horizontally (parallel to the countertop) through the tomatoes. Keep the hand holding the lid out of harm's way.

STEWED TOMATOES OR TOMATOES CREOLE

6 servings

This recipe has been in *Joy* since the beginning. Feel free to pare back the "Cajun holy trinity" in any way you like to make a more restrained pot of stewed tomatoes. Fresh, juicy slicing tomatoes will provide their own cooking liquid. For drier, meatier plum tomatoes, add ½ cup stock or water.

Melt in a large skillet over medium heat:

4 tablespoons butter

Add and cook, stirring, until softened:

1 large onion, chopped
1 large red or green bell pepper, chopped
2 celery ribs, chopped

Add:

2 pounds fresh tomatoes, peeled, 281, if desired, and sliced, halved, or coarsely chopped, or one 28-ounce can whole tomatoes
(4 garlic cloves, minced)
2 teaspoons brown sugar
¾ teaspoon salt

(¾ teaspoon curry powder)
¼ teaspoon sweet paprika

Bring to a simmer over high heat then reduce the heat slightly to keep the mixture bubbling briskly. Cook, stirring occasionally, until tender, 15 to 20 minutes. If desired, add:

(¼ cup heavy cream)

The tomatoes may be thickened with:

(¼ cup dry bread crumbs)

Simmer briefly, until thick and smooth. Taste and add more salt and pepper if needed. Serve hot on:

Toast, cooked white rice, 343, Creamy Grits, 323, or Buttermilk Biscuits, 635

with, if desired:

(Cooked bacon)

Or use the mixture to stuff bell peppers, 262.

FRIED GREEN TOMATOES

6 servings

Though green tomatoes can occasionally be found in supermarkets in regions of the country where the dish is popular, this recipe is most useful for gardeners who cannot bear to waste still-green tomatoes left on the vine in late autumn. For a twist on a classic, make these into BLT sandwiches, 137; fry the bacon first, and use the drippings to fry the tomato slices.

Core, then cut crosswise into ½-inch-thick slices:

2 pounds green slicing tomatoes

Combine in a shallow bowl:

1 cup fine cornmeal
½ cup all-purpose flour
(1 tablespoon minced parsley)
(1 tablespoon minced thyme)
1 teaspoon sweet paprika
1 teaspoon salt
1 teaspoon black pepper

Dip the tomato slices one at a time into:

1 cup milk or buttermilk

and then coat with the cornmeal mixture, shake off the excess, and set on a plate. Heat in a large skillet until hot enough to sizzle a drop of water (about 350°F):

½ inch vegetable oil or bacon fat

Add as many tomatoes as will fit in a single layer and fry until golden and crisp, turning once, 2 to 3 minutes. Drain on paper towels. Repeat with the remaining tomatoes. Serve immediately, plain or, if desired, with:

(Ranch Dressing, 577, Aïoli, 564, or Rémoulade Sauce, 564)

TOMATOES PROVENÇALE

4 servings

Preheat the oven to 350°F. Lightly oil a 13 × 9-inch baking dish. Combine in a small bowl:

½ cup fresh bread crumbs, 957
2 tablespoons grated Parmesan
2 tablespoons chopped parsley
2 tablespoons chopped basil
2 garlic cloves, finely chopped
2 teaspoons olive oil

Halve crosswise, then gently squeeze the seeds from:

4 firm-ripe medium slicing tomatoes

Arrange cut side up in the baking dish and season to taste with:

Salt and black pepper

Spoon the bread crumb mixture over the tomatoes, gently patting it into a dome on each. Drizzle over the tops:

Olive oil

Bake until the bread crumbs are golden and the tomatoes are softened, about 50 minutes.

BROILED TOMATOES

4 servings

Serve as a side dish, place slices on toast rubbed with garlic, or toss with the optional ingredients and serve with pita or crusty bread for a rustic dip.

Position a rack about 5 inches away from the top of the oven and preheat the broiler. Lightly oil a rimmed baking sheet. Core and cut into slices ½ to ¾ inch thick:

2 pounds firm-ripe tomatoes

Season with:

½ teaspoon salt
¼ teaspoon black pepper

Place on the baking sheet. If desired, sprinkle with:

(½ cup grated Parmesan or crumbled feta cheese [2 ounces])

Drizzle with:

2 tablespoons olive oil

Broil until golden on top and heated through, about 5 minutes. Sprinkle or toss with any of the following:

½ cup pitted and chopped olives, such as Kalamata or Castelvetrano
Chopped herbs, such as parsley, thyme, oregano, basil, tarragon, or a combination

Or, if made without cheese, serve with:

Rémoulade Sauce, 564, or Tzatziki, 569

SLOW-ROASTED TOMATOES

2 to 4 servings

Gentle heat and time concentrates the flavor of tomatoes and turns them silky and sweet. Simply running a knife through them results in a rich, chunky sauce. Toss with pasta or use on a pizza.

Preheat the oven to 250°F. Line a rimmed baking sheet with parchment paper. Spread out on the sheet:

2 pounds tomatoes, cut into ¾-inch-thick slices

Combine:

1 teaspoon sugar
½ teaspoon salt
¼ teaspoon black pepper

Sprinkle over the tomatoes. Drizzle with:

Olive oil

Sprinkle with:

Chopped basil, thyme, or other herb of your choice

Bake for 2 hours. Let cool to room temperature.

SCALLOPED TOMATOES

8 to 10 servings

An old-fashioned way to make use of the summer's bounty of fresh tomatoes.

Preheat the oven to 350°F. Grease a 10-inch shallow round baking or quiche dish or pie pan. Peel, halve, and seed, if desired, 281:

3 pounds tomatoes

Chop into ¼-inch pieces (you should have about 4 cups). Melt in a large skillet over medium heat:

2 tablespoons butter

Stir in and cook, stirring constantly, until fragrant and nicely toasted, 4 to 6 minutes:

1½ cups dry bread crumbs

Scrape the crumbs into a bowl and set aside. Return the skillet to medium heat and add:

3 tablespoons butter

Heat until the foam begins to subside, then add:

1 medium onion, finely chopped

1 large red or green bell pepper, finely chopped

Cook, stirring occasionally, until tender and just beginning to brown, about 10 minutes. Add the vegetables to the crumbs along with:

1 tablespoon sugar

¾ teaspoon salt

½ teaspoon black pepper

Mix well. Distribute half of the crumb mixture over the bottom of the baking dish. Cover evenly with the tomatoes and sprinkle lightly with:

Salt and black pepper

Sprinkle the remaining crumb mixture evenly over the top. Bake until the tomatoes are bubbling in the center and the top is richly browned, about 40 minutes.

Sprinkle with:

Chopped parsley

HOT STUFFED TOMATOES

Preheat the oven to 350°F. Cut large hollows in the stem ends of:

Firm-ripe medium tomatoes

Lightly sprinkle with salt and invert them on a rack to drain for about 15 minutes.

Fill the tomato cases with any of the following:

Cheese (fresh goat cheese, mozzarella, or ricotta), bread crumbs, and minced herbs

Browned ground lamb, pine nuts, and cooked rice, 343

Sausage, Onion, and Sage Stuffing, 535, or Rice Dressing with Chorizo and Chiles, 536

Wild Rice with Sautéed Mushrooms, 340, Cajun Dirty Rice, 332, or any cooked grain, 340, seasoned with herbs and salt to taste

Mushroom Filling, 312, or Meat and Spinach Filling, 312, mixed with ricotta

Creamed Spinach, 244, Sautéed Corn, 235, or Creamed Corn, 235, and crumbled crisp cooked bacon

Cover with:

Au Gratin II or III, 958, or grated Parmesan or Romano

Place the cases in a baking pan and bake until soft and browned, about 30 minutes. If they are very ripe, you may bake them in well-greased muffin tins to keep them shapely.

ABOUT TURNIPS

Turnips are the sweet, spicy, white-fleshed root of a plant closely related to mustards and cabbages. The most commonly available turnips are upwards of 2 or 3 inches in diameter and are sold without their greens. Tinged purple where they were exposed to the sky, these are often very firm, fine-grained, and thick-skinned. Younger turnips, often sold in summer with their greens attached, are significantly juicier and more tender. Some varieties—such as the white **Hakurei** or **Tokyo** types—are mild, radish-like, and have tender skin.

Turnips are sweeter and milder when harvested during cool weather. Select firm, unblemished roots that are heavy for their size. Store in an open plastic bag in the refrigerator crisper. If the greens are still attached, remove and store separately. Young turnips should be used within 1 week of purchase; mature turnips will keep for up to 1 month.

To prepare younger turnips, simply wash them well and cut as desired. Peel the tough skin off mature turnips, and pare off any woody areas. Cut into slices, wedges, cubes, or matchsticks. One pound of turnips will yield about 2 cups cooked. The earthy taste of cooked rutabagas and older turnips makes it possible to use them interchangeably in recipes.

Small, tender turnips are best served raw as crudités, 45, sliced or julienned and added to salads, or cooked briefly in stir-fries or as for radishes, 271. Mature turnips can be combined with other root vegetables in a braise, 203, or a puree, 203. A favorite German peasant dish, **Himmel und Erde** (Heaven and Earth), is made of mashed turnips, potatoes, and apples. Turnips are especially good when quartered and scattered around a lamb, beef, or venison roast (see About Vegetables for a Roast, 201). Like their cabbage and mustard relatives, turnips produce tasty tops: Use young, tender greens in salads or lightly wilt, 243; braise tougher, mature greens Southern-Style, 243. The spiciness of turnips can be tempered with cream and butter, or rounded with warm curry spices. Their sweetness can be balanced with lemon, vinegar, or tangy, sharp cheeses. Smoked or cured pork, thyme, parsley, and chervil also pair well with turnips.

To boil or steam mature turnips, peel them, cut into ½-inch slices, and simmer in salted water or steam, 1056, until tender, about 10 minutes.

Pressure-cook whole, mature turnips with 1 inch of water for 8 minutes at 15 psi. Let the pressure release naturally for 10 minutes, then open the valve to release the pressure completely, 1059.

BRAISED TURNIPS WITH LEEKS AND BACON

4 servings

Cook in a large skillet over medium heat until crisp:

4 slices bacon, diced

Transfer the bacon to a plate lined with paper towels to drain, and set aside. Spoon off all but 3 tablespoons of fat from the skillet. Increase the heat to medium-high and add cut side down:

1½ pounds turnips, peeled and cut into ½-inch-thick wedges
Cook until browned on one side, about 7 minutes. Add:
2 large leeks, trimmed, halved lengthwise, well cleaned, and thinly sliced
4 garlic cloves, coarsely chopped
Reduce the heat to medium and cook, stirring, until the leeks have softened, about 5 minutes. Chop and add the bacon along with:
1 cup chicken stock or broth or white wine
(¼ teaspoon red pepper flakes)
Reduce the heat, cover the skillet, and simmer until the turnips are just tender, 15 to 20 minutes. Stir in:
Lemon juice or vinegar to taste
Chopped parsley or thyme
Salt and black pepper to taste

ABOUT WATER CHESTNUTS

Chinese water chestnuts are not chestnuts at all, but rather the enlarged tips of watergrass stems. They resemble chestnuts in shape and color. **Horned water chestnuts,** also known as **caltrops,** are the shiny seeds of another aquatic plant, which can have up to 4 sharp horns. Like lotus root and bamboo shoots, they retain crispness after long braising or simmering, which is why even canned water chestnuts can add crunch to dishes. Fresh water chestnuts have a delicacy not found in the blandly straightforward crunch of canned ones.

Choose firm water chestnuts without soft spots or signs of yellowing. Stored unpeeled and submerged in water, they will keep for at least 2 weeks. To store opened canned water chestnuts, transfer to a container, submerge in fresh water, and refrigerate for 1 week. If they have a metallic taste, boil for 1 minute and drain.

Water chestnuts grow in muddy water; fresh ones must be washed before peeling. Cut the skin off with a sharp knife, paring away any brown spots. Their crisp white flesh will discolor, so drop peeled pieces into a bowl of acidulated water, 951, if not cooking at once. Slice and add to stir-fries or cooked dishes. Though uncooked water chestnuts are edible, ➤ we do not recommend consuming them raw, as their outer layers may harbor waterborne parasites. For use in salads and adding to dumpling fillings, ➤ boil fresh water chestnuts for at least 5 minutes. Drain, let cool, and dice or slice as needed. Wrap slices in bacon with prunes or chicken livers to make Rumaki, 64, or chop and mix into ground meat fillings to add texture to Wontons, 315.

YAMS

See About Sweet Potatoes and Yams, 278.

ABOUT YUCA

Also called **cassava** or **manioc,** this starchy tropical root is refined into **tapioca,** 1023. While the highly productive "bitter" varieties must be processed to remove cyanide compounds before being turned into flour or meal, the "sweet" type available in our markets is cooked as a vegetable. Its bark-like brown skin conceals hard, pure-white flesh that turns yellowish and almost translucent when cooked, with a rich, buttery taste and the texture of a dry, flaky potato. It is tasty in stews or served with garlicky olive oil or fresh salsa.

Yuca roots do not store very well, which is why we find them dipped in wax. The roots should be very firm, with no mold, soft spots, or cracks on the surface; discard those with black streaks running through the flesh. Store at cool room temperature or in the refrigerator crisper and cook as soon as possible. Or freeze peeled raw chunks tightly wrapped in plastic for up to 1 month.

➤ Always peel yuca; not only are they usually covered in wax, but the skin may contain traces of cyanide. Cut the root into 3-inch sections, turn each so that it stands up, and trim off the skin and pinkish inner layer from the white flesh with a sturdy knife. Split the chunks lengthwise and pull out the thin, fibrous core that runs down the center of the root. Rinse well and hold in cold water.

➤ Always cook yuca roots before eating. Yuca is higher in calories than potatoes and quite filling in small portions. In addition to the simple recipe below, you may simmer yuca until tender and mash it, 265, or cut into sticks or batons, and fry as for Pan-Fried Potatoes, 268, or French Fries, 270. Or, slice yuca thinly and fry into chips, 48.

YUCA WITH CITRUS AND GARLIC

6 servings

Cut into 3-inch sections, peel, halve lengthwise, and core, above:
3 pounds yuca
Cut the yuca into ½-inch-thick slices or cubes. Rinse well and place in a pot of cold water to cover. Add:
½ teaspoon salt
Bring to a boil, then reduce the heat, cover, and simmer until the yuca is easily pierced with a fork, 15 to 20 minutes. Meanwhile, prepare:
Mojo, 567
When the yuca is tender, drain well and transfer to a serving bowl. Add the mojo to taste (you do not need to let the mojo cool before adding to the yuca) along with:
Chopped cilantro
Chopped green onion
Salt to taste
Serve immediately.

ABOUT TOFU, TEMPEH, AND OTHER PLANT-BASED PROTEINS

Many satisfying, protein-rich alternatives to meat can be concocted from processed vegetables and pulses. Some of these products, such as tofu and tempeh, were first developed centuries ago in China and Indonesia, respectively. They are enjoyed in their own right, as well as in place of animal protein. Others, like neutral-flavored wheat gluten, were pressed into service as a meat substitute for vegetarians. While Benjamin Franklin mentioned tofu in a letter in 1770, tofu and tempeh did not begin to reach the mainstream in the United States until the 1970s. By that time, modern industrial agriculture was also beginning to introduce foods made from the excess protein and starch resulting from the manufacture of flours and oils. Many of these products were made with the explicit intention of replacing or supplementing meat: **Textured vegetable protein** (TVP) and the mushroom-based **mycoprotein** are specifically engineered to have a meaty, chewy texture.

As vegetarianism, veganism, and a general interest in vegetable-centered diets has spread to a growing number of people, a dizzying selection of new meat-mimicking products has arrived in the marketplace. Some are based on older formulas for repurposed industrial proteins and starches; some utilize natural alternatives, such as marinated, underripe jackfruit, 196. Still others are the result of contemporary research and "disruptive" attempts to supplant meat with more ecologically sustainable alternatives. Vegetable- and grain-based burger patties are mimicking more of the properties of those made from ground beef, including the taste and appearance of blood. Perhaps more significantly, there is now much discussion of "growing" meat in laboratories.

As meat mimicry is a fecund field of study prone to frequent innovation, we will stick to covering a few widely consumed vegetable proteins.

TOFU

Tofu has been unfairly maligned in this country. Often thought of as boring and bland, these blocks of soybean protein are frequently associated with food co-ops and bleak 1970s vegetarian cookery. Regardless of tofu's culinary history in the United States, it is revered throughout Eastern Asia and can be the satisfying star of a dish or play an important supporting role to other flavorful ingredients. Homemade tofu is superior to all but the freshest store-bought tofu. Though tofu making is a little involved, the process is fairly straightforward. ➤ To make your own tofu, see 1019.

Also called **bean curd** and **dofu,** regular tofu is made like cheese: An acid or mineral salt is added to soy milk, which coagulates into curds. These curds are then broken up and drained. If not processed further, the result is **soft** or **silken tofu,** which ranges from soupy to just-set in texture. When pureed, it has the creamy consistency of yogurt and can be used in cream soups, sauces, dips, salad dressings, and desserts like Vegan Chocolate Pudding, 817.

If tofu is placed in molds and pressed, it can become quite dense. Pressed tofu is sold in **medium, firm, extra-firm,** and **super-firm** (or **high protein**) varieties. Firm tofu may also be **smoked,** which adds welcome character. Another tasty variety, **baked tofu,** is sold in smaller, vacuum-sealed slabs (it is not actually baked, just pressed and seasoned with spices, sugar, and soy sauce). Medium tofu is denser than silken, but still delicate; use it in soups, or other dishes that do not require very much stirring or flipping. Firm and extra-firm tofu are very good for stir-frying; the less-common super-firm is positively toothsome. Medium and firm tofu blocks hold their shape well enough to be pressed and made firmer (see below). Freezing and thawing pressed tofu adds even more texture.

Yuba, or **tofu skin,** is worth seeking out at Asian markets. Made from the solids that collect on the surface of simmering soy milk, these thin skins have a light, chewy texture and a yellowish tinge. You may find them fresh, frozen, or dried. They may be added to stir-fries or used as a dumpling skin. Sometimes bite-sized sections are gathered and tied into **soy knots,** which are good for simmering in soups or dishes like Spicy Sichuan Hot Pot, 97.

Do not let the flexibility of tofu—its ability to take on so many textures and flavors—keep you from enjoying it in simpler preparations. You can vary the texture of tofu by garnishing it with something crunchy—like Crispy Fried Shallots, 256, for instance—or by cooking with a method that makes it crispy on the outside, such as pan-frying or applying a crunchy coating and deep-frying.

Please note that tofu package sizes vary widely. In the following recipes, you can use any size package close to the weight indicated. Store tofu refrigerated in its original package. Once opened, discard the liquid and store in fresh water; change the water daily. It will keep for a week or more, depending on its freshness when purchased.

To press a 1-pound block of tofu, cut into thin slices of equal thickness, or cut horizontally into two slabs, each about 1 inch thick. Place on a clean cutting board in one layer. Allow the water to drain off by placing one end of the board over the edge of the sink or on a baking sheet and propping up the other end with a ¼-cup measure. Place a second cutting board or similarly shaped weight over the tofu and let stand for 10 minutes. The sides of the tofu should bulge very slightly, but be careful not to overweight tofu before it has compacted, or it may split. After 10 minutes, add more weight, evenly distributed; a cast-iron skillet or Dutch oven with two or three large cans, or several nested heavy skillets will do the job. Check the weighted tofu for firmness after 30 minutes; if desired, turn the slabs over, replace the weight, and press for an additional 15 to 30 minutes. Refrigerate pressed tofu in a bowl of water; it will not reabsorb water and can be kept for 2 to 3 days if you change the water daily. While some recipes call for pressed tofu, this extra step is not essential, it just adds textural refinement.

Freezing tofu removes even more moisture. Use pressed firm or extra-firm tofu and freeze solid (at least 3 hours). Once thawed, press it gently between your palms to squeeze out excess moisture. Thawed frozen tofu can be cut into cubes and used like other tofu, but the dryness makes it chewier and better able to absorb marinades and sauces. It also crumbles easily, and can mimic the texture of hard-boiled egg whites in a mock egg salad or ground meat in sauces and fillings.

To brine tofu, which makes it fry up very crisp, cut tofu into cubes or slabs and place in a bowl. Bring water to a boil, add 1 tablespoon salt for every quart of water, and pour over the tofu. Let the tofu brine for at least 15 minutes and blot any excess moisture off the surface.

To marinate tofu, press and/or freeze, cut into cubes or slabs, and place in a saucepan. Add a marinade of your choice, 579–82; if the tofu is not submerged, add water to cover. Bring to a simmer over medium heat, reduce the heat so that the marinade gently bubbles, and cook for 15 minutes. Remove from the heat and let cool (refrigerating in the liquid overnight is best). Drain and blot dry before cooking; you may use the marinade to prepare a sauce, or save it to marinate more tofu.

To smoke tofu, see 1067.

To make tofu into cheese, see Tofu Misozuke, 943.

MAPO DOFU (SICHUAN-STYLE TOFU)

4 servings

This dish is traditionally made with tofu and ground beef or pork. However, we often make a vegetarian version by simply omitting the meat.

Warm in a large skillet over medium-high heat:

1 tablespoon vegetable oil

If desired, add:

(½ pound ground beef or pork)

Cook, using a wooden spoon to break up the meat, until cooked through and starting to crisp, about 5 minutes. Add to the skillet:

2 tablespoons Sichuan chili bean paste, 970
(1 tablespoon fermented black beans, rinsed)
1-inch piece ginger, peeled and minced
3 garlic cloves, minced
(¼ teaspoon cayenne pepper)

Cook, stirring, until fragrant, about 1 minute. Carefully pour into the skillet (it may spatter):

1 cup chicken or vegetable stock or broth
1 tablespoon soy sauce

Immediately add to the skillet:

14 ounces soft or medium tofu, cut into ½-inch cubes

Let the sauce simmer without disturbing the tofu for about 3 minutes. Push the tofu to the sides of the skillet and stir into the sauce:

1 tablespoon cornstarch dissolved in 2 tablespoons cold water

Let the sauce thicken, then gently stir the tofu. Remove from the heat and sprinkle with:

½ teaspoon ground Sichuan pepper
1 green onion, thinly sliced

TOFU SCRAMBLE

2 servings

Nutritional yeast and the optional black salt give tofu the savory, sulfur-scented note of scrambled eggs. Consider this a basic blueprint from which you can build a wide variety of breakfast scrambles. Use any vegetable that you like and stir in Pesto, 580, or start with chopped poblano peppers and onions, stir in chili powder, and top with avocado and salsa, 573–74.

Drain, pat dry, and coarsely crumble into a bowl:

14 ounces medium to firm tofu

Toss the tofu with:

2 tablespoons nutritional yeast
½ teaspoon salt
½ teaspoon ground turmeric
(⅛ teaspoon black salt, 1013)

Warm in a large skillet over medium heat:

1 tablespoon vegetable oil

Add and cook until the vegetables are softened:

½ cup chopped vegetables (such as red bell pepper, onion, mushrooms, etc.) or any of the suggestions in Additions to Scrambled Eggs I, 156

Stir in the tofu and cook for 5 minutes without stirring, then give the tofu one good stir and serve.

AGEDASHI TOFU

4 servings

This dish, usually served as an appetizer, is all about contrast: creamy, mild tofu coated with a crisp cornstarch shell, swimming in a salty, savory broth. Make the most of your hot frying oil by preparing tempura-fried vegetables, 204, along with this dish. For a vegetarian version, make a broth with kombu and dried shiitakes and substitute for the dashi. Please read about Deep-Frying, 1051.

Cut into 1-inch cubes:

14 ounces firm silken or medium tofu

Gently toss with:

½ cup cornstarch

Set aside. Heat to 365°F in a deep heavy pot or Dutch oven:

2 inches vegetable oil

Whisk together in a small saucepan:

1 cup Dashi, 78
2 tablespoons soy sauce
2 tablespoons mirin

Heat gently over low heat and keep warm while you fry the tofu. When the oil is hot, fry the tofu in 2 batches until crisp and lightly browned, about 5 minutes. Divide among small bowls, then ladle the dashi mixture into the bowls and top with:

Katsuobushi (dried bonito flakes), 956
Thinly sliced green onion

CRISPY PAN-FRIED TOFU

4 servings

I. This simple treatment does not require any coatings to get a satisfying, crispy result. A perfect way to prepare tofu before adding to a stir-fry.

Cut crosswise into 8 equal slices:

14 ounces firm or extra-firm tofu

Press and freeze, 285, if desired, then brine, 285, the tofu slices for at least 15 minutes. Heat in a large skillet over medium heat:

2 tablespoons vegetable oil

Fry the tofu, in batches if necessary, until browned on the bottom, about 4 minutes, then flip and cook until browned on the second side, about 4 minutes more. If frying in 2 batches, wipe out the skillet between batches and add more oil.

II. A spiced cornmeal coating adds texture and flavor.

Cut crosswise into 8 equal slices:

14 ounces extra-firm tofu

If desired, press and freeze, 285, or marinate, 285. Otherwise, pat dry. Whisk together in a shallow bowl:

¼ cup cornstarch
¼ cup cool water

Whisk together in a second shallow bowl:

½ cup fine cornmeal
1 tablespoon chili powder or curry powder
1 teaspoon salt
1 teaspoon smoked paprika
1 teaspoon sugar

Fry as directed in **version I,** first dipping the tofu in the cornstarch mixture, then in the cornmeal.

BAKED MARINATED TOFU

4 servings

If desired, press, 285:

14 ounces extra-firm tofu

Prepare:

Thai-Style Lemongrass Marinade, 581, Vietnamese-Style Marinade, 581, Balkan Marinade, 580, Becker Chicken or Pork Marinade, 581, or Lemon Marinade, 580

Cut the tofu crosswise into ½-inch-thick slabs and place in a wide saucepan (the tofu can be in more than one layer in the pan). Pour the marinade over the tofu. If the tofu is not submerged, add enough water to barely cover. Bring to a boil over medium-high heat, then cover, reduce the heat, and simmer for 15 minutes. Remove from the heat. Use the tofu immediately, or let it cool completely, then cover and refrigerate for up to 24 hours.

Preheat the oven to 425°F. Lightly grease a baking sheet.

Remove the tofu from the marinade (reserve any leftover marinade for another use), allowing any excess to drip off, and place it on the baking sheet. Bake until the tofu has firmed up and is starting to brown, about 20 minutes.

TEMPEH

Tempeh is a fermented food from Indonesia made from partially cooked beans that have been inoculated with a special mold. As the beans ferment, the mold binds them into a cake and a nutty flavor and firm, meaty texture develops. Soybeans are traditional, and still the most popular bean to use, but tempeh made with other legumes and grains (or a combination of them) is quite common. Though it may not be as versatile as tofu, tempeh is toothsome and has a more assertive, savory flavor—and even the blandest tempeh easily absorbs marinades. These qualities make it a favorite vegetarian protein substitute in many dishes that would normally rely on slices or cubes of meat, poultry, or fish. When crumbled and browned, tempeh is an excellent substitute for ground meat.

Tempeh may be stored refrigerated for up to 10 days in its original packaging or tightly wrapped. If you are able to find unpasteurized tempeh (virtually all commercially available tempeh is pasteurized), its shelf life is very short—about 3 days. Luckily, all tempeh freezes well, for up to 3 months, tightly wrapped. Packages of tempeh should be marked with a freshness date. White mold is to be expected, but ➤ sliminess or signs of darker molds is not desirable, nor is a strong ammonia smell.

Tempeh should be cooked before eating, and is usually cut into slices, strips, and cubes. Crumbled, it makes a fine substitute for ground beef or sausage in dishes like Megan's Vegan Chili, 89. Since the beans and grains used to make tempeh are only partially cooked before being inoculated, ➤ tempeh is much improved by steaming before marinating and grilling, or using in quick-cooking dishes like stir-fries.

To steam tempeh, leave whole or cut into slices or cubes, as desired. Transfer to a steaming basket, place over rapidly boiling water, cover, and cook for 10 minutes.

SAMBAL GORENG TEMPEH

4 servings

In this Indonesian dish, pan-fried tempeh is simmered in a fragrant paste until the mixture is concentrated and almost dry. If you cannot find sweet soy sauce, simply substitute 2 teaspoons regular soy sauce or tamari mixed with 2 teaspoons brown sugar.

Add to a food processor and pulse until finely ground:

1 medium tomato, chopped
1 large shallot, coarsely chopped
4 garlic cloves, chopped
2 fresh red chiles (such as Fresno), stemmed and seeded, or 1 tablespoon chile garlic paste
1-inch piece ginger or galangal, peeled and chopped
1 tablespoon palm sugar or dark brown sugar
1 tablespoon sweet soy sauce (kecap manis), 1020
(½ teaspoon shrimp paste, roasted, 1018)

Set aside. Heat in a large skillet over medium-high heat:

¼ cup vegetable oil

Add and cook, stirring occasionally, until golden brown, about 8 minutes:

14 to 16 ounces tempeh, cut into ½-inch cubes

Transfer to a plate. Add the tomato mixture to the skillet and simmer, stirring frequently, until thickened, about 4 minutes. Add the tempeh, stir to coat the tempeh with the sauce, and cook until heated through and the sauce is almost dry, about 4 minutes. Serve over:

Cooked white rice, 343

SEASONED TEMPEH CRUMBLES

4 servings

Tempeh crumbles make an excellent stand-in for ground meat. Here, they are seasoned like Italian sausage and could easily serve as the basis for a tomato sauce. For use in other dishes, try substituting for ground meat in Picadillo, 503, Spiced Ground Meat for Tacos, 503, Nachos, 57, or Sloppy Joes, 140, adjusting the amount of tempeh accordingly.

Coarsely crumble with your hands:

12 ounces tempeh (steamed, above, if desired)

Warm in a medium skillet over medium heat:

3 tablespoons vegetable or olive oil

Add and cook until fragrant, about 30 seconds:

3 garlic cloves, minced

Stir in the tempeh and cook, stirring frequently, until browned, 8 to 10 minutes. Stir in:

1 teaspoon dried oregano
½ teaspoon red pepper flakes
(½ teaspoon fennel seeds)
½ teaspoon salt

Continue to cook, stirring, until the mixture is fully combined, well browned, and fragrant, about 2 minutes more.

CARAMELIZED TAMARIND TEMPEH

2 to 3 servings

This sticky, sweet-sour dish is one of our favorite ways to prepare tempeh. It comes together as quickly as a pot of rice and Roasted Broccoli, 221, for a healthy weeknight dinner.

Combine in a small bowl:

3 tablespoons orange juice
2 tablespoons lime juice
1 tablespoon water
1 tablespoon coconut sugar or brown sugar
1 tablespoon tamarind paste
2 garlic cloves, grated or minced
1-inch piece ginger, peeled and grated or minced
2 whole star anise
¼ teaspoon salt or 2 teaspoons fish sauce

Cut into ½-inch-thick strips:

8 ounces tempeh (steamed, 287, if desired)

Warm in a large skillet over medium heat:

2 tablespoons vegetable or coconut oil

Add the tempeh to the skillet and cook until golden brown, about 5 minutes. Flip and brown the second side. Add the tamarind sauce to the skillet and allow it to simmer until reduced and thickened, flipping the tempeh once to caramelize both sides, about 3 minutes. When the tempeh takes on a deep mahogany color, remove from the heat. If desired, sprinkle with:

(Sesame seeds)

Serve with:

Coconut Rice, 333

TVP (TEXTURED VEGETABLE PROTEIN)

Unlike tofu and tempeh, **textured vegetable protein,** or **TVP,** is the result of modern industrial agriculture. Also known as **soy meat** or **soy chunks,** this protein-rich meat substitute is made from defatted soybeans—the main byproduct of soybean oil manufacture—which are extensively processed, and spun or extruded and puffed to have a chewy texture. They are sold in dried chunks, slices, flakes, or granules, which will keep for at least a year in a closed container at room temperature. TVP is also rehydrated and used in the formulation of refrigerated and frozen meat-substitute products, often with added seasonings and other ingredients to enhance its texture, such as wheat gluten, below.

Dried TVP must be cooked with a liquid of some sort, and is quite bland without aggressive seasoning. Granules and flakes swell to twice their volume when cooked, taking on the texture of ground meat. To equal the volume of 1 pound ground meat, soak 1 cup textured vegetable protein; use it alone or in combination with ground meat in meat loaves, spaghetti sauce, chili, tacos, Sloppy Joes, or any other recipe where ground meat is used. A meatloaf made with textured vegetable protein will be softer than one made with meat but will firm up to meat texture if refrigerated overnight.

MEATLESS DINNER LOAF

6 servings

The flavor of this loaf is even better the next day. Leftovers make terrific sandwiches.

Preheat the oven to 350°F. Grease a 9 × 5-inch loaf pan.

Combine in a large bowl:

1 cup textured vegetable protein
One 15-ounce can tomato sauce
One 15-ounce can black or pinto beans, drained and rinsed
¾ cup water
1 large egg, beaten
1 small onion, chopped
1 small jalapeño pepper, seeded and minced, or 2 canned chile peppers, drained and chopped
¾ cup dry bread crumbs
⅓ cup all-purpose flour
¼ cup finely chopped cilantro
1 tablespoon chili powder
3 garlic cloves, minced, or 1 teaspoon garlic powder
1½ teaspoons ground cumin
1 teaspoon salt

Pack the loaf mixture into the pan. Cover loosely with foil and bake for 45 minutes. Uncover and bake until set, about 30 minutes. Let stand in the pan on a rack for 5 minutes, then invert onto a serving platter.

WHEAT GLUTEN OR SEITAN

First made in sixth-century China, wheat gluten is the oldest plant-based meat substitute, and was adopted by Buddhist monks to bring much-needed protein to their vegetarian diet—though it still lacks lysine, an essential amino acid present in animal proteins, tofu, and tempeh. Also called **seitan** or **wheat meat,** the firm protein is made by kneading and washing a dough made of wheat flour to develop the gluten and remove its starch. The most convenient way to make your own seitan is by rehydrating and flavoring **vital wheat gluten,** a free-flowing wheat gluten powder. Or, purchase seasoned and ready-to-eat seitan products.

Seitan swells, absorbs flavor, and becomes firm with cooking. Small chunks or cutlets can be pan-fried or lightly battered and deep-fried for appealing crispness. Thin slices can be simmered in a sauce and will indeed have the texture of braised meat, but ➤ lengthy cooking brings out a bitter taste. Chop seitan in a food processor or grind in a meat grinder and use it like ground meat in sauces and mixtures like Picadillo, 503. Obviously, wheat gluten should be avoided by anyone with a gluten allergy or sensitivity, especially those with celiac disease.

SEITAN

About 4 cups or 1½ pounds

Combine in a large bowl:

2 cups vital wheat gluten, 989
1 cup cold vegetable or mushroom stock or broth, store-bought or homemade, 78–79
¼ cup soy sauce or tamari

(Up to 2 tablespoons curry powder, chili powder, Five-Spice Powder, 590, or mixed ground spices such as cumin, coriander, dried thyme, onion and garlic powder, etc.)

Mix until the dry ingredients are completely moistened, then knead the dough until firm and well combined, about 5 minutes. Form the dough into a log and cut into 1- to 2-inch cubes or chunks. Bring to a gentle simmer in a medium saucepan:

4 cups vegetable or mushroom stock or broth, store-bought or homemade, 78–79

Add the seitan pieces, cover, and simmer gently for 45 minutes. The pieces will swell above the level of the stock (this is normal). Remove the seitan from the broth with a slotted spoon if using right away. Let cool slightly, then squeeze to remove some of the liquid the seitan has absorbed. Or, let the seitan cool in the pan, transfer to a container, add broth, and store covered in the refrigerator for up to 5 days.

KUNG PAO SEITAN

4 servings

Cut into ½-inch cubes:

1 pound seitan, store-bought or homemade, 288

Toss the seitan in a medium bowl with:

2 teaspoons soy sauce
2 teaspoons Shaoxing wine, 952, or dry sherry
1½ teaspoons cornstarch

Let sit for 10 minutes. Whisk together in a small bowl:

1 tablespoon soy sauce
2 teaspoons distilled white vinegar
2 teaspoons Shaoxing wine or dry sherry
2 teaspoons sugar
1 teaspoon toasted sesame oil
1 teaspoon cornstarch
½ teaspoon ground Sichuan pepper or black pepper

Set aside. Heat in a large heavy skillet over medium-high heat:

2 tablespoons vegetable oil

Add and stir-fry very briefly, just until fragrant, 15 to 30 seconds:

8 dried red chiles, such as árbol or Kashmiri

Stir in the seitan and stir-fry until lightly browned, 3 to 4 minutes. Stir in:

4 green onions, trimmed and cut into 1-inch lengths
3 garlic cloves, minced
1-inch piece ginger, peeled and grated

Cook, stirring constantly, about 30 seconds or until very fragrant. Give the sauce a good stir, then stir into the seitan mixture until everything is coated. Remove the skillet from the heat and stir in:

⅓ cup unsalted roasted peanuts

Serve with:

Cooked white rice, 343

PECAN AND CHEDDAR "SAUSAGE" PATTIES

8 patties

These patties are based on a thirties-era recipe for "cheese, nut, and bread loaf." We find the mixture much more delicious in patty form, as it browns very nicely and becomes irresistibly crisp.

Pulse in a food processor until finely ground:

1½ cups pecans, toasted, 1005

Transfer to a medium bowl. Heat in a small skillet over medium heat:

1 tablespoon vegetable oil

Add:

½ medium onion, finely chopped

Cook, stirring, until softened, about 5 minutes. Transfer to the bowl with the pecans along with:

1 cup fresh bread crumbs, 957
1 cup shredded sharp Cheddar (4 ounces)
1 large egg
1 teaspoon brown sugar
¾ teaspoon salt
½ teaspoon black pepper
½ teaspoon smoked paprika or ground chipotle chile powder
½ teaspoon dried sage
½ teaspoon dried thyme, crumbled

Mix well and form the mixture into patties, using about ¼ cup per patty. The patties may be refrigerated, covered, for up to 3 days or frozen for up to 3 months. When ready to cook, heat in a medium skillet:

1 tablespoon vegetable oil

Place the patties in the skillet (frozen patties do not need to be thawed before cooking) and cook until browned on one side, then flip and brown the second side.

PASTA, NOODLES, AND DUMPLINGS

From linguine to lo mein and soba, noodles make up one of the largest and richest categories of staple foods in the world. Nearly every culture has a tradition of turning starch and water into some form of noodle or dumpling. Delicious, convenient, and nourishing, they are easily adapted to what cooks have on hand, inviting improvisation and creativity. Though the origins of noodle making are obscure, tracing back at least four thousand years to central Asia and China, we owe much of our modern enthusiasm for noodles to Italian cuisine. But our familiarity with Japanese ramen, Vietnamese *bún*, pad Thai, and Chinese-American favorites like sesame noodles and chow mein signals an ever-growing appreciation for the immense variety of noodle dishes found throughout East Asia (see About Asian Noodles, 300).

ABOUT PASTA AND NOODLES

Although fresh and dried pasta and noodles are quite different, one is not necessarily better than the other. **Dried pasta** is usually made from durum wheat and water. It comes in a wide variety of shapes, from long, thin spaghetti to short, hollow ziti. Many grocers now stock whole-grain pastas, as well as pastas that use less common varieties of wheat such as spelt and farro. Gluten-free pastas are also available, made from grains like rice, corn, and quinoa; starchy vegetables like potatoes; and legumes like chickpeas, soybeans, black beans, and lentils. Dried pasta is convenient, inexpensive, reliable, and has a long shelf life, making it the perfect emergency pantry item to stock for hurried or uninspired moments.

Fresh pasta is usually made with eggs and flour milled from soft wheat. Though making fresh pasta at home is a little time-consuming, it is easier than you might think, and we find it well worth the effort when time allows. Of course, fresh pasta is essential for making filled dumplings at home, 313. Fresh pasta cooks much faster than dried pasta, has a tender texture, and seems to "hold on" to sauces much better.

Egg noodles, a staple of Eastern European cooking, are made with eggs and flour and cut into short, wide strips. They are widely available dried, though they are very good when fresh and homemade.

Asian noodles come in as many varieties as their Italian brethren. They are made from wheat, buckwheat, rice, or starch, and many types may be found fresh or dried. They range in size from thread-thin rice noodles to thick, chewy udon, and they may be flat and wide or rounded. Rice noodles are often pale white, and some are clear, while wheat noodles are opaque or yellow, depending on whether eggs have been added to the dough. There are also the clear, brownish sweet potato starch noodles used in Korean cuisine called *dangmyeon* (see About Asian Noodles, 300).

ABOUT COOKING PASTA

Pasta cooks quickly and is at its best as soon as it is cooked, so have everything ready before you start—the sauce, a large colander set in the sink for draining, and, if possible, a serving bowl or dishes warming in the oven. Plan on cooking ➤ 3 ounces of dried pasta per main-course serving or 4 ounces of fresh pasta per main-course serving.

To avoid pasta or noodles sticking together, cook them in enough boiling salted water for them to move around freely. As a general rule (see One-Pan Pasta with Tomatoes and Herbs, 298, for an exception) ➤ allow 4 quarts water and 2 tablespoons salt per pound of fresh or dried pasta. For a subtle background flavor, we sometimes add a dried bay leaf to the water.

Once the salted water is rapidly boiling, add the pasta all at once; long strands that do not fit under the water should be allowed to soften for a few seconds, then pressed down and stirred in. Give the pasta a stir, partially cover the pot, and let it return to a boil. ➤ Do not cover the pot completely, or it will boil over. When the water is boiling again, uncover. Stir the pasta often to keep it from sticking together.

No matter which pasta you are cooking, ➤ do not overcook. Though cooking times on packages of dried pasta are usually accurate, we recommend lifting a piece from the pot and tasting it—not once, but several times. We think the perfect texture is **al dente**—literally, to the tooth—a tender but firm texture that offers slight resistance to the bite. Remember, ➤ fresh pasta cooks much faster than dried; see Boiled Pasta or Egg Noodles, 295. If desired, you may partially cook the pasta in boiling water, and then finish it in a barely simmering tomato sauce. This allows the pasta to absorb a bit of the sauce as it cooks, and the sauce is enriched and thickened by the starch clinging to the pasta.

Once the pasta is done, ➤ scoop out and reserve a small amount of the cooking water. This starchy liquid helps loosen sauces, gives them body, and helps them adhere to the pasta. It is especially useful for sauces based on garlic and olive oil or sautéed vegetables, where adding more oil instead would make the sauce too heavy.

Empty the pot into the colander and shake the colander to rid the pasta of most of the water. ➤ Rinse pasta only if you want to separate the pieces (for example, for lasagne) or if it is to be eaten cool in a salad. Like pasta water, the starch that clings to unrinsed pasta helps the sauce meld with the hot pasta.

➤ Use some of the reserved cooking water to thin the sauce if needed. Immediately combine the drained pasta with its sauce to finish cooking, as suggested above, or simply toss the hot pasta and sauce in a warmed serving bowl. ➤ Remember that pasta is meant to be moistened with sauce, not swimming in it: You want to taste the pasta as well as the sauce.

SAUCES FOR PASTA

Pasta can be dressed simply or served with a long-simmered ragu. Some of the classics include Pesto, 586, Marinara Sauce, 556, Puttanesca Sauce, 557, and Bolognese Sauce, 558. For a classic, slow-cooked ragu, see Hearty Beef Ragu, 466. Many of the butter sauces, 558, and flavored butters, 559, are excellent with pasta as well. ➤ Have ready ¼ cup of oil- or butter-based sauce per serving of pasta; or up to ½ cup per serving for lighter tomato sauces.

However, don't restrict yourself to sauces. Part of pasta's appeal is that it can help turn odds and ends into dinner. There are many recipes in this book just waiting to be turned into pasta dishes. In the Vegetables chapter, for instance, Braised Baby Artichokes and Peas, 207, Roman-Style Fava Beans, 212, Garlic-Braised Broccoli Rabe, 221, and Ratatouille Provençale, 204, can be easily transformed into pasta dishes. You may need to add pasta water and a healthy grating of cheese to some of these dishes to coax them into mingling with the pasta.

Other good candidates include Mixed Shellfish in Tomato Sauce, 347, Mushroom Ragout, 251, Slow-Roasted Tomatoes, 282, and Shellfish with Mushrooms and Greens, 348. For egg noodles, see Additions to Egg Noodles, 300.

MATCHING PASTA AND SAUCES

There are hundreds of different pasta shapes. With so many possibilities, it helps to remember a basic rule for pairing pasta and sauce: ➤ Match large shapes such as penne and wide, thick rigatoni with sauces with big flavors and bite-sized chunks of vegetables or meats. Ethereal angel hair is best with lighter sauces. Cream or butter sauces go best with egg noodles. Of course, rules can always be broken—for instance, pesto can be at home on both rigatoni and angel hair.

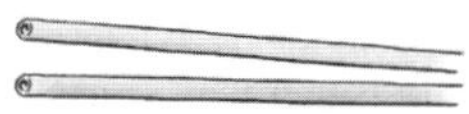
Bucatini

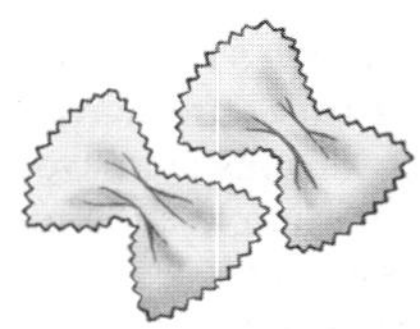
Farfalle

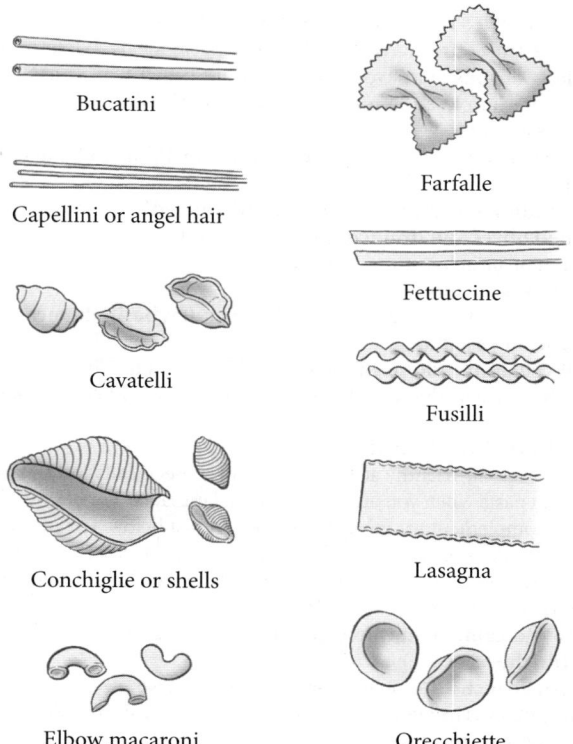

Capellini or angel hair

Fettuccine

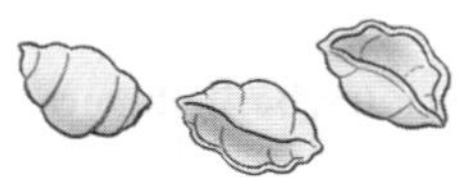
Cavatelli

Fusilli

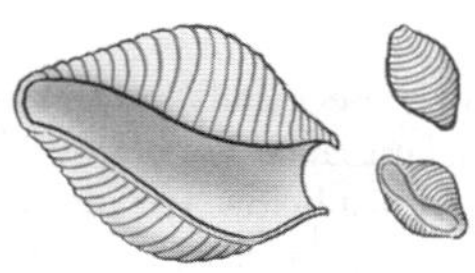
Conchiglie or shells

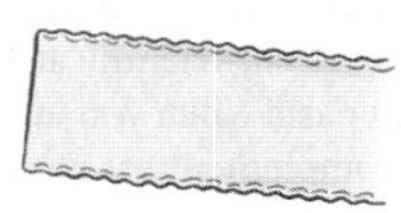
Lasagna

Elbow macaroni

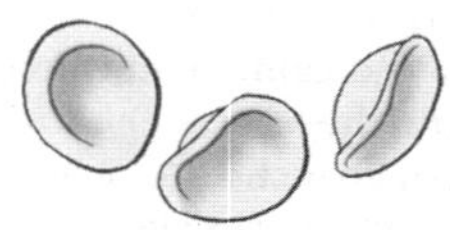
Orecchiette

Orzo

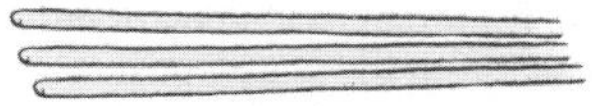

Spaghetti

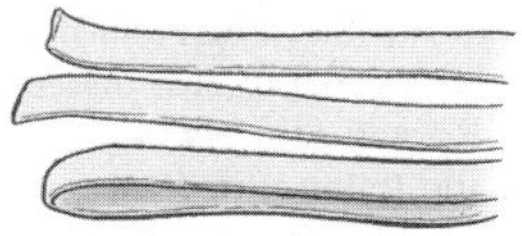

Tagliatelle

Pappardelle

Tubetti or ditaline

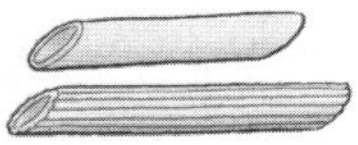

Penne and penne rigate

Vermicelli

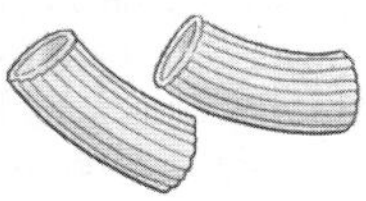

Rigatoni

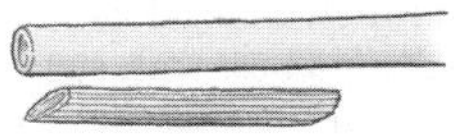

Ziti

DRESSING UP STORE-BOUGHT PASTA SAUCE

Prepared sauces are convenient for quick pasta meals. Look for the simplest versions, and avoid those that are heavy with thickeners and sugar. Simple additions that can boost the flavor of a store-bought sauce are:

A drizzle of extra-virgin olive oil and a sprinkling of black pepper
A handful of mushrooms, sliced and sautéed
Pitted olives and drained capers, chopped
A can or pouch of tuna, drained
Chopped anchovies
A mixture of minced herbs, such as parsley, basil, thyme, and/or rosemary
Minced garlic and/or onion sautéed in olive oil, 255
Browned, crumbled Italian sausage or seasoned ground beef

ADDITIONS TO PASTA

This list of pasta-friendly accompaniments is specifically for dressing plain, hot pasta when you do not wish to make a sauce. For best results, choose complementary ingredients from the list below. For instance, pair ricotta, lemon zest, and fresh herbs with angel hair pasta; or smoked salmon, capers, crème fraîche, and chives with fettuccine.

Extra-virgin olive oil or melted butter
Heavy cream, plain whole milk or Greek yogurt, or crème fraîche
Fresh goat cheese, ricotta, or other soft cheese
Chopped herbs such as oregano, thyme, marjoram, parsley, chives, or mint
Finely grated lemon zest or lemon juice
Chopped sun-dried tomatoes, olives, or capers
Chopped smoked salmon, anchovies, or canned or pouch tuna
Grated hard cheese, such as Romano or Parmesan
Chopped ham, prosciutto, or salami
Sautéed zucchini, roasted eggplant, roasted red bell peppers, cooked peas, or sautéed mushrooms

ABOUT CHEESE FOR PASTA

The combination of pasta and cheese in even the simplest arrangements, such as Fettuccine with Butter and Cheese, 295, can be so superb that it's little wonder the two ingredients are linked in our minds. For the best flavor, ➤ buy cheese in chunks, not preshredded. For robust pasta dishes, use the largest holes of a box grater; for fragile pastas with delicate sauces, use a small hand-held rasp-style grater/zester.

Do not feel obliged, however, to serve grated cheese with every pasta dish. Some are better without it, such as most seafood pasta dishes. Highly seasoned sauces such as those containing olives, capers, or red pepper flakes do not *need* cheese (but who are we to judge?). A common substitute for cheese that adds a pleasing, crunchy texture to pasta is Browned or Buttered Bread Crumbs, 957.

Parmesan cheese is a hard, dry cow's milk cheese with a salty, nutty flavor, and it is the queen of pasta-appropriate cheeses. **Grana Padano, dry Jack, Asiago,** and **Romano** are also excellent for garnishing or tossing with pasta.

Ricotta can be excellent in pasta dishes beyond its usual role in lasagne. We prefer whole-milk ricotta or the very fresh ricotta sold at the cheese counters of some grocery stores (for extra credit, make your own, 965). **Ricotta salata** is simply well-drained, pressed, and salted ricotta—it is hard, dry, salty, and very crumbly. Use as you would Parmesan, for topping pasta dishes.

These suggestions are just that—suggestions. Experiment with different cheeses. For instance, you might add crumbled Gorgonzola to a pasta dish with a rich cream sauce—the piquant flavor of the cheese will add a tangy, salty element. Top baked pasta dishes with sharp white Cheddar or a young Gouda; substitute smoked provolone for half of the usual mozzarella in lasagne. In short, let your cheese drawer and your grocer's cheese selection be your guide.

ABOUT LEFTOVER PASTA

Leftover cooked pasta, with or without sauce, can be reheated in a skillet or casserole or used in a Frittata, 159. To cook in a skillet, add a little olive oil or butter and cook over medium heat until the pieces turn crisp, brown, and chewy. Add a bit of water if necessary to guard against scorching or sticking. Serve the pasta for a quick meal with cooked garlicky kale, chard, or spinach, fried eggs, a sauce, or just a sprinkle of cheese. For a more elaborate treatment, see Frittata di Scammaro, 293. Most leftover tomato sauces and cooked pastas can be combined in Leftover Pasta Casserole, 293. See Additions to Pasta, above, for adding fresh elements to plain leftover pasta.

FRITTATA DI SCAMMARO

4 servings

Despite its name, this fried pasta cake has no eggs. Patience is rewarded when browning the pasta—don't rush it or the seasonings will burn before the cake turns golden. If you have leftover pasta, this is a superb way to use it.

Have ready:

1 pound cooked spaghetti or angel hair pasta (from ½ pound dried)

Heat in a large nonstick skillet over medium heat until hot:

⅓ cup olive oil

Add and cook, stirring, until the garlic is fragrant, about 1 minute:

½ cup black olives, pitted and coarsely chopped
⅓ cup pine nuts
¼ cup golden raisins
3 tablespoons drained capers
4 anchovy fillets, chopped
3 garlic cloves, chopped
½ teaspoon red pepper flakes

Add the cooked pasta and toss with the olive mixture. Reduce the heat to medium-low and allow the pasta to brown, undisturbed, until golden, about 15 minutes. Flip the pasta cake and cook on the second side until browned, about 15 minutes more. Serve cut into wedges, garnished with:

Lemon wedges
Chopped parsley

LEFTOVER PASTA CASSEROLE

4 servings

In the Midwest, this is known as **Johnny Marzetti** when it is made with meat sauce and topped with **1 cup shredded Cheddar or mozzarella (4 ounces)**.

Preheat the oven to 375°F. Butter an 8- to 9-inch square baking dish. Heat in a saucepan:

3 cups pasta sauce, such as Marinara Sauce, 556, Meaty Tomato Sauce, 557, or Puttanesca Sauce, 557

Toss the sauce with:

4 cups leftover pasta

Season to taste with:

Salt and black pepper

Pour the mixture into the prepared baking dish. Sprinkle with:

¼ cup dry bread crumbs
¼ cup grated Parmesan

Dot with:

2 tablespoons butter, cut into small pieces

Bake until the top is browned, about 30 minutes.

ABOUT MAKING FRESH PASTA

Fresh egg pasta has a light, delicate texture and a rich flavor. It is more absorbent than dried pasta and cooks faster. Fresh pasta is generally made with all-purpose flour. That said, you can make it with semolina flour, whole wheat flour, or **00 flour** (a very fine Italian wheat flour produced especially for use in pasta and pizza doughs). Whole eggs, egg yolks, and/or water are used to moisten the flour, and sometimes salt and olive oil are added. Fresh pasta dough is easy to make by hand, or you can mix it in a food processor or mixer. To roll the dough, you will need either a long wooden rolling pin or a pasta rolling machine. You can flavor and color homemade pasta with spinach, 295, or fresh herbs, 295, or add the finely grated zest of a lemon, ¼ cup tomato paste, ¼ cup cooked pureed beet, or 1 tablespoon squid ink to a recipe of Fresh Pasta Dough, 294. You will not need to adjust the amount of flour in the recipe, but you may need a few pinches more when rolling out the dough. ➤ One pound of fresh pasta serves 4 as a main dish.

➤ Letting pasta dough rest, wrapped in plastic, for at least 30 minutes after mixing will make it much easier to work with. To rest the dough for longer, wrap tightly in plastic wrap and refrigerate up to 24 hours or freeze up to 3 months (thaw overnight in the refrigerator). The key to light pasta is gently stretching and pulling the sheet of dough as you roll it thinner and thinner. Whether with a rolling pin or a pasta machine, ➤ work with only one-quarter of the pasta dough at a time, leaving the rest loosely covered.

ROLLING PASTA DOUGH BY HAND

Lightly flour a large surface and use a rolling pin to roll out one-quarter of the dough at a time, repeatedly turning it as the round grows. Continue, flipping the dough over occasionally, until it reaches the desired thickness. ➤ **For ribbon pastas,** such as fettuccine, the dough should be about ⅛ inch thick, thin enough to detect the outline of your hand through it. This thickness is also fine for heartier filled pastas like Baked Cannelloni, 310. ➤ **For tortellini, ravioli,** and other filled dumplings, the sheets should be as thin as possible—sheer enough to see your hand through them.

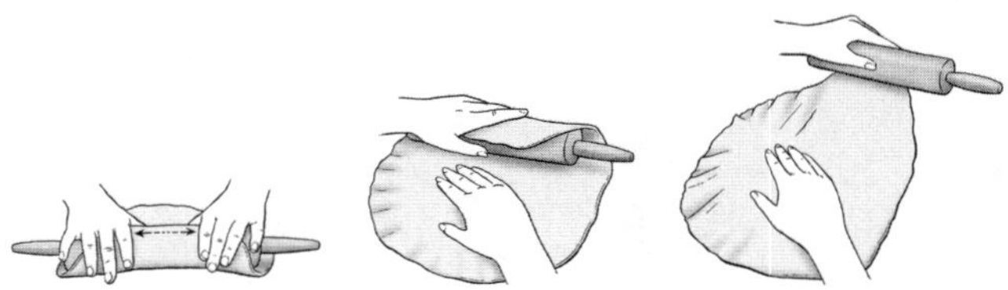

Rolling pasta dough by hand

ROLLING PASTA DOUGH WITH A PASTA ROLLER

Set the machine's rollers at the widest setting. Work with one-quarter of the pasta dough at a time. Lightly flour the dough and pass it through the rollers twice, folding it over onto itself before rolling it each time. Sprinkle flour on the dough any time it threatens to stick. ➤ Guide the dough as it comes out of the rollers with the palm of your hand. Set the rollers one notch closer together and repeat the rolling process. ➤ The dough should go from lumpy and even holey to a satiny sheet. As this happens, begin to stretch the dough gently as it emerges from the rollers. Continue to notch the rollers closer together and roll the pasta through them until the dough reaches the desired thickness.

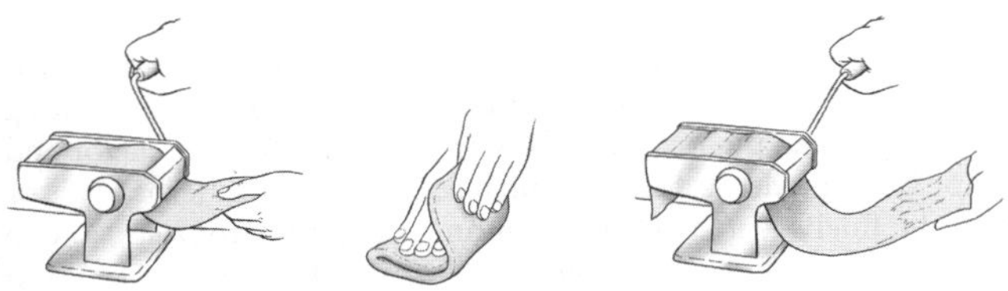

Making pasta with a pasta roller

CUTTING AND MAKING PASTA SHAPES

To cut pasta by hand, ➤ use a sharp knife, pizza cutter, or a pastry wheel. **For filled pasta,** such as ravioli or cannelloni, trim the pasta sheets into long strips about 4 inches wide or leave as wide as the strips come from the machine. For **cannelloni,** cut the strips crosswise into 4-inch squares. For filling and cutting **ravioli** and **tortellini,** see the illustration on 313. ➤ Fill while the dough is still fresh and moist enough to fold and seal.

For unfilled shapes, let the pasta sheet dry on a lightly floured counter until it feels leathery but not at all stiff, about 20 minutes. For **lasagne,** you may trim sheets to the size of your baking dish, or cut into 12 × 4-inch rectangles. For **farfalle** cut the sheet into rectangles about 1½ × 1 inch—use a pastry wheel or pizza cutter—and pinch each one together at the center.

For fettuccine and other ribbon shapes, many pasta machines come with handy cutters that neatly turn dough sheets into long strands of pasta. If working by hand, gently roll up well-floured pasta sheets and cut with a sharp knife to the desired width—about ¼ inch for **fettuccine,** ⅜ inch for **tagliatelle,** and ¾ inch for **pappardelle.** Carefully separate the strips and dust with flour to prevent sticking. Cook the pasta right away or dry it for storage (see below).

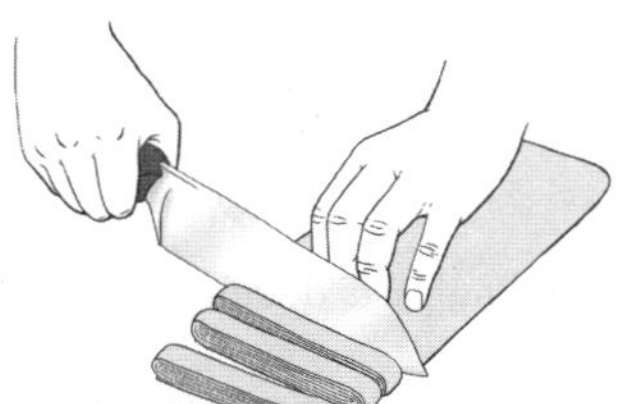

Cutting fresh pasta by hand

STORING FRESH PASTA

To store fresh pasta ribbons, either drape them on a pasta drying rack (we've seen clothes drying racks used in a pinch) or twirl a few strands at a time into loose coils that equal about one serving. Place the coils on wire racks to dry further until needed.

To store ribbon pasta or filled pasta shapes in the refrigerator, dust a large baking sheet with flour and spread out individual pieces (or one-serving coils) so that they do not touch. Refrigerate, covered with plastic wrap. Use within 24 hours.

To freeze fresh pasta, line large baking sheets with parchment or foil. Arrange one-serving coils of fettuccine and other ribbon pastas on the sheets; farfalle, ravioli, and other shapes should be spread out so they do not touch. Freeze unfilled pasta until firm, about 2 hours; freeze filled pastas overnight. Handling carefully, transfer the pasta to heavy-duty freezer bags and seal, leaving some air in the bags to protect the pasta from being crushed. Store in the freezer for up to 2 months. ➤ Frozen pasta can be cooked as is, no thawing necessary (filled shapes will require a few extra minutes to cook).

For longer storage in the pantry, let the pasta dry completely—it should break with a snap—and store in sealed plastic bags. Pasta can also be dried in a food dehydrator. ➤ Make sure it is completely dry before placing in plastic bags, or it will mold. Dried pasta is brittle and breaks easily, so handle carefully.

FRESH PASTA DOUGH

About 1 pound; 6 first-course or 4 main-course servings

Please read About Making Fresh Pasta, 293. Using the larger number of egg yolks will yield a richer pasta. Or, if you have a bunch of egg whites to use up, substitute ½ cup egg whites for the eggs below.

If making by hand, mound on a clean counter:

2 cups all-purpose flour

Make a well in the center and add to the well:

3 large eggs or 2 large eggs and 3 egg yolks
(½ teaspoon salt)
(1 teaspoon extra-virgin olive oil)

Beat the eggs lightly with a fork, drawing in some flour as you go, until the eggs are mixed and slightly thickened. Using the fingertips of one hand, gradually incorporate the flour into the eggs and blend everything into a smooth, not too stiff dough. If the dough feels too dry and crumbly, add a little water as needed. If it is too sticky, add a little more flour. Use a dough scraper to lift and turn the dough if it sticks. Knead the dough for about 10 minutes, or until smooth and pliable.

If using a food processor, combine all the ingredients and pulse until a smooth dough forms, about 1 minute. Remove from the processor and knead for 5 minutes as directed above.

If using a stand mixer, affix the dough hook and mix the ingredients on low speed until they come together into a dough. Increase to medium speed and knead for 2 to 3 minutes. Remove from the mixer and knead for 5 minutes as directed above.

Divide the dough into 4 pieces and wrap the pieces loosely in plastic wrap or cover with an inverted bowl. Let the dough rest at room temperature for at least 30 minutes before rolling it out. Roll out and cut as desired, above.

SEMOLINA PASTA

About 1 pound; 6 first-course or 4 main-course servings

Our preferred dough for lasagna and wide ribbon pasta. Do not roll it to the thinnest setting of a pasta machine, as the semolina flour is somewhat coarse and the dough tends to tear if rolled too thin. Prepare **Fresh Pasta Dough, above,** substituting **1 cup semolina flour** for the same amount of all-purpose flour.

WHOLE WHEAT PASTA

About 1 pound; 6 first-course or 4 main-course servings

Prepare **Fresh Pasta Dough, 294,** substituting **1 cup whole wheat flour** for the same amount of all-purpose flour. This dough may need a little more liquid; if it seems dry and crumbly, add 1 to 2 teaspoons water and knead until blended and smooth.

SPINACH PASTA

About 1 pound; 6 first-course or 4 main-course servings

Blanch, 1047, **10 ounces fresh spinach, trimmed and washed, or frozen spinach leaves.** Drain, transfer to a kitchen towel, and squeeze as much moisture out of the spinach as possible. Very finely mince the spinach. You should have about ½ cup (a little more or less is fine). Prepare **Fresh Pasta Dough, 294,** adding the spinach to the flour with the eggs.

HERB PASTA

About 1 pound; 6 first-course or 4 main-course servings

Have ready ¼ **cup minced strong herbs** (sage, rosemary, thyme, oregano, or marjoram) or ½ **cup minced mild herbs** (basil, chives, parsley, or green onions). Prepare **Fresh Pasta Dough, 294,** adding the herbs to the flour with the eggs.

FRESH EGG NOODLE DOUGH

About 1 pound; 6 side-dish or 4 main-course servings

An all-purpose German-style noodle.

If making by hand, mix together in a large bowl or on the counter, then shape into a mound:

2 cups all-purpose flour
1 teaspoon salt

Make a well in the center of the flour. Lightly beat together and pour into the well:

1 large egg
4 large egg yolks

Beat the eggs with a fork, drawing in some flour as you do so, until they are slightly thickened. Using the fingertips of one hand, gradually incorporate the flour and blend everything into a smooth, not too stiff dough, adding as needed:

1 to 2 tablespoons water

If making in a food processor, combine all the ingredients and process just long enough to blend, 15 to 20 seconds, being careful not to overmix the dough. Once the dough has come together, turn it out onto a lightly floured surface and knead to form a soft dough, about 5 minutes, adding more flour if necessary to keep the dough from sticking.

If using a stand mixer, affix the dough hook and mix the ingredients on low speed until they come together into a dough. Increase to medium speed and knead for 2 to 3 minutes or until smooth.

Divide the dough into 4 pieces and wrap the pieces loosely in plastic or cover them with an inverted bowl. If you have time, let the dough rest at least 30 minutes before rolling it out.

Roll out and cut the dough, 293–94, into fine threads, about ⅛ inch wide, or thick ribbons, about ½ inch wide, then cut into 2-inch pieces.

BOILED PASTA OR EGG NOODLES

6 first-course or 4 main-course servings

Bring to a rolling boil in a large pot:

4 quarts water
2 tablespoons salt
(1 bay leaf)

Drop in:

12 ounces dried or 1 pound fresh pasta or noodles

Return to a boil and cook, stirring frequently, until tender but still firm. Start testing fresh pasta and very thin shapes after about 30 seconds, dried strand pasta after 4 minutes, and macaroni and other short, tubular shapes after 8 minutes. Reserve a cupful of the pasta water and drain the pasta in a large colander. (Rinse the pasta if it is to be used cold.) Quickly transfer to a serving bowl or the empty pot and toss with a sauce (add some of the pasta water if needed).

FETTUCCINE WITH BUTTER AND CHEESE

4 servings

I. Also known as **pasta in bianco** or **fettuccine al burro.** To make it **cacio e pepe,** use Romano cheese and a generous amount of freshly ground black pepper.

Cook in a large pot of boiling salted water:

12 ounces dried fettuccine or tagliatelle or 1 pound fresh

Reserve ½ cup of the pasta water. Drain the pasta, transfer to a serving bowl or back to the pasta cooking pot, and toss with the pasta water and:

1½ cups grated Parmesan or Romano (6 ounces)
4 tablespoons (½ stick) butter, softened
Black pepper to taste

II. Fettuccine Alfredo

Cook the pasta as for **I, above.** While the pasta is cooking, melt in a large skillet over medium heat:

4 tablespoons (½ stick) butter

Drain the pasta and add it to the skillet along with:

1 cup heavy cream
1 cup grated Parmesan (4 ounces)
Salt and black pepper to taste

Toss over low heat until the pasta is well coated.

FETTUCCINE WITH PROSCIUTTO AND PEAS

Prepare **Fettuccine Alfredo, above,** reducing the butter to 1 tablespoon. Melt the butter in a skillet and cook **4 ounces prosciutto, chopped,** until crisp. Add the cream to the skillet and bring to a simmer. Stir in **1 cup fresh or frozen peas** and cook 2 minutes. Stir in the pasta, Parmesan, salt, and pepper.

SPAGHETTI CARBONARA

4 servings

Cook in a large pot of boiling salted water:

12 ounces dried spaghetti or linguine or 1 pound fresh

Meanwhile, cook in a small skillet over medium heat, stirring occasionally, until browned:

6 ounces diced bacon, pancetta, or guanciale

If desired, deglaze the pan with:

(A splash of dry white wine)

Scrape up any browned bits. Set the skillet aside. Beat together in a small bowl:

⅔ cup grated Parmesan or Romano (about 3 ounces)
3 large eggs
¼ teaspoon salt
¼ teaspoon black pepper

Reserve ½ cup of the pasta water. Drain the pasta and return it to the hot pot off the heat. Immediately add the hot bacon and fat and the cheese mixture, stirring to coat thoroughly; the heat of the pasta will cook the eggs. Add the reserved pasta water if necessary to loosen the sauce. Taste and add more salt and pepper, if desired.

SPAGHETTI AGLIO E OLIO (SPAGHETTI WITH GARLIC AND OIL)

4 servings

A simple sauce of olive oil and garlic is one of the purest ways of enjoying good pasta.

Cook in a large pot of boiling salted water:

12 ounces dried spaghetti or linguine or 1 pound fresh

Meanwhile, heat in a large skillet over medium heat:

3 tablespoons olive oil

Add and cook, stirring, until fragrant, about 2 minutes:

3 large garlic cloves, thinly sliced
(1 dried red chile pepper)

Discard the chile pepper, if used. Reserve ½ cup of the pasta water. Drain the spaghetti, add the hot pasta to the skillet along with the pasta water, and toss to combine. Season to taste with:

Salt and black pepper

MACARONI AND CHEESE

6 to 8 side-dish servings

I. Very creamy, very cheesy.

Cook in a large pot of boiling salted water:

2 cups elbow macaroni (8 ounces)

Drain and return to the pot. Add:

4 tablespoons (½ stick) butter, softened

Stir until well blended. Add and stir well:

One 12-ounce can evaporated milk
3 cups shredded extra-sharp Cheddar (12 ounces)
2 large eggs, lightly beaten
½ teaspoon salt, or to taste
(¼ teaspoon cayenne pepper)

Set the pot over low heat and cook, stirring constantly, until the sauce is smooth and the pasta is steaming, about 10 minutes. The sauce should thicken noticeably. Increase the heat slightly if the sauce is still soupy after 5 minutes, but watch it very carefully. Do not overheat, or the sauce will curdle.

II. Prepare **Baked Macaroni and Cheese, below,** but do not preheat the oven or grease a baking dish. Stir all the cheese into the sauce at once. After the pasta is cooked, stir it into the sauce and serve without baking; sprinkle the bread crumbs on top, if desired.

BAKED MACARONI AND CHEESE

6 to 8 side-dish servings

An especially good rendition of a timeless classic. The sauce can be made ahead and combined with the just-cooked macaroni before baking, or the entire casserole can be assembled a day in advance.

Preheat the oven to 350°F. Grease a deep 8- or 9-inch square baking dish. Prepare:

2 cups White Sauce I, 548

Stir in:

½ medium onion, minced
1 bay leaf
¼ teaspoon sweet paprika

Simmer gently, stirring often, for 15 minutes. Have ready:

2 cups grated sharp Cheddar or Colby (8 ounces)

Remove the sauce from the heat, discard the bay leaf, and stir in two-thirds of the cheese. Reserve the rest. Season to taste with:

Salt and black pepper

Meanwhile, cook in a large pot of boiling salted water until tender but firm:

2 cups elbow macaroni, small shells, or tubetti (8 ounces)

Drain the pasta and return it to the hot pot. Stir in the sauce. Pour the mixture into the prepared baking dish and sprinkle with the remaining cheese. Sprinkle over the top:

½ cup Browned or Buttered Bread Crumbs, 957

Bake until the bread crumbs are lightly browned, about 30 minutes. Let stand for 5 minutes before serving.

KIMCHI MAC

Prepare **Macaroni and Cheese I or II, above,** stirring in at the end **1 cup kimchi, store-bought or homemade, 941, drained well and chopped.** Garnish with **chopped green onion.**

MACARONI AND CHEESE FOR A CROWD

14 to 16 side-dish servings

The optional ingredients below are just the beginning. Fresh chorizo (crumbled and browned), Sautéed Onions, 255, Roasted Garlic, 241, blue cheese, or Mushroom Ragout, 251, would also be quite good.

Cook in a large pot of boiling salted water:

1 pound elbow macaroni, small shells, or tubetti

Preheat the oven to 325°F. Grease two 9-inch square baking pans. Have ready:

4 cups grated sharp cheese, such as Cheddar, Gruyère, or Asiago or a combination (1 pound)
1½ cups dry bread crumbs

Mix together half of the cheese and 1 cup of the crumbs in a bowl with:

4 tablespoons (½ stick) butter, melted

Set the bread crumb mixture aside. Drain the pasta, return it to the pasta cooking pot, and mix with:

7 large eggs, beaten
1¾ cups milk
(½ cup chopped olives)

(½ cup chopped ham)
(⅓ cup chopped jarred roasted red bell peppers or pimientos)
(¼ cup finely chopped seeded jalapeños)
(½ cup chopped green onion)
1 teaspoon salt
½ teaspoon black pepper, or to taste

Stir in the remaining cheese and bread crumbs. Divide the mixture between the prepared baking pans. Cover with the reserved bread crumb mixture. Bake until golden brown, about 25 minutes.

FETTUCCINE WITH FRESH HERBS

4 servings

Cook in a large pot of boiling salted water:
12 ounces dried fettuccine or tagliatelle or 1 pound fresh
Meanwhile, rub a warmed serving bowl with:
1 garlic clove, halved
Combine in the bowl:
¼ cup extra-virgin olive oil
About 1 cup chopped fresh herbs (a combination of any of the following: oregano, thyme, basil, tarragon, parsley, sage, mint, and chives)
1 cup grated Parmesan (4 ounces)
Salt and black pepper to taste
Reserve ½ cup of the pasta water. Drain the pasta, add to the bowl, and toss with the herb mixture and reserved pasta water until the cheese is melted and forms a sauce with the oil and herbs.

PASTA PRIMAVERA

4 servings

Any seasonal vegetables can be substituted for the ones used below—just make sure to cut them about the same size. Try sugar snap peas, cooked baby artichokes, green beans, green onions, zucchini, or fava beans.

Bring to a rolling boil in a large pot:
4 quarts water
2 tablespoons salt
Add and cook for 1 minute:
1 small bunch (about 12 ounces) asparagus, trimmed, stems diced, tips left whole
1 small bunch (about 8 ounces) broccoli, cut into very small florets, stems reserved for another use
Scoop out the vegetables with a slotted spoon, transfer to a colander, and rinse under cold water to stop the cooking. Keep the cooking water warm.
Heat in a large skillet over medium heat:
2 tablespoons olive oil
3 tablespoons butter
Add and cook, stirring, until softened, about 5 minutes:
1 large onion, finely chopped
Add the blanched asparagus and broccoli along with:
1 cup fresh or thawed frozen peas
Salt and black pepper to taste
Cook, stirring, until the vegetables are tender. Meanwhile, return the vegetable cooking water to a boil. Drop in and cook until tender but firm:
12 ounces dried fettuccine or tagliatelle or 1 pound fresh
While the pasta is cooking, stir into the skillet with the vegetables and simmer gently until slightly reduced:
1 cup heavy cream
Drain the pasta and add it to the sauce along with:
12 basil leaves, chopped
½ cup grated Parmesan (2 ounces)
Toss to coat over low heat. Serve hot.

PASTA ALLA NORMA (PASTA WITH EGGPLANT AND TOMATO SAUCE)

4 servings

Prepare, using eggplant slices:
Roasted Eggplant II, 238
Meanwhile, heat in a large skillet over medium heat until hot:
2 tablespoons olive oil
Add and cook until fragrant, about 1 minute:
2 garlic cloves, chopped
½ teaspoon red pepper flakes
Stir in, bring to a simmer, and cook, stirring occasionally, until thickened, about 10 minutes:
One 28-ounce can whole tomatoes, chopped, with their juice
Stir in:
8 basil leaves, torn
Salt and black pepper to taste
Cook in a large pot of boiling salted water until tender but firm:
12 ounces dried spaghetti or ziti
Reserve ½ cup of the pasta water. Drain the pasta and toss in a warmed serving bowl with the tomato sauce and pasta water. Add:
½ cup grated ricotta salata or Pecorino Romano (2 ounces)
Toss again. Coarsely chop the eggplant and serve on top of the pasta.

PASTA CON LE SARDE (PASTA WITH SARDINES AND FENNEL)

4 servings

If you are not usually disposed to eating sardines, consider this a "gateway sardine dish."

Combine in a small bowl and set aside:
½ cup dry white wine or ¼ cup warm water
½ teaspoon saffron threads
Heat in a medium skillet over medium heat until hot:
2 tablespoons olive oil
Add and cook, stirring, until well browned:
½ cup dry bread crumbs (preferably coarse)
¼ teaspoon salt
(Finely grated zest of 1 lemon)
Transfer the crumbs to a plate and set aside. Cook in a large pot of boiling salted water until tender but firm:
8 ounces dried bucatini or spaghetti

Reserve ½ cup of the pasta water. Drain the pasta and set aside. Return the empty pasta pot to the heat and add:

3 tablespoons olive oil

Add and cook, stirring, until softened, about 8 minutes:

1 small fennel bulb, thinly sliced, tops reserved
1 small onion, thinly sliced

Stir in and cook until the garlic is fragrant, about 1 minute:

¼ cup golden raisins or dried currants
¼ cup pine nuts
2 garlic cloves, minced
(3 anchovy fillets, rinsed and chopped)

Add the steeped saffron liquid to the pot and cook until reduced by half. Add:

Two 4-ounce tins high-quality sardines (not smoked), drained

Add the pasta and reserved pasta water, tossing with tongs to combine. Cook until the ingredients have melded and everything is heated through. Serve topped with the bread crumbs and:

Chopped fennel fronds
(Grated Romano cheese)

ONE-PAN PASTA WITH TOMATOES AND HERBS

4 servings

A recent "discovery" that has deep roots in Italian home kitchens, this dish flies in the face of the conventional wisdom that pasta must be cooked in a large quantity of water. For a heartier version, brown **8 ounces crumbled Italian sausage, store-bought or homemade, 511,** then transfer to a plate and use 3 tablespoons of the rendered fat (add olive oil if needed) to cook the onions and garlic. Proceed as directed, adding the sausage back in with the basil and cheese.

Warm in a large, deep skillet over medium heat until hot:

3 tablespoons olive oil

Add and cook, stirring, until softened, about 5 minutes:

1 medium onion, thinly sliced
½ teaspoon salt

Add and cook 1 minute more:

3 garlic cloves, thinly sliced
½ teaspoon red pepper flakes
½ teaspoon dried oregano or 1 teaspoon minced fresh oregano

Stir in:

2 tablespoons tomato paste

Allow the tomato paste to brown slightly on the bottom of the skillet, then add:

½ cup dry white wine, water, or chicken or vegetable stock

Scrape any browned bits off the bottom of the skillet. Add:

3 cups water or chicken or vegetable stock
3 Roma or plum tomatoes, chopped, or one 14½-ounce can diced tomatoes
(4 anchovy fillets, minced)

Bring to a boil and add:

12 ounces dried spaghetti, linguine, fettuccine, or bucatini

Boil the pasta, stirring occasionally, until tender, 7 to 10 minutes depending on the pasta shape. If the liquid has evaporated before the pasta is tender, add more liquid and continue cooking. Remove from the heat and stir in:

10 fresh basil leaves, or to taste
Up to ¾ cup grated Parmesan (3 ounces)
Salt and black pepper to taste

FETTUCCINE WITH SALMON AND ASPARAGUS

4 servings

Use spinach fettuccine for an especially attractive dish.

Bring to a rolling boil in a large pot:

4 quarts water
2 tablespoons salt

Add and cook until tender but firm, 1 to 4 minutes, depending on their thickness:

1 pound asparagus, tough ends trimmed, cut into 1-inch pieces

Scoop out the asparagus with a slotted spoon, transfer to a colander, and rinse under cold water to stop the cooking. Add to the boiling water and cook until tender but firm:

12 ounces dried fettuccine or 1 pound fresh

Meanwhile, melt in a large skillet over medium heat:

3 tablespoons butter

Add the asparagus and cook, stirring, just to coat with butter, about 1 minute. Stir in and heat through:

1 cup heavy cream
Finely grated zest of 1 lemon

Drain the pasta and add it to the skillet along with:

4 ounces smoked salmon, cut into thin strips, or cooked fresh salmon, flaked
¼ cup minced chives
¼ cup chopped parsley
(2 to 3 tablespoons capers, to taste, drained)
Salt and black pepper to taste

Toss to combine and serve hot.

LINGUINE WITH CLAM SAUCE

4 to 6 servings

For red clam sauce, add the optional tomatoes. To use canned clams, add **four 6½-ounce cans chopped or whole clams with their juices** to the cooked pasta.

Heat in a large pot over medium-high heat:

1 tablespoon olive oil

Add and cook, stirring, until the onion softens, 3 to 5 minutes:

1 small onion, chopped
1 garlic clove, sliced
½ teaspoon dried oregano
(Pinch of red pepper flakes)

Increase the heat to high and add:

4 pounds small clams (such as littlenecks), scrubbed
1 cup dry white wine

Cover the pot and cook until the clams open. Pour the clams and broth into a large bowl and let cool slightly. Working over the bowl to catch the juices, shuck the clams; if the clams are sandy, rinse

them in the broth as you go. Put the clams in a small bowl, strain the broth, and set aside.
Heat in a large skillet:
2 tablespoons olive oil
Add and cook, stirring, for a few minutes:
(1 large tomato, chopped)
1 large garlic clove, minced
Add the broth and simmer until reduced to about 1 cup. Meanwhile, cook in a large pot of boiling salted water:
1 pound dried linguine or spaghetti
Stir the clams and any liquid into the skillet and stir in:
2 tablespoons butter
¼ cup chopped parsley
Drain the pasta and add to the sauce, tossing to coat. Season to taste with:
Salt and black pepper

PENNE WITH VODKA SAUCE

4 to 6 servings
Heat in a large skillet over medium heat:
3 tablespoons butter or olive oil
Add and cook, stirring, until softened, about 5 minutes:
1 onion, finely chopped
Add and cook, stirring, until fragrant, about 1 minute:
2 large garlic cloves, minced
Stir in:
One 28-ounce can whole tomatoes, drained and chopped
¼ cup vodka
¼ teaspoon red pepper flakes
Simmer briskly for 10 minutes. Stir in and heat through:
½ cup heavy cream
Meanwhile, cook in a large pot of boiling salted water:
1 pound dried penne
Stir into the sauce:
(12 basil leaves, chopped)
Salt and black pepper to taste
Drain the pasta and add to the sauce. If desired, add:
(½ cup grated Parmesan [2 ounces])
Toss well to coat the pasta with the sauce.

TAGLIATELLE WITH WILTED GREENS

4 servings
Cook in a large pot of boiling salted water:
12 ounces dried tagliatelle or fettuccine or 1 pound fresh
Meanwhile, heat in a large skillet over medium heat:
3 tablespoons olive oil
Add and cook, stirring, until barely browned:
½ small onion, chopped
4 garlic cloves, chopped
½ teaspoon red pepper flakes
Increase the heat to high and add:
3 big handfuls arugula leaves or chopped spinach, kale, or mustard greens (about 5 ounces)
Salt and black pepper to taste
Cook, stirring, until the greens are wilted. Reserve ½ cup of the pasta water. Drain the pasta and toss it with the greens, adding:
½ cup grated Romano or Parmesan, or crumbled fresh goat cheese (2 ounces)
and enough of the reserved pasta water to make a cohesive sauce.

PASTA E FAGIOLI (PASTA AND BEANS)

4 servings
This version of pasta and beans is more a thick stew than a soup. If you prefer it thinner, add more stock or broth, or even water. If desired, add a Parmesan rind along with the stock.
Heat in a large saucepan over medium heat:
2 tablespoons olive oil
Add and cook, stirring, until the onion is golden brown, about 8 minutes:
1 medium onion, finely chopped
1 carrot, finely chopped
1 celery rib with leaves, finely chopped
Stir in:
2 large garlic cloves, minced
Cook for 1 minute, then add:
Two 15½-ounce cans cannellini, borlotti, or Great Northern beans, drained and rinsed, or 3 cups cooked white beans
One 14½-ounce can diced tomatoes
Partially mash the beans with the back of a spoon. Add:
2 cups chicken or vegetable stock or broth
Bring to a simmer, partially cover, reduce the heat, and simmer for 5 minutes. Stir in:
1 cup elbow macaroni, ditalini, or other short pasta (4 ounces)
Cook until the pasta is tender. Thin the sauce, if needed, with additional stock, broth, or water. Season to taste with:
Salt and black pepper
Just before serving, stir in:
¼ cup grated Romano
2 tablespoons minced parsley
Ladle into bowls and serve with additional grated cheese.

ORECCHIETTE WITH SAUSAGE AND BROCCOLI RABE

4 to 6 servings
Heat in a large skillet over medium heat:
1 tablespoon olive oil
Add:
1 pound store-bought Italian sausage, removed from its casings, or homemade, 511
Cook, breaking up the meat with a spoon, until nicely browned, about 8 minutes. Stir in and cook for 1 minute:
3 large garlic cloves, minced
¼ teaspoon red pepper flakes
Stir in:
1 large bunch broccoli rabe, trimmed and chopped
Cover and cook just until tender, about 5 minutes. Season to taste with:
Salt and black pepper

Meanwhile, cook in a large pot of boiling salted water:

1 pound orecchiette or cavatelli

Reserve ½ cup of the pasta water. Drain the pasta, add to the skillet along with the pasta water, and toss over low heat. Serve sprinkled with:

Grated Romano

ROSSEJAT DE FIDEOS (SPANISH TOASTED NOODLES)

4 servings

Similar to paella, 334, but made with short, toasted noodles instead of rice. This version is a simple one, but you can dress it up by adding chorizo, a variety of fish and shellfish, chicken thighs, or even rabbit. Flavorful, homemade stock will make this dish truly excellent. To break pasta into small pieces without making a mess, hold them inside a paper bag as you break them apart.

Line a baking sheet with paper towels. Heat in a large skillet or Dutch oven over medium heat:

¼ cup olive oil

Add and cook, stirring occasionally, until toasted and deep brown:

12 ounces dried fideos or angel hair pasta broken into 1-inch pieces

Transfer the pasta to the lined baking sheet. Return the pan to the heat and add:

1 tablespoon olive oil

When hot, add and cook, stirring, until softened:

½ medium onion, diced
½ red bell pepper, diced

Add and cook, stirring, until fragrant, about 1 minute:

4 garlic cloves, chopped
1 teaspoon smoked paprika

Stir in the toasted noodles along with:

3 cups chicken stock, shrimp stock, or clam juice
2 Roma or plum tomatoes, grated on the large holes of a box grater

Bring to a simmer and cook undisturbed and uncovered until most of the stock is absorbed by the noodles, 10 to 15 minutes. Season to taste with:

Salt

If all the liquid has been absorbed, add a splash of stock or water to the pan. Place on top of the pasta:

12 ounces large shrimp (U30), peeled and deveined, 363, or 1 pound mussels or clams in the shell, or a combination

Cover the pan, reduce the heat to medium-low, and cook until the shrimp are cooked through or the mussels or clams have opened, 3 to 5 minutes. Serve with:

Chopped parsley
Aïoli, 564

BUTTERED EGG NOODLES

6 to 8 side-dish servings

Cook in a large pot of boiling salted water:

12 ounces dried egg noodles or 1 pound fresh, 295

Drain and return to the pot. Add:

1 stick (4 ounces) butter, melted or browned, 558
Salt and black pepper to taste

Toss to coat.

ADDITIONS TO EGG NOODLES

Prepare **Buttered Egg Noodles, above**, and add any of the following, alone or in combination:

Up to ½ cup chopped chives, parsley, or dill
1 cup Browned or Buttered Bread Crumbs, 957
Up to ½ cup chopped toasted, 1005, walnuts
Up to 4 slices bacon, cooked until crisp and crumbled
8 ounces cottage cheese, sour cream, plain Greek yogurt, or crème fraîche
2 tablespoons poppy seeds
2 garlic cloves, minced

Or serve buttered egg noodles with:

Boeuf Bourguignon, 465
Beef Stroganoff, 463
Chicken Paprika, 421
Sauerbraten, 464
Coq au Vin, 420

HALUSKI (FRIED CABBAGE AND NOODLES)

6 side-dish servings

File this simple, buttery Polish dish under comfort food. The version below is vegetarian, but slices of pan-fried kielbasa or even crumbled cooked bacon may be stirred in. If adding bacon, use the bacon grease instead of butter to cook the onion.

Melt in a Dutch oven over medium heat:

4 tablespoons (½ stick) butter

Add:

1 large onion, thinly sliced

Cook, stirring, until softened and beginning to brown, about 20 minutes. Reduce the heat if the onion begins to get too dark. Add:

4 tablespoons (½ stick) butter

When the butter is melted, add:

1½ pounds green cabbage, shredded (about 9 packed cups)
½ teaspoon salt

Cover and let steam for 5 minutes to wilt the cabbage. Remove the lid and cook, stirring occasionally, until the cabbage is very soft and starting to brown, about 15 minutes more. While the cabbage cooks, cook until tender in a large pot of boiling salted water:

8 ounces wide dried egg noodles

Drain and add to the cabbage mixture, tossing to combine. Season liberally with:

Black pepper

ABOUT ASIAN NOODLES

After four thousand years of culinary refinement and improvisation, cooks in China, Japan, Thailand, Vietnam, and Korea, among other countries, have developed a wondrous repertoire of noodle dishes. Many of these—yakisoba, sesame noodles, pad Thai, lo mein, and ramen—have become American favorites. Noodles and noodle dishes from Asia—a huge continent with a correspondingly diverse array of cuisines—are plentiful enough for many books to be written on the subject. By including them here in this way, we hope not to pigeonhole them or imply that they can be discussed comprehensively in such a small space, but rather to show that they are in their own class and involve techniques and ingredients that set them apart from their Mediterranean and Eastern European brethren.

These noodles can be categorized by the type of flour or starch with which they are made: wheat or rice; mung bean or sweet potato starch; and buckwheat, to name a few. ➤ When looking for substitutes, choose noodles in the same starch family.

➤ Before stir-frying or pan-frying, cook noodles until tender but firm, rinse under cold water until completely cool, then drain them well.

Chinese egg noodles (*mian*) or *mein* are made with soft wheat flour and eggs. Some are pale yellow in color. **Lo mein noodles,** about 1/8 inch thick, resemble spaghetti and are boiled before stir-frying, pan-frying, or using in cold noodle dishes. **Chow mein noodles** are thinner than lo mein and are often sold parboiled, so they may not need to be boiled before pan-frying or deep-frying. **Wonton noodles** are springy, yellow, and can be very thin and rounded or flat and wide. They are used most often in soups.

Rice noodles are easy to find in dried form, but are increasingly available fresh, especially at pan-Asian grocery stores. Typically, fresh rice noodles need a mere minute or two of cooking. Some fresh or dried rice noodles only need to be rehydrated. Cover with very hot tap water for 10 minutes or until tender (making sure to separate them as they soak by teasing apart the strands with chopsticks), drain, and add to soups or stir-fries. Dried thin rice noodles are the most commonly available (often sold as "rice sticks" or "rice vermicelli"); wider and thicker rice noodles are also worth seeking out for dishes like chow fun.

Starch noodles include so-called cellophane noodles (mung bean or potato starch), Japanese *shirataki* (konjac yam starch), and, our favorite, Korean *dangmyeon* (sweet potato starch). All of them may be added to stir-fries, fried until crisp, or added to soups.

Soba are Japanese noodles made from wheat flour and buckwheat (or buckwheat alone), giving them a slightly nutty flavor and grayish color. Often a course unto itself, soba is traditionally served cold in a square wooden box with a dipping sauce made of Dashi, 78, seasoned with soy sauce and mirin. Do not confuse soba noodles with yakisoba, which is a Japanese dish similar to chow mein using yakisoba or ramen noodles, pork, vegetables, and a flavorful sauce (see Chow Mein, below).

Udon are long, plump Japanese noodles made with wheat flour. Typically served in broth and sprinkled with chopped green onions and shichimi, 1017, these hearty noodles are also quite good when fried like Chow Mein, below. **Somen noodles** are thin—around the size of angel hair pasta—and are often served cold, in the manner of soba. **Ramen noodles** have a springy, chewy texture from being made with alkaline mineral water. They can be found fresh or dried. As any college student or hungry adolescent can attest, dried ramen is tasty, convenient, and economical. With that caveat, we must profess our love for fresh ramen, which is increasingly available refrigerated or frozen in grocery stores. In a pinch, use **yakisoba noodles,** which are similar. Ramen is usually served hot, in satisfying broths adorned with a variety of meats, vegetables, and garnishes. Ramen is also served cold in summer months with a light broth and topped with refreshing garnishes like cucumber and tomato. Hawaiian **saimin noodles** are very similar to ramen, but they are made with more egg and have a firm texture.

LO MEIN

4 servings

Fresh Chinese egg noodles are best in this dish, but any spaghetti-like noodle will work in a pinch. Almost any combination of meat and vegetables can be added. If desired, use leftover meat. Simply slice it and add at the very end, cooking just long enough to reheat it.

Have ready one of the following:

8 ounces boneless, skinless chicken thigh or breast, pork loin, or fresh pork belly, thinly sliced
8 ounces peeled shrimp or scallops, coarsely chopped
8 ounces extra-firm tofu, cut into 1/2-inch cubes

Stir together in a small bowl:

1/2 cup chicken or vegetable stock or broth
3 tablespoons oyster or hoisin sauce
2 tablespoons soy sauce
1 tablespoon sugar
2 teaspoons toasted sesame oil

Cook in a large pot of boiling unsalted water just until tender:

10 ounces dried lo mein or chow mein noodles or spaghetti

Drain, rinse under cold running water, then drain again. Heat a wok or large skillet over medium-high heat. When hot, pour in:

2 tablespoons vegetable oil

Swirl the oil in the pan until shimmering but not smoking. Add the meat, shellfish, or tofu and stir-fry, cooking just until opaque or, for tofu or pork belly, lightly crisped. Add to the pan:

2 cups packed shredded napa cabbage (4 ounces)
1 medium carrot, julienned
3 green onions, cut into 2-inch pieces
4 ounces mushrooms, sliced
1 garlic clove, minced

Stir-fry until the vegetables are softened, about 2 minutes. Pour the stock mixture down the side of the pan, stir, and cook 1 minute. Add the noodles, and toss to combine and heat through. If desired, add and cook for about 30 seconds:

(3/4 cup mung bean sprouts)

Serve hot.

CHOW MEIN

4 servings

Prepare **Lo Mein, above,** using a large nonstick skillet or well-seasoned wok. After cooking the meat or tofu and vegetables, but before adding the stock mixture, transfer them to a plate and set aside. Add **2 tablespoons vegetable oil** to the pan and, when hot, add the cooked noodles. Cook without stirring until they begin to crisp and brown slightly, about 4 minutes. Add the stock mixture and use a spatula to loosen any sticking noodles and toss them with the sauce. Return the meat or tofu and vegetables to the pan and toss to combine.

For **Yakisoba,** substitute **dried yakisoba or ramen noodles** and, if desired, garnish with **(ground nori seaweed [aonori])** and **(beni shoga or pickled ginger).**

BEEF CHOW FUN

4 servings

Broad, pan-fried rice noodles are typical noodle-house fare.

Soak in hot water to cover until softened, about 10 minutes:

8 ounces ½-inch-wide dried rice noodles

Stir together well in a medium bowl:

2 teaspoons soy sauce
1 teaspoon cornstarch

Very thinly slice across the grain:

8 ounces flank steak

Toss the meat in the soy sauce mixture and marinate for 15 minutes. Whisk together in a small bowl:

½ cup chicken stock or broth
¼ cup oyster sauce
2 tablespoons Shaoxing wine, 952, or dry white wine
2 tablespoons soy sauce
2 teaspoons toasted sesame oil
2 teaspoons sugar
2 teaspoons cornstarch

Set aside. Drain the noodles well. Heat a wok or large skillet over high heat. When hot, pour in:

¼ cup vegetable oil

Swirl the oil around the pan until very hot but not smoking. Add the noodles and stir and toss occasionally until some surfaces brown slightly. Transfer to a plate and wipe out the pan. Heat the pan again until hot. Pour in:

2 tablespoons vegetable oil

Swirl the oil around the pan until very hot but not smoking. Add the beef and stir-fry, flipping it in the oil to separate the slices, about 20 seconds. Transfer to the plate with the noodles. Heat the pan again until hot. Pour in:

2 tablespoons vegetable oil

Swirl the oil around the pan until very hot but not smoking. Add and stir briefly:

2 teaspoons fermented black beans
2 garlic cloves, minced
1-inch piece ginger, peeled and grated or minced

Add and toss for 1 minute:

8 ounces green beans, trimmed and cut into 2-inch pieces
1 to 3 Fresno, serrano, or jalapeño peppers, to taste, seeded and cut into thin strips
4 green onions, cut into 2-inch pieces

Return the beef and noodles to the pan and toss to mix thoroughly. Stir in the stock-cornstarch mixture, stirring until the sauce is thickened and the noodles are glazed. Transfer to a serving dish.

SESAME NOODLES

6 servings

These noodles are perfect party or potluck fare: They can be made ahead, hold well, and are best served at room temperature. Chinese sesame paste is ideal for this recipe, but tahini is easier to find and works well.

Whisk together thoroughly in a large bowl:

3 tablespoons soy sauce
2 tablespoons water
2 tablespoons rice vinegar
2 tablespoons smooth unsweetened peanut butter
2 tablespoons seasame paste or tahini
2 tablespoons sugar
1 tablespoon toasted sesame oil
(1 tablespoon chili garlic paste, sriracha, or sambal oelek, 969)
(½ teaspoon ground Sichuan pepper or Five-Spice Powder, 590)
1 garlic clove, minced
1-inch piece ginger, peeled and minced or grated

Set aside. Cook in a large pot of boiling unsalted water until tender:

1 pound dried Chinese egg noodles or spaghetti

Drain in a colander and rinse under cold water until cool. Drain again and add to the bowl of sauce along with:

1 cucumber, peeled, seeded, and julienned
2 carrots, julienned

Toss everything together. Season to taste with more soy sauce and garnish with:

3 green onions, thinly sliced
Chopped roasted peanuts or toasted sesame seeds

DAN DAN NOODLES (SPICY SICHUAN NOODLES)

4 servings

Cook in a large pot of boiling unsalted water until tender:

12 ounces dried Chinese egg noodles or spaghetti

Drain the noodles, rinse under cold water, and drain again. Set aside. Stir together in a small bowl:

¼ cup chicken stock or broth or water
2 tablespoons soy sauce
2 tablespoons chili oil
2 tablespoons Shaoxing wine, 952, or dry sherry
1 tablespoon Chinese black vinegar or unseasoned rice vinegar
2 teaspoons sesame paste or tahini
2 teaspoons toasted sesame oil
2 teaspoons sugar
½ teaspoon ground Sichuan pepper

Set aside. Heat a wok or large skillet over medium heat. When hot, add:

2 tablespoons peanut or vegetable oil

Swirl the oil around in the pan until it shimmers. Add and stir-fry until the garlic browns slightly:

2-inch piece ginger, peeled and minced
2 garlic cloves, minced

Add and cook, breaking up the meat, until no longer pink but not browned:

1 pound ground pork

Drain any excess fat. Stir in the sauce and cook for 2 minutes. Transfer the noodles to a serving plate and pour the pork mixture over them. Garnish with:

Chopped roasted peanuts
Finely chopped green onions

KHAO SOI GAI (THAI CHICKEN CURRY NOODLES)

4 servings

Superlative comfort food from northern Thailand. Tender egg noodles and fall-apart chicken lurk in the coconut-curry broth; the optional crispy fried noodles add crunch. Add more or less curry paste depending on your tolerance for spice and the heat level of the curry paste you have on hand. **Pickled mustard greens** are an optional garnish here, but they add a welcome, tangy complexity to the rich broth. Made from a chunky, thick-leafed variety of mustard, these pickles are available at most Asian markets, either in small cans or plastic pouches (purchase the sour or "acrid" variety).

In a large a pot of boiling unsalted water, cook until just tender:

8 ounces dried Chinese egg noodles or thin egg noodles, or 1 pound fresh wonton noodles

Drain, rinse, and drain again. Set aside. Heat in a large skillet or saucepan over medium heat:

2 tablespoons vegetable oil

Add and fry, stirring, until fragrant and slightly darkened:

2 to 3 tablespoons yellow curry paste or red curry paste, store-bought or homemade, 585

Add:

4 chicken legs, thighs and drumsticks separated, or 2½ pounds bone-in chicken thighs
One 13½-ounce can coconut milk
2 cups chicken stock or broth
¼ cup packed brown sugar or grated palm sugar
2 tablespoons curry powder

Bring to a boil, reduce the heat, and simmer until the chicken is cooked through and tender, about 30 minutes. Meanwhile, if you wish to have a crispy topping for the soup, remove a handful of the cooked noodles and divide the rest among serving bowls. Heat in a small, deep saucepan to 350°F:

(2 inches vegetable oil)

Thoroughly dry the handful of noodles and shape into four "nests." Fry one at a time, turning once, until crispy and golden, about 2 minutes. Drain the nests on a plate lined with paper towels. When the chicken is done, divide it among the bowls. Taste the broth and add:

1 to 2 tablespoons fish sauce, or to taste

Top the noodles with the broth and fried noodles, if using. Serve with:

Lime wedges
Thai fried chili paste, 969, or sambal oelek, 969
Thinly sliced shallots
Chopped cilantro
(Chile-Infused Fish Sauce, 571)
(Chopped pickled mustard greens, see headnote)

PAD THAI

2 or 3 servings

To double this recipe, use two pans, as the ingredients will crowd the pan. Tamarind paste is available in tubs, bottles, or sometimes squeeze tubes at most Asian grocery stores. If you can only find tamarind paste in a block with seeds or need to use a substitute, see About Tamarinds, 195.

Soak in hot water to cover until softened, about 30 minutes:

8 ounces flat, thin dried rice noodles (sometimes labeled "pad Thai noodles")

Meanwhile, stir together in a small bowl:

3 to 4 tablespoons fish sauce, to taste
3 tablespoons palm sugar or brown sugar
2 tablespoons lime juice
2 tablespoons seedless tamarind paste, mixed with 2 tablespoons water

Heat a wok or large skillet over medium-high heat until hot. If desired, cook until toasted and crispy:

(2 tablespoons small dried shrimp, rinsed and dried)

Remove the shrimp, coarsely chop, and set aside. Add to the hot pan:

1 tablespoon vegetable oil

Swirl the oil to coat the pan, then add to the pan and cook, stirring vigorously, until set:

3 eggs, well beaten

Transfer to a plate. Heat the pan until hot again and add:

2 tablespoons vegetable oil

Swirl until very hot but not smoking. Add and cook, stirring constantly, until lightly browned:

6 ounces firm tofu, cut into ½-inch cubes

Transfer the tofu to the plate with the eggs. Add to the pan and cook until pink and cooked through, about 2 minutes:

8 ounces large shrimp, peeled, deveined, 363, and split lengthwise in half

Add the toasted dried shrimp, if using. Drain the noodles well, add to the pan, and toss to coat in the oil. Add the fish sauce mixture and stir well. Return the eggs and tofu to the pan along with:

2 cups mung bean sprouts
4 green onions, cut into 2-inch pieces
½ teaspoon red pepper flakes

Toss with the noodles and cook 2 minutes. Serve with:

Lime wedges
Chopped cilantro
Chopped roasted peanuts
(Finely sliced banana blossom, 955)

KUAYTIAW KHUA KAI (THAI FRIED RICE NOODLES WITH CHICKEN AND ROMAINE)

2 servings

As with pad Thai, if you wish to make this for more people, use two pans to avoid crowding. If desired, substitute **12 ounces fresh rice noodles** (called *sen yai* or chow fun noodles). You do not need to soak or boil fresh noodles.

Soak in warm water for 30 minutes:

6 ounces wide (at least ½ inch) dried rice noodles

Drain well. Bring a pot of water to a boil, add the noodles, and cook for 1 minute. Drain well and rinse under cold water. Whisk together in a small bowl and set aside:

2 large eggs
2 tablespoons oyster sauce
2 tablespoons soy sauce
1 tablespoon sugar
¼ teaspoon ground white pepper

Heat in a wok or a large skillet over medium-high heat:

2 tablespoons vegetable oil or pork fat

Add to the pan and cook, stirring frequently:

8 ounces boneless, skinless chicken thighs, thinly sliced

When cooked through, about 2 minutes, transfer to a plate and set aside. Add the noodles to the pan and allow to cook, undisturbed, for 2 minutes. Add the egg mixture. When the noodles start to brown, flip them. Return the chicken to the pan along with:

2 green onions, thinly sliced
1½ cups coarsely chopped romaine lettuce

With a spatula, break up the noodles and toss everything together. Serve immediately on:

Whole romaine leaves

With:

Chile-Infused Fish Sauce, 571
Thai chile flakes or red pepper flakes
White vinegar

UDON NOODLES IN BROTH

4 to 6 servings

Simplicity itself—freshly cooked noodles in a flavorful broth garnished with green onions and shichimi togarashi.

Bring to a simmer in a large pot over medium heat:

8 cups Dashi, 78, or chicken stock or broth
½ cup soy sauce
½ cup mirin

Cook in a large pot of boiling unsalted water until tender:

1 pound dried udon noodles

Drain the noodles and divide among individual soup bowls. If desired, add to each bowl:

(1 Poached Egg, 153, 4 to 6 eggs total)

Sprinkle with:

Thinly sliced green onions

Ladle 1½ to 2 cups seasoned broth into each bowl. Sprinkle over to taste:

Shichimi togarashi, 1017

SHOYU RAMEN

4 to 6 servings

Bring to a low simmer in a large saucepan over medium heat:

10 cups Poultry Stock, 76, Dashi, 78, or Mushroom Stock II, 79
½ cup soy sauce
½ cup mirin
¼ cup sake
2 garlic cloves, grated
1-inch piece ginger, peeled and grated or minced

In a large pot of boiling unsalted water, cook until tender:

1½ pounds fresh or frozen ramen noodles or 1 pound dried

Divide the noodles among bowls and pour the seasoned stock over them. Top with any of the following:

Chashu Pork, 496, roasted pork, cooked ground pork, or firm tofu
Toasted sesame oil and/or chili oil
Thinly sliced green onions
Corn kernels, bamboo shoots, kimchi, cooked mushrooms, or raw enoki mushrooms
Shichimi togarashi, 1017
Toasted nori seaweed
Hard-Boiled Egg, 151, cooked so that the yolks are runny or barely set

MISO RAMEN

Prepare **Shoyu Ramen, above**, substituting ½ **cup red miso** for the soy sauce, reducing the mirin to ¼ cup, and adding **2 teaspoons toasted sesame oil.**

COLD SOBA NOODLES

4 servings

This is the classic way to eat buckwheat noodles—chilled but accompanied by hot and spicy condiments, creating an appealing contrast. If desired, serve with tempura-battered fried shrimp, 348, or vegetables, 204.

Bring to a gentle boil in a medium saucepan over medium heat:

2½ cups Dashi, 78
½ cup plus 2 tablespoons soy sauce
¼ cup mirin
1 teaspoon sugar

Remove from the heat and let cool to room temperature. Using scissors, cut into fine shreds:

1 sheet toasted nori, 1016

Arrange on a plate:

½ cup sliced green onions
⅓ cup grated daikon radish
2 tablespoons wasabi paste

In a large pot of boiling unsalted water, cook until nearly tender:

12 ounces soba noodles

Drain in a colander and rinse under cold water until cool, swishing the noodles with your hand to rinse well. Divide the noodles among 4 bowls. Sprinkle each serving with nori shreds. Divide the dipping sauce into 4 little bowls and place one beside each serving. Place the plate with wasabi on it within easy reach. To eat, add a little green onion, radish, and wasabi to the dipping sauce, and dip each bite of noodles in the sauce.

JAPCHAE (KOREAN SWEET POTATO NOODLES)

4 side-dish servings or 2 main-course servings

Traditionally, *japchae* is served as a side dish, family-style, at large gatherings, but it makes a lovely vegetarian main dish as well. Many thanks to our friend Yeojin Park for this recipe.

Heat in a large skillet over medium-high heat:

1 tablespoon vegetable oil

Add and cook, stirring, until just tender, about 5 minutes:

½ large onion, thinly sliced
A pinch of salt

Transfer the onions to a large bowl. Add to the skillet:

4 ounces shiitake mushrooms, stems discarded, caps thinly sliced (about 1½ cups sliced)
A pinch of salt

Cook until softened, about 5 minutes. If needed, add a little more oil to the skillet. Transfer the mushrooms to the bowl with the onions. Add to the skillet:

1 tablespoon vegetable oil
1 large carrot, cut into matchsticks
A pinch of salt

Cook, stirring, until barely tender, about 4 minutes. Transfer to the bowl with the other vegetables. Bring a large pot of salted water to a boil and add:

1 bunch mature spinach (about 2 lightly packed cups), well washed

Blanch for 1 minute, then use a slotted spoon or spider to transfer the spinach to a colander to drain. When cool enough to handle, press excess moisture out of the spinach and transfer to the bowl with the other vegetables.

Add to the boiling water:

4 ounces sweet potato starch noodles

Cover the pot, remove from the heat, and let the noodles steep until tender, 7 to 8 minutes. Drain well, shaking the noodles in the colander to remove excess water. Transfer the noodles to the bowl with the vegetables. Add:

2 tablespoons soy sauce
1 tablespoon toasted sesame oil

Toss everything together and taste, adding more soy sauce or sesame oil if needed. Before serving, garnish with:

Sesame seeds
Chopped green onions

BÚN (VIETNAMESE RICE NOODLE BOWLS)

4 servings

Grilled, broiled, and seared meat is excellent in this dish, especially Grilled Vietnamese-Style Pork, 493, Beef Kebabs, 46, Salt-and-Pepper Shrimp, 363, Crispy Pan-Fried Tofu, 286, or Caramelized Tamarind Tempeh, 288. Or simply marinate the desired protein in Vietnamese-Style Marinade, 581, then bake, sauté, or grill.

Prepare and set aside:

Nuoc Cham, 571

Soak in warm water for 30 minutes or until tender:

12 ounces dried, thin rice noodles

Drain well and divide among 4 bowls. Top the noodles with:

2 cups shredded leaf lettuce, romaine, or napa cabbage
1 large cucumber, peeled, seeded, and thinly sliced
1 large carrot, shredded
4 ounces daikon or red radishes, shredded or thinly sliced
5 green onions, chopped

Arrange on top of the vegetables:

1 pound chicken, pork, beef, tofu, shrimp, or a combination, cooked and cut into bite-sized pieces

Serve with the *nuoc cham* to spoon over the bowls and any of the following garnishes:

Lime wedges
Mung bean or radish sprouts
Sprigs of assorted herbs, such as cilantro, mint, and shiso
Sambal oelek, 969, or sriracha
Chopped roasted peanuts

ABOUT DUMPLINGS

There are as many types of dumpling as there are doughs. Dumplings are an ideal accompaniment to broths, soups, and stews, especially since many of them can be whipped up quickly and simply added to the simmering pot. At the risk of sounding indulgent, we must admit that we are partial to sautéing some types of cooked dumplings in butter until crisped and browned, perhaps with a smashed garlic clove, and then tossing them with herbs and cheese (Spätzle, 308, Potato Gnocchi, 306, and Malfatti, 307, are particularly good this way). Of course, you may treat them as you would pasta and simply top them with a hearty tomato sauce or ragu. To learn more about filled dumplings, see 313.

Drop dumplings, which often resemble drop biscuits, tend to expand significantly during cooking. Though they can be cooked in water or stock, we prefer to simmer them on the top of soups, stews, or fricassees.

When cooking dumplings, bring an ample quantity of soup, broth, gravy, or stew to a simmer in a wide pot. To drop dumpling batter from a spoon easily, dip the spoon in the liquid first, then scoop up a spoonful of batter and drop it gingerly into the pot. ➤ Never crowd the pot. Cover and cook as directed. Be sure the pot never exceeds a simmer, or the dumplings may become soggy or even disintegrate. When the dumplings look fluffy, test them for doneness as you would a cake, by inserting a wooden toothpick and seeing that it comes away clean. Serve as soon as they are done, or they will become heavy. Some good additions to drop dumpling dough are parsley or other herbs, cheese, or grated onion. Also see Matzo Ball Soup, 84.

Batter dumplings such as Spätzle, 308, and pasta-like dumplings like Potato Gnocchi, 306, also benefit from the water or broth being at a simmer—not a boil. Unlike drop dumplings, they are not cooked on the surface of a soup or stew, but rather in a pot of salted water. They may be simply tossed with butter or any sauce you might use for pasta, 291, but they are at their best sautéed in butter until browned.

DUMPLINGS

6 to 8 servings

Whisk together in a bowl:

2 cups all-purpose flour
1 tablespoon baking powder
¾ teaspoon salt

Bring just to a simmer in a small saucepan:

1 cup milk
3 tablespoons butter

Add to the dry ingredients. Stir with a fork or briefly knead until the mixture comes together. If desired, mix in:

(1/4 cup finely chopped parsley or 2 tablespoons minced chives)

Gently drop spoonfuls of the batter on top of a simmering stock, broth, or stew. The dumplings should barely touch. Cover them and simmer gently for 10 minutes. Depending on the size of your pot, you may need to cook them in batches. Serve at once.

FARINA DUMPLINGS COCKAIGNE

6 servings

A favorite of Marion Becker's. Farina is often sold under the name "cream of wheat." Though usually cooked and served in soup, these dumplings may be simmered in stock, broth, or water, then served with gravy. Or they may be drained after cooking, placed in a greased baking dish, and covered with Tomato Sauce, 556. Sprinkle the top with 1/4 cup grated Parmesan, dot it with 1 tablespoon butter, and bake in a 350°F oven for about 15 minutes.

Bring to a boil in a medium saucepan:

2 cups milk

Add, stir, and simmer until thick, about 5 minutes:

1/2 cup farina
1 tablespoon butter
1/2 teaspoon salt
1/8 teaspoon sweet paprika
(1/8 teaspoon grated or ground nutmeg)

Remove from the heat and beat in vigorously one at a time:

2 large eggs, at room temperature

The heat of the mixture will thicken and cook the eggs. Moisten your hands with cool water. Shape the dough a generous teaspoon at a time into small balls and drop into a simmering stock, broth, or stew. Cook, covered, about 2 minutes. Depending on the size of your pot, you may need to cook them in batches. Serve at once.

CORNMEAL DUMPLINGS

4 to 6 servings

We believe that dumplings reached their peak in a small Kentucky town when we were served chicken with dumplings—the latter light as thistledown. "Oh, yes," said the hotel proprietress wearily, "they are always like that when our cook is drunk."

Combine in a bowl:

3/4 cup all-purpose flour
1/2 cup fine cornmeal
(2 tablespoons grated onion or minced green onion)
1 teaspoon baking powder
1/2 teaspoon salt
1/4 teaspoon black pepper

Bring to a simmer in a small saucepan:

1/3 cup water or milk
1 tablespoon butter or bacon fat

Pour the milk mixture over the flour mixture and mix together until cool. Add:

3 egg yolks

Knead the yolks into the dough until combined. Gently drop spoonfuls of the batter into a simmering stock, broth, or stew. Simmer the dumplings for about 15 minutes. Depending on the size of your pot, you may need to cook them in batches. Serve at once.

BUTTERKLÖSSE (BUTTER DUMPLINGS)

4 servings

Beat with a handheld electric mixer in a medium bowl until smooth:

2 tablespoons butter, softened

Beat in:

2 large eggs, lightly beaten, at room temperature

Stir in:

1/2 cup all-purpose flour
1/4 teaspoon salt

Drop the batter from a teaspoon into a simmering stock, broth, or stew. Cover and simmer about 5 minutes. Depending on the size of your pot, you may need to cook them in batches. Serve at once.

KARTOFFELKLÖSSE (POTATO DUMPLINGS)

6 to 8 servings

These are light and tender, especially good with a roast and gravy. They are traditional with Sauerbraten, 464. Some cooks like to put a tiny sprig of parsley in the center of each dumpling.

Place in a large pot:

2 1/2 pounds russet potatoes, peeled and quartered

Add water to cover, bring to a boil, then reduce to a simmer and cook until the potatoes are tender, about 20 minutes. Drain and push through a potato ricer or force through a sieve with the back of a spoon onto a baking sheet. Allow the potatoes to cool until just barely warm. Stir in, still on the baking sheet:

2 large eggs
1 cup all-purpose flour
1 1/2 teaspoons salt

Stir with a fork just until the ingredients are blended and fluffy. Gently shape into 1-inch balls. Bring to a simmer in a medium saucepan:

4 quarts water

Working in batches if necessary, drop the dumplings into the liquid and simmer gently for about 10 minutes. Use a slotted spoon to transfer them to a warmed serving dish. Stir together in a bowl:

1 stick (4 ounces) butter, melted, or 1/2 cup hot bacon fat
1 cup dry bread crumbs

Sprinkle the crumbs over the dumplings and serve.

POTATO GNOCCHI

I. TRADITIONAL

About 200 gnocchi; 18 first-course or 10 main-course servings

It is traditional to cook and sauce potato gnocchi like pasta and eat them as a first course or one-dish meal. Once cooked through, gnocchi are also excellent sautéed in butter and garlic, dressed with Parmesan, black pepper or red pepper flakes, and chopped fresh herbs.

Preheat the oven to 400°F. Scrub well:

2 pounds russet potatoes

Prick each potato in a dozen places with a fork. Bake directly on an oven rack until easily pierced with a fork, about 1 hour. While the potatoes are still hot, split them lengthwise and scoop out the pulp into a potato ricer or food mill fitted with the finest disk. Rice or mill the potato onto a baking sheet and spread it out to let as much steam escape as possible. Once all the steam has dissipated, sprinkle and drizzle evenly over the potatoes:

1⅓ cups all-purpose flour
2 egg yolks, beaten
1 teaspoon salt

Mix these ingredients into the potato using a dough scraper or spatula until combined. Turn the dough out onto a floured work surface and briefly knead until smooth. Bring 4 inches of well-salted water to a simmer in a large pot. Have ready:

3 tablespoons butter, melted, or extra-virgin olive oil

Roll about 2 tablespoons of the dough into a ¾-inch-thick log. Cut crosswise into ¾-inch pieces. Press each piece against the tines of a fork, rolling it as you do; this will naturally cause the gnocchi to curl slightly, leaving one side indented and the other ridged. Test the gnocchi by dropping a few into the simmering water and cooking until they float, about 2 minutes. They should hold a firm shape and be chewy to the bite. If they are too soft or disintegrate, knead into the dough:

(Up to 3 tablespoons all-purpose flour)
(Some beaten egg)

Test again. When the dough is right, roll the rest of the dough into three or four ¾-inch-thick ropes. Cut the ropes into ¾-inch pieces, shape the dough on the fork as directed above, letting them drop onto a lightly floured baking sheet. Bring the water back to a simmer. ➤ Do not let the water reach a full boil. Drop one-third to half of the gnocchi into the pot and simmer, uncovered, until they float, then remove with a slotted spoon or skimmer to a wide bowl. ➤ Never drain gnocchi by pouring the contents of the pot into a colander. Drizzle some of the melted butter over the gnocchi. Toss to coat. Repeat until all the gnocchi are done. Serve hot with:

Additional melted butter or olive oil and grated Parmesan, a tomato sauce, 556–58, or Pesto, 586

To make gnocchi ahead, spread uncooked gnocchi on a lightly floured baking sheet and freeze until hard, then transfer to a freezer bag or container; they will keep frozen for up to 1 month. Cook directly from the freezer, adding about 1 minute to the cooking time.

II. QUICK
About 60 gnocchi; 4 servings

Instant potatoes turn gnocchi-making into a breezy, 15-minute affair rather than an hours-long commitment. While we cannot claim that they are equal to their from-scratch brethren in every way, they are tasty in their own right and a great way to get your bearings as you learn how to make gnocchi.

Place in a medium bowl:

1 cup instant mashed potato flakes

Pour over them:

1 cup boiling water

Stir to combine, then stir in:

1 cup all-purpose flour
1 large egg
¾ teaspoon salt

Knead briefly until the mixture is smooth, then shape and cook as described in **version I, 306,** dusting the surface with flour as needed.

MALFATTI (SPINACH-RICOTTA GNOCCHI)
5 side-dish servings

Malfatti means "badly made," so you'll know you've made these properly if they seem a little . . . rustic. Please read about Forming Quenelles, 1046, for guidance on how to use two spoons to shape these, but don't worry about achieving a perfect shape. You may substitute **one 10-ounce package frozen spinach, thawed and squeezed dry,** for the fresh spinach, if desired.

Cook in rapidly boiling water until wilted, less than 1 minute:

1 pound fresh spinach

Transfer to an ice water bath to cool, drain well, then place in a clean kitchen towel and wring out as much moisture as possible. Finely chop the spinach and place in a medium bowl. Add and stir to combine:

1 pound whole-milk ricotta
1 cup all-purpose flour
½ cup finely grated Romano or Parmesan (2 ounces)
2 large eggs
½ teaspoon salt
½ teaspoon black pepper

Bring a large pot of salted water to a simmer. With a spoon, scoop up about 1 tablespoon of the gnocchi mixture. Use a second spoon to shape the mixture into rough ovals or balls, then drop into the simmering water. Cook several at a time until they float. The dumplings will shed a little spinach into the water; this is normal. Never allow the water to boil. Transfer the dumplings with a slotted spoon to a serving dish and repeat with the remaining gnocchi. To serve, top the gnocchi with:

Melted butter or Brown Butter, 558
Bread crumbs

Or place the gnocchi in a lightly greased baking dish, drizzle with butter and finely grated Parmesan, and bake at 400°F until lightly browned, about 15 minutes.

ROMAN-STYLE BAKED GNOCCHI
5 side-dish servings

For a similar dish that uses polenta, see Fried Polenta, 323. After cutting out the gnocchi, there will be scraps. You may place these in a second, small dish, top with cheese, and bake as directed. These make a tasty cook's snack or delicious leftovers.

Bring to a boil in a medium saucepan:

2½ cups milk
1 teaspoon salt

Reduce the heat to medium-low and slowly stream into the milk while stirring:

1 cup semolina flour

Stir until the mixture is very thick, like polenta; this will happen almost immediately. Remove from the heat and stir in:

½ cup finely grated Parmesan (2 ounces)
1 large egg, beaten

Grease a rimmed baking sheet and spread the semolina mixture onto it. Cover with plastic wrap and let set until cool enough to touch. Use your hands to press the mixture into an even layer ½ inch thick. Refrigerate, covered, at least 2 hours or until firm.

Preheat the oven to 400°F. Grease a 9-inch square baking dish. Using a 2-inch round cookie or biscuit cutter or a drinking glass, cut out rounds of the semolina mixture and transfer them to the baking dish, overlapping them slightly. Top with:

½ cup finely grated Parmesan (2 ounces)
2 tablespoons butter, cut into small pieces

Bake until golden brown, about 25 minutes.

BAKED GNUDI WITH BROWN BUTTER AND SAGE

4 side-dish servings

Think of these as lazy, cheesy gnocchi.

Preheat the oven to 400°F. Butter an 8- or 9-inch baking dish or pie plate. Combine in a medium bowl:

1 cup whole-milk ricotta
½ cup finely grated Romano or Parmesan (2 ounces)
⅓ cup all-purpose flour
1 large egg
¼ teaspoon salt
(Pinch of grated or ground nutmeg)

Using two spoons, scoop heaping tablespoons of the mixture into the baking dish, forming rough, irregularly shaped dumplings. Prepare, using 4 tablespoons butter:

Brown Butter, 558

When the butter is browned, remove from the heat and add:

2 tablespoons finely chopped sage

The butter will foam. When the foam subsides, pour the butter over the gnudi. Bake until browned, 15 to 20 minutes. Serve topped with:

Finely grated Romano or Parmesan

GNOCCHI PARISIENNE

6 servings

Prepare, omitting the sugar:

Choux Paste, 697

Stir in:

½ cup finely grated Parmesan (2 ounces)
(Up to 2 tablespoons fresh thyme leaves or minced chives)
(½ teaspoon black pepper)

Bring a large pot of water to a boil. Transfer the dough to a zip-top bag or a pastry bag. Cut a hole in one corner of the bag or pastry bag (there is no need to use a tip if using a pastry bag) about 1 inch wide. Holding the bag over the pot, gently squeeze it. When about 1 inch of dough is extruded, use a sharp knife or scissors to cut it off, letting it fall into the water. Repeat until about 15 or so dumplings are in the boiling water. When the gnocchi float, allow them to cook 2 minutes more, then transfer with a slotted spoon to a plate or baking sheet. Cook the remaining dough in the same way.

Melt in a large skillet, preferably nonstick, over medium heat:

1 tablespoon butter

Add half the gnocchi and sauté, stirring occasionally, until lightly browned. Transfer to a serving dish and repeat with remaining gnocchi and more butter. Top with:

½ cup finely grated Parmesan (2 ounces)

Alternatively, the gnocchi may be layered in a dish with:

Any tomato sauce, 556–58

and sprinkled with:

Grated Parmesan

Bake at 375°F until warmed through and the cheese is melted, about 20 minutes.

SPÄTZLE

4 or 5 side-dish servings

These German egg dumplings are often served alongside a goulash or stew and are particularly welcome next to Wienerschnitzel, 475, or Sauerbraten, 464. Substituting milk for the water produces a richer, if slightly denser, dumpling. If desired, sauté the cooked spätzle in butter until the edges are crisp.

Combine in a bowl:

1½ cups all-purpose flour
¾ teaspoon salt
½ teaspoon baking powder
Pinch of grated or ground nutmeg

Beat together in a small bowl:

2 large eggs
½ cup water or milk

Add to the flour mixture. Beat well with a wooden spoon to create a fairly elastic batter. Bring to a simmer in a large saucepan:

6 cups salted water or chicken stock or broth

Drop small bits of the batter from a spoon into the bubbling liquid, or force the batter through a colander, potato ricer, or spätzle maker to produce strands of dough that will puff into irregular shapes. The spätzle are done when they float to the surface. They should be delicate, light, and slightly chewy. If the first few taste heavy and dense, add a few more drops of water or milk to the batter before continuing. Lift the cooked spätzle from the saucepan with a strainer or slotted spoon. Serve sprinkled with:

Melted butter or ⅓ cup Browned or Buttered Bread Crumbs, 957

Or transfer to a shallow broilerproof baking dish and preheat the broiler. Top the spätzle with:

¼ cup grated mild cheese, such as Swiss, Emmentaler, or Gouda

Broil until the cheese is melted, about 1 minute.

ABOUT BAKED PASTA AND NOODLE DISHES

You can easily make delicious casseroles by tossing cooked pasta or noodles with sauces, meats, vegetables, or cheese. Try one of the following classics like pastitsio or kugel, or improvise by adding leftovers or other ingredients you have on hand. If assembled in advance and refrigerated before baking, ➤ add at least 15 minutes to the baking time. If the top of the casserole is browning too quickly, or if you like a moister baked pasta, ➤ cover the baking dish with foil for all or part of the cooking time. For classic, comforting American fare like Tuna-Vegetable Casserole, see 538.

PASTITSIO

8 to 12 servings

This Greek casserole is a little time-consuming to prepare, but it can be done in stages. In fact, it tastes best when assembled ahead and refrigerated for a day before baking.

Prepare:

3 cups White Sauce I, 548

Heat in a medium saucepan over medium heat:

1 tablespoon olive oil

Add and cook, stirring, until beginning to soften, about 5 minutes:

1 large onion, chopped

Add:

1 pound ground lamb or beef
2 garlic cloves, minced

Cook, stirring to break up the meat, until no longer pink. Stir in:

One 14½-ounce can diced tomatoes
½ cup dry red wine
1 tablespoon tomato paste
1½ teaspoons salt
1 teaspoon ground cinnamon
1 teaspoon dried oregano
½ teaspoon black pepper

Simmer, uncovered, for 15 minutes. Take off the heat and stir in:

¼ cup minced parsley

Meanwhile, cook in a large pot of boiling salted water until slightly undercooked:

1 pound elbow macaroni, penne, or other small pasta

Drain and combine the pasta and meat sauce. (The pasta mixture and the white sauce can be covered and refrigerated for up to 2 days before assembling.)

Preheat the oven to 375°F. Grease a 13 × 9-inch baking dish. Spoon the pasta mixture into the dish. Place the white sauce in a large bowl and mix in:

4 large eggs, beaten
½ cup grated Parmesan (2 ounces)
½ cup crumbled feta cheese

Pour the white sauce over the pasta. Sprinkle with:

½ cup grated Parmesan (2 ounces)

Bake until set and golden, 35 to 40 minutes. Let stand for 10 minutes before cutting.

MUSHROOM-WALNUT NOODLE KUGEL

10 to 12 side-dish servings

Kugel is a type of casserole served at traditional Jewish holiday meals, and there are countless recipes for them, both sweet and savory. For another savory favorite, see Potato Kugel, 268. If you prefer a dish without a crunchy top, bake covered with foil.

Preheat the oven to 350°F. Grease a 13 × 9-inch baking dish.

Heat in a large skillet over medium-high heat:

½ cup vegetable oil

Add and cook, stirring, until golden brown, about 10 minutes:

2 medium onions, thinly sliced

With a slotted spoon, transfer the onions to a bowl. Add to the oil remaining in the skillet:

1 large portobello mushroom cap, cut into 1-inch pieces
8 ounces button mushrooms, sliced
Salt and black pepper to taste

Cook, stirring, until the mushrooms are browned, about 10 minutes. Set the skillet aside. Meanwhile, cook in a large pot of boiling salted water:

12 ounces dried egg noodles

Drain and place in a bowl. Add and stir together well:

5 large eggs, well beaten

Stir in the onions and mushrooms with the oil from the skillet, along with:

¾ cup coarsely chopped toasted, 1005, walnuts

Pour the mixture into the baking dish and bake until lightly browned, about 35 minutes. Let stand 10 minutes before serving.

SWEET NOODLE KUGEL

12 to 14 side-dish servings

Preheat the oven to 325°F. Grease a 13 × 9-inch baking dish. Stir together in a large bowl:

2 cups sour cream
1 pound cottage cheese
1 pound cream cheese, softened
3 large eggs
½ cup sugar
2 teaspoons vanilla
1 teaspoon ground cinnamon
½ teaspoon salt

Cook in a large pot of boiling salted water until slightly undercooked:

1 pound dried egg noodles

Drain, add to the cheese mixture, and stir together well. Pour into the prepared baking dish. Bake for 1½ hours. Meanwhile, stir together in a small bowl:

(¾ cup dark or golden raisins)
½ cup packed dark brown sugar
½ cup chopped toasted, 1005, walnuts
2 tablespoons all-purpose flour
2 teaspoons ground cinnamon
2 tablespoons butter, softened

Sprinkle over the top of the casserole. Bake for 30 minutes more, until browned. Let stand 10 minutes before serving.

BAKED MANICOTTI OR SHELLS

8 servings

If you choose one of the less-cheesy fillings, try topping with **3 cups White Sauce I, 548,** and **1 cup shredded Parmesan (4 ounces)** instead of tomato sauce and mozzarella.

Prepare and have ready:

3 cups any tomato sauce, 556–58
4 cups any pasta filling, 311–12

Preheat the oven to 350°F. Lightly grease a 13 × 9-inch baking dish.

Cook in a large pot of boiling salted water until barely tender:

1 pound manicotti or jumbo shells

Drain. Stuff the pasta with the filling and arrange side by side in the prepared baking dish. (At this point, the dish can be covered and refrigerated for up to 24 hours.) Spoon the tomato sauce over the pasta and sprinkle with:

2 cups shredded mozzarella (8 ounces)
½ cup grated Parmesan or Romano (2 ounces)

Cover with foil and bake until heated through, about 40 minutes. Let stand 10 minutes before serving.

BAKED CANNELLONI OR CRESPELLES

8 servings

For **Cannelloni**, prepare **one recipe of any fresh pasta dough, 294–95, rolled out and cut into 4-inch squares, 293–94.** Leave the pasta squares unboiled. For **Crespelles,** prepare **one recipe of Savory Crêpes, 646.** Prepare the sauces, fillings, and baking dish as for **Baked Manicotti or Shells, 309.** Spread about ¼ cup of filling along one edge of each pasta square or in a line in the center of each crêpe. Roll them up to form a tube shape, and place seam side down in the greased baking dish. Cover with the sauce and cheese and bake as directed.

LASAGNE

8 to 12 servings

Have ready:

7 to 8 cups any tomato sauce, 556–58
15 ounces ricotta
1 pound mozzarella, shredded
1 cup grated Parmesan (4 ounces)

Preheat the oven to 375°F. Grease a deep 13 × 9-inch baking dish, 13 × 9 × 2-inch baking pan, or lasagne pan. Have ready:

12 ounces dried lasagna noodles or 1 pound any fresh pasta dough, 294–95, rolled and cut into 4 × 12-inch sheets, 293–94

For dried noodles, cook in a large pot of boiling salted water until barely tender. Drain the pasta, rinse under cool water, and blot dry. For fresh lasagna noodles, do not boil. Spread a thin layer of sauce over the bottom of the prepared pan. Arrange a single layer of pasta, slightly overlapping, in the bottom of the pan. Spread with one-third of the ricotta. Scatter one-quarter of the mozzarella over the ricotta and sprinkle with ¼ cup of the Parmesan. Reserve 2 cups of the sauce for the top of the lasagne, and spoon about one-third of the remaining sauce into the pan. Add another layer of pasta, and continue layering until you have 4 layers of pasta with 3 layers of filling. Spread the reserved sauce over the top layer of pasta. Sprinkle with the remaining mozzarella and Parmesan. Place the pan on a baking sheet to catch any drips, loosely cover the pan with foil, and bake for 30 minutes. Uncover and continue to bake until golden and bubbling, 20 to 25 minutes more. Let stand 15 minutes before serving.

LASAGNE BOLOGNESE

8 to 10 servings

Prepare the white sauce and meat sauce a day or so ahead, if you like.

Prepare and have ready:

4 cups Bolognese Sauce, 558
3 cups White Sauce I, 548
1 cup grated Parmesan, Romano, Asiago, or dry Jack (4 ounces)

Preheat the oven to 350°F. Grease a deep 13 × 9-inch baking dish, 13 × 9 × 2-inch baking pan, or lasagne pan. Have ready:

12 ounces dried lasagna noodles or 1 pound Spinach Pasta Dough, 295, rolled and cut into 4 × 12-inch sheets, 293–94

For dried noodles, cook in a large pot of boiling salted water until barely tender. Drain the pasta, rinse under cool water, and blot dry. For fresh lasagna noodles, do not boil. If necessary, warm the Bolognese sauce. Spread 1 cup Bolognese sauce over the bottom of the prepared pan. Cover with a layer of pasta, overlapping the noodles slightly. Reserve ¾ cup of the white sauce for the top of the lasagne, spread ¾ cup of the white sauce over the noodles, and top with 1 cup of the meat sauce. Sprinkle with ¼ cup of the cheese. Top with another layer of pasta. Repeat until you have 4 layers of pasta with 3 layers of filling, and top the final layer of pasta with the reserved white sauce and ¼ cup cheese. Place the pan on a baking sheet to catch any drips, loosely cover the pan with foil, and bake for 30 minutes. Uncover and continue to bake until golden and bubbling, 20 to 25 minutes more. Let stand 15 minutes before serving.

ROASTED MUSHROOM LASAGNE

For the most flavor, supplement standard cremini mushrooms with other varieties such as shiitake, chanterelle, maitake, morel, or oyster. But even if you just use creminis, this will still be delicious!

Prepare, using 2 rimmed baking sheets:

Double recipe Roasted Mushrooms, 252

To ensure the mushrooms roast evenly, switch the baking sheets and rotate them halfway through cooking. As the mushrooms roast, heat in a medium saucepan until steaming:

4 cups whole milk
1 ounce dried porcini mushrooms

Cover and remove from the heat. Melt in a large saucepan over medium heat:

1 stick (4 ounces) butter

Whisk in:

½ cup all-purpose flour

Let the flour sizzle in the butter until golden, about 5 minutes. Gradually whisk in the porcini-infused milk (leave the dried porcinis in the milk). Bring to a simmer, whisking frequently, and cook until thickened, about 5 minutes. Remove from the heat. When the mushrooms have finished roasting and cooled slightly, coarsely chop them and stir into the milk mixture, along with:

2 tablespoons fresh thyme leaves

Season to taste with:

Salt and black pepper

Preheat the oven to 375°F. Grease a deep 13 × 9-inch baking dish, 13 × 9 × 2-inch baking pan, or lasagne pan. Prepare:

Cheese Filling, 311

Have ready:

12 ounces dried lasagna noodles or 1 pound any fresh pasta dough, 294–95, rolled and cut into 4 × 12-inch sheets, 293–94

For dried noodles, cook in a large pot of boiling salted water until barely tender. Drain the pasta, rinse under cool water, and blot it dry. For fresh lasagna noodles, do not boil. Spread a thin layer of mushroom sauce on the bottom of the prepared pan. Cover with a layer of noodles, overlapping them slightly. Top with one-third of the ricotta mixture and one-quarter of the mushroom sauce. Repeat three more times, topping the last layer of pasta with the remaining mushroom sauce. Sprinkle on top:

¼ cup grated Parmesan

Cover the lasagne with foil and bake 30 minutes. Remove the foil and bake until well browned and bubbling, about 15 minutes more. Let stand for 15 minutes before serving.

ROASTED VEGETABLE LASAGNE

8 to 12 servings

The vegetables in this meatless lasagne can be prepared a day ahead, covered, and stored in the refrigerator.

Preheat the oven to 450°F. Place in a large bowl:

2 pounds eggplant, quartered lengthwise and cut into ½-inch-thick slices
1 pound zucchini, cut into ½-inch-thick slices
2 red bell peppers, cut into ½-inch-wide slices
1 head garlic, cloves separated and left unpeeled

Add to the vegetables and toss to coat:

¼ cup olive oil
1 teaspoon salt
½ teaspoon black pepper

Divide the vegetables between 2 rimmed baking sheets, spreading them in a single layer. Roast for 20 minutes. Toss the vegetables with a spatula and continue to roast until well browned and soft, about 20 minutes more. Meanwhile, prepare or have ready:

3 cups any tomato sauce, 556–58
4 cups shredded mozzarella (1 pound)
½ cup grated Parmesan (2 ounces)

Reduce the oven temperature to 375°F. Grease a deep 13 × 9-inch baking dish, 13 × 9 × 2-inch baking pan, or lasagne pan. Have ready:

12 ounces dried lasagna noodles or 1 pound any fresh pasta dough, 294–95, rolled and cut into 4 × 12-inch sheets, 293–94

For dried noodles, cook in a large pot of boiling salted water until barely tender. Drain the pasta, rinse under cool water, and blot it dry. For fresh lasagna noodles, do not boil. Peel and chop the roasted garlic cloves. Prepare:

Cheese Filling, below

Mix the chopped garlic into the filling. Spread a thin layer of tomato sauce over the bottom of the prepared pan. Cover with a layer of pasta, slightly overlapping. Spread with one-third of the cheese filling. Spoon one-third of the roasted vegetables on top, then sprinkle one-quarter of the mozzarella and Parmesan over the ricotta. Top with ½ cup sauce. Add another layer of pasta and continue layering the lasagna until you have 4 layers of pasta and 3 layers of filling. Spread the remaining sauce on top and sprinkle with the remaining mozzarella and Parmesan. Place the pan on a baking sheet to catch any drips, loosely cover the pan with foil, and bake for 30 minutes. Uncover and continue to bake until golden and bubbling, 20 to 25 minutes more. Let stand for 15 minutes before serving.

ABOUT STUFFED PASTA

Pasta stuffed with homemade filling is an impressive dish, whether served with a sauce or floating in a rich broth. Making stuffed pasta requires some work, but the filling can be seasoned to taste, and unique combinations can be created. The possibilities extend beyond the fillings listed here; leftovers from a roast or stew can be chopped, seasoned, and quickly turned into a pasta filling. In most cases, ➤ the filling and the sauce can be prepared a day in advance and refrigerated until you are ready to stuff the pasta. Also see Spinach-Ricotta Stuffing, 535.

When filling pasta, ➤ the dough must be filled and shaped while it is still moist, so have the filling prepared before rolling out the pasta. Roll the pasta thin enough so you can see your hand through it, 293, and keep the sheets moist by covering them with plastic wrap as you work. If the pasta is allowed to become too dry, it may be difficult to seal.

➤ *To freeze stuffed pasta,* leave uncooked and place on foil- or parchment-lined baking sheets so they do not touch. Freeze overnight, then transfer to freezer bags for easy storage. This way, you can pull out as many as needed and put them right into a simmering pot of water, broth, or soup. Freeze for up to 3 months.

To cook stuffed pasta, add to simmering salted water. ➤ Most filled pastas will float to the surface when they are done. Frozen pasta will require an extra minute or two, as will any pasta containing raw meat or poultry. ➤ Keep filled pastas cooking at a gentle simmer to prevent ruptures.

Stuffed pastas can be paired with butter, tomato, meat, cream, or white sauces. Match the pasta to the sauce according to your taste and the rest of the menu. In general, the sauce should contrast with the filling. See individual recipes for suggestions.

CHEESE FILLING

About 2¼ cups

A perfect, simple filling for dried pastas such as manicotti or jumbo shells as well as for fresh stuffed cannelloni, ravioli, or tortellini. If you like, add some finely chopped prosciutto or fresh herbs such as oregano, marjoram, or thyme. Pasta stuffed with this filling is perfect with tomato sauces, 556–58, Pesto, 586, or Hearty Beef Ragu, 466.

Mix together in a medium bowl until thoroughly combined:

15 ounces ricotta
½ cup grated Parmesan (2 ounces)
2 large eggs
2 tablespoons minced parsley
½ teaspoon salt
½ teaspoon black pepper
(¼ teaspoon grated or ground nutmeg)

Chill until ready to use. The filling can be covered and refrigerated for up to 2 days.

MUSHROOM FILLING

About 2¾ cups

Mushroom-filled pasta pairs nicely with creamy sauces, or a simple tomato-based sauce.

Rinse and soak in hot water to cover until softened, about 20 minutes:

1 ounce dried mushrooms, such as porcini

Heat in a large skillet over medium heat:

2 tablespoons olive oil

Add and cook, stirring, until the onion is browned:

1 medium onion, finely chopped
2 bay leaves

Lift the mushrooms from the soaking liquid, reserving the liquid, squeeze dry, and finely chop. Add the mushrooms to the skillet along with:

12 ounces any kind of fresh mushrooms, coarsely chopped

Cook the mushrooms, stirring, for 2 minutes. Add:

⅓ cup dry red wine
2 tablespoons tomato paste
2 garlic cloves, minced

Bring to a boil and cook until the pan is almost dry. Line a fine-mesh sieve with dampened paper towels and pour the mushroom soaking liquid through the sieve directly into the skillet. Let it boil until evaporated. Add and let boil until evaporated:

½ cup chicken stock or broth

Season to taste with:

Salt and black pepper

Remove from the heat and let cool; remove and discard the bay leaves. Blend in:

½ to 1 cup grated Parmesan (2 to 4 ounces), to taste

The filling can be covered and refrigerated for up to 3 days.

MEAT AND SPINACH FILLING

About 2 cups

Our favorite filling for ravioli, this is also good in tortellini. Serve the cooked pasta with butter and cheese, or with a tomato sauce, 556–58. For a vegetarian filling, substitute **1 cup finely chopped Sautéed Mushrooms, 251, or Seasoned Tempeh Crumbles, 287,** for the browned meat.

Heat in a medium skillet over medium-high heat:

2 tablespoons butter or olive oil

When the butter or oil is hot, add:

8 ounces ground veal or lean pork

Cook, stirring often and breaking up the ground meat, until the mixture is browned and cooked through, 4 to 5 minutes. Stir in:

¼ cup dry white wine

Bring to a boil, scraping up the browned bits on the bottom of the skillet. Remove from the heat and let cool. Combine in a bowl:

½ cup chopped frozen spinach, thawed, drained, and squeezed dry
2 large eggs
¼ cup fresh bread crumbs, 957, lightly toasted
½ cup grated Romano or Parmesan (2 ounces)
2 teaspoons finely chopped parsley
½ teaspoon dried basil, marjoram, or oregano
1 garlic clove, minced
Salt and black pepper to taste

Stir in:

Enough stock or broth, cream, or gravy to form a stiff paste

The filling can be covered and refrigerated for up to 2 days.

THREE-MEAT FILLING

About 4 cups

Use to fill ravioli, tortellini, or cannelloni. Serve with a tomato sauce, 556–58, or Roasted Red Pepper Sauce, 554.

Heat in a medium skillet over medium-high heat:

2 tablespoons butter or olive oil

When the butter or oil is hot, add:

12 ounces ground chicken, turkey, pork, or a combination
½ small onion, finely chopped
¼ teaspoon salt
¼ teaspoon black pepper

Cook, stirring often and breaking up the ground meat, until the mixture is browned and cooked through, about 5 minutes. Stir in:

¼ cup dry white wine

Bring to a boil, scraping up the browned bits on the bottom of the skillet. Remove from the heat and let cool. Scrape the meat mixture into a food processor along with:

1½ cups grated Parmesan (6 ounces)
4 ounces mortadella or bologna, chopped
3 ounces prosciutto, chopped
Pinch of grated or ground nutmeg

Process until finely chopped and well blended. Taste and adjust the seasonings. The filling can be covered and refrigerated for up to 2 days.

WINTER SQUASH FILLING

About 1¾ cups

Use to stuff ravioli or tortellini. We prefer them with the browned butter and sage mixture from Baked Gnudi with Brown Butter and Sage, 308.

Preheat the oven to 375°F. Line a baking pan with foil.

Halve lengthwise:

1 medium butternut squash (1½ pounds)

Scoop out the seeds and membranes. Place the halves cut side down in the pan. Bake until tender when pierced with a knife, about 1 hour. Let cool slightly, scoop out the pulp, then pass through a ricer or food mill, or puree in a food processor until smooth. You should have about 1½ cups (slightly more or less is fine). Mix the squash with:

½ cup grated Parmesan (2 ounces)
⅛ teaspoon grated or ground nutmeg
Salt to taste

The filling can be covered and refrigerated for up to 4 days.

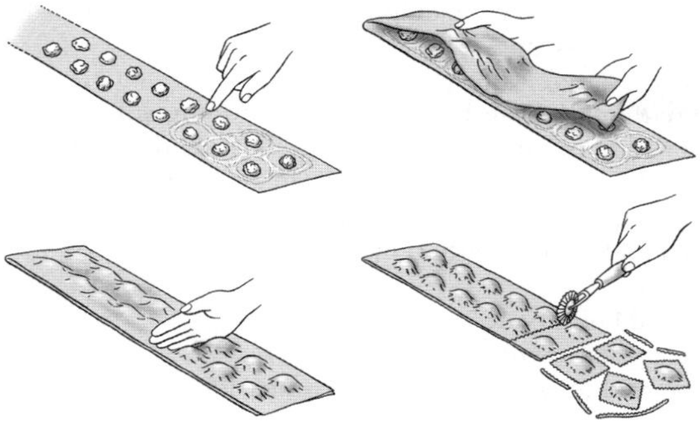

Making ravioli

RAVIOLI

40 ravioli; 8 servings

Often served with a complementary sauce like any other pasta, cooked ravioli may also be sautéed in butter or olive oil until crispy around the edges and seasoned with fresh herbs and grated Parmesan.

Have ready:

Fresh Pasta Dough, 294, rolled and cut into 4-inch-wide sheets, 293–94

1¼ cups any pasta filling, 311–12

Lay the pasta sheet with a long edge parallel to you on a lightly floured surface. On half of the sheet, place ½-teaspoon mounds of the filling spaced 1 inch apart. Dip your finger in water and run it around each mound of filling. Fold the other half of the pasta sheet over, taking care to cover each mound so that no air is trapped. With the side of your hand, press firmly between the mounds of filling to seal. Use a pizza cutter or pastry wheel to cut the sheet into squares or rectangles, checking that each piece is well sealed. (To cut round ravioli, use a cookie cutter or biscuit cutter.) Place the ravioli, not touching one another, on baking sheets dusted with flour. Repeat with the remaining pasta and filling. Let stand 45 minutes to 1 hour at room temperature, turning the pieces occasionally, before cooking. To cook, bring to a boil in a large pot:

4 quarts water

2 tablespoons salt

Add the ravioli, being careful not to crowd the pot; cook them in batches if necessary. Reduce the heat and simmer gently until the ravioli float to the surface, 2 to 3 minutes. Frozen ravioli will require an extra minute or two.

TORTELLINI

48 tortellini; 8 servings

Tortellini are traditionally stuffed with a meat filling, but mushroom, winter squash, or cheese filling is also good. We recommend doubling or tripling this recipe and freezing the extra.

Prepare:

Fresh Pasta Dough, 294, rolled and cut into 4-inch-wide sheets, 293–94

1½ cups any pasta filling, 311–12

Use a 2-inch round cutter to cut out rounds of dough. Place ¼-teaspoon filling in the center of each dough round, and fold the round in half, sealing the edges. Bring the two ends of the half-moon together and pinch them together to form a plump circle. Place the shaped tortellini on a floured baking sheet and loosely cover with a damp kitchen towel. Repeat with remaining dough and filling. Dough scraps may be saved and rerolled once. If the dough becomes too dry to seal, dip your finger in a little water and moisten the edges of the dumplings before sealing. Let the tortellini sit on the baking sheet 45 minutes to 1 hour before cooking. Cook as for **Ravioli, above.**

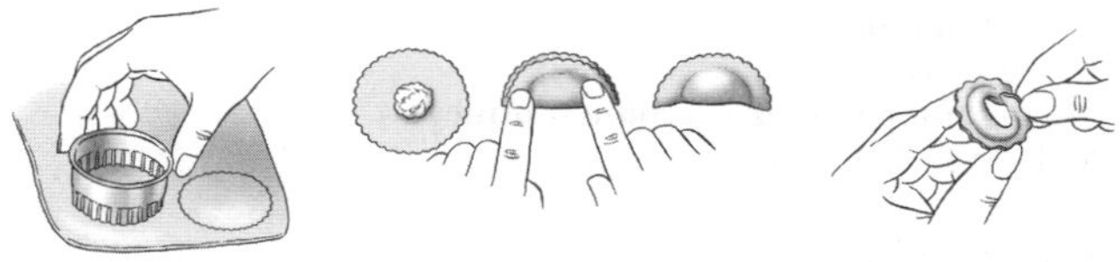

Making tortellini

ABOUT FILLED DUMPLINGS

Meat, cabbage, mushrooms, and cheese are just a few of the ingredients used in Central and Eastern Europe to make filled dumplings. Some, like kreplach and pierogi, have cooked fillings, while others are filled with seasoned raw meat. They improve simple, broth-based soups, but we covet those that are pan-fried after being simmered and served with melted butter or sour cream, dill, and a splash of vinegar.

Asian dumplings typically consist of a thin dough wrapper filled with meat, fish, or vegetables and can be steamed, simmered in soup, or fried (see Pot Stickers or Gyoza, 63, and Fried Wontons, 71). As with filled pastas, extra dumplings made for the freezer are a true asset to harried cooks. To freeze, see About Stuffed Pasta, 311.

POTATO AND CHEESE FILLING

About 2½ cups

Place in a large pot:

1 pound russet potatoes, peeled and quartered

Add cool water to cover, bring to a boil, then reduce the heat to simmer until the potatoes are tender, about 20 minutes. Drain and mash or rice the potatoes into a bowl and mix in:

3 tablespoons butter, softened

½ cup grated sharp Cheddar or Parmesan (2 ounces)

(½ small onion, minced and sautéed)

Salt and black pepper to taste

Allow to cool completely before using.

SAUERKRAUT-MUSHROOM FILLING

About 2 cups

Heat in a large skillet over medium heat:

2 tablespoons butter or olive oil

Add and cook, stirring, until soft:

1 medium onion, finely chopped

Add and cook, stirring, until tender:

1 cup finely chopped mushrooms

Transfer to a bowl and stir in:

1 cup sauerkraut, drained and chopped
Salt and black pepper to taste

Allow to cool completely before using.

SWEET CHEESE FILLING

About 2 cups

Combine in a medium bowl:

12 ounces cottage or farmer cheese, drained
2 large eggs, beaten
1 tablespoon butter, melted
2 tablespoons sugar
½ teaspoon salt
¼ teaspoon grated or ground nutmeg

Chill until ready to use.

SOUR CHERRY FILLING

About 2 cups

As an alternative to this recipe, you may use Sour Cherry Preserves, 918, as a filling.

Combine in a medium saucepan:

1 pound pitted fresh or frozen sour cherries (about 2 cups)
½ cup sugar

Bring to a boil and cook until the juices have reduced and are no longer runny, about 15 minutes. Combine in a small bowl:

1 tablespoon cornstarch
2 tablespoons cold water

Stir the cornstarch slurry into the cherries. Boil to thicken, about 1 minute. Remove from the heat and let cool.

VARENIKI OR PIEROGI

36 dumplings; 4 to 6 servings

Ukrainian **vareniki** and Polish **pierogi** are made from rounds of dough folded around filling into half-moons. Fillings vary from savory ground meat and cabbage to potatoes and cheese, to slightly sweet farmer cheese and berries, the last of which is often served as a dessert. They are delicious sautéed in (or dressed with) butter, topped with sour cream, and served as a substantial first course or light main course.

Have ready:

Fresh Pasta Dough, 294, or Fresh Egg Noodle Dough, 295
Any dumpling filling, above, or Buckwheat Pilaf, 321

Divide the dough into 4 pieces and tightly cover 3 of the pieces with plastic wrap. Use a pasta roller or a rolling pin to roll out one piece of dough as thin as possible, about 1⁄16 inch thick. Use a 3-inch round cutter to cut out rounds of dough. Place a heaping teaspoon of filling slightly off-center on each dough round, and fold the dough over to form a half-moon, sealing the edges. Bring the two ends of the half-moon together and pinch them to form a plump circle. Place the shaped dumplings on a floured baking sheet and loosely cover with a damp kitchen towel. Repeat with the remaining dough and filling. Dough scraps may be saved and rerolled once. If the dough becomes too dry to seal, dip your finger in a little water and moisten the edges of the dumplings before sealing. Let the dumplings rest on the baking sheet for 45 minutes before cooking. To cook, make a soup (such as Hearty Dumpling Soup, 84), or simply bring to a simmer in a large pot:

4 quarts salted water

Add the dumplings in batches to avoid overcrowding, reduce the heat, and simmer until the dumplings float, 2 to 3 minutes. Carefully remove with a strainer or slotted spoon to a warmed bowl. Repeat with the remaining dumplings. Pour over them:

2 to 4 tablespoons butter, melted, to taste

Serve with:

Sautéed Onions, 255
Sour cream or cottage cheese
(Browned or Buttered Bread Crumbs, 957)

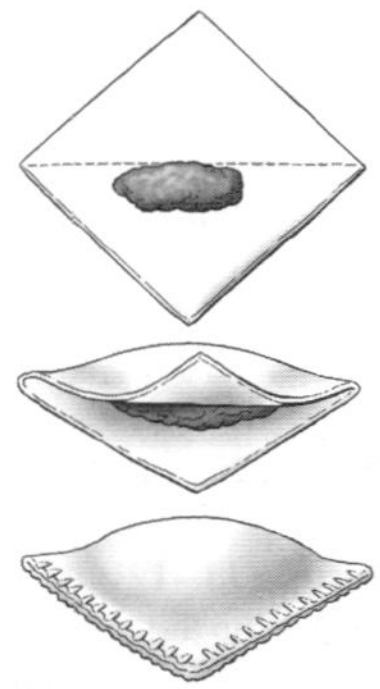

Filling and folding kreplach

KREPLACH

36 dumplings; 6 servings

Jewish kreplach are traditionally cooked and served in a hearty chicken or beef broth. A particularly clever strategy is to mince the chicken or beef you have made the broth with and combine with sautéed onions to fill the dumplings. Other common fillings include leftover Beef Pot Roast, 464, or Sweet-and-Sour Brisket, 469; simply substitute 1 cup minced leftover meat for the chicken or ground beef.

Mix together in a bowl:

1 cup Sautéed Onions, 255, minced
8 ounces browned ground beef, drained, or 1 cup finely chopped cooked chicken
1 egg yolk
2 tablespoons chopped parsley, dill, thyme, or a combination
¾ teaspoon salt
¾ teaspoon black pepper

Prepare:

Fresh Pasta Dough, 294, or Fresh Egg Noodle Dough, 295

Divide the dough into 4 pieces and tightly cover 3 of the pieces with plastic wrap. Use a pasta roller or a rolling pin to roll out one piece of dough as thin as possible, about 1⁄16 inch. Cut the dough into 3-inch squares. Place a heaping teaspoon of filling slightly off-center and fold over to form a triangle. Seal the edges by pressing them with your fingers, then with the tines of a fork. Repeat with remaining dough and filling. Cook as for **Vareniki or Pierogi, above.**

PELMENI

Makes about 100 dumplings; 8 to 10 servings

A Russian favorite, pelmeni hail from Siberia where they were traditionally carried along on winter hunting trips and buried in sacks in the snow, where they would keep for months. We prefer *pelmeni* served on their own with sour cream, but they may also be cooked and served in broth. Because these are a bit labor-intensive to make, find a friend or duty-bound loved one to help. To freeze pelmeni, see 294.

Have ready:

Fresh Pasta Dough, 294

Combine in a medium bowl:

½ pound ground beef
½ pound ground pork
1 small onion, minced
(1 to 2 tablespoons minced dill, to taste)
(2 garlic cloves, minced)
¾ teaspoon salt
½ teaspoon black pepper

Refrigerate the mixture while you roll out the dough. Divide the dough into 4 pieces and tightly cover 3 of the pieces with plastic wrap. Use a pasta roller or a rolling pin to roll out one piece of dough as thin as possible, about 1⁄16 inch. Use a 2- to 3-inch round cutter to cut out rounds of dough. Place a teaspoon of filling slightly off-center on each dough round, and fold the round in half, sealing the edges. Bring the two ends of the half-moon together and pinch them to form a plump circle. Place the shaped pelmeni on a floured baking sheet and loosely cover with a damp kitchen towel. Repeat with remaining dough and filling. Dough scraps may be saved and rerolled once. If the dough becomes too dry to seal, dip your finger in a little water and moisten the edges of the dumplings before sealing. Let the pelmeni rest on the baking sheet for 45 minutes before cooking.

To cook, bring to a boil in a large pot:

4 quarts salted water

Boil as many pelmeni as will fit comfortably in a single layer in the pot—do not crowd. When the pelmeni float, cook for 1 minute more. Cook frozen pelmeni for an additional minute. Remove with a slotted spoon and cook remaining pelmeni. Serve with:

Melted butter
Sour cream
White vinegar

WONTONS

About 35 wontons; 6 to 8 servings

Homemade wontons are fun and easy to prepare. Once assembled, they can be frozen for later use. When cooking wontons, keep the water at a low simmer to prevent them from opening.

Pulse in a food processor until finely chopped:

8 ounces boneless, skinless chicken breast, shrimp, peeled and deveined, 363, or ground pork

Transfer to a bowl and add:

8 canned water chestnuts, minced
1 green onion, thinly sliced
1-inch piece ginger, peeled and minced
1 tablespoon cornstarch
1 tablespoon soy sauce
1 tablespoon Shaoxing wine, 952, or dry sherry
1 teaspoon toasted sesame oil
½ to 1 teaspoon chili oil, to taste
1 teaspoon sugar
½ teaspoon salt
⅛ teaspoon black pepper

Stir together in a small bowl to make an egg wash:

1 large egg
1 tablespoon water

Have ready (but covered):

35 square wonton wrappers

Working in batches, lay out 10 wrappers, arranging them so that one point is facing you. Lightly brush each wrapper with egg wash. Place 1 teaspoon of the filling in the center of each wrapper, as shown. Fold the wonton in half by bringing the bottom corner up to meet the top corner, forming a triangle. Press the edges firmly to seal, squeezing all the air out. Then, bring the two outside points to meet at the center and press to seal. To cook, see Hearty Dumpling Soup, 84, or Fried Wontons, 71. You may also freeze wontons as directed in About Stuffed Pasta, 311.

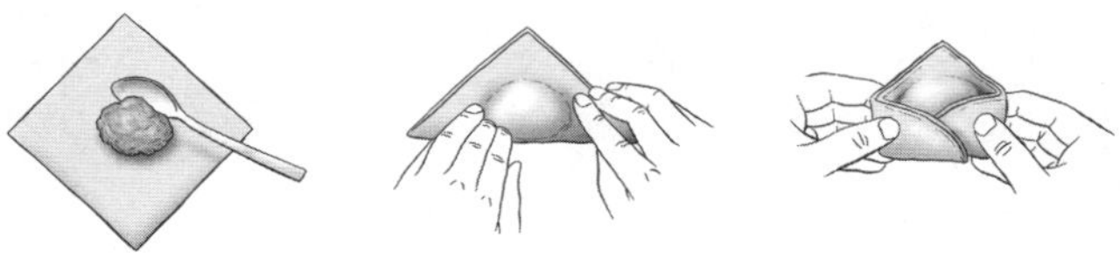

Making wontons

VEGETABLE WONTONS

About 30 wontons; 4 to 6 servings

Heat in a large skillet over medium heat:

1 tablespoon vegetable oil

Add and cook, stirring, until the vegetables are wilted, about 5 minutes:

5 ounces shiitake mushrooms, stems discarded, caps chopped (about 1½ cups)
5 ounces button mushrooms, chopped (about 2 cups)
8 ounces firm tofu, drained and crumbled
2 green onions, chopped
½ cup thinly sliced napa cabbage
1-inch piece ginger, peeled and minced

Transfer to a bowl and let the filling cool. Season the filling, make the egg wash, fill, and fold as for **Wontons, above.**

SEAFOOD OR PORK SHUMAI

32 dumplings; 4 to 6 servings

Combine in a large bowl and mix well:

1 pound shrimp, peeled, deveined, 363, and finely chopped; or ground pork
1 large egg
2-inch piece ginger, peeled and minced
2 tablespoons minced cilantro

1 tablespoon cornstarch
1 green onion, minced
1 tablespoon toasted sesame oil
1 tablespoon rice vinegar
½ teaspoon salt

Have ready:

32 round wonton wrappers

Place a wonton wrapper on a work surface and place 1 tablespoon of the filling in the center. Pick the wrapper up so that it partially surrounds the filling, pleating the edges of the wrapper so that it resembles a cup, as shown; the filling should be exposed at the top and level with the wrapper. Tap the dumpling against the work surface to flatten the bottom. Place on a lightly oiled plate and repeat with the remaining wrappers and filling. Place half the dumplings, without touching each other, in an oiled steamer basket. Bring 1 or 2 inches of water to a boil in a large pot, put the basket on top, cover, and steam until the dumplings are cooked through, about 10 minutes. Transfer to a plate and keep warm. Cook the remaining dumplings in the same way. Serve hot with:

Soy sauce

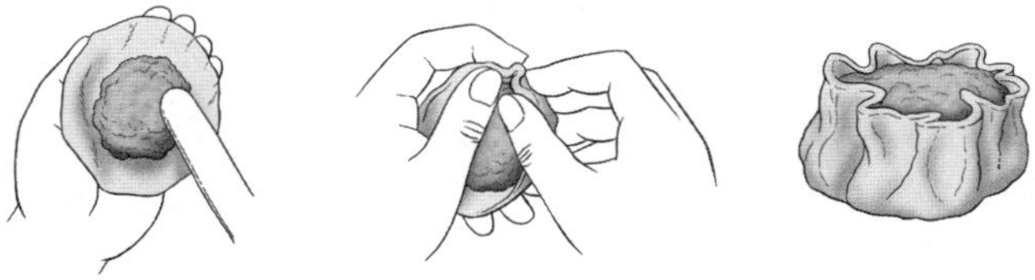

Making shumai

BĀO (CHINESE STEAMED BUNS)

16 buns

Prepare the dough for:

Hard Rolls, 619, using oil instead of shortening and omitting the egg whites

Allow the dough to rise once. Have ready:

About 1½ cups chopped Chashu Pork, 496, filling for Wontons or Vegetable Wontons, 315, or filling for Pork and Mushroom Lettuce Wraps, 63

Cut parchment paper into sixteen 3-inch squares and set aside. Divide the dough in half, covering half with plastic wrap to prevent it from drying out. Shape the other half into a log about 12 inches long. Divide into 8 pieces. Shape each piece into a ball by rolling it on your work surface beneath your palm. Use a rolling pin (a small dowel-like pin works best) to roll each piece into a roughly 5-inch round that is slightly thicker in the center than at the edges. Lay the dough round on your palm and place 1 heaping tablespoon of filling in the middle. Use the thumb of the hand holding the dough to press the filling down as you gather up the edges with your other hand, pleating them as you go. After the last pleat, gently twist the pleated "topknot" of the bun to seal it. Place each filled bun on a square of parchment and cover with a damp kitchen towel while you finish shaping and filling the buns.

Place the buns in a bamboo steamer, cover, and let rise until puffy, about 30 minutes. Pour ½ inch of water into a skillet or wok on top of which the bamboo steamer will sit. Place the steamer on top of the skillet and bring the water to a boil. The steamer should be sitting above, not in, the water. When steam starts to come out the top of the steamer, set a timer for 15 minutes. When the time is up, carefully remove the steamer from the skillet and serve the buns immediately. Leftover buns may be refrigerated for up to 4 days or frozen for up to 2 months. Steam or microwave to reheat.

GRAINS

Our ancestors' cultivation of grains enabled the birth of civilization as we know it. Part of the appeal of grains was nutrient density. Further, grains can be stored for quite a long time under the right conditions, providing food long after the harvest. But our interest in grains today, apart from nutrition and storage capabilities, stems from the fact that their presence is cemented in most of the world's cuisines, and many of us cannot imagine a meal without them.

All true grains are the fruits of grasses. Some **pseudocereals** are covered in this chapter as well. These include buckwheat, quinoa, and amaranth. Though they are not true grains, their preparation and use is very similar.

Whole grain kernels are sometimes called **berries** or **groats.** Most grains are similar in structure to the wheat kernel, see below, being composed of three parts: the **bran,** the **germ,** and the **endosperm.** The tough outer layers, or bran, contain most of the grain's vitamins, minerals, and fiber. The germ, which is only a small part of the kernel, nonetheless contains most of the protein and all of the fat. The endosperm is largely starch, with some protein. Most of the nutritional content and rich, nutty flavor are in the bran and germ. However, it is common practice when processing grain to remove some or all of the bran and germ. The resulting grain is often referred to as **pearled** or **semi-pearled.** White rice, for example, is endosperm only, as is the part of the wheat that is ground into white flour. Semi-pearling leaves some of the bran layer on, which is what gives brown, red, and black rices their distinctive color.

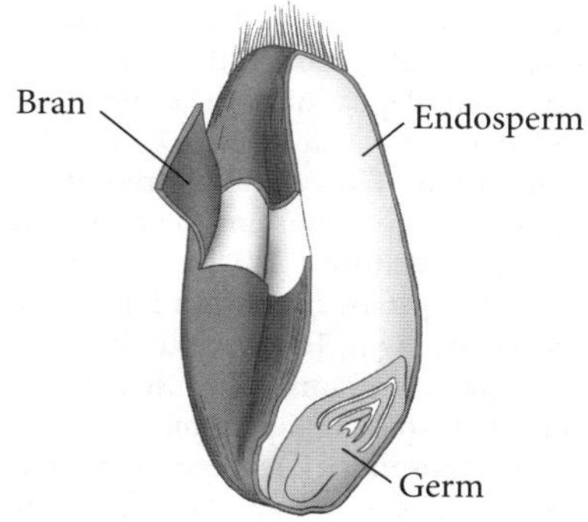

The three basic parts of a wheat kernel

Nutritionally, whole grains are the best choice. Pearled grains and the grits or meal made from them may be enriched with B vitamins and iron to replace what was lost in processing, but the vitamin E and fiber found in whole grains are not typically replaced.

From a convenience perspective, pearled grains are the clear winner: They can be stored for a very long time and lack the tough bran layers, which reduces their cooking time by half or more. Semi-pearled grains are a nice compromise since they cook more quickly than whole grains while retaining some of the nutritional benefits and nutty flavors. Unfortunately, they are just as perishable as whole grains.

ABOUT BUYING AND STORING GRAINS

Any whole or refined grain is vulnerable to insect infestation and rancidity. Since whole grains such as wheat berries and brown rice still have their high-fat germ intact, they are more prone to rancidity than white rice and other pearled grains. For this reason, we recommend ➤ buying whole grains in small quantities and storing them in tightly covered containers in a cool, dry pantry or the refrigerator or freezer. With the exception of wheat germ and buckwheat, ➤ most grains can be stored for up to 6 months in the pantry and up to 1 year in the freezer. Ideally, though, only buy what you will use in 3 months or less for optimum quality. Signs of rancidity are an off odor before cooking or a bitter taste when cooked. If the raw grains clump together, it may be a sign of infestation or spoilage, and at that point, unfortunately, it is best to discard the grain.

PREPARING GRAINS FOR COOKING

While rinsing grains was once commonly advised in older cookbooks to rid them of debris and dirt, most grains now come to us well cleaned, making the rinsing step unnecessary. Even quinoa, which is notable for a high concentration of saponins on its outer hull, is now washed before it appears on store shelves, making rinsing unnecessary. However, it certainly never hurts to rinse grains, and if you buy grains locally from small producers, you may wish to rinse them to remove any dirt, chaff, or other debris. Sometimes rinsing is desirable for other reasons; rinsing rice, for instance, can remove surface starches and keep the grains from sticking together.

To rinse grains, cover them with ample water in a bowl and briefly swish them around. Drain off the water, add more to cover, swish, and drain again. Repeat until the drained water is relatively clear and free of debris.

Soaking whole grains like wheat berries, rye berries, farro, Kamut, spelt, and whole oats shortens their cooking time by up to half and improves their texture.

To soak hard whole grains, cover with 2 inches of water and let soak for 8 hours, or overnight. To reduce cooking time even further, pour boiling water over the grains and let them sit overnight. Grains can be cooked in their soaking liquid, but it will be high in starch and may cause the grains to stick together more during cooking.

Sprouting whole grains is yet another way to enjoy them, and according to scientific research, it can make their nutrients more available for your body to absorb, increase their concentration of antioxidants, increase dietary fiber, and potentially lower the glycemic reaction to eating them. Sprouted grains should be treated like cooked grains when using in recipes. They can be added to baked goods, stir-fries, and salads or cooked into a porridge.

To sprout whole grains, see 1021.

Toasting grains before cooking enhances their flavor and prevents them from clumping together.

To toast grains on the stovetop, spread them in a heavy saucepan or skillet and heat over medium heat, stirring often, until their aroma is released; be careful not to scorch very small grains such as amaranth, millet, and teff. ➤ Heating a little oil or butter in the pan before you toast the grains will add flavor and help keep the kernels separate, promoting a fluffy texture in the cooked dish.

To toast grains in the oven, spread them on a baking sheet and toast in a preheated 350°F oven for about 10 minutes, stirring once.

ABOUT COOKING GRAINS

See the Grains Cooking Chart, 340, for basic cooking guidelines for every grain in this chapter. There are four basic methods of cooking grains. The first is the **absorption method:** Grains are brought to a boil with just enough liquid to hydrate them, then the pan is covered, the heat is reduced, and the grains are gently simmered until they are tender and have absorbed all the liquid in the pan. Often, this method is accompanied by a steaming step where the grains are removed from the heat after they have absorbed most of the liquid, then allowed to sit, covered, for several minutes to finish cooking. Most grains benefit from being fluffed afterward; use a fork to reach to the bottom of the pan and gently pull the grains to the top. If not serving at once, keep covered. Resting grains in the covered pan off the heat for 5 to 10 minutes, either before or after fluffing, allows the grain to absorb the last bits of moisture, resulting in plump grains.

If you add more liquid to the pot than the grains can absorb and continue cooking the grains until starchy and broken down, then you have **porridge.** Starting with pearled, cracked, rolled, or ground grains greatly speeds up this process.

Grains can also be cooked **pasta-style,** meaning simmered in a larger amount of water until tender and then drained. This method has two main advantages. First, there is no need to measure the amount of liquid or grains—simply set a timer and drain the grains when they are tender. Second, when you are cooking tougher whole grains like hominy and wheat berries, you do not need to worry as much about the liquid evaporating before the grains are tender. This is also the ideal method to use if you're after perfectly distinct grains as opposed to sticky, clumped grains (the starch on the surface of the grains dissipates). While most grains can be cooked this way, we do not recommend it for tiny grains like amaranth and teff.

Cooking grains **risotto-style** involves toasting them in oil or butter and then cooking them with a flavorful liquid until they have absorbed it, then adding more liquid a little at a time. This process is repeated until the grains are tender and creamy from the released starch. Though this method takes a bit more effort, the results are very tasty, especially if the cooking liquid is flavorful (constant evaporation will concentrate its flavors). For a shortcut that does not require constant tending, see Pressure-Cooker Risotto, 336.

Though traditionally used to cook specific types of rice, you may cook quinoa, buckwheat, oats, pearl barley, and farro in this way with good results.

Finally, grains may be **steamed.** While you may see recipes for "steamed rice," that is usually something of a misnomer and refers to the absorption method, 318. Glutinous or sticky rice, 343, must be steamed, that is to say cooked above, not in, boiling water.

One common criticism of whole grains is that they take a long time to cook, which supposedly makes them an impractical choice for weeknight meals. There are several ways to get around this. One is to soak them, 318. This dramatically reduces the cooking time of whole grains. Second, there are many appliances that can be used to make cooking whole grains more convenient. A rice cooker reliably turns out well-cooked grains. Stovetop and electric pressure cookers are particularly effective for preparing long-cooking grains such as wheat berries and hulled barley, where the cooking time may be cut in half. See the Grains Cooking Chart, 340, for estimated times, but consult the manufacturer's manual for specific instructions. Tough grains can also be set for a day-long simmer in the slow cooker. ➤ Expect them to take 6 to 8 hours on low heat to become tender.

Finally, you can go the old-fashioned route and cook a large batch of grains on the weekend and use them throughout the week. Or, cook a large pot of grains and freeze them in meal-sized amounts—we recommend freezing for firm, long-cooking grains like brown rice, wheat berries, and hominy, but not delicate rices or small grains like amaranth or quinoa. The day you want to use them, simply take them out of the freezer in the morning, and by dinner all they need is to be reheated and seasoned.

ABOUT COMBINING GRAINS

Using two or three grains in one dish adds flavor and texture. Do this with grains that are cooked in roughly the same amount of time and with similar amounts of liquid. Some examples are brown rice and pearl barley; bulgur and buckwheat; cornmeal and amaranth; hulled barley and wheat berries. When combining grains that require different amounts of cooking, add to the pot sequentially; they will need a little less water together than they do separately because there is less evaporation. Choose a pot big enough to hold both grains, and add more water as needed, ¼ cup at a time, toward the end of cooking until the grains are tender. Our favorite combination is wheat berries and brown rice, 338.

ABOUT PUFFED GRAINS

Popcorn is our most familiar puffed-grain treat, and while it's doubtful than any other grain could upset that status, it is worth noting that most grains can be puffed or popped. Many are readily available for purchase at most grocery stores, such as puffed rice or wheat (look in the breakfast cereal aisle). Others, like puffed sorghum, are available at specialty markets, particularly Indian grocery stores. Look online for puffed grains such as quinoa, amaranth, and Kamut.

Some grains may be easily puffed at home. Popcorn, 47, is the obvious choice, but wild rice is another option. Simply heat a little oil in a skillet over medium-high and add a handful of wild rice grains to the pan (do not use a wild rice blend). Shake to coat with oil, then cover the pan. The rice will puff quickly. When the popping slows dramatically, uncover the pan, transfer the grains to a plate lined with paper towels, and sprinkle with salt. This process also works well with black rice (sometimes sold as Forbidden Rice) and amaranth.

While most puffed grains other than popcorn are not really suited to being eaten on their own, they may be used in a variety of other ways. Puffed grains are excellent sprinkled on salads as a crunchy crouton replacement, mixed into granola, or used as a garnish for cooked vegetables (think crunchy, puffed wild rice on roasted winter squash). We have also sprinkled puffed wild rice on top of chocolate bark with delectable results. There are many Indian snacks made largely of puffed grains, and you can find an assortment of them at Indian markets. **Bhel puri,** a popular street food snack, is a mixture of seasoned puffed rice, chickpeas, cubes of cooked potato, chopped red onion, cilantro, tomatoes, and spices, topped with plain yogurt, a variety of chutneys, and Chaat Masala, 589.

SERVING GRAINS

Serving seasoned grains as a side dish to accompany vegetables and a protein is the obvious choice, and they fill out a dinner plate admirably. Beyond this basic function, grains are incredibly versatile; as a supplement to the recipes in this chapter, here are some strategies for incorporating them into your mealtime repertoire.

Any cold or lukewarm grain can be turned into a salad. See About Grain and Rice Salads, 130, for specific ideas, or improvise: Toss cooked grains with salad dressing or vinaigrette, nearly any cooked vegetable (roast the vegetables for more flavor), fresh herbs, and cheese such as crumbled feta, cubes of browned Halloumi, or finely grated Parmesan. Cold farro, barley, or Kamut is delightful when mixed with thinly sliced fennel, apples, and dill, and drizzled with Herbed Yogurt Dressing, 577.

Grains can also be used to make grain bowls. Top seasoned, cooked grains of any kind with a protein, like baked chicken or baked tofu, 287, cooked or raw vegetables, toasted nuts or seeds, and a simple sauce, dressing, or vinaigrette.

Any leftover grain may be fried as for Fried Rice, 332, or use them make grain cakes: Stir flavorings like herbs, spices, cheese, sautéed onions, and chopped or grated vegetables into the cooked grains and add a binder, like eggs and flour (for a specific formula, see Millet Cakes with Parmesan and Sun-Dried Tomatoes, 326). Serve with a condiment, or top as for Sopes, 612. Other, delectable ways of repurposing leftover grains include Cheesy Millet Spoon Bread with Chiles, 326, and Fried Polenta, 323.

Cooked grains may be stirred into brothy soups a few minutes before they are finished. Stir uncooked grains into soup in time for the grain to cook in the simmering broth; this will also thicken the soup. Or toss grains with seasonings and herbs and stuff into whole fish, halved acorn or delicata squash, portobello mushrooms, or tomatoes and bake or roast until all of the ingredients are tender and heated through (for specific mixtures, see About Grain Stuffings and Dressings, 535).

Stir cooked grains into baked goods like muffins, quick breads, and pancakes. Oats cooked into porridge is a classic breakfast staple, but nearly any grain can be made into a porridge. Prepare quick-cooking grains like bulgur, quinoa, or millet the day you want to eat them, or reheat already cooked grains in a little milk or nondairy milk. Add spices like cinnamon or cardamom and a few drops of vanilla extract. Add a sweetener like honey or chopped dates to the grains as they cook, or serve topped with honey, jam, fresh or dried fruit, a scoop of yogurt, or toasted nuts or seeds. For a savory breakfast porridge, see Congee, 333—and try the suggested list of toppings with other porridge-friendly grains like grits, teff, or rolled oats.

ABOUT STORING AND REHEATING COOKED GRAINS

Cooked grains reheat beautifully. Most cooked grains can be refrigerated for up to 3 days—or a few days longer if cooked in plain water and not with stock or other perishable ingredients. For grains that take a long time to cook, we often prepare more than we need and freeze the leftovers. This works especially well with sturdy grains like wheat berries or hominy.

To reheat in the microwave, spread portions on individual plates, cover with plastic wrap or a moist paper towel, and cook on high for 1 to 2 minutes per serving. To reheat a bowlful, sprinkle the surface lightly with water, cover with plastic wrap or a lid, and heat on high for about 1½ minutes per cup; stir before serving.

To reheat on the stovetop, pour ⅛ inch of water into a saucepan, add the grain, stir, and simmer, covered, over medium heat until hot. Or heat 1 to 2 tablespoons vegetable oil for every 3 cups cold cooked grain in a skillet; add the grain and cook, stirring, until heated through. See Serving Grains, 319, for more ideas on how to use leftover grains.

ABOUT AMARANTH

Native to the tropical Americas and cultivated by the Aztecs more than five thousand years ago, amaranth is tall and leafy, with a shock of magenta, gold, or green flowers that yield innumerable, tiny seeds. Amaranth is not technically a grain, but rather, a pseudocereal.

Tiny, gold, and flecked with black, amaranth seeds have a pleasantly crunchy texture and nutty flavor, with a slight peppery bite. When cooked, the seeds turn shiny. Cooked amaranth is porridge-like and very thick (stir the pot often—amaranth tends to stick to the bottom). Sweetened and seasoned, amaranth makes a delicious breakfast porridge. Its thickening power can be put to good use in soups as well (simply add it to simmering broth). During cooking, amaranth may release a grassy odor, but this will dissipate.

Raw amaranth may be stirred into doughs and batters to add a crunchy texture to baked goods; leftover cooked amaranth may be added to pancakes, quick breads, or muffins. Amaranth is also rolled into flakes, which can be treated like rolled oats. Amaranth can also be puffed like wild rice (see About Puffed Grains, 319). For amaranth greens, see 242. For amaranth flour, see 985. Amaranth is gluten-free.

ABOUT BARLEY

While barley is a rather humble-looking grain, it has an illustrious history. In the thirteenth century, Edward II standardized the English measurement system using 3 grains of barley, set end to end, as representative of an inch, from which followed all other measurements of length. Barley is perhaps most familiar to us in soups such as Beef Barley Soup, 95, and Scotch Broth, 98. But barley's roasted-nut flavor and pleasing, chewy bite make it especially welcome as a side dish or in dishes like Warm Barley, Mushroom, and Asparagus Salad, 131.

Barley is sold three ways: pearled, Scotch, and hulled. The off-white oval kernels commonly sold as **pearl** (or **pearled**) **barley** have had their husk, bran, and germ removed, leaving only the endosperm. This strips the grain of much of its nutrition but makes it faster cooking and gives it a smoother texture than Scotch or hulled barley. Because barley is the highest in fiber of all grains, even pearl barley is relatively high in fiber. **Scotch** or **pot barley** has more of the bran left on, and therefore more fiber, potassium, and B vitamins are retained. It should be soaked, 318, and has a chewier texture than pearl barley. **Hulled, whole,** or **hull-less barley** is the most nutritious, with only the inedible outer husk removed. ➤ It, too, can be soaked and requires longer cooking. It is chewier and grittier than pearl or Scotch barley. Barley is also processed into two quick-cooking forms: **barley grits** and **rolled barley,** or **barley flakes,** which look like rolled oats and can be cooked the same way (see the Grains Cooking Chart, 340). These are generally used to make breakfast cereal. For barley flour, see 485.

BARLEY "RISOTTO" WITH MUSHROOMS

6 to 8 first-course or 4 main-course servings

Cooked in the style of risotto, pearl barley thickens the cooking liquid and becomes rich and creamy (Scotch or hulled barley will not work).

Melt in a large, deep skillet over medium heat until the foam subsides:

4 tablespoons (½ stick) butter

Add and cook, stirring, until tender but not browned, about 7 minutes:

1 large onion, finely chopped

Stir in and cook until softened:

8 ounces shiitake mushrooms, stems discarded, caps diced

Add and stir until glazed with butter:

1 cup pearl barley

Add and cook, stirring, until the liquid is absorbed, about 3 minutes:

⅔ cup dry white wine
2 garlic cloves, minced
(½ teaspoon salt, if using unsalted broth)
½ teaspoon black pepper

Meanwhile, in a medium saucepan, bring to a boil, then reduce the heat to a gentle simmer:

8 cups chicken broth, preferably unsalted

Stir 2 cups of the broth into the barley. Cook at a moderate to brisk simmer, stirring occasionally, until the broth is almost absorbed, 8 to 9 minutes. Add the remaining broth ½ cup at a time, allowing each addition to be absorbed before adding the next and stirring often; it will take 4 to 5 minutes for each addition to be absorbed and a total of 45 to 55 minutes for the barley to become tender. If you run out of broth before the barley is done, finish cooking with hot water. Stir in, if desired:

(½ to 1 cup grated Parmesan [2 to 4 ounces])

Garnish with:

2 to 3 tablespoons chopped parsley or 1 to 2 teaspoons chopped thyme

This can be made up to 4 days ahead. Let cool completely, then cover and refrigerate. Reheat in a skillet over low heat, adding a little water and stirring frequently.

ABOUT BUCKWHEAT

Buckwheat is a pseudocereal, and is more closely related to rhubarb and sorrel than to wheat. In spite of its name, it is safe for those on a gluten-free diet. Buckwheat groats have a delicate nutty flavor, which is often intensified by toasting or roasting, in which case they are called **kasha.** When left whole, the groats are pleasantly chewy. They tend to stick together, and are frequently mixed with an egg and toasted in the pan before cooking. Both untoasted buckwheat and kasha are available cracked to various degrees of fineness, which yields a porridge that can range from grainy to smooth; serve as a nourishing breakfast, or substitute for cornmeal in polenta recipes, 322–23. ➤ As with other grains, cooking buckwheat in broth will add flavor and richness; see Stuffed Cabbage Rolls II, 227. **Buckwheat flour,** 986, is used in breads and pancakes; see Buckwheat Crêpes, 646, Buckwheat Blini, 641, Buckwheat Corn Bread, 630, and Buckwheat Pancakes, 640. For Japanese buckwheat noodles, or **soba**, see 301.

KASHA VARNISHKES (BOW-TIES WITH KASHA)

8 side-dish or 4 main-course servings

Kasha varnishkes is a traditional Eastern European dish. It can be turned into a salad by adding blanched asparagus, broccoli, or other fresh vegetables and tossing with a vinaigrette.

Combine in a large nonstick skillet and cook over medium-high heat, stirring frequently, until the onions are browned, about 10 minutes:

3 tablespoons rendered chicken fat or vegetable oil
2 large onions, coarsely chopped
(2 cups sliced mushrooms)
Salt and black pepper to taste

Add and cook 1 minute more:

2 garlic cloves, minced

Transfer to a large bowl. Wipe out the skillet and set aside. Meanwhile, cook in a large pot of boiling salted water until al dente:

1½ cups bow-tie pasta (6 ounces)

Drain and toss with the onion mixture. In the nonstick skillet, cook:

1 cup whole buckwheat groats

as directed in the Grains Cooking Chart, 340, using instead of water:

2 cups chicken broth

Stir in the pasta mixture. Taste and adjust the seasoning. If the mixture is dry, add:

(¼ cup chicken broth or water)

Sprinkle with:

2 tablespoons chopped parsley

BUCKWHEAT PILAF

About 3½ cups; 4 to 6 servings

This simple side dish may also be used as a filling for Pierogi, 314.

Heat in a large saucepan over medium heat:

1 tablespoon butter or vegetable oil

If desired, add and cook, stirring, until softened, about 1 minute:

(1 garlic clove, minced, or 2 tablespoons minced shallot or onion)

Add and cook, stirring, until toasted and golden, about 3 minutes:

1 cup whole buckwheat groats

Stir in:

2 cups boiling chicken broth or water
½ teaspoon salt

Cover and cook over low heat until the buckwheat is tender and the liquid is absorbed, about 15 minutes. Let stand, covered, for 5 minutes. Fluff before serving.

BULGUR

See About Wheat, 337.

ABOUT CORNMEAL, HOMINY, AND GRITS

All these products are derived from **field corn** varieties, which are starchier and less sugary relatives of the **sweet corn** we eat fresh off the cob and cook as a vegetable, 234. There are several types of field corn: **Dent corn,** named for the indentation in each kernel, is raised for drying and processing as cornmeal or hominy; **flint corn** is even drier and harder than dent corn (the cobs of colorful "Indian corn" you find during the fall are types of flint corn), and is used to make polenta; **flour corn** is grown exclusively for corn flour, 986.

Hominy is corn that has been treated with slaked lime or lye to loosen the hulls and partially soften the kernels, which are then washed and dried. It is often sold under its Mexican name **posole,** which is also the name of a hominy-studded stew, 323–24. Dried hominy comes in a rainbow of colors—white, yellow, blue, and red—and is available whole, cracked, or ground. Whole dried hominy benefits from soaking overnight and must be cooked for a long time to become fully tender. Luckily, cooked whole hominy is available frozen and canned. Freshly treated hominy is ground to make **masa,** the dough for corn tortillas. When masa is dried and ground into a flour, it is called **masa harina,** or instant masa. Fresh masa is well worth seeking out for its remarkable flavor and the velvety texture it lends to homemade Corn Tortillas, 612.

Most **cornmeal** on the market is hulled and degerminated before grinding, then enriched to replace the nutrients removed in processing. Whole-grain cornmeal, however, contains some or all of both the bran and germ. It has a higher fiber and mineral content and richer flavor than degerminated cornmeal. It is usually stone-ground. **Coarse, medium,** and **fine** cornmeal can be used interchangeably in some recipes, but they do respond differently to cooking. For instance, fine cornmeal tends to absorb liquid faster than medium or coarse cornmeal, and coarse cornmeal can be unpleasantly hard or gritty when used in baked goods. **Yellow, white,** and **blue cornmeal** may be used interchangeably.

Two special types of cornmeal are worth noting. **Grits,** a favorite throughout the American South, are usually made from dried and ground dent corn. They are processed and packaged in several ways: **Old-fashioned grits** are coarsely ground, **quick-cooking grits** are more finely ground, and **instant grits** are precooked and dried. **Hominy grits** are ground from dried, treated corn (though it must be noted that the term "hominy" is occasionally applied to grits made from untreated corn as well). **Stone-ground grits** contain the germ and thus have a shorter shelf life but more nutrients and a much richer flavor. Grits are delicious cooked plain, served topped with butter or a Fried Egg, 155, or baked in a casserole, as in Cheesy Baked Polenta or Grits, below.

Polenta differs from grits in that it is exclusively made from flint corn and is milled several times, giving it a more uniform texture than grits, which are typically milled only once. Packaged logs of cooked polenta ready for slicing and browning (see Fried Polenta, 323) can be found in most supermarkets.

Many small farms and gristmills sell cornmeal, polenta, and grits, and they vary widely in how they are processed. We highly recommend seeking out these sources, but keep in mind that there may be fragments of chaff in their products, which will never properly soften, even after hours of simmering. To remove these particles before cooking, cover the grits or polenta with plenty of cold water, swish them around thoroughly, and wait 15 minutes for any particles to rise to the top. Skim off the chaff with a mesh strainer or spoon, and proceed as directed (use the soaking liquid if you want to get every bit of corn flavor in your dish).

To prevent lumps when making polenta, grits, or cornmeal mush, ➤ add the cornmeal in a thin, steady stream to the pot of boiling water or stock, whisking constantly, and continue to stir frequently as it cooks. Alternatively, mix the cornmeal with cold liquid before adding it gradually to boiling liquid. Cooking times will vary depending on the grind.

Favorite cornmeal dishes in other chapters include Megan's Southern Corn Bread, 631, Indian Pudding, 831, Crusty Soft-Center Spoon Bread, 631, Chicken Tamale Pie, 537, Johnnycakes, 641, Cornmeal Dumplings, 306, Cornmeal Waffles, 643, Hushpuppies, 655, and Cornmeal Pancakes, 641.

CORNMEAL MUSH

3½ to 4 cups; 4 to 6 servings

Bring to a boil in a medium saucepan:

4 cups water or 2 cups each water and milk
1 teaspoon salt

Whisk into the boiling liquid in a thin, steady stream:

1 cup fine white or yellow cornmeal

Stir until smooth. Reduce the heat to medium-low, cover, and cook, stirring often, until the cornmeal loses its raw taste, about 30 minutes, stirring in a little more water if the mush becomes too thick. Spoon into bowls and drizzle over the top:

Melted butter
Molasses, maple syrup, sorghum, or honey

CREAMY POLENTA

About 4 cups; 4 to 6 servings

Long cooking yields the traditional, silky-smooth result. For quicker cooking, the night or morning before you wish to cook the polenta, bring 1½ cups water or broth to a boil in a large saucepan and whisk in the polenta. Cover and let sit for up to 12 hours. When ready to cook, add the remaining 2½ cups water or broth to the saucepan, whisk to break up the polenta, and simmer until thickened and the cornmeal has lost its raw taste, 10 to 12 minutes.

Bring to a boil in a large saucepan:

4 cups chicken stock or water or broth
3 tablespoons butter

Pour in very slowly, whisking constantly:

1 cup polenta

Reduce the heat to low and cook, stirring frequently with a wooden spoon, until the polenta is thick and comes away from the sides of the pan as it is stirred and the cornmeal has lost its raw taste, 30 to 40 minutes. Stir in:

½ cup grated Parmesan (2 ounces)
1 teaspoon salt, or to taste

BECKER RUSTIC POLENTA

About 4 cups; 4 servings

Cooking polenta for less time results in a toothsome texture. Some American brands of polenta are done in as little as 5 minutes; Italian polenta may take a bit longer.

Melt in a large saucepan over medium heat:

3 tablespoons butter

Add and cook until translucent:

½ medium onion, finely chopped

Add and bring to a boil:

4 cups chicken stock or broth

Slowly add, whisking constantly:

1 cup polenta
¼ teaspoon salt

Adjust the heat to maintain a low simmer and cook, whisking, until the polenta has lost its raw taste, 5 to 10 minutes. Stir in:

½ cup grated Parmesan (2 ounces)

CHEESY BAKED POLENTA OR GRITS

6 to 8 servings

Preheat the oven to 350°F. Butter a 2-quart or 9-inch square baking dish.

Melt in a large saucepan over medium heat:

4 tablespoons (½ stick) butter

Add and cook, stirring, until translucent, about 5 minutes:

½ medium onion, chopped

Stir in and cook for 1 minute:

1 garlic clove, minced

Add and bring to a boil:

2 cups water, vegetable stock, or chicken stock or broth
2 cups whole milk

Gradually whisk in:

1 cup polenta or old-fashioned or stone-ground grits
1 teaspoon salt

Bring to a rapid boil, then remove from the heat. Stir in:

1½ cups grated Cheddar, Fontina, or Gruyère (6 ounces)
(½ cup grated Parmesan [2 ounces])

Add and stir to combine:

2 eggs, beaten
(2 tablespoons finely chopped thyme or oregano)
(¼ teaspoon cayenne pepper)

Pour the mixture into the prepared baking dish. Bake until firm and golden brown on top, about 1 hour.

SOUFFLÉED BAKED POLENTA OR GRITS

Prepare **Cheesy Baked Polenta or Grits, 322,** but separate the eggs and stir just the yolks in with the optional thyme or oregano and cayenne. Beat the egg whites until soft peaks form, then fold into the polenta or grits just before pouring them into the baking dish. Bake as directed.

FRIED POLENTA

4 servings

In addition to the entrée serving suggestions given below, you may also top these crispy, golden triangles with Roasted Peppers, 262, or a simple dusting of Parmesan and black pepper. Serve as an appetizer, or as an accompaniment to soups, stews, or braised meats. The polenta can be cooked and chilled up to 3 days in advance. Of course, smaller leftover portions of polenta (or grits) can be chilled until set in a smaller vessel and fried as well.

I. PAN-FRIED

Prepare:

Creamy Polenta, 322, using 2 tablespoons Parmesan

Lightly oil a 13 × 9-inch baking dish. Spread the polenta in an even layer in the dish and let cool slightly. Cover and refrigerate until cold and firm, at least 1½ hours. When ready to fry, cut the polenta into 3-inch squares, then cut the squares into triangles.

Heat on a griddle or in a large heavy skillet:

¼ cup olive oil or 4 tablespoons butter

Carefully transfer the polenta to the pan, without crowding (cook in batches if necessary), and brown on both sides. Drain on paper towels. Serve topped with:

Garlic-Braised Broccoli Rabe, 221, a tomato sauce, 556–58, Bolognese Sauce, 558, Mushroom Ragout, 251, or Hearty Beef Ragu, 466

II. OVEN-FRIED

Cook, chill, and cut the polenta as for **version I, above.** Preheat the oven to 425°F. Line a baking sheet with parchment paper and lightly brush it and the polenta pieces with:

Olive oil

Carefully transfer the polenta to the baking sheet. Bake until the bottom is browned, about 15 minutes. Turn the polenta pieces and bake until the other side is browned, about 10 minutes more. Serve as for I.

CREAMY GRITS

About 3 cups; 4 servings

For the Low Country classic Shrimp and Grits, see 364.

I. STOVETOP

Bring to a boil in a heavy-bottomed saucepan:

3¾ cups water
1½ cups milk, cream, or half-and half
3 tablespoons butter
½ teaspoon salt

In a thin, steady stream whisk in:

¾ cup old-fashioned or stone-ground grits

Return to a boil, then reduce the heat to medium-low and simmer, stirring occasionally, until the grits have visibly thickened, about 20 minutes. Reduce the heat to low. Cook, stirring occasionally, until the grits are soft but not runny, about 40 minutes more.

II. SLOW COOKER

Bring just to a boil in a medium saucepan:

3 cups water
1 cup milk, cream, or half-and-half

Pour into a slow cooker set on low. Whisk in:

¾ cup stone-ground grits

Stir in:

3 tablespoons butter, cut into small cubes
½ teaspoon salt

Cover and cook, stirring every hour, until very creamy and tender, about 6 hours.

GREEN POSOLE

8 to 10 servings

For **Vegetarian Posole,** omit the chicken and add **two 15-ounce cans pinto beans, drained.** Reduce the simmering time to 30 minutes. To make with pork, omit the chicken and potatoes and brown 2 pounds cubed pork shoulder as for Red Posole, 324, before adding the onions. Proceed as directed, simmering until the pork is tender, 1½ to 2 hours.

Have ready:

1 pound dried hominy (about 3 cups), cooked, 341, or two 25-ounce cans hominy, drained

Place in a blender and blend until smooth:

1 pound tomatillos, husked and coarsely chopped
1 small bunch sorrel, watercress, or purslane, coarsely chopped
6 serrano or 3 jalapeño peppers, or more to taste, seeded and coarsely chopped
½ cup pumpkin seeds, toasted, 1012
¾ cup water

Heat in a large heavy soup pot over medium heat:

2 tablespoons vegetable oil

Add and cook, stirring occasionally, until tender, 6 to 8 minutes:

1 large onion, chopped

Add and stir until fragrant, about 30 seconds:

4 large garlic cloves, minced

Increase the heat to medium-high and pour in the tomatillo mixture. Cook, stirring, until the mixture is at a brisk simmer and has turned olive green, about 5 minutes. Add the hominy along with:

12 cups chicken or vegetable stock or broth
3 whole chicken legs (about 2 pounds), skin removed
(1 pound red potatoes, diced)
(2 large epazote sprigs, chopped, or 1½ teaspoons dried oregano)

Bring to a boil. Cover, reduce the heat, and simmer until the chicken is cooked through and the potatoes are tender, about 40 minutes. Remove the chicken from the pot and let sit until cool enough to handle. Shred the meat, discarding the bones or reserving them for stock. Return the chicken to the pot and season to taste with:

Salt

Simmer, uncovered, for 10 minutes. Taste and adjust the seasonings. Serve the posole, passing separately:

Minced red onion or chopped green onion
Diced avocado
Chopped cilantro
Crumbled tortilla chips or pork rinds
Shredded romaine lettuce
Thinly sliced red radishes
Lime wedges

RED POSOLE

8 to 10 servings

Have ready:

1 pound dried hominy (about 3 cups), cooked, 341, or two 25-ounce cans hominy, drained

Remove the stems and seeds from:

4 ounces mild dried red chiles such as guajillo, ancho, and New Mexico (preferably a combination)

Toast the chiles in a skillet or in the oven, 969; they should soften but not blacken. Transfer them to a bowl and cover with warm water. Place a plate or bowl on top to keep the chiles submerged and let them soak for 20 minutes.

Meanwhile, sprinkle:

2 pounds pork shoulder, trimmed and cut into 1-inch cubes

with:

1 teaspoon salt

Heat in a large soup pot over medium-high heat until shimmering:

2 tablespoons vegetable oil

Add the pork in batches and brown on all sides. This should take about 20 minutes. Transfer the pork to a plate and drain all but 2 tablespoons of fat from the pot. Add and cook, stirring, until the onion is softened, about 6 minutes:

1 large onion, thinly sliced
4 garlic cloves, smashed

Add the pork back to the pot along with:

10 cups chicken stock or water or broth
1 tablespoon dried oregano
1 teaspoon ground cumin
1 bay leaf

Increase the heat to high. As the mixture heats, drain the soaked chiles and add to a blender, along with:

2 cups chicken stock or water or broth

Puree until the chiles are a smooth paste. Strain the chile mixture through a fine-mesh sieve into the pot with the pork and stir well. Bring to a boil, then reduce the heat to a simmer, partially cover, and cook until the pork is tender, about 1½ hours. Discard the bay leaf. Serve with any of the garnishes from Green Posole, 323.

CHICKEN AND CHEESE TAMALES

16 tamales

Tamales can be wrapped in corn husks or banana leaves (see variation, 325) and baked or steamed. (If neither is available, you can use 8 × 10-inch pieces of parchment paper.) To vary this recipe, use about 2½ cups Picadillo, 503, shredded Braised Carnitas, 495, or leftover shredded cooked chicken dressed with Red Mole, 553, or Green Mole, 554. Or make vegetarian tamales with drained Frijoles de la Olla, 213, and cheese. Season the filling to taste with salt and spices before forming the tamales. ***To use fresh masa,*** substitute 4 cups (2 pounds) fresh masa for the masa harina/liquid mixture, beating it into the shortening or lard as directed and adding baking powder and salt.

Submerge in a bowl of warm water:

About 4 ounces dried corn husks

Let stand until soft and pliable, about 1 hour (you can leave them to soak overnight, if desired).

Combine on a plate:

1 teaspoon ground cumin
1 teaspoon chili powder
1 teaspoon salt
½ teaspoon cayenne pepper

Coat with the seasoning:

1¼ pounds boneless, skinless chicken thighs (about 5 thighs)

Heat in a large skillet over medium heat:

2 tablespoons vegetable oil

Add the chicken thighs and brown lightly on both sides, then cover and cook over medium-low heat until cooked through, about 10 minutes. Transfer to a plate. Add to the skillet and cook, stirring, until softened, about 5 minutes:

1 medium onion, thinly sliced

Add and cook, stirring, for another 2 minutes:

1 to 2 jalapeño or serrano peppers, seeded and finely chopped

Transfer the onions and peppers to a medium bowl. Finely shred the cooked chicken, add it to the bowl with the onions, and set aside.

Stir together in a large bowl until blended:

3 cups masa harina
2¼ teaspoons baking powder
1½ teaspoons salt

Slowly stir in until well combined:

2½ cups chicken broth or water, heated until steaming

Beat in another large bowl with an electric mixer on high speed until fluffy, about 2 minutes:

1 cup lard or vegetable shortening (8 ounces)

Gradually add the masa mixture one golf ball–sized piece at a time while beating on high speed. Once all the masa is added, continue beating until the dough is the consistency of fluffy mashed potatoes. In theory, the dough is ready when ½ teaspoon dropped into a glass of cold water floats, but even if it doesn't, the tamales will still be delicious.

Drain the corn husks and pat dry. Set aside 16 of the biggest ones. Have ready:

1½ cups grated Monterey Jack, pepper Jack, or Oaxaca cheese (6 ounces)

Place a steamer insert or an expandable steamer in a deep stockpot, or use a tamale steamer. Fill the bottom of the pot or steamer with 1 to 2 inches of water (it should not touch the bottom of the steamer insert or rack). Line the bottom and sides of the pot or steamer with two-thirds of the remaining corn husks.

To form the tamales, lay one corn husk rough side up on a work surface, with the pointed end closer to you. Spread ¼ cup masa dough thinly over the wide part of the husk, leaving the pointed end bare. Spoon 2 tablespoons of the chicken mixture in a vertical line down the center of the masa, then sprinkle with 1½ tablespoons of the cheese. Fold over the left and right sides to enclose the filling (if the husk is too small to enclose the filling, wrap with another husk), then fold the pointed end up. If desired, secure the tamale with kitchen string or leave it untied. Stand the tamale in the steamer, open end up. As you form the rest of the tamales, place them in the steamer.

Cover the tamales with the remaining corn husks. Cover the pot, bring to a boil, and steam over medium heat until a husk peels away easily from the filling, about 1 hour. Add more boiling water to the pot during cooking if necessary.

Remove from the heat and let stand, covered, for 5 minutes before serving. Or let cool completely and refrigerate for several days, or freeze for up to 3 months. Reheat in the steamer before serving.

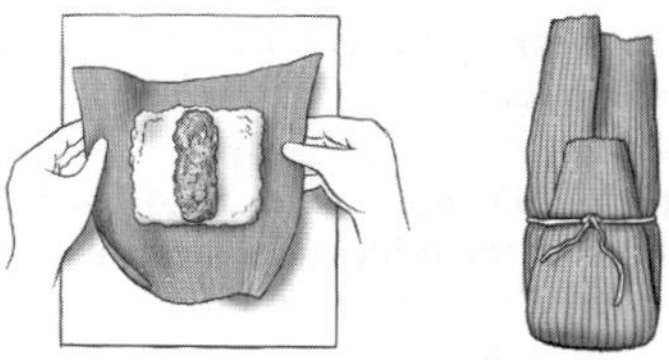

Making tamales

BANANA LEAF TAMALES

While most of us are familiar with corn husk–wrapped tamales, banana leaf tamales are common in the tropical regions of Mexico, such as Oaxaca and the Yucatán Peninsula. You can find banana leaves in the freezer section of most Mexican and Asian supermarkets. See Banana Leaves, 955, for more information.

Have ready **one 1-pound package banana leaves.** If the leaves are frozen, let them thaw at room temperature or thaw them under warm running water. Prepare the desired tamale filling and masa mixture, 324, and have everything ready.

Unfold the banana leaves, wipe them down with a damp cloth, and use kitchen shears to cut them into sixteen 8 × 10-inch rectangles, trimming off the center rib and any outer brown leaf tips and discarding them (or save the center ribs to tie the tamales).

Soften the banana leaf rectangles by briefly running them over a gas flame or warming them in a large, dry skillet over medium heat. The leaves will change color slightly to an olive green when they are ready. This should take only a few seconds on both sides. Fill and fold the leaves as directed in Chicken and Cheese Tamales, 324. You may tie them to hold them together or leave them untied and simply pack them into the steamer so they stay closed. Cook as directed above.

THREE SISTERS TAMALES
16 tamales

"Three sisters" refers to three indigenous North American staple crops that were often grown together—corn, beans, and squash. They make fine companions inside a tamale as well.

Heat in a large skillet over medium heat:

2 tablespoons vegetable oil

Add and cook, stirring occasionally, until the onion is softened and the squash is barely tender, about 8 minutes:

1 medium onion, thinly sliced
1 medium summer squash (about 8 ounces), cut into ½-inch chunks

Stir in:

1 cup cooked or canned pinto or black beans, drained and rinsed
½ cup corn kernels
1 teaspoon ground cumin
1 teaspoon ground coriander
1 teaspoon dried oregano
¾ teaspoon salt

Set aside. Have ready:

About 4 ounces dried corn husks, soaked, 324, or one-pound package banana leaves, prepared as above
1½ cups grated Monterey Jack, pepper Jack, or Oaxaca cheese (6 ounces)

Prepare:

Masa mixture from Chicken and Cheese Tamales, 324

Fill the tamales and steam as directed.

COUSCOUS

See About Wheat, 337.

EINKORN, EMMER, AND FARRO

See About Wheat, 337.

ABOUT JOB'S TEARS

This grain comes from a domesticated type of Asian grass that is closely related to corn. Job's tears also go under the names **coix seeds, adlay,** and (confusingly) **Chinese pearl barley** (they are unrelated). The Japanese call the grain **hato mugi,** and make a semi-pearled type called **yuuki hato mugi.** They resemble pea-sized whole corn grains (though some might be even smaller). With a delicate, nutty taste reminiscent of corn and rice, Job's tears are very high in protein and may be used as a quicker-cooking alternative to hominy in posole, 323–24, or cooked with brown rice and served as a side dish. Look for Job's tears at natural foods stores and Asian markets.

KAMUT OR KHORASAN WHEAT

See About Wheat, 337.

ABOUT MILLET

Millet, one of our oldest cultivated grains, is widely eaten in China, Germany, Russia, India, and Africa. Tiny, rounded, and pale gold or red, millet is gluten-free and always sold hulled. Once cooked, millet makes a fluffy side dish that resembles couscous, with a delicate flavor. It can also be cooked as a porridge, enriched with cream or milk and sugar. Stir it into soups, or use in a grain salad, 130, or stuffing, 535. It is an excellent addition to baked goods and granola, 327, as it can be added raw for a pleasant crunch. ➤ Its flavor becomes fuller and richer when the grain is toasted first in a little oil or butter.

SAFFRON MILLET

4 servings

This recipe was contributed by our friend and cookbook author Maria Speck. It's one of those dishes that is more than the sum of its parts.

Heat a medium saucepan over medium heat. When hot, add:

1 cup millet
¼ teaspoon loosely packed saffron threads

Cook, stirring frequently, until the millet crackles, emits a toasty scent, and starts to turn golden, 2 to 3 minutes. Watch closely so as not to burn the saffron. Add:

1¾ cups water
½ teaspoon salt

Take care as the water will splatter. Bring to a boil. Reduce the heat to maintain a simmer, cover, and cook until the liquid is absorbed, 15 to 20 minutes. If the kernels still have a bit too much crunch for your liking, drizzle on a few more tablespoons of water and cook a few minutes more.

Remove from the heat and distribute across the top of the millet:

2 tablespoons butter, cut into small pieces

Allow it to sit, covered, for 5 minutes. Fluff with a fork and serve immediately.

CHEESY MILLET SPOON BREAD WITH CHILES

6 servings

This recipe, adapted from an older edition of *Joy*, works well with almost any cooked grain. The additions can be varied—try using Gruyère or Swiss cheese instead of Cheddar, and stir in diced ham and Melted Leeks, 247.

Preheat the oven to 350°F. Lightly oil an 8- or 9-inch square baking dish.

Combine in a medium bowl:

2 cups buttermilk
1 cup cooked millet, 342
1 cup shredded Cheddar (4 ounces)
One 4-ounce can diced mild or hot green chiles, drained
2 large eggs, beaten
¼ cup fine or medium yellow or white cornmeal
2 green onions, finely chopped
2 tablespoons butter, melted, or olive oil
¾ teaspoon salt
½ teaspoon baking soda

Scrape the mixture into the prepared dish and bake until set and browned, about 40 minutes.

MILLET CAKES WITH PARMESAN AND SUN-DRIED TOMATOES

4 to 6 servings

Serve with Wilted Tender Greens, 343, and a Fried Egg, 155, as a vegetarian entrée. The millet mixture can be prepared up to 2 days in advance.

Blot with paper towels:

¼ cup diced oil-packed sun-dried tomatoes

Heat in a large skillet or large wide saucepan over medium heat:

2 tablespoons olive oil

Add and cook for 1 minute:

¼ cup finely chopped onion

Add and cook, stirring, over medium heat until the onion and millet are golden, about 4 minutes:

⅓ cup millet
⅓ cup white rice

Add and cook until fragrant, about 30 seconds:

1 garlic clove, minced

Add the sun-dried tomatoes along with:

2 cups chicken or vegetable stock or broth

Bring to a boil, then reduce the heat to medium-low, cover, and cook until the liquid is absorbed and the millet is soft, 25 to 30 minutes. Uncover and stir to break up the grains. Let cool slightly. Add:

¼ cup grated Parmesan
2 large eggs, beaten

Stir until well blended. Dampen your hands with cold water and shape ⅓-cup portions of the millet mixture into small patties about 3 inches in diameter and ½ inch thick. Place on a platter and refrigerate until thoroughly chilled, for 1 hour.

Heat in a large nonstick skillet until hot:

1 tablespoon olive or vegetable oil

Fry the millet cakes until browned on the first side, about 4 minutes. Turn and brown the other side.

ABOUT OATS

Samuel Johnson, in his 1755 dictionary, defines oats as "a grain which in England is generally given to horses, but in Scotland supports the people." A sharp-tongued Scotsman's response to this was "That's why England has such good horses, and Scotland has such fine men." Nutritionally speaking, he may not have been far off the mark with that retort. Oats are highly nutritious, being rich in fiber, which aids digestion and lowers cholesterol. They also happen to be gluten-free—though they are often cross-contaminated because they are often processed in facilities that also process wheat. If you are on a gluten-free diet, purchase only certified gluten-free oats.

All oats, whether whole, crushed, or flaked, are whole grains and still have the bran. **Oat berries** are similar to wheat berries in how they cook. **Rolled oats** have been steamed and then flattened into flakes. They are available as **old-fashioned oats,** which are the largest; **quick-cooking oats,** which are oat berries cut into small pieces before they are rolled; and **instant oats,** which are cut very small, rolled very thin, and precooked. All three types can be cooked in 5 minutes or less. **Oat groats** are whole, hulled oat berries. They may be "steel-cut" (also called Irish oatmeal or Scotch oats) or flattened, or "rolled," as well. Oat groats take longer to cook than rolled oats and yield a delightfully chewy porridge. **Oat bran** is the outer layers of the oat kernels only; it is sold crushed and often cooked as a cereal.

All cooked oatmeal is excellent for breakfast with dried or fresh fruit, spices, brown sugar or maple syrup, and milk or cream. For more oat recipes, see Oatmeal Raisin Cookies, 771, Goetta, 512, Oatmeal Pancakes, 642, Oatmeal Cake, 732, and Oat Bread Cockaigne, 601. For oat flour, see 986.

MEGAN'S SEEDED OLIVE OIL GRANOLA

9½ cups

This full-flavored granola, which is cooked until "well done," has an almost savory quality. We think of it as granola for people who don't like granola.

Preheat the oven to 325°F. Lightly oil 2 large baking sheets (or line 2 baking sheets with parchment paper for easier cleanup).

Toss together in a large bowl:

3 cups old-fashioned rolled oats
¾ cup pumpkin seeds
¾ cup sunflower seeds
¾ cup walnuts or pecans, coarsely chopped
½ cup sesame seeds
(½ cup cacao nibs)

Stir together in a small bowl until combined:

⅓ cup olive oil
⅓ cup packed brown sugar
¼ cup maple syrup
¼ cup sorghum syrup or molasses
¾ teaspoon salt

Stir the wet ingredients into the dry ingredients until fully combined. Spread the granola in a thin layer on the prepared baking sheets. Bake, stirring the granola every 15 minutes and rotating the sheets front to back and switching racks until the granola is a deep, burnished brown, about 1 hour.

Let cool completely, then transfer to an airtight container and store at room temperature for up to 1 month.

LOW-SUGAR GRANOLA

5 cups

This extra-crunchy granola uses pureed ripe banana in place of some of the sugar. The resulting granola is lightly sweet, with no real banana flavor to speak of.

Preheat the oven to 325°F. Lightly oil a large baking sheet or line with parchment paper.

Stir together in a large bowl:

2½ cups old-fashioned rolled oats
½ cup quinoa
½ cup millet
½ cup pumpkin seeds
½ cup pecans, coarsely chopped
1 teaspoon ground cinnamon
½ teaspoon grated or ground nutmeg
½ teaspoon ground cardamom
½ teaspoon salt

Combine in a blender and blend until smooth:

1 large ripe banana
¼ cup maple syrup
¼ cup olive oil or melted coconut oil

Stir the wet ingredients into the dry ingredients until fully combined. Spread the granola in a thin layer on the prepared baking sheet. Bake, stirring every 15 minutes, until golden brown, 50 minutes to 1 hour. Let cool completely. Store in an airtight container at room temperature for up to 1 month.

MUESLI

2 to 4 servings

Muesli, also called **Swiss oatmeal,** was developed in the late nineteenth century by a Swiss physician. Eat it at room temperature or warmed, with milk, yogurt, cream, or sliced fruit on top.

If desired, toast the oats before soaking them. Preheat the oven to 350°F. Spread out on a rimmed baking sheet:

1 cup old-fashioned rolled oats

Toast until fragrant and lightly browned, about 10 minutes. Let cool completely. Or skip straight to soaking. Place the oats in a bowl and add:

1 cup boiling water
¼ teaspoon salt

Cover and soak overnight. Before serving, stir in:

Up to ½ cup chopped dried fruit
⅓ cup chopped toasted, 1005, walnuts, almonds, or pistachios
(½ cup grated tart apple)
(¼ cup flaked or shredded unsweetened coconut, toasted, 973)
2 tablespoons honey or brown sugar, or to taste

BAKED OATMEAL

6 servings

Vary the fruit, nuts, and sweetener to suit your family's tastes.

Preheat the oven to 375°F. Butter an 8-inch square baking dish.

Combine in a medium bowl:

2 cups old-fashioned rolled oats
2 cups milk or nondairy milk
1 cup fresh or frozen berries or ½ cup chopped dried fruit
(½ cup pumpkin or sunflower seeds, walnuts, or almonds, toasted, 1005)
⅓ cup honey, maple syrup, or packed brown sugar

4 tablespoons (½ stick) melted butter or coconut oil
1 large egg
1 teaspoon ground cinnamon
(1 teaspoon vanilla)
½ teaspoon salt

Pour into the baking dish and bake until the top is golden and the oats are set, about 30 minutes.

PUMPKIN BAKED OATMEAL

Prepare **Baked Oatmeal, 327,** substituting for 1 cup of the milk **1 cup pumpkin, sweet potato, or winter squash puree.** Add **1 teaspoon ground ginger, ¼ teaspoon ground allspice,** and **⅛ teaspoon ground cloves.** Stir in **½ cup raisins, currants, or golden raisins** instead of fresh fruit. Bake as directed.

OVERNIGHT STEEL-CUT OATS

4 servings

Sometimes cooking steel-cut oats in the morning can be a little too much to ask. With this method, you are doing your future self a favor: All you have to do in the morning is reheat the oats.

Combine in a medium saucepan:

3 cups water
1 cup steel-cut oats
¼ teaspoon salt

Bring to a boil, cover, then remove from the heat. Let sit overnight. In the morning, reheat and serve with your favorite oatmeal toppings.

ABOUT QUINOA AND CANIHUA

Like amaranth and buckwheat, quinoa (pronounced *keen-wa*) is a pseudocereal we cook and eat as we do grains. Cultivated in the Andes by Inca farmers for thousands of years, quinoa cooks quickly, is high in minerals, and is one of the best sources of plant protein. In fact, it provides a complete protein since it contains all of the essential amino acids. Quinoa is closely related to another pseudocereal called **canihua** or **kaniwa,** which cooks a little differently (see the Grains Cooking Chart, 340).

At one time, quinoa required a thorough rinse under cold running water to remove bitter saponins, but now almost all commercially available quinoa is pre-rinsed. If you buy quinoa from a small farm, you may need to rinse it. When cooked, quinoa uncoils and becomes translucent. Toast quinoa before cooking, with or without butter or oil, for the best flavor; it is especially good with toasted pecans or other nuts and makes a delicious pilaf. Quinoa grows in several colors, but only three are commonly available: gold, red, and black. They are interchangeable in recipes. You may also find rolled **quinoa flakes** available, which make an excellent, almost-instant breakfast that is high in protein.

Quinoa also makes an admirable breakfast porridge, as well as a base for salad (see Quinoa Salad with Broccoli and Feta, 132). Quinoa may also be substituted for bulgur or rice in pilafs and dishes like Tabbouleh, 131. Leftover quinoa is excellent bound with egg, shaped into cakes, and pan-fried.

JEWELED QUINOA

4 to 6 servings

This dish is almost as much about aesthetics as it is about flavor. The orange squash, pink pomegranate seeds, and green herbs and pistachios are as visually enticing as they are flavorsome.

Preheat the oven to 425°F. Toss together on a large rimmed baking sheet:

1 small butternut squash (about 1½ pounds), peeled, seeded, and cut into ¾-inch cubes
2 tablespoons vegetable oil
½ teaspoon salt
½ teaspoon black pepper

Roast until tender and browned, about 25 minutes.

Meanwhile, heat in a large saucepan over medium heat:

2 tablespoons butter or olive oil

Add and cook, stirring, until softened, 6 to 8 minutes:

1 small onion, diced, or 1 small leek, halved lengthwise, well cleaned and thinly sliced

Stir in and cook, stirring occasionally, until fragrant and toasted, about 5 minutes:

1 cup quinoa

Add:

1½ cups unsalted chicken stock or broth or water
½ teaspoon salt

Bring to a boil, then reduce the heat to low, cover, and simmer until tender, about 15 minutes. Let stand off the heat for 5 minutes. Transfer the quinoa to a large bowl, add the squash, and toss to combine. Stir in:

½ cup pomegranate seeds
½ cup packed chopped herbs, such as parsley, dill, mint, or chives, or a combination

Before serving, sprinkle with:

⅓ cup crumbled feta cheese
¼ cup chopped roasted pistachios or toasted, 1012, pumpkin seeds

QUINOA PILAF

About 3 cups; 4 servings

Proceed as for **Buckwheat Pilaf, 321,** using **1 cup quinoa** in place of the buckwheat.

ABOUT RICE

Derived from wild grasses native to Asia and Africa, rice is now an essential ingredient in kitchens throughout the world. **White rice** has had the outer coating—the bran—and the oily germ removed. It cooks quickly and has excellent keeping qualities, remaining fresh for a year or longer at ordinary shelf temperatures. **Brown rice** has the bran and germ still attached, which contain most of the grain's vitamins, minerals, and nutty flavors. Unfortunately, the bran is much slower to tenderize during cooking and the oils contained in the germ can go rancid, which diminishes its shelf life. For this reason, we suggest storing brown rice in the refrigerator, if possible, and using it within a few months. There is an in-between type now available called **haiga** or **germ rice,** which is "half-milled": Only its bran has been removed (the germ is left intact). Tan-colored haiga is a delicious compromise: Partial milling leaves it with more flavor and nutrients than white rice, and the absence of the bran layers makes it much quicker to prepare than brown rice.

Aside from processing methods, fifteen thousand years of cultivation has given rise to many varieties of rice throughout the world. **Long-grain rices** contain less of the starch amylopectin, which is what causes rice grains to stick together. Thus, cooked long-grain rice tends to remain separate and fluffy. **Basmati rice,** whose name means "Queen of Fragrance" in Sanskrit, has an alluring aroma and flavor. Basmati gives Indian pilafs (or *pulaos*) their distinctive fluffy texture and aroma. **Jasmine,** another long-grain rice, is denser when cooked, and has a subtle, perfumed aroma. Several American hybrid aromatic rices have become more widely available. These include **Texmati,** a basmati grown in Texas; **Wehani,** a long-grain reddish-brown rice from California; and **Louisiana Pecan** or **popcorn rice,** named for its nut-like aroma. **Carolina gold,** a unique long-grain variety grown in South Carolina, is one of the only types available originally bred from wild African grasses (all other common rice types originated from central Asian grasses). Though it is not especially fragrant, rice cultivators in the southern United States have bred **Charleston gold,** an aromatic cousin.

Short- and **medium-grain rices** are oval to nearly round in shape and cook up tender and moist. These include Japanese and Chinese white rices, paella rices like **Calasparra, bomba,** and **Valencia,** risotto rices, as well as **Thai sticky** or **glutinous rice** (despite the common name, this rice contains no gluten). In general, medium- and short-grain rice types contain more amylopectin starch, and thus cook up "stickier" than long-grain varieties. This quality is a boon to dishes like sushi, musubi, risotto, and puddings. For more on Italian risotto rices like **Arborio** and **carnaroli,** see About Risotto, 335.

Red and **black rices** have had some or all of their bran left on to retain their unique color. Since they are polished to varying degrees, some will cook more quickly than brown rice and others will require the same long simmering time. If you are unsure how polished your rice is, prepare a small test batch. **Thai black rice** is a whole-grain sticky rice and must be steamed rather than boiled.

Wild rice is not true rice: The seed comes from an American grass. See About Wild Rice, 339.

Parboiled or **"converted" rice** is specially processed with steam pressure before having the bran and germ removed, which effectively transfers some of their nutrients to the white endosperm that remains. It is less prone to becoming sticky or clumpy when cooked than regular white rice. It also requires a bit more liquid and a slightly longer cooking time than white rice but shares the same long shelf life. **Instant rice,** which can be either white or brown, has been cooked and then dehydrated before packaging. It is not as flavorful as conventional rice, but it is convenient because it cooks in just a few minutes.

Rice grains have a tendency to break during milling, which has encouraged industrious cooks (and millers) to come up with ways to prepare (or market) these perfectly edible grain fragments, or "brokens." You may find **broken rice** processed into a uniform shape and sold as **rice grits, rice couscous,** or **rice polenta.** Since the starch within the rice grains has been exposed, it will add body to the liquid in which the grains are cooked, making them especially good for puddings and porridges like Congee, 353. Or, simply cook them as for the grits, polenta, and couscous they are often marketed as.

Some imported rice, and any rice bought in bulk, should be rinsed before cooking. Rinsing rids the rice of most surface starches, promoting distinct, separate grains. However, in recipes such as risotto, where a creamy consistency is desired, or with parboiled rice, rinsing is not recommended.

For basic cooking instructions using the absorption method, see the Grains Cooking Chart, 340. ➤ Rice can also be cooked like pasta if you prefer your grains separate. Bring a large pot of salted water to a boil, add the rice, and boil until tender. Drain and serve. Rice cookers are wonderful devices that make preparing white or brown rice a snap. Follow the manufacturer's instructions. Longer-cooking brown rice may be cooked in a fraction of the time with a pressure cooker (see the brown rice entry on 343).

For more recipes using rice, see Red Beans and Rice, 216, Chicken and Rice Soup, 93, Arroz con Pollo, 131, Rice Salad with Chicken and Olives, 130, Brown Rice Salad with Dates and Oranges, 131, Stuffed Bell Peppers, 262, Chicken Rice Casserole, 537, and About Grain Stuffings and Dressings, 535.

BAKED RICE

4 servings

This recipe is easily doubled. For **Baked Brown Rice,** substitute brown rice for the white rice, increase the chicken broth or water to 2½ cups, and bake for 45 minutes. (For this variation, a loyal reader suggests replacing a quarter of the brown rice with wild rice.)

Preheat the oven to 350°F. Heat in a Dutch oven or 10-inch ovenproof skillet with a lid over medium heat:

1 to 3 tablespoons butter or olive oil (use the greater amount if adding mushrooms)

Add and cook, stirring, until softened, about 5 minutes:

(6 ounces mushrooms, coarsely chopped)
½ medium onion, chopped
(1 garlic clove, minced)

Add and stir until well coated:

1 cup long-grain white rice

Add:

1½ cups chicken broth or water
¼ teaspoon salt

Bring to a boil. Cover, put in the oven, and bake until the rice is tender and the broth has been absorbed, about 20 minutes. Let stand, covered, for 5 minutes before serving.

RICE PILAF

4 servings

Pilafs call for cooking rice briefly in butter or oil before adding broth or water, a technique that ensures that the grains will be fluffy,

separate, and flavorful. For even more flavor, sauté the rice until it browns slightly.
Melt in a large saucepan over medium-low heat:
2 tablespoons butter
Add and cook, stirring, until golden, about 8 minutes:
½ medium onion, chopped
Add and stir until the rice becomes translucent around the edges 3 to 5 minutes:
1 cup basmati rice, or other long-grain rice
Stir in:
1½ cups chicken broth or water
(½ teaspoon salt, if using unsalted broth or water)
Bring to a boil. Stir once, cover, and cook over low heat until the liquid is absorbed and the rice is tender, about 15 minutes. Let stand off the heat, covered, for 5 minutes before serving. Sprinkle with:
2 tablespoons chopped toasted, 1005, walnuts or
2 tablespoons chopped parsley

MUJADARA (LENTILS AND RICE WITH BROWNED ONIONS)

6 servings

Mujadara is a simple, frugal, and satisfying dish that is popular throughout the Levant, particularly as a Lenten staple for Orthodox Christians in Syria and Lebanon. Mujadara may appear homely, but the generous topping of silky browned onions gives the dish an alluring richness. To simplify things a bit, we cook the lentils and rice together, parboiling the lentils before adding the rice to ensure that they cook in the same amount of time.
Have ready:
3 large onions, thinly sliced
Heat in a large skillet over medium heat:
2 tablespoons vegetable oil
Stir two-thirds of the onions into the oil to coat and sprinkle with:
½ teaspoon salt
Cook, stirring occasionally, until the onions are deep golden brown, about 20 minutes, reducing the heat if necessary to keep the onions from burning.
Meanwhile, heat in a large saucepan over medium heat:
2 tablespoons vegetable oil
Add the remaining onions and sauté, stirring occasionally, until translucent, 6 to 8 minutes. Stir in and cook for 1 minute:
3 garlic cloves, minced
1½ teaspoons ground cumin
1 teaspoon salt
1 teaspoon ground coriander
1 teaspoon ground allspice
½ teaspoon ground cinnamon
Add:
1 cup green lentils (Puy lentils)
4½ cups water
Bring to a boil, then reduce the heat slightly, cover, and simmer briskly for 12 minutes. Stir in:
2 cups short- or long-grain white rice
Cover, reduce the heat to medium-low, and simmer until the rice and lentils are tender, about 20 minutes. Let stand off the heat for 5 to 10 minutes, then fluff with a fork. To serve, pile the lentils and rice onto a plate and top with the browned onions. Serve with:
Plain yogurt
Chopped parsley, dill, or cilantro

BECKER RICE AND NOODLE PILAF

4 or 5 servings

If you can find fine egg noodles, use those instead of the angel hair pasta. To break pasta into small pieces without making a mess, hold them inside a paper bag as you break them apart.
Combine in a large, wide saucepan or deep skillet over medium heat and stir until the noodles are toasted and brown:
2 tablespoons butter
2 shallots or ½ medium onion, minced
2 ounces angel hair pasta broken into 1-inch lengths (about ½ cup)
Add and cook, stirring, until the rice is translucent around the edges:
1 cup long-grain white rice
Add and bring to a boil:
2 cups chicken broth
(½ teaspoon salt, if using unsalted broth)
Reduce the heat to low, cover, and simmer gently for 20 minutes. Allow to stand off the heat, covered, 5 minutes before serving. Fluff with a fork.

SPANISH RICE

4 to 6 servings

Preheat the oven to 350°F. Combine in a Dutch oven or 10-inch ovenproof skillet and cook, stirring, over medium heat until the onions are golden, about 8 minutes:
1 tablespoon vegetable oil
2 slices bacon, minced
½ medium onion, chopped
½ green bell pepper, chopped
1 garlic clove, minced
Add and stir until well coated:
1 cup long-grain white rice
Add and bring to a boil:
1¾ cups chicken stock or broth
1 cup drained canned diced tomatoes
½ teaspoon sweet or hot paprika
¼ teaspoon salt
¼ teaspoon black pepper
Stir once, cover, transfer to the oven, and bake until the liquid is absorbed and the rice is tender, about 25 minutes. Uncover and let stand 5 minutes before serving.

HOPPIN' JOHN

6 to 8 servings

Southerners traditionally serve Hoppin' John on New Year's Day as a good luck dish. For a quicker version, use two 15-ounce cans black-eyed peas, drained and rinsed. Add the peas and ham to the rice and cook as directed.

Rinse, pick over, and soak for 6 to 8 hours:

8 ounces dried black-eyed peas (about 1¼ cups)

Drain and rinse thoroughly. Place in an ovenproof pot or Dutch oven and add:

3 cups water
1 large onion, chopped
½ cup diced smoked ham
(2 garlic cloves, minced)
½ teaspoon dried thyme
½ teaspoon red pepper flakes
2 bay leaves

Bring to a simmer and simmer gently, uncovered, just until the peas are tender, 30 to 50 minutes depending on the age of the peas. Drain, reserving the cooking liquid (set the pot aside). Discard the bay leaves. Transfer the peas and ham to a bowl and season to taste with:

Salt and black pepper

Cover and set aside. Add to the reserved cooking liquid, to make 2½ cups:

½ to 1¼ cups chicken stock or broth

Preheat the oven to 325°F. Set the pot you used to cook the peas over medium heat and add:

2 tablespoons butter
2 to 4 slices bacon, diced

Cook, stirring, until the bacon has rendered most of its fat and begun to crisp. Stir in:

1¼ cups long-grain white rice
1 teaspoon salt

Cook, stirring to coat the rice with fat, about 1 minute. Add the pea cooking liquid and the pea-ham mixture and bring to a simmer. Stir once, then cover, and bake until the rice has absorbed the liquid, 20 to 25 minutes. Sprinkle with:

¼ cup minced parsley

Toss lightly with a fork to fluff the rice and mix the ingredients. Let stand uncovered for 10 minutes before serving. Hoppin' John can be made 1 day ahead, covered, and refrigerated. Bring to room temperature, then bake, covered and without stirring, in a 275°F oven just until warmed through.

JAMAICAN RICE AND PEAS

6 to 8 servings

An excellent, satisfying dish that combines creamy coconut milk and the floral, spicy Scotch bonnet chile. Serve with a Caribbean dish such as Jamaican Jerk Chicken, 413, or Guyanese Pepperpot, 468.

Heat in a medium saucepan over medium heat:

1 tablespoon vegetable oil

Add and cook, stirring, until fragrant, about 1 minute:

3 green onions, chopped
2 garlic cloves, minced

Stir in and bring to a boil:

One 13½-ounce can coconut milk
1½ cups unsalted chicken stock or broth or water
2 sprigs thyme
1 Scotch bonnet or habanero chile, minced
1 teaspoon salt
½ teaspoon black pepper

Stir in:

Two 15-ounce cans or 3 cups cooked black-eyed peas or kidney beans, drained and rinsed
2 cups long-grain white rice

Return to a boil. Stir once, reduce the heat to low, cover, and simmer until the rice is tender and has absorbed the liquid, about 20 minutes. Remove from the heat and let stand, covered, for 10 minutes. Remove the thyme sprigs and fluff with a fork before serving.

CHICKEN JAMBALAYA

6 to 8 servings

Season:

2½ pounds bone-in chicken parts

with:

1 teaspoon salt
½ teaspoon black pepper

Heat in a large skillet or Dutch oven over medium heat:

2 tablespoons vegetable oil

Add the chicken and cook, turning once, until browned on all sides, about 10 minutes. Transfer the chicken to a plate. Add to the skillet and brown:

12 ounces andouille sausage, sliced, or 8 ounces smoked ham, diced

Transfer to the plate with the chicken. Drain off all but 2 tablespoons of the drippings. Add and cook, stirring, until softened, about 8 minutes:

1 medium onion, chopped
1 medium green bell pepper, diced
1 celery rib, chopped
3 garlic cloves, minced

Add and cook for 2 minutes, stirring to coat:

1 cup long-grain white rice
2 tablespoons tomato paste
¼ to 1 teaspoon cayenne pepper, to taste

Stir in:

2 cups chicken stock or broth or water
One 14½-ounce can diced tomatoes
½ teaspoon salt
½ teaspoon dried thyme
1 bay leaf

Return the chicken and andouille to the skillet. Cook, covered, over medium-low heat until the liquid is absorbed and the chicken is cooked through, about 20 minutes. Cook, uncovered, until the sauce thickens, 5 to 8 minutes. Discard the bay leaf. Stir in before serving:

¼ cup chopped parsley

CAJUN DIRTY RICE

6 to 8 servings

If you cannot find or do not want to add chicken gizzards, omit and add **12 ounces coarsely chopped mushrooms** with the onions, celery, and pepper. To omit the liver as well, use **12 ounces mushrooms** and **1 pound ground pork, sausage, or tasso ham.**

Prepare for cooking, 444, and pat dry:

1 pound chicken gizzards

Heat in a Dutch oven or large saucepan over medium heat:

2 tablespoons vegetable oil

Add the gizzards and brown on all sides, about 10 minutes. Transfer to a plate. Add to the pot and brown, turning once, about 8 minutes:

½ pound chicken livers, rinsed and patted dry

Set aside with the cooked gizzards. Add to the pot:

½ pound ground pork, bulk sausage, chopped andouille sausage, or chopped tasso ham

Break up the meat with a spoon, and cook until browned, about 6 minutes. Stir in:

1 medium onion, chopped
1 celery rib, chopped
½ green bell pepper or 3 to 5 jalapeños, seeded and chopped

Cook until softened, about 5 minutes, scraping any browned bits off the bottom of the pot.

Finely chop the gizzards and liver and return them to the pot, along with:

5 garlic cloves, chopped
2 teaspoons dried thyme
1 teaspoon salt
(¼ to ½ teaspoon cayenne pepper, to taste)

Cook, stirring occasionally, for another 3 minutes. Add:

3 cups chicken stock or broth, pork stock, or water
1½ cups long-grain white rice

Stir, bring to a boil, then reduce the heat to medium-low, cover, and simmer until the rice is tender and the liquid is absorbed, about 15 minutes. Let stand off the heat for 5 minutes. Stir in:

4 green onions, thinly sliced
½ cup finely chopped parsley

Serve with:

Hot sauce

FRIED RICE

4 servings

This is a delicious way to use leftover rice. In fact, leftover rice works best since its excess moisture has evaporated, making it easier to fry and brown. To improve results with freshly cooked rice, spread the grains out on a baking sheet and let stand for 10 minutes, or until the rice stops steaming. See the additions below for ideas.

Whisk together:

4 eggs
½ teaspoon salt

Heat a large nonstick skillet or wok over medium heat until hot. Pour in, tilting the skillet to coat:

1 tablespoon vegetable oil

Add the eggs all at once. As the eggs set, push the edges toward the center and tilt the skillet to redistribute uncooked egg. When completely set, break the egg into clumps and transfer to a bowl. Pour into the skillet and heat over medium-high heat:

2 tablespoons vegetable oil

Add and cook until fragrant, about 1 minute:

1-inch piece ginger, peeled and minced
2 garlic cloves, minced

Add and cook, stirring frequently, until the peas are thawed and carrots are just tender, about 3 minutes:

1 carrot, finely diced
½ cup frozen green peas

Add and cook, stirring frequently, until the rice is warmed through, about 3 minutes:

3 to 4 cups cold cooked rice

Stir in the cooked eggs, along with:

3 green onions, thinly sliced
2 tablespoons soy sauce, or to taste
1 teaspoon toasted sesame oil, or to taste

ADDITIONS TO FRIED RICE

Add any of the following to the recipe above at the same time as the carrot and peas.

½ cup finely shredded green or red cabbage
½ cup leftover cooked vegetables, such as broccoli, green beans, squash, or corn, diced or cut into bite-sized pieces
½ cup thawed frozen vegetables, such as corn or green beans
½ cup diced Chinese sausage or smoked ham
1 cup chopped cooked chicken, pork, or fish, or cooked small to medium shrimp
¼ cup chopped peanuts or cashews or 1 tablespoon toasted sesame seeds

KIMCHI FRIED RICE

4 servings

Topping this spicy, smoky dish with the optional fried eggs makes it an exemplary breakfast or lunch.

Place in a large skillet over medium heat:

6 slices bacon

Cook until the bacon has rendered its fat and become browned and crisp, about 5 minutes. Transfer the bacon to a plate lined with paper towels. Drain all but 2 tablespoons of the bacon fat from the skillet and add:

1½ cups drained kimchi, coarsely chopped

Cook, stirring, for 3 minutes. Coarsely chop the cooked bacon and add to the skillet, along with:

4 cups cooked white rice (preferably short-grain), 343

Stir to combine and gently press the rice mixture into the skillet with the back of a spatula. Cook, stirring occasionally, until the rice starts to brown and crisp, 6 to 8 minutes. Transfer to plates or bowls and, if desired, top each serving with:

(1 Fried Egg, 155, preferably over easy or sunny-side up)

Garnish with:

Thinly sliced green onion
Drizzle of toasted sesame oil
Toasted sesame seeds

CONGEE

4 servings

Congee, its Thai cousin, *jok*, and its Korean counterpart, *juk*, will win over even the most tender of stomachs. It is considered breakfast food and is a restorative meal for those recovering from a bad cold. Serve congee with any toppings you like—we are fans of cooked chicken, green onion, sesame oil, and soy sauce.

Place in a fine-mesh sieve and rinse:

1 cup short-grain white rice or broken rice

Transfer to a large saucepan and add:

6 cups unsalted chicken stock or broth or water, or a combination
½ teaspoon salt

Bring to a boil, then reduce the heat to medium-low, partially cover, and simmer gently, stirring occasionally, until the rice grains puff, then burst open, and the mixture is thick and porridge-like, about 1 hour. Stir more frequently toward the end of cooking to prevent the rice from sticking to the bottom of the pan. If needed, add a little water to reach a loose, porridge-like consistency.

Ladle the congee into bowls and serve piping hot topped with any of the following:

Thinly sliced green onion or Crispy Fried Shallots, 256
A drizzle of toasted sesame oil and/or soy sauce
Chopped roasted peanuts
Diced pickled mustard greens, 113
Sliced cooked Chinese sausage or diced cooked chicken
Soft-Boiled, 150, Poached, 153, or Fried Eggs, 155
Thai fried chili paste, 969 (use sparingly!), or Spicy Chinese Chile Crisp, 572

PERSIAN RICE

4 to 6 servings

Traditionally Persian rice is cooked slowly in a heavy pot over direct heat so that a delicious crust, called *tahdig*, forms on the bottom. The crust is lifted out and served either on top of the soft cooked rice or in a separate dish. In this simplified version, the rice is baked in a nonstick skillet and inverted like a large pancake, with the crisp rice on top and the soft cooked rice underneath.

Preheat the oven to 350°F. Bring to a boil in a large pot:

3 quarts water
1 tablespoon salt

Stir in:

2 cups white basmati rice
1 cinnamon stick
3 whole cloves
6 black peppercorns
¼ teaspoon cardamom seeds (from about 3 pods)

Cook uncovered, stirring occasionally, until the rice is almost tender, about 10 minutes. Drain and let stand in a sieve until ready to use. (Leave the spices in the rice.) Melt in a large ovenproof nonstick skillet over medium heat:

1 stick (4 ounces) butter

Spoon off 3 tablespoons of the butter and set aside. Add to the skillet:

1 medium onion, thinly sliced
¼ teaspoon saffron threads

Cook, stirring, until the onions are golden, about 8 minutes. Spread the onions in an even layer in the skillet. Stir into the cooked rice:

2 tablespoons diced dried apricots
2 tablespoons dried sweet or sour cherries or golden raisins
1 teaspoon salt

Spoon the rice over the onions. Smooth the top of the rice with the back of a large spoon and press down very firmly to pack it. Drizzle the reserved butter evenly over the top. Cover with a double layer of foil, pressing down on the top and crimping the edges. Transfer to the oven and bake for 1 hour.

Let stand, covered, for 10 minutes. Uncover the rice and invert a large round platter over the skillet. Protecting your hands with a kitchen towel, turn the skillet and platter over, allowing the rice to drop onto the platter. Sprinkle with:

¼ cup chopped pistachios

COCONUT RICE

4 to 6 servings

Bring to a boil in a large saucepan:

1 cup canned coconut milk
1 cup water
1 cup jasmine rice
¾ teaspoon salt

Stir once, cover, and cook over very low heat until the liquid is absorbed and the rice is tender, about 20 minutes. If desired, sprinkle over the cooked rice:

(⅓ cup shredded or flaked unsweetened coconut, toasted, 973)
(Cilantro leaves)

INDIAN LEMON RICE

4 servings

This flavorful South Indian–style rice dish is loaded with fragrant seeds, spices, and fresh curry leaves. While some of the ingredients are hard to find at a regular supermarket, a trip to an Indian grocery store should do the trick. You may also use 3½ to 4 cups leftover rice in this dish, heating until warmed through.

Cook, 343:

1½ cups jasmine rice

Once cooked, but while the rice is still warm, heat in a large skillet over medium heat until shimmering:

2 tablespoons vegetable oil

Add and cook, stirring occasionally, until browned:

3 tablespoons raw peanuts

Stir in and cook, stirring occasionally, until the mustard seeds start to pop:

2 teaspoons chana dal (split chickpeas), urad dal, or split yellow lentils

1 teaspoon brown or yellow mustard seeds
(½ teaspoon cumin seeds)

Cautiously stir in (the leaves may sputter):

15 fresh curry leaves
2 serrano peppers, seeded and minced
(3 dried red Indian chiles)
1 teaspoon ground turmeric
¾ teaspoon salt
(Pinch of asafoetida, 954)

Stir in:

2 tablespoons lemon juice

Immediately add the cooked rice, stirring well to evenly coat the rice with the seasoning mixture. Remove from the heat and garnish with:

Chopped cilantro

PAELLA VALENCIANA

6 servings

Paella gets its name from the broad, shallow pan (*paellera*) traditionally used to cook this classic Valencian dish. True Valencian paella is made with chicken, rabbit, and snails, though we chose not to include snails here.

Combine in a small bowl and set aside:

¼ teaspoon saffron threads
½ cup warm water

Heat in a 12- to 14-inch paella pan or large skillet over medium heat:

¼ cup olive oil

Add and brown in batches:

1 pound bone-in chicken thighs
1 pound rabbit, cut into small serving pieces (or substitute more chicken thighs)

As the chicken and rabbit pieces are browned, transfer them to a plate. Pour off all but 2 tablespoons of fat from the pan. Add:

3 tomatoes, peeled, 281, and chopped
1 medium onion, chopped

Cook, stirring often, until well browned and concentrated, about 15 minutes. Stir in:

2 teaspoons Spanish pimentón or smoked sweet paprika

Pour in the reserved saffron mixture along with:

4 cups hot unsalted chicken stock or broth
1 teaspoon salt

Return the chicken and rabbit pieces to the pan. Simmer, uncovered, for 10 minutes. Remove the chicken and rabbit from the pan once more. Add to the pan:

2 cups Valencia or bomba rice
1 cup frozen, canned, or cooked butter beans or baby limas
8 ounces green beans, trimmed and cut into 1-inch pieces
One 3-inch sprig rosemary

Stir well, making sure the ingredients are well distributed, then nestle the chicken and rabbit in the rice. Cook, uncovered and without stirring, over medium-low heat until the rice is tender and the liquid is absorbed, 20 to 25 minutes. If the liquid evaporates before the rice is done, add more hot stock or water as needed. For the last 5 minutes of cooking, increase the heat to medium-high to brown the bottom of the rice. Do not allow the rice to burn; however, a dark brown crust on the bottom of the pan is desirable. Let stand off the heat for 10 minutes before serving. Discard the rosemary sprig. To serve, cut the chicken and rabbit from the bone, then distribute the meat around the dish.

SHELLFISH PAELLA

Prepare **Paella Valenciana, above,** omitting the rabbit and rosemary, and using Fish Stock, 77, or Shellfish Stock, 78, instead of chicken stock. If desired, add **(4 ounces Spanish chorizo, diced)** along with the onions and tomatoes. After the rice has cooked for 12 minutes, arrange **1 pound large shrimp, peeled and deveined, 281,** on top of the rice in a circular pattern. Cook, uncovered, for 10 minutes more. Arrange **18 mussels, scrubbed and debearded, 351,** on top of the rice, pressing them down slightly to embed them in the rice, and cook until the mussels open, about 5 minutes. Proceed as directed. Serve garnished with **lemon wedges.**

GOHAN (PLAIN JAPANESE RICE)

6½ cups

This rice is the base for all sushi (vinegared rice) dishes.

Place in a bowl with cold water to cover:

3 cups Japanese short- or medium-grain rice (sometimes labeled "sushi rice")

Swish the rice with your fingers vigorously, then drain the rice. Repeat until the water remains almost clear. This usually takes several rinsings. Drain the rice well after the final rinse. Transfer the rice to a straight-sided heavy-bottomed pot, along with:

3 cups plus 2 tablespoons cold water

Let the rice stand for 10 minutes. Cover the pot with a tight-fitting lid and bring to a boil over high heat. Do not remove the lid; instead, watch for the lid to begin to dance. This should take about 5 minutes. Reduce the heat to medium and continue to cook until the water is absorbed, about 5 minutes. Increase the heat to high again for 30 seconds to dry the rice. Remove the pot from the heat and let stand, still tightly covered, for at least 10 minutes, or up to 30 minutes. Use the following amounts to make less rice:

1 cup rice and 1 cup plus 1½ tablespoons water yields a generous 2 cups
2 cups rice and 2 cups plus 2 tablespoons water yields a generous 4 cups

SHARI (SUSHI RICE)

6½ cups

This is the vinegared rice essential to sushi. Use only warm, freshly cooked rice, which will better absorb the seasoned vinegar.

Combine in a small saucepan:

1 cup rice vinegar
2 tablespoons sugar
1 teaspoon salt

Heat, stirring, just until the sugar and salt are dissolved. Set the seasoned vinegar aside. Prepare:

Gohan, above

Spread the hot rice out in a wide bowl. Toss the rice with a spatula or spoon while fanning it with a piece of stiff cardboard to cool it. When steam no longer rises from the rice, gradually sprinkle with 6 tablespoons of the seasoned vinegar, 1 tablespoon at a time, gently folding and tossing with the spatula. Taste and continue to add, again 1 tablespoon at a time, up to 6 tablespoons more seasoned vinegar, or to taste. Cover with a dampened cloth until ready to use.

MAKIZUSHI (ROLLED SUSHI)

10 rolls; 5 to 10 servings

The ingredients in this recipe can be used to make 5 crab, tuna, or salmon rolls and 5 vegetable rolls, or 10 vegetable rolls. For making an entire batch with fish or crab, you will need to double the amount. If the nori is not toasted, cook each sheet for a few seconds under the broiler or pass it back and forth over a gas flame until it stiffens slightly and is fragrant. For safety information for handling fish, see Serving Raw Fish, 377.

Prepare:

Shari, 334

Have ready and, if necessary, cut into 7 × 5-inch rectangles:

10 sheets toasted nori seaweed

Have ready:

(5 ounces lump crabmeat, five 7 × ¼-inch imitation crab sticks, or 4 ounces raw sushi-grade tuna or salmon, sliced into long, ¼-inch-thick pieces)

1 cucumber, peeled, seeded, and cut into ten 7 × ¼-inch strips

1 avocado, peeled, pitted, and sliced lengthwise into 20 strips, dipped in fresh lemon juice

(1 large carrot, julienned)

5 green onions, trimmed and cut lengthwise into 2 pieces each

1½ tablespoons toasted sesame seeds

½ cup radish sprouts

Place a bamboo sushi mat on a work surface with the slats running horizontally. Lay 1 nori sheet shiny side down on the mat with a long side closer to you. Spread ½ cup rice across the entire surface, leaving a 1-inch border at the top of the nori sheet.

To make each crab, tuna, or salmon roll, place 1 ounce crabmeat, 1 strip imitation crab, or 1 strip tuna or salmon across the center of the rice. Add 1 strip of cucumber, 2 strips of avocado placed end to end, carrot strips (if using) placed end to end, and 1 piece of green onion.

To make each vegetable roll, sprinkle the rice with sesame seeds. Top with 1 strip of cucumber, 2 slices of avocado placed end to end, carrot strips (if using) placed end to end, and 1 piece of green onion. Top with radish sprouts.

Beginning with the edge closer to you, roll up each nori sheet, using the sushi mat to squeeze along the length of the sheet to compress it into a compact roll. Continue rolling and squeezing to the end of the nori sheet. The roll should be as tight as possible. Roll back and forth gently to seal the nori. Lay the rolls seam side down on a tray, cover with plastic wrap, and refrigerate until ready to serve. You will have some sushi rice left over.

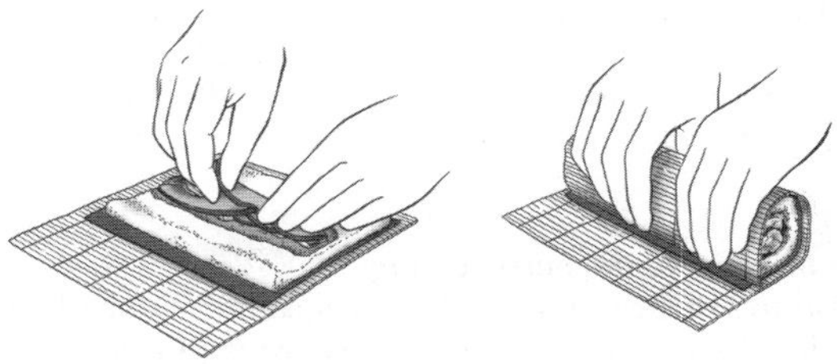

Rolling makizushi

To serve, cut each roll into 8 equal pieces. Serve with:

Pickled ginger, store-bought or homemade, 930

Soy sauce

Wasabi paste

Diners can mix the soy sauce with wasabi, to taste, for dipping.

ABOUT RISOTTO

Risotto, the classic rice dish of northern Italy, is surprisingly easy to prepare. The technique is simple: Gradually stir simmering stock or broth into rice. As the rice absorbs the hot broth it expands, and the friction of constant stirring softens the outer layer of the grain and releases starch, resulting in a creamy consistency.

Medium-grain rices such as **Arborio, Vialone Nano, baldo,** or **carnaroli** contain the proper ratio of starches essential to the texture of classic risotto. In a pinch, Calrose rice makes a decent substitute for the varieties listed above. Arborio rice is notable for its firm center or core (called "chalk") that remains al dente, or firm to the bite, even after prolonged cooking.

Risotto is typically prepared with chicken stock or broth, but a flavorful vegetable broth can also be used. Use a wide, shallow, heavy-bottomed saucepan. Cook the risotto at a simmer, adding ½ to 1 cup of hot broth at a time. Taste the rice frequently while cooking to gauge its tenderness and creaminess, and anticipate about 20 minutes total cooking time once the stock is first added. Let the risotto stand off the heat for a few minutes before serving.

True risotto is made with rice, but other grains can be cooked using this technique. Barley, farro, spelt, quinoa, and einkorn are all good candidates for the risotto method. Firmer grains such as farro, spelt, or einkorn benefit from soaking overnight before being used in this way. You may also wish to crack about one-quarter of the grains in a food processor after soaking to help them release their starch. You can expect 1 cup of the hardier of these grains to take up to 7 cups of stock to become tender. They will still have some chew. Barley will use about the same amount of stock as rice. Quinoa takes about half the amount of stock that rice does.

Regardless of the grain you use, there are many different ways to flavor risotto. Start the process by sautéing minced onion, shallot, or leeks, and sliced mushrooms. Whisk pumpkin, sweet potato, or squash puree into the simmering stock for an autumnal risotto, and top with fried sage leaves, 1013. Toward the end of cooking risotto, stir in quick-cooking vegetables like peas, asparagus, broccoli florets, or chopped zucchini. Alternatively, you can flavor risotto by adorning it with a variety of toppings, such as cubed and roasted winter squash, whole roasted cherry tomatoes, or, for the extravagant, shaved truffles; or try a few Seared Sea Scallops, 356, a few drops of balsamic reduction, and a handful of arugula for a main-course risotto dish.

RISOTTO

6 side-dish or 4 main-course servings

For **Risotto Milanese,** the classic accompaniment to braised meat, especially Osso Buco, 476, steep **3 generous pinches saffron** in 1 cup of the hot broth for 10 minutes and stir into the rice after adding the wine. Proceed as directed below.

Pour into a saucepan, heat, and maintain at a bare simmer:

8 cups chicken broth

Heat in a large heavy saucepan over medium-low heat:

2 tablespoons butter or olive oil

Add and cook, stirring, until soft but not browned:

1 medium onion, minced

(1 teaspoon salt, if using unsalted chicken broth)

Stir in:

2 cups Arborio or other risotto rice

Continue to stir the rice until it is thoroughly coated in fat and almost entirely opaque, 3 to 5 minutes. Add, if desired:

(½ cup dry white wine)

Stir until the wine is absorbed. Stir in the broth 1 cup at a time, waiting for each cup to be absorbed before adding the next. Stir the risotto continuously and maintain a simmer. When 6 cups broth have been absorbed, add the remaining broth ½ cup at a time and start tasting the rice. Take the risotto off the heat when the rice is tender but still has some "bite"; it should be creamy, not stiff. Fold in:

1 to 1½ cups grated Parmesan, to taste (4 to 6 ounces)

2 tablespoons butter

Season to taste with:

Salt and black pepper

RISI E BISI (RICE AND PEAS)

8 to 10 side-dish or 6 to 8 main-course servings

Proceed as for **Risotto, above,** adding with the onion **2 ounces pancetta, minced.** When half the broth has been absorbed, add **1½ pounds fresh or frozen peas, ½ cup coarsely chopped parsley,** and **2 tablespoons chopped fennel tops or 1 teaspoon ground fennel seeds.** Continue cooking. Finish with the Parmesan, butter, and **a generous amount of black pepper.**

RISOTTO WITH MUSHROOMS

6 to 8 first-course or 4 to 6 main-course servings

This makes a satisfying main-course risotto, especially with wild mushrooms such as morels or chanterelles.

Soak in hot water to cover for 20 minutes:

½ cup dried porcini mushrooms (about ½ ounce)

Drain the mushrooms, reserving the soaking liquid, and coarsely chop. Pour into a saucepan, heat, and maintain at a bare simmer:

8 cups chicken broth

Heat in a large saucepan over medium heat:

2 tablespoons olive oil

Add the chopped porcini and:

1 pound mushrooms, sliced

2 shallots, minced

Cook, stirring occasionally, until lightly browned. Stir in:

2 cups Arborio or other risotto rice

Stir the rice until it is thoroughly coated in fat and almost opaque, 3 to 5 minutes. Add the mushroom soaking liquid and boil until it has evaporated. Proceed as for:

Risotto, above

FRESH CORN RISOTTO

6 to 8 first-course or 4 to 6 main-course servings

We like to serve this golden risotto topped with sautéed chanterelle mushrooms and Seared Sea Scallops, 356. If desired, prepare a **corncob broth** to use instead of or combined with the chicken broth: Place spent corn cobs in a pot and add water to cover. Bring to a boil, reduce the heat, and simmer for 45 minutes, then strain.

Bring to a simmer in a medium saucepan:

8 cups chicken broth

Have ready:

2 cups corn kernels (from about 3 large ears)

In a food processor, puree 1 cup of the corn kernels. Set aside.

Heat in a large heavy saucepan over medium heat:

3 tablespoons butter or olive oil

Add and cook, stirring, until translucent, about 5 minutes:

2 medium shallots or 1 small onion, finely chopped

Add:

2 cups Arborio or other risotto rice

Stir until the rice is coated in the fat and almost opaque, 3 to 5 minutes. Add, if desired:

(½ cup dry white wine)

Stir until the wine is absorbed. Stir in the broth 1 cup at a time, waiting for each cup to be absorbed before adding the next. Stir the risotto continuously and maintain a simmer. When 6 cups broth have been absorbed, add the pureed corn. Add the remaining broth ½ cup at a time and start tasting the rice. Take the risotto off the heat when the rice is tender but still has some "bite"; it should be creamy, not stiff. When the rice is tender, stir in the remaining corn. Stir in:

Salt and black pepper to taste

If desired, top with:

(Grated Parmesan)

PRESSURE-COOKER RISOTTO

This method may be used with any risotto recipe. For instance, for Risotto with Mushrooms, above, sauté the mushrooms and shallots before adding the rice and broth. For Risi e Bisi, above, stir in the peas after the rice is fully cooked. Just remember that you will need about 4 cups broth for 2 cups rice.

Set a pressure cooker over medium heat or turn on an electric pressure cooker to the sauté function. Add butter or oil as directed, sauté the onion, and briefly toast the rice. Add the wine (if using) and cook until it has been absorbed. Add only **4 cups chicken broth,** then put the lid on the pressure cooker, seal, and allow it to come up to pressure. Pressure-cook for 7 minutes. Quick-release the pressure by opening the release valve to vent all the steam, 1059. When all the steam is released, open the pressure cooker and stir in the Parmesan and butter as directed. Taste and season with salt and black pepper.

ABOUT RYE

Though it is used to produce robustly flavored breads and spicy whiskeys, rye has a surprisingly mild flavor as a whole grain. Sometimes labeled **rye berries,** the long gray-brown kernels take time to simmer to chewy softness, and they benefit from an overnight soak. Substitute rye berries for wheat berries in recipes. The grains hold up well in grain salads, 130, or serve them warm as a bed for roasted poultry to catch the drippings and juices. Also available are **rye flakes** or **rolled rye,** which look like rolled oats and can be cooked the same way. Rye flakes are generally used to make breakfast porridge or granola, 327. For rye flour, see 988.

RYE PILAF

About 2½ cups; 4 servings

Proceed as for **Buckwheat Pilaf, 321,** using in place of the buckwheat **1 cup rye berries, soaked overnight in water to cover.** Increase the liquid to 2½ cups and increase the cooking time to 25 to 30 minutes.

ABOUT SORGHUM OR MILO

Sorghum is an incredibly important staple crop that originated in Egypt but is now grown across Africa, India, Asia, and the Americas. It is a robust, drought- and heat-tolerant grain that is notable for its use as both a whole grain, flour, and sweetener.

Whole sorghum can be simmered until tender and used as a side dish or in salads or soups. It is available in two forms: Specialty stores usually stock the grain with most of its tan to light-brown bran intact; Asian markets often carry a paler, pearled sorghum. The former cooks slowly into distinct, toothsome grains; the latter thickens the cooking liquid with starch and becomes tender much more quickly (see the Grains Cooking Chart, 340, for cooking times).

Darker, whole-grain sorghum may be popped as for Popcorn, 47—though the pop is not as dramatic. Sorghum may also be found flaked and ground into flour, 1018. For sorghum syrup, see 1018. Sorghum is a gluten-free grain.

SPELT

See About Wheat, 337.

ABOUT TEFF

Teff seeds are very tiny—about the size of poppy seeds—which may explain why their name means "lost" in Amharic. It has a light, nutty flavor and crunchy texture and smells like molasses while cooking. Rich in protein and calcium (teff has the highest calcium content among grains), the kernels have a high bran-to-endosperm ratio, which makes them high in fiber. Teff is best known as the staple grain of Ethiopia, where the flour is turned into a tangy, spongy flatbread called *injera*. In the United States, teff is sold as a flour and a whole grain and is used in many gluten-free products. The kernels naturally clump together. Serve it as a polenta-like side dish topped with braised greens or roasted vegetables, or as breakfast porridge topped with warmed milk and maple syrup. Teff cooked like a porridge (3 parts water to 1 part teff) can be spread in a baking pan while warm, refrigerated, cut into squares or triangles, then baked or fried like polenta (see Fried Polenta, 323). For teff flour, see 988.

ABOUT TRITICALE

A hybrid of wheat (*triticum* in Latin) and rye (*secale* in Latin), triticale was developed in Scotland more than a century ago. Triticale berries are a little larger than wheat berries and are milder in taste but can be soaked and cooked the same way. See the Grains Cooking Chart, 340. Triticale may be substituted in any wheat berry, spelt, or rye recipe. Toast the grains first in a skillet or in the oven to bring out more of their subtle flavor.

ABOUT WHEAT

The wheat family of grains is a large one, encompassing both modern red and white wheats as well as many varieties of ancient wheats, including farro, spelt, einkorn, emmer, and Kamut. Processed wheat in the form of couscous, bulgur, and freekeh are also covered here. Most whole wheat berries can be cooked similarly and used interchangeably in recipes. In addition to the recipes below, use any variety of wheat berry in Wheat Salad with Pesto and Zucchini, 131.

WHEAT BERRIES, CRACKED WHEAT, BULGUR, FREEKEH, AND COUSCOUS

Whole wheat kernels are called **wheat berries.** The wheat berries most often available in markets are hard red winter wheat, but you may also find hard white wheat, which is lower in protein and has a slightly milder flavor. The primary difference between "hard" and "soft" wheats is their protein content and gluten strength. Hard wheats contain more protein, stronger gluten, and are often milled into bread flour, while soft wheat is better suited to making pastries. All of these wheat berry types cook in about the same time. **Durum wheat,** the hardest variety, is exclusively milled into fine durum flour or a coarse flour called **semolina.** For more on wheat flours, see 987.

Milled wheat berries are called **cracked wheat.** If the milling is coarse, the wheat can be cooked like white rice and used in salads and pilafs; if finely ground, it can be added for texture to bread doughs and batters. Either way, cracked wheat tastes better toasted. When wheat berries are steamed, dried, and then milled, the result is **bulgur,** available in fine, medium, and coarse grinds. Fine and medium bulgur—a central ingredient in Tabbouleh, 131—are very convenient, as they only need to be covered with boiling water and left to rehydrate in a covered bowl. Coarse bulgur needs to be simmered for a bit; once cooked, it is often enriched with butter, studded with pine nuts or chopped dried fruit, and served as a side dish. **Freekeh** is wheat (usually spelt) harvested while still green and then parched. This is traditionally accomplished over a smoldering fire, which gives it a slightly smoky flavor. Though occasionally found whole, most freekeh in stores has been cracked and resembles coarse bulgur.

Couscous are tiny pellets made by gradually sprinkling water into durum flour that is being constantly mixed. The mixture is sifted to produce a uniform size. Couscous is most commonly made with semolina, but it can be made from other flours, such as whole wheat or spelt. Couscous is interchangeable with bulgur and other tiny grains, such as quinoa, in soups and salads. It may be served on its own as a side dish, seasoned with flavored butter and chopped fresh herbs or diced cooked vegetables. Couscous is a mainstay of North African cuisines and is eaten throughout the Mediterranean. The couscous commonly sold in the United States has been presteamed and dried before packaging and is simply reconstituted in boiling water; it may be labeled **quick-cooking, precooked,** or **instant.** Couscous that is not presteamed comes in different granulations and requires longer cooking. **Israeli couscous,** which is actually tiny pasta made from a kneaded dough, is roughly the size of barley. It can be cooked in a generous amount of boiling salted water, as for pasta, and is especially good in a pilaf, 339.

FARRO (SPELT, EMMER, AND EINKORN)

While we tend to think of farro as a distinct grain, the word can actually be used to identify three different types of ancient wheat. In Italy, *farro grande* is what we call **spelt,** *farro medio* is **emmer,** and *farro piccolo* is **einkorn.** When you buy grains labeled "farro" in the United States, you are probably, in fact, buying emmer.

All three farros are sold as a whole grain. Though they may be used interchangeably in recipes—or substituted for wheat berries—their cooking times vary widely, with einkorn taking less than half the time of spelt. Occasionally, emmer and spelt can be found in a semi-pearled form. This means that some of the bran layer has been polished or scratched off, which shortens cooking time and allows starch from within the grain to thicken the cooking liquid. To compare simmering times among these types, see the Grains Cooking Chart, 340. Pearled emmer and spelt may be cooked as for risotto (see Farrotto, 339).

Spelt is very high in protein (up to 17 percent by weight) and it is readily available in whole grain and flour form, 988. Einkorn is thought to be the most ancient of wheats, possibly gathered by humans as far back as thirty thousand years ago. Like other varieties of wheat, einkorn's flavor is mild and slightly nutty, and the berries have a nice chewiness.

KAMUT OR KHORASAN WHEAT

Khorasan is the largest of all the wheat relatives, its grains being at least twice as large as modern wheat. It is named for the province of Khorasan, a region in what is now Iran and Afghanistan. "Kamut" is actually a brand name of Khorasan wheat, and its trademark signifies that the grain was grown organically and is not hybridized or genetically modified. It was brought to the United States around 1950, but it was not trademarked as Kamut until 1990. Khorasan wheat is more nutritious than generic wheat berries, and it has a buttery, nutty flavor. Use it as you would wheat or rye berries, spelt, or emmer.

WHEAT BERRIES WITH SAUTÉED ONIONS AND DRIED FRUITS

4 to 6 servings

Heat in a large skillet over medium heat:

2 tablespoons butter or olive oil

Add and cook, stirring, until golden, 8 to 10 minutes:

1 medium onion, chopped

Stir in:

3 cups cooked wheat, spelt, or Kamut berries, 342, or a combination of cooked grains

1 cup mixed dried fruits, such as diced dried apricots or pitted prunes, dark or golden raisins, or dried currants, cherries, or cranberries

1 cinnamon stick

½ cup chicken broth or water

Cover and cook over low heat, stirring once or twice, about 10 minutes. Season to taste with:

Salt and black pepper

If desired, sprinkle with:

(¼ cup chopped toasted, 1005, blanched almonds, walnuts, or pecans)

WHEAT BERRIES AND BROWN RICE

4 servings

This is our favorite combination of grains. The butter and soy sauce give it a rich, savory boost.

Bring to a boil in a medium saucepan:

3 cups water

½ teaspoon salt

Stir in:

½ cup wheat berries

Reduce the heat to a simmer, cover, and cook for 20 minutes. Stir in:

½ cup long-grain brown rice

Continue to simmer, covered, until both grains are tender, about 40 minutes. Remove from the heat and let sit, covered, for 10 minutes. Stir in:

1 tablespoon butter

1 tablespoon soy sauce

FREEKEH WITH GREENS, CHICKPEAS, AND HALLOUMI

4 servings

Freekeh's subtly smoky flavor is an excellent partner to the toasty browned Halloumi in this dish.

Cook as directed, 341:

¾ cup cracked freekeh

While the freekeh cooks, heat in a large skillet over medium heat:

2 tablespoons olive oil

Add:

8 ounces Halloumi, cut into ½-inch cubes

Cook, turning occasionally, until well browned. Transfer to a plate and add to the skillet:

One 15-ounce can chickpeas, drained and rinsed

Cook, stirring occasionally, until the chickpeas start to brown, about 5 minutes. Stir in:

2 garlic cloves, minced
1 teaspoon cumin seeds

Cook, stirring, until fragrant, about 1 minute. Add to the skillet:

2 packed cups greens, such as baby spinach or shredded kale, collards, or chard

Cook, stirring, just until wilted, about 4 minutes.

When the freekeh is cooked, stir it into the chickpea and greens mixture and cook, stirring, until everything is heated through and any residual liquid clinging to the freekeh has evaporated. Stir in the Halloumi. Season with:

2 tablespoons lemon juice
Salt and black pepper to taste

FARROTTO

6 servings

Whole-grain farro will not work very well using this method, so double-check to make sure that the farro you use is labeled "semi-pearled" (or look for pale spots or abrasions on the grain).

Proceed as for **Risotto, 336,** using **2 cups semi-pearled farro** instead of rice. You will likely need to use all 8 cups broth.

COUSCOUS WITH PINE NUTS AND RAISINS

6 to 8 servings

Bulgur can also be used in this recipe, or mix couscous and bulgur together for a tasty variation.

Toss together in a large bowl:

3 cups cooked couscous (about 1⅓ cups uncooked, 341)
Vinaigrette, 575, to taste

Add and toss to combine:

¼ cup pine nuts, toasted, 1012
1 yellow bell pepper, finely diced
6 dried apricots, chopped
⅓ cup golden raisins
2 tablespoons chopped cilantro, parsley, or minced chives

Season to taste with:

Salt

COUSCOUS WITH CHICKEN, LEMON, AND OLIVES

6 to 8 servings

An amalgam of two classic Moroccan chicken stews, one with olives and one with preserved lemon. If you can't find preserved lemon, we encourage you to try making your own, 942.

Combine in a large zip-top bag or a bowl:

4 pounds bone-in chicken parts (skinned, if desired)
2 large garlic cloves, minced
2 tablespoons olive oil
1 teaspoon cracked coriander seeds
1 teaspoon salt
½ teaspoon ground cumin
½ teaspoon ground ginger
½ teaspoon sweet paprika
½ teaspoon black pepper
Pinch of crushed saffron threads

Refrigerate, covered, for at least 1 hour or up to 24 hours, moving the chicken around in the bag or bowl from time to time.

Remove the chicken pieces. Heat in a Dutch oven or other large heavy pot:

2 tablespoons vegetable oil

Add the chicken in batches, without crowding, and brown on both sides. Add:

2 cups water
1 large leek, trimmed, halved, well cleaned, and thinly sliced

Bring to a simmer over medium-high heat, skimming off any foam that rises with a slotted spoon. Reduce the heat, cover, and simmer gently until the chicken is tender, about 40 minutes. Add:

1 preserved lemon, cut into thick slices
⅔ cup green olives, pitted and halved

Simmer until the chicken is falling off the bone, another 10 to 15 minutes.

Meanwhile, cook, 341, omitting the optional butter or oil:

2½ cups couscous

Transfer to a large serving bowl and toss with:

1 tablespoon olive oil

Arrange the chicken, preserved lemons, and olives on top of the couscous. Bring the liquid in the pot to a boil and reduce by half. Stir in:

¼ cup lemon juice, or more to taste
¼ cup chopped parsley

Taste and adjust the seasonings. Pour the sauce over the chicken and garnish with:

2 tablespoons chopped parsley

ISRAELI COUSCOUS PILAF

4 servings

Heat in a saucepan over medium heat:

2 tablespoons butter or vegetable oil

Add and cook, stirring, until softened but not browned:

1 shallot, minced

Stir in:

1 cup Israeli couscous

Cook, stirring, until lightly browned, about 3 minutes. Add:

1¾ cups chicken or vegetable broth or water
½ teaspoon salt

Bring to a boil, then reduce the heat, cover, and simmer until the couscous is tender but still firm and the liquid is absorbed, 15 to 18 minutes.

ABOUT WILD RICE

Wild rice is the seed of a grass native to the Great Lakes region. Most of the wild rice commonly available is now cultivated. ➤ It is a good idea to cover wild rice with cold water before cooking so that bits of hull will float free and can then be skimmed off. The nutty flavor and chewiness of wild rice make it a good match for mushrooms and wild game. See Wild Rice Dressing, 536, and Wild Rice Salad with Sausage, 130. For cooking instructions, see 343. To puff wild rice, see About Puffed Grains, 319.

WILD RICE WITH SAUTÉED MUSHROOMS

4 to 6 servings

Cook, 343:

1 cup wild rice

While the rice is cooking, prepare:

Sautéed Mushrooms, 251, of any kind

Stir the cooked wild rice into the mushrooms and season to taste with:

Salt and black pepper

Sprinkle with:

¼ cup chopped parsley

(¼ cup sliced almonds, toasted, 1005)

GRAINS COOKING CHART

Grain	Amount of Liquid (water, stock, or broth unless otherwise noted)	Method For added flavor, grains may be toasted first, 318. For given quantities, use a small 2-quart pot or saucepan with a tight-fitting lid unless otherwise noted. For pressure-cooking,* always consult the manufacturer's instructions.	Yield and Servings
Amaranth 1 cup	3 cups	Bring amaranth, liquid, and ½ **teaspoon salt** to a boil. Reduce heat to low, cover, and cook 20 to 25 minutes.	3 cups; 3 to 4 servings
Barley, grits 1 cup	3 cups water, or 1½ cups milk and 1½ cups water	Bring liquid and (½ **teaspoon salt**) to a boil and slowly whisk in grits. Reduce heat to low, cover, and cook until water is absorbed, 10 to 15 minutes.	3 cups; 4 servings
Barley, pearl 1 cup	3 cups for firm, chewy texture; 4 cups for softer texture *6 cups for pressure-cooking*	Bring barley, liquid, and ½ **teaspoon salt** to a boil. Reduce heat to low, cover, and cook about 30 minutes. Drain any excess liquid. ***To pressure-cook,**** add barley and liquid to pot along with ➤ **2 tablespoons oil** and bring to pressure; cook until tender, about 15 minutes in a stovetop cooker or 17 minutes in an electric model. Remove from heat and let pressure release naturally for 10 minutes, then quick-release the pressure. Drain excess liquid.	3½ cups; 4 to 6 servings
Barley, rolled or flaked 1 cup	2 cups	Bring liquid and (½ **teaspoon salt**) to a boil. Stir in barley flakes, reduce heat, cover, and simmer, stirring occasionally, 5 to 7 minutes. Remove from heat and let stand for 2 minutes.	2½ cups; 2 servings
Barley, Scotch or hulled 1 cup	4 cups *6 cups for pressure-cooking*	Bring barley and liquid to a boil. Reduce heat to low, cover, and cook about 50 minutes. Drain any excess liquid. ***To pressure-cook,**** add barley, liquid, and ➤ **2 tablespoons oil** to pot and bring to pressure; cook about 20 minutes in a stovetop cooker or 25 minutes in an electric model. Remove from heat and let pressure release naturally for 10 minutes, then quick-release the pressure. Drain excess liquid.	3 cups; 3 to 4 servings
Buckwheat, whole groats 1 cup	2 cups	Bring liquid, ½ **teaspoon salt,** and **1 to 2 tablespoons butter or oil** to a boil. Slowly stir in buckwheat and return to a boil. Reduce heat, cover, and simmer about 10 minutes. Let stand, covered, for 5 minutes and fluff with a fork.	3 cups; 3 to 4 servings
Bulgur, fine and medium 1 cup	2½ cups	Place bulgur in a bowl. Bring liquid and ½ **teaspoon salt** to a boil. Gradually pour into bulgur, stirring. Cover with a plate and let stand until liquid is absorbed, about 30 minutes. Drain excess liquid.	3 cups; 4 servings

*Never fill your pressure cooker to over half of its maximum capacity when cooking grains. Always consult the instructions and guidelines in your pressure cooker's user manual and be sure to increase the amount of oil in the same proportion if cooking more than 1 cup of grains. ➤ Do not omit the oil! It is necessary to keep the grains from foaming, which can interfere with the cooker's ability to vent pressure.

Grain	Amount of Liquid (water, stock, or broth unless otherwise noted)	Method For added flavor, grains may be toasted first, 318. For given quantities, use a small 2-quart pot or saucepan with a tight-fitting lid unless otherwise noted. For pressure-cooking,* always consult the manufacturer's instructions.	Yield and Servings
Bulgur, coarse 1 cup	1½ cups	Bring bulgur, liquid, ½ **teaspoon salt,** and (**2 tablespoons butter**) to a boil. Reduce heat to low, cover, and cook 15 minutes, then let stand off the heat for another 15 minutes. Fluff with a fork before serving.	2½ cups; 3 to 4 servings
Canihua 1 cup	3 cups	Bring liquid and ½ **teaspoon salt** to a boil. Stir in canihua, reduce heat to low, cover, and cook until liquid is absorbed, about 15 minutes.	4 cups; 5 servings
Cornmeal, grits, and polenta see 321			
Couscous, fine 1 cup	1¼ cups	Bring liquid, ½ **teaspoon salt,** and **1 tablespoon butter or oil** to a boil. Stir in couscous, cover, and remove from heat. Let stand for 10 minutes. Fluff with a fork before serving.	3 cups; 3 to 4 servings
Couscous, pearl or Israeli 1 cup	1½ cups	Bring liquid and ½ **teaspoon salt** to a boil. Stir in couscous, reduce heat to low, cover, and simmer for 10 minutes. Drain if necessary.	2 cups; 3 to 4 servings
Einkorn berries 1 cup	2 cups	Bring einkorn, liquid, and ½ **teaspoon salt** to a boil. Reduce heat, cover, and simmer for 20 to 25 minutes. Drain if necessary.	2 cups; 3 to 4 servings
Emmer or farro, semi-pearled and whole berries 1 cup	2 cups	Bring emmer, liquid, and ½ **teaspoon salt** to a boil. Reduce heat to low and cover. Cook semi-pearled emmer for 20 minutes and whole-grain emmer for 45 to 50 minutes. Drain if necessary.	2½ cups; 4 servings
Freekeh, cracked or whole berries 1 cup	2½ cups	Bring freekeh, liquid, and ¼ **teaspoon salt** to a boil. Reduce heat, cover, and simmer 20 minutes for cracked freekeh, or 35 to 40 minutes for whole freekeh.	3 cups; 4 servings
Hominy, whole or cracked 1 cup	8 cups for stovetop or pressure-cooking	To speed cooking, soak the hominy for 8 hours or more in water to cover. Discard soaking liquid. Bring hominy and liquid to a boil. Reduce heat, cover, and simmer until tender and no longer grainy, 1½ to 2 hours (longer if not soaked). Drain. ***To pressure-cook,**** skip soaking the hominy. Add hominy and liquid to pot along with ➤ **1 tablespoon oil** and bring to pressure; cook about 45 minutes to 1 hour in a stovetop cooker or about 1 hour 5 minutes for an electric model. Remove from heat and let pressure release naturally for 10 minutes, then quick-release the pressure. Drain excess liquid.	3 cups; 3 to 4 servings
Job's tears 1 cup	2½ cups	Bring Job's tears, liquid, and ½ **teaspoon salt** to a boil. Reduce heat, cover, and simmer 30 to 50 minutes.	2½ cups; 3 to 4 servings

*Never fill your pressure cooker to over half of its maximum capacity when cooking grains. Always consult the instructions and guidelines in your pressure cooker's user manual and be sure to increase the amount of oil in the same proportion if cooking more than 1 cup of grains. ➤ Do not omit the oil! It is necessary to keep the grains from foaming, which can interfere with the cooker's ability to vent pressure.

Grain	Amount of Liquid (water, stock, or broth unless otherwise noted)	Method For added flavor, grains may be toasted first, 318. For given quantities, use a small 2-quart pot or saucepan with a tight-fitting lid unless otherwise noted. For pressure-cooking,* always consult the manufacturer's instructions.	Yield and Servings
Kamut or Khorasan berries 1 cup	3 cups *6 cups for pressure-cooking*	To speed cooking, soak berries for 8 hours or more in water to cover (use the soaking water for cooking). Bring berries and liquid to a boil. Reduce heat, cover, and simmer until berries absorb liquid, about 45 minutes for soaked grains or 1¼ to 1½ hours, if left unsoaked. ***To pressure-cook,**** skip soaking the berries. Add berries and liquid to pot along with ➤ **1 tablespoon oil** and bring to pressure; cook about 35 minutes in a stovetop cooker or 40 minutes for an electric model. Remove from heat and let pressure release naturally for 10 minutes, then quick-release the pressure. Drain excess liquid.	2½ cups; 3 to 4 servings
Kasha, whole 1 cup	2 cups	Cook as for buckwheat groats, 340.	3 cups; 3 to 4 servings
Kasha, ground 1 cup	2 cups water, or 1 cup water and 1 cup milk	Bring liquid and (**½ teaspoon salt**) to a boil and slowly whisk in ground kasha. Reduce heat to low, cover, and cook, stirring occasionally, until liquid is absorbed, about 10 minutes.	2½ cups; 2 servings
Millet 1 cup	2 cups	Bring liquid and **½ teaspoon salt** to a boil and whisk in millet. Reduce heat to low, cover, and cook 20 minutes. Let stand, covered, for 5 minutes.	3½ cups; 4 to 6 servings
Oats, whole groats 1 cup	3 cups	Bring oats, liquid, and **½ teaspoon salt** to a boil. Reduce heat to low, cover, and cook for 35 minutes for just-tender grains or 1 hour for an oatmeal-like porridge.	2½ cups; 3 to 4 servings
Oats, steel-cut 1 cup	4 cups water, or 2 cups water and 2 cups milk	Bring liquid to a boil and add oats along with (**½ teaspoon salt**). Reduce heat and simmer, uncovered, for 20 minutes, stirring often to keep oats from sticking to the bottom of pan.	3 cups; 3 to 4 servings
Oats, rolled (old-fashioned or quick-cooking) 1 cup	2 cups water, or 1 cup water and 1 cup milk	Bring liquid to a boil and add oats along with (**a pinch of salt**) and (**⅓ cup raisins**). Reduce heat and simmer uncovered, stirring often. Cook "quick-cooking" rolled oats for about 3 minutes and "old-fashioned" rolled oats for about 5 minutes.	2½ cups; 2 to 3 servings
Quinoa 1 cup	1½ cups	Bring liquid and **½ teaspoon salt** to a boil. Stir in quinoa, reduce heat to low, cover, and cook until liquid is absorbed, about 15 minutes.	3½ cups; 4 servings
Rice, black (not glutinous) 1 cup	2 cups	Bring rice, liquid, and (**½ teaspoon salt**) to a boil. Reduce heat to low, cover, and cook 35 to 40 minutes. Fluff with a fork, cover, and let stand 5 minutes before serving.	3 cups; 4 servings

*Never fill your pressure cooker to over half of its maximum capacity when cooking grains. Always consult the instructions and guidelines in your pressure cooker's user manual and be sure to increase the amount of oil in the same proportion if cooking more than 1 cup of grains. ➤ Do not omit the oil! It is necessary to keep the grains from foaming, which can interfere with the cooker's ability to vent pressure.

Grain	Amount of Liquid (water, stock, or broth unless otherwise noted)	Method For added flavor, grains may be toasted first, 318. For given quantities, use a small 2-quart pot or saucepan with a tight-fitting lid unless otherwise noted. For pressure-cooking,* always consult the manufacturer's instructions.	Yield and Servings
Rice, brown 1 cup	2 cups *6 cups for pressure-cooking*	Rinse rice well and drain. Bring rice and liquid to a boil and cook for 1 minute. Reduce heat to low, cover, and simmer long- and medium-grain brown rice for 35 to 40 minutes; short-grain brown rice for 45 to 50 minutes. Remove from heat and let stand another 10 minutes. Fluff with a fork, cover, and let stand 5 minutes before serving. ***To pressure-cook,**** add rice and liquid to pot along with ➤ **1 tablespoon oil** and bring to pressure; cook about 17 minutes in a stovetop cooker or 20 minutes for an electric model. Remove from heat and let pressure release naturally for 10 minutes, then quick-release the pressure. Drain excess liquid.	3 cups; 4 servings
Rice, haiga or half-milled 1 cup	1¼ cups	For separate grains that do not clump, rinse rice in several changes of water and drain. Bring rice, liquid, (½ **teaspoon salt**), and (**2 tablespoons butter**) to a boil. Reduce heat to low, cover, and cook 15 minutes. Remove from heat and let stand another 5 minutes. Fluff with a fork, cover, and let stand 5 minutes before serving.	2½ cups; 2 to 3 servings
Rice, parboiled or converted 1 cup	1½ cups	Bring rice, liquid, (½ **teaspoon salt**), and (**2 tablespoons butter**) to a boil. Reduce heat to low, cover, and cook 25 minutes. Remove from heat and let stand 5 minutes. Fluff with a fork, cover, and let stand 5 minutes before serving.	3½ cups; 4 servings
Rice, red (not glutinous) 1 cup	2 cups	Bring rice, liquid, and (½ **teaspoon salt**) to a boil. Reduce heat to low, cover, and cook 18 to 22 minutes. Fluff with a fork, cover, and let stand 5 minutes before serving.	2½ cups; 2 to 3 servings
Rice, sticky or glutinous 1 cup	—	Cover rice grains with 3 inches warm tap water and let soak for at least 3 hours. Place a steamer basket in a saucepan with 1 inch of water in it. Put soaked rice in the basket, cover pan tightly, and steam until rice is tender, about 20 minutes for white sticky rice or 35 minutes for red or black sticky rice.	2½ cups; 2 to 3 servings
Rice, white 1 cup	1¼ cups for medium- and short-grain rice; 2 cups for long-grain rice	For separate grains that do not clump together, rinse the rice in several changes of water and drain. Bring rice, liquid, (½ **teaspoon salt**), and (**2 tablespoons butter**) to a boil. Reduce heat to low, cover, and cook 15 minutes. Remove from heat and let stand 5 minutes. Fluff with a fork, cover, and let stand 5 minutes before serving.	2½ cups; 2 to 3 servings
Rice, wild 1 cup	3 cups	Rinse and drain rice. Bring rice, liquid, and ½ **teaspoon salt** to a boil. Reduce heat, cover, and cook until rice is tender and grains are splayed, revealing their white interior, 35 minutes to 1 hour.	3 cups; 4 servings

*Never fill your pressure cooker to over half of its maximum capacity when cooking grains. Always consult the instructions and guidelines in your pressure cooker's user manual and be sure to increase the amount of oil in the same proportion if cooking more than 1 cup of grains. ➤ Do not omit the oil! It is necessary to keep the grains from foaming, which can interfere with the cooker's ability to vent pressure.

Grain	Amount of Liquid (water, stock, or broth unless otherwise noted)	Method For added flavor, grains may be toasted first, 318. For given quantities, use a small 2-quart pot or saucepan with a tight-fitting lid unless otherwise noted. For pressure-cooking,* always consult the manufacturer's instructions.	Yield and Servings
Rye berries 1 cup	3 cups *6 cups for pressure-cooking*	To speed cooking, soak berries for 8 hours or more in water to cover (use the soaking water for cooking). Bring berries and liquid to a boil, reduce heat, cover, and simmer until liquid is absorbed, 25 to 30 minutes for soaked grains or 40 minutes, if left unsoaked. ***To pressure-cook,**** skip soaking the berries. Add berries and liquid to pan along with ➤ **1 tablespoon oil** and bring to pressure; cook about 20 minutes in a stovetop cooker or 25 minutes in an electric model. Remove from heat and let pressure release naturally for 10 minutes, then quick-release the pressure. Drain excess liquid.	2½ cups; 4 servings
Sorghum 1 cup	2½ cups *6 cups for pressure-cooking*	Bring sorghum, liquid, and ½ **teaspoon salt** to a boil. Reduce heat to low, cover, and simmer. Cook pale, pearled sorghum for 25 minutes and tan, whole-grain sorghum for 45 minutes. (For more on the difference between these, see 337.) ***To pressure-cook* whole-grain sorghum,*** add grains and liquid to pot along with ➤ **1 tablespoon oil** and bring to pressure; cook about 25 minutes in a stovetop cooker or 30 minutes for an electric model. Remove from heat and let pressure release naturally for 10 minutes, then quick-release the pressure. Drain excess liquid. Pressure-cooking pearled sorghum is not practical.	2½ to 3 cups; 4 servings
Spelt berries 1 cup	3 cups *6 cups for pressure-cooking*	To speed cooking, soak berries for 8 hours or more in water to cover (use the soaking water for cooking). Bring berries and liquid to a boil. Reduce heat, cover, and simmer until liquid is absorbed, 45 to 55 minutes for soaked grains or 1¼ hours, if left unsoaked. Pearled spelt berries do not need soaking and cook much more quickly, 20 to 25 minutes. ***To pressure-cook,**** skip soaking the berries. Add berries and liquid along with ➤ **1 tablespoon oil** and bring to pressure; cook about 35 minutes in a stovetop cooker or 40 minutes for an electric model. Remove from heat and let pressure release naturally for 10 minutes, then quick-release the pressure. Drain excess liquid.	2 to 2½ cups; 4 servings
Teff 1 cup	2½ cups for firm grains; 3 cups for porridge	Bring liquid and ½ **teaspoon salt** to a boil. Gradually whisk in grains, reduce heat to low, cover, and simmer about 15 minutes.	2½ to 3 cups; 2 to 4 servings
Triticale 1 cup	3 cups *6 cups for pressure-cooking*	To speed cooking, soak triticale for 8 hours or more in water to cover (use the soaking water for cooking). Bring triticale, liquid, and ½ **teaspoon salt** to a boil. Reduce heat, cover, and simmer until liquid is absorbed, 30 to 45 minutes for soaked grains or 1 to 1¼ hours, if left unsoaked. ***To pressure-cook,**** skip soaking the triticale. Add triticale and liquid to pot along with ➤ **1 tablespoon oil** and bring to pressure; cook about 25 minutes in a stovetop cooker or 30 minutes for an electric model. Remove from heat and let pressure release naturally for 10 minutes, then quick-release the pressure. Drain excess liquid.	2 to 2½ cups; 4 servings

*Never fill your pressure cooker to over half of its maximum capacity when cooking grains. Always consult the instructions and guidelines in your pressure cooker's user manual and be sure to increase the amount of oil in the same proportion if cooking more than 1 cup of grains. ➤ Do not omit the oil! It is necessary to keep the grains from foaming, which can interfere with the cooker's ability to vent pressure.

Grain	Amount of Liquid (water, stock, or broth unless otherwise noted)	Method For added flavor, grains may be toasted first, 318. For given quantities, use a small 2-quart pot or saucepan with a tight-fitting lid unless otherwise noted. For pressure-cooking,* always consult the manufacturer's instructions.	Yield and Servings
Wheat berries, hard or soft 1 cup	3 cups *6 cups for pressure-cooking*	To speed cooking, soak berries for 8 hours or more in water to cover (use the soaking water for cooking). Bring the berries and liquid to a boil. Reduce heat, cover, and simmer until liquid is absorbed, 40 to 45 minutes for soaked grains or about 1 hour, if left unsoaked. ***To pressure-cook,**** skip soaking the berries. Add berries and liquid to pot along with ➤ **1 tablespoon oil** and bring to pressure; cook about 30 minutes in a stovetop cooker or 35 minutes for an electric model. Remove from heat and let pressure release naturally for 10 minutes, then quick-release the pressure. Drain excess liquid.	2 to 2½ cups; 4 servings

*Never fill your pressure cooker to over half of its maximum capacity when cooking grains. Always consult the instructions and guidelines in your pressure cooker's user manual and be sure to increase the amount of oil in the same proportion if cooking more than 1 cup of grains. ➤ Do not omit the oil! It is necessary to keep the grains from foaming, which can interfere with the cooker's ability to vent pressure.

SHELLFISH

Nothing brings the fragrances of the ocean into our kitchens like cooking shellfish. When we speak of shellfish, we are talking about the edible species of two major groups: crustaceans and mollusks.

Armor-clad **crustaceans** have legs and sometimes claws, and include crab, lobster, shrimp, and crayfish. **Mollusks** tend to live within a protective shell, which deters predators and controls water flow in and out. Two-shelled oysters, clams, scallops, and mussels are collectively known as **bivalves;** the single-shelled conch, abalone, whelk, and snail are called **gastropods.** The most advanced of the mollusks are the **cephalopods,** which includes squid, octopus, and cuttlefish. They evolved, quite literally, out of their shells approximately 500 million years ago, though traces of their primordial shell remain (the "quill" or "cuttlebone" in squid and cuttlefish).

Though turtles and frogs are not shellfish, they are traditionally grouped together in cookery, as they possess some similarities in habitat, preparation, and texture.

SHELLFISH SAFETY

There is a small but present risk of contaminants in shellfish that can cause illness. The biggest cause of foodborne illness in raw shellfish is *Vibrio* bacteria. *Vibrio vulnificus*, and the less-serious *parahaemolyticus* type, thrive in warmer waters and can contaminate most species of shellfish, although most incidents of *Vibrio* poisoning are caused by consumption of raw oysters. ➤ Cooking for a short time will kill *Vibrio* bacteria.

Algal blooms are the second most common cause of shellfish poisoning. The neurotoxins produced by certain types of algae accumulate in shellfish and ➤ cannot be neutralized by cooking. The most notorious of these are the so-called "red tides" along the Eastern seaboard and Gulf of Mexico, and the domoic acid–producing algal blooms along the temperate Pacific coast.

To avoid these dangerous contaminants, ➤ it is imperative that shellfish be purchased from a reputable source. If in doubt, ask to see the tag that, by law, must be affixed to each container of oysters, clams, mussels, and scallops in the shell. The tag will state the date and location of harvest as well as the harvester's registration or identification number. ➤ Take care when gathering shellfish yourself; updated beach closure information is routinely posted online by state authorities and should be heeded without fail. As long as the water is regularly tested and contains no more than the legal limit of harmful bacteria, your risks are minimal.

BUYING AND STORING FRESH SHELLFISH

It bears repeating: Buy shellfish from a reputable source. Aside from lobster and the occasional crab or crayfish, the only types of shellfish commonly sold alive are bivalve mollusks. ➤ Buy live bivalves in intact shells that are tightly closed (or close when tapped) and do not slide side to side. If they gape open even after being handled, they are dead and will spoil quickly if they are not spoiled already.

➤ Store live shellfish refrigerated, preferably at 40°F, in a bowl, deep plate, or rimmed baking sheet and cover with a damp towel. Cook them as soon as possible; store for no longer than 2 days. Crab and lobster will turn docile in the cold, but be sure they are confined. Store oysters cupped side down. Do not let shellfish sit in water (they will drown for lack of oxygen) and ensure they will not slip into the melt water if storing on ice in a cooler. If storing in a plastic bag, open it slightly (or poke holes in the top) so the shellfish can breathe. You may freeze shellfish (once you have determined them to be alive) shucked or whole, but they must be used in cooked dishes thereafter. For tips on buying frozen and processed products, see individual shellfish entries.

If you are unsure of whether shellfish are still good, it is best to err on the side of caution. ➤ If they smell bad or you suspect that they have not been kept cold enough, throw them out.

SERVING RAW SHELLFISH

The beauty of raw shellfish lies in their delicate flavors and textures. This is especially true of oysters. ➤ Remember, whenever you eat raw shellfish, it must be from a safe source (see Shellfish Safety, 346), alive when shucked, properly chilled, and eaten promptly; raw shellfish can cause illness if not handled with care. ➤ If you or any of your dining companions are pregnant or have a compromised immune system, we recommend avoiding the consumption of raw shellfish (pasteurized oysters are a good option, if available).

RAW SHELLFISH ON THE HALF SHELL

Carefully shuck shellfish, preserving as much of their juice as possible—see individual shellfish entries for instructions. Arrange the raw shellfish on the half shell on crushed ice, gently pressing them in so they do not tip over; place any accompanying sauces in the center. Allow 5 to 6 pieces and 1/4 cup of sauce per person. To serve scallops raw, see Scallop Ceviche, 355.

For shellfish, choose:

Raw oysters, hard-shell clams, or mussels

For sauces, we prefer:

Becker Cocktail Sauce, 569
Any Mignonette, 570
Tabasco or other hot pepper sauce

Serve with:

Lemon wedges and grated peeled fresh horseradish
Oyster crackers, rice crackers, Soda Crackers, 49, or Rye Crackers, 50
Endive or radicchio leaves

ABOUT COOKING SHELLFISH

With the notable exceptions of long-simmered squid and octopus, 368, prepare shellfish with a light hand, as most species are easy to overcook and tend to turn rubbery. That said, if you are cooking for persons who are pregnant or have weakened immune systems, cook oysters and other shellfish until their shells are open and their flesh is firm and opaque. You may wish to purchase pasteurized shellfish to be doubly sure.

Another tip that applies to many different kinds of shellfish: When cooking live, in-shell bivalves such as oysters, mussels, and clams, remember that the juice they release when cooked or shucked has a delicious, briny flavor. Collect it whenever possible. In the case of steaming, the liquid and exuded juices are practically a ready-made sauce or broth: A squeeze of lemon, some fresh herbs, and a last-minute addition of butter or cream to thicken and add body are all that is needed. For a more concentrated flavor, you may wish to simmer the liquid until significantly reduced before adding these finishing touches.

The shells of shrimp, crab, and lobster contain lots of flavor, which can be coaxed out of them by briefly simmering in water with aromatics (see Shrimp or Shellfish Stock, 78), or by gently heating with butter as in Shrimp or Lobster Butter, 560. Toasting crustacean shells in the oven prior to simmering or infusing deepens their flavor.

In any case, keep in mind that you can always cheat—or at least stack the odds in your favor—by fortifying the liquid called for in many recipes with bottled clam juice.

Below, find a selection of dishes that use a mix of shellfish or work well for many different types. In addition to these versatile formulas, see Bouillabaisse, 102, Cioppino, 102, Shellfish Paella, 334, and Rossejat de Fideos, 300.

MIXED SHELLFISH IN TOMATO SAUCE

4 to 6 servings

If you are using mostly clams or mussels, use the larger amount suggested. To make this moist enough to serve over pasta, add extra tomatoes or 1/2 cup of the pasta cooking water. Or serve as is with a baguette.

Combine in a large heavy skillet over medium heat:

3 tablespoons olive oil
3 garlic cloves, coarsely chopped
1/2 teaspoon red pepper flakes

Cook, stirring, until fragrant. Add:

3 cups peeled, 281, and chopped tomatoes or one 28-ounce can crushed tomatoes
(1/3 cup dry white wine)
1 teaspoon chopped fresh oregano or 1/2 teaspoon dried oregano

Bring to a simmer and cook, stirring occasionally, until the tomatoes break up. Season to taste with:

Salt and black pepper

Stir in:

2 to 4 pounds mixed shellfish, such as shrimp, peeled and deveined, 363, cleaned squid, 368, mussels, scrubbed and debearded, 350, hard-shell clams, scrubbed, 352, and cooked whelk, 369, or octopus, 368, cut into bite-sized pieces

Cover the skillet, reduce the heat to medium-low, and cook until the shellfish are cooked (or, in the case of whelk or octopus, heated through) and any mussels or clams have opened, 5 to 10 minutes. Garnish with:

Chopped parsley or basil

SHELLFISH WITH MUSHROOMS AND GREENS

4 servings

If you are using mostly clams or mussels, use the larger amount suggested.

Combine in a large heavy saucepan:

¼ cup olive oil
4 ounces mushrooms, chopped
3 garlic cloves, chopped

Cook, stirring, over medium heat, until the mushrooms begin to soften, about 5 minutes. Add:

1 cup packed coarsely chopped greens, such as kale, chard, collards, mustard, or dandelion
2 cups clam juice or 1 cup clam juice and 1 cup dry white wine

Increase the heat and simmer for 5 minutes, or until the greens are tender. Stir in:

2 to 4 pounds mixed shellfish, such as shrimp, peeled and deveined, 363, cleaned squid, 368, mussels, scrubbed and debearded, 350, hard-shell clams, scrubbed, 352, and cooked whelk, 369, or octopus, 368, cut into bite-sized pieces

Cover the pan, reduce the heat to medium-low, and cook until the shellfish are cooked (or, in the case of whelk or octopus, heated through) and any mussels or clams have opened, 5 to 10 minutes. Season to taste with:

Salt and black pepper

Spoon the shellfish, mushrooms, and greens into serving bowls and pour some of the cooking juices over them. Drizzle with:

Extra-virgin olive oil

DEEP-FRIED SHELLFISH

4 servings

Please read about Deep-Frying, 1051.

I. FLOURED OR BREADED

Have ready:

1½ to 2 pounds mixed shellfish, such as shucked clams, 352, shucked oysters, 349, shrimp, peeled and deveined, 363, scallops, side "hinge" removed, 355, and/or squid, cleaned, 368, and cut into pieces

Pat the pieces dry and coat with:

Flour Coating, 658, or Bound Bread Crumb or Cracker Coating, 658

Let the pieces dry on a rack set over a rimmed baking sheet for at least 20 minutes before frying (1 hour in the refrigerator will give crispier results). Heat to 365°F in a deep heavy pot or Dutch oven over medium-high heat:

2 inches vegetable oil

Add several pieces at a time to the oil, without crowding, and cook until golden brown, stirring occasionally (large pieces may need to be turned). Drain on paper towels. Serve with any of the following:

Lemon wedges and hot pepper sauce
Tartar Sauce, 563, Aïoli, 564, or flavored mayonnaise, 563
Marinara Sauce, 556, or Becker Cocktail Sauce, 569

II. BATTERED

Have ready:

1½ to 2 pounds mixed shellfish, such as shucked clams, 352, shucked oysters, 349, shrimp, peeled and deveined, 363, scallops, side "hinge" removed, 355, and/or squid, cleaned, 368, and cut into pieces

Pat the pieces dry. Heat to 365°F in a deep heavy pot or Dutch oven over medium-high heat:

2 inches vegetable oil

While the oil heats, prepare in a medium bowl:

Beer Batter, 657, Tempura Batter, 657, Pakora Batter, 657, or Cornstarch Batter, 657

Test the oil by dripping a few drops of the batter into it: They should sink slightly, then rise and puff quickly, but not brown immediately. Working in batches, dip the shellfish 1 piece at a time into the batter and add to the oil without crowding. Fry, undisturbed, for about 1 minute, then turn and fry for another minute, or until the shellfish is opaque and the batter crisp but barely browned. Drain on paper towels. Serve with any of the following:

Lemon wedges and hot pepper sauce
Tartar Sauce, 563, Rémoulade Sauce, 564, Aïoli, 564, or flavored mayonnaise, 563
Marinara Sauce, 556, Becker Cocktail Sauce, 569, or Tentsuyu, 572

PAN-FRIED SHELLFISH

We find frying in less oil to be more convenient: You can use fats you might hesitate to use in large quantities, such as butter or olive oil. If you are tempted to use flavorful fats like lard or bacon grease, combine them with a more neutral-tasting fat like vegetable oil to avoid overpowering the flavor of the shellfish.

Place a large skillet over medium-high heat. Prepare the shellfish as for **Deep-Fried Shellfish I, above.** Add **½ cup vegetable oil or butter** to the pan. When it shimmers, add the floured or breaded pieces of shellfish without crowding the pan. Cook, in batches if necessary, turning gently once or twice, until golden. Drain on paper towels and serve with any of the condiments and garnishes listed above.

ABOUT OYSTERS

"He was a bold man," declared Jonathan Swift, "that first ate an oyster." And, in our opinion, he must have been quite a determined character just to shuck it. Although edible at any time, these shellfish are best in flavor and of firmer texture when they are not spawning. Wild oysters spawn during summer months, but the overwhelming majority of farmed oysters sold in the summer are bred to be sterile, thus of fine quality year-round. As with any bivalve, summertime oysters should be sourced carefully, as warm waters are more welcoming to bacteria that cause illness (see Shellfish Safety, 346). Oysters in the shell should be alive (there are exceptions, see 349). If they have broken shells or gape and do not close quickly in handling, discard them. These mollusks have one shallow and one deep half shell, and it is in the deeper "cupped" side that they are served raw or baked.

Of the numerous species of oyster, five are important in the United States: the large **Eastern oyster,** the **Pacific oyster,** the **European flat oyster,** the diminutive **Kumamoto oyster,** and the tiny, rare **Olympia oyster.** Within these major species fall the musical names that reflect this bivalve's geographic diversity: **Wellfleet, Chincoteague, Blue Point, Belon, Westcott Bay, Malpeque, Apalachicola, Breton Sound, Hama Hama, Skookum, Mad River,** and **Marennes.** These place names are more than a formality; an oyster's flavor depends on the waters it comes from—salinity, mineral content, and temperature contribute to its texture and taste.

To prepare oysters for shucking or cooking, scrub them thoroughly with a stiff brush under running water.

To shuck oysters, first provide yourself with a small, sturdy oyster knife and a kitchen towel. Fold the towel in half, lay it on a flat surface, and place an oyster "cupped" side down on the towel, with the hinge pointing toward your dominant hand. Fold the towel over the oyster and, keeping the oyster steady with one hand, insert the tip of the oyster knife into the hinge of the shell at a 45-degree angle. Gently press in until you think the knife's tip is far enough in to leverage the shells apart and twist the handle until the hinge gives way. Pry the upper shell high enough to insert the blade, and run the knife between the upper shell and the oyster, severing the adductor muscle that holds them together. Remove the upper shell and, being careful to not spill the juices, run the knife between the oyster and the bottom shell. If you do not have an oyster knife on hand, a flathead screwdriver will suffice.

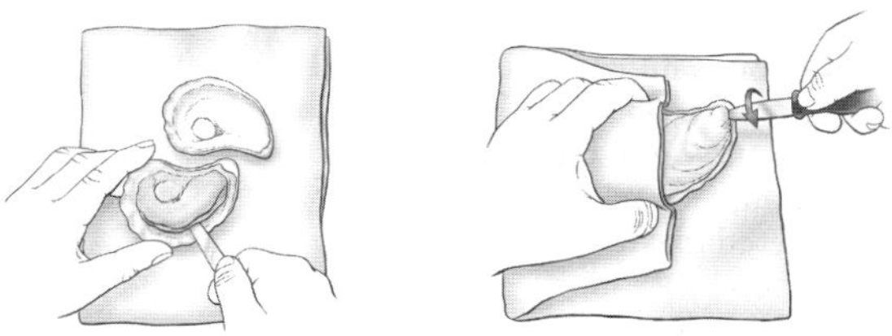

Shucking an oyster

Until you develop the knack, shucking is not easy. Should you grow desperate, you may be willing to sacrifice some flavor for convenience. If so, place the oysters in a 400°F oven for 5 to 7 minutes, depending on size, then drop them briefly into ice water and drain. They should open more easily, but cooking can toughen the muscle that attaches the oyster to its shell, making it more difficult to pry the meat from the shell. A gentler option is to hold them in 140°F water for 5 to 7 minutes, then shock them in ice water (an immersion circulator, 1054, is good for this).

Once open, carefully free the oyster from the shell with a knife, and ➤ examine it to be sure no bits of shell adhere. If you are using the oysters out of the shell, drop them into a sieve, reserving the juice. If the oysters are sandy, you may rinse them in a separate bowl. Before using the oyster liquor in a sauce, be sure it is free of grit. If it is gritty, strain through doubled cheesecloth or a piece of thin kitchen towel.

A handful of processors on the Gulf Coast have started using pasteurization techniques that virtually eliminate the chance of *Vibrio* poisoning in whole, fresh oysters. These processes kill the oyster as well, making them quite easy to shuck. For this reason, they are held together with a band of tape so that the juices do not escape. To date, this is the only form of dead shellfish generally considered safe to eat raw. As with other raw shellfish, pasteurized oysters in the shell must be refrigerated and used within 2 weeks of when they were processed ("use by" dates are available at retailers).

If purchasing shucked oysters, free them of any bits of shell. They should be plump and creamy in color, and the liquor clear, not cloudy, and free from sour or unpleasant odors. Allow ➤ 1 quart undrained shucked oysters for 6 servings. It is hard to estimate amounts for oysters in the shell, as they vary in size—for example, 6 moderate-sized Eastern oysters would equal about 20 of the tiny Olympia oysters.

To store live oysters, see Buying and Storing Fresh Shellfish, 346. Store shucked oysters refrigerated, covered by their liquor, in a closed container. If you bought them fresh, shucked oysters may be stored in this way up to 3 days, or packed in freezer bags and frozen for several months.

In our opinion, it's hard to beat raw oysters on the half shell, 347, simply adorned with lemon and horseradish. Breading and pan-frying them, 348, is also quite delicious. They may also be steamed as for clams, 352, until they start to open, 10 to 20 minutes. For other ideas, see Hangtown Fry, 159, Angels on Horseback, 65, Oyster Stew, 100, Oysters Rockefeller, 66, and Seafood Gumbo, 101.

BROILED OYSTERS

Allow 6 oysters per serving

In a metal pie plate or on a baking sheet, make a thick bed of:

Rock salt

Adjust a rack so it is 5 inches below the heating element. Preheat the broiler. Scrub well, then shuck, above, leaving the oysters in the half shell:

Oysters

Place the oysters on the bed of salt and broil about 2 minutes, until the edges curl. Garnish with:

Minced parsley or Lemon and Parsley Butter, 559

Serve with:

Lemon wedges and grated peeled fresh horseradish

GRILLED OYSTERS

Allow 6 oysters per serving

You may grill many oysters in their shells right on the coals without toughening them, but if you have the smaller Kumamoto or Olympia oysters, put them on a piece of foil before placing them on the grill (and double the number per serving).

Prepare a hot grill fire, 1063. Scrub well:

Oysters

Place them on the grill grate, cupped side down. Grill until the shells pop open. Remove carefully, so as not to spill the juices. Serve with:

Lemon wedges
Melted butter
Hot sauce

BAKED OYSTERS ON THE HALF SHELL

4 servings

For a classic alternative, see Oysters Rockefeller, 66.

Preheat the oven to 475°F. Scrub well, then shuck, 349, leaving the oysters in the half shell and reserving the liquor:

24 large oysters

Use the reserved liquor to prepare:

Double recipe of the sauce for Creamed Oysters, below

Cover each oyster with 1 tablespoon sauce. Sprinkle them with:

Dry bread crumbs

Bake until the bread crumbs are golden, about 10 minutes. Sprinkle with:

Chopped chervil or parsley

OYSTERS MOSCA

2 or 3 servings

A classic New Orleans oyster dish. If desired, leave the oysters on the half shell, top with the bread crumb mixture, and bake as directed.

Preheat the oven to 425°F. Butter a small baking dish or gratin dish (just large enough to hold the oysters in a single layer) and place in the dish:

12 large oysters, shucked, 349, and drained

Heat in a medium skillet over medium heat until shimmering:

⅓ cup olive oil

Add and cook, stirring, until fragrant, about 1 minute:

2 green onions, thinly sliced
3 garlic cloves, minced

Remove from the heat and stir in:

½ cup fine dry bread crumbs or panko
⅓ cup finely grated Pecorino Romano
½ teaspoon dried oregano or 1 teaspoon minced fresh oregano
½ teaspoon red pepper flakes
¼ teaspoon black pepper
¼ teaspoon salt
(⅛ teaspoon cayenne pepper)

Sprinkle the crumb mixture over the oysters and sprinkle with:

1 tablespoon lemon juice

Bake until browned and bubbling, 15 to 20 minutes.

SCALLOPED OYSTERS

6 servings

Preheat the oven to 350°F. Butter a 13 × 9-inch baking dish. Have ready:

1 quart oysters, shucked, 349, with their liquor (about 32 large oysters)

Mix together:

2 cups coarsely crushed soda crackers
1 cup dry bread crumbs
1½ sticks (6 ounces) butter, melted

Combine in a small bowl:

1 cup heavy cream
Pinch of grated or ground nutmeg or ground mace
Salt and black pepper to taste
(Celery salt to taste)

Place a thin layer of the crumb mixture in the bottom of the prepared baking dish. Cover it with half of the oysters. Pour over half of the cream mixture. Follow with three-quarters of the remaining crumbs and the rest of the oysters. Pour the remaining cream over the oysters and cover with the remaining crumbs. Bake until the top is golden and the sauce bubbles, 20 to 25 minutes.

CREAMED OYSTERS

4 servings

New Yorkers may know this dish as an **oyster pan roast,** never mind that they are gently poached. If the shucked oysters you buy are not packed with much of their liquor, add ½ **cup clam juice.** To soak up every drop of sauce, place a slice of toast in each bowl before adding the oysters.

Drain and reserve the liquor from:

1 pint oysters (about 16 large oysters), shucked, 349

Set the oysters aside and pour the liquor through a fine-mesh sieve into a medium saucepan. Add and bring to a simmer over medium-high heat:

1 cup heavy cream or half-and-half
2 tablespoons butter
½ teaspoon salt or celery salt
¼ teaspoon sweet paprika or cayenne pepper
(1 teaspoon curry powder)

Add the oysters and heat through, 1 to 2 minutes; do not allow the sauce to boil. Transfer the oysters to serving bowls with a slotted spoon. If desired, season the sauce with any combination of the following:

(2 tablespoons mild, tomato-based chili sauce)
(1 teaspoon lemon juice)
(½ teaspoon Worcestershire sauce)

Divide the sauce among the bowls and serve at once with:

Hot buttered toast

Sprinkle generously with:

Chopped parsley

ABOUT MUSSELS

Sweet, delicious, and abundant, these mollusks have been called "the oysters of the poor." ➤ Though fresh mussels can be shucked and eaten raw, 347, they deteriorate rapidly and should be treated with caution. Alternatively, they may be steamed, shucked, and served on the half shell as for raw oysters or clams, 347.

To select and store mussels, see Buying and Storing Fresh Shellfish, 346. Green-tipped **New Zealand mussels** look distinctive, and are often larger than the **blue** and **Mediterranean mussels** found on our shores. Some say they are slightly tougher. As with oysters, some mussel farms have become famous for their quality and consistency, such as **Penn Cove** in Washington State or **Prince Edward Island** in eastern Canada.

To prepare mussels for cooking, scrub the shells with a stiff brush under running water. Some mussels are distinguished by a **beard,** a tangle of dark fibers that enables them to cling to rocks. Debeard just before cooking, as the mussels will die soon after it is removed. Simply pull the dark, fibrous strands that emerge from between the shells near the hinge, moving them back and forth until they give way. If desired, shuck as for clams, 352.

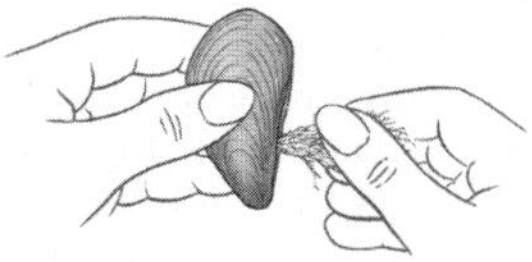

Removing the beard from a mussel

Mussels are also available precooked and shucked, or vacuum-packed and frozen raw, in their shells. The former should never be cooked further, just heated through. Frozen mussels in their shell will open as fresh ones do, and may be steamed from frozen (we do not recommend eating them raw).

➤ For 4 servings, allow about 1 quart shucked mussels or 3 quarts (about 6 pounds) of mussels in the shell. Shucked, they may be fried, 348, or stir-fried, 354. For other mussel ideas, see Billi-Bi (Cream of Mussel Soup), 100, and Shellfish Paella, 334. Mussels are a good alternative in dishes that call for clams, such as Linguine with Clam Sauce, 298, or Clams Casino, 66. Finally, you may grill them as for oysters, 349.

STEAMED MUSSELS

4 servings

Mussels may be steamed in a variety of cooking liquids with succulent results. Don't forget to place a bowl on the table for the empty shells.

I. MOULES MARINIÈRE (MUSSELS STEAMED IN WINE)

Scrub, debeard, above, and set aside:

6 pounds mussels

Bring to a boil in a large pot over high heat and cook for 3 minutes:

2 cups dry white wine
¼ cup minced parsley
2 shallots, minced
3 garlic cloves, chopped
(4 sprigs thyme)
(1 bay leaf)
½ teaspoon salt

Add the mussels, cover the pot, and cook, shaking the pot occasionally, until the mussels have opened, 8 to 10 minutes. Divide the mussels among serving bowls. Discard the thyme and bay leaf, if used, and add to the cooking liquid:

1 stick (4 ounces) butter
(1 tablespoon Dijon mustard)
(1 tablespoon capers)

Stir until the butter has melted and pour the sauce over the mussels. Top with:

Lemon juice
Minced parsley

Serve with:

Crusty bread

Or, for the classic dish **Moules Frites,** serve with:

French Fries, 270, and Aïoli, 564

Use a half shell to spoon up the liquor to the last drop.

II. THAI-STYLE

Prepare **Steamed Mussels I, above,** substituting the following for the white wine mixture:

One 13½-ounce can coconut milk
2 stalks lemongrass, toughest outer leaves removed and the tender part of the stalk sliced
(5 makrut lime leaves, torn)
1 to 2 Thai chiles, to taste, sliced
3 garlic cloves, chopped
2 shallots, finely chopped
½ teaspoon salt

Cook the mussels as directed and serve topped with:

Lime juice to taste
Chopped cilantro

Serve with:

Cooked jasmine or short-grain white rice, 343

III. ITALIAN-STYLE

Prepare **Steamed Mussels I, above,** substituting the following for the white wine mixture:

One 14½-ounce can diced tomatoes
½ fennel bulb, thinly sliced
¼ cup minced parsley
3 garlic cloves, finely chopped
3-inch strip orange zest, removed with a vegetable peeler
½ teaspoon salt
¼ teaspoon saffron threads

Cook the mussels as directed and drizzle with:

Extra-virgin olive oil

Serve with:

Cooked linguine, bucatini, or spaghetti

IV. MUSSELS WITH CIDER AND CREAM

Prepare **Steamed Mussels I, above,** substituting the following for the white wine mixture:

2 cups dry hard cider
¼ cup heavy cream or crème fraîche
2 shallots, thinly sliced
3 garlic cloves, finely chopped
½ teaspoon salt
½ teaspoon black pepper

Cook the mussels as directed and top with:

Minced chives

Serve with:

Crusty bread

BUTTERED BAKED MUSSELS

Allow 10 to 12 per serving

Preheat the oven to 450°F. Place on a large rimmed baking sheet in a single layer:

Mussels, scrubbed and debearded, 350

Heat in the oven just until the shells open; do not overcook. Remove the upper shell from each mussel, working over a bowl to catch the liquor. If any has escaped onto the baking dish, strain and add it to the liquor in the bowl. Serve the mussels on their lower shells accompanied by small dishes of:

Melted butter (flavored with minced garlic, if desired)

Serve the liquor in cups along with the mussels and garnish with:

Lemon wedges

The liquor is delicious to drink, but, to avoid any residue of sand, don't entirely drain the cup.

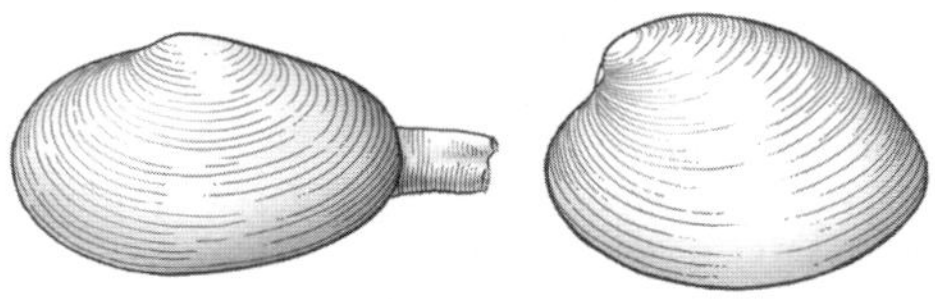

Soft-shell clam Hard-shell clam

ABOUT CLAMS

There are dozens of varieties of clams, but all fall roughly into two distinct types: **soft-shell** and **hard-shell.** Clams are sold alive and fresh in their shells or shucked and frozen or canned. To select and store live clams, see Buying and Storing Fresh Shellfish, 346.

➤ Allow 2 pounds (about 1 quart) of unshucked small clams per person for steamed clams. Eight quarts of clams in the shell will yield about 1 quart shucked.

Canned clams are perfectly acceptable in a pinch and should be a pantry staple. They are sold minced, chopped, or whole and are a good substitute for fresh in chowders. Clams are also available frozen, either shucked or vacuum-packed in their shells. The former are perfect for chowders; the latter are great for steaming and other cooked preparations, but do not eat them raw.

SOFT-SHELL OR LONGNECK CLAMS

Soft-shell or **longneck clams** are perfect for steaming, which is why they are also referred to as **steamers.** Originally native to the Atlantic, longnecks are readily available on the West Coast, joining the **razor, gaper,** and **geoduck** (pronounced "gooey-duck") **clams** native to the region. All soft-shell clams are sandy and need to be purged (see below). Although they are easy to shuck, ➤ soft-shell clams are never eaten raw (with the notable exception of geoduck sashimi). The small varieties are usually steamed or deep-fried.

To purge soft-shell clams before shucking, ➤ scrub and wash them in several changes of cold water, then soak in a cold brine of ½ cup salt per 1 gallon of water for 3 to 12 hours. It may be necessary to rinse cooked clams further to completely rid them of sand. Small soft-shell clams may be steamed unshucked, and the tough skin of the siphon (or neck) can usually be pulled off with the fingers.

To shuck soft-shell clams, run a short sharp knife along the inside of the top shell. Work over a bowl to catch the juices. Cut the meat from the bottom shell. Slit the skin of the siphon and pull off the skin. For razor clams and larger clams, ➤ find the darkly colored stomach and cut or scrape it out. Some clams may contain a clear rod, called a "crystalline style," that helps them digest food. If present, remove before cooking.

To remove the tougher skin of geoduck and gaper clam siphons, cut the siphons off and blanch them in boiling water for 1 minute. Pull off the skin when cooled. Split the siphons down the center, pry them open like a book, and rinse out the contents.

HARD-SHELL CLAMS

The most prevalent type of hard-shell clam on the Atlantic coast is the **quahog.** Quahogs are classified by size. **Littlenecks** and **middlenecks** are the smallest—averaging 8 to 12 clams per pound—and best for steaming. Depending on where you are, **cherrystone** can mean either a small or medium clam. **Top necks** (or **count necks**) and **chowder clams** are large (2 to 4 per pound!) and inexpensive, making them the best choice for (you guessed it) chowder. **Mahogany clams** are ocean-dwelling quahogs and have a more pronounced, briny flavor. **Surf** or **bar clams,** a large, triangular species, are the sandiest of all hard-shell clams. They may be cut into strips and served raw or fried, or used in chowders and broth.

On the Pacific coast, **Manila clams** are the most prolific farmed species. The native Pacific **butter clam** is distinguished by its small size and succulent flavor. Other indigenous Pacific varieties include the sweet and tender **pismo** and the **Pacific littleneck.** All of these varieties are good for steaming or eating raw on the half shell, 347.

The term **cockle** is applied to several species of clam-like mollusks. Most of them are quite small, and tend to be very sandy.

Shucking a hard-shell clam

To shuck hard-shell clams, first scrub them under running water. ➤ With the exception of cockles and surf clams, hard-shelled clams are generally not very sandy and do not need to be purged (for the exceptions noted above, purge as for soft-shell clams, above). Carefully guide a knife between the shells and squeeze the blade into the clam, as shown. After opening, cut through the muscle holding the shells together, working over a bowl to catch any juices. They can be difficult to open, especially larger ones. If you have time, freezing them spread out on a baking sheet for several hours and letting them thaw in the refrigerator makes the job quite easy. Or, if you are in a hurry and using them in a cooked dish, place them in a baking pan in a 350°F oven until they open. ➤ For larger clams, cut open the stomachs and scrape out the contents. Large hard-shell clams have a tough upper portion that may be separated from the tender portion, then chopped, ground, or sliced into strips, and creamed, scalloped, made into fritters, or used in chowders, 103–4.

For other clam recipes, see Clams Casino, 66, Linguine with Clam Sauce, 298, and Bouillabaisse, 102.

STEAMED CLAMS

4 servings

You can steam any clam you like, but soft-shell clams are the traditional steamers, in large part because it is difficult to purge them entirely of sand. Once strained of sand, the resulting broth gives you a flavorful dip in which you can rinse the clams before eating. Since they are not as sandy, ➤ steam hard-shell clams as for mussels, 351.

Place in a large pot with an inch or so of water:

2 quarts small soft-shell clams (about 4 pounds)

Cover the pot, turn the heat to high, and cook, shaking the pot occasionally, until the clams are all open, 5 to 10 minutes. Overcooking makes clams tough. Meanwhile, melt in a small saucepan over low heat:

2 sticks (8 ounces) butter
(3 garlic cloves, minced)

When the clams are cooked, transfer them with a slotted spoon to a large bowl. Strain the broth, then season to taste with:

Salt and black pepper

Pour the butter into separate dishes for each diner. Serve the broth in cups along with the clams and garnish with:

Lemon wedges

To eat the clams, lift them out of the shell by the neck (siphon). Peel off the sheath (tough outer skin) of the neck. Swish the clam in the broth to remove any sand, and then dip in butter. The broth is delicious to drink, but, to avoid any residue of sand, either strain it through a fine-mesh sieve (or don't entirely drain the cup).

BAKED SOFT-SHELL CLAMS

4 servings

Preheat the oven to 425°F. Scrub and purge, 352:

2 quarts small soft-shell clams (about 4 pounds)

To keep the clams steady, line a baking sheet with crumpled foil or a bed of:

Rock salt

Arrange the clams in the foil or salt. Bake about 15 minutes, until the shells open. Remove the top shells carefully, over a bowl. Serve on the half shell on individual plates with any of the following:

Melted butter or any flavored butter, 559–60
Becker Cocktail Sauce, 569

Garnish with:

Lemon wedges

BAKED STUFFED CLAMS (STUFFIES)

5 servings

This recipe is traditionally made with large top neck or chowder clams, which can average 2 to 3 clams per pound. However, it can also be successfully and deliciously made with smaller littleneck clams, if you only have access to those.

Preheat the oven to 375°F. Prepare:

Parsley and Bread Crumb Stuffing, 534, or Bacon Stuffing for Fish, 534

Bring ½ inch water to a boil in a large pot. Add to the pot:

5 pounds hard-shell clams, scrubbed

Steam just until the clams open, 2 to 5 minutes. Remove the clams from the pot, reserving the liquid.

If using large clams, shuck them, reserving one shell from each clam for serving, and chop the clam meat, mixing it into the stuffing. Mound the stuffing onto the reserved shells and place on a baking sheet.

If using littlenecks, carefully remove the top shell, leaving the clam meat inside. Top each clam with 1 teaspoon stuffing and place the clams on a baking sheet.

Bake the clams until the stuffing is well browned, about 10 minutes for littlenecks or 20 minutes for top necks and chowder clams. Serve with:

Lemon wedges and hot pepper sauce

CLAMBAKE

Whatever the size of your bake, buy the clams the day before and scrub them well to remove sand. A big outdoor bake is described in version I; a smaller, home-friendly one in II.

In addition to the food, you will need seaweed for a clambake. Generally speaking, almost any seaweed can be used. However, be aware that seaweeds accumulate toxins, so avoid collecting seaweed from any area where pollution is a concern. If making version I, you will also need enough wood to build a large fire, about 15 large rocks, and a large canvas tarp to place on top of the food so the heat and steam are trapped inside the pit.

I. ***About 20 servings***

Please read about Pit Cooking, 1062.

Dig a pit about 2 feet deep, 2 feet wide, and 3 feet long in the sand. Line the bottom of the pit with large smooth stones, then build a big fire on top of the stones. Feed the fire to keep it going for 1 to 2 hours, then allow it to burn down until all the wood has burned to coals, about 2 hours.

Have ready:

3 pounds potatoes or sweet potatoes, scrubbed
2 pounds large onions, unpeeled
12 bone-in chicken thighs
2 dozen ears corn in the husk, silks removed
(3 pounds spicy sausage links, such as Italian, linguiça, or andouille, wrapped in cheesecloth)
8 quarts littleneck or cherrystone clams (about 16 pounds), scrubbed and rinsed
(8 quarts mussels [about 12 pounds], scrubbed and debearded, 350)

When the fire is all coals, spread out the coals over the stones and cover the coals with a 6- to 8-inch-thick layer of seaweed. Stack the ingredients in the order listed above on top of each other on the seaweed, adding thin layers of seaweed in between. You may wrap ingredients in cheesecloth to make large bundles.

Add:

Twelve 1-pound live lobsters, killed, 360

Top with a 3- to 4-inch layer of seaweed. Pour about 8 cups seawater over the last layer of seaweed. Cover the pit completely with a large canvas tarp that has been thoroughly soaked with seawater. Weight the edges of the tarp with rocks to hold it in place. During the steaming, the tarp will puff up, which is a sign of a satisfactory "bake." Cook 1 to 1½ hours. To test, lift the tarp carefully at one corner, so as not to get sand into the pit, and see if the lobsters are cooked. If so, the whole feast should be cooked to just the right point. Remove the food packets and lobsters from the pit and serve hot, with plenty of paper towels and:

Melted butter

II. ***8 servings***
A more domesticated "bake" can be prepared in a 20-quart stockpot on a stove or outdoor grill.
Add 4 cups water to the largest pot you have and bring to a boil. Add:
2 pounds small red potatoes
8 bone-in chicken thighs
Cover, reduce the heat, and simmer gently for 20 minutes. Add:
Six 1½-pound live lobsters, killed, 36
Cover and cook 8 minutes more. Place on the lobsters:
8 ears corn, shucked
Cook 10 minutes, covered. Add:
4 quarts small clams (about 8 pounds), well scrubbed
Cover and steam until the clams open, 5 to 10 minutes longer. Serve with:
Melted butter

STIR-FRIED CLAMS OR MUSSELS WITH OYSTER SAUCE
4 servings
Have ready:
4 pounds littleneck clams, scrubbed and rinsed, or mussels, scrubbed and debearded, 350
Heat in a wok or large skillet over high heat:
2 tablespoons vegetable oil
Add:
2 garlic cloves, minced
1-inch piece ginger, peeled and minced
and the clams or mussels. Cover and cook 2 minutes. Uncover and cook, stirring, until the mollusks open, a few minutes more. Add:
2 tablespoons soy sauce
2 tablespoons oyster sauce
1 tablespoon Shaoxing wine, 952, dry sherry, or sake
2 tablespoons chopped green onions
Cook, stirring, for about 30 seconds. Stir in:
¼ cup bottled clam juice or water
Transfer the clams or mussels to a serving dish, pour the sauce over them, and garnish with:
Minced green onions and cilantro
Serve with:
Cooked rice, 343

THAI CLAM POT
4 to 6 servings
Place in a heatproof bowl:
8 ounces dried thin or flat rice noodles or rice vermicelli
Pour boiling water over the noodles until they are submerged. Use tongs to push them under the water as they soften. Allow to sit, checking every couple of minutes, until the noodles are limp and tender. If using flat rice noodles, this may take up to 10 minutes, but very thin rice noodles will take considerably less time. Drain the noodles and rinse under cold water. Set aside.
Heat in a heavy pot or Dutch oven over medium-high heat until shimmering:
2 tablespoons vegetable oil
Add and cook, stirring, for about 15 seconds:
8 garlic cloves, thinly sliced
1 stalk lemongrass, tender white part only, thinly sliced
(3 makrut lime leaves, 998)
1 teaspoon red pepper flakes or 2 dried red Thai chiles
Add and bring to a boil:
One 13½-ounce can coconut milk
1 tablespoon brown sugar or palm sugar
Add:
3 pounds small hard-shell clams, scrubbed
Return to a boil, then reduce the heat to medium, cover, and cook just until the clams have opened, 3 to 5 minutes. Stir in:
½ cup cilantro leaves
2 tablespoons fish sauce or salt to taste
Divide the noodles among individual bowls, add the clams, and pour the broth over them. Serve with:
Lime wedges

ABOUT SCALLOPS
These beautiful mollusks, known on French menus as **coquilles St. Jacques,** are traditional emblems of the shrine of St. James in Santiago de Compostela, Spain. Pilgrims who visited ate the mollusks as penance—surely not a rigorous one—and afterward fastened the shells to their hats. Scallops are also responsible for the cooking term "scalloped," which originally meant seafood creamed, heated, and served in a shell.

The scallops available in markets are almost never the whole mollusk but instead are the edible section of its adductor muscle, which controls the animal's movement. Since this muscle does not accumulate any contaminants from the sea, scallops are the safest shellfish to eat raw (see Scallop Ceviche, 355). Nonetheless, as with all shellfish, scallops are still extremely perishable, so use the same caution you would with raw oysters or clams: Source with care and use promptly.

Some prefer the small, tender, creamy pink or tan **bay scallops,** especially the scarce and expensive wild bay scallops of the New England coastline. **Calico scallops** are even smaller, coming in at up to 100 per pound. They are sweet and delicate, but ➤ use extreme care not to overcook them. They are so small that they only need a minute's cooking by most methods. We prefer larger, firmer **sea scallops** (30 to under 10 per pound). They are still sweet and succulent, but they have more texture, and are easier to cook. Larger sea scallops are especially suited to brief, high-heat cooking methods such as grilling, broiling, and searing.

To shuck scallops, scrub them well. Since scallops gape naturally, they are easy to shuck. Open the shell with any sharp knife, then cut out the muscle (and red or white roe, if any). ➤ Discard all else in the shell.

For both in-shell scallops that you shuck as well as for already shucked scallops, remove the tough "hinge" (sometimes called the tendon) that runs down the side of the muscle.

Scallops should have a sweet, pleasant odor. Scallops are sometimes soaked in a bath of water and preservatives to extend their shelf life, and this increases their thawed weight. ➤ Thus, make every effort to buy unsoaked, or "dry packed" scallops. They have a cleaner taste and brown better when sautéed because they contain less water. Avoid scallops sold with the phrase: "water added." Be suspicious of any sea scallops that are pure white, a good indication that they have been soaked; the natural color of sea scallops ranges from off-white to pale shades of orange, pink, and tan. Individually quick frozen (IQF) sea scallops can be a good buy and retain most of their flavor.

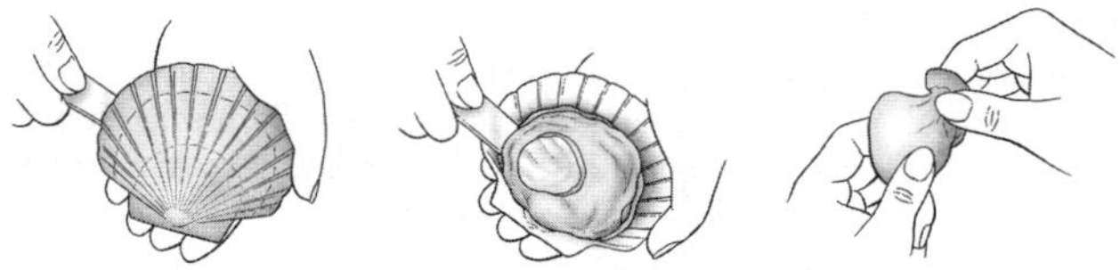

Shucking a scallop and removing the "hinge"

➤ Allow about ⅓ pound of scallops per serving. Seared, grilled, or broiled sea scallops are quite good with a simple squeeze of lemon, a vinaigrette, 575, Beurre Blanc, 558, or Brown Butter, 558. Serve atop a lightly sauced pasta dish or assertive greens like arugula, watercress, or radicchio. Bay scallops or cubed sea scallops are a welcome addition to Fried Rice, 332, chowders, bisques, and clear soups like Tom Yum Goong, 101 (replace the shrimp with scallops), ➤ as long as they are added toward the end of cooking. To use sea scallops in a dish that calls for smaller bay scallops, slice or cube them before cooking. For **dried scallops,** see 1016.

SCALLOP CEVICHE

4 servings

Ceviche is raw shellfish or fish, 377, marinated in an acidic dressing. Though not technically cooked, the acid causes the shellfish to turn opaque and firm up.

Place in a medium bowl:

1 pound whole bay scallops or sea scallops, side "hinge" removed, above, cut into small chunks

Toss with:

¼ cup lemon juice
¼ cup lime juice
1 to 2 serrano peppers or fresh red Thai chiles, very thinly sliced
(¼ medium red onion, sliced paper thin)
¼ teaspoon salt

Refrigerate, stirring occasionally, for at least 2 hours or overnight. Top with:

Chopped cilantro
Drizzle of extra-virgin olive oil

Serve with:

Tostadas or tortilla chips
Sliced avocado

SCALLOPS MEUNIÈRE

4 servings

Dry between towels:

1 pound bay or sea scallops, side "hinge" removed, above

Dip them in:

Bound Bread Crumb or Cracker Coating, 658

Let them dry on a rack about 15 minutes. Melt in a large heavy skillet over medium-high heat:

4 tablespoons (½ stick) butter

When the butter is hot, add the scallops and cook, turning bay scallops frequently and sea scallops just once, until evenly browned on both sides, about 3 minutes for bay scallops, 5 minutes for sea scallops. Just before the scallops are done, sprinkle with:

Fresh lemon juice
Finely chopped parsley
Salt and black pepper to taste

Serve, if desired, with:

(Tomatoes Provençale, 282)

COQUILLES ST. JACQUES (SEA SCALLOP GRATIN)

2 servings

The sauce can be prepared several hours in advance and refrigerated; bring to a simmer before proceeding.

Combine in a bowl and mix well:

½ cup fresh bread crumbs, 957
3 tablespoons grated Parmesan
2 tablespoons butter, melted
1 tablespoon minced parsley
1 teaspoon chopped thyme
⅛ teaspoon salt
Black pepper to taste

Melt in a medium skillet over medium heat:

1 tablespoon butter

Add and cook, stirring, until softened but not browned, about 2 minutes:

2 shallots, minced
2 garlic cloves, minced

Add and cook, stirring occasionally, until the mushrooms are softened, about 7 minutes:

8 ounces small mushrooms, quartered
1 teaspoon salt

Add:

¼ cup dry white wine

Increase the heat and simmer until the wine has almost evaporated, about 3 minutes. Add:

1 cup heavy cream

Bring to a gentle boil and boil until thickened, about 5 minutes. Preheat the broiler. Reduce the sauce to a simmer and add:

12 ounces sea scallops, side "hinge" removed, 354, and halved horizontally

Cook until the scallops are no longer translucent, about 1½ minutes. Remove from the heat and stir in:

1 teaspoon lemon juice

Spoon the mixture into scallop shells or individual gratin dishes. Sprinkle the bread crumb mixture over the scallops and sauce. Broil until golden brown on top and bubbling around the edges, about 1½ minutes.

SEARED SEA SCALLOPS

4 servings

This simple cooking method is our favorite for scallops. The flavor and texture of the scallop are preserved, and the golden crust contrasts delectably with the creamy, sweet flesh.

Pat dry with paper towels:

1 pound dry-packed sea scallops, side "hinge" removed, 354

Lightly season on both sides with:

Salt

Let the scallops sit on a plate while the oil heats. Heat in a large skillet over medium-high heat until just starting to smoke:

1 tablespoon vegetable oil or Clarified Butter, 960

Quickly pat the scallops dry once more and add to the pan without crowding. Cook, undisturbed, until golden brown on the bottom, 1 to 1½ minutes. Flip with a spatula and cook the second side until browned, about 1 minute more. If desired, serve with:

(Beurre Blanc, 558, Chimichurri, 567, Salsa Verde, 567, or Pesto, 586)

ABOUT ABALONE

This delicious, single-shelled gastropod comes to our markets from Australia, Japan, Mexico, and Peru—shelled, pounded, and ready to cook. To aid conservation, the wild abalone native to the shores of Alaska and California can only be harvested for sport when they have reached 7 inches in width. Farmed abalone is smaller and raised on ocean-floor "sea ranches" or in contained systems. The meat is typically sold canned or pounded and frozen (which we favor).

To prepare whole abalone, remove the large edible adductor muscle, or "foot," by running a knife between the shell and meat. A shucked abalone has a crown of organs around the top of the muscle (the side closest to the shell). Cut off this ring of viscera and remove the head, located at the edge of the foot. The black edge of the foot is edible, but can be easily trimmed off. Large, wild abalone needs a prodigious pounding to become tender, but smaller, farmed abalone needs little if any.

To pound abalone, leave it whole or slice across the grain for steaks. Cover both sides with plastic wrap, and beat with a meat pounder using even, measured strokes. The meat is ready to cook when it looks like one of Dalí's limp watches; any more and the texture will be too soft. In addition to sautéing pounded and breaded steaks (below), you may poach thinly sliced abalone just until tender in any flavorful broth or sauce. Or, beat and chop abalone for chowder. ➤ Allow 1 pound for 2 to 3 servings.

SAUTÉED ABALONE

2 to 3 servings

Cut into ⅜-inch-thick steaks across the grain and pound, above:

1 pound abalone

Dip in:

Bound Bread Crumb or Cracker Coating, 658

Heat in a heavy skillet over medium-high heat:

2 tablespoons vegetable oil or Clarified Butter, 960

Add the abalone and cook 1 to 2 minutes on each side. Serve garnished with:

Lemon wedges

ABOUT CRABS

Simply prepared crab is a luxurious eating experience that is hard to improve upon. For most diners, the rich, buttery flesh of a Dungeness or stone crab claw needs little adornment, save a tableside gilding of melted butter or a squeeze of lemon.

Of course, the fact that crab needs no embellishment has not stemmed human ingenuity. Recipes for crab apply to almost all species, but the type of crab or the part of the crab from which the meat is taken may make a difference in color, taste, and texture. As a general rule, meat from the body has a finer texture than leg and claw meat, which is darker and usually has more flavor.

➤ When purchasing live crabs, go for the liveliest—they should react when removed from the tank. If the crabs are placed in a plastic bag, poke holes in it so they can breathe. For the amount of meat to expect from whole crab, see the individual types on 357. Store on ice temporarily if necessary and refrigerate as soon as possible, covered with a damp towel with a tray underneath to catch water. Cook live crabs within a day of purchase. If stored in the refrigerator overnight, be sure all the crabs are still alive before you cook them (they will be lethargic from the cold).

To kill a crab before cooking, you may sedate them first by placing them in the freezer for about 2 hours. Place the crab belly down on a cutting board. Holding it firmly in place, plunge the point of a heavy knife straight down between and slightly behind the eyes. Quickly cut through the head.

Freshly cooked crab is also widely available in the shell. Whole, cooked crabs should feel heavy for their size, smell sweet, have shells free of cracks, and all claws and legs intact. They should be purchased and consumed within 3 days of when they were cooked.

Frozen whole crab and crab legs are usually cooked as well and can last 6 months if stored properly. Frozen crab should be free of freezer burn and any exposed flesh should be white and not dry looking. Thaw frozen crab in a bowl or dish in the refrigerator.

While we are often told that life is about the journey, not the destination, **picked crabmeat** is a wonderful convenience for cooks when time (or patience) is in short supply. Freshly cooked and picked crabmeat is available at many seafood markets; it is the best choice, as very little has been done to mar its natural sweetness and delicate texture. Pasteurized crabmeat, which is packaged in cans or vacuum-sealed in bags and frozen, is an excellent second choice if fresh crabmeat is not available. Fresh and pasteurized crabmeat must be kept refrigerated or frozen. Shelf-stable canned crabmeat is stored at room temperature and usually of lower quality—refrigerate it after opening and use within a few days. ➤ Regardless of type, pick over crabmeat for small bits of shell and cartilage and store in the refrigerator.

The majority of crabmeat sold in this country is picked from blue crabs and graded for quality (other types of crabmeat are not graded). The grading system is based on the size of the chunks, or lumps, of meat. **Collosal** and **jumbo lump** are the highest grades, followed by **backfin;** all consist solely of largely intact body muscles. **Special,** or **flake,** consists of smaller pieces from the body; **claw** is self-explanatory, and not to be scoffed at for its light brown tinge. For most uses, special grade crabmeat is perfectly acceptable; let common sense and your budget guide you.

To remove the meat from cooked crabs, turn the crab onto its back and lift the pointed flap called the **apron** at the base away from the body with a firm hold at the wide end. Slowly twist off the apron, removing the intestinal vein as well. Pull off the large claws at the body, then gently crack the claws with a nutcracker, mallet, or rolling pin and pull out the meat. Remove the legs, then bend each one to break at the joint and remove the upper leg meat. Pull off the top shell, then clean out and discard the feathery gills (also called "dead man's fingers") underneath. Break the body in two and pick out the meat, discarding any bits of shell or cartilage, and remove the **tomalley** (a digestive gland) and **roe.** Reserve the tomalley, if desired, as a rich addition to an accompanying sauce. Avoid eating tomalley when there is a red tide; crabs eat bivalve mollusks, which may be tainted with neurotoxins (the crabmeat is perfectly safe to eat). The roe is a classic addition to Charleston She-Crab Soup, 99. Crab shells can replace the shrimp or lobster shells in Shrimp or Lobster Butter, 560.

To prepare crab shells for stuffing, select large perfect shells and scrub them well with a brush. Place them in a large pot, cover with water, and add 1 teaspoon baking soda. Bring to a boil, then drain, rinse, and dry the shells. They are now ready for filling.

BLUE CRABS

These denizens of the Atlantic, comically skittish on land, efficiently beautiful swimmers in the water, furnish most of the fresh crabmeat in the market. For grades, see above. Male blue crabs, or "jimmies," are generally preferred to "sooks" (females) because they contain more meat. As illustrated, the female has a wider fringed apron than the male. On average, blue crabs weigh in at about 5 ounces a piece. ➤ Expect 15 percent of a blue crab's live weight to be crabmeat. One pound of crabs (about 3) will yield 2¼ ounces of meat.

Male crab and female crab

Blue crabs harvested when they are molting are sold as **soft-shell crabs.** If purchased live, they will not be very active, but they should have a fresh smell. Soft-shells can also be purchased cooked or frozen. Soft-shell crabs are prepared and eaten quite differently from their hard-shelled counterparts.

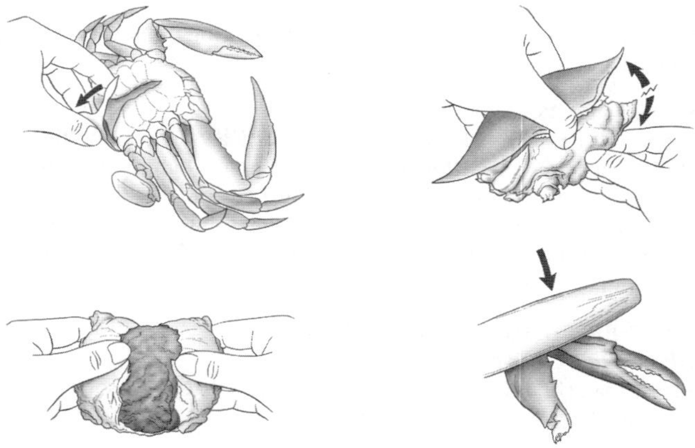

Removing meat from a hard-shell crab

To prepare soft-shell crabs for cooking, wash them in several changes of cold water. Snip off the eyes and mouth with kitchen shears. Lift the tapering points on each side of the top shell and pull out and discard the gills. Turn the crab on its back, lift the apron and, with a firm hold at the wide end, slowly twist and pull it off. Almost every part of a soft-shell crab is edible. They are usually breaded and pan-fried or deep-fried, as in the recipes that follow.

Cleaning a soft-shell crab

DUNGENESS CRABS

Native to the West Coast, this crab is prized for its sweet, lobster-like meat. To protect them from overharvesting, only males with a shell wider than 6 inches can be kept. These usually average 1½ to 2½ pounds, 25 percent of which is crabmeat. **Jonah crabs** are an East Coast relative of the Dungeness crab, with brownish flesh and black-tipped claws. **Atlantic rock crab** (or "**peekytoe crab**") is slightly smaller but similar in texture and flavor. For a recipe that features Dungeness crabs, see Cioppino, 102.

KING CRABS

Mostly from Alaskan waters, king crabs are huge and pinkish in color. Give preference to American-caught crab in the market, as it is subject to more stringent rules designed to prevent overharvesting. Unless you live close to where these crabs are caught, you will almost never find them whole and raw. Rather, the legs are sold on their own, precooked and frozen. Thaw frozen king crab overnight in the refrigerator. Because they are already cooked, they should be served cold or briefly reheated by broiling, steaming, or grilling. **Snow crab,** smaller and less expensive than king crab, is also sold cooked and frozen and may be treated like king crab.

STONE CRABS

From Florida, with pale flesh and a very delicate texture and flavor, stone crabs are valued for their claws. When caught, one or both claws are removed, and the crab is returned to its habitat, where, hopefully, it will grow its claws back—as crabs are quite capable of doing. Sold cooked, stone crabs need no preparation. Crush or crack the claw shell and pick out the meat or reheat as for king crabs, 357.

DEEP-FRIED SOFT-SHELL CRABS

Allow 2 to 3 crabs per serving

Please read about Deep-Frying, 1051. For pan-fried soft-shell crabs, see Fried Soft-Shell Crab Sandwich, 140.

Dry between paper towels:

Soft-shell crabs, cleaned, 357

Dip them in:

Bound Bread Crumb or Cracker Coating, 658

Heat to 365°F in a deep heavy pot or Dutch oven over medium-high heat:

2 inches vegetable oil

Add the crabs a few at a time, without crowding, and fry until golden brown, 3 to 5 minutes, turning once. Drain on paper towels. Season to taste with:

Salt and black pepper

Serve with:

Tartar Sauce, 563, Rémoulade Sauce, 564, or parsley and Brown Butter, 558

GRILLED OR BROILED SOFT-SHELL CRABS

4 servings

Prepare a medium-hot grill, 1063, or preheat the broiler and position an oven rack 2 or 3 inches from the heating element.

Mix in a small bowl:

4 tablespoons (1/2 stick) butter, melted, or olive oil
(1 garlic clove, minced or grated)
(Pinch of cayenne pepper)
Salt and black pepper to taste

Brush the butter mixture over both sides of:

8 soft-shell crabs, cleaned, 357, and patted dry

Grill or broil until firm, about 4 minutes each side, taking care not to burn the shells, especially the claws. They do not turn red as other crabs do. Serve with:

Lemon or lime wedges and hot pepper sauce, or melted butter

STEAMED BLUE CRABS

8 to 10 crabs per person

The traditional and delightfully messy way to serve these crabs is to dump them onto the center of a table covered with newspaper. For cracking, hand out small hammers, pliers, or nutcrackers. For picking out meat, provide wooden skewers, seafood forks, and nut picks. An atmosphere of congeniality and a roll of paper towels or stack of Wet-Naps are key.

Fit a steamer insert into a very large stockpot. Pour into the pot:

2 cups cider vinegar
(12 ounces beer)

Add water to come two-thirds of the way up to the bottom of the insert. Bring the mixture to a boil. Rinse under cold water:

24 live blue crabs

Arrange in no more than 6 layers in the steamer insert, sprinkling each layer with:

1 tablespoon kosher salt (up to 6 tablespoons total)
(1 tablespoon crab boil seasoning or Chesapeake Bay Seasoning, 588 [up to 6 tablespoons total])

Reduce the heat to a rapid simmer, cover the pot tightly, and steam the crabs until they turn bright pink and their legs can be pulled from the sockets fairly easily, 15 to 20 minutes. Serve with:

Melted butter
Lemon wedges

POACHED OR BOILED CRABS

8 to 10 blue crabs per person or one 1½-pound Dungeness crab per person

Serve simply with crab crackers or nutcrackers, plenty of napkins, and melted butter and lemon, or use the picked crabmeat in other recipes.

Fill a large pot two-thirds full with:

Water

Bring to a boil over high heat. Add:

1 tablespoon salt for each quart of water

Using tongs, slide into the water, one at a time, so as not to disturb the boil:

Live hard-shell crabs, rinsed

Reduce the heat to a simmer and cook for about 15 minutes or until their legs can be pulled from the sockets fairly easily. Transfer the crabs to a platter and serve whole with:

Melted butter and lemon wedges

To eat, twist off the claws and set aside. Turn the crab body upside down, remove the apron using a sharp knife, if necessary, and discard. Pry off the top shell as if opening a book, then discard the gills. Break the body in half to pick out the meat. The green tomalley may be eaten or discarded, depending on the preference of the diner. Claw meat can be released with a nutcracker.

CRAB CAKES

4 servings

Mix in a large bowl:

1/4 cup mayonnaise
1 large egg
2 tablespoons minced parsley
1 tablespoon Dijon mustard
(1 teaspoon crab boil seasoning or Chesapeake Bay Seasoning, 588)
(1/4 teaspoon cayenne pepper)
1/4 teaspoon salt
1/4 teaspoon black pepper

Add and gently mix just enough to combine:

1 pound lump crabmeat, picked over for shells and cartilage
1/2 cup fresh, 957, or dry bread crumbs

Shape the mixture into 8 cakes. Place the cakes on a plate lined with wax paper. If desired, cover and refrigerate for up to 8 hours.

Preheat the oven to 200°F. Heat in a large skillet over medium heat:

4 tablespoons (½ stick) butter, Clarified Butter, 960, or vegetable oil

When the fat is hot, add half the cakes to the pan. Reduce the heat to medium-low and cook until browned on both sides, about 5 minutes per side. Keep the finished cakes warm in the oven while the rest cook. Serve hot with:

Lemon wedges
Aïoli, 564, Rémoulade Sauce, 564, or a flavored mayonnaise, 563

SINGAPOREAN CHILLI CRAB

2 servings

Break out the Wet-Naps! This dish is as messy to eat as it is delicious. If you wish, substitute lobster for the crab; cut it up as for Lobster Américaine, 361.

Combine in a medium bowl and set aside:

⅓ cup mild, tomato-based chili sauce or ketchup
¼ cup water
1 tablespoon chili garlic sauce, sriracha sauce, or sambal oelek, 969
1 tablespoon rice vinegar
1 tablespoon brown sugar
1 tablespoon soy sauce

Have ready:

1 live Dungeness crab (2 to 3 pounds), killed, 356

Twist off the claws and crack them once or twice to expose the meat. Remove and discard the top shell, gills, and viscera, and cut the body into 4 pieces. Heat in a wok or large skillet over high heat until shimmering:

2 tablespoons vegetable oil

Add and cook until softened, about 2 minutes:

1 large shallot, minced
3 garlic cloves, minced
1-inch piece ginger, peeled and minced
(1 fresh red chile, minced)
(1 tablespoon fermented black beans)

Add the chili sauce mixture and bring to a boil. Add the crab pieces and stir to coat with sauce. Simmer for 5 minutes. Add and stir, bringing to a rolling boil to thicken:

2 teaspoons cornstarch dissolved in 1 tablespoon cold water

Remove the pan from the heat. Add and stir in to combine:

1 egg yolk, beaten

Transfer the crab to a serving plate, pour the sauce over it, and top with:

2 green onions, chopped

Serve with:

Crusty bread or cooked white rice, 343

ABOUT LOBSTERS

We encounter two types of lobsters in the continental United States. The **American** or **Northern lobster** is caught from Canada to the Carolinas, and is often referred to as Maine lobster. It is mottled dark brown with a blue-green tint and reddish accents.

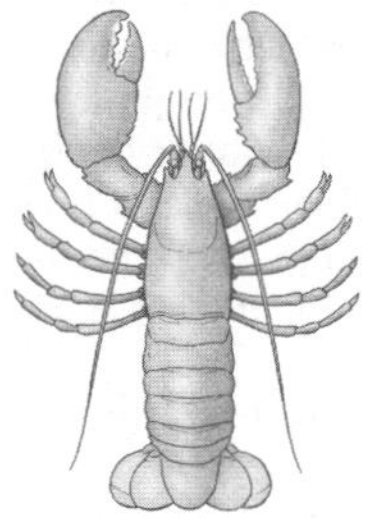

American or Northern lobster

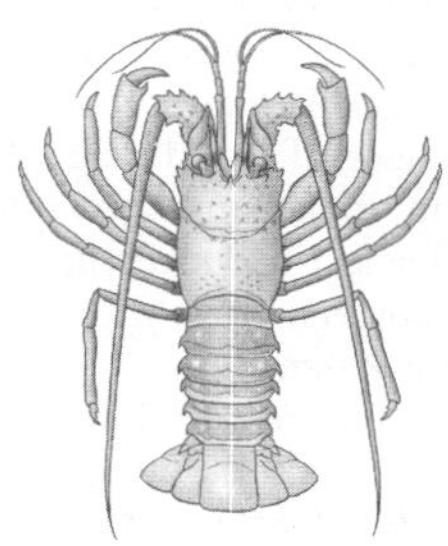

Spiny or rock lobster

The **spiny lobster, rock lobster,** or **langouste** is caught off the shores of Florida and California, as well as Australia, New Zealand, South Africa, and in the Mediterranean. It has extra-long antennae but no claws, and most of the meat is in the heavy tail. Spiny lobster tails marketed as "cold water" are thought to have better flavor. They vary in color from tan to reddish orange to maroon, with light spotting. Spiny lobster tails are usually sold frozen.

Rarely encountered on this side of the Atlantic, the **Norwegian lobster,** a relative of the spiny, is known in France as **langoustine** and is famous in Italy as **scampo** (usually referred to in the plural, **scampi**). The **European lobster** is quite similar to our Northern lobster, though not plentiful enough to export here.

Regardless of type, most lobsters require about the same cooking time and may be cut and cleaned in the same way. But as the lobster ritual is more complicated for the American type, we will discuss it in further detail below.

Some consider female lobsters to be finer in flavor. However, this is often simply due to the presence of **roe,** or **coral,** in the female, which may be eaten along with the meat or used in a sauce. To tell the difference between male and female lobsters, look for soft, leathery, fin-like appendages on the underside, just where the body and tail meet. In the male, these appendages are bony. Female lobsters also have somewhat broader tails, whereas males often have larger claws. The greenish substance in both sexes is the hepatopancreas, or **tomalley,** not attractive but delicious. ➤ However, avoid eating tomalley when there is a red tide. While lobsters are not filter feeders, they do sometimes eat bivalves tainted with neurotoxins during red tides. These neurotoxins accumulate in the tomalley. The meat, however, is perfectly fine to eat.

➤ When purchasing live lobster, be sure they are "alive and lively" when removed from the tank. Allow one 1½- to 2½-pound lobster per serving. ➤ A 2½-pound lobster will yield about 2 cups of cooked meat. Some say that larger lobsters are tough, but that is not the case. In fact, there is a good argument to be made in favor of larger lobsters. They contain proportionally more meat for their size than smaller lobsters. The larger a lobster gets, the more meat it has in those difficult-to-reach parts of the claw and the body that make lobster eating so much fun. If lobster meat is occasionally tough and stringy, it is more likely the result of overcooking than size. The one downside to buying large lobsters is that they are harder to cook evenly.

To store live lobsters until ready to use, place them in the refrigerator on a rimmed baking sheet, wrapped in moistened newspaper or covered with a moist towel. Do not store lobsters directly on ice or in water. The claws should be plugged with a small piece of wood or held together with rubber bands. Before cooking, make sure your lobsters are still active and that the tail snaps back if it is stretched out when you pick up the lobster. To clean lobsters, grasp them firmly at the back and rinse under cool running water.

For some preparations, it is necessary to halve or cut apart a lobster before cooking.

To kill a lobster before cooking, you may sedate them first by placing them in the freezer for about 2 hours. Place the lobster belly down on a cutting board. Holding it firmly in place, find the crosshatch right behind the lobster's head and plunge the point of a heavy knife straight down, as shown below. Cut through the head; this will kill the lobster quickly.

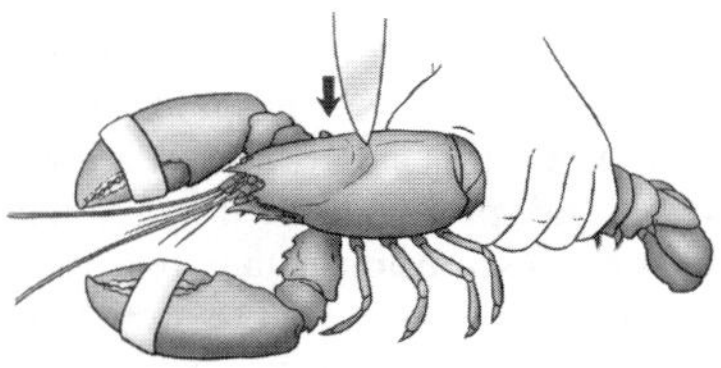

To kill a lobster before cooking it, pierce it behind the head with a sharp, heavy knife.

➤ When using dry-heat cooking methods such as broiling, grilling, and baking, lobster meat has a tendency to stick to the shell. To counteract this, you may blanch the lobsters first by steaming or boiling for 1 minute.

If you buy cooked lobster in the shell, make sure that the color is bright red and that it has a fresh seashore aroma. ➤ Most important of all, the tail—as with the uncooked lobster—when pulled, should roll back into place under the body. This means the lobster was alive, as it should have been, when cooked.

➤ ***To remove the meat from a parboiled or fully cooked lobster,*** twist the claws off the body. Crack the large claws and knuckles with a nutcracker, rolling pin, or the spine of a heavy knife. For the claws, try to hit the shell at the inner hump. This will crack it so that the meat in the entire larger pincer claw is released. Crack off the small pincer shell, and its meat will slide out. We find a wooden skewer helpful for removing meat from the slender interior of the claw. Separate the tail from the body with a twisting motion. Roll the tail on a work surface while gently pressing down until the shell cracks. The tail meat should come out neatly in one piece. If desired, use scissors to cut through the underside of the tail shell to make it easier to extract the meat.

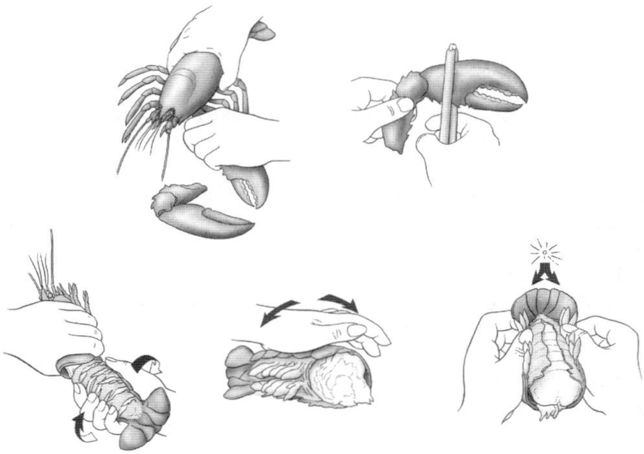

Snap the claws off the lobster and crack them; twist off the lobster tail; roll and press the tail, then peel off the shell.

Snap off the eight legs; on large lobsters, there is good meat in these. Snap each in half and use a skewer to push the meat out. Alternatively, leave them whole, insert the broken end of each in your mouth, and suck out the contents.

There are also small bits of meat in the body. Lift the protective shell, or carapace, from where it met the tail—it should come right off. Crack the body open lengthwise and pick out the meat between the gills and the legs. The tomalley and roe can also be removed. You may use the lobster shells to make Lobster Butter, 560.

For other approaches to serving this precious crustacean, see Lobster Rolls, 138, Lobster Bisque, 100, Lobster Salad Vinaigrette, 121, and Lobster or Shrimp Salad, 124.

STEAMED LOBSTER

This is the easiest method of preparation for the home cook, which also yields a much more concentrated cooking liquid for adding to sauces. If desired, freeze the lobsters for 2 hours to sedate them before cooking.

In a deep stockpot, bring to a boil over high heat:

1½ inches water

(1 cup or more white wine)

Add:

Live lobsters

Cover, weighting the lid to keep in the steam and the lobsters. Steam about 10 minutes for 1½-pound lobsters, plus about 3 minutes for each additional pound, until they turn bright red. Remove with tongs. For larger lobsters to be used for salads, hors d'oeuvre, or sauced dishes, plunge them into ice water to arrest further cooking.

Serve with:

(Individual bowls of the cooking liquid)

Melted butter

Lemon wedges

Provide each person with plenty of napkins, a shell cracker or nutcracker, and a bib. For instructions on how to remove the meat, see 360.

BOILED LOBSTER

There is only one good reason to boil lobsters instead of steaming them: If you are cooking several batches of lobster, the last few batches will be cooking in a lobster stock. Aside from this rare-use case—which is of dubious value—stick with steaming, as it is faster and easier. If desired, freeze the lobsters for 2 hours to sedate them before cooking.

Place in a large heavy pot enough water so the lobsters will be, completely covered when you plunge them in. Add for each quart of water:

1 tablespoon salt

Bring the water to a rolling boil. Carefully immerse, head first because of splashing:

$1\frac{1}{2}$- to $2\frac{1}{2}$-pound live lobsters

Cover, weight the lid, and allow the water to return to a boil. Reduce the heat at once and simmer the lobsters about 8 minutes for $1\frac{1}{2}$-pound lobsters, plus about 3 minutes for each additional pound, until they turn bright red. Drain.

Serve with:

Melted butter
Lemon wedges

Provide each person with plenty of napkins, a shell cracker or nutcracker, and a bib. For instructions on how to remove the meat, see 360.

GRILLED OR BROILED LOBSTER

2 servings

If desired, freeze the lobsters for 2 hours to sedate them before cooking.

Prepare a medium-hot grill fire, 1063, or preheat the broiler. Have ready:

Two $1\frac{1}{2}$-pound live lobsters

Kill them by cutting through the head as directed, 360. Turn the lobsters over and cut through the flesh of each one from head to tail, leaving the top shell intact, and pry the shells open so the lobsters lie flat like open books. Remove and discard the head sacs and tail veins. If broiling the lobsters, you may prepare a stuffing by removing both coral, if present, and tomalley and mixing them together with:

(2 tablespoons fresh bread crumbs, 957)
(2 teaspoons lemon juice or dry sherry)

Stuff it into the cavities. Brush the exposed lobster meat (and the stuffing, if using) with:

Melted butter or olive oil

Season to taste with:

Salt and black pepper

If grilling or broiling unstuffed, place shell side down over indirect heat on the grill or shell side up on a baking sheet under the broiler and cook about 10 minutes. If broiling stuffed, place shell side down on a baking sheet and broil about 10 minutes. Serve with:

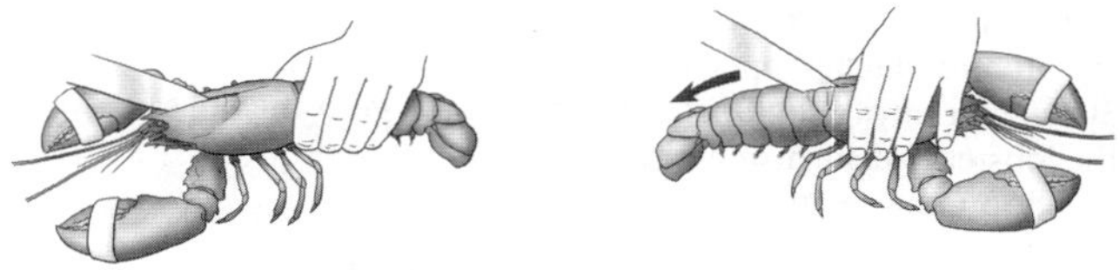

Cut forward through the head; to halve the lobster, cut back through the body and tail.

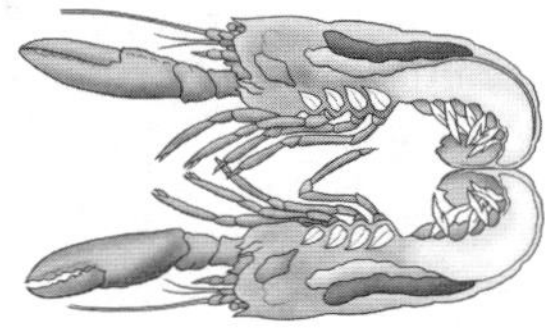

A halved lobster

Lemon wedges
Melted butter

LOBSTER AMÉRICAINE (OR ARMORICAINE)

2 servings

If desired, freeze the lobsters for 2 hours to sedate them before cooking. For a similar treatment with a little more zip, see Singaporean Chilli Crab, 359.

Place on a rimmed baking sheet to catch any juices:

Two $1\frac{1}{2}$-pound live lobsters

Kill them by cutting through the head as directed, 360. Cut through the body and back through the tail, severing the carapace in half. Cut off the claws and crack them once or twice to expose the meat. Remove and discard the head sacs and tail veins. Reserve the coral, if present, and tomalley for the sauce, if desired. Cut the tail halves from the body. Melt in a large skillet over medium heat:

3 tablespoons butter

Add and cook until softened:

2 shallots, chopped
2 garlic cloves, minced

Add the lobster pieces still in the shell. Cook, stirring frequently, until the shells are red, about 4 minutes. Add to the skillet:

3 tablespoons Cognac or brandy

Flambé, 1049. Add to the skillet to extinguish the flames:

1 cup dry white wine
$\frac{1}{2}$ cup fish stock or water
$\frac{3}{4}$ cup tomato puree

Add any reserved lobster juices, the coral, and tomalley, if using. Simmer about 15 minutes. Meanwhile, mash together with a fork until the mixture forms a paste:

2 tablespoons butter
2 tablespoons flour

Transfer the lobster pieces to a serving dish and whisk the butter-flour mixture into the sauce along with:

1 tablespoon chopped tarragon
Salt and black pepper to taste

Simmer briefly to slightly thicken the sauce. Pour the hot sauce over the lobster and garnish with:

Chopped parsley

BAKED STUFFED LOBSTER

2 servings

If desired, freeze the lobsters for 2 hours to sedate them before cooking.

Preheat the oven to 375°F. Toss together in a medium bowl:

1½ cups Browned or Buttered Bread Crumbs, 957
¼ cup chopped parsley
1 garlic clove, minced
½ teaspoon salt
½ teaspoon black pepper
2 tablespoons olive oil

Split lengthwise in half, as for Grilled or Broiled Lobster, 361, working on a rimmed baking sheet to collect the juices:

Two 1½- to 2-pound live lobsters

Remove and discard the head sacs and tail veins. Moisten the stuffing with 2 tablespoons of the lobster juices and, if desired, the flavorful tomalley. Lightly press the mixture into the body cavities and tails. Pour into the baking sheet:

¾ cup dry white wine

Bake the lobsters until the stuffing is very hot and browned on top and the tail meat feels firm when pressed with your finger, 30 to 35 minutes, basting the claws 2 or 3 times with the pan juices. If the stuffing looks dry, moisten it again with pan juices, but do not add more than a teaspoon or two, or the stuffing will become soggy.

LOBSTER THERMIDOR

2 servings

Béchamel is traditional, but crème fraîche is a wonderful shortcut.

Mix together in a bowl:

½ cup crème fraîche or Sauce Béchamel II, 548
1 tablespoon Dijon mustard
(1 tablespoon dry sherry, Madeira, or Cognac)
(¼ teaspoon minced tarragon, chervil, or thyme)

Set aside. Prepare, discarding the tomalley and coral:

2 Broiled Lobsters, 361, unstuffed

When the lobsters are cooked, remove from the oven, leaving the broiler on. Carefully remove the body and tail meat, keeping the shells intact. Snap the claws off, crack them, and pick the meat out. Dice the lobster meat and stir into the crème fraîche mixture along with any accumulated juices. Crumple up a large sheet of foil and spread it out on the baking sheet you used to broil the lobster. Nestle the lobster shells in the foil, cut side up, and fill them with the dressed lobster meat. If desired, sprinkle with:

(Shredded Gruyère)

Return to the broiler and cook until the tops are lightly browned.

LOBSTER NEWBURG

4 servings

You may substitute **2 cups lump crabmeat** for the lobster.

Steam, 360, or boil, 361:

Two 1½- to 2-pound live lobsters

Pick and dice the meat (you should have about 2 cups). Bring to a brisk simmer in a medium skillet over medium-high heat:

4 tablespoons (½ stick) butter
¼ cup Madeira or dry sherry
½ cup heavy cream

Cook for 2 minutes, then reduce the heat to medium-low. When the sauce is barely bubbling, slowly whisk in:

3 egg yolks

Cook, whisking constantly, until thickened. Season to taste with:

Salt

Stir in the diced lobster meat and cook briefly until heated through. Serve at once over:

Hot buttered toast

If desired, lightly sprinkle the smothered toasts with a dash of:

(Smoked paprika)

ABOUT SHRIMP

These small crustaceans are more popular in this country than any other seafood. To meet this insatiable demand and keep costs low, we import most of our shrimp from Asia and South America, where many of them are farm-raised. If your budget allows, try some of the superlative varieties native to our shores: the warm-water brown, white, and pink shrimp found from the Carolinas to the Gulf of Mexico, or the cold-water spot prawns and tiny bay shrimp of the Pacific. While there are slight differences in flavor and texture, all shrimp, including freshwater varieties, may be substituted for one another if size is taken into consideration for serving amounts and cooking time. **Prawn,** though technically a different species, is a term often used for larger shrimp.

When purchasing shrimp, be sure they are free of black spots (spot and tiger prawns are obvious exceptions). They should feel relatively dry and firm—not slimy or "sandy." They should not smell like ammonia or be overly fishy. Nearly all shrimp are frozen immediately after being caught. Unless you find yourself in an area known for shrimping, it follows that shrimp in the freezer section are just as "fresh" as the specimens in the fish case, which can deteriorate quickly in their thawed state. An added bonus: IQF (individually quick frozen) shrimp can be removed one at a time and thawed as needed.

Shrimp are sold by size, or count per pound. **U10** shrimp, under 10 per pound, are huge; **51/60** count, with 51 to 60 shrimp per pound, are quite small. Given that it is best to peel shrimp yourself (the shells make excellent stock, 78; freeze the shells in a plastic bag until you collect enough to make stock), it makes sense to buy the largest shrimp you can afford. Stay with those in the **16/20** or **26/30** count per pound range for a good combination of economy, size, and relative ease of peeling.

Though rare, **head-on shrimp** are available at some markets. For those who are not squeamish, this is good news, as cooked heads are filled with a rich treat (but be careful of their sharp, pointed "noses" or rostrums, which should be snipped off before cooking). If you prefer your meals to be less adventurous, keep in mind that heads add tremendous flavor to simmering stocks, soups, and sauces (freeze them in a bag for future use). Unfortunately, head-on shrimp deteriorate rather quickly. Be doubly sure they are not limp when you purchase them and use as soon as possible, preferably the day of purchase. Spot prawns in particular should either have their heads removed within hours of expiring or be cooked right away.

Three pounds of head-on shrimp will yield about 2 pounds shell-on shrimp. Once peeled, the yield will be about 1½ pounds. ➤ For each serving, plan on 1 pound of head-on shrimp, ⅔ to ¾ pound shell-on shrimp, or ⅓ to ½ pound peeled shrimp.

If you are grilling, broiling, or boiling shrimp, it is ➤ best to buy and cook shrimp in their shells, for it protects the meat from drying out and helps retain maximum flavor. Peeling is easy either before or after cooking. A slight tug releases the body shell from the tail. The small intestinal tract, or "vein," of a shrimp can impart a bitter taste, so deveining is recommended, especially for large shrimp, though not mandatory.

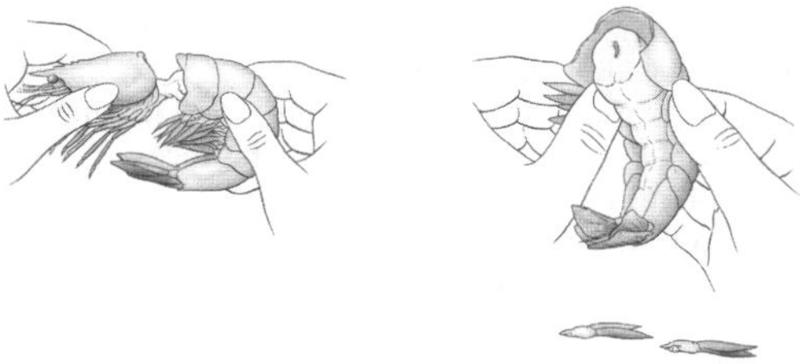

Peeling shrimp

To devein shrimp, make a shallow cut down the back of a peeled shrimp and pull out the vein with the tip of a small-pointed knife or deveining tool while holding the shrimp under running water. If you wish to devein while preserving some of the benefits of cooking in the shell, cut through the back of the shell and into the shrimp with a pair of small scissors, leaving the shell intact and pulling out the vein.

To butterfly shrimp, lay the shrimp peeled or unpeeled, on its side on a work surface. Starting about ¼ inch from the tail, make a cut along the inside curl of the shrimp (through the legs), without cutting the shrimp or shell in half. With your fingers, open the shrimp and flatten it with the palm of your hand so it lies almost flat.

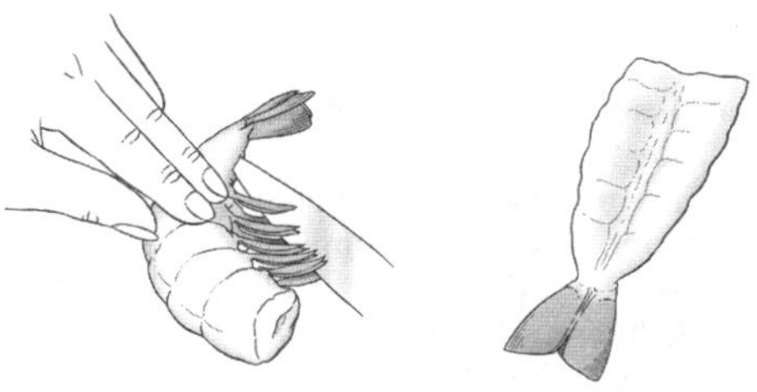

Butterflying shrimp

➤ For instructions on frying shrimp, see Deep-Fried Shellfish, 348, and Pan-Fried Shellfish, 348. For more shrimp recipes, see Satay Skewers, 61, Grilled or Broiled Shrimp Cockaigne, 65, Cajun Popcorn Shrimp, 65, Pickled Shrimp, 65, Rossejat de Fideos, 300, Pad Thai, 303, Tom Yum Goong, 101, Shellfish Paella, 34, Lobster or Shrimp Salad, 124, and The Mallory's Shrimp Salad, 121. For information on **dried shrimp,** see 1016.

QUICK SKILLET SHRIMP

2 servings

Quality, fresh shrimp need little more than brief cooking, butter, and lemon juice.

Place in a large nonstick skillet:

1 to 1½ pounds shell-on shrimp, deveined, above

Cover and cook in their own juices on medium to medium-high heat for 2 minutes. Uncover, stir, and cook until the shells turn pink and the flesh is opaque, an additional 2 minutes. Cover the table with newspaper, get a roll of paper towels, and serve immediately with:

Melted butter
Lemon wedges

BLACKENED SHRIMP

4 servings

A superlative dish for those who do not feel like they're cooking unless the smoke alarm goes off.

Prepare:

Cajun Blackening Spice, 587

Toss in a bowl with:

2 to 2½ pounds shell-on shrimp (preferably 26/30 or larger), deveined, above

Turn on an exhaust fan and open a window. Heat in a large skillet over high heat:

2 tablespoons vegetable oil

When the oil just barely starts to smoke, add the shrimp in a single layer and cook, turning once, until the shells turn pink and the flesh is opaque, about 1 minute per side. Serve with:

Lemon wedges

SALT-AND-PEPPER SHRIMP OR SQUID

4 servings

If using shrimp, the idea is to eat them shell and all. We are especially fond of the crispy shrimp legs after frying. Using head-on shrimp will take this dish from delicious to superb. Please read about Deep-Frying, 1051.

Whisk together in a medium bowl:

⅓ cup flour
⅓ cup cornstarch
2 teaspoons black pepper or ground Sichuan pepper
1 teaspoon salt
½ teaspoon baking soda

Toss in the flour mixture:

2 to 2½ pounds shell-on shrimp, deveined, above, 4 pounds head-on shrimp (sharp "noses" or rostrums cut off), or 1½ pounds squid, 368, cleaned and cut into bite-sized pieces

Shake off excess flour, place on a rack over a baking sheet, and refrigerate while the oil is heating. Heat to 365°F in a deep heavy pot or Dutch oven:

2 inches vegetable oil

In two batches, carefully lower the shrimp or squid into the oil and fry until golden brown and crisp, 2 to 3 minutes. Remove with a spider or slotted spoon to a rack over a baking sheet lined with paper towels to drain. If desired, sprinkle with more:

(Black pepper or ground Sichuan pepper)

POACHED OR "BOILED" SHRIMP

4 servings

This recipe creates a *court bouillon*, 80, a flavorful liquid, that is then used to poach the shrimp. If desired, however, you may simply cook the shrimp in plain, salted water.

Combine in a large saucepan:

2 celery ribs, cut into 2-inch pieces
1 medium onion, cut into eighths
1 small lemon, quartered
½ bunch parsley
8 black peppercorns
2 bay leaves
1 tablespoon salt
½ teaspoon cayenne pepper
10 cups water

Bring to a boil, then reduce the heat and simmer, uncovered, for 10 minutes. Strain the liquid and return it to the pan. Add:

2 to 2½ pounds shell-on shrimp, deveined, 363

Return the liquid to a boil, reduce the heat, and simmer, uncovered, for 2 to 3 minutes or until pink and firm. Drain the shrimp immediately and transfer to a platter to cool. If desired, serve with:

(Becker Cocktail Sauce, 569, Rémoulade Sauce, 564, or Tartar Sauce, 563)

BECKER BARBECUED SHRIMP

4 servings

Crusty bread dipped in the sauce is so tasty it's almost possible to ignore the shrimp. Unpeeled head-on shrimp, if available, are perfect for this recipe, if your guests do not mind making a delicious mess (have extra napkins handy).

Grind in a spice mill or coffee grinder:

2 teaspoons dried rosemary
1 teaspoon dried oregano
1 teaspoon red pepper flakes
1 teaspoon sweet paprika
1 teaspoon black peppercorns
1 teaspoon salt

Melt in a large skillet over medium heat:

4 tablespoons (½ stick) butter

Add the spice mixture and:

4 garlic cloves, minced

Cook, stirring, for 2 minutes. Add and cook for 4 to 5 minutes or until pink, stirring once or twice:

2 pounds large shell-on shrimp (26/30 or larger), peeled and deveined, 363, or 3 pounds unpeeled head-on shrimp (sharp "noses" or rostrums cut off)

Transfer the shrimp to a bowl. Add to the skillet:

½ cup chicken stock or broth
½ cup beer

Bring to a boil over high heat and cook for 1½ to 2 minutes. Remove from the heat and return the shrimp to the skillet to heat through. Season with:

2 tablespoons minced parsley
2 tablespoons lemon juice

Serve with:

Warm crusty bread

SHRIMP AND GRITS

4 servings

Prepare:

Creamy Grits, 323

Have ready:

1½ pounds shell-on shrimp (26/30 or larger), peeled and deveined, 363, reserving the shells

Set the shrimp aside and place the shells in a saucepan with:

2½ cups water

Bring to a boil, reduce the heat, and simmer until the liquid is reduced by half. Strain the liquid into a bowl, pressing on the shells. Discard the shells and set the broth aside. Cook in a large skillet over medium heat until the fat is rendered, 5 to 7 minutes:

4 slices bacon, cut crosswise into ½-inch pieces

Stir in and cook until lightly browned:

1 medium onion, finely chopped

Stir in and cook until fragrant:

2 garlic cloves, minced

Add and cook, stirring, until lightly browned, about 1 minute:

2 tablespoons all-purpose flour

Slowly stir in the reserved broth, then stir in:

(1½ cups chopped, seeded, and peeled, 281, tomatoes or one 14½-ounce can diced tomatoes)
¼ teaspoon salt
⅛ teaspoon cayenne pepper, or to taste

Bring to a simmer. Add the reserved shrimp and cook, stirring occasionally, until they are pink and the liquid is slightly thickened, about 5 minutes. Stir in:

¼ cup heavy cream or half-and-half

Serve the shrimp over the grits. Sprinkle with:

2 tablespoons chopped parsley

CAMARONES A LA DIABLA (SPICY SIMMERED SHRIMP)

4 servings

Add the smaller amount of árbol chiles for less heat. If you cannot find the dried chiles, you may substitute **3 canned chipotle peppers in adobo sauce,** but remove the seeds.

Combine in a medium saucepan:

3 Roma or plum tomatoes, quartered
½ medium onion, coarsely chopped
4 garlic cloves, peeled
4 to 6 dried chiles de árbol, to taste, stemmed
3 dried guajillo chiles, stemmed and seeded
½ teaspoon salt
¾ cup water

Bring to a boil, cover, and simmer until the onion and chiles are softened, about 15 minutes. Puree with an immersion blender (or in a food processor or regular blender) until smooth. Season to taste with:

Salt

Set aside. Heat in a large skillet over medium-high heat until hot:

2 tablespoons vegetable oil

Add the sauce and:

2 pounds medium shell-on shrimp, peeled and deveined, 363

Simmer the shrimp for a few minutes, until firm and pink. Serve in all its saucy glory with:

Cooked white rice, 343
Lime wedges
Chopped cilantro

SHRIMP CREOLE

6 servings

Combine in a heavy skillet over medium heat and cook, stirring frequently, until light brown:

¼ cup vegetable oil or butter
¼ cup all-purpose flour

Add and sauté until softened, about 8 minutes:

1 onion, chopped
1 celery rib, chopped
½ green bell pepper, chopped

Add and cook until fragrant, about 2 minutes:

3 garlic cloves, minced
2 teaspoons dried thyme
1 bay leaf
¼ to ½ teaspoon cayenne pepper, to taste
½ teaspoon salt
½ teaspoon black pepper

Add and stir to combine:

1 cup canned crushed tomatoes
1 cup shrimp or chicken stock or water
2 tablespoons tomato paste

Cover and simmer gently over medium-low heat for 20 minutes. Add:

1½ pounds medium to large shell-on shrimp, peeled and deveined, 363

Cook until the shrimp are firm and pink, about 5 minutes. Remove from the heat and taste the sauce for seasoning. Discard the bay leaf. Serve with:

Cooked white rice, 343
Hot pepper sauce
Chopped parsley

CAMARONES AL MOJO DE AJO (SHRIMP IN GARLIC-CITRUS SAUCE)

4 servings

This is a simpler version of traditional *mojo de ajo*, a sauce made of slowly caramelized garlic, lime juice, and chiles.

Heat in a large skillet over medium heat until shimmering:

¼ cup vegetable oil

Add and cook, stirring, until golden:

8 garlic cloves, finely chopped

Stir in and cook for 30 seconds:

½ teaspoon red pepper flakes

Add:

⅓ cup lime juice
⅓ cup orange juice

Bring to a simmer and cook until reduced by three-quarters—it will look thickened and slightly syrupy. Add:

2 pounds medium shell-on shrimp, peeled and deveined, 363
½ teaspoon salt

Cook, stirring occasionally, until the shrimp are firm and pink, 3 to 4 minutes. Serve with:

Crusty bread

COCONUT SHRIMP

4 servings

Prepare **Deep-Fried Shellfish II, 348,** using shrimp and the beer batter, but substitute **orange juice** for the beer. After dipping the shrimp in the batter, press them into a mixture of **3 cups shredded unsweetened coconut** and **1 cup dry bread crumbs.** Fry as directed. If desired, serve with (**Fruit Salsa, 574**).

SHRIMP SCAMPI

4 servings

Made popular by Italian-American restaurants in the 1950s, this dish deserves its status as a classic, and is equally delicious made with the same amount of bay scallops, cut-up cleaned squid, 368, or precooked octopus, 368.

Combine in a large skillet over medium heat:

3 tablespoons olive oil
3 garlic cloves, minced
½ teaspoon red pepper flakes
¼ teaspoon salt

Cook, stirring, until fragrant, about 1 minute. Increase the heat to medium-high and add:

½ cup dry white wine or chicken broth

Boil until reduced by half, about 3 minutes. Add:

2 pounds large shell-on shrimp, peeled and deveined, 363

Cook, stirring occasionally, until the shrimp are firm and pink, about 5 minutes. Sprinkle with:

¼ cup minced parsley
1 tablespoon lemon juice

Serve with:

Crusty bread, Creamy Polenta, 322, or cooked linguine or bucatini

GRILLED OR BROILED SHRIMP OR SCALLOPS

4 servings

I. BASIC

Feel free to improvise with the seasoning. Many pastes and rubs, 583–87, can be substituted for the simple treatment here.

Prepare a hot grill fire, 1063, or preheat the broiler and place the broiler rack as close to the heat as possible. Toss to coat in a shallow bowl:

2 pounds large shell-on shrimp, peeled and deveined, 363, or sea scallops, side "hinge" removed, 354, or a combination
2 tablespoons olive oil
1 teaspoon salt
1 teaspoon black pepper, sweet paprika, or chili powder
(1 tablespoon sherry vinegar)

If grilling, thread the shellfish onto skewers (or use a grilling basket) to keep them from falling into the fire. Grill or broil, turning the shrimp after the first side turns pink, about 2 minutes; or turn the scallops when the first side becomes opaque, 2 to 3 minutes. Grill or broil until the second side is pink or opaque; test one of the shrimp or scallops by cutting into it to make sure it is cooked through. Serve garnished with:

Lemon wedges, minced parsley or cilantro, and extra-virgin olive oil

Or tossed with:

Vinaigrette, 575, flavored with fresh herbs and made with lemon juice, or Chimichurri, 567

II. GLAZED

Prepare and have ready:

Hoisin-Ginger Glaze, 578, Teriyaki Marinade reduced to a glaze, 582, Chipotle Barbecue Sauce, 582, or Vietnamese Caramel Sauce, 578

Preheat the grill or broiler and season the shrimp as for **I, 365.** Cook for the first 2 minutes, but before turning the shrimp or scallops, brush the top sides with one of the glazes (if using Vietnamese Caramel Sauce, apply it sparingly). Turn and grill or broil for 2 minutes more. Turn again, move the shellfish to a cooler part of the grill or adjust the broiler rack to the center of the oven, and brush again with glaze. Turn and brush every minute or so for 3 to 4 minutes, until the shellfish has developed a nice glaze and is cooked through. Serve with:

Minced green onion

SHRIMP FAJITAS

Prepare **Steak Fajitas, 459,** substituting **1½ pounds peeled and deveined shrimp, 363,** for the steak. Marinate for 30 minutes to 1 hour. Broil or sauté the shrimp until firm and pink, 4 to 5 minutes. Or, to grill, thread onto bamboo skewers that have been soaked in water for 1 hour and grill as directed in Grilled or Broiled Shrimp or Scallops I, 365.

BAKED STUFFED JUMBO SHRIMP

4 servings

We call for two different sizes of shrimp because it is cheaper to buy smaller shrimp for the stuffing mixture. However, if you wish to simplify your grocery list, just buy more jumbo shrimp.

Position a rack in the upper third of the oven. Preheat the oven to 450°F. Butterfly, 363:

2 pounds shell-on shrimp (16/20 or larger)

Prepare:

Stuffing for Baked Stuffed Lobster, 362, using fresh bread crumbs instead of browned and 6 tablespoons melted butter instead of olive oil

Stir in:

4 ounces small shrimp, peeled and chopped

Arrange the large shrimp in a single layer in a shallow baking dish and top with the stuffing, pressing it lightly so it adheres. Pour around the shrimp, just enough to cover the bottom of the baking dish:

Dry white wine or chicken stock or broth

Bake until the shrimp are piping hot, 10 to 12 minutes. Serve immediately.

THAI SHRIMP CURRY

4 servings

We like our curries very spicy, sour, salty, and a little sweet, but feel free to adjust the seasonings to suit your taste.

Heat in a large skillet over medium heat:

1 tablespoon vegetable oil

Add and cook, stirring, until fragrant, about 2 minutes:

3 tablespoons red or green curry paste, store-bought or homemade, 585

Stir in:

1 red or yellow bell pepper, cut into thin strips
2 large shallots or ½ medium onion, thinly sliced
2 garlic cloves, minced

Cook until just starting to soften, about 4 minutes, using a sturdy spatula to scrape up browning curry paste off the bottom of the skillet. Stir in:

One 13½-ounce can coconut milk
1 to 2 tablespoons fish sauce, to taste
1 tablespoon palm sugar or brown sugar

Bring the mixture to a simmer and add:

1½ pounds shell-on shrimp, peeled and deveined, 363

Cook until the shrimp are firm and pink, 2 to 3 minutes. Stir in:

2 tablespoons lime juice
(15 Thai basil leaves)

Taste and add salt, more fish sauce, or more lime juice as desired. Serve with:

Cooked white rice, 343
Chopped cilantro

SHRIMP OR CRAWFISH ÉTOUFFÉE

4 to 6 servings

Melt in a large skillet or Dutch oven over medium heat:

6 tablespoons butter

Gradually whisk in:

¼ cup all-purpose flour

Cook, stirring constantly, until the roux is almost as dark as milk chocolate, about 20 minutes. Stir in:

1 medium onion, chopped
2 celery ribs, chopped
1 small green bell pepper, chopped

Cook, stirring, until the vegetables are softened, 5 to 6 minutes. The roux will continue to darken to a deep mahogany color. Add:

4 garlic cloves, chopped
1 teaspoon dried thyme
1 teaspoon salt
½ teaspoon cayenne pepper

Stir well and cook for 1 minute more. Stir in:

2 cups chicken stock or Shrimp or Shellfish Stock, 78, made from the shrimp shells, or water
2 tablespoons tomato paste
1 tablespoon Worcestershire sauce
¼ teaspoon hot pepper sauce, or to taste

Stirring constantly, bring the sauce to a simmer. Add:

2 pounds medium to large shell-on shrimp, peeled and deveined, 363, or crayfish tails (from 10 pounds head-on crayfish)

Bring the liquid back to a simmer. Reduce the heat so the sauce bubbles gently, cover, and cook until the shrimp or crayfish are firm and pink, about 10 minutes. Add:

4 green onions, finely chopped
¼ cup chopped parsley

Season to taste with:

Salt and black pepper
Hot pepper sauce

Serve with:

Cooked rice, 343

ABOUT CRAYFISH OR CRAWFISH (ÉCREVISSES)

One of the thrills Irma's parents had was to find in Missouri streams the crayfish they had so relished in Europe. These miniature freshwater lobsters were brought to the table in great steaming crimson mounds, garnished with dill or swimming in their own juices—that is, *à la nage*. Peeled crayfish tails lend themselves to all kinds of combinations and sauces, but the connoisseur is happy to consume them *au naturel*, preferably with their juicy heads. Though found in freshwater streams and swamps throughout the country, most commercially available crayfish is farmed in Louisiana and sold live from midwinter through spring. A small percentage is processed and sold frozen. Species native to North America are the size of very large shrimp—from 15 to 20 per pound. Not all crayfish are so diminutive: A single Australian crayfish can top out at 10 pounds or more.

When buying live crayfish, sort out and discard dead ones. For small crayfish, expect about 20 percent of a crayfish's weight to be picked meat, or ➤1 pound of meat for every 4 to 5 pounds of small crayfish. Larger, mature crayfish have larger claws, and can yield as little as 8 percent their weight in tail meat. On average, purchase 3 to 4 pounds of live crayfish per serving.

You can occasionally find fresh, uncooked peeled crayfish tails for purchase at seafood markets. These should be cooked as soon as they are purchased. Whole crayfish are also available precooked and frozen, as are peeled crayfish tails. Unfortunately, this makes them more perishable, so use them within 6 months of their processing date. ➤A 1-pound package of fresh or frozen tails will serve 3 people.

➤ Live crayfish are very perishable and should be eaten as soon as possible. Barring immediate consumption, they may be stored in the refrigerator, covered with a damp cloth or paper towel, for no more than a day. As with other live shellfish, leave the bag or cooler you are storing them in unsealed, otherwise they will suffocate.

To clean crayfish, rinse them well in several changes of cold water until the water stays clear. If they have been kept in fresh running water before you bought them, their guts or "veins" will likely be purged. If not, purge them by soaking in several changes of water over a period of 6 hours, as processors do. If time is of the essence and you still wish to devein crayfish before cooking, you can humanely dispatch them with a sharp knife through the head or by freezing for 2 hours. If you plan to serve the tail meat in a dish like Crawfish Pie, 704, or Shrimp or Crawfish Étouffée, 366, the easiest option is to cook them first, twist the tail from the body, peel, and devein as for shrimp, 363.

BOILED CRAYFISH

Allow about 1 dozen per serving

Have ready:

Fresh crayfish, cleaned, above, or frozen whole crayfish

Fill a large pot with water and add:

1 leek, halved and cleaned, or 1 small onion, chopped
Parsley sprigs
1 carrot, chopped
(3 tablespoons distilled white or cider vinegar)

Bring to a boil. Drop the crayfish one by one into the boiling water at a rate that will not disturb the boil and cook no longer than 5 to 7 minutes, until the shells turn red. Serve in the shell, with plenty of:

Melted butter

seasoned with:

Minced dill or Cajun Blackening Spice, 587

Crayfish are eaten with the fingers; serve with napkins and finger bowls. Separate the tail from the body, and crack open the tail by holding it between the thumbs and forefingers of both hands and forcing it back against the curve of the shell.

CAJUN-STYLE CRAWFISH BOIL

8 servings

True Cajuns may scoff at the suggestion that less than 4 or 5 pounds of crayfish per serving is adequate, but we find these proportions more appropriate for a home crayfish boil.

Pour 5 quarts water into a large stockpot and add:

2 large onions, quartered
2 lemons, quartered
One 6-ounce container crab boil seasoning
¼ cup salt
¼ cup Tabasco sauce
1 head garlic, halved crosswise

Bring to a boil and cook for 10 minutes. Add and simmer for 10 minutes:

2 pounds small red potatoes

Add and simmer for 5 minutes:

3 ears corn, shucked and cut into 3-inch pieces
1½ pounds andouille or Cajun-style boudin sausage, cut into ½-inch pieces

Add and simmer until bright red and cooked through, about 5 minutes:

10 pounds whole crayfish, fresh and cleaned, above, or thawed frozen

Transfer the crayfish, sausage, and vegetables with a slotted spoon to a large platter. Serve on a table covered with newspaper along with bowls of the cooking liquid and:

Crusty French bread
Softened butter
Tabasco sauce

ABOUT OCTOPUS, SQUID, AND CUTTLEFISH

These inkfish belong to the category of odd-looking sea creatures known collectively as cephalopods. They all have long, edible arms, a body that can be formed into a natural sack for stuffing, and an ink-expelling sac, which the creature uses to create an escape screen in the water. **Octopus** and **squid** are found in abundance on both coasts of North America. **Cuttlefish,** similar to squid in the kitchen aside from their large cuttlebones, are imported from across the Atlantic, Asia, and the South Pacific.

Freezing and thawing is common before sale for all inkfish, and does not diminish quality significantly, so long as they remain plump, shiny, and fresh smelling. You may keep them frozen for up to 3 months. Octopus is generally sold between 1 and 4 pounds, with 2 being ideal. Look for small squid and cuttlefish (8 inches long or less), as they are tenderer. Squid is also known as **calamari,** its Italian name. ➤ Allow about ½ pound per serving.

In general, squid and cuttlefish can either be cooked for a very brief time (less than 2 minutes) to a tender-but-snappy texture (no more than a "rare" 130°F internal temperature, though measuring can be difficult), or they must be cooked for quite a while to break down their collagen into gelatin (at least 30 minutes). In between those extremes, they will be tough and chewy. Octopus is often too tough for brief cooking and should first be tenderized by precooking before sautéing, grilling, or frying. Though not as dramatic as pounding with a mallet or hurling against rocks, simmering is the more reliable and convenient method for tenderizing octopus.

To precook octopus, simmer it in water to cover with 1 tablespoon salt, 1 bay leaf, 2 crushed garlic cloves, and a few black peppercorns. Test for tenderness after 45 minutes by piercing it with a knife; ➤ it is ready when the knife meets little resistance, which may take up to 2 hours. Alternatively, octopus may be cooked in a stovetop or electric pressure cooker, at full pressure, for 15 minutes. Allow the pressure to release naturally for 10 minutes, then quick-release the remaining pressure by opening the release valve to vent the steam. If the octopus is still tough, pressure-cook it for 5 minutes more.

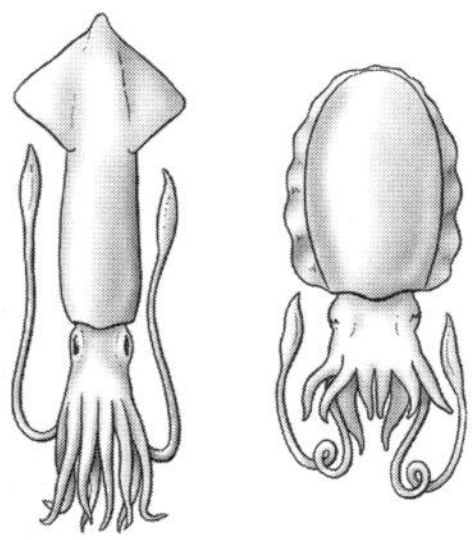

Squid and cuttlefish

Inkfish are generally sold cleaned, but if necessary, cleaning is easy.

To clean fresh octopus, trim off the mouth and eyes, taking care not to pierce the ink sac, which lies close by. Cut off the head, turn it inside out, and rinse away its contents. Remove the hard beak from the body by pushing it through the opening at the end of the body. Massage under running water to remove all mud from the suckers. The skin is edible but most will come off during cooking.

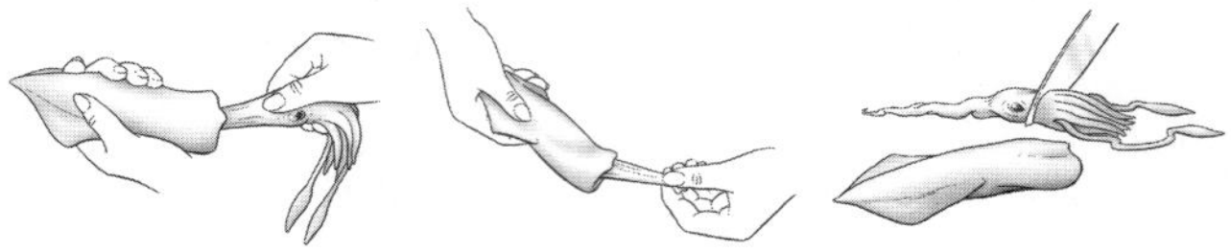

Cleaning a squid

To clean squid, grasp the head and innards by reaching far up inside the body, and pull gently, removing the translucent quill as well. Feel the head for a hard lump. This is the beak. Remove it, then cut off the tentacles below the eyes. Cut off the fins (which are edible, if slightly tougher) and use a dull knife blade to scrape the purplish skin from the body. Turn the body inside out and scrape off any innards. Rinse the body and tentacles. You may leave the body whole for stuffing (the tentacles can be chopped and used in the stuffing), or cut the body into rings and the tentacles into bite-sized pieces. For grilling, broiling, and searing, butterfly the body so that it lies flat, and carefully score the flesh in a diamond pattern with a sharp knife. This simplifies handling, keeps the squid from curling up, and helps marinades and seasonings adhere.

Clean cuttlefish as for squid, except first slice the body lengthwise to make it easier to remove the innards. You may need to cut the cuttlebone out with a knife.

➤ The small gray ink sac of squid or cuttlefish can be carefully cut away and its contents used to lend a saline flavor and inky black color to risotto, 336–37, paella, 334, Rossejat de Fideos, 300, and Fresh Pasta Dough, 294.

Squid responds well to deep-frying, 348, especially when served with Aïoli, 564, or Marinara Sauce, 556. Also see Salt-and-Pepper Shrimp or Squid, 363.

GRILLED OR CHARRED SQUID

4 servings

Prepare a very hot grill fire, 1063, or set a cast-iron skillet over medium-high heat. Toss in a shallow bowl to coat:

2 pounds squid, cleaned, above, tentacles cut off, bodies halved lengthwise
2 tablespoons olive oil
(1 tablespoon sherry vinegar or other vinegar)
½ teaspoon salt

When the fire or pan is good and hot, add the squid and cook about 1 minute, 2 at most, until firm and seared. Turn and cook for another minute. Be careful—overcooking will make the squid tough. Serve immediately with:

Lemon wedges and minced parsley, Salsa Verde, 567, or Vinaigrette, 575, flavored with fresh herbs

STUFFED SQUID

6 servings

Clean, 368:

Twelve 5-inch squid

Chop the tentacles and set aside.

Preheat the oven to 400°F. Prepare:

½ recipe Parsley and Bread Crumb Stuffing, 534

Mix in the chopped tentacles. Stuff each squid body with 2 tablespoons stuffing. Place in a single layer in a baking dish. Combine in a medium bowl:

½ cup dry white wine
½ cup water
¼ cup olive oil
¼ cup tomato sauce or crushed canned tomatoes
¼ cup finely chopped parsley
¼ teaspoon salt

Pour over the squid. Bake until the squid are tender, about 30 minutes. Serve hot or cold.

GRILLED MARINATED OCTOPUS

4 servings

Precook, 368:

One 2- to 2½-pound octopus, cleaned, 368

Separate the tentacles from the body. Combine in a large bowl:

⅓ cup olive oil
⅓ cup red wine vinegar
6 sprigs oregano
(Several sprigs thyme)
3 garlic cloves, smashed
½ teaspoon red pepper flakes
½ teaspoon salt

Add the octopus pieces, tossing to coat with the marinade. Cover and marinate, refrigerated, at least 2 hours and up to 24 hours.

Prepare a hot grill fire, 1063. Remove the octopus from the marinade, allowing excess to drip off. Grill the octopus until well charred on both sides, about 6 minutes per side. Transfer to a cutting board. If desired, leave the tentacles whole or slice into ½-inch-thick pieces. Cut the body into strips or chunks. If desired, serve with:

(Shaved Fennel and White Bean Salad, 129)

Or serve on a bed of:

(Arugula and boiled baby potatoes dressed with some of the octopus marinade)

With:

Crusty bread
Drizzle of extra-virgin olive oil
Lemon wedges

TAKO POKE (KOREAN-STYLE OCTOPUS POKE)

4 servings

Pronounced "poh-kay," this version of the Hawaiian raw tuna preparation (see Tuna or Salmon Poke, 377) is spicier, with a bit of tang from the kimchi. This dish is perfect as a summery appetizer or as part of a main course.

Prepare or purchase:

1 pound cooked octopus, 368, cut into ½-inch cubes

Meanwhile, whisk together in a medium bowl:

3 tablespoons tamari or soy sauce
1 tablespoon gochujang, 970
1 tablespoon toasted sesame oil

Stir in the cooked octopus along with:

½ cup finely chopped kimchi with its juice
2 green onions, thinly sliced, or ¼ cup finely chopped sweet onion
1 teaspoon toasted sesame seeds

Marinate, covered and refrigerated, for at least 10 minutes and up to 1 day before serving. Serve over bowls of:

Cooked short-grain rice, 343

ABOUT CONCH AND WHELK

Conch and whelk are gastropods, or large marine snails. ➤ It is now illegal to harvest live conch in US waters—they are on the endangered species list. Most conch comes from the Caribbean islands. You can order legally harvested, usually farmed, conch from Internet retailers. It should be cooked and frozen. If you have a live conch, ➤ poach in the shell in boiling water for 5 minutes. Once cooked, you can easily grab the meat with a fork or skewer and pull out a substantial—4 ounces or so—piece of meat. Conch and whelk can be cooked the same ways. Both are tender and delicious when raw or cooked minimally; more often their meat is cooked long enough so it toughens and then becomes tender again, like squid.

Conch and whelk can be braised, stewed, or precooked as for octopus, 368, and fried, 348. Because of their mild, sweet clam-like flavor, both can be substituted for clams in chowder and pasta.

CONCH OR WHELK SALAD

4 servings

Trim all the orange and dark flesh from:

4 conchs or whelks, cut into chunks (2 cups)

Bring a large saucepan of water to a boil. Add the conch and simmer for 30 minutes. Drain.

Combine in a large bowl:

1 large tomato, chopped
½ red onion, chopped
½ red bell pepper, chopped
½ cucumber, chopped
1 jalapeño or habanero pepper, seeded and minced
¼ cup chopped cilantro
¼ cup lime juice
2 tablespoons orange juice
2 tablespoons olive oil
Salt and black pepper to taste

Add the conch and toss to mix. Serve over:

Romaine leaves

ABOUT IMITATION CRAB AND LOBSTER (SURIMI)

Surimi, often sold as imitation crab legs or lobster chunks, is a processed form of white fish fillets (usually, but not always, Pacific pollock), shaped and colored to look like crabmeat, which it does—right down to the dyed pinkish red edges. Surimi is best used as a substitute for crab in mayonnaise-based recipes such as salads, creamy dips, and soups. See Lobster or Shrimp Salad, 124, Hot Crab Dip, 52, or Makizushi (Rolled Sushi), 335.

ABOUT TURTLES

In the United States, only farm-raised freshwater turtles and limited species of wild freshwater turtles can legally be used for food. ➤ Sea turtle populations have been protected by the Endangered Species Act since 1973, and the **diamondback terrapin**—once prized for its tender flesh in soup—is now protected by state laws all along the Eastern Seaboard. The turtles most frequently caught or farmed and consumed in temperate North America are **freshwater turtles,** such as the **snapping turtle,** which abound in lakes and streams from North Dakota to Florida. Aptly named as to disposition, they are quite a different kettle of fish: short-tempered and capable of inflicting nasty bites.

➤ We do not recommend attempting to prepare live turtles in the domestic kitchen. For those who remain undiscouraged, we add a word of caution: If catching turtles yourself, make sure they are from a clean, unpolluted area, as they can accumulate toxins. Also keep in mind that the **Eastern box turtle** has been known to consume poisonous mushrooms, making them especially risky to prepare. Most of us are content to eat the highly prized, gelatinous meat of turtles found cooked and canned or raw and frozen from Internet retailers.

TURTLE SOUP

4 to 6 servings

Melt in a heavy saucepan over medium heat:

2 tablespoons butter

Add and brown, about 7 minutes:

1 pound canned or thawed turtle meat, cut into ½-inch chunks

Add and cook until the vegetables soften, about 5 minutes:

1 onion, chopped
3 celery ribs, chopped
3 garlic cloves, minced
1 jalapeño pepper, minced
½ green bell pepper, chopped
1½ teaspoons dried oregano
1½ teaspoons dried thyme
2 bay leaves

Add and bring to a boil:

4 cups beef or veal stock or broth

Reduce the heat and simmer for 25 minutes. Meanwhile, melt in a small saucepan:

4 tablespoons (½ stick) butter

Stir in and cook, stirring, over medium heat until golden brown, about 8 minutes:

¼ cup all-purpose flour

Gradually whisk the roux into the soup and simmer for another 20 minutes, whisking occasionally. Add and simmer for 10 minutes:

1½ cups chopped peeled, 281, tomatoes
¾ cup dry sherry
1 tablespoon hot pepper sauce
1½ teaspoons Worcestershire sauce
Juice of ½ lemon

Discard the bay leaves. Season to taste with:

Salt and black pepper

Garnish with:

Watercress
Chopped Hard-Boiled Egg, 151

ABOUT SNAILS

The Romans, who were passionate about snails, grew them on ranches where they were fed special foods like bay leaves, wine, and spicy soups as a "preseasoning." Some things haven't changed—today most snails are farmed. If you gather them yourself, follow these directions: For 10 days to 2 weeks, feed them on lettuce leaves, removing the old leaves and furnishing new ones every few days. Then, ➤ scrub your wild snails—or purchased ranch-raised snails—until all slime is removed.

Put into a large stainless steel or enameled pot:

50 large snails, well scrubbed

Mix together to dissolve the salt:

1 gallon water
¼ cup distilled white vinegar
½ cup salt

Pour enough of this liquid over the snails to cover them. Swish them around in the pot, then drain and rinse them. Repeat this entire process two more times, or until the water remains clear. Discard any snails whose heads have not by this time popped out of their shells, drain the rest of the snails well, and return them to the pot.

Add enough to cover the snails:

Boiling water

Place the pot over high heat and boil the snails for 5 minutes. Drain and cool, then remove the snails from the shells with a small fork; reserve the shells. Hold the upper part of each snail with your thumb and forefinger and score the lower part of the body so you can pull out the swollen intestinal tube. Discard it. Transfer the snails to a medium saucepan and add:

2 cups light stock or broth or water
2 cups dry white wine

Bring to a boil, then reduce the heat to a simmer, cover, and cook until tender, about 3 hours. Add during the last 30 minutes of cooking:

4 sprigs parsley
3 sprigs thyme
1 bay leaf
¼ teaspoon white or black peppercorns
(2 whole cloves)
2 garlic cloves, smashed

Allow the snails to cool in the liquid and store, refrigerated, for up to 3 days. Drain before using in the following recipe, or in any way you choose.

BAKED BUTTERED SNAILS

8 servings

Prepare snails as described on 370 or have ready:

(50 canned snails, drained and rinsed)

(50 empty, clean snail shells)

Have ready:

Triple recipe of Snail Butter, 560

Dry the snails and shells with a cloth. Pipe 1 teaspoon of the butter into each shell. Place a snail in each shell. Pipe more butter over the snails, generously covering them so that only the herbed butter is visible at the opening. You may refrigerate the snails for later use, or bake them at once. Preheat the oven to 425°F. In a baking dish, spread a layer of:

Rock salt

Arrange the snails in the dish, pressing them gently into the salt. Bake just long enough to get them piping hot, 5 to 7 minutes. Serve in snail dishes.

ABOUT FROG LEGS

Light pink, meaty frog legs, often compared to chicken in texture and flavor, should be gently cooked to preserve their sweetness. They are primarily sold frozen, in pairs attached at the hip, skinned and ready to cook. Fresh frog legs are harvested in the South and Midwest in the spring and summer and some people go frog "gigging" during this time. ➤ Allow 2 to 3 large or 6 small frog legs per person.

To prepare frogs for cooking, cut off and discard the feet; then cut off the hind legs—the only part of the frog used—close to the body. Wash the legs in cold water. Begin at the top and strip off the skin like a glove. Through an experiment with a twitching frog leg, Galvani discovered the electric current that bears his name. Should you prefer keeping your kitchen and your scientific activities separate and distinct, chill the frog legs before skinning.

BRAISED FROG LEGS

2 servings

Rinse and skin, above, if necessary:

8 large frog legs

Combine in a shallow bowl:

½ cup flour

½ teaspoon salt

¼ teaspoon black pepper

Dredge the frog legs in the seasoned flour. Heat in a large skillet over medium heat:

3 tablespoons butter or vegetable oil

Add the frog legs and cook until browned, about 4 minutes per side. Transfer to a plate. Add to the skillet and cook until softened:

½ medium onion, chopped

¼ teaspoon salt

¼ teaspoon black pepper

Return the frog legs to the skillet and pour in:

¾ cup chicken stock or broth

Bring to a boil, then reduce the heat, cover tightly and simmer for 10 minutes.

Meanwhile, melt in a small skillet:

2 tablespoons butter

Add and toast in the butter:

½ cup dry bread crumbs

(¼ cup finely chopped hazelnuts)

Transfer the frog legs to a serving dish. Bring the stock and onion mixture in the skillet to a boil and stir in:

2 tablespoons heavy cream

Cook briefly until thickened and pour the sauce over the frog legs. Sprinkle with the bread crumbs and:

Chopped parsley

DEEP-FRIED FROG LEGS

Please read about Deep-Frying, 1051.

Clean and divide in half at the hip joint:

Frog legs

Dip them in:

Bound Bread Crumb or Cracker Coating, 658

Let dry on a plate or rack for 1 hour. Heat to 365°F in a deep heavy pot or Dutch oven:

2 inches vegetable oil

Fry the frog legs, turning once, until golden. Drain on a plate lined with paper towels. Serve with:

Tartar Sauce, 563

FISH

From beachside shacks and suburban sushi counters to community fish fries and home kitchens, the preparation and presentation of fish is as varied as the myriad types we catch and eat. Unfortunately, fish consumption has become somewhat fraught in the last few decades. Destructive practices have depleted popular fisheries and disrupted ecosystems. Climate change and the warming of the world's oceans have compounded this predicament. In other words, buying and consuming fish is not so carefree as it once was; now, it is best to make considered choices at the fish counter. For guidance on making responsible purchases, see Sustainability, Traceability, and Fish Fraud, 394.

For many, the fear of overcooking or marring the delicate flesh of an increasingly precious protein can be discouraging, even prohibitive. Please take heart and remember that, with a few basic considerations, fish is very easy and quick to prepare, highly nutritious, and can still be consumed in a responsible way.

When in doubt, a trustworthy fishmonger is an invaluable resource in the purchasing and cooking of fish. As many species of fish with healthy populations are likely to be unfamiliar to the average cook, view the fishmonger as a repository of information and, rather than avoiding the unfamiliar, embrace it as an opportunity to learn and try something new. Further, do not view the recipes in this chapter as immutable formulas: Substitute fish based on your budget and what is available; for guidance on how to substitute similar varieties, see Commonly Cooked Fish, 394.

FISH SAFETY AND NUTRITION

Fish are high in protein and omega-3 fatty acids, making them an excellent source of overall nutrition. The catch, so to speak, is the risk posed by **pollutants** in fish—like mercury, industrial chemicals, and pesticides. Mercury and other heavy metals are picked up by smaller, krill-eating fish, which are then eaten by larger fish. When still larger fish eat these, the totality of mercury that has collected in smaller species is passed up the food chain, thus concentrating in the ecosystem's top predators. Over time, the amount of mercury in a long-living predatory fish can become quite high. This is called bioaccumulation.

As a result, ➤ it is best to avoid (or severely limit) eating large or long-lived predatory fish like shark, swordfish, king mackerel, tilefish, marlin, orange roughy, bigeye tuna, and yellowfin (ahi) tuna. A good rule of thumb when buying fish is to purchase those lower on the food chain. Smaller fish are much less likely to contain harmful levels of mercury and other toxins. Another good strategy is to consume a wide variety of fish from several sources, rather than sticking to one favorite type.

➤ The most current FDA recommendations are for adults to eat 2 to 3 servings of low-mercury fish or shellfish per week, 1 to 2 servings for children. These include salmon, pollock, canned "light" tuna, tilapia, catfish, and cod. Some popular pantry staples—like canned white albacore tuna—can be relatively high in mercury, but it is fine to consume them in moderation (about 1 serving per week).

Parasites are also common in fish. These organisms are typically killed either by freezing or by cooking. Most parasites in saltwater fish are not transferrable to humans, meaning that even if you ingest a live one, it will die in the digestion process. Freshwater fish may harbor tapeworms, which, unlike most fish parasites, can infect humans. Fish sold as "sushi grade," meaning it is intended for raw consumption, is frozen at very low temperatures for a specific period of time to kill parasites. Tuna is the rare exception: Its flesh is parasite-free. For all other fish, ➤ if you plan to serve it raw, 377, ask to make sure it is "sushi-grade."

If you catch your own fish, ➤ do not eat it raw unless you are able to freeze it at –4°F or below for at least 7 days (verify this with an accurate freezer thermometer). Be aware that most upright home freezers do not reach these low temperatures (chest freezers will, depending on the make and model).

BUYING AND STORING FISH

As noted at the beginning of the chapter, many popular fisheries are in poor shape, and we urge you to make informed decisions when choosing fish to prepare. For more on sustainable choices, traceability, and farmed or wild fish, see 394. Sourcing aside, there are some simple rules that will help you bring home high-quality fish. First, ➤ buy the fish the day you are going to eat it, or at most the day before. If your plans change and you find you are not going to cook it, freeze it (see below).

➤ For each serving allow: 12 ounces whole fish; 8 ounces if the head, tail, and fins have been removed; or 6 ounces fish steak or fillet.

Fresh fish should positively glisten, have pink or bright red gills, clear eyes that are not sunken in, and firm, almost translucent flesh. It should not have spots of pink (which are usually bruises) or brown (which indicate spoilage). A whitish dry or chalky appearance on the surface of the flesh may indicate moisture loss or freezer burn. It should smell like the sea, even cucumber-y (it will, of course, also smell somewhat like fish, but it should smell fresh). ➤ Fish should be gutted as soon as possible after they are caught. Unless they are straight from a holding tank, do not buy ungutted fish.

After buying fresh fish, keep it on ice or in a cooler on the way home. Home refrigerators are not cold enough for maximum preservation, so ➤ store fillets and steaks in their original wrapping on ice in the refrigerator. Whole fish may be kept directly on ice. A large colander full of ice placed over a bowl works well, or fill a large baking dish or roasting pan with ice for longer whole fish.

FROZEN FISH

Since large fishing boats go out for weeks at a time, fish that is frozen on board these ships will be fresher than any that has merely been chilled. As long as the freezing process is fast (and the thawing gradual), frozen fish can be of very good quality. Buy only solidly frozen packages. They should not be torn, misshapen, show evidence of freezer burn, or have large ice crystals on them. The best frozen fish is likely to be vacuum-sealed or glazed with ice, 887, which prevents freezer burn. Frozen fish should be thawed before cooking in the refrigerator or under cool running water. ➤ Thawed frozen fish should never be refrozen, so it is best to cook and consume it within a day or so.

To freeze fish at home, we highly recommend vacuum-sealing or packing it in freezer bags with the air-displacement method, 881, and quick-freezing it in an icy brine. Though not as effective as commercial blast freezers, this method is best for preserving the texture of fish at home. In a large bowl or stoppered kitchen sink, prepare a brine with 1 pound ice, ½ cup salt, and ½ cup cold water (for freezing large batches of fish, double or triple these amounts). Submerge the bagged fish in the icy brine until frozen solid, then transfer to the freezer.

To freeze fish with an ice glaze, see 887.

ABOUT PROCESSING LIVE OR FRESHLY CAUGHT FISH

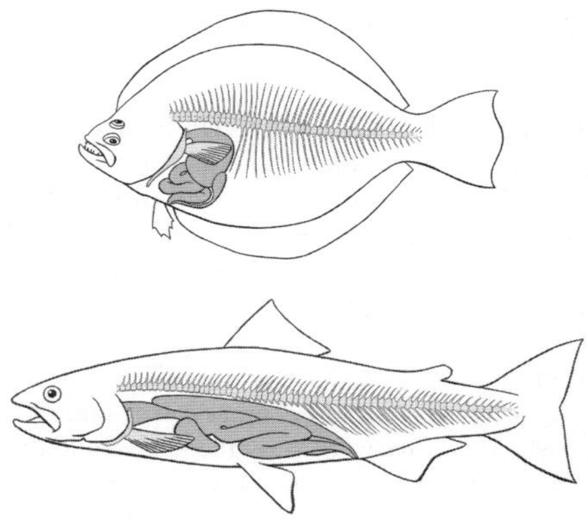

Location of guts and spine in a flatfish and roundfish

For the recreational angler, eating fish caught in the morning can be the fulfilling end to a successful day on the water. In reality, things are not quite so simple. Fish is extremely perishable, and care must be taken to ensure that its quality be preserved by proper handling. In general, the process we recommend goes like this: Kill the fish quickly (see below), let it bleed out, decide whether or not you wish to cook it with the skin on, then scale, 374, if desired, gut the fish, 374, and decide if you want to wait for the fish to go through rigor mortis (see 374).

KILLING FISH

While there is some romance to the angler's creel, fish should never be allowed to simply asphyxiate after being caught. A prolonged death is not only inhumane, it affects the quality of the fish and can lead to off flavors and poor texture. When a fish is first caught, stun it by hitting it over the head with a blunt object and insert a knife through one of the fish's gills, cutting forward toward the spine to sever the main artery. Optionally, turn the fish over and cut through the other gill as well. For especially large fish, cut the fish above the tail and sever the spine to expose the artery there as well. Place the fish in a bucket of cool water and allow it to bleed out.

During rigor mortis, a fish will be stiff and inflexible, its fillets will curl when cooked, and the flesh will be very firm. Fish typically go into rigor in as little as 1 hour or as many as 8 hours after being killed. The exact time varies tremendously based on many factors, but in general the better condition the fish was in while alive, the more quickly it was caught and dispatched, and the better it is stored afterward, the longer it will take for the fish to enter rigor. Waiting for it to come out of rigor means delayed gratification, but a better end result. The only alternative is to cook the fish before it enters rigor, but even then the fish will likely be tougher than if you wait. While waiting for the fish to come out of rigor, keep it well chilled, preferably on ice. This process could take anywhere from 8 hours to several days.

➤ Do not fillet a fish during rigor. You can fillet a fish before it enters rigor, but the fillets may shrink a bit. Do not chill pre-rigor fillets in cold water or in direct contact with ice, as this causes the fillets to shrink more.

PREPARING FISH FOR COOKING

If you merely want skinned fillets, you do not need to scale roundfish, remove its fins, or gut it. Simply skip to the instructions for filleting a roundfish and be especially careful cutting through the scales. (If the scales are particularly thick, scale the portion along the back you plan to cut through).

SCALING FISH

Most fish species have skin that becomes crispy and delicious when cooked properly. If you wish to enjoy the skin, scale the fish before gutting it (it is much easier). If, however, you do not plan to eat the skin, feel free to skip the scaling step. Keep in mind that ➤ some fish, such as mackerel and small trout, have inoffensive scales that can be left on.

To scale a fish, first cut off the fins with kitchen shears so they will not nick you while you work. Or, for the pectoral fins, make shallow incisions on either side, then pull them out. This removes the bones behind the fins as well. If at all possible, scale fish outdoors or, if the fish are small enough, partially fill the kitchen sink with water and scale the fish submerged under the water. To scale larger fish, spread several layers of newspaper on a steady work surface. Rinse the fish briefly in cold water—a wet fish is easier to scale. Grasp the fish firmly with your nondominant hand near the base of the tail or by the head. If it is very slippery, you may want to secure your grip with a dish towel. Beginning at the tail, ➤ run a butter knife blade or a fish scaler over the scales from the tail toward the head, in short strokes to minimize flying scales. Remove the scales around the back of the head.

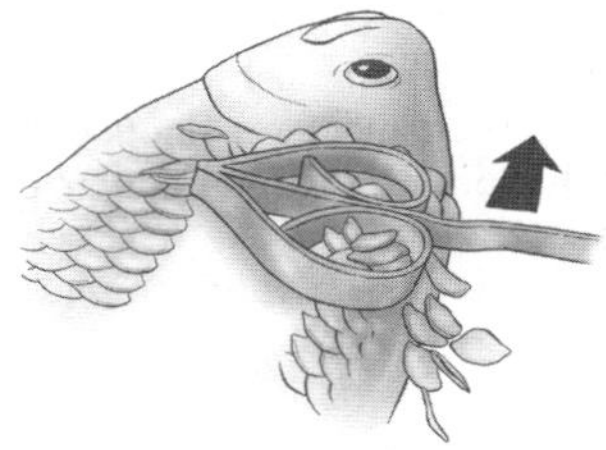

Scaling a fish

GUTTING FISH

➤ All fish should be gutted as soon as possible after being caught. Freshwater fish are especially susceptible to parasites, which can migrate from the guts to the flesh in a remarkably short time. If immediate gutting is not feasible, chilling the fish in ice water slows this process dramatically, which will give you several hours of leeway.

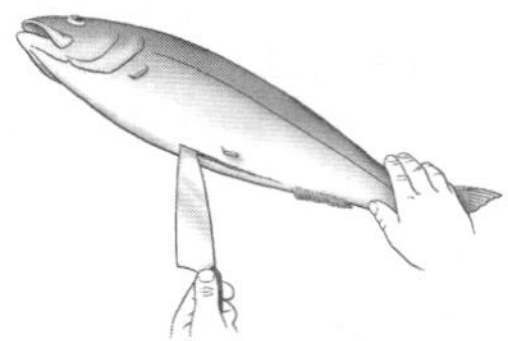

Gutting a roundfish

To gut a roundfish, use a razor-sharp knife to open up the belly, running from the anus (or vent) to just below the gills. Spread open the incision, and pull the guts out all together. Scrape out the kidney, which is attached to the spine. If the fish has one, remove the swim bladder—a small white sac attached to the inside of the fish. Tear or cut out the gills with kitchen shears. Rinse the fish well, inside and out, with cold water. If you plan to cook the fish whole, you are done preparing the fish and may proceed with cooking.

To gut very small roundfish, such as smelts, sardines, anchovies, or sprats, use scissors to cut an incision from just below the head to the vent. Grasp the fish's head and pull down toward the vent in one motion. This removes the head and carries with it most of the innards. You will be left with two tiny fillets joined by the skin.

Be sure to wrap and discard the entrails promptly. Fish guts are stinky; unless your garbage will be collected soon, transfer fish remains to a plastic bag, tie it off, and freeze on a rimmed baking sheet until trash day.

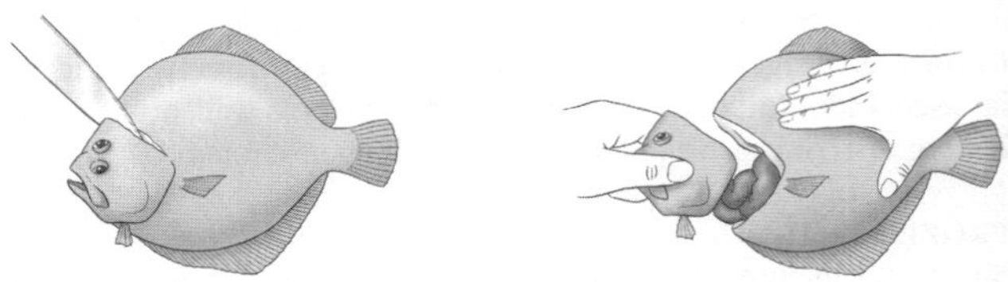

Gutting a flatfish

To gut a flatfish, the easiest way is to remove the head first. Cut around the head and gills, making a V-shaped notch. Pull the head away from the body, twisting it. The guts will come away with the head. Or, if you wish to leave the head on, cut a semicircle starting just under the pectoral fin. Lift up the flap created by the incision and remove the guts. Only buy gutted flatfish.

PREPARING ROUNDFISH FOR COOKING

To remove the head, tail, and fins, first cut the head above the collarbone and break through the backbone by snapping it off on the edge of the work surface. The pectoral fins, if not previously cut off, should come away with the head. Remove the ventral, or belly, fin by slot-cutting around it. To remove the tail, slice just above it. Keep the choicer trimmings—especially the head—for Fish Stock or Fumet, 77. Save the collars and tails from large roundfish, as they may have quite a bit of meat still on them. They may be seasoned, roasted or grilled, and the meat eaten off the bone, like ribs.

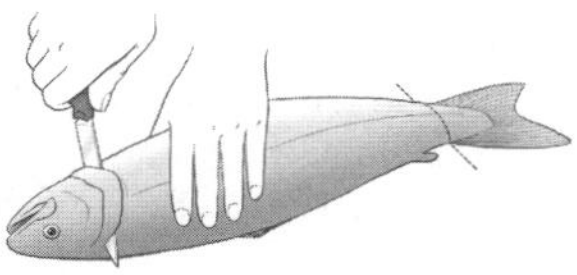
Removing the head and tail

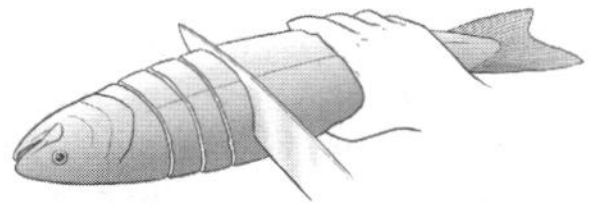
Cutting roundfish into steaks

To cut a large roundfish into steaks, first scale and gut the fish as directed on 374. Beginning at the head end, cut the fish at even intervals with a sharp knife, as shown above, into cross sections at least 1 inch thick. If desired, use a thin, sharp knife to cut just inside the rib bones on either side of each steak as shown below. Pull the rib bones away and cut them free with scissors, or carefully remove the section of spine at the center of the steak as well. Or, for especially large steaks, split them into two boneless portions by cutting the fillet sections from the spine and rib in one cut. Cut off the thin belly ends if desired, shown below. This is our preferred method for fish we plan to grill; steaks are sturdier than fillets and can be cut thicker, giving the fish time to brown without becoming overcooked. Some active, hard-swimming fish like tuna, swordfish, and bluefish may have a strong-tasting, red- or purple-tinged section of muscle called the **bloodline.** If desired, cut this away before cooking.

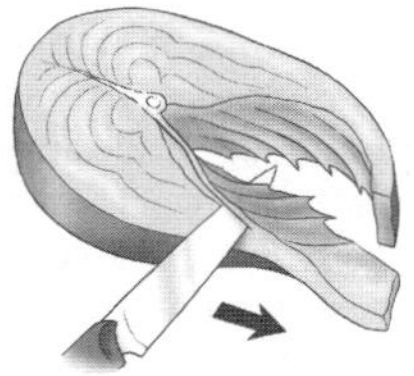
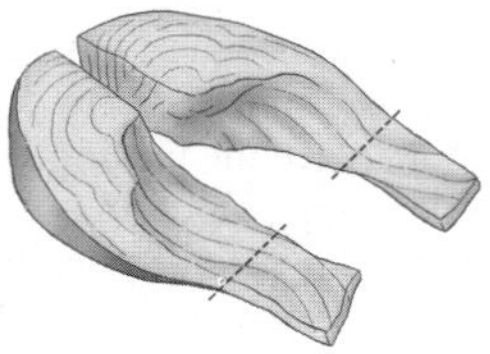
Removing the rib bones from steaks
Cutting into two portions and trimming off the belly ends

To fillet a roundfish, place it on a work surface on several layers of newspaper or brown paper. Cut all around the back of the head and just in front of the tail on either side, then all down the back on either side of the dorsal fin and spine. Then, slice down at a slight angle behind the collarbone. Holding the knife blade parallel to the fish, with the cutting edge toward the tail and the point against the spine, cut with a sliding motion along the backbone until you have freed the fillet all the way to the tail. As you cut, press the blade of the knife against the bones to remove as much flesh as possible. The fillet should come off in one piece. Repeat on the other side to remove the second fillet. If desired, run your fingers along the surface to feel for the tips of the small **pin bones** that run through the fillet, and use fish tweezers or a pair of needle-nosed pliers to pull them out.

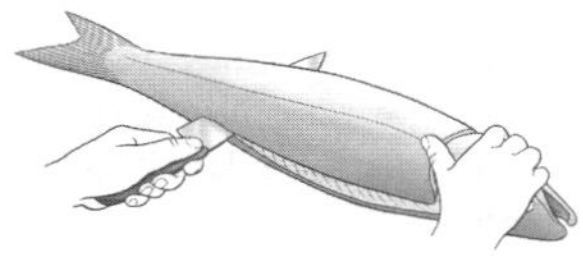
Filleting a roundfish

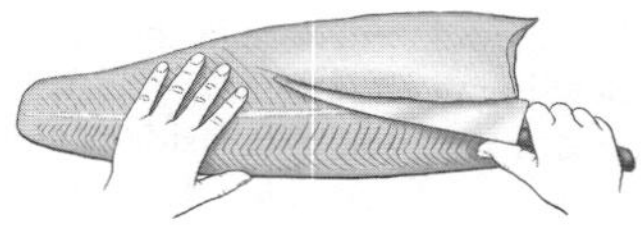
Carving off the rib bones

➤ For a quicker and easier alternative method of filleting that may leave a bit more flesh on the bones, gut the fish and cut down to the spine behind the collar bone. Turn the knife to lay flat against the spine. Firmly grasping the collar bone, slice down the length of the spine from collar to tail, cutting through the rib bones. The rib bones and spine of large grouper and snapper may need a little extra attention: After the fillet has been sliced, tap the knife against the rib bones to cut through them, shown above left. Once cut free, flip the fillet skin side down, then carefully cut the ribs away from the flesh, above right; you may do this easily to small, whole fillets, but we recommend cutting larger fillets like salmon into smaller portions (i.e., shorter than the length of your knife) before removing the rib bones.

To skin whole fillets, place on a cutting board skin side down. Holding the tail end firmly with your free hand, cut through the flesh of the fillet about ½ inch from the tail end. Then flatten the cutting angle of the knife so that it lies flat against the skin. With the blade angled slightly downward, carefully work the knife forward, as shown, keeping it close against the skin while your other hand holds the skin taut from the tail end. At this point, especially thick fillets, such as salmon, may be cut crosswise into 1½- to 2-inch-wide suprêmes, which are ideal for individual portions.

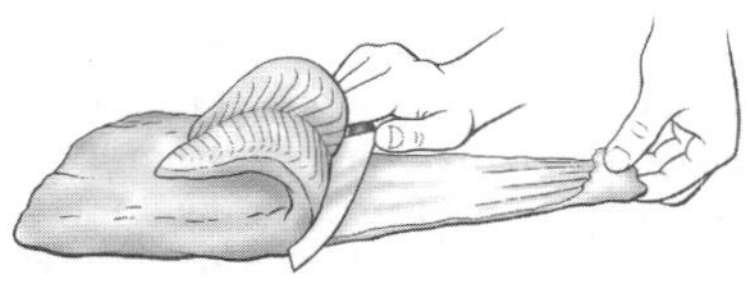
Skinning a fillet

To prepare roundfish for cooking whole, scale it (if you wish to eat the skin), and remove the guts and fins, leaving the bones to remove at the table. Of course, it is gracious to warn everyone first, or serve guests fillet portions (see About Serving Whole Fish, 378).

Butterflied fish are easier to eat, and especially suited to stuffing: The rib bones and spine are removed from the belly side of the fish, thus leaving the fillets connected at the back. The fish may be kept intact for stuffing, or the head and tail can be removed so the fish lies flat, allowing you to cook the fish as though it were one large fillet.

To butterfly a roundfish, scale, gut, and remove the fins as directed. Lay the fish on its side, with the belly facing your dominant hand and tail pointing away from you. Starting at the tail of the fish, carefully slice the top fillet away from the rib bones. Keep the blade as close to the rib bones as possible, working your way down the length of the fish. Starting at the tail again, slice between the bottom row of rib bones and the bottom fillet. At this point, you may cut the tail and head off, if desired. Alternatively, sever the spine at both ends of the fish with kitchen shears or scissors. Open the fish up like a book and spread the fillets flat so that the rib bones stick up. Starting at either end of the fish, place the index and middle finger of one hand on either side of the spine. Holding the fillets in place with your fingers, firmly grasp the rib bones with your other hand and pull up. The spine should come free. Move your fingers down a bit and pull the bones free again; repeat until the spine comes away completely. Remove pin bones as described on 375, if desired.

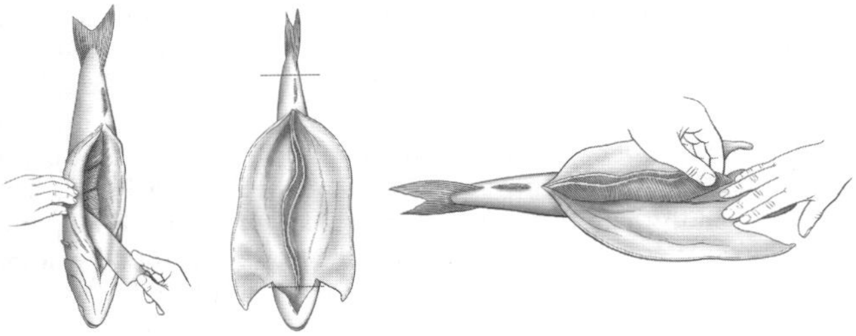

Butterflying a roundfish

PREPARING FLATFISH FOR COOKING

Flatfish yield four fillets each, two from each side of the fish. While the skin on most small flatfish, such as flounder, is delicious, the skin on larger ones, such as halibut, tends to be tough and not worth saving.

To fillet a flatfish, find the faint line that runs down the center of the fish from collar to tail (the **lateral line**). This line marks the location of the spine, and where to separate the two fillets on that side. With a long, sharp fillet knife, cut through the flesh all the way to the rib bones along the spine, and slice from collar to tail. Slip the knife under one of the fillets, angling the blade to cut close to the bone, and gradually free the fillet from the bones, working toward the outside edge of the fish. Repeat with the second fillet on this side, then turn the fish over and repeat on the second side. The fillets from the top of the fish—the side with eyes—will be slightly thicker than those from the bottom. Skin, if desired, as for whole roundfish fillets, 375.

To skin a flatfish for serving whole, cut a gash through the skin above the tail. Peel back about $\frac{3}{4}$ inch of the skin. Grasp the released skin firmly in one hand and hold the tail flat with your other hand while you pull the skin steadily toward the head.

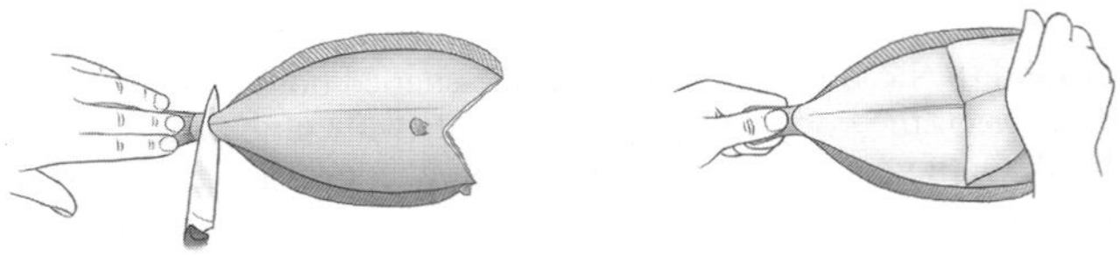

Skinning a flatfish

To "pocket" a midsized flatfish for stuffing, remove the head and gut the fish. Insert a very thin, sharp, long knife in through the hole where the head was, and cut the flesh away from the bones on either side of the spine, making as few cuts as possible and cutting all the way to the tail inside the fish (try not to puncture the skin). Do this on both sides. Use scissors to cut the bones on either side of the spine halfway between the spine and fins. This effectively cuts the skeleton of the fish into three pieces, two of which are attached to the outer fins and one in the center of the fish, which is attached to the tail. Use the scissors to trim off the sharp fins on either side of the fish, then turn the fish inside out, like you would a sock. With the scissors, cut off the spine, which is attached at the tail, as close to the tail as possible, then cut off the bones attached to either side of the fish as close to the outer edge as possible without damaging the flesh of the fish or cutting through the skin. Then turn the fish right side out again. The fish is ready for stuffing.

ABOUT MARINATING AND BRINING FISH

Unlike beef, pork, and chicken, fish flesh has very short muscle fibers and less connective tissue. When you compare a thick beef steak to a thick fish steak you can feel the difference—the beef steak is firm and fairly inflexible while the fish steak is softer and pliable, so much so that fish flesh can be easily damaged by rough handling. What this means for the home cook is that fish should be handled gently and cooked with care to avoid overcooking. It also means that, unlike meat, which can easily spend a day or so in a marinade, ➤ fish needs only 30 minutes to 1 hour. Unless you are making Ceviche, 377, ➤ never use a very acidic marinade, as it will cause fish to become tough and dry.

Most fish benefit from **brining.** The salt not only seasons the fish throughout, but it also strengthens the cell walls and firms up the flesh a bit (ideal for cooking methods such as grilling), and it inhibits the formation of white albumin (the unsightly white goop that fish exudes as it cooks). This last benefit is especially noticeable with salmon, whose pink flesh shows the albumin in high contrast. Brining whole fish is certainly possible but not necessary—the skin, head, and tail give the fish more rigidity and nicely hide any imperfections or leaking albumin.

To make a brine for fish, whisk together 2 cups cool water, $1\frac{1}{2}$ tablespoons salt, and $1\frac{1}{2}$ tablespoons sugar in a medium bowl until the salt and sugar are dissolved. To ensure the brine covers the fish, you may need to double or triple the brine, or simply place the fish steaks or fillets in a gallon zip-top bag, add the brine, and press as much air out of the bag as possible. Lay the bag flat on a baking sheet or in a baking pan and refrigerate thin fillets 15 minutes and thicker fillets and steaks (1 inch thick or greater) for up to 1 hour. Before cooking the fish, pat dry and discard the brine.

➤ We prefer the relative ease of **dry-brining,** or sprinkling fish all over with salt (and sometimes sugar) and letting the salt dissolve and penetrate the flesh for a brief time. Just like brining, dry-brining seasons and firms the flesh of fish while inhibiting the formation of albumin. It is much quicker than whipping up a brine and does not dilute the flavor of the fish.

To dry-brine fish fillets or steaks, the easiest method is to liberally sprinkle the fish on all sides with kosher salt. For the sake of precision and a touch of sweetness, you may mix together ¾ teaspoon table salt (or 1½ teaspoons Diamond kosher salt) and ¾ teaspoon sugar for every pound of fish fillets or steaks. Sprinkle all sides of the fish with the mixture and let sit for 20 minutes in the refrigerator, preferably on a rack over a rimmed baking sheet or plate. Rinse the fish well under cold water, pat dry, and proceed with cooking.

SERVING RAW FISH

Raw fish is enjoyed the world over. It is hard to imagine a better way to appreciate the textures and flavors of pristine fish than by eating it raw. We are perhaps most familiar with Japanese preparations, such as **sushi,** 335, and **sashimi,** or bite-sized slices of raw fish served with soy sauce and garnishes. **Tataki,** a lesser-known Japanese preparation, involves quickly searing a fish steak or loin (usually tuna) over high heat, leaving the inside raw. The rare fish is then sliced and dressed with daikon radish and ponzu sauce, 1020. Italian **pesce crudo** is thinly sliced and simply dressed with good olive oil, lemon juice, and salt. **Carpaccio** is another term that may be applied to Italian-style raw fish, commonly tuna. **Tartare,** the French term classically associated with minced raw beef, may be seen on restaurant menus applied to fish (again, usually tuna). **Poke** is a Hawaiian dish of raw fish mixed with various seasonings. **Ceviche,** a Peruvian specialty, is raw fish marinated in an acidic mixture, usually made with citrus juice, which firms the fish as it sits.

In general, tuna is the best fish for raw preparations at home, since there is no risk of parasites. For all other fish, ➤ you must ensure that it was frozen long enough and at a sufficiently low temperature to kill any parasites (see Fish Safety and Nutrition, 372). ➤ We do not recommend using freshwater fish in any raw preparation. Likewise, ➤ do not eat any fish from the cod family raw (see Cod, 396, for a list of these).

When preparing fish to eat raw, keep it well chilled, preferably on ice, during transport from the grocery store. Plan to eat it the same day you buy it, and keep it in its original wrapper on ice until you are ready to prepare and serve it. For all raw fish dishes except for marinated ones like ceviche and poke, ➤ we recommend brining or dry-brining, 1046; besides seasoning the fish, brining also firms the flesh, which makes it easier to slice and gives it a pleasing texture. Use exceptionally clean knives, cutting boards, and other equipment during preparation, and do not allow the fish to sit out long at room temperature before it is eaten. Normally, we are big advocates of leftovers, but in this case, prepare only what you can eat in one sitting.

CEVICHE

6 servings

Ceviche is raw fish or shellfish marinated in citrus juice. Though the fish is not technically cooked, it turns opaque and firms up due to the acid in the marinade. Serve the ceviche with tostadas or tortilla chips, if desired. ➤ Please read Serving Raw Fish, above, for how to choose and handle fish safely.

Remove the skin and any bones from:

1 pound very fresh firm-fleshed fish fillets such as grouper, halibut, flounder, or snapper

Cut into small cubes, about ⅜ inch, place in a glass or stainless steel bowl, and toss with:

1 cup fresh lime juice

Cover and refrigerate for 30 minutes. Scoop out the fish with a slotted spoon (reserve the lime juice), transfer to another bowl, and mix in:

2 tablespoons chopped cilantro
1 to 2 jalapeño peppers, to taste, seeded and minced
1½ tablespoons olive oil
1 teaspoon dried oregano
½ teaspoon salt, or to taste
(½ to 1 teaspoon sugar, to taste)

Add a little of the reserved lime juice to the fish, to taste. Adjust the seasonings and refrigerate until serving time. Serve garnished with:

Cilantro sprigs
Diced avocado
Pico de Gallo, 573

TUNA OR SALMON POKE

4 servings

Pronounced "poh-kay," this simple Hawaiian preparation can take on scores of different forms, although the original was simple—just raw fish, salt, roasted and ground *kukui* or *candlenuts,* or perhaps seaweed. ➤ Please read Serving Raw Fish, above, for how to choose and handle fish safely. For a spicy version made with cooked octopus, see Tako Poke (Korean-Style Octopus Poke), 369.

Combine in a medium bowl:

1 pound sushi-grade ahi tuna or salmon, cut into ½-inch cubes
3 tablespoons tamari or soy sauce
2 green onions, thinly sliced, or ¼ cup finely chopped sweet onion
1 tablespoon toasted sesame oil
1 teaspoon toasted sesame seeds
(1 teaspoon red pepper flakes or 1 thinly sliced fresh red chile)

Cover and marinate in the refrigerator for at least 10 minutes and up to 1 day before serving. If desired, right before serving, stir in:

(1 avocado, pitted and diced)
(Furikake, 1016, or crumbled toasted nori seaweed)

ABOUT COOKING FISH

Always pat fish dry before cooking. It is not necessary to rinse fish if it smells impeccably fresh; if it does have an odor, rinse it well in cool water (if it still smells very strong, discard it). The main objective with any kind of fish is to avoid overcooking.

To test fish for doneness, insert a thermometer at an angle into the thickest portion of the flesh. ➤ The minimum safe temperature for fish is 120°F, at which point it will be rare. For medium-rare, cook fish to 125°F; for medium, 130° to 135°F; for well-done, 145°F. Once the fish has been removed from the heat, the temperature may rise a little bit as it rests (often called carry-over cooking), but the change is not nearly as dramatic as it can be for meat or poultry.

As you cook more and more fish, you will be able to discern doneness by sight and touch. ➤ The flesh will firm up, start to flake apart, and become opaque. When you suspect that a piece of fish has nearly finished cooking, take a thin knife and gently poke between the flakes of fillets or steaks. If you like salmon, swordfish, or tuna on the rare side, remove the fish from the heat when the interior still has the translucent look of raw fish.

Whether your fish is large or small, round or flat, choose the cooking method most likely to help retain its juiciness. In general, lean fish benefit from gentle, moist-heat cooking methods and more fat—either used during cooking or in the accompanying sauce. Fattier fish, such as black cod (sablefish) and king salmon, can be cooked in a variety of ways and are, in a sense, self-basting. Even slightly overcooked, these fish will be moist and succulent, making them a bit more forgiving for the budding fish cook.

For fish-based dishes other than the ones in this chapter, see About Fish and Shellfish Soups, 99, the suggested fish and shellfish sandwich combinations for cold, 136, and hot, 139, sandwiches, Salade Niçoise, 121, and Pasta con le Sarde, 297. To smoke fish, see Hot-Smoked Salmon, 393.

SAUCES FOR FISH

The best sauces for fish are light and simple. For the ultimate in simplicity, drizzle fish with Brown Butter, 558, or a good olive oil and sprinkle with chopped fresh herbs such as parsley, tarragon, chives, or chervil.

Beurre Blanc, 558, is a classic, rich but unobtrusive sauce for lighter fish such as halibut; adding savory, bold miso paste makes it an excellent pairing for rich fish like salmon or mackerel (see Miso Beurre Blanc, 559). Or pair rich fish with something punchy and acidic such as Sauce Gribiche, 568, or Vinaigrette, 575. White Wine Sauce, 549, and Sauce Ravigote, 550, are natural pairings with almost all fish.

Herb-forward sauces also go very well with most fish; try Salsa Verde, 567, Mojo, 567, Chimichurri, 567, Jen's Basil Oil, 570, Charmoula, 586, and Zhug, 567. Creamy but fresh cold sauces such as Tzatziki, 569, or Herbed Yogurt Dressing, 577, are also excellent with fish. In summer, any salsa, 573–74, makes a refreshing accompaniment to grilled fish, especially Pico de Gallo, 573, and Fruit Salsa, 574. Tomato-Olive Relish, 568, is another excellent pairing for grilled or broiled fish.

ABOUT SERVING WHOLE FISH

To bone a whole, cooked roundfish, remove the skin from one side of the fish. With a narrow blade, cut a line down each side of the spine from head to tail. From both sides of this line, cut pieces 2½ to 3 inches wide and lift them away from the bones. Now, beginning at the tail and holding down the bottom fillet with the knife or the back of a fork, free the backbone. The exposed lower fillet is now ready to be served.

To bone a whole, cooked flatfish, use a knife or spatula to pull away the small bones along the top and bottom edges. Cut along each side of the fish's spine to separate the two fillets on top. Starting at the backbone, gently pull each of these fillets up away from the bones, work a thin spatula underneath them, and transfer to a serving plate. Cut through the backbone at the collar, then lift it up and discard it. This will expose the remaining pair of fillets underneath; slip the spatula between each of them and the skin on the bottom and transfer to the serving plate.

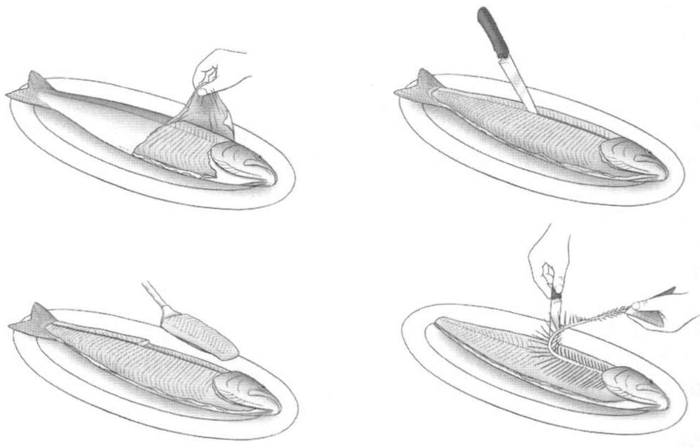

Serving a whole roundfish

ABOUT ROASTING OR BAKING FISH

Roasting and baking are especially convenient methods for cooking large, thick fillets and whole fish: A baking dish or rimmed baking sheet will hold all but the largest specimens, and they will not need to be turned or moved during the cooking process. Slash the skin of whole large fish three or four times before cooking to help the heat penetrate, allow seasonings to flavor the flesh, and prevent the skin from splitting.

Baking at 350°F or lower has the added benefit of promoting even cooking in thick pieces, and gives you a large margin of error when it comes to overcooking the fish. High-heat roasting is faster, of course, and it adds flavor through browning. Generally, roasting is suited to thicker cuts of fish; thin steaks and fillets can be roasted, but do not try to brown them (they will overcook and dry out before they brown). You may roast vegetables and fish together in the same pan, but choose vegetables that either cook quickly—such as asparagus, cherry tomatoes, or small broccoli florets—or precook them as in Fish Boulangère, 380.

BAKED OR SLOW-ROASTED FISH

4 servings

Large whole fish and big fillets may be cooked with this method (figure on 12 ounces per person or 6 ounces per person, respectively). To stuff whole roundfish, butterfly, 376, and add about 10 minutes to the roasting time. Some good stuffings include Parsley and Bread Crumb Stuffing, 534, Bacon Stuffing for Fish, 534, and Green Herb Stuffing, 534. Since the skin will never crisp up with this method, we usually do not scale fish (remove the skin before serving or instruct diners to remove it).

Prepare for cooking, 374–76:

3 pounds whole fish or 1½ pounds fish fillets

For fillets, brine or dry-brine, 377, if desired. If using whole fish, slash the skin a few times on both sides.

Preheat the oven to 325°F. Pat the fish dry and rub generously (inside and out for whole fish) with:

Olive oil, softened butter, or any flavored butter, 559–60
Salt (if the fish has not been brined) and black pepper

Place the whole fish on a greased rack in a baking dish or rimmed baking sheet. For fillets, grease a baking dish or a rimmed baking sheet and place the fillets directly on the bottom. Or, if desired, you may tuck under the fish:

(Fennel fronds, herb sprigs, or thin slices of lemon)

Transfer to the oven and bake for 15 to 30 minutes, depending on the thickness of the fish. The flesh should be firm and opaque throughout, or reach an internal temperature of 125° to 130°F, the latter temperature for flakier fish (for more on how to test for doneness, see 377). Transfer to a serving dish; for serving whole fish, see 378. Garnish with:

Lemon quarters
Sprigs of parsley, basil, or tarragon

Or serve with:

White Wine Sauce, 549, Beurre Blanc, 558, Salsa Verde, 567, Zhug, 567, Sauce Gribiche, 568, or a salsa, 573–74

HIGH-HEAT ROASTED FISH

4 servings

This recipe can be used with fillets larger than those called for; however, for whole fish greater than 3 pounds, stick with slow-roasting to avoid overcooking the outside before the center is done. We do not recommend this method for fish fillets less than 1 inch thick; oven-frying, 380, and pan-frying, 387, are better methods for thin fillets.

If necessary, scale and prepare for cooking, 374–76:

3 pounds whole fish or 1½ pounds fish fillets

For fillets, brine or dry-brine, 377, if desired.

Preheat the oven to 475°F. Rub the fish all over with:

Vegetable oil
Salt (if the fish has not been brined) and black pepper

If whole, slash the skin a few times on both sides. If desired, stuff each whole fish with:

(Several thin slices of lemon or lime)
(Several sprigs parsley, thyme, tarragon, oregano, or cilantro)

Place the whole fish on a greased rack in a baking dish. For fillets, grease a baking dish or rimmed baking sheet and place the fillets directly on the bottom. Roast for 10 to 20 minutes depending on the thickness of the fish. The flesh should be firm and opaque throughout, or reach an internal temperature of 125° to 130°F, the latter temperature for flakier fish (for more on how to test for doneness, see 377). Serve and garnish as directed in Baked or Slow-Roasted Fish, 378.

PAUPIETTES (STUFFED FISH FILLETS)

4 servings

Prepare:

Parsley and Bread Crumb Stuffing, 534

Preheat the oven to 350°F. Have ready:

4 skinned sole or bluefish fillets or other very thin fillets

Coat each of 4 individual 8-ounce molds or ramekins with:

Butter

Line each mold with a fillet. The fillets must be long enough, when folded over, to cover the top. Fill the molds with the stuffing, and fold the ends of the fillets over the top. Place the molds in a water bath or bain marie, 812. Bake until firm and opaque throughout, about 30 minutes. Unmold the paupiettes onto a hot platter. Garnish with:

Lemon wedges
Sprigs of parsley or watercress

Serve with:

Beurre Blanc, 558, made with lemon juice, or White Wine Sauce, 549

FISH EN PAPILLOTE (FISH BAKED IN PARCHMENT)

This method keeps even the leanest fish moist. If necessary, foil may be used instead of parchment. See Additions to Fish Baked in Parchment, below, for flavoring ideas.

Preheat the oven to 425°F. For each serving, place on one side of a large square of parchment paper:

One 6- to 8-ounce fish fillet

Sprinkle with:

Salt and black pepper

Dot with:

½ tablespoon butter or olive oil

Fold the parchment paper over and pleat the edges so it stays closed. Bake until the paper is browned and puffed, about 15 minutes. Unwrap the packet and ensure the fish is firm and opaque throughout, or a thermometer registers 125° to 130°F, the latter temperature for flakier fish (for more on how to test for doneness, see 377). Serve immediately.

ADDITIONS TO FISH BAKED IN PARCHMENT

For each serving, add to the parchment packet:

2 tablespoons thinly sliced leeks, 2 teaspoons white wine, ½ teaspoon fresh herbs (thyme, tarragon, savory, chervil), and ½ garlic clove, thinly sliced
1 tablespoon minced shallots, ¼ cup sliced mushrooms, 2 teaspoons heavy cream, and 2 teaspoons minced parsley or chives
⅓ cup cooked wild rice, 343, ½ garlic clove, thinly sliced, and 2 thin lemon slices
¼ cup halved cherry tomatoes, 2 tablespoons sliced pitted green olives, and 1 teaspoon small capers
⅓ cup cooked jasmine rice, 343, 2 thin lime slices, 1 garlic clove, thinly sliced, 1 teaspoon minced lemongrass, 2 cilantro sprigs, ¼ teaspoon red pepper flakes or ½ Thai chile, thinly sliced, and a dash of fish sauce
⅓ cup cooked couscous, 341, 2 tablespoons Charmoula, 586, and ¼ cup very thinly sliced red onion

OVEN-FRIED FISH FILLETS

4 servings

These flavorful fillets are quick to whip up on a weeknight and can be made with inexpensive white fish.

Position a rack in the upper third of the oven. Preheat the oven to 500°F. Lightly oil a baking sheet. Have ready:

1½ pounds cod, bluefish, grouper, or other flaky white fish fillets, patted dry

Place in a shallow bowl:

½ cup milk or buttermilk

Mix together in a second shallow bowl:

1 cup dry bread crumbs or panko
½ cup finely grated Parmesan (2 ounces)
1 teaspoon sweet paprika or smoked paprika
1 teaspoon garlic powder
1 teaspoon onion powder
¾ teaspoon salt
½ teaspoon black pepper
¼ teaspoon cayenne pepper

Dip the fish fillets in the milk, then coat with the bread crumb mixture, patting to make the crumbs adhere. Place the fillets on the baking sheet and drizzle over them:

2 tablespoons olive oil or melted butter

Roast for 8 to 12 minutes, depending on the thickness of the fillets. The flesh should be firm and opaque throughout, or reach an internal temperature of 125° to 130°F, the latter temperature for flakier fish (for more on how to test for doneness, see 377). Serve hot with:

Salsa Verde, 567, or Tartar Sauce, 563
Lemon wedges

VERACRUZ-STYLE SNAPPER

4 servings

Use "true" cinnamon (Ceylon, or canela, 972) if you have it. Instead of baking the fish in the sauce as directed below, you may grill, broil, or pan-fry the fish and serve the tomato sauce alongside. Any firm-fleshed white fish, such as grouper, cod, or rockfish, may be used in this recipe.

Prepare:

Veracruz-Style Tomato Sauce, 556

While the sauce cooks, preheat the oven to 400°F. Have ready a 13 × 9-inch baking dish. If necessary, scale and prepare for cooking, 374–76:

One whole 2- to 2½-pound red snapper or 1½ to 2 pounds red snapper fillets, cut into 4 equal pieces

Spread a thin layer of the sauce in the bottom of the dish and place the fish on top. Cover the fish with the remaining sauce and bake for 15 to 20 minutes, depending on the thickness of the fish or fillets. The flesh should be opaque and flake apart when prodded with a fork.

FISH BOULANGÈRE (BAKED FISH WITH POTATOES AND PEARL ONIONS)

4 servings

If necessary, scale and prepare for cooking, 374–76:

One whole 3-pound cod or 1½ pounds center-cut cod, haddock, or halibut fillets

Preheat the oven to 350°F. Butter a shallow baking dish.

Combine in a medium saucepan:

16 small gold or red potatoes, peeled if desired
Water to cover

Simmer until tender but not mushy, 15 to 20 minutes. For the last 5 minutes of cooking, add:

12 pearl onions, peeled

Drain well and transfer to a bowl. Pat the fish dry and place in the prepared baking dish. Toss the potatoes and onions with:

2 tablespoons butter, melted
1 teaspoon minced fresh thyme or ½ teaspoon dried thyme
½ teaspoon salt
¼ teaspoon black pepper

Arrange the vegetables around the fish. Brush the fish with:

2 tablespoons butter, melted

Sprinkle with:

Salt and black pepper

Bake for 20 to 30 minutes, depending on the thickness of the fish. The flesh should be firm and opaque throughout, or reach an internal temperature of 125° to 130°F, the latter temperature for flakier fish (for more on how to test for doneness, see 377). Serve in the baking dish; for serving whole fish, see 378. Garnish with:

Chopped parsley
Lemon wedges

FISH BAKED IN SALT

4 servings

Baking fish in coarse salt is one of the finest, simplest, and most flavorful ways to prepare it, for the salt crust acts as a moist "oven," enveloping the entire fish and baking it gently and evenly.

Prepare for cooking, 374–76:

One 3-pound whole fish, such as red snapper, branzino, grouper, porgy, or rockfish, or one 2-pound center-cut salmon fillet

Preheat the oven to 500°F. Cover the bottom of a baking dish just large enough to hold the fish with a ½-inch layer of:

Rock salt or ice cream salt

Pat the fish dry and lay it on the salt. Pour enough salt over and around it to cover all of its surfaces by at least ¼ inch. Bake for 30 minutes. Poke through the salt into the thickest part of the fish with a thermometer. Remove the fish when it has reached 120°F; it will likely take 10 to 15 minutes more to reach this temperature. Remove the dish from the oven and let stand for 5 minutes (the fish will continue to cook).

Crack through the salt and carefully uncover the fish, brushing off all the salt. Transfer with a spatula to a serving platter. For serving whole fish, see 378. Drizzle with:

Extra-virgin olive oil

Serve with:

Lemon wedges

ABOUT STEAMING, POACHING, BRAISING, AND COOKING FISH SOUS VIDE

These moist-heat methods are the best ways to cook delicate, lean fish to retain flavor and prevent drying out. For fish soups and chowders, see 99. **Steaming** is ideal for delicate, mild-fleshed fish. Aromatics are often added to the steaming liquid to perfume the fish. Both fillets and small whole fish may be steamed either in a steamer basket or sitting atop aromatics such as fennel fronds, lemon slices, or seaweed. For especially delicate fish, you may simply set them atop any of these aromatics on a serving plate that will fit inside of the steamer. Or use a bamboo steamer lined with cabbage leaves or softened kombu, 1016.

Poaching involves gently cooking fish in a barely bubbling liquid. This can be wine, stock, butter, olive oil, or a combination of these. Special, oval-shaped fish poachers exist, but they are hardly necessary. Fish fillets can simply be poached in a skillet with high sides or in a baking dish in the oven. Poaching is done at a very low simmer or just below a simmer for about 5 minutes for every ½ inch of thickness. If a fish or shellfish stock is used for the poaching liquid, you may use some of it, either as is or reduced, in the sauce served with the fish (a Court Bouillon, 80, may be too acidic). Strain it into a wide saucepan and simmer until it has thickened to the desired consistency. Whisk in butter off the heat to enrich the sauce and season to taste.

Braising fish, at first glance, is very similar to poaching them: Fish is cooked slowly at a low temperature in liquid. The main difference is that there is less, but more flavorful cooking liquid, which is served as a sauce. However, braising fish is quite different from braising other meats. While beef short ribs are braised for hours, fish is braised for a much shorter time—often just 10 minutes or less. Braising liquids can be anything from tomato sauce to a Thai-style coconut curry sauce. The only necessity is that the liquid be a flavorful one going in (or it should be heavily seasoned and enriched afterward, as for Braised Fish Fillets with Lemon and Capers, 382). Serve braises over pasta or noodles, cooked rice or other grains, polenta or grits, or with toasted bread.

Cooking fish **sous vide** is a little like poaching, but much more precise, and the fish cooks in its own juices.

To cook fish fillets and steaks sous vide, fill a pot or other large vessel with water, and preheat the water bath with an immersion circulator set to the desired temperature. A temperature of 120° to 125°F yields rare to medium-rare fish, and 130°F yields flakier, medium-cooked fish. While the water heats, place the fish fillets in a single layer in zip-top freezer bags or vacuum seal bags. Add a little olive oil or butter to each bag, and seasonings such as salt, pepper, herbs, and a lemon slice or piece of zest (if desired, the fish may be brined or dry-brined, 377; in which case, there is no need to add more salt). Seal the bags, pushing out as much air as possible with the air displacement method, 881, and place in the preheated bath. It should take ½-inch-thick fillets or steaks about 30 minutes to cook; 1-inch-thick fillets or steaks take 40 minutes; and 1½-inch-thick fillets or steaks take about 1 hour. Unlike other methods, there is no danger of overcooking the fish, and it can be held in the bath for up to 30 minutes before serving. You may cook frozen, vacuum-packed fish straight from the freezer by doubling the cooking time. To crisp the skin of fillets after cooking, remove them from the bags and heat a little vegetable oil in a skillet over medium-high heat until very hot. Add the fillets skin side down and cook, undisturbed, until the skin is browned and crisp, 30 seconds to 1 minute. To preserve the crispy skin and show it off when serving, plate the fillets skin side up. For more information on sous vide cooking, see 1054.

POACHED FISH

4 servings

This easy method results in a moist piece of fish, and it works well with all types: whole fish, steaks, or fillets. Choose the smallest pan that will hold the fish comfortably in order to use as little liquid as possible (this will dilute the fish's distinctive flavor less and result in a more flavorful liquid for sauce making).

If necessary, scale and prepare for cooking, 374–76:

3 pounds whole fish or 1½ to 2 pounds fish steaks or fillets

Place in a pan or deep skillet large enough to hold the fish comfortably. Add cold water to barely cover the fish. Remove the fillets from the pan and add to the water:

1 tablespoon salt

Bring the water to a boil over high heat, return the fish to the pan, and immediately remove the pan from the heat. Cover and let stand for 10 minutes for fish or fillets that are 1 inch thick. For thinner fish, check at about 7 minutes. Thicker fish may need up to 15 minutes. The flesh should be firm and opaque throughout, or reach an internal temperature of 125° to 130°F, the latter temperature for flakier fish (for more on how to test for doneness, see 377). Remove the fish from the water, drain well, and serve or refrigerate until ready to serve. Before serving, bring the fish to room temperature, and peel off the skin. Season to taste with:

Salt and black pepper

Serve with one or several of the following:

Mayonnaise, 563, Scandinavian Mustard-Dill Sauce, 566, Beurre Blanc, 558, Herbed Yogurt Dressing, 577, or Green Goddess Dressing, 577

POACHING LIQUIDS FOR FISH

Use any of the following liquids:

Court Bouillon, 80
Fish Stock or Fumet, 77
Quick Seafood Stock, 80
Shrimp or Shellfish Stock, 78
Dashi, 78
Equal parts white wine, red wine, or sake and water

Add any of the following to the fish-poaching liquid and simmer for 5 minutes before adding the fish:

Finely diced onion or shallot, or sliced leeks
Finely diced carrot, celery, or fennel
Bay leaf, thyme sprigs, or fennel fronds
One lemongrass stalk, trimmed and pounded with the spine of a knife until bruised and fragrant
Crushed black peppercorns
Strips of lemon or orange zest, removed with a vegetable peeler
Smashed garlic cloves
A piece of kombu, 1016
Dried chiles

POACHED FISH QUENELLES

4 servings

"Quenelle" refers to the football-like shape of these fish dumplings. All the ingredients should be kept very cold. If possible, put the bowl and blade of the food processor in the freezer for 15 minutes before using.

Combine in a food processor:

1 pound cleaned pike, sole, or any delicate white-fleshed fish, skin removed
1 cup well-chilled heavy cream
1 cup fresh bread crumbs, 957
3 large egg whites
1 tablespoon lemon juice
½ teaspoon salt
¼ teaspoon black pepper
Pinch of grated nutmeg

Process until the mixture is ground into a very smooth paste, about 1 minute, scraping down the sides of the food processor bowl as needed. Cover and chill overnight. The mixture should be very firm.

If broiling the quenelles in sauce, have ready a well-buttered broilerproof pan, large skillet, or individual gratin dishes, and preheat the broiler. Bring to a very gentle simmer in a wide, shallow pan:

Fish Stock or Fumet, 77, Quick Seafood Stock, 80, or salted water

Shape the fish mixture into quenelles, 1046, gently dropping them into the simmering water as you go. Simmer gently for 8 minutes, turning the quenelles over halfway through cooking. Remove with a slotted spoon and place on a baking sheet lined with paper towels or a kitchen towel to absorb any excess liquid. Serve coated with:

Sauce Allemande, 550, or White Wine Sauce, 549

Or if broiling, preheat the broiler and place an oven rack 6 inches from the heating element. Transfer the quenelles to the buttered dish, and cover with the sauce. Broil until browned and bubbling, 2 to 4 minutes.

GEFILTE FISH

10 servings

Combine in a food processor and pulse until finely ground:

3 pounds mixed lean and fat fish, such as whitefish, bluefish, jack, salmon, pike, and/or carp, skinned and cut into 1-inch pieces
1 large onion, coarsely chopped
1 celery rib, coarsely chopped
¼ cup chopped parsley

Transfer the mixture to a bowl and stir in:

3 large eggs, beaten
3 tablespoons matzo meal
1 tablespoon salt
1 tablespoon black or white pepper
1 tablespoon sugar

Add, folding in ¼ cup at a time to create a fluffy texture:

1 cup ice water

Dip your hands in chilled water and shape the mixture into 1-inch balls. Bring to a simmer in a large pot:

4 quarts fish stock, homemade, 77, or store-bought

Gently drop the fish balls into the stock (there should be enough room for them to puff up), along with:

1 carrot, peeled

Cover and simmer for 30 minutes. With a slotted spoon, remove the balls and layer in a large baking dish with high sides, such as a lasagne pan. Cut the carrot into thin round slices and reserve. Reserve the stock. Sprinkle:

2 envelopes (4½ teaspoons) kosher gelatin

over:

½ cup cold water

and allow it to soften for 5 minutes. Measure out 8 cups of the reserved stock and stir the gelatin into it until dissolved. Pour the mixture over the fish balls. If there is any stock left over, it can be frozen. Cover and refrigerate until set, about 2 hours. Serve the fish cold with some of the jelly, topped with a carrot slice. Serve with:

Grated peeled fresh horseradish or prepared horseradish
Sprigs of dill

BRAISED FISH FILLETS WITH LEMON AND CAPERS

4 servings

A simple, quick sauce is made here by swirling butter, lemon juice, and herbs into the braising liquid. Variations on this dependable theme are endless; for inspiration, see Beurre Blanc, 558, and About Flavored Butters, 559.

Preheat the oven to 350°F. Place in a baking dish just large enough to hold the fish:

1½ to 2 pounds haddock, grouper, tilapia, or other fish fillets

Sprinkle the fish with:

½ teaspoon salt
¼ teaspoon black pepper

Pour into the dish:

½ cup dry white wine or chicken or fish stock

Cover tightly with a lid or foil and bake for 15 to 25 minutes, depending on the thickness of the fish. The flesh should be firm and opaque throughout, or reach an internal temperature of 125° to 130°F, the latter temperature for flakier fish (for more on how to test for doneness, see 377). Place the fish on a platter and cover to keep warm. Swirl into the liquid in the baking dish until melted:

3 tablespoons butter, cut into small pieces

Stir in:

2 tablespoons drained small capers
1 tablespoon minced tarragon or chives
2 teaspoons lemon juice
Salt and black pepper to taste

Pour the sauce over the fish.

CHINESE STEAMED FISH

2 to 4 servings

This dish is fast enough to be the backbone of a weeknight meal, but it is truly elegant. The quick cooking method combined with a simple sauce allows the delicate flavor of the fish to come through. If cooking a whole fish, it will serve only 2 to 3 people, whereas fish steaks, because they are all meat, will feed 4.

Combine in a small bowl:

2 tablespoons Shaoxing wine, 952, or dry sherry
2 tablespoons soy sauce
1 tablespoon toasted sesame oil
2 green onions, minced
2 garlic cloves, finely slivered
½ teaspoon sugar

Place on a heatproof plate just large enough to hold them:

Two 1-pound halibut or other white fish fillets or steaks; or one 1½- to 2-pound whole fish, such as sea bass or grouper, scaled and cleaned, 374–76

Cut 2 or 3 slashes in each side of the fish if using whole fish. Pour the sauce over the fish. Scatter over the fish:

2 green onions, halved crosswise, then cut into long, thin slivers
1-inch piece ginger, peeled and cut into thin slivers

If desired, cover the fish and marinate in the refrigerator for up to 2 hours. When you are ready to cook, place a rack in the bottom of a large pot (or use a bamboo steamer). Place the fish, still on the plate, on the rack or in the steamer, cover the pot, and bring the water to a boil. Steam until the fish is cooked through, 10 to 12 minutes for thick steaks, 12 to 15 minutes for whole fish, or until the internal temperature reaches 130°F. Serve the fish with the accumulated juices.

BUTTER- OR OLIVE OIL-POACHED FISH

4 servings

This decadent method of preparing fish infuses it with the rich flavors of the fat. It is ideal for leaner fish like halibut, cod, freshwater bass, or leaner types of salmon. Also try it with scallops.

Dry-brine, 377:

1½ to 2 pounds skinless fish fillets

Preheat the oven to 325°F. Place in a baking dish just large enough to hold the fish:

4 sticks (1 pound) butter, melted, or 2 cups olive oil
(8 sprigs thyme)
(3 garlic cloves, smashed)

Rinse the salt off the fish and pat dry. Place the fish in the baking dish and bake for 20 to 30 minutes, depending on the thickness of the fish. The flesh should be opaque throughout and reach an internal temperature of 130° to 135°F. To serve, remove the fish from the fat, allowing the excess to drip off. Serve immediately. Leftover fat should be strained and refrigerated or frozen. It may be used again for poaching or sautéing.

FISH CURRY

4 servings

This curry is a little thinner than the variety enriched with coconut milk, but the absence of fat lets the flavor of the curry paste and the fish come through. For a coconut-based curry, see Thai Shrimp Curry, 366, which may be made with chunks of any firm-fleshed white fish.

Heat in a large, deep skillet over medium heat until shimmering:

2 tablespoons vegetable oil

Add:

3 tablespoons red, green, or yellow curry paste, homemade, 585, or store-bought
(1 tablespoon ground dried shrimp or 6 anchovy fillets, minced)

The paste will splatter a lot in the oil, so have a splatter screen handy, if possible. Fry the paste, stirring constantly, until the oil is tinted the color of the curry paste and the mixture is very fragrant, about 2 minutes. Stir in:

1½ cups fish or chicken stock or broth

Scrape any browned bits off the bottom of the skillet. Bring to a simmer and add:

2 tablespoons lime juice
Fish sauce to taste

Place in the simmering stock:

1½ pounds firm-fleshed white fish fillets or steaks (skin and bones removed), cut into 2-inch chunks
1 cup bite-sized vegetable pieces such as green beans, peas, bell pepper, zucchini, bamboo shoots, etc.

Simmer gently, turning once if the fish pieces are thick, until the fish is cooked through, 5 to 7 minutes. Serve over:

Cooked short-grain rice, 343, or rice noodles

ABOUT MICROWAVING FISH

The microwave does a fine job of cooking small quantities of fish. The rules are straightforward: First, get used to cooking fish in your microwave, so that you can get a sense of how long the cooking will take (the alternative is opening the door every 30 seconds). ➤ Cook small portions, never more than a pound, and preferably less. Do not use a lot of liquid. Be sparing with added ingredients—the more you include, the more likely this method will result in uneven cooking. You may also cook Fish en Papillote, 379, in the microwave (one packet at a time; do not use foil).

MICROWAVED FISH FILLETS

2 servings

Flaky white fish such as cod, perch, or trout work beautifully in this recipe.

Arrange on a plate with the thickest edge toward the outside:

8 to 12 ounces fish fillets, up to 1 inch thick, preferably in 2 pieces, rinsed and patted dry

Season with:

¼ teaspoon salt
¼ teaspoon black pepper

Sprinkle with:

1 tablespoon fish stock, dry white wine, or lemon or lime juice

Cover with an inverted plate or plastic wrap. Microwave on high for 3 minutes, 2 minutes for flounder or other flatfish, 4 minutes if the fillets approach an inch in thickness. The internal temperature should reach 130°F and the fish should flake apart and appear opaque (for more on how to test for doneness, see 377). If the fish is nearly done, cover it and let it stand for a minute to finish cooking. If it needs more time, continue to microwave in 1- to 2-minute bursts, to avoid overcooking. Drizzle over the fish:

Extra-virgin olive oil or melted butter
Serve with:
Lemon wedges
Chopped fresh herbs

ABOUT GRILLING AND BROILING FISH

"Ruling a large kingdom," observed Lao-tzu, "is like cooking a small fish." What he meant was that both should be delicately handled. In the case of grilling and broiling fish, we respectfully disagree: The intense heat chars the surface of the fish, and in the case of grilling, adds a slight smokiness. Fish fillets and steaks to be grilled or broiled benefit from brining or dry-brining, 377, which firms the flesh and seasons the fish. Fish can also be briefly marinated or sprinkled with a rub before grilling. We are partial to Charmoula, 586, and Jerk Spice Rub, 587.

Broiling is pretty straightforward. For fillets or split whole fish, place the oven rack so the fish will be 2 to 3 inches from the broiler. For thick fish steaks or thick whole fish, place the rack about 6 inches from the source of heat. Preheat the broiler for at least 5 minutes and place fish on a lightly oiled baking sheet or broiler pan, or in a cast-iron skillet. Rub the fish with vegetable oil or Clarified Butter, 960. If the fillets have skin, place them skin side down; it is not necessary to turn them during cooking. Thick steaks and whole fish will need to be flipped at least once. Good fish for broiling include: halibut or salmon steaks, sole, split herring, mackerel, and sea trout. For swordfish steaks, baste with plenty of butter and be vigilant, as they tend to become dry. For more on broiling, see 1050.

For **grilling,** Lao-tzu's advice does make some sense: Fish tends to stick to the grill grate, so it must be finessed. Choose skin-on fillets and whole fish, or thick steaks of firm-fleshed fish such as swordfish, salmon, and tuna. Delicate white fish such as pollock or cod are difficult to grill without using leaves, fronds, or a plank (see Planked Fish, 386). Regardless of what fish you grill, fastidiously clean the grates and brush them with a thin layer of vegetable oil. ➤ For more on preparing a grill fire, see 1063.

Whole fish must be turned at least once on the grill to cook evenly. They do not need to be scaled unless you would like to eat the skin. In fact, the scales give the fish a bit more structure, making them easier to turn. Small firm whole fish such as mackerel, pompano, red snapper, and trout are fairly easy to handle, though we recommend holding them steady with tongs while slipping a thin turner underneath. Specially shaped fish grilling baskets are great for whole fish, especially ones that may be too large for a turner or spatula to support.

➤ Thick fish steaks are our favorite cut to grill: Most fish that are cut into steaks are firm to begin with, and the grain of the muscle makes them less prone to sticking and flaking off. In essence, they may be treated as if you were cooking a rare beef steak.

Thick, skin-on fillets are easy to grill, provided you do not attempt to turn them. ➤ To ensure the fillets remain intact, leave the skin on (scaled, if you eat the skin) and cook them entirely on that side (which is less prone to sticking). Move them to a cooler part of the grill when the skin has browned to your liking and finish cooking with the cover on. If using a kettle-style grill, you can avoid moving larger fillets by rotating the entire grill grate until they are off to the side of the coals. If the worst happens and the skin is firmly melded to the grate, the meat of the fillet can still be freed with a spatula and transferred to a plate.

Skin-on fillets of small fish such as sardines may be skewered and grilled. ➤ Thin or delicate fillets from other fish such as tilapia, sole, and cod are virtually impossible to grill unless they are placed on top of something, such as a soaked wooden plank, 386, banana or fig leaves, seaweed, or fennel fronds. Fillets grilled this way may not have grill marks, but they will pick up smoky flavors (as well as the aroma of the leaves or fronds used). Alternatively, wrap delicate fillets in foil pouches as for Fish en Papillote, 379 (do not use parchment).

GRILLED OR BROILED WHOLE FISH

4 servings

Please read About Grilling and Broiling Fish, above. Trout, mackerel, and black cod (sablefish) are good choices; their scales are practically nonexistent. If you do not have your heart set on eating the skin, there is no need to scale other fish. Another option that quickens cooking and results in boneless fish: Butterfly them, 376, and cook entirely skin side down. ***To grill larger fish,*** build a two-zone grill fire, 1063, cook over the coals on both sides as directed, then move the fish off to the side of the coals. Cover and cook until the internal temperature reaches 125° to 130°F.

If necessary, scale and prepare for cooking, 374–76:
Four 1- to 1½-pound whole fish, such as mackerel, trout, or black cod (sablefish)
Prepare a medium-hot grill fire, 1063, or preheat the broiler (with an oven rack 6 inches from the heating element). Pat the fish dry and brush with:
1 tablespoon vegetable oil
Sprinkle inside and out with:
Salt and black pepper
To grill, place the fish on the grill over direct heat for 5 minutes, then carefully turn the fish and cook until done, about 10 minutes more. ***To broil,*** set the fish on an oiled rimmed baking sheet and place under the broiler. Broil the fish, turning once, until firm and opaque throughout and browned on both sides, about 10 minutes total.
The internal temperature should be 125° to 130°F. Serve immediately with:
Lemon wedges, Salsa Verde, 567, or Charmoula, 586

GRILLED OR BROILED WHOLE TROUT WITH BACON

4 servings

If you catch your own trout, there is nothing better. To ensure that the bacon renders and crisps, don't rush the grilling process. While the drama of cooking over a very hot grill is appealing, indirect heat is the only way to go here. If using the broiler, use the rendered bacon drippings to make Wilted Spinach Salad, 118. Please read About Grilling and Broiling Fish, above.
Prepare for cooking, 374–76:
4 whole trout (12 ounces to 1 pound each)

To remove the bones, butterfly them, 376, if desired.

Prepare a medium-hot grill fire, 1063, or preheat the broiler (with an oven rack 6 inches from the heating element). Pat the fish dry and sprinkle with:

Salt and black pepper

Wrap each fish with:

2 slices bacon (8 slices total)

Use sturdy toothpicks, trimmed wooden skewers, or butcher's twine to hold the bacon in place. ***To grill,*** place the fish on the grill over indirect heat. Cover the grill and cook for about 8 minutes, taking care not to burn the bacon. Uncover and cook the fish, turning every so often, until the bacon is crisp and the flesh is firm and opaque throughout, 12 to 15 minutes more.

To broil, lay the trout on an oiled rack on a rimmed baking sheet and place under the broiler. Broil the fish, turning every 5 minutes, until the bacon is crisp and the fish is cooked, 15 to 20 minutes. If needed, lower the broiler rack.

The internal temperature should be 125° to 135°F.

GRILLED WHOLE STUFFED TROUT

4 servings

This recipe can be adapted for broiling—use Grilled or Broiled Whole Fish, 384, as a guide. Trout are among the easiest fish to grill whole. You may slather the inside with a paste to season the flesh, or stuff with a fragrant bread crumb mixture. Please read About Grilling and Broiling Fish, 384.

Prepare one of the following:

½ cup Green Curry Paste, 585, Mexican Adobo I, 584, Jamaican Jerk Paste, 584, or Chinese Black Bean Sauce, 573, or ⅓ cup Harissa I, 584

1 cup Pesto, 586, Charmoula, 586, or Salsa Verde, 567

1½ cups Parsley and Bread Crumb Stuffing, 534

Prepare a medium-hot grill fire, 1063. Prepare for cooking, 374–76:

4 small trout (about 12 ounces each)

To remove the bones, butterfly them, 376, if desired. Pat the fish dry inside and out. Sprinkle with:

Salt and black pepper

Place one-quarter of the paste or stuffing in the body cavity of each trout. Lash each fish together with three pieces of butcher's twine. Place the trout on the grill and cook for 4 to 5 minutes per side, or until golden brown and blistered on the outside and opaque throughout. The internal temperature should be 125° to 130°F.

SPICE-RUBBED GRILLED OR BROILED FISH

4 servings

Spice rubs add tremendous flavor to grilled or broiled fish. As the fish cooks, the rub forms a dense, flavorful crust on the outside, leaving the inside moist and tender. Please read About Grilling and Broiling Fish, 384.

If necessary, scale and prepare for cooking, 374–76:

Two 1½- to 2-pound whole fish or four 8-ounce fish fillets or fish steaks, cut about 1½ inches thick

Pat dry and rub generously with one of the following:

½ recipe Southern Barbecue Dry Rub, 587

Cajun Blackening Spice, 587

Jerk Spice Rub, 587

Chili powder, store-bought or homemade, 588

You may not need to use all the rub. Set aside. Prepare a medium-hot grill fire, 1063, or preheat the broiler (with an oven rack 3 inches beneath the broiler if the fish is 1 inch thick or less, and 6 inches beneath the broiler if the fish is more than 1 inch thick). If grilling, oil the grill rack. If broiling, place the fish on an oiled baking sheet. Place the fish on the grill over indirect heat or under the broiler and grill or broil for 5 to 10 minutes per side depending on the thickness of the fish, or until opaque throughout and the internal temperature reaches 130°F. Serve at once.

GRILLED FISH STEAKS

4 servings

This recipe can be easily adapted for broiling. We enjoy grilled tuna steaks served on a bun with wasabi-spiked mayonnaise, lettuce, tomato, and avocado. Please read About Grilling and Broiling Fish, 584.

Have ready:

1½ to 2 pounds firm fish steaks, such as tuna, swordfish, or salmon, preferably 1½ to 2 inches thick

If desired, dry-brine, 377, then rinse and pat them dry.

Prepare a medium-hot grill fire, 1063. Brush the fish with:

2 tablespoons vegetable oil

If desired, sprinkle with:

(Salt, if the fish was not brined)

(Black pepper, or a dry rub, 587)

Place on the grill over direct heat and cook, turning once, 4 to 5 minutes per side for rare (120°F), 5 to 7 minutes per side for medium-rare (125°F), or 7 to 9 minutes per side for medium (130°F). If desired, baste the steaks after each turn with:

(Juice of ½ lemon)

Garnish with:

Lemon wedges and chopped herbs

Or serve with a flavorful table sauce such as:

Charmoula, 586, or a salsa, 573–74

For tuna steaks, we recommend serving with the following accompaniments:

A small dish of soy sauce or ponzu sauce, 1020

1 tablespoon wasabi paste

Pickled Ginger, 930

FISH KEBABS WITH VINAIGRETTE

4 servings

Please read About Grilling and Broiling Fish, 384, and Skewer Cooking, 1065.

Cut into 1½-inch cubes:

1½ to 2 pounds thick, firm fish steaks or fillets, such as swordfish or tuna

Brine, 376, if desired. If using bamboo skewers, soak them in water for at least 30 minutes.

Prepare a medium-hot grill fire, 1063, or preheat the broiler (with an oven rack 6 inches from the heating element). Oil the grill rack.
Prepare in a large bowl:

Vinaigrette, 575, with fresh herbs added

Pat the fish cubes dry and add them to the bowl along with:

2 firm-ripe nectarines or peaches, pitted, quartered, and each quarter halved crosswise
2 red bell peppers, quartered and each quarter halved crosswise
2 red onions, cut into 8 wedges each

Toss to combine and thread everything onto 8 metal or wooden skewers; do not crowd. If broiling, place the skewers on a lightly oiled baking sheet. Grill over direct heat or broil, turning as each side browns and brushing occasionally with any remaining marinade, 10 to 15 minutes. Remove from the grill and serve immediately.

TERIYAKI-GRILLED FISH STEAKS

4 servings

The secret to succulent teriyaki is to apply the glaze bit by bit toward the end of the grilling process so that it becomes deeply browned but does not burn. The technique also works well with eel, and boneless chicken breasts or thighs. Please read About Grilling and Broiling Fish, 384.
Prepare:

Teriyaki Marinade, 582

Place in a baking dish or zip-top bag:

Four 6- to 8-ounce salmon, tuna, or other fish steaks, at least 1 inch thick, patted dry

Add the marinade and turn the fish to coat. Marinate for about 15 minutes, turning once. Remove the fish from the marinade, and pat dry. Transfer the marinade to a saucepan and cook, stirring, over medium heat until reduced by half. Pour half of the reduced marinade in a bowl for serving.

Prepare a hot grill fire, 1063, and oil the grill rack or preheat the broiler (with the oven rack 2 to 3 inches from the heating element). If broiling, place the fish on a lightly oiled rimmed baking sheet. Grill or broil for 2 minutes, until the fish begins to brown. Turn and grill or broil for 2 minutes more. Move the fish to a cooler part of the grill, or move the broiler rack down a notch. Brush the fish with the remaining teriyaki mixture and grill or broil, with the glazed surface facing the heat, until the glaze dries, about 1 minute. Brush the other side with more teriyaki and turn so that side faces the heat, cooking until the glaze dries. The fish should be done or nearly so, with an internal temperature of 125° to 130°F. If it needs another few minutes, repeat the brushing and glazing procedure once or twice. Serve with the reserved teriyaki sauce.

PLANKED FISH

4 servings

This cooking method is adaptable to many seasonings, but if you use an aromatic wood such as cedar, try to restrain your creativity and enjoy the lovely aroma it imparts to the fish. We prefer to use cedar and a large salmon fillet that fits neatly on the plank. If you have some open bottles of wine, you may soak the plank in wine instead of water. Please read about Planking, 1064.
Soak in water for at least 6 hours:

A 6 × 12-inch plank of untreated wood such as alder, hickory, maple, or cedar

Have ready:

1½ to 2 pounds fish fillets or steaks, such as salmon, black sea bass, halibut, or monkfish

Brush the fish with:

Olive oil or melted butter

Season with:

Salt and black pepper

Prepare a hot grill fire, 1063. Place the plank on the grill and let it heat until it just begins to smoke. Place the fish in the center of the plank, skin side down. Cover the grill and cook until the fish is opaque throughout, 10 to 15 minutes depending on the thickness. The internal temperature should be about 125°F. Serve with:

Lemon wedges

GRILLED OR BROILED FISH FILLETS

4 servings

If grilling, only use skin-on fillets at least 1 inch thick. If grilling or broiling fillets of oily fish such as bluefish or black cod (sablefish), no oil is needed. Please read About Grilling and Broiling Fish, 384.
Prepare a hot, two-zone grill fire, 1063, or preheat the broiler (with an oven rack 3 inches from the heating element if the fish is 1 inch thick or less, and 6 inches from the heat if the fish is over 1 inch thick). Oil a baking sheet or shallow roasting pan. Brush:

1½ to 2 pounds fish fillets, skin on or off, in 1 or more pieces, patted dry

with:

2 tablespoons olive oil or melted butter

Sprinkle with:

Salt and black pepper

To grill, place the fish skin side down over direct heat and grill undisturbed for 4 minutes. Fillets that are ½ inch thick or less are done as soon as the exterior turns opaque. If they are thicker, check after 6 minutes. Fish up to 1 inch thick will probably be done at this point; thicker fillets will need another couple of minutes. Those over 1½ inches thick should be turned and cooked another 5 or 6 minutes until firm and opaque throughout. If needed, move the fish to the cooler part of the grill or lower the broiler rack to finish cooking.
To broil, place the fish skin side down on the oiled baking sheet and under the broiler. Broil for 4 minutes. The internal temperature should be 125° to 130°F.
Sprinkle with:

Fresh lemon juice

Serve with:

Any of the suggestions in Sauces for Fish, 378

GRILLED OR BROILED FISH FILLETS WITH HERBS

Prepare **Grilled or Broiled Fish Fillets, above.** Stir **2 tablespoons chopped herbs (any combination of parsley, chervil, basil, thyme, and/or fennel fronds)** into the olive oil or melted butter or use **Char-**

moula, 586, instead of the olive oil or butter. If the fillets are ½ inch thick or less, spread this paste on them before broiling. Rub thicker fillets with some olive oil or melted butter before cooking and spread the herb paste on them 3 or 4 minutes before they are done.

BROILED FISH FILLETS WITH BREAD CRUMBS

Prepare **Browned or Buttered Bread Crumbs, 957,** using ¾ cup fresh bread crumbs, 957, and 3 tablespoons olive oil or butter. Prepare broiled fish as directed in **Grilled or Broiled Fish Fillets, 386.** If the fillets are ½ inch thick or less, omit the olive oil or butter and spread the bread crumb mixture on them before broiling. Rub thicker fillets with some olive oil or melted butter and spread the bread crumb mixture on them 3 to 4 minutes before they are done. Serve with **parsley** and **lemon wedges** or **any of the suggestions in Sauces for Fish, 378.**

BLACK COD MISOZUKE

4 servings

This dish is traditionally called *kasuzuke* and is made with sake lees or **kasu,** a byproduct of sake brewing. We use miso because it is much easier to find, though you can sometimes find *kasu* at Japanese grocery stores. To use *kasu,* substitute for the marinade below a mixture of **½ cup sake lees (kasu), ¼ cup mirin, ¼ cup water, 2 tablespoons brown sugar, 2 tablespoons white miso, and 1 tablespoon soy sauce or tamari.** A nice, fatty salmon fillet (preferably king salmon or Chinook) can fill in for black cod.

Place in a gallon zip-top bag:

1½ to 2 pounds black cod (sablefish) fillets, cut into 4 pieces

Mix together in a bowl until smooth:

¼ cup white miso
¼ cup mirin
¼ cup sake (preferably unfiltered)
1 tablespoon soy sauce or tamari
1 tablespoon sugar

Scrape the marinade into the bag, carefully squeeze the air out, and seal it. Gently massage the bag until the fillets are coated with the marinade. Put the bag in a bowl and marinate in the refrigerator for at least 1 hour or overnight.

Preheat the broiler for 10 minutes and place an oven rack as close to the broiler as possible.

Meanwhile, remove the fish from the bag, and wipe off excess marinade with a paper towel. Put the fillets skin side down on a sturdy rimmed baking sheet lined with foil.

Broil until the surface is nicely browned and the fish begins to flake when prodded with a fork, 5 to 6 minutes for 1-inch-thick fillets. Remove from the oven. The broiling causes any pin bones to protrude from the fillets. Remove them. We like to serve the fish with:

Cooked short-grain rice, 343 (mixed with a little rice vinegar, if desired)
Sprouts or tender greens

ABOUT SEARING, SAUTÉING, AND PAN-FRYING FISH

These methods involve cooking fish on the stovetop in a very small to moderate amount of fat. ➤ Always use a fat that can withstand the heat at which the fish will be cooked—refined vegetable oils with a high smoke point, 981, or Clarified Butter, 960, work well for high heat. Dry fish well to reduce splattering caused by surface moisture. We also recommend using a splatter screen for these cooking methods to keep splattering oil burns to a minimum and to avoid making a greasy mess. A slotted fish spatula is another important tool for cooking fish with these methods. It supports the flesh of the fish during turning and is thin and flexible enough to slide easily beneath delicate fillets.

Searing uses the least amount of oil and the highest temperature of these three methods. Use this method for browning and crisping the skin on thick fish fillets, for fish steaks that you plan to serve rare or medium-rare, or for browning the skin of fish that has been cooked sous vide. Use a heavy pan, such as cast iron, to sear fish, and make sure your exhaust fan is on (or that the kitchen is well ventilated). Fish to be seared should be at least 1 inch thick. Heat the skillet over medium-high to high heat until ripping hot (a few drops of water flicked onto the surface should hiss and evaporate immediately), then add a small amount of oil with a high smoke point. Add the fish to the pan and sear until well browned, then flip and sear the second side. The whole process should take a few minutes per side at most. If the fish has been coated with a Cajun blend of spices before searing, it is **blackened,** 389. **Pan-roasting** is a sister technique to searing that works well for thick fish fillets with skin on one side or for whole small fish such as trout. Preheat the oven to a moderate temperature, 350° to 375°F. Sear the skin side of fillets or one side of a whole fish as directed above, then transfer the skillet to the oven to allow the fish to finish cooking. Fillets should be left skin side down, and whole fish should be flipped before placing in the oven.

Sautéing fish is done at a slightly lower temperature than searing and is best suited to firm-fleshed fish. Because of the moderate temperature, butter may be used in sautéing. The butter browns during cooking, giving the fish a lovely nutty flavor. After cooking the fish, the pan juices may be turned into a sauce. Steaks, fillets, and small whole fish can be **pan-fried.** The heat is kept fairly high, and a thin layer of oil is added to the pan. Oils and fats with a high smoke point, 981, are best for pan-frying.

Dredging fish in flour or crumbs before sautéing or pan-frying can give it a fantastic crunch and promotes browning (which is especially useful for quick-cooking fish). Dip it in a bowl of milk, buttermilk, or beaten egg or egg white before dredging in flour or meal to help the coating adhere. The dredge can be as simple as fine cornmeal or flour seasoned with salt and pepper. Or, use a mixture of 3 parts fine cornmeal to 1 part flour. For even crunchier results, try using Bound Bread Crumb or Cracker Coating, 658 (we are partial to panko). For tips on breading and coating fried foods, see 658.

PAN-FRIED FISH FILLETS OR STEAKS

4 servings

Our favorite way to cook salmon fillets. Most of the frying occurs on the skin side, which gets nice and crispy.

Have ready:

1½ to 2 pounds skin-on fish fillets or steaks, at least 1 inch thick

Brine or dry-brine, 376–77, if desired, and pat dry. Sprinkle with:

Salt (if not brined) and black pepper

Heat in a large skillet over medium-high heat until shimmering:

2 tablespoons vegetable oil

For fillets: Lay the fish skin side down in the skillet and press gently on the top of the fillets with a spatula for the first 30 seconds. Cook until the skin is deep brown, 5 to 7 minutes. Turn the fish and cook for about 1 minute more for medium-rare to medium or 2 minutes for well-done.

For steaks: Cook the fish on one side for 4 minutes, turn, and cook for 4 minutes more, or until the internal temperature in the center of the fish reads 125° to 130°F. If desired, serve with:

(Salsa Verde, 567, Yogurt-Dill Sauce, 569, or Fruit Salsa, 574)

BREADED PAN-FRIED FISH

4 servings

This basic recipe is useful for every fish from tiny smelts or sardines to midsized butterfish, bluegills, crappie, and sunfish all the way up to croaker and porgy. Rice flour and cornstarch will produce crispier results; for added crunch, try Bound Bread Crumb or Cracker Coating, 658. Please read About Searing, Sautéing, and Pan-Frying Fish, 387.

If necessary, gut, scale, and prepare for cooking, 374–76:

4 pounds small whole fish, or 1½ pounds ½-inch-thick white-fleshed fish fillets, such as flounder or sole

Pour into a shallow dish:

1 cup milk or buttermilk, or as needed to cover

Add the fish and soak for 15 minutes. Mix in a shallow bowl:

1 cup fine cornmeal, flour, rice flour, or cornstarch or a combination
1 teaspoon salt
1 teaspoon black pepper

Lift the fish out of the liquid, allowing the excess to drip off, coat it with the dredge, and set on a plate. Heat to 375°F in a large skillet over medium-high heat:

½ cup vegetable oil (mixed with bacon drippings, if desired) or lard

When the fat is hot, add the fish in small batches and fry, turning once, until browned on both sides, adjusting the heat so that the fat is always bubbling but not burning the coating. Usually the fish is done when both sides are golden, but check the interior of larger fish to make sure the flesh is firm and opaque throughout. Drain well on paper towels. Serve hot with:

Minced parsley and lemon wedges, Pico de Gallo, 573, or Tartar Sauce, 563

SAUTÉED SMELTS OR ANCHOVIES

4 servings

A superlative appetizer or beer snack; serve with a green salad for a memorable lunch. Please read About Searing, Sautéing, and Pan-Frying Fish, 387.

Prepare for cooking, 374–76:

1½ pounds smelts or fresh anchovies

Pour into a shallow dish:

1 cup milk or buttermilk, or as needed to cover

Mix in a shallow bowl:

1 cup fine cornmeal or flour or a combination
1 teaspoon salt
1 teaspoon black pepper

Preheat the oven to 200°F. Heat in a large skillet over medium heat:

4 tablespoons (½ stick) butter or olive oil

When the fat is hot, dip the fish in the milk, coat it with the dredge, and add to the skillet in batches. Fry, turning occasionally, until both sides are golden brown and the flesh is firm and opaque, 6 to 8 minutes total. Drain on a plate lined with paper towels and keep warm in the oven. Add more butter or oil to the skillet, if needed, and fry the rest of the fish. Serve piping hot with:

Lemon wedges
(Aïoli, 564, Rémoulade Sauce, 564, or Tartar Sauce, 563)

BROOK TROUT MEUNIÈRE

4 servings

Please read About Searing, Sautéing, and Pan-Frying Fish, 387.

Have ready:

4 brook trout, about 8 ounces each

Cut off the fins; leave the heads and tails on. Thoroughly whisk together on a plate:

1 cup flour
1 teaspoon salt
½ teaspoon black pepper

Dredge the trout in the seasoned flour. Heat in a large skillet over medium-high heat:

¼ cup Clarified Butter, 960

When the butter is hot, add the trout and cook, turning once, until firm and nicely browned, about 3 minutes per side. Transfer to a hot platter. Add to the drippings in the skillet:

3 tablespoons butter

Let it brown. Sprinkle the fish with:

Chopped parsley

Pour the browned butter over the fish. Garnish with:

Lemon wedges

PAN-FRIED SKATE WITH BLACK BUTTER

4 servings

Please read About Searing, Sautéing, and Pan-Frying Fish, 387.

Preheat the oven to 200°F. Thoroughly whisk together on a plate:

1 cup flour
1 teaspoon salt
½ teaspoon black pepper

Dredge in the flour mixture:

Four 6-ounce boneless skate wings

Heat a skillet large enough to hold the skate in a single layer over medium-high heat. Add and melt until the foam subsides:

3 tablespoons butter

Add the skate and brown on both sides, 2 to 3 minutes per side; the skate is done when you can begin to separate the segments. Transfer to a platter and keep warm in the oven. Wipe out the skillet and return to medium heat. Cook:

3 tablespoons butter
until the milk solids fall to the bottom of the skillet and turn dark brown, then remove from the heat and stir in:
2 tablespoons drained capers
1 tablespoon white wine vinegar
Let sizzle about 10 seconds. Pour the sauce over the skate and garnish with:
Minced parsley

SAUTÉED PEPPER-CRUSTED FISH STEAKS

4 servings

If desired, substitute ¾ cup chicken stock plus 2 tablespoons lemon juice for the wine in the pan sauce made after cooking the fish. Reduce as directed. Please read About Searing, Sautéing, and Pan-Frying Fish, 387.
Dry-brine, 377:
4 thick tuna or swordfish steaks (6 to 8 ounces each)
Rinse off the salt and pat dry. Press onto both sides of the steaks:
2 tablespoons coarsely cracked black peppercorns or a mixture of cracked black, white, pink, and green peppercorns
Any pepper that does not adhere can be sprinkled onto the fish while it cooks. Heat in a large skillet over medium-high heat:
2 tablespoons vegetable oil
When hot, add the steaks to the skillet and brown them for 2 to 3 minutes on each side, or until the internal temperature is 120° to 125°F for rare to medium-rare. Transfer to a warmed platter and reduce the heat to medium. Add to the skillet:
1 cup dry red or white wine
1 small shallot, minced
Cook, stirring, until the wine is reduced by about one-third and the shallots are softened, about 2 minutes. Remove from the heat and whisk in bit by bit:
2 tablespoons butter, cut into small pieces
Add:
1 teaspoon minced fresh tarragon or a pinch of dried tarragon, or 2 tablespoons minced parsley
Salt to taste
Spoon the sauce over the steaks and serve.

BLACKENED FISH STEAKS OR FILLETS

4 servings

The original blackened fish was redfish. The spice mixture and technique were created in New Orleans by chef Paul Prudhomme. Make this dish with any firm-fleshed steaks or fillets, such as swordfish, red snapper, grouper, or catfish. But do not make the dish unless your stove has a functional exhaust fan. And turn off the smoke detectors (don't forget to turn them back on after cooking!).
Please read about Blackening, 1053. Prepare:
Cajun Blackening Spice, 587
Place a large cast-iron skillet over high heat. Turn on the exhaust fan. Have ready:
½ cup Clarified Butter, 960
1½ to 2 pounds firm-fleshed fish fillets or steaks, patted dry
When the pan is quite hot, after 5 to 8 minutes, brush both sides of the fish with a little of the butter, then lay it in the spice mixture, turning to coat. Place in the pan and drizzle a little butter over each. Cook, turning once, for 3 to 6 minutes, depending on the thickness of the fish, or until the flesh is firm and opaque throughout. Serve with:
Lemon wedges

PAN-FRIED SALMON CAKES

4 to 6 servings

You don't have to remove the bones and skin from the salmon, but do so if you prefer. If desired, make the cakes slightly larger and serve on buns as salmon burgers. These make an excellent quick, affordable dinner.
Combine in a large bowl:
Two 15-ounce cans salmon, drained
½ cup fine bread or cracker crumbs
½ cup shredded sharp Cheddar (2 ounces)
2 large eggs, beaten
2 teaspoons minced fresh thyme or 1 teaspoon dried thyme
¼ teaspoon salt
¼ teaspoon black pepper
Heat in a large skillet (preferably nonstick) over medium heat:
1 tablespoon vegetable oil
Using a ⅓-cup measure, shape the salmon mixture into patties. Cook until browned and firm, flipping once, 3 to 4 minutes per side. Serve with:
Yogurt-Dill Sauce, 569

PAN-FRIED SHAD ROE

2 servings

Shad roe is a sac of tiny eggs held together by a membrane. The two crescent-shaped parts are usually divided and one half will serve one person; it is very rich and filling. The flavor is like nothing else, delicate and not very fishy; the texture is dense and chewy. It is only available in the early spring when the shad are running. Be careful not to overcook, for it continues to cook after being removed from the heat. It should be darker in the center, not uniformly pink throughout.
Prepare the brine for fish, 376. Gently separate the 2 parts and pat dry:
1 pair shad roe
Brine the roe sacs for 2 hours, then drain and pat dry. Whisk together on a plate:
1 cup flour
1 teaspoon salt
Dredge the roe in the flour mixture. Heat in a heavy skillet over medium heat:
3 tablespoons butter or bacon drippings
When the fat is hot, add the roe and cook, turning once, until golden brown on both sides and firm and springy to the touch, about 3 minutes per side. Very large roe sacs may need up to 8 minutes total. Serve on:
Warm toast

Garnish with:

Lemon wedges
Chopped parsley

ABOUT DEEP-FRYING AND SHALLOW-FRYING FISH

In many parts of the country, cooking fish means battering and frying it. Though we would eventually tire of fish if it was always treated in this way, it is impossible to deny its merits: Crispy coatings and fluffy batters add textural contrast and flavor, and the method itself keeps the fish incredibly moist.

The best fish for frying are flaky, white-fleshed fish such as cod, halibut, flounder, dogfish, grouper, and mackerel. Or fry whole fish such as anchovies, herring, sardines, and smelts. The crispiest results are achieved when the fish is coated with flour or crumbs; batters are best for deep-frying fish. For more on these treatments, see About Battering Fried Foods, 656, and About Coating Fried Foods, 658.

For **deep-frying,** the oil should be deep enough that the fish is completely covered. Deep-frying is essential for battered fish: When totally immersed in hot oil, the batter will quickly set on the fish pieces, forming a nice, even layer. Thin fillets can be deep-fried in a skillet with high sides; thick chunks of fish or small whole fish should be fried in a Dutch oven or other heavy, deep vessel. Proper oil temperature is critical: Oil that is too cold will lead to greasy, sodden food, and oil that is too hot risks burning the coating before the food is fully cooked. ➤ For large pieces of fish, an oil temperature of 350°F is ideal; smaller pieces can be fried at higher temperatures, up to 375°F. Use an oil with a high smoke point, 981, to prevent off flavors from developing; do not reuse oil used to fry fish. Please read About Deep-Frying, 1051.

If deep-frying seems wasteful or intimidating because of the amount of oil involved, consider **shallow-frying.** Instead of being completely submerged, oil only comes halfway up the sides of the fish. Consequently, pieces must be carefully turned to cook through and brown evenly on both sides. Use a skillet with high sides, or use a deep pot, which will contain the splattering somewhat. Though deep-frying delivers evenly browned pieces with no turning, we prefer shallow-frying for breaded or coated fish since it uses much less oil. ➤ We do not recommend shallow-frying battered fish; the batter will not set on the exposed surface of fish pieces and slowly drains off into the surrounding oil, leaving the top bare.

When frying several batches of fish, fry a "tester" first to establish a frying time, then keep the temperature of the oil and size of the fish or fillets consistent as you cook. Do not crowd the pan as that will cause the temperature of the oil to drop. Unless the fillet or piece is very thick, the fish will usually be cooked through by the time it is browned on the outside. To test fish for doneness, measure the temperature with an instant-read thermometer—it is cooked through at 125° to 130°F—or cut into a piece and make sure the flesh is opaque and flakes when prodded.

FRIED FISH

Allow about ⅓ pound boneless fish per serving

Use firm-fleshed fish; catfish, snapper, blackfish, dogfish, grouper, and halibut are all good choices. Please read About Deep-Frying and Shallow-Frying Fish, above.

I. DEEP-FRIED

Have ready:

Fillets or chunks of fish, or cleaned small fish

Heat to 370°F in a deep-fryer, deep heavy pot, or Dutch oven over medium-high heat:

3 inches vegetable oil such as peanut or canola

Dip the fish in:

Beer Batter, 657, Tempura Batter, 657, Pakora Batter, 657, Flour Coating, 658, or Bound Bread Crumb or Cracker Coating, 658

Gently lower the fish into the hot fat and fry, without crowding, until golden brown, 5 to 8 minutes. Drain on paper towels or newspaper. Serve very hot, with:

Tartar Sauce, 563, Cilantro-Mint Chutney, 568, Raita, 569, Becker Cocktail Sauce, 569, or the sauce for Pla Raad Prik, 391

II. SHALLOW-FRIED

Have ready:

Fillets or chunks of fish, or cleaned small fish

Heat to 370°F in a heavy skillet with high sides or a Dutch oven:

¾ to 1 inch vegetable oil such as peanut or canola

Dredge the fish in:

Flour Coating, 658, or Bound Bread Crumb or Cracker Coating, 658

Fry, without crowding, until golden brown on both sides, 5 to 8 minutes, turning once. Drain on paper towels or newspaper. Serve very hot, as for version I.

SOUTHERN-STYLE DEEP-FRIED CATFISH

4 servings

Firm catfish fillets are perfect for frying. To serve the fish with Hushpuppies, fry the dough first, drain on a plate or rimmed baking sheet lined with paper towels, and keep warm in a 200°F oven while the fish cooks. Please read About Deep-Frying and Shallow-Frying Fish, above.

Have ready:

1½ to 2 pounds catfish fillets, patted dry

Heat to 350°F in a deep-fryer, deep heavy pot, or Dutch oven over medium-high heat:

2 inches vegetable oil such as peanut or canola

Mix together in a wide shallow dish:

1 cup fine cornmeal
(1 tablespoon chili powder)
1 teaspoon salt
½ teaspoon black pepper

Dredge the fish fillets in the cornmeal mixture, pressing it on so it adheres to the fish. Carefully lower the fish one fillet at a time into the hot oil, without crowding. Cook the fish in batches if necessary—it will not take long. Gently stir once or twice to keep the fillets from sticking. Remove the fillets when they are golden brown, 4 to 5 minutes, and drain on paper towels. Serve immediately with:

Hushpuppies, 655
Tartar Sauce, 563
Lemon wedges

PLA RAAD PRIK (THAI FRIED FISH WITH TAMARIND-GARLIC SAUCE)

2 to 3 servings

This visually stunning dish is topped with a tangy, spicy sauce of tamarind, garlic, and Thai chiles. You will be looking for other things to serve the sauce with. For tips on breading and coating fried foods, see 658. Please read About Deep-Frying and Shallow-Frying Fish, 390.

Heat in a small saucepan over medium-high heat:

1 tablespoon vegetable oil

Add and cook, stirring, until softened:

2 small shallots, minced
3 garlic cloves, minced
2 to 4 fresh red or green Thai chiles, to taste, seeded, if desired, and minced

Stir in:

2 tablespoons tamarind paste, 195, mixed with ¼ cup water
3 tablespoons palm sugar or packed brown sugar
1 tablespoon fish sauce

Remove the tamarind-garlic sauce from the heat. Taste and, if needed, add:

Salt

Have ready:

One 1½- to 2-pound whole fish, such as red snapper, tilapia, or trout, scaled if necessary, 374

With a sharp knife, cut several deep slashes in both sides of the fish running from the dorsal fin to the belly.

Heat to 350°F in a wok, deep heavy pot, or Dutch oven:

2 inches vegetable oil

Mix together well on a large plate or in a shallow baking dish:

½ cup cornstarch or rice flour
1½ teaspoons salt
1 teaspoon white pepper

Dredge both sides of the fish in the cornstarch mixture. When the oil is hot, gently lower the fish into the oil and fry for 4 minutes, then turn the fish with tongs and fry until the fish is cooked through, 4 minutes more. Remove the fish from the oil to drain on paper towels. Serve whole topped with the tamarind-garlic sauce.

FISH AND CHIPS

4 servings

On the East Coast, dogfish (sometimes sold as "cape shark" or "sand shark") is classic, but the deluxe "chipping" fish on the West Coast is halibut. Cod and haddock are also common. Any white-fleshed fish is suitable, but we recommend firmer fillets, as they are less likely to fall apart. Please read About Deep-Frying and Shallow-Frying Fish, 390.

Preheat the oven to 200°F. Cut into thick uniform strips slightly larger than French fries:

4 large russet potatoes, peeled

Soak in cold water for 30 minutes.

Prepare:

Beer Batter, 657

Set aside. Heat to 330°F in a deep-fryer, deep heavy pot, or Dutch oven over medium-high heat:

3 inches vegetable oil such as peanut or canola

Drain and dry the potatoes. Drop the potatoes about 1 cup at a time into the hot oil and fry until the spattering ceases, about 2 minutes. Remove with a slotted spoon and drain on a brown paper bag or paper towels. When finished with the potatoes, increase the temperature of the oil to 365°F. Stir the batter. Dip into it one piece at a time, letting the excess batter drip off:

1½ pounds dogfish, halibut, or other white-fleshed fish fillets, patted dry

Slip the fish carefully into the oil. Adjust the heat, if necessary, to maintain the temperature. The fish is done when golden brown. Drain on paper towels and keep warm in the oven.

To finish the chips, fry the potatoes a second time in small batches until golden brown, 2 to 3 minutes. Drain on paper towels. Arrange the potatoes and fish on a platter and serve with:

Malt vinegar
Lemon wedges
Tartar Sauce, 563

THAI FISH CAKES

4 servings

These are fragrant, spicy, crisp, and fresh tasting. Serve with a spicy, vinegary coleslaw, 119, or Green Papaya Salad, 129. If desired, these cakes may be shallow-fried by flattening them slightly and turning once during cooking. Please read About Deep-Frying and Shallow-Frying Fish, 390.

Combine in a food processor:

1 shallot, chopped
2 garlic cloves, chopped
½-inch piece ginger or galangal, 989, peeled and coarsely chopped
2 tablespoons fish sauce
Finely grated zest of 1 lime
1 teaspoon red pepper flakes
1 teaspoon sugar
½ teaspoon salt

Pulse until finely chopped. Add:

1 pound white-fleshed fish fillets, patted dry and cut into 1-inch chunks
1 large egg

Process to a paste. Add and pulse the machine a few times to combine:

2 tablespoons minced cilantro
2 green onions, coarsely chopped

Transfer to a bowl. Heat to 370°F in a deep-fryer, deep heavy pot, or Dutch oven over medium-high heat:

2 inches vegetable oil such as peanut or canola

Knead the fish mixture until it is smooth, then shape it into 1-inch balls. Carefully add them to the hot oil, adjusting the heat to maintain the temperature if needed. Cook, in batches if necessary, until deeply browned, 2 to 3 minutes. Drain on paper towels. Serve, garnished with:

Cilantro, mint, and/or Thai basil
Lime wedges

ESCABECHE (SPANISH MARINATED FRIED FISH)

4 servings

Firm, white-fleshed fish work well here, but sardine and mackerel fillets are also quite good. Please read About Deep-Frying and Shallow-Frying Fish, 390.

Combine in a small saucepan:

½ cup white wine vinegar
½ cup water
2 garlic cloves, minced
1 small jalapeño pepper or other chile, seeded and minced
1½ teaspoons sugar
½ teaspoon ground cumin
½ teaspoon salt
¼ teaspoon black pepper

Bring to a boil over high heat, then remove from the heat. Thoroughly whisk together on a plate:

½ cup flour
½ teaspoon salt
¼ teaspoon black pepper

Dredge in the flour mixture to coat well:

1 pound skinned cod, snapper, or halibut fillets

Heat in a large skillet over medium-high heat until hot but not smoking:

¼ cup vegetable oil

Fry the fillets until golden brown and opaque at the center, 3 to 4 minutes on each side depending on the thickness. Transfer to a wide shallow bowl. Pour the vinegar mixture on top and sprinkle with:

¼ cup chopped cilantro
2 tablespoons lime juice

Let sit until the fish has cooled completely to allow the marinade to flavor the fish. Serve at room temperature.

FRIED TINY FISH

These fish morsels make a superb appetizer on their own or as part of a Fritto Misto, 658.

Please read About Deep-Frying and Shallow-Frying Fish, 390. Have ready:

Whole whitebait, smelts, or fresh anchovies, or fresh sardine fillets

Whitebait are so small that they may be eaten whole, guts and all; smelts and anchovies should be gutted and have their heads removed, 374. Heat to 375°F in a deep-fryer, deep heavy pot, or Dutch oven over medium-high heat:

2 inches vegetable oil such as peanut or canola

Combine in a medium bowl:

1 cup fine cornmeal, flour, rice flour, or cornstarch
1 teaspoon salt
1 teaspoon black pepper

Gently toss the fish with this mixture, shake off the excess, and fry in batches for 2 to 3 minutes, or until crisp and golden brown. Garnish with:

Lemon wedges

ABOUT SMOKED AND PRESERVED FISH

Fishermen throughout human history have developed strategies to prolong their harvest without the aid of refrigeration. Smoking, drying, salting, and pickling are no longer essential for preserving fish, but the flavors and textures these processes create are remarkable, and worth seeking out. Others are perhaps a little too remarkable for most diners; while we do not discuss lutefisk, *surströmming*, or *hákarl* in these pages, we encourage the adventurous to press onward and investigate their distinctive, limited appeal. For types of preserved fish that are used primarily as a seasoning or ingredient, see Anchovies, 953, Bonito, 956, Bottarga, 1016, and Seafood, Dried, 1016.

Cured salmon, such as the ever-popular bagel topping **lox**, has a mild flavor and delicate texture. Though available at the supermarket, it is a stone-simple process that is easily replicated at home. **Gravlax,** lox's rustic Nordic ancestor, is often flavored with herbs and other aromatics. Though it may have been considered an effective preservation technique when it was first developed by industrious Nordic fishermen—who buried it in the ground to partially ferment—gravlax and lox are perishable, and we recommend storing them for no more than 1 week. Other cured products, like **marinated herring,** 397, can be stored for much longer.

Lox, as well as brined haddock and herring, are often cold-smoked. This imparts a very fine flavor and texture, but takes place at temperatures that do not cook the fish. This process turns cured salmon into **Nova lox** and haddock into **finnan haddie.** A cold-smoked herring is known as a **kipper**—actually a general term for any smoked fish (for more, see 397). ➤ We do not recommend attempting to cold-smoke fish at home due to safety concerns.

Hot-smoking, 1068, cooks fish to doneness. Hot-smoking is particularly suited to fatty, seafaring fish like salmon and black cod (sablefish), as well as freshwater fish like trout, sturgeon, and chub. Indeed, this is by far the most popular style of smoking fish in the salmon-rich Pacific Northwest. All hot-smoked fish is ready to eat and will keep for about the same amount of time as any cooked fish; store all smoked fish refrigerated in covered containers and eat within a week of smoking or purchase.

Curing fish heavily with salt and then air-drying it until rock-hard is a much more effective preservation method. **Salted mackerel** and **herring** can be found from time to time, but the most celebrated and widely available is **salt cod** (now made with other white-fleshed fish like haddock due to the overfishing of cod). All of these are found filleted and bone-free, but they must be soaked in water before cooking to soften and desalt them. For a delicious salt cod appetizer, see Brandade de Morue, 54. For Salt Cod Croquettes, see 655.

To desalt salted fish, soak the fish in several changes of fresh water in the refrigerator for 24 to 48 hours before using.

To flake salt cod, put the desalted fish in cold unsalted Court Bouillon, 80, or just plain water to cover, and bring to a boil, then reduce the heat and simmer for 25 minutes. Drain, remove any skin and bones, and flake. One pound dried salt cod will yield about 2 cups flaked fish.

GRAVLAX (CURED SALMON)

15 servings

This traditional Swedish method of curing salmon is easy to do at home. The fish must be impeccably fresh. Gravlax keeps well, covered and refrigerated, for several days. Please read About Smoked and Preserved Fish, 392. As with raw fish and Ceviche, 377, ➤ use only previously frozen (or "sushi-grade") salmon, as salt-curing alone does not kill parasites. If you wish to cure freshly caught salmon, hot-smoke it instead (see below).

Leaving the skin on, cut into 2 large fillets:

One 4- to 5- pound whole salmon, gutted and cleaned, 374–76

With a sharp knife, score the skin every inch or so, cutting into the flesh as little as possible. Mix together in a medium bowl:

2 cups Diamond kosher salt
1 cup sugar
1 tablespoon black pepper
(1 tablespoon ground fennel)
(1 tablespoon ground coriander)
(Zest of 2 lemons, removed with a vegetable peeler and cut into thin strips)
(Zest of 2 limes, removed with a vegetable peeler and cut into thin strips)

Rub the fillets all over with this mixture. Place one of the fillets flesh side up and lay over the flesh:

2 cups coarsely chopped dill, including stems
(2 medium beets, shredded)

If desired, sprinkle with:

(2 tablespoons aquavit or plain or lemon-flavored vodka)

Lay the other fillet flesh side down on top of the dill-covered fillet. Sprinkle the outside with the remaining sugar mixture and wrap as tightly as possible in several layers of plastic wrap. Place on a platter or baking sheet, cover with a cutting board or second baking sheet, and weight with 4 pounds of cans or other weights. Refrigerate for 3 days. Once a day, remove the weights, flip the salmon packet over, and place the weights back on. The gravlax is done when the flesh is opaque. Remove the salmon from its wrappings and rinse off any remaining cure. Pat dry. Slice thinly.

HOT-SMOKED SALMON

2 pounds

This recipe can be scaled up depending on how much salmon you wish to smoke. Black cod (sablefish), sturgeon, and mackerel are also excellent prepared in this way. Please read about Smoking, 1067.

Combine in a medium bowl:

4 cups cool water
½ cup packed brown sugar
¼ cup pickling or table salt or ½ cup Diamond kosher salt

Whisk until the salt and sugar are dissolved. Use fish tweezers or a clean pair of pliers to remove any bones from:

2 pounds skin-on salmon fillets

Place the salmon in a glass, enamel, or stainless steel pan just large enough to hold it. Alternatively, place in a 1-gallon heavy-duty zip-top bag and place the bag in a bowl in case of leakage. Pour the brine over the salmon, cover the pan or seal the bag, and refrigerate for 8 hours. If the salmon is not completely submerged in the brine, turn it occasionally. When finished brining, pat the salmon dry and place it skin side down on a rack and refrigerate uncovered until dry to the touch, 8 to 12 hours.

Heat a smoker or grill set up for indirect cooking, 1062, to 200°F (preferably with a water pan). Add to the coals:

1 small chunk alder, apple, pecan, maple, or other hard wood

Add the salmon to the cooler side of the smoker or grill, skin side down. Smoke for 45 minutes, then, if desired, baste the fish lightly with:

(Maple syrup or warmed honey)

Continue to smoke, basting every 15 minutes with more syrup, if using, until the internal temperature of the fish reaches 145°F, no more. Remove the fish from the smoker and let cool completely. Wrap tightly and refrigerate for up to 10 days or vacuum-seal and freeze for up to 6 months.

SMOKED SALMON HASH

4 servings

A stellar breakfast or brunch dish courtesy of David Barber, chef and owner of the much-missed Three Square Grill in Hillsdale, Oregon. For a more Scandinavian take, omit the bell pepper, Tabasco sauce, and Worcestershire sauce. Stir in with the salmon: **1 tablespoon prepared horseradish, 1 tablespoon whole-grain mustard,** and **3 tablespoons drained capers.** Top each serving with **1 to 2 tablespoons sour cream or crème fraîche.**

Boil until just tender, 265:

1½ pounds red potatoes

Drain and let cool enough to handle. For small potatoes, lightly flatten them with a glass. Cut larger potatoes into 1-inch cubes. Heat in a large skillet over medium heat:

2 tablespoons vegetable oil

Add and cook, stirring, until the peppers are softened, about 7 minutes:

½ red bell pepper, chopped
1 medium onion, chopped

Add the potatoes, stir, press down firmly with a spatula, and cook undisturbed until browned, about 10 minutes. Scrape up the potatoes, stir, press down, and cook 10 minutes more or until brown. Add and stir to combine:

6 ounces hot-smoked salmon, flaked
Dash of Tabasco sauce
Dash of Worcestershire sauce

Season to taste with:

Salt and black pepper

Divide among plates and top with:

4 Fried Eggs, 155, or Poached Eggs, 153

Garnish with:

Minced parsley
(Lemon wedges)

SALT HERRING AND POTATOES

4 servings

Soak overnight in water or milk to cover:
2 large salt herring (kippered herring)
Drain and split them into 2 fillets. Remove and discard the skin and bones. Cut the fillets into 1-inch-wide pieces. Preheat the oven to 375°F. Butter a 9-inch square baking dish.
Very thinly slice:
6 red potatoes, peeled, if desired
1 medium onion
Arrange the potatoes, onions, and herring in alternating layers in the prepared baking dish, beginning and ending with potatoes. Cover the top with:
Au Gratin II, 958
Bake until the potatoes are tender, about 45 minutes.

KEDGEREE

4 servings

Bring to a boil in a medium saucepan:
½ cup heavy cream
Add and simmer for 2 minutes:
1 teaspoon curry powder
½ teaspoon salt
¼ teaspoon cayenne pepper
Add and heat through:
3 cups cooked basmati or jasmine rice, 343
Meanwhile, thinly slice, keeping the white and green parts separate:
4 green onions
Fold the onion whites into the rice mixture along with:
8 ounces smoked haddock or trout fillets, at room temperature, broken into ½-inch pieces
Transfer the kedgeree to a serving dish. Top with the onion greens and:
3 Hard-Boiled Eggs, 151, chopped

ABOUT ROE AND MILT

The eggs of female fish are known as **roe,** or **hard roe;** the male fish's sperm is known as **milt,** or **soft roe,** as its texture is creamy rather than grainy. Both types are used in cooking, but hard roe is far more popular. It is lightly brined to season and firm. The roe of certain fish is more valued than the fish itself; for **caviar,** see 66. For **shad roe,** see 66.

You may serve the roe or milt of fish such as herring, mackerel, flounder, salmon, carp, or cod as in the recipe for Pan-Fried Shad Roe, 389. The milt of salmon must have the vein removed. Roe may also be served as an appetizer, particularly as a beautiful and delicious topping for canapés, 66, Deviled Eggs, 151, or stuffed potatoes, 59. Or use with sushi, 355 (particularly **cod, flying fish [tobiko], herring** or **salmon roe**).

When buying roe, look for unpasteurized lightly salted roe that has been kept refrigerated.

COMMONLY COOKED FISH

The way we buy and cook fish is changing. Since the advent of commercial fishing, we have approached fish cookery selectively. We have relied upon the bounty of the oceans to supply us with a never-ending stock of a few highly prized species, such as salmon and tuna. That reality is rapidly changing. We have come up against the limits of natural abundance and face a future where we can no longer be so choosy. The old approach of going to the fish counter looking for a specific fish must give way to a spirit of practicality and adaptability, where the fish that are more abundant dictate what and how we cook, rather than the other way around. This may sound dire, but to be honest we have long restricted ourselves to a narrow view of what the piscine world has to offer. There are many incredibly delicious fish out there that suffer from a lack of understanding on the part of the cook, or just sheer unfamiliarity. We have created this guide to help mitigate these problems. Use it to compare fish you already know you enjoy with those you might develop an appreciation for. Many different types of fish can be used interchangeably in recipes, and substituting a more abundant species for an overfished one can be an excellent learning experience while saving you money into the bargain.

SUSTAINABILITY, TRACEABILITY, AND FISH FRAUD

Because of consumer demand for a few fish, the wild populations of our most popular species are in decline. Unfortunately, we cannot categorically point to all but a few outliers and say: "This fish should be avoided at all costs." Sometimes a fish that is overharvested in one area is plentiful and sustainably managed in another. Similarly, the same fish from the same place may be caught with responsible methods or destructive ones.

Aquaculture, once thought to be a panacea for the woes of declining fish stocks, is similarly complicated. The ecological impact of **farmed fish** varies widely within a given fish species depending on what the fish are fed and how their waste is dealt with. The location of the farming operation is also very important; a vivid case in point: the 2017 escape of 250,000 Atlantic salmon from their marine-net confines into the waters of Puget Sound, where wild salmon populations are struggling to survive.

To make matters worse, there have been many well-documented studies and investigations over the last several years that have uncovered rampant **fish fraud** within the industry. That is, selling a less-desirable species under the name of a popular one, or misrepresenting fish as sustainably harvested when they are not. Industry-wide efforts are now being made to implement **traceability** practices, which will (hopefully) allow processors, suppliers, mongers, and consumers to know exactly where and how a particular catch of fish was harvested and follow it through the supply chain.

All of this is to say: Despite initiatives to improve record-keeping, accountability, and supply-chain transparency, there are simply too many global fisheries, fishing practices, variable international regulations, and changes in the marketplace for us to lay out *definitive* best practices for buying fish. One good strategy is to buy fish caught from well-regulated American fisheries rather than those caught elsewhere. This may be harder than it sounds: The majority of the seafood caught by US fisheries is exported, and most of the seafood we consume is imported. Nonetheless, if presented with a clear choice at the market, go with American fish.

All that said, we recommend you look to those with an intimate knowledge of fish for the most up-to-date information. Many smaller fishmongers and some supermarkets have taken proactive stances on these issues by letting shoppers know which fish are harvested or farmed in ways that are better for fish populations and other marine life. There are some labels that indicate a product was raised or harvested via sustainable practices, most notably the easily recognizable ➤ Marine Stewardship Council's Certified Sustainable Seafood label (www.msc.org). There are several certification programs for sustainably farmed fish products, including labels from Aquaculture Stewardship Council (www.asc.org) and Best Aquaculture Practices (www.bap.org). However, it must be said that the standards for specific labels vary; when you encounter an unfamiliar label, maintain a healthy skepticism and do your own research as to the standards by which labels are bestowed. For a list of sustainable choices, visit the websites above or ➤ visit the Monterey Bay Aquarium's Seafood Watch website (www.seafoodwatch.org) for an interactive guide to sustainable fish. There is even a smartphone app available to help you make informed choices while standing at the seafood counter.

ANCHOVY

Anchovies are tiny, filter-feeding saltwater fish with soft flesh. If you are fortunate enough to find fresh anchovies, a rare occurrence indeed, try them breaded and fried whole or gently sautéed with olive oil, garlic, and herbs. Or, should you find yourself with more of them than you know what to do with, use them in Escabeche, 392.

When used to describe the salted, canned product, "anchovy" does not refer to a single type of fish but is rather an aggregate term used to denote any of about twenty different species of small fish or fish fry, that is, baby fish. Canned anchovies should be rinsed of excess salt and oil; use them as a flavoring for sauces, soups, stews, and ragus. When used in small quantities, they add a distinct but ineffable flavor that does not read as "fishy." White anchovies, cured in vinegar and often imported from Spain, are particularly delicate tasting (no need to rinse them). Serve these with good toasted bread and olive oil. For more information on preserved anchovies as an ingredient, see 953.

ARCTIC CHAR

A relative of salmon and trout, with a similar fat content and flavorful pink- to ivory-colored firm flesh, Arctic char is well suited to all preparations. Most char in markets is farmed, but wild Arctic char is found in alpine lakes and coastal Arctic waters. Like salmon, some species of Arctic char migrate from the sea upriver to spawn. **Dolly Varden** and **grayling** are similar fish.

BASS

Bass is often used as more of a generic marketing term for many unrelated types of fish. True ocean-caught bass have wonderfully sweet, fairly firm white flesh and are excellent served whole or in fillets. **Black sea bass** are usually sold at under 3 pounds, though they can be larger. **Striped bass** (often called **rockfish** in the Chesapeake) is a favorite East Coast fish that is commonly available farmed, although wild stocks have recovered thanks to management efforts. Gaining popularity here, **branzino,** also called **European bass** or **sea bass,** has long been prized in the Mediterranean for its white, firm, mildly sweet flesh that is reminiscent of scallops. Sauté them whole in olive oil. **Barramundi** or **Asian sea bass,** mild, white, flaky-fleshed fish, are highly prized in Thailand and are a common farmed species. They are excellent steamed and served in a tangy, fragrant sauce of lime juice, fish sauce, garlic, chiles, and cilantro. Also see **Chilean sea bass,** 396. For **white sea bass,** see croaker, 396.

Groupers are also part of the large sea bass family. Grouper is found in the southern Atlantic, the Gulf of Mexico, and the southern Pacific, in greater quantity in the summer. **Black grouper** and a variety unfortunately called **"gag"** are both typically sold as black grouper. They are very similar fish, so mislabeled gag grouper is not really misleading. **Red grouper** is not quite as firm as black grouper and has a milder flavor, making it a preferred variety. Grouper shows up as meaty white fillets in most markets. Lean and flavorful, the firm, flaky flesh stands up to most treatments, including poaching or braising.

Snappers are favored for their sweet flavor and generally firm, meaty texture. The popular red-skinned **red snapper** has lean white flesh with a touch of sweetness that cooks to large flakes. **Yellowtail snapper,** which are gray with a yellow stripe that runs from head to tail, are milder and have pinkish flesh. There are several other popular species, such as **vermillion snapper,** known as **beeliners,** and **mangrove snapper.** Smaller snappers are well suited to grilling or pan-frying whole, or make Veracruz-Style Snapper, 380.

Pacific rockfish (not to be confused with the colloquial name used in the Chesapeake for striped bass) can be one of a dozen related species. Sometimes sold as **Pacific snapper,** it is affordable, widely available on the West Coast, and has a slightly softer texture than true snapper. The very lean white flesh cooks to small flakes and is perfect for any cooking method.

Smallmouth and **largemouth bass** are among the most popular freshwater sport fish in America. Their moderately firm flesh is suited to broiling, grilling, pan-frying, roasting, and sautéing. Smallmouth are the better of the two for eating, as they live in colder water.

BLACKFISH (TAUTOG)

A popular saltwater sport fish in the wrasse family, blackfish is seen in some East Coast markets in late spring and early fall. The sturdy, lean white flesh should be skinned (the skin can be bitter) before broiling, sautéing, poaching, or frying. It is among the finest fish for chowder. Blackfish is closely related to **hogfish** and **California sheepshead.**

BLUEFISH

Popular among fishermen and sold in markets on the East Coast in the summer, this meaty, oily saltwater fish should be well cleaned as soon as it is caught, kept very cold, and prepared at peak freshness. Smaller, younger bluefish—those under 3 pounds or so—are more succulent and can be cooked in myriad ways. Larger bluefish are best grilled, broiled, or hot-smoked, 393.

BUFFALO FISH

Easily mistaken for carp, these leviathans are native to rivers and streams in the southeastern United States. We experienced their abundance when we lived in East Tennessee where, every spring, much of the small community gathered to watch the "running of the buffalo." The fish flooded the tributaries of the Little Tennessee River, and locals took the opportunity to fish, harpoon, and shoot them in great numbers. Unfortunately, most of the dead fish were left to rot on the riverbank, though some enterprising souls used them as garden fertilizer. They are quite bony, and may be treated as for carp, below.

BUTTERFISH

These small saltwater fish are best served whole, skin-on; their silver skin needs no scaling. Butterfish have delicate off-white flesh and are flavorful and moderate in fat content. They are delicious pan-fried whole.

CARP

These great, languid, soft-finned freshwater fish can be admired swimming in koi ponds or in the tanks from which they are sold live in Asian seafood markets. Carp caught in cold water is very clean tasting, while carp from warm waters can be mushy. The fish should always be skinned before cooking as it is particularly difficult to scale and the skin is not delicious. Fish expert Barton Seaver recommends blanching the fish in boiling water for 30 seconds, then rubbing off the skin and layer of fat underneath. These are not sought-after fish, as they are quite bony and their flavor tends toward the earthy side. In fact, their flesh contains the same flavor compound as beets—geosmin—which is concentrated in the skin and darker flesh. Both the **common carp** and **Asian carp,** including **black, silver, bighead,** and **grass carp,** are considered invasive species in the United States, where they have dominated Midwestern rivers and streams. Carp is best in preparations that tame its strong flavor. Try braising or stewing it in red wine with lots of aromatics, or brine it for a day before cooking. In China, carp are steamed or fried whole. While carp may not be the finest flavored fish, it is worth considering as a food fish due to its abundance. Carp is classic in Gefilte Fish, 382.

CATFISH

Catfish is a common designation for many species, most of which have whisker-like barbels, or sensory organs on the face. **Channel catfish, flathead, white,** and **blue catfish** are among the most prized wild and farmed catfish in the States. Asian catfish, including species of **pangasius** such as **swai, tra, basa,** and **sutchi** catfish are also widely farmed, imported, and consumed in the United States. There are also saltwater catfish, such as the **gafftopsail catfish,** which are excellent, if unloved. Like carp, wild catfish can have a muddy flavor, but if prepared properly they are good eating. Most of the catfish you are likely to encounter in stores is farmed and has a clean, mild flavor and dense, meaty flesh that is ideal for pan-frying, deep-frying, grilling, broiling, sautéing, or braising. Catfish roe is most commonly consumed in Southeast Asia and the southern United States.

CHILEAN SEA BASS (PATAGONIAN TOOTHFISH)

Not really a bass, this delicious white-fleshed saltwater fish became so popular during the late 1990s that it was overfished in the South American waters where it is found. Since then, the fishery has been extensively regulated, and the population has bounced back to a decent degree, enough for some (but not all) fisheries to be found on the Monterey Bay Aquarium's list of sustainably caught fish. "Chilean" is a misnomer, coined by a fish merchant in the 1970s. The Patagonian toothfish is a pelagic fish with a very wide range and is fished from South Korea to South Africa to Australia to France to the Ross Sea in the case of the **Antarctic toothfish.**

COD

While supplies of **Atlantic cod** have dwindled, **pollock, ling, hake, whiting, cusk,** and **haddock** are also members of the cod family. **Scrod** is a term for any fish in this family weighing no more than 2 pounds. Most of these saltwater fish have a delicate flavor and firm to moderately firm white flesh that cooks into large flakes (hake and ling have softer flesh). **Pacific cod** are basically identical to Atlantic cod, and are still fished sustainably. Similarly, there is a huge fishery for **Pacific pollock,** which is used to make fish sticks. Inland, there is one freshwater codfish, the **burbot.** Also called **eelpout, ling, Mariah,** or, interestingly, **lawyer,** this is an ugly but tasty fish that lives in deep, cold lakes.

Prepare cod any way but grilled, as the flesh is too delicate and lean. **Salt cod,** which has been salt-cured and dried until it is quite stiff, is a popular ingredient in Portuguese, French, Spanish, and Italian cooking. Look for thick, white, firm fillets. To use salt cod, see About Smoked and Preserved Fish, 392.

Smoked split haddock, called **finnan haddie,** originated in Scotland. It can be roasted, or creamed, broiled and basted with butter, or simmered in milk, which tempers its flavor. For **black cod,** see sablefish, 398, and for **lingcod,** see 397.

CROAKER OR DRUM (SPOT, SPOTFIN)

Croaker is synonymous with **drum,** and both terms are meant to describe the sound they make under water. **California white sea bass** is a variety of croaker. **Red drum,** or **redfish,** are the drums most likely to be found commercially, other than actual croakers, which are commonly found in markets around the Chesapeake Bay. **Black drum,** when small, are called **puppy drum** and are delicious; fully grown black drum are notoriously wormy. **Weakfish** is a drum but does not resemble red or black drum in shape. It is also called **sea trout** and its Southern cousin the **speckled** or **spotted sea trout,** with good reason, as it is an excellent food fish, fine-textured and delicately flavored like trout. You can also find a little drum called a **spot** in Southeastern markets, and a drum known as **whiting** in Texas. Inland, there is a freshwater drum that is delicious, if unloved. All drums have sweet, mild, white flesh low in fat. These primarily saltwater fish are suitable for many preparations, from pan-frying and deep-frying to braising and roasting. Red drum is the classic fish to use for Blackened Fish Steaks or Fillets, 389, and its bones are excellent in Fish Stock or Fumet, 77. Never use drum raw, as it is susceptible to parasites.

DORY

Dory, also known as **St. Pierre,** is a flattened, odd-looking saltwater fish with a pronounced lower jaw and a black spot on both sides said to represent the thumbprint of St. Peter. The European **John Dory** is the best known, though there is also an American relative known as the **buckler** or **silver dory.** The firm, lean, delicious white flesh should be prepared as fillets, as the fish is bony (its bones are excellent in Fish Stock or Fumet, 77). It is best poached, sautéed, slow-roasted, or used in seafood stews such as Bouillabaisse, 102.

EEL

Eel is a saltwater fish that spawns in the Sargasso Sea in the western Atlantic, and from there travels back to its freshwater haunts in the United States, Europe, or Iceland to mature in the rivers and streams frequented by its parents. This journey can take up to two years. Eels are excellent eating with firm, silky, fatty flesh. They may be seared, broiled, braised, grilled, or smoked to good effect.

Most cooks prefer to buy eel skinned, but for the intrepid, we offer the following method: Throw them in a bucket of salt to kill them. This also removes the slime that makes them so difficult to handle. Then impale the eel through the head on a nail you have set up on a pole for this purpose. Cut through the eel skin all the way around just below the small fins near the head. Peel the skin back with a pair of pliers until the whole skin comes off like a glove. Clean the fish by slitting the white belly and removing the gut, which lies close to the surface.

FLOUNDER

The delicate white flesh of this saltwater flatfish, usually sold filleted, is sometimes marketed as sole. **Gray sole** is actually a flounder with an elongated shape and more delicate flesh. Large flounder may be called **lemon sole** or **sea flounder. Fluke,** or **summer flounder,** are closely related to the **southern flounder** and the **Gulf flounder.** A common catch for recreational fishermen, fluke can weigh in excess of 20 pounds but are more often closer to 5 pounds. Flounder is excellent and perhaps best known in a deep-fried state, but it is a fine eating fish, well suited to baking or sautéing. The thick, flaky white fillets of fluke are particularly able to absorb the flavors of other ingredients. Fluke is wonderful marinated or sauced and can be grilled, pan-fried, sautéed, or roasted. The **California halibut** is a very close cousin and can be cooked in the same ways.

HALIBUT

Atlantic and **Pacific halibut** are the largest flatfish in the world. In fact, just the cheeks from a large halibut can be the size of a saucer. The firm, flaky white flesh is lean, with a very mild flavor. Because of its leanness, it benefits from moist cooking methods such as steaming, poaching, or cooking en papillote, 1057. For many, halibut makes the finest fish and chips. California halibut is actually a flounder (see flounder, above).

HERRING

A small, rich saltwater fish with dark, strong-flavored flesh, herring occasionally passes for sardines in the market, but it is more often found preserved or smoked. Fresh herring are good grilled, broiled, roasted, and fried. Herring has innumerable fine bones. If you split a herring down the center of the back with a sharp knife, lever up the backbone, and carefully pull it out, most of these small bones will come with it. After cleaning, you may cook herring in one piece or split it in two.

Kippered herring have been salted, split, and cold-smoked until they take on a reddish hue (though this is sometimes artificially produced with red food coloring). More lightly salted and briefly smoked, whole silver-colored **bloaters,** so called for their slightly plumped, or bloated, look, can be eaten cold with bread and butter, or broiled in butter.

Marinated herring comes in various disguises. **Rollmops** are fresh boned herring that are rolled, often around a piece of cucumber, held together with a toothpick, and pickled. **Bismarck herring** are skin-on fillets pickled in vinegar, often with onions, sometimes sweetened. **Matjes** or **virgin herring** come in a sweet-sour brine of vinegar and sugar.

JACK

There are twenty-one species of jack; all are saltwater fish. Their firm, flavorful, rich flesh is well suited to grilling or sautéing. One of the best-known members of this fish family is the **pompano.** Ranging from 1 to 3 pounds, whole silver-skinned pompano are best grilled, pan-fried, or sautéed. **Amberjacks,** a favorite of the Gulf of Mexico, are excellent grilled, roasted, smoked, or slow barbecued. Large amberjacks should be cooked through due to a higher incidence of parasites. **Yellowtail amberjack** is a Pacific saltwater fish that is a favorite at sushi restaurants, where it is called **hamachi.**

LINGCOD AND LING

Confusingly, **lingcod** is unrelated to cod (it is a member of the greenling family). It is an elongated, ferocious, toothy monster found only in the North Pacific. It has lean flesh that is sometimes translucent blue; but it cooks up white. Lingcod is firm enough for grilling, soups and stews, and makes excellent fish and chips. **Blue ling** is in the same order as cod and is often described as a type of cod, 396. **Common ling** is an Atlantic cod-like fish that is commonly used for **lutefisk,** a Scandinavian preparation of dried fish that has been treated with lye.

MACKEREL

Mackerel are a family of saltwater fish in the same family as tuna, though most are much smaller and so are treated differently. Because proper handling is especially crucial with mackerel, they have a reputation for being strong-flavored, but when cleaned and kept with care, this fish is exceptionally delicious. **Atlantic mackerel,** practically one and the same as **Atlantic chub mackerel** and **Pacific chub mackerel,** are the most common and have a soft texture, a higher fat content, and almost sweet-tasting flesh. They are well suited to grilling, smoking, broiling, and sautéing. **Spanish mackerel** is a mild-tasting fish well suited to a variety of preparations, including sushi. **King mackerel** is often sold as steaks, and its dense, flaky flesh is ideal for marinating and grilling. It is the best mackerel for smoking. **Wahoo** has pale pink flesh that resembles tuna and turns white when cooked. It is excellent grilled or seared. The rich flesh of mackerels is complemented by citrus juice or vinegar.

MAHI-MAHI (DOLPHINFISH, DORADO)

Unrelated to the marine mammal dolphin, mahi-mahi is fished mostly in the South Atlantic, the Gulf of Mexico, and the Pacific, and is an exciting catch for fishermen; they are most plentiful in the warmer months. Their firm, mild, off-white flesh holds up well to multiple cooking methods, but is especially nice when grilled.

MONKFISH (ANGLERFISH, LOTTE)

These rather terrifying saltwater fish are sometimes called "poor man's lobster." Although the flavor is really quite different, it does have some of the briny sweetness of lobster flesh and is a superb eating fish in its own right. The tail fillets are covered with a thin gray membrane, which must be removed before cooking to prevent the flesh from buckling. Monkfish can be grilled, broiled, roasted, sautéed, or braised. Monkfish liver is highly regarded in Japan and is silky and rich, somewhat like foie gras. Monkfish bones are particularly good for stock.

MULLET

Delicious when extremely fresh, both **striped mullet** and **silver mullet** weigh 4 pounds or less. They are saltwater fish caught along the southern Atlantic coast and the Gulf Coast. Firm and fatty, mullet stands up well to grilling and especially to hot-smoking, though they are wonderful prepared by any method using direct heat. Mullet roe, when salted and dried, is called **bottarga** in Italy and is perhaps most commonly grated over pasta dishes, adding a salty, rich, savory flavor (see 956 for more on its use).

ORANGE ROUGHY

Imported skinless orange roughy fillets from Australia and New Zealand have firm, lean white flesh. They can be pan-fried or cooked with moist heat. It has mild flavor and is a suitable substitute for cod or fillet of sole. A saltwater fish, orange roughy is sturdy enough for most preparations, except grilling.

PANFISH

This category was made up to pay tribute to the little fish, usually freshwater, that we catch as children: **sunfish** (sometimes called **bream**), **bluegills, crappies, bullhead catfish,** and **rock bass.** They account for the greatest proportion of sport fishing in the United States and can be caught in lakes and ponds everywhere. If you don't catch and release, pan-fry them. Small **Pacific surf perch,** of which there are many species, work well in panfish recipes.

PERCH

Only two true perch are seen with any regularity. **Walleye** (sometimes erroneously referred to as walleye pike) has relatively few bones and a delicate flavor, and its sweet, lean flesh can be roasted, pan-fried, or braised. Its cousin the **sauger** can be cooked similarly. **Yellow perch** is a popular sport fish with firm, lean flesh that should be skinned before pan-frying or braising. Walleye and perch are freshwater fish.

PIKE

A sweet, lean freshwater fish, the **Northern pike** can get up to 67 pounds. The larger the pike, the easier it is to find and remove its many bones. **Muskellunge,** the largest member of the family, is a popular game fish but is rarely kept for eating. Pike's little cousin the **pickerel** lives in Eastern lakes and rivers. Very low in fat, pike and pickerel's moderately firm flesh is best for pan-frying, roasting, and sautéing. They are also excellent in soups and chowders.

PORGY

Also known as **sea bream** (the French **dorade** or Italian **orato**), **grunts,** or **scup,** the lean, flaky flesh of these saltwater fish makes up for their boniness with mild, subtle flavor. **Sheepshead** is another member of this family and has sweet flesh that can resemble that of the shellfish they eat. Porgies are good sautéed, grilled whole, or baked.

RED MULLET

Unrelated to true mullet, these European saltwater imports have firm, lean, well-flavored white flesh that can be prepared by most methods but is best pan-fried, grilled, or broiled.

SABLEFISH (ALASKA COD, BLACK COD)

Sometimes mistakenly called **butterfish,** this saltwater fish is not actually a cod. It has flavorful, rich, soft flesh that cooks to thin white flakes, and its high fat content makes it ideal for smoking or broiling (see Black Cod Misozuke, 387).

SALMON

Most salmon are anadromous, meaning they spend their adult lives at sea but return to freshwater rivers and streams to spawn. Salmon can be broken down into Atlantic and Pacific varieties. Its flesh ranges from pale coral to vermilion in color. In some rare cases, white salmon is found. There are five species of Pacific salmon and most in markets will be wild. **Chinook** or **king salmon** is the largest and fattiest, followed by **coho** or **silver salmon.** The flesh of **sockeye** has an incredible, almost neon reddish hue. All boast full-flavored flesh that is more distinctive than that of the farmed Atlantic salmon. Smaller **pink salmon** and **chum** or **keta salmon** are not as highly prized as the fatty, succulent Chinook or coho, but they still have good flavor and are more affordable. In addition, there are popular sport fisheries for landlocked sockeye known as **kokanee,** as well as Chinook salmon in the Great Lakes. Cooking pink or chum salmon with the skin prevents the fish from drying out and gives the meat more flavor from the fat just beneath the skin. One of the country's most popular fish, salmon is suited for almost every cooking technique depending on the type of salmon and the cut, though it is too high in fat to benefit from deep-frying. In general, salmon steaks are best for grilling, and fillets are excellent sautéed or seared. For a more delicate approach, salmon may be poached or cooked en papillote, 1057. Salmon is wonderful both hot- and cold-smoked and cured, as in Gravlax, 393.

SARDINES

True sardines are actually members of the herring family, though more than twenty different species of small, silver fish can be canned and marketed as sardines. Imported European sardines are larger and more flavorful than those caught in the American Atlantic, which are more often canned. Rub off the scales under running water and pull out the gills and innards of whole fresh sardines, then cook them as is, or stuff them. They are excellent grilled or pan-fried. Serve with lemon wedges or in Escabeche, 392, to temper their fatty, full flavor. We adore high-quality canned sardines on toasted bread with Salsa Verde, 567, or on salads with hard-boiled eggs and a citrusy dressing.

SHAD
A herring relative prized for its roe, 394, **American shad** or its cousin the **hickory shad** have sweet, rich, soft flesh that is best purchased filleted, preferably by an expert who can navigate around its many small bones. Shad is excellent smoked, and, once the meat has been flaked away from the bones, makes a wonderful fish cake. Plank-roasting, 386, is a traditional way to prepare whole shad, which is available in the spring. Shad are anadromous, meaning they live in both salt water and fresh water.

SHARK
Shark is usually sold as steaks, with sweet white flesh. **Mako** and **thresher shark** are the most sought-after. The rough gray skin and any dark-colored flesh or bloodlines are usually removed before cooking. The firm meat is similar to swordfish, and will stand up to most cooking methods, particularly grilling and broiling. It is especially good for kebabs as the flesh holds its shape well. A variety of smaller sharks are popular sport fish, notably the **leopard shark** in California and the **bonnet head** in the Southeast. Spiny **dogfish** are widely sold as fish and chips. Shark of any kind is excellent in chowders and stews. Look for light-colored shark meat with no odor of ammonia, and avoid overcooking, as it is prone to dryness.

SKATE (RAY)
You can buy skate wings filleted and skinned, or skin them yourself by freeing the meat off either side of the central line of cartilage, then skinning the meat the same way you would a roundfish fillet, 375. The firm, lean, flavorful meat is a good candidate for pan-frying, deep-frying, and poaching. If you leave the cartilaginous skeleton intact, it provides a silky richness to poaching broth. As skate cools, its gelatinous character intensifies and can feel almost sticky in the mouth; serve skate with something acidic, such as vinaigrette, or just a dash of lemon juice or vinegar, to offset this tendency.

SMELTS
Smelts are very small freshwater fish. Their skinny, near-translucent bodies are mild and sweet. They are wonderful deep-fried and eaten whole as a crispy snack. **Eulachon,** small, short-lived smelt, are stronger flavored and incredibly rich. So rich, in fact, that they are sometimes called **candlefish** because some indigenous peoples in the Pacific Northwest dried the fish and used them as candles. A similar species called the **grunion** can be found on Southern California beaches on certain summer tides. Small whole smelts are ideal for pan-frying or deep-frying. Fatty eulachon may be hot-smoked, 393.

SOLE
Dover sole, also called **channel sole,** is a saltwater fish imported from Europe and correspondingly costly. This firm sole has a delicate flavor that is so popular that imposters such as the inferior Pacific flounder are sometimes marketed as Dover sole. Remove the tough skin before cooking; grill (whole fish only), sauté, roast, or briefly and gently braise. The flatfish caught in American waters and referred to as sole is actually flounder; true sole is found only in European salt waters. Classic recipes calling for sole can be prepared with any firm white fish.

SWORDFISH
Unless you've seen the extremely long sword of this fish displayed on the wall of a seafood restaurant or store, you are not likely to encounter it whole, as these large fish are sold in pieces, the most common being symmetrical steaks, with four sections of meat with concentric whorls around the central vertebra. Steaks or pieces cut from the belly are much fattier than those from other parts of the fish and can be braised successfully. The key thing to look for when buying swordfish is its bloodline—it should be bright red with a brown tinge. It will have a dull, muddy appearance if the fish is not very fresh. Firm and flavorful, swordfish is an ideal candidate for cooking with high heat—grilling, broiling, roasting, or pan-frying. Avoid overcooking swordfish, as it becomes dry and grainy.

TILAPIA
Native to Africa, most tilapia at the market has been farm-raised. It is a mild, all-purpose saltwater or freshwater fish that has lean, fairly firm flesh. While not highly sought-after, it is an abundant, affordable fish with good flavor and texture. Poach, bake, deep-fry, or sauté.

TILEFISH
A firm white saltwater fish with lean flesh and a delicate flavor somewhat resembling shellfish. Tilefish is available on the East Coast or Gulf of Mexico year-round. Sold as fillets or steaks, it is usually very affordable. Almost any cooking method, particularly braising, works well.

TROUT
Part of the salmon family, trout is a milder and, in most cases, leaner fish than salmon. Though farmed trout varies, it can be quite good. Farmed varieties are almost invariably **rainbow trout,** but there are many wild species in North America. Easterners prize the **brook trout,** and Midwesterners the **lake trout,** but neither are actually trout; both are char. Particularly rich specimens respond well to brining and hot-smoking. In fact, this is the single best method for cooking lake trout. When wild rainbow trout head out to sea, they become **steelhead trout,** and are often thought of as a type of salmon, to which they are related so closely they share the same genus. All trout, including **brown, cutthroat, bull** and **golden,** are suited to grilling whole (in a fish basket, if you have one), broiling, pan-frying, and roasting. Steelhead are the only trout that commonly spends time in saltwater, but there are sea-run browns, called **"salmon trout"** in Europe, as well as sea-run cutthroats in British Columbia.

TUNA

Widely distributed and of widely differing characteristics, tuna is a family of pelagic fish ranging in size from the bluefin—a magnificent game fish that can weigh up to 1,500 pounds—to the far smaller skipjack and albacore, whose processed meat often ends up in cans or pouches.

The almost translucent red meat of **bluefin tuna** is enjoyed raw in sushi or sashimi and as tuna tartare; it is firm enough to be cooked with intense heat (grilling, pan-frying, or searing). Red at the center is a good way to enjoy its flavor, provided the fish is very fresh. Currently, bluefin tuna is in decline and extensively managed. As such, we do not recommend purchasing it should you even be able to find it. One notable exception is farmed bluefin tuna, which has the potential to reduce the strain of overfishing wild populations. It commands a premium price and is still fairly rare.

A close second to bluefin, **bigeye tuna** is prized for its rich taste and bright red flesh, which is superb when grilled. **Skipjack** or **oceanic bonito,** are the most abundant of all tunas, are usually under 10 pounds, and have strong-flavored flesh. While most skipjack is canned, it is possible to find small whole fish in markets, and it is used in Japan to make bonito flakes, or katsuobushi, 956, the magical dried fish flakes that are shaved onto Okonomiyaki, 226, and turned into Dashi, 78. Skipjack is excellent in poke, 377. A close relative to the skipjack is the **blackfin tuna,** which is a popular sport fish. **Yellowfin,** also commonly called **ahi,** usually shows up in markets as loins from which steaks can be cut (this is preferable to buying precut steaks, as they will be fresher), and is used in sushi. **Albacore** is the premier tuna of the North Pacific, and can be cooked any way yellowfin can. Tuna are warm-blooded, and when caught can put up so much of a fight that they "cook" themselves from the inside out. This should not be a problem for the average consumer, but always look for consistent coloring in tuna, with no signs of gray near the bloodline. When preparing tuna, you may want to trim away any dark streaks, which have a strong iodine tang.

TURBOT

A prized European saltwater flatfish that inspired the creation of the French cooking vessel called a *turbotière* to accommodate its diamond shape, true turbot has firm and delicate white flesh and is very expensive. It can be cooked in any way you would cook summer flounder.

WHITEFISH

This freshwater salmon relative has silver skin and rich, mild-flavored meat that takes well to smoking. It is too rich to deep-fry. Whitefish roe is highly prized.

POULTRY AND WILDFOWL

Poultry refers to farm-raised birds like chicken, turkey, domestic duck and goose, guinea hen, ostrich, emu, and squab. **Wildfowl,** 436, or game birds, include species that are primarily hunted and are not usually available commercially, such as wild duck, goose, and turkey—all very different birds from their farm-raised counterparts—as well as pheasant, partridge, grouse, quail, dove, pigeon, woodcock, and snipe. Pheasant, quail, and some European species of partridge and grouse are also available farmed, but we discuss both types in wildfowl since they are traditionally thought of as game birds.

ABOUT BUYING POULTRY

The vast majority of poultry sold in grocery stores is from two breeds: the Cornish cross chicken, and the broad-breasted white turkey. These plump, lean, large-breasted birds are the darlings of industrial poultry rearing, and the speed at which they are raised to maturity continues to improve, as does their yield of meat. Indeed, modern rearing of Cornish cross chickens produces birds two and a half times as massive in less than half the time it took to raise chickens to market weight in 1925. Standard grocery store poultry has been domesticated to such an extent that there is very little variation between individual birds.

Poultry raised on small farms, however, may vary quite a bit from the norm, especially if the bird in question is of an **heirloom** or **heritage breed.** These fowl are more likely to have darker meat, larger legs, and smaller breasts; their flavor can be exceptional. Birds sold as **free-range** or **free-roaming** must be given access to the outside, however that is the *only* requirement; the area to which they have access may be small, and consist of gravel and no forage of any kind. The term **pastured** or **pasture-raised** tends to be more meaningful, as this practice can affect the flavor and size of the birds. Pastured birds may be a bit smaller than standard supermarket poultry, and they may have yellow fat and skin from eating grasses and insects (but keep in mind that yellow coloration alone does not prove the poultry was pastured).

Organic poultry must be raised without antibiotics and fed certified organic feed. Organic feed cannot contain animal byproducts, or genetically engineered grains. The term **"natural"** is unregulated and essentially meaningless. According to current USDA standards, no poultry may be given hormones; thus, poultry labeled as **"hormone-free"** is akin to labeling bottled water "no carbs" or "fat free."

Air-chilled poultry is cooled after slaughter with the use of cold air rather than the usual water-chilling method. Water-chilled chicken takes on some water, making the birds slightly less flavorful and more prone to bacterial contamination than their air-chilled counterparts. On the other end of the spectrum are **basted** or **self-basting** chickens and turkeys, which have been injected with a solution containing salt, broth, and sometimes fat. As with brined poultry, 405, these birds will keep moist when roasted, but their texture may be altered for the worse. In general, we recommend avoiding poultry labeled with these terms, or packages that identify a certain percentage of the stated weight as "solution" or "water added."

Kosher poultry must be free of injury or illness and killed in a specific way by a specially trained person called a *shechita*. The bird is then bled out and salted to draw out more blood. **Halal poultry** is handled similarly in that the birds must have their throats slit, then they are bled out. However, halal birds do not have to be salted. Kosher poultry should not be brined, or the result may be too salty.

Regardless of the type of poultry and how it was raised or slaughtered, if the package contains an unusual amount of liquid, feels sticky, or has an off odor, the contents are suspect.

➤ Plan on buying ½ pound boneless or ¾ pound bone-in poultry pieces per serving. For whole birds, estimate about ➤ 1 pound per serving. Keep in mind that larger birds have a higher meat-to-bone ratio.

For making bound salads, casseroles, enchiladas, and the like, remember that 1 pound boneless poultry will yield about ¾ pound cooked meat (or about 2 cups diced or shredded); 1 pound bone-in poultry will yield about ½ pound cooked meat (or about 1 cup diced or shredded).

➤ For more specific information on particular birds, see About Chicken, 406, About Turkey, 426, and About Duck and Goose, 430.

ABOUT STORAGE AND SAFE HANDLING OF POULTRY

Store raw poultry at the back of the refrigerator, on the bottom shelf. ➤ To reduce the chance of contamination, place refrigerated packages of poultry on a rimmed baking sheet; keep other items in the refrigerator from touching poultry, especially foods that will be eaten raw, such as salad greens or fresh fruit. ➤ Cook or freeze poultry within several days of purchase. Never refreeze poultry once it has been thawed.

Assuming a freezer temperature of 0°F or lower, poultry will remain safe to eat for several months, but for the best taste and texture, cook it within 1 month. Frozen poultry should be ➤ thawed either in the refrigerator or in cold water, so when buying especially large birds like turkey, always buy it well in advance. Technically, whole birds destined for roasting may be cooked from frozen, but for best results thaw them first (this will also save you from the chilly task of removing giblets from their icy cavity). We do not advocate buying frozen, prestuffed whole poultry; if you must prepare it, do not thaw prior to cooking and follow the cooking instructions provided.

To thaw frozen poultry, set the bird on a rimmed baking sheet in the refrigerator, still in its original packaging, and allow 1 day for every 4 to 5 pounds. Poultry can appear to be thawed before it really is. Do not assume it is fully thawed until the flesh feels soft and pliable to the touch and the legs and wings move freely at the joints. Should a refrigerator-thawed whole bird prove to be stiff and icy on the day you plan to roast it, you may quicken the process by submerging it in a sink or large bowl full of cold tap water. Keep poultry in its original packaging if it looks water-tight; if not, transfer poultry to a zip-top bag, force out as much air as possible using the air displacement method, 881, and seal tight. Place it in the sink and weight it down with a heavy pot to keep it submerged. Thaw for 1 to 8 hours, depending on the weight, turning the bird and changing the water frequently.

➤ Raw poultry is highly susceptible to spoilage and must be treated carefully. The most common health concern is poor handling, which may contaminate hands and kitchen surfaces with *Salmonella enteridis*. Though salmonella is completely eradicated at the recommended internal temperature for doneness (165°F or above), poultry juices may contaminate uncooked or lightly cooked food that has come into contact with residue on hands, cutting boards, sinks, counters, or knives. After handling raw poultry, ➤ always wash your hands and any surfaces and kitchen tools that have come in contact with the chicken or its juices with hot, sudsy water before preparing other foods. To make doubly sure, wipe everything down with sanitizing solution, xx. ➤ If you wipe your hands on your apron or a dish towel, replace them promptly with clean ones.

➤ Do not rinse poultry. Though it may seem like a good sanitary measure, the exposed surfaces of poultry will be rendered safe during cooking. More important, the rinse water splattering off the carcass will spread contaminated liquid over a large area. Simply pour any standing juices in the package or chest cavity down the drain and pat poultry dry with a paper towel.

ABOUT CUTTING UP RAW POULTRY

Cutting up a bird yourself saves money and ensures you have the right parts cut just the way you want them. There will also be parts, such as the backbone and neck, to add to a stock bag, 73. Though it takes a bit of practice to find the perfect spot in each joint to slide the blade through, a little practice goes a long way. ➤ Use a paper towel to hold the bird during this process for a sure grip. To prepare smaller game birds for cooking, see About Hanging, Plucking, and Dressing Wildfowl, 436.

BONE-IN POULTRY PARTS

This process will turn a whole bird into 8 to 10 pieces for frying, braising, roasting, and grilling. For skinless parts, simply pull the skin off the pieces once they are cut. Though order is not incredibly important, we prefer to remove the wings and wishbone first, followed by the legs, then attending to the backbone and breast.

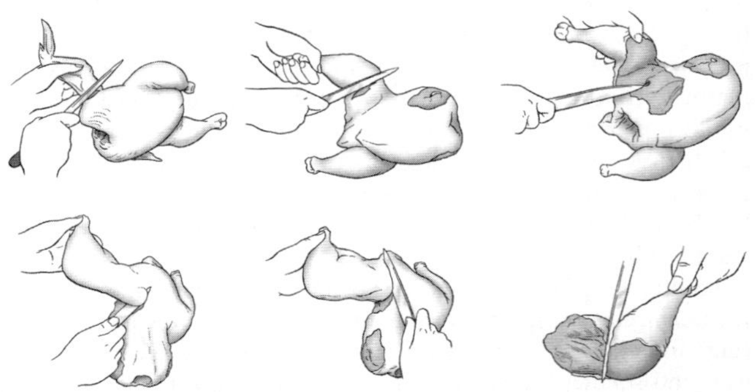

Cutting off the wings and legs; separating the drumstick and thigh

To remove the wings, grasp one wing and lift it up, pulling the skin taut. Make a small incision where the wing meets the breast and locate the joint. With one hand holding the wing and the other grasping the body of the bird, bend the joint backward until the wing pops out of the socket; insert the knife in this gap and slice the wing away. Repeat on the other side. To fashion wings into drumettes, flats (wingettes), and tips, see 404.

To make cutting the breast easier, remove the **wishbone,** a slender, V-shaped bone that runs from the wing joints to the center of the breast near the neck opening. Lay the bird on its back. Find the wishbone, run your knife tip on either side of it, pull it out with your fingers, and cut it free.

To remove the legs, force one leg outward and down. Slash the taut skin above the thigh where it meets the backbone to expose the joint. As with the wings, grasp the leg and the torso and bend the joint backward until the ball of the thigh bone pops out of its socket. Hold the leg up and, starting from the top, slice through the skin and flesh of the thigh as close to the backbone as possible, letting gravity assist you as you work. Try to cut out the **oyster** (a small nugget of meat nestled beside the backbone just above the hip joint) so that it stays attached to the thigh.

To separate the drumstick from the thigh, place the leg on a cutting board with the inner side up and locate the knee joint; a thin line of fat lies directly above it. Slice through the meat to expose the joint, grasp the leg with both hands, and bend the joint backward until it pops open. Slide your knife through the gap and sever the cartilage and remaining flesh.

Large turkey drumsticks (and those of many wildfowl) often have tough **tendons.** Most diners and cooks are perfectly content to eat around them. If you wish, you can remove them by first cutting away the meat around the bone near the bottom of the drumstick. Scrape the meat and skin below your cut with the spine of your knife and find the spots of white tendon in the exposed meat. Pull the tendons out with a pair of pliers.

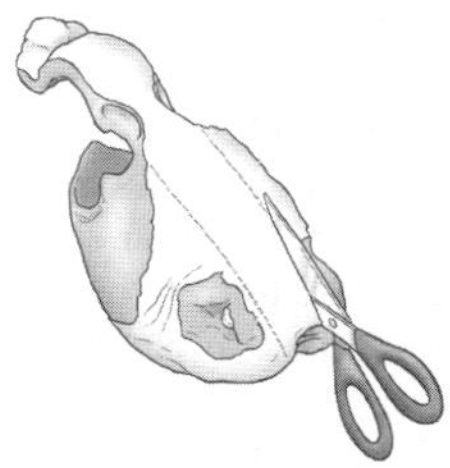

Separating the breast from the back

To remove the backbone, cut through the rib bones on either side with a sharp, heavy knife or kitchen shears. Save the back for the stockpot or stock bag, 73.

To split the breast for bone-in pieces, you have two options. The first method is simple and straightforward but requires a sturdy knife. Turn the breast skin side up and locate the ridge of the breastbone that runs down the center. Slice through the skin and meat on one side of the breastbone, working from the thick to the thin end of the breast. Rest the knife blade on the bone underneath your cut, and apply pressure to the spine of the knife until it crunches through the bone. Repeat on the other side.

Another method involves first removing the ridged portion of the backbone from the other side. Turn the breast skin side down and score the broad inner side of the breastbone lengthwise on either side of center. With thumbs resting on the ribs, grasp the breast with both hands and bend it backward until the breastbone cracks into three pieces. Rotate the breast so the tapered portion points to your dominant hand. Holding the breast firmly in place on either side of the cracks with your other hand, grip the center section of bone that was freed and pull it away. Slice through the skin where the breastbone ridge used to be.

Finally, peel or cut free any flat, flimsy pieces of breastbone that remain from each breast half. If desired, cut each breast half crosswise between the rib bones into 2 equal pieces for 4 total breast pieces.

SPATCHCOCKED (BUTTERFLIED) AND SPLIT

Spatchcocking, or butterflying, whole birds—flattening them by cutting out their backbone—helps them cook more evenly. This technique is especially useful for roasting poultry, or for browning smaller birds skin side down in a pan (see Chicken Under a Brick, 408). Cutting spatchcocked birds down the center and skewering each leg and breast quarter together makes them easier to manipulate on a grill. The wing and hip joints of chickens and Cornish hens are fairly easy to cut through; turkey joints require special care and some elbow grease.

To spatchcock or butterfly poultry, cut through the ribs on either side of the backbone with shears or a heavy knife. When your blade reaches the thigh and wing joints, firmly grasp the torso behind the knife with one hand and twist the knife so that the sharp edge presses against the backbone. Carefully apply pressure until the joint pops out of the socket and cut through the gap. Turn the bird breast side down and score the breastbone down the center with your knife. Turn the bird breast side up, place your palm in the center of the breast, and press hard to flatten the bird out.

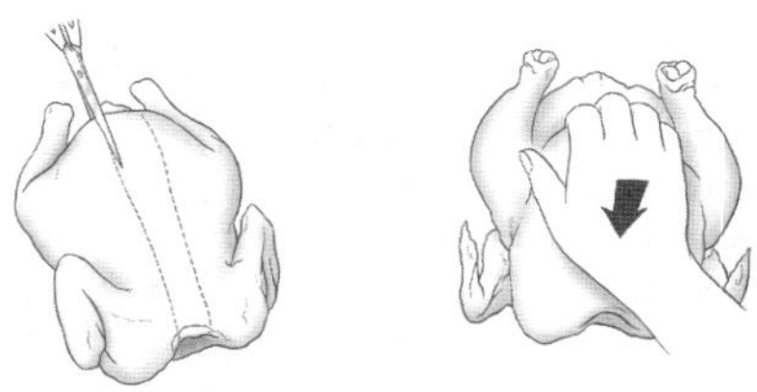

Butterflying a chicken

For very small birds such as squab or partridge, place the bird breast side up, slip a knife into the body cavity with the edge resting on one side of the backbone. Press down on the breast (and the knife underneath), until the knife crunches through the rib bones. Move the knife edge over to the other side of the backbone and cut through the ribs on that side to free the backbone. Flatten the bird as directed above.

To split poultry, remove the backbone and flatten as for butterflying. Cut on either side of the breastbone to halve the bird. Insert one or two long skewers through the thigh and into the breast to hold together the breast and leg (this makes poultry especially easy to maneuver on the grill).

BONELESS PIECES

To prepare boneless breasts, first remove the wings, wishbone, legs, and backbone as described on 402. Make a lengthwise cut on one side of the breastbone from the thick to the thin end of the breast. Angling the knife outward, slice along the rib bones and detach the breast meat from the bones. Repeat on the other side. If desired, peel off the skin.

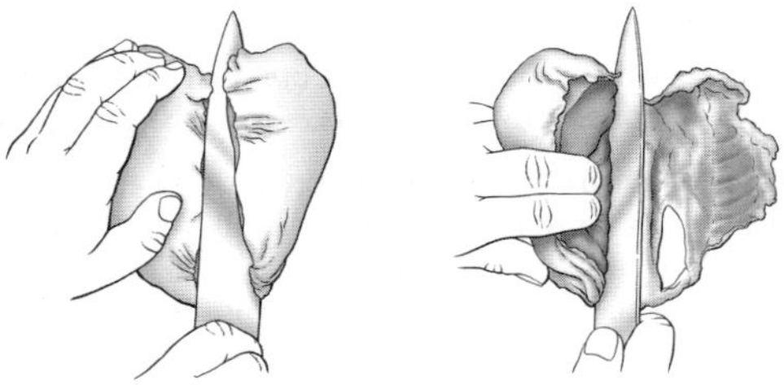

Boning a chicken breast

If desired, you may peel the loosely connected **tender** or **tenderloin** from the cut side of the breast. These slender muscles run along each side of the breastbone and have a white piece of tendon in them. We find this tendon fairly inoffensive, but it is easy enough to remove.

To remove the white tendon from chicken tenders, loosen the exposed flap of tendon at the thick end of the tender, and press it against the cutting board with a finger. Place your knife blade next to your finger, and scrape the blade down the length of the tendon so it is left behind on the cutting board.

To make cutlets, start with a boneless, skinless breast. To turn the breast into one large cutlet, see Pan-Fried Chicken Cutlets, 414. For smaller cutlets (or larger breasts), hold a very sharp knife at a 45-degree angle to the cutting board and slice the breast lengthwise into ½-inch-wide strips (freezing the breasts for 20 minutes makes this easier). Pound the strips gently between sheets of wax paper or pieces of plastic wrap until they are ¼ inch thick. (For tips on pounding, see Mincing, Grinding, and Pounding, 451.)

To prepare boneless chicken thighs, trim off any excess fat or overhanging skin. Place the thigh skin side down on a work surface. Cut through the meat down the center of the bone. Use the blade to pry the meat away and gradually expose the bone, working the knife along both sides and always angling the blade toward the bone to cut the meat cleanly away. Slide the knife under the bone, cutting it away from the meat below, then carefully slice down the length of the bone in both directions, freeing each end of the bone from the meat.

Drumsticks are hardly ever boned, but they may be treated just like thighs. If you go to this trouble, you may wish to pull out any tendons as well with your fingers or a pair of pliers.

DRUMETTES AND FLATS OR WINGETTES

To prepare poultry wings, you may wish to separate them at the first and second joints. The first portion is called the **drumette;** it is the meatiest, and friendliest for eating with your fingers. The middle portion of the wing is called the **flat** or **wingette;** two bones run through it, but it still has a fair bit of meat. Finally there is the **tip,** which is mostly cartilage, skin, and fat. Remove if desired (wing tips may be saved for stock, 73); we enjoy them when they are left attached to the flat and allowed to turn crispy and brown.

ABOUT BONING WHOLE POULTRY

Boning a whole bird so that it can be stuffed and shaped into a facsimile of its original self is less difficult than you might suspect. ➤ During the entire boning job, try not to pierce the skin except for the initial incision. ➤ Always keep the tip of the knife toward the bones.

Place the bird breast down on a cutting board. Cut off the first two joints of each wing (the wing tip and the flat portion adjacent to it) and save them for stock, 73. Use a small, sharp knife to cut two incisions in the front of the breast where the wishbone is. Use your fingers to pull out the wishbone.

Next, make an incision down the entire length of the backbone, through both skin and flesh. Turn the chicken on one side, and pull the skin back to expose the shoulder. Wiggle the drumette to find the joint, then cut in the center of the joint all the way through it. Repeat on the other side.

Stand the bird up with the legs facing down. Grab the drumette on one side with your dominant hand, and use the other hand to firmly grasp the bird's backbone. Pull the drumette down toward the tail of the bird; the breast should peel away from the carcass easily. Keep pulling until the oyster is visible (the small nugget of meat where the thigh meets the backbone). Repeat on the other side.

Put two fingers on either side of the breastbone and pull down to free the breasts from the bottom of the breastbone; the tenders will remain attached to the carcass. At this point, the meat will only be attached to the carcass at the thighs. Lay the chicken on one side. Holding it by the thigh, use a knife to cut in toward the backbone to cut out the oyster. Then bend the leg backward from the inside to pop the hip joint out of the socket, and pull the skin and meat away from the carcass. Repeat on the other side. Run your finger along either side of the breastbone to free the tenders and reserve them. The meat and skin should be completely free of the carcass except for the legs.

To remove the leg bones, find the hip joint and use your knife to scrape some of the thigh meat from the bone. This will give you something to hold on to. Grasping the exposed bone, use the spine of a small knife to scrape downward, scraping the meat from the bone until you reach the joint where the thigh meets the drumstick. Carefully cut around the joint, then again use the spine of the knife to scrape the meat toward the end of the drumstick. The leg is now essentially inside out. Turn it right side out, and use the spine of your knife to break the leg bone where you just finished scraping (near the end of the drumstick). Once the bone is broken, you can pull the leg bones free (the very end of the drumstick bone can be removed after cooking—removing it before cooking can tear the skin, which will shrink during cooking). Repeat on the other side.

Now the only bones left are the joint of the wings closest to the body. To remove these, use a small knife to cut around the joint, then use the spine of the knife to scrape the meat from the bone. Pull out the bone. The wing will now be inside out. Turn it right side out. Repeat on the other side. The bird may now be stuffed, below, tied, and cooked. If you find this confusing (or daunting), we highly recommend scouring the Internet for inspiring clips of Jacques Pépin demonstrating *la technique*.

ABOUT BRINING POULTRY

Brining—that is, soaking in a solution of water and salt—helps poultry retain moisture during cooking and seasons the meat throughout. **Dry-brining** is the act of salting the exterior of a piece of meat and allowing it to sit, uncovered and refrigerated, for several hours or for up to 2 days, depending on the size of the bird.

We confess that brining in liquid is something we rarely do. It requires a large amount of refrigerator space (or dirtying a cooler), and the sloshing liquid has a greater potential to cause cross-contamination. Logistics and safety aside, wet-brining inhibits the browning of poultry skin and gives the meat a firm, "deli meat" texture (many consider this to be a good thing, as it is positively juicy). On the other hand, we dry-brine poultry frequently: It takes up much less space, does not alter the texture of the meat, and encourages surface browning by drying out the skin. ➤ Do not use either brine method on "self-basting" or kosher poultry, 402, as they are already treated with salt.

To brine poultry, measure **¾ cup table salt or 1½ cups Diamond kosher salt for every 1 gallon of very cold water.** Always use a container or stainless steel pot large enough to completely submerge the bird. The amount of brine needed will depend on the brining vessel used. For a 15- to 25-pound turkey, plan on 2 gallons of brine. For a whole chicken, 1 gallon usually suffices. For 4 chicken breasts, you will need about 1 quart. Brine turkeys for 12 to 24 hours, whole chickens for 12 hours, and chicken parts for 30 minutes to 1 hour, always in the refrigerator. You can also experiment with adding flavors to your brine: cracked peppercorns, allspice, brown sugar, apple juice, or bay leaves. While the flavors of these ingredients will not penetrate the meat, they will flavor the surface and interior of the bird. Discard the brine after use. Once the bird is removed from the brine, pat it as dry as possible. If you have time, place the bird on a rack on a rimmed baking sheet and refrigerate, uncovered, up to 24 hours to dry out the skin. This will encourage browning.

To dry-brine poultry, generously sprinkle the surface of the meat and skin with **¾ teaspoon table salt or 1½ teaspoons Diamond kosher salt for every 1 pound** of poultry; for whole turkeys, use **½ teaspoon table salt or 1 teaspoon Diamond kosher salt per pound** (we recommend using kosher salt as it is easier to distribute evenly). Place the poultry on a rack set on top of a rimmed baking sheet and refrigerate, uncovered. Chickens will be seasoned throughout after 24 hours; turkeys after 48 hours.

➤ Reduce or omit the salt in any stuffing destined to be used in brined or dry-brined poultry, as well as in any pan gravy or sauce made from its drippings. Thoroughly pat the cavity dry, as residual brine may make stuffing or gravy too salty.

ABOUT STUFFING AND TRUSSING POULTRY

For an impassioned plea for why you should be baking your stuffing in a casserole dish instead of inside poultry, see About Stuffings and Dressings, 531. ➤ Always wait until just before roasting to stuff a bird. This may not be convenient, but it is the only safe procedure. (When refrigerated, the cold may not fully penetrate the stuffing, and whatever stuffing does become cold will not heat through before the bird is overcooked.)

If, however, you still wish to stuff poultry, place the bird in a large pan and have the stuffing hot or at room temperature. Pack it loosely in the body and neck cavities. Stuff birds only about three-quarters full—the stuffing will expand during cooking. Cover the neck cavity with the neck skin (secure with a small skewer, if desired). Cover the body cavity by tying the drumsticks together over the cavity.

Trussing is rarely a must, but it gives the bird a handsome shape, and makes for easier handling. Fasten the legs close to the body by tying the ends of the drumsticks together. Turn the wings back, pass the string around them, and tie it in front of the breast, as shown.

Performing a simple truss on a chicken

ABOUT CARVING POULTRY

After roasting and resting the bird, remove and set aside any stuffing before carving. We highly recommend carving the bird in the kitchen and then presenting the dark and white meat arranged on a platter for serving. With a large bird such as a turkey, carve one side to begin, then from the other side as needed. If the bird is to be carved at the table, place it breast side up on a large, heated serving platter and garnish with fresh herbs and any vegetables roasted alongside the bird.

There is a subtle, old-fashioned art to tableside carving. A hefty, sharp knife is essential. A two-tined long-handled fork is the traditional prop for tableside carving, but a good pair of tongs may be pressed into service instead.

To remove the leg, secure a drumstick with a carving fork or tongs and pull the leg away from the torso. Cut down and toward the backbone until the hip joint is exposed. To sever the leg, place the knife blade in the center of the joint and make a twisting movement with the knife to pop it loose. In carving a duck or goose, you will find the leg joint more difficult to sever because it is much farther under the bird and somewhat recessed (kitchen shears are a good tool to fall back on if you have too much trouble). Once the leg is free, cut the joint between the thigh and drumstick, again placing the blade in the center of the joint and twisting gently.

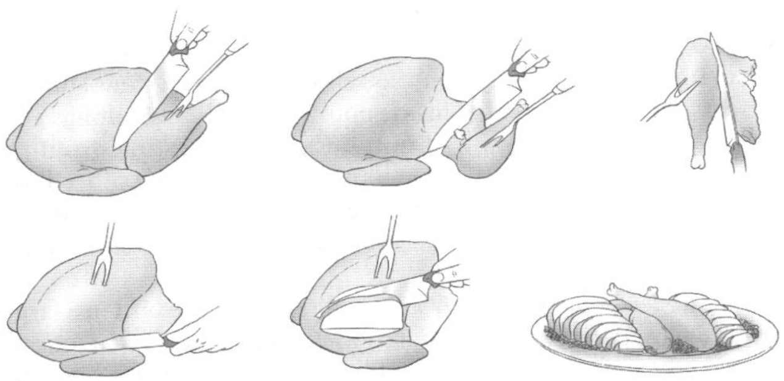

Carving a bird

Proceed to remove the wings in a similar manner. If the bird is large, divide the wings at the second joint as well.

To slice the breast in the kitchen, cut down the entire length of the breast, just to one side of the breastbone. Turn the knife so it is angled away from the breastbone and slice off the breast in one piece, pressing the blade against the rib bones. Once the breasts are removed in this way, cut crosswise slices from them. For a smaller bird, such as a chicken, the breast may be removed in this way, then cut crosswise in half to make 2 servings per breast.

To slice the breast of larger birds at the table, begin at the area nearest the neck and make a cut parallel to the platter, as shown. Then, turn the knife perpendicular to the platter and slice the breast lengthwise, placing the slices on a serving platter as you work.

To carve thighs, slice the meat from either side of the bone. Chicken thighs may be served just like this: two pieces of boneless thigh meat that can be easily eaten with knife and fork, and a meaty bone for diners to eat from with their hands. For large turkey thighs, thinly slice the now-boneless pieces crosswise (and perhaps slice off any meat still clinging to the bone).

To carve large drumsticks, you have two options. The easiest—aside from letting diners fend for themselves—is to grasp the exposed bone and "pull" the meat with a fork, which will easily separate from the tough leg tendons, leaving them attached to the bone. For the prettiest results, remove the tendons first by cutting around the meat closest to the exposed bone and pull them out (a pair of pliers is helpful here). Once removed, grasp the exposed end and cut the meat away down the length of the bone, rotating the drumstick as you go.

Arrange white and dark meat on the serving platter so that diners can easily find their preference.

ABOUT COOKING POULTRY

Recommended cooking times are given in individual recipes, but these times are approximate. Using an accurate instant-read thermometer is the most reliable method for determining doneness, period.

➤ All poultry meat is safe to eat when it reaches an internal temperature of 165°F. The USDA's minimum temperatures are determined by measuring the percentage of pathogens and bacteria that die when exposed to a given temperature for a short time. ➤ 165°F is the maximum temperature we recommend for chicken and turkey breast meat, which will dry out and toughen at higher temperatures. Goose and duck breasts are a completely different story; for more on them, see 431.

Unfortunately, "safe" does not equal "ideal," especially when it comes to dark poultry meat: Thighs and drumsticks cooked to 165°F will seem underdone and chewy. ➤ We recommend cooking the thighs and drumsticks of all poultry to an internal temperature of at least 175° to 180°F, which will make them tender and succulent. As demonstrated by Duck or Goose Confit, 433, dark poultry meat is virtually impossible to overcook, so do not worry about going over this temperature.

Given the sensitivity of breast meat and the imperviousness of dark meat, we recommend checking the temperature of both when roasting whole birds: Remove the bird from the oven and insert a thermometer into the thickest portion of the breast and the inner thigh muscle, taking care that the tip is not in contact with the bone. To achieve a safe final temperature, we consider breast meat to be done when it registers 155° to 160°F and when thighs register 165° to 170°F (the breasts and thighs will finish cooking out of the oven as the bird rests, reaching a final temperature of at least 165°F and 175°F, respectively). ➤ If the breasts are done but the legs require more time, sever the legs at the joint and return them to the oven to finish cooking (loosely cover the rest of the bird with foil to rest and keep warm). For the best way to do this—as well as other methods for getting the breast and legs to cook evenly—see About Roasting Chicken, 407, Turkey, 427, and Ducks and Geese, 431.

If you do not have a thermometer, test for doneness by pricking the thigh to see if the juice runs clear, or jiggle the drumstick to see if the hip joint is loose. Neither of these techniques is a substitute for a good thermometer, but they may be useful in a pinch. Sometimes fully cooked meat remains reddish near the bone. This is the result of red blood cells seeping into the adjacent meat, causing it to look rare. Don't worry—this is normal and completely safe.

For stuffed poultry, ➤ the center of the stuffing should reach at least 165°F. If the bird has finished cooking and the stuffing has not reached 165°F, the best option is to transfer it to a buttered baking dish and return it to the oven to cook through while the bird rests.

ABOUT CHICKEN

Modern chickens are the distant progeny of a game bird native to India and Southeast Asia. It has surpassed all its feathery brethren—all animals, for that matter—to become the most popular animal protein in the world. Of all the breeds raised for meat in the United States, the most common is the large-breasted, fast-growing Cornish cross. Heritage breeds, which are often preferred by smaller poultry farms, tend to have larger legs and smaller breasts. For information regarding labeling standards for organic and free-range chicken, see About Buying Poultry, 401. As a general rule, ➤ figure on 1 pound of whole chicken, 12 ounces of bone-in chicken pieces, or 8 ounces boneless chicken per person.

The most common size of whole chicken available in markets is the **broiler-fryer.** Broilers currently average 4¾ pounds, though the only standard for calling a chicken a broiler or fryer is not weight, but rather age: Broilers must be under 10 weeks old. Chickens harvested between 8 to 12 weeks that weigh 5 pounds or more may be sold as **roasters.** Aside from the number of people they will serve, there is not much difference between broilers and roasters; both types can be roasted, fried, baked, fricasseed, or stewed. The only variable that makes a difference in the kitchen is the thicker breasts and legs of especially large birds, which take longer to cook through.

Roosters and **stewing hens** are much older. In fact, you are likely to only find these birds at farmers' markets and Asian grocery stores. Their dark meat is tougher but highly flavorful. While not suitable for roasting or frying, stewing hens are perfect for braises, fricassees, and soups. To use these older birds in braising and stewing recipes, plan to cook them twice as long as the estimated cooking time (and taste several times after the original cooking time has elapsed to see if the texture is to your liking yet).

Poussins and **Cornish hens** are the smallest chickens available, weighing between 1 and 2 pounds. Poussins can be any young chicken, but Cornish hens must be a Cornish cross breed and harvested before they are five weeks old. They are occasionally sold as "game hens," which is doubly false: They are not game birds, nor are they exclusively female. Much like veal, the meat of these young birds is tender and pale. Their small size means they cook through much faster than full-grown birds, which makes them especially suited to high-heat roasting, 409, broiling, 412, or grilling, 412. Smaller ones are the perfect choice for a single-serving bird; 2-pounders will feed 2 people.

A **capon** is a castrated young male chicken. His loss is the epicure's gain—it causes him to swell to a weight of 6 to 12 pounds, enough for 8 or more generous servings. Traditionally these birds are fed milk or porridge, making the meat extremely white and tender. Reserve them for roasting whole.

When a recipe calls for **chicken parts,** you may include drumsticks, thighs, breasts, or a combination. If you wish to cut up a whole chicken for the recipe, purchase one about 10 ounces larger than the weight of bone-in chicken parts called for. To cut up and debone a whole chicken for use in recipes calling for boneless parts, buy one that is one and a half times heavier than the weight of boneless chicken called for. See About Cutting Up Raw Poultry, 402.

Chicken breasts are made up of white, lean, close-grained meat and may be found whole—that is, two bone-in breasts connected by the breastbone—or cut in half. We prefer bone-in breasts for roasting and grilling. Many prefer boneless skinless breasts, which are especially quick, versatile, and easy to prepare. The inner breast muscles, or **tenders,** are ready to be breaded and fried right out of the package (see Chicken Fingers, 415). Convenience aside, ➤ chicken breast is easy to overcook. Cook breasts just to 165°F, or they will be disappointingly dry and firm. Brining, 405, is a good precaution to take, but this negates the convenience aspect.

Chicken legs, on the other hand, are nearly impossible to overcook (and much more flavorful). Even when cooked to temperatures in excess of 190°F, dark leg meat manages to remain tender and juicy. In the kitchen, this means that legs can be browned to your liking without fear of overcooking—or slow-smoked or stewed until the meat is fall-off-the-bone tender. **Drumsticks** are especially good for frying, as they have a ready-made handle for eating with your fingers. When braised or stewed, their meat easily shreds off the bone, leaving tendons and cartilage attached for easy removal. Chicken **thighs** are much more versatile, as they can be easily boned and cut into cubes or strips. In fact, thighs are increasingly available with the bone and skin removed, which makes them an easy, flavorful alternative to chicken breast in sautés and stir-fries. We use chicken thighs whenever possible for this reason—especially in braises and stews. Once grilled or roasted, we like to cut thighs on either side of the thigh bone, which yields two boneless "fork-and-knife" portions and a center piece that eats like a rib.

For most of us, **chicken wings** are synonymous with the spicy, smothered Buffalo-type we devour by the dozen (see Buffalo Chicken Wings, 60). Domestic chickens are flightless, which means their wing meat is more like white breast meat. However, since their wings have a much higher proportion of skin and cartilage, we tend to fry and roast wings until they are well done, which softens the cartilage and crisps the skin. The high proportion of cartilage also makes wings a good addition to meat stocks, 75–77, to which they add body and richness.

For **ground chicken,** see About Ground Poultry, 430. For **giblets, liver, gizzards,** and **feet,** see About Poultry Offal or Giblets, 444.

ABOUT ROASTING CHICKEN

Whole chickens are best roasted in a shallow roasting pan, on a rimmed baking sheet, or in an ovenproof skillet. For larger chickens, choose a larger skillet with a second "helper" handle (or be prepared to support the pan from underneath with a thick oven mitt). Some cooks like to use a vertical roasting rack. These wire racks have a wide circular base that tapers to fit inside the bird's cavity. The rack promotes even cooking and browning by exposing all sides of the bird to the heat reflected off the oven walls. By opening up the body cavity, the rack also promotes the circulation of hot air inside the bird, helping it cook faster.

Those who prefer crispy, browned skin will be better served by using higher oven temperatures—and smaller chickens, since larger birds cook more evenly at lower temperatures. Spatchcocking, 403, can help achieve this result (especially with larger chickens); flattening the bird shortens the roasting time, promotes even browning of the skin, and hastens the cooking of the legs so they are done at about the same time as the breasts.

Roasting chicken in parts avoids all of these pitfalls by allowing you to easily remove pieces from the oven as they finish cooking. Breast meat, especially with the skin on, is fine to use, but thighs are our preference, since their dark meat remains moist and tender even when they are cooked until crisp and well browned.

ROAST CHICKEN

Variations and tweaks on this theme are seemingly endless, but we find these two basic approaches to be the easiest and most useful. For added flavor, loosen the skin around the breast and thighs and rub any of the mixtures suggested in Additions to Broiled or Grilled Chicken, 411, underneath the skin.

I. HIGH-HEAT

4 to 6 servings

The best method for achieving browned, crispy skin. Use a smaller chicken as indicated (or spatchcock larger ones).

Remove the neck and giblets from:

One 3- to 5-pound chicken

Spatchcock, 403, if desired. Rub the chicken all over with:

2 teaspoons to 1 tablespoon salt (use the smaller amount for a 3- to 4-pound bird)

¾ teaspoon black pepper

If desired, for crispier skin and thorough seasoning, place the chicken on a rack set over a rimmed baking sheet and let it sit overnight, uncovered, in the refrigerator.

Position a rack in the center of the oven. Preheat the oven to 450°F. If desired, place in the body cavity of the chicken:

(6 sprigs parsley, tarragon, thyme, rosemary, sage, or a combination)

(1 small lemon, quartered)

Place breast side up on a rack set in a roasting pan or in an ovenproof skillet large enough to hold the bird. Roast the chicken until the internal temperature of the breast reaches 155°F and the thickest part of the thigh registers 170°F. Begin checking spatchcocked birds after 35 minutes. Smaller whole chickens may take as little as 50 minutes; larger chickens may take up to 1½ hours. Transfer to a platter and let stand 10 to 15 minutes before carving, 405.

II. LOW-HEAT

4 to 8 servings

Our preferred method for evenly cooking large chickens (or capons) and stuffed birds.

If desired, prepare and have hot or at room temperature:

(½ recipe Basic Bread Stuffing or Dressing, 532, or ½ recipe Basic Corn Bread Stuffing or Dressing, 532)

Season and prepare for roasting as for version I:

One 3- to 8-pound chicken

Position a rack in the center of the oven. Preheat the oven to 350°F.

Loosely pack the stuffing, if using, into the body cavity of the chicken. Roast the chicken until the internal temperature of the breast reaches 155°F and the thickest part of the thigh registers 170°F, 1 hour to 2 hours 45 minutes depending on the size of the bird. If the bird is stuffed, the internal temperature of the stuffing should reach 165°F. If the chicken is cooked through but the stuffing is not, transfer the stuffing to a baking dish and return to the oven while the chicken rests. Let the chicken rest 10 to 15 minutes before carving, 405. If desired, preheat the broiler while the bird rests and briefly return it to the oven for several minutes to brown the skin (watch it attentively!).

ROAST CHICKEN WITH VEGETABLES

4 to 8 servings

The vegetables will take about 45 minutes to become tender and browned, so you may need to add them partway through cooking depending on the roasting temperature and approximate cooking time of the bird. We often allow the vegetables to cook just as long as the chicken. They caramelize and crisp in the chicken fat, so while they may technically be overcooked they are deliciously so. Use the greater amount of vegetables for a larger bird.

Season and prepare a whole chicken as for **Roast Chicken I or II, 407.** Toss together in a large roasting pan:

2 to 3 medium red or gold potatoes, quartered

2 to 3 medium carrots, halved lengthwise and cut into 1-inch pieces, or 1 medium celery root, peeled and cut into 1-inch-thick wedges

2 to 3 small onions or large shallots, quartered lengthwise

1 tablespoon vegetable oil

Place a roasting rack on top of the vegetables, and set the chicken on the rack. Roast as directed, using one of the two versions. Stir the vegetables once or twice during roasting. (Though it involves getting an extra pan dirty, we find it convenient to move the chicken—or the entire roasting rack—to a rimmed baking sheet when it is time to stir them.) Remove the chicken and vegetables from the pan and let the meat rest. Taste the vegetables and season if necessary. If there are any browned bits in the pan, pour out any fat and add:

(½ cup hot chicken stock or broth)

Deglaze by scraping the browned bits off the pan, then pour the juices over the vegetables.

CHICKEN UNDER A BRICK

4 servings

Pressing chicken underneath a weight—whether a heavy skillet or a couple of foil-wrapped bricks—pushes the skin against the hot pan, which produces a beautifully burnished exterior. Smaller birds can be cooked this way. Keep in mind that they will cook faster, so have an instant-read thermometer at the ready to test for doneness.

Spatchcock, 403:

One 4-pound chicken

Loosen the skin around the breast and thighs and spread underneath:

Garlic-Herb Rub for Poultry, 587 (reserve the lemons)

Sprinkle all over with:

2 teaspoons salt

1 teaspoon black pepper

For crispier skin and thorough seasoning, place the chicken on a rack set over a rimmed baking sheet and let it sit overnight, uncovered, in the refrigerator. Position a rack in the center of the oven. Preheat the oven to 450°F.

Set a 10- to 12-inch ovenproof (preferably cast iron) skillet over medium-high heat for several minutes. Add to the skillet, swirling to coat:

1 tablespoon vegetable oil

Place the chicken skin side down in the skillet, loosely cover with a small square of foil, and place a second heavy, ovenproof skillet or weight on top. Cook, undisturbed, for 5 minutes, then transfer the skillet to the oven and roast for 15 minutes. Using sturdy oven mitts, remove the chicken from the oven and take the second skillet or weight off. Discard the foil and slide a spatula underneath the skin to make sure it is not sticking to the skillet. Carefully flip the chicken skin side up and return the skillet to the oven, uncovered.

Roast until the skin is deeply browned and the internal temperature of the breast reaches 155°F, 20 to 25 minutes more. Transfer the chicken to a platter and let rest for 10 minutes. As the chicken rests, make, if desired:

(Herb Pan Sauce, 546)

Or place the skillet over medium-low heat and gently fry in the pan drippings:

(Thick slices of country bread)

Cut the bread slices in half. Cut the chicken into pieces and serve over the bread, if using; if you have not made a pan sauce, sprinkle the chicken with the juice of one or both of the zested lemons left from making the rub before serving.

ROAST CORNISH HENS

4 servings

Position a rack in the center of the oven. Preheat the oven to 450°F. Place a wire rack on a large rimmed baking sheet or in a shallow roasting pan large enough to allow several inches of space between the birds.

Have ready:

2 large Cornish hens (about 1¾ pounds each), spatchcocked, 403

Arrange the birds breast-side up on the rack. Brush the skin with:

2 tablespoons vegetable oil

Mix together in a small bowl:

1½ teaspoons dried thyme, crumbled
1 teaspoon salt
1 teaspoon black pepper

Rub the mixture onto both sides of the birds. Roast until the internal temperature of the thickest part of the thigh reaches 170°F and the thigh releases clear juices when pricked, 20 to 30 minutes. Place the birds on a platter, tent with foil, and let stand for 10 minutes. Prepare with the pan juices, if desired:

(Basic Pan Gravy, 545)

GLAZED STUFFED CORNISH HENS

4 servings

Any of the glazes in About Glazes, 578, may be substituted for the jelly mixture below.

Prepare one of the following:

Wild Rice Dressing, 536, Spiced Rice Stuffing, 536, Couscous Stuffing with Apricots and Pistachios, 535, or Rice Dressing with Chorizo and Chiles, 536 (about 2 cups total), warm or at room temperature

Position a rack in the center of the oven. Preheat the oven to 425°F. Remove the neck and giblets from:

Four 1- to 1½-pound Cornish hens

Sprinkle all over with:

Salt

Stuff each bird with ½ cup of the prepared stuffing or dressing. Arrange the birds breast side up on a rack set in a shallow roasting pan. Roast for 25 minutes.

Heat in a small saucepan over low heat and stir until smooth:

⅓ cup jelly, seedless jam, or strained preserves or marmalade
2 tablespoons soy sauce or balsamic vinegar

Set aside. Take the roasting pan out of the oven and brush the birds generously with the glaze. To prevent smoking, pour ⅛ inch water into the roasting pan. Return the birds to the oven and roast until the internal temperature of the thickest part of the thigh reaches 170°F and the stuffing reaches 165°F, 15 to 20 minutes. If the glaze starts to burn, tent the birds with foil. Transfer the birds to a platter and let stand for 10 minutes before serving.

ROASTED CHICKEN PARTS

4 servings

As noted in About Chicken, 406, thighs and drumsticks are very forgiving and may be roasted until they are as browned and crispy as you like. Instead of the simple seasoning given here, try any of the suggestions in Additions to Broiled or Grilled Chicken, 411. For a tasty breaded crust, see Oven-Fried Chicken, 418.

Have ready:

3½ to 4½ pounds bone-in chicken parts

Season the chicken with:

1 tablespoon salt
1 tablespoon black pepper

For crispier skin and thorough seasoning, place the chicken on a rack set over a rimmed baking sheet and let it sit overnight, uncovered, in the refrigerator.

Position a rack in the center of the oven. Preheat the oven to 450°F.

Arrange the chicken skin side up in a shallow roasting pan or rimmed baking sheet and transfer to the oven. Breasts or breast pieces should be removed from the oven when they reach an internal temperature of 160°F, about 30 minutes. Thighs and drumsticks should be baked until they release clear juices when pricked with a fork and the internal temperature registers at least 170°F, about 40 minutes.

CHICKEN BREASTS BAKED ON A BED OF MUSHROOMS

4 to 6 servings

For well-browned, crisp chicken skin, heat 1 tablespoon vegetable oil in a large skillet over medium-high heat and brown the chicken, skin side down, before placing on top of the mushrooms.

Position a rack in the center of the oven. Preheat the oven to 400°F. Lightly oil a baking pan or shallow baking dish just large enough to hold the chicken pieces in a single layer.

Place in the bottom of the baking pan:

1 pound mushrooms (or a mixture), sliced

If using shiitakes, discard the stems or save them for stock, 73. Add to the pan:

1½ cups dry white wine, low-sodium chicken stock, or a combination
3 garlic cloves, thinly sliced
1 tablespoon fresh thyme leaves or 1 teaspoon dried thyme
¼ teaspoon salt
Black pepper to taste

Trim any excess fat from:

4 bone-in or boneless chicken breasts, skin left on (about 2 pounds)

Season with:

1½ teaspoons salt
½ teaspoon black pepper

Lay the chicken breasts skin side up on top of the mushroom mixture. Brush lightly with:

Olive oil

Bake, uncovered, until the internal temperature of the chicken reaches 160°F, 35 to 45 minutes.

Using a slotted spoon, transfer the chicken and mushrooms to a platter, arranging the chicken skin side up on the mushrooms. Pour the pan juices into a small saucepan and skim off the fat with a spoon. Add:

½ cup low-sodium chicken stock or broth
½ cup heavy cream

Boil over high heat until reduced to about 1 cup or until slightly thickened. Taste and adjust the seasonings. Spoon some of the sauce over the chicken and pass the rest separately. If desired, sprinkle the chicken with:

(Minced parsley)

SICILIAN-STYLE STUFFED CHICKEN BREASTS

8 servings

Prepare, omitting the egg and using only ⅓ to ⅔ cup chicken stock or broth:

½ recipe Italian Bread Crumb Stuffing, 533

The stuffing should be just moist enough to hold together in a ball when squeezed firmly; do not overmoisten. Stir in:

¼ cup oil-cured black olives, pitted and chopped
¼ cup raisins or golden raisins, chopped, or dried currants
¼ cup toasted, 1012, pine nuts or finely chopped walnuts
(4 anchovy fillets, rinsed, dried, and finely chopped)
2 tablespoons drained small capers

Position a rack in the center of the oven. Preheat the oven to 350°F. Lightly oil a 13 × 9-inch baking pan.

Trim any fat around the edges of:

8 boneless, skinless chicken breasts (about 3 pounds)

One at a time, place the chicken breasts between sheets of wax paper and pound with a mallet or a rolling pin until about ⅜ inch thick. Season both sides with:

1½ teaspoons salt
1 teaspoon black pepper

Lay the breasts smooth side down on a work surface and place ¼ cup stuffing on the center of each chicken breast, pressing lightly to compact. Bring the ends of the chicken up over the stuffing. Lay the packets seam side down in the prepared baking pan and brush with:

Olive oil

Bake until the chicken is lightly browned and the internal temperature reaches 160°F, 20 to 30 minutes.

MEDITERRANEAN CHICKEN BREAST PACKETS

4 servings

Please read about Cooking en Papillote, 1057. The seasonings can be varied to your taste; for a packet that serves as a whole meal, see Chicken Hobo Packs, 413.

Position a rack in the center of the oven. Preheat the oven to 450°F. Trim any fat around the edges of:

4 boneless, skinless chicken breasts (about 1½ pounds)

Season both sides with:

1 teaspoon salt

Tear off four 18-inch pieces of heavy-duty foil or parchment paper. Lightly oil one side of each. Lay one chicken breast on the oiled side. Divide among the breasts:

10 pitted green or Kalamata olives, finely chopped
1 lemon, very thinly sliced, or 1½ tablespoons minced salt-preserved lemon
2 tablespoons finely chopped oregano, thyme, parsley, or a combination
4 garlic cloves, minced
(1 teaspoon red pepper flakes)

Drizzle over the chicken:

3 tablespoons olive oil

Fold the foil or parchment over the chicken, then crimp the edges to seal tightly. Place on a baking sheet and bake for 20 minutes. Remove from the oven and let stand for 5 minutes. The internal temperature should reach 165°F. To avoid being burned by steam, open carefully.

ABOUT BROILING AND GRILLING CHICKEN

To ensure a moist, flavorful result, we usually brine, 405, rub, 587, or marinate, 579, chicken to be broiled and grilled. Marinades and glazes promote browning (and, ultimately, burning), which is a good thing if you are cooking skewered strips or cubes of chicken, as they have a short broiling or grilling time. On the other hand, bone-in pieces and thicker boneless breasts will likely be charred by the time they finish cooking under a broiler or over direct heat on the grill. There are several ways to avoid this: Use a marinade that does not contain much sugar; brush glazes and sauces on the chicken shortly before it has cooked through, then broil or grill until burnished; or stuff pastes and spice rubs underneath the skin to prevent them from burning. Finally, you may simply move or cover the pieces to protect them from direct heat for a portion of the cooking time.

Broiling: Always broil chicken in a two-piece broiling pan with a slotted or perforated broiling tray, which allows the dripping fat to drain away and collect in the pan below. If broiled in a flat baking pan or on a rack set in a pan, the fat will be directly exposed to the heat and will smoke and may even catch fire. Small chicken pieces are best for broiling, as larger pieces are more likely to burn before they are done. Depending on the broiler, it may be necessary to move the chicken farther from the heat to prevent charring. Thicker pieces may be successfully broiled by placing them on one of the lower racks of the oven at the outset. If they begin to burn before they are cooked through, reduce the heat and protect the chicken with a sheet of foil. To broil a whole chicken, choose the smallest bird you can find and first spatchcock or split it, 403. ➤ Always broil the bone side first, or the skin will become soggy.

Grilling: Simply seasoned boneless, skinless chicken parts and kebabs can be grilled over direct heat from start to finish. Chicken seasoned with a paste, marinade, or rub may burn if left over direct heat for the entire cooking time, so be ready to move it to the side if necessary. Bone-in, skin-on chicken will need longer to cook through, and tends to drip fat, which causes flare-ups when grilled over coals. For these reasons, we recommend starting whole chickens and bone-in, skin-on pieces over indirect heat, 1062, with the cover on. When the chicken is within 20°F of doneness, uncover the grill and move it to sizzle over direct heat to finish, turning until browned all over. If the skin causes a flare-up or the surface starts to char, move the chicken to the cooler side again and finish cooking with indirect heat. If your grill does not have a lid, cut chicken into pieces and cook over a moderate fire, reserving a cooler spot to which pieces can be quickly moved in case of flare-ups—or move them to an elevated rack (if your grill is equipped with this convenience).

ADDITIONS TO BROILED OR GRILLED CHICKEN

Marinate whole chickens for up to 24 hours, and pieces for 6 to 12 hours in any of the following:

Lemon Marinade, 580, Tandoori Marinade, 580, Balkan Marinade, 580, Sinaloan Marinade, 581, Thai-Style Lemongrass Marinade, 581, Becker Chicken or Pork Marinade, 581, and Teriyaki Marinade, 582

As with brining, patting marinated chicken dry will make it easier to brown the skin (refrigerating it uncovered on a rack set in a rimmed baking sheet for at least 4 hours or overnight will help even more).

Chicken may instead be seasoned with a paste, 583–86, or dry rub, 587, up to 24 hours before broiling or grilling. For the best results, stuff herb and spice pastes under the skin to keep them from burning. Mixtures especially suited for chicken include:

Cajun Blackening Spice, 587, Garlic-Herb Rub for Poultry, 587, Sweet and Smoky Spice Rub, 587, and Jerk Spice Rub, 587

Jamaican Jerk Paste, 584, Mediterranean Garlic Herb Paste, 584, Mustard Paste, 584, Green or Red Curry Paste, 585, or Charmoula, 586

During the last 5 minutes or so of cooking, you may glaze the chicken with any glaze, 578–79, but especially:

Hoisin-Ginger Glaze, 578, Bourbon-Molasses Glaze, 579, Honey Glaze I, 579, or Chipotle Barbecue Sauce, 582

If you prefer to serve the chicken with a condiment instead of seasoning it before or during cooking, we recommend the following:

Mojo, 567, Zhug, 567, Chimichurri, 567, Tomato-Olive Relish, 568, Roasted Tomato–Chipotle Salsa, 574, Alabama White Barbecue Sauce, 582, or Honey Mustard Dipping Sauce, 566

BROILED CHICKEN

4 servings

Please read About Broiling and Grilling Chicken, 410. To vary the flavor, see Additions to Broiled or Grilled Chicken, above.

Position an oven rack 8 inches beneath the broiler. Preheat the broiler. Have ready:

One 3½- to 4-pound chicken, 3½ pounds bone-in chicken parts, or 2 pounds boneless chicken parts

If broiling a whole chicken, spatchcock or split it, 403, and make a shallow incision on the inside of each leg at the drumstick/thigh joint to help the heat penetrate. If the chicken was brined or marinated, pat it dry. Arrange the chicken skin side down on a broiler tray and lightly rub with:

Vegetable oil

If the chicken is unseasoned, sprinkle with:

2 teaspoons salt

1½ teaspoons black pepper

Broil for 12 to 15 minutes. Turn the chicken skin side up and broil until the skin is browned and crisp; another 15 to 20 minutes for a bone-in chicken, or 8 to 10 minutes for boneless chicken. If broiling pieces, remove the breasts when they reach an internal temperature of 155°F and thighs or drumsticks at 175° to 180°F. If the skin begins to char before the chicken is done, move the tray farther from the heat or tent it with a sheet of foil. Transfer to a platter and let stand for 10 minutes.

GRILLED CHICKEN

4 servings

Please read About Broiling and Grilling Chicken, 410. Don't forget that chicken can be marinated, brined, or rubbed with spices before cooking, or glazed toward the end of cooking. See Additions to Broiled or Grilled Chicken, above, for details. If grilling boneless, skinless chicken breasts, marinate or brine them, 405, as they tend to dry out on the grill due to their lack of fat.

Have ready:

One 3½- to 4-pound chicken, 3½ pounds bone-in chicken parts, or 2 pounds boneless chicken parts

If grilling a whole chicken, spatchcock or split it, 403. For ease of handling, insert one or two skewers through the thigh and into the breast so that the leg quarters are firmly attached to the breast. Prepare a hot, two-zone grill fire, 1063, or preheat a gas grill on high for 10 minutes. If the chicken was brined or marinated, pat it dry. If the chicken is unseasoned, sprinkle with:

2 teaspoons salt

1½ teaspoons black pepper

If using a gas grill, reduce the heat of one of the burners to low. Place the chicken skin side up on the cooler side of the grill, cover, and cook until it is within 20°F of being done; this can take as little as 10 minutes for thinner boneless pieces, 30 or 40 minutes for bone-in pieces, or 45 minutes to 1 hour for spatchcocked or split birds. For the last 5 minutes of cooking, open the grill and flip the chicken skin side down over direct heat. If using a gas grill, turn the heat down to medium. Cook until the skin is browned and crisp, then turn and brown the other side. If grilling pieces, remove the breasts when they reach 155°F and thighs or drumsticks at 175° to 180°F. For spatchcocked or split birds, remove them when the thigh reaches 170° to 175°F. Once browned, the chicken parts may be brushed with a glaze or sauce, or sprinkle after each turn with:

(Lemon juice)

Let the chicken rest for 10 minutes before serving.

BROILED OR GRILLED BARBECUED CHICKEN

Prepare **Broiled Chicken, 411,** or **Grilled Chicken, 411.** About 2 minutes before the chicken is fully cooked, brush both sides with **1 cup Kansas City Barbecue Sauce, 582,** or **Chipotle Barbecue Sauce, 582.** Return to the broiler skin side up or to the grill skin side down and cook just until the skin and sauce have charred slightly. Serve with additional barbecue sauce.

BROILED OR GRILLED TERIYAKI CHICKEN

Prepare **Broiled Chicken, 411,** or **Grilled Chicken, 411.** Rub the pieces lightly with vegetable oil before broiling or grilling and omit the salt and pepper. Prepare **Teriyaki Marinade, 582,** and simmer, stirring, in a small saucepan over medium heat until slightly thickened. About 2 minutes before the chicken is fully cooked, brush both sides with about ¾ cup of the sauce. Return to the broiler skin side up or to the grill skin side down and cook until the skin is lightly charred. Serve with additional sauce.

SMOKED CHICKEN

4 to 6 servings

Please read about Barbecuing, 1066. To avoid the rigmarole of removing the bird and cutting off the breast meat, you may cut the chicken into pieces beforehand and remove them as they cook through—or simplify things further by using **3 to 4½ pounds chicken thighs or whole legs** instead of a whole chicken.

Remove the neck and giblets from:

One 4- to 6-pound chicken

Rub all over with:

¼ cup Southern Barbecue Dry Rub, 587, or 1 tablespoon salt and 1 tablespoon black pepper

Refrigerate, uncovered, on a wire rack overnight. Heat a smoker or grill set up for indirect cooking to 225° to 250°F, 1068 (preferably with a water pan). Add to the coals:

One small chunk of dry hickory, oak, or mesquite wood

Add the chicken to the cooler side of the smoker or grill and cover so that the top vent pulls smoke across the bird. If possible, position the chicken so that the legs are closer to the coals than the breasts. Adjust the vents to maintain the temperature. If you do not have a water pan inside to keep the smoker or grill humid, baste the meat every 20 minutes with:

(Basic Mop, 583, or Beer Mop, 583)

If you plan to keep the breast meat moist for serving in pieces, transfer the chicken to a rimmed baking sheet when a thermometer inserted in the thickest part of the breast registers 155°F, about 2 hours. Sever the legs at the backbone and return them to the smoker or grill and cook for 20 minutes longer (tent the breast and wing portion with foil to keep warm).

If you plan to pull or shred the meat and dress with a sauce, smoke the bird whole until a thermometer inserted in the thickest part of the inner thigh registers 175°F, 2½ to 3 hours. Transfer to a rimmed baking sheet, loosely cover with foil, and rest for at least 15 minutes.

Cut the bird into serving pieces (see About Carving Poultry, 405) or remove the skin and shred the meat off the bone with a fork. Chop up the skin and add back in, if desired. Dress the pulled chicken or serve the pieces with:

Alabama White Barbecue Sauce, 582, or Chipotle Barbecue Sauce, 582

GAI YANG (THAI-STYLE GRILLED CORNISH HENS)

4 servings

A superlative treatment for poultry that results in deeply browned birds with flavorful meat and skin. This procedure may be used with a whole chicken, but follow the cooking times in Grilled Chicken, 411.

Prepare:

Thai-Style Lemongrass Marinade, 581

Spatchcock, 403:

Two 1½- to 1¾-pound Cornish hens

Toss the hens with the marinade in a large bowl, cover, and marinate, refrigerated, for at least 4 hours or (preferably) overnight.

Prepare a hot, two-zone grill fire, 1063, or preheat a gas grill on high for 10 minutes. Remove the hens from the marinade and pat dry (reserve the marinade). To make the birds easier to manipulate on the grill, insert skewers through the thighs and into the lower breast of each bird.

If using a gas grill, reduce the heat of one of the burners to low. Place the chicken skin side up on the cooler side of the grill, cover, and grill for 20 minutes. Baste with some of the marinade, then move the hens to the hotter side of the grill and cook until browned on that side, about 5 minutes. Flip the hens skin side down, and cook until the skin is lightly browned, about 1 minute. The hens are done when a thermometer inserted in the thickest part of the breast registers 160°F. If it needs more cooking, do so on the cooler side of the grill, covered. Transfer to a platter and let rest for 5 minutes. Serve with:

Green Papaya Salad, 129

Cooked sticky rice, 343

BROILED CORNISH HENS

2 to 4 servings

Position an oven rack 8 inches below the broiler. Preheat the broiler.

Spatchcock or split, 403:

Two 1½- to 1¾-pound Cornish hens

Brush the skin with:

2 tablespoons melted butter or vegetable oil

Rub on both sides with:

¾ teaspoon salt

½ teaspoon black pepper

Place the hens skin side down on a rack set over a large baking sheet. Broil until starting to brown, 10 to 13 minutes. Turn the hens skin side up and broil until browned, 8 to 10 minutes more. Let rest, tented with foil, for 10 minutes before serving.

CHICKEN KEBABS

4 servings

Soak wooden or bamboo skewers in water for at least 30 minutes before use. Almost any vegetable will work, but firm vegetables such as carrots, potatoes, cauliflower, and broccoli should first be steamed until nearly tender. Please read About Broiling and Grilling Chicken, 410, and Skewer Cooking, 1065.

Prepare in a large bowl:

¾ cup Becker Chicken or Pork Marinade, 581, Lemon Marinade, 580, or Tandoori Marinade, 580

Pour half of the marinade into a medium bowl and add:

2 pounds boneless, skinless chicken breasts or thighs, cut into 1-inch cubes

Turn to coat and marinate the chicken in the refrigerator for at least 30 minutes, and for up to 2 hours.

When you are ready to grill, add to the remaining half of the marinade:

1 large red onion, cut into 1-inch chunks, or 1 bunch green onions, cut into 1-inch pieces
16 small mushrooms
16 cherry tomatoes
1 bell pepper, cut into 1-inch squares, or 2 small zucchini, halved lengthwise and sliced ½ inch thick

Prepare a hot, two-zone grill fire, 1063, or preheat a gas grill for 10 minutes on high. Remove the chicken from the marinade and thread it onto the skewers, leaving a little space between the pieces to allow for even cooking. If you thread the pieces onto 2 parallel skewers for each kebab, they will stay put when turned. Skewer the vegetables in the same manner. If using a gas grill, turn one burner down to medium. Arrange the skewers on the hot side of the grill and cook for 4 minutes, then turn and grill until the chicken is well browned and cooked through and the vegetables are just tender and browned along the edges, 3 to 4 minutes more. If any of the skewers start to burn before they are finished cooking, move them to the cooler side of the grill.

JAMAICAN JERK CHICKEN

8 servings

Please read About Broiling and Grilling Chicken, 410.

Prepare in a large bowl:

Jamaican Jerk Paste, 584

Add and toss with the paste:

8 whole chicken legs or 8 bone-in, skin-on chicken breasts

Mix well, spreading the jerk mixture under the skin. Cover and marinate the chicken in the refrigerator for at least 2 hours or (preferably) overnight.

Prepare a hot, two-zone grill fire, 1063, or preheat a gas grill for 10 minutes on high. If using a gas grill, turn one burner down to low and the other burner to medium-high. Arrange the chicken pieces skin side down on the cooler side of the grill. Cover the grill and cook for 20 minutes. Turn the chicken and cook for 15 to 20 minutes more or until the internal temperature of breasts reaches 165°F or the legs reach 175° to 180°F. For the last 5 minutes, move the chicken to the hot side of the grill and carefully brown it, turning once or twice. Serve with:

Jamaican Rice and Peas, 331, or Black-Eyed Peas and Greens, 216

TANDOORI CHICKEN OR CHICKEN TIKKA

4 servings

In Indian cooking, "tandoori" refers to food cooked in a *tandoor*, a fiercely hot charcoal-fired vertical oven. Meats cooked in a *tandoor* are usually marinated in an aromatic and bright orange-yellow mixture of yogurt and spices. An excellent tandoori-style chicken can be prepared in a covered grill using a very hot fire. To turn this recipe into **Chicken Tikka,** substitute **2 pounds boneless, skinless chicken thighs or breasts.** Cut into 1-inch cubes, marinate as directed, and grill as for Chicken Kebabs, 412. Please read About Broiling and Grilling Chicken, 410.

Remove the skin from:

3½ pounds bone-in chicken parts

Season and marinade as directed in:

Tandoori Marinade I, 580

Refrigerate for 4 to 6 hours.

Prepare a hot, two-zone grill fire, 1063, or preheat a gas grill for 10 minutes on high. If using a gas grill, turn one burner down to medium. Arrange the chicken parts skin side up on the cooler side of the grill, cover, and grill for 20 minutes. Move the chicken to the hot side of the grill, without flipping, and cook until lightly charred, about 3 minutes. Flip the pieces and brown on the other side, moving them around to avoid flare-ups if necessary. The chicken is done when the internal temperature of the breasts reaches 155°F and the thighs and drumsticks reach 170°F. If needed, move the chicken once again to the cooler side of the grill, cover, and finish cooking.

CHICKEN HOBO PACKS

6 servings

This is a technique for all seasons—the grill's hot coals, a campfire in summer, or a fireplace in winter, 1068. Bury the chicken in the embers surrounding the fire, not directly under it. If no fire is to be had, bake the packs on a rimmed baking sheet at 350°F for 40 minutes. This recipe can be multiplied to serve many people, but wrap only 2 thighs per packet to guarantee easy handling. If desired, other vegetables may be added to the packets as well, such as broccoli or cauliflower florets, sweet potato chunks, or cherry tomatoes.

Have ready:

1 lemon or lime, very thinly sliced

Combine in a large bowl and toss well:

6 garlic cloves, thinly sliced
⅓ cup chopped cilantro or parsley
¼ cup olive oil
1 jalapeño or serrano pepper, seeded and minced

Remove the skin from:

6 bone-in chicken thighs

Sprinkle generously with:

Salt and black pepper

Add the chicken to the garlic-oil mixture and turn to coat, along with:

12 small new potatoes

Place 2 chicken thighs and 4 potatoes in the center of an 18-inch square of heavy-duty foil and top with 2 or 3 lemon or lime slices.

Cover with a second sheet of foil. Crimp the edges of the two sheets to seal securely, then roll in the edges 3 to 4 inches toward the center. Wrap the package completely in a third sheet of foil to double-seal. Repeat to make 2 more packages.

Prepare a hot grill fire, 1063. Clear a space in the fire and lay the packages in the space. Pile the hot coals over and around the packages. Cook for 30 to 40 minutes. Remove with tongs and let stand 10 minutes. Open carefully to avoid being burned by steam.

ABOUT SAUTÉING AND STIR-FRYING CHICKEN

Sautés and stir-fries are the saviors of weeknight dinner, and boneless, skinless chicken is the default protein for these quick, off-the-cuff preparations. Chicken breast in particular requires no special treatment: Easily cut into strips or pounded into cutlets, it is mild-mannered enough to play well with practically any seasoning, sauce, or vegetable you care to add to the pan.

In spite of the boneless breast's appeal, we recommend branching out and using boneless, skinless thighs instead: They are readily available, much more forgiving, and have more flavor. Of course, they do not hold together well when pounded into cutlets, nor are they amenable to stuffing; for everything else, however, we think thighs are a superior cut.

For tips on pounding chicken breasts into cutlets, see Mincing, Grinding, and Pounding, 451. For more stir-fried chicken dishes, see Lo Mein, 301, and Kuaytiaw Khua Kai, 303.

PAN-FRIED OR SAUTÉED CHICKEN

4 to 6 servings

I. BONE-IN CHICKEN PARTS

Bone-in chicken must finish cooking over lower heat once it has been browned. For chicken with a more substantial crust, see Crispy Deep-Fried Chicken, 418.

Have ready:

3½ to 4½ pounds bone-in chicken parts

Trim off any excess fat and season generously with:

1 tablespoon salt
1 tablespoon black pepper

Heat in a large heavy skillet over medium-high heat:

2 tablespoons vegetable oil

Cooking in batches if necessary, arrange the chicken pieces skin side down in a single layer in the skillet. Fry until the chicken is nicely browned on the first side and detaches easily from the skillet, about 5 minutes. Turn the chicken with tongs and cook until nicely browned on the second side, about 5 minutes more. Transfer to a plate or rimmed baking sheet and brown the rest of the pieces. When all the pieces are browned, return them to the skillet and reduce the heat to medium. Continue to cook the chicken, turning often, until the internal temperature reaches 165°F for the breast pieces, and 175°F for thighs, 15 to 20 minutes depending on the size and thickness of the pieces. Transfer the chicken to a platter.

If desired, prepare in the skillet:

(Basic Pan Gravy, 545, or Herbed Pan Sauce, 546)

II. BONELESS BREASTS OR THIGHS

This chicken should be a rich nut-brown on the outside, tender and juicy inside.

Have ready:

4 boneless, skinless chicken breasts or 6 boneless, skinless chicken thighs (1½ to 2 pounds)

Trim off any fat and sprinkle on both sides with:

2 teaspoons salt
1 teaspoon black pepper

Spread on a plate:

¼ cup flour

Coat the chicken with the flour and shake off the excess. Heat in a large heavy skillet over medium heat until fragrant and nut-brown:

1½ tablespoons butter
1½ tablespoons olive oil

Swirl the butter and oil together. Add the chicken and cook undisturbed until golden brown, 4 to 6 minutes. Turn the chicken and cook until firm to the touch and the internal temperature reaches 155°F for breasts, 170°F for thighs, 4 to 6 minutes more.

If desired, prepare in the skillet:

(Basic Pan Gravy, 545, or Herbed Pan Sauce, 546)

PAN-FRIED CHICKEN CUTLETS

4 servings

The even, solid texture of chicken breasts is ideal here (thighs tend to split when pounded). For tips on pounding chicken into cutlets, see Mincing, Grinding, and Pounding, 451.

I. FLOURED

Have ready:

4 boneless, skinless chicken breasts (about 2 pounds)

Trim any fat around the edges. Butterfly each breast by holding the knife parallel to the work surface and slicing lengthwise through the thicker side. Continue slicing through the breast, stopping ½ inch from the opposite side to form a hinge. Open each breast like a book and flatten it with your hand. Place a butterflied breast between sheets of wax paper and pound with a mallet or rolling pin to flatten to ¼ to ½ inch thick. If the breasts seem too large for the pan once they have been pounded, cut them in half.

Season with:

1½ teaspoons salt
1 teaspoon black pepper

Spread on a plate:

½ cup flour

Preheat the oven to 200°F. Heat in a large heavy skillet over medium-high heat:

3 tablespoons vegetable oil

Working in batches, coat the cutlets with the flour, shake off the excess, and cook until lightly browned, 2 to 3 minutes each side, adding more oil between batches if the skillet looks dry. As they finish cooking, transfer the cutlets to a plate or baking sheet lined with paper towels and keep warm in the oven. Serve immediately or at room temperature.

II. CHICKEN MILANESE

Butterfly and pound chicken breasts as for **version I.** Combine in a wide shallow bowl:

1½ cups dry bread crumbs
(¼ to ½ cup grated Parmesan [1 to 2 ounces])
(1½ teaspoons dried rosemary, thyme, or oregano, crumbled)

1½ teaspoons salt
1 teaspoon black pepper
Whisk together in a shallow bowl:
2 large eggs
1 tablespoon water
Spread on a plate:
½ cup flour
Coat the chicken with the flour and shake off the excess. Dip in the egg mixture, then coat with the bread crumb mixture, patting with your fingers to make the crumbs adhere. Set aside on a plate. Preheat the oven to 200°F.
Pan-fry the cutlets as directed in **version I,** using:
⅓ cup vegetable oil

III. CHICKEN KATSU

These Japanese-style cutlets have an appealing golden-brown panko crust. To make this with the traditional pork, butterfly and pound the pork as directed in Breaded Pork Chops or Cutlets, 493, and substitute for the chicken in this recipe.
Butterfly, pound, season, and flour chicken breasts as for version I.
Whisk together in a shallow bowl:
2 eggs
1 tablespoon water
Add to a second bowl:
1 cup panko bread crumbs
Dip the floured chicken in the egg, then coat with the panko. Place on a plate. Preheat the oven to 200°F.
Pan-fry the cutlets as directed in **version I,** using:
⅓ cup vegetable oil
Serve with:
Katsu Sauce, 572

CHICKEN PICCATA

4 to 6 servings

Prepare and keep warm in a 200°F oven:
Pan-Fried or Sautéed Chicken, 414, or Pan-Fried Chicken Cutlets I, 414
Pour off all but 1 tablespoon of the fat from the skillet. Place the skillet over medium heat and add:
1 small shallot, minced
Cook, stirring, until softened, about 1 minute. Increase the heat to high and add:
1 cup chicken stock or broth
Bring to a boil, scraping the bottom of the skillet with a wooden spoon to loosen the browned bits. Add:
¼ cup lemon juice
2 tablespoons drained small capers
Boil until the sauce is reduced to about ⅓ cup, 3 to 4 minutes. Add any accumulated chicken juices. Take off the heat and swirl in:
3 tablespoons butter, softened
Pour the sauce over the chicken and serve immediately.

CHICKEN MARSALA

4 to 6 servings

Prepare and keep warm in a 200°F oven:
Pan-Fried Chicken Cutlets I, 414
Wipe out the skillet, place over medium heat, and add:
1 tablespoon vegetable oil
Add and cook, stirring, until rendered and browned:
3 ounces diced pancetta or bacon
Transfer to a small bowl and set aside. Pour off all but 1 tablespoon of fat from the skillet and add:
1 small onion, chopped
Cook, stirring, until softened, about 5 minutes. Increase the heat to medium-high and add:
8 ounces button mushrooms, thinly sliced
Cook, until softened, 3 to 5 minutes. Return the cooked pancetta to the skillet, along with:
1 cup chicken stock or broth
⅔ cup dry Marsala
3 garlic cloves, minced
(1 tablespoon tomato paste)
3 sprigs thyme
Bring to a boil and cook until the mixture has reduced to one-quarter of its original volume, about 5 minutes. Add:
¼ cup heavy cream
Boil until the sauce is thick enough to lightly coat a spoon, about 5 minutes. Remove the thyme sprigs and stir in:
2 tablespoons finely chopped parsley
Salt and black pepper to taste
Several drops of lemon juice
Spoon the sauce over the chicken and serve immediately.

CHICKEN PARMIGIANA

4 servings

This Italian-American classic can be assembled early in the day, refrigerated, and baked when needed. Use 3 cups of your favorite store-bought tomato sauce if time is short.
Have ready:
Tomato Sauce, 556
Prepare:
Pan-Fried Chicken Cutlets II, 414
Position a rack in the center of the oven. Preheat the oven to 350°F. Lightly oil a 13 × 9-inch baking dish. Spoon 1 cup of the sauce into the baking dish. Arrange the chicken breasts over the sauce, slightly overlapping them. Sprinkle with:
¼ cup grated Parmesan
Spoon over the remaining sauce. Top with:
1½ cups shredded mozzarella or 6 ounces mozzarella, thinly sliced
½ cup grated Parmesan (2 ounces)
Cover the dish with foil and bake until heated through, 20 to 30 minutes. To brown the top, remove the foil and place the dish briefly under a hot broiler. Serve hot, sprinkled with:
Chopped parsley

CHICKEN FINGERS

4 servings

With a dipping sauce, these make nice hors d'oeuvre, and, of course, children love them.
Have ready:
4 boneless, skinless chicken breasts (about 2 pounds)

If there are tenders, peel them off the underside of the chicken breasts and remove the white tendons, 404. Cut the breasts lengthwise into 6 pieces each. Flour, dip in egg, bread, and cook as directed for **Chicken Milanese, 414,** or **Chicken Katsu, 415.** If desired, serve with:

(Marinara Sauce, 556, Ranch Dressing, 577, or Honey Mustard Dipping Sauce, 566)

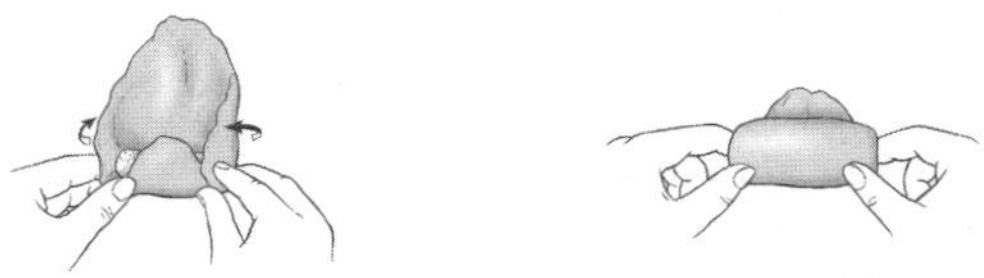

Preparing Chicken Kiev

CHICKEN KIEV

4 servings

This classic consists of pounded boneless, skinless chicken breasts rolled around seasoned butter, then breaded and fried. The key to success is to seal the chicken packets tightly and to bread them well so the butter does not leak out during cooking. You may prepare the chicken a day ahead. For tips on pounding chicken into cutlets, see Mincing, Grinding, and Pounding, 451.

Using the back of a wooden spoon or an electric mixer, beat together in a medium bowl:

1 stick (4 ounces) butter, softened
1 tablespoon lemon juice
1 tablespoon minced parsley
(1 tablespoon minced chives)
1 garlic clove, minced or grated on a rasp grater
½ teaspoon salt
¼ teaspoon black pepper

Shape the butter into a 4 × 3-inch rectangle on a sheet of wax paper. Wrap in the paper and refrigerate for 2 hours. Have ready:

4 boneless, skinless chicken breasts (about 2 pounds)

Trim any fat around the edges. One at a time place the breasts between sheets of wax paper and gently pound with a mallet or a rolling pin until ¼ inch thick. Season both sides with:

Salt and black pepper

Cut the chilled butter crosswise into 4 (1 × 3-inch) fingers. Arrange the chicken smooth side down on a work surface. Place 1 finger of butter crosswise on each breast about one-third of the way up from the narrow end. Fold the narrow end over the butter, as shown, then roll up the butter in the breast, tucking in the sides to enclose completely.

Combine in a wide shallow bowl:

2 cups dry bread crumbs
1 teaspoon salt
1 teaspoon black pepper

Whisk together in another bowl:

2 large eggs
1 tablespoon water

Spread on a plate:

½ cup flour

Coat the chicken packets in the flour, being sure to cover the ends, roll the packets in the egg mixture, and then coat on all sides with the bread crumb mixture, patting with your fingers to make the crumbs adhere. Place the rolls seam side down on a rack set in a baking sheet, cover loosely with plastic wrap, and refrigerate for at least 1 hour and for up to 8 hours.

Heat in a large skillet over medium-high heat to 350° to 365°F:

½ cup vegetable oil

Arrange the rolls seam side down in the skillet and cook until the first side is nut-brown, 2 to 3 minutes. Turn to brown on all sides, 1 to 2 minutes per side. Drain on paper towels and serve immediately.

CHICKEN CORDON BLEU

4 servings

Have ready:

4 boneless, skinless chicken breasts (about 2 pounds)

Trim any fat around the edges. One at a time, place the breasts between sheets of wax paper and pound with a mallet or rolling pin until about ⅜ inch thick. Season both sides with:

1 teaspoon salt
1 teaspoon black pepper

Arrange the chicken smooth side down on a work surface. Cover one half of each breast with:

1 thin slice ham or prosciutto (4 total)

Leaving space around the edges, top the ham slice with:

1 thin slice Gruyère or other Swiss cheese (4 total)

Fold each chicken breast in half over the ham and cheese and press the edges firmly together to seal. Combine in a wide shallow bowl:

1 cup dry bread crumbs
¼ cup minced parsley
1 teaspoon salt
½ teaspoon black pepper

Whisk together in a shallow bowl:

2 large eggs
1 tablespoon water

Spread on a plate:

¼ cup flour

Press both sides of each packet in the flour, then dip in the egg mixture, then coat with the bread crumb mixture, patting with your fingers to make the crumbs adhere. Set aside on a plate. Heat in a large heavy skillet over medium-high heat until shimmering:

3 tablespoons vegetable oil

Place the packets in the skillet and cook until browned on both sides, 3 to 4 minutes each. Drain on paper towels and serve immediately.

STIR-FRIED GARLIC CHICKEN

4 servings

Please read about Stir-Frying, 1052.

Combine in a medium bowl and mix together thoroughly:

1 tablespoon cornstarch
1 tablespoon Shaoxing wine, 952, dry sherry, or dry white wine

2 teaspoons soy sauce
2 teaspoons oyster sauce
1 teaspoon salt
1 teaspoon sugar

Cut into 1½ × ½-inch strips:

1½ pounds boneless, skinless chicken breasts or thighs

Toss in the soy sauce mixture. Cover with plastic wrap and let stand for 20 to 30 minutes. Have ready:

2 garlic cloves, minced
1-inch piece ginger, peeled and minced
⅔ cup chicken stock or broth
½ cup snow peas, trimmed
½ medium onion, cut into ¼-inch slices
3 green onions, halved lengthwise, then cut into 2-inch pieces

Mix well in a small bowl:

1 tablespoon hoisin sauce
1 tablespoon ketchup
2 teaspoons toasted sesame oil
1½ teaspoons soy sauce
½ teaspoon red pepper flakes

Heat a wok or large skillet over high heat until hot. Add:

2 tablespoons vegetable oil

Add the minced garlic and ginger and stir briefly until very slightly browned. Add the chicken and quickly stir and flip it in the oil to separate the pieces. Add the sliced onion, toss, and cook for about 3 minutes. Add the chicken stock and stir until the stock is heated through. Add the snow peas, stir once, cover, and cook for 2 minutes. Add the hoisin sauce mixture and stir gently until all the chicken pieces are thoroughly coated. Sprinkle with the green onions, stir gently, and serve immediately with:

Cooked short-grain rice, 343

ABOUT FRYING CHICKEN

At its best, fried chicken is defined by a crispy, flavorful crust with succulent, juicy chicken underneath. To achieve this ideal there are a few variables to keep in mind.

First, the oil temperature for frying chicken should be hot enough to sizzle appealingly, but not so hot that the crust browns before the chicken is cooked through. The best way to tell when the fat is hot enough is to use an instant-read thermometer: In most scenarios, 350°F is a reasonable oil temperature. The temperature of the oil will drop precipitously when the chicken is added, so keep the burner on high heat until the oil temperature recovers. Monitor the oil temperature frequently to prevent it from overheating or getting too cold. In this vein, ➤ take care not to crowd the pan, which will cause the oil temperature to plummet and take longer to recover. (This can cause the resulting chicken to be greasy.)

Second, the mass of some chicken pieces (bone-in breasts in particular) are so large that getting them to cook through in the time it takes the crust to brown can be a challenge. Cut large chicken breasts crosswise in half to compensate for this. Even when using a thermometer, being vigilant about the temperature of the oil, and cutting the chicken into manageable pieces, you may find that the chicken looks perfectly browned and crisp but is not fully cooked. ➤ Don't panic. Transfer the chicken to an oiled rack set over a baking sheet and place in a 200°F oven until cooked through.

The fat you fry in is important. Some fried chicken connoisseurs use a combination of fats, such as vegetable oil, Clarified Butter, 960, and lard or bacon grease. If you prefer a more neutral flavor, use vegetable oil and/or shortening only. Never use plain butter, as its milk solids will separate out, sink to the bottom of the pan, and burn. Extra-virgin olive oil and other fats with a moderate or low smoke point, 981, should also be avoided.

We highly recommend brining (see About Brining Poultry, 405) or marinating chicken before frying. Buttermilk Marinade, 580, is classic, as it tenderizes the chicken, seasons it, and provides a thick coating that encourages the breading to adhere. Our favorite "ready-made" marinade for fried chicken is dill pickle brine; you may have to go through a few jars of pickles to accumulate enough brine, but the delay helps us check our fried chicken consumption. Do not marinate chicken in pickle brine for more than 4 hours. All that said, even a plain brine will ensure the chicken is evenly seasoned and stays moist during cooking.

As for dredges, seasoned flour is simple, classic, and good, but there are other options. Using part cornstarch or potato starch results in a crispier crust. Fried chicken can get an extra crispy boost from dry bread crumbs, panko, or even crumbled corn flake cereal. ➤ For more on dredges, breading, and coating, see 658. After dredging, you may dry the coating by placing the chicken pieces on a wire rack over a rimmed baking sheet and refrigerating uncovered for 1 hour, or overnight—which will make the coating resilient and extra crispy.

After frying chicken, place it on a rack over a baking sheet to keep it from sitting in its own grease and to allow air circulation around it, preserving its crisp crust. All fried chicken is good both hot and cold, but be aware that leftover fried chicken will lose its alluring crispness. Please read about Deep-Frying, 1051, for more information on deep-frying technique. For fried chicken dishes typically served as appetizers, see Buffalo Chicken Wings, 60, and Thai-Style Chicken Wings, 61.

SKILLET FRIED CHICKEN

4 to 6 servings

This chicken has the crackling crisp skin and distinctive mahogany color that are the hallmarks of the dish. The buttermilk marinade is optional but highly recommended. To vary the results with other marinades, brines, and crusts, see About Frying Chicken, above.

Have ready:

3½ to 4½ pounds bone-in chicken parts

Separate any legs into thighs and drumsticks; cut breasts crosswise in half. If marinating the chicken, prepare:

(Buttermilk Marinade, 580)

Add the chicken and turn to coat well. Cover and refrigerate for at least 4 hours or overnight. Remove the meat from the marinade, allowing any excess to drip off.

Combine in a sturdy paper or zip-top bag and shake to mix:

1½ cups flour
½ cup cornstarch

2 teaspoons salt
1 teaspoon black pepper
(¼ teaspoon cayenne pepper)

Shake the chicken a few pieces at a time in the bag until well coated and let dry on a rack set over a baking sheet at room temperature for 30 minutes or, for a crispier result, refrigerate overnight (bring to room temperature before frying).

Preheat the oven to 200°F. Heat in a deep heavy skillet (preferably cast iron) over medium-high heat:

½ inch vegetable shortening, rendered lard, vegetable oil, or a combination

When the oil is hot enough (about 350°F or when a small corner of a chicken piece dipped into the fat causes vigorous bubbling), gently place the chicken, in batches, skin side down in the hot fat, without crowding. Cook for 10 minutes or until browned on the first side; check after 5 minutes and move the pieces if they are coloring unevenly or turn the heat down if the chicken is browning too quickly. Turn the chicken with tongs and cook until the second side is richly browned, 10 to 12 minutes more. Breast pieces should read 160°F, thighs and drumsticks should reach 175°F. Transfer the chicken to a rack set over a baking sheet lined with paper towels or a brown paper bag and place in the oven to keep warm while you fry the remaining pieces.

After cooking all the chicken, you may pour the fat out of the skillet, retaining the browned bits, and prepare with milk:

(Basic Pan Gravy, 565)

Pass the sauce at the table.

CRISPY DEEP-FRIED CHICKEN

4 servings

Try this recipe if the crust-to-meat ratio of plain fried chicken is simply not high enough. Please read About Frying Chicken, 417, and about Deep-Frying, 1051.

Have ready:

3½ to 4½ pounds bone-in chicken parts

Separate any legs into thighs and drumsticks; cut breasts crosswise in half. Whisk well in a medium bowl:

½ cup milk or buttermilk
2 large eggs
1 teaspoon salt

Mix together on a plate:

1½ cups flour
2 teaspoons salt
2 teaspoons black pepper

Toss the chicken pieces in the flour mixture, then coat with the egg mixture. Lift the pieces out of the egg, letting the excess drip off. Coat with the flour mixture again and transfer the pieces to dry on a rack set over a baking sheet at room temperature for 30 minutes or, for a crispier result, refrigerate overnight (refrigerate the egg mixture along with the chicken; bring both chicken and egg mixture to room temperature before frying).

Preheat the oven to 200°F. Heat in a deep-fryer or deep heavy pot over medium-high heat to 350°F:

3 inches vegetable oil, shortening, lard, or a combination

Toss the breast pieces in the flour mixture, then coat with the egg mixture. Lift the pieces out of the egg, letting the excess drip off, and coat with the flour mixture again. Place in the hot fat and fry until well browned and the internal temperature reaches 160°F, turning the pieces several times with tongs and keeping the fat between 320° and 360°F. Transfer the pieces to a rack set over a baking sheet lined with paper towels or a brown paper bag, and hold in the warm oven. Repeat the double-dredging procedure with the thighs and drumsticks, frying the pieces until browned and the internal temperature reaches 175°F. Serve with, if desired:

(Rémoulade Sauce, 564, or warm honey)

NASHVILLE HOT CHICKEN

4 servings

Pioneered by the owners of Prince's Hot Chicken Shack in Nashville, Tennessee, this chicken is so spectacularly crisp, spicy, and succulent that the first time we ate it we did so in reverent silence. For the full experience, place each serving of the fried chicken on top of the white bread so the bread soaks up the flavorful oil and chicken juices.

Preheat the oven to 200°F. Prepare and keep warm in the oven:

Crispy Deep-Fried Chicken, above

After frying the first batch of chicken, carefully pour ½ cup of the frying oil into a medium heatproof bowl and whisk in:

1 to 4 tablespoons cayenne pepper (know your limits)
1 tablespoon brown sugar
1 teaspoon sweet paprika
1 teaspoon garlic powder
½ teaspoon salt

When all the chicken is fried, brush the spiced oil on each piece (you may not use all the seasoned oil) and serve immediately with:

Slices of untoasted white sandwich bread
Sliced dill pickles

OVEN-FRIED CHICKEN

4 to 6 servings

Have ready:

3½ to 4½ pounds bone-in chicken parts

If using large chicken breasts, cut each one in half crosswise. Prepare:

Buttermilk Marinade, 580

Add the chicken and turn to coat. Cover and refrigerate for at least 4 hours or overnight.

Position a rack in the center of the oven. Preheat the oven to 425°F. Combine in a wide shallow bowl:

2 cups panko bread crumbs
(½ cup finely grated Parmesan, Romano, or pecorino [2 ounces])
1 teaspoon chili powder
1 teaspoon salt
½ teaspoon black pepper

Whisk together in a shallow bowl:

2 large eggs

Place in a third shallow bowl:

¾ cup flour

Remove the chicken from the marinade and shake off the excess. Dip the chicken in the flour, then in the egg, then in the panko mixture, patting with your fingers to make the crumbs adhere. Arrange the chicken skin side up on a wire rack set on a rimmed baking sheet. Drizzle over the chicken:

1 stick (4 ounces) butter, melted, or vegetable oil

Bake until the internal temperature of the breast pieces reaches 160°F, 35 to 40 minutes. Transfer the breast pieces to a platter and, if necessary, bake thighs and drumsticks until they reach 175°F, about 10 minutes more.

ABOUT POACHING, STEWING, AND BRAISING CHICKEN

Poached chicken is not the most exciting dish on its own, but it forms the base of a wide variety of dishes like enchiladas, salads, soups, and casseroles. For poaching poultry in fat, see Duck or Goose Confit, 433. For more on poaching, see 1054.

The world's cuisines boast a wealth of fricassees, stews, and ragouts made with chicken. Definitions of these dishes overlap, but all involve braising chicken in a liquid like wine or stock, often with vegetables or other additions; sometimes, as in fricassees, the meat is sautéed before braising. The braising liquid becomes a flavorful sauce or gravy, which can be thickened or enriched with cream. Some braises—like Coq au Vin, 420—are made with a *garniture*, which is vegetables cooked separately and added near the end of the braising time to provide fresh flavors and a textural contrast to the tender, simmered meat and vegetables.

Any braise may be cooked on the stovetop or in the oven. The oven certainly has a hands-off appeal, as the even heat needs no tending or adjustment. Simply preheat the oven to 300°F, transfer the covered pot to the oven, and cook for the specified time (or until tender). Chicken braises are also perfect for pressure-cooking.

To adapt braised chicken recipes for the pressure cooker, see 1060.

Braised chicken dishes can be served with couscous, rice, egg noodles, Boiled Potatoes, 265, Spätzle, 308, or crusty bread. Aside from the recipes here, see About Poultry Soups, 92, Brunswick Stew, 470, Couscous with Chicken, Lemon, and Olives, 339, and Khao Soi Gai, 303.

POACHED CHICKEN

4 servings

An excellent way to prepare chicken for dishes such as Chicken or Turkey Potpie, 704, Chicken Salad, 123, or enchiladas, 539–40. Turkey is easily substituted here, as is duck or goose. For the last two, please read About Duck and Goose, 430, for a discussion of doneness.

Place in a Dutch oven:

3½ pounds parts bone-in chicken parts or 2 pounds boneless, skinless chicken parts
1 carrot, cut into 2-inch pieces
2 celery ribs, cut into 2-inch pieces
2 cups chicken stock or broth
1 medium onion, quartered
2 sprigs parsley
2 sprigs thyme
1 bay leaf

Add water to cover the pieces by 2 inches. Bring to a simmer, then reduce the heat so the liquid barely bubbles. Partially cover and cook until the meat releases clear juices when pierced with a fork, 20 to 25 minutes for bone-in chicken, about 10 minutes for boneless chicken. The breast meat should reach an internal temperature of 165°F; thighs and drumsticks should reach 175° to 180°F. Remove the meat and let cool. Remove and discard any skin and bones; cut or shred the meat into bite-sized pieces. Skim the fat from the poaching broth with a spoon, then strain the liquid and discard the vegetables. The broth can be used right away or cooled and stored in the refrigerator or freezer for another use.

SHOYU CHICKEN

4 to 6 servings

A comforting Hawaiian dish best served on a steaming mound of rice, which will soak up the rich, sweet, and gingery poaching liquid. We know of few dishes that require as little effort for the enjoyment they offer. Removing the skin will reduce the amount of fat in the poaching liquid, but we enjoy the richness it adds to the resulting sauce (you can split the difference and remove the skin from half of the thighs).

Combine in a Dutch oven or large saucepan:

3½ pounds bone-in chicken thighs, skin removed if desired
1½ cups soy sauce
1 cup water
⅔ cup packed brown sugar
One 2-inch piece ginger, peeled and minced
6 green onions, chopped, dark green parts reserved
4 garlic cloves, smashed

Bring to a simmer over medium-high heat, then reduce the heat so the liquid barely bubbles. Partially cover and cook until the internal temperature of the thighs reaches 175°F, about 30 minutes. Transfer the thighs to a rimmed baking sheet or platter and cover loosely with foil to keep warm. Increase the heat to medium-high and boil the cooking liquid, stirring occasionally, until it is reduced to about half its original volume. Remove the skin and bones from the thighs, if desired, and place atop servings of:

Cooked short-grain white rice, 343

Drizzle liberally with the sauce. Chop the reserved green onion tops and sprinkle on each serving, along with:

Toasted sesame seeds

CREAMED CHICKEN

4 to 6 servings

Poached and shredded poultry in a rich cream sauce (essentially just a very thick white sauce or béchamel) can be served over rice or pasta, on toast, or used as the base for a potpie or casserole.

I. Prepare:

Poached Chicken, 419

Reserve the poaching liquid. After the meat is cut or shredded, melt in a large saucepan over medium-low heat:

4 tablespoons (½ stick) butter

Add and whisk until smooth:

⅓ cup all-purpose flour (for serving over rice, pasta, or toast), or ½ cup (for a potpie or casserole)

Cook, whisking constantly, for 1 minute. Take the pan off the heat. Add 2 cups of the reserved poaching liquid and whisk until smooth. Whisk in:

1½ cups whole milk or half-and-half

Place the pan back on the heat, increase the heat, and bring the mixture to a simmer, whisking constantly. Scrape the inside of the pan and whisk vigorously to break up any lumps. Let simmer for 1 minute. Stir in the cooked chicken, bring to a simmer, and cook for 1 minute more. Take off the heat and season to taste with:

Lemon juice

Salt and white or black pepper

II. WITH LEFTOVER CHICKEN

Prepare **version I** using **4 cups shredded cooked chicken.** In making the sauce, replace the poaching broth with **2 cups chicken broth, store-bought or homemade, 81.**

CHICKEN WITH 40 CLOVES OF GARLIC

6 to 8 servings

Traditionally, this dish is cooked in a covered casserole; the flesh ends up succulent but the skin will not brown. For the sake of flavorful skin, we opt to brown the chicken before cooking. If you are not a chicken skin aficionado, feel free to skip this step.

Position a rack in the center of the oven. Preheat the oven to 375°F. Have ready:

3½ pounds bone-in chicken parts or one 4-pound chicken

If using a whole bird, remove the neck and giblets and cut the chicken into 10 pieces (see About Cutting Up Raw Poultry, 402). Season the chicken with:

1½ teaspoons salt

Heat in a Dutch oven over medium-high heat:

2 tablespoons vegetable oil

Add the chicken pieces in batches and brown well on both sides. Transfer to a plate and add to the pot:

2 cups chicken stock or broth, or as needed

1 cup dry white wine, or as needed

3 heads garlic, cloves separated but not peeled

2 teaspoons fresh thyme leaves or 1 teaspoon dried thyme

2 teaspoons chopped fresh sage or 1 teaspoon dried sage

1 teaspoon minced fresh rosemary or ½ teaspoon dried rosemary

½ teaspoon black pepper

Bring to a boil, using a wooden spoon to scrape any browned bits off the bottom of the pot. Return the chicken pieces to the pot, skin side up, cover, and transfer to the oven. Bake for 20 minutes. Increase the oven temperature to 450°F, uncover the pot, and cook the chicken until the internal temperature of the breast pieces reaches 160°F, about 25 minutes. Transfer to a plate and simmer the thighs and drumsticks until they reach 175°F, about 10 minutes longer. Return the breasts to the pot when all of the pieces are done. Make sure there is always some liquid in the bottom of the pot; add a little more wine or stock if needed.

Remove the chicken and garlic from the pot and keep warm. Skim as much fat as possible from the pan juices with a spoon. If the pan juices are watery or weak in flavor, boil them down over high heat to concentrate. Peel 10 of the garlic cloves and mash to a paste, then stir into the sauce and boil for 1 minute. Take the sauce off the heat. If desired, stir in:

(2 tablespoons minced parsley or 2 teaspoons minced thyme, tarragon, or rosemary)

Season to taste with:

Salt and black pepper

Arrange the chicken on a platter. Spoon the sauce over it and scatter the garlic cloves around it.

COQ AU VIN (CHICKEN BRAISED IN WINE)

4 servings

When the old rooster, or *coq*, lost his crow, he would find himself the main ingredient in this classic French braise. It is commonly made with red wine, but if you would like to try a white, choose one that is fruity, such as riesling or chardonnay. This recipe is written for supermarket chickens, which are uniformly young and tender. If you have a rooster or stewing hen, plan on braising it for much longer than this recipe instructs, until very tender. Any leftover sauce from this recipe can be used to make Oeufs en Meurette, 154.

Have ready:

4 pounds bone-in chicken parts or one 4- to 4½-pound chicken

If using a whole bird, remove the neck and giblets and cut the chicken into 10 pieces (see About Cutting Up Raw Poultry, 402). Season the chicken with:

2 teaspoons salt

1 teaspoon black pepper

Cook in a Dutch oven over medium-high heat until browned:

4 slices thick-cut bacon, cut crosswise into ¼-inch strips

Transfer to a plate. Add as many pieces of chicken to the pot as will fit and cook until browned on both sides, about 7 minutes. Transfer to a plate. Brown the remaining pieces. Pour off all but 3 tablespoons of the fat from the pot. Add:

1 medium onion, chopped

1 carrot, chopped

Cook, stirring occasionally, until softened, about 10 minutes. Stir in:

3 tablespoons all-purpose flour

Reduce the heat to low. Cook, stirring constantly, until the flour just begins to turn light brown, about 5 minutes. Stir in:

3 cups dry red wine

1 cup chicken stock or broth

2 tablespoons tomato paste

2 bay leaves

½ teaspoon dried thyme

½ teaspoon dried marjoram or oregano, crumbled

Increase the heat to high and bring the sauce to a boil, stirring constantly. Return the bacon and chicken, with any accumulated juices, to the pot. Return the sauce to a boil, then reduce the heat so that the liquid barely simmers, cover, and cook until the internal temperature of the breast pieces reaches 160°F, about 25 minutes.

Transfer to a plate and simmer the thighs and drumsticks until they reach 175°F, about 10 minutes longer. Return the breasts to the pot when all of the pieces are done.
Meanwhile, melt in a wide skillet over medium-high heat:

3 tablespoons butter

Add, if desired:

(1½ cups pearl onions, peeled)

Cook, stirring often, until lightly browned and just tender, 5 to 8 minutes. Add:

8 ounces mushrooms, sliced

Cook, stirring, until the mushrooms release their juices. Take the skillet off the heat. Transfer the chicken to a platter and cover with foil. Discard the bay leaves. Bring the sauce to a boil over high heat and reduce until syrupy, using a spoon to skim off the fat as it accumulates. Add the mushrooms and onions, if using, with the pan juices to the sauce and heat through. Season to taste with:

Salt and black pepper

Pour the sauce over the chicken. If desired, garnish with:

(Minced parsley)

FRENCH CASSEROLE CHICKEN

4 to 6 servings

This dish was originally intended for cooking old stewing chickens. Marion Becker's original headnote wryly stated "Whenever we see one of our contemporaries trying to regain her youthful allure with gaudy sartorial trappings, we think of a dish we found in a collection of college alumnae recipes, called 'Suprême of Old Hen.'" These days, most chickens are so young and tender that we have changed the recipe to use all thighs. If you are in fact using a stewing hen, plan on braising it for much longer than this recipe instructs, until very tender.
Have ready:

2½ pounds bone-in chicken thighs or whole legs

Sprinkle with:

2 teaspoons salt
1 teaspoon black pepper

Heat in a large pot or Dutch oven over medium-high heat:

2 tablespoons vegetable oil

Add the chicken in batches and brown on both sides. Transfer to a plate and set aside. Add to the pot and sauté until the onions are translucent, about 10 minutes:

2 tart apples, cored and chopped
4 celery ribs with leaves, chopped
1 onion, chopped
4 sprigs parsley

Add:

⅓ cup dry white wine

Scrape up any browned bits on the bottom of the pot. Add and stir to combine:

3 tablespoons all-purpose flour

Return the chicken to the pot along with:

1½ cups chicken stock or broth

Bring the liquid to a boil, cover the pot tightly, and gently simmer over low heat until the internal temperature of the chicken reaches 175° to 180°F, about 45 minutes.

Transfer the chicken to a serving dish, strain the sauce through a fine-mesh sieve, and return to medium-high heat to reduce the sauce by one-third to thicken. Skim any fat from the surface with a spoon. Take off the heat and whisk in:

½ cup sour cream or crème fraîche
2 teaspoons minced tarragon
Salt and black pepper to taste

Pour the sauce over the chicken and serve.

THAI-STYLE YELLOW CHICKEN CURRY

4 servings

Thai yellow curry tends to be milder than green or red curry and uses *nam prik gaeng karee*, or yellow curry paste. The vegetables in yellow chicken curry are simple—just potatoes and onions—but you can, of course, add other vegetables to the mix, including Thai eggplant, zucchini, or bell pepper. Red curry paste, 585, may be substituted for the yellow, if desired. For a similar noodle dish that uses bone-in chicken, see Khao Soi Gai, 303.
Heat in a large skillet over medium heat:

1 tablespoon vegetable or coconut oil

Add and cook, stirring, until fragrant and starting to brown:

4 tablespoons yellow curry paste

Stir in and bring to a simmer:

One 13½-ounce can coconut milk
½ cup chicken stock or broth
2 tablespoons fish sauce

Stir in:

1 pound yellow or red potatoes, cut into 1-inch chunks
1 medium onion, thinly sliced

Cover and cook until the potatoes are almost tender, about 10 minutes. Stir in:

1 pound boneless, skinless chicken thighs, cut into 1½-inch chunks

Continue to simmer, covered, until the chicken is cooked through, about 6 minutes. Stir in:

1 tablespoon lime juice

Taste and add more fish sauce or salt and lime juice if needed. Serve with:

Cooked jasmine rice, 343

THAI-STYLE GREEN CHICKEN CURRY

Prepare **Thai-Style Yellow Chicken Curry, above,** substituting **green curry paste, store-bought or homemade, 585,** for the yellow curry paste. Omit the potatoes and add along with the onion **½ red bell pepper or 3 Fresno peppers, seeded and coarsely chopped.** Add with the chicken **8 ounces green Thai eggplants, quartered.** Just before serving, stir in **⅓ cup packed Thai or sweet basil leaves, coarsely chopped or torn into pieces.**

CHICKEN PAPRIKA

4 to 6 servings

Serve this flavorful dish with small boiled potatoes or Spätzle, 308.
Have ready:

3½ to 4 pounds bone-in chicken parts

Separate the legs into thighs and drumsticks; cut the breasts in half crosswise. Season with:

2 teaspoons salt
1 teaspoon black pepper

Heat in a large skillet or Dutch oven over medium-high heat:

2 tablespoons vegetable oil or rendered lard

Add the chicken in batches, without crowding, and cook, turning once, until golden, about 5 minutes each side. Transfer the chicken to a plate and brown the remaining chicken. Add to the fat in the pan:

1 large onion, thinly sliced

Reduce the heat slightly and cook, stirring and scraping up the browned bits on the bottom of the pan, until the onion begins to turn golden, about 10 minutes. Add:

1½ cups chicken stock or broth
¼ cup Hungarian sweet paprika, or a combination of sweet and hot
3 large garlic cloves, minced
1 bay leaf

Bring to a boil, stirring constantly. Return the chicken, with any accumulated juices, to the pan. Reduce the heat so that the liquid barely bubbles, cover, and cook, turning the chicken once or twice, until the internal temperature reaches 160°F for the breasts and 175°F for the thighs, 25 to 30 minutes.

Transfer the chicken to a serving platter and cover to keep warm. Discard the bay leaf. Let the sauce stand briefly off the heat, then skim the fat off the surface with a spoon. Bring the sauce back to a boil over high heat and cook until thickened and brick red. Take the pan off the heat and whisk into the sauce:

1 cup sour cream

Season to taste with:

Salt and black pepper
Lemon juice

Pour the sauce over the chicken and serve sprinkled with:

Chopped dill or parsley

CHICKEN FRICASSEE

4 to 5 servings

Have ready:

3½ to 4½ pounds bone-in chicken parts

Separate the legs into thighs and drumsticks; cut each breast in half crosswise through the bone. If desired, remove the skin. Season the chicken with:

Salt and white or black pepper

Melt in a large heavy skillet over medium heat:

4 tablespoons (½ stick) butter

Add the chicken in batches, without crowding, and cook, turning once, until golden, about 5 minutes each side. Transfer to a plate and brown the remaining chicken. Add to the fat in the skillet:

1 large onion, chopped

Cook, stirring occasionally, until tender but not browned, about 5 minutes. Stir in:

⅓ cup all-purpose flour

Cook, stirring, for 1 minute, then reduce the heat to medium-low and whisk in:

1¾ cups chicken stock or broth

Whisking constantly, bring to a boil over high heat. Add:

8 ounces mushrooms, sliced
2 medium carrots, diced
2 medium celery ribs, diced
½ teaspoon dried thyme
1 teaspoon salt
½ teaspoon white or black pepper

Return the chicken pieces, with any accumulated juices, to the skillet and bring to a simmer. Reduce the heat so that the liquid barely bubbles. Cover tightly and cook until the internal temperature of the thigh reaches 175°F, 20 to 30 minutes. Skim off the fat from around the sides of the skillet with a spoon. If desired, stir in:

(¼ to ½ cup heavy cream)

Season to taste with:

Salt and white or black pepper
Lemon juice

CHICKEN AND DUMPLINGS

4 to 5 servings

Prepare:

Chicken Fricassee, above

Push the chicken pieces down so that they are submerged in the sauce. Drop in spoonfuls over the top:

Dumplings, 305, or Cornmeal Dumplings, 306

Cover and cook as directed for the dumplings.

CHICKEN CACCIATORE

6 servings

Cacciatore means "hunter's style" in Italian. There are countless versions of this dish, some made with rabbit (which seems more appropriate to the name). Creamy Polenta, 322, is a traditional companion.

Have ready:

3½ to 4 pounds bone-in chicken parts, preferably thighs

Season with:

1½ teaspoons salt
1 teaspoon black pepper

Heat in a large heavy skillet over medium-high heat:

2 tablespoons olive oil

Add the chicken in batches, without crowding, and cook, turning once, until golden, about 5 minutes each side. Transfer to a plate. Reduce the heat to medium and add to the fat in the skillet:

1 medium onion, finely chopped
1 bay leaf
1½ teaspoons chopped fresh rosemary or ½ teaspoon dried rosemary, crumbled
1 teaspoon minced fresh sage or ½ teaspoon dried sage, crumbled
¼ teaspoon red pepper flakes

Cook, stirring, until the onion is golden brown, about 10 minutes. Add:

8 ounces mushrooms, sliced
2 large garlic cloves, minced

Cook until the mushrooms are softened, about 5 minutes. Pour into the skillet:

½ cup dry red or white wine

Bring to a boil over medium-high heat, scraping up any browned bits on the bottom of the skillet. Return the chicken to the skillet and cook until the wine is nearly evaporated. Add:

One 14½-ounce can diced tomatoes
½ cup chicken stock or broth
(½ cup oil-cured black olives, pitted and sliced)

Bring to a boil, then reduce the heat to low, cover, and simmer gently until the chicken is tender, about 30 minutes. Uncover and boil the pan juices over high heat until slightly thickened, about 10 minutes. Discard the bay leaf. Taste and adjust the seasonings.

CHICKEN MARENGO

6 to 8 servings

According to legend, this braise was served to Napoleon after he had fasted through his victorious battle at Marengo. The dish, composed of ingredients sourced from the nearby countryside, was such a success that Napoleon's chef had to prepare it after every subsequent battle. We like to serve this with cooked white beans or couscous.

Have ready:

3½ to 4 pounds bone-in chicken parts, preferably thighs

Season with:

1½ teaspoons salt
1 teaspoon black pepper

Heat in a Dutch oven over medium-high heat:

2 tablespoons olive oil

Add the chicken in batches, without crowding, and cook, turning once, until golden, about 5 minutes each side. Transfer to a plate. Reduce the heat to medium and add to the fat in the pot:

1 medium onion, thinly sliced

Cook, stirring, until softened, 6 to 8 minutes. Return the chicken pieces to the pot along with:

One 14½-ounce can diced tomatoes
1 cup chicken stock or broth
½ cup dry white wine or additional stock or broth
(2 tablespoons brandy)
2 garlic cloves, minced
1 bay leaf
4 sprigs parsley
½ teaspoon dried thyme

Cover and simmer until tender, about 30 minutes.

While the chicken cooks, melt in a large skillet over medium heat:

4 tablespoons (½ stick) butter

Add and sauté until starting to soften, about 5 minutes:

20 pearl onions, peeled

Stir in and cook until they release their juices:

1 pound mushrooms, sliced

Take the skillet off the heat. When the chicken is done, transfer it to a platter. Remove the bay leaf and parsley sprigs, then bring the sauce to a boil and reduce it for about 5 minutes. Season to taste with:

Salt and black pepper

Stir the mushrooms and onions into the sauce along with:

1 cup pitted black olives, such as Kalamata
2 tablespoons lemon juice

Serve the chicken with the sauce and vegetables. Garnish with:

Chopped parsley

COUNTRY CAPTAIN

4 servings

Cecily Brownstone, a friend of Irma and Marion's, contributed this time-tested formula in the early 1960s. According to her, the dish owes its name not to the sea captain who brought the recipe back to our shores, but to the Indian officer who first introduced him to it. We have since heard several other accounts, but there is little doubt that the dish has become a comfort-food favorite on both sides of the Atlantic. Serve over cooked rice, 343.

Preheat the oven to 350°F. Have ready:

3½ to 4½ pounds bone-in chicken parts

Season with:

1½ teaspoons salt
1 teaspoon black pepper

Lightly coat the chicken in:

Flour

Melt in a large ovenproof skillet or Dutch oven over medium heat:

4 tablespoons (½ stick) butter

Add the chicken in batches, without crowding, and cook, turning once, until golden, about 5 minutes each side. Transfer to a plate. Add to the fat in the pan:

One 14½-ounce can diced tomatoes
1 small onion, diced
½ green bell pepper, diced
3 garlic cloves, minced
1 tablespoon curry powder
½ teaspoon dried thyme

Bring to a simmer, scraping any browned bits from the bottom of the pan. Return the chicken to the pan, skin side up, and bake, uncovered, until the chicken is tender, about 40 minutes. Stir into the sauce:

3 tablespoons dried currants

Garnish with:

Toasted, 1005, slivered almonds

CHICKEN MAKHINI MASALA

4 servings

This dish, contributed by friend and gifted chef Kusuma Rao, is the precursor to the Anglo-Indian favorite **chicken tikka masala,** also known as **butter chicken.** All these dishes start with marinated and grilled chicken, which is then fortified with a creamy, rich tomato sauce. We recommend marinating and grilling a sufficiently large batch of chicken for two meals, then following up with this dish the next day. ➤ If you wish to make the recipe without an intermediate meal, marinate the chicken, then grill or roast it as you make the sauce.

Marinate:

2 pounds bone-in chicken thighs, skin removed

in:

½ recipe Tandoori Marinade I, 580

Grill as for **Tandoori Chicken, 413,** or preheat the oven to 425°F and line a baking sheet with parchment paper. Bake until the internal temperature of the chicken reaches 170°F, about 20 minutes.

Cut the cooked chicken off the bone into bite-sized pieces. Heat in a large heavy skillet over medium-low heat until hot:

2 tablespoons vegetable oil

Add and cook, stirring occasionally, until fragrant:

3 whole cloves
1 cinnamon stick
1 bay leaf
3 cardamom pods

Add and cook until starting to sizzle and just beginning to brown:

1 teaspoon cumin seeds

Add and sauté until very well browned (this can take up to 20 minutes):

1 large onion, finely diced
½ teaspoon salt

Add and cook, stirring, for 20 seconds:

½ teaspoon ground turmeric

Add and cook, stirring frequently, for 3 to 4 minutes:

6 garlic cloves, minced
One 2-inch piece ginger, peeled and minced

Or use:

⅓ cup prepared ginger-garlic paste

Stir in:

1 pound plum or Roma tomatoes, chopped, or one 14½-ounce can diced tomatoes
1 to 3 serrano or jalapeño peppers, to taste, minced
1 tablespoon ground coriander
2 teaspoons ground fennel
2 teaspoons ground cumin
½ to 1 teaspoon cayenne pepper, to taste
½ teaspoon salt

Cook, scraping the skillet frequently, until the tomatoes are completely broken down and the mixture forms a paste, 10 to 15 minutes. (If time allows, add ½ cup water and allow the mixture to simmer, reduce, and become a thick paste again.) If desired, for a very smooth masala, discard the cinnamon and bay leaf and transfer the paste to a blender. Puree until smooth.

If the sauce was blended, scrape it back into the skillet. Stir in:

⅓ cup water

Bring the mixture to a simmer and add:

1 teaspoon garam masala
(1 tablespoon ground dried fenugreek leaves)

Simmer for 10 minutes, adding a little water as needed and scraping the bottom of the skillet constantly to keep it from burning. Add the cooked chicken along with:

3 tablespoons butter

Stir to combine and simmer for another few minutes. If desired, thin out with:

(Up to ½ cup heavy cream)

Taste and add more salt if needed. Serve with:

Cooked jasmine or basmati rice, 343
(Naan, 611)

BASQUE CHICKEN

4 to 6 servings

Have ready:

3½ to 4 pounds bone-in chicken parts

Heat in a Dutch oven over medium-high heat:

2 tablespoons olive oil

Add the chicken in batches, without crowding, and cook, turning once, until golden, about 5 minutes each side. Transfer to a plate.

Reduce the heat to medium and add to the fat in the pot:

1 medium onion, chopped
2 red, yellow, or green bell peppers or 8 ounces Basque or Italian frying peppers, cut into ½-inch-wide strips
4 small jalapeño peppers, seeded and cut into strips
4 ounces cured ham (such as country ham, prosciutto, or serrano), cut into ½-inch dice
6 garlic cloves, chopped
1¼ teaspoons salt
½ teaspoon black pepper

Cook, stirring often, until the peppers are softened, about 10 minutes. Add:

2 pounds fresh tomatoes, chopped, or one 28-ounce can whole tomatoes, crushed

Return the chicken pieces to the pot. Bring the liquid to a simmer, cover, reduce the heat to low to medium-low, and simmer gently until the chicken is cooked through and tender (the thighs should reach 175°F and the breasts about 160°F), about 45 minutes.

Serve over:

Cooked rice, 343

ARROZ CON POLLO (CHICKEN AND RICE)

4 servings

A classic combination with scores of variants around the world. This Spanish-leaning version is tinted with fragrant saffron; for the broth-y, olive-studded Puerto Rican version, see Asopao de Pollo, 93.

Have ready:

3½ to 4½ pounds chicken parts

Season with:

2 teaspoons salt
1 teaspoon black pepper

Heat in a Dutch oven over medium-high heat:

2 tablespoons vegetable oil

Add the chicken in batches, without crowding, and cook, turning once, until golden, about 5 minutes each side. Transfer to a platter.

Reduce the heat to medium and add to the fat in the pot:

1 large onion, chopped
(1 green bell pepper, diced)
4 ounces ham, serrano ham, or cured Spanish chorizo, diced (about ½ cup)

Cook, stirring occasionally, until the onion is just tender, about 5 minutes. Add and stir to coat with fat:

2 cups medium- or long-grain white rice

Add and cook, stirring, for 1 minute:

3 garlic cloves, minced
1 tablespoon sweet paprika
1 teaspoon salt
½ teaspoon black pepper

Add:

3 cups chicken stock or broth
½ teaspoon dried oregano
¼ teaspoon loosely packed saffron threads

Bring to a boil over high heat, scraping the bottom of the pot with a wooden spoon to loosen the browned bits. Place the chicken pieces in the pot and pour in any accumulated juices. Cover the pot and simmer over medium-low heat for 20 minutes. Stir in:

1 cup unthawed frozen peas
⅓ cup drained pimientos or roasted red peppers, cut into thin 1-inch-long strips
¼ cup chopped green olives

Cover and cook until the rice is tender, about 5 minutes more. Taste and adjust the seasonings.

CHICKEN TAGINE WITH CHICKPEAS

4 to 6 servings

A *tagine* (also spelled *tajine*) is an earthenware cooking vessel with a conical lid that is used in Moroccan cuisine to make savory braised dishes like this one. For another take on this, see Couscous with Chicken, Lemon, and Olives, 339.

Remove the skin and pat dry:

3½ to 4½ pounds bone-in chicken parts

Heat in a large skillet or Dutch oven over medium-high heat:

2 tablespoons vegetable oil or Clarified Butter, 960

Add the chicken in batches, without crowding, and cook, turning once, until golden, about 5 minutes each side. Transfer to a plate. Add to the fat in the pan:

1 large onion, sliced

Cook, stirring, until softened, 6 to 8 minutes. Stir in:

One 15-ounce can chickpeas, drained and rinsed
1 cup water or chicken stock or broth
1 medium preserved lemon, 942, pulp discarded, rind thinly sliced
3 garlic cloves, minced
1 teaspoon ground coriander
1 teaspoon ground ginger
¾ teaspoon salt
(½ teaspoon saffron threads)
½ teaspoon ground cinnamon
½ teaspoon black pepper
⅛ to ¼ teaspoon cayenne pepper, to taste

Return the chicken to the pan, skin side up. Bring to a boil, then reduce the heat to a simmer, cover tightly, and cook until the internal temperature of breast pieces reaches 160°F, 25 to 30 minutes, and thighs and drumsticks reach 175°F, about 10 minutes more. (If necessary, transfer breast pieces to a plate and return to the pan when the thighs and drumsticks are done.) Take off the heat and sprinkle with:

½ cup chopped parsley, cilantro, or a combination

Taste the sauce and, if needed, season with more:

Salt and black pepper

Serve with:

Cooked white rice, 343, or couscous, 341

CHICKEN CHILI VERDE

4 to 6 servings

Serve this delicious stew with rice, beans, and tortillas or use as a filling for tamales, burritos, tacos, or enchiladas. You can make a quicker version by skipping the poaching step and using **2 to 3 cups chopped leftover chicken or turkey** and **2 cups chicken stock or broth.**

Place in a medium pot:

2½ pounds bone-in chicken parts

Add:

4 cups chicken stock or broth

Bring to a boil, reduce to a simmer, and cook, partially covered, for 30 minutes or until the breasts reach an internal temperature of 160°F and the thighs reach an internal temperature of 175°F. Take off the heat. Remove the chicken from the broth and reserve the broth. When the chicken is cool enough to handle, remove the skin and bones, keeping the meat in large chunks. Heat in a large skillet or Dutch oven over medium heat:

2 tablespoons vegetable oil

Add and cook, stirring occasionally, until tender, about 5 minutes:

1 medium onion, chopped
3 garlic cloves, minced

Add and cook, stirring, about 1 minute:

2 teaspoons chili powder
1 teaspoon ground cumin
½ teaspoon dried oregano
½ teaspoon salt

Add 2 cups of the reserved poaching broth along with:

4 large or 6 medium tomatillos, husked, rinsed, and diced

Separate the leaves and stems of:

1 large bunch cilantro

Finely chop the leaves and stems separately. Add the stems to the pan along with:

3 Anaheim, Hatch, or poblano peppers, roasted, 262, peeled, and chopped, or one 7-ounce can diced green chiles, drained
(2 jalapeño peppers, seeded and finely chopped)

Bring to a simmer and simmer gently, uncovered, for 10 minutes. Add the chicken and ½ cup of the chopped cilantro leaves along with:

2 tablespoons lime juice

Simmer for 5 to 10 minutes to heat through. Season to taste with:

Salt

Serve garnished with the remaining cilantro leaves.

CHICKEN TINGA

4 or 5 servings

If desired, use 3 canned chipotles in adobo sauce in place of the dried chiles; add them directly to the blender.

Adjust an oven rack so it is 4 inches from the heating element. Preheat the broiler.

Heat in a dry skillet over medium heat:

3 dried chipotle chiles, stemmed and seeded

Press the chiles flat with a spatula. Toast the chiles, turning once or twice, until fragrant, 1 minute or less. Transfer the chiles to a small heatproof bowl and add:

Boiling water to cover

Set aside. Meanwhile, place on a baking sheet:

5 plum or Roma tomatoes
1 small onion, peeled and cut into 4 wedges
4 garlic cloves, unpeeled

Broil, turning the vegetables every 5 minutes. Remove the garlic after 8 to 10 minutes or when the peel is slightly singed. The vegetables are ready when they are soft and charred, 15 to 20 minutes. Peel the garlic. Transfer the tomatoes, onion, and garlic to a blender. Drain the chipotles (reserving the soaking liquid) and add the chiles to the blender along with:

1 teaspoon salt

Puree. Heat in a large skillet over medium heat until shimmering:

2 tablespoons vegetable oil

Add in batches, without crowding, and cook, turning once, until golden, about 5 minutes each side:

2 pounds bone-in chicken thighs, skin removed

Pour the chipotle sauce into the skillet. Add ½ cup reserved chipotle soaking liquid or water to the blender and swish it around to loosen the remaining sauce, then pour it into the skillet. Bring the sauce to a simmer, cover, and cook, simmering gently over medium-low heat, until the chicken is cooked through, about 20 minutes.

Transfer the chicken to a cutting board and use two forks to shred it. Save the bones for stock, 73, or discard them, and return the shredded chicken to the sauce. Serve the chicken in tacos, burritos, tortas, or enchiladas or on tostadas with:

Refried Beans, 215
Crumbled Cotija cheese
Diced avocado

CHICKEN ÉTOUFFÉE

6 to 8 servings

A classic Cajun fricassee.

Please read about Roux, 542. Have ready:

4 to 5 pounds bone-in chicken parts

Mix together in a small bowl:

1 teaspoon sweet paprika
1 teaspoon dried thyme
1 teaspoon salt
½ teaspoon black pepper
¼ teaspoon cayenne pepper

Rub the spice mixture all over the chicken pieces. Pour into a brown paper bag:

1 cup flour

Add the chicken to the bag and shake to coat with flour; shake off the excess. Reserve the flour. Heat in a large heavy skillet or Dutch oven over medium heat:

3 tablespoons vegetable oil

Add the chicken in batches, without crowding, and brown on both sides. Transfer to a plate. Pour off all but about 3 tablespoons of the fat from the pan. Reduce the heat to medium and stir in 3 tablespoons of the reserved flour. Cook, stirring constantly, until the roux is almost as dark as milk chocolate, up to 20 minutes.

Add and cook, stirring, until the vegetables are softened, 6 to 8 minutes:

1 medium onion, chopped
1 celery rib, chopped
½ red or green bell pepper, chopped
¼ cup chopped andouille sausage or smoked ham

Stir in and cook for 1 minute:

3 garlic cloves, finely chopped

Stir in and bring to a simmer, stirring constantly:

2 cups chicken stock or broth
3 tablespoons tomato paste
1 tablespoon Worcestershire sauce
¼ teaspoon hot pepper sauce, or to taste

Return the chicken pieces, with their juices, to the pan and bring to a simmer. Cover and cook, turning occasionally, until the internal temperature of the thighs reaches 180°F, about 30 minutes. Transfer the chicken to a plate. Skim the fat from the sauce with a spoon. Add:

4 green onions, finely chopped
¼ cup chopped parsley

Boil until the sauce is thickened. Taste and add more hot pepper sauce and/or salt and pepper if needed. Return the chicken to the skillet and heat through. Serve with:

Cooked rice, 343

ABOUT TURKEY

Benjamin Franklin wrote in a letter to his daughter, "I wish the bald eagle had not been chosen as the representative of our country. . . . The turkey is a much more respectable character and, withal, a true original native of America." Perhaps Ben would have been pleased that the turkey has taken first place in the holiday feasts of his countrymen.

Nearly all turkeys sold in this country are of one breed: the Broad Breasted White or Bronze. As their names imply, these turkeys are bred to have very large breasts as well as small legs and relatively bland meat. Unless you buy a turkey from a small farmer or a high-end butcher, you are unlikely to encounter any other type of turkey. **Heritage breed turkeys,** while expensive, are more flavorful and have smaller breasts and larger legs, making them ideal for lovers of dark meat. They tend to be smaller than standard grocery-store turkeys, though they come in a range of sizes.

Self-basting turkeys have been injected with broth, vegetable oil or butter, salt, and seasonings to enhance their moistness and flavor. While these birds come out of the oven uniformly moist and seasoned, we find their wet, deli meat–like texture less than desirable. Some swear by the superior flavor of a **fresh turkey.** They are more expensive since they have to be specially ordered, but there may not be an appreciable difference in flavor. **Kosher turkeys** are already salted and should not be brined. Be circumspect in the amount of salt you rub into their skin or add to pan gravies made with their drippings. **Natural turkeys** are simply minimally processed, meaning no water or seasonings have been added to them. The "natural" designation has nothing to do with how the turkeys were raised or what they were fed. For information regarding labeling standards for **organic** and **free-range** poultry, see About Buying Poultry, 401. For information about **wild turkeys,** see 439.

The whole turkeys available at supermarkets generally weigh between 10 and 25 pounds, though the average size purchased by home cooks is 15 pounds. When determining what size turkey to buy, ➤ allow about 1 pound per adult, ½ pound per child, plus, if you wish, a margin for leftovers.

Turkey parts are available, but not nearly as ubiquitous as those of chicken. **Whole turkey breast** can be found in the frozen section of many grocery stores, boneless as well as bone-in. When the back portion, ribs, and breastbone are left on the breast, it is sometimes referred to as a **crown roast** and makes an attractive holiday roast for a smaller dining party. Slices of boneless, skinless turkey breast are sometimes called **turkey cutlets** or, if sliced or pounded very thin, **turkey scaloppine.** These can be used in any recipe calling for chicken, veal, or pork cutlets. Finally, supermarkets sometimes carry packages of **turkey tenderloins** or **tenders,** which are the 4- to 6-ounce strips of breast meat located on either side of the breastbone. These cuts are perfect for skewering, stir-frying, or sautéing. Cook turkey breast to a final temperature of no more than 165°F, or it will turn dry and firm.

Turkey legs, like those of chicken, are more flavorful, and remain moist even after prolonged cooking and high internal temperatures. We recommend they be cooked to a final temperature of at least 175°F. Since they are quite large, turkey legs are not sold whole; packages of **thighs** and **drumsticks** (often called "legs" despite the missing thigh) are sporadically available. They are especially good for braising, stewing, barbecuing, and smoking. Smoked turkey legs are sometimes available, and they are excellent for adding flavor to soups, braised vegetables, and simmered beans (think of them as a substitute for ham hocks). **Turkey wings** have substantially more white meat than those of chicken; they may be cooked as for chicken wings, 60.

Finally, a quick word on **leftover turkey,** which seems almost as essential to our gastronomical experience of Thanksgiving as the roast itself. Many are content with the usual sandwiches or Turkey Tetrazzini, 539, but we also love leftover turkey in burritos or enchiladas, atop Bún, 305, in Asopao de Pollo, 93, and reheated in mole poblano (see Turkey in Red Mole, 430). The carcass can (and should!) be used to make stock (see Poultry Stock, 76). Soups and braises that utilize this stock as well as the leftover meat are especially satisfying; Chicken Noodle Soup, 93, Chicken Chili Verde, 425, Shoyu Ramen, 304, and many other soups and braises can all be modified like this: Simply skip any cooking instructions for the meat, use the stock to build the broth or braising liquid, and add the turkey meat at the last minute to heat through.

ABOUT ROASTING TURKEY

There is perhaps no other roast that causes so much confusion, trepidation, and culinary "Hail Mary"ing as the turkey, leading cooks to do things like brining, injecting, goosing oven temperatures, covering the breast with butter-soaked cheesecloth, turning the bird throughout cooking, basting, rubbing all manner of seasonings under the skin, ad infinitum. While none of these precautionary steps is "wrong," we would like to offer some perspective to ambitious turkey tinkerers by noting that some of the best results we have had were achieved with the simplest recipes.

With that out of the way, we whole-heartedly recommend dry-brining turkey before roasting, 408. Leaving a healthy sprinkle of salt on the turkey for a day or so in advance helps season the meat, keep the meat moist, and dry out the skin, which then browns more evenly. For more flavor, stuff a paste of minced fresh herbs, garlic, lemon zest, and olive oil under the skin before dry-brining. We are especially fond of Garlic-Herb Rub for Poultry, 587 (also see the under-the-skin suggestions in Additions to Broiled or Grilled Chicken, 411).

Many turkeys and whole turkey breasts are sold with a pop-up "thermometer." They are not trustworthy indicators of doneness. ➤ The most reliable test for doneness is to roast turkey until a thermometer inserted into the thickest part of the breast reaches 155°F and the inner thigh registers at least 170°F. (Make sure the thermometer is not touching the bone.) The temperature of the bird will continue to rise 10 to 15 degrees during the 20- to 40-minute resting period after roasting. If the bird is stuffed, be sure the center of the stuffing reaches at least 165°F.

If the breasts are done and the legs are not, carve them off at the hip joint, and return the legs to the oven to finish cooking while the breast rests. Obviously, the downside to this is that you will not be able to present an intact, bronzed bird to your dinner guests, but they will be infinitely more disappointed by overcooked turkey breast. If the worst happens and the breasts overcook, make extra gravy (and thinly slice the breast).

There are several roasting methods that help the turkey cook evenly and intact for carving at the table. For larger turkeys, we recommend turning the roast as directed for High-Heat Roast Turkey, 428. For smaller turkeys, we prefer to spatchcock, 403, the bird and roast at high heat. Once flattened out, a 12- to 14-pound turkey just barely fits on a standard half-size rimmed baking sheet. A larger size of rimmed baking sheet—a two-thirds or three-quarter-size sheet pan—may be used to roast larger spatchcocked birds. Just be sure that the pan will fit in your oven, as they can reach 22 inches in length.

Generally speaking, we do not recommend basting turkey. Opening the oven door frequently causes the temperature to drop, and basting the skin with anything but drippings, oil, or clarified butter will inhibit browning and crisping. That said, if the breast is looking pale and dry, feel free to baste; at the very least, it will keep you busy and attentive.

No beautifully roasted turkey is complete without gravy. If you have gone to the trouble of roasting a turkey, you owe it to yourself to use its drippings in a homemade gravy. Quick Pan Sauce or Gravy, 545, is made entirely in the roasting pan. Turkey Giblet Gravy, 545, requires the preparation of a giblet stock, but this can be done ahead, even a day or two before roasting. The browned bits and sticky brown glaze remaining in the roasting pan when the bird is done are the basis of a perfect gravy, so do not discard them when skimming the fat from the juices.

To roast turkey parts, follow the directions for Roasted Chicken Parts, 409, cooking turkey breasts until the internal temperature reaches 160°F and thighs and drumsticks reach at least 175°F, 45 minutes to 1 hour.

CLASSIC ROAST TURKEY

10 to 25 servings

This is the ideal method to use for birds over 15 pounds in weight, though it works well for smaller birds, too. The lower heat ensures that the bird cooks to doneness relatively evenly. While we give the option to stuff the bird, please be aware that you will have to remove the stuffing and finish cooking it in a baking dish, as it will not cook through at the same rate as the turkey. Please read About Turkey, 426, and About Roasting Turkey, 427.

A day or more before roasting the turkey, you may brine or dry-brine it, 405 (we recommend dry-brining), if desired. If you have wet-brined the bird, pat it dry and allow it to air-dry overnight, uncovered and refrigerated, on a rack set over a baking sheet. It is imperative to dry out the skin to encourage browning.

Position a rack in the lower third of the oven. Preheat the oven to 500°F.

If you wish to stuff the bird, have hot or at room temperature:

(Basic Bread Stuffing or Dressing, 532, or Basic Corn Bread Stuffing or Dressing, 532, with any desired additions)

If you have not done so already, remove the giblets and neck from:

One 10- to 25-pound turkey

If the bird is not kosher, self-basting, or brined, rub all over with:

Salt

Loosely pack the body and neck cavities with the stuffing, if using. Bring the legs together and tie them to hold the stuffing in. Set the turkey breast side up on a V rack in a roasting pan or on a large rimmed baking sheet. Any leftover stuffing can be placed in a buttered baking dish. Brush the turkey's skin all over with:

3 to 6 tablespoons melted butter, depending on the size of the turkey, or as needed

Transfer the turkey to the oven and immediately reduce the oven temperature to 325°F. Roast until the internal temperature of the breast reaches 155°F, and the thickest part of the thigh reaches at least 170°F. (Stuffing must reach 165°F.) This may take as little as 2 hours for a 10-pound turkey and up to 6 hours for a very large turkey. Transfer the turkey to a platter and let rest for at least 20 and up to 40 minutes before carving.

➤ If the breast is done but the thighs are not, take the turkey out of the oven and carve the legs off at the hip joint. Place the legs on a rimmed baking sheet and return to the oven to finish cooking through while the breast and carcass rests. ➤ If the stuffing is not done, spoon it into a buttered baking dish and place in the oven to cook through as the turkey rests.

While the turkey rests, prepare, if desired:

(Quick Pan Sauce or Gravy, 545, or Turkey Giblet Gravy, 545)

Finally, if at the end of cooking you are not happy with the degree of browning, increase the oven temperature to 500°F and let it preheat when you remove the turkey to rest. When the oven is preheated and the gravy made, place the rested turkey back in the pan and roast until the skin is browned, about 10 minutes. To carve, see About Carving Poultry, 405.

HIGH-HEAT ROAST TURKEY

10 to 15 servings

This technique delivers a beautifully browned, intensely flavorful bird. To cook to doneness at a higher heat, the bird should weigh 15 pounds or less. To keep the drippings from burning, the roasting pan must be heavy-gauge. Do not stuff the turkey if using this method. If roasting a turkey 14 pounds or under, you may spatchcock it, 403, and roast it on a wire rack set over a large rimmed baking sheet (be warned that spatchcocking a turkey takes considerable elbow grease). Spatchcocked turkeys do not need to be turned during roasting and will cook faster.

Please read About Turkey, 426, and About Roasting Turkey, 427. A day or more before roasting the turkey, you may brine or dry-brine it, 405. If you have wet-brined the bird, pat dry, and, if possible, allow to air-dry overnight, uncovered and refrigerated, on a rack set over a baking sheet.

Remove the giblets and neck from:

One 10- to 15-pound turkey

Position a rack in the lower third of the oven. Preheat the oven to 425°F.

Rub the turkey all over with:

2 tablespoons vegetable oil

If the bird is not kosher, self-basting, or brined, generously rub it all over with:

Salt

Truss, 405, if desired. Place the turkey on a V rack in a heavy roasting pan and turn the turkey onto its side so one of the legs is facing up. If it topples over, prop it up with crumpled foil. Roast for 30 minutes. Remove the turkey from the oven. Wearing silicone oven mitts (or oven mitts covered in a layer of foil), grasp the turkey at both ends. A set of sturdy tongs is helpful for lifting and balancing the bird. Turn it onto its other side, again propping it up with foil if necessary. Roast for 30 minutes. Turn the bird from side to side every 30 minutes until the internal temperature of the thickest part of the breast registers 155°F and the thigh registers at least 170°F, 1 to 1½ hours more. Transfer the turkey to a platter, loosely cover with foil, and let it rest for at least 20 minutes before carving.

➤ If the breast is done but the thighs are not, take the turkey out of the oven and carve the legs off at the hip joint. Place the legs on a rimmed baking sheet and return to the oven to finish cooking through while the breast and carcass rests.

While the turkey rests, prepare, if desired:

(Quick Pan Sauce or Gravy, 545, or Turkey Giblet Gravy, 545)

To carve, see About Carving Poultry, 405.

ROAST TURKEY BREAST

5 to 9 servings

Please read About Turkey, 426, and About Roasting Turkey, 427.

Position a rack in the center of the oven. Preheat the oven to 425°F.

Have ready:

One 4- to 7-pound whole bone-in turkey breast
Season both sides generously with:
Salt and black pepper
Arrange the breast skin side up on a rimmed baking sheet or in a shallow roasting pan. Brush the skin with:
2 tablespoons melted butter
Roast until the meat releases clear juices when pricked with a knife and the internal temperature of the thickest part reaches 155°F. Smaller turkey breasts may be done in 1 hour; larger ones may take 2 hours. Let stand for 20 minutes before carving. While the turkey rests, prepare, if desired:
(Quick Pan Sauce or Gravy, 545, or Turkey Giblet Gravy, 545)

GRILLED TURKEY

12 servings

Grilling a turkey over indirect heat on a charcoal grill is a good idea for several reasons, most notably because the results are flavorful and different from the usual Thanksgiving roast. An added advantage: It does not take up oven space, leaving you free to roast and bake sides and pies to your heart's content. Turkeys in the range of 10 to 14 pounds work better than larger ones. This method is not appropriate for stuffed birds.

Please read About Broiling and Grilling Chicken, 410, About Turkey, 426, and About Roasting Turkey, 427. A day or more before grilling the turkey, you may brine or dry-brine it, 405. If you have wet-brined the bird, pat dry, and if possible, allow to air-dry overnight, uncovered and refrigerated, on a rack set over a baking sheet.
Remove the neck and giblets from:
One 10- to 14-pound turkey
If the bird is not kosher, self-basting, or brined, generously rub it all over with:
Salt
Arrange the turkey breast side down on a V rack or wire rack set inside a large disposable roasting pan. If you are using a flat rack, you may need to prop the turkey up with crumpled foil. Brush the back and legs with:
2 tablespoons melted butter
Pour ½ cup water into the roasting pan.

Open the bottom vents of the grill completely. Ignite a thick layer of charcoal briquettes and heat until covered with white ash, then push half the coals to each side of the grill. Replace the grill rack and set the turkey, in the pan, in the center of the rack. Cover the grill and open the cover vents completely. Roast for 1 hour.

About 40 minutes into roasting, heat more charcoal in a chimney starter. After 1 hour of roasting, remove the turkey from the grill, remove the grill rack, stir up the coals, and add half of the new hot coals to each pile. Replace the grill cover. Protecting your hands with towels or mitts, grasp the turkey at both ends and turn breast side up. Baste the breast with:
2 tablespoons melted butter
If the pan is dry, add more water. Return the turkey to the center of the grill, replace the lid, and cook until the internal temperature in the thickest part of the thigh reaches 165°F and the breast reaches at least 155°F, 60 to 80 minutes more. Transfer the turkey to a platter and let stand loosely covered with foil for at least 20 and for up to 40 minutes.
Meanwhile, if desired, prepare:
(Quick Pan Sauce or Gravy, 545, or Turkey Giblet Gravy, 545)
To carve, see About Carving Poultry, 405.

DEEP-FRIED TURKEY

12 servings

First, we suggest looking at compilation videos of turkey-frying mishaps to gain an awareness of what you are up against. (Reconsidering is always allowed.) There are many ways to disastrously mess this up, but the most catastrophic outcomes can be avoided by never frying a turkey indoors, on a wooden deck, near anything combustible, or underneath an overhang.

Success is made even more probable by making sure the oil will not overflow the pot. To determine the amount of oil you will need, place the turkey in the frying pot, and add water to cover, recording the amount needed. (A 40-quart pot usually takes 6 gallons of oil to cook a 12-pound turkey.)

Finally, make absolutely sure the turkey is completely thawed and bone dry on the surface. We recommend dry-brining, 405; then pat the turkey dry inside and out. As the turkey is quite heavy to add and remove from a tall pot, this is a cooking technique that is best performed by two people.
Remove the giblets and neck from:
One 12-pound turkey
If the bird is not kosher, self-basting, or brined, you may use a hypodermic meat injector (available at gourmet shops and online retailers) to infuse the bird with seasoning. Allow to steep for at least 1 hour and then pour through a fine-mesh sieve:
(¾ to 1 cup Lemon Marinade, 580, Balkan Marinade, 580, or Becker Chicken or Pork Marinade, 581)
Fill the needle with the strained marinade and inject about 1 ounce of the marinade in each thigh and the front and back of each breast. Let the turkey marinate on a rimmed baking sheet in the refrigerator for at least 2 hours. If the turkey was not dry-brined, you may rub the skin all over with:
(Cajun Blackening Spice, 587, Coffee Spice Rub, 587, or Sweet and Smoky Spice Rub, 587)
Heat to 300°F in an outdoor propane turkey fryer with a 40-quart capacity:
6 gallons vegetable oil
Wearing silicone gloves or mitts, place the turkey in the cooking basket and carefully lower into the hot oil. Stand back as the oil will spit and pop as the cold turkey enters the hot oil. Bring the oil to 350°F over high heat and cook, adjusting the heat to maintain the frying temperature, until the internal temperature of the thickest part of the breast reaches 155°F, about 45 minutes. Turn off the burner and use long-handled tongs to locate the handle of the cooking basket. Slip the lifting rod back under the handle to remove the turkey from the oil. Hold it over the pot and let the excess oil drain, then place the basket and turkey on a rimmed baking sheet. Transfer the turkey to a platter and let stand loosely covered with foil for at least 20 and for up to 40 minutes.

TURKEY IN RED MOLE

6 servings

Pass plenty of hot corn tortillas with this flavorful dish. This is also a great way to use leftover turkey. Simply shred the turkey from the bones (remove the skin) and warm it through in the sauce.

Prepare in a Dutch oven:

Mole Poblano, 553

Preheat the oven to 325°F. Have ready:

2½ to 3 pounds turkey legs or thighs and drumsticks

Sprinkle the turkey parts with:

Salt and black pepper

Heat in a large heavy skillet over medium-high heat until hot:

1 tablespoon vegetable oil

Add the turkey in batches and brown on all sides. Transfer to the pot with the mole. Cover, transfer to the oven, and cook until the internal temperature in the thickest part of the meat reaches 180°F, about 40 minutes. Remove the turkey from the mole and cut into pieces or shred with a fork. Serve with a generous amount of the sauce and a garnish of:

Chopped cilantro
Lime wedges

ABOUT GROUND POULTRY

Ground chicken and turkey make tasty, healthful substitutes for ground beef or pork, particularly in highly seasoned dishes like chili and tacos. ➤ When substituting ground chicken or turkey for beef in milder dishes, you may want to increase the seasonings. You will also likely need to increase the amount of fat when browning ground poultry in recipes that call for beef or pork.

Of all ground poultry, we prefer **ground duck,** which has more flavor (and fat) than chicken or turkey. It makes excellent burgers. Since it is rare to find, you will most likely have to grind it yourself; for detailed instructions, see Grinding Meat at Home, 501. If grinding chicken or turkey, we recommend using dark meat for more flavor and fat. Poultry skin can be ground along with the meat, but make sure it is very well chilled.

CHICKEN AND APPLE SAUSAGE

About 2 pounds

Please read Making Sausage at Home, 509. Although it has much less fat than conventional breakfast sausage, it remains juicy if not overcooked.

Bring to a boil in a small saucepan and boil down to 2 to 3 tablespoons of syrup:

1 cup apple cider

Let cool. Meanwhile, pull off and reserve the skin from:

2¼ pounds bone-in chicken thighs

With a sharp knife, cut the meat off the bones. Cut the chicken into strips, if using a meat grinder, or 1-inch cubes, if using a food processor. Chill the chicken and chicken skin in the freezer for 30 minutes. Grind the chicken and skin together in a meat grinder fitted with a ⅜-inch plate, or coarsely chop by hand or in a food processor, along with:

1½ ounces dried apples

Transfer the chicken and apple mixture to a large bowl and add the cooled cider syrup. Add:

2½ teaspoons salt
1 teaspoon black pepper
1 teaspoon dried sage
½ teaspoon dried thyme
⅛ teaspoon ground cinnamon
⅛ teaspoon ground ginger

Using your hands, knead and squeeze the mixture until well blended. Shape, cook, or store as for **Country Sausage, 510.**

TURKEY OR CHICKEN BURGERS

4 burgers

To grind your own turkey or chicken for these burgers, see Grinding Meat at Home, 501. If possible, use dark meat for more flavor and moisture. Ground duck will also work here.

Combine in a medium bowl:

3 green onions, minced
(2 tablespoons cold butter, cut into small cubes)
(2 teaspoons curry powder, chili powder, or Five-Spice Powder, 590)
½ teaspoon salt
½ teaspoon black pepper

Using your hands, separate into small chunks:

1 pound ground turkey or chicken

Add to the bowl and toss with the seasonings; do not overmix. Shape into 4 patties and grill, broil, or pan-fry as for Hamburger Patties, 504; the internal temperature at the center of the patties should reach 165°F. Serve on toast or buns as for Hamburgers, 144, or Patty Melt, 144.

TURKEY OR CHICKEN LOAF

4 servings

Prepare **Meatloaf, 506**, substituting **1½ pounds ground chicken or turkey** for the beef and cooking until the center of the loaf reaches 165°F.

TURKEY OR CHICKEN MEATBALLS

4 servings

Prepare **Italian Meatballs, 507,** substituting **1 pound ground chicken or turkey** for the beef and cooking until they reach 165°F.

ABOUT DUCK AND GOOSE

Virtually all domesticated ducks are the descendants of mallards; the venerable **Long Island** or **Pekin duck** is the most widely available type. Pekins have plentiful fat and the lightest flesh, which is comparable to the dark meat of chicken. **Rouen ducks** are a French mallard-type breed; they are more flavorful and grow to a larger size than Pekins. **Muscovy ducks** are large, tree-dwelling ducks native to the Americas, and have leaner, darker, gamier meat. **Moulards,** a hybrid of Pekin and Muscovy, offer some benefits of both breeds: a large size, flavorful meat, and plenty of fat. Moulards are also preferred for the production of foie gras, 446.

Pekin and female Muscovy ducks are available whole, weighing between 4 and 6 pounds. Smaller birds may be marked "broiler" or "fryer," and larger ones "roaster," as is the custom for whole chicken. Whole ducks certainly have a centerpiece appeal, but for individual plated servings, perfectly crisped duck breasts are the height of luxury—as is rich, meltingly tender confited leg meat, 433. Moulard breasts (sometimes referred to as **magret**) and leg quarters—as well as the leg quarters of Muscovy ducks—can be found from specialty suppliers. These parts can be especially large: Whereas a Pekin breast is ample for one serving, Moulard breasts can feed two; Muscovy drake legs are nearly twice the size of Pekin legs.

Goose is entirely dark meat, and its flavor is reminiscent of beef. In seventeenth-century England, certain cuts of roast beef were known, fancifully, as goose. Geese are picky eaters and slow growing, which makes them an expensive item. While larger than ducks, geese present similar issues to cooks and should be handled in much the same way. Whole goose or goose parts can be special-ordered from most grocery stores, or from a local farm. The most prevalent breed is the white Embden, which is available from 8 to more than 15 pounds.

There are two basic issues cooks need to come to terms with when cooking ducks and geese. First: Most ducks and geese have a ton of fat directly underneath their skin. Getting this fat to render is a bit difficult, but can be overcome with a few tricks. To encourage a rendered, crisp result when roasting, see About Roasting Ducks and Geese, below; for the best way to treat breasts, see Pan-Seared Duck Breasts, 432. Save any rendered fat for other cooking projects—duck and goose fat are true delicacies.

Second, and perhaps more intractable: Goose and duck breasts have the best texture and flavor when cooked to medium-rare, or 135°F. This is a problem for several reasons, the most obvious being that the USDA recommends cooking all poultry to 165°F, or well-done (which effectively means that you must ruin the breast meat to be safe). Here, we can only say that those who wish to risk their safety will have a very pleasant meal; those who adhere to USDA guidelines will likely develop a hatred for duck and goose breast.

Perhaps less obvious is the difficulty this poses for those who wish to roast their duck or goose whole: Like other poultry, duck and goose legs are best when cooked to at least 170°F. With no intervention, the breast will be dry and overcooked by the time the legs have finished cooking. For strategies to prevent this, see the section on roasting below.

Since these birds have both a heavy frame and a high fat content, ➤ allow 1½ pounds of whole duck or goose per serving. Ducks and geese are very richly flavored birds when compared to chicken. The meat itself is flavorful, and the thick cap of fat under the skin contributes to this richness even further. To balance their richness, serve duck and goose with something acidic, whether mustard, Braised Sauerkraut, 225, or a tart or fruity sauce, such as Gastrique, 565, Fig and Red Wine Sauce, 552, English Cumberland Sauce, 566, or Sweet-Sour Orange Pan Sauce, 546. For a hearty, duck-laden winter dish, see Cassoulet, 216.

ABOUT ROASTING DUCKS AND GEESE

For information on roasting wild waterfowl, see 438. Ducks and geese share one notable problem with other poultry: that of achieving simultaneous doneness in the breasts and legs. However, to complicate matters further, duck and goose breasts are best cooked to 135°F, when they are still pink inside (like other birds, their legs are best cooked to above 170°F). On top of that, there is the issue of their fatty skin, which must be rendered properly.

With chicken and turkey, the easiest solution is to roast the bird until the breasts are done, remove the legs, and continue roasting the legs until they reach 170°F or above while the breasts rest. However, since the hip joints of waterfowl are harder to get at, the best strategy is to carve the breasts off the bone, leaving the legs attached, and place the rest of the carcass back in the oven to finish cooking. (If the wings are in danger of getting singed, wrap them in a layer of foil.)

Once the legs have finished cooking, game enthusiast and food writer Hank Shaw recommends reheating the breasts by quickly searing them skin side down in a skillet over medium-high heat for several minutes just before serving. The breasts—which have cooled while the legs finished cooking—are well insulated by their fatty skin and crisp nicely in the pan without overcooking.

No matter how you choose to roast a duck or goose, the fat should be trimmed and the skin pricked or carefully scored to promote rendering. Pull out large pieces of fat and cut away any flaps of excess skin from the openings of the body and neck cavities. Then prick the bird lightly all over to allow rendering fat to escape: Insert a skewer, needle, or slender knife through the skin and into the fat, without puncturing the meat itself. (Puncturing the skin at a shallow angle can help prevent this from happening.) Alternatively, you may score the skin covering the breasts with shallow, parallel cuts at ½-inch intervals. Use an especially sharp knife to slice through the skin and a portion of the fat, but ➤ do not cut into the breast meat.

If you have time, dry-brine, 405, the bird. For some preparations, such as Chinese-style roast duck, the bird is scalded and dried before roasting, either by dunking it briefly in very hot water or by ladling hot water over the skin.

To scald a duck or goose, fill a large pot one-half to two-thirds full of water and bring to a rolling boil. Protecting your hands with rubber gloves, submerge the neck end of the bird in the boiling water for 1 minute. Remove the bird, let the water come to a boil once more, then submerge the tail end for 1 minute. Drain the bird and pat as dry as possible inside and out. Set the bird breast side up on a wire rack set in a roasting pan and refrigerate, uncovered, for 24 to 48 hours to dry the skin.

Duck and goose are carved in the same basic way as chicken and turkey, 405, except their leg and wing joints are located closer to the back and are harder to get at. For this reason, duck and goose are best carved in the kitchen rather than at the table (but do exhibit it at the table first), since disjointing the bird is inevitably a bit of a struggle.

Rendered duck and goose fat, or schmaltz, 1015, is delicious and should never be discarded. Strain it into a clean container and keep it to make Duck or Goose Confit, 433, or for frying most anything—especially potatoes.

ROAST DUCK OR GOOSE

2 to 4 servings

Please read About Duck and Goose, 430. For **duck à l'orange,** after roasting the duck, prepare Sweet-Sour Orange Pan Sauce, 546, with the pan juices.

I. For leaner ducks, like Muscovy

Remove the neck and giblets from:

One 4½- to 5½-pound duck

Snip the wing tips off and reserve them with the giblets. Pull out any lumps of fat from around the cavities and cut away excess flaps of skin. Using a skewer, needle, or knife tip, prick the skin all over, especially over the thighs and breast. Avoid puncturing the meat.

If desired, dry-brine, 405, the bird for up to 2 days.

Preheat the oven to 450°F. If the bird was not dry-brined, sprinkle liberally with:

Salt and black pepper

If it was dry-brined, sprinkle it with black pepper only. Place the bird breast side up on a V rack in a roasting pan or on a vertical poultry roasting rack set on a rimmed baking sheet. Transfer to the oven and reduce the temperature at once to 350°F. Roast for about 20 minutes per pound, or until the internal temperature of the thigh reaches 170°F. If desired, remove the bird from the oven and carve off the breasts when they reach 135°F, then return the bird to the oven to finish cooking. Let stand for 10 to 15 minutes. If the breasts were separated from the rest of the bird, heat a dry heavy skillet over medium-high heat. Place the duck breasts in the skillet skin side down and cook until deeply browned, 3 to 5 minutes.

If desired, while the bird is roasting, use the reserved neck, giblets, and wing tips to prepare:

(Turkey Giblet Gravy, 545)

up through the step where it is thickened with roux. Once the bird is done, finish the gravy as directed. Alternatively, serve the bird with:

(Quick Orange Sauce for Duck, 553)

II. For geese and fattier ducks like Pekin and Rouen

Trim, prick, and dry-brine or season the duck as directed in version I. Preheat the oven to 325°F. Place the bird breast side up on a V rack in a roasting pan or on a vertical poultry roasting rack set in a roasting pan. Roast for about 20 minutes per pound, or until the internal temperature of the thigh reaches 170°F. If desired, remove the bird from the oven and carve off the breasts when they reach 135°F, then return the bird to the oven to finish cooking. Let stand for 10 to 15 minutes. If the breasts were separated from the rest of the bird, heat a dry heavy skillet over medium-high heat. Place the duck or goose breasts in the skillet skin side down and cook until deeply browned, 3 to 5 minutes.

GLAZED ROAST DUCK OR GOOSE

2 to 4 servings

Prepare any of the glazes from About Glazes, 578–79. Prepare and cook **Roast Duck or Goose, above,** until it reaches the right internal temperature. Remove the bird from the oven and increase the oven temperature to 500°F. Transfer the rack holding the bird onto a rimmed baking sheet and pour the fat out of the pan, then return the rack to the pan. If you have removed the breasts, place them back on the bird without browning them in a skillet. Coat the bird with the glaze, then return it to the oven until caramelized, 5 to 10 minutes. Let stand for 10 to 15 minutes before carving, 405.

CHINESE ROAST DUCK

2 to 4 servings

With its crispy, lacquered-looking skin, this is similar to the famous Peking duck but requires much less time and effort. Please read About Roasting Ducks and Geese, 431.

Remove the neck and giblets from:

One 4½- to 5-pound duck

Pull out the large pieces of fat from the openings of the body and neck cavities. Place the duck on a rack set in a roasting pan. Combine in a large saucepan and bring to a boil:

5 cups water
½ cup soy sauce
¼ cup honey

Ladle the boiling mixture over the duck, turning the duck to scald both sides. Pour off the liquid and pat the duck dry. Place the duck on a wire rack set on a rimmed baking sheet. Refrigerate, uncovered, for 24 to 48 hours. Or set the duck in front of an electric fan in a cool basement or garage for 2 to 3 hours to dry the skin well.

Prick the duck skin all over with a knife tip or sharp skewer, being careful not to pierce the meat. Position a rack in the lower third of the oven. Preheat the oven to 425°F.

Place the duck breast side up on a V rack or on a vertical poultry roasting rack set in a roasting pan. To prevent the fat from smoking, pour 2 cups water into the pan. Roast the duck for 20 minutes, then turn breast side down and roast for 20 minutes more. Remove from the oven and reduce the oven temperature to 350°F. Pour all the fat and water out of the roasting pan, then turn the duck breast side up. Stir together in a small bowl:

¾ cup orange juice
¼ cup rice vinegar
3 tablespoons soy sauce
2 tablespoons honey
(½ teaspoon Five-Spice Powder, 590)

Brush the duck with the orange juice mixture. Roast for 20 minutes. Turn the duck breast side down, brush again with the mixture, and roast for 20 minutes. Turn the duck breast side up again, give it another brushing, and roast for 20 minutes more. Let the duck rest for 10 minutes before carving, 405.

PAN-SEARED DUCK BREASTS

6 servings

Duck breasts are best served rare or medium-rare. This technique is best with breasts from leaner ducks, such as Muscovies and Moulards. In addition to the French-inflected sauces on 433, consider serving these with Mole Poblano, 553, seasoned to taste with lime juice and salt.

Have ready:

6 boneless, skin-on duck breasts

Use a sharp knife to cut a ½-inch crosshatch pattern into the skin and fat (without cutting the meat). Sprinkle them liberally with:

Salt

Place the duck breasts skin side down in a dry, large heavy skillet and place over medium heat. Cook until the skin is golden brown, 10 to 15 minutes. Turn and cook until the internal temperature reaches 130°F for rare to 140°F for medium, 2 to 3 minutes more. If desired, prepare in the skillet:

(Herb Pan Sauce, 546, Wine and Sour Cherry Pan Sauce, 547, or Sweet-Sour Orange Pan Sauce, 546)

Or serve with:

(Quick Orange Sauce for Duck, 553, Fig and Red Wine Sauce, 552, or Gastrique, 565)

GRILLED DUCK BREASTS WITH HOISIN-GINGER SAUCE

4 servings

Grilling duck breast presents a challenge. The fat renders out as it cooks and causes flare-ups. Thus, we recommend a two-zone fire. Move the duck to the cooler side of the grill as flare-ups occur. Please read about Grilling, 1050.

Prepare a medium-hot, two-zone grill fire, 1063, or preheat a gas grill on medium heat for 10 minutes, then turn off one side. Combine in a small saucepan and mix well:

½ cup hoisin sauce
¼ cup rice vinegar
1 tablespoon soy sauce
(1 tablespoon sambal oelek, 969)
1-inch piece ginger, peeled and minced
2 teaspoons toasted sesame oil
2 green onions, thinly sliced

Bring to a simmer and cook, stirring occasionally, for 5 minutes. Reduce the heat to low and cover to keep warm. Have ready:

4 boneless, skin-on duck breasts

Score the skin in a ½-inch crosshatch pattern (without cutting the meat). Sprinkle with:

Salt and black pepper

Arrange the duck breasts skin side down over direct heat and grill until starting to brown, about 4 minutes. Transfer the breasts, still skin side down, to indirect heat and cook until the internal temperature reaches 130° to 135°F for medium-rare, about 5 minutes more. Transfer to a platter and let stand for 10 minutes, then thinly slice on the diagonal. Spoon the sauce over the slices and serve.

FESENJOON (PERSIAN DUCK AND POMEGRANATE STEW)

6 servings

Fesenjoon is a Persian stew, or *khoresh*, of duck in a tangy sauce redolent of pomegranate molasses and toasted walnuts. This dish is often made with chicken instead of duck. Substitute 3 pounds chicken leg quarters or bone-in chicken thighs for the duck (remove the skin and any excess fat). Braise the chicken until tender, about 40 minutes.

Preheat the oven to 350°F. Spread out on a baking sheet:

2 cups walnuts

Toast the nuts until well browned, 12 to 16 minutes. Let cool, then transfer to a food processor and pulse until very finely ground. Melt in a large skillet or Dutch oven over medium heat:

4 tablespoons (½ stick) butter

Add and cook, stirring frequently, until the onions are very soft and brown, about 15 minutes:

1 large onion, thinly sliced
1 teaspoon salt

Stir in the ground walnuts along with:

¾ cup pomegranate molasses, store-bought or homemade, 193
4 cups chicken stock or broth or water
2 tablespoons sugar or honey
1 teaspoon ground turmeric

Bring to a boil, then reduce the heat to low, cover, and simmer, stirring occasionally, for 1 hour. This prolonged simmering period allows the flavors of the sauce to meld and draws out the oil in the walnuts.

Add:

3 pounds duck legs (about 6 large legs), skin and excess fat removed

Bring back to a simmer, cover, and cook very slowly until the duck is very tender, about 2 hours. Remove the duck from the sauce and tent with foil to keep warm. Increase the heat to high and boil the sauce until reduced and thickened, 10 to 15 minutes. Taste the sauce and add salt as needed. Serve the duck and sauce over:

Cooked white basmati rice, 343

Garnish with:

Pomegranate seeds

DUCK OR GOOSE CONFIT

4 to 6 servings

A classic ingredient in Cassoulet, 216, well-browned confit can also be used in hash, 473, as a topping for a salad of sturdy greens, or added to a bowl of simmered white beans. To make confit without having to add fat, see version II. You can also achieve similar results by seasoning the legs as directed and then braising and browning them as for Braised Carnitas, 495 (using the garlic, shallots, zest, and herbs given on 434).

I. TRADITIONAL METHOD

Since this method essentially poaches the legs in fat, they must be dry-brined first (otherwise, the salt used to season them would disperse in the fat). The method described in II, 434, is more convenient since it does not require this extra step, nor the large amount of fat. But remember: Herb- and spice-infused duck fat has many uses, and can be stored away for a special batch of fried potatoes—or another round of confit.

Have ready:

2½ to 3 pounds skin-on duck or goose legs

Combine in a small bowl:

1½ tablespoons table salt or 3 tablespoons Diamond kosher salt
1 tablespoon black pepper

Rub the mixture evenly over the duck or goose legs. Place them in a bowl or container, cover tightly, and refrigerate for 1 to 2 days.

Preheat the oven to 250°F.

Combine in a Dutch oven:

4 cups duck or goose fat, lard, olive oil, or a combination (about 1½ pounds)
2 shallots, sliced
6 garlic cloves, peeled
5 sprigs fresh thyme or ½ teaspoon dried thyme
(2 strips lemon or orange zest, removed with a vegetable peeler)
2 whole cloves
1 bay leaf

Stir over low heat until the fat melts. Remove from the heat. Slip the duck or goose legs into the fat. They should be completely submerged. If they are not, add more fat. Cover the pot and transfer to the oven. Cook until the meat is very tender, to the point of falling off the bone when prodded with a fork, 2 to 3 hours.

If not using right away, transfer the duck or goose legs to a storage container, then strain the fat over them, making sure they are covered. Let cool to room temperature, then refrigerate for up to a month. To freeze, gingerly transfer the legs to zip-top bags after they have cooled to room temperature. Add enough fat to completely coat the legs and then seal the bag, forcing as much air out as possible. Freeze for up to 6 months.

When ready to use, warm until the legs are easily removed from the fat. Adjust an oven rack so it is 6 to 8 inches from the heating element. Preheat the broiler. Transfer the legs to a rimmed baking sheet skin side up and broil, turning once, until the skin is crisp and the legs are heated through, 6 to 8 minutes. Alternatively, pan-fry the legs skin side down in a skillet over medium heat, turning once, 5 to 6 minutes or until crisp and heated through. Be careful when turning the meat, as it is very tender.

II. SOUS VIDE METHOD

Cooking the legs sous vide, 1054, offers two advantages: No extra fat is necessary and, since the salt will not be dispersed in fat, there is no need to dry-brine the legs overnight to season the interior of the meat.

Preheat a water bath to 165°F with an immersion circulator. Season the legs as directed in version I, and add all the ingredients listed except for the fat to a gallon-sized zip-top bag or vacuum bag. Seal it using the air displacement method, 881, or with a vacuum sealer. Add to the water bath, cover the bath with plastic wrap to prevent excessive evaporation, and cook for 12 hours. Cool the bags completely and refrigerate for up to 1 month or freeze for up to 6 months. When ready to serve, broil or pan-fry the legs as directed above.

DUCK OR GOOSE RILLETTES

6 to 8 servings

Prepare **Pork Rillettes, 514,** substituting **3½ pounds duck or goose legs** for the pork and simmering until tender, about 1½ hours. Discard the skin, shred the meat off the bones, and proceed as directed.

ABOUT GUINEA FOWL

The guinea fowl, or **guinea hen,** was originally domesticated in Africa and has since been raised for meat in many parts of the world. Their tender flesh is lean, light, and delicate, with a taste similar to that of pheasant. Since guinea fowl has less than half the fat of chicken, the bird is usually barded, 1046, before roasting, or braised, stewed, or sautéed to ensure it remains moist and tender. Any recipe for pheasant or for braised or fried chicken will work for guinea fowl. Just keep in mind that they are generally smaller than chickens, and will cook more quickly. For this reason, they are usually sold whole rather than broken down into breasts and leg quarters (to cut them into parts, see About Cutting Up Raw Poultry, 402). ➤ Smaller birds will serve two, larger ones will serve four.

ROAST GUINEA FOWL

About 4 servings

The hens may be prepared up to 2 hours ahead and refrigerated until ready to roast.

Prepare:

¼ cup Chile Butter, 560, Green Butter, 560, or Snail Butter, 560

Preheat the oven to 450°F.

Have ready:

One 3-pound guinea hen

Being careful not to tear it, loosen the skin around the breast and thighs, then force the butter under the skin with your fingertips. Rub any remaining butter on the outside of the bird. Place it breast side down on a V rack in a roasting pan and roast for 20 minutes. Reduce the oven temperature to 350°F and turn the bird breast side up. Add to the pan, if desired:

(½ cup dry white wine)

Roast until the internal temperature of the thickest part of the thigh reaches 165°F and the juices from the thigh run clear when the skin is pierced, 25 to 30 minutes more. Transfer to a cutting board, cover loosely with foil, and let stand for 10 minutes before carving. Carve the bird and pour the pan juices over the meat.

ABOUT SQUAB

Squab are farm-raised **pigeons** harvested at 4 weeks of age, before they have learned to fly. Their meat is dark, rich, tender, and succulent. Squab adapts well to many cooking methods, whether roasted whole or split and broiled, grilled, or sautéed. Like duck or goose breast, squab is best when cooked to medium-rare, or 135°F, throughout; at this stage the juices run pink and the meat remains slightly rosy and moist. When cooked further, squab can taste livery; this taste dissipates if they are braised until the meat falls from the bone. Strangely, it is the squab's legs that are prone to drying out rather than the breast. ➤ Squab generally weigh ¾ to 1 pound—enough to serve 1 per person. They may also be split for an appetizer for 2.

GRILLED OR BROILED SQUAB

2 servings

Position an oven rack 4 inches from the heating element and grease a broiler pan. Preheat the broiler. Or prepare a medium-hot grill fire, 1063. Spatchcock, 403:

Two 1-pound squab

Lay the squab skin side up on the broiler pan, if broiling, or on a work surface. Brush well with:

2 tablespoons melted butter

Sprinkle with:

Salt and black pepper

Broil or grill (starting skin side down, if grilling) until the internal temperature of the breasts and thighs reaches 135° to 140°F and the juices from the thighs are light pink when the skin is pierced, 12 to 18 minutes. When grilling, turn the squab once halfway through cooking. If desired, serve on:

(Buttered toast)

Pour any pan drippings over the squab. Serve immediately.

SALMI OF SQUAB

4 servings

This rich ragu-like dish is much simpler than the traditional French *salmi*, which involves a gruesome tool called a duck press (used to extract the juices from the carcass for enriching the sauce). Other game birds can be substituted. If you aren't saving the backbones for stock, they can be added to the pot with the squab to enrich the sauce, then removed before serving.

Remove the backbone and split in half at the breastbone, 403:

Two 1-pound squab

Season on both sides with:

Salt and black pepper

Heat in a large skillet over medium-high heat:

2 tablespoons vegetable oil

Working in batches, add the squab skin side down and cook until browned, about 5 minutes. Turn over and cook for 2 to 3 minutes more. Transfer to a plate. Add to the skillet and cook, stirring, until they begin to brown, about 8 minutes:

1 large shallot, thinly sliced
1 pound mushrooms, sliced
1 tablespoon fresh thyme leaves or 1 teaspoon dried thyme

Reduce the heat to medium and cook, stirring, until the mushrooms are softened, about 5 minutes. Add and cook, stirring to loosen the browned bits, until almost evaporated:

3 tablespoons Cognac or other brandy

Add and cook until reduced by half:

1½ cups dry red wine
1½ cups game, beef, or chicken stock or broth

Return the squab to the skillet and simmer gently, covered, until the meat begins to fall from the bone, 20 to 25 minutes, turning the birds halfway through cooking. Remove the skillet from the heat and transfer the birds to a plate to cool slightly. Pull off and discard the skin of the birds, then pull the meat from the bones and add it to the skillet. Stir in:

(2 tablespoons butter)
Salt and black pepper to taste
2 tablespoons chopped parsley

Serve over:

Creamy Polenta, 322, cooked pasta, or thick pieces of toast

CHINESE-STYLE SMOKED SQUAB

4 servings

You can smoke any small bird in this way, but be careful not to overcook it or the meat will dry out.

Please read about Smoking, 1067. Combine in a large shallow pan:

Finely grated zest of 1 lemon
Finely grated zest of 1 orange
½ cup light soy sauce, 1020
⅓ cup oyster sauce
2 tablespoons honey
1-inch piece ginger, peeled and minced
2 garlic cloves, minced
½ teaspoon black pepper

Add to the pan, turning to coat:

Four 1-pound squab, whole or backbone removed and split, 403

Marinate in the refrigerator for 6 hours or overnight. Remove the squab from the marinade and reserve it for basting. Pat the birds dry and let the surface of the birds dry even further by placing them on a rack set over a rimmed baking sheet and refrigerating uncovered for several hours before smoking. Heat a smoker or grill for hot-smoking, 1068, with a target temperature of 225°F. Add to the fire:

1 small chunk of hardwood, such as apple, cherry, or oak

Add the squab and smoke, basting with the marinade several times, until the internal temperature of the meat reaches 135°F, about 1 hour. Serve immediately.

ABOUT OSTRICH AND EMU

Ostrich and emu are ratites, or flightless, long-legged birds. Unlike chickens and other domesticated birds that do not generally fly around, ratites have evolved over millennia to thrive on the ground, and no longer have the skeletal structure to support winged flight. They taste and are cooked very much like venison. Both of these large, farm-raised birds have deep-red, lean meat. The main difference between the two is that the meat of the emu, which is a smaller animal, is finer grained. Although the different cuts of ostrich and emu can be confusing, ➤ the most tender portions are the cuts referred to as the **fan fillet, inside strip, tenderloin,** and **oyster;** next in tenderness are the **tip, top loin,** and **outside strip.** The tougher cuts, as one might imagine, come from the leg area, thus ostrich leg meat is usually ground. **Ground ostrich** makes fine burgers, though they are best cooked to medium-rare to preserve juiciness. ➤ Use recipes for venison, 528–29, or lean beef in preparing ostrich or emu. The best cooking methods are sautéing or quickly grilling to medium-rare. As with venison and buffalo, overcooking turns the meat dry and tough.

EMU OR OSTRICH FILLETS

4 servings

Pat dry:

1½ pounds ostrich or emu meat, cut into 4 fillets

Season all over with:

1½ teaspoons salt
1 teaspoon black pepper

Heat in a large skillet:

2 tablespoons vegetable oil

Add the fillets to the pan, in batches if necessary, and sear for 3 minutes per side for medium-rare, or until the internal temperature reaches 130° to 135°F.

Serve with:

Herb Pan Sauce, 546, or Sauce Marchand de Vin, 551, or Sauce Chasseur, 551

ABOUT WILDFOWL

Much like game, the birds referred to as "wildfowl" were once exclusively hunted. Today, however, many species of wildfowl are available farm-raised. Unless you hunt or have generous friends who do, you will probably be working with the latter type: Only farm-raised wildfowl or species hunted in Europe and imported to the United States may be sold in grocery stores. For information on cooking domesticated ducks and geese, see 431.

There are two basic categories of wildfowl: waterfowl and upland game birds. **Waterfowl** include wild ducks and geese. **Upland game birds** form a much larger category, including pheasant, dove, pigeon, quail, snipe, woodcock, wild turkey, and others.

Wildfowl are, with the exception of some ducks and geese, leaner than chicken and turkey. For this reason, special care should be taken during cooking to avoid drying out the meat. Another important consideration: The meat of wildfowl is denser than domesticated poultry, and the connective tissues holding them together are far, far tougher. Wild birds are athletes, and their musculature reflects that. Some birds, such as wild duck and goose, have almost beefy flesh. This is all to say that the normal rules of cooking poultry do not necessarily apply to game birds. Further, regardless of how the birds are cooked, you should expect the meat to have a taste and texture different from store-bought poultry.

Wild birds lead uncontrolled lives and reveal little history until inspected during preparation. What the bird has been feeding on, how old it is, and how those both affect the overall health of the bird is not certain at the point of pulling the trigger. The intrepid can even open and inspect the contents of the crop—the pouch at the base of their neck where food is temporarily stored. Generally speaking, ➤ birds that have eaten grain are much more palatable than those feeding on fish eggs, amphibians, shellfish, aquatic plants, and algae. Thus, if birds are harvested near waterways or in coastal areas, there is a greater chance their meat or fat will carry off-flavors. Conversely, birds shot near fields of grain crops are much more likely to be tasty (and fattier). If the bird appears sickly—with discolored meat or putrid odor—do not eat it.

To determine the age of wildfowl, look at the small covert feathers on the leading edge of the wings forward of the big flight feathers. If these feathers have buff-colored edges, the bird is likely younger than one year old. If the color goes all the way to the edge of the feather, the bird is older. Spurs on pheasants and turkeys are a good marker, too: Worn-down spurs indicate an older animal. The presence of pinfeathers is not a good indicator, as all birds molt at certain times and even older birds can be shot shortly after new feathers grow in; for example, grouse shot in September tend to be loaded with pinfeathers.

ABOUT HANGING, PLUCKING, AND DRESSING WILDFOWL

How you handle birds in the field (or marsh) depends on how you wish to treat and cook them. The most important thing is to keep them in a cool, dry place. Cooling is an essential part of good game care. If you have several birds, ➤ keep them in the shade in a cool place and do not pile the birds on top of one another. If it is hot out, a cooler with ice is a good idea, but keep the birds away from the melt water.

HANGING

Hanging game birds such as geese, ducks, and pheasant is an aging process that breaks down tissue, tenderizing it and enhancing flavor. Of course, it is not necessary. Some of the benefits of hanging can be achieved by refrigerating the whole birds for a couple of days, but the enzymes that cause tissue to break down work very slowly at refrigerator temperatures. ➤ Never hang a gut-shot bird—they should be plucked, dressed, and cooked as soon as possible.

To hang birds, do not gut or pluck them, as odd as that may sound. The major exception is geese and wild turkeys, which should be gutted immediately. Hang them by the feet or neck between 45° and 55°F. Wild ducks and geese should only be hung for a few days, but birds like pheasant may be hung for up to 1 week. Small birds such as quail, dove, woodcock, and snipe are perfect after only a few days—never hang them for more than a week. Another factor is age: Younger, tender birds should not be hung as long as older, tougher ones. Regardless of age, species, or size, keep in mind that the flavor and texture will improve in as little as 1 day of hanging; in other words, if you are a little squeamish about the process, start small.

After hanging, ➤ all birds should be dry-plucked or skinned and refrigerated or frozen until they are cooked.

PLUCKING

Unless you intend to skin the bird, plucking is necessary. Upland game birds may be dry- or wet-plucked. **Dry-plucking** is ➤ easiest if the bird has been hung or refrigerated for at least 48 hours, and preferably 72; this allows the bird to go through rigor mortis, and the feathers will pull out more easily. Pull the feathers by hand from the body down to the knee joint on the legs, and to the first joint of the wings. Take extra care, as the skin can be thin and fragile. After plucking the bird, remove any pinfeathers with a pair of tweezers, or just pull them out with your fingers. After removing the coarser feathers, those remaining will be downy or small. You can then ➤ singe the bird all over with a lighter or torch to remove these last feathers.

Wet-plucking is the best method to use for waterfowl. Because these birds have a very fine layer of down under their large feathers, the easiest way to remove most of the feathers in one fell swoop is to use wax.

To wet-pluck upland game birds, heat a pot of water until steaming (it should not be simmering or boiling) and dunk the birds—one at a time—in the water for about 3 seconds. Drain the bird and repeat this dunking several times, until a wing or tail feather pulls out easily. They should come out with minimal resistance. If they are still hard to remove, keep dunking the bird. Pluck the bird quickly, while it is still warm.

To wet-pluck waterfowl, start by plucking the largest feathers on the wings, tail, and body. Heat a large pot of water until steaming, and add paraffin wax (available in the canning section of most grocery stores). You will need more wax for larger birds—about one 1-pound block for a single large duck or goose. Also prepare an ice water bath large enough to hold the bird. When the wax has melted, hold the bird by the head and feet and rotate the body on the surface of the water so the wax coats it. Then transfer the bird to the ice bath and dunk it completely. This will cause the wax to harden. Drain the bird for a few minutes, then gently peel away the wax-matted feathers from the skin.

DRESSING

To dress whole birds, cut off the head, pull down the neck skin, and cut off the neck close to the body. The neck may be saved for stock or soup. Then cut off the feet and wingtips (for very small birds, cut off the wings entirely) with a cleaver or heavy-duty shears.

Lay the bird breast side up and, taking great care not to pierce the innards, make a shallow incision across the carcass just below the breastbone. Make a second incision, cutting from the vent up to the breastbone incision so the cuts form a T shape. Insert your fingers into the cavity and pull free the internal organs, if not already removed in the field. Explore carefully to ensure the removal of every bit of the viscera from the cavity, as well as surplus fat. ➤ Among the edible viscera of a wildfowl is the heart, which needs no further prep. The liver and gizzard are edible, but need to be cleaned.

Should you choose to use the giblets, start by slicing off the top of the heart above the fat ring. Cut or pull the green sac, or gallbladder, away from the liver very carefully and discard it. Do this under cold, running water so if it breaks, you won't get green bile on the liver. If the liver looks spotted or is a color other than red-to-beige, discard it. Sever the intestines from the gizzard and remove the fat from it. To clean the liver, heart, and gizzards for cooking, see About Poultry Offal or Giblets, 444.

Before cooking, rinse the bird thoroughly inside and out under running water and pat dry with a paper towel. Sometimes you will see patches of clotted blood near shot holes. Use a small, sharp knife to gently scrape it away if you can, lifting the skin if necessary.

Breasting-out birds is a convenient technique often used for small game birds such as dove, band-tail pigeon, quail, and woodcock. These birds are so small that any meat besides the breast can be minimal. It is also useful for fish-eating waterfowl like sea ducks: These birds have fishy skin and fat, but their breast meat is much milder and worth salvaging.

To breast-out a bird, remove the feathers from the breast and, with a sharp knife, cut each breast away from the breastbone and ribs. (This is much like boning a chicken breast, 404, only here you are working on a whole bird to remove just the breast.) Often it is not necessary to keep the breast skin; see individual recipes.

COOKING WILDFOWL

The ideal criterion for doneness of any meat is internal temperature, but the flesh of some wildfowl, particularly smaller birds, is thin, making thermometers impractical to use. Instead, observe the approximate cooking times we recommend, and if necessary, prick the meat or cut into it carefully to determine if more time is required. Remember that meat will continue to cook when removed from the heat (the larger the bird, the more the internal temperature will rise during the resting period). Also, remember that ➤ most game is better on the rare side. Meat can always be returned for continued cooking; it is impossible to undo overcooking.

The age and diet of any bird affects the flavor and determines how it should be cooked. To determine the age of a bird, see 436. Younger birds and small, farmed birds can be roasted, fried, or grilled successfully. In general, braise or stew older birds for the best results. In the case of dark-meat birds, the breasts should be cooked to a different level of doneness than the legs. For ducks, geese, and dark-meat grouse, the breasts should be served rare or medium-rare, and the legs should be cooked longer until tender. This means that, for best results, the breasts of large ducks and geese should be separated from the legs at some point during cooking to ensure that they are not overcooked but that the legs are given adequate time to become succulent and tender (for small ducks, doves, and pigeons, this mid-cook butchery is not as practical; these birds should be left whole if roasting). Duck and goose breasts, once removed from the bird, should be allowed to rest. Then sear them skin side down over very high heat just before serving to crisp the skin.

As the legs of waterfowl benefit from longer, slower cooking, you may save up the legs from several birds and confit them, 443. This process renders them exceptionally tender, moist, and flavorful.

For the recipes in this section that call for wild ducks, geese, pheasant, and quail, their farmed counterparts may be used with some caveats. When you kill a game bird, you have no idea what you will find once the bird is plucked and gutted. It may have been feeding well, or it may be very lean. It may be a young bird, or, depending on the type, it may be quite old. Farmed birds are much more consistent. They will have had a reliable diet of grains, they will never be very old, and they will not have worked nearly as hard to make a living as their wild counterparts. This makes them milder, fatter, and with softer, less-developed muscles. In general, this means that farmed game will tend to cook more quickly than wild, and taste milder.

➤ Wildfowl is incredibly variable, which means you will have to use your judgment to cook them properly. Bear in mind these four pieces of advice: One, smaller birds may be cooked with a higher heat than larger ones. Two, wildfowl breasts need less cooking than thighs. Three, thighs are often best braised. Four, the drumsticks of larger birds, such as pheasants and wild turkeys, are best cooked slowly until the meat falls off the bone.

Barding, 1046, is sometimes a good option for lean wildfowl. The advantage of barding is clear: It adds fat to an otherwise lean meat and protects and bastes the bird as it roasts—which is especially important if the birds have been skinned. On the other hand, if your bird still has its skin, barding prevents it from browning and crisping up. Barding is completely unnecessary for duck and goose with the skin on—unless they are conspicuously thin. However, for upland game birds or any skinned bird, barding can be a good strategy. To encourage some browning of the surface of the meat, you may remove the barding toward the end of cooking.

An alternative to barding is to rub the bird all over with butter or drizzle with olive oil before roasting. A flavored butter, 559–60, may be used to baste the bird, or the skin can be loosened around the breast and thighs of the bird and the softened butter worked under the skin as well. Butter not only helps keep the bird moist but it also promotes browning of the skin and adds flavor.

ABOUT WILD DUCK AND GOOSE

The flavor of wild ducks and geese depends very much on what species you have and how they have been feeding. Shallow-water or dabbler types may feast in grain fields and be very succulent. They may also feed on algae and other less than tasty morsels, in which case they will not be nearly as delicious. Dabblers include **mallard, black duck, pintail, baldpate or widgeon, gadwall, teal, shoveler,** and **wood duck.** Diving ducks, which thrive on aquatic vegetation, include the **redhead, ruddy, bufflehead, golden-eye, scaup, canvasback,** and **ring-neck.** Sometimes these varieties feed on fish or shellfish, a diet that can make them less than palatable. The **red, hooded,** and **American mergansers** or other habitual fish eaters will taste of their feed and are not the most delicious for eating.

Wild geese are similar to ducks in that their flavor depends on what they eat. **Canada geese,** while much maligned for their tendency to foul up golf courses and parks, can be quite tasty if they have eaten a lot of grain. **Specklebelly geese** are the most prized wild species in North America. They are excellent roasted whole. **Snow** and **Ross's geese** are often very lean, and can be hard to pluck. Most times they are best skinned before cooking, making them best for confit, 443.

To test the palatability of wild waterfowl, remove a piece of the fat and heat it over medium-high heat in a small skillet. If the fat smells clean and nutty, you are most likely in for a treat. If it smells fishy, the best course of action is to breast-out the bird, 437, or at least remove its skin and all visible fat before cooking. Orange or bright-yellow fat can also be a sign of a serial fish-eater.

For cooking ideas beyond the ones given here, see About Duck and Goose, 430. To determine the age of ducks and geese, see 436. Remember that wild birds will be less fatty, smaller, and tougher than their domesticated counterparts; cook them accordingly. Duck or goose legs are excellent braised until tender in any flavorful liquid: Use recipes like Coq au Vin, 420, or Turkey in Red Mole, 430, as a base, and substitute duck or goose legs for the chicken or turkey. Because wild ducks and geese have very dark meat, they are excellent paired with strong flavors like Dijon mustard, horseradish, or sauerkraut. The strong, fatty meat benefits tremendously from acidity, so sauces like Gastrique, 565, pair especially well with these birds. The rich meat is also delicious offset by a little sweetness, so serve duck or goose with roasted fruit or fruit-based sauces like English Cumberland Sauce, 566. Rich, wine-based sauces are another good option. See Fig and Red Wine Sauce, 552. Also see Wild Turkey or Goose Legs Braised in Red Wine, 439.

ROAST WILD DUCK

4 servings

Wildfowl is variable in size and a hunt may net only one bird; feel free to halve the sauce mixture. In general, for whole wild ducks and geese, plan on serving 1⅓ to 1½ pounds per person.

Please read About Roasting Ducks and Geese, 431, and About Wild Duck and Goose, above. Preheat the oven to 500°F. Bring to room temperature and pat thoroughly dry inside and out:

2 wild ducks such as mallards, pintail, or black ducks (about 6 pounds)

Sprinkle liberally with:

1½ teaspoons salt
1 teaspoon black pepper

Rub the birds inside and out with:

Softened butter or duck fat

Place the ducks on a rack in a roasting pan and place in the oven. Roast until the internal temperature reaches 130° to 135°F for rare to medium-rare; start checking the bird's temperature at 15 minutes. Spoon off all but about 2 tablespoons of the fat from the roasting pan. Place the pan over 2 burners on the stovetop over medium heat, then add:

½ cup dry white wine
½ cup chicken or veal stock
2 teaspoons cider vinegar
1 teaspoon sugar

Scrape up any browned bits from the bottom of the pan, then transfer the liquid to a small saucepan. Bring the liquid to a boil and reduce by about half, until thickened, then take off the heat and whisk in, if desired:

(2 tablespoons heavy cream, sour cream, or crème fraîche)

Season the sauce to taste, carve the ducks, and serve.

SEARED WILD DUCK OR GOOSE BREASTS

Skin-on breasts are essential here, so do not use meat from a bird that does not pass the palatability test, above. Because wild ducks and geese are so variable in size, we do not give a yield here. Plan on about 6 ounces of meat per serving. Please read Cooking Wildfowl, 437, and About Wild Duck and Goose, above.

Have ready:

Boneless, skin-on duck or goose breasts

Use a sharp knife to score the skin in a ½-inch crosshatch pattern (without cutting the meat). Season generously with:

Salt and black pepper

Place in a heavy skillet:

1 tablespoon duck fat or vegetable oil

For large duck or goose breasts, place the breasts skin side down in the skillet and turn the heat up to medium-high. For small duck breasts, preheat the skillet over medium-high heat until the fat shimmers, then add the breasts. Let the breasts cook, undisturbed, until the skin is golden brown and crispy, 3 to 12 minutes (the lesser amount of time for very small duck breasts, and the greater amount of time for goose breasts). During the first couple minutes of cooking, use a spatula to press down on the breasts to ensure the entire surface of the skin is in contact with the skillet. Flip the breasts and cook 1 to 8 minutes (the lesser amount of time for very small duck breasts, and the greater amount of time for goose breasts), or until the internal temperature reaches 125° to 130°F. Transfer the breasts to a plate, tent with foil, and let rest for 2 to 10 minutes depending on the size of the breasts. Serve immediately.

WILD DUCK FRICASSEE

4 servings

Please read Cooking Wildfowl, 437, and About Wild Duck and Goose, 438.

Pat dry:

1½ pounds skin-on boneless wild duck breasts

Sprinkle with:

1 teaspoon salt

½ teaspoon black pepper

Heat a large skillet over medium-high heat until hot. Add the breasts skin side down and cook until the skin is crisp and browned, about 6 minutes. Turn and cook until the breasts are medium-rare, about 2 minutes more. Transfer the duck to a platter and cover to keep warm. Pour off all but 2 tablespoons of the fat from the skillet. Add and cook, stirring, until softened, 6 to 8 minutes:

1 large leek, trimmed, well-cleaned, and thinly sliced

Add and cook, stirring, until the mushrooms are softened and have released their juices, about 5 minutes:

8 ounces mushrooms, sliced

Add and stir to coat the vegetables:

2 tablespoons all-purpose flour

Cook, stirring, until fragrant, about 2 minutes more. Add:

2 cups chicken stock or broth

2 teaspoons chopped thyme

Bring to a boil, then reduce the heat to medium-low, and simmer until the liquid has reduced by half, about 10 minutes. Whisk in:

2 tablespoons butter, cut into cubes

Season the sauce to taste with:

Salt and black pepper

Return the duck breasts to the skillet and heat until warmed through, 2 to 3 minutes.

GLAZED GRILLED DUCK LEGS

4 to 8 servings

Prepare **Chashu Pork, 496,** substituting **2 to 4 pounds duck legs** for the pork belly. Cook until tender, 3 to 4 hours. Remove the duck legs from the sauce, discard the green onions, and reduce the sauce until slightly thickened and syrupy. Prepare a hot grill fire, 1063. Brush the duck legs with the reduced sauce, place on the grill, and cook briefly just until charred on all sides, about 5 minutes total. Serve with **cooked jasmine rice, 343.**

ABOUT WILD TURKEY

Wild turkeys are leaner and have more leg meat and less breast meat than most domestic breeds, and their dark meat tends to be much darker than that of store-bought birds. The average live weight of a wild turkey is 17 pounds for toms, 9 pounds for hens. You can determine the age of a male wild turkey by looking at its beard: A three-year-old turkey will have a beard that is 8 inches long or greater. A shorter beard means a younger turkey. To determine the age of a female, see 436.

Younger birds may be slow-roasted (high-heat roasting is not advisable for these birds, as they dry out quickly). Jakes, which are young males, are excellent fried. Turkeys of any age are excellent braised or poached, and you are less likely to dry out the meat. An old tom is best smoked (see Smoked Chicken, 412) or braised until tender. Consider braising in flavorful sauces, such as Mole Poblano, 553, or go the simpler route and gently poach the breasts in a rich chicken or turkey stock. Their legs and thighs make an excellent confit, 433. Wings are white meat, and, once braised until tender, are fantastic grilled or barbecued. If roasting whole, we recommend barding, 1046, the breast to keep the lean meat moist. ➤ Figure on serving 1 to 1½ pounds bone-in wild turkey per person.

WILD TURKEY ROASTED IN A BAKING BAG

6 to 10 servings

Roasting wild turkey in a bag keeps it from losing precious juices. Please read About Wildfowl, 436, and About Wild Turkey, above. If desired, wet-brine, 405, the turkey for up to 24 hours. Preheat the oven to 375°F. Have ready a large roasting bag. Pat dry:

One 6- to 10-pound wild turkey

Rub with:

Salt and black pepper

Generously slather the turkey with:

4 tablespoons (½ stick) butter, softened

If desired, stuff with:

(3 celery ribs, cut into 1-inch pieces)

(1 onion, quartered)

Tie the legs together. Put the turkey in the roasting bag, tie the bag closed, and place it in a roasting pan. Roast until the internal temperature of the breast reaches 155°F and the juices from the thigh are just slightly pink when the skin is pierced, about 10 minutes per pound. Remove the turkey from the oven and let stand for about 20 minutes before removing from the roasting bag and carving. If you would like a gravy, use the juices to prepare:

(Basic Pan Gravy, 545)

WILD TURKEY OR GOOSE LEGS BRAISED IN RED WINE

4 servings

Please read Cooking Wildfowl, 437, and About Wild Turkey, above. Have ready:

2½ to 3½ pounds wild turkey or goose legs, separated into thighs and drumsticks

Prepare, substituting the turkey or goose for the chicken:

Coq au Vin, 420

Cook until tender, 2 to 3 hours. Serve with:

Cooked egg noodles

ABOUT PHEASANT

Pheasant, which has been farm-raised for centuries in both Europe and America, is one of the most popular game birds. Although it is considered an "exotic" meat, pheasant really does resemble chicken.

The pinkish-white meat of farm-raised birds is especially reminiscent, with its mild, delicate flavor and slightly denser texture.

Younger wild pheasants will have a flexible breastbone, gray legs, and a large pointed terminal feather in its wings. Young roosters have short, sharp spurs; older roosters have long, well-worn spurs. You may roast or broil young pheasants. Old birds should be braised. Alternatively, wild pheasant can be cut up so that dark and white meat can be cooked separately: Tougher thighs and legs are best braised or stewed; tender breast meat is best fried, grilled, sautéed, or roasted.

Whole pheasants ➤ weigh between 2 and 4 pounds and will serve 2 people. Their small bones mean a high ratio of meat to bone. The leg and thigh meat is darker, firmer, and stronger in flavor than the breast meat. To give the bird both flavor and tenderness, ➤ pheasants should be hung, 436, up to 1 week or kept in the refrigerator in the feathers for about 3 days. Pheasants ➤ can be used in most chicken recipes with the understanding that it is quite a bit leaner than chicken, so avoid overcooking, which renders the meat dry and tasteless. To cook pheasants with dry-heat methods like roasting, wet-brining, 405, the birds first is good insurance against dryness. Pheasant breast meat is excellent in stir-fries, such as Stir-Fried Garlic Chicken, 416.

ROAST PHEASANT

2 servings

Roasted whole pheasant is traditionally stuffed with wild rice and mushrooms and served with Sauce Chasseur, 551. We think this classic preparation can barely be improved upon if you find yourself in possession of a beautiful, perfect bird. We, however, opt to serve the bird with dressing on the side. Filling the cavity of the pheasant prevents even cooking and can lead to the breast meat drying out before the interior is fully cooked.

Please read About Wildfowl, 436, and About Pheasant, 439. If desired, wet-brine, 405, the pheasant up to 8 hours before proceeding. Remove the pheasant from the brine, pat dry, and let sit on a rack set over a baking sheet in the refrigerator for at least 2 hours and for up to 6 hours to dry the skin.

Preheat the oven to 400°F. Pat dry:

One 2- to 3-pound young pheasant

Season inside and out with:

1 teaspoon salt
½ teaspoon black pepper

Rub the bird with:

3 tablespoons butter, softened

Place it on a rack in a roasting pan, set the pan in the oven, and reduce the oven temperature to 350°F. Roast until the internal temperature of the thigh reaches 155°F, 35 to 40 minutes. When pierced, the juices from the thigh should run faintly pink but not red. Let stand, loosely tented with foil, about 20 minutes before carving. If desired, serve with:

(Sauce Chasseur, 551)
(Sausage, Onion, and Sage Stuffing, 535, or Wild Rice Dressing, 536)

PHEASANT BRAISED WITH GIN AND JUNIPER

3 to 4 servings

While there is quite a bit of gin in the braising liquid, do not worry: The sauce does not come out tasting like a cocktail. Please read About Wildfowl, 436, and About Pheasant, 439.

Pat dry:

One 3- to 3½-pound pheasant

Cut the bird into 6 pieces—2 legs and 4 breast pieces (cut each breast crosswise in half). Season with:

Salt and black pepper

Heat in a Dutch oven over medium-high heat:

2 tablespoons vegetable oil

Working in batches, brown the pheasant on both sides. Transfer to a plate. Add to the pot and cook, stirring, until softened:

2 shallots, thinly sliced

Add:

1½ cups chicken stock or broth
⅔ cup gin
¼ cup dry sherry
½ teaspoon juniper berries, crushed
1 bay leaf

Scrape up any browned bits on the bottom of the pot. Add the pheasant legs to the pot, reserving the breasts. Bring the liquid to a boil, then reduce the heat to maintain a very gentle simmer, cover the pot, and cook at a bare simmer for 30 minutes. Add the breasts to the pot, cover, and cook until the pheasant is tender and the juices from the breast run light pink or clear when pierced, about 15 minutes more. Transfer the pheasant to a plate and loosely cover with foil.

If desired, strain the sauce and return to the pot, or simply remove the bay leaf. Boil over medium-high heat until reduced and slightly syrupy, 6 to 8 minutes. Take the pot off the heat and stir in:

2 tablespoons minced parsley
(1 tablespoon butter, cut into cubes)
Salt and black pepper to taste

Serve the pheasant with the sauce.

BRAISED PHEASANT WITH APPLES

4 servings

Delicious anytime, but especially evocative of autumn. Please read About Wildfowl, 436, and About Pheasant, 439.

Pat dry:

One 2- to 3-pound young pheasant

Cut into 4 pieces—2 breasts and 2 legs—and sprinkle with:

Salt and black pepper

Cook in a heavy pot or Dutch ove large enough to hold the pheasant comfortably over medium heat:

3 slices bacon, cut crosswise into strips

Stir occasionally until browned and rendered. Use a slotted spoon to transfer the bacon to a small bowl. If needed, add vegetable oil so there is 1 tablespoon of fat in the pot. Lightly brown the pheasant in the fat on both sides, 5 to 7 minutes. Transfer the pheasant to a plate. Add to the pot:

2 large shallots, thinly sliced
2 Granny Smith apples, peeled, cored, and cut into ½-inch slices

Cook, stirring occasionally, until the shallot is softened, 6 to 8 minutes. Stir the bacon back into the shallots and apples, and return the pheasant legs (reserve the breasts) to the pot, along with:

1½ cups chicken stock or broth
¼ cup brandy, Calvados, or apple cider
1 tablespoon cider vinegar
1 teaspoon fresh thyme leaves or ½ teaspoon dried thyme
1 teaspoon minced fresh sage or ½ teaspoon dried sage

Bring to a simmer, then cover tightly and simmer very gently over low heat for 20 minutes. Add the breasts to the pot and continue to gently simmer until the pheasant breasts release light pink juices when the skin is pierced, 20 to 25 minutes more. Transfer the pheasant to a platter and loosely tent with foil. Place the pot over medium-high heat and bring the pan juices to a simmer. Whisk together in a medium bowl:

¼ cup heavy cream
2 teaspoons all-purpose flour

Slowly stir the cream mixture into the pan juices. Cook, stirring constantly, until the sauce thickens slightly. Season to taste with:

Salt and black pepper

Serve the pheasant with the sauce, accompanied by:

Cooked wild rice, 343, or Potato Gnocchi, 306

ABOUT PARTRIDGE AND GROUSE

Most **farm-raised partridge** is the variety known as **chukar partridge.** The common wild partridge varieties are chukar and **Hungarian partridge.** These small birds are appreciated for their tender, tasty, lean breast meat, which is similar to that of pheasant but a little firmer and less delicate. Farm-raised partridges generally weigh a bit less than 1 pound apiece, so ➤ serve 1 bird per person. They can be roasted as for grouse, below, or cut into serving pieces and grilled, sautéed, or braised. They may also be cooked as for Cornish game hen, 409.

Grouse, a close cousin of partridge, is not farmed and remains a true game bird; any found in US markets is imported. It is considered by many to be the finest of game birds, often with more flavorful meat than partridge. In the United States we hunt **ruffed, sooty, dusky, spruce, sage, ptarmigan,** and **sharp-tailed grouse,** and **prairie chicken.**

Sharp-tailed grouse, spruce grouse, ptarmigan, and prairie chicken all have darker meat. Strangely, prairie chicken and sage grouse have dark-meat breasts and lighter thigh meat. Grouse may range from less than a pound for a ptarmigan to 5 or 6 pounds for sage grouse roosters; whatever the size of the bird, about ➤ 1 pound per person is a generous helping of this rich and delicious bird.

As with all game birds, diet and age of a grouse or partridge affect the flavor and texture of the meat. In the early fall, ruffed grouse are often found in apple orchards or feeding on other fruits such as wild grapes. This diet makes the ruffed grouse particularly delectable. Spruce grouse, as their name implies, live in spruce forests and eat spruce needles. They have the bad reputation of tasting "sprucey." In the late fall and winter months, when their feed is limited, they do depend heavily on spruce and are less tasty than in the early fall. In general, no matter the species, ➤ early-season birds that are well fed and eating a range of foods are preferable for the hunter's table.

If roasting grouse or partridge, wet-brining them, 405, beforehand gives you a little more leeway with cooking time. A trick to get the birds to cook more evenly is to spatchcock, 403, them before roasting or grilling. ➤ Grouse and pheasant may be substituted for each other; partridge and quail recipes are interchangeable.

ROASTED GROUSE

4 servings

Please read About Wildfowl, 436, and About Partridge and Grouse, above.

If desired, wet-brine, 405, the grouse for up to 4 hours, then pat dry and let sit on a rack set over a rimmed baking sheet in the refrigerator for 4 to 8 hours. Preheat the oven to 500°F. Pat dry:

Four 1-pound grouse

Season inside and out with:

Salt and black pepper

Place the birds on a rack in a roasting pan, set the pan in the oven, and roast until the juices from the thigh are light pink when the skin is pierced, 10 to 15 minutes. Transfer the birds to a platter, loosely tent with foil, and let rest for 10 minutes. Prepare:

Herb Pan Sauce, 546, or Sweet-Sour Orange Pan Sauce, 546

Serve with, if desired:

(Uncooked Cranberry Relish, 180)

PORT-MARINATED PARTRIDGE OR GROUSE

2 servings

Please read Cooking Wildfowl, 437, and About Partridge and Grouse, above.

Pat dry:

2 small partridge or grouse

With kitchen shears, cut out the backbone and discard or save for stock, 73. Cut each bird into 2 halves by cutting through the breastbone. Place them in a deep bowl or baking dish just large enough to hold them.

Combine in a bowl:

2 cups port
1 small onion, chopped
1 garlic clove, sliced
1 bay leaf
¾ teaspoon salt
½ teaspoon black pepper

Pour over the birds. Cover and refrigerate for 24 hours. If the marinade does not completely cover the bird, turn the pieces every so often.

Preheat the oven to 325°F.

Remove the birds from the marinade and pat dry. Strain the marinade into a medium saucepan and heat until steaming. Melt in a Dutch oven just large enough to hold the partridge over medium heat:

2 tablespoons butter

Add the bird halves skin side down and cook until browned. Turn skin side up, pour the marinade over them, and bake, covered, for 30 minutes. Uncover and cook until tender, 30 to 45 minutes. Transfer the birds to a platter and loosely tent with foil. Pour the pan juices into a small saucepan and boil over high heat until reduced to about 1 cup of sauce with a slightly syrupy consistency. Season to taste with:

Lemon juice

Pour the sauce over the birds. Serve with:

Cooked wild rice, 343, or egg noodles

ROASTED SHARPTAIL GROUSE, PTARMIGAN, OR PRAIRIE CHICKEN

Allow 1 bird per person

If desired, wet-brine, 405, the birds for up to 4 hours, then pat dry and let sit on a rack set over a baking sheet in the refrigerator for 4 hours. Preheat the oven to 300°F. Pat dry:

Sharptail grouse, ptarmigan, or prairie chicken

Sprinkle with:

Salt and black pepper

Rub each bird with:

1 tablespoon butter, softened

Place on a rack in a roasting pan and roast until cooked to medium-rare, 30 to 45 minutes—the meat should be pale pink. Remove the birds from the oven and increase the temperature to 500°F.

Let the birds rest, loosely tented with foil, for 15 minutes. Once the oven is preheated, place the birds back in the oven and roast until browned, no more than 10 minutes.

ABOUT QUAIL

Quail is exceptionally sweet and tender. Since it is widely farm-raised, it is readily available. Quail is one of the smallest game birds commonly eaten in the United States, weighing between 4 and 8 ounces, with only a few ounces of meat per bird. ➤ Two quail make a main course, one an appetizer. We love quail served hot off the grill or spit, to be picked up and eaten with the fingers, but they can be roasted whole or split lengthwise and broiled, sautéed, or braised.

"Boned" or "semiboned" quail has the backbone and breastbone removed, but the tiny wing and leg bones remain. This product is widely available and, from both a cook's and a diner's standpoint, very convenient.

Wild quail has delicious white meat. In the United States, we hunt **bobwhite, California, scaled, Mearn's, mountain,** and **Gambel's quail** and all are roughly the same size, with the mountain quail being the largest—almost the size of a partridge. All are larger than their farm-raised cousins, which are normally a Japanese breed called **coturnix.** If you can find farm-raised bobwhites, buy them as they are the best farm-raised birds available. Like all wild birds, wild quail have unpredictable diets and have more flavor than those purchased from the grocery store.

Wild and farmed quail can be treated identically in the kitchen. If roasting whole, quail benefit, like many game birds, from wet-brining, 405, for up to 4 hours. Be sure to dry the bird well afterward, letting it sit on a rack set over a baking sheet for several hours in the refrigerator to dry the skin. Serve roasted quail with Quince Preserves, 918, or Sweet-Sour Orange Pan Sauce, 546; watercress and lemon wedges; roasted root vegetables; baked pears or apples; or Spätzle, 308, or Potato Gnocchi, 306. If you broil the quail, brush it with Snail Butter, 560, or any glaze, 578–79, before and after cooking.

SPICY MAPLE-ROASTED QUAIL

8 first-course or 4 main-course servings

Serve these as an appetizer on their own or as a main course accompanied by sautéed greens and rice. The marinade may be used with Cornish hens, chicken, and pork tenderloin as well.

Pat dry:

8 quail

Whisk together in a shallow bowl:

⅓ cup maple syrup
¼ cup soy sauce
2 tablespoons red wine vinegar
2 tablespoons chile garlic paste or ¼ teaspoon cayenne pepper
8 garlic cloves, minced or grated
½ teaspoon Five-Spice Powder, 590

Add the quail, turning to coat. Marinate, covered and refrigerated, for 4 to 8 hours.

Preheat the oven to 500°F.

Drain the quail, reserving the marinade. Pat dry, and place on a rack in a roasting pan. Fold the wingtips under the birds and tie the legs together. Roast until the juices from the thigh are slightly pink when the skin is pierced and the flesh is still juicy, 12 to 20 minutes.

While the quail roast, transfer the reserved marinade to a small saucepan and bring to a boil. Reduce to a sticky glaze and reserve.

When the quail are finished cooking, brush them with the glaze, cover loosely with foil, and let stand for 5 minutes before serving. Serve quail with any leftover glaze.

ABOUT SMALL GAME BIRDS

The birds discussed here are of many kinds: **woodcock, coots** (not the sea ducks that are called coots, but small rail-like birds), **doves, pigeon, snipe, rails,** and **gallinules.** While snipe, coots, and gallinules are technically water birds, these birds are grouped together on the basis of size and therefore similar treatment and the fact that they are served one or more to a person. All of these birds have dark meat. Doves, pigeons and snipe are all highly regarded game birds, while gallinules, rails, and coots are not as prized. American woodcock is a true epicurean delight and is many a game bird aficionado's favorite bounty. Its dark, rich meat is like no other and ➤ should always be prepared rare. It is occasionally served "in the round"—whole bird with entrails and head. Smaller than its European cousin, it is a migratory bird that is only available in the wild, and there are small limits on the number that can be taken each day. One bird per person is barely a meal—so often the hunter returns with only enough woodcock to serve as an appetizer or hors d'oeuvre. Curiously, woodcock, like prairie chickens and sage grouse, is an "opposite" bird, with dark meat breasts and light meat legs and thighs.

You may cook and serve game birds whole, or breast them out, 437. ➤ Small birds should be barded, 1046, rubbed generously with butter or oil, or wrapped in fig or grape leaves. All lend themselves to roasting, skewering and grilling, or broiling; allow from 3 to 10 minutes to cook through.

ROASTED SMALL GAME BIRDS

3 to 6 servings

Please read About Small Game Birds, 442.

If desired, the birds may be seasoned and rubbed with butter, then broiled 6 inches from the heat, turning frequently, until cooked, 4 to 10 minutes.

Preheat the oven to 500°F. Pat dry:

6 small game birds

Sprinkle with:

Salt and black pepper

Rub the birds with:

3 tablespoons butter, softened

Place on a rack in a roasting pan. Roast for 5 to 12 minutes, depending on the size of the birds. The juices should run light pink when the meat is pierced. Let rest loosely tented with foil for 5 minutes before serving.

Serve with:

Basic Pan Gravy, 545, or Wine and Sour Cherry Pan Sauce, 547

Serve the birds on:

Toasted buttered bread

Pour the gravy over them. Garnish with:

Chopped parsley

WINE-BRAISED SMALL GAME BIRDS

3 to 6 servings

For this recipe, the birds can be skinned and in parts.

Please read About Small Game Birds, 442. Preheat the oven to 300°F.

Have ready:

6 small game birds

Prepare the wine sauce for:

Coq au Vin, 420

Place the birds in an ovenproof pan or Dutch oven just large enough to hold them in a single layer and pour the hot wine sauce over them. Cover, transfer to the oven, and bake until tender, about 30 minutes. While the birds cook, prepare the pearl onions and mushrooms as directed in Coq au Vin. Transfer the birds to a plate and loosely tent with foil. Reduce the sauce until syrupy, then stir in the onions and mushrooms. Pour the sauce over the birds and garnish with:

Chopped parsley

Serve with:

Cooked egg noodles or toasted bread

SKEWERED SMALL BIRDS

Please read About Small Game Birds, 442.

Pat dry, salt and pepper, rub with softened butter, and wrap in grape or fig leaves:

Small birds

or bard them, 1046, with very thin slices of:

(Pancetta or prosciutto)

Prepare a hot grill fire, 1063. Skewer and cook on the grill until browned, 8 to 12 minutes.

DOVES AND NOODLES

6 servings

Please read About Small Game Birds, 442. For this recipe, the doves can be skinned and cut into pieces.

Rinse, pat dry, and place in a large pot:

12 doves, whole or cut up

Add:

Chicken stock, water, or a combination, to cover
1 tablespoon salt
1 tablespoon sugar

Bring to a bare simmer and poach the doves until tender, 8 to 15 minutes. Drain, and discard the skin, if any. Let cool, then take the meat off the bones and reserve. Preheat the oven to 350°F.

Melt in a medium saucepan over medium heat:

2 tablespoons butter

Add and cook, stirring, until softened, 6 to 8 minutes:

1 small onion, finely chopped

Add and cook until the mushrooms release their juices, about 8 minutes:

8 ounces mushrooms, thinly sliced
1 garlic clove, minced

Stir in:

2 tablespoons all-purpose flour

Gradually add:

1 cup sour cream
1 cup milk
½ teaspoon salt
¼ teaspoon black pepper

Combine the sauce in a 13 × 9 × 2-inch baking dish with:

4 cups cooked egg noodles (8 ounces dried)

Mix in the dove meat. Cover with foil and bake until bubbling, 30 to 40 minutes. Sprinkle with:

Chopped parsley

SMALL BIRDS IN ROSEMARY CREAM SAUCE

8 to 10 first-course or 2 to 4 main-course servings

Serve this as an appetizer or over angel hair pasta as a main course.

Rinse, pat dry, and breast-out, 437, or, if boned, slice into strips:

4 woodcock, dove, squab, or other small birds

Heat in a large skillet over medium-high heat:

2 tablespoons vegetable oil

Add the meat and cook, stirring, for about 1 minute. It should still be pink. Transfer to a warm platter. Add to the skillet:

1 shallot, minced

Cook, stirring to scrape up any browned bits, until the shallots have softened, about 5 minutes. Stir in:

3 tablespoons Armagnac or other brandy

Once the brandy is reduced by half, add:

½ cup heavy cream
1½ teaspoons chopped rosemary
(1½ teaspoons juniper berries, crushed)

Bring to a boil and simmer until the sauce has thickened and reduced by half.

Season to taste with:

Salt and black pepper

Pour the sauce over the meat.

ABOUT POULTRY OFFAL OR GIBLETS

Some of us know **giblets** (pronounced JIB-lets)—an opaque term for organ meats—simply as a bag of gory bits that must be removed from birds before roasting. For others, these odd bits are indispensable for making Thanksgiving gravy, 545, pâtés and mousses, rich stocks, and specialties like Cajun Dirty Rice, 332. Here we discuss the best ways to prepare poultry organ meats and provide a handful of recipes that celebrate them. For more on rendered poultry fat, or **schmaltz,** see 1015. For preparing the organ meats of cows, sheep, goats, and pigs, please see About Offal and Variety Meats, 514.

Livers, especially chicken livers, are perhaps the most plentiful and common giblet to find. Milder than the livers of cows and other animals, chicken livers are sold in tubs; they may be displayed in the poultry case of your grocery store or hiding in the freezer aisle. Aside from being ground up into pâtés and whipped into mousse, chicken livers are most often browned quickly in fat or breaded and fried. Once browned, they may be added to dishes like Cajun Dirty Rice, 332, or to a filling for Kreplach, 314. Turkey livers can be substituted in any recipe, but they will need to be cut into several pieces (they can reach 4 times the size of a chicken liver). For the glamorous (and infamous) livers of domesticated ducks and geese, see About Foie Gras, 446.

To prepare poultry livers for cooking, remove the greenish gall bladder if it is still attached (cut it off without puncturing). Peel off the outer membranes, trim away any fat, and separate into lobes.

Gizzards are a portion of the bird's digestive tract, a second stomach or "gastric mill" for the hard seeds and grain it consumes. They are composed of two semicircular halves of dark meat connected by a tough layer of tendon that acts like a grinding plate when it is filled with grit. The muscles that power the "mill" work hard, and have a firm, snappy texture. This texture is appreciated for its own sake in stir-fries, but gizzards can also be made tender by braising, using for confit, 446, or chopping the meat fine as for Cajun Dirty Rice, 332.

To prepare gizzards for cooking, use a small sharp knife to cut each half of meat away from the center grinder plate. Discard the plate, and carefully slice the silver skin off the two meaty bits.

Hearts are by far the easiest giblet to like, as they require next to no trimming, cook quickly, are mild in flavor, and do not have a curious texture like gizzards. The key is to cook them only to medium-rare, as they will toughen when cooked further. To brown them quickly, skewer whole hearts and grill them as for Chicken Yakitori, 445 (marinate them with the mixture for Anticuchos de Corazón, 518, before grilling, if desired).

Feet, like wings, are rich in collagen and used to add body to poultry stocks, broths, stews, and braising liquids. Many Chinese recipes fry and then braise feet—called "phoenix claws"—in a highly seasoned liquid until they are very tender. For many, they are a prized dim sum item, while others are not as fond of their gelatinous texture. In fact, we think braised chicken feet are perhaps the best example of how our appreciation of a food's texture is dictated by cultural norms. If you enjoy the soft-but-firm quality of simmered beef tendon or pig's feet, you will certainly like chicken feet. If not, you may reverse the procedure employed by Chinese cooks: Braise the feet until tender, dry them well, and then deep-fry them until they puff, crisp, and turn golden brown. Or, simply toss them in vegetable oil, season, and roast them in a 450°F oven, flipping occasionally, until they are nicely browned.

To prepare poultry feet for cooking, scrub them well with a brush and trim off the claws.

The enthusiasm of some diners may wane when we look to the **neck** and head of poultry, but many find these parts very useful, if not delectable. Whole birds sold with giblets usually come with the neck, which is best browned in a pan and added to poultry stocks, especially those destined for making gravy, 545. **Duck tongues** are sold by the pound in some Asian grocery stores. These are typically simmered until tender, which makes it relatively easy to pull out the bony piece of cartilage that runs through them. Afterward, the tongues can be skewered and grilled as for Chicken Yakitori, 445, breaded and pan-fried as for Chicken Fingers, 415, or deep-fried until they puff and become shatteringly crisp (dry the tongues and fry as for Pork Rinds, 520).

To prepare duck tongues, bring them to a simmer in Court Bouillon, 80, white wine, or the mixture for Shoyu Chicken, 419, and cook for 30 minutes, or until tender. While the tongues are still warm, squeeze the cut side, grasp the protruding cartilage, and pull it free. If you have any difficulty, you can always butterfly the tongues to get the cartilage out.

Cockscombs are the crests of red flesh that crown a chicken's head. Cockscombs have been appreciated since ancient times—usually as a garnish for chicken dishes. Like other collagen-rich cuts, they must be simmered for a bit, after which they can be browned in a pan or fried until golden. Remove any tough bits from the base of these and prepare as for duck tongues, above.

Skin is sometimes thought of as an inconvenience, a bit of fatty "wrapping" to be removed and discarded. We could not disagree more: Poultry skin takes well to seasoning and browns beautifully when roasted, grilled, or fried. In some instances, however, we understand the impulse to trim off skin, especially before adding pieces to braises and fricassees, which can turn the skin soggy and result in excess fat that must be skimmed from the stew. To utilize chicken or turkey skin that would otherwise be thrown away, we highly recommend making Crispy Chicken Skins, 445 (lightly seasoned pieces of skin oven-fried until crisp). The result can be used as a crispy garnish for the dish the skinless poultry was used to make, or used as an alternative to croutons on a green salad.

SAUTÉED CHICKEN LIVERS

4 servings

The trick to sautéing chicken livers is to cook them in small batches in a very hot skillet using an ample quantity of fat. This ensures that they will brown lightly and cook evenly.

Rinse lightly in a colander:

1 pound chicken livers

Remove the connective strings, separating the lobes. Pat as dry as possible. Season with:

1 teaspoon salt
½ teaspoon black pepper

Melt in a large skillet over medium-high heat until lightly browned and fragrant:

3 tablespoons butter, or as needed

Add half of the livers to the skillet in a single layer (be careful—they will cause the fat to sputter; if you have a splatter screen now is the time to use it). Cook undisturbed for 1 minute, then flip them and cook until firm and beginning to release juices into the skillet, 1 to 2 minutes more. Transfer to a plate and cook the remaining livers in the same way, adding more butter if needed.

Reduce the heat to medium and add to the fat remaining in the skillet:

1 small onion or large shallot, minced

Cook, stirring, until softened, about 4 minutes. Stir in:

½ cup dry white wine
½ cup chicken stock or broth
1 tablespoon minced sage

Bring to a boil, scraping the browned bits from the bottom of the skillet, and boil until the liquid is reduced by half and slightly syrupy. Return the livers and their accumulated juices to the skillet and heat, stirring, just until the sauce bubbles. Take off the heat and stir in:

2 tablespoons minced parsley

Season with:

Salt and black pepper to taste
Several drops of lemon juice, white wine vinegar, or sherry vinegar

FRIED CHICKEN LIVERS

3 to 4 servings

Rinse lightly in a colander:

1 pound chicken livers

Remove the connective strings, separating the lobes. Pat as dry as possible.

Combine in a medium bowl:

½ cup flour
1 teaspoon salt
1 teaspoon black pepper

Toss the livers in the flour mixture to coat. Heat in a deep heavy skillet:

1 inch vegetable oil

Add the livers to the hot oil in batches, without crowding, and fry until browned on the first side, about 3 minutes. Turn and brown the other side. Drain on paper towels and serve immediately.

CHICKEN YAKITORI

4 servings

Yakitori, or chicken cooked on skewers, is an excellent way to prepare quick-cooking chicken giblets. It is also a good approach for feeding the offal-averse: The familiar flavors of the teriyaki glaze help offset the trepidation many feel toward odd bits. Of course, you may avoid controversy altogether by substituting **1½ pounds boneless, skinless chicken thighs, cut into bite-sized pieces.**

Prepare and reduce to a thick glaze:

Teriyaki Marinade, 582

Rinse and pat dry:

1½ pounds chicken hearts, duck hearts, chicken livers, or a combination

Season with:

1 teaspoon salt
1 teaspoon black pepper

Have ready:

10 green onions, cut into 1½-inch pieces

Prepare a hot grill fire, 1063. If using wooden skewers, fold two 12-inch lengths of foil lengthwise into 3 or 4 layers. Thread the meat onto the skewers, interspersing the meat with the green onion pieces (if the skewers are wooden, leave the same amount of bare skewer at the tops and bottoms of all the skewers). Position the folded foil strips parallel to each other on the grill so that the tips and ends of the skewers rest over the foil but the meat and green onions are exposed to the fire (this will keep the ends of the skewers from burning). Place the skewers on the grill and cook for 6 minutes, turning once. Transfer the skewers to a rimmed baking sheet, brush on both sides with the teriyaki glaze, and return to the grill for another minute, turning once. Serve with any extra glaze.

CRISPY CHICKEN SKINS

Braising bone-in chicken pieces but want crispy skin? Remove the skin from the chicken pieces, crisp in the oven, and serve on top of the finished dish. This requires at least one pair of rimmed baking sheets that nest, or one that can lie flat inside of a larger baking sheet.

Preheat the oven to 350°F. Have ready:

Chicken skin

Line a rimmed baking sheet with parchment paper and stretch the pieces of skin out on the parchment, making sure the pieces do not overlap. Lightly sprinkle each piece of skin with:

A pinch of salt and black pepper

Avoid the temptation to generously season the skin—a little salt goes a long way here. Place another sheet of parchment paper over the skin and nest a rimmed baking sheet on top so the pieces are pressed flat. Bake until the skin is golden brown and crisp, about 40 minutes.

GIZZARD CONFIT

5 servings

Gizzards have tremendous flavor, and the long, slow cooking softens their characteristic "snap." In fact, even the layer of tendon is tender enough to eat (though you may still want to trim it off).

Prepare **Duck or Goose Confit, 433,** substituting **2 pounds duck**

or chicken gizzards, trimmed, if desired. Cook until tender, 3 to 4 hours. Store and brown as directed.

ABOUT FOIE GRAS

Foie gras is French for "fat liver," and it is, indeed, the liver of a duck or goose that has been enlarged to stupendous proportions by means of force-feeding (or *gavage*). Perhaps no food is as controversial as foie gras, though it is also one of the most sought-after by gourmands and acolytes of French culinary tradition.

Foie gras is very mild in taste, more like butter than liver. Grade A foie gras is large, smooth, and unblemished. It is the finest available and is best sautéed or used in preparations where its smooth, creamy texture and appearance can be appreciated. Grade B foie gras is still of good quality, though somewhat smaller, softer, and darker in color, with more pronounced veins. It is excellent for pâtés, terrines, and mousses, though it can be sliced and seared like Grade A foie gras. Grade C is the lowest, and should only be used in terrines and mousses. Goose foie gras is larger and milder than that of duck; it is not available in the United States.

Foie gras must be special-ordered or bought online and is always very expensive. Usually it is sold whole, but you can sometimes buy either the larger or the (less desirable) smaller lobe separately. Foie gras is usually vacuum-packed and will keep for several weeks if unopened (use open packages within 2 days). In handling foie gras, remember that it is largely fat. It will chip and crumble if cut when too cold and will simply melt away to nothing if cooked too much.

To prepare foie gras for cooking, leave it at room temperature for about 1 hour to soften slightly. Carefully pull apart the 2 lobes with your hands and pull out as much of the connective matter as you can with your fingers.

Grade A foie gras destined for pan-searing needs no advance preparation other than to be sliced. Grade B foie gras should be deveined and may then be soaked in ice water for an hour or so to draw out excess blood. Once foie gras has been cleaned, it can be tightly wrapped in plastic and refrigerated for a day before cooking.

Before slicing foie gras, let it stand at room temperature for 1 hour. (If you are proceeding directly from cleaning to slicing without an intermediary soaking, it has already softened enough.) Provide yourself with a pitcher filled with very hot water, a stack of paper towels, and a thin sharp knife. Cut each lobe crosswise into slices a little over ½ inch thick, dipping the knife in hot water each time and thoroughly wiping the knife clean after each cut. Arrange the slices in a single layer on a baking sheet lined with wax paper. If you are not going to cook the foie gras at once, cover it with another sheet of wax paper, and refrigerate it for up to 12 hours.

Cold foie gras is traditionally served with a very sweet white wine, such as Sauternes, but hot foie gras is equally good with other sweet or semisweet white wines, especially German Riesling.

PAN-SEARED FOIE GRAS

8 to 10 first-course servings

Pan-seared foie gras is always served rare and creamy in the center. It cooks in a flash and must be served at once, so have all ingredients, cooking equipment, and serving plates—as well as your guests—assembled before you begin. Pan-seared foie gras should be served simply: either on small thin rounds of toasted brioche or with a fruit sauce or compote or a sweet-sour sauce such as Gastrique, 565, or Fig and Red Wine Sauce, 552.

Clean, and, if you wish, soak, as above:

1 whole duck foie gras

If it has been chilled, let the foie gras stand at room temperature for 1 hour. Cut into slices a little more than ½ inch thick. Season generously with:

Salt and black pepper

Have ready a large, warmed plate on which to put the foie gras slices as they are cooked and a bowl into which you can drain excess fat. Heat the skillet over high heat for a few minutes until very hot. Place 4 to 6 slices of foie gras in the skillet (they should sizzle briskly as soon as they hit the skillet) and cook just until the foie gras pulls in slightly on the underside and releases fat into the skillet, 15 to 30 seconds. Turn the slices with a spatula and cook 15 to 30 seconds on the second side, until well browned but not overcooked. Transfer the foie gras to the plate and pour the fat into the bowl. Repeat until all the foie gras is cooked. Moisten the foie gras with a sauce, if using (see headnote), and serve at once.

FOIE GRAS TERRINE

10 to 12 servings

Of all the ways to celebrate such a prized ingredient, this preparation is probably the most foolproof and straightforward. The result is a first course that showcases foie gras in all its glory, without anything else to get in the way. Serve it with a sweet white wine such as Sauternes, or, to play up the luxury factor even more and provide a refreshing, effervescent counterpoint to the foie gras, with flutes of Champagne.

Have ready a 3- to 4-cup terrine mold or small glass or ceramic loaf pan (a small metal pan may be used, but line it with plastic wrap so it extends over the sides generously). Cut a piece of thick cardboard to fit just inside the top of the mold. Wrap the cardboard in foil, then in several layers of plastic wrap. Set aside.

Let sit at room temperature for about 1 hour so it can soften for easier handling:

1 whole grade A or B duck foie gras (about 1½ pounds)

Separate the lobes and remove any prominent veins. Try to keep the foie intact. Some pieces will likely break off—this is okay. The pieces can be used to fill any gaps in the mold.

Preheat the oven to 200°F.

Sprinkle the foie all over with:

1½ teaspoons salt
½ teaspoon black pepper

Pour into the bottom of the terrine mold or loaf pan:

1 tablespoon Sauternes, Moscato d'Asti, or other sweet white wine

Place the large lobe of the foie smooth side down in the terrine mold. Sprinkle with:

1 tablespoon Sauternes, Moscato d'Asti, or other sweet white wine

Place the small lobe of the foie on top, smooth side up. Use any broken pieces of foie to fill gaps in the mold. Wrap the top of the terrine mold tightly with plastic wrap to seal, then place the mold in a deep ovenproof pan, such as a roasting pan, with a thin kitchen towel lining the bottom. Add enough hot, not boiling, water to come halfway up the sides of the mold and place in the oven. Cook until the internal temperature of the foie gras reaches 125°F, about 1½ hours.

Place the mold on a small rimmed baking sheet or plate. Place the foil-wrapped piece of cardboard on top of the foie gras in the mold. Set a 2- to 3-pound weight on top, such as a couple of cans. Let sit for 30 minutes. Remove the weight(s) and the cardboard, smooth the fat on top of the terrine, wrap tightly, and refrigerate for 2 days.

To unmold, invert the terrine onto a plate. Wrap the bottom of the terrine mold in a kitchen towel dampened with hot water and wait for the terrine to fall out of the mold. Cut the terrine into thin slices and sprinkle lightly with:

Salt and black pepper

Serve with:

Toasts

Fig jam, or Fig and Red Wine Sauce, 552

MEAT

In *Joy's* 1975 edition, Marion wrote: "A reappraisal of meat and its role is due in this protein-hungry world . . . [many] see meat as a wasteful commodity whose production costs far exceed those of grains, which, if skillfully combined and supplemented, can furnish us with adequate nourishment. For many, too, meat eating provokes ethical considerations." These concerns may have been on the fringe when Marion expressed them, but they are now commonplace—and increasingly urgent—for many, well-documented reasons ranging from the ecological and economic to the ethical.

We like to believe that there is a "middle ground"—a conscientious way to savor meat in moderation. For us, this means reappraising how we choose cuts, as well as how we prepare and serve them. One strategy is to treat meats as Marion suggests: as a flavoring, ingredient, or supporting element rather than the focal point of the plate. Delicious feasts can be made by stretching an economical cut in a curry or ragu. As luck would have it, the cheapest, toughest cuts are also the most flavorful (and the most abundant in the livestock we eat). By all means: Continue to grill steaks and chops, but try to think of these treatments as an indulgence rather than a well-worn path to weeknight dinner. In the end, this strategy will save you money—which you can use to splurge on tastier, ethically raised and harvested meat.

ABOUT MEAT CUTS

The nomenclature used to refer to different cuts of meat can be confusing: Names for the same cut differ from animal to animal; the same cut may go by several names; and sometimes one term can refer to two different cuts. Much of this has to do with the idiosyncrasies of the butchering trade over time, but some recent, industry-led merchandising efforts have not helped matters. For cuts specific to each animal, see our entries on Beef Cuts, 454, Veal Cuts, 473, Lamb Cuts, 477, and Pork Cuts, 486. For the organ meats and odd bits of these animals, see About Offal and Variety Meats, 514.

Ambiguous names aside, we can all agree that **roasts** are large portions of meat meant to be cooked whole and sliced or shredded before serving. The term **steak** also remains uncontroversial: a slab of meat, either a slender muscle or a larger one cut across the grain to a thickness ranging from ¾ inch to 3 inches. If this slab contains bone, it may be referred to as a **chop;** if cut thinner, it may be called a **cutlet.**

Generally speaking, when choosing a cut of meat there is a trade-off between tenderness and flavor: ➤ Tender muscles are leaner and have less flavor; rich, flavorful cuts are tougher. The tenderest cuts generally lie in the section of the animal where the least movement and stress occur. For cows, hogs, and other four-legged animals, this area is close to the spine, between the shoulder and rump. Since they have little connective tissue and fine-grained muscle fibers, these cuts respond well to faster, dry-heat processes, such as roasting, grilling, broiling, searing, sautéing, and stir-frying, 1050–52. They may also be gently poached or cooked sous vide, 1054. Regardless of the method, these tender cuts only need to be cooked long enough to reach a safe internal temperature, or until the desired doneness is reached (see Recommended Final Internal Temperatures for Meats, 453).

Cuts from the neck, shoulder, belly, and legs contain more connective tissue and have coarse-grained muscle fibers. Generally, these cuts must be cooked for quite a while—well past the point of a medium-rare steak—so that the collagen-rich connective tissue breaks down and the fibers become tender. For long, slow cooking, moist-heat processes like braising, stewing, and pot-roasting keep the meat from drying out, 1057. Cooking these cuts sous vide, 1054, offers its own distinct advantages as well.

Of course, there are many notable exceptions to the rule: The most tender muscle in a side of beef (the teres major) is actually nestled next to the shoulder blade; the heart—a lean muscle that is continuously exerted—is delectable when seared over high heat and served rare. And then there are the time-honored ways to intervene and change the texture of meat before it is cooked; see Mincing, Grinding, and Pounding, 451.

ABOUT BUYING MEAT

American consumers benefit from two forms of protection enforced by the US Department of Agriculture (USDA). First, all meat processed for sale across state lines is subject to daily government inspection for wholesomeness and cleanliness. (So-called "custom" facilities, which process animals for local hunters and farmers, are not subject to daily inspection, though they are still inspected periodically.) Second, some meats are graded for quality in accordance with federal standards by government-employed inspectors. Though several metrics are used for grading different animals, graders are primarily concerned with **marbling,** or the presence of intramuscular fat. The logic goes: The more a muscle is shot through with tiny veins of fat, the more tender, juicy, and flavorful it is once cooked. Grading is voluntary, and many processors choose not to have their meats graded. This is not a reflection of lower quality, but it does mean a greater degree of uncertainty for shoppers who are not savvy enough to recognize a good piece of meat. For further details on grading, see individual meat entries in this chapter.

There is more to meat than cuts and grades. How the animals are fed, how long the meat has been held and at what temperature, whether or not it was treated with preservatives, and when it was packaged are all variables unknown to the consumer. You must rely on your experience and the integrity of your butcher. Read labels carefully, ask questions, and stay informed.

For labeling terms applied to specific meats, see their individual entries in this chapter. Some general standards and labeling that are applied to all meat include **organic** certification, which means that the animal ate 100 percent organically grown feed. **Kosher** and **halal** meats are processed according to rabbinical or Islamic law, respectively. The term **"natural"** is allowed on packaging, but it means next to nothing: The law only requires that meat not be "fundamentally altered" during processing and not contain artificial flavorings, colorings, preservatives, or other synthetic ingredients (all fresh meat falls into this category).

In general, ➤ we do not recommend purchasing premarinated meats, especially those that are vacuum-packed with their marinades at a packing facility. If your grocery store or butcher marinates meats on-premises, purchase a small quantity first to determine whether or not they can be trusted—both with the seasoning and the quality of the meat used (which is harder to inspect once marinated). ➤ We also discourage purchasing cuts of meat that have been tenderized via puncturing with a Jaccard-style meat tenderizer, 451; though efforts are made to keep the process sanitary, we feel the risk of contamination is too great. (Meat tenderized in this way will have tiny, regularly spaced holes all over its surface.)

When comparing prices at the butcher counter, bear in mind that cuts with the smallest percentage of bone and fat yield the most meat. While the price per pound may go down for bonier cuts with more fat, the amount you need per serving goes up. This is not to say bony cuts cannot be a bargain—they frequently are—but try to account for the proportion of trim when cost is driving your decision.

SERVING SIZES

When buying ➤ boneless meat, allow ¼ to ⅓ pound per serving. This category includes ground meat; boneless stew meat; boned roasts and steaks; tenderloin; and most variety meats. ➤ When buying meat with some bone, allow ⅓ to ½ pound per serving. These cuts include rib roasts, bone-in steaks and chops, and hams. For ➤ bony cuts, allow ¾ to 1 pound per serving. In this bracket are short ribs, spareribs, shanks, hocks, and bone-in cuts from the shoulder, breast, and plate.

STORING RAW AND COOKED MEATS

Raw meat must be cooked or frozen promptly. ➤ Take special care to avoid cross-contamination by washing hands and sanitizing work surfaces immediately before and after handling raw meat, xx. Ground meat, fresh sausage, and organ meats are among the most perishable types of meat. Cook them within 24 hours of purchase. Cubed meat should be used within 48 hours. Steaks and chops will hold for 2 to 4 days, roasts for 3 to 5 days. The date on vacuum-packed meats will indicate when it is best cooked by. Store all raw meat on the bottom shelf of the refrigerator. We like to place packages of raw meat on a quarter sheet pan (readily available at restaurant supply stores) so that any leaked juices do not come in contact with the refrigerator shelf or other foods.

Any raw meats that cannot be cooked within the recommended time should be frozen immediately after purchase. For storage times and tips on maintaining the quality of frozen meats, ➤ see About Freezing Meat, Poultry, Fish, and Seafood, 887. To safely thaw frozen meats, see 887.

Prepackaged cured or smoked meat and sausages may be stored refrigerated for a week in their original wrappers. Once the package is opened, exposed surfaces should be protected. In checking for spoilage, be sure the meat is not slimy to the touch, and that there is no off odor.

Cooked meats are best stored in a covered container in the refrigerator; they will keep for 3 to 4 days. For roasts, drain off any hot gravy or pan juices and allow it to cool separately. Cooked meat can be frozen for 2 to 3 months, but we can only recommend freezing stewed dishes like chili and ragu, or rich, resilient cuts like pork shoulder (their abundance of gelatin and fat helps them withstand thawing and reheating). Cooked meat—especially large roasts—tend to become dry on reheating. To reheat, thinly slice the meat and warm a sauce or gravy just until steaming. This might be the pan sauce you served with the roast or a freshly made sauce; for inspiration, see About Cooked Sauces, 552, and Becker Pork Hash, 491. ➤ For a primer on the myriad ways to repurpose leftover meat, see xli.

BRINING, MARINATING, AND SEASONING MEAT

Lightly season all meat before cooking with salt (and pepper, if desired), then finish the dish with seasoning to taste. For chops, steaks, and roasts that are destined for the grill, roasting pan, skillet, or any other dry-heat method, you may improve their juiciness by brining them first. We prefer salting and letting the meat rest for an extended period, which is often referred to as **dry-brining.**

To dry-brine meat, liberally sprinkle it all over with salt, and let it sit uncovered on a wire rack set in a rimmed baking sheet in the refrigerator overnight for small cuts, and up to 2 days for large roasts. We recommend using **1 teaspoon table salt or 2 teaspoons Diamond kosher salt for every 1 pound of meat** (in this instance, we recommend using kosher salt as it is easier to distribute evenly). The salt penetrates deeply and bonds to water in the meat, which helps it stay moist during cooking. At the same time, the salting and prolonged exposure to air helps dry out the surface, which aids browning.

Wet-brining, 1046, is another method that promotes a moist, juicy result. However, we find that submerging some meats in brine gives them a springy "deli-meat" texture, dilutes the flavor of the meat, and offers no real advantage over dry-brining with regard to retaining juiciness. On the other hand, we do like the results of brining leaner pork loin chops and roasts.

Marination is the process of enhancing the texture and flavor of meat by soaking it in a liquid containing salt, aromatic seasonings, and almost always an acid, such as vinegar, wine, lemon juice, buttermilk, or yogurt. For many years, it has been commonly accepted that the flavor of marinades penetrates below the surface of meat. We now know that little besides the salt seasons or tenderizes meat deeper than ⅛ inch. The tissue structure of some muscles—such as beef brisket and skirt steak—actually do absorb and hold on to marinades very well. Of course, cutting meat thinly, pounding it flat, or deeply scoring it can boost the efficacy of marinades. For more on this subject, see About Marinades, 579.

Meat injectors (also called **meat pumps**) are one way to disperse brines, marinades, and fat throughout a large roast. They are especially popular with barbecue enthusiasts. To increase a roast's juiciness, use a rich broth. Or, for especially lean meats, you may inject seasoned oil, a vinaigrette, 575, or melted butter. Using ¼ cup of fat or broth for every pound of meat, insert the needle as close to the center of a roast as you can and inject a small amount of liquid. Retract the needle halfway, nudge it to one side or another, push farther in to create a separate "pocket," and inject a little more. Repeat a few more times, and then move to a new injection point. Try to distribute the liquid evenly throughout the roast. When injecting brines and marinades, keep their salt content in mind; taste the mixture, and inject sparingly if you even suspect that it may be too much (salt can always be added later). Any added seasonings must be fine enough to travel through the syringe needle.

Rubs and pastes, 583–87, can be applied immediately before cooking or a day or two in advance. The spice rub or paste will result in a highly flavorful, slightly crunchy crust on roasted or barbecued meats. Unless you are intentionally blackening, 1053, a steak or chop, try to keep the rub or paste from burning, which will turn them bitter. Using indirect heat on the grill, 1062, and moderate roasting temperatures are the best strategies for avoiding burnt bits.

There are other ways to add flavor to meats. Large roasts may be butterflied, slathered with an aromatic filling, and then rolled up and tied (see About Stuffing Roasts and Thin Meats, 452). Small incisions can be made over the surface of a large cut of meat and stuffed with slivers of garlic, anchovies, or a mix of spices and herbs. These little pockets will add flavor to the surrounding meat when cut.

TENDERIZING TOUGH MEATS

Tough meat is primarily caused by the presence of connective tissue, coarse muscle fibers, and/or a lack of intramuscular fat. There are many tricks for tenderizing tough cuts, but the easiest approach is to cook them low and slow with a moist-heat method; for a general discussion, see Braising, Stewing, and Pot-Roasting, 1057, and Barbecuing, 1066. Sous vide cooking, 1054, a relative newcomer, uses even lower heat and a slower cooking process to achieve completely different results. Since these methods allow for easy reheating and holding, try to plan ahead and give yourself time to ➤ sample the texture of the dish and cook longer if needed.

The low-and-slow solution is good for most tough meats, but sometimes fine-grained muscles that are largely free of connective tissue can still turn out chewy or dry if they are very lean. Larding, 451, and barding, 1046, can help make up somewhat for this lack of fat. Of course, by the time you know a cut would benefit from larding, it may be too late; ➤ if the worst has happened and chewy meat must be served, thinly slice steaks and roasts across the grain, and dress with plenty of pan juices or a rich sauce.

TENDERIZERS

Acidic marinades have a tenderizing effect since they add moisture and begin to break down tissue; however, prolonged exposure denatures the proteins in the meat, causing it to "cook" and toughen. Some fruits, like Asian pear, pineapple, kiwi, and papaya, contain protease enzymes, which naturally tenderize meat. Any of these can be added to a marinade or paste, but they will render the surface of meats mushy if left on for too long. **Papain,** a protease enzyme found in papaya fruit, is the active ingredient in commercial meat tenderizing powders. To use a commercial meat tenderizer, sprinkle it on both sides of the meat right before cooking, allowing 1 teaspoon tenderizer per pound. Prick the meat all over with a fork after applying the tenderizer.

MINCING, GRINDING, AND POUNDING

These are the most common methods of mechanical tenderization, where meat fibers are loosened or severed. The results of mincing and grinding meat are quite different. **Minced meat**—which is best achieved by freezing the meat for 30 minutes, then using a very sharp knife and a lot of patience to dice the meat very fine—results in distinct, sharply cut bits that remain separate in further preparation. On the other hand, **ground meat,** especially if run through the grinder multiple times, will bind together into clumps. If mixed further, ground meat will become stickier and take on a springy, snappy texture—this is how emulsified sausages like bologna and hot dogs are created (for more on this effect, see Grinding Meat at Home, 501). ➤ For information on choosing and storing ground meat, see 501.

Pounding loosens and breaks down tough meat fibers. It may be done with a **wooden, metal,** or **rubber mallet,** or a **meat pounder.** Slightly moistening the mallet makes the meat less likely to stick. To discourage tearing, ➤ strike the meat with a glancing motion rather than applying force in a straight downward motion, working from the center of the cut to the edge. ➤ For delicate cuts like veal scallops, put the meat between sheets of plastic wrap or wax paper. These precautions will keep the meat intact even when pounded paper-thin. Trim off any fat, and if any membrane adheres, slash it in a number of places so the meat will not curl up during cooking.

CUBING AND JACCARDING

These two mechanical methods require special tools. **Cubing**—not the knife cut, but the process that gives us cube steak, 455—involves running a steak or cutlet from a lean, tough muscle through a pair of rollers fitted with many short, wide blades. These blades slash through the meat's muscle fibers, making it seem tender and easier to chew. Cube steak is tender enough to cook with dry-heat methods (as in Chicken-Fried Steak, 461).

A related technique involves the use of a **Jaccard-type meat tenderizer,** which punctures meat with dozens of tiny blades. Like cubing, these blades sever muscle fibers and connective tissue. Unfortunately, there is one major drawback: While the interior of the meat is effectively sterile before Jaccarding, any bacteria on the surface will be pushed inside by the Jaccarding process. If the meat is cooked well done, this is not an issue, but Jaccarded cuts cooked only to medium-rare can be hazardous (the bacteria potentially introduced from the blades will not be killed at lower temperatures). ➤ We recommend using Jaccard tenderizers exclusively on steaks freshly cut from a roast and then only on the freshly cut sides. Or, you may sterilize the outside of thicker steaks and roasts with a 30-second blanch in boiling water, or briskly flame the surface with a propane torch. ➤ Take special care to clean the instrument before each use with a sanitizing solution, xx.

LARDING

Larding is traditionally accomplished by inserting strips of pork fat or bacon, called **lardoons,** into lean roasts, which enhances their juiciness and flavor. **Larding needles** are of two types: Those used for larding near the surface are very thin, pinpointed models with a hinged top that can be pried open to insert a lardoon and then hold it as the needle is drawn through the meat at a shallow angle, shown below. The second type is inserted through the entirety of a roast, with an open channel that runs the entire length of the shaft. This type is slightly more versatile, as the channel may also be filled with a flavored butter, 559–60, and chilled in the refrigerator until firm. ➤ For larding, use 2 ounces of fat per pound of meat. To use a meat injector to inject flavored oil or melted fat into meat, see Brining, Marinating, and Seasoning Meat, 450.

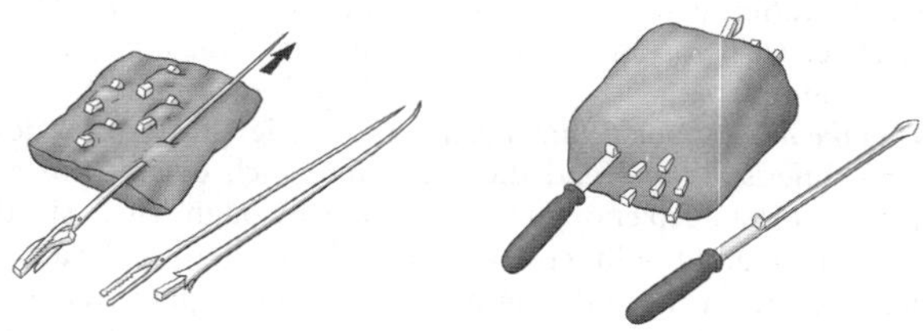

Inserting short and long lardoons into meat with larding needles

LARDOONS

Enough for 2 to 2½ pounds meat

For scaling to different sizes of roasts, remember to use about 2 ounces of fat for 1 pound of lean meat. Salt pork may be blanched briefly to desalt it, then left to dry.

I. WITH PORK FAT

Cut into ⅛- to ¼-inch-thick batons, 201:

4 ounces salt pork, slab bacon, or fatback

Toss in a bowl with any of the following:

3 garlic cloves, minced
1 tablespoon minced herbs such as parsley, thyme, oregano, or chives
1 teaspoon black pepper
A few tablespoons brandy
A pinch of grated or ground nutmeg or cloves

Insert short lengths near the surface with a thin larding needle as shown above. Longer lengths can be inserted across a roast, with the needle parallel to the grain (they will show up when the meat is sliced across the grain).

II. WITH FLAVORED BUTTER

Seasoned butter is excellent for larding meats that you do not plan to turn over during roasting; just remember to insert it on a diagonal as directed below or it may leak out.

Prepare:

A flavored butter, 559–60

While the butter is still soft, carefully spoon it into a channeled larding needle, making sure that it is evenly distributed. Freeze the filled needle for 20 minutes, or until the butter is firm. Insert the needle halfway up the side of the roast, parallel to the grain, and angled downward (this will discourage the butter from leaking out). Push the needle until it is just short of going through the other side. Stick a narrow object (like the handle of a spoon) into the channel of butter right at the meat's surface and pull the needle from the roast. Repeat at intervals down the roast, refrigerating the roast while freezing more butter in the needle if needed. If you do not have a larding needle, you may also make a slender incision diagonally into a roast so that the opening is on the top and work softened butter into the pocket with a teaspoon.

ABOUT STUFFING ROASTS AND THIN MEATS

Stuffing roasts with a flavorful mixture is a classic embellishment used to deeply season the meat with an herb paste or fortify it with stuffing. Long, roughly cylindrical, boneless roasts like pork loin or beef strip loin, chuck eye, and eye of round, can be **butterflied** or **Y-cut,** stuffed with a filling, rolled up, and tied. The latter is so named because if you could see a cross-section of the meat, it would look like an inverse Y.

To make a Y-cut for filling a roast, make a lengthwise cut down its centerline; start and end the incision ½ inch or so from each end, and cut just deep enough to go halfway through. Then, starting inside that cut and holding the knife at a slight angle, make a cut to the left and then a cut to the right, both deep enough to go halfway from the base of the initial cut to the surface. Stuff your filling into the cavities and tie the roast with butcher's twine at 2-inch intervals.

To butterfly a roast, place the roast on a cutting board so that a short side faces you. Make a cut down the entire length of the roast between ½ to 1 inch from the side closest to your cutting hand. Once the knife is ½ to 1 inch from the cutting board, rotate the blade toward the inside of the roast so that it remains parallel to the outside of the roast and the cut portion is of an even thickness. As you slice, "unroll" the uncut center portion. When the meat unfurls into a sheet, you may pound it to even it out, or leave as is. Spread your filling evenly over the meat, leaving a good 1½- to 2-inch border of bare meat on the side you cut first. Roll up the meat, starting at the edge that was cut last, and tie at 2-inch intervals. Large, flat, inexpensive cuts like beef flank and skirt steak may be stuffed as well: See Flank Steak with Dressing, 472.

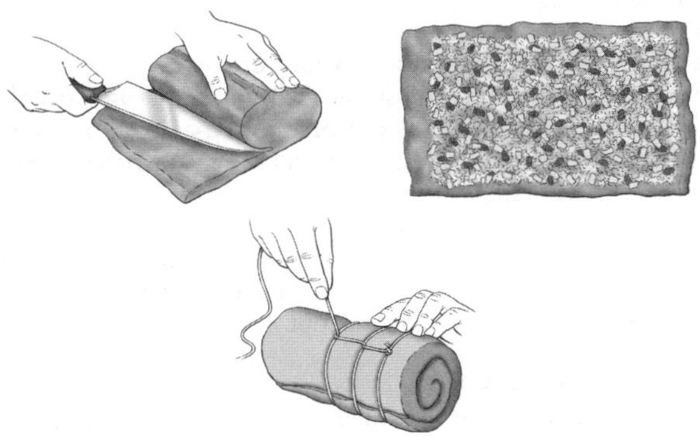

Cutting the roast open, spreading stuffing over the meat, and tying the rolled-up roast

Finally, slender cutlets from a larger muscle can be pounded thin and rolled up with or wrapped around an aromatic filling and then tied. **Rolls, roulades,** and **rouladen** are made by spreading the filling over the meat and then rolling them up. **Paupiettes** and **braciole** are made by wrapping a filling in pounded meat and tying it into a parcel. The meat for a paupiette is often drawn together around the filling and tied; braciole tend to be rolled up with the sides tucked in, much like a burrito, 147. Large or small, rolled or wrapped, these meaty parcels are then browned all over and braised in a flavorful liquid, which is then used to sauce the meat. For directions on pounding meat, see 451.

TIMING AND DONENESS

Recommended cooking times are given in the individual recipes. Remember ➤ meat cooking times are approximate at best, for there are many factors that make precision impossible—the temperature of the meat at the outset of cooking, its shape and thickness, the presence of large bones, and the accuracy of your oven thermostat or grill thermometer are but a few.

For this reason (we cannot emphasize this enough) ➤ use an accurate, instant-read thermometer to determine when steaks, chops, and roasts are done. (To test the accuracy of your thermometer, see 1043.) Insert the probe into the center of the meat, away from fat or bone. When measuring the temperature of thin foods, such as pork chops or hamburger patties, insert the thermometer horizontally through the side, so the sensing area is in the center of the food. Some thermometers are designed to be left in the meat during cooking; these can be useful—especially when tending a temperamental fire for smoking meats—but they are hardly necessary.

The following chart gives you the *final* temperatures that tender cuts of meat should reach to be considered safe to eat. We emphasize "final," because when a steak or roast is removed from the heat, it is customary to let it **rest** or **stand** for 5 to 10 minutes after cooking. As the meat rests, it will continue to "cook" as the higher temperature of the outer layer moves toward the center of the chop, steak, or roast (this is known as **carry-over cooking**). The thicker the piece of meat, the more heat it will absorb, and the more its core temperature will rise as it rests.

Though carry-over cooking makes determining when to remove meat from the heat a bit tricky, in general, we recommend that you ➤ remove meat from the oven, pan, or grill when a thermometer registers 5 to 10 degrees less than the chart on 453 specifies for a given level of doneness (5 degrees less for thinner cuts and 10 degrees less for large cuts and roasts). Most of our recipes factor this in and are written accordingly. If the worst has happened and the roasting or grilling meat has reached the desired temperature listed on the chart, ➤ you can keep the meat from cooking further by slicing it immediately into serving pieces (just be sure to do so on a rimmed baking sheet or deep plate to collect any juices).

RECOMMENDED FINAL INTERNAL TEMPERATURES FOR MEATS

Type of Meat	Recommended Temperature	Color (if cut open)
Beef, veal, or lamb (roasts, steaks, chops)		
Rare	125°F*	Deep, purplish red
Medium-rare	135°F*	Reddish pink
Medium	140°F*	Pink
Medium-well	145°F	Grayish pink
Well-done	155°F	Brownish gray
Fresh pork (including raw or uncooked, smoked hams)		
Medium	145°F	Pale, with a rosy blush
Well-done	155°F	Off white
Ground beef, veal, lamb, or pork (including fresh sausage)	160°F	
Precooked ham, sausages, and hot dogs	140°F	

*According to the USDA, red meats must be cooked to 145°F, or medium-well, to be considered safe. We are confident that properly stored and handled roasts, chops, and steaks cut from beef, veal, and lamb are safe to eat when cooked rare or medium-rare.

Note that the temperatures in the chart are the *minimum* temperatures for tender cuts cooked by conventional methods; the USDA arrives at their recommended temperatures by determining the percentage of potential pathogens and bacteria that will perish when exposed to a given temperature for a short time. Tougher cuts—beef brisket, pork shoulder roasts, and lamb shanks for instance—must be cooked much longer and well beyond these temperatures to become fully tender (they may be safe to eat at the minimum temperature listed, but they will be difficult to chew).

Finally, if you have no thermometer, there are a couple of time-honored methods for estimating doneness, such as pressing the surface of the steak or roast with your finger. If the meat feels soft yet resilient—if it dents easily and at once resumes its shape—it is cooked to medium-rare; if the meat remains firm under finger pressure, it is well-done. A much more reliable test is to make a small incision in the meat and check the center for the desired color of doneness (see the right-hand column in the chart). Again, remember that the meat will continue to cook for a short time after being taken off the heat.

ABOUT BEEF

Though our appetite for chicken in the United States has eclipsed our consumption of beef, no animal protein is as highly revered, or provokes as much gustatory enthusiasm. For many of us, a thick T-bone is emblematic of carnivorism—and hedonistic excess—writ large. It follows that such enthusiasm has led to a high degree of specificity with how beef is bred, raised, harvested, and stored.

Cattle breeds, such as Japanese **wagyu** and Scottish **Angus cattle,** are held in very high esteem since they are genetically predisposed to heavy marbling. **Piedmontese cattle** are desirable for the opposite reason: Their meat is lower in fat while retaining tenderness. Similarly, **grass-fed cattle** are almost always leaner, and often touted as more nutritious and flavorful than fattier **grain-fed** (or grain-finished) **cattle.** A few things to remember: The "grass-fed" label is no longer regulated by the USDA, the term has no direct bearing on the overall quality of the meat, and grass-feeding does not mean the cattle were raised in idyllic pastures. On the other hand, the authentically raised wagyu available from high-end butchers and wholesalers (sometimes wrongly referred to as **Kobe beef**) has a comparatively luxurious lifestyle, eating an abundance of supplementary grain and grain products. The result is an extreme level of marbling.

Beef is voluntarily submitted for USDA quality grading; ungraded beef is not necessarily inferior and may meet or exceed these standards. **Prime** grade represents about 2 percent of graded beef and is generally commandeered by restaurants and specialty markets. It is abundantly marbled, tender, well-flavored, and fine-textured. **Choice** grade is of high quality but has somewhat less marbling (it is usually the highest grade available in the supermarket). **Select** grade beef is still relatively tender, with even less marbling and a higher ratio of lean meat to fat. **Standard, Commercial, Utility, Cutter** and **Canner** grades are given to meat with a coarser appearance and little marbling. These grades are mainly ground or used in processed meat products.

Well-marbled, Prime-grade beef is very forgiving: Tender cuts from the rib and loin are predisposed to be moist and juicy, even if they get overcooked slightly when roasted or grilled. Leaner cuts of Choice-grade beef should be watched carefully, as the margin between done and dry and overcooked is narrower. Since Select-grade cuts have less fat on the outside and are generally less juicy and flavorful, we prefer using them for stir-fries, marinated dishes like Carne Asada, 459, or in braises and stews, 463.

Other, newer certifications include the USDA's **Tender** and **Very Tender** labels, which must be earned by submitting steaks and roasts to testing by an instrument that measures the force required to bite through them. High-quality wagyu is sometimes labeled by the Japanese grading system (A1 through A5, with 5 being the highest quality).

Finally, the manner in which beef is stored can have a drastic effect on its quality (and price). **Wet-aged beef** accounts for most beef sold; it is processed as quickly as possible, vacuum-packed in bags, and chilled for shipping. During this time, enzymes within the meat begin to break down its proteins, making the meat more tender. **Dry-aged beef** is kept in a locker with precise climate control for weeks, sometimes even months. As the beef ages, it loses moisture through evaporation, which concentrates its flavors as enzymes tenderize the interior. When the process is complete, the dried outer layers are trimmed off. Between moisture loss and trimming off this outer layer, dry-aged beef may lose more than one-quarter of its original weight. The result is full-flavored, highly sought after, and priced accordingly.

BEEF CUTS

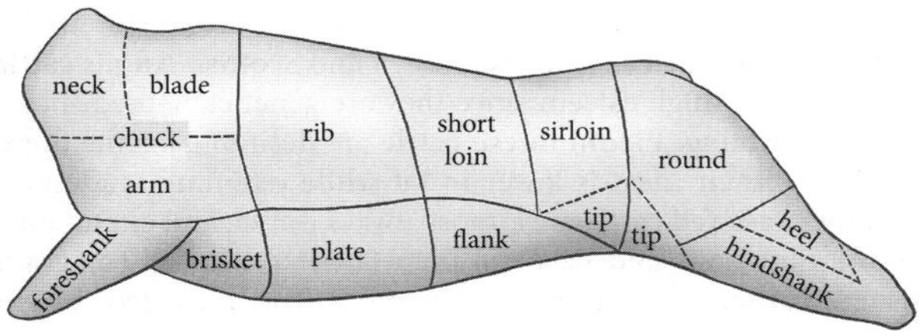

Major cuts of beef

The muscles that get worked the most—those from the chuck, brisket, plate, round, and shanks—are generally tougher, but more flavorful. The rib, short loin, and sirloin sections are the most tender. All these areas—both tough and tender—are worth examining, so we proceed from nose to tail, and from roast to steak. For organ meats, including the heart, see 514.

Cows are ruminants, so it makes sense that their **cheeks** and **tongue** are worked continuously, making them tough and collagen-rich. With long, slow cooking, beef cheek can be transformed into some of the most flavorful stews and braises we have ever tasted. Since tongue requires special treatment, we deal with it elsewhere, 516.

The **chuck** is another cut that is traditionally stewed, braised, or pot-roasted. This is especially true of the hard-working muscles that make up the **neck**, the thick, crosscut **arm roast** and **7-bone roast** (named for the cut shape of one its bones), as well as the **chuck short ribs.** If the chuck short ribs are boned, the resulting cut is called the **chuck flap** (or **country-style beef ribs** when cut into strips). However, many tender steaks and roasts may be cut from the chuck area: The **shoulder tender,** also known as the **teres major** or **petite tender roast,** which lies along the shoulder blade, is one of the tenderest muscles in the entire cow (do not confuse it with the poorly named **chuck tender,** which is not). More common is the adjacent **flat-iron** or **top blade steak;** it is very tasty and often compared to the much more expensive strip loin steak. A layer of connective tissue runs at a frustrating diagonal through this cut; since it is difficult to remove, we recommend first cooking flat-irons and then carving it out once they have rested (or simply warning diners of its presence). The **underblade flap** is a well-marbled, tender cut from the other side of the shoulder blade, and may be found cut across the grain and sold as **Denver steaks.** The underblade is one of several muscles that make up the **chuck eye roll,** which is composed of many of the same muscles found in the more expensive rib-eye portion. Like the rib eye, it is tender, has lots of flavor, and is best roasted whole or cut into steaks for grilling, searing, pan-frying, or broiling.

The front legs, or **foreshanks**, are especially rich with collagen, and must be braised or stewed; if cross-cut into steaks, you may treat them as for Osso Buco, 476. The **brisket** is composed of two portions: the larger, lean **flat** portion (also called **first cut**) and the rich, fatty **point** or **deckle** (often sold as **second cut**). Either cut of brisket is wonderful for braising (keep in mind that a second cut braise will require thorough skimming). For Smoked Brisket, 469, and Pastrami, 938, we highly recommend choosing the second cut portion, or a roast cut from a whole brisket that has some of the point muscle still attached (it has a fuller flavor and stays moist). For Corned Beef, 472, the leaner flat portion is best.

Behind the shoulder is the uniformly tender and well-marbled **rib** section. If trimmed of excess fat and bone, it becomes the **standing rib roast,** or **prime rib.** If left whole, this roast has 7 ribs, but smaller roasts may be cut from it, or it may be cut to the thickness of a bone or less to make bone-in **rib-eye** or **cowboy steaks.** If this roast has the ribs removed, it may be called a **rib-eye roast;** boneless steaks cut from this are sometimes called **Delmonico steaks. Beef back ribs** are trimmed to between 6 and 8 inches wide and come in slabs of 4 to 8 ribs, which makes them an impressive cut to barbecue (see Smoked Beef Ribs, 470). Nearly all of their meat is between the bones, making them much less efficient in servings per pound than pork ribs and beef short ribs (not surprisingly, they are also much cheaper). Sometimes the thin outer muscle of the rib-eye roast is removed and sold as the **rib-eye cap** (which is considered by some to be the most luxurious cut of beef).

Starting at the front of the hind quarter is the **short loin.** The top portion contains the same muscles found in the rib eye; it is well-marbled and exceptionally tender. If left whole, it is called the **strip** or **top loin roast** (the ribs may be left on or removed). When cut, the result is **New York strip steak,** also known as **Kansas City, shell,** or **club steak.** On the other side of the vertebrae is the aptly named **tenderloin** or **fillet,** a lean and fine-grained muscle. The strip and tenderloin may be left on the bone and cut into **T-bone steaks** and **porterhouse steaks;** the only difference is the porterhouse's bigger portion of tenderloin (it is cut from farther back, where the tenderloin is thickest). When fashioned into a roast, the narrow portion of tenderloin is sometimes folded back and tied to promote even cooking. If the thick, center section is cut into a large roast or into 2- or 3-serving portions, it is referred to as a **Châteaubriand.** If the tenderloin is portioned, the tips are discarded or used for kebabs, the narrow section is cut into thick steaks (sometimes called **tournedos**), and steaks from the larger portion are called **filet mignons.** Last but not least, is the **hanger steak,** an absolutely fantastic grilling cut with a full, rich, deep flavor and tender texture, especially when sliced across its prominent grain. We hesitate to say more, as doing so may contribute to its growing popularity (and end its reasonable pricing once and for all).

The thick end of the tenderloin runs into the **sirloin** portion of the animal. Though leaner and less coveted than the rib or short loin, the sirloin contains many desirable cuts and has more flavor. The best steaks come from the upper portion of the sirloin, which is sold as **top sirloin** (or **top butt sirloin**). The outermost muscle is sold as the **top sirloin cap** or **coulotte**—both as a triangular roast and as steaks (also called **picanha**), which are especially popular for grilling. The other portion, or **center-cut top sirloin,** is lean and strikes a good balance between flavor and tenderness. From the **bottom sirloin,** or **bottom butt,** comes the increasingly popular **tri-tip,** or **triangle steak,** another favorite for grilling. On the bottommost portion of the sirloin is the **sirloin flap** or **bavette.** Shaped like flank steak (see below), the sirloin flap is decently marbled and perfect for grilling (especially as Carne Asada, 459).

Traditionally, the regions beneath the rib and loin have been neglected by shoppers and were quite economical. This is still true of some cuts, but for most the secret is out. The **plate** sits right below the rib section, and the upper portion is where most **short ribs** are cut from. Short ribs can be individually cut lengthwise (**English-style**) or crosscut into 1-inch (**flanken**) or ¼-inch strips (**Korean-style** or **Kalbi,** 459). Though traditionally thought of as a braising cut, short ribs are excellent on the grill; they can be cooked as for steak or smoked. Below that is the **navel,** a flavorful, thin cut generously layered with fat (it is, after all, the beefy equivalent of bacon). Traditionally, the navel was cured in a brine, rubbed with spices, and smoked to make Pastrami, 938, though most pastrami is now made with the leaner brisket. The plate is also home to the **inner** and **outer skirt steaks.** Both skirt steaks are long, thin, marbled, and very flavorful; their open grain absorbs marinades and holds on to rubs well, which makes them a favorite for grilling. Underneath the loin is the **flank** portion. **Flank steak** is a lean, flat, boneless cut with tremendous flavor; it can be grilled whole and thinly sliced across the grain, or braised and shredded (see Ropa Vieja, 471).

At the rear of the animal is the **round,** which starts at the pelvis and includes the entire hind leg. Though these muscles support a lot of weight, they are not as well-used as the chuck, and therefore leaner and moderately tender. The **top round** is the most tender portion and may be cut into lean steaks and roasts. A thin muscle covering the top round is sometimes available under the name **Santa Fe steak,** which can be grilled whole like flank steak. Though often used for kebabs, stir-frying strips, pot roasts, and ground meat, some parts from the **bottom round** are cut into steaks as well. ➤ For grilling or broiling, avoid the lean, tough **eye of round steaks.** The **knuckle** portion of the round lies above the kneecap and is also known as **round tip** or **sirloin tip** (this last name is used since the muscles here reach their full size in the sirloin portion). Steaks are cut from the knuckle and the tougher **outside round** that covers it, such as **sirloin tip** and **Western tip steaks,** respectively (the latter may need to be marinated or tenderized). Meat from this area may also be thinly sliced and used for dishes like Beef Braciole, 470, or Philly Cheese Steak, 140. Practically any steak cut from the top or bottom round may be tenderized with a special machine and turned into **cube steak;** the divots and increased surface area of cube steak makes it ideal for flouring and frying (see Chicken-Fried Steak, 461). The **heel** portion of the round has a lot of sinew and is very tough, making braising or stewing a necessity. Buried deep within the heel, there is one tender muscle called the **merlot steak,** which is suitable for grilling or searing (you will probably have to ask a specialty butcher to cut it from the heel).

Finally, for using the tough **hindshanks,** find cross-cut slices to prepare Osso Buco, 476, or cut the meat off the bone and use in stews. To use **oxtails** and **marrow bones,** see 519 and 520 respectively.

ABOUT ROASTING BEEF

For a primer on roasting, see 1050. We highly recommend roasting naturally tender beef cuts. The most prized (and most expensive) are the standing rib roast or boneless rib roast, strip loin roast, and tenderloin. Chuck eye roasts are cut from the same muscle group as the rib roast but are much more affordable. Top sirloin, tri-tip, sirloin tip, and top round roasts are also worth looking at. ➤ Do not cook tenderloin or roasts from the sirloin and round past medium-rare (their leanness and/or relative toughness will give a dry result). Of course, you may lard, 451, lean roasts to lend them juiciness and a richer flavor.

To prepare a roast for cooking, pat it dry and season liberally with salt and pepper. If you have the time, we highly recommend dry-brining, 451, beef roasts to increase flavor and promote browning. You may also wish to season the roast with a rub, 587. Boneless rib roast, strip loin, chuck eye, top round, and the thicker end of the tenderloin can be butterflied or Y-cut and stuffed with a filling (see About Stuffing Roasts and Thin Meats, 452).

When choosing the cooking method, remember: ➤ The thicker the roast, the gentler the heat should be for the majority of the cooking time. The same goes for roasts that taper in thickness, like tri-tip and coulotte. Lower heat will result in more evenly cooked meat (the same principle is at work in sous vide cooking, 1054). To a certain degree, this is a matter of preference: Some relish edge-to-edge medium-rare, others like a gradient of doneness (sometimes, to appease all diners, an unevenly cooked roast is just the thing). But there is no doubt that cooking large roasts at a consistently high temperature results in a thicker layer of overdone meat, which will be especially tough in roasts from the sirloin, round, or any cut of Select-grade beef.

Of course, high temperatures are needed to brown the surface of roasts. For small roasts like tenderloin, you may brown them quickly in a large skillet and finish them in the oven, as for Pan-Roasted Beef, 456. Increasing the oven temperature at the beginning or end of the cooking process gives slightly different results. Browning at the beginning is more convenient, since the cooking is done when the roast reaches the preferred temperature. Browning at the end, sometimes called **reverse searing,** takes a little extra time and effort, but results in more evenly cooked meat.

To carve roasts, steady the roast with a meat fork and slice the meat off any bones in one chunk. Then set the roast fat side up and cut it vertically into slices as thick or as thin as you like. A second method for rib roasts, shown below, is to set the roast on its side and cut it horizontally from the fat side toward the rib into thicker slices, removing the rib bones one at a time with a vertical cut as you carve off the slices.

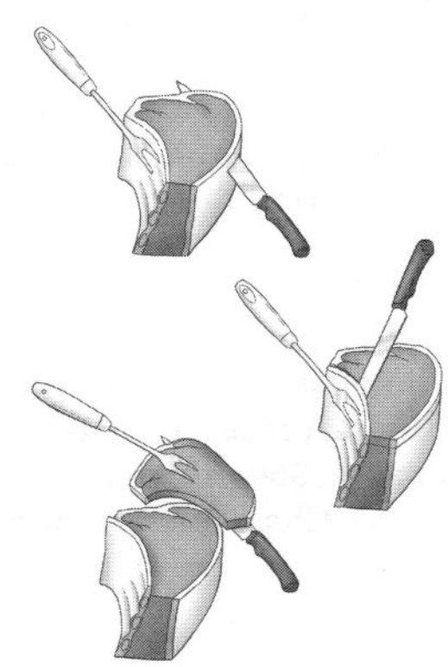

Carving a rib roast

MAKING A JUS

A simple method for boosting the flavor and enhancing the juiciness of roast beef is to make a quick **jus** (or juice) with the pan drippings as soon as the roast comes from the oven. Remove the cooked roast from the roasting pan and set it aside, loosely covered, to rest. Pour or spoon off any excess grease from the pan drippings.

Place the roasting pan over medium heat and add:

½ to ¾ cup of any flavorful stock, 75–79, preferably beef or mushroom

Bring the liquid to a boil and scrape the bottom of the pan with a wooden spoon until all the browned bits are dissolved. Season to taste with:

Salt and black pepper

Drizzle the jus over the sliced beef—or use the jus as the basis for (or enhancement of) a more robust sauce. For several options, see About Gravies and Pan Sauces, 544.

ROAST BEEF

2 servings per pound for bone-in roasts; 3 servings per pound for boneless roasts

This technique yields classic results in the shortest time. The roast will be pink in the center, with a bit of medium to medium-well done beef toward the crusty exterior. We recommend this method only for well-marbled cuts from the rib or loin. For a slower technique that results in more evenly cooked meat, see Slow-Roasted Beef, below.

Trim all but a ¼-inch thickness of fat from:

One beef roast from the rib or loin, bone-in or boneless

Season the roast liberally with:

About ½ teaspoon salt and ¼ teaspoon black pepper per pound of meat

Place fat side up on a rack set in a shallow roasting pan and refrigerate uncovered for at least 1 hour or up to 2 days to dry out the surface of the meat (this will promote browning).

When ready to cook, set the roast out at room temperature for 30 minutes and preheat the oven to 450°F.

Place the pan in the oven and roast for 20 minutes. Reduce the oven temperature to 300°F and roast until a thermometer inserted in the center of the thickest part registers between 120° and 130°F for rare to medium-rare (for other temperatures, see chart, 453). Begin checking smaller roasts after 20 minutes; thicker roasts may take 1½ hours. Transfer the meat to a platter, cover loosely with foil, and let stand for 15 to 20 minutes before carving (the temperature will rise 5 to 10 degrees during this time). If desired, make a jus, above, or:

(Basic Pan Gravy, 545)

Carve the roast into ⅛- to ½-inch slices as desired. Drizzle the jus or gravy over the slices. If not using either, serve with:

Chimichurri, 567, Salsa Verde, 567, Horseradish Sauce, 566, Z.26 Steak Sauce, 569, Béarnaise Sauce, 561, Sauce Meurette, 553, Sauce Chasseur, 551, or Sauce Marchand de Vin, 551

SLOW-ROASTED BEEF

2 servings per pound for bone-in roasts; 3 servings per pound for boneless roasts

As the name implies, this method takes longer, but yields consistent doneness from the center of the roast to near its surface. Use this method for any cut of beef; it is especially suited to thick roasts—which are prone to turning well-done on the outside before they cook all the way through—or smaller roasts of varying thicknesses like tri-tip and coulotte.

Trim all but a ¼-inch thickness of fat from:

One beef roast, bone-in or boneless

Season the roast liberally with:

About ½ teaspoon salt and ¼ teaspoon black pepper per pound of meat

Place fat side up on a rack set in a shallow roasting pan and refrigerate uncovered for at least 1 hour and up to 2 days to dry out the surface of the meat (this will promote browning).

Preheat the oven to 250°F.

Place the pan in the oven and roast until a thermometer inserted in the center of thickest part registers between 120° to 130°F for rare to medium-rare (for other temperatures, see chart, 453). For a thick roast, this may take 5 hours or more; for a tri-tip, begin checking the temperature after 30 minutes. Remove from the oven and let rest uncovered (the temperature will rise 5 to 10 degrees during this time). Meanwhile, increase the oven temperature to 500°F.

Once the meat has rested, return it to the hot oven and roast until the outside is well browned, about 10 minutes more. If desired, make a jus, gravy, or sauce as directed in Roast Beef, above. Carve the roast into ⅛- to ½-inch slices as desired. Drizzle any jus or gravy over the slices or serve with sauce on the side.

PAN-ROASTED BEEF

4 to 5 servings

Browning thicker steaks and smaller roasts in a skillet and then finishing them in a moderate oven results in a nice crust and an evenly cooked interior. Thicker roasts may also be cooked this way, as long as they comfortably fit in the pan. ➤ For steaks less than 2 inches thick, grill, pan-sear, or sauté them instead, 460–61.

Preheat the oven to 300°F. Pat dry:

One 1½-pound beef tenderloin roast or a large beef steak, 2 inches or more thick

Season with:

¾ teaspoon salt

½ teaspoon black pepper

If using the tapered end of the tenderloin, fold the thinner "tail" end of the tenderloin back along itself so that the roast is an even thickness; tie every 2 inches with butcher's twine. Heat in a large ovenproof skillet over medium-high heat:

1½ teaspoons vegetable oil, bacon fat, or lard

Add the beef and brown well on all sides, about 8 minutes. Transfer the skillet to the oven and roast until a thermometer inserted in the thickest part of the meat registers 120° to 130°F for rare to medium-rare, about 15 minutes for thick steaks and 20 to 25 minutes for tenderloin roasts (for other temperatures, see chart, 453).

Transfer to a plate and let stand for 5 to 10 minutes before slicing. Meanwhile, if desired, pour off all the fat from the skillet, place over medium-high heat, and make:

(Herb Pan Sauce, 546, or the pan sauce for Steak au Poivre, 461, or Steak Diane, 461)

Slice the meat and arrange on a platter. Spoon the pan sauce or any accumulated juices over the slices (or serve with any of the sauces suggested for Roast Beef, 456, on the side).

STUFFED EYE OF ROUND OR TOP ROUND ROAST

8 to 10 servings

Stuffing is a good way to boost the flavor of economical roasts while making them seem more tender and moist. Instead of using a simple Y-cut as directed below, you may butterfly the roast, 452, for a pinwheel effect.

Heat in a medium skillet over medium heat:

2 tablespoons olive oil

Add and cook, stirring, until softened, 6 to 8 minutes:

2 medium onions, chopped

Add and cook, stirring, until heated through, about 5 minutes:

1 cup finely chopped pancetta or ham (about 4 ounces)
1 cup cooked spinach, well drained and chopped
⅓ cup chopped green or black olives
2 garlic cloves, chopped
2 tablespoons chopped basil
2 teaspoons chopped parsley
1 teaspoon black pepper
½ teaspoon salt

Let cool, then stir in:

⅔ cup fresh bread crumbs, 957

Set aside. Have ready:

One 4-pound boneless beef eye of round or top round roast, trimmed of excess fat

Make a Y-cut as described on 452. Fill the cavities with the spinach mixture. Reshape the roast and tie it at 1½-inch intervals.

Season all over with:

1½ teaspoons salt
1 teaspoon black pepper

Place on a rack set in a shallow roasting pan and preheat the oven to 450°F.

Rub the surface of the meat with:

2 tablespoons vegetable oil

Transfer to the oven and roast for 15 minutes. Reduce the oven temperature to 325°F and cook until a thermometer inserted in the thickest part of the meat registers 120° to 130°F for rare to medium-rare (for other temperatures, see chart, 453). This should take 20 to 30 minutes. Remove the roast from the oven, cover loosely with foil, and let stand for 15 to 20 minutes before carving (the temperature will rise 5 to 10 degrees during this time). Cut into ¾-inch slices and serve.

BEEF WELLINGTON

6 to 8 servings

There are many steps and several components to this classic recipe, but the result never fails to impress: moist, rosy-centered beef tenderloin surrounded by a rich, concentrated filling of mushrooms and foie gras or pâté—all encased in a crisp pastry crust. A roast of uniform thickness is crucial to success. To prepare foie gras for cooking, see 446.

Pat dry:

One 3-pound center-cut beef tenderloin roast, well trimmed

Season with:

1 teaspoon salt
1 teaspoon black pepper

Place fat side up on a rack set over a rimmed baking sheet and refrigerate uncovered for at least 1 hour and up to overnight.

Heat in a heavy skillet over medium-high heat:

2 tablespoons vegetable oil

When the fat smokes, add the tenderloin roast and sear on all sides for about 8 minutes. Transfer to a plate and place in the refrigerator for at least 30 minutes. Meanwhile, prepare:

Triple recipe Duxelles, 252 (about 1½ cups)

After cooking the mixture as directed, keep the duxelles in the skillet and stir over low heat until it becomes dry, about 5 minutes more. Transfer to a medium bowl and add:

5 ounces (½ cup) foie gras, Pâté de Campagne, 513, Chicken Liver Pâté, 62, or store-bought liverwurst, mashed until smooth
3 tablespoons Madeira, sherry, or vermouth

Mix together until thoroughly combined and set aside. Position a rack in the center of the oven. Preheat the oven to 400°F.

Roll out to a ¼-inch-thick square large enough to wrap easily around the meat with some overlap:

1 pound Puff Pastry, 691, lightly chilled, or a 14 × 10-inch sheet frozen puff pastry, thawed

Whisk together in a small bowl:

1 egg
1 tablespoon water
1 tablespoon milk

Distribute dollops of the duxelles mixture over the pastry and spread evenly with a spatula, leaving a 1-inch border around the edges. Place the browned tenderloin in the center and gently drape the pastry around the roast, wrapping it in a neat package. Trim off and set aside any excess dough and seal the edges by brushing them with the egg wash and pressing them together. Lightly grease a rimmed baking sheet. Place the wrapped beef seam side down on the sheet and brush the top with egg wash. Use the reserved dough trimmings to make decorative leaves or scrolls, if desired. Cut 2 or 3 small evenly spaced neat holes in the top of the pastry to allow steam to escape and to allow you to insert a meat thermometer without breaking the crust. Bake until the crust is golden brown and a thermometer inserted in the thickest part of the roast registers 120° to 130°F for rare to medium-rare (for other temperatures, see chart, 453). Start checking the temperature after 25 minutes. If the pastry begins to get too brown during baking, cover it loosely with foil. Remove the roast from the oven and let stand, uncovered, for 15 to 20 minutes. Slice the roast at the table, using a serrated knife to cut ¾-inch-thick slices. If desired, serve with:

(Sauce Meurette, 553, Sauce Madeira, 551, or Sauce Marchand du Vin, 551)

CHUCK ROAST IN FOIL

10 to 16 servings

Wrapping a roast in foil: the everyman's Wellington. If your company is informal, do not cut the foil until you are at the table and ready to carve. The sudden burst of fragrance adds to the anticipation.

Preheat the oven to 300°F. Have ready:

One 5- to 8-pound bone-in chuck roast, such as a 7-bone chuck roast or arm roast

Place the roast on a double thickness of heavy-duty foil large enough to envelop it. Combine in a small bowl:

2 packages dried onion soup mix

1 teaspoon black pepper

Sprinkle the meat with half this mixture, then turn over and sprinkle with the remaining mix. Wrap the roast carefully in the foil, sealing it tightly so that no juices can escape. Place in a roasting pan and bake until a thermometer inserted in the thickest part of the roast registers 125° to 130°F for medium-rare, about 3½ to 4 hours (for other temperatures, see chart, 453). Let the meat rest for 10 minutes. Carefully unwrap the roast with tongs to allow the steam to escape. Carve into slices and serve with:

Mashed Potatoes, 265, or Spätzle, 308

Drizzle each serving with some of the pan juices.

ABOUT GRILLING, BROILING, AND SAUTÉING BEEF

These high-heat methods require tender cuts of beef, ideally those with some marbling. Steaks from the rib and loin are the classic choices here, though flat-iron, skirt, flank, hanger, bavette, and chuck eye steaks are all good choices, especially for the grill. For searing and sautéing, stick with boneless, crosscut steaks; their flat surface will make full contact with the pan and brown evenly. For hamburgers, see 144. For more on setting up a grill, or tips on sautéing, searing, and broiling, see the corresponding sections in Cooking Methods and Techniques, 1042.

Since a steak of average thickness will take 10 minutes or less to cook through, ➤ it is imperative that the surface of the meat be as dry as possible and the heat high in order to form a nice crust before the interior overcooks. This rule applies to browning steaks after sous vide cooking as well, 1054. Since high heat produces a lot of smoke, ➤ when broiling or searing, turn on an exhaust fan at its highest setting, open any windows or doors, and temporarily deactivate your smoke detector, if feasible (do not forget to turn it back on when you're done). When we lived in an apartment without an exhaust fan, we opened the kitchen window and placed a fan set on high speed in the kitchen doorway to blow any smoke out the window. Not a perfect setup, but it worked.

For sautéing steaks, a stainless steel sauté pan or skillet is best, since it will not react with wine or any other acidic ingredients you use to make pan sauces. For searing, a cast-iron skillet or flat griddle is ideal (we do not recommend grill pans). If broiling, use a broiler pan set on the top-most rack position.

For grilling roasts and thicker steaks, set up a two-zone fire, 1063. This way, if the beef has browned but not cooked through, it can be transferred to the cooler side, covered, and cooked the rest of the way with indirect heat. Of course, you can reverse this procedure (as is done in the oven for Slow-Roasted Beef, 456): Roasts and thicker steaks may be cooked on the cooler side of a covered grill until they are nearly done, rested, and then browned directly over the flames.

A quick way to cook beef is to cut any tender steak into cubes or strips and sauté or stir-fry over high heat. In addition to being convenient, such dishes are popular with those who enjoy the taste of beef but find a large slab of steak daunting or dull. Because the beef is cooked quickly over high heat, ➤ success depends on starting with naturally tender cuts, such as top loin or sirloin, or slicing tougher cuts such as hanger steak, flat-iron steak, skirt steak, and flank steak across the grain after cooking.

GRILLED BEEF ROAST

8 to 12 servings

Searing a beef roast over a hot fire, then finishing with indirect heat on the cooler side of a covered grill gives it a deliciously crusty exterior and a tender, moist interior. Drizzling the roast with the optional lemon juice deposits sugars on the surface—which helps it brown—while adding a nice flavor. If using a tenderloin, do not trim any of its fat (it will add to the wonderful charbroiled flavor). Though we prefer grilling smaller roasts, large roasts can be cooked in the same way. For especially even doneness, reverse the process and start large roasts on the cooler side of the grill with a medium-hot fire, then sear at the end directly over the flames (if the roast takes a long time to cook through to the desired doneness, a fresh load of hot charcoal may be added for the browning step).

Pat dry:

One 3- to 5-pound beef tenderloin or tri-tip roast

Season with:

1 tablespoon salt

2 teaspoons black pepper

If cooking a tenderloin, fold the thinner "tail" end back onto the roast to give it even thickness and tie it every 2 inches with butcher's twine. Set the roast aside on a rack. Prepare a hot, two-zone grill fire, 1063, or preheat a gas grill on high for 10 minutes. If using a gas grill, reduce the heat of one of the burners to low. Brown the beef well on both sides over the hotter side of the grill, about 5 minutes per side. With each turn, you may squeeze over the surface:

(Juice of ½ lemon)

Move the meat to the cooler side of the grill, cover, and cook until a thermometer inserted in the thickest part of the meat registers 120° to 130°F for rare to medium-rare (for other temperatures, see chart, 453). Place the meat on a platter, cover loosely with foil, and let stand for 10 minutes before carving. Cut the roast into ½-inch slices (with tri-tip, try to slice the meat across the grain). If desired, serve with:

(Chimichurri, 567, Horseradish Sauce, 566, Sauce Meurette, 553, or a flavored butter, 559–60)

GRILLED OR BROILED STEAK

4 servings

Cooking times for grilling and broiling are approximate and depend on the many variables of steaks and cooking temperatures. The best way to ensure proper doneness is with a good thermometer. Squeezing the optional lemon juice on the steaks is highly recommended: in addition to seasoning the steaks, the sugars left on the surface once the juice evaporates helps them brown.

Pat dry:

4 small or 2 large beef steaks, 1 to 2 inches thick

Season both sides of the steaks with:

2 teaspoons salt
1 teaspoon black pepper

Place the steaks on a rack set over a rimmed baking sheet or plate and refrigerate uncovered for at least 1 hour and up to overnight to dry out the surface of the meat (this will promote browning).

Prepare a hot grill fire, 1063, or place a broiler pan on a rack and preheat the broiler. If broiling, a 1-inch-thick steak should be about 2 inches from the heat; for 2-inch-thick steaks, lower the rack so the surface of the meat is 4 or 5 inches from the heat source.

Grill or broil the steaks, turning 1-inch-thick steaks once just past the halfway point in the cooking time; turn 2-inch-thick steaks more frequently. With each turn, you may squeeze over them:

(Juice of ½ lemon)

Cook until a thermometer inserted in the center of the steak registers 120° to 130°F for rare to medium-rare (for other temperatures, see chart, 453). If grilling thicker steaks, they may become sufficiently browned before reaching the desired doneness. If this happens, move them to a cooler section of the grill or farther from the broiler to complete cooking. Let rest 5 minutes before serving. If desired, serve with:

(Chimichurri, 567, Z.26 Steak Sauce, 569, Horseradish Sauce, 566, or a flavored butter, 559–60)

CARNE ASADA

4 servings

Spanish for "grilled meat," this flavorful, Mexican preparation is usually made with skirt steak. It can be done with other cuts, but few absorb marinades as well as skirt steak. For a spicier result, you may rub the steak with Mexican Adobo I, 584, instead of using the marinade below. Or, if time is of the essence, you may skip the marinade altogether and liberally sprinkle the steak with **2 tablespoons chili powder** and **1 teaspoon salt** (and squeeze the **juice of ½ lime** over the meat after each turn on the grill).

Combine in a food processor or blender:

½ cup orange juice
1 small onion, chopped
1 cup chopped cilantro leaves and stems
¼ cup lime juice
2 tablespoons distilled white or cider vinegar
2 tablespoons soy sauce
5 garlic cloves, chopped
1 teaspoon salt
1 teaspoon ground cumin
1 teaspoon black pepper

Process or blend until smooth and combined. Transfer to a large bowl and add:

1 to 1½ pounds skirt steak, flank steak, or sirloin flap (bavette)

Marinate in the refrigerator for at least 2 hours but no more than 5 hours. Remove the steak from the marinade, allowing the excess to drip off. If you have time, let the meat dry in the refrigerator, uncovered, on a rack set over a baking sheet for 1 hour.

Prepare a hot grill fire, 1063.

Grill the steak over the hottest part of the grill, turning occasionally until cooked to the desired degree of doneness (see chart, 453). Transfer to a cutting board and let rest for 5 minutes. Thinly slice the meat across the grain. Serve in Tacos, 146, Burritos, 147, or Tortas, 143.

STEAK FAJITAS

4 servings

Prepare the meat and set up the grill for:

Carne Asada, above

While the grill heats up, heat in a large skillet over medium-high heat:

2 tablespoons vegetable oil

Add and cook, stirring, until tender and browned, about 7 minutes:

2 medium onions, halved and thinly sliced
2 green bell or poblano peppers, or a combination, cut into strips
½ teaspoon salt

Toss with:

1 teaspoon dried oregano

Remove from the heat and cover to keep warm. Grill the meat as directed. While the meat rests, warm on the grill:

Twelve 6-inch flour tortillas

Slice the steak across the grain into thin strips. Serve with the tortillas and:

Pico de Gallo, 573, Table Salsa, 573, or other salsa of choice
Guacamole, 51
Sour cream

To assemble, place some steak and sautéed onions and peppers on each tortilla, and top as desired.

KALBI (KOREAN GRILLED SHORT RIBS)

4 servings

Unlike the fall-off-the-bone braised short ribs most of us are familiar with, Korean-style short ribs are cut crosswise through the rib bones into thin strips, and are then marinated and grilled until nicely charred. Serve with rice and lettuce or shiso leaves and tuck pieces of meat and clumps of rice inside the leaves to make **ssam.** If you cannot find crosscut short ribs that are sliced thin enough (look for them at Korean or pan-Asian supermarkets), you may slice **2 pounds beef brisket** across the grain into ¼-inch-thick slabs (to make slicing easier, first freeze the brisket for 30 minutes).

Have ready:

3 pounds short ribs, crosscut into ¼-inch-thick slices
Sprinkle the ribs with:
⅓ cup sugar
Rub the sugar all over the ribs and refrigerate for 1 hour. Meanwhile, whisk together in a medium bowl:
2 cups water
1 cup soy sauce
2 large garlic cloves, minced or grated on a rasp grater
1 tablespoon brown sugar
1 tablespoon black pepper
Place the short ribs in the marinade. Cover and refrigerate at least 1 hour and up to 2 days, turning the short ribs occasionally so that they marinate evenly.

Prepare a hot, two-zone grill fire, 1063.

Remove the ribs from the marinade and shake off any excess (do not rinse the ribs). Grill over the cooler part of the grill, turning once or twice, until well browned on both sides, about 8 minutes. Transfer to the hot side and let cook, covered, for 5 minutes more. Serve immediately with:
Cooked short-grain white rice, 343
Kimchi, store-bought or homemade, 941
Butter lettuce, romaine lettuce, or shiso leaves

BEEF KEBABS

4 to 6 servings

For more on kebabs, please read Skewer Cooking, 1065. If using wooden skewers, soak them in water for at least 1 hour.
Prepare one of the following:
Vietnamese-Style Marinade, 581, Thai-Style Lemongrass Marinade, 581, Balkan Marinade, 580, Beer Marinade, 581, or any paste, 583–86, or any dry rub, 587
Cut into 1-inch cubes:
1½ pounds boneless beef top loin, sirloin, or hanger steak
Combine the beef in a bowl with:
1 onion, cut into small wedges
(1 bell pepper, cut into 1-inch pieces)
Add the marinade, paste, or rub and toss to coat. Cover and marinate in the refrigerator for at least 2 hours.

Place a broiler pan on a rack set 3 to 4 inches below the heat and preheat the broiler and broiler pan; or prepare a medium-hot grill fire, 1063. Thread the meat and vegetables onto skewers. Broil or grill for 8 to 10 minutes, turning the skewers occasionally. Make a small incision in a cube of meat and check the center: It should be slightly less done than desired, for it will continue to cook somewhat off the heat. Serve immediately with:
Coconut Rice, 333, Rice Pilaf, 329, or Crispy Smashed Potatoes, 268
Or use as a filling for:
Flatbread or Pita Sandwiches, 145

LONDON BROIL

4 to 6 servings

Flank steak is the traditional cut for London broil, but much confusion has been created by butchers selling thickly sliced chuck roasts and top round roasts under the same name. Thus, it is best to think of London broil as a cooking method: Tough beef normally reserved for braising and stewing is quickly broiled until rare or medium-rare and then thinly sliced across the grain. Both of these measures keep the result tender and juicy. ➤ Never cook these cuts beyond medium-rare, or they will become tough and dry.
Have ready:
1 beef flank steak or a 1½-inch-thick boneless slab of chuck arm roast or top round roast (about 2 pounds)
If desired, marinate the beef for at least 2 hours in:
(Lemon Marinade, 580, Balkan Marinade, 580, Teriyaki Marinade, 582, or the marinade for Carne Asada, 459)
Pat the meat dry. If not using a marinade, season with:
1½ teaspoons salt
1 teaspoon black pepper
Place an ovenproof skillet or roasting pan on a rack set 3 to 4 inches below the heat and preheat the broiler and skillet. Once the skillet is hot, add the beef and broil on one side for 5 minutes. Turn it over and broil on the other side until a thermometer inserted in the thickest part of the meat registers 120° to 130°F for rare to medium-rare. Start checking for doneness after 3 to 4 minutes. Transfer the steak to a platter, let it rest for 5 minutes, then carve it across the grain into ¼-inch-thick slices. Serve with any of the suggested sauces for Grilled or Broiled Steak, 459.

PAN-SEARED STEAK

4 servings

Searing is an excellent method for achieving a crisp, browned crust on any steak up to 1½ inches thick; larger ones benefit from searing and then transferring to the oven to cook through (see Pan-Roasted Beef, 456). Unfortunately, the high heat creates smoke and splattering, so use your exhaust fan and open a window. If you would like to serve your steak with a pan sauce, consider lowering the heat a bit and sautéing them instead (see 461). For **Blackened Steaks,** season them with **¼ cup Cajun Blackening Spice, 587,** and omit the salt and pepper below.
Pat dry:
4 small or 2 large beef steaks, ¾ to 1½ inches thick
Season both sides of the steaks with:
2 teaspoons salt
1 teaspoon black pepper
Place the steaks on a rack set over a rimmed baking sheet or plate and refrigerate uncovered for at least 1 hour and up to overnight to dry out the surface of the meat (this will promote browning).

When ready to cook, preheat a large cast-iron skillet or griddle over medium-high heat for 10 minutes. Once the skillet has preheated, take the steaks out of the refrigerator (starting with cold steaks helps prevent overcooking). If the meat is very lean, lightly brush the steaks with:
(Vegetable oil or warmed rendered bacon, duck, or beef fat)
Add the steaks to the skillet, leaving plenty of space between them. Sear, uncovered, for about 5 minutes. Turn and sear the other side for 3 to 6 minutes. A thermometer inserted in the center of the steak should register 120° to 130°F for rare to medium-rare (for other

temperatures, see chart, 453). Turn the steaks more than once if one side gets too brown before they are done. Pour off any fat that accumulates during cooking. Serve with any of the suggested sauces for Grilled or Broiled Steak, 459.

SAUTÉED STEAK

4 servings

This technique produces steaks with a nicely browned exterior. Since the heat is slightly lower than it is for searing, the browned bits left in the skillet do not become black and bitter, and can be used to make a tasty pan sauce (see the recipes that follow). For more sauce ideas, please read About Gravies and Pan Sauces, 544.

Pat dry:

4 beef steaks, ¾ to 1½ inches thick

Season both sides of the steaks with:

2 teaspoons salt
1 teaspoon black pepper

Heat in a large stainless steel skillet over medium-high heat:

1 tablespoon vegetable oil or rendered bacon, duck, or beef fat

When the fat begins to smoke, add the steaks to the skillet without crowding. Cook for 5 to 7 minutes on each side, or until they reach 120° to 130°F for rare to medium-rare (for other temperatures, see chart, 453). Transfer the steaks to a warmed platter and let stand for 5 minutes before serving. Meanwhile, if desired, pour off any fat from the skillet and make:

(A pan sauce, 545–47)

STEAK DIANE

4 servings

This dish was created to entertain restaurant patrons with a tableside flambé. If you want to play with fire, after adding the brandy to the skillet, warm it for 10 seconds, and light with a long match, a long lighter, or a propane torch. Shake the skillet until the flames go out and then add the stock and the remaining ingredients. This pan sauce is also delicious with venison steaks or pork chops.

Prepare:

Sautéed Steak, above

While the steaks stand, pour off any fat in the skillet and return the skillet to medium-high heat. Melt:

2 tablespoons butter

Add and cook, stirring, until softened, about 2 minutes:

½ cup finely chopped shallots or green onions (white part only)

Stir in:

¼ cup brandy
¼ cup beef stock or broth
1 tablespoon Dijon mustard
2 teaspoons lemon juice
1 teaspoon Worcestershire sauce
Salt and black pepper to taste

Boil for 1 to 2 minutes, scraping up any browned bits. Add any juices from the steaks. If desired, remove from the heat and add bit by bit, swirling the skillet until melted:

(2 tablespoons butter)

Stir in:

2 tablespoons minced chives
2 tablespoons chopped parsley

Pour the sauce over the steaks and serve immediately.

STEAK AU POIVRE (PEPPERED STEAK WITH CREAM SAUCE)

4 servings

A French bistro classic.

Pat dry:

2 boneless beef strip steaks, cut in half, or 4 filet mignon steaks, 1½ inches thick

Press onto both sides of the steaks, working the seasonings into the meat:

¼ cup cracked black peppercorns
1 tablespoon salt

Heat a large stainless steel skillet over medium-high heat. Once the skillet is hot, add:

2 tablespoons vegetable oil

Add the steaks to the skillet, without crowding, and cook for 5 to 7 minutes on each side, or until they reach 120° to 130°F for rare to medium-rare (for other temperatures, see chart, 453). Transfer the steaks to a warmed platter and let stand, loosely covered. Pour off any excess fat from the skillet and add:

1 tablespoon butter
¼ cup minced onion or shallot

Cook, stirring, until just barely softened, about 1 minute. Remove the skillet from the heat and carefully add:

¼ cup brandy

Return the skillet to the heat and cook until the liquid is almost evaporated. Add and boil until reduced by half, about 5 minutes:

1 cup beef or veal stock or broth

Add and boil until reduced by half, about 4 minutes more:

¼ cup heavy cream

Stir in:

2 tablespoons chopped parsley
Salt and cracked black peppercorns to taste

Serve immediately over the steaks.

CHICKEN-FRIED STEAK

4 servings

Instead of pounding the steak, you may substitute **1½ pounds cube steak**. For tips on pounding meat, see 451.

Pound to ⅓ inch thick:

One 1½-pound beef round or rump steak

Cut into 4 serving pieces. Mix in a shallow bowl:

1 cup flour
2 teaspoons black pepper
1½ teaspoons salt
¾ teaspoon cayenne pepper

Whisk together in a second shallow bowl:

¼ cup milk
1 egg

Coat each steak with the seasoned flour, dip into the egg mixture, coat with the seasoned flour again, and shake off any excess. Let dry on a rack for 15 minutes.
Heat in a large heavy skillet over medium-high heat:
½ inch vegetable oil, vegetable shortening, or lard
Add the steaks and fry, turning once, until golden brown, 2 to 3 minutes each side. Transfer to a warmed platter and cover loosely. Pour off all but 2 to 3 tablespoons of fat from the skillet and set back on the heat. Add and cook, stirring, about 5 minutes:
1 onion, thinly sliced
Add and cook, stirring, for 2 to 3 minutes:
2 tablespoons all-purpose flour
Stir in and bring to a boil, scraping up any browned bits:
1 cup milk
Reduce the heat and simmer until thickened, 3 to 5 minutes. Season with:
Salt and black pepper to taste
(Dash of hot pepper sauce)
Pour over the steaks.

BEEF AND BROCCOLI STIR-FRY
4 to 6 servings
Please read about Stir-Frying, 1052. If desired, substitute asparagus, trimmed and cut into 2-inch pieces, for the broccoli.
Combine in a medium bowl:
¼ cup soy sauce
2 tablespoons Shaoxing wine, 952, or dry sherry
1 tablespoon water
1 tablespoon sugar
1 tablespoon cornstarch
2 teaspoons toasted sesame oil
Add and toss to coat:
1 pound boneless beef steak, such as flank steak, sliced across the grain into ½-inch-thick strips
Marinate for at least 20 and up to 30 minutes. Meanwhile, prepare:
1 pound broccoli, trimmed and cut into bite-sized florets
6 green onions, cut into 2-inch pieces
1 red bell pepper, thinly sliced
1 cup sliced mushrooms, preferably shiitake caps
Combine in a small bowl:
1-inch piece ginger, peeled and minced
3 garlic cloves, minced
(1 teaspoon red pepper flakes or Sichuan peppercorns)
Heat in a wok or large heavy skillet over high heat until shimmering:
2 tablespoons vegetable oil
Add the ginger-garlic mixture and cook, stirring constantly, until fragrant but not browned, about 30 seconds. Add the beef and its marinade and cook, stirring to separate the slices, until browned, about 2 minutes. Transfer the beef mixture to a plate. Wipe out the pan and reheat over high until shimmering:
2 tablespoons vegetable oil
Add the vegetables and stir-fry until crisp-tender, about 2 minutes. Return the meat and any accumulated juices to the pan and toss together for 10 seconds to heat through and combine. Serve with:
Cooked white rice, 343

SUKIYAKI
4 servings
Japan's famous "friendship dish" is prepared ceremoniously at table in an electric skillet or wok—or, less festively, in the kitchen in a wok or heavy skillet. Sukiyaki is traditionally served with beaten raw egg for dipping the cooked ingredients in. **Shungiku,** or **chrysanthemum greens,** are traditional to cook with this dish. Gathered from the crown daisy, they have a nice grassy, herbal flavor. Use the leaves as well as the crispy stems. Young, tender leaves (and flowers) can be added to salads, but the larger, mature greens should be cooked as they are here, stir-fried, or chopped and added as a garnish for hot soups.
For easy slicing, freeze for 20 minutes:
2 pounds boneless beef rib-eye steak
Slice ⅛ inch thick across the grain and arrange on a platter. Also arrange attractively on the platter:
4 green onions, cut into 1-inch pieces on the diagonal
8 shiitake mushrooms, stems discarded, caps thinly sliced, or 1 bunch enoki mushrooms
1 generous cup coarsely chopped shungiku or chrysanthemum greens or chopped napa cabbage
About 7 ounces firm tofu, pressed, 285, if desired, and cut into ¾-inch cubes
½ cup canned bamboo shoots, rinsed and thinly sliced
14 ounces shirataki (konjac) noodles
Combine in a small bowl:
½ cup sake
½ cup soy sauce
½ cup mirin
½ cup water
2 tablespoons sugar
Heat in a wok or skillet over medium heat until shimmering:
2 tablespoons vegetable oil
Add the beef and cook, turning frequently, without browning, about 3 minutes. Transfer the meat to a small plate. Add the sake mixture to the wok, cover, and bring to a simmer. Make neat little piles of the green onions, mushrooms, cabbage, tofu, bamboo shoots, and shirataki in the wok. Braise just until the mushrooms have softened; the vegetables should retain their crispness and color. As the ingredients cook through, remove them with a pair of chopsticks and divide among plates. Add the meat back to the broth as needed to reheat and season it. After all the ingredients have been eaten, if desired, add to the sauce remaining in the wok:
(4 ounces udon noodles, cooked)
The noodles will become coated with the sauce.

BECKER MONGOLIAN BEEF
4 servings
Stir together in a small bowl:
3 tablespoons soy sauce
2 tablespoons hoisin sauce or brown sugar
2 tablespoons rice vinegar
2 tablespoons water
1 tablespoon cornstarch
½ teaspoon sambal oelek, 969, sriracha, or 2 dashes hot pepper sauce

Heat in a large skillet over medium heat:

2 tablespoons vegetable oil

Add and cook, stirring, for about 2 minutes:

4 garlic cloves, thinly sliced

1-inch piece ginger, peeled and julienned

With a slotted spoon, transfer the garlic and ginger to a plate. Increase the heat to medium-high and brown in batches:

1 pound beef flank steak, skirt steak, or sirloin flap (bavette), cut into thin strips

Transfer the meat to the plate as each batch is browned. When all the meat is browned, return it to the skillet, along with the soy sauce mixture, the garlic, and ginger. Cook, stirring, over medium heat for 3 to 4 minutes to thicken the sauce. Stir in:

8 green onions, thinly sliced on the diagonal

Remove from the heat, cover, and let stand for 5 minutes to wilt the green onions. Serve over:

Cooked rice, 343

BEEF STROGANOFF

4 servings

This dish is traditionally made with tenderloin, but we prefer less expensive cuts that have more flavor. If you do use tenderloin, try to find the less expensive tips, the tapered "tail," or a portion from the sirloin or butt end. Seasoning and browning the beef in chunks and then cutting them into strips before adding back to the pan ensures a nice, browned crust and perfectly done meat.

Cut into 2-inch cubes or chunks:

1 pound beef tenderloin, top loin, sirloin tip, or hanger steak

Season with:

¾ teaspoon salt

½ teaspoon black pepper

Heat in a large skillet over medium-high heat:

1 tablespoon vegetable oil

Add the meat in batches, cooking until well browned on all sides, about 6 minutes per batch. Transfer to a cutting board. Pour out any excess fat, reduce the heat to medium, and melt in the skillet:

2 tablespoons butter

Add and cook, stirring until softened, about 5 minutes:

1 small onion or 2 medium shallots, chopped

Use a wooden spatula to scrape the browned bits off the bottom of the skillet as the moisture from the onions loosens them. Add:

8 ounces mushrooms, sliced

Cook, stirring, until the liquid released by the mushrooms has evaporated, about 8 minutes. Add:

1 cup beef stock or broth

(1 tablespoon Cognac)

Simmer for 10 minutes. Meanwhile, cut each browned beef cube into three slabs and then slice into ¼-inch-thick strips. Stir into the liquid in the skillet:

¾ cup sour cream

1½ teaspoons Dijon mustard

Return the meat and any accumulated juices to the skillet. Simmer—do not boil—until the meat is heated through but still medium-rare, about 2 minutes. Stir in:

1 tablespoon chopped dill, parsley, chives, or a combination

Salt and black pepper to taste

Serve immediately over:

Cooked egg noodles

ABOUT BRAISING, STEWING, AND BARBECUING BEEF

Braises and stews may seem time-consuming, but they actually involve very little active work: With a few hours of hands-off cooking, tough, economical cuts of beef reward with deeper flavors and a richly textured cooking liquid that can be served as a broth or easily turned into a sauce. Of course, pressure-cooking, 1059, and slow cooking, 1058, add much to the convenience side of the equation. For more on the basic technique, see Braising, Stewing, and Pot-Roasting, 1057. Though we often group barbecuing with grilling, smoking meats in a moist environment has much more in common with braising, as both transform tough cuts with slow, gentle heat and yield tender, flavorful, fall-off-the-bone results. For some guidance on setting up a smoker, see Barbecuing, 1066.

For braises and stews we recommend meat from the chuck, short rib, cross-rib, brisket, and bottom round. If you can find them, meat from the neck, cheeks, and shank are even better. ➤ If you substitute cheeks, heel, or shank for the cuts specified in these recipes, they may take longer to become tender. To add body to the braising liquid, consider substituting oxtails for a portion of the meat. For more on oxtails, see About Offal and Variety Meats, 514.

As with many full-flavored, slow-cooked dishes, beef stews are better one or two days after being made. Reheat stews gently, adding a bit more liquid if necessary. Serve in wide bowls with pasta, rice, potatoes, fresh bread, dumplings, or biscuits.

For stew, we recommend buying steaks or roasts and trimming and cutting them yourself into ½- to 3-inch cubes. Packaged, precut meat labeled "beef stew meat" is often more expensive per pound, and you never know what cut of beef you are getting. Small cubes will cook more quickly and give the stew a thicker, more homogeneous character, while large chunks maintain their shape. Large or small, the meat is done when tender enough to cut with a fork. For a fresher flavor, add more vegetables or herbs toward the end of cooking, giving them just enough time to cook through. ➤ To adapt a braising or stewing recipe to use a slow cooker, see 1058; for pressure-cooking, see 1059.

The most celebrated cut of beef to barbecue or smoke is the brisket, preferably whole or cut from the marbled point end. Brisket is notoriously temperamental and may take a very long time to become tender, but for the barbecue cook it is the ultimate cut to master (and it must be said that a well-prepared smoked brisket is truly a thing of beauty). For those looking to get their feet wet but are not quite ready to tackle brisket, a tied chuck roast may be smoked until tender in the same way as brisket, 469. Beef chuck has the advantage of being more uniformly marbled than brisket and is thus not as likely to dry out. Beef back ribs and short ribs are also more forgiving and comparatively speedy (see Smoked Beef Ribs, 470).

BEEF POT ROAST
6 to 10 servings
The key to a moist and tender pot roast is to cook the meat at a bare simmer. If your pot and lid are ovenproof, you may cook the roast on the bottom rack of a preheated 300°F oven.
Pat dry:
One 3- to 5-pound boneless beef chuck or bottom round roast
Season with:
1½ teaspoons salt
1 teaspoon black pepper
If possible, place the roast on a rack set in a rimmed baking sheet and refrigerate uncovered overnight to dry out the surface of the meat (this will promote browning).
Heat in a large Dutch oven over medium-high heat:
3 tablespoons vegetable oil
Add the roast and patiently brown it on all sides, about 20 minutes. You want a nice, dark brown color, but do not let it scorch. Transfer the meat to a plate. Pour off all but 2 tablespoons of fat from the pot and add:
2 onions, chopped
2 celery ribs, chopped
1 carrot, chopped
(1 turnip, chopped)
Cook, stirring occasionally, just until the vegetables begin to color, about 5 minutes. Add:
2 cups beef or chicken stock or broth, dry red wine, beer, water, or a combination
Bring to a boil and add:
1 bay leaf
1½ teaspoons chopped fresh thyme or ½ teaspoon dried thyme
Return the roast to the Dutch oven and cover. Reduce the heat under the pot to its lowest setting, so that the liquid just barely simmers. Cook, turning the roast every 30 minutes or so, until fork-tender. Flat roasts will take 1½ to 2½ hours; round or oblong roasts can take as long as 4 hours. Make sure there is always some liquid in the pot; add more as needed. When the meat is fork-tender, transfer it to a platter and cover with foil to keep warm. Skim off any fat from the surface of the liquid and strain the liquid, making sure to remove the bay leaf. Serve the pan juices as is, or to thicken the sauce, bring the liquid to a simmer and add:
(Kneaded Butter, 544, made with 1 tablespoon butter and 1 tablespoon all-purpose flour)
Whisk the mixture into the liquid and simmer, stirring constantly, until thickened.

STRACOTTO (ITALIAN POT ROAST)
8 to 10 servings
Traditionally made with Barolo, but good with any dry robust red wine. This is a fantastic dish for a Sunday supper, giving you left-overs to look forward to all week. The braising juices can be used to sauce pasta, and the meat, moistened with the pan sauce, makes excellent hot sandwiches on chewy rolls. If your pot and lid are not ovenproof, you may cook this on the stovetop at a low simmer.
Pat dry:
One 4-pound boneless beef chuck or bottom round roast
Season with:
1½ teaspoons salt
1 teaspoon black pepper
If possible, place the roast on a rack set in a rimmed baking sheet and refrigerate uncovered overnight to dry out the surface of the meat (this will promote browning).
Preheat the oven to 300°F.
Mince together (this may be done in a food processor):
5 garlic cloves
¼ cup packed parsley leaves
4 fresh sage leaves or 1 teaspoon dried sage
1 tablespoon fresh rosemary or 1 teaspoon dried rosemary
Set aside. Heat in a Dutch oven over medium-high heat:
3 tablespoons vegetable oil
Add the roast and brown it well on all sides, about 20 minutes. Transfer the roast to a plate and pour off all but 2 tablespoons of the fat. Return the pot to the heat and add:
1 onion, chopped
1 carrot, chopped
1 celery rib with leaves, chopped
1 bay leaf
Cook, stirring, until the onion is lightly browned. Stir in the herb mixture and cook for 30 seconds. Add and boil until the pot is almost dry:
½ cup dry red wine
2 tablespoons tomato paste
Stir in and bring to a simmer, scraping any browned bits from the bottom of the pot:
2 cups dry red wine
1 cup beef or chicken stock or broth
One 14½-ounce can crushed or diced tomatoes
Add the roast to the pot, bring to a gentle simmer, and cover. Transfer to the oven and cook until the meat is very tender, 2½ to 3 hours. Transfer the meat to a platter and cover with foil to keep warm. Skim off any fat from the surface of the liquid and remove the bay leaf. Taste and adjust the seasonings. If the sauce seems thin, simmer to reduce and thicken it. Carve the meat into ¼-inch-thick slices and moisten it with the braising liquid. Serve with:
Creamy Polenta, 322

SAUERBRATEN
8 servings
This sweet-sour pot roast has been in *Joy* from the beginning. Irma was never "brave enough" to add gingersnaps to the gravy, but we think it gives the dish a nice flavor.
Combine in a medium saucepan and heat, stirring, until the sugar is dissolved:
2 cups distilled white or white wine vinegar
2 cups water
1 medium onion, sliced
¼ cup sugar
(2 teaspoons caraway seeds)

1 teaspoon black peppercorns
6 whole cloves
(4 juniper berries)
4 allspice berries
2 bay leaves

Let cool, then transfer to a large, heavy-duty zip-top bag or a large bowl. Add and turn to coat:

One 4- to 5-pound boneless beef chuck, top round, or bottom round roast, trimmed of excess fat

Cover and refrigerate for 2 days, turning the roast once a day.

When ready to cook, drain the meat, reserving the marinade, and pat dry. Strain the marinade and reserve the liquid. Season the meat with:

2 teaspoons salt
1 teaspoon black pepper

Heat in a large heavy pot or Dutch oven over medium heat:

2 tablespoons vegetable oil

Add the roast and brown on all sides, about 20 minutes. Remove the meat and pour off all but 2 tablespoons of fat from the pot. Add and cook, stirring, until the vegetables begin to soften, about 5 minutes:

1 onion, chopped
1 carrot, chopped
1 celery rib, chopped

Add the roast and half of the reserved marinade (discard the rest). Add enough:

Chicken or beef stock or broth

to come halfway up the sides of the meat. Bring to a boil, then reduce the heat, cover, and simmer (or place in a preheated 300°F oven) until the meat is completely tender, 2½ to 3 hours. Transfer the meat to a platter and cover to keep warm. Skim the fat from the cooking liquid and reduce the liquid over high heat to about 2½ cups. Stir in:

¼ cup crushed gingersnaps or dried rye bread crumbs

Cook, stirring, until the sauce begins to thicken, about 5 minutes. If desired, whisk in off the heat:

(¾ cup sour cream)

Slice the meat and serve with the gravy and:

Potato Dumplings, 306, Latkes, 269, or cooked egg noodles

BEEF STEW

6 to 8 servings

As with all stews, the flavors deepen if chilled overnight and reheated. Also, once chilled, the fat is easily skimmed from the top.

Trim, pat dry, and cut into 2-inch cubes:

2 pounds boneless beef stew meat, such as chuck, brisket, or bottom round

Season with:

1 teaspoon salt
½ teaspoon black pepper

Dredge in:

½ cup flour

Shake off any excess flour. Heat in a Dutch oven over medium-high heat:

2 tablespoons vegetable oil or rendered bacon or beef fat

Add the meat in batches and brown on all sides, being careful not to crowd the pot or scorch the meat. Remove with a slotted spoon. Pour off all but 2 tablespoons of fat from the pot (or add more if needed). Add:

1 onion, chopped
1 carrot, chopped
1 celery rib, chopped
4 garlic cloves, chopped

Cover and cook, stirring often, over medium heat until the onions are softened, 6 to 8 minutes. Return the meat to the pot and add:

3 cups beef or chicken stock or broth, dry red or white wine, beer, or a combination
2 bay leaves
1 teaspoon dried thyme, oregano, savory, marjoram, or a combination
½ teaspoon salt
½ teaspoon black pepper

Bring to a boil, then reduce the heat, cover, and simmer gently (or place in a preheated 300°F oven) until the meat is fork-tender, 1½ to 2 hours. Add:

2 carrots, cut into 1-inch chunks
4 medium red or gold potatoes, peeled and cut into 1-inch chunks
(2 small turnips, peeled and cut into 1-inch chunks)
(2 small parsnips, peeled and cut into 1-inch chunks)

Cover and cook until the vegetables are tender, 35 to 40 minutes. Remove the pot from the heat and remove the bay leaves. Chill the stew overnight, if desired. Skim off any fat from the surface of the stew and return to a faint simmer over medium-low heat (if necessary). Taste and adjust the seasonings. If desired, to thicken the sauce, whisk into the stew:

(Kneaded Butter, 544, made with 1 tablespoon butter and 1 tablespoon all-purpose flour)

Simmer, stirring, until thickened. Garnish with:

Chopped parsley

BOEUF BOURGUIGNON

6 to 8 servings

This robust stew typifies the earthy, full-flavored cooking of Burgundy, France. Choose a light, dry red wine such as pinot noir (the grape of Burgundy) or Beaujolais and marinate the beef overnight for the most flavor.

Cut into 2-inch cubes:

3 pounds boneless beef stew meat, such as chuck, brisket, or bottom round

Place the meat in a large bowl and add:

One 750ml bottle dry red wine
2 tablespoons olive oil
1 onion, cut into wedges
1 carrot, thickly sliced
1 celery rib, thickly sliced
3 garlic cloves, smashed
4 sprigs parsley

3 sprigs fresh thyme or ½ teaspoon dried thyme
1 teaspoon cracked black peppercorns
1 bay leaf
½ teaspoon salt

Stir to combine and coat the meat. Cover and marinate in the refrigerator for at least 2 hours, but preferably overnight.

Drain the beef, reserving the marinade, and pat dry. Strain the marinade and reserve the liquid and the vegetables separately. Heat in a large Dutch oven over medium heat:

4 ounces bacon, diced

Cook until the bacon is browned and rendered. Transfer the bacon to a plate, leaving the fat in the pot. You should have 2 tablespoons. If not, add vegetable oil as needed. Add the meat in batches and slowly brown on all sides. Transfer to the plate with the bacon. Add the reserved vegetables to the pot and cook until lightly browned, about 8 minutes. Stir in:

2 tablespoons all-purpose flour

Cook, stirring, until beginning to brown, about 1 minute. Stir in the reserved marinade and return the browned beef and bacon to the pot. If the marinade does not cover the beef and vegetables, add:

Additional wine or water

Bring to a boil. Reduce the heat, cover, and simmer gently (or place in a preheated 300°F oven) until the meat is fork-tender, 1½ to 2 hours. Remove the herb sprigs and bay leaf. Chill the stew overnight, if desired. Skim off any fat from the surface of the stew and return to a faint simmer over low heat (if necessary).

Meanwhile, melt in a large skillet over medium heat:

3 tablespoons butter

Add and cook, stirring often, until lightly browned and just tender, 5 to 8 minutes:

2 cups pearl onions, peeled

Add and cook, stirring, until the mushrooms release their juices:

8 ounces mushrooms, sliced

Add the mushrooms and onions to the stew, along with:

¼ cup chopped parsley
Salt and black pepper to taste

If you wish to thicken the sauce, whisk in:

(Kneaded Butter, 544, made with 1 tablespoon butter and 1 tablespoon all-purpose flour)

Simmer, stirring, until thickened. Serve with:

Thick, toasted slices of baguette or other crusty bread

CARBONNADE FLAMANDE (BELGIAN BEEF AND BEER STEW)

4 to 6 servings

Pat dry and cut into 1½-inch cubes:

2 pounds boneless beef stew meat, such as chuck, brisket, or bottom round

Season with:

½ teaspoon salt
½ teaspoon black pepper

Melt in a large Dutch oven over medium heat:

2 tablespoons butter

Add the meat in batches and brown on all sides. Transfer to a plate. Drain all but 2 tablespoons of the fat from the pot (if necessary, add more fat). Add and cook, stirring, until soft, about 8 minutes:

1 medium onion, thinly sliced

Mix in and cook, stirring occasionally, for an additional 2 minutes:

2 tablespoons all-purpose flour

Add:

2 cups beer, such as a dark lager
1 garlic clove, minced
½ teaspoon sugar
½ teaspoon salt

Return the meat to the pot. Bring to a boil, then reduce the heat, cover, and simmer gently (or place in a preheated 300°F oven) until the meat is tender, 2 to 2½ hours. Transfer the meat to a platter and strain the sauce through a medium-mesh sieve. If desired, stir into the sauce:

(½ teaspoon cider vinegar or sherry vinegar)

Serve the meat with the sauce and:

Boiled new potatoes, 265, garnished with parsley or dill

HEARTY BEEF RAGU

8 to 10 servings

The flavors of this ragu will deepen if chilled overnight and reheated. Also, once chilled, the fat is easily skimmed from the top. We love to substitute lamb shoulder chops or country-style pork ribs for the beef (a combination of meats is also quite good). For a ragu based on ground meat, see Bolognese Sauce, 558 (and Cincinnati Chili Cockaigne, 502, or Keema Alu, 503, if we're allowed to be indulgent with the term "ragu").

Preheat the oven to 300°F.

Pat dry:

2 pounds boneless chuck, brisket, neck, or bottom round, cut into 1-inch cubes, or 3 pounds bone-in short ribs, crosscut shank, or oxtails

Heat in a Dutch oven or heavy pot over medium-high heat:

2 tablespoons vegetable oil

Add the meat in batches and brown on all sides. Transfer to a plate. Pour off all but 2 tablespoons of fat from the pot (or add more if needed). Add:

1 large onion, finely chopped
1 medium carrot, finely chopped
1 medium celery rib with leaves, finely chopped
4 garlic cloves, chopped

Cook, stirring occasionally, until the vegetables soften, 8 to 10 minutes. Stir in:

2 tablespoons tomato paste

Cook, stirring, until the tomato paste has browned and is sticking a little to the bottom of the pot. Add:

1 cup dry red or white wine

Bring to a boil, scraping to release the browned bits on the bottom of the pot. Stir in:

Two 28-ounce cans whole tomatoes
1½ teaspoons dried oregano
½ teaspoon red pepper flakes

1 bay leaf
(4 anchovy fillets, chopped)

Bring to a simmer, crushing some of the tomatoes against the side of the pot with a spoon or spatula. Return the meat to the pot, cover, and transfer to the preheated oven. Cook until the meat is very tender, 3 to 4 hours.

Remove the bay leaf. If using bone-in cuts, transfer them to a rimmed baking sheet. When cool enough to handle, shred the meat from the bone, discarding any gristly bits, and return to the pot. Chill the ragu overnight, if desired. Skim off any fat from the surface of the stew, return to a faint simmer over low heat (if necessary), and season to taste with:

Salt and black pepper

Serve with:

Cooked pasta, such as ziti, penne, or pappardelle

Top each serving with:

Chopped parsley, oregano, or a combination
Grated Parmesan or Romano

BEEF RENDANG (INDONESIAN DRY CURRY)

6 servings

Think of rendang as a concentrated, caramelized coconut curry. Once the meat is tender, the coconut milk is briskly reduced. When all the water boils off, the meat, sugars, curry paste, and coconut solids start to fry in coconut oil. This caramelizes the mixture and turns the stew a deep brown. The only downside to this fantastically delicious dish is that ➤ rendang requires vigilance and frequent stirring, especially toward the end when the mixture tends to scorch if not tended to (we also highly recommend using a splatter screen). The payoff is well worth it.

Soak in water for 30 minutes:

8 small dried chiles, such as bird's eye or chiles de árbol, stemmed and seeded

Drain the chiles and place in a food processor along with:

8 ounces shallots, chopped
2 stalks lemongrass, white part only, thinly sliced
6 garlic cloves, peeled
1-inch piece ginger, peeled and chopped
(1-inch piece galangal, peeled and chopped)
1-inch piece turmeric root, peeled and chopped, or ½ teaspoon ground turmeric
(¼ teaspoon grated or ground nutmeg)

Process to a thick paste, scraping down the sides of the bowl as needed. Heat in a large skillet or Dutch oven over medium-high heat until shimmering:

3 tablespoons vegetable oil

Add the paste and fry until browned and fragrant, about 5 minutes. Add:

2 pounds chuck roast, bottom round, or boneless short ribs, cut into 1-inch cubes

Mix the beef together thoroughly with the paste, then add:

Two 13½-ounce cans coconut milk
1 tablespoon seedless tamarind pulp or tamarind paste, 195
1 tablespoon coconut sugar or dark brown sugar
1 stalk lemongrass, bruised
2 whole star anise
One 2- to 3-inch cinnamon stick
4 whole cloves
3 green cardamom pods, lightly crushed

Bring the mixture to a simmer. Cover, reduce the heat to low, and simmer, stirring occasionally, until the beef is nearly tender, about 1 hour. Uncover, increase the heat to medium-high, and bring to a lively simmer. Reduce the mixture until the coconut milk has nearly evaporated and the paste and beef start to fry and turn brown, 25 to 30 minutes. ➤ Stir the mixture every 2 minutes as the liquid reduces, scraping the bottom and sides of the pan to make sure the sauce does not scorch. It will sputter, so partially cover the pan or use a splatter screen. ➤ For the last 10 minutes, reduce the heat to medium and stir more frequently. If the thickening liquid bubbles too violently, or if it starts to brown more quickly than you care to scrape the pan, reduce the heat. When the mixture stops sputtering and starts frying, break up the meat a bit with a spatula and fry over medium-low until the rendang is mahogany-brown. Push the meat to one side, tilt the pan, and spoon off as much fat as possible. Pick out the whole spices and discard. Stir in:

(6 makrut lime leaves, stems removed, very thinly sliced)
¼ cup flaked unsweetened dried coconut, toasted, 973

Season to taste with:

Salt

Serve immediately over:

Cooked white rice, 343, or Coconut Rice, 333

HUNGARIAN GOULASH (PÖRKÖLT)

6 servings

Beef shank meat is a common ingredient in this dish, as is veal—substitute at will.

Pat dry and cut into 1-inch cubes:

2 pounds boneless beef chuck, brisket, or bottom round

Toss with:

1 teaspoon salt
½ teaspoon black pepper

Heat in a Dutch oven over medium-high heat:

¼ cup vegetable oil or bacon fat

Add the meat in batches and brown on all sides. Transfer to a plate. Drain all but 2 tablespoons fat from the pot (if necessary, add more fat), reduce the heat to medium, and add:

2 large onions, thinly sliced

Cook, stirring, for 5 minutes. Add and cook for 5 minutes more:

8 ounces Hungarian wax peppers or 1 green or red bell pepper, chopped
6 garlic cloves, coarsely chopped

Return the meat to the pot along with:

2 cups beef stock, chicken stock, or tomato juice
1 cup red wine
¼ cup Hungarian sweet paprika
2 tablespoons tomato paste
1 teaspoon dried marjoram or ¾ teaspoon dried oregano

(½ teaspoon caraway seeds)
1 bay leaf

Cover the pot and simmer until tender, about 1½ hours. Skim any fat from the surface and remove the bay leaf. Serve over:

Spätzle, 308, Potato Gnocchi, 306, Malfatti, 307, or boiled new potatoes, 265

If desired, garnish each serving with:

(A dollop of sour cream)
(Chopped parsley or dill)

GUYANESE PEPPERPOT

6 to 8 servings

This richly spiced dish is traditionally served on Christmas morning in Guyana. **Cassareep** is a thick, dark, heavily seasoned, molasses-like syrup made from yuca, 284. Though scarce in this country, it is worth seeking out for the irresistible flavor it adds to this stew. Order cassareep online, or find it at well-stocked Caribbean markets. If you cannot find it, substitute ⅓ **cup molasses, 1 tablespoon soy sauce,** and **1 tablespoon Worcestershire sauce.** Pork, lamb, or mutton shoulder may be substituted for the beef.

Pat dry and cut into 1½-inch pieces:

3 pounds boneless beef stew meat, such as chuck, brisket, or bottom round

Season with:

1 teaspoon salt
½ teaspoon black pepper

Heat in a large pot or Dutch oven over medium heat:

1 tablespoon vegetable oil

Add the meat in batches and brown on all sides. Transfer to a plate. Drain all but 1 tablespoon of fat from the pot (if necessary, add more fat) and add:

1 large onion, chopped
4 garlic cloves, chopped

Cook, stirring, until softened, about 6 minutes. Return the meat to the pot along with:

½ cup cassareep (see headnote)
2 habaneros or 3 to 4 wiri wiri peppers, left whole, or seeded and chopped
2-inch piece ginger, peeled and minced
3 tablespoons brown sugar
Two 3-inch strips orange zest, removed with a vegetable peeler
4 sprigs thyme
One 2- to 3-inch cinnamon stick
(¼ teaspoon ground allspice)
3 whole cloves

Add enough water to the pot to just cover the meat. Bring to a boil, then reduce the heat, cover, and simmer gently over medium-low heat until the meat is completely tender, about 3 hours. Remove the cinnamon stick, herb sprigs, and orange zest (and peppers, if left whole) and serve as a stew with:

Crusty white bread

Or, to serve over rice, transfer the meat to a plate with a slotted spoon. Reduce the liquid in the pot over medium-high heat until it has thickened into a sauce. Return the meat to the pot, let stand for a few minutes, and serve with:

Cooked rice, 343, Coconut Rice, 333, or Jamaican Rice and Peas, 331

Garnish with:

Chopped cilantro

BEEF MASSAMAN CURRY

5 to 6 servings

Fully cooked chunks of potato are sometimes added to this richly spiced Thai curry at the end, but we like to cook the potatoes in the sauce so they soak up the flavors of the curry while lending it body.

Combine in a deep heavy skillet, pot, or Dutch oven:

½ cup canned coconut milk
¼ cup Massaman curry paste, store-bought or homemade, 585

If using store-bought paste, also add:

(One 2-inch cinnamon stick)
(1 whole star anise)
(4 green or 2 black cardamom pods)

Cook over medium heat, stirring frequently and scraping up the curry paste from the bottom of the pan, until the coconut milk reduces, the oil separates out of the coconut milk, and the curry paste begins to fry. Stir in:

1½ pounds beef chuck, cut into ¾-inch cubes
1¼ cups canned coconut milk
1 cup water
3 large shallots, thinly sliced
2 tablespoons coconut sugar or brown sugar
2 tablespoons fish sauce
¼ teaspoon salt

Bring to a boil, cover, and reduce the heat to simmer gently until the beef is very tender, about 1 hour. Remove any whole spices, if used.

Add to the pan:

12 ounces gold or red potatoes, cut into ½-inch chunks
2 tablespoons tamarind paste or concentrate, 195

Simmer, covered, until the potatoes are tender, 20 to 25 minutes.

Stir in:

¼ cup roasted unsalted peanuts, coarsely chopped

Serve with:

Cooked short-grain rice, 343

Garnished with:

Chopped cilantro or Thai basil leaves

CHILI CON CARNE

6 to 8 servings

A classic Texas dish of stewed, spiced beef chunks (for chilis that use ground meat, see 502–3). To combine Texas classics, try making this dish with leftover Smoked Brisket, 469: Start by cooking the onions, garlic, and peppers. When the mixture has simmered for 30 minutes, cut the brisket into 1-inch cubes, add to the pot, and cook for another 30 minutes. To make a **Frito pie** or **walking taco,** open an individual package of corn snacks on one side with scissors, ladle ½ cup warm chili over the Fritos in the bag, and top with finely chopped onion and shredded Cheddar to taste. Serve with hot sauce.

Pat dry:

3 pounds boneless beef chuck, trimmed and cut into ½- to 1-inch cubes

Season with:

1½ teaspoons salt

Heat in a large skillet over medium-high heat:

2 tablespoons vegetable oil

Add the meat in batches and brown on all sides. Transfer to a plate. Pour off all but 2 tablespoons oil from the skillet (if necessary, add more fat). Add:

2 large onions, chopped
10 garlic cloves, chopped
2 to 6 jalapeño peppers, seeded and chopped
½ teaspoon salt

Cook, stirring often, until the vegetables are softened, 6 to 8 minutes. Stir in:

½ cup chili powder, store-bought or homemade, 588

Cook for 2 minutes. Return the meat to the skillet along with:

One 28-ounce can whole tomatoes
4 cups water
1 tablespoon red wine vinegar or cider vinegar

Simmer uncovered, stirring occasionally, until the meat is tender and the sauce is reduced and thickened, 1½ to 2 hours. While the chili simmers, crush the tomatoes against the side of the skillet with the back of a wooden spoon. Season to taste with:

Salt

SWEET-AND-SOUR BRISKET

6 to 8 servings

You can serve this immediately, but it is much better if prepared a day ahead, chilled, and reheated, as directed in this recipe.

Preheat the oven to 350°F.

Pat dry:

One 3½- to 4-pound beef brisket flat portion (or "first cut"), trimmed

Season with:

1½ teaspoons salt
1 teaspoon black pepper

Heat in a roasting pan over medium-high heat:

2 tablespoons vegetable oil

Brown the brisket, about 5 minutes each side, then transfer to a plate. Reduce the heat to medium, add more oil if needed, and add:

2 large onions, sliced

Cook the onions until golden brown, about 10 minutes. Add:

½ cup dry red wine
½ cup beef stock or broth

Cook for 1 minute, scraping up the browned bits. Stir in:

1 cup mild, tomato-based chili sauce
½ cup cider vinegar
½ cup packed dark brown sugar
1 bay leaf

Taste the sauce and adjust the seasoning. Return the meat to the pan and spoon the sauce over it. Cover the pan tightly with foil, transfer to the oven, and cook until the brisket is fork-tender, 2 to 3 hours. Remove the pan from the oven, uncover, and let cool in the pan, then refrigerate overnight. Remove the bay leaf, slice the meat, and return it to the sauce. Reheat in a 350°F oven for 25 to 30 minutes.

SMOKED BRISKET

10 to 16 servings

For feeding a crowd, you can special order a whole "packer" brisket, which weighs 10 to 15 pounds and serves at least 12. Smoking whole brisket is notoriously difficult to master, and it can take upward of 16 hours to properly barbecue. To be safe, give yourself 20 hours from the time a whole brisket goes on the grate to when guests arrive; if done well ahead of time, wrap tightly in foil, place on a rimmed baking sheet, and keep warm in an oven set to its lowest temperature. Of course, smaller portions cut from the brisket are much more manageable. The easiest to find is the brisket flat, or "first cut," which runs from 6 to 8 pounds. Unfortunately, the flat is very lean, which is why we recommend finding the marbled point end, or "second cut." At an average of 3 to 4 pounds, they are relatively small, so you will need 2 or 3 to feed a crowd. If, heaven forbid, you have leftovers, cut the meat into 1-inch cubes and use to make a batch of Chili con Carne, 468.

Please read about Barbecuing, 1066. Trim all but ¼ inch of fat from:

1 whole beef brisket, 1 brisket flat ("first cut"), or 2 or 3 point-end ("second cut") portions

Rub all over with:

½ cup Southern Barbecue Dry Rub, 587, Coffee Spice Rub, 587, or ½ teaspoon each salt and black pepper for every pound of meat

Place on a rack set in a rimmed baking sheet and refrigerate uncovered overnight, or for up to 2 days.

Heat a smoker or grill set up for barbecuing, 1067, to 225° to 250°F (preferably with a water pan). Add to the coals:

One small chunk of dry hickory, oak, or mesquite wood

Add the brisket to the cooler side of the smoker or grill and cover so that the top vent pulls smoke across the meat. Adjust the vents to maintain the temperature (this is difficult and may take practice, or, in the worst case, a fresh load of charcoal). You may add another small chunk of hickory wood every hour for the first 4 hours. If you do not have a water pan inside to keep the smoker or grill humid, baste the meat every 2 hours with:

(Basic Mop, 583, or Beer Mop, 583)

Smoke the brisket until it has reached an internal temperature of 200° to 205°F in its thickest part, or until the meat wants to shred easily when lightly prodded with a fork; this can take 10 to 14 hours for a brisket flat or point-end portions, and up to 20 hours for a whole brisket. To quicken the pace somewhat, you may wrap the brisket in a double thickness of foil when it reaches 150°F and return it to the smoker to finish cooking (keep in mind that this will soften the brisket's crunchy, spice-rubbed surface, or "bark").

When the brisket is tender, transfer to a rimmed baking sheet or large platter, remove any foil (save the juices!), and rest for at least 15 minutes. Slice across the grain and serve with:

Chipotle Barbecue Sauce, 582, Kansas City Barbecue Sauce, 582, or another sauce of your choosing

If you have wrapped the brisket in foil, be sure to stir some of the accumulated juices into the sauce. For serving as sandwiches, set the barbecue sauce at the table and provide:

10 to 16 warmed hamburger buns or soft white bread
A coleslaw, 119–20

Bread-and-Butter Pickles, 924, Pickled Peppers, 927, or Taqueria Pickles, 930

Or serve as part of a "meat-and-three" with the toast and coleslaw along with two (or more) of the following:

Southern-Style Greens, 243, Frijoles de la Olla, 213
Creamy Potato Salad, 127, German Potato Salad, 127

SMOKED BEEF RIBS

5 or 6 servings

Much less troublesome than brisket, quicker to prepare, and assuredly delicious. Do not balk at the amount of back ribs called for; their long, thick bones account for most of their weight. When scaling up, be sure your smoker can accommodate the number of back rib slabs you wish to serve.

Please read about Barbecuing, 1066. Pat dry:

10 to 12 pounds beef back ribs (about two 7-bone slabs) or 4 to 5 pounds beef short ribs, as bone-in slabs or cut into individual ribs

If using back ribs, be sure the membrane on the concave side of the ribs has been removed. To peel the membrane from the ribs, see 487. If using short ribs, trim off all but a thin layer of fat from their meaty side. Rub on all sides with (using the lesser quantities for short ribs):

⅓ to ½ cup Southern Barbecue Dry Rub, 587, Coffee Spice Rub, 587, or 1 to 2 tablespoons each salt and black pepper

Place on a rack set in a rimmed baking sheet and refrigerate, uncovered, overnight and for up to 2 days. Heat a smoker or grill set up for barbecuing, 1067, to 300°F (preferably with a water pan). Add to the coals:

One small chunk of dry hickory, oak, or fruitwood such as apple or cherry

Add the ribs to the cooler side of the smoker or grill and cover so that the top vent pulls smoke across the meat. Adjust the vents to maintain the temperature (this is difficult and may take practice, or, in the worst case, a fresh load of charcoal). You may add another small chunk of hickory wood every hour for the first 4 hours. If you do not have a water pan inside to keep the smoker or grill humid, baste the meat every 2 hours with:

(Basic Mop, 583, or Beer Mop, 583)

Cook the ribs until they are tender and their bones wiggle, about 4 hours for back ribs, and up to 9 hours for short ribs. ➤ Do not cover the ribs in foil to shorten the cooking time. If desired, brush the ribs for the last hour of cooking with:

(Kansas City Barbecue Sauce, 582, Chipotle Barbecue Sauce, 582, or Kentucky-Style Mutton Dip, 583)

BRUNSWICK STEW

10 servings

A smokehouse classic. In the words of Southern humorist Roy Blount Jr., "Brunswick stew is what happens when small mammals carrying ears of corn fall into barbecue pits." For ease of sourcing, our version is made with chicken and leftover smoked meat (a defining feature of the dish in North Carolina). If you happen to have hunters in the family, feel free to substitute small game like rabbit and squirrel, 524, with the understanding that wild meats may take longer to become tender.

Remove the skin from:

2½ pounds bone-in chicken thighs or whole legs

Season with:

1½ teaspoons salt
½ teaspoon black pepper

Heat in a Dutch oven over medium-high heat:

2 tablespoons bacon fat or vegetable oil

Add the chicken and brown on all sides. Transfer to a plate. Add enough oil or fat to the pot to equal 2 tablespoons, and reduce the heat to medium. Add:

1 large onion, chopped
2 celery ribs, chopped

Cook, stirring occasionally, until tender, 6 to 8 minutes. Return the chicken and any accumulated juices to the pot along with:

One 28-ounce can whole tomatoes, chopped, with their juice
3 cups fresh or frozen lima beans
2 cups chopped leftover barbecue, such as smoked brisket, pork shoulder, mutton, or rib meat
2 cups chicken stock or broth or water
1 cup diced red or gold potatoes
(1 cup barbecue sauce, store-bought or homemade, 582–83)
3 garlic cloves, minced
2 bay leaves
¼ teaspoon cayenne pepper

Bring slowly to a boil. Reduce the heat at once and simmer for about 45 minutes. Transfer the chicken to a cutting board, remove any bones, and shred the meat with two forks. Add it back to the stew along with:

3 cups fresh or frozen corn kernels
(1 cup sliced okra, fresh or frozen)

Simmer uncovered for 10 minutes. Remove the bay leaves. Season the stew with:

Salt, black pepper, and cayenne pepper to taste
Several dashes of Worcestershire sauce
Several dashes of hot pepper sauce

BEEF BRACIOLE

4 servings

Braciole, an Italian specialty, is best made from pounded slices of beef rump, top round, or bottom round. Pounded pork or veal cutlets may also be used. The individual slices are stuffed, rolled, tied, and braised in a combination of wine, stock, and tomatoes. For tips on pounding meat, see 451.

Purchase from a butcher or slice from a roast:

Four ¼-inch-thick slices rump, bottom round, or top round steak (4 to 5 ounces each)

Pound the slices to about ⅛ inch thick, taking care not to tear the meat. Trim any excess fat and pat dry. Season with:

½ teaspoon salt
½ teaspoon black pepper

Mix together in a medium bowl:

1 cup fresh bread crumbs, 957
4 ounces ground beef, veal, or pork
½ cup grated Parmesan (2 ounces)
¼ cup chopped parsley
¼ cup finely chopped prosciutto or ham
1 large egg, lightly beaten

Spread the stuffing evenly over the meat, leaving at least a 1-inch border all around. Roll up, tucking in the sides to form a tight, neat packet. Tie securely with butcher's twine, both crosswise and lengthwise. Dredge the rolls in:

½ cup flour

Heat in a large heavy skillet over medium-high heat:

2 tablespoons olive oil

Add the meat packets and brown carefully on all sides. Remove the rolls with a slotted spoon. Pour off all but 2 tablespoons of fat from the skillet (if necessary, add more fat). Add to the skillet:

½ cup finely chopped onion
¼ cup finely chopped carrot
2 teaspoons minced garlic

Cover and cook over medium heat for 5 minutes. Add and bring to a boil:

½ cup beef stock or broth
½ cup dry red wine
½ cup tomato puree or 2 tablespoons tomato paste
1 bay leaf

Return the beef rolls to the skillet, reduce the heat, cover, and simmer until the beef is fork-tender, 1 to 1½ hours.

Transfer the rolls to a platter and cover to keep warm. Remove the bay leaf. Skim off the fat from the surface of the liquid. Reduce, if necessary, over high heat just until syrupy. Season to taste with:

Salt and black pepper

Remove the strings from the rolls and cut into 1-inch slices or leave whole. Pour the sauce over the meat.

ROPA VIEJA (CUBAN BRAISED AND SHREDDED BEEF)

6 to 8 servings

The name translates as "old clothes," which the shreds of beef and strips of onion and pepper are said to resemble. Like Puerto Rican Asopao de Pollo, 93, and Veracruz-Style Snapper, 380, this dish combines tomatoes, warm spices, and piquant olives. It is mildly spiced, but flavor-packed. Serve with rice, Tostones, 263, and Frijoles de la Olla, 213. Leftovers are superb in sandwiches.

Cut parallel to the grain into 3-inch-wide pieces:

2 pounds trimmed flank steak, bottom round, or lean brisket

Pat dry and sprinkle all over with:

1 teaspoon salt

Heat in a large ovenproof skillet or Dutch oven over medium-high heat:

2 tablespoons vegetable oil or rendered beef fat

Add the beef in batches, browning on all sides. Transfer to a platter and pour off all but 1 tablespoon of the fat. Reduce the heat to medium and preheat the oven to 300°F. Add to the pan:

2 large onions, thinly sliced
2 large bell peppers, any color, thinly sliced

Cook until the onions and peppers have softened, about 7 minutes. Add and scrape up any browned bits:

1 cup dry red or white wine

Return the beef to the pan along with:

One 14½-ounce can diced tomatoes
6 garlic cloves, smashed
2 tablespoons tomato paste
2 teaspoons dried oregano
1½ teaspoons ground cumin
¼ teaspoon ground allspice
2 bay leaves
One 2-inch cinnamon stick (preferably canela, 972)

Bring to a simmer over high heat, cover the pan with a tight-fitting lid, and transfer to the oven. Cook until the beef easily shreds with a fork, 1½ to 2 hours.

Remove the pan from the oven and transfer the meat to a cutting board. Remove the cinnamon and bay leaves. Remove any fat from the surface of the braising liquid. Once cool, shred the meat with a fork into thin strands and stir back into the sauce along with:

1 cup chopped green olives

Stir and heat through over medium-low heat for 5 minutes, or until bubbling. Season to taste with:

Salt and black pepper
Lemon juice or distilled white vinegar

Serve garnished with:

Chopped parsley or cilantro

BRAISED SHORT RIBS

4 servings

Unlike back ribs, which are mostly bone, short ribs offer a good amount of rich-tasting meat. We prefer English-style short ribs, 455, for this recipe, but flanken, 455, will work in a pinch.

Preheat the oven to 300°F.

Pat dry:

3 pounds beef short ribs, excess fat trimmed

Season with:

1 teaspoon salt
½ teaspoon black pepper

Heat in a Dutch oven or large ovenproof skillet over medium-high heat:

2 tablespoons vegetable oil, beef fat, or bacon fat

Add the ribs in batches and brown well on all sides. Transfer to a plate. Pour off all but about 2 tablespoons fat from the pan. Reduce the heat to medium and add:

2 onions, chopped
2 celery ribs, chopped
1 large carrot, chopped
6 garlic cloves, lightly smashed

Cook until lightly browned, about 10 minutes, scraping up any browned bits from the bottom of the pan. Add:

2 cups beef stock, poultry stock, dry white wine, red wine, or a combination

5 sprigs thyme, rosemary, oregano, parsley, or a combination
2 bay leaves
(½ ounce dried porcini mushrooms, coarsely chopped)

Return the short ribs to the pan and bring to a boil over high heat. Cover the pan, transfer to the oven, and cook until the ribs are fork-tender, about 2 hours.

Transfer the ribs to a platter and cover to keep warm. Skim off any fat from the surface of the liquid and remove the herbs. If you wish to thicken the sauce, reduce it over high heat until it is the desired consistency. Season to taste with:

Salt and black pepper
Red wine vinegar or sherry vinegar

Pour the sauce over the ribs and top with:

Chopped parsley
(Crispy Fried Shallots, 256)

Serve with:

Creamy Polenta, 322, or Mashed Potatoes, 265

FLANK STEAK WITH DRESSING

4 to 6 servings

This pinwheeled roast has been in *Joy* since 1936.

Pat dry:

One 2- to 2½-pound flank steak

Place the flank steak on a cutting board so that the tapered portion is pointing toward you and the thinner side is facing your knife hand. With your knife parallel to the cutting board, carefully cut the flank steak horizontally, stopping ½ inch away from the opposite edge. Open the flank steak like a book and pound it to an even thickness.

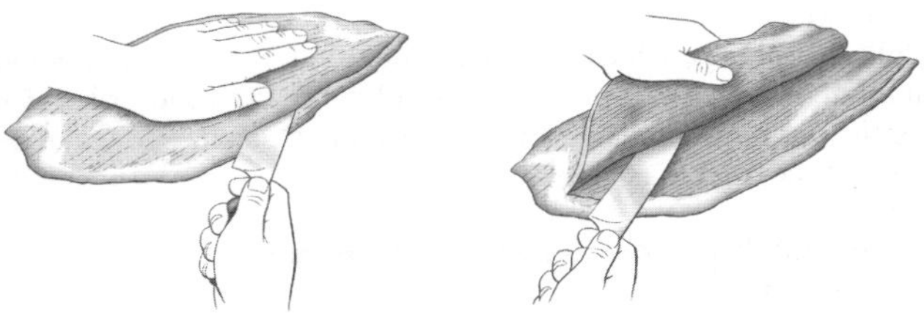

Slicing the flank steak and opening it like a book for stuffing

Season both sides with:

1 teaspoon salt

Melt in a Dutch oven or large skillet over medium heat:

4 tablespoons (½ stick) butter

Add and sauté until soft and golden:

1 small onion, finely chopped
1 celery rib, finely chopped
2 garlic cloves, minced

Transfer the sautéed vegetables to a bowl and mix in:

1 cup dry bread crumbs
1 large egg, beaten
2 tablespoons chopped parsley
1 teaspoon sweet paprika
1 teaspoon Worcestershire sauce
¼ teaspoon dry mustard

Spread this stuffing over the steak. Starting at the tapered end, roll the steak up loosely and tie it at 2-inch intervals. Preheat the oven to 300°F.

Wipe out the pan and heat over medium-high heat:

3 tablespoons vegetable oil

Brown the rolled steak on all sides in the hot oil. Transfer to a plate and reduce the heat to medium. Whisk into the oil:

2 tablespoons all-purpose flour

Cook, stirring, until the flour takes on a nutty smell, about 2 minutes. Gradually whisk in:

2 cups dry red wine, beef stock, tomato juice, or a combination
¼ teaspoon salt

Bring to a simmer. When thickened, return the steak to the pan and spoon the sauce over the meat. Cover and bake until the internal temperature of the meat reaches 130° to 135°F, about 1 hour.

Let the meat rest for 10 minutes. Cut into ½-inch-thick slices and place on a serving plate. Pour some of the sauce over the meat; transfer the remaining sauce to a gravy boat or bowl for passing around the table.

CORNED BEEF

8 to 10 servings

The term "corned" refers to the kernel-sized crystals of salt once used to cure large cuts of beef brisket. In most supermarkets, corned beef is sold in vacuum-sealed bags that contain some of the brine and seasonings used during curing; it needs to be cooked before serving. To make your own corned beef from scratch, see 937. To make **New England Boiled Dinner,** use the corned beef cooking liquid to simmer an assortment of sturdy vegetables such as peeled chunks of parsnips, turnips, potatoes, carrots, small onions, and cabbage wedges until tender. Leftover corned beef makes great sandwiches (see Reuben Sandwich, 141) and, of course, superlative hash, 473.

Rinse under running water to remove the surface brine from:

One 4-pound corned beef brisket, store-bought or homemade, 937

Place the brisket in a large pot and add water to cover along with:

20 black peppercorns
2 bay leaves

Bring to a boil, reduce the heat, cover, and simmer until a fork can easily penetrate to the center, about 3 hours.

Remove the meat and let stand for 15 minutes. For an attractive presentation, you may brown the outside of the corned beef on a baking sheet in a 350°F oven for 15 minutes after coating the surface with:

(Brown Sugar Glaze, 578, or Honey Glaze, 579)

Cut the brisket into thin slices across the grain and transfer to a platter. Serve with:

Horseradish Sauce, 566, or prepared horseradish
Coarse whole-grain mustard or hot English-style mustard
Boiled Potatoes, 265

CORNED BEEF HASH

4 to 5 servings

This is a chunky hash, just the way we like it. To make **Red Flannel Hash,** replace half the potatoes with **8 ounces beets, cooked, 219, peeled, and cut into ½-inch cubes.**

Heat in a large heavy skillet over medium-high heat:

3 tablespoons vegetable oil or beef fat

Add and cook, stirring, until the onion is just beginning to brown, about 5 minutes:

1 large onion, chopped
(2 jalapeño peppers, seeded and diced)

Add and cook, stirring, for 5 minutes.

1 pound red or gold potatoes, boiled, 265, and cut into 1-inch chunks (about 3 cups)

Add and cook, stirring, until the potatoes and meat are browned around the edges, about 5 minutes:

2 to 3 cups coarsely shredded or cubed cooked corned beef

Stir in:

3 tablespoons beef or chicken broth or water
(2 tablespoons ketchup or mild, tomato-based chili sauce)
(½ teaspoon dried thyme or sage)
Salt and black pepper to taste

Reduce the heat to medium. Lightly mash the potato pieces with the edge of a spatula. Cook, stirring frequently, until all the ingredients are nicely browned, about 10 minutes. Firmly press the hash into a cake with the back of the spatula, then cook, pressing occasionally, until the bottom is well browned, 10 to 15 minutes. Loosen the bottom of the cake with the spatula, then slide or invert onto a serving plate and cut into wedges. Sprinkle with:

Chopped parsley

Serve with, if desired:

(Fried Eggs, 155, or Poached Eggs, 153)

ABOUT VEAL

Veal is harvested from young calves, aged 3 to 5 months. Though it was once cheap and plentiful in grocery stores, veal has plummeted in popularity since its heyday in the 1940s. Traditionally, veal calves were raised solely on milk and confined to keep their muscles underdeveloped, which gave their meat a pale appearance, mild flavor, and bad reputation. Keep in mind these two observations when considering veal: First, calves are no longer confined to the degree they once were, and milk has been replaced or supplemented with a more nutritionally balanced formula. Second, veal calves are predominantly the unwanted male offspring of dairy cows. If not raised for veal, these animals are often dispatched on the spot. Veal calves are a byproduct of something many people value and take for granted, and they will be killed one way or another.

Many veal calves are pastured before slaughter and have pink flesh from their grazing diet (their meat is commonly sold as **pastured** or **rose veal**). Though better from an ethical perspective, veal that has taken on a red tint is sometimes from older calves rather than pastured ones and may be a bit more like beef (and more flavorful as a result). Veal is rarely sold graded; if you do encounter it, the grading criteria are similar to beef (though veal is invariably leaner). Veal bones should be white on the outside and bright red at the center.

VEAL CUTS

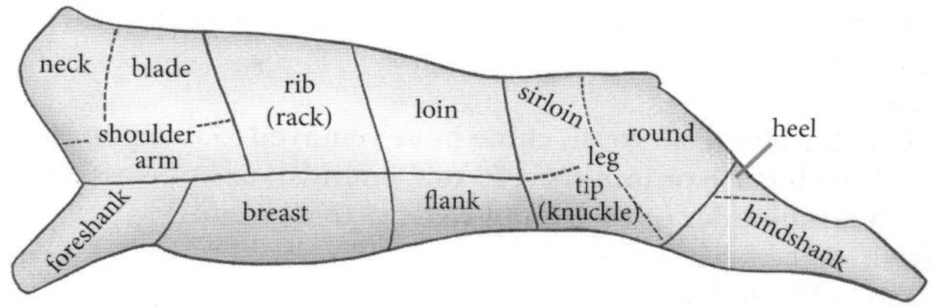

Major cuts of veal

Obviously, veal cuts are generally the same as beef, but since the animals are smaller, fewer roasts and individual muscles are separated from the major cuts. The **veal breast** encompasses the same area as the beef brisket and plate and is often stuffed and roasted whole, 474. The **foreshank** and **hindshank** are usually crosscut into thick slabs and braised (most famously in Osso Buco, 476). The veal shoulder is sold in several large cuts, most commonly the **arm roast** and **blade roast,** or cut into **blade, arm,** or **shoulder chops;** these may be roasted but are best braised.

As with beef, roasts and chops cut from the veal **rib** and **loin** are tender enough to roast, grill, broil, sear, or pan-fry just until they reach a safe internal temperature (see chart, 453). Leave at least ¼ inch of fat to keep the lean chops moist during cooking. **Medallions** are cut from the boneless top loin or tenderloin, which have been trimmed of fat and connective tissue.

The **flank, sirloin tip,** and **round** portion of veal are primarily turned into thin **cutlets** or **scallops** (also called **scaloppine**), which are often pounded, floured or breaded, and sautéed or pan-fried, 474–75. The most prized meat for veal scallops comes from the long eye of round muscle of the leg freed from its membrane and tough connective tissue. Cutlets, also cut from the bottom round, are usually cut ½ to ¾ inch thick, with the small round bone intact. After the bone is removed, they are often pounded thin. Of course, veal sirloin and any of the leg muscles may be sold as roasts; see Beef Cuts, 454, for more on these (the veal cuts will obviously be smaller, leaner, and more tender).

ABOUT ROASTING VEAL

Because veal is lean, roasting it can be a challenge. The best roasts are from the rib and loin; we recommend cooking them no further than medium-rare. Though rib and loin roasts may be cooked at higher oven temperatures, they are prone to drying out. Thus, we prefer cooking all veal at lower roasting temperatures, regardless of how tender they may be. If you have the time and inclination, lean veal roasts benefit from larding, 451. Veal breast, on the other hand, has several layers of fat. Unlike almost every other cut of meat, veal breast is traditionally stuffed with the bone in: A long, deep pocket is cut next to the ribs starting at the thicker brisket end and extending toward the plate or belly end.

SLOW-ROASTED VEAL

6 to 8 servings

Since veal tends to leanness, we recommend slow-roasting even the tenderest roasts from the loin and rib. If you have leftovers, make the Italian classic **Vitello Tonnato Freddo** by thinly slicing chilled veal roast and serving cold, topped with Tonnato Sauce, 564, and garnished with lemon wedges.

Have ready:

One 6-rib veal rib roast, chine bone removed (5 to 6 pounds), boneless rib or loin roast (3 to 4 pounds), or boneless tied veal shoulder or top round roast (3 to 4 pounds)

Season and cook as for:

Slow-Roasted Beef, 456

Serve with a jus, 456, made from the drippings, or prepare:

Basic Pan Gravy, 545, or Herb Pan Sauce, 546, made with white wine

STUFFED ROASTED VEAL BREAST

15 to 20 servings

Whole veal breast is the most cumbersome roast that can still fit in a standard oven. You will need a pan that is at least 17 × 11½ inches to accommodate the entire veal breast. Preparing the breast for stuffing is a bit involved; try to get a butcher to cut the pocket for you.

Prepare:

Basic Bread Stuffing or Dressing, 532

Preheat the oven to 325°F. Pat dry:

One 12- to 14-pound whole veal breast

Starting from the wider end of the roast, use a sharp paring knife to carefully slice the meat away from the bones to within 1 to 1½ inches of each side, forming a pocket. Lifting the meat with one hand, carefully slice the meat away from each bone. Work slowly, turning the blade to slice toward each side, until the pocket extends down the length of the roast. For ease of serving, turn the roast bone side up and cut through the rigid cartilage between the ribs without cutting into the meat. This makes carving the roast easier. Season the outside with:

Salt and black pepper

Fill the pocket with the stuffing, spreading it in an even layer. Place the breast in a large roasting pan. Brush with:

Olive oil

Roast, uncovered, until the inside is no longer pink when you make a small incision near the bone, 2½ to 3 hours. Transfer the meat to a platter and let stand for 15 to 20 minutes. Skim the fat from the pan juices in the roasting pan and add:

2 cups dry white wine or chicken stock or broth

Set the roasting pan over high heat and bring to a boil. Reduce the heat and simmer until the sauce is reduced by half. Season to taste with:

Salt and black pepper

Slice the veal and spoon the sauce over the slices.

ABOUT GRILLING, BROILING, AND SAUTÉING VEAL

The best veal cuts for high-heat methods are chops from the rib and loin, or medallions cut from the tenderloin. Chops for grilling and broiling are best cut about 1½ inches thick; pan-fried chops are ideal cut 1 inch thick. Veal medallions are generally sliced about ¾ inch thick and cook quickly in a hot skillet. Grilled veal chops can be cooked and served simply with a wedge of lemon, or served with a vinaigrette, chutney, relish, or other sauce. Sautéing or pan-frying chops and medallions is also a great option, since the lean, mild meat can be embellished with a quick, flavorful pan sauce, 544.

Some of the most famous veal dishes are made by sautéing thinly pounded cutlets, especially those from veal leg. Pounded-and-fried veal preparations are found on practically every side of the Alps: Italy has *scaloppine* and the famous, breaded *Milanese*; Austria has *Wienerschnitzel*; Germans relish pork *schnitzel*. There are countless variations on this theme.

GRILLED OR BROILED VEAL CHOPS

4 servings

Prepare a hot grill fire, 1063, or place a broiler pan on an oven rack set 3 to 4 inches from the heating element and preheat the broiler. Pat dry:

4 rib or loin veal chops, 1¼ to 1½ inches thick

Rub with:

2 tablespoons olive oil

Sprinkle with:

Salt and black pepper

Place the chops on the grill rack over direct heat or on the broiler pan and cook for 5 minutes on each side until they register 120° to 130°F for rare to medium-rare. For medium, cook 1 minute more or until 135°F. Transfer to a platter or plates and serve with:

Lemon wedges or Salsa Verde, 567

SAUTÉED VEAL CHOPS

4 servings

Pat dry:

4 rib or loin veal chops, 1 inch thick

Season with:

Salt and black pepper

Melt in a large skillet over medium-high heat:

2 tablespoons butter

Add the chops and sear both sides, each about 2 minutes. Reduce the heat to medium and cook, turning once, until they register 120° to 130°F for rare to medium-rare, about 4 minutes more. For medium, cook 1 minute more or until 135°F. Transfer to plates and let stand. Serve as for Grilled or Broiled Veal Chops, above, or drain off most of the fat and prepare, if desired:

(Herb Pan Sauce, 546)

Spoon over the chops and serve.

SAUTÉED VEAL CUTLETS OR SCALOPPINE

4 servings

Serve simply, as in this recipe, or try any of the variations that follow. For tips on pounding veal into cutlets, see 451.

Preheat the oven to 180°F. Have ready an ovenproof platter. Pound to slightly less than ¼ inch thick:

1 pound veal cutlets

Season with:

½ teaspoon salt
½ teaspoon black pepper

Dredge in:

½ cup flour

Shake off the excess. Heat in a large skillet over medium-high heat:

1 tablespoon olive oil
1 tablespoon butter

Brown the cutlets in batches, being careful not to crowd the skillet, and cook quickly, 30 to 60 seconds each side. Transfer to the platter as the cutlets brown and keep warm in the oven. Add more oil and butter to the skillet as needed. You may serve the cutlets simply seasoned to taste with:

Salt and black pepper
Lemon juice

Or keep them warm in the oven, drain off most of the fat, and make, if desired:

(Herb Pan Sauce, 546)

Pour the sauce over the veal and, if desired, serve garnished with:

(Sautéed Mushrooms, 251, or Garlic-Braised Broccoli Rabe, 221)

VEAL PICCATA

4 servings

Prepare through the browning step:

Sautéed Veal Cutlets or Scaloppine, above

Add to the skillet:

¼ cup dry white wine
⅓ cup lemon juice

Bring to a boil, scraping up the browned bits with a wooden spoon. Reduce the heat and simmer until slightly reduced, about 5 minutes. Remove from the heat and quickly whisk in:

4 tablespoons (½ stick) butter, softened
2 tablespoons chopped parsley
(1 tablespoon capers)
Salt and black pepper to taste

Spoon the sauce over the veal and serve immediately.

WIENERSCHNITZEL (BREADED VEAL CUTLETS)

4 servings

An Austrian specialty that is worthy of mimicking with thin portions of all manner of meats, fowl, and fish. To make these **Wienerschnitzel à la Holstein,** top each cutlet with a **Fried Egg, 155, 2 anchovy fillets,** and ½ **teaspoon drained capers.** For other schnitzels, see Breaded Pork Chops or Cutlets, 493, and Pan-Fried Chicken Cutlets II, 414. For tips on pounding veal into cutlets, see 451.

Preheat the oven to 180°F. Have ready an ovenproof platter. Pound to slightly less than ¼ inch thick:

1 pound veal cutlets

Season with:

½ teaspoon salt
½ teaspoon black pepper

Spread on a plate:

½ cup flour

Beat together in a shallow bowl:

2 eggs
1 tablespoon milk

Spread on another plate:

2 cups dry bread crumbs or 2½ cups fresh bread crumbs, 957

Dredge the veal lightly in the flour and shake off the excess. Dip into the egg mixture, then coat with the bread crumbs, pressing down on the crumbs slightly to help them adhere to the veal. Heat in a large skillet over medium-high heat:

3 tablespoons vegetable oil or Clarified Butter, 960

Cook the cutlets in batches, adding more oil or butter to the skillet as needed. Fry until nicely browned, 1 to 1½ minutes each side. Transfer to paper towels to drain as they brown, then keep warm on the platter in the oven. Sprinkle the cutlets to taste with:

Salt and black pepper

Serve simply with:

Lemon wedges

VEAL PARMIGIANA

4 servings

Pound **1 pound veal cutlets** to a thickness of ¼ inch and use them instead of chicken to prepare **Chicken Parmigiana, 415.**

VEAL SALTIMBOCCA

4 servings

Saltimbocca means "jump into the mouth," which is precisely what these delicious stuffed and sauced cutlets do. Prosciutto and sage are the traditional stuffing, but a slice of cheese is often added as well. If desired, use chicken or turkey breast instead of veal. For tips on pounding veal into cutlets, see 451.

Pound to slightly less than ⅛ inch thick:

1 pound veal cutlets

Season with:

½ teaspoon salt
½ teaspoon black pepper

Lay the scaloppine out flat and top each with:

1 paper-thin slice prosciutto (about 2 ounces total)
2 large fresh sage leaves (about 16 total)

Roll the veal around the filling and secure with toothpicks. Heat in a large heavy skillet over medium-high heat:

1 tablespoon olive oil
1 tablespoon butter

Add the veal packets and cook, turning once, until lightly browned, about 1½ minutes on each side. Transfer to a platter and cover with foil to keep warm. Add to the hot skillet:

½ cup dry white wine

Bring to a boil, scraping the bottom of the skillet with a wooden spoon to loosen the browned bits, and boil until the wine is almost evaporated. Add:

1 cup chicken or veal stock or broth
1 tablespoon lemon juice

Boil over high heat until reduced to about ½ cup. Remove the skillet from the heat and stir in:

2 tablespoons butter, softened

Taste and adjust the seasonings, adding a bit more lemon juice to taste. Pour the sauce over the veal packets.

PAPRIKA SCHNITZEL

4 to 5 servings

Prepare:

Sautéed Veal Cutlets or Scaloppine, 475

After browning the cutlets, wipe out the skillet and melt:

2 tablespoons butter

Add and cook, stirring, until lightly browned:

1 small onion, thinly sliced

Add and simmer for 5 minutes:

1 cup chicken stock or broth
3 tablespoons sweet paprika

Stir in:

½ cup sour cream

Add the veal and just heat through. Do not boil. Season to taste with:

Salt and black pepper

Garnish with:

2 tablespoons chopped parsley
(1 tablespoon capers or chopped anchovies)

Serve with:

Spätzle, 308, or Buttered Egg Noodles, 300

ABOUT BRAISING AND STEWING VEAL

As with beef, the best cuts of veal for stewing and braising come from the neck, shoulder, breast, round, and shank (see Veal Cuts, 473). To braise larger cuts, look for whole pieces of boneless chuck or breast, which can be braised bone-in or boneless or rolled and tied—ideal for stuffing. Veal shanks should be crosscut into thick slices to expose the marrow, which is considered a special treat for spreading on toast. As always, browning the meat thoroughly translates into a better braise. For more information on braising and stewing, see 1057. ➤ To adapt a braising or stewing recipe to use a slow cooker, see 1058; for pressure-cooking, see 1059.

OSSO BUCO (BRAISED VEAL SHANKS)

6 servings

Literally translated, *osso buco* means "bone with a hole," and in veal shanks, that hole contains marrow, 520. If possible, choose crosscut slices of veal hind shank, which are meatier than those from the foreshank. Or, you may substitute crosscut beef foreshank, lamb hindshank, or pork foreshank.

Preheat the oven to 300°F. Pat dry:

6 slices veal shank, 1½ inches thick (about 3 pounds)

Season with:

2 teaspoons salt
1 teaspoon black pepper

Heat in a large Dutch oven over medium-high heat:

2 tablespoons vegetable oil

Add the shanks in batches and brown well on all sides, adding more oil as needed. Transfer to a plate. Reduce the heat to medium-low and add to the pot:

1 carrot, chopped
1 onion, chopped
½ celery rib, chopped
4 garlic cloves, minced
3 sprigs parsley
4 sprigs thyme
1 bay leaf

Cook, stirring, until the vegetables are softened. Return the shanks to the pot, arranging in a single layer. Add:

1 cup dry white wine
1 cup veal or chicken stock or broth, or as needed

The liquid should reach about halfway up the shanks. Increase the heat to high and bring to a boil. Cover, transfer to the oven, and braise for 1 hour. Turn the slices over and add if needed to keep the level of the liquid halfway up the shanks:

(1 to 2 cups veal or chicken stock or broth)

Braise until the meat is tender, about 1 hour more. Turn off the oven, remove the shanks to an ovenproof serving platter and place in the turned-off oven to keep warm. Spoon off any fat from the braising juices, strain the juices into a saucepan, and boil over high heat until slightly thickened. Before serving, stir in:

Gremolata, 587
Salt and black pepper to taste

Spoon the sauce over the meat and serve with:

Risotto, 336, or Creamy Polenta, 322

Scoop the marrow from the bones with a small spoon to eat or spread on:

Toast

ABOUT LAMB AND MUTTON

The meat of young sheep, or **lamb,** usually comes to market when it is between 6 and 8 months of age. Domestic American lambs are much larger than New Zealand lambs, and have a bit more fat from their grain-supplemented diet. **Yearling mutton,** or **hogget,** is harvested at 12 to 18 months; mutton is 18 months old or older. The smallest lamb, sometimes referred to as **hothouse** or **milk-fed lamb,** are 6 to 8 weeks old and weigh as little as 15 pounds. Lambs of this size are generally roasted whole. Other small lambs, between 20 and 50 pounds, are often sold as **spring** or **Easter lamb** (though they are available year-round).

Mutton, or mature sheep, is darker in color and richer in flavor than lamb. Though not as tender, we think mutton is underrated and we seek it out for specific dishes: It makes especially fine curries, ragus, and braises. Western Kentuckians take advantage of mutton's robust flavor by barbecuing it with a Worcestershire-based mop (see Kentucky-Style Mutton Dip, 583). Look for mutton at halal markets or inquire with a butcher who buys directly from farmers. ➤ Mutton tends to have more fat than lamb and should be well trimmed before cooking—especially if you wish to reduce its gaminess. Prepare mutton as for lamb or goat, allowing extra cooking time for larger cuts. If mutton is appealing to you but unavailable, try looking for goat instead, 484.

Lamb may be voluntarily submitted for grading by the USDA as Prime, Choice (the most common at grocery stores), or Good. Mutton is graded the same, except it cannot score a Prime grade. Marbling of the muscles with fat is not as large a factor in grading lamb or mutton as it is with beef. Again, grading is voluntary, thus ungraded lamb is common as well (and not necessarily of poor quality). Look for meat that is deeply colored; it may range from rose to red, depending on the age of the animal (mutton can be dark red). The fat should be waxy white.

In addition to the dishes here, substitute lamb or mutton cuts for corresponding ones in beef recipes (we are especially fond of mutton in Guyanese Pepperpot, 464).

LAMB CUTS

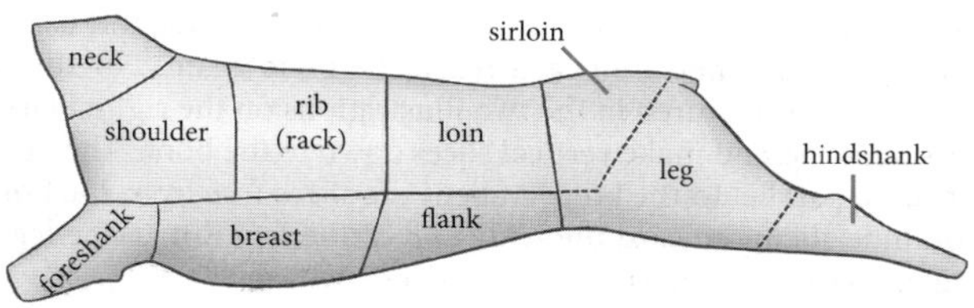

Major cuts of lamb

The sides of larger lamb cuts facing the skin may have a thick, white, fatty layer of connective tissue called **fell.** Be sure to remove any if present.

Use lamb **shoulder** for braising and stewing, especially when cut into **blade** and **arm chops,** which allow for efficient browning (simply brown them like steaks and cut them into chunks later). If boned, it may be tied into a roast or cut into chunks for stew meat. **Shoulder ribs,** a 4-rib slab cut from the lower shoulder, are very meaty and perfect for barbecuing (they are rare, so grab them if you see them). Lamb **neck** is especially rich in collagen, which lends body and richness to braises, stews, and stocks; like the shoulder, we prefer crosscut neck chops since their shape makes browning easy (since they are cut with a band saw, wipe off any white specks).

Lamb **breast** is the long section of the lower chest and rib bones, which have several layers of meat and fat. Boned breast is sometimes referred to as lamb **belly.** Traditionally, boned breast is rolled, tied, and roasted or braised. But, as the name implies, it can be cooked in many of the ways pork belly can, even cured into bacon, 497. We prefer lamb breast when it is left on the bone and trimmed into a neat slab for barbecuing like pork spareribs (these are often referred to as **Denver ribs**). Be sure to peel off their inner membranes as for pork, 487.

Lamb **shank** is a popular braising cut with lots of flavor; the foreshanks are smaller than the meaty hindshanks. Both can be found whole, and occasionally crosscut (the latter is wonderful when cooked as for Osso Buco, 476).

The **rib** (or **rack**) may be sold whole or cut into **rib chops.** In either form, it is best cooked with dry-heat methods such as roasting, broiling, sautéing, or grilling. We recommend cooking rack of lamb to rare or medium-rare, or 120° to 130°F before the meat rests (for other temperatures, see chart, 453). Whole racks usually have 7 rib bones, although some butchers include an eighth rib from the shoulder end. The ribs are often **frenched,** or trimmed and scraped to expose the bone. ➤ An average trimmed rack weighs between 1¼ and 2½ pounds; the larger size will feed 2 or 3 people, figuring 2 or 3 chops per serving; for the smaller size of rack, figure on ➤ 3 or 4 chops per person.

To french a rack of lamb, place the rack bone side down on a cutting board and, with a sharp knife held perpendicular to the rib bones, make a long cut through the fat layer about 2 inches from the end of the bones and above the eye meat. Angle the knife into the cut and slide the knife away from the eye meat toward the ends of the bones. Keep the blade flush with the bones and remove the layer of fat covering them. Cut out the meat between the bones. Scrape the exposed bone free of any fat or connective tissue, which will otherwise burn during roasting.

The lamb **loin** runs from the last rib to the hip, or sirloin. If both loin muscles are still attached to the backbone, the resulting roast is called a **saddle.** If the saddle is split through the backbone and cut into slices, the result is **loin chops,** which look like miniature T-bone steaks. A single trimmed loin ranges in size from ¾ pound for New Zealand or baby lamb to 2 pounds for domestic lamb. For this reason, a boneless loin roast is often fashioned by carefully boning the saddle so that the two loins are still connected, or by tying two loins together to form one roast (see Pan-Roasted Loin of Lamb, 479). The **sirloin** portion, which runs farther back along the top of the lamb, is usually cut into **sirloin chops,** but it may be boned and tied into a roast as well. They are comparable to loin or rib chops but are often much cheaper. Lamb loin and sirloin should be cooked no more than medium-rare.

Below the loin is the **flank** portion, which is relatively rare to find intact. Unlike the larger flank steak muscles found in beef, lamb flanks are thin and small, usually with plenty of fat attached. Like boned breast, the fat can be left on and the whole flank turned into bacon, 497. Otherwise, we suggest trimming the fat away and using in Carne Asada, 459, or slicing across the grain for use in stir-fries.

Lamb **leg** is lean, flavorful, and surprisingly tender. It is best roasted, grilled, or sautéed to medium-rare, but older yearling mutton or mutton legs may be fatty enough to roast or braise until the meat is tender and falls off the bone. Crosscut **leg chops,** or **leg steaks,** are increasingly common in grocery stores. When cut into strips or chunks, leg is also the best choice for kebabs and stir-fries. The leg is made up of several muscles, which have an intermuscular membrane called **silverskin.** The silverskin holds the leg together; if you plan to cook the leg as a whole piece, it is best left on. Some cooks remove the silverskin before cooking since it can be chewy; for instructions, see Preparing Venison for Cooking, 527.

The **bone-in leg roast** is a festive centerpiece, but a **butterflied** leg has a few advantages: Any fat in the center of the leg can be removed, a boneless roast is easier to carve at the table, and it can be stuffed or seasoned throughout. If left untied, a butterflied leg can be grilled or roasted very quickly, like a gigantic steak.

To bone a whole leg of lamb, first trim away any thick layers of fat or fell. If the leg has a sickle-shaped pelvic or aitch bone attached, place the leg on a cutting board with the bone facing up. Cut around the aitch bone, always angling the blade toward the bone to keep from cutting into the muscle. Continue scraping away meat and connective tissue from the bone until you reach the hip joint. Lift and bend the aitch bone until the joint is fully exposed and slip your knife between the ball and socket to cut the ligament inside. Remove the aitch bone and, starting at the ball joint, make an incision down the center of the leg along the femur bone (if the shank is attached, you can remove it or make a new cut along that bone as well). Run the tip of your knife on either side of the bones, angling the blade toward it to avoid cutting into the muscle. Once the sides of the leg bones are exposed, go back to the ball joint at the top of the leg and carefully cut underneath the bone. As you cut, lift the ball joint with your other hand, let the meat drape downward, and cut the bone free (always angle the blade toward the bone).

To butterfly a lamb leg, lay the boneless leg flat with the outward-facing side down. Two muscles on either end of the leg muscles are especially thick; to achieve an even thickness, split these large muscles by cutting them parallel to the cutting board, starting at the side facing the rest of the leg muscles and to within an inch of the other side. Open the muscles like a book; the entire leg should now be roughly the same thickness.

ABOUT ROASTING LAMB

Leg of lamb is by far the most popular cut to roast, but slow-roasting shoulder is economical and yields richer results. Lamb rib racks and loin roasts are wonderfully tender, but they are also small and relatively expensive; save these roasts for intimate dinners among close friends and family. For more on these, see Lamb Cuts, 477; for more on the technique, see Baking, Roasting, and Pan-Roasting, 1050.

ROAST LEG OF LAMB

8 to 10 servings

A bone-in leg of lamb raised in the United States generally weighs 8 to 10 pounds; those raised in Australia and New Zealand can weigh 7 pounds or less. ➤ Figure on ¾ to 1 pound per person of bone-in lamb. Each leg has 2 or 3 bones: the hip or pelvis, the femur or thigh, and the shank. A butcher may remove all or some of these; we recommend asking them to remove the hip bone to make carving easier.

Preheat the oven to 450°F. Pat dry, trim, and prepare:

One 8- to 10-pound bone-in leg of lamb

Rub the surface of the roast with:

3 tablespoons olive oil

Combine in a small bowl:

1 tablespoon salt

1 tablespoon finely minced fresh rosemary or 1½ teaspoons finely crumbled dried rosemary

2 teaspoons black pepper

Rub this mixture all over the leg, or, if desired, reserve half of the seasoning and toss with:

(4 large garlic cloves, cut lengthwise into slivers or slices)

(1 tablespoon olive oil)

Cut 15 to 20 evenly spaced slits in the roast, and insert the seasoned garlic slivers. Arrange the leg meatier side up on a rack in a roasting pan. Place it in the oven and immediately reduce the oven temperature to 325°F. Roast until a thermometer inserted in the thickest part of the meat registers 125° to 130°F for medium-rare, 1¾ to 2½ hours (the temperature will rise about 5 degrees out of the oven). Remove from the oven, cover loosely with foil, and let stand for 15 to 20 minutes.

To carve a lamb leg, you have a choice. For large, thin, flat slices, consult the illustration shown below on the left: Grab the shank, or narrow end, of the roast with a kitchen towel and raise the leg at an angle off the platter. With a sharp carving knife held parallel to the bone, cut ¼-inch-thick slices from the meatiest part of the leg, continuing until you reach the bone. Turn the leg over and use the same slicing method until you reach the bone again. For thicker slices, carve as pictured in the two illustrations on the right: Start at the shank end and make vertical slices down to the bone. Then turn the knife parallel to the bone and cut the slices free from the bone. Continue slicing toward the wide end of the leg. Rotate the leg as you go to carve the meat off all the sides.

Serve with:

Mint Sauce, 567, Salsa Verde, 567, or Avgolemono, 552

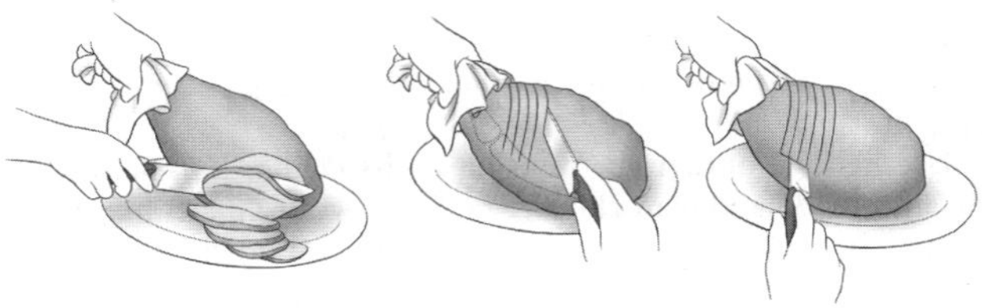

Two methods of carving a leg of lamb

ROASTED LAMB SHOULDER

8 to 10 servings

Once boned and tied, shoulder roasts are easy to accommodate in most pans. Do not miss the opportunity to season throughout with a seasoning or paste (see 479). To cook a bone-in lamb shoulder, see Kentucky-Style Smoked Mutton Shoulder, 484.

Have ready:

One 4- to 5-pound boneless, tied shoulder roast

Season and cook as for:

Slow-Roasted Beef, 456

Start checking the temperature of boneless roasts after 1 hour and bone-in roasts after 1½ hours; remove, rest, and brown at a higher temperature as directed. Serve with any of the suggested sauces for Roast Leg of Lamb, above.

STUFFED LAMB ROAST

8 to 10 servings

Removing the bones from a lamb leg or shoulder is an opportunity to add flavor to the inside of the roast. Leg roasts in particular are great for stuffing with a grain- or bread crumb–based mixture. Shoulder roasts have a more haphazard arrangement of muscles and will hold less stuffing; we prefer to season their interior with an herb or spice paste.

Pat dry:

One 4- to 5-pound butterflied, 478, leg of lamb or boneless lamb shoulder roast, trimmed to an even thickness of 2 to 2½ inches

To season the inside with a paste, prepare:

½ cup Mediterranean Garlic Herb Paste, 584, Jamaican Jerk Paste, 584, Harissa I, 584, Charmoula, 586, Mexican Adobo I, 584, or the mixture from Lamb Shawarma, 480 (grate the onion instead of slicing it)

Spread this mixture evenly on the boned side of the meat.

To fill with a stuffing, season the boned side of the meat with:

1 teaspoon salt

½ teaspoon black pepper

Spoon evenly over the seasoned surface, using the lesser amount for a shoulder roast:

2 to 4 cups any bread crumb– or grain-based stuffing, 533–37, but especially Couscous Stuffing with Apricots and Pistachios, 535, and Spiced Rice Stuffing, 536

Tightly roll or fold the roast back together; for leg roasts, roll up the lamb starting at the longer side. Tie the roast securely at 2-inch intervals to give it a snug, compact, cylindrical shape. For shoulder roasts, be easier on yourself: They will never look tidy. Scrape any bits of paste or stuffing from the surface of the tied roast and season the outside with:

1 teaspoon salt

(½ teaspoon black pepper)

Refrigerate for at least 3 hours and preferably overnight to allow the flavors to meld.

Roast as for **Roast Leg of Lamb, 478**, or **Roasted Lamb Shoulder, 478**.

PAN-ROASTED RACK OF LAMB

2 to 3 servings

Searing the rack of lamb before roasting browns it and helps melt any untrimmed fat.

Preheat the oven to 425°F.

Pat dry:

1 rack of lamb (7 or 8 ribs), trimmed, leaving a thin layer of fat on the surface

Season with:

1 teaspoon salt

½ teaspoon black pepper

Heat a large heavy ovenproof skillet over medium-high heat. When the skillet is hot, add and quickly swirl around:

1 tablespoon vegetable oil

Add the lamb meat side down and brown well, about 2 minutes. Turn it and brown the other side, 2 minutes more. Pour off any fat in the skillet, then set the lamb bone side down in the skillet and transfer to the oven. Roast until a thermometer inserted in the thickest part of the meat registers 125° to 130°F for rare or medium-rare, 15 to 20 minutes (the temperature will rise 5 to 10 degrees out of the oven). Remove from the oven, cover loosely with foil, and let stand for 5 to 10 minutes. Cut between the bones and serve 2 or 3 chops per person. If desired, serve with:

(Wine and Sour Cherry Pan Sauce, 547, Herb Pan Sauce, 546, Charmoula, 586, Chimichurri, 567, or Salsa Verde, 567)

PAN-ROASTED LOIN OF LAMB

4 servings

Boned lamb loins can be quite small. You may special order a roast where both loins are left attached and the backbone removed. They are then trimmed and tied together into a tidy, thick, cylindrical roast with a layer of fat all around, which keeps the loins from drying out and prevents overcooking. To order this from a butcher, specify a **double boneless loin roast** (the cooking time will be 5 to 10 minutes longer). Alternatively, if you have two boneless loins that are under 1 pound, you may tie them together into one roast. Even when roasting a single loin, tie it with butcher's twine so that it holds its shape. Leave a ¼-inch layer of fat on the roast to keep it moist while roasting. Rubbing the roast with olive oil before roasting is also a good idea.

Preheat the oven to 300°F.

Pat dry:

One 1½- to 2-pound boneless loin of lamb, trimmed and tied at 1½-inch intervals

Season with:

1 teaspoon salt

½ teaspoon black pepper

Heat in a large ovenproof skillet over medium-high heat:

1½ teaspoons vegetable oil, bacon fat, or lard

Brown the lamb loin on all sides, about 5 minutes. Place the skillet in the oven and roast until a thermometer inserted in the thickest part of the meat registers 125° to 130°F for rare or medium-rare, about 15 minutes (the temperature will rise 5 degrees out of the oven). Remove from the oven, cover loosely with foil, and let stand for 5 to 10 minutes. Remove the strings and cut the lamb into ¾- to 1-inch-thick medallions. If desired, serve with:

(Wine and Sour Cherry Pan Sauce, 547, Herb Pan Sauce, 546, Sauce Meurette, 553, or Sauce Marchand de Vin, 551)

ABOUT GRILLING, BROILING, AND SAUTÉING LAMB

The best cuts of lamb for these dry-heat methods come from the rib, loin, sirloin, and leg, 477. Shoulder chops, though a bit chewier, have plenty of flavor; they are great on the grill, as are sirloin chops, leg chops, and butterflied leg; we prefer to marinate all of these (or season them with a paste, 584–86) for several hours before cooking. Grilled or broiled chops from the rib and loin are a special treat; lightly season them before cooking and serve with a sauce.

Trim most of the fat from lamb chops that are to be sautéed, especially if you plan to make a pan sauce. We recommend sautéing chops from the rib and loin; leg chops should be cut off the bone into steaks to promote even browning. For stir-frying, leg meat is the best choice; if you have the time, remove as much of the silverskin as possible (see Preparing Venison for Cooking, 527, for detailed instructions).

GRILLED OR BROILED BUTTERFLIED LEG OF LAMB

8 to 10 servings

Pat dry:

One 4- to 5-pound butterflied, 478, leg of lamb, trimmed to an even thickness of 2 to 2½ inches

Rub the entire surface with:

½ cup Jamaican Jerk Paste, 584, Charmoula, 586, Mexican Adobo I, 584, or Sweet and Smoky Spice Rub, 587

or a mixture of:

3 tablespoons minced fresh rosemary or 1 tablespoon dried rosemary
6 garlic cloves, minced
2 teaspoons salt
1 teaspoon black pepper

Place on a baking sheet and let sit, uncovered, in the refrigerator for at least 1 hour, and up to 24 hours.

Prepare a medium-hot grill fire, 1063, or place a broiler pan on an oven rack set 4 to 5 inches below the heat. Preheat the broiler. Place the lamb boned side up on the grill rack or boned side down on the broiler pan. Cook, turning once, until well browned but still juicy and pink on the inside, about 10 minutes on each side or until the internal temperature registers 130°F for medium-rare. Cook for a few minutes more on each side until 135°F for medium. Cover loosely with foil and let stand for 6 to 8 minutes, then cut into ½-inch-thick slices. If desired, serve with:

(Red Onion Marmalade, 568, or Roasted Tomato–Chipotle Salsa, 574)

GRILLED OR BROILED LAMB CHOPS

4 servings

Rib and loin chops are the most tender, but do not discount leg, sirloin, and shoulder chops—especially the latter, which are streaked with fat and very flavorful. Shoulder chops benefit from the tenderizing effect of a marinade, especially Tandoori Marinade, 580. Grill or broil lightly seasoned chops 3 to 4 inches from the heat so they brown well; cook marinated chops a bit farther away to prevent burning.

Prepare a hot grill fire, 1063, or place a broiler pan on an oven rack set 3 to 4 inches below the heat. Preheat the broiler. Pat dry:

2 to 2½ pounds lamb chops, about 1 inch thick

Rub both sides with:

1 teaspoon salt
½ teaspoon black pepper

Place the chops on the grill rack over direct heat or on the broiler pan and cook for 5 minutes on each side to until the internal temperature reaches 120° to 130°F for rare to medium-rare. Cook 1 minute more to 135°F for medium. Rest the chops for 5 minutes before serving. If desired, top with:

(Flavored butter, 559–60, Mint Sauce, 567, Charmoula, 586, or Chimichurri, 567)

GRILLED RACK OF LAMB

2 to 3 servings

Pat dry:

1 rack of lamb (7 or 8 ribs), trimmed, leaving a thin layer of fat on the surface

Season with:

1 teaspoon salt
½ teaspoon black pepper

Prepare a medium-hot, two-zone grill fire, 1063, or preheat a gas grill on high for 10 minutes. If using a gas grill, reduce the heat of one of the burners to low. Place the lamb meat side down to the hotter side of the grill and cook for 2 minutes. Flip the rack over and squeeze with:

Juice of 1 lemon

Cook for another minute over direct heat and transfer to the cooler side of the grill. Cover and cook until the internal temperature registers 120° to 130°F for rare to medium-rare, about 15 minutes more. Serve with:

Salsa Verde, 567, made with mint, or Chimichurri, 567

SAUTÉED LAMB CHOPS

4 servings

Pat dry:

2 pounds lamb rib, loin, or leg chops, about 1 inch thick

Season with:

1 teaspoon salt
½ teaspoon black pepper

Heat in a large heavy skillet over medium-high heat until the butter begins to turn light brown:

1 tablespoon butter
1 tablespoon olive oil

Arrange the lamb chops in the skillet. Sear for 4½ to 5 minutes on each side until the internal temperature reaches 120° to 130°F for rare to medium-rare. Cook 1 minute more to 135°F for medium. You may pour off most of the fat and make:

(Herb Pan Sauce, 546)

Or serve with:

(Charmoula, 586, or Salsa Verde, 567)

LAMB SHAWARMA

4 servings

This recipe is an accessible imitation of the original, in which spiced lamb or beef is layered on a vertical rotisserie, shaved off as it browns, and served in flatbreads. The flavors of the dish can be re-created by marinating thinly sliced lamb shoulder and onions for several hours, then briefly pan-frying them until cooked through. For a more browned result, use the marinade to make Lamb Kebabs, 481, cutting the onion into wedges and interspersing pieces on the skewers with the cubes of meat.

Place on a rimmed baking sheet and freeze for 30 minutes:

1½ pounds boneless lamb shoulder, trimmed of excess fat

Meanwhile, combine in a medium bowl:

1 medium onion, halved lengthwise and thinly sliced
¼ cup vegetable oil

Finely grated zest of 1 lemon
(Finely grated zest of ½ orange)
2 tablespoons lemon juice
1 tablespoon minced parsley, mint, or a combination
1 teaspoon salt
1 teaspoon black pepper, white pepper, or a combination
1 teaspoon dried thyme, oregano, or a combination
1 teaspoon ground allspice
(½ teaspoon ground sumac)
½ teaspoon ground cinnamon
½ teaspoon ground cumin, fennel, or a combination
¼ teaspoon ground coriander
(¼ teaspoon ground cardamom)

Thinly slice the chilled shoulder into ¼-inch strips, add to the bowl, and toss to coat. Marinate in the refrigerator for at least 2 hours and up to overnight.

Transfer the strips of lamb to a plate, leaving the onion slices in the bowl (if some onion is left with the lamb, all is not lost; do the best you can). Heat in a large skillet or wok over medium-high heat:

2 tablespoons vegetable oil

Fry the lamb strips in several batches, turning once or twice, until cooked through and beginning to brown, about 4 minutes. Do not crowd the pan; if the browned bits on the bottom threaten to burn, reduce the heat. As each batch finishes, transfer to a bowl and cover to keep warm (add more oil to the pan if necessary). When all of the lamb is cooked, reduce the heat to medium and, if the pan is dry, add enough oil to cover the bottom. Spread the marinated onions in the pan in an even layer and cook for 2 minutes without stirring. Scrape any browned bits off the bottom of the pan and cook, stirring frequently, until the onions are soft and caramelized, about 4 minutes longer. Stir in the cooked lamb. Use shawarma as a filling for:

Flatbread or Pita Sandwiches, 145

Or over:

Rice Pilaf, 329

Or, to serve as part of a mezze, 46, prepare:

Hummus, 52

Spread the hummus in a shallow bowl, top with the shawarma, and serve with:

Warmed pita bread

LAMB KEBABS

4 servings

For more on kebabs, please read about Skewer Cooking, 1065. If using wooden skewers, soak them in water for at least 1 hour.

Cut into 1-inch cubes:

1½ pounds boneless lamb leg, sirloin, or shoulder

Combine the lamb in a bowl with:

Balkan Marinade, 580, Tandoori Marinade, 580, or the marinade for Lamb Shawarma, 480

Toss to coat. Cover and marinate in the refrigerator for 4 to 12 hours.

Place a broiler pan on an oven rack set 3 to 4 inches below the heat. Preheat the broiler; or prepare a medium-hot grill fire, 1063. Thread the meat and vegetables onto skewers. Broil or grill for 8 to 10 minutes, turning the skewers occasionally. Make a small incision in a cube of meat and check the center: It should be slightly less done than desired, for it will continue to cook somewhat off the heat. Serve immediately with:

Rice Pilaf, 329, Mujadara, 330, Couscous, 341, or Fattoush, 128

Or use as a filling for:

Flatbread or Pita Sandwiches, 145

ABOUT BRAISING, STEWING, AND BARBECUING LAMB

The best meat for these moist-heat methods comes from the shoulder, neck, breast, and shanks, 477. These flavorful, collagen-rich cuts are simmered until the meat is thoroughly cooked and fall-off-the-bone tender. We do not recommend braising leg meat; it can become dry when stewed or braised. Flavorful, mature mutton, 476, shines in braised dishes and is worth seeking out.

A whole shoulder, boned and rolled, can be braised slowly as for Beef Pot Roast, 464, or Stracotto, 464. Shoulder chops are ideal for braising, even if you plan to serve the meat in a chunky stew or curry: Simply bone, trim, and cut the cooked meat into bite-sized pieces when it is tender. Lamb neck pieces are another fine choice for slow, moist cooking; though they are less meaty than some cuts, their flavor is tremendous. In addition to the recipes that follow, lamb can be substituted for beef, pork, veal, and goat in any slow-cooked stew or braise. We are especially fond of using lamb neck, shoulder, or shank in Boeuf Bourguignon, 465, Hearty Beef Ragu, 464, and Goat Birria, 485. For more information on the basic technique, see Braising, Stewing, and Pot-Roasting, 1057. ➤ To adapt a braising or stewing recipe to use a slow cooker, see 1058; for pressure-cooking, see 1059.

BRAISED LAMB SHOULDER

8 servings

Preheat the oven to 300°F.

Pat dry:

One 4- to 5-pound boneless lamb shoulder roast, rolled and tied

Season with:

2 teaspoons salt
1 teaspoon black pepper

Heat in a Dutch oven over medium-high heat:

2 tablespoons vegetable oil

Add the lamb and brown on all sides. Remove the lamb from the pot and pour off all but 2 tablespoons of oil (add more oil if needed) and reduce the heat to medium. Add:

1 large onion, chopped
1 celery rib, chopped
1 carrot, diced
(1 small fennel bulb, chopped)

Cook, scraping up any browned bits, until the vegetables are softened, about 10 minutes. Add:

2 cups dry red or white wine, beef or lamb stock, or a combination
6 garlic cloves, smashed
(4 anchovy fillets, chopped)

3 sprigs fresh oregano or marjoram or 1 teaspoon dried oregano or marjoram
3 sprigs fresh thyme or 1 teaspoon dried thyme
3-inch sprig fresh rosemary or 1 teaspoon dried rosemary
1 teaspoon red pepper flakes
1 bay leaf

Return the lamb to the pot and bring to a simmer over high heat. Cover, transfer to the oven, and cook until the meat is fork-tender, 2 to 2½ hours. Remove the meat from the pot and keep warm. Skim off the fat from the surface of the sauce and remove the herb sprigs and bay leaf. Taste and adjust the seasonings. Cut the strings from the meat and serve it in chunks or slices, with plenty of sauce.

BRAISED LAMB SHOULDER OR NECK CHOPS

4 servings

Pat dry:

2½ to 3 pounds lamb shoulder or neck chops, about 1 inch thick

Season with:

1 teaspoon salt
½ teaspoon black pepper

Heat in a large heavy skillet over medium-high heat:

2 tablespoons vegetable oil

Brown the lamb chops in batches, about 4 minutes each side. Transfer the chops to a plate and pour off all but about 1 tablespoon of fat from the skillet. Add:

1 large onion, thinly sliced
3 garlic cloves, lightly smashed

Cook, stirring, until the onions have softened, 6 to 8 minutes. Add:

2 cups dry white wine, lamb or chicken stock, or a combination
2 sprigs fresh oregano or ¼ teaspoon dried oregano
2 sprigs fresh thyme or ¼ teaspoon dried thyme
(¼ teaspoon red pepper flakes)
1 bay leaf

Scrape up any browned bits, return the chops to the skillet, and bring to a simmer over high heat. Reduce the heat to low, cover, and simmer, turning once, until the chops are tender, 40 to 45 minutes. Remove from the heat and transfer the chops to a platter. Remove the herb sprigs and bay leaf and skim off any fat from the surface of the sauce. Add, if desired:

(½ cup Kalamata olives, pitted and halved)

Taste and adjust the seasonings. Garnish with:

Chopped parsley

BRAISED LAMB SHANKS WITH CHICKPEAS

4 servings

Shanks contain a good deal of connective tissue, which, when braised, produces a velvety sauce.

Preheat the oven to 300°F.

Trim most of the external fat from:

4 meaty lamb shanks (3 to 4 pounds)

Season with:

1 teaspoon salt
½ teaspoon black pepper

Heat in a Dutch oven over medium-high heat:

2 tablespoons vegetable oil

Add the shanks and brown on all sides. Transfer the shanks to a plate and pour off the fat. Reduce the heat to medium and add:

2 tablespoons olive oil
2 onions, halved and thinly sliced
6 garlic cloves, smashed

Cook, stirring often, until the onions are soft. Add:

2 cups chicken or lamb stock or broth or water
1 cup dry white wine
One 14½-ounce can diced tomatoes
(1 tablespoon chopped Salt-Preserved Lemon, 942)
1 teaspoon ground coriander
1 teaspoon ground cumin
Pinch of saffron threads or ground allspice
One 2- to 3-inch cinnamon stick
1 bay leaf

Return the lamb shanks to the pot and bring to a boil over high heat. Cover, transfer to the oven, and cook for 1½ hours. Remove from the oven and add:

One 15-ounce can chickpeas, drained
2 medium carrots, sliced
2 cups diced peeled winter squash, such as butternut

Cover and bake until the carrots are tender and the meat shreds easily, about 30 minutes more. Remove the meat and vegetables to a platter and cover to keep warm. Skim off the fat from the surface of the sauce, remove the cinnamon and bay leaf, and add:

2 tablespoons chopped mint
(2 tablespoons chopped cilantro)
(1 tablespoon Harissa I, 584, or to taste)
Lemon juice to taste

Taste and adjust the seasonings. Pour the sauce over the meat and vegetables. Serve with:

Rice Pilaf, 329, Couscous, 341, or cooked orzo

NAVARIN PRINTANIÈRE (SPRING LAMB STEW)

8 to 10 servings

As with all stews, the flavors deepen if chilled overnight and reheated. Also, once chilled, the fat is easily skimmed from the top.

Trim the fat from:

2 pounds boneless or 3 pounds bone-in lamb shoulder, neck, breast, shank, or a combination

If the lamb is boneless, cut into 1½-inch pieces. Sprinkle with:

1½ teaspoons salt
1 teaspoon black pepper

Heat in a Dutch oven over medium-high heat:

2 tablespoons vegetable oil

Add the meat in batches and brown on all sides. Transfer the meat as it browns to a platter. Reduce the heat to medium and add:

8 ounces spring, small cipollini, or pearl onions, peeled with ends trimmed
(1 leek, halved lengthwise and well cleaned)

Brown until golden, then transfer the onions to the platter with a slotted spoon and drain off any fat from the pot. If using, cut the leek into bite-sized pieces. Melt in the pot:

2 tablespoons butter
Gradually whisk into the butter:
2 tablespoons all-purpose flour
Cook, stirring, until the flour is golden and fragrant, about 5 minutes. Slowly whisk in:
2 cups dry white wine
Increase the heat to high, scraping the bottom to release any browned bits. Let the wine reduce by about half and then return the meat and onions to the pot along with:
3 cups chicken stock or broth
(2 tablespoons tomato paste)
4 garlic cloves, minced
1 bay leaf
Bring to a simmer, cover, and cook until the lamb is fork-tender, about 1½ hours. Add to the pot:
8 ounces small red potatoes, halved
6 young or slender carrots, peeled
2 small turnips, peeled and cut into ½-inch wedges
2 sprigs thyme
Cover and simmer until the vegetables are tender, about 20 minutes longer. Remove the bay leaf and thyme sprigs. If using bone-in cuts, transfer them to a baking sheet. When cool enough to handle, remove any bones, discard any gristly bits, cut into chunks, and return the meat to the pot. Chill the stew overnight, if desired. Skim off any fat from the surface of the stew, return to a faint simmer over low heat (if necessary), and stir in:
1 cup fresh or frozen green peas
8 ounces green beans, such as haricots verts, steamed until crisp-tender, and thinly sliced on the diagonal
Heat through and serve at once, sprinkled with:
Finely chopped parsley

IRISH STEW

4 to 6 servings

A winter favorite, especially when prepared with mutton chops. The meat is traditionally not browned here, but you may brown the meat first (use oil rather than butter) for deeper flavor. If you choose not to brown the meat, be especially diligent when trimming fat from the lamb.
Preheat the oven to 300°F.
Heat in a Dutch oven over medium heat:
2 tablespoons vegetable oil or butter
Add and cook, stirring, until beginning to soften, about 5 minutes:
2 onions, chopped
Add and cook, stirring, until the flour is beginning to brown, about 5 minutes:
2 tablespoons all-purpose flour
Stir in:
2½ pounds boneless lamb shoulder, cut into 1½-inch cubes, or 3½ to 4 pounds bone-in lamb shoulder or neck chops, trimmed of excess fat
3 cups lamb stock, chicken stock, Irish stout, water, or a combination
5 sprigs fresh thyme or ¾ teaspoon dried thyme
1 teaspoon salt
½ teaspoon black pepper
Bring to a simmer over high heat, cover, and transfer to the oven. After 1 hour, remove from the oven and stir in:
2 pounds gold potatoes, peeled and quartered
2 carrots, cut on the diagonal into thick slices
Cover, return to the oven, and cook until the meat is fork-tender, 1 to 2 hours more.

Remove the thyme sprigs and skim the fat from the top of the stew. If using shoulder or neck chops, transfer them to a baking sheet. When cool enough to handle, transfer any bones, discard any gristly bits, cut into chunks, and return the meat to the pot. Chill the stew overnight, if desired. Skim off any fat from the surface of the stew and return to a faint simmer over low heat (if necessary). Taste and adjust the seasoning. Garnish each serving with:
Chopped parsley
Minced chives

LAMB CURRY WITH TOMATO

4 servings

This hot red curry has a rich, reduced tomato sauce perfect for serving over rice.
Drain, reserving the juice, and coarsely chop:
One 28-ounce can whole tomatoes
Heat in a Dutch oven over medium heat:
2 tablespoons vegetable oil
Add and cook, stirring, until softened and starting to brown, about 8 minutes:
1 medium onion, thinly sliced
Increase the heat to medium-high, add, and cook, stirring, for 30 seconds:
2 teaspoons ground coriander
2 teaspoons ground cumin
3 garlic cloves, minced
1-inch piece ginger, peeled and minced
1 teaspoon ground turmeric
¾ teaspoon salt
¼ to ½ teaspoon cayenne pepper
Add ½ cup of the chopped tomatoes and ¼ cup of the reserved tomato juice along with:
1½ pounds boneless lamb shoulder, trimmed and cut into 1- to 1¼-inch cubes
Simmer, stirring occasionally, until the liquid is reduced and thickened slightly, 5 to 7 minutes. Stir in the remaining tomatoes and juice, cover, reduce the heat to maintain a simmer, and cook until the lamb is tender, 45 to 60 minutes.

Remove the meat with a slotted spoon and keep warm. Skim any fat from the surface of the liquid, increase the heat, and simmer briskly until the sauce is thickened. Return the meat to the sauce. Serve with:
Cooked basmati rice, 343
Garnish each serving with:
Chopped cilantro

LAMB SAAG (CURRIED LAMB AND GREENS)

6 to 8 servings

Use any combination of sturdy cooking greens as a substitute for the spinach and mustard: Amaranth, lamb's quarters, collards, turnip greens, and kale are all good choices. Mutton and goat shoulder are excellent substitutes for the lamb.

Trim off excess fat from:

2½ to 3 pounds lamb shoulder or neck chops, or 2 pounds boneless lamb shoulder

If using boneless shoulder, cut the meat into 1½-inch pieces. Toss the lamb in a bowl with:

1½ teaspoons salt

Heat in a Dutch oven over medium-high heat:

2 tablespoons vegetable oil or Ghee, 960

Add the lamb in batches and brown on all sides. Transfer the browned lamb to a plate. Reduce the heat to medium, drain off any fat, and add:

¼ cup vegetable oil or Ghee, 960
2 teaspoons cumin seeds
1 teaspoon yellow or black mustard seeds

When the seeds become fragrant and start to pop, add:

3 dried Kashmiri chiles or chiles de árbol, seeded and stemmed
2 bay leaves

Cook until the chiles and bay leaves crisp and darken, about 30 seconds more. Add:

2 large onions, chopped
6 garlic cloves, chopped
1 to 3 serrano peppers, seeded and chopped
1-inch piece ginger, peeled and minced
2 teaspoons ground turmeric
1 teaspoon ground coriander
½ teaspoon ground fenugreek
(¼ teaspoon ground cloves)

Cook, stirring, until the onions are soft and translucent, about 10 minutes. Add:

2 cups water
One 14½-ounce can diced tomatoes
1½ pounds chopped fresh spinach, or one 10-ounce package frozen spinach
1 pound mustard greens, chopped

Bring to a simmer, reduce the heat, cover, and cook until the meat is tender, about 1½ hours.

Uncover and simmer for another 20 or 30 minutes to thicken the curry. Remove the bay leaves. If using shoulder or neck chops, transfer them to a baking sheet. When cool enough to handle, shred the meat, discarding any bones or gristly bits, and return the meat to the pot. Stir in:

⅓ cup plain yogurt
Salt and cayenne pepper to taste

Serve with:

Cooked basmati rice, 343

Garnish each serving with:

Chopped cilantro

KENTUCKY-STYLE SMOKED MUTTON SHOULDER

8 servings

Whereas beef and pork barbecue are common in many regions of the United States, mutton is unique to several counties of western Kentucky, where it was once the most economical protein. Mutton or yearling mutton shoulder will have more flavor, but lamb is perfectly acceptable; mutton can be special ordered or found at halal and Latino markets.

Please read about Barbecuing, 1066. Trim all but ¼ inch of fat from:

One 8-pound bone-in lamb or mutton shoulder

Rub all over with:

1½ tablespoons salt
1 tablespoon black pepper

Place on a rack set in a rimmed baking sheet and refrigerate, uncovered, overnight, or for up to 2 days.

Heat a smoker or grill set up for barbecuing, 1067, to 225° to 250°F (preferably with a water pan). Add to the coals:

One small chunk of dry hickory wood

Add the brisket to the cooler side of the smoker or grill and cover so that the top vent pulls smoke across the meat. Adjust the vents to maintain the temperature (this is difficult and may take practice, or, in the worst case, a fresh load of charcoal). You may add another small chunk of hickory wood every hour for the first 4 hours. Baste the meat every 2 hours with:

Kentucky-Style Mutton Dip, 583

Cook until the meat is tender and a thermometer inserted in the thickest part registers 200°F, 8 to 10 hours.

Transfer to a platter or baking sheet, cover with foil, and let the meat rest for at least 15 minutes. Meanwhile, put the remainder of the mutton dip in a small saucepan over medium heat and simmer for 5 minutes, or until thickened to your liking. Take the meat off the bone and thinly slice, pull, or chop it. Dress with enough sauce to lightly coat the meat (place the rest of the sauce on the table for use as a condiment). Serve as part of a "meat-and-three" (see Smoked Pork Shoulder, 496). Or, to serve in sandwiches, provide:

8 warmed hamburger buns or 16 slices toasted white or rye bread
Lettuce
Tomato slices
Dill pickle slices

ABOUT GOAT OR KID

In this country, goat meat continues to linger in obscurity; it is nearly impossible to find goat in large chain grocery stores, and we rarely encounter it in restaurants. Despite this, US production of meat goats has increased in the last thirty years. We hope this presages our joining the rest of the world in the "goat fan club": Young goats are slow-roasted for Easter and Christmas feasting in many parts of Europe, and there are countless goat dishes in the cuisines of the Caribbean, Latin America, Africa, and India.

Goat's rich flavor is only one aspect of its appeal: Though similar to lamb and mutton in many ways, goat is dramatically lower in calories and fat. Indeed, along with red game meats like venison, buffalo, and yak (see Processing Large Game, 526), goat meat is less fatty and calorie-dense than beef, pork, and even chicken breast.

Young goat, or **kid,** is usually harvested at 3 to 5 months (in Latino markets, kid may be marked as **cabrito**). As with lamb and veal, smaller kids are more tender and have a subtler flavor. Adult goat meat is usually sold without any special labeling, though the Spanish **chivo** may be used, or the term **chevon** (a combination of the French for "goat," *chèvre*, and mutton, the English term for the meat of older sheep). Mature goat is tough, but flavorful, making it ideal for braises and stews.

Goat is sold in the same cuts as lamb and mutton, 477. You can find goat at Latino, Greek, West Indian, or halal markets; kid may be found around Easter in these establishments, though premium markets occasionally sell it as well. The tender rib and loin chops of kid may be roasted or grilled as for lamb; since it is incredibly lean, do not cook goat above medium-rare, or 130° to 135°F. Use adult goat meat in any stewed or braised lamb or beef recipe; you may need to cook goat for longer than estimated for the lamb or beef. We especially love using goat for Guyanese Pepperpot, 468, Beef Rendang, 467, and Hearty Beef Ragu, 466.

A word of caution: We regularly encounter goat meat for sale that has been cut with a band saw from bone-in goat shoulder. These bony chunks definitely improve the flavor of curries and stews, but the finished dish may have ➤ small, sharp bone fragments, which can be treacherous when you are not expecting them. So, if you choose to go ahead with using bone-in goat stew meat, advise diners to be wary of bones.

➤ To adapt a braising or stewing recipe to use a slow cooker, see 1058; for pressure-cooking, see 1059.

JAMAICAN CURRIED GOAT

4 to 6 servings

This curry owes its fragrant heat to Scotch bonnet peppers, the Caribbean relative of the habanero. Lamb or pork can be substituted for the goat.

Combine in a large bowl and toss to coat evenly:

2 pounds boneless goat shoulder, trimmed and cut into 1-inch cubes
1 teaspoon salt
1 teaspoon black pepper

Heat in a Dutch oven over medium-high heat:

3 tablespoons vegetable oil

Add the meat in batches and brown on all sides, about 8 minutes. Remove the browned meat with a slotted spoon and pour off all but 2 tablespoons oil from the pot (add more oil if needed). Add to the pot and cook over medium heat, stirring often, until the onion begins to brown, about 8 minutes:

1 large onion, chopped
1 celery rib, chopped

Return the goat to the pot along with:

2½ cups chicken stock or water
4 garlic cloves, chopped
1 to 3 Scotch bonnet or habanero peppers, seeded and minced
1-inch piece ginger, peeled and minced
3 tablespoons curry powder, store-bought or homemade, 588
4 sprigs fresh thyme or 1 teaspoon dried thyme
(½ teaspoon ground cinnamon or allspice)
1 bay leaf

Bring to a boil, then cover and simmer over low heat for 1 hour. Add:

1 pound gold or red potatoes, peeled and cut into 1-inch quarters or chunks

Cover and cook until the potatoes and meat are fork-tender, 35 to 45 minutes.

Remove from the heat and skim off any fat from the surface of the sauce. Remove the bay leaf and thyme sprigs. Taste and adjust the seasonings. Garnish, if desired, with:

(Chopped cilantro)

Serve with:

Cooked rice, 343, Coconut Rice, 333, Jamaican Rice and Peas, 331, or Fried Plantains, 263

GOAT BIRRIA

8 to 10 servings

This rich adobo from Jalisco, Mexico, is perfect for stewing cuts of lamb and beef as well. We serve this with corn tortillas, but leftovers are an excellent filling for enchiladas, 539–40, Burritos, 147, and Tortas, 143. If needed, omit any chiles you cannot find and substitute a little more of the ones you can. If using goat stew meat, be sure to check for bone fragments and warn diners (see About Goat, 484).

Stem, seed, and toast, 262:

5 guajillo chiles
4 ancho chiles
2 dried chipotles

Place in a small bowl, cover with water, and soak for 30 minutes. Meanwhile, toast in a Dutch oven over medium heat until fragrant:

1 teaspoon cumin seeds
(2 whole cloves)
(One 2- to 3-inch cinnamon stick)

Transfer the spices to a blender. Roast in the Dutch oven until charred on all sides:

1 medium onion, halved
8 unpeeled garlic cloves
2 to 4 fresh serrano chiles, left whole

Remove to a small plate and let cool. Add to the pot:

1 tablespoon vegetable oil or lard

Add:

4 pounds goat shoulder chops, or 3 pounds boneless goat stew meat

Brown on all sides, in batches, about 10 minutes. As the goat browns, peel the roasted garlic and remove the stem and seeds from the charred serranos. Add to the blender along with the drained, soaked chiles, charred onion halves, and:

¼ cup cider vinegar or distilled white vinegar

Puree until smooth. When the goat is browned, transfer to a plate, scrape the pureed chile mixture into the pot, and fry, stirring, for 30 seconds. Add:

One 28-ounce can whole tomatoes, or 2 pounds fresh tomatoes, coarsely chopped
One 12-ounce bottle Mexican lager or 1½ cups water
1 teaspoon dried oregano
1 bay leaf

Return the goat to the pot and bring to a simmer over medium-high heat. Reduce the heat to low, cover, and simmer until the goat is very tender, about 3 hours.

Remove the bay leaf. Transfer the goat to a plate and skim off any fat from the surface. Increase the heat to medium-high and reduce the braising liquid by two-thirds. As the liquid reduces, shred the meat, removing any bones or gristly bits. When the liquid is thick and reduced, remove from the heat and return the meat to the pot. Taste and adjust the seasoning with:

Salt
Cider vinegar or distilled white vinegar

Serve with:

Corn tortillas, store-bought or homemade, 612
Lime wedges
Chopped cilantro and green onions

ABOUT PORK

At the risk of evoking the uncle who holds forth at every holiday meal about how everything once tasted better and cost less than it does today, we must observe that American pork is not the same meat it used to be. In response to increasingly health-conscious consumers demanding leaner proteins—like chicken—commodity pork has been exclusively bred for the last three decades to produce higher yields of lean meat. Pork loin used to be rich and marbled, but modern pork loin has the same fat content as skinless chicken. While this is a victory for modern breeding practices, it can end in tragedy for cooks: The fattier pork loins of yore were much more forgiving in the kitchen, and yielded moister, tastier results. Now, we must take care to treat pork loin and other tender cuts with a light hand, as overcooking them for a few extra minutes can result in tough, dry, and flavorless meat.

Luckily, there are signs that the tide of lean commodity pork may be ebbing; the calculated value of lean loins continues to decrease as cooks look elsewhere for better-tasting protein that does not turn dry after a moment's inattention. Just as the desire for healthier foods changed the industry, our desire for tastier pork may as well—in time. Additionally, so-called **heritage breeds** of hog—that is, traditional breeds that have not had the fat bred out of them—are available at farmers' markets and are making inroads at specialty markets. A decade ago, pork breeds were practically anonymous; now, the labels on chops and roasts may boast of their breed or the feed they are finished on. Berkshire, Duroc, and Mangalitsa are but a few of these, and many are **pastured** for at least some of their lives. Though heritage pork breeds are certainly not a guarantee of quality, the odds are much greater that they will be more flavorful than commodity pork. Unfortunately, you will have to pay a premium to find out. For information on **boar,** the destructive, free-ranging brethren of domesticated hogs, see 529.

Suckling pigs are less than 2 months old; they range in weight from 15 to 30 pounds and are more uniformly tender than full-grown hogs. Roasted whole, they make one of the most dramatic holiday centerpieces. Suckling pigs can usually be ordered in advance from a local butcher, bought from Internet retailers, or ordered directly from farms.

Pork is currently not graded for quality, but the USDA has proposed a voluntary grading scheme with Prime, Choice, and Select grades. These grades would be determined by marbling and color—pale pork is very soft, while darker flesh can be tough and dry. In lieu of grades, remember that the best pork has a moderate, reddish-pink hue and at least a hint of marbling (the more the better). In general, lighter pork tends to be more tender. Any exterior fat should be smooth and white.

Dry-heat cooking methods, such as roasting, grilling, sautéing, pan-frying, and stir-frying are reserved for naturally tender cuts from the loin and tenderloin. For best results, cook these cuts to medium, with a faint blush of pink, or ➤ an internal temperature of 140° to 145°F (the temperature will continue to rise 5 to 10 degrees once off the heat). Brining is also a good strategy to ensure lean chops and roasts remain moist and have a nice, firm texture. Make a brine as directed, 1046, add the pork to the brine, and refrigerate, allowing 3 hours for thick pork chops and 6 to 12 hours for roasts, depending on their thickness.

Pork may remain pink even when the meat is cooked to the correct internal temperature. The tendency to cook pork until gray and dry came from a fear of trichinosis, once associated with eating undercooked pork. ➤ But trichinosis is eradicated in less than a minute in meat that has reached or exceeded 140°F.

Of course, tough stewing cuts from the shoulder, leg, and shanks will be chewy and unpalatable unless cooked for much longer by the slow heat of braising, stewing, and smoking or slow-roasting.

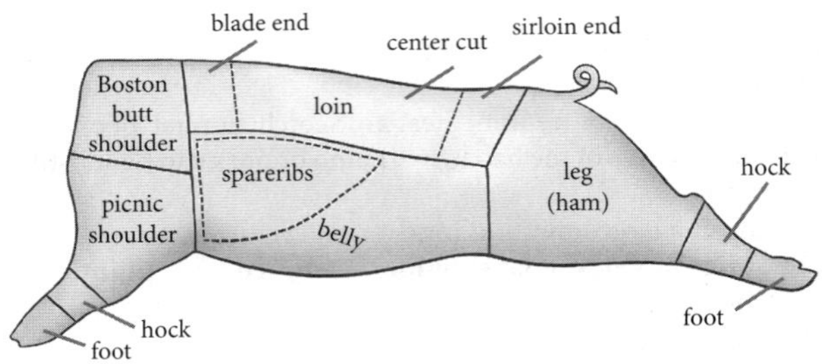

Major cuts of pork

PORK CUTS

Though pigs do not chew cud as cattle do, their **cheeks** are exceptionally dense and rich with flavor. These small medallions are perfect for long-simmering stews and braises. Covering the cheeks is the **jowl,** a very fatty cut with several layers of meat; it is most often cured (Italians call it *guanciale*, 498) and used like bacon or pancetta in pasta and vegetable dishes.

On a hog, the **shoulder** includes the neck, upper arm, chest, and shoulder blade section. The muscles here work hard, thus they have more flavor and a higher fat content. The shoulder is usually split into two halves: The upper section includes the shoulder blade and neck; it is often referred to as the **Boston butt.** With the vertebrae, or **neck bones** removed, the butt portion may be sold as a bone-in roast (our preferred cut for barbecuing; see Smoked Pork Shoulder, 496) or boned and tied into a roast. Bone-in **shoulder blade chops** (also known as **butt steaks**) are ideal for braising. You can occasionally find the upper portion of the butt fashioned into a fantastic, cylindrical roast and sold as a **Danish collar, shoulder eye,** or **coppa roast.** Analogous to the beef chuck eye roll, 454, this roast contains some of the same muscles that run down the loin, making it relatively tender compared to the rest of the shoulder. Below the butt is the chest and upper arm, referred to collectively as the **picnic** portion, which may be sold whole with the skin on, cut into large **arm roasts,** or cut into steaks. Like the butt, roasts from the picnic may be found bone-in or boned and tied. Sometimes the pectoral muscle is cut from the picnic and sold as **pork brisket.**

Pig's feet, or **trotters,** are loaded with collagen, which lends body to stocks, soups, or stews like Feijoada, 214. Once the feet are removed from the lower portion of the arm, what is left is called the **foreshank.** The foreshanks, as well as the **hindshanks,** are usually crosscut into several pieces and sold as **hocks.** Shanks are the toughest and most flavorful cut of pork. Along with the neck bones, they are often cured and smoked for use as a flavoring in braised greens, beans, and soups.

The most popular cuts of pork come from the **loin**—the meat that runs along either side of the backbone, starting in the shoulder blade area and running all the way to the hip bone. The loin is 15 ribs (or vertebrae) long and consists of a thick bundle of muscles that covers the top of the ribs, and a slender tenderloin muscle tucked underneath the lumbar portion, which gets thicker as it runs to the leg (for more on the tenderloin, see below). These muscles may be cut off the bone and fashioned into roasts or, if left on the bone, the whole loin may be cut into chops. Retail cuts from the loin are divided into several areas. The **blade end** consists of the first two ribs; a portion of the shoulder blade or scapula runs through it. The blade end is usually cut into **loin blade chops,** or sliced so that they open into long pieces, or **country-style ribs** (this is a fairly loose term that can apply to slender cuts from the shoulder as well). Like shoulder blade chops, these are very flavorful and good for braising; country-style ribs are particularly convenient as they need little to no trimming and need only be cut into chunks for a curry or stew (see Red Posole, 324).

The **center-cut** portion of the loin is where **rib roasts** are cut from; these are usually 8 or 9 ribs long. The ribs may be removed for cutting boneless roasts (if cut from the front end, it may be referred to as a **rib-eye roast**). The slab of meaty rib bones that remain are sold as **back ribs.** Two bone-in rib roasts may be frenched and tied together to form a **crown roast,** 489. The lumbar portion of the center-cut loin has no rib bones, but small "finger bones" project upward from the spine; when the loin is boned, these are sometimes sold as **button ribs** or **riblets.**

Chops cut from the center loin portion used to be known simply as **loin chops,** but the pork industry has introduced new labeling terms borrowed from beef butchery in a bid to make them sound more exciting. Chops cut from the front section, once referred to as **rib chops,** may now be labeled **rib-eye chops.** As with beef steaks from the same area, rib chops tend to have a bit more intermuscular fat (when choosing chops from leaner hogs, these are our favorite). **Center-cut chops** come next, followed by **T-bone chops,** which have a very small portion of tenderloin attached. **Porterhouse chops** are cut from the last few ribs of the center-cut portion and contain a larger medallion of tenderloin. When the top loin is separated from the ribs and cut into steaks, they may be marked as **New York chops,** as they are the equivalent of beef strip steaks, or the more generic **boneless loin chop.** Of course, any of these may be cut into thicker, or **double-cut chops.**

Finally, bridging the loin and leg is the **sirloin.** The sirloin contains a part of the pelvic bone, and the loin and tenderloin muscles are joined by tougher ones that help support the animal's weight. It may be sold as a roast or cut into **sirloin chops.** In any form, sirloin is often a good value when compared to other portions of the loin.

The **tenderloin** is routinely cut off the loin and sold as a slender roast; it is very low in fat and very tender, with a mild flavor. Tenderloins can be cooked whole or cut into medallions, which may be butterflied and pan-fried, 494, or pounded into thin cutlets, 493. Cut these slices from the thicker end of the tenderloin and save the narrow end for pan-frying or pan-roasting in one piece (see Pan-Roasted Pork Tenderloin, 489). Tenderloin (over)cooks quickly and is best suited to searing, pan-roasting, frying, stir-frying, broiling, and grilling.

Below the loin is the **belly,** from which comes bacon, salt pork, side meat, and other cured treasures, 497. Our insatiable demand for bacon has kept fresh pork belly out of American meat cases, but this is beginning to change; if you would like to try roasting or braising fresh belly and you cannot find any, most butchers and markets will be able to procure it, if not cut it to order. There are wonderful cuts lurking in the belly that may occasionally be found at specialty shops, including pork **skirt steaks** and pork **flank steaks;** like their beefy counterparts, both are perfect for grilling (see Carne Asada, 459). The larger outside skirt is sometimes referred to by the intriguing Spanish butchery term **secreto.**

When the layers of fat and meat are removed to make bacon, all that is left are the rib bones, the cartilaginous area adjacent to the sternum, and the meat in between. If left whole, these are referred to as **spareribs;** if the bottom portion is cut away, they are referred to as **St. Louis–style ribs** (the bottom trim is occasionally sold as **rib tips**). Though they may have less meat than country-style ribs and baby back ribs, spareribs are considered by many to be the best for barbecuing. If it has not been removed already, do your best to ➤ carefully peel away the tough membrane that covers the inside of the ribs (it will not soften, no matter how long it is cooked).

To peel the membrane from ribs, first slip the tip of a knife underneath the membrane at the end of each rib and work it slowly down the length of the bones. As you work the knife in, gently pry the membrane up until you can grasp it with your fingers. Peel the membrane off; if necessary, hold the membrane in one hand and slice along where it meets the bone until it pulls away freely.

Pork **leg,** or **fresh ham,** is occasionally found whole, with a good portion of the shank attached; for information on cured pork leg, ➤ see About Ham, 499. If a leg is sold as "semiboneless," this means that the pelvic and tail bones have been removed, but not the femur, kneecap, or shank bone. Around ham-centric holidays, you may find whole fresh hams with all the bones removed and tied into tidy, festive roasts. For most of the year, it is much more common to find fresh pork leg cut into steaks and smaller roasts. Bone-in or boned leg may be crosscut into large steaks and sold as **center leg slices.** The upper inside portion of the leg is partially covered by the thin, well-marbled **leg cap steak,** which is reminiscent of beef skirt steak; it is best grilled or pan-fried. The **eye of leg** or **Des Moines roast** is well-marbled and responds well to high-heat roasting or grilling. The small **sirloin tip,** or **leg tip,** is leaner, but still tender enough to be roasted whole—or cut into medallions, butterflied, and pan-fried like pork tenderloin (see Country-Fried Pork Tenderloin with Gravy, 494). The two largest leg muscles, the **top leg roast** and **bottom leg roast,** are lean and flavorful; both are at their best when sliced into thin cutlets, pounded flat, breaded, and pan-fried (see Breaded Pork Chops or Cutlets, 493).

ABOUT ROASTING AND BAKING PORK

From crisp-skinned suckling pig to a simple herbed loin, roasting pork can yield an impressive holiday centerpiece or a tasty weeknight repast. Loin is by far the most common roast to find at the butcher counter, followed by shoulder. Because it is so lean, loin requires attention to prevent overcooking. To hedge against this outcome, brine loin roasts, 1046, before cooking, then dry them thoroughly. Choosing a loin roast with a fair amount of fat left on will also help (any excess can always be trimmed off). Pork shoulder has no trouble staying moist and tender but needs to be roasted for much longer. Pork belly benefits from a longer roasting time as well, which renders some of its fat and crisps the outside. Leftover roast pork of any kind is perfect for Becker Pork Hash, 491.

PORK LOIN ROAST

6 to 8 servings

Pork loin is best slow-roasted to ensure the outer layer of the roast does not turn dry before the center cooks through. For an especially even doneness, you can cook the loin roast at the lower temperature until it reaches 140°F, remove from the oven and rest for 30 minutes, and brown it at 500°F (as is done with Slow-Roasted Beef, 456). Boneless roasts cook a little faster, but bone-in roasts are tastier and make for a nice presentation. Rib roasts will often have the back bone (or chine bone) removed. If it has not been removed, ask the butcher to cut through the chine bone for easier portioning. (If all else fails, you may unceremoniously cut the loin completely off the bone before carving.) To promote juiciness, brine the loin, 1046, and omit the salt below.

Preheat the oven to 500°F.

Trim all but a thin layer of fat from the top of:

One 3-pound boneless or 5-pound bone-in center-cut pork loin roast

Dry thoroughly and rub with:

1 tablespoon olive oil
1 teaspoon salt
½ teaspoon black pepper

Place the meat on a rack in a roasting pan, fatty side up. Roast for 10 minutes. Reduce the oven temperature to 250°F and roast until a thermometer inserted in the thickest part of the meat registers 140° to 145°F (the temperature will rise 5 to 10 degrees as the roast rests). Cooking times vary depending on the thickness of the roast; begin checking after 45 minutes (and expect around 1½ hours total cooking time). Transfer to a cutting board, cover loosely with foil, and let stand for 10 minutes. Skim off the fat from the pan juices and reserve. If desired, prepare:

(Basic Pan Gravy, 545, or Herb Pan Sauce, 546)

For rib roasts, you may cut the loin off the bones in one piece and slice into ¼- to ½-inch slices or cut between the ribs into thicker chops. For a special treat, top the slices with:

(Double recipe Duxelles, 252)

Arrange the slices so that they overlap on a platter and spoon the pan juices or pan sauce over them.

HERBED PORK SHOULDER ROAST

6 to 8 servings

Rubbed with lemon zest, fresh herbs, garlic, and fennel, the seasoning for this butterflied shoulder roast is based on Italian specialties like porchetta (a boneless loin rolled up in the belly, which is still attached) and *arista di maiale* (the classic Florentine loin roast). Since the former is hard to obtain at the meat counter and the latter can be pricey and temperamental, we prefer the richness, convenience, and outstanding flavor of a boneless shoulder roast. If desired, you may use a boneless loin roast: Butterfly, 452, rub the cut side with the seasoning, tie, and roast as directed in Pork Loin Roast, above. Leftover slices are superb when reheated and crisped up in a skillet. Serve with Garlic-Braised Broccoli Rabe, 221.

Have ready:

One 4-pound boneless pork shoulder roast

Untie the roast and butterfly further if some portions seem uneven. Trim any fat or gristle from the inside. Mix together in a bowl:

8 garlic cloves, minced
Finely grated zest of 1 lemon
(1 tablespoon minced fennel fronds)
1 tablespoon minced rosemary
1 tablespoon minced sage
1 tablespoon olive oil
1 teaspoon ground fennel
1 teaspoon red pepper flakes
½ teaspoon salt
½ teaspoon black pepper

Spread this mixture evenly on the interior of the roast. Roll the shoulder into a roughly cylindrical shape and tie at 1½-inch intervals with butcher's twine. Season the outside of the roast with:

1½ teaspoons salt
1 teaspoon black pepper

Place on a rack set in a rimmed baking sheet and refrigerate uncovered for at least 3 hours, and preferably overnight (this will promote browning).

Preheat the oven to 325°F.

Place the roast on a rack in a roasting pan and transfer to the oven. Roast until a thermometer inserted in the thickest part of the meat registers 180°F, 3 to 3½ hours. Transfer the roast to a platter, tent loosely with foil, and let rest for 20 minutes. If desired, pour off the fat from the pan and use the pan juices to make:

(Basic Pan Gravy, 545)

PAN-ROASTED PORK TENDERLOIN

3 to 4 servings

Tenderloin needs special treatment to get browned to our liking. If you find a pork loin roast that will fit comfortably in an ovenproof skillet, you may use this technique for it as well. ➤ For tenderloins less than 1½ inches thick, grill or sauté them as for pork chops, 492–93. If desired, first brine, 1046, the tenderloin and omit the salt below.

Preheat the oven to 300°F.

Pat dry:

One 1- to 1½-pound pork tenderloin

Season with:

1 teaspoon salt

½ teaspoon black pepper

If the tenderloin is too long to fit in the skillet you plan to use, you may either bend it into a crescent shape or cut it in half crosswise. Fold the thinner end of the tenderloin back along the roast and tie with 2 lengths of butcher's twine so the pork is of an even thickness.

Heat in a large ovenproof skillet over medium-high heat:

1 tablespoon bacon fat, lard, or vegetable oil

Brown the tenderloin well on all sides, 6 to 8 minutes. Transfer to the oven and roast until a thermometer inserted in the thickest part of the meat registers 145°F, 12 to 15 minutes. Transfer to a plate, cover loosely with foil, and let stand for 5 to 10 minutes before slicing. If desired, pour off all the fat from the skillet, place over medium-high heat, and make:

(Herb Pan Sauce, 546, or the pan sauce for Steak au Poivre, 461, or Steak Diane, 461)

Bring to a boil, scraping up any browned bits from the bottom. Slice the meat, spoon the sauce over the tenderloin, and serve.

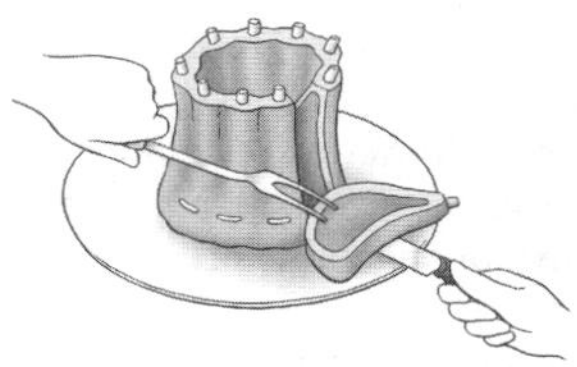

Carving a crown roast of pork

CROWN ROAST OF PORK

12 to 15 servings

Most butchers will prepare a crown roast for you from two loin racks, but make sure the loins used are of uniform size so that it cooks evenly.

Prepare:

Basic Bread Stuffing or Dressing, 532 (made with sausage and apples, if desired; see Additions to Bread Stuffing, 532)

Preheat the oven to 350°F.

Mix together in a small bowl:

2 tablespoons vegetable or olive oil

4 teaspoons dried thyme

4 teaspoons ground allspice

2 teaspoons salt

1 teaspoon black pepper

Rub the mixture all over the surface of:

One 12-pound crown roast of pork

Place in a roasting pan and roast for 1 hour.

Fill the center with the stuffing, placing any stuffing that will not fit in the roast in a separate buttered baking dish. Continue to roast until a thermometer inserted in the thickest part of the meat registers 145°F, 1 to 2 hours more (the temperature will rise 5 to 10 degrees as the roast rests). If the top of the stuffing starts to brown too much before the roast is done, cover just the stuffing with foil. Transfer the finished roast to a cutting board, cover loosely with foil, and let stand for 15 minutes. Place the roasting pan over 2 burners on medium-high heat and add to the pan:

½ cup Madeira or dry white wine

Bring to a simmer, scraping up the browned bits on the bottom of the pan. Strain into a saucepan and add:

1½ cups chicken stock or broth

Bring to a boil, then boil to concentrate the flavor if the juices taste thin and weak. To thicken the juices for gravy, reduce the heat and add to the simmering juices, whisking until smooth:

Kneaded Butter, 544, made with 1 tablespoon butter and 1 tablespoon all-purpose flour

Simmer to thicken and adjust the seasonings. Carve the roast into individual chops as shown and serve with the sauce and stuffing.

CRISPY PAN-ROASTED PORK BELLY

6 to 8 servings

Pork belly roasted with the rind on is a memorable treat. The thicker, meatier end of the pork belly is ideal here. If your knife is not sharp enough to score the skin, a box cutter fitted with a fresh blade works well.

Preheat the oven to 375°F.

Pat dry:

One 2-pound portion pork belly, skin attached

Using a very sharp knife, slice through the skin at ½-inch intervals in a crosshatch pattern; try not to cut into the meat underneath. Mix together in a bowl:

1 teaspoon salt

½ teaspoon pepper

½ teaspoon minced rosemary or thyme and ½ teaspoon minced lemon zest, or 1 teaspoon five-spice powder

Sprinkle both sides of the pork belly with this mixture, rubbing it into the crevices of the cut skin. Heat in a large ovenproof skillet over medium heat:

1 teaspoon vegetable oil or lard

Place the belly in the skillet skin side down and cook until the skin is golden, about 5 minutes. Carefully slide a thin spatula underneath the belly so that the skin does not stick to the skillet. Turn the belly skin side up and transfer the skillet to the oven. Roast until a thermometer inserted in its thickest part registers 180°F, about 1 hour.

Cut into thick slabs and serve with:

Garlic-Braised Broccoli Rabe, 221, and Mashed Potatoes, 265

BAKED PORK RIBS

6 to 8 servings

For a sublime variation, marinate overnight in a double recipe of the mixture for Five-Spice Ribs, 61.

Pat dry:

2 racks St. Louis–cut pork spareribs or 3 racks back ribs (6 to 8 pounds)

If the racks still have the tough membrane that covers their concave side, you will need to peel it off, 487. Rub both sides with:

⅔ cup to 1 cup Sweet and Smoky Spice Rub, 587, Southern Barbecue Dry Rub, 587, or Coffee Spice Rub, 587

Refrigerate uncovered for at least 1 hour, or, for a stronger flavor, wrap in plastic and refrigerate overnight and then uncover.

Position a rack in the center of the oven. Preheat the oven to 325°F.

Arrange the rib slabs on one or two rimmed baking sheets, cover with foil, and bake for 1½ hours. While the ribs cook, you may make:

(A mop or barbecue sauce, 582–83)

When the baking time is up, remove the sheet(s) from the oven. Uncover the ribs, drain any fat from the sheet(s), and continue baking, uncovered, basting every 15 minutes with the mop or sauce (if using), until tender, about 1 hour more. Twist one of the rib bones: It should feel loose and give a little. Loosely cover the ribs with foil and let stand for 15 minutes before serving. If desired, swab the ribs lightly and/or serve with:

(Barbecue sauce, 582–83)

LATIN ROASTED PICNIC SHOULDER

8 to 10 servings

The picnic shoulder is among the tastiest of pork roasts. Try to find a whole picnic roast with the skin left on. Brushing it with water during roasting keeps the skin tender enough to eat. If your knife is not sharp enough to score the skin, a box cutter fitted with a fresh blade works well.

Gather the ingredients for:

Double recipe Mojo, 567

Instead of simmering, add the mojo ingredients to a blender or food processor and puree until smooth. Have ready:

One 8-pound bone-in, skin-on pork picnic shoulder

Using a very sharp knife, slice through the skin at 1-inch intervals in a crosshatch pattern; try not to cut into the meat underneath. Push your fingers between the muscles exposed on the cut side of the roast and work them open so that more of the interior will be exposed to the marinade. Place the roast in a bowl just big enough to fit it, or in a large zip-top bag or oven bag set in a baking dish. Add the marinade, cover the bowl or close the bag, and refrigerate overnight and for up to 2 days. If the pork is not fully submerged in the marinade, turn it several times so that all sides are equally exposed.

Preheat the oven to 350°F.

Drain the marinade into a bowl and set aside. Pat the roast dry and place on a rack in a roasting pan. Roast until a thermometer inserted in the center registers 185°F, 4 to 4½ hours, brushing the skin every 30 minutes with cold water.

Transfer the roast to a cutting board, cover loosely with foil, and let stand for 20 minutes. Meanwhile, skim off the fat from the pan juices. Place the roasting pan over 2 burners on medium-high heat and add the reserved marinade. Bring to a boil, scraping up the browned bits on the bottom of the pan. Once deglazed, transfer the marinade to a saucepan and simmer for an additional 5 minutes, or until the sauce has thickened to your liking. Season to taste with:

(Chopped parsley, cilantro, oregano, or a combination)
Salt and black pepper

Remove the crispy squares of skin and slice the meat; arrange the slices on a platter and pour the sauce over them. Arrange the cracklings around the meat and serve.

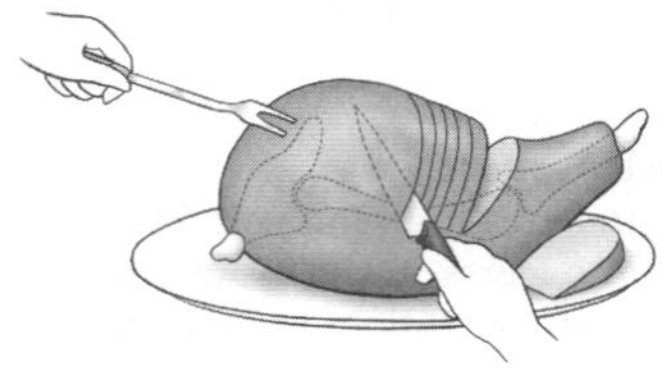

Carving a whole ham

ROAST FRESH HAM OR LEG OF PORK

15 to 20 servings

A whole pork leg, also known as **fresh uncured ham,** is perfect for feeding a large crowd and great for holidays. Cooking times are approximate because the weight of fresh hams is variable. Plan on about 1 pound per person, less if there are numerous side dishes. Ask your butcher to remove most of the skin, leaving it around the shank. Or, if you wish to present cracklings with the meat, leave it on and score at 1-inch intervals as for Latin Roasted Picnic Shoulder, above.

Preheat the oven to 350°F.

If the butcher has not done so, remove the skin up to, but not including, the shank from:

One 15- to 20-pound bone-in fresh ham

Place the ham in a large roasting pan. Mix together in a small bowl:

2 tablespoons olive or vegetable oil
1 tablespoon salt
2 teaspoons dried sage, thyme, crumbled rosemary, or a combination
2 teaspoons black pepper

Rub this mixture over the entire surface of the pork. Place the pork in the oven and roast for 1 hour. Pour into the roasting pan:

3 cups dry white wine

Return to the oven and roast, basting every 30 minutes until a thermometer inserted in the thickest part of the meat registers 140°F (the temperature will rise about 10 degrees out of the oven). Add water if necessary so the pan juices do not scorch. This may take 3½ hours or more for very large hams; start checking smaller hams at 2 hours. Transfer the ham to a large platter, cover loosely with foil, and let stand for 30 minutes. Meanwhile, if desired, add enough stock or broth to the pan juices to make 4 cups and prepare:

(Quadruple recipe Basic Pan Gravy, 545)

To carve the meat, cut it into slices starting at the shank end, keeping the knife perpendicular to the bone. Then make one long slice along the bone to separate the slices from the leg. Arrange the slices on a platter and serve with the pan gravy, if using, or one or more of the following sauces (be sure that you have at least 3 cups of sauce to serve with the ham):

(Horseradish Sauce, 566, Scandinavian Mustard-Dill Sauce, 566, Bavarian Apple and Horseradish Sauce, 567)

ROAST SUCKLING PIG

8 to 12 servings

Sucking pig must be special ordered. Have the butcher prepare the pig for you by cleaning it well and removing all the organs. A 20-inch roasting pan is ideal. Do not use a disposable aluminum pan, as it will collapse. If your knife is not sharp enough to score the skin, a box cutter fitted with a fresh blade works well.

The day before or just before roasting, prepare one of the following stuffings (you will need 12 cups):

1½ recipes Basic Bread Stuffing or Dressing, 532, Basic Corn Bread Stuffing or Dressing, 532, or a double recipe Apple and Cherry Bread Stuffing, 533

Position a rack in the lowest position in the oven. Preheat the oven to 450°F.

Generously oil a 20-inch-long roasting pan. If the pan is smaller (no smaller than 17 inches), have ready a loaf pan and lots of heavy-duty foil.

Place on a work surface:

One 15- to 20-pound suckling pig

Check to make sure that no bristles or hairs remain; if any do, shave them off with a safety razor or singe them with a torch. Thoroughly pat the pig dry inside and out. On a work surface, turn the pig on its back and fill the cavity loosely with the stuffing. Truss with butcher's twine or skewers about 2 inches apart. Skewer the legs into position, pulling the forelegs forward and bending the hindlegs into a crouching stance. Turn the pig over. Using a very sharp knife, score the skin on either side of the backbone at 1-inch intervals in a crisscross pattern; you may cut into the fat underneath, but avoid slicing the meat. Put a block of wood or ball of foil in its mouth to hold it open. Mix together in a small bowl:

¼ cup olive oil
2 tablespoons salt
1 tablespoon black pepper

Rub the mixture over the entire pig. Place the pig in the prepared roasting pan, resting it on its haunches and keeping it upright. If your pan is too small, arrange the pig diagonally in the pan and prop its head up with the loaf pan under its chin. Slip heavy-duty foil extending out from the roasting pan under the head and loaf pan to catch the juices and let them flow back into the pan during cooking. If the pig has a tendency to lean to one side, prop it up with balls of foil. Cover the ears and tail with pieces of foil. Place the pig in the oven, uncovered, and roast for 30 minutes. Reduce the oven temperature to 350°F and pour into the roasting pan:

3 cups dry white wine

Continue to cook, basting the pig every 30 minutes with the wine and pan juices. Roast until a thermometer inserted in the thickest part of the rump registers 145° to 150°F, 2 to 2½ hours more (the temperature will rise 5 to 10 degrees out of the oven).

Place the pig on a platter and let stand for 30 to 60 minutes. Skim off the fat from the pan juices, place the roasting pan over medium-high heat, and add:

2 cups chicken stock or broth

Bring to a simmer, stirring to scrape up the browned bits on the bottom of the pan. Simply serve with the pan juices. Or make a gravy by mixing together in a small bowl until well combined:

(¼ cup cornstarch)
(3 tablespoons cold water)

Pour the pan juices into a saucepan, bring to a simmer, and whisk in the cornstarch mixture. Bring to a boil and reduce the liquid until it has thickened. Season to taste with:

Salt and black pepper

Remove the foil from the pig's ears and tail. Gently roll it on its side and remove the string and/or skewers. Return the pig to its right side-up position. Remove the wooden block or foil ball from the pig's mouth. Place in the mouth, if desired:

(1 apple, lemon, or lime)

and in the eyes:

(Prunes or grapes)

Garnish the platter with:

A bed of watercress or other greens, Baked Apples Stuffed with Sausage, 175, or Tomatoes Provençale, 282

After presenting the pig at the table, carve it by removing the forelegs and hindquarters and arranging these on a platter. Cut the skin into squares. Remove the loin meat and cut into slices. Separate the ribs. Arrange the slices and skin on the platter and let the guests pick at the rest. Pass the platter with the gravy.

BECKER PORK HASH

3 or 4 servings

Homemade hashes—seasoned mixtures of chopped vegetables and cooked meat—are the convenience foods of yesteryear: a quick meal made of leftover roasts. Pan-fried, potato-laden versions (like Corned Beef Hash, 473) have aged well and continue to endure as a hearty breakfast go-to. Gravy-style hashes like this one are much better for repurposing meats that tend to dry out when reheated, such as pork loin, turkey, and chicken breast. Sadly, they have fallen out of favor. Regardless of these long-term trends, we count this recipe among our favorites for serving leftover pork roast—or turkey after Thanksgiving.

Melt in a large skillet over medium heat:

2 tablespoons butter

Add and cook, stirring, until the carrots are tender and the onion translucent, 5 to 7 minutes:

1 large onion, chopped
2 medium carrots, diced

Stir in:

8 ounces mushrooms, chopped

Increase the heat to medium-high and cook, stirring often, until the liquid the mushrooms release has evaporated, about 5 minutes. Add:

1½ cups chicken stock, leftover pan juices, or a combination
½ cup heavy cream
¼ cup port or Marsala
1 tablespoon soy sauce
2 garlic cloves, minced
1½ teaspoons fresh thyme leaves or ½ teaspoon dried thyme

Bring to a simmer, reduce the heat, and cook, stirring occasionally, for 10 minutes. Meanwhile, mix together into a paste in a small bowl:

2 tablespoons butter, softened
2 tablespoons all-purpose flour

When the simmering time is up, gradually whisk in the butter-flour mixture and simmer until thickened, an additional 2 minutes. Add and heat through, without simmering:

2 to 3 cups diced leftover roast pork
(One 10-ounce package frozen green peas)

Season to taste with:

Black pepper

Serve over:

Buttered egg noodles or toast

Garnish each serving with:

Chopped parsley

ABOUT GRILLING, BROILING, AND SAUTÉING PORK

These high-heat methods are perfect for loin chops and tenderloin, since they promote the formation of a brown crust before the meat overcooks and dries out. Tender parts of the pork shoulder, especially steaks cut from the collar or coppa area, 486, are also a fine choice and can be grilled, broiled, or sautéed as for loin chops. Other parts of the shoulder are too tough for this treatment. On the other hand, shoulder portions sliced across the grain into ½-inch strips are perfect for marinating, threading on skewers, and grilling.

To prepare pork for direct-heat grilling, trim most of the fat to keep flare-ups to a minimum. Some flare-ups are to be expected, even desirable (for that char-grilled flavor); just keep an eye on the meat and be ready to move it to cooler areas of the grill if it begins to char excessively. When purchasing pork chops to sear or sauté, do not shy away from those that have a nice layer of fat along the side: Trim off the excess, render it, and then cook the chops in their own fat.

GRILLED PORK TENDERLOIN

4 servings

Grill tenderloin whole to keep it from drying out. For tenderloins less than 1½ inches thick, treat as for chops, below. To ensure juiciness, first brine, 1046, the tenderloin and omit the salt below.

Prepare a medium-hot grill fire, 1063. Pat dry:

One 1- to 1½-pound pork tenderloin

Season with:

1 teaspoon salt
½ teaspoon black pepper

If the tenderloin is much thinner at one end, fold the thin end back along the roast and tie with two lengths of butcher's twine. Grill, turning every 2 minutes or so, until a thermometer inserted in the thickest part of the meat registers 140°F, 12 to 15 minutes (the temperature will rise 5 degrees off the grill). Loosely cover with foil and let stand for 5 to 10 minutes before slicing. Serve with:

A barbecue sauce, 582–83, Mojo, 567, Chimichurri, 567, or Vinaigrette, 575

GRILLED OR BROILED PORK LOIN CHOPS

4 servings

Pat dry:

4 bone-in or boneless center-cut pork loin chops, ¾ to 1½ inches thick

Rub with:

2 tablespoons vegetable oil

Season with:

1 teaspoon salt
½ teaspoon black pepper

Prepare a hot grill fire, 1063, or place a broiler pan on an oven rack set 3 to 4 inches below the heating element and preheat the broiler. Place the chops on the grill over direct heat or under the broiler. Cook thinner chops for about 8 minutes, turning once or twice. Thicker chops may need an extra minute or two. After each turn, sprinkle the chops with:

Juice of ½ lemon

The chops are done when a thermometer inserted in the center of the meat (near but not touching any bones) reads 145°F. For especially thick "double-cut" chops, you may wish to move them to a cooler area of the grill once browned (or to a lower oven rack if broiling), give them another spritz of lemon juice, cover the grill (or loosely cover with foil), and cook until done.

PORK SOUVLAKI

6 to 8 servings

For some of us, a pita filled with souvlaki is quintessential fair food. Feel free to substitute lamb shoulder or beef chuck for the pork.

Prepare:

Balkan Marinade, 580

and reserve the zested lemons. Slice across the grain into ¼- to ½-inch-thick slabs:

2½ pounds boneless pork shoulder, large streaks of fat removed

Cut these slabs into 1-inch-wide strips; cut any strip over 6 inches in half. Add the meat to a bowl or zip-top bag along with the marinade. Marinate in the refrigerator, covered, for at least 3 hours and up to 8 hours.

An hour before grilling, if using wooden skewers, soak them in water. Prepare a medium-hot, two-zone grill fire, 1063. Thread the pork onto skewers. Sear the skewers on one side until browned around the edges, about 3 minutes. Turn the skewers, drizzle with juice from one of the reserved lemons, and brown on the other side, another 2 to 3 minutes. As the skewers brown, pile them on top of one another on the cooler side of the grill; when the last skewers are

browned, sprinkle the remaining lemon over the pile and cover the grill. Cook 10 minutes more.
Use as a filling for:
Flatbread or Pita Sandwiches, 145
Or serve the skewers with:
Greek Salad, 117
Warmed pita bread or Crispy Smashed Potatoes, 268
Tzatziki, 569

GRILLED VIETNAMESE-STYLE PORK
4 servings

One of our favorite toppings for Bún (Vietnamese Rice Noodle Bowls), 305. Thick, center-cut, or sirloin pork chops are great here, but we are fond of using thinner chops or thin, skewered slices of pork shoulder, too.
Have ready one of the following:
4 bone-in or boneless center-cut pork loin chops, ¾ to 1½ inches thick
1½ pounds boneless pork shoulder, large streaks of fat removed
If using pork shoulder, slice it across the grain into ¼- to ½-inch-thick slabs.
Prepare:
Vietnamese-Style Marinade, 581, or Thai-Style Lemongrass Marinade, 581
Combine the pork with the marinade in a zip-top bag or bowl. Refrigerate for at least 2 hours and up to overnight, turning occasionally so it marinates evenly. If using wooden skewers, soak them in water for at least 1 hour.

Transfer the pork to a rack, wiping excess marinade back into the bag or bowl with your fingers and reserving it. Pat the meat dry. If using pork shoulder, thread the meat onto skewers. Transfer the marinade to a small saucepan and bring to a boil, then simmer over medium heat for 10 minutes, or until it reaches a sauce-like consistency.

Prepare a hot grill fire, 1063. For pork chops, cook as directed for **Grilled or Broiled Pork Loin Chops, 492.** For pork shoulder skewers, cook as directed for **Pork Souvlaki, 492.** Serve drizzled with the reduced sauce and garnish with:
Lime wedges

SAUTÉED PORK CHOPS
4 servings

This method works well for chops up to 1½ inches thick. For thicker, double-cut chops, treat as for Pan-Roasted Pork Tenderloin, 489. Preheat the oven to 350°F, brown the chops as described below using an ovenproof skillet, then transfer them to the oven to finish cooking.
Pat dry:
4 bone-in or boneless pork loin chops, 1 inch thick (about 1½ pounds)
Season with:
1 teaspoon salt
½ teaspoon black pepper
If possible, place the chops on a rack set in a rimmed baking sheet and refrigerate uncovered for at least 1 hour (this will promote browning).
Heat in a large skillet over medium-high heat:
1 tablespoon vegetable oil
Add the chops and cook until a thermometer inserted in the center of each chop registers 145°F, 4 to 5 minutes per side. Transfer to a warmed platter or plates to rest for 5 minutes. Meanwhile, if desired, pour off all but 1 tablespoon of fat from the skillet and make:
(A pan sauce, 545–46, or the sauce for Steak Diane, 461)
Serve with the chops.

BREADED PORK CHOPS OR CUTLETS
4 servings

For tips on pounding pork chops and steaks into thin cutlets, see 404.
Pat dry:
1½ pounds thinly sliced pork leg steaks or 4 boneless pork loin chops (¾ to 1 inch thick)
If using loin chops, butterfly each one by slicing lengthwise through the fatty, curved side of the chop, holding the knife parallel to the work surface. Continue slicing through the chop, leaving ½ inch of the meat intact on the opposite side to form a hinge. Open each chop like a book and flatten it with your hand. Pound to an even thickness of about ¼ inch. If the pieces seem too large for the pan once they have been pounded, cut them in half.

Proceed to bread and fry as for **Wienerschnitzel, 475.** Or, for **Pork Milanese,** proceed as for **Pan-Fried Chicken Cutlets II, 414.**

SWEET-AND-SOUR PORK
4 servings

The Chinese-American take-out classic. Please read about Deep-Frying, 1051.
Heat in a large saucepan or a wok over medium heat:
2 inches vegetable oil
Whisk to combine in a medium bowl:
¼ cup all-purpose flour
¼ cup cornstarch
2 large eggs
¼ teaspoon salt
1 tablespoon water
Add to the batter, stirring to coat:
1 pound pork loin, cut into ¾-inch cubes
When the oil reaches 365°F, fry the pork in batches until light golden brown and crisp, 3 to 4 minutes per batch. Use a slotted spoon or spider to transfer the pork to a rack set over a baking sheet to drain. (Pour the frying oil into a heatproof bowl or container and set aside to cool before discarding or recycling.) Whisk together in a medium bowl:
6 tablespoons pineapple juice
2 tablespoons cider vinegar
1 tablespoon brown sugar
2 teaspoons cornstarch

2 teaspoons soy sauce
2 teaspoons Worcestershire sauce

Place the pan back over medium heat and add:

1 tablespoon vegetable oil

When the oil shimmers, add:

2 large garlic cloves, smashed

Cook, stirring, until fragrant, about 1 minute. Add:

1 red or green bell pepper, cut into ¾-inch chunks
1½ cups ¾-inch pineapple chunks

Cook, stirring, until starting to soften, about 4 minutes. Stir in the sauce and the pork and cook briefly, stirring constantly to coat the pork and vegetables with the sauce, just until heated through and the sauce has thickened. Serve with:

Cooked rice, 343

Garnish with:

Thinly sliced green onion

COUNTRY-FRIED PORK TENDERLOIN WITH GRAVY

6 to 8 servings or 12 pieces for biscuit sandwiches

This spicy pork dish is sometimes served at breakfast, and it also makes a tasty sandwich.

Combine in a small bowl:

1 tablespoon sweet paprika
1½ teaspoons salt
1½ teaspoons black pepper
½ teaspoon garlic powder
½ teaspoon dried sage
½ teaspoon dried oregano
½ teaspoon dry mustard
½ teaspoon cayenne pepper

Pat dry:

1½ pounds pork tenderloin, cut crosswise into 12 pieces

Butterfly each piece by placing it cut side down and, with the knife held parallel to the work surface, cut horizontally toward the other side, leaving ½ inch of the meat intact to form a hinge. Open each piece like a book and flatten it with your hand. Rub the pork with the spice mixture, transfer to a baking sheet, and refrigerate uncovered for 1 hour.

Heat in a large skillet over medium-high heat:

¼ inch vegetable oil

Dredge the tenderloin pieces in:

½ cup flour

Shake off the excess. Add to the skillet in batches and fry until browned on one side, 3 to 4 minutes. Turn and fry on the other side for 3 to 4 minutes. Remove the pork to a platter and cover to keep warm. For the gravy, pour off all but 2 tablespoons of the fat from the skillet. Whisk in:

2 tablespoons all-purpose flour

Whisk in slowly:

1 cup milk

Heat just to a boil, scraping up any browned bits on the bottom of the skillet. Season the gravy to taste with:

Salt and black pepper

Pour the gravy over the pork. Serve with:

Biscuits, 635–37, or soft rolls

ABOUT BRAISING, STEWING, AND BARBECUING PORK

These gentle, moist-heat cooking methods are used for less tender cuts of pork from the shoulder, leg, shanks, and belly. The cuts from either end of the loin—the blade end or the sirloin end—can be braised as well. Along with shoulder steaks, we appreciate the ease with which they can be browned, and bones add flavor to the braising liquid. ➤ To adapt a braising or stewing recipe to use a slow cooker, see 1058; for pressure-cooking, see 1059.

Low-and-slow barbecuing is also a moist-heat method, since frequent basting or a water pan, 1066, keeps the humidity of the grill or smoker elevated. Shoulder and spareribs are our favorite cuts to barbecue, though back ribs and rib tips have their own appeal. If you must choose between the butt and picnic portion of the shoulder, keep in mind that the butt will yield the most meat.

PORK BRAISED IN MILK

6 servings

Our absolute favorite cut to use here is the collar, or coppa roast, 486.

Heat in a Dutch oven over medium heat:

2 slices bacon or pancetta

Cook until the fat renders and the slices are browned. Remove the bacon (reserve it for serving) and add to the pot:

One 2½-pound boneless pork shoulder or sirloin roast or one 3-pound bone-in pork loin roast

Brown the meat on all sides, about 15 minutes total, and transfer to a plate. Add to the pot:

1 small onion, diced
(1 small fennel bulb, diced)
1 celery rib, diced
1 carrot, diced
6 garlic cloves, smashed

Cook until the vegetables begin to brown, about 8 minutes. Add:

3 cups whole milk
6 sage leaves
2 bay leaves
2 large strips lemon zest, removed with a vegetable peeler
3-inch sprig rosemary

Return the pork to the pot, bring to a simmer over high heat, then cover and reduce the heat to low. Simmer, turning the meat occasionally, until the pork is very tender when pierced with the tip of a sharp knife, 1½ to 2 hours.

Transfer the meat to a platter and cover with foil to keep warm; remove the herbs and zest. Skim as much fat from the surface of the braising liquid as possible and bring to a boil over medium-high. Cook, stirring occasionally, until reduced by half, about 15 minutes. If desired, you may strain the vegetables out or blend the sauce for a smoother texture. Season to taste with:

Salt and black pepper

Slice the meat and arrange on a platter. Spoon the sauce over the meat. Crumble the cooked bacon or pancetta and sprinkle over the top along with:

Chopped parsley

BRAISED STUFFED PORK CHOPS COCKAIGNE

4 servings

Preheat the oven to 350°F.

Prepare:

Italian Bread Crumb Stuffing, 533

Trim off the excess fat from:

4 pork rib chops, about 1½ inches thick

Holding the knife parallel to the work surface, cut a large gash or pocket in one side of each chop and stuff with the stuffing. Skewer closed with wooden skewers or toothpicks. Heat in a large heavy skillet over medium-high heat:

1 tablespoon vegetable oil

Add the chops to the skillet and sear on each side. Arrange the chops in a single layer in a lidded baking dish. Pour in:

¼ inch milk or chicken stock or broth

Cover and bake until tender, about 1 hour 15 minutes. If desired, skim any fat from the cooking liquid and use it to make:

(Basic Pan Gravy, 545)

in the skillet used to brown the chops. Or serve with:

(Cranberry Sauce, 179)

BRAISED PORK WITH SAUERKRAUT

8 servings

The addition of fresh cabbage to the traditional pairing of pork and sauerkraut gives this dish another dimension of flavor.

Pat dry:

One 4-pound boneless pork shoulder roast, excess fat trimmed

Mix together in a small bowl:

2 teaspoons sweet paprika
1 teaspoon salt
1 teaspoon black pepper
½ teaspoon dried sage
½ teaspoon dried thyme
¼ teaspoon dry mustard

Rub the spice mix all over the pork. Transfer to a rack set in a rimmed baking sheet and refrigerate uncovered for at least 2 hours (or overnight).

Preheat the oven to 325°F.

Heat in a Dutch oven over medium heat:

2 tablespoons olive oil or bacon fat

Add the meat and brown on all sides. Transfer to a plate. Pour off all but 2 tablespoons of the fat from the pot and add:

4 cups shredded cabbage
1 onion, thinly sliced
1 carrot, diced
1 leek, trimmed, halved, well cleaned, and thinly sliced

Cover the pot and cook, stirring occasionally, until the vegetables are softened and the cabbage is wilted, about 10 minutes. Add and cook for 1 minute more:

2 garlic cloves, minced

Add:

1 pound sauerkraut, drained
1 cup chicken stock or broth
One 12-ounce bottle dark beer
1 teaspoon caraway seeds
(1 teaspoon dried savory)
2 bay leaves

Bring to a boil. Return the meat to the pot, nestling it into the cabbage mixture, and cover the pot. Transfer to the oven to braise until the meat is fork-tender, 2 to 3 hours. Remove the meat from the pot and remove the bay leaves. Skim off any fat from the pan juices. Slice the meat and serve with the vegetables and juices.

BRAISED PULLED PORK

12 servings

Though no substitute for real-deal Smoked Pork Shoulder, 496, this indoor method is much easier and quicker. The shoulder braises in its own juices and becomes meltingly tender. Properly sauced on a bun, even the pickiest barbecue connoisseur should be won over, or at least appeased. To give the pork a smoky flavor, use smoked salt in the rub, or replace half of the paprika with smoked paprika.

Trim off and reserve the excess fat from:

One 4-pound boneless pork shoulder butt or blade roast

Rub the roast with:

Southern Barbecue Dry Rub, 587

The meat can be cooked at once or wrapped in 2 layers of foil and refrigerated for up to 24 hours. Position a rack in the center of the oven. Preheat the oven to 325°F.

Heat a Dutch oven (or other heavy ovenproof pot large enough to hold the meat) over medium heat. Add the reserved pork trimmings and render until you have 2 tablespoons fat. Alternatively, use:

(2 tablespoons rendered bacon fat or vegetable oil)

Add the meat and brown well on all sides. Cover the pot tightly with a lid or foil, transfer to the oven, and bake until the meat is tender enough to be shredded with a fork, 3 to 3½ hours. Transfer the roast to a large baking dish or platter and skim the fat from the pan juices. Shred the meat with a fork and mix together with the pan juices. Dress and serve as for **Smoked Pork Shoulder, 496.**

BRAISED CARNITAS

6 servings

Carnitas are traditionally made by frying pork from start to finish in a lazily bubbling bath of lard, or *manteca*. The results are spectacular, but famed author Diana Kennedy's home kitchen-friendly method is almost as delicious and much more convenient: Pork shoulder is braised until tender, the braising liquid is allowed to evaporate, and the cubes of pork fry in their own rendered fat.

Place in a Dutch oven:

3 pounds untrimmed boneless pork shoulder, cut into 1½-inch cubes
2 cups water
5 unpeeled garlic cloves, lightly smashed
Zest of 1 orange, removed in wide strips with a vegetable peeler
2 bay leaves
1 tablespoon salt

Bring to a boil, reduce the heat, and simmer, covered, for 1½ hours. Uncover the pot and remove the garlic cloves, zest, and bay leaves.

Increase the heat to medium and cook, stirring occasionally, until all of the water has evaporated. Immediately reduce the heat to medium-low and fry the pork in its own fat until golden and crispy. Serve in Tacos, 146, or Tortas, 143, or accompanied with:

Frijoles de la Olla, 213, or Refried Beans, 215
Cooked long-grain rice, 343, or tortillas
Any salsa, 573–74, Mexican Adobo Sauce, 585, or Habanero-Citrus Hot Sauce, 571
Cilantro sprigs
Sliced avocado
Lime wedges

PORK ADOVADA

6 servings

In this popular New Mexican stew, meat is marinated in a paste made from dried chiles. In the Southwest, this stew is typically served with rice and Sopapillas, 654, but flour or corn tortillas can be substituted.

Combine in a small bowl:

6 dried New Mexico chiles
Hot water to cover

Keep the chiles submerged by placing a saucer or small pot lid over them and let soak for 20 minutes. Drain the peppers, reserving the water. Slit the peppers open and discard the stems and seeds. Put the peppers and ¼ cup of the soaking liquid in a food processor or blender. Add:

⅓ cup cider vinegar
4 garlic cloves, peeled
1 teaspoon salt
1 teaspoon cumin seeds
½ teaspoon dried oregano
½ teaspoon black pepper
¼ teaspoon ground coriander
Pinch of ground cinnamon

Process to a smooth paste. Pour the paste into a large bowl and add:

3 pounds boneless pork shoulder or country-style ribs, trimmed and cut into 1½-inch pieces, or 3½ pounds pork shoulder steaks

Toss to coat the meat with the marinade. Cover and refrigerate for at least 12 hours and up to 3 days, turning the meat occasionally.

Heat in a Dutch oven over medium heat:

2 tablespoons vegetable oil

Add and cook, stirring often, until softened but not browned, about 5 minutes:

1 large onion, chopped

Add the pork and its marinade along with:

One 28-ounce can whole tomatoes

Reduce the heat, cover, and simmer until the pork is tender, 1½ to 2 hours.

Transfer the meat to a rimmed baking sheet. If using shoulder steaks, remove any bones and cut the meat into chunks. Skim the fat from the sauce, then boil the sauce over medium-high heat to thicken, stirring occasionally. Taste and adjust the seasonings. Return the pork to the pot, stir to coat, and heat through. Serve as for **Braised Carnitas, 495.**

SMOTHERED COUNTRY-STYLE RIBS

6 to 8 servings

After 4 hours of cooking, these ribs become fall-apart tender and deeply infused with the flavor of the sauce.

Position a rack in the center of the oven. Preheat the oven to 350°F.

Arrange in a large baking dish:

4 pounds country-style ribs

Whisk together in a bowl:

1½ cups barbecue sauce, 582–83
1 cup water

Pour the sauce over the ribs and turn them to coat. Cover with foil and bake for 3 hours. Uncover and bake the ribs for 30 minutes. Turn them and continue to bake until fork-tender, about 30 minutes more. Transfer the ribs to a platter and let stand for 15 minutes. Skim the fat from the sauce and drizzle on or serve alongside the ribs.

CHASHU PORK (JAPANESE BRAISED PORK BELLY)

8 servings

Ask your butcher to roll and tie the pork belly for you if possible. If that's not an option, rolling the belly is much easier with two people: One person holds the belly in place while someone else ties it with butcher's twine. Chashu pork is perhaps best known for its role as a garnish for ramen, 304, but leftovers can be used anywhere from sandwiches to stir-fries. (Simply slice to the desired thickness and griddle until browned and heated through.)

Preheat the oven to 250°F.

Tightly roll into a cylinder with the skin side facing out, and tie at 2-inch intervals:

One 2-pound slab pork belly, skin attached

Bring to a simmer in a Dutch oven:

1 cup sake
1 cup mirin
¼ cup soy sauce
5 garlic cloves, smashed
1 bunch green onions, whole

Add the pork belly, cover, and transfer to the oven. Cook until a skewer into the center of the meat offers very little resistance, 4 to 5 hours.

Allow the meat to rest for 20 minutes before slicing very thin. Reserve the cooking liquid, discarding the green onions. Once cool, skim off the fat and use as a seasoning for the broth used to make ramen, 304, rice dishes, or other braises.

SMOKED PORK SHOULDER

8 to 10 servings

In many parts of the country, "barbecue" means spice-rubbed pork shoulder, smoked over hickory until it has a rosy smoke ring, fork-tender meat, and a nice crusty bark. It is customary to finely chop or pull (that is, shred) the pork, moisten with barbecue sauce, and serve on warm buns as suggested on 497. That said, any sauce or method of serving will shine here: Toss with New Mexico Green Chile Sauce, 554, Mexican Adobo Sauce, 585, or a judicious splash of Habanero-Citrus Hot Sauce, 571, for serving in Tacos, 146, and Tortas, 143; or season with Nuoc Cham, 571, or top with a drizzle of Vietnamese Caramel Sauce, 578, for filling Banh Mi, 139. Since leftovers are likely, try a few of these suggestions for the sake of variation, or use the pork as a filling for enchiladas, 539–40. For a smokeless, cheater's version, see Braised Pulled Pork, 495.

Please read about Barbecuing, 1066. Trim all but ¼ inch of fat from:

One 6- to 8-pound pork shoulder butt roast, bone-in or boneless and tied

Rub all over with:

½ cup Southern Barbecue Dry Rub, 587, or ½ teaspoon each salt and black pepper for every pound of meat

Place on a rack set in a rimmed baking sheet and refrigerate uncovered overnight or for up to 2 days.

Heat a smoker or grill set up for barbecuing, 1067, to 225° to 250°F (preferably with a water pan). Add to the coals:

One small chunk of dry hickory or apple wood

Add the pork shoulder to the cooler side of the smoker or grill and cover so that the top vent pulls smoke across the meat. Adjust the vents to maintain the temperature (this is difficult and may take practice, or, in the worst case, a fresh load of charcoal). You may add another small chunk of hickory wood every hour for the first 4 hours. If you do not have a water pan inside to keep the smoker or grill humid, baste the meat every 2 hours with:

(Basic Mop, 583, Beer Mop, 583, or North Carolina–Style Barbecue Sauce, 583, with no added ketchup)

Cook the pork shoulder until a thermometer inserted in the thickest part registers 200°F, or until the meat wants to shred easily when lightly prodded with a fork and the shoulder bone wiggles when shaken with tongs. This can take 10 to 14 hours. To quicken the pace somewhat, you may take the pork shoulder out when it reaches 150°F, wrap it in a double thickness of foil, and return to the smoker to finish cooking (keep in mind that this will soften the shoulder's crunchy, spice-rubbed surface, or "bark").

When the pork is tender, transfer to a rimmed baking sheet or large platter and carefully remove any foil, pouring off the juices into a measuring cup. Rest the pork for at least 15 minutes. Some prefer to pull the pork apart in irregular, bite-sized clumps, others shred it with a fork, or chop it finely; we prefer the chunkier approach. If you have cooking juices from wrapping the pork, skim as much fat as you can from the surface of the juices (or use a gravy separator), then add some of the juices to the pork. Moisten the pork with:

North Carolina–Style Barbecue Sauce, 583, or a barbecue sauce of your choice, 582–83

Toss together, adding more sauce bit by bit, until it is seasoned to your taste; keep in mind that whoever wants more sauce can add it later, to their taste. For serving as sandwiches, provide more barbecue sauce for the table and:

8 to 10 warmed hamburger buns
Coleslaw, 119
Bread-and-Butter Pickles, 924, or another pickle of your choice

Or serve as part of a "meat-and-three" with a coleslaw as above and two (or more) of the following:

Southern-Style Greens, 243, Baked Beans, 215, or Black-Eyed Peas and Greens, 216
Hushpuppies, 655, Southern Corn Bread, 630, or Baked Macaroni and Cheese, 296

BARBECUED PORK RIBS

6 to 8 servings

We prefer smoking pork with hickory wood chunks, but pecan and fruitwoods work well here, too. Please read about Barbecuing, 1066. Pat dry:

3 racks St. Louis–cut pork spareribs or 4 racks back ribs (7 to 9 pounds)

If the racks still have the tough membrane that covers their concave side, you will need to peel it off, 487. Rub both sides with:

⅔ to 1 cup Southern Barbecue Dry Rub, 587, or Coffee Spice Rub, 587

Refrigerate for at least 1 hour or, for a stronger flavor, wrap in plastic and refrigerate overnight.

Heat a smoker or grill set up for barbecuing, 1067, to 225° to 250°F (preferably with a water pan). Add to the coals:

One small chunk of dry hickory wood

Arrange the rib slabs side by side on the cooler side of the smoker or grill and cover so that the top vent pulls smoke across the meat. Adjust the vents to maintain the temperature (this is difficult and may take practice, or, in the worst case, a fresh load of charcoal). You may add another small chunk of hickory wood every other hour. If you do not have a water pan inside to keep the smoker or grill humid, baste the ribs every 2 hours with:

(Basic Mop, 583, or Beer Mop, 583)

Cook until the ribs are tender. A good way to tell is to twist one of the rib bones: It should feel loose and give a little. Back ribs may be done in 3 hours; spareribs make take up to 6 hours. Place the ribs on a baking sheet or platter, cover tightly with foil and let stand for at least 15 minutes before serving. If you wish, swab the ribs lightly or serve with:

A barbecue sauce, 582–83

ABOUT BACON, SALT PORK, AND FATBACK

Bacon is usually made from fat-streaked pork belly. The best bacon is dry-cured and then smoked; however most bacon available at the supermarket has been injected with brine and smoke flavoring. You can distinguish dry-cured bacon from the other, lesser bacon because it is firmer, and will not exude liquid or shrink as much when cooked. Despite this state of affairs, bacon is universally loved, and even the wateriest slices can be coaxed to browned, savory goodness with a pan and a little patience. To make your own bacon, see 497.

Most bacon is made with curing salt, which contains sodium nitrite. A traditional preservative, curing salt is also responsible for the characteristic flavor and pinkish color of bacon, ham, corned beef, and other cured meats. Unfortunately, studies have found that there is a risk of sodium nitrite forming minute amounts of carcinogenic nitrosamines when fried. In response to this health concern, some bacon is now made without the use of curing salts, and may be labeled as **uncured** or **"no nitrates or nitrites added."** Uncured bacon may simply be pork belly that has been heavily salted (which tastes like salty roasted pork and fools no one), or it may be brined with a mixture that contains celery juice powder, a vegetable-based source of nitrites. Though the latter product is essentially cured with chemically similar methods as normal bacon, celery juice powder is not recognized as an effective curing agent by the USDA, and bacon, ham, or sausage made with it must be labeled uncured. For more on curing salts, see 936.

Most bacon sold in this country is sold sliced. Unsliced **slab bacon** is ideal for fashioning thick pieces to use for larding, 451, or for *lardons*, the French term for bacon that has been cubed or sliced, blanched, and fried until crisp. Bacon streaked with a good proportion of lean meat is best for serving as a breakfast meat. We prefer thick-sliced bacon, and especially enjoy peppered bacon.

You may find irregular pieces for sale called **bacon ends;** trimmed from the sides of the belly, they are especially smoky. Though not the best choice for breakfast, bacon ends are perfect for flavoring braises, stews, and simmering beans with smoky bacon essence. On the other end of the spectrum is **pancetta,** an unsmoked Italian bacon that has been cured with bay leaves, thyme, black pepper, and other spices. Unlike regular bacon, pancetta is virtually guaranteed to be dry-cured. You may find pancetta in the standard slab shape, but it is more commonly rolled and tied, which makes for spiraled slices. When cooking presliced pancetta, keep in mind that it is much quicker to brown than bacon (it is usually sliced thinner and contains less water). You may substitute bacon for pancetta; if desired, blanch the bacon first in boiling water to subdue the smoky flavor and make it more pancetta-like.

Not all bacon comes from the belly. Italian **guanciale** is made from fatty, full-flavored pork jowls. Guanciale is primarily used as an ingredient in vegetable dishes, stews, and pasta dishes like Spaghetti Carbonara, 295. **Back bacon,** or **Canadian bacon,** is made with brined, smoked pork loin. Canadian bacon is so lean it resembles ham more than bacon. Like "partially cooked" ham, 499, it has been held at temperatures above 137°F for an extended time to eradicate *Trichinella* contamination. In order to be safe to eat, however, it must be cooked to an internal temperature of 145°F. The rarely seen unsmoked variety, sometimes referred to as **peameal** or **cornmeal bacon,** has not been cooked at all; it comes rolled in cornmeal and is typically baked whole, or cut into slices and pan-fried or grilled.

When the fattier parts of the belly are dry-cured in large chunks and left unsmoked, they are called **salt pork,** or **side meat,** which may or may not have a "streak of lean" running through it. Salt pork is commonly rendered in a pan for cooking; it is occasionally added in large chunks to simmering chowders, stews, or beans, which lends richness to the entire dish. As the name implies, it is heavily salted; hold off on seasoning dishes with more salt until the end of cooking (if desired, soak overnight before using to reduce the saltiness).

The thick layer of fat that runs the length of the hog above the loin is called **fatback.** Pieces of fatback may be rendered in a pan for cooking, or rendered in larger quantities to make lard, 451. Less often, it is cut into thin strips and used to lard meats, 451. **Cracklings** are slices or cubes of skin-on fatback and pork belly that have been rendered and fried until golden and crispy. They are an excellent addition to corn bread, 630, or finely chopped and sprinkled on a green salad or Larb, 122. When left uncured, fatback has a pure, mellow flavor. Though occasionally made into salt pork in the United States, cured fatback is much more prevalent in Europe. Italian **lardo** is similar to salt pork, but it is made exclusively from slabs of fatback and cured with rosemary, pepper, garlic, and other spices for 6 months or more. In Eastern Europe, a similar product is called **salo.** Both may be thinly sliced (freezing briefly makes this easier) and consumed raw—much like dry-cured ham or salami—or ground, seasoned, and whipped into an unctuous, butter-like spread.

To remove excess salt from bacon, place it in a cold skillet, cover with ½ inch water, and cook over medium heat until the water evaporates. At this point, you may remove it and let it cool for use in a recipe (for serving slices with breakfast or in sandwiches, just continue to fry the bacon until golden brown).

COOKING BACON

2 or 3 slices thick-cut bacon per serving

I. BAKED

This is our preferred method for cooking slab bacon, especially for several servings or more. All of the slices brown evenly in one batch, there is no splatter, and pieces remain relatively flat.

Preheat the oven to 400°F. Have ready a rimmed baking sheet. For easier cleanup, line the baking sheet with parchment paper or foil.

Place on the sheet in one even layer so they do not overlap:

Slices of bacon

Bake for 10 minutes, then remove the sheet from the oven and turn the slices. If any of them are browning faster than the others, rearrange them to cook evenly. Return to the oven and bake until browned to your liking, 5 to 10 minutes longer. Drain on paper towels.

To candy the bacon, pour off the rendered fat from the baking sheet. Liberally brush or sprinkle both sides of each bacon slice with **honey, sorghum syrup, maple syrup,** or **brown sugar.** Return the bacon to the baking sheet and return the sheet to the oven for another 5 minutes.

II. PAN-FRIED

The key to well-rendered crispy bacon on the stovetop is low heat and patience: The longer bacon cooks, the more fat is rendered out of it. Of course, some misguided souls prefer theirs "flubbery"; so cook to your own personal taste. If frying lean Canadian bacon, add 1 tablespoon butter or oil to the skillet.

Place in a large cast-iron or other heavy skillet:

Slices of bacon

Do not overlap the slices; if needed, cut them in half to fit more in the skillet. Place the skillet over medium-low heat and slowly cook until the bacon is browned. Turn often and monitor the heat to avoid burning it. Transfer to paper towels to drain. If cooking in batches, pour the grease into a coffee mug between batches to prevent excess popping and splattering.

III. MICROWAVED

Since microwaves vary in power and efficiency, the method below provides only an approximate time. Practice to find the timing and desired degree of doneness for your own oven.

Spread 2 layers of paper towels on a plate and arrange on the towels:

Slices of bacon

Place in the microwave and cook on high for 3 minutes. Touch the bacon; if it is not crisp enough, continue cooking, checking for doneness every 30 seconds. Pat the surface of the bacon with paper towels and serve.

ABOUT HAM AND HAM HOCKS

Someone once defined eternity as a ham and two people. The definition probably dates from the days when the term applied to the small mountain of meat we now call a **whole ham,** which is the entire back leg portion of the hog, cured or smoked. Today the term "ham" is used for a variety of pork products fashioned from the leg and shoulder that have been cured and sometimes smoked or aged (or both). For "fresh ham," or raw pork leg that has not been smoked or cured, see 487. In general, there are two categories of ham: brined or brine-cured hams and dry-cured hams.

BRINE-CURED HAMS

Also referred to as **deli hams,** or **city hams,** this is the most common category of hams available to us. These are the moist honey-glazed hams that grace our holiday tables and stock our deli cases, waiting to be sliced to order. ➤ They must be refrigerated. City hams have been submerged in or injected with a brine and then cooked through. Sometimes they are smoked, or they may simply have smoke flavor added to the brine. In response to health concerns, city hams are now available "uncured," meaning they have been made with celery juice powder rather than standard curing salt (for more on this, see About Bacon, 497). **Partially cooked hams** have been cooked to a temperature between 137° and 145°F for an extended period to destroy *Trichinella* parasites. ➤ They must be cooked to an internal temperature of 145°F to be safe to eat. **Fully cooked hams**—also labeled "ready to eat" or "ready to serve"—can be eaten, with no further preparation, but they will taste better and have a more appealing presentation if warmed through to 145°F and glazed (see Baked Ham, 500). These may be found spiral-cut so that they hold together for a dramatic presentation and are easy to serve as well.

Bone-in city ham comes in several forms. A whole ham includes the entire hind leg with the hip and leg bones intact, averages between 15 and 20 pounds, and will serve at least 20 people generously, with leftovers (do not neglect the bones, which may be added to Pork Stock, 76). For smaller crowds, you can buy a section of a whole ham, either the rounded upper thigh portion, or **rump half,** or the lower **shank half.** The rump half is meatier and has less fat, but it is somewhat difficult to carve because of the hip bone (see the illustration on 490 for guidance). Either section can weigh from 5 to 8 pounds—enough to serve 8 to 12 people. Smaller steaks and ham roasts are also available cut from the center of the leg. These **center ham slices** or **roasts** generally weigh under 2 pounds and are quick to cook and serve; see Broiled Ham Steak, 501.

Boneless city ham is available in many shapes and sizes: whole, halved, shaped, or in chunks. Oblong deli hams are meant to be thinly sliced for sandwiches; they are made with lean cured meat with most of the external fat removed. Some boneless hams are formed from chunks of leg meat and may contain added water and phosphates. The best boneless hams have no water or other ingredients added; these are simply labeled "ham." Others, in descending order of quality, are "ham with natural juices," "ham with water added," and "ham-and-water product." Unfortunately, the texture of **canned hams** leaves much to be desired. When you buy them, check the label for perishability and suggested refrigeration.

Besides the traditional hind leg, there are hams from the shoulder that tend to cost less while providing excellent flavor. **Picnic ham** is fashioned from the lower portion of the shoulder; it is very tasty but tends to be slightly tougher than ham from the hind leg. Because it contains more fat and connective tissue in proportion to lean meat, ➤ you should figure on almost a pound of picnic ham on the bone per serving. Another shoulder ham, known as the **smoked shoulder roll, cottage ham,** or **daisy ham,** comes from the upper blade portion of the shoulder; though tender and tasty, it may be quite fatty. Cut into slices, it makes a delicious alternative to bacon. **Tasso ham**—a Louisiana specialty made by curing pork shoulder with a piquant mix of spices and then hot-smoking it—is often chopped and added for flavor to gumbo, jambalaya, étouffée, and other Creole and Cajun dishes.

Aside from filling sandwiches, city ham is added as a main ingredient or flavoring in countless dishes; for some examples, see Chicken Cordon Bleu, 416, Chef's Salad, 120, and Asopao de Pollo, 93. For serving as an appetizer, see About Party Platters, 45, Deviled Ham, 62, and Corn and Ham Fritters, 654.

DRY-CURED HAMS

Dry-cured hams are raw, trimmed hog legs that have been covered with a salt cure and left to age for 6 months or more. This causes the ham to lose at least one-fifth of its weight from water loss, which concentrates its flavor and firms its texture. Aged hams also undergo enzymatic changes, which produce a host of interesting flavors; the longer a ham is aged, the funkier and more pronounced these flavors become. Dry-cured hams are sometimes cold-smoked before aging, or left unsmoked for a milder, purer flavor. High levels of salt and lowered water activity, 934, allow whole dry-cured hams to be stored at room temperature for long periods without spoiling. Especially well-aged specimens are fantastic when sliced paper-thin and eaten raw.

Hams have been dry-cured in Virginia, Kentucky, and Tennessee for generations. Though many of these hams bear the name of the state or community they are crafted in (such as **Smithfield**), they are collectively referred to as **country hams.** Some country hams are smoked (usually over hickory), others are just cured and aged (6 months minimum, and for as long as 2 or 3 years). Whole bone-in or boneless country hams are available for purchase directly from the producer. If you wish to slice country ham paper-thin for eating raw, purchase a boneless one as it is much easier to slice across the grain. Most producers do not trim off the skin or desiccated outer surface of the exposed meat (called the "face"). These crusty, mold-blemished areas are inedible and must be trimmed off. ➤ Once the interior of the ham has been exposed, it should be tightly wrapped (or, ideally, vacuum-packed) and refrigerated or frozen. To bake a whole country ham, see 500.

Thin "biscuit slices" and thicker steaks or center slices can be found at some grocery stores, especially in the South. The biscuit slices are meant to be pan-fried and eaten as a salty breakfast meat; thicker steaks are intended to be braised or desalted and pan-fried. Either product (used in moderation) makes a fine substitute for ham hocks or bacon as a flavoring in braises and stews. We do not recommend eating biscuit or center slices raw, as their thick cuts make them chewy.

Europe is the birthplace of numerous varieties of dry-cured hams, many of which can be found stateside in local stores and online. Italian **prosciutto** and Spanish **serrano ham** are perhaps the best known to us. Though most prosciutto and serrano sold is of high quality, some special types are very distinctive. In the Parma region, prosciutto is made from hogs that have been fed whey from Parmesan cheese production; Ibérico ham, a type of serrano, is made from a special breed of black hogs that are pastured in acorn-strewn forests before slaughter. These practices give the ham a unique richness. French **Bayonne ham** and Germany's smoked **Westphalian ham** are also available. Though the term **"Black Forest ham,"** denotes a dry-cured, smoked ham in Europe, the label can be applied to just about any ham product in this country. Italian **speck** is made with portions from the leg, which are dry-cured with juniper, bay leaves, and other spices and lightly smoked. **Coppa,** or **capicola,** is made from a tender, boneless portion of the shoulder, 487, and dry-cured in a piquant or mild mix of spices.

With the exception of country ham, dry-cured hams are usually reserved for slicing thin and eating raw. We prefer them sliced across the grain, but many serrano enthusiasts prefer their ham sliced with the grain, which gives it a slight chew. For ideas on how to serve fine ham as an appetizer or light meal, see About Party Platters, 45. Thinly sliced cured ham is wonderful wrapped around ripe melon slices, 58, or halved figs.

Any dry-cured ham can be used as a seasoning in cooked dishes; just be sure to keep in mind how salty the ham is and moderate (or compensate) accordingly. Dry-cured and smoked **ham hocks** are a much more common ingredient in our kitchens. Since the hock area is the hardest-working, these contribute a deep flavor to slow-cooked stews and bean soups, as well as enriching the texture of the cooking liquid or broth with gelatin. For cooking uncured pig's feet, see 519.

BAKED HAM

2/3 pound bone-in ham or 1/2 pound boneless ham per person

Preheat the oven to 325°F.

Have ready:

1 ham, partially or fully cooked

If the ham has skin or rind attached and you wish to make it crisp and serve with the ham, take a sharp knife and carefully score the skin at 1-inch intervals in a crisscross pattern; if your knife is not sharp enough, a box cutter fitted with a fresh blade works well. Slice through the skin and some of the fat, but try to keep from cutting into the muscle underneath. Place on a rack set in a shallow roasting pan, skin side up; if the ham has been spiral-cut, cover the pan tightly with foil to keep it from drying out. Bake until a thermometer inserted in the center of the thickest portion of the ham (next to but not touching any bones) registers 145°F. For a whole 10- to 15-pound ham, allow 18 to 20 minutes per pound; for a half—5 to 7 pounds—about 20 minutes per pound; or for a shank or butt portion weighing 3 to 4 pounds, about 35 minutes per pound.

To glaze the ham, remove it from the oven about 30 minutes before it is done, unwrap if necessary, and increase the oven temperature to 425°F. If you have chosen not to serve the skin, remove it now and slash the fat underneath in a crisscross pattern. Cover the surface with:

Honey Glaze II, 579, Bourbon-Molasses Glaze, 579, or Pineapple Glaze, 579

Or mix together in a small bowl:

1 1/3 cups packed brown sugar
3 tablespoons cider vinegar, wine, or ham drippings
2 teaspoons dry mustard

You may stud the fat at the intersections of the slashes with:

(Whole cloves)

For a festive, kitschy touch, festoon the ham with:

(Pineapple rings studded with maraschino cherries)

Return the ham to the oven, reduce the oven temperature to 325°F again, and cook until the ham is nicely browned, about 30 minutes. Serve on a platter.

BAKED COUNTRY HAM

20 to 25 servings

Soaking country hams in several changes of water reduces their saltiness. Some especially well-cured specimens may take a very long time to soak. Please keep in mind that even after soaking, country ham will always be saltier than baked city ham, so make portions smaller accordingly—and always slice across the grain.

Place in a large stockpot, with the shank end facing up:

One 14- to 17-pound bone-in country ham

Add cold water to cover. Let soak for 24 hours, or 48 hours for especially aged hams, changing the water every 6 hours or so. Scrub the ham well, using a stiff brush to remove any mold, trim off all dried meat that was exposed to the air during aging, and rinse thoroughly. The best way to determine if the ham is soaked long enough is to go by taste (properly cured country hams are safe to eat raw). Make a slender V-shaped notch cut 2 inches deep into the larger muscle exposed by trimming. Taste the meat at the interior edge of this "core sample" for saltiness. If the ham is still too salty to your taste, thoroughly clean the pot out and soak for longer.

Once soaked to your liking, drain off the water, clean the stockpot, and return the ham to it, shank end up. Add water to cover (it is fine if the tough shank end rises above the water). Bring to a boil, reduce the heat to maintain a low simmer, cover if possible, and cook until the meat reaches an internal temperature of 145°F (about 15 minutes for every pound of ham). Add more boiling water if necessary.

Preheat the oven to 375°F.

Drain the ham, transfer to a work surface, and remove the skin while it is still warm. Trim the fat so that it is no more than ¼ inch thick. Mix together in a small bowl:

¼ cup brown sugar
¼ cup fine cornmeal
2 tablespoons dry mustard

Dust the surface of the ham with this mixture and place on a rack in a roasting pan. Transfer to the oven and bake until the outside is golden and beginning to brown, about 15 minutes. Cut the ham in slices perpendicular to the bone (or carve off large portions from the bone and slice on a cutting board across the grain). For the most tender results, make the slices very thin. Serve warm or at room temperature.

BROILED HAM STEAK

8 ounces ham per person

A delicious treatment for brine-cured ham. To use country ham, reduce its saltiness as suggested in Country Ham Steak with Red-Eye Gravy, below.

Adjust an oven rack so it is 3 inches below the heating element and preheat the broiler.

Slash in several places the fat edge of:

1 ham steak, about 1 inch thick

Place it on a broiler pan and broil for 10 minutes on each side, or until browned. If desired, glaze the ham toward the end of cooking with a mixture of:

¼ cup grape jelly, melted
1 tablespoon lemon juice
1 teaspoon dry mustard

Serve with:

Fresh Corn Fritters, 236, or Broiled Tomatoes, 282

COUNTRY HAM STEAK WITH RED-EYE GRAVY

4 servings

A Southern classic. To reduce the saltiness of the country ham steak, add it to the skillet first and cover with water. Bring to a boil and simmer for 5 minutes. Transfer the steak to a plate, discard the water, wipe out the skillet, and proceed as directed.

Melt in a large skillet over medium-high heat:

1½ teaspoons butter

Add:

One ¾- to 1-inch-thick country ham steak (1½ to 2 pounds)

Cook the steak until nicely browned, 3 to 5 minutes on each side. Remove to a platter and season to taste with:

Black pepper

Return the skillet to the heat and add:

1 cup coffee

Boil, stirring, until it turns slightly red. Add:

½ cup heavy cream

Reduce the heat and simmer until slightly thickened, about 10 minutes. Season to taste with:

Salt and black pepper

Serve the ham with the gravy, preferably over:

Warm biscuits, 635–37

ABOUT GROUND MEAT

Mincing, chopping, and grinding meat are time-honored techniques for selling tougher, less-desirable cuts, as well as the leaner trim from roasts and steaks that would otherwise be thrown out. ➤ For instructions on grinding your own meat, see Grinding Meat at Home, below. At the grocery store, ground meat is an economical, convenient protein. Fat content is an important consideration in buying ground meat, as it not only affects its nutritional value, but also bears heavily on your chosen cooking method. Lean ground beef, for instance, makes for dry, sad hamburgers and is better suited for fillings where rendered fat might pose a problem, in braises and chilis where its tendency toward dryness will be masked, or in flavorful, bound mixtures like meatloaves and meatballs.

Beef is by far the most popular meat to grind. By law, it cannot contain more than 30 percent fat, and most supermarkets and butcher shops sell several grades of ground beef labeled according to their percentage of fat, their percentage of lean meat, or both. Some stores may instead label beef as **ground chuck, ground sirloin,** and **ground round,** with round being the leanest of the three (though not necessarily the leanest available, which can reach 5 percent fat or less). Burger patties—whether grilled or pan-fried—are best when made from ground chuck, or any ground beef containing 15 percent fat or higher.

Other ground meats are rarely marked with their percentage of fat to lean, so we must rely on our senses. Ground **veal** should be a pale pink. Generally, veal contains very little fat and is usually combined with beef or pork to make up the difference. Ground **lamb** should be pale red or dark pink. Ground **pork** should be pink. Pale or whitish pork is potentially high in fat and is not recommended for meatballs and meatloaf; it can be used for pâtés and terrines, 513, made into Country Sausage, 510, or browned, rendered, and drained for dishes like Mapo Dofu, 286. For ground turkey and chicken, ➤ see About Ground Poultry, 430.

Store raw ground meat for no more than 24 hours in the refrigerator. It is safe to freeze, but its texture will suffer; as ground meat thaws, it exudes most of its moisture, which will result in a drier texture.

GRINDING MEAT AT HOME

Meat can be ground at home for use in patties, balls, loaves, and sausage links. The best methods require dedicated equipment—or a very sharp knife and a surplus of time. Remember these rules for safety and hygiene: ➤ Keep the meat refrigerated before and between all steps. ➤ Wash all utensils, equipment, and work surfaces before and after grinding meat; use dish soap as well as a sanitizing solution, xx. ➤ Wash your hands frequently.

Aside from studiously sanitizing all equipment and work surfaces, the biggest concerns when grinding meat are **smear** and **springiness.** Fat that is closer to room temperature is more likely to be "smeared" into a paste (especially by a dull blade), which will then render very quickly when cooked. Springiness, on the other hand, is usually caused by grinding meat with a dull blade or handling it excessively once ground. The more meat is ground or handled afterward, the more myosin is released. **Myosin,** the main type of protein in muscle fibers, acts as an emulsifying agent and helps bind together the water and fat present in the meat. The resulting emulsion is sticky, and functions like a binder or glue. This effect can be exploited for **emulsified sausages** like Boudin Blanc, 512, or as a binder for Swedish Meatballs, 508, but it must be carefully controlled when grinding meat for use in burgers and coarse-textured sausages, which can quickly become too dense. To reduce smear and springiness, grind the meat with sharp, clean-cutting tools and keep the meat and fat well chilled at all times.

Electric meat grinders are ideal, as their motors are up to the task, and the metal grinding parts can be chilled to keep smear to a minimum. Hand-cranked grinders are also excellent, since they generate the least heat. They are less than convenient for obvious reasons, as is cutting by hand—though results from hand-cutting can be exceptional, provided you have a sharp knife, a keen eye, and the time for several chilling breaks in the freezer. Grinding attachments for stand mixers can produce good results, but plastic grinder parts are not as durable (and their parts cannot be chilled).

To grind meat with a meat grinder, first cut the meat and any fat into chunks small enough to comfortably fit into the grinder chute, place the meat on a rimmed baking sheet, and thoroughly chill in the freezer for 30 minutes. While the meat chills, set up your grinder by placing a bowl or rimmed baking sheet underneath to collect the ground meat. For most applications, we recommend using a medium-sized, ➤ ¼-inch grinding plate. Sometimes, juices may squirt out of the grinding plate; to keep this from causing a (contaminated) mess, tape a sheet of paper so that it drapes over the grinding plate to limit any splatter.

Once the meat is chilled, run it through the grinder (for a stand mixer attachment, set the speed to low). ➤ When grinding a large batch of meat, remove it from the freezer in small batches as needed. If a finer texture is desired, chill the ground meat for 15 minutes and grind it again. For a firm-but-coarse texture, double-grind half and gingerly mix it back in with the coarser meat.

To grind meat with a food processor, first cut it (along with any fat, if making sausage) into ¾-inch cubes and freeze for 30 minutes on a rimmed baking sheet. Working with 8 ounces at a time, place the meat in the food processor bowl. Pulse several times, stir the meat in the bowl, and repeat until it is the desired texture. ➤ Use caution, as the food processor will grind the meat quickly, making it easy to overprocess. For best results, stop processing the meat while the largest pieces are around ¼ inch in size. Transfer the meat to a bowl. Proceed with grinding the remaining meat in 8-ounce batches.

MACLEID'S ROCKCASTLE CHILI

8 to 10 servings

This deluxe chili was refined by noted camp chef Matthew T. MacLeid, Esq. on his countless sojourns in Kentucky's Rockcastle River Gorge. Cubed chuck or brisket can be substituted for the ground beef.

Cook in a Dutch oven or large heavy pot over medium heat until rendered and golden brown:

8 ounces bacon, diced

Remove the bacon with a slotted spoon. Add to the pot:

1½ pounds ground beef
2 large onions, chopped
6 to 12 large garlic cloves, coarsely chopped

Cook, stirring, until the beef is no longer pink and the onions have softened, about 10 minutes. Add, scraping up the browned bits on the bottom of the pot, and stir until the foam disappears:

One 12-ounce bottle dark beer

Stir the bacon back in along with:

One 28-ounce can whole tomatoes
One 15-ounce can kidney beans, with their liquid
One 15-ounce can Great Northern beans, with their liquid
One 15-ounce can pinto beans, with their liquid
One 12-ounce bottle dark beer or 1½ cups water
6 tablespoons ancho chile powder
2 tablespoons ground cumin
1 tablespoon black pepper

Simmer until the flavors have melded, about 1 hour, stirring occasionally to prevent sticking. Season to taste with:

Salt and black pepper
Hot pepper sauce

CINCINNATI CHILI COCKAIGNE

6 servings

There are hundreds of so-called original recipes for John Kiradjieff's chili, which he served in Cincinnati's first chili parlor, The Empress. We particularly like this version and can guarantee without question that it is a faithful rendition. For skeptical or puzzled readers who have trouble squaring this chocolate-laced spaghetti topping with their notions of what a chili ought to be: We suggest you think of it as a Macedonian Bolognese sauce instead. In addition to the five "ways" of topping pasta with this chili, use as a filling for cheese Coneys, 144.

Bring to a boil in a large pot:

4 cups water

Add:

2 pounds ground beef chuck

Stir until separated, and reduce the heat to a simmer. Add:

2 medium onions, finely chopped
5 to 6 garlic cloves, chopped
One 15-ounce can tomato sauce
2 tablespoons cider vinegar
1 tablespoon Worcestershire sauce
2 teaspoons salt
2 teaspoons ground cinnamon
1 teaspoon cayenne pepper
1 teaspoon ground cumin
¼ teaspoon black pepper
¼ teaspoon ground allspice
¼ teaspoon ground cloves
1 large bay leaf
½ ounce unsweetened chocolate, finely chopped

Bring to a boil, then reduce the heat to a simmer and cook for 2½ hours. Cool, uncovered, and refrigerate overnight. The next day, skim off all or most of the fat and remove the bay leaf. Reheat the chili over medium-low heat.

To serve as a **2-Way,** spoon the chili over:

Cooked spaghetti

For a **3-Way,** add:

Grated medium or sharp Cheddar

For a **4-Way,** sprinkle on top of the cheese:

Chopped onions

For a **5-Way,** layer between the spaghetti and chili:

Cooked red kidney beans, 213

Traditional sides include:

Oyster crackers
Hot pepper sauce

OHIO FARMHOUSE SAUSAGE CHILI

4 to 6 servings

Crumble into a large skillet:

1 pound bulk pork sausage or Country Sausage, 510

Cook over medium-high heat, stirring and breaking up the sausage with a spatula until it is rendered and nicely browned, about 6 minutes. Transfer the sausage to a plate and drain all but 2 tablespoons of fat from the skillet. Add:

1 large onion, chopped
(½ green bell pepper, chopped)
1 celery rib, diced

Cook, stirring, until the vegetables are softened, about 8 minutes. Return the sausage to the skillet along with:

Two 14½-ounce cans diced tomatoes
2 cups tomato juice or chicken broth, or a combination
1 to 2 tablespoons maple syrup or molasses, to taste
2 teaspoons ground cumin
1½ teaspoons ground sage
½ teaspoon black pepper

Simmer for 20 minutes. Add and simmer 15 minutes more:

Two 14½-ounce cans red kidney beans, drained and rinsed, or 3½ cups cooked, 213

SPICED GROUND MEAT FOR TACOS

4 servings

The irresistible smell of chili powder–spiced ground beef and frying onions announces "Taco Night" for countless families. This crowd-pleasing mixture has been a Mexican-American restaurant staple for nearly a century. For other ground meat mixtures to fill tacos and burritos with, see Picadillo, below, as well as Fresh Chorizo Sausage, 513.

Heat in a medium skillet over medium heat:

2 tablespoons vegetable oil

Add and cook, stirring often, until softened, 4 to 5 minutes:

1 medium onion, chopped

Increase the heat to medium-high, add and cook, breaking up the meat with a wooden spoon, until it is no longer pink, about 5 minutes:

1 pound lean ground beef, pork, chicken, or turkey

Add and cook, stirring, for 30 seconds:

1 to 3 garlic cloves, minced
1 tablespoon chili powder
2 teaspoons ground cumin
(2 teaspoons ground coriander)

Add, reduce the heat to low, and cook, stirring occasionally, for 10 minutes:

1 cup canned crushed tomatoes or tomato juice

Season to taste with:

Salt or hot sauce

Use as a filling for Tacos, 146, and Burritos, 147, as a topping for Nachos, 57, or let the meat cool and use it to stuff Chiles Rellenos, 263.

PICADILLO

4 to 6 servings

This dish is sometimes served as is, with bowls of garnishes such as grated cheese, shredded lettuce, guacamole, and chopped tomatoes on the side. It is also a tasty filling for Burritos, 147, Tacos, 146, Tostadas, 147, enchiladas, 539–40, or Chiles Rellenos, 263.

Add to a large skillet over medium-high heat:

1 pound lean ground beef
8 ounces fresh chorizo

Cook, crumbling the meat with a spatula, until the mixture is nicely browned, 8 to 10 minutes. Transfer the meat to a plate and drain all but 2 tablespoons of fat from the skillet. Add:

1 onion, chopped

Cook until the onions have softened, scraping up any browned bits off the bottom of the skillet. Return the browned meat to the skillet along with:

2 garlic cloves, minced
1 cup chopped fresh tomatoes, or one 14½-ounce can diced tomatoes, drained
1 tablespoon cider vinegar
1 teaspoon ground cinnamon
¼ teaspoon ground cumin
Pinch of sugar
Pinch of ground cloves
1 bay leaf

Simmer, covered, for 30 minutes. Add:

½ cup raisins
(½ cup slivered almonds)
(½ cup pitted green olives, chopped)

Cook, uncovered, for 10 minutes more. Remove the bay leaf before serving.

KEEMA ALU (INDIAN SPICED BEEF WITH POTATOES AND SPICES)

4 servings

This dish makes a satisfying meal when paired with cooked lentils and Naan, 611.

Heat in a large cast-iron or other heavy skillet over medium-high heat:

3 tablespoons vegetable oil

Add and cook, stirring, until golden brown:

1 medium onion, finely chopped

Add and cook briefly, stirring, just until well mixed:

2 garlic cloves, minced
1-inch piece ginger, peeled and minced
2 teaspoons ground cumin
2 teaspoons ground coriander
1 teaspoon ground turmeric
¼ teaspoon cayenne pepper, or to taste

Add and cook, stirring, until the meat is no longer pink and all the liquid is evaporated, 8 to 10 minutes:

1 pound lean ground beef, lamb, or chicken
½ cup chopped canned tomatoes
¾ teaspoon salt

Add:

12 ounces red or gold potatoes, peeled and cut into ½-inch cubes
1 cup water

Cover, reduce the heat to low, and simmer until the potatoes are tender, 15 to 20 minutes. Uncover, increase the heat, and cook until all the water is evaporated. Taste and adjust the seasonings. Sprinkle with:

Chopped cilantro

If desired, serve over:

Cooked basmati rice, 343

ADANA-STYLE LAMB KEBABS

4 servings

The ground meat for these kebabs must be kneaded to develop the myosin, 502, which will help bind it to the skewers. Wide, flat metal skewers are best for these, but they may be made with slender ones (use a metal spatula to help move and flip them on the grill).

Prepare:

Quick-Pickled Onions, 930

Set aside to cool. Meanwhile, combine in another bowl:

1 pound ground lamb
2 tablespoons grated onion
2 tablespoons ground sumac
2 garlic cloves, minced
2 tablespoons Urfa, Aleppo, or Marash chile flakes, 968
¾ teaspoon salt
1 teaspoon ground cumin

Knead together with your hands until the mixture is smooth and very sticky, about 3 minutes. Divide the meat into 4 equal portions and pack onto 4 skewers in oblong, sausage-like shapes. If using wooden skewers, protect the protruding ends with foil. Prepare a hot grill fire, 1063, or preheat a gas grill on high for 10 minutes.

Place the skewers on the grill. Cook, turning once or twice, until the kebabs are well browned all over, about 8 minutes. Drain the pickled onions and mix in a bowl with:

½ cup chopped parsley
1 tablespoon ground sumac
1 tablespoon olive oil

Use the kebabs and pickled onion mixture as a filling for:

Flatbread or Pita Sandwiches, 145

Or serve over:

Rice Pilaf, 329, or Fattoush, 128

ABOUT GROUND MEAT PATTIES

At home, hamburgers are usually grilled, but a hot skillet or griddle can yield excellent results. In fact, if you care more about getting a good crust on your burger than grill marks or smoky flavor, you will likely prefer griddled burgers.

As noted in About Ground Meat, 501, beef marked "ground chuck"—or any ground meat with 15 percent fat or greater—is best for hamburgers. We prefer to evenly sprinkle salt and pepper on formed patties rather than mixing in flavorings, as overhandling the ground meat tends to make it "springy." That said, some people enjoy adding spices and aromatics to their patties. Just be sure to cook any raw ingredients, such as diced onion, and let cool before you add them (the beef will be overcooked by the time they have a chance to lose their raw bite and crunch).

Unless you are smashing them (see Hamburger Patties II, below), you will need to form the patties; if they will be served on a bun, we recommend they be shaped no wider than their serving vessel. For patties that cook up relatively flat, shape the top of the patties so that they are slightly concave (they tend to swell in the center as they cook). When shaping patties for burgers, handle the meat lightly, compacting it just enough so it holds its shape. Our favorite method is to use gravity: Hold a vaguely round, patty-sized portion of meat above a clean work surface and let it drop from a height of 8 inches or so. Turn the patty flat side up and drop again, then pat the sides to get an evenly rounded shape, gently pinching the edges so that they are slightly raised.

Some like their burgers thick, juicy, and still pink inside, while others enjoy thin, well-browned patties. Preferences aside, please keep in mind that ➤ the USDA recommends cooking all ground meats to an internal temperature of 160°F.

For vegetable-based burgers and fashioning your cooked meat into sandwiches, see About Burgers, 144.

HAMBURGER PATTIES

4 servings

To form patties, please read About Ground Meat Patties, above.

I. GRILLED OR BROILED

Prepare a hot grill fire, 1063, or place a broiler pan on an oven rack set 3 to 4 inches below the heating element. Preheat the broiler. Divide into 4 equal portions and form into ¾-inch-thick patties:

1¼ pounds ground beef chuck

Sprinkle with:

Salt and black pepper

Grill or broil, flipping once, about 3 minutes on each side for rare, 4 minutes for medium, or 5 minutes for well-done. For a **Cheeseburger,** after flipping the patty, place on top:

(Slices of American, Cheddar, Swiss, or other melty cheese)

Serve on buns with toppings of your choice (see About Burgers, 144).

II. GRIDDLED OR SMASHED

Heat in a heavy skillet (preferably cast iron) over medium-high heat:

2 teaspoons vegetable oil

Turn on an exhaust fan or open a window. Prepare the patties as in version I. When the oil just starts to smoke, add the patties to the skillet and cook, flipping once, to the desired degree of doneness. If desired, use a wide metal spatula to press down on the burgers and flatten them to about ½-inch thick; if smashing the burgers in this way, you will not need to cook them as long. Cook until a deep brown crust has formed, then flip and brown the second side (top with cheese, if desired). Serve on buns with toppings of your choice (see About Burgers, 144).

BECKER BURGERS

4 servings

These braised burgers are flavorful, juicy, and tender. Serve on top of whole wheat toast, with the pan juices poured over the burgers.

Divide into 4 equal portions and form each into a patty about ¾ inch thick:

1½ pounds ground round or sirloin

Heat in a heavy skillet over medium-high heat:

2 tablespoons bacon fat, lard, Clarified Butter, 960, or vegetable oil

Add the patties and cook for 2 minutes. Turn and cook on the other side for 4 minutes for medium-rare. Sprinkle the burgers generously with:

Black pepper

and then:

2 tablespoons soy sauce
2 tablespoons port
Several drops of hot pepper sauce

Remove the skillet from the heat, cover, and let stand for 5 minutes before serving.

BECKER LAMB PATTIES

4 servings

Combine in a large bowl and mix, using your hands, until just combined:

1 pound ground lamb
Finely grated zest and juice of ½ lemon
2 teaspoons sherry
2 teaspoons soy sauce
2 garlic cloves, minced
1 teaspoon dried thyme, crumbled
1 teaspoon salt
1 teaspoon black pepper
2 dashes hot pepper sauce

For use in flatbread sandwiches, shape the mixture into twelve 2-inch-wide patties; for serving like a hamburger, form the mixture into four 1-inch-thick patties. Heat in a large skillet over medium-high heat:

2 tablespoons vegetable oil

Fry the 2-inch patties for 2 minutes on each side; fry the larger burgers for 3 minutes on each side for rare, 4 minutes for medium, or 5 minutes for well-done. Serve as a filling for:

Flatbread or Pita Sandwiches, 145

Or as for:

Hamburgers, 144

BEET AND CAPER BURGERS

4 servings

The combination of earthy beets, rich beef, and briny capers in these patties is inspired by Biff à la Lindström, a classic Swedish dish. These are a bit simpler to make, with a more straightforward texture.

Combine in a bowl:

1 pound ground beef chuck or ground lamb
½ cup finely chopped pickled or cooked beets
¼ cup drained capers
2 garlic cloves, minced or grated
½ teaspoon salt
½ teaspoon black pepper

Mix together until just combined. Form the meat into four 1-inch-thick patties and cook as for Hamburger Patties, 504. Serve as a sandwich, or with dressed greens and:

Crispy Smashed Potatoes, 268

In either case, try them with:

(Scandinavian Mustard-Dill Sauce, 566)

ABOUT MEATLOAF AND MEATBALLS

Meatloaf may be shaped by hand and baked on a rimmed baking sheet or packed into a loaf pan. Hand-formed loaves will brown more effectively in the oven, but loaves baked in a pan will be juicier and attractively shaped. You may pour about ½ cup ketchup or mild, tomato-based chili sauce in the bottom of the pan before filling it with the meat; or glaze the top of the loaf with either when it is half-baked. This gives it a good flavor and a light crust.

Do not overcook; a thermometer should read 160°F when inserted in the center of the loaf. Meatloaf should be firm but not dry. To bake individual meat loaves, use a greased muffin tin; they will cook through in 20 to 30 minutes. Once baked, you may turn them out onto a rimmed baking sheet, coat them with a glaze, 578–79, and broil until nicely browned. Thick slices of leftover meatloaf make fantastic sandwiches: Reheat by pan-frying in a nonstick pan with a little butter until browned on both sides.

Meatballs are similar to meatloaf in everything but form. Some types, like Swedish Meatballs, 508, are given a chewy, snappy texture by kneading or mixing for several minutes. Meatballs can be simmered in stock or browned and then added to a sauce or gravy. To freeze meatballs, cook them, whether by simmering, pan-frying, or broiling, and freeze in zip-top bags—preferably in sauce. The sauce reduces the amount of air in the bag, thus protecting the meatballs from freezer burn. The meatballs can then be thawed and gently reheated in the sauce. ➤ Any meatloaf recipe can be used for meatballs. For meatloaf and meatballs made with turkey or chicken, see About Ground Poultry, 430.

MEATLOAF

6 servings

As noted on 505, meatballs and loaves are very similar; in addition to this formula, you may try substituting 1½ recipes of the mixture for Italian Meatballs, 507, or Keftedes, 62. For the best flavor do not let ground veal exceed one-quarter of the total amount of meat. To keep the meatloaf from being overly greasy, limit the sausage to a quarter of the total as well.

Preheat the oven to 350°F. Lightly grease a 9 × 5-inch loaf pan.

Heat in a large skillet over medium heat:

2 tablespoons vegetable oil

Add and cook, stirring, until softened, 6 to 8 minutes:

1 large onion, finely chopped

Add and cook, stirring, 1 minute more:

3 garlic cloves, finely chopped

Transfer the onion mixture to a large bowl and add:

1½ pounds ground meat: beef, veal, pork, bulk sausage, lamb, or a combination
1 cup quick-cooking rolled oats or dry bread crumbs
⅔ cup ketchup or mild, tomato-based chili sauce
½ cup chopped parsley
(½ cup finely grated Parmesan [2 ounces])
3 large eggs, lightly beaten
1 teaspoon dried thyme
(1 teaspoon smoked paprika)
1 teaspoon salt
½ teaspoon black pepper

Knead the mixture with your hands just until well blended. Fill the prepared loaf pan with the meat mixture, mounding the top. Place the pan on a baking sheet and bake until the meatloaf is firm to the touch and has shrunk from the sides of the pan or a thermometer inserted in the center reads 160°F, 1 hour to 1 hour 15 minutes. Pour off the excess fat and let stand for 15 minutes before serving. If desired, brush the loaf before serving with:

Ketchup or barbecue sauce

ADDITIONS TO MEATLOAF

If you are experimenting, first mix a very small batch and fry a patty of the mixture to taste before mixing and cooking an entire loaf. For each 9 × 5-inch loaf, add any of the following or a combination:

½ cup finely grated carrots, potatoes, or sweet potatoes
½ cup Sautéed Mushrooms, 251
¼ cup coarsely chopped toasted, 1005, almonds, pecans, or walnuts
2 teaspoons Worcestershire sauce
1 tablespoon Dijon mustard or drained prepared horseradish
1 tablespoon chopped thyme, oregano, basil, dill, or minced chives

Marion was especially partial to adding:

¼ cup chopped green olives and ¼ cup chopped water chestnuts

SHEPHERD'S PIE

4 servings

Finely chopped or ground lamb covered with mashed potatoes is a favorite pub food in England and Ireland. Substituting chopped or ground beef for the lamb makes the dish **Cottage Pie.** For the sake of variation, try any of the Additions to Mashed Potatoes, 265, in your topping. We especially like adding a head of roasted garlic or up to ½ cup fresh goat cheese and a couple tablespoons minced chives.

Prepare and set aside:

Mashed Potatoes, 265

Preheat the oven to 400°F. Grease a 9-inch pie plate or an 8 × 8-inch baking dish.

Combine in a large skillet over medium heat:

3 tablespoons vegetable oil
1 onion, chopped
1 carrot, chopped
1 celery rib, chopped

Cook, stirring occasionally, until the vegetables are tender but not browned, 10 to 15 minutes. Increase the heat to medium-high and add:

1 pound ground lamb

Cook, breaking up the meat with a wooden spoon, until the lamb and vegetables are beginning to brown, about 5 minutes. Skim off any excess fat. Stir in:

1 tablespoon all-purpose flour

Cook, stirring, for 2 minutes. Add:

¾ cup beef or chicken broth
1½ teaspoons chopped fresh thyme or ½ teaspoon dried thyme
1½ teaspoons chopped fresh rosemary or ½ teaspoon dried rosemary
Pinch of grated or ground nutmeg
Salt and black pepper to taste

Reduce the heat to low and cook, stirring occasionally, until thickened, about 5 minutes. Transfer to the prepared pie plate or baking dish. Spread the mashed potatoes over the top, making peaks or a pattern with a fork. Scatter over the top:

2 tablespoons butter, cut into small pieces

Bake until the potatoes are browned and the dish is heated through, 30 to 35 minutes. Let cool slightly, then serve directly from the pie plate or baking dish.

HAMBURGER PIE

4 servings

This pie originally appeared in Irma's 1939 cookbook *Streamlined Cooking*, her paean to the convenience of canned foods. Dress this up or down as you see fit, but do not deny the genius of shingling a pie with buttered toast squares!

Preheat the oven to 400°F.

Combine in a large skillet over medium heat:

1 pound ground beef chuck
1 medium onion, chopped

Cook, breaking up the beef with a wooden spoon, until it is browned and the onion softened, about 10 minutes. Stir in and cook, stirring, 1 minute:

2 tablespoons all-purpose flour
1 tablespoon chili powder

Stir in, bring to a simmer, and cook 3 minutes:

One 14½-ounce can diced tomatoes
One 15¼-ounce can corn kernels, drained, or one 10-ounce package frozen corn
2 garlic cloves, minced
(1 teaspoon brown sugar)

Season to taste with:

Salt and black pepper

Transfer the mixture to a 9-inch glass pie pan or an 8 × 8-inch baking dish. Trim the crusts from:

7 slices white sandwich bread

Spread one side of the slices with:

2 tablespoons butter, softened

Cut each bread slice into 4 equal squares. Arrange the bread buttered side up over the meat mixture, overlapping the pieces by about ½ inch and covering the mixture completely. Gently press the bread down to anchor it to the filling. Bake until the crust is browned, 12 to 15 minutes.

KÖNIGSBERGER KLOPS (GERMAN MEATBALLS)

About twenty 2-inch meatballs

Sometimes we all need to be coddled by a meal's warm embrace. Think of it as caloric self-care. Smothered meatballs and bread crumb–topped egg noodles is old-fashioned German comfort food. Be well! For the best flavor, do not let veal exceed one-quarter of the ground meat used.

Combine and let soak in a bowl:

One 1-inch-thick slice bread
Water, milk, or stock to cover

In another bowl, have ready:

1½ pounds ground beef, veal, pork, or a combination

Beat well and add to the meat:

2 large eggs

Melt in a medium skillet over medium heat:

1 tablespoon butter

Add and sauté until golden, about 8 minutes:

1 medium onion, finely chopped

Add the sautéed onion to the meat. Wring the liquid from the soaked bread, tear it into little pieces, and add to the meat. Add:

3 tablespoons chopped parsley
1¼ teaspoons salt
¼ teaspoon sweet paprika
Finely grated zest of 1 lemon
1 teaspoon lemon juice
1 teaspoon Worcestershire sauce, or 2 anchovies, minced
(A small grating of nutmeg)

Combine the ingredients lightly with your hands. Shape lightly into 2-inch balls. Bring to a simmer in a large saucepan:

5 cups chicken or vegetable stock

Drop the meatballs in, cover, and simmer for 15 minutes. Remove the meatballs from the stock with a slotted spoon and transfer the stock to a bowl. In the same pan, make:

Basic Pan Gravy, 545, using 10 tablespoons butter, ⅔ cup all-purpose flour, and all of the reserved stock

Cook and stir the gravy until smooth. Add:

2 tablespoons capers, chopped pickles, or sour cream
2 tablespoons chopped parsley

Add the meatballs to the gravy and cook to reheat. Serve with a platter of:

Cooked egg noodles or Spätzle, 308

Cover generously with:

Buttered Bread Crumbs, 957

ITALIAN MEATBALLS

About twenty 1½-inch meatballs

I. SHALLOW-FRIED

The tried and true way to brown meatballs is in a skillet. Feel free to experiment with the meats used; the classic beef-pork-veal meatloaf combination is wonderful here, too.

If desired, prepare:

(A tomato sauce, 556–58)

Bring to a low simmer, cover, and have at the ready. Otherwise, preheat the oven to 200°F.

Combine in a large bowl:

1 pound ground beef, half ground beef and ground pork, or 12 ounces lean ground beef and 4 ounces hot or mild Italian sausage, removed from its casings
2 garlic cloves, minced
½ cup chopped parsley
½ cup grated Parmesan (2 ounces)
1 medium onion, finely chopped
½ cup fresh bread crumbs, 957
1 large egg, beaten
(3 tablespoons dry red wine)
2 tablespoons tomato paste
1 teaspoon salt
¼ teaspoon black pepper
½ teaspoon dried oregano

Mix with your hands. Scoop out the mixture in heaping tablespoons and form into 1½-inch balls. (You may form 2-inch balls or larger, but after browning them you will need to cook them further—either by simmering or baking—until they reach 160°F in the center.)

Dredge the meatballs in:

½ cup flour

Heat in a large skillet over medium heat:

¼ inch olive or vegetable oil

When the oil shimmers, fry the meatballs in uncrowded batches, turning them several times so that they brown evenly. As the meatballs finish browning, transfer them to the warmed tomato sauce, if using. If not serving with a sauce, place the browned meatballs in a baking dish and transfer to the oven to keep warm.

II. BROILED

This method is quicker, less messy, and mostly hands-off.

Prepare the mixture for **I, above,** and set aside. Adjust an oven rack so it is 8 inches below the heat. Preheat the broiler. Line a large rimmed baking sheet with foil. Form the meat mixture into 1½-inch balls (omitting the flour dredge) and place them on the baking sheet in rows so they do not touch. Broil for 10 minutes and remove the baking sheet from the oven. Turn the balls with tongs, return to the oven, and broil until they are nicely browned all over and a thermometer inserted in the center registers at least 160°F, another 5 to 10 minutes.

SWEDISH MEATBALLS

About 25 small meatballs; 5 servings

Melt in a small skillet over medium heat:

1 tablespoon butter

Add and cook, stirring until soft, 3 to 4 minutes:

¼ cup minced onion

Set aside. Combine in the bowl of an electric mixer and let stand until soft, about 2 minutes:

⅔ cup fresh bread crumbs, 957
⅓ cup milk

Add the sautéed onions along with:

12 ounces lean ground beef
12 ounces lean ground pork
1 large egg
1 teaspoon salt
¼ teaspoon black pepper
¼ teaspoon ground allspice
¼ teaspoon grated or ground nutmeg

Beat on low speed until smooth, then turn the mixer to high speed and beat until light and fluffy, about 2 minutes. Shape the meat into 1- to 1½-inch balls. Melt in a large skillet over medium heat:

4 tablespoons (½ stick) butter

Brown the meatballs in batches, then remove and drain on paper towels. If the butter in the skillet has burned after cooking all the meatballs, pour it out and discard it, leaving any browned bits in the skillet. Add to the skillet if needed:

(4 tablespoons butter)

Add to the skillet and cook, stirring, until lightly browned:

2 tablespoons all-purpose flour

Slowly add while whisking:

2 cups beef stock or broth

Cook, whisking, until the gravy is thick and smooth. Return the meatballs to the skillet, cover, and cook until the meatballs are heated through, about 5 minutes. Remove them to a platter and whisk into the sauce:

⅓ cup sour cream or heavy cream
(2 tablespoons lingonberry or red currant jelly)

Pour the sauce over the meatballs.

ABOUT SAUSAGE

Here we discuss store-bought sausage; for making your own, see 509.

FRESH SAUSAGE

Fresh sausage is sold raw. It can be bought in bulk—a loose mixture that can be formed into patties or crumbled and browned—or in casings. **Country-style** or **breakfast sausage** and spicy **fresh chorizo** can easily be found in bulk in the meat cases of most grocery stores. Among the many fresh sausages found in casings, the most common are slender **breakfast links,** and the thicker **bratwurst** and **Italian sausages** (the latter may be found in bulk as well). Of course, any sausage in casings may be cut open, crumbled, and cooked like bulk sausage.

When shopping for fresh sausage links, we try to avoid those that contain corn syrup. Though the sugar aids browning, we do not like the burnt residue corn syrup leaves after grilling or pan-frying. If serving in buns or as a main-dish protein, allow about 1 pound fresh sausage for 4 people.

➤ Fresh sausage must be cooked to a temperature of 160°F to be safe to eat. After handling raw sausage, wash your hands and any utensils or surfaces you have used. ➤ Fresh sausage is very perishable; refrigerate immediately and cook within 2 days.

Fresh bulk sausage is best shaped into patties and pan-fried or used as an ingredient in dishes like Picadillo, 503, or Italian Meatballs, 507. Sausage links respond well to poaching, pan-frying, broiling, and grilling—especially grilling. Poaching fresh sausage links before grilling helps prevent flare-ups, makes cooking a large number of sausages more efficient, and allows you to do tasty things, like infuse bratwurst with butter and beer before grilling (see Bratwurst, 512). We do not recommend microwaving fresh sausages (they tend to burst).

PRECOOKED SAUSAGES

These range from springy, fine-textured emulsified sausages, 509, like **hot dogs, bologna, mortadella,** and **knockwurst,** to coarser types like **andouille, smoked kielbasa,** and **salami cotto.** Precooked sausages are completely safe to eat as is, but most are vastly improved if heated through before eating. Since these sausages are perishable, they should be refrigerated immediately and eaten within 3 to 5 days of purchase, or by the use-by date.

Precooked sausages can be reheated with any of the methods given for fresh. They are obviously more carefree, as all you must do is make sure they are warmed through and browned to your liking. If you must microwave precooked sausages, it is best to submerge them in stock or water in a closely covered container to keep the skin from turning tough.

CURED SAUSAGES

These are made like fresh sausage, but with the important addition of curing salt, 936. They are then inoculated with a specific strain of *Lactobacillus* bacteria, left to ferment in a high-humidity environment, cold-smoked (or not), and then dried under climate-controlled conditions for up to 3 months. The result of this careful combination of salting, acidification, and dehydration is a dense, highly flavored sausage that will keep at room temperature. (For more on this process, see About Curing Meats, 936.)

Fully cured sausages like **finocchiona, soppressata,** and **Spanish chorizo** keep unrefrigerated for several months but will eventually dry out if not kept in their packaging (or a humid environment). **Semi-dry** or **partially cured sausages** are dried for less time—usually no more than 1 week—which gives them a moister texture and shortens their effective storage time. **Summer sausage** and tangy, pizza-destined **pepperoni** are perhaps the most popular examples, but this category also includes **Thuringer** and the delectable Pennsylvania-Dutch favorite **Lebanon bologna.** Though some semi-dry sausages are safe to store at room temperature, we recommend keeping them refrigerated for no more than 3 weeks (or store as directed on the package).

Whether fully cured or semi-dry, ➤ once a sausage has been cut into, tightly wrap and refrigerate any that is left over to maintain its quality and prevent surface mold. Thinly sliced, semi-dry sausage is a classic filling for submarine sandwiches, 138. Both types can be eaten raw as part of a charcuterie platter, 45, or used as an ingredient in dishes like paella, 334, pizza, 613–16, or calzones, 707.

COOKING SAUSAGE LINKS

4 to 6 servings

For turning cooked sausages into sandwiches, see About Hot Dogs, 143. A quality sausage is well seasoned and needs little embellishment to be satisfying, but a pile of sauerkraut or some creamy mashed potatoes and a good whole-grain mustard never hurt. If cooking crépinettes, 510, we recommend pan-frying and grilling.

I. POACHED

Bring 8 cups water to a boil in a medium pot. Add:

8 fresh or precooked sausages

Bring to a very low boil, then reduce the heat to maintain a faint simmer. Cook until the center of the sausages registers 160°F, 10 to 15 minutes.

II. PAN-FRIED

Place in a large skillet over medium heat:

1 teaspoon vegetable oil

8 fresh or precooked sausages

Cover and cook, turning often, until evenly browned. Precooked sausages will take 5 to 6 minutes to brown and warm through; fresh sausages will take 10 minutes or so to cook through completely and brown.

III. SPLIT AND GRIDDLED

This is our preferred method for cooking hot dogs indoors. We highly recommend using an extra skillet or grill press to weight the hot dogs down as they cook.

Preheat the oven to 200°F.

Split lengthwise without cutting all the way through:

8 hot dogs or other precooked or smoked sausage

Melt in a large skillet or griddle over medium heat:

2 tablespoons butter

Add half the sausages, opening each one like a book, placing them cut side-down in the pan, and pressing down with a spatula so they lie flat. Occasionally press down on them as they cook, or weight them down with another skillet or a grill press so the entire cut surface is in contact with the pan. Cook until browned, about 6 minutes or to your liking. Transfer to a plate and keep warm in the oven. Add more butter to the pan and brown the remaining sausages.

IV. GRILLED

Hot dogs and precooked sausages are a brown-and-serve affair—about 5 minutes over direct heat will usually do the trick. Grilling fresh sausages is a little trickier, since they need to be cooked through and contain fat that renders out and causes flare-ups. Cooking them through with indirect heat before browning them over the flames is relatively foolproof. If you have a gas grill that can maintain a low heat—or the ability to cook items 8 inches or more from the hot coals—you may cook the sausages over direct heat the whole time, which will lend them an especially smoky flavor. For another approach, see Bratwurst, 512.

Prepare a hot, two-zone grill fire, 1063, or preheat a gas grill on high for 10 minutes. If using a gas grill, reduce the heat of one of the burners to low. Place on the cooler side of the grill:

8 fresh sausages

Cover the grill and cook until they are firm and register an internal temperature of about 160°F, about 8 minutes for 1-inch-thick sausages. Move them over direct heat and cook until nicely browned, turning occasionally.

MAKING SAUSAGE AT HOME

It is quite easy to make fresh sausage at home. The advantage of making your own sausage is that you control everything: the amount of fat and salt, the quality and type of meat, and the spice blend. A meat grinder (or grinding attachment) produces the best texture. A food processor may be used for bulk sausage; it will also work for emulsified sausage links like Boudin Blanc, 512. However, ➤ we do not recommend using a food processor to make bratwurst and other coarse-textured sausage links. ➤ Chilling or partially freezing the meats and fats before grinding is especially important for coarse-textured sausages: smearing, 501, causes the fat to render faster and leak out of the casings, causing flare-ups and shrunken links.

Sausage stuffers can be stand-alone, lever-operated devices; casing is loaded onto the stuffing tube (sometimes referred to as a stuffing horn) and tied into a knot. A vented piston then forces the sausage mixture out of the tube. As the meat is extruded through the tube, more casing is pulled off the tube as needed. The filled casing is then pinched at intervals and tied or twisted to form links. Many electric grinders and grinding attachments have a stuffing tube that can be swapped out for the grinding plate and blade.

Sausage casings can reach gargantuan sizes, but the ones we use most often are ¾ to 1½ inches in diameter. Smaller sizes are better for breakfast links and highly flavored mixtures like Fresh Chorizo Sausage, 511, and Merguez Sausage, 511; larger sizes are ideal for bratwurst and the like. **Collagen** casings are very convenient, since they need no soaking, but many swear by the snap of **natural** casings, which are made from the salted small intestines of sheep and hogs. (If using collagen casings, make sure they are of the edible kind, as some are designed for making dry salami.) Sheep casings average ¾ inch to just over 1 inch in diameter; hog casings are a bit larger, averaging around 1¼ inches. Some of these may be available at a grocery store or butcher that makes sausage links in-house; all types are easily found on the Internet.

➤ If you are just beginning your sausage-making journey and do not want to purchase a stuffer, try shaping the sausage mixture into patties and wrapping them in caul fat to make **crépinettes** (see 510). Though disc-shaped, the caul fat casing keeps the sausage nice and juicy, and they are easily handled on the grill. For more on caul fat, see 518.

GRINDING AND MIXING SAUSAGE

To make bulk sausage with a food processor, first cut all the meat and fat called for in a recipe into 1-inch cubes or smaller (smaller is better). Freeze the cubes on a rimmed baking sheet for 30 minutes. As the meat chills, prepare any seasonings and aromatics. Process the meat in batches as directed in Grinding Meat at Home, 501. Transfer each batch to a bowl and sprinkle a portion of the seasonings over the ground meat. Repeat until all the sausage has been processed, layering more seasoning over each batch. Gingerly mix the sausage together to evenly distribute the seasonings. When adjusting seasonings, ➤ fry a small patty, taste, and tweak the mixture as needed. Cover the sausage and place in the refrigerator. You can use the mixture immediately for pan-fried patties or as an ingredient. Unless making Boudin Blanc, 512, or another emulsified sausage link, ➤ we do not recommend using food-processed sausage for stuffing casings; the texture is not uniform, the myosin is probably overdeveloped (which causes a "snappy" texture where it is not wanted), and the fat has likely been smeared (which causes it to render prematurely and leak out). None of this is necessarily detrimental for patties, but may lead to mealy, deflated links.

To grind sausage with a meat grinder, first cut all the meat and fat called for in a recipe into 1-inch cubes. Trim off any connective tissue and freeze the cubes on a rimmed baking sheet for 30 minutes. As the meat chills, prepare the other ingredients and set up equipment as directed in Grinding Meat at Home, 501. Mix the chilled cubes together with the seasonings in a bowl and grind the meat as directed. If stuffing the sausage into casings, you may need to grind the sausage twice (see individual recipes). As noted above, pan-fry a small portion to check the seasonings before stuffing.

STUFFING SAUSAGE

To stuff sausage links, first prepare the casings by setting out the length you will need; ➤ for every pound of sausage, measure out 2½ feet of 1-inch casings or 2 feet of 1½-inch casings (this allows for extra to work with if the casing tears or bursts). Soak salt-packed sheep casings for at least 30 minutes in a bowl of warm water so they become pliable (hog casings are thicker, and should be soaked in the refrigerator overnight). Holding one end open under a faucet, run warm tap water through the casing, flushing out any salt. Squeeze excess water out of the casing and carefully work the whole length onto the stuffing tube, being careful not to tear it. Remove the sausage mixture from the refrigerator, add to the stuffer, and push the mixture through slowly so that it just begins to come out of the tube. Pull the end of the casing over the stuffer and tie it into a knot, keeping as much air out as possible. Push more sausage into the casing, gradually pulling more casing off the tube as the meat emerges. ➤ Do not overfill the casing; it should be slightly limp and pliable to the touch. Once the casing has been filled, pull off several extra inches of casing, cut off the rest, and transfer the coil to a work surface. Starting at the knotted end, pinch the filled casing at even intervals to get the desired length of link; make them any length you like, but we recommend 3 to 4 inches for breakfast sausages or 5 to 6 inches for bratwurst and Italian sausages. Beginning at the knotted end, twist the length in one direction several times. ➤ Do not overtwist; the formed link should still be soft enough to show an indent after being pressed with a thumb. Repeat with the next link, but switch the twisting direction (this way, the links are not so easy to unravel). ➤ If the casing bursts, simply cut out the damaged section, knot the casing again on either side of the blow out, and proceed with twisting the rest of the links. When you get to the last two links, tie a knot at the open end before pinching between them. Though not necessary, you can ensure the links hold their shape by tying each twisted portion with a length of butcher's twine. Transfer to the refrigerator on a rimmed baking sheet until ready to cook. For best results, let the sausage rest overnight, refrigerated and uncovered, before cutting the links apart (the casings and sausage will meld together). To prepare and serve, see Cooking Sausage Links, 509.

To make crépinettes, first thaw and unroll a portion of caul fat, 518. Form the sausage mixture into equally sized patties; do not worry about compacting the mixture as you might for burgers. We like the size of crépinettes made by portioning the sausage with a ⅓-cup measure and shaping it into a 1-inch-thick patty. Place the patties over the stretched-out caul fat and cut around the patty with a pair of scissors leaving enough of a border so that the fat can be folded over the top and overlap slightly (for ⅓-cup-sized patties, figure on 5-inch squares). Gently press the overlapping portion to seal. Repeat, unrolling more caul fat as needed. When all the patties are wrapped, place on baking sheets in one layer and let the sausage rest overnight in the refrigerator, uncovered, for the tightest seal. To pan-fry crépinettes, see Country Sausage I, below; to grill, see Cooking Sausage Links, 509.

COUNTRY SAUSAGE

About 2 pounds or eight 5-inch sausages

I. FRESHLY GROUND

The seasonings below are our favorite for a savory breakfast sausage. For one tasty alternative, see Chicken and Apple Sausage, 430. Please read Making Sausage at Home, 509, and Grinding Meat at Home, 501.

Cut and chill as directed in Grinding and Mixing Sausage, above:

1½ pounds pork shoulder, trimmed of connective tissue
8 ounces leaf lard or pork fatback, rind removed

As the meat and fat chill, mix together in a bowl:

2 crushed ice cubes, if using a meat grinder, or ¼ cup cold water
2 teaspoons salt
2 teaspoons coarsely ground black pepper
2 teaspoons minced fresh sage or ½ teaspoon dried sage
2 teaspoons minced fresh marjoram or thyme, or ½ teaspoon dried marjoram or thyme
(2 teaspoons minced fresh savory or ½ teaspoon dried savory)
(1 teaspoon red pepper flakes, or ¼ teaspoon cayenne pepper)
(¼ teaspoon ground bay leaf)
(Pinch of ground cloves)

Grind the chilled meat with a food processor or a meat grinder fitted with a 1/4-inch plate (if using a food processor, mix the meat with the seasonings after grinding; if using a meat grinder, mix them before grinding). Fry a small piece of the mixture in a skillet, taste, and adjust the seasonings if needed, being careful not to overmix. Form into patties or stuff into:

(6 feet of 3/4-inch sausage casings, 4 feet of 1 1/2-inch sausage casings, or 2 square feet of caul fat, prepared as described in Stuffing Sausage, 510)

If you used a food processor to grind the meat, do not stuff it into casings.

To fry sausage patties and crépinettes, arrange in uncrowded batches in a cold, ungreased skillet and place over medium heat. Cook until well-done and browned on both sides, draining excess fat as necessary. To cook links, see 509; remember that crépinettes can also be grilled. The sausage can be refrigerated for up to 3 days or tightly wrapped and frozen for up to 3 months.

II. PREGROUND

For a good, casual compromise between homemade and store-bought bulk sausage, start with ground pork and add seasonings as desired. Buy pork that is pale pink, or 25 to 30 percent fat. (If the ground pork looks really lean, replace up to a quarter of it with finely chopped bacon.)

Prepare the seasoning mixture for **Country Sausage I, 510,** and place in a bowl. Add **2 pounds ground pork** to the seasonings in small clumps. Toss these clumps with the seasoning, then lightly knead until well mixed. Form the mixture into patties or crépinettes, 510. We do not recommend stuffing preground pork into casings.

FRESH CHORIZO SAUSAGE

About 2 pounds or eight 5-inch sausages

Mexican-style chorizo is a versatile mixture, and we would not know what to do without it. Pan-fry and substitute for bulk sausage to spice up dishes like Basic Corn Bread Stuffing, 532, and stuffed peppers, or form into patties and pan-fry as a breakfast meat. Of course, when broken up and browned in a skillet, drained chorizo is a perfect filling for Tacos, 146, Burritos, 147, and Tortas, 143, or as a topping for pizza, 613–16, and Nachos, 57.

I. RED

Prepare **Country Sausage I or II, 510**, substituting the following mixture for the ice/water, salt, herbs, and spices:

3 tablespoons New Mexico, guajillo, or ancho chile powder, or a combination
4 garlic cloves, minced
2 tablespoons cider vinegar
1 tablespoon dried oregano
2 teaspoons salt
(1 teaspoon chipotle chile powder)
1/2 teaspoon ground cumin
1/2 teaspoon ground allspice
1/4 teaspoon ground cloves

II. GREEN

We are confident that those who try this less-common chorizo will be instant converts.

Roast, 262:

1 poblano pepper
2 to 4 serrano peppers

Peel and seed the peppers and place on a cutting board along with:

1/3 cup pumpkin seeds, toasted, 1012
1/4 cup finely chopped cilantro stems

Chop these ingredients together until finely minced. Prepare **Red Chorizo, above,** substituting this roasted pepper/pumpkin seed mixture for the 3 tablespoons chile powder.

ITALIAN SAUSAGE

About 2 pounds or eight 5-inch sausages

Prepare **Country Sausage I or II, 510,** substituting the following mixture for the ice/water, salt, herbs, and spices:

2 tablespoons red wine
4 garlic cloves, minced
1 tablespoon dried oregano
(2 teaspoons dried sage or basil)
2 teaspoons salt
1 1/2 teaspoons black pepper
(1 teaspoon to 1 tablespoon red pepper flakes)
1 teaspoon fennel seeds, lightly crushed, or 1/2 teaspoon ground fennel

MERGUEZ SAUSAGE

2 1/2 pounds or ten 5-inch sausages

A lamb sausage with North African spices. We particularly enjoy merguez as a breakfast meat with Shakshouka, 154, with Tuscan Beans, 213, or Ful Medames, 214, or grilled and served in Flatbread or Pita Sandwiches, 145. Please read Making Sausage at Home, 509, and Grinding Meat at Home, 501.

Cut and chill as directed in Grinding and Mixing Sausage, 510:

2 pounds lamb shoulder, trimmed of connective tissue
8 ounces leaf lard, pork fatback, lamb suet, 1023, or beef suet

As the lamb and fat chill, mix together in a bowl:

2 garlic cloves, minced
2 tablespoons sweet paprika (half may be smoked)
1 tablespoon salt
1 tablespoon ground sumac
1 1/2 teaspoons ground cumin
1/2 teaspoon ground fennel, preferably toasted first, 1021
1/4 teaspoon ground allspice
1/4 teaspoon cayenne pepper, or more to taste

Grind the chilled meat with a food processor or a meat grinder fitted with a 1/4-inch plate (if using a food processor, mix the meat with the seasonings after grinding; if using a meat grinder, mix them before grinding). Fry a small piece of the mixture in a skillet, taste, and adjust the seasonings if needed, being careful not to overmix. Form into patties or stuff into:

(5 feet of 1 1/2-inch sausage casings or about 2 1/2 square feet of caul fat, prepared as described in Stuffing Sausage, 510)

To fry sausage patties and crépinettes, see Country Sausage I, 510. To cook links, see 509; remember that crépinettes can also be grilled.

The sausage can be refrigerated for up to 3 days or tightly wrapped and frozen for up to 3 months.

BRATWURST

About 3 pounds or twelve 5-inch sausages

Like Boudin Blanc, below, this recipe is for sausage links only, and thus requires a meat grinder and a sausage stuffing tube. For a bit of heat, we sometimes season the sausage mixture with **2 teaspoons red pepper flakes.** Please read Making Sausage at Home, 509, and Grinding Meat at Home, 501.

Cut into ¾-inch cubes and chill as directed in Grinding and Mixing Sausage, 510:

1½ pounds pork shoulder, fat trimmed and discarded
1 pound veal or beef shoulder, fat trimmed and discarded
8 ounces leaf lard or pork fatback

As the meat chills, combine in a bowl:

1 tablespoon salt
(4 garlic cloves, minced or pressed)
2 teaspoons ground white pepper
1 teaspoon dried marjoram
½ teaspoon caraway seed
½ teaspoon ground or grated nutmeg
½ teaspoon ground allspice
¼ teaspoon ground ginger

Thoroughly mix the chilled cubes with the seasoning and run the mixture in batches through a meat grinder fitted with a ¼-inch plate. For a snappier sausage with a finer texture, divide the mixture in half and reserve one portion in the refrigerator. Run the other half through the grinder a second time, thoroughly mix the two portions together, and refrigerate. Fry a small piece of the mixture in a skillet, taste, and adjust the seasonings if needed. If necessary, soak and rinse, 510:

6 feet 1¼- or 1½-inch diameter sausage casings

Stuff the casings as directed, twisting into 5-inch links. Refrigerate the links for at least 2 hours and up to overnight before cutting the links apart. Cook as for any sausage link, 509.

To prepare bratwurst **Sheboygan-style,** bring to a low simmer in a large saucepan or Dutch oven:

6 cups beer, preferably a German lager
1 cup (2 sticks) butter
2 large onions, one grated, the other thinly sliced
3 garlic cloves, smashed
(1 tablespoon red pepper flakes)
1 teaspoon salt
½ teaspoon black pepper
1 bay leaf

Prepare a medium grill fire, 1063. Add the bratwurst to the simmering liquid, cover, and poach or braise over low heat until they are cooked through. Brown the cooked bratwurst on the grill, turning frequently. When the brats are evenly browned, transfer them to their warm beer-butter-onion bath to keep warm. Serve the brats in:

Split crusty buns

With a pair of tongs, drain the braised onion slices and place on top of the brats. Serve with:

Sauerkraut
Whole-grain mustard

BOUDIN BLANC (FRENCH WHITE SAUSAGE)

About 1½ pounds

This is an emulsified sausage with a smooth, springy texture. Please read Making Sausage at Home, 509, and Grinding Meat at Home, 501. Chill and grind as directed in Grinding and Mixing Sausage, 510, using a ¼-inch grinder plate:

8 ounces pork loin, cut into ¾-inch cubes
8 ounces chicken breast or rabbit meat, cut into ¾-inch cubes
4 ounces leaf lard or pork fatback, cut into ¾-inch cubes

Toss in a large bowl with:

2 cups chopped onions
½ cup fresh bread crumbs, 957
2 teaspoons salt
1 teaspoon white pepper
¼ teaspoon ground cinnamon
⅛ teaspoon ground cloves
⅛ teaspoon grated or ground nutmeg
⅛ teaspoon ground ginger

Chill in the refrigerator for at least 30 minutes and grind the mixture again. Blend together with:

¼ cup cream
3 large eggs, beaten

Return the mixture to the refrigerator. If necessary, soak and rinse, 510:

4 feet of 1-inch-diameter sausage casings

Stuff the casings as directed, 510, forming 6-inch links. Poach the sausages, 509; if any rise to the surface, puncture them with a small skewer to release the air and prevent bursting. Cool and store for up to 3 days. When ready to serve, brush with:

Melted butter

and sauté or grill until golden brown.

GRAPES AND SAUSAGES

4 servings

Preheat the oven to 500°F.

Prick all over with a fork to prevent bursting:

1½ pounds mild Italian sausages

Heat in a large heavy skillet over medium heat:

2 tablespoons olive oil or butter

Add the sausages and cook, turning occasionally, until browned, about 10 minutes. Mix in a baking pan:

12 ounces seedless grapes, halved if large
2 teaspoons minced rosemary

Lay the sausages over the grapes and pour any drippings from the skillet into the pan. Roast until the grapes are beginning to brown, about 20 minutes. Season with:

Salt and black pepper to taste
(Dashes of balsamic vinegar)

PORK SCRAPPLE OR GOETTA

About 6 servings

These grain-filled regional specialties represent a rare style of sausage-making. If you use cornmeal, call it **scrapple;** if you use oats, call it **goetta.**

Combine in a large pot and bring to a boil:

6 cups water
1 onion, sliced
6 black peppercorns
1 small bay leaf

Add:

2 pounds pork neck bones or spareribs

Reduce the heat and simmer until the meat falls from the bones, about 1½ hours. Strain, reserving the liquid and meat separately.

For scrapple, measure out 4 cups of the reserved liquid, adding additional water or stock if necessary. Use this liquid to prepare:

Cornmeal Mush, 322

For goetta, use 3 cups of the reserved liquid to cook, 342:

1 cup old-fashioned rolled oats

Remove all the meat from the pork bones and finely chop. Add it to the cooked cornmeal mush or oatmeal. Season with:

2 tablespoons grated onion
1 teaspoon salt
½ teaspoon dried thyme or sage
A grating of nutmeg
⅛ teaspoon cayenne pepper

Pour the mixture into a loaf pan that has been rinsed with cold water. Refrigerate until cold and firm, unmold, and cut into thick slices. To serve, pan-fry the slices until brown in:

Melted butter or bacon fat

ABOUT PÂTÉS AND TERRINES

Pâtés and terrines are stars of the charcuterie board, and they are nearly as easy to make as meatloaf. What distinguishes them is the luxurious quality of their ingredients. The richness of a pâté can come from liver, cream, or eggs. The texture may be smooth, if all the meat is finely ground, or coarse-textured. Pâté may be studded with toasted nuts, thinly sliced truffles, or diced cured ham. Lean meats such as chicken and rabbit can be used, but they require the addition of fatback, pork belly, or another fatty cut. Pâtés are traditionally wrapped in yet more luxurious fat to preserve their moistness and ensure that they are easy to unmold. The loaf pan or mold may be lined with slices of pork belly, pancetta, or bacon—the latter will add a smoky flavor. These should be removed before serving or peeled away as needed—the pale belly meat has a poor texture and any bacon or pancetta flavor has been drawn into the pâté. Caul fat, 518, is another option; though harder to find, it does not need to be peeled off before serving, and the stencil of lacy fat adds a decorative touch.

The ingredients of pâtés and terrines should be very fresh, especially liver, which should be handled and prepared with special care (see About Liver, 514). Some of the meats can be bought ground, or you can ask your butcher to grind them for you. To grind your own meats, see 501. A properly made pâté or terrine will safely keep for 7 to 8 days in the refrigerator. Also see Chicken Liver Pâté, 62.

PÂTÉ DE CAMPAGNE

10 servings

For a great first course, serve slices of this fancy meatloaf with cornichons, crusty bread, and whole-grain mustard. Our version has a slightly smoky flavor from the bacon. If you can find caul fat, you may line the pan and cover the pâté with a large piece of it (about 20 × 20 inches) instead of bacon or belly, folding the edges over the meat, and trimming the excess. To prepare pork or calves' liver, see About Liver, 514; for chicken livers, see 445.

Melt in a small skillet over medium heat:

2 tablespoons butter

Add and cook until softened, 6 to 8 minutes:

1 small onion, finely chopped

Add and cook, stirring, 1 minute more:

3 garlic cloves, minced

Set the onion mixture aside to cool. Preheat the oven to 325°F. Line the bottom and sides of a terrine mold or 9 × 5-inch loaf pan with:

12 to 16 slices pork belly or bacon

Cut and chill as directed in Grinding Meat at Home, 501:

1¼ pounds pork shoulder, cut into 1-inch chunks
6 ounces well-trimmed pork, veal, or chicken liver
4 ounces pork fatback, cut into 1-inch chunks

To use a food processor, pulse the chilled meat and fat in small batches, scraping the bowl frequently, until the largest pieces are about ⅓ inch across. Transfer each batch of ground meat to a large bowl as you go.

To use a meat grinder, use a ⅜- or ½-inch grinding plate and run the chilled meat and fat through as directed in Grinding Meat at Home, 501. Add the cooled onions and garlic to the bowl along with:

2 large eggs, lightly beaten
½ cup heavy cream
(½ cup hazelnuts, toasted, 1005, and coarsely chopped)
2 tablespoons Cognac
1 tablespoon chopped parsley
2 teaspoons fresh thyme leaves, minced
1½ teaspoons salt
1½ teaspoons white or black pepper
½ teaspoon ground allspice
(⅛ teaspoon grated or ground nutmeg)

Mix until well combined. Fill the lined loaf pan with the mixture and spread evenly. Place over the top:

5 or 6 slices pork belly or bacon

Butter a piece of foil and cover the pan tightly. Place the loaf pan in a roasting pan and place the roasting pan on a pulled-out oven rack. Fill the roasting pan with warm water to come halfway up the sides of the pâté. Bake until the juices run clear and a thermometer inserted in the center registers 160°F, about 2 hours.

Transfer to a rimmed baking sheet or pour the water out of the roasting pan and place the pâté back in it. Place a small board or another loaf pan on top of the foil and weight down with a 2- or 3-pound can or other weight. Let cool, then refrigerate until firm, at least 12 hours and for up to 2 days.

To serve, remove the belly or bacon from the top of the pâté. Run a sharp knife around the edges, and turn the pâté out onto a serving platter or cutting board (if the pâté sticks, set the bottom of the pan in warm water until it releases). Remove the bacon from the bottom and sides of the pâté, and serve in thick slices.

PORK RILLETTES

2½ to 3 cups

Here, a rich cut of pork is cooked until tender, shredded, and then whipped with some of the cooking liquid into a delicious spread. For a similar, quicker result, see Deviled Ham, 62.

Cut into 1½-inch cubes:

2 pounds fatty pork shoulder or pork belly, or 1½ pounds lean pork shoulder or leg roast plus 8 ounces diced fatback

Place in a large saucepan or Dutch oven along with:

Stock or water to barely cover
1½ tablespoons salt
1 teaspoon black peppercorns
5 whole cloves
5 allspice berries
3 sprigs thyme
1 bay leaf

Bring to a boil. Reduce the heat to maintain a simmer, cover, and cook until the meat is fall-apart tender, about 3 hours.

Transfer the cubes of pork to a bowl and strain the fat and cooking liquid into a measuring cup. When the pieces have cooled somewhat, shred them with a fork and mix vigorously with a wooden spoon, adding a bit of the cooking liquid so that the mixture resembles a chunky spread. Sample the mixture and season to taste with:

Salt and black or white pepper

Pack the mixture into ramekins or crocks and transfer to the refrigerator. At this point you can simply cover or wrap the ramekins, but it is traditional to "seal" them with a layer of:

(Rendered lard or duck fat)

Let the rillettes sit overnight in the refrigerator before serving; they will keep refrigerated for up to 1 week or frozen in sealed bags for up to 3 months. Let come to room temperature before serving with:

Sliced baguette or crackers, pickles, and whole-grain mustard

ABOUT OFFAL AND VARIETY MEATS

Despite being relatively inexpensive thanks to the "miracles" of large-scale modern agriculture, our tendency to buy tenderloins and rib roasts is, in many ways, a demonstration of excess and extreme luxury. The cuts most consumers gravitate to represent a tiny fraction of an animal's dressed weight. As we have tried to emphasize throughout this chapter, the practice of buying only the "best" cuts of the animal is deeply flawed from a culinary standpoint: Simply put, we neglect some of the most flavorful portions of the animal for often trivial reasons. Some of these reasons are legitimate—beef cheeks take much longer to cook than a filet mignon—while others are less defensible, such as our tendency toward revulsion at the slightest reminder that a meal has been made of a living animal. The abstract fantasy we are afforded by sterile, plastic-wrapped retail packages of portioned meat is much harder to maintain when you know that a particular cut was fashioned from a cow's head, a hog's foot, or a lamb's liver. Though very little is wasted in the modern slaughterhouse, we think it is important to acknowledge and celebrate these "odd bits." The culinary traditions surrounding them run deep for reasons other than mere frugality: Many of these cuts are very tasty.

Most variety meats are not difficult to prepare at home. ➤ It is essential that variety meats be purchased very fresh or well-frozen, as they are highly perishable. We recommend ordering ahead from a full-service meat market or shopping for them at pan-Asian markets (especially busy ones) and cooking promptly.

Beef cheeks, lamb neck, and other muscular cuts are often considered variety meats, but since they require no special treatment, we have placed them in the preceding sections of this chapter; see Beef Cuts, 454, Lamb Cuts, 477, and Pork Cuts, 486, for more information. For avian odd bits, see About Poultry Offal or Giblets, 444.

ABOUT LIVER

Livers from young animals are smaller, milder, and more tender. Calf's liver is delicate, delicious, and fairly expensive. It is paler in color and milder than mature beef liver, which is a dark brownish-red and strong in flavor. Lamb liver is tender like calf's. Pork liver is strong in taste, though very tender, and well worth the added effort of trimming out the tough fibers. For utmost freshness, we recommend purchasing whole liver with its outer membrane intact, rather than packages of sliced liver.

To prepare liver for cooking, wipe it first with a damp cloth. If the green-hued gallbladder is still attached, cut it off and discard. Remove the outer membrane covering the liver, as well as any veins; these can be easily peeled from fresh liver. ➤ To lessen the flavor of strong-tasting beef and pork livers, you may soak them in ice water or milk for several hours or overnight; gently blot dry before cooking.

➤ Do not overcook liver; it will toughen and turn chalky. To nudge the odds in your favor, do not slice liver thinner than ½ inch thick for sautéing or pan-frying. Liver has an affinity with Madeira, white wine, sour cream, nutmeg, and thyme. ➤ The drippings in which liver has cooked may taste bitter; taste them before using for a pan sauce, 546. Serve liver with Béarnaise Sauce, 561, Sauce Lyonnaise, 551, an herbed Beurre Blanc, 558, or a mustard-laced Vinaigrette, 575.

SAUTÉED CALF'S LIVER

4 servings

This classic presentation reminds us that simplicity is often the best approach. However, you may augment and garnish this basic recipe as you please; for the classic combination of **Liver and Onions,** first prepare a double batch of Sautéed Onions, 255, then transfer them to a platter and keep warm in a 200°F oven. Using the same skillet, proceed to cook the liver as directed on 515. Combine and serve.

Remove the membrane and cut into ½-inch-thick slices:

1 pound calf's liver

Season with:

1 teaspoon salt
½ teaspoon black pepper

Dredge both sides in:

Flour

Heat in a large heavy skillet over medium-high heat:

2 tablespoons vegetable oil or butter, or a combination, or as needed

Add the liver in batches and brown quickly, about 2 minutes on each side; do not overcook. Do not crowd the skillet, and add more oil or butter as needed. Transfer to a warmed platter and serve with any of the suggested sauces in About Liver, 514. Or, if the drippings are not bitter, cover the liver to keep warm, drain off excess fat, and prepare:

(Pan sauce for Veal Piccata, 475)

ABOUT SWEETBREADS

Neither leavened nor sweet, these paired lobes are actually the thymus gland, which is located near the animal's throat. They are knobby and oblong in appearance. The smooth-surfaced, round lobes of the pancreatic gland are sometimes sold as sweetbreads as well, but they are considered inferior. Veal and lamb sweetbreads are those most favored; they are rich, tender, creamy, and mild. Like all organ meats, ➤ sweetbreads are highly perishable and should be prepared for use as soon as possible after purchasing.

To prepare sweetbreads for cooking, first soak them in a large quantity of cold water in the refrigerator for at least 1 hour to draw out any blood, changing the water 2 or 3 times.

Place the sweetbreads in a pot or saucepan and cover with cooled Court Bouillon, 80, or acidulated water, 951. Slowly bring to a boil over medium heat and simmer uncovered until the sweetbreads are slightly firm to the touch; they should still give slightly to pressure—as British offal enthusiast Ferguson Henderson explains, "think of the finger that pushes the Pillsbury Doughboy's tummy." Smaller sweetbreads may be firm by the time the liquid boils; larger ones may take up to 5 minutes of simmering. Remove the sweetbreads with a slotted spoon and transfer at once to a bowl of ice water. When they have cooled somewhat but are still warm to the touch, drain again and trim by removing any cartilage, tubes, connective tissue, and any tougher outer layers of their membranous covering—do not remove too much, or they will not retain their shape. To expel more water and firm them up for cooking, place the sweetbreads in a pie dish or on a plate, top with another plate or pie dish, and weight down with a heavy can. Refrigerate, weighted, for several hours.

Leave them whole or slice or break them into smaller sections, being careful not to disturb the very fine membrane that surrounds the smaller lobes. Once prepared, you may pan-fry sweetbreads as directed below, deep-fry them, or season well and cook over a hot grill fire on skewers until they are nicely browned.

PAN-FRIED SWEETBREADS

4 to 6 servings

Cut into ¼-inch-thick slices:

1 pound sweetbreads, prepared as directed above

Whisk together in a shallow bowl:

1 large egg, lightly beaten
1 tablespoon milk or water

Spread in a second shallow bowl:

¾ cup dry bread crumbs

Spread in a third shallow bowl:

½ cup flour

Pat the sweetbread slices dry and season with:

Salt and black pepper

Dredge the slices lightly in the flour and shake off the excess. Slide the flour-coated slices through the egg mixture, making sure the entire surface is covered, then coat with the bread crumbs, pressing the crumbs with your fingers so they adhere. Handle very gently so that the coating does not crack. Heat in a medium skillet over medium-high heat:

½ inch vegetable oil

When the oil shimmers, add the sweetbreads in batches and cook until browned on the first side, 1½ to 2 minutes. Turn and brown on the other side, about 30 seconds. Drain on paper towels and cover to keep warm while cooking the remaining sweetbreads. Serve garnished with:

Lemon wedges

Or spoon over the top:

Brown Butter, 558, Beurre Blanc, 558, made with fresh herbs, or Gastrique, 565

ABOUT BRAINS

Brains are the most delicate and creamy organ meat. They contain no muscle fiber at all and are extremely high in fat—much of it saturated. They can have a texture almost like a very thick sauce. As with practically all organ meats, calves' brains are held in the highest esteem, but those of goat, lamb, pork, and beef are also eaten.

➤ A note on health risks: In our previous edition, we discouraged readers from preparing the brains of cows, sheep, or pigs, citing the health risks posed by Bovine Spongiform Encephalopathy, or BSE (commonly known as "mad cow" disease). Once BSE-tainted brain or spinal material is consumed, there is a small likelihood of contracting the human equivalent, Creutzfeldt-Jakob Disease (or CJD). The last known instances of this disease in US cattle were in 2003 and 2017; both atypical cases in older dairy cows that were not being considered for slaughter. BSE is spread in cattle if they are fed meat-and-bone meal of an infected animal—a practice that is now highly regulated—and easily avoided altogether by purchasing offal from a trusted source of ethically raised meat. Calves are also less likely to be infected. In other words, the initially small odds of contracting CJD from consuming brains have plummeted and are even lower when some basic precautions are taken. The question that remains for adventurous cooks and eaters is: Why incur this risk for the opportunity to eat something as neutral-flavored, "delicately" textured, and cholesterol-heavy as brains? Having been forewarned from a gastronomic and health-risk perspective, our (current) final word on this is: To each their own.

As noted, try to source brains from young, pastured, ethically raised animals to minimize health risks. Brains should be symmetrical, compact, and pale pink or white in color with very little blood or discoloration. They should smell clean and fresh, not sour; they will be soft to the touch but should not be mushy. Like other organ meats, brains are extremely perishable; keep refrigerated and cook within 24 hours of purchase. They are very delicate and tend to fall apart, so handle them with care.

To prepare brains for cooking, soak them in a brine, 1046, in the refrigerator for 6 hours and up to overnight, changing the brine several times (this will rid them of any trace of blood). For a creamier result, they may be cooked at this point. To give them more texture, put the brains in a saucepan, cover with cooled Court Bouillon, 80, or acidulated water, 951, and slowly bring to a simmer over medium heat. Cook at the gentlest simmer until they are slightly firm to the touch, which can take anywhere from 5 to 15 minutes depending on size. Drain thoroughly. Like sweetbreads, it is best to place the poached brains between two plates or pie dishes, weight them down with a heavy can, and refrigerate for several hours, which will firm them up further and rid them of excess moisture.

Once poached and pressed, we recommend cutting the brains in pieces and pan-frying as for sweetbreads, 515. It is also traditional to serve them cooked with scrambled eggs.

ABOUT KIDNEYS

Kidneys are maligned for their abject function, but some discerning eaters relish them for their "fine tang of faintly scented urine." Regardless of your gastronomic leanings, know that fresh kidneys should be firm and shiny, with no discolored spots or ammonia odor. Calf or veal kidneys are the most tender and delicious, as are those of lamb, which are somewhat softer. Lamb and pork kidneys are the exact shape and color of kidney beans; calf and beef kidneys are untidy bundles of irregular nodules. Veal and pork kidneys should be pinkish brown in color; beef and lamb kidneys are a darker reddish brown. All kidneys are encased in leaf lard, 997, or suet, 1023, both of which are especially firm and highly prized; some of this fat may still cling to their outer membranes.

To prepare kidneys for cooking, first peel off any fat—you may use it to sauté the kidneys or save for another purpose. Peel off the outer membranes and split the kidneys: for lamb and pig kidneys cut them in half starting on the side that bulges outward, leaving the opposite side intact, and open like a book to reveal their fatty core. For veal and beef kidneys, cut along the midline between the nodules until the tubes at their center are exposed. Remove any fat, veins, or tubes from the interior and rinse well. Smaller kidneys can be patted dry and cooked at this point. Large beef and pork kidneys tend to be strong in flavor and should be left to soak for at least 2 hours in a brine, 1046, or milk.

Veal and lamb kidneys should be cooked for a brief time over brisk heat. When grilling or broiling smaller kidneys, keep them from curling by threading them onto skewers after opening them. Cook over a hot grill fire as for Chicken Yakitori, 445, exposing the cut side to the heat first. ➤ Do not overcook: The center should be slightly pink. Kidneys are often mixed with other ingredients, as in a stew of mushrooms and wine or in a creamy sauce of mustard and shallots. Never allow them to boil in a sauce, as this hardens them. Pour the hot sauce over them or toss them in it for a moment or two off the heat.

SAUTÉED KIDNEYS WITH MUSTARD

4 servings

A traditional French treatment. In Britain, the sauce is likely to be finished with dashes of Worcestershire sauce and a pinch of cayenne. Prepare as above:

1 veal or 6 lamb kidneys (about 1½ pounds)

Cut veal kidneys crosswise into ½-inch slices or lamb kidneys lengthwise in half. Season with:

1 teaspoon salt
½ teaspoon black pepper

Heat in a large heavy skillet over medium-high heat:

2 tablespoons vegetable oil

When the oil smokes, add the kidneys in batches and brown well, about 1½ minutes on each side. Transfer to a plate and keep warm, reduce the heat to medium, and pour off any fat. Add to the skillet:

2 tablespoons butter
½ cup finely chopped shallots or onion
2 garlic cloves, minced

Cook, stirring until softened, 3 to 4 minutes. Add:

1 cup dry white wine, or ½ cup wine and ½ cup chicken stock
(2 tablespoons Cognac)
1 teaspoon thyme leaves, coarsely chopped
1 bay leaf

Bring to a boil, scraping up the browned bits on the bottom of the skillet, and reduce to about ⅓ cup. Remove from the heat and discard the bay leaf. Stir in and mix thoroughly:

2 tablespoons heavy cream
2 teaspoons Dijon or whole-grain mustard

Season to taste with:

Salt and black pepper

Return the kidneys and their juices to the skillet and stir gently to coat with the sauce. Top with:

Minced chives, chopped parsley, or a combination

ABOUT TONGUE

In 1963, Marion began this section with the statement: "Lucky indeed is the cook with the gift of tongues!" This enthusiasm has caused consternation in the minds of many readers, some of whom ascribe Marion's alien sentiment to a bygone age when tongue was held in higher regard. But anyone familiar with the more adventurous end of a taco truck's menu will probably recognize Marion as one of their own, a like-minded contemporary who would ravenously dig in to a mess of rich, tender, and irresistibly beefy *tacos de lengua.*

You may find tongues fresh or frozen, and occasionally smoked or pickled. Smaller veal and lamb tongues have the mildest flavor and finest texture, but we prefer beef tongues for their richness; for the best texture, purchase beef tongues that weigh no more than 3 pounds.

To prepare tongue for cooking, first scrub its pebbly skin under running water. Place the tongue in a pot and cover with Court Bouillon, 80, or water. Bring to a simmer, cover, and cook until the tongue is tender and the skin peels easily from the meat, 2 to 3 hours.

Remove from the cooking liquid and let both cool separately; when the tongue is cool enough to handle, peel the skin off—do not let it cool completely, as it will not peel as easily. Trim and discard any cartilage, small bones, and gristle from the tongue's base and store the meat in its cooking liquid until ready to slice or cook further.

To slice tongue, start at the base, making your cuts perpendicular to the work surface and parallel to the base. Toward the tip, cut slices holding the knife at an angle to the work surface.

For the longest time, we have recommended simply carving cooked tongue into slices and serving—either cold or reheated in the cooking liquid—with an assertive sauce, perhaps between slices of bread. Without a doubt, this is still to our minds a good preparation and it is loved by many. Sauce Piquant, 551, Horseradish Sauce, 566, or Salsa Verde, 567, are all good options. The preparation below, however, is our favorite.

CRISPY PAN-FRIED TONGUE WITH ONIONS AND JALAPEÑOS

5 or 6 servings

The most common argument against tongue has nothing to do with its superlative flavor, but its uniquely tender texture. The best antidote—the one that will make tongue-haters into tongue-seekers—is to cook the tongue to tenderness, then grill or pan-fry for a crispy contrast. Serve this beguiling mixture in Tacos, 146, burritos, 147, and Tortas, 143.

Scrub and simmer until tender as described on 516:

2 to 3 pounds fresh beef, veal, or lamb tongue

Once cooled, peeled, and trimmed, slice the tongue across the grain into ½-inch-thick slices. Sprinkle the slices with:

1 teaspoon salt

Set aside. Place in a large, dry skillet over medium heat:

4 jalapeño peppers, left whole

4 spring onions or large green onions, green tops trimmed and reserved, or 4 small unpeeled shallots

Pan-roast them, turning occasionally, until the peppers and onions are blackened on all sides and beginning to shrivel. Transfer the vegetables to a cutting board. Increase the heat to medium-high and add:

3 tablespoons vegetable oil, lard, or drippings

When the fat shimmers, brown the tongue slices in batches, about 4 minutes on each side. As they brown, transfer them to a platter and add more fat to the skillet if necessary. When all the slices are browned, reduce the heat to medium. Discard the stems and seeds from the jalapeños and coarsely chop them with the roasted onions and reserved onion greens. Add the vegetables to the skillet along with:

2 garlic cloves, finely chopped

1 tablespoon chopped fresh oregano or 1 teaspoon dried oregano

Cook until fragrant, about 2 minutes more. Coarsely chop the browned tongue into slender, bite-sized pieces (or smaller for filling tacos) and return to the skillet. Season to taste with:

Salt and black pepper

ABOUT HEART

The heart is a fickle muscle, requiring quick, high heat or a long, steamy braise. When trimmed of exterior fat, heart is very lean; despite this, it is full-flavored, and not in the polarizing way liver and kidney are. Of course, it can be ground into submission (see Grinding Meat at Home, 510) and added to a hamburger mixture, or minced into tartare, 64, if it is impeccably fresh.

To prepare heart for cooking, thoroughly rinse and trim it of all arteries or tubes, tough tissues, veins, and blood clots. Since beef heart is so large, you will need to butterfly it along the seams of connective tissue running through it; if you wish to tie it back together and cook it whole, leave the exterior membrane intact (many traditional recipes call for stuffing heart, and then browning and braising until tender). Dry thoroughly. A heart weighs 4 to 5 pounds for beef, about 1 pound for veal, and 10 to 12 ounces for pork and lamb. Because so much trimming is required, a beef heart will serve about 5; a veal heart will serve 1. A pork heart must be cooked to 145°F (and braised for much longer to become tender); beef, veal, and lamb hearts can be braised as well, or cooked to rare or medium-rare (see chart, 453).

ANTICUCHOS DE CORAZÓN (PERUVIAN BEEF HEART SKEWERS)

4 servings

This method is approachable for fledgling explorers of heart cookery. The delectable marinade and steak-like results are easy for the less adventurous to embrace. The key is a very hot fire and a very short cooking time. Grill the skewers within 4 inches of the coals for the best results.

Prepare for cooking as directed above:

1 beef or 4 veal hearts

Cut 1½ to 2 pounds of the trimmed meat into ½-inch-wide strips (the strips do not have to be of uniform length). Mix in a large bowl:

½ cup red wine vinegar

¼ cup olive oil

2 tablespoons ground red chiles, such as ají panca, ancho, or chiles de árbol, or a combination

4 garlic cloves, minced

1 tablespoon ground cumin

1 teaspoon dried oregano

1 teaspoon black pepper

1 teaspoon salt

(½ teaspoon ground annatto seeds)

Add the heart strips and marinate for 3 hours and up to overnight.

If using wooden skewers, soak them in water to cover for 1 hour before you cook the heart. Prepare a hot grill fire, 1063. Thread the meat onto the skewers and grill for 3 to 4 minutes, turning once. ➤ Do not cook beyond medium-rare. Serve at once, garnished with:

A salsa, 573–74, or Habanero-Citrus Hot Sauce, 571

Or on top of:

Becker House Salad, 116

ABOUT CAUL FAT

Caul fat is a diaphanous, intricately patterned sheet of fatty tissue cut from the peritoneum, a sac that secures the stomach and intestines to the abdominal wall. Sheep and hogs have caul fat, but cows have much more of it, making it the most common to find. Though you will have to call ahead to order caul fat, it is well worth seeking out. In essence, it is nature's ready-made barding fat, 1046, as it can be draped on or wrapped around all manner of fish and fowl or used to line a loaf pan for baking pâtés (see Pâté de Campagne, 513). This lacey web of fat clings to a translucent membrane. This membrane is somewhat delicate, but when intact it does not readily leak juices. In fact, ➤ caul fat is an incredible boon to anyone who wishes to experiment with sausage-making but does not own a stuffer or want to fiddle with casings; for more, see our instructions for making crépinettes, 510.

Dealing with caul fat is much like using plastic wrap: The thin sheet is generally inclined to stick to things—including itself—and must be unrolled to lie flat. The trick is to be gentle and avoid tearing holes in the membrane; as you unroll portions, gently pick up and drape the caul fat farther from the roll and out to the sides to keep it from bunching up. For lining molds or loaf pans, drape the fat over the vessel, leaving plenty of overhang. Gently nudge the fat into the corners of the pan and press it against the sides. Trim any excess fat, leaving a large enough border so that it can be folded over to cover the top of a pâté or terrine mixture. To bard or encase, lay the item on top of the unrolled caul fat and cut around it with scissors, again leaving plenty to fold over the top and envelop the item. Press gently to seal the caul fat to itself.

ABOUT TRIPE

Tripe is the smooth muscle lining the four stomachs of ruminants. Cattle provide most of the tripe available with their comparatively large stomachs. From the first stomach, or rumen, we derive **blanket** or **smooth tripe;** it is the largest, mildest, and relatively fatty. From the second stomach (reticulum) comes tender **honeycomb tripe,** the most commonly found type. Next is the many-layered **book** or **bible tripe** from the third stomach (omasum). Finally, the last stomach is called the abomasum, which gives us the wrinkled, rarely seen **reed tripe.** ➤ Since tripe is very perishable, it should be kept refrigerated and used as soon as possible with the exception of pickled tripe, which can be found in some markets.

Though sometimes sold as "fresh," packaged tripe has been blanched, treated with bleach to lighten its color, and parboiled. It still must be simmered for several hours to become tender.

To prepare store-bought tripe, rinse thoroughly. If it has an off odor or smells of bleach, cover with cold water in a pot, bring to a simmer, and immediately drain (repeat if necessary). Once cool, cut into pieces, and proceed with your recipe.

To prepare freshly butchered tripe, first scrub it thoroughly under water to get rid of any foreign material that may be trapped in its nooks and crannies. Cover with cold water in a pot, bring to a simmer, and immediately drain. Rinse the tripe again and soak it overnight in acidulated water, 951, refrigerated. The next day, simmer the tripe in brine, 1046, for 15 minutes. Rinse well and drain once more. If the tripe smells neutral, cut it up for cooking; if not, repeat the steps above as necessary.

As tripe cooks, its texture changes from slightly crunchy to soft and gristle-like, and finally to meltingly tender. When braised in a seasoned liquid or broth, tripe handily takes on its flavor; in addition to the recipes below, see Pho Bo, 96, and Pepper Pot, 99.

FRIED TRIPE

6 servings

First included in the 1936 edition, this dish can be a decadent first course if thick blanket tripe is used; honeycomb tripe is more reminiscent of fried calamari (we prefer this kind for tacos). Please read about Deep-Frying, 1051.

Prepare as directed above:

2 pounds tripe

Cut into bite-sized squares or strips and wash well. Transfer to a pot and add:

Court Bouillon, 80, or water to cover
1 tablespoon salt

Bring to a boil, reduce the heat, cover, and simmer the tripe until very tender, about 3 hours.

Drain and set aside to cool. Mix together in a large bowl:

1 cup flour
1½ teaspoons salt
1 teaspoon cayenne pepper

When cool enough to handle, add the tripe to the bowl and toss to coat. Preheat the oven to 200°F.

Heat to 370°F in a deep-fryer, deep heavy pot, or Dutch oven:

2 inches vegetable oil or lard

Fry the tripe in batches until golden brown, adjusting the heat to maintain the right temperature. Transfer the fried tripe to a baking sheet lined with paper towels and transfer to the oven to keep warm while the other batches fry. Serve hot in:

Tacos, 146

Or serve as an appetizer with:

Salsa Verde, 567, or Horseradish Sauce, 566

Or simply garnished with:

Lemon wedges and chopped parsley

ITALIAN-STYLE TRIPE

6 servings

Prepare as directed, above:

2 pounds honeycomb tripe

Cut into bite-sized squares or strips and wash well. Transfer to a pot and add:

Court Bouillon, 80, or water to cover
1 tablespoon salt

Bring to a boil, reduce the heat, cover, and simmer the tripe until tender, about 2 hours. Drain and set aside.

While the tripe simmers, prepare:

Tomato Sauce, 556

Add the tripe to the sauce, cover, and simmer 15 minutes more. If the sauce is too dry, add:

(¼ to ½ cup dry red wine)

If wine is added, simmer it briefly to cook off the alcohol. Top with:
Grated Parmesan

ABOUT CHITTERLINGS AND HOG MAWS

The small and large intestines of sheep, cows, and pigs are used to encase sausages, but those of pigs are also enjoyed singly after being simmered until tender in a highly seasoned liquid. The well-cleaned small intestines of hogs are known as chitterlings—commonly spelled and pronounced as **chitlins.** Chitterlings must be soaked in several changes of water, trimmed of most of their fat, and cut into small pieces.

Hog maw, also called **buche,** is the outer layer of pork stomach; it is often cut into pieces and treated in the same way as chitterlings, though it is sometimes left whole and filled with a stuffing (much like the infamous Scottish sheep-stomach preparation, haggis). Hog maws are a bit thicker than chitterlings and require a more thorough cleaning.

These odd bits are most appreciated in the American South, Pennsylvania Dutch country, and in Mexican cuisine. In France, chitterlings (and tripe) are cooked, chopped, and used to fill sausages.

A word of caution: Raw intestines can harbor dangerous bacteria, including *Yersinia interocolitica*, an organism that causes gastrointestinal distress and other, more serious symptoms in many people every year, especially small children. Since chitterlings require extensive preparation where surfaces may be splattered and cross-contaminated, ➤ please take special caution to clean all surfaces and disinfect with a sanitizing solution, xx. Wash hands especially well before and after preparing the chitterlings.

To prepare chitterlings and hog maws, wash well in several changes of cold water and soak, refrigerated, in brine, 1046, to cover for 24 hours. Wash them again in 5 or 6 changes of water. If chitterlings are still whole, split them in half lengthwise to expose their inner surface. Peel off and discard the thin, transparent layer of fat and cut into bite-sized pieces. Hog maws must be simmered in water for 30 minutes before cleaning; peel away most of the fat, and trim out any discolored portions or cartilaginous chunks.

STEWED CHITTERLINGS OR HOG MAWS

4 to 6 servings

Put in a large pot with water to cover:
2 pounds chitterlings, cleaned and cut into 2-inch pieces
1 large onion, sliced
¼ cup cider vinegar
(3 dried ancho or New Mexico chiles, seeded and stemmed)
2 tablespoons salt
2 teaspoons dried thyme
(½ teaspoon ground cloves)
½ teaspoon black pepper
1 garlic clove
1 bay leaf

Bring slowly to a boil. Cover, reduce the heat, and simmer until tender, 3 to 4 hours. Stir occasionally to prevent sticking.

SAUTÉED CHITTERLINGS

4 to 6 servings

Prepare:
Stewed Chitterlings, above

When the chitterlings are tender, drain and dry well. Heat in a large skillet over medium-high heat:
2 tablespoons vegetable oil

Add the chitterlings and sauté until golden brown, 5 to 8 minutes. Season to taste with:
Cider vinegar and salt or hot sauce

Serve with:
Black-Eyed Peas and Greens, 216
Southern Corn Bread, 630
Hot pepper sauce

ABOUT SKIN, EARS, TAILS, AND FEET

Though they take a long time to prepare, these extremities are beloved for their unctuous, decadent texture when cooked until tender and the flavorful meat shreds easily from the bone. The cartilaginous goodness of ears, feet, and tails can be exploited to give dishes—even a large pot of stock—a silken texture.

Among these cuts, **oxtails** are the most familiar (and highest in price). They add incredible depth and body to soups like Pho Bo, 96, and are a favorite for braising. Oxtails are usually sold crosscut, making them easy to brown as well as eat; if you manage to find a whole oxtail, they are relatively easy to cut into sections or medallions (just slice at the indentations into 1- to 2-inch lengths). **Pig's tails** are much smaller, less meaty, and significantly harder to find. Look for hairs on the skin and shave with a safety razor if necessary. Pig's tails add flavor and body to braises and stews; add them whole, cook until soft, and pick the meat off the bone at the end of cooking.

Pig's feet (or **trotters**) and **calf's feet** can be treated in the same way. Or, to use them as the main ingredient of a meal rather than a gelatin-rich ingredient, try to find trotters with the hock still attached (they will have more meat). Simmer the feet until tender as for Stewed Chitterlings, above. Most feet will be tender after 4 hours of cooking. You may pick off the meat and dress with a sauce, or leave them whole and crisp up their skin in a 400°F oven. We prefer to serve the meat already picked; it can always be crisped up afterward as for Sautéed Chitterlings, above, or Crispy Pan-Fried Tongue, 517.

Pig's ears must be brined overnight and simmered for a long time as well, but the core of cartilage running through them will always be a bit snappy. Once simmered until tender, we prefer them deep-fried, as for tripe, 518.

The only skin we use in the kitchen is from hogs. Small strips of trimmed **pig skin** can be added to dishes in the manner of pig's tails: as a gelatin-boosting ingredient that adds body to braises and stews. Some even brine and smoke pig skin to give it a ham hock–like flavor. The most memorable (and involved) preparation of pig skin results in crunchy **Pork Rinds** or **Chicharrones,** 520.

BRAISED OXTAILS (OXTAIL STEW)

4 servings

Oxtails need the gentle, slow heat of a braise to soften their connective tissue. The result is a dish with a rich beef flavor and a velvety sauce. Oxtails are usually sold in 1- to 3-inch cross sections; because of the amount of bone, you should buy at least 1 pound per person. Pieces from the very narrow tip of the tail yield almost no meat and are best saved for the stockpot.

Preheat the oven to 300°F.

Heat in a Dutch oven or large ovenproof skillet:

¼ cup vegetable oil, lard, or beef fat

Whisk together in a large bowl:

2 cups flour
1 tablespoon black pepper
1 tablespoon salt

Dredge:

4 pounds oxtails, crosscut into 1- to 2-inch-long pieces

in the seasoned flour. Brown the oxtails in batches, transferring them to a plate as they finish. Pour off the fat and add to the pan:

½ cup white wine

Scrape up any browned bits and let the wine cook off a bit. Add:

3 cups beef stock, chicken stock, or water

Return the oxtails to the pan and bring to a boil over high heat. Cover, transfer the pan to the oven, and cook until the oxtails are very tender, 4 to 5 hours, adding more stock if needed. During the last 45 minutes of cooking, add:

2 large onions, chopped
3 carrots, chopped
3 celery ribs, chopped
4 garlic cloves, chopped

Transfer the oxtails and vegetables to a platter with a slotted spoon and skim off as much fat as possible (a gravy separator comes in handy here). Reduce the liquid over medium-high heat until it thickens somewhat, or add:

(Kneaded Butter, 544, made with 2 tablespoons butter and 2 tablespoons all-purpose flour)

Season to taste with:

Salt and black pepper
Chopped parsley

Pour the sauce over the oxtails and serve with:

Mashed Potatoes, 265

PORK RINDS OR CHICHARRONES

Here, pig skin is trimmed, simmered, scraped, baked overnight in a low oven, and deep-fried. The water trapped inside the skin boils and evaporates, causing the skin to puff up and expand. For those wondering why they should bother with such a time-consuming process, we must report that turning a discarded bit of trim into an impossibly crunchy snack is very satisfying. Freshly fried rinds are magical when served warm, showered with salt, and chili powder. Portland chef Aaron Barnett serves his magnificent fresh pork rinds with Aleppo pepper and warmed maple syrup, and we heartily recommend you do the same. Please read about Deep-Frying, 1051.

Pat dry:

Fresh pig skin

Cut the skin into 4 × 12-inch pieces. Working with one piece at a time, place the skin fat side up on a cutting board. Pressing down on the fat at one end, carefully slice into the fat at an angle until the blade is very close to the skin. Turn the blade so that it is parallel to the skin, and continue carefully slicing away as much fat as possible, being sure not to cut through the skin. When you have sliced through to the other end, turn the piece and slice away the fat from the end you started at. Repeat with the remaining skin. Transfer the skin to a pot and add:

Water to cover by several inches

Bring to a boil, reduce the heat to a simmer, cover, and cook until the skin is tender and easily torn, 1½ to 2 hours.

Transfer with a slotted spoon to a plate. Preheat the oven to 200°F.

Once the skin is cool enough to handle (but still warm), transfer to a cutting board, pat dry, and spread out fat side up. Using a bench scraper or the flat edge of a metal spatula, gently scrape any remaining fat from the skin (leaving some on is fine, but they will not puff as well). Cut the skin into smaller pieces: 4-inch squares or larger are impressive, but bite-sized, 1-inch pieces are best for serving a crowd. Spread the pieces flat on a wire rack set over a rimmed baking sheet (make sure they do not overlap). Bake for at least 8 hours, or overnight for the puffiest results. The skin should be light brown and very hard.

Once oven-dried, the rinds can be kept in a closed container and refrigerated for up to 2 weeks. Fry them as needed.

When ready to serve, heat to 375°F in a deep-fryer, deep heavy pot, or Dutch oven:

3 inches vegetable oil

Fry the pieces in batches until they puff and expand, about 30 seconds. Transfer to a plate lined with paper towels and sprinkle liberally with:

Salt
Chili powder

Serve while hot as an appetizer or snack. Crumbled or chopped pork rinds may also be used as a crunchy topping for dishes like Larb, 122.

ABOUT MARROW BONES

Marrow is found in the center of the long leg bones of most animals, but the most common marrow bones are from cows and calves. Sometimes they are found whole, but more often they are crosscut into 3-inch pieces or cut into longer pieces and split down the middle (also known as **canoe cut**). Cut marrow bones should be very clean, free of any whitish specks on the cut surfaces, as well as any blood. The marrow itself is slightly off-white in color and should be firm to the touch.

To prepare marrow bones for cooking, rinse several times, cover in cold brine, 1046, and soak in the refrigerator for 24 hours, changing the brine several times (this will draw out any blood that remains). From here you can roast the marrow bones (see 521) or remove the marrow to enrich a sauce, such as Sauce Bordelaise, 551.

To remove marrow before cooking, let the bones sit at room temperature for 20 minutes. If the bones are whole, use the back of a heavy knife to crack the bone, then pull it apart; remove the marrow from the center. For bones that have been crosscut, run a thin knife around the marrow at each opening and slowly push out the marrow with your finger. For canoe-cut marrow bones, slide a knife underneath the marrow and pop it out. Chill until ready to use.

To roast marrow bones, brine them as directed on 520 and preheat the oven to 450°F. Season the marrow bones liberally with salt and pepper and place on a baking sheet with the cut sides up. Roast until the marrow is softened and warm, about 20 minutes. ➤ Do not overcook marrow; it is very fatty and simply melts under too much heat. Serve with toast rounds as a decadent appetizer. Provide marrow spoons or other long spoons to enable diners to scoop out the marrow.

ABOUT BLOOD

There is perhaps no other odd bit that American cooks and diners approach with more trepidation than blood. Most Americans, in fact, have likely never knowingly eaten it or even had it offered to them. Our own first experience with blood was in a restaurant specializing in the Vietnamese soup *bún bò Huế*. Tucked in among the rice noodles, thin slices of beef, pork knuckles, oxtails, and paper-thin sliced onion were two brick red cubes of coagulated pig blood. We found the flavor to be remarkably mild, with just a little iron tang and with the texture of firm tofu. In fact, the flavor of blood is milder than that of liver.

Vietnam isn't the only place where blood is enjoyed. Nordic cooks make blood pancakes; France has *boudin noir*, or blood sausage; Ireland's County Cork boasts *drisheen*, a blood pudding; and in the Philippines *dinuguan* is a popular stew of offal, blood, and chiles. There are good reasons blood is almost universally appreciated. Apart from being an affordable, nutrient-rich foodstuff, blood adds richness to dishes and can be used to thicken soups and stews, giving them an almost custardy quality (overcooked blood, however, tends to be grainy).

The most widely available type of blood is pig's blood. You may find it liquid, coagulated in cakes, or frozen. Liquid blood is necessary for most blood-related recipes. Use cubes of coagulated blood in soups and add them at the end of cooking. When buying blood, look for a reddish-brown color. There should be almost no odor at all. Use blood soon after buying, preferably within a day, or freeze it for up to 3 months. Before working with blood, stir it well, and strain out any clots through a medium-mesh sieve. When cooking with blood, be aware that it will not keep its bright color (it turns dark brown).

GAME AND EXOTIC MEATS

Historically, "game" has been used to refer solely to animals hunted or caught in the wild. For a century, it has largely been illegal to sell hunted game in the United States, which has led to the advent of farmed and ranched game. Thus, the term "game" now includes ranched and domesticated animals from species that were once exclusively wild, such as elk. Since other unfamiliar animals like yak are also available—and have a similarly novel appeal—we cover them in this chapter as well.

Wild game hunted in this country is prohibited for resale and must be hunted by the cook or received as a gift from a generous hunter. In the kitchen, wild game can be unpredictable: The animals' diet, sex, age, and stress level when harvested can have a profound effect on flavor and texture. **Ranched game,** which has come to include deer, elk, bison, and exotics like African antelope, is raised under free-range conditions. Ideally, their surroundings provide them with a ranging area and diet comparable to that of their natural habitat, which helps them develop a more complex flavor. **Farmed game** animals, such as penned rabbits and pastured deer, elk, and bison, are fed a specific diet rather than foraging for themselves. They are typically milder in taste, more tender, and somewhat fattier than their wild counterparts. Though ranched and farmed game may lack the assertive character of wild meat, it is a much more consistent ingredient to work with in the kitchen (and infinitely more convenient for those of us who do most of our hunting in grocery stores).

ABOUT BUYING GAME

With the exception of a few Texas-based distributors of boar meat and one purveyor of nonnative axis deer from Hawaii, it is illegal to sell wild game meat that has been hunted in the United States. Other countries, notably the United Kingdom, do allow commercial hunting, and the meat may be imported and sold, but the majority of game for sale has been ranched or farmed. Some grocery stores stock game meats; if they do, it will most likely be in the frozen foods aisle. Many meat departments and butcher shops can special-order several types of game with a few days' notice. There are also several distributors of game that accept retail orders online and will deliver frozen meat to your door. For best results, ➤ thaw frozen game slowly in the refrigerator (for more guidance on storage, see Storing Raw and Cooked Meats, 449).

WILD GAME AND FOOD SAFETY

Though we provide some guidance on how to process game in individual entries in this chapter, we must emphasize: ➤ Contact your local cooperative extension service or state and federal fish and wildlife agencies for information on the proper handling of the species you plan to hunt. Hunters must become familiar with seasons, bag limits, and possession laws, as well as how to clean, cut, and store the fruit of their efforts.

Large game should be ➤ immediately **field-dressed,** or have its abdominal cavity cut open and internal organs removed to aid cooling and prevent contamination. This holds true for small game in warm conditions, too. Once the animal is dead, the carcass needs to be cooled as quickly as possible. If it is warm out, this means skinning the animal as well as eviscerating it. Prompt dressing, quick cooling, and scrupulous cleaning are not just good food safety practices—these measures enhance the flavor of the animal.

Those who handle game in the wild need to be aware of the potential risks posed by organisms that can cause illness during dressing and butchering. ➤ Wild game meat may be contaminated with several pathogens that can be transmitted by skin contact alone. Brucellosis can occur in bison, venison, and boar; tularemia occurs in rabbits, hares, muskrats, beavers, and squirrels; armadillos may carry leprosy; wild boar meat may be contaminated with parasites, which can enter the bloodstream through cuts in your hands. Thus, hunters should always ➤ wear disposable rubber or nitrile gloves when dressing or handling rabbit, hare, squirrel, beaver, muskrat, armadillo, and boar. There is less risk of contracting an illness by handling venison and wild bison meat, but we recommend gloves for those as well.

Other harmful bacteria such as *E. coli* and *Salmonella enterica* have been detected in game animals' digestive tracts, but this is rare. *Trichinella* parasites are another concern in some species of wild game, especially bear and boar. These organisms must be ingested to cause illness or infection (with the notable exception of tularemia and *Trichinella*, which can be contracted by handling if you have cuts or scrapes on your hands).

Luckily, ➤ all of these bacteria and parasites are uncommon in game meats, and may be neutralized by carefully handling the carcass and cooking meat until it reaches an internal temperature of 160°F or more.

Many state agencies are concerned about the spread of another illness, one caused by infectious proteins or prions, which infect brain and spinal tissue. In venison, these prions can cause Chronic Wasting Disease, or CWD. Though the prions associated with CWD have yet to cause health complications in humans, many are concerned that they may at some point. Since prions are not wiped out by cooking temperatures, the only way to control exposure is to refrain from preparing dishes with the bones or brains of animals that may be infected. If the minute risk of CWD concerns you, consult local authorities on the current status of infections in your area and guidelines for identifying and avoiding infected animals. Also consider purchasing farmed or ranched venison (all venison sold comes from animals inspected for CWD).

ABOUT COOKING GAME

Hunting wild game involves a great expenditure of time and effort. Farmed and ranched game can command a high price. Thus, masking the distinctive flavors of such a precious protein with an overly assertive sauce or lengthy bath in a marinade seems like a supreme waste. Instead, we recommend celebrating and enhancing game's unique flavors.

Our recipes are written for the ranched or farmed game that is most widely available. Wild game is almost always a bit leaner than ranched and farmed game, though the difference in cooking is minimal. Of course, the age of hunted game is also more variable, and the tougher cuts of mature animals will need to be cooked longer to make them tender.

Since game is generally lower in fat than other meats, tender cuts threaten to turn dry and chewy very quickly—especially red meats like bison and venison—when cooked beyond medium. This is very hard to square with USDA guidelines, which call for cooking wild and ranched game meat until the thickest part registers 160°F. While this conservative temperature does not bother us for small game, bear, and boar, we prefer bison and venison cooked medium-rare. If bucking this rule with regard to venison and bison will cause you to lose sleep—or, more important, if you are cooking for people with immune deficiencies—please overcook the meat as per the USDA's recommendations.

Overcooking is certainly not a problem for tough braising and stewing cuts. However, unlike many tough cuts from farmed livestock, those of wild animals may lack fat. One option is to lard, 451, or bard, 1046, them; another is to enrich their braising liquids, or serve them with a velvety sauce. ➤ If game meat does have fatty trimmings, they may not taste good. To be sure, render a small portion of the fat first to make sure it does not have any off flavors or odors.

Gaminess is a frequent complaint among hunters, especially those who prioritize adorning their walls over replenishing their freezer. Coveted trophy animals—large, mature males with impressive hides or large antlers—tend to be the gamiest. Diet can also contribute to off flavors: bears and raccoons may subsist on refuse; deer may nibble lichen. Harvesting any animal when they are in rut, or immediately afterward, can also drastically affect their flavor. These natural "seasonings" can be amplified by poor field-dressing or inadequate chilling post-slaughter. In some cases, the majority of these off flavors reside in the animals' fat. If you suspect wild game of having too much character, cook a small portion. If the meat is in need of mellowing, the first step to salvaging it is to remove all fat and connective tissue. If this does not work, consider soaking the trimmed meat in a Wine Marinade, 580, Buttermilk Marinade, 580, or brine, 1046. These treatments may also help tenderize the meat, but other strategies are more effective; for especially tough game, see Tenderizing Tough Meats, 450.

Another time-honored strategy for serving highly flavored wild game is to pair it with a full-bodied, full-flavored braising liquid or sauce. In addition to the traditional formulas given in this chapter, you may substitute tough cuts of gamey meat in any of the flavorful braises from other chapters, such as boar in Pork Adovada, 496, moose in Massaman Curry, 468, hare in Chicken Chili Verde, 425, or bear in Beef Rendang, 467, or Guyanese Pepperpot, 468. For tender steaks and chops that remain gamey, try pairing with Wine and Sour Cherry Pan Sauce, 547, English Cumberland Sauce, 566, or a traditional French brown sauce like Sauce Madeira, 551, Sauce Chasseur, 551, Sauce Demi-Glace, 551, or Sauce Marchand de Vin, 551.

ABOUT SMALL GAME

Small game has long been part of America's culinary traditions. Since rabbit is the most common small game animal to find in stores, we devote an entire section to them below, along with hare—known in the United States as jackrabbit. The rest of these mammals are hunted or trapped only. Animals caught in the wild should be dressed as soon as possible. ➤ Handle all small wild game with rubber or nitrile gloves to prevent against the danger of tularemia infection (or, in the case of armadillos, leprosy).

Squirrel has mild meat the color of a chicken thigh. Gray and fox squirrels have a steady diet of nuts, and are much better eating than red squirrels, which eat pine buds and can have an off flavor. Young squirrels may be fried as for rabbit; larger squirrels should be braised until tender. In addition to being fried and fricasseed, squirrel is traditionally stewed, either by itself or in communal pot dishes like Burgoo and Brunswick Stew, 470. Megan's grandfather Bryan has sworn to us that squirrel produces the finest gravy. Squirrel should be skinned following the directions for rabbit, below.

Opossums and **raccoons** are opportunistic eaters. After trapping opossums, it's a good idea to feed them wholesome scraps, milk, and grains for at least several days (ideally a week or more) before slaughter (do not attempt this with raccoons). If you still want to eat your cute, furry captives, dispatch them quickly and humanely. Rinse the carcass of any dirt and skin promptly by cutting off the feet and tail and carefully slicing down the center of the animal's abdomen, being careful not to puncture the abdominal wall. Carefully peel the skin away, slicing along the seam of skin and meat until you reach the spine. Push the legs inward, turning the furry "sleeves" inside out. Finally, grasp the skin near where the tail was and pull toward the front of the animal. When the skin is pulled as far as the neck and ears, sever the head. Remove glands from the area under the forelegs, hind legs, and the small of the back. Proceed dressing as for rabbit, below. ➤ Trim all excess fat.

Since their diets are less varied and never involve trash, **muskrat, woodchuck,** and **beaver** do not require feeding in captivity to become palatable. Skin and dress as for opossum or raccoon; after skinning, carefully remove any glands without puncturing them. Beavers have very large castor glands just below their anus; muskrat and woodchuck have numerous glands on the back and under the legs. ➤ Trim all excess fat. All these creatures have dark meat and benefit from braising and stewing until tender (see the Poultry and Meat chapters for inspiration). Keep in mind that muskrats are strong tasting, almost "pond-y," and are best brined, 1046, or soaked in acidulated water, 951, before cooking.

ABOUT RABBIT AND HARE

Rabbits are farmed and widely available; their meat is lean, mild, and often as pale as chicken breast. Commercial rabbit breeds grow large quickly: Younger animals weighing less than 5 pounds are sold as **fryers; roaster** rabbits are full-grown, and weigh between 5 and 8 pounds. Younger rabbits are more tender and, as the labeling implies, best for quick cooking methods like frying; roaster rabbits are more suited to fricassees and braises, but can also be fried. Despite their commercial abundance, wild rabbit is still a favorite game animal to hunt. The most common type to find in the wild is the **Eastern cottontail,** which averages 2½ pounds and serves two. **Marsh rabbits** are the same size, while **desert cottontails** are a bit smaller. The **swamp rabbit** of the Deep South is much larger, averaging 5 pounds. The **common** or **European rabbit** was introduced to a few areas of North America and is now considered an invasive species.

Hares are a closely related species found exclusively in the wild (though hunted hare meat is imported and may be ordered from online retailers). The **snowshoe hare**—sometimes called the **varying hare,** since they turn from brown to white in the winter months—is only slightly larger than the Eastern cottontail, averaging 3 to 4 pounds. Other species, such as **white-tailed** and **black-tailed jackrabbits** average 8 to 12 pounds, with the white-tailed jack being heavier on average. The largest native species is the **Arctic hare,** which routinely tops 10 pounds. Generally, hare has darker, tougher, and more flavorful meat. Though small, young specimens (called leverets) may be cooked as for rabbit, fully grown hare responds best to slow, moist-heat cooking methods and aggressive seasoning. Hasenpfeffer, 525, and other traditional preparations often call for marinating hare overnight in wine or vinegar.

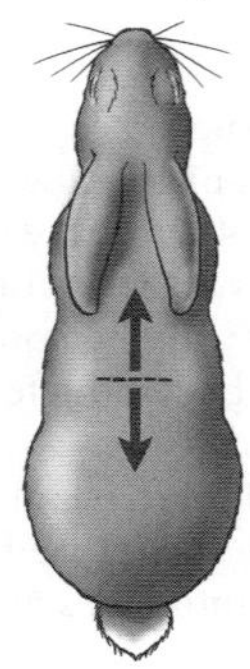

Skinning a rabbit or hare

To skin and dress rabbit or hare, first put on disposable rubber or nitrile gloves to avoid possible tularemia infection. Pinch the skin along the center of the spine and make a perpendicular cut big enough to fit two fingers in. Insert the index and middle fingers of both hands into the incision and forcefully pull the skin apart; the pelt should peel off neatly. When the pelt pulls away from the hind legs, sever the feet at the joint and discard with the attached skin. Then, attend to the front: When the neck and forelegs are exposed, sever the head and feet, discarding them with the front half of the pelt. Slice open the rabbit's paunch, taking care not to nick the intestines. Remove the entrails and discard them, except for the heart, kidneys, and liver (to prepare and cook them, see About Poultry Offal or Giblets, 444). ➤ Rinse the carcass inside and out, then dry carefully.

To cut apart a rabbit for cooking, lay the skinned and cleaned rabbit on its back and cut off the two hindquarters (back legs and thighs). Next remove the two forequarters (right and left front legs and ribs). What remains is the **saddle**—the loin meat that runs along the backbone, below the ribs and stomach and above the hind legs. Remove the silverskin on top of the saddle (for instructions, see Preparing Venison for Cooking, 527). For recipes that call for 7 serving pieces, cut the saddle into 3 pieces.

FRIED RABBIT

2 servings

Prepare **Pan-Fried or Sautéed Chicken I, 414,** or **Skillet Fried Chicken, 417,** substituting **one 3-pound fryer rabbit, cut into 7 serving pieces, above.** Do not attempt to use larger rabbits or hare. (If pan-fried, you may drain off the fat from the skillet and make **Herb Pan Sauce, 546**). Serve with **lemon wedges or hot sauce.**

FRICASSEE OF RABBIT

4 servings

Cut into 7 serving pieces, above:

One 3½-pound rabbit

Whisk together on a plate:

1 cup flour
1 teaspoon salt
½ teaspoon black pepper

Dredge the rabbit in the flour to coat. Melt in a large skillet or Dutch oven over medium heat:

4 tablespoons (½ stick) butter

Or cook until rendered and beginning to crisp:

6 ounces diced bacon

Remove the bacon, if using, and set aside on a plate. Fry the rabbit pieces, in batches if necessary, until lightly browned all over, about 5 minutes each side. Transfer the rabbit to the plate with the bacon. Add to the pan and cook until softened, about 10 minutes:

1 shallot or small onion, diced
2 celery ribs, diced

Return the rabbit (and bacon if using) to the pan. If desired, flambé, 1049, the rabbit with:

(¼ cup brandy)

When the flames subside, add:

1½ cups chicken stock or dry white wine
1 large strip lemon zest, removed with a vegetable peeler
(3 fresh sage leaves)
2 sprigs parsley

Cover and simmer the meat until done, about 15 minutes. Do not let the liquid boil at any time. Meanwhile, melt in a skillet over medium heat:

2 tablespoons butter

Add and cook, stirring, until lightly browned, about 15 minutes:

1 cup pearl onions, peeled
8 ounces mushrooms, quartered

When the rabbit is tender, remove the herbs and lemon zest; young rabbits will take 25 to 30 minutes. Transfer the rabbit to a hot serving dish. Stir the browned pearl onions and mushrooms into the braising liquid and reduce for 5 minutes over medium heat. Pour the sauce over the rabbit and sprinkle with:

Chopped parsley, chervil, tarragon, or a combination

HASENPFEFFER

6 servings

This dish is the traditional German treatment for mature wild rabbits and hares. To use farmed rabbit, we recommend finding a mature roaster.

Heat in a large skillet over medium-high heat:

2 tablespoons vegetable oil

Add and cook, stirring, until the onion is golden:

1 large onion, chopped
3 celery ribs, chopped
2 carrots, chopped

Add:

3 cups fruity red wine such as gamay, pinot noir, or merlot
1 cup red wine vinegar
½ cup coarsely chopped parsley
6 garlic cloves, smashed
1 teaspoon dried thyme
1 teaspoon crushed black peppercorns
1 teaspoon whole cloves
½ teaspoon allspice berries
½ teaspoon juniper berries
2 bay leaves

Bring to a boil, then reduce the heat and simmer for 1 hour. Strain and cool.

Cut into 7 serving pieces, above:

One 6- to 8-pound roaster rabbit or mature hare

Place the pieces in a bowl, add the cooled liquid, and marinate in the refrigerator overnight.

Drain the rabbit and reserve the marinade. Pat the pieces of rabbit dry and whisk together on a plate:

1 cup flour
1 teaspoon salt
½ teaspoon black pepper

Dredge the pieces in the flour to coat. Heat in a Dutch oven over medium-high heat:

3 tablespoons bacon fat or vegetable oil

Brown the rabbit pieces on both sides, in batches if necessary. Transfer the pieces to a plate, discard the fat, and reduce the heat to medium. Melt in the pot:

2 tablespoons butter

Add and cook until translucent and beginning to brown, about 6 minutes:

1 large onion, chopped

Add the reserved marinade and browned rabbit. Bring to a simmer, cover, and cook until the meat is done throughout and tender; roaster rabbits will take about 40 minutes, tougher wild rabbits and hares may take up to 2 hours. Serve with:

Buttered egg noodles, Spätzle, 308, or Potato Dumplings, 306

BRAISED MARINATED RABBIT WITH PRUNES

6 servings

Combine in a large bowl:

3 cups dry red wine
1 tablespoon olive oil
1 medium onion, diced

1 carrot, diced
2 sprigs thyme
1 bay leaf

Cut into 7 serving pieces, 525:

One 3½-pound rabbit

Add the rabbit to the bowl, cover, and marinate in the refrigerator for at least 6 and up to 24 hours.

Cook in a Dutch oven or heavy pot over medium heat until browned and rendered:

6 ounces bacon, diced

Transfer with a slotted spoon to paper towels to drain. Remove the rabbit from the marinade (reserve the marinade) and pat dry. Season with:

1 teaspoon salt
½ teaspoon black pepper

Add the rabbit pieces to the pot and lightly brown on both sides. Transfer to a plate. Reduce the heat to low and cook, stirring, until starting to brown slightly:

2 tablespoons all-purpose flour

Slowly whisk in the reserved marinade. Bring to a boil and return the bacon and rabbit to the pan. Reduce the heat, cover, and simmer for 25 minutes. Add:

1½ cups pitted prunes

Cover and simmer until the rabbit is tender, about 20 minutes more. Meanwhile, melt in a skillet over medium heat:

2 tablespoons butter

Add and cook, stirring until lightly browned, about 15 minutes:

1 cup pearl onions, peeled
8 ounces mushrooms, quartered

Transfer the rabbit and prunes to a deep serving dish and cover to keep warm. Discard the thyme sprigs and bay leaf. Scoop out about ½ cup of the sauce from the Dutch oven and add to the skillet with the mushrooms, scraping the skillet with a wooden spatula to loosen any browned bits. Add the pearl onions, mushrooms, and pan juices to the sauce in the Dutch oven and boil over high heat until slightly thickened and the pearl onions are tender, 5 to 8 minutes. Season with:

2 tablespoons lemon juice or sherry vinegar
(2 teaspoons red currant jelly or apricot preserves)
Salt and black pepper to taste

Simmer, stirring, for 5 minutes more. Pour the sauce over the rabbit and serve immediately, sprinkled with:

Chopped parsley, tarragon, or a combination

LAPIN À LA MOUTARDE (RABBIT WITH MUSTARD)

4 to 6 servings

Serve this French bistro classic with a salad, plenty of crusty bread, and dry white wine.

Cut into 7 serving pieces, 525:

One 3- to 3½-pound rabbit

Generously brush the pieces with:

⅓ cup Dijon mustard

Season with:

1 teaspoon salt
½ teaspoon black pepper

Heat in a large skillet over medium heat:

3 tablespoons vegetable oil

Add the rabbit pieces, in batches if necessary, and lightly brown on each side. Transfer the rabbit to a platter. Discard the oil, reduce the heat to medium-low, and melt in the skillet:

2 tablespoons butter

Cook, stirring, until lightly browned:

1 small onion or large shallot, finely chopped

Add and bring to a boil, scraping up the browned bits:

1½ cups dry white wine, chicken stock, or a combination

Return the rabbit to the skillet along with:

½ cup heavy cream
2 sprigs each parsley and thyme

Cover and simmer gently until the rabbit is tender but still moist, about 45 minutes. Transfer the rabbit to a platter and cover to keep warm; discard the herb sprigs. Bring the sauce to a boil and cook until reduced enough to coat the back of a spoon. Stir in:

2 tablespoons chopped parsley, chives, tarragon, chervil, or a combination
1 tablespoon Dijon mustard
Lemon juice or white wine vinegar to taste
Salt and black pepper to taste

Spoon the sauce over and around the rabbit.

PROCESSING LARGE GAME

Game shot cleanly in an unsuspecting moment is milder, more tender, and will deteriorate more slowly than game that has been chased. ➤ Immediate and careful gutting, removal of all hair near exposed flesh, and timely skinning are essential.

To field-dress a large, freshly killed game carcass, it is convenient to hang it from the feet or neck so that you are able to work at a comfortable standing posture. Make a lengthwise incision just underneath the breastbone, cutting just deep enough to penetrate the abdominal cavity. Once the cut has been started, slice through the abdominal wall toward the genitals, using just the knife tip; hold the blade so that the cutting edge faces outward so as not to pierce any internal organs. The stomach, intestines, and bladder must be removed with special care so that they do not rupture and spill their contents, which can contaminate the meat, hasten spoilage, or cause off flavors. When cutting out the bladder, pinch the connecting tube to contain any urine. Cut away and discard any glands you may find. Any edible organ meats should be used at once or frozen right away. For directions on cooking them, see About Offal and Variety Meats, 514.

Work, if possible, in such a way that after the removal of the internal organs, you will merely have to wipe the cavity with a dry cloth. If fluids from internal organs or blood have touched the flesh, or the flesh has been bullet-pierced, scrape or cut the areas as cleanly as possible. Do not allow any blood to remain, as it will produce off flavors. Wipe such areas with snow or water or, if available, salt water. Dry thoroughly.

Once the animal is dressed, the carcass needs to be cooled as quickly as possible. Skinning helps speed cooling tremendously. In icy conditions, or if you have access to a meat locker, leaving the skin on is a good idea until you are ready to butcher the carcass. When skinning, try to keep loose hairs away from the flesh, as they are hard to remove later. ➤ Be careful not to cut into the tarsal glands on the inside of the hind legs; they're typically marked with black fur. To further shorten cooling time, the body cavity can be propped open with sticks; larger animals like elk and moose are best quartered; bags of ice can be put into the body cavity (leave the ice in the bags). Once the carcass is back home, promptly cool to below 40°F and let the meat rest for a minimum of 24 hours before butchering (by then, the carcass should no longer be in rigor mortis). The flavor and texture of venison improves markedly if allowed to age for a week or two at 34° to 38°F before cooking or portioning and freezing.

ABOUT VENISON

Though frequently used to refer to deer meat, the term "venison" (derived from the Latin *venari*, or "to hunt") encompasses the meat of all large, antlered game animals, including **moose, elk, caribou, antelope, pronghorn,** and **deer.** With the exception of moose, pronghorn, and caribou, these species are ranched or farmed commercially in the United States. As with all game, ranched venison is more consistent in size, quality, and taste than wild venison, which can have a strong, gamey flavor. Regardless of species and rearing, all venison is red meat, and tends to be very lean.

Deer remains the most popular and common of venison animals to hunt and raise for meat. **White-tailed deer** are the most common species in the eastern United States; **mule** or **black-tailed deer** are the most common from the Rocky Mountains westward. Much of the venison available today is the meat of farm-raised **red deer** from New Zealand. **Fallow deer** is also farm-raised. Asian species such as the spotted **axis** or **chital deer** and **sika deer,** are also ranched extensively. Meat from hunted axis deer in Hawaii is one of the only truly wild meats available for purchase.

Antelope meat is delicately flavored and a bit lighter than other venison. Indian **nilgai** (or **nilgi**) and **blackbuck antelope** are ranched in Texas; the former is larger and has a milder flavor. **Pronghorns** are native to North America and are often called pronghorn antelope or "speed goats." Strangely, they are more closely related to giraffes than either antelopes or goats.

Moose and **elk** are the largest species of North American venison; they are considered by many to yield the best-tasting meat, which frequently draws comparisons to beef. Moose is not available for purchase, but elk is farmed extensively. **Caribou** range throughout the subpolar regions of the northern hemisphere. **Reindeer** are close, semidomesticated relatives of caribou; their meat is available from Alaskan ranches. Both caribou and reindeer are mild-flavored and beef-like.

PREPARING VENISON FOR COOKING

For instructions on dressing and chilling wild venison, please read Processing Large Game, 526.

The individual muscles of all mammals are sheathed in a tough, sinewy covering called **silverskin.** Since cuts from the shoulder and neck need prolonged cooking, their silverskin is not as much of a worry to cooks, because it takes long, moist cooking to soften. However, we recommend carefully trimming as much silverskin as possible from the outside of tender roasts, medallions, and chops cut from the saddle and hind leg. Leg roasts and steaks are particularly troublesome, which is why savvy venison processors offer the Denver leg (see 528).

To remove silverskin, use a long, thin-bladed knife such as a fillet or boning knife. Pierce the silverskin with the point of the knife and carefully work a flap of the silverskin free. Keeping pressure on the silverskin and not the meat, slice it away—the action is very much like cutting the skin off a fish fillet, 376. If the area to be cleaned is fairly straight—like the side of a loin muscle, for example—you may remove it exactly like fish skin by turning the meat so the silverskin side is against the cutting board. Slip your knife between a flap of silverskin and muscle, pin the loose silverskin to the cutting board with your fingers, and slice off the remaining silverskin by cutting down the length of the muscle, angling the blade slightly away from the meat to minimize waste.

Wild venison harvested in arid regions of the West may taste of the sagebrush that deer and antelope herds frequently nibble on. When the flavor is subtle, this natural seasoning can be an asset; when strong, it is less than desirable (and occasionally renders older animals unpalatable). In more temperate climates, lichen and other forage may add their own subtle (or overt) character. If any of these flavors is too pronounced, see About Cooking Game, 523, for ways of lessening it. If the animal is mature and tough, see Tenderizing Tough Meats, 450.

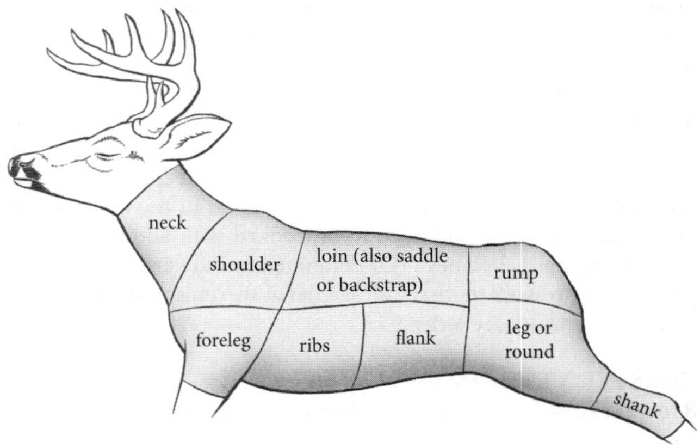

Venison cuts

COOKING VENISON

The USDA advises cooking all wild and ranched game meat until its thickest part registers 160°F. This is unfortunate, as venison lacks fat marbling. Without any fat to coat its proteins, venison steak quickly turns tough and chewy when cooked above medium. The risk of eating venison rare or medium-rare—especially farmed and ranched venison, which is processed in an inspected butchering facility—seems acceptable to us. If you would like to err on the side of eating quality rather than food safety, we offer this simple advice: ➤ Roast, broil, grill, or sauté tender cuts from the loin and hind leg area until medium-rare; stew, braise, or slowly roast tougher cuts from the neck, shoulder, and shanks until tender.

As with all four-legged animals, the most tender meat is found in the loin, which lies along the back between the shoulder and hip. This area comprises the **backstrap,** or top loin, and **tenderloin.** The rib area behind the shoulder may be fashioned into a 4- or 8-rib roast. Individual chops may also be cut from this area, or the top loin muscle may be cut off the ribs entirely and sliced into steaks. Thicker loin chops or steaks from deer, elk, and moose can be substituted in any recipe for beef steaks, 459–61. The tenderloin may be sold whole (which is our preference since it is harder to overcook) or cut into medallions. Cook it gently, as for Becker Venison Medallions, 529, or pan-roast it until medium-rare.

Venison from the **sirloin** and **leg** may be cut into steaks or sold as roasts. Many processors conveniently remove the bones from the leg, seam-cut the individual muscles, and trim off any silverskin. Referred to as the **Denver leg,** this treatment results in a convenient assortment of 7 or 8 muscles, which are easily cut into steaks, medallions, or strips.

Cuts from the **shoulder** can occasionally be found sold as boneless roasts. The **neck** and **forelegs** are sometimes crosscut into slices and may be cooked as for Osso Buco, 476; to cook whole shanks, substitute venison in Braised Lamb Shanks with Chickpeas, 482. Venison **flank steaks** are quite a bit smaller than beef flanks—unless they're from elk or moose; season (or marinate as for Carne Asada, 459) and sear or grill them very quickly over high heat. Serve sliced thinly across the grain. Game processors who cater to hunters often cut these portions into stew meat—a perfect stand-in for beef, lamb, and goat in stews and chilis.

Ground venison can be fashioned into burger patties, as well as used in ground meat dishes like Bolognese Sauce, 558, Keema Alu, 503, Picadillo, 503, meatballs, 507–8, or sausages, 510–12. When substituting for beef and other ground meats, keep in mind that unless your processor included pork or beef fat in the initial grind, pure ground venison will need to be cooked with additional fat to compensate for its leanness. (Or combine ground venison with fatty ground beef to avoid this issue altogether as in Venison Burgers, 528.)

To dry venison, see Jerky, 947.

ROASTED VENISON

8 to 12 servings if boneless, 6 to 8 servings if bone-in

Use this recipe for large bone-in or boneless roasts. For backstrap roasts, tenderloins, and other small roasts that fit easily in a skillet, cook as for Pan-Roasted Beef, 456.

Remove as much silverskin, 527, as possible from the outside of:

1 venison roast, boneless or bone-in

If desired, lard, 451, the roast. Season the outside liberally with:

Salt and black pepper (about ½ teaspoon salt and ¼ teaspoon black pepper per pound of meat)

Place fat side up on a rack in a shallow roasting pan and refrigerate uncovered for at least 1 hour and up to 2 days (the longer the better).

When ready to cook, set the roast out at room temperature and preheat the oven to 250°F. Brush the top of the roast with:

Vegetable oil, Clarified Butter, 960, or warmed lard

Place the pan in the oven and roast until a thermometer inserted into the center of the thickest part registers between 120° and 130°F for rare to medium-rare (or, to comply with USDA safety guidelines, cook to 160°F). For a thick roast, this may take 2 hours or more; for a boneless loin roast, begin checking the temperature after 30 minutes. Remove from the oven and let rest uncovered for 30 minutes (the temperature will continue to rise 5 to 10 degrees during this time). Meanwhile, set the oven to 500°F.

Once the meat has rested, return it to the hot oven and roast until the outside is well browned, about 10 minutes more. Transfer the roast to a platter and cover to keep warm. Drain all fat from the roasting pan, set over medium-high heat, and add:

3 cups game or chicken broth

Boil, scraping up any browned bits, until the sauce is reduced to 1½ to 2 cups. Transfer to a saucepan set over high heat and add:

¼ cup red currant jelly

¼ cup Cognac or other brandy

Boil until slightly thickened, 2 to 3 minutes. Season to taste with:

Salt and black pepper

Carve the roast into ⅛- to ½-inch slices. Add any juices that have accumulated on the platter to the sauce and serve on the side.

VENISON POT ROAST

For less tender cuts of farmed venison, such as shoulder and neck roasts or shanks, prepare as for **Beef Pot Roast, 464,** or **Stracotto, 464.** For mature, tough wild venison roasts, prepare as for **Sauerbraten, 464,** or **Boeuf Bourguignon, 465** (letting the venison marinate overnight for the latter). Cook as directed until tender; the length of time will depend on the size and shape of the roast (and how mature the animal was when harvested).

SAUTÉED VENISON STEAKS

4 servings

Use steaks cut from the loin or tender portion of the leg for this recipe.

Have ready:

Four 6- to 7-ounce venison steaks from the loin or leg

Season on both sides with:

1½ teaspoons salt

1 teaspoon black pepper

Heat in a heavy skillet over high heat:

3 tablespoons vegetable oil, bacon drippings, or Clarified Butter, 960

Quickly brown the meat, 2 to 3 minutes each side or until the internal temperature of the meat reaches 120° to 130°F for rare to medium-rare. Transfer to a plate. If desired, prepare:

(Herb Pan Sauce, 546, Wine and Sour Cherry Pan Sauce, 547, or the pan sauce for Steak Diane, 461, or Steak au Poivre, 461)

Or, you may serve the steaks with:

(Chimichurri, 567)

Or top each steak with a thin slice or dollop of a:

(Flavored butter, 559–60)

VENISON BURGER

4 servings

Ground venison is very lean and is best when combined with a bit of fattier ground beef.

Combine:

10 ounces ground venison

6 ounces ground chuck

Or chill and grind together, 501:

14 ounces venison, cut into chunks and trimmed of connective tissue

3 ounces beef suet

Shape, season, cook, and serve as for **Hamburger Patties, 504.** Alternatively, substitute the venison mixture for the ground beef in **Becker Burgers, 505,** or **Beet and Caper Burgers, 505.**

BECKER VENISON MEDALLIONS

4 servings

Gentle cooking—and lots of butter—is sometimes the best approach for treasured backstrap and tenderloin medallions.

Place one at a time between sheets of wax paper and gently pound until 1/4 inch thick:

1 pound venison medallions

Season to taste with:

Salt and black pepper

Melt in a large heavy skillet over medium heat:

6 tablespoons (3/4 stick) butter

Add the medallions, in batches, and cook until browned, 1 to 2 minutes per side. Transfer the meat to a platter. Add to the skillet:

3 tablespoons port or Madeira

Warm the sauce for about 1 minute, then stir in any accumulated juices from the venison. Pour over the medallions and serve with:

Sautéed Mushrooms, 251

ABOUT WILD SHEEP AND GOATS

Wild sheep and goats live in rugged terrain in the western part of the United States and Canada. There are several species referred to as bighorn sheep, including **Rocky Mountain, Dall's,** and **stone sheep.** The **desert bighorn** is on the endangered list, but other populations are sufficient to sustain a limited hunting season (the proceeds of which go to conservation efforts). Wild sheep, as well as the **Rocky Mountain goat,** have distinctive and flavorful meat. Cook these animals as you would domestic lamb and goat, 478–85.

Less common is the **muskox,** an enormous, shaggy relative that lives in the subpolar Arctic. Successfully reintroduced to several areas of Alaska, its meat is extremely well marbled—more so than most grades of beef. Cook tender cuts as you would prime grade beef from the rib or loin.

For instructions on dressing and chilling, please read Processing Large Game, 526.

ABOUT BOAR AND JAVELINA

Most "wild boar" are domesticated hogs that escaped captivity and have turned feral. Once in the wild, the piglets from former barnyard hogs grow straight tails, stiff, upright ears, and long tusks rather quickly, which they use to root through soil (these are often called **razorback** hogs). The **Eurasian wild boar** (or **Russian boar**) was specifically released in North America for sport. Both have since spread wildly out of control. These populations are considered an invasive species wherever they are present, destroying large swaths of farmland and natural habitat every year. For this reason, wild hogs are one of the only meats hunted in this country that may be sold to consumers—currently only in Texas, and from processors subject to state inspection.

The **collared peccary** or **javelina,** is native to the southwestern United States, and from the Caribbean to northern Argentina. Though not technically a pig, javelinas closely resemble them and have been grouped with wild pigs until recently. Unlike boars, javelina are primarily vegetarian, and consequently run a much lower risk of harboring trichinosis parasites.

For instructions on dressing and chilling, please read Processing Large Game, 526. Due to the risk of possible infection, ➤ always wear disposable rubber or nitrile gloves when handling wild boar meat. When field-dressing javelina, be wary of the gland tucked into the skin at the small of the back. Do not pierce the gland, or it will contaminate the meat with its funky fragrance.

Boar meat is leaner and darker than most pork and can range in flavor from mild to distinctly pungent depending on the animal's age, sex, and diet, as well as when it was killed. In general, younger pigs are preferred for flavor and tenderness; this is especially so with boars, as older ones develop an offensive taste and odor known as "boar taint." Sows are, as a rule, milder in flavor. To deal with off-flavors and gaminess, see 523.

Boar is sold in familiar pork cuts, and may generally be prepared like pork, 486–97. Since wild pigs are much more likely to carry trichinosis than farm-raised pork, ➤ cook it to an internal temperature of at least 160°F. Use shoulder roasts in any braised pork recipe, especially Pork Braised in Milk, 494, and Braised Pork with Sauerkraut, 495 (or substitute for beef in Stracotto, 464). You may also cut boar shoulder into chunks for Braised Carnitas, 495, Pork Adovada, 496, or Boeuf Bourguignon, 465. Ground boar is best used in Italian Sausage, 511, or Fresh Chorizo Sausage, 511.

ABOUT BEAR

Though many children grow up hugging stuffed miniatures of these charismatic animals, bear has been hunted and eaten in North America since prehistoric times. Unlike most wild game, bear can be incredibly fatty—both in marbling and fatty trim. This means that bear meat may be braised, stewed, or pot-roasted as for beef or pork, but any braising liquid or broth should be skimmed especially well of rendered fat (chilling overnight for easy removal is highly recommended).

Though they mostly eat berries and other wholesome vegetarian forage, bears may also eat other animals, living and dead. As a result, ➤ bear meat has a high probability of harboring trichinosis parasites and must be cooked until the thickest portion reads 160°F on a thermometer.

Since bears are opportunistic omnivores, it is hard to generalize with regard to what they have eaten, what they will taste like, or if they will even be palatable. In general, bears harvested in coastal areas and near rivers during a salmon run will probably taste of the fish they catch and shellfish they forage. Bears taken near popular camping areas or suburban communities may have eaten refuse from dumpsters. Do not be surprised if their meat tastes unsavory as a result. Other, subtler diet choices may flavor bear meat in ways that can be managed; for lessening gaminess, see 523.

Bear fat is prized among some bakers. To determine its suitability, first melt a portion of the fat in a skillet. If the fat has a relatively mild odor and taste, render the rest of it promptly, 982, and freeze in ice cube trays. Thaw cubes as needed in the refrigerator for cutting into biscuit doughs or using in other flaky pastries.

BRAISED BEAR

6 to 8 servings

Heat in a large pot or Dutch oven:

¼ cup vegetable oil

Brown in batches:

4 pounds boneless bear meat, cut into 2-inch cubes

Transfer to a platter and set aside. Drain off any fat and add to the pot:

2 tablespoons butter

When the butter has melted, add and cook, stirring, until softened, about 5 minutes:

2 carrots, chopped
1 large onion, chopped
2 celery ribs, chopped

Add the browned meat, along with:

2 cups dry red wine
1 cup chicken stock or broth
8 garlic cloves, smashed
1 bay leaf
1 teaspoon dried thyme

Bring to a boil, then reduce to a simmer, cover, and simmer until the meat is fork-tender, about 2½ hours. Transfer the meat to a plate, discard the bay leaf, and thoroughly skim off any fat. If desired, reduce the braising liquid over high heat until it has thickened, or mash together with a fork in a small bowl:

(2 tablespoons butter)
(2 tablespoons all-purpose flour)

Whisk the mixture into the braising liquid. Season to taste with:

Salt and black pepper

Return the meat to the sauce and heat through. Serve over:

Creamy Polenta, 322

Garnish with:

Gremolata, 587, or chopped parsley, chives, or savory

ABOUT BISON, YAK, AND ALPACA

American buffalo, or **bison,** is an animal indigenous to North America that once roamed in huge herds over the plains of this country, providing both food, clothing, and shelter for Native Americans. After being hunted to the brink of extinction by settlers and the US government, wild buffalo populations have rebounded somewhat. Buffalo is also raised for meat on ranches around the United States and is much like beef: well flavored and relatively mild with red, dense meat. Bison may be used in virtually any beef recipe. It is sold in many of the same cuts as beef, but bison cuts are larger in size.

Yak, a distant Asian relative to the muskox and bison, is much easier to ranch, and is becoming more popular to raise for meat in the United States. Yak meat is similar to that of bison, but redder in appearance, leaner, nutty-tasting, and a bit sweet. The camel-related **alpaca** is primarily raised for fiber, but its meat may be available for purchase from farmers' markets and Internet retailers. Alpaca has lean, red meat that is very similar to bison. Cuts are similar to bison and beef, but they will be smaller.

Buffalo, yak, and alpaca have significant nutritional advantages over beef for those who are concerned about fat: Their meat is high in protein and extremely low in cholesterol (about 30 percent lower than beef), and it has about half the calories and fat of beef. More important, it is delicious in its own right. The result is an experience comparable to eating a beef steak, but with roughly the same nutritional profile as eating a skinless chicken breast.

Though the meat itself is lean, bison steaks and roasts may have a rind of fat; it is usually a bit gamey, and we recommend trimming it before cooking. As with all wild and farmed game, the USDA recommends cooking bison to a minimum temperature of 160°F. We imagine the same to be true for yak and alpaca, though guidelines for these meats are seemingly nonexistent. Since all of these animals have lean meat, tender loin and leg meat will be rendered dry and chewy at this temperature. If you would like to flaunt the rules for an acceptable risk, we recommend ➤ roasting, broiling, grilling, or sautéing tender cuts from the rib, loin, and sirloin area until medium-rare; stew, braise, or slowly roast tougher cuts from the neck, shoulder, and shanks until tender. For burgers, the ground meat from these lean animals should be combined with ground beef, or ground with beef fat (see Venison Burgers, 528).

BUFFALO ROAST WITH BOURBON-MOLASSES GLAZE

10 to 14 servings

Trim all but a ¼-inch thickness of fat from:

One 7- to 9-pound boneless buffalo rib or top sirloin roast

Season all over with:

1½ tablespoons salt
1 tablespoon black pepper or 1½ tablespoons Chili Powder, 588

If desired, tie securely every 2 inches so that the roast holds its shape. Place fat side up on a rack in a shallow roasting pan and refrigerate uncovered for at least 1 hour and up to 2 days.

When ready to cook, set the roast out at room temperature and preheat the oven to 250°F. Place the pan in the oven and roast until a thermometer inserted in the center of the thickest part registers 120° to 130°F for rare to medium-rare, 1¼ to 2 hours. As the roast cooks, prepare:

Bourbon-Molasses Glaze, 579

Remove from the oven and let rest uncovered for 30 minutes (the temperature will continue to rise 5 to 10 degrees during this time). Meanwhile, set the oven to 500°F.

Once the meat has rested, brush it all over with the glaze, return to the oven, and roast for 5 minutes. Take the roast out, glaze it again, and cook until nicely browned, about 5 minutes more. Slice the roast and, if desired, top each slice with a generous dollop of:

(Chile Butter, 560)

STUFFINGS AND CASSEROLES

Stuffing is—with the possible exception of gravy—the most esteemed dish on the holiday table. While the standard seasoned bread variety is the best known and most coveted of the category, grain stuffings can be nearly as delectable given the right treatment. All stuffings are elevated and enriched by savory, aromatic ingredients like celery, onions, spices, herbs, oysters, giblets, sausage, mushrooms, nuts, and dried fruits. Stuffings and dressings get the most attention around the holiday season, but we think they should be considered viable side dishes the rest of the year. They are also good for stuffing items beyond poultry. Bake flavorful stuffings in vegetable cases like acorn or delicata squash, bell peppers, tomatoes, and onions.

The popularity of **casseroles,** 537—a diverse collection of mixtures named after the dish they are baked in—seems to have waned in recent years. Despite being passé in some circles, casseroles are truly the foods of community and sharing, and when prepared with a little extra care, they can be worthy of that honor. We heartily recommend them to cooks looking to feed the masses at potlucks, barbecues, and receptions. They also make sturdy, filling, reheatable meals for families with newborns.

ABOUT STUFFINGS AND DRESSINGS

Is there a difference between stuffing and dressing? They are, after all, composed of the same ingredients. Here, we base the distinction on how they are used: **Stuffing** refers to a mixture stuffed inside a bird, roast, fish, or vegetable; **dressing** is cooked in a baking dish. Almost any "dressing" can be used as a stuffing, and many stuffings make good dressings. They differ in the ingredients used in only one way: ➤ We do not use eggs in stuffing, but we do use them in dressing to bind the ingredients.

Most people come to appreciate bread stuffings for their instrumental role on the Thanksgiving table. Here we must issue a warning: ➤ Stuffings baked inside poultry must be cooked to an internal temperature of 165°F. This necessary safety precaution prevents salmonella contamination from the poultry's juices, which soak into the stuffing. For this reason, and several more to follow, ➤ we recommend baking stuffing mixtures separately (i.e., as dressings) to serve alongside the Thanksgiving turkey. While stuffing that has soaked up turkey juices has great appeal, coaxing turkey breast and stuffing to simultaneous doneness is very difficult. One must either overcook the bird or remove the hot stuffing, transfer it to a baking dish, and finish cooking it through as the bird rests. Further, unless cooking for a very small crowd, the amount of stuffing that will fit inside a bird is unlikely to align with the number of guests. Finally, dressings develop a crispy crust, as opposed to stuffings, which tend to moistness. Because we prefer the flavor of a well-browned dressing, we recommend baking it in a dish. Right after the bird or roast comes out of the oven, moisten the cooked dressing with the pan juices. Using homemade chicken or turkey stock in dressings improves the flavor even further.

For those who remain determined to stuff their roast, ➤ figure on approximately ½ cup stuffing for each pound of whole bird or fish. Should there be extra stuffing that does not fit in the cavity of the item being stuffed, cook it separately in a greased baking dish. Always stuff foods just before cooking. ➤ Pack stuffings lightly so as not to compact them, and allow a little unfilled space inside the stuffed item to allow the stuffing to expand. For stuffed poultry, remove all the stuffing before carving. For instructions on preparing a bird for stuffing, see About Stuffing and Trussing Poultry, 405.

➤ If a bird is done before the stuffing has reached 165°F, remove the pan from the oven and scoop the stuffing into a buttered baking dish. As the bird rests, return the stuffing to the oven and bake until it has reached 165°F.

Dressing can be assembled 1 day ahead of time and go directly from the refrigerator to the oven. Or, you may prepare and refrigerate the bread and aromatics in a container or a zip-top bag up to 3 days in advance. ➤ Add any liquids such as stock or melted butter just before baking. Refrigerated stuffing should be tempered before stuffing into any kind of meat: Remove the stuffing from the refrigerator about 30 minutes before using, or preheat it until lukewarm in a 300°F oven.

ABOUT BREAD STUFFINGS AND DRESSINGS

"No more turkey," announced the little boy at the Thanksgiving dinner table, "but I'd like another helping of that bread he ate." We all know that the real allure of Thanksgiving dinner is not the tradition-hallowed main dish, no matter how burnished its skin or moist its meat. In our experience, bread stuffings are the leftovers everyone volunteers to take home first.

If you prefer a dry stuffing, add enough stock so the bread barely sticks together when firmly squeezed and bake it uncovered. For a moister texture, add enough stock so that the bread holds together readily when pressed and bake covered with foil (uncover the dish for the last 15 minutes of baking to brown the top slightly).

Allow about ¾ cup dressing per person. ➤ A 1-pound loaf of bread yields about 10 cups of fresh bread cubes, including the crust, which should be used unless otherwise specified in the recipe. To toast bread cubes for stuffing, see Croutons IV, 638.

BASIC BREAD STUFFING OR DRESSING

About 10 cups; 13 servings

For a note on the wisdom of stuffing poultry, please read About Stuffings and Dressings, 531. This recipe yields enough to fill a 13 × 9-inch baking dish, or one 14- to 17-pound turkey with enough left over for a small baking dish. To stuff a chicken or 6 to 8 Cornish hens, halve the recipe. For a larger turkey, increase the ingredients by half.

Preheat the oven to 400°F. Toast on a large baking sheet, stirring several times, until golden brown, 5 to 10 minutes:

1 pound firm white sandwich, French, or Italian bread, including crusts, cut into ½-inch cubes (10 cups lightly packed)

Transfer to a large bowl and reduce the oven temperature to 350°F, if baking in a dish; if stuffing a bird, preheat the oven to the temperature indicated in the recipe. Melt in a large skillet over medium-high heat until the foam subsides:

4 to 8 tablespoons (½ to 1 stick) butter

Add and cook, stirring, until tender, 6 to 8 minutes:

1 large onion, chopped
2 celery ribs, finely chopped
(Liver, heart, and gizzard from the turkey or chicken to be stuffed, finely chopped)

Remove from the heat and stir in:

½ cup minced parsley
1 tablespoon minced fresh sage or 1 teaspoon dried sage
1 tablespoon minced fresh thyme or 1 teaspoon dried thyme
¾ teaspoon salt
½ teaspoon black pepper
¼ teaspoon grated or ground nutmeg
⅛ teaspoon ground cloves

Add to the bread cubes and toss until well combined. Stir in, a little at a time, until the stuffing is lightly moist but not packed together:

½ to 1 cup chicken stock or broth, or as needed

Adjust the seasonings. If you desire a firm dressing and are baking in a dish, toss with:

(2 large eggs, well beaten)

If stuffing poultry, spoon the stuffing into the bird(s). For dressing, transfer to a buttered 13 × 9-inch baking dish and drizzle with:

1 to 1½ cups chicken stock or broth, or as needed

For soft dressing, cover the dish with foil. For crispy, browned dressing, leave the dish uncovered and dot with:

Up to 3 tablespoons butter, cut into pieces

If the stuffing is in a dish, bake until browned as desired, 30 to 45 minutes. If the stuffing is inside a bird, ensure that the internal temperature of the stuffing reaches 165°F.

BASIC CORN BREAD STUFFING OR DRESSING

About 8 cups; 10 servings

A regional variation that is now widely traveled. Any corn bread will work in this recipe. Please read About Bread Stuffings and Dressings, 531.

Prepare **Basic Bread Stuffing or Dressing, above,** substituting **1 recipe Southern Corn Bread, 630, or other corn bread, cubed (8 cups)** for the bread cubes. Leave all other ingredient quantities the same, but omit the nutmeg and cloves.

ADDITIONS TO BREAD STUFFING

Toss any of the following alone or in combination into the stuffing mixture at the same time as the herbs and spices:

Up to 1 cup walnuts, pecans, or Brazil nuts, toasted, 1005, and coarsely chopped
1½ cups cooked, canned, or frozen chestnuts, coarsely chopped
1 cup dried fruit (such as raisins, cranberries, cherries, or diced prunes)
24 shucked, 349, or 1 pint raw oysters, drained, and liquid reserved (use the liquid to moisten the stuffing, if desired)

4 cups diced peeled green apples, such as Granny Smith
¼ teaspoon cayenne pepper

The following additions must be cooked before tossing with the bread and seasonings:

1 pound bulk pork sausage, Italian sausage, or fresh chorizo, browned in a skillet (replace up to half of the butter with the rendered fat to cook the onions and celery, if desired)
1 pound button or wild mushrooms, sliced and sautéed in butter along with the onions
1 red or green bell pepper, diced, sautéed along with the onions

APPLE AND CHERRY BREAD STUFFING

About 7 cups; 9 servings

Perfect for pork. Please read About Bread Stuffings and Dressings, 531.

If baking separately as a dressing, preheat the oven to 350°F and butter a 9-inch square baking dish. Melt in a large skillet over medium heat until the butter foams:

4 tablespoons (½ stick) butter

Add and cook, stirring, until translucent, about 5 minutes:

2 celery ribs, chopped
1 medium onion, chopped

Remove from the heat and add:

4 cups cubed stale white or whole wheat bread, corn bread, or plain croutons
1 large apple, cored, peeled, and diced
¾ cup dried tart cherries
½ cup port or Madeira
¼ cup raisins
(1 tablespoon minced rosemary)
1 teaspoon black pepper
½ teaspoon salt

If baking as a dressing, add:

(1 large egg, well beaten)

Moisten with:

Up to ½ cup chicken stock or broth, or as needed

Spoon the stuffing into the bird. For the dressing, transfer to the prepared baking dish and moisten with:

Up to 1 cup chicken stock or broth, or as needed

Bake the dressing until browned as desired, 30 to 45 minutes. If stuffing inside meat, ensure that the internal temperature of the stuffing reaches the minimum safe internal temperature for that particular meat (165°F for poultry; 145°F for pork).

CORN BREAD STUFFING WITH ROASTED PEPPERS

10 to 12 cups; 13 to 16 servings

Two drained 4-ounce cans diced mild green chiles can be substituted for the roasted peppers.

Prepare:

Basic Corn Bread Stuffing or Dressing, 532

Roast, 262:

4 poblano peppers or 8 Anaheim peppers
3 jalapeño peppers

Peel, seed, and chop the peppers and add to the stuffing along with:

1 teaspoon ground cumin
1 teaspoon dried oregano
1 cup frozen, canned, or fresh corn kernels

Toss the corn bread with the seasonings and bake as directed.

APPLE AND PRUNE DRESSING

About 4½ cups; 6 servings

Excellent with roasted pork, goose, or duck.

If baking separately as a dressing, preheat the oven to 350°F and butter an 8-inch square baking dish. Combine in a bowl:

3 cups cubed white bread (crusts removed)
1 cup diced peeled tart apples
¾ cup chopped pitted prunes
½ cup chopped toasted, 1005, walnuts or pecans
1 stick (4 ounces) butter, melted, or ½ cup bacon drippings or duck or goose fat
1 tablespoon lemon juice
1 teaspoon salt

Spoon the stuffing into the bird. If baking as a dressing, add:

(1 large egg, well beaten)

Transfer to the prepared baking dish and moisten with:

½ cup chicken, pork, duck, or goose stock or broth

Bake the dressing until browned, about 30 minutes. The stuffing is done when it reaches an internal temperature of 165°F.

ABOUT BREAD CRUMB STUFFINGS

Practically any kind of bread can be used to make bread crumb stuffings, whether Italian or French bread, homemade sandwich bread, or corn bread. Whatever the bread, if the crumbs are stale or toasted (what we refer to as "dry bread crumbs"), the stuffing will be drier and firmer; when crumbs are left soft and untoasted (what we call "fresh bread crumbs"), the stuffing will be moist and dense. For tips on making bread crumbs, see 957.

Unseasoned packaged bread crumbs can be used in any recipe, but ➤ increase the stock called for in the recipe by one-third. ➤ A 1-pound loaf of bread yields about 6 cups fresh bread crumbs, including the crust, which should be used unless otherwise specified in the recipe.

ITALIAN BREAD CRUMB STUFFING

About 4 cups; 5 servings

This may be used to stuff boneless chicken breasts, zucchini, or a roast chicken. ➤ If using as a stuffing, do not use the eggs. Please read About Bread Crumb Stuffings, above.

If baking separately as a dressing, preheat the oven to 350°F and butter a 4-cup baking dish.

Melt in a small skillet over medium-high heat until the foam begins to subside:

4 tablespoons (½ stick) butter

Add and cook, stirring, until tender but not browned, about 5 minutes:

1 medium onion, finely chopped

Stir in and cook for 30 seconds:

2 garlic cloves, minced

Transfer to a bowl and stir in:

2 cups dry bread crumbs
½ cup grated Parmesan (2 ounces)
¼ cup finely chopped parsley
½ teaspoon dried rosemary, crumbled
½ teaspoon dried sage
½ teaspoon salt
½ teaspoon black pepper

Stir in, adding enough to make the stuffing just moist enough to hold together in a crumbly ball when squeezed firmly in your hand:

1 to 1½ cups chicken stock or broth, or as needed

If baking as a dressing, add:

(1 large egg, well beaten)

Spoon the stuffing into the meat or vegetable case. For a dressing, transfer to the prepared baking dish and moisten with:

½ cup chicken stock or broth

Bake the dressing until browned, about 30 minutes, or, for stuffing inside a chicken, until the internal temperature reaches 165°F.

PARSLEY AND BREAD CRUMB STUFFING

About 2 cups

This delicate, buttery stuffing can be used to stuff a range of seafood, from sole fillets to whole baked trout; it also makes a fine stuffing for chicken breasts or even for topping baked oysters. This recipe makes enough to stuff 4 servings, or 2 pounds fish fillets or steaks or 3 to 4 pounds whole fish. For a more decadent stuffing, add to the mixture below **1 cup cooked lobster, lump crabmeat, or drained raw oysters, finely chopped.** Please read About Bread Crumb Stuffings, 533.

Melt in a medium skillet over medium heat:

6 tablespoons (¾ stick) butter

Add and cook, stirring, until tender but not browned, about 10 minutes:

½ cup finely chopped onions
½ cup finely chopped celery

Remove from the heat and stir in:

1½ cups fresh bread crumbs, 957
3 tablespoons finely chopped parsley
(½ cup cooked spinach, drained and chopped)
(2 tablespoons drained small capers)
(2 teaspoons minced fresh tarragon or dill or ½ teaspoon dried tarragon or dill)

Season with:

½ teaspoon lemon juice
¼ teaspoon salt
¼ teaspoon black pepper
(¼ teaspoon dry mustard)

BACON STUFFING FOR FISH

About 3 cups

A savory stuffing that can stand up to the flavors of rich-tasting fish such as trout, salmon, bluefish, and mackerel. This stuffing can also be used to enrich lean fish, like tilapia.

Cook in a large skillet until crisp:

12 slices bacon

Drain the bacon on paper towels. Omitting the butter and using the bacon fat to cook the vegetables, prepare:

Parsley and Bread Crumb Stuffing, above

Add the crumbled bacon. If desired, stir into the stuffing:

(3 tablespoons finely chopped toasted, 1005, pecans)

SEAFOOD STUFFING

About 2½ cups

This dressing has a smoky bacon flavor and the consistency of spoon bread, 631. Spread it on top of thick fish fillets or steaks before baking (thin pieces of fish will overcook by the time the stuffing is cooked through) or use it as a filling for bell peppers or other vegetable cases. Please read About Bread Crumb Stuffings, 533.

Melt in a skillet over medium heat:

2 tablespoons butter

Add and cook, stirring, until the vegetables are tender but not browned, 7 to 10 minutes:

1 celery rib, finely chopped
½ small onion or 1 shallot, finely chopped
2 slices bacon, minced

Add and cook, stirring, for 1 minute:

1 cup fresh bread crumbs, 957

Remove from the heat and let cool for 10 minutes. Combine in a medium bowl:

1 cup cooked or canned crabmeat, picked over for shells and cartilage, or 1 cup chopped peeled cooked shrimp
(2 large eggs, well beaten)

Stir in the bread crumb mixture. Then stir in:

1 tablespoon dry sherry
Finely grated zest of 1 lemon

GREEN HERB STUFFING

About 1½ cups

This has a tempting green color and a lightly tangy flavor. It is excellent with fish or poultry. If using with fish, omit the egg. For a chicken that is larger than 3 pounds, double the recipe.

Melt in a small skillet over medium heat:

2 tablespoons butter

Add and cook, stirring, until translucent, about 4 minutes:

2 tablespoons chopped shallots

Remove from the heat and cool slightly. Combine in a food processor:

½ cup chopped tender inner celery ribs with leaves
½ cup coarsely chopped parsley
¼ cup watercress leaves
½ teaspoon salt

1 teaspoon minced fresh basil or tarragon or ¼ teaspoon dried basil or tarragon
(1 large egg)
Add the shallots and pulse until a paste forms. Tear into small crumbly pieces:
2 slices white sandwich bread, crusts removed
Place in a medium bowl, add the herb paste, and blend lightly with a fork. Add:
¼ cup roasted unsalted pistachios, chopped
If using to stuff poultry or the optional egg was added, cook until it reaches an internal temperature of 165°F.

SAUSAGE, ONION, AND SAGE STUFFING

About 5½ cups; 7 servings

If baking separately as a dressing, preheat the oven to 350°F and butter an 8-inch square baking dish.
Cook in a medium skillet over medium heat, breaking up the meat with a spoon, until browned:
8 ounces bulk breakfast or Italian sausage
Using a slotted spoon, transfer the meat to a plate lined with paper towels to drain. Pour off all but 2 tablespoons of fat from the skillet. Add and cook until softened:
1 large onion, finely chopped
1 celery rib, finely chopped
Transfer the onion mixture to a bowl and add the sausage along with:
3 cups dry bread or corn bread crumbs
2 teaspoons chopped fresh sage or 1 teaspoon dried sage
1 teaspoon dried thyme
1 stick (4 ounces) butter, melted
¾ teaspoon salt
¼ teaspoon black pepper
(½ cup chopped tart apple)
If baking as a dressing, also add:
(1 large egg, well beaten)
Stir to combine. Moisten with:
½ cup chicken stock or broth
Spoon the stuffing into the meat or vegetable being stuffed. For a dressing, transfer to the prepared baking dish and bake until browned, about 30 minutes. If using to stuff poultry, cook until it reaches an internal temperature of 165°F.

SPINACH-RICOTTA STUFFING

About 2 cups

Stuff this well-seasoned mixture under the skin of chicken parts or a spatchcocked, 403, whole bird. It also makes a nice filling for pasta, 311.
Heat in a medium skillet over medium heat:
1 tablespoon olive oil
Add and cook, stirring, until softened, about 5 minutes:
½ small onion, finely chopped
1 garlic clove, minced
Meanwhile, squeeze almost dry and place in a medium bowl:
12 ounces spinach, cooked as directed in Wilted Tender Greens, 243, and coarsely chopped, or one 10-ounce package frozen chopped spinach, thawed
Add the onion and garlic to the spinach, then mix in:
1 cup ricotta
½ cup fresh bread crumbs, 957
2 tablespoons grated Parmesan
½ teaspoon salt
¼ teaspoon black pepper
Pinch of grated or ground nutmeg

ABOUT GRAIN STUFFINGS AND DRESSINGS

Almost any grain is suitable for a stuffing. In fact, many of the recipes in the Grains chapter, 317, can be used either as stuffings or dressings. Indian Lemon Rice, 333, Wheat Berries with Sautéed Onions and Dried Fruits, 338, Couscous with Pine Nuts and Raisins, 339, and Wild Rice with Sautéed Mushrooms, 340, all make excellent stuffings for meat or for vegetable cases. The reverse is also true: Many of these stuffings make for an excellent grain side dish.

Interesting variations on the recipes that follow may be made by substituting one grain for another. Consider using barley, farro, freekeh, or even quinoa as the base of a stuffing (for changes in cooking times, see the Grains Cooking Chart, 340). Grains like quinoa, freekeh, and bulgur are especially nice in stuffings because they readily soak up the juices and flavors of the food they are stuffed inside.

COUSCOUS STUFFING WITH APRICOTS AND PISTACHIOS

About 4 cups

Use as a stuffing for small birds such as Cornish hens, poussins, or squab, or serve as a side dish for roasted or grilled lamb. If desired, replace some of the apricots with finely diced dates.
Melt in a large saucepan over medium heat:
2 tablespoons butter
Add and cook, stirring, until tender, about 5 minutes:
½ small onion, finely chopped
Stir in:
1½ cups chicken stock or broth
½ cup finely chopped dried apricots
(1 tablespoon chopped Salt-Preserved Lemons, 942)
½ teaspoon salt
¼ teaspoon black pepper
Pinch of ground cinnamon
Pinch of ground ginger
Bring to a boil and stir in:
1 cup quick-cooking couscous
Remove from the heat, cover, and let stand for 5 minutes. Fluff with a fork and stir in:
½ cup chopped pistachios, whole pine nuts, or slivered toasted, 1005, almonds
¼ cup minced parsley
Spoon the stuffing into the bird before cooking, or serve immediately as a side. If stuffed in a bird, the stuffing is done when it reaches an internal temperature of 165°F.

RICE DRESSING WITH CHORIZO AND CHILES

About 4 cups

This is wonderful as a stuffing for chicken or bell peppers, but it also makes a great side dish if the egg is omitted. **One 4-ounce can diced mild green chiles, drained,** can be substituted for the poblano or Anaheim peppers. If using as a stuffing for meat, omit the optional egg.

If baking separately as a dressing, preheat the oven to 350°F and grease a shallow 8-inch square baking dish.

Cook in a large skillet over medium heat, breaking up the meat with spoon, until cooked through and browned, 8 to 10 minutes:

1 pound bulk fresh chorizo

With a slotted spoon transfer the chorizo to a plate lined with paper towels. If the meat did not leave behind much fat, add to the skillet:

A little vegetable oil

Add and cook, stirring, until tender, about 5 minutes:

1 onion, finely chopped
4 garlic cloves, minced

Transfer to a large bowl and add the chorizo along with:

3 cups cooked white rice, 343
(1 large egg, lightly beaten)
2 poblano peppers or 4 Anaheim peppers, roasted, 262, peeled, seeded, and chopped
4 green onions, chopped
½ cup chopped cilantro leaves and stems
¼ teaspoon salt, or to taste
¼ teaspoon black pepper, or to taste

If using as a stuffing, spoon into the meat or vegetables before cooking. For a dressing, transfer to the prepared baking dish, cover, and bake until browned as desired, 20 to 30 minutes. If using to stuff poultry or the optional egg was added, cook until it reaches an internal temperature of 165°F.

SPICED RICE STUFFING

About 4 cups

This aromatic stuffing goes well with Cornish hens, partridge, or quail. Baked in a casserole, it also makes a good side dish with grilled chicken, fish, or lamb.

If baking separately as a dressing, preheat the oven to 350°F and grease a shallow 8-inch square baking dish.

Heat in a large skillet over medium heat:

2 tablespoons olive oil

Add and cook, stirring, until tender, about 5 minutes:

1 medium onion, finely chopped

Add and stir until well blended:

1 cup medium- or long-grain rice
3 garlic cloves, minced
1 teaspoon salt
½ teaspoon ground cumin
½ teaspoon ground coriander
½ teaspoon ground turmeric
½ teaspoon sweet paprika
½ teaspoon ground ginger
½ teaspoon black pepper

Stir in and bring to a simmer:

1½ to 2 cups chicken stock or broth (2 cups if using long-grain rice)

Reduce the heat to low and simmer, covered, until the rice is tender and all the liquid is absorbed, about 20 minutes. Turn the mixture into a large bowl and let cool slightly, then stir in:

¼ cup golden raisins
¼ cup diced pitted prunes
¼ cup toasted, 1005, slivered almonds
Finely grated zest of 1 lemon
2 tablespoons lemon juice

If baking as a dressing, add:

(1 large egg, well beaten)

Adjust the seasonings. If using as a stuffing, spoon into the meat or vegetables before cooking. For a dressing, transfer to the prepared baking dish, cover, and bake until browned as desired, 20 to 30 minutes. If used to stuff poultry or the optional egg was added, cook until it reaches an internal temperature of 165°F.

WILD RICE DRESSING

3 to 4 cups

This is the perfect stuffing or accompaniment to wild game birds, venison, or winter squash. A wild rice blend can be substituted.

If baking separately as a dressing, preheat the oven to 350°F and grease a shallow 8-inch square baking dish.

Combine in a medium saucepan:

3½ cups chicken stock or broth
(Heart, gizzard, and neck from the bird or birds to be stuffed, finely diced or cut into 1-inch pieces)

Bring to a boil, then reduce the heat and simmer, covered, for 15 minutes. Uncover, increase the heat to high, and bring to a rolling boil. Stir in:

1 cup wild rice
(1 ounce dried porcini mushrooms, finely chopped or ground)

Reduce the heat to low and simmer, covered, until tender, 30 to 50 minutes. About 5 minutes before the rice is done, if desired, stir in:

(Livers from the bird or birds to be stuffed, finely diced)

If they were used, discard the neck(s). Set the rice aside. Melt in a large skillet over medium heat:

4 tablespoons (½ stick) butter

Stir in and cook until soft, about 5 minutes:

1 small onion or large shallot, finely chopped
1 celery rib, finely chopped

Add and cook, stirring, until barely soft, about 3 minutes:

4 ounces mushrooms, chopped
2 garlic cloves, minced
(¼ cup chopped toasted, 1005, pecans or hazelnuts)
(¼ cup drained canned water chestnut slices)

Add the hot rice and mix well. Add:

¼ cup minced parsley
1½ teaspoons minced fresh thyme or ½ teaspoon dried thyme

1½ teaspoons minced fresh sage or ½ teaspoon dried sage
Salt and black pepper to taste

Spoon the stuffing into the bird before cooking. For a dressing, transfer to the prepared baking dish, cover, and bake until browned as desired, 20 to 30 minutes. If used to stuff poultry, cook until it reaches an internal temperature of 165°F.

SAUERKRAUT STUFFING FOR WILDFOWL

About 5 cups

Ideal for stuffing roast duck or goose.

If baking separately as a dressing, preheat the oven to 350°F and grease a shallow 9-inch square baking dish.

Heat in a large skillet over medium heat:

2 tablespoons vegetable oil or duck or goose fat

Add and cook, stirring, until softened, 6 to 8 minutes:

1 medium onion, thinly sliced
1 Granny Smith apple, cored, peeled, and chopped
(½ cup canned water chestnuts, drained and chopped)
2 garlic cloves, minced

Stir in:

4 cups drained sauerkraut, store-bought or homemade, 940
(¼ cup dried currants)
1 teaspoon chopped fresh thyme or ½ teaspoon dried thyme
½ teaspoon caraway seeds
(½ teaspoon lightly crushed juniper berries)
Salt and black pepper to taste

Cook until heated through, about 5 minutes. If using as a stuffing, spoon into the bird before cooking. For a side dish, transfer to the prepared baking dish and bake for 20 minutes before serving. If used to stuff poultry, cook until it reaches an internal temperature of 165°F.

ABOUT CASSEROLES

The recipes here are known by the name of the vessel they are baked in. Thus any mixture of vegetables, meat, grains, pasta, or dairy baked in a large, shallow dish could be termed a casserole. This presents us with endless possibilities; casseroles also go by the name "hot dish," which is appropriately inclusive and vague.

Our common understanding of what constitutes a casserole is more specific than the name suggests. A particular type of casserole became popular in the 1930s, when brands selling convenience foods were trying to gain a foothold in grocery stores. Many of us grew up with noodle casseroles made with canned condensed soup, and many of us have fond memories of those dishes. Versatile for their ability to be prepared in advance (often with leftovers), reheated, and shared without losing their essence, casserole dishes populate many a groaning buffet table at community events, such as potlucks, church suppers, and funerals.

Despite the canned-soup origins of many of these casseroles, we have decided to take a more homemade approach in the recipes below. We find that using these products does not save all that much time, and the results of preparing a quick béchamel sauce are much tastier. For those who cannot imagine making their favorite casserole without them, we provide canned soup substitutions as well.

For other casserole recipes, see Leftover Pasta Casserole, 293, Macaroni and Cheese for a Crowd, 296, Pastitsio, 309, Mushroom-Walnut Noodle Kugel, 309, lasagne, 310–11, Green Bean Casserole, 210, Broccoli-Cheese Casserole, 221, Moussaka, 239, Potato Kugel, 268, and Mashed Potato Casserole for a Crowd, 266. We have also included enchiladas here. While we do not really think of them as casseroles, they seemed most at home in this crowd-friendly section.

CHICKEN RICE CASSEROLE

8 servings

Cooked turkey may be used instead of chicken. Use any type of cooked rice. If desired, substitute **two 10¾-ounce cans condensed cream of mushroom or chicken soup** mixed with **½ cup milk** and **½ cup chicken broth** for the butter/mushroom/flour/chicken broth/milk mixture.

Preheat the oven to 400°F. Grease a 13 × 9-inch baking dish.

Melt in a large saucepan over medium heat:

6 tablespoons (¾ stick) butter

Stir in and cook until softened, about 5 minutes:

8 ounces mushrooms, sliced (3 cups)

Stir in until well blended:

½ cup all-purpose flour

Slowly add while whisking:

2 cups chicken stock or broth
1½ cups whole milk or half-and-half

Bring to a boil, reduce the heat, and cook until the sauce is thickened and smooth, about 5 minutes. Mix in:

4 cups chopped or shredded cooked chicken (from about 2 pounds boneless, skinless raw chicken)
3 cups cooked rice, 343
(½ cup chopped toasted, 1005, walnuts, almonds, or pecans)

Pour into the prepared dish. Mix together and sprinkle on top:

½ cup dry bread crumbs
2 tablespoons grated Parmesan
1 tablespoon butter, melted

Bake until the sauce is bubbling and the topping is golden brown, 25 to 35 minutes.

CHICKEN TAMALE PIE

8 to 10 servings

This dish can be baked 3 days ahead, cooled, and kept covered in the refrigerator, then reheated in a 350°F oven for 25 minutes.

Heat in a large skillet over medium-high heat:

1 tablespoon vegetable oil

Add and brown, breaking up the meat with a wooden spoon:

1½ pounds ground chicken or turkey

Stir in:

3 cups salsa, drained of excess liquid
½ cup sliced pimiento-stuffed green olives
1 tablespoon chili powder
1 tablespoon ground cumin
½ teaspoon ground cinnamon

Bring to a simmer, then reduce the heat to low and simmer gently, stirring occasionally, for 10 minutes to allow the flavors to blend. Remove from the heat.

Preheat the oven to 400°F. Grease a 13 × 9-inch baking dish.

Bring just to a boil in a small saucepan:

1⅓ cups water
1 cup vegetable or chicken stock or broth

Remove from the heat. Mix together in a large bowl:

3 cups fine cornmeal
⅓ cup vegetable oil
2 teaspoons baking powder
1½ teaspoons salt

Stir until all the cornmeal is coated with the oil. Add the hot stock mixture and stir well. Let the batter stand for 5 minutes, then mix in:

2 large eggs, well beaten

Reserve 1½ cups of the batter. Spread the remaining batter evenly over the bottom of the prepared dish. Spoon in the chicken filling. Cover with:

3 cups grated Cheddar (12 ounces)

Stir into the reserved batter:

¼ cup hot water

Spread in a thin, even layer over the top of the pie. (The batter will blend with the cheese.) Bake until browned, about 40 minutes. Let stand 15 minutes before cutting.

CORN BREAD TAMALE PIE

6 servings

This updated recipe dates back to *Joy*'s 1936 edition, in which the filling is completely enclosed in a cornmeal crust.

Combine in a large skillet over medium-high heat:

1 pound ground beef
1 medium onion, chopped

Sauté until the meat is browned and the onion translucent, about 10 minutes. Add:

1 cup canned black beans, drained and rinsed
1 cup drained canned or frozen corn
1 cup tomato sauce
1 cup beef or chicken stock or broth or water
(½ cup diced green bell pepper)
1 tablespoon chili powder
½ teaspoon ground cumin
1 teaspoon salt
¼ teaspoon black pepper

Simmer for 15 minutes. Set aside.

Preheat the oven to 425°F. Grease a shallow 2-quart casserole.

Whisk together in a medium bowl:

¾ cup fine cornmeal
1 tablespoon all-purpose flour
1 tablespoon sugar
1½ teaspoons baking powder
½ teaspoon salt

Whisk together in a small bowl until well blended:

1 large egg
⅓ cup milk
1 tablespoon vegetable oil

Pour the wet ingredients over the dry and whisk until well combined. Spread the meat mixture in the prepared casserole and cover with the cornmeal batter. The batter will disappear into the meat mixture but will rise during baking and form a layer of corn bread. Bake until the corn bread is browned, 20 to 25 minutes.

KING RANCH CHICKEN CASSEROLE

8 servings

To prepare the authentic recipe, substitute **two 10¾-ounce cans condensed cream of chicken soup** for the flour, chicken stock, and sour cream.

Preheat the oven to 375°F. Lightly grease a 13 × 9-inch baking dish.

Have ready:

12 corn tortillas
2 cups shredded Monterey Jack or Oaxaca cheese (8 ounces)

Melt in a large skillet over medium heat:

6 tablespoons unsalted butter

Add and cook, stirring, until softened, 10 to 12 minutes:

1 medium onion, finely chopped
1 red bell pepper, finely chopped
1 poblano pepper, finely chopped
(2 jalapeño peppers, seeded, if desired, and finely chopped)

Stir in and cook for 1 minute:

3 garlic cloves, minced
1 tablespoon chili powder
(¼ to ½ teaspoon cayenne pepper, to taste)

Add and cook, stirring, for 2 minutes:

⅓ cup all-purpose flour

Gradually stir in:

2 cups chicken stock or broth

Bring to a simmer and cook, stirring, until thickened, about 5 minutes. Remove from the heat and stir in:

3 to 4 cups cubed or shredded cooked chicken (from 1½ to 2 pounds boneless, skinless raw chicken)
1 cup sour cream or crema
Salt and black pepper to taste

Spread a thin layer of chicken sauce on the bottom of the prepared dish and top with 6 of the tortillas. Spread half the remaining chicken sauce over the tortillas, then sprinkle with half the cheese. Top with the remaining 6 tortillas, then the remaining sauce, then the remaining cheese. Bake until browned on top and bubbling, 40 to 45 minutes. Let cool 10 minutes before serving.

TUNA-VEGETABLE CASSEROLE

4 to 6 servings

If desired, substitute **one 10¾-ounce can condensed cream of mushroom soup** mixed with **¾ cup milk** for the butter/mushroom/onion/flour/milk mixture.

Preheat the oven to 375°F. Grease an 8-inch square baking dish.

Cook in a large pot of boiling salted water:

4 ounces dried egg noodles
Drain well. Melt in a medium saucepan over medium heat:
4 tablespoons (1/2 stick) butter
Add and cook, stirring occasionally, until the vegetables are just tender, about 5 minutes:
6 ounces mushrooms, sliced
(1/2 red or green bell pepper, diced)
1 small onion, finely chopped
Stir in and cook for 1 minute:
1/4 cup all-purpose flour
Gradually whisk in:
2 1/2 cups milk
Bring the sauce to a boil, whisking, then turn the heat down and simmer for 10 minutes. Remove from the heat and add, whisking until hot:
1 cup shredded Cheddar (4 ounces)
12 ounces canned or pouch tuna, drained and flaked
Add the drained pasta to the sauce along with:
(1/2 cup frozen green peas)
1/4 cup minced parsley
Salt and black pepper to taste
Stir together well. Pour the mixture into the prepared baking dish. Mix together and sprinkle over the top:
1/2 cup dry bread crumbs, fine cracker crumbs, crushed cornflakes, or crushed plain potato chips
2 tablespoons butter, melted
Bake until browned on top, 25 to 35 minutes.

TURKEY TETRAZZINI

8 servings

If desired, substitute **two 10 3/4-ounce cans condensed cream of mushroom or chicken soup** mixed with **1/2 cup milk** and **1/2 cup chicken broth** for the butter/mushroom/flour/chicken broth/milk mixture. If you are using leftover pasta, you will need about 4 cups. Cooked chicken may be substituted for the turkey.
Preheat the oven to 400°F. Grease a 13 × 9-inch baking dish.
Cook in a large pot of boiling salted water:
8 ounces dried spaghetti, macaroni, or egg noodles
Meanwhile, melt in a saucepan over medium heat:
6 tablespoons (3/4 stick) butter
Add and cook, stirring, until softened, about 5 minutes:
8 ounces mushrooms, sliced
Stir in until well blended:
1/2 cup all-purpose flour
Slowly add while whisking:
2 cups chicken stock or broth
1 1/2 cups whole milk or half-and-half
(1/4 cup dry sherry)
Bring to a boil, reduce the heat, and cook until the sauce is thickened and smooth, about 5 minutes. Mix in:
4 cups chopped cooked turkey (about 1 1/4 pounds)
Drain the pasta and gently mix into the turkey mixture. Pour into the prepared dish. Mix together in a small bowl:
1/2 cup grated Parmesan (2 ounces)
1/2 cup dry bread crumbs
Sprinkle the mixture over the casserole and dot with:
2 tablespoons butter, cut into small cubes
Bake until the sauce is bubbling and the topping is golden brown, 25 to 35 minutes.

CHICKEN ENCHILADAS

4 to 6 servings

If time is of the essence, use **4 cups store-bought red enchilada sauce** instead of freshly cooked sauce. For a spicier take, prepare Mexican Adobo II, 585 (with the greater amount of liquid), or a double batch of New Mexico–Style Chile Sauce I, 554, and substitute for the sauce below. For the chicken, feel free to use shredded store-bought rotisserie chicken or leftover chicken; if starting from scratch, prepare Poached Chicken, 419, then shred.
Heat in a large skillet over medium-high heat:
2 tablespoons vegetable oil
Add and cook, stirring frequently, until the onions are translucent and just beginning to brown around the edges, about 7 minutes:
1 large onion, chopped
2 jalapeño peppers, seeded and chopped
4 garlic cloves, finely chopped
Add and cook for 1 minute, stirring constantly:
1/4 cup chili powder
2 teaspoons ground cumin
Add, bring to a simmer, and cook for 5 minutes, stirring frequently:
One 28-ounce can diced tomatoes, drained
(2 canned chipotle peppers in adobo sauce, chopped)
1 teaspoon salt
Transfer the mixture to a blender or food processor and puree until very smooth. Taste and add more salt if needed. Transfer 1/2 cup of the enchilada sauce to a medium bowl and add:
2 1/2 cups shredded cooked chicken (from about 1 1/2 pounds boneless, skinless raw chicken)
Set aside. Preheat the oven to 400°F. Spread a thin layer of enchilada sauce over the bottom of a 13 × 9-inch baking dish. Have ready:
12 corn tortillas or eight 7- to 8-inch flour tortillas
Return the rest of the enchilada sauce to the large skillet and keep warm over medium heat. Working with a few tortillas at a time, use tongs to dip the tortillas in the warm sauce so it coats both sides. Allow the tortillas to sit in the sauce briefly, just long enough to warm them and make them pliable. Then transfer the tortillas to a plate. Spoon 2 to 3 tablespoons of the chicken mixture down the center of each tortilla, then roll into a cylinder. If using corn tortillas, be aware that they will crack—this is okay. Arrange the enchiladas seam side down in the baking dish. Cover with the remaining enchilada sauce, then sprinkle with:
1 cup shredded Cheddar, Monterey Jack, or Oaxaca cheese (4 ounces)
Bake until the sauce begins to bubble, about 15 minutes. Serve with:
Sour cream
Chopped green onion
Chopped cilantro

CHEESE ENCHILADAS

Prepare **Chicken Enchiladas, 539,** substituting **2½ cups additional shredded Cheddar, Monterey Jack, Oaxaca cheese, or a combination (10 ounces)** for the chicken.

BEEF OR PORK ENCHILADAS

Prepare **Chicken Enchiladas, 539,** substituting **2½ cups shredded leftover pot roast or leftover cooked pork shoulder** for the chicken.

ENCHILADAS VERDES

4 to 6 servings

Prepare:

New Mexico–Style Chile Sauce II, 554, or ½ recipe (2½ cups) Roasted Tomatillo Spinach Sauce, 555

Preheat the oven to 400°F. Lightly oil a 13 × 9-inch baking dish. Combine in a bowl:

2½ cups shredded cooked chicken (from about 1½ pounds boneless, skinless raw chicken)
½ cup sour cream
4 green onions, finely chopped
¼ cup minced cilantro
1 teaspoon ground cumin
Salt to taste

Set out:

12 corn tortillas or eight 7- to 8-inch flour tortillas

Stack the tortillas, wrap in foil, and bake until soft and pliable, about 5 minutes. Spread a thin layer of the sauce in the bottom of the prepared baking dish. For each enchilada, spoon about 3 tablespoons of the chicken mixture down the center of a tortilla, then roll the tortilla up into a cylinder. Arrange the enchiladas seam side down in the baking dish and cover with the remaining sauce. Sprinkle on top:

1 cup shredded Cheddar, Monterey Jack, or Oaxaca cheese (4 ounces)

Bake until the sauce begins to bubble, about 15 minutes. Serve with:

Sour cream

NEW MEXICO–STYLE ENCHILADA STACKS

4 servings

Rather than tortillas rolled around a filling, then topped with sauce, New Mexico enchiladas are stacked, with layers of tortilla, chile sauce, cheese, and fillings. They can be as simple as cheese and chile sauce or they can incorporate more substantial fillings.

Have ready:

12 corn tortillas

Heat in a medium skillet over medium heat (dip the edge of a tortilla in the oil and it should sizzle):

½ inch vegetable oil

Fry the tortillas briefly, flipping once, until they have puffed slightly on both sides, about 30 seconds total. Transfer to paper towels to drain. Have ready:

(2 cups any of the suggested Fillings for Tacos and Burritos, 146)
2 cups New Mexico–Style Chile Sauce, 554
3 cups shredded Monterey Jack, mozzarella, or Oaxaca cheese (12 ounces)

Adjust a rack so it is 6 to 8 inches below the heating element. Preheat the broiler. Line a large baking sheet with foil.

To make the enchilada stacks, set 4 tortillas on the baking sheet. Top each with ¼ cup filling, if using, then 2 heaping tablespoons of the sauce, followed by ¼ cup of the cheese. Top each stack with a second tortilla, ¼ cup optional filling, 2 heaping tablespoons sauce, and ¼ cup cheese. Top each stack with a third tortilla, then divide the remaining sauce and cheese among them.

Broil until the cheese is melted, 3 to 5 minutes.

SAVORY SAUCES, SALAD DRESSINGS, MARINADES, AND SEASONING BLENDS

Life without these elixirs would be very dull. Nearly all of our foods depend upon them at one stage of cooking or another, from condiment to essential ingredient to cooking medium. Indeed, for many of us, these preparations are the most rewarding, as they can fundamentally alter our experience of a meal.

ABOUT SAUCES

Whether as embellishment or defining element, sauces succeed when they enhance the flavors of the food they accompany. They may deepen and amplify flavors already present in the food: A sauce based on demi-glace adds even more meatiness to a slice of prime rib; hoisin and fish sauce accentuate the savoriness of a bowl of **pho.** In other instances, a sauce can balance or contrast with food: Hollandaise adds richness and acidity to the fresh, green flavor of asparagus; the dry starchiness of potatoes can be offset by a meaty gravy or a tart vinaigrette; acidic, piquant sauces like gastrique, mojo, and salsa verde cut through the richness of fatty meats.

Sauces also moisten foods, whether it's a pan of enchiladas, eggs Benedict, or hot buttermilk biscuits. Sauces can be an afterthought or garnish, like bottled steak sauce or hot sauce. In other contexts, they are integral to the meal, such as turkey gravy on Thanksgiving, a rich peanut sauce for satay, dressing for a pile of greens, or a bright puttanesca tossed with pasta. But one thing sauces should never do is instill fear in the cook. On the whole, they are simple and an area of cooking in which it is easy to excel.

The trepidation many home cooks feel when it comes to sauce making is probably largely due to the influence of French cuisine. Classic French sauces such as espagnole and béchamel have a reputation for complexity and difficulty. Indeed, some classic French sauces can take many hours to make, require cooking flour to very specific shades of brown, or involve a lot of whisking. The good news is that only a handful of these classic sauces deserve their reputation for fussiness. More important, though we cannot imagine life without them, French sauces represent only a tiny fraction of those we now enjoy. In fact, the world is full of delectable sauces that go far beyond the flour- and butter-heavy classics. Many culinary traditions balance disparate flavors in one sauce, such as pairing tart tamarind with earthy, warm spices in a chutney, or pungent shrimp paste with aromatic lemongrass, lime, and cilantro in a Thai curry. In some Chinese and Southeast Asian sauces, umami-rich ingredients like fermented black beans, fish sauce, and soy sauce boost their savory appeal. Many Indian sauces rely on spices for much of their flavor, and different flavor profiles are achieved by using spices whole, coarsely ground, or finely ground; toasted, tempered, or raw.

In short, there are many paths to sauce making, and exploring them can give you a better sense for cooking and flavor than any other kitchen exercise. When choosing a sauce to accompany a dish, whether a rich velouté, a spicy chutney, or an herbaceous chimichurri, remember that it should complement the food it accompanies.

ABOUT SAUCE TOOLS

Saucepans, ideally with sloping sides (in which case they are called *sauciers*), are especially good tools for making all types of cooked sauces, but especially the classic French repertoire. They are excellent for reducing or cooking down sauces to concentrate flavor, as they allow liquids to boil down quickly, and the slanted sides facilitate whisking and stirring. Those made of stainless steel are less likely to be scratched from whisking or deglazing and scraping; avoid aluminum, which may react with acidic ingredients.

Simple tools within easy reach of the stove smooth the process of sauce making. **Whisks** are vital for emulsifying sauces such as vinaigrette, hollandaise, and mayonnaise and for avoiding lumps in roux-based sauces and gravies. A **rasp grater,** often referred to by the most widespread brand name Microplane, is our preferred tool for quickly and easily grating lemon zest, nutmeg, or cloves of garlic destined for uncooked vinaigrettes, salsas, and table sauces. We prefer the ease of an **immersion blender** for pureeing simmered sauces (a potato masher or the back of a spoon is helpful for breaking up tomatoes for a chunkier texture). For especially smooth sauces, you may want to invest in a conical, fine-mesh **chinois** sieve, through which you can strain sauces or press mixtures using a scraper or wooden pestle designed specifically for the purpose. A **double boiler** is used to make some delicate egg-based sauces—a stainless steel bowl set over a saucepan of simmering water works well in its place.

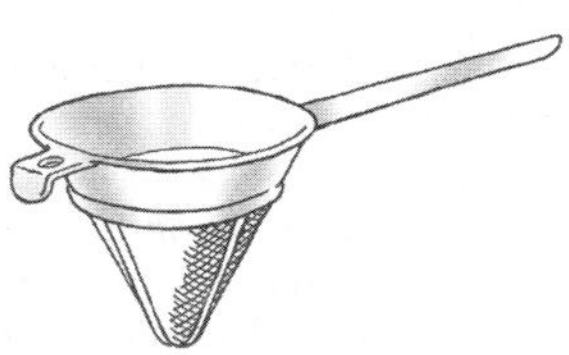

Chinois

Electric **blenders** and **food processors** are great labor-savers when making emulsified sauces and many condiments. They can, however, change the texture and flavor of a sauce somewhat, as they whip in a good deal of air, which tends to make thickened sauces foamy and less intense and lightens the color of some other sauces. These appliances are fine to use for pesto and other pastes, but many cooks swear by a **mortar and pestle** for making herb and spice pastes, as grinding releases more flavor compounds from ingredients than the cutting action of a blender or processor.

KEEPING SAUCES

You can keep most sauces, including white sauces, veloutés, tomato sauces, brown sauces, and gravies, in the refrigerator for up to 4 or 5 days. In general, we do not recommend keeping sauces made with eggs, cream, or milk for more than 2 or 3 days in the refrigerator—the exception to this rule being mayonnaise, which can be kept refrigerated for 1 week.

Luckily, you can freeze many of these sauces in ice cube trays and then, after removing the cubes from the tray, keep the cubes in the freezer in a zip-top bag, taking out as many as you need for immediate use. They can be melted in a double boiler—4 large cubes melt down to about ½ cup sauce. You can even freeze Hollandaise, 561, and Béarnaise Sauce, 561, but be very careful when reheating. ➤ A double boiler or water bath of warm or barely simmering water is the best way to reheat delicate sauces. Do not freeze mayonnaise; it will separate.

Vinaigrettes can be kept for weeks in the refrigerator, although those made with fresh herbs, cheese, or vegetables other than garlic taste best soon after they are made. Acidic or cooked condiments, such as barbecue sauce, may be kept refrigerated for a month or longer.

ABOUT THICKENERS FOR SAUCES

Sauces are generally thickened just enough to lightly enrobe food, or to "coat the back of a spoon." Do not add powdered thickeners such as flour or cornstarch directly to the hot liquid or lumps that cannot be smoothed will form. ➤ First mix the starch with fat or a cold liquid, then whisk it into the sauce.

ROUX

The most common thickener for savory sauces is a roux: a mixture of fat and flour, usually in equal amounts. The fat lubricates and smooths the flour so it does not form lumps when combined with the liquid. The fat may be butter, schmaltz, 1015, rendered meat drippings, or oil. A roux is made by melting or heating the fat, adding the flour, and cooking over low heat while whisking or stirring constantly. If a roux cooks too quickly, the resulting mixture will be grainy and is more susceptible to burning. If the fat floats to the top, the roux has separated; if this happens, there is nothing to do but to throw out the roux and start over.

There are three types of roux: white, blond, and brown. **White roux,** used to make béchamel, is cooked just until the butter and flour are evenly incorporated, then liquid is whisked in before the roux begins to color. **Blond roux,** used in gravies, velouté sauces, and some cream soups, is cooked until it begins to give off a faint nutty aroma and turns an ivory color. **Brown roux,** basic to Cajun and Creole cooking, is cooked until it is a dark, reddish brown and has a strong nutty fragrance. Be very attentive to roux cooked to this stage; a minute too long, and the roux will burn and turn bitter. Though it may take longer, ➤ cooking roux to darker stages is much easier to do over medium or medium-low heat. ➤ The browner you cook a roux, the less thickening power it has (heat eventually breaks down the starch in the flour).

When the desired color of roux has been reached, slowly whisk in the milk, stock, or other liquid. If you have made the roux in advance, it is important to first warm either it or the liquid to be added to it. Avoid combining a very hot roux and a very hot liquid, which can spatter and cause burns, or a cold roux and a cold liquid, which can become lumpy. Once the roux and liquid are combined, whisk constantly until the sauce is thickened and comes to a simmer. Once it has thickened, use gentle cooking to reduce the sauce to the desired consistency. Any trace of a floury taste should disappear after a few minutes of slow simmering. If lumps do appear, strain the sauce through a fine-mesh sieve before proceeding with the recipe.

To save time, consider making a large batch of roux in advance and freezing it for up to several months. When the roux has been cooked to the desired color and is still soft, spoon it into an ice cube tray and freeze. Transfer the frozen cubes to a zip-top bag and store in the freezer. To thicken a sauce, drop the frozen cubes into the hot liquid—1 cube or 2 tablespoons of blond roux will thicken approximately 1 cup liquid—until the desired thickness is achieved.

FILÉ POWDER

Filé powder is made from ground sassafras leaves. For thickening and flavor, add filé to gumbos. The powder has a tendency to become stringy when heated, so add after the gumbo is removed from the heat. In fact, filé is often added at the table. Filé does not reheat well, so thicken only the portion of gumbo that will be eaten.

FLOUR

Flour mixed with water can be used to thicken gravies and sauces, but the results are never so palatable as when a roux is used. Whisk together 1 part flour and 2 parts cold water or stock to make a smooth paste. Stir as much of the paste as needed into the boiling stock or pan drippings or juices. Let the sauce heat until it thickens, and simmer at least 3 minutes more to cook the flour, whisking frequently. Cake and pastry flours have lower protein contents and will produce a smooth gravy in less time. Instant flour, 988, which goes by the brand name Wondra, can be mixed directly into gravies and sauces without first being mixed with water and does not need to be cooked further once the mixture has thickened. Roughly 2 tablespoons flour and ¼ cup water mixed into a paste thickens 1 cup liquid.

BROWNED FLOUR

This is a variant used in gravies that enhances color and flavor. The slow—but inexpensive—procedure by which it is made is worth trying. Preheat the oven to 250°F. Place about 1 cup flour in a thin, even layer in a heavy pan. Bake, shaking the pan periodically so the flour browns evenly. The flour, when ready, will be golden brown and smell nutty and baked. Do not let it get too dark or, as with brown roux, it will become bitter and lose its thickening power altogether. Even properly browned flour has only about half the thickening power of regular flour. It can be stored in a tightly covered jar and used in flour paste, above.

CORNSTARCH

Cornstarch is an excellent thickening agent. With almost twice the thickening power of flour, cornstarch gives a glossy, translucent appearance to sauces. If introduced directly into a hot liquid, lumps are formed that cannot be smoothed. Mix a small amount of cold liquid with the cornstarch to form a **slurry.** Whisk the slurry into a simmering sauce at the last minute. Cornstarch thickens almost immediately, allowing you to easily judge the amount needed. One teaspoon cornstarch dissolved in 2 tablespoons cold water thickens 1 cup liquid. ➤ Overheating will thin a cornstarch-thickened sauce. Also see Cornstarch, 974.

ARROWROOT

Of all the thickeners, arrowroot makes the most delicately textured sauces. It performs much like cornstarch when dissolved in cold liquid and whisked in at the last moment to thicken a sauce, making it shiny and glossy, but it has a bit more thickening power than cornstarch, and it is less likely to thin out if overheated. ➤ However, arrowroot should be used only when the sauce is to be served within 10 minutes of preparation. It will not hold, nor will it reheat. Since the flavor of arrowroot is neutral and it does not have to be cooked to remove rawness, as does flour, and since it thickens at a lower temperature than either flour or cornstarch, it is ideal for use in egg-based sauces and other sauces that should not boil. Use 1 tablespoon arrowroot dissolved in 2 tablespoons cold water to thicken 1 cup liquid. Do not use arrowroot to thicken dairy-based sauces. Also see Arrowroot, 954.

POTATO STARCH

Preferred by some cooks to flour as a thickener in certain delicate sauces. Mix it with a cold liquid and add to simmering stock. When it is used, less simmering is required than for flour, and the sauce gains some translucency. ➤ If overheated, the sauce will thin out. Use potato starch as for cornstarch, above. Also see Potato Starch, 1023.

TAPIOCA STARCH

Tapioca starch is derived from the cassava root, 1023. It is used for thickening sauces, clear fruit glazes, and fruit fillings, particularly those intended to be served cold or frozen, as it does not break down when frozen the way flour-thickened sauces do. ➤ Do not boil a liquid that has been thickened with tapioca flour; it will become stringy. Once the liquid begins to simmer, remove it from the heat and let it sit for 15 minutes, stirring only once or twice during the first 5 minutes, and the sauce will set. Use 1 teaspoon tapioca flour dissolved in 1 tablespoon cold water to thicken 1 cup liquid. Also see Tapioca Starch, 1023; ➤ do not confuse tapioca starch with cassava flour, 986.

EGG YOLKS

Egg yolks not only thicken but also enrich sauces. Yolks contain a high proportion of fat and protein, as well as lecithin, a fat-like molecule. These all contribute to the yolk's ability to thicken and emulsify sauces. ➤ Never add egg yolks directly to hot liquid. Always temper them by first mixing them in a separate bowl with a small quantity of hot liquid. Then incorporate a little more of the hot liquid. Off the heat, stir this mixture into the remainder of the hot liquid and then stir over low heat until the sauce thickens. ➤ Do not allow the sauce to boil, or it will curdle. If this happens, strain it. Unless you can control the heat source very precisely, it is generally safer to add egg yolks to a mixture in a double boiler. Two or 3 egg yolks will lightly thicken 1½ cups liquid.

Melted butter or oil added very slowly to egg yolks with constant whisking will produce an emulsion that is quite thick. Suitably seasoned, this becomes the base for Hollandaise, 561, or Mayonnaise, 563.

REDUCTION

Another classic way to thicken sauces and intensify their flavor. Sauce demi-glace and sauce espagnole may be thickened during very slow simmering by the evaporation of liquid. ➤ If you intend to thicken a sauce by reduction, season after you have brought it down to the right consistency, or you may find it unpleasantly salty. Reduce any thick sauce over very low heat to avoid scorching.

BUTTER SWIRLS

While it does not technically thicken sauces, swirled in bit by bit, butter enriches and gives body to sauces. After adding butter, the sauce must be served at once, and it can't be reheated. To finish a sauce with butter, strain, if desired, heat gently, and add cold butter bit by bit, gently stirring the sauce in a circular motion so that the butter makes a visible spiral as it melts. Remove the pan from the heat before the butter is fully melted and continue to stir. About 1 tablespoon butter is generally used to finish 1 cup sauce. Flavored butters, 559–60, can also be used when their flavors are appropriate. Perhaps the most obvious example of a sauce finished with butter is Beurre Blanc, 558.

BEURRE MANIÉ (KNEADED BUTTER)

Beurre manié is something of a panacea for thickening thin sauces at the end of the cooking process. After adding kneaded butter, ➤ do not boil the sauce. Simmer only long enough to dispel the floury taste and thicken the liquid. To make it, work 2 tablespoons softened butter and 2 tablespoons flour together with a fork. Drop pea-sized amounts of it into the hot liquid, whisking constantly until the ingredients are well blended and the sauce thickens. This amount will be sufficient for about 1 cup liquid.

BREAD CRUMBS AND GROUND NUTS

Finely ground bread crumbs and nuts can be used to add texture and thickness to sauces. Pesto, 586, Romesco Sauce, 570, and green and red mole, 553–54, are thickened with ground nuts or seeds; bread crumbs add body to the spicy Mediterranean mayonnaise known as Rouille, 565. Corn tortillas are sometimes used to thicken sauces like Red Mole, 553.

CREAM AND CRÈME FRAÎCHE

Heavy cream can be used as a thickener if it is first simmered to reduce its volume. This can be done directly in the sauce, as in a gravy or pan sauce, or the cream can be reduced separately and then added to the sauce. In either case, ➤ use a deep heavy-bottomed pan so that the cream will not boil over, and let the cream simmer until it is reduced by about half its original volume. Reduced cream can be used in large amounts for white sauces or in small doses to add a satiny finish to almost any other sauce. Crème fraîche can be spooned directly into a simmering sauce to add body, richness, and a subtle tangy flavor. While crème fraîche and sour cream have a similar consistency, crème fraîche will not separate if boiled, whereas sour cream will.

PUREES

Purees of cooked vegetables, fruits, and rice are an excellent way to add body and flavor to a sauce. The puree can be very smooth or slightly chunky. Starchy vegetables, such as potatoes or white beans, will make a sauce quite thick, while other vegetables and fruits, such as roasted pepper or stewed onions, will thicken it only slightly.

XANTHAN GUM

Xanthan gum may be used in very small amounts to thicken sauces, and it has the advantage of neither altering the flavor nor the color of the sauce. Xanthan gum does not need to be hydrated like cornstarch—it can be whisked or blended directly into hot or cold liquid. When using xanthan gum to thicken a sauce, it is important to keep the sauce moving quickly in order to disperse the xanthan gum. This can be done with a whisk, but it is better to use an immersion blender or a blender: Place the sauce in an immersion blender's cup container (or a deep, narrow bowl or glass jar) or a blender. With the blender running, lightly sprinkle in ¼ teaspoon xanthan gum per 2 cups sauce. Blend for about 30 seconds to fully disperse the xanthan gum. It is better to add too little xanthan gum than too much, as this can result in a slimy, gloppy consistency. If the sauce is still too thin after adding a little xanthan gum, add more, ⅛ teaspoon at a time, until thickened to the desired consistency. For more information on xanthan gum, see 992.

SERVING SAUCES

The venerable gravy boat is the traditional way to serve hot sauces tableside, but ramekins and other small heatproof containers will work. Miniature individual pitchers and pots are appropriate when lobster, artichokes, or asparagus is on the menu, allowing guests to dip (and double-dip, if they want) their food in their own personal supply of sauce. Like the food it accompanies, sauce, if it is meant to be served hot, should—you guessed it—be kept hot. Sauces on the buffet table may be kept hot in small saucepans, placed on a heating stand set over a candle, or in chafing dishes. Or prepare a hot water bath by setting a container of sauce in a basin of hot water, refreshing the hot water as needed. Be especially careful with egg-based sauces, as they tend to scorch or separate if placed over too high a heat. Keep in mind that ➤ sauces will not keep indefinitely on a buffet table or in a chafing dish, and no sauce should ever sit out for more than 2 hours.

Sauces that need to be kept cold, such as yogurt- and cream-based sauces and mayonnaise, may be kept chilled in containers placed over or partially submerged in ice.

ABOUT GRAVIES AND PAN SAUCES

Gravies and pan sauces are made from the pan drippings of roasted, pan-fried, or sautéed meat or poultry. While a traditional gravy is thickened with flour, a pan sauce is not. Delectable residues and browned bits from sautéing, roasting, or browning, known as the *fond* (bottom, or base), make up the base of pan sauces to be served with poultry and meat dishes. Note that *fond* is also used to refer to stocks.

Whether you intend to thicken your sauce with flour or not, the first step is to remove the meat or poultry from the pan and **degrease** the pan. There are several ways to do this quickly. One is to pour any juices left in the pan into a heatproof glass container and submerge it in cold water. The fat will rise quickly and can be spooned off. You can also use a **gravy or fat separator.** Another method, if there is more fat than pan juices, is to use a baster: Tip the pan and siphon off the good juices from underneath the top layer of grease.

The second step is to **deglaze** the pan by adding ¼ cup water, wine, or stock and stirring and scraping the browned bits from the pan's bottom and sides (if the pan is on the heat and the liquid evaporates before you can scrape off all the bits, add more). If the pan you are deglazing is a skillet or Dutch oven, you may start this task by leaving a little fat in the pan and adding finely chopped onions or shallots. Cook them over medium heat, stirring, until they sweat. Their liquid, combined with stirring and scraping, will release the tasty bits from the pan. At this point, you may add more wine or stock to the pan, or simply add the defatted pan juices back to the pan. Use stock appropriate to the meat or poultry the sauce will accompany, or wine that will complement any to be served at the table.

If making a pan sauce from meat cooked in a skillet, the sauce may be made in the skillet as well. Roasting pans, on the other hand, are not ideal vessels for preparing a sauce; it's easier to employ your saucepan for the purpose. First, pour any fat or pan juices from the roasting pan and degrease as described above. Deglaze the roasting pan with a flavorful liquid. If using a roux, 542, to thicken your pan sauce into a gravy, prepare it in the saucepan (you may use the fat you have skimmed from the juices to make the roux, if desired), then whisk in the deglazed pan juices and simmer to thicken. If you choose not to make a roux, gravies and pan sauces can be thickened with cream, kneaded butter, or cornstarch, or finished with a butter swirl, 544. To be sure there is enough gravy to go around for a big occasion, you can increase the yield by adding more butter to supplement the fat in the pan, more flour, and additional warm stock to multiply the recipe accordingly.

The liquid from a braise may also be turned into a sort of pan sauce. Remove the meat and any large chunks of vegetables, and skim off as much fat as possible. If desired, strain or puree the sauce to make it perfectly smooth, then return to the heat, bring to a simmer, and reduce until it has thickened, or whisk in kneaded butter, 544, until the sauce reaches the desired thickness.

BASIC PAN GRAVY

About 1 cup

A roux-based gravy suitable for poultry, beef, pork, and milder lamb and venison. If desired, you may strain the drippings first and remove excess fat, then return some of the fat to the pan to make the roux. To use a thickener other than flour, please see About Thickeners for Sauces, 542, for the correct amount to add for the amount of liquid below. This method works best for smaller cuts cooked in a skillet such as steaks, chops, or chicken parts. If the meat has been cooked in a roasting pan, see About Gravies and Pan Sauces, 544, for the easiest way to proceed.

Remove the meat or poultry from the pan, place it on a platter, and keep warm. Pour off all the pan juices, leaving behind or adding:

Fat from the pan drippings or butter to make 2 tablespoons

Place the pan over medium-low heat (melt the butter, if using). Gradually whisk in:

1 to 2 tablespoons all-purpose flour (the larger amount for a thicker sauce)

Cook, whisking constantly, until the roux is smooth and the flour is nutty and fragrant, about 5 minutes. Gradually whisk in:

The degreased pan juices plus enough stock, wine, beer, cream, milk, or water to make 1 cup

Simmer gently until thickened, up to 10 minutes. Season to taste with:

Salt and black pepper
(Minced fresh or crumbled dried herbs, such as thyme, rosemary, or sage)
(Finely grated lemon zest or lemon juice)

Strain the gravy, if desired, and reheat before serving.

QUICK PAN SAUCE OR GRAVY

About 1 cup

This sauce is a simple accompaniment to roast chicken, turkey, or pork loin. Unlike the roux-based gravy above, this can be left unthickened, although the addition of kneaded butter, 544, will give it a gravy-like body without the hassle of making a roux. The amounts given here are for a small chicken. For a **Quick Turkey Gravy** deglaze the roasting pan with **½ cup white wine, sherry, stock, or water,** use **4 cups chicken or turkey stock,** and thicken the mixture with **4 tablespoons softened butter** and **¼ cup flour** mixed together into a paste.

After transferring the meat to a platter, pour into the roasting pan:

¼ cup dry white wine, sherry, port, Madeira, or water

Place the roasting pan on 2 burners over medium-high heat. Bring the juices to a simmer and, using a wooden spoon, scrape up the browned bits in the bottom of the pan. Pour the mixture into a heatproof glass container and let the fat rise to the top, then skim off the fat and discard. (You can also use a gravy separator.) Transfer the mixture to a small saucepan. Add the juices that have accumulated around the meat along with:

¾ cup chicken or turkey stock or broth

Bring to a simmer. If desired, to thicken the sauce into a gravy, mix to a smooth paste:

(1 tablespoon butter, softened)
(1 tablespoon all-purpose flour)

Whisk the paste bit by bit into the simmering sauce and cook until thickened. Season with:

Several drops of lemon juice or vinegar
Salt and black pepper to taste

TURKEY GIBLET GRAVY

About 4 cups

This classic accompaniment to roasted turkey, 428, benefits from a rich, brown giblet stock and a blond roux (for an easier option, see Quick Turkey Gravy, above). This gravy can be prepared as the turkey roasts, or up to 2 days ahead of time, and the pan juices added

when they are ready. Confirm that your turkey comes with giblets, which are typically wrapped in paper or plastic and tucked inside the cavity; if it does not, you will need to buy them separately. Even if your turkey does include giblets, you may need to buy extra if you are increasing this recipe by half or doubling it.
Rinse and pat dry:

1 turkey neck, heart, gizzard, and liver

Chop the neck into 2-inch pieces. Cut the heart lengthwise in half, and divide the gizzard at the lobes. Remove any connective strings and excess fat from the liver and set aside. Heat in a large, wide saucepan over medium heat:

2 tablespoons vegetable oil

Add the turkey parts (except for the liver) to the pan, then scatter around them:

1 small onion, chopped

Cook, without stirring, until the turkey parts are richly browned on the first side, 5 to 10 minutes; reduce the heat slightly if the ingredients begin to burn. Turn and brown the second side in the same manner. Add:

4 cups turkey or chicken stock or broth
½ cup dry white or red wine or additional broth
(¼ cup finely chopped carrots)
(¼ cup finely chopped celery)
(2 sprigs parsley)
1 large bay leaf
2 or 3 sprigs fresh thyme or ½ teaspoon dried thyme
(4 whole cloves or allspice berries or a pinch of ground cloves or allspice)

Partially cover the pan and simmer very slowly until the meat is tender, about 1 hour. Add the reserved liver and simmer until firm, about 5 minutes.

Strain the stock through a fine-mesh sieve and add to measure 4 cups:

Additional stock, broth, or water

Finely chop the neck meat and giblets and add to the stock. Discard the strained vegetables and herbs. Melt in the saucepan over medium heat:

4 tablespoons (½ stick) butter

Gradually whisk in:

⅓ cup all-purpose flour

Cook, stirring constantly, until the mixture has browned slightly and smells nutty, about 10 minutes. Remove the pan from the heat. For an especially silky gravy, transfer the stock to a saucepan and bring it to a furious boil, then pour it all at once into the roux, whisking as you pour. Otherwise, simply whisk the warm stock into the roux, blending thoroughly. Whisking constantly, bring the gravy to a simmer over medium heat and cook for 1 minute. Remove from the heat and cover. If you will be finishing and serving the gravy within 1 hour, let it stand at room temperature; otherwise, let it cool and refrigerate.

When the turkey is done, transfer it to a platter to rest, and begin warming the gravy over low heat. Remove the rack from the roasting pan. If the juices have evaporated, leaving only fat and browned bits on the bottom of the pan, carefully pour out the fat and discard it, retaining all the browned bits. If there are juices left, tilt the pan and skim off as much fat as possible with a spoon (or pour the fat and juices into a cup, let the fat rise to the top, and skim it off). Set the pan on 2 burners over medium heat. Pour in:

1 cup dry white wine, sherry, Madeira, port, or water

Bring to a simmer, scraping the bottom of the pan with a wooden spoon to loosen the browned bits. Pour the drippings into the gravy. Place the gravy over medium heat and simmer, stirring occasionally, for 5 minutes to blend the flavors. Season to taste with:

Salt and black pepper

Pour into a gravy boat and serve immediately.

HERB PAN SAUCE

About ⅔ cup

A bright and lively sauce for beef, lamb, pork, or chicken. This sauce can also be made without pan drippings, in which case, cook the shallots first in oil or butter.
After pan-frying steaks, lamb chops, pork chops, or chicken pieces, transfer them to a platter and keep warm. Pour off most of the excess fat and set the pan over medium heat. Add:

½ cup minced onion or shallot

Cook, stirring, until softened but not browned. Increase the heat to medium-high and add:

⅔ cup dry white or red wine, hard cider, or chicken stock or broth

Stir with a wooden spoon to loosen and dissolve any browned bits, then bring to a boil and add:

1 tablespoon lemon juice, white wine vinegar, or Cognac, or to taste
(4 teaspoons Dijon mustard)
(1 bay leaf)
Salt and black pepper to taste

Cook, stirring occasionally, until slightly reduced and thickened, 1 to 2 minutes. If desired, add and cook until reduced by about half, 1 to 2 minutes:

(½ cup heavy cream)

Take off the heat and swirl in bit by bit:

1½ teaspoons butter

Remove the bay leaf, if used, or, for a perfectly smooth sauce, strain it through a fine-mesh sieve. Stir in:

2 tablespoons minced herbs such as parsley, tarragon, thyme, or a combination

Spoon the sauce over the meat and garnish with:

Minced fresh herbs

SWEET-SOUR ORANGE PAN SAUCE

About 1½ cups

This sauce is particularly nice with game birds. To turn this into a true **Bigarade Sauce** for duck or goose, use the zest and juice from a Seville (bitter) orange and omit the lemon juice.
With a fork, mash together in a small bowl until combined:

2 tablespoons unsalted butter, softened
2 tablespoons all-purpose flour

Set aside. Using a vegetable peeler, remove strips of zest from:

1 navel orange

Cut the zest into slivers about 1/8 inch wide and 1 inch long. Place the zest in a small saucepan, add 4 cups cold water, and bring to a boil over high heat; cook 1 minute. Drain the zest in a sieve, rinse with cold water, and pat dry.

Transfer the roasted bird(s) to a platter and keep warm. Pour off the fat from the roasting pan. Pour into the pan:

1 cup game or chicken stock or broth

Set the pan over medium heat (on 2 burners if necessary) and bring to a simmer, scraping the pan bottom with a wooden spoon to dissolve the browned bits. Remove the pan from the heat and set aside. Combine in a small heavy saucepan and cook over medium heat, stirring, until a light brown, caramel color:

2 tablespoons white wine vinegar
2 tablespoons sugar

Add the contents of the roasting pan and simmer for 5 minutes. Whisk in the orange zest along with:

½ cup strained orange juice
2 tablespoons orange liqueur
1 tablespoon lemon juice
Salt and black pepper to taste

Bring to a simmer, stir the softened butter and flour mixture into the sauce, and simmer for 1 minute or until thickened. Spoon the sauce over the bird(s) and garnish with:

Orange sections

WINE AND SOUR CHERRY PAN SAUCE

About ⅔ cup

After pan-frying steak, venison steaks, or pork chops, transfer them to a platter and keep warm.

Pour off all but 1 tablespoon fat from the skillet and set it over medium heat. Add and cook, stirring, until just starting to soften and brown:

⅓ cup minced onions or shallots

Meanwhile, combine and set aside:

½ cup chicken stock or broth or water
⅓ cup dried tart cherries

Add to the onions:

¼ cup dry red or white wine

Bring to a boil, stirring with a wooden spoon to loosen and dissolve any browned bits, and cook for 1 minute. Add the stock and dried cherries along with:

One 2-inch-long strip lemon zest, removed with a vegetable peeler
1 teaspoon light brown sugar
(½ teaspoon balsamic vinegar)
½ teaspoon fresh thyme leaves

Bring to a boil over high heat and cook, stirring often, until reduced by half and thickened, about 2 minutes. Remove the zest. Stir in any accumulated juices from the meat. Season with:

Salt and black pepper to taste
(A few drops of lemon juice)

If desired, for a velvety texture, swirl in bit by bit:

(1 tablespoon butter)

Arrange the meat on plates and spoon over the sauce.

SAUSAGE GRAVY

About 2½ cups

Known in the South by the names **sawmill gravy, white gravy,** and **cream gravy,** this fortifying mixture, served atop freshly baked biscuits, 634–37, has fueled many a hard day's work. For a spicier result, use **8 ounces Fresh Chorizo Sausage, 511, diced andouille sausage, or tasso ham.**

Brown in a large skillet, breaking up the meat with a spatula or spoon:

8 ounces store-bought bulk sausage or Country Sausage, 510

Using a slotted spoon, transfer to paper towels to drain. Pour off all but 2 tablespoons drippings from the skillet. If necessary, add enough:

Butter

to make 2 tablespoons. Stir into the drippings and whisk until the roux is smooth:

2 tablespoons all-purpose flour

Whisking constantly, add and cook until thickened, about 5 minutes:

2 cups milk

Season with:

½ teaspoon salt
½ teaspoon black pepper, or to taste
2 dashes hot pepper sauce

Fold the reserved sausage into the sauce.

MUSHROOM GRAVY

About 1½ cups

This vegetarian gravy is the perfect substitute for sausage gravy on warm buttermilk biscuits.

Heat in a small saucepan over medium heat:

2 tablespoons olive oil or butter

Add and cook until softened, about 4 minutes:

1 shallot, minced

Add and cook, stirring, until they start to brown, about 4 minutes:

4 ounces shiitake or cremini mushrooms or a combination, chopped

Stir in and cook, stirring, for 1 minute:

3 tablespoons all-purpose flour

Slowly whisk in:

1 cup vegetable stock
½ cup half-and-half, milk, or unsweetened almond or soy milk
(1 tablespoon ground dried mushrooms such as porcini or shiitake)

Increase the heat to medium-high, bring to a simmer, and cook, stirring, until the gravy thickens, about 5 minutes. Season to taste with:

Salt and black pepper

ABOUT FRENCH MOTHER SAUCES

Most classic French sauces are based on "mother sauces," or *fonds de cuisine* (foundations of cooking). First codified by chef Marie-Antoine Carême in the eighteenth century, then updated by chef Auguste Escoffier in the nineteenth century, the mother sauces were the foundations for dozens of derivative sauces. The idea was that one could prepare a large batch of *sauce béchamel* or *sauce velouté* and have at one's fingertips a dozen different sauces that could be built on that base. Even though, to our modern eyes, many of these sauces appear fussy and outdated, they were actually a simplification of much more expensive and time-consuming sauces from the days when noble houses had a battalion of cooks to labor over complex preparations.

These mother sauces were not originally intended for home cooks, but mastering them is easy enough, and will enable you to prepare a large number of sauces. While they are not as important in modern cooking culture as they once were, we appreciate them and the extraordinary tradition of French cooking they represent. More important, they are reliably delicious when prepared well.

Below, find roux-based mother sauces and a handful of their variations; for other classic foundational sauces, see About Hollandaise and Béarnaise, 561, and About Tomato Sauce, 556.

ABOUT WHITE SAUCES

White sauces are comprised of a lightly cooked roux (or blond roux, 542) to which milk or a light stock is added and simmered until thick. *Béchamel*, which uses milk, is useful not only for adding richness to foods like vegetables and chicken, but also serves as a base for many other sauces and dishes such as Macaroni and Cheese, 296, Chicken Pot Pie, 704, Lasagne Bolognese, 310, and Moussaka, 239. *Sauce velouté* is made with a light stock (which often matches what you intend to serve the sauce with) and thickened with a blond roux. The resulting sauce is more ivory colored than a béchamel and slightly translucent. White sauce and velouté can be refrigerated for up to 3 days or kept warm in the top of a double boiler for up to 1 hour. Place a piece of wax paper or plastic wrap directly on the surface of the sauce to prevent a skin from forming.

WHITE SAUCE OR BÉCHAMEL

About 1 cup

I. To add flavor to this delicate sauce, you may infuse the milk first: Bring it to a boil in a medium saucepan over medium heat with **1 bay leaf** and **1 thick onion slice stuck with 2 whole cloves.** Immediately take off the heat, cover, and let stand for 15 minutes. Fish out the onion and bay leaf and proceed as directed.

Melt in a medium saucepan over medium-low heat:

2 tablespoons butter

Whisk in until well blended and smooth, about 1½ minutes:

2 tablespoons all-purpose flour

Remove the pan from the heat and slowly whisk in:

1 cup milk

Return the pan to the heat and bring to a simmer, whisking constantly to prevent lumps. Continue to cook, whisking, until the sauce is smooth and hot and has thickened, 1 to 2 minutes. If you are using this sauce as is, season to taste with:

Salt and black or white pepper
Grated or ground nutmeg

II. THICK BÉCHAMEL

Prepare **White Sauce I, above,** using **3 tablespoons butter, 3 tablespoons all-purpose flour,** and **1 cup milk.**

ADDITIONS TO WHITE SAUCE

Whisk into **White Sauce I or II, above,** one of the following:

Up to 3 tablespoons drained prepared horseradish
2 tablespoons Shrimp or Lobster Butter, 560
1 tablespoon Dijon mustard
1 to 2 tablespoons minced herbs, such as chives, parsley, tarragon, or thyme
3 to 5 anchovy fillets, minced, or 1 to 2 teaspoons anchovy paste
2 teaspoons curry powder or sweet paprika
1 teaspoon lemon juice
1 teaspoon sherry
½ teaspoon Worcestershire sauce

VEGAN WHITE SAUCE OR BÉCHAMEL

About 1 cup

I. Prepare **White Sauce I, above,** using **2 tablespoons olive or vegetable oil or vegan butter,** and substituting **1 cup unsweetened soy milk** for the milk.

II. VEGAN AND GLUTEN-FREE

Pureeing rice with stock produces the look and feel of heavy cream. Add seasonings and herbs to serve with pasta or vegetables, or use as an ingredient in casseroles and soups.

Heat in a medium saucepan over medium heat:

1 tablespoon olive oil

Add and cook, stirring, until softened:

¼ cup minced onions

Add and cook, stirring constantly, for 2 minutes:

3 tablespoons white rice, preferably medium- or short-grain

Add:

½ cup dry white wine
⅓ cup vegetable stock

Bring to a simmer, then cover, reduce the heat, and simmer gently until the liquid is almost absorbed and the rice is very soft, about 35 minutes. Let cool slightly, then transfer to a blender or food processor and puree until smooth. With the machine running, add until the desired consistency is reached:

Up to ¾ cup more vegetable stock

Season with:

1½ teaspoons lemon juice
Salt and black pepper to taste
(Minced herbs such as thyme or tarragon)

SAUCE MORNAY (CHEESE SAUCE)

About 1 cup

Desperate parents have been hiding nutritious vegetables under a cloak of Mornay for decades, and it is the backbone of a good Macaroni and Cheese, 296. It can be spread over everything from cauliflower to lobster, then browned in the oven or under a broiler.

Using equal parts Gruyère and Parmesan is traditional, but practically any aged cheese, alone or in combination, can be very good. Try Swiss or Cheddar, or mix milder cheeses with sharper pungent ones like Gorgonzola, Roquefort, and Stilton. For a richer, cheesier sauce for broccoli or baked potatoes, use the larger amount of cheese listed below.

Prepare:

White Sauce I, 548

When it is smooth and hot, reduce the heat to low and stir in:

¼ to 1 cup firmly packed finely grated cheese (1 to 4 ounces)

Cook, stirring, just until the cheese is melted, or the cheese may turn stringy. Season with:

Salt to taste
Pinch of cayenne pepper or hot paprika
Pinch of grated or ground nutmeg or mace

Should the sauce become stringy, bring it just to a simmer and whisk in:

(A few drops of dry white wine or lemon juice)

then remove from the heat.

SAUCE SOUBISE (ONION SAUCE)

About ¾ cup

For fish, veal, sweetbreads, lamb, or main-course vegetables.

Combine in a medium heavy saucepan over medium-low heat:

1 large onion, chopped
2 tablespoons butter

Cover and cook, stirring occasionally, until the onions are tender but not browned, about 25 minutes. Stir in:

2 tablespoons all-purpose flour

Cook, stirring, until smooth, about 1½ minutes. Whisk in:

1 cup milk

Bring to a simmer and cook, stirring frequently, until thick, 1 to 2 minutes. Strain through a medium-mesh sieve into a small saucepan. The sauce will be thick. Set over low heat and slowly whisk in until the desired consistency is reached:

2 to 4 tablespoons heavy cream or milk

Season with:

Salt and white pepper to taste
Pinch of grated or ground nutmeg

SAUCE VELOUTÉ

About 1¾ cups

For a more flavorful velouté, start with up to twice as much stock as is called for below and reduce it to the specified volume before whisking into the roux. If serving this sauce with fish or shellfish you may substitute **3 tablespoons Shrimp or Lobster Butter, 560,** for the butter in the roux.

Heat in a small saucepan over medium heat, stirring occasionally, until hot:

2½ cups veal stock, or chicken, fish, or vegetable stock

Meanwhile, melt in a medium saucepan over medium-low heat:

3 tablespoons butter

Stir in:

3 tablespoons all-purpose flour

Reduce the heat to low and cook, stirring constantly, until the roux smells nutty and is ivory colored, about 6 minutes. Remove from the heat and let cool for 2 minutes. Gradually whisk the warm stock into the roux. Return the saucepan to the heat and bring the sauce slowly to a simmer, whisking to prevent lumps. Cook over medium-low heat, stirring often and skimming any skin that forms on the surface, until thick enough to coat the back of a spoon, about 20 minutes; do not boil.

If desired, strain through a fine-mesh sieve and, just before serving, whisk in:

(1 to 2 tablespoons butter or any flavored butter, 559–60, softened)

If you are using this sauce as is, season to taste with:

(Salt and white pepper)

SAUCE SUPRÊME (ENRICHED VELOUTÉ)

About 2½ cups

Best with chicken, fish, or vegetables.

Prepare:

Sauce Velouté, above

and with the following additions: If desired, lightly sauté in the butter before adding the flour:

(½ cup minced mushrooms)

Add to the saucepan along with the stock:

¾ cup heavy cream

Just before adjusting the seasoning and serving, whisk in:

2 tablespoons heavy cream or crème fraîche
(2 tablespoons butter, softened)
(Lemon juice, to taste)

WHITE WINE SAUCE

About 1¼ cups

Few of us may have to worry about what to do with leftover Champagne, but should that dilemma ever be yours, you may use it here instead of white wine.

Prepare, but do not season:

½ recipe Sauce Velouté, above

using Fumet, 77, to replace the stock, if desired, if serving with fish.

Have ready:

1 stick (4 ounces) butter, cut into 6 pieces

Combine in a medium saucepan and boil until reduced almost to a glaze:

1 cup dry white wine or Champagne
¼ cup minced shallots

Remove the wine mixture from the heat and, stirring with a wooden spoon, add the butter piece by piece so that it softens but does not liquefy and the sauce retains a creamy texture. Add:

1½ teaspoons chopped tarragon

Meanwhile, heat the velouté sauce until hot but not boiling. Whisk in the butter mixture. Season to taste with:

Salt and white pepper

Serve at once.

SAUCE RAVIGOTE

About 1 cup

Serve lukewarm over fish, light meats, or poultry.

Combine in a small saucepan:

2 shallots, very finely chopped
1 tablespoon tarragon vinegar

Bring to a boil and cook, stirring constantly, until the vinegar has almost evaporated, about 1 minute. Add:

1 cup Sauce Velouté, 549

Simmer gently for about 10 minutes, stirring frequently. Season to taste with:

Salt and black pepper

Cool the sauce to lukewarm, then add:

1½ tablespoons chopped parsley
1 tablespoon chopped drained capers
2 teaspoons minced chives
½ teaspoon chopped tarragon

SAUCE ALLEMANDE (EGG-THICKENED VELOUTÉ)

About 1½ cups

An enriched velouté to be used with poached chicken or vegetables. It becomes **Poulette Sauce** if, as a final step, you add finely chopped parsley. When serving with fish or lamb, we like to stir in a generous tablespoon of chopped drained capers. ➤ Do not let the sauce boil after the egg is added or it will curdle.

Prepare:

Sauce Velouté, 549, with chicken stock

Remove the velouté from the heat and stir in:

1 large egg yolk, beaten with 2 tablespoons heavy cream

Return the sauce to low heat and cook until slightly thickened. Just before serving, stir in:

1 tablespoon lemon juice
1 tablespoon butter
Salt and black pepper to taste
Pinch of grated or ground nutmeg

ABOUT BROWN SAUCES

Sauce espagnole, along with *sauce demi-glace*, are the fundamental starting points for seemingly endless variation. Their color and deep, savory character come from the use of a dark, nutty roux, flavorful brown stocks, and reduction. Though brown sauces are more time-consuming than others, their flavor and texture are well worth the effort. For the most complex and compelling sauces, different liquids (wine, stock, or juice, for example) and savory ingredients (onions, chopped ham, and herbs, to name a few) are added at intervals and allowed to cook down and concentrate before the next is added, creating layers of flavor.

The best brown sauces begin with high-quality brown stock, preferably homemade. If you find the flavor of either your stock or sauce a bit pale, add a spoonful or two of meat glaze, store-bought or homemade, 76, to the sauce as it simmers. The wines used in these sauces should be of good quality, especially any that are added close to the end of cooking. Do not attempt to produce brown sauces that are as thick as béchamels or veloutés; they will only be sticky and unappealing. Stop cooking when the sauce has reached the consistency of heavy cream. A swirl of butter at the end will add a sheen to these sauces while enriching their flavor. Herbs, spices, and mushrooms are frequent additions to any brown sauce. Brown sauces can be refrigerated for 4 to 5 days or frozen for 3 months.

SAUCE ESPAGNOLE (BROWN SAUCE)

About 5 cups

To increase the usefulness of this time-consuming sauce, prepare it and freeze in cubes (see Keeping Sauces, 542) or 1-cup amounts, then reheat and use as is or as a base for any of the brown sauce variations that follow.

Heat in a large heavy saucepan or Dutch oven:

1 stick (4 ounces) butter or ½ cup beef or veal drippings or bacon fat

Add and cook, stirring, until beginning to brown:

½ cup finely chopped onions
¼ cup finely chopped carrots
¼ cup finely chopped celery

Add and cook, stirring until the flour is thoroughly browned:

½ cup all-purpose flour

Stir in:

10 black peppercorns
2 cups drained and finely chopped canned whole tomatoes or 2 cups tomato puree
½ cup coarsely chopped parsley

Add:

8 cups Brown Beef Stock, 75

Increase the heat to high and bring to a boil, then reduce the heat and simmer until reduced by half, 2 to 2½ hours. Stir occasionally and skim off the fat as it rises to the top. The sauce should be the consistency of heavy cream, and no thicker.

Strain the sauce through a fine-mesh sieve into a bowl. Stir occasionally as the sauce cools to prevent the formation of a skin. If necessary, thin with additional stock or water. If you are using this sauce as is, season to taste with:

(Salt and black pepper)

QUICK BROWN SAUCE

About 3¼ cups

Prepared in about 30 minutes, this sauce makes the wonders of brown sauce much more accessible. If made with mushroom stock, it is vegetarian.

Melt in a large wide saucepan over medium-high heat:

4 tablespoons (½ stick) butter

Add and cook, stirring, until well browned, about 10 minutes:

2 large onions, finely chopped

Reduce the heat to medium and add:

2 tablespoons sugar
(2 tablespoons tomato paste)

Cook, stirring, until the sugar and tomato paste, if using, are deeply browned (do not burn them). Carefully whisk in:

½ cup dry red or white wine

Bring to a boil and boil until reduced by half, 2 to 3 minutes. Whisk in:

6½ cups Brown Beef Stock, 75, Brown Poultry Stock, 76, or Mushroom Stock I, 79
¼ cup porcini mushroom powder or 1 ounce dried porcini mushrooms, finely ground
½ teaspoon dried thyme

Bring to a rolling boil over high heat and boil for 4 minutes. Strain through a fine-mesh sieve into a heatproof bowl and set aside. Melt in the same saucepan over medium heat:

3 tablespoons butter

Whisk in and cook, stirring, until the roux is walnut brown, 5 to 8 minutes:

¼ cup all-purpose flour

Whisk in the strained stock along with:

2 tablespoons port
¼ teaspoon black pepper

Bring to a boil, whisking, and simmer briskly until it is the consistency of heavy cream, 15 to 20 minutes. Strain again, if desired, and if using as is, blend in:

(Salt to taste)
(1 tablespoon butter)

SAUCE DEMI-GLACE

About 4½ cups

A brown sauce made thicker and more flavorful by additional stock and reduction, 542. Serve with filet mignon or game or use as a base for other sauces.

Combine in a large heavy saucepan or Dutch oven over medium heat:

4 cups Sauce Espagnole, 550
4 cups Brown Beef Stock, 75, or Brown Poultry Stock, 76
½ cup chopped mushrooms

Bring to a simmer, then reduce the heat slightly and simmer gently, uncovered, skimming often to remove fat and scum, until reduced by half, 2 to 2½ hours.

Strain through a fine-mesh sieve into a clean saucepan. Stir in over very low heat:

½ cup dry port, Madeira, or dry sherry
Salt and black pepper to taste

If desired, just before serving, whisk in, small pieces at a time:

(2 to 4 tablespoons unsalted butter, softened)

SAUCE MADEIRA

About 1¼ cups

A wonderful accompaniment to game or beef filet. Dry sherry or port may be substituted for the Madeira. For **Sauce Périgueux,** stir in **1 tablespoon minced black truffles** before adding the butter.

Bring to a simmer in a medium saucepan:

1 cup Sauce Espagnole, 550, Quick Brown Sauce, 550, or Sauce Demi-Glace, above
¼ cup Madeira
(1 teaspoon Meat Glaze, 76)

Simmer until reduced to 1 cup. Add:

¼ cup Madeira
Salt and black pepper to taste

Swirl in bit by bit, if desired:

(1 tablespoon butter)

SAUCE LYONNAISE (BROWN ONION SAUCE)

About 1½ cups

A good choice for hearty meats. For **Sauce Piquant,** stir in with the herbs **1 tablespoon chopped drained capers** and **1 tablespoon chopped cornichons, or other sour pickles.**

Melt in a medium saucepan over medium heat:

1 tablespoon butter

Add and cook, stirring, until golden brown:

¼ cup finely chopped onions

Add and simmer until reduced by two-thirds:

½ cup dry white wine
2 tablespoons white wine vinegar
2 sprigs thyme

Add and simmer for 15 minutes:

1 cup Sauce Espagnole, 550, Quick Brown Sauce, 550, or Sauce Demi-Glace, above

Just before serving, add:

1 tablespoon finely chopped parsley, or a combination of parsley and tarragon or chervil
Salt and black pepper to taste

SAUCE CHASSEUR (HUNTER'S SAUCE)

About 2 cups

Traditionally served with game, this sauce is also delectable with roasted meats or poultry, steaks, or chops.

Melt in a medium heavy saucepan over medium heat:

2 tablespoons butter

Add and cook, stirring, until softened:

2 tablespoons minced shallots

Add and cook, stirring, until lightly browned, about 5 minutes:

1 cup sliced mushrooms

Add and simmer until reduced by half:

⅓ cup dry white wine
(2 tablespoons brandy)

Add and simmer for 5 minutes:

1 cup Sauce Espagnole, 550, Quick Brown Sauce, 550, or Sauce Demi-Glace, above
(½ cup tomato puree)
Salt and black pepper to taste

Just before serving, stir in:

1 tablespoon minced parsley
(1 tablespoon minced chervil or tarragon)

Swirl in bit by bit, if desired:

(2 tablespoons butter)

SAUCE MARCHAND DE VIN (RED WINE SAUCE)

About 1 cup

Serve with steak, sweetbreads, chops, or game. For **Sauce Bordelaise,** omit the butter and swirl in **¼ cup diced prepared beef marrow, 520,** just before serving.

Combine in a small heavy saucepan over medium-high heat:

1 cup dry red wine
¼ cup sherry vinegar or red wine vinegar
1 shallot, minced
1 sprig thyme
1 sprig parsley
½ bay leaf
4 black peppercorns

Bring to a simmer and cook until reduced by three-quarters. Strain through a fine-mesh sieve into a medium saucepan. Place over medium heat and stir in:

1 cup Sauce Espagnole, 550, Quick Brown Sauce, 550, or Sauce Demi-Glace, 551

Simmer for 15 minutes. Just before serving, stir in:

2 teaspoons minced parsley
Salt and black pepper to taste

ABOUT COOKED SAUCES

Though drippings and cooked flour are fantastic bases for a sauce, they are hardly necessary. Here are a handful of sauces made without pan drippings or roux that do not fall neatly into other categories. Most begin with sautéing shallots or onions, then proceed as for standard pan sauces. Layers of flavor come from successive additions of aromatic ingredients and liquids such as wine, stock, or juice. Unlike the roux-based mother sauces above, these simpler formulas are thickened by simmering until reduced, or made with pureed nuts, fruits, or vegetables. Others may be thickened with cornstarch, a last-minute swirl of butter, or cheese.

BASIC CREAM SAUCE

About 1 cup

A simpler alternative to Béchamel, 548. This rich sauce is especially delicious with sautéed wild mushrooms or pasta.

Combine in a medium saucepan:

2 cups heavy cream
2 tablespoons chopped thyme or rosemary
(2 tablespoons lightly crushed juniper berries)

Bring to a rolling boil, stirring occasionally with a whisk only to prevent boiling over. Reduce the heat slightly and reduce by half. Strain through a fine-mesh sieve. Season to taste with:

Salt

AVGOLEMONO (GREEK LEMON-EGG SAUCE)

About 2¼ cups

This Greek sauce is good with lamb or green vegetables. For other hot egg sauces, see Sauce Allemande, 550, and About Hollandaise and Béarnaise, 561.

Bring to a simmer in a small saucepan and keep warm:

1 cup vegetable or chicken stock or broth

Beat in a medium bowl until thickened:

3 large eggs

Beat in:

¼ cup lemon juice

Beat half of the hot stock into the egg mixture, then whisk this mixture back into the remaining stock. Cook, stirring constantly, over medium-low or low heat until the sauce is thick and creamy and coats the back of the spoon; do not let the sauce boil, or it will curdle. Remove from the heat and season to taste with:

Salt and black pepper

Serve immediately.

STIR-FRY SAUCE

About ¼ cup

For about 1 pound of vegetables. Delicious mixed with chicken or tofu and vegetables and served over rice.

Blend until smooth in a small bowl:

2 teaspoons cornstarch
2 tablespoons cold water

Add:

4 teaspoons soy sauce
1½ teaspoons rice vinegar
1 teaspoon brown sugar
¼ teaspoon salt
(2 teaspoons finely grated peeled ginger)

Pour over the cooked vegetables in the pan. Stir well until the whole mixture comes just to a boil and the sauce thickens, then take it off the heat at once.

WINE PLUM SAUCE

About 1 cup

A deeply flavored sauce for roast chicken, duck, or goose.

Combine in a medium saucepan and bring to a boil over medium-high heat:

8 ounces red or purple plums, pitted and sliced
1 cup dry red wine

Boil until reduced to a syrup, about 15 minutes. Let cool for 10 minutes, then pass through a food mill or puree in a blender or food processor and strain through a fine-mesh sieve. Return the puree to the pan and stir in:

¼ cup honey
¼ cup chicken or vegetable stock or broth
1 tablespoon soy sauce

Simmer until thickened, about 10 minutes. Season to taste with:

Salt and black pepper

FIG AND RED WINE SAUCE

About 2 cups

This sauce can be made a week ahead. If possible, use large dried Calimyrna figs rather than the smaller, darker Mission figs. This sauce is perfect for Pan-Seared Duck Breasts, 432.

Combine in a medium saucepan:

2 cups fruity dry red wine, such as zinfandel
¼ cup duck or chicken stock or broth or water
2 tablespoons sugar
½ teaspoon dried thyme
One 2-inch-long strip lemon zest, removed with a vegetable peeler
1 large garlic clove, minced
1 bay leaf
Pinch of ground cloves or allspice

Bring to a boil over high heat, stirring occasionally. Add:

16 dried figs, stems removed

Return to a boil. Reduce the heat, cover, and simmer gently until the figs are very soft but still retain their shape, about 45 minutes. If the liquid reduces to less than 1 cup before the figs are soft, add a little water.

Remove from the heat and discard the lemon zest and bay leaf. Puree 3 of the figs with ½ cup of the liquid in a food processor or blender until very smooth. Stir the puree back into the figs. If needed, thin the sauce with:

(Additional wine, stock, or water)

Or, if the sauce is a little thin, boil and reduce it until syrupy.

QUICK ORANGE SAUCE FOR DUCK

About ½ cup

Combine in a small saucepan:

½ cup orange marmalade
2 tablespoons soy sauce
2 tablespoons orange liqueur or orange juice
1 tablespoon white wine vinegar

Bring to a boil over medium heat and cook just until the sauce is the consistency of light syrup. If it becomes too thick, dilute it with stock or water. Season to taste with:

Salt and black pepper

SAUCE MEURETTE (BURGUNDIAN RED WINE SAUCE)

About 1½ cups

A much quicker alternative to time-consuming brown sauces. This deeply flavored, magenta-colored sauce is silky and rich. Serve with beef, roasted poultry, or Poached Eggs, 153.

Melt in a large, wide saucepan over medium heat:

4 tablespoons (½ stick) butter

Add and cook, stirring occasionally, until the vegetables soften, about 10 minutes:

1 cup chopped carrot
1 cup chopped celery
1 cup chopped onion
4 garlic cloves, smashed
½ cup chopped ham or pancetta

Add, bring to a simmer, and cook for 30 minutes:

4 cups dry red wine or 2 cups red wine and 2 cups Brown Beef Stock, 75
1 bay leaf
2 sprigs thyme
2 sprigs parsley

Strain, discard the solids, and return the liquid to the saucepan. Boil until reduced to 1 cup, about 15 minutes. While the sauce reduces, mash together with a fork until the mixture forms a paste:

1 tablespoon butter, softened
1 tablespoon all-purpose flour

Whisk the butter-flour mixture into the sauce at the last second, simmer briefly until thickened, and remove from the heat. If desired, stir into the sauce:

(1 cup Sautéed Mushrooms, 251)

Season with:

Salt and black pepper to taste
(A dash of red wine vinegar)
(A dash of brandy)

MOLE POBLANO (RED MOLE)

About 5 cups

Mole comes from *molli*, the Nahuatl word for "sauce." Many used to think the word was derived from the Spanish verb *moler*, or "to grind." Both, however, are accurate: Moles are as variable as the word "sauce" suggests, and are made from ground or pureed chiles, vegetables, spices, nuts, and, occasionally, chocolate. Serve this red mole with chicken, turkey, or pork. Leftover sauce can be frozen, but to regain the smooth texture, you may need to puree it in a blender before reheating it.

Heat in a medium heavy skillet or griddle (preferably cast iron), over medium heat:

8 large unpeeled garlic cloves

Roast, turning occasionally, until soft and charred on all sides, about 15 minutes. Let cool, then peel. Meanwhile, remove the stems and seeds from:

8 medium dried ancho chiles (4 ounces), or a combination of dried ancho, mulato, pasilla, and chipotle seco chiles

Tear the chiles into flat pieces. Lightly toast the chiles in the hot skillet, pressing them flat with a metal spatula, for about 10 seconds on each side (you may also toast them in the oven, 969). Transfer to a bowl, add hot water to cover, and submerge them with a plate. Let soak for 30 minutes. Drain the chiles and place in a blender along with the garlic. Add:

⅔ cup chicken stock or broth
1½ teaspoons dried oregano
½ teaspoon black pepper
⅛ teaspoon ground cloves

Blend the mixture until smooth, then press it through a medium-mesh sieve into a bowl and set aside. Heat in a Dutch oven over medium heat until hot:

1½ tablespoons vegetable oil

Add and cook, stirring constantly, until lightly toasted, about 3 minutes:

½ cup almonds

With a slotted spoon, transfer the almonds to the blender. Add to the hot oil remaining in the pot:

1 small onion, thinly sliced

Cook, stirring occasionally, until nicely browned, about 8 minutes. With the slotted spoon, transfer the onion to the blender. Add to the hot pot:

¼ cup raisins

Cook, stirring constantly, until puffed, about 30 seconds. Scoop the raisins into the blender. Add to the blender:

2 slices white bread or 2 corn tortillas, toasted until charred and torn into pieces
1 cup chicken stock or broth
½ cup drained canned whole tomatoes, chopped

¼ cup chopped unsweetened chocolate or 2 tablespoons unsweetened cocoa powder
¼ teaspoon ground cinnamon

Blend until very smooth. Heat in the Dutch oven over medium heat until hot:

1 tablespoon vegetable oil

Add the reserved ancho mixture and cook, stirring, until it darkens and becomes very thick, about 5 minutes. Stir in the almond mixture and cook until very thick, about 5 minutes. Stir in:

4 cups chicken stock or broth

Bring to a boil, then reduce the heat to low, partially cover, and simmer, stirring often, for 45 minutes. Season with:

Salt to taste
1 tablespoon sugar, or to taste

GREEN MOLE

About 2 cups

This rich, buttery Guanajuato-style mole gets much of its flavor from toasted sesame and pumpkin seeds. It is delicious served with a wide variety of meats and vegetables, and we love to reheat shredded leftover chicken or pork directly in the simmering mole. Or, toss meat to be used in tamales, 324–25, in the mole to flavor it.

Heat in a medium skillet over medium heat:

¾ cup pumpkin seeds

Toast, stirring frequently, until browned and fragrant, about 4 minutes. Transfer to a bowl. Place the skillet back on the heat and add:

½ cup sesame seeds

Toast, stirring frequently, until lightly browned, about 5 minutes. Transfer to the bowl with the pumpkin seeds. Place in a blender:

½ pound tomatillos, husked and rinsed
6 green onions or ½ medium onion, chopped
1 small bunch cilantro, chopped (about 1 cup packed)
6 romaine lettuce leaves, chopped
2 serrano peppers, seeded
2 garlic cloves, peeled
1 teaspoon salt

Add the pumpkin and sesame seeds and blend until completely smooth, adding a little water if necessary to blend. The mixture will be very thick. At this point, the mole can be kept refrigerated for up to 5 days or used immediately. Transfer the mole to a medium saucepan and whisk in:

1 cup chicken stock or water

If the sauce is very thick, add more chicken stock or water to reach the desired consistency. Bring to a simmer. Serve with:

Braised Pulled Pork, 495, Braised Carnitas, 495, Roast Chicken, 407, or Poached Chicken, 419

NEW MEXICO–STYLE CHILE SAUCE

Whether made with fresh or dried chiles, this sauce is perfect on top of enchiladas, 539, and Huevos Rancheros, 156, or diluted with water or stock and used as a braising liquid for cubes of pork shoulder. Although it is not traditional, we sometimes substitute a can of Mexican lager for some of the water or stock.

I. DRIED CHILES

About 2 cups

If desired, you may use **2½ ounces dried whole New Mexico chiles** instead of chile powder. Remove their stems and seeds, toast them, 262, break them into pieces, and add with the liquid. Simmer for 15 minutes as directed below, then puree in a blender until completely smooth (note that if using dried chiles, the sauce won't thicken to a gravy-like consistency until after pureeing).

Heat in a large skillet over medium heat:

2 tablespoons vegetable oil, bacon fat, or lard

Add and cook, stirring, until softened, about 5 minutes:

1 medium onion, finely chopped

Add and cook 1 minute more:

2 garlic cloves, minced

Stir in and cook for 1 minute:

½ cup red or green New Mexico chile powder

Stir in:

3 cups water, beef stock, or chicken stock
½ teaspoon salt
½ teaspoon dried oregano

Bring to a simmer, then reduce the heat to maintain a slow bubble. Cook, stirring frequently, until thickened to a gravy-like consistency, about 15 minutes. Season to taste with:

Salt

II. FRESH GREEN CHILES

About 3 cups

One of our favorites for Huevos Rancheros, 156.

Have ready:

1½ pounds Hatch, NuMex, or Anaheim green chiles, roasted, 262, or 1½ cups canned or jarred green chiles, drained

Peel, seed, and chop the roasted chiles. Prepare **version I, above,** through sautéing the onion and garlic. Stir in:

2 tablespoons all-purpose flour or 3 tablespoons masa harina

Add the roasted chiles instead of the chile powder. Add only 2 cups water or stock, and season as directed. Increase the heat to medium-high and simmer until thickened, about 5 minutes.

ROASTED RED PEPPER SAUCE

About 1¾ cups

Serve this deeply flavored sauce with roasted or grilled meats, chicken, fish, or pasta.

Heat in a large heavy skillet over medium heat:

2 tablespoons olive oil

Add and cook, stirring often, until lightly browned, 5 to 7 minutes:

1 medium onion, chopped

Stir in and cook, stirring, for 1 minute:

1½ pounds red bell peppers, roasted, 262, peeled, seeded, and coarsely chopped, or 2 cups jarred roasted red peppers, drained and chopped
2 garlic cloves, minced
1 tablespoon sweet paprika
¼ teaspoon ground cinnamon
⅛ to ¼ teaspoon cayenne pepper, to taste

Add:

1½ cups vegetable stock or broth
1 cup water

Bring to a boil, then reduce the heat to medium-low, partially cover, and simmer for 20 minutes. Puree the sauce in a blender or food processor. Season to taste with:

Salt and black pepper

ROASTED TOMATILLO SPINACH SAUCE

About 5 cups

Perfect for Enchiladas Verdes, 540. You can use this technique with almost any vegetable to create a range of vibrant sauces: Simply roast the vegetables until they are soft and beginning to caramelize and then puree the hot vegetables in a blender or food processor along with all their cooking juices, a bit of stock, and seasonings to match.

Preheat the oven to 400°F.

Spread in a single layer in an oiled baking pan:

2 pounds tomatillos, husked and rinsed
2 medium poblano or Anaheim peppers, halved and seeded
1 large onion, quartered
12 garlic cloves, peeled

Roast until very soft, 40 to 45 minutes. Transfer the vegetables, including the pan juices, to a blender or food processor and add:

1¼ cups coarsely chopped spinach
⅓ cup chopped cilantro
¼ cup chicken or vegetable stock or broth, or as needed
Salt and black pepper to taste

Pulse until smooth, adding more stock if necessary to make a medium-bodied sauce. Reheat gently in a small saucepan and serve or store, refrigerated, for up to 2 days. Reheat before serving.

ABOUT TOMATO SAUCES

Although tomatoes are indigenous to the Americas, our favorite tomato sauces have made long round-trips to our kitchens. Italy is largely responsible for the diverse family of sauces we use to dress pasta. A smooth, roux-thickened sauce, or *sauce tomate*, is one of the five French mother sauces, 547, though we rarely use it today. Ketchup, our ubiquitous national condiment, is descended from more pungent Asian and English forbearers. (For recipes, see Quick Ketchup, 565, and Tomato Ketchup, 931.) For more traditional American tomato sauces, see salsas, 573–74.

Tomatoes can be used raw or cooked, pureed or coarsely chopped, as a backdrop for other ingredients or on their own, to produce a range of vibrant sauces. Their juiciness makes them ideal for creating sauces without the broth or stock that so many other sauces depend on. They also provide their own acidity and sweetness, and the cook can play to either of those elements in sauce making.

Most tomato sauce recipes invite improvisation, but no matter what other ingredients eventually find their way into the sauce, the best sauces begin with good fresh or canned tomatoes. If using **fresh tomatoes,** ➤ we highly recommend purchasing plum types (such as Romas) for simmering in sauces; they are usually less expensive, contain fewer seeds, and are less variable in quality. ➤ Much of a tomato's flavor is found in the gel-like liquid surrounding their seeds. For this reason, we never seed our tomatoes (unless making a garnish like concassé, 281). Tomato sauces can be put through a food mill to remove seeds without wasting the flavorful gel, but we find it to be more trouble than it's worth. Of course, choosing sauce-friendly plum tomatoes will also keep sauces from being overly seedy. Peeling tomatoes, 281, is a matter of preference, but we recommend it for sauces that will not be pureed or passed through a food mill.

Canned tomatoes are one of the few ingredients that are just as useful and delicious as fresh ones, and we recommend them, without reservation, for tomato sauces. Though they need a little attention to break down into smaller chunks, we prefer buying canned tomatoes whole rather than diced or pureed. After 15 minutes of simmering, they are quite easy to smash against the side of a saucepan with a wooden spoon, which results in a wonderfully hearty and rustic texture. A potato masher is an excellent way to achieve the same end (and has less potential to get messy). Do not assume that imported canned tomatoes are best; several brands of domestic tomatoes are as good as and sometimes better than imported varieties. ➤ One 28-ounce can of tomatoes is roughly equivalent to 2 pounds fresh tomatoes, and they may be substituted for one another bearing in mind that fresh tomatoes may require a little more simmering than canned, as they tend to be firmer and less concentrated.

Dried tomatoes and tomato paste are two well-loved additions that can improve the flavor of a sauce. For quick-cooking sauces, sun-dried tomatoes should be soaked in hot water until softened and plump, diced, and added with the other tomatoes. For long-simmering ragus, you may snip them into small pieces with a pair of scissors and add them dry (they should be tender by the time the sauce is done). Oil-packed dried tomatoes can be added to sauces without plumping or prolonged simmering. **Tomato paste** may be added at any point and does not require special treatment. For richer sauces and braises, we like to add it during the last few minutes of browning the onions, carrots, or celery; the paste's sugars caramelize and add depth to the sauce. Stir frequently and add liquid as soon as the paste is uniformly browned; do not let the paste scorch.

The faster a tomato sauce is cooked, the fresher and brighter its flavor; hence we prefer using a wide saucepan or a skillet, which promotes evaporation. On the other hand, when generous amounts of aromatic vegetables and seasonings are part of a recipe, a longer simmer encourages flavors to unfold and meld together. Meat-based tomato sauces often cook longer still, and for these a Dutch oven or large heavy saucepan is the best cooking vessel.

If serving on pasta, 3 cups tomato sauce will be enough for about 1 pound dried pasta. Tomato sauces need not be restricted to pasta and pizza—use them on meats, poultry, fish, and vegetables. There are classic pairings like Eggplant Parmigiana, 238, and Chicken Parmigiana, 415, and less classic but equally delicious pairings such as sautéed pork medallions or mild fish steaks with Puttanesca Sauce, 557. In addition to topping or accompanying foods, tomato sauces can be used as a braising liquid for large roasts (Stracotto, 464) and whole fish (Veracruz-Style Snapper, 38), or smaller items like Beef Braciole, 470, and Stuffed Cabbage Rolls, 226.

Tomato sauce can be kept in the refrigerator for up to 1 week or frozen for up to 6 months.

TOMATO SAUCE

About 3 cups

Don't bother peeling the tomatoes if you plan to put the sauce through a food mill. Furthermore, if you don't mind a chunky tomato sauce, there is no need to peel the tomatoes or food-mill the sauce. For a classic, roux-thickened French tomato sauce (called **Sauce Tomate**), replace the olive oil with **2 tablespoons butter,** then add **2 tablespoons flour** to the softened vegetables and cook, stirring, until the flour is nutty and fragrant. Proceed as directed and pass the sauce through a food mill.

Heat in a large skillet over medium heat:

2 tablespoons olive oil

Add:

1 small onion, finely chopped
(1 small carrot, finely chopped)
(1 small celery rib with leaves, finely chopped)

Cover, reduce the heat to low, and cook, stirring occasionally, until the vegetables are very soft, about 15 minutes. Add and cook, stirring, for 30 seconds:

2 garlic cloves, minced
(1 tablespoon chopped basil, rosemary, sage, or thyme)

Stir in:

2 pounds fresh plum or Roma tomatoes, peeled, 281, and coarsely chopped, or one 28-ounce can whole tomatoes
(½ cup sun-dried tomatoes, soaked in boiling water until soft, and finely chopped)
2 teaspoons tomato paste
¾ teaspoon salt, or to taste
¼ teaspoon black pepper, or to taste

Simmer, uncovered, crushing the tomatoes with a potato masher or a wooden spoon to break them up, until the sauce is thickened, 15 to 20 minutes. Pass through a food mill for a smooth sauce.

MARINARA SAUCE

About 2¼ cups

The simplest sauce for seafood and pastas.

Combine in a large saucepan and bring to a simmer over medium-low heat:

2 pounds fresh plum or Roma tomatoes, peeled, 281, and coarsely chopped, or one 28-ounce can whole tomatoes
⅓ cup olive oil
3 to 6 garlic cloves, to taste, halved or lightly smashed
6 sprigs basil
6 sprigs parsley
(½ teaspoon red pepper flakes)

Simmer, uncovered, crushing the tomatoes with a potato masher or a wooden spoon to break them up, until the sauce is thickened, about 10 minutes. For a smoother texture, you may pass the sauce through a food mill or puree in a blender or a food processor. Season to taste with:

Salt and black pepper

PIZZA SAUCE

About 3 cups

This raw puree "cooks" on the pie. You might be tempted to add raw garlic here, but pizzas bake through before the garlic can mellow out, leaving a harsh flavor. If garlic is a must in your pizza sauce, use pureed Marinara Sauce, above.

Puree in a blender or food processor until mostly smooth:

One 28-ounce can whole tomatoes, drained
2 tablespoons olive oil
3 fresh basil leaves
(¼ teaspoon red pepper flakes)
(¼ teaspoon dried oregano)
¼ teaspoon salt

NO-COOK TOMATO SAUCE

About 6 cups

Make this easy formula when you can get juicy fresh tomatoes and the weather is too hot for simmering sauces. It's good on bruschetta as well as over pasta. If serving with pasta, we like to toss the hot pasta with small cubes of fresh mozzarella cheese before adding the tomato sauce and sprinkle each portion with 1 to 2 teaspoons balsamic vinegar.

Drain in a colander for 20 minutes:

5 large tomatoes (about 2½ pounds), finely diced

Transfer to a large bowl and stir in:

½ cup fresh basil or parsley leaves, or ¼ cup oregano leaves, finely chopped
(½ cup pitted oil-cured or brined olives, chopped)
3 tablespoons extra-virgin olive oil
2 garlic cloves, minced
(1 small fresh chile pepper, seeded and minced, or ¼ teaspoon red pepper flakes)
Salt and black pepper to taste

Let stand for at least 30 minutes. Serve at room temperature.

GRILLED TOMATO SAUCE

About 3½ cups

Prepare a medium-hot grill fire, 1063, or position an oven rack 6 inches from the heat. Preheat the broiler.

Place on the grill or under the broiler:

12 plum or Roma tomatoes or 6 large tomatoes (about 3 pounds)

Turn with tongs as the skin chars. When lightly charred all over, cool, then puree or chop in a food processor or blender. Transfer to a medium bowl and stir in:

¼ cup extra-virgin olive oil
2 tablespoons chopped basil
Salt and black pepper to taste

VERACRUZ-STYLE TOMATO SAUCE

About 4 cups

The combination of cinnamon, bay leaf, garlic, olives, and pickles in a tomato sauce may seem odd, but this sauce is irresistible with grilled fish and pork. For a braised dish that uses this sauce, see Veracruz-Style Snapper, 380. Use "true" cinnamon or canela, 972, for the best result.

Heat in a medium saucepan over medium heat:

¼ cup olive oil

Add and cook, stirring, until softened, about 5 minutes:

1 medium onion, chopped

Add and cook 1 minute more:

4 garlic cloves, chopped

Stir in:

2 pounds fresh plum or Roma tomatoes, chopped, or one 28-ounce can whole tomatoes, chopped

Bring to a simmer and cook, stirring occasionally, until slightly thickened, about 10 minutes. Tie together tightly into a bundle:

4 sprigs flat-leaf parsley
2 sprigs thyme
(2 sprigs marjoram)
2 sprigs oregano

Add the bundle to the pan along with:

1 cup sliced pimiento-stuffed green olives
½ cup dry white wine
(½ cup sliced pickled jalapeños, seeded)
1 teaspoon capers or 2 large caper berries, chopped
1 bay leaf
One 2-inch cinnamon stick

Bring to a simmer and cook, stirring, until the sauce is thick but not pasty, 15 to 20 minutes. Discard the herb bundle, bay leaf, and cinnamon. Season to taste with:

Salt

AMATRICIANA SAUCE

About 2 cups

This sauce is the perfect partner for bucatini; shave a little Pecorino Romano on top.

Place in a large heavy skillet over medium heat:

6 slices bacon, cut into ¼-inch dice

Or use instead of the bacon:

2 tablespoons olive oil
6 ounces pancetta, cut into ¼-inch dice

Cook, stirring, until the bacon or pancetta has rendered most of its fat and turned deep golden brown, about 10 minutes. Remove with a slotted spoon and set aside. Pour off all but 2 tablespoons fat from the skillet. Return the skillet to medium heat. Add and cook, stirring, until golden brown:

1 large onion, finely chopped

Add and cook, stirring, for 1 minute, being careful not to burn the garlic:

1 large garlic clove, minced
1 dried red chile pepper or ¼ teaspoon red pepper flakes

Increase the heat to high and add:

2 pounds fresh plum or Roma tomatoes, peeled, 281, and chopped, or one 28-ounce can whole tomatoes

Stir in the bacon or pancetta and simmer, crushing the tomatoes with a potato masher or a wooden spoon, until thickened, about 5 minutes. Season to taste with:

Black pepper
Red pepper flakes

PUTTANESCA SAUCE

About 3 cups

Puttanesca, or "streetwalker's" sauce, is assembled from pantry items and ready in minutes, making it ideal for busy cooks drawn to the spicy, punchy combination of olives, capers, anchovies, and dried chiles. An inspired choice for dressing pasta or as a topping for white-fleshed fish, sautéed chicken breasts, or Roasted Cauliflower Wedges, 229.

Heat in a large skillet over medium heat:

¼ cup olive oil

Add and cook, stirring, just until the garlic is pale blond, about 30 seconds:

2 large garlic cloves, minced
1 dried red chile pepper or ¼ teaspoon red pepper flakes

Stir in and cook for about 30 seconds:

1 cup oil-cured black olives, pitted and chopped
6 anchovy fillets, rinsed
½ teaspoon dried oregano

Stir in:

2 pounds fresh tomatoes, peeled, 281, if desired, and chopped, or one 28-ounce can whole tomatoes

Simmer, uncovered, crushing the tomatoes with a potato masher or a wooden spoon, until the sauce is thickened, about 5 minutes. Stir in:

3 tablespoons minced parsley
2 tablespoons drained capers

Season to taste with:

Salt and black pepper

MEATY TOMATO SAUCE

About 4 cups

A simple and relatively quick sauce. For a deluxe, long-simmered upgrade, see Hearty Beef Ragu, 466.

Add to a large heavy saucepan or skillet:

2 tablespoons olive oil
(2 ounces pancetta or bacon, diced)

If using pancetta or bacon, cook over medium heat, stirring, until it renders its fat, and drain off all but 2 tablespoons. Increase the heat to medium-high and add:

½ pound ground beef, lamb, pork, or mild or hot Italian sausage, store-bought or homemade, 511

Cook, stirring, until the meat browns, about 7 minutes. Transfer the meat to a plate and pour off all but 2 tablespoons fat from the pan. Add and cook, stirring, until softened, about 5 minutes:

1 medium onion, chopped

Add and cook, stirring, for 2 minutes:

4 garlic cloves, minced
1 tablespoon tomato paste
(¼ teaspoon red pepper flakes)

Add the reserved meat and:

One 28-ounce can whole tomatoes
(1 teaspoon fresh thyme or oregano leaves or ½ teaspoon dried thyme or oregano)
½ teaspoon salt
¼ teaspoon black pepper
Pinch of sugar

Cook, uncovered, crushing the tomatoes with a potato masher or a wooden spoon, until they have cooked down and smell very fragrant, about 15 minutes. Cover and cook over low heat, stirring often, until the sauce is thickened, about 30 minutes. Stir in:

3 tablespoons slivered basil or chopped parsley
Salt and black pepper to taste

BOLOGNESE SAUCE

About 4½ cups

While beef and pork are the main ingredients in this long-simmered ragu, we have given it a home near its tomato-rich, pasta-friendly brethren. (For Cincinnati's version of Bolognese, see Cincinnati Chili Cockaigne, 502.) For a chunkier ragu of braised lamb or beef, see Hearty Beef Ragu, 466.

Heat in a large saucepan over medium-low heat:

3 tablespoons olive oil
1 ounce pancetta or bacon, finely chopped

Cook, stirring, until the pancetta or bacon releases its fat but is not browned, about 8 minutes. Increase the heat to medium and add:

1 large carrot, minced
2 small celery ribs, minced
½ medium onion, minced

Cook, stirring, until the onions are translucent, about 5 minutes. Add and brown:

1¼ pounds coarsely ground beef chuck, ground pork shoulder, or a combination

Stir in:

¾ cup chicken or beef stock or broth
⅔ cup dry white wine
2 tablespoons tomato paste

Reduce the heat to low and simmer gently, partially covered, skimming off the fat occasionally. From time to time as the sauce simmers, add 2 tablespoons at a time:

1½ cups whole milk

Cook until the sauce is the consistency of thick soup, about 2 hours. Remove from the heat and let cool. Cover and refrigerate for up to 24 hours.

Skim the fat off the top before reheating. Serve over wide noodles like tagliatelle, with Tortellini, 313, or in Lasagne Bolognese, 310.

TOMATO SAUCE WITH MEATBALLS

Enough for 1 pound pasta

Prepare:

Tomato Sauce, 556
Italian Meatballs, 507

Brown the meatballs as directed and transfer to the simmering tomato sauce. If the meatballs are large and have not reached 160°F in the center, gently simmer until they are cooked through, about 15 minutes.

ABOUT BUTTER SAUCES

The simplest of these sauces is nothing more than seasoned butter cooked until it begins to brown and take on a rich, nutty flavor. Beurre Blanc, below, is an equally simple concept, but slightly trickier to prepare, since it derives its smoothness from whisking butter into wine bit by bit just before serving. Unlike mayonnaise or vinaigrette (for which you make an emulsion from scratch), here you are essentially melting the butter chunks in liquid over a gentle heat so that the butter's emulsified structure is not destroyed. The result: a flavorful, thinned-out butter with the consistency of heavy cream. The ideal temperature for keeping beurre blanc stable is around 125°F—if allowed to cool, the fat will begin to solidify; at 135°F, the butterfat will leak out of the emulsion and break into a greasy pool on the top of the sauce. If this seems too delicate a balance for a hurried weeknight, flavored butters, 559–60, are much more forgiving and can be made well ahead of time.

BROWN BUTTER

About ⅓ cup

Make this quickly in the same skillet you cooked fish in and serve it over the fish, or make it separately to use as a sauce for green vegetables.

Melt in a small skillet over medium-low heat:

5 tablespoons butter, preferably unsalted

Cook slowly until the butter becomes light brown and smells nutty, shaking the pan or stirring occasionally so it cooks evenly. Watch as the butter begins to foam; it can burn easily. When the foaming subsides a bit, swirl the pan. You should see browned bits on the bottom of the pan. Remove the butter from the heat. It can be used as is or season with:

(1 tablespoon finely chopped parsley)
(1 teaspoon white wine vinegar or lemon juice)
(Salt and black pepper to taste)

Serve immediately.

BLACK BUTTER

Delicious against the light flavor of sautéed fish such as sole, cod, or skate.

Prepare **Brown Butter, above,** allowing it to cook until it is dark brown.

BEURRE BLANC (WHITE BUTTER SAUCE)

About ½ cup

Rich and refined, beurre blanc is traditionally served with fish, but is also excellent drizzled on seared scallops; grilled or sautéed chicken or pork chops; Roasted Asparagus, 208; or grilled artichokes, 206. Adding a small amount of cream before adding the butter helps keep the sauce stable.

Combine in a small skillet over medium heat:

6 tablespoons dry white wine
2 tablespoons white wine vinegar
3 tablespoons minced shallots
Salt and white pepper to taste

Bring to a simmer and simmer, uncovered, until reduced by three-quarters. Stir in:

1 tablespoon heavy cream

Remove from the heat and add one piece at a time, whisking constantly, until the sauce is creamy and pale:

1 stick (4 ounces) cold butter, preferably unsalted, cut into 8 pieces

Add each piece before the previous one has completely melted, or the sauce will separate. If you need a bit more heat to soften the butter, set the pan briefly over very low heat. Strain through a fine-mesh sieve, if desired. Season to taste with:

Salt and black pepper

Use immediately. If there is any delay, try to keep the sauce around 125°F to prevent it from congealing or separating.

VARIATIONS OF BEURRE BLANC

Cider: For the wine, substitute **6 tablespoons dry hard cider.**

Citrus: Substitute **2 tablespoons lemon, lime, orange, or grapefruit juice** for the vinegar and add **½ teaspoon finely grated zest** with the shallots.

Herbs: Stir into the finished sauce **1 to 2 tablespoons minced herbs, such as tarragon, fennel fronds, chervil, chives, parsley, or a combination.**

For serving with shellfish: you may replace half of the butter with **4 tablespoons Shrimp or Lobster Butter, 560, chilled until solid and cut into 4 pieces** (add the plain butter first or the sauce will not thicken).

MISO BEURRE BLANC

About ¾ cup

This salty, tangy, buttery sauce is excellent served with green vegetables like asparagus or as a lily-gilding accompaniment to a perfectly cooked steak or chop.

Whisk together in a medium saucepan:

¼ cup white miso
2 tablespoons lime juice
2 tablespoons dry sake
2 teaspoons Dijon mustard

Bring to a boil, then remove from the heat and whisk in one piece at a time:

6 tablespoons cold unsalted butter, cut into 6 cubes

Serve immediately.

ABOUT FLAVORED BUTTERS

A pat or dollop of flavored butter (also called *beurre composé* or **compound butter**) placed on top of hot foods quickly melts into a lush sauce. These mixtures have much to recommend them: Most are simple to make, they can be prepared well ahead of time, and they do not require any finesse or attention before serving. They are also an excellent means of using and preserving the flavor of fresh herbs that might otherwise be fleeting. Extra thyme or rosemary in the crisper is an excellent excuse to make flavored butter, as is a bumper garden crop of basil or tarragon. Compound butters freeze well so don't hesitate to make more than needed for immediate use, especially if your aim is to make use of a surplus of herbs. To flavor oils, see 1008. To infuse butter with the flavor of truffles, see 1029.

Flavored butters can, of course, be used immediately while they are still soft for dipping radishes and other vegetables in, or for spooning on top of hot fish, seared steaks, baked potatoes, or warm dinner rolls. They may also be melted and served as a finishing sauce for meat or vegetables, or chilled, sliced thinly, and placed on foods to melt. Finally, they may be used in recipes such as Chicken Kiev, 416, or Baked Buttered Snails, 371, where butter is integral to the flavor of the dish.

To store flavored butter, roll it into a cylinder in wax paper, parchment paper, or plastic wrap and refrigerate for 1½ to 2 hours or freeze for several months. Herbed butters ➤ should not be refrigerated for longer than 24 hours, as the herbs deteriorate quickly. Slice thin rounds from the butter as needed.

ADDITIONS TO FLAVORED BUTTER

Flavored butters are a blank slate for all kinds of ingredients. We recommend seasoning them with a heavy hand since they are not intended to be eaten on their own, but rather used as a flavoring for other foods.

Place in a bowl:

1 stick (4 ounces) softened butter, preferably unsalted

Stir in any of the following:

½ cup toasted, 1005, almonds, hazelnuts, pistachios, walnuts, or pecans, pulsed in a food processor until very finely ground
¼ cup black caviar and 1 tablespoon lemon juice
1 tablespoon Harissa I, 584
6 anchovy fillets, minced, and ½ teaspoon lemon juice, or to taste
Up to 3 garlic cloves, mashed to a paste, or cloves from 1 head black garlic, 990, finely chopped, or from 1 head Roasted Garlic, 241, mashed
¼ to ½ cup minced fresh herbs (use the smaller amount for more pungent herbs like rosemary or tarragon)
Finely grated zest of 1 orange or lemon and 1 tablespoon orange or lemon juice
¼ cup drained capers, finely chopped
¼ cup white miso
1 tablespoon curry powder or Garam Masala, 588, or to taste

Mix in:

Salt to taste

Use immediately or roll, chill, and store as directed, above.

LEMON AND PARSLEY BUTTER

About ½ cup

Also called *beurre maître d'hôtel*, this is delicious over grilled or broiled steak.

Beat together in a medium bowl:

1 stick (4 ounces) butter, softened
2 tablespoons finely chopped parsley
1½ to 2 tablespoons lemon juice, to taste
Salt to taste

Use immediately or roll, chill, and store as directed, above.

SNAIL BUTTER

About ⅔ cup

The traditional name for this mixture does not do it justice for most readers. Make no mistake: This is the butter you're looking for. As the name suggests, many use it for dressing *escargot*, but it is also good on warm bread, as a spread for cold sandwiches, or atop grilled lamb chops or fish steaks.

Beat together in a medium bowl:

1 stick (4 ounces) butter, softened
¼ cup minced shallots or green onions (white part only)
(2 tablespoons minced celery)
2 tablespoons minced parsley
(2 tablespoons lemon juice)
2 to 3 garlic cloves, to taste, mashed to a paste with
1 teaspoon salt
Black pepper to taste

Use immediately or roll, chill, and store as directed, 559.

MONTPELLIER BUTTER

About 2 cups

This flavorful compound butter is a little fussy to make, but it compensates by being incredibly delicious. Serve it with grilled meats or fish, especially salmon.

Have a bowl of ice water ready. Bring a large saucepan of water to a boil. Add to the boiling water and blanch for 30 seconds:

1 cup lightly packed watercress leaves (1 ounce)
1 cup lightly packed parsley leaves (1 ounce)
1 cup lightly packed spinach leaves (1 ounce)
½ cup lightly packed chervil leaves (½ ounce) or substitute more parsley
⅓ cup lightly packed tarragon leaves (½ ounce)
⅓ cup chopped chives (½ ounce)

With a spider or slotted spoon transfer the herbs immediately to the ice water to cool. Drain the herbs well, lightly pressing out any excess water. Spread the herbs on half of a kitchen towel, fold the other half over them, and roll up the towel like a jelly-roll, lightly pressing it to blot the herbs dry. Transfer the herbs to a food processor and pulse until very finely chopped. Add to the food processor and pulse until finely chopped:

(Yolks from 3 Hard-Boiled Eggs, 151)
4 to 6 anchovy fillets, to taste, rinsed and patted dry
2 tablespoons drained capers
2 to 3 cornichons, to taste, coarsely chopped
1 garlic clove, coarsely chopped
½ teaspoon salt
¼ teaspoon black pepper

Add and pulse until very smooth, scraping down the sides of the bowl as needed:

1 stick (4 ounces) unsalted butter, softened

With the machine running, add in a thin, steady stream:

¼ cup olive oil
1 teaspoon lemon juice

Use immediately or roll, chill, and store as directed, 559.

SHRIMP OR LOBSTER BUTTER

½ to ⅔ cup

Delicately pink and deliciously flavored. Unlike the butters above, which are generally used as a sauce or condiment, shellfish butter is primarily used as a last-minute addition to sauces to be served with fish or shellfish (sometimes the very same creatures used to make the butter).

Spread on a baking sheet and dry in a 250°F oven for 30 minutes:

Shells (raw or cooked) from 1½ to 2 pounds shrimp or crayfish or from one 1½- to 2-pound lobster, rinsed and drained

When cooled, place the shells in a towel, fold the towel over, and break them up as fine as possible with a mallet or rolling pin. Melt in the top of a double boiler over simmering water:

2 sticks (8 ounces) butter

Add the shells and cook over the simmering water for 10 minutes. Set aside for 20 minutes to allow the flavors to infuse. Pour into a fine-mesh sieve set over a bowl; let stand for up to 20 minutes to drain off all the butter. Refrigerate until chilled. Skim off the butter when the mixture has solidified; discard any liquid.

Use immediately, or let the butter soften and roll, chill, and store as directed, 559.

KIMCHI BUTTER

About ¾ cup

This spicy and tangy butter is excellent with grilled steaks or chops, roasted cauliflower, green peas, or roasted cabbage.

Beat together in a medium bowl until thoroughly combined:

1 stick (4 ounces) unsalted butter, softened
¼ cup very finely chopped, well-drained kimchi
2 tablespoons minced chives

Use immediately or roll, chill, and store as directed, 559.

CHILE BUTTER

About ⅔ cup

Heat in a small skillet over medium heat:

2 tablespoons olive oil

Add and cook, stirring, until softened:

½ cup minced shallots or green onions
4 garlic cloves, finely chopped

Transfer to a small bowl and let cool. Stir in:

4 tablespoons (½ stick) butter, softened
2 tablespoons minced cilantro, parsley, or a combination
1½ tablespoons chipotle, ancho, or Urfa chile powder
1 tablespoon lemon juice
½ teaspoon ground cinnamon
½ teaspoon ground cumin
Salt and black pepper to taste

Use immediately or roll, chill, and store as directed, 559.

GREEN BUTTER

About ⅔ cup

Use for broiled fish, steamed vegetables, or chicken, or to give white or cream sauces a light green color and some added zing.

Have a bowl of ice water ready. Bring a large saucepan of water to a boil. Place in a fine-mesh sieve:

1 shallot, chopped, or 1 tablespoon chopped onion
1 tablespoon fresh tarragon leaves
1 tablespoon fresh chervil leaves
1 tablespoon fresh parsley leaves

Lower the sieve of shallot and herbs into the water and blanch for 10 seconds. Lift the sieve out of the boiling water and lower it into the ice water. Drain, transfer to a kitchen towel, and pat dry. Pound to a paste in a mortar, or grind to a paste in a small food processor. Gradually blend in:

4 tablespoons (½ stick) butter, softened
Salt to taste

Use immediately or roll, chill, and store as directed, 559.

ABOUT HOLLANDAISE AND BÉARNAISE

Smooth, velvety, and rich, hollandaise and béarnaise transform the plainest and simplest cooked vegetables, well-browned steaks, or fish into superb dishes. These emulsified sauces—meaning the state where one liquid is forcefully dispersed into another one it normally would not mix with—are close cousins of mayonnaise and vinaigrette, though they are served hot. Professional chefs will make these sauces in a pan directly over low heat, but we strongly recommend using a double boiler or—better yet—a stainless steel bowl set over a saucepan holding about 1½ inches of water. The advantage of the bowl is that its shape gives you plenty of room to whisk. Whichever method you choose, ➤ the water in the bottom pan should barely simmer, not boil, and the water should not touch the bottom of the bowl or pan above. Remove the bowl or top of the double boiler from the heat if you feel that the sauce is getting too hot; whisk until the sauce cools slightly, then put it back over the heat to continue. For preparations that do not require as much attention, see the blender-friendly recipes below, as well as the thinner Avgolemono Sauce, 552, and Sauce Allemande, 550.

The most critical stage in making hollandaise or béarnaise by hand is the initial whipping and cooking of the egg yolks. Begin by whisking the yolks and water off the heat until light and frothy. Then, warm the yolks over the barely simmering water as you continue to whisk vigorously. They will become pale yellow, thicker, and expand to three or four times their original volume.

Remove the yolks from the heat and add the warm—not hot—melted butter in a steady trickle, whisking constantly. Scrape the sides and bottom of the bowl or pan as you go to keep the sauce smooth. Do not let the sauce or butter cool too much as you whisk, or the butter will begin to harden and thicken; add a few drops of warm water if this happens. If at any point the sauce looks as if it is about to separate, immediately whisk in a few tablespoons of cold heavy cream or water. If it separates, all is not lost: Simply whisk another yolk in a clean bowl, then slowly pour this yolk into the broken sauce, whisking constantly, to re-form the emulsion. Hollandaise and béarnaise can be frozen. To thaw, reheat very gently in a double boiler, stirring briskly and frequently to preserve its consistency.

HOLLANDAISE

Generous 1 cup

Melt over low heat:

1¼ sticks (5 ounces) butter

Keep warm. Place in a large stainless steel bowl or the top of a double boiler:

3 large egg yolks
1½ tablespoons cold water

Off the heat, beat the yolks with a whisk until light and frothy. Place the bowl or the top of the double boiler over barely simmering water and continue to whisk until the eggs are thickened, 3 to 5 minutes, being careful not to let the eggs get too hot. If needed, remove the bowl or pan and whisk to cool the mixture slightly. Whisking constantly, very slowly add the butter, leaving the white milk solids behind. Whisk in:

½ to 2 teaspoons lemon juice, to taste
(A dash of hot pepper sauce)
Salt and white pepper to taste

If the sauce is too thick, whisk in a few drops of warm water. Serve immediately or cover and keep warm for up to 30 minutes by placing the bowl or pan in warm (not hot) water.

BLENDER HOLLANDAISE

About ½ cup

Here, the heat of the warmed butter cooks and thickens the egg. While much easier, the blender method results in a slightly pale and less flavorful sauce. ➤ Do not make in a smaller quantity than given here—there will not be enough heat to cook the eggs properly. This may also be made with an immersion blender.

Warm a blender container by filling it with hot water and allowing it to sit for 5 minutes. Pour out the water and dry well. Add to the blender:

3 large egg yolks, at room temperature
1½ to 2 teaspoons lemon juice, to taste
¼ teaspoon salt
Pinch of cayenne pepper

Melt in a small saucepan until bubbling:

1 stick (4 ounces) unsalted butter

Remove from the heat. Blend the egg yolks on high for 3 seconds; with the blender running, pour in the butter in a steady stream. By the time all the butter is poured in—about 30 seconds—the sauce should be finished. If not, blend on high about 5 seconds longer. If the sauce is too thick, add a few drops of warm water. Taste and adjust the seasoning with salt and lemon juice, if necessary. Serve at once or keep warm for up to 30 minutes by immersing the blender container in warm water.

BÉARNAISE SAUCE

About 1 cup

Heavenly on grilled steak and fish. Substituting fresh mint for the tarragon makes a **Paloise Sauce,** but parsley, basil, thyme, chives, or sage may also be used.

Pick the leaves from:

4 sprigs tarragon

Chop the leaves and set aside. Place the stems in a small saucepan and add:

3 tablespoons dry white wine
3 tablespoons tarragon or white wine vinegar
1 tablespoon minced shallot
8 black peppercorns, lightly cracked

Bring to a simmer and simmer, uncovered, until reduced by two-thirds. Discard the tarragon stems and reserve the liquid and shallot mixture. Melt in a small saucepan over low heat:

1¼ sticks (5 ounces) butter

Keep warm. Place in a large stainless steel bowl or the top of a double boiler:

3 large egg yolks
1½ teaspoons cold water

Off the heat, whisk the egg mixture until light and frothy. Place the bowl or the top of the double boiler over barely simmering water and whisk until the eggs are thickened, 3 to 5 minutes, being careful not to let the eggs get too hot. Remove the bowl or pan from the heat. Whisking constantly, very slowly add the melted butter, leaving the white milk solids behind in the pan. Whisk in the reserved tarragon leaves and the reduced liquid and shallot mixture gradually, to taste. Season to taste with:

Salt and white pepper

If the sauce is too thick, thin it with a few drops of the reserved liquid or warm water. Serve immediately or keep warm for up to 30 minutes by placing the pan or bowl in warm water.

BLENDER BÉARNAISE SAUCE

About ¾ cup

Combine in a small saucepan over low heat and simmer until reduced to about 1 tablespoon:

2 tablespoons dry white wine
2 tablespoons tarragon or white wine vinegar
1 tablespoon minced shallot
½ teaspoon chopped tarragon
4 black peppercorns, lightly cracked

Strain through a fine-mesh sieve and let cool. Stir the liquid to taste into:

Blender Hollandaise, 561, made with water instead of lemon juice

Stir in:

½ teaspoon minced tarragon, or more to taste

Taste and adjust the seasonings. Serve immediately.

ABOUT MAYONNAISE

If you are accustomed to store-bought mayonnaise, your first taste of the homemade stuff will be a pleasant surprise. Many who claim to despise mayonnaise change their mind after tasting the real article, which is silky, light, tangy, and quick to make. Like vinaigrette, hollandaise, and béarnaise, mayonnaise is an emulsion, or a mixture of two types of liquid that typically don't mix—one water-based (egg yolk and lemon juice or vinegar), the other oil-based. These liquids are forced to comingle by one of them being gradually beaten into the other with a whisk, which causes smaller and smaller droplets to form and disperse throughout the sauce. Egg yolks contain proteins and lecithin (a fat-like molecule) that act as emulsifiers, encouraging the liquid and oil in mayonnaise to come together and thicken.

The oil you choose will be the predominant flavor in your mayonnaise. Strongly flavored extra-virgin olive oil, for example, will make a pungent mayonnaise. For general use, a balance of fruity and mild oils, such as olive and vegetable, is most satisfying. Usually 3 parts mild to 1 part fruity oil is about right, although some prefer half-and-half. Since mayonnaise is mostly oil, ➤ the oil must be very fresh: Even a tinge of rancidity will make the sauce all but inedible, so taste the oil before you start. (Older or improperly stored oil can also cause mayonnaise to separate.)

There are several ways to make mayonnaise: in a bowl with a whisk; in a stand mixer with the whisk attachment; with an immersion blender; or in a food processor or blender. Of the machine-based methods, we prefer using a stand mixer as it is quick and nearly foolproof; blenders and food processors can overheat, causing the mayonnaise to break. Mayonnaise made by machine tends to have a greater volume and a fluffy texture, but it cannot duplicate the smoothness and the rich sheen of the hand-beaten product.

➤ Ingredients at room temperature emulsify more readily than cold ones, so start by bringing the eggs to room temperature by briefly submerging them in hot water before cracking. ➤ To be certain of success, bear in mind that you need 3 times as much oil as other liquid ingredients, including egg yolks.

To fix a separated mayonnaise, place a fresh egg yolk in a small clean bowl and slowly add the separated mayonnaise, drizzling it and whisking it in as you first did with the oil. You may need to add more oil to compensate for the extra yolk. If the mayonnaise is too thick for your taste, thin it with a little water.

Mayonnaise can be flavored in many ways. Add herbs, spices, flavored vinegars, and/or dry mustard or Dijon to the yolks at the start (mustard not only flavors the mayonnaise—it also helps with emulsification). Lemon juice and wine vinegar are classic, but other citrus juices and most mild vinegars can be used. If you know you will be adding liquid flavorings, use 1 to 2 tablespoons extra oil to make a thicker mayonnaise.

Store homemade mayonnaise tightly covered in the refrigerator for up to 1 week. If it contains fresh herbs, use within 2 days. Mayonnaise does not freeze well. When serving homemade mayonnaise and any food containing it, keep track of the time it spends outside the refrigerator. Because raw eggs contain microorganisms that start multiplying above 40°F, the maximum time mayonnaise should be out of the refrigerator is 2 hours—or, when the temperature is 85°F or above, 1 hour. When the risk of salmonella in raw eggs is a concern, use pasteurized eggs, 977.

To perk up store-bought mayonnaise, see the flavorful additions listed on 563. Beating in 1 to 2 tablespoons good olive oil until all trace of it has disappeared will make store-bought mayonnaise stiffer and heavier and improve its flavor.

MAYONNAISE

About 1 cup

I. WHISK OR STAND MIXER METHOD

Use a ceramic, glass, or stainless steel bowl (aluminum and copper will react with the acid and affect the color and flavor of the sauce). For easier hand-whisking, place the bowl on a damp kitchen towel to prevent it from rocking or spinning as you work.

Have ready a balloon whisk and a medium bowl or affix the whisk attachment to a stand mixer. Whisk together until smooth and light:

2 large egg yolks, at room temperature
1 to 2 tablespoons lemon juice or white wine vinegar, to taste
¼ teaspoon salt
Pinch of white pepper
(Up to 1½ teaspoons Dijon mustard)

If using a stand mixer, increase the speed to medium-high. Very gradually whisk in:

1 cup vegetable oil, or ¾ cup vegetable oil and ¼ cup olive oil

As the mixture thickens—when about one-third of the oil has been added—whisk in the oil more steadily, making sure each addition is thoroughly blended before adding the next. Should the oil stop being absorbed, stop pouring the oil and whisk vigorously before adding more. Whisk in:

Salt and white pepper to taste

Serve immediately, or refrigerate for up to 1 week.

II. IMMERSION BLENDER METHOD

Place all the ingredients from **version I, above,** in a narrow jar just wide enough to fit the end of an immersion blender (most immersion blenders come with such a jar—use it if possible). Place the end of the blender into the jar so it touches the bottom. Start the blender on medium speed, keeping it at the bottom of the jar until you can see the mixture form a vortex, thicken, and become opaque. Slowly lift the blender up and pulse it a couple times up and down to make sure all the oil is incorporated.

BLENDER MAYONNAISE

About 1½ cups

This mayonnaise differs from the above recipe in that it uses a whole egg and starts off with oil already added to the egg, with lemon juice added later (both of these tweaks help the emulsion form in the blender). Compared to the other methods, this one consistently produces the stiffest texture. You can also make this version in a food processor; use the plastic blade if you have one, as it seems to make a slightly lighter sauce.

Add to a blender:

1 large egg, at room temperature
¼ cup vegetable oil
1 teaspoon dry mustard
1 teaspoon salt
1 teaspoon sugar
Pinch of cayenne pepper

Cover and blend on high until thoroughly combined. With the blender running, slowly add in a thin, steady stream:

½ cup vegetable oil

and then:

3 tablespoons lemon juice

until thoroughly blended. Slowly add:

½ cup vegetable oil

and blend until thick. You may have to stop and start the blender occasionally to scrape down the sides.

ADDITIONS TO MAYONNAISE

Whisk any of the following into 1 cup homemade or store-bought mayonnaise:

2 tablespoons curry powder, warmed in 2 tablespoons vegetable oil over medium heat until fragrant
Cloves from 1 head Roasted Garlic, 241, mashed (see Aïoli, 564, to use raw garlic)
1 teaspoon dry mustard or up to 3 tablespoons Dijon or whole-grain mustard
1 tablespoon minced chipotle peppers in adobo sauce, plus 1 tablespoon of the adobo sauce
2 to 3 tablespoons minced herbs, such as tarragon, basil, chervil, chives, parsley, and/or oregano
¼ cup finely chopped watercress
Up to ½ cup ketchup
2 tablespoons white miso
Up to 2 tablespoons drained prepared horseradish
½ cup plain yogurt
½ cup heavy cream, whipped to soft peaks

SAUCE PARISIENNE (EGGLESS MAYONNAISE)

About 1 cup

This rich, tangy French sauce is traditionally made with petit-suisse cheese, but cream cheese is a good substitute. Serve well chilled.

Process in a food processor until smooth and creamy:

5 ounces cream cheese, Neufchâtel, or petit-suisse cheese
(¼ teaspoon sweet or hot paprika)

With the machine running, add in a slow, steady stream:

5 tablespoons vegetable oil

Add in a slow, steady stream:

2 tablespoons lemon juice

Blend in:

½ teaspoon salt
½ teaspoon white or black pepper

Stop the machine and scrape down the sides. Taste and adjust the seasonings. Transfer to a bowl, cover, and chill. The sauce will keep, covered and refrigerated, for 2 weeks.

Stir in before serving, if desired:

(2 tablespoons chopped chervil)

TARTAR SAUCE

About 1⅓ cups

A good standby for fried fish. Try replacing the parsley with other herbs, such as tarragon or chives.

Stir to combine in a medium bowl:

1 cup mayonnaise, store-bought or homemade, above
(1 Hard-Boiled Egg, 151, finely chopped)

1 tablespoon drained sweet pickle relish or finely chopped sweet pickles
1 tablespoon chopped drained capers
1 tablespoon finely chopped parsley
(1 tablespoon chopped green olives)
1 teaspoon Dijon mustard
1 teaspoon minced shallot
Salt and black pepper to taste
(1 garlic clove, minced)
(Cayenne pepper or hot pepper sauce to taste)

You may thin the sauce with:

(A little wine vinegar or lemon juice)

SAUCE LOUIS

About 1 cup

Especially good with stuffed artichokes, steamed asparagus, or crab; see Crab Louis, 121.

Whisk together in a medium bowl:

½ cup Vinaigrette, 575
¼ cup mayonnaise, store-bought or homemade, 563
¼ cup mild, tomato-based chili sauce
1 teaspoon Worcestershire sauce
Salt and black pepper to taste

RÉMOULADE SAUCE

About 1½ cups

This French classic is marvelous with salads, vegetables, cold meats, French Fries, 270, or fried fish and shellfish.

Stir to combine in a medium bowl:

1 cup mayonnaise, store-bought or homemade, 563
1 tablespoon minced cornichons
1 tablespoon drained small capers, finely chopped
1 tablespoon chopped parsley
1½ teaspoons chopped tarragon
1 small garlic clove, minced
½ teaspoon Dijon mustard
Salt and black pepper to taste
(1 Hard-Boiled Egg, 151, finely chopped)

CREOLE RÉMOULADE SAUCE

Prepare **Rémoulade Sauce, above,** omitting the cornichons, capers, and tarragon. Add **1 tablespoon prepared horseradish, 1 tablespoon minced green onion, 1 tablespoon minced celery, 1 tablespoon minced green bell pepper, 1 tablespoon ketchup, 1 teaspoon Worcestershire sauce,** and **1 teaspoon sweet paprika.**

TONNATO SAUCE (TUNA SAUCE)

About 2 cups

This tangy sauce is traditionally served with veal, but we also love it with cold poached chicken, roast pork, or grilled or roasted vegetables.

Combine in a food processor or blender:

One 5- to 6-ounce can tuna packed in oil, drained
1 cup mayonnaise, store-bought or homemade, 563
5 anchovy fillets, finely chopped, or 2 teaspoons anchovy paste
3 tablespoons drained capers
3 tablespoons lemon juice
Black pepper to taste

Process until smooth, 30 seconds to 1 minute, scraping down the sides as needed. Transfer to a bowl, cover, and refrigerate. To serve, thinly slice the cold meat or chicken and arrange, overlapping, on a platter. Pour the sauce over and sprinkle with:

Chopped parsley

AÏOLI (GARLIC MAYONNAISE)

About 1 cup

Very popular in France, where it is sometimes referred to as *beurre de Provence*. In some areas of the Mediterranean, egg yolks are not used, which can make for a runnier sauce. Spread aïoli on a sandwich as you would mayonnaise; use as a dipping sauce for crudités; serve with Steamed Mussels I, 351, and French Fries, 270; or serve over cold poached salmon, grilled and roasted meats, or cold boiled potatoes.

Mince or mash to a paste:

4 to 6 garlic cloves, to taste

Place in a bowl and whisk together with:

2 large egg yolks, at room temperature
⅛ teaspoon salt
(White pepper to taste)

Very slowly, and whisking constantly, add, as for Mayonnaise I, 563:

1 cup olive oil (preferably ¾ cup refined olive oil and ¼ cup extra-virgin olive oil)

Whisk in:

1 teaspoon lemon juice
½ teaspoon cold water

SKORDALIA (POTATO-GARLIC MAYONNAISE)

About 1½ cups

Here the richness of mayonnaise is tempered by the addition of cooked, mashed potato and/or ground nuts. Both versions are excellent as a garnish for soups or served with grilled meats.

I. WITH POTATO

This version is good as a sauce or for binding dishes such as crab cakes.

Prepare:

Aïoli, above

Whisk in:

½ cup lukewarm mashed cooked, 265, potatoes

blending well, but not more than necessary. Season to taste with:

Salt and/or lemon juice

If the sauce is extremely thick, whisk in water until it is the desired consistency.

II. WITH NUTS

The addition of ground nuts makes this an excellent dip.

Prepare:

Aïoli, above

After the sauce has thickened, add:

¼ cup ground toasted, 1005, almonds or walnuts
1 small boiled potato, 265, riced, or ¼ cup fresh bread crumbs, 957
2 tablespoons chopped parsley
1 tablespoon lemon juice
¼ teaspoon salt, or to taste

ROUILLE (RED PEPPER–GARLIC MAYONNAISE)

Rouille is French for "rust," and this golden red, strongly flavored condiment is a natural with octopus or grilled vegetables, but is most famous for being dolloped on toast to accompany bouillabaisse.

I. *About ⅔ cup*

This version is traditionally made with a bit of the saffron-scented broth from Bouillabaisse, 102. You may also make and serve it with Cioppino, 102, or another soup.

Process in a food processor or pound together in a bowl or mortar to a smooth paste:

½ roasted red bell pepper, 262, or 1 pimiento, drained
1 dried red chile, softened in hot water for 30 minutes, or a dash of hot pepper sauce
¼ cup fresh bread crumbs, 957, soaked in water and squeezed dry
2 garlic cloves, minced or grated on a rasp grater
¼ teaspoon salt

Very gradually whisk in:

¼ cup olive oil, vegetable oil, or a combination

Should the oil stop being absorbed, stop pouring the oil and whisk vigorously before adding more. Just before serving, thin the sauce with:

2 to 3 tablespoons of the soup you are serving

II. *About 1¼ cups*

This saffron–red pepper aïoli is the perfect accompaniment to fried shellfish, 348; Grilled Squid, 368, Grilled Marinated Octopus, 369; or chilled crab.

Prepare:

Mayonnaise, 563

Set aside. Process in a blender or food processor or pound together in a bowl or mortar to a smooth paste:

1 roasted red bell pepper, 262, or 2 jarred pimiento or piquillo peppers, drained
1 dried red chile, softened in hot water for 30 minutes, or ⅛ teaspoon cayenne pepper
2 garlic cloves, minced or grated on a rasp grater
½ teaspoon saffron threads, crumbled

Gently fold the mixture into the prepared mayonnaise.

ABOUT TABLE SAUCES, DIPPING SAUCES, AND CONDIMENTS

Like mayonnaises and flavored butters, most of these sauces and condiments are passed at the table. Some, such as Salsa Verde, 567, and Chimichurri, 567, are scooped over foods. Others, like Mojo, 567, and Habanero-Citrus Hot Sauce, 571, are thinner and drizzled on. Of course, many sauces—ketchup, tamarind chutney, and peanut sauce, to name a few—are usually for dipping (for thicker, heartier ones, see About Dips, 50). For barbecue sauces, see 582. For making your own mustard, see 1003. For large-batch condiments suitable for storing, see Pickles, 922.

QUICK KETCHUP

About ¾ cup

Ketchup is perhaps as ubiquitous in modern American cuisine as Sauce Espagnole, 550, was in Escoffier's France: Countless sauces are born of this foundational condiment. This version is quickly assembled out of pantry staples—a boon for those who don't like to have a ketchup bottle languishing in the refrigerator, taking up precious shelf space (or those looking for a less sugary alternative to store-bought ketchup). For a smoky flavor, substitute smoked paprika or chipotle chile powder for the cayenne pepper. To make a much larger batch of ketchup from fresh tomatoes and peppers, see 931.

Combine in a small bowl:

One 6-ounce can tomato paste
¼ cup cider vinegar or malt vinegar
1 tablespoon mild honey, agave nectar, or Simple Syrup, 16
1 teaspoon salt
½ teaspoon garlic powder
⅛ teaspoon ground allspice
⅛ teaspoon cayenne pepper
Pinch of ground cloves

Whisk together thoroughly. Slowly whisk in:

Up to 2 tablespoons water

until the sauce is the desired consistency.

GASTRIQUE (SWEET-SOUR VINEGAR SAUCE)

About ½ cup

Also known as **agrodolce,** this sticky, tangy sauce is meant to be used in tiny amounts. It perfectly complements the flavors of rich meats like duck, goose, lamb, and venison, or hearty vegetables like roasted winter squash and grilled or roasted mushrooms. Play with different vinegars, 1029, and sweeteners depending on what you plan to serve this with, and feel free to start the sauce by sautéing some minced shallot or garlic, throw in herb sprigs, or add dried fruits like cherries, currants, or chopped figs.

Stir together in a medium saucepan:

½ cup sugar, brown sugar, honey, or maple syrup
1 tablespoon water

Place over medium-high heat and bring to a boil. Cook until the sugar turns a deep amber or, if using brown sugar, honey, or maple syrup, simply bring to a boil. Remove from the heat and carefully stir in:

½ cup white wine vinegar

Return to the heat and reduce, swirling the pan frequently, until syrupy, 3 to 5 minutes.

SWEET-AND-SOUR SAUCE

About 1 cup

The Chinese-American takeout classic.

Whisk together in a small bowl:

2 teaspoons cornstarch
2 tablespoons water

Combine in a medium saucepan:

½ cup pineapple juice
¼ cup packed light brown sugar
¼ cup rice or cider vinegar
3 tablespoons ketchup
1 tablespoon soy sauce

Bring to a boil over medium-high heat, stirring frequently. When the sugar is dissolved, stir the cornstarch slurry and add it to the sauce, stirring until combined. Cook until thickened and remove from the heat. Allow to cool. Season to taste with:

Salt

TAMARIND CHUTNEY

About 1 cup

This sweet-sour chutney is perfect with Pakoras, 203. This recipe calls for tamarind concentrate or tamarind paste, which makes a thinner chutney than if using tamarind pulp. To use tamarind pulp (brick tamarind) instead, prepare it using the same quantities and method as directed in About Tamarinds, 195, before proceeding with the recipe.

Mix together in a small saucepan:

1 cup water
¼ cup tamarind paste or concentrate

Add:

⅓ to ½ cup brown sugar or jaggery, to taste
(2 garlic cloves, minced or grated on a rasp grater)
1 teaspoon ground ginger or a 1-inch piece fresh ginger, peeled and minced
½ teaspoon cayenne pepper
½ teaspoon cumin seeds, toasted, 1005, and ground
½ teaspoon salt
(⅛ teaspoon asafoetida, 954, or black salt, 1013)

Simmer until the sugar is dissolved, about 3 minutes. Allow the chutney to sit for at least 1 hour before serving to allow the flavors to mellow and meld.

ENGLISH CUMBERLAND SAUCE

About ⅔ cup

A red currant sauce particularly suited to serving with venison. It is best served cold.

Bring a medium saucepan of water to a rolling boil and add:

One 2 × ¾-inch strip orange zest, removed with a vegetable peeler and thinly sliced crosswise into slivers

Blanch for 3 minutes, then drain. Dry the pan and add the blanched zest back to it along with:

½ cup red currant jelly
⅓ cup port
½ teaspoon dry mustard
¼ teaspoon salt
Black pepper to taste

Place over medium heat and bring to a simmer, whisking frequently. Reduce the heat and simmer gently for 5 minutes. Let cool completely and refrigerate until cold before serving.

HORSERADISH SAUCE

I. WHIPPED CREAM-BASED

About 1⅓ cups

This light condiment is a particular delight with hot roast beef, but it is also good with cold meats.

Beat in a medium bowl to stiff peaks, 791:

½ cup cold heavy cream

Gradually, beat in:

3 tablespoons lemon juice or distilled white or cider vinegar
2 tablespoons grated peeled fresh or drained prepared horseradish
¼ teaspoon salt
Pinch of cayenne pepper

Chill for at least 30 and for up to 60 minutes. Stir gently before serving.

II. MAYONNAISE-BASED

About 1¾ cups

A richer sauce perfect for serving with Crudités, 45, slathering on pastrami and corned beef sandwiches, or serving with roasted beets or parsnips.

Stir together thoroughly in a medium bowl:

1 cup mayonnaise, store-bought or homemade, 563
½ cup sour cream
3 to 4 tablespoons grated peeled fresh or drained prepared horseradish, to taste

Add:

1 to 2 teaspoons cider vinegar or lemon juice, to taste
¼ teaspoon salt, or to taste
(Pinch of sugar)

HONEY MUSTARD DIPPING SAUCE

About ⅔ cup

This simple sauce is especially good with fried chicken or fish.

Stir together well in a small bowl:

6 tablespoons honey
¼ cup Dijon mustard
Cayenne pepper to taste

Serve at room temperature. The sauce will keep, covered and refrigerated, for up to 1 month.

SCANDINAVIAN MUSTARD-DILL SAUCE

Generous ½ cup

Traditional with Gravlax, 393, this can also be served with other smoked, grilled, sautéed, or poached fish.

Whisk together in a medium bowl until smooth:

6 tablespoons Swedish or Dijon mustard
¼ cup minced dill
2 to 4 tablespoons sugar, to taste
¼ cup lemon juice or red wine vinegar, or to taste

Salt and black pepper to taste
Generous pinch of ground cardamom

Cover and let stand for 2 hours to allow the flavors to develop. Serve at room temperature or chilled. The sauce will keep, covered and refrigerated, for up to 2 days.

BAVARIAN APPLE AND HORSERADISH SAUCE

¾ to 1 cup

Delightfully simple, and a marvelous accompaniment for sausages, pork, beef, or fish.

Stir together well in a medium bowl:

⅓ cup grated peeled fresh or drained prepared horseradish
⅓ cup finely grated peeled tart green apple
2½ tablespoons lemon juice
½ teaspoon sugar
½ teaspoon salt

Cover and let stand for 30 minutes to allow the flavors to develop.

You may serve this as is as a relish-type condiment. For a creamier sauce, stir in:

(¼ cup sour cream or crème fraîche)

Garnish with:

1 teaspoon minced parsley
(1 teaspoon minced dill or chives)

Serve immediately.

MOJO

About 1 cup

This Cuban table sauce is briefly cooked to bring out the full flavor of the garlic. Serve with grilled beef, chicken, pork, or fish, or use as a marinade for any of these. Mojo is best served fresh, but the sauce will keep, covered and refrigerated, for up to 3 days.

Heat in a medium saucepan over medium heat:

½ cup olive oil

Add and cook until fragrant but not browned, 20 to 30 seconds:

8 garlic cloves, minced

Carefully stir in and bring to a boil:

1 cup sour orange juice, or ½ cup orange juice and ½ cup lime juice
1 tablespoon minced fresh oregano or 1 teaspoon dried oregano
¾ teaspoon ground cumin
½ teaspoon salt
¼ teaspoon black pepper

Reduce the heat to simmer gently for 10 minutes. Let cool and serve at room temperature.

MINT SAUCE

About 2 cups

A tradition with roasted lamb, this sauce is thin and sprightly—a refreshing change from Mint Jelly, 911.

Stir together in a bowl until the sugar has dissolved:

1½ cups malt vinegar or other strong vinegar
½ cup sugar

Stir in:

1 cup loosely packed mint leaves, minced

Let stand for 2 hours. The sauce will keep, covered and refrigerated, for up to 2 days.

CHIMICHURRI

About 1¼ cups

A tangy, spicy Argentinian sauce to serve with grilled or roasted meat.

Whisk together thoroughly in a small bowl:

½ cup olive oil
¼ cup red wine vinegar

Stir in:

⅓ cup finely chopped onion, shallot, or green onion
⅓ cup finely chopped parsley
4 garlic cloves, finely chopped
(1 tablespoon finely chopped oregano)
¼ teaspoon cayenne pepper, or to taste
¼ teaspoon black pepper, or to taste
Salt to taste

Cover and let stand for 2 hours to allow the flavors to develop. The sauce will keep, covered and refrigerated, for up to 2 days.

SALSA VERDE (ITALIAN GREEN SAUCE)

About ¾ cup

This classic green sauce—not to be confused with Mexican *salsa verde* (or tomatillo salsa; see 573)—is traditionally served with braised meats, fried calamari, grilled fish, and roasted cauliflower or eggplant. For a thicker texture, add ½ **cup dry bread crumbs** to the mixture below and puree until smooth and creamy, adding a little water if needed to make a paste.

Combine in a food processor:

1 cup packed fresh parsley leaves
½ cup extra-virgin olive oil
3 tablespoons drained capers
(Up to 6 anchovy fillets)
2 garlic cloves, chopped
1 tablespoon red wine vinegar or lemon juice
½ teaspoon whole-grain mustard
(½ teaspoon red pepper flakes)
Salt to taste

Blend to a uniform consistency, but do not process to a puree. Adjust the seasonings. The sauce will keep, covered and refrigerated, for up to 1 week. Serve at room temperature.

ZHUG (YEMENI CILANTRO-CHILE SAUCE)

About 1 cup

With the lesser amount of chiles, *zhug* is somewhat like Salsa Verde or Chimichurri, above: It's a perky, herbal accompaniment to grilled meats and falafel, a dipping sauce, or a last-minute "enlivener" for soups and braises. With the larger amount of chiles, it's better to think of *zhug* as a chunky hot sauce or relish. We like to add ground black cardamom seeds, which lend a subtle smoky, aromatic flavor.

Coarsely chop:

2 to 8 serrano peppers, seeded
4 garlic cloves

Add to a food processor and pulse a few times until finely chopped. Add and pulse into a chunky paste:

1½ cups packed coarsely chopped cilantro leaves and stems
½ cup packed coarsely chopped parsley leaves and stems
¼ cup olive oil
1 tablespoon lemon juice
½ teaspoon salt
½ teaspoon black pepper
½ teaspoon ground green or black cardamom seeds
½ teaspoon ground cumin
(½ teaspoon ground caraway)

The sauce will keep, covered and refrigerated, for up to 5 days.

CILANTRO-MINT CHUTNEY

About 1½ cups

This bright, herb-packed sauce is our preferred condiment for samosas, 68, and Pakoras, 203.

Combine in a food processor or blender:

1 cup lightly packed fresh mint leaves
½ cup lightly packed fresh cilantro leaves
½ cup coarsely chopped onion
3 green onions, coarsely chopped
3 jalapeño peppers, seeded and coarsely chopped
2 garlic cloves, coarsely chopped
3 tablespoons water
2 to 3 tablespoons lemon juice, to taste
¼ teaspoon salt

Puree, stopping to scrape down the sides as needed. Cover and refrigerate for up to 3 days.

SAUCE GRIBICHE

About ⅔ cup

This tangy sauce is excellent for vegetables that need perking up, like boiled potatoes or cauliflower, but it also stands up to strongly flavored foods, such as Raddicchio and Treviso, 114.

Whisk together in a medium bowl:

2 tablespoons red wine vinegar
1 tablespoon Dijon mustard

Gradually whisk in:

¼ cup olive oil

Stir in:

1 Hard-Boiled Egg, 151, minced or pressed through a fine-mesh sieve
2 tablespoons minced cornichons
1 tablespoon drained capers, minced
2 teaspoons minced tarragon
2 teaspoons minced parsley
(2 teaspoons minced chervil)
¼ teaspoon black pepper

This sauce is best the day it's made, but you may refrigerate it for up to 3 days.

CORN AND TOMATO RELISH

About 3½ cups

This relish goes particularly well with pork. If you wish, you can use 1½ cups thawed frozen corn, but be sure to use only good-quality fresh tomatoes.

Shuck and remove the silks from:

3 ears corn

Cook in boiling salted water to cover for 1 minute, then drain, and cut off the kernels. Place the corn kernels in a small bowl and add:

2 tomatoes, finely diced
1 small red onion, finely diced
½ cup cider vinegar
¼ cup diced sweet pickles
1 tablespoon sugar
1 teaspoon celery salt
½ teaspoon black pepper, or to taste

Mix together well, cover, and refrigerate for at least 1 hour before serving to let the flavors meld. This relish will keep, covered and refrigerated, for up to 1 week.

TOMATO-OLIVE RELISH

About 2½ cups

Make this fresh, bright-tasting relish when tomatoes are at their prime. Serve it with grilled fish steaks or chicken, or on crostini.

Mix well in a medium bowl:

1 large tomato, diced
½ red onion, diced, or 4 green onions, thinly sliced
½ cup pitted Kalamata olives, halved lengthwise
¼ cup extra-virgin olive oil
¼ cup lemon juice
¼ cup chopped basil
1 garlic clove, minced
Salt and black pepper to taste

Let sit for 30 minutes at room temperature for the flavors to meld. Store, refrigerated, for up to 3 days.

RED ONION MARMALADE

About 1½ cups

Wonderful with roasted meats, and a good alternative (or supplement) to Cranberry Sauce, 179, for serving with a Thanksgiving turkey.

Combine in a medium saucepan over low heat:

4 large red onions, halved lengthwise and thinly sliced
½ cup dry red wine
½ cup red wine vinegar
⅓ cup packed light brown sugar
¼ cup honey

Cook, stirring, until the sugar is dissolved, then simmer, stirring often, until the mixture has the consistency of marmalade, about 1½ hours. Stir in:

1 tablespoon orange juice
1 tablespoon lemon juice

Cook, stirring, until blended, about 3 minutes more. Let cool. The marmalade will keep, covered and refrigerated, for up to 3 weeks. Serve at room temperature.

TZATZIKI (GREEK YOGURT SAUCE)

About 2 cups

A cool companion to fried foods or grilled meat, and a fine dip on its own with pita bread.

Stir together in a small bowl:

1 cup plain Greek yogurt
½ cucumber, peeled, seeded, and finely diced
1 tablespoon extra-virgin olive oil
1 tablespoon chopped dill
1 tablespoon chopped mint
1 tablespoon red wine vinegar or lemon juice
1 garlic clove, minced
½ teaspoon salt

Let sit, stirring occasionally, for 15 minutes to allow the flavors to meld. Store, refrigerated, for up to 3 days.

YOGURT-DILL SAUCE

About 1 cup

Serve this simple sauce with salmon, especially Pan-Fried Salmon Cakes, 389, and roasted carrots and beets.

Whisk together in a medium bowl:

1 cup plain yogurt
1 tablespoon minced dill
1 tablespoon grated peeled fresh or drained prepared horseradish
1 tablespoon stone-ground mustard
1 garlic clove, minced or grated on a rasp grater

Serve immediately or store, refrigerated, for up to 5 days.

RAITA (INDIAN YOGURT SALAD)

About 1¾ cups

Serve this cooling condiment alongside spicy meats, fish, poultry, or vegetarian entrées. For a change, substitute **¾ cup peeled, shredded daikon radish** for the cucumber (or use a combination).

Stir together in a small bowl:

1 cucumber, peeled, seeded, and finely chopped
1 cup plain yogurt
1 tablespoon finely chopped mint
¼ teaspoon ground cumin
¼ teaspoon salt
(1 jalapeño or serrano pepper, seeded and diced)

Raita is best served fresh, but it can be prepared ahead and refrigerated, covered, for up to 1 day.

TOMATO ACHAR

About 2¼ cups

Serve this Indian pickle with Dal, 218, rice, or Naan, 611. If desired, the recipe may be halved, but we have never had trouble finding uses for this flavorful condiment.

Have ready:

2 pounds tomatoes, quartered
1 head garlic, peeled and chopped
4 serrano peppers, seeded and chopped

Heat in a large saucepan over medium heat:

⅓ cup vegetable or mustard oil

When the oil is hot, add and fry for 30 seconds:

1½ teaspoons black or yellow mustard seeds
1½ teaspoons fenugreek seeds
½ teaspoon fennel seeds
(½ teaspoon ajwain seeds, 951)
(½ teaspoon nigella seeds, 1004)
(3 whole dried Kashmiri or árbol chiles)

Standing back to avoid the sputtering oil, add:

12 fresh curry leaves, 975, coarsely chopped
1 bay leaf

Add the garlic and serranos and cook for 2 minutes. Stir in the tomatoes and:

2 teaspoons salt
(¼ teaspoon asafoetida, 954)

Bring to a simmer and cook, stirring occasionally, over medium-low heat until most of the liquid has been cooked off, about 1½ hours. You will need to stir more frequently as the mixture reduces to prevent it from sticking to the pot and burning. Remove from the heat, remove the bay leaf, and let cool. Season to taste with:

Salt

Store, refrigerated, for up to 1 month.

BECKER COCKTAIL SAUCE

About 1 cup

This family favorite makes a lively dunking sauce for seafood.

Stir together well in a small bowl:

1 cup mild, tomato-based chili sauce or ketchup
¼ cup finely grated peeled fresh horseradish
1 teaspoon curry powder
(1 tablespoon soy sauce)
(1 to 2 garlic cloves, to taste, minced)
Hot pepper sauce to taste
Black pepper to taste
Finely grated zest of 1 lemon
Lemon juice to taste

The sauce will keep, covered and refrigerated, for up to 1 week. Serve at room temperature.

Z.26 STEAK SAUCE

About 2½ cups

Based on English "brown sauce," this dark and tangy condiment is best served with nicely charred red meat.

Heat in a medium saucepan over medium-high heat:

2 tablespoons vegetable oil

Add and cook, stirring, until browned, 8 to 10 minutes:

1 large onion, chopped

Add and cook, stirring, about 1 minute more:

5 garlic cloves, chopped

Stir in:

⅔ cup malt vinegar
¼ cup tomato paste
¼ cup raisins
¼ cup molasses

¼ cup Worcestershire sauce
2 tablespoons orange marmalade
2 tablespoons tamarind pulp, seeds removed, 195, or 1 tablespoon tamarind concentrate or extract
1 teaspoon salt
½ teaspoon white pepper
¼ teaspoon each ground allspice, cinnamon, and cloves

Bring to a boil, then reduce the heat and simmer gently for 10 minutes. Transfer to a blender and puree until smooth. Thin the sauce to the desired consistency with:

Up to ½ cup water

Let cool completely. Store refrigerated for up to 6 months.

MIGNONETTE SAUCE

About ½ cup; enough for 24 oysters

Classic with oysters on the half shell, 347, this sauce is good with any raw shellfish. Many different types of vinegar can be substituted for the red wine vinegar. Try sherry, vermouth, or Banyuls vinegar, or an infused vinegar, 103–31.

Mix together in a small bowl:

½ cup red wine vinegar
4 teaspoons minced shallots
(1 tablespoon finely chopped parsley)
2 teaspoons cracked black peppercorns
¾ teaspoon salt

Serve chilled or at room temperature.

CHAMPAGNE MIGNONETTE

Substitute ¼ **cup Champagne** and ¼ **cup Champagne or white wine vinegar** for the red wine vinegar in **Mignonette Sauce, above.**

MIGNONETTE GRANITÉ

To add flavor and texture to oysters on the half shell, 347, freeze **Mignonette Sauce** or **Champagne Mignonette, above,** as for Berry Granita, 849, and scoop small mounds of the ice onto the oysters.

GARLIC AND WALNUT SAUCE

About 1⅓ cups

This is a version of one of the dozens of walnut sauces found in the cuisine of Georgia (that is, the country in Eastern Europe between the Black Sea and Caspian Sea). Serve with cucumbers, tomatoes, roasted beets, poached chicken or turkey, or as a dipping sauce for bread. The sauce can be thicker, almost like hummus, or runny, like heavy cream, depending on what you intend to serve it with. You can increase the amount of spices to taste, if desired.

Combine in a food processor and process until finely ground:

1 cup walnuts, toasted, 1005
3 garlic cloves, coarsely chopped

Add and pulse to combine:

3 tablespoons minced cilantro or parsley
2 teaspoons lemon juice or red wine vinegar
¼ teaspoon ground coriander
¼ teaspoon cayenne pepper, or to taste
¼ teaspoon ground turmeric
(¼ teaspoon ground blue fenugreek leaves)

Thin the sauce to the desired consistency with:

Up to ¾ cup chicken or vegetable stock

Transfer to a bowl. Serve at room temperature. Store, refrigerated, for up to 1 week.

JEN'S BASIL OIL

About ½ cup

Our friend Jen Bryman makes this flavorful, bright-green sauce in the summer when basil is plentiful. It is thicker than most flavored oils, and even more straightforward than Pistou, 586. As with pesto, you may replace the basil with arugula for a more peppery effect. We love this sauce with asparagus, on salads, dotted on fresh cheeses, and drizzled over pasta dishes.

Combine in a blender:

1 cup lightly packed basil leaves
¼ cup extra-virgin olive oil
2 tablespoons water
1 tablespoon lemon juice
¼ teaspoon salt

Blend until smooth. Let sit, refrigerated, for at least 30 minutes before using to allow the flavors to meld. Keep refrigerated for up to 5 days.

ROMESCO SAUCE

About 2½ cups

To simplify this recipe slightly, you may skip the roasting step and use **1 cup canned whole tomatoes, drained,** instead of fresh, **½ cup drained jarred roasted red peppers** instead of fresh, and **1 garlic clove, minced,** instead of the roasted garlic.

Position an oven rack 4 inches below the heat. Preheat the broiler. Line a rimmed baking sheet with foil and place on the baking sheet:

1 large red bell pepper
1 pound Roma or plum tomatoes, halved, cut sides up
4 to 6 unpeeled garlic cloves, to taste

Broil, turning the pepper occasionally, until the tomatoes are blackened in spots and the pepper is well blackened all over, about 15 minutes. The garlic will be done (charred and soft) before the pepper and tomatoes. Transfer the pepper to a bowl and cover with a plate. Let steam until cool enough to handle, then peel off the blackened skin, remove the stem, and scrape out the seeds. Peel the garlic cloves.

Meanwhile, add to a small heatproof bowl:

2 dried ñora chiles, or 1 dried ancho chile and 1 dried guajillo chile, stemmed and seeded

Cover with boiling water and soak for 15 minutes.

Add to a food processor and pulse until finely chopped:

½ cup hazelnuts, toasted, 992

Drain the soaked chiles well and add them to the food processor along with the bell pepper, tomatoes, garlic, and:

1 to 2 tablespoons sherry vinegar, to taste
1½ teaspoons smoked paprika
½ teaspoon salt

Process into a chunky paste. With the machine running, slowly pour in:

½ cup olive oil

Season to taste with:

Salt

Store, refrigerated, for up to 1 week.

HABANERO-CITRUS HOT SAUCE

About 1 cup

This thin and punchy Yucatecan-style hot sauce is the perfect accompaniment to Braised Carnitas, 495, or any grilled or broiled fish, poultry, or meat. We also enjoy it with raw oysters on the half shell, 347, or mashed into an avocado. Pan-roasting and steeping the habaneros in citrus juice makes them surprisingly mellow. That said, this is a truly hot sauce, so use carefully.

Place in a medium dry skillet over medium heat:

4 green onions, white parts only (reserve the green tops)
6 unpeeled garlic cloves
2 to 4 habanero peppers, to taste

Cook the onions, garlic, and habaneros, turning occasionally, until blackened on all sides and the garlic is softened. They may not cook at the same rate, so remove them from the skillet as they are done. Peel the garlic and remove the stems from the habaneros. Add them to a blender, along with the green onion bottoms and reserved green tops and:

¾ cup sour orange juice, or equal parts orange juice and lime juice
¼ cup distilled white vinegar
1 teaspoon salt

Blend until smooth. Let stand at least 30 minutes before serving.

NAM PRIK (THAI-STYLE RELISH)

About ¼ cup

Nam prik, which translates as "pepper water," is a traditional table sauce of Thailand, where there are dozens of variations on the recipe. Some are very thin while others are thick and chunky relishes. They may contain shrimp paste, 1018, fried shallots, fish, and even ground pork. *Nam prik* is served with vegetables, stirred into soups, and used as a sauce for rice, noodles, meat, or fish. The sauce is best if allowed to stand for a day or two, and it keeps well for several weeks in the refrigerator.

Combine in a food processor or a mortar and process or pound to a paste:

18 tiny dried shrimp, toasted, 1016, and chopped
4 small dried Thai or árbol chiles, seeded, if desired, and crumbled
4 garlic cloves, chopped
2 tablespoons lime juice
1 tablespoon fish sauce

Stir in:

3 small red or green serrano peppers or Thai chiles, seeded, if desired, and finely chopped
Chopped cilantro to taste
(Palm sugar, 1025, or brown sugar to taste)

Cover and refrigerate for at least 1 day before serving.

PEANUT DIPPING SAUCE

About 1¾ cups

Some version of this sauce is served all over Southeast Asia, with the small skewers of meat and chicken known as satay, 61, or with many other dishes from Summer Rolls, 71, to grilled meats.

Combine in a medium saucepan:

1 cup canned coconut milk
½ cup smooth peanut butter
4 teaspoons palm sugar, 1025, or brown sugar
1 tablespoon fish sauce
1 tablespoon soy sauce
1 tablespoon red curry paste or Massaman curry paste, store-bought or homemade, 585

Whisk in thoroughly:

½ cup hot water

Cook, stirring occasionally, over low heat until the flavors are well blended, about 15 minutes. Stir into the peanut sauce:

2 teaspoons lime juice or rice vinegar, or to taste

NUOC CHAM

About 1 cup

This all-purpose Vietnamese condiment can be used as a dipping sauce for spring rolls or skewers of grilled meat, or to dress Vietnamese bún bowls, 305.

Stir in a small bowl until the sugar has dissolved:

½ cup water
⅓ cup lime juice, distilled white vinegar, or a combination
3 tablespoons sugar, or to taste
2 to 6 tablespoons fish sauce, to taste

Add:

1 or 2 Thai chiles or serrano peppers, to taste, thinly sliced
(3 garlic cloves, minced)

Let stand for at least 10 minutes before serving to allow the flavors to develop. The sauce will keep, covered and refrigerated, for up to 2 days if made with lime juice, or for 6 days if made with vinegar.

CHILE-INFUSED FISH SAUCE

About ½ cup

You will find this condiment on the table at most Thai and Vietnamese restaurants. It is just the thing to add depth, salt, and heat to bowls of Pho Bo, 96 and dishes like Thai fried rice noodles (Kuaytiaw Khua Kai, 303).

Combine in a small bowl:

½ cup fish sauce
10 Thai chiles, thinly sliced

Let sit for at least 30 minutes to give the chiles time to infuse the fish sauce, then use immediately or refrigerate for up to 1 week.

SSAMJANG (KOREAN DIPPING SAUCE)

About ⅓ cup

This salty sauce is usually served with *ssam* (green leafy vegetables, such as lettuce and shiso, wrapped around a filling, often meat). If you prefer a sweeter *ssamjang*, add honey to taste. The yield of this recipe is small, but remember: A little goes a long way (you can also thin it out with a little water or additional vinegar).

Stir together in a medium bowl:

¼ cup doenjang, 970
1½ tablespoons gochujang, 970
1½ teaspoons toasted sesame oil
1 teaspoon distilled white vinegar
2 garlic cloves, minced or grated on a rasp grater
1 green onion, finely chopped

Taste and adjust the seasonings if needed. Sprinkle on top:

1 teaspoon toasted sesame seeds

TENTSUYU (TEMPURA DIPPING SAUCE)

About 1½ cups

The classic accompaniment to tempura.

Combine in a small saucepan:

1 cup Dashi, 78, or 1 cup water and 1 teaspoon instant dashi granules
¼ cup mirin
2 tablespoons soy sauce
Pinch of sugar

Bring to a boil and remove from the heat. Serve warm. If desired, just before serving, stir in:

(¼ cup grated daikon radish)
(½-inch piece ginger, peeled and minced or grated)

KATSU SAUCE

About ½ cup

Specifically for Chicken Katsu, 415, we think of this tangy, salty sauce as a cousin to steak sauce. Serve it with almost any fried food or use it as a glaze for ribs.

Whisk together in a small bowl:

¼ cup ketchup
2 tablespoons oyster sauce
4 teaspoons Worcestershire sauce
1 tablespoon mirin or 2 teaspoons sugar
¼ teaspoon garlic powder

DIPPING SAUCE FOR DUMPLINGS

About 1 cup

Serve this sauce with Pot Stickers, 63, Fried Wontons, 91, or Seafood or Pork Shumai, 315.

Bring to a boil in a small saucepan:

½ cup rice vinegar
¼ cup mirin
¼ cup soy sauce
1½ tablespoons lemon juice
2 garlic cloves, minced
3 green onions, thinly sliced
1 teaspoon toasted sesame oil

Let cool slightly and transfer to a small bowl.

SPICY CHINESE CHILE CRISP

About 2 cups

Chile crisp, or Lao Gan Ma, was invented by a woman named Tao Huabi in Guizhou, China, in 1997. We developed this recipe out of necessity: We routinely crave Lao Gan Ma, but its growing popularity in the United States has led to shortages. For an even crispier texture, fry the shallots called for here separately as for Crispy Fried Shallots, 256, and proceed as directed, adding them to the food processor with the other ingredients. Serve this condiment with rice, noodles, dumplings, stir-fries, and soups.

Combine in a large saucepan:

1 cup vegetable oil
6 ounces shallots (3 to 4 large), thinly sliced
5 large garlic cloves, thinly sliced
1¼ ounces dried red chiles (such as árbol), toasted, 969, stemmed, seeded, and broken into pieces (or ½ cup red pepper flakes)
¼ cup roasted peanuts or soy nuts
2 tablespoons fermented black beans, 983
(2 tablespoons Sichuan chili bean paste, 970)
(2 tablespoons chopped dried shrimp or anchovies, 1016)

Heat over medium heat until just beginning to simmer, then reduce the heat to maintain a lazy bubble. Cook until the shallots have softened and shrunk and the whole mixture has darkened somewhat and become very fragrant, 20 to 25 minutes. Remove the pan from the heat and let cool for 10 minutes. Stir in:

1½ teaspoons ground Sichuan peppercorns
1 teaspoon salt, MSG, or mushroom seasoning, 984
½ teaspoon sugar

Once cool, transfer the mixture to a food processor and pulse until ground into a chunky paste (about 3 long pulses). Transfer to a glass jar or container. Store refrigerated.

SRIRACHA

About 2 cups

Almost any fresh red chile will do, but we have had especially good luck with what are known as "red finger hots." Red jalapeños or Fresnos will work as well. Though you may be tempted to use red Thai chiles, fight this impulse! They are incredibly difficult to seed and, if used whole, will make the sauce way too spicy.

Wearing gloves, stem, seed, and coarsely chop:

1½ pounds fresh red chiles

Transfer the chiles to a medium saucepan and add:

½ cup water
⅓ cup rice or coconut vinegar
¼ cup packed grated palm sugar, 1025, or packed dark brown sugar
4 to 6 garlic cloves, to taste
1 teaspoon salt

Bring the mixture to a boil, simmer for 10 minutes, and remove from the heat. When cool, transfer to a blender or food processor and puree until smooth. Add water or a touch of vinegar if the mixture is too thick; it should be the consistency of ketchup. Season to taste with:

Salt

Transfer to a bottle or jar. Store in the refrigerator. The sauce will keep for at least 1 month.

CHINESE BLACK BEAN SAUCE

About ½ cup

This sauce can be rubbed on fish or shellfish before steaming or served as a condiment with the finished dish.

Mash to a paste with a fork in a small bowl or chop in a food processor:

3 tablespoons fermented black beans

Stir in or pulse in:

2 green onions, finely chopped
2 tablespoons soy sauce
2 tablespoons Shaoxing wine, 952, or dry sherry
4 garlic cloves, finely chopped
2 teaspoons vegetable oil
2 teaspoons toasted sesame oil
2 teaspoons finely chopped peeled ginger
Salt and cracked black peppercorns to taste

Serve at room temperature. The sauce will keep, covered and refrigerated, for up to 6 days.

ABOUT SALSAS

Salsa means "sauce" in both Italian and Spanish, and in these languages, the word can apply to everything from creamy white sauce to brown gravy. Still, when we hear the word "salsa," it is usually the tomato- and chile-based type that springs to mind.

Raw salsas are best made with ripe summer tomatoes. During winter months, we opt for canned tomatoes (see Table Salsa, below) or roasted ones (see Roasted Tomato–Chipotle Salsa, 574). If the taste of raw onion in salsa is off-putting to you, place the chopped onions in a fine-mesh sieve and pour boiling water over them. Or sprinkle with lime juice and let them "pickle" for 15 minutes before combining with the other ingredients.

We like to pan-roast these ingredients in a dry cast-iron skillet over medium heat, turning occasionally, until they are blackened all over. Dry-roasting ingredients such as fresh and dried chiles, unpeeled garlic cloves, whole small tomatoes, tomatillos, and green onions is a staple technique of Mexican cooking.

When removing the lid of the blender or food processor after grinding mixtures that include chiles, avert your face—the fumes are powerful.

Allow at least ¼ cup salsa per serving. Aside from those containing avocado, most salsas can be refrigerated in a covered container for 5 to 7 days.

PICO DE GALLO (FRESH SALSA)

About 2 cups

This recipe is easily doubled or tripled, but make only as much as you will use immediately, as it loses its texture and the heat increases on standing. To make the spicy Yucatecan salsa called **xni pec,** or "dog's nose," substitute **2 habaneros** for the serranos or jalapeños, and substitute **1 tablespoon lime juice** plus **2 tablespoons orange juice** for the lime juice. Pico de gallo complements everything from tacos to grilled meat and vegetables.

Combine in a medium bowl:

2 large tomatoes or 3 to 5 plum or Roma tomatoes, seeded if desired and finely diced
½ small white or red onion, finely chopped, rinsed, and drained, or 8 green onions, chopped
¼ to ½ cup chopped cilantro leaves and tender stems, to taste
3 to 5 serrano or jalapeño peppers, to taste, seeded and minced
(6 radishes, finely chopped)
2 tablespoons lime juice
(1 garlic clove, minced)

Stir together. Season to taste with:

Salt

Serve immediately.

SALSA VERDE CRUDA (RAW TOMATILLO SALSA)

About 2 cups

This intensely fresh, herbal salsa is especially good with fish, chicken, roasted vegetables, and eggs. For a richer salsa, you may roast half of the tomatillos as for Roasted Tomato–Chipotle Salsa, 574, or the peppers and onions as for Table Salsa, below.

Combine in a food processor or blender and coarsely puree, leaving the mixture a little chunky:

8 ounces tomatillos, husked, rinsed, and chopped
4 green onions, chopped
1 to 3 serrano or jalapeño peppers, to taste, seeded and chopped
(1 garlic clove)
¼ cup finely chopped cilantro

Transfer to a medium bowl and stir in enough cold water to loosen the mixture to a sauce-like consistency. Season to taste with:

Salt

Serve immediately.

TABLE SALSA

About 2½ cups

This is our favorite salsa for everyday use: It is flavorful, convenient, and ready in the time it takes to drink a beer. Because it is made with canned tomatoes, this is the perfect salsa to make when tomatoes are not in season.

Add to a dry, medium heavy skillet over medium heat:

3 green onions, white parts only (reserve the green tops)
3 garlic cloves, unpeeled
2 or 3 fresh chiles such as serrano, jalapeño, habanero, manzana, or a combination, to taste

Cook, turning the pieces occasionally, until the contents of the skillet are lightly charred all over, about 15 minutes. Meanwhile, drain off about half of the juice from:

One 28-ounce can whole tomatoes

Add 2 of the tomatoes to a food processor along with:

1 tablespoon lime juice
1 teaspoon distilled white or cider vinegar

½ teaspoon salt
½ teaspoon ground cumin, toasted before grinding, 1021, if desired
½ teaspoon ground coriander, toasted before grinding, 1021, if desired
½ teaspoon oregano, preferably Mexican
(¼ teaspoon cayenne pepper or chipotle chile powder)

When the vegetables are charred, peel the garlic cloves, remove the stems and seeds from the chiles, and cut them into chunks, along with the green onion bottoms. Add the garlic, chiles, and green onion bottoms to the food processor and pulse until finely chopped. Add the rest of the canned tomatoes along with:

¼ cup packed coarsely chopped cilantro
Reserved green onion tops, thinly sliced

Process until well combined but still a little chunky. Adjust seasonings to taste with:

Lime juice
Salt

Serve immediately or keep refrigerated for up to 1 week.

CORN, TOMATO, AND AVOCADO SALSA

About 3½ cups

Combine in a medium bowl:

16 cherry tomatoes, halved
Kernels from 2 ears corn
1 avocado, pitted, peeled, and chopped
½ small red onion, finely diced, rinsed, and drained
1 garlic clove, finely chopped
1 to 3 jalapeño peppers, to taste, seeded and finely chopped
¼ cup chopped basil
2 tablespoons vegetable oil
¼ cup lime juice, or to taste
½ teaspoon salt
¼ teaspoon black pepper

Stir together well. This salsa will keep, covered and refrigerated, for up to 3 days.

GUASACACA SAUCE (VENEZUELAN AVOCADO SALSA)

About 1½ cups

This smooth avocado sauce can be treated as a dip, similar to Guacamole, 51, or it can be used as a sauce for grilled meats or vegetables.

Combine in a food processor:

1 large avocado, pitted and peeled
¼ cup finely chopped onion
¼ cup finely chopped green bell pepper
1 jalapeño or serrano pepper, seeded if desired
1 garlic clove, peeled
¼ cup packed fresh parsley leaves
¼ cup packed fresh cilantro leaves
2 tablespoons distilled white vinegar or white wine vinegar
1 tablespoon lime juice
¼ teaspoon salt

Pulse until very finely chopped, scraping down the bowl as needed. With the motor running, add in a thin, steady stream:

¼ cup olive oil

Adjust the seasoning to taste with:

Salt
Vinegar or lime juice

The salsa will keep, covered and refrigerated, for up to 3 days.

ROASTED TOMATO-CHIPOTLE SALSA

About 4 cups

Tomatoes take on a deeper flavor when roasted. This salsa is particularly good with grilled chicken, fish, or lamb and with tacos or enchiladas.

Prepare a medium-low grill fire, 1063, or position an oven rack as close to the heat as possible. Preheat the broiler.

Place on the grill or a foil-lined rimmed baking sheet:

6 medium tomatoes, halved

Grill or broil, turning as needed, until the skins are blackened in spots and slightly softened, about 5 minutes on each side on the grill, slightly less time under the broiler. When cool enough to handle, peel and coarsely chop the tomatoes. Put them in a medium bowl and stir in:

1 small onion, finely chopped, rinsed, and drained
¼ cup coarsely chopped cilantro
3 tablespoons lime juice, or to taste
2 tablespoons olive oil
2 garlic cloves, finely chopped
1 canned chipotle pepper in adobo sauce, finely chopped, or to taste
1 teaspoon ground cumin
Salt to taste

Serve immediately or store, refrigerated, for up to 1 week.

FRUIT SALSA

About 3 cups

We generally aren't fans of fruit salsa, but we love this one. It avoids being overly sweet and has just enough spice to keep things interesting. It is wonderful with many things, but particularly with grilled or sautéed fish. We highly recommend adding the optional avocado.

Combine in a large bowl:

1½ cups diced peeled mango, papaya, pineapple, peaches, or a combination
½ cup diced red bell pepper
(1 large avocado, pitted, peeled, and chopped)
3 green onions, chopped, or ⅓ cup diced red onion
¼ cup coarsely chopped cilantro
2 tablespoons orange juice
2 tablespoons lime juice
1 garlic clove, minced or grated on a rasp grater
1 jalapeño, serrano, or habanero pepper, seeded and minced
¼ teaspoon salt, or to taste

The salsa will keep, covered and refrigerated, for up to 3 days.

ABOUT VINAIGRETTES AND SALAD DRESSINGS

Vinaigrettes are emulsions of oil and vinegar or citrus juice. Like mayonnaise, emulsifying these two incompatible liquids by vigorously whisking the oil into the vinegar thickens vinaigrettes, but most are only thick enough to lightly cling to the leaves they are tossed with. Mustard is a classic addition that helps vinaigrettes form a good emulsion. Other vinaigrette-like dressings, such as the one for Caesar Salad, 117, rely upon egg yolks. Still-thicker ones use mayonnaise, pureed vegetables, nut butters, or cheese and other dairy products for body. Whether simple or rich and complex, salad dressings, with the rarest exceptions, should never repeat in their composition the materials they grace. For instance, pair a very bright vinaigrette with a rich salad of avocados or roasted beets, or use a rich, creamy dressing for a salad of bitter greens.

Classic vinaigrette proportions are 3 to 4 parts oil to 1 part acid, such as lemon juice, lime juice, or vinegar, with salt and pepper to taste. The recipes below generally adhere to this rule, but we must confess to preferring a tarter ratio, like the one called for in Megan's Lemon-Dijon Dressing, below. Be sure your oil is fresh, as any off notes will make the dressing inedible. After preparing any vinaigrette or salad dressing, dip a lettuce leaf in the dressing and taste it to gauge whether it is salty or acidic enough. Adjust the seasonings accordingly.

Traditionally, vinaigrettes are whisked in a bowl, but we find that adding all the ingredients to a jar with a tight-fitting lid and shaking the jar vigorously is quicker and easier. Give them a good shake immediately before dressing salads. For a longer-lasting emulsion, prepare vinaigrettes in a blender, a food processor, or with a hand blender.

Dressings are best made the same day they are to be used. Those that do not contain fresh herbs will keep in the refrigerator for up to 1 week. For more information on dressing salads, see About Dressing and Serving Salads, 115. In general, for each cup of greens you will need about 1 tablespoon vinaigrette or 1½ tablespoons of a creamy dressing. For more on selecting ingredients for use in vinaigrettes, see Oils, 1006, and Vinegar, 1029. Most of the thicker, creamy dressings that follow also make excellent dips for crudités, 45.

VINAIGRETTE

About 1 cup

In addition to the variations suggested below, keep in mind that it is worth experimenting with most vinegars and citrus juices in vinaigrettes.

Combine in a medium bowl:

¼ cup red or white wine vinegar, balsamic vinegar, sherry vinegar, or lemon juice
(1 teaspoon minced shallot)
(1 small garlic clove, minced, grated on a rasp grater, or mashed to a paste)
(½ to 1 teaspoon Dijon or whole-grain mustard, to taste)
½ teaspoon salt
⅛ teaspoon black pepper, or to taste

Whisk until blended. Add gradually, whisking constantly after each addition:

¾ cup olive oil

If made in advance, cover and refrigerate. Shake well before using.

ADDITIONS TO VINAIGRETTE

Whisk any of the following into Vinaigrette, above.

¼ cup minced herbs such as basil, dill, parsley, chives, tarragon, or a combination
½ cup finely chopped watercress leaves
¼ cup minced preserved lemon
1 to 2 teaspoons cracked black peppercorns, to taste, and the finely grated zest of 1 lemon
1 tablespoon grated peeled fresh or drained prepared horseradish, or to taste
1 tablespoon honey
1 plum or Roma tomato, grated on the large holes of a box grater
¼ to ⅓ cup crumbled Roquefort or other blue cheese, to taste
¼ cup finely grated Parmesan or Romano cheese
4 anchovy fillets, minced, or up to 1 tablespoon anchovy paste

MEGAN'S LEMON-DIJON DRESSING

About 1 cup

This tart formula is our favorite for almost any green salad.

Combine in a pint jar with a tight-fitting lid:

¾ cup extra-virgin olive oil
(Finely grated zest of 1 lemon)
¼ cup plus 1 tablespoon lemon juice
2 teaspoons Dijon mustard
1 garlic clove, minced or grated on a rasp grater
½ teaspoon salt
½ teaspoon black pepper

Shake vigorously to combine.

WALNUT VINAIGRETTE

About ¾ cup

Serve over mixed greens or spinach with goat cheese or grilled chicken.

Whisk together in a small bowl:

3 tablespoons balsamic or red wine vinegar, or to taste
2 tablespoons minced toasted, 1005, walnuts
2 teaspoons Dijon mustard
1½ teaspoons minced shallot

Add in a slow, steady stream, whisking constantly:

⅓ cup extra-virgin olive oil
⅓ cup walnut oil (or use an additional ⅓ cup extra-virgin olive oil)

Taste and adjust the seasonings.

POPPY SEED–HONEY DRESSING

About ⅔ cup

This dressing is a favorite for salads that combine greens and fruit.

Whisk together in a small bowl until smooth:

¼ cup honey
3 tablespoons cider or other fruit vinegar
1 small shallot, minced
2 teaspoons Dijon mustard
1 teaspoon poppy seeds
Salt and black pepper to taste

Gradually add, whisking constantly:

2 tablespoons olive oil

Taste and adjust the seasonings.

ROASTED RED PEPPER DRESSING

About 1¼ cups

Combine in a blender or food processor:

One 6½-ounce jar roasted red peppers, drained
6 tablespoons olive oil
2 tablespoons lemon juice
2 tablespoons white wine vinegar
3 tablespoons chopped shallots
1 tablespoon ground cumin
1 garlic clove, chopped
Salt and black pepper to taste
Pinch of cayenne pepper

Blend until smooth.

JAPANESE STEAKHOUSE GINGER DRESSING

About 1½ cups

Combine in a blender and process until thick and smooth:

½ cup coarsely chopped carrots
¼ cup coarsely chopped celery
¼ cup vegetable oil
¼ cup rice vinegar
2 tablespoons chopped peeled ginger
2 tablespoons chopped onion
2 tablespoons sugar
1 tablespoon soy sauce
2 teaspoons ketchup
2 teaspoons lemon juice
1 teaspoon salt
½ teaspoon black pepper
2 dashes hot pepper sauce

ROASTED GARLIC DRESSING

About ¾ cup

Preheat the oven to 400°F. Place on a doubled piece of foil:

1 head garlic, top third cut off and loose skin removed
2 shallots, loose skin removed

Drizzle with:

2 tablespoons olive oil

Wrap and seal tightly. Place on a baking sheet and roast for 1 hour.

Remove the package from the oven, carefully open, and let cool. When cool enough to handle, squeeze the garlic and shallots from their skins into a small food processor or a blender. Add and process to a puree:

2 tablespoons olive oil
1 tablespoon lemon juice
1 tablespoon white wine vinegar
1 teaspoon Dijon mustard
1 teaspoon fresh thyme leaves
1 teaspoon minced rosemary
Salt and black pepper to taste

With the machine running, add in a slow, steady stream, processing until smooth:

6 tablespoons olive oil

Taste and adjust the seasonings. Use immediately, or cover and refrigerate for up to 5 days.

MISO DRESSING

About ⅔ cup

This dressing is perfect for cold noodle salads, in chicken salad, or with spicy greens like arugula.

Whisk together in a medium bowl:

¼ cup white miso
3 tablespoons vegetable oil
2 tablespoons white wine or rice vinegar
1 teaspoon toasted sesame oil
1 garlic clove, minced or grated on a rasp grater

Whisk in until the desired consistency is reached:

Up to ¼ cup water

TAHINI DRESSING

About 1 cup

Tahini, or sesame seed paste, is a staple of Middle Eastern cooking. This dressing goes especially well with Falafel, 214, and chickpea salads.

Whisk together in a small bowl:

½ cup tahini
½ cup water
2 tablespoons lemon juice
(1 garlic clove, minced or grated on a rasp grater)
(½ teaspoon ground cumin)
¼ teaspoon salt

RUSSIAN DRESSING

About 1⅓ cups

This sauce is better known as a condiment than a salad dressing. Use it to flavor the yolks for Deviled Eggs, 151, drizzle over a Reuben Sandwich, 141, or serve as a dipping sauce with fried foods.

Whisk together in a small bowl:

1 cup mayonnaise, store-bought or homemade, 563
1 tablespoon grated peeled fresh or drained prepared horseradish
(1 teaspoon Worcestershire sauce)
¼ cup mild, tomato-based chili sauce or ketchup
1 teaspoon grated onion
(1 teaspoon hot pepper sauce)

Chill before using.

THOUSAND ISLAND DRESSING

About 1½ cups

A relative of Russian dressing, Thousand Island is a classic topping for a wedge of iceberg lettuce. Without the hard-boiled egg, it also makes a good "special sauce" for burgers and sandwiches.

Stir together in a small bowl until well blended:

1 cup mayonnaise, store-bought or homemade, 563
¼ cup mild, tomato-based chili sauce or ketchup
(1 Hard-Boiled Egg, 151, chopped)
2 tablespoons pickle relish, minced pickles, or minced green olives
1 tablespoon grated or minced onion
1 tablespoon minced chives

1 tablespoon minced parsley
Salt and black pepper to taste

Taste and adjust the seasonings. Use immediately, or cover and refrigerate for up to 5 days.

RANCH DRESSING

About 1½ cups

The original version was created at the Hidden Valley Guest Ranch in Santa Barbara, California, in the 1950s. For a modern, lighter version, substitute plain Greek yogurt for the sour cream or mayonnaise.

Whisk together in a medium bowl until well blended:

⅔ cup sour cream or mayonnaise, store-bought or homemade, 563
½ cup buttermilk
2 to 3 tablespoons lemon or lime juice, to taste
1 tablespoon minced cilantro or parsley
1 tablespoon minced chives
1 tablespoon minced dill
1 garlic clove, mashed to a paste or grated on a rasp grater
Salt and black pepper to taste

Taste and adjust the seasonings. Use immediately, or cover and refrigerate for up to 5 days. The flavor will improve over the course of an hour or so.

GREEN GODDESS DRESSING

About 1¾ cups

Like ranch dressing, this lesser-known classic hails from California. Use with robust greens, such as romaine, drizzle over roasted vegetables, or serve with crudités, 45.

Combine in a medium bowl:

1 cup mayonnaise, store-bought or homemade, 563
1 garlic clove, minced or grated on a rasp grater
3 anchovy fillets, minced
½ cup sour cream
¼ cup minced chives or green onions
¼ cup minced parsley
1 tablespoon lemon juice
1 tablespoon tarragon or white wine vinegar
½ teaspoon salt
Black pepper to taste

Taste and adjust the seasonings. Use immediately, or cover and refrigerate for up to 3 days.

HERBED YOGURT DRESSING

About 1 cup

This creamy bright-green dressing pairs well with bitter or hearty greens like radicchio or kale.

Combine in a blender:

½ cup plain yogurt
2 green onions, finely chopped
¼ cup packed chopped cilantro
2 tablespoons minced chives
2 tablespoons minced parsley
1 tablespoon lemon juice
1 garlic clove, chopped
½ teaspoon salt

Blend until smooth. With the blender running, add in a slow, steady stream:

¼ cup olive oil

Use immediately, or cover and refrigerate for up to 3 days.

CREAMY BLUE CHEESE DRESSING

About 1 cup

Combine in a blender:

⅓ cup crumbled blue cheese
2 ounces cream cheese
¼ cup buttermilk
1 tablespoon red wine vinegar
¼ teaspoon salt
¼ teaspoon black pepper

Blend until smooth. If the dressing is too thick, add a little more buttermilk to reach the desired consistency. Transfer to a bowl and stir in:

¼ cup crumbled blue cheese

Season to taste with:

Salt and black pepper

Use immediately, or refrigerate for up to 5 days.

FETA OR GOAT CHEESE DRESSING

About 1¼ cups

Serve with a Greek-style salad or pasta salad, over sliced tomatoes, or as a dip for crudités, 45.

Combine in a blender:

1 cup crumbled feta or fresh goat cheese (4 ounces)
2 tablespoons red wine vinegar
2 tablespoons extra-virgin olive oil
1 teaspoon minced fresh oregano or ½ teaspoon dried oregano
¼ teaspoon salt
¼ teaspoon black pepper

Blend until smooth. With the machine running, add in a slow, steady stream, blending until smooth:

⅓ cup milk

If the dressing is too thick, add a little more milk as needed. Taste and adjust the seasonings. Use immediately, or cover and refrigerate for up to 5 days.

BUTTERMILK-HONEY DRESSING

About 1¼ cups

Whisk together in a small bowl:

¼ cup rice vinegar
¼ cup sour cream
¼ cup buttermilk
2 to 3 tablespoons honey, to taste
1 garlic clove, minced or grated on a rasp grater
1 green onion, minced
Pinch of cayenne pepper
½ teaspoon salt
¼ teaspoon black pepper

Add in a slow, steady stream, whisking constantly:

½ cup olive oil

Use immediately, or refrigerate for up to 5 days.

CREAMY HORSERADISH DRESSING

About ⅔ cup

Whisk together in a small bowl:

¼ cup heavy cream
2 tablespoons drained prepared horseradish
4 teaspoons red wine vinegar
½ teaspoon salt

Gradually whisk in until well blended:

¼ cup plus 2 tablespoons vegetable oil

Use immediately, or refrigerate for up to 5 days.

CREAMY PARMESAN DRESSING

About ¾ cup

Called "Half-and-Half Dressing" in previous editions of *Joy*, this dressing is a fine compromise between creamy and tangy and just happens to be an excellent substitute for the dressing in Caesar Salad, 117.

Whisk to combine in a medium bowl:

½ cup Vinaigrette, 575
½ cup grated Parmesan (2 ounces)
¼ cup mayonnaise, store-bought or homemade, 563
1 garlic clove, minced or grated on a rasp grater
(1 to 3 anchovy fillets, to taste, minced)

Use immediately, or refrigerate for up to 5 days.

ABOUT GLAZES

The savory glazes in this section impart color and flavor to meats, fish, and vegetables. The sheen they provide usually comes from some form of melted and browned sugar. Glazes should be thick enough to paint on the food without dripping. They are usually applied to food during the last several minutes of cooking, but a quick final coating of glaze may be brushed on just before serving. Some glazes can be passed as dipping sauces at the table.

In general, apply glaze during the last 15 to 45 minutes of cooking, the timing depending on the heat of the oven or grill, the sweetness of the sauce, and the size of the piece of meat. The hotter the oven or grill, the less time it will take for glaze to caramelize.

To glaze smaller pieces on a hot grill, move the pieces off direct heat, apply the glaze, and move them back over the flames a few at a time, watching them carefully.

To glaze roasting poultry, take poultry parts out of the oven and brush the glaze on 5 to 10 minutes before they are finished cooking. For whole poultry, depending on size, wait until 15 to 30 minutes before the end of cooking to glaze—the smaller the bird, the shorter the time.

To glaze a large ham, remove it from the oven about 45 minutes before it is done. Score the fat on top in any pattern, stud with whole cloves, if desired, and brush with the glaze, then return to the oven.

Most glazes keep, refrigerated, for at least 1 week. Reheat gently over medium-low heat before using. Teriyaki Marinade, 582, may also be used as a glaze, as can any barbecue sauce, 582–83 (aside from North Carolina–style sauce, which is too thin).

VIETNAMESE CARAMEL SAUCE

About ¾ cup

This rich, savory caramel may be used as a last-minute glaze for grilled skewers of meat, tofu, and poultry or added in small amounts to sauces and braised dishes for extra depth of flavor.

Combine in a small saucepan:

1 cup sugar
⅓ cup water

Set over medium heat and stir until the sugar has dissolved. Increase the heat to medium-high and bring to a boil (do not stir once the mixture is boiling). Simmer until the mixture is amber colored, or has reached 375°F on a thermometer. Take the pan off the heat and, being careful of splatters, add:

½ cup fish sauce or ¼ cup fish sauce and ¼ cup water

After the mixture has stopped foaming vigorously, stir until it is smooth. Once cool, skim off any remaining foam. Use immediately, or store refrigerated in a covered container for up to 6 months.

HOISIN-GINGER GLAZE

About 1 cup

An umami-rich glaze for salmon, duck breast, pork loin, or chicken. For **Miso Glaze,** omit the soy sauce and substitute **¼ cup red or white miso** for the hoisin sauce and **¼ cup sake** for the wine.

Whisk to combine in a small bowl:

½ cup hoisin sauce
(2 tablespoons chile garlic paste or sriracha)
2 tablespoons honey or brown sugar
2 tablespoons Shaoxing wine, 952, or dry sherry
2 tablespoons rice vinegar
1 tablespoon soy sauce
1-inch piece ginger, peeled and minced or grated on a rasp grater
2 garlic cloves, minced or grated on a rasp grater
(1 teaspoon toasted sesame oil)

BROWN SUGAR GLAZE

About ¾ cup

For baked ham, grilled or roasted poultry, or grilled sausages.

Mix together in a bowl with your fingers, breaking up any lumps:

¾ cup packed light brown sugar
2 teaspoons dry mustard

Slowly stir in until the paste is of spreading consistency:

Orange juice, rum, or bourbon

CRANBERRY GLAZE

About 1½ cups

Best used for baked ham.

Combine in a small saucepan over medium-low heat:

1 cup canned jellied cranberry sauce
½ cup packed brown sugar
2 tablespoons lemon juice

Briefly heat, stirring occasionally, to dissolve the sugar and make of spreading consistency.

MARMALADE GLAZE

For baked ham or poultry.

Briefly heat if necessary to make of spreading consistency:

¾ cup orange, lemon, ginger, pineapple, or other marmalade

If desired, stir in:

(2 tablespoons Cognac or bourbon)

PINEAPPLE GLAZE

About ⅔ cup

A sweet glaze for baked ham.

Stir together in a medium saucepan over low heat until the sugar is dissolved:

¾ cup packed light brown sugar
½ cup finely chopped fresh or drained canned crushed pineapple
½ teaspoon ground ginger

Cook over medium-low heat, stirring frequently, until the sugar is dissolved and the glaze is smooth, about 10 minutes.

BOURBON-MOLASSES GLAZE

About 1 cup

A boozy glaze for baked ham, roast chicken, grilled salmon, or pork chops.

Combine in a small saucepan:

1 cup bourbon
1 cup light molasses, maple syrup, sorghum syrup, or honey, or a combination
1 tablespoon Worcestershire sauce
(1 tablespoon Dijon mustard)
One 3-inch-long strip orange zest, removed with a vegetable peeler
¼ teaspoon ground cloves or allspice
1 bay leaf

Simmer over medium heat until the mixture has reduced by half and coats the back of a spoon, about 15 minutes. Remove the orange zest and bay leaf before using.

HONEY GLAZE

I. FOR MEATS AND VEGETABLES

About ½ cup

Stir together in a small bowl:

¼ cup honey
¼ cup soy sauce
1 teaspoon dry mustard

II. FOR BAKED HAM

About 1¼ cups

Combine in a medium saucepan:

½ cup honey
½ cup packed brown sugar
¼ cup orange juice
2 tablespoons cider vinegar
2 teaspoons dry mustard
½ teaspoon ground cloves
½ teaspoon ground allspice
½ teaspoon salt

ABOUT MARINADES

These aromatic seasoned liquids are used to flavor meat, poultry, fish, or vegetables before cooking. Because nearly all contain some type of acid, such as wine, vinegar, citrus juice, or yogurt or buttermilk, they also "tenderize" the surfaces of meat, fish, and poultry. ➤ Marinades containing raw alcohol, much like those containing citrus juice or vinegar, can "cook" the outside of meat marinated in it, causing it to develop a mushy texture if marinated for too long.

Most flavor compounds are too large to permeate the interior of a piece of meat. Thus, marinades can only impart flavor to the outermost layer of tissue. The exception to this is salt, which is very small and can penetrate deeper. Nevertheless, marinades do noticeably alter the flavor of foods. Thinly sliced meats are particularly good at picking up marinades. Certain cuts of meat, such as skirt steak and brisket, are structured in a way that helps them absorb and retain marinades better. If you would like to flavor the interior of a cut of meat, try injecting, 45, flavorful liquids into the meat. Another option is to make deep incisions in larger pieces of meat so that more surface is exposed to the marinade.

Though the shape of foods and marinating vessels make estimates difficult, we recommend you ➤ prepare at least ½ cup marinade for every 1 pound food. Marinade containers should be made of food-grade plastic, glass, or a nonreactive metal such as stainless steel. Less marinade is needed to cover if the meat, poultry, or fish is placed in a container just large enough to hold it. Large zip-top bags are ideal for the same reason: Very little marinade is needed when the air is forced out of them before sealing. For larger items that will not fit in gallon-sized zip-top bags, oven bags are a readily available substitute. In either case, place marinating bags in a bowl, baking dish, or roasting pan so that they do not leak in the refrigerator. (For slender objects like hanger steaks and kalbi-cut short ribs, a loaf pan can be ideal.)

The marination period may vary from only a few minutes to many hours; always refrigerate marinating foods. Stir or turn the meat occasionally during the process. Unless directed otherwise, avoid letting meats sit in acidic marinades for more than 2 or 3 hours, or they may give the surface a mealy or mushy texture. Fish should never be marinated for long, or it will toughen and turn into Ceviche, 377.

Store-bought and homemade vinaigrettes, 575, may be used as marinades, but in general, we recommend avoiding mixtures that contain large quantities of sugar or oil for foods that are to be grilled over direct heat. Excess oil will cause flare-ups, and though a small amount of sugar promotes browning, too much can cause foods to burn before they cook through. The amount of sugar in a marinade should be in inverse proportion to how long an item takes to cook. For instance, a marinade with more sugar might be okay for thinly sliced meat that will cook in a short time (see Kalbi, 45, for a good example of this), but not for a whole chicken or large pieces of meat, which take much longer to cook through and thus risk burning. ➤ Do not use extra-virgin olive oil in marinades: It will solidify at refrigerator temperatures and its nuances will be completely lost on grilled foods.

➤ Always drain marinated foods and pat them dry if they are to be browned. Drying for an hour or more on a wire rack set above a rimmed baking sheet is ideal, especially if the item is to be smoked, 1067, or barbecued, 1066. After a thorough simmering, some marinades are suitable for using as a sauce. Indeed, several classic dishes are built upon the reuse of marinades, such as Boeuf Bourguignon, 64, Hasenpfeffer, 525, and Sauerbraten, 464.

LEMON MARINADE

About 1 cup

Best with chicken, vegetables, and stronger fish. Do not marinate fish for more than 30 minutes or meats for longer than 4 hours.

Whisk together in a small bowl:

½ cup vegetable oil
Finely grated zest of 1 lemon
⅓ cup lemon juice
(2 tablespoons Dijon mustard)
(2 tablespoons finely chopped thyme, oregano, rosemary, marjoram, tarragon, or a combination)
6 garlic cloves, minced
1 teaspoon salt
1 teaspoon black pepper

WINE MARINADE

Generous 2 cups

Cooking the marinade evaporates much of the wine's alcohol, which keeps the mixture from prematurely "cooking" meats. Red wine is excellent for red meat or game; white wine is better for fish, pork, and poultry.

Combine in a medium saucepan and simmer over medium-low heat for 5 minutes:

2 cups dry red or white wine
1 small red onion, thinly sliced
2 tablespoons vegetable oil
2 garlic cloves, minced
1 teaspoon fresh thyme leaves
6 black peppercorns, cracked
1 small bay leaf
(2 whole cloves)
1 teaspoon salt

Let cool before using. The marinade will keep, covered and refrigerated, for up to 1 week.

TANDOORI MARINADE

In Indian cooking, chicken and lamb are marinated in this aromatic mixture of yogurt and spices before they are cooked in the extremely high heat of a *tandoor*, 413. The marinade is often tinted with a natural dye, which gives tandoori chicken its characteristic orange-yellow color.

I. FOR MEATS

About 1 cup; enough for 3 to 4 pounds of meat

Our friend Kusuma Rao insists that coating the meat with salt, citrus, and spices first is crucial: It changes the texture of the meat, improves the color, and helps the spices adhere better. If you would rather skip this step, use version II, below.

Place the meat to be marinated in a bowl and sprinkle evenly with:

1½ to 2 teaspoons salt (½ teaspoon per pound of meat)

Add and thoroughly combine with:

1 teaspoon Kashmiri chili powder or cayenne pepper
Finely grated zest of 3 lemons
⅓ cup lemon juice

Add and toss to coat with:

¾ cup plain whole-milk Greek yogurt
2 tablespoons dried fenugreek leaves, 983, ground or finely crumbled with your fingers
1 tablespoon Garam Masala, 588
1½ teaspoons ground turmeric
(½ to 1 teaspoon Kashmiri chili powder or cayenne pepper)

Cover and marinate, refrigerated, for at least 2 hours and up to overnight (or as directed in individual recipes). Before cooking the meat, use your fingers to wipe off excess marinade.

II. FOR VEGETABLES

About 1¼ cups

When roasting and broiling indoors, we use smoked paprika in place of the sweet paprika to make up for the lack of grilled flavors.

Whisk together in a large bowl:

1 cup whole-milk plain yogurt
Finely grated zest of 1 lemon
¼ cup lemon juice
2 tablespoons Garam Masala, 588, or curry powder
6 garlic cloves, minced or grated on a rasp grater
One 2-inch piece ginger, peeled and minced or grated on a rasp grater
2 tablespoons sweet paprika
1 tablespoon ground turmeric
2 teaspoons salt
(1 teaspoon ground fenugreek leaves)
1 teaspoon cayenne pepper

Use to marinate as directed in version 1, above.

BUTTERMILK MARINADE

About 2 cups

A classic, tenderizing treatment for chicken pieces before they are dredged and fried (see Skillet Fried Chicken, 417). Marinate chicken for up to 24 hours in this marinade.

Combine in a medium bowl:

2 cups buttermilk or 1½ cups yogurt and ½ cup water
4 garlic cloves, minced
2 tablespoons sugar
(2 tablespoons curry powder or chili powder)
2 teaspoons salt
1 teaspoon black pepper

BALKAN MARINADE

About ¾ cup

This is a marinade for Pork Souvlaki, 492, but it is also good for grilled chops or cubes of lamb, and vegetable kebabs. If marinating meats longer than 4 hours, make the marinade less acidic by increasing the olive oil to 1 cup.

Combine in a medium bowl:

½ cup red wine vinegar, lemon juice, or a combination
½ cup olive oil
6 garlic cloves, minced
2 tablespoons minced fresh oregano or 2 teaspoons dried Greek oregano
2 tablespoons minced fresh thyme leaves or 2 teaspoons dried thyme
1 tablespoon black pepper
(1 tablespoon red pepper flakes)
(1 teaspoon minced fresh rosemary or ½ teaspoon dried and crumbled rosemary)
1 teaspoon salt
Finely grated zest of 2 lemons
2 fresh bay leaves, torn in half and bruised, or 1 dried bay leaf, left whole

SINALOAN MARINADE

About 4 cups; enough for 1 chicken

We are lucky to live near a food truck that serves Sinaloan-style grilled chicken (Sinaloa is a state in northwestern Mexico). The chickens are butterflied, 403, marinated in this sweet and tangy marinade, and grilled over a charcoal fire until well bronzed. This is one of our favorite meals when paired with a stack of warm corn tortillas, Frijoles de la Olla, 213 and rice. Marinate chicken for up to 12 hours in this marinade.

Combine in a blender:

1 large onion, cut into chunks
Cloves from 1 head garlic, peeled
1½ cups orange juice or pineapple juice
½ cup lime juice
¼ cup vegetable oil
2 tablespoons chopped oregano
1 tablespoon chopped thyme
(1 tablespoon ancho chile powder)
(1 bay leaf)
(Pinch of ground cloves or allspice)
2 teaspoons salt

Blend until completely smooth.

THAI-STYLE LEMONGRASS MARINADE

About 1 cup

This marinade is excellent with chicken, pork, or shrimp. Marinate shrimp no more than 2 hours, and chicken or pork for up to 8 hours.

Combine in a food processor:

1 medium shallot, coarsely chopped
½ cup chopped cilantro leaves and stems
¼ cup packed grated palm sugar, 1025, or light brown sugar
¼ cup lime juice
¼ cup fish sauce
6 garlic cloves, coarsely chopped
3 lemongrass stalks, tender bottom portion only, thinly sliced
(4 makrut lime leaves, thinly sliced)
2 fresh or dried Thai chiles, stemmed, or 1 teaspoon red pepper flakes
½ teaspoon white pepper

Pulse until finely ground.

VIETNAMESE-STYLE MARINADE

About 1⅔ cups

For grilled pork, chicken, or shrimp. The sugar in this marinade will brown quickly, so it is best used with thin, quick-cooking cuts, or for larger cuts cooked over indirect heat. To use leftover marinade as a finishing sauce, see Grilled Vietnamese-Style Pork, 493.

Whisk together in a medium bowl:

1 large onion, grated
⅓ cup rice vinegar
¼ cup sugar or Vietnamese Caramel Sauce, 578
(1 tablespoon minced lemongrass or the finely grated zest of 1 lime)
¼ cup fish sauce
1 teaspoon ground white or black pepper
(1 teaspoon chile garlic paste, ½ teaspoon red pepper flakes, or ¼ teaspoon fried chile paste)

BEER MARINADE

About 1⅔ cups

For beef or pork.

Combine in a medium bowl:

1½ cups beer
¼ cup orange marmalade
3 tablespoons soy sauce
2 tablespoons sugar or honey
1 tablespoon dry mustard
1 teaspoon ground ginger
2 garlic cloves, minced
½ teaspoon salt
⅛ teaspoon hot pepper sauce

BECKER CHICKEN OR PORK MARINADE

About 1 cup

Whisk together in a small bowl until well blended:

¼ cup red wine
¼ cup red wine vinegar
¼ cup vegetable oil
2 tablespoons balsamic vinegar
2 teaspoons soy sauce
Finely grated zest of 1 lemon
1½ tablespoons lemon juice
2 tablespoons chopped thyme
1 tablespoon chopped rosemary
4 to 6 garlic cloves, to taste, minced
2 teaspoons salt
2 teaspoons black pepper
3 dashes hot pepper sauce

TERIYAKI MARINADE

About 2 cups

This classic marinade for meat, poultry, and firm-fleshed fish is also basted on items once they have browned. If reduced until syrupy, it can be used as a glaze for chicken and other proteins.

Combine in a small saucepan over medium heat and cook, stirring, until the sugar is dissolved:

⅔ cup sake
⅔ cup mirin
⅔ cup soy sauce
2 tablespoons sugar

Use the hot mixture immediately as a light sauce or glaze, or chill to use as a marinade. **For a glaze** suitable for Chicken Yakitori, 445, simmer over medium heat until the mixture has reduced by half.

ABOUT BARBECUE SAUCES AND MOPS

Whether based on ketchup, mustard, or vinegar, barbecue sauce is a beloved condiment that adds welcome acidity, sweetness, and savor to all kinds of smoked and grilled meats. Though there are plenty of purists out there who prefer their ribs "naked" and their brisket unadulterated, most of us cannot imagine a backyard cookout without them. South Carolina is known for its mustard-based sauces, while in neighboring North Carolina, tangy, vinegar-heavy sauces predominate, sometimes with a ketchup bottle waved over them for a little extra depth. Memphis, Kansas City, and Eastern Texas barbecue sauces tend to be sweeter and tomato-based, sometimes with a spicy kick. And in Kentucky, Worcestershire-based sauces (called "dip") can be found alongside barbecued mutton or pork.

Barbecue sauces may be added during cooking, applied at the last minute as a glaze, or simply served alongside grilled or barbecued meat—in some cases, they are used in all of these ways. If applying sauce to the meat while it is cooking, consider the oven, grill, or broiler temperature, the sweetness of the sauce, and the size of what you are cooking to determine when to baste. Mops and thinner sauces like Kentucky-Style Mutton Dip, 583, and North Carolina–Style Barbecue Sauce, 583, can be used to baste meats throughout their time on the smoker or grill. When cooking at high temperatures, either under the broiler or on the grill over direct heat, apply coatings of thicker, sweeter sauces during the last 5 to 10 minutes of cooking (and be ready to move meats to the cooler side of the grill or farther away from the broiler if the sauce starts to burn). Like any condiment, the sauce should complement rather than obscure the smoky flavor of the meat. Serve extra sauce at the table.

Many cooks like to baste the meat with a tangy, flavorful liquid, called a "mop" or mopping sauce. Though mops certainly season the meat, the moisture they add is also very beneficial when smoking meats: As the mop evaporates, the humidity of the smoker increases, which helps the smoke flavor adhere to the meat. (This is why we suggest using them in recipes if you do not have a water pan to keep the smoking environment humid.) Beyond smoking, mops can be used to baste grilling meats; just be sure to ➤ brush them on food only after it has browned to your liking.

KANSAS CITY BARBECUE SAUCE

About 3 cups

In general, barbecue sauces become sweeter and thicker as you travel farther west across the United States, and this style is at the western edge of the barbecue-style map. For most, this recipe is the Platonic ideal of barbecue sauces: It's sweet, spicy, and tangy and works well on just about any meat you slather it on.

Stir together in a medium bowl:

2 cups ketchup
½ cup cider vinegar
½ cup packed brown sugar
⅓ cup yellow mustard
¼ cup molasses
2 tablespoons chili powder
2 tablespoons sweet paprika
¼ teaspoon cayenne pepper or 1 teaspoon hot pepper sauce

Heat in a medium saucepan over medium heat:

3 tablespoons butter or vegetable oil

Add and cook, stirring, until softened, about 5 minutes:

½ medium onion, minced

Add and cook until fragrant, about 1 minute more:

4 garlic cloves, minced or grated on a rasp grater

Stir in the ketchup mixture and bring to a simmer. Reduce the heat to medium-low and simmer gently for 15 minutes. Season to taste with:

Salt and black pepper

CHIPOTLE BARBECUE SAUCE

About 3 cups

Canned chipotle peppers in adobo sauce are ideal for adding heat and smoke to barbecue sauce.

Combine in a medium saucepan:

1½ cups ketchup
1 cup cider vinegar
½ cup packed brown sugar
4 to 6 canned chipotles peppers in adobo sauce, chopped, plus 2 tablespoons adobo sauce, or ¼ cup Mexican Adobo I, 584
(1 tablespoon ground cumin, toasted before grinding, 1021, if desired)
2 garlic cloves, minced or grated on a rasp grater

Bring to a simmer over medium heat, reduce the heat to low, and cook for 10 minutes.

ALABAMA WHITE BARBECUE SAUCE

About 1½ cups

This unusual barbecue sauce is specifically for grilled or smoked chicken, but it also works as a dressing for Classic Coleslaw, 119, or as a dipping sauce.

Whisk together in a medium bowl:

1 cup mayonnaise
½ cup cider vinegar
2 garlic cloves, minced or grated on a rasp grater, or 1 tablespoon garlic powder

1 tablespoon yellow mustard
1 tablespoon drained prepared horseradish
½ teaspoon salt
½ teaspoon black pepper
¼ teaspoon cayenne pepper

Cover and refrigerate for up to 5 days.

SOUTH CAROLINA–STYLE MUSTARD BARBECUE SAUCE

About 3 cups

This sauce can serve as a glaze for ribs, a condiment for fried chicken, or a sauce for pulled pork.

Whisk together in a medium bowl:

1½ cups yellow mustard
½ cup ketchup
½ cup cider vinegar
½ cup sugar
2 tablespoons Worcestershire sauce
1 tablespoon black pepper
2 teaspoons garlic powder
2 teaspoons onion powder

Allow to sit at least 1 hour before using. Store, refrigerated, for up to 1 month.

NORTH CAROLINA–STYLE BARBECUE SAUCE

About 1½ cups

This thin, spicy vinegar mixture is used as a mop as well as a sauce for Smoked Pork Shoulder, 496. Once shredded or chopped, the pork absorbs the sauce, which balances its richness. In the Piedmont region, up to ½ **cup ketchup, tomato puree, or tomato juice** may be added. Though not traditional, we like to steep ½ **teaspoon mustard seeds** and **1 or 2 minced garlic cloves** in the mixture overnight before using.

Whisk to combine in a medium bowl:

¾ cup distilled white vinegar
¾ cup cider vinegar
1 tablespoon hot pepper sauce, or more to taste
1 tablespoon sugar
2 teaspoons red pepper flakes
1 teaspoon black pepper
½ teaspoon salt

KENTUCKY-STYLE MUTTON DIP

About 5 cups

Our friend Wes Berry, author of *The Kentucky Barbecue Book*, shared this recipe with us, which we have tweaked and scaled down for home use. Much like North Carolina–Style Barbecue Sauce, above, this "dip" is used to baste meats as they cook and is also served alongside as a thin table sauce. Though traditionally used for lamb or mutton, this sauce is also excellent for basting and saucing a beef shoulder roast, short ribs, or a venison haunch.

Combine in a medium saucepan:

1½ cups Worcestershire sauce
1½ cups water
(1 small onion, grated)
One 6-ounce can tomato paste
½ cup packed brown sugar
¼ cup distilled white or cider vinegar
4 tablespoons (½ stick) butter or bacon fat
2 tablespoons lemon juice
2 teaspoons black pepper
1 teaspoon salt
½ teaspoon ground allspice

Bring to a simmer and cook for 5 minutes, stirring to dissolve the sugar and tomato paste.

BASIC MOP

About 2 cups

Whisk together in a bowl until the salt dissolves:

2 cups distilled white vinegar
2 teaspoons salt
1 teaspoon black pepper, or to taste
1 teaspoon red pepper flakes, or to taste

Stir in:

1 small onion, thinly sliced
1 jalapeño pepper, thinly sliced

Use the same day.

BEER MOP

About 10 cups

Combine in a saucepan and bring to a simmer:

Six 12-ounce bottles dark beer
1 cup cider vinegar
½ cup packed dark brown sugar
1 large red onion, chopped
4 garlic cloves, chopped
2 serrano peppers, chopped
2 bay leaves
2 teaspoons salt
1 teaspoon black pepper

Simmer for 15 minutes. Remove from heat, remove the bay leaves, and cool before using.

ABOUT PASTES

Some of these pungent mixtures are used as a kind of concentrated marinade. Some, such as Pesto, 586, are enjoyed as sauce-like condiments. Others, like the Thai pastes here, are used as seasoning ingredients, and are fried in oil at the outset of curry making to soften their flavors and add complexity. For information on chile paste products available in stores, see 969.

Pastes may simply be a spice blend or dry rub that has been moistened with oil, but they usually include fresh aromatic ingredients as well, such as fresh ginger, shallots, garlic, and lemongrass. Though most pastes are traditionally made in a mortar and pestle, we find that they are easier to assemble in a blender or food processor (though their flavor and texture might differ). For tips on using both methods, see 1045.

You can keep any unused pastes refrigerated for up to 1 week in tightly covered small jars, but ➤ discard or thoroughly simmer any that have come into contact with raw poultry, fish, or meat (to avoid this, simply measure out the amount you think you will need and reserve the rest). Many of these pastes can be frozen as well with little impact on their quality; they are especially convenient if frozen in cubes—we have a dedicated ice cube tray for this purpose, as plastic tends to absorb flavors and colors. Once frozen, pop out the paste cubes and store in a freezer bag for up to 2 months.

JAMAICAN JERK PASTE

About 1¼ cups

This is traditionally used to marinate pork and chicken, but it is also a good flavoring for goat, mutton, or lamb steaks and chops. The meat was traditionally grilled on an open fire with pimento (allspice) wood, and the allspice in this rub is intended to re-create that effect. For a rub with similar spices, see Jerk Spice Rub, 587.

Combine in a food processor or blender and puree:

⅓ cup lime juice
2 tablespoons distilled white vinegar
(2 tablespoons orange juice)
Up to 10 Scotch bonnet or habanero peppers
3 green onions, coarsely chopped
2 tablespoons dried basil
2 tablespoons dried thyme
2 tablespoons yellow mustard seeds or 1 tablespoon dry mustard
2 teaspoons ground allspice
1 teaspoon ground cloves
1 teaspoon salt
1 teaspoon black pepper

The mixture should have the consistency of thick tomato sauce. If necessary, thin with additional:

(Lime juice, vinegar, or orange juice)

MEDITERRANEAN GARLIC HERB PASTE

About 1½ cups

This is wonderful on grilled and roasted vegetables, fish, lamb, and beef.

Combine in a blender or food processor and coarsely puree, leaving the mixture a little chunky:

2 cups loosely packed mixed fresh herb leaves (parsley, sage, rosemary, thyme, basil, and/or oregano)
10 garlic cloves, coarsely chopped
½ cup olive oil
1 tablespoon red pepper flakes
1 tablespoon black pepper
1 teaspoon salt
Finely grated zest of 1 lemon

MUSTARD PASTE

About ⅔ cup

This is equally suited to roast lamb, beef, rabbit, and chicken, and it gives the meat a gilded finish.

Stir together well in a small bowl:

½ cup Dijon or brown mustard
2 tablespoons dry white wine
(1 garlic clove, minced)
1 tablespoon minced fresh herbs or 1 teaspoon dried herbs (use rosemary for lamb, thyme for beef, or tarragon for chicken or rabbit)
1 teaspoon minced peeled fresh ginger or ¼ teaspoon ground ginger

HARISSA

I. PASTE

About ⅓ cup

This fiery pepper paste from North Africa is stirred into seafood stews, soups, herb salads, and vegetable dishes; tossed with black olives; and used as an ingredient in sauces for brochettes, tagines, and couscous. We also love it as a sandwich spread; an addition to mayonnaise or hummus; or thinned with good olive oil to use as a topping for white-fleshed fish.

Toast in a small, dry skillet over medium heat, shaking the pan often to prevent burning, until very aromatic, 2 to 3 minutes:

1 teaspoon caraway seeds
1 teaspoon coriander seeds
½ teaspoon cumin seeds

Transfer the seeds to a plate and let cool, then grind to a fine powder with a mortar and pestle or in a spice mill or coffee grinder. Transfer the ground spices to a small bowl and stir in:

¼ cup olive oil
3 tablespoons sweet paprika
2 teaspoons smoked hot paprika
2 garlic cloves, minced or grated on a rasp grater
¼ teaspoon cayenne pepper
¼ teaspoon salt

The harissa will be very thick and dry. To store, transfer the paste to a small jar and top with a thin film of:

Olive oil

It will keep, covered and refrigerated, for up to 3 months.

II. SAUCE

About ¾ cup

When the pungent heat of harissa is stretched and bulked up with roasted pepper and tomato, the result is more of a dipping sauce or spread.

Prepare **version I, above,** and transfer to a food processor. Add **½ cup drained jarred roasted red bell pepper** and **1 canned whole tomato.** Process until smooth.

MEXICAN ADOBO

A basic, flexible formula that can be made with most dried chiles, such as guajillo, ancho, cascabel, and chipotle. We recommend using a variety of different types for greater complexity. (For an example of a balanced mix, see Goat Birria, 485.)

I. PASTE

About 1 cup

Toast, 969, briefly in a large, dry skillet over medium heat:

2 ounces dried chiles, stemmed and seeded

Transfer to a bowl, breaking up if necessary, and add hot water to cover. Let soak for 15 minutes. Drain and transfer to a blender or food processor along with:

½ cup water, stock, or Mexican lager
2 tablespoons cider vinegar, distilled white vinegar, lime juice, or orange juice
(2 garlic cloves)
½ teaspoon sugar
½ teaspoon salt
(Pinch of ground cumin, cinnamon, clove, and/or black pepper)

Puree until very smooth, adding water if necessary.

II. SAUCE

2 to 3 cups

Use this sauce for enchiladas or as a condiment for grilled meats, fish, or roasted vegetables. Or, dilute it even further for use as a braising liquid for pork, lamb, or beef.

Prepare **version I, 584,** using **1 to 2 cups water, stock, tomato juice, or Mexican lager.** For a moderately thick sauce: Use the smaller amount of liquid, transfer to a medium saucepan and bring to a simmer over medium heat. Reduce the heat and cook for 5 minutes. For a braising liquid: Use the larger amount of liquid (skip the simmering as the liquid will cook during braising). In either case, add more **vinegar or lime juice** and **salt to taste.**

GREEN CURRY PASTE

About 1¼ cups

A fragrant, spicy paste for use in Thai curries, and also an excellent seasoning paste for meats and seafood. Because making curry paste requires some scouting for ingredients, we like to make extra and freeze it in cubes as described in About Pastes, 583. When you're ready to make curry, start with one frozen cube (about 2 tablespoons) for a moderately spicy, deeply flavorful curry that will generously serve 2 people. If you like very spicy curries, you may work up to 2 cubes. To get the best flavor from curry paste, fry it in a couple tablespoons of the fat that collects at the top of coconut milk cans (or use oil) before adding the other ingredients.

Combine in a small, dry skillet over medium heat and toast, shaking the pan often to prevent burning, 2 to 3 minutes:

1 tablespoon coriander seeds
1½ teaspoons cumin seeds
1½ teaspoons white peppercorns

Transfer to a plate and let cool to room temperature. Transfer the spices to a blender or food processor along with:

½ cup tightly packed fresh cilantro leaves and stems or 3 ounces coriander root, 973
4 ounces green Thai chiles or serrano peppers, seeded, if desired, and chopped
3 shallots, coarsely chopped
Cloves from 1 head garlic, coarsely chopped
2 tablespoons chopped peeled galangal, 989, or ginger
1½ tablespoons chopped peeled fresh turmeric
1 stalk lemongrass, tender bottom portion only, chopped
2 makrut lime leaves or the finely grated zest of 2 limes
(1½ teaspoons shrimp paste)
¾ teaspoon salt

Blend or process until homogenous and fairly smooth. The paste will be very thick. As you blend, the shallots and chiles will release some liquid, but use the blender's tamper to help the ingredients blend evenly. If using a food processor, scrape down the sides of the bowl regularly to ensure a smooth paste.

RED CURRY PASTE

Soak **1 ounce dried red chiles, such as Thai or árbol, stemmed and seeded,** in hot water for 1 hour, then drain. Prepare **Green Curry Paste, above,** substituting the soaked red chiles for the fresh green ones.

MASSAMAN CURRY PASTE

About 1¼ cups

A specialty of southern Thailand traditionally used in a curry made with beef and potatoes (see Beef Massaman Curry, 465). To store and use excess paste, see About Pastes, 583.

Combine in a large heavy skillet over medium heat and toast, stirring, until fragrant, about 3 minutes:

One 3-inch cinnamon stick, cracked into several pieces
4 green cardamom pods (for a smokier flavor, use black cardamom)
½ whole nutmeg, cracked into large chunks

Add:

½ ounce dried small red chiles such as Thai or árbol (about ½ cup), stemmed and seeded
2 tablespoons coriander seeds
2 teaspoons cumin seeds
2 teaspoons black peppercorns
6 whole cloves

Toast until slightly darkened and fragrant, 2 to 3 minutes, shaking the pan to prevent scorching. Pour the chiles and spices into a bowl and let cool. Add to the dry skillet:

Unpeeled cloves from 1 head garlic
2 large shallots, peeled and halved lengthwise, or 4 small shallots, unpeeled and whole
One unpeeled 2-inch piece galangal, 989, or ginger
1 stalk lemongrass, tender bottom portion only

Cook, stirring, until everything is lightly charred and softened, 15 to 20 minutes. Transfer to a bowl and let cool. Meanwhile, crack the cardamom pods by pounding them under the side of a knife. Collect the seeds within and discard the pods. Grind the seeds with all the other spices in a mortar and pestle or spice grinder. If desired, transfer to a food processor. When the garlic is cool enough to handle, peel and add to the mortar or food processor. Peel the shallots, if necessary, and the galangal. Slice the shallots, galangal, and lemongrass and add them to the mortar or food processor along with:

2 ounces coriander root, 973, or ½ cup chopped cilantro stems
¼ cup unsalted roasted peanuts
(1 teaspoon shrimp paste)
½ teaspoon ground turmeric
1 teaspoon salt

Process or grind until smooth, scraping down the sides as needed. Store refrigerated for up to 2 weeks or freeze for up to 6 months.

CHARMOULA (MOROCCAN HERB PASTE)

About 1½ cups

Charmoula's consistency is between a chunky paste and a thick relish or sauce. It is traditionally used to flavor fish before or after cooking. We also like to pass it at the table as a condiment.

Stir together well in a small bowl:

⅓ cup finely chopped parsley
⅓ cup finely chopped cilantro
2 tablespoons olive oil
2 tablespoons lemon juice
2 garlic cloves, finely chopped

Grind to a fine powder in a spice mill, coffee grinder, or blender, or with a mortar and pestle:

1 teaspoon coriander seeds
1 teaspoon cumin seeds
12 white or black peppercorns
1 teaspoon red pepper flakes
(Generous pinch of saffron threads)

Add the ground spices to the herb mixture along with:

1 medium onion, finely chopped
1 teaspoon hot or sweet paprika
Salt to taste
Cayenne pepper to taste

Stir together well. To store, transfer to a small jar and top with a thin film of:

Olive oil

It will keep, covered and refrigerated, for 4 days.

PESTO AND PISTOU

About 1 cup

Italian for "paste," pesto is a popular Ligurian sauce made with fresh basil and pine nuts. Of course, it is not the only pesto, and we often find ourselves using what we have on hand, whether it is arugula and toasted hazelnuts; parsley, carrot tops, and almonds; or kale, oregano, and walnuts. To make the French condiment **pistou,** omit the nuts.

I. FOOD PROCESSOR METHOD

Combine in a food processor and process to a rough paste:

2 cups loosely packed fresh basil leaves
½ cup grated Parmesan or Pecorino Romano (2 ounces)
⅓ cup pine nuts, toasted, 1012
2 garlic cloves, chopped

With the machine running, slowly add:

½ cup extra-virgin olive oil

The pesto should be a thick paste. If it seems dry, add a little more olive oil. Season to taste with:

Salt

Use immediately, or pour a very thin film of olive oil over the top, cover, and refrigerate for up to 1 week.

II. MORTAR AND PESTLE METHOD

For a more robust texture, use a mortar and pestle.

Using the ingredients and quantities from **version I, above,** pound the pine nuts until very fine. Add the garlic and pound until ground to a paste. Add the basil and a pinch of salt. Pound until ground to a paste. Stir in the cheese and pound until incorporated. Stir in the oil and season to taste.

SPICY CARROT TOP PESTO

About 1 cup

If you purchase carrots that still have fresh greens attached, try making this pesto. Use as a sandwich spread, slather on toast with sliced tomatoes and avocado, or thin it out with more oil and lemon juice to make a quick sauce for vegetables.

Trim the tops from:

1 large bunch carrots

Pick the frond-like leaves from the tough stems and discard the stems. Measure the leaves. You should have about 2 packed cups. If not, you can fill out the rest with **fresh parsley leaves** or simply make a half-batch of this recipe. Place the leaves in a food processor along with:

½ cup grated Pecorino Romano, Manchego, or Parmesan (2 ounces)
⅓ cup pumpkin seeds, toasted, 1005
1 garlic clove, coarsely chopped
½ to 1 teaspoon red pepper flakes, to taste
(½ teaspoon Espelette, Urfa, or Marash chile flakes, 968)
¼ teaspoon salt

Process to a coarse paste. With the machine running, slowly add:

½ cup extra-virgin olive oil

Use within 1 week.

SUN-DRIED TOMATO PESTO

About 1⅓ cups

Spread this on bruschetta or pizza, toss it with pasta, or serve it with grilled poultry or seafood.

Combine in a small saucepan:

⅓ cup chopped, drained oil-packed sun-dried tomatoes
Water to cover

Bring to a boil, then remove from the heat and let stand for 20 minutes.

Meanwhile, combine in a food processor:

1 cup loosely packed fresh basil leaves
⅓ cup grated Parmesan
1 large garlic clove, chopped

Pulse until finely ground. With the machine running, pour into the food processor in a slow, steady stream:

¼ cup extra-virgin olive oil

Drain the tomato mixture, reserving the liquid. Add the tomato mixture to the processor and finely chop. Blend in ⅓ cup of the reserved soaking liquid. Season to taste with:

Salt and black pepper

PERSILLADE

½ to ¾ cup

From *persil*, the French word for "parsley," persillade is a mixture of chopped parsley and garlic that is used as a garnish to add flavor and color to pan-fried potatoes, sautéed pork chops, or baked chicken legs. Add the optional bread crumbs to form a crust for fish fillets, rack of lamb, or broiled shrimp.

Mix together in a small bowl:

½ cup chopped parsley
2 garlic cloves, minced
(⅓ cup fresh bread crumbs, 957)
2 tablespoons olive oil, or enough to make a paste

GREMOLATA

About 3 tablespoons

A mixture of seasonings used to garnish Osso Buco, 476, gravies, pan sauces, and roasted or grilled meats.

Mix together well in a small bowl:

2 tablespoons finely chopped parsley
2 garlic cloves, minced
2 teaspoons finely grated lemon zest

Sprinkle this mixture on during the last 5 minutes of cooking.

GARLIC-HERB RUB FOR POULTRY

About 3 tablespoons

Use these proportions for a chicken weighing about 4 pounds. Double the ingredients for a larger bird. Note that this does not contain any salt, so you will still need to salt the skin of the chicken.

Mix together in a small bowl:

4 garlic cloves, minced
Finely grated zest of 2 lemons
1 teaspoon olive oil
1 teaspoon minced rosemary
1 teaspoon dried oregano, thyme, sage, or a combination
(1 teaspoon red pepper flakes)

Carefully loosen the skin around the breast, thighs, and drumsticks with your fingers and spread the herb mixture under the skin.

ABOUT DRY RUBS

A dry rub is a blend of herbs, spices, and sugar that is rubbed on food—especially meat and poultry—before grilling, searing, sautéing, pan-frying, or roasting. To use a dry rub, simply rub the mixture over the entire surface of the food, using enough pressure to make sure that an even layer adheres. Some seasonings produce a handsome dark finish and some create a tasty crunchy crust, especially during grilling, searing, or pan-frying. Unused rubs will keep at room temperature, tightly sealed, for 6 weeks. ➤ Omit salt from the rub if you have marinated, brined, or dry-brined your meat.

CAJUN BLACKENING SPICE

About ⅓ cup

This mix can be rubbed on chicken, fatty fish, steaks, or vegetables before blackening, 1053, broiling, grilling, or sautéing in a cast-iron pan. It will transform into a flavorful, deeply caramelized crust as the food cooks. Expect the spices to smoke some during cooking; we advise turning on an exhaust fan and opening a window.

Mix together in a small bowl:

2 tablespoons sweet paprika
2 teaspoons dried thyme
2 teaspoons dried oregano or marjoram
2 teaspoons cayenne pepper
2 teaspoons coarsely cracked black or white peppercorns
1 teaspoon salt

SOUTHERN BARBECUE DRY RUB

About 2 cups

Southern barbecue chefs rub spice mixtures like this one onto pork or beef before starting the long, slow cooking that will transform it into barbecue. By the end of cooking, it will have produced a dark, crusty "bark" that is loaded with flavor.

Stir together well in a small bowl:

½ cup sweet or hot paprika
¼ cup packed brown sugar
¼ cup chili powder
¼ cup salt
¼ cup cracked black peppercorns
2 tablespoons cayenne pepper
2 tablespoons ground cumin
1 teaspoon ground mace

COFFEE SPICE RUB

Generous 1 cup

An excellent rub for steak.

Mix together well in a small bowl:

¼ cup ancho chile powder
¼ cup finely ground espresso-roast coffee beans
2 tablespoons sweet paprika
2 tablespoons dark brown sugar
1 tablespoon dry mustard
1 tablespoon salt
1 tablespoon black pepper
1 tablespoon dried oregano
1 tablespoon ground coriander
2 teaspoons ground ginger
2 teaspoons ground chile de árbol or other pure ground chile powder

SWEET AND SMOKY SPICE RUB

About 1 cup

Rub on chicken, beef, lamb, or pork as well as salmon and bluefish.

Mix together well in a small bowl:

¼ cup smoked paprika
¼ cup packed brown sugar
¼ cup black pepper
2 tablespoons ground cumin
2 tablespoons salt

JERK SPICE RUB

About ⅔ cup

In addition to pork or chicken, this rub is also good for seasoning shrimp and fish with jerk-type flavors. When grilling jerk-rubbed items, baste them with lime juice periodically, or after each turn.

Mix together well in a small bowl:

3 tablespoons dried thyme, crumbled
2 tablespoons brown sugar

2 tablespoons red pepper flakes
1 tablespoon salt
1 tablespoon black pepper
1 tablespoon dry mustard
2 teaspoons ground allspice
1 teaspoon ground ginger
¼ teaspoon ground cloves

ABOUT HERB AND SPICE BLENDS

Like sauce making, there is a certain alchemy and intrigue that surrounds herb and spice blends. Some of this mystery is due to the complex, varied, and sometimes unfamiliar culinary traditions these mixtures come from. Some may be due to the secrecy with which popular, commercially available blends are shrouded. Regardless of this enigmatic aura, many complex or simple flavorings can be easily concocted from ingredients found at your grocery store. Still more are within reach after a quick trip to a specialty market or Internet retailer, 1077. When made fresh from whole spices (and in modest quantities, so they do not go stale), these blends will surpass nearly anything you can buy. For information on toasting and grinding spices, see 1020. Store all spice blends in airtight containers in a cool place away from direct sunlight, if possible. ➤ Use freshly ground blends within 3 months.

CHESAPEAKE BAY SEASONING

About ½ cup

This recipe makes enough for boiling a dozen crabs, 358, but we also use it for seasoning popcorn, French Fries, 270, and Potato or Root Vegetable Chips, 48.

Grind to a fine powder in a spice grinder:

10 bay leaves
1 tablespoon black peppercorns
1 teaspoon white peppercorns

Transfer to a small bowl and add:

3 tablespoons celery salt
2 tablespoons sweet paprika
1 tablespoon dry mustard
2 teaspoons ground ginger
⅛ teaspoon each ground mace or nutmeg, cinnamon, allspice, cayenne pepper, and cloves

Mix until thoroughly combined.

CHILI POWDER

About ⅔ cup

Essential for many Southwestern and Mexican dishes, but also a wonderful seasoning for sprinkling on at the table. Chili powders vary, but they are generally based on a combination of ground chiles, cumin, coriander, oregano, and black pepper.

I. WITH TOASTED CHILES OR WHOLE SPICES

Toast, 1021, on the stovetop or in the oven:

2½ ounces dried whole chiles, stemmed, seeded, and flattened

Let cool and set aside. Toast until fragrant and browned in a dry skillet over medium heat:

1 tablespoon cumin seeds
1 tablespoon coriander seeds
(1 tablespoon black peppercorns)

Transfer to a bowl. Once cool, crush the chiles and add them along with the spices to a spice grinder or mortar and pestle. Add:

1 tablespoon dried oregano, preferably Mexican

Grind the ingredients into a fine powder. If using as a condiment, grind in:

(1 tablespoon garlic powder)
(1 tablespoon onion powder)

II. WITH GROUND SPICES

Prepare **version I, above,** substituting ½ **cup ancho, chipotle, or other pure ground chile powder** for the whole chiles and **1 tablespoon each ground cumin, ground coriander, and black pepper** (if using) for the whole spices.

MADRAS CURRY POWDER

About 1⅓ cups

In India, there is no such thing as a singular "curry powder," but this blend of spices has come to be a fixture in many kitchens.

Combine in a dry skillet and toast over medium heat until fragrant and a shade darker, about 4 minutes:

6 tablespoons coriander seeds
¼ cup cumin seeds
3 tablespoons chana dal (yellow split peas)
1 tablespoon black peppercorns
1 tablespoon mustard seeds
5 dried small red chile peppers
(10 fresh or dried curry leaves)

Transfer to bowl and stir in:

2 tablespoons fenugreek seeds

Let the spices cool completely. Working in batches, grind the spices to a powder in a spice mill or coffee grinder. Return to the bowl and mix well. Stir in:

3 tablespoons ground turmeric

Store in an airtight container in a cool place.

GARAM MASALA

The term "garam masala" refers to a large family of spice blends that differ depending on the region and the cook. They play an important role in the characteristic flavor of many Indian dishes. While making them takes a little time and potentially some ingredient hunting, once they are prepared they provide the cook with an easy means of adding tremendous complexity and richness to dishes of all kinds.

I.

About ½ cup

This blend is balanced to the "cool" side with a healthy dose of cardamom.

Place inside a thin, folded kitchen towel and smash with a rolling pin or a heavy skillet until lightly crushed:

¼ cup green or black cardamom pods

Collect the cardamom seeds and discard the pods. Alternatively, use:

1 tablespoon plus 1 teaspoon cardamom seeds

Combine the seeds in a spice grinder with:

2 tablespoons cumin or black cumin seeds
2 tablespoons black peppercorns
Two 2½- to 3-inch cinnamon sticks, broken into shards
1 tablespoon whole cloves
(2 mace blades)
1 teaspoon grated or ground nutmeg

Grind the mixture to a powder. Store in an airtight container.

II.

About ⅓ cup

This blend is heavier on warm spices: cinnamon, cloves, and ginger. Add ½ teaspoon or so to dishes like Chana Masala, 217, Palak Paneer, 245, or Spinach Pakoras, 245.

Place inside a thin, folded kitchen towel and crack into pieces with a rolling pin or a heavy skillet:

Two 2½- to 3-inch cinnamon sticks
½ whole nutmeg

Place a large skillet over medium heat and add the cinnamon and nutmeg pieces along with:

2 tablespoons coriander seeds
1 tablespoon cumin seeds
8 green cardamom pods
1 teaspoon whole cloves
1 teaspoon black peppercorns
1 teaspoon fennel seeds

Toast, stirring frequently, until the spices are fragrant and browned. Transfer to a plate to cool completely. Fish out the cardamom pods, crack them open by pounding them under the side of a knife. Collect the seeds within, and discard the pods. Place the seeds in a spice grinder along with all the other toasted spices. Add:

2 teaspoons ground ginger
2 bay leaves, crumbled

Grind into a powder.

CHAAT MASALA

About ⅓ cup

This salty, tangy blend is sprinkled on street food snacks—called *chaat*—all across India. Use it on Pakoras, 203, Popcorn, 47, or even French Fries, 270.

Place a small skillet over medium heat and add:

1 tablespoon cumin seeds
(1½ teaspoons fennel seeds)

Toast, stirring frequently, until the seeds are fragrant and toasted. Transfer to a spice grinder and let cool completely. Add to the spice grinder:

1 tablespoon plus 1 teaspoon dried mango powder (amchur, 953)
1 tablespoon black salt, 1013
½ teaspoon salt
(¼ teaspoon asafoetida, 954)

Grind into a fine powder.

BAHARAT

About ⅓ cup

Use *baharat* as a rub for meats and fish, or as an ingredient in pilafs, couscous, or other grain or lentil dishes.

Place inside a thin, folded kitchen towel and break into pieces with a rolling pin or a heavy skillet:

Two 2½- to 3-inch cinnamon sticks
1 nutmeg

Transfer to a spice grinder. Crack open by pounding with the side of a knife:

4 green cardamom pods

Collect the seeds within, and discard the pods. Add to the grinder along with:

1 tablespoon cumin seeds
2 teaspoons coriander seeds
2 teaspoons black peppercorns
(2 teaspoons dried rose petals)
1 teaspoon whole cloves
1 teaspoon allspice berries
(1 teaspoon dried mint)

Grind into a fine powder.

DUKKAH

About 1¼ cups

Dukkah is a condiment often served with bread in its native Egypt, but we love it on salads, roasted vegetables (especially winter squash), and hummus.

Place a large skillet over medium heat. When hot, add and roast, stirring frequently, until browned:

½ cup hazelnuts, pistachios, almonds, walnuts, cashews, or a combination

Transfer the nuts to a food processor and let cool slightly. Add to the skillet:

¼ cup sesame seeds
¼ cup coriander seeds
2 tablespoons cumin seeds
(1 teaspoon ajwain, 951, or fennel seeds)

Toast, stirring frequently, until fragrant and the seeds begin to make popping sounds. Transfer to the food processor and let cool for 5 minutes. Add to the food processor:

2 teaspoons dried thyme or marjoram
1 teaspoon dried oregano
(1 teaspoon dried mint)
½ teaspoon salt
½ teaspoon black pepper
½ teaspoon red pepper flakes
(½ teaspoon ground black lime, 956, or sumac)

Pulse until the mixture is ground to the consistency of coarse bread crumbs. Do not process to a powder; it should have some texture.

ZA'ATAR

About ¼ cup

This toasty, tart, and herbal Middle Eastern blend may be sprinkled on grilled flatbread, roasted vegetables, salads, kebabs, or hummus. For the herb callez za'atar, see Marjoram, 1000.

Place a small skillet over medium heat and add:

2 tablespoons dried thyme
(2 teaspoons dried marjoram)

Toast, stirring frequently, until fragrant, about 2 minutes. Transfer to a spice grinder and let cool completely. Add to the spice grinder:

1 tablespoon ground sumac

Grind until fine. Transfer to a small bowl and stir in:

1 tablespoon toasted sesame seeds

BERBERE

About ½ cup

This spice blend is essential for many traditional Ethiopian stews, but it may be used on everything from chicken to vegetables, or mix it into olive oil with salt as a dipping sauce for bread.

Place a large skillet over medium heat and add:

2 tablespoons coriander seeds
5 dried chiles de árbol, piri piri peppers, or bird's eye chiles, stemmed and seeded
1 teaspoon cumin seeds
½ teaspoon fenugreek seeds
½ teaspoon black peppercorns
(¼ teaspoon ajwain seeds, 951)
3 black cardamom pods
3 allspice berries
1 whole clove

Toast, stirring frequently, until the spices are fragrant and lightly browned. The chiles will be ready before the rest of the spices, so remove them when they start to blacken even slightly. Transfer to a plate and let cool completely. Crack open the cardamom pods by pounding them under the side of a knife. Collect the seeds within, and discard the pods. Transfer the seeds and other spices to a spice grinder along with:

3 tablespoons sweet paprika
(1 tablespoon dried holy basil or dried basil)
¼ teaspoon ground cinnamon
¼ teaspoon ground ginger
¼ teaspoon grated or ground nutmeg

Grind into a fine powder.

EVERYTHING SEASONING

About ½ cup

Best known for bestowing "everything" on bagels, this mixture of seeds, dried alliums, and salt works wonders when used as a topping for dinner rolls or sandwich bread, a coating for cheese balls, 55, or sprinkled on avocado toast.

Add to a medium skillet over medium heat:

2 tablespoons sesame seeds
2 tablespoons poppy seeds
2 tablespoons dried onion flakes
1 tablespoon dried garlic flakes
(1 tablespoon fennel seeds)

Toast, stirring frequently, until the mixture is fragrant and lightly browned. Transfer to a plate to cool completely, then stir in:

1 tablespoon flaky sea salt

Store in an airtight container.

RAS EL HANOUT

About ⅔ cup

This Moroccan spice mix typically contains many different elements, including seeds, leaves, flowers, roots, and barks. It is usually added by the pinch or ½ teaspoon to stews of meat and poultry and to couscous dishes.

Toast in a small skillet over medium heat until fragrant, about 5 minutes:

2 tablespoons coriander seeds
1 tablespoon cumin seeds
1 tablespoon black peppercorns
1 tablespoon fennel seeds
(2 teaspoons cubeb, long pepper, grains of paradise, or a combination)
2 teaspoons allspice berries
1 teaspoon mustard seeds
1 teaspoon caraway seeds
8 green cardamom pods
5 whole cloves
3 mace blades
One 2-inch cinnamon stick, preferably canela, 972

Let the spices cool completely. Crack the cardamom pods by pounding them under the side of a knife. Collect the seeds within, and discard the pods. Transfer the seeds and other toasted spices to a mortar or spice grinder along with:

(1 tablespoon dried rosebuds)
2 teaspoons ground turmeric
2 teaspoons ground ginger
1 teaspoon grated or ground nutmeg
½ teaspoon cayenne pepper

Grind to a fine powder.

FIVE-SPICE POWDER

About ¼ cup

This pungent, slightly sweet mixture of ground spices sometimes contains cardamom or ginger, and black peppercorns can be substituted for the Sichuan peppercorns. Use sparingly when preparing roasted meats or poultry.

Grind into a powder in a spice grinder:

6 whole star anise
1 tablespoon fennel seeds
1 tablespoon Sichuan peppercorns
1 teaspoon whole cloves (about 20)
1 cinnamon stick, preferably cassia, 962, crushed into shards

Store in an airtight container.

SICHUAN PEPPER SALT

About 1/3 cup

Combine in a small, dry skillet and toast over medium heat, shaking the pan, until the peppercorns begin to smoke:

2 tablespoons Sichuan peppercorns
1 teaspoon white peppercorns

Transfer to a mortar or spice grinder and grind to a coarse powder. Add:

3 tablespoons Diamond kosher salt

QUATRE ÉPICES (SPICE PARISIENNE)

This mixture is a favorite for stews and sweets. It may vary in ingredients according to the will of the *épicier* or the whim of his customer, and frequently contains more than four *(quatre)* spices. Marie-Antoine Carême, the famous French chef who is considered the father of haute cuisine, concocted a formula for **épices composées** that included dried thyme, bay leaves, basil, sage, a little coriander, and mace, and—at the end—the addition of one-third part ground black pepper.

Store these in an airtight container.

I.

Mix together well in a small bowl:

1 tablespoon ground cinnamon
1 teaspoon ground cloves
1 teaspoon grated or ground nutmeg
1 teaspoon ground ginger

II.

Mix together well in a small bowl:

1 teaspoon white pepper
1/2 teaspoon grated or ground nutmeg
1/2 teaspoon ground ginger or cinnamon
1/4 teaspoon ground cloves

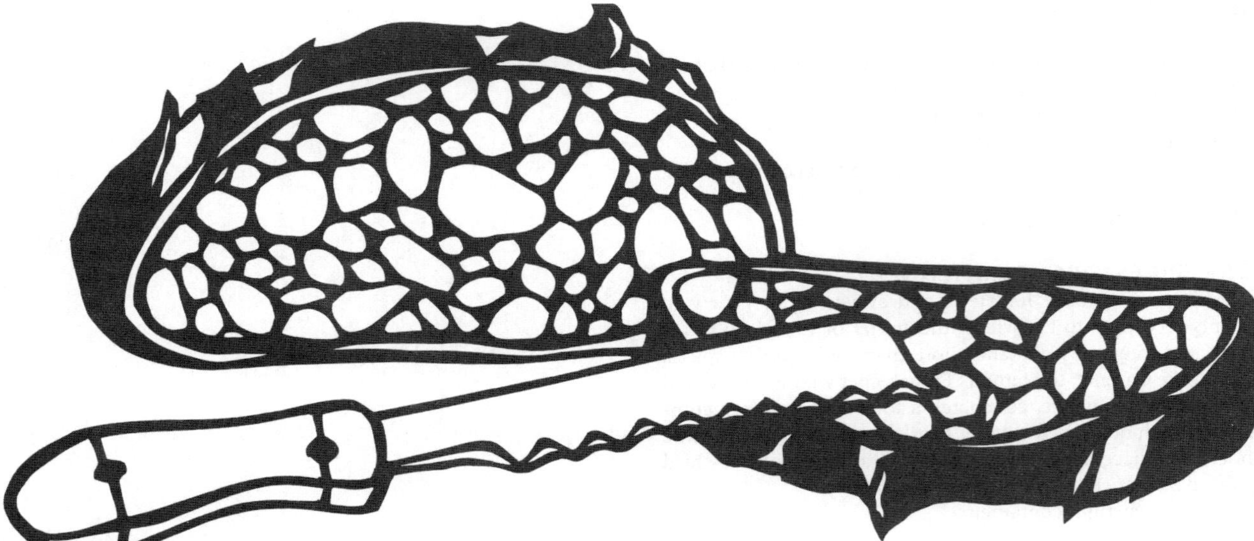

BREADS AND COFFEE CAKES

The importance of bread was probably realized in tandem with the delight of it. Bread is one of our oldest foods, and perhaps the most fundamental. Transforming flour and water into bread is not only something like shaking hands with our history, but it's also, as every baker discovers, a return to real flavor and a satisfying, meditative process.

Bread is made from flour or meal of nearly every kind, from wheat to barley to buckwheat to corn. It may be leavened with yeasts from the air or from a store-bought packet. Other breads get their rise from chemical sources like baking powder and baking soda. Then there are the breads that are not leavened at all but are rolled thin and baked into large sheets of pliable or crisp flatbread.

For the new baker, we recommend beginning with quick breads, 655, skillet breads such as corn bread, 630, griddle breads like English Muffins, 621, and flatbreads, 610. Then there are the relatively straightforward but more time-intensive yeast breads made with commercial yeast. For the seasoned baker, baking with a sourdough starter, 608, can provide new challenges and rewards. No matter which you choose to make, the fuller flavors and diverse textures of homemade breads easily repay the effort it takes to make them.

ABOUT YEAST BREAD

If you have never made yeast bread before, behold one of the great dramas of the kitchen! Do not be intimidated by the process. All breads are made from just a handful of simple ingredients.

YEAST

Yeast is a living organism. As it feeds on the natural sugars found in the flour in the dough, it multiplies, releasing carbon dioxide. It is this gas, trapped within a web of gluten strands, that causes dough to rise. This rising agent is sold in envelopes or jars as **active dry** and **instant** or **quick-rising** granules. For **fresh,** or **"compressed," yeast,** which requires slightly different handling, see 1034.

➤ The key is first to ensure the yeast is alive and well, and then to provide an environment where the yeast can thrive. To satisfy the former requirement, many recipes call for "activating" the yeast before mixing it into the dough. If you know your yeast is fresh (for instance, if you just bought the yeast, or if it is well shy of its use-by date), this step is unnecessary. However, if your yeast has been in the pantry or freezer for some time, this is a good precautionary step to take to avoid wasting ingredients should the yeast be expired. When placed in water with a pinch of sugar, yeast should dissolve and start to bubble very slightly after about 10 minutes. If, however, you know your yeast to be fresh, mix it right into the dry ingredients whether it is active dry or instant (while it was once the case that active dry yeast had to be dissolved in liquid before mixing it in, this is no longer true, though in many of our recipes we still prefer to dissolve the yeast in water to ensure that it is well dispersed in the dough).

To provide an environment where yeast can thrive, pay attention to temperature. Yeast must not be exposed to too much heat. If it is, it will die, and the bread will not rise at all. For recipes where active dry yeast is dissolved in warm liquid, take care not to heat the liquid beyond 115°F. Some types of yeast, specifically "instant" yeast, benefit from temperatures between 120° and 130°F. Yeast starts to die at 140°F and up. Many bread recipes instruct you to keep the dough warm through the rising process. This promotes yeast activity and hastens the rise. However, warmer is not always better. In recent years, slow-rising bread has come back into fashion. The doughs for these breads are often "retarded," or kept at cool temperatures to slow yeast development. This process takes a lot longer from start to finish, but the resulting breads tend to have a much more complex flavor and better texture. For breads using a sourdough starter instead of commercial yeast, see 608. For more information about yeast, see 1034.

FLOUR

In most recipes, the flour used is either all-purpose flour or bread flour. These flours are ideal for bread because they're rich in two proteins—glutenin and gliadin—that, when combined with liquid and stirred or kneaded, produce gluten, an elastic matrix that traps the gas released by the yeast. Gluten provides structure to dough and gives bread its characteristic texture. The more the gluten is developed, the chewier the bread will be. **Bread flour** has an especially high protein content and is therefore ideal for hearty breads. **All-purpose flour,** which has slightly less protein than bread flour, will produce satisfactory results in all recipes and is better for some rolls and breads that are more delicate in texture. **Whole wheat flour** and other whole-grain flours are often used in combination with all-purpose or bread flour to keep the loaf from being too dense. However, these flours are well worth incorporating into your breads as they provide much more flavor, texture, and nutrients than white flour. Delicious breads may be made with flours made from other grains, such as **rye, oats, cornmeal,** or **buckwheat.** Some flours that have little or no gluten-producing capabilities may be used in combination with all-purpose or bread flour.

When replacing wheat flour with other flours or grains in any of our recipes, please observe the following guidelines: ➤ When adding buckwheat, barley, cornmeal, millet, white or brown rice flour, or any combination of these, use wheat flour for at least half of the flour called for in the recipe. If adding bran or soy flour, use wheat flour for at least three-quarters of the flour called for.

For information on making gluten-free breads, see 605. For a diagram of a grain kernel, see 317.

LIQUIDS

Water and milk are the typical liquids used to bind the flour into a dough and to create steam when the bread is baked. Water tends to produce a chewy bread, milk a more tender and cakelike one. Most breads made with milk, such as White Bread, 599, can be made with water instead. The resulting loaf will be chewier. Do not, however, substitute water for milk in rolls, holiday breads, or coffee cakes, or the breads will be coarse and tough.

One important thing to consider when making bread is **hydration.** Obviously, liquid is necessary to bind the dry ingredients together, but the degree to which a dough is hydrated makes a huge difference in the outcome of the bread. Some breads, such as most sandwich breads, have a low hydration, meaning that just enough water is used to bring the dough together. These breads tend to have a close, fine crumb with small, even air bubbles. Other breads, like Ciabatta, 604, have a high hydration, where so much water is used that the dough is very sticky and slack. These breads tend to have a more open crumb structure with larger, irregular air bubbles. Because a higher hydration helps with gluten formation, these breads are often chewier than their low-hydration counterparts. For the effects of soft and hard water in baking, see Water, 1032.

Eggs are sometimes added to doughs, and technically they are a liquid, contributing to the doughs' hydration. However, eggs also contain protein and fat. These characteristics promote tenderness and make breads light and puffy. For this reason, they are often used in rich breads like Challah, 602, which would otherwise be dense. Eggs inhibit the action of yeast, and thus egg-rich doughs are slow to rise.

FATS

Many of the recipes in this chapter contain no added fat. These doughs are referred to as "lean." This category encompasses many old-fashioned breads, including rustic sourdoughs, baguettes, ciabatta, and the like. Other recipes, such as sandwich breads and brioche, call for shortening, oil, or butter. Even a small amount of fat makes bread more tender by inhibiting gluten formation, resulting in shorter gluten strands (hence the term "shortening"). A large amount makes bread so tender and close-grained that it has nearly the texture of cake. And, of course, some fats, particularly butter, add flavor.

ADDITIONS TO YEAST DOUGHS

Salt and **sugar** are added to breads for flavor. Salt is a yeast inhibitor, but it is never added to bread in quantities large enough for that to be an issue. In small quantities, sugar is a yeast promoter, but in larger quantities (over ½ cup per 4 cups flour), sugar slows yeast down. Sugar is hygroscopic, meaning it is attracted to water on a molecular level. In doughs, sugar competes with yeast for water. Enough added sugar can dehydrate the yeast cells by pulling water from them. When large quantities of sugar are used, the dough will hardly rise at all unless special procedures are followed (usually this amounts to adding a higher proportion of yeast). This is why even the sweetest yeast breads are never as sweet as cake. Sugar may be reduced by up to half in many recipes without negative consequences. Lower-sugar breads are drier than high-sugar breads, but not to a dramatic degree.

There are quite a few other ingredients that can add depth and variety to breads. Nuts, dried fruit, herbs, olives, sautéed or caramelized onions, roasted garlic, dried fruit, sprouted grains or beans, cracked wheat, leftover cooked grains, cheese, and spices are common additions to yeast breads. If the additions are dry you can practically add as much as good taste allows so long as the dough can bind them. ➤ Any of these additions should be mixed into the dough after the initial mixing and autolyse, 595. Some bread recipes call for a "soaker," or grains that have been soaked in water until plump. Wet additions should be accounted for when considering the hydration of the dough. Depending on the water content, you may wish to reduce the liquid called for in the recipe. Although very wet doughs are harder to handle, they can produce exceptional breads.

EQUIPMENT

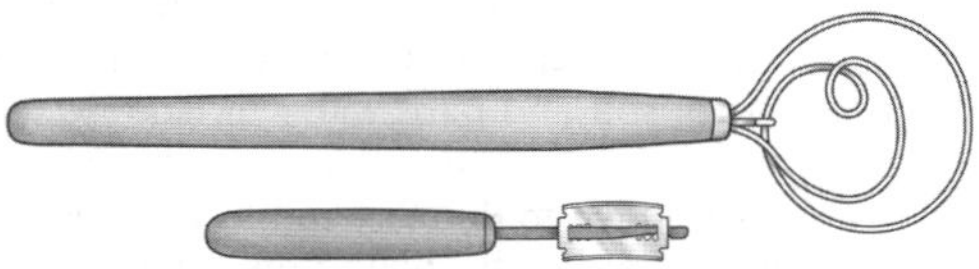

Dough whisk and lame

Bread is so simple that the budding baker can get by with no more than a countertop and their hands. However, there are some tools that make the process easier. Our favorite bread-making tool is a **bench scraper,** 660. It is ideal for scraping very wet, sticky doughs from the work surface, cutting dough into portions, and helping to shape dough. **Bowl scrapers** are flexible pieces of plastic that make scraping wet doughs from bowls an easy task. **Dough whisks** are effective, affordable tools for mixing dough if you do not have a mixer. If you wish to score dough before baking, a common practice for rustic breads, the best tool for the job is a **lame** (pronounced "lahm"), which consists of a razor blade attached to a handle. To help high-hydration doughs keep their shape during proofing, you may wish to invest in **bannetons,** or special baskets created expressly for this purpose. **Proofing cloths** are linen cloths that are used to help baguettes keep their shape during rising.

Baking stones and **baking steels** are favored by many bakers who make hand-shaped loaves. They are placed in the oven during preheating, and they not only promote good ovenspring, 597, in the dough, they also help regulate the temperature of the oven, lessening fluctuations caused by opening the oven door or from the oven cycling on and off during baking. They also result in a thick, crisp, deeply browned crust. **Dutch ovens** are now a common tool for baking breads. They have the same advantages of baking stones and steels, but they have the added benefit of trapping the steam released by the dough in the initial phase of baking. The steam prevents the crust from setting until the loaf has expanded to its maximum height. At this point, the lid is removed and the bread is baked until the crust is set and dark brown.

Combo cooker

A "combo cooker"—a cast-iron Dutch oven whose lid also serves as a skillet—is especially useful for bread baking, since the deeper Dutch oven can be inverted over the dough so it can be baked on the shallow skillet ("lid") part. This is easier and safer than trying to lower dough down into a piping hot Dutch oven.

For mixing doughs, a **heavy-duty stand mixer** equipped with a **dough hook** significantly reduces the time and physical labor involved. Bear in mind that the motor can burn out if the dough is too tough or if too much dough is mixed at once. The dough can be mixed and kneaded from start to finish using the dough hook, but it is quicker to do the initial mixing with the paddle attachment and then change to the hook when the ingredients are fully mixed. ➤ A large batch of dough may require a little kneading by hand to become truly smooth. Never walk away and leave a mixer unattended. It may "walk" off the countertop, or the dough may climb up the hook and gum up the gears. See Mixing Bread Dough, below, for instructions on using a stand mixer to mix dough.

Food processors can be used for mixing, but many are not strong enough to knead bread dough, and many that *do* have the strength do not have the capacity to handle doughs made with more than 3 or 4 cups of flour. Check the manufacturer's instructions regarding capacity. See Mixing Bread Dough, below, for instructions on using a food processor to mix dough.

MIXING BREAD DOUGH

Dry yeast does not need to be mixed with liquid before using, but if you would like to "prove" your yeast, dissolve it in liquid between 105° and 115°F and let stand for 5 minutes. For compressed fresh yeast, dissolve it in 85°F liquid and let stand, without stirring, for 10 minutes.

Many yeast breads are made with **pre-ferments,** that is, a portion of the dough started some time before the dough as a whole is mixed. These may be leavened naturally—like sourdough, 608—or with commercial yeasts. See About Starters or Pre-Ferments for more information, 606.

The **conventional** or **straight dough method** is the easiest and most familiar mixing method for home bakers. It does not require the preparation of a pre-ferment, but rather involves simply mixing the dry ingredients with the wet ingredients, kneading the dough, and allowing it to rise once or twice before baking.

To mix dough by hand, combine the liquids and softened or melted fat, if applicable, in a large bowl, then add all but 1 cup of the flour. Stir with a wooden spoon or a dough whisk until the dough comes together. Add the reserved flour little by little until the dough is pliable but neither dry nor very sticky (or as described in the recipe). At this point, all yeast doughs benefit from autolyse, or resting, below.

To use a heavy-duty stand mixer, combine part of the flour, the yeast, sugar, and salt in the mixer bowl and combine briefly at low speed. Add the liquids and softened or melted fat, if applicable, and beat as indicated in the recipe. Gradually add enough flour to make a soft dough. Let the dough rest, as below. After resting, knead with a dough hook until the dough is smooth and elastic, about 10 minutes or as directed.

To mix dough in a food processor, combine the lesser amount of flour called for in the recipe, the remaining dry ingredients, and the softened or melted fat, if applicable, in the work bowl and process until well mixed, about 20 seconds. Have the liquid ingredients at refrigerator temperature, as the food processor tends to overheat doughs. With the machine running, add the liquid ingredients through the feed tube. Process until the dough cleans the sides of the bowl, 45 to 60 seconds, stopping the machine once or twice and adding a little flour if the dough seems sticky. ➤ Do not process for longer than 60 seconds total, or the gluten may begin to break down. If, for some reason, the dough appears to require more kneading after 60 seconds, finish it by hand.

AUTOLYSE, OR RESTING THE DOUGH

Autolyse is a French term coined by baking professor Raymond Calvel in his 2001 book *The Taste of Bread* for the resting period immediately following the mixing of the dough. At this point the dough will still be somewhat shaggy, rough, and unpromising. Simply cover the dough and leave it for at least 20 minutes and up to 40 minutes. During this time the flour hydrates, gluten begins to form, and enzymes that promote elasticity are activated. Giving the dough this head start before kneading makes the kneading process more efficient, and the dough will be easier to handle into the bargain.

KNEADING YEAST DOUGH

Kneading makes dough smooth and elastic by developing gluten. Yeast causes the dough to ferment, which produces carbon dioxide; this gas gets trapped in the gluten strands as bubbles, which causes the dough to rise. Kneading may be done with an appliance, but because the process is rhythmic and relaxing, many prefer to knead by hand. Even those who enjoy hand-kneading, however, may find that kneading by machine is preferable for very wet or sticky doughs, such as rye dough.

Generally speaking, doughs vary in moisture content and only experience can tell you exactly how much flour to add during the kneading process. Further, ambient humidity can significantly affect the amount of flour you will need. Thus, some variations in the amount of flour are indicated in the individual recipes. We will say, however, that one of the most common mistakes made by novice bread makers is adding too much flour during kneading, which results in dry, dense loaves. During kneading, only dust the work surface with a very light coating of flour, and opt to flour your hands rather than the dough itself, if things get sticky. Use a bench scraper to help pry stubborn doughs from the work surface.

Kneading can be done on any countertop of a reasonable size or even a large cutting board. Very lightly flour the surface and place the dough on it. To knead, fold the dough on top of itself toward you, then press it away from you with the floured heel of your hand, as shown; give it a quarter turn, fold it, and press away again. More flour may be necessary, but again, flour your hands rather than the dough itself. Initially, very soft doughs, like Brioche, 603, are not really kneaded but are peeled or scraped off the work surface and folded over onto themselves, as shown. ➤ Bench scrapers are particularly helpful for kneading these soft doughs. As the gluten develops through sustained kneading, the dough will become smooth and elastic. Kneading should be thorough, but not heavy or rough, and should take about 10 minutes.

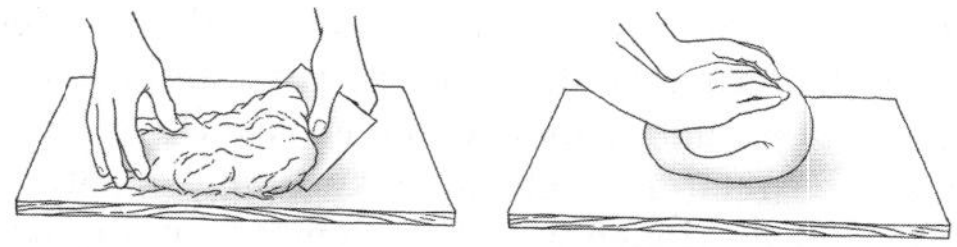

Kneading yeast dough

When the dough is smooth, elastic, and satiny, and air blisters appear just under the surface, it is ready. The dough at this point should no longer stick to the work surface or your hands. ➤ To test its elasticity, slowly and gently stretch a small piece of dough, turning it in a circular motion as you pull so that it stretches evenly. The dough should hold together without tearing until it forms a sheer membrane, thin enough to let light come through. This is called the **windowpane test.** Alternatively, test the temperature of the dough with an instant-read thermometer; the center of the dough should register 77° to 80°F.

There is a new school of thought when it comes to kneading dough. **No-knead breads** have become popular, particularly with home bakers, for obvious reasons: They are easier to make and produce less mess. Surprisingly, the results of this low-effort method can rival or exceed many kneaded breads in flavor and texture. Some recipes call for extended fermentation with periodic gentle stretching and folding, so while the dough is not technically "no-knead," it is minimally handled. This may seem counterintuitive, as it is commonly thought that kneading is the best and primary way to encourage gluten development. However, as discussed in Autolyse, or Resting the Dough, above, letting dough sit for extended periods of time is hugely beneficial for gluten development and decreases the amount of handling needed to produce a first-rate loaf. No-knead doughs often use less yeast than standard doughs due to a longer fermentation, and they often have a higher hydration to promote gluten formation with minimal handling. In short, extended periods of kneading are used in many recipes to compensate for a very short fermentation time, whereas no-knead doughs rely on time for their texture.

RETARDING DOUGH

Bread baking is interesting because it is not like most cooking where one process follows immediately behind another until the dish is done. When you make yeast bread, you are working with living organisms that are subject to their environment. By manipulating this environment, you can hasten or delay the process to a great degree. As discussed in Yeast, 592, warm temperatures speed yeast activity, and cool temperatures slow it down. Placing the dough in a cool environment retards, or slows, yeast development, thus delaying the rising process.

The most obvious benefit to slowing down yeast is the flexibility it adds to the process: Bread-baking is hard to fit into a busy schedule, and retarded doughs can be made in the evening, refrigerated, and baked the next day. It's also very convenient to be able to pop dough into the refrigerator if something comes up and you can't tend to it right away. Further, chilling makes the dough easier to handle.

Though less evident, we value this technique primarily for the improvement in flavor and texture it lends to the finished bread. By extending the fermentation time, the yeast and bacteria in the dough are able to produce a more complex flavor.

Dough can be retarded right after kneading or after the first rise. Simply cover the dough well to prevent it from drying out and refrigerate it. The amount of time it can be refrigerated varies, but generally doughs refrigerated during their bulk fermentation, below, can be left for up to 2 days with no ill effects. Before baking, shape the dough while it is cold, then allow it to come to room temperature for an hour, or until it rises the desired amount, before baking.

Covering the dough to rise, testing for properly risen dough, punching down the dough

THE FIRST RISE OR BULK FERMENTATION

After kneading comes the first rise. This is really as simple as letting the dough sit, covered, in a bowl until nearly doubled in size. Yeast dough rises most efficiently in a draft-free place at a temperature of 75° to 85°F. If the room is cold, you can place the bowl of dough on a rack over a pan of warm water; near, but not on, a radiator; or in an oven heated for less than 1 minute, until you can just feel warmth, and then turned off. The bulk rise can be very slow without affecting the quality of the bread (a long, slow fermentation equals better flavor and texture), so if you have the time there is no need to speed the process by keeping the dough warm.

The first time the dough rises it should be allowed to nearly double in bulk, which generally takes 1 to 2 hours at warm room temperature. ➤ Never allow a dough to rise so much during bulk fermentation that it begins to deflate, as this will result in a bread with a coarse, close texture. To make sure the dough has risen sufficiently, press it firmly with your fingertips. ➤ The imprint of your fingertips should remain in the dough, as illustrated, above.

DIVIDING AND PRESHAPING THE DOUGH

Before shaping, many bread recipes call for "punching down" the dough. However, there is never any reason to take this literally. In fact, after bulk fermentation, yeast doughs should be handled with care to avoid deflating the many bubbles you and the yeast have worked so hard to create. Simply turn the dough out of the bowl onto a very lightly floured work surface. If it sticks to the bowl, use a flexible plastic bowl scraper to help you.

Yeast breads divide into two basic types: those baked in a pan, like White Bread, 599, and those baked free-form, like Rustic French Bread, 606. Each type requires a different shaping procedure. Because most recipes for yeast breads yield more than one loaf, divide the dough into the number of pieces called for in the recipe. If desired, weigh the dough before dividing it, then use the scale to divide the dough precisely. Lightly form the dough into balls (see below), cover with a clean cloth, and allow to rest for at least 10 and up to 30 minutes.

To "round" portioned dough into balls, lightly cup your hands around the dough and pull the dough toward you, using the friction of the dough against the work surface to help shape it into a ball.

THE FINAL SHAPE

Shaping plays a truly important role in baking and our enjoyment of the final loaf. Some breads, like the baguette, have a higher ratio of crust to crumb, making them exceptionally chewy, crusty, and flavorful from the browning of the surface of the bread. Others, like the boule or round loaf, have a lower crust-to-crumb ratio, which helps them stay moist and fresh for longer.

Breads explicitly for making sandwiches are often baked in loaf pans so their even shape makes perfect, consistent slices. Different types of bread pans promote distinctive crusts. A standard aluminum bread pan, either bare metal or nonstick, will promote a thin, golden crust. Glass, dark-finished aluminum, ceramic, and enamel pans produce a thick, dark crust. ➤ For glass and enamel pans, reduce the oven temperature by 25°F. Unless the recipe indicates otherwise, the pan(s) should be greased.

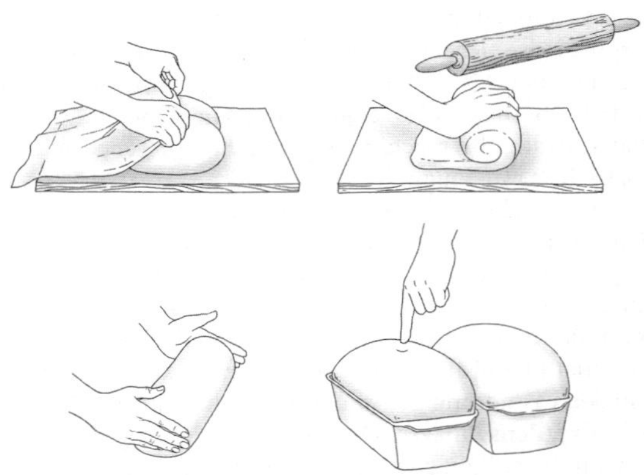

Covering the dough to rest, forming the loaf, and shaping pan-baked bread

To form a loaf for pan-baking, place one of the pieces of rested dough on a work surface. Use a rolling pin or your palm to flatten it slightly into a rectangle. Starting with a long side, roll the dough tightly, somewhat like a jelly-roll. To complete the roll, seal the seam by pressing the dough together and place, seam side down, on the surface. Then, with your hands at either end of the roll, compress the ends of the loaf as shown, 596, folding under any excess as you slide the dough, seam side down, into the greased pan.

Since free-form loaves are not supported by the sides of a pan, they must be formed especially tightly if they are to hold their shape. Thus the shaping of free-form loaves is something of an art and the knack comes with practice. Do not be too critical of your results. Even bakers with years of experience find that their free-form loaves sprawl a bit. This is part of the charm of these rustic loaves.

To form a round loaf or boule, place the dough on a lightly floured work surface. Cup your hands around the far side of the dough with the pinky sides of your hands resting on the work surface. ➤ Exert pressure on the lower portion of the loaf as you pull the dough toward you against the work surface so that a small portion of dough is tucked underneath the loaf and the surface of the loaf tightens. Rotate the loaf a quarter-turn and repeat. Keep pressing and rotating until the loaf is round and the surface becomes smooth and taut. This should only take a minute or so. Let the loaf rest for about 10 minutes, loosely covered with a clean cloth, and then ➤ give it a few more turns to tighten the loaf. Transfer to a baking sheet, banneton, or as directed in the recipe.

There are scores of different free-form shapes beyond the boule, and we do not have the space to cover them all; for two other shapes, see Quick French Bread, 604, and Ciabatta, 604.

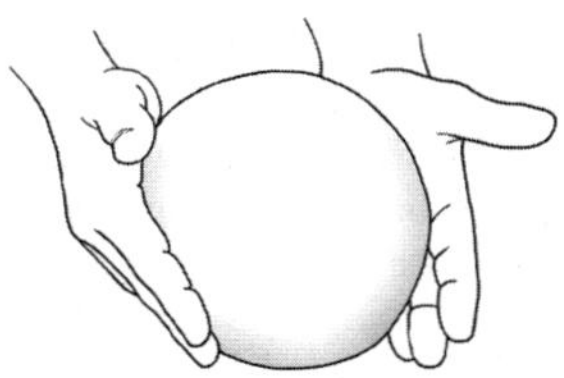

Forming a round loaf

PROOFING DOUGH OR THE FINAL RISE

Proofing is the final rise before baking. After being handled and deflated somewhat in the shaping process, the dough needs time to recover its loft before baking sets the shape of the bread. For many breads, such as most sandwich breads, this final rise is fairly short—45 minutes to 1 hour or so. Other breads, like sourdough, have a much longer proof. As with the first rise, there is no need to keep the dough in a warm place unless your kitchen is very cold. Warmer temperatures will speed the rise, but cool room temperatures are perfectly adequate for proofing. In fact, some prefer to proof their breads in the refrigerator. As you might imagine, this takes quite a bit longer, but the resulting flavor of the bread will be much more complex than one that was baked after a quick final proof.

To proof the dough, cover the dough with a clean cloth. If the dough is in a pan, it will eventually fill in the corners of the pan. While it is rising, preheat the oven. When ready to bake, the loaf will be symmetrical and ➤ a slight impression will remain when you press it lightly with your fingertips. Do not permit a loaf to overrise, or an air space may form beneath the top crust.

SCORING LOAVES

Most free-form loaves and some pan-baked loaves are **scored,** or cut across the top, immediately before baking. Scoring is both to aid rising and for decoration. The amount that bread rises in the oven is called **ovenspring.** Ovenspring is the result of the water in the dough turning to steam, the acceleration of yeast activity as the dough heats up, and gases expanding. If bread is baked without scoring, the pressure of the expanding dough may tear the crust in an irregular pattern—or, worse, the dough may be trapped by the solidifying crust and rise very little in the oven. Slashes may be made with a lame, 594, a single-edged razor blade, or a very sharp knife. The slashing tool is typically held at a 45-degree angle, and the cut goes ¼ to ½ inch into the dough. This angle creates a cut that allows the dough to expand to its maximum potential before the crust sets and prevents any further rise. Do not cut too deep, as this can result in the cut flap of dough collapsing onto itself and setting before ovenspring is complete.

For round loaves, you may make a single crescent-shaped cut about two-thirds of the way around the top of the loaf. Or make a crisscross pattern by cutting about 6 slashes, 1 inch apart, across the top of the loaf and then 6 more slashes perpendicular to or diagonal to these. Or cut 4 slashes in a square pattern on top of the loaf. The very ends of the slashes should overlap. Mark baguettes with diagonal slashes on an acute angle. ➤ Regardless of the loaf or slash pattern, never cut into the sides or the ends of the loaf, or you will release the surface tension and the loaf will not hold its shape.

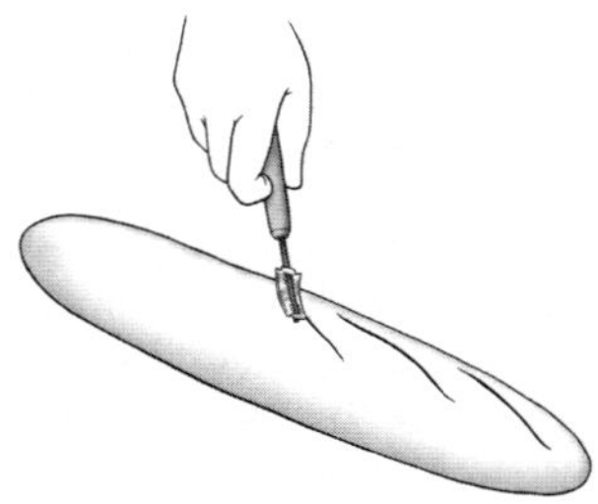

Scoring a baguette

ABOUT BAKING BREAD

As with every other stage of the bread-making process, how you go about baking bread depends on the results you want to achieve and the type of bread you are making. For instance, sandwich loaves are baked at a lower temperature than rustic breads because you want a lighter, thinner crust on a sandwich loaf and a thicker, crustier one on a rustic loaf. Individual recipes will direct you as to the particulars.

When loaves in pans have doubled or nearly doubled in size,

they are ready for the oven. Bake a single loaf in the middle of the preheated oven. Bake two loaves side by side. When baking more than two loaves, switch racks from top to bottom during baking and rotate the pans front to back so they brown evenly (see the proper oven placement illustration on 1071).

Controlling heat and humidity in the oven is essential for successful bread baking. Most oven surfaces are made of light sheet metal, which retains heat poorly; every time the oven door is opened, the temperature drops and the bread suffers. Placing a baking stone or steel on the bottom rack helps regulate the oven temperature. Because a stone or steel takes a long time to heat up, start preheating the oven at least 45 minutes before baking.

When free-form loaves are done proofing, turn them out of their proofing basket, seam side down, onto a baking sheet or baker's peel well sprinkled with a thin, even layer of flour or cornmeal. If you are setting more than one loaf on a baking sheet or baking stone, bear in mind that the loaves will increase in size by almost half, so leave plenty of space—almost the size of a whole loaf—in between.

Humidity promotes ovenspring by keeping the crust of free-form loaves from setting too quickly. Professional ovens have steam injectors, but at home you can improvise with a pan and some water. Place a heavy pan in the bottom of the oven or on the lowest rack before preheating. Pour 1 cup hot water into it right after loading the breads into the oven. The water should sizzle and steam dramatically as soon as it hits the hot pan. Close the oven door as quickly as possible to trap the steam.

Another method for trapping steam is to bake the bread inside a Dutch oven or combo cooker, 594. This technique only works for round loaves, but it produces spectacular results. Preheat the Dutch oven or combo cooker in the oven for at least 30 minutes. Carefully turn the loaf into the hot Dutch oven or onto the skillet part of the combo cooker, cover with the lid or the deeper part of the combo cooker, and return to the oven. The loaf will bake covered for the first half of baking, which traps the steam and prevents the crust from setting, ensuring maximum ovenspring. Then the lid or top is removed for the last half of baking, allowing the crust to set and become deep golden brown.

Some loaves are "washed" before baking to help with browning or to produce a shiny crust. Milk, either used in the dough or brushed on toward the end of the baking period, gives a good all-over brown color. Cream or butter may also be brushed on 5 to 10 minutes before the end of baking for color. For a glossy, golden crust, you may brush the top toward the end of baking with egg wash: 1 egg yolk beaten with 1 tablespoon water or milk.

Some breads are garnished with seeds, such as sesame or poppy seeds. Seeds should be applied after brushing the dough with either milk, egg wash, or plain water, and before baking. To keep the crust of sandwich loaves soft, brush the crust with melted or softened butter after the bread is baked and out of the pan, then cover it with a clean cloth.

TESTING BREADS FOR DONENESS

The easiest way to determine whether a loaf has finished baking is to insert an instant-read thermometer into the center; sandwich breads and other soft, enriched breads should read 185° to 190°F. Rustic, crusty breads should reach at least 200°F. Pan-baked breads will shrink from the sides of the pan when they are approaching doneness. Another time-honored test is to tap the bottom of a baked loaf with your finger; if the loaf makes a hollow sound, it is done. If necessary, return the loaf to the oven, in or out of the pan, for a few minutes until it is finished.

Exceptions to these rules are especially dense, moist breads, such as country breads made with starters like Rye Bread with a Sponge Starter, 607, and Sourdough Rye Bread, 610. Even though these breads may look done and sound hollow when tapped, they need to reach an internal temperature of 210°F in order to evaporate moisture and ensure a crackling crisp crust. ➤ Turn the oven off and let the loaves remain in the oven for 10 minutes. This cool-down technique will dry the bread without overbaking or burning it.

COOLING AND STORING BREAD

When the bread has finished baking, remove it at once from the pan and place it on a wire rack. Rustic, crusty loaves emit a "song" as they cool: Put your ear next to the loaf and listen for gentle crackling sounds. ➤ Let the bread cool completely before wrapping, storing, or freezing. There should be no warmth radiating from the loaf. If it is wrapped while still warm, condensation may encourage mold. ➤ Do not cut into a loaf until it has been out of the oven for at least 20 minutes, and wait an hour if possible (less for rolls and small breads). Bread always tastes best after it has cooled to an internal temperature of 85°F or less.

While it is considered "best practice" to store bread in a paper bag, we usually keep ours in a plastic bag. Being a household of two, it is impossible for us to finish a loaf before it becomes hard when stored in a paper bag. While storing in plastic does soften the crust, we typically toast bread before eating it, making softening less of a concern. Whether storing in paper or plastic, there are trade-offs. Most breads stored in a breadbox, a ventilated drawer, or a loosely closed paper bag will remain fresh for 3 to 5 days but will become more and more stale. (Breadboxes and drawers should be periodically wiped with a mild baking soda or bleach solution to kill mold spores.) Bread stored in a plastic bag or wrapped in plastic wrap will remain fresh somewhat longer, though the crust will soften. ➤ Refrigeration dries bread out. To store bread for a prolonged period, freeze well-wrapped loaves for up to 3 months. ➤ Once thawed, frozen bread stales quickly, so do not thaw more than you can consume within a day. Frozen bread can be quickly revived by lightly sprinkling it with water, loosely wrapping it in foil, and baking it at 350°F until warm. See About Uses for Leftover Breads, 638, for some ideas for using stale bread.

▲ BREAD BAKING AT HIGH ALTITUDES

At high altitudes, use one-quarter less active dry yeast than called for. Avoid instant or rapid-rise yeast, which can make bread rise too fast, sacrificing flavor and texture. It is fine for sea-level baking but is less successful at altitude because reduced air pressure encourages rapid yeast expansion. Alternatively, allow the first rise (bulk fermentation) to take place in the refrigerator to slow the rise and help with flavor development.

At 5,000 feet and above, some breads, such as White Bread, below, benefit from increasing the baking temperature about 25°F above that at sea level; baking times at altitude may stay the same as sea level or take slightly longer. At 10,000 feet, the ovenspring is enhanced if you preheat the oven 25° to 50°F above the baking temperature, then reduce the heat at least 25°F (or to the temperature specified in the recipe) when the bread is put in the oven.

WHITE BREAD

Two 9 × 5-inch loaves

This perfect white bread first appeared in *Joy* in 1931. It is an even-grained all-purpose bread that stales slowly and cuts well for sandwiches. Add the optional eggs for a richer bread with a more golden color. For **Rich White Bread,** replace the water with 1 cup (235g) milk, add the optional eggs, and increase the sugar to ⅓ cup (65g).

Whisk to combine in a medium bowl:

1 cup (235g) lukewarm (80° to 90°F) milk
1¼ cups (295g) lukewarm (80° to 90°F) water
2 tablespoons sugar (25g) or honey (40g)
2 tablespoons (30g) butter, melted
1 envelope (2¼ teaspoons) active dry yeast

Have ready in a large bowl or a stand mixer fitted with the dough hook:

6 cups (750g) all-purpose flour
1 tablespoon salt

Add the lukewarm milk mixture along with, if desired:

(2 large eggs, well beaten)

Stir until just combined, adding up to ½ cup more flour if the dough is extremely sticky. Cover and let the dough rest for at least 15 and up to 30 minutes.

Knead the dough on a lightly floured work surface or with the mixer on medium-low speed until smooth and elastic, about 10 minutes, adding more flour if needed. Transfer the dough to an oiled bowl and turn once to coat with oil. Cover and let rise in a warm place (75° to 85°F) until doubled in bulk, at least 1 hour.

Grease two 9 × 5-inch loaf pans. Divide the dough in half, shape into 2 loaves for pan-baking, 597, and place in the pans. Cover with oiled plastic wrap and let rise again until almost doubled in bulk, 1 to 1½ hours.

While the dough rises, preheat the oven to 450°F.

Bake the bread 10 minutes. Reduce the heat to 350°F and bake until the crust is golden brown and the bottom sounds hollow when tapped, about 30 minutes longer. Immediately turn the loaves out of the pans onto a wire rack to cool completely.

WHOLE WHEAT SANDWICH BREAD

Two 9 × 5-inch loaves

Prepare **White Bread, above,** using **2 cups (260g) whole wheat flour, 4 cups (500g) all-purpose flour,** and **1½ cups (355g) water.**

SPROUTED WHOLE WHEAT BREAD

Coarsely chop **2 cups sprouted wheat, soybeans, lentils, wheat berries, or chickpeas, 1021,** in a food processor. Prepare **White Bread, above,** using **2 cups (260g) whole wheat flour, 4 cups (500g) all-purpose flour,** and a total of **2 envelopes (1½ tablespoons)** active dry yeast. Add the chopped, sprouted grains to the flour along with the liquid and proceed as directed.

CINNAMON RAISIN BREAD

Two 9 × 5-inch loaves

Prepare the dough for:

Rich White Bread, above, through the first rise

While the dough is rising, place in a small saucepan with enough cold water to cover by ½ inch:

1½ cups raisins or golden raisins

Bring to a boil, then drain well and let cool. Stir together in a small bowl:

½ cup (100g) sugar
2 tablespoons ground cinnamon

Grease two 9 × 5-inch loaf pans. Divide the dough in half. Using a rolling pin, roll the dough into two 8 × 18-inch rectangles about ½ inch thick. Brush the surface of the dough with:

1 tablespoon butter, melted

Sprinkle all but 4 teaspoons of the cinnamon sugar over the rectangles, then spread the raisins evenly over the surface. Starting from one 8-inch side, roll up the dough tightly, like a jelly-roll. Pinch the seam and ends closed. Place seam side down in the pans. Cover loosely with oiled plastic wrap and let rise until doubled in bulk, 1 to 1½ hours.

While the dough rises, preheat the oven to 375°F.

Whisk together and brush over the top of the loaves:

1 large egg
Pinch of salt

Sprinkle the top of the dough with the reserved cinnamon sugar. Bake until the crust is deep golden brown and the bottom sounds hollow when tapped, 40 to 45 minutes. Immediately turn the loaves out of the pans onto a wire rack. While the bread is still hot, brush the tops with:

4 teaspoons butter, melted

Let cool completely.

PIMIENTO CHEESE BREAD

1 large round loaf

For variation, add minced fresh or dried herbs, such as thyme or marjoram, minced green onion, or chopped green olives to the dough.

Combine in a large bowl or a stand mixer fitted with the paddle attachment:

¾ cup (185g) room-temperature (70° to 75°F) buttermilk
2 tablespoons (30g) butter, melted
1 tablespoon (10g) sugar
1½ teaspoons salt
(1 teaspoon coarsely ground black pepper)

Combine in a small bowl and let stand until the yeast is dissolved, about 5 minutes:

¼ cup (60g) warm (105° to 115°F) water
1 envelope (2¼ teaspoons) active dry yeast

Stir the yeast mixture into the buttermilk mixture. Add and stir until smooth:

1 large egg
3/4 cup shredded extra sharp Cheddar (3 oz or 85g)
One 2-ounce jar chopped pimientos, well drained

Stir in well, on low speed if using a stand mixer:

1½ cups (200g) bread flour

If using a mixer, remove the paddle and attach the dough hook. Add and continue stirring until the dough begins to leave the sides of the bowl:

1 to 1½ cups (125 to 190g) all-purpose flour

Knead by hand or with the mixer on medium-low speed until the dough is smooth and elastic, about 10 minutes. Transfer the dough to an oiled bowl and turn to coat with oil. Cover and let rise in a warm place (75° to 85°F) until doubled in bulk, about 1 hour.

Shape into a round loaf, 597. If desired, sprinkle the shaped loaf with:

(½ cup shredded extra sharp Cheddar [2 oz or 55g])

Cover the dough lightly with oiled plastic wrap and let rise again until nearly doubled in bulk, 45 minutes to 1 hour.

While the dough rises, preheat the oven to 375°F.

If the loaf was not sprinkled with cheese, brush with:

Melted butter

Bake until the crust is golden brown and the bottom sounds hollow when tapped, 35 to 40 minutes. Transfer to a rack to cool completely.

DILL BATTER LOAF

One 9 × 5-inch loaf

This dill-flecked loaf begs to be spread with cream cheese and topped with cucumbers, but it also pairs perfectly with salted butter. Because the dough is sticky, this bread is easiest made in a stand mixer, but it can be kneaded by hand if ¼ cup extra flour is worked into the dough.

Combine in a large bowl or in a stand mixer fitted with the paddle attachment:

3 cups (375g) all-purpose flour
½ cup finely chopped green onions
½ cup chopped dill
1 envelope (2¼ teaspoons) instant yeast
1 teaspoon salt

Mix briefly to combine. Add:

1 cup (235g) cottage cheese
½ cup (120g) water or buttermilk
1 large egg
2 tablespoons (25g) olive oil

Mix, on low speed if using a mixer, until the dough comes together. If using a mixer, remove the paddle and attach the dough hook. Knead by hand or with the mixer on medium-low speed until the dough is smooth and elastic, about 10 minutes. Transfer the dough to an oiled bowl and turn to coat with oil. Cover and let rise in a warm place (75° to 85°F) until doubled in bulk, 1 to 1½ hours.

Grease a 9 × 5-inch loaf pan. Form the dough into a loaf for pan-baking, 597, and place seam side down in the pan. Cover with oiled plastic wrap and let rise in a warm place (75° to 85°F) until doubled in bulk, about 1 hour.

While the dough rises, preheat the oven to 350°F.

If desired, brush the top of the loaf with:

(1 egg, lightly beaten, or 1 tablespoon butter, melted)

Sprinkle lightly with:

(½ teaspoon flaky sea salt)

Bake until the crust is deep golden brown and the bottom sounds hollow when tapped, 35 to 40 minutes. Immediately turn the loaf out of the pan onto a wire rack to cool completely.

ALL WHOLE WHEAT BREAD COCKAIGNE

Two 9 × 5-inch loaves

A heavier, coarser bread than those made partly with white flour, but one with excellent flavor.

Combine in a large bowl or a stand mixer fitted with the paddle attachment:

6 cups (785g) whole wheat flour
½ cup (45g) dry milk powder
1 envelope (2¼ teaspoons) active dry yeast

Stir in:

2¼ cups (530g) warm (105° to 115°F) water or milk
¼ cup (85g) molasses or honey
2 tablespoons (30g) butter, melted
1 tablespoon salt

Mix briefly, adding a little flour or liquid if necessary, just until the dough comes together. Cover and let the dough rest for at least 15 and up to 30 minutes.

If using a mixer, remove the paddle and attach the dough hook. Knead the dough by hand or with the mixer on medium-low speed until smooth and elastic, about 10 minutes. Transfer the dough to an oiled bowl and turn to coat with oil. Cover and let rise in a warm place (75° to 85°F) until doubled in bulk, about 1½ hours.

Grease two 9 × 5-inch loaf pans. Divide the dough in half, shape into loaves for pan-baking, 597, and place in the pans. Cover loosely with oiled plastic wrap and let rise until almost doubled in bulk, about 1 hour.

While the dough rises, preheat the oven to 350°F.

Bake until the crust is golden brown, the bottom sounds hollow when tapped, and the internal temperature reaches 205°F, about 45 minutes. Immediately turn the loaves out of the pans onto a wire rack to cool completely.

LIMPA (SWEDISH RYE BREAD)

Two 9-inch round or oval loaves

The dough for this lightly sweet bread is very sticky, so if you have a stand mixer, use it. We like to eat toasted slices of this hearty loaf with the strange and delicious Norwegian cheese called *gjetost*, or brown cheese.

Combine in a large bowl or a stand mixer fitted with the paddle attachment:

1½ cups (355g) warm (105° to 115°F) water
⅓ cup (65g) sugar
¼ cup (85g) molasses
Finely grated zest of 1 orange
1 tablespoon fennel seeds

1 tablespoon caraway seeds
1 envelope (2¼ teaspoons) active dry yeast
2 teaspoons salt

Stir in until smooth:

2½ cups (300g) dark rye flour

Add:

2½ cups (315g) all-purpose flour

Knead in the flour or mix on low speed until the dough just comes together. Cover and let rest for at least 15 and up to 30 minutes.

If using a mixer, remove the paddle and attach the dough hook. Knead the dough on a lightly floured work surface or with the mixer on medium-low speed until smooth and elastic, 8 to 10 minutes. Transfer the dough to an oiled bowl and turn to coat with oil. Cover and let rise until puffy and increased in volume, 1½ to 2 hours.

Lightly grease a baking sheet and dust with:

Cornmeal

Divide the dough in half. Shape each half into a round loaf, 597, and place on the prepared baking sheet. Loosely cover with a cloth or oiled plastic wrap and let rise until puffy and a fingertip lightly pressed into the dough leaves an indentation, about 1½ hours.

While the dough rises, preheat the oven to 375°F.

Make three diagonal slashes in the top of the loaves with a sharp knife or lame. Bake until the crust is set and the internal temperature reaches 205°F, 40 to 50 minutes. Turn off the oven and leave the loaves in for 10 minutes more. Transfer the loaves to a wire rack to cool completely before slicing. Serve with:

Salted butter and jam

CRACKED-WHEAT BREAD

Two 9 × 5-inch loaves

Place in a medium bowl:

1 cup (155g) fine bulgur

Pour over it:

Boiling water to barely cover

Let sit, covered, for 10 minutes to soften. If all the water is not absorbed, drain off any excess. Stir in:

1 cup (235g) milk
3 tablespoons sugar (35g) or honey (65g)
2 tablespoons vegetable oil (25g) or butter (30g), melted
1 tablespoon (20g) molasses
1 tablespoon salt

Let cool.

Meanwhile, combine in a large bowl or a stand mixer fitted with the paddle attachment and mix well:

4 cups (500g) all-purpose flour
2 cups (260g) whole wheat flour
2 envelopes (1½ tablespoons) active dry yeast

Add the bulgur mixture to the flour mixture and stir just until the dough comes together. Cover and let the dough rest for 20 minutes.

If using a mixer, remove the paddle and attach the dough hook. Knead the dough on a lightly floured work surface or with the mixer on medium-low speed until smooth and elastic, about 10 minutes. Transfer the dough to an oiled bowl and turn to coat with oil. Cover and let rise in a warm place (75° to 85°F) until doubled in bulk, about 1 hour.

Grease two 9 × 5-inch loaf pans. Divide the dough in half and shape into loaves for pan-baking, 597. Place in the pans, loosely cover with oiled plastic wrap, and let rise until doubled in bulk, about 45 minutes.

While the dough rises, preheat the oven to 350°F.

Bake until the crust is golden brown, the bottom sounds hollow when tapped, and the internal temperature reaches 205°F, 35 to 40 minutes. Immediately turn the loaves out of the pans onto a wire rack to cool completely.

OAT BREAD COCKAIGNE

Two 9 × 5-inch loaves

Combine in a large bowl or a stand mixer fitted with the paddle attachment:

2 cups (470g) warm (105° to 115°F) milk
1 cup (100g) old-fashioned rolled oats
2 large eggs, lightly beaten
½ cup packed (115g) brown sugar
¼ cup (50g) vegetable oil
2 teaspoons salt

Stir in until just combined:

3 cups (375g) all-purpose flour
2 cups whole wheat (260g) or dark rye flour (240g)
1 cup (110g) soy flour
¼ to ½ cup (20 to 40g) wheat germ
2 envelopes (1½ tablespoons) active dry yeast

Cover and let the dough rest for 15 to 30 minutes.

Replace the paddle attachment with the dough hook. Knead the dough on a lightly floured work surface or with the mixer on medium-low speed until smooth and elastic, about 10 minutes. Transfer the dough to an oiled bowl and turn once to coat with oil. Cover and let rise in a warm place (75° to 85°F) until doubled in bulk, about 1 hour.

Grease two 9 × 5-inch loaf pans. Divide the dough in half and shape into loaves for pan-baking, 597. Place in the pans, loosely cover with oiled plastic wrap, and let rise again until doubled in bulk, about 45 minutes.

While the dough rises, preheat the oven to 350°F.

Brush the top of the loaves with:

1 egg, lightly beaten with a pinch of salt

If desired, sprinkle with:

(2 tablespoons old-fashioned rolled oats)

Bake until the crust is golden brown, the bottom sounds hollow when tapped, and the internal temperature reaches 205°F, about 1 hour. Immediately turn the loaves out of the pans onto a wire rack to cool completely.

ENGLISH MUFFIN BREAD

One 9 × 5-inch loaf

Prepare the dough for:

English Muffins, 621, through the first rise

Grease a 9 × 5-inch loaf pan and dust with:

Cornmeal

Transfer the dough to the pan (no need to shape the dough into a loaf) and cover with oiled plastic wrap. For more flavor, refrigerate for 8 to 12 hours, or let rise in a warm place (75° to 85°F) until the dough fills the pan and is light and puffy, 30 to 45 minutes.

While the dough rises, preheat the oven to 400°F.

Bake the bread until golden brown and the internal temperature reaches 195°F, about 25 minutes. Immediately turn the loaf out of the pan onto a wire rack to cool completely.

BUTTERMILK POTATO BREAD

Two 9 × 5-inch loaves

This dough can also be used to make rolls (to shape, see About Yeast Rolls, 617).

Prepare:

¾ cup riced or mashed freshly boiled russet potatoes, 265

Place the still-warm potatoes in a large bowl or in a stand mixer fitted with the paddle attachment and mix in:

1 stick (4 oz or 115g) unsalted butter, very soft

Add and mix well:

2 cups (485g) room-temperature (70° to 75°F) buttermilk
2 envelopes (1½ tablespoons) active dry yeast
2 large eggs, lightly beaten
2 tablespoons (25g) sugar
2½ teaspoons salt

Replace the paddle attachment with the dough hook and gradually stir in until the dough is moist but not sticky:

6¼ to 6½ cups (820 to 855g) bread flour

Cover and let the dough rest for 15 to 30 minutes.

Knead the dough on a lightly floured work surface or with the mixer on medium-low speed until smooth and elastic, about 10 minutes. Transfer the dough to an oiled bowl and turn once to coat with oil. Cover and let rise in a warm place (75° to 85°F) until doubled in bulk, 1 to 1½ hours.

Grease two 9 × 5-inch loaf pans. Divide the dough in half and shape into loaves for pan-baking, 597. Place in the loaf pans, loosely cover with oiled plastic wrap, and let rise until doubled in bulk, about 1 hour.

While the dough rises, preheat the oven to 375°F.

Brush the top of the loaves with:

1 egg, lightly beaten with a pinch of salt

If desired, sprinkle with:

(1 tablespoon poppy seeds)

Bake until the crust is golden brown, the bottom sounds hollow when tapped, and the internal temperature reaches 205°F, 40 to 45 minutes. Immediately turn the loaves out of the pans onto a wire rack to cool completely.

CHALLAH

1 braided loaf

This traditional Jewish Sabbath egg bread is similar to Brioche, 603.

Combine in a large bowl or a stand mixer fitted with the dough paddle attachment:

½ cup (120g) warm (105° to 115°F) water
½ cup (65g) bread flour
2 large eggs, lightly beaten
2 large egg yolks, lightly beaten
3 tablespoons (40g) vegetable oil
3 tablespoons (35g) sugar
1 envelope (2¼ teaspoons) active dry yeast
1¼ teaspoons salt

Mix by hand or on low speed until thoroughly blended. Gradually stir in:

2½ cups (330g) bread flour

Mix until the dough just comes together. Cover and let the dough rest for at least 15 and up to 30 minutes.

Replace the paddle attachment with the dough hook. Knead the dough on a lightly floured work surface or with the mixer on medium-low speed until smooth and elastic, 8 to 10 minutes. Transfer the dough to an oiled bowl and turn to coat with oil. Cover and let rise in a warm place (75° to 85°F) until doubled in bulk, 1 to 1½ hours.

Knead the dough briefly and return to the bowl. Refrigerate, covered, until it has nearly doubled in bulk (a three-quarter rise is sufficient), 2 to 12 hours. The dough is now ready to be shaped.

Divide the dough into 3 pieces. On an unfloured work surface, roll into balls. Let rest, loosely covered with plastic wrap, for 10 minutes.

Grease a baking sheet and sprinkle it with:

Cornmeal

Roll each ball into a 14-inch-long rope, about 1½ inches thick and slightly tapered at the ends. Dust the 3 ropes lightly with flour, so they will be distinctly separated when baked. Place the ropes side by side and pinch the top ends together. Braid the dough strands until you reach the other ends. Tuck the ends of the braid underneath the loaf and set it on the baking sheet.

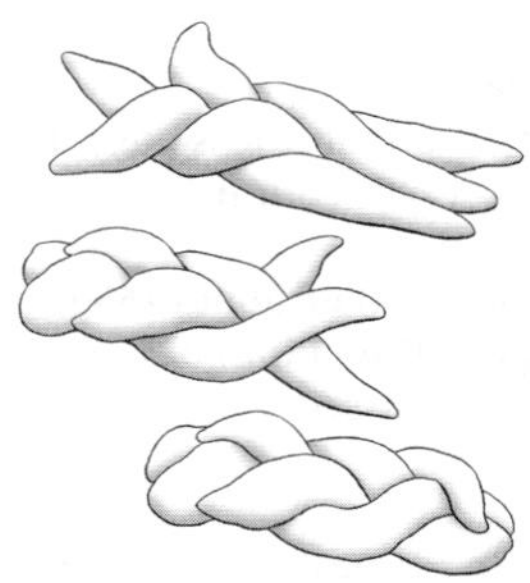

Braiding three-strand challah

Brush over the top of the loaf:

1 egg, beaten with a pinch of salt

Reserve the egg wash. Loosely cover the braid with lightly oiled plastic wrap and let rise in a warm place (75° to 85°F) until not quite doubled in bulk, about 45 minutes.

While the dough rises, preheat the oven to 375°F.

Brush the loaf again with egg wash. If desired, sprinkle with:

(1 tablespoon poppy or sesame seeds)
Bake until the crust is golden brown and the bottom of the loaf sounds hollow when tapped, 30 to 35 minutes. Let cool completely on a rack.

BRIOCHE
1 loaf or 10 small rolls
This classic is a simple yeast dough enriched with eggs and lots of butter; use it for loaves, plain rolls, and rolls stuffed with fruit, meat, or cheese, or bake in special fluted brioche tins (see Brioche à Tête, 621). The high butter content gives the impression that the dough is wetter than it actually is, leading to the temptation—which you must resist—to add more flour. This dough is easily braided: follow the directions for **Challah, 602.**
Combine in a large bowl or a stand mixer fitted with the paddle attachment and let stand until the yeast is dissolved, about 5 minutes:
⅓ cup (80g) warm (105° to 115°F) whole milk
1 envelope (2¼ teaspoons) active dry yeast
Mix in by hand or on low speed:
1 cup (125g) all-purpose flour
3 large eggs, lightly beaten
1 tablespoon (10g) sugar
1 teaspoon salt
Gradually stir in:
1 to 1¼ cups (125 to 155g) all-purpose flour
Mix for about 5 minutes, until all the ingredients are blended. Cover and let the dough rest for 20 minutes.

Replace the paddle attachment with the dough hook. Knead by hand for about 15 minutes or with the mixer on medium-low speed for 7 to 10 minutes, until the dough cleans the sides of the bowl. Because this is a sticky dough, kneading by hand requires a particular technique: Slap the dough down on the work surface, lift half of it up with both hands (part of it will remain stuck to the table, which is fine), and slap it down over onto itself (keep a bench scraper handy to help). Repeat this until the dough is smooth and elastic. Have ready:
1½ sticks (6 oz or 170g) unsalted butter, softened

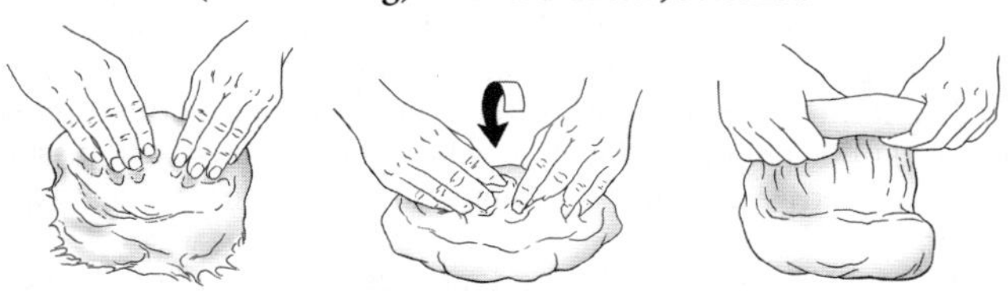
Kneading brioche

Vigorously knead or mix in the butter 1 tablespoon at a time, waiting until each piece of butter is nearly incorporated before adding the next. Continue to mix until the butter is completely incorporated and the dough is once again smooth. Butter a large bowl. Place the dough in the bowl, cover with plastic wrap, and let rise in a warm place (75° to 85°F) until doubled in bulk, about 1½ hours.

Knead the dough briefly a second time, just enough to deflate it, then refrigerate, covered, for 8 to 12 hours or until doubled.

For a loaf, butter a 9 × 5-inch loaf pan and shape the dough into a loaf for pan-baking, 597. Alternatively, for a sectioned loaf (see illustration below for one example of this), divide the dough into 4 or 8 equal pieces, round the dough into balls (follow the instructions in About Yeast Rolls, 617), and place them in 1 or 2 rows in the loaf pan. For brioche rolls, divide the dough into 10 equal pieces and shape into rolls, 617. Loosely cover the loaf or rolls with lightly oiled plastic wrap and let rise in a warm place (75° to 85°F) until not quite doubled in bulk, about 1 hour.

Preheat the oven to 375°F.
Brush the dough with:
1 egg yolk, beaten with 1 tablespoon water or milk
Bake until the crust is a deep golden brown and a knife inserted in the center of one brioche comes out clean, about 20 minutes for rolls and 35 to 40 minutes for a loaf. Unmold or transfer the brioche(s) onto a wire rack to cool. Serve slightly warm or cool.

Making a sectioned brioche loaf

CHOCOLATE-WALNUT BABKA
1 loaf
Babka can be made with a variety of fillings, from a simple cinnamon-sugar mixture to the nut-chocolate mixture here. If the brioche dough is too sticky to work with at any point during the shaping process, cover and refrigerate for 20 to 30 minutes to help it firm up.
Prepare the dough for:
Brioche, above, through the first rise
Refrigerate the dough for 1 hour. Stir together in a small bowl:
6 tablespoons (85g) unsalted butter, melted
¼ cup (50g) sugar
3 tablespoons (20g) unsweetened cocoa powder, Dutch process or natural
½ teaspoon ground cinnamon
¼ teaspoon salt
Set aside. Prepare and set aside:
Streusel II, 800
Have ready:
3 ounces semisweet or bittersweet chocolate, finely chopped
½ cup chopped walnuts, toasted, 1005
Transfer the dough to a lightly floured work surface. Roll it out into a roughly 20 × 10-inch rectangle and spread evenly with the cocoa-butter mixture. Sprinkle evenly with the chopped chocolate

and walnuts. With a long edge closest to you, roll up the dough into a cylinder. Slice the cylinder in half lengthwise to expose the layers of filling. Twist the two lengths of dough around each other to form a simple braid shape, then fold the braid in half and place in a generously buttered 9 × 5-inch loaf pan. Brush the loaf with:

1 large egg, well beaten with a pinch of salt

Sprinkle with the streusel, cover, and let rise until puffy and increased in volume, 1 to 1½ hours.

While the loaf is rising, preheat the oven to 350°F.

Bake the babka until golden brown, 50 to 55 minutes. Let cool in the pan on a rack for 15 minutes, then use a thin offset spatula to help release it from the pan. Let cool completely on a rack.

QUICK FRENCH BREAD

3 baguettes

Quicker than Rustic French Bread, 606, this bread has a good flavor and an even crumb.

Combine in a large bowl or a stand mixer fitted with the paddle attachment:

1½ cups (355g) lukewarm (80° to 90°F) water
1 teaspoon active dry yeast

Let stand for 5 minutes, then add:

3¼ cups (405g) all-purpose flour
¼ cup (35g) whole wheat flour
1½ teaspoons salt

Mix with a wooden spoon or on low speed until the dough just comes together. Cover and let rest for 20 minutes.

Replace the paddle attachment with the dough hook. Knead on a lightly floured work surface or with the mixer on medium-low speed until smooth and elastic, about 10 minutes. Transfer the dough to an oiled bowl and turn to coat with oil. Cover and let rise in a warm place (75° to 85°F) until doubled in bulk, about 45 minutes.

Knead the dough briefly a second time, about 3 minutes, then preshape the dough into a ball, return to the oiled bowl, cover, and let rise again until doubled in bulk, about 1 hour.

Turn the dough out onto a lightly floured work surface and divide it into 3 equal pieces. Gently shape each piece into a roughly 10 × 8-inch rectangle. Working with one rectangle at a time, with a long edge facing you, fold the top third of the dough toward you, then fold the bottom third (the edge closer to you), over the first fold and seal the edge (like a business letter). Fold the dough in half lengthwise while simultaneously rolling it away from you so the seam ends up on the bottom. Use your palms to roll the dough into a roughly 14-inch rope that tapers slightly at the ends. Repeat with the remaining pieces of dough.

Transfer the dough to a metal baguette pan or dust a thin kitchen towel with flour. Place one baguette on the floured towel and bunch up the towel down the length of one side of the loaf. Place the second baguette next to the first on the towel, with the bunched-up bit of towel separating them. Bunch up the towel next to the second baguette, and place the third baguette next to it. Roll up 2 more towels and place one on either side of the outer baguettes to help them keep their shape. Let rise until doubled in bulk, about 1 hour.

Preheat the oven to 450°F. If using a baking stone or steel, preheat them with the oven. Place a metal baking pan or cast-iron skillet on the bottom rack and preheat it as well.

Transfer the baguettes to a floured peel if using a baking stone or steel. If not, transfer the baguettes to a cookie sheet. If using a baguette pan, there is no need to transfer the baguettes. Score the baguettes with 3 long, diagonal cuts each, 597. Slide the baguettes onto the baking stone or steel, or place the cookie sheet or baguette pan in the oven. Immediately pour 1 cup hot water into the preheated baking pan or skillet and close the oven door. Bake the baguettes until deeply golden brown, 25 to 30 minutes. Let cool completely on a rack before cutting.

CIABATTA

1 roughly 12 x 8-inch loaf

This Italian bread is made with a fairly wet dough. It must be kneaded extensively to develop the gluten necessary to provide structure to its many irregular air bubbles, which create ciabatta's distinctive open crumb and contribute to its pleasing, chewy texture.

Combine in a stand mixer fitted with the paddle attachment:

2 cups (265g) bread flour
1 cup (235g) lukewarm (80° to 90°F) water
1 teaspoon active dry yeast

Mix until the ingredients are just combined. Let the dough rest for 20 minutes. Turn the mixer back on medium speed and mix about 2 minutes until the dough has gathered around the paddle. With the mixer running, gradually add:

2 tablespoons (30g) lukewarm (80° to 90°F) water

Mix until the dough is gathered around the paddle again. Switch to the dough hook and add:

1 teaspoon salt
1 teaspoon olive oil

Mix on medium-high speed until the dough cleans the sides of the bowl and makes a slapping sound against the side of the bowl, 8 to 10 minutes. The dough will be wet and sticky but should look smooth and shiny. Transfer it to a lightly oiled bowl and cover with plastic wrap. Let it rise in a warm place for 45 minutes.

With the dough still in the bowl, lift up one side of the dough, stretch it gently, then fold it over on itself. Repeat this stretching and folding technique 3 more times, then flip the dough so the seam is down. At this point, the dough may be tightly covered with plastic wrap and refrigerated up to 24 hours to allow it to develop more flavor.

Alternatively, cover and let the dough rest, 45 more minutes, then fold it again, 4 more times, in the same way as before. Cover and let it rise 45 minutes more. Gently turn the bubbly dough out onto a well-floured countertop and gently shape into a rectangle using a bench scraper. Lightly cover with oiled plastic wrap and let rest for 30 minutes.

Meanwhile, preheat the oven to 450°F, with a baking stone or steel or a baking sheet on the center rack and a metal baking pan or cast-iron skillet on the bottom rack. Place a piece of parchment paper on a baking peel, cookie sheet, or an inverted baking sheet and lightly flour the parchment. With a bench scraper and a floured hand, gingerly transfer the dough to the parchment paper by gathering it up from each side and, in one quick motion, flipping it onto the parchment. Gently reshape the dough into a roughly 12 x 8-inch rectangle.

Slide the parchment onto the stone, steel, or baking sheet and immediately add 1 cup hot water to the baking pan or skillet. Bake for 10 minutes. Take out the pan or skillet, turn the bread by rotating the parchment paper 180 degrees, and bake, about 10 more minutes, or until the bread is crusty and brown. Let cool completely, then tap off the excess flour.

ABOUT GLUTEN-FREE YEAST BREADS

Making gluten-free yeast breads is a very different process from that of the standard loaf. Gluten-free baking presents a notable challenge, as the thing that literally binds almost all baked goods—gluten—is completely absent. Making gluten-free bread is entirely possible, but there is a different set of rules. For starters, the lack of gluten must be mitigated by something. Usually, this is a blend of very starchy flours (rice flour, potato starch, cornstarch, and tapioca starch) and less starchy ones (quinoa, millet, brown rice, sorghum, and buckwheat flours). Often, other ingredients are added to help bind the dough. These include xanthan gum, 544, and eggs. Powdered milk is often added to enrich gluten-free breads and provide protein without adding extra liquid, helping with the structure of the bread.

Gluten-free bread is usually not kneaded, since the primary goal of kneading is to develop gluten structure. The "doughs" for gluten-free breads are often more like batters, making them either difficult or impossible to knead in the traditional sense. However, these breads should be well mixed and allowed to hydrate. Mix the ingredients just until they come together, then cover and let rest for 10 minutes. After the rest, continue mixing for another 3 minutes or so. Since they lack gluten and are very wet, these breads do not hold their shape well and are most successful when baked in a pan. It is possible to make free-form gluten-free breads, but they will not be as shapely. ➤ Because gluten-free bread doughs are very wet and dense, bake them until the internal temperature reaches 210°F, and always let the bread cool completely on a rack before cutting into it. Gluten-free breads tend to dry out faster than wheat breads, so store them tightly wrapped. Gluten-free breads freeze well. For more information on specific flours, see 985. See also Gluten-Free Pizza, 615.

GLUTEN-FREE SANDWICH BREAD

One 9 × 5-inch loaf

Slices of this light, tender bread are even better toasted. The "dough" is very wet—more like a thick batter. This recipe is written to use fine white rice flour, available at Asian markets. Stone-ground rice flour is coarser and will not work in this recipe.

Whisk to combine in a medium bowl:

1 cup (235g) lukewarm (80° to 90°F) milk
½ cup (120g) lukewarm (80° to 90°F) water
2 large eggs, well beaten
1 tablespoon sugar (10g) or honey (20g)
1 tablespoon (15g) butter, melted
1 envelope (2¼ teaspoons) active dry yeast

Whisk together in a large bowl or a stand mixer fitted with the paddle attachment:

1 cup (110g) white rice flour
1 cup (125g) tapioca starch
½ cup (70g) brown rice flour
½ cup potato starch (85g) or cornstarch (65g)
2 teaspoons xanthan gum
1½ teaspoons salt

Add the milk mixture and beat until combined. Cover the bowl and let the dough rise for 1 hour.

Grease a 9 × 5-inch loaf pan. Scrape the dough into the pan, cover with oiled plastic wrap, and let rise again until the batter rises just above the rim of the pan, about 45 minutes.

While the dough rises, preheat the oven to 350°F.

Bake the bread until the internal temperature reaches 210°F, about 40 minutes. Immediately turn the loaf out of the pan onto a wire rack to cool completely.

GLUTEN-FREE WHOLE-GRAIN BREAD

One 9 × 5-inch loaf

A slightly heartier loaf than Gluten-Free Sandwich Bread, above, but still light and moist. Brown rice and sorghum flours give the bread a more complex flavor.

Whisk to combine in a large bowl or a stand mixer fitted with the paddle attachment:

2 cups (285g) brown rice flour
½ cup (60g) sorghum flour
⅓ cup potato starch (55g) or tapioca starch (40g)
⅓ cup (45g) cornstarch
2 tablespoons (15g) ground flaxseeds
2 teaspoons xanthan gum
2 tablespoons sugar (25g) or brown sugar (30g)
1½ teaspoons salt

Whisk together in a medium bowl:

1 cup (235g) lukewarm (80° to 90°F) milk
3 large eggs, at room temperature
¼ cup (50g) vegetable oil, or 4 tablespoons (55g) unsalted butter, melted
1 envelope (2¼ teaspoons) active dry yeast

Add the milk mixture to the dry ingredients and mix well or beat on medium-low in the mixer for about 3 minutes. The dough will be very wet and sticky. If desired, mix in the following (choose one, a combination, or all):

(¼ cup sunflower seeds, toasted, 1027)
(¼ cup pumpkin seeds, toasted, 1005)
(3 tablespoons toasted sesame seeds)
(2 tablespoons poppy seeds)

Cover the bowl and let the dough rise for 1 hour.

Grease a 9 × 5-inch loaf pan. Scrape the dough into the pan and smooth the top. Cover the pan with oiled plastic wrap and let rise again until the dough rises just above the edge of the pan, about 1 hour.

While the dough rises, preheat the oven to 350°F.

Bake until golden brown and the internal temperature of the loaf reaches 210°F, about 45 minutes. If the bread browns too quickly, tent it with foil. Immediately turn the loaf out of the pan onto a wire rack to cool completely.

ABOUT STARTERS OR PRE-FERMENTS

A **starter** is a fermented batter or dough that is used in place of yeast to make bread rise. **Pre-ferment** is just another name for starter, but one that gets at the heart of what a starter is. The purpose of all pre-ferments is to allow for more flavor development through the cultivation of yeasts and bacteria, the hydration of the flour, and the breakdown of complex starches into simpler ones by enzymes. Pre-ferments also enhance the final texture of the bread by extending the amount of time the dough spends in active fermentation. There are many different terms for starters, and they can be quite confusing, but they all do the same thing.

Sourdough starters, 608, are a type of pre-ferment, but one that is maintained over a long period of time. Pre-ferments have a range of hydration levels, from the very dry, dough-like **pâte fermentée,** which is simply a piece of dough reserved from a previous batch of bread, to the very wet **poolish,** which has a batter-like consistency. A **biga** is a dry pre-ferment like *pâte fermentée*, but it usually contains no salt.

Sponge starters are the quickest to make and tend to be wet or batter-like. Depending on the sponge, it may be ready for use in as little as an hour. Any bread using the straight dough method can be converted to use a sponge. Simply combine all the liquid and yeast called for in a bread recipe with one-quarter of the flour. Let the sponge sit at room temperature until bubbling and tripled in volume. Then combine the other ingredients with the sponge and proceed with the recipe. For other bread recipes using a sponge, see Stollen, 624, and Panettone, 624.

RUSTIC FRENCH BREAD

2 round loaves or 3 baguettes

Leavened with a sponge starter, above, these free-form loaves are crusty and have a moist, chewy crumb.

Stir together well in a medium bowl:

¾ cup (100g) bread flour
½ cup (120g) lukewarm (80° to 90°F) water
½ teaspoon active dry yeast

Cover the bowl tightly with plastic wrap and let rise at room temperature (about 70°F) until bubbling and tripled in volume, 5 to 6 hours; or let rise for about 14 hours in the refrigerator.

Pour the sponge into a large bowl or a stand mixer fitted with the dough hook. Stir in:

5 to 5½ cups (655 to 725g) bread flour, or as needed
1¾ cups (415g) room-temperature (70° to 75°F) water (or warm water [105° to 115°F] if the dough has been refrigerated)
2 teaspoons salt

Mix until the dough cleans the sides of the bowl. If necessary, adjust the consistency by adding flour or water. The dough should feel sticky to the touch but should not actually stick to your hands. Cover and let the dough rest for 20 minutes. Knead the dough on a lightly floured surface or with the mixer on medium-low speed until smooth and elastic, about 10 minutes.

Transfer the dough to an oiled bowl and turn once to coat with oil. Cover and let rise until doubled in bulk, about 3 hours in a warm place (75° to 80°F) or about 6 hours at cooler room temperature.

Divide the dough in half for round loaves or into 3 pieces for baguettes. Preshape each piece into a ball, 596, cover, and let rest for 15 minutes. Shape the dough into round loaves, 597, or baguettes (for baguettes, follow the shaping instructions in Quick French Bread, 604). For round loaves, transfer them bottom side up to floured bannetons if you have them. Otherwise place the shaped loaves on a parchment-lined baking sheet. Cover with plastic wrap and let rise at room temperature until doubled in bulk, 1½ to 3 hours.

Position racks in the center and lower third of the oven. Place a metal baking pan or cast-iron skillet on the lower rack. Preheat the oven to 450°F. If using a baking stone or steel, preheat it on the center rack for 45 minutes.

For round loaves, turn them out of the bannetons, if using, onto the preheated baking stone or steel or a parchment-lined baking sheet. For baguettes, if using a baking stone or steel, slide them with their parchment onto the stone or steel; or, simply bake them on the baking sheet they rose on. Score, 597, the tops of the risen loaves. Place the loaves on the center rack. Pour 2 cups boiling water into the preheated pan on the lower rack. Bake until the loaves are browned, the bottoms sound hollow when tapped, and the internal temperature reaches 210°F, about 35 minutes for baguettes, or about 40 minutes for round loaves. To further set the crust, turn off the oven and leave the baked loaves in the oven for 5 minutes.

Let cool completely on a wire rack.

FOUGASSE

4 loaves

Prepare the sponge for **Rustic French Bread, above,** and when making the dough (when the sponge is mixed with more flour, water, and salt), add **½ cup coarsely chopped pitted black olives such as Kalamata** and **2 tablespoons minced rosemary.** When it is time to divide the dough, divide it into 4 equal pieces. Roll each piece of dough into a rough triangular shape about ½ inch thick. Use a knife, pizza cutter, or bench scraper to cut one lengthwise slash in the dough starting 1 inch below the tip of the triangle and ending 1 inch above the base of the triangle. Cut 3 diagonal slashes on either side of the longer central slash (like drawing the veins on a leaf). Gently stretch the dough on all sides to open up the slashes and prevent them from sealing themselves during rising and baking. Cover the loaves and let rise until puffy, 1½ to 2 hours. Before baking, spritz the loaves lightly with water. Set up the oven racks and water pan as directed above and bake 2 loaves at a time, until golden brown, about 30 minutes per batch. Skip the crust-setting step.

WHITE BREAD MADE WITH A SPONGE STARTER

2 round loaves or sandwich loaves

This sponge-based version of basic white bread is more flavorful than that made by the straight dough method, 594. Please read About Starters or Pre-Ferments, 606.

Combine in a medium bowl and stir well:

¾ cup (100g) bread flour
½ cup (120g) lukewarm (80° to 90°F) water
½ teaspoon active dry yeast

Cover the bowl tightly with plastic wrap and let rise at room temperature (about 70°F), until bubbling and tripled in volume, about 6 hours; or let the starter rise for about 14 hours in the refrigerator.

Transfer the sponge to a large bowl or a stand mixer fitted with the dough hook and add:

4½ cups (590g) bread flour
2 cups (475g) room-temperature (70° to 75°F) water (or warm water [105° to 115°F] if the dough was refrigerated)
1 tablespoon salt

Mix until the dough just comes together, then cover and let rest for 20 minutes. Knead by hand or with the mixer on medium-low speed until the dough is smooth and elastic, about 10 minutes. If necessary, adjust the consistency of the dough by adding flour or water. The dough should feel tacky but not actually stick to your hands. Transfer the dough to an oiled bowl and turn to coat with oil. Cover the bowl with plastic wrap and set aside to let rise until doubled in bulk, about 3 hours in a warm place (75° to 80°F) or about 6 hours at a cooler room temperature.

Divide the dough in half and shape each half into a round loaf or loaves for pan-baking, 597. Place the shaped loaves in bannetons or bowls lined with floured thin kitchen towels or in 2 oiled 9 × 5-inch loaf pans. Cover with oiled plastic wrap and let rise at room temperature until doubled in bulk, 2 to 4 hours.

Preheat the oven to 450°F. Place a rack in the bottom third of the oven and a rack in the center of the oven. Place a metal baking pan or cast-iron skillet on the bottom rack. For round loaves, you may use a baking stone or steel. Preheat it on the center oven rack for 45 minutes. If you do not have a baking stone or steel, have ready a large baking sheet lined with parchment paper.

For round loaves, flip the risen loaves onto the hot baking stone or steel or parchment-lined baking sheet, spacing them several inches apart.

Score, 597, the round loaves. Slide the loaves into the oven (if baking sandwich loaves, set the loaf pans directly on the center rack). Pour 1 cup hot water into the pan or skillet. Bake until the loaves are browned and the bottoms of the loaves sound hollow when tapped, about 40 minutes. To further set the crust, turn off the oven and leave the baked loaves in the oven for 5 minutes. Let cool completely on a rack.

RYE BREAD WITH A SPONGE STARTER

2 round loaves

Use dark rye flour, which has more rye flavor than white rye flour. Also, please read About Starters or Pre-Ferments, 606.

Combine in a medium bowl and let stand until the yeast is dissolved, about 5 minutes:

½ cup (120g) warm (105° to 115°F) water
½ teaspoon active dry yeast

Add:

¾ cup (100g) bread flour

Stir rapidly with a wooden spoon until you notice elastic strands pulling away from the sides of the bowl, about 2 minutes. Cover the bowl tightly with plastic wrap and let rise at room temperature until bubbling and tripled in volume, about 6 hours; or let the starter rise for about 14 hours in the refrigerator.

Scrape the sponge into a large bowl or a stand mixer fitted with the paddle attachment and add:

2½ cups (590g) room-temperature (72° to 75°F) water (or warm water [105° to 115°F] if the dough has been refrigerated)
3½ cups (420g) dark rye flour
3½ cups (460g) bread flour
(2 tablespoons caraway seeds)
(2 tablespoons sesame seeds)
½ teaspoon active dry yeast

Stir rapidly with a wooden spoon or mix on medium-low speed until the dough just comes together. Adjust the consistency of the dough by adding more bread flour or water. Switch to the dough hook. Work in by hand or with the mixer for 2 minutes:

1 tablespoon salt

Knead by hand or with the mixer on medium-low speed until the dough is smooth, elastic, and firm, 7 to 10 minutes. Transfer the dough to an oiled bowl and turn to coat with oil. Cover the bowl tightly with plastic wrap and let rise in a warm place (75° to 85°F) for 1½ hours. The dough will rise only very slightly; do not leave it longer, or it will overferment the starter, which will make the bread heavy (yeast cells eat rye flour very quickly).

Grease a large baking sheet and sprinkle with:

Cornmeal

Divide the dough in half and shape each half into a round loaf, 597. Place the loaves on the baking sheets, leaving space between them. Cover with oiled plastic wrap and let rise in a warm place (75° to 85°F) for 1½ hours.

Position racks in the center and lower third of the oven. Place a metal baking pan or cast-iron skillet on the lower rack. Preheat the oven to 450°F.

Place the loaves on the center rack. Immediately pour 2 cups boiling water into the pan or skillet on the lower rack. Bake until well browned, the loaves sound hollow when tapped on the bottom, and the internal temperature reaches 105° to 110°F, about 45 minutes. To further set the crust, turn the oven off and let the loaves remain in the oven for 10 minutes. Let cool completely on a rack.

MOLASSES BREAD

One 9 × 5-inch loaf

This bread, a hybrid of a yeast bread and a quick bread, is inspired by one from the Otis Café in the tiny town of Otis, Oregon. Serve with plenty of salted butter.

Stir together in a small bowl:

½ cup (65g) all-purpose flour
⅓ cup (80g) lukewarm (80° to 90°F) water
½ teaspoon active dry yeast

Cover tightly and let rise at room temperature until bubbling and nearly tripled in volume, about 6 hours; or let rise for 14 hours in the refrigerator.

Preheat the oven to 350°F. Transfer the sponge to a large bowl. Add and mix until smooth:

1 cup (245g) room-temperature (72° to 75°F) buttermilk
¾ cup (255g) molasses
1 large egg

Stir in:

2½ cups (330g) whole wheat flour
1 cup (125g) all-purpose flour
1 teaspoon baking soda

Butter a 9 × 5-inch loaf pan and scrape the batter into the pan. Bake until the bread is firm to the touch and a skewer inserted in the center comes out clean, 60 to 70 minutes. Let cool in the pan on a rack for 10 minutes, then turn out onto the rack to cool completely. If desired, while the bread is still warm, brush the top with:

(1 tablespoon butter, softened)

ABOUT SOURDOUGH STARTERS

There is perhaps no other cooking-related subject so fraught with mysticism as the sourdough starter. Perhaps this is because the way we cook most often feels very controlled: One step follows another, and there is little guesswork involved. Sourdough starters, however, harness wild yeasts, incorporating them into a microbe-rich stew that is used to seed dough that eventually, hopefully, becomes bread. As discussed with regard to yeast, 592, these microbes are affected by their environment, and this is nowhere so evident as with a sourdough starter. For all the uncertainties of baking with a sourdough starter, once you get a feel for working with it you will find that there really is no mystery, and the rewards of baking with a starter are readily apparent in the flavor and texture of the finished loaf.

WHAT IS A SOURDOUGH STARTER?

A sourdough starter, called a *levain* in French, begins with flour and water. Any type of flour may be used, even gluten-free flours, but we normally use a combination of all-purpose and whole wheat flours. Sourdough starters can have varying hydration levels, some being wet and batter-like, others being thick and dough-like. When we keep an active starter, we prefer a wet one, as it is easier to mix fresh flour and water into a wet starter, and it is easier to mix the starter into the other ingredients for bread dough. Dry starters are excellent for longer storage, such as when you are keeping your starter dormant in the refrigerator, as the higher proportion of flour slows fermentation.

MAKING A SOURDOUGH STARTER

While sourdough starters can be jump-started with store-bought yeast, it is unnecessary. The bacteria and yeast needed for a starter live in the air and will readily colonize a starter because it contains all the things they need to thrive: carbohydrates and water. The process of getting a sourdough starter going may take anywhere from a few days to a week or more, but it will happen. Bubbling is a good indication that the starter is becoming active. During this period, the starter should be "refreshed" or fed daily. In this early phase, it is important to be consistent about feeding. Over time, the starter's activity will increase, and eventually it will rise and fall predictably. At this point, the starter is ready for baking. For instructions on feeding a starter, see Sourdough Starter, 609.

USING DISCARDED STARTER

Each time the starter is fed, most of it is discarded. This discarded portion can be used in other baked goods (keep in mind how much water and flour is in the starter and subtract that from the recipe it is added to). One of our favorite things to do with discarded starter is to make a simple pancake batter: Add an egg or two to the starter, a pinch each of salt and sugar, and enough flour to get the mixture to a pancake batter consistency (cook a small test pancake if you are unsure about the consistency of the batter). Or add enough flour to the starter to make a stiff dough that can be rolled, then roll it out very thin, top with seeds and sea salt, and bake into rustic crackers. Also see Sourdough Chocolate Cake, 729.

KEEPING A STARTER

A well-established starter may be refrigerated between bread-baking days. In the refrigerator, a starter's rate of fermentation slows drastically, and the starter requires only occasional feeding.

To store a sourdough starter, simply place it in a container, cover it tightly, and place it in the coldest part of the refrigerator. Here it can stay a month or more without being fed at all. Refrigerated starters may develop a thin layer of ugly, brownish liquid on top called hooch. It is harmless and should be discarded before using the starter. A starter may also be frozen indefinitely.

To revive a dormant starter, take it out of the refrigerator and feed it as directed in Sourdough Starter, 609, but twice daily for 3 days. On the third day, the second feeding should be based on the recipe you plan to use to bake bread (in other words, follow the instructions in the recipe for feeding the starter the last time). This 3-day period is not set in stone, however. Look for a return to the starter's normal behavior of rising and falling predictably. If the starter is still erratic after 3 days of being fed regularly, give it more time. Let frozen starters sit at least 24 hours first in the refrigerator, then leave at room temperature for at least 2 hours before feeding to revive it. Proceed as for a refrigerated starter.

Regardless of whether the starter has been kept at room temperature, in the refrigerator, or in the freezer, the easiest way to tell if it is ready for mixing with the other ingredients to make dough is the **float test:** Drop a small spoonful of the starter into a bowl of water. It should float. If it doesn't, give it more time.

CONVERTING A STARTER

You will inevitably run across recipes that call for a starter different from the one you have. Some recipes call for a stiff starter and others call for a liquid starter.

To convert a stiff starter to a liquid starter, combine 2 tablespoons active starter with equal parts flour and water by weight.

To convert a liquid starter to a stiff starter, combine 2 tablespoons active starter with 2 parts flour to 1 part water by weight. You may also wish to make sourdough breads that are made with flours other than the flour contained in your starter. Do you need to use a rye-based starter to make sourdough rye? The short answer is no. You can make a perfectly wonderful rye bread using a white flour starter. You may use rye flour to feed the starter before making a loaf of rye bread, but it is not necessary.

Converting a bread recipe that uses commercial yeast into a sourdough-raised bread requires a scale, a bit of math, and tweaking according to your judgment. In order to do the math and make the tweaks, consider these facts: 1 cup active starter has about the same rising potential as 1 envelope of yeast. A liquid starter contains roughly equal parts water and flour by weight. A stiff starter contains 2 parts flour to 1 part water by weight.

To replace one envelope of commercial yeast in a bread recipe, measure out 1 cup starter and weigh it on a scale. If you have a liquid starter, divide the weight by 2 and subtract an equal weight of flour and liquid from the bread recipe. If you have a stiff starter, subtract two-thirds its weight from the flour and one-third from the water. The ratios can be tweaked to your liking: Some prefer a wetter dough when baking *levain*-raised breads, so you might subtract more flour than water from the recipe to change the hydration.

Another thing to take into account is that *levain*-raised breads take a lot longer to rise. Your favorite sandwich bread may be ready to go into the oven after 3 hours of rising, but when converted to use a starter it will take much, much longer. Of course, the vast majority of this time is hands-off. Generally, plan on an 8- to 12-hour rise. Further, there's no need to go through the double rising that most bread recipes call for (the first rise in a bowl and the second in the loaf pan). Simply shape the kneaded dough, place it in the loaf pan, and allow it to rise once.

SOURDOUGH STARTER (LEVAIN)

A sourdough starter is like your own personal collection of microorganisms that you can use to jump-start doughs without commercial yeast. But even more important, a starter brings the tremendous flavor that can only come from time and patience. Please read About Sourdough Starters, 608, before beginning.

Whisk together well in a large bowl:

4 cups (525g) whole wheat flour
4 cups (500g) all-purpose flour

Transfer to a bag or an airtight container. This is the flour blend you will use to feed your starter. Measure 1¼ cups of this flour blend into a medium container such as a quart jar or a plastic container with about a 4-cup capacity. Add to the flour:

¾ cup (175g) lukewarm (80° to 90°F) water

Stir together until smooth. Cover with a piece of thin, clean kitchen towel or fabric, and secure the fabric with a rubber band. Let the starter sit at room temperature, out of direct sunlight, for several days. Check it daily. You should start to see bubbles after 3 to 5 days. If a crust forms on top, that's okay. If the starter smells cheesy, yeasty, or nose-tinglingly sharp, your starter is alive. The only thing to look out for is mold. If any mold grows on the starter, discard it and start again.

When you see signs of fermentation, the starter is ready to be fed. It will need several more days—maybe even a week or more—of consistent feedings before it is ready to make bread.

To feed the sourdough starter, every day at roughly the same time, discard all but about ¼ cup of the starter (or see Using Discarded Starter, 608). Add to the remaining ¼ cup starter in the container:

1¼ cups (160g) whole wheat/all-purpose flour blend, from above
¾ cup (175g) water

Adding a precise amount of flour and water is not as important as feeding the starter regularly: As long as most of the previous day's starter is discarded and enough flour and water are added to make a thick paste, you're doing it right. Once you get a feel for it, you may choose not to measure the flour and water at all.

As you feed the starter, try to get a sense of its behavior. It should increase in volume for several hours after being fed. At some point it will start to deflate. The smell of the starter will also change—right after feeding, it should smell mild. As the starter approaches the time for its next feeding, it will smell sharper and more acidic. Sometimes it may even smell like nail polish remover.

The starter is ready for baking when it rises and falls consistently for a few days. At least 12 hours before you plan to start making bread, discard all but about 1 tablespoon of the starter (the starter clinging to the sides and bottom of the container will be enough). *For a liquid starter,* stir in:

1¾ cups (225g) whole wheat/all-purpose flour blend, from above
1 cup (235g) lukewarm (80° to 90°F) water

For a stiff starter, use:

2½ cups (305g) whole wheat/all-purpose flour blend, from above
⅔ cup (155g) lukewarm (80° to 90°F) water

Cover and let sit until the starter has increased in volume, 8 to 12 hours. To test for readiness, drop a spoonful of starter in a cup of water. It should float. If the starter does not float, cover it and wait until it is ready. In very warm conditions, the starter may have already peaked and deflated at 8 hours. In cool conditions, it may take longer (in this case, try to place the starter in a warm location). Working with a starter is all about learning how to read its signs. This is a skill you will pick up over time.

When the starter is ready, proceed with one of the recipes below or any sourdough recipe calling for a liquid starter (for those calling for a stiff starter, see Converting a Starter, 608).

RUSTIC NO-KNEAD SOURDOUGH BREAD

2 round loaves

While this recipe is long, the process is really quite simple. There are different stages at which the dough can be retarded if you need to walk away from it for a while. If desired, any of the additions to yeast doughs, 593, may be added at the same time as the salt.

Mix together in a large bowl or a stand mixer fitted with the dough hook:

1½ cups active Sourdough Starter, above (it should pass the float test, 608)
1½ cups (355g) lukewarm (80° to 90°F) water

Add:

4 cups (525g) bread flour
½ cup (65g) whole wheat flour

Mix by hand or on low speed until a sticky dough forms. Cover the bowl and let the dough rest for 30 minutes.

Mix in by hand or with the dough hook until combined:

¼ cup (60g) lukewarm (80° to 90°F) water
1 teaspoon salt

Transfer to a bowl just large enough to hold the dough with a little room to spare. Let the dough rise in a draft-free place until increased in volume (it will not double in volume like doughs made with commercial yeast), 3 to 4 hours. If the dough is in a glass or clear plastic container, you will be able to see air bubbles. Alternatively, after mixing in the salt, cover the dough tightly and refrigerate for 12 to 14 hours.

Turn out the dough onto a very lightly floured work surface. Divide it into 2 equal pieces, and round the dough into balls, 596. Cover and let rest for 15 minutes. Give the dough a final shape into rounds, 597. Lightly flour 2 thin kitchen towels (flour sack towels work nicely) and use them to line 2 bannetons or bowls just large enough to hold the dough. Transfer the shaped rounds, seam side up, to the baskets or bowls, cover, and let rise until a finger gently pressed into the dough leaves an imprint that does not spring back, 3 to 4 hours. Or cover and refrigerate the loaves up to 12 hours.

To bake the loaves in a Dutch oven or combo cooker, 594, preheat the oven to 500°F for 45 minutes with the Dutch oven or combo cooker in the oven as it preheats. Uncover one of the loaves and gently remove it from the basket or bowl. Use lightly floured hands to transfer it carefully, seam side down, to the hot Dutch oven (be careful not to burn your hands or arms) or skillet part of the combo cooker. Score the dough with a lame, 594, or a very sharp knife, cover with the lid or the deeper part of the combo cooker, and return it to the oven. Bake for 15 minutes, then remove the lid, reduce the heat to 450°F, and bake until deeply browned, 15 to 20 minutes more. Transfer the bread to a rack to cool completely. Return the empty Dutch oven or combo cooker to the oven, increase the oven temperature to 500°F, and let the Dutch oven or combo cooker preheat for at least 10 minutes before baking the second loaf.

To bake the loaves on a baking stone, steel, or baking sheet, position racks in the center and lower third of the oven. Preheat the oven to 450°F. Place the stone, steel, or baking sheet on the center rack to preheat. Place a metal baking pan or cast-iron skillet on the lower rack. Once hot, take the stone, steel, or baking sheet out of the oven. Turn out the loaves, seam side down, onto the stone, steel, or pan, score them, and place in the oven. Immediately pour 1 cup hot water into the baking pan or skillet on the lower rack and close the oven door. Bake until deeply golden brown, 35 to 40 minutes. Transfer to a rack to cool completely.

SOURDOUGH RYE BREAD

2 loaves

Place in a medium bowl:

⅓ cup active Sourdough Starter, 609

Feed the starter with:

1½ cups (180g) dark rye flour
1¼ cups (295g) water

Stir until smooth. Combine and sprinkle over the top of the starter:

1¾ cups (210g) dark rye flour
1¾ cups (220g) all-purpose flour

Cover tightly with plastic wrap and let ferment until the starter has risen and created a network of cracks in the flour sprinkled over it, 4 to 5 hours.

Mix until smooth and then stir in:

1¼ to 1¾ cups (155 to 220g) all-purpose flour
1 cup (235g) water
1 tablespoon caraway seeds
1½ teaspoons salt

The dough should be neither very dry nor very wet. If necessary, add a little more flour or water to adjust the consistency. Let the dough rest for 20 minutes. Turn the dough out onto a lightly floured work surface and knead until smooth and pliable, working in more all-purpose flour if it is too sticky (the dough will be tacky, but it should not stick aggressively to your hands). Divide the dough into 2 equal pieces, and shape into rounds, 597. Place the loaves on a greased baking sheet, cover loosely with a cloth, and let rise until increased but not doubled in bulk. A fingertip pressed gently into the dough should leave an imprint that does not spring back right away. This should take 3 to 4 hours.

Position racks in the center and lower third of the oven. Preheat the oven to 425°F. Place a metal baking pan or cast-iron skillet on the lower rack.

Score, 597, the loaves if desired, place on the center rack in the oven, and immediately pour 1 cup hot water into the baking pan or skillet. Bake until the internal temperature of the loaves reaches at least 110°F, 50 to 60 minutes. To further set the crust, turn the oven off and let the loaves remain in the oven for 10 minutes. Transfer to a rack to cool completely.

ABOUT FLATBREADS

While flatbreads are perhaps not as visually impressive as their puffy, loaved counterparts, they are no less beloved. These breads are some of the oldest formulas, many of them (such as pita, lavash, and matzo) originating from the cradle of civilization. Others, like pizza, are so popular that they need no introduction. For the home baker, flatbreads are doubly enticing. Preparing them has all the tactile appeal of bread making, but they are generally easier and quicker to make and don't require the shaping skills of other doughs. Additionally, any lack of skill on the part of the cook is handily concealed by the rustic charm of the end result. These breads proof very quickly, if at all, and bake in a flash. The results are by turns crusty, crispy, irregular, and completely irresistible.

PITA BREAD

8 pitas

Excellent for sandwiches and scooping up dips and sauces—especially Hummus, 52, or Baba Ghanoush, 53. You can substitute whole wheat flour for any portion of the white flour, according to your preference, although the dough may require additional water to be soft and pliable.

Combine in a large bowl or a stand mixer fitted with the dough hook:

1 cup (235g) room-temperature (70° to 75°F) water
2 tablespoons (25g) olive oil

1 tablespoon (10g) sugar
1 envelope (2¼ teaspoons) active dry yeast

Add:

3 cups (395g) bread flour
1½ teaspoons salt

Mix by hand or on low speed for about 1 minute or until the dough comes together. Knead for about 10 minutes by hand or with the dough hook on medium-low speed for 8 minutes until the dough is smooth, soft, and elastic. Add flour or water as needed; the dough should be slightly tacky but not sticky. Transfer the dough to an oiled bowl and turn to lightly coat with oil. Cover with plastic wrap and let rise until nearly doubled in bulk, 1 to 1½ hours.

Position a rack in the lower third of the oven. Preheat the oven to 500°F.

Meanwhile, transfer the dough to a lightly floured work surface and divide equally into 8 pieces. Roll the pieces into balls. Cover and let rest for 20 minutes.

Roll out each ball of dough into a 6- to 7-inch round ⅛ inch thick. Take care not to roll the center of the rounds too thin—the dough should be a uniform thickness. Gently transfer 4 of the rounds to a large, lightly greased baking sheet. Bake until the dough rounds puff into balloons, about 4 minutes, then bake 30 seconds longer and immediately transfer the breads to a rack to cool. If you leave the breads in the oven too long, they will become dry and will not deflate to flat disks. Bake the remaining rounds.

NAAN

4 oval breads

This delicious, soft Indian flatbread is traditionally baked in red-hot tandoor ovens. At home, a preheated baking stone or steel can yield good results. If desired, substitute Ghee, 960, for the butter.

Combine in a large bowl or a stand mixer fitted with the dough hook:

2 cups (265g) bread flour
½ teaspoon salt
1⅛ teaspoons active dry yeast

Add:

¾ cup plain yogurt (180g) or buttermilk (185g), at room temperature
2 tablespoons butter (30g), melted
1 teaspoon to 1 tablespoon water, as needed

Mix by hand or on low speed until a soft ball of dough forms. Knead for about 10 minutes by hand or on low to medium speed, until the dough is smooth and elastic. Transfer the dough to an oiled bowl and turn once to coat with oil. Cover with plastic wrap and let rise until nearly doubled, about 1½ hours.

Position a rack in the lowest position in the oven and place a baking stone, steel, or inverted heavy-gauge baking sheet on the rack. Preheat the oven to 475°F for 45 minutes.

Meanwhile, divide the dough into 4 equal pieces. Roll into balls, cover, and let rest for 10 minutes. Roll out each ball of dough on a very lightly floured surface to an oval 8 to 10 inches long and ¼ inch thick. Brush the tops with:

2 tablespoons butter, melted

If desired, sprinkle on top:

(2 tablespoons minced green onions or garlic)

Place as many dough ovals as will fit without touching each other directly on the baking stone, steel, or sheet and bake until each oval is puffy and deeply browned on the bottom, 6 to 7 minutes. Remove from the oven. If desired, brush the naan with:

(Melted butter)

Place in a cloth-lined basket and keep covered. Bake the remaining breads. Serve warm.

LAYERED PARATHA

Makes eight 8-inch parathas

Brushing the rolled-out dough with ghee and coiling it up creates flaky layers in these unleavened Indian flatbreads.

Combine in a medium bowl:

1 cup (125g) all-purpose flour
1 cup (130g) whole wheat flour
½ teaspoon salt

Add:

⅔ cup (160g) warm water
1 tablespoon (15g) Ghee, 960, or butter, melted

Mix until the dough is very smooth. Cover and let the dough rest for 20 minutes.

Melt and keep warm:

4 tablespoons (55g) Ghee, 960, or butter

Divide the dough into 8 equal pieces. Working with one piece at a time (keep the remaining pieces covered), roll out the dough as thinly as possible into a round. Brush with the melted butter, then roll up jelly-roll style. Wind the resulting log of dough around itself into a coil. Roll out the dough into a roughly 6- to 7-inch round. You may find it easier to use your fingers and the heel of your hand to spread the dough into a round. Do not overflour the work surface; some sticking is fine as it will help you roll the dough thinner. Brush both sides of the round with melted butter. Repeat with the remaining dough, stacking the parathas on top of one another with pieces of parchment or wax paper in between.

Heat a dry skillet over medium heat until hot. Place one paratha in the skillet and cook until unevenly browned on the bottom, about 2 minutes. Flip and brown the second side. Repeat with the remaining parathas.

LEFSE

Sixteen 6-inch flatbreads

These Norwegian flatbreads are often served around the holidays with butter, sugar, and cinnamon, although we fill them with savory fillings, too. If desired, use 2 cups leftover mashed potatoes instead of the freshly boiled potatoes. If you're a true rebel, you can even make these with instant mashed potatoes.

Place in a pot and add cool water to cover:

1 pound (455g) russet potatoes, peeled and cut into quarters

Bring to a boil, then reduce the heat to a simmer and cook until very tender, about 15 minutes. Drain the potatoes well and put them through a ricer into a large bowl (alternatively, mash the potatoes until very smooth). Add:

4 tablespoons (55g) unsalted butter, softened
¼ cup (60g) milk or heavy cream
½ teaspoon salt
½ teaspoon sugar

Taste and adjust the seasonings if needed. Cover and refrigerate until cold, at least 4 hours or overnight. Add to the potatoes:

1¼ cups (155g) all-purpose flour

Mix in until combined, then transfer the dough to a lightly floured work surface and knead briefly until smooth and pliable, adding a little extra flour if needed. Divide the dough in half, roll each half into a 1-inch-thick log, and cut each log crosswise into 8 pieces.

Heat a dry skillet over medium heat until hot.

Working with 1 piece of dough at a time and keeping the rest covered, roll out each piece of dough into a round as thin as possible, flouring the surface and the dough lightly as needed; some sticking is fine. Transfer the dough to the skillet (a bench scraper can help lift up the tender dough) and cook until browned in spots, 1 to 2 minutes. Flip and cook the second side, 1 to 2 minutes more. Transfer to a plate and cover with a kitchen towel to keep warm. Repeat with the remaining dough.

FLOUR TORTILLAS

Eight 6- to 8-inch tortillas

Flour tortillas are very easy to make and much tastier than store-bought tortillas.

Combine in a large bowl or a stand mixer fitted with the dough hook:

2 cups (265g) bread flour
1 teaspoon baking powder
1 teaspoon salt
¼ cup (50g) vegetable shortening or lard
¾ cup (175g) hot (115° to 130°F) water

Mix by hand or on low speed until the dough comes together. Knead by hand or on low to medium speed until smooth, 4 to 6 minutes.

Divide the dough into 8 pieces and roll them into balls. Cover and let rest for 20 minutes.

Roll out each ball of dough into a 6- to 8-inch round about ⅛ inch thick. If a dough round is resistant, move to the next piece and return later to finish rolling.

Heat a large cast-iron or nonstick skillet over medium heat. Slide the tortillas into the skillet one by one, cooking until brown spots appear, about 30 seconds on the first side, 15 seconds once flipped. Cover the cooked tortillas to keep warm while you cook the rest. Serve warm.

CORN TORTILLAS

Sixteen 5-inch tortillas

This dough dries out quickly; the unused portion should be kept wrapped or covered until ready to use; you may always readjust the consistency by kneading it with additional water if necessary—extra kneading does not harm the finished product. If you can find it, fresh masa makes remarkable tortillas, and it requires even less work. Simply knead the masa with a little water if it is crumbly and proceed to cook them as directed below.

Mix in a bowl with your hands, adjusting the quantity of water as necessary to form a soft dough:

2 cups (210g) masa harina
1¼ to 1⅓ cups (295 to 315g) hot (120° to 125°F) water

Cover with plastic wrap and let rest at least 30 minutes.

Knead the rested dough, adjusting the consistency with additional water or masa as necessary, until it is soft, smooth, and pliable but neither sticky nor crumbly.

Place 2 heavy ungreased skillets on the stove or use a griddle large enough to cover two burners. Adjust the heat under 1 skillet (or one side of the griddle) to medium-low and the second to medium-high.

Form the dough into 1½-inch balls. Keep covered with a damp clean towel while you press the tortillas. Place a dough ball between 2 pieces of sturdy plastic or wax paper (plastic grocery bags work remarkably well). Using a tortilla press or the bottom of a pie plate, press the dough firmly, turning it 180 degrees and pressing again as necessary, until it is uniformly 1/16 inch thick. (If the tortilla crumbles when you pick it up, the dough is too dry; if it sticks badly to the plastic, the tortilla is too thin or the dough is too wet. Adjust the consistency of the rest of the dough accordingly before continuing to shape the tortillas.) Peel off the top piece of plastic or wax paper, turn the tortilla over onto your hand, and peel off the bottom piece of plastic or wax paper.

Lay the tortilla in the cooler of the 2 skillets until it begins to release itself from the pan but the edges have not begun to curl, about 20 seconds. Flip the tortilla over onto the hotter skillet and cook until the underside is lightly browned in spots, 20 to 30 seconds. Flip the tortilla over and finish browning the first side. If the pan is hot enough and the dough properly moist, the tortilla should puff up (you may encourage this by pressing it with your fingers or the back of a spatula). When it is browned, transfer the tortilla to a clean towel (it will deflate) and cover it. Form and cook the remaining tortillas, stacking them on top of each other and covering the stack each time. Serve warm. Reheat leftovers wrapped in foil in the oven until soft and pliable.

SOPES

8 sopes (4 servings)

These quick little masa cakes are hearty and can be filled with a variety of things. In their simplest form, they are topped with Frijoles de la Olla, 213, or Refried Beans, 215, shredded lettuce, *crema* or sour cream, and grated cheese.

Combine in a medium bowl:

2 cups (210g) masa harina
¾ teaspoon salt

Add:

1¼ cups (295g) lukewarm (80° to 90°F) water

Stir until the dough comes together. It should be smooth and pliable; not crumbly or sticky. It may need an extra splash of water or a sprinkle of masa to reach the right consistency. Divide the dough into 8 pieces. Place each piece between 2 layers of sturdy plastic or wax paper (a plastic grocery bag also works well) and flatten with a tortilla press or a heavy skillet into a ¼-inch-thick round. Heat a large, heavy, dry skillet over medium heat until hot. Add the *sopes* in batches and cook about 1 minute or until the bottom looks dry, then flip and cook 1 minute more. Flip one final time and let cook about 30 seconds. Transfer to a plate and cover with a kitchen towel to keep warm.

When the *sopes* are cool enough to handle but still warm, pinch them all the way around the edge to create a rim. The *sopes* will look like little round boats. Add to the hot skillet:

¼ cup (50g) vegetable oil

When the oil shimmers, return the *sopes* to the pan in batches. Cook, turning once, just until golden on both sides, about 1 minute per side. Drain on a plate lined with paper towels. Serve with toppings. For ideas, see Fillings for Tacos and Burritos, 146.

AREPAS

8 arepas (4 servings)

From Venezuela and Colombia, arepas are made with precooked corn flour, the most widely available brand being P.A.N. Stuffed arepas, like the ones in this recipe, are Venezuelan.

Combine in a medium bowl:

2 cups (305g) precooked corn flour
2 cups (475g) lukewarm (80° to 90°F) water
¾ teaspoon salt

Stir until a smooth dough forms. You may need to add a little more water to achieve a pliable, moist (but not sticky) dough. If desired, stir in:

(1 cup shredded mozzarella, queso blanco, or other mild cheese [4 oz or 115g])

Divide the dough into 8 pieces and shape them into balls. Flatten into discs just over ½ inch thick. Heat in a nonstick skillet over medium heat:

¼ cup (50g) vegetable oil

When the oil shimmers, add the arepas in batches and cook, turning once, until golden brown on both sides, about 5 minutes per side. Transfer to a plate lined with paper towels to drain. To serve, cut halfway through the arepas horizontally, leaving them in one piece but with a pocket for stuffing. Fill with any of the following, or a combination:

Shredded cheese, such as mozzarella or queso blanco
Braised Carnitas, 495, Braised Pulled Pork, 495, or any shredded and cooked beef or chicken
Cooked black beans

FOCACCIA

Two 8- or 9-inch round breads or one large bread

Prepare:

Pizza Dough, 614, through the first rise

Divide the dough in half, roll each piece out to a ½-inch-thick round, and transfer to 2 well-oiled 8- or 9-inch round cake pans or square baking pans. Alternatively, keep the dough in one piece, roll it out into a ½-inch-thick rectangle, and use a large baking sheet. Cover with oiled plastic wrap and let rise until puffy, 1 to 1½ hours.

Preheat the oven to 400°F.

Ten minutes before baking, press the dough with your fingertips to make indentations all over. Drizzle with:

Up to ½ cup (100g) olive oil

Top with any of the following, or a combination:

2 tablespoons grated cheese, such as Romano, Parmesan, or Asiago
1 teaspoon crumbled dried herbs, such as rosemary, thyme, or oregano, or up to 1 tablespoon fresh herb leaves or minced herbs
½ teaspoon coarse or flaky salt
Slices of sun-dried tomatoes, olives, Caramelized Onions, 255, diced roasted potato, roasted garlic cloves, 241, or grapes

Bake until golden brown, about 25 minutes. Turn out of the pans and onto a wire rack. Serve warm or at room temperature, as is, or sliced open horizontally to use as a sandwich bread.

KHACHAPURI (GEORGIAN CHEESE-FILLED BREAD)

1 large khachapuri or 4 servings

This boat-shaped bread is a version of the many different types of *khachapuri* found across Georgia. Common to all of them is an ample quantity of cheese.

Prepare:

½ recipe Pizza Dough, 614

Once the dough has risen, preheat the oven to 375°F. Line a large baking sheet with parchment paper.

On a lightly floured surface, shape the dough into a ball. Roll the dough into a 12-inch round. Cover and let rest for 10 minutes.

Meanwhile, mix together in a medium bowl:

1 cup shredded mozzarella (4 oz or 115g)
½ cup crumbled feta cheese (2 oz or 55g)
1 large egg
1 tablespoon (15g) butter, softened

Transfer the dough to the lined baking sheet. Sprinkle the cheese filling over the dough, spreading the filling to within 1 inch of the edge. Tightly roll one side of the dough round one-third of the way toward the center, then roll the opposite side of the dough round one-third of the way toward the center. Gently form the bread into a boat-like shape that is open in the middle and joined at both ends. At each end, pinch the joined dough together to prevent it from unrolling and twist each end gently. Brush the dough with:

1 egg yolk, well beaten

Bake until the cheese is bubbling and browned, about 25 minutes. Remove from the oven and crack into the center of the bread:

1 large egg

Return to the oven until the white is set but the yolk is still runny, 4 to 6 minutes. As soon as the bread comes out of the oven, place on top of the egg:

1 tablespoon butter, softened

To eat, stir the runny yolk and butter into the melted cheese. Tear off pieces of the bread and dip them in the molten cheesy mixture.

ABOUT PIZZA

Pizza is simply a round of yeast dough rolled to any thickness, topped with a wide variety of toppings, and baked. But then, nothing is truly simple about pizza. It ranges in style from thicker Sicilian-style sheet pan pies to deep-dish Chicago-style pizza to enormous thin-crusted New York–style pizza. Pizzas may be found topped with nearly anything you can think of, although we think the best ones are those not overburdened by vast quantities of toppings.

Home pizza baking has taken a turn for the better over the past ten years or so. Instead of quick-rising yeast doughs, many home pizza bakers now prefer slower rising doughs that are allowed to sit overnight in the refrigerator, offering up a chewier crumb and better flavor. Many of us have also discovered the thick steel plates, or baking steels, made specifically for baking pizzas in home ovens. When preheated to a high temperature, these plates provide a consistent high heat that results in a deeply browned crust. Unlike baking stones, the steel may be used in tandem with the broiler setting to produce exquisitely melty, bubbling, browned pies that seem to defy what we once thought of as homemade pizza.

Baking stones may be used with good results, but never use the broiler setting or subject them to extreme changes in temperature or they may crack. Cast-iron pizza pans are another good option, although the results are not quite as good as with a baking steel. Pizza may also be grilled, 616.

PIZZA DOUGH

Two 12-inch crusts

As you become an avid pizza baker, you will no doubt come up with your own style of crust and your own favorite toppings. For topping ideas, see Pizza Combinations, below. For baking instructions, see Pizza Margherita, below. If desired, substitute 00 flour, 985, for half the all-purpose flour.

I. QUICK-RISING

Combine in a large bowl or a stand mixer fitted with the dough hook and let stand until the yeast is dissolved, about 5 minutes:

1⅓ cups (315g) warm (105° to 115°F) water
1 envelope (2¼ teaspoons) active dry yeast

Add:

3½ to 3¾ cups (440 to 470g) all-purpose flour
2 tablespoons (25g) olive oil
1¼ teaspoons salt

Mix by hand or on low speed for about 1 minute. Knead for about 5 minutes by hand or on low to medium speed until the dough is smooth and elastic, working in a little flour if needed. Transfer the dough to a bowl lightly oiled with olive oil and turn to coat with the oil. Cover and let rise in a warm place (75° to 85°F) until doubled in bulk, 1 to 1½ hours.

Preheat the oven to 500°F. Position a rack in the bottom third of the oven. Place a baking stone or steel in the oven and preheat it for 45 minutes, if using. Or grease 2 baking sheets and dust with:

Cornmeal

Divide the dough in half. Roll each piece into a ball and let rest, loosely covered with plastic wrap, for 15 minutes. Prepare the desired toppings (see Pizza Combinations, below).

One at a time, flatten each ball of dough on a lightly floured work surface into a 12-inch round, rolling and stretching the dough. Or stretch the dough in the air, allowing the weight of the dough to help stretch it out, rotating the dough as you stretch. As the dough gets thinner, drape it over the backs of your hands as you turn it to avoid tearing holes in it. Place each dough round on a prepared baking sheet, or, if using a baking stone or steel, place them on cookie sheets or a baker's peel dusted with flour. The dough is now ready to be topped and baked (see Pizza Margherita, below).

II. SLOW-RISING

Prepare **Pizza Dough, above,** using only ¼ **teaspoon active dry yeast.** Once the dough comes together, knead for 3 minutes. Divide the dough in half, shape into balls, wrap tightly in plastic wrap, and refrigerate for at least 12 hours or for up to 3 days. Let the dough sit at room temperature for 30 minutes before shaping, topping, and baking.

PIZZA MARGHERITA (PIZZA WITH TOMATO SAUCE AND MOZZARELLA)

Two 12-inch pizzas

This classic pizza has a medium-thick crust topped with tomato sauce, cheese, and basil.

Prepare:

Pizza Dough, above, or two 1-pound packages store-bought refrigerated pizza dough

Preheat and prepare the oven and form two 12-inch rounds of dough as directed. Spread in an even layer over both pizzas, leaving a ½-inch border all around:

½ cup Marinara Sauce, 556, or Pizza Sauce, 556

Sprinkle with:

1½ cups shredded mozzarella (6 ounces)
½ cup coarsely chopped basil or whole basil leaves
Salt and black pepper to taste

Bake one pizza at a time. If baking the pizzas on baking sheets, bake them on the bottom rack. If using a baking stone or steel, place the pizza on a floured baker's peel or cookie sheet. Gently shake the peel or cookie sheet back and forth until the dough slides a bit. If the dough is sticking, lift it up gently and throw a little more flour underneath it. Quickly slide the pizza off the peel onto the baking stone or steel (this move takes practice—consider working on your technique a good excuse to make pizza more often). Bake until the crust is browned and the cheese is golden, about 12 minutes. If using a baking steel, after the pizza has cooked for 5 minutes, you may turn on the broiler and broil the pizza until browned and bubbling. Turn the temperature back to 500°F before baking the next pizza.

PIZZA COMBINATIONS

Topping a pizza is a matter of taste. In Russia, pizza may be topped with red herring or *mackba* (a mixture of sardines, salmon, mackerel, tuna, and onions). Indians top pizza with ginger, minced mutton, and paneer. In Japan, squid and *"mayo jaga"* (mayonnaise, potato, and bacon) are popular. The "Double Dutch" is a favorite in the Netherlands: double cheese, double onions, and double beef. The important thing to remember is that in order to prevent a soggy pizza, some toppings must be precooked to release their excess fat or liquid. Listed below are a few of our favorite topping combinations. ➤ The amounts given will make two pizzas. For sauce, cheese, and basil amounts, use Pizza Margherita, above, as a guide.

Toppings	Sauce	Cheese
6 ounces pepperoni, thinly sliced	Tomato	Mozzarella
12 ounces hot or mild Italian sausage, crumbled, browned, and drained on paper towels; 1 small yellow or red onion, very thinly sliced; (sliced pickled peppers)	Tomato	Mozzarella
12 ounces fresh chorizo, crumbled, browned, and drained on paper towels; coarsely chopped green onion; 1½ cups Pan-Fried Potatoes, 268	None	Mozzarella or Oaxaca cheese
4 ounces very thinly sliced pancetta; fresh basil leaves	Tomato	Mozzarella
4 ounces very thinly sliced prosciutto or Canadian bacon; 1 cup fresh pineapple chunks	Tomato	Mozzarella
4 ounces very thinly sliced prosciutto; 1 cup drained marinated artichoke hearts, quartered; ½ cup Kalamata or other brine-cured black olives, pitted and sliced	Tomato	Mozzarella
1 medium zucchini or 5 trimmed asparagus spears, shaved into thin ribbons with a vegetable peeler; ½ cup Kalamata olives, pitted and sliced; 16 sage leaves tossed with 1 teaspoon olive oil	½ cup Pesto, 586	½ cup crumbled feta cheese; 1 cup mozzarella
1 cup Caramelized Onions, 255; ½ cup Kalamata or other brine-cured black olives, pitted; 4 teaspoons finely chopped fresh rosemary or 2 teaspoons dried rosemary	None, or Béchamel II, 548, flavored with 1 garlic clove, minced	None
60 shucked or drained canned littleneck clams; 3 garlic cloves, minced; 2 tablespoons olive oil. After baking, top with 1 tablespoon chopped parsley.	None	1 cup Pecorino Romano
6 ounces picked crabmeat; black pepper	None	2 ounces Taleggio, cut into small chunks; 1 cup mozzarella
2 portobello mushrooms or 10 to 15 button mushrooms, thinly sliced and sautéed; 1 red onion, thinly sliced and sautéed with 3 minced garlic cloves; ½ teaspoon dried thyme	None	1 cup crumbled fresh goat cheese (chèvre)
1 cup Melted Leeks, 247; 8 ounces maitake mushrooms, broken into small "florets" and tossed with 2 tablespoons olive oil	None	2 ounces Taleggio, cut into small chunks; 1 cup mozzarella
1 small Granny Smith or Honeycrisp apple, cored and thinly sliced; black pepper. After baking, drizzle lightly with honey and top with 2 cups arugula.	None	3 ounces Gorgonzola, crumbled; 1 cup mozzarella

GLUTEN-FREE PIZZA

Enough dough for one 12- to 14-inch pizza

This recipe is written to use fine white rice flour, available at Asian markets. Stone-ground rice flour is coarser and will not work. ➤ There is enough dough for one pizza, so adjust topping quantities accordingly.

Mix together in a large bowl or a stand mixer fitted with the paddle attachment:

¾ cup (95g) tapioca starch
½ cup (70g) brown rice flour
½ cup (55g) white rice flour
¼ cup (40g) potato starch
1½ teaspoons xanthan gum
½ teaspoon salt

Add and stir or mix in on low speed for 1 minute:

1 cup (235g) lukewarm (80° to 90°F) water
1 egg, at room temperature
2 tablespoons (25g) olive oil
1¼ teaspoons active dry yeast

Increase the speed to medium-high and mix for 4 minutes or stir the dough until smooth. Grease a large baking sheet or a 12- to 14-inch pizza pan and sprinkle with:

2 tablespoons cornmeal

With an oiled spatula, spread the sticky dough evenly onto the pan as thinly as possible (about ¼ inch). Cover loosely with oiled plastic wrap and let rise until puffy, about 45 minutes.

Preheat the oven to 425°F.

Prick the pizza crust all over with a fork and bake for 12 to 15 minutes. Cover with:

Any of the pizza toppings (see Pizza Combinations, 614)

Return to the oven and bake until the cheese is melted and the dough is browned, 5 to 8 minutes. Let cool about 5 minutes before cutting into slices.

CHICAGO-STYLE DEEP-DISH PIZZA

5 to 6 servings

Just like other kinds of pizza, Chicago-style pizzas can have a wide variety of toppings, such as peppers and onions, pepperoni or salami, Italian sausage, spinach, or really anything you like. The recipe below is just a blueprint. The key is to use plenty of cheese and put the sauce on top.

Prepare:

Pizza Dough I, 614

Adding to the dough along with the olive oil:

2 tablespoons (30g) unsalted butter, melted

Let the dough rise as directed. Meanwhile, prepare:

Marinara Sauce, 556

Preheat the oven to 425°F. Grease a 12-inch cast-iron skillet, a deep 12-inch cake pan, or 2 deep 9-inch cake pans with:

2 tablespoons butter, softened

Dust the pan(s) with:

Medium-grind cornmeal

Shake out any excess cornmeal.

Once the dough has doubled in bulk, transfer it to a lightly floured work surface and stretch it out into a 14-inch round if using a 12-inch skillet or cake pan. If using 9-inch cake pans, divide the dough in half, shape each half into a ball, 596, and stretch out the dough into 11-inch rounds. Take care not to stretch the crust too thin. Transfer the dough to the pan(s), pressing it gently into the corners and up the sides of the pan(s). Top the dough with:

12 ounces cheese, preferably a combination of sliced provolone and shredded mozzarella

(1 cup sliced pepperoni or salami, or 1 pound Italian sausage, crumbled, cooked, and drained)

Top the filling with the marinara sauce. Sprinkle on top of the sauce:

½ cup finely grated Parmesan (2 ounces)

Cut off any overhanging dough where it meets the pan rim, or fold it over and pinch it at the edge to form a thicker crust. Drizzle the top of the pizza(s) with:

1 tablespoon olive oil

Bake the pizza(s) until the crust is a deep golden brown, about 35 minutes. Sprinkle with:

1 tablespoon finely chopped parsley

Let cool for 10 minutes before cutting and serving.

GRANDMA-STYLE PAN PIZZA

6 servings

There are different ways to assemble a grandma-style pizza depending on your preference. Some build these pies much like a standard pizza, with sauce directly on top of the dough, then toppings, then cheese. Others spoon the sauce on top of the cheese in diagonal lines. Both ways are excellent, so the choice is yours.

Prepare:

Pizza Dough I, 614

Let the dough rise as directed. Meanwhile, prepare and have ready:

Marinara Sauce, 556

2 cups shredded mozzarella (8 ounces)

½ cup finely grated Parmesan (2 ounces)

(Any desired toppings from Pizza Combinations, 614)

Preheat the oven to 425°F.

Grease a large rimmed baking sheet (about 18 × 13 inches). Stretch and pull the dough into a rectangular shape. Cover and let rest for 10 minutes. Stretch it out again to cover the bottom of the baking sheet. If the dough springs back, let it rest another 10 minutes and try again. There is no need to press the dough up the sides of the pan. Top the dough with the sauce, cheeses, and any desired toppings in the order you prefer. Bake the pizza until the cheese is melted and the crust is well browned, 20 to 25 minutes. If desired, turn on the broiler for a few minutes to brown the cheese. If desired, top with:

(Fresh basil leaves)

GRILLED PIZZA

Grilled pizza is simple to make and has a crisp yet chewy crust. Making grilled pizzas can be the basis for a summer party. Make smaller crusts for individual pizzas. Grill both sides of the dough, and have a basket full of grilled pizza crusts alongside a variety of toppings when guests arrive. Each person tops his or her own, and you heat them on the grill. Both charcoal and gas grills work well.

I. OVER DIRECT HEAT

Prepare a hot grill fire, 1063. Have ready:

Pizza Dough, 614, risen, or two 1-pound packages store-bought refrigerated pizza dough

Shape the dough as for Pizza Margherita, 614. Place one piece of dough at a time on a lightly floured cookie sheet or a baker's peel. Gently shake the cookie sheet or peel back and forth until the dough slides a bit. If the dough is sticking, lift it up gently and throw a little more flour underneath it. Slide the dough directly onto the grill grate. Watch for the dough to firm up as the bottom cooks. When it is firm enough, about 5 minutes, flip it over, leave it on the grill, and top with your selected ingredients; or place it cooked side up on a floured surface (to prevent sticking), add the toppings, and then return to the grill. ➤ Use less topping on a grilled pizza than one baked in an oven to ensure heating throughout. ➤ To cook the topping and melt the cheese, cover the grill.

II. ON A STONE OR STEEL

Another grilling method that produces an incredibly crisp crust requires a pizza stone or baking steel.

Prepare a hot grill fire, 1063, and place a baking stone or steel on the grill grate, cover the grill, and preheat for 45 minutes to 1 hour. Have ready:

Pizza Dough, 614, risen, or two 1-pound packages store-bought refrigerated pizza dough

If using a charcoal grill, at this point you need to add more coals: Carefully remove the grate and stone or steel, add another chimney of lit coals (oven or pit gloves are essential here), then replace the grate and stone. Shape the dough as for Pizza Margherita, 614, place on a lightly floured cookie sheet or baker's peel, and add the desired toppings. Gently shake the cookie sheet or peel back and forth until the dough slides a bit. If the dough is sticking, lift it up gently and throw a little more flour underneath it. Slide the pizzas onto the stone or steel, cover the grill, and check for doneness every 5 minutes. The pizza is done when the crust is well browned, the toppings are cooked or warmed through, and the cheese is melted.

ABOUT YEAST ROLLS

The visual appeal of crusty, golden brown rolls is a stimulant to the appetite, especially if they are still warm from the oven. There is little difference between making bread and rolls, so if you are a novice, ➤ please read About Yeast Bread, 592. In fact, most recipes for loaf breads can be used to make rolls. The classic roll shape is a simple ball, but also see the illustrations throughout this section for more creative shapes.

To shape yeast rolls into balls, first divide the dough into the number of pieces specified in the recipe. This can be accomplished by eyeballing them or by weighing the total amount of dough, then dividing that by the recipe yield and weighing each piece of dough accordingly to ensure they are all the same size. Fold the corners of each piece of dough into the center, pressing them lightly together. Turn the dough over so the seam side is facing down, and use a cupped palm to roll the dough against the lightly floured countertop. The action of the dough clinging lightly to the surface will help shape it into a tight round.

Vary the flavor of rolls with any of the additions to yeast doughs, 593. Sprinkle the tops with seeds: poppy, celery, fennel, caraway, or lightly toasted sesame. Because freshly baked rolls are ideal with dinner, read Retarding Dough, 595. It's much easier to make the dough ahead of time, refrigerate it until it is needed, and shape and bake the rolls just before dinner.

PARKER HOUSE ROLLS

Thirty 2-inch rolls

This is a basic, not-too-sweet dough that can be used for variously shaped dinner rolls.

Combine in a small bowl and stir to dissolve the sugar and melt the butter:

1 cup (235g) warm (105° to 115°F) milk
2 tablespoons (30g) butter, softened
1 tablespoon (10g) sugar
3/4 teaspoon salt

Combine in a large bowl and let stand until the yeast is dissolved, about 5 minutes:

2 tablespoons (30g) warm (105° to 115°F) water
1 envelope (2 1/4 teaspoons) active dry yeast

Stir the milk mixture into the yeast. Beat in:

1 large egg

Have ready:

3 1/3 to 3 2/3 cups (415 to 460g) all-purpose flour

Stir in part of the flour, then transfer the dough to a work surface and knead in the rest, using only enough to form a dough that can be handled easily. Place in an oiled bowl. Brush the top with:

Melted butter

Cover and let the dough rise in a warm place (75° to 85°F) until doubled in bulk, about 1 hour.

Roll the dough out into a 30-inch-long log and cut into 1-inch pieces. Roll each piece into a ball and flatten into a 2-inch round. Dip the handle of a wooden spoon in flour or rub flour on a rolling pin and use it to make a deep crease across the middle of each roll. Fold the rolls over on the crease and press the edges together lightly. Place about 2 inches apart in rows on greased baking sheets. Let rise in a warm place (75° to 85°F) until puffy, about 35 minutes.

While the dough rises, preheat the oven to 425°F.

Bake until golden brown, 15 to 18 minutes. Transfer the rolls to a wire rack to cool.

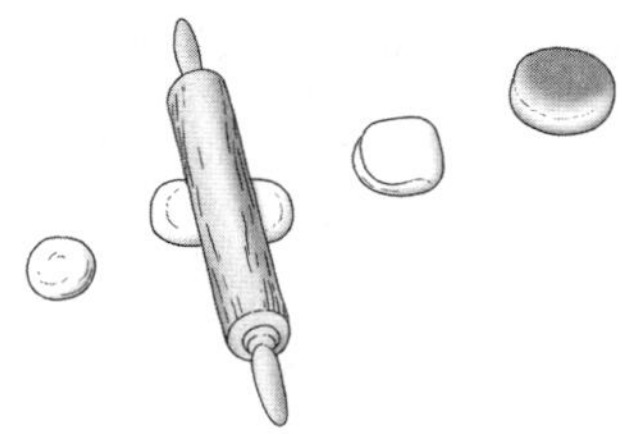

Forming Parker House rolls—a baked Parker House roll is at far right

CLOVERLEAF ROLLS

Twenty-four 2-inch rolls

Prepare the dough for **Parker House Rolls, above.** After the first rising in the bowl, grease 2 standard muffin tins. Divide the dough into 24 pieces. For each roll, divide one piece of dough into 3 pieces, roll into small balls, and place in a muffin cup, as shown. Brush the tops with **melted butter.** Let rise, covered, in a warm place until about doubled in bulk, about 30 minutes. Preheat the oven to 425°F. Bake until golden brown, 15 to 18 minutes. Transfer the rolls to a wire rack to cool.

Shaping cloverleaf rolls

NO-KNEAD REFRIGERATOR ROLLS

15 rolls

Nearly any yeast roll can be prepared using this method.

Combine in a large bowl and let stand until the yeast is dissolved, about 5 minutes:

½ cup (120g) warm (105° to 115°F) water
1 envelope (2¼ teaspoons) active dry yeast

Stir into the dissolved yeast:

1 cup (235g) lukewarm (80° to 90°F) milk
6 tablespoons (85g) unsalted butter, melted and slightly cooled
¼ cup (50g) sugar
1 large egg
1 teaspoon salt

Add and beat in until a soft dough forms:

About 3½ cups (440g) all-purpose flour

Transfer the dough to a large oiled bowl and turn once to coat with oil. Cover tightly and refrigerate for at least 12 hours and up to 3 days. When ready to bake, remove the dough from the refrigerator and allow it to rest, covered, for 30 minutes.

Punch down the dough, divide it into 15 equal portions, and round them into balls, 617. Place the rolls in 2 cake pans or one larger baking pan and allow to rise until doubled in bulk, 45 minutes to 1 hour.

While the dough rises, preheat the oven to 425°F.

Bake the rolls until golden brown, about 15 minutes. If desired, brush the tops with:

(Melted butter)

BUTTERMILK ROLLS (FAN-TANS)

24 rolls

These rolls are so rich they need not be buttered.

Have ready:

1½ cups (365g) room-temperature (70° to 75°F) buttermilk

Pour ⅓ cup of the buttermilk into a glass measure. Add and let stand until dissolved, about 5 minutes:

1 envelope (2¼ teaspoons) active dry yeast

Pour the remaining buttermilk into a large bowl. Add the dissolved yeast along with:

¼ cup (50g) sugar
2 teaspoons salt
¼ teaspoon baking soda

Stir in:

4 cups (500g) all-purpose flour
2 tablespoons (30g) butter, melted

Transfer to a work surface and knead until smooth and elastic. Transfer the dough to an oiled bowl and turn once to coat with oil. Cover with a clean cloth and let rise until slightly more than doubled in bulk, about 1 hour.

Divide the dough in half. Roll each half into a 9 × 18-inch rectangle about ⅛ inch thick. Let rest 10 minutes.

Brush the dough with:

2 tablespoons butter, melted

Cut each rectangle lengthwise into 6 strips 1½ inches wide. Make 2 stacks of 6 strips each and use a bench scraper or a string (see the illustration below) to cut each stack into twelve 1½-inch lengths (a total of 24 rolls). Place the rolls in 2 buttered muffin tins, one cut side facing up. Loosely cover with oiled plastic wrap and let rise in a warm place (75° to 85°F) until doubled in bulk, 45 minutes to 1 hour.

While the rolls rise, preheat the oven to 400°F.

Bake until well browned, 15 to 20 minutes. Transfer the rolls to a wire rack to cool.

Making buttermilk rolls (fan-tans)

BUTTERMILK POTATO ROLLS

About 48 rolls

Prepare the dough for:

Buttermilk Potato Bread, 602, through the first rise

While the dough rises, preheat the oven to 425°F.

After rising, shape and let rise as for Cloverleaf Rolls, 617. If desired, glaze the tops of the rolls with:

(1 egg yolk, beaten with 1 to 2 tablespoons water or milk)

If desired, sprinkle with:

(Poppy seeds)

Bake until browned, 15 to 18 minutes. Transfer the rolls to a wire rack to cool.

CHEESE ROLLS

12 rolls

Prepare the dough for **Pimiento Cheese Bread, 599.** Let rise once, then divide the dough evenly into 12 pieces. Round each piece into a ball, 617, and place on a lightly oiled baking sheet, spacing them evenly. Sprinkle with cheese as directed. Let rise, and bake as directed for 15 to 20 minutes or until golden. Transfer the rolls to a wire rack to cool completely.

WHOLE WHEAT ROLLS

About forty 2-inch rolls

Prepare the dough for:

All Whole Wheat Bread Cockaigne, 600, or Oat Bread, 601, through the first rise

Divide the dough into 40 pieces and round each piece into a ball, 617. Cover, and let rise until almost doubled in size, about 1 hour.

While the dough rises, preheat the oven to 425°F.

Brush the tops of the rolls with:

4 tablespoons (½ stick) butter, melted

If desired, sprinkle with:

(Flaky sea salt, chopped walnuts, or rolled oats)

Bake until browned, 12 to 18 minutes. Transfer the rolls to a wire rack to cool.

HARD ROLLS

Twelve 2¼-inch rolls

These rolls are wonderfully crusty. The beaten egg whites give them a light, soft crumb. If desired, brush the rolls with **1 egg yolk, beaten with 1 to 2 tablespoons water or milk,** and sprinkle with **Everything Seasoning, 590.**

Stir together in a large bowl or a stand mixer fitted with the dough hook:

1¼ cups (295g) warm (105° to 115°F) water
2 tablespoons (25g) vegetable shortening
1 tablespoon (10g) sugar
1 envelope (2¼ teaspoons) active dry yeast

Add:

2½ cups (315g) all-purpose flour
1¼ teaspoons salt

Mix by hand or on low speed until thoroughly blended. In a separate bowl, beat until soft peaks form, 977:

2 large egg whites

Fold into the dough. Gradually stir in until the dough is moist but no longer sticky:

1¾ to 2 cups (220 to 250g) all-purpose flour

Knead for about 7 minutes by hand or with the dough hook on low to medium speed until the dough is smooth and elastic. Transfer the dough to an oiled bowl and turn once to coat with oil. Cover with plastic wrap and let rise in a warm place (75° to 85°F) until doubled in bulk, 1 to 1½ hours.

Punch down the dough, knead it briefly, and let rise again until doubled, about 1 hour.

Punch down the dough and divide it into 12 pieces. On an unfloured work surface, round each piece into a ball, 617. Lightly dust a baking sheet with:

Cornmeal

Place the rolls 2 inches apart on the baking sheet. Loosely cover with oiled plastic wrap and let rise in a warm place (75° to 85°F) until doubled in bulk, about 1 hour.

Position racks in the center and bottom third of the oven and place a 13 × 9-inch baking pan on the lower rack. Preheat the oven to 425°F.

Place the rolls on the center rack and immediately pour 2 cups boiling water into the hot baking pan. Bake the rolls until golden brown and crusty, about 20 minutes. Serve freshly baked and warm, or reheat for about 5 minutes in a 400°F oven.

HAMBURGER BUNS

8 buns

These soft, pillowy, golden hamburger buns put mass-produced ones to shame.

Prepare the dough for:

½ recipe White Bread, 599, through the first rise

Divide the dough into 8 equal pieces and round them into balls, 617. Place on a lightly greased baking sheet, cover with oiled plastic wrap, and let rise until puffy, about 30 minutes.

Preheat the oven to 375°F. Brush the buns with:

1 large egg, beaten with 1 tablespoon water

If desired, sprinkle with:

(2 tablespoons sesame seeds)

Bake until golden brown, 15 to 18 minutes. Remove from the oven and brush with:

3 tablespoons butter, melted

Transfer the buns to a wire rack to cool.

HOT CROSS BUNS

18 buns

These originated in medieval England to commemorate Good Friday.

Prepare the dough for:

Parker House Rolls, 617, increasing the sugar to ¼ cup

After stirring in part of the flour, add to the remaining flour:

¼ cup currants or chopped raisins
(2 tablespoons finely chopped candied citron)
¼ teaspoon ground cinnamon
⅛ teaspoon grated or ground nutmeg

Knead in the remaining flour. After the first rising, punch down the dough and divide into 18 pieces. Round each piece into a ball, 617, and place in rows on greased baking sheets so the buns barely touch one another. Cover and let rise until almost doubled in bulk, 45 minutes to 1 hour.

While the buns rise, preheat the oven to 425°F.

Bake until golden brown, about 20 minutes.

While the rolls bake, stir together in a small bowl:

½ cup powdered sugar
1 tablespoon lemon or orange juice or milk

While the rolls are still slightly warm, decorate each one with glaze in the shape of a cross.

PALM LEAF ROLLS (SOUR CREAM ROLLS)

About 36 rolls

Sweet enough for a dessert if you add a bit more sugar. Serve with coffee and fruit.

Combine in a small bowl and let stand until the yeast is dissolved, about 5 minutes:

¼ cup (60g) warm (105° to 115°F) water
1 envelope (2¼ teaspoons) active dry yeast

Stir together in a large bowl until blended:

3 cups (375g) all-purpose flour
1½ teaspoons salt

Cut in with a pastry blender or your fingers until reduced to pea-sized bits:

1 stick (4 oz or 115g) cold unsalted butter, cut into pieces

Stir in:

2 large eggs, beaten
1 cup (230g) sour cream
1 teaspoon vanilla

Blend in the dissolved yeast. Cover the dough and refrigerate for 2 to 12 hours.

Have ready:

1 cup Vanilla Sugar, 1026

or a mixture of:

1 cup sugar

2 teaspoons ground cinnamon

Sprinkle a work surface with half the sugar mixture. Divide the dough in half. Roll one half into a 6 × 18-inch rectangle. Fold the 2 short sides of the rectangle in toward the center (as shown top left, below), bringing the ends to within about ¾ inch of each other. Repeat this folding again (as shown top right). Fold the two halves together, slice into ¼-inch-thick "palm leaves," and arrange 1 inch apart on a greased baking sheet. Repeat this process with the other half of the dough, first sprinkling the board with the remaining sugar mixture. Cover with plastic wrap and let rise until puffy, about 20 minutes.

While the rolls rise, preheat the oven to 375°F.

Bake until golden brown, about 20 minutes. Transfer the rolls to a wire rack to cool.

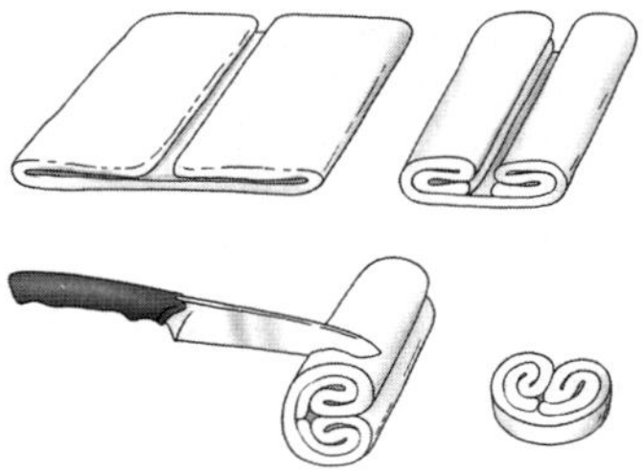

Folding and cutting palm leaf rolls

KOLACHES

About thirty-six 2-inch rolls

Prepare and refrigerate the dough for:

Palm Leaf Rolls, 619

Roll the dough into 2-inch balls, 617, and place 2 inches apart on greased baking sheets. The dough will be very sticky; flour your hands as necessary. Have ready one or more of the following:

Any of the fillings for coffee cakes, 803–4, jam, or chopped fruit (1½ to 2¼ cups total)

Press an indentation into the center of each roll, making a ¼-inch rim. Fill each one with 2 teaspoons to 1 tablespoon of a filling. Cover and let rise until puffy and nearly doubled, about 40 minutes. While the rolls rise, preheat the oven to 375°F.

Bake the rolls until well browned, about 20 minutes. Transfer the rolls to a wire rack to cool. If desired, sprinkle with:

(Powdered sugar)

OVERNIGHT SWEET CRESCENT ROLLS

About 48 rolls

This sweet dough is good for rolls, buns, and coffee cakes. It is designed to be made the night before, then shaped and baked for breakfast. However, the dough can be mixed and allowed to rise at room temperature if desired. This dough can also be shaped into filled pinwheels; see the illustration and shaping technique, 696, for Danish Pastry Dough.

Stir in a saucepan over low heat until the shortening melts:

1 cup (235g) milk

½ cup (95g) vegetable shortening or lard

Let cool. Meanwhile, combine in a large bowl and let stand until the yeast is dissolved, about 5 minutes:

2 tablespoons (30g) warm (105° to 115°F) water

1 envelope (2¼ teaspoons) active dry yeast

2 teaspoons sugar

Beat the milk mixture into the yeast mixture, along with:

½ cup (100g) sugar

3 large eggs, beaten

1 teaspoon salt

Gradually stir in

4½ cups (565g) all-purpose flour

Transfer the dough to a work surface and knead until smooth, about 5 minutes. Transfer the dough to an oiled bowl and turn to coat with oil. Cover tightly with plastic wrap and refrigerate for 12 to 24 hours.

Divide the dough into 3 portions. Roll each one into a round about 9 inches in diameter. Brush the rounds with:

2 tablespoons butter, melted

and dust each round with a mixture of:

¼ cup sugar

1 teaspoon ground cinnamon

or top with:

¾ cup any coffee cake filling, 803–4

Cut each round into 16 wedges. Roll up each piece beginning at the wider end, stretching the dough a bit as you roll it. Brush the rolls with:

1 large egg, beaten with 1 tablespoon water or milk

Arrange the rolls 2 inches apart on greased baking sheets, seam side down. Loosely cover with oiled plastic wrap and let rise until doubled in bulk, about 1½ hours.

While the rolls rise, position a rack in the center of the oven and preheat the oven to 375°F.

Bake the rolls one sheet at a time until browned, 15 to 18 minutes. Take care—they burn easily. Transfer the rolls to a wire rack to cool.

STICKY BUNS

Eight 4-inch buns

The ultimate sticky bun, chewy and decadent.

Prepare the dough for:

Yeasted Coffee Cake, 623, through the first rise

Butter a 13 × 9-inch baking pan. Bring to a boil in a small saucepan over medium heat, stirring to dissolve the sugar:

1 cup packed dark brown sugar

1 stick (4 oz or 115g) unsalted butter

¼ cup (80g) honey

Remove from the heat. If desired, stir in:

(2 cups pecans, toasted, 1005, and chopped)

Pour the hot syrup into the baking pan and spread it evenly. Let cool.

Roll out the dough to a 16 × 12-inch rectangle. Brush with:

1 tablespoon butter, melted

Sprinkle with a mixture of:

⅓ cup packed dark brown sugar

2 teaspoons ground cinnamon

Starting from a long side, roll up the dough into a cylinder. Cut crosswise into 8 slices. Arrange the slices cut side down in the prepared pan, spacing them evenly. Cover with oiled plastic wrap and let rise until doubled in bulk, about 1 hour.

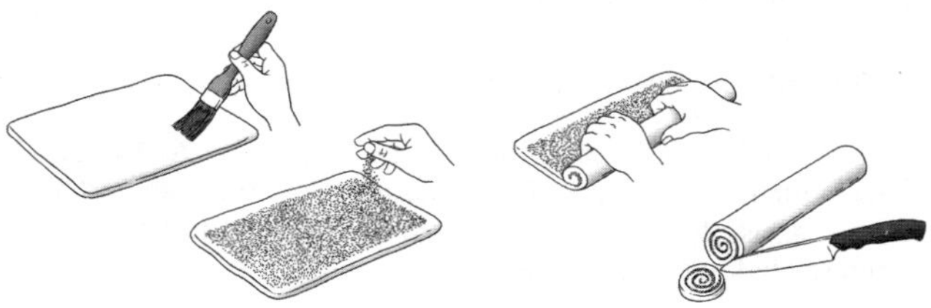

Preparing sticky buns

While the buns rise, preheat the oven to 350°F.

Bake until the buns are golden brown and the syrup is bubbling hot, about 30 minutes. Let the buns cool in the pan for 5 minutes, then invert the pan onto a rimmed baking sheet; you may want to line the sheet with foil or parchment for easier cleanup. Serve warm or at room temperature, pulling the sticky buns apart at the seams.

CINNAMON ROLLS

12 cinnamon rolls

Prepare the dough for:

Yeasted Coffee Cake, 623, through the first rise

While the dough rises, beat in a large bowl or a stand mixer fitted with the paddle attachment until smooth and creamy:

1 stick (4 oz or 115g) unsalted butter, softened

½ cup packed brown sugar

1 tablespoon ground cinnamon

¼ teaspoon salt

Butter a 13 × 9-inch baking dish. Roll out the dough on a lightly floured work surface into a 16 × 12-inch rectangle. Spread evenly with the butter mixture. Starting from a long side, roll up the dough tightly into a cylinder. Cut crosswise into 12 slices. Arrange the cinnamon rolls cut side up in the buttered baking dish, cover with plastic wrap, and let rise for 1 hour at room temperature or overnight in the refrigerator.

Prepare:

½ recipe Cream Cheese Frosting I, 792

When ready to bake, preheat the oven to 350°F. Bake the cinnamon rolls until golden brown and puffy, 25 to 30 minutes if at room temperature or 40 to 45 minutes if baking straight from the refrigerator. Transfer the pan to a rack and let cool 15 minutes before spreading with the cream cheese frosting. Serve warm.

BRIOCHE À TÊTE (TOPPED BRIOCHE)

10 rolls

A *brioche à tête*, literally, brioche with a head, has a small topknot that sits on a larger base. These are traditionally baked in fluted molds that flare at the top.

Prepare the dough for:

Brioche, 603, through the 8- to 12-hour refrigeration

Roll the dough on an unfloured work surface into a ball. Cover and let rest for 10 minutes. Butter ten 4-ounce fluted brioche molds, muffin cups, or ramekins (if using brioche molds or ramekins, place them on a baking sheet). Divide the dough evenly into 10 pieces and roll each piece into a ball, 617. Using the edge of your hand (like a karate chop), partially divide each ball (without going all the way through) into 2 parts, one twice as big as the other—like a small snowman. Set each piece of dough into a mold with the larger (base) part on the bottom; push the top section down so that it is deeply nestled in the base. Brush over the dough:

1 egg, beaten with a pinch of salt

Cover loosely with oiled plastic wrap and let rise in a warm place (75° to 85°F) until doubled in bulk, about 1 hour.

While the rolls rise, preheat the oven to 375°F.

Bake until deeply golden, about 20 minutes. Immediately turn out of the molds onto a wire rack to cool.

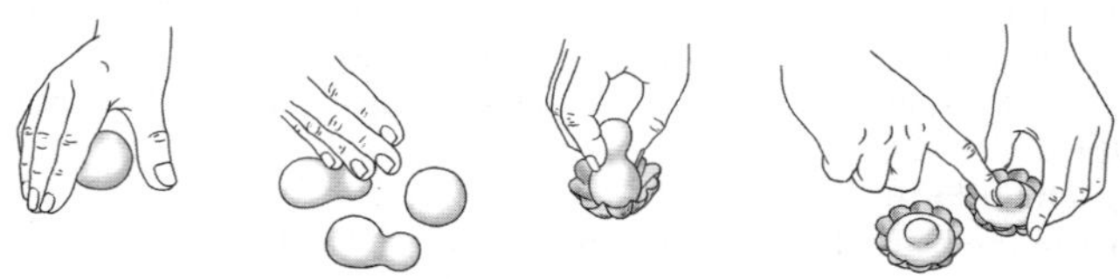

Forming a brioche à tête

ENGLISH MUFFINS

About twenty 3-inch muffins

Stir together in a bowl:

2¾ cups (345g) all-purpose flour

¾ cup (100g) whole wheat flour

2 tablespoons (25g) sugar

2 teaspoons salt

1 envelope (2¼ teaspoons) active dry yeast

Whisk together in a small bowl:

2 cups (485g) lukewarm (80° to 90°F) buttermilk

3 tablespoons (45g) unsalted butter, melted

Stir the buttermilk mixture into the flour mixture. Mix until the dough comes together in a smooth, cohesive mass. Cover the bowl with plastic wrap and let rise at room temperature until puffy, about 1 hour; or refrigerate for 8 to 12 hours.

When ready to cook, spread evenly on a rimmed baking sheet:

1 cup coarse cornmeal

Using a large spoon, scoop the dough onto the baking sheet ⅓ cup at a time into 20 mounds, leaving space between them. Sprinkle the tops with more cornmeal.

Heat a cast-iron skillet or griddle over medium-low heat until warm. Place as many of the English muffins in the skillet as will fit comfortably, without touching. Cook on one side for 5 minutes—the heat should be so low that there is no browning during this step. After 5 minutes, turn the heat up very slightly, enough to encourage browning. Cook, flipping when the first side is browned, until light brown on both sides. The slow cooking process allows them to rise and expand. Transfer to a wire rack. Reduce the heat to medium-low and let the skillet or griddle cool for 5 minutes, then repeat the cooking process with the remaining English muffins.

To separate the muffins before toasting, hold 2 forks back to back, insert them into the muffins, and pry them open. Toast, and butter generously. The uneven browning gives them great charm.

CRUMPETS

About 15 crumpets

Crumpets are similar to English muffins, but they are made from a batter rather than a dough. Classically, crumpets are baked in greased muffin rings, but they may also be dropped free-form, as here. Crumpets are eaten warm but need not be split or toasted.

Prepare the dough for:

English Muffins, 621

with these changes: Omit the whole wheat flour and use only **2½ cups (315g) all-purpose flour.** Use **1 cup (245g) buttermilk** and **1 cup (235g) water** for the liquid. Mix until smooth, cover, and let stand until the batter rises and then falls, 1½ to 3 hours.

Heat a skillet or griddle over medium-low heat. Lightly grease the skillet with:

Oil or butter

Drop the batter by ¼-cup spoonfuls onto the skillet or griddle to make 4-inch cakes. (They will not be even in shape.) Cook until the bottom is lightly browned and the top is bubbling, flip with a spatula, and cook until cooked through, about 2 minutes per side. If needed, increase the heat slightly to encourage browning. If not serving at once, wrap and refrigerate. To serve, toast or wrap in foil and reheat in a warm oven.

BAGELS

8 bagels

Our favorite accompaniment is cream cheese and lox or smoked salmon. Try sprinkling poppy or sesame seeds, freeze-dried onions, Everything Seasoning, 590, or coarse salt on top of the dough before baking.

Combine in a large bowl or a stand mixer fitted with the dough hook:

1 cup plus 2 tablespoons (265g) warm (105° to 115°F) water
1 envelope (2¼ teaspoons) active dry yeast
2½ teaspoons sugar

Stir in:

1 cup (130g) bread flour
1 tablespoon (10g) vegetable shortening, melted
1¾ teaspoons salt
1½ teaspoons malt syrup or sugar

Gradually stir in:

3 to 3½ cups (395 to 460g) bread flour

Cover and let rest for 20 minutes. Knead for about 10 minutes by hand or on low to medium speed until the dough is smooth and elastic. Let rest, covered, 15 to 20 minutes.

Divide the dough into 8 equal pieces. Roll each piece into a rope about 10 inches long, tapering the ends. Wet the ends to help seal, and form into rings, stretching the top end over and around the bottom end and pinching them together underneath. Let rise, covered, on a lightly floured surface until puffy, about 15 minutes.

Preheat the oven to 425°F.

Bring to a boil in a large pot:

4 quarts water
1 tablespoon malt syrup or sugar
½ teaspoon salt

Drop the rings 4 at a time into the boiling water. As the bagels surface, turn them over and cook about 45 seconds longer. Skim out the bagels, allowing the water to drain off them, and place on an ungreased baking sheet coated with:

Cornmeal

Sprinkle with toppings of choice, if desired. Bake until golden brown and crisp, 20 to 25 minutes, turning after 15 minutes.

BIALYS

8 bialys

A cousin of the bagel, a bialy is a chewy, flat roll with a depression in its center filled with a mixture of onions and poppy seeds. Originally from Bialystok, Poland, these exceptional little breads are difficult to find in the United States outside New York City.

Prepare the dough for:

Bagels, above, through the resting period

Divide the dough into 8 equal pieces and roll each piece into a ball, 617. Place on an oiled baking sheet, cover loosely with plastic wrap, and let rise until puffy, about 1 hour.

Meanwhile, heat in a medium skillet over medium heat:

1 tablespoon vegetable oil

Add and cook, stirring, until very soft and just starting to brown:

1 medium onion, very finely chopped

Remove from the heat and stir in:

1 tablespoon poppy seeds
¼ teaspoon salt
¼ teaspoon black pepper

Preheat the oven to 450°F.

When the dough is ready, stretch each piece of dough into a roughly 6-inch round. Use your fingers to press the dough thinner in the center than at the edges. Place the bialys on 2 greased baking sheets. Spoon about 1 teaspoon of the onion filling onto the center of each bialy, where the dough is thinner, and spread out the filling so it covers the thinner part of the dough. Bake until the bialys are golden brown, 10 to 12 minutes. Transfer to a wire rack to cool.

PRETZELS

Twelve 5-inch pretzels

A chewy pretzel that is easy to make. Baking the baking soda (used in the water bath for the pretzels), a trick from food scientist Harold McGee, creates a stronger alkali, which gets these pretzels closer to authentic lye-bathed ones without all the hazards that come with using lye.

Preheat the oven to 250°F. Line a baking sheet with foil and spread out in an even layer on the foil:

½ cup (135g) baking soda

Bake the baking soda for 1 hour. Set aside.

Combine in a large bowl or a stand mixer fitted with the dough hook:

1 cup (235g) warm (105° to 115°F) water
1 envelope (2¼ teaspoons) active dry yeast

Add:

1½ cups (190g) all-purpose flour
1½ cups (200g) bread flour
2 tablespoons butter (30g) or shortening (25g), melted
1 tablespoon (10g) sugar
½ teaspoon salt

Mix by hand or on low speed, adding more flour or water if needed to make a moist but not sticky dough. Knead for about 10 minutes by hand or on low to medium speed until the dough is smooth and elastic. Transfer the dough to an oiled bowl and turn once to coat with oil. Cover with plastic wrap and let rise in a warm place (75° to 85°F) until doubled in bulk, 1 to 1½ hours.

Divide the dough into 12 equal pieces. On an unfloured work surface, roll each piece into a ball. Loosely cover with oiled plastic wrap and let rest for 10 minutes.

Grease 2 baking sheets. Roll each ball into an 18-inch-long rope, working from the center outward and slightly tapering the ends. Bring the ends of each rope of dough to meet in front of you and form an oval, but do not join the ends. Lift the two ends and twist the dough ropes around each other about 3 inches from the ends. Gently press one end into the dough at 2 o'clock and the other at 10 o'clock. Place the pretzels on the baking sheets, cover, and let rise in a warm place (75° to 85°F) until nearly doubled in bulk, about 35 minutes.

While the pretzels rise, preheat the oven to 400°F. Bring to a boil in a big pot or deep skillet:

10 cups water

Add the baked baking soda to the water and reduce the heat to maintain a simmer. Using a slotted spoon, gently slide several pretzels at a time into the water. Simmer for 30 seconds, then flip them over and continue to simmer until puffed, about 30 seconds longer. Drain off any excess water and pat the pretzels dry. Return to the greased baking sheets. Sprinkle with:

Coarse salt or pretzel salt

Bake until deep golden brown, about 15 minutes. Let cool completely and store in an airtight container for up to 3 days.

ABOUT YEASTED COFFEE CAKES

Yeasted coffee cakes are most commonly enjoyed around the holidays. They neatly straddle the line between yeast bread and cake, with all the complex flavors of the former and the buttery sweetness of the latter (though yeasted coffee cakes never contain as much sugar as cakes). Because sugar and fat inhibit yeast development, allow plenty of time for the dough to rise, preferably in a warm place.

Remember when you are baking bread and rolls that many of those doughs can be made into coffee cakes and sweet rolls. Try some with the special fillings suggested on 803–4.

YEASTED COFFEE CAKE

1 loaf

A simple multipurpose yeasted coffee cake dough made as a breakfast loaf with a streusel topping.

Combine in a large bowl or a stand mixer fitted with the dough hook and let stand until softened, about 5 minutes:

¼ cup (60g) warm (105° to 115°F) water
1 envelope (2¼ teaspoons) active dry yeast

Add:

½ cup (65g) all-purpose or bread flour
⅓ cup (65g) sugar
¼ cup (60g) milk
2 large eggs
1 teaspoon vanilla
1 teaspoon salt

Mix by hand or on low speed until blended. Gradually stir in:

2 to 2¼ cups all-purpose flour (250 to 280g) or bread flour (265 to 295g)

Mix for 1 minute, or until the dough comes together. Let sit for 15 minutes. Knead by hand for about 10 minutes or on low to medium speed for 5 to 7 minutes, until the dough is smooth and elastic and no longer sticks to your hands or the bowl. Add:

6 tablespoons (3 oz or 85g) unsalted butter, very soft

Knead in the butter until completely incorporated and the dough is once again smooth.

Transfer the dough to a large buttered bowl. Cover with plastic wrap and let rise in a warm place (75° to 85°F) until doubled in bulk, about 1½ hours.

Knead the dough briefly a second time and refrigerate, covered, until doubled again, for 4 to 12 hours.

Butter a 9 × 5-inch loaf pan. Prepare:

⅔ cup Streusel, 800

Punch down the dough and roll out to a 16 × 9-inch rectangle about ⅓ inch thick. Brush the surface with:

1½ teaspoons butter, melted

Sprinkle evenly with half the streusel topping, along with, if desired:

(⅓ cup chopped toasted, 1005, nuts, such as pecans or walnuts)

Starting from one short side, roll up the dough as you would a jelly-roll. Place seam side down in the loaf pan, cover loosely with plastic wrap, and let rise in a warm place (75° to 85°F) until doubled in bulk, about 1½ hours.

While the loaf rises, preheat the oven to 375°F.

Brush over the top of the loaf:

1 egg yolk, beaten with 1 to 2 tablespoons water or milk

Sprinkle the remaining streusel topping over the dough. Bake the loaf until golden brown and a knife inserted in the center comes out clean, about 45 minutes. Turn the loaf out of the pan onto a wire rack to cool.

FILLED COFFEE CAKE

2 loaves

Prepare the dough for:

Buttermilk Potato Bread, 602

with these changes: Steep the buttermilk with **¼ teaspoon saffron** before adding (this gives the breads a golden color). Increase the sugar to **6 tablespoons (75g).** Let the dough go through the first rise as directed.

Meanwhile, prepare:

Any filling for coffee cakes, 803–4

Roll the dough out to a 22 × 11-inch rectangle, spread with the filling, then form and let rise as for Danish Coffee Cake, below. Bake as for Yeasted Coffee Cake, 623. If desired, glaze with:

(Quick Translucent Sugar Glaze I or II, 799)

DANISH COFFEE CAKE

One 10-inch ring

Scandinavians have among the highest coffee consumption in the world, so it's understandable that they have also created some of the best pastries, especially this light confection, which falls between a rich coffee cake and a rich pastry (a fine place to be if ever there was one). If desired, glaze the finished coffee cake, 799.

Prepare:

½ recipe Danish Pastry Dough, 696

Roll the chilled dough out on a lightly floured surface into a rectangle about 29 × 11 inches and about ⅜ inch thick. Trim any folded edges that might keep the dough from rising. Spread it with:

Any filling for coffee cakes, 803–4

and starting from the short side, roll the dough into a cylinder. Bring the two ends of the roll together, and press to seal using a little water for glue. Lift the ring onto a greased baking sheet. With floured scissors held perpendicular to the roll, cut gashes 1 to 2 inches apart through the outer rim of the ring, cutting to within 1 inch of the inner rim. As you cut, turn each partially cut slice flat onto the baking sheet. Brush the top of the dough with:

1 egg yolk, beaten with 1 to 2 tablespoons water or milk

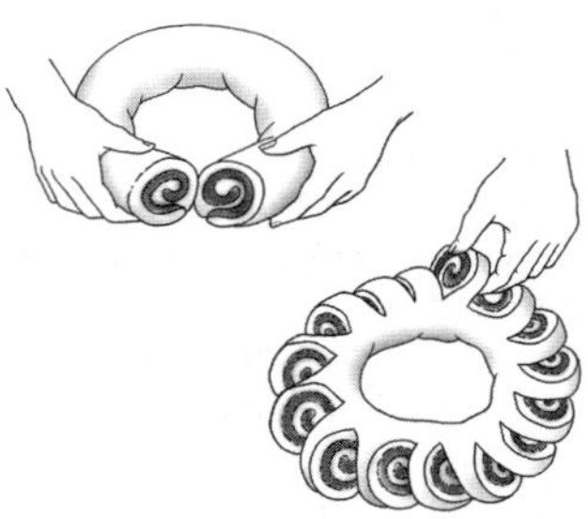

Forming Danish coffee cake

being careful not to cover the cut portions, as the glaze could inhibit the rising of the dough. Cover with a clean cloth and let rise until doubled in bulk, about 25 minutes.

While the coffee cake rises, preheat the oven to 400°F.

Bake until golden brown, about 25 minutes.

PANETTONE (ITALIAN CHRISTMAS BREAD)

2 tall round loaves

If baked in greased coffee cans or specially made panettone molds and attractively enveloped, these cakes make wonderful gifts.

Combine in a medium bowl:

1 cup (125g) all-purpose flour
1 cup (235g) warm (105° to 115°F) water
1 envelope (2¼ teaspoons) active dry yeast

Cover this sponge and let rise in a warm place (75° to 85°F) for about 30 minutes or until very bubbly.

Meanwhile, beat in a large bowl or a stand mixer fitted with the paddle attachment until light and creamy:

1 stick (4 oz or 115g) unsalted butter, softened
½ cup (100g) sugar

Beat in one at a time:

2 large eggs

Add:

1 teaspoon salt
2 teaspoons grated lemon zest

Beat in the sponge. If using a stand mixer, switch to the dough hook.

Gradually beat in:

3½ cups (440g) all-purpose flour

Beat or mix the dough for 5 minutes more. Add:

1 cup golden raisins
½ cup chopped candied citron, orange peel, ginger, or pineapple

Cover the bowl with a clean cloth and let the dough rise until almost doubled in bulk, about 2 hours.

Divide the dough in half. Place in 2 greased 9-inch tube pans, 6-cup coffee cans, or panettone molds and let rise until puffy, 30 minutes to 1 hour.

While the cakes rise, preheat the oven to 350°F.

Lightly brush the tops of the cakes with:

Melted butter

If desired, sprinkle the tops with:

(½ cup slivered almonds)
(¼ cup sugar)

Bake until golden, about 30 minutes. Immediately turn the cakes out of the pans and let cool completely (cakes baked in panettone molds do not need to be removed). If you didn't use the almonds and sugar, spread on, if desired:

(Quick Translucent Sugar Glaze I or II, 799)

STOLLEN (GERMAN CHRISTMAS LOAF)

2 long loaves

Stollen is traditionally served during the Christmas holidays. The shape and folds of the dough are said to represent the folds of the blanket of the baby Jesus. Stollen is similar to brioche, but it has a slightly coarser texture and contains more sugar, as well as nuts and candied fruit.

Combine in a medium bowl and let stand until the yeast is dissolved, about 5 minutes:

1½ cups (355g) warm (105° to 115°F) water or milk
2 envelopes (1½ tablespoons) active dry yeast

Add:

1 cup (125g) all-purpose flour

Cover this sponge and let it rest in a warm place until light and foamy, about 1 hour.

Beat in a large bowl until light and creamy:

3 sticks (12 oz or 340g) unsalted butter, softened
¾ cup (150g) sugar
Beat in one at a time:
3 large eggs
Add:
¾ teaspoon salt
¾ teaspoon grated lemon zest
Beat in the sponge, then gradually knead in:
5 to 7 cups (625 to 875g) all-purpose flour
Knead until the dough is smooth and elastic but not dry or stiff. Cover and let rise until doubled in bulk, 1 to 1½ hours.
Toss together in a small bowl:
1½ cups raisins
1½ cups chopped or slivered blanched almonds
(½ cup chopped candied fruits)
Flour (just enough to coat)
Transfer the dough to a floured work surface. Knead in the fruit and nut mixture. Divide the dough into 2 equal pieces. Working with one at a time (and keeping the other covered), roll a piece of dough into an oval about 16 inches long, 9 inches wide, and ½ inch thick. Do not roll out to the edges of the oval—the edges should be thicker than the center. Brush the top of the dough with half of:
2 tablespoons butter, melted
Fold the oval slightly less than half lengthwise so the long edges of the dough are about ½ inch apart. Tuck the two short ends (about 1 inch on each end) underneath the loaf. Place the stollen on a greased baking sheet. Shape the other piece of dough in the same way. Loosely cover both loaves with oiled plastic wrap and let rise in a warm place (75° to 85°F) for about 45 minutes. The dough does not have to fully double in volume; a three-quarter rise is enough.

While the stollens rise, position a rack in the center of the oven and preheat to 350°F.

Bake the loaves until deep golden brown and a knife inserted in the center comes out clean, 50 to 60 minutes.
Brush the loaves with:
3 tablespoons butter, melted
Sift over the top:
¼ cup powdered sugar
Return to the oven for 3 minutes. Sift over the top:
¼ cup powdered sugar
Transfer to a rack to cool.

KUGELHOPF

1 ring

This slightly sweet decorative loaf comes from the Alsace region of France. Kugelhopf is baked in a tall fluted mold. An earthenware mold is traditional, but metal or glass molds work just as well. You can also use a plain or fluted tube pan. This makes wonderful breakfast bread.
Place in a small saucepan with enough cold water to cover by ½ inch:
½ cup dried currants
Bring to a boil, then drain well. Transfer the currants to a small bowl and sprinkle with:
2 tablespoons rum or orange juice
Cover and let soak for at least 1 hour, or up to 3 days.
Prepare the dough for:
Brioche, 603, through the 8- to 12-hour refrigeration
Butter a 7- to 8-cup kugelhopf mold or tube pan. Sprinkle the bottom of the mold with:
¼ cup slivered almonds
Or place in the indentations in the bottom of the mold:
Whole blanched almonds
Knead the currants and any unabsorbed liquid into the dough. Tear off chunks of dough, form them into balls, and press into the bottom of the mold, covering the almonds completely. Press the remaining dough over the top, as evenly as possible. Cover with oiled plastic wrap and let rise in a warm place (75° to 85°F) until doubled in bulk, 1 to 1½ hours.

While the kugelhopf rises, preheat the oven to 375°F.

Bake the kugelhopf until golden brown and a knife inserted in the middle of the loaf comes out clean, about 45 minutes. Immediately turn out of the pan onto a wire rack. Dust the top with:
Powdered sugar
Let cool completely. Just before serving, dust a second time with:
Powdered sugar

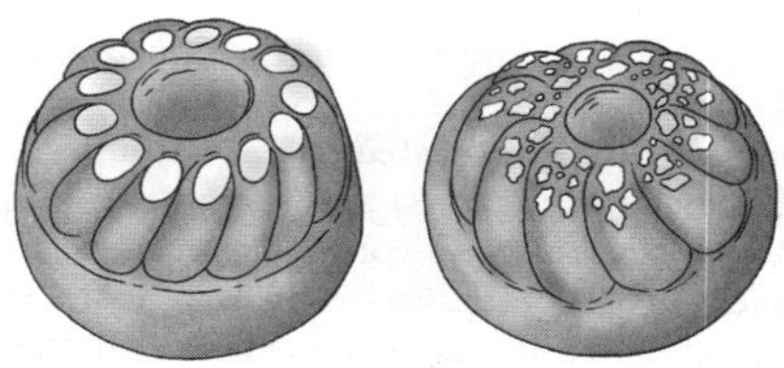

Baked kugelhopf

ABOUT QUICK BREADS AND COFFEE CAKES

These breads are ideal for the baker who can't quite commit to yeast breads. A counterpoint to the drama and mystery of the yeast-risen loaf, quick breads are reliable, sturdy, and no-nonsense. These breads are made with batters rather than dough, and they tend to be dense and moist as a result. In fact, quick breads probably have more in common with cakes than breads.

When making quick breads, have all ingredients at room temperature. Quick breads made with oil keep well, but butter-based breads should be served immediately after baking; they fade fairly soon. Moist quick breads should be stored in the refrigerator if not eaten within a couple days, but quick breads made with butter should be kept at room temperature.

▲ Quick breads are leavened with baking powder and/or baking soda. Both need to be reduced as altitude increases. Baking soda produces carbon dioxide and also neutralizes acidity in the batter. ➤ At high altitudes, the more acidic a batter, the more quickly it will set in the oven's heat—a great advantage. For some recipes, it is best to leave more of a batter's acidity intact by removing a little more baking soda (but don't cut it out) or replacing part of it with baking powder or reworking the balance between the two.

DATE NUT BREAD

One 9 × 5-inch loaf or four 5½ × 3-inch loaves

Choose relatively dry dates, rather than Medjools, which are too soft here.

Position a rack in the lower third of the oven. Preheat the oven to 350°F. Grease one 9 × 5-inch loaf pan or four 5½ × 3-inch loaf pans.

Cut into quarters (sixths if large) and place in a medium bowl:

1½ cups packed pitted dates

Stir in:

1 cup (235g) boiling water
1 teaspoon baking soda

Let stand until the mixture is lukewarm, about 20 minutes. Whisk together thoroughly in a medium bowl:

1⅔ cups (210g) all-purpose flour
½ teaspoon salt
½ teaspoon baking powder

Whisk together in a large bowl:

2 large eggs
1 cup packed (230g) brown sugar
¼ cup (50g) vegetable oil
1 teaspoon vanilla

Stir in the cooled date mixture. Stir in the flour mixture just until blended. Fold in:

2 cups coarsely chopped toasted, 1005, walnuts

Scrape the batter into the pan(s) and spread evenly. Bake until a toothpick inserted in the center comes out clean, 35 to 40 minutes for small loaves, 55 to 65 minutes for the large loaf. Let cool in the pan(s) on a rack for 10 minutes, then turn out onto the rack to cool completely.

SALLY LUNN BREAD

One 9 × 5-inch loaf

This light, tender little loaf is a cross between a quick bread and a yeast bread. Serve it with butter, jam, and cups of black tea.

Butter a 9 × 5-inch loaf pan. Whisk together in a medium bowl:

2 cups (250g) all-purpose flour
2 teaspoons baking powder
1 teaspoon salt

Combine in a small bowl and let sit until the yeast dissolves, about 5 minutes:

¾ cup (175g) lukewarm (80° to 90°F) milk
1 teaspoon active dry yeast

Beat in a large bowl with an electric mixer on medium-high speed until light and fluffy, about 3 minutes:

1 stick (4 oz or 115g) unsalted butter, softened
½ cup (100g) sugar

Beat in one at a time:

2 large eggs, at room temperature

On low speed, add the flour mixture to the batter in about 3 parts, alternating with the milk in 2 parts. Beat the batter just until it looks smooth. Scrape into the prepared pan, cover, and let rise for 30 minutes.

While the batter rises, preheat the oven to 375°F.

Bake until a toothpick inserted into the center comes out clean or the cake begins to pull away from the sides of the pan, 35 to 40 minutes. Turn the bread out of the pan onto a wire rack to cool.

ORANGE BREAD

One 9 × 5-inch loaf

This is an easily made bread. If desired, slice it and eat it while hot, with lots of good butter. You'll find this bread easier to slice on the second day.

Preheat the oven to 350°F. Grease a 9 × 5-inch loaf pan.

Whisk together in a large bowl (using the larger amount of sugar for a more cakelike result):

3 cups (375g) all-purpose flour
½ to ¾ cup (100 to 150g) sugar
1 tablespoon baking powder
½ teaspoon salt

Beat together in a medium bowl:

1¼ cups (295g) milk
Finely grated zest of 1 orange
¼ cup (60g) orange juice
1 large egg
2 tablespoons (25g) vegetable oil

Pour the liquid mixture into the dry ingredients and combine with a few swift strokes. Stir lightly until barely blended. If desired, fold in:

(1 cup chopped toasted, 1005, walnuts or pecans)
(⅓ cup finely chopped dried cranberries or apricots)

Scrape the batter into the prepared pan. Bake until a toothpick inserted in the center comes out clean, about 50 minutes. Let cool for 10 minutes in the pan on a rack, then turn out onto the rack to cool completely.

BANANA BREAD COCKAIGNE

One 9 × 5-inch loaf

This is Marion Becker's banana bread, and we think it is just about perfect.

Preheat the oven to 350°F. Grease a 9 × 5-inch loaf pan.

Whisk together in a medium bowl:

1½ cups (190g) all-purpose flour
1½ teaspoons baking powder
½ teaspoon salt

Beat in a large bowl, with an electric mixer on medium speed, until creamy:

⅔ cup (130g) sugar
⅓ cup vegetable shortening (65g) or 6 tablespoons (3 oz or 85g) unsalted butter, softened
Finely grated zest of 1 lemon

Beat in:

2 large eggs, beaten
1 cup mashed ripe bananas (2 to 3)

Add the dry ingredients and stir just until combined. If desired, fold in:

(½ cup chopped toasted, 1005, walnuts)
(¼ cup finely chopped dried apricots or candied ginger)

Scrape the batter into the prepared pan. Bake until a toothpick inserted in the center comes out clean, about 1 hour. Let cool for 10 minutes in the pan on a rack, then turn out onto the rack to cool completely.

MARBLED BANANA BREAD

Prepare the batter for **Banana Bread Cockaigne, 626.** Divide the batter evenly between two bowls. Add **3 tablespoons (20g) unsweetened cocoa powder, sifted** and **½ cup chocolate chips or chunks** to one bowl, and fold in just until combined. Alternate dollops of plain and chocolate batter in the prepared loaf pan, and use a butter knife or spatula to swirl the batter. Bake as directed.

PUMPKIN BREAD

One 9 × 5-inch loaf

This loaf can be made with any cooked mashed winter squash or sweet potatoes.

Preheat the oven to 350°F. Grease a 9 × 5-inch loaf pan.

Whisk together in a medium bowl:

1½ cups (190g) all-purpose flour
1½ teaspoons ground cinnamon
1 teaspoon baking soda
1 teaspoon salt
1 teaspoon ground ginger
½ teaspoon grated or ground nutmeg
¼ teaspoon baking powder
¼ teaspoon ground cloves

Whisk together in a large bowl until smooth:

1⅓ cups sugar (265g) or 1 cup sugar (200g) plus ⅓ cup packed (75g) brown sugar
1¼ cups cooked or canned unsweetened pumpkin puree
¾ cup (155g) vegetable oil
2 large eggs
½ teaspoon vanilla

Add the flour mixture to the pumpkin mixture and stir just until smooth. If desired, fold in:

(½ cup coarsely chopped toasted, 1005, walnuts or pecans)
(½ cup chocolate chips or white chocolate chips)

Pour into the prepared pan and spread evenly. If desired, for a crunchy, sparkling top crust, sprinkle with:

(2 teaspoons sugar)

Bake until a toothpick inserted in the center comes out clean, about 1 hour. Let cool in the pan on a rack for 10 minutes, then turn out onto the rack to cool completely.

ZUCCHINI BREAD

One 9 × 5-inch loaf

For **Carrot Bread**, replace the grated zucchini with **1½ cups grated carrots.**

Preheat the oven to 350°F. Grease a 9 × 5-inch loaf pan.

Whisk together in a medium bowl:

1½ cups (190g) all-purpose flour
1 teaspoon baking soda
1 teaspoon baking powder
¼ teaspoon ground cinnamon

Blend well in a large bowl:

¾ cup (150g) sugar
2 large eggs, beaten
½ cup (105g) vegetable oil
1 teaspoon vanilla
½ teaspoon salt

Stir the flour mixture into the egg mixture. Add and blend in with a few swift strokes:

1 cup grated zucchini
(1½ cups chopped toasted, 1005, pecans or walnuts or chocolate chips)

Scrape the batter into the prepared pan. Bake until the bread pulls away from the sides of the pan, about 45 minutes. Let cool in the pan on a rack for 10 minutes, then turn out onto the rack to cool completely.

LEMON BROWN BUTTER LOAF

One 9 × 5-inch loaf

This rich, tender, lemon-scented quick bread almost has the texture of pound cake. The simple glaze adds a hit of fresh, bright lemon flavor.

Preheat the oven to 350°F. Grease a 9 × 5-inch loaf pan.

Whisk to combine in a large bowl:

1½ cups (190g) all-purpose flour
1 teaspoon baking powder
½ teaspoon salt
¼ teaspoon baking soda

Combine in a medium bowl or food processor:

1 cup (200g) sugar
Finely grated zest of 2 lemons

Pulse or mix until the zest is dispersed and the mixture is fragrant. Add:

2 sticks (8 oz or 225g) unsalted butter, browned, 558, and cooled for 15 minutes
4 large eggs
¼ cup (60g) buttermilk
2 tablespoons (30g) lemon juice
1 teaspoon vanilla

Mix or pulse until combined. Stir the wet ingredients into the dry ingredients until just combined. Scrape the batter into the prepared pan. Bake until golden brown and a toothpick inserted in the center of the loaf comes out clean, 50 to 55 minutes. Let cool in the pan on a rack for 10 minutes, then turn out onto the rack to cool completely. Prepare:

Quick Translucent Sugar Glaze II, 799, using lemon zest and juice

Drizzle the glaze over the cooled loaf.

BEER BREAD

One 9 × 5-inch loaf

Serve with hearty soups or stews and mild or strong cheeses. Slices are good toasted, or you can rewarm the whole loaf in the oven for a crisp outer crust. This bread keeps for two to three days.

Preheat the oven to 400°F. Grease a 9 × 5-inch loaf pan.

Whisk together thoroughly in a large bowl:

3 cups (375g) all-purpose flour
½ cup (50g) old-fashioned rolled oats
2 tablespoons sugar (25g) or honey (40g)
1 tablespoon baking powder
1 teaspoon salt

Add:

1½ cups (one 12-ounce bottle) light or dark beer, cold or at room temperature, but not flat
2 tablespoons unsalted butter (30g), melted, or olive oil (25g)

Fold just until the dry ingredients are moistened. Scrape the batter into the prepared pan and spread evenly. Bake until a toothpick inserted in the center and all the way to the bottom of the pan comes out clean, 35 to 40 minutes. Let cool in the pan on a rack for 10 minutes, then turn out onto the rack to cool completely.

BEER, CHEESE, AND SCALLION BREAD

Prepare **Beer Bread, 627,** adding to the flour mixture **½ cup finely diced sharp Cheddar** or **aged Monterey Jack, ¼ cup sliced green onions,** and **(2 teaspoons caraway seeds).**

ROSEMARY-OLIVE BREAD

One 9 × 5-inch loaf

This savory quick bread is just the thing with a bowl of soup.

Position a rack in the lower third of the oven. Preheat the oven to 350°F. Grease a 9 × 5-inch loaf pan.

Whisk together in a large bowl:

1½ cups (190g) all-purpose flour
¾ cup (100g) whole wheat flour
2½ teaspoons baking powder
2 teaspoons chopped rosemary
½ teaspoon salt

Whisk together in a large bowl:

1 cup (235g) milk
2 large eggs
¼ cup (50g) olive oil

Add the milk mixture to the flour mixture and stir until most of the flour is moistened. Stir in:

⅓ cup finely chopped toasted, 1005, walnuts
⅓ cup chopped pitted Kalamata olives

Stir just until the olives and nuts are evenly distributed. The batter will be stiff. Scrape the batter into the pan and smooth the top. Bake until a toothpick inserted in the center comes out clean, 40 to 45 minutes. Let cool in the pan on a rack for 10 minutes, then turn out onto the rack to cool completely.

IRISH SODA BREAD

One 8-inch round loaf or 9 × 5-inch loaf

When this batter is made with the greater amount of sugar and buttermilk and baked in a loaf pan, it becomes a fine crusty tea bread that stays moist for three to four days.

Preheat the oven to 375°F for a round loaf, 350°F for a tea bread. Grease a large baking sheet or a 9 × 5-inch loaf pan.

Whisk together thoroughly in a large bowl:

2 cups (250g) all-purpose flour
2 tablespoons (25g) sugar, or ⅓ cup (65g) for the tea bread
1 teaspoon baking powder
½ teaspoon baking soda
½ teaspoon salt

Stir in:

1 cup raisins
(2 teaspoons caraway seeds)

Whisk together in another bowl:

⅔ cup (160g) buttermilk, or 1 cup (245g) for the tea bread
1 large egg
2 tablespoons (30g) butter, melted

Add the buttermilk mixture to the flour mixture and stir just until the dry ingredients are moistened. The batter will be stiff but sticky. Scrape the batter onto the baking sheet in a mound 6 to 7 inches in diameter, or scrape it into the loaf pan and spread evenly. For the round loaf, use a sharp knife to slash a large "X" about ½ inch deep on top of the batter. Bake until golden brown and a toothpick inserted in the center comes out clean, 25 to 30 minutes for the round loaf, 45 to 50 minutes for the tea bread. Transfer the round loaf to a rack to cool completely before serving. Or, for the tea bread, let cool in the pan on a rack for 10 minutes, then turn out onto the rack to cool completely.

POPPY SEED LOAF

Position a rack in the lower third of the oven. Preheat the oven to 350°F. Grease a 9 × 5-inch loaf pan. Prepare **Irish Soda Bread, above,** using the greater amount of sugar and buttermilk. Substitute **2 tablespoons poppy seeds** for the raisins and caraway seeds. Scrape the batter into the pan and bake as above, but for 35 to 40 minutes.

BROWN BREAD

2 round or cylindrical loaves

Grease two 4-cup molds, such as pudding molds, small heatproof bowls, or 28-ounce cans. Have ready a pot or Dutch oven large enough to hold both molds. Place a rack, trivet, or folded towel in the pot. Bring a separate large pot of water to a boil while you prepare the batter.

Whisk together thoroughly in a large bowl:

1 cup (160g) fine yellow cornmeal
1 cup (120g) dark rye flour
1 cup (130g) whole wheat flour
2 teaspoons baking soda
1 teaspoon salt

Whisk together in another bowl:

2 cups (485g) buttermilk
1 cup raisins or currants
¾ cup (255g) molasses

Add the buttermilk mixture to the flour mixture and stir until well blended. Divide the batter between the molds. If the pudding molds have lids and clips, grease the inside of the lids and secure the clips. Otherwise, cover the molds with a double thickness of greased foil, greased side down, and secure tightly with kitchen string.

Set the molds in the prepared pot. Pour boiling water into the pot until it reaches halfway up the sides of the molds. Cover the pot and set it over high heat. When the water comes back to a boil, adjust the heat so that the water simmers gently. Steam until a toothpick inserted in the center comes out clean and the breads pull away from the sides of the molds, about 1 hour, replenishing the water in the steamer as necessary.

Transfer the molds to a rack, uncover the breads, and let cool for about 20 minutes before unmolding. If the breads were steamed in cans and they prove difficult to unmold, remove the bottom of the can with a can opener and push the breads out. Serve warm, or let cool completely on the rack before wrapping to store. To slice without crumbling, use a tough string or unflavored dental floss and a sawing motion.

QUICK COFFEE CAKE

One 9-inch square coffee cake

Perfect for a Sunday brunch.

Preheat the oven to 375°F. Grease a 9-inch square baking pan and line with parchment paper so the parchment comes above the rim of the pan on 2 opposite sides.

Whisk together in a medium bowl:

1½ cups sifted (180g) all-purpose flour
2 teaspoons baking powder
½ teaspoon salt

Beat in a large bowl or stand mixer fitted with the paddle attachment until light and fluffy:

4 tablespoons (2 oz or 55g) unsalted butter, softened
½ cup (100g) sugar

Beat in:

Finely grated zest of 1 lemon or orange
½ teaspoon vanilla

Beat in:

1 large egg

Beat in the flour mixture in 2 additions, alternating with:

⅔ cup (155g) milk

Stir or mix until smooth. Spread the batter in the prepared pan. If desired, toss together and sprinkle over the batter:

(1¼ cups berries, pitted cherries, fresh or frozen cranberries, or diced apples)
(⅓ cup sugar)

Then sprinkle with:

Streusel, 800

Bake until a toothpick inserted in the center of the cake comes out clean or with moist crumbs attached, about 25 minutes if covered with streusel alone, 25 to 30 minutes if covered with fruit and streusel. Let cool in the pan on a rack.

COFFEE CAKE WITH MARBLED FILLING

1 large ring

Grease an 8- to 10-cup fluted tube or Bundt pan. Prepare:

Chocolate Fruit Filling, 804

Prepare the batter for:

Quick Coffee Cake, above

Spoon one-quarter of the batter into the pan and spread evenly. Sprinkle with half of the filling. Top with half of the remaining batter and sprinkle with the remaining filling. Top with the remaining batter. Marble the cake and filling with a small spoon, scooping batter from the bottom of the pan up to the top 5 or 6 times and moving around the tube with each scoop. Spread the surface of the batter evenly. Bake until a toothpick inserted in the center comes out clean, 45 to 50 minutes. Let cool in the pan on a rack for 10 minutes. Rotate and tap the pan until the cake is loosened on all sides, then invert the cake onto the rack to cool. Serve warm or at room temperature, sprinkled with:

Powdered sugar

DELUXE CRUMB CAKE

One 10-inch cake

This is a moist coffee cake with a crumbly top. For a raspberry variation, spread ½ **cup seedless raspberry jam** over the batter before sprinkling the streusel on top.

Have all ingredients at room temperature, about 70°F. Preheat the oven to 350°F. Generously grease the bottom and lightly grease the sides of a 10-inch springform pan. Line the bottom with a round of parchment.

Whisk together in a large bowl until well blended:

2 cups (250g) all-purpose flour
1 cup plus 2 tablespoons (225g) sugar
1 teaspoon salt

Add and cut in with a pastry blender or your fingers until the mixture resembles coarse crumbs:

10 tablespoons (5 oz or 140g) unsalted butter

Measure out 1 cup of the crumbs and set aside for the streusel. To the mixture remaining in the large bowl, add and whisk thoroughly:

1 teaspoon baking powder
½ teaspoon baking soda

Stir in until smooth:

¾ cup buttermilk (185g) or plain yogurt (180g)
1 large egg
1 teaspoon vanilla
(1 teaspoon almond extract, if using almonds in the streusel topping)

Scrape the batter into the prepared pan and smooth the top. For the streusel topping, add to the small bowl of reserved crumbs:

¾ cup walnuts, pecans, or almonds, toasted, 1005, and finely chopped
½ cup packed brown sugar
1 egg yolk
1 teaspoon ground cinnamon

Toss with a fork until blended, then sprinkle the streusel over the batter. Bake until the center of the cake is firm, 50 to 65 minutes. Let cool in the pan on a rack for 10 minutes. Slide a slim knife around the cake to release it from the pan. Remove the pan sides. Let cool on the rack at least 30 minutes before serving.

DELUXE COCONUT CHOCOLATE CHIP COFFEE CAKE

Prepare **Deluxe Crumb Cake, above,** stirring into the batter **1 cup mini chocolate chips.** For the streusel topping, reduce the nuts to ½ cup, omit the cinnamon, and add **1 cup lightly packed flaked sweetened or unsweetened coconut.**

ABOUT CORN BREADS

Anyone who grew up on Southern corn bread hankers for a golden brown crust, crunchy edges, and a light but slightly gritty bite. This style of corn bread is best made with stone-ground cornmeal and baked in a preheated cast-iron pan to create a thick, burnished crust. Northern-style corn bread tends to be sweeter, paler, thicker, and cakier.

Whether you bake corn muffins, corn sticks, or corn bread, you can vary the cornmeal and flour proportions to your own taste. See Corn Bread, Corn Muffins, or Corn Sticks, below, for a fairly light corn bread. For the stalwart corn bread lover, Southern Corn Bread, below, is the way to go. ➤ Coarse-ground cornmeal is too gritty for corn bread; opt for medium- or fine-grind cornmeal. As far as sweeteners go, we typically skip the sugar, but just a touch can enhance the flavor of the cornmeal. You can also substitute oil, bacon grease, or other fats for the butter in most corn bread recipes. For Johnnycakes, see 641.

▲ To make corn bread at high altitudes, see About Quick Breads and Coffee Cakes, 625.

ADDITIONS TO CORN BREAD

3 to 4 drained and finely chopped chipotle peppers in adobo
1 to 2 jalapeño peppers, seeded and minced
Up to one 4-ounce can mild green chile peppers, drained and diced
1 poblano pepper, roasted, 262, peeled, seeded, and diced
½ cup diced drained oil-packed sun-dried tomatoes
Up to 1 cup fresh or frozen corn kernels
Up to 1 cup (4 ounces) grated Cheddar or Monterey Jack
1 medium onion, chopped and sautéed, 255
½ cup crumbled crisp bacon
½ cup sunflower seeds or roasted pumpkin seeds

CORN BREAD, CORN MUFFINS, OR CORN STICKS

One 8-inch square or 10-inch round bread, about fifteen 2-inch muffins, or about 20 sticks

Have all ingredients at room temperature, about 70°F. Preheat the oven to 425°F. Grease an 8-inch square pan, a 9- or 10-inch ovenproof skillet (such as cast iron), 2 muffin tins, or 3 corn stick pans (or bake the corn sticks in batches) with butter, oil, or bacon fat. Place in the oven until sizzling hot.

Whisk together in a large bowl:

1¼ cups (200g) fine yellow or white cornmeal, preferably stone-ground
¾ cup (95g) all-purpose flour
1 to 4 tablespoons (10 to 50g) sugar, to taste
2½ teaspoons baking powder
¾ teaspoon salt

Add:

1 cup (235g) milk
2 large eggs, beaten
3 tablespoons bacon fat, vegetable oil (40g), or butter (45g), melted

Combine with a few rapid strokes. Scrape the batter into the hot pan(s). Bake until nicely browned, about 12 minutes for corn sticks, 15 to 18 minutes for corn bread or muffins. Serve immediately.

BUCKWHEAT CORN BREAD

One 8-inch square bread

Prepare **Corn Bread, above,** substituting for ½ **cup of the cornmeal** ½ **cup (60g) buckwheat flour** and adding (½ **cup sunflower seeds, toasted, 1027**). Bake in an 8-inch square pan.

SOUTHERN CORN BREAD

One 9-inch round bread

Southern corn bread is traditionally made with white cornmeal, buttermilk, eggs, leavening, and salt—and little, if any, flour or sugar. Some cooks stir in a tablespoon of bacon fat to enrich the batter. The resulting bread is moist and crusty. Rush this bread from oven to table. The batter may be baked in a muffin or corn stick pan, adjusting the baking time accordingly (see Corn Bread, Corn Muffins, or Corn Sticks, above).

Preheat the oven to 450°F. Place a 9-inch heavy ovenproof skillet in the oven as it preheats.

Whisk together thoroughly in a large bowl:

1¾ cups (280g) fine cornmeal, preferably stone-ground
(1 tablespoon [10g] sugar)
1 teaspoon baking powder
1 teaspoon baking soda
1 teaspoon salt

Whisk together in another bowl:

1½ cups (365g) buttermilk
2 large eggs

Add the buttermilk mixture to the cornmeal mixture and whisk just until blended. Take the skillet out of the oven and add to it:

1 tablespoon bacon fat, lard, oil, or vegetable shortening

Swirl to coat the skillet with the fat and pour in the batter all at once. Bake until the top is browned and the center feels firm when pressed, 20 to 25 minutes. Serve immediately from the skillet, cut into wedges or squares, along with:

Butter

Leftovers, though dry, are nice enough if wrapped in foil and rewarmed in a low oven. Megan likes to crumble leftover corn bread into a tall glass and pour buttermilk over it. Think of it as Southern breakfast cereal.

CRACKLING CORN BREAD

One 9- or 10-inch round bread

Try eating just one piece.

Preheat the oven to 450°F.

Rinse, then pat dry:

4 ounces fatty salt pork or slab bacon

Slice off and discard the rind, if present, then cut the pork into ¼-inch dice. (If the pork is too soft to cut easily, freeze it for 30 minutes.) Place in a 9- or 10-inch heavy ovenproof skillet (preferably cast iron) and cook over medium heat until the fat is rendered and the cracklings are very browned and crisp. Remove from the heat.

Prepare the batter for:

Corn Bread, Corn Muffins, or Corn Sticks, 630, or Southern Corn Bread, 630

If using the Corn Bread, Corn Muffins, or Corn Sticks recipe, omit the fat. Fold in the cracklings and all but 1 tablespoon of the fat from the skillet. Set the skillet over high heat until the fat smokes. Remove from the heat and pour in the batter all at once. Transfer to the oven and bake until a toothpick inserted in the center comes out clean, 18 to 22 minutes. Serve at once, either plain or with:

(Jam or sorghum syrup)

MEGAN'S SOUTHERN CORN BREAD

One 9-inch round bread

The soaking process is what makes this corn bread special, so don't be tempted to skip it. It makes for an incredibly moist crumb and softens the coarser cornmeal. If you want corn bread for dinner, simply start soaking the cornmeal in the morning before you leave for work (a process that takes 5 minutes), then finish the corn bread when you get home.

Stir together in a small bowl:

1¼ cups (200g) fine yellow or white cornmeal, preferably stone-ground
½ cup (75g) medium-grind cornmeal or polenta

Pour over the cornmeal:

1½ cups (355g) boiling water

Stir to make sure all the cornmeal is wet, then cover and let soak for 4 to 12 hours.

Preheat the oven to 450°F with a 9-inch cast-iron skillet inside. Add to the soaked cornmeal and stir to incorporate:

1 teaspoon baking powder
1 teaspoon baking soda
1 teaspoon salt

Stir in:

2 large eggs
½ to ¾ cup (120 to 185g) buttermilk

Use the larger amount of buttermilk if the batter seems too thick after adding ½ cup. The batter should be fairly loose, almost like pancake batter. Remove the hot skillet from the oven and add:

1 tablespoon bacon fat, lard, or vegetable oil

Swirl the fat around in the skillet to coat it, then pour in the batter. Be careful—it will sizzle dramatically. Return the skillet to the oven and bake until deep golden brown and firm, 20 to 25 minutes. Turn the corn bread out onto a plate and serve immediately.

CORN ZEPHYRS COCKAIGNE

About thirty 2½-inch puffs

These little corn cakes don't look like much, but they are strangely addictive. They may also be cooked in a little fat in a skillet on the stovetop until golden.

Combine in a large saucepan:

1 cup (160g) fine cornmeal, preferably stone-ground white
1 tablespoon (10g) lard or vegetable shortening
1 teaspoon salt

Pour over:

4 cups (945g) boiling water

Cook over low heat for 30 minutes, stirring frequently. Remove from the heat and lightly butter the top to keep it from crusting. Cool to room temperature.

Preheat the oven to 350°F. Grease a large baking sheet.

Beat the cornmeal mixture well. In a large bowl beat until stiff but not dry, 978:

4 large egg whites

Fold them lightly into the cornmeal mixture. Drop the batter by the tablespoon onto the baking sheet. Bake until firm, about 30 minutes.

ABOUT SPOON BREAD

This Southern specialty has a texture between corn bread and custard that is somewhat like Yorkshire Pudding, 634 (albeit without as dramatic a puff). As the name implies, these breads are soft enough to eat with a spoon, although some speculate that the name comes from suppawn, an indigenous dish that was similar to cornmeal mush. Any of the Additions to Corn Bread, 630, may be added to spoon breads as well, as may leftover cooked grains. Also see Cheesy Millet Spoon Bread with Chiles, 326.

CRUSTY SOFT-CENTER SPOON BREAD

6 servings

Using stone-ground cornmeal will result in a more soufflé-like texture.

Preheat the oven to 375°F.

Whisk together in a large bowl:

¾ cup (120g) fine yellow cornmeal, preferably stone-ground
¼ cup (30g) all-purpose flour
1 tablespoon (10g) sugar
1 teaspoon salt
1 teaspoon baking powder

Stir in until well blended:

1 cup (235g) milk
1 large egg

Melt in an 8-inch square baking dish in the oven:

2 tablespoons butter

Swirl the butter in the dish to coat the inside, then pour the butter into the batter and stir to combine. Pour the batter into the hot dish, then pour over the top:

½ cup (120g) milk

Bake until good and crusty on top, about 45 minutes.

BUTTERMILK SPOON BREAD

4 servings

Preheat the oven to 350°F.

Place in a large bowl:

1 cup (160g) fine white cornmeal, preferably stone-ground

Pour over:

1½ cups (355g) boiling water

Mix well, and cool slightly. Beat well in a medium bowl:

1 cup (245g) buttermilk
1 large egg
1 tablespoon (15g) butter, melted

1 teaspoon baking soda
¾ teaspoon salt

Add the buttermilk mixture to the cornmeal mixture and mix well. Heat a greased 8-inch square baking dish in the oven until hot. Pour in the batter and bake until lightly puffed and set, 30 to 40 minutes. If you wish to keep the top soft, add from time to time, while the bread is baking, a few tablespoons of milk, using in all:

(½ cup milk or half-and-half)

If you opt for adding the milk or half-and-half, it will take the spoon bread longer to bake, about 1 hour.

ABOUT MUFFINS

Muffin batters are easily made. ➤ To mix, add the liquid ingredients to the dry ones in a few swift strokes. This will leave some lumps. Overmixed batter results in muffins that are coarse and full of tunnels. Good muffins should be rounded on top, with the grain of the muffin uniform and the crumb moist. A weary muffin peak is caused by oven heat that is too low, and a wobbly peaked, asymmetrical shape is caused by uneven oven heat. This is remedied by rotating the muffin tin halfway through baking. Sometimes muffins on the outside edges of the pan finish baking before the innermost muffins are done. To avoid overbaking, remove the fully cooked muffins from the tin (easier if paper liners were used), and return the tin to the oven to finish baking the stragglers.

Fill muffin cups two-thirds to three-quarters full of batter. Any muffin recipe can be used to make miniature or jumbo muffins. Batter for 12 standard muffins will make 24 to 32 miniature muffins or 6 to 8 jumbo muffins. ➤ Mini muffins will take 10 to 12 minutes to bake; ➤ jumbo muffins require 22 to 25 minutes. In addition to the recipes in this section, any quick bread, coffee cake, or corn bread batter can be baked in a muffin tin.

The richer and sweeter the muffin, the longer it will stay moist. Muffins that contain only 4 tablespoons or less butter or oil are best consumed freshly baked or as soon as possible, for they go stale quickly. When adding berries to muffins, opt for frozen ones if possible. They are easier to mix in and less likely to turn the batter an unappetizing color.

Most muffin batters can be mixed, spooned into the pan, covered, and refrigerated overnight, then baked in the morning. Muffins can also be frozen either before or after baking. To freeze before baking, simply scoop the batter into paper-lined muffin tins and freeze. Transfer the frozen muffins to a plastic freezer bag, with a note to remind you of the oven temperature and baking time called for in the recipe. To bake, plop the still-frozen muffins into a muffin tin and bake for about 5 minutes longer than specified in the recipe, to compensate for the cold batter. To freeze baked muffins, cool thoroughly, then bag and freeze. To reheat, place the frozen muffins on a baking sheet in a 350°F oven or in a toaster oven for 5 to 10 minutes, until hot. Microwave heating is also effective, but you will not have a crisp crust or crunchy edges.

ADDITIONS TO MUFFINS

Have these additions ready before beginning and fold them into the batter at the end of mixing. For muffins with savory additions, use only 2 tablespoons sugar in the basic recipe for Muffins, below. For more ideas, see Additions to Yeast Doughs, 593, and Additions to Corn Bread, 630.

Use any of the following, alone or in combination:

Up to 1½ cups fresh or frozen chopped fruit or berries
¼ to ½ cup chopped toasted, 1005, nuts, dried apricots, prunes, dates, or figs
1 cup coarsely chopped fresh cranberries plus 2 teaspoons finely grated orange zest
1 cup chopped roasted pears, 171, and ½ cup chopped toasted, 1005, walnuts
½ cup chopped dark chocolate and the finely grated zest of 1 orange
½ cup mashed ripe bananas, ½ cup toasted, 973, coconut flakes, and 1 tablespoon dark rum
½ cup very well drained canned crushed pineapple
6 to 8 slices bacon, cooked until crisp and crumbled
1½ cups grated sharp Cheddar (6 ounces) and ¼ cup chopped chives

MUFFINS

12 muffins

With this recipe, you can create myriad muffins by adding any of the Additions to Muffins, above. You can substitute up to 1 cup (130g) whole wheat flour or whole wheat pastry flour for an equal measure of all-purpose flour. Note that the liquid ingredient is your choice, from low-fat milk to cream. The flexible amount of butter or oil allows for control of the richness with the following advice: Muffins intended to be eaten warm from the oven are perfectly delicious made with ¼ cup butter or oil. If muffins must be baked hours before they will be consumed, or even the day before, use ½ cup butter or oil.

Position a rack in the center of the oven. Preheat the oven to 400°F. Grease a standard 12-muffin tin or line with paper liners.

Whisk together thoroughly in a large bowl:

2 cups (250g) all-purpose flour
1 tablespoon baking powder
½ teaspoon salt
(¼ teaspoon grated or ground nutmeg)

Whisk together in another bowl:

1 cup milk (235g) or cream (230g)
2 large eggs
⅔ cup sugar (130g) or packed light brown sugar (155g)
4 to 8 tablespoons (2 to 4 oz or 55 to 115g) unsalted butter, melted, or ¼ to ½ cup (50 to 105g) vegetable oil
1 teaspoon vanilla

Add the milk mixture to the flour mixture and mix together with a few light strokes just until the dry ingredients are moistened. The batter will not be smooth. Divide the batter among the muffin cups. If desired, top the muffins with:

(Streusel, 800)

Bake until a toothpick inserted in 1 or 2 of the muffins comes out clean, about 17 minutes (or longer for variations with fruit). Let cool for 2 to 3 minutes in the pan. If not serving hot, transfer the muffins to a wire rack to cool. Serve as soon as possible, preferably within a few hours of baking.

SOUR CREAM MUFFINS

Prepare **Muffins, 632,** using 4 tablespoons butter, adding **½ teaspoon baking soda** to the flour mixture, and substituting **1 cup sour cream (230g), buttermilk (245g), or plain yogurt (240g)** for the milk or cream.

LEMON–POPPY SEED MUFFINS

Prepare **Muffins, 632,** adding **1½ tablespoons poppy seeds** to the flour mixture and the **finely grated zest of 1 lemon** to the milk mixture.

PUMPKIN OR SWEET POTATO MUFFINS

16 muffins

Prepare **Muffins, 632,** adding **1 teaspoon ground cinnamon** and **1 teaspoon grated or ground nutmeg** to the flour mixture. Add **⅓ cup (65g) additional sugar** and **1 cup cooked or canned unsweetened pumpkin puree** or **1 cup cold mashed sweet potatoes** to the milk mixture. If desired, stir **(1 cup chopped toasted, 1005, pecans)** or **(1 cup white chocolate chips)** into the batter.

BLUEBERRY MUFFINS

Prepare **Muffins, 632,** or **Corn Bread, 630,** using ½ cup (100g) sugar and folding into the batter **1½ cups fresh or frozen blueberries.** If desired, also add the **(finely grated zest of 1 lemon).**

DOUBLE-CHOCOLATE MUFFINS

Prepare **Muffins, 632,** reducing the flour to 1½ cups (190g) and adding **½ cup (40g) unsweetened cocoa powder, sifted.** Use 1 stick (4 oz or 115g) unsalted butter, melted, and fold **1 cup chocolate chips or chunks** into the batter.

HERB AND ROASTED GARLIC MUFFINS

Prepare **Southern Corn Bread, 630,** folding into the batter **3 tablespoons chopped chives, tarragon, or dill,** or **1 tablespoon minced rosemary,** and **the mashed cloves from 1 head Roasted Garlic I, 241,** plus the **finely grated zest of 1 lemon.**

BRAN MUFFINS

16 muffins

Preheat the oven to 350°F. Grease 16 cups of two standard muffin tins or line with paper liners.

Whisk together in a large bowl:

- **2 cups all-purpose (250g) or whole wheat flour (260g)**
- **1½ cups oat bran (160g) or wheat bran (85g)**
- **2 tablespoons (25g) sugar**
- **(Finely grated zest of 1 orange)**
- **1¼ teaspoons baking soda**
- **¼ teaspoon salt**

Beat in another bowl:

- **2 cups (485g) buttermilk**
- **½ cup (170g) molasses**
- **1 large egg**
- **2 to 4 tablespoons (30 to 55g) butter, melted**

Add the buttermilk mixture to the flour mixture and combine with a few swift strokes. Fold in, before the dry ingredients are entirely moist:

- **1 cup chopped toasted, 1005, walnuts or pecans**
- **½ cup raisins or chopped dates**

Divide the batter among the muffin cups. Bake until a toothpick inserted in 1 or 2 of the muffins comes out clean, about 25 minutes. Let cool for 2 to 3 minutes in the pans. If not serving hot, transfer the muffins to a wire rack to cool. Serve within a few hours of baking.

SUNRISE MUFFINS

12 muffins

Loaded with shredded carrots and apple, nuts, and dried fruit, these muffins are downright wholesome. Fortunately, they make up for their healthfulness by being undeniably tasty.

Preheat the oven to 350°F. Grease a standard 12-muffin tin or line with paper liners.

Whisk together thoroughly in a large bowl:

- **1 cup whole wheat (130g) or spelt flour (125g)**
- **1 cup all-purpose flour (125g), almond meal or almond flour (90g), or oat flour (105g)**
- **1½ teaspoons ground cinnamon**
- **2 teaspoons baking soda**
- **½ teaspoon salt**

Whisk together in a medium bowl:

- **3 large eggs**
- **½ cup vegetable oil (105g) or coconut oil (115g), melted**
- **½ cup (155g) maple syrup or ⅓ cup (110g) honey**
- **(Finely grated zest of 1 orange)**
- **2 teaspoons vanilla**

Stir into the wet ingredients:

- **1 cup grated carrot (about 3 medium)**
- **1 cup grated cored apple (about 1 large)**
- **½ cup walnuts or pecans, toasted, 1005, and coarsely chopped**
- **½ cup raisins, golden raisins, or other dried fruit**
- **(½ cup bittersweet chocolate chips or chopped dark chocolate)**

Stir the wet ingredients into the flour mixture just until combined. Divide the batter among the muffin cups, filling them almost to the brim. Bake until golden brown and a toothpick inserted in 1 or 2 of the muffins comes out clean, 20 to 25 minutes. Let cool in the pan for 10 minutes, then transfer the muffins to a wire rack to cool completely.

APPLE-WALNUT MUFFINS

12 muffins

Preheat the oven to 400°F. Grease a standard 12-muffin tin or line with paper liners.

Whisk together thoroughly in a medium bowl:

- **1½ cups (190g) all-purpose flour**
- **2 teaspoons baking powder**
- **1 teaspoon baking soda**
- **¼ teaspoon salt**
- **1½ teaspoons ground cinnamon**

Combine in a large bowl and let stand for 10 minutes:

- **1½ packed cups coarsely grated or finely chopped cored apples or pears (about 2 medium)**
- **¾ cup (150g) sugar**

Stir into the fruit mixture:

2 large eggs, lightly beaten
5 tablespoons (70g) butter, melted
½ cup chopped toasted, 1005, walnuts

Add the flour mixture and fold just until the dry ingredients are moistened. The batter will not be smooth. Divide the batter among the muffin cups. Bake until a toothpick inserted in 1 or 2 of the muffins comes out clean, 14 to 16 minutes. Let cool for 2 to 3 minutes in the pan. If not serving hot, transfer the muffins to a wire rack to cool. Serve as soon as possible, preferably the day they are baked.

BANANA MUFFINS

12 muffins

Preheat the oven to 350°F. Grease a standard 12-muffin tin or line with paper liners. Prepare the batter for **Banana Bread Cockaigne, 626.** Divide the batter among the muffin cups and bake until a toothpick inserted in 1 or 2 of the muffins comes out clean, 15 to 20 minutes. Let cool for 2 to 3 minutes in the pan before transferring to a wire rack.

POPOVERS

8 large or 12 medium popovers

Have all ingredients at room temperature, about 70°F. Preheat the oven to 450°F. Grease a popover tin, a standard 12-muffin tin, or eight 6-ounce custard cups. If using custard cups, grease them lightly and, depending on what you are serving with the popovers, dust with sugar, flour, or grated Parmesan. This will give the batter something to cling to.

Beat together in a medium bowl just until smooth:

1 cup (235g) milk
1 tablespoon (15g) butter, melted
1 cup (125g) all-purpose flour
¼ teaspoon salt

Beat in one at a time, but do not overbeat:

2 large eggs, beaten

The batter should be no heavier than whipping cream. Fill the popover tin, muffin cups, or custard cups no more than three-quarters full. Don't overload—too much batter in the pans will give the popovers a muffinlike texture. ➤ Bake at once. After 15 minutes, reduce the heat ➤ without peeping, to 350°F and bake about 20 minutes longer. To test for doneness, remove a popover and check to be sure the side walls are firm. If not cooked long enough, the popovers will collapse. After baking, you may want to insert a sharp paring knife gently into the popovers to allow the steam to escape. Serve immediately.

CHEESE POPOVERS

Combine in a bowl **½ cup (2 ounces) grated sharp Cheddar or Parmesan, ¼ teaspoon black pepper,** and **⅛ teaspoon cayenne pepper.** Prepare the batter for **Popovers, above.** Pour about 1 tablespoon batter into each cup and divide the cheese among the cups. Add the remaining batter. Bake as directed.

YORKSHIRE PUDDING

6 servings

It was customary to cook this old and delicious dish in the pan with the roast, letting the drippings fall upon it. As many of us now cook roast beef in a low oven and no longer have extravagant drippings, we prepare the pudding separately in the hot oven required to puff it up and brown it quickly. Serve it from the dish in which it was baked, cut into squares. It was traditionally served before the meat, but we prefer to substitute the pudding for the usual starch served with the main course.

Have all ingredients at room temperature, about 70°F. Preheat the oven to 400°F.

Sift into a bowl:

¾ cup plus 2 tablespoons (110g) all-purpose flour
½ teaspoon salt

Make a well in the center and pour in:

½ cup (120g) milk

Stir in the milk. Beat in:

2 large eggs, beaten

Add:

½ cup (120g) water

Beat the batter until large bubbles rise to the surface. (The batter can be covered and refrigerated for 1 hour, then beaten again before cooking.) Pour into an 11 × 7-inch baking dish or 6 regular muffin cups:

¼ inch hot beef drippings or melted butter

Heat the dish or pan in the oven until hot. Pour in the batter and bake for 20 minutes. Reduce the oven temperature to 350°F and bake until puffed and golden brown, 10 to 15 minutes longer. Serve immediately.

ABOUT BISCUITS AND SCONES

Biscuits are small, savory quick breads. Sweetened biscuits made to be served as part of a dessert are sometimes called shortcakes. Scones are sweet, rich biscuits that are usually made with cream as well as (or instead of) butter. Eggs add flavor, rich color, and a slightly cakey texture. Scones are often cut into triangles, although round, biscuit-like scones are not uncommon.

If you approach biscuit making with an easygoing attitude, light, fluffy, golden biscuits are sure to follow. If there is a single rule by which to make all biscuits and scones, it is "do not worry." The less the dough is handled and fussed over, the better. All biscuits and scones can be made successfully with all-purpose flour, but the secret to truly feather-light biscuits is low-protein flour. It can be hard to find these flours outside the South, but pastry flour is a good stand-in, and can often be found in the bulk section of large supermarkets.

CUTTING IN THE FAT

When a recipe directs you to "cut in" butter or another fat, this can be accomplished in a few different ways.

To cut fat into a flour mixture for biscuits or scones, first be sure the fat is very cold. Butter may be used straight from the refrigerator; shortening and lard are best when frozen for 20 minutes. Cut the fat into small pieces or cubes with a knife (you may also freeze the fat and grate it on the large holes of a cheese grater). Toss the fat with the flour mixture, then use your hands, a pastry blender, or stand mixer fitted with the paddle attachment to mix and "cut" the fat into smaller pieces. Mixing until the fat resembles coarse crumbs will result in soft, fluffy biscuits; leaving the fat in larger, flattened chunks (this is easiest if you use your hands) results in flaky biscuits. When the liquid is added, only mix it in enough to moisten all the flour, not enough to bring it fully together into a solid mass. At this point, transfer the rough dough to a lightly floured work surface and press the dough together into an irregular ball.

To cut fat into a flour mixture for biscuits or scones with a food processor, cut the fat into small pieces or cubes and freeze until hard, about 20 minutes. Pulse the dry ingredients in the food processor briefly. Add the frozen fat cubes. For scones or for biscuits with a flaky, layered structure, pulse just until the largest butter pieces are the size of peas and the smallest resemble bread crumbs. For fluffy biscuits, pulse until all the pieces of fat are the size of bread crumbs. Add the liquid and pulse just until the dough barely comes together, not longer. Do not allow the butter to form a blended paste with the flour. Turn the dough out onto a lightly floured work surface and press it together with your hands, then continue as directed.

ROLLING OUT AND CUTTING THE DOUGH

Typically, scones are not rolled out; see individual recipes for instructions on shaping. When rolling out biscuit dough, don't roll it too flat; we find a 3/4- to 1-inch thickness perfect for tall, golden biscuits. Some prefer thinner biscuits, which is fine, but be careful not to overbake them, as thin biscuits quickly turn into pucks in the oven.

➤ For extra flaky biscuits, borrow a technique usually associated with laminated doughs like croissant dough: Once the biscuit dough is slightly flattened on your work surface, fold it in thirds (like a business letter). Then, rotate the dough 90 degrees and repeat this folding once more before rolling out the dough and cutting it.

To cut the dough into rounds, use a biscuit cutter that has been dipped in flour; ➤ do not twist the cutter (this inhibits the biscuits' rise). There are shapes other than the traditional round biscuits: We like square and rectangular shapes because they leave no dough scraps. Dough scraps may be pressed together (again, do not knead), re-rolled, and cut out once. Any further gathering and re-rolling will result in denser and tougher biscuits, although we often bake all the scraps and snack on them regardless.

If desired, you may fill rolled biscuits before baking: Roll the dough into a square or rectangle 1/4 inch thick. Cut in half and spread or sprinkle one half with any flavorful sweet or savory mixture, such as jam or preserves, Streusel, 800, any coffee cake filling, 803–4, nuts, dried fruit, chutney, Pesto, 586, Tapenade, 54, goat cheese, or herbs. Top with the second half of the dough, then cut and bake. For a simpler approach, you can make depressions in the center of cut biscuits with your fingers—press as deeply as you can without pushing through the dough—and fill the nooks with jam or any of the moist fillings listed above.

For a golden brown finish, brush the tops of biscuits or scones with milk or butter. Scones and sweet biscuits may be sprinkled with sugar or turbinado sugar for a sparkling, crunchy top crust. Place biscuits 1 inch apart if you like them crusty all over, close together if not. We have had great success baking biscuits on a preheated baking stone or skillet. This approach not only promotes high-rise biscuits, but it also crisps and browns the bottoms nicely. Otherwise, a simple baking dish or baking sheet works perfectly well.

▲ At high altitude, baking powder biscuits should require no adjustment of the leavening.

ADDITIONS TO BISCUITS AND SCONES

Additions should be mixed in after cutting in the butter and before adding the liquid. Adding them after the dough comes together can result in overkneading, which will toughen the dough.

Incorporate any of the following alone or in combination:

Up to 6 slices bacon, cooked until crisp and crumbled
1/2 cup chopped sautéed, 255, or caramelized, 255, onion
Up to 1/3 cup finely chopped ham or prosciutto
Up to 1/3 cup finely chopped, drained oil-packed sun-dried tomatoes
1/4 cup finely chopped parsley, dill, or chives
2 tablespoons minced rosemary, thyme, or sage
Up to 1/2 cup grated Parmesan or crumbled Roquefort; reduce the salt slightly
Up to 3/4 cup finely shredded Cheddar or Monterey Jack
Up to 1/3 cup drained canned diced green chile peppers or pimientos

BUTTERMILK BISCUITS

About twelve 2 1/2-inch biscuits

To make biscuits with milk, substitute whole milk for the buttermilk and omit the baking soda.

Preheat the oven to 425°F. Line a large baking sheet with parchment paper or have ready a 10-inch cast-iron skillet.

Whisk to combine in a large bowl:

3 cups (375g) all-purpose flour
1 tablespoon baking powder
1 teaspoon salt
3/4 teaspoon baking soda

Add:

1 1/2 sticks (6 oz or 170g) cold unsalted butter, cut into cubes

Cut in the butter, 634, using a pastry blender or your fingers to work it into the flour until it is in small, flattened pieces and the mixture is crumbly. Stir in:

1 1/4 cups (305g) buttermilk

Stir just until the dough comes together. Transfer the dough to a lightly floured surface, and knead very briefly just to bring the dough together. Pat the dough out into a 3/4-inch-thick round. Use a floured biscuit cutter (any size cutter will work) to cut out biscuits as close together as possible. Do not twist the cutter—just push it down into the dough. Transfer the biscuits to the prepared baking sheet or skillet with the sides of the biscuits touching. Brush the tops with:

2 tablespoons butter, melted

Bake until golden brown, 15 to 20 minutes.

ANGEL BISCUITS

Angel biscuits are made with yeast, making them extra light and with a subtle yeasty flavor similar to that of a buttery roll. Combine **1½ teaspoons active dry yeast** with **¼ cup (60g) warm (100°F) water** in a small bowl and let sit until the yeast is dissolved, about 5 minutes. Prepare the dough for **Buttermilk Biscuits, 635,** substituting the yeast-water mixture for ¼ cup (60g) of the buttermilk. Cover the dough tightly and refrigerate for 4 hours or overnight. When ready to bake, preheat the oven, roll out, cut, and bake as directed.

SWEET POTATO BISCUITS

Whisk together **1 cup sweet potato puree (canned or homemade), ½ cup (120g) buttermilk,** and **2 tablespoons (30g) brown sugar** in a medium bowl. Prepare the dough for **Buttermilk Biscuits, 635,** substituting the sweet potato mixture for the buttermilk. Roll out, cut, and bake as directed.

CORNMEAL BISCUITS

Prepare **Buttermilk Biscuits, 635,** reducing the flour to 2½ cups (315g) and adding **½ cup (80g) fine cornmeal** and **2 tablespoons (25g) sugar** to the dry ingredients. Roll out, cut, and bake as directed.

WHOLE-GRAIN BISCUITS

Prepare **Buttermilk Biscuits, 635,** reducing the flour to 2 cups (250g) and adding **1 cup whole wheat flour (130g), dark rye flour (120g), spelt flour (125g), or buckwheat flour (120g)** and **1 tablespoon (10g) sugar.** Roll out, cut, and bake as directed.

BISCUIT STICKS

Prepare the dough for **Buttermilk Biscuits, 635.** Roll the dough ½ inch thick and cut into 3 × ½-inch sticks. Place the sticks on an ungreased baking sheet and brush with **melted butter.** Reduce the baking time slightly. To serve, stack log-cabin fashion.

QUICK DROP BISCUITS

No kneading or rolling necessary. Preheat the oven to 450°F. Prepare **Buttermilk Biscuits, 635,** and increase the buttermilk to 1½ cups (365g). Stir until the dough comes together. Drop large spoonfuls of dough onto an ungreased baking sheet and bake until lightly browned, 12 to 15 minutes.

STICKY BREAKFAST PULL-APART BREAD

10 to 12 servings

Preheat the oven to 400°F. Generously butter a 10-inch Bundt pan (preferably nonstick). Prepare **½ recipe of the topping for Sticky Buns, 620,** stirring in at the end **¼ cup (60g) heavy cream.** Set aside. Prepare the dough for **Buttermilk Biscuits, 635.** When the dough comes together, form or cut it into 16 pieces. Roll the pieces in **4 tablespoons (2 oz or 55g) melted butter** then in **½ cup (100g) sugar** mixed with **1 teaspoon ground cinnamon,** and nestle them in the prepared pan. Pour the sticky syrup evenly over the biscuits. Bake until browned and a skewer inserted in the center comes out clean, 30 to 35 minutes. Turn the bread out onto a serving platter while it is still hot, being careful not to burn yourself with the molten sugar syrup.

QUICK CREAM BISCUITS OR SHORTCAKES

Eight 3-inch shortcakes

The cream in this recipe replaces the butter in a standard biscuit dough, resulting in biscuits that are quicker and easier to make but with all the richness you expect in a biscuit.

Preheat the oven to 450°F. Lightly grease a baking sheet.

Whisk together thoroughly in a large bowl:

2 cups (250g) all-purpose flour
(2 to 4 tablespoons [25 to 50g] sugar, to taste)
2½ teaspoons baking powder
½ teaspoon salt

Add all at once:

1½ cups (345g) heavy cream

Mix just until most of the dry ingredients are moistened. Scoop up big spoonfuls of the dough, roughly form them into biscuit shapes, and place on the baking sheet. For shortcakes, if desired, sprinkle on top of the biscuits:

(4 teaspoons sugar)

Bake until very lightly browned, 12 to 15 minutes. Serve warm.

EASTER BUNNY BISCUITS

Preheat the oven to 425°F. Grease a baking sheet. Prepare the dough for **Quick Cream Biscuits or Shortcakes, above,** adding the optional sugar to the dough. Roll out the dough to a thickness of ½ inch. Cut the dough with 3 sizes of round cutters: 3 inches, 1½ inches, and about ¾ inch. For each bunny, cut 1 large round, 3 medium, and 1 small round. Assemble, using the large biscuit for the body, one of the medium ones for the head, and the small one, rolled into a ball, for the tail. Flatten the remaining 2 medium biscuits slightly and shape into ovals for the ears. Place the bunnies on the baking sheet. Bake until lightly browned, about 15 minutes.

GRIDDLE BISCUITS

Prepare any rolled biscuit dough, 635–36. To cook, place 1 inch apart on a lightly greased griddle over medium heat. Brown them on one side for 5 to 7 minutes, then turn and brown on the other side.

MEGAN'S CHEDDAR-SCALLION BISCUITS

6 large or 8 medium biscuits

Scattering grated cheese on the baking sheet before placing the biscuits on top results in crispy, toasty "feet."

Preheat the oven to 425°F. Line a baking sheet with parchment paper.

Whisk to combine in a large bowl:

2 cups (250g) all-purpose flour
2 teaspoons baking powder
¾ teaspoon baking soda
¾ teaspoon black pepper
½ teaspoon salt

Add:

1 stick (4 oz or 115g) cold unsalted butter, cut into cubes

Cut in the butter, 634, using a pastry blender or your fingers to work it into the flour until it is in small, flattened pieces and the mixture is crumbly. Stir in:

½ cup grated sharp Cheddar (2 oz or 55g)
4 green onions, thinly sliced

Add and stir just until the dough comes together:

¾ to 1 cup (185 to 245g) buttermilk

Use the larger amount of buttermilk if the dough is crumbly and dry after adding ¾ cup. Transfer the dough to a lightly floured surface and knead very briefly just to bring the dough together. Pat the dough out into a rectangle. Starting at a short end, fold one-third of the dough toward the center, then fold the opposite end over the first folded end (a business letter fold). Pat out the dough into a rectangle again and give it one more business letter fold. Pat the dough out into a 6 × 9-inch rectangle ¾ to 1 inch thick. Using a sharp knife, cut the dough into 6 square or 8 rectangular biscuits. Sprinkle in small mounds on the baking sheet, one mound for each biscuit:

½ cup grated sharp Cheddar (2 ounces)

Place each biscuit on a mound of cheese on the baking sheet. If needed, scatter the cheese a bit so it sticks out from under each biscuit (this ensures that every biscuit has crispy cheese "feet"). Brush the biscuits with:

1 tablespoon unsalted butter, melted

Bake until golden brown, 15 to 20 minutes.

BEATEN BISCUITS

To win unending gratitude, serve these to any homesick Southerner (for extra points, serve with country ham and pepper jelly). To ensure the tender, fine-grained texture characteristic of these biscuits, the dough must be thoroughly beaten. This is a labor of love, although version II makes the process much easier. Beaten biscuits can be stored, airtight, at room temperature for up to 3 weeks.

I. BY HAND

About fifty 1½-inch biscuits

Stir together thoroughly in a large bowl:

4 cups (500g) all-purpose flour
1 teaspoon salt
1 teaspoon baking powder

Add:

½ cup (95g) chilled lard or vegetable shortening

Cut in the fat, 634, with a pastry blender or your fingers until the consistency of cornmeal. Add, stirring to make a stiff dough:

About 1 cup (235g) ice water

Transfer the dough to a lightly floured work surface. Beat the dough with a rolling pin until it is blistered, folding it over frequently. This is a long process, requiring 30 minutes or more or about 500 whacks. Meanwhile, preheat the oven to 325°F.

When the dough is smooth, roll it to a thickness of ½ inch and cut it with a floured 1½-inch biscuit cutter. Knead the scraps together, then roll, fold, and cut in the same manner. Place the biscuits on an ungreased baking sheet and brush the tops with:

Melted butter

Pierce each biscuit with a fork in 3 places. Bake until lightly browned on the bottom and golden brown on top, about 30 minutes.

II. FOOD PROCESSOR METHOD

About fifteen 2-inch biscuits

Preheat the oven to 400°F.

Combine in a food processor and process for 5 seconds:

2 cups (250g) all-purpose flour
½ teaspoon salt
¼ teaspoon baking powder

Add and process until the mixture resembles coarse crumbs, about 10 seconds:

¼ cup (50g) chilled lard or vegetable shortening

Add and process for 3 minutes:

½ cup (120g) ice water

The dough will be soft and putty-like, something like melted mozzarella. Wrap in plastic and let rest for 10 minutes.

On an unfloured surface, roll the dough out to a little more than ⅛ inch thick. Fold it in half, making 2 layers, and roll lightly, just enough to make the dough layers adhere to one another. Cut out 2-inch rounds with a floured biscuit cutter. Knead the scraps together, then roll, fold, and cut in the same manner. Arrange the biscuits on an ungreased baking sheet so they are close together but not touching. Prick each biscuit with a fork 3 times. Bake until the tops are golden brown and the bottoms are deep brown, 18 to 22 minutes.

CLASSIC SCONES

8 to 12 scones

For the easiest prep and richest scones, make **Cream Scones** by increasing the heavy cream to 1¼ cups (290g) and omitting the butter and egg.

Preheat the oven to 450°F.

Whisk together in a large bowl:

2½ cups (315g) all-purpose flour
2¼ teaspoons baking powder
¼ cup (50g) sugar
½ teaspoon salt

Add and cut in, 634, until the size of small peas:

4 tablespoons (2 oz or 55g) cold unsalted butter

Beat together in a small bowl to combine:

1 cup (230g) heavy cream
1 large egg
(1 teaspoon vanilla)

Make a well in the flour mixture. Pour in the cream mixture and combine with a few swift strokes. Handle the dough as little as possible. Turn it out onto a lightly floured work surface. To make the classic wedge shape, pat into an 8-inch round and then cut into 8 to 12 wedges; or cut into 2½-inch rounds with a floured biscuit cutter, or cut as for Biscuit Sticks, 636. Place on an ungreased baking sheet. Brush with:

Heavy cream

If desired, sprinkle with:

(Granulated or turbinado sugar)

Bake until golden, about 15 minutes. Serve warm or at room temperature.

LEMON-BLUEBERRY SCONES

Prepare **Classic Scones or Cream Scones, 637,** adding the **finely grated zest of 1 lemon** with the cream mixture. Then add **1½ cups frozen blueberries** to the dough before it is fully mixed. Sprinkle with the optional sugar before baking.

CHOCOLATE-ORANGE SCONES

Prepare **Classic Scones or Cream Scones, 637,** adding the **finely grated zest of 1 orange** with the cream mixture. When the cream mixture is partially stirred in, add **½ cup semisweet chocolate chips or chopped dark chocolate** and knead briefly to incorporate.

ABOUT USES FOR LEFTOVER BREADS

A bread surplus can be put to many good uses—so don't throw a piece away! It can be used for French Toast, 644, Bostock, 645, or Crostini, 49; for stuffings, 531; as a thickener in soups—see Pappa al Pomodoro, 91, and Sopa de Ajo, 91; and for sauces—see Rouille I, 565, and Salsa Verde, 567. Bread crumbs also feature in Stuffed Artichokes alla Romana, 207, Brussels Sprout Gratin, 222, and Tomatoes Provençale, 282.

CROUTONS

These dried or fried seasoned bread morsels come in all sizes. In small dice, they add crunch and heft to salads and soups. Larger toasts can serve as a resting place for grilled meats, soaking up errant juices. Also see Crostini, 49. For salads, we recommend approximately ⅓ cup bread cubes per serving.

I. PAN-FRIED

Cube or coarsely tear:

Bread, fresh or stale

Add to a large skillet:

Butter, olive oil, or a combination (about 1 tablespoon per cup of bread cubes)
(1 to 3 garlic cloves, smashed)
(One 3-inch sprig rosemary)

If using garlic or rosemary, let them lightly sizzle in the fat over medium-low heat for 5 minutes. Increase the heat to medium, add the bread cubes, and cook, turning or tossing occasionally, until evenly brown, turning down the heat if needed to avoid burning. Remove the rosemary sprig if it is too far gone, otherwise strip the crispy leaves from the stem and toss with the bread cubes. When browned, take off the heat and sprinkle the croutons with:

Salt and black pepper

II. BAKED

If desired, you may infuse the fat used here with garlic or rosemary first, as described above.

Preheat the oven to 375°F. Toss together on a baking sheet:

½-inch cubes bread or corn bread
Olive oil or melted butter (about 1 tablespoon per cup of bread cubes)

Bake, shaking the pan once or twice, until the croutons are golden brown, 10 to 15 minutes. Sprinkle while still warm with:

Salt and black pepper

III. SEASONED

After 2 to 3 cups croutons have been sautéed or baked, above, drop them while still hot into a bag containing:

1 teaspoon salt
1 teaspoon sweet paprika or ½ teaspoon red pepper flakes
¼ cup finely grated Parmesan
2 to 3 tablespoons or more finely chopped parsley, thyme, sage, oregano, or a combination

Close the bag and shake it until the croutons are evenly coated. Transfer to a plate or baking sheet to cool and crisp.

IV. DRY CROUTONS FOR STUFFINGS AND DRESSINGS

Preheat the oven to 200°F. Cut into small cubes:

Bread or corn bread

Place in a single layer on a baking sheet and bake, stirring occasionally, for 1 to 2 hours until dry and golden brown.

GARLIC BREAD

6 servings

Serve this extra buttery, extra garlicky bread alongside spaghetti with tomato sauce—perhaps with Italian Meatballs, 507. Any leftovers make deluxe croutons for a Caesar salad.

Position an oven rack in the center of the oven and preheat the broiler.

Cut in half horizontally:

1 baguette

Combine in a small saucepan:

4 tablespoons (½ stick) unsalted butter
¼ cup olive oil
4 garlic cloves, minced or grated on a rasp grater

Heat over medium-low heat until the butter is melted and the garlic sizzles, about 1 minute. Place the baguette on a baking sheet, cut sides up, and brush with the butter mixture. Sprinkle with:

¼ cup minced parsley
3 tablespoons finely grated Parmesan

Broil until the bread is lightly toasted. To serve, cut into pieces.

MELBA TOAST

Cut into the thinnest possible slices:

White or other bread

Remove the crusts. Place on a baking sheet and toast in a 250°F oven until crisp and a light golden brown.

PANCAKES, WAFFLES, DOUGHNUTS, AND FRITTERS

From johnnycakes to crêpes, *panisses*, and *dosas*, the satisfying simplicity of fried and griddled batters has made them an essential feature of cuisines throughout the world. They may be topped or layered with savory or sweet ingredients, or folded around them like a flatbread—though in these cases they tend to be more delicate and thus confined to eating off (or directly over) a plate. Small pancakes, like Buckwheat Blini, 641, are a bit more portable and may serve as a base for canapés as well.

This chapter also covers the many delicious fried doughs we refer to as doughnuts. Some thick batters, such as Choux Paste, 697, are fried (see Pets de Nonne, 654), but most doughnuts are made with thick doughs. Croquettes, 654–55, on the other hand, are mixtures of cheese, vegetables, or meats bound together, usually with béchamel sauce, shaped, and deep-fried.

Finally, as many of us know from attending state fairs, nearly anything can be battered or breaded and then fried. Find the batters and coatings for doing so at the end of this chapter, 656–59.

ABOUT PANCAKES OR GRIDDLE CAKES

Pancakes, blintzes, crêpes, or griddle cakes: No matter what they are called, all are simple to make. ➤ There are two equally important things to control in producing them: the consistency of the batter and the heat of the griddle or pan.

When mixing pancake batter, quickly incorporate liquid ingredients into dry ingredients until just combined—and no more. Resist the temptation to overmix the batter; there will almost always be some lumps, but they will not be noticeable after cooking. ➤ It is always wise to cook one test pancake to make sure the consistency of the batter is correct. If the batter is too thick and does not spread enough to make a cake of the desired thickness, dilute it with a little water or milk. If too thin, add a little flour.

To prepare the griddle or pan, preheat it for several minutes. Test the heat of the griddle or pan by sprinkling a few drops of cold water on it. If the water bounces and sputters, the pan is ready to use (see illustration, 640). If the water just sits and boils, the pan is not hot enough and the pancakes will spread too much. If the water evaporates instantly, the pan is too hot. When the pan is at the right temperature, lightly grease it. One of the most common pancake mistakes is using too much oil for cooking. If using a nonstick cooking surface, add a little oil to a small bowl, then saturate part of a paper towel with the oil. Brush the pan lightly with the paper towel before cooking each batch of pancakes. Cast-iron pans may require a bit more oil, but not much more—the idea is to griddle the pancakes, not fry them. Spoon, ladle, or pour batter from a few inches above the pan. Make the cakes large or small, as you like, but make sure there is enough space for the batter to spread.

▲ At high altitudes, decrease the baking powder and/or soda called for in the following recipes by about one-quarter.

Making pancakes

PANCAKES OR GRIDDLE CAKES

About sixteen 4-inch pancakes

Please read About Pancakes or Griddle Cakes, 639. This recipe, perhaps more than any other in this book, has garnered lifelong *Joy* fans. For thicker, fluffier pancakes, use up to 1 tablespoon baking powder. For **silver dollar pancakes,** use only 1 tablespoon batter per pancake.

Preheat the oven to 200°F. Whisk together in a large bowl:

1½ cups (190g) all-purpose flour
3 tablespoons (35g) sugar
2 teaspoons baking powder
¾ teaspoon salt

Combine in another bowl, using the smaller amount of milk to start:

1 to 1¼ cups (235 to 295g) milk
3 tablespoons (45g) butter, melted
2 large eggs
(½ teaspoon vanilla)

Mix the liquid ingredients into the flour mixture just until combined. If the batter still seems thick, whisk in the remaining ¼ cup (60g) milk. Place a large nonstick skillet over medium heat or preheat a griddle to medium-hot (about 325°F). When the skillet is hot, lightly brush the surface with a paper towel dipped in:

Vegetable oil

From just a few inches above the surface, ladle the batter onto the skillet or griddle using ¼ cup batter for each 4-inch pancake. Cook undisturbed until bubbles form and pop on the surface of the pancakes and the bottom is golden brown, 2 to 3 minutes. Flip the pancakes and cook until browned on the second side, 1 to 2 minutes more. Transfer the pancakes as they finish cooking to a platter or rimmed baking sheet and keep warm in the oven. Serve immediately with:

Softened butter
Maple syrup

BUTTERMILK PANCAKES

About sixteen 3-inch pancakes

Prepare **Pancakes or Griddle Cakes, above.** Add **½ teaspoon baking soda** to the flour mixture. Decrease the baking powder to 1 teaspoon. Substitute **buttermilk** for the milk.

BUCKWHEAT PANCAKES

Prepare **Pancakes or Griddle Cakes, above,** using **¾ cup buckwheat flour** and **¾ cup all-purpose flour.**

ADDITIONS TO PANCAKES

Gently stir any of the following into the pancake batter after the liquid and dry ingredients have been mixed together:

1 cup shredded sharp Cheddar (4 oz or 115g)
¾ cup fresh or unthawed frozen blueberries or raspberries
¾ cup finely diced or mashed ripe bananas
¾ cup unsweetened pumpkin puree
½ cup raisins or any finely diced soft dried fruit
½ cup finely chopped toasted, 1005, walnuts or pecans
½ cup crumbled cooked bacon
½ cup shredded sweetened coconut
½ cup chocolate chips or chopped chocolate

YEASTED PANCAKES

About twenty 4-inch pancakes

Though not a must, an overnight rest takes these tangy, moist pancakes from really good to great. This batter also makes superb waffles.

Whisk together in a large bowl:

½ cup (120g) warm (105° to 115°F) water
1 envelope (2¼ teaspoons) active dry yeast

Let stand until the yeast is dissolved, about 5 minutes.

Combine in a small saucepan:

1½ cups (355g) milk
3 tablespoons (45g) butter

Heat until the butter is melted. Let cool to between 105° and 115°F, then whisk into the yeast mixture. Whisk in until a smooth batter forms:

2 cups (250g) all-purpose flour
3 tablespoons (35g) sugar

Cover the bowl tightly with plastic wrap and set in a warm place until the mixture increases in volume by at least half and forms bubbles, about 1 hour.

Stir the batter down, then cover and let rise for at least 3 hours and up to 48 hours in the refrigerator.

When ready to cook, let the batter stand at room temperature for 20 minutes. Stir the batter to deflate, then whisk in:

2 large eggs
½ teaspoon salt

Cook, keep warm, and serve as for **Pancakes or Griddle Cakes, 640.**

FOUR-GRAIN FLAPJACKS

About eighteen 4-inch pancakes

Whisk together in a large bowl:

1 cup (130g) whole wheat flour
¾ cup (95g) all-purpose flour
⅓ cup (55g) fine cornmeal
¼ cup (25g) old-fashioned or quick-cooking rolled oats
2 teaspoons baking powder
¾ teaspoon salt
½ teaspoon baking soda
(½ teaspoon ground cinnamon)

Combine in another medium bowl:

1½ cups (355g) milk
4 tablespoons (2 oz or 55g) butter, melted
¼ cup (80g) honey
3 large eggs

Quickly mix the liquid ingredients into the flour mixture. Cook, keep warm, and serve as for **Pancakes or Griddle Cakes, 640.**

CORNMEAL PANCAKES

About sixteen 4-inch pancakes

These golden pancakes have the hearty taste and texture of a corn muffin and a slightly irregular shape. If desired, omit the sugar for savory pancakes.

Combine in a large bowl:

1 cup (160g) fine cornmeal
1 to 2 tablespoons honey, maple syrup, or sugar, to taste
¾ teaspoon salt

Slowly stir in:

1 cup (235g) boiling water

Cover and let stand 10 minutes. Add and whisk well:

½ cup (120g) milk
2 tablespoons (30g) butter, melted
2 teaspoons baking powder

Add and whisk well:

1 large egg

Whisk in with a few quick strokes:

½ cup (65g) all-purpose flour

If desired, fold into the batter:

(¾ cup fresh, thawed frozen, or drained canned corn kernels)

Cook as for **Pancakes or Griddle Cakes, 640,** using 3 tablespoons batter for each pancake.

JOHNNYCAKES

About twelve 3-inch cakes

These corn cakes are crusty on the outside, moist on the inside. Johnnycakes can be eaten at breakfast with maple syrup or butter and jam. They are also delicious with Beef Pot Roast, 464, or Chicken Fricassee, 422.

Preheat the oven to 200°F. Stir to combine in a large bowl:

1½ cups stone-ground fine (240g) or medium-grind (225g) cornmeal
1 teaspoon salt
1 teaspoon sugar

Pour in slowly, stirring constantly to prevent lumps:

2¼ cups (530g) boiling water

Set aside for 10 minutes. Set a large skillet over medium heat or preheat a griddle to medium-hot (about 325°F). Melt in the skillet or on the griddle:

1 tablespoon butter

When the butter begins to brown, add the batter, using ¼ cup per cake. Flatten the batter slightly with the back of a spatula and cook until the undersides of the cakes are deep golden brown. Cut into extremely thin pats:

1½ tablespoons butter

Place one pat on each cake, flip with a spatula, and cook on the other side until deep golden brown. Keep warm in the oven, and repeat with the remaining batter, using more butter as needed.

BUCKWHEAT BLINI

About twenty-four 2½-inch blini or eight 8 to 9-inch thin blini

These yeast-raised buckwheat pancakes may be served with butter and jam or with savory accompaniments like Sautéed Mushrooms, 251, or smoked fish and sour cream. For best results, cook in cast-iron. For **miniature blini,** which make excellent bases for canapés or for serving with caviar, 66, use a heaping teaspoonful of batter for each blini.

Combine in a small saucepan:

¾ cup (175g) milk
3 tablespoons (45g) butter

Heat until the butter is melted. Let cool to between 105° and 115°F. Stir in:

1 teaspoon active dry yeast

Let stand 5 minutes, then stir until the yeast is completely dissolved. Whisk together in a large bowl:

½ cup (65g) all-purpose flour
½ cup (60g) buckwheat flour
1 tablespoon (10g) sugar
½ teaspoon salt

Whisk the milk mixture into the flour mixture until well combined. Cover tightly with plastic wrap and let rise in a warm place until doubled in volume, about 1 hour.

Make the blini immediately or stir the batter down and refrigerate, covered, for up to 8 hours. If the batter has been refrigerated, let stand at room temperature for 20 minutes before proceeding.

Stir to deflate the batter, then whisk in:

2 large eggs

Let the batter stand 5 minutes. To cook, follow the instructions in **Pancakes or Griddle Cakes, 640,** using a heaping tablespoon of batter for each blini. If the batter becomes puffy, gently stir it down before making more cakes. To make larger, crêpe-like blini, whisk an additional:

¼ cup (60g) milk

into the batter. Use 1/3 cup batter per pancake and tilt the skillet to allow the batter to spread into an 8- to 9-inch round. Cook, turning once, until browned on both sides.

OATMEAL PANCAKES

About twenty 3½-inch pancakes

Whisk together in a large bowl:

½ cup (65g) all-purpose flour
1 teaspoon baking powder
½ teaspoon salt

Beat in a separate medium bowl:

2 large eggs

Stir into the eggs:

1½ cups cooked oatmeal, 342 (from ¾ cup old-fashioned rolled oats)
½ cup (120g) milk or buttermilk
2 tablespoons melted butter or bacon fat

Quickly stir the oatmeal mixture into the flour mixture. The batter may appear lumpy. Cook, keep warm, and serve as for **Pancakes or Griddle Cakes, 640.** Lightly stir the batter each time before ladling to make sure the oatmeal is evenly distributed among the cakes.

LEMON–SOUR CREAM PANCAKES

About twelve 4-inch pancakes

Delicious with honey, sweetened sour cream, Crème Fraîche, 974, or Blueberry Compote, 178.

Whisk together in a large bowl:

1 cup (125g) all-purpose flour
¼ cup (50g) sugar
1½ teaspoons baking powder
½ teaspoon baking soda
¼ teaspoon salt

Combine in another medium bowl:

¾ cup (180g) sour cream
⅓ cup (80g) milk
Finely grated zest of 2 lemons
¼ cup (60g) lemon juice
3 tablespoons (45g) butter, melted
1 large egg
1½ teaspoons vanilla

Quickly mix the liquid ingredients into the flour mixture. The batter will be thick and bubbly. Cook, keep warm, and serve as for **Pancakes or Griddle Cakes, 640.**

COTTAGE CHEESE PANCAKES

About twenty-two 4-inch pancakes

Cottage cheese gives these pancakes a tender crumb. Serve them straight off the griddle for the best texture. These pancakes are excellent with cherry jam or a fruit compote.

Whisk together in a large bowl:

1⅓ cups (165g) all-purpose flour
¼ cup (50g) sugar
2 teaspoons baking powder
½ teaspoon baking soda
¼ teaspoon salt

Whisk together in a separate medium bowl:

1 cup (235g) milk
1 cup (235g) cottage cheese
3 tablespoons (45g) butter, melted
2 large egg yolks
1 teaspoon vanilla

Gently whisk the wet ingredients into the dry ingredients until just combined. Beat until stiff but not dry, 978:

2 large egg whites

Fold into the batter. Cook, keep warm, and serve as for **Pancakes or Griddle Cakes, 640.**

ABOUT WAFFLES

The pleasure of eating waffles more than justifies the special equipment required to make them. Pocked with perfect, crisp squares, waffles are geometrically satisfying to behold. But they aren't merely aesthetically pleasing. The large surface area of a waffle ensures maximum crispiness, and their depressions can hold a prodigious amount of melted butter and syrup.

Most waffle batters are similar to pancake batters. However, they are distinct in one way: Waffles are always made with a fair amount of butter or fat to promote a crisp, light texture and to ensure that the waffles release easily from the iron. (➤ Pancake batter may be used to make waffles, provided you add 2 tablespoons melted butter or oil to the batter.) The richer the batter, the crisper the waffle. If desired, substitute 3 tablespoons vegetable oil for every 4 tablespoons butter, but do not expect the same richness of flavor. ➤ For a superbly light result, beat the egg whites separately, 977, and fold them into the batter. ➤ Keep waffles tender by not overbeating or overmixing the batter.

Recipe yields will vary depending on the size of your waffle iron. For example, irons for Belgian waffles, which have very deep plates, will produce only about half as many waffles as conventional waffle irons. The yields of our recipes are based on a standard iron, with a plate divided into 4 × 4½ × ½-inch grids.

Leftover waffles can be cooled, wrapped in plastic, and stored in the refrigerator for 3 days or frozen for several months. To reheat, bake them, unthawed, on a rack set on a baking sheet in a 350°F oven for about 10 minutes, or toast in the toaster at the lowest setting for 5 minutes.

▲ At high altitudes, decrease the baking powder and/or soda called for in the following recipes by about one-quarter.

WAFFLES

About 6 waffles

If serving these with savory food, omit the sugar. When mixing the batter, use 4 tablespoons butter for a leaner waffle, 8 tablespoons (1 stick) for a classic light and fluffy waffle, or 2 sticks (8 ounces) for the crunchiest, most delicious waffle imaginable.

Preheat a waffle iron.

Whisk together in a large bowl:

1¾ cups (220g) all-purpose flour
2 tablespoons (25g) sugar
1 tablespoon baking powder
½ teaspoon salt

Thoroughly blend in another medium bowl:

3 large eggs
4 to 16 tablespoons (2 to 8 oz or 55g to 225g) unsalted butter, melted
1½ cups (355g) milk

Make a well in the center of the flour mixture and pour in the wet ingredients. Whisk the wet ingredients into the flour mixture with a few swift strokes. If desired, gently stir in one of the:

(Additions to Pancakes, 640)

Preheat the oven to 200°F. Ladle enough batter into the center of the waffle iron to cover about two-thirds of the grid surface. Close the lid and wait about 4 minutes. When the waffle is ready, steam will stop emerging from the cracks of the iron. If you try to lift the top of the iron and it shows resistance, it probably means the waffle is not quite done. Allow it to cook slightly longer and try again. As the waffles finish cooking, transfer them to a rimmed baking sheet and keep them warm in the oven. To preserve their crispiness, set a rack in the baking sheet first, or just put the waffles directly on the oven racks. Serve with:

Maple syrup, honey, chopped fresh fruit, or a sweet sauce, 805–11

BUTTERMILK WAFFLES

Prepare **Waffles, 642.** Add ¼ **teaspoon baking soda** to the flour mixture. Decrease the baking powder to 2 teaspoons. Substitute **buttermilk** for the milk.

CORNMEAL WAFFLES

About 6 waffles

Terrific with syrup and sausages, these can also be cut into wedges and paired with fried chicken, 417–18.

Preheat a waffle iron.

Whisk together in a large bowl:

1 cup (125g) all-purpose flour
1 cup (160g) fine cornmeal
2 teaspoons baking powder
¾ teaspoon salt
½ teaspoon baking soda

Whisk together in another medium bowl:

2 cups (485g) buttermilk
5 tablespoons (70g) unsalted butter, melted
¼ cup (80g) maple syrup
2 large egg yolks (whites reserved)

Make a well in the center of the dry ingredients and pour in the wet ingredients. Whisk the wet ingredients into the flour mixture with a few swift strokes. Beat until stiff but not dry, 978:

2 large egg whites

Fold into the batter. Cook, keep warm, and serve as for **Waffles, 642.**

BACON CORNMEAL WAFFLES

Prepare **Cornmeal Waffles, above.** Cook until crisp **3 thin slices bacon.** Crumble into the batter and proceed as directed.

CHOCOLATE WAFFLES

About 8 waffles

Delectable with vanilla ice cream. These waffles are delicate, so remove them from the iron carefully.

Preheat a waffle iron.

Whisk together in a large bowl:

1½ cups (190g) all-purpose flour
1 cup (200g) sugar
½ cup (40g) unsweetened cocoa powder, sifted if lumpy
2 teaspoons baking powder
½ teaspoon salt

Whisk in a medium bowl until frothy:

2 large eggs

Whisk in:

1 cup (235g) milk
1½ sticks (6 oz or 170g) unsalted butter, melted
1 teaspoon vanilla

Whisk the wet ingredients into the flour mixture with a few swift strokes. If desired, fold in:

(½ cup mini chocolate chips)

Cook, keep warm, and serve as for **Waffles, 642.** This batter tends to thicken up as it stands. If needed, add about 1 tablespoon additional milk to the batter to loosen it.

GOLDEN SWEET POTATO WAFFLES

6 servings

These beautiful waffles are excellent served with warm Applesauce, 174.

Preheat a waffle iron.

Whisk together in a large bowl:

1 cup (125g) all-purpose flour
2 tablespoons (25g) sugar
2 teaspoons baking powder
1 teaspoon ground cinnamon
½ teaspoon salt
(½ teaspoon ground cardamom)

Whisk together in a medium bowl:

1 cup (235g) milk
3 large eggs
½ cup mashed sweet potatoes or canned sweet potato puree
2 tablespoons (30g) butter, melted
1 teaspoon vanilla

Fold the wet ingredients into the flour mixture just until combined. Cook, keep warm, and serve as for **Waffles, 642.**

YEASTED BELGIAN WAFFLES

About 12 waffles

Serve these waffles with Whipped Cream, 791, and sliced strawberries.

Preheat a waffle iron.

Whisk together in a large bowl:

3 cups (705g) warm (105° to 115°F) milk
1 envelope (2¼ teaspoons) active dry yeast

Let stand until the yeast is dissolved, about 5 minutes, then stir until smooth. Whisk in:

1½ sticks (6 oz or 170g) unsalted butter, melted and cooled to lukewarm
½ cup (100g) sugar
3 large egg yolks (whites reserved)
2 teaspoons vanilla
1½ teaspoons salt

Add in 3 parts, beating with a spoon until smooth after each addition:

4 cups (500g) all-purpose flour

Cover tightly with plastic wrap and let rise at room temperature until doubled in volume, 1 to 1½ hours. Stir to deflate the batter. Beat until soft peaks form, 977:

3 large egg whites

Fold into the batter. Cook and keep warm as for **Waffles, 642.** Sprinkle with:

Powdered sugar

LIÈGE-STYLE WAFFLES

10 waffles

These waffles are one of the quintessential Belgian street foods, served straight from the iron and glistening with caramelized pearl sugar. Pearl sugar can be hard to find, but it is usually available at specialty markets that sell European foods. In a pinch, use sugar cubes crushed into pearl-sized bits.

Prepare the dough for:

Brioche, 603

through the refrigeration step. Fold or knead in:

½ cup pearl sugar

Divide the dough into 10 pieces.

Preheat a waffle iron. Preheat the oven to 200°F.

Depending on the size of your waffle iron, you may be able to cook multiple waffles at a time, or as few as two. Place the balls of dough in the waffle iron and cook until deeply browned and caramelized. Transfer to a baking sheet and place in the oven while you cook the remaining waffles. Serve warm, as is (the waffles are sweet and rich enough to need no adornment), or topped with any of the following:

(Whipped Cream, 791)
(Powdered sugar)
(Nutella and sliced bananas)

ABOUT FRENCH TOAST

The French name for this specialty is *pain perdu*, meaning "lost bread." As the name indicates, "lost" or stale bread is ideal for making French toast, but fresh bread is perfectly serviceable. Any bread may be used for French toast, but soft, white sandwich bread, brioche, and challah are best. Though most commonly cooked in a skillet or on a griddle, you may cook French toast in a waffle iron, which will improve its syrup- and sauce-holding abilities: Coat the bread slices in the egg mixture, then cook the bread in a preheated waffle iron until golden. Finally, French toast can be arranged in a baking dish and baked, which is simply a bread pudding, 829, by another name. Regardless of what you wish to call it, the advantages to baking French toast include easy, make-ahead preparation and an especially soft, custard-like texture.

FRENCH TOAST

4 servings

Whisk together in a shallow bowl:

⅔ cup (155g) milk or half-and-half
4 large eggs
2 tablespoons sugar (25g) or maple syrup (40g)
1 teaspoon vanilla or 1 tablespoon rum
¼ teaspoon salt

One at a time, soak both sides in the egg mixture:

8 slices white sandwich bread

Melt in a preheated nonstick skillet or griddle over medium heat:

1 tablespoon butter

Once melted, add the bread in batches and cook, turning once, until browned on both sides. Repeat with the remaining bread, adding more butter to the pan as needed. Serve hot. If desired, sprinkle with:

(Powdered sugar)

SAVORY FRENCH TOAST

Prepare the batter for:

French Toast, above, omitting the sweetener and vanilla or rum

Whisk into the batter:

½ cup finely grated Parmesan (2 ounces)
2 teaspoons minced oregano, rosemary, or thyme
(½ teaspoon red pepper flakes)
¼ teaspoon black pepper

Proceed as directed. If desired, serve topped with:

(Fried Eggs, 155)
(Sliced avocado)

STUFFED FRENCH TOAST

8 servings

Preheat the oven to 400°F. Lightly butter a large baking sheet.

Beat together in a large bowl until smooth:

8 ounces (225g) cream cheese, softened
¼ cup packed (60g) brown sugar
¼ cup honey (85g) or maple syrup (80g)
1 teaspoon vanilla
(Finely grated zest of 1 orange)
½ teaspoon ground cinnamon
¼ teaspoon salt

Trim the ends and crusts from:

One 1-pound loaf white sandwich bread or brioche, unsliced

Cut the loaf into 8 thick slices. Carefully cut into one side of each slice to create a pocket that you can open with your fingers. Spoon or pipe an equal amount of the filling into each pocket. Mix together in a shallow bowl:

1 cup (235g) milk
3 large eggs
¼ cup (30g) all-purpose flour
3 tablespoons (35g) sugar
2 teaspoons baking powder
2 teaspoons vanilla
¼ teaspoon salt

One slice at a time, soak the stuffed bread in the egg mixture until thoroughly coated but not falling apart and transfer to a plate before browning. Melt in a large skillet over medium-low heat:

2 tablespoons butter

Working in batches, add the stuffed bread and brown on both sides, adding more butter to the skillet as needed. Transfer to the prepared baking sheet. When all the stuffed slices are browned, bake until fragrant and golden brown all over, about 6 minutes. Serve immediately.

BAKED FRENCH TOAST

4 servings

Whisk together in large bowl:

1 cup heavy cream (230g) or milk (235g)
6 large eggs
¼ cup (80g) maple syrup
2 tablespoons (30g) brown sugar
1 teaspoon vanilla
¼ teaspoon salt

Trim the crusts from:

8 slices white sandwich bread or challah

One slice at a time, turn the bread in the egg mixture to coat it, then fit the coated bread into an 8-inch baking dish, making a double layer. Very gently press the bread to compress the slices slightly. Cover with plastic wrap and refrigerate overnight.

Preheat the oven to 400°F.

Lightly butter a rimmed baking sheet, preferably nonstick. Using a wide spatula—or, if you find it easier, your hands—lift the bread, slice by slice, out of the soaking mixture, allowing the excess liquid to drip back into the dish, and place on the baking sheet. Bake until puffed and golden, 12 to 15 minutes, turning the slices halfway through baking. Serve immediately with:

Maple syrup
(Sliced fresh fruit)

BOSTOCK

8 servings

Bostock is brioche brushed with an orange-flavored syrup and apricot jam, then slathered with frangipane, an almond and butter filling. During baking, the frangipane becomes golden and crusty. It is an excellent treat for those who think brioche is not rich enough.

Preheat the oven to 375°F.

Have ready:

Eight ½- to ¾-inch-thick slices brioche (from 1 loaf)
Frangipane, 802, at room temperature
½ recipe Simple Syrup, 16
¾ cup sliced almonds
½ cup apricot jam

Whisk into the simple syrup:

1 tablespoon orange liqueur, such as Cointreau or Grand Marnier
1 teaspoon orange flower water

Place the brioche slices on a baking sheet. Brush them with the simple syrup (you will not use all the syrup). Spread each slice with 1 tablespoon apricot jam, then with 3 tablespoons frangipane. Sprinkle with the sliced almonds. Bake until golden brown, about 25 minutes. Before serving, sprinkle with:

Powdered sugar

ABOUT CRÊPES

Crêpes are very thin, delicate pancakes. In the United States, we tend to think of crêpes as sweet, but savory crêpes are beloved in France, where they are sometimes called *galettes*. In some cases, these savory crêpes are made with buckwheat flour and may be filled with ham and cheese, mushrooms, or eggs cooked over easy. Unlike pancakes, crêpes require a very smooth batter, which is most easily achieved in a blender, although whisking in a bowl works fine. Crêpe batter can be made up to 2 days ahead and refrigerated in a covered container. Before using a refrigerated batter, gently stir and let stand at room temperature for 30 minutes.

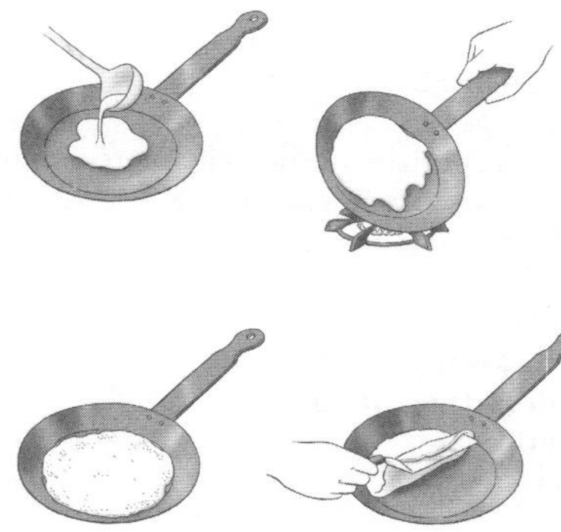

Making crêpes

Crêpes can be made in a well-seasoned crêpe pan or in a regular small to medium nonstick skillet. While a spatula may be used to flip crêpes, we recommend working up the confidence to try flipping them with a flick of the wrist.

To store crêpes, place them in a stack on a plate, cover tightly with plastic wrap, and refrigerate for up to 24 hours. Or wrap the stack in foil, seal in a plastic bag, and freeze for up to 1 month. To thaw frozen crêpes, place in the refrigerator for about 12 hours or thaw at room temperature just until they are soft enough to peel them apart without tearing.

SAVORY OR SWEET CRÊPES

About 12 crêpes

Savory crêpes make an elegant brunch, lunch, or supper dish when rolled around a filling; see Filled Savory Crêpes, 646. Sweet crêpes may be treated as lavish desserts or simply sprinkle them with sugar and lemon juice or spread with warmed preserves and eat for breakfast.

I. SAVORY

Combine in a large bowl or blender and mix or blend until smooth:

1 cup (125g) all-purpose flour
1 cup (235g) milk
½ cup (120g) lukewarm water

4 large eggs
4 tablespoons (2 oz or 55g) butter, melted
½ teaspoon salt

Place a medium nonstick skillet over medium heat. Have ready:

2 tablespoons butter

Add ½ teaspoon butter to the skillet and swirl to coat. Pour enough batter into the skillet to cover the bottom with a very thin coating (about ¼ cup). Tilt and rotate the skillet to cover the bottom with batter, and cook until the crêpe bubbles and the bottom is lightly browned, 1 to 1½ minutes. Turn the crêpes with a long, thin spatula or flip it with a quick flick of the wrist. Cook the second side until browned (it will not brown evenly but will be nicely speckled). Slide the crêpe onto a plate and repeat with the remaining batter, adding more butter after cooking each crêpe.

II. SWEET

Prepare the batter as above, adding **3 tablespoons (35g) sugar** and decreasing the salt to ⅛ teaspoon.

BUCKWHEAT CRÊPES

About ten 9-inch crêpes

Buckwheat crêpes, a specialty of the Brittany region of France, are larger and a little thicker than regular crêpes with an assertive flavor from the buckwheat flour. Buckwheat crêpes are typically filled with savory mixtures.

Combine in a blender:

½ cup (60g) buckwheat flour
½ cup (65g) all-purpose flour
1 cup (235g) milk
¾ cup (175g) water
3 large eggs
2 tablespoons (25g) vegetable oil
½ teaspoon salt

Blend until combined, then scrape down the sides of the container and blend about 15 seconds more or until smooth. Cook, keep warm, and serve as for **Savory or Sweet Crêpes, 645,** using about ⅓ cup batter for each crêpe.

FILLED SAVORY CRÊPES

10 to 12 crêpes

The traditional pairing for savory crêpes is hard apple cider.

Prepare:

Savory Crêpes, 645, or Buckwheat Crêpes, above

Preheat the oven to 400°F. Lightly butter a 13 × 9-inch baking dish. Have ready one of the following:

About 4 cups Creamed Mushrooms, 251, or Mushroom Ragout, 251
About 4 cups Creamed Spinach, 244
20 to 24 slices ham and 10 to 12 slices Swiss cheese or 2½ to 3 cups shredded Gruyère or Emmenthaler (10 to 12 ounces)

Spread about ¼ cup of filling (or, for the ham and cheese, 2 slices of ham and 1 slice or ¼ cup of shredded cheese) in the center of the pale side of each crêpe, leaving a 1-inch border all around, then roll up the crêpes. Arrange seam side down in a single layer in the prepared baking dish. Brush with:

3 tablespoons butter, melted

Sprinkle with:

½ cup grated Parmesan (2 ounces)

Bake until lightly browned, about 20 minutes.

FILLED SWEET CRÊPES

12 crêpes

These are filled and rolled; an alternative way to present sweet crêpes is to spread them with the filling, then fold them in half, then in half again into a triangular shape.

Prepare:

12 Sweet Crêpes, above

Have ready 4 cups of one of the following or a combination:

Any fruit, poached, 170, roasted, 171, or sautéed, 172
Any flavor Pastry Cream, 801–2
Whipped Cream, 791
Applesauce, 174
Jam or preserves
Lemon Curd, 802
Chocolate Ganache, 797

Spread 3 to 4 tablespoons of filling in the center of the pale side of each crêpe, leaving a 1-inch border all around, then roll up the crêpes. Arrange seam side down on a serving platter. Brush with:

3 tablespoons butter, melted

Dust with:

Powdered sugar

CRÊPES SUZETTE

12 crêpes

Please read Flambéing or Flaming, 1049.

Prepare:

12 Sweet Crêpes, above

Place in a large skillet over medium heat:

4 tablespoons (2 oz or 55g) butter
(Finely grated zest of 1 orange)
½ cup (120g) orange juice
⅓ cup (65g) sugar
1 teaspoon lemon juice

Bring to a boil, stirring to melt the sugar, then continue to boil until slightly thickened, 2 to 3 minutes. Stir in:

2 tablespoons Grand Marnier
2 tablespoons Cognac or other brandy

Return the sauce to a boil and boil for 30 seconds. Using tongs, add a crêpe to the skillet or chafing dish and soak in the sauce about 15 seconds, then fold it in half twice so it is triangular in shape with the browner side out. Lay the folded crêpe against the inside of the skillet while you continue to soak and fold the remaining crêpes, laying each against the inside of the skillet as you go. When all are folded, arrange the crêpes over the bottom of the skillet and pour over them:

½ cup Grand Marnier

Cook about 15 seconds, spooning the sauce over the crêpes. Standing back, carefully ignite with a long lighter or wooden match. Serve still flaming.

CRÊPES WITH CARAMELIZED APPLES

12 crêpes

The apples, which can be refrigerated for a week, are delicious on any pancake or waffle. If desired, make the crêpes and apples up to 2 days ahead of time.

Prepare:

12 Sweet Crêpes, 646

Set aside. Combine in a small saucepan:

1 cup apple cider
3 tablespoons light corn syrup
1 tablespoon light brown sugar
1 tablespoon lemon juice

Simmer over medium heat until the mixture is reduced by half, about 10 minutes. Stir in:

3 medium Golden Delicious apples, peeled, cored, and cut into 12 wedges each
2 tablespoons cold butter

Continue to simmer until the apples are tender and the syrup is very thick, about 15 minutes.

Preheat the oven to 350°F. Line a large baking sheet with parchment paper.

Have ready:

3 tablespoons butter, melted

Brush the crêpes lightly with the butter and arrange on the prepared baking sheet, overlapping as necessary. Bake until warmed through, about 5 minutes. Fill the crêpes with the apples and sauce. If desired, top with:

(Whipped Cream, 791, or vanilla ice cream)

CRÊPE CAKE

6 servings

For an especially dramatic cake that will serve 10 to 12 people, prepare a double recipe of crêpes. If flaming the cake, please read Flambéing or Flaming, 1049.

Prepare:

12 Sweet Crêpes, 646

Spread 11 of the crêpes with a very thin layer of:

Jelly or jam, Chocolate Ganache, 797, or any flavor Pastry Cream, 801–2

Stack the coated crêpes like a layer cake on a flameproof platter, and top with the uncoated crêpe. Sprinkle the top with:

Powdered sugar

Set aside at room temperature for up to 8 hours.

Preheat the oven to 250°F.

If you would like to flame the dessert, heat in a small saucepan until just warm:

(¼ cup brandy or rum)

Pour over the crêpes and, standing back, carefully ignite with a long lighter or wooden match. To serve, place the crêpe cake in the oven until warmed through, about 15 minutes. Cut into wedges. If desired, serve with:

(Whipped Cream, 791)

BLINTZES

About twelve 7½-inch blintzes

Blintzes, much like crêpes, are very thin pancakes, but the name can also refer to the dish that results when blintzes are stuffed with a filling. See Sweet Cheese Blintzes, below, and Blueberry Blintzes, 648.

Combine in a blender or food processor and blend or process until smooth:

1 cup (125g) all-purpose flour
1 cup (235g) milk
3 large eggs
2 tablespoons (30g) butter, melted
2 teaspoons sugar
Pinch of salt

Place a medium nonstick skillet over medium heat. Have ready:

2 tablespoons butter

Add ½ teaspoon butter to the skillet and swirl to coat. Pour 3 tablespoons of batter into the skillet, tilting and rotating the skillet to cover the bottom. Cook without turning until the batter is dry and set and the underside is golden, about 3 minutes. Slide the blintz onto a plate and repeat with the remaining batter, adding more butter after cooking each blintz.

SWEET CHEESE BLINTZES

12 blintzes

The classic accompaniment to sweet cheese blintzes is poached sour cherries, 170. Also delicious are mixed fresh berries, a warm Dried Fruit Compote, 169, or Applesauce, 174. Cheese blintzes can be made with either small-curd cottage cheese or farmer cheese. If using cottage cheese, first drain it for 1 hour in a sieve set over a bowl.

Prepare:

12 Blintzes, above

Combine in a food processor and process until smooth:

1 pound small-curd cottage cheese, drained, or farmer cheese
3 ounces cream cheese
2 large eggs
2 tablespoons sugar
1 teaspoon vanilla
½ teaspoon salt
(Finely grated zest of 1 orange)

Transfer to a medium bowl and stir in, if desired:

(½ cup raisins)

Spoon 3 tablespoons of the filling onto the center of the pale side of a blintz. Fold the two sides in to cover the filling, then fold the bottom up. Starting at the folded bottom, roll the blintz up to form a rectangular package. Continue with the remaining blintzes and filling. (The filled blintzes can be wrapped airtight and frozen for up to 1 month. Thaw in the refrigerator.) Melt in a large skillet, preferably nonstick, over medium heat until the bubbles have subsided:

3 tablespoons butter

Add the blintzes to the skillet, seam side down, and cook, turning once, until golden brown on both sides. Serve immediately.

BLUEBERRY BLINTZES

6 blintzes

Prepare:

6 Blintzes, 647

Combine in a medium saucepan:

1 cup fresh or unthawed frozen blueberries
Finely grated zest and juice of ½ lemon
2 tablespoons sugar
(Pinch of ground cinnamon)

Bring to a boil over medium heat, stirring constantly, then continue to boil until the mixture is the consistency of jam. Add:

1 cup fresh or unthawed frozen blueberries

Cook and stir for 1 minute. Transfer to a bowl and let cool to room temperature.

Spoon 2 generous tablespoons of the filling onto the center of the pale side of each blintz. Fold and roll each into a rectangular package as for Sweet Cheese Blintzes, 647. Cook or store as directed. Serve immediately with:

Sour cream, Crème Anglaise, 806, or Lemon Curd, 802

PALATSCHINKEN (VIENNESE-STYLE CRÊPES)

8 rolled pancakes

Prepare the batter for:

Blintzes, 647

Cook on both sides as for **Savory or Sweet Crêpes, 645,** using ¼ cup batter for each pancake. Cool, then wrap until ready to serve.

Preheat the oven to 350°F. Line a large baking sheet with parchment paper.

Brush the pancakes lightly with:

2 tablespoons butter, melted

Arrange on the prepared baking sheet, overlapping slightly if necessary. Bake until warmed through, about 5 minutes. Meanwhile, combine in a small saucepan and bring to a boil:

1 cup apricot jam
1 tablespoon brandy

Remove from the heat. Spread each pancake with 2 tablespoons of the jam mixture and roll up. Transfer to individual plates and sprinkle with:

½ cup finely chopped toasted, 1005, walnuts
Powdered sugar

If desired, serve with:

(Whipped Cream, 791)

DOSAS (INDIAN RICE AND LENTIL PANCAKES)

About ten 9-inch dosas

Dosas are thin, crêpe-like Indian pancakes. They may be very thin, dry, and crisp, or softer and thicker. This version is made with rice and black gram (sold as *urad dal* at Indian grocery stores) and makes a very thin, crisp *dosa*. The usual accompaniments to *dosa* are *sambar* (a thin lentil soup not unlike dal) and chutney, though the *dosas* are sometimes wrapped around a spiced potato and onion filling. If desired, prepare the filling for Quick Phyllo Samosas with Potatoes and Peas, 68, and wrap the *dosa* around it.

Combine in a medium bowl:

½ cup (100g) basmati rice
½ cup (105g) urad dal or yellow split peas

Add:

Water to generously cover

Let sit for at least 12 hours and up to overnight.

Drain the rice and peas well and transfer to a blender along with:

1½ cups (355g) water
1 teaspoon cumin seeds
½ teaspoon fenugreek seeds
¼ teaspoon salt
(Pinch of asafoetida, 954)
(Pinch of cayenne pepper)

Blend until very smooth. Strain through a fine-mesh sieve into a bowl, tightly cover with plastic wrap, and let sit in a warm place, such as on top of the refrigerator, for 24 hours to ferment slightly.

Heat a large nonstick skillet over medium-low heat for 5 minutes. When the skillet is ready a few drops of water sprinkled on its surface will sizzle and evaporate almost instantly. Whisk the batter well—it should be very frothy and light. Whisk in:

¼ cup (60g) water

The batter should be thin enough to run in a ribbon from a spoon. Take the preheated skillet off the heat. Pour ⅓ cup batter into the center of the skillet and use the bottom of the measuring cup to spread it very thinly, working in a circular motion from the center outward, into an 8- to 9-inch round. This spreading action takes some practice, so do not be discouraged if the first few *dosas* look rough. The key is to apply the right amount of pressure to the measuring cup—too little and the batter will not spread effectively; too much and it will scrape the set batter from the skillet and create large holes. Place the skillet back on the heat. Sprinkle over the *dosa*:

1 teaspoon vegetable oil

Let cook until the *dosa* is set and the surface is covered in tiny holes from where bubbles appeared and burst, 3 to 4 minutes. Flip the *dosa* and cook until done on the second side, about 1 minute more. Loosely roll up the *dosa* and place it seam side down on a rack. Repeat the process with the remaining batter, taking the skillet off the heat each time to spread the batter, then placing it back on the heat to cook the *dosa*. Serve with:

Dal, 218
Cilantro-Mint Chutney, 568

BÁNH XÈO (SAVORY VIETNAMESE FILLED CRÊPES)

4 servings

Because these crêpes must be cooked one at a time, invite guests to start eating as soon as the crêpes come out of the skillet. To eat, cut off pieces of the crêpe, fold them along with the herbs in the romaine leaves, and dip in the *nuoc cham*.

Whisk to combine in a medium bowl:

1½ cups (170g) rice flour
1 cup (235g) water
½ cup (115g) canned coconut milk
2 green onions, thinly sliced
½ teaspoon salt
½ teaspoon ground turmeric

Set aside while you prepare the remaining ingredients. Prepare and lay out on a large plate or rimmed baking sheet:

8 ounces pork shoulder, sliced as thinly as possible and cut into 1-inch pieces
½ medium onion, very thinly sliced
8 ounces medium shrimp, peeled, deveined, 363, and halved lengthwise
2 cups packed mung bean sprouts

Heat in a large nonstick skillet over medium-high heat:

2 teaspoons vegetable oil

Add one-quarter of the pork and onion and cook, stirring, until the pork is no longer pink, about 1 minute. Add one-quarter of the shrimp and spread the pork, shrimp, and onion evenly in the skillet. Pour ½ cup of the batter into the skillet and quickly tilt and rotate the skillet to coat it with batter. Cook the crêpe until it just appears set, about 1 minute. Scatter ½ cup of the bean sprouts on half of the crêpe, and cover the skillet. Cook until the sprouts are slightly translucent, about 1 minute. Uncover the skillet and drizzle around the edge of the crêpe so it runs beneath the crêpe, not on top of it:

2 teaspoons vegetable oil

Continue to cook until the crêpe is crispy, 1 to 2 minutes more. Fold the crêpe in half in the skillet to cover the bean sprouts, then slide it onto a plate. Repeat this process three more times with the remaining fillings, batter, and more oil. Serve the crêpes with:

16 romaine lettuce leaves
1 English cucumber, thinly sliced on the diagonal
½ bunch cilantro, stems trimmed
1 small bunch mint
(1 small bunch Vietnamese coriander, 973)
Nuoc Cham, 571

ABOUT OVEN-BAKED PANCAKES

Dutch babies, *pfannkuchen*, and *nöckerl* are "pancakes" if the phrase is taken literally—they are, after all, cakes cooked in a pan. And yet they bear little resemblance to other pancakes: Their light texture and dramatic puff are much more like that of Popovers, 634, or soufflés, 161–62. Though traditionally served as dessert, they are quite popular when served at breakfast or brunch. Sturdier, chickpea-based Socca, 650, does not puff, and is perfect for topping with savory ingredients.

DUTCH BABY

2 to 4 servings

Sometimes called a **puff pancake,** this impressive confection emerges from the oven puffed and golden, like a giant popover. The traditional topping of powdered sugar and lemon juice is hard to beat, but butter and maple syrup, fruit preserves, or Sautéed Apple Rings, 174, are worthy embellishments. We sometimes top Dutch babies with savory toppings like sautéed greens and fried eggs.

Position a rack in the lower third of the oven. Preheat the oven to 425°F. Whisk together in a medium bowl:

½ cup (120g) milk
2 large eggs, at room temperature
¼ teaspoon salt

Add and whisk until smooth:

½ cup (65g) all-purpose flour

Melt in a 10-inch cast-iron skillet or other ovenproof pan over medium heat:

4 tablespoons (½ stick) butter

Tilt the skillet so that the butter coats the sides. Pour the egg mixture into the skillet, place the skillet in the oven, and bake for 15 minutes. Reduce the temperature to 350°F and bake until the pancake is puffed and richly browned, 10 to 15 minutes more. Sprinkle with:

Powdered sugar
Lemon juice

Serve immediately, straight from the skillet, before the pancake falls.

PFANNKUCHEN (GERMAN PANCAKE)

4 servings

Our recipe is based on one by Henriette Davidis, nineteenth-century Germany's greatest cookbook author.

Preheat the oven to 400°F.

Whisk vigorously in a medium bowl until thickened and lemon colored, 1 to 2 minutes:

4 large egg yolks (whites reserved)
3 tablespoons (35g) sugar
⅛ teaspoon salt

Whisk in:

¼ cup (60g) milk
¼ cup (60g) lukewarm water
Finely grated zest of 1 lemon
(¼ teaspoon vanilla)

Add and whisk until smooth:

½ cup (65g) cornstarch

Beat until stiff but not dry, 978:

4 large egg whites

Add to the yolk mixture, gently whisking until the whites are incorporated but not deflated; the batter should have the appearance of a light foam. Immediately melt in a 10-inch heavy ovenproof skillet, preferably nonstick, over medium heat:

3 tablespoons butter

When the bubbles subside, pour in the batter. Cook until the pancake looks golden brown on the underside when pried back from the skillet with a knife, about 2 minutes. Place the skillet in the oven and bake until the pancake has puffed and the top feels dry and set when gently touched, about 5 minutes. Immediately slide the pancake onto a serving platter and sprinkle with:

Powdered sugar
(Ground cinnamon)

Serve at once, accompanied with:

⅔ cup warmed apricot or cherry preserves

NÖCKERL (AUSTRIAN PANCAKES)

4 servings

When in Salzburg, few visitors fail to indulge in one or more of these souffléed globular puffs. To be fair, they are more akin to free-form soufflés than pancakes.

Preheat the oven to 350°F.
Combine in a medium bowl and whisk until thickened and pale:

2 large egg yolks (whites reserved)
1 tablespoon (10g) sugar
(Finely grated zest of 1 lemon)

Beat in a large bowl until almost stiff, 977:

3 large egg whites

Gradually beat in:

¼ cup (50g) sugar

Beat until the whites are very stiff and shiny, then beat in:

½ teaspoon vanilla

Sift over, then gently fold in with a silicone spatula:

2 tablespoons (15g) all-purpose flour

Gently fold in the egg yolk mixture. Immediately melt in a large ovenproof skillet over medium-high heat:

2 tablespoons butter

When the butter smells fragrant and is just beginning to color, spoon four 1-cup mounds of the mixture into the skillet, heaping them high and spacing them as far apart as possible. Cook until the pancakes are lightly colored on the bottom, about 3 minutes. Transfer the skillet to the oven and bake the pancakes until lightly brown and puffed but still soft in the center, 10 to 12 minutes. Sprinkle generously with:

Powdered sugar

Serve at once. If desired, accompany with:

(Warmed preserves or Fresh Berry Coulis, 805, made with raspberries)

SOCCA (SAVORY CHICKPEA PANCAKE)

4 servings

These simple pancakes are called *socca* in Nice, France, and *farinata* or *cecina* in Italy. They are traditionally baked in wood-fired ovens, so if you happen to have a backyard wood oven or a charcoal grill, try cooking the pancake in one of those for an added smoky flavor. *Socca* is typically a snack, but we sometimes like to serve it for breakfast topped with sautéed greens and sunny-side up eggs.

Whisk to combine in a medium bowl:

1 cup (115g) chickpea flour
1 cup (235g) water
1 tablespoon (15g) olive oil
¼ teaspoon salt

The batter should be the consistency of thin pancake batter. If needed, add a little more water to reach the right consistency. Let the batter rest for 30 minutes.

Position a rack in the center of the oven and place a large cast-iron or other ovenproof skillet on the rack. Preheat the broiler for 10 minutes. Heat in the skillet taken from the oven:

1 tablespoon olive oil

Tilt the skillet to coat it with oil, then pour in the batter. Return the skillet to the oven and broil until the pancake is cooked through and browned around the edges, 4 to 7 minutes. Loosen the pancake with a spatula and slide it onto a plate. Cut into pieces and drizzle with:

Extra-virgin olive oil

Sprinkle to taste with:

Salt and black pepper

ABOUT DOUGHNUTS

It seems to us that the various forms of fried dough enjoyed by people across the globe may well have been invented to assuage the ills of the human condition. Dutch settlers brought doughnuts to America in the form of what was called *olykoeks* (oily cakes). Over the course of a couple hundred years, doughnuts were transformed into their modern incarnation.

There is not much to making doughnuts, but there are a few important things to keep in mind. When mixing doughnut doughs, ➤ have all the ingredients at room temperature, and stir the wet and dry ingredients together quickly just until well blended. This prevents the development of gluten in the dough, which will toughen the doughnuts. Many doughnut doughs are soft and sticky when first mixed, but when chilled for at least 2 hours before cutting, they become firm enough to handle easily. These doughs can be refrigerated up to 2 days before shaping and frying. In addition to the recipes given here, also see Brioche, 603, for a rich dough that is excellent when shaped and fried.

To form doughnuts, roll the dough ½ inch thick (unless otherwise specified) on a lightly floured work surface or on floured wax paper. In most cases, it is easier to roll the dough to an even thickness if you divide it in half before rolling. ➤ Cut out doughnuts either with a well-floured doughnut cutter or with 2 sizes of round biscuit or cookie cutters, using a smaller cutter for the doughnut holes. ➤ Our recipes are developed for a 3½-inch cutter with a 1-inch hole. If you use a smaller cutter, the yield will be greater than that given in the recipe (a 2½-inch cutter, for example, will yield nearly twice as many doughnuts). Using a spatula or your hands, transfer the cut doughnuts to a sheet of wax or parchment paper that has been generously floured. Press the scraps together, handling them as little as possible, then roll and cut out more doughnuts. Scraps of scraps will make tough doughnuts, so use these instead to make "holes," which you can either cut with a 1-inch cutter or form with your hands.

Before beginning, ➤ please read about Deep-Frying, 1051. Fry the doughnuts in a heavy pot or Dutch oven, using about 3 inches vegetable oil or melted shortening. Whichever fat you use, it must be fresh, not recycled. The oil or fat should hover between 360° and 375°F. To keep the fat at a constant temperature, ➤ never crowd the fryer. The easiest and safest way to transfer doughnuts to the pot is to ➤ slide them in one at a time using a long metal spatula that has been dipped in the hot fat. A deep golden brown color is the best indicator of doneness. To be sure that you are gauging doneness correctly, cut into one doughnut from the first batch to be sure the inside is done. If it is underdone, the remaining doughnuts should be cooked longer. Remove the doughnuts with tongs or a wooden chopstick inserted through the hole in each one, holding them briefly over the pot to allow excess fat to drip off. Place the cooked doughnuts on a triple layer of paper towels, then immediately turn them to blot fat from the second side.

Homemade doughnuts are best eaten on the day they are made,

though they will remain reasonably moist for up to 2 days if stored in a tightly sealed container at room temperature. Doughnuts can also be frozen in a zip-top freezer bag for up to 1 month and eaten immediately after thawing.

▲ Recipes for yeast-raised doughnuts require no adjustment at high altitudes. For other doughnuts, reduce the baking powder or baking soda by one-quarter, ➤ but do not reduce baking soda to below ½ teaspoon per each cup of buttermilk or sour cream used.

CAKE DOUGHNUTS

About 18 doughnuts

Please read About Doughnuts, 650.

Whisk together in a medium bowl until thoroughly mixed:

4 cups (500g) all-purpose flour
4 teaspoons baking powder
¾ teaspoon ground cinnamon
(¾ teaspoon grated or ground nutmeg)
¾ teaspoon salt

Beat well in a large bowl with an electric mixer:

2 large eggs

Add slowly and beat until thick and creamy:

1 cup (200g) sugar

On low speed, add and beat until blended:

1 cup (235g) milk
5 tablespoons (70g) unsalted butter, melted
1 teaspoon vanilla

Mix the wet ingredients into the flour mixture with a spoon just until blended. The dough will be soft and sticky. Cover the bowl tightly with plastic wrap and refrigerate for at least 2 hours and up to 24 hours.

Roll out the dough on a lightly floured surface to ½ inch thick and cut out the doughnuts. Let them rest, loosely covered with oiled plastic wrap, for 30 minutes.

Heat to 365°F in a deep-fryer, deep heavy pot, or Dutch oven:

3 inches vegetable oil or shortening

Fry in batches, flipping halfway through, until golden, about 4 minutes. Drain briefly on a baking sheet lined with paper towels, turning them to blot fat from the second side. While still warm, toss in a bowl with:

Flavored Sugars, 1026

Or let cool and glaze with:

Any icing or glaze, 798–800

YEAST DOUGHNUTS

About 24 doughnuts

Please read About Doughnuts, 650.

Whisk together in a stand mixer (or a large bowl):

1 cup (235g) warm (105° to 115°F) water
2 envelopes (2¼ teaspoons each) active dry yeast

Let stand until the yeast is dissolved, about 5 minutes. Add and stir in until smooth:

1 cup (125g) all-purpose flour

Cover the bowl tightly with plastic wrap and let stand at room temperature until bubbling, about 30 minutes.

Mix in with the paddle attachment (or by hand):

⅔ cup (130g) sugar
1¼ sticks (5 oz or 140g) butter, softened
3 large eggs
2 teaspoons vanilla
1 teaspoon salt
(Finely grated zest of 1 lemon or orange)

Add:

3½ cups (440g) all-purpose flour

Switch to the dough hook and knead on medium-low speed until the dough wraps around the hook and comes away from the sides of the bowl. (Or mix the flour in with a spoon, then knead the dough until smooth and elastic.) Cover the mixer bowl with plastic wrap. (If you kneaded the dough by hand, transfer it to a bowl and cover tightly.) Let the dough rise at room temperature until tripled in volume, 1½ to 2 hours.

Knead the dough very briefly to deflate it, return it to the bowl, cover tightly, and refrigerate for at least 3 hours and up to 16 hours.

Roll out the dough on a lightly floured surface to ⅜ inch thick and cut out the doughnuts. Let the doughnuts rise, uncovered, at room temperature until soft and puffy, about 1 hour.

Fry, drain, and coat or glaze as for **Cake Doughnuts, above.** Begin frying the doughnuts as soon as they have risen, or they will overrise, and the taste and texture will change for the worse.

SOUR CREAM DOUGHNUTS

About twelve 2¾-inch doughnuts

Please read About Doughnuts, 650.

Whisk together in a medium bowl:

2 cups (250g) all-purpose flour
2½ teaspoons baking powder
½ teaspoon baking soda
½ teaspoon salt
½ teaspoon ground cinnamon

Beat in a large bowl until foamy:

2 large eggs

Gradually add and beat until thoroughly blended:

½ cup (100g) sugar

Stir in until blended:

½ cup (120g) sour cream
1 teaspoon vanilla

Add the flour mixture to the egg mixture and stir just until incorporated. The dough will be very soft. Pat the dough into a disc, wrap in plastic wrap, and refrigerate for at least 2 hours and up to 2 days.

Roll out, cut, rest, and fry as for **Cake Doughnuts, above.** Drain well on paper towels and either dust with:

Powdered sugar

or toss in a bowl with:

Flavored Sugars, 1026

Serve while still warm.

BUTTERMILK POTATO DOUGHNUTS

About 20 doughnuts

Please read About Doughnuts, 650.

Prepare:

2 cups riced boiled russet potatoes, 265

Whisk together thoroughly in a medium bowl:

3¾ cups (470g) all-purpose flour
2½ teaspoons baking powder
1 teaspoon salt
½ teaspoon baking soda
¼ teaspoon grated or ground nutmeg or cinnamon

Beat in a large bowl, with an electric mixer at high speed, until foamy, about 1 minute:

2 large eggs

Gradually add and beat until thick and creamy:

¾ cup (150g) sugar

On low speed, add and beat until blended:

1 cup (245g) buttermilk
4 tablespoons (2 oz or 55g) butter, melted
1 teaspoon vanilla

Beat in the riced potatoes. Using a large spoon, stir in the flour mixture. The dough will be very soft. Wrap in plastic and refrigerate for at least 2 hours and up to 24 hours.

Roll out, cut, rest, and fry as for **Cake Doughnuts, 651.** Drain briefly on a baking sheet lined with paper towels, then, while still warm, toss in a bowl with:

Flavored Sugars, 1026

Or let cool and glaze with:

Any icing or glaze, 798–800

CHOCOLATE DOUGHNUTS

About 14 doughnuts

Please read About Doughnuts, 650.

Combine in a large bowl:

⅔ cup (65g) Dutch-process cocoa powder
4 tablespoons (2 oz or 55g) butter, cut into small pieces

Pour in and whisk until smooth:

⅔ cup (160g) boiling water

Let stand 5 minutes. Whisk in until thoroughly blended:

1 cup (200g) sugar
⅔ cup (160g) sour cream
2 large eggs
2 teaspoons vanilla
1 teaspoon salt
1 teaspoon baking powder
½ teaspoon baking soda

Add:

4¼ cups (530g) all-purpose flour

Stir until the flour is absorbed and a soft dough forms. Wrap the dough in plastic and refrigerate for at least 2 hours and up to 24 hours.

Roll out, cut, rest, and fry as for **Cake Doughnuts, 651.** The doughnuts are cooked through when they have become several shades darker and are not raw when cut into. If desired, when the doughnuts have cooled, dip one side of each doughnut into:

(Bittersweet Chocolate Glaze or Frosting, 798)

Place on a rack, glazed side up. Let stand until the glaze is dry, about 1 hour.

DROPPED DOUGHNUTS

About sixty 1½-inch balls

Without the characteristic hole, these are lighter in texture. If you dip the spoon into the frying oil before spooning up each gob of batter, the doughnuts will slide easily into the pot. Please read About Doughnuts, 650.

Prepare the dough for either of the following, decreasing the flour by ½ cup:

Cake Doughnuts, 651, or Chocolate Doughnuts, above

Do not refrigerate the dough. Cover it and set aside at room temperature for 30 minutes.

Heat to 375°F in a deep-fryer, deep heavy pot, or Dutch oven:

3 inches vegetable oil or shortening

Slide about 1 tablespoon dough for each doughnut into the fat, adding 5 or 6 at a time, and fry about 3 minutes. Drain briefly on a baking sheet lined with paper towels, then, while still warm, toss in a bowl with:

Flavored Sugars, 1026

JELLY DOUGHNUTS

About 24 doughnuts

Be sure to let these rise until very light and puffy or air pockets will develop around the jelly centers. Please read About Doughnuts, 650.

Prepare the dough for:

Yeast Doughnuts, 651

Working with one-quarter of the dough at a time, on a lightly floured work surface roll out the dough to a little more than ⅛ inch thick. Cut into rounds using a 3- to 3½-inch round cookie or biscuit cutter (do not cut holes out of the rounds). Gather, re-roll, and cut the scraps. You should have about 48 rounds altogether. Have ready:

About ¾ cup jelly or jam

Place a heaping teaspoon of jam or jelly in the center of half of the rounds. Brush the edges of these filled rounds with:

1 large egg white, lightly beaten

Top each filled round with a plain round of dough and pinch the edges together to seal. Transfer to well-floured wax paper and let rise until light and puffy, about 1 hour.

Fry and drain as for **Cake Doughnuts, 651.** Begin frying the doughnuts as soon as they have risen, or they will overrise and the taste and texture will change for the worse. Dust with:

Powdered sugar

HONEY-DIPPED DOUGHNUTS

About 24 doughnuts

Prepare the dough, cut out, and fry:

Yeast Doughnuts, 651

Meanwhile, set a wire rack over a baking sheet. Combine in a large saucepan:

4 cups powdered sugar (about 1 pound)
⅓ cup honey
¼ cup water

Cook the glaze over medium heat, whisking constantly, until the mixture just begins to simmer and is completely smooth. Remove the pan from the heat.

While the fried doughnuts are still warm, drop them into the glaze one at a time, turning to glaze both sides. Using a chopstick or long skewer, transfer the doughnuts to the wire rack. If the glaze stiffens while you are dipping the doughnuts, warm it briefly over low heat. Let the doughnuts stand about 15 minutes, or until the glaze is dry.

CRULLERS

About 24 crullers

Crullers were brought to America by Dutch immigrants. They have a twisted or knotted shape and are richer than doughnuts. Please read About Doughnuts, 650.

Whisk together thoroughly in a medium bowl:

4 cups (500g) all-purpose flour
(1 teaspoon grated or ground nutmeg)
¾ teaspoon ground cinnamon
2 teaspoons baking powder
¾ teaspoon salt

Add:

8 tablespoons (4 oz or 115g) unsalted butter, softened

Rub with your hands until the butter has completely disappeared into the dry ingredients, without a speck of unblended butter remaining. The mixture should feel soft and slightly greasy and should hold together in a crumbly mass when grasped. Beat in a medium bowl, with a mixer at high speed, until very foamy:

4 large eggs

Gradually beat in until thick and creamy:

¾ cup (150g) sugar

Beat in on low speed:

2 tablespoons (30g) milk

Stir the egg mixture into the flour mixture with a spoon until a soft dough forms. Wrap the dough in plastic wrap and refrigerate for at least 2 hours and up to 24 hours.

Using 1 level tablespoon for each, roll the dough between your hands into 48 balls. Do not flour the dough; if it becomes too soft to handle, refrigerate it briefly. Place the balls on a baking sheet covered with wax or parchment paper, cover with plastic wrap, and refrigerate for at least 1 hour.

Line a baking sheet with parchment paper and sprinkle generously with flour. Work with just a few balls at a time, leaving the rest in the refrigerator. On unfloured wax or parchment paper, roll 2 balls under your palms into 5-inch ropes. Place the ropes side by side, pinch one end to seal, then twist the ropes a few times and seal the other end. Transfer to the prepared baking sheet. Repeat to make 24 crullers. Let stand at room temperature, uncovered, for 30 minutes.

Fry, drain, and coat or glaze as for **Cake Doughnuts, 651.**

NEW ORLEANS BEIGNETS

About thirty 2½-inch beignets

New Orleans is famous for these puffy, crusty treats, which go well with the city's renowned chicory-flavored coffee. Please read About Doughnuts, 650.

Combine in a large bowl:

¾ cup (175g) lukewarm (105° to 115°F) water
1 teaspoon active dry yeast

Let stand 5 minutes, then whisk until the yeast is dissolved. Whisk in, blending well:

½ cup (125g) evaporated milk
¼ cup (50g) sugar
1 large egg
½ teaspoon salt

Beat in with a spoon until a smooth batter forms:

2 cups (250g) all-purpose flour

Beat in:

3 tablespoons butter (45g), softened, or vegetable shortening (35g)

Beat in thoroughly:

2 cups (250g) all-purpose flour

Cover the bowl tightly with plastic wrap and refrigerate for at least 12 hours and up to 24 hours.

Heat to 365°F in a deep-fryer, deep heavy pot, or Dutch oven:

3 inches vegetable oil or shortening

While the oil heats, form the beignets: Punch the dough down, divide it in half, and return one half to the refrigerator. On a lightly floured work surface, roll the dough ⅛ inch thick and, using a sharp knife, cut into 2½-inch squares. Then immediately roll and cut the other half of the dough; do not permit the beignets to rise. Starting with the beignets you cut first, fry 5 or 6 beignets at a time until golden brown, 1 to 2 minutes on each side. Drain on paper towels. Dust with:

Powdered sugar

Serve as soon as possible, preferably while still warm.

CALAS (CREOLE RICE FRITTERS)

About 20 fritters

These old-fashioned fritters were once sold by street vendors—many of them slaves, former slaves, or the descendants of slaves—in New Orleans. While they have fallen out of favor when compared to the beignet, we think they are worth remembering. Please read about Deep-Frying, 1051.

Heat to 365°F in a deep-fryer, deep heavy pot, or Dutch oven:

2 inches vegetable oil

Meanwhile, mix together in a large bowl:

2 cups cooked white rice, 343
3 large eggs
½ cup (100g) sugar
2¼ teaspoons baking powder
1 teaspoon vanilla
½ teaspoon ground cinnamon
(½ teaspoon grated or ground nutmeg)

Add:

¾ cup (95g) all-purpose flour

Stir to combine. Carefully drop 1 tablespoon of batter for each doughnut into the fat, adding 5 or 6 at a time. Fry until golden. Drain on paper towels or a rack set over a baking sheet. Sprinkle with:

Powdered sugar

PETS DE NONNE (FRENCH-STYLE BEIGNETS)

About 28 small beignets

Light as air, these beignets are actually small, deep-fried cream puffs. Their French name translates as "nun's farts." Please read about Deep-Frying, 1051.

Prepare:

Choux Paste, 697

Add, if desired:

(Finely grated zest of 1 lemon or ½ orange)

Heat to 365°F in a deep-fryer, deep heavy pot, or Dutch oven:

3 inches vegetable oil or shortening

Drop level tablespoons of the dough into the fat, adding 6 or 8 at a time. As soon as they are cooked enough on one side, they will turn themselves over. When browned on both sides, 4 to 5 minutes total, remove from the fat with a slotted spoon and drain on paper towels. Sprinkle with:

Powdered sugar

Serve at once.

ROSETTES

About forty-eight 3 × ½-inch rosettes

Rosettes are shaped with a special long-handled mold. They are fried in deep fat to ensure that the mold doesn't touch the bottom of the pot when submerged in the oil. As a rule of thumb, the depth of the fat should be about 3 times the height of the mold. Since only one rosette is fried at a time, a narrow pot and a relatively small amount of fat may be used. Please read about Deep-Frying, 1051.

Whisk in a medium bowl until blended:

2 large eggs
1 tablespoon sugar
1 teaspoon vanilla
¼ teaspoon salt

Whisk gradually into the egg mixture, alternating between the flour and milk:

1¼ cups (155g) sifted all-purpose flour
1 cup (235g) milk

Pour the batter into a deep bowl just wide enough to dip the iron into.

Heat to 365°F in a small, deep heavy pot:

3 inches vegetable oil or shortening

Dip the iron into the hot fat for 15 seconds, then dip it into the batter only deep enough to come halfway up the sides of the iron, then immediately return the iron to the fat, immersing it but being sure not to touch the bottom of the pot. Cook until the rosette is golden brown and crisp, 30 to 45 seconds. Remove the rosette from the iron with a fork or skewer and place it hollow side down on paper towels to drain. Dip the iron in the fat again and repeat the process. Dust the rosettes with:

Powdered sugar

SOPAPILLAS

12 breads

Serve as a snack or a dessert. Please read about Deep-Frying, 1051.

Whisk together in a medium bowl until well blended:

2 cups (250g) all-purpose flour
1 tablespoon baking powder
1 tablespoon sugar
¾ teaspoon salt

Add and stir until a soft dough forms:

¾ cup (175g) warm water
1 tablespoon (15g) vegetable oil

With lightly floured hands, knead the dough just until smooth and slightly elastic, about 1 minute. (If kneaded too much, the dough will be difficult to roll out later.) Place the dough in an oiled bowl and refrigerate for at least 1 hour and up to 2 hours.

Heat to 375°F in a 10-inch-wide heavy pot or deep skillet:

2 inches lard or vegetable oil

While the lard or oil heats, roll out the dough on a lightly floured surface to just over ⅛ inch thick and cut into 3-inch squares.

Fry in batches until puffy and light brown, about 1 minute per side, turning with tongs. Drain on paper towels. Drizzle with:

Honey

Or sprinkle with:

Powdered sugar

ABOUT SAVORY FRITTERS AND CROQUETTES

The term "fritter" refers to several types of savory fried foods. There are simple fried batters, like Hushpuppies, 655, and then there are those studded with fresh or precooked bits of meat, fish, and vegetables. The term may also refer to large batter-dipped and deep-fried pieces of meat, poultry, fish, and vegetables (see About Battering Fried Foods, 656). In addition to the mixtures below, see Thai Fish Cakes, 391, as well as pan-fried recipes like Fresh Corn Fritters, 236, and Sauerkraut Fritters, 225, which are flat and thin like pancakes.

Croquettes are made from thick mixtures that are shaped and then coated with bread crumbs or flour. When well made, these fried cakes or balls are crunchy on the outside, creamy on the inside, and deserving of their status as a classic. Because their cooking time is short—2 to 4 minutes—recipes nearly always call for precooked foods or ingredients such as cheese that only need to be heated through. ➤ The food added to the mixture should be well drained and patted dry if needed.

Fritters and croquettes are best served immediately after frying. If necessary, hold cooked fritters and croquettes on a rack above a rimmed baking sheet in a 200°F oven. If the worst has happened and the fritters have gone cold, you may reheat and re-crisp them in a 400°F oven for 5 minutes.

CORN AND HAM FRITTERS

6 servings

Please read about Deep-Frying, 1051.

Whisk together in a medium bowl:

1⅓ cups (165g) all-purpose flour
2 teaspoons baking powder

¾ teaspoon salt
¾ teaspoon sweet paprika

Whisk together in another medium bowl until well blended:

2 large egg yolks (whites reserved)
½ cup (120g) milk
½ cup canned cream-style corn

Whisk the wet ingredients into the flour mixture until barely blended, leaving the batter lumpy. Fold in:

¾ cup finely diced deli ham or ½ cup finely diced country ham
2 tablespoons minced onion or green onion
2 tablespoons minced parsley

Beat until stiff but not dry, 978:

2 large egg whites

Fold the whites into the batter.

Heat to 365°F in a deep-fryer, deep heavy pot, or Dutch oven:

3 inches vegetable oil or shortening

Drop the batter by 3-tablespoon dollops, a few at a time, into the hot oil and fry until golden brown, 3 to 4 minutes. Drain on a rack or paper towels.

HUSHPUPPIES

About 50 hushpuppies

These morsels of fried cornmeal batter are flavored with onion and have a crusty, golden brown exterior. Traditionally fried alongside fish, they are also a popular side dish at barbecue establishments throughout the South. Please read about Deep-Frying, 1051.

Preheat the oven to 200°F.

Whisk together thoroughly in a large bowl:

1⅔ cups fine (265g) or medium-grind cornmeal (250g)
⅓ cup (40g) all-purpose flour
2 teaspoons baking powder
1 teaspoon sugar
1 teaspoon black pepper
¾ teaspoon salt
½ teaspoon baking soda
⅛ teaspoon cayenne pepper

Whisk together in medium bowl:

2 large eggs
1 cup (245g) buttermilk
½ cup grated onion

Add to the cornmeal mixture and stir just until combined.

Heat to 365°F in a deep-fryer, deep heavy pot, or Dutch oven:

2 inches vegetable oil or shortening

Using a measuring tablespoon, gently drop the batter into the hot fat. Fry in batches, turning once, until golden brown, 1½ to 2 minutes. Transfer to a baking sheet lined with paper towels and place in the oven to keep warm. Serve warm.

CHEESE CROQUETTES COCKAIGNE

16 croquettes

Please read about Deep-Frying, 1051.

Melt in a medium saucepan over medium heat:

3 tablespoons butter

Gradually stir in, then cook for 2 minutes, stirring constantly:

¼ cup all-purpose flour

Whisk in and cook, whisking frequently, until very thick, about 5 minutes:

⅔ cup milk

Reduce the heat to low and stir in:

1¼ cups grated Swiss cheese or Gruyère (5 ounces)
½ teaspoon salt
¼ teaspoon black pepper
(Pinch of cayenne pepper)

Remove from the heat and stir in until blended:

2 large egg yolks

Spread the mixture in a well-oiled 8-inch square baking dish. Cover and chill until firm, about 1 hour in the freezer or 2 to 3 hours in the refrigerator.

Turn the mixture out onto a work surface and cut into 2-inch squares.

Heat to 365°F in a deep-fryer, deep heavy pot, or Dutch oven:

2 inches vegetable oil

While the oil heats, flour your hands and dredge the croquettes in:

Flour

Let the croquettes dry on a rack for 10 minutes, then coat with the flour again. Fry the croquettes in batches until golden, 2 to 4 minutes. Drain on paper towels and serve with:

Tomato Sauce, 556

SALT COD CROQUETTES

6 servings

Please read about Deep-Frying, 1051.

Prepare the mixture for:

Brandade de Morue, 54, reducing both the cream and olive oil to ¼ cup

Mix in:

2 large eggs

Shape the mixture into 2-inch balls with an ice cream scoop or 2 spoons (using about 2 tablespoons of the mixture for each croquette), place on a baking sheet lined with parchment paper, and refrigerate while the oil heats.

Heat to 365°F in a deep-fryer, deep heavy pot, or Dutch oven:

2 inches vegetable oil

Roll the cod balls in:

1½ cups fine dry bread crumbs

Fry the croquettes in batches, without crowding, until golden brown and cooked through, about 4 minutes. Drain on paper towels and serve with:

Aïoli, 564
Lemon wedges

SALMON CROQUETTES

About 16 croquettes

Please read about Deep-Frying, 1051.

Combine in a medium bowl:

1½ cups flaked cooked or canned salmon, bones and skin removed (from about 1 pound salmon)

1½ cups mashed Boiled Potatoes, 265, using russets, or leftover mashed potatoes
1 large egg, beaten
1 tablespoon minced parsley
1 tablespoon minced chives
1 tablespoon minced dill
2 green onions, thinly sliced
½ teaspoon salt
¼ teaspoon cayenne pepper

Spread in separate shallow bowls:

1 cup flour
2 cups fresh bread crumbs, 957

Whisk together in a third shallow bowl:

3 large eggs

Form the balls from ¼-cup scoops of the salmon mixture. Gently roll each ball in the flour until coated, dip in the beaten egg, then roll in the bread crumbs until coated. Set aside on a plate to dry for 10 minutes.

Heat to 375°F in a deep-fryer, deep heavy pot, or Dutch oven:

3 inches vegetable oil or shortening

Gently drop 4 croquettes at a time into the hot fat and fry until deeply browned on all sides, about 2 minutes. Remove with a slotted spoon and drain on paper towels.

ABOUT FRUIT FRITTERS

It is very important that fruit used for fritters be ripe but not mushy. Fruit slices or chunks should be no thicker than ½ inch. Use apples—cored and cut into rings—pineapple wedges, orange segments, halved small apricots, bananas cut into 3 or 4 diagonal pieces, and halved figs.

Fruit for fritters may be marinated for up to 2 hours in wine, kirsch, rum, or brandy. After marinating, ➤ drain the fruit well and dust it with powdered sugar just before immersing it in the batter. Either dust fruit fritters with powdered sugar or serve with a sauce.

In season, try making **flower fritters** from the fuzzy white clusters of elderberry blossoms. Dusted with powdered sugar and sprinkled with kirsch, they are dreamy. Other unsprayed flowers—such as squash, pumpkin, nasturtium, day lily, or yucca blossoms—may also be frittered. For a savory treatment, see Squash Blossoms Stuffed with Cheese and Herbs, 277.

FRITTER BATTER FOR FRUIT

Enough to coat 2 cups fruit

This batter can be used either to encase about 2 cups diced fruit or to hold the same amount of small fruits and berries that are mixed directly and gently into it. Please read about Deep-Frying, 1051.

Whisk together in a medium bowl until blended:

1 cup (125g) all-purpose flour
2 tablespoons (25g) sugar
1½ teaspoons baking powder
¼ teaspoon salt

Add and whisk until the batter is smooth:

⅔ cup (155g) milk
1 large egg yolk
1 tablespoon (15g) butter, melted, or vegetable oil

Beat until stiff but not dry, 978:

2 large egg whites

Gently fold the egg whites into the batter with a spatula.

Heat to 365°F in a deep-fryer, deep heavy pot, or Dutch oven:

3 inches vegetable oil or shortening

Pat the fruit dry with paper towels. Drop 3 to 4 pieces of fruit into the batter at a time and turn gently to coat well. Using tongs, lift the fruit from the batter and drop gently into the hot fat. Do not crowd the pan. Fry until golden brown, 3 to 5 minutes, turning once or twice. Drain on a rack or on paper towels. Dust with:

Powdered sugar

or serve with:

Hot Lemon or Lime Sauce, 805, Crème Anglaise, 806, Fresh Berry Coulis, 805, or Orange Liqueur Sauce, 811

APPLE FRITTERS

About 36 small fritters

These bite-sized fritters are soft and loaded with apple bits. For a sweet and salty treat, stir **4 ounces (115g) sharp Cheddar, cut into small cubes,** into the batter along with the apples. Please read about Deep-Frying, 1051.

Mix together in a medium bowl:

1⅓ cups (165g) all-purpose flour
¼ cup (50g) sugar
1½ teaspoons baking powder
1 teaspoon ground cinnamon
(½ teaspoon ground cardamom)
¼ teaspoon salt

Whisk together in another medium bowl:

⅔ cup (155g) milk
1 large egg yolk (white reserved)
1 tablespoon (15g) butter, melted

Stir the wet ingredients into the flour mixture until smooth. Pour into a shallow baking dish:

3 tablespoons lemon juice

Add and toss to coat:

4 large firm apples, peeled, cored, and cut into ⅜-inch cubes

Heat to 365°F in a deep-fryer, deep heavy pot, or Dutch oven:

3 inches vegetable oil

Beat until stiff but not dry, 978:

2 large egg whites

Fold the egg whites into the batter, then gently fold in the apples. Drop the batter into the oil a heaping tablespoon at a time, being sure to scoop up some of the apples each time. Fry in batches, turning once, until golden brown and puffed. Drain on paper towels. Dust with:

Powdered sugar

Or toss in:

Flavored Sugar I, 1026

ABOUT BATTERING FRIED FOODS

Pat dry any food to be battered and fried with paper towels. While not necessary, a light dusting of flour may help the batter adhere. When the surface of the food is dry, the batter will adhere if it passes this easy test: Hold a generous spoonful of the batter above the mixing bowl. Rather than running from the spoon in a broad shining ribbon, the batter should start to run for just about a 1½-inch length, then drop in successive long splats. If the batter proves too thin, stir in a bit more flour. If you have time, refrigerate the batter, covered, for at least 2 hours and up to overnight, then beat until very smooth. This resting period allows the starch to absorb the liquid in the batter while simultaneously allowing the gluten to relax. If you do not have time to let the batter rest, mix it to smoothness with as few strokes as possible so as not to build up the gluten in the flour. Before frying, please read about Deep-Frying, 1051. As with all fried foods, pay close attention to the temperature of the oil, keeping it as close to the target temperature as possible and allowing the oil temperature to recover between batches. Do not crowd the fryer.

BEER BATTER

Enough to coat 2 cups food

Try this beer batter with thin slices of zucchini, eggplant, sweet potato, or pumpkin; whole mushrooms; asparagus spears; 2-inch pieces of green onions; scallops; chicken strips; or shrimp, shelled, with the tail left on. The beaten egg whites will produce a lighter batter, but they are not absolutely necessary. Please read about Deep-Frying, 1051.

Whisk together in a medium bowl until blended:

1 cup (125g) all-purpose flour
1 teaspoon salt
¼ teaspoon black pepper

Whisk together in another medium bowl until blended:

2 large egg yolks
1 tablespoon (15g) butter, melted

Whisk in:

¾ cup (175g) beer, poured and settled

Whisk the wet ingredients into the flour mixture just until smooth. If time permits, cover the bowl with plastic wrap and let stand for up to 2 hours at room temperature or for up to 12 hours in the refrigerator. If refrigerated, bring the batter to room temperature before proceeding.

If desired, beat until stiff but not dry, 978:

(2 large egg whites)

Fold the egg whites gently but thoroughly into the batter.

To fry, follow the directions in the specific recipe. Or, for a general procedure, heat to 365°F in a deep-fryer, deep heavy pot, or Dutch oven:

3 inches vegetable oil

Pat the food dry and drop 3 to 4 pieces at a time into the batter and turn to coat well. Using tongs, lift the food from the batter and drop gently into the hot fat. Do not crowd the pot. Fry until golden brown, 3 to 5 minutes, turning once or twice. Drain on a rack or on paper towels.

TEMPURA BATTER

Enough to coat 4 cups food

Have all your vegetables and meat ready to go and the oil preheated before making this batter. The key to light, crisp tempura is a very light hand when mixing the batter and keeping it very cold. Some cooks even place the bowl of tempura batter in an ice water bath to keep it chilled. Please read about Deep-Frying, 1051.

Heat to 365°F, or as directed in specific recipes, in a deep-fryer, deep heavy pot, or Dutch oven:

3 inches vegetable oil

Spread on a plate and set aside:

½ cup cake flour

Whisk together in a medium bowl:

1½ cups (165g) cake flour
½ cup (65g) cornstarch
½ teaspoon salt

Combine in a large bowl:

1½ cups (355g) ice-cold club soda
2 large egg yolks

Add the cake flour/cornstarch mixture all at once to the club soda and gently mix in (do not use a whisk—a fork or a few chopsticks are ideal) as quickly but gently as possible. There will still be lumps in the batter and some undissolved bits of flour—this is what you want.

To fry, follow the directions in the specific recipe. Or, for a general procedure, pat the food dry. Dredge 3 to 4 pieces of food in the reserved cake flour, then dip in the batter and immediately place in the hot oil. Do not crowd the pot. Fry in batches until golden and crisp, then drain on a rack or on paper towels.

PAKORA BATTER

Enough to coat 4 cups food

Please read about Deep-Frying, 1051.

Combine in a medium bowl:

2½ cups (290g) chickpea flour
½ cup (65g) all-purpose flour
1 tablespoon garam masala, 588, or curry powder
2 teaspoons salt

Whisk in until smooth, adding the amount needed to reach the consistency of pancake batter:

1¾ to 2 cups (415 to 475g) water

To fry, follow the directions in the specific recipe. Or, for a general procedure, heat to 365°F in a deep-fryer, deep heavy pot, or Dutch oven:

3 inches vegetable oil

Pat the food dry. Drop 3 to 4 pieces of food into the batter at a time and turn to coat. Using tongs, lift out the food and drop gently into the hot fat. Do not crowd the pot. Fry until golden brown, 3 to 5 minutes, turning once or twice. Drain on a rack or on paper towels.

CORNSTARCH BATTER

Enough to coat 4 cups food

This batter does not brown very much but turns into a light, crisp, thin shell when fried. Please read about Deep-Frying, 1051.

Whisk together in a large bowl:

¾ cup (95g) all-purpose flour
¾ cup (95g) cornstarch
1 teaspoon salt
(½ teaspoon black pepper)

Whisk in until smooth:

1 cup (235g) water

To fry, follow the directions in the specific recipe. Or, for a general procedure, heat to 365°F in a deep-fryer, deep heavy pot, or Dutch oven:

3 inches vegetable oil

Pat the food dry and drop several pieces at a time into the batter and turn to coat well. Using tongs, lift the food from the batter and drop gently into the hot fat. Do not crowd the pot. Fry until golden brown, 3 to 5 minutes, turning once or twice. Drain on a rack or on paper towels.

FRITTO MISTO

4 servings

This Italian "mixed fry" can be composed of a wide variety of vegetables and seafood. We recommend always including the sage and lemon slices. Please read about Deep-Frying, 1051.

Preheat the oven to 200°F.

Prepare:

Cornstarch Batter, 657, or Beer Batter, 657

Set aside. Have ready about $1\frac{1}{2}$ pounds total of a combination of any of the following:

Medium shrimp, peeled and deveined, 363
Fresh sardines, fresh or marinated white anchovies, or other tiny fish
Baby octopus or squid tentacles
Maitake or enoki mushrooms, broken apart into small clusters
Baby artichokes, halved, or drained and dried marinated artichoke hearts
Asparagus or slender green beans, cut into 2-inch pieces
Thinly sliced onion or red onion, or green onions cut into 2-inch pieces
Thinly sliced fennel bulb
Sage leaves
Thin lemon slices, seeds discarded

Heat to 365°F in a deep-fryer, deep heavy pot, or Dutch oven:

2 inches vegetable oil

Dip the vegetables and fish or seafood in the batter and fry, in batches, until lightly browned and crisp, 3 to 5 minutes. It is easier to fry one ingredient at a time than to mix them together, as they cook at different rates. Lemon slices and sage leaves cook especially quickly. Use a slotted spoon or spider to transfer the food to a rack set over a baking sheet. Sprinkle the food immediately after it is removed from the oil with:

Salt

Keep warm in the oven while you fry the rest of the food. Serve with:

Lemon wedges

ABOUT COATING FRIED FOODS

Dredging, that is, coating food with flour or crumbs—or enrobing it with a more elaborate "bound" coating—can produce the crispiest results when fried (especially when pan-frying or shallow-frying). The classic coatings to use are seasoned bread crumbs, flour, and fine cornmeal. Even crispier crusts can be achieved by using finer flours and starches, such as rice flour, cornstarch, masa harina, and potato starch. Dipping items in a bowl of thin batter, buttermilk, or beaten eggs and then dredging them in coarser bread crumbs like panko—or crushed crackers—adds a satisfying crunch. Hard, aged cheeses like Romano and Parmesan add flavor and richness; dried herbs and ground spices of all sorts may be employed. We encourage you to experiment and let your taste buds guide future research.

The main thing to remember is that you want an even and unbroken covering that adheres well. Any food that is excessively moist should be patted dry first. If the food is not fragile, simply put a small quantity of the seasoned coating in a paper or plastic bag with the food you want to cover, and shake. You will find this method quickly gives you a very even coating.

Coating food in a bag

➤ For the sturdiest and crispiest coating, place coated or breaded foods on a wire rack set above a rimmed baking sheet and refrigerate for at least 1 hour and up to overnight before frying. The coating will have time to absorb any moisture and dry out, which will make it adhere better and brown up beautifully.

FLOUR COATING

Pour into a shallow bowl:

$1\frac{1}{2}$ cups milk or buttermilk

Mix in a second shallow bowl:

2 cups flour, or $\frac{1}{2}$ cup flour and $1\frac{1}{2}$ cups fine cornmeal
$1\frac{1}{2}$ teaspoons salt
1 teaspoon black pepper

Dip the piece of food to be fried in the milk and hold it above the bowl for several seconds to drain. Coat with the seasoned flour, shaking off the excess. Repeat with the remaining food items.

BOUND BREAD CRUMB OR CRACKER COATING

I. BATTER

Pat the food dry. Whisk together in a shallow bowl:

1 cup all-purpose flour
$1\frac{1}{4}$ cups water

Mix in a second shallow bowl:

$1\frac{1}{2}$ cups Seasoned Crumbs, 659

Dip each piece of food to be fried in the thin batter, then place the food in the crumbs. See that the crumbs adhere evenly to all the edges of the food as well as to its larger surfaces. If you see any vacant places, sprinkle a few crumbs onto them. Pat on any loose crumbs that might fall off and brown too rapidly, thus discoloring the frying fat. ➤ Place on a rack set over a rimmed baking sheet to dry for at least 20 minutes before frying (refrigerating for at least 1 hour and up to overnight will produce better results).

II. EGG WASH

Pat the food dry. Have ready a shallow bowl of:

1 cup flour
1 teaspoon salt
½ teaspoon black pepper

Combine in a second shallow bowl:

1 large egg, slightly beaten
1 tablespoon water or milk

Stir together. Place in a third bowl:

1½ cups Seasoned Crumbs, below, or other crumbs

Dredge each piece of food in the flour: Toss it lightly from one palm to the other, patting it gently all over, and shake off any excess flour, as shown. Then, slide the flour-coated food through the egg mixture, making sure the entire surface is coated; allow any excess moisture to drip off. Place the food in the crumbs. See that the crumbs adhere evenly to all the edges of the food as well as to its larger surfaces. If you see any vacant places, sprinkle a few crumbs onto them. Pat on any loose crumbs that might fall off and brown too rapidly, thus discoloring the frying fat. ➤ Place on a rack set over a rimmed baking sheet to dry for at least 20 minutes before frying (refrigerating for at least 1 hour and up to overnight will produce better results).

Applying bound breading or coating

SEASONED CRUMBS

Seasoning crumbs is a matter of personal taste. Besides salt and pepper, try spice blends such as chili powder or Garam Masala, 558, minced herbs, white pepper, curry powder, or red pepper flakes.

I. BASIC

Mix together:

1 cup dry bread crumbs, panko, or finely crushed cornflakes or crackers
1 teaspoon salt
½ teaspoon black pepper or ½ teaspoon sweet paprika

II. CHEESE AND HERB

Mix together:

1 cup dry bread crumbs, panko, or finely crushed cornflakes or crackers
3 tablespoons grated Parmesan or Romano
1 teaspoon minced fresh herbs (such as thyme, basil, chives, savory, or tarragon) or ½ teaspoon dried, or a pinch of minced rosemary

PIES AND PASTRIES

The pie as we know it dates back to medieval Europe, where a wide array of ingredients was baked inside thick pastry shells. Centuries later, Americans have made a national study of this dish. Pies vary across America almost as much as the terrain, from Floridian Key lime pies to Pennsylvania Dutch shoofly pies to Pacific Northwest marionberry pies.

Pie's most challenging component—the crust—weds it to the other pastries we discuss here, among them puff pastry and croissants. While these delicacies require a bit of practice and patience to master, we think they are well worth the effort. There is nothing quite like a flaky, homemade pastry redolent of browned butter. And above all, nothing compares to the feeling of serving a pie or pastry to a table of appreciative eaters.

ABOUT EQUIPMENT FOR PIES AND PASTRIES

While pie can be made under humble circumstances (we have substituted a wine bottle for a rolling pin more than once), having proper equipment will go far in creating praiseworthy pastries.

There are two styles of **rolling pins** used in crust making—the **standard pin** with handles, and the **pastry pin,** or **French pin,** which can have a tapered or uniformly cylindrical shape and no handles. Choose a pin of a size and weight you find comfortable. We have come to prefer French pins for their maneuverability and because they are generally lighter in weight. Wood is the perfect material for all rolling pins. Hollow metal pins filled with ice water sweat, and glass pins are beautiful but fragile. While marble pins are heavy, some bakers prefer them because they help to keep the dough cool and are easy to clean.

Mixing the dough can be accomplished by hand or by machine. A **pastry blender,** with 5 or 6 bowed metal blades for cutting butter into flour, is the best tool for the hand method, but a **food processor** also makes good and speedy dough. If you lack both of those, your hands make an admirable substitute provided care is taken to work quickly to ensure that the dough does not become too warm. Other useful tools include a **ruler,** to measure the thickness and diameter of dough; a **fluted pastry wheel** or **pastry jagger** (a pizza wheel works as well), for cutting lattices; and a metal **dough scraper** (also called a **bench scraper**). For weighting unfilled, or blind-baked, crusts, use **pie weights** or uncooked dried beans, rice, or granulated sugar. Some bakers cover the edge of a pie crust with a **metal shield** to prevent overbrowning, but the same benefit can be achieved with strips of foil shaped into a ring.

Pie pans come in two standard diameters, 9 and 10 inches; ➤ the former has a capacity of around 4½ cups, the latter 6 cups. Standard pie pans are approximately 1¼ inches deep; deep-dish pie pans are 1½ inches deep. Glass pie pans produce wonderfully brown, crisp crusts, but you may need to reduce the baking time by 20 to 25 percent. Heavy metal pans, whether matte, shiny, or black finish, make for well-browned crusts. Ceramic pans are beautiful, but they insulate the crust, resulting in slower baking and a tendency toward a soggy bottom crust. No matter the material of your preferred pie pan, it is more than possible to bake perfect pies in it with a little practice. The only material we do not recommend for pies with a pastry crust is disposable aluminum, as it causes crusts to bake unevenly.

For tarts, use a two-piece **tart pan** (a tart pan with a removable bottom to allow unmolding for serving), or a **tart ring** coupled with a baking sheet wide enough to hold it. ➤ A pan or ring measuring 9½ to 10 inches across and about 1 inch deep holds 4 to 4½ cups filling; an 11-inch pan or ring of the same depth will hold 4½ to 6 cups filling. You may also use several small tartlet pans or rings measuring about 4½ inches for individual tartlets (they will hold ¾ to 1 cup filling each).

In theory, you may bake most pies either in one large pan or divide the dough and filling among several small pie or tart pans. However, it is best to bake fruit pies, like apple or cherry, in a large format, as the longer baking time allows the fruit to cook and thicken properly. Pies with custard-based fillings can be equally delicious in a large or small format.

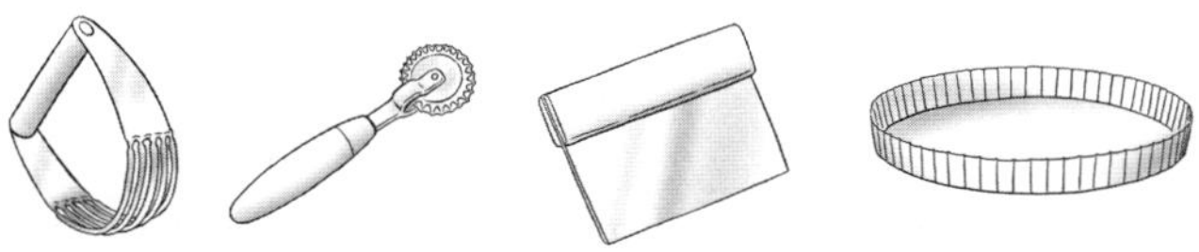

Pastry blender, fluted pastry wheel, bench scraper, two-piece tart pan

CHOOSING A PIE DOUGH RECIPE

Any flaky pastry dough, such as Basic Pie or Pastry Dough, 664, or All-Butter Pie or Pastry Dough, 664, works well with most pies, but especially double-crust fruit pies because these doughs are particularly sturdy. Otherwise, pair the pie dough to the filling as you like. The basic dough made with lard is particularly good with apple pies. Cream Cheese Pastry Dough, 665, is excellent with sweet fruit pies like blueberry or cherry; Cornmeal Pie or Pastry Dough, 665, works well with blueberry or blackberry pies; and Nutty Pie or Pastry Dough, 665, pairs beautifully with stone fruits, such as peaches, apricots, or plums. Be aware, however, that nut doughs tend to leak during baking. Sweet Dough for Tarts, 665, while excellent for single-crust tarts and pies, is not good for covered fruit pies, as it is likely to char during the long baking.

ABOUT MAKING PIE DOUGH

There are two important things to bear in mind when making pie dough. ➤ Keep the dough and the ingredients used to make it well chilled, and handle the dough lightly but confidently to inhibit excessive gluten development. Chilled ingredients will yield a buttery, flaky crust, rather than a greasy one; though some gluten development is necessary, being careful not to overwork the dough ensures a tender crust.

To make pie dough by hand, begin by cutting the cold fat into roughly ½-inch chunks. Cut the fat into the dry ingredients with a pastry blender or your fingers. If using your fingers, rub the butter into the flour, flattening the pieces of fat between your fingers. ➤ As you do this, it can help to think about the role butter plays in pie crusts. The ideal pie crust is tender and flaky, not dense, greasy, or crumbly. To achieve a flaky texture, you want the butter to be in flat sheets coated in flour. Working the butter into the flour until it is in tiny, crumb-like pieces is not necessarily a bad thing, but your crust will be less flaky and more crumbly—closer to shortbread than pastry. (Some pie crusts combine these two strategies to achieve a balance of flakiness and tenderness.) Continue to work until all the pieces of fat are flattened and well incorporated into the flour. Getting all the pieces of fat to the same size is unnecessary—in fact, if you do, you will likely overwork the mixture and heat up the fat too much. The fat should be in firm, separate pieces, some fine and crumb-like, some the size of peas or a little larger, and some larger, flattened pieces.

Next, bind the dough with ice water. The trick is to ➤ add enough water to make the dough hold together but not so much as to make it sticky. The flour and fat mixture should be moistened only to the point where it appears "shaggy" but holds together when squeezed and is not dry or crumbly. The amount of water required varies and depends on the protein content of the flour, the type of fat used, the degree of blending of fat and flour, the temperature of the fat and water, and the ambient humidity. In other words, you must go by feel rather than exact measurements. If the mixture gathers into a mass on its own, without pressure, it is too wet. However, beginners should probably err on the side of overmoistening, as a very dry dough tends to split or crumble when rolled. ▲ When making pies at high altitudes, where evaporation is greater, you may achieve better results with pastry if you add a bit more liquid. Our best advice to would-be pie makers is to practice making pie dough regularly to get a feel for the process. Perfect pie crust is well within reach with practice and proper technique.

Cutting the fat into the dry ingredients with a pastry blender

If you have made enough dough for a double-crust pie, divide the dough into 2 equal parts, or as directed in the recipe. At this point you may go in one of two directions, each of which has advantages and disadvantages.

One option is to wrap the dough in plastic and refrigerate for at least 30 minutes before rolling it out. Letting the dough rest can make it easier to work with, as it allows the gluten to relax and gives the flour time to absorb the water evenly. If needed, you can keep the dough, well wrapped, in the refrigerator or store as directed below. If the dough has been chilled for longer than 30 minutes, it may need to sit at room temperature until it feels firm yet pliable, like modeling clay, when pressed. If it is too cold, the dough will crack around the edges when rolled.

Another option is to roll out the dough immediately, fit it into the pie pan, and then chill it. The principle advantage to this method is that the dough is supple right after being made. If your kitchen is very warm, however, you are better off refrigerating the dough before rolling and then again after it is in the pie pan.

To store pie dough, tightly wrap single-crust portions of dough in plastic wrap and refrigerate for up to 3 days. To freeze dough, either shape it into a disk and double-wrap it or roll out and shape the dough in the pie pan, then wrap tightly and freeze for up to 3 months. Refrigerated dough may need to sit at room temperature for a few minutes to become pliable. Dough frozen in a disk should be allowed to thaw completely in the refrigerator before rolling and shaping. Dough frozen in a pie pan can be baked from frozen. You may need to add a few extra minutes of baking time.

MIXING PIE DOUGH USING A FOOD PROCESSOR

Pie dough may be made in less than a minute with this appliance. Combine the dry ingredients in the food processor and process for 5 seconds. Cut the cold butter, fat, or cream cheese into cubes and scatter over the dry ingredients. Pulse in 1- to 2-second bursts until most of the fat is the size of peas. With the machine turned off, drizzle some ice water evenly over the top. Pulse until no dry patches remain. Continue adding water in small amounts and pulsing until the dough holds together when squeezed and is neither crumbly nor wet. Do not allow the dough to gather into a single mass during processing. Turn the dough out of the processor bowl, press and gather the dough into a ball, then flatten into a disk. Wrap, refrigerate, and proceed as directed.

MIXING PIE DOUGH USING A STAND MIXER

Combine the dry ingredients in the bowl of a mixer fitted with the paddle attachment and mix at low speed for a few seconds, then add the cold fat or cream cheese. Beat at medium-low speed until the mixture is the consistency of coarse crumbs. Add the ice water and mix until the dough begins to cling to the paddle. Should the dough be too crumbly, incorporate 1 to 3 teaspoons water with your hands so that the dough comes together when pressed.

ROLLING PIE DOUGH

You can roll dough on a pastry cloth, pastry board, marble slab (which retains cold and helps keep the dough from softening) or on a clean smooth countertop. Do not roll dough next to the oven or in a hot corner of the kitchen or the fat will melt. If the dough becomes too soft during rolling, loosen it from the work surface, slide a cookie sheet beneath it, and refrigerate until it firms up.

Place the dough in the center of a lightly floured work surface and lightly flour the dough as well. Roll out the dough from the center outward, stopping just short of the edge. Pause after each stroke of the pin to rotate the dough a quarter turn to prevent sticking. This is crucial. One of the most common mistakes in this step of the process is the cook moving around the dough, approaching it warily from every direction. Move the dough rather than letting the dough move you. At any sign of sticking, throw a little flour underneath the dough and keep going. At first, this will feel awkward, but you will come into your own soon enough and the process will become rhythmic.

While you roll, seal cracks and splits by pushing the dough together with your fingers. It's best to fix cracks as soon as they appear, as small cracks become large ones. Patch any holes, tears, or thin spots with dough scraps, dabbing them on one side with cold water and firmly pressing them, moistened side down, into place.

Very fragile doughs may be rolled out between two pieces of parchment paper. As you roll the dough, periodically peel off the top piece of parchment paper, place it back on top of the dough, flip the whole arrangement over, and peel off the back piece of parchment paper, replacing it before proceeding with rolling.

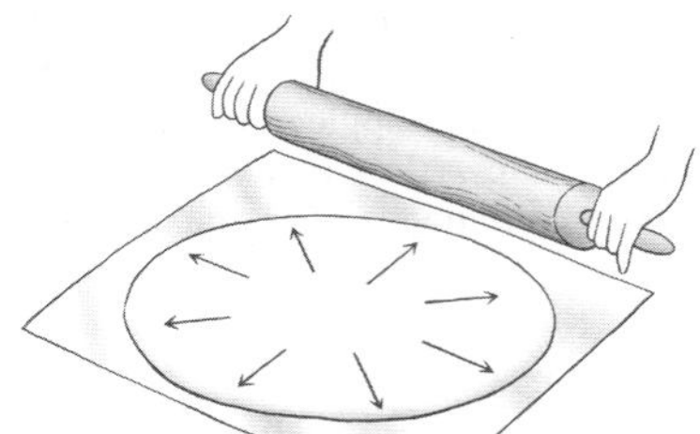

Rolling pie dough

LINING A PIE OR TART PAN WITH DOUGH

Roll the dough into a round roughly 3 to 4 inches larger than the diameter of your pan. This will allow plenty of dough with which to construct a rim. To calculate the size by eye, place the pan (right side up for a tart pan, inverted for a pie pan) in the center of the dough. To transfer the rolled dough to the pan, roll it loosely around the pin, and starting over one side of the pan, unroll the dough. If the dough is off-center, gently slide it into position with your hands. Ease the dough into the pan loosely and then, using your fingertips, press it firmly into the pan. Cover any gaps in the overhang by patching with dough scraps lightly moistened on one side with cold water. Trim the edges of the dough with scissors or a small paring knife, leaving a 1-inch overhang. Dough trimmings can be used to make a decorative edge for single-crust pies or decorative shapes for the top of a double-crust pie; or they can be given to kids for "play dough" or sprinkled with sugar and cinnamon and baked.

FORMING SINGLE-CRUST PIES

For a single-crust pie, tuck the overhanging dough underneath itself to make a doubled edge that rests on the rim of the pie pan. This "rim" of dough is important, as it will help to hold the juices in the pie—and it's pretty to look at once it is crimped or fluted.

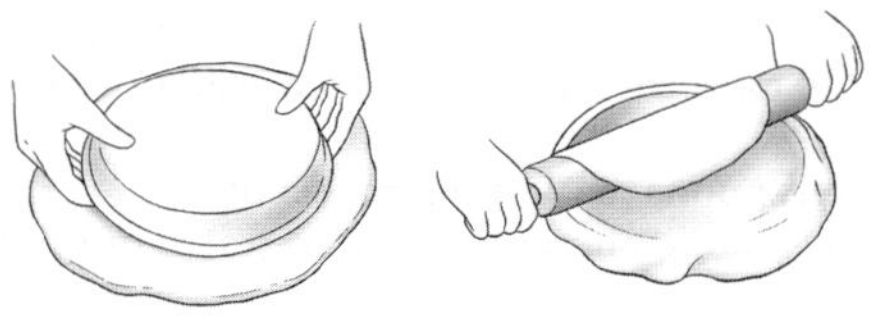

Checking the size of the pie dough and transferring it to the pie pan with the rolling pin

To make a crimped rim, press it all around with the tines of a fork.

To make a fluted rim, press your thumb and index finger, held about 1 inch apart, against the outside of the rim, then press a dent in the dough from the inside with the index finger of your other hand.

To make a coiled or braided design, roll dough trimmings into long thin ropes, then twist or braid the ropes to your choosing. Flatten the rim of the pie crust against the edge of the pan, brush with cold water, and press the rope into place.

➤ Freeze the crust for 15 minutes or refrigerate for 1 hour.

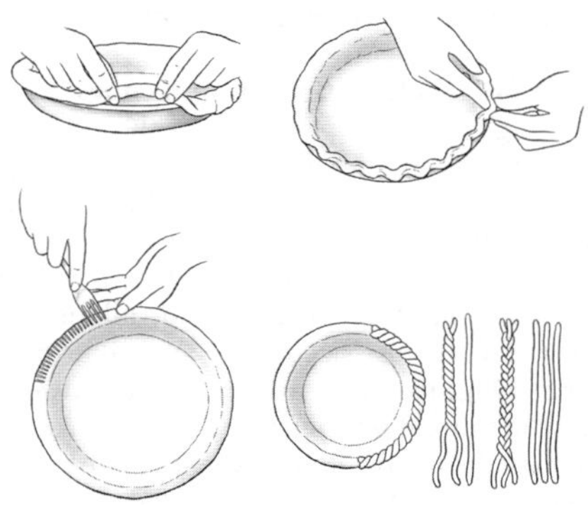

Tucking the overhanging dough underneath itself to make a double layer, forming a fluted rim, crimping the rim, or making coiled rims by twisting or braiding dough ropes and pressing them along the rim of the pan

FORMING TART CRUSTS

For a tart, fold the overhanging dough back onto itself, doubling the thickness of the upper part of the crust, and press firmly against the inside rim of the tart pan. Squeeze any noticeably thicker parts of the sides with your fingers to even them, then trim excess dough flush with the top using scissors or a paring knife or roll a rolling pin across the top of the pan.

➤ Freeze the crust for 15 minutes or refrigerate for 1 hour.

For individual pies, use a muffin tin or, for deeper shells, custard cups. You may also use small tart or pie pans, tart rings, or even miniature cast-iron skillets. Cut rounds of dough 4½ or 5½ inches in diameter and fit them into the molds. Chill as directed above.

To form a double-crust pie, see below.

ABOUT CRUSTS BAKED WITH FILLINGS

For some pies, the crust is baked at the same time as the filling. This is true of all double-crust pies, and some single-crust pies, depending on the recipe. Before filling and baking, ➤ freeze the crust for 15 minutes or refrigerate for 1 hour. Do not prick the bottom of the crust. ➤ If the pie filling is juicy, sprinkle the bottom of the crust lightly with a mixture of equal parts flour and sugar to prevent sogginess.

FORMING DOUBLE-CRUST PIES

Line the pie pan with the bottom crust as directed above, but do not trim, fold, and crimp the overhanging dough. Refrigerate until the filling is ready. Roll out the top crust as indicated below and refrigerate while you fill the bottom crust as directed in the recipe.

To make a solid top crust, roll the second dough disk into a round about 2 inches larger than the diameter of the pie pan. Brush the overhanging edge of the bottom crust lightly with cold water. Place the top crust over the pie. Firmly pinch the edges of both crusts together with your fingers to seal. Trim the doubled edge to an even overhang of 1 inch, then tuck the overhang underneath itself so that the folded edge is flush with the rim of the pie pan. Crimp or flute the rim as for a single-crust pie, above; a high fluted rim will help to contain any juices that bubble through the top crust. To allow the steam to escape during baking, prick the top crust with a fork in several places or, using a sharp paring knife, make three or four 2-inch vents or slashes in it. You may cut scraps of dough into decorative shapes, brush lightly with cold water or an egg wash of beaten egg or egg yolk mixed with a little water, and press onto the top crust.

To make a plain lattice top for a 9-inch pie, roll the dough for the top crust into a 13½-inch round. Cut plain strips of dough with a knife or pastry wheel, or roll pieces of dough into ropes, then twist and weave or arrange the plain strips or ropes in a crisscross. The strips may be skinnier or wider depending on the look you want. You may even alternate thin and wide strips on the same pie. Spoon the filling into the bottom crust and brush the edge of the bottom crust lightly with cold water. Place half of the dough strips on top of the filled pie, leaving space between them, then arrange the remaining dough strips over these, either on a diagonal or in a perpendicular crisscross pattern. Trim the lattice strips, leaving a ½-inch overhang at each end. Press the strips against the bottom crust. Fold the overhanging edges of the lattice and the bottom crust underneath itself so that the folded edge is flush with the rim of the pan and the lattice strips are secured. Crimp or flute the edge as desired, above.

To make a woven lattice top for a 9-inch pie, roll the dough and cut strips as directed above. Place half of the dough strips at least ½ inch apart on top of the pie or on a cookie sheet (weaving the lattice on a cookie sheet then transferring it to the pie is less messy). Weave in the remaining dough strips in an over-under-over-under basket-weave pattern. If you worked on a cookie sheet, slide the lattice off the cookie sheet onto the pie (chilling the lattice for a few minutes first will make the transfer easier). Trim the lattice strips, leaving a ½-inch overhang at each end. Press the strips against the bottom crust. Fold the overhanging edges of the lattice and the bottom crust underneath itself so that the folded edge is flush with the rim of the pan and the lattice strips are secured. Crimp or flute the edge as desired, 663.

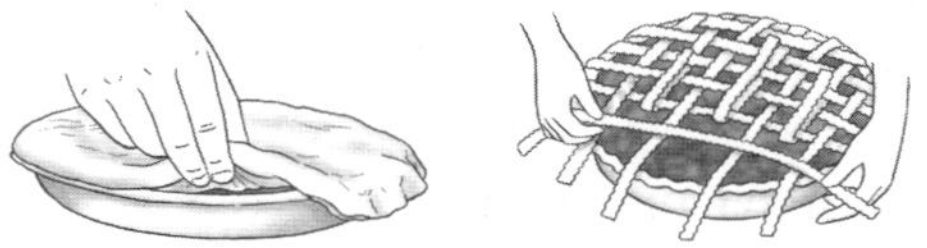

Shaping dough for a double-crust pie: Fold over the excess dough on a double-crust pie or form a woven lattice

To decorate the top with "shingles" of pie dough, first line the pie pan with the bottom crust and shape the rim as desired; see Lining a Pie or Tart Pan with Dough, 662. Cut the rolled out top crust into rounds, squares, diamonds, or another shape with a cookie cutter. Place them on top of the pie filling so they overlap slightly, in shingle fashion. The shingles should sit on top of the filling, not the rim. This style of crust is easy to put together and can be quite eye-catching.

Finally, to give any double, lattice, or shingled crust a glossy, golden, sparkling finish, ➤ brush the top with an egg wash of egg beaten with a little water, milk, or heavy cream, and sprinkle with granulated or turbinado sugar.

ABOUT BLIND BAKING CRUSTS

Blind baking—or baking pie or tart shells without filling—ensures a crisp, perfectly baked crust for baked fillings or precooked or no-cook fillings. Fit the bottom crust into the pie pan, trim the overhang, and crimp or flute the edge; see Lining a Pie or Tart Pan with Dough, 662. Prick or "dock" the dough generously with a fork. ➤ Freeze the dough in the pan for 15 minutes or refrigerate it for 1 hour (if you have time, refrigerating it for 1 hour is preferred). Line the dough with parchment paper, then ➤ fill it to the brim with dried beans or pie weights. (Do not be tempted to scrimp on the pie weights. Underweighted crusts tend to shrink.) Cookbook author Stella Parks uses granulated sugar as a pie weight, which fills the crust nicely and can be used in baking afterward. Press down gently on the weights to push them into the corners of the crust. This keeps the dough from buckling and baking unevenly.

To blind bake pie shells, place the chilled, weighted shells in a preheated 375°F oven, unless otherwise noted, for about 25 minutes or until the edge is dry to the touch and light brown. Remove the parchment paper and weights and bake 8 to 10 minutes longer until the bottom of the crust is light golden brown and dry to the touch. Cool the crust unless otherwise directed. If baking small, individual pie shells, keep in mind that the baking time will be less than for a large pie crust.

ADDITIONS TO PIE DOUGH

Vary a basic pie or pastry dough for a double crust by adding to the dry ingredients one of the following:

Up to 1 tablespoon poppy or caraway seeds
1 tablespoon chopped fresh herbs, such as thyme or rosemary
Finely grated zest of 1 lemon or orange or 2 limes
1 cup grated hard cheese, such as Parmesan or Romano (4 oz or 115g)
Up to 3 tablespoons toasted sesame seeds
½ teaspoon ground cinnamon and/or grated or ground nutmeg
2 tablespoons (10g) unsweetened natural or Dutch-process cocoa powder

BASIC PIE OR PASTRY DOUGH

One 9- or 10-inch double crust

For a 9-inch single-crust pie, make half the recipe (or make the full amount and wrap half of the dough and refrigerate or freeze for future use).

Whisk together in a medium bowl or pulse briefly in a food processor:

2½ cups (315g) all-purpose flour
(1 teaspoon sugar, for sweet pies)
½ teaspoon salt

Have ready:

¾ cup chilled lard (155g) or vegetable shortening (145g), cut into small pieces
3 tablespoons (45g) cold butter, cut into cubes

If mixing the dough by hand, place half of the cubes on the flour mixture and using a pastry blender or fingertips, lightly work it in, 661, until it has the consistency of oats. Add the remaining pieces of fat and rub into the flour, flattening them between your fingers until they are roughly pea-sized or a little larger with some larger, flattened pieces. If using a food processor, add all the fat at once and pulse until most of it is in pea-sized pieces. Sprinkle the dough with:

6 tablespoons (90g) ice water mixed with 1 tablespoon distilled white or cider vinegar

Blend the water gently into the dough with a silicone spatula or pulse until it just holds together. If the dough is still dry and crumbly, add:

1 to 3 teaspoons ice water

The dough should not be wet or sticky but should hold together when squeezed. Divide the dough in half, shape each into a disk, and roll out immediately as directed in Rolling Pie Dough, 662, or wrap in plastic wrap and refrigerate for at least 30 minutes or up to 3 days. Prepare as directed in Lining a Pie or Tart Pan with Dough, 662. To fill and bake, see individual recipes. For a baked shell, see About Blind Baking Crusts, above.

ALL-BUTTER PIE OR PASTRY DOUGH

One 9- or 10-inch double crust

This is our all-time favorite pie dough recipe. We find that all-butter doughs taste better and are easier to handle than doughs with a combination of butter and shortening. For a 9-inch single-crust pie, make half the recipe (or make the full amount and wrap half of the dough and refrigerate or freeze for future use).

Whisk together in a medium bowl or pulse briefly in a food processor:

2½ cups (315g) all-purpose flour
(1 teaspoon sugar, for sweet pies)
½ teaspoon salt

Add:

2 sticks (8 oz or 225g) cold unsalted butter, cut into cubes

If mixing the dough by hand, work in the butter, flattening the pieces between your fingers until they are roughly pea-sized or a little larger with some larger, flattened pieces. If using a food processor, add all the fat at once and pulse until the butter pieces are mostly pea-sized. Sprinkle the dough with:

6 tablespoons (90g) ice water mixed with 1 tablespoon distilled white or cider vinegar

Blend the water gently into the dough with a silicone spatula or pulse until it just holds together. If the dough is still dry and crumbly, add:

1 to 3 teaspoons ice water

The dough should not be wet or sticky but should hold together when squeezed. Divide the dough in half, shape each into a disk, and roll out immediately as directed in Rolling Pie Dough, 662, or wrap in plastic wrap and refrigerate for at least 30 minutes or up to 3 days. Prepare as directed in Lining a Pie or Tart Pan with Dough, 662. To fill and bake, see individual recipes. For a baked shell, see About Blind Baking Crusts, 664.

CHEDDAR PIE OR PASTRY DOUGH

Delicious for savory pies, like quiche, or for Apple Pie, 670.

Prepare **All-Butter Pie or Pastry Dough, 664,** cutting in with the butter **2 cups shredded sharp or medium Cheddar (8 oz or 225g).** Proceed as directed. The dough will be a little more crumbly than regular pie dough.

CORNMEAL PIE OR PASTRY DOUGH

Cornmeal adds both crunch and lightness to crusts. Use this for fresh fruit tarts made with berries, peaches, or nectarines.

Prepare **All-Butter Pie or Pastry Dough, 664.** Add **⅓ cup (35g) powdered sugar** to the dry ingredients and substitute **¾ cup (120g) fine yellow cornmeal** for ¾ cup (95g) of the flour.

NUTTY PIE OR PASTRY DOUGH

Prepare **All-Butter Pie or Pastry Dough, 664.** Add **½ cup finely chopped walnuts or pecans** (grind them in a food processor), **⅓ cup (35g) powdered sugar,** and **(1 teaspoon finely grated lemon zest)** to the dry ingredients.

WHOLE-GRAIN PIE OR PASTRY DOUGH

Prepare **All-Butter Pie or Pastry Dough, 664.** Add to the dry ingredients **⅓ cup (35g) powdered sugar** and substitute **1 cup whole wheat pastry flour (120g), buckwheat flour (125g), spelt flour (125g), or dark rye flour (120g)** for 1 cup (125g) of the all-purpose flour. For extra tenderness, beat **1 large egg yolk** with **⅓ cup (80g) ice water** and add it to the dough in place of the 6 tablespoons water.

SWEET DOUGH FOR TARTS

Two 10-inch tart shells or ten 3-inch tartlet shells

This sugar cookie–like dough has a crumbly, melt-in-your-mouth texture when baked. Use it for any of the tarts in this chapter, 674–77. For a single tart shell, make half the recipe (or make the full amount and wrap half of the dough and refrigerate or freeze for future use).

Whisk together in a medium bowl:

2¾ cups (345g) all-purpose flour
¼ teaspoon salt

Beat in a large bowl or the bowl of a stand mixer until smooth:

2 sticks (8 oz or 225g) unsalted butter, softened

Add and beat until smooth:

¾ cup (75g) powdered sugar

Scrape down the sides of the bowl. Beat in until combined:

1 teaspoon vanilla

Scrape down the sides of the bowl again and add the flour mixture. Mix on low speed until the butter and flour are combined and crumbly, but do not mix so long that the dough is a completely smooth mass. Add:

1 large egg, beaten

Mix on low speed until the dough comes together. Divide the dough in half for large tarts or into 10 equal pieces for tartlets. Flatten each into a disk and wrap tightly in plastic wrap. Refrigerate for at least 2 hours or overnight. Before using, allow the dough to sit at room temperature until pliable but not soft.

Roll out the dough between two pieces of parchment paper. Transfer to one or two 10-inch tart pan(s) or ten 3-inch tartlet pans or rings and press the dough gently into the corners. Fit the dough into the pan as directed in Lining a Pie or Tart Pan with Dough, 662. Prick the dough all over with a fork and freeze for 30 minutes.

Preheat the oven to 350°F.

Line the tart shell(s) with parchment paper and fill halfway with pie weights or dried beans. Bake until golden, about 25 minutes. Remove the parchment paper and weights and bake 5 minutes more. Let cool completely before filling.

CREAM CHEESE PASTRY DOUGH

One 9-inch single pie crust or eight 3-inch tart or individual pie shells

This deliciously rich, slightly tangy dough makes excellent tart shells or turnovers, 687.

Whisk together in a medium bowl:

1 cup (125g) all-purpose flour
¼ teaspoon salt

Cut in until well blended:

1 stick (4 oz or 115g) cold unsalted butter, cut into cubes
4 ounces (115g) cold cream cheese, cut into cubes

Shape the dough into a disk, wrap in plastic wrap, and refrigerate for at least 1 hour.

Roll out as described in Rolling Pie Dough, 662, and prepare as directed in Lining a Pie or Tart Pan with Dough, 662. To fill and bake, see individual recipes. For a baked shell, see About Blind Baking Crusts, 664.

To use for individual pies or tarts, divide the dough into 8 pieces and roll out, 662. Line muffin tins or 3-inch tartlet pans or rings with dough and freeze for 15 minutes or refrigerate for 1 hour. Blind bake, 664, at 375°F for 15 to 20 minutes or until dry to the touch and golden brown.

PHYLLO PIE CRUST

One 9- or 10-inch crust

For a sweet pie, sprinkle sugar lightly over each layer of buttered phyllo. For a savory pie, you may crush a garlic clove and let it steep in the melted butter over low heat for 10 minutes, and sprinkle minced fresh herbs between the layers.

Have ready:

10 sheets phyllo dough, thawed if frozen
4 tablespoons (½ stick) butter, melted
(⅓ cup sugar, or any Flavored Sugar, 1026)

Keep phyllo sheets covered with a dry kitchen towel topped with a damp towel while you work. Place 1 sheet of phyllo on a work surface and brush with melted butter. If desired, sprinkle lightly with sugar. Place a second sheet of phyllo over the first, staggering the corners slightly. Brush with butter and sprinkle with sugar, if using. Repeat with the remaining phyllo, butter, and sugar, staggering each sheet so it doesn't match up perfectly with the last. Transfer the dough to a lightly oiled 9- or 10-inch pie pan, pressing it evenly into the bottom and up the sides of the pan. Fold any dough edges extending beyond the rim of the pie pan underneath. The edge will have a slightly rumpled look.

For pies with unbaked fillings, preheat the oven to 375°F, line the shell with parchment paper, and fill halfway with pie weights or beans. Bake until browned and crisp, about 15 minutes.

For pies with baked fillings, fill and bake as directed in the recipe, covering the crust rim with foil if it starts to brown too quickly. Phyllo crusts are best the day they're made.

MERINGUE PIE SHELL

One 9- or 10-inch pie crust

Sweet, crisp meringue makes an excellent crust for tarts made with fresh fruit and whipped cream. Meringue shells can be made in pans of any size or formed on a baking sheet using a spoon or a pastry bag. To cut the sweetness, flavor the meringue with coffee or cocoa. Position a rack in the lower third of the oven. Preheat the oven to 225°F. Very generously grease both the inside and the rim of a 9-inch pie pan, preferably glass, with vegetable shortening. Dust the pan with flour, tilt in all directions to coat, and then tap out the excess.

Prepare:

French Meringue, 794, using 3 egg whites and ¾ cup sugar

Spread the meringue over the bottom and up the sides of the prepared pie pan with the back of a spoon. Bake until the interior of the meringue seems just slightly sticky when probed with the tip of a paring knife, 1½ to 2 hours. Turn off the oven and let the crust cool completely in the oven. Fill the shell just before serving to prevent sogginess.

ABOUT PAT-IN-THE-PAN CRUSTS

If you have anxiety about rolling out pie dough, these crusts are for you! Pat-in-the-pan doughs are soft and supple, making them easy to handle and shape. They have a crumbly and pleasantly crunchy, rather than flaky, texture. Pat-in-the-pan crusts do not need to be weighted. They cannot be used to make covered fruit pies, though shortbread pat-in-the-pan doughs can be used to good effect in making flat free-form dessert tarts such as galettes and crostatas, 689. Crumb and nut crusts, 667, can be considered pat-in-the-pan crusts, though they can only be used for single-crust pies.

To shape pat-in-the-pan doughs for a pie or tart, butter and flour a 9-inch pie pan or a 9½- or 10-inch two-piece tart pan. Pat the dough evenly over the bottom and up the sides of the pan. Alternatively, roll it with a rolling pin between sheets of parchment paper and flip it into the pan, sealing any cracks with your fingers. If making a pie, crimp or flute the rim, 663. Thoroughly prick the sides and bottom of the crust with a fork. For individual pies or tartlets, divide the dough into 8 pieces and press it into muffin tins or molds. Refrigerate the crust(s) for 30 minutes.

To bake pat-in-the-pan pie or tart shells that are to be filled with a mixture that needs no further baking, place in a preheated 425°F oven (400°F for shortbread) until the crust is golden brown, 18 to 22 minutes, pricking the bottom once or twice if it bubbles. If filling the shell with an uncooked mixture that requires baking, bake the crust for 15 minutes, whisk together 1 large egg yolk and a pinch of salt, and brush the warm crust with this glaze, then return to the oven and bake until the glaze sets, 1 to 2 minutes. Fill the pie or tart shell and bake as directed.

To bake individual pat-in-the-pan pies or tartlets that are to be filled with a mixture that needs no further baking, place the muffin tin or molds in a preheated 425°F oven (400°F for shortbread) and bake until firm and golden brown, 12 to 15 minutes, pricking the crusts once or twice if they bubble. If filling the shells with an uncooked mixture that requires baking, bake them for 9 minutes. Whisk together 1 large egg yolk and a pinch of salt, brush the warm crusts with this glaze, then return to the oven and bake until the glaze sets, 1 to 2 minutes. Fill the pie or tartlet shells and finish baking as directed.

Forming a pat-in-the-pan pie crust and shaping the rim

PAT-IN-THE-PAN BUTTER DOUGH

One 9-inch single pie crust or 9½- or 10-inch tart shell or eight 3½-inch tartlet shells

Whisk together in a bowl or process in a food processor for 10 seconds:

1½ cups (190g) all-purpose flour
½ teaspoon salt

Add:

1 stick (4 oz or 115g) unsalted butter, cut into 8 pieces, softened

Mash with the back of a fork or process until the mixture resembles coarse crumbs. Drizzle over the top:

2 to 3 tablespoons (30 to 45g) heavy cream

using the smaller amount of cream to start. Stir or process until the crumbs look damp and hold together when pinched, adding the additional tablespoon of cream if necessary to bring the dough together. To shape and bake, see About Pat-in-the-Pan Crusts, 666.

PAT-IN-THE-PAN SHORTBREAD DOUGH

One 9-inch single pie crust or 9½- or 10-inch tart shell or eight 3-inch tartlet shells

When baked, this rich, sweet dough resembles a shortbread cookie. Use it for cream pies, lemon tarts, fresh fruit tarts with pastry cream, or any other pie or tart with a creamy or buttery filling.

Whisk together in a bowl or process in a food processor for 10 seconds:

1¼ cups (155g) all-purpose flour
⅓ cup (65g) sugar
(Finely grated zest of 1 small lemon)
¼ teaspoon salt

Add:

1 stick (4 oz or 115g) unsalted butter, cut into 8 pieces, softened

Mash with the back of a fork or process until the mixture resembles coarse crumbs. Add:

1 large egg yolk

Stir or process just until the dough comes together in a ball. If the dough is too soft and sticky to work with, wrap it and refrigerate for at least 30 minutes (up to 2 days). To shape and bake, see About Pat-in-the-Pan Crusts, 666.

ABOUT CRUMB CRUSTS

These crusts, mixed and patted into the pan, are a pie-making shortcut. Graham cracker crumbs are the traditional base, but chocolate and vanilla wafers, gingersnaps, zwieback, animal crackers, speculoos, and biscotti also make wonderful crumbs for crusts. If you are starting with whole crackers or cookies, grind them in a food processor or put them in a sturdy plastic bag and pulverize them with a rolling pin until fine. After mixing the crumbs with butter and sugar as directed, press the mixture evenly into the bottom and up the sides of a pie pan, using the bottom of a drinking glass to help, if desired.

To bake an unfilled crumb crust, preheat the oven to 350°F and bake for 10 to 12 minutes. Cool the baked shell before filling. Note that Nut Crust, below, is not baked before filling but, rather, frozen.

Fill the chilled or baked shell with a chiffon filling, 682–83, or Bavarian cream or mousse, 822–24, and top with Whipped Cream, 791. Or fill with custard or fruit fillings and top with meringue, 793–95.

CRUMB CRUST

One 9- or 10-inch crust plus topping

The flavor of the filling should determine which cracker or cookie to crumble.

Put in a medium bowl, reserving a tablespoon or two for topping, if desired:

1½ cups (215g) fine graham cracker, vanilla wafer, chocolate wafer, or gingersnap crumbs

Add and stir until well blended:

¼ to ½ cup (50 to 100g) sugar, depending on sweetness of the cookies
6 tablespoons (3 oz or 85g) unsalted butter, melted and cooled
(1 teaspoon ground cinnamon)

To shape the shell and bake, see About Crumb Crusts, above. When the pie is filled, scatter reserved crumbs as a topping.

CORNFLAKE PIE CRUST

One 9-inch crust

This crust pairs nicely with citrusy fillings, like the one for Lemon Meringue Pie, 681, or use Lemon Curd, 802, and whipped cream.

Grind until fine in 2 batches in a food processor:

6 cups cornflakes

Transfer to a large bowl and add:

6 tablespoons (3 oz or 85g) unsalted butter, melted
¼ cup (50g) sugar

Stir until well blended. Press evenly into a 9-inch pie dish and bake as directed in About Crumb Crusts, above.

NUT CRUST

One 9- or 10-inch crust

To make this crust in a food processor, combine all the ingredients and pulse until the nuts are finely chopped.

Chop to the consistency of coarse crumbs:

2 cups walnuts or pecans

Combine in a large bowl with:

4 tablespoons (2 oz or 55g) unsalted butter, softened
3 tablespoons (35g) sugar
¼ teaspoon salt

Mix with a fork until uniformly moistened. Press the nut mixture evenly over the bottom and up the sides of a 9-inch pie pan. Do not bake the crust before filling, but freeze it for 20 minutes.

COCONUT CRUST

One 9- or 10-inch crust

Pair this crust with Lemon Curd, 802, and Whipped Cream, 791, Key Lime Pie filling, 682, or Old-Fashioned Chocolate Pudding, 817, or use it to make the ultimate Coconut Cream Pie, 680.

Preheat the oven to 350°F.

Knead together in a medium bowl until the mixture comes together:

3 lightly packed cups (340g) shredded sweetened coconut
1 stick (4 oz or 115g) unsalted butter, softened

Press evenly into a 9- or 10-inch pie pan. Bake until the crust is golden brown and fragrant, 20 to 25 minutes. Let cool completely before filling.

ABOUT FRUIT PIES

Fruit pies are typically double-crusted, lattice-topped, or streusel-topped. Other than the fruit, which may be canned, frozen, dried, precooked, or fresh and raw, the filling usually contains sugar and a thickener such as flour or cornstarch. Canned fruits, preferably packed in unsweetened juice, make acceptable pies; see Berry or Cherry Pie with Canned or Bottled Fruit, 669, and Peach Custard Pie Cockaigne, 671.

Start with ➤ 5 cups raw or 4 cups cooked fruit for a 9-inch pie, or even more in the case of apples, to ensure that the filling will seem ample and the top crust will not sink. The measuring cup should be leveled, not heaped.

Ideally, the amount of sugar and thickener added to the filling should be adjusted according to the sweetness, acidity, and juiciness of the fruit, and your personal taste. Deciding how much thickener to add is tricky. Technically, each batch requires a different amount of thickening, depending on the variety of fruit and how ripe it is. In general, we lean toward the lesser quantity of thickener when there is a choice given in the recipes. However, if you are partial to pies that slice neatly and you are willing to risk a slightly solid filling, add the greater amount of thickener called for.

Any fruit pie can be thickened with flour, but cornstarch and tapioca starch produce glossy, clear fillings with a smoother consistency. However, apple pie benefits from the thickening that flour imparts, making the filling more opaque and creamy in appearance. ➤ In general you will need about 1/3 cup cornstarch or tapioca starch for juicy berry pies but only about 2 tablespoons for apple pies, as apples will release less water and contain more pectin, which helps the pie filling set up. If using flour, you will need about 1½ tablespoons more flour than cornstarch or tapioca starch no matter what kind of fruit you are using.

Fruit pies should be baked (or frozen) as soon as they are filled and assembled, or the filling will begin to soften the bottom crust. Preheat the oven before assembling your pie, and place the pie on the lowest oven rack to brown and crisp the bottom crust and prevent the upper crust from browning too quickly. ➤ Do not declare a pie done until the top has turned a deep, rich brown, almost the color of a hazelnut shell, and thick juices bubble through the steam vents or lattice. Remember that pies glazed with egg, milk, or cream will often brown within the first 30 minutes of baking, long before they are baked through. You can slow, but not stop, the browning process by laying a sheet of foil loosely over the top crust or by shaping strips of foil into a ring and placing them on top of the crust rim.

To bake fresh fruit pies, place in a 400°F oven for about 1 hour 15 minutes, unless directed otherwise in the recipe. If you glaze the pie with cream or egg wash and sugar, you will need to tent it with foil partway through baking.

▲ When baking double-crust apple pies above 7,000 feet, it is nearly impossible to bake through a tall pile of packed apple slices (or other hard fruit) before the crust begins to burn. Since water boils at a lower temperature at higher elevations, it takes a very long time to get enough heat into the fruit to soften it. To remedy this, use soft eating apples such as McIntosh, Golden Delicious, or Cortland instead of green cooking apples (or use a combination), or precook a portion of the apples with sugar and spices on top of the stove, then layer them with thin-sliced raw apples to build up a mound before covering with pastry.

FROZEN-FRUIT PIES

To use frozen fruits in pie filling, choose those that are "individually quick frozen" (IQF) or "dry-packed," meaning they have been processed without sugar and come in loose pieces rather than a block. Follow any recipe calling for fresh fruit, substituting an equal volume of frozen fruit. Separate the pieces, but do not thaw before measuring the fruit. Toss the still-frozen fruit with the other ingredients, using about 1 tablespoon extra thickener, and spoon the filling into the crust at once. Set the pie dish on a baking sheet to catch any drips,

To bake pies made with frozen fruit, place in a 400°F oven for 50 minutes, then reduce the heat to 350°F and bake until thick juices bubble through the vents, 25 to 30 minutes more. If you glaze the pie with cream or egg wash and sugar, you will need to tent it with foil partway through baking.

GUIDELINES FOR FRESH OR FROZEN FRUIT PIE FILLING

If you don't find the fruit combination you are looking for in the following recipes, feel free to experiment with fillings. Use these suggestions as a guide to some good beginnings, referencing the information above for baking instructions. If using frozen fruit, do not thaw before measuring.

Mix together 5 cups sliced fruit or whole berries in one of the following combinations:

3½ cups sliced peeled pears and 1½ cups raspberries, cranberries, or raisins
3½ cups sliced peeled, 167, peaches and 1½ cups blueberries or raspberries
3 cups sliced peeled apples and 2 cups sliced green tomatoes
3½ cups sliced peeled apples and 1½ cups raspberries, blackberries, cranberries, or fresh currants
2½ cups chopped hulled strawberries and 2½ cups diced rhubarb, pitted sour cherries, or gooseberries

with:

¾ to 1¼ cups (150 to 250g) sugar depending on the sweetness of the fruit
1/3 cup tapioca starch (40g) or cornstarch (45g), or 1/3 cup plus 1½ tablespoons (55g) all-purpose flour (for apple pies, use only 2 tablespoons tapioca or cornstarch or 3 tablespoons flour)
1 to 2 tablespoons (15 to 30g) lemon juice
¼ teaspoon salt
2 to 3 tablespoons (30 to 45g) butter, cut into small pieces

FRESH BERRY PIE

One 9-inch double-crust pie

For blackberries or blueberries, we like to use Cornmeal Pie or Pastry Dough, 665. Please read About Crusts Baked with Fillings, 663.

Line a 9-inch pie pan with:

1 recipe Basic Pie or Pastry Dough, 664, All-Butter Pie or Pastry Dough, 664, or a double recipe Cream Cheese Pastry Dough, 665

Toss together in a large bowl:

5 cups fresh gooseberries, currants, blackberries, raspberries, blueberries, huckleberries, loganberries, cut-up hulled strawberries, or a combination

(1½ tablespoons [25g] lemon juice, if using sweet fruit)

Combine in a small bowl:

⅔ to 1 cup (130 to 200g) sugar, or more to taste

⅓ cup tapioca starch (40g) or cornstarch (45g)

(½ teaspoon ground cinnamon)

Sprinkle this mixture over the berries and stir gently until well blended. Let stand 15 minutes.

Turn the fruit into the pie shell. Dot with:

2 tablespoons butter, cut into small pieces

Cover with a pricked or vented top crust or a lattice, 663, and freeze the pie for 15 minutes or refrigerate for 1 hour to chill the crust. Position a rack in the lower third of the oven. Preheat the oven to 400°F.

For a bronzed crust, brush the top of the pie with:

(1 large egg, beaten with 1 teaspoon water)

Place the pie on a baking sheet and bake until golden brown, about 1 hour 15 minutes. Let cool completely on a rack.

BERRY OR CHERRY PIE WITH CANNED OR BOTTLED FRUIT

One 9-inch double-crust pie

Please read About Crusts Baked with Fillings, 663.

Prepare:

1 recipe Basic Pie or Pastry Dough, 664, All-Butter Pie or Pastry Dough, 664, or a double recipe Cream Cheese Pastry Dough, 665

Line a 9-inch pie pan with half the dough.

Drain, reserving the juice:

Three 15- to 16-ounce cans or bottles sweet or sour cherries or berries, preferably packed in unsweetened juice

Measure 3½ cups fruit and ½ cup juice and combine in a bowl with:

½ to ¾ cup (100 to 150g) sugar

¼ cup (30g) tapioca starch or cornstarch

2 tablespoons (30g) lemon juice

Let the mixture stand, stirring occasionally, for 15 minutes, then pour into the bottom crust. Dot with:

2 tablespoons butter, cut into small pieces

Cover with a pricked or vented top crust or a lattice, 663, and freeze the pie for 15 minutes or refrigerate for 1 hour to chill the crust. Position a rack in the lower third of the oven. Preheat the oven to 400°F.

For a bronzed crust, brush the top of the pie with:

(1 large egg, beaten with 1 teaspoon water)

Place the pie on a baking sheet and bake until thick juices bubble through the vents, about 1 hour 15 minutes. Let cool completely on a rack.

BLUEBERRY PIE

One 9-inch double-crust pie

Please read About Crusts Baked with Fillings, 663. To use frozen blueberries, see Frozen-Fruit Pies, 668.

Prepare:

1 recipe Basic Pie or Pastry Dough, 664, All-Butter Pie or Pastry Dough, 664, Cornmeal Pie or Pastry Dough, 665, or a double recipe Cream Cheese Pastry Dough, 665

Line a 9-inch pie pan with half the dough.

Combine in a large bowl and let stand for 15 minutes:

5 cups blueberries, picked over

¾ to 1 cup (150 to 200g) sugar

⅓ cup tapioca starch (40g) or cornstarch (45g)

1 tablespoon (15g) lemon juice

(Finely grated zest of 1 lemon)

¼ teaspoon salt

Pour the mixture into the bottom crust and dot with:

2 tablespoons butter, cut into small pieces

Cover with a pricked or vented top crust or a lattice, 663, and freeze for 15 minutes or refrigerate for 1 hour to chill the crust. Position a rack in the lower third of the oven. Preheat the oven to 400°F.

For a bronzed crust, brush the top of the pie with:

(1 large egg, beaten with 1 teaspoon water)

Place the pie on a baking sheet and bake until thick juices bubble through the vents, about 1 hour 15 minutes. Let cool completely on a rack.

FRESH CHERRY PIE

One 9-inch double-crust pie

This cherry pie is so good it'll kill ya. Sour cherries, like Montmorency, make the best pie, but ripe Bing or Rainier cherries will certainly do. Please read About Crusts Baked with Fillings, 663.

Prepare:

1 recipe Basic Pie or Pastry Dough, 664, All-Butter Pie or Pastry Dough, 664, or a double recipe Cream Cheese Pastry Dough, 665

Line a 9-inch pie pan with half the dough.

Combine in a large bowl and let stand for 15 minutes:

5 cups pitted sour, Bing, or Rainier cherries (2 to 2½ lb or 910g to 1.135kg)

1¼ cups (250g) sugar for sour cherries, ¾ cup (150g) for Bing or Rainier cherries

⅓ cup tapioca starch (40g) or cornstarch (45g)

1 to 2 tablespoons (15 to 30g) lemon juice (use the smaller amount for tart cherries)

(¼ teaspoon almond extract)

Pour the mixture into the bottom crust and dot with:

2 tablespoons butter, cut into small pieces

Cover with a pricked or vented top crust or a lattice, 663, and freeze the pie for 15 minutes or refrigerate for 1 hour to chill the crust. Position a rack in the lower third of the oven. Preheat the oven to 400°F.

For a bronzed crust, brush the top of the pie with:

(1 large egg, beaten with 1 teaspoon water)

Place the pie on a baking sheet and bake until thick juices bubble through the vents, about 1 hour 15 minutes. Let cool completely on a rack.

GLAZED BERRY PIE

One 9-inch single-crust pie

Create a high rim with the crust to hold the generous filling.

Line a 9-inch pie pan with:

½ recipe Basic Pie or Pastry Dough, 664, or Pat-in-the-Pan Butter Dough, 666

Chill and bake the crust as directed in About Blind Baking Crusts, 664, or About Crumb Crusts, 667.

Pick over:

6 cups strawberries or red or black raspberries

Hull the strawberries; cut very large ones in half. Measure 4 cups of berries and put in a large bowl. Puree the remaining 2 cups berries in a blender or food processor. Strain, if desired. Whisk together in a medium saucepan:

1 cup (200g) sugar
¼ cup (30g) cornstarch
⅛ teaspoon salt

Whisk in:

½ cup (120g) water
2 tablespoons (30g) lemon juice

Stir in the pureed berries. Bring the mixture to a simmer over medium-high heat, stirring constantly, and cook for 1 minute. Add to the reserved berries, and stir gently to combine. Pour into the crust. Refrigerate the pie for at least 4 hours to set.

This pie is best served the day it is made. Serve with:

Whipped Cream, 791

APPLE PIE

Top your pie with ice cream and call it *à la mode*, if you will; call it paradise when you use firm, flavorful apples like Granny Smith, Rome Beauty, Braeburn, and Winesap. Apple pie is especially fine when made with Cheddar Pie or Pastry Dough, 665. Please read About Crusts Baked with Fillings, 663.

I. CLASSIC (UNCOOKED FILLING)

One 9-inch double-crust pie

Prepare:

Basic Pie or Pastry Dough, 664, or All-Butter Pie or Pastry Dough, 664

Line a 9-inch pie pan with half the dough. Peel, core, and slice ¼ inch thick:

2½ pounds (1.13kg) tart apples (5 to 6 large)

Whisk together in a large bowl:

¾ cup (150g) sugar
3 tablespoons (25g) all-purpose flour or 2 tablespoons cornstarch (15g)
½ teaspoon ground cinnamon
¼ teaspoon salt

Stir in the apples along with:

1 tablespoon (15g) lemon juice

Let stand for 15 minutes, stirring several times, so that the apples soften slightly.

Pour the filling into the bottom crust and gently level with the back of a spoon. Dot the top with:

2 tablespoons butter, cut into small pieces

Cover with a pricked or vented top crust, 663, and freeze for 15 minutes or refrigerate for 1 hour to chill the crust. Position a rack in the lower third of the oven and preheat it to 425°F.

For a bronzed crust, brush the top of the pie with:

(1 large egg, beaten with 1 teaspoon water)

Sprinkle with:

2 teaspoons sugar
(⅛ teaspoon ground cinnamon)

Place the pie on a baking sheet and bake for 30 minutes. Reduce the oven temperature to 350°F and bake until the fruit feels just tender when a knife is poked through a steam vent and juices have begun to bubble through the vents, 30 to 45 minutes more. Let cool completely on a rack, 3 to 4 hours.

The pie is best the day it is baked, but it can be kept at room temperature for 2 to 3 days. If you wish to serve the pie warm, place it in a 350°F oven for about 15 minutes.

II. PRECOOKED FILLING

One 9-inch double-crust pie

Precooking the filling eliminates any gap between it and the top crust when baked and produces a beautifully full, compact pie that slices like a dream.

Prepare:

Basic Pie or Pastry Dough, 664, or All-Butter Pie or Pastry Dough, 664

Line a 9-inch pie pan with half the dough. Peel, core, and slice a little thicker than ¼ inch:

3 pounds tart apples (6 to 8 medium)

Melt in a large, deep skillet or Dutch oven over high heat until sizzling and fragrant:

3 tablespoons butter

Add the apples and toss until glazed. Reduce the heat to medium, cover tightly, and cook, stirring frequently, until the apples are softened on the outside but still slightly crunchy, 5 to 7 minutes. Stir in:

¾ cup (150g) sugar
½ teaspoon ground cinnamon
¼ teaspoon salt

Increase the heat to high and cook the apples at a rapid boil until the juices become thick and syrupy, about 3 minutes. Immediately spread the apples in a thin layer on a baking sheet, and let them cool to room temperature.

Spoon the apple mixture into the bottom crust. Cover with a vented top crust or a lattice, 663, and freeze the pie for 15 minutes or refrigerate for 1 hour to chill the crust. Position a rack in the lower third of the oven. Preheat the oven to 350°F.

For a bronzed crust, brush the top of the pie with:

(1 large egg, beaten with 1 teaspoon water)

Bake until the crust is richly browned and the filling has begun to bubble, 30 to 40 minutes. Let cool completely on a rack, 3 to 4 hours.

The pie is best if eaten promptly, but it can be kept at room temperature for 2 to 3 days. If you wish to serve the pie warm, place it in a 350°F oven for about 15 minutes.

III. STREUSEL-TOPPED

One 9-inch single-crust pie

Prepare **I or II, above,** using:

½ recipe Basic Pie or Pastry Dough, 664, or All-Butter Pie or Pastry Dough, 664

In place of an upper crust, top with a sprinkling of:

Streusel, 800

Bake as directed. If the streusel starts to become too brown, loosely cover with foil until the apples are tender. Let cool completely on a rack.

PEACH CUSTARD PIE COCKAIGNE

One 9-inch single-crust pie

Prepare:

½ recipe Basic Pie or Pastry Dough, 664, or All-Butter Pie or Pastry Dough, 664

Position a rack in the lower third of the oven and preheat the oven to 375°F.

Line a 9-inch pie pan with the dough. Chill and blind bake as directed in About Blind Baking Crusts, 664. Brush the baked crust with:

1 egg yolk, beaten

Return the crust to the oven until the glaze is set, about 3 minutes. Reduce the oven temperature to 350°F. Whisk together in a medium bowl until well blended:

1 large egg or 2 large egg yolks
⅓ cup (65g) sugar
6 tablespoons (3 oz or 85g) unsalted butter, melted
3 tablespoons (25g) all-purpose flour
½ teaspoon vanilla
¼ teaspoon salt

Arrange in a single layer, cut side down, in the bottom of the pie shell:

3 fresh peaches, peeled, 167, halved, and pitted, or 6 drained canned peach halves

Pour the egg mixture over the peaches. Bake the pie until the custard is browned and crusty on top and appears firmly set in the center when the pan is nudged, 40 to 45 minutes. Let cool on a rack. Serve warm or at room temperature. The pie can be refrigerated for up to 2 days. If desired, garnish with:

(Whipped Cream, 791)

PEACH PIE

One 9-inch double-crust pie

Please read About Crusts Baked with Fillings, 663. To use frozen peaches, see Frozen-Fruit Pies, 668.

Prepare:

1 recipe Basic Pie or Pastry Dough, 664, All-Butter Pie or Pastry Dough, 664, Nutty Pie or Pastry Dough, 665, or a double recipe Cream Cheese Pastry Dough, 665

Line a 9-inch pie pan with half the dough.

Peel, 167, pit, and slice ¼ thick:

2½ pounds (1.13kg) peaches

Place the peaches in a large bowl and add:

½ to ¾ cup (100 to 150g) sugar
¼ cup (30g) tapioca starch or cornstarch
3 tablespoons (45g) lemon juice
(¼ teaspoon almond extract)
¼ teaspoon salt

Let stand for 15 minutes, stirring occasionally. Pour the filling into the bottom crust and dot with:

2 tablespoons butter, cut into small pieces

Cover with a pricked or vented top crust or a lattice, 663, and freeze the pie for 15 minutes or refrigerate for 1 hour to chill the crust. Position a rack in the lower third of the oven. Preheat the oven to 400°F. For a bronzed crust, lightly brush the top of the pie with:

Milk or cream

Sprinkle with:

2 tablespoons sugar

Place the pie on a baking sheet and bake until thick juices bubble through the vents, about 1 hour 15 minutes. Let cool completely on a rack.

STRAWBERRY RHUBARB PIE

One 9-inch double-crust pie

This springtime pie is our very favorite fruit pie. If desired, make it all rhubarb by substituting more chopped rhubarb for the strawberries, and increase the sugar to 1⅓ cups. For a special twist, try adding **2 teaspoons Angostura bitters** to the filling. Please read About Crusts Baked with Fillings, 663.

Prepare:

1 recipe Basic Pie or Pastry Dough, 664, All-Butter Pie or Pastry Dough, 664, or a double recipe Cream Cheese Pastry Dough, 665

Line a 9-inch pie pan with half the dough.

Combine in a large bowl and let stand for 15 minutes, stirring occasionally:

2½ cups coarsely chopped rhubarb (¾ to 1 lb or 340 to 455g)
2½ cups halved hulled strawberries (about ¾ lb or 340g)
¾ to 1 cup (150 to 200g) sugar, depending on tartness of fruit
¼ cup (30g) tapioca starch or cornstarch
(Finely grated zest of 1 orange)
¼ teaspoon salt

Pour the filling into the bottom crust and dot with:

2 tablespoons butter, cut into small pieces

Cover with a pricked or vented top crust or a lattice, 663, and freeze the pie for 15 minutes or refrigerate for 1 hour to chill the crust. Position a rack in the lower third of the oven. Preheat the oven to 400°F.

For a bronzed crust, lightly brush the top of the pie with:

Milk or cream

Sprinkle with:

2 teaspoons sugar

Place the pie on a baking sheet and bake until thick juices bubble through the vents, about 1 hour 15 minutes. Let cool completely on a rack.

CONCORD GRAPE PIE

One 9-inch double-crust pie

This old-fashioned pie is time-consuming, but the result is a heavenly slice of Americana. You may substitute **2 pounds (910g) muscadine or scuppernong grapes** for the Concords, or any other variety whose skins slip off when pinched. Please read About Crusts Baked with Fillings, 663.

Prepare:

Basic Pie or Pastry Dough, 664, or All-Butter Pie or Pastry Dough, 664

Rinse, stem, and pick over:

4 cups Concord grapes (about 2 lb or 910g)

One at a time, pinch the grapes to slip off the skins; reserve both skins and pulp separately. Simmer the pulp in a medium saucepan over medium heat until the seeds loosen, about 5 minutes. Run the pulp through a food mill or strain through a coarse sieve into a bowl and discard the seeds. Add the skins to the pulp, then stir in:

¾ to 1 cup (150 to 200g) sugar, depending on tartness of fruit
2 tablespoons (30g) butter, cut into small pieces
1 tablespoon (15g) lemon juice
¼ teaspoon salt

Let cool, then stir in:

¼ cup (30g) tapioca starch or cornstarch

Line a 9-inch pie pan with half the dough. Pour the filling into the bottom crust. Cover with a pricked or vented top crust or a lattice, 663, and freeze the pie for 15 minutes or refrigerate for 1 hour to chill the crust. Position a rack in the lower third of the oven. Preheat the oven to 400°F.

For a bronzed crust, brush the top of the pie with:

(1 large egg, beaten with 1 teaspoon water)

and sprinkle with:

(2 teaspoons sugar)

Place the pie on a baking sheet and bake until thick juices bubble through the vents, about 1 hour 15 minutes. Let cool completely in the pan on a rack.

MINCEMEAT PIE

One 9-inch double-crust pie

Please read About Crusts Baked with Fillings, 663.

I. MOCK

This *Joy* classic originally appeared in the 1931 edition.

Coarsely chop:

1½ cups raisins

Peel, core, and slice ¼ inch thick:

4 Granny Smith apples or a combination of apples and green tomatoes (3 cups)

Combine the raisins and apples in a large saucepan. Add:

Finely grated zest of 1 orange
½ cup orange juice
½ cup apple cider or other fruit juice

Cover and simmer until the apples are very soft. Stir in until well blended:

¾ cup sugar
¼ teaspoon each ground cinnamon and cloves
3 tablespoons finely crushed soda crackers

This mixture will keep for several days. Shortly before using the filling, add, if desired:

(1 tablespoon brandy)

Prepare:

Basic Pie or Pastry Dough, 664, or All-Butter Pie or Pastry Dough, 664

Line a 9-inch pie pan with half the dough. Pour the filling into the pie shell. Cover with a pricked or vented top crust or with a lattice, 663, and freeze the pie for 15 minutes or refrigerate for 1 hour to chill the crust. Position a rack in the lower third of the oven. Preheat the oven to 400°F.

For a bronzed crust, brush the top of the pie with:

(1 large egg, beaten with 1 teaspoon water)

Bake until deep golden brown, 50 to 60 minutes.

II. OLD-FASHIONED

Stir together in a large bowl:

2 Granny Smith apples, cored and chopped
½ cup ground or chopped beef suet, 1023
½ cup raisins, chopped
½ cup dried currants
½ cup chopped toasted, 1005, walnuts
½ cup packed brown sugar
(¼ cup chopped candied citron)
(¼ cup chopped candied orange peel)
(¼ cup chopped candied lemon peel)
¼ cup brandy
Finely grated zest and juice of 1 lemon
Finely grated zest of 1 orange
1 teaspoon ground cinnamon
(½ teaspoon ground mace)
(½ teaspoon ground coriander)
½ teaspoon salt
¼ teaspoon ground cloves
¼ teaspoon black pepper
¼ teaspoon grated or ground nutmeg

Cover tightly and refrigerate for at least 3 days to allow the flavors to meld and develop. Prepare a crust and bake as for Mock Mincemeat Pie, above.

RAISIN PIE

One 9-inch double-crust pie

Please read About Crusts Baked with Fillings, 663.

Prepare:

1 recipe Basic Pie or Pastry Dough, 664, All-Butter Pie or Pastry Dough, 664, or a double recipe Cream Cheese Pastry Dough, 665

Combine in a medium saucepan and bring to a boil over high heat:

4 cups (1½ lb or 680g) raisins or 2 cups dark raisins plus 2 cups golden raisins
2½ cups (590g) water

Reduce the heat and simmer gently for 5 minutes. Remove from the heat. Mix thoroughly, then stir into the raisins:

1 cup packed (230g) brown sugar
¼ cup (30g) all-purpose flour
(¾ teaspoon ground cinnamon)
½ teaspoon salt

Add and bring to a simmer over medium heat, stirring constantly:

3 tablespoons (45g) butter, cut into small pieces
1 tablespoon (15g) lemon juice or any kind of vinegar

Continue to simmer for 1 minute. Let cool to room temperature.

Line a 9-inch pie pan with half the dough. Pour the filling into the bottom crust. Cover with a pricked or vented top crust or a lattice, 663, and freeze the pie for 15 minutes or refrigerate for 1 hour to chill the crust. Position a rack in the lower third of the oven. Preheat the oven to 400°F.

For a bronzed crust, brush the top of the pie with:

(1 large egg, beaten with 1 teaspoon water)

Bake the pie until the crust is richly browned and the filling is bubbly, 40 to 45 minutes. Let cool completely on a rack. The pie can be stored at room temperature for up to 2 days. Serve with:

Whipped Cream, 791, or vanilla ice cream

DEEP-DISH FRUIT PIE

12 to 15 servings

A deep-dish pie is the perfect pièce de résistance when a regular pie just won't do. Follow this recipe using a variety of different fruits for an absolutely stunning dessert: Use 1½ recipes of any of the fruit fillings in this chapter with the exception of uncooked apple pie filling. Please read About Crusts Baked with Fillings, 663.

Have ready a 9-inch deep-dish pie pan or a 9-inch springform pan.

Prepare:

Double recipe All-Butter Pie or Pastry Dough, 664

Divide the dough in half, and divide one of those halves in half again. Shape the two smaller pieces of dough into disks, wrap tightly, and refrigerate. Dust a work surface with flour and roll out the large piece of dough into a large round ¼ to ⅓ inch thick. Transfer the dough to the pie pan or springform pan, pressing it into the corners and up the sides. Fold any overhanging dough back and tuck it under to make a thick edge that sits just on top of the pan rim. Chill the dough while you prepare the filling and top crust.

Toss together in a large bowl:

8 cups berries, pitted and halved cherries, or sliced pitted peaches, plums, or apricots (2½ to 3 lb or 1.133 to 1.36kg)
2 to 2½ cups (395 to 495g) sugar, depending on sweetness of fruit
½ cup tapioca starch (60g) or cornstarch (65g)
3 tablespoons (45g) lemon juice
¼ teaspoon salt

Roll out one of the smaller pieces of dough into a round ¼ to ⅓ inch thick (save the other small piece for decorative accents on the top crust, or store it in the freezer for future use, 662). Pour the filling into the bottom crust. Place the dough round over the filling and fold the overhanging edge under the bottom crust. Flute or crimp the rim, 663, and cut steam vents in the top crust. Freeze the pie for 20 minutes. Position a rack in the lower third of the oven. Preheat the oven to 400°F.

Brush the top crust with:

2 tablespoons heavy cream

Sprinkle with:

Sugar or turbinado sugar

Place the pie on a baking sheet and bake until golden brown and the filling is thick and bubbles up through the crust vents, about 1 hour 20 minutes. Let cool completely on a rack before slicing, 4 hours.

FRUIT SLAB PIE

12 servings

Slab pies are ideal for potlucks, or if you simply prefer a higher crust to filling ratio. Any of the fruit fillings in this chapter can be used to make a slab pie. Please read About Crusts Baked with Fillings, 663.

Prepare:

Double recipe All-Butter Pie or Pastry Dough, 664

Divide the dough in half and shape each into a rectangular brick. Wrap each in plastic wrap and refrigerate 1 hour.

Toss together in a large bowl:

6 cups berries, pitted and halved cherries, or sliced pitted peaches, plums, or apricots (2 lb or 910g)
1 to 1¼ cups (200 to 250g) sugar, depending on sweetness of fruit
⅓ cup tapioca starch (40g) or cornstarch (45g)
2 tablespoons (30g) lemon juice
¼ teaspoon salt

Position a rack in the lower third of the oven. Preheat the oven to 400°F.

Roll out half the dough into a roughly 18 × 13-inch rectangle about ¼ inch thick. Transfer the dough to a jelly-roll pan (15 × 10 inches) and trim the edge so there is about a ¾-inch overhang. Pour the filling into the bottom crust. Roll out the remaining dough into a roughly 16 × 11-inch rectangle about ¼ inch thick. Place the dough over the filling and fold the overhanging edges back underneath themselves so a thick edge of dough rests on the rim of the pan. Crimp or flute the edge, 663, and cut steam vents in the top crust. Brush with:

1 large egg, beaten with 1 teaspoon water

Sprinkle with:

Sugar or turbinado sugar

Bake until golden brown and the filling is thick and bubbles up through the crust vents, 35 to 40 minutes. Let cool on a rack for 1 hour before slicing.

TARTE TATIN

One 10- or 11-inch tart

This classic French upside-down apple tart is named for the Tatin sisters, who served it at their hotel in the Loire Valley. When the tart is turned out of the skillet, the top crust—an overlapping ring of golden, caramelized apples—is an enticing sight. Prepare the tart in any deep, heavy ovenproof skillet, such as cast-iron, measuring 7 to 8 inches across the bottom and 10 to 11 inches across the top. Pans made especially for tarte Tatin are available online and at some cookware stores. Please read Rolling Pie Dough and Lining a Pie or Tart Pan with Dough, 662.

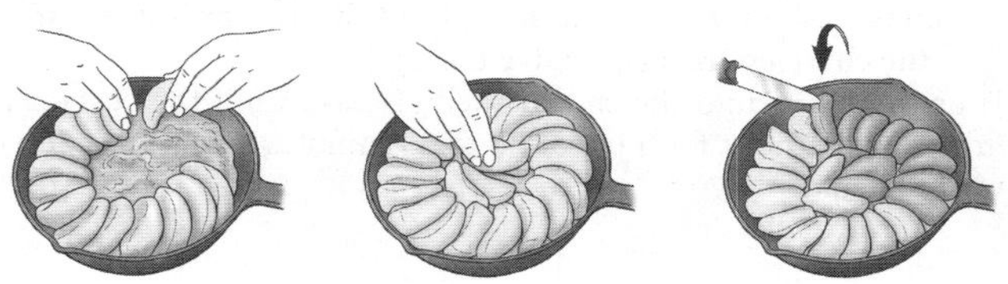

Assembling a tarte Tatin

Have ready:

8 ounces puff pastry, store-bought or homemade, 691, Rough Puff Pastry, 692, or ½ recipe All-Butter Pie or Pastry Dough, 664

Roll or cut the dough into a 12-inch round, slip a cookie sheet beneath it, and refrigerate.

Position a rack in the upper third of the oven. Preheat the oven to 375°F.

Peel, core, and quarter:

6 firm medium apples such as Braeburn, Granny Smith, or Honeycrisp (about 3 pounds or 1.36kg)

Melt in a skillet (see note, 673, for skillet size and type):

1 stick (4 oz or 115g) unsalted butter

Remove from the heat and sprinkle evenly over the bottom:

1 cup (200g) sugar

Arrange a ring of apple quarters around the outer edge of the skillet, standing the apples on the thin edge of their cut side and propping them up against one another so as to fit as many as possible. Fill in the center of the skillet with the remaining apple quarters. (You may have a piece or two of apple left over.) Place the skillet over high heat and cook until the juices turn from butterscotch to deep amber, 10 to 12 minutes.

Remove the skillet from the heat, spear the apples with a fork or the tip of a paring knife, and flip them onto their uncooked sides. Return the skillet to high heat and cook 5 minutes more. Remove the skillet from the heat and slide the prepared crust onto the apples. Being careful not to burn your fingers, gently tuck the edges of the dough against the inner sides of the skillet. Transfer to the oven and bake until the crust is richly browned, 25 to 35 minutes. Let cool on a rack for 20 minutes.

Loosen the sides of the tart with a knife and invert the tart onto a heatproof serving plate. Return any apples that stick to the skillet to their proper place on top of the tart. Serve immediately, or let stand at room temperature for up to 8 hours. When ready to serve, warm the tart to tepid in an oven heated at the lowest setting.

SOUR CREAM CHERRY OR BERRY PIE OR TARTLETS

One 9-inch single-crust pie or four 3½-inch tartlets

Line a 9-inch pie shell or four 3½-inch tartlet shells with:

Crumb Crust, 667, made with graham crackers

Freeze the shell(s) for 20 minutes.

Preheat the oven to 325°F.

Beat in a medium bowl:

3 large eggs

Stir in:

¾ cup (150g) sugar

¾ cup (180g) sour cream

2 cups fresh or drained canned pitted cherries or berries (if the cherries are large, halve them)

Pour the filling into the chilled shell(s). Bake until the custard is firm, about 1 hour for a pie or 30 to 35 minutes for tartlets. Serve warm or cold.

ABOUT TARTS

While the difference between a pie and a tart can be nebulous, tarts are generally characterized by having a single, bottom crust and being shallower than a pie. They are baked in two-piece tart pans or in tart rings placed on a baking sheet. Any pie dough can be used to make tarts, although tart dough is typically crumblier than pie dough. Sweet Dough for Tarts, 665, is ideal, but if you are using a two-piece pan, pat-in-the-pan doughs, 666–67, work as well. For more information on tart pans and rings, including filling capacities, see About Equipment for Pies and Pastries, 660.

BITTERSWEET CHOCOLATE TART

One 9½- or 10-inch tart

Best served the day it is baked.

Line a 9½- or 10-inch two-piece tart pan with:

½ recipe Sweet Dough for Tarts, 665, or 1 recipe Pat-in-the-Pan Shortbread Dough, 667

Chill and bake as directed in the dough recipe, or in About Pat-in-the-Pan Crusts, 666. Position a rack in the lower third of the oven. Adjust the oven temperature to 375°F.

Bring to a simmer in a small saucepan:

1 cup (230g) heavy cream

Remove from the heat and add:

8 ounces (225g) semisweet or bittersweet chocolate, finely chopped

Whisk gently until the chocolate is completely melted and the mixture is smooth, then whisk in:

1 large egg, lightly beaten

Pour the chocolate mixture into the tart shell. Bake until the center seems set but still quivers, like gelatin, when the pan is nudged, 15 to 20 minutes. Let cool in the pan on a rack.

Serve slightly warm or at room temperature with:

Whipped Cream, 791

Store in the refrigerator.

CHOCOLATE-GLAZED CARAMEL TART

One 9½- or 10-inch tart

Serve this tart in small slices. It is like a candy bar in pie form.

Line a 9½- or 10-inch two-piece tart pan with:

½ recipe Sweet Dough for Tarts, 665, or 1 recipe Pat-in-the-Pan Shortbread Dough, 667

Chill and bake as directed in the dough recipe, or in About Pat-in-the-Pan Crusts, 666. After removing the pie weights, if using, or a few minutes before the crust is fully baked, glaze the crust with:

1 large egg yolk, beaten

Return the crust to the oven until golden brown, 5 to 8 minutes. Position a rack in the lower third of the oven. Reduce the oven temperature to 325°F.

Stir together in a medium heavy saucepan:

1½ cups (300g) sugar

½ cup (120g) water

Place the pan over medium heat and stir until the sugar dissolves. It is important that the sugar be dissolved before the boil is reached, so slide the pan off and on the burner as necessary. Increase the heat to high and bring the syrup to a rolling boil. Cover the pan tightly and boil for 2 minutes. Uncover the pan and cook until the caramel begins to darken. Gently swirling the pan, cook until the caramel turns a deep amber. Remove the pan from the heat. Standing back to avoid spatters, pour in:

1¼ cups (290g) heavy cream

Stir until smooth. If the caramel remains lumpy, place the saucepan over low heat and stir until smooth. Let cool for 10 minutes. Whisk until frothy in a medium bowl:

1 large egg
1 large egg yolk
1 teaspoon vanilla
¼ teaspoon salt

Gradually whisk the caramel mixture into the egg mixture. Pour the filling into the prepared tart shell. Bake until the edges darken and begin to bubble and the center looks almost set, 45 to 55 minutes. Let cool completely in the pan on a rack.

Spread over the caramel filling:

½ recipe Chocolate Ganache, 797

Sprinkle with:

½ cup slivered almonds, toasted, 1005, and chopped

Refrigerate the tart until firm, at least 4 hours, or for up to 2 days. Serve chilled with:

Whipped Cream, 791

SALTED CARAMEL NUT TART

One 9-inch tart

In this rich tart, nuts are enrobed in amber caramel and baked to sticky perfection.

Line a 9-inch two-piece tart pan or ring with:

½ recipe Sweet Dough for Tarts, 665, or 1 recipe Pat-in-the-Pan Shortbread Dough, 667

Chill and bake as directed in the dough recipe, or in About Pat-in-the-Pan Crusts, 666. While the tart shell bakes, prepare:

Salted Caramel Sauce, 809

Stir into the finished sauce:

½ cup cashews, coarsely chopped
½ cup walnuts, coarsely chopped
½ cup pecans, coarsely chopped
½ cup slivered almonds

Increase the oven temperature to 400°F if necessary. Pour the caramel-nut mixture into the tart shell and bake until very bubbly and deeply browned, 15 to 20 minutes. Let cool completely in the pan on a rack.

LEMON TART

One 9½- or 10-inch tart

This elegant classic is simple to prepare, and much richer than cornstarch-thickened lemon pies, 681.

Line a 9½- or 10-inch two-piece tart pan with:

½ recipe Sweet Dough for Tarts, 665, or 1 recipe Pat-in-the-Pan Butter Dough, 666

Chill and bake as directed in the dough recipe, or in About Pat-in-the-Pan Crusts, 666. After removing the pie weights, if using, or a few minutes before the crust is fully baked, glaze the crust with:

1 large egg yolk, beaten

Return the crust to the oven until golden brown, 5 to 8 minutes. Position a rack in the center of the oven. Reduce the oven temperature to 350°F if necessary.

Combine in a medium heatproof bowl:

1 cup (200g) sugar
1 stick (4 oz or 115g) unsalted butter, cut into small pieces

Bring 1 inch of water to a bare simmer in a skillet. Set the bowl in the skillet and stir until the butter is melted. Remove the bowl from the skillet. Add to the bowl and beat until no yellow streaks remain:

8 large egg yolks

Stir in:

½ cup (120g) strained lemon juice (from 2 to 3 lemons)

Return the bowl to the skillet and, stirring gently, heat the mixture until thickened to the consistency of heavy cream (it will lightly coat a spoon), 6 to 8 minutes. Strain through a fine-mesh sieve into a medium bowl, then stir in:

1 tablespoon finely grated lemon zest

Pour the filling into the tart shell. Bake until the center is set when the pan is nudged, 15 to 20 minutes. Let cool completely in the pan on a rack. Lightly press a sheet of oiled plastic wrap directly on the filling. The tart can be refrigerated for up to 1 day. Let warm to room temperature before serving. If desired, serve with:

(Fresh Berry Coulis, 805 made with raspberries)
(Whipped Cream, 791)

FRESH FRUIT TART

One 9½- or 10-inch tart

The same formula can also be used for smaller tartlets, but slightly more or less glaze, pastry cream, and fruit may be needed.

Line a 9½- or 10-inch two-piece tart pan with:

½ recipe Sweet Dough for Tarts, 665, or 1 recipe Pat-in-the-Pan Shortbread Dough, 667

Chill and bake as directed in the dough recipe, or in About Pat-in-the-Pan Crusts, 666. After removing the pie weights, if using, or a few minutes before the crust is fully baked, glaze the crust with:

1 large egg yolk, beaten

Return the crust to the oven until golden brown, 5 to 8 minutes. Let cool completely.

Brush over the bottom of the crust:

3 tablespoons currant, raspberry, or strawberry jelly, melted

Refrigerate the shell for 10 minutes to set the glaze. Spread evenly in the crust:

1 cup Pastry Cream, 801, or Frangipane Pastry Cream, 801

Arrange over the cream in a single layer:

2 cups whole small berries, sliced hulled strawberries, or thinly sliced fruit, such as apricot, kiwi, or mango

If desired, brush the fruit lightly with:

(3 tablespoons currant, raspberry, or strawberry jelly, melted)

Or, just before serving, dust the tart very lightly with:

(Powdered sugar)

If not serving immediately, store in the refrigerator for no longer than 6 hours.

RASPBERRY STREUSEL TART

One 9½- or 10-inch tart

You can make this tart with any summer berry or with a mixture of berries.

Line a 9½- or 10-inch two-piece tart pan with:

½ recipe Sweet Dough for Tarts, 665, or 1 recipe Pat-in-the-Pan Shortbread Dough, 667

Chill and bake the crust as directed in the dough recipe, or About Pat-in-the-Pan Crusts, 666. After removing the pie weights, if using, or a few minutes before the crust is fully baked, glaze the crust with:

1 large egg yolk, beaten

Return the crust to the oven until golden brown, 5 to 8 minutes. Let cool completely. Position a rack in the center of the oven. Reduce the oven temperature to 350°F if necessary.

Stir together in a large bowl just until combined:

3 cups raspberries or other berries
½ cup (100g) sugar
2 tablespoons (15g) cornstarch
1 tablespoon (15g) lemon juice

Distribute the raspberry mixture evenly in the tart shell. Sprinkle over the berries:

Streusel I, 800

Bake until the streusel has browned and thick juices bubble up near the center, 50 to 60 minutes. Let cool completely in the pan on a rack.

APPLE TARTLETS

Five 4-inch or eight 2¾-inch tartlets

Position a rack in the lower third of the oven. Preheat the oven to 375°F.

Line 8 standard muffin cups or 5 individual 4-inch pie pans with:

Basic Pie or Pastry Dough, 664, or All-Butter Pie or Pastry Dough, 664

Fill with:

4 cups thinly sliced, cored, peeled apples (see Apple Pie headnote, 670, for apple variety suggestions)

Whisk to combine in a medium bowl:

1 cup (230g) heavy cream
½ cup (100g) sugar
2 large eggs, lightly beaten
2 tablespoons (30g) butter, melted
1 tablespoon (15g) lemon juice
(½ teaspoon ground cinnamon)
(⅛ teaspoon grated or ground nutmeg)

Pour the mixture over the fruit. Bake until golden brown and bubbling, 30 to 40 minutes. Let cool completely in the pan(s) on a rack.

LINZERTORTE

One 9½-inch torte

Named after the Austrian town of Linz, the traditional linzertorte is a lattice-top tart made with a rich nut crust and filled with raspberry or currant jam. Other jams, preserves, and marmalades can be substituted, as can fruit butters. Linzertorte improves in flavor if it stands for 2 to 3 days after baking, and it keeps for at least 1 week.

Whisk thoroughly in a large bowl:

1⅓ cups (165g) all-purpose flour
1 cup slivered almonds or whole hazelnuts, toasted, 1005, and finely ground in a food processor
½ cup (100g) sugar
(1 tablespoon unsweetened cocoa powder)
1 teaspoon ground cinnamon
¼ teaspoon ground cloves
¼ teaspoon salt

Add and mix on low speed with an electric mixer until a smooth dough forms:

1¼ sticks (5 oz or 140g) unsalted butter, softened
2 large egg yolks
Finely grated zest of 1 lemon

Press the dough into a flat disk, wrap in plastic, and refrigerate for at least 2 hours, or for up to 2 days. Let the dough stand at room temperature until malleable but firm, about 30 minutes.

Position a rack in the center of the oven. Preheat the oven to 350°F. Butter and flour a 9½- or 10-inch two-piece tart pan.

Set aside one-quarter of the dough for the lattice. Press the remaining dough evenly into the bottom and up the sides of the tart pan. Roll the remaining dough between 2 sheets of plastic wrap or wax paper into a 10-inch square. Remove the top sheet of plastic or paper and cut the dough into 8 to 12 strips of equal width. If the strips are too soft to handle, refrigerate or freeze them until firm.

Spread evenly over the tart shell:

1 to 1½ cups raspberry jam

The layer of jam should be about ¼ inch thick. Carefully arrange half of the dough strips on the tart at equal distance from each other; pinch the ends onto the bottom crust. Arrange the remaining strips on top at right angles to those beneath, forming a crisscross lattice. If the strips break during handling, simply piece them together; they will fuse during baking. Bake until the lattice is golden brown, 40 to 45 minutes. Let cool completely in the pan on a rack.

The torte can be wrapped airtight, still on the pan bottom, and stored in the refrigerator for up to 1 week or frozen for up to 1 month. Serve at room temperature.

BAKEWELL TART

One 9-inch tart

In this classic British dessert, a layer of tart jam is topped with a rich almond filling and sliced almonds. It is a gloriously elegant dessert, and sturdy enough to take on a picnic.

Butter and flour a 9-inch two-piece tart pan or tart ring. Line with:

½ recipe Sweet Dough for Tarts, 665, or 1 recipe Pat-in-the-Pan Shortbread Dough, 667

Chill and bake as directed in the dough recipe or in About Pat-in-the-Pan Crusts, 666. After removing the pie weights, if using, or a few minutes before the crust is fully baked, glaze the crust with:

1 large egg yolk, beaten

Return the crust to the oven until golden brown, 5 to 8 minutes. Let cool for 10 minutes. Adjust the oven temperature to 375°F.

Prepare:

Frangipane, 802

Spread over the crust:

⅓ cup raspberry jam

Scoop the frangipane in dollops over the jam and spread evenly in the tart shell using a small offset spatula. Sprinkle over the top:

½ cup sliced almonds

Return to the oven and bake until the frangipane is set and browned, 30 to 35 minutes. Let cool completely in the pan on a rack. Before serving, dust with:

Powdered sugar

MEGAN'S FRANGIPANE FRUIT TARTS

One 9-inch tart or five 3- to 4-inch tartlets

These tarts are excellent made with just about any fruit. Part of their appeal is the way the frangipane bubbles up around the fruit, partially engulfing it and turning golden brown.

Have ready:

½ recipe Sweet Dough for Tarts, 665, or ½ recipe All-Butter Pie or Pastry Dough, 664

Frangipane, 802

Butter and flour a 9-inch two-piece tart pan or tart ring for one large tart, or 5 tart rings placed on a large baking sheet for tartlets. Line the tart pan with the dough for the tart; or divide the dough into 5 pieces and roll into small rounds for the tartlets. Chill and bake as directed in the dough recipe, or in About Blind Baking Crusts, 664. Cool completely.

Preheat the oven to 375°F. Fill the crust(s) with the frangipane and arrange on top in a decorative pattern one of the following:

3 to 4 plums, apricots, nectarines, or pluots, sliced

12 fresh figs, stemmed and halved

2 cups fresh berries, halved or sliced if using strawberries

2 cups cherries, pitted and halved

2 large stalks rhubarb, cut into ½-inch slices

Sprinkle the tart(s) lightly with:

Turbinado sugar

Bake until the filling is browned and set and the fruit is lightly caramelized, 45 minutes for a single large tart, 30 to 35 minutes for small tartlets. Let cool completely in the pan(s) on a rack before serving.

ABOUT TRANSPARENT PIES

There is a whole galaxy of pie fillings based on brown sugar, molasses, and corn syrup or maple syrup. These pies seem born of scarcity and frugality. In fact, they are closely related to so-called "desperation pie," which is made with eggs, sugar, vinegar, and not much else. While transparent pies are made of humble ingredients, they are some of our favorite pies to eat and to make.

Chess pie, a type of transparent pie, is generally considered a Southern specialty, although it has traveled widely. The true genesis of the name is lost to history, but our favorite origin story is that of the frugal housewife who, when asked what was in store for dessert, replied simply, "Jes' pie." Perhaps the most notable thing about chess pie is its range. It may be made in a wide variety of flavors by changing the sweetener (white or brown sugar, maple syrup, molasses, sorghum syrup, or honey) or adding nuts, citrus zests, dried or fresh fruits, bourbon, or rum. No matter the flavor, store chess pies in the refrigerator, but let them come to room temperature before serving. While we recommend blind baking the pie crusts, 664, before filling for the crispest results, these pies can be baked in a raw crust as well.

PECAN PIE

One 9-inch single-crust pie

This pie has a mild, sweet, buttery flavor. For a dark pecan pie with caramel notes, use light or dark brown sugar and dark corn syrup. We have also substituted sorghum syrup, 1018, or maple syrup for part of the corn syrup with very good results. For even more flavor, brown the butter before adding to the filling (see the instructions in Brown Butter, 558). If you are not a traditionalist, black walnuts instead of pecans make a piquant substitution.

Line a 9-inch pie pan, preferably glass, with:

½ recipe All-Butter Pie or Pastry Dough, 664, or 1 recipe Pat-in-the-Pan Butter Dough, 666

Bake the crust as directed in About Blind Baking Crusts, 664, or About Pat-in-the-Pan Crusts, 666. After removing the pie weights, if using, or a few minutes before the crust is baked, glaze the crust with:

1 large egg yolk, beaten

Return the crust to the oven until golden brown, 5 to 8 minutes. Reduce the oven temperature to 375°F if necessary. Position a rack in the center of the oven.

Whisk in a large bowl until blended:

4 large eggs

1 cup sugar (200g) or packed brown sugar (230g) or a combination

¾ cup (260g) light corn syrup or golden syrup

5 tablespoons (70g) unsalted butter, melted

1 teaspoon vanilla or up to 3 tablespoons bourbon or dark rum

½ teaspoon salt

Stir in:

2 cups pecans, toasted, 1005

Pour the filling into the pie crust. Bake until the edges are firm and the center seems set but quivery, like gelatin, when the pan is nudged, 35 to 40 minutes. Let cool on a rack for at least 1½ hours.

Serve warm or at room temperature. The pie can be stored in the refrigerator for up to 2 days, but let come to room temperature or warm in a 275°F oven for 15 minutes before serving.

TRANSPARENT PIE

We have encountered this great Southern favorite at all sorts of gatherings, from parties to funerals. There are many variations, but we like to use our recipe for **Pecan Pie, above,** omitting the pecans and replacing the vanilla with **a grating of nutmeg or 1 tablespoon (15g) lemon juice.**

CHOCOLATE CHIP OR CHUNK PECAN PIE

Prepare **Pecan Pie, above,** reducing the pecans to 1 cup and stirring in **1 cup chocolate chips or 6 ounces (140g) dark or milk chocolate, or a combination, cut into ¼-inch chunks,** along with the nuts. Bake until set, 35 to 40 minutes. Refrigerate the cooled pie until cold and hard, then slice. To serve, warm the slices in a 275°F oven until the chocolate just begins to soften.

SHOOFLY PIE

One 9-inch single-crust pie

There are both "dry bottom" and "wet bottom" versions of this Pennsylvania Dutch specialty. The dry-bottom pie is almost like soft gingerbread in a crust, while the "wet" one, as in our version, consists of a molasses custard topped with crumbs.

Line a 9-inch pie pan with:

½ recipe All-Butter Pie or Pastry Dough, 664, or 1 recipe Pat-in-the-Pan Butter Dough, 666

Bake the crust as directed in About Blind Baking Crusts, 664, or About Pat-in-the-Pan Crusts, 666. Position a rack in the center of the oven. Adjust the oven temperature to 400°F.

Combine in a medium bowl:

1 cup (125g) all-purpose flour
⅔ cup packed (155g) dark brown sugar
5 tablespoons (70g) unsalted butter, softened

Mash with a fork or chop with a pastry blender until crumbly. Beat in a separate medium bowl until blended:

1 cup (340g) molasses
1 large egg
1 teaspoon baking soda

Stir in thoroughly:

1 cup (235g) boiling water

Stir half of the crumb mixture into the molasses mixture, and pour into the prepared crust. Sprinkle the remaining crumb mixture evenly over the top. Bake for 10 minutes. Reduce the oven temperature to 350°F and bake until the edges are firm, 20 to 30 minutes more. Let cool completely on a rack.

The pie can be stored at room temperature for up to 3 days. Serve accompanied with:

Whipped Cream, 791

CHESS PIE

One 9-inch single-crust pie

Line a 9-inch pie pan with:

½ recipe All-Butter Pie or Pastry Dough, 664

Bake the crust as directed in About Blind Baking Crusts, 664. After removing the pie weights, glaze the crust with:

1 large egg yolk, beaten

Return the crust to the oven until golden brown, 5 to 8 minutes. Reduce the oven temperature to 325°F. Whisk in a large heatproof bowl just until no yellow streaks remain:

⅔ cup heavy cream (155g) or buttermilk (160g)
6 tablespoons (3 oz or 85g) unsalted butter, melted
1 large egg
3 large egg yolks
½ cup (100g) sugar
½ cup packed (115g) brown sugar
1 tablespoon (10g) fine yellow or white cornmeal
1 tablespoon distilled white or cider vinegar
(1 teaspoon vanilla)
½ teaspoon salt

Pour the filling into the crust. Bake until the edges are firm and the center seems set but quivery, like gelatin, when the pan is nudged, 40 to 50 minutes.

CHOCOLATE CHESS PIE

Prepare **Chess Pie, above,** adding **½ cup natural (40g) or Dutch-process (50g) cocoa powder, sifted,** to the filling. Add the optional vanilla and omit the vinegar. If desired, dust the cooled pie with **(cocoa powder)** before serving.

PUMPKIN OR SQUASH CHESS PIE

Prepare **Chess Pie, above,** adding **1 cup pumpkin, squash, or sweet potato puree** to the filling and, if desired, **(½ teaspoon each ground cinnamon and cardamom)**. If desired, grate **(nutmeg)** over the cooled pie.

ANGOSTURA CHESS PIE

This is an unusual pie for those who like a little bitter with their sweet. Prepare **Chess Pie, above,** using **1 cup (200g) white sugar** instead of a mixture of white and brown sugar, omitting the vinegar, and adding **1 tablespoon Angostura bitters** to the filling.

LEMON CHESS PIE

Prepare **Chess Pie, above.** Substitute **½ cup (100g) additional white sugar** for the brown sugar. Omit the salt and add the **finely grated zest of 1 lemon.** Use **⅓ cup (75g) heavy cream plus ⅓ cup (80g) fresh lemon juice** instead of cream or buttermilk. Reduce the baking time to 30 to 40 minutes.

CHESS TARTLETS

Five 3-inch tartlets

If you use the filling for Chess Pie, above, these are very much like **Canadian butter tarts,** which also sometimes contain walnuts, pecans, or raisins.

Prepare:

½ recipe All-Butter Pie or Pastry Dough, 664, or Sweet Dough for Tarts, 665

Line five 3-inch tartlet pans with the dough and bake as directed in the dough recipe or in About Blind Baking Crusts, 664. Reduce the oven temperature to 325°F. Fill with the filling for:

Chess Pie or any variation, above

Bake until set, about 20 minutes. When cool, top with:

Whipped Cream, 791

HONEY, SORGHUM, OR MAPLE SYRUP PIE

One 9-inch single-crust pie

By simply varying the syrup in this pie, you can achieve a range of flavors.

Line a 9-inch pie pan with:

½ recipe Basic Pie or Pastry Dough, 664

Bake as directed in About Blind Baking Crusts, 664. Reduce the oven temperature to 350°F. Whisk together in a medium bowl:

¾ cup maple syrup (235g), honey (250g), or sorghum syrup (255g)
½ cup (115g) heavy cream
½ cup (100g) sugar

5 tablespoons (70g) unsalted butter, melted
3 large eggs
1 tablespoon all-purpose flour or fine cornmeal
¼ teaspoon salt

Pour the filling into the crust. Bake until the center seems set but still quivers, like gelatin, when the pan is nudged, 45 to 55 minutes. Let cool completely on a rack.

Serve with:

Whipped Cream, 791

ABOUT CUSTARD AND CREAM PIES

Like all custards, fillings for custard pies need to be baked at a relatively low temperature to keep from curdling, but the crust tends to become soggy unless the pie is baked at a high heat. The trick is to have both custard and crust hot when the pie is assembled. This allows the custard to set quickly at the comfortably low temperature it favors, and thus the crust does not become soaked. To prevent the filling from overcooking and turning grainy around the edges, ➤ custard pies must be removed from the oven when the center is still quivery, like gelatin. The filling will continue to cook on stored heat as the pie stands and will thicken further upon cooling.

Because custard and cream pies are highly susceptible to spoilage, refrigerate them as soon as they have cooled to room temperature. Serve within a day of baking, or the crust will soften. Custard pies can be served cold, at room temperature, or slightly warm. Cream pies must be served chilled.

CUSTARD PIE

One 9-inch single-crust pie

Line a 9-inch pie pan, preferably glass, with:

½ recipe Basic Pie or Pastry Dough, 664, or All-Butter Pie or Pastry Dough, 664

Bake as directed in About Blind Baking Crusts, 664. After removing the pie weights, glaze the crust with:

1 large egg yolk, beaten

Return the crust to the oven and bake until golden brown, 5 to 8 minutes. Reduce the oven temperature to 350°F.

While the crust bakes, prepare the filling. Whisk together in a large bowl just until blended:

3 large eggs
3 large egg yolks
½ cup (100g) sugar
1 teaspoon vanilla
⅛ teaspoon salt

Bring to a simmer in a medium saucepan over medium heat:

2 cups (460g) half-and-half or heavy cream

While gently whisking, gradually add the hot cream to the egg mixture. Strain through a fine-mesh sieve. Immediately pour the hot custard into the warm crust. If desired, dust the top with:

(¼ to ½ teaspoon grated or ground nutmeg)

Bake until the center of the custard seems set but quivery, like gelatin, when the pan is nudged, 40 to 50 minutes. Let cool completely on a rack. Serve plain or with:

Sugared fresh fruit

or garnished with:

Chocolate shavings

JAM CUSTARD PIE

This simple variation adds a touch of color and tartness to traditional custard pie. Prepare **Custard Pie, above,** spreading **½ cup strawberry, raspberry, or apricot jam** on the crust before gently ladling the hot custard filling on top. Bake as directed.

CHOCOLATE-GLAZED CUSTARD PIE

Prepare **Custard Pie, above,** omitting the optional nutmeg. Let the pie cool to room temperature. Meanwhile, prepare **Chocolate Ganache, 797.** Let the ganache cool slightly, then spread it over the top of the pie. Refrigerate until the glaze sets.

VANILLA CREAM PIE

One 9-inch single-crust pie

If you plan to cover the pie with meringue instead of whipped cream, read About Meringue, 793.

Line a 9-inch pie pan with:

½ recipe All-Butter Pie or Pastry Dough, 664, or 1 recipe any pat-in-the-pan dough, 666–67, or Crumb Crust, 667

Bake the crust as directed in About Blind Baking Crusts, 664, About Pat-in-the-Pan Crusts, 666, or About Crumb Crusts, 667. If topping the pie with meringue, adjust the oven temperature to 375°F if necessary.

Whisk in a medium heavy saucepan until well blended:

⅔ cup (130g) sugar
¼ cup (30g) cornstarch
¼ teaspoon salt

Gradually whisk in:

2½ cups (590g) whole milk

Vigorously whisk in until no yellow streaks remain:

5 large egg yolks (whites reserved if making meringue)

Stirring constantly with a silicone spatula, bring to a simmer over medium heat. Remove from the heat, scrape the corners of the saucepan, and whisk until smooth. Return to the heat and, whisking constantly, bring to a sputtering simmer and cook for 1 minute. Off the heat, whisk in:

3 tablespoons (45g) butter, cut into small pieces
1½ teaspoons vanilla

Spoon the filling into the prepared crust.

To cover the pie with meringue, proceed at once, while the filling is still hot, to prepare:

Italian Meringue, 794

Spread the meringue over the top of the hot pie, anchoring it to the crust rim all around. Bake the pie until the meringue is browned, 15 to 20 minutes, let cool completely on a rack, and refrigerate.

To cover the pie with whipped cream, press a sheet of plastic wrap directly on the surface of the filling. Refrigerate the pie for at least 3 hours to firm the filling. Shortly before serving, remove the plastic wrap and cover the pie with:

Whipped Cream, 791

COFFEE CREAM PIE

Prepare the crust and filling for **Vanilla Cream Pie, above.** Whisk **2 tablespoons instant coffee or espresso powder** into the sugar and cornstarch mixture, and, if desired, substitute **(1 tablespoon rum)** for the vanilla. Top with **Whipped Cream, 791.**

CHOCOLATE CREAM PIE

One 9-inch single-crust pie

I.

Line a 9-inch pie pan with:

½ recipe All-Butter Pie or Pastry Dough, 664, or 1 recipe any pat-in-the-pan dough, 666–67, or Crumb Crust, 667

Bake the crust as directed in About Blind Baking Crusts, 664, About Pat-in-the-Pan Crusts, 666, or About Crumb Crusts, 667. If topping the pie with meringue, adjust the oven temperature to 375°F if necessary.

Whisk in a medium heavy saucepan until well blended:

¾ cup (130g) sugar
¼ cup (30g) cornstarch
¼ teaspoon salt

Gradually whisk in:

2½ cups (590g) whole milk

Bring just to a simmer, then take off the heat and whisk in until melted:

2 ounces (55g) unsweetened chocolate, chopped

Vigorously whisk in until no yellow streaks remain:

5 large egg yolks (whites reserved if making meringue)

Stirring constantly with a silicone spatula, bring to a simmer over medium heat. Remove from the heat, scrape the corners of the saucepan, and whisk until smooth. Return to the heat and, whisking constantly, bring to a sputtering simmer and cook for 1 minute. Off the heat, whisk in:

3 tablespoons (45g) butter, cut into small pieces
1½ teaspoons vanilla

Spoon the filling into the prepared crust, then proceed as for Vanilla Cream Pie, 679.

II.

Fill any blind-baked pie crust with:

Chocolate Pots de Crème, 815, Chocolate Mousse, 822, or Milk or White Chocolate Mousse, 823

Refrigerate until chilled, or until ready to serve. Garnish with:

Whipped Cream, 791

BANANA CREAM PIE

One 9-inch single-crust pie

Prepare the crust and filling for **Vanilla Cream Pie, 679,** blending the sugar, cornstarch, salt, milk, and egg yolks in a blender with **2 very ripe bananas** until completely smooth. Transfer the mixture to a saucepan and cook as directed, until thickened, stirring in the butter and vanilla at the end. Transfer to a bowl, press a piece of plastic wrap directly on the surface of the custard, and let cool completely.

Peel and thinly slice **2 firm-ripe bananas.** Place half of the bananas in the bottom of the pie crust, and spoon half of the cooled custard over the bananas. Scatter the remaining bananas over the top, and top with remaining custard. Top the pie with **Whipped Cream, 791.**

BUTTERSCOTCH CREAM PIE

One 9-inch single-crust pie

Line a 9-inch pie pan with:

1 recipe Nut Crust, 667, or Crumb Crust, 667, or ½ recipe All-Butter Pie or Pastry Dough, 664

Bake or chill the crust as directed in the recipe, About Crumb Crusts, 667, or About Blind Baking Crusts, 664.

Combine in a medium heavy saucepan and cook over medium heat, stirring, until melted and bubbling, 3 to 5 minutes:

6 tablespoons (3 oz or 85g) unsalted butter
1 cup packed (230g) light brown sugar

Remove from the heat and gradually stir in:

½ cup (115g) heavy cream

If necessary, return briefly to the heat to melt the butterscotch. Let cool slightly. Whisk in a separate medium heavy saucepan until well blended:

¼ cup (30g) cornstarch
¼ teaspoon salt

Gradually whisk in:

2 cups (470g) whole milk

Whisk in the butterscotch. Whisk in until no yellow streaks remain:

5 large egg yolks

Stirring constantly with a silicone spatula, bring to a sputtering simmer over medium heat. Simmer for 1 minute, scraping the corners of the pan well. Off the heat, stir in:

1½ teaspoons vanilla
(1 tablespoon bourbon or whiskey)

Spoon the filling into the crust and press a sheet of plastic wrap directly on the surface. Refrigerate the pie for at least 3 hours to firm the filling. Shortly before serving, remove the plastic wrap and cover the pie with:

Whipped Cream, 791

COCONUT CREAM PIE

If desired, substitute canned coconut milk for half of the whole milk. In a medium saucepan bring **2½ cups (590g) whole milk** to a simmer. Remove from the heat and stir in **1 cup flaked or shredded unsweetened coconut, toasted, 973.** Cover and let steep for 30 minutes, then strain. If desired, you may leave the toasted coconut in the milk rather than straining it out. Prepare the crust and filling for **Vanilla Cream Pie, 679,** using the coconut-infused milk instead of plain milk. Top the cooled pie with **Whipped Cream, 791,** and sprinkle with ½ **cup flaked or shredded unsweetened coconut, toasted, 973.**

ABOUT PUMPKIN, SQUASH, AND SWEET POTATO PIES

Pies made from cooked vegetable purees such as pumpkin or sweet potato should be handled somewhat like custard pies: gently baked and ➤ removed from the oven while the filling is still quivery, like set gelatin. If starting from fresh vegetables, you will need 5 to 6 pounds of pumpkin or squash to make 4 cups of puree, enough for 2 pies. Look for pie pumpkins—a smaller, sweeter variety with finer-textured flesh than decorative jack-o'-lanterns—or squash such as Hubbard, kabocha, buttercup, or butternut. In fact, the best "pumpkin" pie we have ever made was with butternut squash.

To prepare fresh pumpkin or squash puree, wash and split the pumpkins or squash into quarters with a cleaver or heavy knife. Cut out the stem, scrape out the stringy pulp and seeds, and cut into 4-inch pieces. Place the pumpkin or squash rind side down in an oiled roasting pan, cover tightly with foil, and bake at 325°F until very soft, about 1½ hours. Scrape the flesh free of the rind and puree in a food processor, or force it through a food mill. Scrape the puree into a colander lined with a thin kitchen towel, bring the ends of the towel up over it, and let the pumpkin or squash drain for 1 hour, stirring it occasionally.

PUMPKIN, SQUASH, OR SWEET POTATO PIE

One 9-inch single-crust pie

Use 3 eggs for a soft, custardy filling, 2 for a firmer pie with a pronounced pumpkin flavor. To prepare this with sweetened condensed milk, substitute **1½ cups (455g) sweetened condensed milk** for the heavy cream and do not add the white sugar.

I. CLASSIC

Line a 9-inch pie pan with:

½ recipe All-Butter Pie or Pastry Dough, 664

Bake as directed in About Blind Baking Crusts, 664. After removing the weights, glaze the crust with:

1 large egg yolk, beaten

Return the crust to the oven until golden brown, 5 to 8 minutes. Leave the oven on. Whisk thoroughly in a large bowl:

2 cups pumpkin, squash, or sweet potato puree, canned or prepared, above
1½ cups heavy cream (345g) or evaporated milk (370g)
½ cup (100g) sugar
2 to 3 large eggs
⅓ cup packed (75g) brown sugar
1 teaspoon ground cinnamon
1 teaspoon ground ginger
½ teaspoon grated or ground nutmeg
¼ teaspoon ground cloves or allspice
½ teaspoon salt

Warm the pie crust in the oven until it is hot to the touch, but leave the filling at room temperature. Pour the pumpkin mixture into the crust and bake until firm, 35 to 45 minutes. Let cool completely on a rack.

The pie can be refrigerated for up to 5 days. Serve cold or at room temperature, accompanied with:

Whipped Cream, 791 (flavored with 2 tablespoons bourbon)

II. WITH SOUR CREAM

Follow the directions in **I, above,** omitting the milk and adding **2 tablespoons (45g) molasses** and **1½ cups (360g) sour cream.**

ABOUT LEMON AND LIME PIES

These zingy pies deserve fresh citrus juice and zest. Citrus zest, with its pungent oils, is essential to a well-flavored filling, and fresh juice tastes better than frozen or bottled juices, whose flavor is compromised by pasteurization and preservatives (the exception to this is bottled Key lime juice, which is so much easier to use than having to juice Key limes that any flavor nuances lost in bottling seem a reasonable price to pay for the convenience). For an equally pleasing, crowd-friendly alternative, see Lemon Bars, 767.

LEMON MERINGUE PIE

One 9-inch single-crust pie

If meringue is not your thing, feel free to top this pie with Whipped Cream, 791. For a dessert with a richer filling, see Lemon Tart, 675. Read About Meringue, 793.

Line a 9-inch pie pan with:

½ recipe All-Butter Pie or Pastry Dough, 664

Bake the crust as directed in About Blind Baking Crusts, 664. Leave the oven on. Combine in a medium saucepan:

1½ cups (300g) sugar
6 tablespoons (50g) cornstarch
¼ teaspoon salt

Gradually blend in until smooth:

½ cup (120g) cold water
½ cup (120g) lemon juice

Add, blending thoroughly:

3 large egg yolks, well beaten

Add:

2 tablespoons (30g) unsalted butter, cut into small pieces

Stirring constantly, gradually add:

1½ cups (355g) boiling water

Bring to a full boil over medium-high heat, stirring gently. Once it begins to thicken, reduce the heat and simmer slowly for 1 minute. Remove from the heat and stir in:

Finely grated zest of 1 lemon

Pour into the baked pie shell. Prepare:

Soft Meringue Topping I or II, 795, or Italian Meringue, 794

Spread a band of meringue around the perimeter of the filling, anchoring it to the crust at all points. Dollop the remaining meringue over the center and smooth the top. Bake the pie until the meringue is browned, 15 to 20 minutes. If using Italian meringue, you may brown it with a propane torch instead of in the oven. Let cool completely on a rack. Serve or refrigerate for up to 5 days.

OHIO SHAKER LEMON PIE

One 9-inch double-crust pie

The very tart filling in this favorite consists of paper-thin lemon slices macerated in sugar until tender and sweet. It may sound odd, but don't be afraid—it is as delicious as it is unusual. Please read About Crusts Baked with Fillings, 663.

Finely grate and reserve the zest from:

2 large lemons

Slice the lemons paper-thin, discarding the seeds. Combine the lemon slices and zest in a medium bowl with:

2 cups (395g) sugar
¼ teaspoon salt

Cover and let stand at room temperature for 2 to 24 hours (the longer the better), stirring occasionally.

Prepare:

Basic Pie or Pastry Dough, 664, or All-Butter Pie or Pastry Dough, 664

Line a 9-inch pie pan with half the dough. Position a rack in the lower third of the oven. Preheat the oven to 425°F.

Whisk in a large bowl until frothy:

4 large eggs

Whisk in:

4 tablespoons (2 oz or 55g) butter, melted
3 tablespoons (25g) all-purpose flour

Stir in the lemon mixture. Pour the filling into the bottom crust and level with the back of a spoon. Cover with a pricked or vented top crust or a lattice, 663. Bake the pie for 30 minutes. Reduce the oven temperature to 350°F and bake until a knife inserted into the center comes out clean, 20 to 30 minutes more. Let cool completely on a rack.

The pie can be refrigerated for up to 5 days, but it should be served at room temperature.

KEY LIME PIE

One 9-inch single-crust pie

This pie owes its distinctive character to the citrus variety called the Key lime, which, while not native to Florida, is called the Key lime in the United States because it has been grown in the Florida Keys since the 1800s. Bottled Key lime juice is perfectly acceptable when fresh Key limes are not available, or, in a pinch, just use regular limes (but don't tell anyone). Read About Meringue, 793.

Line a 9-inch pie pan with:

½ recipe Basic Pie or Pastry Dough, 664, or 1 recipe Crumb Crust, 667, made with graham crackers

Bake the crust as directed in About Blind Baking Crusts, 664, or About Crumb Crusts, 667.

Reduce the oven temperature to 325°F. Whisk together in a medium bowl until well blended:

One 15-ounce can sweetened condensed milk
4 large egg yolks
½ cup (120g) Key lime juice (from 12 to 14 Key limes)
(3 to 4 teaspoons finely grated Key lime zest)

Pour the filling into the pie crust. If not topping the pie with meringue, bake the pie until the center looks set but quivers when the pan is nudged, 15 to 17 minutes. Let cool completely on a rack, then refrigerate for up to 1 day. Serve with:

Whipped Cream, 791

If topping the pie with meringue, bake the pie until the filling thickens just enough to support the topping, 5 to 7 minutes, but no longer. Meanwhile, prepare:

Soft Meringue Topping I or II, 795, or Italian Meringue, 749

Spread a band of meringue around the perimeter of the filling, anchoring it to the crust at all points. Dollop the remaining meringue over the center and smooth the top. Bake the pie until the meringue is browned, about 20 minutes more. If using Italian meringue, you may also brown it with a propane torch instead of in the oven, but first bake until the filling is set. Let cool completely on a rack, then refrigerate for up to 5 days.

NO-BAKE LEMON OR LIME PIE

One 9-inch single-crust pie

This is a pie for the hottest of summer days, when firing up the oven is the last thing you want to do.

Line a 9-inch pie pan with:

Crumb Crust, 667, made with graham crackers

Or have ready a store-bought graham cracker crust. Freeze for 20 minutes.

Beat or process until smooth with a hand mixer, stand mixer, or food processor:

1 pound (455g) cream cheese
Finely grated zest of 2 limes

Add and beat to combine:

One 14-ounce can sweetened condensed milk

Scrape down the sides of the bowl as needed. Add:

⅓ cup (80g) lime juice (from 2 to 3 large limes)
1 teaspoon vanilla

Beat until very smooth. Pour the filling into the crust and smooth it out. Refrigerate at least 3 hours. Serve with:

Whipped Cream, 791, and long strands of lime zest removed with a citrus zester
(Mango slices, fresh raspberries, or Fresh Berry Coulis, 805, made with raspberries)

ABOUT CHIFFON AND MOUSSE PIES

These pies have a light and airy texture imparted by whipped cream or beaten egg whites. If the filling is based on a custard sauce stiffened with gelatin, you have a **chiffon pie;** otherwise the filling is a **mousse.** The secret is a gentle hand in folding the whipped cream, egg whites, or other aerated mixture into the filling. Mousse pies soften quickly at room temperature and become difficult to slice neatly, so leave them in the refrigerator until just before serving.

Many chiffon pies call for raw egg whites, so please see the note on uncooked eggs, 977, or use egg whites from pasteurized eggs, if safety is a concern. Any mousse or Bavarian cream, 822–23, can also be served in a baked pie shell.

LEMON OR LIME CHIFFON PIE

One 9-inch single-crust pie

To make **Orange Chiffon Pie,** substitute **orange juice** for the water and lemon juice, and **orange zest** for the lemon zest.

Line a 9-inch pie pan with:

½ recipe All-Butter Pie or Pastry Dough, 664, or 1 recipe any pat-in-the-pan dough, 666–67, or Crumb Crust, 667

Bake the crust as directed in About Blind Baking Crusts, 664, About Pat-in-the-Pan Crusts, 666, or About Crumb Crusts, 667.

Combine in the top of a double boiler or a medium heatproof bowl:

½ cup (100g) sugar
⅔ cup (160g) water
⅓ cup (80g) lemon or lime juice
4 large egg yolks (whites reserved)
1 tablespoon unflavored gelatin

Cook and stir these ingredients over simmering water until thick. Add:

1 tablespoon finely grated lemon or lime zest

Refrigerate the mixture until it forms little mounds when dropped from a spoon. Be careful not to chill the mixture until it is fully set or it will be impossible to fold in the egg whites. Beat in a large bowl until soft peaks form, 977:

4 large egg whites

Beat in gradually and continue beating until the peaks are stiff but not dry, 978:

⅓ cup (65g) sugar

Fold the egg whites into the lemon mixture. Fill the pie crust and chill until set, 4 to 6 hours.

BLACK BOTTOM PIE

One 10-inch single-crust pie

Line a 10-inch pie pan with:

Crumb Crust, 667, preferably made with gingersnaps

Bake as directed in About Crumb Crusts, 667, and let cool completely. Pour into a small cup:

¼ cup (60g) cold water

Sprinkle over the top and let stand for 5 minutes:

1½ teaspoons unflavored gelatin

Place in a medium bowl:

6 ounces (170g) semisweet or bittersweet chocolate, finely chopped, or 1 cup semisweet chocolate chips

Whisk together thoroughly in a medium heavy saucepan:

⅓ cup (65g) sugar
4 teaspoons (10g) cornstarch

Gradually whisk in:

2 cups half-and-half (470g) or 1 cup whole milk (235g) plus 1 cup heavy cream (230g)

Vigorously whisk in until no yellow streaks remain:

4 large egg yolks (whites reserved)

Stirring constantly, bring to a simmer over medium heat and cook for 30 seconds. Immediately stir 1 cup of the mixture into the chocolate. Add the softened gelatin to the mixture remaining in the pan and stir for 30 seconds to dissolve the gelatin. Vigorously stir the chocolate mixture until smooth (if the chocolate fails to melt completely, set the bottom of the bowl in very hot water). Spread the chocolate mixture evenly over the bottom of the pie crust and refrigerate. Stir into the custard still in the pan:

2 teaspoons vanilla
(2 tablespoons dark rum or Grand Marnier)

Beat in a large bowl until foamy:

3 large egg whites

Add:

¼ teaspoon cream of tartar

Continue to beat until soft peaks form, 977, then gradually beat in:

⅓ cup plus 1 tablespoon (80g) sugar

Increase the speed to high and beat until the peaks are stiff and glossy, 977. Gently fold the egg whites into the custard mixture. Spoon the filling over the chocolate mixture in the pie crust. Refrigerate for at least 3 hours, or up to 1 day before serving.

Top with:

Whipped Cream, 791

If you wish, sprinkle with:

(1 ounce semisweet or bittersweet chocolate, grated or shaved)

The pie can be refrigerated for up to 5 days.

PUMPKIN CHIFFON PIE

One 9-inch single-crust pie

Line a 9-inch pie pan with:

½ recipe All-Butter Pie or Pastry Dough, 666, or 1 recipe Crumb Crust, 667, made with graham crackers

Bake the crust as directed in About Blind Baking Crusts, 664, or About Crumb Crusts, 667.

Pour into a small cup:

¼ cup (60g) cold water

Sprinkle over the top and let stand for 5 minutes:

1 tablespoon unflavored gelatin

Lightly beat in the top of a double boiler or large heatproof bowl:

3 large egg yolks (whites reserved)

Add:

1¼ cups unsweetened pumpkin puree, homemade or canned
½ cup (120g) milk
½ cup white (100g) or packed brown (115g) sugar
½ teaspoon salt
¼ teaspoon ground cinnamon
¼ teaspoon grated or ground nutmeg
¼ teaspoon ground ginger

Cook and stir over, not in, simmering water until thickened. Stir in the softened gelatin until dissolved. Refrigerate until the mixture thickens but is not completely set.

Whip in a large bowl until soft peaks form, 977:

3 large egg whites

Gradually beat in:

½ cup (100g) sugar

Beat the egg whites until stiff but not dry, 978. Fold into the pumpkin mixture and fill the pie shell. Refrigerate several hours to set.

Serve garnished with:

Whipped Cream, 791

PEANUT BUTTER PIE

One 10-inch single-crust pie

This rich but mousse-like pie is a great favorite with children and the grown-ups who cook for them.

Line a 10-inch pie pan with:

Crumb Crust, 667, made with graham crackers or chocolate wafers

Bake the crust as directed in About Crumb Crusts, 667. Let cool completely on a rack.

Beat in a large bowl just until smoothly blended:

8 ounces (225g) cream cheese, softened
1 cup (235g) chunky or smooth peanut butter
½ cup (100g) sugar
2 teaspoons vanilla

Beat in a medium bowl until stiff peaks form:

1 cup (230g) cold heavy cream

Using a large silicone spatula, fold half of the whipped cream into the peanut butter mixture to lighten it, then fold in the remaining cream. Spread the mixture evenly in the cooled pie crust. Press a sheet of plastic wrap directly on the surface and refrigerate until firm, about 4 hours.

Prepare:

Chocolate Ganache, 797

Let cool to lukewarm, then pour the glaze over the top of the pie and spread evenly. If desired, sprinkle with:

(⅓ cup chopped salted peanuts)

Refrigerate for at least 1 hour, or for up to 3 days.

RUSTIC FRUIT DESSERTS

Here we include cobblers, crisps, brown Betties, slumps, grunts, buckles, and sonkers. This family of desserts is based on biscuit or pie dough, dumplings, bread crumbs, or crumbled toppings; the fruit may be cooked under, over, or inside the dough, or between dough layers. A few are adapted from European pastries, but most are American inventions born of simple home cooking. These desserts are generally best the day they're made, served warm with cold heavy cream, Whipped Cream, 791, Vanilla Bean Crème Anglaise, 806, vanilla ice cream, or plain or vanilla whole-milk yogurt.

BLUEBERRY AND PEACH BUCKLE

One 10-inch round or 9-inch square buckle

These are so named because the fruit causes the surface of the batter to buckle during baking. While this dessert is suspiciously like a cake, we think its fruity unctuousness has earned it a place among the pies.

Position a rack in the lower third of the oven. Preheat the oven to 350°F. Butter and flour a 10 × 2-inch round cake pan or 9-inch square baking dish.

Prepare:

Streusel, 800

Halve, pit, and cut into small chunks:

1 large peach

Combine with:

1½ cups blueberries or boysenberries

Whisk together in a medium bowl:

1¾ cups (220g) all-purpose flour
2 teaspoons baking powder
½ teaspoon salt

Combine in another large bowl and beat until slightly fluffy:

4 tablespoons (2 oz or 55g) butter, softened
1 cup (200g) sugar
1 large egg

Gradually beat into the butter-sugar mixture:

½ cup (120g) milk

Add the flour mixture and stir just until the dry ingredients are moistened and the batter is smooth. Gently fold in the fruit. Spoon into the prepared pan and spread evenly. Sprinkle the streusel topping evenly over the batter. Bake until the top springs back when touched and a toothpick inserted in the center comes out clean, 50 to 55 minutes. Let cool in the pan on a rack for at least 20 minutes before serving.

FRUIT CRISP

6 to 8 servings

If using apples, select tart, crisp ones to balance the sweetness of the topping. Gravenstein, Pippin, and Braeburn are all good choices.

Preheat the oven to 375°F. Have ready an unbuttered 2-inch-deep 2-quart baking dish.

Peel, core, and cut into 1-inch chunks:

2½ pounds (1.13kg) tart apples (about 8 medium)

Or use the same amount of:

Berries, pitted cherries, rhubarb, cut into chunks, peaches or plums, pitted and cut into chunks

Spread the fruit evenly in the baking dish and toss with:

¼ cup (50g) sugar
2 tablespoons (30g) lemon juice
2 tablespoons (15g) cornstarch or tapioca starch

Combine in a medium bowl or food processor:

¾ cup (95g) all-purpose flour
½ cup packed (115g) brown sugar
1 teaspoon ground cinnamon or cardamom
½ teaspoon salt
(¼ teaspoon grated or ground nutmeg)

Add:

1 stick (4 oz or 115g) cold unsalted butter, cut into small pieces

Cut in the butter or pulse until the mixture resembles coarse bread crumbs. If desired, stir in:

(½ cup sliced almonds)

Scatter the topping evenly over the fruit. Bake until the topping is golden brown, the juices are bubbling, and the apples are tender, 50 to 55 minutes (start checking at 40 minutes if using a tender fruit). Serve hot or at room temperature.

GINGER CRISP

Prepare **Fruit Crisp, above,** substituting **1½ cups crushed gingersnap cookies** (from one 9-ounce box gingersnaps) for the flour and reducing the sugar in the topping to ⅓ cup (65g).

STRAWBERRY SONKER

8 to 10 servings

This specialty of Surry County, North Carolina, where Megan's family is from, is made with many different fruits and with different styles of crust. We are partial to this version, in which a thin batter is poured over juicy cooked fruit. In the oven, the fruit rises up oozingly around the batter (or maybe the batter sinks into the fruit—we aren't entirely sure), creating the effect of sweet biscuit islands in a sticky strawberry sea.

Preheat the oven to 350°F. Place in a 13 × 9 × 2-inch baking dish:

1 stick (4 oz or 115g) unsalted butter, cut into chunks

Place the baking dish in the oven until the butter is completely melted. Remove from the oven, tilt the dish so the butter coats the inside, and set aside.

Combine in a large saucepan:

4 generous cups sliced hulled strawberries (from about 5 cups whole berries)
¼ cup (50g) sugar

Bring to a boil over high heat, then reduce the heat to a simmer, stirring frequently, until very juicy, about 10 minutes. Whisk together in a medium bowl:

1 cup (125g) all-purpose flour
1 cup (235g) milk
¾ cup (150g) sugar
1½ teaspoons baking powder
¼ teaspoon salt

Pour the hot strawberry mixture into the baking dish, then pour the batter as evenly as possible over the strawberries. It will look messy and imperfect—this is what you want! Bake until browned, 40 to 45 minutes. Serve warm.

SOUR CHERRY AMARETTI CRISP

6 servings

Cherries and almonds are closely related. Marasca cherries and apricots are distant cousins as well, and all four are used to concoct this dessert—the latter two in the forms of bitter maraschino liqueur and crunchy amaretti cookies (traditionally made from apricot kernels). The result is rich, fruity, and tart.

Preheat the oven to 375°F.

Toss together in a 9-inch square baking dish:

1½ pounds (680g) fresh or frozen pitted sour cherries
2 tablespoons (15g) cornstarch
¼ cup (50g) sugar
(2 tablespoons maraschino liqueur or kirsch)

Combine in a small bowl:

1 cup finely ground amaretti cookie crumbs (from about 18 cookies)
½ cup (50g) old-fashioned rolled oats
⅓ cup sliced almonds
¼ teaspoon salt

Stir in:

6 tablespoons (3 oz or 85g) unsalted butter, melted

Sprinkle the mixture over the cherries and bake until the cherries are bubbling and the juice looks thick, about 40 minutes. If the top is browning too quickly, cover loosely with foil. Let cool for at least 15 minutes before serving.

APPLE, PEACH, OR APRICOT BROWN BETTY

6 servings

A brown Betty is both layered and topped with sweet buttered crumbs, which absorb the fruit juices and help thicken them.

Preheat the oven to 350°F. Have ready an unbuttered 8-inch square baking dish.

Core or pit and slice:

1 pound apples, peaches, or apricots

Stir together with a fork in a small bowl:

1½ cups dry bread crumbs
6 tablespoons (3 oz or 85g) unsalted butter, melted

Whisk together in a large bowl:

1¼ cups packed (290g) dark brown sugar
1 teaspoon ground cinnamon
¼ teaspoon grated or ground nutmeg
¼ teaspoon ground cloves

Stir the fruit into the sugar and add:

3 tablespoons (45g) lemon juice

Spread one-third of the crumb mixture evenly in the bottom of the baking dish and distribute half of the fruit mixture over the crumbs. Spread another third of the crumb mixture evenly on top of the fruit and distribute the remaining fruit mixture over the crumbs. Spread the remaining crumbs on top. Cover the dish with foil and bake until the fruit is tender, about 40 minutes. Uncover the dish, increase the oven temperature to 400°F, and bake until browned, 10 to 15 minutes. Serve warm.

FRUIT COBBLER

6 to 8 servings

A cobbler is much like a deep-dish pie made with a rich biscuit dough and fruit. While neither tidy nor shapely, it is indisputably tasty. Although almost any type of fruit or combination of fruits may be used, berries are traditional. Frozen berries can be substituted when fresh ones are out of season; use them directly from the freezer without thawing, and increase the baking time as needed to cook the dough through.

Position a rack in the lower third of the oven. Preheat the oven to 375°F. Have ready an unbuttered cast-iron, enameled cast-iron, earthenware, or glass baking dish of about 2-quart capacity and 2 inches deep.

Prepare in any combination:

6 cups berries, hulled and halved strawberries, and/or sliced peaches, plums, or apricots

Combine the fruit in a large bowl and toss with:

½ cup (100g) sugar
2 tablespoons (15g) cornstarch or ¼ cup (30g) all-purpose flour
Finely grated zest of 1 lemon or lime

Spread the fruit mixture evenly in the baking dish. Prepare the dough for:

Buttermilk Biscuits, 635, Quick Cream Biscuits or Shortcakes, 636, Quick Drop Biscuits, 636, or Cornmeal Biscuits, 636

If using drop biscuit dough, simply drop spoonfuls of dough on the fruit. For other doughs, dust the dough with a little flour, then roll or pat it with your hands to the shape of the top of the baking dish and between ¼ and ½ inch thick. Cut the dough into rounds, squares, rectangles, or wedges and place the dough on the fruit. You may also gently roll pieces of the dough into balls, flatten each one slightly, and place them on the fruit. Lightly brush the dough with:

2 tablespoons melted butter, heavy cream, or milk

Sprinkle with:

1 tablespoon sugar

Bake until the top is golden brown and the juices have thickened slightly, 45 to 50 minutes. Let cool for 15 minutes before serving.

CHOCOLATE COBBLER

8 servings

We have taken to calling this gooey, intensely chocolaty dessert a "molten brownie." The process for making it is unusual, but do not stray from the instructions and you will be rewarded.

Preheat the oven to 350°F. Place in an 8- or 9-inch square baking dish:

4 tablespoons (2 oz or 55g) butter

Place in the oven until the butter is melted, then remove and set aside.

Whisk together in a medium bowl:

1 cup (125g) all-purpose flour
½ cup packed (115g) brown sugar
¼ cup (20g) unsweetened cocoa powder
1½ teaspoons baking powder
½ teaspoon salt

Pour the melted butter out of the baking dish into the flour mixture and whisk in, along with:

½ cup (120g) milk
1 teaspoon vanilla
(Finely grated zest of 1 orange)

Spread the flour mixture in the baking dish and sprinkle with:

4 ounces (115g) semisweet, bittersweet, or dark chocolate (up to 70% cacao), chopped

Mix together in a medium bowl:

½ cup (100g) sugar
½ cup packed (115g) brown sugar
¼ cup (20g) unsweetened cocoa powder

Sprinkle the sugar mixture over the chocolate in the baking dish. Pour over the top, but do not mix in:

1¼ cups (295g) boiling water

Bake until barely set in the middle, 30 to 35 minutes. Let cool for 10 minutes before serving.

APRICOT-CHERRY SLUMP

6 to 8 servings

Slumps are cooked in a covered saucepan and served in bowls—like a hot, sweet soup or stew with buttery dumplings.

Whisk together thoroughly in a medium bowl:

1½ cups (190g) all-purpose flour
2 teaspoons baking powder
½ teaspoon salt

Add and stir just until the dry ingredients are moistened:

1 cup (235g) milk
4 tablespoons (2 oz or 55g) butter, melted

Combine in a large heavy saucepan or Dutch oven with a tight-fitting lid and stir until the sugar is dissolved:

1 cup (235g) water
½ cup (100g) sugar

Add to the sugar water:

1 pound (455g) apricots, halved and pitted
1 pound (455g) cherries, pitted

Cover and bring to a boil over high heat. Reduce the heat and simmer for about 10 minutes. Remove the lid and quickly cover the fruit with spoonfuls of the batter. Replace the lid and simmer over low heat for 20 minutes. Check the dumplings for doneness. They should look firm and feel dry to the touch. If not, cover and continue steaming for 5 to 10 minutes more. Serve immediately.

BLACKBERRY-RASPBERRY GRUNT

6 to 8 servings

Grunts are steamed in a mold in a pot of water and inverted when served—somewhat resembling a warm fruit shortcake. Also try this with blueberries or strawberries.

Butter a 1½-quart baking dish, such as a soufflé dish or pudding mold. Have ready a Dutch oven or a lidded pot large enough to hold the dish or mold with ample room around it. Toss together in a medium bowl:

1 pint raspberries
1 pint blackberries
½ cup (100g) sugar

Pour the fruit into the buttered mold and spread evenly. Whisk together thoroughly in a small bowl:

1¼ cups (155g) all-purpose flour
2 tablespoons (25g) sugar
1¼ teaspoons baking powder
½ teaspoon salt

Add:

3 tablespoons (1½ oz or 45g) cold butter, cubed

Using a pastry blender or your fingertips, cut the butter into the dry ingredients until the mixture resembles coarse crumbs. Add:

½ cup (120g) milk

Stir just until the dry ingredients are moistened. Lightly flour your hands and gather the dough into a ball. Knead it gently against the sides of the bowl, turning and pressing any loose pieces into the dough until they adhere. Dust the top and bottom of the dough with a little flour. On a work surface, pat the dough into a round just large enough to cover the top of the fruit. Cover the fruit with the dough. Tear off a piece of foil large enough to cover the top and reach halfway down the sides of the mold. Butter an area in the center of the foil the same size as the dough. Cover the mold with foil, butter side down, and press the foil against the outside of the mold. Tie a string around the foil to secure it. Place a second piece of foil, folded in half, in the bottom of the pot. Set the mold on the foil. Place a plate on top of the mold. Place the pot over low heat and pour in:

Boiling water

to come halfway up the sides of the mold. Cover the pot with a tight-fitting lid and simmer for 1½ hours, replenishing the water as needed to maintain the water level.

Carefully remove the mold from the pot. Remove the plate. Cut the string and carefully remove the foil. Run the knife around the biscuit topping to loosen it from the sides of the dish. Carefully unmold the dessert onto a large platter deep enough to hold the juices. Serve warm.

APPLE OR PEAR PANDOWDY

6 to 8 servings

This is best served warm on the day it's made.

Position a rack in the lower third of the oven. Preheat the oven to 400°F. Have ready an unbuttered 8-inch square baking dish.
Prepare:

½ recipe All-Butter Pie or Pastry Dough, 664, or Basic Pie or Pastry Dough, 664

On a lightly floured surface, roll the dough into a 9-inch square. Place on a cookie sheet and refrigerate while you prepare the filling.
Peel, core, and cut into ¼-inch-thick slices:

2 pounds (910g) apples or ripe pears

Combine the fruit in a large bowl with:

½ cup maple syrup (155g), molasses (170g), packed brown sugar (115g), or white sugar (100g)
2 tablespoons (15g) cornstarch or 3 tablespoons (25g) all-purpose flour
½ teaspoon ground cinnamon
¼ teaspoon grated or ground nutmeg
¼ teaspoon salt
⅛ teaspoon ground allspice

Spread the fruit mixture evenly in the baking dish. Dot with:

2 tablespoons unsalted butter, cut into small pieces

Remove the dough from the refrigerator and let stand for a few minutes, until pliable, then arrange the dough over the top of the apples. Tuck the edges of the dough into the dish. Bake until the top has browned lightly, about 30 minutes. Remove the dish from the oven and reduce the oven temperature to 350°F.

With a knife, score the crust into 2-inch squares. Baste the crust squares by tilting the pan and spooning the juices over them; or submerge the squares in the juices with the back of a spoon. Return the dish to the oven and bake until the fruit is tender when pierced with a skewer, the filling has thickened slightly, and the crust is golden brown, about 30 minutes more. Let cool for 15 minutes before serving.

BERRY PANDOWDY

Prepare **Apple or Pear Pandowdy, 686,** using **½ recipe Cornmeal Pie or Pastry Dough, 665,** for the crust. Substitute **3 pints blueberries, raspberries, or blackberries, or a combination,** for the apples/pears, and use **white or light brown sugar.** Use **¼ teaspoon ground cinnamon** and omit the nutmeg and allspice.

CHERRY CLAFOUTIS

6 to 8 servings

A clafoutis is a simple French country dessert. It is similar to an old American dessert called **batter pudding** and is made by pouring batter over fresh fruit. Clafoutis is traditionally made with unpitted cherries, but we err on the side of dental safety. Raspberries or blackberries may be substituted for the cherries with great success.
Preheat the oven to 375°F. Butter a 10-inch deep-dish pie pan.
Beat in a medium bowl until frothy, about 2 minutes:

4 large eggs
¾ cup (150g) sugar

Add and beat until smooth:

1 cup (235g) milk
1½ teaspoons vanilla
(1 tablespoon Cognac or rum)

Stir in:

¾ cup (95g) all-purpose flour
Pinch of salt

Distribute over the bottom of the prepared pie pan:

1 pound sweet cherries, pitted (frozen cherries, thawed and patted dry, or canned cherries, drained and dried, can be used)

Pour the batter over the cherries and place the pie pan on a baking sheet. Bake the clafoutis for 10 minutes. Reduce the oven temperature to 350°F and bake until the top has puffed (it will sink on cooling) and a toothpick inserted in the center comes out clean, about 35 minutes. Let cool for about 20 minutes before serving.

FAR BRETON

6 servings

A clafoutis, but with Armagnac-soaked prunes instead of fresh fruit.
Preheat the oven to 375°F. Lightly butter a 10-inch deep-dish pie pan or a deep cake pan.
Combine in a small saucepan:

24 medium pitted prunes
½ cup Armagnac, Cognac, rum, or whiskey

Bring to a simmer over medium heat, then reduce the heat to cook very gently until the prunes are plump and the liquor is mostly absorbed. Scatter the prunes evenly over the bottom of the prepared pan. Set aside.
Prepare the batter for:

Cherry Clafoutis, above

Pour the batter over the prunes. Bake until browned and set, 25 to 30 minutes.

ABOUT FRUIT DUMPLINGS, TURNOVERS, AND HAND PIES

Any pie dough, puff pastry, or biscuit dough can be used to make fruit dumplings or turnovers. **Dumplings** are formed by gathering the edges of the dough up around the filling like a purse or pouch; the resulting packets may be baked or simmered. **Turnovers** are made by folding the dough over the filling and can be formed in any size from miniature to large. **Hand pies** are very similar to turnovers, but they may be made by folding the dough over the filling or by sandwiching the filling between 2 pieces of dough. See below for more information on hand pies. The dough can be made well ahead and kept chilled until ready to use. These little "pies" are best eaten the day they are baked.

Almost all the fruit pie recipes in this chapter can be made in hand pie form. The process is simple and flexible.

To form hand pies or turnovers, roll out your choice of dough (All-Butter Pie or Pastry Dough, 664, is our favorite) to a ⅛-inch thickness. Cut into small or large rounds, squares, or rectangles. If desired, hand pies can be formed by sandwiching filling between two pieces of dough, or one round piece of dough can be folded over the filling to form half-moon pies. For the filling, fruit should be chopped smaller than for large pies. Apples and pears should be diced, peaches, apricots, and plums should be chopped, and strawberries should be quartered. Small berries are fine to leave whole. Most fruits do not need to be precooked, but we recommend precooking fillings made from apples and pears due to the shorter baking time hand pies require.

Place a small mound of filling on top of the dough, leaving a ½-inch border all the way around the edge. Very lightly brush the edges with water, and place another piece of dough on top, or fold the dough over if making half-moon pies. Flute or crimp the edge of the pies and cut a small slit or two in the top to allow steam to escape. If desired, brush the pies with cream and sprinkle with sugar.

To bake hand pies or turnovers, place on a baking sheet and bake at 375°F until golden brown, 20 to 30 minutes depending on the filling and size of the pies. Hand pies can also be deep-fried or pan-fried.

To deep-fry hand pies, first read about Deep-Frying, 1051. Use a precooked filling or cut the fruit—especially apples and pears—into fine dice. After shaping the pies do not cut a slit in the top. Refrigerate the pies while you heat 3 inches of vegetable oil in a deep, heavy pot to 350°F. Fry the pies a few at a time, being sure not to crowd the pan, until golden brown, turning once during cooking, 1½ to 2 minutes per side. Transfer to a baking sheet lined with paper towels to drain. Serve hot.

To pan-fry hand pies, see the method for Treva's Fried Apple Pies, 689.

APPLE DUMPLINGS

6 dumplings

This is, hands down, one of our favorite recipes in this entire book. On the first chilly autumn day, there is nothing that can compete with these warming pastries.

Prepare:

1 recipe Cream Cheese Pastry Dough, 665, ½ recipe All-Butter Pie or Pastry Dough, 664, or 1 recipe of the dough for Quick Cream Biscuits or Shortcakes, 636

Refrigerate at least 30 minutes.

Preheat the oven to 425°F. Generously butter a baking dish large enough to hold the dumplings with 1 to 2 inches between each one, such as an 11 × 7-inch dish or a 12-inch oval gratin dish. Peel and core (leaving them whole):

6 small apples (about 4 ounces each)

Or peel, halve lengthwise, and core:

3 large apples (about 8 ounces each)

Mix with a fork in a small bowl until blended:

½ cup packed (115g) dark brown sugar
1 teaspoon ground cinnamon
¼ teaspoon salt

Add and mix well:

4 tablespoons (2 oz or 55g) butter, softened

Fill the whole apples with the mixture and pat any remaining mixture on top of the fruit, or, if using apple halves, fill the hollows with the mixture and reserve any remaining. Set aside. On a lightly floured surface, roll the dough into an 18 × 12-inch rectangle about ⅛ inch thick. Cut into six 6-inch squares, then roll each square a little larger, into a 7-inch square. Lightly brush with:

1 large egg, lightly beaten

Place an apple in the middle of each square. If using apple halves, place cut side down and spread the remaining sugar mixture over the rounded tops of the apples. For each square, bring the 4 corners of the dough up around the apple and pinch the corners and edges of the dough together. Prick the top of each pastry several times with a fork. Place the dumplings in the baking dish and bake for 10 minutes. While the dumplings bake, make the syrup. Combine in a small saucepan:

1 cup (235g) water
½ cup packed (115g) light brown sugar
1 small lemon, thinly sliced and seeded
2 tablespoons (30g) unsalted butter
1 teaspoon ground cinnamon
¼ teaspoon salt

Stir until the sugar is dissolved, bring to a boil, and boil for 5 minutes. Pour the boiling syrup over the dumplings when they begin to color, 10 to 15 minutes into the cooking time. Reduce the oven temperature to 350°F and bake until the apples are tender when pierced with a small knife, 30 to 35 minutes more. Baste the apples with the syrup every 10 minutes or so to form a glaze and flavor the crust. If the dumplings start to brown too quickly, loosely cover with foil. Let cool slightly. Serve warm with:

Heavy cream (softly whipped, 791, if desired) or vanilla ice cream

SWEET FRUIT TURNOVERS

For more information on shaping, read About Fruit Dumplings, Turnovers, and Hand Pies, 687.

Prepare:

Puff pastry, store-bought or homemade, 691, Rough Puff Pastry, 692 or All-Butter Pie or Pastry Dough, 664

To form the turnovers, 687, roll out and cut the dough as directed into rounds, squares, or rectangles of the desired size (anywhere from 3 to 6 inches). Place in the center of each pastry one of the following:

Well-flavored applesauce
Preserves or jam (only use for very small turnovers)
Filling for Mock Mincemeat Pie, 672
Any fruit pie filling, 668–74

Use enough filling so that it is mounded slightly, but not so much that it distorts the pastry. Brush the edges of each turnover lightly with water. Fold the dough over into half-moons, triangles, or rectangles and press the edges to seal. Arrange the turnovers at least 1 inch apart on 2 ungreased baking sheets, and refrigerate for 30 minutes.

Position a rack in the lower third of the oven. Preheat the oven to 400°F.

Brush the tops of the turnovers with:

1 egg yolk, beaten with 2 tablespoons heavy cream

Bake until golden brown, about 20 minutes. While they are still warm, dust the pastries with:

Powdered sugar

APPLE OR PEAR TURNOVERS

8 turnovers

Prepare:

½ recipe Puff Pastry, 691, 1 pound store-bought puff pastry, thawed, or a double recipe Rough Puff Pastry, 692, or 1 recipe All-Butter Pie or Pastry Dough, 664

Divide the dough in half and roll each portion into an 11-inch square, about ⅛ inch thick. Place on a baking sheet and refrigerate.

Peel, core, and cut into ¼-inch dice:

1 pound (455g) apples or pears

Place in a medium bowl and toss well with:

¼ cup (50g) sugar
1 teaspoon all-purpose flour
1 teaspoon lemon juice
½ teaspoon ground cinnamon
Pinch of salt

Transfer the pastry squares to a cutting board and trim ½ inch from all sides to make two 10-inch squares. Cut each into four 5-inch squares (or rounds if you prefer, using a large cutter). Spoon the apple mixture, dividing it equally, onto the center of the pastry squares. Lightly brush a ½-inch border on 2 adjacent edges of each pastry square with:

1 large egg, lightly beaten

Form a triangular turnover by folding the dry corner of each square over the apples to the egg-washed corner; press the edges together with the tines of a fork to seal them. Brush the top of each turnover with egg wash, and cut 3 small slits in the top of each one. Arrange the turnovers at least 1 inch apart on 2 ungreased baking sheets and refrigerate for 30 minutes.

Position a rack in the lower third of the oven. Preheat the oven to 425°F.

Bake the turnovers until they begin to brown, about 15 minutes. Reduce the oven temperature to 350°F and bake until golden, 15 to 20 minutes more. Serve warm.

TREVA'S FRIED APPLE PIES

6 hand pies

Megan's great-grandmother, Treva Martin, made these pies every fall. She used dried apples exclusively, but we like to throw in some fresh, tart apple as well. After frying, these pies should be rustic-looking and unevenly browned. That is part of their charm.

Prepare:

All-Butter Pie or Pastry Dough, 664, or Basic Pie or Pastry Dough, 664

Divide the dough in half, wrap tightly, and refrigerate. While the dough chills, prepare the filling. Place in a medium saucepan:

1½ cups lightly packed (about 3¾ oz or 105g) dried apples, chopped
¾ cup (175g) water
1 small tart apple, cored and finely diced
½ cup (100g) sugar
2 tablespoons (15g) all-purpose flour
1 teaspoon ground cinnamon
Pinch of salt

Bring to a boil over medium heat and cook, stirring, until the water is almost completely evaporated and the fresh apples are crisp tender. Transfer the mixture to a plate to cool completely.

Working with half of the dough, roll out ⅛ inch thick. Cut the dough into 6½- to 7-inch rounds using a small plate as a template. Place ⅓ cup of the filling on half of the dough, leaving a ½-inch border. Brush the edge of the dough lightly with water. Fold the bare half of the dough over the filling to make a half-moon shape and press it closed with the tines of a fork. Repeat with the remaining dough and filling, rerolling any dough scraps one time. You should get 6 pies in total. Refrigerate the pies for 20 minutes.

Meanwhile, heat in a large skillet over medium heat:

¼ cup vegetable shortening or leaf lard

When the fat is hot, add 2 pies to the skillet. Cook until browned on the bottom, about 5 minutes. Flip and brown the second side, about 4 minutes more, adjusting the heat as needed to prevent the pies from browning too quickly. Transfer to a baking sheet lined with paper towels. Repeat with the remaining pies, adding more shortening to the skillet as needed or wiping out the skillet between batches if the flour particles start to burn. Serve warm or at room temperature.

ABOUT GALETTES AND CROSTATAS

A galette (French) or crostata (Italian) is a free-form tart baked on a cookie sheet rather than in a pie or tart pan. Galettes and crostatas may be made with a flat crust of pastry, baked with sweetened fruit on top. Or, if the fruit is juicy, the sides of the pastry can be folded over part of the fruit filling to keep in the juices. Most galettes are large, but you can also make individual-sized galettes.

Any of the pie or pastry doughs in this chapter may be used to make these rustic pies, including Rough Puff Pastry, 692. In fact, some of the more fragile doughs, such as Whole Grain Pie or Pastry Dough, 665, are excellent in this application. To use Pat-in-the-Pan Shortbread Dough, 667, roll it out between two sheets of parchment paper, then fill with the fruit and shape as directed.

The tops of galettes and crostatas are usually left bare, but we sometimes top them with Streusel, 800. To help the pastry brown and to add extra crunch, we also like to brush the crust edges with a beaten egg or heavy cream and sprinkle them with turbinado or regular sugar.

FRUIT GALETTE OR CROSTATA

8 servings

Prepare:

½ recipe All-Butter Pie or Pastry Dough, 664, or 1 recipe Rough Puff Pastry, 692

Position a rack in the lower third of the oven. Preheat the oven to 375°F.

Roll the dough into an 11-inch round, 662. Lift the dough onto a large baking sheet. Leaving a 1-inch border all around the edge, spread evenly over the dough:

¼ cup raspberry or other jam

Toss together in a medium bowl:

4 plums or apricots, or 2 peaches or nectarines, pitted and cut into ½-inch slices (about 1 pound)

(½ cup raspberries or blueberries)
2 tablespoons sugar
4 teaspoons all-purpose flour

Distribute the fruit mixture over the jam, in a decorative pattern or in a heap. Fold in the border of dough to form a rim. Bake until the crust is golden brown and the fruit juices have thickened, 25 to 35 minutes. Serve warm.

APPLE GALETTE OR CROSTATA

8 servings

Prepare:

½ recipe All-Butter Pie or Pastry Dough, 664, or 1 recipe Rough Puff Pastry, 692

Position a rack in the lower third of the oven. Preheat the oven to 425°F.

Roll the dough into an 11- to 12-inch round, 662. Transfer the dough to a baking sheet. Brush the pastry with a thin coat of:

3 tablespoons unsalted butter, melted and cooled to lukewarm

Reserve the rest of the butter. Sprinkle the pastry with:

1 tablespoon sugar

Peel, core, and slice ⅛ inch thick:

2 large firm apples, such as Pink Lady or Granny Smith

Leaving a 1-inch border all around the edge, arrange the apple slices in slightly overlapping concentric rings on the pastry. Fold the border of dough over the edges of the apples. Brush or drizzle all but about 2 teaspoons of the remaining melted butter over the apples. Combine in a small bowl:

3 tablespoons sugar
⅛ teaspoon ground cinnamon

Sprinkle the cinnamon sugar over the apples. Bake until the pastry begins to brown, 15 to 20 minutes. Reduce the oven temperature to 350°F and bake until the pastry is golden brown, 5 to 10 minutes more. Brush the apples with the reserved butter. Serve warm or at room temperature.

ABOUT PASTRIES

Like pies, pastries are made with patience and lots of butter. In the case of croissants and puff pastry, the dough is much flakier than that used for a pie, with many distinct layers of butter created by **lamination,** the process of repeated rolling and folding. During baking the water contained in the layers of butter evaporates. This creates air pockets, which gives croissants a flaky, honeycombed texture and puff pastry a shatteringly crisp one.

But the term "pastry" encompasses much more than just laminated doughs. Choux pastry is made by beating eggs into a cooked dough, which yields tender, hollow pastries when baked. Strudel is made with a pliable dough stretched extremely thin and brushed with butter. Phyllo is paper-thin sheets of dough brushed with butter and layered, creating a kind of pseudo-lamination effect. What all these pastries have in common is a light-as-a-feather richness that we crave.

ABOUT LAYERED OR LAMINATED DOUGHS

In the making of any kind of layered dough—such as Puff Pastry, 691, dough for Croissants, 694, or Danish Pastry Dough, 696—a large block of butter is wrapped in the dough like a package, then the dough is rolled out and folded, rerolled, and refolded. The idea is to create thin, even layers of butter between distinct layers of dough, rather than integrating dough and butter as you do in making pie dough. For this process to work, ➤ the butter must be at around 55° to 60°F so that it is cool enough that it doesn't melt during rolling but warm enough that it doesn't crack. Cold, hard butter may break under the pressure of the rolling pin instead of rolling out into a smooth sheet between the layers of dough. If the butter breaks and is pushed through the dough layer, the dough and butter layers will be uneven, and butter may even leak out of the dough during baking. Fortunately, if this happens, it is possible to see and feel the butter cracking in the dough as it is rolled out, enabling you to stop and let the dough rest (and the butter soften a bit) until it can be rolled out smoothly. Butter that is too soft is even worse, as the dough and butter merge under pressure from the rolling pin instead of maintaining their separate identities. If the butter begins to melt, the pastries will be greasy and dense rather than flaky. If the dough seems squishy and/or the butter oozes from it as you roll, stop and refrigerate it until firm but still pliable.

To roll out laminated dough, flour the work surface and the dough lightly. Always position the dough with a short side facing you. Roll the dough with even pressure to maintain an even thickness. Keeping the pin parallel to the work surface, roll from the center of the dough away from you and then from the center of the dough back toward you, lifting the pin after each roll. (Rolling back and forth without lifting the pin can overdevelop the gluten in the dough, making it tough.) Never roll the pin over the edges of the dough. Roll the dough the long way to the desired length and then adjust the width if necessary. As you roll, try to keep the corners square, the sides of the dough as straight as possible, and the thickness even. Straighten the sides of the dough occasionally with your hands, as though straightening a stack of papers, or press the sides with a bench scraper or the rolling pin. If a small area of butter becomes uncovered as you roll the dough, gently pat a little flour over the butter spot, and brush off any excess. ➤ Brush excess flour from the dough with a dry pastry brush before folding.

As in all wheat flour doughs, gluten in the dough is developed as the dough is handled or rolled. To avoid excess gluten development and a tough dough, rotate it ninety degrees after every fold so that the gluten strands are stretched in a different direction with each successive turn (a **"turn"** is accomplished each time the dough is rolled out and folded; the number of turns is specified in each recipe). After each turn, the dough should be wrapped in plastic wrap, refrigerated, and allowed to rest. This relaxes the gluten strands and lets them adjust to their new length; chilling firms the butter, which keeps the layers of dough and butter distinct. Do not allow the butter to turn hard or brittle; if this occurs, let the dough sit on the counter for 10 minutes or so until the butter reaches a pliable state. Depending on the temperature of your kitchen, you may be able to make 2 turns back to back rather than chilling the dough between each turn. It can take a bit of practice to become a good judge of when the dough is too cold, too warm, or just right. Sometimes the finished dough is chilled again after it has been rolled into a sheet, before it is cut into shapes—and often again just before baking. See specific instructions in each recipe. It is surprisingly easy to lose track of how many turns you have given the dough as it rests. To keep count of the turns, make a shallow fingertip imprint in the dough—one for each turn—before refrigerating the dough for each rest period.

ABOUT PUFF PASTRY

Puff pastry is the flakiest pastry imaginable, which is not surprising when you consider that it is made up of hundreds of layers and contains just as much butter as flour, if not more. The tools and equipment required are the same as those needed for pie crusts, 660; a cool marble work surface is ideal, but not essential. To roll puff pastry, see About Layered or Laminated Doughs, 690, and the specific recipes for instructions.

Puff pastry can be cut into myriad shapes or sizes and filled to create countless desserts and savory foods, from appetizers, like Brie Baked in Pastry, 57, to main courses, like Beef Wellington, 457, to desserts, like Mille-Feuille (Napoleon), 693. Save all puff pastry scraps, trimmings, and unused dough and freeze according to the instructions below. The accumulated scraps can be rolled together once thawed, then folded as if you were giving the dough a single turn before rolling out and using. Rolled scraps of puff pastry are best used for napoleons, twists, mini tarts, palm leaves, or any other pastry for which full height is not crucial.

To cut and dock puff pastry dough, roll it out to the desired thickness, trim the edges, and cut into desired shapes. Always cut puff pastry with a sharp knife, pressing straight down through the dough. Dragging the knife prevents the edges of the pastry from rising evenly or to full capacity. **Docking** (or pricking) is the term for piercing a pastry all over with the tines of a fork, or a tool called a **pastry docker,** to allow steam to escape and prevent the dough from bubbling up unevenly. Napoleon layers are docked to keep them very thin but still flaky; the centers of patty shells (bouchées) are docked so the sides will rise but the interiors will remain thin.

To store puff pastry dough, wrap tightly in plastic and then foil, then slip the packets into a zip-top bag, pressing out the air before sealing. Refrigerate for up to 2 days or freeze for up to 6 months. Before using, thaw the dough, still wrapped, overnight in the refrigerator.

Puff pastry can also be frozen after it is rolled out, either in sheets or cut into shapes. After rolling, chill on a baking sheet until firm; cut into shapes if desired or leave sheets whole, and wrap. Stack cut pieces with wax paper between each layer for wrapping and freezing. For the best rise, bake frozen (unfilled) cut pieces without thawing. If freezing sheets, thaw them overnight in the refrigerator before cutting. Unbaked filled puff pastry shapes such as turnovers can be covered and refrigerated for up to 8 hours before baking.

PUFF PASTRY

About 2¾ pounds

In this modernized puff pastry recipe, both the dough and the butter block are mixed separately in the food processor. To make puff pastry the old-fashioned way, mix the dough by hand or in a stand mixer and beat the 3½ sticks of butter with a rolling pin, working in the cup of flour, until the butter is pliable but not soft or sticky. Please read About Layered or Laminated Doughs, 690, and About Puff Pastry, above.

Pulse to combine in a food processor:

2⅓ cups (290g) all-purpose flour
1¼ teaspoons salt

Scatter over the flour:

5 tablespoons (70g) cold unsalted butter, cut into ½-inch cubes

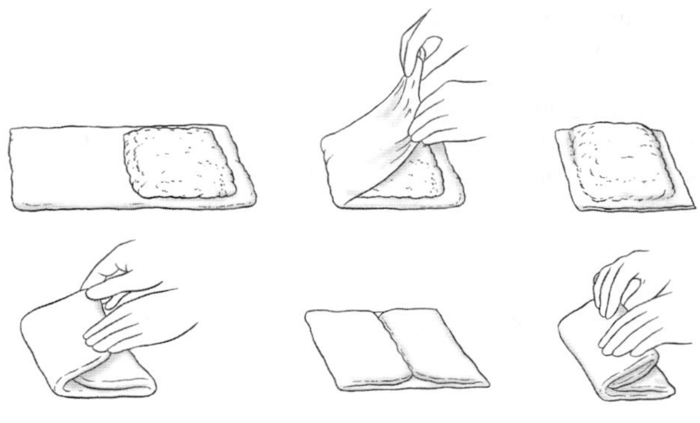

Folding puff pastry

Pulse until the mixture resembles coarse crumbs. Drizzle over:

¾ cup (175g) ice water

Pulse just until the dough begins to come together, 10 to 15 seconds. Scrape the dough onto a sheet of plastic wrap and form it into a 5-inch square. Wrap the dough and refrigerate for 1 hour.

Meanwhile, cut into ½-inch slices and freeze for 2 minutes:

3½ sticks (14 oz or 395g) unsalted butter

Place in the food processor:

1 cup (125g) all-purpose flour

Distribute the butter slices over the flour and pulse just until the mixture looks like fine gravel. Scrape the mixture down from the processor sides and process just until smooth. Scrape onto a sheet of plastic wrap and shape the butter into a 6-inch square. Wrap the butter block tightly and refrigerate while you roll out the dough.

Place the dough square on a lightly floured surface and roll into a 13 × 8-inch rectangle. Brush off the excess flour. Remove the butter block from the refrigerator and unwrap it. As shown in the top three illustrations, above, center it on one half of the dough; fold the dough over the butter, completely covering it; press the dough together to seal on the three open sides. Turn the dough a quarter turn counterclockwise.

Roll the dough package into a 17 × 7½-inch rectangle, keeping a short side facing you. Fold the bottom third of the dough up over the center of the dough. Fold the top third of the dough down over top of the first third, as though you were folding a business letter. This is called a single turn (shown on the bottom left, 691). Rotate the dough a quarter turn counterclockwise and roll the dough once more into a 17 × 7½-inch rectangle. This time fold the bottom end up and the top end down to meet in the center (do not overlap), then fold the dough in half, to make 4 layers of dough, as shown on bottom center and right, 691. This double fold is the second turn. Mark the dough with 2 finger imprints to remind yourself that you have given the dough 2 turns. Wrap the dough tightly and refrigerate for 45 minutes.

With the folded edge on the left, roll the dough out again to 17 × 7½ inches. Make another double fold, for the third turn. Mark with 3 finger imprints, wrap the dough, and refrigerate for 45 minutes.

Roll the dough out and make another double fold for the fourth turn. Mark the dough with 4 imprints, wrap, and refrigerate for at least 1 hour before using. Or wrap and store as directed in About Puff Pastry, 691.

CHOCOLATE PUFF PASTRY

Prepare **Puff Pastry, 691.** Add to the butter-flour mixture for the butter block **1 cup (100g) Dutch-process cocoa powder.** Proceed as directed.

Folding rough puff pastry

ROUGH PUFF PASTRY

About 12 ounces

This vastly easier version of puff pastry is perfect for free-form fruit tarts or Tarte Tatin, 673. Please read About Layered or Laminated Doughs, 690, and About Puff Pastry, 691.

Combine in a medium bowl:

1 cup (125g) all-purpose flour
¼ teaspoon salt

Add and toss to coat with flour:

1 stick (4 oz or 115g) very cold unsalted butter, cut into cubes

Pour in a little at a time:

¼ cup (60g) ice water

Stir until the mixture just comes together, adding more water in small increments if needed. It should not be sticky. It will look like butter cubes barely held together by a shaggy dough. Transfer the lumpy mass of dough onto a piece of plastic wrap, wrap tightly, flatten it, and shape into a square 1 inch thick by tapping the dough on the countertop on 4 sides. Refrigerate for 15 minutes.

Lightly flour a work surface and unwrap the dough. Roll the dough out into a rectangle ¼ inch thick, lifting the dough as you roll to ensure it isn't sticking to the surface. At first this will feel very awkward, and the dough will be chunky and want to break apart, but keep rolling, flouring the dough if it sticks. Make a double fold: With a short side facing you, fold the top edge of the dough in so the edge meets the center of the rectangle (as shown, left). Fold the bottom of the dough in to meet the top edge in the center without overlapping (center). Fold the dough in half again, closing it like a book (right). Mark the dough with 1 finger imprint to remind yourself that you have given the dough 1 turn. Wrap the dough tightly in plastic wrap and refrigerate for 15 minutes.

With the folded edge on the left, again roll the dough out into a rectangle ¼ inch thick and make another double fold. Mark the dough with 2 imprints, wrap it tightly in plastic wrap, and refrigerate for 15 minutes.

Roll out and double fold once more; the dough should be smooth. Wrap the dough tightly in plastic wrap and chill for 30 minutes before using.

To use the dough, roll out to a ⅛-inch thickness and cut into the desired shapes.

PALMIERS

About forty-eight 3-inch cookies

Store-bought puff pastry may also be used to make these shatteringly crisp cookies. Spices or flavorings, such as cinnamon, vanilla bean seeds, or citrus zest, may be mixed into the sugar for added flavor.

Have ready:

1 cup (200g) sugar

Lightly sugar a work surface and roll out into a 12 × 5½-inch rectangle:

8 ounces puff pastry, store-bought or homemade, 691

Sprinkle about ¼ cup of the sugar over the dough and roll over it lightly with the rolling pin to imbed the sugar in the dough. With a short side facing you, fold the bottom third up over the center and the top third down over the center, like a business letter. Turn the dough so the folded edge is on the left and roll out into a 13 × 7-inch rectangle, with a short side facing you. Sprinkle about 2 tablespoons sugar over the dough and roll over it lightly with the rolling pin. Fold each long side of the dough over toward the center, leaving a ¼-inch space in the middle (as shown, 693). Lightly brush the top of one folded side with:

1 large egg white, lightly beaten

Sprinkle the other folded side with 1 tablespoon sugar. Fold the dough lengthwise in half, so that the sugared surface meets the egg white, and press together. Place the pastry on an ungreased baking sheet. Cover and refrigerate for at least 30 minutes, or wrap airtight and freeze until ready to use.

Position a rack in the lower third of the oven. Preheat the oven to 425°F. Line 2 baking sheets with parchment paper or silicone liners or generously grease them.

If the dough is frozen, let it thaw for 5 to 10 minutes before cutting. Spread some of the remaining sugar in a shallow bowl. Transfer the dough to a cutting board and cut crosswise into ¼-inch slices. Press one cut side of each slice into the sugar and place the cookies sugar side down and at least 3 inches apart on the prepared baking

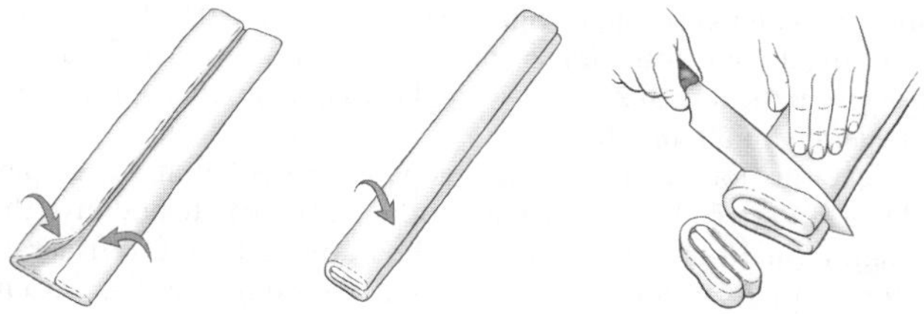

Folding and slicing palmiers

sheets. If necessary, push each slice back into shape. Sprinkle more sugar over the tops.

Bake one sheet at a time, until the cookies begin to brown around the edges, about 5 minutes. Turn each cookie over with a spatula and bake until golden brown and caramelized all over, 2 to 5 minutes longer. Watch carefully, for the cookies can burn quickly. Transfer to a rack and let cool completely.

PATTY SHELLS

Small patty shells—deep shells of puff pastry baked and then filled with sweet or savory fillings—are called *bouchées* (mouthfuls). Very small hors d'oeuvre–sized patty shells are called *petites bouchées*, or "little mouthfuls." Our favorite filling is Gruyère and Caramelized Onions, 255. Other good savory fillings include Mushroom Ragout, 251, Ratatouille Provençale, 204, Melted Leeks, 247, and Chicken or Turkey Salad, 123. As for sweet fillings, we recommend Pastry Cream, 801, and fresh fruit, or Fruit Fool, 173.

I. SMALL

Eighteen 2-inch shells

Prepare:

Puff Pastry, 691

Divide the dough into thirds. Working with one piece at a time (keep the remainder refrigerated), roll the dough out to a 14 × 6½-inch rectangle. Using a 2-inch cutter, cut out 12 rounds. Arrange 6 rounds upside down on an ungreased or parchment paper– or silicone-lined baking sheet, about 2 inches apart. Using a 1-inch round cutter, cut out the centers of the remaining 6 rounds to make rings. (Save the centers for another use.) Turn the rings upside down and position them on top of the rounds on the baking sheet. Using the back of a table knife, press an indentation every ¼ inch around the outside edge of the rounds to flute them. With a fork, prick only the centers of the shells, not the rings. Cover and refrigerate while the oven preheats.

Preheat the oven to 425°F. Using a sharp knife, score a circle on the bottom piece of dough following the inside edge of the ring.

Bake until puffed and golden brown, about 20 minutes. As soon as the patty shells come from the oven, cut out the inner rounds that have puffed out from the center of each shell and set aside (you will use these as lids). Transfer to a rack to let cool.

II. MEDIUM

Six 4-inch shells

Proceed as directed for **Small Patty Shells, above,** rolling each third of the dough into a 13 × 9-inch rectangle. Cut out the rounds using a 4-inch cutter, and use a 2-inch cutter to make the rings. Assemble and bake as directed.

III. LARGE OR VOL-AU-VENT

One 8-inch shell

Prepare as directed for **Small Patty Shells, above,** dividing the dough in half and rolling each half to a 10-inch square. Cut out 2 rounds using an 8-inch cutter, the removable bottom of an 8-inch tart pan, or an 8-inch cake pan, then cut out the center of one with a 6-inch cutter or pan. Assemble as directed. Bake at 425°F for 20 minutes, then reduce the heat to 350°F and continue baking until puffed and golden brown, about 20 minutes.

MILLE-FEUILLE (NAPOLEON)

6 to 8 servings

Could the Emperor conceivably have had these in mind when he contended that "an army marches on its stomach"? A classic napoleon, or *mille-feuille* (thousand-leaf), is made up of 3 layers of puff pastry filled with vanilla pastry cream. Serve the napoleon within a few hours of making it. If you make the napoleons with saved puff pastry scraps, you do not need to weight the layers during baking. For an easier approach, see Phyllo Napoleons, 701.

Prepare and chill:

Pastry Cream, 801

Roll out to a 17½ × 13½-inch rectangle 1/16 to ⅛ inch thick:

½ recipe Puff Pastry, 691

Transfer the pastry to an ungreased baking sheet. Prick it all over with a fork. Cover and refrigerate for at least 30 minutes, or wrap airtight and freeze until ready to use.

If the dough is frozen, let it thaw for a few minutes before trimming. Transfer the dough to a cutting board and trim the sides to make a 16 × 12-inch rectangle. Return it to the baking sheet and the refrigerator while the oven preheats.

Position a rack in the lower third of the oven. Preheat the oven to 400°F.

Invert a wire rack and place it directly on the dough to prevent it from rising in the oven while baking. Bake for 10 minutes, remove the rack and prick the pastry all over, then replace the rack and bake until golden brown, 10 to 15 minutes more. Remove the rack for the final 2 to 3 minutes to dry and cook the top layers. Slide the pastry onto a wire rack and let cool.

Using a sharp serrated knife, saw the pastry gently lengthwise into 3 equal strips. Brush 2 of the strips with:

1½ tablespoons apricot jam, warmed

Spread half of the pastry cream over one of the (jam-covered) pastry strips. Place the second (jam-covered) piece on top and cover with the remaining pastry cream. Turn the last puff pastry strip upside down and place it over the pastry cream. Refrigerate until ready to serve, but no longer than 6 hours.

Use a sharp serrated knife and a sawing motion to cut the napoleon into individual servings. Dust the top of each serving with:

Powdered sugar

CROISSANTS

Eighteen 3½-inch-long croissants

Croissant is the French word for "crescent." Rich, somewhat troublesome, but unequaled by any other form of roll, a croissant can be made plain or baked with a filling, such as jam, almond paste, or even savory ingredients like ham and cheese. Filled with chocolate, it is called *pain au chocolat* (chocolate bread). Please read About Layered or Laminated Doughs, 690.

Place on a work surface:

3 sticks (12 oz or 340g) cold unsalted butter

Measure:

3 tablespoons all-purpose flour

Sprinkle the butter with a little of the flour and begin to beat it with a rolling pin. Scrape the butter from the work surface and the rolling pin as needed and fold it over itself into a heap. Continue to work the butter, adding in the flour gradually, until it is a smooth and malleable mass. Place the butter on a sheet of plastic wrap and shape it into a 9 × 6-inch rectangle. Wrap and refrigerate the butter while you make the dough.

Whisk together in a small bowl and let stand until the yeast is dissolved, about 5 minutes:

1 cup (235g) warm (105° to 115°F) whole milk
1 envelope (2¼ teaspoons) active dry yeast
1 tablespoon (10g) sugar

Mix together in a large bowl:

2¾ cups (345g) all-purpose flour
2 tablespoons (30g) unsalted butter, cut into small pieces, softened
1 teaspoon salt

Make a well in the center of the flour mixture and add the warm milk mixture. Mix with a fork or your fingers to make a dough. Transfer to a lightly floured surface and knead for a few seconds, until smooth. Shape into a ball, wrap tightly in plastic wrap, and refrigerate the dough for 15 minutes.

Sprinkle the top of the dough with flour and roll into a 15½ × 8-inch rectangle, sprinkling additional flour underneath it as needed to prevent sticking. Position the dough so that one of the short sides is facing you. Cover the upper two-thirds of the dough with the rectangle of butter, leaving a 1-inch border of dough on the sides and at the top. Fold the bottom third of the dough over half of the butter. Fold the top third of the dough, with the butter on it, down over the first third, as if you were folding a business letter. Press the edges of the dough together on all 3 open sides to seal in the butter. Rotate the dough so that the folded edge is on the left and the sealed edge is on the right.

Sprinkle the dough lightly with flour and press it gently with the rolling pin to flatten it slightly. Keeping the short side of the dough facing you, roll into an 18 × 8-inch rectangle. Fold the bottom third up and the top third down again. (This rolling and folding is called a single turn.) Rotate the dough so that the folded edge is on the left and the open edge is on the right (like a book about to be opened). Give the dough one more single turn, rolling it into an 18 × 8-inch rectangle and folding it in thirds. Sprinkle the work surface lightly with flour as needed to prevent the dough from sticking; if at any time the butter gets soft, refrigerate the dough for 10 to 15 minutes. Mark the dough with 2 finger imprints to remind yourself that you have given the dough 2 turns. Wrap the dough loosely in plastic and refrigerate for 30 minutes.

Place the dough so the folded edge is on the left and the open edge is on the right, and give it another turn. Rotate and give the dough a final turn. If at any time the butter gets soft, refrigerate it for 10 to 15 minutes. (At this point the dough can be frozen, wrapped in plastic, then foil, then a zip-top bag with the air pressed out. If frozen, thaw overnight in the refrigerator before proceeding.)

Roll the dough into a 24 × 12-inch rectangle, about ¼ inch thick. Let stand for 5 minutes to relax the gluten and prevent shrinking when cut.

Cut the dough lengthwise into two 24 × 6-inch strips. Refrigerate 1 strip on a baking sheet. Position the remaining rectangle with one long side facing you. Starting from the left, mark the bottom edge of the dough by nicking it with a knife at 4½-inch intervals. Mark the top edge of the dough 2¼ inches from the left edge, then continue to mark it at 4½-inch intervals. To cut the dough into triangles, cut from the bottom left corner of the dough to the first mark at the top, then from that mark to the first mark at the bottom, then from the first mark at the bottom to the second mark at the top, and so forth, until you have 9 triangles. Make a ¼-inch-long nick in the middle of the base of each triangle.

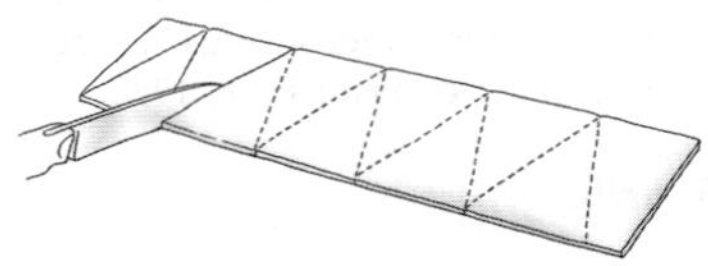

Cutting triangles for croissants

To form a croissant, stretch the base of a triangle by pulling the corners gently as you begin to roll the stretched edge tightly (but not too tightly) toward the opposite point of the triangle. Finish rolling the croissant so that the point of the triangle is on the bottom of the roll. Shape the other triangles in the same manner. Place the croissants at least 2 inches apart on ungreased baking sheets, curving the ends to form crescent shapes. Repeat the procedure with the second rectangle of dough. (Unbaked croissants can be refrigerated, covered, overnight; they will rise partially, for the yeast continues to work slowly in the chilled environment. Let them finish rising at room temperature before baking. They can also be frozen; thaw overnight in the refrigerator before proceeding.)

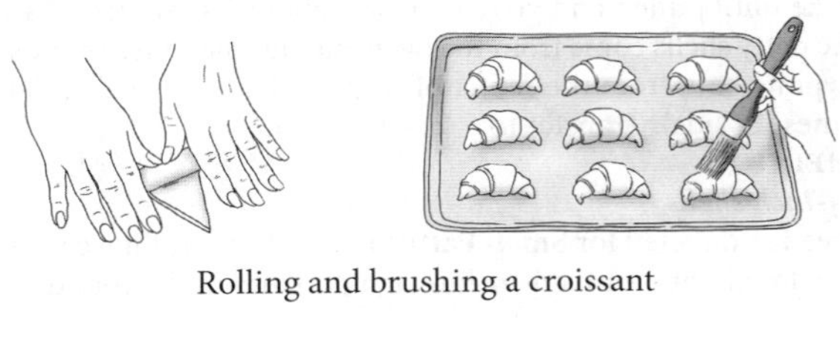

Rolling and brushing a croissant

Cover the croissants with a clean cloth or plastic wrap. Let rise at room temperature until increased in volume by almost half, 1 to 1½ hours.

Position a rack in the lower third of the oven. Preheat the oven to 375°F.

Brush the croissants lightly with:

1 large egg, beaten with 1 teaspoon water

Bake until golden brown, 20 to 25 minutes. Transfer the croissants to a rack and let cool completely. Croissants are best served the day they are baked, but they may be frozen for 1 month in a sealed zip-top bag. Reheat in a preheated 300°F oven for 5 minutes.

RASPBERRY CROISSANTS

Any jam may be used in place of the raspberry jam—try apricot, blueberry, or black currant jam or apple butter.

Prepare **Croissants, 694,** through cutting into triangles. Place **1½ teaspoons raspberry jam (9 tablespoons total)** ¾ inch from the nick at the base of each triangle before rolling up the croissant. On the first roll, pinch the dough around the jam to seal it in.

ALMOND CROISSANTS

Prepare **Croissants, 694,** through cutting into triangles. Place **1½ teaspoons Frangipane, 802 (9 tablespoons total)** ¾ inch from the nick at the base of each triangle before rolling up the croissant. After brushing with the egg wash, sprinkle the tops with **sliced almonds.** After baking, dust liberally with **powdered sugar.**

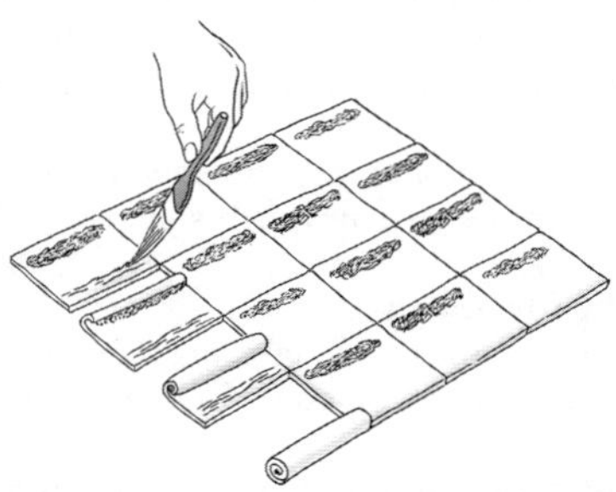

Cutting, filling, and shaping *pains au chocolat*

PAIN AU CHOCOLAT

About thirty-two 3½-inch-long rolls

Little flaky rolls of croissant pastry filled with dark chocolate are a traditional French *goûter*—teatime or after-school snack.

Have ready:

12 ounces (340g) semisweet or bittersweet chocolate, coarsely chopped, or 12 ounces large chocolate chips

Prepare the dough for:

Croissants, 694

Proceed with the recipe through all four turns, as directed. After chilling the dough, divide it in half, and return one half to the refrigerator. Roll the other half into a 16-inch square. Cut into sixteen 4-inch squares. Arrange ½ ounce of the chocolate in a 2-inch-long mound in each square, parallel to and about ½ inch in from one edge of the square. Lightly brush the opposite edge of the square with a ½-inch band of:

1 large egg, lightly beaten

Fold the edge of the dough closest to the chocolate over the chocolate and continue to roll the dough up into a cylinder. Place the rolls seam side down at least 2 inches apart on ungreased baking sheets. Repeat with the remaining dough and chocolate.

Let rise and bake as for Croissants, 694.

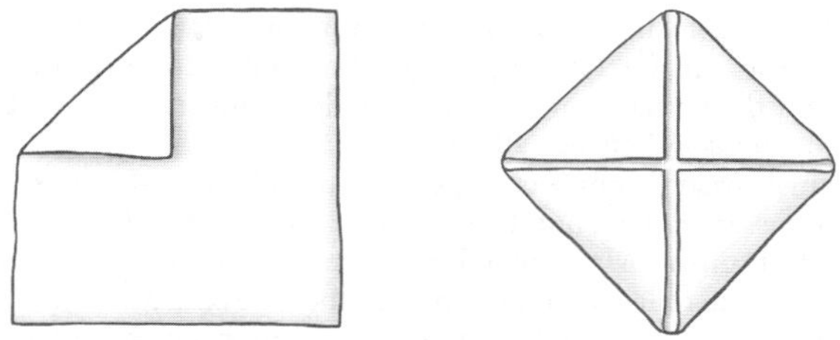

Folding dough for kouign amanns

KOUIGN AMANN

18 kouign amanns

A type of Breton pastry, a kouign amann is somewhat similar to a croissant, but sprinkled with sugar and shaped differently. During baking, the sugar caramelizes, yielding a flaky, butter-and-sugar-bronzed pastry that can only be described as ambrosial. To vary the flavor, use vanilla sugar or rub the zest of 2 oranges or lemons into the sugar. Or tuck a small spoonful of jam into the center of each pastry before folding the corners into the center.

Prepare the dough for:

Croissants, 694

Proceed with the recipe through the first two turns, as directed. After chilling the dough, roll it out into an 18 × 12-inch rectangle and sprinkle with:

⅓ cup (65g) sugar

Press the sugar into the dough. Fold the dough into thirds, giving it another turn. Roll out the dough once more, into an 18 × 12-inch rectangle, and sprinkle with:

⅓ cup (65g) sugar

Press the sugar into the dough again, fold the dough into thirds, and chill for 15 minutes. Liberally butter 18 cups of two standard 12-cup muffin tins. Lightly dust a work surface with flour and roll the dough into a 24 × 12-inch rectangle, about ¼ inch thick. Let stand for 5 minutes. Trim any irregular edges and cut the dough into 4-inch squares. Fold the four corners of each square of dough into the center, pressing them gently to get them to stick (see above). Fit the pastries into the muffin cups and sprinkle with:

¼ cup (50g) sugar

Cover loosely with plastic wrap and let rise until puffy, 30 to 45 minutes.

Preheat the oven to 400°F.

Place the pastries in the oven and reduce the heat to 375°F. Bake until deep golden brown and caramelized, 30 to 35 minutes, rotating the pans from front to back and switching racks halfway through baking. Remove from the oven and let cool in the pan for 5 minutes, then transfer to a rack to cool, using a small offset spatula to help pry the pastries from the muffin tin. ➤ Do not let the pastries cool completely in the tin or they will stick badly.

DANISH PASTRY DOUGH

Enough for about twenty-four 3-inch pastries

This buttery pastry, a cross between a rich bread and puff pastry, is a revelation, so much better than store-bought Danish as to seem like a different thing altogether. For more information on rolling, see instructions for Puff Pastry, 691. Remember to refrigerate the dough if the butter becomes soft. The ideal temperature for letting the dough rise is between 70° and 80°F.

Danish pastry dough is egg-enriched and somewhat less flaky than croissant dough, but the procedure for making it is quite similar. Bake Danish pastries on unbuttered baking sheets unless you are making filled, rolled, and sliced ones, which are baked on their sides with the filling touching the baking sheet—in this case, buttered or parchment paper–lined pans are essential. Danish pastries are best eaten the day they are baked.

Place on a work surface:

2 sticks (8 oz or 225g) cold unsalted butter

Measure:

2 tablespoons all-purpose flour

Sprinkle the butter with a little of the flour and begin to beat it with a rolling pin. Scrape the butter from the work surface and the rolling pin as needed and fold it over itself into a heap. Continue to work the butter until it is a smooth and malleable mass. Knead the rest of the flour into the butter with your hands, working quickly to keep the butter cold. Place the butter on a sheet of plastic wrap and shape it into an 8 × 5½-inch rectangle. Wrap and refrigerate the butter while you make the dough.

Whisk together in a small bowl and let stand until the yeast is dissolved, about 5 minutes:

½ cup (120g) warm (105° to 115°F) whole milk
1 envelope (2¼ teaspoons) active dry yeast
1 tablespoon (10g) sugar

Mix together in a large bowl:

2 cups plus 2 tablespoons (265g) all-purpose flour
2 tablespoons (25g) sugar
½ teaspoon salt
½ tablespoon unsalted butter, cut into small pieces, softened

Make a well in the center of the flour mixture and pour the yeast mixture into it. Mix lightly with a fork to form a thin batter in the well. Beat together and add to the well:

1 large egg
1 large egg yolk

Then mix with a fork or your fingers to make a dough. Transfer to a lightly floured work surface and knead for a few seconds, until smooth. Let the dough rest for 5 minutes.

Sprinkle the top of the dough with flour. Roll out into a 14 × 8-inch rectangle, sprinkling additional flour underneath it as needed to prevent sticking. Position the dough so that one of the short sides is facing you. Cover the upper two-thirds of the dough with the rectangle of butter, leaving a 1-inch border of dough on the sides and at the top. Fold the bottom third of the dough over the butter. Fold the top third of the dough, with the butter on it, down over the first third, as if you were folding a business letter. Press the edges of the dough together on all 3 open sides to seal in the butter. Rotate the dough so that the folded edge is on the left and the sealed edge is on the right.

Sprinkle the dough lightly with flour and press it gently with the rolling pin to flatten it slightly. Keeping the short side of the rectangle facing you, roll into a 16 × 8-inch rectangle. Fold the bottom third up and the top third down again. (This rolling and folding is called a single turn.) Rotate the dough so that the folded edge is on the left and the open edge is on the right (like a book about to be opened). Give the dough one more single turn, rolling it into a 16 × 8-inch rectangle and folding it in thirds. Sprinkle the work surface lightly with flour as needed to prevent the dough from sticking. If at any time the butter gets soft, refrigerate the dough for 10 to 15 minutes. Mark the dough with 2 finger imprints, to remind yourself that you have given the dough 2 turns. Wrap the dough loosely in plastic wrap and refrigerate for 30 minutes.

Give the dough 2 more single turns, always making sure that the folded edge is on the left and the open edge is on the right before beginning the next roll. Make 4 imprints, wrap in plastic, and refrigerate for 30 minutes.

Give the dough a final single turn, wrap, and refrigerate it for at least 30 minutes. (At this point, the dough can be frozen or refrigerated overnight. Before freezing, wrap in plastic, then foil, then airtight in a zip-top bag; thaw overnight in the refrigerator before rolling.)

For classic square danishes, roll the dough into an 18 × 9-inch rectangle and cut into eighteen 3-inch squares. Lightly brush the squares with:

1 large egg, lightly beaten

Bring each corner into the center, pressing them into the middle so they stick. Place a scant tablespoon of any of the following in the center of each square:

2 cups any coffee cake filling, 803–4, filling for Sweet Cheese Blintzes, 647, Frangipane, 802, or jam

Place the danishes 2 to 3 inches apart on ungreased baking sheets. Let rise until puffy, 30 to 60 minutes. Preheat the oven to 375°F. Bake until golden brown, 20 to 30 minutes.

For pinwheels, see the illustration, 697. Roll the dough out into an 18 × 9-inch rectangle. Cut into eighteen 3-inch squares. Lightly brush the squares with egg, as above, and make a 1½-inch slit from each corner toward the center. Starting at the bottom left, fold one corner of each triangle to the center and press it down, forming a pinwheel. Place a scant tablespoon of any filling listed above in the center, and sprinkle lightly with sugar. Place the pinwheels 2 to 3 inches apart on ungreased baking sheets. Let rise until puffy, 30 to 60 minutes. Preheat the oven to 375°F. Bake until golden brown, 20 to 30 minutes.

For spirals, divide the dough in half, and roll each half into a 17 × 12-inch rectangle. Spread a thin layer of filling over each rectangle of dough, leaving a ¼-inch border on all sides. Roll the dough into a log, starting on one long side. Place the log seam side down on a buttered baking sheet and freeze for 15 minutes. Place each log on a cutting board and trim the ends by ½ inch. Cut each log into sixteen 1-inch-thick slices. Arrange the slices 2 to 3 inches apart on the baking sheet. Let rise until puffy, 30 to 60 minutes. Brush the pastries with beaten egg, 696, and bake at 375°F until golden brown, 15 to 20 minutes.

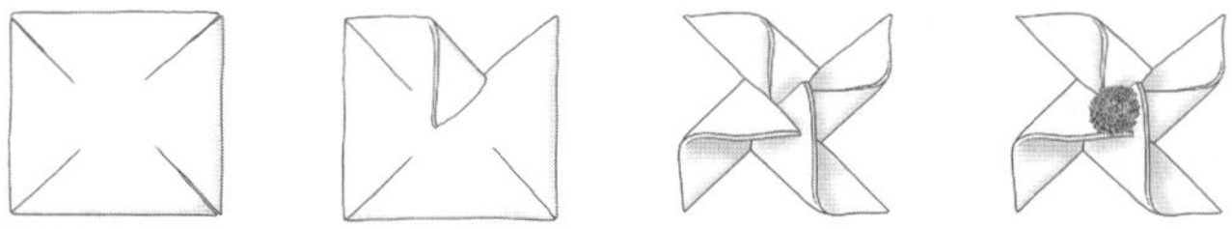

Forming pinwheels

BEAR CLAWS

6 claws

Prepare:

½ recipe Danish Pastry Dough, 696

Cut the dough into 3 pieces. Roll each into an 18 × 9-inch rectangle. Brush them with:

6 tablespoons butter, melted

Mix together in a small bowl:

½ cup chopped walnuts, toasted, 1005
¼ cup chopped dates
2 tablespoons sugar
½ teaspoon ground cinnamon

Sprinkle the mixture evenly over the rolled-out dough. Fold each rectangle of dough lengthwise into thirds, pinching the edges together to hold in the filling. Cut each piece in half crosswise. Place them seam side down on a greased baking sheet. Make 3 slashes in the folded side of each, as shown below, to make the "claws." Brush with:

3 tablespoons butter, melted

Cover and let rise until puffy, about 45 minutes.

Preheat the oven to 375°F.

Bake until golden, about 25 minutes. If desired, drizzle with:

(Quick Translucent Sugar Glaze I or II, 799)

And sprinkle with:

(Sliced almonds)

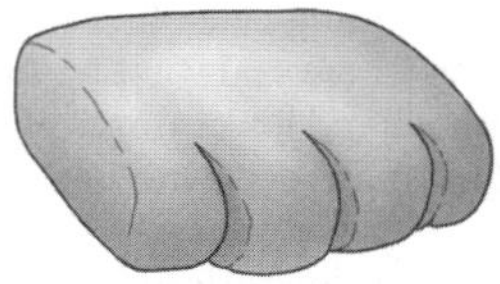

Bear claw

ABOUT CHOUX PASTE (PÂTE À CHOUX)

Choux is French for "cabbages," and these little dollops of puff paste indeed expand in the oven to resemble tiny cabbage heads. Choux paste can be formed into a variety of shapes and filled with an even greater variety of fillings both sweet and savory. It is also the basis for cream puffs, éclairs, and Gougères, 70.

Like other pastry doughs, choux paste consists of flour, butter, and water or milk, but it is cooked on top of the stove before it is shaped and baked. For golden, tender puffs, use milk as the liquid. For lighter, crisp choux puffs that hold up better over time, use water. After cooking, the paste must be allowed to cool slightly before the eggs are added to prevent the eggs from cooking; but if the paste is too cold when the eggs are added, they will not blend in smoothly. The finished paste should be shiny, smooth, and very thick but not stiff. The paste is baked in a hot oven for the first few minutes to cause quick expansion; the temperature is then reduced to finish the baking and dry out the hollow shells.

Once baked and filled, choux pastries should be served immediately or refrigerated and served within a few hours. However, unfilled baked shells can be frozen for up to 1 week in an airtight container. Thaw overnight in the refrigerator. Before filling, you may wish to re-crisp them for a few minutes in a 375°F oven.

CHOUX PASTE

About 2½ cups

Use the sugar if the choux paste will be used in a sweet application. Measure and have ready:

1 cup (125g) all-purpose flour

Combine in a large saucepan:

1 cup (135g) milk or water, or ½ cup each milk and water
1 stick (4 oz or 115g) unsalted butter, cut into small pieces
(1 tablespoon [10g] sugar)
½ teaspoon salt

Bring the mixture to a full boil over medium heat. Add the flour all at once and stir vigorously with a wooden spoon. The mixture will look rough at first but it will suddenly become smooth, at which point you should stir faster. The butter may ooze out, which is fine. In a few minutes, the paste will become dry and not cling to the spoon or the sides of the pan, and when the spoon is pressed on it lightly, it will leave a smooth imprint. Do not overcook or overstir at this point, or the dough will fail to puff. Transfer the dough to a large bowl or the bowl of a stand mixer and let cool for 5 minutes, stirring occasionally with a spoon or with the paddle attachment.

Add one at a time, beating vigorously after each addition with a wooden spoon, or on low speed with a mixer:

4 large eggs, at room temperature

Make sure that the paste is smooth each time before adding the next egg. Continue to beat until the dough is smooth and shiny. The proper consistency has been reached when a small quantity of the dough will stand erect if scooped up on the end of a spoon. The paste can be covered and refrigerated for up to 4 hours; you do not need to bring the paste to room temperature before shaping.

ABOUT FILLINGS FOR CREAM PUFFS AND ÉCLAIRS

Use plain or flavored Whipped Cream, 791, puddings, 816–18, any flavor of Pastry Cream, 801, almost any of the fillings for cakes,

801–3, or any ice cream, 840–44. Fill as close to serving time as possible to avoid sogginess. In any case, ➤ remember that cream-based and egg-based fillings must be kept refrigerated. See Stuffed Choux Puffs, 69, for savory filling ideas.

CREAM PUFFS

About 15 puffs

These large shells are a very quick way to make an attractive dessert. Fill just before serving, set the tops slightly askew, and dust with powdered sugar. Please read About Choux Paste, 697.

Position a rack in the lower third of the oven. Preheat the oven to 400°F. Line a baking sheet with parchment paper.

Prepare:

½ recipe Choux Paste, 697, using the optional sugar

Scoop the paste into a pastry bag fitted with a ½-inch plain tip. Hold the tip close to the baking sheet. Do not move it up as you pipe. Simply let the paste bubble up around it until the mounds are about 2½ inches wide and 1 inch high. Space the mounds about 2 inches apart on the baking sheet. Before baking, lightly sprinkle a few drops of water over the shapes on the sheet for a light, airy texture. Bake for 10 minutes. Reduce the heat to 350°F and bake until golden brown and very firm to the touch, about 25 minutes more. Transfer to a rack, poke a small hole in the side of each puff with a skewer or the tip of a knife, and let cool completely.

Prepare:

2 cups lightly sweetened Whipped Cream, flavored or plain, 791, or any flavor Pastry Cream, 801

Slice the tops from the puffs. Fill with the cream, place the tops slightly askew, and dust the puffs with:

Powdered sugar

CHOCOLATE ÉCLAIRS

8 to 10 large or 24 miniature éclairs

Please read About Choux Paste, 697.

Position a rack in the lower third of the oven. Preheat the oven to 400°F. For large éclairs, line one baking sheet with parchment paper; for miniature éclairs, line 2 baking sheets with parchment paper.

Prepare:

Choux Paste, 697, using the optional sugar

Scoop the paste into a large pastry bag fitted with a 1-inch tip for large éclairs or a ½-inch tip for miniatures. Shape the paste into 8 to 10 large (5 inches long and 1½ inches wide) or 24 miniature (2½ inches long and ½ inch wide) éclairs by drawing the tip of the pastry bag along the pan while extruding the dough, finishing with a lifting reverse motion. Before baking, lightly sprinkle a few drops of water over the shapes on the sheet for a light, airy texture. Bake for 10 minutes. Reduce the heat to 350°F and bake until golden brown and very firm to the touch, about 25 minutes more, or 15 to 20 minutes for the miniature éclairs. Transfer the éclairs to a rack, poke a small hole in one end of each éclair with a skewer or the tip of a knife, and let cool completely.

Prepare:

2 cups Vanilla Pastry Cream, Chocolate Pastry Cream, or Mocha Pastry Cream, 801, Whipped Cream, 791, or Whipped Crème Fraîche, 791

Fill a pastry bag fitted with a ¼-inch tip with the cream. Poke the pastry tip into the hole in each éclair and pipe in the filling. Or cut off the top third of the éclairs with a serrated knife (reserve the lids), remove any excess dough, and spoon the filling into the éclairs; this method works best for whipped cream. Dip the top of each éclair (either the whole éclair or the lid) into:

Bittersweet Chocolate Glaze or Frosting, 798, or Chocolate Ganache, 797

Replace the lids on the cut éclairs and refrigerate until the glaze is set, up to 3 hours.

PROFITEROLES

24 profiteroles; 6 servings

A profiterole is a miniature cream puff. It can be filled with any sweet or savory mixture, though it is usually associated with dessert. Vanilla ice cream is traditional, but any flavor can be used.

Position a rack in the lower third of the oven. Preheat the oven to 400°F. Line 2 baking sheets with parchment paper.

Prepare:

½ recipe Choux Paste, 697, using the optional sugar

Scoop the paste into a pastry bag fitted with a ½-inch plain tip. Shape the paste as for Cream Puffs, above, into 24 mounds 1 inch wide and 1 inch high. Before baking, lightly sprinkle a few drops of water over the shapes on the sheet for a light, airy texture. Bake for 10 minutes. Reduce the heat to 350°F and bake until golden brown and very firm to the touch, about 25 minutes more. Transfer to a rack, poke a small hole in the bottom of each profiterole with a skewer or the tip of a knife, and let cool completely.

Prepare:

Chocolate Ganache, 797

Whisk until smooth. Keep warm in the top of a double boiler (or reheat in a microwave just before serving). To serve, slice the shells horizontally in half. Remove any excess dough. In each bottom half, place a small scoop of:

Ice cream or Whipped Cream, 791

Cover with the top halves and place 4 profiteroles on each plate. Drizzle with some of the ganache. Serve immediately, with the remaining ganache on the side.

CROQUEMBOUCHE

8 to 10 servings

This whimsical tower of choux puffs crowned with spun sugar is the French equivalent of a wedding cake. It is also an excellent dessert to serve at any gathering where you want to make an impression.

Position racks in the upper and lower thirds of the oven. Preheat the oven to 400°F. Line 2 baking sheets with parchment paper.

Prepare:

Choux Paste, 697, using the optional sugar

Scoop the paste into a piping bag fitted with a ½-inch plain tip and pipe the dough into ½-inch mounds on the baking sheets, leaving about 1 inch between them. Use a lightly dampened finger to smooth the tops of the puffs. Bake until browned, about 25 minutes, switching racks and rotating the sheets front to back halfway through. Transfer to a wire rack, poke a small hole in the bottom of

each puff with a skewer or the tip of a knife, and let cool completely. At this point the puffs may be frozen for up to 1 month.
Prepare:

Double recipe any flavor pastry cream, 801–2

Let cool completely and refrigerate for at least 1 hour. Transfer the pastry cream to a piping bag fitted with a ¼-inch plain tip. Poke the tip into the holes made by the paring knife or skewer and fill with the cream.

Have a serving platter ready. Fill the sink or a large bowl with cold water. Prepare:

Caramelized Sugar, 857

When the syrup reaches a dark amber color remove from the heat and dip the bottom of the pan into the cold water bath to stop the cooking. Working quickly, dip the bottom of each puff in the sugar syrup and affix it to the serving plate in an 8-inch circle. Continue, building up the tower of puffs into a conical shape by gradually making the ring of puffs smaller and smaller as the cone gets taller. If the syrup starts to harden too much to work with, gently warm it until liquid and proceed until you have made a tall cone of puffs.

To finish the croquembouche, dip 2 forks into the sugar syrup, and wave them over the tower of puffs. The syrup will fall onto the puffs in long strands, creating a spun sugar halo. Continue until all the syrup is used. Serve within 2 hours.

PARIS-BREST
8 to 10 servings

This classic French dessert was created in honor of the Paris-Brest bicycle race, the circular shape of the dessert representing a wheel. It is a ring of choux pastry topped with almonds and filled with a praline-flavored buttercream. We can think of nothing but good things to say about such a dessert.

Preheat the oven to 400°F. Line a large baking sheet with parchment paper. Draw an 8-inch circle on the parchment paper and flip it over.
Prepare:

Choux Paste, 697, using the optional sugar

Scoope the paste into a pastry bag fitted with a ¾-inch star or plain tip. Pipe a ring of choux paste onto the parchment paper along the circle, then pipe another ring just inside the first. The two rings should touch so they fuse together during baking. Pipe a third ring on top of the first two, along the seam made where the first two rings meet. Brush with:

1 large egg, beaten with 1 teaspoon water

Sprinkle generously with:

¼ cup sliced almonds

Bake for 15 minutes. Reduce the oven temperature to 350°F and bake until golden and puffed, about 20 minutes more. Transfer to a rack to cool completely.
While the pastry cools, prepare:

Praline or Nut Buttercream, 797

With a serrated knife, slice the choux pastry ring horizontally in half like you would a cake layer. Transfer the pastry cream to a piping bag fitted with a ¾-inch star tip. Pipe the filling in a decorative pattern on the bottom ring of choux pastry. Place the top ring on top of the filling and dust with:

Powdered sugar

Serve immediately or refrigerate, covered, for up to 1 day. Allow the dessert to sit at room temperature for 30 minutes before serving.

ABOUT STRUDEL

When Marion Becker was a small child in the early 1900s, she remembered Janka, the family's Hungarian laundress, sometimes finding the time to make strudel. First, she draped a round table with a fresh cloth. The neighborhood children gathered around, and their eyes would pop as she rolled the dough, no larger than a softball, into a big thin round. Then, hands lightly clenched, palms down, working under the sheet of dough and from the center out, she stretched it with the flat planes of her knuckles. She would play it out, so to speak, not so much pulling it as coaxing it with long, even friction, moving round and round the table as she worked, until the dough was thin enough to read a newspaper through. From beginning to end, the process had masterly craftsmanship. Would that we could give you her skill as easily as we give you this recipe.

In Marion's memory, the filling was invariably apple. But whether you make strudel dough yourself or buy it, there are endless possibilities: Poppy seeds, cherries, ground meat mixtures, cheese, or even cabbage can be tucked into the flaky layers of a strudel. For Savory Cabbage Strudel, see 703.

APPLE STRUDEL
10 to 12 servings

The strudel can be formed, wrapped tightly in buttered foil, and frozen for up to 2 months before baking, but the pastry will not bake up quite as crisp. Although strudel is best served on the day it is made, you can freeze baked strudel; after thawing, reheat it in a 350°F oven for 15 to 20 minutes.

Cover a table at least 3 feet square with a clean cloth or sheet. Make sure there is enough room to walk around the table. Do not flour the cloth.

Melt and set aside in a small bowl:

1 stick (4 oz or 115g) unsalted butter

Sift together into a large bowl:

1½ cups (200g) bread flour
½ teaspoon salt

Whisk together in a separate small bowl with 1 tablespoon of the melted butter:

1 large egg
⅓ cup (80g) room-temperature water
1 teaspoon cider vinegar

Make a well in the center of the flour mixture and pour the egg mixture into the well. Working from the inside of the well, mix the wet ingredients quickly into the dry ingredients with your fingers or a fork. When all the liquid is incorporated, knead the dough on a lightly floured work surface until it is silky, pliable, and no longer sticky, about 10 minutes. Form the dough into a ball and brush with some of the melted butter. Let rest in a covered bowl in a warm place for at least 30 and for up to 60 minutes.

Have ready:

8 cups chopped, peeled tart apples, such as Gravenstein, Braeburn, or Granny Smith (about 6 large apples)

Preheat the oven to 350°F.

Spread on a rimmed baking sheet and toast in the oven until browned, 10 to 15 minutes:

¾ cup coarse fresh bread crumbs, 957

Transfer half of the bread crumbs to a medium bowl. Add to the bowl and stir together:

1 cup (200g) sugar
½ cup walnuts, toasted, 1005, and finely chopped
⅓ cup dried currants
1 tablespoon finely grated lemon zest
2 teaspoons ground cinnamon

Increase the oven temperature to 400°F. Brush a baking sheet with some of the melted butter.

Roll the dough as thin as possible, then transfer it to the cloth-covered table: Lightly flour the surface only as necessary as you roll the dough; try rolling it without flour. The dough will be soft and responsive to the touch. Remove any rings or bracelets and drape the edges of the dough over the backs of your hands (palms facing down and fingers halfway clenched). Stretch the dough gently at the table, pulling it away from the center and moving your hands apart at the same time. Stretch one section of the dough at a time, and work slowly around the table. Take your time; patience will reward you with a thinner dough. Try not to tear the dough or make holes in it. Stretch the dough into a square 30 to 35 inches on each side, letting it drape over the edges of the table if it is bigger. Anchor each corner of the dough with a small plate if the square stretches back a bit while you work on the other edges. Trim the thicker edges of dough with scissors and use the trimmings to patch any holes. Let the dough dry for 10 minutes so that it will not stick to itself during rolling.

Brush the entire surface of the dough lightly with some of the melted butter. Leaving a 3-inch border of dough along one edge, sprinkle the remaining toasted bread crumbs in a strip next to the border, covering one-third of the dough. Mix the apples with the sugar mixture. Again leaving the 3-inch border of dough along the edge, spread the apple filling over the crumbs. Fold the 3-inch border over the filling. Pick up one end of the cloth underneath the strudel with both hands, one on either side, and let the strudel roll slowly over onto itself, brushing the dough that was on the underside (and thus unbuttered) with melted butter as you roll. Continue to lift the cloth underneath the strudel and let the strudel roll onto itself to the end. Place the rolled strudel on the prepared baking sheet, curving it into a horseshoe shape.

Brush the strudel with two-thirds of the remaining melted butter. Bake for 20 minutes. Brush with the remaining butter and rotate the baking sheet front to back for even browning. Bake until golden brown, 20 to 25 minutes more. Slide onto a rack and let cool.

Dust the strudel with:

Powdered sugar

Slice on the diagonal with a serrated knife. Serve with:

Whipped Cream, 791

ABOUT PHYLLO

Phyllo, or filo, is the tissue-thin pastry used in Greece and much of the Middle East to create delectably crisp pastries. The simplest of ingredients, flour and water, are so skillfully kneaded, rested, and stretched as almost to defy amateur reproduction.

Phyllo—the word means "leaf" in Greek—can be made by hand, but we do not recommend it; it is an arduous and tricky process that yields results no better than what is commercially available frozen in most grocery stores or fresh from Greek and Middle Eastern bakeries.

Store-bought phyllo is easy to work with, but it is essential to keep the thin sheets from drying out. ➤ If using frozen phyllo, thaw it in its package in the refrigerator for several hours, or overnight. Once thawed, unwrap the phyllo and remove only the number of sheets required for the recipe; rewrap the remaining sheets in plastic wrap and return them to the refrigerator or freezer. Stack the sheets to be used on a tray or a sheet of plastic wrap and immediately cover the stack with a dry towel or a piece of plastic wrap, then a damp towel. (Do not allow the damp towel to touch the phyllo, or it will dissolve into paste.) A sheet of phyllo left uncovered dries out in just a minute and will crack when you try to use it. Remove from the covered stack only the number of sheets of phyllo immediately called for and quickly re-cover the stack before proceeding.

Other recipes using phyllo include Phyllo Pie Crust, 666, Spinach or Mushroom Phyllo Triangles, 68, Quick Phyllo Samosas with Potatoes and Peas, 68, Spanakopita, 706, and Savory Cabbage Strudel, 703.

BAKLAVA

About 30 squares or diamonds

Baklava is popular in Greece and throughout the Middle East. Layered with nuts and drenched in sugar syrup or honey, it is the best known of all phyllo pastries. In Greece, it was originally an Easter specialty, made with forty layers of pastry representing the forty days of Lent. Chopped nuts are the traditional filling, but dried fruits, sesame seeds, or coconut may be substituted for a nontraditional version.

Preheat the oven to 325°F. Butter a 13 × 9-inch baking pan.

Finely chop or coarsely grind:

3 cups coarsely chopped, toasted, 1005, nuts (walnuts, pistachios, almonds, and/or pecans)

Stir together in a small bowl:

¼ cup sugar
1 teaspoon finely grated lemon zest
½ teaspoon ground cinnamon

Melt:

2 sticks (8 oz or 225g) unsalted butter

Unfold and stack on a work surface:

1 pound phyllo dough, thawed if frozen

Trim the phyllo into 13 × 9-inch sheets; save the scraps for another use, if desired. Keep the stack covered with plastic wrap and a damp towel. Place 2 phyllo sheets in the baking pan and brush the top sheet evenly with melted butter. Add 2 more sheets and brush with butter, then repeat once more, for a total of 6 sheets. Sprinkle with half of the nuts and then half of the sugar mixture. Cover the filling with 2 phyllo sheets, butter the top sheet, and repeat until there are 6 sheets on top of the filling. Cover with the remaining nuts and sugar mixture. Cover with all of the remaining phyllo sheets, adding them 2 at a time and buttering only the second sheet each time. Brush the top with the remaining butter. Using a sharp serrated knife, cut through all of the layers to make 2-inch diamonds or squares. This is important, because you will not be able to cut the baklava once it is baked without crushing the pastry; it also allows the syrup to soak in and around each piece.

Bake for 30 minutes. Increase the oven temperature to 375°F. Continue to bake until the baklava is golden brown, 20 to 25 minutes.

Meanwhile, combine in a small saucepan:

1⅓ cups sugar
1⅓ cups water
⅓ cup honey
1 tablespoon lemon juice
Zest of 1 orange, removed in large strips with a vegetable peeler

Bring the mixture to a gentle boil, stirring to dissolve the sugar, then reduce the heat and simmer, uncovered, for 15 minutes.

Strain the hot syrup and pour evenly over the baked baklava. Let cool completely on a rack at least 4 hours before serving.

PHYLLO CUPS

6 cups

Individual phyllo cups are versatile. To maintain their crispness, spoon a sweet or savory filling into them just before serving. Unfilled baked phyllo cups can be stored in an airtight container for up to 2 days before using.

Position a rack in the lower third of the oven. Preheat the oven to 350°F. Butter the insides and rims of 6 standard muffin cups.

Melt:

4 tablespoons (2 oz or 55g) butter

Have ready:

¼ cup sugar (for sweet fillings only)

Unfold and stack, then cover with a dry towel and then a damp towel:

4 sheets phyllo dough, thawed if frozen

Place 1 sheet of phyllo on a work surface. Brush the sheet evenly with one-quarter of the melted butter. If using sugar, sprinkle 1 tablespoon of it evenly over the dough. Cover with a second sheet of phyllo and butter and sugar it in the same manner. Repeat with the remaining sheets of phyllo, ending with a layer of butter and sugar. Cut the stack of phyllo sheets into twelve 4½-inch squares (3 strips down and 4 across). Place a square stack in one side of a muffin cup, easing it in with the backs of your fingers so that it covers half the bottom and rises to hang over one side of the cup. Ease in a second stack, slightly overlapping the first, to cover the other half of the bottom and hang over the other side of the muffin cup. Repeat to make 5 more phyllo cups.

Bake until the pastry is golden brown, 10 to 15 minutes. Carefully remove from the muffin cups and let cool before filling.

PHYLLO NAPOLEONS

9 servings

These informal pastries are much easier to make than their puff pastry counterpart, Mille-Feuille, 693. They can be filled as directed with pastry cream, but feel free to improvise, using flavored pastry cream and adding fresh fruit, such as raspberries or sliced strawberries, between the layers.

Prepare and chill:

Any flavor pastry cream, 801–2

Preheat the oven to 400°F. Have 2 ungreased baking sheets ready.

Have ready:

½ pound phyllo dough, thawed if frozen
1 stick (4 oz or 115g) unsalted butter, melted

Lay the phyllo flat on a work surface and cover with a dry towel, then with a damp towel while you work. Place 2 sheets of phyllo on top of one another on a work surface. Brush the top sheet of phyllo with butter, and, if desired, sprinkle lightly with:

(Sugar or any flavored sugar, 1026)

Place two more sheets of phyllo on top, brush with butter, and sprinkle with sugar, if desired. Repeat this, buttering and sugaring every other sheet of phyllo, until there are 8 layers. Brush the top layer with butter, and, if desired, sprinkle with more sugar. Cut the phyllo in half lengthwise to create 2 long rectangles. Cut the rectangles crosswise into 2-inch-wide rectangles. Transfer to the baking sheet and nest a second baking sheet directly on top to press the phyllo flat and prevent it from warping during baking.

Bake until the phyllo is browned and crisp, 11 to 13 minutes. Transfer to a cooling rack. Repeat the process with remaining phyllo sheets, butter, and sugar, if using.

To assemble each napoleon, spread or pipe pastry cream in a ½-inch layer on top of one phyllo rectangle, then top with a second piece of phyllo. Spread or pipe another ½-inch layer of pastry cream, then top with a third and final layer of phyllo. Repeat with remaining phyllo rectangles and pastry cream. Dust the tops of the napoleons with:

Powdered sugar

ABOUT SAVORY PIES AND PASTRIES

Many savory pies were born of convenience and portability. A hearty filling encased in dough was both a meal and a lunchbox of sorts, providing laborers with sustenance that did not require utensils. Others, such as spanakopita and potpies, are not intended to be transported, but rather portioned and shared at the table. For other savory pies, see About Quiche, 162, Corn Bread Tamale Pie, 538, and Shepherd's Pie, 506.

CORNISH PASTIES

About 9 servings

Pasties are meat hand pies, originally from Cornwall, England. They were a portable lunch for miners and other laborers who needed a hearty meal that was easy to transport. This tradition of hand-held meat pies traveled to northern Michigan with Cornish immigrants, and these pies are now beloved by miners and regular folk alike.

The addition of curry powder is nontraditional, but we appreciate the extra spice.

Whisk together in a medium bowl or pulse in a food processor to combine:

4 cups (500g) all-purpose flour
2 teaspoons baking powder
½ teaspoon salt

Add and work in with a pastry blender or your fingers or pulse until the fat is in very small pieces and the dough is crumbly:

4 ounces (115g) leaf lard or suet or 1 stick (4 oz or 115g) cold unsalted butter

Add and stir in or pulse until the dough just comes together in a shaggy ball:

¾ cup (175g) ice water
2 large egg yolks

Knead the dough briefly until it forms a smooth ball. Flatten into a 1-inch-thick disk, wrap tightly in plastic wrap, and refrigerate for at least 1 hour or overnight.

Mix together in a medium bowl and set aside:

¾ pound skirt, sirloin, or hanger steak, finely chopped (pieces should be about ½ inch)
½ cup finely diced russet potato
½ cup finely chopped onion
½ cup finely diced turnip or rutabaga
2 tablespoons all-purpose flour
(2 tablespoons minced herbs such as thyme, parsley, savory, or chives)
(1 tablespoon curry powder or garam masala, store-bought or homemade, 558)
1¼ teaspoons salt
½ teaspoon black pepper

Preheat the oven to 350°F. Lightly grease a large baking sheet.

Unwrap the dough and place on a lightly floured work surface. Divide the dough in half and keep half tightly wrapped. Lightly flour the top of the dough and roll out to just over ⅛ inch thick. Use a small plate to cut out 6-inch rounds of dough. Gather the dough scraps into a ball and roll out again, cutting out as many dough rounds as possible. Repeat with the second half of the dough. You should have about 9 rounds. Scoop ⅓ cup filling onto each piece of dough, leaving a ½-inch border around the edges. Lightly brush the edges with:

1 large egg, beaten with 1 teaspoon water

Bring the edges together and crimp them or use a fork to press them together. Cut a few small slits in the top of the pasties or prick a few times with a fork. Place the pasties on the prepared baking sheet and brush with egg wash. Bake until golden brown and firm, about 50 minutes. Let cool about 10 minutes before serving.

EMPANADAS WITH PICADILLO

15 empanadas

Empanadas come in an astonishing array of shapes, with all manner of fillings and doughs. Try using Chicken Chili Verde, 425, Chili Con Carne, 468, or even Sautéed Corn, 235, with shredded mozzarella or Oaxaca cheese instead of the picadillo and hard-boiled eggs. You can also use fresh masa or the dough for Corn Tortillas, 612, if desired.

Prepare the dough for:

No-Knead Refrigerator Rolls, 618, omitting the yeast and using lard or shortening instead of butter

Cover and let the dough rest while you prepare:

Picadillo, 503
4 Hard-Boiled Eggs, 151, peeled and quartered

Divide the dough into 15 pieces and shape into balls. Use as little extra flour as possible during the shaping process.

Position racks in the upper and lower thirds of the oven. Preheat the oven to 400°F. Lightly grease 2 baking sheets or line with parchment paper.

Flatten the balls of dough into disks, then roll out to a ⅛-inch thickness. Scoop a scant ¼ cup picadillo onto half of each dough round, leaving a ½-inch border, and top with a hard-boiled egg quarter. Fold the plain half of the dough over the filling to form a half-moon shape. Crimp the edge or press closed with the tines of a fork. Place the empanadas at least 1 inch apart on the prepared baking sheets and brush lightly with:

1 egg, beaten with 1 teaspoon water

Bake until golden, about 25 minutes, rotating the baking sheets front to back and switching oven racks halfway through. Let cool for 5 minutes before serving.

FATAYER BI SABANEKH (LEBANESE SPINACH PIES)

About 25 small pies

These sumac-scented pies are a favorite of ours. They make a wonderful addition to a mezze platter, 46, accompanied by a bowl of Tahini Dressing, 576. For a larger, flakier spinach pie, see Spanakopita, 706.

Set aside in a colander to thaw and drain:

12 ounces frozen spinach

Prepare the dough for:

½ recipe No-Knead Refrigerator Rolls, 618, using olive oil instead of butter or shortening and using 1 egg yolk instead of 1 egg

Proceed through the first rising, and do not refrigerate.

While the dough rises, prepare the filling. Press the thawed spinach in the colander to get out as much liquid as possible. Transfer to a medium bowl and stir in:

½ cup finely chopped onion
(⅓ cup crumbled feta)
¼ cup pine nuts or coarsely chopped slivered almonds, toasted, 1005
2 tablespoons ground sumac or the finely grated zest of 1 lemon plus 2 tablespoons lemon juice
2 tablespoons olive oil
¾ teaspoon salt (½ teaspoon if using feta)

Position racks in the upper and lower thirds of the oven. Preheat the oven to 400°F. Lightly grease 2 baking sheets or line with parchment paper.

Transfer the dough to a lightly floured work surface and knead it briefly to deflate it. Roll it out to a ⅛-inch thickness. Cut into

3- to 4-inch rounds with a biscuit cutter. Gather the dough scraps into a ball and wrap in plastic wrap. Place 1 scant tablespoon filling in the center of each dough round. To shape, bring three sides of the dough together in the center and pinch them closed to form a triangle. Repeat with the remaining dough and filling. You may re-roll the dough scraps up to 3 times to cut out more rounds. Place the pies on the prepared baking sheets and brush with:

Olive oil

Bake until golden brown, about 15 minutes, rotating the baking sheets front to back and switching oven racks halfway through. Serve hot, warm, or cold.

PIROSHKI

About 20 piroshki

Piroshki, or pirozhki, are part of a large family of predominantly savory pies that hail from Russia to Central and East Asia, the Balkans, and Iran. There are many popular fillings, both savory and sweet, but ground beef is among the most common, at least in Russia.

Prepare the dough for:

Parker House Rolls, 617

Let rise one time.

While the dough rises, prepare the filling. Heat in a large skillet over medium heat:

1 pound ground beef
3/4 teaspoon salt
1/2 teaspoon black pepper

Cook, breaking up the meat, until cooked through, about 10 minutes. Transfer to a medium bowl with a slotted spoon. Pour off all but 2 tablespoons of fat from the skillet and add:

1 large onion, finely chopped

Cook, stirring, until softened, about 8 minutes. Stir the onion into the bowl with the cooked beef along with:

2 Hard-Boiled Eggs, 151, finely chopped
1/4 cup finely chopped dill
3 tablespoons sour cream

Season to taste with:

Salt and black pepper

Let cool completely.

Lightly oil a large baking sheet or line with parchment paper. Divide the dough into 20 pieces. Keep the dough balls lightly covered while you work to prevent them from drying out. On a lightly floured work surface, roll each ball of dough out into a 3- to 4-inch round. Place a heaping tablespoon of filling in the center. Bring 2 sides of the dough up to meet in the center over the filling and press to seal. Gently use your palm to flatten slightly into a plump, oblong dumpling shape, like a flattened football. Place seam side down on the prepared baking sheet. Cover and let rise until puffy, about 30 minutes.

Preheat the oven to 350°F.

Brush the piroshki with:

1 egg, beaten with 1 teaspoon water

Bake until golden brown, 25 to 30 minutes.

POTATO KNISHES

8 knishes

Knishes can be stuffed with a wide variety of fillings, including sauerkraut, kasha, and cheese, but potato and onion—preferably cooked in schmaltz, 1015—is one of the most popular fillings.

Prepare the dough for:

Apple Strudel, 699, substituting 1 tablespoon vegetable oil for the butter

While the dough rests, prepare the filling. Peel and quarter:

2 pounds russet potatoes (about 3 medium)

Place in a large pot and cover with cool water. Bring to a boil over high heat, then reduce the heat to maintain a gentle simmer. Simmer until the potatoes are tender, 15 to 20 minutes.

While the potatoes cook, heat in a large skillet over medium heat:

1/4 cup chicken, duck, or goose fat or vegetable oil

Add and cook, stirring, until softened and starting to brown, about 15 minutes:

2 large onions, chopped

When the potatoes are tender, drain well. Rice or mash the potatoes until smooth and stir in the cooked onions. Add:

1 1/4 teaspoons salt, or to taste
1/2 teaspoon black pepper, or to taste

Preheat the oven to 375°F. Lightly oil a large baking sheet.

Divide the dough in half. Roll and stretch out one piece of dough very thin, into a roughly 12-inch square. You should not need to use any flour during the rolling process. In fact, you want the dough to stick a little to the surface to help stretch it thin enough. Place half the potato filling in a 3-inch-wide mound along the bottom edge of the dough, leaving 1 inch of bare dough on the right and left sides and about 2 inches of bare dough along the bottom edge. Roll up the dough loosely like a jelly roll. Use the side of your hand, like a karate chop motion, to press the filling down every 3 inches, then use a knife to cut through the dough in those places. Seal one side of each knish, then turn so the seam is on the bottom. Close the top of the knishes as best as you can and squish them gently to make the sides bulge out a bit, giving them a plump shape. Place on the prepared baking sheet. Repeat with the remaining dough and filling.

Brush the knishes with:

1 egg, beaten with 1 teaspoon water

Bake until golden brown, about 40 minutes. Serve warm or at room temperature with:

Spicy mustard

SAVORY CABBAGE STRUDEL

10 to 12 servings

We like savory strudels just as much as their sweet counterparts. If you make the strudel dough, you will end up with one large, horseshoe-shaped strudel. If you use phyllo dough, this recipe makes 2 smaller, rectangular strudels.

Prepare:

The dough for Apple Strudel, 699

Alternatively, you may use:

1 package store-bought phyllo dough, thawed if frozen

To prepare the filling, melt in a Dutch oven or large pot:

4 tablespoons butter

Add little by little:

4 pounds green cabbage, cored and shredded
1¼ teaspoons salt

Cook each addition of cabbage until slightly softened before adding the next. If necessary, add a few tablespoons of water to the pot and cover to help speed the process. Once all the cabbage is added and wilted, add:

⅓ cup dry white wine

Cover and cook the cabbage until very tender, about 10 minutes. Stir in:

1 tablespoon poppy seeds
1 teaspoon caraway seeds
½ teaspoon black pepper

Taste for seasoning. Pour the cabbage into a colander and allow it to drain and cool completely. Press the cabbage to extract as much moisture as possible.

Preheat the oven to 400°F.

Melt in a small saucepan:

1½ sticks (6 oz) unsalted butter

If using strudel dough, stretch it out as directed, 700. If using phyllo dough, lay sheets out on a cloth-covered work surface, allowing the sheets to overlap by 2 inches, to make two roughly 16 × 35-inch rectangles. Lightly brush the phyllo sheets with butter, then add another layer of phyllo to each rectangle. Brush with butter and repeat two more times. There should be 4 layers of phyllo in each rectangle. Brush the top layer of phyllo with butter.

Leaving a 3-inch border along one long edge of the strudel dough or each phyllo rectangle, sprinkle in a strip next to the border, covering one-third of the dough:

¾ cup dry bread crumbs (divided if using phyllo)

Spread over the bread crumbs:

1½ cups sour cream (divided if using phyllo)

Spread the cooled cabbage filling over the sour cream. Fold the 3-inch border over the filling. If using strudel dough, pick up the edge of the cloth underneath the strudel and use it to help the strudel roll slowly over onto itself, brushing the dough with melted butter as you roll. Continue rolling the dough and brushing it with butter until it is completely rolled up. Place the strudel on a baking sheet, curving it into a horseshoe shape and brush it with butter. If using phyllo, simply roll up the dough with your hands, brushing it with butter as you roll. Place the two rolls side by side on the baking sheet.

Bake for 20 minutes. Brush again with butter and return to the oven until deep golden brown, 20 to 25 minutes more. Serve immediately, sliced with a serrated knife.

BEEF POTPIE

6 to 8 servings

Prepare:

Beef Stew, 465
½ recipe Basic Pie or Pastry Dough, 664, ½ recipe All-Butter Pie or Pastry Dough, 664, or the dough for Buttermilk Biscuits, 635, or Quick Drop Biscuits, 636

Position a rack in the upper third of the oven. Preheat the oven to 400°F.

Grease a 13 × 9-inch baking dish and add the stew. If using buttermilk biscuit dough, pat out the dough as directed in the biscuit recipe, cut the dough into biscuits, and arrange on top of the stew, overlapping the biscuits if necessary. If using drop biscuit dough, simply drop the dough in walnut-sized pieces on top. If using pie dough, roll it out into the shape of the dish, place on top of the stew, and tuck the edges down in against the sides of the dish. Brush the top with:

1 large egg, beaten with 1 teaspoon water

Bake until the pie is bubbling and the crust is nicely browned, 30 to 40 minutes. Let cool for 15 minutes before serving.

CHICKEN OR TURKEY POTPIE

6 to 8 servings

Leftover or store-bought, precooked chicken or turkey breast is perfect here.

Prepare:

Creamed Chicken, 419, made with ½ cup flour

Prepare the dough for:

Buttermilk Biscuits, 635, Quick Drop Biscuits, 636, ½ recipe Basic Pie or Pastry Dough, 664, or ½ recipe All-Butter Pie or Pastry Dough, 664

Position a rack in the upper third of the oven. Preheat the oven to 400°F. Grease a 13 × 9-inch baking dish.

Melt in a large skillet over medium-high heat:

2 tablespoons butter

Add and cook, stirring often, about 5 minutes:

1 medium onion, chopped
3 medium carrots, sliced
2 small celery ribs, sliced

Stir the vegetables into the creamed chicken along with:

¾ cup frozen peas
3 tablespoons minced parsley

Pour the mixture into the prepared dish. If using buttermilk biscuit dough, pat out the dough as directed in the biscuit recipe, cut the dough into biscuits, and arrange on top of the chicken, overlapping the biscuits if necessary. If using drop biscuit dough, simply drop the dough in walnut-sized pieces on top. If using pie dough, roll it out into the shape of the dish, place on top of the chicken, and tuck the edges down in against the sides of the dish. Brush the top with:

1 large egg, beaten with 1 teaspoon water

Bake until the sauce is bubbling and the topping is browned, 30 to 40 minutes. Let cool for 15 minutes before serving.

CRAWFISH PIE

6 servings

Crawfish pie can be found with a single or double crust, or as hand pies. We have opted for a single crust on top of the pie for convenience's sake, but feel free to experiment to suit your own taste (you will need to decrease the liquid by at least half and cool the filling before making hand pies, 687). If you are itching to make this pie but cannot find crawfish, substitute peeled and deveined shrimp, 363.

Prepare:

½ recipe Basic Pie or Pastry Dough, 664, or All-Butter Pie or Pastry Dough, 664

Preheat the oven to 375°F.

Heat in a 10-inch ovenproof skillet (preferably cast-iron) over medium heat until shimmering:

2 tablespoons vegetable oil

Add and sauté until soft, 6 to 8 minutes:

1 onion, chopped
1 celery rib, chopped
½ green bell pepper, chopped

Stir in and sauté 1 minute more:

4 green onions, chopped
4 garlic cloves, finely chopped
2 teaspoons fresh thyme or 1 teaspoon dried thyme
½ teaspoon sweet paprika
½ teaspoon black pepper
½ teaspoon salt
¼ teaspoon cayenne pepper

Add and stir until the vegetables are coated with flour:

2 tablespoons all-purpose flour

Stir in:

½ cup heavy cream
½ cup chicken stock or broth or clam juice

Bring to a simmer and cook until slightly thickened. Stir in and cook for 5 minutes:

1 pound fresh or thawed frozen crawfish tail meat

Remove from the heat. Roll out the dough into a round large enough to fit into the skillet and place on top of the crawfish, tucking in any overhanging edges. Cut a few slits in the crust and brush with:

1 large egg, beaten with 1 teaspoon water

Bake until golden brown and bubbling, 25 to 30 minutes. Let cool for 15 minutes before serving.

STEAK AND KIDNEY PIE

6 to 8 servings

Classic recipes for this old English favorite often call for beef kidneys. If they are used, they should be soaked, 516, and the cooking time must be increased to ensure tenderness. If you'd rather not use kidneys, substitute the same amount of sliced mushrooms. Rather than encasing the stew in dough, we recommend a topping only.

Prepare:

½ recipe All-Butter Pie or Pastry Dough, 664

Cut into ½-inch cubes:

1½ pounds boneless round steak or other steak

Wash, remove the membranes, and thinly slice:

12 ounces veal or lamb kidneys

Melt in a large saucepan or skillet over medium-high heat:

3 tablespoons butter or beef fat

Add the kidneys and:

½ cup chopped onion

Cook, stirring, until the onion is tender, about 5 minutes. Meanwhile, mix together in a wide, shallow bowl:

½ cup flour
½ teaspoon salt
¼ teaspoon black pepper

Dredge the beef in the flour mixture and add the beef cubes to the pan. Cook, stirring, until browned, 8 to 10 minutes. Add:

2 cups beef stock or broth
1 cup dry red wine or beer

Bring to a boil, then reduce the heat and simmer, stirring occasionally, until the beef is tender, about 1 hour.

Preheat the oven to 425°F.

Transfer the meat mixture to a 9-inch skillet, pie dish, or baking dish. Roll out the dough into an 11-inch round and place on top of the steak and kidneys, tucking in any overhanging edges. Cut a slit in the dough to allow steam to escape. Brush the dough with:

1 large egg, beaten with 1 teaspoon water

Bake until the crust is browned, 15 to 20 minutes. Let cool for 15 minutes before serving.

TOURTIÈRE (FRENCH CANADIAN MEAT PIE)

8 servings

This richly spiced pie is traditionally served at Christmas in Québécois households.

Prepare:

All-Butter Pie or Pastry Dough, 664, or Basic Pie or Pastry Dough, 664

While the dough is chilling, place a Dutch oven over medium heat and add:

1 pound ground beef
1 pound ground pork

Cook, stirring and breaking up the meat with a wooden spoon, until browned and cooked through, about 10 minutes. Transfer the meat to a bowl, leaving behind as much fat as possible. Pour off all but 2 tablespoons fat from the pot. Add:

1 large onion, chopped

Cook, stirring, until softened, about 5 minutes. Add:

1 medium russet potato, diced
1 teaspoon salt
½ teaspoon black pepper
½ teaspoon ground cinnamon
½ teaspoon grated or ground nutmeg
¼ teaspoon ground allspice
¼ teaspoon ground cloves
1 bay leaf

Stir until the potatoes and onions are coated with the spices. Return the beef and pork to the pot along with:

1 cup beef or pork stock or water

Bring to a simmer, cover, and reduce the heat to simmer gently for 30 minutes. Uncover and continue to simmer until all the liquid has evaporated. Transfer the mixture to a small baking sheet, discard the bay leaf, and cool completely.

Roll out half the dough into a ⅛-inch-thick round and transfer to a 9-inch skillet or deep-dish pie pan. Press the dough evenly into the corners and up the sides of the pan. Pour the beef and pork mixture into the pan. Roll out the second half of the dough into a roughly 11-inch round and place on top of the filling. Fold the overhanging edge of the top crust inside the skillet, between the skillet and the bottom crust. Crimp the edges together to seal them. Freeze the pie for 15 minutes or refrigerate for 1 hour. Preheat the oven to 375°F.

Brush the crust all over with:

1 egg yolk, well beaten

Cut a few steam vents in the top crust or cut a decorative hole in the center. Bake until golden brown, 45 to 50 minutes. Let cool for 10 minutes before serving.

SPANAKOPITA (GREEK SPINACH PIE)

About thirty 2-inch squares or diamonds

If desired, substitute about **15 ounces frozen spinach, thawed**, for the fresh. The important thing is to press as much liquid out of the spinach as possible to ensure a crisp crust.

Stem, wash well, and coarsely chop:

2 pounds spinach

Heat in a large skillet over medium heat:

2 tablespoons olive oil

Add and cook until softened, 5 to 7 minutes:

1 large onion, finely chopped

Add the spinach a handful at a time. Cook until the spinach is wilted and the liquid is released, about 5 minutes. Increase the heat to high and cook, stirring often, until the liquid is evaporated and the spinach is dry, 7 to 10 minutes. Stir in:

¼ cup minced dill or parsley

Let stand until cool enough to handle, then transfer to a colander and squeeze to remove the excess liquid. Beat in a medium bowl:

4 large eggs

Add the spinach mixture along with:

8 ounces feta, crumbled
2 tablespoons grated Kefalotiri or Parmesan cheese
½ teaspoon salt

Lightly oil a 13 × 9 × 2-inch baking dish. Melt:

1 stick (4 oz or 115g) unsalted butter

Unroll on a dry work surface:

1 pound phyllo dough, thawed if frozen

Trim the dough into a 9 × 13-inch rectangle. Cover with a dry towel and cover the dry towel with a damp towel. Lay 1 sheet of phyllo in and up the sides of the prepared baking dish and brush lightly with butter. Top with 7 more phyllo sheets, brushing each lightly with butter. Spread the spinach mixture over the phyllo. Top with 8 more sheets, brushing each with butter. Roll the overhanging phyllo from the sides to form a border all the way around. With a thin, sharp knife, cut the pie into squares or diamonds, but do not cut through the bottom or the filling will leak onto the pan. Refrigerate for 30 minutes.

Preheat the oven to 375°F.

Bake the pie until crisp and golden, about 45 minutes. Remove from the oven and let cool for a few minutes. Cut the squares or diamonds right through to the bottom and serve.

TOMATO COBBLER

6 servings

This is the perfect savory cobbler to make in late summer, when your garden is overrun by cherry tomatoes. We like to use drop biscuits for the topping, and we add a handful of chopped herbs, such as thyme and chives, and some grated Cheddar to the dough.

Heat in a large ovenproof skillet over medium heat until shimmering:

2 tablespoons olive oil

Add and cook, stirring, until softened, about 5 minutes:

1 medium onion, chopped

Add and cook, stirring, 1 minute more:

3 garlic cloves, finely chopped
1 tablespoon fresh thyme leaves or 1 teaspoon dried thyme
2 teaspoons minced fresh oregano or ½ teaspoon dried oregano
½ teaspoon salt
¼ teaspoon black pepper
¼ teaspoon red pepper flakes

Remove the skillet from the heat and add:

2 pounds cherry tomatoes, mixed red and yellow if possible

Stir the tomatoes into the onions and seasonings until combined. Set aside.

Preheat the oven to 375°F.

Prepare the dough for:

Quick Drop Biscuits, 636, or Cornmeal Biscuits, 636

Roll out the dough as directed (unless using drop biscuit dough), and cut into 2- to 3-inch biscuits. Place the biscuits or drop the biscuit dough in walnut-sized pieces on top of the tomatoes, allowing some of the tomato mixture to peek through. Place the skillet in the oven and bake until the biscuits are golden brown and the tomato mixture is bubbling, 35 to 40 minutes. Let cool for 10 minutes before serving.

TOMATO-RICOTTA TART

6 servings

This tart is perfect for celebrating the last of the summer heirloom tomatoes, after you've had your fill of tomato salads and sandwiches. It is also an excellent vegetarian main dish when served with a butter lettuce salad.

Preheat the oven to 375°F.

Prepare:

½ recipe All-Butter Pie or Pastry Dough, 664

Line a 9-inch pie or tart pan with the dough. Bake as directed in About Blind Baking Crusts, 664. Meanwhile, combine in a medium bowl:

15 to 16 ounces whole-milk ricotta
2 large eggs
⅓ cup chopped basil
½ cup grated Parmesan (2 ounces)
Finely grated zest of ½ lemon
1 tablespoon lemon juice
½ teaspoon salt
½ teaspoon black pepper

When the crust is ready, fill it with the ricotta mixture. Arrange over the top, allowing the slices to overlap slightly in a circular pattern:

3 small to medium heirloom tomatoes, cut into ½-inch-thick slices

Season the tomatoes lightly with:

Salt and black pepper

Bake the tart until the tomatoes start to shrivel and have released most of their watery juices, 40 to 45 minutes. Let cool 10 minutes before serving.

CALZONES

Eight 8-inch calzones

A calzone is somewhat like a savory turnover. The possibilities for calzone fillings are many; see the chart of suggested pizza toppings, 614, for ideas. You will need about 4 cups filling or ½ cup per calzone.

Prepare through the first rise:

Pizza Dough, 614, or two 1-pound packages refrigerated pizza dough

Preheat the oven to 450°F. Lightly grease 2 baking sheets.

Divide the dough into 8 balls. Place on a lightly floured work surface, sprinkle with flour, and cover with a kitchen towel or plastic wrap. Let stand for 20 minutes.

Meanwhile, coarsely chop:

2 cups any combination of pizza toppings

Mix with:

2 cups shredded mozzarella (8 ounces)

Shape each ball of dough into a thick disk and let stand for about 5 minutes, then roll each disk into an 8-inch round. Divide the filling among the rounds, placing it on one half of each. Fold the bare half of the dough over, making a half-moon, moisten the edges with water, and tightly seal with your fingertips. Cut a 1-inch slit in the top of each calzone, place on the prepared baking sheets, and transfer to the oven. Reduce the oven temperature to 400°F and bake until nicely browned, about 25 minutes. Serve hot or at room temperature, with:

Marinara Sauce, 556

STROMBOLI

Two 12-inch stromboli

The fillings for stromboli are as variable as those for pizza; see the chart of suggested pizza toppings, 614, for ideas.

Prepare through the first rise:

Pizza Dough, 614, or two 1-pound packages refrigerated pizza dough

Preheat the oven to 400°F. Lightly grease 2 baking sheets or line with parchment paper.

Divide the dough in half if using homemade dough. Form each piece into a ball. Place on a lightly floured work surface, sprinkle with flour, and cover with a kitchen towel or plastic wrap. Let stand for 20 minutes.

Shape each ball of dough into a thick disk and let stand for about 5 minutes, then roll into 8 × 12-inch rectangles. Leaving a ½-inch border on one long side, spread each with:

¼ cup Tomato Sauce, 556, or Marinara Sauce, 556 (½ cup total)

Divide between the pieces of dough, keeping the ½-inch border:

10 ounces sliced provolone
6 ounces sliced salami
4 ounces sliced pepperoni

Starting from the long side opposite the border, tightly roll each rectangle up into a 12-inch log. Pinch the ends closed and place the logs seam side down on the prepared baking sheets. Cut a few diagonal slits in the top of each log. Bake the stromboli until firm and lightly browned, about 20 minutes. Cut into 1-inch slices and serve hot or at room temperature.

CAKES AND CUPCAKES

Whether you bake a cake for a birthday, whip up a batch of cupcakes for a bake sale, or hand a pan of gingerbread over a back fence, the gesture is one of fellowship that enriches your life and the lives of those around you.

In earlier editions, Irma devoted *Joy*'s cake chapter to light and airy cakes at least 3 layers tall and almost invariably made by separating eggs and folding in the whites for lightness. These cakes can be excellent, but we find the modern home baker is less enamored of whipping egg whites and far more interested in rich, moist cakes that are easy to make. We have made room for both types of cakes here and appreciate them for the very different experiences they bring to the table. From featherlight Angel Food Cake, 719, to buttery, fine-textured Pound Cake, 726, and rich, ever-popular cheesecakes, 752–54, this chapter will help you find your ideal cake—the recipe you keep in your back pocket for all kinds of occasions.

For all cakes, start with high-quality ingredients. Because a cake baker is unable to taste and correct along the way, pay careful attention to ➤ pan sizes, measurements, and the temperature of everything, including the ingredients and the heat of the oven. ➤ Pay attention also to the physical states you induce by stirring, creaming, and folding. Our drawings and descriptions will get you off to a flying start, but you will learn to recognize the proper "look" of critical stages in cake making most effectively through practice.

For the sake of accuracy and for those readers who prefer to use the metric system when baking, we now include gram quantities for dough and batter ingredients; for more information on measuring by weight and volume, see Measuring Ingredients, 1042.

CAKE TYPES

Angel food and **sponge cakes** are sometimes called **foam cakes** because they depend exclusively on the expansion of the air trapped in their egg-rich batters for leavening. Angel food cakes use only egg whites and so have a very light, fluffy crumb and an almost dry texture. Sponge cakes, though also light in texture, contain an appreciable amount of fat by way of their yolk content, giving them a slightly moister texture. **Génoise** cakes use warmed, whipped whole eggs for loft, but they also contain melted butter, which lends them a light texture and the rich flavor of a butter cake. **Tortes** often depend on egg yolks for their fat content and on egg whites for their leavening; ground nuts and bread crumbs replace flour as their base, so these cakes tend to be close-grained and crumbly.

Most **butter cakes** use baking powder and/or baking soda for leavening, with the notable exception of pound cakes. They also employ a technique called creaming, 723, in which softened butter and sugar are beaten together until smooth, very light, and fluffy. The sharp-edged sugar crystals and the action of beating encourage the formation of air pockets, which ultimately add loft to the resulting cake. This action is a means of mechanical leavening, as opposed to chemical leavening from baking powder and baking soda.

Oil cakes are some of the easiest cakes to make. They are usually mixed in one bowl and do not require beating eggs or egg whites or creaming butter and sugar. Oil cakes do not have the irresistible buttery flavor of a butter cake, but they are generally very moist (and keep longer).

Cheesecakes resemble baked custards more than the other cake types in this chapter; see About Cheesecakes, 752, for more information.

ABOUT THE TEMPERATURE OF INGREDIENTS

Before starting to bake, all ingredients should be at room temperature (68° to 70°F; butter can be a little cooler, as noted just below). This is especially important for butter cakes, where the butter, liquid, and eggs form an emulsion during mixing. Emulsions can break or curdle (like a sauce) if some ingredients are colder than the others. When this happens, the batter loses its ability to trap air, and the cake will be heavy.

Butter should still be cool—from 65° to 70°F—but malleable when squeezed, not soft and squishy. Butter that is too soft or melted will not trap air and the batter will collapse with prolonged beating. Very warm butter can also lead to greasy baked goods. An easy way to soften butter is to cut it into small cubes and spread them out on a plate. Within 15 to 20 minutes at average room temperature it will be warm enough for baking.

Cold eggs do not increase in volume as much as room-temperature or warm eggs when beaten, and they won't blend smoothly into batters containing large quantities of melted chocolate. To bring eggs to room temperature quickly, place them in a bowl and cover with warm water. In 10 minutes or so they will be ready.

Transform cold dairy products into room-temperature ingredients quickly by judiciously using the microwave, a few seconds at a time, on low power or "defrost." Liquids at 68° to 70°F feel quite cool, not warm, to the touch. If you are not sure of what this temperature feels like, an inexpensive instant-read thermometer can be used to verify your judgment. Cold liquids like milk may be left on the countertop until warmed slightly or place them in a bowl or measuring cup set inside a hot water bath.

MIXING CAKE BATTERS

Whether you mix a cake by hand or with an electric mixer, mixing affects leavening and, therefore, the volume and texture of a cake. Different methods of mixing, creaming, stirring, beating, and folding are used for different ingredients and to achieve different goals.

There are two kinds of electric mixers: **stand mixers** and **handheld mixers.** Mixing times vary depending on the mixer. For instance, it will take longer to whip egg whites with a hand mixer than it will with a stand mixer. Handheld mixers are fine for most jobs, but ➤ some cakes—such as sponge cakes, which are made by whipping whole eggs into a foam—are much better when made with a stand mixer. The high speed of a stand mixer can incorporate more air into egg whites or butter and sugar than hand mixers or a whisk, resulting in lighter, loftier foams.

In recipes, we provide mixing times and speeds for guidance, but the most important signals are in the bowl. Learning to bake is learning to recognize when egg yolks and sugar are "thick and pale yellow" or when butter beaten with sugar has "lightened in color and texture," regardless of the clock or the mixer setting. ➤ One of the foremost keys to smooth, light, and even cake batters is to scrape down the sides of the bowl, and the beater(s), frequently during the mixing process. For detailed information on creaming butter and sugar, see About Butter Cakes, 723. For tips on whipping and folding in egg whites, see Beating Eggs, 977. For more on sifting ingredients, see Sifting, 1045.

Creaming and mixing cake batter by hand

Stirring is used to incorporate dry and/or wet ingredients gently but thoroughly into another mixture without overmixing or beating.

To stir cake batter by hand, use a wooden spoon or silicone spatula. Begin at the center of the bowl, mixing with a circular motion; widen the circle as the ingredients become blended. Scrape the sides of the bowl from time to time as necessary. The entire operation of adding and blending the dry and liquid ingredients should not take more than 2 minutes.

To stir cake batter by machine, mix at low speed, just until the ingredients are smoothly blended. Do not overmix.

Folding in egg whites is a delicate operation. The object is to blend thoroughly yet not lose any of the air you have incorporated into the ingredients. It is always done by hand, with a silicone spatula.

Folding egg whites into cake batter

To fold in egg whites, make sure the bowl is large enough. Scoop one-third of the beaten whites onto the cake batter. Use the edge of a spatula to cut down through the middle of the egg whites to the bottom of the bowl. Sweep the spatula toward you up against the side of the bowl, scooping up batter from the bottom of the bowl and bringing it to the top. Repeat the folding stroke, rotating the bowl slightly with the other hand each time you repeat the folding motion until the egg whites are incorporated. Then add the remaining whipped egg whites and repeat the folding motion until the batter is lightened and the egg whites are dispersed throughout. For most batters, it is fine to leave some white streaks of egg whites showing.

ABOUT CAKE PANS

Cake pans come in a variety of materials. For a thin, evenly browned crust, ➤ sturdy medium-weight aluminum pans with dull surfaces or nonstick finishes are best. Avoid stainless steel, which does not conduct heat evenly. Heavy dark metal and glass pans absorb and hold more heat, resulting in heavier, darker crusts. If you bake in these pans, ➤ reduce the oven temperature by 25°F but expect the baking time to be approximately the same. In any case, pan materials affect baking time, so always check cakes early to be safe.

The best results in each recipe will be achieved by using the pan size(s) specified. When baking layer cakes, use pans with straight sides. Cake pans with tall sides are fine to use for any cake so long as the diameter is appropriate. If you bake in a larger pan, the cake will be thinner and will bake in less time; batter baked in a pan that is too small may overflow the pan and may not bake evenly. ➤ If you do not have a pan that corresponds to the size and shape called for in the recipe, see the next section and the chart below to substitute a different pan that will hold the same volume as the pan the recipe calls for.

Should a square or rectangular pan be too large, you can reduce the size of it with a divider made of folded foil, as shown. The batter holds the divider in place on one side. Dried beans or rice can be used to support the other side.

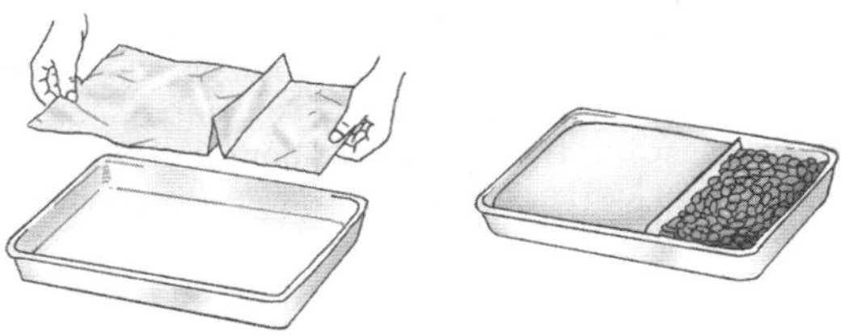

Reducing the pan size with a foil divider, weighted on one side

The texture of butter cakes, especially, varies with the depth of the batter in the pan. Thin layers baked in separate pans turn out with a lighter texture but are prone to drying out. The same cakes baked in loaf pans or tube pans, either plain or fluted, are usually moister and denser. ➤ If you prefer a moist, dense-textured cake, you can bake many-layer cakes in one 3-inch-deep springform pan of the same diameter as the pans called for in the recipe. The finished cake, 2 to 3 inches tall, may be cut horizontally into thin layers or left as a thick, single-layer cake, which has the advantage of being easier to frost. Remember that the baking time for a deeper cake will be longer.

ABOUT CAKE PAN SIZES AND CAPACITIES

Fill pans no more than one-half to two-thirds full. Loaf and tube pans can be filled to a slightly higher level. ➤ To determine how much batter to mix for an oddly shaped pan, first measure the volume of the pan with water. Using a liquid measuring cup, pour water by the cupful into the pan until it is full to the brim. Then calculate two-thirds of that amount for your batter.

To translate a recipe made for one size pan to use a different size pan, calculate the volume of the pans the recipe calls for, then calculate the volume of the pans you'd like to use (see the chart below for help with this). Divide the volume of the pans you want to use by the volume of the pans called for in the recipe. The resulting number is what you should multiply the ingredients in the recipe by in order to fill the desired pan. Of course, this multiplication will be much easier if you use weight rather than volume.

If you scale up a recipe baked in, say, three 8-inch round cake pans to use a Bundt pan, keep in mind that you will need to bake the Bundt cake longer than the 8-inch cakes. Always use a toothpick or skewer to test whether the batter is fully set rather than relying upon a time estimate alone. Depending on the oven temperature, keep an eye on the cake to make sure it does not brown too quickly (place a piece of foil over the cake to slow browning).

Pans from different manufacturers differ in exact measurement, and pan capacities vary depending on whether the pan sides are straight or flared. For the chart below, pans are measured across the top between the inside edges. The capacities are approximate.

COMMON BAKING PAN VOLUMES

To substitute one pan for another (or more than one), the easiest way is to substitute those of equal volume. Keep in mind that ➤ large changes in the depth of batter in the pan will affect baking times and the finished texture. For baking thin sheet cakes, see 746.

Volume	Equivalent
16 cups (up to 10½ cups cake batter)	One 10 × 4-inch tube pan One 13 × 9 × 2-inch baking pan Two 9 × 2-inch round cake pans Two 9 × 1½-inch square baking pans Two 9 × 5-inch loaf pans 30 to 36 standard cupcakes
12 cups (up to 8 cups cake batter)	One 9-inch tube pan One 10-inch Bundt pan One 10-inch springform pan One 17½ × 11½-inch jelly-roll pan Two 8 × 2-inch round cake pans Two 8 × 1½-inch square baking pans Two 8½ × 4½-inch loaf pans Two 9 × 1½-inch round cake pans Three 8 × 1½-inch round cake pans 18 to 24 standard cupcakes
10 cups (up to 6½ cups cake batter)	One 9 × 2-inch round cake pan One 9 × 2-inch square baking pan One 15½ × 10½-inch jelly-roll pan
8 cups (up to 5⅓ cups cake batter)	One 9 × 2-inch round cake pan One 9 × 1½-inch square baking pan One 9 × 5-inch loaf pan Two 6 × 2-inch round cake pans Two 8 × 1½-inch round cake pans Two 8 × 4-inch loaf pans 12 to 18 standard cupcakes

ABOUT PAN PREPARATION

Angel food cakes, chiffon cakes, and most sponge cakes and tortes are baked in pans with ungreased sides so that the batter can climb up and cling to the sides of the pan for support during baking and cooling. Most other types of cakes are baked in greased or greased and floured pans. As an added precaution, ➤ we recommend lining the bottoms of round cake pans with parchment paper. Parchment rounds are available for purchase, or simply place a pan on top of parchment paper and trace around the pan with a pencil. Cut out the shape and fit it into the greased pan.

Fluted tube (Bundt) pans and decorative molds are prepared differently. These must be greased and floured carefully, including in all grooves and crevices, so that the cake will release without the aid of a knife, which will damage its surface. The same is true for layer cakes that will not be iced on the sides.

To grease and flour a pan, make a paste of 2 parts solid vegetable shortening and 1 part flour (or cocoa powder if the cake is chocolate) and apply to the inside of the pan in a thin, even layer with a paper towel, pastry brush, or your fingers. Butter, oil, nonstick spray, and margarine may be used, but they do not release cakes as well as shortening does. A layer cake pan requires 1½ teaspoons shortening plus ¾ teaspoon flour or cocoa powder, a small plain or fluted tube pan needs 1 tablespoon shortening plus 1½ teaspoons flour or cocoa powder, and a large plain or fluted tube pan needs 2 tablespoons shortening plus 1 tablespoon flour or cocoa powder.

If using nonstick pans, parchment paper can still be used in the bottom, for insurance. Tube pans should be greased and floured even if they are nonstick. For pan placement in the oven, see 1071.

ABOUT TESTING CAKES FOR DONENESS

Some cakes, such as Individual Molten Chocolate Cakes, 743, are ready to be removed from the oven when they are still gooey in the center. Most, however, can be tested for doneness with the following methods. Insert a cake tester—such as a thin metal or wooden skewer or a toothpick—in the center of the cake; if it emerges perfectly clean, or with a few moist crumbs, the cake is done. The cake should be lightly browned, beginning to shrink from the sides of the pan, and should not jiggle at all. If pressed lightly with a finger, it should feel firm to the touch and spring back into shape at once, except in very rich cakes and chocolate cakes, which may dent slightly and still be done.

After removing it from the oven, cool the cake briefly in the pan on a rack—10 to 15 minutes—and then cool completely out of the pan, on a rack (except for sheet cakes, which are typically cooled in the pan unless otherwise directed). If cakes are left in the pan too long, they can become soggy and difficult to remove. To unmold, turn the pan over another rack, or put a plate on top of the pan and flip gently. Remove the parchment paper, if used, then repeat the action to transfer the cake back to the original rack so it is right side up. For exceptions, see About Angel Food Cakes, 718, About Sponge Cakes, 719, and Génoise, 721.

PREPARING A LAYER CAKE FOR FILLING AND FROSTING

Cakes should be completely cool before being trimmed, cut, and filled. Warm cake layers melt fillings and cause layers to slip and slide. In fact, cakes that are refrigerated until well chilled are easier to handle, fill, and frost. They also tend to be less crumbly, an advantage when trying to avoid errant crumbs in a beautifully iced cake.

First, ➤ if the cake is freshly baked and very tender, place it in the freezer for 20 minutes.

To level cake layers, trim their tops level with a long, serrated knife. During frosting and filling, place all the layers cut side down, since it is easier to spread frosting on an uncut and very level surface. Cake layers that are only very slightly domed on top may not need to be leveled. Place the bottom and middle layers dome side down and the top dome side up.

To cut cake horizontally into thinner layers, set the cake on a piece of foil, parchment paper, or a decorating turntable or lazy Susan. If the cake is not level, trim it now (see above). Cut a shallow notch down one side of the cake so that you can line up the layers when you assemble the cake.

Now, place one hand flat on top of the cake. Hold the blade of a long, serrated knife against the side of the cake where you wish to cut it. Turn the cake counterclockwise (clockwise if you are left-handed) while you saw a shallow groove all around the cake, always at an equal distance from the top of the cake so the layer will be even. Do not try to cut all the way through the cake the first time around.

After you have cut the groove, continue to rotate the cake while cutting deeper and deeper into the groove until the layer is free. Alternatively, once the groove is cut, wrap a length of strong thread or dental floss around the groove, cross the ends in front, and pull them until the layer is cut through. Slide a piece of cardboard or a cookie sheet under the new layer, lift it up, and set it aside.

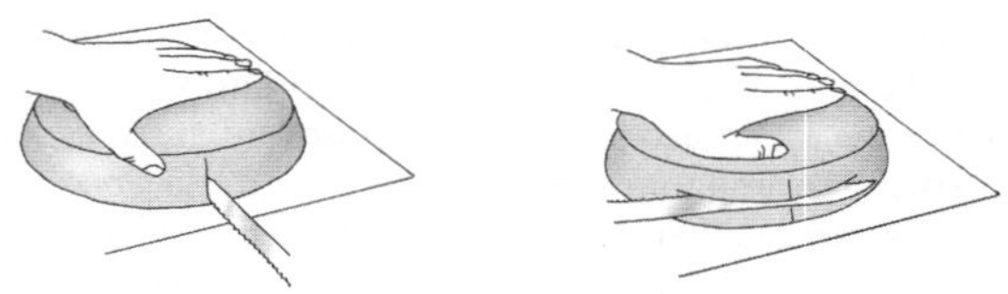

Cutting a single cake into layers

To create a base for the cake, use a cardboard cake round or springform pan bottom the same diameter as the cake. This will allow you to move the cake safely after you have completed it. Anchor the cake to the base with a dab of frosting. Otherwise, assemble and frost the cake directly on the serving platter. Slide 4 wide strips of wax or parchment paper under the edges of the cake on all sides to keep the platter clean. Remove the strips after the cake is frosted.

ABOUT FILLING AND FROSTING CAKES

Choosing the filling and frosting for a cake is similar to choosing a sauce to garnish a dish. There is the complementary approach of pairing like with like—for instance, a light Angel Food Cake, 719, topped with Whipped Cream, 791, or Devil's Food Cake Cockaigne, 728, slathered with rich Chocolate Sour Cream Frosting, 793. Or contrast the cake and the frosting, using chocolate frosting for a yellow cake, or Fluffy White Frosting, 795, on a rich chocolate torte. There is no single perfect formula for a good layer cake, and you may be pleasantly surprised by going off-script.

Refrigeration is another point to consider when pairing cakes with fillings and frostings. Sponge cakes, chiffon cakes, and angel food cakes do not harden in the refrigerator, so they are compatible with fillings and frostings that require refrigeration, such as citrus curds, whipped cream, or buttercreams. Any cake filled or frosted with buttercream should be removed from the refrigerator an hour or more in advance of serving to restore its creamy glory. Butter cakes and rich chocolate tortes are diminished by refrigeration; flavor and fragrance are lost, and their velvety-rich textures harden. Should you pair one of these cakes with a filling or frosting that requires refrigeration, frost it at the last minute, or remove the chilled cake from the refrigerator well in advance of serving. Quick powdered sugar–based icings like Peanut Butter Frosting, 792, or glazes, 799–800, do not require refrigeration, which makes them especially compatible with butter cakes.

Icing and frosting yields in this book are given in cups, so consider the size of the cake, the number of layers, and the richness of the cake and the frosting when determining how much frosting you will need. You may have to double or even triple the frosting or icing recipe. See the Frosting Cakes chart, 713, for more information.

While you may choose to fill your layer cake with one mixture and frost it with another, most frostings and icings moonlight as fillings, too. This simplifies things greatly for the cook. To use frosting between the layers as well as on the top and sides of the cake, use one-quarter to one-third of the total frosting between the layers. Then, slather the remaining frosting on the top and sides of the cake.

The amount of filling used for a particular cake depends on the style of cake and the richness of the filling. Fluffy frostings and whipped cream are spread thicker than dense buttercreams. Buttercream between several thin cake layers (such as the layers of a torte) should be spread less than ⅛ inch thick (only ⅓ cup of buttercream between 8-inch layers; ⅓ to ½ cup between 9-inch layers). Fillings between thicker cake layers (such as those comprising a standard layer cake) can be spread up to ¼ inch thick (up to 1 cup between layers). In other words, if the layers are thin, spread the filling thin; if the layers are thicker, spread the filling thicker. Each time you set a layer in place, make sure it is centered on the layer beneath it and line up the notch if the layers were cut.

The Frosting Cakes chart, 713, offers general guidelines on how much frosting and filling to use for different size cakes. Also consider your own taste as well as the flavor, richness, and sweetness of the cake layers and the frosting when determining how much frosting to use. Whipped cream and egg white-based frostings are quite fluffy, and you can use the higher suggested amounts—or even more. For rich chocolate glazes or buttercreams in European-style tortes with thin layers, work with the smaller amounts. Please read About Cake Fillings, 801, for more information on selecting cake fillings.

EQUIPMENT

A stainless steel **frosting spatula** (offset or flat) with a narrow 8-inch blade is an excellent all-purpose tool for spreading frostings on cakes. The spatula enables you to spread a frosting smooth or to decorate with swirls or with raised spikes; it also facilitates the spreading of poured chocolate glazes. Small offset spatulas are ideal for detail work. A **cake comb** (described in About Angel Food Cakes, 718) or **serrated knife** can be used to texture the sides and/or top of a cake. Perhaps not surprisingly, a perfectly smooth coat of frosting is the hardest texture to master. If you are determined to learn this technique, it is worth purchasing a **decorating turntable** or a **lazy Susan,** which will allow you to rotate the cake while holding the spatula steady as you smooth the frosting. Any frosting or icing that is smooth and holds a shape can be piped with a **pastry bag** fitted with a **decorative pastry tip.**

ADJUSTING THE CONSISTENCY OF FROSTINGS

The consistency of the frosting is critical to achieving the effect you want. Frosting that is too thick or stiff will tear the cake and pull up crumbs. Frosting that is too thin will collapse into a puddle when piped and may even slide off the cake. Modify the consistency of the frosting according to need. Frostings rich in butter or chocolate can be softened or stiffened by placing the bowl in a pan of either warm water or ice water and stirring until the frosting reaches the desired consistency. Treat powdered sugar icings the same way or beat in extra liquid a few drops at a time to soften, powdered sugar to stiffen.

Whipped cream frosting works a little differently; do not try to soften or stiffen it once it is made or you will break down the cream. When you plan to frost with whipped cream (or whipped ganache), underwhip the cream slightly. Spreading and smoothing the cream as you frost the cake will stiffen it adequately. If the cream is stiff before you begin, your finished frosting will look and taste overbeaten and grainy, but you may briefly whisk in some extra heavy cream to loosen the whipped cream if needed. See Decorative Treatments for Cakes, 714.

FROSTING A CAKE

Brush loose crumbs from the cake layers as necessary before you begin. If you begin frosting the cake and the frosting is so thick that it tears the cake and creates crumbs, adjust the consistency as directed above. Keep crumbs from "contaminating" the frosting in the bowl by scraping the spatula against another container each time before dipping it back into the frosting. Or divide the frosting between two bowls and work out of one for the "crumb coat" (see below), saving the other for the final frosting.

To keep crumbs from marring the finished frosting or glaze, seal the cake first. Some cakes are sealed with hot strained jam or preserves; heat 2 cups jam or preserves, strain through a sieve, and brush a thin layer over the cake. Or apply a **crumb coat** to the cake by first spreading a very thin coating of frosting all over to

FROSTING CAKES

These amounts are approximate. For richer buttercream frostings and ganache, reduce these amounts by 25 percent. For sugary glazes, use only half the amount.

CAKE SIZE	AMOUNT OF FROSTING		
13 × 9 × 2-inch sheet cake	3½ cups for top and sides (2½ cups for top only)		
9½ × 5½ × 3-inch loaf cake	2½ cups for top and sides (1¼ cups for top only)		
9- or 10-inch tube or Bundt cake	3½ cups		
12 standard cupcakes	1½ cups		
8-inch round cake	Top and sides	Top, sides, and filling	Filling only
1 standard layer	2 cups		
2 standard layers	2¾ cups	3½ cups	⅓ to ¾ cup
3 standard layers	3½ cups	5 cups	⅔ to 1½ cups
9-inch round cake			
1 standard layer	2½ cups		
2 standard layers	3½ cups	4½ cups	½ to 1 cup
3 standard layers	4½ cups	6½ cups	1 to 2 cups
17½ × 11½-inch roll cake	1⅓ to 3 cups	3 to 6 cups	1½ to 3 cups

smooth the surface and secure any crumbs. It is fine to use frosting "contaminated" with crumbs for the crumb coat. For best results, refrigerate the cake for a few minutes to set the jam or crumb coat before the final frosting. For chocolate butter glazes and ganaches, cool the glaze to the consistency of frosting for the crumb coat, then gently warm the remaining glaze to the correct temperature and fluidity for glazing.

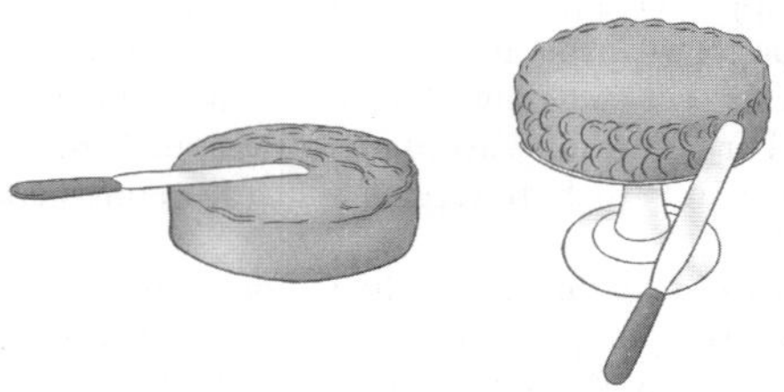

The frosting spatula enables you to apply a smooth or textured frosting

Use a clean, crumb-free spatula for the final frosting. Start by frosting the top of the cake, using a frosting spatula to evenly apply the frosting and pushing excess toward the edge of the cake. Then frost the sides of the cake, using excess frosting from the top of the cake plus any remaining frosting. If you have a decorating turntable, spin it while smoothing the sides of the cake with a bench scraper, 661, or icing smoother. Let the bottom edge of the bench scraper or icing smoother rest on the turntable. Sweep a frosting spatula across any ridges of frosting along the top edge of the cake to smooth them, passing the spatula from the edge to the center of the top of the cake. You can texture the sides with a cake comb, or coat with chopped nuts, or use the back of a spoon or an offset spatula to make peaks, valleys, and swirls in the frosting—see 714 for decorating techniques. To help smooth frostings, sometimes it is helpful to dip the blade of the spatula in hot water, then dry it. The warm spatula will soften the frosting slightly and encourage it to smooth out. Do not warm the spatula if using whipped cream to frost a cake as the heat will cause the cream to break down.

COATING A CAKE WITH CHOCOLATE GLAZE

Unlike lavishly spread frostings, which cover a multitude of imperfections on the surface of a cake, a chocolate glaze, 797, poured over a cake reveals all of them. There are a few secrets to a perfectly glazed chocolate cake or torte: the preparation of the cake shape, the temperature of the cake, and the temperature of the glaze.

The cake must be level. If necessary, level, 711, sponge or butter cake layers. To level chocolate or nut tortes that have a slightly sunken center, press the edges and invert the cake as directed in About Tortes, 741. Place the cake on a rigid base such as a cardboard cake round or the bottom of a springform pan so that the glaze will not crack or buckle when the cake is moved.

The cake surface must be smooth before glazing. In some classic European desserts, a coat of hot strained apricot or red currant jam is used to seal the cake or torte before glazing. An even more effective technique is to frost the cake thinly with a little chocolate glaze that has been cooled to the consistency of frosting. This is called crumb-coating, 712. Once the jam or crumb coat is applied, a cake should be refrigerated for 5 to 10 minutes to set it before glazing.

To glaze the cake, place it on a rack over a rimmed baking sheet or on a decorating turntable. Reheat the remaining glaze, if necessary, just until it is pourable (about 85°F). If it is too cool, it will immediately turn dull; if it is too warm, it will pour off the cake before coating it thickly enough. Pour the glaze onto the top of the cake and use a metal spatula to coat the top and sides completely, as shown. Gaps in coverage can be fixed by dipping the spatula into the excess glaze on the turntable or baking sheet and touching the bare spot. Avoid spreading the glaze as it dries—this will dull the surface and cause streaks. The glaze on a cold cake will start to set immediately, so you must work quickly. For a room-temperature cake, let the glaze set naturally at room temperature; do not refrigerate the cake at any time. For cold cakes, return them to the refrigerator immediately after glazing and leave there until needed.

Dull, mottled, or streaked glazes are caused by glazes poured at the wrong temperature or by cakes at the wrong temperature before or after glazing. Following these instructions will ensure gleaming, mirror-smooth glazed cakes.

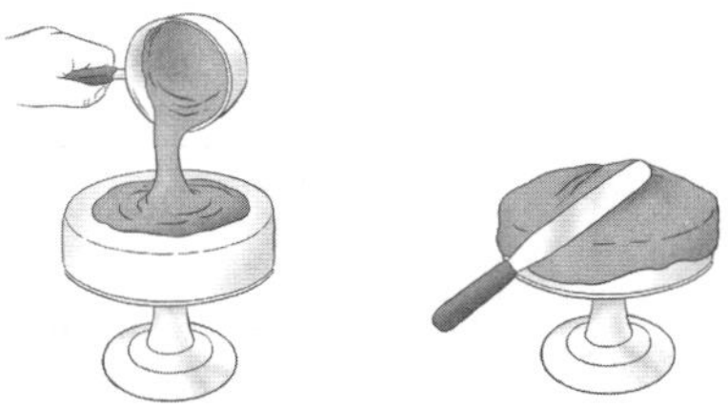

Pouring a glaze in the center of the cake and spreading it with a spatula

DECORATIVE TREATMENTS FOR CAKES

To texture the top and sides of a frosted cake, while the frosting is still soft, dip a cake comb or serrated knife in hot water and wipe it dry. Hold it gently against the side of the cake at a 90-degree angle and, if you are using a turntable, rotate it slowly while holding the comb or knife steady; otherwise, gently sweep it around the sides of the cake.

To stencil the top of a cake, refrigerate the cake to firm the frosting, if used (plain cakes may also be stenciled; they do not need to be refrigerated first). Use a paper doily or make a hand-cut stencil: Fold a round of wax or parchment paper slightly larger than the surface of the cake into eighths or sixteenths and cut out small shapes along the folds (as for paper snowflakes). The shapes need not be specific or symmetrical. The advantage of a hand-cut stencil is that the cutouts will be larger and more distinct than those of a lace doily and thus the design will show up better. No special design talent is necessary, and you can even enlist children to do the cutting. Flatten the stencil under a heavy book, if necessary, before using. Place the doily or stencil on top of the cake and use a fine-mesh sieve to sift a thin, even coating of powdered sugar or cocoa over it. Use both hands to lift the stencil carefully off the cake, in a straight upward motion without disturbing the pattern. Stencil cakes shortly before serving: the design will fade as the sugar or cocoa is absorbed by the frosting.

Stenciling the top of a cake

To pipe borders, rosettes, stars, or other larger motifs with frostings, use a cloth, plastic, or disposable pastry bag. If you choose cloth, use it with the ragged fabric seam facing out. If desired, fit the pastry bag with a metal decorating tip. You will need to cut a hole in the tip of disposable pastry bags for the decorating tip to fit through.

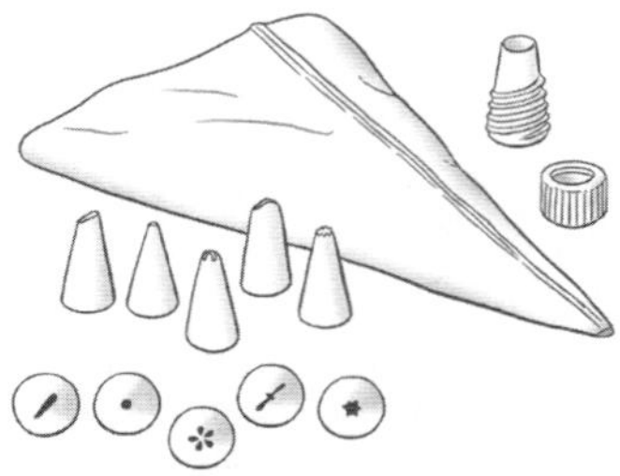

Pastry bag, tips, and coupler

Frostings to be piped should be stiff enough to hold a crisp shape. Stir them with a silicone spatula until smooth before filling the bag. Whipped cream should be slightly underwhipped before piping, as forcing it through the bag will stiffen it further; stiffly whipped cream will come out of a pastry bag looking grainy and overbeaten. For best results, avoid piping whipped cream through a tip smaller than ¼ inch. If needed, adjust the consistency of the frosting, 712.

To fill a pastry bag, turn down the top of the bag to form a cuff and place the pastry bag, tip down, inside a tall measuring cup or glass to hold it steady and upright while you fill it. Use a small spatula to push icing well down into the point of the bag, filling the bag about two-thirds full. Before you begin, press the bag to equalize the icing and to force any air bubbles toward the tip so that they will not destroy the smoothness of your decorations. Unfold the top cuff of the pastry bag and gather it together just above the level of the frosting, being careful not to capture any large air bubbles inside the bag. Twist the top of the bag to compress the frosting and move it down to the tip. As the frosting is expelled, instead of pressing the frosting down, use the action of twisting the top of the bag to compress the frosting as you work. Piping bags made with parchment paper (see How to Make Your Own Pastry Bag, 715) are handled a little differently. The top of the bag should be rolled down as you work to compress the frosting.

To make several colors of frosting or icing for decoration, divide the frosting among several small bowls and tint with paste or liquid food coloring, then transfer them to piping bags. For colors that are needed only in small quantities, use smaller amounts of frosting and smaller bags.

For practice, apply the icing on an inverted cake pan until you are comfortable with the piping bag and the action of making different designs. The icing (although not whipped cream) can be scraped off repeatedly and reused.

When you are ready to decorate the cake, it is helpful if the cake is on a decorating turntable or lazy Susan. In any case, when working on the sides, try to have the cake just above elbow level. Pressure and movement are controlled by your writing hand. Your other hand is used only for steadying. As shown in the first two illustrations (below), grasp the bag lightly but firmly in the palm of your hand with your thumb resting on top, leaving your fingers free to press the bag as you turn your hand and wrist to form designs. For cloth or plastic piping bags, use the dominant hand to twist the top of the bag as icing is expelled. For a homemade parchment paper piping bag, as icing is expelled, fold the top of the bag down to compress the remaining icing. As shown in the second pair of illustrations, sometimes you will rest the tip of the bag in a scissorlike V of your first two fingers; at other times you will merely guide the bag (as shown in the last illustration below).

Icing designs are the result of three factors: the angle of the bag and tip with respect to the surface of the cake, the timing and pressure of the squeeze, and the direction and speed of the stroke or movement. The bag and tip are held at either a 45-degree angle to the surface of the cake or a 90-degree angle (straight up and down). Start to squeeze the bag a split second before starting to move the tip, and stop squeezing a split second before coming to a stop. The amount of squeezing before you begin to move the tip determines how full and fanned out the shape will be at the start. If your designs trail off with an extra tail, it is because you are continuing to squeeze as you finish the stroke. When you decrease pressure as you finish the stroke, it tapers off. If you have trouble getting the shape, try altering any of these three variables.

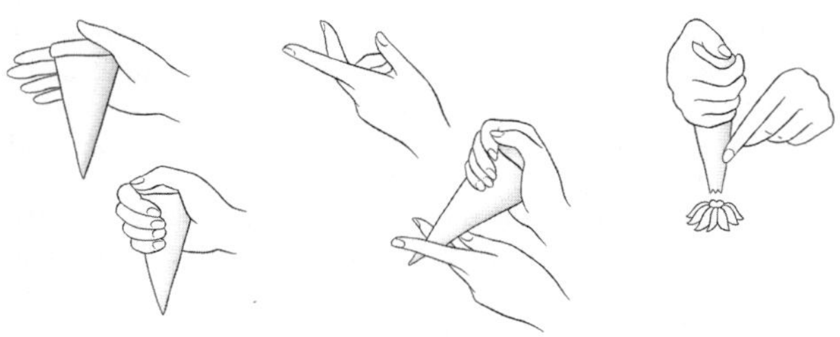

Holding a pastry bag to pipe designs

Practice is really the only way to perfect piping. There are two inexpensive and sturdy mixtures that can be used over and over to practice. ➤ Mix instant mashed potatoes with water to the desired consistency. As you practice, adjust the consistency of the potatoes with water as needed. Alternatively, make practice "buttercream" by beating 4 cups (1 pound) powdered sugar into $1\frac{1}{2}$ cups vegetable shortening mixed with 2 tablespoons water and 1 tablespoon corn syrup.

Some simple decorations for cakes

As in any work of art, the concept should make you forget technique. Make a sketch first of what you want to do or have it clearly in mind. The patterns shown above are conventional ones; try them, then develop your own style.

It is a great temptation when decorating cakes to overload them. Instead, try out some asymmetrical compositions, leaving plenty of undecorated space to set them off. At first you may want to make some of the more complicated designs separately on a piece of wax paper and let them dry before applying them to the cake. For those items made separately, let the icing stiffen on the paper (this can be aided by refrigerating or freezing them), then gently peel off the paper, and use a little reserved icing as adhesive to affix it to the cake.

Another simple cake decorating idea is to press chopped nuts or coconut onto a frosted cake, as shown below.

Coating the sides of a cake with nuts

HOW TO MAKE YOUR OWN PASTRY BAG

Following the illustrations, 716, cut a rectangle of parchment paper about 15 × 11 inches (*top left*). Fold the paper diagonally in half (*top center*), with the folded edge farthest from you. Hold the paper tightly between two fingers at the center point of the long fold (*top right*) and pull point "A" down to meet point "B" and start to roll the paper from right to left into a cornucopia. The spot on the folded edge you were holding should form a tight point. Continue to roll the paper (*bottom left*) until the cornucopia is complete. Turn it point down and with the seam toward you and the tall side (where "A" and "B" are touching) away from you (*bottom, second from left*). The seam should lie in direct line with the point of one of the highest peaks of the bag. Fold down the shorter peaks on the seam side (where "C" and "D" are touching) to stabilize the shape of the cornucopia and the seam (*bottom, third from left*). If you could see through the lower one, you would find the hollow cone ready to receive the icing. Before filling, press the tip of the paper cone flat and cut off the end. If you plan to use a metal tip from your pastry bag kit, be sure the opening is large enough to hold the tip but not so large that it will slip through under pressure. If you plan to use the tip of the paper cone itself rather than a metal tip to make the designs, make a separate paper cone for each type of "tip": Cut the tip straight across to make a small round opening; clip it with a single notch for a star tip, or with a double notch for a rose tip. After filling, turn the peaks on both sides of the bag inside and double fold the top of the bag to tightly close it (*bottom right*); this helps make the cornucopia leakproof at the top when pressure is applied.

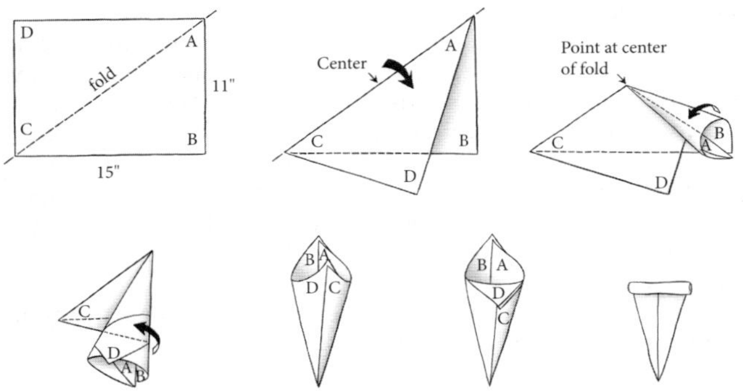

Making your own pastry bag

FRESH FLOWERS FOR CAKES

Cake decorations can be made from edible flowers, if you are sure ➤ they were not sprayed. Choose flowers such as hollyhocks, chamomile, nasturtiums, pansies, violets, borage, and roses. Field daisies and African daisies hold up well. Long sprays of amaranth can be draped so they fall down the sides of cakes, or they may be arranged where one tier meets another on a tiered cake. Other flowers, such as strawflowers, that are not exactly edible but that are not poisonous may also be used. Add sprays of herbs, fennel fronds, and nonpoisonous leaves such as geranium or even spruce tips for visual interest. ➤ Beware of flowers like lilies of the valley or crocus, which are poisonous. To prepare flowers for decorating, remove the stamens and cut off all but ¾ inch of the stems. Arrange the flowers on the iced cake just before serving it.

ABOUT STORING AND FREEZING CAKES

Unadorned cakes and those covered with an icing or glaze can be safely stored at room temperature under a cake dome. After several days, they will begin to dry out. If the cake has been cut, you can press a piece of plastic wrap or wax paper against the cut sides, which will help keep it moist. Oil-based cakes will keep moist longer than those made with butter.

Any cake filled or frosted with whipped cream, meringue, pastry cream, or cream cheese or buttercream frosting must be refrigerated. Refrigerated cakes are best stored in airtight plastic containers to keep them from absorbing odors and flavors from other foods and to keep them from drying out (wax paper pressed against cut sides is helpful here, too). Let refrigerated cakes come to room temperature for 1 hour before serving. Oil cakes may be served straight from the refrigerator if desired.

Most cakes can be frozen with little loss of quality. The richer the cake, the better it will retain flavor and texture after freezing and thawing. ➤ Moist oil-based cakes, butter cakes, cheesecakes, and rich chocolate tortes may be frozen for up to 3 months. ➤ Cakes with little or no fat, such as angel food cakes and sponge cakes, start to dry out and lose quality in as little as a week. Cakes such as tortes and génoise that will be brushed with a syrup during assembly are best for freezing, as you aren't relying on the cake itself for moisture. Spice cakes may diminish in flavor after about 6 weeks in the freezer. Fully frosted cakes may also be frozen—choose moist cakes with high-fat frostings such as cream cheese frosting or buttercream. Meringue-based icings do not freeze well.

The tighter a cake is wrapped and the faster it is frozen, the better results you will have. To this end, chill cakes before freezing, then wrap airtight first in plastic wrap and then in heavy-duty foil or plastic freezer containers or bags for a second barrier. For frosted cakes, assemble and chill them well before wrapping.

Thaw cakes without unwrapping or removing them from their container, so that condensation collects on the surface of the wrapper or container rather than on the cake. Thaw cakes that are to be served cold in the refrigerator; cakes that are to be served at room temperature should be thawed at room temperature.

ABOUT WEDDING AND OTHER LARGE CAKES

For any large cake, choose a cake recipe that can be doubled or tripled successfully. In this book, we have had success with White Cake, 724, in particular. It is surprisingly easy to make a large white cake with three 2-layer tiers for about 75 guests. For up to 25 additional servings, make a 2-layer "back-up" sheet cake by baking an additional triple batch of the cake in two 13 × 9-inch pans and frosting it with 4 to 5 cups frosting. For large cake layers (over 12 inches in diameter), lower the indicated oven temperature by 25°F and increase the baking time as needed. For more even baking, swap the position of the pans in the oven, 1071, and rotate them front to back about halfway through.

Many different kinds of cakes can be scaled up into wedding cakes. Opt for a firm cake, rather than an extremely moist or dense one. Cutting through a dense cake can cause the filling to leak out. Very moist cakes can be difficult to handle, tier, and transport. To translate a recipe made for one size pan to use a different size pan, see About Cake Pan Sizes and Capacities, 710.

To make the cake tiers: Grease and flour the sides of two

12 × 2-inch round pans, two 9 × 2-inch round pans, and two 6 × 2-inch round pans and line the bottoms with rounds of parchment paper. Mix and bake 3 separate recipes of White Cake, 724: One recipe makes enough batter for one 12-inch layer plus one 6-inch layer or two 9-inch layers. Measure the batter into the pans: 6 cups for the 12-inch pan, 4 cups for the 9-inch pans, and 2 cups for the 6-inch pan. Bake the 6-inch layers for 10 to 20 minutes, the 9-inch layers for 25 to 30 minutes, and the 12-inch layers for 40 to 50 minutes.

To select filling and frosting for a wedding cake, first, keep the weather in mind. If the wedding is indoors in a climate-controlled area, the frosting options are a bit more flexible. If outdoors during a potentially warm or hot time of year, stick to buttercream. You'll need 16 cups Meringue Buttercream I or II, 796, or Quick Vanilla Butter Frosting, 792 (4 to 5 cups to fill the layers and 10 to 11 cups to frost the cake and pipe the borders). Make 5 recipes of Meringue Buttercream I or II, or 8 recipes of Quick Vanilla Butter Frosting, allowing 1 pound powdered sugar for every 2 recipes for the latter. If desired, the cake may be filled with something other than icing (in this case you will only need 11 cups frosting). Lemon Curd, 802, or Lime Curd, 802, make for a lively flavor contrast to buttercream; thick Chocolate Ganache, 797, with a thin layer of raspberry preserves adds richness and a truffle-like appeal; Salted Caramel Sauce, 809, and sliced bananas can be combined for something a little different. Any fillings that will be apt to ooze out from between the layers—like lemon curd—can be kept in place with a "dam" of icing on the outer edge of the cake layer.

To fill and crumb-coat the layers and assemble the tiers, cool the cake layers completely before assembly. Even better, chill the layers before filling and frosting. This firms the cakes, making them easier to move and frost. Slide a cookie sheet under large cake layers to move them without cracking. If the layers are not flat, or if the top crust is tough or dry, level them, 711, with a serrated knife. You will assemble each tier on cardboard cake rounds and stack them with the rounds in place, so you don't have to worry about lifting and moving them around without any support.

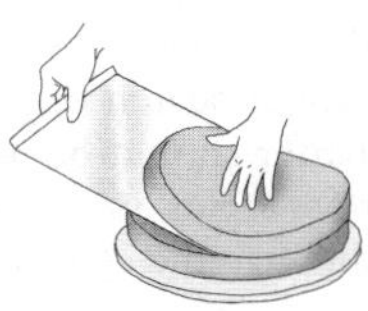

Using a cookie sheet to move large layers

To assemble the 12-inch tier, dab frosting on the center of a 12-inch cardboard cake round to keep the cake from sliding. Center one of the 12-inch layers right side up on the cardboard. Spread with 2 to 2½ cups frosting. Top with the second cake layer, upside down. Brush away any stray crumbs clinging to the top and sides of the cake. Spread a very thin crumb coat, 712, over the top and sides of the cake to cover cracks and secure crumbs. Refrigerate to set the frosting.

Assemble the 9-inch tier on a 9-inch cardboard round, filling the layers with about 1¼ cups frosting and then crumb-coating. Assemble the 6-inch tier on a 6-inch cardboard round, filling with about ⅓ cup frosting and then crumb-coating. Refrigerate or put in a cool place.

To frost the tiers, place 3 or 4 pieces of double-sided adhesive tape on the cake plate or presentation board about 4 inches in from the edges. (To make a presentation board, wrap an 18-inch plywood round with florist's foil or foil wrapping paper. Secure the foil to the underside of the board with tape.) Frost the 12-inch tier, either as smoothly as possible or with swirls using a large offset spatula. A long extra-wide spatula with a stiff blade is best for lifting and transferring tiers. Otherwise, slide a sturdy metal spatula under the tier and tilt it up so that you can slide your hands under for support. Lift the tier over the center of the plate or presentation board. Set the edge farthest from you down first, 2 inches from the edge of the plate or board. Pivot the cake to center it, if necessary, before lowering the back edge. Refrigerate or put in a cool place to set the frosting. Frost the top and sides of the other 2 tiers and refrigerate or put in a cool place. If you are transporting the cake to a venue, you may wish to transport it in tiers and assemble onsite. Take extra frosting to touch up the cake if needed.

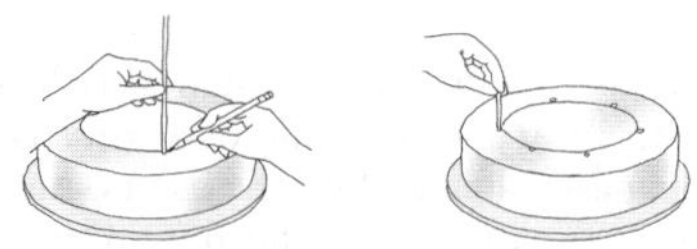

Marking the dowel at the surface of the frosting and inserting the supports into the cakes at even intervals

To stack the tiers, cut a round of wax or parchment paper 7 inches in diameter. Center it on top of the 12-inch tier. Insert a plastic drinking straw or ¼-inch wooden dowel straight down into the cake at one edge of the paper round. Mark the straw or dowel with a pencil or edible marker at the surface of the frosting, remove it, and cut at the mark to make a support. Cut 5 more identical lengths of straws or dowels. Insert the supports into the cake, evenly spaced around the perimeter of the paper round. Put a generous teaspoon of frosting in the center of the paper round.

Cut a round of wax or parchment paper 4 inches in diameter. Center it on top of the 9-inch tier. Mark and cut 4 or 5 drinking straw or dowel supports and insert them evenly around the perimeter of the paper round. Put a small dollop of frosting in the center of the paper round.

Lift the 9-inch tier with the long pancake turner or your hand and hold it centered over the paper round on the 12-inch tier. Lower the front edge (opposite you) first, with a friend guiding you if possible. Then, once the cake is lowered about an inch above the bottom tier, replace your hand and the spatula with a small offset spatula, which will be easier to remove without damaging the frosting on the lower tier; lower the tier into place. Carefully remove the offset spatula.

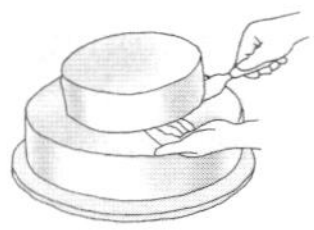

Lowering the 9-inch onto the 12-inch tier

Transfer the 6-inch tier to the center of the 9-inch tier, using the procedure described on 717. If you are transporting the cake after assembly, you may wish to "stake" it for added stability. Cut a length of ¼-inch wooden dowel slightly shorter than the height of the cake. Whittle a long sharp point on one end or use a pencil sharpener. Drive the stake straight down into the center of the cake, tapping with a hammer; use a length of dowel to help you push the support down the last inch or so. You will cover the hole later with decoration.

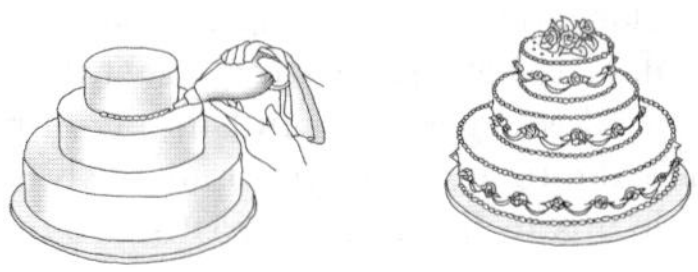

Piping frosting to cover the seams; completed wedding cake

To decorate the cake, adjust the consistency of the frosting or buttercream, 712, if necessary so that it holds a stiff shape when piped. Fit a star tip into a pastry bag and fill the bag no more than half full with buttercream or frosting. Pipe a border around the base of the top tier where it meets the tier below. Pipe a similar border to cover the seam between the 9-inch tier and the bottom tier. Refrigerate the cake to set the frosting before decorating. The cake is now ready to decorate with buttercream designs, Crystallized Flowers, 876, or edible flowers (see Fresh Flowers for Cakes, 716).

To cut the cake, whether it is round or rectangular, begin at the lowest tier. To make the cuts even in depth, run a knife vertically through the bottom tier, where it abuts the second tier. Continue this process at each tier. Cut successive slices until a cylindrical central core remains, crested by the ornate top. Remove and save the top or freeze it for the first anniversary party. Then finish slicing the central core, beginning at the top.

ABOUT TWO-PIECE CAKE MOLDS

To use a two-piece cake mold, such as a lamb, bunny, or Santa, grease the mold with vegetable shortening, using a pastry brush and being rather lavish, then dust with flour. Prepare the **batter for White Cake, 724.** Fill the face side of the mold with batter (or simply fill the pan two-thirds full if using a pan designed to clip together before filling). Any leftover batter may be used for cupcakes. If the mold has steam vents, fill the solid section with the batter to just below the joint. (Using these directions, we have baked successfully in cake molds even when they had no steam vents.) Move a long offset spatula gently through the batter to release any air bubbles; ➤ be careful not to disturb the greased and floured surface of the mold. For structural stability, you may place wooden toothpicks into the batter in any weak spots, such as ears where they join the head (with some molds, this will not be possible), ➤ but remember to remove them when you cut the cake. Put the lid on the mold, if applicable, making sure it locks, and tie or wire together so the steam of the rising batter will not force the two sections apart.

Put the mold on a rimmed baking sheet and bake for 40 minutes to 1 hour. Test as you would any cake, inserting a skewer through a steam vent or hole in the mold. Cool the cake in the mold on a rack for about 15 minutes. Carefully remove the top of the mold and let cool about 5 minutes more to allow the cake to firm up a little, then unmold and cool completely on the rack. ➤ Do not try to stand it upright until it is cool. If the cake has constitutional weaknesses, reinforce it with a wooden or metal skewer before icing. Ice with **Fluffy White Frosting, 795.** For woolly or angora effects (particularly nice for a lamb mold), press into the icing **½ to 1 cup shredded sweetened coconut.** To accentuate the features, use **raisins, nuts, cherries, and/or gumdrops.**

ABOUT ANGEL FOOD CAKES

Angel food cakes have no chemical leaveners such as baking powder or baking soda. The main sources of leavening are air and steam, so the volume of air beaten into the egg whites is of supreme importance, as is the care with which other ingredients are folded into them. See Beating Eggs, 977, for detailed information on whipping egg whites.

The choice of pan and its careful preparation are essential to good results. Choose a tube pan with a removable bottom. The central tube gives the light batter additional support during baking. ➤ Do not grease or flour the pan. A clean, dry, grease-free pan is essential for the cake to rise properly.

The egg whites should be at least 3 days old (if using store-bought eggs, this should not be an issue), at about 60°F, and separated just before use. Overbeating the whites is the single most common mistake in the production of angel food cakes. Unlike the whites in most other meringues, egg whites for angel food cakes should be beaten just short of stiff. If using a stand mixer, once the egg whites are beaten, give them a few swift strokes by hand with a whisk to incorporate any unbeaten egg whites at the bottom of the bowl. The finished batter should be just soft enough to pour into the cake pan. Cream of tartar, 975, is used to keep angel food cakes lily white and to stabilize the egg whites, helping them hold their lofty foam.

Let angel food cakes cool completely, upside down, before frosting or wrapping airtight. They keep well for 2 to 3 days. They do not freeze as well as butter cakes or other sponge cakes; ➤ avoid freezing them for more than a week.

It is best to cut an angel food cake with a special **angel food cake cutter,** which resembles a giant metal comb with several widely spaced long, thin prongs. If you do not want to purchase a single-use tool, you can simply insert 2 forks back-to-back to pry the cake gently apart. Or use a very sharp serrated knife and a gentle sawing motion to avoid compacting the tender cake. Angel food cakes are best served with fresh fruit, especially macerated strawberries, 181, and softly whipped cream. Alternatively, use angel food cake cubes in Trifle, 827, or cut the cake into fingers to use in Tiramisù, 826. Leftover angel food cake can be sliced and toasted in a little butter to revive it; or treat it like French Toast, 644.

ANGEL FOOD CAKE

One 10-inch tube cake; about 16 servings

A very tall, moist, and tender cake. ➤ For a thin sheet for roll cakes and charlottes, bake as for Cake Sheet for Roll Cakes, 746. ▲ For a high-altitude version of this cake, see 756.

Position a rack in the lower third of the oven. Preheat the oven to 350°F. Have ready a clean, dry, ungreased 10-inch angel food cake pan or tube pan.

Sift together 3 times:

1 cup sifted (100g) cake flour
¾ cup (150g) sugar
½ teaspoon salt

Combine in a large bowl or in a stand mixer with the whisk attachment and beat on low speed for 1 minute:

1½ cups (365g) egg whites (about 11 large whites) at around 60°F
1 tablespoon (15g) water
1 teaspoon cream of tartar
1 teaspoon vanilla
(¼ teaspoon almond extract)

Increase the speed to medium-high and beat until the mixture increases 4 to 5 times in volume and resembles a bowl of soft foam. (This takes anywhere from 3 to 5 minutes.) The foam will hold a very soft, moist shape when the beaters are lifted. On medium-high speed, beat in 1 tablespoon at a time, taking 2 to 3 minutes:

¾ cup (150g) sugar

When all the sugar has been added, the foam will be creamy white and hold soft, moist, glossy peaks that bend over at the points; do not beat until stiff. If the mixer bowl is nearly full, transfer the mixture to a wide 4- to 6-quart bowl for easier folding. Sift one-quarter of the flour mixture evenly over the whipped egg whites and fold gently with a silicone spatula only until the flour is almost incorporated; do not stir or mix. Repeat 3 more times, folding in the last addition until no traces of flour are visible. Pour the batter into the pan and tilt or spread to level the top. Bake until a cake tester inserted in the center comes out clean, 35 to 40 minutes.

Invert the cake immediately and cool upside down in the pan to prevent it from sinking. If using an angel food cake pan, set it on the feet of the pan to hold it above the surface of the table or if using a regular tube pan, prop it higher by resting the tube on a bottle or inverted metal funnel. Let the cake cool for at least 1½ hours, until it is thoroughly set.

Slide a thin knife around the cake to detach it from the pan. Using the same procedure, detach the cake from the center tube. If the pan has a removable bottom, pull the tube up to lift the cake from the pan sides. Slide the knife under the cake to detach it from the bottom. If the pan does not have a removable bottom, invert the pan and tap it against the counter to loosen the cake. Allow the cake to drop onto a rack or serving platter.

COFFEE ANGEL FOOD CAKE

Prepare **Angel Food Cake, above.** In a small bowl whisk together the 1 tablespoon water called for in the recipe with **1 tablespoon instant espresso powder,** and add it to the egg whites. Proceed as directed.

COCONUT ANGEL FOOD CAKE

Prepare **Angel Food Cake, above,** adding **½ teaspoon coconut extract** to the unbeaten egg whites. Fold into the batter with the last addition of flour **½ cup shredded sweetened coconut.**

LEMON OR ORANGE ANGEL FOOD CAKE

Prepare **Angel Food Cake, above.** Stir the **finely grated zest of 1 lemon or orange** into the flour mixture and substitute **1 teaspoon lemon or orange extract** for the almond extract.

CHOCOLATE ANGEL FOOD CAKE

▲ For a high-altitude version of this cake, see 757.

Prepare **Angel Food Cake, above.** Substitute **½ cup (40g) unsweetened cocoa powder, preferably Dutch-process,** for ½ cup (50g) of the sifted cake flour. If desired, dissolve in the 1 tablespoon water **(1 teaspoon instant espresso powder),** then add it to the egg whites. Fold into the batter with the last addition of cocoa and flour **2 ounces (55g) semisweet or bittersweet chocolate, finely chopped or grated.**

MARBLE ANGEL FOOD CAKE

Whisk together the flour mixture for **Angel Food Cake, above.** Transfer one-half of the flour mixture to another medium mixing bowl and whisk in **¼ cup (20g) unsweetened cocoa powder.** Set both flour mixtures aside. Beat the egg whites as directed. Once they are fully beaten and all the sugar is incorporated, transfer half the egg white mixture to a large bowl. Fold the plain flour mixture into one of the bowls of egg whites in 3 parts. Fold the flour-cocoa powder mixture into the other bowl of egg whites in 3 parts. Alternate the batters in the tube pan, either by layering the batters or by alternating blobs of each batter into the pan, and then swirling with a knife to marble.

ABOUT SPONGE CAKES

Sponge cakes are similar to angel food cakes, but the yolks and whites are beaten separately, then folded together. There are two styles of sponge cakes: American sponge cakes are sweet and moist; European sponge cakes—like French *biscuit*, 74—tend to be less sweet and a bit drier because they are usually enriched after baking with a Moistening Syrup, 800, or filling.

Since the leavening of these cakes relies largely on whipping the eggs into a stiff foam, all the suggestions for trapping air given in About Angel Food Cakes, 718, apply here—with this added admonition: Egg yolks beat to a greater volume if they are at about 70°F. An electric mixer, preferably a stand mixer with the whisk attachment, must be used to beat the egg and sugar mixtures in order to achieve proper volume. If using a stand mixer, once the egg whites are beaten, give them a few swift strokes by hand with a whisk to incorporate any unbeaten egg whites at the bottom of the bowl. ➤ Follow instructions in the recipes as to whether the pan should be greased and floured. Many of these sponge cakes require a grease-free pan—or grease-free sides, at the least—in order to rise properly.

SPONGE CAKE

One 10-inch tube cake or one 10-inch round cake; 12 to 16 servings

➤ For roll cakes, see Sponge Cake Sheet, 747. ▲ For a high-altitude version of this cake, see 758.

Have all ingredients at room temperature, about 70°F. Preheat the oven to 325°F. Have ready a clean, dry, ungreased 10-inch tube pan or a 10-inch round cake pan lined with a round of parchment paper.

Sift together:

1 cup (110g) cake flour
1½ teaspoons baking powder

Combine in a large bowl or in a stand mixer with the whisk attachment:

⅔ cup (130g) sugar
7 large egg yolks
1 teaspoon vanilla

Beat on high speed until thick and pale yellow, 2 to 3 minutes. Beat in:

2 tablespoons (30g) orange juice or water
(1 teaspoon finely grated lemon zest)
(1 teaspoon finely grated orange zest)
¼ teaspoon salt

Sift the flour mixture evenly over the top, but do not mix it in. Using clean beaters, beat in a large bowl on medium speed until soft peaks form, 977:

7 large egg whites
1 tablespoon (10g) sugar
½ teaspoon cream of tartar

Gradually add, beating on high speed:

⅓ cup (65g) sugar

Beat until the peaks are stiff but not dry, 978. Use a silicone spatula to fold one-quarter of the egg whites into the egg yolk mixture, then fold in the remaining whites. Scrape the batter into the tube pan or cake pan, and spread evenly. Bake until the top springs back when lightly pressed and a cake tester inserted into the center comes out clean, 40 to 50 minutes.

Cool and remove from the pan as for Angel Food Cake, 719.

Serve unadorned or frost with:

Fluffy White Frosting, 795, flavored with lemon or orange

or serve with:

Fresh fruit and whipped cream

PASSOVER CITRUS SPONGE CAKE

One 10-inch tube cake; 12 to 16 servings

Have all ingredients at room temperature, about 70°F. Preheat the oven to 350°F. Have ready a clean, dry, ungreased 10-inch tube pan.

Whisk together thoroughly in a medium bowl:

⅔ cup (80g) matzo meal
⅓ cup (55g) potato starch
¼ teaspoon salt

Beat in a large bowl or in a stand mixer with the whisk attachment, on high speed until thick and pale yellow, about 2 minutes:

9 large egg yolks
1 cup (200g) sugar

Beat in:

Finely grated zest of ½ orange
Finely grated zest of 1 lemon
¼ cup (60g) strained orange juice
1 tablespoon (15g) strained lemon juice

Gradually add the matzo mixture to the egg yolk mixture, beating on low speed just until smooth. Using clean beaters, beat in a large bowl on medium speed until soft peaks form, 977:

9 large egg whites
½ teaspoon cream of tartar

Gradually add, beating on high speed:

½ cup (100g) sugar

Beat until the peaks are stiff but not dry, 977. Use a silicone spatula to fold one-quarter of the egg whites into the egg yolk mixture, then fold in the remaining whites. Spoon the batter gently into the tube pan and spread evenly. Bake until the top springs back when lightly pressed and a cake tester inserted into the center comes out clean, 40 to 45 minutes.

Cool and remove from the pan as for Angel Food Cake, 719.

PASSOVER NUT SPONGE CAKE

Prepare **Passover Citrus Sponge Cake, above,** folding in with the second addition of egg whites **1 cup finely chopped or ground toasted, 1005, walnuts, pecans, or almonds.**

CHOCOLATE SPONGE CAKE

One 10-inch tube cake; 12 to 16 servings

You can cut this cake into layers, sprinkle the layers with rum or a liqueur of choice, if desired, and spread them with Whipped Ganache Filling, 803. Dust lightly with powdered sugar or frost with Whipped Cream, 791.

Have all ingredients at room temperature, about 70°F. Preheat the oven to 350°F. Have ready an ungreased 10-inch tube pan.

Sift together 2 times, then return to the sifter:

⅔ cup sifted (65g) cake flour
½ cup (40g) unsweetened Dutch-process cocoa powder
¼ teaspoon salt

Combine in a stand mixer with the whisk attachment:

6 large eggs
2 teaspoons vanilla
2 teaspoons instant espresso powder

Beat on high speed until the consistency of softly whipped cream, about 10 minutes. Gradually beat in 1 tablespoon at a time, beating for about 3 minutes in all:

1 cup (200g) sugar

Sift about one-third of the cocoa mixture over the top and fold in. Sift and fold in the remaining cocoa mixture in 2 more additions. Scrape the batter into the tube pan and spread evenly. Bake until the top springs back when lightly pressed and a cake tester inserted into the center comes out clean, about 45 minutes.

To cool and unmold, see Angel Food Cake, 719. Serve plain or with:

Whipped Cream, 791

TRES LECHES CAKE

One 9-inch square cake or one 11 × 7-inch cake; about 12 servings

This Latin American sponge cake is drenched with a sweet mixture of two types of milk and heavy cream. It is traditionally topped with sweet soft meringue; replace the meringue with whipped cream, if you prefer.

Have all ingredients at room temperature, about 70°F. Preheat the oven to 350°F. Grease a 9-inch square pan or an 11 × 7-inch baking pan.

Sift together:

1 cup (125g) all-purpose flour
2 teaspoons baking powder

Combine in a large bowl or in a stand mixer with the whisk attachment and beat on medium speed until soft peaks form, 977:

3 large egg whites
1/8 teaspoon cream of tartar

Gradually add, beating on high speed:

1 cup (200g) sugar

Beat in one at a time:

3 large egg yolks
(Finely grated zest of 1 orange)

Add one-quarter of the flour mixture at a time, beating on low speed or stirring with a silicone spatula just until incorporated and scraping the sides of the bowl as necessary. Add and beat just until the batter is smooth:

1/4 cup (60g) milk

Scrape the batter into the prepared pan and spread evenly. Bake until the top springs back when lightly pressed and a toothpick inserted into the center comes out clean, 25 to 30 minutes.

Let cool in the pan on a rack for 10 minutes.

Meanwhile, whisk together in a medium bowl:

3/4 cup (185g) evaporated milk
3/4 cup (228g) sweetened condensed milk
1/2 cup (115g) heavy cream
(2 tablespoons dark rum)

Leaving the cake in the pan, prick it with a toothpick at 1-inch intervals. Pour the milk mixture slowly over the cake, including the edges and the corners. Let cool, then refrigerate for at least 1 hour, or overnight, before serving.

For the topping, prepare:

Soft Meringue Topping I or II, 795

To serve, leave the cake in the pan or slide a slim knife around the cake to detach it from the pan, and invert the cake onto a large shallow serving platter with enough of a rim to hold the excess milk that will gradually collect around the cake like a sauce. Spread or pipe the meringue topping over the cake. Cut into squares to serve. Refrigerate any leftovers and eat within 24 hours.

FRENCH SPONGE CAKE (BISCUIT)

Two 9-inch round layers or one 10-inch round cake

Biscuit (bee-SKWEE) is a classic air-leavened sponge cake used to make the fancy European-style layered cakes called tortes. This light, dry-textured cake is meant to be soaked with syrups before being filled with buttercream, mousse, or other filling. This recipe yields two 1-inch layers or one 2-inch layer that can be sliced into 2 or 3 thin layers. ➤ To make a thin sheet for roll cakes and charlottes, bake as for Cake Sheet for Roll Cakes, 746.

Have all ingredients at room temperature, about 70°F. Preheat the oven to 325°F. Grease and flour the bottom(s) of two 9 × 2-inch round cake pans or one 10-inch springform pan. Line the bottom(s) with rounds of parchment paper.

Measure and return to the sifter:

1 cup plus 2 tablespoons sifted (115g) cake flour

Combine in a large bowl or in a stand mixer with the whisk and beat on high speed until thick and pale yellow, 2 to 3 minutes:

6 large egg yolks
1/4 cup (50g) sugar
1 teaspoon vanilla

Sift the flour evenly over the top but do not mix it in. Using clean beaters, beat in another large bowl on medium speed until soft peaks form, 977:

6 large egg whites
1/4 teaspoon cream of tartar

Gradually add, beating on high speed:

1/3 cup (65g) sugar

Beat until the peaks are stiff but not dry, 978. Use a silicone spatula to fold one-third of the egg whites not quite thoroughly into the egg yolk mixture. Fold in the remaining whites in 2 additions. Scrape the batter into the pan(s) and spread evenly. Bake until the top springs back when lightly pressed and a toothpick inserted into the center comes out clean, 20 to 25 minutes in cake pans, 35 to 40 minutes in a springform pan.

Let cool in the pan(s) on a rack for 10 minutes. Slide a thin knife around the cake to detach it from the pan(s); remove the ring of the springform pan, if using. Invert the cake and remove the paper liner(s). Let cool right side up on the rack.

GÉNOISE

Two 9-inch layers or one 9-inch round cake

Enriched with a little butter, this is a rich, moist cake of Italian origin, and has no equal for versatility—excellent with fruit fillings, as a roll cake with cream fillings, or as a foil for a simple glaze or fresh fruit. This recipe makes two 1-inch layers or one 2-inch layer that can be split into 3 or 4 thin layers. Clarified butter, 960, gives a superior result, but regular butter will do. You'll need to begin with a bit more butter to get the 5 1/3 tablespoons needed if you choose to clarify it. ➤ To make a thin sheet for roll cakes and charlottes, bake as for Cake Sheet for Roll Cakes, 746.

Have all ingredients at room temperature, about 70°F. Preheat the oven to 350°F. Grease and flour the bottom(s) of two 9 × 2-inch round cake pans or one 9-inch springform pan and line the bottom(s) with rounds of parchment paper.
Sift together 3 times and return to the sifter:

1¼ cups sifted (125g) cake flour
¼ cup (50g) sugar

Melt in a small saucepan:

5⅓ tablespoons (75g) unsalted butter, preferably clarified, 960

Set aside. Whisk together in a large heatproof bowl or a stand mixer bowl:

6 large eggs
¾ cup (150g) sugar

Set the bowl in a skillet of barely simmering water and whisk constantly until the mixture is warm to the touch (about 110°F). Remove the bowl from the heat and beat on high speed with a hand mixer, or in a stand mixer with the whisk attachment, until the mixture is lemon colored, has tripled in volume, and has reached the stage known as **au ruban**—like a continuous flat ribbon when dropped from a spoon (about 5 minutes in a stand mixer, 10 to 15 minutes with a handheld mixer). In 3 additions, sift the flour mixture over the top and fold in very gently with a silicone spatula. Reheat the butter until it is hot and transfer to a medium bowl. Fold about 1½ cups of the egg mixture into the butter until completely incorporated, along with:

1 teaspoon vanilla

Scrape the mixture onto the remaining egg mixture and fold in. Scrape the batter into the pan(s) and spread evenly. Bake until the cake begins to pull away from the sides of the pan(s) and the top springs back when lightly pressed, about 15 minutes in cake pans, 30 minutes in a springform pan.

Let cool in the pan(s) on a rack for 10 minutes. Slide a thin knife around the cake to detach it from the pan(s); remove the ring of the springform pan, if using. Invert the cake and remove the paper liner(s). Let cool right side up on the rack.

CHOCOLATE GÉNOISE

Prepare **Génoise, 721,** reducing the flour to ½ cup plus 1 tablespoon sifted (105g) cake flour. Sift it together 3 times with **½ cup plus 1 tablespoon (45g) unsweetened cocoa powder** and return to the sifter. Do not sift any of the sugar with the flour mixture; instead, whisk together all the sugar (1 cup total or 200g) with the eggs. Proceed as directed.

ABOUT CHIFFON CAKES

With a very light, fluffy, and tender texture, chiffon cakes are less sweet than angel food cakes and moister than sponge cakes. They are also the easiest type of foam cake to master, with a little less drama than angel food cakes but a reliably light, tender crumb. Chiffon cakes contain oil instead of butter. Whipped egg whites and baking powder and/or soda provide leavening. Egg yolks add richness and a little color to the batter.

In theory any oil may be used in sponge cakes. While the neutral-tasting vegetable oils are often preferred, more pronounced oils can be added for a subtle flavor boost. Try a grassy extra-virgin olive oil, or mildly nutty walnut oil or pistachio oil. While it is tempting, do not substitute melted butter, shortening, or coconut oil for the oil. Since oil does not contribute flavor the way butter does, chiffon cakes are often flavored with tangy citrus juice and zest, spices, chocolate or cocoa, or toasted nuts. Customize these cakes by varying the spices, extracts, and citrus zest, changing the liquid from water to fruit juice or coffee, or adding finely chopped nuts or miniature chocolate chips.

➤ Do not grease or flour the pan. A clean, dry, grease-free pan is essential for the cake to rise properly. Remove chiffon cakes from the pan as you would Angel Food Cake, 719. All chiffon cakes can be served with a simple dusting of powdered sugar, or drizzle with a citrus or liquor-flavored sugar glaze (see Quick Translucent Sugar Glazes, 799). Oil keeps chiffon cakes soft even when refrigerated, tender even when frozen. Thus, a chiffon cake is a good choice for filling or layering with ice cream: Slice a chiffon cake horizontally into 3 layers and fill with softened ice cream, sorbet, or frozen yogurt. Refreeze for at least several hours, or overnight, before serving with a chocolate or fruit sauce or with whipped cream and toasted nuts.

CHIFFON CAKE

One 10-inch tube cake or 13 × 9-inch cake; 12 to 16 servings

➤ To make a thin sheet for roll cakes and charlottes, bake as for Cake Sheet for Roll Cakes, 746.
Have all ingredients at room temperature, about 70°F. Preheat the oven to 325°F. Have ready an ungreased 10-inch tube pan or 13 × 9-inch baking pan.
Whisk together thoroughly in a large bowl:

2¼ cups sifted (225g) cake flour
1¼ cups (250g) sugar
1 tablespoon baking powder
1 teaspoon salt

Add and beat on high speed until smooth:

5 large egg yolks
¾ cup (175g) water
½ cup (105g) vegetable oil
(Finely grated zest of 1 lemon)
1 teaspoon vanilla

Using clean beaters, beat in another large bowl, or in a stand mixer with the whisk attachment, on medium speed until soft peaks form, 977:

8 large egg whites
½ teaspoon cream of tartar

Gradually add, beating on high speed:

¼ cup (50g) sugar

Beat the whites until they're so stiff they begin to lose their gloss. Use a silicone spatula to fold one-quarter of the egg whites into the egg yolk mixture, then fold in the remaining whites. Scrape the batter into the pan and spread evenly. Bake until the top springs back when lightly pressed and a toothpick inserted into the center comes out clean, 55 to 65 minutes for a tube pan or 30 to 35 minutes for a baking pan.

Cool and unmold as for Angel Food Cake, 719; rest the 13 × 9-inch pan upside down on 4 glasses.

Ice with:

Quick Lemon Frosting, 792, or Fluffy White Frosting, 795, flavored with orange

or serve with:

Fresh berries and Whipped Cream, 791

ORANGE CHIFFON CAKE

Prepare **Chiffon Cake, 722,** substituting for the water and lemon zest the **finely grated zest of 1 orange** and **3/4 cup (185g) strained orange juice.**

MOCHA CHIFFON CAKE

One 10-inch tube cake; 12 to 16 servings

Have the eggs at room temperature, about 70°F. Preheat the oven to 325°F. Have ready an ungreased 10-inch tube pan.

Whisk together in a medium bowl until smooth:

3/4 cup (175g) boiling water
1/2 cup (40g) unsweetened cocoa powder
1 tablespoon plus 1 teaspoon instant coffee or espresso powder

Let cool, then whisk in:

1/2 cup (105g) vegetable oil
5 large egg yolks
1 teaspoon vanilla

Whisk together thoroughly in a large bowl:

1 3/4 cups sifted (175g) cake flour
1 1/4 cups (250g) sugar
2 teaspoons baking powder
1/2 teaspoon salt
1/4 teaspoon baking soda

Add the cocoa mixture and whisk until smooth. Using clean beaters, beat in another large bowl, or in a stand mixer with the whisk attachment, on medium speed until soft peaks form, 977:

8 large egg whites
1/2 teaspoon cream of tartar

Gradually add, beating on high speed:

1/4 cup (50g) sugar

Beat until the peaks are very stiff, 978. Use a silicone spatula to fold one-quarter of the egg whites into the cocoa mixture, then fold in the remaining whites. Scrape the batter into the pan and spread evenly. Bake until the top springs back when lightly pressed and a toothpick inserted into the center comes out clean, 55 to 65 minutes.

Let cool and unmold as for Angel Food Cake, 719.

Ice with:

Fluffy White Frosting, 795, flavored with orange or coffee, Quick Mocha Frosting, 792, any chocolate frosting, 793, or plain or flavored Whipped Cream, 791

ABOUT BUTTER CAKES

Butter cakes are the glory of the American cake repertoire. For flavor and texture, butter is our strong preference, as it has been for generations of bakers back to the eighteenth century. Butter cake began as "pound cake," because it called for a pound each of four ingredients—butter, flour, eggs, and sugar. A lot of experience, a little imagination, and a bit of baking powder have given us lighter and more sophisticated versions of butter cakes ever since.

Because butter cakes rely on butter for both their flavor and texture ➤ it is of the utmost importance that the butter be at room temperature: 70°F (65°F in a very hot kitchen or climate) is ideal. Butter at this temperature is pliable but still cool, not melted, squishy, or greasy. Cold butter will not disperse properly in the batter; melted or oversoftened butter will lead to a greasy, heavy cake. Either extreme inhibits the formation of air bubbles during the creaming process, ultimately affecting the texture of the finished cake. See About the Temperature of Ingredients, 709.

Creaming is the crucial first step in mixing butter cakes: Butter and sugar are beaten together until they appear lighter in color, smooth, even, and fluffy. As they are mixed together, the sugar crystals cut holes in the fat; these holes, or air bubbles, are essential because they will expand with gases during baking, enabling the cake to rise. ➤ Regular granulated sugar, not powdered or superfine sugar, must be used. Well-creamed butter and sugar create the initial structure of the batter, enabling other ingredients to be added without causing that structure to collapse.

To cream by hand, mash the butter against the side of the bowl with the back of a wooden spoon, using a gliding motion and keeping the butter in a limited area of the bowl rather than spreading it all over. Scrape the mass together as necessary and repeat the gliding motion until the butter is softened. Add the sugar gradually and work the butter and sugar together until the mixture is light in color and smooth, even, and creamy in texture. It will look like sugary frosting. If it looks curdled or frothy, or begins to ooze melted butter, you have worked it too long or the butter is too warm. The result will be a coarse-grained or greasy cake. Correct the situation by refrigerating the mixture for 5 to 10 minutes before continuing to beat.

To cream with an electric mixer, beat the butter at low speed for about 30 seconds, until creamy. Add the sugar gradually and beat at medium-high speed until the mixture is light in color, smooth, even, and creamy in texture and resembles a sugary frosting. This usually requires from 3 to 10 minutes, depending on quantities and the type of mixer. For a heavy-duty mixer, use the paddle and beat on medium speed for less time, usually 4 to 7 minutes.

Room-temperature eggs are added to the creamed sugar and butter ➤ gradually to preserve the volume and avoid breaking the emulsion of the ingredients. If the eggs are added too fast, or if they are too cold, the emulsion with the butter "breaks" and the mixture looks curdled. If this happens, volume may be lost and the cake may suffer in texture (that said, cakes with this deficiency are rarely outright failures). Turning the mixer briefly to a higher speed can sometimes smooth out the batter and restore the emulsion. There is no advantage to beating the eggs any longer than it takes to incorporate them. The goal is to retain as much of the air whipped into the butter and sugar as possible.

After the eggs are incorporated, the dry ingredients are usually added in 3 parts, alternating with 2 additions of the wet ingredients. To keep the mixture as stable as possible, start and end with the dry ingredients. Use low speed to incorporate the dry and wet ingredients, and scrape the sides of the bowl frequently to ensure that the creamed butter is evenly mixed into the batter. Mix the added ingredients only enough to incorporate; ➤ overmixing during this stage can develop too much gluten in the flour, toughen the cake, and result in too fine a crumb. For this reason, some careful bakers like to mix in the dry and wet ingredients by hand with a silicone spatula. If nuts and other lumpy ingredients are to be added, fold them in lightly at the end of the mixing process.

➤ Most butter cakes that are baked in round layers can also be baked in loaf or tube pans, or as a single thick layer in a deep cake pan or springform pan. As a rule of thumb, fill loaf and tube pans two-thirds full. For a more precise strategy, measure the batter and choose an appropriate pan (or combination of pans) from the chart on page 710. ➤ Baking time will be longer than for thin layers. Loaves often take 50 to 60 minutes or longer to bake; 8 × 2- and 9 × 2-inch round pans filled two-thirds full may take 40 to 50 minutes. Cakes baked in 9- and 10-inch plain tube pans and 9-inch Bundt pans take close to 1 hour, or more. To test for doneness, insert a toothpick or skewer into the center of the cake: The toothpick should come out clean or with only a few moist crumbs adhering to it. Always check for doneness at the low end of the time range given in the recipe. The texture of cakes baked in deeper pans will be more close-grained and velvety, like moist pound cake, than those baked in thin layers. You can also bake butter cake batter in individual pans or molds, such as cupcake tins, tartlet, or madeleine pans.

WHITE CAKE

Three 8-inch round layers; 12 to 16 servings

This recipe is very forgiving in that it can be multiplied by 8 and still give as good a result as when made in the smaller quantity below. We once saw a wedding cake made from this recipe that contained 130 eggs and was big enough to serve 400 guests. See instructions under About Wedding and Other Large Cakes, 716. ▲ For a high-altitude version of this cake, see 757.

Have all ingredients at room temperature, about 70°F. Preheat the oven to 350°F. Grease and flour three 8-inch round cake pans and line the bottoms with rounds of parchment paper.

Whisk together thoroughly in a medium bowl:

3½ cups sifted (350g) cake flour
1 tablespoon plus 1 teaspoon baking powder
½ teaspoon salt

Combine in a separate bowl or liquid measuring cup:

1 cup (235g) milk
1 teaspoon vanilla

Beat in a large bowl, or in a stand mixer with the paddle attachment, until creamy:

2 sticks (8 oz or 225g) unsalted butter, softened

Gradually add and beat until light and fluffy, 3 to 5 minutes:

1⅔ cups (335g) sugar

On low speed, add the flour mixture to the batter in 3 parts, alternating them with the milk mixture in 2 parts, beating until smooth. Using clean beaters, beat in another large bowl, or in a stand mixer with the whisk attachment, on medium speed until soft peaks form, 977:

8 large egg whites
½ teaspoon cream of tartar

Gradually add, beating on high speed:

⅓ cup (65g) sugar

Beat until stiff but not dry, 978. Use a silicone spatula to fold one-quarter of the egg whites into the batter, then fold in the remaining whites. Divide the batter among the pans and spread evenly. Bake until a toothpick inserted into the center comes out clean, 15 to 20 minutes.

Cool the cakes in the pans for 10 minutes, then run a knife around the cakes and invert them onto a rack to cool completely. When cool, frost the cake with your choice of frosting, 792, buttercream, 795, or icing, 798.

CONFETTI CAKE

Prepare the batter for **White Cake, above,** folding in with the second addition of egg whites **¾ cup multicolored sprinkles** (not nonpareils; elongated rainbow sprinkles work best). Let cool. Fill and frost the cake with **a double recipe Quick Vanilla Butter Frosting, 792,** and decorate with **multicolored sprinkles.**

LEMON COCONUT LAYER CAKE

Prepare **White Cake, above.** Let cool. Fill with **Citrus Custard Filling, 802, or Lemon Curd, 802.** Cover the top and sides with **Fluffy White Frosting, 795.** Press into the frosting **1½ cups shredded sweetened coconut.**

COCONUT MILK CAKE COCKAIGNE

One 8-inch 3-layer cake; 12 to 16 servings

Have all ingredients at room temperature, about 70°F. Preheat the oven to 350°F. Grease and flour three 8-inch round cake pans and line the bottoms with rounds of parchment paper.

Whisk together in a medium bowl:

2¾ cups (345g) all-purpose flour
2 teaspoons baking powder
½ teaspoon salt

Beat in a large bowl, or in a stand mixer with the paddle attachment, until creamy:

1½ sticks (6 oz or 170g) unsalted butter, softened

Gradually add and beat until very light and fluffy, about 5 minutes:

2 cups (400g) sugar

Beat in:

1 teaspoon vanilla
(½ teaspoon coconut extract)

Beat in one at a time, scraping down the sides of the bowl after each addition:

3 large eggs

On low speed, add the flour mixture in 3 parts, alternating with:

¾ cup (180g) canned coconut milk

in 2 parts, beating just until smooth. With the last addition of flour, fold in:

¾ cup shredded unsweetened coconut

Scrape the batter into the prepared pans. Bake until a toothpick inserted in the center comes out clean, 20 to 25 minutes.

Let cool in the pans on a rack for 15 minutes, then invert the cakes onto the rack, peel off the parchment, and turn them right side up to cool completely. Spread between the layers:

Lime Curd, 802

Frost the outside of the cake with:

1½ recipes Whipped Cream, 791, or Stabilized Whipped Cream, 791

Sprinkle around the edge of the top of the cake:

½ cup flaked unsweetened coconut, toasted, 973

Refrigerate for at least 1 hour and serve within 2 days.

BUTTERMILK LAYER CAKE

One 8-inch 2-layer cake; 12 to 16 servings

Have all ingredients at room temperature, about 70°F. Preheat the oven to 350°F. Grease and flour two 8 × 2-inch round cake pans and line the bottoms with rounds of parchment paper.

Whisk together in a medium bowl until thoroughly blended:

2⅓ cups sifted (235g) cake flour
1½ teaspoons baking powder
½ teaspoon baking soda
¼ teaspoon salt

Beat in a large bowl, or in a stand mixer with the paddle attachment, until creamy:

1½ sticks (6 oz or 170g) unsalted butter, softened

Gradually add and beat on high speed until light and fluffy, 3 to 5 minutes:

1⅓ cups (265g) sugar

Whisk together, then gradually beat in, taking about 2 minutes:

3 large eggs
1 teaspoon vanilla

Beating on low speed, add the flour mixture in 3 parts, alternating with:

1 cup (245g) buttermilk

in 2 parts, beating until smooth and scraping the sides of the bowl as necessary. Divide the batter between the pans and spread evenly. Bake until a toothpick inserted into the center comes out clean, 30 to 35 minutes.

Let cool in the pans on a rack for 15 minutes, then invert the cakes onto the rack, peel off the parchment, and turn them right side up to cool completely.

Fill and frost with:

Chocolate Satin Frosting, 793, Chocolate Mousse Frosting, 793, or a double recipe Chocolate Sour Cream Frosting, 793

RED VELVET CAKE

One 8-inch 2-layer cake; 12 to 16 servings

This smooth and rich chocolaty cake has a distinctive red color. Prepare **Buttermilk Layer Cake, above.** Add to the flour mixture **1 tablespoon (10g) unsweetened cocoa powder.** Add **1 to 3 tablespoons red food coloring** with the first addition of buttermilk. Fill and frost with a **double recipe Cream Cheese Frosting, 792.**

FOUR-EGG YELLOW CAKE

Three 8- or 9-inch round layers; about 16 servings

▲ For a high-altitude version of this cake, see 756.

Have all ingredients at room temperature, about 70°F. Preheat the oven to 350°F. Grease and flour three 8- or 9-inch round cake pans and line the bottoms with rounds of parchment paper.

Whisk together well in a medium bowl:

2⅔ cups sifted (265g) cake flour
2¼ teaspoons baking powder
½ teaspoon salt

Combine in another bowl or in a liquid measuring cup:

1 cup (235g) milk
1½ teaspoons vanilla

Beat in a large bowl, or in a stand mixer with the paddle attachment, until creamy.

2 sticks (8 oz or 225g) unsalted butter, softened

Gradually add and beat on high speed until light, 3 to 5 minutes:

1¾ cups (350g) sugar

Beat in one at a time:

4 large eggs

On low speed, add the flour mixture in 3 parts, alternating with the milk mixture in 2 parts, beating until smooth. Divide the batter among the pans and spread evenly. Bake until a toothpick inserted into the center comes out clean, 25 to 30 minutes.

Let cool in the pans on a rack for 15 minutes, then invert the cakes onto the rack, peel off the parchment, and turn them right side up to cool completely. Fill, 801, and frost, 792, as desired.

EIGHT-YOLK GOLD CAKE

One 9-inch 3-layer cake; about 16 servings

Nicely complemented by any orange or chocolate filling or frosting.

Have all ingredients at room temperature, about 70°F. Preheat the oven to 350°F. Grease and flour three 9-inch round cake pans and line the bottoms with rounds of parchment paper.

Whisk together thoroughly in a medium bowl:

2½ cups sifted (250g) cake flour
2½ teaspoons baking powder
¼ teaspoon salt

Whisk together in a small bowl:

8 large egg yolks
2 teaspoons vanilla

Beat in a large bowl, or in a stand mixer with the paddle attachment, until creamy:

1½ sticks (6 oz or 170g) unsalted butter, softened

Gradually add and beat on high speed until light and fluffy, 3 to 5 minutes:

1¼ cups (250g) sugar

Beat in the yolk mixture. On low speed, add the flour mixture in 3 parts, alternating with:

¾ cup (175g) milk

in 2 parts, beating until smooth. Divide the batter among the pans and spread evenly. Bake until a toothpick inserted into the center comes out clean, 18 to 20 minutes.

Let cool in the pans on a rack for 15 minutes, then invert the cakes onto the rack, peel off the parchment, and turn them right side up to cool completely.

Fill and frost with:

Chocolate Fudge Frosting, 792, Chocolate Cream Cheese Frosting, 792, Chocolate Satin Frosting, 793, or Chocolate Sour Cream Frosting, 793

FRESH FRUIT KUCHEN

One 9-inch round cake; about 12 servings

Position a rack in the lower third of the oven. Preheat the oven to 350°F. Grease a 9-inch springform pan and line the bottom with a round of parchment paper.

Prepare and set aside:

Streusel, 800

Spread evenly in the pan:

1 pound peaches, nectarines, apricots, or plums, pitted and sliced; cherries, pitted and halved; or raspberries or blueberries (about 3 cups)

Whisk together in a medium bowl:

1 cup (125g) all-purpose flour
1½ teaspoons baking powder
¼ teaspoon salt

Beat in a large bowl, or in a stand mixer with the paddle attachment, until fluffy:

1 stick (4 oz or 115g) unsalted butter, softened
¾ cup (150g) sugar
(Finely grated zest of 1 lemon)
1 teaspoon vanilla or ½ teaspoon almond extract

Beat in one at a time just until blended:

2 large eggs

Stir in the flour mixture just until incorporated. Scrape the batter into the pan and spread evenly. Scatter the streusel on top. Bake until the topping is golden brown and a toothpick inserted in the center of the cake comes out clean, 40 to 45 minutes.

Let cool in the pan on a rack for 15 minutes, then remove the pan ring and let cool completely.

POPPY SEED CUSTARD CAKE COCKAIGNE

One 9-inch 2-layer cake; 12 to 16 servings

Have all ingredients at room temperature, about 70°F.

Combine in a small bowl and soak for 2 hours:

1 cup (235g) milk
⅔ cup poppy seeds
1 teaspoon vanilla

Preheat the oven to 350°F. Grease and flour two 9-inch round cake pans and line the bottoms with rounds of parchment paper.

Whisk together thoroughly in a medium bowl:

2 cups sifted (200g) cake flour
2½ teaspoons baking powder
½ teaspoon salt

Beat in a large bowl, or in a stand mixer with the paddle attachment, until creamy:

1 stick plus 3 tablespoons (5½ oz or 160g) unsalted butter, softened

Beat in:

1½ cups (300g) sugar

Beat until light and fluffy, scraping down the sides of the bowl a few times during mixing, about 5 minutes. Beat in one at a time until combined, scraping down the sides of the bowl frequently:

3 large eggs

Add the flour mixture in 3 parts, alternating with the milk mixture in 2 parts, scraping down the sides of the bowl after each addition. Beat until just combined. Scrape the batter into the prepared pans. Bake until a toothpick inserted in the center comes out clean, 15 to 20 minutes.

Let cool in the pans on a rack for 10 minutes, then invert the cakes onto the rack, peel off the parchment, and turn them right side up to cool completely. Spread between the layers:

Citrus Custard Filling, 802

Dust the top with:

Powdered sugar

POUND CAKE

Two 9 × 5-inch loaves or one 10-inch tube cake; about 16 servings

Have all ingredients at room temperature, about 70°F. Preheat the oven to 325°F. Grease and flour two 9 × 5-inch loaf pans or one 10-inch tube pan.

Beat in a large bowl, or in a stand mixer with the paddle attachment, at medium-high speed for 1 minute:

4 sticks (1 lb or 455g) unsalted butter, softened

Gradually add and beat until light, 5 to 7 minutes:

2 cups (400g) sugar

Beat in one at a time, beating well after each addition:

8 large eggs

Beat in:

2 teaspoons vanilla

On low speed, add slowly, mixing only until thoroughly blended:

4 cups sifted (400g) cake flour
½ teaspoon salt

Scrape the batter into the pan(s). Bake until a toothpick inserted into the center comes out clean, about 1 hour for loaf pans, about 15 minutes longer for a tube pan.

Let loaves cool in the pans on a rack for 10 minutes, a tube cake for 15 minutes. Turn the cake(s) out of the pan(s). Turn loaves right side up to cool. Let a tube cake cool upside down.

LIQUOR-SOAKED POUND CAKE

Prepare **Pound Cake, above,** as 9 × 5-inch loaves. While the cakes are baking, combine in a medium saucepan **2⅔ cups (330g) sugar** and **1⅓ cups (315g) water.** Bring to a boil over medium heat, stirring until the sugar dissolves. Boil for 1 minute, let cool until just warm, then stir in **1⅓ cups dark rum, brandy, or bourbon.** Poke holes halfway through the warm cakes with a skewer, spacing ½ inch apart. Pour the syrup over the cakes and let cool completely before removing from the pans.

MIMOSA POUND CAKE

One 9- or 10-inch Bundt cake; about 16 servings

We have always wondered what those tiny bottles of sparkling wine are for. The answer came to us when Megan developed the recipe for this meltingly tender cake.

Have all ingredients at room temperature, about 70°F. Preheat the oven to 325°F. Grease and flour a 9- or 10-inch Bundt pan.

Beat in a large bowl, or in a stand mixer with the paddle attachment, until smooth:

2 sticks (8 oz or 225g) unsalted butter, softened
½ cup (95g) vegetable shortening
Finely grated zest of 1 orange
(1 teaspoon orange extract)
1 teaspoon vanilla
½ teaspoon salt

Add and cream until very fluffy, 5 to 7 minutes:

3 cups (600g) sugar

Add one at a time, beating until combined:

5 large eggs

Add in 3 parts:

3 cups cake (330g) or pastry flour (360g)

alternating with, in 2 parts:

1 cup sparkling wine, poured and settled

Beat until just combined. Scrape the batter into the prepared pan and bake until a skewer inserted in the center comes out with moist crumbs attached, about 1 hour 10 minutes.

Let the cake cool in the pan for 10 minutes. Unmold onto a rack to cool completely.

Meanwhile, to prepare the glaze, beat together in a medium bowl:

3 cups (300g) powdered sugar, sifted
Finely grated zest of 2 oranges
¼ to ⅓ cup sparkling wine, or enough to reach a thick but pourable consistency

Place a piece of parchment paper under the rack the cake is sitting on. Pour the glaze over the cake. Let set for 10 minutes.

CHOCOLATE POUND CAKE

Two 9 × 5-inch loaves or one 9- or 10-inch tube cake; about 16 servings

Have all ingredients at room temperature, about 70°F. Preheat the oven to 325°F.

Mix together into a paste in a small bowl:

2 tablespoons (30g) unsalted butter, softened
2 tablespoons (10g) cocoa powder

Use this mixture to grease two 9 × 5-inch loaf pans or one 9- or 10-inch tube pan. Whisk together in a medium bowl:

2½ cups sifted (250g) cake flour
¾ cup (60g) unsweetened natural or Dutch-process cocoa powder
1 teaspoon salt

Set aside. Have ready:

8 ounces (225g) bittersweet chocolate, melted, 972, and cooled to about 80°F

Beat in a large bowl, or in a stand mixer with the paddle attachment, until creamy:

3 sticks (12 oz or 340g) unsalted butter, softened

Gradually add and beat until light and fluffy, 5 to 7 minutes:

2¼ cups (450g) sugar

Beat in:

2 teaspoons vanilla

Beat in the melted chocolate until combined. Beat in one at a time until combined, scraping down the sides of the bowl frequently:

8 large eggs

Gently mix in the flour mixture in 3 parts, alternating with:

1 cup (240g) sour cream

in 2 parts. Mix just until combined. Scrape the batter into the prepared pan(s). Bake until a toothpick inserted in the center comes out clean, about 1 hour for the loaf pans, about 15 minutes longer for the tube pan.

Let loaves cool in the pans on a rack for 10 minutes; a tube pan for 15 minutes. Turn the cake(s) out of the pan(s). Turn loaves right side up to cool. Let a tube cake cool upside down.

LEMON–POPPY SEED POUND CAKE

One 9 × 5-inch loaf; about 8 servings

This beautiful pound cake is from cake maven Rose Levy Beranbaum.

Have all ingredients at room temperature, about 70°F. Preheat the oven to 350°F. Grease and flour a 9 × 5-inch loaf pan.

Whisk together thoroughly in a large bowl, or in a stand mixer with the paddle attachment:

1½ cups sifted (150g) cake flour
¾ cup (150g) sugar
3 tablespoons poppy seeds
Finely grated zest of 2 lemons
¾ teaspoon baking powder
¼ teaspoon salt

Whisk together thoroughly in a medium bowl:

3 large eggs
3 tablespoons (45g) milk
1½ teaspoons vanilla

Add half of the egg mixture to the flour mixture along with:

1 stick plus 5 tablespoons (6½ oz or 185g) unsalted butter, softened

Beat on low speed until the dry ingredients are moistened. Increase the speed to high and beat for exactly 1 minute. Scrape the sides of the bowl. Gradually add the remaining egg mixture in 2 parts, beating for 20 seconds after each addition. Scrape the sides of the bowl. Scrape the batter into the pan and spread evenly. Bake until a toothpick inserted into the center comes out clean, 55 to 65 minutes.

Shortly before the cake is done, combine in a small saucepan and stir over low heat until the sugar is dissolved:

⅓ cup (65g) sugar
¼ cup (60g) lemon juice

As soon as the cake comes out of the oven, place the pan on a rack, poke the cake all over with a wooden skewer, and brush it with half of the syrup. Let cool in the pan on the rack for 10 minutes.

Slide a slim knife around the cake to detach it from the pan. Invert onto the rack. Poke the bottom of the cake with the skewer and brush with some of the syrup. Turn on one side and brush with half of the remaining syrup, then turn on the other side and brush with the remaining syrup. Let cool completely, then wrap airtight and store for at least 24 hours before serving.

SOUR CREAM POUND CAKE

One 10-inch Bundt or one 9-inch tube cake; about 16 servings

This rich, golden cake stays moist for close to a week.

Have all ingredients at room temperature, about 70°F. Preheat the oven to 325°F. Grease and flour a 10-inch Bundt pan or 9-inch plain tube pan.

Whisk together in a medium bowl until thoroughly blended:

3 cups sifted (300g) cake flour
¼ teaspoon baking soda
¼ teaspoon salt

Combine in a small bowl:

1 cup (240g) sour cream
2 teaspoons vanilla

Beat in a large bowl, or in a stand mixer with the paddle attachment, until creamy:

2 sticks (8 oz or 225g) unsalted butter, softened

Gradually add and beat on high speed until light and fluffy, 3 to 5 minutes:

2½ cups (500g) sugar

Beat in one at a time:

6 large eggs

On low speed, add the flour mixture in 3 parts, alternating with the sour cream mixture in 2 parts, beating until smooth and scraping the sides of the bowl with a silicone spatula as necessary. Scrape the batter into the prepared pan and spread evenly. Bake until a toothpick inserted into the center comes out clean, 70 to 80 minutes.

Let cool in the pan on a rack for 10 minutes. Slide a thin knife around the cake to detach it from the pan, invert the cake, and let cool completely.

THE ROMBAUER SPECIAL CHOCOLATE CAKE

One 13 × 9-inch cake; 16 to 20 servings

Dating back to the 1931 edition of *Joy*, this was Irma's go-to recipe for family birthdays. It is a light chocolate sheet cake by today's standards, but pleasing nonetheless and made elegant with a coating of marshmallow-like frosting.

Have all ingredients at room temperature, about 70°F. Preheat the oven to 350°F. Grease a 13 × 9-inch pan.

Whisk together thoroughly in a medium bowl:

1¾ cups sifted (175g) cake flour
1 tablespoon baking powder
½ teaspoon salt
(1 teaspoon ground cinnamon)
(¼ teaspoon ground cloves)
(1 cup coarsely chopped toasted, 1005, walnuts or pecans)

Melt in a double boiler or heatproof bowl over a pan of barely simmering water:

2 ounces (55g) unsweetened chocolate, finely chopped

Whisk into the melted chocolate:

⅓ cup (80g) boiling water

Beat in a large bowl, or in a stand mixer with the paddle attachment, on high speed until creamy:

1 stick (4 oz or 115g) unsalted butter, softened

Add and beat until light and fluffy, about 5 minutes:

1½ cups (300g) sugar
1 teaspoon vanilla

Beat in, one at a time:

4 large eggs

Add the cooled chocolate mixture. Beating on low speed, add the flour mixture to the butter mixture in 3 parts, alternating with:

½ cup (120g) milk

in 2 parts. Beat the batter until smooth after each addition, scraping down the sides of the bowl a few times. Scrape the batter into the prepared pan and bake until a cake tester inserted in the center comes out clean, about 30 minutes.

Let the cake cool in the pan on a rack.

When cool, spread with:

Fluffy White Frosting, 795

Drizzle over the frosting:

4 ounces (115g) semisweet or bittersweet chocolate, melted, 972, and cooled

DEVIL'S FOOD CAKE COCKAIGNE

One 9-inch 2-layer cake; 12 to 16 servings

Have all ingredients at room temperature, about 70°F. Preheat the oven to 350°F. Grease and flour two 9-inch round cake pans and line the bottoms with rounds of parchment paper. ▲ For a high-altitude chocolate cake, see 757.

Melt in a double boiler or heatproof bowl set over a pan of barely simmering water:

4 ounces (115g) semisweet or bittersweet chocolate, chopped

Sift together in a medium bowl:

1½ cups (190g) all-purpose flour
½ cup (40g) unsweetened cocoa powder
1 teaspoon baking soda
¾ teaspoon salt

Combine in a measuring cup:

1 cup (245g) buttermilk
¼ cup (60g) brewed coffee

Beat in a large bowl, or in a stand mixer with the paddle attachment, until creamy:

2 sticks (8 oz or 225g) unsalted butter, softened

Add and beat until very fluffy, about 5 minutes:

1 cup (200g) sugar
½ cup packed (115g) brown sugar

Scrape down the sides of the bowl and add:

1 teaspoon vanilla

Add one at a time until fully combined:

3 large eggs

Scrape down the sides of the bowl. On low speed, add the flour mixture to the butter-sugar mixture in 3 parts, alternating with the milk mixture in 2 parts, beating until smooth. Fold in the melted chocolate. Scrape the batter into the prepared pans, smoothing the top. Bake until a toothpick inserted into the center comes out clean, 25 to 30 minutes.

Let cool in the pans on a rack for 10 minutes. Invert the cakes onto the rack, peel off the parchment, and turn right side up to cool completely.

Fill and frost with:

Double recipe Quick Chocolate Butter Icing, 799, Peanut Butter Frosting, 792, or Chocolate Mousse Frosting, 793

CHOCOLATE COCONUT ICEBOX CAKE

One 9-inch 4-layer cake; 16 servings

This tall cake is a tour de force, based on one made by Megan's grandmother.

Prepare and bake as 4 layers:

Double recipe Devil's Food Cake Cockaigne, 728

Let the cakes cool completely. Have ready:

Triple recipe Whipped Cream, 791, or Whipped Crème Fraîche, 791

4 cups shredded sweetened coconut

Cut each chocolate cake layer horizontally in half, 711, to make 8 thin layers. Set aside 3½ cups of the whipped cream for frosting the cake and 2¼ cups coconut for decorating the outside of the cake. Place one layer on a serving platter and top with a thin layer of whipped cream and ¼ cup coconut. Repeat with the remaining layers. After placing the final layer on top, frost the top and sides of the cake with the reserved whipped cream, and press the reserved coconut into the whipped cream all over the cake. Cover and refrigerate for at least 8 hours and up to 24 hours. Let sit at room temperature for 30 minutes before serving.

CHOCOLATE BLACKOUT CAKE

One 9-inch 3-layer cake; about 16 servings

This is the ultimate chocolate cake, made with layers of devil's food cake, chocolate pudding, and ganache. Make it at your own peril.

Prepare, substituting **Dutch-process cocoa powder** for the regular cocoa powder and using **2 teaspoons baking powder** instead of baking soda:

Devil's Food Cake Cockaigne, 728

Let the cakes cool completely.

Prepare:

Old-Fashioned Chocolate Pudding, 817, using Dutch-process instead of regular cocoa powder

Transfer the pudding to a bowl, place plastic wrap directly on the surface of the pudding, and refrigerate until completely cooled and set, at least 4 hours.

Prepare:

Chocolate Ganache, 797

When the chocolate is melted, whisk in:

½ cup (120g) sour cream

3 tablespoons (45g) butter, cut into small cubes

Let the ganache stand until spreadable and no longer runny.

To assemble the cake, use a serrated knife or dental floss to cut the cake layers in half horizontally, 711. Crumble one layer into fine crumbs and reserve. Place one of the remaining layers on a plate or cake stand. Top with half the pudding, spreading it to the edge. Top with a second cake layer, then spread the remaining pudding over it. Top with the last cake layer. Frost the top and sides of the cake with the cooled ganache. Press the crumbs from the crumbled cake layer into the sides and top of the cake. Serve immediately or refrigerate up to 1 day. Keep any leftovers refrigerated.

CHOCOLATE MAYONNAISE CAKE

One 13 × 9-inch cake or one 9-inch 2-layer cake; 16 to 20 servings

Have all ingredients at room temperature, about 70°F. Preheat the oven to 350°F. Grease and flour a 13 × 9-inch pan or two 9-inch round cake pans, and line the bottoms with parchment paper.

Whisk together in a medium bowl:

2 cups (250g) all-purpose flour

1 teaspoon baking soda

½ teaspoon baking powder

Melt in a double boiler or heatproof bowl set over barely simmering water:

4 ounces (115g) unsweetened chocolate, finely chopped

Set aside to cool slightly. Beat in a large bowl, or in a stand mixer with the paddle attachment, at medium-high speed until light, about 3 minutes:

1⅔ cups (330g) sugar

3 large eggs

1 teaspoon vanilla

Add to the melted chocolate, mixing until smooth:

¾ cup mayonnaise

Beat the chocolate-mayonnaise mixture into the batter. On low speed, add the flour mixture in 3 parts, alternating with:

1⅓ cups (315g) water

in 2 parts, beating until smooth. Scrape the batter into the prepared pan(s). Bake until a toothpick inserted in the center comes out clean, 30 to 40 minutes.

Let the 13 × 9-inch cake cool in the pan on a rack. For round layers, let cool in the pans on a rack for 10 minutes, then remove from the pans, peel off the parchment, and let cool on the rack.

Fill and frost with:

3 cups any chocolate frosting, 793

SOURDOUGH CHOCOLATE CAKE

One 9-inch cake; about 12 servings

A great way to use up extra sourdough starter. We love this extra tall single-layer cake simply dusted with powdered sugar, but it can be frosted or cut into layers, then filled and frosted.

Have all ingredients at room temperature, about 70°F. Preheat the oven to 350°F. Coat a 9-inch springform pan with cooking spray and line the bottom with a round of parchment paper.

Whisk together in a medium bowl:

1½ cups (190g) all-purpose flour

¼ cup (20g) unsweetened cocoa powder

1 teaspoon baking soda

½ teaspoon salt

Beat in a large bowl, or in a stand mixer with the paddle attachment, until light and fluffy, about 5 minutes:

6 tablespoons (3 oz or 85g) unsalted butter, softened
1 cup (200g) sugar

Beat in one at a time just until combined:

2 large eggs

Whisk together in a medium bowl:

1 cup liquid Sourdough Starter, 609
¾ cup (175g) milk
4 ounces (115g) semisweet chocolate, melted, 972, and slightly cooled
1 teaspoon vanilla

Add the flour mixture to the butter in 3 parts, alternating with the sourdough mixture in 2 parts, mixing until just combined and scraping down the sides of the bowl several times. Scrape into the prepared pan and bake until a toothpick inserted in the center comes out clean, about 40 minutes.

Let cool in the pan for 15 minutes. Run a thin knife around the inside of the pan to loosen the cake, then remove the pan ring. Cool the cake completely, then transfer to a serving platter. Before serving, dust with:

Powdered sugar

GERMAN CHOCOLATE CAKE

One 8- or 9-inch 3-layer cake; 12 to 16 servings

This well-loved American cake is so-named because it was originally made with a specific type of sweet chocolate invented by a man named German.

Have all ingredients at room temperature, about 70°F. Preheat the oven to 350°F. Grease and flour three 8- or 9-inch round cake pans and line the bottoms with rounds of parchment paper.

Whisk together in a medium bowl until thoroughly blended:

2¼ cups sifted (225g) cake flour
1 teaspoon baking soda
½ teaspoon salt

Combine in a small bowl and stir until the chocolate is melted and smooth:

4 ounces (115g) semisweet or bittersweet chocolate, finely chopped
½ cup (120g) boiling water

Stir in:

1 teaspoon vanilla

Beat in a large bowl, or in a stand mixer with the paddle attachment, until creamy, about 30 seconds:

2 sticks (8 oz or 225g) unsalted butter, softened

Gradually add and beat on high speed until light and fluffy, 4 to 6 minutes:

2 cups (400g) sugar

Beat in one at a time:

4 large eggs

On low speed, add the melted chocolate to the butter-sugar mixture and beat just until incorporated. Add the flour mixture in 3 parts, alternating with:

1 cup buttermilk (245g) or sour cream (240g)

in 2 parts, beating until smooth and scraping the sides of the bowl with a silicone spatula as necessary. Divide the batter among the pans and spread evenly. Bake until a toothpick inserted into the center comes out clean, 25 to 35 minutes.

Let cool in the pans on a rack for 10 minutes. Invert the cakes onto a rack, peel off the parchment, and turn right side up to cool completely.

Spread between the layers and on the top, leaving the sides bare:

Coconut-Pecan Filling, 803

MARZIPAN CAKE

One 8-inch cake; 8 to 12 servings

The crunchy almond topping is all the decoration this cake needs. Serve with fresh fruit or Fresh Berry Coulis, 805, made with raspberries.

Have all ingredients at room temperature, about 70°F. Preheat the oven to 325°F.

Toast on a rimmed baking sheet until lightly browned, 8 to 10 minutes:

⅔ cup sliced almonds

Let cool. (Leave the oven on.) Grease an 8-inch round cake pan liberally with:

2 tablespoons (30g) unsalted butter, softened

Line the bottom of the pan with a round of parchment paper and butter the parchment as well. Press the toasted nuts into the butter on the bottom and sides of the pan. Sprinkle evenly with:

1 tablespoon (10g) sugar

Crumble into a large bowl, or a stand mixer with the paddle attachment:

7 to 8 ounces (200 to 225g) Almond Paste, 873, or marzipan

Add and beat in until soft and well blended:

6 tablespoons (3 oz or 85g) unsalted butter, softened

Gradually add and beat on high speed until light, 2 to 3 minutes:

½ cup (100g) sugar

Whisk together in a small bowl:

3 large eggs
(1 tablespoon kirsch or brandy)
¼ teaspoon almond extract

Gradually beat the egg mixture into the butter-sugar mixture just until combined. Whisk together in another small bowl:

⅓ cup (40g) all-purpose flour
¼ teaspoon baking powder
¼ teaspoon salt

Add to the butter mixture and mix in just until combined. Scrape the batter into the prepared pan and bake until a toothpick inserted into the center comes out clean, 35 to 40 minutes.

Let cool in the pan on a rack for 10 minutes. Run a thin knife around the cake to loosen it from the pan, then invert the cake onto the rack. Peel off the parchment paper and cool completely.

VELVET SPICE BUNDT CAKE

One 8- or 9-inch Bundt cake; 12 to 16 servings

This cake has a very delicate, moist crumb. Its flavor is unequaled among spice cakes.

Have all ingredients at room temperature, about 70°F. Preheat the oven to 350°F. Grease and flour an 8- or 9-inch Bundt pan.

Whisk together in a medium bowl until thoroughly blended:

2⅓ cups sifted (235g) cake flour
1½ teaspoons baking powder
1 teaspoon grated or ground nutmeg
1 teaspoon ground cinnamon
½ teaspoon baking soda
½ teaspoon ground cloves
½ teaspoon salt

Beat in a large bowl, or in a stand mixer with the paddle attachment, until creamy, about 30 seconds:

1½ sticks (6 oz or 170g) unsalted butter, softened

Gradually add and beat on high speed until light and fluffy, 2 to 4 minutes:

1½ cups packed (345g) brown sugar
(Finely grated zest of 1 orange)

Beat in one at a time:

3 large eggs

On low speed, add the flour mixture in 3 parts, alternating with:

¾ cup plus 2 tablespoons plain yogurt (210g) or buttermilk (215g)

in 2 parts, beating until smooth and scraping the sides of the bowl with a silicone spatula as necessary. Scrape the batter into the pan and spread evenly. Bake until a toothpick inserted into the center comes out clean, 45 to 55 minutes.

Cool in the pan on a rack for 15 minutes, then invert onto the rack to cool completely.

BURNT SUGAR CAKE

One 9-inch 2-layer cake; 12 to 16 servings

The caramelized flavor of this *Joy* classic from 1931 is a taste sensation.

Have all ingredients at room temperature, about 70°F. Preheat the oven to 375°F. Grease and flour two 9-inch round pans and line the bottoms with rounds of parchment paper.

Melt in a large saucepan over medium heat, stirring occasionally:

½ cup (100g) sugar

The sugar will melt unevenly in the pan, so stir the melted sugar into the unmelted sugar and repeat until all the sugar is melted. At this point, it should be very dark brown. Remove from the heat and add very slowly and carefully, stirring with a long-handled spoon until smooth:

½ cup (120g) boiling water

If the sugar seizes up, place it back over medium heat and melt, stirring constantly. Cool the syrup until it has the consistency of molasses.

Whisk together in a medium bowl until thoroughly blended:

2½ cups sifted (250g) cake flour
2½ teaspoons baking powder
¼ teaspoon salt

Beat in a large bowl, or in a stand mixer with the paddle attachment, at medium-high speed until creamy:

1 stick (4 oz or 115g) unsalted butter, softened

Gradually add and beat until light and fluffy, about 5 minutes:

1½ cups (300g) sugar
1 teaspoon vanilla

Beat in one at a time:

2 large eggs

On low speed, add the flour mixture in 3 parts, alternating with:

1 cup (235g) water

in 2 parts, beating until smooth. Beat in:

3 tablespoons of the caramel (reserve the remaining caramel)

Spread the batter in the prepared pans, smoothing the top. Bake until a toothpick inserted into the center comes out clean, about 25 minutes.

Let cool in the pans on a rack for 15 minutes. Invert onto the rack, peel off the parchment paper, and turn right side up to cool completely.

Fill and frost the cake with:

Fluffy White Frosting, 795, or 2 cups Quick Vanilla Butter Frosting, 792

flavored with:

4 teaspoons reserved caramel

Store any remaining caramel in a closed jar; it will keep indefinitely.

FIG AND BROWN BUTTER SPICE CAKE

One 9-inch Bundt cake; 12 to 16 servings

This rich, golden cake is deeply flavored and irresistibly moist. It makes a stunning holiday dessert.

Have all ingredients at room temperature, about 70°F. Preheat the oven to 350°F. Coat a 9-inch Bundt pan with cooking spray.

Combine in a medium saucepan:

1 cup dried figs, chopped
½ cup Cognac or brandy

Bring to a simmer over medium-high heat, then cover, take off the heat, and let sit for 30 minutes. Melt in a medium skillet:

1½ sticks (6 oz or 170g) unsalted butter

Cook over medium heat until the butter crackles and foams and the milk solids turn golden brown (keep a close eye on it, as it can burn quickly). Immediately transfer the brown butter to a large mixing bowl or a stand mixer with the paddle attachment, using a spatula to scrape the brown bits on the bottom of the skillet into the bowl. Beat on medium-low speed until cooled. Sift together into a medium bowl:

2 cups (250g) all-purpose flour
2 teaspoons baking powder
½ teaspoon baking soda
½ teaspoon salt
½ teaspoon ground cinnamon
¼ teaspoon ground cloves

Add to the cooled browned butter and beat until smooth:

1 cup packed (230g) brown sugar

Beat in:

1 teaspoon vanilla

Beat in one at a time:

2 large eggs

Add the flour mixture to the butter mixture in 2 parts, alternating with:

1 cup buttermilk (245g) or plain yogurt (240g)

Beat until just combined. Fold in the figs along with any unabsorbed Cognac. Scrape the batter into the prepared pan. Bake until a toothpick inserted into the center comes out clean, about 45 minutes.

Let cool in the pan on a rack for 30 minutes. Invert onto the rack to cool completely. Serve with:

Whipped Cream, 791, flavored with Cognac or brandy

APPLESAUCE CAKE

One 8-inch square cake or one 9 × 5-inch loaf; 8 to 10 servings

The 8-inch square pan yields the lightest-textured cake; the loaf is denser.

Have all ingredients at room temperature, about 70°F. Preheat the oven to 350°F. Grease and flour an 8-inch square baking pan or a 9 × 5-inch loaf pan.

Whisk together thoroughly in a medium bowl:

1¾ cups sifted (210g) all-purpose flour
1 teaspoon baking soda
1 teaspoon ground cinnamon
½ teaspoon ground cloves
½ teaspoon salt
(½ teaspoon ground allspice)
(¼ teaspoon grated or ground nutmeg)

Beat in a large bowl, or in a stand mixer with the paddle attachment, until creamy, about 30 seconds:

1 stick (4 oz or 115g) unsalted butter, softened

Gradually add and beat on high speed until lightened in color and texture, 3 to 5 minutes:

1 cup white (200g) or packed light brown sugar (230g)

Beat in:

1 large egg

On low speed, add the flour mixture in 3 parts, alternating with:

1 cup (225g) unsweetened applesauce

in 2 parts, beating after each addition just until incorporated and scraping the sides of the bowl with a silicone spatula as necessary. If desired, stir in:

(1 cup finely chopped toasted, 1005, walnuts or pecans)
(1 cup raisins, golden raisins, or dried currants)

Scrape the batter into the pan and spread evenly. Bake until a toothpick inserted into the center comes out clean, 25 to 30 minutes in a square pan, 1 hour to 1 hour 10 minutes in a loaf pan.

Let cool in the pan on a rack for 15 minutes, then invert onto the rack to cool completely.

Frost with:

Quick Butterscotch (Penuche) Icing, 799, or Quick Brown Butter Icing, 799

or sprinkle with:

Powdered sugar

ROMBAUER JAM CAKE

One 8- or 10-inch Bundt cake or one 9-inch tube cake; 12 to 16 servings

Have all ingredients at room temperature, about 70°F. Preheat the oven to 350°F. Grease and flour an 8- or 10-inch Bundt pan or a 9-inch plain tube pan.

Whisk together thoroughly in a medium bowl:

1½ cups sifted (180g) all-purpose flour
1 teaspoon baking powder
1 teaspoon ground cinnamon
1 teaspoon grated or ground nutmeg
½ teaspoon baking soda
½ teaspoon ground cloves
½ teaspoon salt

Beat in a large bowl, or in a stand mixer with the paddle attachment, until light and fluffy, about 5 minutes:

⅔ cup packed (155g) dark brown sugar
1 stick plus 2 tablespoons (5 oz or 140g) unsalted butter, softened

Beat in one at a time:

3 large eggs

Beat in:

¼ cup (60g) milk

On low speed, beat in the flour mixture until barely blended. Beat in:

⅔ cup seedless raspberry or blackberry jam
(½ cup coarsely chopped toasted, 1005, walnuts or pecans)

Scrape the batter into the pan, spreading it evenly. Bake until a toothpick inserted into the center comes out clean, about 30 minutes.

Let cool in the pan on a rack for 10 minutes, then tap the pan against the countertop to loosen the cake, invert onto the rack, and let cool.

Ice with:

Quick Brown Butter Icing, 799, or Quick Butterscotch (Penuche) Icing, 799

OATMEAL CAKE

One 13 × 9-inch cake; 16 to 20 servings

This sweet, moist cake with its unusual brûléed topping is an excellent potluck companion. Make it a day or two before serving for best flavor.

Have all ingredients at room temperature, about 70°F. Preheat the oven to 350°F. Grease a 13 × 9-inch baking pan.

Combine in a medium bowl and let stand for 20 minutes:

1 cup (100g) old-fashioned rolled oats
1½ cups (355g) boiling water

Meanwhile, whisk together thoroughly in another medium bowl:

1⅓ cups (165g) all-purpose flour
1 teaspoon baking soda
1 teaspoon ground cinnamon
½ teaspoon grated or ground nutmeg
½ teaspoon salt

Beat in a medium bowl, or in a stand mixer with the paddle attachment, on high speed until light and fluffy, 4 to 6 minutes:

1 stick (4 oz or 115g) unsalted butter, softened
1 cup (200g) sugar
1 cup packed (230g) brown sugar
Beat in:
2 large eggs
1 teaspoon vanilla
Beat in the oat mixture on low speed, then beat in the flour mixture. Scrape the batter into the pan and spread evenly. Bake until a toothpick inserted in the center comes out clean, about 30 minutes. Let cool briefly in the pan on a rack. While still warm, ice with:
Double recipe Brûléed Icing, 800
Broil as directed.

TOMATO SOUP CAKE (MYSTERY CAKE)

One 9-inch square cake; about 12 servings

This combination of ingredients makes a surprisingly good cake. But why shouldn't it? The "mystery" element is tomato, which is, after all, a fruit.
Have all ingredients at room temperature, about 70°F. Preheat the oven to 350°F. Grease a 9-inch square baking pan.
Whisk together thoroughly in a medium bowl:
2 cups sifted (240g) all-purpose flour
1 teaspoon baking soda
1 teaspoon ground cinnamon
½ teaspoon grated or ground nutmeg
½ teaspoon ground cloves
½ teaspoon salt
Beat in a large bowl, or in a stand mixer with the paddle attachment, at high speed until light and fluffy, about 5 minutes:
4 tablespoons (2 oz or 55g) unsalted butter
1 cup (200g) sugar
On low speed, beat in the flour mixture in 3 parts, alternating with:
One 10¾-ounce can condensed tomato soup
in 2 parts, beating until smooth. Fold in:
1 cup chopped toasted, 1005, walnuts or pecans
1 cup raisins
Scrape the batter into the prepared pan, smoothing the top. Bake until a toothpick inserted into the center comes out clean, about 45 minutes.
Let the cake cool in the pan on a rack.
Spread with:
Fluffy White Frosting, 795, or Cream Cheese Frosting, 792
or dust with:
Powdered sugar

BANANA CAKE COCKAIGNE

One 9-inch 2-layer cake or one 10-inch cake; 12 to 16 servings

If served very fresh, this cake is good without icing, just sprinkled with powdered sugar.
Have all ingredients at room temperature, about 70°F. Preheat the oven to 350°F. Grease and flour two 9-inch round cake pans or one 10-inch springform pan and line the bottom(s) with rounds of parchment paper.
Whisk together thoroughly in a medium bowl:
2¼ cups sifted (225g) cake flour
¾ teaspoon baking soda
½ teaspoon baking powder
½ teaspoon salt
Combine in a medium bowl:
1 cup lightly mashed ripe bananas (about 2 large)
¼ cup (60g) plain yogurt or buttermilk
1 teaspoon vanilla
Beat in a large bowl, or in a stand mixer with the paddle attachment, until creamy:
1 stick (4 oz or 115g) unsalted butter, softened
Gradually add and beat until light and fluffy, about 5 minutes:
1 cup plus 2 tablespoons (225g) sugar
Beat in one at a time:
2 large eggs
On low speed, add the flour mixture in 3 parts, alternating with the banana mixture in 2 parts, beating until smooth. Scrape the batter into the pan(s), smoothing the top. Bake until a toothpick inserted into the center comes out clean, 30 to 45 minutes.
Let cool in the pan(s) on a rack for 10 minutes. Invert onto the rack, peel off the parchment paper, and turn right side up to cool completely.
For a 2-layer cake, arrange between the layers:
2 ripe bananas, sliced
For either the 2-layer cake or the single-layer cake, frost with:
Cream Cheese Frosting, 792, or Chocolate Sour Cream Frosting, 793

ST. LOUIS GOOEY BUTTER CAKE

One 13 × 9-inch cake; 12 to 16 servings

This St. Louis classic consists of a lightly sweet yeasted dough topped with a rich, buttery layer. The key to this cake is not overbaking it. The topping should be pale and still a bit jiggly in the center when you take it out of the oven.
Combine in a small saucepan:
⅓ cup (80g) milk
2 tablespoons (15g) all-purpose flour
Cook over medium heat, stirring constantly, until a thick paste forms. Let cool until just warm. Mix together in a small bowl and let sit for 5 minutes:
⅓ cup (80g) warm (105° to 115°F) milk or water
1 teaspoon active dry yeast
Transfer the yeast to a stand mixer with the dough hook. Add the milk-flour paste along with:
2¼ cups (280g) all-purpose flour
3 tablespoons (35g) sugar
1 large egg
½ teaspoon salt
Knead on low speed for about 5 minutes until smooth, then add:
4 tablespoons (2 oz or 55g) unsalted butter, softened
Knead on low to medium speed until the dough is smooth and elastic, 8 to 10 minutes. Cover and let rise until doubled, 1 to 2 hours.
Coat a 13 × 9-inch baking pan with cooking spray and line with parchment paper so that it extends up the long sides of the pan.

Press the dough evenly into the pan. Cover and let rise again until puffy, 1 to 2 hours.

Preheat the oven to 350°F.

In a stand mixer with the paddle attachment, beat together until very light and fluffy, about 5 minutes:

1 stick plus 2 tablespoons (5 oz or 140g) unsalted butter, softened
1½ cups (300g) sugar
½ teaspoon salt

Beat in until smooth:

1 large egg

Stir together in a small bowl:

¼ cup (90g) light corn syrup
2 tablespoons (30g) water
2 teaspoons vanilla
(½ teaspoon almond extract)

Add the corn syrup mixture to the butter-sugar mixture alternating with:

1½ cups (190g) all-purpose flour

Scoop the topping onto the risen dough in spoonfuls and gently spread it all over the dough, taking care not to deflate the dough too much. Bake until the cake is golden around the edges, 20 to 25 minutes. It should still be very soft in the center.

Let cool completely, then cut into squares. Dust with:

Powdered sugar

ABOUT QUICK OR ONE-BOWL CAKES

We all want a good cake in a hurry. Quick cakes are great favorites, not only for their ease of preparation but also for their delicious flavors and hearty, satisfying textures. These cakes tend to be more moist and dense than butter cakes or foam cakes. Feel free to make them even when you are not in a hurry. They also happen to be excellent recipes for teaching children to bake. The batter for all of these cakes can be mixed in one bowl in a matter of minutes. Many are just as easy to mix by hand as with an electric mixer.

BLITZKUCHEN (LIGHTNING CAKE)

One 8-inch cake; 8 to 10 servings

This *Joy* classic can be baked with or without the almond topping. Either approach produces a beautifully tender cake.

Have all ingredients at room temperature, about 70°F. Preheat the oven to 350°F. Grease and flour an 8 × 2-inch round cake pan and line the bottom with a round of parchment paper.

Whisk together thoroughly in a medium bowl:

1 cup (125g) all-purpose flour
1 teaspoon baking powder
¼ teaspoon salt

Beat in a large bowl, or in a stand mixer with the paddle attachment, until creamy:

1 stick (4 oz or 115g) unsalted butter, softened

Gradually add and beat on high speed until light and fluffy, 3 to 5 minutes:

1 cup (200g) sugar

Beat in one at a time:

3 large eggs

Beat in:

Finely grated zest of 1 lemon
2 tablespoons (30g) lemon juice

Stir in the flour mixture just until combined. Scrape the batter into the pan and spread evenly. If desired, sprinkle the top with a mixture of:

(⅓ cup sliced almonds)
(1 heaping tablespoon sugar)

Bake until a toothpick inserted into the center comes out clean, 30 to 35 minutes.

Let cool in the pan on a rack for 10 minutes. Loosen the sides with a knife, invert onto the rack, peel off the parchment paper, and turn right side up on the rack to cool. Frost with any frosting, 792–93.

FRENCH YOGURT CAKE

One 9 × 5-inch loaf; about 8 servings

This super simple loaf cake is just the thing to make when you want a little something sweet. It also travels well.

Preheat the oven to 350°F. Coat a 9 × 5-inch loaf pan with cooking spray and line the bottom and sides with parchment paper.

Whisk to combine in a medium bowl:

1½ cups (190g) all-purpose flour
1½ teaspoons baking powder
½ teaspoon salt

Whisk to combine in a large bowl:

1 cup (200g) sugar
3 large eggs
½ cup (120g) whole-milk plain yogurt
½ cup (105g) vegetable or mild olive oil
1½ teaspoons vanilla
(Finely grated zest of 1 lemon or orange)

Add the flour mixture to the wet ingredients and fold in until just combined. Scrape the batter into the prepared pan. If desired, for a frosted look, dust the top of the cake with:

(1 tablespoon sugar)

Bake until a toothpick inserted into the center comes out clean, 50 to 55 minutes.

Let cool in the pan on a rack for 10 minutes. Invert the cake onto the rack, peel off the parchment paper, if used, and turn right side up to cool completely. Serve with:

Cut-up fresh fruit or Macerated Fruit, 167

CHOCOLATE SHEET CAKE (TEXAS SHEET CAKE)

One 13 × 9-inch cake; 20 to 30 servings

Serve this cake straight from the pan.

Have all ingredients at room temperature, about 70°F. Preheat the oven to 375°F. Grease a 13 × 9-inch pan.

Whisk together in a large bowl until well blended:

2 cups (400g) sugar
2 cups (250g) all-purpose flour
1 teaspoon baking soda
½ teaspoon salt

Combine in a medium saucepan and bring to a boil, stirring constantly:

1 cup (235g) water or coffee
½ cup (100g) vegetable oil
1 stick (4 oz or 115g) unsalted butter
½ cup (40g) unsweetened cocoa powder

Pour the hot mixture over the dry ingredients and stir together just until smooth. Let cool for 5 minutes, then whisk in:

2 large eggs
½ cup (120g) buttermilk
1 teaspoon vanilla

Scrape the batter into the pan and spread evenly. Bake until a toothpick inserted into the center comes out clean, 20 to 25 minutes.

Let cool completely in the pan on a rack.

If desired, spread with:

(1½ to 2 cups Quick Mocha Frosting, 792, Quick Chocolate Butter Icing, 799, or Chocolate Satin Frosting, 793)

MISSISSIPPI MUD CAKE

One 13 × 9-inch cake; 16 to 20 servings

Prepare:

Chocolate Sheet Cake, 734

As soon as the cake comes out of the oven, cover the top evenly with:

3½ cups miniature marshmallows

Sprinkle the marshmallows with:

1 cup chopped pecans

Return the cake to the oven until the marshmallows soften and puff, 2 to 3 minutes. Remove from the oven and spread over the top:

2 to 3 cups Chocolate Satin Frosting, 793, to taste

Spread the frosting gently so as not to dislodge the marshmallows and nuts. Cool the cake in the pan on a rack until the topping is set.

VEGAN CHOCOLATE CAKE

One 8-inch square cake; about 16 servings

This is a delightfully simple and tasty chocolate cake, whether or not you happen to be vegan.

Preheat the oven to 375°F. Grease and flour an 8-inch square baking pan and line the bottom with a square of parchment paper.

Whisk together in a large bowl until well blended:

1½ cups (190g) all-purpose flour
1 cup plus 2 tablespoons (225g) sugar
⅓ cup plus 1 tablespoon (30g) unsweetened cocoa powder
1 teaspoon baking soda
½ teaspoon salt

Add:

1 cup (235g) cold water
¼ cup (50g) vegetable oil
1 tablespoon (15g) distilled white vinegar
2 teaspoons vanilla

Whisk until smooth. Scrape the batter into the pan and spread evenly. Bake until a cake tester inserted into the center comes out clean, about 30 minutes.

Let cool in the pan on a rack for 10 minutes. Slide a thin knife around the cake to detach it from the pan. Invert the cake, peel off the paper liner, then turn right side up on the rack to cool.

Serve plain, dusted with:

Powdered sugar

or frost with:

Vegan Chocolate Frosting, 793

OLIVE OIL CAKE

One 9-inch cake; 12 to 16 servings

One of our all-time favorite cakes. It is thick, golden, and rich with olive oil. It reminds us a bit of pound cake, but with an Italian twist.

Preheat the oven to 350°F. Coat a 9-inch springform pan with cooking spray and line the bottom with a round of parchment paper.

Whisk together in a medium bowl:

1½ cups (190g) all-purpose flour
½ cup fine cornmeal (80g) or almond flour (45g)
¾ teaspoon salt
½ teaspoon baking powder
½ teaspoon baking soda

Whisk together in a large bowl:

1½ cups (300g) sugar
1¼ cups (265g) extra-virgin olive oil
1¼ cups (300g) plain yogurt
3 large eggs
Finely grated zest of 1 orange or lemon
½ cup (120g) orange or lemon juice

Fold the flour mixture into the olive oil mixture just until combined, and scrape the batter into the prepared pan. Bake until a toothpick inserted into the center comes out clean, about 1 hour 15 minutes.

Let cool in the pan on a rack for 30 minutes. Run a thin knife around the inside of the pan, and remove the pan ring. Let the cake cool completely on the pan base. Serve with:

Whipped Cream, 791

ORANGE RUM CAKE

One 8-inch round cake; about 12 servings

This orange cake has the lightness of a sponge cake and the butteriness of a pound cake.

Have all ingredients at room temperature, about 70°F. Preheat the oven to 375°F. Grease and flour an 8 × 2-inch round cake pan and line the bottom with a round of parchment paper.

Melt and let cool:

3 tablespoons (45g) unsalted butter

Beat in a large bowl, or in a stand mixer with the whisk attachment, on high speed until thick and pale yellow, about 4 minutes:

1 cup (200g) sugar
3 large eggs
Finely grated zest of 1 orange
¼ teaspoon salt

Sift over the top and fold in:

1¼ cups (155g) all-purpose flour
1½ teaspoons baking powder

Stir in the melted butter along with:

⅓ cup (75g) heavy cream

Scrape the batter into the pan and spread evenly. Bake until a toothpick inserted into the center comes out clean, 30 to 35 minutes.

Let cool in the pan on a rack for 10 minutes. Puncture the cake all over with a wooden skewer. Spoon over:

½ cup dark rum

Let cool completely in the pan.

Glaze with:

Bittersweet Chocolate Glaze or Frosting, 798

or dust with:

Powdered sugar

ORANGE ALMOND CAKE

Prepare the crunchy almond topping as directed in **Marzipan Cake, 730,** in the cake pan before making **Orange Rum Cake, 735,** adding to the batter along with the orange zest **¼ teaspoon almond extract**.

VEGAN ORANGE CAKE

One 8-inch round cake; 8 to 10 servings

A deeply flavored cake needing only a light dusting of powdered sugar for garnish.

Preheat the oven to 350°F. Coat an 8-inch round cake pan with cooking spray and line the bottom with a round of parchment paper.

Whisk together in a large bowl:

1½ cups (190g) all-purpose flour
¾ cup (150g) sugar
1 teaspoon baking powder
½ teaspoon baking soda
¼ teaspoon salt

Whisk together in a medium bowl until smooth:

Finely grated zest of 1 orange
1 cup (245g) orange juice
⅓ cup (70g) vegetable or olive oil
1 teaspoon vanilla

Fold the orange juice mixture into the flour mixture just until combined. Scrape the batter into the prepared pan. Bake until a toothpick inserted into the center comes out clean, 35 to 40 minutes.

Let cool in the pan on a rack for 10 minutes. Slide a thin knife around the cake, invert it, peel off the parchment paper, and turn the cake right side up on the rack to cool completely. Dust with:

Powdered sugar

APPLE CAKE

One 8-inch square cake; about 16 servings

We like to use tart green apples with the peels left on.

Preheat the oven to 350°F. Grease and flour an 8-inch square baking pan and line the bottom with parchment paper.

Whisk together thoroughly in a large bowl, pinching out any lumps in the brown sugar:

1½ cups (190g) all-purpose flour or 1 cup (125g) all-purpose flour plus ½ cup (65g) whole wheat flour
1 cup packed (230g) brown sugar
1 teaspoon baking soda
1 teaspoon ground cinnamon
½ teaspoon ground cloves
½ teaspoon grated or ground nutmeg
½ teaspoon salt

Add and stir together until smooth:

1 cup (245g) buttermilk
½ cup (105g) vegetable oil
(2 tablespoons rum or brandy)
1 teaspoon vanilla

Stir in:

1 cup diced cored apples
½ cup chopped toasted, 1005, walnuts or pecans

Scrape the batter into the pan and spread evenly. Bake until a toothpick inserted into the center comes out clean, 40 to 45 minutes.

Let the cake cool in the pan on a rack. Serve warm, plain, or cool, unmold, and frost with:

Quick Vanilla Butter Frosting, 792, or Quick Butterscotch (Penuche) Icing, 799

CARROT CAKE

One 9-inch 2-layer cake, one 8-inch 2-layer cake, or one 13 × 9-inch cake; 16 to 20 servings

Moist and flavorful enough to enjoy plain, but everyone knows it's best with cream cheese frosting.

Have all ingredients at room temperature, about 70°F. Preheat the oven to 350°F. Grease and flour two 9-inch round cake pans, two 8-inch square pans, or one 13 × 9-inch pan.

Whisk together thoroughly in a large bowl:

1⅓ cups (165g) all-purpose flour
1 cup (200g) sugar
1½ teaspoons baking soda
1 teaspoon baking powder
1 teaspoon ground cinnamon
½ teaspoon ground cloves
½ teaspoon grated or ground nutmeg
½ teaspoon ground allspice
½ teaspoon salt

Whisk together well in a small bowl:

⅔ cup (140g) vegetable oil
3 large eggs

Stir this into the flour mixture until just combined. Stir in:

1½ cups shredded carrots
1 cup chopped toasted, 1005, walnuts
(1 cup golden raisins)
(½ cup canned crushed pineapple, drained)

Scrape the batter into the pan(s) and spread evenly. Bake until a toothpick inserted into the center comes out clean, 25 to 30 minutes in round or square pans, 30 to 35 minutes in a 13 × 9-inch pan.

Let the 13 × 9-inch cake cool in the pan on a rack. For round or square pans, cool in the pans for 10 minutes, then turn out onto the rack to cool completely.

Frost with:

Cream Cheese Frosting, 792, Quick Vanilla Butter Frosting, 792, or Quick Brown Butter Icing, 799

Or sprinkle the sheet cake with:

Powdered sugar

HUMMINGBIRD CAKE

One 9-inch 3-layer cake; about 16 servings

This Jamaican specialty, now a popular dessert in the South, was originally known as **Doctor Bird Cake,** named for the red-billed streamertail hummingbird that is indigenous to Jamaica. It is made extra moist by the addition of banana and pineapple. To decorate the top of the cake, either arrange whole pecans in a circle around the edge of the cake or sprinkle chopped pecans evenly over the top.

Preheat the oven to 350°F. Coat three 9-inch round cake pans with cooking spray and line the bottoms with rounds of parchment paper.

Whisk to combine in a large bowl:

3 cups (375g) all-purpose flour
2 teaspoons baking powder
1 teaspoon ground cinnamon
1 teaspoon salt
¾ teaspoon baking soda
½ teaspoon ground allspice

Whisk to combine in a medium bowl:

2 cups mashed ripe banana (about 3 large)
One 8-ounce can crushed pineapple with juice
1 cup (200g) sugar
1 cup packed (230g) brown sugar
1 cup (210g) vegetable oil
3 large eggs
2 teaspoons vanilla

Add the banana-pineapple mixture to the flour mixture and stir just until combined. Fold in:

1 cup chopped toasted, 1005, pecans

Divide the batter among the prepared pans and bake until a toothpick inserted into the center comes out clean, 25 to 30 minutes.

Let cool in the pans on a rack for 10 minutes. Invert the cakes onto the rack, peel off the parchment paper, and turn right side up to cool completely.

Fill and frost with:

Double recipe Cream Cheese Frosting, 792

Garnish the top of the cake with:

12 whole pecans, toasted, 1005, ¾ cup chopped toasted pecans

FRESH GINGER CAKE

One 9-inch square cake; about 12 servings

A food processor makes quick work of mincing the fresh ginger for this cake. (No, the amount of ginger is not a typo.)

Preheat the oven to 350°F. Grease and flour a 9-inch square baking pan and line the bottom with a square of parchment paper.

Whisk together thoroughly in a medium bowl:

1½ cups (190g) all-purpose flour
1 teaspoon baking soda
¼ teaspoon salt

Whisk together in a large bowl:

½ cup packed (115g) light or dark brown sugar
½ cup (170g) molasses
½ cup minced peeled ginger (from about 4 ounces [115g] unpeeled ginger)
1 large egg

Combine in a medium saucepan and heat until the butter is melted:

1 stick (4 oz or 115g) unsalted butter
½ cup (120g) water

Whisk into the molasses mixture. Stir the flour mixture into the molasses-butter mixture just until smooth. Scrape the batter into the pan. Bake until a toothpick inserted into the center comes out clean, 25 to 30 minutes.

Let cool in the pan on a rack for 10 minutes. Slide a thin knife around the cake to detach it from the pan. Invert the cake onto the rack, peel off the parchment paper, and turn right side up to cool completely. Serve dusted with:

Powdered sugar

APPLE STACK CAKE

One 9-inch 5-layer cake; 16 to 20 servings

This unusual cake is an old-timey Appalachian specialty. The layers are very thin—more like large cookies than cake—and the filling is a rustic, apple butter-like mixture made from dried apples. The cake will be best 2 or 3 days after it is assembled, so don't rush it. For a tasty, nontraditional variation, use dried figs instead of the dried apples, and serve the cake with whipped cream. For a shortcut, use prepared apple butter instead of the homemade apple filling below. The recipe calls for 5 cake pans, but the cakes may be made in batches if you don't have enough pans. Or to go really old-school, bake the cakes a single layer at a time in a cast-iron skillet.

Preheat the oven to 350°F. Grease five 9-inch round cake pans liberally with:

Unsalted, softened butter or shortening

Dust lightly with:

All-purpose flour

For the filling, combine in a large saucepan:

12 ounces (340g) dried apples
⅓ cup packed (75g) dark brown sugar
¾ teaspoon ground cinnamon
½ teaspoon ground ginger
¼ teaspoon ground allspice
Water to just cover the apples

Bring the mixture to a boil, then reduce the heat to simmer, partially covered, until the apples are very soft and the liquid is reduced to the consistency of apple butter. Use a potato masher to mash the filling into a rough, chunky paste.

While the filling cooks, make the cakes. Whisk together in a large bowl:

5 cups (625g) all-purpose flour
1 teaspoon baking powder
1 teaspoon baking soda
1 teaspoon salt

Whisk together in a medium bowl:

1 cup (340g) molasses or sorghum syrup, 1018
1 cup (245g) buttermilk
½ cup (100g) sugar

½ cup packed (115g) dark brown sugar
½ cup (105g) vegetable oil or melted shortening
2 large eggs

Add the molasses-buttermilk mixture to the flour mixture and stir until combined. The dough will be very thick—almost like gingerbread dough. Divide the dough in 5 pieces. Press each piece of dough into a prepared cake pan (if baking in batches, keep the unused dough covered while the other pieces bake). Bake until slightly risen and the cakes are firm to the touch, 12 to 15 minutes. The cakes will be very flat. Remove from the pans and let cool completely on a wire rack.

Place one cake layer on a plate. Spread one-quarter of the filling onto the top of the layer to the edge. Top with a second cake layer and another one-quarter of the filling. Repeat until the cakes and filling are all used, ending with a cake layer. Wrap the cake tightly and refrigerate for at least 2 days before serving.

If desired, before serving dust the cake with:

Powdered sugar

APPLE, PEACH, OR PLUM CAKE COCKAIGNE

One 9- or 10-inch round cake; about 12 servings

A family favorite, we especially love this cake made with purple plums for their gorgeous color.

Preheat the oven to 425°F. Grease a 9- or 10-inch round cake pan.

Sift together into a bowl:

1 cup (125g) all-purpose flour
2 tablespoons (25g) sugar
1 teaspoon baking powder
¼ teaspoon salt

Add:

3 tablespoons (45g) cold unsalted butter, cut into cubes

Using a pastry blender or 2 forks, cut the butter into the dry ingredients until the mixture resembles coarse cornmeal. Beat well in a measuring cup:

1 large egg
½ teaspoon vanilla

Add:

Enough milk to make ½ cup

(If the fruit to be used is very juicy, reduce the liquid by 1 tablespoon.) Stir into the flour and butter to make a stiff dough. Pat or spread the dough into the prepared pan. Arrange on top of the dough in tight overlapping rows:

4 cups sliced peeled apples or peaches or sliced pitted plums

Combine and sprinkle over the fruit:

1 cup white (200g) or packed brown sugar (230g)
2 teaspoons ground cinnamon
3 tablespoons (45g) unsalted butter, melted

Bake until a toothpick inserted into the center comes out clean, about 25 minutes. Serve warm.

PINEAPPLE UPSIDE-DOWN CAKE

One 9-inch cake; 8 to 10 servings

Traditionally baked in a cast-iron skillet, this cake was devised to promote canned pineapple. The pineapple rings and maraschinos may be replaced with wedges of fresh apricots, peaches, or plums, if desired. ➤ For a gooier topping (one of the joys of this cake), you have two options: Either increase the butter in the pan to 6 tablespoons (85g) and the brown sugar to 1 cup (230g), or bake the cake in an 8-inch pan and increase only the butter to 4 tablespoons (55g). Have all ingredients at room temperature, about 70°F. Preheat the oven to 350°F. Have ready a 9-inch skillet or a 9 × 2-inch round cake pan.

Drain and place in 1 layer on paper towels to absorb the excess juice:

7 slices canned unsweetened pineapple (from a 20-ounce can)

Place in the skillet or cake pan:

3 tablespoons (45g) unsalted butter

Place the skillet in the oven until the butter is melted, or melt it on top of the stove. Tilt to coat all sides with butter. The extra butter will settle at the bottom of the skillet. Sprinkle evenly over the bottom of the skillet:

¾ cup packed (175g) brown sugar

Place 1 pineapple ring in the center of the skillet and arrange 6 more around it. Place in the center of each ring and in the spaces between them:

19 maraschino cherries

Whisk together in a small bowl with a fork:

2 large eggs
2 tablespoons (30g) buttermilk
½ teaspoon vanilla

Whisk together in a large bowl, or a stand mixer with the paddle attachment:

1 cup (125g) all-purpose flour
¾ cup (150g) sugar
¾ teaspoon baking powder
¼ teaspoon baking soda
¼ teaspoon salt

Add:

6 tablespoons (3 oz or 85g) unsalted butter, softened
6 tablespoons (90g) buttermilk

Beat on low speed just until the flour is moistened, then increase the speed to medium, or high if using a handheld mixer, and beat for exactly 1½ minutes. The batter will be stiff. Add the egg mixture in 3 parts, beating for exactly 20 seconds and scraping the bowl after each addition. Scrape the batter over the fruit in the skillet and spread evenly. Bake until a toothpick inserted into the cake comes out clean, 35 to 40 minutes.

Remove the cake from the oven and tilt the skillet in all directions to detach the cake from the sides of the skillet. Let cool for 2 to 3 minutes before unmolding. Invert a serving platter on top of the skillet. Cover your hands with oven mitts and turn the cake onto the platter. Lift off the skillet. If any fruit pieces are askew, use a fork to push them back into place. If any brown sugar is left in the skillet, spoon it over the cake. Serve warm or cool.

GUY FAWKES DAY CAKE

One 8-inch square cake; 16 servings

Also called **parkin,** this not-too-sweet cake is the traditional gingerbread of northern England. It is perfect with a dollop of Whipped Cream, 791.

Preheat the oven to 350°F. Grease an 8-inch square baking pan.

Melt and stir together in a saucepan:

1 stick (4 oz or 115g) unsalted butter
⅔ cup (230g) molasses

Remove from the heat. Whisk together thoroughly in a large bowl:

1 cup (125g) all-purpose flour
⅔ cup (65g) old-fashioned rolled oats
1 tablespoon (10g) sugar
1 teaspoon ground ginger
¼ teaspoon ground cloves
½ teaspoon salt
½ teaspoon baking soda
(Finely grated zest of 1 lemon)

Stir the melted butter mixture into the flour mixture in 2 parts, alternating with:

⅔ cup (155g) milk

Stir just until the dry ingredients are moist. The batter will be thin. Pour into the pan and bake until the cake begins to pull away from the sides of the pan, about 35 minutes.

Let the cake cool in the pan on a rack.

LEKACH (JEWISH HONEY CAKE)

One 13 × 9-inch cake; 16 to 20 servings

Preheat the oven to 300°F. Grease a 13 × 9-inch glass baking pan.

Combine in a medium saucepan and cook, stirring gently, over medium-low heat until well blended:

1½ cups (505g) honey
1 cup (235g) brewed coffee
¾ cup (155g) vegetable oil
2 teaspoons vanilla

Remove from the heat and set aside to cool. Whisk together thoroughly in a large bowl:

3¾ cups (470g) all-purpose flour
1½ teaspoons baking soda
1 teaspoon baking powder
2 teaspoons ground cinnamon
½ teaspoon ground ginger
(¾ cup raisins)
(¾ cup chopped toasted, 1005, walnuts)

Beat in a medium bowl, or in a stand mixer with the whisk attachment, on high speed until thick and pale yellow, 4 to 5 minutes:

3 large eggs
¾ cup (150g) sugar

Beat the cooled honey mixture into the eggs. Add the flour mixture and beat until well blended. Scrape the batter into the pan and spread evenly. Bake until a toothpick inserted into the center comes out clean, 40 to 45 minutes.

As soon as the cake is removed from the oven, use a fork to prick holes all over the surface. Heat to lukewarm:

¼ cup (85g) honey

Using a large spoon, pour and spread the honey over the surface of the cake. Let the cake cool completely in the pan on a rack before cutting.

BIENENSTICH (BEE STING CAKE)

One 9-inch cake; about 10 servings

A German yeasted cake with a caramelized honey and almond topping and a custardy filling.

Grease a 9-inch springform pan. Using **2 tablespoons (25g) sugar, 1 large egg,** and **1½ cups (190g) flour,** prepare the dough for:

½ recipe Parker House Rolls, 617

Place the dough in the prepared pan, pressing it gently but evenly into the pan. Cover and let rise until almost doubled, about 45 minutes. Preheat the oven to 350°F.

While the dough rises, combine in a medium saucepan:

1 stick (4 oz or 115g) unsalted butter, cut into small cubes
⅓ cup (110g) honey
¼ cup (50g) sugar
¼ teaspoon salt

Bring to a boil over medium-high heat, stirring constantly until the sugar dissolves. Stir in:

1½ cups sliced almonds

Let the mixture boil until the sugar turns amber, 2 to 4 minutes. Remove from the heat and stir in:

2 teaspoons vanilla

Allow the almond mixture to cool slightly—it should be spreadable but not piping hot. Spread the mixture evenly over the top of the dough to the edge. Bake until well browned and a toothpick inserted into the center of the cake comes out clean, 25 to 30 minutes.

Let cool in the pan for 15 minutes, then remove the pan ring. Prepare:

Pastry Cream, 801

Let cool completely, then cover and refrigerate until chilled, at least 2 hours.

When the cake is completely cooled, use a serrated knife to cut it in half horizontally. Fill the cake with the chilled pastry cream and place the almond-topped layer back on top. Serve immediately or cover and refrigerate up to 1 day before serving. Store any leftovers refrigerated for up to 4 days.

ABOUT FRUITCAKES

The archetypal fruitcake—studded with unearthly green and red candied fruit and heavy enough to serve as a doorstop—is what comes to mind for many of us when we think of this oft-maligned category of cake. The reality, though, is that those notorious loaves are a shadow of what a good fruitcake can be. While both heavily spiced dark fruitcakes and light ones can be excellent, we have come to prefer light ones. We make our fruitcakes a month or more in advance of when they are to be served or gifted. When doused with rum, bourbon, or brandy, they improve greatly with age. We have kept such fruitcakes, wrapped in liquor-soaked cloth and then refrigerated in a plastic bag, for well over a year.

Fruitcakes are essentially butter cakes with just enough batter to bind the fruit and nuts. The usual candied fruits may be used, but we prefer to replace them with chopped dried fruits such as apricots, dates, cherries, and candied ginger along with the traditional raisins or currants. If you do like glacéed or candied fruits, you will be rewarded by spending a little extra on the best quality, often available from specialty stores. Larger pieces rather than finely diced candied fruits are usually fresher and better. Slicing candied or dried fruits can be a sticky procedure at best; use oiled scissors or lightly oil the blade of a very sharp knife.

For fruitcakes, use shiny metal pans rather than dark or glass ones. This will prevent excessive browning of the cake and any fruit pieces that touch the pan during the long, slow baking period. Line the pans with parchment paper that extends over the 2 long sides to ensure that the heavy but fragile cake emerges from the pan without sticking or breaking. For a tube pan, line the bottom with paper by cutting a hole to allow for the tube, and use wide strips of paper to line the sides and tube as well. Grease pans first to hold the paper in place. If desired, grease the paper as well, though it is not absolutely necessary.

The amount of batter for two 9 × 5-inch loaf pans can be baked in one 10-inch tube pan; the baking time will be about twice as long. Miniature loaf pans, small fluted molds, or disposable aluminum pans are the perfect size for gift loaves. Grease and flour fluted molds generously, as they cannot be lined with paper. As a general rule, pans can be filled to within ¾ inch of the top, as fruitcake batters rise very little during baking.

➤ When the cake is cool, you can puncture it several times with a skewer and very slowly pour or brush on up to 1 cup liquor—such as brandy, bourbon, or dark rum—allowing the cake to absorb the liquid. To store, wrap tightly in plastic wrap and then place inside a plastic bag if possible. Or, if you prefer, wrap in brandy- or liquor-soaked linens, such as pieces of flour sack towel or muslin, and place in a resealable plastic bag. Fruitcakes can be stored for about 1 month at room temperature or for at least 6 months in the refrigerator. Liquor-soaked cakes keep for at least 1 year.

FRUITCAKE COCKAIGNE

Two 9 × 5-inch loaves

This light fruitcake is our favorite. Once cooled, we soak it with brandy. Please read About Fruitcakes, above.

Have all ingredients at room temperature, about 70°F. Preheat the oven to 325°F. Grease two 9 × 5-inch loaf pans and line with parchment paper so it extends over the long sides of the pans.

Measure into a large bowl:

4 cups sifted (480g) all-purpose flour

Mix ½ cup (60g) of the sifted flour in a medium bowl with:

1 cup chopped toasted, 1005, slivered almonds or hazelnuts
1 cup golden raisins
½ cup chopped dried apricots
(½ cup shredded or flaked unsweetened coconut)
(¼ cup thinly sliced candied citron or candied orange or lemon peel)
(¼ cup finely chopped dried cherries)

Whisk into the remaining flour:

1 teaspoon baking powder
½ teaspoon salt

Beat in another large bowl, or in a stand mixer with the paddle attachment, until creamy:

1½ sticks (6 oz or 170g) unsalted butter, softened

Gradually add, beating on high speed, and beat until light and fluffy, 5 to 7 minutes:

2 cups (400g) sugar

Beat in one at a time:

5 large eggs

Beat in:

1 teaspoon vanilla

On low speed, gradually beat in the flour mixture until thoroughly combined. Fold in the nuts and fruits. Divide the batter between the pans and spread evenly. Bake until a toothpick inserted into the center comes out clean, about 1 hour.

Let cool in the pan on a rack for 30 minutes. Carefully transfer to the rack, peel off the parchment paper, and cool completely. To store, see About Fruitcakes, 739.

DARK FRUITCAKE

Two 9 × 5-inch loaves or one 10-inch tube cake

This is best stored for at least 1 month before serving, but we have enjoyed it fresh as well. Please read About Fruitcakes, 739.

Have all ingredients at room temperature, about 70°F. Preheat the oven to 300°F. Grease two 9 × 5-inch loaf pans or one 10-inch tube pan and line with parchment paper so it extends over the long sides of the pans (for a tube pan, line the bottom with a parchment round with a hole in the center, and line the sides of the pan with a long strip of parchment).

Sift together into a large bowl:

3 cups (375g) all-purpose flour
1 teaspoon baking powder
1 teaspoon ground cinnamon
1 teaspoon grated or ground nutmeg
½ teaspoon baking soda
½ teaspoon ground mace
½ teaspoon ground cloves
¼ teaspoon salt

Beat in another large bowl, or in a stand mixer with the paddle attachment, until creamy:

2 sticks (8 oz or 225g) unsalted butter, softened

Gradually add and beat on high speed until lightened in color and texture, 3 to 5 minutes:

2 cups packed (460g) dark brown sugar

Beat in one at a time, scraping the sides of the bowl as necessary:

6 large eggs

Beat in:

½ cup (170g) molasses
Finely grated zest of 1 orange
⅓ cup (80g) orange juice
Finely grated zest of 1 lemon
3 tablespoons (45g) lemon juice

On low speed, add the flour mixture in 3 parts, alternating with:

½ cup brandy

in 2 parts. Beat just until blended and scrape the sides of the bowl as necessary. Fold in:

2½ cups diced mixed candied and/or dried fruit (citron, pineapple, cherries, apricots, ginger, and/or orange and lemon peel)
2 cups coarsely chopped toasted, 1005, walnuts
1½ cups chopped dates
1½ cups dried currants
1½ cups golden raisins

Scrape the batter into the pan(s) and spread evenly. Bake until a toothpick inserted into the center comes out clean, about 1½ hours for loaf cakes, 2½ to 3 hours for a tube cake. (If the cake is getting too dark on top, tent it loosely with foil for the last 30 to 60 minutes.)

Let cool in the pan on a rack for about 1 hour. Invert the cake and peel off the parchment paper. Let cool right side up on the rack. To store, see About Fruitcakes, 739.

ABOUT TORTES

A nut torte is simply a sponge cake in which the flour is replaced with dry bread or cake crumbs and nuts ground to a fine meal. The technique for preparing nut tortes is just like that of sponge cakes: Egg yolks and sugar are beaten until thick and pale yellow before flavorings and nuts are added. Stiffly beaten egg whites are folded in, providing most of the leavening.

➤ Do not use ground commercial bread crumbs; they are too fine. Prepare your own, 957, by crushing dry crustless white bread in a plastic bag using a rolling pin, or in a food processor.

To grind nuts for tortes, use a small coffee/spice grinder with a sharp blade or a food processor. Nuts must never be ground to the point where they become oily. Do not grind more than ¼ cup at a time to avoid overheating the nuts and to ensure they become meal rather than nut butter. Alternatively, you may use store-bought almond meal (also called almond flour).

Because nut tortes are often too delicate in texture to withstand much handling, they are baked in springform pans or tube pans with removable bottoms. ➤ Only the bottoms of the pans are greased and floured, as tortes require the sides of the pan to be dry and free of grease in order to rise properly. ➤ Let these cakes cool completely in the pan before removing them from the pan.

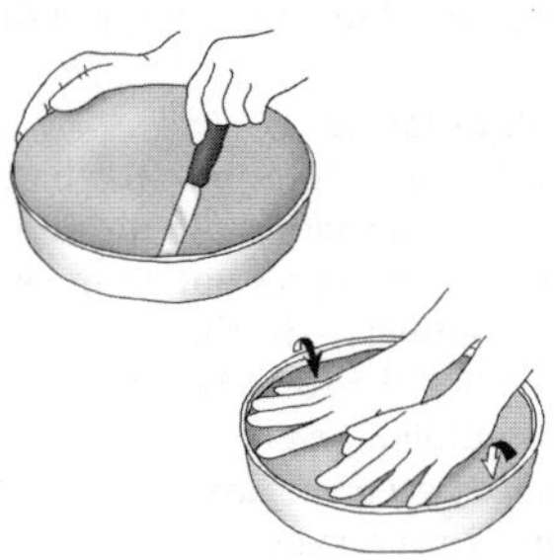

Removing a torte from a springform pan

To unmold a torte made in a springform pan, slide a thin flexible knife or small metal spatula around the edges of the cake, pressing it against the pan to avoid tearing the torte. If desired, with the cake still in the pan, level the torte by pressing down gently and compacting the edges with your fingers, so the center and edges are the same height, as shown. Remove the sides of the pan and invert. Remove the paper liner, if using, then turn right side up.

ALMOND TORTE COCKAIGNE

Two 8-inch round layers or one 8-inch cake; about 12 servings

This is the classic German *mandeltorte*—a not-too-sweet almond cake with just a hint of citrus. The extra egg white makes a lighter cake. Pecans may be substituted for the almonds. Please read About Tortes, above.

Have all ingredients at room temperature, about 70°F. Preheat the oven to 325°F. Grease and flour the bottom(s) of two 8 × 2-inch round cake pans or one 8-inch springform pan and line the bottom(s) with rounds of parchment paper.

Grind to a fine meal in a food processor or coffee/spice grinder:

¾ cup whole raw almonds

Beat in a large bowl, or in a stand mixer with the whisk attachment, on high speed until thick and pale yellow, about 2 minutes:

¾ cup (150g) sugar
6 large egg yolks (whites reserved)

Fold in the almonds, along with:

½ cup toasted, 957, or dry white bread crumbs
Finely grated zest of 1 lemon or orange
3 tablespoons (45g) lemon or orange juice
1 teaspoon ground cinnamon
1 teaspoon almond extract

Using clean beaters, beat in another large bowl on medium speed until soft peaks form, 977:

6 large egg whites
¼ teaspoon cream of tartar

Gradually add, beating on high speed:

¼ cup (50g) sugar

Beat until the peaks are stiff but not dry, 978. Use a silicone spatula to fold one-quarter of the egg whites into the almond mixture, then fold in the remaining whites. Scrape the batter into the pan(s) and spread evenly. Bake until a toothpick inserted into the center comes out clean, about 20 minutes in round pans, 50 to 55 minutes in a springform pan.

Let cool completely in the pan(s) on a rack; the center will sink as it cools. To level and remove from the pan, see About Tortes, above. Frost (and fill, if baked in layers) with:

Whipped Cream, 791, or any flavored whipped cream, Quick Chocolate Butter Icing, 799, or Bittersweet Chocolate Glaze or Frosting, 798

Or leave unfrosted and fill layers with:

Whipped Cream, 791, a mixture of whipped cream and Lemon Curd, 802, or Citrus Custard Filling, 802

and sprinkle with:

Powdered sugar

PASSOVER ALMOND TORTE

Prepare **Almond Torte Cockaigne, 741,** substituting **½ cup (60g) matzo meal** for the bread crumbs.

HAZELNUT TORTE

One 10-inch cake; about 12 servings

Toasted, 992, hazelnuts will yield a more intense flavor. Please read About Tortes, 741.

Have all ingredients at room temperature, about 70°F. Preheat the oven to 350°F. Grease and flour the bottom of a 10-inch springform pan and line with a round of parchment paper.

Beat in a large bowl, or in a stand mixer with the whisk attachment, at medium-high speed for 1 minute:

12 large egg yolks (8 whites reserved)

Gradually add and beat well until thick and lemon colored:

1 cup (200g) sugar

Fold in, blending well:

1 cup hazelnuts, finely ground, 741
1 cup pecans or walnuts, finely ground, 741

Using clean beaters (or clean the whisk attachment, transfer the yolk mixture to another bowl, and clean the mixer bowl), beat in a large bowl at medium-high speed until stiff but not dry, 978:

8 large egg whites
½ teaspoon cream of tartar

Fold one-quarter of the egg whites into the batter, then fold in the remaining whites. Scrape the batter into the pan. Bake until a toothpick inserted into the center comes out clean, about 40 minutes.

Let cool in the pan on a rack; the center will sink. To level and unmold, see About Tortes, 741.

Serve with:

Whipped Cream, 791, or any flavored whipped cream

or spread the cake with:

Quick Mocha Frosting, 792

CHOCOLATE WALNUT TORTE

One 9-inch cake; about 12 servings

Please read About Tortes, 741.

Have all ingredients at room temperature, about 70°F. Preheat the oven to 325°F. Grease and flour the bottom of a 9-inch springform pan and line with a round of parchment paper.

Beat in a large bowl, or in a stand mixer with the whisk attachment, at medium-high speed for 1 minute:

6 large egg yolks (whites reserved)

Gradually add, beating until thick and pale:

¾ cup plus 2 tablespoons (175g) sugar

Fold in, blending well:

¾ cup finely chopped toasted, 1005, walnuts
½ cup finely crushed plain cracker crumbs
2 ounces (55g) unsweetened chocolate, grated
2 tablespoons brandy or dark rum
½ teaspoon baking powder
(½ teaspoon ground cinnamon)
(¼ teaspoon ground cloves)
(¼ teaspoon grated or ground nutmeg)

Using clean beaters (or clean the whisk attachment, transfer the yolk mixture to another bowl, and clean the mixer bowl), beat in a large bowl at medium-high speed until stiff but not dry, 978:

6 large egg whites
¼ teaspoon cream of tartar

Fold one-quarter of the egg whites into the batter, then fold in the remaining whites. Scrape the batter into the pan. Bake until a toothpick inserted into the center comes out clean, about 1 hour.

Let cool in the pan; the center will sink. To level and unmold, see About Tortes, 741.

Spread with:

Quick Chocolate Butter Icing, 799, or Bittersweet Chocolate Glaze or Frosting, 798

or serve with:

Crème Anglaise, 806

SACHERTORTE

One 9-inch 2-layer cake; 12 to 16 servings

The definition of the sachertorte is very strictly regulated in Austria. We make no claims that our recipe would pass muster in its home country, but we think it a fine example of its kind. Adding the extra egg white makes a lighter cake. Please read About Tortes, 741.

Have all ingredients at room temperature, about 70°F. Preheat the oven to 325°F. Grease and flour the bottom of a 9-inch springform pan and line with a round of parchment paper.

Grate:

6 ounces (170g) semisweet or bittersweet chocolate

Beat in a large bowl, or in a stand mixer with the paddle attachment, at medium-high speed until light and creamy, about 3 minutes:

½ cup (100g) sugar
1 stick (4 oz or 115g) unsalted butter, softened

Beat in one at a time:

6 large egg yolks (whites reserved)

Add the grated chocolate and:

¾ cup dry bread crumbs
¼ cup (25g) finely ground blanched almonds or almond meal
¼ teaspoon salt

Using clean beaters (or transfer the yolk mixture to another bowl, clean the stand mixer bowl, and switch to the whisk), beat in a large bowl at medium-high speed until stiff but not dry, 998:

6 egg whites
½ teaspoon cream of tartar

Fold one-quarter of the egg whites into the batter, then fold in the remaining whites. Scrape the batter into the pan. Bake until a toothpick inserted into the center comes out clean, 50 minutes to 1 hour.

Let the cake cool completely in the pan on a rack. Remove the sides of the pan and slice the torte horizontally into 2 layers, 711. Should the top be mounded, reverse the layers so the finished cake has a flat top. Spread between the layers:

1 cup apricot jam or preserves

Cover the cake with:

Bittersweet Chocolate Glaze or Frosting, 798

For a really Viennese effect, garnish each slice with a great gob of *schlag*, or:

(Whipped Cream, 791)

ABOUT FLOURLESS CHOCOLATE CAKES

These dense cakes are similar to nut tortes in that the leavening and much of the structure are provided by eggs. All these cakes tend to sink in the center as they cool and remain moister than other cakes. They are very rich, not only from the eggs and butter, but also from gratuitous amounts of chocolate. Choose a fine-quality chocolate, as it is the star ingredient. Chocolate with a 54 to 65% cacao content will work in these recipes. Higher-percentage chocolate will require the addition of more sugar and potentially more liquid. For more information on substituting one type of chocolate for another, see Chocolate and Cacao, 970.

INDIVIDUAL MOLTEN CHOCOLATE CAKES

9 small cakes

You can make the batter for these ultrarich cakes, scrape it into the muffin tin, cover, and refrigerate overnight before baking. Please read About Flourless Chocolate Cakes, above.

Have all ingredients at room temperature, about 70°F. Preheat the oven to 400°F. Butter 9 cups of a standard muffin tin. Sprinkle inside the muffin cups:

Sugar

Shake the sugar around the inside of the muffin cups to coat, then dump out any excess sugar.

Heat in the top of a double boiler or a heatproof bowl set over barely simmering water:

6 ounces (170g) semisweet or bittersweet chocolate, coarsely chopped

1 stick plus 2 tablespoons (5 oz or 140g) unsalted butter

Remove from the heat. Sift into the chocolate-butter mixture:

¼ cup (20g) unsweetened cocoa powder

2 tablespoons (15g) cake flour

¼ teaspoon salt

Stir until smooth. Stir in:

4 large egg yolks (whites reserved)

Beat in a medium bowl on medium speed until soft peaks form, 977:

4 large egg whites

¼ teaspoon cream of tartar

Gradually add, beating on high speed until the peaks are stiff but not dry, 978:

¼ cup (50g) sugar

Use a silicone spatula to fold one-quarter of the egg whites into the chocolate mixture, then fold in the remaining whites. Fill the muffin cups about three-quarters full. Bake until the cakes look set on top but are still gooey in the center, 5 to 6 minutes (a minute or so longer if the batter has been refrigerated). Let sit for 2 to 3 minutes; the cakes will shrink slightly from the sides of the tin. Place a rack over the cakes and invert to unmold. Serve hot, accompanied with:

Whipped Cream, 791

FLOURLESS CHOCOLATE DECADENCE

One 8-inch round cake; 12 to 14 servings

Serve cut into very small wedges with whipped cream and fresh raspberries or Fresh Berry Coulis, 805. Please read About Flourless Chocolate Cakes, above.

Have all ingredients at room temperature, about 70°F. Preheat the oven to 325°F. Grease an 8 × 2-inch round cake pan (not a springform) and line the bottom with a round of parchment paper.

Combine in a large heatproof bowl:

1 pound (455g) semisweet or bittersweet chocolate, coarsely chopped

1 stick plus 2 tablespoons (5 oz or 140g) unsalted butter, cut into small pieces

Set the bowl over a large skillet of barely simmering water and stir often until the chocolate and butter are warm, melted, and smooth. Remove from the heat and whisk in:

5 large egg yolks (whites reserved)

Beat in large bowl, or in a stand mixer with the whisk attachment, on medium speed until soft peaks form, 977:

5 large egg whites

¼ teaspoon cream of tartar

Gradually add, beating on high speed until the peaks are stiff but not dry, 978:

1 tablespoon (10g) sugar

Use a silicone spatula to fold one-quarter of the egg whites into the chocolate mixture, then fold in the remaining whites. Scrape the batter into the pan and spread evenly. Set the pan in a large shallow baking dish or roasting pan, set the baking dish on a pulled-out oven rack, and pour in enough boiling water to reach halfway up the sides of the cake pan. Bake for exactly 30 minutes; the top of the cake will have a thin crust and the interior will still be gooey.

Set the cake pan on a rack to cool completely, then refrigerate until chilled, or overnight.

To unmold, slide a thin knife around the cake to detach it from the pan. Invert the cake and peel off the paper liner. Reinvert onto a serving platter. Sprinkle with:

Powdered sugar

Store in the refrigerator, but remove 1 hour or more before serving to soften. Cut with a hot knife, wiping off the knife between cuts.

CHOCOLATE MOUSSE CAKE

One 8-inch round cake; 12 to 14 servings

Only 1 to 1½ inches tall, this confection has the texture of mousse, with the intensity of a bittersweet chocolate truffle. Please read About Flourless Chocolate Cakes, above.

Have all ingredients at room temperature, about 70°F. Preheat the oven to 350°F. Grease the sides of an 8-inch round cake pan and line the bottom with a round of parchment paper.

Place in a large heatproof bowl:

5 ounces (140g) semisweet or bittersweet chocolate, coarsely chopped

Combine in a small heavy saucepan:

⅔ cup (130g) sugar

½ cup (40g) unsweetened Dutch-process cocoa powder

2 tablespoons (15g) all-purpose flour

Whisk in just enough milk to make a paste, then whisk in the rest:

¾ cup (175g) milk

Bring to a simmer over medium heat, stirring constantly with a wooden spoon to prevent scorching. Reduce the heat and simmer very gently, stirring constantly, until slightly thickened, about

1 minute. Immediately pour the hot mixture over the chopped chocolate and whisk until the chocolate is melted and the mixture is completely smooth. Whisk in:

2 large egg yolks (whites reserved)
1 teaspoon vanilla

Beat in a large bowl, or in a stand mixer with the whisk attachment, on medium speed until soft peaks form, 977:

4 large egg whites
¼ teaspoon cream of tartar

Gradually add, beating on high speed until the peaks are stiff but not dry, 978:

¼ cup (50g) sugar

Use a silicone spatula to fold one-quarter of the egg whites into the chocolate mixture, then fold in the remaining whites. Scrape the batter into the pan and spread evenly. Bake, cool, and unmold as for Flourless Chocolate Decadence, 743.

If desired, sprinkle with:

(Powdered sugar)

Or serve with:

(Vanilla ice cream, Fresh Berry Coulis, 805, or Whipped Cream, 791)

Cut with a hot knife, wiping off the knife between cuts.

ABOUT FILLED CAKES

These extravagant cakes are beautiful, decadent, and, let's be honest, complicated. Best to consider them a challenge and embrace complexity! The key is patience—while it may be tempting to rush through the process, thorough cooling of the cake layers, fillings, and assembled cakes is extremely important. Take extra care with these cakes, as any shortcut shows. The reward for all your patience, bravery, and hard work will be a magnificent centerpiece that will look almost too beautiful to eat, but that will somehow get eaten anyway.

To go off-recipe, you may fill any angel food cake, 718–19, as shown. Begin by marking the topmost 1-inch portion of the cake with toothpicks. Using the toothpicks as guides, cut all around the cake with a serrated knife. Cut completely through the cake with a delicate sawing motion and set this 1-inch-thick slice aside to serve as the lid. Then, start to cut a channel to hold the filling: Make two vertical incisions in the cake, curving the blade so that it remains 1 inch from the inner and outer surfaces of the cake. Cut to within 1 inch of the bottom, but no more. To remove the cake from the channel, insert the knife diagonally in the outer incision and slice all around toward the inner incision. Then reverse the action and repeat the cut from the inside incision toward the outside incision. These two cuts will bisect each other in an X and give you 3 loose triangular sections that are easily removed. The fourth triangle attached to the base can be cut free with a curved grapefruit knife or carefully scooped out with a grapefruit spoon.

For lining molds (see About Charlottes, 824), use any sponge cake, 719–22, or angel food cake, 718–19, Génoise, 721, or torte, 741–42. Stabilized fillings (those made with gelatin) are best for filled molds and cakes. See the recipes for Bavarian creams and mousses, 822–24, in the Desserts chapter.

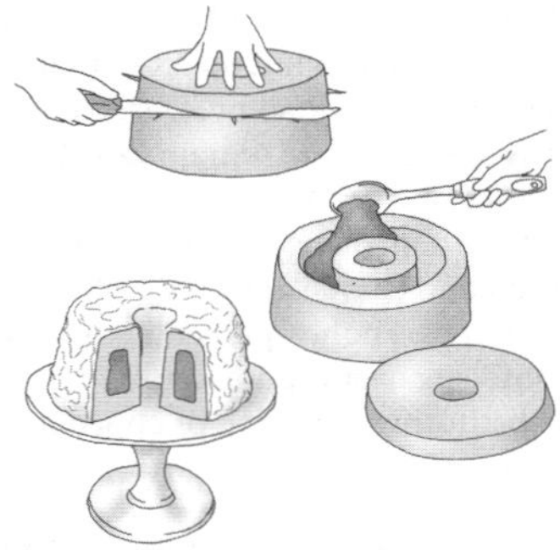

Making a filled cake

SICILIAN CASSATA

One 8-inch cake; about 16 servings

Cassata is Sicily's over-the-top special-occasion cake. Sponge cake is flavored with sweet rum syrup and filled with ricotta cheese studded with candied citron, cinnamon, and vanilla. The whole cake is enveloped in sheets of marzipan and gilded with candied fruits.

Prepare:

Sponge Cake Sheet, 749

Have ready an 8-inch springform pan. Puree in a food processor until perfectly smooth, 3 to 4 minutes:

2 pounds (905g) whole-milk ricotta

Add and pulse until combined:

1 cup (100g) powdered sugar
⅔ cup finely chopped candied citron or candied orange peel
1 teaspoon vanilla
(¼ teaspoon ground cinnamon)

Cut two 8-inch round layers and two 13 × 1½-inch strips from the cooled sponge cake. Brush with:

¼ cup rum

Place one cake layer, moist side up, in the bottom of the springform pan. Line the sides of the pan with the strips, moist sides facing in. Trim the strips to fit snugly and cut level with the pan rim. Scrape the ricotta filling into the pan and spread evenly. Place the second cake layer, moist side down, on top of the filling. Press to level. Cover the pan with plastic wrap and refrigerate for at least 2 hours, or overnight.

Remove the pan ring and invert the cake onto a serving platter (or leave it on the pan bottom). Refrigerate until needed.

Combine in a small saucepan and bring to a simmer:

⅔ cup apricot jam
3 tablespoons (45g) water

Strain through a sieve into a bowl. Knead until smooth and pliable:

14 ounces (395g) marzipan, homemade, 873, or store-bought

Use a rolling pin to roll a little less than half of the marzipan between 2 sheets of parchment paper into a smooth 9½-inch round; to avoid creases, peel off and reposition the parchment paper now and then. Brush the top and sides of the cake generously with the warm apricot glaze. Center the marzipan, best side facing up, on top of the cake, smoothing the surface and pressing the edges over and against the sides of the cake. Roll the remaining marzipan into a rough 12 × 8-inch rectangle. Cut 4 neat strips, each 7 inches long and exactly as wide as the cake is tall. One by one, press the strips smoothly against the sides of the cake, overlapping the edges neatly. Arrange on top of the cake in a geometric pattern:

Candied fruit

sticking the fruit in place with a little apricot jam or light corn syrup. Refrigerate for at least 2 hours, or up to 8 hours before serving.

BOSTON CREAM PIE

One 8- or 9-inch 2-layer cake; about 12 servings

Traditionally called a pie because of the pans the layers were originally baked in, this is really a layer cake. Use sponge cake for light, airy layers or butter cake for a richer, denser cake.

Have ready 2 layers of:

Sponge Cake, 720, Four-Egg Yellow Cake, 725, or Buttermilk Layer Cake, 725

Fill with:

About 1½ cups Pastry Cream, 801

Leave the sides exposed, but pour over the top:

Bittersweet Chocolate Glaze or Frosting, 798

BLACK FOREST CAKE

One 9-inch 3-layer cake; about 16 servings

Prepare:

One 9-inch Chocolate Génoise, 722, cut into 3 layers

Combine in a small bowl:

½ cup Moistening Syrup, 800
¼ cup kirsch

Thaw and drain:

Two 10- to 12-ounce packages (565 to 680g) frozen unsweetened cherries

Combine in a small heatproof bowl:

6 ounces (170g) semisweet or bittersweet chocolate, finely chopped
¼ cup (60g) boiling water

Stir until the chocolate is melted and the mixture is smooth. If the chocolate does not melt completely, place it in a skillet of barely simmering water and stir constantly until melted. Place 1 cake layer in the bottom of a 9-inch springform pan. Brush liberally with kirsch syrup. Whip in a large bowl until soft peaks form, 977:

4 cups (925g) cold heavy cream or 2 cups (460g) heavy cream and 2 cups (460g) crème fraîche
⅓ cup (65g) sugar
2 teaspoons vanilla

Fold ⅓ cup of the whipped cream into the chocolate mixture, then fold in another ½ cup. Immediately spread the chocolate cream over the moistened cake. Moisten the top of another layer with syrup and place it moist side down on the chocolate cream. Press to level. Moisten the top of the layer. Arrange a single layer of cherries without packing them tightly, on top; you will have some cherries left over. Spread about 2 cups of whipped cream over and between the cherries. Moisten the last cake layer and place it moist side down on the cherries and cream; press gently to level. Refrigerate the cake, as well as the remaining whipped cream and cherries, until firm, at least 30 minutes.

Frost the top and sides of the cake with the remaining whipped cream. Use a pastry bag fitted with a large star tip to pipe 12 to 16 whipped cream rosettes or a border of whipped cream around the top edge of the cake. Blot the remaining cherries dry and place 1 on each rosette. Decorate the center of the cake with:

Chocolate shavings

Refrigerate for at least 12 hours, or for up to 24 hours, before serving.

CHOCOLATE RASPBERRY CREAM CAKE

Prepare **Black Forest Cake, above.** Substitute **2½ cups fresh raspberries** for the cherries and ¼ cup **framboise** (raspberry eau-de-vie) for the kirsch. Or substitute **¾ cup raspberry liqueur** for the kirsch mixture.

ICEBOX CAKE

15 servings

An icebox "cake" is a no-bake dessert made from thin wafer cookies, such as graham crackers, whipped cream, and fruit. It's about as easy as cake making gets. The only catch is that it needs time to sit in the fridge for a couple of hours to allow the cookies to soften. Use your imagination with the filling, pairing complementary flavors like chopped mango and pineapple, toasted coconut, and whipped cream with added lime zest. Other things can be used in the layers as well, like chopped chocolate, thinly spread jam or preserves, or even pudding.

Prepare:

Triple recipe Whipped Cream, 791

Have ready:

One box (14 to 15 ounces) graham crackers, 2 packages (18 ounces) chocolate wafer cookies, or other thin, crisp cookies
4 cups prepared fresh fruit such as sliced hulled strawberries, chopped ripe peaches, or halved pitted cherries
(1 cup finely chopped toasted, 1005, nuts such as almonds, hazelnuts, or pecans)

Spread a very thin layer of whipped cream in the bottom of a 13 × 9-inch baking dish. Top with a layer of cookies. Divide the remaining whipped cream into quarters. Top the cookies with one-quarter of the whipped cream and one-quarter of the fruit (and nuts, if using). Top with another layer of cookies. Repeat the layering process, ending with a fruit layer. Cover with plastic wrap and refrigerate for at least 2 and up to 8 hours before serving. Eat within 2 days.

ABOUT SAVARINS AND BABAS

The same featherlight yeast-raised dough is used for both savarins and babas, but the shapes are different, and babas contain raisins or currants. Savarins, which can be large or small, may be baked in individual doughnut-shaped molds or in large savarin molds or tube pans. Babas are baked in individual cup-shaped molds. These cakes are thoroughly soaked in a sugar syrup and doused with rum or other spirits. The finished product is deliciously moist. A flavorful dark rum from Martinique or Jamaica is traditional, but babas and savarins also can be flavored with any fruit brandy such as kirsch, Poire Williams, framboise, or mirabelle.

SAVARIN

One 8-inch fluted tube cake; 8 to 10 servings

Combine in a large bowl, or in a stand mixer, and let stand until the yeast is dissolved, about 5 minutes:

1 envelope (2¼ teaspoons) active dry yeast
¾ cup (175g) warm (105° to 115°F) water

Add to the yeast mixture and mix until blended:

1⅓ cups all-purpose (165g) or bread flour (175g)
1 tablespoon (10g) sugar
½ teaspoon salt

Gradually stir in:

2 large eggs, lightly beaten
1⅓ cups all-purpose (165g) or bread flour (175g)

Mix until the dough comes together, about 2 minutes. Knead by hand for 10 minutes or with the dough hook for about 6 minutes, until the dough is smooth and elastic and no longer sticks to your hands or the bowl. Gradually knead in:

4 tablespoons (2 oz or 55g) unsalted butter, melted and cooled

Continue to knead until the butter is completely incorporated and the dough is soft and pliable. Place the dough in a large oiled bowl, cover with plastic wrap, and let rest in a warm place (75° to 80°F) for about 15 minutes.

Lightly oil a savarin mold or an 8-inch fluted tube or Bundt pan (oil is used because butter can pit the surface of the savarin). Gently place the dough in the mold, spreading it with your fingers so it fills the mold evenly. Cover with plastic wrap and let rise in a warm place (75° to 85°F) until doubled in volume, about 1 hour.

Preheat the oven to 350°F.

Place the pan on a baking sheet and bake until the savarin is golden brown all over, including the sides, and a knife inserted in the center comes out clean, about 45 minutes.

Immediately unmold the savarin onto a rack and let cool completely. (The savarin can be stored in a well-sealed plastic bag for up to 4 days in the refrigerator or up to 2 weeks in the freezer.)

About 15 minutes before serving, bring to a boil in a saucepan, stirring to dissolve the sugar:

1 cup (200g) sugar
2 cups (475g) water
Finely grated zest of 1 lemon
(1 vanilla bean, split)

Remove from the heat and stir in:

½ cup dark rum or fruit brandy
(1 teaspoon vanilla, if not using vanilla bean)

Transfer the savarin to a plate and place the plate on a rack. Place the rack on a baking sheet. Ladle the hot syrup over the top (which was the bottom as it baked) until the entire savarin is well soaked with the syrup. The syrup must be hot so the savarin can quickly absorb it without becoming soggy or losing its shape; the syrup that runs off can be rewarmed and ladled over the cake again. Let the thoroughly moistened savarin drain for about 10 minutes.

Just before serving, fill the center of the savarin with:

Whipped Cream, 791

Top with:

Whole or sliced strawberries, other fresh fruits, or Macerated Fruit, 168

BABA AU RHUM

12 servings

Combine in a small saucepan:

½ cup dried currants or raisins
Enough cold water to cover the fruit by ½ inch

Bring to a boil, then drain well. Transfer to a small bowl and sprinkle with:

¼ cup rum

Cover and let soak for at least 30 minutes, or up to 3 days.

Prepare the dough for:

Savarin, above

kneading the drained currants into the dough by hand or with the dough hook just after the butter. Let rest in a warm place (75° to 80°F) for about 15 minutes.

Lightly oil 12 traditional baba molds or 12 cups of a standard muffin tin. Divide the dough into 12 pieces and fill each cup. Cover loosely with oiled plastic wrap and let rise in a warm place until the dough has doubled in bulk and fills the molds, about 30 minutes.

Preheat the oven to 350°F. Bake until golden brown and a knife inserted into the center comes out clean, about 30 minutes. Immediately unmold the babas onto a rack and let cool completely. (The babas can be stored like Savarin, above.) Prepare the syrup for:

Savarin, above

About 15 minutes before serving, steep the cooled babas in the syrup. Serve the soaked babas plain, or fill by cutting them horizontally in half and spreading the bottom layer with:

(Whipped Cream, 791, or Pastry Cream, 801)

Cover with the top baba layers.

ABOUT ROLL CAKES

Almost any angel food, sponge, or chiffon cake can be made into a sheet for roll cakes. There is even a special size of rimmed baking sheet—called a jelly-roll pan—made for this very purpose. Most agree that jelly-roll pans are 15½ × 10½ × 1-inch, but many manufacturers have not received this memo: Some examples measure a diminutive 13 × 9 inches, others may reach 17½ × 11½ inches. To ensure no one comes up short, our cake sheet recipes assume the largest size pan, which holds about 8 cups cake batter. ➤ If your jelly-roll pan is smaller, use less cake batter, evenly spreading it to two-thirds the height of the pan. Extra batter may be baked as cupcakes.

Grease the pan and always line with parchment paper. Spread the batter evenly with an offset spatula. Cake sheets are easy to overbake, which dries them out and makes them prone to cracking when the cake is rolled. To avoid this, test for doneness early, and ➤ take the cake out of the oven as soon as the top springs back when lightly pressed. A properly baked cake sheet can be allowed to cool flat, even in the pan, and still remain flexible enough to roll.

CAKE SHEET FOR ROLL CAKES

One 17 × 11-inch sheet, for an 11-inch roll

Practically any variation on the batters on 747 will work here; if using a smaller 15½ × 10½-inch jelly-roll pan, halve the batter recipes.

Preheat the oven to 325°F. Grease a 17½ × 11½ × 1-inch rimmed baking sheet and line the bottom with parchment paper.

Prepare the batter for one of the following:

Any chiffon cake, 722–23
Angel Food Cake, 719
Génoise, 721, or Chocolate Génoise, 722
French Sponge Cake (Biscuit), 721

Scrape the batter into the pan, spreading evenly, until it is two-thirds full (there may be a cup or two of batter leftover). Bake until the top springs back when lightly pressed, 15 to 20 minutes.

While the cake is still warm, run a knife along the edges to release it from the pan. Immediately invert the cake onto a sheet of parchment paper and remove the pan. Let the cake cool completely before peeling off the paper liner.

Peel off the paper liner and place a fresh sheet of parchment paper on top. Flip the cake and peel off the parchment paper the cake was cooled on, removing the brown "skin" from the cake as you do so.

➤ If using French Sponge Cake, Génoise, or Chocolate Génoise, brush the cake with:

(½ cup Moistening Syrup, 800, flavored with 2 to 5 tablespoons liquor or liqueur if desired)

Spread it with:

1½ to 2 cups desired filling, 801–3, or frosting, 792–93

using the smaller amount for richer fillings or frostings and the larger amount for fluffier, lighter fillings or frostings. Starting on a short side, fold and press an inch or so of the cake firmly up over the filling to get started. Keep these first turns tight; cracking will diminish as the diameter of the roll increases. Use the parchment under the cake to help roll the cake. Once the cake is rolled, use two hands to move the roll carefully back to the center of the parchment. Wrap the back of the parchment over the cake so that it overlaps the front portion of parchment, covering the roll completely. Place the edge of a cookie sheet right next to the long side of the cake roll, where it meets the parchment, and tighten the cake roll by pressing the baking sheet at an angle toward the counter while you grasp the bottom sheet of parchment, shown below. Then wrap the tightened cake roll in the parchment and fold the ends. Refrigerate at least 1 hour to firm the roll before unwrapping and serving.

If desired, sift over the cake before serving:

(Powdered sugar)

Tightening the cake roll

SPONGE CAKE SHEET

One 17 × 11-inch sheet, for an 11-inch roll

A delightfully tender, moist, close-grained sponge that rolls beautifully without cracking.

Have all ingredients at room temperature, about 70°F. Preheat the oven to 400°F. Grease a 17½ × 11½-inch rimmed baking sheet and line the bottom with parchment paper.

Measure and return to the sifter:

¾ cup sifted (75g) cake flour

Heat in a small saucepan until the butter is melted:

¼ cup (60g) milk
3 tablespoons (45g) unsalted butter

Combine in a large bowl, or in a stand mixer with the whisk attachment, and beat until light-colored, tripled in volume, and the consistency of softly whipped cream (about 5 minutes in a stand mixer, 7 to 10 minutes with a handheld mixer):

¾ cup (150g) sugar
5 large eggs

Beat in:

1 teaspoon baking powder

Reheat the butter and milk until steaming hot. Sift the flour mixture in 3 additions over the top of the egg mixture and fold in. Add the hot milk mixture all at once and fold in until well combined. Scrape the batter into the pan and spread evenly. Bake until the top is golden brown and springs back when lightly pressed, 8 to 10 minutes. While the cake is still hot, run a knife along the edges to release it from the pan. Immediately invert the cake onto a sheet of parchment paper on top of a sheet pan or cutting board and remove the pan. Let the cake cool completely before peeling off the paper liner.

Peel off the paper liner and place a fresh sheet of parchment paper on top. Flip the cake and peel off the parchment paper the cake was cooled on, removing the brown "skin" from the cake as you do so.

Spread the cake with:

1½ to 2 cups filling, 801–3

Roll, wrap, and refrigerate as for Cake Sheet for Roll Cakes, 746.

If desired, frost with:

(Any frosting, 792–93)

or sift over the cake before serving:

(Powdered sugar)

JELLY ROLL

One 11-inch roll; about 10 servings

Prepare **Sponge Cake Sheet, above.** Spread the cooled sheet with **¾ to 1 cup jam or jelly, such as raspberry, blackberry, or apricot.** Roll, wrap, and refrigerate as for Cake Sheet for Roll Cakes, 746. Dust with **powdered sugar.**

CREAM ROLL

One 11-inch roll; about 10 servings

Prepare **Cake Sheet for Roll Cakes, 746.** Spread the cooled sheet with **2 to 2½ cups plain or flavored Whipped Cream, 791, or Whipped Crème Fraîche, 791, or 1½ to 2 cups Pastry Cream, 801.** Roll, wrap, and refrigerate as for Cake Sheet for Roll Cakes. If desired, sift **(powdered sugar)** over the cake before serving.

LEMON ROLL

One 11-inch roll; about 10 servings

This is superb made with angel food cake baked as a sheet, and the cake conveniently yields surplus yolks for the curd or custard filling.

Prepare **Cake Sheet for Roll Cakes, 740.** Spread the cooled sheet with **1½ cups Citrus Custard Filling, 802,** or **Lemon Curd, 802.** Roll, wrap, and refrigerate as for Cake Sheet for Roll Cakes. If desired, sift (**powdered sugar**) over the cake before serving.

CHOCOLATE-FILLED ROLL

One 10- or 11-inch roll; about 10 servings

Prepare **Cake Sheet for Roll Cakes, 746.** Spread the cooled sheet with **3 cups Whipped Ganache Filling, 803, or Whipped Cream, 791, flavored with cocoa powder and/or espresso powder** or **1½ to 2 cups Chocolate Buttercream, 797, Chocolate Pastry Cream, 801, or Mocha Pastry Cream, 801.** Roll, wrap, and refrigerate as for Cake Sheet for Roll Cakes. If desired, sift **(powdered sugar or cocoa powder)** over the cake before serving.

BÛCHE DE NOËL (YULE LOG CAKE)

One 11-inch roll; about 10 servings

This makes a stunning holiday centerpiece.

Have ready:

Sponge Cake Sheet, 747, or Chocolate Génoise, 722, baked and cooled as for Cake Sheet for Roll Cakes, 746

Filling: 2 cups Chocolate Mousse Frosting, 793, Whipped Cream, 791, flavored with cocoa powder, Meringue Buttercream I or II, 796, flavored with espresso powder or Whipped Ganache Filling, 803

Frosting: Chocolate Satin Frosting, 793, Chocolate Ganache cooled to frosting consistency, 797, or Milk Chocolate Mocha Glaze or Frosting, 803

Combine:

½ cup Moistening Syrup, 800

¼ to ⅓ cup brandy or dark rum, to taste

Place the sheet cake right side up on a large sheet of parchment paper. Brush generously with the syrup. Spread with the 2 cups filling. Roll and wrap as for Cake Sheet for Roll Cakes, 746. For easiest handling, freeze for at least 3 hours until semifrozen. It will keep, frozen, for up to 3 months.

When ready to decorate, let the frosting come to room temperature and stir or beat until smooth. Spread most of it over the cake roll, then texture it with a fork to look like tree bark. Use a sharp knife dipped in hot water to cut a 2-inch slice from each end of the roll. Set the cake roll on a serving plate. Place the reserved slices on either side of the cake roll to resemble stumps, using any remaining frosting to cover the joints. If serving immediately, decorate the log with:

Meringue Mushrooms, 751

Or refrigerate for up to 48 hours, remove from the refrigerator 2 to 3 hours before serving, and then decorate with the mushrooms.

ABOUT CUPCAKES AND MINIATURE CAKES

You can transform nearly any cake batter into cupcakes by baking it in a muffin pan lined with paper liners or greased and floured (even for sponge and angel cake batters, which are normally baked in ungreased pans). Paper liners are easy and neat; they also keep cupcakes moist and fresh longer. Children enjoy eating cupcakes that have been baked in flat-bottomed ice cream cones (set the cones inside the cups of a muffin tin before baking).

Fill muffin tins (or plain ice cream cones) about two-thirds full and bake at 350°F. Baking time is usually 15 to 20 minutes. It is always best to check early and watch carefully. Bake until the tops spring back when pressed and a toothpick inserted into the center of a cupcake comes out clean. Let cool in the pan for about 5 minutes before unmolding.

You can also transform rich butter cake batters into sophisticated miniature cakes, to be eaten like cookies. Bake in small decorative molds such as round or rectangular tartlet pans or madeleine molds. Grease and flour the molds and fill them about half full. Baking time will be about 10 minutes, more or less, depending on the size of the

CUPCAKE SUGGESTIONS

BATTER	FROSTING	TOPPING (OPTIONAL)	YIELD
Four-Egg Yellow Cake, 725 Eight-Yolk Gold Cake, 725	Chocolate Cream Cheese Frosting, 792, or Quick Chocolate Butter Icing, 799	Sprinkles	About 18
Blitzkuchen, 731	Plain or flavored Fluffy White Frosting, 795, or powdered sugar	Sprinkles or chocolate shavings	About 12
Sponge Cake, 720			About 20
Angel Food Cake, 719	Any buttercream, 795–97	Toasted coconut	About 40
Devil's Food Cake Cockaigne, 728	Quick Mocha Frosting, 792, or Quick Chocolate Butter Icing, 799	White chocolate curls or sprinkles	About 24
Rombauer Jam Cake, 732	Quick Butterscotch (Penuche) Icing, 799	Ground cinnamon or chopped toasted nuts	About 20
Carrot Cake, 736, or Red Velvet Cake, 725	Quick Brown Butter Icing, 799, or Cream Cheese Frosting, 792	Toasted pecans or walnuts	24 to 30

molds. Serve sprinkled with powdered sugar or glaze with Citrus Glaze, 799, Liqueur Glaze, 799, or Quick Lemon Frosting, 792, and serve with coffee or tea.

Choose any icing, 798–99, or frosting, 792–93, for cupcakes or refer to the chart on 748 for specific suggestions. Stiff or creamy icings can be spread with a small knife or spatula. To apply a thin glaze, hold cupcakes upside down and dip the tops. For a pointed swirl on top, dip into a soft, fluffy topping such as Fluffy White Frosting, 795, and twist as you lift and turn the cupcake right side up.

Icing cupcakes

PETITS FOURS

About eighty 1-inch squares

Traditional petits fours are made of small cubes of white cake, pound cake, or sponge cake split and filled with jam and iced with fondant. However, if you are willing to experiment, you can create interesting and elegant petits fours from almost any cake, filling, and frosting you choose.

Prepare the batter for:

Sponge Cake Sheet, 747, Génoise, 721, or Chocolate Génoise, 722, or Pound Cake, 726

Bake in a 13 × 9-inch baking pan greased, floured, and lined with parchment paper, at the temperature recommended for the cake; baking time will be 28 to 30 minutes. Bake just until the top of the cake springs back when lightly pressed and a toothpick inserted into a few places comes out clean. Let cool completely in the pan on a rack before filling and frosting.

If the finished cake is 1 or more inches tall, cut it into three large pieces to make it easier to handle, then cut each piece horizontally into two layers with a serrated knife. If less than 1 inch tall, cut the whole cake horizontally in half. Spread the cut side of the bottom layer(s) with:

1 cup jam, heated and strained or pureed for easy spreading, or a filling, 801–3, or any buttercream, 795–97

Stack the layers, placing the uncoated piece(s) on top of the filling. Transfer to a cookie sheet and cover the top and sides with plastic wrap. Place a second cookie sheet on top and weight with canned goods to level and compact the layers so they will not come apart when cut into small shapes. Refrigerate for several hours, until firm, or wrap and freeze for up to 3 months.

To glaze and coat with marzipan, if desired, first brush over the filled cakes:

(Hot strained preserves)

and top with:

(A 1/8-inch-thick layer of rolled marzipan, homemade, 873, or store-bought)

Glazing petits fours

Cut the cake into small squares or bars with a sharp serrated knife; 1-inch squares will yield the classic two-bite-size cake. Or, with cookie or canapé cutters, cut the cake into small squares or diamonds, rounds or hearts, or other shapes.

If not glazed with preserves and covered with marzipan, you can spread a thin coat of:

(Any buttercream, 795–97)

on the tops and sides. Refrigerate to set the coating before glazing.

Place the cakes 1 inch apart on a wire grid or a rack set on a rimmed baking sheet. Spoon over each cake:

Bittersweet Chocolate Glaze, 798, Chocolate Ganache, 797, or Fondant icing, 800

as shown (you will need 4 pounds of fondant to coat 80 petits fours). Chill or let stand to set the coating. Once the glaze is set, decorate the petits fours with:

Candied violets, rose petals, or edible flowers, candied fruits, dragées, sliced almonds, pistachios, or toasted, 973, flaked coconut

If you like, serve in pleated paper cups. Petits fours can be completed up to 24 hours in advance.

MADELEINES

About 20 tea cakes

These buttery French tea cakes, something between a sponge cake and a butter cake in texture, are traditionally baked in scallop-shaped madeleine molds, but you can use miniature muffin tins or small tartlet pans in any shape.

Have all ingredients at room temperature, about 70°F.

Sift together and then return to the sifter:

1 1/2 cups sifted (150g) cake flour
1/2 teaspoon baking powder
1/4 teaspoon salt

Mash and beat in a medium bowl with a wooden spoon or silicone spatula until the consistency of mayonnaise:

1 1/2 sticks (6 oz or 170g) unsalted butter, softened

Beat in a large bowl, or in a stand mixer with the whisk attachment, on high speed until thick and pale yellow, 2 to 5 minutes:

3 large eggs
1 large egg yolk
3/4 cup (150g) sugar
1 1/2 teaspoons vanilla

Sift the flour mixture over the top and fold in with a silicone spatula. Fold a dollop of the egg mixture into the butter to lighten it, then scrape the butter mixture back into the remaining egg mixture and fold together. Let rest for 30 minutes.

Preheat the oven to 450°F. Using melted butter, generously grease 1 or 2 madeleine pans with 12 molds each.

Fill the molds three-quarters full; set any remaining batter aside. Bake until the cakes are golden on the top and golden brown around the edges, 8 to 10 minutes. Immediately loosen each cake with the tip of a slim knife and unmold onto a rack to cool. If necessary, wipe the molds clean and let cool, rebutter them, fill with the remaining batter, and bake. These are best the day they are made but they can be stored in an airtight container for a day or two.

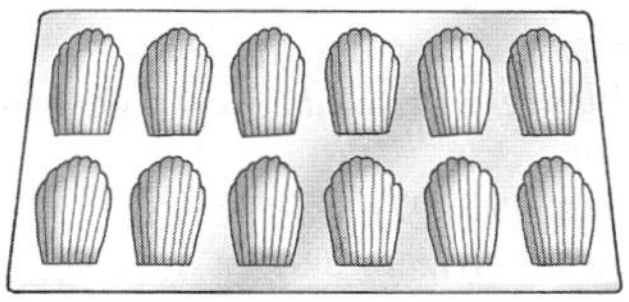

Madeleine pan

CANNELÉS DE BORDEAUX

About sixteen 1¾-inch tall cannelés

Cannelés are a specialty of the Bordeaux region of France. These little cakes have a custardy center with a deeply browned, burnished crust. They can be finicky to make, and the copper molds used to bake them are expensive. However, if you are a cannelé devotee, they are worth the price. Silicone cannelé molds may be used, but they do not produce results as irresistible as those baked in copper molds.

Combine in a medium saucepan:

1½ cups (355g) milk
3 tablespoons (45g) unsalted butter

Place over medium heat until the butter is melted and the milk is just steaming, not simmering or boiling. Combine in a food processor and pulse together:

¾ cup (150g) sugar
¾ cup (95g) all-purpose flour
¼ teaspoon salt

Add and pulse until incorporated:

1 large egg
2 large egg yolks

Transfer the hot milk to a liquid measuring cup with a pouring lip. With the machine running, add the hot milk through the feed tube until incorporated. Add:

2 tablespoons dark rum
1 teaspoon vanilla extract or paste

Pulse briefly to incorporate. Let the batter cool, then refrigerate, covered, overnight.

Position racks in the upper third and center of the oven. Preheat the oven to 400°F. Let the batter come to room temperature while the oven preheats. If using copper molds, place them on a baking sheet and heat them in the oven for 10 minutes. When ready to bake, coat each mold with cooking spray or brush lightly with:

Vegetable oil or Clarified Butter, 960

Stir the batter well, then fill the molds three-quarters full. Bake on the center rack for 10 minutes, then rotate the pan front to back in the oven, reduce the temperature to 350°F, and bake for 30 minutes. Move the cannelé molds to the top oven rack and bake until deeply browned, 30 to 40 minutes more. Remove the cannelés from the molds immediately to cool completely on a rack.

FINANCIERS

16 small cakes

Financiers are a ubiquitous French treat available at nearly every bakery. They are so easy to whip up and so supremely tasty that we wonder why they aren't as popular in the United States.

Preheat the oven to 375°F. Grease 16 cups of a mini muffin tin.

Whisk to combine in a medium bowl:

1 cup (90g) almond or hazelnut meal
½ cup (100g) sugar
¼ cup (30g) all-purpose flour
¼ teaspoon salt

Add and mix in until smooth:

2 large eggs
5 tablespoons (70g) unsalted butter, melted
1 teaspoon vanilla or ½ teaspoon almond extract

Divide the batter among the muffin cups, filling them three-quarters full. Bake until risen and browned, 12 to 15 minutes.

Let cool completely in the muffin tin on a rack, then remove the cakes from the tin.

LADYFINGERS

Thirty-six 4-inch ladyfingers

These light sponge fingers are a delicious nibble to serve with coffee, but most find their way into refrigerator desserts such as Tiramisù, 826, or Charlotte Russe, 825.

Preheat the oven to 350°F. Grease and flour 2 large baking sheets or line the bottoms with parchment paper.

Prepare the batter for:

French Sponge Cake (Biscuit), 721

Scrape the batter into a large pastry bag fitted with a ⅝-inch plain tip. Pipe 4-inch-long fingers at least 1 inch apart on the baking sheets. Sift lightly over the ladyfingers:

Powdered sugar

Bake until golden brown, 10 to 15 minutes.

Transfer the ladyfingers to a rack, or slide the parchment paper onto the rack, and cool completely. Store in an airtight container for up to 5 days.

ABOUT BAKED MERINGUE AND DACQUOISE

Meringue is a subject that covers a lot of ground. Meringue can be baked into crisp cookies (Meringue Kisses, 775), poached in milk to make ethereal desserts (Floating Islands, 815), formed into nests for cradling whipped cream and fruit (Pavlova, 826), used as a pie topping (Lemon Meringue Pie, 681) or a pie shell (Meringue Pie

Shell, 666), or even slathered on cakes as frosting (Fluffy White Frosting, 795). As all meringues and variations are based on beaten egg whites, see Beating Eggs, 977, for the proper beating technique. ➤ For detailed information on meringue as a whole, see About Meringue, 793.

Here we are concerned with baked meringue. Baked meringues can be crisp and dry throughout, like Meringue Kisses, 725, crisp on the outside and marshmallowy within, like Pavlova, 826, and Macarons, 782, or dry with a cake-like texture. Dacquoise, below, is a crisp sheet of meringue made with ground nuts and a little flour or cornstarch. Meringue and dacquoise may be used as cake layers on their own or alternated with thin sponge or génoise layers. Filled and frosted with buttercream, these make elegant layer cakes.

Meringues are crisp or soft depending upon the ratio of sugar to egg whites and the temperature at which the meringue is baked; a higher ratio of sugar to egg whites and a lower baking temperature makes for crisper meringues.

Crisp baked meringue shells or layers to be filled with whipped cream, custard, mousses, or any other moist fillings should be filled just before serving if they are to remain crisp. Meringues filled with ice cream or frozen desserts are called *meringues glacées* and can be filled in advance and returned to the freezer for up to 4 days before serving. Crisp meringue or dacquoise layers layered with buttercreams retain much of their crispness because the high fat content of the buttercream protects the layers from moisture.

BAKED MERINGUE

Two 8- or 9-inch rounds, three 7-inch rounds, or twelve 3-inch meringue shells

Please read About Baked Meringue and Dacquoise, 750.

Have all ingredients at room temperature, about 70°F. Preheat the oven to 200°F for larger shapes and 225°F for smaller shapes. Line cookie sheets with parchment paper for free-form meringues or individual meringue shells. Or, for layers, trace two 8- or 9-inch or three 7-inch circles on the parchment (the easiest way to do this is to find a cake pan of the desired size and trace around the bottom), leaving an inch between them, and turn the parchment upside down so that the tracing shows through but cannot transfer to the meringue.

Prepare:

French Meringue, 794, Swiss Meringue, 794, or Italian Meringue, 794

To make free-form meringue shells, simply spoon heaps of meringue onto a baking sheet lined with parchment paper, making a depression in the center of each one with the back of the spoon.

To form meringue layers with a spatula, divide the meringue evenly among the circles and spread into rounds with an offset spatula, making sure that the thickness of the meringue is as uniform as possible. Neaten the edges of each round by tracing around them with your finger, if desired.

To form meringue layers with a pastry bag, scrape the meringue into a large pastry bag fitted with a ⅜- to ½-inch plain tip. Starting in the center of each circle, pipe a widening spiral of meringue until each round is covered with a coiled rope of meringue.

Bake until completely dry but not at all browned, up to 2½ hours. To check for doneness, remove a test shape from the oven and let it cool for 5 minutes. If it is dry and crisp to the bite, then meringues of similar size are done. Larger meringues can also be tested by probing with the tip of a sharp paring knife. If the center of the meringue seems only slightly sticky, it will crisp as it cools.

Let cool in the turned-off oven to ensure dryness; an overnight rest in an oven with a pilot light is the sure way to get perfect meringues. If not using immediately, store airtight for several weeks. Do not refrigerate or freeze. Meringue layers are fragile. Cut the excess parchment paper from around each one and store still attached to the paper for protection. To remove it from the parchment, slide a slender metal spatula under each layer.

DACQUOISE

Two 8- or 9-inch rounds or three 7-inch rounds

Use the larger amount of nuts for more flavor. Please read About Baked Meringue and Dacquoise, 750.

Have all ingredients at room temperature, about 70°F. Preheat the oven to 200°F. Line cookie sheets with parchment paper. Trace two 8- or 9-inch or three 7-inch circles on the parchment, leaving at least an inch between them, and turn the parchment upside down so that the tracing shows through but cannot transfer to the meringue.

Combine in a food processor:

½ to ¾ cup toasted, 1005, cooled nuts (whole or pieces), such as hazelnuts and almonds
⅓ cup (65g) superfine sugar
1 tablespoon (10g) cornstarch

Pulse until the mixture has the consistency of fine cornmeal; do not overprocess, or the nuts will become oily. Beat in a large bowl, or in a stand mixer with the whisk attachment, on medium speed until soft peaks form, 977:

4 large egg whites
½ teaspoon cream of tartar

Very gradually add, 1 tablespoon at a time, beating on high speed:

½ cup (95g) superfine sugar

Beat until the meringue holds very stiff peaks. Fold in the nut mixture. Shape and bake the layers as directed in Baked Meringue, above.

MERINGUE MUSHROOMS

48 to 60 mushrooms

Though you should feel free to eat or serve these adorable mushrooms as you see fit, they are the traditional decoration for a Bûche de Noël, 748. Please read About Baked Meringue and Dacquoise, 750.

Preheat the oven to 200°F. Line 2 baking sheets with parchment paper.

Prepare:

Swiss Meringue, 794

Scrape the meringue into a large pastry bag fitted with a ½-inch plain tip. Pipe thin pointed "kiss" shapes about 1 inch tall onto the baking sheets to make mushroom stems. Pipe round button shapes in different sizes to make mushroom caps. Use a lightly moistened or damp finger to smooth the tops of the caps if necessary. Dust lightly with:

Unsweetened cocoa powder

Bake until crisp and completely dry, about 2 hours.

Let cool overnight in the turned-off oven.

Melt in a double boiler or a heatproof bowl set over a pan of barely simmering water:

2 ounces (55g) semisweet or bittersweet chocolate, coarsely chopped

Use a sharp knife to cut off and discard the pointed ends of the meringue stems. Spread a little melted chocolate on the flat side of each meringue mushroom cap and attach the stems while the chocolate is still soft. Let stand until the chocolate is set. The mushrooms can be stored in an airtight container for up to 4 weeks.

FRESH STRAWBERRY MERINGUE OR DACQUOISE

One 9-inch cake; about 12 servings

Crunchy and creamy, sweet and tart, this is a grand dessert. Have your way with it: Vary the nuts in the dacquoise, omit the chocolate coating on the layers, or substitute whole raspberries for the sliced strawberries.

Prepare and bake three 9-inch layers using:

1½ recipes Baked Meringue, 751, or Dacquoise, 751, made with almonds

Choose 12 of the best-looking berries from:

2 pints strawberries, hulled

Dip them halfway into:

1 cup Bittersweet Chocolate Glaze, 798

Set on a cookie sheet lined with wax or parchment paper and refrigerate. Spread both sides of each meringue or dacquoise layer with the remaining glaze. Set the coated layers on wax or parchment paper and refrigerate to set the chocolate.

Slice the remaining strawberries. Whip until thickened:

2 cups (460g) heavy cream or 1 cup (230g) heavy cream and 1 cup (230g) crème fraîche

Add and beat just until almost stiff:

1 to 2 tablespoons (25g) sugar

1 teaspoon vanilla

Fold the sliced berries into 2 cups of the whipped cream. Spread 1 chocolate-coated layer with about half of the strawberry filling. Top with a second layer. Spread with the remaining filling. Top with the third layer. Frost the top and sides of the stack with the plain whipped cream. Press into the sides:

¾ cup sliced almonds, toasted, 1005

If there is any cream remaining, use a pastry bag fitted with a medium star tip to pipe a border of rosettes around the top edge of the cake. Decorate the top with the chocolate-coated strawberries. Refrigerate for at least 2 and for up to 4 hours before serving.

ABOUT CHEESECAKES

Cheesecakes are really very rich custards, not cakes at all. As such, they require low heat and proper timing to avoid the most common pitfalls: cracking, shrinkage, and overbaking around the edges.

Cheesecake batter should be well mixed but not overbeaten, which can lead to a cake that puffs dramatically during baking and falls and cracks as it cools. While the food processor is excellent for transforming cottage cheese, ricotta, and other curd cheeses into perfectly smooth purees, it is not ideal for mixing cream cheese and other ingredients, as overprocessing can break down the cheese and produce a thin, heavy batter that does not rise at all. During mixing, scrape the sides of the mixing bowl and the beaters frequently, as the stiffer cheese mixture clinging to the beaters or bowl will not blend with the thinner mixture after the eggs and liquids are added. Before mixing cheesecake batter, ensure the cream cheese is at room temperature to avoid lumps. Trying to beat lumps out of cold cream cheese can easily lead to overbeating.

Most cheesecake failures are caused by baking too long or at too high a temperature and/or cooling too quickly. Unfortunately, cracking and shrinking do not become obvious until the cheesecake is out of the oven and cooling, by which time the only answer is to hide any blemishes as described at the end of this discussion. To avoid these problems in the first place ➤ take care to grease the sides of the pan before filling it so that the cake lets go of the pan as it cools and shrinks instead of cracking in the center; ➤ keep baking temperatures low (300° to 325°F, with some exceptions), and take the cake out of the oven when it is set around the edge but still jiggly in the center.

Another way to guard against cracking is to bake cheesecakes in a **water bath,** or bain-marie, which insulates the cake and allows the center and the edges to cook at about the same rate. It virtually guarantees that the cake will be as creamy around the sides as it is in the center, and it promotes a gentle, even rise with very little shrinkage. The water bath is very forgiving: Even 10 minutes of extra baking is unlikely to damage the texture of the cake. ➤ To bake in a water bath, see the recipe for Creamy Water-Bath Cheesecake, 753 (for more information on the technique, see About Custards, 812).

You may ask why we do not recommend baking all cheesecakes in a water bath. Cheesecake crusts do not emerge as crisp if baked in a water bath, and some cheesecake lovers prefer a dense, dry, creamy texture and intense cheese flavor that cannot be produced with a water bath. To each cheesecake maven his or her own, and *vive la différence*!

➤ Cheesecakes do not set until completely cool or even chilled. Cool a cheesecake slowly on the counter with a large bowl or pot inverted over it to keep the environment warm and moist. Some prefer to let cheesecakes cool in the turned-off oven with the door cracked or propped open with a wooden spoon.

➤ The flavor and texture of all cheesecakes profit from thorough chilling before serving, for at least 24 hours, or, preferably, 48 hours; longer chilling intensifies the cheese flavor and the density of the cake. Store cheesecakes, covered, in the refrigerator. Remove an hour or so before serving to bring out the flavor and soften the texture.

Remember: A cracked cheesecake is not the end of the world! Our favorite remedy is to stir some sour cream with a little sugar and vanilla and spread the mixture over the chilled cheesecake. Decorate with a little fresh fruit, and no one will be the wiser.

ADDITIONS TO CHEESECAKE

Vary the flavor of the crust by adding:

Finely ground toasted, 1005, nuts

Spices such as ground cinnamon, cardamom, allspice, and ginger

Gingersnaps or chocolate wafer cookies instead of graham crackers

Fold into plain cheesecake batter:

Fresh berries rolled in sugar

Liquor-soaked chopped dried fruit or minced crystallized ginger

Flavor batters with:

French Praline, 873

Cocoa or instant coffee powder

Finely grated citrus zest

Liquors or liqueurs

Marble them with:

Lemon Curd, 802, or Lime Curd, 802

Jams or preserves

Top baked cheesecakes with:

Bittersweet Chocolate Glaze, 798

Lemon Curd, 802, or Lime Curd, 802

Salted Caramel Sauce, 809

Fresh fruit

Preserves

CHEESECAKE COCKAIGNE

One 10-inch cheesecake; 12 to 16 servings

One of the simplest and best. This old-fashioned sour cream-topped cake is only about 1¼ inches tall.

Lightly grease a 10-inch springform pan. Press evenly into the bottom of the pan:

Crumb Crust, 667, made with graham crackers

Bake as directed in About Crumb Crusts, 667.

Have all ingredients at room temperature, about 70°F. Preheat the oven to 300°F.

Beat in a medium bowl, or in a stand mixer with the paddle attachment, until creamy:

1½ pounds (three 8 oz packages or 680g) cream cheese, softened

Gradually beat in:

1 cup (200g) sugar

1 teaspoon vanilla or ¼ teaspoon almond extract

Beat in one at a time just until incorporated, scraping the sides of the bowl and the beaters after each addition:

3 large eggs

Scrape the batter into the crust and smooth the top. Place on a cookie sheet. Bake until the center just barely jiggles when the pan is tapped, 45 to 55 minutes.

Let cool in the pan on a rack for at least 1 hour.

Combine and spread over the cake:

1 cup (240g) sour cream

¼ cup (50g) sugar

1 teaspoon vanilla

⅛ teaspoon salt

Let cool completely in the pan on a rack before removing the pan ring. Cover and refrigerate for at least 3 hours, preferably 24 hours, before serving. Serve with:

Fresh strawberries

NEW YORK–STYLE CHEESECAKE

One 9-inch cheesecake; 16 to 20 servings

Do not be afraid of the extreme oven temperature—the surface of the cake will be golden, with a creamy interior.

Preheat the oven to 400°F. Lightly grease a 9-inch springform pan.

Prepare:

Pat-in-the-Pan Shortbread Dough, 667

Press one-third of the dough, or slightly less, over the bottom of the pan as evenly as possible. Prick the dough all over with a fork. Bake until the crust is light golden brown, 10 to 15 minutes. Let cool completely on a rack.

Press the remaining dough about ⅛ inch thick around the sides of the pan, making sure that it is attached to the bottom crust all around. Brush the bottom and sides of the crust with:

1 egg white, well beaten

Refrigerate the crust if you are not filling it right away.

Have all ingredients at room temperature, about 70°F. Preheat the oven to 500°F.

Beat in a large bowl, or in a stand mixer with the paddle attachment, until smooth and creamy:

2½ pounds (five 8 oz packages or 1.135kg) cream cheese, softened

Scrape the sides of the bowl and the beaters well. Gradually add and beat until smooth and creamy, 1 to 2 minutes:

1¾ cups (350g) sugar

(Up to 3 tablespoons [25g] all-purpose flour, for a denser texture)

Beat in:

Finely grated zest of 1 lemon

½ teaspoon vanilla

Beat in one at a time just until incorporated, scraping the sides of the bowl and the beaters after each addition:

5 large eggs

2 large egg yolks

On low speed, beat in:

½ cup (115g) heavy cream

Scrape the batter into the crust and smooth the top. Bake for 15 minutes at 500°F, then reduce the oven temperature to 200°F and bake for 1 hour more.

Turn the oven off, prop the oven door ajar with the handle of a wooden spoon, and let the cake cool in the oven for 30 minutes.

Transfer to a rack and let cool completely in the pan before removing the pan ring. Cover and refrigerate for at least 6 hours, preferably 24 hours, before serving. The cheese flavor is even more intense after 48 hours.

CREAMY WATER-BATH CHEESECAKE

One 9-inch cheesecake; 12 to 16 servings

Baking in a water bath yields an ultracreamy cheesecake with a texture that is consistent from the edges to the center. You can bake any crustless cheesecake this way.

Have all ingredients at room temperature, about 70°F. Preheat the oven to 325°F.

Coat the bottom and sides of a 9-inch springform pan with:

1 tablespoon (15g) unsalted butter

Sprinkle with:

¼ cup graham cracker crumbs

Tilt and tap the pan to spread the crumbs evenly over the bottom and sides. Set the pan on a length of wide heavy-duty foil. Fold the foil carefully up against the sides of the pan without tearing it.

Beat in a large bowl, or in a stand mixer with the paddle attachment, just until smooth:

2 pounds (four 8 oz packages or 905g) cream cheese, softened

Scrape the sides of the bowl and the beaters well. Gradually add and beat until smooth and creamy, 1 to 2 minutes:

1⅓ cups (265g) sugar

Beat in one at a time just until incorporated, scraping the sides of the bowl and the beaters after each addition:

4 large eggs

Add and beat on low speed just until mixed:

¼ cup (60g) heavy cream
¼ cup (60g) sour cream
2 teaspoons vanilla
Finely grated zest of 1 lemon

Scrape the batter into the pan and smooth the top. Set the pan in a large baking dish or roasting pan. Set the baking dish on a pulled-out oven rack and pour in enough boiling water to reach halfway up the sides of the cheesecake pan. Bake until the edges of the cheesecake look set but the center jiggles slightly when the pan is tapped, 55 to 60 minutes.

Turn off the oven, prop the door ajar with the handle of a wooden spoon, and let the cake cool in the oven for 1 hour.

Transfer to a rack and let cool completely in the pan before removing the pan ring. Cover and refrigerate for at least 6 hours, preferably for 24 hours, before serving.

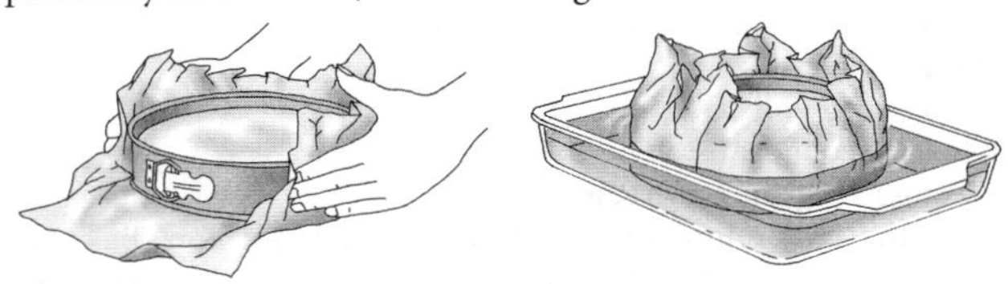

The water-bath method

CHOCOLATE CHEESECAKE

One 9-inch cheesecake; about 16 servings

Richer than rich; for chocolate lovers only.

Lightly grease a 9 × 2-inch springform or round cake pan. Press evenly into the bottom of the pan:

Crumb Crust, 667, made with chocolate wafers

Bake as directed in About Crumb Crusts, 667. Let cool.

Have all ingredients at room temperature, about 70°F. Place a loaf pan or cake pan filled halfway with hot water on the bottom rack of the oven. Preheat the oven to 350°F.

Place in a small heatproof bowl:

8 ounces (225g) semisweet or bittersweet chocolate, finely chopped

Add:

⅓ cup (80g) boiling water

Stir until the chocolate is melted and smooth. Beat in a large bowl, or in a stand mixer with the paddle attachment, just until smooth:

1 pound (two 8 oz packages or 455g) cream cheese, softened

Scrape the sides of the bowl and the beaters well. Gradually add and beat until smooth and creamy, 1 to 2 minutes:

⅔ cup (130g) sugar
1 teaspoon vanilla

Beat in one at a time just until incorporated, scraping the sides of the bowl and the beaters after each addition:

3 large eggs

Beat in:

2 cups (480g) sour cream
1 tablespoon (10g) unsweetened cocoa powder

Add the warm chocolate mixture and beat on low speed just until well blended. Scrape the batter into the crust and smooth the top. Place on a baking sheet and bake until the edges of the cake have puffed but the center still looks moist and jiggles when the pan is tapped, 40 to 45 minutes.

Turn off the oven, prop the door ajar with the handle of a wooden spoon, and let the cake cool in the oven for 1 hour.

Transfer to a rack and let cool completely in the pan before removing the pan ring (if a cake pan was used, do not unmold it). Cover and refrigerate for at least 6 hours, preferably 24 hours, before serving. The flavors are even more intense after 48 hours.

PUMPKIN CHEESECAKE

One 8-inch cheesecake; 10 to 12 servings

We like to serve this golden cheesecake on Thanksgiving as a pleasing contrast to the usual pumpkin pie.

Lightly grease an 8 × 2-inch springform or round cake pan. Press evenly into the bottom of the pan:

Crumb Crust, 667, made with graham crackers or gingersnaps, or Nut Crust, 667, made with pecans

Bake as directed in About Crumb Crusts, 667, or chill as directed in the Nut Crust recipe. Let cool.

Have all ingredients at room temperature, about 70°F. Place a metal loaf pan or cake pan filled halfway with hot water on the bottom rack of the oven. Preheat the oven to 350°F.

Combine in a small bowl:

⅔ cup packed (155g) brown sugar
¾ teaspoon ground cinnamon
¼ teaspoon ground cloves
¼ teaspoon ground ginger
⅛ teaspoon grated or ground nutmeg

Beat in a large bowl, or in a stand mixer with the paddle attachment, just until smooth:

1 pound (two 8 oz packages or 455g) cream cheese, softened

Scrape the sides of the bowl and the beaters well. Gradually add the sugar mixture and beat until smooth and creamy, 1 to 2 minutes. Beat in one at a time until well blended, scraping the sides of the bowl and the beaters after each addition:

2 large eggs
2 large egg yolks

Add and beat in just until mixed:

1 cup canned or cooked unsweetened pumpkin puree

Scrape the batter into the crust and smooth the top. Set the pan on a baking sheet. Bake for 30 minutes at 350°F, then reduce the oven temperature to 325°F and bake until the edges of the cheesecake are puffed but the center still looks moist and jiggles when the pan is tapped, 10 to 15 minutes more.

Meanwhile, whisk together in a small bowl until well blended:

1½ cups (360g) sour cream

⅓ cup packed (75g) light brown sugar

1 teaspoon vanilla

Spread on top of the hot cake and smooth with an offset spatula. Return to the oven for 7 minutes. Remove the pan from the oven and place on a rack, then cover the pan and rack with a large inverted bowl or pot so that the cake cools slowly. Let cool completely before removing the pan ring (if a cake pan was used, do not unmold it). Cover and refrigerate for at least 6 hours, preferably 24 hours, before serving.

▲ ABOUT HIGH-ALTITUDE CAKE BAKING

Cakes baked at high altitudes are subject to pixielike variations that often defy general rules. Cakes begin to react strongly to atmospheric changes at elevations around 3,000 feet above sea level and changes grow more intense as elevation increases: Cakes may rise fast, then fall flat, or cool with a bowl-shaped depression in the center. They may crust over on top and have a sodden center or a coarse and heavy crumb. They may overflow the pan or stick to it.

As for remedies, the only real rule is, alas, that there is no rule. There are some adjustment guidelines, but each recipe requires its own individual changes. To adapt your favorite sea-level recipes, read the advice below, then launch forth on your own, taking notes until you know what gives you the greatest success.

When baking at altitude, take extra care greasing, flouring, and lining pans. Cakes tend to stick to their pans, especially above 7,000 feet, so generously grease and flour all pans, and line them with parchment paper wherever possible.

The higher in elevation you go above sea level, the less the air pressure, so leavening gases (air, carbon dioxide, water vapor) in baked goods expand more quickly. In most recipes, baking powder and/or baking soda must be reduced or rebalanced for proper rise. ➤ Acidity helps a batter set in the heat of the oven, so sometimes you need to reduce the amount of baking soda (which neutralizes the acidity of certain ingredients) more than you would expect in order to leave some of the batter's acidity intact. ➤ Buttermilk is preferred to regular milk above 5,000 feet, because it provides acidity as well as contributing to moisture, richness, and tenderness. With reduced air pressure, whipped egg whites tend to rise spectacularly and then fall flat unless beaten with special care (see the next paragraph). Sometimes adding an extra egg white will improve a sea-level recipe by contributing moisture and strength, but too many whites can dry out a batter, so use caution. For best results, follow our high-altitude recipes exactly as written.

When whipping egg whites at altitudes above 3,000 feet, ➤ you do *not* want stiff peaks; whip the whites on high speed just until you begin to see beater tracks on the surface. At this point, start watching carefully until the whites are smooth, glossy, and form soft, gently droopy peaks when the beaters are lifted. Soft peaks have room to expand and hold shape when baked. At high altitudes, stiff peaks are overwhipped—as they expand when baked, they will burst and the baked goods will collapse.

➤ The higher the elevation, the lower the boiling point of water (see the table, 1070). This makes it harder to deliver enough heat to the center of dense wet cake batter to make it rise. Every 500-foot increase in altitude causes the boiling point of water to drop about 1°F. ➤ The higher the elevation, the longer it takes to bake some cakes and the longer it takes to cook foods in or over liquid; custards take longer to set, cornstarch takes longer to gelatinize and thicken.

When baking cakes, sometimes it is advisable to raise the oven temperature by about 25°F. However, in some cases this can cause the cake to crust over on top before the center bakes through—the solution then is to lower the temperature and bake longer. ➤ An easy fix for loaf cakes and tea breads is to replace the traditional loaf pan with a tube pan in order to deliver heat to the batter's center. The resulting cake won't be as tall but is guaranteed to bake through.

➤ Liquids evaporate faster at higher elevations, leaving behind higher concentrations of sugar and fat. Excess sugar coarsens a cake's texture. Excesses of both sugar and fat reduce the strength of gluten in wheat flour, leaving a weakened structure that can cause a cake to fall. ➤ At high altitudes, many recipes call for reducing the sugar, and some butter-rich recipes also need a slight reduction in fat. ➤ Be sure to use the type of flour called for in a high-altitude recipe: All-purpose flour is often used instead of cake flour because its slightly higher protein content contributes to a stronger batter structure, preventing the cake from collapsing when it cools.

Drier air in mountainous elevations means that ➤ flour often needs more liquid blended into it (although it is primarily the type of flour that governs water requirements—high-protein flour absorbs more liquid than all-purpose flour, which absorbs more water than cake flour). Lower humidity also means that the surfaces of baked goods dry out and cool off more quickly. Baked meringues stay crisp longer, but other baked goods grow stale faster than at sea level. At high altitudes, always double-wrap baked goods airtight as soon as they are completely cool. For freezing, double-wrap airtight, then wrap again with heavy-duty foil or place in a freezer-weight zip-top bag.

Directions for every elevation work approximately 1,500 feet above and below that elevation. For example, recipes for 7,000 feet work up to about 8,500 feet. The recipes in this section are written for 5,000 feet, with adjustments given for higher altitudes. The modifications given in the chart on 756 are simply suggestions, not absolute rules. Because high altitude baking can be mercurial, try the adjustments one at a time when tweaking a recipe, and only after establishing that the recipe needs to be tweaked in the first place. Unfortunately, there are no quick fixes for high-altitude baking (short of using the specially formulated recipes in this section), and trial and error is the best approach.

SPECIFIC ALTITUDE ADJUSTMENTS FOR CAKE BATTERS

ALTITUDE	3,000 FEET	5,000 FEET	7,500 FEET	10,000 FEET
Oven temperature	Increase by 25°F	Increase by 25°F	Bake at 350°F until done	Bake at 350°F until done
Increase each cup flour by	0 to 1 tablespoon	0 to 2 tablespoons	2 to 4 tablespoons	2 to 4 tablespoons
Reduce each teaspoon baking powder or soda by	⅛ teaspoon	⅛ to ¼ teaspoon	¼ to ½ teaspoon	½ to ⅔ teaspoon
Reduce each cup sugar by	0 to 1 tablespoon	0 to 2 tablespoons	2 to 4 tablespoons	3 to 4 tablespoons
Increase each cup liquid by	0 to 2 tablespoons	2 to 4 tablespoons	3 to 4 tablespoons	3 to 4 tablespoons
Reduce each cup fat by	—	—	—	1 to 2 tablespoons

▲ HIGH-ALTITUDE CLASSIC 1-2-3-4 CAKE (OR CUPCAKES)

Two 9-inch round layers, or one 13 × 9-inch cake, or about twenty-four 2¾-inch cupcakes; 16 to 24 servings

This easy-to-remember formula was originally designed—at sea level—for reliability: 1 cup butter, 2 cups sugar, 3 cups flour, 4 eggs. At higher elevations, because adjustments are needed, the numbers and proportions change, as you will see below. You can vary the flavor, keeping the vanilla, by adding orange, lemon, or almond extract. Please read About High-Altitude Cake Baking, 755, and About Butter Cakes, 723. This recipe is designed for baking at 5,000 feet.

If baking at 7,000 feet, reduce the oven temperature to 350°F. Add 2 tablespoons (15g) flour, reduce the sugar by 1 tablespoon (10g), and add 2 tablespoons (30g) buttermilk. Bake layers for 22 to 27 minutes, a sheet cake for 30 to 32 minutes, or cupcakes for 22 to 25 minutes.

If baking at 10,000 feet, preheat the oven to 375°F, then reduce the temperature to bake at 350°F. Add 2 tablespoons (15g) flour and 3 tablespoons plus 1 teaspoon (50g) buttermilk; reduce the baking powder by ½ teaspoon and the sugar by 1 tablespoon (10g). Bake layers for 28 to 30 minutes, sheet cake for 30 to 35 minutes, or cupcakes for 28 to 30 minutes.

Have all ingredients at room temperature, about 70°F. Preheat the oven to 375°F. Thoroughly grease and flour two 9-inch round cake pans, one 13 × 9-inch baking pan, or two 12-cup muffin tins. Line round cake pans with parchment paper and muffin tins with paper liners.

Whisk together thoroughly in a medium bowl:

3 cups plus 1 tablespoon sifted (370g) all-purpose flour
2 teaspoons baking powder
¾ teaspoon salt

Beat in a large bowl, or in a stand mixer with the paddle attachment, until well blended:

2 sticks (8 oz or 225g) unsalted butter, softened
2 cups minus 1 tablespoon (390g) sugar
2 teaspoons vanilla
(1 teaspoon almond or other extract)

Scrape down the bowl and beat for 1 minute. Add 2 at a time, beating well after each addition:

5 large eggs

Scrape down the bowl. (Don't worry if the batter looks curdled.) On low speed, add the flour mixture in 2 parts, alternating with:

1 cup plus 2 tablespoons (275g) buttermilk

in 2 parts, blending well. Then beat on high speed for about 1 minute or until the batter is smooth and creamy. Divide the batter between the round pans, scrape into the baking pan, or, for cupcakes, fill the cups almost three-quarters full. Bake until a toothpick inserted into the center comes out clean, 22 to 25 minutes for layers, 30 to 33 minutes for the sheet cake, or 20 to 22 minutes for cupcakes.

Let cool in the pans on a rack for about 15 minutes. Unmold if applicable and cool completely. (The sheet cake can be cooled in and served from the pan.)

▲ HIGH-ALTITUDE ANGEL FOOD CAKE

One 10-inch tube cake

Please read About High-Altitude Cake Baking, 755, and About Angel Food Cakes, 718. This recipe is designed for baking at 5,000 to 7,000 feet.

If baking at 10,000 feet, reduce the oven temperature to 350°F. Add 2 tablespoons (15g) flour, ½ teaspoon cream of tartar, and 1 more teaspoon almond or orange extract, if using. Bake for 30 to 35 minutes.

Have all ingredients at room temperature, about 70°F. Preheat the oven to 375°F. Have ready an ungreased 10-inch tube pan.

Sift together and return to the sifter:

1 cup plus 2 tablespoons sifted (115g) cake flour
½ cup (50g) powdered sugar

Beat in a large bowl, or in a stand mixer with the whisk attachment, until foamy:

1½ cups (365g) egg whites (about 11 large whites)
1½ teaspoons cream of tartar
½ teaspoon salt

Gradually add and beat on high speed until soft, slightly droopy peaks form:

¾ cup (145g) superfine sugar

Fold in:

2 teaspoons vanilla
(1 teaspoon almond or orange extract)
2 tablespoons (30g) water

Add the dry ingredients one-quarter at a time, sifting them over the whites and gently folding them in, until no flour is visible. Scoop the batter into the tube pan. Gently run a knife through the batter once to burst any large air bubbles. Bake until a cake tester inserted into the center comes out clean, 25 to 30 minutes.

To cool and unmold, see Angel Food Cake, 719. Top the cake with a little sifted:

Powdered sugar

▲ HIGH-ALTITUDE CHOCOLATE ANGEL FOOD CAKE

Prepare **High-Altitude Angel Food Cake, 756,** reducing the cake flour to 1 cup (100g) and adding **¼ cup sifted (20g) unsweetened Dutch-process cocoa powder.** Increase the sugar by ¼ cup (50g).

▲ HIGH-ALTITUDE WHITE CAKE

Two 8- or 9-inch round layers

The batter rises higher in 8-inch pans than in 9-inch pans, but the latter is fine if you don't mind a cake with 1-inch-high layers. Please read About High-Altitude Cake Baking, 755, and About Butter Cakes, 723. This recipe is designed for baking at 5,000 feet.

If baking at 7,000 feet, preheat the oven to 350°F. Reduce the baking powder by ¼ teaspoon and the sugar creamed with the butter by 2 tablespoons (30g). Add ¼ teaspoon cream of tartar and replace the milk with buttermilk and increase by 1½ tablespoons (25g). Bake about 25 minutes.

If baking at 10,000 feet, bake at 375°F. Use a blend of 1¼ cups plus 1 tablespoon sifted (130g) cake flour and 1¼ cups plus 1 tablespoon sifted (160g) all-purpose flour. Reduce the baking powder by ¼ teaspoon, the butter by 1 tablespoon (15g), and the sugar creamed with butter by ¼ cup (50g). Add ¼ teaspoon salt, ¼ teaspoon cream of tartar, and ½ teaspoon each vanilla and almond extract. Replace the milk with buttermilk and increase by ¼ cup (60g). Bake about 27 minutes.

Have all ingredients at room temperature, about 70°F. Preheat the oven to 375°F. Thoroughly grease and flour two 8- or 9-inch round cake pans and line with rounds of parchment paper.

Whisk together thoroughly in a medium bowl:

2½ cups sifted (250g) cake flour
1½ teaspoons baking powder
¼ teaspoon salt

Beat in a large bowl, or in a stand mixer with the whisk attachment, until foamy:

4 large egg whites
¼ teaspoon cream of tartar

Gradually add and beat on high speed until soft, slightly droopy peaks form:

⅓ cup (65g) sugar

Beat in another large bowl (or transfer the egg whites to another bowl and reuse the stand mixer bowl with the paddle attachment) until well blended:

1 stick (4 oz or 115g) unsalted butter, softened
1 cup (200g) sugar
1 teaspoon vanilla
(1 teaspoon almond or other extract)

On low speed, add the flour mixture in 3 parts, alternating with:

1¼ cups (295g) milk

in 2 parts, scraping down the bowl after each addition. Beat on high about 30 seconds, until smooth and creamy. Gently fold the whites into the batter in 3 additions with a silicone spatula. Divide the batter between the pans. Bake until a cake tester inserted into the center comes out clean, 25 to 27 minutes.

Let cool in the pans on a rack for 10 to 15 minutes. Invert the cakes out of the pans, remove the paper liners, and set right side up on the rack to cool completely.

▲ HIGH-ALTITUDE FUDGE CAKE

Two 9-inch round layers, one 13 × 9-inch cake, or about twenty-four 2¾-inch cupcakes; 16 to 24 servings

This cake has a rich chocolate flavor and moist tender crumb. Unsweetened chocolate gives a slightly deeper chocolate flavor but you can also use semisweet chocolate chips. Please read About High-Altitude Cake Baking, 755, and About Butter Cakes, 723. This recipe is designed for baking at 5,000 feet.

If baking at 7,000 feet, replace the cake flour with sifted all-purpose flour (240g) and reduce the baking powder by ½ teaspoon. Replace the regular milk with buttermilk and increase it by 1 tablespoon (15g). Reduce the sugar beaten into the whites to 2 tablespoons (25g). Bake layers or a sheet cake for 35 to 40 minutes, cupcakes for 15 to 20 minutes.

If baking at 10,000 feet, replace the cake flour with sifted all-purpose flour and increase by 1 tablespoon (250g total), and reduce the baking powder by ¾ teaspoon. If using unsweetened chocolate, reduce the sugar beaten with the butter by ½ cup (100g); if using semisweet chocolate, reduce it by ¾ cup (150g). Replace the milk with buttermilk and increase it by 2 tablespoons (30g). Bake layers about 33 minutes, a sheet cake about 42 minutes, or cupcakes 25 minutes.

Have all ingredients at room temperature, about 70°F. Preheat the oven to 350°F. Thoroughly grease and flour two 9-inch round cake pans, one 13 × 9-inch baking pan, or two 12-cup muffin tins. Line round cake pans with parchment paper and muffin tins with paper liners.

Melt, stirring constantly, in a double boiler or heatproof bowl over barely simmering water:

4 ounces (115g) unsweetened chocolate, chopped, or 1 cup semisweet chocolate chips

Whisk together thoroughly in a medium bowl:

2 cups sifted (200g) cake flour
2 teaspoons baking powder
½ teaspoon salt

Beat in a large bowl, or in a stand mixer with the whisk attachment, until foamy:

3 large egg whites
¼ teaspoon cream of tartar

Gradually add and beat on high speed until soft, slightly droopy peaks form:

¼ cup (50g) sugar

Set aside. Beat in another large bowl (or transfer the egg whites to another bowl and reuse the stand mixer bowl with the paddle attachment) until light and fluffy:

1 stick (4 oz or 115g) unsalted butter, softened
2 cups (400g) sugar (reduce to 1½ cups [300g] if using chocolate chips)
2 teaspoons vanilla

Scrape down the bowl and beat a few seconds longer. Beat in, blending well:

3 large egg yolks

Beat in the melted chocolate. Scrape down the bowl. On low speed, add the flour mixture in 3 parts, alternating with:

1½ cups (355g) milk

in 2 parts, scraping down the bowl and beating well after each addition. Gently fold in the whites by hand in 3 additions until the batter no longer looks streaky. Divide the batter between the round pans, scrape into the baking pan, or, for cupcakes, fill cups almost three-quarters full. Bake until a cake tester inserted into the center comes out clean, 35 to 40 minutes for layers or a sheet pan, 15 to 20 minutes for cupcakes.

Let cool in the pan(s) on a wire rack for 10 to 15 minutes. Then unmold and cool completely. (The sheet cake can be cooled in and served from the pan.)

▲ HIGH-ALTITUDE CITRUS SPONGE CAKE

One 10-inch Bundt cake

Please read About High-Altitude Cake Baking, 755, and About Butter Cakes, 723. This recipe is for baking at 5,000 through 7,000 feet. ***At 10,000 feet,*** reduce the oven heat to 350°F. Reduce the butter by 2 tablespoons (30g), use only 7 yolks, and reduce the sugar beaten into the yolks by 2 tablespoons (25g). Increase the flour by 2⅓ tablespoons (20g) and the cream of tartar by ½ teaspoon. Bake 25 to 30 minutes, then (without cooling first) immediately invert onto a rack, unmold, and cool completely.

Have all ingredients at room temperature, about 70°F. Preheat the oven to 375°F. Grease a 10-inch Bundt pan generously and dust with flour; tap out excess flour.

Combine in a medium bowl:

3 tablespoons (45g) unsalted butter
Finely grated zest of 2 lemons
Finely grated zest of 1 orange
¼ cup (60g) lemon juice
2 teaspoons lemon extract
1 teaspoon vanilla

Sift together and return to the sifter:

1¼ cups plus 1 tablespoon sifted (130g) cake flour
½ teaspoon salt

Beat in a large bowl, or in a stand mixer with the whisk attachment, until foamy:

7 large egg whites
½ teaspoon cream of tartar

Gradually add and beat on high speed until soft, slightly droopy peaks form:

½ cup (100g) sugar

Beat in another large bowl (or transfer the egg whites to another bowl and reuse the stand mixer bowl and the whisk) on high speed until the batter is thick and a pale lemony color and forms a continuous flat ribbon when dropped from the beaters:

8 large egg yolks
½ cup (100g) sugar

Reserve about 1½ cups of the egg whites. Fold the remaining whites into the batter in 2 additions alternating with the flour in 2 additions (sift the flour on top and then fold in). Stir the melted butter–lemon juice mixture and fold into the reserved whites; try to maintain volume in the whites while blending in the liquid. Fold the lemon mixture into the batter; make sure no liquid pools in the bottom of the bowl. Scrape the batter into the pan and run a knife through the batter once to release any large air bubbles. Bake until a cake tester inserted into the center comes out clean, 20 to 25 minutes.

Let cool in the pan on a rack for about 10 minutes. Run a knife between the cake sides and tube, top with a plate, invert, and unmold. Let cool completely.

Just before serving, sprinkle with:

Powdered sugar

Slice with a serrated knife.

▲ HIGH-ALTITUDE CARROT CAKE

One 9½- or 10-inch Bundt or plain tube cake

The best-ever carrot cake—not too sweet and packed with nuts, raisins, and sunflower seeds. Top it with a simple dusting of powdered sugar, or spread with the traditional Cream Cheese Frosting, 792. Please read About High-Altitude Cake Baking, 755. This recipe is designed for baking at 5,000 feet.

If baking at 7,000 feet, reduce the oven temperature to 350°F. Reduce the sugar by ¼ cup (50g), and add 2 tablespoons (15g) flour and ¼ teaspoon ginger. Bake for 35 to 40 minutes.

If baking at 10,000 feet, preheat the oven to 375°F, then reduce the temperature to bake at 350°F. Reduce the oil by ¼ cup (50g), the sugar by ½ cup (100g), and the baking soda by ¼ teaspoon. Add 1 large egg plus 1 yolk, ¼ cup (30g) flour, and ¼ teaspoon each nutmeg and ginger. Bake for 55 to 58 minutes.

Have all ingredients at room temperature, about 70°F. Preheat the oven to 375°F. Liberally grease and flour a 9½- or 10-inch Bundt or plain tube pan.

Toss together in a medium bowl:

3 cups grated carrots
1 cup chopped walnuts
(¼ cup sunflower seeds)
(⅓ cup raisins or dried currants)
¼ cup wheat germ (20g), wheat bran (15g), or oat bran (25g)

Whisk together in a large bowl:

2 cups (400g) sugar
1½ cups (315g) vegetable oil
6 large eggs
2 teaspoons vanilla

Place a large sieve over the bowl with the oil-egg mixture and measure into it:

2 cups plus 1 tablespoon sifted (250g) all-purpose flour
2 teaspoons ground cinnamon
1½ teaspoons baking soda
1 teaspoon salt
¾ teaspoon grated or ground nutmeg
½ teaspoon ground ginger
½ teaspoon ground allspice

Sift the dry ingredients into the oil-egg mixture and stir to combine. Stir in the carrot-nut mixture. Scrape the batter into the pan and bake until a toothpick inserted into the center comes out clean, 42 to 45 minutes.

Let cool in the pan on a rack for about 25 minutes, or until the pan bottom is almost comfortable to touch. Unmold and let cool completely.

▲ HIGH ALTITUDE PEACH-PECAN UPSIDE-DOWN CAKE

One 9- or 10-inch round cake

This delicious peach variation on traditional pineapple upside-down cake has a lightly spiced cake and buttery honey-cardamom sauce. Fresh or whole frozen raspberries can be substituted for the nuts. Replace the peaches with nectarines, or use fresh or canned apricots, pears, or whole frozen berries. Please read About High-Altitude Cake Baking, 755. This recipe is for baking at 5,000 feet.

If baking at 7,000 feet, reduce the oven temperature to 325°F and bake for 40 minutes.

If baking at 10,000 feet, bake at 350°F. Reduce the sugar in the topping by 1 tablespoon (10g). Reduce the sugar in the batter by 2 tablespoons plus 2 teaspoons (30g) and the baking powder by ½ teaspoon; add 2 tablespoons (15g) flour and ¼ teaspoon salt. Bake for 45 to 48 minutes.

Have all ingredients at room temperature, about 70°F. Preheat the oven to 350°F.

Have ready:

30 slices peeled fresh peaches (3 or 4 medium to large), 30 frozen (or partially thawed) peach slices, or 30 canned peach slices (from two 15-ounce cans in light syrup), drained on paper towels

Combine in a 10-inch ovenproof skillet and stir over medium heat until the butter is melted:

5 tablespoons (70g) unsalted butter
⅔ cup packed (155g) light brown sugar (or slightly less if fruit is very juicy)

Add, stirring until smooth and just beginning to bubble:

¼ cup (85g) honey
¼ teaspoon grated or ground nutmeg
¼ teaspoon ground cardamom
Pinch of salt

Remove from the heat. Arrange the peach slices in the syrup in a pinwheel pattern. Tuck in around the peaches:

½ cup pecan halves or pieces, toasted, 1005

Whisk together thoroughly in a medium bowl:

1½ cups (190g) all-purpose flour
1½ teaspoons baking powder
1½ teaspoons ground ginger
1 teaspoon ground cardamom
½ teaspoon ground cinnamon
½ teaspoon grated or ground nutmeg
¼ teaspoon salt

Beat together in a large bowl, or in a stand mixer with the paddle attachment:

½ cup (100g) sugar
5⅓ tablespoons (75g) unsalted butter, melted
⅓ cup (80g) buttermilk
¼ cup (85g) honey
2 large eggs
1 teaspoon vanilla

Add the flour mixture to the butter-sugar mixture and stir well to blend. Spoon the batter over the fruit in the skillet. (Don't worry if the batter looks skimpy; it spreads as it bakes.) Set the skillet on a cookie sheet and bake until a cake tester inserted into the center comes out clean or with a few moist crumbs, 35 to 40 minutes.

Let cool in the skillet on a rack for about 5 minutes, or until the juices stop bubbling. Cover the cake with a serving plate that has a lip to catch the sauce, and invert with a sharp downward shake. Lift off the skillet and reposition any fruit stuck to the skillet. Let cool about 5 minutes and serve warm, if desired, with:

(Whipped Cream, 791)

▲ HIGH-ALTITUDE SOUR CREAM STREUSEL COFFEE CAKE

One 9- or 9½-inch Bundt cake

This rich moist cake, layered with crunchy cinnamon-nut crumbs is wonderfully satisfying. It's everyone's favorite at a brunch or picnic and tastes even better the day after it is baked. Please read About High-Altitude Cake Baking, 755, and About Butter Cakes, 723. This recipe is designed for baking at 5,000 feet.

If baking at 7,000 feet, reduce the oven temperature to 350°F. Add 2½ tablespoons (40g) milk or buttermilk. Bake for 50 to 55 minutes.

If baking at 10,000 feet, reduce the oven temperature to 350°F. Add 3 tablespoons (25g) flour, 1 tablespoon (10g) sugar, and 2 tablespoons plus 1 teaspoon (35g) milk or buttermilk. Bake for 55 to 58 minutes.

Have all ingredients at room temperature, about 70°F. Preheat the oven to 375°F. Liberally grease and flour a 9- to 9½-inch Bundt pan.

Combine in a small bowl:

¾ cup chopped toasted, 1005, walnuts
⅓ cup (65g) sugar
¾ teaspoon ground cinnamon

Whisk together thoroughly in a medium bowl:

3 cups sifted (360g) all-purpose flour
1 teaspoon baking powder
1 teaspoon salt
½ teaspoon baking soda

Beat in a large bowl, or in a stand mixer with the paddle attachment, until well blended:

1¼ cups (250g) sugar
1½ sticks (6 oz or 170g) unsalted butter, softened
2 teaspoons vanilla

Scrape down the sides of the bowl and the beaters and beat for 1 minute. Add 2 at a time, beating well after each addition:

5 large eggs

Scrape down the bowl and beat in:

1½ cups (360g) sour cream
3 tablespoons (45g) milk or buttermilk

On low speed, gradually add the flour mixture. Scrape down the bowl and beat just until smooth, thick, and creamy; don't overbeat. Sprinkle over the bottom of the prepared baking pan:

¼ cup chopped toasted, 1005, walnuts

Spoon about 2 cups batter over the nuts, covering them completely. Sprinkle on about half the cinnamon-nut crumbs, taking care not to spread them quite to the pan edges. Top with about 2 more cups of batter, add the remaining crumbs, and top with the remaining batter. Bake until a toothpick inserted into the center comes out clean, 45 to 50 minutes.

Let cool in the pan on a rack for about 25 minutes, or until the pan feels comfortable to touch. Unmold and cool completely.

▲ HIGH-ALTITUDE GINGERBREAD

One 9-inch square cake

This moist, tender gingerbread has a wonderfully spicy kick. Serious ginger lovers can also add grated fresh ginger. Please read About High-Altitude at Cake Baking, 755, and About Butter Cakes, 723. This recipe is for baking at 5,000 feet.

If baking at 7,000 feet, reduce the oven temperature to 350°F. Add ¼ teaspoon salt and increase the hot water by 2 tablespoons (30g). Bake 40 to 45 minutes.

If baking at 10,000 feet, bake at 375°F. Omit the baking powder and reduce the baking soda by ¼ teaspoon and the sugar by 2 tablespoons (25g). Bake for 42 to 45 minutes.

Have all ingredients at room temperature, about 70°F. Preheat the oven to 375°F. Grease and flour a 9-inch square baking pan and line the bottom with parchment paper.

Whisk together thoroughly in a medium bowl:

2½ cups sifted (300g) all-purpose flour
1½ tablespoons ground ginger
1 teaspoon ground cinnamon
¾ teaspoon baking soda
½ teaspoon baking powder
½ teaspoon salt
½ teaspoon grated or ground nutmeg
¼ teaspoon black or white pepper

Beat in a large bowl, or in a stand mixer with the paddle attachment, until well blended:

1 stick (4 oz or 115g) unsalted butter, softened
½ cup plus 2 tablespoons (125g) sugar

Add one at a time, beating well after each addition:

2 large eggs

Scrape down the sides of the bowl and the beaters and beat in:

⅔ cup (160g) sour cream
(1-inch piece ginger, peeled and grated)

Combine in a 2-cup measure with a pouring lip and stir until dissolved:

1 cup (235g) very hot water
½ cup (170g) molasses

On lowest speed, add the flour mixture in 4 parts, alternating with the molasses mixture in 3 parts, scraping down the bowl after each addition and beating until smooth. The batter will be quite runny. Pour the batter into the pan and bake until a toothpick inserted into the center comes out clean, 35 to 40 minutes.

Let cool in the pan on a rack. Serve from the pan, topped with:

(Whipped Cream, 791)

▲ HIGH-ALTITUDE CHOCOLATE SPONGE ROLL

One 15 × 10-inch sheet, for a 10-inch roll

Using natural cocoa, which is slightly more acidic, gives the best results. Fill this cake with your favorite preserves, sweetened whipped cream, or any buttercream icing, 795–97. For Christmas, this can be made into a Bûche de Noël, 748. Please read About High-Altitude Cake Baking, 755, and About Roll Cakes, 746. This recipe is designed for baking at 5,000 feet.

If baking at 7,000 feet, add ½ teaspoon cream of tartar. Bake for 9 to 10 minutes.

If baking at 10,000 feet, reduce the oven temperature to 350°F. Add 1 tablespoon flour, reduce the baking powder by ⅛ teaspoon, and increase the cream of tartar to 1 teaspoon. Bake for 9 to 10 minutes.

Have all ingredients at room temperature, about 70°F. Preheat the oven to 375°F. Grease a 15½ × 10½-inch jelly-roll pan, line the bottom with parchment paper, generously grease the paper, and dust with flour. This recipe will also work with a 17½ × 11½ × 1-inch pan, but the cake will be slightly thinner (check the cake for doneness early).

Whisk together thoroughly in a medium bowl:

¼ cup sifted (25g) cake flour
¼ cup (20g) unsweetened cocoa powder, sifted
½ teaspoon baking powder
¼ teaspoon salt

Beat in a large bowl, or in a stand mixer with the whisk attachment, until foamy:

6 large egg whites
¼ teaspoon cream of tartar

Gradually add and beat on high speed until soft, slightly droopy peaks form:

3 tablespoons (35g) sugar

Set aside. Beat in another large bowl (or transfer the egg whites to another bowl and reuse the stand mixer bowl with the whisk attachment) on high speed until the batter is thick and a pale lemony color and forms a continuous flat ribbon falling back on itself when dropped from the beaters:

6 large egg yolks
3 tablespoons (35g) sugar
½ teaspoon vanilla

Fold in about one-third of the egg whites. Sprinkle about one-quarter of the cocoa-flour mixture onto the batter and fold in with a light touch to avoid losing volume. Repeat, alternately folding in the whites and cocoa-flour mixture; don't worry if there are still a few streaks of white. Scrape the batter into the pan and spread it evenly. Bake until the top is springy to the touch and a toothpick inserted into the center comes out clean, 5 to 7 minutes; don't overbake, or the cake will be dry.

Meanwhile, sift onto a clean kitchen towel in an area the size of the baking pan:

⅓ cup (25g) unsweetened cocoa powder

As soon as the cake is baked, invert the pan over the cocoa, lift off the pan, and peel off the paper liner. With a serrated knife, trim off about ⅛ inch of the crusty cake edges. Leave the cake flat until it cools completely, then spread with the desired filling, roll, see Cake Sheet for Roll Cakes, 746, wrap, and refrigerate for at least 1 hour, or until firm. If not filling immediately, wrap tightly in plastic wrap to prevent it from drying out.

COOKIES AND BARS

Marion Becker marked the recipes that emerged from her kitchen with the appellation "Cockaigne," the medieval French name of a mythical land of abundance where rivers run with wine, houses are made of cake, and roast fowl roam the streets, asking to be eaten (for a quintessentially American twist on this, listen to the song "Big Rock Candy Mountain"). It is no accident that the word "cookie" comes from the same root word as Cockaigne; we imagine Marion's modest kitchen was often enveloped in the scent of baking cookies, a singular pleasure that conjures a sense of comfort, home, and sated appetites. The simplicity and ease of baking cookies only adds to this sense of abundance: With knowledge of a few straightforward techniques, basic cupboard ingredients, and a few baking sheets, cookies can be effortlessly churned out of the humblest of kitchens.

ABOUT COOKIE DOUGH

Some cookie dough ingredients are stirred together; some are creamed to combine, 709, and others are blended like pastry, 661. Unless otherwise specified, ➤ let your ingredients warm almost to room temperature. And once you add the flour to the wet ingredients in a recipe, don't overbeat the dough: This can result in tough cookies.

While nothing compares to the flavor of a cookie made entirely with butter, lard, shortening, and coconut oil can be substituted with limited success. Butter is 85 percent fat and 15 percent water. Some margarines have the same ratio of fat to water (see the nutritional facts panel to see if your product is one of these). To get similar results from pure shortening, you will need to substitute 7 tablespoons (85g) shortening and 1 tablespoon water for every 1 stick (4 oz or 115g) butter. ➤ Do not use reduced-fat tub margarines and "spreads" when making cookies.

Using a shortening or margarine formulated to melt at the same temperature as butter will help as well. Butter melts at 90° to 95°F, about the same as lard; virgin coconut oil melts at 76°F, which means that it needs to be chilled slightly to be creamed (or confined to recipes that call for melted butter or oil) and will produce a dough that spreads faster, resulting in thinner and crispier cookies. On the other hand, vegetable shortening usually melts at 117°F (though some organic brands are formulated to melt at around 100°F; check the label or consult the manufacturer's website), which will keep the dough from spreading, resulting in thicker, paler cookies with a softer texture.

Our recipes call for all-purpose flour, and you can use bleached or unbleached. Keep in mind that ➤ too much flour makes cookies tough and dry; too little makes them spread and lose their shape. You may want to combine different flours. In general, we suggest substituting no more than half whole wheat flour or nonwheat alternatives, 985, for the all-purpose flour in a recipe. It is possible to use all whole wheat flour in some recipes, but expect the cookies to be a bit dense and dry. Whole wheat pastry flour, which is milled from a softer wheat, and white whole wheat flour, milled from white rather than red wheat, are better options, and will produce tender cookies. If using whole wheat flour, you will likely need to increase the liquid in the recipe slightly (whole wheat flour absorbs more water). Add a small amount of water or milk to help bring the dough together if needed. Richly flavored doughs made with molasses, chocolate, or peanut butter produce the best whole wheat cookies.

In recipes with additions to the cookie dough such as nuts, dried fruits, or chocolate chips, changes in these ingredients are easy. Experimentation is the best teacher. Substitute dried fruit for nuts, nuts for dried fruit, or use a combination of both. If you have a favorite type of nut, use it instead of the one called for. The same goes for extracts, chocolate chips, or coconut.

DECORATING COOKIES

We've always liked the idea of decorations that provide a clue to a cookie's flavor—a sprinkling of cinnamon and sugar to advertise a hint of spices, for example, or a few coconut shreds to signal a coconut filling. Whatever you choose for decoration, it is best to keep it simple.

Before baking, you may shower the dough with flavorful, crunchy sugar, such as turbinado, or a judicious sprinkle of flaky salt. To ensure that nonpareils and other garnishes will stay on top of cookies, press them firmly into the dough (use a wide-bladed spatula if the cookies are flat).

Some decorations can be added in the final minutes of baking: Try adding small chunks of bittersweet chocolate or caramel candy to the top of cookies and briefly return them to the oven to soften them.

Of course, you may decorate the cookies after baking by securing garnishes with Royal Icing, 798. Or dip them in melted or tempered chocolate, 858, and sprinkle the chocolate with chopped nuts, coconut, flaky sea salt, or crushed peppermint sticks.

ABOUT BAKING COOKIES

Always preheat the oven at least 20 minutes before baking. If you use a convection oven to bake cookies, set it 25°F lower than the recipes call for or follow the manufacturer's instructions. Choose a medium- to heavy-gauge baking sheet or cookie sheet. Do not use pans with high sides, as they not only deflect the heat but make the cookies hard to remove. The very best aluminum sheets have a shiny baking surface and specially dulled bottoms to produce even browning. If you have only thin dark sheets, you can place a second empty sheet under the first while baking, for insulation.

Some cookies—such as shortbread and others that have a high amount of fat, for instance—can be baked on ungreased baking sheets. Unless the recipe specifies otherwise, grease baking sheets with butter, shortening, or a coating of cooking spray, or use parchment paper. Silicone liners work best for doughs that are very sticky or have very little fat, or for cookies that are very thin and delicate. Avoid using silicone liners unless called for, as they inhibit browning; ➤ for most cookies, we prefer lining with parchment paper. Try to keep cookies a uniform size and thickness and space them as directed.

Because many factors can affect baking time, you will find a range of suggested times in our recipes. Set your timer to the minimum time specified. If necessary, reset it and bake for the additional time. It takes only a matter of moments for cookies to bake too long or burn (especially cookies containing molasses or brown sugar). ➤ If you are baking more than 1 sheet of cookies at a time, switch the sheets from rack to rack and also rotate them front to back halfway through baking so they cook evenly.

Within 2 to 3 minutes after cookies have finished baking, use a wide, thin-bladed spatula to lift the cookies and place them on racks to cool. If the cookies cool and stick to the sheet, return them to the oven for a few minutes to heat and soften again. Between batches, baking sheets should be cooled for a bit to ensure that the next batch doesn't overspread. If you have one or two extra baking sheets on hand, you can bake cookies more efficiently by loading them while the others bake off. ➤ When baking several batches of cookies it is best to keep the dough in the refrigerator while waiting for the cookies in the oven to bake. Leaving the dough out in a warm kitchen can cause the cookies to spread more and more as time goes on.

▲ BAKING COOKIES AT HIGH ALTITUDES

Between sea level and 3,000 feet, simple sugar cookies may not require any adjustments, but above that altitude, many types begin to show some changes. At 5,000 feet and above, cookies tend to spread more and get tougher or overcrisp. To control spread, strengthen the batter by adding a little flour and/or decreasing sugar. You may also try slightly reducing the amount of baking powder, baking soda, or cream of tartar. Oven temperature can be increased 15° to 25°F in some cases, though other cookies benefit from longer baking at moderate temperature; there is no single fix. If the texture is too dry, add a tablespoon or more liquid or another egg yolk or a little dark corn syrup. In high dry air, cookies stale quickly and must be stored airtight as soon as they are completely cooled.

STORING BAKED COOKIES

Cookies tend to dry out or go limp if not properly stored. Keep cookies in tightly covered plastic storage containers, cookie tins, or resealable plastic bags. ➤ Never put cookies in any kind of container until they have cooled completely. Warm cookies will produce steam, which will cause the entire batch to soften, and eventually to spoil. And if the cookies have been iced, let the icing set and dry completely before storing them. Pack each type of cookie in its own container to prevent the mingling of flavors and changes in moisture content.

Most cookies can be stored at room temperature for 1 to 2 weeks. To restore freshness, cookies can be heated briefly before serving. Cookies that have dried out and hardened may be refreshed by placing a piece of apple in the container of cookies. Close the lid tightly, and in a day or two, the cookies will have softened.

Most cookies freeze well for a month if packed airtight. Brownies, chocolate chip and sugar cookies, and thin, crispy varieties freeze particularly well. If freezing bar cookies, freeze them uncut, then cut into servings when partially thawed. Cookies should be frozen without icing or decorations. Allow them to thaw completely before sugar-coating, glazing, or frosting. When setting cookies out to thaw, it is best to partially unwrap them so they can breathe and so condensation won't build up. If you want to eat frozen cookies right away, lay them on baking sheets and warm in a preheated 300°F oven for a few minutes.

ABOUT STORING COOKIE DOUGH

Cookie dough can be frozen for 2 months or refrigerated for 3 days with or without rolling, dropping, or shaping. ➤ If you want fresh cookies on short notice, your best bet is to freeze cut or portioned dough. Or, use the "icebox cookie" method: Roll the dough into an even cylinder, wrap it in plastic, freeze it, and cut discs from the dough as needed (see About Icebox or Refrigerator Cookies, 780). Drop-cookie dough can be portioned, frozen on a baking sheet, then put in a zip-top bag and baked as needed. Roll-cookie dough can be rolled out between parchment paper, frozen, then wrapped well in plastic wrap. You can cut out the shapes before or after freezing. For tender or sticky roll-cookie doughs, it is often easier to roll out and cut the dough (without removing the cut-outs), freeze the whole sheet of dough, and then pop the shapes out for baking. Store bar-cookie dough covered tightly in the container in which it will be baked. ➤ To bake frozen cookie dough, simply use the temperature as directed in the recipe, and add a few minutes to the cooking time if needed.

ABOUT PACKAGING COOKIES FOR SHIPPING AND GIFT GIVING

If you are mailing cookies, the best choices are bar cookies or small to medium cookies that are at least ¼ inch thick and firm in consistency. More delicate varieties can be shipped successfully if they are packed in tins or sturdy plastic boxes with crumpled wax or parchment paper to protect them. Extremely thin, brittle cookies and tender, crumbly ones do not travel well, nor do cookies with sticky glazes or with moist fillings or glazes. Meringue kisses and other egg white cookies are also an unwise choice.

After placing the cookies in durable rigid containers, pack them in larger boxes filled with bubble wrap, crumpled newspaper, or popcorn (Marion's favorite) to cushion the goodies from bumps and knocks.

If you plan to personally deliver your cookies to their recipients, cookie tins, ceramic cookie jars, clear glass storage jars, and decorative wooden boxes all make a gift of home-baked cookies more special. Secure loose lids by tying the containers up with ribbons. If you have sewing skills, you can also present cookies in fabric sacks tied with ribbon or fancy twist-ties made with wire ribbon. (Slip a plastic bag, cut down to size, inside for an airtight liner.) Small, dainty cookies can be tucked into colored candy papers or mini cupcake cups in flat candy boxes. For a special touch, when you tie the ribbon around the gift bag or box, secure a cookie cutter in the bow, and include the recipe.

ABOUT CHRISTMAS COOKIES AND COOKIE ORNAMENTS

Christmas and cookies are inseparable. Stars, angels, bells, and trees are all time-honored shapes for holiday treats. You may already have a collection of cookie cutters that you use at this special time of year, or you may cut your own shapes. Christmas classics include Zimsterne, 779, Mexican Wedding Cakes, 773, Pfeffernüsse, 772, Spekulatius, 779, Springerle, 779, Lebkuchen, 768, Rolled Sugar Cookies, 776, Gingerbread Men, 776, Linzer Hearts, 785, Viennese Crescents, 777, and Spritz Cookies, 780.

To prepare a cookie for hanging as an ornament, use a sturdy dough, such as the dough for Gingerbread House, 787. Use the end of a straw to cut a hole through the uncooked shaped dough. Be sure the hole is far enough from the top so that the cookie is strong enough not to break when it hangs. Bake the cookies until firm, and when cooled, loop ribbon, string, or lace trim through the hole in each cookie and tie. If you want a decoration for the table or mantelpiece, the Gingerbread House is charming, and a perfect project to do with children.

ABOUT BARS OR SQUARES

The quickest and most easily made cookies are squares and bars. Bake them in greased pans at least 1½ inches deep. ➤ Pay close attention to the size of the pan called for in each recipe—variations will throw off the baking time, and the thickness of the batter in the pan affects texture. A too-large pan will give a dry, brittle result. A pan smaller than indicated in the recipes will give a cakey result—not a chewy one.

For easy removal after baking, line the pan with parchment paper, leaving enough overhang on two opposite sides to use as handles. Once the bars have cooled completely, the entire slab can be lifted from the pan to a board for cutting, making cleanup easy as well. Whether you cut them in the pan or out, always cool bars completely before cutting with a knife into bars, squares, or triangles. To store, see Storing Baked Cookies, 763.

BROWNIES COCKAIGNE

Sixteen to twenty-four 2-inch squares

Almost everyone has their own take on this classic American confection. This is the classic, lighter brownie that has appeared in *Joy* since 1931.

Preheat the oven to 350°F. If you want chewy and moist brownies, use a 13 × 9 × 2-inch pan; if cakey, a 9-inch square pan. Grease the pan and line with parchment paper so it extends over the long sides.

Melt in a small saucepan:

1 stick (4 oz or 115g) unsalted butter
4 ounces (115g) unsweetened chocolate, finely chopped

Let cool. If you don't, your brownies will be heavy and dry. Beat in a large bowl until light in color and foamy in texture:

4 large eggs
¼ teaspoon salt

Gradually add and continue beating until thick:

2 cups (400g) sugar
1 teaspoon vanilla

With a few swift strokes, stir in the cooled chocolate mixture just until combined. Even if you are using an electric mixer, switch to a wooden spoon for this. Stir in just until combined:

1 cup (125g) all-purpose flour

If desired, gently stir in:

(1 cup chopped toasted, 1005, pecans)

Scrape the batter into the prepared pan. Bake about 25 minutes or until a toothpick inserted in the center comes out clean or with moist crumbs attached. Let cool completely in the pan on a rack. Serve garnished with:

Whipped Cream, 791, ice cream, 840–44, or an icing, 798–99

FUDGY BROWNIES

Sixteen 2-inch squares

Darker, richer, and fudgier than Brownies Cockaigne, 764, this is our idea of the perfect, modern brownie.

Preheat the oven to 350°F. Grease a 9-inch square baking pan and line with parchment paper so it extends over 2 sides.

Melt, stirring frequently, in a large saucepan over low heat:

1 stick (4 oz or 115g) unsalted butter, cut into cubes
1 cup (170g) semisweet chocolate chips

Whisk in until the sugar is dissolved:

½ cup (100g) sugar
½ cup packed (115g) brown sugar

Whisk in until just combined:

2 large eggs
(2 teaspoons espresso powder)
1 teaspoon vanilla

Stir in just until combined:

¾ cup (95g) all-purpose flour
⅓ cup (25g) unsweetened cocoa powder
¼ teaspoon salt

Scrape into the prepared pan. If desired, sprinkle over the top:

(½ teaspoon flaky sea salt)

Bake until a toothpick inserted in the center comes out with moist crumbs attached, 18 to 20 minutes. Let cool completely in the pan on a rack before cutting.

CHEESECAKE BROWNIES

Sixteen 2-inch squares

Prepare using a 9-inch square baking pan:

Fudgy Brownies, above

After scraping the batter into the prepared pan, beat in a large bowl until blended and smooth:

8 ounces (230g) cream cheese, softened
¼ cup (50g) sugar
1 large egg
1 teaspoon vanilla

Spread the mixture on top of the brownie batter in an even layer and bake until a toothpick inserted in the center comes out with moist crumbs attached, about 40 to 45 minutes. Let cool completely in the pan on a rack before cutting.

BUTTERSCOTCH BROWNIES OR BLONDIES

Sixteen 2-inch squares

Preheat the oven to 350°F. Grease an 8-inch square baking pan and line with parchment paper so it extends over 2 sides.

Whisk together thoroughly in a medium bowl:

1 cup (125g) all-purpose flour
¼ teaspoon baking powder
⅛ teaspoon baking soda
⅛ teaspoon salt

Melt in a large heavy saucepan over medium heat:

1 stick (4 oz or 115g) unsalted butter

Let the butter brown, stirring occasionally, until light golden brown and fragrant, about 4 minutes. Remove from the heat and stir in until well blended:

⅔ cup (155g) packed light brown sugar
¼ cup (50g) sugar

Let cool to barely warm. Stir in until well combined:

1 large egg
1 large egg yolk
1 tablespoon (25g) light corn syrup
1½ teaspoons vanilla

Stir the flour mixture into the wet ingredients. If desired, stir in:

(1 cup chopped pecans, toasted, 1005, 1 cup semisweet chocolate chips, or ⅔ cup shredded sweetened coconut)

Scrape into the pan. Bake until the top is golden brown and a toothpick inserted in the center comes out clean, 25 to 30 minutes. Let cool completely in the pan on a rack before cutting.

CHOCOLATE-GLAZED TOFFEE BARS

Twenty-four 2 × 1⅓-inch bars

A chewy brown sugar–pecan toffee layer spread over shortbread and topped with chocolate. These bars are best made a day ahead.

Preheat the oven to 350°F. Grease an 8-inch square baking pan and line with parchment paper so it extends over 2 sides.

Prepare the dough for:

½ recipe Scotch Shortbread, 780

Press the dough firmly into the bottom of the pan to form a smooth, even layer. Bake the dough for 15 minutes. Set aside on a rack (and leave the oven on).

Combine in a medium heavy saucepan and bring to a boil over medium heat, stirring frequently:

5 tablespoons (70g) unsalted butter, cut into pieces
½ cup (115g) packed light brown sugar
2 tablespoons (40g) clover or other mild honey
1 tablespoon (15g) milk
⅛ teaspoon salt

Boil, uncovered, for 3 minutes. Remove from the heat and stir in:

1½ cups chopped toasted, 1005, pecans
1 teaspoon vanilla

Spread the nut mixture evenly over the baked crust. Return the pan to the oven and bake until bubbling, golden brown, and just slightly darker at the edges, about 20 minutes. Place the pan on a rack and sprinkle over the top:

⅓ cup semisweet or bittersweet chocolate chips

Let stand until the chocolate chips partially melt, then spread evenly with a table knife or offset spatula. Sprinkle over the top:

2 tablespoons finely chopped toasted, 1005, pecans

Let the chocolate cool until beginning to set but still slightly soft. Cut into 24 bars, then let cool completely in the pan before removing the bars.

CHRISTMAS CHOCOLATE BARS COCKAIGNE

Fifty-four 2 × 1-inch bars

If you can, make these ahead of time—the flavor improves immensely after 2 days.

Preheat the oven to 350°F. Grease a 13 × 9 × 2-inch baking pan and line with parchment paper so it extends over the 2 long sides.

Whisk together in a medium bowl:

1½ cups (190g) all-purpose flour
1½ teaspoons ground cinnamon
¾ teaspoon ground cloves
½ teaspoon baking soda
½ teaspoon salt
¼ teaspoon ground allspice

Beat in a large bowl until thick and pale:

1⅓ cups packed (305g) brown sugar
3 large eggs

Add the flour mixture to the batter in 2 parts, alternating with:

¼ cup honey (80g) or molasses (85g)

Stir in:

1¼ cups mixed dried cherries, golden raisins, and chopped blanched almonds
2 ounces (55g) unsweetened chocolate, finely chopped

Spread the batter evenly into the prepared pan. Bake until set, about 20 minutes. Place the pan on a rack. While still warm, spread evenly with:

Citrus Glaze, 799, made with lemon juice

Let stand until completely cool and the glaze is set, then cut into bars.

GOOEY CHOCOLATE OAT BARS

Fifty-four 2 × 1-inch bars

Add the optional coconut flakes, and you may call these **Magic Cookie Bars.**

Preheat the oven to 350°F. Grease a 13 × 9 × 2-inch baking pan and line with parchment paper so it extends over the 2 long sides.

Beat together in a large bowl:

1½ sticks (6 oz or 170g) unsalted butter, softened
1 cup (230g) packed brown sugar

Beat in:

1 large egg
1 large egg yolk
1½ teaspoons vanilla

Set aside. Whisk together in a medium bowl:

1¾ cups (220g) all-purpose flour
¾ teaspoon baking soda
¾ teaspoon salt

Stir in:

2¼ cups (225g) old-fashioned rolled oats

Stir the flour-oat mixture into the butter-sugar mixture until combined. Press two-thirds of the mixture into the prepared pan and set the rest aside. Combine in a medium saucepan and stir over low heat until smooth:

1½ cups (255g) semisweet chocolate chips
1 cup (305g) sweetened condensed milk
1½ tablespoons (25g) unsalted butter
Pinch of salt

Stir in:

¾ cup chopped walnuts or pecans

Spread the chocolate mixture over the crust, then dot with the remaining flour-oat mixture. If desired, sprinkle with:

(½ cup shredded or flaked sweetened coconut)

Bake until set, about 25 minutes. Let cool completely in the pan on a rack before cutting into bars.

RASPBERRY STREUSEL BARS

Twenty 2½ × 2-inch bars

Any sort of jam you have on hand will work in this recipe, so don't feel boxed in by the title.

Preheat the oven to 375°F. Grease a 13 × 9 × 2-inch baking pan and line with parchment paper so it extends over the 2 long sides.

Whisk together in a medium bowl:

3 cups (375g) all-purpose flour
½ cup (100g) sugar
½ teaspoon salt

Add:

2 sticks (8 oz or 225g) cold unsalted butter, cut into small pieces

Using a pastry blender or your fingertips, cut or rub in the butter until it is the size of small peas (or, combine the flour, sugar, and salt in a food processor, sprinkle the butter over the top, and process until well blended). Stir together in a small bowl:

¼ cup (60g) milk
1 large egg yolk
1 teaspoon almond extract

Add the milk mixture to the flour mixture and stir or pulse until the dough begins to hold together. Press two-thirds of the dough into the bottom of the prepared pan. Bake until barely firm in the center, 12 to 15 minutes. Set the pan on a rack (leave the oven on) and spread evenly over the hot crust:

1 cup raspberry jam

Add to the reserved dough:

½ cup sliced almonds
⅓ cup (35g) old-fashioned rolled oats
½ teaspoon ground cinnamon

Work in with your hands until just combined. Sprinkle the streusel evenly over the jam, leaving some clumps large and some small. Bake until the streusel is browned and the raspberry jam is bubbling, 25 to 30 minutes. Let cool completely in the pan on a rack before cutting into bars.

PECAN OR ANGEL SLICES

Twelve 3 × 2¼-inch bars

Many a copy of *Joy* has been sold on the strength of this recipe.

Preheat the oven to 350°F. Grease a 9-inch square baking pan and line with parchment paper so it extends over 2 sides.

Beat in a medium bowl until well blended:

4 tablespoons (½ stick or 55g) unsalted butter, softened
2 tablespoons (25g) sugar
1 large egg yolk
¼ teaspoon vanilla

Stir in until well blended and smooth:

¾ cup (95g) all-purpose flour

Press the dough evenly into the baking pan. Bake for 10 minutes and remove from the oven (leave the oven on). Meanwhile, beat in a medium bowl until well combined:

2 large eggs
1 cup packed (230g) light brown sugar
1½ tablespoons all-purpose flour
1½ teaspoons vanilla
¼ teaspoon baking powder
⅛ teaspoon salt

Stir in:

1½ cups chopped toasted, 1005, pecans or walnuts
1 cup flaked or shredded sweetened or unsweetened coconut, lightly toasted, 973

Spread the mixture evenly over the hot baked crust. Return to the oven and bake until the top is firm and golden brown and a toothpick inserted in the center comes out slightly wet, 20 to 25 minutes. Set the pan on a rack. If desired, while still warm, spread evenly with:

(Citrus Glaze, 799, made with lemon juice)

Let stand until completely cool and the glaze is set before cutting into bars.

NANAIMO BARS

Twenty-four 2¼ × 1½-inch bars

Nanaimo is a small town in British Columbia best known for these rich bars (and an annual bathtub race).

Preheat the oven to 350°F. Lightly grease a 9-inch square pan and line with parchment paper so it extends over 2 sides.

Prepare:

Crumb Crust, 667, using ¼ cup (50g) sugar and 1 stick (4 oz or 115g) unsalted butter

Stir into the crust mixture:

1 cup shredded unsweetened coconut
½ cup walnuts, toasted, 1005, and finely chopped
¼ cup (20g) unsweetened cocoa powder, sifted

Press into the prepared pan and bake until lightly browned, about 10 minutes. Allow to cool completely.

Meanwhile, for the filling, beat together in a medium bowl, or in a stand mixer with the paddle attachment, until creamy:

1 stick (4 oz or 115g) unsalted butter, softened
2 cups (200g) powdered sugar
2 tablespoons custard powder or instant vanilla pudding mix
¼ teaspoon salt

Beat in until completely smooth:

¼ cup (60g) whole milk or heavy cream

Spread the filling over the crust and refrigerate. Melt in a double boiler (or a heatproof bowl set over a pan of barely simmering water):

4 ounces (115g) semisweet chocolate, finely chopped
¼ cup (60g) heavy cream

Stir frequently until smooth, then pour over the filling. Refrigerate until the chocolate topping is set, about 30 minutes. Cut into squares or bars and serve, or store, refrigerated, for up to 1 week.

PB&J BARS

Twenty-four 2¼ × 1½-inch bars

A lunchbox classic in bar cookie form.

Preheat the oven to 375°F. Lightly grease a 9-inch square baking pan and line with parchment paper so it extends over 2 sides.

Prepare the dough for:

Peanut Butter Cookies, 771

Press two-thirds of the dough into the prepared pan. Spread over the dough:

¾ cup grape jelly, or raspberry or strawberry jam

Crumble the remaining dough over the jam or jelly. Sprinkle on top:

⅓ cup roasted peanuts, coarsely chopped

Bake until firm, about 25 minutes. Let cool completely in the pan on a rack before cutting into bars. Store in an airtight container for up to 2 weeks.

LEMON BARS

Eighteen 3 × 2-inch bars

Preheat the oven to 325°F. Have ready an ungreased 13 × 9 × 2-inch baking pan.

Whisk together in a medium bowl:

1½ cups (190g) all-purpose flour
¼ cup (25g) powdered sugar
Pinch of salt

Add:

1½ sticks (6 oz or 170g) cold unsalted butter, cut into small pieces

Using a pastry blender or your fingertips, cut or rub in the butter until it is the size of small peas. Press the dough into the bottom and ¾ inch up the sides of the baking pan. Bake until golden brown, 25 to 30 minutes. Transfer the pan to a rack and reduce the oven temperature to 300°F.

Whisk together in a large bowl until well combined:

6 large eggs
3 cups (600g) sugar

Stir in:

Finely grated zest of 1 lemon
1 cup plus 2 tablespoons (270g) fresh lemon juice (from about 5 lemons)

Sift over the top and stir in until well blended and smooth:

½ cup (65g) all-purpose flour

Pour the batter over the baked crust. Return to the oven and bake until the topping is set, about 35 minutes. Let cool in the pan on a rack before cutting into bars.

LEBKUCHEN (GERMAN HONEY BARS)

Thirty-six 2¼ × 1½-inch bars

Lebkuchen recipes are many and diverse—some are flourless, made with almond and hazelnut meal; some are made in bar form and others in cookie form; some are glazed with chocolate and others with a thin lemon glaze. This recipe is based on one given to us by the president and CEO of our publishing house, Carolyn Reidy, whose mother, Mildred Kroll, was a prolific cookie baker. We like to age the dough for up to two months before baking to allow the flavors to develop (the sugar and honey keep the egg from spoiling). After baking, these resilient cookies can be stored in an airtight container for at least a month more.

Heat in a large heavy saucepan until runny:

1 cup (320g) honey
2 tablespoons (30g) water

Remove from the heat and stir in until melted:

6 tablespoons (¾ stick or 85g) unsalted butter, cut into cubes

Transfer to a large bowl and stir in:

¾ cup packed (175g) brown sugar
2 large eggs, lightly beaten
Finely grated zest of 1 lemon
1 tablespoon (15g) lemon juice

Whisk together in a medium bowl:

2½ cups sifted (300g) all-purpose flour
½ teaspoon baking soda
1 tablespoon ground cinnamon
1 teaspoon ground cloves
½ teaspoon grated or ground nutmeg
¼ teaspoon ground cardamom
¼ teaspoon ground anise
½ teaspoon salt

Add the flour mixture to the honey mixture and stir just until combined. Add:

⅓ cup chopped blanched almonds
⅓ cup chopped citron
⅓ cup chopped candied orange peel

Stir until the dough is smooth. Cover the dough tightly with plastic wrap and refrigerate at least 24 hours or up to 1 month.

When ready to bake, preheat the oven to 375°F. Grease a 13 × 9 × 2-inch baking pan and line with parchment paper so it extends over the 2 long sides.

Firmly press the dough into the prepared pan to form a smooth, even layer. Bake until a toothpick inserted in the center comes out almost clean, about 30 minutes. While the lebkuchen is still warm, spread evenly over the top:

Citrus Glaze, 799, made with lemon juice

Mark into bars by cutting into the lebkuchen about ¼ inch deep with a knife. Decorate, if desired, by placing in the center of each bar:

(1 candied cherry)

And arrange around each cherry:

(4 whole blanched almonds)

Let stand in the pan on a rack until completely cool and the icing is set. Using the overhanging parchment as handles, transfer to a cutting board. Cut into bars. If possible, let the cookies age for at least 2 weeks to allow the spices to ripen. Lebkuchen will keep for months in an airtight container.

ABOUT DROP COOKIES

Irma was a drop cookie enthusiast. In the 1936 edition she proclaimed that "whoever invented drop cakes deserves a decoration . . . they are delicious to eat, fine to keep on hand, and painless to manufacture." We wholeheartedly agree!

Unless otherwise indicated, dough for drop cookies should be dropped from a measuring teaspoon or tablespoon. This is for the sake of precision, as it helps ensure that recipe yields and baking times are accurate. Drop cookie doughs vary in texture. Some fall easily from the spoon and flatten into wafers in baking. Stiffer doughs need a push with a finger or a second spoon to release them.

When chilled, these doughs may be formed into balls and flattened between your palms. First dampen your hands or dust them with flour or powdered sugar, or, if the cookies are a chocolate or other dark dough, with cocoa powder. To flatten balls on the baking sheet, use the bottom of a glass that has been lightly greased or dusted with flour, powdered sugar, or cocoa. Or, to give a crisscross effect, you may flatten them by pressing with a fork dipped in flour.

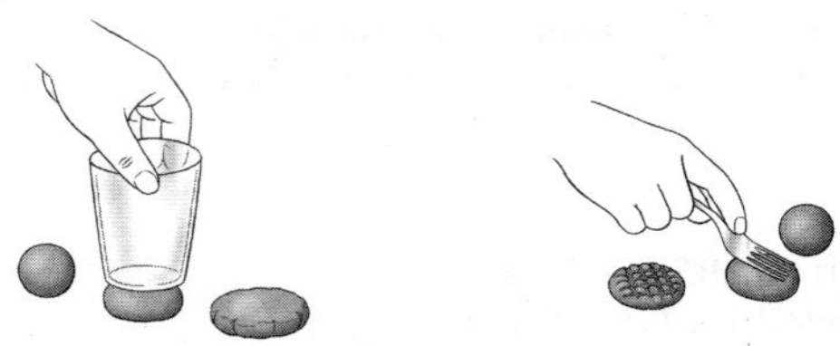

Two ways to flatten drop cookies

Unless otherwise directed, drop cookies should be cooled on the baking sheets 1 to 2 minutes before transferring them to a rack to cool completely. Please see About Baking Cookies, 763.

SOFT AND CHEWY SUGAR COOKIES

About 35 cookies

Preheat the oven to 375°F. Lightly grease or line 2 baking sheets or cookie sheets with parchment paper.

Sift together into a medium bowl:

2½ cups (315g) all-purpose flour
1½ teaspoons baking powder
¾ teaspoon salt
(¼ teaspoon ground cinnamon or ½ teaspoon grated or ground nutmeg)

Beat in a large bowl, or in a stand mixer with the paddle attachment, until light and fluffy:

1¼ cups (250g) sugar
1½ sticks (6 oz or 170g) unsalted butter, softened

Add and beat to combine:

2 teaspoons vanilla
(Finely grated zest of 1 lemon)

Beat in:

1 large egg

Add the flour mixture and beat until the dough is smooth. Portion the dough by the rounded tablespoon and roll into balls, then roll the balls in:

Sugar

Place about 1 inch apart on the baking sheets, then flatten the balls with a glass, 768. Bake until set and barely light brown around the edges, about 10 minutes, switching oven racks and rotating the sheets halfway through. Let cool for 2 or 3 minutes on the sheets, then transfer to a wire rack to cool completely.

CHEWY CHOCOLATE SUGAR COOKIES

About 24 cookies

Prepare the dough for **Soft and Chewy Sugar Cookies, 768,** using **2 cups (250g) all-purpose flour** and **½ cup (40g) unsweetened cocoa powder.** Portion the dough using a ¼-cup measure. Break the resulting dough balls in half and roll into balls (each cookie will use 2 tablespoons dough). Flatten the dough balls on the baking sheets and, if desired, lightly sprinkle with sugar. Bake until barely set, 8 to 10 minutes, switching oven racks and rotating the sheets halfway through. Let cool as directed above.

DOUBLE-CHOCOLATE PEPPERMINT COOKIES

About 26 cookies

Prepare the dough for **Soft and Chewy Sugar Cookies, 768,** using **2 cups (250g) all-purpose flour** and **½ cup (40g) unsweetened cocoa powder.** Substitute **peppermint extract** for the vanilla and add **¾ cup (130g) semisweet chocolate chips** after stirring in the flour mixture. Portion the dough using a ¼-cup measure. Break the resulting dough balls in half and roll into balls (each cookie will use 2 tablespoons dough). Flatten the dough balls on the baking sheets and, if desired, lightly sprinkle with sugar. Bake until barely set, 8 to 10 minutes, switching oven racks and rotating the sheets halfway through. Let cool as directed above.

CRUNCHY SUGAR COOKIES

About 65 cookies

This light, crunchy sugar cookie is from Megan's great-grandmother Treva Martin.

Preheat the oven to 350°F. Line 2 baking sheets or cookie sheets with parchment paper.

Whisk together in a medium bowl:

2 cups (250g) all-purpose flour
½ teaspoon baking soda
½ teaspoon cream of tartar
½ teaspoon salt

Beat in a large bowl until smooth:

1 stick (4 oz or 115g) unsalted butter, softened
½ cup (105g) vegetable oil
½ cup (100g) sugar
½ cup (50g) powdered sugar

Beat in:

1 teaspoon vanilla

Beat in one at a time:

2 large eggs

Beat in the flour mixture just until combined. Drop by the rounded teaspoon onto the prepared baking sheets about 1½ inches apart. Bake until golden brown around the edges, about 12 minutes, switching oven racks and rotating the sheets halfway through. Let cool for 5 minutes on the sheets, then transfer to a wire rack to cool completely. Store in an airtight container for up to 1 month.

SNICKERDOODLES

About thirty-six 3-inch cookies

Preheat the oven to 350°F. Grease or line 2 baking sheets or cookie sheets with parchment paper.

Whisk together in a medium bowl until well blended:

2¾ cups (345g) all-purpose flour
2 teaspoons cream of tartar
1 teaspoon baking soda
¼ teaspoon salt

Beat in a large bowl until light and fluffy:

2 sticks (8 oz or 225g) unsalted butter, softened
1½ cups (300g) sugar

Add one at a time and beat until well incorporated:

2 large eggs

Stir in the flour mixture until just combined. Combine in a small bowl:

¼ cup (50g) sugar
1 tablespoon ground cinnamon

Shape the dough into 1¼-inch balls, roll in the cinnamon sugar, and arrange about 2¾ inches apart on the prepared baking sheets. Bake until the cookies are light golden brown at the edges, 12 to 14 minutes, switching oven racks and rotating the sheets halfway through. Let cool on the sheet for 2 or 3 minutes, then transfer to a wire rack to cool completely.

CHOCOLATE CHIP COOKIES

About thirty-six 2½-inch cookies

Created in the 1930s by Ruth Wakefield of the Toll House Inn in Whitman, Massachusetts, the original recipe calls for cutting bars of semisweet chocolate into small chunks. Chocolate chips were first sold in 1939 to streamline this step—*Joy*'s 1943 recipe spread the good news: "a specially prepared chocolate may be bought for use in cookies." We occasionally like to use coarsely chopped chocolate instead. These cookies tend to turn out best when baked on dark metal baking sheets.

Preheat the oven to 375°F. Grease or line 2 baking sheets or cookie sheets with parchment paper.

Whisk together in a bowl:

1 cup plus 2 tablespoons (140g) all-purpose flour
½ teaspoon baking soda

Beat in a large bowl until well blended:

1 stick (4 oz or 115g) unsalted butter, softened
⅓ cup (65g) sugar
⅓ cup packed (75g) light brown sugar

Add and beat until well combined:

1 large egg
½ teaspoon salt
1 teaspoon vanilla

Beat the flour mixture into the butter-sugar mixture until well blended and smooth. Stir in:

1 cup (170g) semisweet chocolate chips or chopped chocolate
(¾ cup chopped toasted, 1005, walnuts or pecans)

Drop the dough by the heaping teaspoon for smaller cookies, or by the tablespoon for larger cookies, 2 or 3 inches apart onto the prepared baking sheets. Bake until the cookies are just slightly golden on top and the edges are browned, 8 to 10 minutes, switching oven racks and rotating the sheets halfway through. Let cool on the sheets for 2 to 3 minutes, then transfer to a wire rack to cool.

SKILLET CHOCOLATE CHIP COOKIE

8 to 10 servings

This giant cookie can also be baked over a campfire in a Dutch oven. We recommend dousing the finished cookie with whole milk or a big scoop of vanilla ice cream.

Prepare the dough for **Chocolate Chip Cookies, 769,** and press evenly into a 10-inch cast-iron skillet. If desired, sprinkle with **(flaky sea salt)**. Bake until golden brown, 20 to 25 minutes. Allow to cool slightly, then cut into pieces for serving, or drizzle **½ cup whole milk** over the cookie, pass around spoons, and eat warm right out of the skillet.

NORA'S CHOCOLATE CHIP COOKIES

About 30 cookies

Our friend Nora Mace developed this recipe as a thicker, chewier alternative to our classic chocolate chip cookie recipe. These cookies benefit from letting the dough rest overnight in the refrigerator, but they're excellent baked right away, too.

Preheat the oven to 350°F. Grease or line 2 baking sheets or cookie sheets with parchment paper.

Whisk together in a medium bowl:

1⅔ cups (210g) all-purpose flour
1 teaspoon salt
½ teaspoon baking soda

Set aside. Beat in a large bowl, or in a stand mixer with the paddle attachment, until light and fluffy, about 4 minutes:

1½ sticks (6 oz or 170g) unsalted butter, softened
⅔ cup (130g) sugar
½ cup packed (115g) brown sugar

Scrape down the sides of the bowl and beater regularly. Beat in:

1 teaspoon vanilla

Add and beat just until combined:

1 large egg
1 large egg yolk

Stir the flour mixture into the butter-sugar mixture until well blended and smooth. Stir in:

1½ cups (255g) semisweet or bittersweet chocolate chips

Drop the dough by the level tablespoon about 2 inches apart onto the prepared baking sheets. Bake until the edges are browned but the centers are still pale, about 12 minutes, switching oven racks and rotating the sheets halfway through. Let cool on the sheets for 2 to 3 minutes, then transfer to a wire rack to cool completely.

WHITE CHOCOLATE MACADAMIA COOKIES

About seventy-five 2½-inch cookies

If desired, use heaping tablespoons of batter to make slightly larger, chewier cookies. For very large cookies, use a ⅓-cup measure, drop the dough 3 inches apart on the baking sheets, and bake for 18 to 20 minutes. You will have about 14 cookies.

Preheat the oven to 350°F. Grease or line 2 baking sheets or cookie sheets with parchment paper.

Whisk together in a medium bowl:

2½ cups (315g) all-purpose flour
1 teaspoon baking soda
¼ teaspoon salt

Beat in a large bowl, or in a stand mixer with the paddle attachment, until light and fluffy:

2 sticks (8 oz or 230g) unsalted butter, softened
1⅓ cups (265g) sugar
⅔ cup packed (155g) dark brown sugar

Beat in one at a time:

2 large eggs
1 teaspoon vanilla
(Finely grated zest of 1 lemon)

Stir the flour mixture into the butter-sugar mixture. Stir in:

1 cup coarsely chopped macadamia nuts (about 4 oz or 115g)
1 cup coarsely chopped white chocolate (about 4 oz or 115g)

Drop the dough by the heaping teaspoon about 1½ inches apart onto the prepared baking sheets. Bake until golden brown, 13 to 15 minutes, switching oven racks and rotating the sheets halfway through. Let cool on the sheets for 2 to 3 minutes, then transfer to a wire rack to cool completely.

CHOCOLATE KRINKLES

About 40 cookies

The dough for these rich chocolate cookies is rolled in powdered sugar, then baked, resulting in a crackle-patterned exterior. We think of this cookie as a modern classic.

Preheat the oven to 350°F. Line 2 baking sheets or cookie sheets with parchment paper.

Melt gently in a double boiler or a heatproof bowl set over a pan of barely simmering water:

6 ounces (170g) bittersweet chocolate, finely chopped, or
1 cup (170g) semisweet chocolate chips

Set aside to cool slightly. Whisk together in a medium bowl:

1¼ cups (155g) all-purpose flour
¼ cup (20g) unsweetened cocoa powder
2 teaspoons baking powder
¼ teaspoon salt

Beat in a large bowl, or in a stand mixer with the paddle attachment, until light and fluffy:

1 stick (4 oz or 115g) unsalted butter, softened
¾ cup (150g) sugar

Beat in:

1 teaspoon vanilla

Beat in one at a time just until combined:

2 large eggs

Beat in the melted chocolate and the flour mixture until combined. Using a tablespoon, portion the dough and roll in:

½ cup (50g) powdered sugar

Place on the prepared baking sheets 1½ inches apart. Sprinkle the top of each cookie with a pinch of powdered sugar. Bake until the cookies are cracked and slightly firm, about 10 minutes, switching oven racks and rotating the sheets halfway through. Let cool on the sheets for 2 to 3 minutes, then transfer to a wire rack to cool completely.

PEANUT BUTTER COOKIES

About sixty 1½-inch cookies

For those who dote on peanut butter cookies, try these rich and crumbly ones, first published in the 1936 edition. Peanut butters vary in oil content, so start with the smaller amount of flour and add until the dough is satiny (but not dry).

Preheat the oven to 375°F. Grease or line 2 baking sheets or cookie sheets with parchment paper.

Beat in a large bowl, or in a stand mixer with the paddle attachment, until soft:

1 stick (4 oz or 115g) unsalted butter, softened

Add gradually and blend until creamy:

½ cup (100g) sugar
½ cup packed (115g) brown sugar

Beat in:

1 large egg
1 cup (240g) peanut butter (smooth or chunky)
½ teaspoon vanilla
½ teaspoon baking soda
½ teaspoon salt

Gradually mix in:

1¼ to 1½ cups (155 to 190g) all-purpose flour

Shape into 1-inch balls and arrange about 2 inches apart on the prepared baking sheets. Press flat with a fork, as shown on 768. Bake until firm, 10 to 12 minutes, switching oven racks and rotating the sheets halfway through. Let cool on the sheets for 2 to 3 minutes, then transfer to a wire rack to cool completely.

OATMEAL RAISIN COOKIES

About forty-eight 3-inch cookies

Preheat the oven to 350°F. Grease or line 2 baking sheets or cookie sheets with parchment paper.

Whisk together in a medium bowl:

1¾ cups (220g) all-purpose flour
¾ teaspoon baking soda
¾ teaspoon baking powder
½ teaspoon salt
½ teaspoon ground cinnamon
½ teaspoon grated or ground nutmeg

Beat in a large bowl, or in a stand mixer with the paddle attachment, until well blended:

2 sticks (8 oz or 225g) unsalted butter, softened
1½ cups packed (345g) brown sugar
¼ cup (50g) sugar
2 large eggs
2½ teaspoons vanilla

Stir the flour mixture into the butter-sugar mixture. Stir in:

3½ cups (350g) old-fashioned rolled oats
1 cup raisins, chopped
(¾ cup chopped toasted, 1005, walnuts)

Shape the dough into generous 1½-inch balls and place about 2 inches apart on the prepared baking sheets. Flatten the balls into ½-inch-thick rounds. Bake until the cookies are lightly browned all over, 12 to 14 minutes, switching oven racks and rotating the sheets halfway through. Let cool on the sheets for 2 to 3 minutes, then transfer to a wire rack to cool completely.

COWBOY COOKIES

About forty 3-inch cookies

We like to improvise with this recipe depending on the ingredients we have on hand. Crushed pretzels, crisp cereal, dried cranberries, white chocolate or peanut butter chips, and bourbon-soaked raisins are all good substitutions for the chocolate, pecans, and/or coconut.

Prepare **Oatmeal Raisin Cookies, above,** omitting the nutmeg, substituting for the raisins **1 cup semisweet chocolate chips,** decreasing the oats to 1½ cups (150g), and adding **1 cup pecans, toasted, 1005, and chopped,** and **1 cup shredded or flaked sweetened coconut.**

ANZAC BISCUITS

About 45 biscuits

ANZAC is an acronym for the Australian and New Zealand Army Corps, and these biscuits were sent to soldiers abroad during World War I. They can be soft or crunchy. For soft cookies, bake them for the shorter amount of time. These cookies were designed to hold up well over a long period of time, so you can store them in an airtight container for up to 1 month.

Preheat the oven to 350°F. Line 2 baking sheets or cookie sheets with parchment paper.

Stir together in a large bowl:

2 cups (250g) all-purpose flour
2 cups (200g) old-fashioned rolled oats
1 cup (200g) sugar
1 cup shredded sweetened coconut
½ cup packed (115g) light brown sugar
½ teaspoon salt

Melt in a small saucepan over medium heat:

1½ sticks (6 oz or 170g) unsalted butter
2 tablespoons (40g) honey or golden syrup

Stir together in a small bowl until dissolved:

1 teaspoon baking soda
6 tablespoons (90g) boiling water

Stir the baking soda mixture into the butter mixture. Add the butter mixture to the dry ingredients and stir to combine. Scoop the dough by the rounded tablespoon onto the prepared baking sheets about 2 inches apart and flatten them with a glass, 768. Bake until golden brown and dry to the touch, 15 to 20 minutes, switching oven racks and rotating the sheets halfway through. Let cool on the sheets for 2 to 3 minutes, then transfer to a wire rack to cool completely.

GINGERSNAPS

About forty 2¼-inch cookies

For crunchy cookies, overbake slightly; for more tender ones, underbake by a minute or two.

Preheat the oven to 350°F. Grease or line 2 baking sheets or cookie sheets with parchment paper.

Whisk together in a large bowl:

1½ cups (190g) all-purpose flour
1 cup (200g) sugar
1 teaspoon ground ginger
1 teaspoon baking soda
½ teaspoon ground cloves
½ teaspoon salt

Add and beat until well combined:

½ cup (95g) vegetable shortening, melted and cooled
¼ cup (85g) dark molasses or sorghum syrup
1 large egg

If desired, stir in:

(¾ cup [75g] old-fashioned rolled oats)

You may bake the cookies immediately or refrigerate the dough overnight to allow the flavors to meld (the cookies will also spread less on the baking sheet if the dough is cold). Use a tablespoon to portion the dough, roll into balls, and place 2 inches apart on the prepared baking sheets. Lightly dampen the bottom of a small drinking glass, then dip it in:

Sugar

Press down on each ball of dough to flatten, dipping the glass in sugar before pressing each cookie. Bake until browned, 10 to 12 minutes, switching oven racks and rotating the sheets halfway through. Let cool on the sheets for 2 to 3 minutes, then transfer to a wire rack to cool completely.

PFEFFERNÜSSE (PEPPERNUTS)

About sixty 1-inch cookies

As with Lebkuchen, 768, these cookies will keep for a very long time in an airtight container. In fact, we think the flavor and texture improve over time.

Whisk together in a medium bowl:

1 cup plus 1 tablespoon (135g) all-purpose flour
1 teaspoon ground cinnamon
½ teaspoon ground cardamom
¼ teaspoon baking powder
¼ teaspoon ground cloves
¼ teaspoon grated or ground nutmeg
⅛ teaspoon baking soda
⅛ teaspoon salt
⅛ teaspoon black pepper

Beat in a large bowl, or in a stand mixer with the paddle attachment, until very fluffy:

4 tablespoons (½ stick or 55g) unsalted butter, softened
½ cup (100g) sugar

Add and beat until well combined:

1 large egg yolk

Stir in:

¼ cup slivered almonds, finely chopped
¼ cup finely chopped candied orange peel
Finely grated zest of 1 lemon

Stir in the flour mixture in batches, alternating with:

3 tablespoons (60g) molasses
3 tablespoons (45g) brandy

Cover and refrigerate the dough for at least 8 hours, or for up to 2 days, to allow the flavors to blend.

Preheat the oven to 350°F. Grease or line 2 baking sheets or cookie sheets with parchment paper.

Shape the dough into ¾-inch balls and arrange about 1 inch apart on the prepared baking sheets. Bake until the cookies are lightly browned, 12 to 14 minutes, switching oven racks and rotating the sheets halfway through. Let cool for 2 to 3 minutes on the sheets, then roll the still-warm cookies in:

⅔ cup powdered sugar

Transfer to a wire rack to cool completely.

HERMITS

About forty 2-inch cookies

Many hermit recipes include molasses, but this recipe hews closer to the nineteenth-century New England originals. Irma was fond of adding hickory nuts to her hermits. If you are lucky enough to find these elusive nuts—and determined enough to shell them—consider stretching your haul by adding them to these classic dried-fruit-and-spice cookies.

Preheat the oven to 375°F. Grease or line 2 baking sheets or cookie sheets with parchment paper.

Whisk until blended in a medium bowl:

1⅓ cups (165g) all-purpose flour
¾ teaspoon ground cinnamon
½ teaspoon ground cloves
Finely grated zest of 1 orange
¼ teaspoon baking soda
Pinch of salt

Beat in a large bowl, or in a stand mixer with the paddle attachment, until creamy:

1 stick (4 oz or 115g) unsalted butter, softened
1 cup packed (230g) light brown sugar

Beat in:

1 large egg
½ cup sour cream (115g), yogurt (115g), or buttermilk (120g)

Add the flour mixture to the butter-sugar mixture and beat until smooth. Stir in:

½ cup chopped raisins, currants, dried figs, dried apricots, candied citron, or a combination
(¼ cup chopped nuts or shredded coconut)

Drop the dough by the teaspoon about 3 inches apart onto the prepared baking sheets. Bake until the cookies are browned, about 10 minutes, switching oven racks and rotating the sheets halfway through. Let cool on the sheets for 2 to 3 minutes, then transfer to a wire rack to cool completely. If desired, spread thinly over the cookies:

(Quick Butterscotch Icing (Penuche), 799)

MEXICAN WEDDING CAKES

About sixty 1¼-inch cookies

Preheat the oven to 350°F. Grease or line 2 baking sheets or cookie sheets with parchment paper.

Beat in a large bowl, or in a stand mixer with the paddle attachment, until well blended:

2 sticks (8 oz or 230g) unsalted butter, softened
½ cup (50g) powdered sugar
2 teaspoons vanilla
¼ teaspoon salt

Stir in:

1 cup pecans, toasted, 1005, cooled, and finely ground in a food processor

Stir in until well blended:

2 cups (250g) all-purpose flour

Shape into 1-inch balls and arrange about 1¼ inches apart on the prepared baking sheets. Bake until the cookies are lightly browned, 12 to 15 minutes, switching oven racks and rotating the sheets halfway through. Let cool on the sheets for 2 to 3 minutes, then transfer to a wire rack to cool completely. Roll the cooled cookies in:

¾ cup powdered sugar

ABOUT THIN COOKIES

Most of these cookies are fragile, but if made small and baked on a baking sheet lined with parchment paper or a silicone liner, as directed, they are easy to remove. ➤ Should they harden on the pan, return the baking sheet to the oven for a moment before trying to remove them. Because these cookies are so fragile, store them between layers of parchment or wax paper in an airtight container.

BENNE (SESAME SEED) WAFERS

About fifty 2½-inch wafers

Benne seeds are an early heirloom variety of sesame seeds, brought by enslaved West Africans to South Carolina's Lowcountry. The plants thrived in the humid climate, and benne seeds were used extensively to enrich baked goods and candies, as well as savory dishes, with their deeply nutty, slightly bitter flavor. Though regular sesame seeds will work here, we highly recommend seeking out benne seeds, which are available for purchase online. These thin, crisp cookies will be irresistable either way.

Preheat the oven to 375°F. Line 2 baking sheets or cookie sheets with parchment paper or silicone liners.

Beat in a large bowl until light:

2 large eggs

Gradually beat in until well blended:

1⅓ cups packed (305g) light brown sugar

Add:

5 tablespoons (40g) all-purpose flour
1 teaspoon vanilla
⅛ teaspoon salt
⅛ teaspoon baking powder

Beat the batter until smooth, then add:

½ cup benne seeds or white sesame seeds, toasted

Drop the batter by the teaspoon about 2 inches apart onto the prepared baking sheets. Bake 1 sheet at a time until the cookies are just browned at the edges, about 8 minutes, rotating the sheet halfway through. Let cool on the sheets for 2 to 3 minutes, then transfer to a wire rack to cool completely.

PECAN LACE

About sixty 3-inch wafers

Much of the appeal of these see-through wafers is in their brittle, caramelized texture, so be sure to make them on a dry day.

Preheat the oven to 375°F. Line 2 baking sheets or cookie sheets with parchment paper or silicone liners.

Melt in a medium saucepan:

1¼ sticks (5 oz or 145g) unsalted butter

Simmer the butter gently, stirring occasionally, until the solids on the bottom of the pan turn light brown, 3 to 4 minutes. Remove from the heat and stir in until blended:

1 cup packed (230g) light brown sugar
¼ cup (90g) light corn syrup
1 tablespoon (15g) milk
¼ teaspoon salt

Stir in until combined:

1½ cups (150g) old-fashioned rolled oats
½ cup finely chopped toasted, 1005, pecans
2 tablespoons (15g) all-purpose flour
2 teaspoons vanilla

Drop the batter by the teaspoon about 3½ inches apart onto the baking sheets. Bake 1 sheet at a time until the cookies are lightly browned, 12 to 14 minutes, rotating the sheet halfway through. Let cool on the sheet for 2 to 3 minutes, then transfer to a wire rack to cool completely.

OATMEAL LACE COOKIES

About sixty 2-inch cookies

These are grown-up oatmeal cookies. Because they are so fragile, some will inevitably break, and when they do, crumble them over ice cream.

Stir together in a medium bowl until well blended:

¾ cup (95g) all-purpose flour
½ cup (100g) sugar
½ cup packed (115g) light brown sugar
½ teaspoon baking soda
½ teaspoon salt
1 stick (4 oz or 115g) unsalted butter, melted
1 large egg
1 tablespoon (15g) milk
(Finely grated zest of 1 lemon)
½ teaspoon vanilla or almond extract

Stir in:

1 cup (100g) old-fashioned rolled oats

Refrigerate the batter for 1 hour.

Preheat the oven to 400°F. Line 2 baking sheets or cookie sheets with parchment paper or silicone liners.

Drop the batter by the teaspoon onto the baking sheets and bake 1 sheet at a time, rotating the sheet halfway through, until golden brown, 10 to 12 minutes. Let cool completely on the sheet on a wire rack.

LEMONY BUTTER WAFERS

About forty-eight 2-inch wafers

These delicate, lemon-scented cookies are among our favorites in this chapter.

Preheat the oven to 375°F. Grease or line 2 baking sheets with parchment paper.

Beat in a medium bowl, or a stand mixer with the paddle attachment, until light and fluffy:

1 stick (4 oz or 115g) unsalted butter, softened
½ cup (100g) sugar

Beat in:

1 teaspoon vanilla
Finely grated zest of 1 lemon

Add and beat until combined:

1 large egg

Stir in:

¾ cup sifted (75g) cake flour
Pinch of salt
(1½ tablespoons poppy seeds)

Drop the cookies by the teaspoon 3 inches apart onto the prepared baking sheets. Bake until the edges brown, 6 to 7 minutes, switching oven racks and rotating the sheets halfway through. Let cool on the sheets for 2 to 3 minutes, then transfer to a wire rack to cool completely.

FLORENTINES COCKAIGNE

About fifteen 3-inch cookies

Marion considered these "the height of elegance." We are especially fond of Florentines made with candied ginger, candied citron or orange peel, and dried apricots.

Preheat the oven to 350°F. Line 2 baking sheets with parchment paper or silicone liners.

Toss together in a small bowl until the fruit is separated:

1¼ cups packed chopped mixed candied and/or dried fruit
½ cup (65g) all-purpose flour

Transfer the fruit mixture to a food processor and add:

½ cup slivered almonds
¼ cup packed (60g) light brown sugar
¼ cup (80g) honey
½ teaspoon vanilla
⅛ teaspoon salt

Pulse until the fruit and nuts are about ¼ inch in size. Add:

4 tablespoons (½ stick or 55g) unsalted butter, melted

Process briefly, until the fruit and nuts are about ⅛ inch in size. Transfer to a bowl. Shape into 1-inch balls and place about 3 inches apart on the baking sheets. Flatten the balls into 2½-inch discs. Bake 1 sheet at a time until golden brown, 7 to 9 minutes, rotating the sheet halfway through. Let cool on the sheet for 2 to 3 minutes, then transfer to a wire rack to cool completely.

Dip the bottoms of the cookies in:

4 ounces (115g) semisweet or bittersweet chocolate, melted

Place on baking sheets lined with parchment paper and refrigerate to set the chocolate. Store in an airtight container at room temperature.

GINGER THINS

About four hundred ¾-inch wafers

These little cakes will be the size of a quarter when baked. Our recipe tester told us she fantasized about piling them into a bowl, topping with milk, and eating them like cereal. We think this is a fabulous idea.

Preheat the oven to 325°F. Line 2 baking sheets or cookie sheets with parchment paper or silicone liners.

Sift together into a medium bowl:

1½ cups (190g) all-purpose flour
½ teaspoon baking soda
½ teaspoon ground cinnamon
½ teaspoon ground cloves
½ teaspoon ground ginger
¼ teaspoon salt

Beat in a large bowl, or in a stand mixer with the paddle attachment, until light and fluffy:

1½ sticks (6 oz or 170g) unsalted butter, softened
1 cup packed (230g) brown sugar
1 large egg, beaten
¼ cup (85g) molasses

Stir the flour mixture into the butter-sugar mixture until smooth. You may portion the cookies by dropping ⅛-teaspoon dots of dough 1 inch apart onto the baking sheets. Or, for an easier time, transfer the cookie dough to a pastry bag fitted with a small plain tip or a zip-top bag with one corner cut off, and pipe the dough into ⅛-teaspoon mounds onto the sheets. Bake until crisp, 5 to 6 minutes, switching oven racks and rotating the sheets halfway through. Let cool on the sheets for 2 to 3 minutes, then transfer to a wire rack to cool completely.

ALMOND MACAROONS

About 30 cookies

I. Known in Italy as **amaretti.** A very light, fine-textured macaroon. For the French filled cookie, see Macarons, 782.

Combine in a food processor:

1 cup (275g) almond paste, store-bought or homemade, 873
1 cup (100g) powdered sugar
Pinch of salt

Pulse until finely crumbled. With the machine running, slowly add and process until the mixture is smooth, about 1 minute:

3 large egg whites
(¼ teaspoon almond extract)

Transfer the mixture to a large heavy saucepan and cook, stirring constantly, over medium heat until slightly thickened, about 4 minutes. Transfer to a bowl and refrigerate until cooled and slightly firm, 20 to 30 minutes.

Preheat the oven to 350°F. Grease or line 2 baking sheets or cookie sheets with parchment paper.

Drop the dough by the heaping teaspoon about 2 inches apart onto the prepared baking sheets. Bake until the cookies are tinged with brown, 15 to 17 minutes, switching oven racks and rotating the sheets halfway through. Let cool on the sheets for 2 to 3 minutes, then transfer to a wire rack to cool completely.

II. A richly flavored macaroon made with freshly ground blanched almonds for a more rustic texture. This is our preferred cookie for serving with Affogato, 851.

Preheat the oven to 350°F. Line 2 baking sheets or cookie sheets with parchment paper.

Grind in two batches in a food processor until finely ground but not powdery:

1 pound blanched slivered almonds

Transfer to a medium bowl. Stir in:

2 cups (200g) powdered sugar
2 egg whites
1 teaspoon vanilla
½ teaspoon almond extract
½ teaspoon salt

The mixture will be crumbly but should hold together when squeezed. Drop by the tablespoon in mounds 1 inch apart onto the baking sheets. Bake until lightly browned, 15 to 18 minutes, switching oven racks and rotating the sheets halfway through. Let cool on the sheets for 2 to 3 minutes, then transfer to a wire rack to cool completely.

COCONUT MACAROONS

About thirty-six 1½-inch cookies

Preheat the oven to 325°F. Line 2 baking sheets or cookie sheets with parchment paper.

Stir together in a large bowl until combined:

⅔ cup (205g) sweetened condensed milk
1 large egg white
1½ teaspoons vanilla
⅛ teaspoon salt

Stir in until blended:

3½ cups flaked or shredded sweetened coconut

Add more condensed milk if the coconut seems especially dry. Drop the dough by the tablespoon about 2 inches apart onto the baking sheets. Bake until golden brown, 20 to 24 minutes, switching oven racks and rotating the sheets halfway through. Let cool on the sheets for 2 to 3 minutes, then transfer to a wire rack to cool completely.

CHOCOLATE COCONUT MACAROONS

Prepare **Coconut Macaroons, above.** For chocolate-coated macaroons, simply dip the baked macaroons in melted or tempered chocolate, 858. For chocolate macaroons, combine the condensed milk with **3 tablespoons unsweetened cocoa powder or 1 ounce unsweetened chocolate, chopped,** in a small saucepan. Heat over low heat, stirring until the cocoa is dissolved or the chocolate is melted. Let cool before making the rest of the dough. Bake as directed.

MERINGUE KISSES

About forty-eight 1½-inch cookies

For tips on working with egg whites, see Beating Eggs, 977. To make **chocolate meringue kisses**, whisk **¼ cup unsweetened cocoa powder** into the sugar.

Preheat the oven to 225°F. Line 2 baking sheets or cookie sheets with parchment paper.

Prepare:

French Meringue, 794, using the optional vanilla

If desired, fold in:

(¾ cup finely ground toasted, 1005, pecans, almonds, pistachios, or hazelnuts)

Using a pastry bag fitted with a ½-inch open star tip or a zip-top bag with a bottom corner snipped off, pipe the batter into 1¼-inch kisses about 1 inch apart on the baking sheets. (Or, drop heaping teaspoons of batter in peaked mounds.) Bake for 45 minutes, switching oven racks and rotating the sheets halfway through. Turn the heat off and let the cookies stand in the oven for 30 minutes, or until cool.

ABOUT ROLLED, MOLDED, AND SHAPED COOKIES

Shaped cookies are such fun to make that they are the perfect enticement to get children in the kitchen to help with molding the dough and decorating the finished cookies. When rolling out cookie dough, use as little extra flour as possible. Alternatively, dust your work surface with powdered sugar. To prevent most cookie doughs from sticking to your work surface and rolling pin, ➤ roll the dough between sheets of parchment or wax paper. We like to roll dough right out of the mixing bowl while it is still pliable, then freeze or refrigerate it before cutting and baking. Of course, you may also refrigerate dough before rolling, but you may need to let it warm up slightly before rolling to prevent cracking. ➤ Cookie dough can be refrigerated, tightly wrapped, for up to 2 days or frozen up to 1 month.

When cutting or shaping cookies, ➤ try to keep them all about the same size and thickness so that they will bake evenly. And remember that if you choose to make cookies larger or smaller than the recipe specifies, the amount of spreading, the baking time, and the recipe yield may vary. Use cutters dipped in flour or powdered sugar and handle the dough as little as possible.

Other cookies are formed by hand, with molds, presses (see Spritz Cookies, 780), or other special equipment. Traditional cookie molds can also be used for firm dough like shortbread and springerle; ➤ they must be well oiled and floured to ensure easy removal. To shape dough into balls, use a small cookie scoop or lightly floured hands. If the dough is very soft or sticky, refrigerate it for a few minutes.

As for cookie cutters, amusing ones lurk in antique shops and cookware stores. You may also find a roller cutter—a progression of shapes on a wheel that is mounted on a handle. The cutter is rolled across the dough and spins out shapes with great rapidity.

ROLLED SUGAR COOKIES

About thirty-six 2- to 3-inch cookies

This is the ideal dough for decorated sugar cookies, but they also have a lovely flavor without any icing whatsoever.

Beat in a large bowl, or in a stand mixer with the paddle attachment, until creamy:

2 sticks (8 oz or 225g) unsalted butter, softened
⅔ cup (130g) sugar

Add and beat until combined:

1½ teaspoons vanilla or almond extract
(Finely grated zest of 1 lemon)

Beat in:

1 large egg

Stir in until blended:

2½ cups (315g) all-purpose flour
½ teaspoon salt
¼ teaspoon baking powder

Divide the dough into thirds, shape into disks, and wrap in plastic. Refrigerate for at least 1 hour or for up to 1 day.

Preheat the oven to 350°F. Grease or line 2 baking sheets or cookie sheets with parchment paper.

Working with 1 portion of dough at a time, roll out ¼ inch thick. Cut out cookies using 2- or 3-inch cutters and arrange about 1 inch apart on the prepared baking sheets. Gather the scraps and reroll one time to cut more cookies. If desired, sprinkle the cookies very lightly with:

(Colored sprinkles, decorating sugar, or nonpareils)

Bake until the cookies are lightly colored on top and slightly darker at the edges, 10 to 12 minutes, switching oven racks and rotating the sheets halfway through. Let cool on the sheets for 2 to 3 minutes, then transfer to a wire rack to cool completely. If desired, decorate the cooled cookies with:

(Royal Icing, 798)

SAND TARTS

About sixty 1½-inch cookies

When Marion and John were traveling in Normandy, they sampled a famous local specialty, **sablés** (*sablé* is French for "sandy"). Marion immediately recognized a familiar cookie, which she had always known as sand tarts. You may substitute brown sugar for the sugar, if desired.

Whisk together in a medium bowl:

2 cups (250g) all-purpose flour
½ teaspoon salt

Beat in a large bowl, or in a stand mixer with the paddle attachment, until creamy:

1½ sticks (6 oz or 170g) unsalted butter, softened

Gradually add and beat until light and fluffy:

¾ cup (150g) sugar

Beat in:

1 large egg yolk (reserve the white)
1 teaspoon vanilla
(Finely grated zest of 1 lemon)

Gradually stir the flour into the butter-sugar mixture until well blended and briefly knead to bring the dough together. Divide the dough in half and roll each half into a 1½-inch-diameter log. Tightly wrap the logs in parchment paper and freeze for 2 hours.

Preheat the oven to 375°F. Line 2 baking sheets or cookie sheets with parchment paper (you may use the parchment paper you wrapped the cookie dough in).

Working with 1 log of dough at a time, slice the log into ¼-inch-thick rounds and place 1 inch apart on the baking sheets. Bake as is or, if desired, brush the tops of the cookies with:

(1 large egg white, beaten)

And sprinkle with:

(Sugar or superfine sugar)

Place in the center of each:

(1 almond slice)

Bake until very light golden, about 8 minutes, switching oven racks and rotating the sheets halfway through. Let cool on the sheets for 2 to 3 minutes, then transfer to a wire rack to cool completely.

MORAVIAN MOLASSES THINS

About sixty-five 2½-inch cookies

These paper-thin cookies are traditional in American communities settled by Moravian immigrants from central Europe.

Whisk together in a medium bowl:

1 cup (125g) all-purpose flour
1½ teaspoons ground cinnamon
1 teaspoon ground ginger
½ teaspoon baking soda
½ teaspoon ground cloves
¼ teaspoon ground cardamom
¼ teaspoon salt

Beat in a medium bowl, or in a stand mixer with the paddle attachment, until blended:

½ cup packed (115g) dark brown sugar
⅓ cup (115g) molasses
¼ cup (50g) vegetable shortening or lard
1 teaspoon vanilla

Stir the flour mixture into the sugar mixture, then knead until smooth. Divide the dough into thirds, shape into disks, and wrap in plastic. Let stand at room temperature for at least 6 hours or, preferably, 12 hours. (The dough can also be refrigerated for up to 4 days; return to room temperature before using.)

Preheat the oven to 300°F. Grease or line 2 baking sheets or cookie sheets with parchment paper.

Working with 1 portion of the dough at a time, roll as thin as possible (about ⅛ inch). Cut out the cookies using a 2¼-inch fluted or plain round cutter and arrange about 1 inch apart on the prepared baking sheets. Bake until the edges of the cookies are just barely browned, 6 to 9 minutes, switching oven racks and rotating the sheets halfway through; don't overbake, or the cookies will be bitter. Let cool on the sheets for 2 to 3 minutes, then transfer to a wire rack to cool completely.

GINGERBREAD MEN

About thirty 4-inch gingerbread men

Preheat the oven to 350°F. Grease or line 2 baking sheets or cookie sheets with parchment paper.

Whisk together in a medium bowl:

3½ cups (415g) all-purpose flour
1 tablespoon ground ginger
2 teaspoons ground cinnamon
1 teaspoon baking soda
½ teaspoon salt
¼ teaspoon ground cloves

Beat in a large bowl, or in a stand mixer with the paddle attachment, until creamy:

½ cup (100g) sugar or ½ cup packed (115g) brown sugar
4 tablespoons (½ stick or 55g) unsalted butter, softened

Beat in:

½ cup (170g) molasses

Add the flour mixture to the butter-sugar mixture in two parts, alternating with:

⅓ cup (80g) water

Use the dough immediately or refrigerate for up to 4 days. Let the dough come to room temperature before rolling. Divide the dough in half. Cover one half with plastic wrap and roll out the other half between two pieces of parchment paper to ¼ inch thick. Cut out cookies using a 4- to 5-inch-tall cutter and arrange 1½ inches apart on the prepared baking sheets. Gather the scraps and reroll one time to cut out more cookies. Bake until the edges of the cookies have just barely darkened, 8 to 10 minutes, switching oven racks and rotating the sheets halfway through. Let cool on the sheets for 2 to 3 minutes, then transfer to a wire rack to cool completely. Decorate the cooled cookies with:

Royal Icing, 798

Pipe the icing using a pastry bag fitted with a ⅛-inch round tip, and apply the icing with a wooden pick or a small knife for additional garnishes—caps, hair, mustaches, belts, etc.

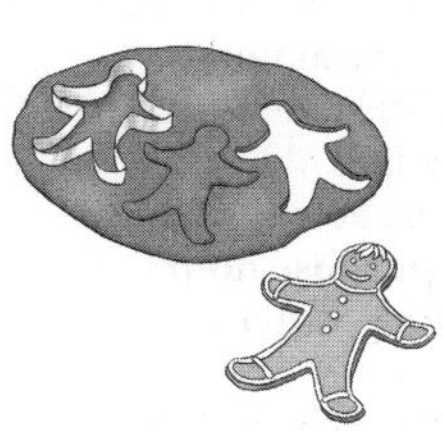

Cutting out gingerbread men

VIENNESE CRESCENTS

About forty-eight 2¼-inch cookies

Preheat the oven to 350°F. Grease or line 2 baking sheets or cookie sheets with parchment paper.

Beat in a large bowl, or in a stand mixer with the paddle attachment, until creamy:

2 sticks (8 oz or 225g) unsalted butter, softened

Add and beat until well combined:

¾ cup (75g) powdered sugar

Beat in:

1 cup (90g) finely ground walnuts or almond meal or flour
2 teaspoons vanilla
(1 teaspoon ground cinnamon)

Stir in until well blended:

2 cups (250g) all-purpose flour

Chill the dough for 1 hour. If using a crescent cookie cutter, roll the dough to the thickness of ¼ inch. If shaping into crescents, roll 1-tablespoon pieces of dough into short ropes, then form them into crescents (see below). Arrange about ¼ inch apart on the prepared baking sheets. Bake until the crescents begin to brown, 13 to 15 minutes, switching oven racks and rotating the sheets halfway through. Let cool on the sheets for 2 to 3 minutes, then transfer to a wire rack to cool completely. Roll the cooled cookies in:

⅔ cup powdered sugar

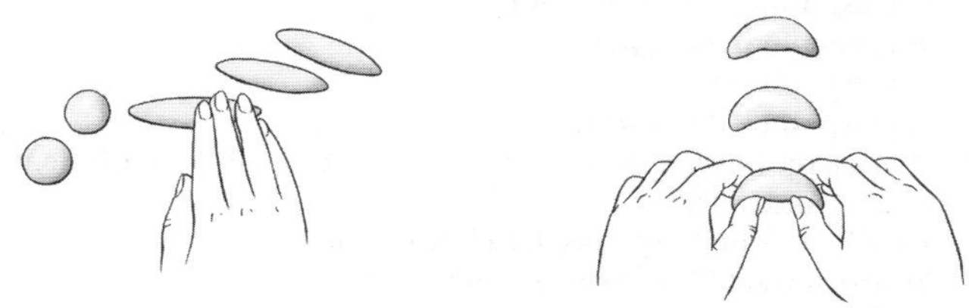

Rolling and shaping Viennese crescents

MANDELPLÄTTCHEN (ALMOND PRETZELS)

Forty-eight 3-inch pretzels

Whisk together in a medium bowl:

2½ cups (315g) all-purpose flour
2 teaspoons ground cinnamon
(Finely grated zest of 1 lemon)
1 teaspoon baking powder
Pinch of salt

Beat in a large bowl, or in a stand mixer with the paddle attachment, until blended:

2 sticks (8 oz or 225g) unsalted butter, softened
1 cup (200g) sugar

Beat in:

¼ cup (60g) sour cream
2 large eggs
1 large egg yolk
1 teaspoon vanilla
(¼ teaspoon almond extract)

Stir the flour mixture into the butter-sugar mixture. Divide the dough in half, shape into disks, and wrap in plastic. Refrigerate until firm enough to handle, about 2 hours.

Preheat the oven to 375°F. Grease or line 2 baking sheets or cookie sheets with parchment paper.

Working with 1 disk at a time, divide the dough into 24 equal pieces. Shape into long thin ropes, twist into pretzel shapes, 623, and arrange about 2 inches apart on the prepared baking sheets. Brush the pretzels with:

1 large egg yolk, beaten

Sprinkle the tops with:

Chopped blanched almonds
Sugar

Bake until the edges are tinged with brown, 10 to 12 minutes, switching oven racks and rotating the sheets halfway through. Let cool on the sheets for 2 to 3 minutes, then transfer to a wire rack to cool completely.

GRAHAM CRACKERS

Twenty 2 × 3½-inch crackers

Homemade graham crackers taste a bit like childhood, but better. You can cut these grahams into any size crackers. For small children, make them bite-sized.

Whisk together in a medium bowl:

1 cup (130g) graham or whole wheat flour
½ cup (65g) all-purpose flour
½ teaspoon ground cinnamon
½ teaspoon baking powder
½ teaspoon salt
¼ teaspoon baking soda

Beat in a large bowl, or in a stand mixer with the paddle attachment, until light and fluffy:

1 stick (4 oz or 115g) unsalted butter, softened
⅓ cup packed (75g) brown sugar
2 tablespoons (40g) honey

Beat in:

1 teaspoon vanilla

Stir the flour mixture into the butter-sugar mixture until the dough comes together. Transfer the dough to a lightly floured surface and knead briefly just until smooth, then divide in half. Roll each piece of dough into a 7 × 10-inch rectangle between two sheets of parchment paper. Peel off the top piece of parchment paper but leave the dough on the bottom piece of parchment. Use a knife or pastry cutter to trim the edges of the dough, then cut each rectangle crosswise into five 2-inch strips, then in half lengthwise to make ten 2 × 3½-inch crackers. Use a fork to dock each cracker 4 times (there is no need to separate the crackers). Stack the rolled out and cut dough between layers of parchment paper on a baking sheet and freeze for 30 minutes.

Preheat the oven to 350°F.

Place the chilled dough still on the parchment paper on 2 baking sheets or cookie sheets and bake until golden brown, 12 to 14 minutes, switching oven racks and rotating the sheets halfway through. Let cool on the sheets for 2 to 3 minutes, then transfer to a wire rack to cool completely. Break the cooled cookies apart along the cut lines.

WHOLE-GRAIN SEED WAFERS

About sixty 2- to 2½-inch cookies

These not-so-sweet cookies are a superb way to try out different whole-grain flours such as buckwheat, Kamut, spelt, rye, corn, or whole wheat. Because they straddle the line between savory and sweet, they are excellent served as part of a cheese platter, 45.

Preheat the oven to 350°F. Line 2 baking sheets or cookie sheets with parchment paper.

Beat together in a medium bowl, or in a stand mixer with the paddle attachment, until smooth:

2 sticks (8 oz or 225g) unsalted butter, softened
⅔ cup (130g) sugar

If desired, beat in:

(Finely grated zest of 1 lemon or 1 orange)

Whisk together in a medium bowl:

2 cups (250g) all-purpose flour
1 cup (130g) whole-grain flour (see headnote above for ideas)
1 teaspoon baking powder
1 teaspoon salt
1 teaspoon ground fennel, coriander, or caraway, or ½ teaspoon ground cardamom

Add the flour mixture to the butter-sugar mixture, stirring until crumbly. Add:

6 to 7 tablespoons (30 to 45g) half-and-half, milk, or water

stirring in just enough so the dough comes together. Transfer the dough to a lightly floured work surface and lightly knead it to bring it together. Roll it out to a ⅛-inch thickness and cut out with a 2- to 2½-inch cutter. Place the cookies 1 inch apart on the baking sheets.

Whisk together in a small bowl:

¼ cup (50g) sugar
2 tablespoons coarsely ground fennel, coriander, or caraway seeds, or 1 tablespoon coarsely ground cardamom seeds

Whisk in a second small bowl:

1 egg white
1 teaspoon water

Brush the cookies with the egg white, then sprinkle with the sugar mixture. Bake until set and lightly browned, 10 to 12 minutes, switching oven racks and rotating the sheets halfway through. Let cool on the sheets for 2 to 3 minutes, then transfer to a wire rack to cool completely.

ANISE-ALMOND BISCOTTI

About forty-two 3 × ½-inch biscotti

For a pistachio variation, omit the anise, use vanilla extract, and substitute pistachios for the almonds.

Preheat the oven to 375°F. Grease or line a baking sheet or cookie sheet with parchment paper.

Whisk together in a large bowl:

3⅓ cups (415g) all-purpose flour
2½ teaspoons baking powder
½ teaspoon salt

Beat in a large bowl until blended:

1¼ cups (250g) sugar
¼ cup (50g) vegetable oil
2 large eggs
2 large egg whites
2 teaspoons anise seed, finely ground
1 teaspoon vanilla or almond extract
Finely grated zest of 1 lemon
Finely grated zest of ½ orange

Add the flour mixture to the sugar-egg mixture along with:

1 cup almonds, coarsely chopped

Stir until blended. Divide the dough in half. Shape each half into a smooth 11 × 1½-inch log by wrapping the log in plastic and rolling it back and forth until smooth, or by shaping it with lightly floured hands. Arrange the logs as far apart from each other as possible on the prepared baking sheet and press to flatten slightly. Bake for 25 minutes. Transfer the baking sheet to a wire rack (leave the oven on).

When the logs are cool enough to handle, carefully transfer to a cutting board and cut on a slight diagonal into ⅜-inch-thick slices. Lay the slices flat on the baking sheet, return to the oven, and bake for 10 minutes. Turn the slices over and bake until lightly browned, 5 to 10 minutes more. Transfer the biscotti to wire racks to cool.

CHOCOLATE-ORANGE BISCOTTI
About forty-two 3 × ½-inch biscotti

If you gild the lily as a matter of course, add ½ **cup chopped toasted, 992, hazelnuts** to the dough along with the chocolate chips.

Preheat the oven to 375°F. Line a baking sheet with parchment paper.
Whisk together in a medium bowl:

2½ cups (315g) all-purpose flour
¾ cup (60g) unsweetened cocoa powder
2 teaspoons baking powder
(2 teaspoons instant espresso powder)
½ teaspoon salt

Beat in a large bowl, or in a stand mixer with the paddle attachment, until smooth:

1 stick (4 oz or 115g) unsalted butter, softened
1¼ cups (250g) sugar

Add:

2 teaspoons vanilla
Finely grated zest of 1 orange

Beat in:

2 large eggs

Add the flour mixture to the butter-sugar mixture and stir in until almost fully combined. Add:

¾ cup chopped dark chocolate or mini semisweet chocolate chips (4 oz or 115g)

Stir to bring the dough together. Shape, bake, and cool as for Anise-Almond Biscotti, 778. If desired, dip half of each cookie in:

(6 ounces [170g] semisweet or bittersweet chocolate, melted)

ZIMSTERNE (CINNAMON-ALMOND STARS)
About thirty-six 1½-inch stars

Deservedly one of the most popular German Christmas cookies. The dough is very fragile and sticky, but the results will make your perseverance worthwhile. If desired, the dough can also be shaped into 1-inch balls and flattened slightly.

Preheat the oven to 300°F. Grease or line 2 baking sheets or cookie sheets with parchment paper.

Whip to medium-firm peaks, 977, in a large bowl:

3 large egg whites
⅛ teaspoon salt

Gradually beat in:

1⅓ cups (135g) powdered sugar
1¼ teaspoons ground cinnamon
Finely grated zest of 1 lemon

Beat until stiff and glossy. Transfer one-third of the egg white mixture to another bowl and set aside. Fold into the remainder:

2⅓ cups whole raw almonds, finely ground

Dust a work surface lightly with powdered sugar. Pat the dough out to a thickness of ⅓ inch; it is too delicate to roll. If it sticks, dust your palms with powdered sugar. Cut using a 1½-inch star cutter. Arrange on the prepared baking sheets about 1½ inches apart. Brush the tops with the reserved egg white mixture. Bake until the tops look dry and slightly crackled, about 20 minutes, switching oven racks and rotating the sheets halfway through. Let cool on the sheets for 2 to 3 minutes, then transfer to a wire rack to cool completely.

SPRINGERLE (MOLDED ANISE COOKIES)
About 30 assorted 2- to 4-inch cookies

These famous German anise cookies are stamped with a wooden mold or roller into quaint designs and figures. If you have no mold, cut the dough into ¾ × 2½-inch bars. For a more pronounced anise flavor, add 1 to 2 teaspoons anise seeds to the storage container.

Whisk together in a medium bowl:

3¼ cups (405g) all-purpose flour
¼ teaspoon baking powder

Lightly beat in a large bowl:

4 large eggs

Add and beat until blended:

1⅔ cups (330g) sugar
Finely grated zest of 1 lemon
1 teaspoon anise extract

Stir the flour mixture into the egg-sugar mixture until well blended. Grease or line 2 baking sheets or cookie sheets with parchment paper. Sprinkle a clean work surface with:

¼ cup all-purpose flour

Turn out the dough onto the work surface and sprinkle with a little more flour. Knead in enough flour to firm the dough and make it manageable. Divide the dough in half and wrap one half in plastic (do not refrigerate). Roll out the remaining dough to ¼ inch thick. Lightly dust a carved springerle rolling pin or cookie mold with flour; tap off the excess. Firmly roll the rolling pin over the dough to imprint designs, or press the mold firmly into the dough, then lift off. Cut the designs apart using a pastry wheel or sharp knife and arrange about ½ inch apart on the prepared baking sheets. Set the cookies aside, uncovered, for 10 to 12 hours.

Preheat the oven to 300°F. If desired, sprinkle the cookies with:

(2 to 3 tablespoons whole or crushed anise seeds)

Bake until the cookies are almost firm but not browned, 18 to 25 minutes, switching oven racks and rotating the sheets halfway through. Let cool on the sheets for 2 to 3 minutes, then transfer to a wire rack to cool completely.

SPEKULATIUS
About twenty-eight 2 × 4-inch cookies

Spekulatius are rich cookies of German origin, with Christmas symbols pressed into them by special carved wooden molds.

Pulse in a food processor or whisk together in a medium bowl:

1½ cups (190g) all-purpose flour
½ cup packed (115g) brown sugar
¼ cup (25g) almond meal or flour

1 teaspoon ground cinnamon
¼ teaspoon ground cloves or cardamom

Add and pulse or work into the flour with your fingers until the butter is in tiny pieces:

6 tablespoons (¾ stick or 85g) cold unsalted butter, cut into cubes

Add and pulse just until a crumbly dough forms:

1 large egg
2 tablespoons (30g) heavy cream

Flatten the dough into a disc, wrap tightly, and refrigerate for 12 to 24 hours.

Preheat the oven to 350°F.

Roll the dough ⅛ inch thick between two pieces of parchment paper. Remove the top piece of parchment paper and stamp the dough with 2 × 4-inch floured molds or cut the dough into 2-inch squares or 2 × 4-inch rectangles if you do not have molds. If the dough becomes too sticky, freeze briefly until stiff. Slide the parchment with the cut-out cookies onto a baking sheet or cookie sheet. Separate the cookies slightly, leaving about ½ inch between them. Brush the cookies lightly with:

1 egg white, beaten

If making cookies that are not stamped, sprinkle with:

(½ cup sliced almonds)

Bake until the cookies are dry and lightly browned, 12 to 15 minutes, rotating the sheet halfway through. Let cool on the sheet for 2 to 3 minutes, then transfer to a wire rack to cool completely.

SPRITZ COOKIES

About sixty 2-inch cookies

Some spritz cookies are soft and tender to the point of being cake-like, but these are crisp-tender. If desired, sprinkle with colored sugar before baking or dip them halfway in melted chocolate after cooling. You can also sandwich 2 spritz cookies together with any buttercream, 796–97, in between.

Sift together into a medium bowl:

2¼ cups (280g) all-purpose flour
½ teaspoon salt

Beat in a separate medium bowl, or in a stand mixer with the paddle attachment, until light and fluffy:

2 sticks (8 oz or 225g) unsalted butter, softened
¾ cup (150g) sugar

Add and beat until combined:

2 large egg yolks
1 teaspoon vanilla or almond extract

Stir the flour mixture into the butter-sugar mixture until the dough is smooth. Chill the dough for 1 hour.

Preheat the oven to 350°F. Line a baking sheet or cookie sheet with parchment paper.

Put the dough through a cookie press onto the prepared sheet, leaving 1 inch between the cookies. The dough should be pliable enough to be put through the press fairly easily, but if it becomes too soft, rechill it slightly. Bake until lightly browned, about 10 minutes, rotating the sheet halfway through. Let cool on the sheet for 2 to 3 minutes, then transfer to a wire rack to cool completely.

CHOCOLATE SPRITZ COOKIES

We didn't think spritz cookies could be more charming, but we were willing to test our assumptions. These brownie-flavored cookies proved us wrong.

Prepare the dough for **Spritz Cookies, above,** using **2 cups (250g) flour** and **½ cup (40g) unsweetened cocoa powder.** Proceed as directed.

SCOTCH SHORTBREAD

Twenty-four 2 × 1⅓-inch bars

If desired, substitute ⅓ **cup (40g) rice flour or cornstarch** for an equal amount of the all-purpose flour, which produces an especially crumbly and tender shortbread.

Preheat the oven to 300°F. Have ready an ungreased 8-inch square baking pan or a rectangular shortbread mold.

Beat in a large bowl until smooth:

1½ sticks (6 oz or 170g) unsalted butter, softened
¼ cup (25g) powdered sugar
¼ cup (50g) sugar
¼ teaspoon salt

Stir in:

1½ cups (190g) all-purpose flour

Lightly knead until blended. Press the dough evenly into the baking pan or shortbread mold. If baking in a pan, pierce the dough deeply with a fork all over in a decorative pattern. If desired, sprinkle with:

(2 teaspoons sugar)

Bake until the shortbread is lightly browned and darker at the edges, 45 to 50 minutes. Cut into bars while still warm, then let cool in the pan or mold.

ABOUT ICEBOX OR REFRIGERATOR COOKIES

We have been extolling the virtues of these cookies since 1931. They store nicely and do not involve rolling, shaping, or scoop portioning. More important, you can slice off as many discs of dough as you want and freshly bake small batches directly from the freezer. Of all the recipes in this chapter, these are the easiest to make ahead of time. After mixing the dough, form it into a 2-inch-diameter roll on a piece of parchment or wax paper, and wrap it securely. Use the straight edge of a bowl scraper or bench scraper to tighten the paper around the roll. See page 747 for an illustration of this technique (note that instead of using a cookie sheet to tighten the roll, you will be using a bowl scraper or bench scraper for the cookie dough).

Chill the roll 4 to 12 hours, after which time it can be very thinly sliced with a sharp knife. You may hasten the chilling by placing the roll in the freezer. If you want to make up a batch and bake them immediately, they can be baked as drop cookies, 768, without chilling.

VANILLA ICEBOX COOKIES

About forty 2½-inch cookies

This dough also makes a good filled cookie, or rich drop cookie; see About Drop Cookies, 768, or About Filled Cookies, 781.

Whisk together in a medium bowl:

1½ cups (155g) all-purpose flour
1 teaspoon baking powder
½ teaspoon salt

Beat in a large bowl, or in a stand mixer with the paddle attachment, until fluffy:

1 stick (4 oz or 115g) unsalted butter, softened
⅔ cup (70g) powdered sugar

Add and beat until combined:

1 large egg
1 teaspoon vanilla or vanilla bean paste
(Finely grated zest of 1 lemon)

Stir the flour mixture into the butter-sugar mixture until blended. Shape the dough into an even 11-inch-long log and wrap tightly in parchment paper. Refrigerate or freeze until firm.

Preheat the oven to 375°F. Grease or line 2 baking sheets or cookie sheets with parchment paper.

Cut the log into scant ¼-inch-thick slices and arrange about 1 inch apart on the prepared baking sheets. Bake until the cookies are lightly browned, 8 to 10 minutes, switching oven racks and rotating the sheets halfway through. The longer the baking time, the crisper the cookies. Let cool on the sheets for 2 to 3 minutes, then transfer to a wire rack to cool completely.

ADDITIONS TO ICEBOX COOKIES

- Add **2 teaspoons loose Earl Grey tea, finely ground,** and the **finely grated zest of 1 orange** along with the vanilla
- Substitute ⅓ **cup packed (75g) brown sugar** for half of the powdered sugar and add **1 cup mini semisweet chocolate chips** along with the flour mixture
- Omit the lemon zest and add **4 ounces (115g) semisweet or bittersweet chocolate, melted and cooled,** before adding the egg
- Add the **finely grated zest of 1 orange** to the butter-sugar mixture and ½ **cup finely chopped dark chocolate** along with the flour mixture
- Add the **finely grated zest of 1 lemon** and **2 tablespoons poppy seeds** along with the vanilla
- Add ½ **cup chopped toasted, 1005, nuts** along with the flour mixture
- Add ⅓ **cup cocoa nibs** along with the flour mixture
- Substitute **rose water** for the vanilla, and add ⅓ **cup finely chopped pistachios** along with the flour mixture
- Add the **finely grated zest of 2 limes** and ½ **teaspoon ground cardamom** along with the vanilla
- Add ⅓ **cup finely chopped candied ginger** along with the flour mixture
- Substitute **packed brown sugar** for the powdered sugar, substitute **1 tablespoon coffee liqueur** for the vanilla, and add **1 tablespoon instant espresso powder** along with the liqueur
- Substitute **packed brown sugar** for the powdered sugar and add ¾ **teaspoon ground cinnamon,** ½ **teaspoon ground ginger,** ¼ **teaspoon grated or ground nutmeg,** ¼ **teaspoon ground allspice,** and ⅛ **teaspoon ground cloves** to the flour mixture

PINWHEEL ICEBOX COOKIES

Two sheets of different colored doughs may be rolled together, as shown below. When sliced, these become pinwheel cookies. Prepare **Vanilla Icebox Cookies, 780,** omitting the lemon zest. Divide the dough in half. Knead or gently mix into half the dough **2 ounces (55g) semisweet or bittersweet chocolate, melted.** If the dough is soft, chill until firm. Roll the vanilla and chocolate doughs separately into equal-sized ⅛-inch-thick rectangles. Layer the chocolate dough over the vanilla dough and roll up like a jelly-roll. Chill, slice, and bake as directed above.

Making pinwheel icebox cookies

ABOUT FILLED COOKIES

Fillings can be as simple as store-bought jam tucked in the indentations of thumbprint cookies or thin chocolate mints sandwiched between golden wafers. You may also use flavored fondant, buttercream icing, 796–97, Chocolate Ganache, 797, or other thick frostings, 792–93, to fill cookies. Since there is so much variety in the shaping, handling, and baking of filled cookies, few rules apply. Simply follow the directions in each recipe and study the illustrations, 782, for inspiration.

FILLED COOKIES

About forty 2-inch cookies

In addition to the fillings on 782, these cookies may be filled with Chopped Fruit Filling, 802, Toasted Walnut or Pecan Filling, 803, Nut Fillings, 803, or any thick preserve.

Prepare the dough for:

Rolled Sugar Cookies, 776, or Vanilla Icebox Cookies, 780

Preheat the oven to 350°F. Line 2 baking sheets or cookie sheets with parchment paper.

Form the dough into 1-inch balls and make an imprint with your thumb to hold a filling, as shown, 782. Or roll out the dough on a lightly floured work surface to ⅛ inch thick and cut into 2-inch rounds.

For turnovers, use a single round of dough for each cookie and a scant 1 teaspoon filling; fold over and seal the edges firmly by pressing them with a floured fork.

For closed tarts, use 2 rounds of dough for each cookie; place 1 teaspoon filling on one and cover with the other, then seal.

For see-through tarts, use 2 rounds of dough for each cookie, cutting a hole in the center of half of the rounds with a small round cutter. Place 1 teaspoon filling on the bottom dough rounds, and cover with the cut-out rounds. Seal the outer edges in the same way.

Place cookies 1 inch apart on the baking sheets. Bake until lightly browned and set, 15 to 18 minutes, switching oven racks and rotat-

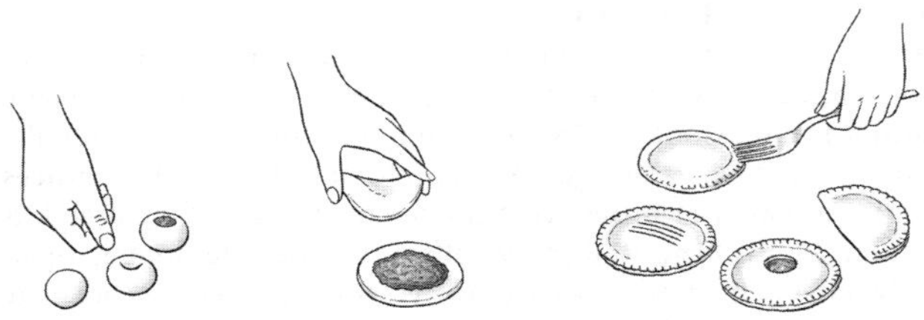

Filled cookies

ing the sheets halfway through. Let cool for 2 to 3 minutes on the sheets, then transfer to wire racks to cool completely.

FILLINGS FOR FILLED COOKIES

I. DRIED FRUIT

Combine in a small heavy saucepan and bring to a boil:

1 cup chopped raisins, dried figs, dates, or apricots
6 tablespoons (70g) sugar
5 tablespoons (75g) water
Finely grated zest of 1 lemon or orange
1 tablespoon (15g) lemon juice or ¼ cup (60g) orange juice
1 tablespoon (15g) unsalted butter
⅛ teaspoon salt

Boil, stirring, until thickened. Cool before using.

II. COCONUT

Combine in a bowl:

1½ cups flaked or shredded coconut, chopped
½ cup packed (115g) brown sugar
1 large egg, lightly beaten
1 tablespoon (10g) all-purpose flour
Finely grated zest and juice of 1 lime

III. MINCEMEAT

Use **about ¾ cup drained store-bought mincemeat** or prepare half the amount of filling for **Mock Mincemeat Pie, 672.**

ALFAJORES DE DULCE DE LECHE

About 20 sandwich cookies

These decadent Argentinian sandwich cookies are typically made with cornstarch-laden cookies that are very soft. We prefer the flavor of buttery icebox cookies; once stored for a day or two, they become meltingly soft all on their own.

Prepare the dough for:

Vanilla Icebox Cookies, 780

Shape, cut, and bake as directed. Prepare or have ready:

Easy Dulce de Leche, 809, or store-bought cajeta or dulce de leche

Let the cookies cool completely, then flip half of them over so the bottom is facing up. Top with 1½ to 2 teaspoons dulce de leche and top with a second cookie. If desired, dust the cookies with:

(Powdered sugar)

Or roll the sides in:

(Shredded coconut)

Store in an airtight container in the refrigerator for up to 1 week.

MACARONS

About 30 macarons

These delicate and beautiful cookies are notoriously difficult to get right. Our best advice is to take your time. Do not rush any stage of the process and be willing to practice. It may take a few tries to achieve picture-perfect macarons. The good news is the results will be delicious regardless of how they look.

Line 2 baking sheets with parchment paper. Mix together with a spatula in a medium bowl until completely smooth:

1½ cups (140g) blanched almond meal or flour, sifted
1¼ cups (125g) powdered sugar, sifted
2 large egg whites

Whip in a stand mixer with the whisk on medium speed until frothy:

2 large egg whites

Beat in:

2 tablespoons (25g) sugar
(½ teaspoon vanilla or almond extract)

Continue to beat on medium speed until soft peaks form, 977, then turn off the mixer. Combine in a medium saucepan:

¾ cup (150g) sugar
3 tablespoons (45g) water

Stir together over medium-low heat until the sugar is dissolved, then increase the heat to medium-high and cook until the syrup reaches 230°F. Turn the mixer on medium-high and add the syrup in a thin, steady stream, pouring it between the whisk and the side of the bowl. Once all the syrup is added, continue beating the egg whites until the mixer bowl is barely warm to the touch. Fold one-third of the egg whites into the almond meal mixture to lighten it, then fold the almond meal mixture into the remaining beaten egg whites along with, if desired:

(3 to 4 drops food coloring)

Fold until the mixture is smooth and homogenous and falls in ribbons off the spatula. It will feel like you are overfolding the mixture, and it will deflate. The batter should resemble lava. Transfer half of the batter to a pastry bag fitted with a ¼- to ½-inch plain tip or a zip-top bag with one corner cut off. Pipe the mixture onto the baking sheets into 1½-inch rounds spaced about 1 inch apart. Repeat with the remaining batter. Firmly tap the baking sheets on the work surface 3 times to remove any air bubbles. Let sit at room temperature until a skin forms on the top of the macarons, about 45 minutes. (Touch one lightly with a fingertip—it should not stick to your finger. If it does, let them dry a bit longer.) If you have a ceiling fan, turn it on. It will help dry out the surface of the macarons.

Preheat the oven to 300°F while the macarons dry.

Bake the macarons one sheet at a time until set, 14 to 16 minutes, rotating the sheets halfway through. Let cool completely on the sheets. Turn half the macarons upside down and top with:

1 teaspoon filling, such as any jam, citrus curd, 802, any buttercream icing, 796–97, chocolate-hazelnut spread, ganache, 797, or any sweetened nut butter (about ⅔ cup total)

Top with a second cookie. Place the macarons in a single layer in airtight containers and freeze overnight or for up to 2 days. Bring to room temperature to serve.

FLAVORED MACARONS

Chocolate: Add **3 tablespoons (15g) unsweetened cocoa powder** to the almond meal mixture and use **Chocolate Ganache, 797,** for the filling.

Lemon: Add the **finely grated zest of 1 lemon** along with the vanilla, use **3 to 4 drops yellow food coloring,** and use **Lemon Curd, 802,** or **Citrus Buttercream, 797,** for the filling.

Pistachio: Use **3 to 4 drops green food coloring** and use **pistachio paste** for the filling.

Coffee: Add **2 teaspoons instant espresso powder** to the almond meal mixture and use **Coffee Buttercream, 797,** for the filling.

Strawberry: Add **3 tablespoons finely ground freeze-dried strawberries** to the almond meal mixture and use **strawberry jam or Meringue Buttercream, 796,** for the filling.

BACI DI DAMA (CHOCOLATE-FILLED HAZELNUT COOKIES)

About 45 sandwich cookies

These "ladies' kisses" are perfect, tiny Italian treats that melt in your mouth.

Preheat the oven to 350°F. Grease or line 2 baking sheets or cookie sheets with parchment paper.

Using roasted and skinned hazelnuts, 992, instead of pecans, prepare the dough for:

Mexican Wedding Cakes, 773

Using level teaspoons of dough, shape the dough into balls, place about 1 inch apart on the prepared baking sheets and bake until light golden brown on the bottom, 10 to 12 minutes, switching oven racks and rotating the sheets halfway through. Let cool on the sheets for 2 to 3 minutes, then transfer to a wire rack to cool completely. Do not roll in powdered sugar. Melt gently in a double boiler (or a heatproof bowl set over a pan of barely simmering water):

3 ounces (85g) bittersweet chocolate, finely chopped

Allow the chocolate to cool slightly so it is thick but still liquid. Spoon a tiny dollop of chocolate onto the underside of half of the cookies, then top with a second cookie to sandwich the chocolate filling. Place the cookies on their sides and let the chocolate set. Store the cookies in an airtight container at room temperature for up to 1 week.

RUGELACH

About 30 rolled rugelach or 24 large or 48 small crescents

Use jam or preserves—not jelly. We have found store-bought chocolate hazelnut spread to be delicious as well. The dough can be refrigerated for up to 1 week or packed airtight and frozen for up to 1 month.

Beat in a large bowl, or in a stand mixer with the paddle attachment, until blended:

2 sticks (8 oz or 225g) unsalted butter, softened
6 ounces (170g) cream cheese, softened

Add and beat until blended:

2¼ cups (280g) all-purpose flour

Divide the dough into thirds. Flatten into 6 × 4-inch rectangles if making rolled rugelach, or into 6-inch disks if making crescents. Wrap in plastic and refrigerate for at least 1 hour.

Preheat the oven to 350°F. Grease or line a large baking sheet or cookie sheet with parchment paper.

Whisk together in a small bowl:

⅓ cup (65g) sugar
1 teaspoon ground cinnamon
Pinch of salt

Work with 1 portion of dough at a time, leaving the remainder refrigerated. Generously flour the work surface and the top of the dough.

For rolled rugelach, roll each portion into a 16 × 10-inch rectangle about ⅛ inch thick. Brush the excess flour from the top and bottom of the dough and work surface, and turn the rectangle so a long side faces you. Leaving a ¼-inch border, spread each rectangle with:

¼ cup raspberry jam or apricot preserves (¾ cup total)

Place in a line along the edge of the jam on the side nearest you:

¼ cup currants, raisins, semisweet chocolate chips, or finely chopped dark chocolate (¾ cup total)

Sprinkle the exposed jam with 2 teaspoons of the cinnamon sugar and:

2½ tablespoons very finely chopped walnuts (½ cup total)

Roll the dough, starting at the long edge nearest you, gently tucking and tightening it as you go. Turn the roll seam side down. Cut into 1½-inch-thick slices and arrange seam side down about 1 inch apart on the prepared baking sheet.

For crescent rugelach, roll each dough portion into a round about 14 inches in diameter and ⅛ inch thick. Using the amounts listed above, spread the jam in a thin layer, leaving a ¼-inch border; then sprinkle the entire surface with the raisins, cinnamon sugar, and chopped nuts. Cut the round into wedges like a pizza—cutting 8 for large cookies or 16 for small cookies—as shown. Roll each one up from the wide end to the point, tucking the point under. Place seam side down on the prepared baking sheet.

Sprinkle each cookie with ⅛ teaspoon of the remaining cinnamon sugar. Bake until the bottoms are lightly browned, about 25 minutes, rotating the sheet halfway through. Let cool on the sheet for 2 to 3 minutes, then transfer to a wire rack to cool completely.

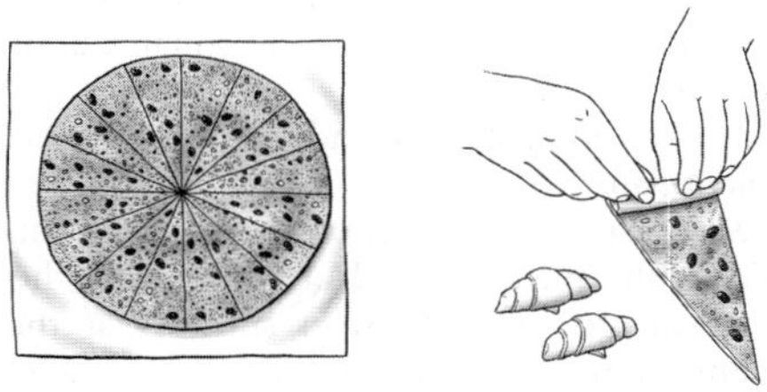

Making rugelach crescents

HAMANTASCHEN

About 20 cookies

The traditional filling for these triangular filled cookies is poppy seed, but we are partial to a dried fruit filling made with apricots.

Prepare the dough for:

Rolled Sugar Cookies, 776

Divide the dough in half, wrap tightly, and refrigerate for at least 1 hour.

Have ready:

A generous 3/4 cup Fillings for Filled Cookies I or II, 782, any of the fillings for coffee cakes, 803–4, the filling for Fig Keplers, below, or any jam or jelly

Preheat the oven to 350°F. Line 2 baking sheets or cookie sheets with parchment paper.

Working with 1 portion of dough at a time, roll out to 1/4 inch thick. If the dough is too cold, it may crack, so let it soften for a few minutes before rolling. Cut out cookies using a 3- to 3½-inch round cutter. Gather the scraps and reroll one time to cut out more cookies. Place the rounds about 1 inch apart on the baking sheets. Place 2 teaspoons filling in the center of each dough round, then fold three sides in toward the center to make triangle-shaped cookies with a triangle of filling showing in the center. Pinch the corners to seal. (If the dough becomes too sticky at any point, place it in the freezer for a few minutes to firm up.) Bake the cookies until light golden brown, 15 to 18 minutes, switching oven racks and rotating the sheets halfway through. Let cool on the sheets for 2 to 3 minutes, then transfer to a wire rack to cool completely.

FIG KEPLERS

About 30 cookies

Megan developed this recipe to re-create her favorite childhood cookie.

Prepare the dough for:

Vanilla Icebox Cookies, 780

with these changes: Use **packed brown sugar** instead of powdered sugar and add along with the vanilla:

Finely grated zest of 1 orange

Divide the dough into quarters, wrap tightly, and refrigerate until firm, about 1 hour.

Meanwhile, for the filling, combine in a medium saucepan:

1 pound (455g) dried figs, chopped

1/2 cup (120g) water

Bring to a boil, cover the pan, and simmer until all the water has been absorbed. Scrape the figs into a food processor and puree, scraping down the sides of the bowl occasionally, until no chunks remain. Let cool.

Preheat the oven to 325°F. Line a baking sheet or cookie sheet with parchment paper.

Place a piece of parchment paper on a work surface and dust with flour. Working with 1 piece of dough at a time, shape the dough into a rectangle by squaring it on the work surface (tap the 4 sides on the surface until they form a rectangle). Roll the dough, checking frequently to make sure it isn't sticking to the parchment paper, into a 4 × 12-inch rectangle. Scoop the fig filling into a pastry bag or a zip-top bag with one corner cut off and pipe in a 1-inch-wide strip lengthwise down the center of the dough. Flatten the filling a bit with wet fingers. Fold one side of the dough over the filling, then the other. Press down on the seam to close it. Using the parchment paper, flip the cookie roll over onto the baking sheet so the seam side is facing down. Refrigerate while you repeat this step with the other 3 pieces of dough.

Bake until the dough is no longer tacky and has begun to brown around the edges, about 16 minutes, rotating the sheet halfway through. While the cookie rolls are still warm, either transfer them to a cutting board (with the help of a large spatula) or cut them directly on the baking sheet. Cut into 1½-inch cookies. You may need to wipe off your knife every so often—the filling is rather sticky. Transfer the cookies to a wire rack and cover with a kitchen towel (this keeps the cookies soft as they cool). Cool the cookies completely. Store the cooled cookies in an airtight container at room temperature for up to 2 weeks.

PECAN TASSIES

24 tarts

Prepare the dough for:

Vanilla Icebox Cookies, 780

Refrigerate the dough for 12 hours.

Meanwhile, prepare using chopped pecans:

1/2 recipe of the filling for Pecan Pie, 677

Preheat the oven to 350°F. Lightly grease 24 cups of a mini muffin tin.

Place 1 tablespoon of the dough in each muffin cup and press it into the bottom and up the sides. Fill the shells with the pecan filling. Bake until set, 15 to 20 minutes, rotating the tin halfway through. Let cool in the tin on a wire rack.

JELLY TOTS

About forty-two 1½-inch cookies

You may call these **thimble cookies, deep-well cookies**, or **thumbprint cookies**, but a rose by any other name . . .

Prepare the dough for:

Rolled Sugar Cookies, 776

Roll the dough into a ball, wrap, and refrigerate for 30 minutes for easier handling.

Preheat the oven to 375°F. Grease or line 2 baking sheets with parchment paper.

Form the dough into 1-inch balls. Roll them in:

Sugar

Or, for a fancier cookie, roll in:

1 egg white, slightly beaten

and then in:

1 cup finely chopped toasted, 1005, nuts

Place the cookies about 1 inch apart on the prepared baking sheets. Depress the center of each cookie with your thumb and fill the centers of the cookies with:

About 3/4 cup any flavor preserves or jam

using about 1 teaspoon per cookie. Bake until set, 12 to 15 minutes, switching racks and rotating the sheets halfway through. Let cool for 2 to 3 minutes on the sheets, then transfer to a wire rack to cool completely.

QUICK PB&J THUMBPRINTS

About 24 cookies

These lightly sweetened cookies are wholesome enough to tuck into your little one's lunch box, and easy enough that a child could make them.

Preheat the oven to 325°F. Line a baking sheet with parchment paper.

Mix together in a medium bowl:

1 cup (240g) smooth unsweetened peanut butter
1 large egg
2 tablespoons (30g) packed brown sugar
2 tablespoons (15g) whole wheat or all-purpose flour

Portion the dough by the heaping teaspoon, roll the dough into balls, and place 1½ inches apart on the baking sheet. With your finger, press an indentation into the middle of each ball of dough. The dough is crumbly and will crack—this is okay. Fill each indentation with:

½ teaspoon strawberry jam (¼ cup total)

Bake until the cookies are set and lightly browned around the edges, 12 to 15 minutes. Let cool completely on the sheet on a rack. Store in an airtight container for up to 1 week.

MACAROON JAM TARTS

About 18 cookies

Irma was quite fond of these: "The star of stars. Quite the best I know how to make. This macaroon tart calls for two kinds of cake—a rich cookie as a base and an almond macaroon as a topping. Add to this thick, good jam—strawberry or plum—and you have as delicious a combination as can be found."

Beat in a medium bowl until creamy:

1 stick (4 oz or 115g) unsalted butter, softened
2 tablespoons (25g) sugar

Beat in:

1 large egg yolk
1½ teaspoons lemon juice
Finely grated zest of 1 lemon

Stir together in a small bowl:

1½ cups (190g) all-purpose flour
¼ teaspoon salt

Add the flour mixture to the butter-sugar mixture in batches, alternating with:

2 tablespoons (30g) cold water

Shape the dough into a disk, wrap in plastic, and refrigerate for 12 hours.

Preheat the oven to 325°F. Grease or line a baking sheet or cookie sheet with parchment paper.

Roll out the dough ⅛ inch thick. Using a round cookie or biscuit cutter, cut into 3-inch rounds, and place on the prepared baking sheet about 1 inch apart. Gather the scraps and reroll up to two more times to cut out more cookies. Whip in a medium bowl until soft peaks form, 977:

3 large egg whites

Gradually beat in:

1⅓ cups (135g) powdered sugar
1 teaspoon vanilla

Beat the meringue until stiff and glossy. Fold in:

2 cups (185g) almond meal or flour

Transfer the mixture to a pastry bag fitted with a medium plain tip or a zip-top bag with one corner cut off. Pipe the meringue mixture in a ½-inch-wide ring around the edges of each dough round. Fill the center of each cookie with:

1 teaspoon any thick jam (about 6 tablespoons total)

Use a small offset spatula to spread the jam evenly. If you like, add two crossed lines of meringue on top, shown below. Bake until lightly browned and the meringue is set, 20 to 25 minutes, rotating the sheet halfway through.

Piping the meringue for Macaroon Jam Tarts

LINZER HEARTS

About 26 sandwich cookies

Prepare the dough for:

Viennese Crescents, 777, using almond meal or flour

Divide the dough in half, wrap tightly, and refrigerate for 1 hour.

Preheat the oven to 350°F. Line 2 baking sheets or cookie sheets with parchment paper.

Working with 1 piece of dough at a time, roll out to a ¼-inch thickness and cut out with a 1½-inch cutter. Use a small round or heart-shaped cutter to cut out the center of half of the cookies. Gather the scraps and reroll one time to cut out more cookies. Arrange on the baking sheets 1 inch apart and bake until golden, 12 to 15 minutes, switching racks and rotating the sheets halfway through. Let cool for 2 to 3 minutes on the sheets, then transfer to a wire rack to cool completely.

Boil for 2 minutes in a small saucepan:

¾ cup seedless raspberry preserves

Cool to lukewarm. Sift over the cookies with the cut-out centers:

Powdered sugar

Turn the solid cookies over, so the bottom side is facing up. Place a small dollop of preserves on the solid cookies. Place a sugar-dusted cut-out cookie over the jam-topped cookies.

ABOUT CURLED COOKIES

Some curled cookies are simply dropped onto the baking sheet; others require a special iron. In either case, they are very elegant—whether they make a tube or cornucopia or are just partially curled after being shaped over a rolling pin or wooden spoon handle while still warm. Filled just before serving, they make a complete dessert. Use flavored or plain Whipped Cream, 791, Chocolate Ganache,

797, or sweetened cream cheese or ricotta. For a festive look, dip the edges of the filled cookies in ground nuts, chocolate sprinkles, or melted dark or white chocolate.

Making krumkakes

BUTTER KRUMKAKES

About thirty 5-inch wafers

To make these fabulously thin Scandinavian wafers, you will need a krumkake iron, which fits over a gas or electric burner. Electric krumkake irons are also available. For a toasted sesame seed effect, a *Joy* fan suggests sprinkling ¼ teaspoon sesame seeds over the batter each time before closing the iron.

Beat in a medium bowl, or in a stand mixer with the whisk attachment, until light:

2 large eggs

Slowly add and beat until pale and the batter falls off the whisk like a glossy ribbon:

⅔ cup (130g) sugar
(Finely grated zest of 1 lemon)

Slowly add with the mixer running:

1 stick (4 oz or 115g) unsalted butter, melted and cooled
1 teaspoon vanilla

Fold in until well blended:

1½ to 1¾ cups (190g to 220g) all-purpose flour

The batter can be quite variable, so do not add all the flour called for in the recipe to start. Test the batter for consistency by baking one test krumkake. To bake, preheat the krumkake iron over medium-low heat for several minutes, then lightly rub with:

Unsalted butter

You should not need to grease the iron again unless the krumkakes stick. Use 1 tablespoon batter for each wafer. The batter should spread easily over the whole surface of the iron but not run over the sides when the top is pressed down. If the batter is too thin, add more flour. Should any batter drip over, lift the iron off its frame and cut off the excess batter along the edge with a knife. Cook each wafer until barely browned, about 2 minutes on each side. As soon as you remove it from the iron, roll it up on a wooden spoon handle or cone form, as illustrated. Or you may prefer to leave these cookies flat to use as sandwich cookies; see Stroopwafels, below.

When cool, fill the cookies (for filling suggestions, see About Curled Cookies, 785).

ALMOND KRUMKAKES

About thirty 5-inch wafers

Prepare **Butter Krumkakes, above,** adding **3 tablespoons (20g) almond meal or flour** along with the sugar and **¼ teaspoon almond extract** along with the vanilla. Bake, form, and fill as directed.

STROOPWAFELS

About 1 dozen sandwich cookies

Stroopwafels are a classic Dutch treat, *stroop* meaning "syrup." The syrup in question is sandwiched between two waffle cookies. As the cookies and syrup cool, the waffles soften slightly, and the syrup becomes chewy. There are special irons you can buy to make these, but pizzelle irons work well, too. Any cookies not eaten right away can be stored up to a week. To rewarm the cookie and soften the syrup inside, set a stroopwafel on the rim of a hot cup of coffee.

Combine in a medium saucepan:

½ cup packed (115g) dark brown sugar
½ cup (175g) dark corn syrup
3 tablespoons (45g) unsalted butter
½ teaspoon ground cinnamon
¼ teaspoon salt

Bring the syrup to a rapid boil, stirring to dissolve the sugar, then immediately remove from the heat and set aside while you make the cookies.

Prepare the dough for:

Butter Krumkakes, above

Cook the batter in a Belgian or Dutch cookie iron, a French gaufrette iron, or a pizzelle iron. For stovetop irons, use medium-low to medium heat, adjusting the heat as needed to brown the cookies without burning them. Depending on the size of the iron, you may need to use more or less batter per cookie, 1 to 2 tablespoons. If your iron is specifically made for stroopwafels, trim the rough edges from the browned cookies with a large round cutter, and split the cookies in half like you would a cake layer. If using a gaufrette or pizzelle iron, the cookies will be too thin to split. Spread a thin layer of the syrup on one cookie (or the cut side of one cookie), then place a second cookie or cookie half on top.

ICE CREAM CONES

10 large or 20 small cones

If made on a krumkake iron, as shown above, this dough can be rolled into delicious thin-walled cones or molded over small ramekins for ice cream bowls. If made on a rectangular waffled gaufrette iron, they will become the typical French honeycombed wafer or *gaufrette*. The Italians know them as *pizzelle*, and you can also use a pizzelle iron.

Preheat an electric iron according to the manufacturer's instructions. If using a stovetop iron, preheat it over medium-low for several minutes. Beat in a medium bowl until stiff but not dry, 978:

2 large egg whites, at room temperature

Gradually fold in:

¾ cup (75g) powdered sugar
¼ teaspoon vanilla
⅛ teaspoon salt

Fold in:

½ cup (65g) all-purpose flour

Stir in gently:

4 tablespoons (½ stick or 55g) unsalted butter, melted and cooled

Spoon 1 tablespoon of the batter into the preheated iron and close the iron. After about 1½ minutes, turn the iron if necessary and cook the second side until beige in color. Remove and, while still warm, shape it over upside-down ramekins or form it into a cone (see illustration, 786). Or let it cool flat. If formed into a shape, fill as directed in About Curled Cookies, 785, and serve. Or serve with ice cream.

FORTUNE COOKIES

About 24 cookies

These cookies and Almond Krumkakes, 786, may be made into fortune cookies for a party. Print the fortunes on small strips of paper. Shaping the cookies is best done by two people, as the cookies cool quickly and then become impossible to shape.

Preheat the oven to 350°F. Line 2 baking sheets or cookie sheets with parchment paper or silicone liners.

Stir together in a medium bowl:

3 large egg whites
⅔ cup (130g) sugar
⅛ teaspoon salt

Stir in one at a time, beating until blended after each addition:

1 stick (4 oz or 115g) unsalted butter, melted and cooled slightly
½ cup (65g) all-purpose flour
(⅓ cup [30g] almond meal or flour)
¼ teaspoon vanilla or 1½ teaspoons lemon juice

Drop by the tablespoon about 4 inches apart onto the baking sheets. Bake 1 sheet at a time until the edges are golden brown, about 10 minutes, rotating the sheet halfway through. While the cookies are still warm, turn over one cookie at a time, place a fortune in the center, letting part of the paper stick out, and fold the cookie in half. Pinch closed and lift the cookie and bring the corners together to make a C shape. Set on a rack to cool. If some of the cookies cool too much to shape, return the sheet to the oven briefly to warm and soften them.

BRANDY SNAPS

About twenty 3½-inch cookies

Preheat the oven to 300°F. Line 2 baking sheets with parchment paper (do not use silicone liners).

Combine in a medium heavy saucepan:

1 stick (4 oz or 115g) unsalted butter
½ cup (100g) sugar or ¼ cup (50g) sugar plus ¼ cup packed (60g) maple sugar
⅓ cup (115g) molasses
½ teaspoon ground cinnamon
Finely grated zest of 1 lemon or ½ orange
¼ teaspoon ground ginger
Pinch of salt

Stir over low heat until the butter is melted and the mixture is smooth. Remove from the heat and stir in:

1 cup (125g) all-purpose flour
2 teaspoons brandy

Let cool until firm enough to shape. Roll into ¾-inch balls and arrange about 2 inches apart on the prepared baking sheets. Bake 1 sheet at a time until browned on the edges, 12 to 15 minutes, rotating the sheet halfway through. Let cool on the sheet for 2 or 3 minutes, then roll up each still-warm cookie on the handle of a wooden spoon. If some of the wafers cool too much to shape, return the sheet to the oven briefly to warm and soften them.

MAPLE CURLS

About fifteen 3-inch curls

These first appeared in *Joy* in 1963.

Preheat the oven to 350°F. Grease or line a baking sheet or cookie sheet with parchment paper. Have ready several rolling pins or bottles of about the same size to shape the wafers.

Combine in a medium saucepan, bring to a hard boil, and cook for 30 seconds:

½ cup (160g) maple syrup
4 tablespoons (½ stick or 55g) unsalted butter

Remove from the heat and stir in:

½ cup (65g) all-purpose flour
¼ teaspoon salt

When well blended, drop the dough by the tablespoon 3 inches apart onto the prepared baking sheet. Bake until the cookies are browned, 12 to 16 minutes, rotating the sheet halfway through. Let cool on the sheet for 2 or 3 minutes, then mold each still-warm cookie over a rolling pin or glass bottle. If some of the wafers cool too much to shape, return the sheet to the oven briefly to warm and soften them.

TUILES (FRENCH ALMOND WAFERS)

About thirty 3-inch wafers

Almost paper-thin, with a subtle almond flavor, tuiles are curled by being draped, while still warm and pliable, over a rolling pin or glass bottle until cool and firm.

Preheat the oven to 350°F. Generously grease or line 2 baking sheets or cookie sheets with parchment paper or silicone liners. Have ready several rolling pins or bottles of about the same size to shape the wafers.

Coarsely chop and set aside:

⅔ cup sliced almonds

Whisk together in a medium bowl until frothy:

2 large egg whites
⅓ cup plus 1 tablespoon (75g) sugar
½ teaspoon vanilla
(¼ teaspoon almond extract)
⅛ teaspoon salt

Sift over the egg white mixture, then whisk in:

½ cup (55g) cake flour

Whisk in until well blended and smooth:

5 tablespoons (70g) unsalted butter, melted and cooled slightly

Drop by the heaping tablespoon about 3 inches apart onto the prepared baking sheets. Using a small offset spatula, spread each portion into a 3-inch round. Sprinkle with the nuts. Bake 1 sheet at a time until golden brown around the edges, 6 to 9 minutes, rotating the sheet halfway through. Let cool on the sheet for a few seconds, then working quickly, use a small offset spatula to lift the still-warm cookies, bottom side down, onto the rolling pins or glass bottles, and let cool completely. If some of the wafers cool too much to shape, return the sheet to the oven briefly to warm and soften them.

GINGERBREAD HOUSE

One gingerbread house (about 5½ inches wide × 7 inches high) on a 9-inch square base, plus 10 to 15 cookies

Connecticut cookbook author and baking teacher Susan G. Purdy has been using this recipe to make festive gingerbread houses with adult-child teams for more than thirty years, as well as at home, with her daughter, Cassandra (now a chef). Make this a family holiday tradition in your home, too. The gingerbread can be baked up to a week in advance of assembling.

Melt in a medium saucepan:

2 sticks (8 oz or 225g) butter or margarine

Add and stir over low heat until the sugar is dissolved and the mixture no longer feels gritty:

1 cup (200g) sugar
1 cup (340g) molasses

Remove from the heat and set aside to cool to lukewarm. Whisk together in a large bowl:

4½ cups (565g) all-purpose flour
1 tablespoon ground ginger
1 teaspoon baking soda
1 teaspoon salt
1 teaspoon ground cinnamon
1 teaspoon grated or ground nutmeg

Make a well in the center of the dry ingredients, pour in the lukewarm butter mixture, and beat to blend everything together. Work in:

½ cup (65g) all-purpose flour

beating until the dough forms a ball and pulls away from the sides of the bowl. Remove the dough from the bowl and knead 3 or 4 times on the counter, until smooth and pliable. Wrap well and refrigerate until the dough is thoroughly cool. (The dough can be prepared several days in advance.) After refrigerating, if the dough feels too soft to roll out, work in a tiny bit more flour.

To make the pattern pieces: Draw the pattern pieces onto stiff cardboard and cut them out. You should have 7 pieces: 2 sides, 1 front, 1 back, 2 roof panels, and 1 base. Rub flour over both sides of the pattern pieces to prevent the dough from sticking to them.

To cut out and bake the gingerbread house: Position oven racks to divide the oven into thirds. Preheat the oven to 350°F.

With a lightly floured rolling pin, roll out about one-third of the dough directly on an ungreased cookie sheet to about ¼ inch thick. Lightly dust the dough with flour. Position as many pattern pieces as will fit comfortably on top of the rolled dough, leaving about ¾ inch between them to allow for spreading during baking. Cut around the patterns with a sharp paring knife. Lift off the pattern pieces. Peel away the dough between the cut pieces. Gather the scraps and reroll one time to cut out more. Repeat with a second and third cookie sheet if needed, using the remaining dough and cutting out all the pieces. Cut around, but ➤ do not lift out, the windows and the front door (if they are removed now, the shapes will warp). Roll out the scraps and use cookie cutters or a paring knife to cut out gingerbread people, fence posts, animals, and other designs.

Bake the gingerbread pieces until the color darkens slightly and the pieces feel nearly stiff (they will firm completely as they cool), 12 to 15 minutes, switching racks and rotating the sheets halfway through. (If the pieces are not crisp when completely cool, return them to the oven and bake a few minutes longer.)

As soon as they come out of the oven, set the sheets on a heatproof surface and immediately, while the dough is still hot, place the pattern pieces on top of the corresponding pieces of hot gingerbread. One at a time, placing a potholder over each shape to protect your hand, cut around each pattern with a paring knife (trimming all the house edges will make them fit together more neatly). Lift off and save the scraps for decorations. Cut out and remove the door and windows. While the dough is still warm, you can halve each cut-out piece of window to make shutters. Save the door cut-out, too. Once the shapes are rigid but still slightly warm, transfer them to wire racks to cool completely. Store them flat on a tray or in a sturdy box in a cool, dry place until ready to assemble.

To assemble the house, prepare:

A double or triple recipe of Royal Icing, 798, or Quick Cookie Icing, 799

The house will require 2 to 6 cups icing, depending on the style of the decorations. Leave about half the icing in the bowl for assembling the house, and use the rest for decorations. Scoop the remaining icing into cups or small bowls, mixing in:

Drops of food coloring

Immediately cover the bowls of icing with plastic wrap so they don't dry out; keep tightly covered when you are not using the icing.

Set the gingerbread base right side up on a tray. (The right side of each piece is the side facing up when baked.) Center the front, back, and side pieces, right side down, on top of the base, with the bottom corners touching.

Place some of the white icing in a pastry bag fitted with a plain ¼- to ½-inch tip or a zip-top bag with a ¼-inch hole cut in one corner, and pipe out a thick ½-inch-deep line of icing around the foundation lines. One at a time, lift the side pieces into place and, with the pastry bag or your fingertip, pipe or spread a generous line of icing along both side edges of each piece. Repeat with the front and back pieces, icing their side edges and standing them up in the foundation icing next to the sides. Gently press all the iced edges of the house together. If the icing is thick enough, the house should now stand up unaided. If it is wobbly, support it on all 4 sides with jars or cans until the icing dries, 1 hour to overnight, depending on the humidity. Do not attempt to add the roof until the icing is dry and the structure feels solid. Note: Don't worry if the icing shows, especially along the seam joints, as it will be covered with "icicles" or other decorations.

To attach the roof, spread icing generously along the top edges of each house piece and along one long edge of each roof panel. Press the roof panels in place, touching each other at the peak. Use your fingertip to smooth all the joints where the pieces meet; add extra icing if necessary for stability. If the roof panels droop, support them with jars or cans until the icing sets. Don't decorate the roof until the icing is set, or the weight of the decorations may cause it to collapse.

To decorate the house, use icing to glue on the window shutters and position the front door ajar. Using icing as glue, decorate the house with:

Jelly beans, gumdrops, candy-coated chocolate pieces, nonpareils, jellied wintergreen leaves, hard round peppermint candies, candy canes, silver dragées, cinnamon red hots, colored sugar wafers, ring-shaped hard candies, caramels, "stone" candies, mini shredded wheat cereal, toasted oat cereal, red shoestring licorice, marshmallows, mini pretzels and pretzel rods, colored sugars, sunflower and pumpkin seeds, dried fruits, raisins, and/or nuts

Make a chimney from flat candies glued together with icing and stacked up on the roof ridge line. To prevent sticking, oil the scissors before cutting soft candies. After the shutters, door, and chimney are in place, add a little water to some of the white icing, making it runny enough to drip. Use the piping bag to pipe drippy icicles along the edges of the roof. For snow, sift over the top of the house and the base a light dusting of:

Powdered sugar

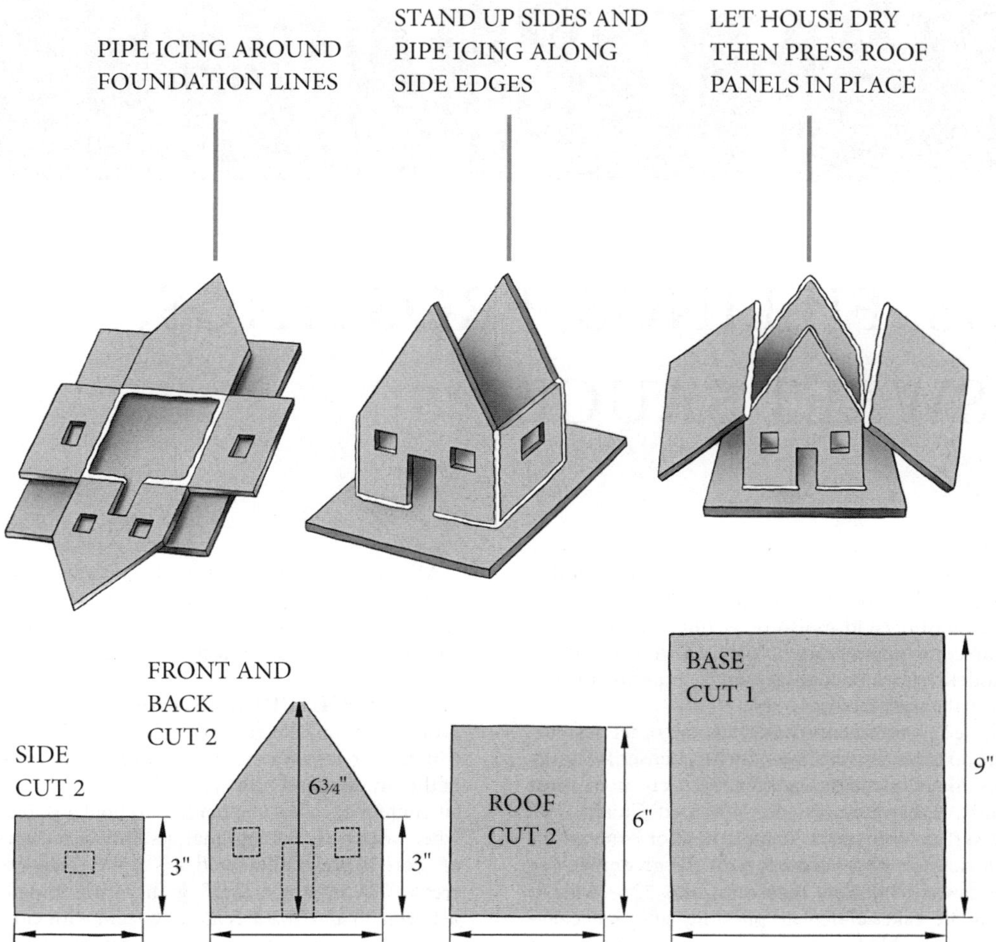

Blueprints for a gingerbread house; cut windows in both side pieces, but cut windows and door in front piece only

ICINGS, FILLINGS, FROSTINGS, AND SWEET SAUCES

Icings, fillings, frostings, glazes, and sauces are the party clothes that transform simple cakes and desserts into celebration-worthy centerpieces. These mixtures add moisture, richness, flavor, visual appeal, and, of course, the opportunity to personalize your efforts. While we offer guidelines, we encourage you to experiment with combinations that strike your fancy.

When pairing these accoutrements with cakes and other desserts, think about flavors, textures, and richness. Richer, denser frostings, fillings, and sauces like Chocolate Ganache, 797, are used more sparingly than fluffy, light mixtures like Whipped Cream, 791. When creating dessert combinations, complement or contrast the flavor, texture, and richness of the dessert with the accompanying filling, frosting, or sauce. Chocolate Blackout Cake, 729—with its rich layers of chocolate cake, chocolate pudding, and ganache—amply demonstrates the sublime results to be had by reinforcing the same flavor and degree of richness. A dense cheesecake with a drizzle of raspberry coulis is equally impressive for its sharp contrast of flavors.

Most of the recipes in Breads and Coffee Cakes, 592, Cakes and Cupcakes, 708, Cookies and Bars, 762, Desserts, 812, and Ice Cream and Frozen Desserts, 836, that reference recipes in this chapter offer pairing suggestions, but feel free to experiment.

ABOUT WHIPPED CREAM

From topping hot, rich beverages to filling and frosting cakes, whipped cream—or *crème Chantilly*, as the French call it—is one of the simplest and most versatile preparations. Cream must have a fat content of at least 30 percent to hold a stable, unseparated foam when whipped. For optimal stability, a fat content of 36 percent or more is preferable—sold as "heavy cream" or "heavy whipping cream." "Whipping cream," or "light whipping cream," can contain between 30 and 36 percent fat. Cream with closer to 30 percent fat will make a lighter but slightly less stable whipped cream, and cream with a higher fat content makes very stable but denser whipped cream.

The cream must be cold before whipping, or the fat will melt and the cream will not aerate, thicken, and expand. When the weather is hot, it is a good idea to put the bowl and the beaters in the freezer for 5 minutes before beating. If your kitchen is very warm, set the bottom of the bowl of cream in ice water as you beat.

Cream can be whipped by hand using a large balloon whisk, but it is certainly easier to use an electric mixer or stand mixer instead. Cream can also be whipped in a glass jar with a tight-fitting lid. Simply fill the jar a little less than half full (use a pint or quart jar depending on how much whipped cream you need), add sugar and vanilla to taste, and shake until softly whipped (the whole process takes less than 2 minutes).

Perfectly whipped cream—billowy and stiff but still smooth—is frequently on its way to becoming butter by the time one has frosted or filled a cake with it, spread it over a cake sheet for a jelly-roll, or forced it through a pastry bag to make rosettes. This is because any manipulation of whipped cream, including stirring, spreading, or forcing it through a small opening, has the same result as continuing to beat it. The solution is to ➤ slightly underwhip any cream to be used as a frosting, filling, or piped decoration. It is also advisable to underwhip cream whenever it must be refrigerated for several hours before use; then whisk the cream briefly to the desired consistency just before use, to reincorporate any liquid that may have separated from it. A cake frosted or filled with whipped cream is best served the day it is made.

➤ To rescue whipped cream that has been overwhipped and appears grainy, add a little more liquid cream and whip it briefly or until very smooth and soft. Whipped cream that has been overwhipped to the point of turning into butter cannot be salvaged for use as whipped cream (although it may be whipped further and made into butter, 958). It is best, at that point, to start over.

For use as a cake filling or frosting, or if the whipped cream needs to stand up for a while, make Stabilized Whipped Cream, below. We have also found that Whipped Crème Fraîche, below, has a more stable foam than plain whipped cream.

WHIPPED CREAM

2 to 2½ cups

This recipe gives you the option of sweetening the whipped cream or not. Unsweetened whipped cream is excellent on very sweet desserts where you want the richness of the cream without any more sugar. For lightly sweet desserts or to use the whipped cream as a cake filling or frosting, add a sweetener as desired.

Beat in a large bowl (chill the bowl if your kitchen is very warm) with a hand mixer or balloon whisk or in a stand mixer set at medium-high speed, until stiff and billowy but not grainy:

1 cup cold heavy cream
(2 teaspoons to 2 tablespoons sugar, 1 to 4 tablespoons sifted powdered sugar, or 2 teaspoons honey, to taste)
(½ teaspoon vanilla)

Use immediately.

STABILIZED WHIPPED CREAM

For a long-lasting whipped cream that does not weep, we recommend adding a stabilizer. Gelatin gives whipped cream a firm, mousse-like texture. It must still be stored in the refrigerator, but it will hold up longer at room temperature, and you can fill or frost a cake with it a day in advance without worry.

Pour **1 tablespoon cold water** into a heatproof cup. Sprinkle with **½ teaspoon unflavored gelatin.** Let the gelatin soften, without stirring, for 5 minutes. Place the cup in a pan of simmering water until the gelatin is melted and the liquid is clear. Let cool to room temperature. Prepare **Whipped Cream, above,** adding the cooled (but not cold) gelatin mixture while you beat as the cream begins to thicken. Stabilized whipped cream can be flavored according to the additions below, but do so as soon as possible—before the gelatin sets.

WHIPPED CRÈME FRAÎCHE

About 2 cups

With a little more complexity than plain whipped cream, this lightly tangy version is excellent served with everything from fresh fruit desserts to pies to puddings. It also holds up better than regular whipped cream over time.

Combine in a large bowl or a stand mixer:

½ cup cold heavy cream
½ cup cold crème fraîche or mascarpone
2 tablespoons sugar
1 teaspoon vanilla or vanilla bean paste

Beat with a hand mixer or balloon whisk or in the stand mixer set at medium speed until light and fluffy.

ADDITIONS TO WHIPPED CREAM

You may flavor cream by infusing it as directed in Flavorings for Custard Bases, 813, then chill the cream thoroughly and proceed as for Whipped Cream, above.

Or, prepare Whipped Cream, above, adding any of the following along with the vanilla and sugar:

2 teaspoons instant coffee or espresso powder
1 to 1½ tablespoons liquor or liqueur, such as Grand Marnier, framboise, or Frangelico
½ teaspoon ground cinnamon
Finely grated zest of 1 lemon or lime and 2 teaspoons lemon or lime juice

Or, before whipping, stir one of the following into a small portion of the cream until smooth, then pour into the rest of the cream and whip as directed:

2 tablespoons unsweetened cocoa powder (use ⅓ cup sifted powdered sugar to offset the bitterness of the cocoa)
2 tablespoons unsweetened cocoa powder plus 2 teaspoons instant coffee or espresso powder (use 2 to 3 tablespoons sugar)

Or use one of the following instead of vanilla:

½ teaspoon rose water or peppermint extract
¾ teaspoon orange flower water

Or, replace the sugar with:

Maple syrup, sorghum syrup, maple sugar, coconut sugar, or Vanilla Sugar, 1026

Or fold any of the following into the finished whipped cream:

¼ cup Lemon Curd, 802, or Lime or Grapefruit Curd, 802
¼ cup French Praline, 873
¼ cup jam, marmalade, or cooled Cooked Fruit Puree, 172

ABOUT FROSTINGS

The terms "frosting" and "icing" are used interchangeably by bakers, but here we take frosting to mean a thicker, fluffier mixture that is spread more generously on cakes. They are typically used in thicker layers than icing, and they tend not to harden. The quick frostings included in this section do dry out on the surface when exposed to air, forming a thin crust, but beneath they stay creamy. These frostings are ideal for cupcakes or quick cakes, or anytime you need a fast, flavorful frosting to slather on something from the oven.

QUICK VANILLA BUTTER FROSTING

About 2 cups

Perhaps the simplest frosting to make.

Combine in a medium bowl and beat together on medium speed:

4 cups (1 pound) powdered sugar, sifted
1 stick (4 ounces) unsalted butter, softened

Add and beat until smooth, starting with the smaller amount of liquid:

4 to 6 tablespoons milk, dry sherry, rum, or coffee
2 teaspoons vanilla or vanilla bean paste
¼ teaspoon salt

If the frosting seems too thick, add more liquid a few drops at a time to reach a smooth, spreadable consistency. If it seems too thin, allow the frosting to sit for 15 minutes. These frostings tend to thicken on their own over time. If it is still too thin, add more powdered sugar. To store, cover the surface of the icing with plastic wrap. This keeps for up to 3 days at room temperature or for up to 3 weeks refrigerated. Soften and stir or beat until smooth before using.

QUICK LEMON FROSTING

Prepare **Quick Vanilla Butter Frosting, above,** adding the **finely grated zest of 1 lemon** to the powdered sugar mixture and use **1 to 2 tablespoons fresh lemon juice, plus milk as needed** for the liquid.

QUICK ORANGE FROSTING

Prepare **Quick Vanilla Butter Frosting, above,** adding the **grated zest of 1 orange** to the powdered sugar mixture and use **4 to 6 tablespoons orange juice** for the liquid.

QUICK MOCHA FROSTING

Prepare **Quick Vanilla Butter Frosting, above,** reducing the powdered sugar to 3½ cups and adding **¼ cup unsweetened cocoa powder** and **1 to 2 teaspoons instant coffee or espresso powder, to taste,** to the mixture. Use milk or coffee for the liquid.

CHOCOLATE FUDGE FROSTING

About 2½ cups

On any chocolate or yellow layer cake, old-fashioned fudge frosting fits the bill. This is also quite tasty on cookies and doughnuts.

Prepare **Chocolate Fudge, 863,** omitting the optional walnuts or reserving them to sprinkle on top of the cake. In the final stage of beating, when the fudge begins to thicken and loses its sheen, beat in **1 tablespoon half-and-half** just until blended. Use a silicone spatula to scrape down the sides and bottom of the bowl, then let the frosting stand and stiffen for 4 to 5 minutes before correcting the consistency. Adjust, if necessary, by stirring in a little more **half-and-half** 1 teaspoon at a time, until the perfect spreading consistency is obtained. Use immediately, or cover the surface with plastic wrap. This keeps for about 1 week at room temperature or for up to 3 weeks refrigerated; or freeze for up to 6 months. Soften and stir until smooth before using.

CREAM CHEESE FROSTING

About 2 cups

There are two secrets to making perfectly smooth cream cheese frosting with enough body to swirl onto a cake or pipe through a pastry bag: Do not overbeat, and use cold—not softened—cream cheese. Feel free to vary the amount of powdered sugar to suit your taste.

I. FOOD PROCESSOR METHOD

The fastest method of all.

Combine in a food processor and pulse just until smooth and creamy:

8 ounces cold cream cheese, cut into cubes
(6 tablespoons [¾ stick] unsalted butter, softened)
2 teaspoons vanilla
3 cups powdered sugar, sifted

If the frosting is too stiff, pulse for a few seconds longer; do not overprocess. If desired, stir in additional flavoring to taste, such as:

(Grated lemon or orange zest, ground cinnamon, or liqueur)

II. MIXER METHOD

Beat in a medium bowl, or in a stand mixer with the paddle attachment, at low speed just until blended:

8 ounces cold cream cheese, cut into cubes
(5 tablespoons unsalted butter, softened)
2 teaspoons vanilla

Add one-third at a time and beat just until smooth and the desired consistency:

4 cups (1 pound) powdered sugar, sifted

If the frosting is too stiff, beat for a few seconds longer; do not overbeat. If desired, stir in additional flavoring to taste (see version I).

CHOCOLATE CREAM CHEESE FROSTING

About 2⅔ cups

Prepare **Cream Cheese Frosting, above.** Melt in a double boiler (or heatproof bowl set over a pan of barely simmering water) **5 ounces semisweet or bittersweet chocolate (up to 64% cacao), chopped,** with **3 tablespoons water or coffee,** stirring often until smooth. Let cool to lukewarm, then stir into the frosting.

PEANUT BUTTER FROSTING

About 2 cups

Stir in chopped roasted peanuts to taste, or sprinkle them over the finished cake, if desired. This is excellent with chocolate cake.

Beat in a medium bowl, or in a stand mixer with the paddle attachment, just until blended:

½ cup smooth peanut butter
3 ounces cold cream cheese, cut into cubes

3 tablespoons heavy cream or milk
1½ tablespoons unsalted butter, softened
1 teaspoon vanilla

Add one-third at a time and beat just until smooth and the desired consistency is reached:

2⅔ cups powdered sugar, sifted

If the frosting is too stiff, add, but do not overbeat:

1 to 2 tablespoons heavy cream or milk, or as needed

SALTED CARAMEL FROSTING

About 2⅓ cups

This frosting is rich and sweet. It is best applied in a thin layer on chocolate cakes, spice cakes, and apple cake.

Prepare:

Salted Caramel Sauce, 809

Transfer the sauce to a large bowl or a stand mixer fitted with the paddle attachment. Let cool until the bottom of the bowl is completely cool to the touch, 30 to 45 minutes. Beat on medium-high speed, adding gradually:

2 to 2½ cups powdered sugar, sifted

The frosting should be thick but spreadable and creamy. If the frosting thickens too much, beat in:

1 to 2 tablespoons heavy cream

CHOCOLATE SATIN FROSTING

About 3 cups

Both kids and adults love this shiny, dark, sweet chocolate frosting, which is easily made in a food processor. Keep any extra in a jar in the refrigerator and melt it for a quick ice cream sauce, or spread it on graham crackers or cookies.

Bring to a boil in a small saucepan:

1 cup evaporated milk or heavy cream

Remove from the heat and add:

6 ounces unsweetened chocolate, coarsely chopped

Cover and let stand, without stirring, for 10 minutes. Scrape into a food processor or blender and add:

1½ cups sugar
6 tablespoons (¾ stick) unsalted butter, cut into small pieces
1 teaspoon vanilla or other extract such as peppermint or orange

Process until the mixture is perfectly smooth, 1 minute or more. Transfer to a bowl. If necessary, let stand for a few minutes (longer if you used cream), until thickened to the desired spreading consistency. This keeps, refrigerated, for up to 1 week if made with cream, or for up to 3 weeks if made with evaporated milk.

CHOCOLATE SOUR CREAM FROSTING

About 2 cups

Bittersweet and glossy. Use this to fill and frost any chocolate butter cake. Prepare just before using. Melt in a double boiler, a heatproof bowl set over a pan of barely simmering water, or in a microwave-safe bowl:

10 ounces semisweet or bittersweet chocolate (up to 64% cacao), coarsely chopped

Melt, stirring frequently. If using a microwave, melt on 50 percent power in 20-second bursts, stirring after each interval. Remove from the heat and stir in—do not beat—just until combined:

1 cup sour cream

Use immediately. If the frosting becomes too stiff or loses its gloss at any time, set the bowl in a larger pan of hot water for a few seconds and stir to soften. This keeps, refrigerated, for up to 1 week.

WHITE CHOCOLATE FROSTING

An excellent frosting for Carrot Cake, 736.

Prepare **Chocolate Sour Cream Frosting, above,** substituting **12 ounces white chocolate** for the semisweet or bittersweet chocolate.

CHOCOLATE MOUSSE FROSTING

About 3½ cups

This frosting has an appealing mousse-like texture. Try it between layers of any angel food cake, 719, a moist sponge cake, 720–22, or Devil's Food Cake Cockaigne, 728.

Whisk together in a medium heatproof bowl, preferably stainless steel:

2 large eggs
2 cups powdered sugar, sifted
½ cup milk, coffee, or water
⅛ teaspoon salt

Set the bowl in a large skillet of barely simmering water and heat, stirring constantly, until the mixture registers 160°F on an instant-read thermometer. Remove from the heat and stir in:

4 ounces unsweetened chocolate, finely chopped
6 tablespoons (¾ stick) unsalted butter, cut into small pieces
1 teaspoon vanilla

Stir until the chocolate and butter are melted and the mixture is smooth. Set the bowl in a larger bowl of ice water and beat on high speed until the frosting holds a shape, 7 to 10 minutes. This keeps, refrigerated, for up to 4 days.

VEGAN CHOCOLATE FROSTING

About 3½ cups

This creamy frosting is deeply chocolatey and perfect for making dramatic swoops and swirls on a cake.

Prepare **Vegan Chocolate Pudding I, 817,** increasing the chocolate to 12 ounces. Chill for 30 minutes before using.

ABOUT MERINGUE

Meringue loosely refers to any mixture of beaten egg whites and sugar. For tips on handling and beating egg whites, see Beating Eggs, 977. For baked meringues, see 750. For Meringue Kisses, see 775.

Meringue is incredibly versatile. Raw meringue is folded into cake batters, mousses, pancakes, and other mixtures that need an infusion of lightness. Raw meringue may also be used as a pie topping. Cooked meringues, such as Swiss Meringue, 794, and Italian Meringue, 794, may be used as toppings or frostings.

Meringue's most popular use (at least in this country) is as a pie topping. While the image this iconic dessert conjures up is one of a perfectly golden crimped crust ringing a mound of bronzed, fluffy meringue, that ideal can be a challenge to achieve. Meringue pie toppings tend to weep beads of brown syrup, and a sticky puddle tends to form between pie filling and meringue. The culprit is uneven heat. Spreading meringue over a cool or lukewarm pie filling and then browning the topping in an oven simply results in undercooked (or uncooked) egg white on the bottom and overcooked egg white on top. The undercooked part of the meringue melts as the pie stands, resulting in a slippery puddle between filling and topping. Meanwhile, the overcooked meringue on the surface breaks down and weeps beads of sticky syrup.

The melting of the meringue along the bottom is easily prevented by having the filling hot, not warm, when you apply the meringue, so that the bottom of the meringue cooks in the heat of the filling. This does require a bit of a cooking balancing act, getting the filling and topping ready at roughly the same time.

Rather than perform feats of culinary prowess, ➤ we have come to prefer using stabilized meringue toppings instead. This can be achieved in a couple different ways. Heating meringue over hot water, as one does in the making of a Swiss Meringue, below, or adding a hot sugar syrup to beaten egg whites as for Italian Meringue, below, serves to stabilize the egg whites and make the meringue less prone to weeping. You can also stabilize meringue with a cooked cornstarch paste, as in Soft Meringue Topping I, 795. While these options have more steps, they allow you to make your pie filling well ahead of time or to let the meringue topping sit while you prepare the filling, meaning you don't have to multitask. And because Swiss and Italian meringues are cooked, there is no need to worry about raw egg whites or cooking the meringue all the way through. You simply need to brown the top to your liking.

When applying meringue to a pie or pudding, ➤ spread a band of topping around the edge of the crust or dish before you fill in the center. If you cover the center first, you are likely to displace some of the filling and cause it to spill over. ➤ If it does not adhere well to the edges at all points, it may pull away during baking. When applying meringue to a crustless pudding, spread the topping to the edge of the dish.

Meringue safety: To be certain that any possible pathogens in the egg whites have been killed, you must heat the meringue to 160°F. The easiest option is to use Swiss Meringue or Italian Meringue, below, both of which are cooked in the course of making them. These are the preferred toppings to use for desserts that are not baked for very long (in fact, if you have a propane torch you need not bake them at all). Otherwise, follow the recipes as written, being sure that your pie filling is piping hot when you spread on the topping. After 20 minutes of baking, carefully insert an instant-read thermometer sideways into the center of the meringue. If the temperature is shy of the mark, bake the meringue a little longer. Be careful, though, not to go much beyond 165°F, or the meringue will begin to break down even if stabilized by cornstarch.

FRENCH MERINGUE

Enough meringue to cover one 9-inch pie or to make twelve 3-inch meringue shells

This is the simplest meringue to make. It bakes up into shatteringly crisp cookies—Meringue Kisses, 775—thanks to its high sugar content. To experiment with different meringue flavors, substitute other extracts for the vanilla, such as peppermint, orange, or rose. Have all the ingredients at room temperature, about 70°F. Beat in a large bowl, or in a stand mixer with the whisk attachment, on medium speed until soft peaks form, 977:

4 large egg whites (about ½ cup)
(1 teaspoon vanilla)
½ teaspoon cream of tartar or 1 teaspoon lemon juice

Very gradually add, 1 tablespoon at a time, beating on high speed:

1 cup superfine or granulated sugar

Beat until the meringue holds very stiff peaks (when the whisk or beater is dipped into the meringue and lifted out of the bowl, the meringue should not droop at all when held sideways or straight up). Shape and bake as directed in the individual recipe.

SWISS MERINGUE

Following the ingredient amounts for **French Meringue, above,** place the egg whites, vanilla, if using, cream of tartar, and sugar in a large heatproof bowl or the bowl of a stand mixer. Set the bowl in a skillet of barely simmering water and whisk until the whites are warm, not hot, to the touch (110° to 115°F). Remove the bowl from the skillet and beat on high speed (with the whisk if using a stand mixer) until the whites are stiff.

ITALIAN MERINGUE

About 5 cups; enough for one 9-inch pie

Italian meringue is similar to Swiss meringue in that it is cooked, but instead of using the double boiler method this meringue uses a cooked sugar syrup to stabilize the egg whites. This light, glossy, marshmallowy meringue is our favorite meringue to use as a pie topping.

Stir in a small heavy saucepan until the sugar is dissolved, then bring to a boil over high heat:

1 cup sugar
½ cup water

In the meantime, beat in large bowl, or in a stand mixer with the whisk attachment, at medium-high speed until nearly stiff:

4 large egg whites (about ½ cup)
⅛ teaspoon cream of tartar or ½ teaspoon lemon juice

When the egg whites are nearly stiff, turn the mixer down to the lowest speed and continue to beat while the syrup cooks.

When the syrup has reached a boil, turn the heat down to medium-low, cover the pan, and simmer for 1 minute to allow the steam to wash down any crystals that may have formed on the sides of the pan. Uncover and brush the sides of the pan with a wet pastry brush. Cook the syrup until a thermometer reads 238° to 240°F, the soft-ball stage, 857. Beating the whites at high speed, add the syrup in a slow, thin stream down the side of the bowl. ➤ Avoid pouring the hot syrup onto the spinning whisk. Continue to beat for 10 minutes, or until the bowl of the mixer is no longer warm. Use as directed in individual recipes.

COFFEE-FLAVORED MERINGUE

Prepare **French Meringue, 994,** or **Swiss Meringue, 794.** Stir **2½ teaspoons instant espresso powder** into the sugar before adding it to the egg whites.

COCOA MERINGUE

Prepare **French Meringue, 794,** or **Swiss Meringue, 794.** Stir **3 tablespoons unsweetened cocoa powder** into the sugar before adding it to the egg whites.

SOFT MERINGUE TOPPING

Enough to cover one 9-inch pie

I. Stabilized with cornstarch, this meringue topping will not weep, leak, or deflate, even when refrigerated for several days. Since the pie filling should be piping hot when the meringue is applied, measure out the meringue ingredients and prepare the cornstarch paste before embarking on the filling.

Mix thoroughly in a small saucepan:

1 tablespoon cornstarch
1 tablespoon sugar

Gradually stir in, making a smooth, runny paste:

⅓ cup water

Bring to a boil over medium heat, stirring briskly all the while, then boil for 15 seconds. Remove the thick paste from the heat and cover. Prepare:

French Meringue, 794, using only ½ cup sugar

Beat on high speed until the peaks are very stiff and glossy but not dry. Reduce to the lowest speed and beat in the cornstarch paste 1 tablespoon at a time. When all the paste is incorporated, increase the speed to medium and beat for 10 seconds. Spread over a hot pie filling (or pudding) and bake as directed in the recipe.

II. This conventional soft meringue topping is more quickly made than version I but is not as stable. It is best served the day it is made. Measure out the meringue ingredients before you start to make the filling.

Prepare:

French Meringue, 794, using only ½ cup sugar

Spread over the hot filling (or pudding) and bake as directed in the recipe.

ABOUT MERINGUE-BASED FROSTINGS

These frostings were referred to as **boiled icings** in previous editions of *Joy*. We felt, however, that this moniker was not only misleading (these frostings are not really boiled) but unappealing as well. In reality, these frostings are prepared exactly like Italian Meringue, 794, and give silky, fluffy, and shiny results. They are what you would expect from a good meringue, but made specifically for the purpose of frosting cakes.

Just as in candy making, success with these frostings depends on low humidity and recognizing certain stages in preparing sugar syrup (see The Stages of Cooked Sugar Syrup, 856). Use a candy thermometer to accurately determine the temperature of the syrup. If the syrup was overcooked and the frosting is too stiff to spread, beating in a teaspoon or two of boiling water or a few drops of lemon juice will restore it.

FLUFFY WHITE FROSTING

About 3⅔ cups

Stir in a small heavy saucepan until the sugar is dissolved, then bring to a boil over high heat:

1 cup sugar
½ cup water

Reduce the heat to low, cover, and simmer to allow the steam to wash down any sugar crystals on the sides of the pan. In the meantime, beat in a stand mixer with the whisk attachment at medium-high speed until stiff:

3 large egg whites
⅛ teaspoon cream of tartar

Turn the mixer down to the lowest speed and continue to beat. Uncover the syrup and cook to 235° to 240°F, the soft-ball stage, 857. Beating the whites at high speed, add the syrup in a slow, thin stream down the side of the bowl. ➤ Avoid pouring the hot syrup onto the spinning whisk. Add:

1 teaspoon vanilla

Continue to beat at high speed until the icing has cooled, 7 to 10 minutes. Reduce the speed to medium and beat 1 more minute. Use at once.

LUSCIOUS ORANGE ICING

About 4 cups

Stir in a small heavy saucepan until the sugar is dissolved, then bring to a boil over high heat:

1 cup sugar
½ cup water
1 tablespoon light corn syrup

Reduce the heat to low, cover, and simmer to allow the steam to wash down any crystals that may have formed on the sides of the pan. In the meantime, beat in a stand mixer with the whisk attachment at medium-high speed until stiff:

3 large egg whites
⅛ teaspoon cream of tartar

Turn the mixer down to the lowest speed and continue to beat. Uncover the syrup and cook until a thermometer reads 235° to 240°F, the soft-ball stage, 857. Beating the egg whites at high speed, add the syrup in a slow, thin stream down the side of the bowl. ➤ Avoid pouring the hot syrup onto the spinning whisk. Beat for 10 minutes, until cooled. Add:

¼ cup powdered sugar, sifted
Finely grated zest of 1 orange
1 tablespoon orange juice or ¾ teaspoon vanilla

Beat the icing to a spreading consistency and use immediately.

ABOUT BUTTERCREAM

Buttercreams are a small but highly regarded family of frostings perhaps best known for their appearance on wedding cakes. In fact, buttercream frosting is ideal for that particular application because it holds up remarkably well under all sorts of conditions. These frostings are durable, easy to handle, and delicious.

French buttercream is prepared somewhat like Italian Meringue, 794, in that it involves preparing a cooked sugar syrup that is beaten into a mixture of whole eggs or egg yolks. Softened butter is beaten in after the sugar syrup is incorporated. **Swiss or Italian meringue buttercreams** use either Swiss Meringue, 794, or Italian Meringue, 794, as a base. For Swiss meringue buttercream, egg whites are whipped over barely simmering water, then beaten until stiff. The resulting meringue is beaten into softened butter. For Italian meringue buttercream, egg whites are beaten, then a cooked sugar syrup is slowly added. Finally, softened butter is beaten in. **Crème mousseline** (sometimes called **German buttercream**) is a mixture of Pastry Cream, 801, and softened butter. It is exceptionally rich and silky.

If all this sounds complicated, just remember to take things one step at a time. Have all ingredients measured and ready to go before you begin. Gather any equipment or utensils you will need and have them on standby. Finally, take the time to read through the recipe a few times until you know the basic process and sequence.

➤ The usual cause of buttercream failures is that the butter or buttercream mixture is either too warm or too cold. Usually, it's a case of working in a warm kitchen, where the ambient temperature easily creeps up above ideal working temperatures for buttercream. First, the softened butter used in making buttercream should never be greasy or mushy. When pressed with a fingertip, the butter should be yielding but still firm. ➤ If you have a thermometer, take the temperature of the butter. It should be around 66° to 69°F. If during the course of making buttercream the frosting seems loose or even soupy, put the whole mixing bowl in the refrigerator for 20 to 30 minutes. Then beat the buttercream for a few minutes on high speed with the whisk attachment. If the frosting is still too soft, repeat this process. If after two tries the frosting still isn't right, there are likely more fundamental problems and your best course of action is to start over.

For lumpy, stiff buttercream, the likely problem is that the mixture is too cold. Either allow the mixture to sit at room temperature until it softens and try beating again, or place the bowl of buttercream over a pot of steaming—not boiling—water in short increments of 15 to 30 seconds. Whip the buttercream vigorously after each interval until it becomes smooth and silky.

For the ultrasimple butter frosting sometimes referred to as **American buttercream,** see Quick Vanilla Butter Frosting, 792.

FRENCH BUTTERCREAM

About 3 cups

This recipe requires the simultaneous preparation of a sugar syrup and the beating of eggs or egg yolks. If the syrup heats up too quickly before the eggs are whipped, take it off the heat to delay the cooking. The eggs or yolks may also be whipped until thick before beginning the sugar syrup. In that case, turn the mixer back on high speed when the syrup is almost ready. Have all the ingredients at room temperature, 68° to 70°F.

Combine in a medium heavy saucepan and cook, stirring, over medium heat until the mixture begins to simmer:

1 cup sugar
½ cup water
¼ teaspoon cream of tartar

Stop stirring, cover, and simmer for 2 minutes to dissolve the sugar. Uncover and wash any sugar crystals from the sides of the pan with a wet pastry brush. Cook, uncovered, until the syrup reaches 235° to 240°F (soft-ball stage, 857) on a candy thermometer.

Meanwhile, in a large bowl, or in a stand mixer with the whisk attachment, beat on high speed until thick and pale yellow:

2 large eggs or 5 large egg yolks

Just before the syrup is ready, begin beating the eggs again on medium speed. Beating constantly, pour the hot syrup in a thin steady stream into the eggs, avoiding the beaters or whisk. Beat the hot mixture until the bottom of the bowl, when touched, no longer feels warm. Beat in 1 tablespoon at a time:

3 sticks (12 ounces) unsalted butter, softened

beating until the buttercream is smooth and spreadable. If the mixture looks curdled at any time, simply continue beating until smooth. If the butter is added too quickly or the ambient temperature is very warm, the mixture may become soupy; refrigerate it for 20 to 30 minutes, then resume beating.

This keeps, refrigerated, for up to 6 days; or freeze for up to 6 months. To soften chilled or frozen buttercream, break it into chunks with a fork. Place it in a large bowl or the bowl of a stand mixer and allow it to come to room temperature. Then beat until smooth and creamy.

MERINGUE BUTTERCREAM

Please read About Buttercream, 795.

I. SWISS

3 to 3½ cups

This egg white buttercream does not require a cooked syrup. Have the butter and egg whites at room temperature, 68° to 70°F.

Have ready:

3 sticks (12 ounces) unsalted butter, softened

Whisk together in a large stainless steel bowl or the bowl of a stand mixer:

4 large egg whites
¾ cup sugar
2 tablespoons water
¼ teaspoon cream of tartar

Set the bowl in a deep skillet filled with about 1 inch of simmering water. Make sure the water level is at least as high as the depth of the egg whites in the bowl. Beat the whites constantly on low speed with a hand mixer or a whisk until the mixture reaches 160°F on an instant-read thermometer. Do not stop beating while the bowl is in the skillet, or the egg whites will overcook. If you cannot hold the thermometer in the egg whites while continuing to beat, remove the bowl from the skillet just to read the thermometer, then immediately return the bowl to the skillet. Remove the bowl from the skillet and add:

1 teaspoon vanilla

If using a stand mixer, attach the bowl to the mixer and use the whisk attachment to beat on high speed until thick, glossy, and stiff. Continue to beat until the bottom of the bowl is no longer warm, about 10 minutes. Switch to the paddle attachment and beat in the softened butter a couple of tablespoons at a time, waiting until each addition is fully incorporated before adding the next. Beat until smooth. This keeps, refrigerated, for up to 6 days; or freeze for up to 6 months. Soften as for French Buttercream, above.

II. ITALIAN

About 4 cups

We find this buttercream, made with a cooked sugar syrup, to be slightly easier than Swiss meringue buttercream. If the frosting looks broken, don't panic. Just keep beating until smooth.

Have ready:

3 sticks (12 ounces) unsalted butter, softened

Prepare:

Italian Meringue, 794

When the bowl of the mixer is no longer warm, beat in the softened butter about a tablespoon at a time until the frosting is very smooth and creamy.

LIQUOR-FLAVORED BUTTERCREAM

Prepare **Meringue Buttercream I or II, 796.** At the very end, beat in **up to ¼ cup liquor or liqueur,** such as bourbon, dark rum, Grand Marnier, or elderflower liqueur.

COFFEE BUTTERCREAM

Dissolve **1 tablespoon instant coffee or espresso powder** in 1½ teaspoons water. Prepare **French Buttercream, 796, or Meringue Buttercream I or II, 796.** Beat most of the espresso mixture into the buttercream, then add the rest as desired, to taste.

MOCHA BUTTERCREAM

Melt **2 ounces semisweet or bittersweet chocolate (up to 64% cacao), chopped,** and let cool to lukewarm. Beat into **Coffee Buttercream, above,** along with **(2 tablespoons coffee liqueur)**, if desired.

CHOCOLATE BUTTERCREAM

About 4½ cups

Melt **8 to 12 ounces semisweet or bittersweet chocolate (up to 64% cacao), chopped,** with 1 tablespoon water for every 2 ounces chocolate. Let cool to lukewarm. Using a silicone spatula, stir into **French Buttercream, 796, or Meringue Buttercream I or II, 796.**

PRALINE OR NUT BUTTERCREAM

Stir **⅓ to ½ cup French Praline, 794, finely chopped toasted, 1005, nuts, or sweetened or unsweetened canned chestnut puree** into **French Buttercream, 796, or Meringue Buttercream I or II, 796.** If desired, stir in **(1 to 2 tablespoons Frangelico)**.

CITRUS BUTTERCREAM

Beat the **finely grated zest of 1 orange, 2 lemons, or 3 limes** and **(1 to 2 tablespoons orange liqueur or limoncello)** into **French Buttercream, 796, or Meringue Buttercream I or II, 796.**

CRÈME MOUSSELINE (GERMAN BUTTERCREAM)

About 3½ cups

This buttercream variation is exceptionally silky smooth and rich. It is very important that the pastry cream and butter be roughly the same temperature before beating them together.

Prepare and let cool to room temperature:

Pastry Cream, 801, using an extra ¼ cup sugar

Have ready:

2 sticks (8 ounces) unsalted butter, softened

In a large bowl, or in a stand mixer with the paddle attachment, beat the pastry cream until smooth. With the mixer running on medium speed, beat in the butter slowly, a couple tablespoons at a time, beating after each addition until fully incorporated and smooth before adding the next. It should take about 3 minutes to incorporate all the butter. Beat until silky smooth. Use right away, cover and refrigerate for up to 5 days, or freeze for up to 3 months. Before using, let it come to room temperature, then beat well until smooth.

ABOUT GANACHE AND CHOCOLATE GLAZES

Ganache is a French term that refers to any combination of chocolate and cream. Ganache is simple and quick to make, smooth on the tongue, and rich in flavor. Butter and, occasionally, eggs or egg yolks, may be included; butter used in place of cream makes a variant of ganache. Ganaches are versatile, used as fillings, frostings, and glazes. Often the very same recipe can be used as a pourable glaze at 85°F or as a spreadable frosting when cooled to room temperature. Or, the same ganache could be chilled and scooped to make truffles, 859–60.

Since ganache relies solely on chocolate for its flavor, use decent-quality chocolate (this is not the time for run-of-the-mill baking chocolate). However, be aware that if using very dark chocolate (above 72% cacao) you may need to use slightly more hot cream to make a smooth ganache. Start by using the amount of cream called for in the recipe, then gradually add more, 1 tablespoon at a time, until the ganache is smooth. Ganache made with darker chocolate may also need a touch more sugar to compensate for the smaller amount of sugar in the chocolate. Simply stir in a little sifted powdered sugar to taste. To use a lower percentage chocolate (around 60% cacao), decrease the amount of hot cream added by 1 tablespoon. To glaze a cake with chocolate, see 713. For more on the properties of chocolate, see Chocolate and Cacao, 970.

CHOCOLATE GANACHE

About 1½ cups

To infuse this mixture with mint, coffee, and other ingredients, follow the instructions in Flavored Ganache, 860, using half the amounts listed.

Bring to a boil in a small saucepan:

¾ cup heavy cream

Remove from the heat and add:

8 ounces semisweet or bittersweet chocolate (60 to 70% cacao), finely chopped

Stir until most of the chocolate is melted. Cover and let stand for 10 minutes, then stir gently until completely smooth.

For a pourable glaze, let cool at room temperature, stirring occasionally, until the ganache reaches about 85°F. For frosting, let cool further until spreadable. If the ganache becomes too stiff, set the pan in a larger pan of hot water and stir until softened; or remelt and then cool to 85° to 95°F for use as a glaze. This keeps for up to 3 days at room temperature or for up to 1 week refrigerated.

BITTERSWEET CHOCOLATE GLAZE OR FROSTING

About 1½ cups

A sophisticated glaze or frosting for rich chocolate or nut tortes. For an even more bittersweet effect, substitute 1 ounce unsweetened chocolate for 1 ounce of the semisweet or bittersweet chocolate. Using water results in a clean-tasting chocolate glaze, which is a nice option if the chocolate you use is especially good.

Melt in a double boiler, a heatproof bowl set over simmering water, or in a microwave on 50 percent power in 20-second bursts, stirring often just until smooth:

6 ounces semisweet or bittersweet chocolate (60 to 70% cacao), coarsely chopped
⅓ cup coffee or water
(Pinch of salt)

Remove from the heat. With a silicone spatula, stir in 2 or 3 pieces at a time:

6 tablespoons (¾ stick) unsalted butter, cut into small pieces

Continue to stir—do not beat—until perfectly smooth.

For a pourable glaze, let cool at room temperature, stirring occasionally, until the mixture reaches 90°F. For frosting, let cool further until spreadable. If the frosting becomes too stiff, set the bowl in a larger pan of hot water and stir until softened; or remelt and then cool to 90°F for use as a glaze. This keeps for up to 3 days at room temperature or for up to 3 weeks refrigerated.

MILK CHOCOLATE MOCHA GLAZE OR FROSTING

About 1¾ cups

Place in a small heatproof bowl:

9 ounces milk chocolate, finely chopped

Combine in a medium saucepan and bring to a simmer:

⅔ cup heavy cream
1 tablespoon light corn syrup
1 tablespoon instant coffee or espresso powder

Immediately pour the hot cream mixture over the chocolate. Stir until the chocolate is melted and the mixture is smooth. For a pourable glaze, let cool just to 100°F. For a frosting, let cool to room temperature and stir with a silicone spatula until spreadable. If the frosting becomes too stiff, set the bowl in a larger pan of hot water and stir gently until softened; or remelt and then cool to 100°F for use as a glaze. This keeps for up to 3 days at room temperature or for up to 3 weeks refrigerated.

ABOUT ICINGS AND GLAZES

These icings should be spread thinly on cakes and cookies. Some of the icings below, such as Creamy Decorating Icing, are best used to pipe intricate decorations on cakes rather than as the primary frosting for the cake as a whole. Royal Icing in particular should be used only for decoration. The glazes in this section are composed primarily of powdered sugar, as opposed to the richer chocolate glazes immediately preceding this section.

CREAMY DECORATING ICING

Enough to frost and lightly decorate a 9-inch layer

A highly manageable icing for intricate, precise decorations that keeps well if stored tightly covered. To use a pastry bag, see Decorative Treatments for Cakes, 714.

Sift into a large bowl:

4 cups (1 pound) powdered sugar

Add and mix well with a hand mixer:

½ cup vegetable shortening
2 to 4 tablespoons milk or heavy or light cream
1 teaspoon vanilla or ½ teaspoon vanilla and ½ teaspoon almond extract

Continue beating until the icing is smooth. It will be slightly stiff. Add more liquid for the proper consistency for making decorations.

ROYAL ICING

This decorative icing dries hard like plaster and is pure white unless tinted with food coloring. It is stiff enough to pipe and makes beautiful filigree, lace, tiny dots, and string work on wedding cakes. Adjust the consistency by adding more or less powdered sugar or a little water. The icing is mostly sugar and not especially delicious, though it is ideal for decorative sugar cookies. Our advice is to use it only when decoration is more important than taste and/or in very small quantities. To avoid the naturally grayish tone that develops during preparation, add to any portion that you want to keep white a slight amount of blue food coloring. Do not use blue in any icing that you plan to color yellow, orange or any other pale, warm tint.

I. RAW EGG WHITE

About 2 cups

Sift together into a medium bowl:

3½ cups powdered sugar
⅛ teaspoon cream of tartar

Beat in a large bowl, or in a stand mixer with the whisk attachment, until stiff but not dry, 978:

2 large egg whites

Gradually add the sifted sugar mixture and:

2 tablespoons lemon juice

until it is of a good consistency to spread. Cover with a damp cloth until ready to use.

To apply as piping or for decorative effects, use a piping bag fitted with a fine plain tip, or cut off the corner of a zip-top bag or the tip of a parchment paper cone, 715. Should you want the icing stiffer, add a little more sifted sugar. To make it softer, thin it very gradually with lemon juice or water.

II. PASTEURIZED EGG WHITE

About ¾ cup

Stir together in a microwave-safe bowl until thoroughly combined:

1 large egg white
⅓ cup powdered sugar

Microwave until the mixture reaches 160°F on a thermometer (it should not exceed 175°F), 30 to 60 seconds. (If you need to take more than one temperature reading, wash the thermometer thoroughly or dip it into a mug of boiling water before taking additional readings.) Add and beat on high speed until the icing is cool and holds stiff peaks:

⅔ cup powdered sugar, sifted
If the icing is not stiff enough, add more sugar. Color, if desired, with liquid, powdered, or paste food coloring; the color will intensify as the icing stands. The icing can be stored in a covered container for up to 3 days; press a piece of wax or parchment paper directly against the surface to prevent drying. The icing can be rebeaten if necessary. To pipe, see version I.

QUICK COOKIE ICING
About 1 cup

This is the ideal icing for rolled sugar cookies. It can be tinted with food coloring. Mix up a thick batch for piping out of zip-top bags (cut off one bottom corner) or piping bags.

Stir together in a medium bowl until smooth:
4 cups (1 pound) powdered sugar, sifted
3 to 4 tablespoons water or lemon juice
If necessary, adjust the consistency with more:
(Powdered sugar or water)
Color as desired. To store, cover the surface of the icing with plastic wrap. This keeps for up to 4 days at room temperature or for about 1 month refrigerated.

HARD-SAUCE ICING
About 1 cup

Break up **Hard Sauce, 810, made with brandy,** with a fork into pieces and let come to room temperature until soft enough to whip. Beat in a large bowl, or in a stand mixer with the paddle attachment, until smooth. Apply in a thin layer to any cooled cake, cookie, or bar.

QUICK BUTTERSCOTCH (PENUCHE) ICING
About 1½ cups

This creamy icing is a pale coffee color with a brown sugar flavor.

Heat in a medium saucepan over medium heat, stirring until smooth:
½ cup packed brown sugar
⅓ cup light cream or evaporated milk
4 tablespoons (½ stick) unsalted butter
⅛ teaspoon salt
Remove from the heat, scrape into a medium bowl, and let cool for about 5 minutes. Gradually add, beating until spreadable:
3 cups powdered sugar, sifted
½ teaspoon vanilla or 1 teaspoon dark rum
If the icing seems thin, set the pan in a larger pan of ice water and beat until spreadable. If necessary, add more:
(Powdered sugar)

QUICK CHOCOLATE BUTTER ICING
About 1¼ cups

Melt in a double boiler (or a heatproof bowl set over a pan of simmering water):
3 ounces unsweetened chocolate, coarsely chopped
3 tablespoons unsalted butter
Remove from the heat and stir in:
¼ cup hot coffee, cream, or milk
1 teaspoon vanilla
Gradually add, beating until spreadable:
2 cups powdered sugar, or to taste, sifted

QUICK BROWN BUTTER ICING
About ¾ cup

Use this icing, flecked with golden brown, on spice cakes.

Melt in a medium skillet over medium heat:
6 tablespoons (¾ stick) unsalted butter
Heat, swirling the skillet occasionally, until the butter crackles, then foams and turns deep golden (it will smell nutty and you will see browned flecks on the bottom of the skillet when swirled). Transfer the butter to a medium bowl and gradually beat in:
1¼ cups powdered sugar, sifted
1 teaspoon vanilla
Beat until smooth and spreadable; do not attempt to thin with liquid. If needed, add a little more powdered sugar to thicken. Use immediately.

QUICK MAPLE ICING
About 1 cup

This icing is quite sweet but very good on spice cakes.

Beat together in a medium bowl, or in a stand mixer with the paddle attachment:
2 cups powdered sugar, sifted
1 tablespoon unsalted butter, softened
½ teaspoon vanilla
¼ teaspoon salt
Add, beating until spreadable:
About ½ cup maple syrup

QUICK TRANSLUCENT SUGAR GLAZES

Just after these glazes are applied, decorate the cake or pastry with nuts or dried or candied fruits, if desired. When it dries, the glaze will hold the decorations in place.

I. MILK
About 1 cup

This can be used as a substitute for fondant on small cakes such as petits fours. Add more sugar or milk as needed to reach the desired consistency.

Beat together in a medium bowl until smooth:
1½ cups powdered sugar, sifted
2 tablespoons milk
¾ teaspoon vanilla

II. CITRUS
About ½ cup; enough to lightly glaze four 8-inch square cakes

Beat together in a medium bowl until smooth:
1¼ cups powdered sugar, sifted
(Finely grated zest of 1 lemon, ½ orange, or 1 lime)
2 tablespoons lemon, orange, or lime juice
½ teaspoon vanilla

III. LIQUEUR
About ⅔ cup

Beat together in a medium bowl until smooth:
2 cups powdered sugar, sifted
3 tablespoons liqueur
2 tablespoons unsalted butter, melted

HONEY BEE GLAZE FOR COFFEE CAKES

Enough for two 9-inch square cakes

Spread this glaze on top of any coffee cake before baking.
Combine in a small saucepan and bring to a boil over medium heat, stirring to dissolve the sugar:

½ cup sugar
¼ cup milk
4 tablespoons (½ stick) unsalted butter
¼ cup honey
½ cup chopped toasted, 1005, nuts

ABOUT FONDANT ICING

Fondant icing is fondant, 865, warmed and thinned to pouring or spreading consistency. Properly applied, it makes a satiny finish on Petits Fours, 749, and cakes. The temperature and consistency of the fondant icing is important, as is the preparation of the items to be glazed. It takes a little practice to apply the icing perfectly.

For best results, warm Fondant, 866, or store-bought fondant very gently in a heatproof bowl set in a skillet of 110°F water. Stir the fondant gently, to avoid creating air bubbles, with a silicone spatula, until it reaches a temperature between 98° and 105°F. Stir in food coloring, if desired, and flavor to taste with extracts, lemon juice, instant espresso powder dissolved in a few teaspoons of water, liqueurs, and the like. If necessary, thin the fondant judiciously with warm water until it is the desired consistency—thinner for pouring over small sweets such as petits fours, thicker for spreading on the tops of cakes. You can test the icing on a spare piece of cake or a cookie.

Fondant icing will not hide cracks, unevenness, crumbs, or other imperfections, so cakes and petits fours must be neat and smooth before the icing is applied. A smooth, thin coat of buttercream or hot apricot glaze spread or brushed on the top and sides of each item is the usual preparation. Chill or freeze (briefly) the items to be coated with fondant so that the surface is firm. The fondant will set quickly.

To store fondant icing, cover the surface with plastic wrap. It keeps for up to 1 week at room temperature or for up to 6 months refrigerated.

To cover petits fours or other pastries with fondant icing, line them up, with spaces between them, on a wire grid or rack set on a baking sheet to catch the excess, which can be scraped up and reused as long as it is crumb free. Warm the fondant as directed above, then pour it with a small liquid measuring cup with a pouring lip, or use a spoon. If it is necessary to spread the fondant with a spatula, do so with a quick, sure stroke, as the fondant glazes over quickly and should not be reworked. Apply any decorations while the fondant is still wet. If you have only a few cakes to glaze, place them one at a time on a slotted pancake turner or spoon held over the pan and ice them individually.

BRÛLÉED ICING

About 1 cup; enough for one 8-inch square cake

Spread on a cake or coffee cake, or on cookies, while still warm, leaving the cake in the pan, if applicable.

Adjust a rack so it's 3 to 5 inches below the heat. Preheat the broiler. Combine in a medium bowl, stirring until smooth:

⅔ cup packed brown sugar
½ cup shredded sweetened coconut or chopped nuts
3 tablespoons unsalted butter, melted
3 tablespoons heavy cream
⅛ teaspoon salt

Spread on the cake and broil until the icing is bubbling all over the surface; take care that it does not burn.

STREUSEL

Use streusel to top coffee cakes, muffins, pies, crumbles, or crisps.

I. SANDIER

⅔ to ¾ cup

Combine in a small bowl and blend until crumbly:

⅓ cup sugar
2 tablespoons all-purpose or rice flour
2 tablespoons unsalted butter
½ teaspoon ground cinnamon

Add, if desired:

(¼ to ½ cup chopped toasted, 1005, nuts)

Sprinkle the streusel over the batter or dough and bake as directed.

II. CRUMBLIER

Whisk to combine in a medium bowl:

½ cup all-purpose flour
½ cup sugar
(½ teaspoon ground cinnamon)
(¼ teaspoon ground cardamom)
¼ teaspoon salt

Add:

5 tablespoons cold unsalted butter, cut into small cubes

Work the butter into the flour with your fingers until the mixture forms medium-sized clumps. Refrigerate until ready to use. Sprinkle the streusel over the batter or dough and bake as directed.

ABOUT MOISTENING SYRUPS FOR CAKES

Moistening syrups are brushed on cake layers, such as Génoise, 721, to add moisture and flavor. They are often combined with liquor or liqueurs for greater complexity of flavor, but they may be flavored in other ways, too. Substitute citrus juice, coffee, tea, or spirits such as dark rum or brandy for the water, or infuse the finished syrup with citrus zest, loose-leaf tea, fresh herbs, whole spices, and the like.

MOISTENING SYRUP

About 1 cup

Combine in a small saucepan:

1 cup sugar
⅔ cup water

Cook, stirring gently, over low heat just until the sugar is dissolved; the syrup does not have to come to a simmer. Remove from the heat and let cool, uncovered, before using. This keeps in a covered jar for up to 3 weeks at room temperature or for up to 6 months refrigerated.

LEMON SYRUP

Prepare **Moistening Syrup, 800,** substituting ⅔ **cup lemon juice** for the water. Heat the mixture just until the sugar is dissolved. Do not simmer, as simmering mars the lemon flavor.

ABOUT CAKE FILLINGS

Making cake fillings can be almost as elaborate an affair as baking the actual cake; however, this need not be the case. We provide a range of fillings in this section, but also see About Whipped Cream, 790—or simply fill layer cakes with the frosting that will cover them. There's no real secret to selecting the filling for a cake. Simply choose something that complements the cake's flavor and level of richness. A rich chocolate cake can benefit from a lightly sweetened stabilized whipped cream filling, just as a light and fluffy yellow cake is complemented by a chocolate pastry cream.

Also consider the time factor. Many cooks like to make cakes ahead of time to avoid being rushed right before serving them. Some fillings stand up well over time, while others are more fragile. Any buttercream, 796–97, or butter-based icing can stand the test of time, as can thick chocolate icings or ganache. Whipped cream, pastry cream, and the like are a bit more delicate. Cakes with these fillings can still be prepped largely ahead of time but are best assembled closer to when they will be served.

You do not always need a separate filling and frosting or icing. In many, if not most, cases the frosting also serves as the filling. Or you can opt for a filling that requires almost no effort. Jams, preserves, marmalades, and conserves all make excellent cake fillings; but spread them thinly or pair them with whipped cream, as they are very sweet. Any cornstarch-thickened pudding, 816–18, or cream pie filling, 679–80, can be used as a cake filling as well. Prepare the pudding or filling as directed, reducing the milk by ½ cup to make it thicker. Allow it to cool completely, then refrigerate for at least 4 hours before using.

PASTRY CREAM (CRÈME PÂTISSIÈRE)

About 2 cups

This is the vanilla custard filling used for many cakes as well as Boston Cream Pie, 745, Chocolate Éclairs, 698, Fresh Fruit Tart, 675, and countless other desserts. You can add 1 to 2 tablespoons liqueur to any variation of this custard along with the vanilla, if desired. For a lighter but richer filling, fold up to ¾ cup Whipped Cream, 791, into this or any of the variations that follows.

Whisk together in a medium heatproof bowl until smooth:

½ cup sugar
2 tablespoons cornstarch
3 large egg yolks
1 large egg
¼ teaspoon salt

Bring to a simmer in a medium saucepan:

1½ cups whole milk
(1 vanilla bean, split lengthwise)

If using, remove the vanilla bean and set aside. Slowly pour half the hot milk over the egg mixture while whisking it constantly. Whisk the tempered egg mixture into the saucepan with the remaining milk and cook, stirring constantly, over medium-low heat until the cream thickens, about 2 minutes. Immediately scrape the custard into a clean bowl and stir in:

2 tablespoons cold unsalted butter, cut into small pieces

If you used a vanilla bean, scrape the seeds from the pod and stir into the pastry cream. If you did not use vanilla bean, stir in, if desired:

(1 teaspoon vanilla)

Place a piece of plastic wrap directly on the surface of the pastry cream to prevent a skin from forming. Let cool, then refrigerate before using. This keeps, refrigerated, for up to 2 days. When ready to use, transfer the pastry cream to a bowl, or a stand mixer with the paddle attachment, and beat on low speed until smooth and creamy.

CHOCOLATE PASTRY CREAM

Prepare **Pastry Cream, above.** Fold **3 to 5 ounces semisweet or bittersweet chocolate (up to 64% cacao), finely chopped,** into the hot custard. Stir gently just until the chocolate is melted and well blended.

COFFEE PASTRY CREAM

Prepare **Pastry Cream, above.** Stir into the hot milk **2 to 3 teaspoons instant coffee or espresso powder.**

MOCHA PASTRY CREAM

Prepare **Pastry Cream, above.** Stir into the hot milk **2 teaspoons instant coffee or espresso powder.** Once the custard is made, fold **3 ounces semisweet or bittersweet chocolate (up to 64% cacao), finely chopped,** into the hot custard. Stir gently just until the chocolate is melted and well blended.

BANANA PASTRY CREAM

Prepare **Pastry Cream, above,** but before whisking together the egg yolk mixture, place the milk and vanilla bean in a saucepan with **2 ripe but not soft bananas, coarsely chopped.** Bring to a simmer, remove from the heat and let steep at least 1 hour (or transfer to a bowl and chill overnight). When ready to make the pastry cream, strain the milk through a fine-mesh sieve (discard the bananas or save them for another use; scrape the seeds from the vanilla bean, and stir them into the milk). Whisk the egg yolk mixture, heat the milk, and make the pastry cream as directed. If desired, stir into the hot custard (**1 to 2 tablespoons dark rum, to taste).** Just before using, fold **2 ripe but firm bananas, diced** into the cold custard.

FRANGIPANE PASTRY CREAM

Prepare **Pastry Cream, above,** folding into the hot custard ⅓ **cup almond meal or flour** and ¼ **teaspoon almond extract.**

BUTTERSCOTCH PASTRY CREAM

Prepare **Pastry Cream, above,** substituting **brown sugar** for the sugar. Stir in ½ **cup butterscotch chips** along with the butter until melted.

PRALINE PASTRY CREAM

Prepare **Pastry Cream, 801.** Fold **⅓ cup crushed French Praline, 873,** into the cold custard just before using.

LEMON CURD

About 1⅔ cups

Tart and tangy, this makes a sensational filling for sponge rolls or Angel Food Cake, 719. You can also swirl it into a plain cheesecake before baking.

Whisk together in a medium saucepan until light in color:

3 large eggs
⅓ cup sugar
Finely grated zest of 1 lemon

Add:

½ cup strained lemon juice
6 tablespoons (¾ stick) unsalted butter, cut into small pieces

Cook, whisking, over medium heat until the butter is melted. Then whisk constantly until the mixture is thickened and simmers gently for a few seconds. Using a silicone spatula, scrape the filling into a medium-mesh sieve set over a bowl and strain the filling into the bowl. Stir in:

½ teaspoon vanilla

Let cool, cover, and refrigerate to thicken. This keeps, refrigerated, for about 1 week.

LIME OR GRAPEFRUIT CURD

Prepare **Lemon Curd, above,** substituting the **finely grated zest of 2 limes or 1 grapefruit** for the lemon zest, and using **½ cup strained lime or grapefruit juice** instead of lemon juice.

ORANGE CURD

Prepare **Lemon Curd, above,** substituting the **finely grated zest of 1 large orange** for the lemon zest and using **¼ cup lemon juice** and **¼ cup orange juice** in place of the lemon juice.

FRANGIPANE

About 2½ cups

Because this filling contains raw eggs, it must be baked before using. It is most commonly used in tarts, such as Megan's Frangipane Fruit Tarts, 677, and Bakewell Tart, 676, but it may also be baked on its own in mini muffin tins, perhaps with a single berry or small spoonful of jam in the middle, for tiny dessert cakes.

Beat in a large bowl, or in a stand mixer with the paddle attachment, until fluffy:

1½ sticks (6 ounces) unsalted butter, softened
1 cup sugar

Beat in:

½ teaspoon almond extract

Beat in one at a time:

2 large eggs

Add and mix until combined:

1⅓ cups almond meal or flour
⅔ cup all-purpose flour
¼ teaspoon salt

Use immediately or store refrigerated in an airtight container for up to 4 days.

BUTTERSCOTCH FILLING

About 3 cups

Prepare the filling for **Butterscotch Cream Pie, 680,** reducing the whole milk to 1½ cups.

CITRUS CUSTARD FILLING

About 1⅓ cups

Whisk together in a medium saucepan:

¾ cup sugar
2 tablespoons cornstarch
⅛ teaspoon salt

Whisk in until smooth:

3 large egg yolks

Whisk in:

½ cup strained orange juice
Finely grated zest of 1 lemon
¼ cup strained lemon juice

Cook over medium-low to medium heat, stirring constantly with a silicone spatula and scraping the bottom and corners of the pan to prevent scorching. When the mixture comes to a simmer and thickens, continue to cook, stirring briskly, for about 30 seconds. Transfer the filling to a medium bowl, straining it through a medium-mesh sieve, if desired. Place a piece of plastic wrap directly on the surface of the filling and refrigerate until chilled. Stir gently before using, but do not beat. This keeps, refrigerated, for up to 2 days.

APRICOT CUSTARD FILLING

About 1½ cups

Combine in a small saucepan and simmer gently for 25 minutes:

½ cup loosely packed dried apricots
1 cup water

Stir in:

1 tablespoon sugar

Simmer until the liquid is reduced to a glaze, 3 to 5 minutes. Puree the mixture in a food processor until smooth. Prepare:

Citrus Custard Filling, above

Stir the apricot puree into the hot filling, then strain and chill as directed.

CHOPPED FRUIT FILLING

I. ***About 1¾ cups***

Combine in a double boiler, or a heatproof bowl set over a pan of simmering water, and stir until the sugar dissolves:

¾ cup evaporated milk
¾ cup sugar
¼ cup water
⅛ teaspoon salt

Add and cook, stirring occasionally, until thick:

¼ cup finely chopped dates
¼ cup finely chopped dried figs

Let cool, then add:

½ cup chopped toasted, 1005, nuts, such as walnuts or pecans
1 teaspoon vanilla

II. *About 2 cups*
Combine in a small saucepan and simmer gently for 25 minutes:
½ cup loosely packed dried apricots
1 cup water
Increase the heat to high and boil until nearly all the liquid has evaporated. Puree in a food processor. Return the mixture to the saucepan. Stir in:
⅔ cup sugar
Cook over low heat until it thickens, about 3 minutes. Remove from the heat and stir in:
Finely grated zest of 1 orange
2 tablespoons orange juice
¾ cup chopped golden raisins
¼ cup finely chopped candied ginger

TOASTED WALNUT OR PECAN FILLING
About 1½ cups
Brown sugar and toasted nuts make a superb filling.
Combine in a small saucepan:
1 cup packed light brown sugar
4 tablespoons (½ stick) unsalted butter, cut into small pieces
2 tablespoons water
¼ teaspoon salt
Cook over low heat, whisking, until the butter is melted and the mixture begins to simmer. Remove from the heat. Whisk in a small bowl:
2 large egg yolks
Add a little of the hot brown sugar mixture to the yolks to warm them, whisking constantly, then whisk the tempered yolks into the saucepan. Return to low heat and cook, whisking constantly, until thickened, 1 to 2 minutes. Remove from the heat and stir in:
1½ cups chopped toasted, 1005, walnuts or pecans
Use immediately.

ALMOND OR HAZELNUT CUSTARD FILLING
About 1½ cups
Combine in a double boiler, or a heatproof bowl set over a pan of simmering water, and cook, stirring, until slightly thickened:
1 cup sugar
1 cup sour cream
1 tablespoon all-purpose flour
Meanwhile, beat in a small bowl:
1 large egg
Whisk about one-third of the hot sour cream mixture into the egg to warm it, then scrape the tempered egg back into the double boiler. Stir in:
1 cup very finely chopped toasted, 992, hazelnuts or blanched almonds
Stir and cook the custard until thick. Remove from the heat, scrape into a clean bowl, and stir in:
½ teaspoon vanilla or 1 tablespoon almond or hazelnut liqueur

COCONUT-PECAN FILLING
About 3¼ cups
Sweet and delicious, this is the traditional German Chocolate Cake, 730, filling and topping.
Combine in a medium saucepan:
1 cup sugar
1 cup evaporated milk or heavy cream
3 large egg yolks
1 stick (4 ounces) unsalted butter, cut into small pieces
Cook over medium heat, stirring constantly, until the mixture is thickened and bubbling gently around the edges. Reduce the heat to low and cook, stirring, for 1 to 2 minutes more. Remove from the heat and stir in:
1⅓ cups flaked sweetened coconut
1⅓ cups chopped toasted, 1005, pecans
Let cool until spreadable. This keeps, refrigerated, for about 1 week. Soften at room temperature before using.

WHIPPED GANACHE FILLING
About 3 cups
This is a light-colored but rich and creamy chocolate filling. This fills a 17½ × 11½-inch jelly-roll generously. If you whip it until it is too stiff, warm the spatula with hot water to help in spreading. Start this a few hours in advance of when it is needed. For a **Mocha Ganache Filling,** add **2 teaspoons instant espresso or coffee powder** to the cream, and use bittersweet, semisweet, or milk chocolate.
Bring to a boil in a medium saucepan:
2 cups heavy cream
Remove from the heat and whisk in:
8 ounces semisweet or bittersweet (up to 64% cacao), milk, or white chocolate, finely chopped
Cover and let stand for 10 minutes. With a silicone spatula, stir the mixture until perfectly smooth, scraping the bottom of the pan to be sure all the chocolate is melted. Cover and chill for at least 2 hours. (The ganache can be refrigerated for up to 5 days or frozen for up to 6 months.) To use, in a large bowl, or in a stand mixer with the paddle attachment, beat on low to medium speed just until the ganache is thickened and begins to hold a shape; do not overbeat (this happens very quickly if using semisweet or bittersweet chocolate, so watch it carefully). Use immediately.

ABOUT FILLINGS FOR COFFEE CAKES AND PASTRIES
These fillings are specifically for yeasted, filled coffee cakes, 623, and other filled pastries such as danishes, 696. You may add distinction to fillings with lemon juice, citrus zest, dried fruits of all kinds, finely chopped citron, finely chopped chocolate, or jam or marmalade. ➤ A 9-inch ring-shaped coffee cake needs about 1 cup-plus of filling; individual rolls or pastries about 2 teaspoons.

NUT FILLINGS
I. *Enough for one 9-inch ring*
Combine in a medium bowl:

½ cup ground toasted, 1005, hazelnuts, almonds, or other nuts
½ cup sugar
(2 tablespoons finely chopped candied citron, candied orange peel, or candied ginger)
2 teaspoons ground cinnamon
½ teaspoon vanilla

Add:

1 large egg, well beaten

Thin with:

Milk, half-and-half, or cream

until of the right consistency to spread over the dough.

II. *Enough for one 9-inch ring*

Have ready:

¼ cup chopped toasted, 1005, nuts
¼ cup chopped citron, candied orange peel, or candied ginger
¼ cup chopped raisins or golden raisins

Melt in a small saucepan:

4 tablespoons (½ stick) unsalted butter

After rolling the dough, spread it with the melted butter, sprinkle with the chopped ingredients and, if desired:

(Sugar)
(Ground cinnamon)

III. *Enough for three 9-inch rings*

Prepare:

Frangipane, 802

Spread over the dough before baking, or use as directed.

APPLE FILLING

Enough for two 9-inch rings

Combine in a large saucepan and boil until the juices are thick and sticky, at least 4 minutes:

2½ cups chopped peeled apples
1 cup packed brown sugar
1 cup raisins
6 tablespoons (¾ stick) unsalted butter
½ teaspoon ground cinnamon
½ teaspoon salt

Let cool slightly before spreading over the dough.

DRIED FRUIT FILLING

Enough for one 9-inch ring

Combine in a medium saucepan and bring to a boil:

8 ounces pitted prunes, dried apricots, dried figs, or dried dates, chopped
1 cup water, apple cider, or orange juice
¼ cup sugar
Pinch of salt

Reduce the heat and simmer until the fruit is very soft, 20 to 30 minutes. Some fruits are drier than others—add more liquid and cook a bit longer, if necessary. Stir in:

2 tablespoons lemon juice
(2 tablespoons Armagnac or Cognac)

Transfer to a blender or food processor and puree. Transfer to a bowl and cool before using.

POPPY SEED FILLING COCKAIGNE

Enough for one 9-inch ring

Grind in a spice grinder:

½ cup poppy seeds

Put the poppy seeds in a small saucepan and add:

¼ cup milk

Bring to a boil, then remove from the heat and stir in:

⅓ cup packed brown sugar
2 tablespoons butter

Stir in:

2 large egg yolks

Heat over medium-low heat, stirring constantly, until the mixture thickens slightly. Let cool slightly, then add:

⅓ cup almond paste, store-bought or homemade, 873, or
½ cup almond meal or flour
(3 tablespoons chopped candied citron)
(2 teaspoons lemon juice or 1 teaspoon vanilla)

Let cool completely before using.

CHEESE FILLINGS

Enough for one 9-inch ring

I. RICOTTA-GOLDEN RAISIN

Blend in a food processor until smooth:

1½ cups whole-milk ricotta

Transfer to a bowl. Add and mix well:

½ cup golden raisins or sultanas
¼ cup sugar
1 large egg
Finely grated zest of 1 lemon

II. CREAM CHEESE

Blend in a food processor until smooth:

4 ounces cream cheese, cut into cubes
3 tablespoons sugar
(½ teaspoon ground cinnamon)
Finely grated zest of 1 lemon
1 tablespoon heavy cream

Use immediately or refrigerate for up to 3 days.

CHOCOLATE FRUIT FILLING

Enough for one 9-inch ring

Stir together in a small bowl until thoroughly combined:

⅓ cup finely chopped toasted, 1005, walnuts or pecans
⅓ cup packed light brown sugar
3 tablespoons finely chopped dark chocolate
2 tablespoons finely chopped dried cranberries, cherries, or apricots
1 tablespoon unsweetened cocoa powder
1 tablespoon instant coffee or espresso powder
1 teaspoon ground cinnamon

ABOUT SWEET SAUCES

Serving a sauce with dessert can be the luxurious extra touch that makes it memorable. Sauces can create a pleasing contrast or they can complement the dessert they are served with. For example, try pairing rich mousses, custards, and ice creams with a tart fruit sauce. With fruit desserts, consider creamy but light-tasting sauces like Whipped Cream, 791, or sabayon, 807. Cakes and bread puddings take well to sauces that soak in. Sometimes gilding the lily is called for. A rich chocolate cake is divine with an equally rich caramel, white chocolate, or Southern whiskey sauce.

ABOUT FRUIT SAUCES

These sauces range from bright, fresh-tasting coulis made with raw fruit to thicker, richer cooked fruit sauces that are usually served hot. Other fruit-based preparations that may be used as sauces include Blueberry Compote, 178, Cooked Fruit Puree, 172, citrus curds, 802, and Fruit Shrub, 16. Also be aware that nearly any fruit juice or nectar may be boiled down, sweetened, if necessary, and thickened with cornstarch to make an impromptu fruit sauce. If desired, enrich these off-the-cuff sauces by whisking in a tablespoon or two of butter at the end of cooking.

FRESH BERRY COULIS

About 1 cup

Puree in a blender or food processor:

1 pint raspberries, blackberries, blueberries, or strawberries, hulled, or 12 ounces frozen dry-pack raspberries, blackberries, strawberries, or blueberries, thawed
3 tablespoons sugar, or more to taste
2 teaspoons strained lemon juice, or more to taste

Use a silicone spatula to push the pulp through a fine-mesh sieve into a bowl. Press firmly, and periodically scrape the inside of the sieve clear of seeds, which will otherwise plug up the holes. Do not waste any of the precious pulp. Continue to press until you are left with just a heaping tablespoon of stiff, clumped-together seeds. Taste the pulp, then stir in a little more sugar or lemon juice, if needed. Serve, at room temperature or chilled. Cover and refrigerate for up to 3 days.

MANGO COULIS

About 1¼ cups

This tropical sauce is especially nice with banana and coconut desserts.

Peel, pit, and dice:

1 large ripe but firm mango

Puree in a blender or food processor with:

2 tablespoons sugar, or more to taste
2 tablespoons water
1 tablespoon strained lime or lemon juice

If needed, thin with a bit more water and adjust sugar and acidity. Serve, at room temperature or chilled. Cover and refrigerate for up to 3 days.

HOT LEMON OR LIME SAUCE

About 1⅓ cups

This sauce is excellent with gingerbread, pound cake, and angel food cake. It is also delicious with desserts containing blueberries or coconut.

Combine in a small heavy saucepan:

⅔ cup sugar
Grated zest of 1 lemon or lime
¼ cup strained lemon or lime juice
2 tablespoons water

Whisk in until thoroughly blended:

3 large egg yolks

Add:

1 stick (4 ounces) unsalted butter, cut into pieces

Set over low heat. Stirring constantly but gently, bring to a simmer and cook until thickened, about 1 minute. Strain through a fine-mesh sieve. Serve at once, or let cool, then cover and refrigerate for up to 3 days. Reheat over low heat, stirring.

CHERRY SAUCE

About 2 cups

Serve over vanilla or chocolate ice cream, chocolate cake, or cheesecake.

Combine in a medium saucepan:

1 pound fresh sweet red cherries, such as Bing, or 2 cups well-drained canned or bottled sweet cherries, halved and pitted
¾ cup sugar
(⅓ to ½ cup kirsch or amaretto, to taste)
3 tablespoons strained lemon juice

Cover and let stand for at least 30 minutes, or up to 3 hours, stirring occasionally. Set the saucepan over medium-high heat. Bring to a boil and cook until the juices are red and syrupy, about 5 minutes. Add:

½ cup brandy or bourbon

Standing back, carefully ignite with a long match or lighter. Let the flames die off, then continue to boil to a thick, syrupy sauce. If the sauce foams up, reduce the heat and continue to simmer, stirring often. If serving the sauce with a warm or room-temperature dessert, take the saucepan off the heat and stir in until incorporated:

(3 tablespoons unsalted butter)

For a cold, warm, or room-temperature dessert, stir in:

(½ teaspoon almond extract)

Serve at once, or let cool. Cover and refrigerate for up to 3 days. Reheat over low heat.

BUTTERED CIDER SAUCE

About 1 cup

This sauce is terrific on gingerbread, pumpkin pie, or apple crisp.

Without peeling or coring, chop into ¼-inch pieces:

1 large Granny Smith or other firm apple

Melt in a medium heavy saucepan:

1 tablespoon unsalted butter

Add the chopped apple and cook over medium heat, stirring occasionally, until softened, about 5 minutes. Add:

1½ cups apple cider or unsweetened apple juice
¼ cup sugar
2 tablespoons honey

Simmer until the apple pieces are translucent, about 15 minutes. Transfer the apple mixture to a sieve set over a bowl. Return the liquid to the saucepan, then force the apple pulp through the sieve. Discard the skin and core. Stir the apple pulp into the liquid and boil rapidly over high heat, stirring, until reduced to about 1 cup. Remove from the heat and stir in:

3 tablespoons unsalted butter, softened
¼ teaspoon grated or ground nutmeg
⅛ teaspoon salt

When the butter is melted, if desired, add:

(2 tablespoons brandy, applejack, or Calvados)

Serve at once, or let cool. Cover and refrigerate for up to 1 week. Reheat over low heat.

COCONUT JAM

About 4½ cups

This thick "jam" is good over rice pudding. Turn it into a sauce by combining it with a puree of tart fruit such as guava.

Combine in a large saucepan and bring to a simmer over medium heat, stirring until the sugar is dissolved:

4 cups water
3 cups sugar
½ cup light corn syrup

Cook until the syrup reaches 220°F on a candy thermometer. Add:

Freshly grated meat of 1 coconut, 184, or 1 cup shredded unsweetened coconut

Cook slowly until the mixture thickens and again reaches 220°F, about 40 minutes. Cool completely and pack into airtight containers. Refrigerate for 1 month or freeze for up to 3 months.

ABOUT CRÈME ANGLAISE (CUSTARD SAUCE)

Although made from the same basic ingredients as crème brûlée, flan, and other dessert custards (see About Custards, 812), custard sauce has a very different consistency because the sauce is prepared on top of the stove and is stirred constantly. This disrupts the protein matrix of the eggs and results in a liquid rather than semisolid custard. A custard sauce can be made with milk alone, but a sauce enriched with cream is superb, especially with simple fruit desserts.

Custard sauce must be heated to about 170°F to thicken, but never past 175°F to avoid curdling. It should be thick enough to coat the back of a spoon—lightly if made with milk alone and fairly heavily if made in part with cream. Running a finger across the back of the spoon will leave a clean line. One of the first signs that the sauce is about to thicken is the dissipation of the foam on top—the sauce will acquire body and a slight sheen. You can return the sauce to the heat if it seems too thin, but remember that it will thicken when chilled.

These sauces can be made in a double boiler, but we prefer to use a heavy pan that diffuses the heat evenly. Stir with a silicone spatula over medium-low heat constantly but *gently* as the sauce heats, sweeping the entire pan bottom and reaching into the corners of the pan. Hard stirring will yield a runny sauce. If the sauce becomes grainy and dull as you stir, signs that it has begun to overheat, immediately pour it through a fine-mesh sieve into a bowl. A slightly overcooked sauce will still be delicious, even if not entirely smooth. Processing it in a blender will partially restore its creaminess.

CRÈME ANGLAISE (CUSTARD SAUCE)

About 2⅔ cups

Lightly beat in a medium bowl:

5 large egg yolks
⅓ to ½ cup sugar
⅛ teaspoon salt

Heat in a medium saucepan over medium heat until bubbles form around the edges:

2 cups whole milk, 1 cup whole milk plus 1 cup heavy cream, or 2 cups half-and-half

Slowly whisk the hot milk into the egg yolk mixture to warm it. Return this mixture to the saucepan and place over medium-low heat. Stir the sauce gently but constantly with a silicone spatula, sweeping the entire pan bottom and reaching into the corners. As soon as the custard is thickened enough to coat the back of a spoon and reaches 170° to 175°F on an instant-read thermometer, pour it through a sieve into a bowl and stir in:

1 teaspoon vanilla, rum, or dry sherry, or a little grated lemon zest

Serve warm or cold. If serving cold, let the sauce cool thoroughly before covering and refrigerating. Condensation will cause it to thin. The sauce can be covered and refrigerated for up to 3 days. To reheat, scrape the sauce into a double boiler over warm (165°F) water and stir occasionally until warmed through.

VANILLA BEAN CRÈME ANGLAISE

Prepare **Crème Anglaise, above.** Before heating the milk or cream, cut **1 vanilla bean** lengthwise in half. Scrape out the seeds with the tip of a spoon and add them along with the pod to the milk. Bring to a simmer. Remove from the heat, cover, and steep for 15 minutes. Rewarm the milk, then proceed with the recipe, using only **½ teaspoon vanilla** and removing the vanilla pod.

COFFEE CRÈME ANGLAISE

Prepare **Crème Anglaise, above,** adding **1 teaspoon instant espresso powder** to the milk or cream. If desired, add **(1 tablespoon coffee liqueur)** to the sauce.

CHOCOLATE CUSTARD SAUCE

About 2 cups

Heat in a medium heavy saucepan, stirring, until the chocolate is melted:

2 cups whole milk, 1 cup whole milk plus 1 cup heavy cream, or 2 cups half-and-half
2 ounces unsweetened chocolate, chopped

Meanwhile, beat well in a medium bowl:

4 large egg yolks
¾ cup sugar
⅛ teaspoon salt

Slowly whisk the hot milk into the egg yolk and sugar mixture. Return this mixture to the saucepan, set over medium-low heat, and stir the sauce gently but constantly, until the custard reaches 170° to 175°F on an instant-read thermometer and coats the back of a spoon. Immediately strain the sauce into a bowl. Stir in:

1 teaspoon vanilla

Serve hot or cold.

ABOUT SABAYON AND ZABAGLIONE

Zabaglione is an Italian dessert made by whisking egg yolks, sugar, and Marsala in a double boiler until the mixture thickens into a foamy cream that is served as soon as it is made. *Sabayon* is the French name for zabaglione and a term that designates a range of desserts and sauces, both savory and sweet. Success hinges on heating these mixtures slowly to a temperature of 160°F. If warmed too quickly, the foam will not thicken properly or acquire maximum volume. If overheated, the sauce will become heavy and sticky and eventually curdle. Thus, cooking the mixture in a double boiler is best. If your double boiler is wider than 6 inches, be sure to use very gentle heat, as the mixture will be spread thin and thus be especially prone to overcooking. Madeira, sherry, or any sweet wine can be used in place of the Marsala.

Sabayon or zabaglione should be made the day it is to be used. Zabaglione is traditionally served warm, but it may be cooled and folded together with whipped cream. This has the effect of stabilizing the sauce, allowing you to keep it chilled for several hours before serving. Serve these sauces with biscotti or amaretti cookies, crostata or galette slices, or on their own with fresh seasonal fruit.

ZABAGLIONE

4 servings

Combine in the top of a double boiler or a heatproof bowl, off the heat:

4 large egg yolks
¼ cup sugar

Whisk vigorously until thick and pale yellow. Whisking constantly, gradually add:

½ cup dry Marsala

Scrape the sides of the double boiler top clean with a silicone spatula, then set over very gently simmering water. Whisking constantly, heat to 160°F on an instant-read thermometer, by which point it will have increased several times in volume and become thick enough to mound very softly on a spoon. The cooking should take 5 to 10 minutes. If the zabaglione appears to be heating too quickly, periodically remove it from the water and whisk vigorously to cool. Serve the zabaglione warm or cool.

For a lighter zabaglione, set the top of the double boiler in ice water and gently whisk the sauce until cool to the touch. Beat in a medium bowl until stiff peaks form:

½ cup heavy cream

and fold into the cooled custard. Spoon into cups or stemmed glasses and serve immediately.

SABAYON WITH WHITE WINE OR ORANGE LIQUEUR

About 2 cups

Prepare:

Zabaglione, above

replacing the Marsala with:

½ cup sweet white wine or ¼ cup orange liqueur plus ¼ cup water

Serve at once, or set the top of the double boiler in ice water and gently whisk the sauce until cool to the touch. Fold in the whipped cream, if desired.

LEMON SABAYON

About 2 cups

Grand on a vanilla or lemon soufflé, 818–19, an almond-flavored tart or cake, or berries.

Whisk together vigorously in the top of a double boiler off the heat until slightly thickened:

2 large eggs
2 large egg yolks
⅓ cup plus 1 tablespoon sugar

Whisking constantly, slowly add:

¼ cup water
Finely grated zest of 1 lemon
3 tablespoons strained lemon juice

Cook as for Zabaglione, above.

ABOUT CHOCOLATE SAUCES

Chocolate sauces are best made from high-quality chocolate—deep and rich in flavor and smooth on the tongue. Whether made with dark, milk, or white chocolate, many chocolate sauces are ganaches, 797, which are emulsions of chocolate and cream. One notable exception is hot fudge sauce, which is closer to a sugar syrup with added chocolate.

For a dairy-free chocolate sauce, make Cocoa Syrup, 9, omitting the optional malted milk powder. Also see Ganache for Hot Chocolate, 9. For more information on chocolate, see 970.

CHOCOLATE SAUCE

About 1 cup

To make in a food processor, grind the chocolate to crumbs and then, with the motor running, add the simmering cream mixture. By the time the last of the cream has been added, the chocolate will be melted and the sauce will be smooth.

Combine in a medium heavy saucepan:

½ cup light cream or ¼ cup heavy cream plus ¼ cup whole milk
1 tablespoon sugar
1 tablespoon unsalted butter

Bring to a rolling boil, stirring constantly. Remove from the heat and immediately add:

4 ounces semisweet or bittersweet chocolate (up to 64% cacao), milk chocolate, or white chocolate, finely chopped

Let stand for 1 minute, then whisk until smooth. Whisk in:

1 teaspoon vanilla or 1 tablespoon dark rum or Cognac

Serve warm or cold; the sauce will thicken as it cools and take on the consistency of ganache after a day in the fridge. Cover and refrigerate for up to 2 weeks. Reheat over low heat, whisking in a little hot water if the sauce looks oily.

HOT FUDGE SAUCE

About 2¾ cups

This sauce becomes firm and chewy when served over ice cream.
Mix in a large heavy saucepan:

½ cup sugar
¼ cup unsweetened cocoa powder
¼ teaspoon salt

Whisk in until well blended:

½ cup water

Bring to a simmer over medium-high heat. Remove from the heat and whisk in:

1 cup heavy cream
1 cup light corn syrup
2 ounces semisweet or bittersweet chocolate (up to 64% cacao), coarsely chopped
¼ teaspoon distilled white vinegar

Return to medium-high heat and boil, whisking frequently, until the bubbles become small and the syrup is thick and sticky (about 225°F on a candy thermometer), 5 to 8 minutes. Remove from the heat and add:

2 ounces semisweet or bittersweet chocolate (up to 64% cacao), finely chopped
4 tablespoons (½ stick) unsalted butter, softened
1 tablespoon vanilla

Whisk until smooth. Serve at once, or let cool. Cover and refrigerate for up to 2 weeks. Reheat in a heavy saucepan over low heat.

MOCHA SAUCE

About 1½ cups

Combine in a small heavy saucepan:

⅔ cup espresso or strong coffee
3 tablespoons sugar
¼ teaspoon salt

Cook, stirring, over very low heat until the sugar is dissolved and the mixture is steaming hot. Add off the heat:

8 ounces semisweet or bittersweet chocolate (up to 64% cacao), finely chopped

Whisk until the chocolate is melted and the sauce is smooth. Whisk in:

2 tablespoons unsalted butter, softened
(1 teaspoon instant espresso powder)

Serve at once. Cool, cover, and refrigerate for up to 2 weeks. Reheat over low heat, adding a little warm water if the sauce becomes oily.

DAIRY-FREE MOCHA SAUCE

Prepare **Mocha Sauce, above,** substituting for the butter **2 tablespoons coconut oil.**

QUICK CHOCOLATE MINT SAUCE

About 1½ cups

Combine in a microwave-safe bowl or a heatproof bowl:

One 12-ounce bag chocolate peppermint patties, chopped
⅓ cup heavy cream
Pinch of salt

Heat in a microwave in 30-second bursts, stirring after each interval, or over a pot of simmering water, stirring frequently until melted and smooth. Serve warm over ice cream.

CHOCOLATE-CARAMEL SAUCE

About 1½ cups

Prepare **Salted Caramel Sauce, 809,** using **4 tablespoons (½ stick) unsalted butter.** After the vanilla is incorporated add **3 ounces semisweet or bittersweet chocolate (up to 64% cacao), finely chopped,** and stir until melted. Serve warm.

CHOCOLATE SHELL

About 2 cups

When poured over ice cream, this chocolate sauce hardens into a shell that can be broken with the back of a spoon into tasty chocolate shards.
Combine in a double boiler or heatproof bowl set over a pan of barely simmering water:

8 ounces semisweet chocolate, finely chopped, or chocolate chips
¾ cup refined coconut oil

Stir frequently until the chocolate is fully melted. Let cool slightly and use right away or transfer to a dry container and store at room temperature. To remelt the chocolate, either transfer the mixture to a double boiler and melt over simmering water, or microwave in 30-second bursts, stirring after each one, until fully melted.

ABOUT CARAMEL AND BUTTERSCOTCH SAUCES

Caramel is simply sugar cooked to the point where it melts and begins to burn (for the stages of this process, see 856). Old cookbooks refer to it, appropriately enough, as burnt sugar. **Butterscotch** is similar, except that butter is added to the sugar as it caramelizes, resulting in the characteristic deep, nutty taste of browned butter combined with caramel. To convert caramel and butterscotch into sauces, a mixture of butter and cream, and/or water or other liquid is added while the syrup is still hot—otherwise, the syrup, once cooled, will become a hard candy.

While caramel can be made by stirring dry sugar in a pot over heat, a more foolproof way is to mix the sugar with a little water. ➤ It is important that the sugar be fully dissolved before the syrup is allowed to boil: Otherwise, the sugar may recrystallize once it reaches 238°F, leaving the cook with a white rock in the pan. (Actually, if the cook breaks the rock up with a spoon and continues cooking, caramel will eventually ensue, although this can be more trouble than it's worth.) As the syrup approaches the caramelization point, the bubbles in the saucepan will become smaller and quieter. Then, around the edges of the pan, the first signs of darkening will appear. Swirl the pan by the handle to disperse these hotter areas of syrup. Cook the syrup until it becomes a deep amber color, but be careful not to scorch it or the caramel will taste bitter. Be prepared for the caramel to sputter and foam when butter and/or cream are added. For this reason, it is always a good idea to use a deeper pan than seems necessary, a long-handled wooden spoon, and oven mitts to protect your hands and forearms. If the caramel seizes after adding the liquid, return it to medium-low heat, stirring constantly, until liquefied.

➤ If you find caramelizing sugar daunting, melt **8 ounces store-bought chewy caramel candies** in **⅓ cup heavy cream** in a saucepan over medium heat, stirring to combine. Add more cream if necessary to get the desired consistency.

SALTED CARAMEL SAUCE

About 1½ cups

Instead of adding cream, you may add apple cider, orange juice, or practically any other fruit juice or strained fruit puree. Or, after stirring in the cream until smooth, stir in ¼ **cup bourbon, Scotch, or dark rum.**

Combine in a deep heavy saucepan:

¼ cup water
1 cup sugar

Set over medium-high heat and stir gently until the sugar is dissolved and the syrup is clear. Do not let the syrup boil until the sugar is completely dissolved. Cover the saucepan and boil the syrup for 1 minute. Uncover and boil the syrup until it begins to darken around the edges. Continue to cook, swirling the saucepan, until the syrup turns deep amber. Remove from the heat and add:

1 stick (4 ounces) unsalted butter, cut into pieces

Gently stir until the butter is incorporated. Stir in:

½ cup heavy cream

If the sauce seizes, set the saucepan over low heat and stir until smooth. Remove from the heat and stir in:

1 teaspoon vanilla
¼ teaspoon fine sea salt

Serve warm or at room temperature. If the sauce seems too thick, stir in while still hot:

(¼ cup heavy cream)

Cover and refrigerate for up to 1 month. Reheat in a double boiler or in a heavy saucepan over low heat.

CARAMEL SYRUP

About ¾ cup

Adding water to hot caramel yields a thick syrup that is irresistible on ice cream, custard, or poached or sautéed fruit.

Prepare **Salted Caramel Sauce, above,** omitting the butter and cream. Instead, combine the sugar and water and caramelize as directed, then remove from the heat and, standing back, add ⅓ **cup water.** Stir until smooth. If the caramel remains lumpy, stir briefly over low heat. Remove from the heat and add the vanilla and salt. Serve at once or let cool. Cover and refrigerate for up to 6 months. Reheat over low heat, stirring in a little water if needed.

BUTTERSCOTCH SAUCE

About 1½ cups

This old-fashioned favorite is made with virtually the same ingredients as caramel sauce but is cooked in a different way.

Cook, stirring, in a medium heavy saucepan over medium heat until the butter is melted and the mixture is combined:

1 stick (4 ounces) unsalted butter
¼ cup water
2 tablespoons light corn syrup

Add and stir until dissolved:

1 cup sugar

Increase the heat to medium-high and, without stirring, boil the mixture until it begins to color around the edges, 4 to 8 minutes. Continue to cook, stirring until the mixture turns light brown. Remove from the heat and, standing back, pour in:

½ cup heavy cream

Stir until smooth. If the sauce remains lumpy, stir briefly over low heat. Remove from the heat and stir in:

1 teaspoon vanilla, whiskey, or Scotch
¼ teaspoon salt

Serve at once, or let cool, then cover and refrigerate for up to 1 month. Reheat in a double boiler.

EASY DULCE DE LECHE

About 1⅓ cups

This is the easiest path to homemade **dulce de leche,** which is traditionally made by simmering sweetened milk for many hours until it caramelizes and thickens—constantly stirring all the while to make sure the milk on the bottom does not scorch. Simmering condensed milk inside the can means minimal mess, no stirring, and the results are outrageously good.

Remove the label from:

One 14-ounce can sweetened condensed milk

Place the can, unopened, in a pot or deep saucepan. Add water to cover by 1 inch. Bring to a boil, reduce the heat, cover, and simmer on medium-low heat for 3 to 4 hours (the longer the cooking time, the darker the dulce de leche will be). Check the pot occasionally to make sure the water level stays above the top of the can. Carefully remove the can from the water. The contents of the can will be under pressure so ➤ allow the can to cool completely before opening.

VANILLA SAUCE

About 1¼ cups

Perfect drizzled on bread puddings or chocolate custards or soufflés.

Combine in a small heavy saucepan:

¼ cup sugar
1 tablespoon cornstarch
1 cup cool water

Cook over medium heat, stirring, until as thick as heavy cream, about 10 minutes. Remove from the heat. Stir in until smooth:

3 tablespoons unsalted butter
⅛ teaspoon salt
Seeds scraped from 2-inch piece vanilla bean
(2 tablespoons dark rum)

Serve warm or at room temperature.

MARSHMALLOW SAUCE

About 5 cups

Wonderful on a hot fudge sundae or chocolate cake.

Combine in a medium heavy saucepan:

1/3 cup water
2/3 cup sugar

Stirring, bring to a rolling boil. Remove from the heat and immediately add:

20 large marshmallows

Stir gently until the marshmallows are melted. Stir in:

1 teaspoon vanilla

Cover and set aside. Proceed at once to make a water bath: Heat 1 inch of water in a large skillet over very low heat until it reaches 155° to 160°F and keep at this temperature. Combine in a heatproof bowl or the bowl of a stand mixer, stirring to dissolve the cream of tartar:

3 tablespoons water
1/4 teaspoon cream of tartar

Whisk in thoroughly:

3 large egg whites
1/3 cup sugar

Set the bowl in the water bath and, whisking frequently, heat the mixture to 140°F. Whisk gently to maintain the mixture between 140° and 155°F for 5 minutes, moving the sauce off and on the heat as needed to maintain the temperature. Remove the bowl from the water bath and beat the egg white mixture on high speed (with the whisk if using a stand mixer) until the bottom of the bowl no longer feels warm, 4 to 8 minutes. Add the marshmallow mixture and beat for 30 seconds more. Use at once, or cool and cover tightly and refrigerate for up to 2 weeks.

ABOUT BOOZY SAUCES

This category encompasses hard sauces and those obscure but outstanding custard-like sauces favored by the British a few generations ago. **Hard sauce** is a mixture of powdered sugar, butter, and spirits, usually brandy or dark rum. Classic hard sauce is, as the name implies, a hard cake of butter and sugar that can be cut with a knife. Hard sauce may be served cold and hard, or it can be softened and whipped into a fluffy cream like a buttercream frosting. See Fluffy Hard Sauce, below. All these sauces are traditionally used on steamed puddings, 832–33, but they are excellent companions to bread puddings, 829–30, Fresh Ginger Cake, 737, or even an autumn take on shortcake with Quick Cream Biscuits or Shortcakes, 636, and buttery sautéed apples.

HARD SAUCE

Generous 3/4 cup

A classic accompaniment to Steamed Plum Pudding, 833.

Beat in a medium bowl, or in a stand mixer with the paddle attachment, until creamy:

5 tablespoons unsalted butter, softened

Gradually add and beat until well blended and fluffy:

1 cup powdered sugar, sifted

Add and beat until very smooth:

1 teaspoon vanilla or 1 tablespoon brandy, rum, whiskey, or coffee
1/8 teaspoon salt

Use as is or chill thoroughly before using.

FLUFFY HARD SAUCE

About 3 3/4 cups

Combine in a large bowl or a stand mixer:

2 sticks (8 ounces) unsalted butter, softened
3 cups powdered sugar, sifted
2 teaspoons vanilla
1/2 teaspoon grated or ground nutmeg

Beat on high speed (with the paddle attachment if using a stand mixer) until light and fluffy but thick enough to hold a firm shape, 6 to 10 minutes. With the beaters running, slowly add:

1/4 cup brandy, Cognac, dark rum, or orange juice

If desired, add:

(Grated zest of 1 orange)

Use at once or cover and refrigerate for up to 3 days. Soften the cold sauce at room temperature until spreadable before serving.

SOUTHERN WHISKEY SAUCE

About 1 1/2 cups

For a milder sauce, replace up to half the whiskey with water; for a very potent sauce, replace the water with whiskey.

Melt in a small heavy saucepan over low heat:

1 stick (4 ounces) unsalted butter

Stir in:

1 cup sugar
1/4 cup bourbon or other whiskey
2 tablespoons water
1/4 teaspoon grated or ground nutmeg
1/8 teaspoon salt

Cook, stirring, until the sugar is dissolved. Remove from the heat. Whisk in a medium bowl until frothy:

1 large egg

Slowly whisk the butter sauce into the egg to warm it, then return this mixture to the saucepan. Set over medium heat and, stirring gently, bring to a simmer. Cook until thickened, about 1 minute. Serve at once or set aside at room temperature for up to 1 hour. Let cool, cover, and refrigerate for up to 3 days. Reheat over low heat, stirring; if the sauce separates, remove it from the heat and whisk in a little warm water.

HOT BRANDY SAUCE

Thanksgiving will never be the same once you try this on pumpkin pie.

Prepare **Southern Whiskey Sauce, above,** substituting **1/4 cup brandy or Cognac** for the bourbon.

HOT BROWN SUGAR SAUCE

A nonalcoholic alternative to traditional whiskey sauce.

Prepare **Southern Whiskey Sauce, above,** substituting **1 cup packed light brown sugar** for the sugar, omitting the bourbon, and increasing the water to 1/3 cup. When the sauce is done, remove from the heat and stir in **1 tablespoon vanilla.**

ORANGE LIQUEUR SAUCE

About 1¾ cups

Lovely with any chocolate or orange dessert, especially soufflés.

Combine in a small heavy saucepan:

⅔ cup sugar
⅓ cup Grand Marnier or other orange liqueur
⅓ cup heavy cream

Whisk in until thoroughly blended:

3 large egg yolks

Add:

1 stick (4 ounces) unsalted butter, cut into pieces

Set over medium-low heat. Stirring constantly, cook the sauce until thick enough to coat the back of a spoon; do not let the sauce simmer. Strain through a fine-mesh sieve. Serve at once, or let cool, cover, and refrigerate for up to 3 days. Reheat over low heat or over hot water. If the sauce separates, remove it from the heat and whisk in a little hot water.

HOT WINE OR PLUM PUDDING SAUCE

Generous 2⅓ cups

Combine in the top of a double boiler or a heatproof bowl:

1 stick (4 ounces) unsalted butter, softened
1 cup sugar

Using a hand mixer, beat on medium-high speed until fluffy and lightened in color. Beat in:

2 large eggs, beaten

Beat in:

¾ cup dry sherry or Madeira
Finely grated zest of 1 lemon
(¼ teaspoon grated or ground nutmeg)

The sauce may look curdled at this point but will smooth out once cooked. Cook over simmering water, beating constantly, until the sauce reaches 160°F, about 5 minutes.

HOT BUTTERED MAPLE SAUCE

About 1⅓ cups

For a delicious dessert, put a scoop of vanilla ice cream on a waffle and top with this sauce.

Combine in a medium heavy saucepan:

1 cup maple syrup
⅓ cup sugar

Stirring constantly, bring to a boil and cook until the last drop of sauce that falls from the spoon makes a short thread (230° to 234°F). Remove from the heat and add:

6 tablespoons (¾ stick) unsalted butter, cut into pieces
2 tablespoons water
⅛ teaspoon salt

Stir briskly until the butter is melted and the sauce is thick and creamy. Whisk in a medium bowl until light and frothy:

1 large egg

Slowly whisk the hot maple syrup mixture into the egg. Rinse out the saucepan, making sure to dissolve any sugar crystals, then dry the saucepan thoroughly. Return the sauce to the saucepan and cook, stirring constantly, over medium heat until the sauce comes to a simmer and is thickened. If desired, stir in:

(¼ cup chopped toasted, 1005, pecans or walnuts)

Serve at once, or let cool, cover, and refrigerate for up to 3 days. Reheat over low heat, stirring; if the sauce separates, remove it from the heat and whisk in a little hot water.

DESSERTS

From a simple selection of cheeses to flaming puddings, molten chocolate fondue, and ethereal soufflés, the ending of a meal can be as premeditated or off-the-cuff as you like. This chapter is home to the many and varied after-dinner treats that do not fall neatly into the realms of cakes, pies, cookies, or ice creams. These sweet misfits include some of our favorite finales to an evening, and carry with them some of our fondest food memories.

ABOUT CUSTARDS

Custards are made by heating eggs, cream, and sugar until they have thickened and form a gel when cooled. If a custard exceeds 180° to 185°F, the egg proteins will begin to shrivel into tiny lumps, giving the custard a grainy consistency. For this reason, they must be heated very gently in an oven or stirred over low heat.

With **baked custards,** ingredients are simply whisked together and poured into custard cups, then gently baked until they come up to temperature. We prefer glazed ceramic ramekins or cups, but any heatproof vessel can work, including wide-mouth half-pint canning jars. A **water bath,** also known as a **bain-marie,** is the cook's most convenient means of managing heat during the cooking of custards. Baking a dish of custard in a larger pan of water insulates the custard from the oven's heat and thereby protects it from overcooking.

To prepare a water bath, choose a pan large enough to accommodate the cups comfortably—they should not touch one another or the pan sides. Arrange the custards in the empty pan, place the pan on a pulled-out rack in a preheated oven, and immediately pour enough scalding-hot tap water into the pan to come one-half to two-thirds of the way up the sides of the custard dishes. An electric kettle makes this step even easier. By pouring the water into the pan after setting it in the oven, you avoid the treacherous dance of carrying a pan full of water from countertop to oven.

To test baked custards for doneness, gently shake a cup, and as soon as the center appears quivery, like firm gelatin, remove them from the oven. Or insert a knife near the edge of the cup; if the blade comes out clean, the custard will be set all the way through when cooled.

Stirred custards, such as the thinner, sauce-like Crème Anglaise, 806, are heated slowly and constantly stirred over low heat until they have thickened. Since baked custards do not require constant attention and are harder to overcook, all of our custard dessert recipes are written for the oven. That said, any of these custards may be prepared on the stovetop by carefully heating the custard base in a double boiler until thickened. ➤ To tell when a stirred custard is done, use an instant-read thermometer and remove it from the heat when it has reached 175° to 180°F. The mixture should coat the back of a spoon. We recommend straining stirred custards for the silkiest texture possible, but it is not absolutely necessary.

Many custard recipes, whether baked or stirred, call for **tempering** the eggs. This is accomplished by whisking a small amount of the hot milk or cream into the eggs to warm them, then gradually adding the "tempered" egg mixture to the rest of the custard base. This will keep the eggs from curdling as they heat up to the temperature of the hot milk or cream.

➤ Allow time to chill the baked custards thoroughly before serving. Always store cooled custards or custard-based dishes tightly covered in the refrigerator, as they readily take on the flavors of strong-smelling foods.

Baking custards in a water bath

Perhaps the most foolproof method for making perfectly set custards is to use an immersion circulator, 1054, which allows you to set a water bath to a very precise temperature, making it virtually impossible to accidentally overcook your custards.

To cook custards using an immersion circulator, pour the custard base into ½- or ¼-pint canning jars, place the lids on top, and screw on the rings (do not overtighten; the rings should be fingertip-tight). Place an immersion circulator in a vessel big enough to accommodate the circulator and the custards (a stockpot works well). Fill the vessel with enough water to cover the jars by 1 inch and set the circulator to 180°F. When the water is preheated, lower the custards into the water bath and cook for 45 minutes. Remove the custards, let cool on a rack for 30 minutes, and chill completely in the refrigerator. Alternatively, you may pour the custard base into a zip-top freezer bag and cook as above. Once cooked, gently shake the bag to ensure the contents are mixed. Cut off a corner of the bag, pipe the base into serving cups, cover, and chill.

BAKED CUSTARD

5 servings

This simple, comforting custard can be readied for the oven in only a few minutes. To flavor, see Flavorings for Custard Bases, below.

Preheat the oven to 325°F.

Whisk in a medium bowl until just blended:

3 large eggs
¼ teaspoon salt

Heat in a small saucepan just until steaming and the sugar is dissolved:

2 cups half-and-half
½ cup sugar

Gradually whisk the hot milk into the egg mixture. Strain through a fine-mesh sieve into a bowl or large measuring cup with a pouring lip. Stir in:

1 teaspoon vanilla or seeds scraped from a 1½-inch piece vanilla bean

Pour into five 6-ounce custard cups or ramekins. If desired, dust with:

(Grated or ground nutmeg)

Set the custards in a deep pan large enough to accommodate them without touching each other or the sides of the pan. Set the pan on a pulled-out oven rack and pour enough scalding-hot tap water into the pan to come one-half to two-thirds of the way up the sides of the custard cups. Bake until set but still quivery in the center when the cups are shaken, 30 to 40 minutes.

Remove the custards from the water bath and let cool on a wire rack for 30 minutes, then cover each one tightly with plastic wrap and refrigerate for at least 2 hours before serving. You may store them in the refrigerator for up to 2 days. If desired, serve with:

(Maple syrup, berries, or a fruit sauce, 805–6)

FLAVORINGS FOR CUSTARD BASES

I. You may infuse the milk or cream by gently heating it with the sugar until steaming and stirring in one of the following:

2 tablespoons herbs, such as dried lavender blossoms, or ½ cup fresh mint leaves, or 2 fresh or dried bay leaves
A pinch of saffron threads
A 1½-inch piece of vanilla bean, split lengthwise (scrape the seeds into the milk after infusing)
Spices such as 6 crushed green cardamom pods, 1 cinnamon stick, or 2 star anise
Toasted, 1005, nuts such as ½ cup almonds, hazelnuts, pistachios, or unsweetened coconut flakes
2 tablespoons tea leaves such as Earl Grey or jasmine
1 cup fresh elderflower blossoms
1 stalk lemongrass, bruised with the spine of a knife and cut into 1-inch pieces
3 fig or pandan leaves, cut into 1-inch pieces

Cover the saucepan and allow to steep for at least 15 minutes. Strain the flavorings out and proceed as directed.

II. Other flavorings may be simply whisked in with the sugar:

¼ cup malted milk powder
2 teaspoons matcha powder

III. Other ingredients may be whisked in off the heat after the custard base is cooked:

2 tablespoons bourbon, rum, Cognac, Grand Marnier, or other liqueur
1 to 2 teaspoons orange flower or rose water, to taste

CARAMEL CUSTARD

5 servings

Proceed as for **Baked Custard, above,** omitting the sugar. Heat the half-and-half gently but do not combine yet with the eggs and salt.

To prepare the caramel, heat **¾ cup sugar, ¼ cup water,** and **¼ teaspoon lemon juice or vinegar** in a deep heavy saucepan (use one that seems larger than necessary, as the caramel will bubble up quite a bit) over medium heat, stirring until the sugar is dissolved. Increase the heat to high and bring the syrup to a rolling boil; cover the pan and boil for 2 minutes. Uncover the pan and cook until the caramel begins to darken. When the caramel turns deep amber, remove from the heat and add a little of the half-and-half, stirring. Be careful—the caramel will bubble furiously. Continue adding the half-and-half a little at a time until completely incorporated. If the caramel seizes up, return to low heat and stir until dissolved.

Let the caramel mixture cool for 10 minutes, then whisk into the eggs as directed above and add the vanilla. Strain the custard through a fine-mesh sieve. Proceed as directed, baking the custards for 25 to 30 minutes. When ready to serve, sprinkle the tops of the custards with **(flaky sea salt),** if desired.

Ovenproof ramekin and custard cup

COFFEE CHOCOLATE CUSTARD

5 servings

An updated take on our recipe from the 1963 edition. The espresso powder accentuates the flavor of the chocolate.

Preheat the oven to 325°F. Place in a medium heatproof bowl:

2 ounces bittersweet chocolate (up to 70% cacao), finely chopped
1 tablespoon instant espresso powder

Heat in a small saucepan just until steaming:

2 cups heavy cream

Pour over the chocolate, let sit 2 minutes, then whisk until smooth. Add:

1 large egg plus 2 large egg yolks, beaten together
⅓ cup sugar
¼ teaspoon salt

Whisk until completely smooth and pass through a fine-mesh sieve. Divide among five 6-ounce custard cups or ramekins. Set the custards in a deep pan large enough to accommodate them without touching each other or the sides of the pan. Set the pan on a pulled-out oven rack and add enough scalding-hot tap water to come one-half to two-thirds of the way up the sides of the custard cups. Bake until set but still quivery in the center when the cups are shaken, 25 to 35 minutes.

Remove the custards from the water bath and let cool on a wire rack for 30 minutes. Cover each custard with plastic wrap and refrigerate for at least 2 hours before serving. You may store them in the refrigerator for up to 2 days. If desired, serve with:

(Whipped Cream, 791 [preferably flavored with whiskey], or Whipped Crème Fraîche, 791)

FLAN OR CRÈME CARAMEL

6 to 8 servings

Flan is a custard baked in a dish with caramel on the bottom. When cooled and inverted onto a serving plate, the caramel enrobes the custard. Flan is the preeminent dessert of Spain and Latin America. It is also a favorite in France, where it is known as *crème caramel.*

Preheat the oven to 325°F. Have ready six 6-ounce custard cups or ramekins or a 9-inch round baking dish.

Prepare the caramelized sugar as directed in **Caramel Custard, 813,** using a small heavy saucepan (do not whisk in the half-and-half). When the caramel turns deep amber, pour into the cups or baking dish. Using a potholder, immediately tilt the cups or dish to spread the caramel over the bottom and halfway up the sides.

Whisk in a large bowl just until blended:

4 large eggs plus 2 large egg yolks
¾ cup sugar
⅛ teaspoon salt

Heat in a medium saucepan just until steaming:

3 cups whole milk

Gradually whisk the hot milk into the egg mixture and stir until the sugar is dissolved. Strain the mixture through a fine-mesh sieve into a bowl or large measuring cup with a pouring lip. Stir in:

¾ teaspoon vanilla

Pour into the caramel-lined cups or dish. Set the cups or dish in a deep pan large enough to accommodate them without touching each other or the sides of the pan. Set the pan on a pulled-out oven rack and add enough scalding-hot tap water to come one-half to two-thirds of the way up the sides of the cups or dish. Bake until firmly set in the center, 50 to 60 minutes for individual cups, 1 to 1½ hours for a single dish.

Remove the custard(s) from the water bath, let cool on a wire rack until barely warm, loosen the edges of the flan with a knife, and invert onto individual plates or a large plate (the plate for a large flan must be either broad or deep to catch all the caramel). If not serving right away, you may refrigerate, covered, for up to 2 days. To unmold, dip the cups or dish briefly in hot water before proceeding as above.

FLAN WITH CONDENSED MILK

6 to 8 servings

In Latin America, flan is made by simmering milk and sugar until reduced to a thick cream, then adding eggs. Since the cooking of the milk and sugar takes as long as an hour, many prefer to make this with sweetened condensed milk.

Preheat the oven to 325°F. Have ready six 6-ounce custard cups or ramekins or a 9-inch round baking dish.

Prepare the caramelized sugar as directed in **Caramel Custard, 813,** using a small heavy saucepan (do not whisk in the half-and-half). When the caramel turns deep amber, pour into the cups or baking dish. Using a potholder, immediately tilt the cups or dish to spread the caramel over the bottom and halfway up the sides.

Combine in a small saucepan and bring to a boil:

One 14-ounce can sweetened condensed milk
1½ cups water

Zest of ½ lime, removed in large strips with a vegetable peeler
1 cinnamon stick
Pinch of salt

Reduce the heat and simmer gently for 5 minutes. Remove from the heat, cover, and let stand until just warm. Strain the mixture through a fine-mesh sieve into a bowl.

Meanwhile, whisk in a large bowl just until blended:

4 large eggs plus 3 large egg yolks
¾ teaspoon vanilla

Gradually whisk the warm milk mixture into the egg mixture. Pour or ladle into the caramel-lined cups or dish. Set the cups or dish in a deep pan large enough to accommodate them without touching each other or the sides of the pan. Set the pan on a pulled-out oven rack and add enough scalding-hot tap water to come one-half to two-thirds of the way up the sides of the cups or dish. Bake until firmly set in the center, 40 to 55 minutes for individual cups, 50 to 70 minutes for a single dish. Let cool, store, and unmold as for Flan, 814.

VANILLA POTS DE CRÈME

6 servings

Instead of vanilla, you may infuse the cream with **a 1½-inch piece vanilla bean, split lengthwise.** Scrape the vanilla seeds into the milk, add the bean pod, and heat the milk to a simmer. Cover, remove from the heat, and allow to infuse for 15 minutes. Remove the vanilla bean pod, heat to a simmer again, and proceed as directed.

Preheat the oven to 325°F.

Whisk in a medium bowl just until blended:

6 large egg yolks
⅓ cup sugar

Bring just to a simmer in a small saucepan:

2 cups whole milk or half-and-half

Gradually whisk the warm milk into the egg yolk mixture. Strain through a fine-mesh sieve into a bowl or large measuring cup with a pouring lip. Skim off any foam with a spoon. Stir in:

1 teaspoon vanilla

Pour the mixture into six 4-ounce ramekins. Cover each ramekin tightly with a piece of foil to prevent a skin from forming. Set the custards in a deep pan large enough to accommodate them without touching each other or the sides of the pan. Set the pan on a pulled-out oven rack and add enough scalding-hot tap water to come one-half to two-thirds of the way up the sides of the ramekins. Bake until set but still quivery in the center when shaken, 40 to 50 minutes.

Remove the custards from the water bath and let cool on a wire rack for 30 minutes, then refrigerate, covered, for at least 2 hours before serving. You may store them in the refrigerator for up to 2 days.

COFFEE POTS DE CRÈME

Prepare **Vanilla Pots de Crème, above,** using **½ cup sugar,** and adding **4 teaspoons instant coffee powder or 1 tablespoon instant espresso powder** to the hot milk or half-and-half.

CHOCOLATE POTS DE CRÈME

Prepare **Vanilla Pots de Crème, above.** When the milk or half-and-half starts to steam, remove from the heat and whisk in **5 ounces bittersweet chocolate (up to 64% cacao), finely chopped.** Proceed as directed. The custards will be set in 25 to 30 minutes.

CRÈME BRÛLÉE

4 to 6 servings

Truly the queen of custards, famous for the incomparable thrill of breaking its burnt sugar crust with a spoon.

Preheat the oven to 325°F.

Prepare the custard base for **Vanilla Pots de Crème, above,** using **2 cups heavy cream** instead of milk or half-and-half. Pour into four 6-ounce or six 4-ounce custard cups or ramekins. Set the custards in a deep pan large enough to accommodate them without touching each other or the sides of the pan. Set the pan on a pulled-out oven rack and add enough scalding-hot tap water to come one-half to two-thirds of the way up the sides of the custards. Bake until the custards are set but still slightly quivery in the center when gently shaken, 30 to 35 minutes.

Remove the custards from the water bath and let cool on a wire rack for 30 minutes. Cover each one and refrigerate for at least 2 hours, or for up to 2 days. Shortly before serving, uncover the custards and gently blot any liquid that has formed on the surface with a paper towel. Sprinkle each of the custards with:

1 tablespoon granulated sugar, light brown sugar, or turbinado sugar (4 to 6 tablespoons total)

Use a propane torch to melt and caramelize the sugar. Hold the flame about 2 inches above the surface of a custard. Move the flame in small circles to melt and color the sugar as evenly as possible; some sugar will remain unmelted and some spots will char; this is part of the charm. Alternatively, if you do not have a torch, arrange the custards on a baking sheet and place directly under the broiler. Broil until the sugar melts and bubbles, turning the sheet and/or moving the custards around if some brown more quickly than others. Serve at once.

MAPLE CRÈME BRÛLÉE

Prepare **Crème Brûlée, above,** substituting **⅔ cup maple syrup** for the sugar in the custard.

RASPBERRY CRÈME BRÛLÉE

Prepare **Crème Brûlée, above,** placing **4 raspberries (16 to 24 total)** in each cup before pouring in the custard.

FLOATING ISLANDS

4 servings

Countless desserts are known as floating islands, or snowy eggs—*îles flottantes* or *oeufs à la neige* in French. All consist of some sort of puffy confection, typically a meringue, 793, floated on a liquid custard or other dessert sauce.

Separate:

5 large eggs

Put the whites in a large bowl; reserve the yolks. Whip the whites until stiff. Gradually beat in:

⅔ cup sugar

Bring to just under a simmer in a large skillet:

2 cups whole milk

Drop half of the meringue mixture from a tablespoon into 4 mounds on the milk (or shape them into quenelles, 1046). Poach them gently, without letting the milk boil, for about 4 minutes, turning them once. Lift them out carefully with a skimmer and place a towel beneath the skimmer and meringue to soak up the excess milk. Repeat with the remaining meringue mixture, placing the poached meringues on a plate or baking sheet. Set aside.

Use the milk and the reserved egg yolks to make:

Crème Anglaise, 806

Pour into a wide bowl and refrigerate until the bottom of the bowl is no longer warm, about 30 minutes. Place the meringues on top. If desired, just before serving, drizzle over the tops of the islands:

(Caramelized Sugar, 857, or Fresh Berry Coulis, 805)

LEMON OR ORANGE SPONGE CUSTARD

6 servings

The batter of this dessert is homogenous when put into the baking dish, but then magically divides during cooking into a layer of quivery custard on the bottom and a light and spongy cake on top. If you serve it from the dish, the sponge will form a decorative top, or you may unmold it. If you prefer a meringue-like quality for the topping, reserve ¼ cup of the sugar to beat slowly into the stiff egg whites before folding them into the egg yolk mixture.

Preheat the oven to 325°F. Lightly butter a 9 × 2-inch round cake pan or six 6-ounce custard cups or ramekins.

Combine in a medium bowl and mash together with the back of a wooden spoon:

⅔ cup sugar
2 tablespoons unsalted butter, softened
⅛ teaspoon salt

Beat in:

3 large egg yolks (whites reserved)

Add and mix until smooth:

3 tablespoons all-purpose flour

Gradually beat in:

Finely grated zest of 1 lemon or orange
¼ cup strained lemon juice or ⅓ cup strained orange juice

Stir in:

1 cup whole milk

Beat in a large bowl on medium-high speed until stiff but not dry, 978:

4 large egg whites, at room temperature

Gently whisk the whites into the milk mixture, blending just until no large lumps of whites remain. Ladle (do not pour) the batter into the prepared pan or cups; it may reach the top. Set the custards in a deep pan large enough to accommodate them without touching each other or the sides of the pan. Set the pan on a pulled-out oven rack and add enough scalding-hot tap water to come one-half to two-thirds of the way up the sides of the custards. Bake until the tops are puffed and golden brown and spring back when pressed lightly with a finger, 30 to 40 minutes for both small and large custards. Let stand for 10 minutes in the water bath. Serve warm, at room temperature, or chilled, in the mold(s) or turned out. If you wish, accompany with:

(Fresh Berry Coulis, 805, using raspberries, or Whipped Cream, 791)

POSSET

6 servings

This simple pudding is made by curdling cream with citrus juice. The absence of eggs or starches makes for a surprisingly light, bright-tasting dessert that pairs perfectly with fresh or roasted fruit.

Bring to a simmer in a wide saucepan:

2 cups heavy cream
½ cup sugar
Pinch of salt

Simmer gently for 5 minutes, watching the pan so the cream doesn't boil over. Remove from the heat and stir in:

6 tablespoons lemon or lime juice
(Finely grated zest of 1 lemon or lime)

Divide among six 4-ounce ramekins and refrigerate until set, about 4 hours or overnight. If desired, serve topped with:

(Fresh Berry Coulis, 805, Roasted Fruit, 171, or citrus segments, 182)

ABOUT CORNSTARCH PUDDINGS

This beloved treat is made by cooking milk, sugar, cornstarch, and sometimes eggs together until thickened into a smooth, satiny cream. It is as simple as it is delicious, and enduringly memorable.

To avoid scorching, prepare cornstarch puddings in a heavy-bottomed saucepan, which will provide gentle, even heat. The best stirring implement is a large, heatproof silicone spatula. ➤ To avoid lumps, gradually and thoroughly whisk the milk into the cornstarch mixture.

On occasion, puddings that have thickened properly in the saucepan will thin out during storage. To avoid this, ➤ do not vigorously stir puddings after they have set. ➤ If the pudding recipe uses eggs, bring the mixture to a boil after adding the eggs to prevent an enzyme in the eggs from breaking the cornstarch bonds, 1022.

Pudding can be served from a single large dish or in individual cups. To prevent a skin from forming, press a piece of plastic wrap directly onto the surface of the warm pudding before chilling, unless, of course, the skin is your favorite part!

VANILLA PUDDING

4 servings

For a speckled vanilla pudding, add the seeds from **a 1½-inch piece vanilla bean, split lengthwise and scraped,** instead of the vanilla.

Have ready a 3-cup bowl or four 5- to 6-ounce cups or ramekins.

Mix thoroughly in a medium heavy saucepan:

¼ cup sugar
3 tablespoons cornstarch
⅛ teaspoon salt

Gradually whisk in:

2 cups milk

Stirring constantly, heat over medium heat until the mixture just comes to a simmer. Remove from the heat and stir ½ cup of the milk mixture slowly into:

1 large egg, well beaten

Stir this back into the milk mixture, bring to a boil over medium heat, and continue to cook for 1 minute, stirring constantly. Remove from the heat. Stir in:

2 teaspoons vanilla

Pour the pudding into the bowl or cups, then press plastic wrap directly onto the surface. Refrigerate for at least 2 hours, or for up to 2 days.

BUTTERSCOTCH PUDDING

6 servings

Have ready a 3-cup bowl or mold or six 5- to 6-ounce cups or ramekins. Prepare the filling for **Butterscotch Cream Pie, 745.** Taste the pudding and add an extra pinch of salt, if desired. Finish and store as for Vanilla Pudding, 816.

OLD-FASHIONED CHOCOLATE PUDDING

4 servings

Have ready a 3-cup bowl or mold or four 5- to 6-ounce cups or ramekins. Whisk together in a medium heavy saucepan:

½ cup sugar
3 tablespoons unsweetened cocoa powder
3 tablespoons cornstarch
¼ teaspoon salt

Whisk in gradually:

2 cups whole milk

Cook over medium heat, stirring occasionally, until the mixture comes to a simmer, and continue to cook for 1 minute. Remove from the heat and stir in:

2 ounces unsweetened or bittersweet chocolate, chopped
1 teaspoon vanilla

Stir until the chocolate is completely melted. Finish and store as for Vanilla Pudding, 816.

VEGAN CHOCOLATE PUDDING

4 servings

The first version is a ridiculously easy, no-cook pudding that gets its richness from silken tofu. The second version has a more traditional texture.

I. Have ready a 4-cup bowl or four 5- to 6-ounce cups or ramekins. Combine in a food processor or blender:

1 pound silken tofu, drained
4 to 6 ounces bittersweet or dark chocolate (up to 72% cacao), melted
2 tablespoons unsweetened cocoa powder, sifted
(1 to 2 tablespoons vegan powdered sugar, sifted)
1 tablespoon vanilla

Blend until completely smooth. Finish and store as for Vanilla Pudding, 816.

II. Prepare **Old-Fashioned Chocolate Pudding, above,** substituting **2 cups unsweetened almond, soy, or beverage-style coconut milk** for the milk.

BANANA PUDDING

8 to 10 servings

For even more banana flavor, puree **2 very ripe bananas** with the milk before making the pudding, and use **¼ cup cornstarch.** For individual banana puddings, assemble this dessert in small cups, glasses, or ramekins.

Mix together thoroughly in a medium heavy saucepan:

½ cup sugar
3 tablespoons cornstarch
⅛ teaspoon salt

Gradually whisk in:

3 cups whole milk

Whisk in thoroughly:

4 large egg yolks

Add:

3 tablespoons unsalted butter, cut into pieces

Stirring constantly, heat over medium heat until the mixture just comes to a simmer. Reduce the heat to low and cook for 2 minutes, stirring briskly. Remove from the heat, and stir in:

1½ teaspoons vanilla

Press plastic wrap directly onto the surface of the pudding and set aside. Have ready:

60 to 70 vanilla wafers

Peel and cut into ¼-inch-thick slices:

4 to 5 large firm-ripe bananas

Line the bottom and sides of a 9-inch square baking dish with the wafers. Cover with half the pudding and bananas. Arrange a layer of wafers over the top, then cover with the remaining pudding and bananas. Press plastic wrap directly onto the surface of the pudding and refrigerate for at least 2 hours. Just before serving, cover with:

Whipped Cream, 791

BANANA PUDDING WITH MERINGUE

Have **Soft Meringue Topping I or II, 795,** and **¼ to ½ cup finely crushed vanilla wafers** ready before assembling **Banana Pudding, above.** Preheat the oven to 425°F. Form the pudding layers as quickly as possible, using a heatproof dish. Scatter a thin, even layer of the crushed cookies over the hot pudding. Spread the meringue topping over the hot pudding to touch the sides of the dish. Brown the meringue in the oven for 5 minutes. Alternatively, brown the meringue with a propane torch. Let the pudding cool to room temperature, then refrigerate for at least 2 hours, or for up to 24 hours.

TEMBLEQUE (COCONUT MILK PUDDING)

8 servings

A creamy Puerto Rican coconut pudding that "trembles" when turned out of the mold.

Grease a 1½-quart soufflé dish or mold. Combine in a large heavy saucepan:

4½ cups canned unsweetened coconut milk
½ cup sugar
¼ teaspoon salt

Heat over medium-low heat, stirring, until the sugar is dissolved. Mix together in a small bowl until smooth:

½ cup canned unsweetened coconut milk
½ cup cornstarch

Stir the cornstarch mixture slowly into the hot coconut milk mixture. Stirring constantly, heat over medium heat until the mixture just comes to a simmer. Reduce the heat to low and continue to cook for 1 minute, stirring constantly. Remove from the heat. If desired, stir in:

(1 teaspoon orange flower water)

Pour the pudding into the prepared dish, cover with plastic wrap, and refrigerate for at least 3 hours. Invert onto a plate and unmold. Garnish with:

Chopped pineapple, papaya, and/or mango
Ground cinnamon

ABOUT DESSERT SOUFFLÉS

If you have never made a soufflé, ➤ please read About Soufflés, 161. Soufflés are perhaps the most misunderstood desserts of all. They have a reputation for difficulty, but it's undeserved—they are quite easy to prepare. Like their savory counterparts, dessert soufflés are made by folding stiffly beaten egg whites into a thick, flavorful base. In traditional recipes, this base is a pastry cream, but the base may also be nuts, a fruit puree, or fruit juice mixed with egg yolks and sugar. For fruit and nut soufflés, the proper beating of the egg whites and the right oven temperatures are especially important. If the egg whites are under- or overbeaten or the baking heat is too high, the soufflé will have the look and texture of old leather. If mixed and baked with care, though, these ingredients result in a delicacy and strength that remind us of dandelion seed puffs just before they blow.

To prepare a mold for a sweet soufflé, pay careful attention to the size of the dish called for, as this affects the lightness and volume of the result. Brush the mold with a thick coat of softened butter, then sprinkle generously with sugar. Tilt the mold in all directions to spread the sugar evenly, then invert the mold and tap out the excess sugar. When prepared in a properly coated mold, a soufflé will rise tall, straight, and even and, even better, it will emerge from the oven with a delightfully crunchy, lightly caramelized crust.

A well-cooked soufflé should be firmly set but still moist and creamy in the center. At the minimum estimated baking time, open the oven door slightly and peek in. If the soufflé has risen about 2½ inches and is deep golden brown on top, you can assume that it has set firm enough not to fall when tested. To test, first touch the top of the soufflé lightly with your hand. If it feels firm, the soufflé may well be cooked through. To be sure, insert a skewer at a 45-degree angle from near the edge of the soufflé toward the center. Remove the soufflé when the skewer comes out dry, or, if you prefer a creamy center, the skewer should be just slightly moist with a bit of thick batter adhering. If it comes out wet, the soufflé needs to be baked longer. A baked soufflé will stay fully risen for at least a minute or two, giving you plenty of time to rush it to the table.

If desired, after bringing the soufflé to the table, open a slit in the top of the soufflé with 2 forks held back to back and pour in a custard sauce, 806. Or, if serving individual soufflés, slit open and tuck a chocolate truffle, 859–60, into each.

To glaze a soufflé, dust it with powdered sugar 2 or 3 minutes before it is done. The soufflé should have ➤ doubled in height and be firm before the sugar is applied. Watch it closely with the oven door partially open. The glaze will remain fairly shiny when the soufflé is served.

VANILLA SOUFFLÉ

6 to 8 servings

This soufflé tastes remarkably like a sugar cookie. You may use **2 vanilla beans** in place of the vanilla extract. Gently heat the heavy cream and sugar until steaming in a small saucepan. Split the vanilla beans lengthwise, scrape the seeds into the cream, and add the pods. Cover, remove from the heat, and let stand for 30 minutes. Remove the vanilla bean pods and proceed as directed.

Position a rack in the lower third of the oven. Preheat the oven to 375°F. Prepare a 9-inch or 2-quart soufflé mold, above.

Melt in a medium saucepan over medium heat:

3 tablespoons unsalted butter

Whisk in until smooth:

2 tablespoons all-purpose flour

Cook, stirring, for 1 minute. Remove from the heat and stir in:

1 cup heavy cream
⅓ cup sugar

Return to the heat and bring to a boil, whisking constantly, then remove from the heat. Whisk in a large bowl until well blended:

4 large egg yolks (whites reserved)

Very gradually whisk in the hot cream mixture, then stir in:

5 teaspoons vanilla

Beat in another large bowl on medium speed until foamy:

5 large egg whites, at room temperature

Add and beat until soft peaks form, 977:

½ teaspoon cream of tartar
⅛ teaspoon salt

Increase the speed to high and beat until the peaks are stiff but not dry, 978. Using a large silicone spatula, gently stir one-quarter of the egg whites into the egg yolk mixture, then fold in the remaining whites. Turn the batter into the prepared soufflé mold and smooth the top. Bake until the soufflé is well risen and the top is deep golden brown, 25 to 30 minutes. Serve at once with:

Any custard sauce, 806, sabayon, 807, or Fresh Berry Coulis, 805

GRAND MARNIER SOUFFLÉ

Prepare **Vanilla Soufflé, above,** adding the **grated zest of 1 large orange** to the cream and sugar before bringing to a boil. Replace the vanilla with **3 tablespoons Grand Marnier.** Serve with **Crème Anglaise, 806.**

CHOCOLATE SOUFFLÉ

4 servings

Unlike most chocolate soufflés, this is made without milk or starch. It is light yet moist, with an exceptional chocolate taste.

Position a rack in the lower third of the oven. Preheat the oven to 375°F. Prepare a 7-inch or 1½-quart soufflé mold, above.

Combine in a medium heatproof bowl:

6 ounces semisweet or bittersweet chocolate (up to 64% cacao), chopped
6 tablespoons (3/4 stick) unsalted butter
2 tablespoons rum, coffee, or water

Set the bowl in a skillet of hot but not simmering water and stir until the mixture is smooth. Let cool for 10 minutes, then whisk in:

3 large egg yolks (whites reserved)

Beat in a large bowl on medium speed until soft peaks form, 977:

4 large egg whites, at room temperature
1/4 teaspoon cream of tartar

Increase the speed to high and gradually beat in:

1/4 cup sugar

Beat until the peaks are stiff but not dry, 978. Using a large silicone spatula, stir one-third of the egg whites into the chocolate mixture, then fold in the remaining whites. Pour the batter into the prepared soufflé mold and smooth the top. (The soufflé can be set aside at room temperature, covered with an inverted bowl, for up to 1 hour; or cover with plastic wrap and refrigerate for up to 24 hours before baking.)

Bake until the soufflé is risen and set, 25 to 30 minutes. Serve at once with:

Fresh Berry Coulis, 805, made with raspberries

LEMON SOUFFLÉ

6 to 8 servings

Position a rack in the lower third of the oven. Preheat the oven to 375°F. Prepare a 9-inch or 2-quart soufflé mold, 818.

Melt in a medium saucepan over medium heat:

3 tablespoons unsalted butter

Whisk in until smooth:

1/4 cup all-purpose flour

Cook, stirring, for 1 minute. Remove from the heat and stir in:

1 cup half-and-half
1/2 cup sugar
Grated zest of 2 lemons

Return to the heat and bring just to a boil, whisking constantly. Remove from the heat. Whisk in a large bowl until slightly thickened:

5 large egg yolks (whites reserved)

Very gradually whisk in the cream mixture, then stir in:

1/3 cup strained lemon juice

Beat in another large bowl on medium speed until soft peaks form, 977:

6 large egg whites, at room temperature
1/2 teaspoon cream of tartar
1/8 teaspoon salt

Increase the speed to high and beat until the peaks are stiff but not dry, 978. Using a large silicone spatula, gently fold one-third of the egg whites into the egg yolk mixture, then fold in the remaining whites. Turn the batter into the prepared soufflé mold and smooth the top. Bake until the soufflé is well risen and the top is deep golden brown, 25 to 35 minutes. Serve at once with:

Lemon Sabayon, 807, or Fresh Berry Coulis, 805, made with raspberries

APRICOT SOUFFLÉ

6 to 8 servings

This is the best fruit soufflé we know; the concentrated flavor of the dried apricots adds a surprising richness.

Combine in a medium saucepan:

1 1/2 cups water
1 cup packed moist dried apricots
1/2 cup sugar

Bring to a simmer, cover, and cook for 20 minutes. Let cool, still covered, at least 30 minutes.

Preheat the oven to 350°F. Prepare as for a soufflé mold, 818, six 8-ounce ramekins or eight 6- to 7-ounce ramekins.

Transfer the apricots and syrup to a blender. Add:

2 tablespoons lemon juice

Puree until perfectly smooth, scraping the sides of the blender. If needed, add a tablespoon or two of water. Transfer the puree to a large bowl. Beat on medium speed until soft peaks form, 977:

5 large egg whites, at room temperature
1/4 teaspoon cream of tartar
1/4 teaspoon salt

Increase the speed to high and gradually beat in:

1/4 cup sugar

Beat until the peaks are stiff but not dry, 978. Fold one-third of the egg whites into the apricot puree, then fold in the remaining whites. Divide the batter equally among the prepared ramekins and smooth the tops. They should be filled to the brim. Transfer the ramekins to a baking sheet and bake just until well risen and beginning to brown, 11 to 15 minutes for the larger soufflés, 10 to 13 minutes for the smaller soufflés. Be careful not to overbake or they will fall and turn soupy in the center. If desired, open a slit in the top of each soufflé with 2 forks held back to back and spoon in:

(Crème Anglaise, 806)

SOUR CREAM APPLE SOUFFLÉ CAKE COCKAIGNE

8 servings

The specialty of Irma's grandmother who came from Lübeck, Germany. This is not at all like a standard soufflé, nor is it like a cake. But like so many desserts that defy labels, it is one of our absolute favorites.

Peel, core, and thinly slice:

4 apples

Melt in a large heavy skillet:

4 tablespoons (1/2 stick) unsalted butter

Add the apples and cook over medium heat, stirring often, until tender, about 5 minutes; do not let them brown. Reduce the heat to low. Combine in a medium bowl and pour over the apples:

8 large egg yolks, beaten
1 cup sugar, or more if the apples are very tart
1/2 cup sour cream
(1/2 cup sliced almonds)
2 tablespoons all-purpose flour
Grated zest and juice of 1 lemon
1/4 teaspoon salt

Stir until thickened. Transfer to a large bowl to cool.

Preheat the oven to 325°F. Grease a 13 × 9-inch baking dish. Whip in a large bowl until stiff but not dry, 978:

8 large egg whites

Gently fold the beaten egg whites into the apple mixture. Spread in the prepared baking dish. Combine and sprinkle over the top:

2 tablespoons dry bread crumbs
2 tablespoons slivered almonds
2 tablespoons sugar
1½ teaspoons ground cinnamon

Bake until the top is a deep golden brown and springs back when pressed, about 45 minutes. The cake may be served hot, but it is best very cold, covered with:

Whipped Cream, 791, flavored with vanilla

ABOUT GELATIN DESSERTS

These desserts are some of the most maligned preparations in American culinary history, and yet for many, they remain an important fixture at family dinners, potlucks, and church picnics. Some of the more baroque gelatin centerpieces of the 1950s and '60s are best left to an earlier era, when it was fashionable to suspend almost anything, in almost any combination, in gelatin. However, with a little restraint, a gelatin dessert can be refreshing, beautiful, and delicious.

For some of these time-honored baroque effects, remember that certain ingredients naturally come to rest either at the top or bottom of a gelatin dessert, and you can achieve interesting layered effects by manipulating nuts and fruits of different weights and porosity. Put them in a slightly jelled mixture—about the consistency of unbeaten egg whites—and let them find their own levels. Apple cubes, banana slices, grapefruit sections, pear slices, strawberry halves, nuts, and marshmallows will all float in gelatin, while fresh orange slices, fresh grapes, and canned apricots, cherries, peaches, pears, pineapple, and plums will settle lower in the mold.

Certain fruits, ➤ such as fresh pineapple, kiwi, figs, and papaya, contain enzymes that prevent gelatin from setting. These fruits must be peeled and cooked first in a sugar syrup until completely tender to make them safe to use in gelatin. Canned pineapple is precooked and does not pose a problem. Strong acids can also weaken the effects of gelatin, as can salt. However, sugar, milk, and alcohol all increase the strength of gelatin to a point.

Almost any bowl that splays outward is suitable for a gelatin dessert mold. For straight-sided gelatin desserts, use a springform pan.

To prepare a mold for a gelatin dessert, rinse the mold with water and shake out the excess unless instructed otherwise. Gelatin desserts usually become firm within 3 to 4 hours of refrigeration. Small desserts set in simple molds may be unmolded at this point. Gelatin terrines and large gelatins made in tall or intricate molds should be refrigerated for at least 8 hours, preferably 1 day. Gelatin continues to stiffen over a 24-hour period. Although gelatins must be refrigerated, ➤ they cannot be frozen. (A related exception to this rule is Bavarians, 822.)

To unmold a gelatin dessert, dip the mold into a sink filled with very hot tap water. Dip metal molds for no longer than a couple of seconds; thick molds of glass or ceramic may need to be dipped for up to 10 seconds before they release. Invert a plate over the top of the mold and then turn both over together. If the dessert is reluctant, tilt the mold up slightly at one side and pry a little part of the top away from the mold with a knife. Quickly withdraw the knife as soon as the dessert begins to descend. Desserts set in ring, heart, or star molds are less likely to end up rumpled if you lightly oil the top—which will become the bottom—before unmolding.

Gelatin desserts are delicious served with custard sauces, 806, fruit sauces, 805–6, or Whipped Cream, 791. Pour the sauce over individual servings, or pass a pitcher at the table. For more detail about working with gelatin, see Gelatin, 996. For very rich gelatin desserts, see Bavarian creams, 84, and mousses, 822–23.

MAKING VEGAN MOLDED DESSERTS

To prepare vegan molded desserts, substitute agar, 992, for gelatin; it will not produce a texture exactly like that of gelatin, but the effect is similar. Agar comes in powdered and flake form and may be found at natural foods stores, in the natural foods section of large supermarkets, or at Asian markets.

For firm agar desserts that can be unmolded and hold their shape, ➤ use 1 teaspoon powdered agar per cup of liquid or use 1 tablespoon flakes per cup of liquid. **For soft agar desserts** that have a more gelatin-like texture but are too fragile to unmold, ➤ use ½ teaspoon powdered agar per cup of liquid or 1½ teaspoons flakes per cup of liquid.

Agar must be hydrated for it to create a gel. To do this, combine agar powder or flakes with ½ cup of the liquid used in the recipe. Bring it to a boil, cover, reduce the heat, and simmer for 3 minutes for powder and 10 minutes for flakes or until the agar is dissolved. Then proceed as directed in the recipes.

ADDITIONS TO GELATIN

If you wish to add fresh pineapple, kiwi, figs, or papaya, cook them first in sugar syrup until tender. When choosing additions, bear in mind how the flavors will complement one another.

Prepare any recipe for gelatin, below. Chill the mixture in a bowl, stirring frequently, until it is the thickness of unbeaten egg whites and falls from a spoon in sheets. If you inadvertently let the gelatin set, simply melt it over gently simmering water and start again. Stir into the gelatin or arrange artfully in the mold up to 1½ cups total:

Whole berries, sliced stone fruit, citrus suprêmes, 182, etc.
Nuts, such as pistachios, walnut halves, pecan halves, etc.
Mini marshmallows

Pour the mixture into a wet 3- to 4-cup mold. Refrigerate until set, about 4 hours, before serving.

LEMON OR LIME GELATIN

4 servings

Pour into a medium bowl:

3 tablespoons cold water

Sprinkle over the top:

1 envelope (2¼ teaspoons) unflavored gelatin

Let stand for 5 minutes. Add and stir to dissolve the gelatin:

1⅓ cups boiling water

Add and stir until dissolved:

3/4 cup sugar

1/4 teaspoon salt

Add:

1/3 cup strained lemon or lime juice

Pour the mixture into a wet 3- to 4-cup mold. Refrigerate until set, about 4 hours. If desired, when the mixture is set to the thickness of unbeaten egg whites, stir in:

(1 teaspoon grated lemon or lime zest)

Unmold and serve with:

Whipped Cream, 791, or Crème Anglaise, 806

ORANGE OR GRAPEFRUIT GELATIN

4 servings

Prepare **Lemon or Lime Gelatin, 820,** using only 1/2 cup sugar. For orange gelatin, dissolve the gelatin and sugar in **1 1/3 cups boiling strained orange juice** instead of water (add the lemon or lime juice as directed). For grapefruit gelatin, omit the lemon or lime juice and dissolve the gelatin and sugar in **1 2/3 cups boiling strained grapefruit juice** instead of water. If using zest, substitute **1 teaspoon orange or grapefruit zest.**

FRUIT GELATIN

4 servings

Pour into a small bowl:

3 tablespoons cold water

Sprinkle over the top:

1 envelope (2 1/4 teaspoons) unflavored gelatin

Let stand for 5 minutes. Meanwhile, bring to a simmer in a medium saucepan:

2 cups cranberry, grape, or apple juice

(1 to 3 tablespoons sugar, to taste, depending on the tartness of the juice used)

Remove from the heat, add the softened gelatin, and stir 1 minute to dissolve the gelatin thoroughly. Set the bottom of the saucepan in a bowl of cold water and let the gelatin cool to lukewarm. Meanwhile, prepare:

1 to 1 1/2 cups fruit, such as thinly sliced apples, sliced strawberries, or whole blueberries or raspberries

For a dessert with fruit on the top, divide the fruit among wet 6-ounce bowls or cups, or place it in a wet 4-cup mold, and ladle the gelatin over. If you want the fruit suspended in the dessert, chill the gelatin in a bowl until it is the thickness of unbeaten egg whites. Then stir in the fruit and pour the gelatin into the wet mold(s). Refrigerate until set, about 4 hours.

Unmold. If desired, serve with:

(Heavy cream or Whipped Cream, 791)

CHAMPAGNE OR ROSÉ GELATIN WITH RASPBERRIES

6 servings

Gelatin desserts are not just for children.

Have ready:

One 750 ml bottle Champagne, sparkling rosé, or other dry sparkling wine

Pour 1 cup of the Champagne into a bowl and sprinkle over the top:

2 envelopes (4 1/2 teaspoons) unflavored gelatin

Let stand 5 minutes to soften. Pour the remaining Champagne into a medium saucepan and let settle. Add:

1/3 cup sugar

Bring to a boil, then immediately remove from the heat. Add the gelatin and stir to dissolve. Stir in:

3 tablespoons strained lemon juice

Divide the mixture among 6 wet 6-ounce ramekins, molds, Champagne flutes, or glass tumblers, or one larger mold such as a Bundt pan or bowl. Refrigerate. When the mixture is set to the thickness of unbeaten egg whites, divide among the ramekins or place in the mold:

1 cup fresh raspberries

Unmold and serve with:

Whipped Cream, 791

PANNA COTTA

6 servings

Italian panna cotta is a rich but light, smooth gelatin cream. For a panna cotta with little flecks of vanilla bean dispersed throughout, rather than concentrated on the bottom, refrigerate the panna cotta mixture until it has the consistency of unbeaten egg whites, then give it a good stir and divide among the molds. Like custard, panna cotta invites experimentation and you may flavor it in a variety of ways (see Flavorings for Custard Bases, 813). If desired, substitute 1 cup buttermilk for the whole milk, but stir it in along with the vanilla. Buttermilk will curdle if heated.

Lightly oil six 4- to 6-ounce custard cups or ramekins. Pour into a small bowl:

3 tablespoons cold water

Sprinkle over the top:

1 envelope (2 1/4 teaspoons) unflavored gelatin

Let stand for 5 minutes to soften. Meanwhile, combine in a saucepan:

1 1/2 cups heavy cream

1 cup whole milk

1/2 cup sugar

(1 vanilla bean, split lengthwise, seeds scraped into the pan)

Bring to a boil, stirring, over medium-high heat. Remove from the heat and remove the vanilla bean, if using. Add the softened gelatin and stir for 1 minute until completely dissolved. Stir in:

1 teaspoon vanilla, if not using vanilla bean

(1/2 teaspoon almond extract)

Pour into the prepared cups and refrigerate until firmly set, about 4 hours. If not serving at once, press plastic wrap directly onto the surface of each cream and refrigerate for up to 3 days. Unmold onto plates and serve with:

Kumquat Compote, 184, or sliced fresh fruit and/or fruit sauce, 805–6

YOGURT AND HONEY PANNA COTTA

4 servings

A light and tangy take on the classic. The use of less gelatin makes for a very creamy, barely set dessert. It should be enjoyed straight from the ramekin, and is particularly good when the cream is infused with elderflower blossoms (see Flavorings for Custard Bases, 813).

Pour into a medium saucepan:

1 cup heavy cream or whole milk

Sprinkle over the cream or milk:

1 teaspoon unflavored gelatin

Let stand for 5 minues to soften. Place the saucepan over medium heat and bring to a simmer, whisking until the gelatin is dissolved, about 2 minutes. Remove from the heat and whisk in:

⅓ cup honey

Whisk until dissolved. Whisk in:

1 cup whole-milk plain Greek yogurt
1 teaspoon vanilla
Pinch of salt

If desired, pass the mixture through a fine-mesh sieve. Divide the mixture among four 4-ounce ramekins, glasses, or teacups and refrigerate until set, at least 4 hours. Serve with:

Fresh berries or Fresh Berry Coulis, 805

ABOUT MOUSSES AND BAVARIAN CREAMS

These are soft, light, airy desserts made with beaten egg whites or whipped cream. **Mousse** means "froth" or "foam" in French. Any dessert or savory dish that has a frothy or foamy texture may be dubbed a mousse. Mousse made with gelatin is firm enough to be unmolded. Mousses are traditionally made with raw eggs. If you wish to make a traditional recipe but have concerns about serving raw eggs, use pasteurized eggs, 977.

A **Bavarian cream** is a specific kind of mousse composed of two to three elements: a gelatin-thickened custard (which gives the dessert its firmness and stability), whipped cream, and sometimes beaten egg whites. When set in a towering, crenulated mold and turned out onto a polished silver tray, a Bavarian makes a spectacular finale for a formal dinner party. Bavarians and mousses may be served frozen, which results in a lovely, smooth-textured alternative to ice cream.

A **cold soufflé** is in fact simply a mousse molded in a ramekin or serving dish wrapped with a paper collar. The collar helps the mousse hold its shape above the rim of the dish, and when it is removed the dessert resembles a baked soufflé.

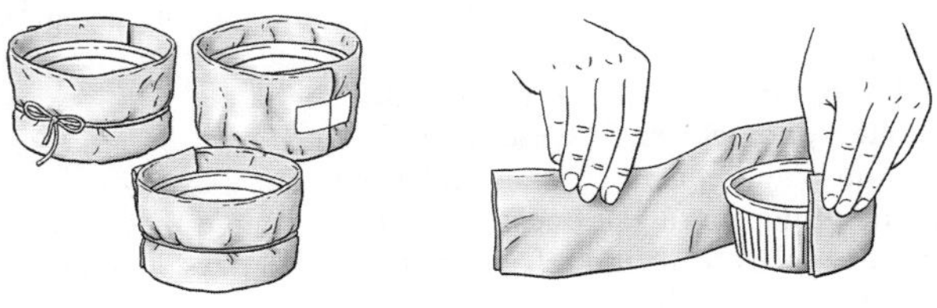

Make a collar with folded wax paper and secure with kitchen string, a rubber band, or tape

Serve mousses and Bavarians in individual bowls, ramekins, wine goblets, Champagne flutes, or wide-mouth half-pint canning jars. Or, create a single large dessert, either in a glass bowl or as for charlottes, 824. Keep in mind that you can also use mousses and Bavarians as pie fillings (crumb or nut crusts, 667–68, are especially nice filled with mousses or Bavarians) or to fill individual tart shells.

Bavarians and mousses may be stored in the freezer for 3 to 4 days. The gelatin in these desserts prevents the formation of coarse crystals.

To unmold a mousse or Bavarian, dip the mold into warm water for a few seconds, place a serving plate over the mold, and flip both over.

CHOCOLATE MOUSSE

6 servings

The director of a boys' camp in Maine once told us about the crestfallen faces in the dining room when it turned out that the "moose" promised for evening dessert had emerged from the pages of *Joy* instead of from the woods.

I. A traditional raw-egg mousse. If using pasteurized eggs, 977, they will require more whipping to form stiff peaks.

Combine in the top of a double boiler or a large heatproof bowl:

6 ounces semisweet or bittersweet chocolate (up to 64% cacao), chopped
2 tablespoons liquor, liqueur, or coffee
2 tablespoons water

Set the bowl over a pan of barely simmering water and stir until the chocolate is melted. Whisk in:

3 large egg yolks

Set aside. Beat in a medium bowl on medium speed until soft peaks form, 977:

3 large egg whites
¼ teaspoon cream of tartar

Gradually beat in:

3 tablespoons sugar

Increase the speed to high and beat until the peaks are stiff but not dry, 978. Fold one-third of the egg whites into the chocolate, then fold the chocolate mixture into the remaining whites. Divide among 6 ramekins or custard cups and refrigerate for at least 4 hours and for up to 24 hours.

II. This mousse uses cooked eggs.

Combine in a large heatproof bowl:

6 ounces semisweet or bittersweet chocolate (up to 64% cacao), chopped
2 tablespoons liquor, liqueur, or coffee
2 tablespoons water

Set the bowl over a pan of barely simmering water and stir until the chocolate is melted. Set the bowl aside (keep the pan of water). Whisk together thoroughly in another heatproof bowl:

3 large eggs
3 tablespoons coffee or water
3 tablespoons sugar

Set the bowl over the simmering water and, stirring constantly with a silicone spatula, heat the mixture until it reaches 160°F. Remove the bowl from the pan of water and beat with a hand mixer until the mixture is light and fluffy, about 5 minutes. Fold one-third of the egg mixture into the chocolate mixture, then fold the chocolate mixture into the remaining egg mixture. Divide among 6 ramekins or custard cups and refrigerate for at least 4 hours and for up to 24 hours.

MILK OR WHITE CHOCOLATE MOUSSE

6 servings

Using whipped cream instead of eggs highlights the flavors of these lighter chocolates. Because white and milk chocolate are much more prone to overheating and seizing up during melting than bittersweet chocolate, be vigilant and make sure the water never simmers.

Heat a saucepan of water until the water is steaming, not simmering. Combine in a medium heatproof bowl:

8 ounces milk or white chocolate, finely chopped
3 tablespoons liquor, liqueur, or water

Remove the saucepan from the heat, place the bowl of chocolate over the steaming water, and stir until the chocolate is completely melted. If needed, set the pan back on the heat to reheat the water. Depending on the chocolate, it may be very thick and pasty after melting. If so, stir in hot water a teaspoon at a time until the chocolate flows smoothly from a spoon held above the bowl. Set aside. Beat in a large bowl, or in a stand mixer with the whisk attachment, until soft peaks form, 977:

1¼ cups heavy cream

Fold one-third of the whipped cream into the chocolate, then fold the chocolate into the remaining whipped cream. Divide the mousse among 6 ramekins or custard cups and refrigerate for at least 2 hours or for up to 24 hours. Alternatively, layer the mousse in glasses with:

(Fresh raspberries or Fresh Berry Coulis, 805, using raspberries)

then refrigerate. Or simply serve the chilled mousse with the berries or coulis.

CHOCOLATE MOUSSE WITH GELATIN

6 servings

When stiffened with a small amount of gelatin, chocolate mousse can be set in a mold and unmolded or used as a filling for a chocolate charlotte or a mousse cake.

Pour into a small cup:

2 tablespoons water

Sprinkle over the top:

1½ teaspoons unflavored gelatin

Let stand for 5 minutes. Prepare:

Chocolate Mousse I or II, 822, or Milk or White Chocolate Mousse, above

with these changes: Substitute the gelatin-water mixture above for an equal amount of the liquid added to the melting chocolate. Fold the whipped eggs or cream in very thoroughly. Spoon the mousse mixture into 6 ramekins or cups or a 5-cup mold or bowl (if you want to unmold the mousse, oil the mold or bowl first). Refrigerate for at least 6 hours to set.

RUM CHOCOLATE MOUSSE

6 servings

This simple, not-too-sweet mousse is adapted from *Joy*'s 1963 edition. If using pasteurized eggs, 977, they will require more whipping to form stiff peaks.

Stir together in a small saucepan over low heat until dissolved:

¼ cup sugar
¼ cup dark rum

Melt in a double boiler or a heatproof bowl set over a pan of barely simmering water:

4 ounces bittersweet chocolate (up to 64% cacao), chopped

When the chocolate is melted, whisk in:

3 tablespoons heavy cream

Gradually whisk the rum syrup into the chocolate until smooth. Let cool. Beat in a medium bowl until stiff but not dry, 978:

2 egg whites
⅛ teaspoon cream of tartar
⅛ teaspoon salt

Fold one-third of the egg whites into the chocolate, then fold in the remaining whites. Whip in a separate bowl until firm peaks form, 977:

1 cup cold heavy cream

Fold the whipped cream into the chocolate mixture. Divide among 6 glasses or cups and refrigerate for at least 2 hours before serving.

CHOCOLATE TERRINE

12 to 16 servings

Made like a chocolate mousse, this rich loaf is firm enough to be cut into slices and served with a sauce. The terrine can be tightly wrapped and frozen for up to 1 month. Let stand at room temperature for 1 hour before slicing and serving.

Lightly oil an 8½ × 4½-inch loaf pan and line with plastic wrap, pressing it firmly into the corners and against the sides.

Melt in a large heatproof bowl set over a pan simmering water, stirring until smooth:

1 pound semisweet or bittersweet chocolate (up to 64% cacao), chopped
2 sticks (8 ounces) unsalted butter, cut into chunks

Set the bowl aside (keep the pan of hot water). Whisk together in a large heatproof bowl:

8 large egg yolks (whites reserved)
⅓ cup cooled strong coffee or ¼ cup water plus 1½ tablespoons liquor or liqueur
½ cup sugar

Place the bowl over the simmering water and whisk constantly until thick, puffy, and shiny, like marshmallow sauce, at least 10 minutes. Remove from the heat and whisk in the chocolate mixture until thoroughly combined. The mixture will deflate a bit. If there is any sign of separation, whisk in cold water, 1 teaspoon at a time, until the mixture is smooth. Beat in a large bowl on medium speed until soft peaks form, 977:

4 large egg whites, at room temperature
¼ teaspoon cream of tartar

Gradually sprinkle in:

1 tablespoon sugar

Increase the speed to high and beat until the peaks are stiff but not dry, 978. Fold one-third of the egg whites into the chocolate mixture, then fold in the remaining whites. Turn the mixture into the prepared pan and cover with plastic wrap. Refrigerate for at least 8 hours. Remove the plastic from the top, invert the terrine onto a serving plate, and peel off the plastic liner. Cut crosswise into slices and serve with:

Crème Anglaise, 806, and/or Fresh Berry Coulis, 805

LEMON OR LIME COLD SOUFFLÉ OR BAVARIAN CREAM

8 servings

If making a cold soufflé, tie paper collars around eight 6-ounce ramekins or one 1½-quart soufflé dish (see illustration, 822). For a Bavarian cream, oil eight 8-ounce custard cups or ramekins or a 2½-quart charlotte or other mold.

Combine in a medium heatproof bowl:

1 tablespoon finely grated lemon or lime zest
½ cup strained lemon or lime juice, chilled

Sprinkle over the top:

1 envelope (2¼ teaspoons) unflavored gelatin

Let stand for 5 minutes. Whisk in a large bowl just until combined:

5 large egg yolks
⅓ cup sugar

Heat in a medium heavy saucepan:

1 cup whole milk

Gradually whisk the hot milk into the egg yolk mixture, then return this mixture to the saucepan. Cook over very low heat, stirring gently, until the mixture is thickened enough to coat the back of a spoon and reaches 175°F on an instant-read thermometer. Immediately pour the hot custard over the gelatin mixture and stir to completely dissolve the gelatin. If desired, strain the mixture. Set the bowl in a pan of cool water and stir until the custard is no longer warm and has thickened slightly. Whip until soft peaks form, 977:

¾ cup cold heavy cream
⅓ cup sugar

If the custard has stiffened, whisk until smooth. Whisk in one-third of the whipped cream and then gently fold in the rest. Turn into the prepared mold(s). Refrigerate for at least 6 hours, or for 10 hours if you plan to unmold the Bavarians. Remove the collar(s) or unmold onto plates. Serve with:

Whipped Cream, 791, or Fresh Berry Coulis, 805

ORANGE COLD SOUFFLÉ OR BAVARIAN CREAM

Combine **2 tablespoons grated orange zest** and **1½ cups strained orange juice** in a small nonreactive saucepan and simmer until reduced to just under ½ cup. Let cool completely, then add **1 tablespoon strained lemon juice.** Prepare **Lemon or Lime Cold Soufflé or Bavarian Cream, above,** substituting the orange reduction for the lemon or lime zest and juice.

CHOCOLATE OR COFFEE BAVARIAN CREAM

8 servings

Without eggs, this and the recipe that follows are not classic but are nevertheless quite good.

Pour into a bowl:

3 tablespoons cold milk

Sprinkle over the top:

1 envelope (2¼ teaspoons) unflavored gelatin

Let stand for 5 minutes. Bring to just under a simmer in a small saucepan:

1½ cups milk or ½ cup milk plus 1 cup heavy cream

Remove from the heat and add, stirring to dissolve the sugar:

4 ounces semisweet or bittersweet chocolate (up to 64% cacao), finely chopped, or 1 tablespoon instant coffee powder
¼ to ⅓ cup sugar (the larger amount, if using coffee)
⅛ teaspoon salt

Stir in the gelatin until dissolved. Stir in:

1 teaspoon vanilla

Chill until the mixture is the thickness of unbeaten egg whites. Whisk the gelatin mixture until fluffy. Whip until firm peaks form:

1 cup cold heavy cream

Fold the cream into the gelatin mixture. Pour into a wet or lightly oiled 4-cup mold. Or, if desired, alternate the cream in layers (in a 5- to 6-cup mold) with:

(6 crumbled macaroons or ladyfingers, soaked in rum or dry sherry, and ½ cup ground nuts, preferably almonds)

Chill for at least 8 hours if you plan to unmold the cream. Serve with:

Whole or crushed berries or sliced fresh fruit and Whipped Cream, 791

BAVARIAN BERRY CREAM

8 servings

Crush in a large bowl:

1 quart strawberries, hulled, or raspberries

Add:

½ cup sugar

Let stand for 30 minutes.

Pour into a small bowl:

3 tablespoons cold water

Sprinkle over the top and let stand for 5 minutes:

2 teaspoons unflavored gelatin

Add and stir to dissolve the gelatin:

3 tablespoons boiling water

Stir the gelatin mixture into the berries. If desired, add:

(1 tablespoon lemon juice)

Refrigerate the gelatin mixture until it is the thickness of unbeaten egg whites. Meanwhile, whip until firm peaks form:

1 cup cold heavy cream

Gently fold the whipped cream into the berry mixture. Pour into a lightly oiled or wet 1½-quart mold. Refrigerate for 8 hours if you plan to unmold the cream.

Serve with:

Fresh Berry Coulis, 805, made with strawberries

ABOUT CHARLOTTES

A charlotte consists of a mousse corseted in ladyfingers or slices of cake or jelly roll and served unmolded. The filling can be any mousse or pudding, including the ones below, but the best choices are those that are stabilized with gelatin. It is important to distinguish between this type of charlotte and another in which a stiff fruit puree, typically apple, is encased in buttered bread strips and baked.

For the classic charlotte, you will need a mold with a flat bottom and straight or only gently sloping sides. For most of our recipes, you will need a mold that measures about 7 inches across the top and has a capacity of 2 to 2½ quarts. ➤ Charlottes can also be prepared in 9 × 5-inch loaf pans, 2- to 2½-quart soufflé dishes, 8-inch square baking pans, 9 × 2-inch round cake pans, or 8 × 3-inch springform pans.

The simplest cake linings are made with thin sheets of Génoise, 721, French Sponge Cake (Biscuit), 721, or Sponge Cake, 720. Cut the cake into long strips and arrange them along the inside of the mold and, if desired, line the bottom with a single large piece cut to fit. If you are using a charlotte mold, soufflé dish, or other deep round mold, the top (which is to say, the bottom of the mold) is prettiest when left bare, and, if desired, adorned after the dessert is turned out of the mold. If you are working with a shallow mold, you will probably want to line the bottom of the mold so that the top of the dessert is covered.

Instead of cake, you may also use filled slices of Jelly Roll, 747, or ladyfingers to line the mold. If using ladyfingers, you will need 3- to 4-inch soft ladyfingers, store-bought or homemade, 750. If you make the ladyfingers yourself, pipe them close together (about ¼ inch apart) on the baking sheet so that they fuse during baking, then simply fit a strip of ladyfingers into the mold. For a shallow mold, cut the ladyfingers in half and arrange them cut ends up around the edges of the mold. Brush the ladyfingers with Moistening Syrup, 800, or the syrup specified in the recipe. Do not use the hard, dry, crunchy ladyfingers often used for tiramisù.

You do not have to cover the top (which will be, after unmolding, the bottom), but if you have ladyfingers or cake to spare, it is a good idea to do so. Charlottes that rest on a solid base are more stable and make neater slices than those with unlined bottoms. Trim the ladyfingers or cake as necessary to make a neat fit. Use the leftover scraps from lining the bottom and sides of the mold as well. Then trim the side lining flush with the bottom lining. If you have any moistening syrup left over, brush it over the bottom lining.

Lining a charlotte mold with slices of jelly roll

Charlottes can also be made in individual sizes. Oil eight to ten 8-ounce soufflé ramekins or small charlotte molds and line with wax or parchment paper. Line the sides with ladyfingers that have been cut crosswise in half, arranging them cut side up; leave both bottom and top bare.

Refrigerate individual desserts for 3 to 4 hours and large desserts for at least 4 hours. If the mold is tall, narrow, or complex, allow at least 12 hours.

To unmold a charlotte, dip the mold into warm water for a few seconds, place a serving plate over the mold, and flip both over.

CHARLOTTE RUSSE

8 to 10 servings

For more information on alternate molds and cake linings, see About Charlottes, 824.

Have ready:

18 to 36 soft ladyfingers, store-bought or homemade, 750

If desired, brush the ladyfingers with:

(⅓ cup brandy, Grand Marnier, framboise, or coffee)

Lightly oil a 2- to 2½-quart charlotte mold and line the sides (and, if desired, the bottom) with the ladyfingers, trimming them, if needed, to fit inside the mold. Pour into the top of a double boiler or a heatproof bowl:

3 tablespoons cold water

Sprinkle over the top:

1½ teaspoons unflavored gelatin

Let stand for 5 minutes, then whisk in:

6 large egg yolks
½ cup sugar

Set the top of the double boiler or bowl over a pan of simmering water and, whisking constantly, heat the mixture until thick and puffy, like marshmallow sauce. (If you are concerned about eating uncooked eggs, periodically insert an instant-read thermometer off the heat, until the mixture reaches 160°F.) Set the double boiler top or bowl in cold water and, whisking now and then, cool to room temperature. Stir in:

2 tablespoons brandy, Cognac, or water
2 teaspoons vanilla

Beat in a separate large bowl on medium speed until light and fluffy:

4 tablespoons (½ stick) unsalted butter, softened
¼ cup sugar
⅛ teaspoon salt

Beat in the cooked egg yolk mixture by heaping tablespoons. Whip in a separate bowl until firm peaks form, 977:

1½ cups cold heavy cream

Using a silicone spatula, stir ½ cup of the whipped cream into the egg yolk mixture, then gently fold in the remaining whipped cream. Turn the mixture into the prepared mold. Cover the top with additional ladyfingers, if you have them, and brush with additional liquor or coffee, if using. Refrigerate for at least 8 hours, or for up to 3 days. Unmold the charlotte, above, onto a plate. Serve with:

Fresh Berry Coulis, 805, using raspberries, or Cherries Jubilee, 181

CHOCOLATE CHARLOTTE

8 servings

For more information on alternate molds and cake linings, see About Charlottes, 824.

Have ready:

18 to 36 soft ladyfingers, store-bought or homemade, 750, or Génoise, 721, Biscuit, 721, or Sponge Cake Sheet, 747, cut into strips to fit the mold being used

Stir together in a small bowl until the sugar is dissolved:

¼ cup hot water or coffee
2 tablespoons sugar

Let cool to lukewarm, then stir in:

¼ cup liquor, liqueur, or coffee

Lightly oil a 2- to 2½-quart charlotte mold and line the sides (and, if desired, the bottom) with the ladyfingers or cake. Brush the coffee syrup onto the ladyfingers or cake strips. Prepare:

Chocolate Mousse with Gelatin, 823

If you wish, fold in:

(½ cup chopped toasted, 1005, nuts)

Fill the lined mold with the mousse. Cover the top with additional ladyfingers or cake scraps, if you have them, then brush with any remaining syrup. Refrigerate for at least 4 hours, or for up to 3 days. Unmold the charlotte, 825, onto a plate. Serve with:

Whipped Cream, 791, Coffee Crème Anglaise, 806, or a chocolate sauce, 807–8

COFFEE CHARLOTTE

6 servings

Prepare **Chocolate Charlotte, 825,** substituting **Coffee Bavarian Cream, 824,** for the chocolate mousse. Serve with **Crème Anglaise, 806, flavored with rum,** or **Chocolate Sauce, 807.**

TIRAMISÙ

10 to 12 servings

Tiramisù is Italian for "pick me up"—and how could ladyfingers soaked in espresso and brandy and slathered with Marsala-laced mascarpone fail to do so? Feel free to use the crunchy, store-bought variety of ladyfingers (do not bake further).

Have ready:

24 ladyfingers, store-bought or homemade, 750, or Génoise, 721, baked in two 8-inch square pans

Preheat the oven to 350°F.

If using the génoise, use only 1½ layers. Cut the whole layer into 8 strips and the half layer into 4 (reserve the remainder for another use). Cut all the strips widthwise in half. Arrange the ladyfingers or génoise strips on a baking sheet. Bake until golden brown and crisp, 8 to 10 minutes. Let cool. Meanwhile, prepare:

Zabaglione, 807

Let the zabaglione cool for about 15 minutes. Combine in a large bowl and whip until the mixture holds soft peaks, 977:

12 ounces mascarpone, softened
½ cup heavy cream
2 teaspoons vanilla

Fold the zabaglione into the whipped mascarpone and set aside. Combine in a shallow dish:

1½ cups cooled espresso or extra-strong coffee
3 tablespoons Marsala, rum, or brandy
3 tablespoons sugar

Have ready:

4 ounces semisweet or bittersweet chocolate (up to 64% cacao), grated

Dip half of the ladyfingers or génoise strips into the espresso mixture and arrange in a 2- to 3-quart serving bowl, leaving a little space between them. Spread half of the mascarpone filling over and between them. Sprinkle with half of the grated chocolate. Dip the remaining ladyfingers or génoise strips into the remaining espresso mixture and arrange on top. Spread the remaining filling over and between them, and sprinkle with the remaining chocolate. Sift over the top:

1 tablespoon unsweetened cocoa powder

Cover and refrigerate for at least 1 hour, or for up to 24 hours before serving.

ETON MESS

6 servings

Named for the British boarding school Eton College where it originated, this is an unruly, summery dessert of crushed meringues and berries folded into whipped cream. It is the perfect dessert for peak strawberry season, although raspberries make an admirable stand-in. If desired, you may use store-bought meringue cookies in this recipe. Crumble 12 small meringues and fold them into the whipped cream. Serve garnished with additional meringues.

Prepare:

Meringue Kisses, 795

Combine in a medium bowl:

1 quart strawberries, hulled and coarsely chopped
2 tablespoons to ¼ cup sugar, depending on the sweetness of the berries
(2 tablespoons framboise, kirsch, or maraschino liqueur)

Allow to macerate at least 15 minutes. Prepare:

Whipped Cream, 791, or Whipped Crème Fraîche, 791

To serve, crumble one-third of the meringues and fold them into the whipped cream, then fold in half the strawberries (if the berries have exuded a lot of liquid, leave most of it behind in the bowl and save it to drizzle over the finished desserts). Divide the mixture among 6 dessert bowls or cups and garnish each with a whole meringue kiss and some of the remaining strawberries (store any leftover kisses in an airtight container for another use). Serve immediately.

PAVLOVA

6 servings

Pavlova is the larger, statelier cousin of Eton Mess, above. Named after Russian ballerina Anna Pavlova, it is widely believed to have originated in Australia or New Zealand, although some say it was created in the United States. Regardless, it is delicious, and can be made using almost any fruit. You may bake the meringue base several hours ahead of time, but do not top with whipped cream and fruit until the moment before serving.

Preheat the oven to 300°F. Line a baking sheet with parchment paper. Place a 9-inch round cake pan on top of the parchment and trace around it with a pencil. Flip the parchment over so the tracing shows through.

Prepare, using **¾ cup sugar** and whisking **2 teaspoons cornstarch** into the sugar before adding to the egg white mixture:

French Meringue, 794

Scrape the meringue onto the baking sheet within the traced circle and spread it into a disk with a slight depression in the center. Place in the oven and reduce the temperature to 250°F. Bake until the meringue is set, about 1 hour. Turn the oven off and let the meringue cool completely in the oven, about 1 hour more.

While the meringue bakes, prepare one of the following:

Macerated Fruit, 167, Fresh Berry Coulis, 805, or Lemon Curd, 802

Or, if desired, have ready:

(2 cups raspberries, blackberries, halved or quartered hulled strawberries, blueberries, diced mango, passion fruit, sliced kiwi, halved cherries, or a combination)

Transfer the baked meringue to a serving platter. Prepare:

Whipped Cream, 791

Spread the whipped cream over the meringue and top with your choice of fruit topping. Serve immediately.

TRIFLE

12 to 14 servings

Prepare:

Double recipe Crème Anglaise, 806

Refrigerate until cold. Have ready:

24 to 30 ladyfingers, store-bought or homemade, 750, Génoise, 721, or any sponge cake, cut into pieces of any size
¾ cup fruit preserves
2 cups berries or sliced fruit
¼ cup sliced or slivered almonds, toasted, 1005

Arrange half of the ladyfingers or cake pieces in the bottom of a 2- to 3-quart serving bowl. If the bowl is glass, make sure that each layer of ingredients touches the sides of the bowl so that the contrasting layers can be seen. Sprinkle with, if desired:

(3 tablespoons sweet wine [such as port, cream sherry, or Marsala], brandy, whiskey, or rum)

Spread with half the preserves. Sprinkle with half the berries or fruit slices. Top with half the crème anglaise and sprinkle with half the nuts. Top with the remaining ladyfingers, more liquor, if using, and the remaining preserves, fruit, and crème anglaise. Whip until the mixture holds soft peaks, 977:

¾ cup cold heavy cream
1 tablespoon sugar
½ teaspoon vanilla

Spread the whipped cream or pipe it decoratively on top of the trifle. Sprinkle with the remaining nuts. Cover and refrigerate for at least 3 hours, or, preferably, for up to 24 hours before serving.

MONT BLANC

6 servings

You can find many sophisticated versions of this dessert in pastry shops across France. The versions that follow are very simple and rustic: a mountain of chestnut puree topped with a snowy peak of whipped cream.

I. HOMEMADE

You may also use **1 pound vacuum-packed, precooked chestnuts** for this, in which case you do not need to cook them in milk. Simply begin with the sugar syrup step and proceed as directed.

Have ready:

2 pounds unshelled chestnuts

Cut an X on the flat side of each nut. Cook in a saucepan of boiling water to cover for 5 minutes. Turn off the heat. Remove a few nuts at a time and peel off the outer shell and inner membrane. Place the nuts in a medium saucepan with:

4 cups whole milk

Cook at a low simmer until very tender, about 30 minutes. Drain, discarding the milk (or reserve it for another use). Bring to a simmer in another medium saucepan:

1 cup water
1 cup sugar

Add the softened chestnuts and cook until the syrup is reduced and thick enough to coat the nuts, about 15 minutes. Cool until just warm and puree the chestnuts and syrup in a food processor until smooth. Press the chestnut paste through a ricer onto a serving plate in a big mound. Do not mash or compact the chestnuts. Prepare:

Whipped Cream, 791

Place the cream on the chestnut mound and let it flow down the sides. Chill well before serving. Just before serving, grate over the top:

Bittersweet chocolate

And then, as our dear old French friend would have said, "I'd be so pleased, I would not thank the King to be my uncle."

II. STORE-BOUGHT

Mont Blanc is easier to make with store-bought sweetened chestnut puree, but because of its remarkable viscosity the puree needs to be lightened up before it will pass through a ricer. We like to use pastry cream for that purpose.

Prepare:

½ recipe Pastry Cream, 801, or Chocolate Pastry Cream, 801

Allow the pastry cream to cool. Beat in a stand mixer on medium speed until loosened up:

1 cup store-bought sweetened chestnut puree

Gradually beat in ½ cup of the pastry cream, beating until the mixture is smooth. Press the chestnut mixture through a ricer onto a serving plate in a big mound. Top with whipped cream and chocolate as in version I, above.

ABOUT RICE AND TAPIOCA PUDDINGS

Rice puddings may never win any awards for comeliness, but they are the pinnacle of childhood comfort food. Short- and medium-grain white rices are high in starch and thus give puddings an especially smooth and creamy texture. Aromatic long-grain rices, such as basmati and jasmine, add their own characteristic flavors. Brown rice may be used for stovetop pudding, but it will need to simmer longer to become tender. Do not use instant rice. See About Rice, 328. Rice puddings are enhanced by flavorings such as nutmeg, anise, cloves, cinnamon, cardamom, vanilla, and orange zest. You may also add dried fruits such as currants, raisins, chopped apricots, dates, or figs.

For tapioca puddings, you may use any size of tapioca pearl that suits you, but for a traditional tapioca pudding, we recommend small or medium pearls. Keep in mind that the larger the pearls, the longer the cook time. Unless you purchase "minute" or quick-cooking tapioca, ➤ we recommend soaking the pearls for at least 1 hour before cooking, although an overnight soak is optimal.

➤ Whether you are using pearls or quick-cooking tapioca, cook only until the tapioca is translucent and no longer gritty. At this point the pudding may still look thin, but it will continue to set up as it cools. For more information on tapioca, see 1027.

Rice and tapioca puddings are easily made dairy- and egg-free. You may substitute soy, almond, cashew, or beverage-style coconut milk for the dairy milk, and eggs can be left out entirely, if desired—rice and tapioca contain a lot of starch and do not require eggs to produce a thick consistency.

BAKED RICE PUDDING

6 to 8 servings

Preheat the oven to 325°F. Butter a 1½-quart shallow baking dish or six 6-ounce custard cups or ramekins. If desired, coat the bottom and sides with:

(Fine cake or cookie crumbs)

Place in a large bowl:

2 cups cooked short- or medium-grain white rice, 343

Beat together in a medium bowl until well blended:

1⅓ cups whole milk
2 large eggs
6 tablespoons sugar or brown sugar
2 tablespoons unsalted butter, softened
1 teaspoon vanilla
⅛ teaspoon salt

Add the milk mixture to the rice. If desired, also add:

(⅓ cup raisins or golden raisins)
(Finely grated zest of ½ lemon)
(1 teaspoon lemon juice)

Stir lightly with a fork to combine. Spread the rice in the prepared baking dish or cups. Bake until a knife inserted in the center comes out clean, about 40 minutes for the large pudding or 25 minutes for the smaller puddings. Serve warm with:

Cream or a fruit sauce, 805–6

STOVETOP RICE PUDDING

6 to 8 servings

For a dairy-free rice pudding, substitute beverage-style coconut milk for the milk in this recipe.

Combine in a large heavy saucepan:

4½ cups whole milk
¾ cup white rice
¼ cup sugar
¼ teaspoon salt
(1 wide strip lemon zest, removed with a vegetable peeler)

Bring to a simmer over medium-high heat, then reduce the heat to low and cook, stirring frequently, until the rice is very tender and the pudding is thick and creamy, about 45 minutes. Remove from the heat and stir in:

2 teaspoons vanilla or 1 teaspoon vanilla and the finely grated zest of 1 lemon

Spoon into a serving bowl or individual cups or ramekins. Serve warm or cold. If storing or serving chilled, press plastic wrap directly onto the surface. If desired, top the pudding(s) with:

(Jam, marmalade, or a fruit sauce, 805–6)
(Whipped Cream, 791)
(Brown sugar)
(Ground cinnamon)

RICE PUDDING BRÛLÉE

Prepare **Stovetop Rice Pudding, above,** and transfer to heatproof ramekins, or make individual **Baked Rice Pudding, above,** omitting the crumb topping. Refrigerate the puddings until cold. Sprinkle each pudding with **2 to 3 teaspoons light brown sugar.** Broil or torch the puddings to caramelize as for **Crème Brûlée, 815.**

SPICED RICE PUDDING

This recipe is based on the Indian dessert *kheer*, a rice pudding flavored with cardamom and saffron.

Proceed as for:

Stovetop Rice Pudding, above

Adding along with the milk and sugar:

1 teaspoon ground cardamom

About 10 minutes before the rice has finished cooking in the milk, add:

¼ teaspoon saffron threads

When the rice has finished cooking, remove from the heat and stir in:

⅓ cup roasted, unsalted pistachios, chopped
(¼ cup slivered almonds, chopped)
(1 teaspoon rose water)

Omit the vanilla, if using.

COCONUT STICKY RICE WITH MANGO

4 to 6 servings

This Thai specialty is very easy to make at home. Purchase 1 mango for every 2 servings.

Soak in water to cover by 2 inches for at least 3 hours or overnight:

2 cups Thai sweet or sticky rice

Drain the rice. Place a steamer basket or steamer insert in a saucepan with 1 inch of water in it. Put the soaked rice in the basket, cover the pan tightly, and steam until the rice is tender, about 20 minutes. While the rice cooks, combine in a small saucepan:

One 13½-ounce can unsweetened coconut milk
⅓ cup packed palm sugar or dark brown sugar
1 teaspoon salt

Stir over medium-low heat until the sugar is dissolved and the mixture is steaming.

Once the rice is cooked, transfer to a bowl and stir in ¾ cup of the coconut milk mixture. Cover and let sit for 10 minutes. Pack the rice into small bowls and unmold into neat mounds on plates. Serve with:

2 or 3 ripe mangos, sliced

Drizzle with more of the coconut milk mixture. If desired, sprinkle with:

(Toasted sesame seeds)

TAPIOCA PUDDING

4 to 6 servings

Using brown sugar adds a hint of caramel flavor.

Whisk together thoroughly in a large heavy saucepan:

2½ cups whole milk
⅓ cup sugar or ½ cup packed brown sugar
¼ cup quick-cooking tapioca
⅛ teaspoon salt

Let stand for 10 minutes, then slowly bring to a simmer over medium heat, stirring constantly. Simmer, stirring, for 2 minutes. If desired, gradually whisk about half of the pudding into:

(1 large egg, well beaten)

Then thoroughly stir the egg mixture into the remaining pudding. Cook, stirring, over low heat just until you see the first sign of thickening, about 3 minutes. Remove from the heat and stir in:

1 teaspoon vanilla

Let cool in the saucepan for 30 minutes; the pudding will thicken considerably. Spoon into cups or bowls. Serve warm or chilled. If you wish, accompany with:

(Whipped Cream, 791, or a fruit sauce, 805–6)
(Cream, fresh berries, crushed or canned fruit, or a chocolate sauce, 807–8)

BAKED PEARL TAPIOCA PUDDING

8 servings

Combine in a bowl:

½ cup small or medium pearl tapioca
1 cup whole milk

Cover and refrigerate overnight. Transfer the tapioca and milk to a heavy saucepan and stir in:

3 cups whole milk

Bring to a boil over medium-high heat, then reduce the heat to low and simmer, stirring frequently, until the mixture is translucent and beginning to thicken, about 12 minutes. Transfer to a large bowl to cool slightly.

Preheat the oven to 325°F. Butter a 2½- to 3-quart baking dish. Beat together in a small bowl:

5 large egg yolks
¾ cup sugar
Grated zest of 1 lemon and juice of ½ lemon, or 1½ teaspoons vanilla

Stir the egg yolk mixture into the cooled tapioca mixture. Beat until stiff but not dry, 978:

5 large egg whites

Fold into the tapioca mixture and pour into the prepared baking dish. Bake until the top is puffed and golden brown and the pudding jiggles when the dish is lightly shaken, about 40 minutes. Serve hot or cold. If desired, serve with:

(Any cooked fruit sauce, 805–6)

COCONUT TAPIOCA PUDDING

6 servings

This pudding is exceptionally good when made with pearl tapioca, however, you can substitute quick-cooking tapioca: Reduce the amount of tapioca to ⅓ cup, soak it for only 10 minutes, and cook the pudding for just 2 minutes at a rolling boil. If desired, substitute beverage-style coconut milk for the milk.

Combine in a large heavy saucepan:

⅔ cup small or medium pearl tapioca
2¾ cups whole milk

Cover and refrigerate for at least 8 hours, or overnight. Stir into the tapioca:

One 13½-ounce can coconut milk
½ cup sugar
⅛ teaspoon salt

Bring to a simmer over medium-high heat, then reduce the heat and gently simmer, stirring constantly, until the pearls are translucent and no longer gritty, about 15 minutes. Be careful not to overcook the pudding, or it will be gluey. Remove from the heat. Whisk in a small bowl until frothy:

1 large egg

Gradually whisk in 1 cup of the hot pudding. Whisk this mixture into the remaining pudding in the pan and let stand for 5 minutes, covered. (The pudding will still be hot enough to cook the egg.) Just before serving, stir in:

⅔ cup shredded or flaked sweetened or unsweetened coconut, toasted, 973

Transfer to a bowl or individual cups and sprinkle with more:

Toasted coconut

Serve warm with:

Fresh tropical fruit such as mango and pineapple, or a fruit sauce, 805–6

ABOUT BREAD PUDDING

Soaking stale bread in a custard base and then baking it is a clever way to transform leftovers into something new and delicious. As with baked custards, bread puddings that are rich in eggs turn grainy and watery unless baked in a water bath. Those made with enough bread to soak up the custard do not need to be baked in a water bath.

Bread puddings may be made with virtually any bread or roll. Egg breads such as challah or brioche produce bread puddings with a light texture. We like to add raisins, chopped dried apricots, toasted nuts, chocolate chips, grated orange or lemon zest, or a few tablespoons of bourbon, brandy, or rum.

These recipes can be baked in a muffin tin to create easy-to-serve individual bread puddings (more crusty, browned surfaces are an added bonus). Simply divide the bread and custard mixture among the muffin cups and halve the baking time.

Bread puddings are best served warm and are especially good served with cream or sweet sauces, as suggested in the recipes below. Most bread puddings can be made 2 to 3 days in advance of serving and reheated in a 300° to 325°F oven for 15 to 30 minutes. Alternatively, you may cut the chilled pudding into thick slabs and reheat them in a buttered nonstick skillet over medium heat until lightly toasted on both sides.

BREAD PUDDING

8 servings

Butter a 2-quart baking dish. Trim the crusts and cut into ½-inch cubes:

12 to 16 ounces sliced white bread, stale but not hard

You should have 5 lightly packed cups. Spread the bread in the prepared baking dish. If desired, scatter over the top:

(¾ cup raisins or other dried fruit)

Whisk together thoroughly in a large bowl:

4 large eggs
3 cups whole milk
¾ cup sugar
1 teaspoon vanilla
¾ teaspoon ground cinnamon
¼ teaspoon grated or ground nutmeg
Pinch of salt

Pour the mixture over the bread and let stand for 30 minutes, periodically pressing the bread down with a spatula to help it absorb the liquid.

Preheat the oven to 350°F.

Bake the pudding in a water bath, 812, until a knife inserted in the center comes out clean, 55 minutes to 1 hour. Serve warm with:

Whipped Cream, 791, or cream

CHOCOLATE-BANANA BREAD PUDDING

10 to 12 servings

Prepare **Bread Pudding, 829,** using **Banana Bread Cockaigne, 626, cut into ½-inch cubes.** Toss **1 cup chocolate chips or chunks** with the bread cubes before pouring the custard into the baking dish. Bake as directed and serve warm. If desired, top with **(Southern Whiskey Sauce, 810, or warm Chocolate Sauce, 807, made with white chocolate)**.

NEW ORLEANS BREAD PUDDING

10 to 12 servings

Spread over the bottom of a 13 × 9-inch baking dish:

3 tablespoons unsalted butter, softened

Cut into ½-inch-thick slices:

1¼ pounds French or Italian bread (1½ to 2 loaves)

Arrange the slices almost upright in tightly spaced rows in the prepared dish. Tuck between the slices:

1 cup raisins

Whisk in a large bowl until frothy:

3 large eggs
4 cups whole milk
2 cups sugar
2 tablespoons vanilla
1 teaspoon ground cinnamon

Pour the liquid over the bread and let stand for 1 hour, periodically pressing the bread down with a spatula to wet the tops of the slices.

Preheat the oven to 375°F.

Bake the pudding until the top is puffed and lightly browned, about 1 hour. When it comes out of the oven, cover with:

Southern Whiskey Sauce, 810

Let cool on a rack for 30 to 60 minutes, then cut into squares and serve.

ABOUT BAKED PUDDINGS

These desserts are firmer and more substantial than cornstarch puddings, because they contain a high proportion of flour, bread crumbs, grains, or some other starch. Baked puddings can be served cold or hot, and they can be prepared in advance and reheated at serving time. While not obligatory, a sauce or accompaniment such as Southern Whiskey Sauce, 810, a custard sauce, 806, or Hot Lemon Sauce, 805, is traditional with most baked puddings. For Baked Rice Pudding, see 826. For a so-called batter pudding, see Cherry Clafoutis, 687.

BAKED FIG PUDDING

14 servings

A rich, dense molasses pudding with hints of warm spice. We love to serve it warm with vanilla ice cream and a sprinkling of whiskey.

Preheat the oven to 325°F. Grease a 9-inch springform pan.

Beat in a large bowl, or in a stand mixer with the paddle attachment, until smooth:

1 stick (4 ounces) unsalted butter, softened

Add and beat until fluffy:

2 large eggs
1 cup molasses

Add:

2 cups finely chopped dried figs
½ teaspoon grated lemon zest
1 cup buttermilk
(½ cup chopped walnuts)

Set aside. Whisk together thoroughly in another large bowl:

2½ cups all-purpose flour
2 teaspoons baking powder
1 teaspoon salt
1 teaspoon ground cinnamon
½ teaspoon grated or ground nutmeg
½ teaspoon baking soda

Stir the flour mixture into the fig mixture until combined. Pour the mixture into the prepared pan. Bake until a toothpick inserted into the pudding comes out clean, about 1 hour. Serve hot with:

Hard Sauce, 810, Salted Caramel Sauce, 809, or a custard sauce, 806

PERSIMMON BUTTERMILK PUDDING

8 servings

A soft pudding with an old-fashioned flavor. Be sure to use very ripe, mushy persimmons.

Preheat the oven to 400°F. Butter a shallow 3-quart baking dish.

Cut lengthwise in half:

6 very ripe large persimmons

Remove any seeds, then scrape the pulp from the skins with a spoon. Puree the pulp in a blender or food processor. If it looks stringy, force it through a sieve with the back of a spoon. Measure 1½ cups pulp. Whisk in a large bowl until light:

4 large eggs

Whisk in the persimmon pulp, then whisk in:

2½ cups buttermilk
4 tablespoons (½ stick) unsalted butter, melted

Whisk together thoroughly in a separate medium bowl:

1½ cups all-purpose flour
1 cup sugar
1½ teaspoons baking powder

1 teaspoon baking soda
½ teaspoon ground cinnamon
½ teaspoon grated or ground nutmeg
½ teaspoon salt

Add the flour mixture to the persimmon mixture and whisk until well blended. Pour the batter into the prepared dish. Bake until the top is deep golden brown and springs back when lightly pressed, about 50 minutes. Serve the pudding warm or cold with:

Whipped Cream, 791, or Hot Lemon Sauce, 805

PUMPKIN BUTTERMILK PUDDING

Prepare **Persimmon Buttermilk Pudding, 830,** substituting **1½ cups canned unsweetened pumpkin puree** for the persimmon pulp. Serve with **Hot Brandy Sauce, 810, Whipped Cream, 791, or vanilla ice cream.**

INDIAN PUDDING

6 to 8 servings

A truly warming dessert, with a taste and texture somewhat like pumpkin pie. This dish is a descendant of the British "hasty pudding." Early American settlers substituted cornmeal, or "Indian meal," for the traditional wheat, as cornmeal was much more readily available.

Preheat the oven to 325°F. Generously butter a 1½- to 2-quart baking dish.

Measure into a large heavy saucepan:

⅔ cup cornmeal

Stir in, very gradually at first to prevent lumps:

4 cups whole milk

Stirring constantly, bring to a boil over medium-high heat. Reduce the heat to low and simmer, stirring frequently, until thick, about 5 minutes. Remove from the heat and whisk in:

⅓ cup sugar
¼ cup molasses
2 large eggs
2 tablespoons unsalted butter, cut into pieces
1 teaspoon ground cinnamon
1 teaspoon vanilla
½ teaspoon ground ginger
⅛ teaspoon grated or ground nutmeg
⅛ teaspoon salt

Turn the pudding into the prepared dish. Bake in a water bath, 812, until the center looks firm but still slightly quivery when the dish is shaken, about 1 hour 10 minutes. A dark crust will form on top. Serve warm with:

Vanilla ice cream or cream

STICKY TOFFEE PUDDING

8 servings

Preheat the oven to 350°F. Butter and flour eight 6-ounce ramekins or a 9 × 2-inch square baking pan.

Combine in a small saucepan:

1½ cups pitted dates, coarsely chopped
1½ cups water

Bring to a boil, then reduce the heat and simmer, uncovered, for 5 minutes. Remove from the heat and stir in:

1¼ teaspoons baking soda

Set aside. Whisk together in a small bowl:

2 cups all-purpose flour
¼ teaspoon baking powder

Beat in a large bowl on high speed until lightened in color and fluffy:

1¼ cups packed light brown sugar
6 tablespoons (¾ stick) unsalted butter, softened

Beat in one at a time:

3 large eggs

Beat in:

1½ teaspoons vanilla

Gradually add the flour mixture, beating on low just until mixed. Stir in the date mixture until just combined. Pour into the prepared ramekins or pan. If using ramekins, put them on a baking sheet. Bake until the pudding is a deep golden brown and a skewer comes out moist but clean, 20 to 25 minutes for ramekins, about 35 minutes for a single large pan. Cool on a rack for 10 minutes. Run a knife around the edge of the ramekins or pan, then turn out the pudding(s) and invert onto the rack, right side up, to cool slightly. Serve warm, each serving covered generously with warm:

Butterscotch Sauce, 809

ABOUT STEAMED PUDDINGS

Steamed puddings form a diverse group of dense, often heavily spiced desserts hailing from England. Some of these taste much like fruitcake, while others have moist, soufflé-like textures. If you do not have a pudding basin—a deep bowl of heatproof ceramic—you may use any heatproof bowl of the same capacity called for in a recipe with equally good results. Grease metal bowls especially well, as the puddings are more prone to sticking to metal than to glass or ceramic. Some specialty cookware stores sell fancy pudding molds. These are usually a tube design and come with a cover that snaps on tightly. Only plum pudding or other very firm puddings should be prepared in such molds. Lighter, more fragile steamed puddings, such as Steamed Chocolate Feather Pudding, 832, will stick hopelessly and may collapse (or, worse, explode) if cooked tightly covered. ➤ Whatever mold you choose, be sure to fill it only two-thirds full to account for any rise during cooking.

To steam a pudding on the stovetop, find a pot large enough to hold the pudding basin or bowl comfortably. If you are steaming several small plum puddings, a covered turkey roaster, set over two burners, is convenient. To insulate the bottom of the pudding, set a trivet, rack, or folded kitchen towel in the bottom of your pot. Place the pudding in the pot, then pour in enough *boiling* water to reach one-half to two-thirds the way up the sides of the pudding bowl. Bring the water back to a boil over high heat, then reduce the heat to a brisk simmer. Cover the pot tightly and steam the pudding until done, checking the pot every 30 minutes and replenishing with boiling water as needed. When removing the cooked pudding from the pot, protect your hands with oven or silicone mitts.

You may also steam puddings in the oven using a water bath—an especially convenient option if your pudding basin or molds will not fit in your largest pot.

To steam puddings in the oven, preheat the oven to 350°F. Choose a Dutch oven, or a roasting or baking pan large enough to accommodate the pudding mold(s) comfortably. Individual molds should not touch each other or the pan sides. Arrange the pudding in the pan and fashion a large, double-layer sheet of foil that will form a tent over the pudding and extend past the pan edges. Fold the foil around the lip of the pan to form as tight a seal as you can, leaving one corner open for pouring water into. Bring a large pot or kettle of water to a boil. Open the oven door and pull out an oven rack, place the pan on it, and immediately pour enough boiling water into the pan to come two-thirds of the way up the sides of the pudding(s). Carefully crimp the foil over the remaining corner, close the oven, and steam for the same amount of time called for in the recipe, checking the water level every 30 minutes by carefully lifting a corner of the foil with a pair of tongs. To cook evenly, steam must circulate over the top of larger puddings, but smaller puddings may be individually covered with foil or wax paper and cooked in a water bath as for baked custards, 812.

▲ At high altitudes, reduce the leavening for these puddings by half.

STEAMED CHOCOLATE FEATHER PUDDING

8 to 10 servings

Reminiscent of a chocolate soufflé, but more substantial.

Preheat the oven to 350°F.

Spread on a baking sheet:

1 cup fine dry bread crumbs

Toast, stirring 2 or 3 times, until lightly golden, about 3 minutes. Let cool completely. Very generously butter a 2-quart heatproof bowl or pudding basin. Sprinkle the inside of the bowl with 2 tablespoons of the toasted crumbs, tilting to coat. Combine in a large heatproof bowl:

8 ounces semisweet or bittersweet chocolate (up to 64% cacao), chopped
½ cup heavy cream
4 tablespoons (½ stick) unsalted butter
2 tablespoons dark rum or strong coffee
Finely grated zest of 1 orange

Set the bowl in a skillet of almost simmering water and stir until the mixture is smooth. Remove from the heat and whisk in:

6 large eggs
½ cup sugar
1 tablespoon vanilla
1 teaspoon ground cinnamon

Sprinkle the remaining bread crumbs over the chocolate mixture along with:

2 tablespoons unsweetened cocoa powder

Fold until the crumbs and cocoa powder are incorporated. Turn the batter into the prepared mold and cover with an inverted plate. Set a rack or folded kitchen towel in the bottom of a pot large enough to hold the pudding comfortably. Set the pudding inside and pour enough boiling water into the pot to come halfway up the sides of the mold. Bring the water to a brisk simmer over medium-high heat and tightly cover the pot. Replenishing the water as needed, steam the pudding until the top has flattened and the center feels firm, about 1 hour 15 minutes. Turn off the heat and let the pudding stand in the covered pot for 15 minutes. Invert the pudding onto a platter and serve with:

Whipped Cream, 791, or Salted Caramel Sauce, 809

STEAMED CARAMEL PUDDING

10 to 12 servings

Ground almonds give this moist, flavorful pudding a fine-grained texture.

Preheat the oven to 350°F.

Spread on a baking sheet:

2 cups slivered almonds

Toast, stirring 2 or 3 times, until golden brown, 5 to 7 minutes. Let cool completely, then grind in a food processor until fine but not at all oily. Generously butter a 2-quart heatproof bowl or pudding basin. Sprinkle the inside of the bowl with 3 tablespoons of the ground almonds, tilting to coat. Heat in a heavy saucepan over medium-high heat:

1½ cups sugar
3 tablespoons very hot water

Stir until the sugar is dissolved. Boil until the syrup begins to darken around the edges. Gently swirl the pan until the caramel turns deep amber. Remove from the heat and carefully stir in:

1 cup heavy cream
6 tablespoons (¾ stick) unsalted butter, cut in pieces

If necessary, heat briefly over low heat to melt the caramel, stirring until smooth. Transfer the caramel to a large bowl and let cool to lukewarm. Beat the remaining ground almonds into the caramel along with:

6 large egg yolks
⅓ cup all-purpose flour
1 tablespoon vanilla
¾ teaspoon salt

Beat in a large bowl on medium speed until foamy:

6 large egg whites, at room temperature

Add:

½ teaspoon cream of tartar

Beat until soft peaks form, then increase the speed to high and beat until the peaks are stiff but not dry, 977. Using a large silicone spatula, stir one-quarter of the egg whites into the caramel mixture to lighten it, then gently but thoroughly fold in the rest. Turn the batter into the prepared mold and cover the top with an inverted plate or cake pan. (The uncooked pudding can be refrigerated for up to 4 hours before steaming.)

Set a rack or folded kitchen towel in the bottom of a pot large enough to hold the pudding comfortably. Set the pudding inside and pour enough boiling water into the pot to come halfway up the sides of the mold. Bring the water to a brisk simmer over medium-high heat and tightly cover the pot. Replenishing the water as needed, steam the pudding until a skewer inserted in the center comes out with only a few moist crumbs clinging to it, about 2 hours. Turn off the heat and let the pudding stand in the covered pot for 15 minutes. Invert the pudding onto a platter and serve with:

Whipped Cream, 791

STEAMED PLUM PUDDING

1 large or 2 or 3 small puddings; 12 to 16 servings

A festive Christmas dish that contains no plums (the English, who created it, called most dried fruits plums). Making it requires patience: Slow cooking is necessary so that the suet melts before the flour particles expand. If cooked too fast, the pudding will be hard. Many cooks set aside a calm day early in the holiday season for this project, for the pudding will only improve and mature while stored. An Irish friend's mother steams her pudding a year in advance and stores it covered in the refrigerator, "feeding" it whiskey every other month (for more, see About Fruitcakes, 739).

To make a single large pudding, use a 3-quart pudding mold, a 3-quart pudding basin, or a deep heatproof glass or ceramic bowl with a capacity of 3 to 3½ quarts. To make smaller puddings, use 2 or 3 molds, basins, and/or baking dishes with a total capacity of 3 to 4 quarts. Very generously grease the mold(s) with vegetable shortening.

Bring to a boil in a large saucepan:

2½ cups raisins
2 cups dried currants
2 cups water

Cover tightly and simmer gently for 20 minutes, then uncover and cook, stirring, until nearly all the liquid has evaporated. Let cool to room temperature. Combine in a large bowl:

1½ cups all-purpose flour
8 ounces ground or finely chopped beef suet, 1023

Rub together lightly with your hands just until the suet particles are separated. Add:

1 cup firmly packed dark brown sugar
1½ teaspoons ground cinnamon
1½ teaspoons ground ginger
½ teaspoon ground cloves
½ teaspoon salt

Rub together just until blended. Whisk together thoroughly in a separate bowl:

4 large eggs
⅓ cup brandy or Cognac
⅓ cup cream sherry

Stir the egg mixture into the flour mixture, then stir in the raisin mixture. If desired, also stir in:

(½ cup finely chopped dates)
(½ cup finely chopped candied citron)

Pour the batter into the prepared mold(s), leaving at least 1 inch of headspace for expansion. If you are using a pudding mold with a cover, grease the inside of the cover and snap it in place. Otherwise, crimp a sheet of foil over the rim of each mold allowing little or no overhang down the sides, and cover with an inverted plate.

Set a rack or folded kitchen towel in the bottom of a pot large enough to hold the pudding comfortably. Set the pudding inside and pour enough boiling water into the pot to come two-thirds of the way up the sides of the mold(s). Cover the pot tightly. Bring the water to a boil over high heat, then adjust the heat to maintain a brisk simmer. Replenishing the pot with boiling water as necessary, steam a single large pudding for 6 to 7 hours, 2 smaller puddings for 4 to 5 hours, or 3 small puddings for 3 to 4 hours. When done, the pudding should be very dark in color nearly to the center. At this point, a large pudding can be kept warm in the covered pot, with the heat off, for 3 hours; smaller puddings for about 1½ hours.

Remove the pudding(s) and let stand at room temperature for 20 minutes, then invert onto a platter. If you wish to flame the pudding, warm to barely lukewarm in a small saucepan:

½ cup brandy or Cognac

Drizzle the liquor over the pudding and then, standing back, ignite with a long match, lighter, or torch. Serve with:

Crème Anglaise, 806, Hot Wine or Plum Pudding Sauce, 811, or Fluffy Hard Sauce, 810

To store the pudding, cool to room temperature in the mold(s), then turn out. Wrap first in plastic, then in foil; refrigerate for up to 1 year—the pudding will become softer, darker, and more flavorful with age. To reheat, return the pudding to its original mold, well greased, and steam again in briskly simmering water for 1½ to 2 hours for a large pudding, about 1 hour for smaller puddings, or until a knife inserted in the center for 15 seconds comes out hot.

ABOUT PANCAKE AND WAFFLE DESSERTS

There are a delicious handful of recipes in the pancakes and waffles chapter that make sweet endings to a meal: Crêpes Suzette, 646, Crêpes with Caramelized Apples, 647, Crêpe Cake, 647, and Palatschinken, 648, a traditional Austrian dessert. Don't be limited to just these, however, for any pancake or waffle can be dressed up and served for dessert, topped with any of the following:

Sour cream, crème fraîche, or Whipped Cream, 791
Strawberry or other preserves
Chocolate Sauce, 807, or Chocolate Custard Sauce, 806
Coffee Crème Anglaise, 806
Hard Sauce, 810, or Southern Whiskey Sauce, 810
Butterscotch Sauce, 809
Hot Buttered Maple Sauce, 811
Cherries Jubilee, 181, Fresh Berry Coulis, 805, or Mango Coulis, 805
Ice cream, 838–44

CHOCOLATE FONDUE

Use for dipping fruit—pieces of pineapple, banana, or orange—or small squares of cake.

I. *1⅔ cups*

Combine in a small saucepan and stir over low heat until smooth:

1½ cups semisweet chocolate chips
¾ cup evaporated milk
(5 large marshmallows or ½ cup mini marshmallows)

Keep warm in a fondue pot.

II. *1½ cups*

Heat in a small saucepan over medium-low heat until warm:

¾ cup whole milk, light or heavy cream, coffee, or sherry

Add and cook over low heat, stirring until smooth:

4 ounces unsweetened chocolate, chopped
1 cup sugar
1 teaspoon vanilla or rum
¼ teaspoon salt

Keep warm in a fondue pot.

COEUR À LA CRÈME

8 servings

Think of this as a barely sweet, crustless, no-bake cheesecake; a perfect, creamy pedestal for ripe, seasonal fruit. If you have the traditional heart-shaped molds with perforated bottoms, line them with dampened cheesecloth and drain the cream directly in the molds for 24 hours.

Have ready:

1 cup sour cream or Whipped Cream, 791

Beat in a separate medium bowl until combined:

1 pound cream cheese, softened
¼ cup powdered sugar
2 tablespoons heavy cream
⅛ teaspoon salt

Fold the sour cream or whipped cream into the cream cheese mixture. Line a sieve with moistened cheesecloth and set it over a bowl. Spoon the mixture into the sieve and refrigerate for 24 hours to drain. Divide the cheese among 8 small ramekins or other molds and refrigerate for 1 hour.

Unmold and serve with:

Strawberries, raspberries, or other fresh fruit or fruit sauce, 805–6

POACHED PEARS IN RED WINE

4 servings

Combine in a saucepan or pot just large enough to hold the pears in one layer lying on their sides:

1½ cups dry red wine
1 cup sugar
One 2-inch strip lemon zest (removed with a vegetable peeler)
2 tablespoons lemon juice
1 cinnamon stick
6 whole cloves or 4 cardamom pods, lightly crushed

Bring to a boil, then reduce the heat to low and simmer, covered, for 5 minutes. Peel and slice ½ inch from the bottom of:

4 whole pears such as Bosc or Anjou

Add the pears to the pot, keeping the liquid at a low simmer. Poach, uncovered, until tender, 10 to 20 minutes, turning frequently. The pears can be set aside at room temperature in the poaching liquid, covered, for up to 12 hours, or refrigerated for up to 3 days. The longer they sit, the more deeply they will color; turn them periodically to tint them evenly.

Serve the pears upright on the plate. They are delicious warm, at room temperature, or chilled, with a few spoonfuls of the poaching liquid. If desired, also serve with:

(Crème Anglaise, 806)

For an elegant presentation, remove the pears from the syrup and boil the syrup over high heat until reduced to about ⅔ cup of thick glaze. Strain to remove the spices. Serve the pears on plates, drizzled with the glaze.

STRAWBERRY SHORTCAKE

8 shortcakes

Have ready:

8 Quick Cream Biscuits or Shortcakes, 636, or Classic Scones, 637, or sixteen 2½-inch squares or rounds of Sponge Cake, 720, or Pound Cake, 726
Double recipe Macerated Fruit, 167, using strawberries

Just before serving, reheat the biscuits or scones in a 250°F oven for 10 minutes. (Do not heat sponge cake or pound cake, if using.)

Meanwhile, prepare:

1½ recipes Whipped Cream, 791

Split each warm biscuit in half with a fork. Place the bottom of each biscuit (or a layer of sponge cake or pound cake) on each of 8 dessert plates. Spoon the berry mixture over and top with the biscuit tops or another layer of cake. Spoon a generous dollop of cream on top of each shortcake. Serve immediately.

FLAMBÉED FRUIT

3 servings

Melt in a large skillet over medium-low heat:

3 tablespoons butter

Add and stir until dissolved and bubbling thickly:

3 tablespoons brown sugar

Add 2 of the following:

3 bananas, halved lengthwise
3 mangoes, pitted and sliced
3 peaches, pitted and sliced
Three ½-inch-thick slices pineapple

Simmer until tender, basting occasionally and turning the fruit pieces to caramelize both sides. Add:

2 ounces warmed brandy, dark rum, or liqueur

Cover the skillet for about 30 seconds to heat everything through, then remove the lid, light the liquor with a long match or lighter, and let it flame until it extinguishes itself. If needed, cover the skillet with a lid to extinguish the flames. Serve immediately.

THE CHEESE COURSE

The cheese course may be served after the main course or after a salad that follows the main course. Cheese may also be served following dessert or instead of it, with fresh, ripe fruit. ➤ Cheeses should always be served at room temperature. Any that are best when *coulant*, or runny, should be removed from the refrigerator 1 hour before serving. Softened cultured butter may also be served with a cheese course.

An ideal cheese course includes ➤ around 3 to 5 cheeses. These should be of different types that contrast with one another in texture and flavor. For instance, one fresh goat cheese; one bloomy-rind cheese, such as Brie or Camembert, or a washed-rind cheese such as Pont-l'Évêque or Époisses; and one blue-veined cheese such as Roquefort, Gorgonzola, or Stilton. Alternately, a single cheese may be served: irregular chunks of crumbly high-quality Parmigiano-Reggiano drizzled with high-quality balsamic vinegar or glaze, for example; a ripe whole Brie, or a wheel of Stilton soft enough to be scooped out with a spoon. Ask a dedicated cheesemonger to help you select cheeses that complement one another.

Serve with fresh or dried fruit such as pears, grapes, figs, or dried apricots. Good bread or crackers are also essential. Our favorite bread to serve with cheese is walnut bread. Unsalted toasted or freshly shelled nuts or roasted chestnuts are pleasant accompaniments. Also include a fruit chutney or Italian *mostarda* with sharp Cheddar; Membrillo (Quince Paste), 194, with Manchego or fresh goat cheese; and fig preserves with any aged, sharp cheese.

If desired, serve cheese with wine, 34. For more general information on serving cheese, see Cheese Platters, 45, in the Appetizers chapter. For more on different cheeses, see Cheese Styles and Types, 962.

ICE CREAM AND FROZEN DESSERTS

Considering the relatively recent advent of refrigeration technology, one might think frozen desserts an invention of the modern world. In reality, humans have craved cold treats for centuries—and have gone to extraordinary lengths to procure them. In King Solomon's day, peasants ferried snow from the mountains to ice the drinks of royalty and the very wealthy. In the third century, during the reign of the Chinese Emperor King Tang of Shang, an iced dessert was made from buffalo milk, camphor, and flour. Ancient examples such as these are many, though it was not until the eighteenth century that the French developed the frozen, custard-based treat we think of as ice cream. It is around this period that ice cream and frozen desserts made the jump from the food of royalty and the nobility to a treat for the masses. As the science of refrigeration advanced, ice cream followed along right behind it. Ice cream's biggest breakthrough in the United States came in the 1840s when Nancy Johnson invented the hand-crank ice cream maker, effectively democratizing ice cream.

Today, ice cream is not so rare and special a treat as it once was. Every grocery store carries dozens of flavors, as well as countless other frozen treats. In spite of ice cream's ubiquity, savvy cooks pass up the ultrasmooth, stabilized supermarket variety for homespun treats made with better ingredients and more character. And no store-bought stand-in can elicit a fraction of the excitement and anticipation from adults and children alike as the noisy ice cream maker churns away on the countertop or back porch, spinning simple ingredients into a sublime summer dessert.

ABOUT ICE CREAM

Ice cream can be made either from a mixture of heated cream, milk, and sugar or a rich egg custard, 812. Both types, before freezing, are referred to as the **ice bream base.** The first, eggless type is known as **Philadelphia-style ice cream,** the second as **frozen custard** or **French-style ice cream.** The natural emulsifiers in egg yolks give custard-style ice creams their fine texture. Philadelphia-style ice cream is not as luxuriously creamy as custard-style, but some prefer it for its lighter texture and the way it allows other flavors to shine through. Regardless of which type you are making, remember that ➤ making the ice cream base ahead of time and refrigerating overnight will improve its flavor and texture.

There are many factors that contribute to an ice cream's texture beyond whether or not the base contains eggs. The amount of fat, the type and quantity of sugar, the air incorporated by the churning process, and the addition of alcohol (which keeps ice creams softer since alcohol does not freeze)—are all variables that affect the final texture. Finally, the speed with which the ice cream base is frozen can alter the size of the ice crystals that form, which will also impact texture. Tinkering with these elements and tasting the results can be an excellent, and very tasty, science lesson.

There are two distinct freezing techniques. **Churned ice creams** employ hand-cranked or electric machines that incorporate air into the base and break up ice crystals to produce a smooth consistency. **Still-frozen desserts, 852,** are made by placing the mixture in a mold in the freezer and allowing it to freeze completely, without stirring or using any special equipment. These desserts require a different formulation of ingredients to ensure their smoothness.

ABOUT CHURN-FREEZING

Churned desserts, including most kinds of ice cream, sherbets, frozen yogurts, and sorbets, require an ice cream maker capable of producing subzero temperatures, because the sugar in the base lowers the freezing point of the liquids from 32°F to around 26°F. The faster an ice cream maker is able to freeze the base, the smaller the ice crystals will be, and the smoother the end result. This is why it is always a good idea to thoroughly chill the ice cream base before churning it.

To quick-chill an ice cream base in an ice water bath, pour it into a thin-walled metal bowl or transfer to a zip-top bag. Make an ice water bath in a sink or larger bowl, adding enough water so that it comes three-quarters of the way up the side of the bowl, or high enough to submerge the zip-top bag. Set the bowl in the ice water and stir the base occasionally until it registers a temperature of 36°F or lower (zip-top bags do not need to be fussed with).

There are three commonly available types of ice cream makers: bucket-type machines that use an ice-salt brine to freeze the base (these may be hand-cranked or electric), frozen-canister models, and electric machines with built-in compressors.

BUCKET-STYLE ICE CREAM MAKERS

These consist of a metal canister into which the ice cream base is poured, set in a larger bucket filled with ice and salt. The stirring mechanism, turned by hand or an electric motor, controls the **dasher** or paddle inside the canister. The salt lowers the temperature of the brine well below 32°F, chilling the metal canister and freezing the mixture inside as it is agitated by the dasher. The principal advantages of these ice cream makers are that they are very affordable and they usually have a capacity of at least 2 quarts, which is ideal for large families or parties.

To use this type of ice cream maker, allow 4 parts ice cubes to 1 part rock salt. Position the chilled metal canister filled with the ice cream base inside the bucket, then pack alternating layers of salt and ice around the canister until the bucket is full. Spin the ice cream as directed in the user's manual. ➤ On a hot day, the temperature of the brine in the bucket-style type is likely to rise more quickly and it may therefore be necessary to add more salt and ice.

FROZEN-CANISTER ICE CREAM MAKERS

These feature a smaller metal canister, 1 to 1½ quarts, with a coolant in its hollow walls. The coolant's temperature is lowered by freezing the canister overnight (or longer). The canister is then filled with the chilled ice cream base and fitted on the appliance or a dasher is fitted inside the canister, and either the canister or the dasher rotates, creating the churning action. ➤ The metal canister must be frozen for at least 12 hours between uses, which means you are limited to one batch of ice cream a day (unless you have multiple canisters). With these types of machines, it is especially important to ➤ thoroughly chill the ice cream base before churning. Otherwise, the ice cream may not freeze properly before the canister thaws.

COMPRESSOR-COOLED ICE CREAM MAKERS

These deluxe models have a built-in freezer that efficiently chills the ice cream base as it churns. They are relatively large (about the size of a small microwave), heavy, and significantly more expensive than the frozen-canister type. On the other hand, they are much more convenient: Once the base is poured into the machine's bowl, it can take as little as 25 minutes to churn, and the resulting texture is excellent. Unlike frozen-canister types, these machines can churn one batch after another. If you make ice cream often, they are a worthwhile investment.

CHURN-FREEZING WITH DRY ICE

Ice cream can be churned without a specialized appliance. All you need is a stand mixer or handheld mixer and dry ice. This method of churn-freezing quickly became our favorite when we lived in a small apartment and had no room for an extra appliance but craved homemade ice cream. The process freezes ice cream in minutes, yielding a silky-smooth texture.

There are a few important safety points to bear in mind when working with dry ice. ➤ Never put dry ice in your mouth or touch it with bare hands; always wear insulated gloves or oven mitts. Dry ice doesn't melt—it sublimates, meaning it turns from a solid directly into carbon dioxide gas. While you are unlikely to work with dry ice in quantities large enough for this to be a problem in an enclosed space, it is best to take precautions. When making ice cream with dry ice, work in a well-ventilated area (most kitchens are). If in doubt, open a window. ➤ Finally, do not eat the ice cream immediately after freezing it. Let it set in the freezer for an hour to allow any residual dry ice to sublimate.

To churn-freeze with dry ice, first have the ice cream base prepared and chilled before procuring the dry ice. Set out a bowl and a hand mixer or use a stand mixer fitted with the paddle attachment. If you can find it, pelletized dry ice is the easiest to use, but blocks of dry ice are more readily available. Cover blocks of dry ice with a towel and break them into smaller pieces with a heavy cast-iron skillet, meat pounder, or hammer. Transfer the chunks to a food processor or blender and pulse them until ground into a powder (alternatively, continue to pound the chunks of dry ice until fine). Transfer the ice cream base to the bowl or the stand mixer and turn the mixer on to a low speed. Gradually add small spoonfuls of powdered dry ice, waiting for each spoonful to disappear before adding the next. Repeat this process, scraping down the sides of the bowl several times, until the mixture is frozen but still malleable (unlike other methods, it is possible to freeze ice cream hard as a brick with dry ice). Transfer it to a container, place a piece of wax or parchment paper directly on the surface of the ice cream, cover, and freeze for at least 1 hour before serving. For several hours after making the ice cream, you may notice a slightly metallic or "carbonated" aftertaste. This flavor is usually very faint and will dissipate with time (dry ice continues to sublimate at freezer temperatures).

ABOUT STORING AND SERVING ICE CREAM AND FROZEN DESSERTS

When the machine has finished its work, the ice cream will still be comparatively soft. Most ice creams benefit from being packed into containers and frozen for at least a few hours to firm them up. This is necessary if you wish to scoop the ice cream into cones. Pack the ice cream tightly into a freezer container, leaving no air pockets. Level the top and place a piece of parchment or wax paper directly on the surface of the ice cream before you snap on the lid.

If the ice cream is too hard to scoop directly from the freezer, let it soften on a refrigerator shelf for 20 to 30 minutes, or on a kitchen counter for up to 10 minutes. Melting and refreezing causes ice crystals to form, so if making a large batch of ice cream to be eaten over several days, freeze it in multiple smaller containers rather than one large container. That way, one container can be taken out, softened, and eaten in its entirety without compromising the texture of the whole batch.

Most homemade ice creams start to lose quality in 5 to 7 days from when they were spun. This is simply the nature of homemade ice cream, as it contains no stabilizers, and home freezers do not stay as cold as commercial ones. Our best advice is to make batches small enough that they will be eaten within a week. If possible, store ice cream in a dedicated upright or chest freezer. If keeping in a refrigerator's freezer, place the ice cream in the top or coldest section.

It is difficult to prevent the development of large ice crystals in sorbets, sherbets, and other lower-fat frozen desserts during storage. They will turn icy after a short time. If this happens, chop the dessert into small pieces, puree in a food processor, and serve immediately.

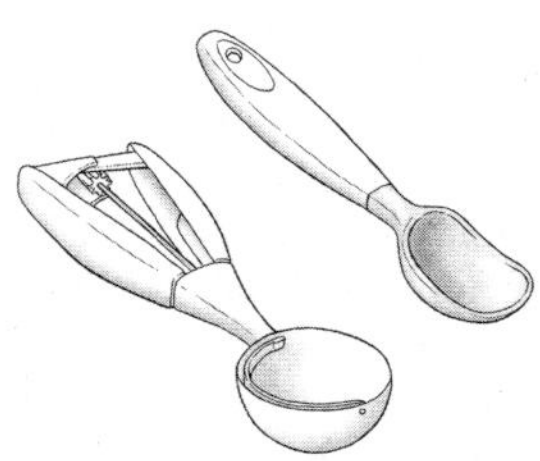

Spring-release and standard ice cream scoop

To scoop ice cream, there are a few options. The standard ice cream scoop is useful for forming perfect round balls of ice cream. Some of these scoops have heat conductive liquid in the handle, which transfers heat from the hand to the scoop, helping the ice cream release from the scoop. A spring-release scoop may also be used, although these scoops tend to break if used with very hard ice cream. Spade-style scoops are excellent for scooping ice cream from large containers or for scooping hard ice cream (they provide more leverage). Regardless of the type, wet the scoop in hot water between dips.

FLAVORING ICE CREAMS

Ice cream bases can be infused with ingredients such as lemon zest, vanilla bean, pandan or fig leaves, toasted coconut, or coffee grounds. Bring the base with the flavoring ingredients just to a boil, then remove the pan from the heat and cover. Allow the base to steep for about 30 minutes, then strain the flavorings out. See Flavorings for Custard Bases, 813, for inspiration.

Flavor can be added by incorporating **mix-ins** like crushed cookies, crumbled brittle, or chopped nuts. Two flavors of ice creams or other frozen desserts can be layered, or **marbled** together to create enticing combinations. Finally, ice creams may be **rippled** with sweet sauces, melted chocolate, jam or preserves, even marshmallow creme.

To incorporate mix-ins, use up to 1 cup chopped, crushed, or whole small ingredients per 1 quart ice cream. Most frozen canister and compressor-type ice cream makers feature a small hatch that can be opened while the machine is still running, allowing you to add mix-ins at the end of churning. Gradually add them to the churning ice cream base when it is nearly frozen—but still soft enough for the mix-ins to be distributed throughout; do not add them too early or they risk impeding proper churning. Alternatively, sprinkle the mix-ins into the churned ice cream while transferring it to a container to freeze.

To marble ice cream, layer two kinds of soft ice cream or other frozen dessert in a shallow storage container, alternating ½-inch-thick layers of each one. Freeze the layered mixture until firm enough to scoop. When you draw the scoop through the layers, the ice cream will have a marbleized effect. Combine two flavors of the same type of frozen dessert, such as vanilla and coffee ice creams, peach and raspberry sorbets, or strawberry and banana frozen yogurts. Or mix and match styles and textures, such as toasted coconut ice cream and mango sorbet, cranberry sherbet and lime sorbet, or chocolate ice cream and hazelnut gelato.

To ripple ice cream, use between ½ and 1 cup sauce or preserves per 1 quart ice cream. Alternate layers of soft ice cream with thin layers of sauce (Chocolate Sauce, 807, Salted Caramel Sauce, 809, Butterscotch Sauce, 809, Marshmallow Sauce, 809, or fruit jam, for example) in a storage container. Freeze until firm enough to scoop. Some good rippled combinations are Spiced Pumpkin Ice Cream, 843, with caramel sauce or apple butter; Vanilla Frozen Yogurt, 846, with chocolate sauce; and Chocolate Ice Cream, 841, with apricot or raspberry jam.

The chart on the next page offers suggestions for suitable mix-ins, ripples, toppings, and accompaniments for many popular ice cream flavors.

GARNISHES AND ADDITIONS TO ICE CREAM			
MIX-INS (up to 1 cup per quart)	**RIPPLES (up to 1 cup per quart)**	**TOPPINGS**	**ACCOMPANIMENTS**
Vanilla, Sweet Cream, and Other Mild Flavors			
Chopped peanut brittle, toffee, or butterscotch Chopped or miniature peanut butter cups Crushed chocolate sandwich cookies or gingersnaps Cubes of Biscuit, 721, Génoise, 721, Brownies Cockaigne, 764, or Blondies, 765 Rosemary and Brown Sugar Nuts, 46 Cocoa nibs	Roasted Fruit, 171 Cherry Sauce, 805 Fresh Berry Coulis, 805 Any jam or preserve Melted chocolate or milk chocolate	Chocolate Shell, 805 Hot Fudge Sauce, 808 Sprinkles Roasted Fruit, 171 Flambéed Fruit, 834 Fresh fruit	Stroopwafels, 786 Lemony Butter Wafers, 774 Florentines Cockaigne, 774 Maple Curls, 787
Chocolaty Flavors			
Torched Marshmallows, 868 Crumbled Amaretti or Almond Macaroons, 774 Crushed espresso beans Chopped chocolate Chopped or miniature peanut butter cups	Cherry Sauce, 805 Easy Dulce de Leche, 809	Whipped Cream, 791, Whipped Crème Fraîche, 791 Marshmallow Sauce, 809	Tuiles, 787 Vanilla Icebox Cookies, 780
Caramel Ice Cream			
Toasted, 1005, pecans, hazelnuts, or peanuts Toffee Torched Marshmallows, 868 Crumbled chocolate cookies Sautéed Apple Rings, 174 Candied bacon, 937	Salted Caramel Sauce, 809 Melted dark chocolate	Toasted, 1005, nuts Bananas Foster, 176 Buttered Cider Sauce, 806 Megan's Seeded Olive Oil Granola, 327	Baked Apples, 174 Fresh Ginger Cake, 737 Blondies, 765
Coconut Ice Cream			
Toasted, 973, flaked coconut Roasted strawberries, pineapple, or banana, 171	Mango Coulis, 805 Lime Curd, 802 Melted dark chocolate Salted Caramel Sauce, 809	Mango Coulis, 805 Fresh Berry Coulis made with raspberries, 805 Chocolate Sauce, 807 Toasted, 973, flaked coconut	Raspberry Streusel Bars, 766 Benne Wafers, 773 Chocolate Angel Food Cake, 719 Fig and Brown Butter Spice Cake, 731
Peach, Mango, and Berry Flavors			
Chopped dark chocolate Roasted Fruit, 171 Crumbled Amaretti or Almond Macaroons, 774	Melted white chocolate Fresh Berry Coulis, 805	Chocolate Shell, 807 Vanilla Sauce, 809 Roasted Fruit, 171 Toasted, 1005, sliced almonds	Anise-Almond Biscotti, 778 Scotch Shortbread, 780 Quick Cream Biscuits or Shortcakes, 636

VANILLA ICE CREAM

About 1 quart

I. PHILADELPHIA-STYLE

Combine in a medium saucepan and bring to a simmer over medium heat, stirring to dissolve the sugar:

1 cup heavy cream
¾ cup sugar
⅛ teaspoon salt

Pour into a medium bowl and stir in:

2 cups heavy cream
1 cup whole milk
2 teaspoons vanilla

Refrigerate the ice cream base until cold, overnight if possible, or quick-chill in an ice water bath, 837.

Pour the mixture into an ice cream maker and freeze as directed. Transfer to a container with a tight-fitting lid and freeze for at least 4 hours to harden.

II. FRENCH VANILLA (CUSTARD-STYLE)

Combine in a medium saucepan and bring to a simmer over medium heat, stirring to dissolve the sugar:

1½ cups whole milk
¾ cup sugar
1 vanilla bean, split lengthwise (seeds scraped into milk and pod added)
⅛ teaspoon salt

Beat together in a medium bowl:

3 large egg yolks

Slowly stir about ½ cup of the hot milk mixture into the beaten egg yolks. Then stir the egg mixture back into the milk. Cook over medium-low heat, stirring constantly, until the custard reaches 175°F and coats the back of a spoon. Do not allow the mixture to boil. Strain through a fine-mesh sieve into a medium bowl and stir in:

2 cups heavy cream

Refrigerate the ice cream base until cold, overnight if possible, or quick-chill in an ice water bath, 837.

Remove the vanilla bean pod. Pour the mixture into an ice cream maker and freeze as directed. Transfer to a container with a tight-fitting lid and freeze for at least 4 hours to harden.

MINT CHOCOLATE CHIP ICE CREAM

About 1½ quarts

Though optional, crème de menthe adds a second level of mint flavor, softens the texture, and lends the ice cream a pretty, pale-green color.

Prepare **Vanilla Ice Cream, above,** omitting the vanilla or vanilla bean. Bring the cream or milk mixture to a simmer as directed and stir in **1 cup chopped mint.** Remove the pan from the heat, cover, and let steep for 30 minutes. Strain the mixture into a medium bowl, pressing firmly to extract all the liquid; discard the mint. Proceed as directed. If desired, add **(1 to 2 tablespoons crème de menthe)** just before refrigerating the ice cream base. When the ice cream is almost frozen, stir in **3 to 4 ounces semisweet or bittersweet chocolate, chopped.**

COFFEE ICE CREAM

About 1 quart

Prepare **Vanilla Ice Cream, above,** omitting the vanilla or vanilla bean. Bring the cream or milk mixture to a simmer as directed and add **¼ cup crushed or coarsely ground coffee beans.** Remove from the heat, cover, and steep for 30 minutes. Strain into a medium bowl; discard the coffee beans. Proceed as directed.

RUM RAISIN ICE CREAM

About 1 quart

Gently warm **½ cup dark rum** and **¾ cup raisins** in a small saucepan over low heat until just starting to steam. Remove from the heat, cover, and steep for 20 minutes. Drain the raisins, reserving both the rum and raisins. Prepare **Vanilla Ice Cream, above,** substituting 1 tablespoon of the rum for the vanilla or vanilla bean. When the ice cream is almost frozen, add the raisins.

TEA-FLAVORED ICE CREAM

About 1 quart

Prepare **Vanilla Ice Cream, above.** Bring the milk or cream mixture to a simmer as directed and add **2 tablespoons tea leaves or 6 tea bags, such as green tea, Earl Grey, or rooibos.** Remove from the heat, cover, and steep for 30 minutes. Strain, pressing firmly to extract all the liquid; discard the tea leaves or bags. Proceed as directed.

MATCHA ICE CREAM

About 1 quart

Proceed as for **Vanilla Ice Cream II, above,** omitting the vanilla bean. Once the ice cream base reaches 175°F and coats a spoon, place **2 tablespoons matcha powder** in a medium bowl. Gradually whisk the heavy cream into the matcha until there are no lumps, then whisk this into the ice cream base along with **1 teaspoon vanilla.** Proceed as directed.

CARAMEL ICE CREAM

About 5 cups

Heat the milk or cream mixture as directed in:

Vanilla Ice Cream, above

Omit the vanilla bean, if using version II. Keep warm over low heat. Combine in a small heavy saucepan:

¾ cup sugar
¼ cup water

Set over medium-high heat and swirl the saucepan gently until the sugar is dissolved and the syrup is clear. Don't let the syrup boil until the sugar is completely dissolved. Cover the pan and let the syrup simmer for 1 minute. Uncover and continue to boil until it begins to darken around the edges. Gently stir the pan until the caramel turns deep amber. When the caramel is ready, remove from the heat, stand back, and immediately stir in the warm milk or cream mixture until thoroughly blended. Be careful: It will sputter. If the caramel hardens, place the pan over low heat and stir until it softens and blends with the cream. Remove from the heat and proceed with the ice cream recipe as directed. If using version I, reduce the vanilla to 1 teaspoon.

CRÈME FRAÎCHE ICE CREAM

About 1 quart

This is an exceedingly delicious, lightly tangy take on vanilla ice cream.

Combine in a blender:

2 cups milk
1½ cups Homemade Crème Fraîche, 974
¾ cup sugar
2 teaspoons vanilla or vanilla bean paste
⅛ teaspoon salt

Blend just until completely smooth and the sugar is dissolved, about 30 seconds. Refrigerate until cold, overnight if possible, or quick-chill in an ice water bath, 837.

Pour the mixture into an ice cream maker and freeze as directed.

BUTTERMILK ICE CREAM

Prepare **Crème Fraîche Ice Cream, above,** substituting **2 cups buttermilk** for the milk and **1½ cups heavy cream** for the crème fraîche.

SWEET CREAM ICE CREAM

About 1 quart

This is the tastiest, easiest vanilla ice cream recipe we know.

Combine in a blender:

1½ cups heavy cream
1 cup whole milk
One 14-ounce can sweetened condensed milk
2 teaspoons vanilla or vanilla bean paste
Pinch of salt

Blend just until smooth. Refrigerate the ice cream base until cold, overnight if possible, or quick-chill in an ice water bath, 837.

Pour the base into an ice cream maker and freeze as directed. Transfer to a container with a tight-fitting lid and freeze for at least 4 hours to harden.

FUDGE SWIRL ICE CREAM

About 5 cups

Prepare ½ **recipe Hot Fudge Sauce, 808.** Let cool completely. Prepare **Vanilla Ice Cream, 840.** When the ice cream is churned, spread a thin layer of room-temperature fudge sauce on the bottom of the container you wish to store the ice cream in. Top with one-third of the ice cream, then spread or drizzle half of the remaining fudge sauce on top. Repeat this layering with the remaining ice cream and fudge sauce, ending with a layer of ice cream on top. Freeze until firm, for at least 4 hours. When scooped, the fudge ripple will show.

PEPPERMINT STICK ICE CREAM

About 1 quart

This recipe is a quick route to a positively festive peppermint ice cream.

Place in a medium heatproof bowl:

1 cup finely crushed hard peppermint candy

Bring just to a simmer in a medium saucepan:

1½ cups whole milk
1½ cups heavy cream

Pour the hot milk-cream mixture over the candy, let cool, then cover and refrigerate for 12 hours.

Stir the mixture well, then pour into an ice cream maker and freeze as directed. If desired, when the ice cream is almost completely frozen, stir in:

(⅓ cup coarsely crushed hard peppermint candy or miniature chocolate chips)

CHOCOLATE ICE CREAM

About 5 cups

Whisk together in a medium saucepan:

½ cup sugar
⅓ cup unsweetened cocoa powder
¼ teaspoon salt

Gradually whisk in:

2 cups whole milk

Bring to a simmer over medium heat, stirring occasionally to dissolve the sugar. Whisk together in a medium heatproof bowl:

4 large egg yolks
¼ cup sugar

Slowly pour about half the hot milk mixture into the eggs, whisking constantly. Pour this mixture back into the saucepan and cook over medium-low heat, stirring constantly, until the custard reaches 175°F and coats the back of a spoon. Do not allow the mixture to boil. Remove the pan from the heat and strain the custard through a fine-mesh sieve into a medium bowl. Stir in:

1 cup heavy cream
1 teaspoon vanilla

Refrigerate the ice cream base until cold, overnight if possible, or quick-chill in an ice water bath, 837.

Pour the base into an ice cream maker and freeze as directed. If desired, when the ice cream is almost frozen, stir in:

(3 to 4 ounces semisweet or bittersweet chocolate, chopped, or 1½ cups ½-inch cubes Fudgy Brownies, 765, completely cooled)

Transfer to a container with a tight-fitting lid and freeze for at least 4 hours to harden.

ROCKY ROAD ICE CREAM

Prepare **Chocolate Ice Cream, above**. When the ice cream is almost frozen, stir in **1 cup miniature marshmallows** and ½ **cup chopped toasted, 1005, walnuts or almonds**.

MALTED MILK CHOCOLATE ICE CREAM

Prepare **Chocolate Ice Cream, above,** whisking into the sugar–cocoa powder mixture ¾ **cup malted milk powder.** Proceed as directed. If desired, when the ice cream is nearly frozen, stir in **(1 cup malted milk balls).**

DARK CHOCOLATE ICE CREAM

About 1 quart

Combine in a medium saucepan and bring to a simmer over medium heat, stirring to dissolve the sugar:

1½ cups whole milk
½ cup sugar
⅛ teaspoon salt

Beat together in a medium heatproof bowl:

3 large egg yolks

Slowly stir about ½ cup of the hot milk mixture into the beaten egg yolks. Stir the egg mixture back into the milk. Cook over medium-low heat, stirring constantly, until the custard reaches 175°F and coats the back of a spoon. Do not allow the mixture to boil. Remove from the heat and stir in until smooth:

¾ cup Cocoa Syrup, 9
¼ cup semisweet or bittersweet chocolate chips or 1½ ounces chopped semisweet or bittersweet chocolate

Stir in:

1½ cups heavy cream

Mix well to combine. Refrigerate the ice cream base until cold, overnight if possible, or quick-chill in an ice water bath, 837.

Pour the base into an ice cream maker and freeze as directed. Transfer to a container with a tight-fitting lid and freeze for at least 4 hours to harden.

PISTACHIO ICE CREAM

About 1 quart

For green pistachio ice cream, add **2 to 4 drops green food coloring** after the almond extract.

Finely grind in a food processor, but not to a paste:

1 cup pistachios, toasted, 1005
1 cup sugar

Transfer to a medium saucepan and add:

2 cups heavy cream
1½ cups whole milk

Bring just to a simmer over medium-low heat, stirring to dissolve the sugar. Remove from the heat, cover, and let steep for 1 hour. Strain through a fine-mesh sieve into a medium bowl, pressing firmly to extract all the liquid; discard the nuts in the sieve. Stir in:

1 teaspoon vanilla
½ teaspoon almond or pistachio extract

Refrigerate the ice cream base until cold, overnight if possible, or quick-chill in an ice water bath, 837.

Pour the base into an ice cream maker and freeze as directed. When the ice cream is almost frozen, add:

½ cup pistachios, toasted, 1005, and finely chopped

Transfer to a container with a tight-fitting lid and freeze for at least 4 hours to harden.

BUTTER PECAN ICE CREAM

About 1 quart

We like to use salted nuts in this classic ice cream.

Combine in a small saucepan and bring to a boil, stirring to dissolve the sugar:

1 cup packed light brown sugar
½ cup water
⅛ teaspoon salt or smoked salt

Boil the syrup for 2 minutes. Meanwhile, beat in a double boiler top or medium heatproof bowl:

4 large egg yolks

Slowly beat the hot sugar syrup into the egg yolks. Cook over simmering water, stirring constantly, until the mixture reaches 175°F and coats the back of a spoon. Do not allow the mixture to boil. Add and stir until melted:

2 tablespoons butter

Strain through a sieve into a medium bowl, then stir in:

1 cup whole milk
1 cup heavy cream
1 teaspoon vanilla
(1 tablespoon sherry or bourbon)

Refrigerate the ice cream base until cold, overnight if possible, or quick-chill in an ice water bath, 837.

Pour the base into an ice cream maker and freeze as directed. When the ice cream is almost frozen, add:

½ cup chopped toasted, 1005, pecans, or roasted, salted pecans

Transfer to a container with a tight-fitting lid and freeze for at least 4 hours to harden.

PEANUT BUTTER ICE CREAM

About 1 quart

For a truly moreish treatment, serve topped with Chocolate Shell, 808, and flaky sea salt. For this recipe, use creamy, no-stir peanut butter; "natural" peanut butter tends to separate.

Combine in a blender:

1 cup whole milk
¾ cup creamy peanut butter
¾ cup sugar
1½ teaspoons vanilla
Pinch of salt

Blend until completely smooth. Transfer to a bowl and whisk in:

1½ cups heavy cream

Refrigerate the ice cream base until cold, overnight if possible, or quick-chill in an ice water bath, 837.

Pour the base into an ice cream maker and freeze as directed. If desired, when the ice cream is almost frozen, fold in:

(1 cup chopped roasted peanuts)

Transfer to a container with a tight-fitting lid and freeze for at least 4 hours to harden.

COCONUT ICE CREAM

About 1 quart

Toast, 973:

2 cups shredded sweetened coconut

Combine in a medium saucepan and bring to a simmer over medium-low heat, stirring to dissolve the sugar:

¾ cup whole milk
¾ cup canned coconut milk
½ cup sugar
⅛ teaspoon salt

Stir in 1 cup of the toasted coconut, remove from the heat, cover, and steep for 30 minutes.

Strain the milk through a fine-mesh sieve into a bowl, pressing firmly on the coconut to extract all the liquid; discard the coconut. Return to the saucepan and bring to a simmer over medium-low heat. Beat together in a medium heatproof bowl:

3 large egg yolks

Slowly stir in about ½ cup of the milk mixture, then stir the egg mixture into the rest of the milk. Cook over low heat, stirring constantly, until the custard reaches 175°F and coats the back of a spoon. Do not allow the mixture to boil. Transfer to a bowl and refrigerate the ice cream base until cold, overnight if possible, or quick-chill in an ice water bath, 837.

Stir in:

2 cups heavy cream

Pour the base into an ice cream maker and freeze as directed. When the ice cream is almost frozen, stir in the remaining 1 cup toasted coconut. Transfer to a container with a tight-fitting lid and freeze for at least 4 hours to harden.

OLIVE OIL ICE CREAM

About 1 quart

There is perhaps no better way to showcase the flavor of a really good olive oil than this savory-sweet ice cream. We recommend using a buttery olive oil rather than a peppery one.

Combine in a medium saucepan and bring to a simmer over medium heat, stirring to dissolve the sugar:

2 cups whole milk
¾ cup sugar
⅛ teaspoon salt

Beat together in a medium heatproof bowl:

3 large egg yolks

Slowly stir about ½ cup of the hot milk mixture into the beaten egg yolks, then stir the egg mixture back into the milk. Cook over medium-low heat, stirring constantly, until the custard reaches 175°F and coats the back of a spoon. Do not allow the mixture to boil. Strain through a fine-mesh sieve into a blender or a deep bowl if using an immersion blender. Combine in a measuring cup or pitcher with a pouring lip:

¾ cup heavy cream
½ cup high-quality extra-virgin olive oil

For a blender, slowly pour the cream-oil mixture in a thin stream into the ice cream base with the machine running on medium speed. For an immersion blender, slowly pour the cream-oil mixture into the bowl with the custard while blending on high speed. The ice cream base should be emulsified. Refrigerate the ice cream base until cold, overnight if possible, or quick-chill in an ice water bath, 837.

Pour the base into an ice cream maker and freeze as directed. Transfer to a container with a tight-fitting lid and freeze for at least 4 hours to harden. If desired, serve scoops of this ice cream lightly sprinkled with:

(Smoked flaky sea salt)

SPICED PUMPKIN ICE CREAM

About 1½ quarts

Combine in a medium saucepan and bring to a simmer over medium-low heat, stirring occasionally to dissolve the sugar:

1½ cups whole milk
¼ cup sugar
½ teaspoon ground cinnamon
½ teaspoon ground ginger
Pinch of grated or ground nutmeg

Beat together in a medium heatproof bowl:

4 large egg yolks
½ cup sugar

Slowly whisk half the hot milk mixture into the beaten egg yolks, then pour this mixture back into the rest of the milk. Cook over low heat, stirring constantly, until the custard reaches 175°F and coats the back of a spoon. Do not allow the mixture to boil. Remove the pan from the heat and strain the custard through a fine-mesh sieve into a medium bowl. Whisk in:

1¼ cups heavy cream
1 cup cooked or canned unsweetened pumpkin puree
1 teaspoon vanilla

Refrigerate the ice cream base until cold, overnight if possible, or quick-chill in an ice water bath, 837.

Pour the base into an ice cream maker and freeze as directed. If desired, when the ice cream is almost frozen, stir in:

(1 cup coarsely crushed graham crackers or gingersnaps)

Transfer to a container with a tight-fitting lid and freeze for at least 4 hours to harden.

MOLASSES ICE CREAM

About 1 quart

This super simple and unusual vegan ice cream is from our friend Helena Root. If desired, fold in up to **(1½ cups ½-inch cubes gingerbread or spice cake)** after churning the ice cream.

Add to a blender and puree until completely homogenous:

1 cup molasses or sorghum syrup
Two 13½-ounce cans full-fat coconut milk

Pour into a bowl and refrigerate the ice cream base until cold, overnight if possible, or quick-chill in an ice water bath, 837.

Pour the base into an ice cream maker and freeze as directed. Transfer to a container with a tight-fitting lid and freeze for at least 4 hours to harden.

DAIRY-FREE VANILLA ICE CREAM

About 1 quart

This base can be tweaked to create different flavors. Any of the suggestions from the Garnishes and Additions to Ice Cream chart, 839, may be mixed into the base, the base may be heated and infused with different flavors as for Mint Chocolate Chip Ice Cream, 84, or Coffee Ice Cream, 840, or stir in caramelized sugar as for Caramel Ice Cream, 840. The optional citric acid does not make the ice cream taste sour at all—it simply adds a little complexity.

Combine in a medium bowl:

1 cup raw cashews
Water to cover

Let sit overnight. Drain the cashews and transfer to a blender. Add:

One 13½-ounce can coconut milk, well shaken
1 cup water
½ cup sugar
(2 tablespoons light corn syrup)
2 teaspoons vanilla or vanilla bean paste
(⅛ teaspoon citric acid)
¼ teaspoon salt

Blend until very smooth, scraping down the sides of the blender as needed. Unless you have a high-powered blender, strain the ice cream base through a fine-mesh sieve. Transfer to a bowl and refrigerate the ice cream base until cold, overnight if possible, or quick-chill it in an ice water bath, 837.

Pour the base into an ice cream maker and freeze as directed. Transfer to a container with a tight-fitting lid and freeze for at least 4 hours to harden.

PEACH, APRICOT, OR NECTARINE ICE CREAM

About 1 quart

Preheat the oven to 350°F.

Pit and halve or quarter:

1 pound apricots, peaches, or nectarines

Toss the fruit in a 13 × 9-inch baking dish with:

½ cup sugar
1 teaspoon lemon juice

Roast, stirring every 10 minutes, until the fruit is extremely soft and broken down, about 45 minutes. Let cool completely in the dish, then slip the skins off the fruit.

Scrape the fruit and its juices into a blender and puree until smooth, or use an immersion blender. Transfer to a medium bowl and whisk in:

2 cups heavy cream
(1 tablespoon peach schnapps or vodka)
½ teaspoon almond extract
Pinch of salt

Refrigerate the ice cream base until cold, overnight if possible, or quick-chill in an ice water bath, 837.

Pour the base into an ice cream maker and freeze as directed. Transfer to a container with a tight-fitting lid and freeze for at least 4 hours to harden.

STRAWBERRY ICE CREAM

About 1 quart

Combine in a food processor:

1 pint strawberries, hulled and sliced
¼ cup plus 2 tablespoons sugar
1 teaspoon vanilla

Pulse about 10 times, just until the fruit is crushed. Transfer to a bowl and refrigerate for 1 hour.

Stir in:

1 cup heavy cream
½ cup whole milk

Stir until the sugar is dissolved, 2 to 3 minutes. Refrigerate the ice cream base until cold, overnight if possible, or quick-chill in an ice water bath, 837.

Pour the base into an ice cream maker and freeze as directed. Transfer to a container with a tight-fitting lid and freeze for at least 4 hours to harden.

BLACKBERRY OR RASPBERRY ICE CREAM

About 1 quart

You may substitute 1 cup (about 9 ounces) thawed frozen berry puree for the homemade puree in this recipe.

Combine in a food processor:

1 pint blackberries or raspberries
½ cup sugar

Pulse until the fruit is crushed and very juicy. Transfer to a small bowl and refrigerate for 1 hour. Strain the mixture through a fine-mesh sieve, pressing firmly to extract all the berry juices; discard the seeds. Add:

1½ cups heavy cream
½ cup whole milk
1 teaspoon vanilla
(1 tablespoon framboise or vodka)

Stir until the sugar is dissolved, 2 to 3 minutes. Refrigerate the ice cream base until cold, overnight if possible, or quick-chill in an ice water bath, 837.

Pour the base into an ice cream maker and freeze as directed. Transfer to a container with a tight-fitting lid and freeze for at least 4 hours to harden.

ORANGE ICE MILK

About 3 cups

Ice milk is less creamy than ice cream, but it is also more refreshing.

Combine in a small bowl and stir until the sugar is dissolved:

Finely grated zest of 1 orange
¾ cup orange juice
⅔ cup sugar
2 tablespoons fresh lemon juice
1 teaspoon vanilla
Pinch of salt

Place in a medium bowl:

2 cups very cold whole milk

Gradually stir the orange juice mixture into the milk. If the milk looks slightly curdled, it will not affect the texture of the ice milk. Pour into an ice cream maker and freeze as directed.

Transfer to a container with a tight-fitting lid and freeze for at least 4 hours to harden.

PINEAPPLE ICE MILK

About 1 quart

Rather than buying pineapple juice, you may use the juice drained from the can of crushed pineapple.

Combine in a small bowl and stir until the sugar is dissolved:

⅔ cup unsweetened pineapple juice
½ cup sugar

½ cup drained canned crushed pineapple
Finely grated zest of 1 lemon
2 tablespoons lemon juice
⅛ teaspoon salt

Place in a medium bowl:

3 cups very cold whole milk

Stir the pineapple juice mixture into the milk. Pour into an ice cream maker and freeze as directed.

Transfer to a container with a tight-fitting lid and freeze for at least 4 hours to harden.

CHOCOLATE CUPS

8 to 10 cups

If the chocolate is at the correct temperature, it will take only one dip to evenly coat a balloon. If the chocolate is too cold, then the coating will be too thick; too hot, and the balloon will likely need more than one dip. Keep leftover chocolate to fill any holes in the cups.

Line a baking sheet with parchment paper or a silicone liner. Inflate to about 5 inches in diameter:

8 to 10 small balloons

Temper, 858, and pour into a medium bowl:

1 pound semisweet or bittersweet chocolate (up to 64% cacao)

Dip the bottom third to half of one balloon into the chocolate, moving it from side to side to coat evenly. Lift the balloon and allow the excess chocolate to drip off, then place, dipped end down, on the prepared baking sheet. Repeat with remaining balloons and chocolate. Refrigerate until set, about 30 minutes. Prick each balloon with a pin to release the air and gently peel the deflated balloon from the chocolate cup. Holes can be patched with the remaining chocolate. Return the bowls to the refrigerator until ready to serve.

ABOUT GELATO

Gelato is simply the Italian word for "ice cream." Originally, gelato was just as rich, if not more so, than ice cream from anywhere else. Now, however, it is thought of as a lower fat type of ice cream. Here we use the term to mean a specific churned or stir-frozen dessert with more milk and egg yolks and less cream. The lower fat content is not intended for the sake of having "low fat" ice cream recipes, but rather to create cleaner, more intense flavors. Gelato is best served at around 15°F. Let it stand at room temperature for 5 to 10 minutes before scooping, or serve it straight from the ice cream maker.

HAZELNUT GELATO

About 1 quart

Preheat the oven to 350°F.

Place on a rimmed baking sheet:

2 cups hazelnuts

Toast until golden brown and fragrant, 10 to 12 minutes. Wrap the nuts in a kitchen towel, rub vigorously to remove as much of the skins as possible, then finely grind them in a food processor, but not to a paste. Bring just to a simmer in a medium saucepan:

3 cups whole milk

Add the nuts. Remove from the heat, cover, and steep for 30 minutes.

Strain the milk into a double boiler or heatproof bowl, pressing firmly to extract as much liquid as possible; discard the nuts. Add:

½ cup sugar

Place the double boiler or bowl over simmering water, stirring occasionally to dissolve the sugar. Meanwhile, beat together in a medium heatproof bowl:

6 large egg yolks
¼ cup sugar

When the milk mixture is steaming, slowly whisk about half of it into the beaten eggs, then stir the egg mixture back into the remaining milk. Cook in the double boiler over a gentle simmer, stirring constantly, until the custard reaches 175°F and coats the back of a spoon. Strain the custard through a fine-mesh sieve into a medium bowl. Stir in:

¼ cup heavy cream
¼ teaspoon vanilla
(1 tablespoon Frangelico or other hazelnut liqueur)

Refrigerate the gelato base until cold, overnight if possible, or quick-chill in an ice water bath, 837.

Pour the base into an ice cream maker and freeze as directed. Transfer to a container with a tight-fitting lid and freeze for at least 4 hours to harden.

GIANDUJA GELATO (CHOCOLATE-HAZELNUT GELATO)

Prepare **Hazelnut Gelato, above,** beating **¼ cup Dutch-process cocoa powder** into the egg yolk mixture before adding the hot milk.

FIOR DI LATTE GELATO

About 1 quart

Fior di latte means "flower of milk." It is an incredibly simple flavor that relies solely upon the highest quality milk you can buy. Grass-fed milk and cream from a local dairy will be your best bet. This is the perfect gelato to serve with seasonal fruit.

Combine in a medium saucepan over medium heat and cook, stirring frequently, until the sugar is dissolved:

1 cup best-quality heavy cream
1 cup sugar
⅛ teaspoon salt

Transfer to a medium bowl and stir in:

2½ cups best-quality whole milk

Refrigerate the gelato base until cold, overnight if possible, or quick-chill in an ice water bath, 837.

Pour the base into an ice cream maker and freeze as directed. Transfer to a container with a tight-fitting lid and freeze for at least 4 hours to harden.

ABOUT FROZEN YOGURT

Frozen yogurt is made with Greek or drained yogurt, sometimes whole milk or cream, sugar, and flavorings. Always use plain, unsweetened yogurt—full-fat yogurt works best. ➤ If using yogurt other than Greek, drain off some of the yogurt's liquid first (see the headnote in Vanilla Frozen Yogurt, 846). Even after being drained, the excess water in yogurt can contribute to iciness. Gelatin can be added to improve the texture, since it traps water and reduces crystallization.

For frozen yogurt that approximates the texture of commercial soft-serve yogurt, serve it fresh out of the ice cream maker. Once it has been frozen for a few hours, it will become firm. As with other frozen desserts, add ingredients such as chopped nuts, chocolate chips, or crumbled cookies when freezing is almost complete. For ideas and recommended amounts, see Flavoring Ice Creams, 838.

VANILLA FROZEN YOGURT

About 1 quart

The optional honey or syrup will yield a slightly smoother, less icy texture. For a vegetarian version, the gelatin may be omitted (use 1¾ cups milk total). This recipe calls for Greek yogurt; to make it with regular yogurt, you will need to drain it first. Line a fine-mesh sieve with cheesecloth or a flour sack towel and set over a bowl. Spoon **2 cups plain whole-milk yogurt** into the sieve. Refrigerate and allow to drain for 2 hours. Scrape the yogurt into a medium bowl; discard the liquid.

Place in a small cup:

¼ cup whole milk

Sprinkle with:

1 teaspoon unflavored gelatin

Let stand for 5 minutes to soften. Combine in a medium saucepan:

1½ cups whole milk
¾ cup sugar
(2 tablespoons honey, light corn syrup, or light cane syrup)

If using, split lengthwise in half:

(½ vanilla bean)

Scrape the seeds into the milk mixture. Add the pod and bring just to a simmer over low heat, stirring occasionally to dissolve the sugar. Remove from the heat and let cool for 5 minutes, then add the gelatin and milk mixture, stirring until the gelatin dissolves completely. Let cool to room temperature.

Place in a medium bowl:

1½ cups plain whole-milk Greek yogurt or drained regular yogurt, see headnote above

Gently whisk the milk mixture into the yogurt. Stir in:

1½ teaspoons vanilla (if not using vanilla bean)

Refrigerate the frozen yogurt base until cold, overnight if possible, or quick-chill in an ice water bath, 837.

Remove the vanilla pod, if you used it. Pour the base into an ice cream maker and freeze as directed. Serve immediately or transfer to a container with a tight-fitting lid and freeze.

CHOCOLATE FROZEN YOGURT

Prepare **Vanilla Frozen Yogurt, above,** omitting the vanilla bean and adding ½ **cup Dutch-process cocoa powder** to the hot milk mixture; whisk until smooth. Proceed as directed, adding the vanilla.

STRAWBERRY FROZEN YOGURT

About 5 cups

For a vegetarian version, the gelatin may be omitted (reduce the milk to 1 cup total).

Place in a food processor:

1 pint strawberries, hulled and sliced

Pulse about 10 times, just until the fruit is crushed; do not puree. Transfer to a large bowl and stir in:

¼ to ⅓ cup sugar, to taste
1 teaspoon vanilla
Pinch of salt

Cover and let stand at room temperature for 1 hour.

Place in a small cup:

¼ cup whole milk

Sprinkle with:

1 envelope (2¼ teaspoons) unflavored gelatin

Let stand for 5 minutes to soften. Combine in a medium saucepan:

¾ cup whole milk
¼ cup plus 2 tablespoons sugar

Bring just to a simmer, stirring occasionally to dissolve the sugar. Remove from the heat and let cool for 5 minutes, then add the gelatin mixture, stirring until it dissolves completely. Let cool to room temperature.

Gently whisk the milk mixture into the strawberries. Whisk in:

1½ cups plain whole-milk Greek yogurt or drained regular yogurt (see Vanilla Frozen Yogurt headnote, above)

Refrigerate the frozen yogurt base until cold, overnight if possible, or quick-chill in an ice water bath, 837.

Pour the base into an ice cream maker and freeze as directed. Serve immediately or transfer to a container with a tight-fitting lid and freeze.

MANGO FROZEN YOGURT

About 1 quart

Canned sweetened Alphonso mango puree can be found at Indian markets. It has a glorious tart-sweet flavor and a stunning orange color.

Place in a medium bowl:

1½ cups plain whole-milk Greek yogurt or drained regular yogurt (see Vanilla Frozen Yogurt headnote, above)

Whisk in:

1⅓ cups canned sweetened Alphonso mango puree
½ cup whole milk
2 tablespoons lime juice

Refrigerate the frozen yogurt base until cold, overnight if possible, or quick-chill in an ice water bath, 837.

Pour the base into an ice cream maker and freeze as directed. Serve immediately or transfer to a container with a tight-fitting lid and freeze.

ABOUT SORBET

Sorbet is a churned or stir-frozen mixture of fresh fruit juice or puree, sugar, and sometimes a little alcohol, resulting in a frozen dessert with an intense fruit flavor. ➤ For an even more intense flavor, substitute orange juice, lemonade, or limeade for the water in the recipes that follow (adjust the added sugar accordingly to account for the sugar in these liquids). Jeni Bauer of Jeni's Splendid Ice Creams uses fruity lambic beer instead of water in some of her sorbets—a particularly good idea, as the alcohol in the lambic will also soften the texture of the sorbet.

Like other churned desserts, sorbet will be soft when it comes out of the ice cream machine. A few hours in the freezer will harden it somewhat, but sorbet should be scoopable right from the freezer, without softening. The key to this consistency is the amount of sugar (and alcohol, if used), which lowers the freezing point of the sorbet and prevents it from getting too hard. Another way to achieve soft-textured sorbet is to use the dry ice method of churn-freezing, 837.

The sweetness of fresh fruit varies, so taste the sorbet before freezing. ➤ It should taste a little too sweet, as freezing dulls both the fruit and sugar flavors. If extra sweetness is needed, add extra sugar a tablespoon at a time, stirring until completely dissolved. If the mixture tastes flat, add lemon juice to taste.

RASPBERRY SORBET

About 2 cups

Combine in a blender:

1½ pints raspberries
1 cup sugar
½ cup water

Puree, then strain through a fine-mesh sieve into a medium bowl, pressing firmly to extract as much juice as possible; discard the seeds. Stir in:

1 tablespoon lemon or lime juice
(1 tablespoon framboise or vodka)

Refrigerate the sorbet base until cold, overnight if possible, or quick-chill in an ice water bath, 837.

Taste and add more sugar or lemon juice if needed, stirring until the sugar is completely dissolved, 2 to 3 minutes. Pour the base into an ice cream maker and freeze as directed. Serve immediately or transfer to a container with a tight-fitting lid and freeze.

BLACKBERRY SORBET

Prepare **Raspberry Sorbet, above,** substituting **1½ pints blackberries** for the raspberries. Add the framboise or vodka, if desired, or substitute **(kirsch)**.

BLUEBERRY SORBET

Prepare **Raspberry Sorbet, above,** substituting **2½ cups blueberries** for the raspberries. Use lemon juice and increase it to 2 tablespoons. If desired, substitute **(crème de cassis or kirsch)** for the framboise or vodka.

STRAWBERRY SORBET

Prepare **Raspberry Sorbet, above,** substituting **1 pound strawberries, hulled and sliced,** for the raspberries. If desired, substitute **(kirsch or amaretto)** for the framboise or vodka.

MANGO SORBET

Prepare **Raspberry Sorbet, above,** substituting **3 medium mangoes, peeled and pitted** for the raspberries. Reduce the sugar to ¾ cup. Use **2 tablespoons lime juice.** If desired, substitute **(Grand Marnier, tequila, or dark rum)** for the framboise or vodka.

PEACH SORBET

Prepare **Raspberry Sorbet, above,** substituting **1½ pounds soft, ripe peaches, peeled and pitted** for the raspberries. Use **2 tablespoons lemon juice** and add it to the peaches before they are pureed. Taste the mixture after chilling and add more lemon juice if needed. If desired, substitute **(amaretto or peach brandy)** for the framboise or vodka.

LEMON SORBET

About 1 quart

Fresh lemon juice and strips of lemon zest are essential for this recipe. If you have access to Meyer lemons, this sorbet will highlight their natural sweetness.

Combine in a small saucepan:

2¼ cups water
2 cups sugar
Zest of 1 lemon, removed in wide strips with a vegetable peeler

Bring to a boil over medium heat, stirring occasionally to dissolve the sugar. Remove the pan from the heat, cover, and steep for 30 minutes.

Strain the sugar syrup into a medium bowl and stir in:

¾ cup lemon juice
(1 tablespoon lemon vodka or limoncello)

Refrigerate the sorbet base until cold, overnight if possible, or quick-chill in an ice water bath, 837.

Taste and add more sugar if needed, stirring until the sugar is completely dissolved, 2 to 3 minutes. Pour the base into an ice cream maker and freeze as directed. Serve immediately or transfer to a container with a tight-fitting lid and freeze.

LIME SORBET

Prepare **Lemon Sorbet, above,** substituting the **finely grated zest of 1 lime** and **¾ cup lime juice** for the lemon zest and juice. If desired, substitute **(1 tablespoon tequila or rum)** for the vodka or limoncello.

ORANGE SORBET

About 1 quart

Combine in a small saucepan:

¾ cup orange juice
1½ cups sugar
Zest of 1 medium orange, removed in wide strips with a vegetable peeler

Heat over medium heat, stirring, just until the sugar is dissolved. Do not boil. Remove the pan from the heat, cover, and steep for 15 minutes. Strain into a medium bowl. Stir in:

$2\frac{1}{4}$ cups orange juice
2 tablespoons lemon juice
(1 tablespoon Grand Marnier, white Curaçao, or vodka)

Refrigerate the sorbet base until cold, overnight if possible, or quick-chill in an ice water bath, 837.

Taste and add more sugar or lemon juice if needed, stirring until the sugar is completely dissolved, 2 to 3 minutes. Pour the base into an ice cream maker and freeze as directed. Serve immediately or transfer to a container with a tight-fitting lid and freeze.

PINK GRAPEFRUIT SORBET

Pink grapefruits are sweeter than white ones, though still tart enough to make this pale pink sorbet supremely appealing.

Prepare **Orange Sorbet, 847,** omitting the lemon juice and substituting **the zest of 1 pink grapefruit** and **3 cups pink grapefruit juice** for the orange zest and juice. If desired, substitute **(1 tablespoon tequila)** for the Grand Marnier, white Curaçao, or vodka.

WATERMELON SORBET

Remove the rind and seeds from **4 pounds red or yellow watermelon.** Puree in a blender until smooth, then strain through a fine-mesh sieve; discard the pulp. Prepare **Orange Sorbet, 847,** omitting the orange zest and substituting 3 cups watermelon juice for the orange juice. Increase the lemon juice to 3 tablespoons. If desired, substitute **(1 tablespoon Campari)** for the Grand Marnier, white Curaçao, or vodka. Add more lemon juice to taste, if needed.

CHOCOLATE SORBET

About 3 cups

Chocolate sorbet is a bit of a head trip. The rich chocolate flavor will have your brain screaming "ice cream!" even though there's not a drop of cream in sight. In fact, the absence of dairy is what shows the chocolate flavor to its best advantage, so choose high-quality cocoa powder and chocolate. For more information on the difference between standard cocoa powder and superb high-fat cocoa powder, see 970.

Place in a medium saucepan:

$\frac{3}{4}$ cup unsweetened cocoa powder

Gradually whisk in until smooth:

1 cup water

Whisk in:

$1\frac{1}{2}$ cups water
1 cup sugar
$\frac{1}{4}$ teaspoon salt

Bring just to a simmer, whisking frequently. Remove from the heat and add:

4 ounces semisweet or bittersweet chocolate (up to 64% cacao), finely chopped

Let sit for 5 minutes, then whisk until the chocolate is melted and the mixture is smooth. Refrigerate the sorbet base until cold, overnight if possible, or quick-chill in an ice water bath, 837.

Pour the base into an ice cream maker and freeze as directed. Serve immediately or transfer to a container with a tight-fitting lid and freeze.

CHAMPAGNE SORBET

About 3 cups

This refreshing sorbet makes a fine ending to a rich meal, or scoop the sorbet into glasses and pour more sparkling wine over it for an adult sorbet float.

Combine in a medium saucepan over medium heat:

$1\frac{1}{4}$ cups sugar
1 cup water

Cook, stirring, until the sugar is dissolved. Bring to a boil, cover, and boil for 5 minutes. Let cool completely, then stir in:

$1\frac{1}{2}$ cups Champagne or other dry sparkling wine
3 tablespoons lemon juice

Refrigerate the sorbet base until cold, overnight if possible, or quick-chill in an ice water bath, 837.

Pour the base into an ice cream maker and freeze as directed. Serve immediately or transfer to a container with a tight-fitting lid and freeze.

INSTANT SORBET

This is a quick and easy ice dessert that doesn't require an ice cream maker. The secret is canned fruit in heavy syrup. The higher proportion of sugar in the heavy syrup means the texture of the sorbet is soft and creamy even after a couple days in the freezer. Fruit in a light syrup can be used, but the final texture will be icier. Bananas may also be frozen and blended. They do not need additional sugar to achieve a creamy texture. If desired, freeze two or more different types of sorbets, then layer them in clear glasses. A 15- to 16-ounce can will yield $1\frac{1}{2}$ to $1\frac{3}{4}$ cups frozen sorbet; layer the sorbet from two cans of this size for 6 to 8 servings.

Puree in a food processor or blender:

One 15- to 16-ounce can fruit in heavy syrup, undrained

Pour the puree into a zip-top freezer bag and freeze flat overnight. Repeat with as many different fruits as desired. When ready to serve, remove the fruit from the bag, cut into pieces, and place in the food processor. Add, if desired:

(2 to 3 teaspoons liqueur)

Pulse until the mixture is almost smooth—some chunks of frozen fruit should remain. Scrape down the sides once or twice. Repeat with each frozen puree. Layer the fruit sorbets in clear parfait glasses or wineglasses. If desired, top with:

(Whipped Cream, 791)

ABOUT SHERBET

Sherbet is a churned or stir-frozen dessert somewhat similar to sorbet in that the flavors are often fruit-based. However, sherbet falls between ice cream and sorbet in terms of richness. Sherbet often contains whole milk or gelatin and sometimes egg whites. As with frozen yogurt, gelatin is the key to smooth, creamy sherbets. The gelatin granules swell, trapping water in a protein matrix, which prevents ice crystals from becoming large.

As the gelatin sherbet base cools, it may begin to set and become lumpy. Don't worry—it will smooth out when churned. As with ice cream, sherbet emerges from the ice cream maker fairly soft. Freeze it for several hours if you prefer it firm. Sherbet is best served at around 20°F, so soften it slightly before serving.

RASPBERRY OR STRAWBERRY SHERBET

About 5 cups

Place in a small cup:

1 tablespoon cold water

Sprinkle with:

1 teaspoon unflavored gelatin

Let stand for 5 minutes to soften. Combine in a small saucepan:

1 cup water or ½ cup water plus ½ cup pineapple juice

¾ to 1 cup sugar, to taste

Bring to a boil, stirring to dissolve the sugar. Boil, covered, for 5 minutes without stirring. Add:

1 to 2 tablespoons lemon juice, to taste

Dissolve the gelatin in the heated syrup. Refrigerate the sherbet base until cold, overnight if possible, or quick-chill in an ice water bath, 837. Puree in a food processor:

1 quart strawberries, hulled, or raspberries

Strain through a fine-mesh sieve into a bowl. Stir in the gelatin mixture. Pour the base into an ice cream maker and freeze as directed. Serve immediately or transfer to a container with a tight-fitting lid and freeze.

ORANGE SHERBET

About 5 cups

Place in a small cup:

¼ cup cold water

Sprinkle with:

1 envelope (2¼ teaspoons) unflavored gelatin

Let stand for 5 minutes to soften. Combine in a medium saucepan:

Zest of 1 orange, removed in wide strips with a vegetable peeler

1¾ cups orange juice

¾ cup sugar

Bring to a simmer, stirring occasionally to dissolve the sugar. Strain through a sieve into a bowl; discard the zest. Add the gelatin, stirring until it is completely dissolved. Stir in:

1 cup whole milk

Refrigerate the sherbet base until cold, overnight if possible, or quick-chill in an ice water bath, 837.

Pour the base into an ice cream maker and freeze as directed. Serve immediately or transfer to a container with a tight-fitting lid and freeze.

LEMON SHERBET

About 5 cups

Prepare **Orange Sherbet, above,** substituting **the zest of 1 lemon** for the orange zest and **¾ cup lemon juice and 1¼ cups water** for the orange juice. Increase the sugar to 1 cup.

LIME SHERBET

About 5 cups

Prepare **Orange Sherbet, above,** substituting **the zest of 1 lime** for the orange zest. Substitute **½ cup lime juice and 1¼ cups water** for the orange juice. Increase the sugar to 1 cup.

CRANBERRY SHERBET

About 5 cups

Try this tart sherbet as a palate cleanser. Frozen cranberries may be used here—do not thaw. A 12-ounce bag yields 3 cups cranberries, so buy two and freeze the leftovers for another use.

Place in a small cup:

¼ cup water

Sprinkle with:

1 envelope (2¼ teaspoons) unflavored gelatin

Let stand 5 minutes to soften. Combine in a medium saucepan:

4½ cups cranberries

1½ cups water

Bring to a simmer and cook over medium heat until the berries have popped, about 10 minutes. Let cool slightly. Puree the cranberry mixture in a blender or food processor until smooth. Strain through a fine-mesh sieve into a bowl, pressing firmly to extract as much juice as possible; discard the pulp. Combine in a small saucepan:

1½ cups sugar

½ cup water

Heat, stirring, until the sugar is dissolved. Stir into the cranberry puree. Add the gelatin, stirring until dissolved. Stir in:

1 cup whole milk

Refrigerate the sherbet base until cold, overnight if possible, or quick-chill in an ice water bath, 837.

Pour the base into an ice cream maker and freeze as directed. Serve immediately or transfer to a container with a tight-fitting lid and freeze.

ABOUT GRANITA

Granita is the Italian word for a dessert ice, made from a flavored sugar-syrup base that is frozen solid, then scraped or shaved to produce its characteristically coarse texture of ice crystals. Granitas tend to contain less sugar than sorbets and taste strongly of their flavoring.

Classic granita is stirred and broken up as it freezes. As soon as the granita has properly solidified, it should be scooped into individual bowls or goblets and served immediately. If you start the granita several hours before dinner, the timing should work. For less work, try ➤ the food processor method.

To make granita in the food processor, pour the cooled granita base into two ice cube trays and freeze for at least 3 hours. (The cubes can be transferred to a zip-top freezer bag and frozen for up to 1 week.) Just before serving, puree the cubes in a food processor. Process only as many cubes at a time as will fit in a single layer in the processor bowl, and pulse just until the granita is smooth. Granita will become slushy if pureed too long.

BERRY GRANITA

About 2½ cups

Combine in a small saucepan:

½ cup water

½ cup sugar, or to taste

Cook over medium heat, stirring, just until the sugar is dissolved. Let cool. Puree in a food processor or blender:

4 cups berries, hulled if necessary and sliced if large

Strain through a fine-mesh sieve into a bowl; discard the seeds or skins. Stir the puree into the cooled syrup. Refrigerate until cold or quick-chill in an ice water bath, 837.

Pour the granita base into a 13 × 9 × 2-inch baking dish. Place in the freezer. Every 30 minutes, scrape the mixture with a fork, stirring the frozen crystals from the edges of the dish back into the liquid, loosening and breaking up the crystals. Repeat until the mixture is completely frozen, about 3 hours.

ESPRESSO OR COFFEE GRANITA

About 3 cups

A classic Italian dessert, served with unsweetened whipped cream. Very strong brewed coffee may be used in place of the espresso.

Combine in a medium bowl:

2 cups hot espresso or strong coffee
1/4 to 1/2 cup sugar, to taste
(1 tablespoon amaretto, Frangelico, or sambuca)

Stir until the sugar is dissolved, then refrigerate until cold or quick-chill in an ice water bath, 837. Freeze as described in Berry Granita, 849.

CAFFÈ LATTE GRANITA

About 3 cups

Prepare **Espresso or Coffee Granita, above,** using only 1 cup espresso or coffee. After dissolving the sugar, add **1 cup whole milk.** Proceed as directed.

CITRUS GRANITA

About 2 cups

Combine in a small saucepan:

1 1/2 cups water
1/2 cup sugar
Zest of 1 lemon, lime, or pink grapefruit, removed in wide strips with a vegetable peeler

Bring to a boil over medium heat, stirring occasionally to dissolve the sugar, then cover and boil 5 minutes without stirring. Remove the pan from the heat and let steep for 15 minutes.

Strain into a medium bowl; discard the zest. Let cool to room temperature, then stir in:

1/2 cup fresh lemon, lime, or pink grapefruit juice

Refrigerate until cold or quick-chill in an ice water bath, 837. Freeze as described in Berry Granita, 849.

FRUIT ICE POPS

Eight 3-ounce pops

Stir together well in a medium bowl:

2 cups pureed fresh, frozen, or canned fruit, such as pineapple, berries, mango, peaches, or watermelon
1 cup orange juice
2 tablespoons sugar, or to taste

Pour the mixture into 3-ounce plastic or paper cups or molds made especially for ice pops. If using plastic or paper cups, place them on a rimmed baking sheet and cover with a sheet of plastic wrap after filling. Poke small holes in the plastic wrap above each cup and insert ice pop sticks into the holes. The plastic wrap will hold the sticks in place. Transfer the molds to the freezer. Freeze until solid, for at least 8 hours. Unmold the pops by briefly running the outside of the cups or molds under cool water or by dipping the molds in cool water until the pops easily release from the molds.

ORANGE CREAM POPS

Eight 3-ounce pops

Stir together well in a medium bowl:

1 cup plus 2 tablespoons orange juice
1 1/2 cups whole-milk plain yogurt
1/3 cup sugar, or to taste
1 teaspoon vanilla

Freeze and unmold as described in Fruit Ice Pops, above.

ROASTED BANANA–COCONUT POPS

About ten 3-ounce pops

Roasting the bananas gives them a deeper, richer flavor.

Preheat the oven to 400°F.

Place on a baking sheet:

3 ripe bananas, unpeeled

Roast until very soft and mushy, about 25 minutes.

Let cool slightly, then peel over a blender container, letting the banana pulp fall into the blender; discard the peels. Add to the blender:

One 13 1/2-ounce can coconut milk
1/2 cup packed brown sugar
1 tablespoon lime juice
1 teaspoon vanilla
1/8 teaspoon salt
(1 tablespoon dark rum)

Freeze and unmold as described in Fruit Ice Pops, above. If desired, to coat the pops with chocolate, prepare:

(Chocolate Shell, 808)

Transfer the chocolate shell to a tall glass or container. Dip the unmolded pops in the chocolate, either halfway or to cover completely. Alternatively, drizzle the pops with the chocolate. Place the coated pops on a baking sheet lined with parchment paper and freeze solid, then transfer to a zip-top bag to store.

CHOCOLATE PUDDING POPS

About eight 3-ounce pops

Whisk together in a medium saucepan:

1/2 cup sugar
1/4 cup Dutch-process cocoa powder, sifted
2 tablespoons cornstarch
1/4 teaspoon salt

Whisk into the sugar mixture:

1 cup milk
1 cup heavy cream

Bring to just under a simmer over medium heat, whisking constantly. When the mixture thickens, remove from the heat and whisk in:

2 ounces semisweet or bittersweet chocolate (up to 64% cacao), chopped
1 teaspoon vanilla

Let cool completely. Freeze and unmold as described in Fruit Ice Pops, 850.

SNOW CREAM

After the first two hours of snowfall, snow is clean and usable for this favorite childhood treat. Do not use snow gathered off the ground.

Place in a chilled bowl:

8 cups fresh snow

Stir in:

½ cup heavy cream
¼ cup plus 2 tablespoons sugar
½ teaspoon vanilla

ABOUT ICE CREAM DESSERTS

Thanks to a great appreciation for sugar and fat, humans have had no trouble concocting a plethora of over-the-top ice cream treats. These include classics like the hot fudge sundae and banana split as well as large-format desserts like ice cream pies and cakes. See Garnishes and Additions to Ice Creams, 839, for a comprehensive list of potential sundae toppings and pairing suggestions.

For other ice cream desserts, see Ice Cream Float, 13, Milk Shake, 13, Fruit Milk Shake, 13, and Strawberries Romanoff, 178.

HOT FUDGE SUNDAE

2 servings

Place in a dessert glass or bowl:

3 scoops any ice cream, 840–44

Top with:

2 to 4 tablespoons Hot Fudge Sauce, 808

If desired, drizzle over the top:

(2 to 4 tablespoons Marshmallow Sauce, 809)

Top with:

Whipped Cream, 791
2 tablespoons chopped toasted, 1005, nuts
1 maraschino cherry

AFFOGATO

Affogato is a simple dessert, but one that hits all the right notes: It is creamy and sweet, but with a good dose of bitterness from the espresso. It is the perfect way to end a special meal without serving a heavy-handed dessert. While technically any ice cream can be used in affogato, we recommend keeping it simple with flavors like vanilla, 840, chocolate, 841, or caramel, 840.

For each serving, place in a small glass or cup:

1 scoop ice cream

Pour over it:

1 ounce (2 tablespoons) freshly brewed espresso or double-strength brewed coffee (follow the brewing instructions in Drip Coffee, 4, using twice the amount of coffee)

If desired, garnish with:

(Chopped toasted, 1005, nuts)

Or serve with:

(Almond Macaroons, 774, or Anise-Almond Biscotti, 778)

BANANA SPLIT

2 servings

Stand up on either side of an oblong dish:

1 banana, split lengthwise in half

Place in between the banana halves:

1 scoop Vanilla Ice Cream, 840
1 scoop Chocolate Ice Cream, 841
1 scoop Strawberry Ice Cream, 844

Spoon the following over the ice cream, using a different topping for each scoop:

2 tablespoons Chocolate Sauce, 807, Mocha Sauce, 808, or Chocolate Shell, 808
2 tablespoons Butterscotch Sauce, 809, or Salted Caramel Sauce, 809
2 tablespoons Marshmallow Sauce, 809, or Fresh Berry Coulis, 805

Top with:

Whipped Cream, 791

If desired, scatter over the top:

(2 tablespoons chopped toasted, 1005, nuts)

Top with:

2 maraschino cherries

ICE CREAM SANDWICHES

For each sandwich, spoon partially softened ice cream between two cookies, then refreeze. Some favorite combinations are:

Chocolate Chip Cookies, 769, and Vanilla Ice Cream, 890
Chewy Chocolate Sugar Cookies, 769, and Peppermint Stick Ice Cream, 841
White Chocolate Macadamia Cookies, 770, and Coconut Ice Cream, 842
Peanut Butter Cookies, 771, and Vanilla Ice Cream, 840, or Chocolate Ice Cream, 841

Roll the sides in:

Shredded coconut, toasted, 973, or chopped toasted, 1005, nuts
Chocolate or multicolored sprinkles
Miniature chocolate chips

ICE CREAM PIE

10 to 12 servings

Do not be limited by the combinations here. You can mix any ice cream with these crusts. Ice cream pies are easiest to cut with a knife dipped in hot water and dried before each cut.

I. Prepare, bake, cool, and freeze until very cold, at least 20 minutes:

Meringue Pie Shell, 666, or Crumb Crust, 667

Fill with:

Vanilla Ice Cream, 840, or Butter Pecan Ice Cream, 842

Top with:

Hot Fudge Sauce, 808, Salted Caramel Sauce, 809, Butterscotch Sauce, 809, or Marshmallow Sauce, 809

Freeze until firm, about 1 hour.

II. Prepare, bake, cool, and freeze until very cold, at least 20 minutes:

Crumb Crust, 667, made with chocolate cookies

Fill with:

Mint Chocolate Chip Ice Cream, 840

If desired, top with:

(Hot Fudge Sauce, 808)

Freeze until firm, about 1 hour. Serve with:

Whipped Cream, 791

III. Prepare and freeze until very cold, at least 20 minutes:

Nut Crust, 667

Fill with:

Spiced Pumpkin Ice Cream, 843

If desired, top with:

(Salted Caramel Sauce, 809)

Freeze until firm, about 1 hour. If not topped with caramel sauce, serve with, if desired:

(Hot Buttered Maple Sauce, 811)

ABOUT STILL-FROZEN DESSERTS

Still-frozen desserts are made by allowing the mixture to freeze without stirring or using any special equipment. Still-frozen desserts ➤ need an emulsifying agent or binder—heavy cream, egg yolks, gelatin, cornstarch, or corn syrup—to keep large ice crystals from forming during the freezing process. Count on a very different texture in these desserts from those made by churning. Any of the Bavarian cream recipes, 824, or mousse recipes, 822–23, may be turned into still-frozen desserts.

Freeze these desserts in metal molds and unmold as for **bombes,** 853. Or make individual French-style **parfaits,** frozen in and served from tall parfait glasses, goblets, or wineglasses. Layer the ice cream or other frozen mixture with fruits, nuts, and sauces if desired. Just before serving, top with whipped cream and a cherry. ➤ For the best texture, do not store more than 24 hours.

To remove frozen desserts from a mold, whether from a loaf pan, Bundt pan, or small individual molds, simply dip the mold in cool water until the dessert releases from the mold when inverted onto a serving plate. Lining the mold with plastic wrap before filling it can help with unmolding but is not necessary.

FROZEN BERRY MOUSSE

6 servings

Prepare:

Bavarian Berry Cream, 824, increasing the sugar to 1 cup

Pour into a 1½-quart mold or 6 individual parfait glasses and freeze until firm, about 6 hours for a single mold or 3 hours for glasses.

Top with:

Whipped Cream, 791
Fresh berries

COFFEE PARFAIT

6 to 8 servings

Combine in the top of a double boiler or a heatproof bowl placed over a saucepan or pot of barely simmering water:

⅔ cup sugar
2 tablespoons cornstarch
⅛ teaspoon salt

Stir in:

2 tablespoons whole milk
2 large egg yolks, beaten
1 cup espresso or very strong coffee

Cook, stirring constantly, until the custard coats the back of a spoon. Pour into a medium bowl and refrigerate until cold.

Whip to soft peaks:

1½ cups heavy cream

Fold into the coffee mixture. Divide among parfait glasses and freeze for at least 4 to 5 hours. If frozen longer, let stand at room temperature for 5 to 10 minutes before serving topped with:

Whipped Cream, 791
(Grated chocolate)

HAZELNUT SEMIFREDDO

6 servings

Preheat the oven to 350°F.

Spread on a rimmed baking sheet:

2 cups hazelnuts

Toast until fragrant, stirring occasionally, 10 to 15 minutes. Immediately transfer the nuts to a clean kitchen towel. Wrap the nuts in the towel and rub vigorously to remove as much of the skins as possible. Let cool completely.

Reserve 6 hazelnuts for garnish. Finely grind the remaining nuts in a food processor, but not to a paste. Bring almost to a simmer in a medium saucepan:

3 cups whole milk

Stir in the ground nuts. Remove the pan from the heat, cover, and steep for 30 minutes.

Strain the milk into a bowl, pressing on the nuts to extract as much liquid as possible; discard the nuts, and return the milk to the saucepan. Add:

⅓ cup sugar

Bring to a simmer, stirring occasionally to dissolve the sugar. Beat in a medium heatproof bowl:

4 large egg yolks
½ cup sugar

Slowly whisk half the hot milk mixture into the eggs. Pour this mixture back into the saucepan and cook over low heat, stirring constantly, until the custard reaches 175°F and coats the back of a spoon. Do not allow the mixture to boil. Remove the pan from the heat and strain the custard through a fine-mesh sieve into a large bowl. Chill thoroughly. Whip to soft peaks:

1 cup heavy cream

Gently stir one-quarter of the whipped cream into the chilled custard, then fold in the remaining whipped cream. Spoon the mixture into 6 individual goblets. Place plastic wrap directly on the surface of the custards. Freeze until firm, for at least 3 hours. Garnish each goblet with a hazelnut. Serve immediately.

CHOCOLATE SEMIFREDDO

12 to 16 servings

Line a 9 × 5-inch loaf pan with plastic wrap, allowing the excess to hang over the edges. Beat in a stand mixer with the whisk on medium-high speed, 2 to 3 minutes:

4 large eggs

Combine in a small saucepan:

¼ cup water
¾ cup sugar

Simmer over medium heat until the syrup is clear. Continue to cook until the sugar reaches 243°F on a candy thermometer. With the mixer running on medium-high speed, slowly add the hot sugar syrup to the eggs, pouring it down the side of the bowl and avoiding the whisk. Beat on high speed until light and fluffy and cooled to room temperature, 5 to 10 minutes.

Gently fold in:

6 ounces bittersweet or dark chocolate, melted
1 teaspoon vanilla

Whip to soft peaks:

1 cup heavy cream

Gently fold the cream into chocolate mixture. Pour into the prepared pan and place plastic wrap directly on the surface. Freeze until firm, for at least 8 hours.

Remove the plastic covering and unmold the semifreddo onto a serving platter. Peel away the plastic wrap, slice, and serve immediately. Alternatively, the semifreddo may be scooped from the pan with an ice cream scoop.

SPUMONI

8 to 10 servings

Authentic Italian *spumone* is essentially an unmolded bombe, below, usually with a center of soft semifreddo or pastry cream, often flavored with amaretti cookies and studded with candied fruit.

Line a 9 × 5-inch loaf pan with plastic wrap, allowing the excess to hang over the edges. Spread evenly in the bottom of the pan:

2 cups Chocolate Ice Cream, 841, softened

Freeze until firm enough to hold the next layer, about 30 minutes.

Spread evenly on top of the first layer:

2 cups Pistachio Ice Cream, 842, softened

Freeze as for the first layer.

Beat together in a medium bowl:

2 cups Vanilla Ice Cream, 840, softened
½ cup maraschino cherries, drained and chopped
½ cup sliced almonds, toasted, 1005
(A few drops red food coloring, to reach desired color)

Spread over the pistachio ice cream and freeze until hard, for at least 2 hours.

Unmold and remove the plastic wrap. Slice and serve with:

Whipped Cream, 791
(Chocolate Sauce, 807)

PISTACHIO AND ROSE WATER KULFI

Eight 3-ounce servings

Kulfi is an Indian still-frozen dessert traditionally made by cooking milk down until rich and concentrated. It is common, however, to use evaporated milk and cream for a speedier procedure. For information on rose water, see Extracts and Flavorings, 980.

Combine in a medium saucepan:

One 12-ounce can evaporated milk
1 cup heavy cream
½ cup sugar
3 cardamom pods, crushed

Bring just to a simmer, stirring to dissolve the sugar, then take off the heat, let cool, and refrigerate overnight.

Strain the mixture; discard the solids. Stir in:

¼ cup pistachios, very finely chopped
1 tablespoon rose water

Pour the mixture into kulfi molds or small paper cups, transfer to the freezer, and allow to freeze solid, overnight. To unmold, run the molds under cool water until the ice cream pops out. If using paper cups, simply peel the paper away from the ice cream and invert onto a plate.

ABOUT BOMBES

A bombe is a molded dessert layered with different flavors of ice cream, frozen yogurt, semifreddo, sherbet, or sorbet. Bombes are traditionally made with still-frozen desserts, but churned or store-bought ice creams and sorbets may be used. Most bombes consist of one or two outside layers and one center layer. Use flavors and textures that will complement one another. Combine ice cream with a sorbet or a sherbet with a semifreddo. Any of these layers may be made with mix-ins, 839, or add crunchy morsels between the layers.

Choose a mold made of stainless steel or tin; it is difficult to unmold a bombe from a glass mold. Oval molds with ridges or melon molds are classic, but loaf pans, bowls, charlotte molds, or springform pans will work as well. Chill the mold in the freezer for 30 minutes before filling. If using homemade ice cream or sorbet, make the bases ahead, then churn each one as needed so that you will be assured of a soft, easy-to-spread consistency. Alternatively, you may soften frozen ice cream in the refrigerator until it is spreadable. Spread in the mold to a thickness of ¾ to 1 inch, one layer at a time. ➤ Each layer must be thoroughly frozen before the next layer is added. Use the back of a serving spoon and pack the ice cream firmly and evenly so there are no air pockets.

After the mold is filled, it must be frozen until solid, for at least 6 hours, or up to 24 hours. ➤ Do not store bombes much longer than this, as the texture may start to coarsen and turn icy.

To unmold a bombe, ➤ invert onto a chilled plate or platter. Place a hot, wet kitchen towel over the mold for 30 seconds, then give the platter a rap on the counter to release the bombe. Once the bombe is unmolded, immediately place back in the freezer to firm the outside layer. To slice, let soften in the refrigerator for 20 to 30 minutes before serving. You also may cut into slices using a sharp knife and arrange on a platter; rinse the knife in hot water and wipe it dry after each slice. Let the slices stand in the refrigerator for 5 to

10 minutes and then serve. A bombe is best when just beginning to melt slightly.

Bombes may be served with fresh berries, Fresh Berry Coulis, 805, or Whipped Cream, 791.

Below are some good combinations for bombes. The first in each list is the outside layer:

Vanilla Ice Cream, 840, and Strawberry Sorbet, 847, or Peach Sorbet, 847

Chocolate Ice Cream, 840, and Caramel Ice Cream, 840, or Coffee Ice Cream, 840

Pistachio Ice Cream, 842, and Cranberry Sherbet, 849, or Raspberry Sherbet, 849

Coconut Ice Cream, 842, and Mango Sorbet, 847, or Mango Frozen Yogurt, 846

BAKED ALASKA

10 to 16 servings

This marvelous construction is a show-stopping finale to a celebratory meal. Though it needs last-minute preparation, it isn't very difficult to make. Miraculously, a little cake on the bottom and a covering of soft meringue is enough to insulate the ice cream while the topping is browned in a hot oven. Of course, if you are in possession of a propane torch, putting the finishing touch on this dessert will be its finest hour. A layer of brownies can be substituted for the cake, if desired. If you wish to use multiple flavors of ice cream in the same dessert, mold the ice cream as directed in About Bombes, 853.

Line a dome-shaped bowl with plastic wrap. Depending on the size of the bowl, fill it with:

1½ pints to ½ gallon ice cream, softened just enough to be spreadable

Smooth the ice cream so the top is flat, and freeze solid. Have ready a round of:

Génoise, 721, Angel Food Cake, 719, or Sponge Cake, 720

at least ½ inch thick and cut slightly larger than the diameter of the bowl in which the ice cream was molded. If desired, sprinkle it lightly with:

(Rum or brandy)

Position the cake on top of the ice cream in the bowl, making sure no plastic wrap comes between the ice cream and the cake. Cover and freeze until needed.

Invert and unmold the dessert onto a serving platter (if using a propane torch to toast the meringue) or a foil-lined baking sheet (if toasting the meringue in the oven). Use any overhanging plastic wrap to help coax the ice cream out of the bowl. If needed, drape a hot, wet kitchen towel over the bowl until the ice cream releases from the bowl. Place the unmolded dessert in the freezer for 20 minutes to set the outside layer.

If you do not plan on using a propane torch to brown the meringue, preheat the oven to 450°F.

Prepare:

Double recipe Italian Meringue, 794, French Meringue, 794, or Soft Meringue Topping I, 795

Spread the meringue over the dessert so the surface is entirely coated with a ¾-inch thickness of meringue, bringing the meringue right down to the surface of the platter or baking sheet. Swirl the topping decoratively with the back of a spoon, or reserve some of the meringue in a pastry bag and pipe on fluted edges and patterns. Bake for 5 minutes, watching carefully, to lightly brown the meringue. Alternatively, evenly brown the outside with a propane torch. Serve immediately, with, if desired:

(Chocolate Sauce, 807, Fresh Berry Coulis, 805, or Salted Caramel Sauce, 809)

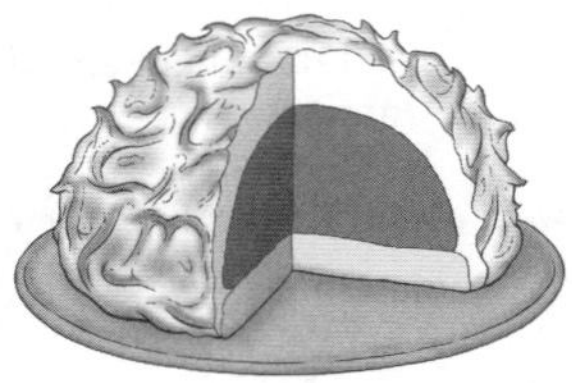

Interior of a Baked Alaska

BISCUIT TORTONIS

12 servings

These old-fashioned Italian desserts get their almond flavor from amaretti cookies, which are traditionally made from apricot kernels.

Combine in a medium bowl:

¾ cup crushed amaretti or Almond Macaroons, 774

¾ cup heavy cream

¼ cup powdered sugar

Pinch of salt

Let stand 1 hour. Whip to soft peaks:

1 cup heavy cream

Fold in the cookie mixture and:

1 teaspoon vanilla

Divide among 12 paper muffin cups set in a muffin tin or on a baking sheet. Before freezing or when partly frozen, decorate the tops with:

Finely chopped toasted, 1005, almonds (about ½ teaspoon per tortoni; 2 tablespoons total)

(Candied cherries)

Freeze until firm, for about 3½ hours.

CANDIES AND CONFECTIONS

Making candy is probably the closest most home cooks get to alchemy. Indeed, the transformation of sugar into stretchy taffy, chewy caramels, shatteringly crisp brittle, and fluffy marshmallows can seem like magic. But really, candy making boils down to sugar (or chocolate), temperature, and time. A basic understanding of crystallization, 856 (or in the case of chocolate, tempering, 858), will prepare you for almost all candy making.

Two variables that are beyond the control of the confectioner, however, are weather and altitude. Heat, humidity, and how high above sea level your kitchen is all play important roles in obtaining the best results when making candy. On humid days, candy must cook longer, to a temperature at least 2 degrees higher than on dry days. Making candy that requires drying time on a rack—chocolate-dipped fondant, hard candy, divinity, nougat, and taffy—should be confined to moderately cool, dry days (or to kitchens with ample air conditioning). ▲ For tips on making candy at high altitudes, see About High-Altitude Candy Making, 857.

ABOUT EQUIPMENT

➤ Always choose large, nonreactive, heavy-bottomed pans with a capacity of three to four times the volume of the ingredients to leave plenty of room for boiling up. ➤ To keep from burning yourself, use a long wooden spoon or a silicone spatula. These tools will not heat up during the prolonged cooking time. Further, when a cold metal spoon is plunged into hot sugar syrup, it may cause the syrup around the spoon to cool slightly, thus leading to undesirable crystallization.

For chocolate work, a **double boiler** is the best tool for melting chocolate without scorching it. You can improvise with a pot or saucepan and a heatproof bowl, but be sure the bowl fits snugly over the saucepan to prevent water from bubbling into the chocolate and causing it to seize. **Immersion circulators** are also wonderful tools for melting and tempering chocolate: They can easily temper smaller amounts of chocolate at a time, do not require constant attention, and are less messy. See About Tempering Chocolate, 858, for the procedure.

Offset spatulas have long, angled, flexible blades and are particularly useful for tasks like spreading chocolate on a marble slab or scraping excess chocolate from chocolate molds. **Parchment paper** is ideal for lining baking sheets and making piping cones. **Silicone liners** are excellent for easy cooling and removal of candies from baking sheets, especially brittles and toffees. **Piping bags and tips** are handy for piping out truffle mixtures and candy fillings. Wash and dry the bags thoroughly after each use to prevent them from souring or purchase disposable, plastic piping bags or use parchment paper to fashion low-budget pastry cones, 716. **Zip-top bags** are an alternative to piping bags. Fill a plastic sandwich or storage bag no more than two-thirds full with the piping mixture, twist the top, and cut a small hole in one bottom corner.

A **candy scraper,** a flat sheet of metal with a handle, is a great tool (a **bench scraper,** 661, is a good multipurpose alternative). Use it to move, scrape, and divide warm masses of candy and dough. Also have on hand a **pastry brush** with natural (not plastic) bristles; a **bowl scraper,** made of thin and flexible plastic; and a **thermometer** for gauging the temperature of sugar syrups and chocolate. Glass candy thermometers are readily available, but we recommend an instant-read digital thermometer (preferably a leave-in thermometer that can be fitted to the side of the pot), which will serve you well whether you're making caramels or prime rib.

Candy scraper, offset spatula, double boiler, candy and truffle dippers

For the avid candy maker, there is no shortage of specialty equipment. **Candy and truffle dippers** are helpful if you make chocolate-dipped candies regularly. Or you can make your own dipping tool by breaking out the two middle tines of a plastic fork. Those who make candy frequently will appreciate a **marble slab** or **granite countertop.** For candies that require rapid cooling, this material absorbs heat quickly and evenly, but not so rapidly as to hasten crystallization. The next best base is a heavy stoneware platter or a rimmed baking sheet elevated on a cooling rack so that air can circulate around it.

For making molded candies, inexpensive plastic or silicone **molds** are available in a multitude of designs and sizes. ➤ Never use an abrasive when cleaning those molds, as chocolate will stick to a scratched surface.

ABOUT CRYSTALLIZATION

The confectioner's success depends on crystallization, but it must happen at the right time and in the right way. Unless you're making rock candy, where large sugar crystals are desirable, the best candies have a fine crystal structure. This can be achieved by paying attention to a few things.

First, ➤ prevent seed points from forming. Larger sugar crystals grow from a seed point. Stray sugar crystals on the side of the pan or on the spoon may become seed points. This is why many candy recipes instruct you to wash down the inside of the pot with a wet brush. Before beginning to work with sugar, make sure all your equipment and utensils are very clean.

Second, ➤ avoid stirring the syrup once it begins to boil. (The rare exceptions to this rule are noted in individual recipes.) Stirring the boiling syrup forces small sugar crystals to bump into one another, forming larger and larger crystals. This is why many candy recipes explicitly tell you not to stir the syrup. If, due to hot spots on your stovetop, the syrup starts to caramelize in one area faster than another, carefully swirl the syrup in the pan rather than stirring it.

Third, ➤ do not be tempted to substitute other products for the granulated white sugar or corn syrup in candy recipes. Granulated white sugar is incredibly pure compared to so-called "raw" sugar and evaporated cane juice products. If these are substituted, their impurities may cause premature or excessive crystallization. Corn syrup plays a crucial role in candy making by preventing crystallization and, sometimes, promoting a chewy texture. In some cases, other liquid sweeteners, such as honey or brown rice syrup, may be substituted for corn syrup with success (caramel candies, for instance, are more forgiving), but in general, follow the recipes exactly as written for best results.

Finally, when pouring or molding the finished syrup, ➤ avoid scraping the dregs from the pan. The crystallization rate of the syrup nearest the bottom of the pan, which has been exposed to the greatest heat, is faster than that of the free-flowing syrup from the upper portion. Adding the former to the latter can cause the entire batch to crystallize.

Some candies, such as fudge, are cooled rapidly, then stirred constantly to create a very fine crystal structure. This is an example of harnessing crystallization to create a desired texture. For more information on crystallization in different types of candies read the individual sections in this chapter.

ABOUT CANDY THERMOMETERS

Candy thermometers are designed to clip to the side of a pot and read the stages of cooked sugar in at least 2-degree gradations between 100° and 400°F. An instant-read digital thermometer is also a good option—just make sure it will read temperatures up to 400°F. Some digital thermometers are short and stubby, which is problematic when dealing with molten sugar syrups and hot steam, so try to find one with a longer probe, and preferably one that can be clipped to the side of the pot. Leaving the probe in the syrup for the duration of the cooking period is the best way to get accurate temperature readings. Ultimately, purchasing an instant-read digital thermometer that can be used in day-to-day cooking as well as candy making is a better investment than buying separate thermometers for different tasks. To test a thermometer's accuracy and calibrate it, see page 1043.

THE STAGES OF COOKED SUGAR SYRUP

As sugar syrup boils, its temperature will rise above the boiling point of water as the water in the syrup evaporates. The temperature will appear stalled at or below 230°F for some time, but after that it will rise quickly. At 330°F, the syrup will have concentrated to over 99 percent sugar. If taken further, the syrup will cease boiling and begin to rapidly break down, producing progressively darker shades of caramel.

Before kitchen thermometers were commonplace, candy makers used cold water to determine when a sugar syrup had reached a desired concentration or "stage." We recommend always using a thermometer, but if you find yourself enamored of candy making, learning how to judge the different stages of sugar syrup by sight is a useful tool to add to the repertoire. The classic way to confirm the stages of cooked sugar syrup is the **cold water test.** ➤ Before performing this test, remove the pan from the heat so as not to overcook the syrup; just a few extra degrees can bring the candy up into the next sugar syrup stage.

To perform the cold water test, use a clean wooden or silicone spoon to drop a small quantity of sugar syrup—less than a teaspoon—into a small container of cold tap water. The temperature to which the sugar has been cooked can be identified by the way the syrup reacts; see below. Use fresh, cool water for each test.

As the water in a sugar syrup heats and evaporates, the concentration of sugar in the syrup rises. The higher the concentration of sugar, the harder the mixture will be upon cooling. Thus chewy candy, like caramel, is cooked to a lower temperature than crunchy or hard candies, like toffee. The stages of cooked sugar syrup, shown below, describe the temperature range for each one, the visual characteristics of each, and a few of the candies that are cooked to that stage.

THREAD—223° to 234°F
Makes a brittle thread that runs off the end of the spoon.

SOFT BALL—235° to 244°F
Syrup dropped into chilled water forms a limp, sticky ball that flattens when removed from the water and rolled between the fingers.
Fluffy White Frosting, 795, Chocolate Fudge, 863, Caramel Corn, 865, Fondant, 866, Peppermint Patties, 866

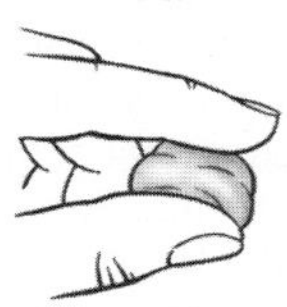

FIRM BALL—245° to 249°F
Syrup dropped into chilled water forms a ball that holds its shape and will not flatten unless pressed with fingers.
Caramels, 864–65, Sesame Halvah, 874, Marshmallows, 868, Marzipan, 873

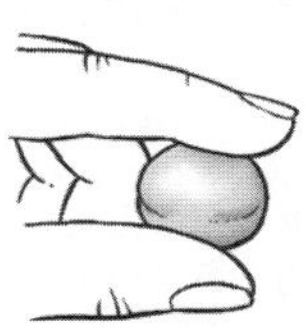

HARD BALL—250° to 265°F
Syrup dropped into chilled water forms a ball that is more rigid but still pliable.
Divinity, 867, Pulled Mints, 869, Taffy, 869, Rock Candy, 872

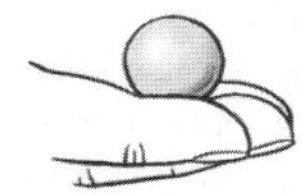

SOFT CRACK—270° to 290°F
Syrup dropped into chilled water separates into hard threads, which, when removed from the water, will bend.
Nougat, 867, Taffy, 869, English Toffee, 870

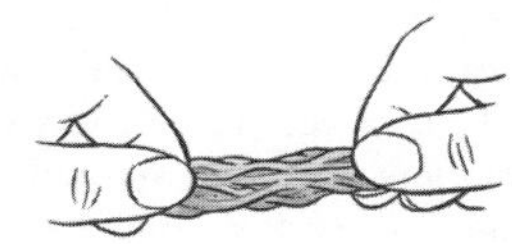

HARD CRACK—300° to 310°F
Syrup dropped into chilled water separates into threads that are hard and brittle.
Butterscotch, 871, Coffee Drops, 871, Peanut Brittle, 870, Lollipops, 872

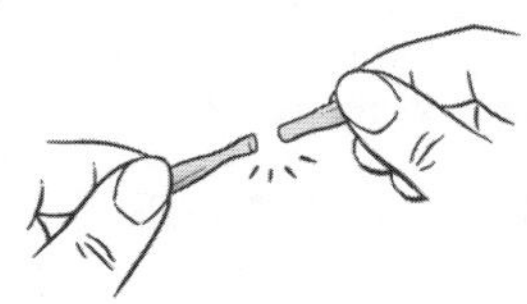

CARAMELIZED SUGAR

For more on the chemical process behind caramelization, see 1024.

Above 330°F
Syrup changes from honey colored to light brown
Sesame Seed Brittle, 870

355° to 360°F
Syrup turns a medium brown color
French Praline, 873, spun sugar, caramel cages

375° to 380°F
Syrup turns a dark brown color
Coloring agent for sauces

410°F
The syrup turns black and then decomposes
None

▲ ABOUT HIGH-ALTITUDE CANDY MAKING

As with baking, altitude can make a difference in candy making. If you live above sea level, cook sugar syrups 1 degree lower than indicated in candy recipes for each increase of 500 feet above sea level. For instance, if you're making fudge, which needs to cook to a minimum of 238°F, your syrup should "fudge" at 230° to 234°F at 2,000 feet, or at 224° to 228°F at 5,000 feet.

ABOUT WRAPPING, STORING, AND SERVING CANDY

To protect candy and preserve its freshness, use precut squares of wax paper, colored foil, and cellophane to wrap hard candies, taffies, and caramels. Or cut long narrow strips of parchment paper, then lay out pieces of candy, generously spaced, along the strips. Seal in the candy by twisting the strip sausage fashion, then cut between the candies to separate them.

Different types of candies benefit from different storage conditions. See individual sections and recipes for specific storage instructions. In general, chocolate candies or candies coated in chocolate should be stored in the refrigerator or freezer in an airtight container. Hard candies, caramels, taffies, and divinity will stay fresh and keep their texture best when individually wrapped and stored in airtight containers at room temperature for no longer than 3 weeks. Do not refrigerate, because they are highly hygroscopic—meaning they attract and absorb moisture and become soft, crumbly, and very sticky.

All candies taste best at room temperature. After refrigerating candies, let them stand at room temperature for at least 20 minutes before serving. Thaw frozen candies in the refrigerator for at least 24 hours before serving, then let them stand at room temperature for at least 20 minutes. Sudden changes in temperature can cause chocolate coating to crack and discolor.

ABOUT CHOCOLATE CANDIES

Chocolate candies are a great introduction to candy making. They tend to be easier to make and less intimidating than candies that require molten sugar syrups. Furthermore, almost everyone loves chocolate. Having said that, working with chocolate can be quite complicated, which is why we devote ample space to a discussion of tempering, below.

In the recipes that follow, we call for bittersweet, dark, milk, or white chocolate. ➤ Do not substitute chocolate chips (they do not melt easily) or compound chocolate (it does not behave or temper like true chocolate, as it is often made with cocoa powder and lacks cocoa butter) in these recipes. For more on chocolate types, see 970.

To store chocolate candies, layer them between sheets of wax paper in an airtight container and place them away from strong-flavored foods—chocolate easily absorbs other flavors, even when covered. Most chocolate candies keep up to 3 weeks in the refrigerator and can be frozen for up to 2 months. For long-term freezing, wrap plastic containers in several layers of foil.

ABOUT TEMPERING CHOCOLATE

The subtitle to this section should be "It's Complicated." As with sugar syrup–based candies, controlled crystallization is key when creating chocolate confections. This is accomplished by tempering, a process of heating and cooling melted chocolate to specific temperatures so that the finished chocolate has a glossy surface, a smooth texture, and a nice snap. ➤ Tempering is only necessary when using high-quality, pure chocolate. Baking chocolate, chocolate coatings, compound chocolate, and chocolate chips cannot be tempered. Many so-called "white chocolate" products do not actually contain any cocoa butter. If a chocolate product contains no cocoa butter, it cannot and does not need to be tempered. Tempering is not required when melted chocolate is used as an ingredient in a recipe (to melt chocolate on the stovetop or in the microwave, see 972).

All good chocolate contains cocoa butter, which is composed of fat molecules that link together to create six different forms of crystals. The most stable of these forms, and the one that we want when tempering chocolate, is form V, or "beta 2." When tempering chocolate, you hold melted chocolate at a temperature conducive to the formation of these beta 2 crystals—82° to 90°F. Once these crystals start to get established, they encourage the formation of more beta 2 crystals. When chocolate is properly tempered, enough beta crystals are present that, as the chocolate cools and hardens, more and more beta crystals form, resulting in glossy, smooth, snappy chocolate.

Chocolate is tempered when it leaves the factory, and with proper handling and storage, it should still be "in temper" when purchased. At this point, the cocoa butter in the bar is completely crystallized and will not turn into a liquid until the crystals are melted, which happens when they are heated above 100°F. Once chocolate is melted, all the beta 2 crystals are destroyed. The chocolate is no longer in temper and must be retempered in order to be used for dipping confections, molding shapes, and making fanciful decorations; in fact, if making molded chocolates, you must temper the chocolate so that they will release easily from the molds.

THE SEED METHOD

This is the most common way of tempering chocolate. After the chocolate is melted—thus destroying all the crystals—you start to cool it by "seeding" it with chunks of solid chocolate that are already in temper. The solid chocolate brings with it plenty of beta 2 crystals to jump-start the formation of more beta 2 crystals in the melted chocolate. When cooled to 88° to 90°F, the combination of stirring and adding in solid chocolate will have promoted the formation of enough crystals to bring the chocolate in temper. ➤ Stirring the chocolate is just as important to the formation of beta 2 crystals as seeding and heating and cooling it to the prescribed temperatures. Finally, be very careful that water does not drip into the chocolate during the tempering process, or the chocolate will seize.

To temper chocolate using the seed method, set aside:

4 ounces high-quality dark, milk, or white chocolate, grated or finely chopped

Place in the top of a double boiler:

1 pound high-quality dark, milk, or white chocolate, grated or finely chopped

Melt the chocolate very slowly over barely simmering water. (If you do not have a double boiler, a heatproof bowl over a pot of water works just as well.) Stir the chocolate constantly until its temperature reaches 115°F. Take the top of the double boiler or the bowl off the pot of steaming water, and wipe off any condensation on the bottom to prevent water from coming in contact with the chocolate. Scrape the chocolate into another bowl and cool, stirring, to 100°F. Add the reserved chocolate chunks and stir until the temperature cools to 88°F for milk and white chocolates and 90°F for dark chocolate. To speed up the process, you may dip the bottom of the bowl of melted chocolate in a shallow ice water bath for several seconds at a time, stirring constantly. Measure the temperature of the chocolate frequently, cleaning off the end of the thermometer between each use. Once the temperature is reached, remove any unmelted chunks of chocolate, place them on a baking sheet lined with wax or parchment paper or a silicone liner, and refrigerate until solid; they are reusable. The chocolate is now in temper and ready to be tested as below and used.

IMMERSION CIRCULATOR METHOD

Using an immersion circulator, 1054, to temper chocolate is much easier as it does not require constant stirring or attention and creates less mess. Place the chocolate in a heavy-duty zip-top freezer bag (do not use regular zip-top bags, as they are not sturdy enough) or vacuum bag but do not close it yet if using a zip-top bag (seal vacuum bags with a vacuum sealer). Fill a stockpot or heatproof container two-thirds full with water. Partially submerge the bag of chocolate in the water, forcing out as much air from the bag as possible without getting the seal wet. Zip the bag shut and clip it to the side of the container or pot. For a sealed vacuum bag, submerge the bag and clip it to the side of the pot. Place the circulator in the water, secure it to the side, and set it to 115°F. Heat the chocolate for 1 hour, massaging the bag every 20 minutes to make sure it is evenly melted. Set the temperature to 81°F and gradually add ice to the water bath to reduce the temperature quickly. After 5 minutes at 81°F, set the circulator to 90°F. Periodically massage the bag to promote even heating. After 10 minutes at 90°F, the chocolate should be in temper and ready for use. Alternatively, you can combine this technique with the seed method, above, by melting the chocolate at 115°F, cooling it to 90°F, and then "seeding" the bag with 25 percent of the melted chocolate's weight in grated, tempered chocolate. Be extremely careful not to get any water in the bag as you do this. When you are ready to use the chocolate, dry the bag completely. You may place the bag in a bowl to help it stay upright and dip items into it or transfer the chocolate to a small bowl. For applying chocolate to Chocolate-Pecan Tortoises, 865, or to drizzle it over candies, simply cut off a corner of the bag and use it as you would a piping bag.

TESTING THE TEMPER AND KEEPING WARM

➤ No matter what method you use to temper chocolate, do not assume it is properly tempered simply because it reached the prescribed temperatures. The chocolate should be tested to ensure that it is properly tempered.

To test tempered chocolate, place a dab of the chocolate on the blade of a butter knife and let set for 3 minutes in a cool area. If it is dry to the touch and evenly glossy with no white streaks, the chocolate is ready to use. If it does not pass the test, hold the chocolate at 90°F (or 88°F for white or milk chocolate) and stir it constantly, then retest after several minutes (if it still fails, start the tempering process over again).

To maintain the temper of a bowl of chocolate over an extended period, place it in a pan of warm water and maintain the temperature of the chocolate at around 90°F. Be careful; if the chocolate exceeds 93°F the chocolate will go out of temper and you will have to begin again. If you tempered the chocolate with an immersion circulator, simply hold the water bath at 88°F for milk and white chocolates and 90°F for dark, unsweetened, or bittersweet chocolate. Keep the chocolate submerged in the bag as long as needed. Bear in mind that there is a limit to how long you can keep chocolate melted and in temper: Eventually, the cocoa butter will grow too many crystals and become too thick to work with easily. The simplest remedy is to transfer half of the chocolate to a bowl and heat it above 100°F in a double boiler, which will destroy the crystals. Mix it back into the tempered chocolate, wait 5 minutes, and it should flow more easily.

DARK CHOCOLATE TRUFFLES

About 1½ pounds; about 80 pieces

Truffles are one of the easiest chocolate candies to make. Named whimsically after the savory black truffle, these candies have centers of plain or flavored ganache, which is a mixture of chocolate and cream. The ganache centers may be dipped in chocolate or coated with a variety of ingredients. Ganache will keep, refrigerated, for up to 1 month, and, frozen, for up to 3 months. Use the best-quality chocolate you can afford.

Place in a heatproof medium bowl or in a 1-quart microwave-safe glass bowl:

12 ounces high-quality dark, semisweet, or bittersweet chocolate (up to 72% cacao), very finely chopped

Measure out:

1¼ cups heavy cream

To make on the stovetop: Heat the cream to just under a simmer in a small saucepan over medium heat and pour all at once over the chocolate. Stir gently in a circular motion until the mixture is smooth and thoroughly blended.

To make in the microwave: Pour the cream over the chocolate in the glass bowl and microwave on high in 30-second increments until melted and smooth, gently stirring after each interval, 1½ to 2½ minutes total.

Let cool to room temperature, stirring occasionally, then refrigerate for 3 to 4 hours, until the ganache is thick and quite stiff. Refrigerate a baking sheet lined with wax or parchment paper or a silicone liner until cold. Use a small, 2-teaspoon portion scoop, melon baller, or a piping bag fitted with a ½-inch plain tip to scoop or pipe out balls of ganache about ¾ inch in diameter onto the chilled baking sheet. Cover loosely with plastic wrap and refrigerate until firm, about 2 hours. When firm, roll the balls between your palms to smooth them out.

For coated truffles, proceed as for:

Coated Chocolate Truffles, 860

For dipped truffles, proceed as for:

Dipped Chocolate Truffles, 860

Serve right away or store, 858.

MILK OR WHITE CHOCOLATE TRUFFLES

About 1 pound; about 54 pieces

Substitute **12 ounces high-quality milk or white chocolate** for the dark chocolate in **Dark Chocolate Truffles, above,** and reduce the amount of cream to ½ cup. Use the microwave method described above, or combine the chocolate and cream in the top of a double boiler or a heatproof bowl placed over hot, not boiling, water and stir frequently until the chocolate is melted and smooth. Let cool, form, and store as directed.

VEGAN CHOCOLATE TRUFFLES

About 1 pound; about 55 pieces

Prepare **Dark Chocolate Truffles, 859,** using **12 ounces vegan dark chocolate (up to 72% cacao), very finely chopped,** and **¾ cup canned coconut milk.** Let cool, form, and store as directed.

FLAVORED GANACHE

Ganache can be flavored by simply adding ingredients to the chocolate/cream mixture or by infusing the cream first. Adding liqueur requires a small adjustment to recipes; see Boozy Chocolate Truffles, below.

Before proceeding with a truffle recipe, heat the cream or coconut milk to just under a simmer and add one of the following (halve the amounts for Milk or White Chocolate Truffles):

1 cup fresh mint leaves or 2 sprigs rosemary
¼ cup crushed coffee beans
8 cardamom pods, crushed, 1 teaspoon fennel seeds, or 1 cinnamon stick
Zest of 1 lemon, orange, or lime, removed in wide strips with a vegetable peeler
1 vanilla bean, split lengthwise
1 tablespoon dried lavender
1 tablespoon Earl Grey tea

Cover, remove from the heat, and allow to steep for 30 minutes. Strain and reheat before adding to the chocolate.

Or, after combining the cream and chocolate, stir one of the following into the ganache while it is still warm:

⅔ cup nuts, toasted, 1005, and finely chopped
2 teaspoons vanilla
1 tablespoon plus 2 teaspoons instant espresso powder
¼ cup raspberry jam
¼ cup tahini
¼ teaspoon chipotle chile powder

BOOZY CHOCOLATE TRUFFLES

Truffles are even more indulgent with a splash of spirits. Bourbon, rum, Cognac, framboise, kirsch, and Grand Marnier are all good choices. Prepare **Dark Chocolate Truffles, 859, Milk or White Chocolate Truffles, 859,** or **Vegan Chocolate Truffles, above,** increasing the amount of chocolate in the ganache to 14 ounces. Once the cream and chocolate are melted, stir in **¼ cup liquor for dark chocolate or 2 tablespoons for milk and white chocolate.** Let cool, form, and store as directed.

DIPPED CHOCOLATE TRUFFLES

In addition to dipping truffles, you may use this procedure to dip squares of nougat, 867, fudge, 862, Honeycomb Candy, 871, or any other type of candy center. If you wish to skip the rigmarole of tempering, there are chocolate coating products available that need only be melted (such as compound chocolate), though their flavor is not as rich as real chocolate. If desired, after dipping, garnish the truffles to indicate the flavor of the filling or simply for decoration. For example, top truffles with pieces of candied citrus peel, a toasted whole nut, freeze-dried fruit, pink peppercorns, a toasted coconut flake, flaky sea salt, or bee pollen.

Prepare the ganache for:

Any of the truffles, 859–60

Temper, 858:

1 pound high-quality dark, milk, or white chocolate

Before dipping into chocolate, be sure the ganache centers are about 70°F. Otherwise the chocolate may streak with gray. Line a baking sheet with wax or parchment paper. Using a fork or a candy dipper, dip the centers, one by one, in a small quantity of the tempered chocolate. Lift them out with the fork and allow excess chocolate to drip off. Place the truffles on the prepared baking sheet and refrigerate until set, about 20 minutes. Serve right away or store, 858.

COATED CHOCOLATE TRUFFLES

Rolling the ganache centers in a coating rather than dipping them in chocolate is a simple, delicious method of finishing truffles. Cocoa powder, meant to suggest the earth that clings to real truffles when they are dug, is classic.

Prepare the ganache for:

Any of the truffles, 859–60

After rolling the ganache centers until smooth, transfer them to a pan lined with wax or parchment paper or a silicone liner. Have ready another lined pan. Spread in a pie plate or shallow bowl one or more of the following (if using more than one coating, place them in separate bowls):

1 cup sifted unsweetened cocoa powder
1 cup sifted unsweetened cocoa powder, mixed with 2 teaspoons ground cinnamon
1 cup powdered sugar, sifted
1 cup powdered sugar, sifted with 1 tablespoon matcha
1 cup shredded coconut, toasted, 973
1 cup nuts, toasted, 1005, and finely chopped

Drop one truffle into the bowl of coating, and shake the bowl to coat it. Chunkier coatings, like chopped nuts, may need to be gently pressed into the truffles to make them adhere. Lift the truffle out and place it on the lined pan. Repeat with the remaining truffles. Serve right away or store, 858.

CHOCOLATE BARK OR BARS

About 1¼ pounds

The easiest chocolate candy to make is also infinitely variable. Pair the type of chocolate with compatible fruits and nuts. For instance, white chocolate with pistachios and dried cherries or dark chocolate with candied ginger.

Line a baking sheet with foil. Temper, 858:

1 pound semisweet, bittersweet, milk, or white chocolate

For bark: Spread the chocolate with an offset spatula about ¼ inch thick on the lined baking sheet. Tap the pan on the work surface to release any air bubbles. Sprinkle on top:

2 cups chopped toasted, 1005, nuts, dried fruit, mini marshmallows, or a combination

For bars: Mix together the tempered chocolate and nuts or fruit and pour into bar-shaped molds.

Refrigerate until firm, about 15 minutes. Then let stand in a cool place to set completely, 30 minutes to 1 hour. Bars are ready to unmold when they have shrunk somewhat from the sides of the molds.

To serve bark, hold the chocolate with the foil to avoid getting fingerprints on it and break into bite-sized irregular shapes. For bars, unmold as for Small Solid Chocolates, below. Serve right away or store, 858.

CHOCOLATE CLUSTERS

About 1 pound; about twenty-five 1-inch clusters

Line a baking sheet with wax or parchment paper or a silicone liner. Temper, 858:

8 ounces high-quality semisweet or bittersweet chocolate

Stir into the chocolate until combined:

1 cup dried fruit, finely chopped if pieces are larger than ½ inch

1 cup nuts, toasted, 1005, and coarsely chopped

Spoon out 1-inch clusters onto the lined baking sheet. Chill the clusters in the freezer for 20 minutes to set the chocolate. Serve right away or store, 858.

SMALL SOLID CHOCOLATES

About 1 pound

Before beginning, you may want to polish your molds with a cotton cloth; this will lower the incidence of air bubbles and produce glossy, smooth chocolates.

Temper, 858:

1 pound high-quality semisweet, bittersweet, milk, or white chocolate

Spread the chocolate over the top of the mold with an offset spatula. Lightly tap the mold on the work surface to release any air bubbles. Scrape any excess chocolate into an empty bowl. This may be melted and reused.

Place the mold on a baking sheet in the freezer for about 15 minutes to set. The chocolates are ready to unmold when they have shrunk somewhat from the sides of the molds.

To unmold, invert the mold over a plate or pan lined with wax or parchment paper and twist it slightly (like an ice cube tray) to release the chocolates. They should come out easily. If not, return to the freezer for 10 minutes more and try again. Serve right away or store, 858.

FILLED CHOCOLATES

About 1 pound

Temper, 858:

1 pound high-quality semisweet, bittersweet, milk, or white chocolate

Spread the chocolate over each mold and scrape the excess into an empty bowl with an offset spatula. Lightly tap the mold on the work surface to release any air bubbles. Let the mold sit for up to 2 minutes, or until the edges of the chocolate start to look as if they are setting and turn dull in color.

Set a fine-mesh wire rack over a large bowl. Invert the mold onto the rack and let the still-melted chocolate drip from the mold for 3 to 5 minutes or until no longer dripping. Repeat the spreading and dripping process several times, until the chocolate shells are as thick as you desire.

Place the mold on a baking sheet in the freezer to set for 10 minutes. Have ready one of the following:

Salted Caramel Sauce, 809, or Easy Dulce de Leche, 809
Marzipan, 873
Peanut butter or chocolate-hazelnut spread
Any flavored ganache, 860, or Chocolate Ganache, 797
Nougat, 867, or Fondant, 866

The filling should be warm and pliable enough to pipe or spoon into the chocolate-lined molds without melting the chocolate. Fill the molds with your choice of filling and tap on the work surface to remove bubbles. Refrigerate for 5 minutes to firm the filling. Spread tempered chocolate over the filling with an offset spatula, scraping the excess into a bowl. Return the filled molds to the refrigerator for 10 minutes.

Gently unmold the chocolate, taking care not to crack it; turning it out onto a clean kitchen towel will help reduce the odds of cracking. Serve or store, 858.

PEANUT BUTTER CUPS

About 1 pound; about 24 cups

One of our favorite chocolate candies. Stir the peanut butter before using if the oil has separated.

Have ready two 11- or 12-cavity peanut butter cup molds lined with 1½-inch fluted paper cups. Or place fluted foil cups in a mini muffin tin. Make 3 parchment paper pastry cones, 716, or use zip-top bags. Temper, 858:

1 pound milk, bittersweet, or white chocolate

Pour half of the chocolate into one of the parchment paper cones or plastic bags. Snip off a ¼-inch opening at the tip of the cone or from a bottom corner of the bag and pipe chocolate into each cup, filling it about one-third full. Let set for 8 to 10 minutes.

Fill the second parchment paper cone or plastic bag with:

¾ cup smooth peanut butter, at room temperature

Snip off a ½-inch opening and pipe peanut butter into the center of each chocolate cup, filling them no more than three-quarters full. Be careful not to pipe the peanut butter to the edges of the mold, or the chocolate will not seal around it. Fill the third parchment paper cone or plastic bag with the remaining chocolate, snip off a ¼-inch opening, and pipe chocolate into each cup, filling it to the top. Tilt the mold as necessary so the chocolate completely fills in any spaces. Alternatively, use an offset spatula to spread the chocolate across the top of the mold and scrape the excess into a bowl. Lightly tap the filled molds on the work surface to release any air bubbles.

Place the molds on a baking sheet and chill in the freezer for 20 minutes to set the chocolate. To unmold, see Small Solid Chocolates, above. Serve right away or store, 858.

BUCKEYES

About 45 pieces

Named after its resemblance to the nuts of the buckeye, Ohio's state tree. Tempering the dipping chocolate will make for a prettier buckeye, but these down-home confections do not need to be fussed over.

Combine in a large bowl or a stand mixer:

1 cup smooth peanut butter
4 tablespoons (½ stick) unsalted butter, softened
1 teaspoon vanilla
¼ teaspoon salt

Beat on medium speed until smooth. Add:

2 cups powdered sugar, sifted

Beat on low to combine, then increase the speed to medium until completely smooth. Line a baking sheet with parchment paper. Portion out the mixture in heaping teaspoons onto the lined sheet. Roll between your palms into smooth balls. Freeze for 15 minutes. Meanwhile, temper, 858, or simply melt in a double boiler:

8 ounces semisweet, bittersweet, or milk chocolate, chopped

Poke a skewer into the top of a peanut butter ball, using it to pick up and dip the candies three-quarters of the way into the chocolate, leaving a round "eye" of peanut butter exposed on top. Place the dipped buckeyes back on the baking sheet and use the tip of your finger to smooth over the hole left by the skewer. Refrigerate until firm, about 30 minutes. Store refrigerated in an airtight container.

JOY OF COCONUT

About 1½ pounds; sixty-four 1-inch squares

Inspired by a popular candy, these coconut-and-almond-filled chocolate squares require no dipping.

Toast, 973:

2½ cups shredded unsweetened coconut

Once toasted to your liking, transfer to a bowl and add:

1 cup light corn syrup
1 tablespoon coconut oil

Stir well and let stand for 1 hour for the coconut to absorb the corn syrup. Line an 8-inch square baking pan with parchment paper or foil. Temper, 858:

12 ounces milk chocolate

Pour half of the chocolate into the lined pan and keep the remaining half warm, 859. Transfer the pan to the refrigerator and let firm up for 15 minutes. Evenly spread the coconut mixture over the hardened chocolate. Starting ½ inch from the top left corner, push halfway into the coconut filling at 1-inch intervals:

64 whole roasted almonds

so the almonds are lying flat. Pour the remaining tempered chocolate over the top of the nut filling. Place in the refrigerator for 30 minutes to set the chocolate. Unmold the slab, let it sit at room temperature for 10 minutes, then carefully cut it (between the almonds) into 1-inch squares. Serve immediately or store, 858.

ABOUT FUDGE

Fudge is a semisoft candy made from a cooked sugar syrup enriched with cream or butter. In the innocent days of the late nineteenth and early twentieth century, fudge making was a collegiate craze, particularly at Vassar, where Marion Becker went to school. Students made batches of fudge in their dorm rooms, sometimes over very rudimentary alcohol burners. While fudge has a reputation for being tricky to make, we think that if college students could make it under such unlikely circumstances, there's no reason the average home cook shouldn't be successful as well. For those who are in a hurry, see Quick Chocolate Fudge, 863, which does not even require a thermometer.

As with any candy, fudge can overcook in the time it takes to retrieve the correct spatula, so have all ingredients and equipment at the ready. Fudge must be cooked slowly over medium heat to the soft-ball stage, 857, so ➤ resist the temptation to increase the heat in an effort to quicken the process, as this often results in a scorched flavor and overly grainy texture. Remember, though, that the soft-ball stage only begins at 235°F; professional candy makers expect their fudge to come in at 238°F, but on occasion, on a very humid day, for instance, it can refuse to ball until the syrup is as hot as 242°F.

To cool fudge in a water bath, place the pan in a second pan of cold water or in a sink with enough cold water to come about an inch up the sides of the fudge pan. ➤ Do not stir the fudge as it cools, as this will result in a grainy texture. At this point, professional candy makers will often add ¼ cup store-bought or homemade Fondant, 866, to ensure the fudge has a fine, smooth texture. Let it cool undisturbed until you can comfortably touch the bottom of the pan with your hand, about 110°F.

To cool fudge on a marble slab, pour the syrup onto a marble slab or baking sheet set on a wire rack. If any butter, vanilla, and salt are used in the recipe, float them on top. The advantage of marble is that it absorbs heat evenly and quickly—but not too quickly. (A 24 × 18-inch slab will hold up to 2 pounds of fudge.)

Regardless of how you cool it, ➤ do not scrape the bottom of the pan when you pour the fudge out, as the sugar mixture on the bottom, cooked to a higher temperature than the rest, could crystallize the rest of the batch.

When the fudge has cooled to 110°F, it needs to be stirred. If the fudge was cooled in a pan, transfer the mixture to a stand mixer and beat it with the paddle attachment on low speed. Alternatively, transfer to a mixing bowl and stir it with a wooden spoon in a slow, gentle figure-eight pattern. If the fudge was cooled on a marble slab, use a candy or bench scraper to work the fudge by lifting and folding, always from the edges to the center. Continue to fold or mix until the fudge thickens, loses its sheen, and begins to hold peaks. Pour the fudge into a buttered pan. ➤ Watch the fudge very carefully—if you neglect it for a moment, it may thicken too much and become hard and unworkable.

To store fudge, wrap it tightly or store in an airtight container to keep it from drying out. The flavor of fudge matures after a day or so, and the texture improves. Don't wait too long to enjoy it, though: If stored longer than 10 days at room temperature or 1 month in the refrigerator, it will develop white spots, known as bloom. These won't affect the flavor, but they give it an unappetizing look. Like all candies, fudge tastes best served at room temperature.

CHOCOLATE FUDGE

About 1½ pounds; 64 pieces

The batches of fudge our grandmothers made were lighter on the chocolate than this smooth and creamy recipe. Personally, we think you should go "all in" on the chocolate if you're going to the trouble of making fudge.

Please read About Fudge, 862. Combine in a large heavy saucepan:

2 cups granulated white sugar
½ cup half-and-half
½ cup heavy cream
¼ cup light corn syrup

Stir over low heat until the sugar is dissolved, about 5 minutes. Bring to a boil and cook, without stirring, for 1 minute. Brush down the sides of the pan with a pastry brush dipped in warm water to remove any sugar crystals that have formed, and remove from the heat. Stir in until melted and completely smooth:

6 ounces semisweet or bittersweet chocolate, chopped

Brush down the sides of the pan again, then set the pan over medium heat and cook, without stirring, until the mixture reaches 238°F, the soft-ball stage. Remove from the heat. Float on top, but do not stir in (stirring at this point can cause graininess):

2 tablespoons butter, softened
1 teaspoon vanilla
⅛ teaspoon salt

Cool the candy to 110°F, without stirring, by placing the bottom of the pan in cold water to stop the cooking. To cool on a marble slab, see About Fudge, 862. When it is cool, stir the fudge with a wooden spoon just until it "snaps" and begins to lose its sheen. Or transfer the cooled fudge to a stand mixer and beat on low speed using the paddle attachment until the fudge begins to thicken and lose its sheen, 5 to 10 minutes. Watch the mixture carefully or it may thicken too much and become unworkable.

If desired, stir in:

(1 to 1½ cups walnuts, pecans, or hazelnuts, toasted, 1005, and coarsely chopped)

Turn the fudge out into an 8-inch square pan lined with parchment paper or buttered foil that extends over two sides. Smooth the top with an offset or silicone spatula, dipping it in hot water as needed. Let stand for at least 1 hour. Remove the fudge from the pan and peel off the foil or parchment paper. Cut the fudge into 1-inch squares and store, 858.

QUICK CHOCOLATE FUDGE

About 1½ pounds; 64 pieces

This is the easiest fudge we know. It requires no thermometer or special cooling technique; just melt everything together, pour into a pan, and let the mixture cool.

Line an 8-inch square pan with parchment paper or buttered foil that extends over two sides. Place in a heatproof bowl or microwave-safe glass bowl:

12 ounces chopped bittersweet chocolate or chocolate chips
One 14-ounce can sweetened condensed milk
4 tablespoons (½ stick) butter

Heat over a pan of hot water, stirring until melted, or microwave on high in 30-second increments until melted and smooth, gently stirring after each interval, 1½ to 2½ minutes total. If desired, stir in:

(1½ cups walnuts or pecans, toasted, 1005, and coarsely chopped)

Transfer the fudge to the prepared pan and smooth the top with an offset spatula, dipping it in hot water as needed. Let stand for at least 1 hour. Remove the fudge from the pan and peel off the foil or parchment paper. Cut the fudge into 1-inch squares and store, 858.

PENUCHE (BROWN SUGAR FUDGE)

About 1 pound; 64 pieces

Penuche, whose name comes from the Spanish word for raw sugar, is simply fudge made with brown sugar—which gives it a rich molasses-like flavor and a grainy texture. Pecans are traditional in penuche, but we also love coconut.

Line an 8-inch square pan with parchment paper or buttered foil that extends over two sides. Combine in a large heavy saucepan:

3 cups packed light brown sugar
½ cup half-and-half
½ cup heavy cream
⅛ teaspoon salt

Stir over low heat until the sugar is dissolved, about 5 minutes. Brush down the sides of the pan with a pastry brush dipped in warm water. Increase the heat to medium and cook, without stirring, until the mixture reaches 238°F, the soft-ball stage. Remove from the heat. Add but do not stir in (stirring at this point can cause graininess):

2 tablespoons butter, softened
1 teaspoon vanilla

Let cool and beat as described in About Fudge, 862. Stir in:

1 cup pecans, toasted, 1005, and coarsely chopped
(1 cup shredded unsweetened coconut, lightly toasted, 973)

Transfer the fudge to the prepared pan. Smooth the top with an offset spatula, dipping it in hot water as needed. Let stand for at least 1 hour. Remove the fudge from the pan and peel off the foil or parchment paper. Cut into 1-inch squares and store, 858.

JAMONCILLO DE LECHE (MEXICAN MILK FUDGE)

About 1½ pounds; 64 pieces

Milk fudge is similar to dulce de leche, 809, but in solid form. The fudge is rich with the flavor of caramelized sugar and browned butter.

Line an 8-inch square pan with buttered parchment paper or foil that extends over two sides. Bring to a boil in a large pot or Dutch oven over medium-high heat:

4 cups whole milk
2 cups granulated white sugar
1 tablespoon butter
1 teaspoon baking soda
½ teaspoon salt
1 cinnamon stick (preferably canela, 972)

Watch carefully—the mixture has a tendency to boil over. Boil, stirring frequently. At about 10 minutes, the mixture will start to turn a light caramel color. At about 20 minutes it will be a deep caramel color. Continue to cook until the mixture reaches 240°F, 40 to 45 minutes total. Remove from the heat and stir in:

2 teaspoons vanilla
(1 cup chopped, toasted, 1005, pecans or lightly toasted pine nuts)

Discard the cinnamon stick. Transfer the mixture to a stand mixer or a bowl and beat on medium speed, using the paddle attachment, a handheld electric mixer, or a wooden spoon, until visibly thickened and no longer shiny but not hard or clumpy, 3 to 5 minutes. Transfer the fudge to the prepared pan. The mixture will be quite thick, so you may need to press it into the pan. Let stand for at least 1 hour. Remove the fudge from the pan and peel off the foil or parchment paper. Cut the fudge into 1-inch squares and store, 858.

MAPLE CANDY

About 1 pound; forty-five 1-inch squares

This Vermont favorite is one of the simplest candies we know and has a texture similar to fudge. The added butter or oil prevents the syrup from foaming up.

Have candy molds ready or line a 9 × 5-inch loaf pan on all sides with buttered parchment paper or foil. Bring to a boil in a large, deep saucepan over medium-high heat:

2 cups maple syrup
½ tablespoon vegetable oil or butter

Boil without stirring until the mixture reaches 238°F, the soft-ball stage, about 15 minutes. Remove from the heat and transfer to a bowl to cool for 10 minutes. Using a wooden spoon, stir the mixture until it loses its sheen and looks creamy. Pour the mixture into the molds or the lined pan. Allow to cool completely and cut into squares or release the candies from molds and store in an airtight container at room temperature.

PEANUT BUTTER OR TAHINI FUDGE

About 1½ pounds; 64 pieces

If using tahini, stir it well to incorporate any oil that has separated out. For another fudge-like tahini candy, see Sesame Halvah, 874.

Line an 8-inch square pan with buttered parchment paper or foil that extends over two sides. Combine in a large saucepan:

2½ sticks (10 ounces) unsalted butter
1¼ cups smooth peanut butter or tahini

Cook over medium heat until the mixture comes to a boil. Remove from the heat and add:

1½ teaspoons vanilla
¼ teaspoon salt

Stir in:

4½ cups powdered sugar, sifted

Mix well to combine. Pour the mixture into the prepared pan. Cover the fudge directly with a piece of plastic wrap. Chill until firm. Cut the fudge into 1-inch squares and store, 858.

ABOUT CARAMEL CANDIES

Caramels are one of our favorites. Unlike tooth-achingly sweet fudge or divinity, caramels are rich, buttery, and complex, and a healthy dose of salt makes them all the more mouthwatering. Despite their name, caramels are only cooked to the firm-ball stage, which means that the temperature of the sugar never gets high enough to start caramelizing. Their characteristic flavor comes from browning, or the Maillard reaction, 1048, rather than caramelization.

Caramels are cooked slowly over medium heat. Resist the temptation to increase the heat to quicken the process, as this can result in a scorched flavor and grainy texture. The temperature to which the caramels are cooked determines their ultimate texture: The higher the temperature, the firmer they are. The length of cooking determines their flavor and color: The longer they cook, the more their flavor develops and their color deepens. Patience is key. It can take from 25 to 45 minutes, depending on the quantity, to cook a batch of caramels.

You may **flavor caramels** by infusing warmed cream for 30 minutes as for Flavored Ganache, 860, and straining before use. For fruit-flavored caramels, substitute fruit puree or juice for up to half of the heavy cream. You may also mix toasted nuts and seeds into caramels or dip them, once cooled and cut, into tempered chocolate (see Dipped Chocolate Truffles, 860).

To set and cut caramels, immediately pour the mixture, without stirring or scraping the bottom of the pan, into an 8-inch square pan lined with buttered parchment paper or foil that extends over two sides. Let cool completely at room temperature or in the refrigerator. When firm, invert the candy onto a cutting board and peel away the parchment paper or foil. Oil a sharp heavy knife and cut into pieces.

To store caramels, wrap them individually in cellophane squares or wax paper, or store them between layers of cellophane or wax or parchment paper in an airtight container. They keep well at room temperature for about 2 weeks or refrigerated for up to a month.

BUTTERSCOTCH CARAMELS

About 2 pounds; seventy to eighty 1-inch pieces

Brown sugar and dark corn syrup combine to produce a deep butterscotch flavor.

Please read About Caramel Candies, above. Line an 8-inch square pan with buttered parchment paper or foil that extends over two sides and set aside. Combine in a large heavy saucepan over medium heat:

2¼ cups packed light brown sugar
2 sticks (8 ounces) unsalted butter, cut into pieces
1 cup heavy cream
½ cup dark corn syrup
¼ cup light corn syrup

Stir with a wooden spoon until the sugar is dissolved, about 5 minutes, then wash down the sides of the pan with a pastry brush dipped in warm water. Cook, stirring constantly, until the mixture comes to a boil. Increase the heat to medium-high and wash down the sides of the pan again. Cook to 248°F, the firm-ball stage. Remove the pan from the heat and quickly stir in:

2 teaspoons vanilla
¼ teaspoon salt

Pour into the prepared pan. Let cool until firm, 4 to 12 hours, then use the foil or parchment paper to lift the caramels out of the pan. Cut, wrap, and store, above.

SALTED CARAMELS

About 1¼ pounds; 64 pieces

Please read About Caramel Candies, 864.

Line an 8-inch square pan with buttered parchment paper or foil that extends over two sides and set aside. Warm over medium-low heat until the butter is melted:

¾ cup heavy cream
4 tablespoons (½ stick) butter

Remove from the heat and set aside. Combine in a large heavy saucepan:

1½ cups granulated white sugar
½ cup light corn syrup, light cane syrup, or brown rice syrup

Stir over medium-low heat until the sugar is dissolved, then wash down the sides of the pan with a pastry brush dipped in warm water. Increase the heat to medium-high and cook until the mixture comes to a boil. Wash down the sides of the pan again. Cook, swirling the pan occasionally, until the caramel is deep golden brown, 7 to 10 minutes. Remove from the heat and slowly stir in the cream mixture. Be careful—it will bubble up furiously. Return to the heat and cook, stirring frequently, to 248°F, the firm-ball stage. Remove the pan from the heat and quickly stir in:

½ teaspoon salt

Pour into the prepared pan. Let cool 10 minutes, then sprinkle on top, if desired:

(¼ teaspoon flaky sea salt or smoked sea salt)

Let cool until firm, 4 to 12 hours, then use foil or parchment to lift the caramels out of the pan. Cut, wrap, and store, 858.

CHOCOLATE CREAM CARAMELS

About 1¾ pounds; 64 pieces

Prepare **Salted Caramels, above.** Stir in **8 ounces bittersweet chocolate, finely chopped** with the salt. To set, cut, wrap, and store, see About Caramel Candies, 864.

CHOCOLATE-PECAN TORTOISES

About 2 pounds; 35 pieces

Lightly grease 2 baking sheets or line them with silicone liners. Arrange on the sheets in groups of 4:

2 cups pecan halves, toasted, 1005

Prepare:

½ batch Butterscotch Caramels, 864

Transfer the caramel to a small bowl for 10 to 15 minutes to cool slightly. Working quickly and using a greased spoon, spoon a scant tablespoon of caramel over the center of each pecan group. Let the caramel cool for 30 minutes.

Temper, 858, or melt:

6 ounces semisweet or milk chocolate

Spoon a scant teaspoon of chocolate over each caramel candy. If desired, sprinkle each candy with a pinch of:

(Flaky sea salt)

Refrigerate for 20 minutes to set the chocolate. Store the candies between layers of wax or parchment paper in an airtight container in the refrigerator for up to 3 weeks or in the freezer for up to 2 months. If frozen, thaw for 24 hours in the refrigerator. Remove the tortoises from the refrigerator 30 minutes before serving.

CARAMEL CORN

About 8 cups

This is the sticky-sweet confection of the circus and boardwalk. If desired, add **1 cup Spanish peanuts.**

Line a baking sheet with parchment paper. Pop, 47:

½ cup popcorn kernels (8 cups popped corn)

Transfer to a large bowl. Melt in a medium heavy saucepan:

2 tablespoons butter

Add and stir over low heat until the sugar is dissolved:

2 cups packed light brown sugar
½ cup water
½ teaspoon salt

Bring to a boil over medium heat, then wash down the sides of the pan with a pastry brush dipped in warm water. Cook, without stirring, to 245°F, the firm-ball stage. Pour over the popcorn. Stir gently with a wooden spoon until the corn is well coated, then turn it out onto the prepared baking sheet. When cool enough to handle, lightly butter your fingers and separate any large chunks. Or, squeeze by the handful into balls around the ends of lollipop or popsicle sticks. Candied popcorn keeps well in an airtight container for about 1 week.

ABOUT FONDANT

Fondant is both a candy in itself and a filling or coating for other candies. Fondant centers can be dipped in chocolate, and melted fondant can be used as an icing and poured over pastries and confections (especially the little cakes called Petits Fours, 749). You can enrich fondant by using milk, cream, or strong coffee in place of the water, or by substituting brown sugar or maple sugar for half of the white sugar. ➤ Do not use unrefined, raw sugars, as they will cause graininess. One of the charms of fondant is that a batch can be made and ripened and then used over a period of weeks, with varying flavors, colors, and shapes to suit the occasion.

The process of making fondant is actually quite similar to that of fudge: The key to both is controlled crystallization induced by stirring or kneading. This creates tiny sugar crystals that cause the syrup to turn from clear to opaque to a glossy, smooth white. After fondant is kneaded, "ripening" makes it more malleable and slightly easier to work with.

To ripen fondant, form it into a ball, let it cool completely to room temperature, and seal it tightly in plastic wrap or a zip-top plastic bag. Fondant may be stored in the refrigerator indefinitely, but bring it to room temperature, covered, before using.

To dip candy centers in fondant, liquefy the fondant in the top of a double boiler or a heatproof bowl over barely simmering water, stirring frequently and making sure that the temperature doesn't rise above 140°F. Remove the double boiler from the heat, but keep the top of the double boiler with the fondant over the hot water to keep it liquid. Drop a candy center into the fondant and turn to coat it completely. Lift out the candy using a candy dipper or fork, let the excess drip off, and place it on a baking sheet lined with wax paper. Refrigerate the dipped candies for 15 to 20 minutes to firm up.

FONDANT

About 1½ pounds

Have ready a nonporous surface, such as a marble slab or a baking sheet placed on a wire rack and sprinkled with cold water. Combine in a large heavy saucepan:

3 cups granulated white sugar
½ cup water
⅓ cup light corn syrup

Bring to a boil over medium heat, stirring occasionally, until the sugar is dissolved. Brush down the sugar clinging to the sides of the pan with a pastry brush dipped in warm water. Cook, without stirring, to 243°F. Immediately pour the syrup onto the prepared surface. ➤ Do not scrape the bottom of the pan. Let the syrup cool to 110°F, 15 to 20 minutes.

Use a candy or bench scraper or a metal spatula to work the syrup by lifting and folding, always from the edges toward the center. Continue to mix until the syrup turns opaque and white and the mass becomes thickened but pliable, about 15 minutes. Alternatively, transfer the syrup to a stand mixer fitted with the paddle attachment and beat on low speed until the fondant becomes thick and opaque, 5 to 8 minutes.

At this stage, the fondant should resemble a stiff dough. Knead it well with your hands, dusting them with powdered sugar. Gather the fondant into a ball, then push it outward with the heel of your hand. Draw it back in with a candy or bench scraper and repeat the process until the surface is smooth and creamy looking. Use immediately, or tightly cover the ball with plastic wrap or place it in a zip-top plastic bag. You may let the fondant ripen in a cool place overnight; it gets better day by day. To keep the fondant for several weeks or months, store it in the refrigerator.

➤ If you accidentally overcook the fondant, and it becomes too hard to knead, cook it again: Place it in the top of a double boiler over simmering water, add ⅔ cup hot water, and cook, stirring constantly, until it has thoroughly liquefied. Then pour it into a clean heavy saucepan and heat it to the boiling point again. Wash down the sides of the pan with a pastry brush dipped in warm water and cook the mixture, uncovered and without stirring, to 243°F. Let cool, stir, and knead as above.

To color fondant, have at hand:

Powdered sugar
Paste food coloring

Place the fondant on a work surface dusted with the sugar. Make several slashes in the fondant and use a toothpick to dot in a few drops of paste food coloring. One-eighth teaspoon will create vivid color in this recipe. Knead and fold the fondant to distribute the color evenly.

To flavor fondant, dust a work surface with powdered sugar as above, and have ready one of the following:

1 to 2 teaspoons flavoring extract, such as vanilla, almond, or peppermint, or rose or orange flower water
3 to 5 drops food-grade essential oil, such as peppermint, anise, orange, or bergamot
1 tablespoon Grand Marnier, kirsch, framboise, or other liqueur
2 teaspoons finely grated orange or lemon zest
½ cup shredded coconut
2 to 4 ounces semisweet, bittersweet, milk, or white chocolate, melted
⅓ cup smooth peanut, almond, or hazelnut butter
½ cup almonds or walnuts, toasted, 1005, and finely chopped
⅓ cup finely chopped dried cherries, candied orange peel, or candied ginger

Work in the flavoring by kneading and folding the fondant. You may want to use a stand mixer fitted with a dough hook at first, then knead by hand.

To shape the fondant, be sure it is at room temperature. Dust the work surface generously with powdered sugar. You may find it easier to work with half of the fondant at one time. Form it into a long cylinder by rolling it under your palms, then cut into candy-size pieces, or mold it into shapes.

To use fondant as a coating or glaze, see About Fondant Icing, 800.

QUICK FONDANT

About 1½ pounds; about seventy-five 1-inch balls

This uncooked version of fondant is very fast and foolproof, but not quite as creamy as the cooked variety. It can be colored or flavored in the same way, but it will not work for coating and glazing. Kids love to model this fondant (or Marzipan, 873) into pumpkins, turkeys, Christmas trees, or other shapes. The texture is like that of clay—but it tastes a lot better!

Add to a large bowl:

1 stick (4 ounces) unsalted butter, softened
¾ teaspoon vanilla
¼ teaspoon salt
(Any flavoring for Fondant, above)

Beat until smooth. Add very slowly and beat until very light:

⅔ cup sweetened condensed milk

Add cup by cup:

5 cups powdered sugar, sifted

Dust a work surface with:

1 cup powdered sugar, sifted

Turn the fondant out onto the work surface and work in the sugar. Shape it into 1-inch balls. Raisins, nuts, or bits of candied fruit may be used as centers, if desired. At this point, you may temper, 858:

1 pound high-quality semisweet, bittersweet, milk, or white chocolate

Dip the fondant into the chocolate, allow any excess to drip off, and place on a parchment-lined baking sheet. Refrigerate for 15 minutes to set the chocolate.

PEPPERMINT PATTIES

About 2 pounds; about forty-eight 2-inch patties

We love these refreshing candies. They taste even better when frozen and eaten cold.

Prepare:

Fondant, above, using ½ cup heavy cream instead of water, or Quick Fondant, above

Once cooled and kneaded, flavor the fondant with:

½ teaspoon peppermint oil or 1 teaspoon peppermint extract, or to taste

Shape the fondant into thin 2-inch disks, place flat on a parchment-lined baking sheet, cover tightly, and refrigerate until firm, about 1 hour.

Temper, 858:

1 pound semisweet, bittersweet, milk, or white chocolate

Remove the patties from the refrigerator and brush the tops with the melted chocolate. Return to the refrigerator until the chocolate has hardened, about 10 minutes. Remove from the refrigerator once more, flip the candies with a small offset spatula and brush the second side liberally with melted chocolate, allowing it to run down the sides a little. Return to the refrigerator until set. Store between layers of wax or parchment paper in an airtight container at room temperature for up to 10 days or in the refrigerator for up to 2 months.

ABOUT NOUGAT

Nougat is a chewy nut candy, sometimes with added candied fruit, made from a cooked sugar syrup combined with stiffly whipped egg whites. If desired, nougat can be left plain, without the addition of nuts or fruit, and used in making homemade candy bars. Nougat layered with roasted peanuts and caramel, and then dipped in chocolate makes for a truly transcendent candy bar. Or use nougat instead of peanut butter as a filling in Peanut Butter Cups, 861, for a light, fluffy treat.

Nougat is traditionally pressed between layers of edible paper (made of rice, wheat, or potato starch), which can be sourced at some candy-making or cake-decorating shops or online. Nougat is very sensitive to humidity, which turns it soft and soggy, so make it on a dry day and store it in an airtight container.

NOUGAT WITH FRUIT AND NUTS

About 1¼ pounds; twenty-four 2½ × 1-inch bars

This recipe is simpler than traditional nougat, which requires two different sugar syrups to be cooked to different temperatures. The same quantity of any nut or fruit may be substituted for the almonds, pistachios, and dried fruit in this recipe—for instance, use macadamia nuts, toasted coconut, and candied ginger. Once the nougat is set, you may dip the cut pieces in chocolate (see Dipped Chocolate Truffles, 860).

Please read About Nougat, above. Line an 8-inch square pan on all sides with edible rice paper or well-buttered foil. Place in a stand mixer fitted with the whisk attachment:

2 large egg whites, at room temperature

Beat the egg whites until soft peaks form, then turn off the mixer. Combine in a small heavy saucepan:

1½ cups granulated white sugar
1 cup light corn syrup
½ cup water
¼ cup honey

Place over medium-low heat and stir until the sugar dissolves. Increase the heat to medium-high and bring to a boil, washing down the sides of the pan with a pastry brush dipped in warm water. Cook, without stirring, to 260°F for soft nougat (ideal for making candy bars), or 275°F for firm nougat (best eaten on its own). As the syrup nears its final temperature, turn up the mixer speed so the egg whites reach stiff peaks at the same time that the syrup reaches 260° or 275°F.

With the mixer running on high speed, pour the syrup into the beaten whites in a slow, steady stream, being careful to avoid hitting the whisk. Do not scrape the pan. Continue to beat until the mixer bowl is warm but no longer hot to the touch, 10 to 12 minutes.

Beat in:

2 tablespoons butter, cut into small pieces, softened

Fold into the nougat:

1 cup sliced almonds, lightly toasted, 1005
½ cup pistachios, toasted, 1005
½ cup chopped dried or candied cherries or candied orange peel

Spread the mixture evenly in the prepared pan—you may need to use your hands to spread it evenly. Cover the top with another layer of edible paper or generously buttered foil, then place a second 8-inch square pan on top and press lightly to even out the mixture and make the edible paper adhere. Fill the top pan with cans or other heavy weights, and let stand overnight at room temperature.

Remove the top pan and weights, run a thin knife around the edges of the pan to loosen the nougat, and invert onto a cutting board. If foil was used, peel it off. With a lightly oiled knife, cut the nougat into bars. Wrap each bar in cellophane or plastic wrap. Store in an airtight container at room temperature for 1 week or in the refrigerator for up to 3 weeks. Serve at room temperature.

CHOCOLATE NOUGAT

Prepare:

Nougat, above

After the syrup has been incorporated into the egg whites, beat in with the butter:

8 ounces dark or bittersweet chocolate, melted

Continue as directed.

DIVINITY

About 1½ pounds; about thirty 1½-inch rounds

Divinity is a classic Southern candy that has a reputation for being difficult to make, but it's actually very easy if you have a stand mixer—and work on a dry day with low humidity. **Sea Foam** is simply divinity made with brown sugar in place of white and dark corn syrup in place of light. For a spirited Southern touch, plump the raisins in **⅓ cup bourbon** over low heat. Drain off any excess bourbon and cool the raisins before adding them to the candy.

Place in a stand mixer fitted with the whisk attachment:

2 large egg whites, at room temperature

Beat the whites at medium speed just until they hold soft peaks. Turn off the mixer. In a large heavy saucepan over medium heat, cook, stirring, until the sugar is dissolved:

2 cups granulated white sugar
½ cup water
½ cup light corn syrup

Bring to a boil. Wash down any sugar crystals that have formed on the sides of the pan with a pastry brush dipped in warm water. Cook the syrup over medium heat, without stirring, to 250° to 255°F, the hard-ball stage.

With the mixer running on high speed, pour the syrup into the beaten egg whites in a slow, steady stream, being careful to avoid hitting the whisk. Do not scrape the pan. Reduce the speed to medium and beat until the mixture is thick, fluffy, and the bottom of the mixer bowl is only slightly warm, 12 to 15 minutes.

Lightly grease a baking sheet. Fold into the divinity mixture:

1 cup chopped, toasted, 1005, pecans or walnuts
(1 cup golden raisins)
1 teaspoon vanilla

Quickly drop the mixture by the spoonful onto the baking sheet, forming 1½-inch mounds. You may need to use a second spoon to help push the sticky mixture onto the pan. Let cool.

Divinity dries out quickly and does not store well. Store between layers of wax or parchment paper in an airtight container at room temperature for several days.

MARSHMALLOWS

About 1¼ pounds; about sixty-four 1-inch squares

Homemade marshmallows are extra fluffy, have an almost creamy texture, and can be made in a host of different flavors. Don't attempt to make marshmallows unless you have a stand mixer to handle the beating for you. If desired, substitute honey or agave syrup for the corn syrup.

Sift together in a medium bowl:

¼ cup cornstarch
¼ cup powdered sugar

Dust a lightly oiled 9-inch square baking pan with some of the mixture. Reserve the remaining mixture to dust the finished marshmallows.

Pour into the bowl of a stand mixer:

½ cup cool water

Sprinkle over the water:

4 envelopes (3 tablespoons) unflavored gelatin

Stir the gelatin into the water to moisten it, and let stand 5 minutes. Place the bowl over a pot of simmering water and stir just until the gelatin dissolves. Place the bowl on the mixer stand and fit the mixer with the whisk attachment.

Combine in a large heavy saucepan:

2 cups granulated white sugar
¾ cup light corn syrup
½ cup water
¼ teaspoon salt

Cook over medium heat, stirring until the sugar is dissolved. Increase the heat to medium-high and bring to a boil. Wash down the sides of the pan with a pastry brush dipped in warm water. Cook, without stirring, to 245°F, the firm-ball stage. Do not allow the temperature to rise any higher, or the marshmallows will be tough. Remove the syrup from the heat.

With the mixer running at medium speed, pour the syrup into the gelatin in a slow, steady stream, being careful to avoid hitting the whisk. Do not scrape the pan. Beat until the mixture is thick and fluffy but still warm and thin enough to pour, about 8 minutes. Beat in:

2 teaspoons vanilla or vanilla bean paste

Transfer the mixture to the prepared pan and spread evenly. Let cool completely, then cover very loosely with foil and let dry until firm enough to cut, 4 to 6 hours.

Dust the top of the marshmallows with some of the reserved cornstarch-sugar mixture, remove them from the pan, and cut into 1-inch squares (or smaller to float in cocoa), using kitchen scissors dusted with:

Cornstarch

Dust the marshmallows with the remaining cornstarch-sugar mixture. Store between layers of wax or parchment paper in an airtight container at room temperature.

SALTED CARAMEL MARSHMALLOWS

Prepare **Marshmallows, above,** through melting the gelatin. Have the corn syrup, water, and salt ready, and increase the salt to ½ teaspoon. Place the 2 cups sugar in a large heavy saucepan and melt over medium heat. Allow the sugar to caramelize, swirling the pan to dissipate any hot spots, until very dark (you want the caramel to be on the ragged edge between very dark caramel and burnt sugar). Very carefully (there will be lots of hot steam!), pour the water, corn syrup, and salt into the caramelized sugar. The caramel may seize up. This is okay—simply remove it from the heat and stir until the caramel re-melts. Return the pan to the heat, increase to medium-high, and boil the syrup until it reaches 245°F, the firm-ball stage. Proceed as directed.

FLAVORING MARSHMALLOWS

Marshmallows are fun to make, in part because they can be flavored in dozens of different ways. Below are some ideas for tweaking the basic recipe above.

Chocolate: Beat in ½ **cup sifted cocoa powder** along with the vanilla; add ¼ **cup sifted cocoa powder** to the cornstarch mixture for dusting the marshmallows

Fruit: Beat in ¼ **cup powdered freeze-dried fruit, such as raspberries or strawberries,** along with the vanilla; add ¼ **cup powdered freeze-dried fruit** to the cornstarch mixture for dusting the marshmallows (about 4 ounces total freeze-dried fruit)

Honey and Rose or Orange Flower: Substitute **honey** for the corn syrup, and substitute **2 teaspoons rose water or orange flower water** for the vanilla

Maple: Substitute **maple syrup** for the corn syrup

Coconut: Substitute **1 teaspoon coconut extract** for the vanilla and roll the cooled and cut marshmallows in **toasted, 973, shredded coconut**

Chocolate-Dipped Peppermint: Substitute ¾ **teaspoon peppermint extract** for the vanilla; dip the set marshmallows in **(tempered chocolate, 858)**, if desired

Honey-Saffron: Substitute **honey** for the corn syrup and steep ¼ **teaspoon saffron** in the water for 5 minutes before adding the gelatin

Coffee: Substitute **cooled strong coffee** for the water for softening the gelatin and **1 teaspoon coffee extract** for the vanilla
Matcha: Beat in **2 tablespoons matcha** along with the vanilla
Bourbon: Substitute **bourbon** for the water in the sugar syrup

ABOUT TAFFY

If you hanker to re-create an old-time candy pull, be sure you have a stout pair of arms. However, should you decide to make taffy-pulling a frequent practice, you may find that a candy hook is well worth the investment. The hook is normally placed at least 6 feet from the floor. The rope of candy is thrown over it repeatedly, and gravity does the rest. ➤ Do not attempt to make taffy on very humid days.

When the syrup has cooled to room temperature, sprinkle any flavorings over it. Start pulling it with your fingertips, allowing a spread of about 18 inches between your hands, then fold it back on itself. Repeat this motion rhythmically. As the mass changes from a somewhat sticky side-whiskered affair to a glistening crystal ribbon, start twisting, while folding and pulling. ➤ Pull until the ridges of the twist begin to hold their shape. The candy will become opaque, firm, and elastic but will retain its satiny finish. Depending on the cooking, the weather, and your pulling skill, this process may take from 5 to 20 minutes.

After cutting, wrap the taffies immediately in wax paper and store in an airtight container.

VANILLA TAFFY

About 12 ounces; about 60 pieces

Have ready an oiled marble slab or a chilled and oiled rimmed baking sheet set on a wire rack. Combine in a medium heavy saucepan:

1 cup granulated white sugar
1/4 cup water
1/4 cup light corn syrup

Stir over medium heat until the sugar is dissolved. Wash down the sides of the pan with a pastry brush dipped in warm water. Increase the heat to medium-high and cook, uncovered, without stirring, to 265°F, the high end of the hard-ball stage. (For a softer taffy, cook the mixture to 250°F; or for a firmer texture, cook to 270°F, the soft-crack stage.)

Remove from the heat and quickly stir in with a wooden spoon until completely absorbed:

2 tablespoons butter, softened
1/4 teaspoon salt

Carefully pour the syrup onto the marble slab or chilled baking sheet. Do not scrape the saucepan. Allow the mixture to sit until cooled to room temperature. Sprinkle any of the following over the mixture (food coloring is purely optional):

2 teaspoons vanilla
Up to 5 drops cinnamon oil (and 3 drops red food coloring)
Up to 5 drops citrus or banana oil (and 3 to 5 drops yellow food coloring)
Up to 6 drops peppermint or spearmint oil (and 3 to 5 drops green food coloring)

With a candy or bench scraper or metal spatula, start to fold the edges of the mixture into the center. Keep scraping and folding until the mixture is firm enough to handle. Then gather it up into a ball with oiled or buttered fingertips and begin pulling, folding, and twisting until the taffy is opaque and firm and holds thin ridges. Dust a work surface with:

Powdered sugar or cornstarch

Form the taffy into a long 3/4-inch-thick rope, letting it fall onto the work surface. Cut into 1-inch pieces with buttered kitchen shears. Immediately wrap each piece of taffy in squares of wax paper and store in an airtight container.

CHOCOLATE TAFFY

Prepare **Vanilla Taffy, above,** cooking the syrup only to 258°F; the addition of chocolate will harden the final mixture considerably. After pouring the syrup onto the baking sheet and allowing it to cool for 5 minutes, sprinkle **3 ounces grated bittersweet, semisweet, or milk chocolate** over it. Proceed as directed.

PULLED MINTS

About 1 pound; about 40 pieces

These are like the little old-fashioned mint cushions that melt in your mouth.

Have ready an oiled marble slab or a chilled and oiled rimmed baking sheet set on a wire rack. Bring to a boil in a large heavy-bottomed saucepan:

1 cup water

Add and stir until the sugar is dissolved:

2 cups granulated white sugar
1/4 teaspoon cream of tartar

Wash down the sides of the pan with a pastry brush dipped in warm water. Cook over medium heat until the syrup comes to a boil, then wash down the sides of the pan again. Increase the heat to medium-high, and cook, without stirring, to about 265°F, the hard-ball stage (for a firmer texture, cook to 270°F, the soft-crack stage). Remove from the heat. Carefully pour the syrup onto the marble slab or chilled baking sheet. Do not scrape the saucepan. Let the syrup cool until heat no longer rises from it and an indentation holds when it is pressed with a fingertip. Sprinkle with:

6 to 8 drops peppermint oil

Using a candy or bench scraper, bring the syrup into a mass, lifting, turning, and folding it. Keep scraping and folding until the mixture is firm enough to handle. Then gather it up into a ball with oiled or buttered fingertips and begin pulling, folding, and twisting until the mixture is opaque and firm and holds thin ridges.
Dust a work surface with:

Powdered sugar or cornstarch

Form the mixture into a long 3/4-inch-thick rope, letting it fall onto the work surface. Cut into 1-inch pieces with buttered scissors. Place between layers of wax paper in an airtight container and let sit at least 30 minutes to as long as overnight until the candies are firm but melt in the mouth. Wrap individually in wax paper and store in an airtight container at room temperature.

ABOUT HARD CANDIES

Hard candies are cooked to high temperatures, mostly the hard-crack stage (300° to 310°F). Some are cooked to an even higher temperature, to light caramel (about 320°F). Humidity is no friend of hard candies—you may need to cook the sugar syrup as much as 10 degrees higher to compensate under such conditions, so we recommend that you don't even try to make hard candies on a rainy or very humid day.

To flavor the candies, use the concentrated oils that have been developed specifically for hard candies, found at specialty candy- or cake-making supply shops and some craft stores. Their flavor can stand up to the high heat of the syrups. Use paste food coloring for lollipops and other colored hard candies.

Wrap hard candies in squares of cellophane or plastic wrap when they are cool and store them in an airtight container at room temperature. Hard candies absorb moisture easily from the air and turn sticky or soft and crumbly but, if well sealed, will keep for 2 to 3 weeks.

PEANUT BRITTLE

About 1¼ pounds

Many brittle connoisseurs use raw nuts, which cook in the syrup; others prefer the roasted kind. For a delicious variation on this recipe, stir in ½ **cup raw cacao nibs** along with the peanuts.

Have ready a marble slab or a large baking sheet lined with buttered parchment paper or a silicone liner and set on a wire rack. Combine in a large heavy saucepan:

2 cups granulated white sugar
1 cup light corn syrup
½ cup water
¼ teaspoon cream of tartar

Bring to a boil over medium-high heat, stirring until the sugar is dissolved. Boil, without stirring, to 265°F, the hard-ball stage. Stir in:

2 cups raw peanuts

Continue cooking, stirring as seldom as possible and only to prevent hot spots from burning, until the syrup reaches 300°F, the hard-crack stage. Remove from the heat and stir in:

3 tablespoons butter, cut into small pieces
1 teaspoon vanilla
¾ teaspoon salt
¼ teaspoon baking soda

As soon as the butter is melted and incorporated, turn out onto the slab or baking sheet. Place a silicone liner on top, put oven mitts on your hands, and press the brittle to the thickness of one nut. Allow to cool completely. Break the brittle into pieces, then store between layers of wax or parchment paper in an airtight container at room temperature for up to 1 month.

MEGAN'S PUMPKIN SEED BRITTLE

About 3 pounds

The espresso and salt in this brittle balance out the sugar, making for a complex twist on a classic confection.

Preheat the oven to 350°F.

Spread on a baking sheet and toast until browned and fragrant, 10 to 12 minutes:

3 cups raw pumpkin seeds

Combine in a small bowl:

2 tablespoons butter, cubed
2 teaspoons vanilla
1 teaspoon baking soda
1 teaspoon instant espresso powder
½ teaspoon salt

Have ready a large baking sheet lined with buttered parchment paper or a silicone liner. Add to a deep, heavy pot:

2 cups packed light brown sugar
1 cup water
1 cup light corn syrup

Cook, stirring, over medium heat until the sugar is dissolved. Increase the heat to high and cook, without stirring, until the syrup reaches 285°F, the soft-crack stage. Stir in the toasted pumpkin seeds and continue cooking, stirring constantly, until the mixture reaches 300°F, the hard-crack stage. Remove from the heat and add the baking soda mixture, stirring until the butter is melted. Pour the brittle as thinly as possible onto the greased or lined baking sheet—do not spread with a spatula. If desired, sprinkle with:

(Flaky sea salt)

Let cool completely, break the brittle into pieces, and store between layers of wax or parchment paper in an airtight container at room temperature for up to 1 month.

SESAME SEED BRITTLE

About 1¾ pounds

Have ready a marble slab or a large baking sheet lined with buttered parchment paper or a silicone liner and set on a wire rack. Combine in a large heavy saucepan:

1½ cups granulated white sugar
¾ cup light corn syrup
4 tablespoons (½ stick) butter, softened

Stir over medium heat until the sugar is dissolved. Wash down the sides of the pan with a pastry brush dipped in warm water. Increase the heat to medium-high, bring the mixture to a boil, and cook, without stirring, to 330°F, the light-caramel stage.

Remove from the heat and quickly stir in:

2 cups toasted sesame seeds
1½ teaspoons vanilla

Carefully pour the mixture out onto the slab or baking sheet. Place a second silicone liner or piece of generously buttered parchment paper on top of the brittle. Cover your hands with oven mitts and press the brittle into a thin, even layer. Let cool completely. Break the brittle into pieces. Store between layers of wax or parchment paper in an airtight container at room temperature for up to 1 month.

ENGLISH TOFFEE

About 1½ pounds

Though toffee is harder than taffy, it is still chewy and sticky—which is why a friend calls it "the dentist's special."

Line a large baking sheet with a silicone liner or well-buttered heavy-duty foil, leaving a 2-inch overhang of foil at the two short ends of the pan.

Combine in a large heavy saucepan:

1¾ cups granulated white sugar
1 cup heavy cream
1 stick (4 ounces) unsalted butter
⅛ teaspoon cream of tartar

Stir over medium heat until the sugar is dissolved. Wash down the sides of the pan with a pastry brush dipped in warm water. Increase the heat to medium-high, bring to a boil, and boil for 3 minutes. Cook, stirring frequently, to about 280°F, the soft-crack stage. The syrup will be light-colored and thick.

Remove from the heat and stir in:

2 teaspoons vanilla or 1 tablespoon dark rum

Pour the candy onto the prepared pan. Do not scrape the bottom of the pan. Let cool for 3 minutes. Sprinkle the hot toffee with:

4 ounces semisweet, bittersweet, or milk chocolate, finely chopped or grated

Let stand for 1 to 2 minutes, then spread the chocolate evenly across the toffee with a small offset spatula. Sprinkle on top:

½ cup finely chopped almonds, toasted, 1005

Refrigerate the toffee for 20 minutes to set the chocolate. Break the toffee into pieces. Store between layers of wax or parchment paper in an airtight container at room temperature for up to 1 month.

BUTTERSCOTCH

About 1¼ pounds; about 80 pieces

Butterscotch begins to solidify immediately after it's cooked and may be scored or shaped before it cools. Work quickly for best results.

Line a large baking sheet with a silicone liner or well-buttered heavy-duty foil, leaving a 2-inch overhang of foil at the two short ends of the pan.

Combine in a large heavy saucepan:

2 cups granulated white sugar
⅔ cup dark corn syrup
¼ cup water
¼ cup heavy cream

Stir over medium heat until the sugar is dissolved. Wash down the sides of the pan with a pastry brush dipped in warm water. Increase the heat to medium-high and stir constantly until the mixture comes to a boil. Cook, swirling the pan as needed to prevent hot spots, to 300°F, the hard-crack stage. Pour the candy onto the prepared pan. Do not scrape the bottom of the saucepan. Let cool for 3 to 4 minutes.

Score the candy into 1-inch pieces with a buttered knife. Let cool completely.

Break the butterscotch into pieces along the scored lines. Wrap each piece in cellophane, or store between layers of wax or parchment paper in an airtight container at room temperature for up to 1 month.

HONEYCOMB CANDY

About 1 pound

This crisp, light candy is an architectural masterpiece of crunchy candy honeycombed with air bubbles. We have also made this candy with great success using sorghum syrup instead of honey. Because honeycomb candy is highly susceptible to humidity, if you live in a humid area we recommend dipping it in tempered chocolate, which serves as a moisture barrier.

Have ready a large baking sheet lined with buttered parchment paper or a silicone liner. Whatever you do, do not attempt to make this without some kind of barrier between the candy and the baking sheet or you will rue the day you were born.

Combine in a large heavy pot:

1½ cups granulated white sugar
¼ cup water
¼ cup light corn syrup
1 teaspoon lemon juice or cider vinegar

Stir the mixture over medium-high heat until the sugar is dissolved. Bring to a boil and cook, without stirring, to 265°F. Add:

¼ cup honey

This will reduce the heat of the syrup considerably. Continue to boil, without stirring, until the syrup reaches 300°F, the hard-crack stage. Immediately remove from the heat and sift over the syrup:

2 teaspoons baking soda

Stir vigorously to disperse the baking soda. It will bubble dramatically. Pour the mixture onto the lined baking sheet. Do not spread the candy with a spatula or you will destroy the honeycomb structure. Let cool completely.

Break the candy into pieces for a rustic look, or use a serrated knife to saw it into uniform pieces. If desired, you may coat the candies in chocolate as for:

(Dipped Chocolate Truffles, 860)

While the chocolate is still wet, sprinkle the candies very sparingly with:

(Flaky sea salt)

Refrigerate to set the chocolate. If covered in chocolate, store as for chocolate candies, 858; if the honeycomb is plain, store in an airtight container at room temperature for up to 1 week.

COFFEE DROPS

About 1¼ pounds; 80 pieces

When buying glycerin, make sure the bottle does not say "for external use only"; you want edible glycerin, which can be found online and at many natural foods stores.

Arrange individual ¾-inch foil candy cups on a baking sheet or simply line it with a silicone liner or lightly buttered foil or parchment paper. Combine in a small bowl and set aside:

¼ cup instant coffee powder
3 tablespoons water
1 tablespoon cider vinegar
½ teaspoon edible glycerin

Prepare:

Butterscotch, above

As soon as you remove the pan from the heat, sprinkle the coffee mixture over the surface of the syrup and stir in gently but thoroughly. Drop the syrup from the edge of the spoon into ¾-inch-wide patties onto the baking sheet, or drop into the foil cups.

When cool, wrap the candies individually in cellophane. Store in an airtight container at room temperature for up to 1 month.

MEXICAN ORANGE CANDY COCKAIGNE

About 2 pounds

This recipe is one of Marion's, presumably written after a trip to Mexico. It is essentially milk fudge, but made by creating an orange-flavored caramel at the start of the cooking process.

Line an 8-inch square pan with parchment that extends over two sides. Heat in a small saucepan over medium heat until steaming but not boiling:

1 cup evaporated milk

Meanwhile, melt in a deep saucepan over medium-high heat:

1 cup sugar

Cook the sugar until it turns a rich brown. Slowly and carefully stir in (there will be lots of very hot steam!):

¼ cup strained orange juice

The sugar may seize up—simply keep stirring over the heat until the syrup becomes liquid again. Slowly add the hot milk and stir until fully combined. Add and stir in until dissolved:

2 cups granulated white sugar

Bring to a boil, cover, and cook 2 minutes, or until the steam washes down any crystals on the sides of the pan. Reduce the heat to medium and cook, uncovered, without stirring, to 238°F, the soft-ball stage. Transfer to a bowl or the bowl of a stand mixer fitted with the paddle attachment. Do not scrape the bottom of the pan. Let cool for 15 minutes. Add:

¼ teaspoon salt
Finely grated zest of 2 oranges

Beat the mixture with a wooden spoon or on low speed until it loses its sheen, begins to look creamy, and is getting just a little harder to stir. Stir in:

1 cup chopped toasted, 1005, pecans or pumpkin seeds

Transfer the mixture to the prepared pan and spread it evenly. Let cool completely before cutting into squares. Store in an airtight container at room temperature for up to 1 month.

LOLLIPOPS

About 1½ pounds; about 24 lollipops

To increase the intensity of flavor in lollipops, use candy flavoring oils rather than extracts. You can stick to classic lollipop flavors such as cherry, lime, lemon, and orange, or opt for more unusual ones, like cinnamon or anise. To color lollipops, use paste food coloring rather than liquid colorings.

Lightly coat lollipop molds with cooking spray and insert sticks. Or, for free-form candies, lightly oil a marble slab or line a baking sheet with a silicone liner or lightly oiled foil or parchment paper. Line up lollipop sticks on the marble or baking sheet with ample space between them. Bring to a boil in a large heavy saucepan:

1 cup water

Remove from the heat. Add:

2 cups granulated white sugar
¾ cup light corn syrup
1 tablespoon butter

Return to low heat and stir gently until the sugar is dissolved. Wash down the sides of the pan with a pastry brush dipped in warm water. Increase the heat to high and cook, without stirring, to 300°F, the hard-crack stage. Remove from the heat and let cool to 160°F. Stir in any of the following:

¼ teaspoon peppermint or cinnamon oil
½ teaspoon orange, lime, or spearmint oil
⅛ teaspoon anise oil

To heighten the fruit flavors and add acidity, stir in:

(1 teaspoon powdered citric acid)

To color the lollipops, stir in:

3 or 4 dots paste food coloring

If using molds, fill them with the hot syrup. If making free-form lollipops, drop a tablespoonful of the mixture over the top of each lollipop stick. As soon as the lollipops are firm and cool, wrap individually in cellophane. Store in an airtight container at room temperature for up to 1 month.

ROCK CANDY

About 1 pound

Rock candy looks like sparkling, sugary diamonds. This is an excellent candy-making project to do with children, and a good lesson on crystallization.

Punch 7 or 8 holes ½ inch up 2 opposite sides of an 8-inch square foil pan, and lace kitchen twine from one side to the other. Place the laced pan in a larger pan at least 1 inch deep to catch leaking syrup. Combine in a medium heavy saucepan:

2½ cups granulated white sugar
1 cup water
Pinch of cream of tartar

Making rock candy

Stir over medium heat to dissolve the sugar. Wash down the sides of the pan with a pastry brush dipped in warm water. Increase the heat to medium-high and cook, without stirring, until the mixture reaches 250°F, the hard-ball stage. Remove from the heat and, if desired, quickly stir in with a wooden spoon:

(3 or 4 dots paste food coloring)

Carefully pour the syrup into the laced pan. Do not scrape the bottom of the saucepan. The syrup should come ½ to ¾ inch over the strings. Cover the pan with a piece of plastic wrap, so that you can see what's happening without jostling the pan. Place in a warm, dry, draft-free place, such as an oven. Watch and wait. Within 36 to 48 hours, you should see crystallization begin. When all the syrup has crystallized, lift out the laced pan. This can take days. Cut the strings and dislodge the rock candy from the pan. Put on a baking sheet in a 200°F oven to dry for 2 hours. Store in an airtight container at room temperature.

ABOUT PRALINE

Two distinct candies go by the name praline. The one pronounced "PRAH-leen" is a patty-shaped pecan candy from New Orleans. French-style praline (spelled *pralin* in French and pronounced "PRAY-leen" in English) is a clear nut brittle made with almonds or hazelnuts that is pulverized into a fine powder for use in various confections or as a garnish for plated desserts. New Orleans pralines have an unmistakable graininess, much like fudge, that comes from beating the sugar mixture while it's warm; that and the city's notorious humidity have resulted in a soft, fudge-like candy.

NEW ORLEANS–STYLE PECAN PRALINES

About forty-two 2-inch pieces

Have ready:

2 cups pecan halves or pieces, toasted, 1005

Line a baking sheet with a silicone liner, lightly buttered foil, or parchment paper. Combine in a large heavy saucepan:

2 cups granulated white sugar
1 cup buttermilk
½ cup packed light brown sugar
4 tablespoons (½ stick) butter
1 teaspoon baking soda
Pinch of salt

Stir over medium heat until the sugar is dissolved. Wash down the sides of the pan with a pastry brush dipped in warm water. Increase the heat to medium-high and cook, without stirring, until the mixture reaches 238°F, the soft-ball stage. Remove from the heat. Quickly stir in the toasted pecans and:

1 teaspoon vanilla

Beat with a wooden spoon for about 1 minute, or until the mixture begins to thicken and become opaque. Drop by the tablespoon onto the prepared baking sheet, forming patties about 2 inches in diameter. Let stand until completely cool, about 30 minutes. Store between layers of wax or parchment paper in an airtight container for up to 3 days.

FRENCH PRALINE (PRALINE POWDER)

About ½ pound

Praline is used not only as an ingredient in other confections, but also as a garnish for desserts. It is superb sprinkled over vanilla ice cream, and can be mixed into frostings and baked goods.

Have ready a marble slab or a large baking sheet lined with buttered parchment paper or a silicone liner. Combine in a small heavy saucepan:

1 cup granulated white sugar
½ cup water
⅛ teaspoon cream of tartar

Stir over medium heat until the sugar is dissolved. Wash down the sides of the pan with a pastry brush dipped in warm water. Increase the heat to medium-high, bring mixture to a boil, and cook, without stirring, until the mixture reaches 356°F, the medium-caramel stage. Add and stir quickly to coat:

1 cup blanched whole almonds or hazelnuts, or a combination of the two, lightly toasted, 1005

Immediately turn out onto the slab or prepared pan. Let cool completely. Break the praline into small pieces. Crush with a rolling pin or pulverize in a food processor. Store in an airtight container in the freezer for up to 1 year.

ABOUT ALMOND PASTE AND MARZIPAN

Almond paste and marzipan are both made from a mixture of finely ground almonds and sugar. Almond paste has a higher proportion of nuts to sugar and is uncooked; marzipan is made with a cooked sugar syrup. Almond paste tends to be slightly grainier and stickier than marzipan, which is very smooth and pliable. Traditionally both sweet and bitter almonds are used in these mixtures. Bitter almonds are seldom used by home cooks because they contain the toxin hydrocyanic acid. To compensate for the milder taste of sweet almonds, we add a dose of almond extract. Both marzipan and almond paste can be colored and flavored by kneading in the colorings and flavorings.

ALMOND PASTE

About 1 pound

The high proportion of nuts to sugar makes this paste a good choice for flavoring cake batters (see Marzipan Cake, 730) and for the centers of bonbons (simply dip 1-inch balls of it in tempered chocolate, 858); or use it to stuff the cavities of dried dates. This recipe can be doubled and processed in batches or in a large-capacity food processor.

Combine in a food processor:

1½ cups blanched whole almonds
¾ cup powdered sugar
½ cup granulated white sugar

Process until the nuts are very finely ground. Add:

¼ cup light corn syrup
½ teaspoon almond extract

Process until the mixture is thoroughly blended and moist enough to hold together when pressed in your hand. If it seems a bit dry, add a teaspoon or so of water and process to combine.

Remove the paste from the processor and knead several times, just to bring the paste together, on a surface dusted with:

Powdered sugar

The paste is now ready for use. Or store at room temperature, wrapped tightly in plastic, for 1 week; for long-term storage, refrigerate for up to 4 weeks, or freeze for up to 3 months. Bring to room temperature before using. If the paste seems very hard, knead in by hand, or beat in with a stand mixer fitted with the paddle attachment:

Corn syrup (or liquid flavoring such as rose water, orange flower water, or liqueur)

MARZIPAN

About 1½ pounds

Marzipan is often molded into elaborate shapes such as fruits, flowers, and animals. Humble disks, balls, and logs of flavored marzipan are just as delicious—especially when dipped in chocolate. Modeling marzipan into various forms either with your hands or in molds is great fun. Paint molded forms with liquid food coloring, if desired.

Combine in a food processor:

1½ cups blanched whole almonds
1¼ cups powdered sugar

Process until the nuts are very finely ground. Leave the nuts in the processor. Combine in a large heavy saucepan:

1¾ cups granulated white sugar
¼ cup light corn syrup
¼ cup water

Stir over medium heat with a wooden spoon until the sugar is dissolved. Wash down the sides of the pan with a pastry brush dipped in warm water. Increase the heat to medium-high and cook, without stirring, until it reaches 245°F, the firm-ball stage.

Remove from the heat, turn on the food processor, and immediately pour in the sugar syrup. Grind to a fine paste, then add:

1½ teaspoons almond extract

Pulse to blend, then transfer the paste to a medium bowl that has been lightly coated with cooking spray. The mixture will be runny, but it will thicken as it cools. Place a damp kitchen towel over the top to keep the paste from drying out and let cool.

The marzipan is now ready for use. If you like, knead in a few drops of food coloring or a little extra flavoring, such as rose or orange flower water or a fruit liqueur. Marzipan can be stored at room temperature, tightly wrapped in plastic and in an airtight container, for 2 to 3 months. It can also be frozen for up to 6 months. Thaw and bring to room temperature before using.

Marzipan shapes can be formed by hand or with the decorative plastic molds used for chocolate. Coat the mold lightly with cooking spray. Pinch off pieces of marzipan, knead for a moment to make them pliable and smooth, and press into the mold. Use a small sharp knife to trim any excess so that the marzipan is level with the surface of the mold (be careful not to scratch the decorative depressions of the mold). Turn the mold over and rap sharply on the counter—the marzipan pieces should fall out; if not, gently prod them out with the tip of a knife.

Kids are great at modeling free-form shapes and enjoy making fanciful creatures and surreal fruits. Shape marzipan by hand just as you would modeling clay, and use a tiny dab of light corn syrup to affix one shape to another. Use whole cloves for fruit stems or the rough side of a grater to create the stippled skin of an orange—just look in your kitchen cupboards for inspiration. Marzipan can also be rolled out on a surface dusted with powdered sugar and cut into various shapes with miniature cookie cutters.

To paint molded marzipan, use regular liquid food coloring. Place a few tablespoons of clear brandy (such as kirsch, framboise, or grappa) in a small bowl or cup and add food coloring little by little until you like the color. Prepare as many colors as you like in this manner. Use a tiny watercolor brush to paint the marzipan. Let dry for 1 hour. For a sparkling finish and to help preserve its moistness, make a glaze for coating the shapes. Combine in a small saucepan:

⅓ cup water
⅓ cup light corn syrup

Bring just to a boil, then remove from the heat. While the glaze is still hot, lightly brush the candies with the glaze. Let stand for 30 minutes, or until completely dry. Store in an airtight container at cool room temperature or in the refrigerator for up to 1 month.

SESAME HALVAH

About one hundred 1-inch pieces

Halvah was originally a generic Arabic term for "sweetmeat." There are many types of halvah, but the one we know the best is a dense, chewy mixture of tahini and sugar syrup. Much like fudge, the texture of halvah improves over several days.

Coat a 9 × 5-inch loaf pan with cooking spray and line with parchment paper that extends over the two long sides. Stir together in a medium saucepan:

One 16-ounce jar or can tahini
1½ teaspoons vanilla
½ teaspoon salt

Stir over medium heat until the tahini reaches 120°F. Remove from the heat and set aside. Combine in a medium heavy saucepan:

1¾ cups granulated white sugar
½ cup honey
½ cup water

Stir gently over medium heat until the sugar is dissolved. Wash down the sides of the pan with a pastry brush dipped in warm water. Increase the heat to medium-high and bring to a boil. Cook, without stirring, to 246° to 248°F, the firm-ball stage.

Remove from the heat and stir in the tahini mixture just until combined. You should still be able to see some of the streaks from the sugar syrup. Pour the mixture into the prepared pan. Let cool completely at room temperature, then cover tightly and refrigerate for at least 24 hours.

Turn the halvah out onto a cutting board and cut into pieces with a lightly oiled knife. If desired, dip in tempered chocolate, 858. Store in the refrigerator between layers of wax or parchment paper in an airtight container for up to 3 months.

GINGERBREAD HALVAH

Prepare **Sesame Halvah, above.** Add to the tahini along with the vanilla and salt, **1 teaspoon ground cinnamon, 1 teaspoon ground ginger, ¼ teaspoon ground cardamom, ¼ teaspoon ground allspice,** and **⅛ teaspoon ground cloves.** Proceed as directed.

CHOCOLATE SWIRL HALVAH

Prepare **Sesame Halvah, above.** Add **4 ounces dark or bittersweet chocolate, melted,** to the sugar syrup after adding the tahini mixture. Stir gently, just enough to swirl the chocolate in—there should still be streaks. Pour the mixture into the prepared pan. Proceed as directed.

FRUIT JELLIES

Sixty-four 1-inch squares

Packed with the bright flavor of fruit, these jewel-colored candies are a welcome change from chocolate. Almost any fresh or thawed frozen fruit may be used, and two or more fruits may be combined.

Line an 8-inch square baking pan with lightly oiled parchment paper or a silicone liner that extends over two sides. Or, have ready silicone molds. Place in a medium heavy-bottomed saucepan:

3 cups fresh or frozen raspberries, halved and hulled strawberries, blackberries, or blueberries

Cook the berries over medium heat until they release their juices, about 5 minutes. Strain the berries through a fine-mesh sieve into a medium bowl, pressing against them with a silicone spatula to extract all the juice. Measure out ⅔ cup puree (save the remainder for another use) and transfer to a large bowl.
Stir into the puree:
2 tablespoons lemon juice
Sprinkle over:
4 envelopes (3 tablespoons) unflavored gelatin
Stir the gelatin into the mixture, then set aside to allow it to soften. Combine in a large heavy saucepan:
3 cups granulated white sugar
1 cup water
Cook over medium heat, stirring, until the sugar dissolves. Brush down the sides of the pan with a pastry brush dipped in warm water. Increase the heat to high and cook, without stirring, to 236°F, the soft-ball stage. Remove from the heat and add the gelatin mixture, stirring until the gelatin is completely dissolved. Return the pan to the heat and cook, stirring constantly, to 224°F. Immediately pour the jelly into the prepared pan or molds. Let the jelly sit at room temperature for 12 hours before cutting it.

Invert the candy onto a cutting board and peel off the paper. Use an oiled, sharp heavy knife to cut the candy into 1-inch squares. Alternatively, use small, oiled cookie cutters to cut out shapes. Roll or dip the jellies in:
¾ to 1 cup superfine sugar
coating them completely. Spread out on wax paper to air-dry. Store between layers of wax or parchment paper in an airtight container for up to 1 week at room temperature or up to 2 weeks in the refrigerator. Serve at room temperature.

CITRUS FRUIT JELLIES

Prepare **Fruit Jellies, 874,** substituting **⅔ cup strained lemon, lime, orange, tangerine, or grapefruit juice** for the berry puree and omitting the lemon juice.

BOURBON OR RUM BALLS

About sixty 1-inch balls

Many of our readers don't think it's Christmas without this cherished classic. These get even better as they age.
Sift together into a medium bowl:
1 cup powdered sugar
2 tablespoons unsweetened cocoa powder
Whisk together in a small bowl until well mixed:
¼ cup bourbon or dark rum
2 tablespoons light corn syrup
Stir the rum mixture into the cocoa mixture and set aside. Combine in a medium bowl:
2½ cups vanilla wafer crumbs (from one 11-ounce box)
1 cup coarsely chopped pecans, toasted, 1005
Stir into the cocoa mixture. If the mixture seems dry, add up to 1 tablespoon bourbon or rum a few drops at a time until the mixture holds together.

Roll the mixture into balls between your palms (the balls do not have to be even). Roll in:
½ cup powdered sugar
Or, if desired, dip in:
(Tempered chocolate, 858)
Store between layers of wax paper in an airtight container at room temperature for up to 3 weeks.

CANDIED APPLES

5 candied apples

Combine in a medium heavy saucepan:
2 cups granulated white sugar
⅔ cup light corn syrup
1 cup water
(1 cinnamon stick)
Cook, stirring, over medium heat until the sugar has dissolved. Bring to a boil. Cover and cook for about 3 minutes, until the steam has washed down any crystals on the sides of the pan. Uncover and cook, without stirring, nearly to the hard-crack stage, 290°F.
Meanwhile, insert a wooden skewer in the stem end of each of:
5 medium apples, washed and dried
Remove the cinnamon stick from the syrup if used. Add:
A few drops of red food coloring
Transfer the syrup to the top of a double boiler over boiling water. Working quickly, dip the apples in the syrup, turning to coat, and stand them on a metal flower holder or a baking sheet lined with wax or parchment paper or a silicone liner to harden, see below. Or, to make the apples easier to handle after dipping, roll the tops in:
(Finely chopped nuts)
and stand on a piece of foil or parchment paper.

Making candied and caramel apples

CARAMEL APPLES

5 caramel apples

Insert a wooden skewer in the stem end of each of:
5 medium apples, washed and dried
Place in the top of a double boiler over simmering water:
1 recipe Salted Caramels, 865, or 1 pound store-bought soft caramels
2 tablespoons water
Heat and stir until the caramels melt into a smooth coating. Dip the skewered apples into the sauce, twirling them until completely coated. Dry and garnish as directed in Candied Apples, above. If refrigerated, they will harden in a few minutes.

CANDIED ORANGE SLICES

About 36 slices

Sugar-glazed citrus slices are an old Mediterranean tradition. Half-moons or chunks of fresh pineapple may be treated the same way.

Cut crosswise into 3/8-inch-thick slices, discarding the ends and any seeds:

3 large unpeeled navel or blood oranges

Combine in a large heavy pot or a Dutch oven:

4½ cups granulated white sugar
4 cups water

Stir over medium-low heat to dissolve the sugar. Increase the heat to medium and bring just to a boil. Brush down the sides of the pan with a pastry brush dipped in warm water.

Meanwhile, arrange the orange slices loosely overlapping on a metal rack that will fit into the pot or Dutch oven, and attach twine to the rack for easy removal.

Lower the rack into the pot of syrup. Press a round of parchment paper on top. Bring the syrup slowly back to a simmer. Let simmer—do not boil—until the slices are translucent and soft, 10 to 15 minutes. Remove the pan from the heat and let the oranges steep, covered, at room temperature for 24 hours.

Using the twine, lift out the rack with the fruit onto a rimmed baking sheet and let drain until dry, 3 to 5 hours. The surface of the slices should be completely dry and hard.

Store between layers of wax or parchment paper in an airtight container at room temperature for up to 1 week or refrigerate for up to 3 weeks.

CANDIED CITRUS PEEL

About 2 cups

Candied citrus peel can be nibbled on its own or dipped in chocolate, and it makes a bright, flavorful addition to other desserts. It can be finely chopped and folded into cheesecake, gingerbread batter, and even ice cream. This recipe is easily doubled.

Scrub:

3 oranges, 2 grapefruit, or 6 lemons

Remove large strips of zest and pith with a vegetable peeler, place in a medium saucepan, and add cold water to cover. Bring to a simmer and simmer for 30 minutes. Drain, cover with cold water again, and simmer until tender. Drain again. Remove any remaining pulp or stringy white pith by scraping it away with a spoon. Cut the peel into strips 2 inches long and ¼ inch wide.

Combine in a large heavy saucepan:

1 cup granulated white sugar
3 tablespoons light corn syrup
¾ cup water

Stir over medium heat until the sugar has dissolved. Wash down the sides of the pan with a pastry brush dipped in warm water. Add the fruit peel and cook very gently over medium heat until most of the syrup has been absorbed. Remove from the heat, cover, and let stand overnight.

Bring to a simmer again, then let cool a little and drain. Place in a large bowl:

1 cup sugar

Toss the drained peel in the sugar until well coated. Transfer to a sheet of wax or parchment paper and let air-dry for at least 1 hour. If desired, dip one half of each candied peel in:

(Tempered chocolate, 858)

Transfer to another sheet of wax or parchment paper and let dry until the chocolate is set. Store between layers of wax or parchment paper in an airtight container in the refrigerator for up to 4 months.

CANDIED GINGER

About 1 pound; about 3 cups

Serve candied ginger as a confection, unadorned or with one half dipped in chocolate, or as an ingredient in other candies or desserts. Fresh young ginger, which has very thin, almost translucent, pink-tinged skin, is best for this recipe, but fibrous, brown-skinned mature ginger is fine to use. Young ginger can sometimes be found at Asian markets.

Peel and trim:

1¼ pounds ginger

Cut across the grain into 1/8-inch-thick slices. If desired, cut the slices into thin slivers.

Place the ginger in a medium heavy saucepan and add water to cover generously. Bring to a boil, then reduce the heat and simmer, stirring occasionally, until the ginger is tender when pierced with a fork, 30 to 40 minutes. Drain and set aside.

Combine in the saucepan:

2 cups granulated white sugar
2 cups water

Stir over low heat until the sugar is dissolved, about 5 minutes. Wash down the sides of the pan with a pastry brush dipped in warm water. Increase the heat to medium-high, bring to boil, and add the ginger. Reduce the heat to maintain a low simmer and cook, stirring occasionally, until the liquid has nearly boiled away, 1½ to 2 hours.

Drain the ginger and arrange on a baking sheet lined with parchment paper or a silicone liner. Let dry overnight. Or, toss the ginger with:

(Superfine or granulated sugar)

while still lukewarm, then dry as directed.

Store in an airtight container at room temperature for up to 1 year.

CRYSTALLIZED FLOWERS

Blossoms encased in a sheer, sparkling coat of sugar make an elegant decoration for cakes or almost any other kind of dessert. Not just any flowers can be used, however: Some species are toxic (among others, delphinium, foxglove, and lily-of-the-valley should be avoided); to be doubly sure, consult a current botanical reference book. ➤ Stay away from sprayed or treated flowers. Farmers' markets are a good source for edible flowers, but ask the farmer if they are organic and untreated. Of course, the best source is your own garden, where you can be sure that they're untreated and can pick them at their optimum point, just as they blossom. Whatever their source, make sure the flowers are clean and dry. This technique also works to frost **mint leaves** with a sparkly sugar coating.

Place in a small bowl:

Pasteurized powdered egg whites, 977

Stir in just enough water to form a thin paste (do not beat the white, as froth is undesirable).

Spread on a small plate:

Superfine or granulated sugar

Hold the flower (or petal or leaf) to be candied with tweezers and using a small watercolor brush, lightly coat the entire surface with the egg white. Hold the flower over the plate of sugar and gently spoon sugar over it, allowing the excess to fall back onto the plate. ➤ It is imperative that you cover every surface with egg white and sugar, for exposed surfaces will decompose—if you missed a spot, simply touch it up with the brush and a little more sugar. Gently tap the tweezers on the side of the plate to knock off excess sugar.

Set the flower, petal, or leaf on a baking sheet lined with parchment paper or a silicone liner and continue with the remaining flowers. When you have finished, check the candied blossoms for any spots that may need touching up.

Set the baking sheet in a warm, dry place to dry for several days, turning the flowers, petals, or leaves once a day to ensure that they dry evenly (this is especially important with whole flowers, for their weight can prevent moisture from evaporating from the bottom). When the flowers are very dry, they will be crisp.

Store them between layers of parchment paper in an airtight container in a cool, dry spot. If dried and stored properly, these will keep for 3 to 6 months or more.

KEEPING AND STORING FOOD

Storing food is all about the delicate balance between shelf life, flavor retention, and maintaining texture. Here, we discuss best practices for storing food in the pantry, refrigerator, freezer, and root cellar. For information on ripening and storing specific fruits or vegetables, see their respective chapters. For meat handling and storage, see Storing Raw and Cooked Meats, 449. For preservation techniques beyond long-term freezing, see the following chapters on canning, salting, fermenting, and drying.

The way in which foods are packaged for storing can greatly affect their shelf life and quality over time. With careful packaging, clear labeling, and efficient organization, the pantry, refrigerator, freezer, and root cellar can be great assets for the home cook. If items are not packaged and organized with care, these spaces are easily sabotaged over time—which can lead to hidden foods that spoil.

Regardless of storage technique, ➤ when foods show the slightest signs of spoilage, such as off odors, mold, moths or other insects, bubbling, unnaturally cloudy liquids, bulging or rusty cans, or liquid that spurts out when a can is opened, please accept the best advice we know: **If in doubt, throw it out.** Do not taste even the smallest bit of the contents.

ABOUT EXPIRATION DATES

Purchased prepared foods are generally marked with "use by" or "sell by" dates. While it is good to pay attention to them, do not take them as absolutes. With the exception of baby formula, expiration dates do not mean that a food is bad after that date, but merely that it may no longer be at its best. In general, use common sense rather than expiration dates to determine when a food is no longer good to eat. Any sign of spoilage, such as the ones mentioned in the above paragraph, should be taken as a self-evident expiration date.

THE PANTRY

Store any staples that are not refrigerated in the darkest, driest area you have, preferably with a constant temperature of no more than 70°F. Items that should be stored in the pantry include bread and crackers; less perishable fruit like bananas, citrus, tomatoes, pineapples, and melons; hardy vegetables like rutabagas, avocados, onions, garlic, potatoes, and winter squash; unshelled nuts; dried foods; tea; cocoa; sugar; chocolate; flours; cooking oils; vinegars; honey, molasses, corn syrup, and sorghum; Worcestershire and vinegar-based hot pepper sauces; flavoring extracts; nonfat dry milk; canned goods; and jars of herbs and spices. All fruits and vegetables must be whole; once they're cut, refrigerate them.

Since heat rises, an improvised cool place can be a low cupboard under your kitchen counter. If you have a few cubic feet of free space against a northern wall not far from the kitchen, consider turning it into a mini larder. Close it off from the adjacent warm area with a thick door, vented at the top. If possible, fit the area with shelves of slate or marble for maximum cooling.

For pantry storage, ➤ use rigid plastic, glass, or metal containers. Glass and plastic have the advantage of being see-through, but all pantry items should be labeled regardless. Make sure all containers have tight-fitting lids. For those who buy dry goods in bulk and need larger storage solutions, there are airtight, threaded lids available for standard 5-gallon plastic buckets that prevent pests from getting inside (make sure the buckets are food-safe). Several tightly closed bags of flour or grains can be stored in each bucket.

The greatest downfall of the pantry is disorganization. Items in the pantry should be rotated so that new foods are placed at the back of shelves and older purchases are in front. Any items purchased in bulk should be transferred to containers with tight-fitting lids and labeled with the name of the item and the date of purchase.

A cluttered, disorganized pantry is an invitation for pantry moths. There are various deterrents and pesticides available for dealing with these pests, but the easiest way to avoid them is to use airtight containers for storage, and ➤ buy only what you will use within 6 months of purchase. For longer-term storage of nuts, flours, cornmeal, and grains, store in the freezer.

The storage guidelines below assume optimum packaging and storing conditions. If your pantry is often warmer than 70°F, the storage time will be shorter than stated. If temperatures are lower than 70°F but still above freezing, the permissible storage period for most of these items is longer. Keep in mind that these guidelines are for ensuring optimum quality; food may be safe to eat beyond the times given, but they may not be as flavorful or nutritious.

➤ About 5 years: properly packaged dehydrated foods; salt, sugar

➤ 2 to 3 years: whole spices, most store-bought canned goods, nonfat dried milk, dried pasta without eggs

➤ About 18 months: dried legumes stored in airtight containers; properly packaged freeze-dried foods; unopened nut butters

➤ About 12 months: home-canned foods, shortening and refined oils, flour, ready-to-eat dry cereals stored in stainless or plastic containers, unopened cereals and whole grains, canned or packaged nuts, baking soda and baking powder, evaporated milk, dried fruits, canned citrus fruits and juices

➤ About 6 months: dry whole milk, unrefined oils, ground spices.

To store water, see 1033.

➤ If insect infestation occurs in your pantry, killing those you can see is not enough. Immediately throw away any opened containers of grain, meal, or flour, even if they are tightly wrapped, and thoroughly clean the storage area. Plastic bags are not impervious to pests. ➤ For a period of several weeks after an infestation, use the pantry to store unopened foods only. (Store opened containers in the refrigerator or freezer.) For those interested in long-term storage, consider 5-gallon plastic buckets with threaded lids.

Recommended refrigerator placement for common foods

THE REFRIGERATOR

At temperatures below 40°F, the growth of bacteria, mold, and yeast is inhibited and enzymes are slowed. ➤ The main compartment of your refrigerator should register 35° to 40°F, with the meat drawer (if there is one) just above the freezing point of 32°F. The overall goal is to keep all food temperatures at 40°F or below. If your refrigerator does not have a built-in thermometer, buy one and place it in the coldest part of the refrigerator. They are inexpensive and will let you know if something is wrong. The coldest place in the main compartment differs in each model, but it is usually at the back of the bottom shelf. When the freezing unit is inside the refrigerator, the coldest place is on the shelf closest to it. The warmest place in any refrigerator is the shelves on the door, which are exposed to warm air every time the door is opened. The less often you open the door, the more economically and efficiently the refrigerator will operate.

For storage in the refrigerator, ➤ glass or plastic containers are ideal for leftovers. Also keep on hand some zip-top food storage bags. Produce bags from the supermarket can be reused if turned inside out, rinsed, and dried well between uses.

Most of the rules for a clean pantry apply to the refrigerator as well. Do not crowd foods or allow them to touch the interior walls anywhere, as the cold air must circulate to do its job. Packing the refrigerator too full can inhibit air flow, causing some foods to freeze and others to be too warm. Keep the most perishable foods front and center, where you can see them and remember to use them. Label and date leftovers. Any foods that need to be used within 2 days can be marked with a piece of colored masking tape—red, for instance.

How long food will keep in the refrigerator has a great deal to do with how it has been packaged. Refrigerated air has a drying effect, and foods need to be protected from it. **Fruits and vegetables** need air and are best stored in a moist environment—the crisper or produce drawer. Crispers are most efficient when at least two-thirds full. Even when stored in the crisper, some vegetables, such as greens, will wilt. Wrap greens and leafy vegetables in a paper towel and place in a plastic bag. If your refrigerator has no crisper, or the crisper is full, store fruits and vegetables in their plastic produce bags (place a towel in bags of greens to control moisture). For

RECOMMENDED STORAGE OF FRESH FRUITS AND VEGETABLES		
Storage Location	**Fruits**	**Vegetables**
Refrigerator	Apples, apricots, Asian pears, berries, cherries, cut fruits, figs, grapes	Artichokes, asparagus, fresh snap and shell beans, beets, broccoli, Brussels sprouts, cabbage, carrots, cauliflower, celery, corn, cut vegetables, green onions, greens, herbs (not basil), leeks, mushrooms, peas, peppers, radishes, sprouts, summer squash
Ripen on counter, then store refrigerated	Avocados, kiwis, nectarines, peaches, pears, plums	
At room temperature	Bananas, citrus, mangoes, melons, papayas, persimmons, pineapple, plantains, pomegranates	Basil (in water), cucumbers, eggplant, garlic, ginger, jicama, potatoes, storage onions, sweet potatoes, tomatoes, winter squash

specific recommendations on storing different types of fruits and vegetables, see the chart, above.

➤ To keep fresh herbs or any vegetable with a stalk—such as asparagus or celery—crisp, put their stems in a jar with 1 inch of water and tent the leaves or tops with a plastic bag. This gives them water and oxygen but shields them from drying air. Set the jar in a place where it is not likely to be knocked over. Fresh basil should be kept this way, but at room temperature.

Store raw meats, fish, and poultry on the bottom shelf, placing them in pans or on a rimmed baking sheet so their juices cannot drip onto other foods or the refrigerator itself. **Meat** can be refrigerated as it came from the market if it will be used in 1 to 2 days. For **fresh fish** that is to be stored more than 1 day, wrap in plastic wrap and lay it on crushed ice in a pan large enough to accommodate it. For **live shellfish**, fill a pan with ice, cover the ice with a kitchen towel, place the shellfish on top, then cover with a second, damp kitchen towel. Serve or cook within 1 to 2 days. Opened packages of **luncheon meats** and hot dogs should be placed in an airtight container and used within a week. While it is tempting to store **dairy products** such as milk in the door of the refrigerator, the door is the warmest place. Keep milk, cream, and yogurt on the top shelves, preferably toward the back, and store away from strong-smelling foods. Wrap all **cheeses** in an inner layer of wax or parchment paper and an outer layer of plastic wrap. Discard any moldy dairy products (except cheese with natural molds) *without tasting*. Store **eggs** in the coldest part of the refrigerator. **Condiments** are best stored in the door. Maple syrup must be kept refrigerated.

Once a can of food has been opened, transfer any leftovers to a food storage container. Do not store in the opened metal can: Exposed to air, the metal can affect the color and flavor of the food.

Modern home refrigerators have the capacity to cool food rapidly. Putting a small amount of loosely covered, moderately hot food in the refrigerator—a custard sauce, for instance—won't do any harm; but very hot food or a large quantity of warm food should be quickly cooled to room temperature before refrigerating, otherwise it will raise the temperature of the interior and could warm the already cooled stored foods in the refrigerator to an unsafe level. To speed the cooling of larger amounts of food, chill them in an ice bath or spread them out in a thin layer so they can cool rapidly.

Keep your refrigerator clean. Get in the habit of wiping off containers with a damp cloth before they go in. If something spills, clean it up at once, or the dry air will dehydrate it quickly, making it hard to remove. If there has been moldy food in any part of the refrigerator, wash the surfaces down with a sanitizing solution, xx. We recommend regularly checking all foods for spoilage, giving a baking soda wash to the shelves, and carefully drying all the surfaces with a clean cloth. An opened box of baking soda in the refrigerator absorbs some odors, but it is no substitute for regular cleaning.

THE FREEZER

Freezing is a comparatively easy and time-saving method of both longer-term food preservation as well as short-term storage. Meats, fish, poultry, some fruits, and precooked foods may be frozen without further treatment. Vegetables, because of the need for blanching, require more time and attention during preparation. Even so, ➤ freezing can take a third to half the amount of time and labor involved in canning, and a fresher flavor can be obtained in most foods by freezing instead of canning. In general, treat your freezer as you would your pantry—label and date all foods, and rotate them regularly, with the oldest foods in close reach to ensure they are used first.

ENSURING QUALITY IN FROZEN FOOD

Only freeze high-quality foods. Freezing should not be viewed as a means of saving nearly spoiled food. Fruit should be ripe but still firm, never mushy or moldy. Vegetables should be fresh, tender, and young. Fruits and vegetables should be frozen as soon as possible after harvest to preserve maximum nutrients and flavor. For this reason, freezing makes the most sense for home gardeners, visitors to "U-pick" berry farms, and farmers' market bargain hunters. ➤ Food should go from preparation to freezer as quickly as possible and then freeze as quickly as possible. This is especially true for meat and fish; see the quick-freeze ice-brine method, 882.

For freezer storage, wrap all foods tightly in foil, freezer paper, plastic freezer wrap, or wax paper, then place in zip-top bags. We do not recommend freezing in glass containers, due to the likelihood of breakage, but tempered glass containers specifically made for freezing are available. Food expands as it freezes, so no matter the container, leave an inch or so of headspace.

To combine several servings of meat, cookies, or other small items in each package, separate them with two thicknesses of wax or freezer paper or folded foil.

The best storage solution for the freezer is vacuum bags, as they exclude air and prevent freezer burn. Home vacuum-sealing machines are available with an assortment of bag sizes, rolls of plastic to make your own bags, and canisters. To approximate vacuum-sealing without buying such an appliance, use zip-top freezer bags and the ➤ **air displacement method.**

To seal a zip-top bag with the air displacement method, place foods in the bag and fill a sufficiently large bowl or sink with enough water to submerge them. Seal the bag up to the last inch or so, and pinching the zip-top, lower into the water until only your fingertips and the unsealed corner of the bag remain exposed (below). The water pressure will force out the air. Seal the bag closed by pulling the remaining corner through your pinched finger and into the water. Very little air, if any, will be left inside.

The economics of keeping a well-stocked freezer can be negated if it is used for miserly hoarding. Foods stored too long will lose their quality and eventually even their desirability, and freezers can quickly become graveyards for forgotten food if they are packed too full. ➤ Never overload your freezer or add more than 3 pounds food for each cubic foot of freezer space during a 24-hour period. When preparing a quantity of foods to be frozen, the temperature control for the freezer should be put at the coldest setting several hours before loading the new foods.

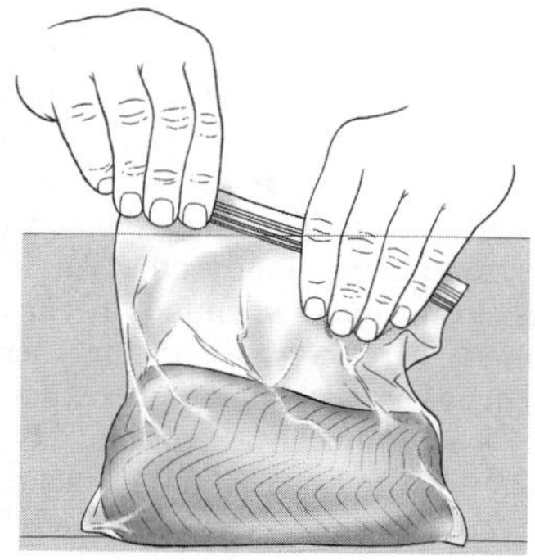

Displacing the air and sealing the bag shut

CHOOSING WHAT TO FREEZE			
	Freezes well	**Does not freeze well**	**Thaw first or cook from frozen?**
Vegetables	Snap and snow peas, young okra, corn, tomatoes, and green beans Cooked and mashed carrots, sweet potatoes, rutabaga, parsnips, turnips, and winter squash	Lettuce and other salad greens, sorrel, sprouts, celery, cabbage, cucumbers, endive, radishes, cardoons, potatoes, yuca, Jerusalem artichokes, jicama, salsify, taro root, truffles, and water chestnuts	Best cooked from frozen
Fruit	Berries, mango, pineapple, cherries, banana, peach slices Juices: apple, raspberry, plum, cherry, and grape	Cherimoyas, citrus, melons, prickly pears, sapotes, star fruit, tamarind	For whole small berries used in quick breads or fruit for smoothies, use frozen; otherwise, thaw
Meat	Most meats, fish, and shellfish freeze well if properly handled and quick-frozen, see 887		Best thawed
Dairy	Butter, milk, heavy cream, soft and hard cheeses	Yogurt, buttermilk, sour cream	Thaw
Other	Baked quick or yeast breads or coffee cakes; unbaked or baked scones or biscuits; unbaked and portioned cookie dough; unbaked fruit pies; baked quiches; baked cake layers; unfilled baked pie shells; cakes frosted with buttercream or cream cheese frosting; nuts, seeds, and grains	Gelatin, mayonnaise, meringues, cooked pasta and rice, milk-based sauces, custards, yeast doughs, cake batters	Cook unbaked pastries, pies, cookies, and baked quiches from frozen

THE FREEZING PROCESS

Food freezes in a sort of chain reaction. The water in the open spaces between cells freezes first. Next, these frozen sections pull water out of the cells, and then that freezes. When food is frozen fast, the crystals that form are many and tiny. ➤ Tiny crystals do a minimum of damage to cell structure and result in thawed food with the finest texture. When food is frozen slowly, on the other hand, large needle-like crystals form (this also happens when food is partially thawed and refrozen several times). Large crystals puncture membranes and cell walls and result in thawed food with a coarse texture. This is why it is important to freeze food as quickly as possible.

Since commercial blast freezing is not a practical alternative for most cooks, we recommend the **ice-brine method,** especially for fish and boneless cuts of meat and poultry. Salt lowers the freezing point of water, and a mixture of ice and brine can reach temperatures below 0°F.

➤ ***To quick-freeze with the ice-brine method,*** prepare individual foods as described in the following sections. Place in vacuum bags and seal them, or use zip-top bags and close with the air displacement method, above. Prepare a brine with 1 pound ice, ½ cup salt, and ½ cup cold water. Submerge the bags in the icy brine until frozen, then transfer to the freezer.

Microorganisms are not destroyed by freezing, but merely held at bay, and enzymes are slowed, not inactivated. Enzymes are inactivated by boiling temperatures, however, which is why all vegetables and some fruits are blanched before freezing. While freezing does not destroy microorganisms, it can destroy other organisms. The parasite in pork that causes trichinosis is killed if held at 5°F for 20 days, for example, and parasites in fish are killed by freezing at −4°F or below for at least 7 days.

FREEZING FOR LONG-TERM STORAGE AND PRESERVATION

The sections below deal specifically with freezing as an alternative preservation technique to canning. Because foods deteriorate much more quickly when improperly stored in the freezer, their preparation and packaging are extremely important to ensure high quality. For long-term storage, a dedicated freezer is essential. Because the freezer attached to your refrigerator is opened often, temperature fluctuations can cause deterioration to occur much more quickly than in a rarely opened chest or upright freezer.

Freezer burn occurs when foods are stored in the freezer for too long, are not tightly wrapped and are exposed to air, and/or are subjected to fluctuations in temperature. To avoid freezer burn, wrap and package all foods properly following the guidelines in this chapter. Do not treat the freezer like a science fiction stasis chamber. Foods still go bad in the freezer, so make an effort to rotate foods and use them within a year. See Ensuring Quality in Frozen Food, 880, as well as the individual sections below for more information.

ABOUT FREEZING FRUIT

Enzymes that naturally occur in fruit will cause some more sensitive types to oxidize and turn brown upon exposure to air. An **antibrowning solution** will prevent this from happening. When preparing a large quantity of apples, apricots, bananas, melons, nectarines, peaches, and pears, ➤ place the peeled and cut fruit in a solution of ½ **teaspoon or 1,500 mg ascorbic acid per 2 quarts water** as you work. Ascorbic acid is available in powder form from a pharmacy, or you can finely crush tablets of vitamin C. You may also add ascorbic acid to the syrup or fruit juice the fruit is packed in.

Commercial ascorbic acid mixtures are available, found with the canning supplies at the grocery store; follow the directions on the label. Citric acid and lemon and lime juice prevent oxidation, but they are less effective, so more is required—which may alter the flavor of the fruit.

Raw fruit can be frozen whole or cut up without cooking or adding a sweetener. This is called the **dry-pack method** or **tray-freezing.** Fruit frozen by this method will be very soft and juicy when thawed.

To tray-freeze fruit, first treat with an antibrowning solution, if necessary. Spread the fruit in a single layer on rimmed baking sheets and freeze until firm. Transfer the pieces to zip-top freezer bags, shaking down the pieces to pack closely. Return to the freezer.

The **sugar-pack method** is also used to freeze uncooked fruits. This method not only sweetens fruit, but stiffens cell walls and keeps ice crystals small.

To sugar-pack fruit, first treat with an antibrowning solution, if necessary. Transfer the fruit to a large bowl, add the required amount of sugar (listed in the chart on 883), and toss to evenly coat. Allow the fruit to macerate or soften until part or all of the sugar is dissolved. Pack the fruit immediately into zip-top freezer bags or containers and place in the freezer in one layer on a rimmed baking sheet.

Fruits destined for compotes and other sweet sauces benefit from the **juice-pack method.**

To juice-pack fruit, first treat with an antibrowning solution, if necessary, and pack whole fruit or cut-up pieces into zip-top freezer bags or containers and cover with juice of the same or a complementary fruit. Seal and place in the freezer in one layer on a rimmed baking sheet.

For uncooked desserts and garnishes, a fruit's flavor, shape, and texture are preserved best and for the longest time using the **syrup-pack method.**

To syrup-pack fruit, make a sugar syrup (see chart, 883) with a sugar percentage that balances the fruit's tartness—usually 20 percent for sweet fruits, 30 percent for tart fruits, or 40 percent for very sour fruits. You can use the fruit's own juice—or a complementary fruit juice—instead of water. Chill the syrup thoroughly, adding any ascorbic acid or vitamin C just before using. Add the fruit to a freezer container or bag, then add the syrup, pressing the fruit down and covering it with additional syrup if needed. Seal and place in the freezer in one layer on a rimmed baking sheet.

➤ For fruits that tend to go soft, such as strawberries and peaches, use the **pectin syrup-pack method.**

To pectin syrup-pack fruit, blend 1 box (1.75 ounces) or ⅓ cup regular powdered pectin with 1 cup water in a small saucepan. Stirring constantly, bring to a boil over high heat and boil for 1 minute. Turn off the heat and add ½ cup sugar. Stir until the sugar is dissolved, then remove from the heat and pour into a 2-cup glass measure. Stir in enough cold water to make 2 cups, then chill thoroughly. Add ascorbic acid or vitamin C if necessary. Pack and freeze the fruit as for syrup-pack, above.

Some fruits can be pureed and frozen. Plums, papayas, mangoes, persimmons, and melons should be pureed uncooked. Use a

PROCEDURES FOR FREEZING SPECIFIC FRUITS		
Fruit	**Preparation**	**Preservation Methods**
Apples and quince	Peel, if desired. Core and cut into ½-inch-thick slices. To sugar- or dry-pack, water-blanch, 884, slices for 2 minutes, then drain.	Dry-pack; sugar-pack using ½ cup sugar to 4 cups fruit; 40-percent syrup-pack; juice-pack; prepare Applesauce, 174, and pack into rigid freezer containers
Apricots, nectarines, and peaches	Peel, or water-blanch, 884, for 30 seconds. Drain, cool quickly, halve, and pit. Quarter or slice, if desired.	Dry-pack; sugar-pack using ½ cup sugar to 4 cups fruit; 20-percent syrup-pack; juice-pack; pectin syrup-pack
Bananas	Peel before tray-freezing. Freeze whole or sliced, after dipping in antibrowning solution.	Dry-pack
Berries	Leave whole; do not wash berries for dry-pack.	Dry-pack; sugar-pack using ¾ cup sugar to 4 cups fruit; 20- to 40-percent syrup-pack; pectin syrup-pack (especially for raspberries, blackberries)
Cherries	Stem and pit	Dry-pack; sugar-pack using ¾ cup sugar to 4 cups fruit; 40-percent syrup-pack; juice-pack; pectin syrup-pack
Citrus fruits (except navel oranges)	Cut into segments, 182, or juice.	40-percent syrup-pack; juice-pack
Coconut	Grate the meat, 973.	Juice-pack with coconut water; dry-pack; sugar-pack using ½ cup sugar to 4 cups coconut
Cranberries	Leave whole	Dry-pack; 50-percent syrup-pack
Currants	Stem	Dry-pack; sugar-pack using ¾ cup sugar to 4 cups fruit; 50-percent syrup-pack
Feijoa	Halve, scoop out the pulp, and mash.	Add sugar to taste to the mashed pulp and pack into rigid freezer containers
Figs	Leave whole	Dry-pack; sugar-pack using ¾ cup sugar to 4 cups fruit; 40-percent syrup-pack; juice-pack
Gooseberries	Top and tail, 180.	Dry-pack; 40-percent syrup-pack; juice-pack
Grapes	Leave whole	Dry-pack; 40-percent syrup-pack; juice-pack
Kiwi	Peel and cut into ¼-inch slices.	Dry-pack
Mango	Peel, pit, and slice.	Dry-pack; sugar-pack using ⅓ cup sugar to 1 cup fruit; 30-percent syrup-pack
Papaya	Remove the seeds and peel and cut into ¾-inch cubes or balls.	30-percent syrup-pack
Passion fruit, persimmons, guavas	Leave whole	Dry-pack
Pears	Peel and halve, quarter, or slice. Heat in simmering juice or 40-percent sugar syrup, 896, for 1 to 2 minutes; let cool.	40-percent sugar syrup-pack; juice-pack
Pineapple	Peel, core, and cut up as desired.	Dry-pack
Plums	Leave whole or halve, pit, and cut into pieces.	Dry-pack; 50-percent syrup-pack; juice-pack; pectin syrup-pack
Rhubarb	Cut the trimmed stalks into desired lengths. Remove and discard all leaves.	Dry-pack; 40-percent syrup-pack; juice-pack

food processor or blender for smooth purees or a potato masher for chunky purees. Add citrus juice to taste to prevent browning. Apples should be cooked into applesauce, 174, and frozen. Use frozen purees within 4 months. All fruit purees may be packaged without sugar. To sweeten purees, allow ½ to 1 cup of sugar per pound of fruit depending on the sweetness of the fruit.

For **fruit juices,** add ½ teaspoon ascorbic acid or 2 teaspoons lemon juice to each gallon of cherry or apple juice. For tomato juice, prepare as you would for canning, 901. Pack into rigid freezer containers; leaving at least 1 inch headspace in the container; freeze.

Any juices or syrups left over from thawed frozen fruit can be whisked with other juices for drinking, added to punch, used as a flavored syrup, or used as a poaching liquid for fresh fruits.

➤ Most fruits can be kept in the freezer for 9 to 12 months without significant loss of quality, though bananas and dry-packed fruits will degrade in as little as 4 months. Citrus fruits and juices will lose quality after 6 months. Juice- and syrup-packed fruits will store better and are less susceptible to freezer burn.

ABOUT FREEZING HERBS

If you have an herb garden you are likely familiar with the problem of having a glut of herbs in the summer but very few in the winter. Or perhaps you've had store-bought herbs go bad in your crisper one too many times. It is, surprisingly, possible to freeze herbs, and very good results can be obtained.

For tough herbs like rosemary and thyme, tray-freeze still on the stems, then transfer to bags. For tender herbs like basil, cilantro, and parsley, water-blanch, below, for 10 seconds, then cool rapidly in an ice water bath. Drain and remove as much excess water as possible by rolling up the herbs in kitchen towels. Finely chop or mince in a food processor, then pack into ice cube trays. Cover the herbs with a neutral oil and freeze. Transfer the frozen cubes to bags.

Herb-heavy mixtures such as Pesto, 586, and curry pastes, 585, freeze especially well in ice cube trays. Or prepare an herb compound butter using softened, salted butter and minced fresh herbs—use ½ cup minced fresh herbs per 8 ounces of butter. Place the butter on a piece of parchment paper and form into a log. Wrap tightly and freeze in the parchment. Cut off a piece of butter when needed to add flavor to soups, sauces, and fresh vegetables.

Herbs frozen in oil or in pastes will store for up to 8 months.

ABOUT FREEZING VEGETABLES

Most vegetables freeze well when dry-packed or tray-frozen as described in About Freezing Fruit, 882. If they are garden-fresh and properly processed, their taste, when served, is excellent. ➤ Choose young, tender vegetables. Starchy ones such as peas, corn, and lima beans are best when slightly immature.

Wash, trim, and prepare all vegetables before freezing, as you would if you were cooking them. Cut vegetables into uniform pieces. Most vegetables should be blanched before freezing. See the chart, below, for instructions for specific vegetables.

Water-blanching provides the fastest penetration of heat, is most effective against enzymes and microorganisms, and takes the least time. **Steam-blanching** vegetables offers fresher flavor and preserves more of their water-soluble C and B vitamins, but steaming takes longer than blanching in boiling water. In either case, vegetables need to be chilled quickly in an ice bath after they are blanched.

To set up an ice bath, fill a large bowl with ice and water, using about 1 pound of ice per pound of vegetables. Immediately after blanching, plunge the vegetables into the ice water to stop the cooking. When they have cooled, lift the vegetables out and drain well. Gently pat dry. Pack blanched vegetables into zip-top freezer bags or rigid freezer containers and freeze immediately, or tray-freeze, 882, then pack when frozen.

To water-blanch vegetables, fill a large pot with 4 quarts unsalted water (or Acidulated Water, 951, for vegetables that tend to oxidize and turn brown). Bring to a boil and drop 1 pound vegetables into the water, stir once, cover with a tight-fitting lid, and set the timer. Keep the heat on high. The water should return to a boil immediately. Lift the lid and stir the vegetables once more. Remove the vegetables from the water with a skimmer the instant the timer rings and immediately plunge into the ice bath to cool.

To steam-blanch vegetables, bring 2 to 3 inches water to a rolling boil in a large saucepan with a tight-fitting lid. Arrange the vegetables in a single layer in a wire basket and set the basket above the water. Cover tightly, keeping the heat on high. When steam starts to escape, set the timer. Lift the lid and shake the basket a few times for even penetration of steam. Remove the vegetables from the heat the instant the timer rings and immediately plunge into the ice bath to cool.

➤ The shelf life of frozen vegetables is 8 to 12 months, except for mashed avocados, which should be used within 2 months. To use frozen vegetables, see About Cooking Frozen Vegetables, 201.

PROCEDURES FOR FREEZING SPECIFIC VEGETABLES

Vegetable	**Preparation**	**Preservation Method**
Artichoke hearts	Trim and cut into pieces, 205.	Water-blanch, 884, in Acidulated Water, 951, for 7 minutes. Let cool, drain, and tray-freeze, 882, then pack into bags and freeze.
Asparagus	Trim off tough parts of the stalks.	Water-blanch, 884, thin stalks for 2 minutes, medium to thick stalks for 3 minutes; add 1½ minutes to each for steam-blanching. Let cool, drain, pack into freezer bags, and freeze.
Avocados	Select unblemished, slightly soft fruits. Peel, pit, and mash.	Add 1 tablespoon fresh lemon juice for every 2 avocados. Pack into containers or bags and freeze.
Beans, lima, shell, and black-eyed peas	Select pods whose beans are plump but not hard. Shell and sort by size.	Water-blanch, 884, small beans for 2 minutes, medium beans for 3 minutes, large beans for 4 minutes; add 1 minute to each for steam-blanching. Let cool, tray-freeze, 882, pack into bags, and return to the freezer.
Beans, snap	Trim and, if necessary, string, but do not halve.	Water-blanch, 884, for 3 minutes, or steam-blanch for 5 minutes; fleshy beans require 30 seconds longer. Let cool, pack into bags, and freeze.
Beans, soy and fava	Select tender pods whose beans are developed but not hard.	Water-blanch, 884, for 4 to 5 minutes, depending on size and tenderness. Let cool and shell the beans. (Peel the favas, if desired.) Pack into bags and freeze.
Beets	Trim and fully cook whole and unpeeled by steaming or simmering, 218, then peel, cool, and slice or cube.	Pack into bags and freeze.
Broccoli and cauliflower	Cut florets and stalks into 1-inch pieces.	Water-blanch, 884, for 3 minutes, or steam-blanch for 5 minutes. Let cool, pack into bags, and freeze.
Brussels sprouts	Trim stem ends, then sort for size.	Water-blanch, 884, small heads for 3 to 4 minutes; add 2 minutes for steam-blanching. Let cool, pack into bags, and freeze.
Carrots	Trim, wash, and peel. Leave small carrots whole; cut larger carrots into cubes, slices, or strips. Or cook until tender, puree and lightly season.	For cubes, slices, or strips, water-blanch, 884, for 2 minutes. For small, whole carrots, water-blanch for 5 minutes. Tray-freeze, 882, pack into containers, and return to the freezer. For puree, let cool, pack into containers, and freeze.
Corn	Shuck, remove the silks, trim the ends, and rinse the ears.	**For corn on the cob,** water-blanch, 884 (up to 1½ inches in diameter, 9 minutes; larger ears, 11 minutes; add 4 to 5 minutes for steam-blanching). Let cool, pack into bags, and freeze. Or simply remove the silks and freeze the ears in their husks without blanching; place in bags and freeze. **For cream-style kernels,** water-blanch the ears for 4 minutes or steam-blanch for 6 minutes. Let cool. Cut and scrape the kernels and juices from the cobs. Pack into containers and freeze.
Greens (collards, chard, kale, mustards, spinach, broccoli rabe)	Remove any tough midribs and stems, but retain those that are tender.	Water-blanch, 884, collards and tough mustard greens for 3 minutes, more tender leaves for 2 minutes. Or stir-fry over high heat until the leaves are wilted, 2 to 3 minutes. Let cool, pack into containers, and freeze.

PROCEDURES FOR FREEZING SPECIFIC VEGETABLES		
Vegetable	**Preparation**	**Preservation Method**
Mushrooms	Rinse, trim, pat dry. Small mushrooms can be frozen whole; cut large caps into ¼-inch slices. Or cook in butter over high heat until almost cooked.	Soak in 1 teaspoon fresh lemon juice per 2 cups water. Steam-blanch, 884, whole large mushrooms for 5 minutes, buttons or large quarters for 3½ minutes, slices for 3 minutes. Let cool. **For cooked mushrooms,** pack in their cooking juice in containers and freeze.
Okra	Wash, then sort by size.	Water-blanch, 884, pods under 4 inches for 3 minutes, longer pods for 5 minutes; add 2 to 3 minutes for steam-blanching. Let cool quickly. Tray-freeze, 882, pack into bags, and return to the freezer.
Parsnips, turnips, and rutabagas	Peel and cut into ½-inch cubes. Or cook until tender, mash, and season.	Water-blanch, 884, cubes for 2 minutes. For either cubes or puree, let cool, pack into containers, and freeze.
Peas, green	Shell and sort the peas by size.	Water-blanch, 884 small peas for 2 minutes or large peas for 3 minutes; add 2 minutes for steam-blanching. Let cool, pack into bags, and freeze.
Peas, snap and snow	Trim and string.	Water-blanch, 884, small pods for 1½ minutes or large pods for 2 minutes; add 2 minutes for steam-blanching. Let cool and tray-freeze, 882, then pack into bags and return to the freezer.
Peppers, bell and chile	Cut into halves, rings, or strips. Peppers also can be roasted, 262.	Dry-pack raw peppers in bags without blanching. If roasting peppers, pack into bags, close, and let them cool. Crack the bags open, squeeze out as much air as possible, seal, and freeze. (The skin will peel off easily once they thaw.)
Squash, spaghetti	Bake, 276. Use a fork to pull out the strands.	Let cool, then pack into containers and freeze.
Squash, summer	Cut into ½-inch-thick slices or shred with a spiralizer, 276.	For slices, water-blanch, 884, for 3 minutes. Let cool, pack into bags, and freeze. For shredded zucchini, steam-blanch, 884, for 1 to 2 minutes. Let cool, pack into bags, and freeze. Use in zucchini breads and cakes. Thaw the shreds enough to squeeze out the excess moisture before measuring.
Squash, winter and pumpkin	Wash, cut into wedges, remove seeds and pulp, and bake at 350°F until tender. Mash or puree.	Let cool quickly, pack into containers, and freeze.
Sweet potatoes	Bake unpeeled until soft. Scoop the flesh from the skins and mash or puree.	Let cool quickly, pack into containers, and freeze.
Tomatillos	Remove the husks, place in a pan, and cover with water. Cover and simmer until tender.	Let cool quickly, pack into rigid freezer containers, and freeze.
Tomatoes, green	Wash, core, and cut into ¼-inch-thick slices.	Pack into containers with freezer paper between the slices. Freeze.
Tomatoes, ripe	Leave whole and unpeeled. Or cook and puree. To save space, simmer, uncovered, until thick or reduced to a paste. Or, prepare Stewed Tomatoes, 281.	For raw, whole tomatoes, tray-freeze, 882, and dry-pack. For cooked, let cool, pour into containers, and freeze.

ABOUT FREEZING MEAT, POULTRY, FISH, AND SEAFOOD

The same advice for all frozen produce applies to the choice of meats: Only freeze fresh, high-quality meat. For best quality, pack it airtight, preferably in vacuum bags (or in zip-tops using the air displacement method, 881), and chill and freeze it as quickly as possible (for best results, use the ice-brine method, 882). All meat, poultry, and seafood should be divided into meal-sized quantities for packaging. Freeze all meats unseasoned.

For **meat and game,** remove any excess fat. Assuming the freezer is 0°F or lower, the quality of beef, lamb, veal, and venison steaks or roasts will keep for 1 year; pork chops and roasts 4 to 6 months; ground meat 3 months; and sausage for 2 months.

Freeze **poultry and game birds** whole or in parts, but always freeze innards separately, and ➤ do not stuff a whole bird before freezing (the stuffing can spoil). Leave the skin on. Chill poultry thoroughly before freezing, allowing 2 days for a whole chicken. For best quality, freeze poultry and game birds no longer than 4 months

Fish weighing 2 pounds or less before cleaning should be frozen whole. Fish fillets that are ½ inch thick or more freeze best. To preserve quality, just before freezing, dip lean fish for 30 seconds in a brine of ¼ cup pickling salt to 4 cups cold water with 2 tablespoons pure ascorbic acid. For freezing for just a week or two, wrap in plastic freezer wrap. For longer storage of small to medium whole fish, steaks, and fillets, we recommend either vacuum packing or sealing them in zip-top bags with the air displacement method, 881, and quick-freezing them with an ice brine, 882. Alternatively, give them an **ice glaze.** Regardless of which method you use, remember that frozen fish begins to lose quality after 3 months.

To glaze fish with ice, dip whole fish, steaks, or fillets in ice water, then tray-freeze, 882, until the water is frozen. Repeat the dipping and freezing until the pieces are glazed with ice ⅛ to ¼ inch thick.

Wash and clean all **shellfish, squid, and octopus.** Clams, oysters, scallops, and mussels can be tray-frozen live in the shell or shucked. Or steam mussels or clams open and remove their meat. Boil crabs for 5 minutes, cool quickly, and freeze meaty pieces in the shell. Similarly, steam or boil lobster, 360–61, cool quickly, and freeze in the shell. For the longest storage life, freeze shrimp raw in their shells, with heads removed. Shucked clams, scallops, oysters with their liquor, and squid and octopus are best packed in rigid freezer containers and covered in water, leaving ½-inch headspace. Freeze up to 3 months.

For **offal,** freeze livers, kidneys, hearts, and tongue raw; cook sweetbreads and tripe (515 and 518, respectively) before freezing.

THAWING FROZEN MEAT, GAME, POULTRY, FISH, AND SHELLFISH

Most frozen meats, game, poultry, and fish can be cooked thawed or unthawed, but we recommend fully thawing meat and poultry before cooking for best quality. Cooking unthawed meat can take 1½ times as long as cooking it fresh, and the cooking can be uneven. (Not to mention underseasoned.) ➤ Variety meats, foods to be cooked in breading or dredging, and all seafood except shrimp must be thawed completely. Shrimp only needs thawing if it is to be deep-fried.

➤ Always place thawing meat on a rimmed baking sheet or in a wide, shallow bowl to contain any juices and prevent cross-contamination. If you have the time, the easiest way to thaw frozen meat is in the refrigerator, in its package. Steaks and chops will thaw in 1 day; larger roasts may take up to 3 days.

To quickly thaw meats, place them in a sealed, waterproof bag with all of the air expelled (if the meat is not vacuum-packed, use the air displacement method, 881, for getting the air out). Put the bagged meat into a large bowl and fill it with cold water. Drain and refill the bowl with fresh water every 30 minutes until the meat has thawed; steaks may take as little as 1 hour, small roasts 2 to 3 hours. For whole turkeys, figure on 30 minutes per pound.

Smaller cuts may also be thawed in a microwave. Set the microwave at 50 percent power for 2 minutes, separate any pieces, flip them over, and microwave at 30 percent power, checking ground meat and fish every 30 seconds and steaks, chops, and chicken pieces every minute to see if they have thawed. Keep in mind that many microwaves cycle on and off when set to partial power levels, thus making them prone to partially cooking meats even when set to "thaw." Inverter-equipped microwaves are better at maintaining a consistent low output.

ABOUT FREEZING AND THAWING EGGS

Eggs must be removed from the shell before freezing. Yolks and whites may be stored separately or the eggs may be beaten and frozen together. The whites may be packed in small tightly sealed one-recipe-sized containers, perhaps in the exact amount for a favorite angel cake (yes, thawed frozen egg whites will whip). ➤ Yolks should be stabilized with salt or sugar, or they will become pasty and hard to mix after freezing. If yolks are to be used for unsweetened food, add ½ teaspoon salt to each 1 cup; if for desserts, add 1½ teaspoons sugar or honey to each 1 cup. Label the yolks accordingly. To use, ➤ thaw in the refrigerator for 8 to 10 hours.

To freeze whole eggs, stir 1½ teaspoons sugar or 1 teaspoon salt into every 2 cups of beaten eggs, depending on how you will be using them. Incorporate as little air as possible when beating the eggs. When packing, allow ½-inch headspace for expansion during freezing. Thaw eggs before using in recipes. **For each whole egg called for in a recipe, use 3 tablespoons thawed egg.** To replace a whole egg in a recipe using separately packed frozen whites and yolks, allow 1 tablespoon plus 1 teaspoon yolk and 2 tablespoons white.

ABOUT FREEZING DAIRY PRODUCTS

Salted butter freezes well for 6 months, but freeze unsalted butter for only 3 months. ➤ Heavy cream may be frozen for up to 2 months. When thawed, the uses for heavy cream are limited to making frozen desserts and using small amounts in vegetables and casseroles. It will not whip well. Do not freeze sour cream, buttermilk, or yogurt. Freeze milk for only 3 months.

Some cheeses may be frozen successfully. Cream cheese and soft, unaged cheeses like chèvre and fromage blanc lose very little quality when frozen. Pack these cheeses tightly into plastic containers, leaving as little airspace as possible. Hard cheeses are also good candidates for freezing. The best method is to vacuum-seal them, though they may also be tightly wrapped in plastic wrap and frozen in freezer bags. Store cheese in the freezer for up to 6 months. Soft-ripened cheeses, like Brie, and washed rind cheeses should never be frozen.

Thaw milk, cream, and cheese in the refrigerator. You may cut off chunks of frozen butter to use immediately in cooking or thaw in the refrigerator.

ABOUT FREEZING PRECOOKED FOODS

Savory and sweet pies, cakes, breads, casseroles, lasagne, chilis, thick stews, stocks and broths, meat ragus, and enchilada or tomato sauces freeze very well. Fried foods, or starchy ones such as cooked pasta and potatoes do not freeze well (the exception being baked noodle or potato casseroles). Toothsome cooked grains like wheat berries, hominy, and brown rice may be frozen and thawed for reheating, but tender rices and small grains like quinoa do not fare as well. Egg-based sauces or foods containing large quantities of celery, cabbage, peppers, garlic, and onion do not freeze well.

Freeze baked foods in pans they can be baked in, such as disposable foil pans. Soups, stews, and stocks may be frozen in rigid containers or freezer bags. Regardless of the food or the container it is stored in, cool cooked dishes completely, then chill in the refrigerator before freezing. Try to use frozen precooked foods within 1 month.

➤ Reheat all frozen precooked foods at moderate heat to an internal temperature of at least 165°F before serving. Most foods can be reheated without thawing first, but they will take more time to warm through.

A NOTE ON POWER OUTAGES

➤ If it is not opened, a fully packed chest or upright freezer will usually keep food safely frozen for about 3 days without electricity. Food in a half-full freezer may last for 1 day. In a sparsely filled freezer, quickly pack everything close together, then close the door and keep it closed or transfer the food to a cooler that will hold it snugly. When the power comes back on, quickly check the food. ➤ If the food is refrigerator-cold (40°F or lower) or if you can feel or see ice crystals, you may refreeze it, but its quality will be lessened. ➤ If the food is at room temperature and you do not know whether it has been that warm for more than 2 hours, discard it without tasting. When discarding potentially dangerous food, wrap it so no person or animal can ingest it.

ABOUT ROOT CELLARS AND WINTERING OVER FRESH PRODUCE

The earliest agricultural societies realized how urgent it was to protect seed grains from deterioration between harvest and planting time, and they developed many ingenious storing methods for protecting them against rodents, rain, insect infestation, and decay. The same enemies plagued them that plague us in our effort to winter over fresh produce: to find areas cool enough to stave off enzymatic action and ventilated sufficiently to prevent decay. **Root cellars** with stone walls and earthen floors are still the most practical solution if the climate is not too cold, too damp, or too dry, since they allow easy access and adequate space in which to segregate fruits from vegetables. When floors and walls are of concrete, produce must be stored away from these surfaces to prevent mildew. Should a basement area be heated, through proximity to a furnace or otherwise, it is not ideal for root cellaring.

Crops that mature late in the season are best for wintering over, but they should not be overripe. Harvest crops on a dry day; most should be allowed to cool in the field (or garden) overnight. There are some exceptions: Onions, for example, need to be cured for about a week after harvesting to attain regular storage status. With root vegetables like carrots, beets, rutabagas, and kohlrabi, leave on an inch of the tops, discarding the rest. The simplest method of all for storing root vegetable crops is to leave them in the ground where they were grown and cover them with 15 to 18 inches of straw. This mulch applied on late crops just before frost should keep the ground from freezing hard. Mark rows with tall poles and keep a plan of your planting to easily locate the vegetables.

For the most part, produce keeps best in a relatively humid environment at temperatures between 35° and 40°F. Sweet potatoes and winter squash respond best to somewhat higher temperatures—50° to 60°F. They need moderately dry storage, as do onions and garlic. A tall shelving unit in the root cellar can provide storage for a range of foods. Keep in mind that shelves near the floor will be cooler and moister, and shelves near the top will be warmer and drier.

Some people prefer to wash vegetables before storing; others refrain. In any case, ➤ the surface of the produce should be dry before storage. It can be insulated and kept at more even temperatures if packed in sawdust. Fruits such as apples and pears may be wrapped individually in paper to keep down contact spoilage from any unnoticed bruises. Whatever material is used, packing should be relegated to the compost heap after one season's use.

CANNING

Canning used to be an essential strategy for preserving the harvest. Today, most of us do not can because we must, but rather because we want to. Enthusiastic canners love the ritual of it; the thick bubbling of fragrant jams, the satisfying "pop" of sealing jars, and the sight of pantry shelves loaded with brightly colored pickles and preserves. In some cases, the quality and economy of home-canned items exceeds what is available at grocery stores. Regardless, canning is a useful skill to have when the backyard apple tree is loaded with far more fruit than may be eaten out of hand, a farmer offers blemished tomatoes for a bargain, or a friend lands a bountiful catch of salmon or tuna.

Canning may seem like a complex procedure, but it is quite easy once you get the hang of it. Though we spend considerable space in this chapter warning about the potential dangers of improperly canned food, please try to keep in mind that canning is absolutely safe as long as you follow safe practices and use tested, up-to-date recipes—such as the ones provided in this book, as well as the USDA's latest *Complete Guide to Home Canning* (see the bibliography, 1077). Read the information in this chapter carefully before beginning your home-canning project. For those who have never attempted to can before, ➤ we suggest your first attempt be a modest batch of pickles, 922, which will help familiarize you with the process and is unlikely to overwhelm.

ABOUT CANNING

The term "canning" is somewhat misleading, since what it usually refers to is preserving in specially designed glass jars rather than metal cans. In a nutshell, raw or hot cooked food is packed into hot jars with enough liquid to eliminate most of the air space. The jars are then covered with a self-sealing lid and are heated, or processed, in a **boiling water bath,** an **atmospheric steam canner**, or a **pressure canner** until they are thoroughly heated through.

HEAT PROCESSING

The heat produced by the canning process kills microorganisms and enzymes that cause spoilage and that are present in all fresh foods. Of special concern is killing off microorganisms that may cause illness. The length of time required to process food is determined by the density of the food, how it is packed, the volume and shape of the jars, the method of processing, and ▲ the altitude, 894. As the jars are heated, the air inside expands and is expelled. As the jars cool, the difference in pressure between the outside and inside of the jars creates a **vacuum seal.** This all-important seal keeps the foods free from bacteria that would otherwise enter the jars, contaminate the contents, and cause illness.

The temperature of a pressure canner, 240°F, is high enough to **sterilize** the contents of jars (i.e., eradicate all living microorganisms present)—as long as they are processed long enough to be heated all the way through. Thus, pressure-canning can be used as the sole preservation step when done properly (see Pressure Canning, 894). The temperature of a boiling-water bath, 212°F, is high enough to **pasteurize** jars (i.e., kill off *most* organisms inside), but if the contents are not acidic enough, the food will be unsafe to store at room temperature. Heating and sealing foods in jars is only one of several strategies canning recipes use to ensure shelf-stability. All recipes for water bath–canned foods must manipulate other factors to be safe to eat, see below.

ACIDITY

Acidity is an essential factor in canning, as lowering the pH of foods to below 4.6 prevents the growth of bacteria known to thrive in low-oxygen environments and survive the heat of water-bath canning, notably *Clostridium botulinum*, the culprit behind **botulism.** Sometimes acidic ingredients must be added to lower the pH, as is the case when vinegar is added to vegetables for pickles and relishes. Sometimes the pH of the food itself is enough to make a food safe in conjunction with controlling another factor, as is the case with jams and jellies made with acidic fruits. In addition to its role as a preservative, adding acids to preserves enhances their flavor and helps retain the color of some foods.

When using lemon juice to boost acid content, ➤ use only commercially **bottled lemon juice**—its acidity is constant, whereas that of fresh juice varies. **Citric acid,** which is derived from citrus fruits, is sold in crystal form, sometimes labeled as "sour salt." Unlike lemon juice, it adds tang without clouding the liquid or imparting a lemon flavor.

For pickling, always use **vinegar** with a content of at least 5 percent acetic acid (sometimes labeled 50 grain). Cider vinegar and distilled white vinegar are both recommended. ➤ Most important, never deviate from the amount and type of acid called for in canning recipes.

WATER ACTIVITY, SUGAR, AND SALT

Without water, bacteria cannot survive or reproduce. Thus, controlling the **water activity**—the amount of water available to bacteria—is very important in the canning process. In jams and jellies, **sugar** is used to reduce the water activity. Sugar is hygroscopic, meaning it attracts water molecules and bonds to them, making them unavailable for microorganisms to consume. When sugar is boiled with the watery juices of cooked fruit, water that cannot be absorbed into the sugar will eventually evaporate, thereby lowering the jam or jelly's water activity to a point that nothing can grow inside. Not only does sugar reduce the water activity in preserves, but it also binds with pectin to help preserves set up, or jell, 908.

Normally, white sugar is used, but you may find recipes calling for brown sugar, honey, or other sweeteners or sugar substitutes; for more, see Using Alternative Sweeteners, 907. Again, it is best to follow recipes as they are written. ➤ Never substitute maple syrup for sugar in canning recipes, as it has a pH higher than 4.6 and may render your preserves unsafe.

Like sugar, **salt** is hygroscopic, and adding lots of it to food reduces its water activity, which helps prevent the growth of microorganisms. In some cases, salt is essential to successful preservation, especially for curing, 934, and fermentation, 938. In most recipes for canned goods, however, salt is simply added to flavor the contents. For pressure-cooked foods, salt can be added directly to the jars before applying the lids. For pickles, salt is added to the brine. Do not can with iodized salt or salt substitutes—the heat of canning may turn them bitter. ➤ Use canning or pickling salt, 1014, to avoid discoloration or precipitation from additives that may be present in other salts.

PICKLES AND JAMS VERSUS LOW-ACID FOODS

Most of our favorite canning recipes achieve their shelf-stability by carefully balancing the factors described above. For instance, a preserve such as strawberry jam has high acidity and low water activity from the added sugar. And cucumber pickles, because they are nonacidic, are canned in a highly acidic brine. Thus, increasing acidity and/or lowering water activity by adding sugar results in a finished product that is safe after being processed in a boiling water bath.

On the other hand, ➤ **low-acid foods** like tuna fillets and green beans canned in water must be processed in a pressure canner at a temperature of 240°F (see Pressure Canning, 894).

RULES FOR SAFE CANNING

After abstractly discussing these factors and processing methods, perhaps the biggest take-away is that ➤ canning recipes are a calculated balancing act and should not be carelessly altered or improvised upon. Before you start a canning project, read through the recipe twice and collect the necessary ingredients, equipment, and utensils. ▲ Be aware of the altitude and make note of any adjustments to processing time or pressure you will need to make during canning, 894. Follow the recipes in this book to the letter; they adhere to USDA guidelines.

Be meticulously clean. Make sure everything that touches the food to be canned is spotless. Wash food thoroughly and measure and cut it according to the recipe. ➤ Can only as the recipe directs, and do not use a mixture of foods or substitutions. Improvisation and safe canning are incompatible (with a few exceptions, 895).

Do not can pureed low-acid foods, such as vegetables, bananas, figs, ripe mangoes, or papayas, and do not thicken liquids with flour or cornstarch before canning. ➤ The density of pureed or thickened food makes it difficult for the heat to penetrate the contents of the jar. Puree or thicken canned foods just before serving, if desired.

Prepare only as many jars as will fit in the canner in one load. Larger water-bath canning pots and pressure canners can sometimes accommodate two layers of jars. Straddle one jar on top of two, staggering them. A rack set between the layers may be helpful.

➤ Be extra cautious when canning low-acid foods to prevent the development of the potentially lethal botulin toxin. Because the spores of *Clostridium botulinum* that produce the toxin may survive 212°F—the temperature of boiling water—even after many hours, ➤ **low-acid foods must be processed in a pressure canner** at a temperature of 240°F.

Botulin toxins are difficult—usually impossible—to detect in canned foods. They may be present even if no odor, gas, color change, or softness in food texture is discovered. ➤ The first indicator of any spoilage to look for is a broken seal or bulging lid. However, the toxin can still be present without any signs if low-acid food is not processed correctly. A sealed jar is not a guarantee of safety either; how the food in the jar was prepared and heated is just as important. Become familiar with the guidelines in Checking for Spoilage, 895, and ➤ never test suspicious canned food by tasting it. The safest rule of thumb is **when in doubt, throw it out.**

Having said this, many novice canners are unreasonably afraid of botulism. As long as you follow trusted, up-to-date recipes and safe procedures for canning, there is absolutely no reason to worry about botulin toxins in jams, jellies, and other sweetened, acidic fruit preserves, or in pickles, relishes, or other acidified or high-acid foods.

Over the years, many unsafe, unapproved canning practices have developed. No matter what your grandmother or an old cookbook may tell you, **do not:** can without heat-processing (the so-called open-kettle method); or process jars in an oven, a microwave, an electric pressure cooker, a slow-cooker, a dishwasher, or under the sun. Do not use aspirin or so-called canning powders as preservatives in lieu of processing correctly. Finally, ➤ never improvise on recipes except in the limited ways suggested in About Improvising, 895.

Preparing a canning work station

HOW TO PROCESS

This is a brief overview of the canning process to help you organize your workspace and thoughts before and during a canning project. As you move through these steps, please consult the detailed information and procedures in the sections below, and in the other canning chapters in this book.

1. Set aside enough time to complete the canning project you have chosen. Rushing through the canning process is not recommended, and you will enjoy your experience much more if you can proceed at a leisurely pace.
2. Read through the recipe at least twice. Look up any unfamiliar terms. Make sure you have all the necessary equipment and ingredients.
3. Prepare a work station.
   a) Gather all recommended utensils, 892, and any specialized ones needed for making jelly, etc.
   b) Fill your canning vessel with water and place a rack in the bottom of the pot. Start to heat the water.
   c) Place a clean kitchen towel on a work surface beside the stove and have another towel ready.
   d) Lightly moisten a paper towel and have it ready for wiping jar rims clean.
4. Clean your jars and lids. Wash them in hot, soapy water, and rinse well. If the processing time in the recipe is less than 10 minutes you will also need to sterilize the jars, 893. Keep jars hot until you are ready to fill them.
5. Assemble and prep the ingredients for your recipe. Proceed to make the jam, jelly, pickle, relish, or preserve following the recipe, or pack low-acid foods as directed.
6. Fill the hot jars, leaving the recommended amount of headspace.
7. Use a tool, such as a small silicone spatula or chopstick, to remove air bubbles from the jars. Wipe the jar rims clean with the damp paper towel. Place lids on jars and screw on rings until fingertip-tight, 833.
8. Place the jars in the prepared water bath or pressure canner. For water-bath canning, make sure the level of the water is at least 1 inch above the jars.
9. Bring the water in the canning pot to a full boil (or follow the instructions for pressure canning, 892). Set a timer for the amount of time specified in the recipe as soon as the water reaches a rolling boil. After processing as directed, take the pot off the heat and let the jars sit in the hot water for 5 minutes before transferring them to the kitchen towel on your work surface.
10. Let the jars cool completely, then remove the rings, check to make sure all the jars have sealed, 894, and store as directed, 895.

CANNING EQUIPMENT

WATER-BATH CANNERS

These are readily available in kitchen and hardware stores, but any large pot will do, as long as it's at least 2½ inches taller than the jars—1 inch to accommodate the boiling water covering the jars, 1 inch to allow for the splashing water as it boils, and ½ inch for the rack placed under the jars. While metal jar racks are available specifically for canning, we have also used a silicone trivet to good effect. The pot should fit over just one burner, although the bottom may be several inches wider than the burner. (If a large pan is set over two burners, the jars in the middle may not receive adequate heat.) The pan lid must be either tight fitting or heavy enough to stay in place over briskly boiling water.

Water-bath canner

ATMOSPHERIC STEAM CANNERS

Until very recently, steam canners were not approved by the USDA, but thanks to research published by the University of Wisconsin we may now safely add atmospheric steam canners to our arsenal of canning tools. Steam canners are composed of a shallow pan that holds water, a perforated metal plate that sits over the water and that holds the jars, and a large cover that fits over the jars and holds in the steam. Some steam canners are equipped with a built-in thermometer. The water reservoir of a steam canner can run dry in 20 minutes, so ▲ they are not ideal for canning at higher altitudes.

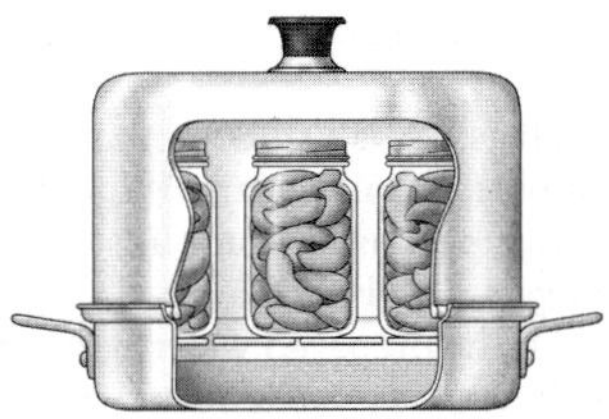

Atmospheric steam canner

PRESSURE CANNERS

These canners are more complicated and expensive than a large pot of boiling water, but they are essential for canning low-acid foods safely. Pressure canners have a locking, vented lid that allows the steam generated inside to build pressure and reach temperatures of 240°F. In order to maintain this temperature at sea level, the canner must reach 10 psi (pounds per square inch). Since the boiling point of water decreases as altitude increases, you will need to increase the pressure of your canner—even up to 15 psi for especially high altitudes, 894. Before proceeding, read any directions or documentation that came with the canner.

The pressure inside a canner is controlled manually by regulating the heat of the burner. Fitted into the cover is either a weighted pressure gauge or a dial-pressure gauge (some pressure canners have both gauges). A **weighted gauge** regulates the pressure inside the canner by allowing small amounts of steam to escape each time the gauge rocks or whistles during processing. These gauges are reliable and trouble-free. Their only disadvantage is that ▲ they offer fewer options at altitudes above 1,000 feet, because the only choices are 10 psi below 1,000 feet or 15 psi at any altitude over 1,000 feet. ➤ All pressure canners should be kept at full steam for 10 minutes before applying the weight.

A **dial gauge,** on the other hand, gives you a precise reading of the pressure inside the canner at any altitude. Dial gauges must be checked annually for accuracy; many county cooperative extension service centers have equipment to check the accuracy of the gauge. Otherwise, check with hardware stores in your area. If your gauge registers more than 2 pounds higher at 5, 10, or 15 psi, order a new one.

➤ **Do not use electric countertop pressure cookers for processing at any altitude;** most of them do not reach a high enough pressure (or temperature) to sterilize foods and are not approved by the USDA. Only buy a canner that was made after 1970 and bears the Underwriter's Laboratory (UL) seal of approval. We do not recommend using antique or hand-me-down canners that predate 1970. The USDA says that to be considered a canner, the pot should hold at least four 1-quart jars. Otherwise, it is too small to use as a canner. Smaller pressure cookers are unsafe for canning. Always thoroughly check and clean the canner according to the manufacturer's instructions before each use.

Pressure canner

JARS

The only jars recommended for home canning are mason-type jars manufactured in the United States specifically for canning. Made of tempered glass, mason jars are designed to withstand the intense heat of processing. They are composed of three parts—the jar itself, a metal lid ringed on the underside with a rubbery sealing compound, and a metal ring. The jars may be reused as long as they are in perfect condition, do not have uneven rims, and are free of chips, cracks, nicks, and scratches. Lids should be used only once. Rings may be reused until they rust or warp.

Jars used for commercially canned foods are intended to be used only once and are unsuitable for home canning. Antique and decorative canning jars, as tempting as they may be, should be avoided because they may be improperly tempered or brittle or have flaws that will cause them to break in processing.

Canning jars come in standard sizes ranging from quarter-pints to quarts. Half-gallon jars are also available but are difficult to handle; we avoid using them for anything but very acidic juices. In fact, the USDA does not condone processing any other type of food in half-gallon jars. Canning jars may be wide- or narrow-mouthed. Wide-mouthed jars are easier to fill and empty.

Another type of attractive canning jar sold under the brand name "Weck" is popular in Europe and becoming increasingly available in the United States. As of now, the USDA does not consider them safe for home canning as they have yet to complete the approval process. If you are determined to use these jars, pack, seal, and store them according to the manufacturer's instructions, but use an approved recipe for the preserve itself (and be especially observant for signs of spoilage, 895).

UTENSILS

In addition to the many standard kitchen tools you will use in the course of a canning project—such as a ladle, wooden spoon, kitchen timer, potholders, clean kitchen towels, and the like—there are a few tools specific to canning that are highly recommended. A **jar lifter** is essential for removing jars from the canner; a **canning funnel** keeps rims clean when filling jars; a long, thin, nonmetallic **spatula** helps remove air bubbles from filled jars. For hot-packing foods, you will need a **wide, heavy-bottomed stainless steel saucepan** to cook foods evenly. Also useful for preparing food for canning is an accurate **instant-read thermometer.** If you do a lot of canning and are of a scientific mind-set, you may wish to purchase a **pH meter.** While this certainly falls in the category of bonus, unnecessary canning equipment, it is a fun tool to have.

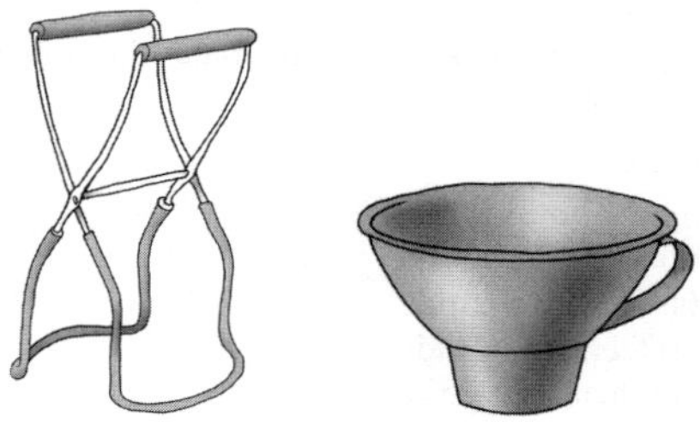

Jar lifter and canning funnel

PREPARING JARS FOR CANNING

The first step in any canning project is to wash the canning jars, new lids, and metal rings in hot soapy water or the dishwasher, then rinse them thoroughly. ➤ Food that will be processed for less than 10 minutes—all jellies and some juices—must go into sterilized jars. Otherwise, the jars do not need to be sterilized—just washed and rinsed well.

To sterilize jars, place them upright in the canner, cover them with hot water, and boil vigorously for 10 minutes at altitudes of 1,000 feet or less. ▲ At higher elevations, boil 1 additional minute for each 1,000 feet. Leave the jars in the hot water until needed. They can be left for several hours, but in that case bring to a boil again before filling.

While it was once necessary to heat canning jar lids in hot water, new lids do not require any pretreatment other than washing.

PACKING JARS

There are two basic techniques for packing jars: raw-pack and hot-pack. Rely upon recipes to tell you which method to use.

With **the raw-pack method,** hot jars are filled with raw or partially cooked food and covered with boiling liquid.

The hot-pack method involves filling hot jars with hot precooked food or jams, jellies, and other fruit preserves. If liquid is added to the jars, such as for pickles, it must be boiling. If food for a hot-pack falls below a simmer as you fill the jars, bring it back to a boil.

Always pack solids first, then add the boiling liquid. With both methods of filling jars, ➤ pack the foods firmly, but not so tightly that the produce is crushed. Pack halves and slices of fruit or vegetables in overlapping layers for the best fit. If the last jar is only partially filled, refrigerate it and eat the contents within a few days.

Headspace, the pocket of air between the top of the food in the jar and the underside of the rim, allows room for food to expand as it heats in processing. Individual recipes will instruct you on how much headspace to leave.

Before putting on lids, ➤ make sure that any air that is trapped in the liquid is expelled. Run a long thin spatula or chopstick down between the inside of the jar and the produce, changing the position of the contents enough to release any trapped air. Then carefully wipe the top of the jar before lidding. Set the lids on top of the jars and screw the rings on firmly, but ➤ stop turning as soon as you feel resistance. This is called **"fingertip-tight."**

WATER-BATH CANNING

The boiling-water method is used for high-acid fruits, fruit preserves, and pickled vegetables. Unless your canner has a jar rack that will securely hold the jars, place a rack in the bottom of the canner to keep the jars from touching the pot or each other. Fill the canner halfway with hot water and bring to a boil over high heat. Have a kettle of boiling water on hand to top off the canner once the jars are loaded. Lower the filled and capped jars onto the rack in the canner, allowing space for the boiling water to circulate between the jars. Add or remove boiling water so the level is at least 1 inch above the jars. Once the water has returned to a rolling boil, set a timer for the required processing time, noting any adjustment for ▲ altitude, 894. Check the water level periodically, and keep a kettle of boiling water handy in case the water falls below 1 inch above the jars.

LOW-TEMPERATURE CANNING

This method was recently approved by the USDA for pickling cucumbers and gives especially crisp results. ➤ Only use this method when a recipe indicates, and never use it for low-acid or nonacid foods. Place filled jars in a canner filled halfway with warm (140°F) water, then add enough hot water to bring the level 1 inch above the jars. Heat the water to 180° to 185°F and maintain this temperature for 30 minutes. ➤ Do not allow the heat to exceed 185°F or fall below 180°F. While adjusting the heat on a stovetop to maintain a steady temperature can be a bit tedious, this method is made simple by using an immersion circulator, 1054. Do not use this method for any pickle except cucumber pickles.

ATMOSPHERIC STEAM CANNING

Instead of being immersed in boiling water, this method of canning envelopes jars in steam. As with the boiling-water method, only use this canning method to preserve high-acid foods such as pickles, jams, jellies, and the like. Also ➤ be sure the processing time for a recipe is under 20 minutes (the steam reservoir may run dry). If the water runs dry, the jars will be underprocessed (your best option is to start the whole process over again, 894).

Be sure the bottom reservoir is filled with water as directed, and bring it to a full, rolling boil. Wait until a column of steam 6 to 8 inches tall is emitted from the holes in the plate before placing the jars on the plate. Cover with the lid and start the timer. Processing times are the same as for water-bath canning. Do not remove the lid at any time during processing. The canner must be adjusted to emit enough steam to maintain a temperature of 212°F during processing. To be certain, you can measure the temperature with a thermometer placed in the steam port. Finally, the booklets that come with atmospheric steam canners may contain potentially dangerous, unapproved instructions for processing. Do not follow them. Just to be clear, ➤ never use steam canners as a substitute for pressure canners.

PRESSURE CANNING

➤ Pressure canning at a temperature of 240°F—10 psi for a weighted gauge or 11 psi for a dial gauge at sea level—is the only safe canning method for nonacid fruits, unacidified vegetables, fish, and meats (for ▲ high altitude pressure adjustments, see below). Detailed directions for the use of a pressure canner are furnished by the manufacturer and should be followed carefully—especially with regard to the checking of the gauge.

Place a rack in the bottom of the canner. Then add 2 to 3 inches of hot water and, if desired, 2 tablespoons white vinegar to help prevent staining on the canner and jars. Lower the filled and capped jars into the canner with a jar lifter or tongs, allowing space between the jars for the steam to circulate. Fit the lid on the canner and lock securely, leaving the vent wide open. Increase the heat to high, and when steam begins to escape, let it vent for 10 minutes. After this venting, close the vent and bring the canner up to pressure.

With a weighted gauge, use the appropriate number of weights, or marked setting, consulting the manufacturer's instructions to learn how your weight should behave when full pressure is reached. With a dial gauge, bring the pressure to 2 to 3 pounds below the goal over high heat, then turn the heat down to medium until the correct pressure is reached. With either type of gauge, ▲ adjust for higher altitudes, as indicated below. Start timing the moment the recommended pressure has been reached. Always monitor the pressure gauge. You can hear the rocking of a weighted gauge, but a dial gauge must be watched.

Should the pressure drop below your target at all, ➤ you must regain the full recommended pressure and then start timing again from the beginning. If the pressure goes past the optimum point, reduce the heat a little. ➤ Turning the burner up and down, producing big fluctuations of pressure, can draw food out of the jars and ruin the seals. Try to keep the pressure from exceeding 15 pounds.

When the timer rings, turn off the heat. Remove the canner from the burner. Let the canner cool until the pressure registers 0—depending on the amount of pressure and size of the canner, this may take up to an hour. Then open the vent or remove the weight. Wait a few minutes more before removing the lid. This cool-down period is calculated into processing time, and shortened or sudden cooling may result in spoilage and broken jars.

▲ HIGH-ALTITUDE CANNING

Canning recipes have been formulated for sea level. At higher altitudes, the temperature of both boiling water and steam is lower. ➤ This means that, in order to can foods safely, the processing time must be increased for water-bath or atmospheric steam canning, or the pressure must be increased for pressure canning. Since atmospheric steam canners can run dry in as little as 20 minutes, they quickly become useless at higher altitudes.

WATER-BATH AND ATMOSPHERIC STEAM CANNING

1,001–3,000 feet, add 5 minutes
3,001–6,000 feet, add 10 minutes
6,001–8,000 feet, add 15 minutes
8,001–10,000 feet, add 20 minutes

PRESSURE CANNING

Use the timing given for sea level but make the following adjustments in pounds of pressure:

DIAL GAUGE

0–2,000 feet: 11 pounds
2,001–4,000 feet: 12 pounds
4,001–6,000 feet: 13 pounds
6,001–8,000 feet: 14 pounds
8,001–10,000 feet: 15 pounds

WEIGHTED GAUGE

0–1,000 feet: 10 pounds
1,001–10,000 feet: 15 pounds

COOLING THE JARS

After processing (and, if pressure canning, depressurizing), let the jars sit undisturbed for 5 minutes. Use a jar lifter to remove them from the canner, and set them upright on a cloth or a rack. Leaving hot jars in the canner can induce spoilage. Food that has been pressure-canned will continue to boil vigorously in the jars for a short time. Place the jars with at least an inch between them to allow air circulation, but do not put them in front of an open window or in a draft.

Do not tighten the metal rings at this point, as this could damage the sealing compound and ruin the seal. As each jar cools, you should hear a hollow popping sound, indicating that the vacuum has pulled the lid down into place. Let the jars stand at room temperature for 12 to 24 hours before testing the seals.

TESTING THE SEALS

Remove the metal rings and check to see if the lids curve down slightly. Then press the center of each lid: It should not move. If the lid depresses and pops back up, the seal has failed. Another test is to lift the jar by the lid with your fingertips a few inches above a work surface. The lid should not pop off. Jars that did not seal properly should be refrigerated at once. They may be safely reprocessed within 24 hours of the original processing time.

To reprocess jars, first remove the lid and discard it. Check the rim of the jar where the lid sits for any small nicks that may have caused the seal to fail. Prepare a new lid, and a new jar if necessary, for processing. Process the same way, for the same amount of time. Reprocessed food will be somewhat diminished in quality.

If you choose not to reprocess, you can store low-acid or nonacid foods in the refrigerator for a few days. Jams, jellies, pickles, and relishes will keep for up to a month. You may freeze jars of any item for up to a month, so long as they have at least 1½ inches headspace to allow for expansion.

LABELING AND STORING CANNED GOODS

➤Always store jars with the rings off. This makes it easy to detect a failed seal, prevents problems later on with corroded or stubborn metal rings, and also lets you check to see whether any food is caught between the lid and rim. If you see food on the rim but the seal is secure, simply mark the jar and serve it sooner rather than later.

Label jar lids in permanent marker with the contents and the date of canning. Store jars in a cool, dark, dry place. Storage temperatures between 45° and 60°F maintain good color and are generally suitable for all properly heat-processed foods. Dampness can corrode the lids and seals. Heat from a radiator, stove, furnace, or the sun will cause spoilage. Do not store jars at temperatures over 95°F. If the storage place is likely to approach freezing temperatures, wrap the jars in newspapers, set them in heavy crates or boxes, and cover with newspapers and blankets. ➤ For best results, use within a year. After a year, chemical changes will begin to diminish the taste, appearance, and nutritional value of canned foods.

CHECKING FOR SPOILAGE

Before serving home-canned food, inspect for spoilage. Make sure that the lids are tight and that they are still depressed at the center, indicating a good seal. If any of the following indications of spoilage is evident, **do not taste the food,** and immediately follow the directions given under Handling Contaminated Food and Jars, below.

Before opening the jar, check to see if: the lid is swollen or no longer depressed in the center; there are streaks of dried food on the outside that originate at the top of the jar; there is mold on the outside of the jar; bubbles are rising in the jar; liquid or food is seeping from the jar; the color of the food is unnatural, or much darker than it ought to be; or the liquid is unnaturally cloudy. **Do not open** if you see any of these signs of spoilage.

When opening a properly sealed jar, you should hear a reassuring "whoosh" as you pry off the lid. Sniff for unnatural or disagreeable (cheesy or sour) odors; look for spurting liquid, gas, or other signs of fermentation; check for mold—any color, even tiny flecks—on the surface of the food and under the lid; and examine the food with a fork for sliminess or other unnatural texture. Discard the jar without tasting as directed below if any of these are apparent. Sometimes, however, the top of canned fruit darkens because there is too much headspace and the fruit is sitting above the level of the liquid. This is harmless if there are no other signs of spoilage. Likewise, dark deposits on the underside of the lid are corrosion from acids and salts and are harmless.

HANDLING CONTAMINATED FOOD AND JARS

Treat any jar with any of the above conditions as though it contained botulin toxins. **Do not taste!** Handle the jar so no part of it comes in contact with a surface that may later touch food. If the lid of the jar is still sealed, wrap the jar in a heavy garbage bag and place in a garbage container with a tight-fitting cover. ➤If the jar is unsealed, open, or leaking, you must detoxify the food before disposing of it, to be certain that no child, pet, or unwary wild animal is accidentally poisoned.

To detoxify an opened, contaminated jar of food, wear plastic or rubber gloves. Carefully lay the jar on its side in a canner. Without splashing, add water to cover the jar by at least 1 inch. Cover the pot and boil for 30 minutes. Wash your hands or the gloves you used thoroughly. The food has now been detoxified, ➤ **but it remains inedible.** When cool, wrap the jar in a heavy garbage bag and dispose of it in a garbage can with a tight-fitting lid.

Prepare a solution of 1 part chlorine bleach to 5 parts water, and use it to thoroughly wash anything—including your hands—that may have come in contact with the jar and its contents before you detoxified it. Wet surfaces and equipment with the solution and let stand for 5 minutes before rinsing. Wrap sponges, cloths, or other materials you used in cleaning in a garbage bag and discard. Wash your hands again.

ABOUT IMPROVISING

As a general rule, ➤ do not tamper with the amounts of fruits or vegetables, sugar, or acid in any canning recipe. With this rule firmly in mind, you *can* play a bit with the flavor of your preserves. Try adding spices to jams, jellies, or pickles. For instance, throw a cinnamon stick into a batch of blueberry jam, ground cardamom and a star anise pod or two into pear butter, or a vanilla bean into apricot preserves (add whole spices in a cheesecloth sachet if you wish to remove them before processing). Citrus zest and fresh herbs are easy ways to add brightness and flavor to any pickle or preserve. Or, for the bold, add a halved habanero pepper to simmering peach jam or the brine for bread-and-butter pickles, or stir a couple tablespoons of liquor into any jam at the end of cooking.

ABOUT CANNING FRUIT

Unless otherwise specified, select firm fruit of perfect quality at its peak of ripeness. ➤ The pieces should be as similar in size as possible. Wash thoroughly by scrubbing sturdy fruits with a brush under cold running water and shaking berries and other delicate fruits in a colander in several changes of cool water. Some fruits benefit from briefly simmering before being canned. See the individual fruits below for instructions.

Fruit may be canned in water, fruit juice, or sugar syrup, with slightly different results. When fruit is canned in plain water, the texture softens and the color diminishes within months. A little sweetening helps canned fruit retain color, flavor, and shape, but too much sugar can overwhelm a fruit's natural flavors. We recommend adding the least amount of sugar you find palatable.

A **light sugar syrup** is very close to the natural sweetness of most fruits and will preserve the quality of the fruit without adding much more than a tablespoon of sugar to each pint jar. Syrup made with white sugar is the most common. The sugar's lack of color and flavors brings the natural flavors of the fruit into sharp focus.

Brown sugar has caramelized undertones that complement some fruits. **Mild honey** or **light corn syrup** can be used to replace one-third to one-half the sugar in the syrup, but be aware that honey has its own flavor and that corn syrup is super sweet.

Unsweetened **apple or white grape juice** may be used in place of a light sugar syrup. ➤ Putting up fruit in its own juice is also permissible as long as the juice is finely strained and is no thicker than the thickest syrup recommended.

Sucralose is a sugar substitute that can withstand the heat of canning and be substituted to taste for sugar. It will not provide the protection to texture and color that sugar does in the canning of fruits, but it will sweeten the food. If you prefer to use other sugar substitutes, can the fruit without them and then add the sweetener when serving.

SUGAR SYRUP FOR CANNING FRUITS

Percent Sugar	Intensity of Sweetness	Amount of Sugar per Quart of Water
10	**Very light:** close to the natural sweetness of most fruits	Heaping 1/3 cup
20	**Light:** satisfying with lightly tart fruits	Heaping 3/4 cup
30	**Medium:** perfect for most tart-sweet fruits	1 1/4 cups
40	**Heavy:** needed only for very tart fruits	1 2/3 cups
50	**Very heavy:** cloying	2 cups

Prepare the syrup before you prepare the fruit, so the syrup will be ready when the fruit is. Place the sugar in a 1-quart measuring cup or pitcher. Add enough cold water to make 1 quart and stir until the sugar is dissolved. Allow 3/4 to 1 cup sugar syrup per pint of fruit. Fill jars of fruit with sugar syrup to within 1/2 inch of the top.

ANTIBROWNING SOLUTIONS FOR CANNING FRUITS

To prevent light-colored fruits from discoloring after being cut, give the pieces a 15-minute soak in one of the following solutions:

- **I.** Crush and dissolve six 500 mg tablets vitamin C (ascorbic acid) in 1 gallon water. Vitamin C is most effective with the largest number of fruits.
- **II.** Use a commercial antibrowning product, following the manufacturer's instructions.
- **III.** Dissolve 1 teaspoon citric acid or 1/4 cup lemon juice in 1 gallon water. Always drain fruits—but do not rinse—before canning.
- **IV.** Prepare a solution of 4 teaspoons salt to 1 gallon water. Rinse the fruit before canning.

APPROXIMATE YIELD OF COMMON FRUITS

Type of Fruit	Pounds of Fruit Needed per Quart Jar	Quart Jars Needed per Bushel of Fruit
Apples	2 1/2 to 3	16 to 20
Apricots	2 to 2 1/2	20 to 25
Berries	1 1/2 to 3	18 to 24
Cherries (lug)	2 to 2 1/2	8 to 12
Peaches	2 to 3	18 to 24
Pears	2 to 3	20 to 25
Plums	1 1/2 to 2 1/2	24 to 30
Tomatoes	2 1/2 to 3 1/2	15 to 20

GUIDE TO CANNING FRUITS

We note superior canning varieties for each fruit as a guide only; other varieties may be canned successfully. ▲ To adjust for higher altitudes, see 894.

➤ Please read the directions for safe and proper canning, 890, before proceeding.

APPLES

Select crisp, juicy apples, a mix of sweet and tart. *Recommended liquids:* 10- to 30-percent sugar syrup, 896, made with up to one-third mild honey; or unsweetened apple juice.

Wash, peel, and core; slice into 1/4-inch-thick wedges. Place slices in Antibrowning Solution IV, above, as they are cut. Drain and rinse.

Boil gently in the desired liquid (a little cinnamon, allspice, or nutmeg can be added) for 5 minutes. Ladle apples into clean, hot half-pint, pint, or quart jars. Add the hot cooking liquid, leaving 1/2 inch headspace, 893. Remove any trapped air from the jars, 893, and adjust the liquid level if needed. Wipe the rims. Place lids on jars and screw on rings until fingertip-tight, 893. Process all jar sizes for 20 minutes in a water-bath canner, 893. Let cool completely and store as directed, 895.

APPLESAUCE

Prepare the apples as above, peeling only if desired. Place in a pan with just enough water or unsweetened apple juice to keep the apples from sticking (1/2 to 1 cup liquid per quart of sliced apples). Bring to a boil over high heat and cook, stirring frequently, until very soft, 5 to 20 minutes. Mash or puree; sweeten to taste, if desired. A little cinnamon, allspice, or nutmeg can be added. Bring to a rolling boil and ladle into clean, hot half-pint, pint, or quart jars, leaving 1/2 inch headspace, 893. Remove any trapped air from the jars, 893, and adjust the liquid level if needed. Wipe the rims. Place lids on jars and screw on rings until fingertip-tight, 893. Process half-pints and pints for 15 minutes (quarts for 20 minutes) in a water-bath canner, 893. Let cool completely and store as directed, 895.

APRICOTS, NECTARINES, AND PEACHES

Clingstone peaches hold their shape best. *Recommended liquids:* Unsweetened white grape juice; or 10- to 30-percent sugar syrup, 896.

Dip peaches in boiling water; slip off the skins. Wash apricots and nectarines well—there is no need to peel them. Halve and pit. If desired, scrape the red from the cavities—it darkens in canning. For easy packing, cut large halves crosswise into 4 wedges. Place the fruit in an antibrowning solution, 896, as you cut. Drain.

Place the fruit in a pan without crowding, cover with the desired liquid, and bring to a boil. Ladle the hot fruit into clean, hot half-pint, pint, or quart jars, packing the halves in layers, cut side down. Add the liquid, leaving ½ inch headspace, 893. Remove any trapped air from the jars, 893, and adjust the liquid level if needed. Wipe the rims. Place lids on jars and screw on rings until fingertip-tight, 893. Process half-pints and pints for 20 minutes (quarts for 25 minutes) in a water-bath canner, 893. Let cool completely and store as directed, 895.

BERRIES

All canned berries soften, but their flavors remain delicious. They are especially good as a dessert topping for cakes, ice cream, and waffles. *Recommended liquids:* Sweetened juice; water; or 30- to 40-percent sugar syrup, 896.

Working with 1 to 2 quarts of berries at a time, stem, wash, drain, and hull as needed. Halve any strawberries that are much larger than the rest. ***For hot-pack,*** heat berries in boiling liquid for 30 seconds and drain. Ladle the hot berries into clean, hot half-pint, pint, or quart jars and add liquid to cover, leaving ½ inch headspace, 893. Remove any trapped air from the jars, 893, and adjust the liquid level if needed. ***For raw-pack,*** fill hot jars with berries, shaking down while filling, and cover with hot liquid, leaving ½-inch headspace, 893. Wipe the rims. Place lids on jars and screw on rings until fingertip-tight, 893. Process half-pints, pints, and hot-packed quarts for 15 minutes (raw-packed quarts for 20 minutes) in a water-bath canner, 893. Let cool completely and store as directed, 895.

CHERRIES

Sweet and tart cherries are both excellent canned, and make superb pie fillings. *Recommended liquids:* Water; unsweetened apple juice or white grape juice; or 30-percent sugar syrup, 896.

Stem and wash. Cherries retain their color and shape best when unpitted, but they may be pitted. To prevent unpitted cherries from splitting when processed, prick each cherry with a clean pin.

In a pan without crowding, combine ½ cup desired liquid for each quart of cherries and quickly bring to a boil. Pack cherries into clean, hot half-pint, pint, or quart jars, and add the hot liquid, leaving ½ inch headspace, 893. Remove any trapped air from the jars, 893, and adjust the liquid level if needed. Wipe the rims. Place lids on jars and screw on rings until fingertip-tight, 893. Process half-pints and pints for 15 minutes (quarts for 20 minutes) in a water-bath canner, 891. Let cool completely and store as directed, 895.

CRANBERRIES

Although they are firmer when frozen, canned cranberries make excellent cranberry sauce. *Recommended liquid:* 40-percent sugar syrup, 896.

Stem and wash. Bring the syrup to a boil, add the berries, and boil for 3 minutes. Pack the hot cranberries into clean, hot half-pint, pint, or quart jars, and add the boiling syrup, leaving ½ inch headspace, 893. Remove any trapped air from the jars, 893, and adjust the liquid level if needed. Wipe the rims. Place lids on jars and screw on rings until fingertip-tight, 893. Process all jar sizes for 15 minutes in a water-bath canner, 893. Let cool completely and store as directed, 895.

CRANBERRY SAUCE, JELLIED

The classic accompaniment to Thanksgiving turkey, this is also wonderful served chilled for dessert. Slice and top with whipped cream and chopped toasted walnuts. *Recommended liquid:* Water.

Stem and wash. In a pan without crowding, combine each quart of cranberries with 1 cup water. Cook until soft, then run through a food mill and return to the pan.

For each original quart of berries, stir in 3 cups sugar. Boil for 3 minutes, stirring. Ladle the hot sauce into clean, hot wide-mouthed half-pint or pint jars, leaving ½ inch headspace, 893. Remove any trapped air from the jars, 893, and adjust the liquid level if needed. Wipe the rims. Place lids on jars and screw on rings until fingertip-tight, 893. Process all the jar sizes for 15 minutes in a water-bath canner, 893. Let cool completely and store as directed, 895.

FIGS

Canned figs have a beautiful appearance and an excellent texture, but their flavor can fade. Select firm fruits without splits. Acid must be added because figs have only borderline acidity. *Recommended liquid:* 20-percent sugar syrup, 896, made with up to one-third mild honey.

Do not stem or peel. Wash. Cover with water and boil gently for 2 minutes; drain.

Bring the syrup to a boil, add the figs, and boil gently for 5 minutes. Pack the hot figs in clean, hot half-pint, pint, or quart jars. Add ¼ teaspoon citric acid or 1 tablespoon bottled lemon juice to each pint jar, or twice this amount to each quart jar. Add the hot cooking liquid, leaving ½ inch headspace, 893. Remove any trapped air from the jars, 893, and adjust the liquid level if needed. Wipe the rims. Place lids on jars and screw on rings until fingertip-tight, 893. Process half-pints and pints for 45 minutes (quarts for 50 minutes) in a water-bath canner, 893. Let cool completely and store as directed, 895.

FRUIT PUREES AND BABY FOOD

Puree any fruit except bananas, cantaloupe and other melons, coconut, figs, mangoes, papayas, and Asian pears, which are insufficiently acidic. (Do not can pureed tomatoes by these directions either.) If necessary, sweeten the fruit puree to taste with sugar or honey. **If making a fruit puree for baby food, however, do not use honey,** as it can cause botulism in babies and children under one year of age. *Recommended liquid:* Water.

Stem, wash, pit, peel, and/or core the fruit as needed. Place in an antibrowning solution, 896. Drain.

Slightly crush or coarsely chop the fruit. Mix in a pan with 1 cup hot water for each quart of fruit. Cook slowly until soft, stirring frequently. Press through a sieve, or puree using the fine blade of a food mill. Sweeten to taste. If using honey, bring to a boil, stirring. If using sugar, boil until the sugar dissolves. Ladle into hot half-pint or pint jars, leaving ¼ inch headspace, 893. Remove any trapped air from the jars, 893, and adjust the liquid level if needed. Wipe the rims. Place lids on jars and screw on rings until fingertip-tight, 893. Process all jar sizes for 20 minutes in a water-bath canner, 893. Let cool completely and store as directed, 895.

GRAPES

Superior canning varieties are Flame, Glenora, Reliance, seedless Concord, and Thompson. *Recommended liquids:* 10- to 20-percent sugar syrup, 896; or unsweetened white grape juice.

Select tight-skinned seedless grapes, ideally picked about 2 weeks before peak ripeness. Wash and stem. Bring the liquid to a boil in one pot and 1 gallon of water to a boil in a separate pot. Drain the grapes, put in a blanching basket or a sieve, and dip in the boiling water for 30 seconds. Drain.

Pack into clean, hot half-pint, pint, or quart jars and add the hot liquid, leaving ½ inch headspace, 893. Remove any trapped air from the jars, 893, and adjust the liquid level if needed. Wipe the rims. Place lids on jars and screw on rings until fingertip-tight, 893. Process all jar sizes for 10 minutes in a water-bath canner, 893. Let cool completely and store as directed, 895.

ORANGES, MANDARINS, GRAPEFRUITS, AND POMELOS

Raw-pack only. While mandarin segments are perfectly delicious on their own, we like canning equal parts orange and grapefruit for more flavor. *Recommended liquid:* 10- to 30-percent sugar syrup, 896.

Wash, peel, and cut off the white pith. Cut between segments and discard the seeds and membrane.

Bring the syrup to a boil. Pack the fruit into clean, hot half-pint, pint, or quart jars. Add the hot syrup, leaving ½ inch headspace, 893. Remove any trapped air from the jars, 893, and adjust the liquid level if needed. Wipe the rims. Place lids on jars and screw on rings until fingertip-tight, 893. Process all jar sizes for 10 minutes in a water-bath canner, 893. Let cool completely and store as directed, 895.

PAPAYAS

The texture and color of canned papayas are excellent, and the flavor is intensified. Papayas have borderline acidity, making it necessary to add acid. *Recommended liquid:* 20- to 30-percent sugar syrup, 896.

Wash and peel. Halve, remove the seeds, and cut the fruit into ½-inch cubes.

Place the syrup and fruit in a saucepan without crowding and bring to a simmer. Cook gently for 2 to 3 minutes. Ladle the fruit into clean, hot pint or quart jars. Add ¼ teaspoon citric acid or 1 tablespoon bottled lemon juice to each pint jar, or twice this amount to each quart jar. Add the hot syrup, leaving ½ inch headspace, 893. Remove any trapped air from the jars, 893, and adjust the liquid level if needed. Wipe the rims. Place lids on jars and screw on rings until fingertip-tight, 893. Process pints for 15 minutes (quarts for 20 minutes) in a water-bath canner, 893. Let cool completely and store as directed, 895.

PEARS

One of the most successfully canned of all foods. Large pieces are rich in flavor and not too soft. Superior canning varieties are Bartlett, Clapp's Favorite, Duchess, Kieffer, and Moonglow. *Recommended liquids:* Water; unsweetened apple juice or white grape juice; or 10- to 30-percent sugar syrup, 896.

Wash and peel. Halve or quarter and core. Place in Antibrowning Solution IV, 896. Drain and rinse.

Boil the fruit gently in the desired liquid for 5 minutes. Ladle into clean, hot half-pint, pint, or quart jars. Add the hot liquid, leaving ½ inch headspace, 893. Remove any trapped air from the jars, 893, and adjust the liquid level if needed. Wipe the rims. Place lids on jars and screw on rings until fingertip-tight, 893. Process half-pints and pints for 20 minutes (quarts for 25 minutes) in a water-bath canner, 893. Let cool completely and store as directed, 895.

PINEAPPLE

Recommended liquids: Water; pineapple juice; or 10- to 30-percent sugar syrup, 896, made with up to one-third mild honey.

Wash, then remove the peel and eyes. Quarter lengthwise and slice out the core. Cut into ½-inch-thick slices or wedges or 1-inch chunks.

Simmer fruit in the desired liquid for 10 minutes. Ladle the hot fruit into clean, hot half-pint, pint, or quart jars. Add the hot liquid, leaving ½ inch headspace, 893. Remove any trapped air from the jars, 893, and adjust the liquid level if needed. Wipe the rims. Place lids on jars and screw on rings until fingertip-tight, 893. Process half-pints and pints for 15 minutes (quarts for 20 minutes) in a water-bath canner, 893. Let cool completely and store as directed, 895.

PLUMS

Superior canning varieties are Burbank, Early Italian, Fellenberg, Greengage, Italian Prune, Laroda, Mount Royal, Nubiana, Santa Rosa, Satsuma, Seneca, Stanley, and Victoria; also wild plums. *Recommended liquids:* Water; or 20- to 30-percent sugar syrup, 896.

Stem and wash. Most plums are best canned whole. Prick skins with a fork to prevent bursting.

Boil fruit gently for 2 minutes in the desired liquid, then cover the pan and let stand for 20 to 30 minutes off the heat. Ladle the hot plums into clean, hot half-pint, pint, or quart jars. Add the liquid, leaving ½ inch headspace, 893. Remove any trapped air from the jars, 893, and adjust the liquid level if needed. Wipe the rims. Place lids on jars and screw on rings until fingertip-tight, 893. Process half-pints and pints for 20 minutes (quarts for 25 minutes) in a water-bath canner, 893. Let cool completely and store as directed, 895.

RHUBARB, STEWED

Recommended liquids: The fruit's own juice; or water.

Select tender bright red stalks. Discard the leaves and green parts. Wash and cut into 1-inch pieces. In a large pan without crowding, combine each quart of chopped rhubarb with ½ to 1 cup sugar, to taste. Let stand until the juices flow, but no more than 4 hours, stirring occasionally.

Slowly bring to a boil. Using a slotted spoon, pack the hot fruit into clean, hot half-pint, pint, or quart jars. Add boiling water if needed, leaving ½ inch headspace, 893. Remove any trapped air from the jars, 893, and adjust the liquid level if needed. Wipe the rims. Place lids on jars and screw on rings until fingertip-tight, 893. Process all jar sizes for 15 minutes in a water-bath canner, 893. Let cool completely and store as directed, 895.

GUIDE TO CANNING FRUIT JUICES

Canning fruit juices is practically as simple and every bit as safe as canning whole fruits. Besides the fact that they are refreshing and nutritious, home-canned juices can be sweetened to your taste. Select fully ripe but firm fruit.

A **juicer** makes quick work of the task; if you don't have one, simmer the cut-up fruit according to the recommendation in each recipe and strain it through a jelly bag or a colander lined with 4 layers of dampened cheesecloth or a flour sack towel. For the clearest juice, refrigerate the strained juice for 24 hours, then pour off the clear juice, leaving the sediment behind, and strain it again through a damp coffee filter.

Pour the strained juice into a heavy-bottomed saucepan, set over low heat, and add sugar to taste, if desired. Stir until the sugar is dissolved. Increase the heat to high and cook, stirring frequently, until the juice almost boils. Overcooking or boiling fresh juice causes the flavor and nutrients to deteriorate, and we recommend temperatures no higher than 190°F. Pour the hot juice immediately into hot pint or quart jars, observing the headspace noted in the recipe. Juices that will be processed for less than 10 minutes must go into sterilized jars. Adjust the lids and process according to the directions for canning high-acid foods in a water-bath canner, 893. Cooking and processing times for clear fruit juices are brief because liquid absorbs heat much faster than whole foods.

Steam juicers are the most efficient way to juice fruit for canning. They resemble a percolator in some ways, but they have a drip pan with a spigot and hose for collecting and dispensing the juice. Not only can they juice a lot of fruit at one time (and with practically no effort), but the juice that emerges from its dispensing tube is already pasteurized, which means that it can be poured directly into sterilized jars and canned. There are a few drawbacks: Steam juicers are large, and though manufacturers claim they are good for general steaming tasks, we would never be tempted to get one out for anything except juicing. Further, to take advantage of their dispense-into-jars convenience while sweetening the juice with sugar, you must sprinkle the sugar into the fruit before juicing. This means that you cannot sweeten (or acidify) to taste, unless you go through the procedure above, which somewhat negates the steam juicer's convenience. Consult the manufacturer's instructions for more details.

Processing times are calculated for sea level. ▲ To adjust for higher altitudes, see 894.

APPLE JUICE OR CIDER

Combine very juicy apples, both sweet and sharp, for the best flavor.

Wash and remove the stem and blossom ends. Juice the fruit with a juicer or steam juicer, above. If you have neither, finely chop the fruit, or use a food processor. You may then use a cider press to extract the juice or simply simmer the apples until soft and strain out the solids. Heat the juice to 190°F and then pour into hot, sterilized, 893, pint, quart, or half-gallon jars, leaving ¼ inch headspace, 893. Wipe the rims. Place lids on jars and screw on rings until fingertip-tight, 893. Process pints and quarts for 5 minutes (half-gallons for 10 minutes) in a water-bath canner, 893. Let cool completely and store as directed, 895.

APRICOT, NECTARINE, OR PEACH NECTAR

Can in pint jars only.

Wash, pit, and coarsely chop. Juice the fruit with a juicer or steam juicer, above. If you have neither, mix 1 cup water for every 1 quart chopped fruit and bring to a simmer. Reduce the heat and cook at below a simmer until soft, stirring frequently, and pass through a sieve, or the fine blade of a food mill. Add 2 tablespoons bottled lemon juice per quart of nectar. Sweeten to taste. Immediately pour the hot nectar into hot, sterilized, 893, pint jars, leaving ¼ inch headspace, 893. Wipe the rims. Place lids on jars and screw on rings until fingertip-tight, 893. Process for 5 minutes in a water-bath canner, 893. Let cool completely and store as directed, 895.

BERRY, CHERRY, OR CURRANT JUICE

Use sweet or tart varieties.

Wash, stem, and crush berries; or wash, stem, pit, and chop cherries. Juice the fruit with a juicer or steam juicer, above. If you have neither, cook at below a simmer until soft, crushing and stirring frequently; add water as needed to prevent sticking. Strain and heat to 190°F. Sweeten to taste. Immediately pour the juice into hot, sterilized, 893, pint, quart, or half-gallon jars, leaving ½ inch headspace, 893. Wipe the rims. Place lids on jars and screw on rings until fingertip-tight, 893. Process pints and quarts for 5 minutes (half-gallons for 10 minutes) in a water-bath canner, 893. Let cool completely and store as directed, 895.

CRANBERRY JUICE

Much fresher tasting than commercially canned juice.

Wash, stem, and pick over the fruit, discarding softened or discolored berries. Juice the fruit with a steam juicer, above, or simply place the berries in a pan, cover with 1 inch water, and bring to a boil. Reduce the heat and cook at below a simmer until all the berries have popped. Strain and heat to 190°F. Sweeten to taste. Immediately pour the juice into hot, sterilized, 893, pint, quart, or half-gallon jars, leaving ¼ inch headspace, 893. Wipe the rims. Place lids on jars and screw on rings until fingertip-tight, 893. Process pints and quarts for 5 minutes (half-gallons for 10 minutes) in a water-bath canner, 893. Let cool completely and store as directed, 895.

GRAPE JUICE

Remove large stems. Wash. Juice the fruit with a juicer or steam juicer, above. If you have neither, cover with boiling water in a pan and cook at below a simmer until soft, crushing frequently; avoid crushing the seeds (they are bitter), whether extracting with a juicer or cooking. Strain. Refrigerate the strained juice overnight, then pour off the clear juice from the sediment. (This is essential for grape juice—otherwise, tartrate crystals will form in the juice.) Strain again and heat to 190°F. Sweeten to taste. Immediately pour the hot juice into hot, sterilized, 893, pint, quart, or half-gallon jars, leaving ¼ inch headspace, 893. Wipe the rims. Place lids on jars and screw on rings until fingertip-tight, 893. Process pints and quarts for 5 minutes (half-gallons for 10 minutes) in a water-bath canner, 893. Let cool completely and store as directed, 895.

GRAPEFRUIT OR GRAPEFRUIT-ORANGE JUICE

For a grapefruit-orange blend, use equal amounts of each juice.

Wash. Halve and extract the juice. Strain and sweeten to taste. Heat to 190°F and hold for 5 minutes at 190°F. Immediately pour the hot juice into hot, sterilized, 893, pint, quart, or half-gallon jars, leaving ¼ inch headspace, 893. Wipe the rims. Place lids on jars and screw on rings until fingertip-tight, 893. Process pints and quarts for 5 minutes (half-gallons for 10 minutes) in a water-bath canner, 893. Let cool completely and store as directed, 895.

PLUM JUICE

Wash, pit, and chop. Juice the fruit with a juicer or steam juicer, 899. If you have neither, mix 1 quart water for every 1 quart chopped fruit in a pan and cook below a simmer until soft, stirring frequently. Strain and heat to 190°F. Sweeten to taste. Pour the hot juice into hot, sterilized, 893, pint, quart, or half-gallon jars, leaving ¼ inch headspace, 893. Wipe the rims. Place lids on jars and screw on rings until fingertip-tight, 893. Process pints and quarts for 5 minutes (half-gallons for 10 minutes) in a water-bath canner, 893. Let cool completely and store as directed, 895.

RHUBARB JUICE

This juice makes a tangy summer cooler.

Select tender bright red stalks. Discard the leaves and green parts. Chop. Juice the fruit with a steam juicer, 899. To make without a steam juicer, cut rhubarb stalks into small chunks and add to a pan, along with 1 quart water for every 5 pounds of fruit. Heat quickly until the water just begins to boil, cover, reduce the heat, and simmer until soft. Strain and heat the juice to 190°F, adding sugar to taste. Immediately pour the hot juice into hot, sterilized, 893, pint, quart, or half-gallon jars, leaving ¼ inch headspace, 893. Wipe the rims. Place lids on jars and screw on rings until fingertip-tight, 893. Process pints and quarts for 5 minutes (half-gallons for 10 minutes) in a water-bath canner, 893. Let cool completely and store as directed, 895.

GUIDE TO CANNING TOMATOES AND TOMATILLOS

Tomatoes are the all-time favorite fruit for home canning. They're abundant in their season, extremely versatile, and easy to can. Tomatillos, which can be especially prolific plants, add a welcome tang to sauces, salsas, and braised dishes like Chicken Chili Verde, 425.

Tomatoes and tomatillos can be processed by either the boiling-water or pressure method. While the boiling-water method gives good results, we recommend pressure canning for better flavor and nutritional value. Select perfect, firm, ripe—not overripe—tomatoes without soft spots, bruises, mold, or broken skin. Do not can tomatoes from dead or frost-killed vines. Wash until the rinsing water is clear. Tomatoes should be peeled before canning; see About Tomatoes, 280, for detailed peeling instructions. Cherry and grape tomatoes do not can successfully.

Though tomatillos and unripe, green tomatoes are consistently high in acid, ripe tomatoes are unpredictable (even old-fashioned varieties with a high-acid reputation). To be safe, add acid to ripe tomatoes (it isn't necessary for green tomatoes or tomatillos). We prefer to use citric acid, but bottled lemon juice can also be used. ➤ After packing the tomatoes into jars, add ¼ teaspoon citric acid or 1 tablespoon bottled lemon juice to each pint jar, twice this amount to each quart jar. A little sugar can be blended into the tomatoes to balance tartness, if necessary, but do not add vegetables or other ingredients that would lower the level of acid. A single small washed fresh herb leaf, like sweet basil, is acceptable; its flavor will intensify with time.

➤ Please read the directions for safe and proper canning, 890, before proceeding. Hot-pack all forms of tomatoes in pint or quart jars. Processing times are calculated for sea level. ▲ To adjust for higher altitudes, see 894.

TOMATOES, CRUSHED

Wash, peel, and cut out the cores. Trim away any bruised or discolored portions and quarter. ➤ Do not prepare more tomatoes than can fit in one canner load at a time. Working quickly once the tomatoes are cut, place only one layer of tomatoes in a large pan. Set over high heat and crush with a potato masher to prevent sticking, then stir until boiling. If desired, sprinkle with salt as you go. Gradually add the remaining pieces, stirring constantly—no need to crush. When all the tomatoes have been added, boil gently for 5 minutes, stirring frequently.

Pack the hot tomatoes into clean, hot pint or quart jars, leaving ½ inch headspace, 893. Remove any trapped air from the jars, 893, and adjust the liquid level if needed. Add ¼ teaspoon citric acid or 1 tablespoon bottled lemon juice to each pint jar, twice this amount to each quart jar. Wipe the rims. Place lids on jars and screw on rings until fingertip-tight, 893. Process pints for 35 minutes (quarts for 45 minutes) in a water-bath canner, 893; or process either size jar for 15 minutes in a pressure canner, 894. Let cool completely and store as directed, 895.

TOMATOES PACKED IN WATER

This process is only for tomatoes packed in water. For other methods of packing whole, halved, or quartered tomatoes, consult the USDA's *Complete Guide to Home Canning* (see the bibliography, 1077).

Wash, peel, and cut out the cores. To can whole tomatoes, select small, meaty ones of uniform size. To can halves, cut the tomatoes on a plate to catch the juice. Put in a pan without crowding, add the juices and water to cover, and boil gently for 5 minutes.

Pack the hot tomatoes into clean, hot pint or quart jars. Add ¼ teaspoon citric acid or 1 tablespoon bottled lemon juice to each pint jar, twice this amount to each quart jar, and salt to taste. Add the hot cooking liquid, leaving ½ inch headspace, 893. Remove any trapped air from the jars, 893, and adjust the liquid level if needed. Wipe the rims. Place lids on jars and screw on rings until fingertip-tight, 893. Process pints for 40 minutes (quarts for 45 minutes) in a water-bath canner, 893; or process either size jar for 10 minutes in a pressure canner, 894. Let cool completely and store as directed, 895.

TOMATO JUICE OR SOUP

Wash, stem, and trim off bruised or discolored portions. To prevent the juice from separating, quarter only about 1 pound of the tomatoes at a time, on a plate to catch the juice. Place in a pan over high heat and crush the tomatoes with a potato masher as they come to a boil. Boil constantly and vigorously while slowly quartering, adding, and crushing the rest of the tomatoes and juices. The mixture should maintain a boil all the time. If desired, sprinkle with salt as you go. When all the tomatoes have been added, simmer for 5 minutes, stirring frequently.

Press while hot through a sieve or food mill and return to the pan. Quickly bring the juice to a boil, and immediately fill clean, hot pint or quart jars, leaving ½ inch headspace, 893. Add ¼ teaspoon citric acid or 1 tablespoon bottled lemon juice to each pint jar, twice this amount to each quart jar. Wipe the rims. Place lids on jars and screw on rings until fingertip-tight, 893. Process pints for 35 minutes (quarts for 40 minutes) in a water-bath canner, 893; or process either size jar for 15 minutes in a pressure canner, 894. Let cool completely and store as directed, 895.

If making tomato soup, do not add a thickener or cream. This must be done after opening jars, at the time of serving.

TOMATO-VEGETABLE JUICE OR SOUP

Weigh the tomatoes, then wash, stem, trim, quarter, crush, and boil as for juice, above. For every 5½ pounds tomatoes, blend in up to, but no more than, ¾ cup finely chopped mixed carrots, celery, onions, and/or bell or hot peppers. Simmer for 20 minutes, stirring frequently.

Press while hot through a sieve or food mill and return to the pan; discard the solids. Rapidly bring the juice to a boil and immediately fill clean, hot pint or quart jars, leaving ½ inch headspace, 893. Add ¼ teaspoon citric acid or 1 tablespoon bottled lemon juice to each pint jar, twice this amount to each quart jar. Wipe the rims. Place lids on jars and screw on rings until fingertip-tight, 893. Process pints for 35 minutes (quarts for 40 minutes) in a water-bath canner, 893; or process either size jar for 15 minutes in a pressure canner, 894. Let cool completely and store as directed, 895.

If making soup, do not add a thickener or cream. This must be done after opening jars, at the time of serving.

TOMATILLOS PACKED IN WATER

Tomatillos have a consistently high acid level and do not need any added lemon juice or citric acid. Select firm underripe fruit. Peel off and discard the husks, then rinse. Cut the fruits in half, or run a clean needle all the way through whole fruit to prevent bursting. Put in a pan without crowding, add water to cover, and boil gently for 5 minutes.

Pack the hot tomatillos into clean, hot pint or quart jars. Add the hot cooking liquid, leaving ½ inch headspace, 893. Remove any trapped air from the jars, 893, and adjust the liquid level if needed. Wipe the rims. Place lids on jars and screw on rings until fingertip-tight, 893. Process pints for 40 minutes (quarts for 45 minutes) in a water-bath canner, 893; or process either size jar for 10 minutes in a pressure canner, 894. Let cool completely and store as directed, 895.

ABOUT CANNING VEGETABLES

The most important thing to keep in mind when canning vegetables is that they are low in acid, making them highly susceptible to the growth of harmful bacteria, and therefore ➤ must be pressure-canned, 894.

The following vegetables are better pickled, frozen, or eaten fresh and ➤ **should not be canned:** artichokes, broccoli, Brussels sprouts, cabbage, cauliflower, cucumbers, eggplant, and any root vegetables not mentioned in this chapter.

Select ripe but firm vegetables of good quality, as close to the same size as possible. Reject any with soft spots, bruises, mold, or broken skin. Scrub sturdy vegetables, such as carrots, potatoes, and squashes, under cold running water until clean. Shake and stir small but firm vegetables, such as shelled peas, in a colander under cold running water. Rinse delicate vegetables in several changes of tepid water until the water is free of sand and impurities. Rinse vegetables after peeling or shelling as well.

Most vegetables benefit from brief precooking before canning. Follow the precooking instructions in the recipes below. ➤ You may add salt to canned vegetables at the rate of 1 teaspoon per quart.

APPROXIMATE YIELD OF COMMON VEGETABLES

Raw Vegetable	Pounds per Quart Jar	Quart Jars per Bushel
Beans, lima, in the pod	4 to 5	6 to 8
Beans, snap	1½ to 2	15 to 20
Beets	2½ to 3	17 to 20
Carrots	2½ to 3	16 to 20
Corn cut off cob	7 ears	8
Greens	2 to 3	6 to 9
Okra	1½ to 2	17
Peas in the pod	2 to 2½	5 to 10
Squash, summer	2 to 2½	16 to 20
Sweet potatoes	2½ to 3	18 to 22
Tomatoes	2½ to 3½	15 to 20

GUIDE TO CANNING VEGETABLES

Please read the directions for safe and proper canning, 890, before proceeding. **If using a dial-gauge pressure canner at sea level, can all vegetables at 11 psi. If using a weighted-gauge pressure canner at sea level, can all vegetables at 10 psi.** ▲ Adjust the pressure as directed for higher altitudes, 894.

ASPARAGUS

Select thick, tight-tipped spears. Wash. For whole stalks, cut 1 inch shorter than the height of the jars. For pieces, peel the tough skin, trim the ends, and cut into 1-inch pieces. ***For hot-pack***, boil the asparagus gently in water for 2 to 3 minutes. Loosely pack the hot asparagus into clean, hot pint or quart jars, whole stalks tips up, and add the boiling cooking liquid, leaving 1 inch headspace, 893. Remove any trapped air from the jars, 893, and adjust the liquid level if needed. ***For raw-pack,*** fill hot pint or quart jars with raw asparagus, packing tightly, and add boiling water, leaving 1 inch headspace, 893. Wipe the rims. Place lids on jars and screw on rings until fingertip-tight, 893. Process pints for 30 minutes (40 minutes for quarts) in a pressure canner, 894. Let cool completely and store as directed, 895.

BEANS, FRESH SHELLED

Select plump, tender pods. Shell and wash thoroughly. Sort sizes, if necessary. ***For hot-pack,*** bring the beans to a boil in water, loosely pack the hot beans into clean, hot pint or quart jars, and add the boiling cooking liquid (if canning fresh kidney beans, drain them and use fresh boiling water to cover instead of the cooking liquid). ***For raw-pack,*** fill hot pint or quart jars with raw beans. Do not press or shake down. Add boiling water to cover. For small beans such as black-eyed or crowder peas, leave 1 inch headspace for pints and 1½ inches for quarts, 893. For large beans such as limas or favas, leave 1 inch headspace for pints and 1¼ inches for quarts. Remove any trapped air from the jars, 893, and adjust the liquid level if needed. Wipe the rims. Place lids on jars and screw on rings until fingertip-tight, 893. Process pints for 40 minutes (50 minutes for quarts) in a pressure canner, 894. Let cool completely and store as directed, 895.

BEANS, GREEN, SNAP, OR WAX

Select crisp, tender, meaty pods. Wash. Remove the tips and any strings. Leave whole, or break or cut into uniform pieces. ***For hot-pack,*** boil the beans gently in water for 5 minutes. Loosely pack the hot beans into clean, hot pint or quart jars, standing whole beans on end. Add the boiling cooking liquid, leaving 1 inch headspace, 893. Remove any trapped air from the jars, 893, and adjust the liquid level if needed. ***For raw-pack,*** fill hot pint or quart jars with raw beans, and add boiling water, leaving 1 inch headspace, 893. Wipe the rims. Place lids on jars and screw on rings until fingertip-tight, 893. Process pints for 20 minutes (25 minutes for quarts) in a pressure canner, 894. Let cool completely and store as directed, 895.

BEETS

Select crisp beets up to 3 inches in diameter. Wash and trim, leaving 1 inch of the roots and stems. Boil gently in water just until the skins loosen, about 20 minutes. Let cool slightly, trim off the roots and stems, and remove the skins. Baby (1-inch) beets may be left whole. Cut beets into ½-inch cubes or slices (halve or quarter very large slices). Pack the hot beets into clean, hot pint or quart jars. Add fresh boiling water, leaving 1 inch headspace, 893. Remove any trapped air from the jars, 893, and adjust the liquid level if needed. Wipe the rims. Place lids on jars and screw on rings until fingertip-tight, 893. Process pints for 30 minutes (35 minutes for quarts) in a pressure canner, 894. Let cool completely and store as directed, 895.

CARROTS

Select sweet, crisp young carrots up to 1¼ inches in diameter. Wash, peel, and wash again. Cut into ½-inch-thick sticks, slices, or chunks. ***For hot-pack,*** boil the carrots gently in water for 5 minutes. Pack the hot carrots into clean, hot pint or quart jars and add the boiling cooking liquid, leaving 1 inch headspace, 893. ***For raw-pack,*** fill hot pint or quart jars tightly with raw carrots and add boiling water, leaving 1 inch headspace, 893. Remove any trapped air from the jars, 893, and adjust the liquid level if needed. Wipe the rims. Place lids on jars and screw on rings until fingertip-tight, 893. Process pints for 25 minutes (30 minutes for quarts) in a pressure canner, 894. Let cool completely and store as directed, 895.

CORN, CREAM-STYLE

Only use pint jars, because the mixture is so dense.

Remove the silks and husks and wash the corn. Drop into boiling water and blanch for 3 minutes. Cut the kernels from the cobs at half the depth of the kernels. Scrape off the remaining kernels and "milk" with a table knife, but do not include any cob material.

In a pan, mix 2 cups boiling water for every 4 cups corn and scrapings. Bring to a boil, stirring. Ladle the hot mixture into clean, hot pint jars, leaving 1 inch headspace, 893. Add ½ teaspoon salt to each pint jar, if desired. Remove any trapped air from the jars, 893, and adjust the liquid level if needed. Wipe the rims. Place lids on jars and screw on rings until fingertip-tight, 893. Process pints for 1 hour 25 minutes in a pressure canner, 894. Let cool completely and store as directed, 895.

CORN, WHOLE-KERNEL

Home-canned corn is crisp and sweet. Super sweet or underripe kernels may turn brown, but this is not harmful. Remove the husks and silks. Wash the corn. Drop into boiling water and blanch for 3 minutes. Cut the kernels from the cobs at about three-quarters the depth of the kernels. Do not scrape the cob—the cob material will cloud the jars and add starch that can create a food safety hazard.

For hot-pack, in a pan, mix 1 cup boiling water for every 4 cups kernels and bring to a boil. Simmer for 5 minutes. Loosely pack the hot kernels into clean, hot pint or quart jars and add the boiling cooking liquid, leaving 1 inch headspace, 893. ***For raw-pack,*** fill hot pint or quart jars with corn kernels. Do not pack down. Add boiling water, leaving 1 inch headspace, 893. For either pack method, add ½ teaspoon salt to each pint jar or 1 teaspoon to each quart jar if desired. Remove any trapped air from the jars, 893, and adjust the liquid level if needed. Wipe the rims. Place lids on jars and screw on rings until fingertip-tight, 893. Process pints for 55 minutes (1 hour 25 minutes for quarts) in a pressure canner, 894. Let cool completely and store as directed, 895.

OKRA

Canned whole okra pods are soft but not slimy, and the flavor is excellent.

Select young, tender pods. Wash and leave whole. Boil gently for 2 minutes. Pack the hot pods upright into clean, hot pint or quart jars and add the hot cooking liquid, leaving 1 inch headspace, 893. Remove any trapped air from the jars, 893, and adjust the liquid level if needed. Wipe the rims. Place lids on jars and screw on rings until fingertip-tight, 893. Process pints for 25 minutes (quarts for 40 minutes) in a pressure canner, 894. Let cool completely and store as directed, 895.

PEAS, GREEN

We recommend freezing peas, 886. Can only as a last resort.

Use young, tender small to medium sweet peas. Shell and wash thoroughly. ***For hot-pack,*** bring peas to a rolling boil in water and boil for 2 minutes. Pack as for fresh beans and peas, leaving 1 inch headspace, 893. ***For raw-pack,*** fill hot pint or quart jars with raw peas and add boiling water, leaving 1 inch headspace, 893. Do not shake or press down peas. Remove any trapped air from the jars, 893, and adjust the liquid level if needed. Wipe the rims. Place lids on jars and screw on rings until fingertip-tight, 893. Process either size jar for 40 minutes in a pressure canner, 894. Let cool completely and store as directed, 895.

PEPPERS, HOT OR SWEET

Only can peppers with thick flesh—the rest are too delicate to peel. Use only pint jars or smaller.

Select crisp, meaty peppers of any color. Wash, roast, 262, and peel the peppers. Remove the cores and seeds. Leave small peppers whole, slashing twice lengthwise with a knife. Quarter or flatten large peppers. Fit the peppers into clean, hot half-pint or pint jars, adding ¼ teaspoon salt per pint. Add boiling water, leaving 1 inch headspace, 893. Remove any trapped air from the jars, 893, and adjust the liquid level if needed. Wipe the rims. Place lids on jars and screw on rings until fingertip-tight, 893. Process either size jar for 35 minutes in a pressure canner, 894. Let cool completely and store as directed, 895.

POTATOES

Canned potatoes are firm and sweet.

Select small to medium firm, waxy potatoes. Wash, peel, and rinse. Leave smaller potatoes (up to 2 inches in diameter) whole; cut larger ones into halves, quarters, or ½-inch cubes. Gently boil larger pieces and whole potatoes in water for 10 minutes; boil ½-inch cubes for 2 minutes. Drain. Pack the hot potatoes into clean, hot pint or quart jars. Add fresh boiling water, leaving 1 inch headspace, 893. Remove any trapped air from the jars, 893, and adjust the liquid level if needed. Wipe the rims. Place lids on jars and screw on rings until fingertip-tight, 893. Process pints for 35 minutes (quarts for 40 minutes) in a pressure canner, 894. Let cool completely and store as directed, 895.

Note: Potatoes that have been stored below 45°F before processing may discolor when canned, but this is harmless.

POTATOES, SWEET

Caution: Do not mash or puree pieces, or the product may be unsafe to can, as the density of mashed sweet potatoes makes it difficult for the heat to penetrate to the center of the jars.

Select small to medium, firm tubers. If desired, prepare a 20-percent sugar syrup, 896. Wash the potatoes. Boil gently, or steam until the skins loosen, about 15 minutes. Peel and cut into quarters or smaller so that the sweet potatoes fit efficiently in the jars. Pack the hot sweet potatoes into clean, hot pint or quart jars. Add the boiling syrup or boiling water, leaving 1 inch headspace, 893. Remove any trapped air from the jars, 893, and adjust the liquid level if needed. Wipe the rims. Place lids on jars and screw on rings until fingertip-tight, 893. Process pints for 1 hour 5 minutes (quarts for 1 hour 30 minutes) in a pressure canner, 894. Let cool completely and store as directed, 895.

SQUASH, WINTER AND PUMPKIN

Caution: Do not mash or puree pieces, or the product may be unsafe to can, as the density of mashed winter squash makes it difficult for the heat to penetrate to the center of the jars.

Select small squashes or pumpkins with hard rinds and dry, thick, fine-grained (not stringy) flesh. Wash, remove seeds, cut into 1-inch-wide slices, and peel. Cut into 1-inch cubes. Boil gently in water for 2 minutes. Pack the hot squash into clean, hot pint or quart jars, and add boiling cooking liquid, leaving 1 inch headspace, 893. Remove any trapped air from the jars, 893, and adjust the liquid level if needed. Wipe the rims. Place lids on jars and screw on rings until fingertip-tight, 893. Process pints for 55 minutes (quarts for 1 hour 30 minutes) in a pressure canner, 894. Let cool completely and store as directed, 895.

SUCCOTASH

This traditional American dish cans well. The tomato is optional.

Use freshly shelled lima beans and freshly cut whole corn kernels (and, if desired, tomatoes as directed for crushing, 900), and prepare as directed for each vegetable, 902. In a pan, combine 4 parts lima beans, 3 parts corn, and, if using, 2 parts crushed tomatoes. Boil gently for 5 minutes. Pack the hot mixture into clean, hot pint or quart jars and add the boiling cooking liquid, leaving 1 inch headspace, 893. Remove any trapped air from the jars, 893, and adjust the liquid level if needed. Wipe the rims. Place lids on jars and screw on rings until fingertip-tight, 893. Process pints for 1 hour (quarts for 1 hour 25 minutes) in a pressure canner, 894. Let cool completely and store as directed, 895.

TURNIPS

Sweet, crisp young turnips remain tasty and firm when canned.

Select tender young turnips no more than 3 inches in diameter. Wash thoroughly and peel. Cut into 1-inch cubes, or slice. Boil gently in water for 5 minutes. Ladle into clean, hot pint or quart jars and add the hot cooking liquid, leaving 1 inch headspace, 893. Remove any trapped air from the jars, 893, and adjust the liquid level if needed. Wipe the rims. Place lids on jars and screw on rings until fingertip-tight, 893. Process pints for 30 minutes (quarts for 35 minutes) in a pressure canner, 894. Let cool completely and store as directed, 895.

ABOUT CANNING MEAT, POULTRY, GAME, AND FISH

The canning of meats, poultry, and game at home can be both a safe and more convenient procedure than the old-fashioned methods of preservation by salting and smoking, 934. ➤ All these foods must be processed in a pressure canner. Make sure that the pressure reaches at least 10 psi (or 240°F) during processing, using an accurate gauge on your pressure canner, and ▲ making any necessary altitude adjustments, 894. To freeze meat, poultry, game, and seafood, see 887.

Jars of canned meat and fish will likely need to be washed after they have sealed and cooled to remove any oils or residue (some leakage will occur during canning; it is harmless). Place jars in a single layer in the sink, and fill the sink with very hot, soapy water up to the rims of the jars. Let soak for 15 minutes, then use a rough-textured sponge or plastic scrubbing pad to scrub any residue off the jars and lids.

It is best to can only fresh, not brined or salted, meats. For brined or salted meats, smoking is a more satisfactory method of preserving than canning. ➤ Please read the directions for safe and proper canning before proceeding, 890.

CANNING RAW MEATS AND POULTRY

Since hot-packed (i.e., precooked) meats must be processed for the same length of time as raw-packed meats, we prefer the raw-pack method.

To raw-pack fresh meats and poultry, first prepare the jars, 891. Cut the meat from the bones. (Save the bones and scraps for stock, 73.) For chicken, separate the pieces at the joints. ➤ Trim the fat carefully from both meats and poultry, as it could cause the meat to have a strong flavor after canning. You may brine strongly flavored game meats for 1 hour in a brine made of 1 tablespoon salt per quart of water. Cut meats across the grain into 1-inch strips or chunks. Pack tightly into clean, hot pint or quart jars. Do not add liquid. ➤ Never use a thickened gravy, as it is unsafe for the canning process. You may add ½ teaspoon salt to each pint jar or 1 teaspoon to each quart for seasoning. Allow 1 inch headspace for meat pieces and 1¼ inches headspace for poultry, 893. Wipe the rims. Place lids on jars and screw on rings until fingertip-tight, 893.

Pint jars may be stacked in the pressure canner, but stagger them, with jars on top straddling two jars below. Secure the lid on the canner. Set the canner over medium-high heat and bring the water inside to a boil (very high heat can cause jars to crack at this stage). Allow the pressure canner to vent for 10 minutes, then cover the steam vent. Process in a dial-gauge steam-pressure canner at 11 psi or in a weighted-gauge pressure canner at 10 psi if you live below 1,000 feet altitude. ▲ To adjust for higher altitudes, see 894. Process pints for 1 hour 15 minutes (quarts for 1 hour 30 minutes). Let the canner cool and depressurize naturally. Remove the jars from the canner, let cool, and store as directed, 895.

For chicken with bones, process pints for 1 hour 5 minutes (quarts for 1 hour 15 minutes). **For chicken without bones,** process pints 1 hour 15 minutes (quarts for 1 hour 30 minutes). Gizzards and hearts may be canned together, in pints only, in boiling chicken broth to cover, but should be packed separately from the meat. Process pints for 1 hour 15 minutes. ➤ Let the canner cool and depressurize naturally. Remove the jars from the canner, let cool, and store as directed, 895.

Liquids cook out of meat and poultry during processing. Sometimes there is not enough after processing and some pieces are no longer covered by liquid. These pieces may darken and dry out somewhat in storage, so use those jars first.

CANNING PRECOOKED MEATS AND POULTRY

You may pressure-can roasted or stewed cuts of meat or sautéed sausages and ground meat (loose or shaped into patties or meatballs).

To hot-pack fresh meats, precook the meat until rare by roasting, stewing, or browning in a small amount of fat. If dealing with whole roasts or larger pieces, cut meat into strips, cubes, or chunks. Remove the bones, gristle, and all surface fat. Ground meats or sausage may be shaped into small patties or balls; cased sausage links should be 3 to 4 inches long. Cook until lightly browned. Ground meat may also be sautéed without shaping. Remove excess fat after precooking ground meats.

Pack tightly, while still hot, into clean, hot pint or quart jars with any meat juices. Add enough boiling water or stock to cover the meat in the jars, leaving 1 inch headspace, 893. ➤ Never use a thickened gravy. Remove any trapped air, 893, and adjust the liquid level if needed. Wipe the rims. Place lids on jars and screw on rings until fingertip-tight, 893. Pint jars may be stacked in the pressure canner, but stagger them, with jars on top straddling two jars below. Secure the lid on the canner. Set the canner over medium-high heat and bring the water inside to a boil (very high heat can cause jars to crack at this stage). Allow the pressure canner to vent for 10 minutes, then cover the steam vent. Process in a dial-gauge pressure canner at 11 psi or in a weighted-gauge pressure canner at 10 psi if you live below 1,000 feet altitude. ▲ To adjust for higher altitudes, see 894. Process pints for 1 hour 15 minutes (quarts for 1 hour 30 minutes). Let the canner cool and depressurize naturally. Remove the jars from the canner, cool, and store as directed, 895.

CANNING MEAT STOCK OR BROTH

Prepare beef or poultry stock or broth, 75–81. Strain the stock, discarding the bones, and cool completely. Refrigerate overnight, then skim off all fat. Reheat the broth to boiling, then fill clean, hot pint or quart jars, leaving 1 inch headspace, 893. Wipe the rims. Place lids on jars and screw on rings until fingertip-tight, 893. Process in a dial-gauge pressure canner at 11 psi or a weighted-gauge pressure canner at 10 psi if you live below 1,000 feet altitude. ▲ To adjust for higher altitudes, see 894. Process pints for 20 minutes (quarts for 25 minutes). Let the canner cool and depressurize naturally. Remove jars from the canner, let cool, and store as directed, 895.

CANNING FISH

This procedure may be used for bluefish, mackerel, salmon, trout, tuna, and other fatty fish. Take care to only can fish that have been cleaned within 2 hours of being caught and kept on ice, refrigerated, or frozen until ready to can.

Rinse the fish and remove the head, tail, fins, and scales. Most fish can be canned with the skin and bones intact (the canning process softens the bones), but for tuna, usually only the boneless, skinless loin is canned. For halibut, remove the bones. Wash and remove all blood. Keep fish stored on ice, with some kind of barrier between the fish and ice (such as a plastic bag), until ready to pack in jars. You may thaw and can frozen fish as long as it has been properly frozen and stored, 887.

Cut fish into pieces small enough to fit inside pint or half-pint jars. Fill sterilized jars as tightly as possible, leaving 1 inch headspace for pints, $3/4$ inch for half pints, 893. If desired, add $1/8$ teaspoon salt to each half-pint or $1/4$ teaspoon salt per pint. You may also add 1 teaspoon olive oil to each jar. Do not add liquid. Wipe the rims clean. Place lids on jars and screw on rings until fingertip-tight, 893. Add 2 to 3 inches of boiling water and 2 tablespoons distilled white vinegar to a pressure canner, then place the jars inside, leaving a little space between the jars. Jars may be stacked, but stagger them, with jars on top straddling two jars below. Secure the lid on the canner. Set the canner over medium-high heat and bring the water inside to a boil (very high heat can cause jars to crack at this stage). Allow the pressure canner to vent for 10 minutes, then cover the steam vent. Process in a dial-gauge pressure canner at 11 psi or a weighted-gauge pressure canner at 10 psi if you live below 1,000 feet altitude. ▲ To adjust for higher altitudes, see 894. Process pints and half-pints for 1 hour 40 minutes. Let the canner cool and depressurize naturally. Remove jars from the canner, let cool, and store as directed, 895.

JAMS, JELLIES, AND PRESERVES

Jellies, jams, preserves, conserves, marmalades, fruit butters, and jellied fruit sauces are all based on the principle of preserving fruit by cooking it with a sweetener (usually sugar) until it forms a gel. Often an acidic ingredient like lemon juice is included to help the gel form—and occasionally powdered or liquid pectin, 1011.

Jelly is fruit juice cooked with sugar until it forms a clear gel. **Jams, butters,** and **jellied fruit sauces** are cooked fruit purees of progressively increasing density; jams are lightly set, butters are thick but still spreadable, and jellied fruit sauces are thick enough to slice (stiff "fruit cheeses," like Membrillo, 194, are even thicker). **Preserves** are similar to jam but chunkier and more rustic. **Marmalades** are almost always made of citrus fruits and consist of a clear jelly studded with thinly sliced citrus peel. **Conserves** are bits of fruit cooked to translucence in heavy syrup, often with dried fruit and nuts stirred in.

EQUIPMENT

Gather all your equipment before you begin to cook the jelly, jam, or preserves. In addition to equipment essential for water-bath canning, 893, a **heavy, wide 8- to 10-quart stainless steel pot** or a **5- to 6-quart enameled Dutch oven** are good vessels for simmering preserves as their width allows water to evaporate more quickly than narrow pans and stockpots. Quicker evaporation means less time simmering, which results in more flavorful preserves. Specialized, flared **jam pans** are ideal, but they are large, have but one purpose, and are hardly necessary. Stay away from uncoated aluminum, iron, thin enamel, or galvanized pots. A **jelly bag** (see illustration, 909) is the best tool for straining juice for jelly; though a sieve or colander lined with a clean, thin cotton kitchen towel may be substituted in a pinch. Have ready a 4- to 8-ounce **ladle** and a **long-handled spatula** or **wooden spoon** that is safe to scrape against the bottom of your pan. The longer the handle, the better; molten sputters of hot jam and fruit butter are nothing to scoff at. Also helpful are a **kitchen scale, digital thermometer, food mill, potato masher, cherry pitter, citrus juicer,** and **rasp grater.**

SELECTING FRUIT

Choose only the freshest and most flavorful fruit. The canning pot is not a receptacle for fruit past its prime. The only true test is to smell and taste—if the fruit lacks full flavor, your results will disappoint. ➤ Slightly underripe to firm-but-ripe fruit is ideal, but a combination of underripe and ripe fruit also works well. Overly ripe fruit has little pectin, which can lead to problems with texture and spoilage. Use fresh fruit as soon as possible after purchase. Or macerate the fruit with the sugar called for in the recipe and refrigerate for up to 5 days before boiling down and processing. If you are too busy to preserve your favorite fruit when it is in season, tray-freeze it, 882, and preserve later when you have time. This solution is most successful with berries and cherries.

When preparing fruit for preserving, remove as little from the fresh fruit as possible, peeling the skin when the recipe directs and cutting away any bruised or soft spots. In all the recipes, it is essential to wash the fruits before you begin.

PECTIN

Pectin is a type of fiber found in the skin, seeds, and flesh of fruit. In the presence of sugar and acid, pectin forms a thick gel. The correct amount of pectin is crucial to the success of jellies, marmalades, and jellied fruit sauces, but is less important for softer-textured jams, conserves, and fruit butters. Natural pectin quantities vary depending on the variety and ripeness of the fruit. As fruit ripens, pectin breaks down. If you are relying on the pectin in fruits to achieve a firm gel, supplement ripe fruits with some slightly underripe ones. See Pectin Content of Fruits, below, to determine whether the fruit you are processing is high or low in pectin.

An easy way to make firm preserves with low-pectin fruit is to combine the fruit with an equal amount of grated tart apples, which contain a large quantity of pectin. Grating the apples ensures that they cook quickly and thicken the preserves without affecting the flavor or texture of the preserve.

If your fruit does not have enough pectin for jelly, you may use **commercial pectin,** 1011. No matter what form of pectin you use, do not rely on the package directions to determine when the preserve is finished cooking. Always use the wrinkle test, 908, to confirm that the preserve has reached the jelling point.

PECTIN CONTENT OF FRUITS

As stated above, fruits should be barely ripe to firm-ripe (or a combination of underripe and ripe, soft fruit).

High-Pectin Fruits	Low-Pectin Fruits
• Tart apples, crab apples, and quinces • Damson and other tart plums • Cranberries, currants, gooseberries, and loganberries • Lemons, limes, grapefruits, and oranges • Concord, Muscadine, and Scuppernong grapes	• Apricots, peaches, nectarines, and cherries • Italian plums and other sweet varieties • Strawberries, blackberries, blueberries, raspberries, and elderberries • Pears, figs, guavas, pineapples, pomegranates, and rhubarb • All grapes except those listed to the left

ACID

Unlike pectin, the acid content of a fruit is easily determined by taste. If the fruit tastes as tart as a green apple or rhubarb, there is sufficient acid present to thicken the preserves, given the proper proportions of pectin and sugar. Lemon juice must be added to recipes for slightly less tart fruits, such as sour cherries, elderberries, table grapes, and sweet plums. Low-acid fruits, including sweet cherries, figs, nectarines, peaches, pears, and strawberries, require even more lemon juice. In addition to the juice's role in helping preserves set, a few drops of lemon or orange juice perk up the flavor of the fruit. Keep in mind that underripe and just-ripe fruits are highest in acid as well as pectin. Since fresh lemon juice varies in acidity from fruit to fruit, ➤ always use bottled lemon juice to acidify preserves. While it is important never to decrease the amount of acid called for in a recipe, you may add more than directed, to taste. We like our preserves on the tart side, so we always taste the mixture right before ladling it into jars and add more lemon juice to taste if needed.

SUGAR AND OTHER SWEETENERS

The role of sugar goes beyond that of a sweetener in making jellies and jams. Not only does sugar preserve fruit by inhibiting the growth of bacteria, it helps set jellies and jams by drawing water away from the pectin molecules, so they can form a gel. High-pectin fruits yield the best-set jellies, but only in the presence of enough sugar. ➤ Decreasing the sugar in a recipe, while possible, can drastically reduce shelf life.

It takes very little sugar to bring out a fruit's flavor. Finding the right amount of sugar is a balancing act. Less sugar means less preserves and they will keep for a shorter time, but the fruit flavors will be brighter. However, you may notice that low-sugar preserves lose their vibrant color faster, and they do not keep as long once opened.

USING ALTERNATIVE SWEETENERS

Brown sugar: For a deeper flavor with molasses and caramel notes, substitute brown sugar for up to half of the white sugar in a recipe. Brown sugar is especially delicious with peach, apple, and pear preserves. In fact, apple butter may be made entirely with brown sugar.

Honey and agave syrup: In any recipe without commercial pectin the sugar may be replaced with mild honey or agave syrup. Because both are sweeter than sugar, reduce the total amount of sweetener by one-third. We love using honey as a sweetener in melon and apricot preserves.

Fruit juice: 100% apple juice, apple juice concentrate, or white grape juice concentrate may be used to sweeten preserves and fruit butters. Because fruit juices contain less sugar, you must use low-sugar pectin in any recipe that requires pectin.

Maple syrup: ➤ Do not substitute maple syrup for sugar called for in a recipe, as it has a pH above 4.6. This higher pH can render preserves unsafe for canning, as only foods with a pH less than 4.6 are safe to can using the water-bath method.

Nonnutritive, artificial sweeteners: Sweeteners such as stevia or xylitol will work in preserves, but you will need to purchase pectin specifically made for low-sugar or sugar-free preserves, see Pectin, 1011. Keep in mind that ➤ anything made with a nonnutritive sweetener will lack the preserving power of sugar and will need to be processed in a water-bath canner for 15 minutes. Even then, the preserves will not keep for as long as sugar-sweetened preserves.

THE JELLING POINT

Most of the recipes in this chapter are based on the principle of boiling sweetened fruit or juice until enough moisture has evaporated and the pectin, acid, and sugar have concentrated. This point is referred to as **the jelling point** and is ➤ best reached by rapid boiling, because the elements that make preserves jell—pectin, sugar, and acid—interact most effectively over intense heat (prolonged cooking at lower temperatures deteriorates pectin). Rapid boiling also tends to keep jellies clearer than slow cooking, while retaining the flavor of the fresh fruit. ➤ Do not double the amounts in these recipes; doubled recipes will not always jell properly and they take significantly longer to cook down, which can damage the flavor of the fruit.

The jelling point can be unpredictable, so it is a good idea to start testing for it early and often while cooking, as described below. A good visual indicator to start testing is when the boiling preserves settle down somewhat and the surface is covered in smaller bubbles.

There are several tests for determining when jams and jellies are approaching the jelling point. ➤ They are best used in conjunction with one another, especially if you are making jam or jelly for the first time. Remove the pan from the heat while performing jelling tests; you can do this as many times as necessary and quality will not be affected. Once the desired consistency has been reached, ➤ immediately remove the pan from the heat.

The wrinkle test (sometimes called the **quick-chill test**) is the most accurate because you actually see how the finished product will jell. We recommend that you start by using the temperature or spoon test, below, as an indication of progress and then, as the preserves begin to thicken, use the wrinkle test to determine whether or not the preserves have reached the jelling point. Before you start cooking, place a couple of saucers in the freezer. ➤ Remove the pan from the heat each time you do this test, or the preserves may overcook. Drop a small amount of syrup onto a chilled saucer and return it to the freezer. After about 3 minutes, pull a finger through the center of the chilled preserves. ➤ For a soft set, the sides should glide back together slowly. For a tender-firm set, the sides should not move and the surface should wrinkle when gently pushed.

The spoon test works best for jellies but is also effective for all but the thickest fruit purees. Scoop up a little boiling syrup or some of the thinnest part of the fruit mixture with a cool, dry stainless steel spoon. Hold it over the pot, but out of the steam, then turn it so that the syrup falls back into the pan from the spoon's side. At first the drip will be light and syrupy. As the syrup continues to cook and thickens, 2 large drops will form along the spoon's edge. ➤ When the drips slide together and fall as one, jelling has begun. For a tender-firm set, wait until these drops are heavy. When the drips glide together and hang off the edge of the spoon a moment before dropping, **the sheeting stage** has been reached, and this will make as firm a gel as the pectin can give. To be doubly sure, we recommend performing the wrinkle test, above, as well.

If you are working with a thick jam or preserve (or doubt your spoon-testing intuition) we recommend using **the temperature test** to gauge when the jelling point is close. ➤ Use a candy thermometer or instant-read digital thermometer. The jelling point is 8 to 10 degrees higher than the boiling point of water, which is 212°F at sea level, for a jelling temperature of 220° to 222°F. (▲ For higher elevations, see High-Altitude Preserving, 909.) For a very soft gel, stop the cooking 2 to 3 degrees lower. For a very firm gel, boil to 3 to 4 degrees higher. Again, we recommend performing the wrinkle test, above, to check the final consistency.

In some cases, jams and jellies may appear to be runny after canning, but will jell over the course of a week or two. If a preserve still has not set to your liking after several weeks, do not despair: Runny, undercooked preserves can always be cooked further until set. Simply empty the jars into a pot, cook them until they pass the wrinkle test, and process again (for jellies, see Troubleshooting, 909).

If you have overcooked your preserves and the gel is very firm, you may either treat the preserves as a jellied fruit sauce and serve, sliced, as part of a cheese plate, or gently warm the preserves with a little water in a saucepan, stirring constantly, until loosened enough to spread.

STORING PRESERVES

For the complete procedure on water-bath canning, please read How to Process, 891. Once canned, preserves will keep up to 18 months in a cool, dark place. Once opened, all preserves need to be refrigerated. To slow the growth of mold, minimize the time the jar stays open or out of the refrigerator, and use preserves within 1 month of opening.

Of course, water-bath canning is not the only way to store jams and jellies. If you wish to avoid processing all of your batch and keep some or all of it around for the short-term, you may simply pour hot preserves into sterilized jars, 893, cover, let cool, and refrigerate. ➤ The shelf life of refrigerated preserves depends on the amount of sugar in the recipe—preserves made with one-half to two-thirds as much sugar as fruit will keep in the refrigerator for at least 2 to 3 weeks. Those made with equal amounts of sugar and fruit will last for 2 months or more.

Most jellies and marmalades do not freeze well. All other preserves will keep for 6 months packed in freezer containers (clearly label them with the contents and the date frozen). Leave ½ inch headspace in containers; leave the same headspace in freezer bags, but force out the air.

➤ Discard preserves that exhibit any of the following: mold (rare in unopened canned preserves, inevitable at some point in refrigerated preserves), fermentation, bubbling, or an unpleasant sour smell. If you have doubts about a preserve, err on the side of caution; see Checking for Spoilage, 895, and Handling Contaminated Food and Jars, 895.

ABOUT YIELDS

Because fresh produce is variable, all recipe yields for preserves are approximate. You may find that after boiling the fruit to the jelling point you have fewer or more jars than the yield specified. This is perfectly normal. ➤ Always wash and sterilize an extra jar or two to account for this variability. When making jams and jellies, we also prepare a tiny quarter-pint jar, as there is often just a bit more jam than can fit inside the recommended number of jars. This tiny jar can be processed along with the rest or stuck in the refrigerator to enjoy right away.

▲ HIGH-ALTITUDE PRESERVING

As altitude increases, so does the length of time preserves will need to be boiled. Below are approximate jelling-point temperatures for higher altitudes. Do not rely on these numbers alone; ➤ always confirm the jelling point by using the wrinkle test, 908.

Altitude above Sea Level	Jelling Point Temperature	Canning Time Adjustment
1,000 feet	218° to 220°F	Add 5 minutes
2,000 feet	216° to 218°F	
3,000 feet	214° to 216°F	Add 10 minutes
4,000 feet	212° to 214°F	
5,000 feet	211° to 212°F	
6,000 feet	209° to 211°F	Add 15 minutes
7,000 feet	207° to 209°F	
8,000 feet	205° to 207°F	Add 20 minutes
9,000 feet	203° to 205°F	
10,000 feet	201° to 203°F	

ABOUT MAKING JELLY

A good jelly is a bright, clear, tender-set gel made from strained fruit juice, wine, spirits, or even herb infusions. Two cooking processes are involved. First, juice is extracted from the fruit. Then, after the juice is strained through a jelly bag, it is boiled with sugar until firm enough to hold its shape when cold. Picture-perfect jelly takes time to make and is dependent on the right proportions of pectin, sugar, and acid. Jelly making takes a little practice, but once you have mastered it, the results are beautiful and elegant.

PREPARING THE FRUIT

When selecting fruits for jelly, in general, ➤ mix one-quarter slightly underripe fruit and three-quarters firm-but-ripe fruit. The underripe fruit provides pectin, and the ripe fruit contributes flavor. With low-pectin fruits, 907, however, pectin must always be added, so use fully ripe fruit for the deepest flavor. Also ➤ weigh and record how much low-pectin fruit you start with to calculate the amount of pectin you should add later (see Cooking Jelly, below). Skins, cores, and seeds should not be removed, because they contribute pectin and flavor and will be strained out in the end.

EXTRACTING THE JUICE

Place the prepared fruit in a large saucepan. Add enough water to barely cover, unless the fruit is very juicy, in which case mash the fruit in the pan first thing and only add a splash of water to prevent burning. ➤ In general, add only enough water as is necessary. Cover the pan and bring to a boil over high heat, lifting the lid and mashing and stirring the fruit frequently. Turn down the heat and simmer until the fruit is thoroughly soft, mashing and stirring until the fruit is completely broken down.

Ladle the resulting juice and mashed fruit into a jelly bag (see below) or a colander or sieve lined with a clean thin cotton kitchen towel (not terrycloth). The bag or colander should be left to drip for 3 to 4 hours—rarely more than a spoonful of extra juice will come after that. ➤ For the clearest jelly, do not squeeze the bag or press the fruit against the cloth, as doing so inevitably squeezes tiny particles of fruit into the juice. These particles, while harmless, will cloud the jelly.

Straining fruit juice with a ready-made jelly bag and a colander lined with a thin cotton towel

COOKING JELLY

Please read How to Process, 891, before proceeding. The yield for jelly generally equals the amount of strained fruit juice, so have the right number of jars ready. Since jellies are processed for less than 10 minutes, you must ➤ sterilize the jars and lids to ensure the preserve is safe, 893. Have a thermometer and chilled saucers on hand for the wrinkle test, 908. The syrup will boil up high, so use a pan at least 4 times taller than the syrup is deep.

Measure the juice and pour it into a heavy saucepan. The recipes below give specific amounts, but as a general rule, add **¾ to 1 cup sugar for every 1 cup juice** for any type of jelly. ➤ High-pectin fruit, 907, will not require any commercial pectin and you may simply add lemon juice to taste. ➤ Low-pectin fruit, 907, will require **one 3-ounce pouch liquid pectin or 2 tablespoons powdered pectin, 1011, for every 2 pounds fruit** and **1½ teaspoons bottled lemon juice per 1 cup juice.**

If using powdered pectin, whisk into the sugar. Bring the juice to a boil and cook over high heat, stirring frequently. ➤ When the syrup thickens noticeably, or reaches 218° to 220°F, add liquid pectin (if using) and start testing for the jelling point, 908. If a skin forms while the pan is off the heat waiting for the wrinkle test, stir it back in. When the syrup reaches the jelling point, ➤ immediately remove from the heat and skim off any foam.

Pour the hot jelly into ➤ hot sterilized half-pint jars, leaving ¼ inch headspace, 893. Process in a water-bath canner for 5 minutes, 893. Jelly may be refrigerated, but it does not freeze well.

TROUBLESHOOTING

If the canned jelly is runny or too soft, remember that some mixtures do not fully set for 2 weeks. You may simply refrigerate a preserve once open to make it firmer, but ➤ the surest way of fixing runny jelly is to boil it again with a mixture of 1 tablespoon sugar, 1 tablespoon water, and 1 teaspoon powdered pectin for each 1 cup jelly—cooking no more than 1 quart at a time. Melt the soft jelly by slowly warming if necessary. Bring the sugar, water, and pectin mixture to a boil over high heat, stirring constantly. Add the runny or melted jelly, bring to a full boil, and boil for just 30 seconds, stirring constantly. Remove from the heat, skim off any foam, and pour into sterilized jars, then process again. Or, easiest of all, label runny jelly as syrup and use as a topping or glaze or stir it into beverages or cocktails.

GOOSEBERRY OR CURRANT JELLY

About 3 half-pint jars

Please read About Making Jelly, 909, and How to Process, 891.

Wash and drain, then thoroughly crush in a large heavy saucepan:

3 pounds gooseberries or currants (about 3¾ pounds with stems attached)

1 cup water

Cover and bring to a boil, then reduce the heat to low and simmer for 10 minutes, mashing frequently. Extract the juice, 909. While the juice drains, prepare a water-bath canner, 891, gather all your canning equipment, 891, put a couple of saucers in the freezer, and have ready 3 sterilized, 893, hot half-pint jars.

Measure the strained juice, transfer to a large saucepan, and add:

¾ to 1 cup sugar for every 1 cup juice

Boil rapidly, stirring constantly, until the mixture reaches the jelling point, 908. Remove the jelly from the heat and skim off any foam. Pour into the prepared jars, leaving ¼ inch headspace, 893. Wipe the rims. Place lids on jars and screw on rings until fingertip-tight, 893. Process for 5 minutes. Let cool completely and store as directed, 908.

BLACKBERRY JELLY

About 3 half-pint jars

Almost any sort of blackberry works for this jelly, but boysenberries, loganberries, Marionberries, and olallieberries work especially well. One form of blackberry or another is in season from June through mid-September. No water is added to this pure-berry jelly, and there is just enough sugar to firm it up. Please read About Making Jelly, 909, and How to Process, 891.

Wash and drain, then thoroughly crush in a large heavy saucepan:

4 pounds blackberries

Bring to a boil, stirring to prevent sticking. Cover, reduce the heat, and simmer until soupy, about 10 minutes, mashing frequently. Extract the juice, 909. While the juice drains, prepare a water-bath canner, 891, gather all your canning equipment, 891, put a couple of saucers in the freezer, and have ready 3 sterilized, 893, hot half-pint jars.

Measure the strained juice, transfer to a large saucepan, and add:

¾ cup sugar for every 1 cup juice

Bring to a boil and cook over high heat, stirring frequently, until the mixture reaches the jelling point, 908. Remove the jelly from the heat and skim off any foam. Pour into the prepared jars, leaving ¼ inch headspace, 893. Wipe the rims. Place lids on jars and screw on rings until fingertip-tight, 893. Process for 5 minutes. Let cool completely and store as directed, 908.

GRAPE JELLY

Prepare **Blackberry Jelly, above,** substituting **Concord, Muscadine,** or **Scuppernong grapes** for the blackberries. After straining, transfer the juice to a glass container and refrigerate until the sediment has settled. Strain the clear juice through a cloth-lined strainer to eliminate tartrate crystals, 975, leaving any sediment behind in the glass container. Proceed as directed.

APPLE, CRAB APPLE, OR QUINCE JELLY

About 4 half-pint jars

This delicately flavored jelly is invaluable for its versatility. Use it as a glaze for chicken or pork, to glaze a fruit tart, or to serve over pancakes. Choose aromatic apples such as Gravenstein, Wealthy, or Cox's Orange Pippin, when available. All crab apples and quinces are excellent. They are extra rich in pectin and have a full, spicy flavor. Please read About Making Jelly, 909, and How to Process, 891.

Combine in a large heavy saucepan:

3 pounds unpeeled apples, crisp crab apples, or quince, quartered

3 cups water for apples or crab apples, 6 cups water for quince

Cover and bring to a boil, then reduce the heat and simmer, mashing and stirring frequently, until the fruit is thoroughly soft, 20 to 25 minutes for apples, 25 to 30 minutes for crab apples, and 30 minutes for quince. Extract the juice, 909. While the juice drains, prepare a water-bath canner, 893, gather all your canning equipment, 891, put a couple of saucers in the freezer, and have ready 4 sterilized, 893, hot half-pint jars.

Measure the strained juice, transfer to a large saucepan, and add:

1 cup sugar for every 1 cup juice

2 tablespoons bottled lemon juice

Bring to a boil and cook over high heat, stirring frequently, until the mixture reaches the jelling point, 908. Remove from the heat and skim off any foam. Pour into the prepared jars, leaving ¼ inch headspace, 893. Wipe the rims. Place lids on jars and screw on rings until fingertip-tight, 893. Process for 5 minutes. Let cool completely and store as directed, 908.

APPLE-BOURBON JELLY

The combination of apples and bourbon always makes us think of drinking spiked apple cider on crisp fall days. Prepare **Apple, Crab Apple, or Quince Jelly, above,** using apples and proceeding through adding the sugar and lemon juice. Once the juice reaches 220°F, stir in **½ cup bourbon or Scotch.** Bring the mixture back to a boil, cook to the jelling point, and proceed with the recipe.

APPLE-ROSE JELLY

Fragrant rose petals are a welcome addition to apple jelly, as apples and roses are closely related. Prepare **Apple, Crab Apple, or Quince Jelly, above.** Add along with the sugar and lemon juice **2 tablespoons dried rose petals or ¼ cup fragrant, fresh organic rose petals.** Before pouring into jars, strain the jelly through a fine-mesh sieve into a large liquid measuring cup with a pouring lip. Proceed as directed.

HERB OR SCENTED JELLY

Prepare **Apple, Crab Apple, or Quince Jelly, 910.** While the jelly simmers, bruise the leaves and bind together with kitchen twine **a bunch of mint, basil, tarragon, thyme, lemon verbena, or unsprayed rose geranium leaves.** After testing for jelling but before removing the jelly from the heat, hold the bunch by the stem ends and pass the leaves through the jelly repeatedly until the desired strength of flavoring is reached. Remove from the heat, skim off any foam, and proceed as directed.

GUAVA JELLY

About 3 half-pint jars

Prepare **Apple, Crab Apple, or Quince Jelly, 910,** substituting **3 pounds slightly underripe guavas, coarsely chopped,** for the apples. Simmer until soft, about 30 minutes. Proceed as directed, substituting **2 tablespoons bottled lime juice** for the lemon juice.

TART PLUM JELLY

About 3 half-pint jars

Prepare **Apple, Crab Apple, or Quince Jelly, 910,** substituting **3 pounds tart plums, coarsely chopped,** for the apples and using **1½ cups water.** Simmer for 15 to 20 minutes. Proceed as directed, omitting the lemon juice.

ROSE HIP JELLY

Yield varies

Rather than call for a specific amount of rose hips, we have opted to make this an open-ended recipe, allowing you to make as much or as little as you can based on the quantity of rose hips you pick. Please read About Making Jelly, 909, and How to Process, 891.

Place in a large heavy saucepan:

Fresh, ripe, unsprayed rose hips, 195
1 tart or green apple, such as Granny Smith, or 1 quince, coarsely chopped, for every 1 pound rose hips

Add water to cover and bring to a boil. Cover and simmer until the rose hips are very soft, adding a little water if needed to keep them submerged. The time it takes the rose hips to become tender will depend on their size and ripeness, so check on them every 15 minutes. When they are very soft, remove the pan from the heat and mash the rose hips with a potato masher. Extract the juice, 909. While the juice drains, prepare a water-bath canner, 893, gather all your canning equipment, 891, put a couple of saucers in the freezer, and have ready sterilized, 893, hot half-pint jars.

Measure the strained juice, transfer to a large saucepan, and add:

1 cup sugar for every 1 cup juice

Bring to a boil and cook over high heat, stirring frequently, until the mixture reaches the jelling point, 908. Remove from the heat. Pour into the prepared jars, leaving ¼ inch headspace, 893. Wipe the rims. Place lids on jars and screw on rings until fingertip-tight, 893. Process for 5 minutes. Let cool completely and store as directed, 908.

PARADISE JELLY

About 7 half-pint jars

This delicate jelly with its exquisite rose color is a family favorite. Please read About Making Jelly, 909, and How to Process, 891.

Combine in a large heavy saucepan:

3 pounds unpeeled green apples, finely chopped
1½ pounds unpeeled quinces, finely chopped
3½ cups water

Bring to a boil, then reduce the heat and simmer for 15 minutes. Stir in:

8 ounces cranberries, picked over, washed, and coarsely chopped

Simmer until the fruit is thoroughly soft, mashing frequently, about 10 minutes more. Extract the juice, 909. While the juice drains, prepare a water-bath canner, 893, gather all your canning equipment, 891, put a couple of saucers in the freezer, and have ready 7 sterilized, 893, hot half-pint jars.

Measure the strained juice, transfer to a large heavy saucepan, and add:

1 cup sugar for every 1 cup juice

Bring to a boil and cook over high heat, stirring frequently, until the mixture reaches the jelling point, 908. Remove from the heat and skim off any foam. Pour into prepared jars, leaving ¼ inch headspace, 893. Wipe the rims. Place lids on jars and screw on rings until fingertip-tight, 893. Process for 5 minutes. Let cool completely and store as directed, 908.

HOT PEPPER JELLY

About 3 half-pint jars

The balanced hot and sweet flavors are delicious with corn bread or biscuits. Ripe red bell peppers give the jelly a translucent orange-red appearance. Please read About Making Jelly, 909, and How to Process, 891.

Combine in a large heavy saucepan:

1 pound red bell peppers, seeded and minced
8 ounces jalapeño peppers, minced (seeded, if desired)
1½ cups white wine vinegar

Stir and bring to a boil, reduce the heat to a simmer, then simmer until the peppers are thoroughly soft, 10 to 12 minutes. Extract the juice, 909. While the juice drains, prepare a water-bath canner, 893, gather all your canning equipment, 891, put a couple of saucers in the freezer, and have ready 3 sterilized, 893, hot half-pint jars.

Measure the strained juice: You should have about 2 cups; add water if necessary. Return the juice to the saucepan and add:

2½ cups sugar

Bring to a boil, stirring constantly. Add:

6 tablespoons liquid pectin, 1011

Boil hard for 1 minute. Remove from the heat and skim off any foam. Use the wrinkle test, 908, to make sure the mixture has reached the jelling point. Pour into the jars, leaving ¼ inch headspace, 893. Wipe the rims. Place lids on jars and screw on rings until fingertip-tight, 893. Process for 5 minutes. Let cool completely and store as directed, 908.

MINT JELLY

About 4 half-pint jars

The classic accompaniment to roast lamb. Make this jelly in the summer when mint is plentiful and aromatic. Please read About Making Jelly, 909, and How to Process, 891.

Place in a large heavy saucepan and thoroughly crush:

1½ cups packed mint leaves, well washed
1½ cups apple juice
½ cup bottled lemon juice

Bring to a boil over high heat. Remove from the heat, cover, and let stand for 10 minutes. Extract the juice, 904. While the juice drains, prepare a water-bath canner, 893, gather all your canning equipment, 891, put a couple of saucers in the freezer, and have ready 4 sterilized, 893, hot half-pint jars.

Measure the strained juice: You should have about 1¾ cups; add water if necessary. Return the mint juice to the saucepan and add:

3½ cups sugar
¾ teaspoon salt
(4 drops green food coloring)

Bring to a boil, stirring constantly. Add:

6 tablespoons liquid pectin, 1011

Boil hard for 1 minute. Remove from the heat and skim off any foam. Use the wrinkle test, 908, to make sure the mixture has reached the jelling point. Pour into the jars, leaving ¼ inch headspace, 893. Wipe the rims. Place lids on jars and screw on rings until fingertip-tight, 893. Process for 5 minutes. Let cool completely and store as directed, 908.

PRICKLY PEAR JELLY

About 5 half-pint jars

Please read About Prickly Pears, 193, About Making Jelly, 909, and How to Process, 891. Wear gloves when handling prickly pears.

Combine in a large heavy saucepan:

4½ pounds ripe prickly pears, coarsely chopped
1 cup water

Bring to a boil, stirring frequently, then reduce the heat to simmer for 5 minutes, mashing the fruit into a pulp with a potato masher. Remove from the heat and extract the juice, 909. While the juice drains, prepare a water-bath canner, 893, gather all your canning equipment, 891, put a couple of saucers in the freezer, and have ready 5 sterilized, 893, hot half-pint jars.

Measure the strained juice: You should have about 3 cups; add water if necessary. Pour the juice into a large heavy saucepan. Add:

6 tablespoons bottled lime juice
2 tablespoons strained orange juice

Stir and bring to a boil over high heat. Whisk together in a medium bowl and stir into the boiling juice:

4 cups sugar
One 1.75-ounce package powdered pectin (5 tablespoons)

Stirring constantly, return to a boil and boil according to the package directions. Use the wrinkle test, 908, to make sure the mixture has reached the jelling point. Pour into jars, leaving ¼ inch headspace, 893. Wipe the rims. Place lids on jars and screw on rings until fingertip-tight, 893. Process for 5 minutes. Let cool completely and store as directed, 908.

ABOUT MAKING JAM

Jam contains lightly jelled whole, crushed, or chopped fruit. It is the simplest and most forgiving of sweet preserves to make and is economical as it uses the fruit pulp. There is a lot of leeway in consistency, and most fruits need little preparation. Use firm-but-ripe fruit sliced or chopped ¼ to ½ inch thick unless otherwise noted. Please read the directions for safe and proper canning, 890, before proceeding.

RED RED STRAWBERRY JAM

About 4 half-pint jars

Use this recipe with only the ripest, most flavorful seasonal fruit. The large amount of sugar reduces the overall boiling time, which will help retain the flavor and color of the fruit. Please see How to Process, 891. Prepare a water-bath canner, 893, gather all your canning equipment, 891, place a couple of saucers in the freezer, and have ready 4 clean, hot half-pint jars, 893.

Combine in a wide heavy pot or Dutch oven:

5 cups sugar
3½ pounds strawberries, hulled and coarsely chopped
¼ cup bottled lemon juice
(1 vanilla bean, split lengthwise)

Stir the fruit gently with a wooden spoon over low heat until it has "juiced up." Then increase the heat to medium-high and stir constantly until the sugar is dissolved. Boil rapidly, stirring frequently, until it reaches the jelling point, 908. Take the pot off the heat. If using the vanilla bean, remove the pod, scrape any vanilla seeds from the pod and add them back to the pot, then discard the pod. Ladle the jam into the prepared jars, leaving ¼ inch headspace, 893. Wipe the rims. Place lids on jars and screw on rings until fingertip-tight, 893. Process for 10 minutes. Let cool completely and store as directed, 908.

STRAWBERRY ROSÉ JAM

About 6 half-pint jars

This ruby-red jam combines our favorite summer wine with our favorite summer fruit. The rosé adds a subtle perfume to a delicious strawberry jam. Please read How to Process, 891.

Combine in a wide heavy pot:

4 pounds strawberries, hulled and coarsely chopped
2½ cups sugar
1 bottle (750 ml) dry rosé wine
Juice of 1 lemon (about 2 tablespoons)
(1 vanilla bean, split lengthwise)

Bring to a boil over high heat. Immediately remove from the heat, transfer to a bowl, and let cool completely. Refrigerate overnight.

Prepare a water-bath canner, 893, gather all your canning equipment, 891, place a couple of saucers in the freezer, and have ready 6 clean, hot half-pint jars, 893.

Strain the berry mixture in a sieve set over a deep, wide pot. Reserve the berries. Boil the rosé syrup until it reaches 215°F and the liquid is reduced by about half, 15 to 20 minutes. Add the strawberries to the syrup and continue to boil, stirring frequently, until the mixture is thick and very dark red and reaches the jelling point, 908, 25 to 30 minutes.

Fish out the vanilla bean, if using, scrape any vanilla seeds from the pod and add them back to the pot, then discard the pod. Ladle the jam into the prepared jars, leaving ½ inch headspace, 893. Wipe the rims. Place lids on jars and screw on rings until fingertip-tight, 893. Process for 10 minutes. Let cool completely and store as directed, 908.

BERRY JAM

About 5 half-pint jars

This is a flexible berry jam recipe that can be used for blackberries (and blackberry relatives), cranberries, elderberries, raspberries, and blueberries. If using half-ripe blueberries, at the red instead of blue stage, the result is a jam far more flavorful than usual—almost like one made with Scandinavian lingonberries. Depending on the tartness of the fruit, you may or may not need to add lemon juice. Add it to taste. Please read How to Process, 891.

Prepare a water-bath canner, 893, gather all your canning equipment, 891, place a couple of saucers in the freezer, and have ready 5 clean, hot half-pint jars, 893.

Combine in a wide, heavy pot or Dutch oven:

8 ounces tart green apples, peeled, cored, and grated
2 pounds berries (see headnote)
(2 tablespoons lemon juice)
3 cups sugar

Bring to a boil, crushing one-quarter of the berries in the pan. Boil, stirring frequently, until it reaches the jelling point, 908. Remove from the heat and skim off any foam. Ladle into prepared jars, leaving ¼ inch headspace, 893. Wipe the rims. Place lids on jars and screw on rings until fingertip-tight, 893. Process for 10 minutes. Let cool completely and store as directed, 908.

GOOSEBERRY JAM

About 3 half-pint jars

Prepare **Berry Jam, above,** omitting the apples and using **2 pounds gooseberries.** If available, cook with **(6 elderflowers tied in a sachet)**. Squeeze their syrup into the jam, then discard the flowers before ladling into jars.

FIVE-FRUIT JAM COCKAIGNE

About 9 half-pint jars

A superlative combination well worth the extra effort required to gather all five types of fruit (an easy way to assemble these ingredients is to freeze them as you find them). Please read How to Process, 891.

Prepare a water-bath canner, 893, gather all your canning equipment, 891, place a couple of saucers in the freezer, and have ready 9 clean, hot half-pint jars, 893.

Combine in a large, wide heavy pan:

1½ pounds strawberries, hulled and coarsely chopped
1 pound red currants
1 pound sweet cherries, stemmed and pitted
1 pound gooseberries, trimmed
1 pound raspberries
7 cups sugar

Bring to a boil, stirring frequently, and boil rapidly, stirring and lightly crushing the fruit, until it reaches the jelling point, 908. Remove from the heat and skim off any foam. Ladle into prepared jars, leaving ¼ inch headspace, 893. Wipe the rims. Place lids on jars and screw on rings until fingertip-tight, 893. Process for 10 minutes. Let cool completely and store as directed, 908.

HONEY-MELON JAM

About 3 half-pint jars

Make this jam with only the most flavorful melons. We like to use fragrant Charentais melons when we can find them. Please read How to Process, 891.

Prepare a water-bath canner, 893, gather all your canning equipment, 891, place a couple of saucers in the freezer, and have ready 3 clean, hot half-pint jars, 893.

Combine in a heavy pot:

3 pounds ripe, fragrant cantaloupe or muskmelon, seeded and finely diced
1 cup honey
Finely grated zest of 1 lemon
¼ cup bottled lemon juice
(1 vanilla bean, split lengthwise)

Bring to a boil and boil rapidly, stirring frequently, until it reaches the jelling point, 908. Remove from the heat. Fish out the vanilla bean, if using, scrape any vanilla seeds from the pod and add them back to the pot, then discard the pod. Ladle jam into the prepared jars, leaving ¼ inch headspace, 893. Wipe the rims. Place lids on jars and screw on rings until fingertip-tight, 893. Process for 10 minutes. Let cool completely and store as directed, 908.

FIG JAM

5 or 6 half-pint jars

This chunky jam is perfectly delicious using only figs, sugar, and lemon juice, but add any of the optional aromatics for extra depth and complexity.

Mix together in a large bowl:

3 pounds ripe figs, stemmed and chopped
2 cups sugar
¼ cup bottled lemon juice

Cover and let the fruit steep for at least 1 hour at room temperature or overnight in the refrigerator.

Prepare a water-bath canner, 893, gather all your canning equipment, 891, place a couple of saucers in the freezer, and have ready 6 clean, hot half-pint jars, 893.

Transfer the steeped figs and their juices to a pot and add any of the following, if desired:

(3 × 1-inch strip orange zest, removed with a vegetable peeler)
(1 cinnamon stick)
(1 star anise)
(3 sprigs thyme or one 5-inch sprig rosemary)

Bring the mixture to a boil and cook, stirring frequently, until the figs have broken down and the mixture reaches the jelling point, 908. Remove from the heat and discard any herb sprigs, whole spices, and zest if you used them. If desired, stir in:

(2 tablespoons orange liqueur)

Ladle into prepared jars, leaving ½ inch headspace, 893. Wipe the rims. Place lids on jars and screw on rings until fingertip-tight, 893. Process for 10 minutes. Let cool completely and store as directed, 908.

PLUM JAM

About 4 half-pint jars

Juicy greengages, damsons, mirabelles, Shiros, and many wild plums make excellent jam. Leave the skin on for maximum flavor. Please read How to Process, 891.

Prepare a water-bath canner, 893, gather all your canning equipment, 891, place a couple of saucers in the freezer, and have ready 4 clean, hot half-pint jars, 893.

Combine in a large heavy saucepan:

2 pounds plums, pitted and coarsely chopped
2½ cups sugar
¼ cup bottled lemon juice

Lightly crush, then bring to a boil, stirring frequently, until it reaches the jelling point, 908. Remove from the heat and skim off any foam. Ladle into prepared jars, leaving ¼ inch headspace, 893. Wipe the rims. Place lids on jars and screw on rings until fingertip-tight, 893. Process for 10 minutes. Let cool completely and store as directed, 908.

SMOKY TOMATO JAM

4 or 5 half-pint jars

Please read How to Process, 891.

I. ROASTED, WITH SMOKED PAPRIKA

In this recipe, smoked paprika and optional chipotle add smokiness and a little heat. Oven-roasting the tomatoes removes much of their moisture, decreasing the amount of time you'll have to cook them down on the stovetop.

Preheat the oven to 400°F. Lightly oil 2 large baking sheets or, for easier cleanup, line the baking sheets with parchment paper. Place in a single layer on the baking sheets, cut side up:

5 pounds Roma, San Marzano, Amish Paste, or other sauce tomatoes, halved

Roast until the tomatoes are shriveled and lightly browned, 35 to 40 minutes. If desired, slip the skins off the tomatoes.

Transfer the tomatoes to a large heavy pot and stir in:

2 cups sugar
⅓ cup bottled lemon juice
1 tablespoon smoked paprika
2 teaspoons pickling salt
1 teaspoon red pepper flakes
1 teaspoon black pepper
(½ teaspoon chipotle chile powder)

Bring to a boil, then reduce the heat to medium-low to simmer, stirring frequently, until thick, 30 to 40 minutes. When placed on a plate, a spoonful of the jam should stay in a mound and not exude watery liquid.

While the jam cooks, prepare a water-bath canner, 893, gather all your canning equipment, 891, and have ready 5 clean, hot half-pint jars, 893.

Ladle jam into prepared jars, leaving ½ inch headspace, 893. Wipe the rims. Place lids on jars and screw on rings until fingertip-tight, 893. Process for 20 minutes. Let cool completely and store as directed, 908.

II. WITH SMOKED TOMATOES

This version takes longer to cook down than version I but has a lovely, lightly smoked flavor.

Prepare a smoker, 1067. Place cut side up on the grate of the smoker or on a rack:

5 pounds Roma, San Marzano, Amish Paste, or other sauce tomatoes, halved

Smoke between 225° and 250°F for 1 hour. If desired, peel the skins off the tomatoes.

Transfer the tomatoes to a large pot and stir in:

2 cups sugar
⅓ cup bottled lemon juice
2 teaspoons pickling salt
1 teaspoon black pepper
1 teaspoon ground coriander
1 teaspoon ground cumin

Bring to a boil, then reduce the heat to medium-low to simmer, stirring frequently, until thick, 30 to 40 minutes. When placed on a plate, a spoonful of the jam should stay in a mound and not exude watery liquid. Ladle into prepared jars and process as directed in version I, above.

GOLDEN CHERRY TOMATO AND GINGER JAM

About 3 half-pint jars

These golden preserves are almost tropical in flavor. Serve slathered on grilled cheese sandwiches, with a cheese plate, or like any other jam, on buttered toast. Please read How to Process, 891.

Combine in a medium bowl:

2 pounds yellow or orange cherry tomatoes, halved
2 cups sugar

Steep, 917, covered and refrigerated, overnight.

Prepare a water-bath canner, 893, gather all your canning equipment, 891, place a couple of saucers in the freezer, and have ready 3 clean, hot half-pint jars, 893.

Transfer the tomatoes to a large heavy saucepan and stir in:

4 ounces ginger, peeled and cut into thin matchsticks
Finely grated zest and juice of 2 large lemons

Bring to a boil, then boil rapidly until it reaches the jelling point, 908. Remove from the heat and skim off any foam. Ladle into prepared jars, leaving ¼ inch headspace, 893. Wipe the rims. Place lids on jars and screw on rings until fingertip-tight, 893. Process for 10 minutes. Let cool completely and store as directed, 908.

ABOUT FREEZER JAMS

The principal advantage of freezer jams is that there is no cooking or canning required, and the resulting jams taste like fresh fruit. While we still prefer the flavor of traditional, cooked jams, this technique is worth a gander if you're short on time and long on fruit and freezer space. Many freezer jams use standard powdered pectin with heaps of sugar, but we prefer to use "instant" freezer jam pectin and less sugar for even more fresh fruit flavor. Thaw frozen jam overnight in the refrigerator, then store refrigerated.

BASIC FREEZER JAM

About 5 half-pint jars

Whisk together in a medium bowl:

2 cups sugar

8 tablespoons instant or freezer jam pectin, 1011

Stir in:

4 cups crushed, finely chopped, or grated fresh fruit, such as berries of all kinds, peaches, mangoes, plums, pears, etc.

Let the mixture sit, stirring occasionally, for 10 minutes. Taste and add if needed:

(Lemon or lime juice to taste)

Ladle into clean plastic or glass freezer jars, leaving ½ inch head-space, 893, and let sit at room temperature until thickened, about 30 minutes. Place lids on jars, label and date them, and refrigerate for up to 3 weeks or freeze for up to 1 year.

MAKING FRUIT BUTTERS AND JELLIED FRUIT SAUCES

Fruit butters are purees that are cooked slowly and thickened by the evaporation of water, resulting in deeply concentrated fruit flavors. They earn their name from their smooth, spreadable consistency. We don't let an autumn go by without making at least one batch of apple butter, which is the classic fruit butter, but we have found that blueberries, peaches and apricots, and plums make excellent butters as well.

Born of thrift, fruit butters contain the least added sugar of all preserves. They are often accented with spices. ➤ The challenge in making fruit butters is to cook them slowly for several hours without scorching. This is commonly done on the stovetop, but the oven works just as well. In fact, we have come to prefer cooking our fruit butters in the oven as it is more hands-off and doesn't turn the stovetop into a splattered, sticky mess. That said, be prepared to cook fruit butters much longer in the oven than you would on a stovetop, as evaporation is slower.

Jellied fruit sauces or, as the British call them, fruit "cheeses," are simply fruit butters that have been cooked down even further, resulting in a very thick, jellied puree. It's best to age jellied fruit sauces for at least 6 months before serving—their flavor develops for up to 2 years and they keep for up to 3 years. To serve, run a knife around the inside of the jar, shake out the jellied sauce, and slice ½ inch thick. Jellied fruit sauce makes a superb dessert, or serve with cheese or roasted meats. For another classic jellied sauce, see Cranberry Sauce II, 179. ➤ Please read the directions for safe and proper canning, 890, before proceeding.

APPLE BUTTER

About 8 half-pint jars

This recipe may be made with any quantity of apples using the proportions below, but keep in mind that larger quantities will take much longer to cook. Please read Making Fruit Butters and Jellied Fruit Sauces, above, and How to Process, 891.

Place in a large heavy pot:

5 pounds unpeeled apples, quartered

4 cups water

Bring to a boil, then reduce the heat and simmer, covered, until very soft, about 20 minutes. Put the fruit through a food mill fitted with the medium disk. Measure the puree.

To bake the butter, preheat the oven to 300°F. Transfer the puree to a roasting pan. Stir in for every 1 cup puree:

½ cup sugar

1 tablespoon bottled lemon juice

¼ teaspoon ground cinnamon

Pinch of ground cloves

Pinch of ground allspice

Bake, stirring every hour, until the apple butter is thick, 3 to 3½ hours.

To make on the stovetop, place the ingredients in a large, wide pot and cook over medium-low heat, stirring frequently and adjusting the heat to prevent scorching, until the butter is thick and can be mounded on a spoon, about 2 hours. It should not exude any thin liquid.

While the butter cooks, prepare a water-bath canner, 893, gather all your canning equipment, 891, and have ready 8 clean, hot half-pint jars, 893.

Ladle the butter into prepared jars, leaving ½ inch headspace, 893. Wipe the rims. Place lids on jars and screw on rings until fingertip-tight, 893. Process for 15 minutes. Let cool completely and store as directed, 908.

PEAR BUTTER

Prepare **Apple Butter, above,** using **5 pounds pears, quartered,** After running the fruit through a food mill, stir in the sugar and lemon juice as directed, and substitute for the spices **2 teaspoons ground cardamom** and **1 teaspoon ground ginger.** Partway through cooking, puree with an immersion blender or in batches in a blender (pears are more grainy than apples, and this step results in a much smoother fruit butter). Continue to cook until thick and process as directed.

SMOKED APPLE BUTTER

Yield varies

This apple butter is an excellent accompaniment to roast pork, as it veers more toward savory than sweet, but we still enjoy it swirled into yogurt and spread on sourdough toast with salted butter. Please read How to Process, 891.

Weigh:

Unpeeled apples, quartered

Record the weight. Prepare a smoker, 1067. Place apples on the rack in the smoker. Smoke at 225° to 250°F for 1 hour. Transfer the apples to a large pot and add:

1 cup water for every 2 initial pounds apples

Bring to a boil and cook, stirring occasionally, until the apples are very soft, about 15 minutes. Run through a food mill fitted with the medium disk and measure the puree. Transfer the puree to a pot or roasting pan.

Add for every 1 cup puree:

½ cup white or brown sugar

1 tablespoon cider vinegar or bottled lemon juice

1/8 teaspoon salt
(1 sprig rosemary; do not use more than 3 sprigs rosemary)

Bring to a boil and simmer over medium-low heat or bake in a 300°F oven, stirring every hour, until the butter is thick and can be mounded on a spoon. It should not exude any thin liquid.

While the butter cooks, prepare a water-bath canner, 893, gather all your canning equipment, 891, and have ready clean, hot half-pint jars, 893 (about 2 half-pint jars per every initial pound of apples).

Ladle the butter into prepared jars, leaving 1/2 inch headspace, 893. Wipe the rims. Place lids on jars and screw on rings until fingertip-tight, 893. Process for 15 minutes. Let cool completely and store as directed, 908.

BLUEBERRY BUTTER

About 4 half-pint jars

If you love blueberry jam, you will adore blueberry butter. Use it on top of oatmeal, between layers of buttermilk cake, or with lemon curd on individual Pavlovas, 826. Please read How to Process, 891.

Puree in batches in a food processor:

3 pounds blueberries

Transfer the puree to a heavy pot or roasting pan and add:

3 cups sugar
1/4 cup bottled lemon juice
(1/4 cup crème de cassis)
(1 teaspoon ground cinnamon)
Finely grated zest of 1 lemon

Bring to a boil and simmer, stirring frequently, over medium-low heat or bake in a 300°F oven, stirring every hour, until the butter is thick and can be mounded on a spoon, 2 1/2 to 3 hours on the stovetop or 3 to 3 1/2 hours in the oven. It should not exude any thin liquid.

While the butter cooks, prepare a water-bath canner, 893, gather all your canning equipment, 891, and have ready 4 clean, hot half-pint jars, 893. Ladle the butter into prepared jars, leaving 1/2 inch headspace, 893. Wipe the rims. Place lids on jars and screw on rings until fingertip-tight, 893. Process for 15 minutes. Let cool completely and store as directed, 908.

PLUM BUTTER

Yield varies

While any plum will make delicious butter, we recommend damson or Italian plums. Please read How to Process, 891.

Weigh and record the weight of:

Ripe plums

Wash, quarter, and pit the plums and place in a large pot along with:

1/2 cup water for every initial 1 pound fruit

Bring to a boil, cover, and reduce the heat to simmer until the plums are very soft, about 15 minutes. Run the pulp through a food mill fitted with the medium disk. Discard the skins and measure the puree. Transfer the puree to a pot or roasting pan and add:

3/4 cup sugar for every 1 cup puree

Bring to a boil and simmer over medium-low heat or bake in a 300°F oven, stirring every hour, until the butter is thick and can be mounded on a spoon. It should not exude any thin liquid, but keep in mind that plum butter will not be quite as thick as apple butter.

While the butter cooks, prepare a water-bath canner, 893, gather all your canning equipment, 891, and have ready clean, hot half-pint jars, 893 (you should get 3/4 to one half-pint jar of finished butter for every 1 cup puree).

Ladle the butter into prepared jars, leaving 1/2 inch headspace, 893. Wipe the rims. Place lids on jars and screw on rings until fingertip-tight, 893. Process for 15 minutes. Let cool completely and store as directed, 908.

PEACH OR APRICOT BUTTER

About 4 half-pint jars

Summer can't last forever, but opening a jar of this butter in January or February gives winter a run for its money. Please read How to Process, 891.

Place in a large heavy pot:

4 pounds peaches or apricots, pitted and coarsely chopped
1/4 cup water

Simmer very slowly until very soft, about 20 minutes. Run the pulp through a food mill fitted with the medium disk and measure it. Transfer the puree to a largae pot or roasting pan. Add:

1/2 cup sugar for every 1 cup puree
3 tablespoons bottled lemon juice
1 vanilla bean, halved lengthwise

Bring to a boil and simmer over medium-low heat or bake in a 300°F oven, stirring every hour, until the butter is thick and can be mounded on a spoon. It should not exude any thin liquid.

While the butter cooks, prepare a water-bath canner, 893, gather all your canning equipment, and have ready 4 clean, hot half-pint jars, 893.

Remove from the heat. Remove the vanilla bean, scrape any vanilla seeds from the pod and add them back to the pot, then discard the pod. Ladle the butter into prepared jars, leaving 1/2 inch headspace, 893. Wipe the rims. Place lids on jars and screw on rings until fingertip-tight, 893. Process for 15 minutes. Let cool completely and store as directed, 908.

JELLIED DAMSON SAUCE (DAMSON "CHEESE")

About five 1-pint jars

Please read Making Fruit Butters and Jellied Fruit Sauces, 915. The method and ratios of fruit to sugar used here also work well with other tart plums, as well as with tart green apples, barely ripe quinces, cranberries, and tart blackberries. This jellied sauce is typically served turned out of the jar (like the canned cranberry sauce of Thanksgiving notoriety), sliced, and served either with a cheese plate or as a simple dessert when topped with whipped cream and toasted almonds.

Preheat the oven to 275°F. Place in a 4 1/2-quart baking dish or roasting pan:

6 pounds damson plums, stemmed

Cover and bake until simmering and syrupy, about 2 1/2 hours. Let sit until cool enough to handle, then pinch the pits from the plums (discard the pits). Divide the plum pulp and juice between 2 wide, heavy 7- to 8-quart saucepans. Prepare a water-bath canner, 893,

gather all your canning equipment, 891, and have ready 5 clean, hot pint jars, 893.
Divide between the 2 saucepans:
8 cups sugar
Bring the puree to a simmer, stirring frequently, over medium heat. When the sugar dissolves, boil vigorously over medium-high heat, stirring almost constantly, until a spoon dragged over the bottom of the pan leaves a trail, 9 to 12 minutes. Ladle into the prepared jars, leaving ½ inch headspace, 893. Wipe the rims. Place lids on jars and screw on rings until fingertip-tight, 893. Process for 15 minutes. Let cool completely and store as directed, 908.

To remove the sauce from the jar, run a small offset spatula or a thin, flexible knife around the inside edge of the jar, coaxing the jellied sauce away from the sides. Invert onto a serving plate, tapping gently to get the sauce to fall from the jar.

ABOUT MAKING PRESERVES

Although the general term "preserves" can be used to refer to the entire category of foods in this chapter, here preserves has a specific meaning: bits of fruit cooked to a translucent state in a thick syrup. Preserves are similar to jam, but chunkier. They are found in two styles. In one, the fruit is denser and thick enough to spread. In the other, more European style, distinct bits of fruit are suspended in a syrup that may drip off toast. Runny preserves are perfect for spooning over pancakes and waffles, ice cream, yogurt, puddings, and cakes.

Whichever style you choose, use the finest fruits to make preserves. Fruits for preserves can be just ripe to fully ripe, since jelling is less important.

STEEPING AND PLUMPING

Because of their unique texture, ➤ preserves benefit from both **steeping** and **plumping** the fruit before canning.

To steep fruit, gently mix the raw fruit and sugar in a stainless steel or glass bowl, cover, and let sit in a cool place to steep for at least 4 hours (or in the refrigerator for up to 5 days). Steeping draws moisture out of the fruit, allowing it to boil off more quickly during the cooking process. After steeping, cook the preserves at a brisk simmer until they reach the jelling point, 908. At this point you may process and can the preserves, or you can plump them.

To plump preserves, after they've reached the jelling point, pour them into a shallow dish, cover loosely, and let sit overnight in the refrigerator. This step is optional, but we recommend plumping to ensure tender fruit that will not float to the top of the jars. The next day, return the preserves to a rolling boil before canning.

STRAWBERRY PRESERVES

About 4 half-pint jars

Please read About Making Preserves, above, and How to Process, 891.
Combine in a medium bowl:
2 pounds firm-ripe strawberries, hulled
3 cups sugar
Crush half the berries for a more spreadable preserve. Cover and steep, above.

Unless you plan to plump the preserves, above, overnight, prepare a water-bath canner, 893, gather all your canning equipment, 891, place a couple of saucers in the freezer, and have ready 4 clean, hot half-pint jars, 893.
Transfer the strawberry mixture to a wide heavy pot and stir in:
¼ cup bottled lemon juice
Boil rapidly, stirring frequently, until it reaches the jelling point, 908. Remove from the heat and skim off any foam. If not plumping the preserves, ladle into prepared jars, leaving ¼ inch headspace, 893. Wipe the rims. Place lids on jars and screw on rings until fingertip-tight, 893. Process for 10 minutes. Let cool completely and store as directed, 908.

If plumping the preserves, the next day return them to a boil before processing and canning.

APRICOT, PEACH, OR NECTARINE PRESERVES

About 6 half-pint jars

Please read About Making Preserves, above, and How to Process, 891.
Combine in a large bowl:
5 pounds unpeeled firm-ripe apricots, peaches, or nectarines, halved and pitted
6 cups sugar
Cover and steep, above.

Unless you plan to plump the preserves, above, overnight, prepare a water-bath canner, 893, gather all your canning equipment, 891, place a couple of saucers in the freezer, and have ready 6 clean, hot half-pint jars, 893.
Transfer the fruit mixture to a large heavy pot and stir in:
¼ cup bottled lemon juice
¼ cup strained orange juice
Boil rapidly, stirring frequently, until it reaches the jelling point, 908. Remove from the heat and skim off any foam. If not plumping the preserves, ladle into prepared jars, leaving ¼ inch headspace, 893. Wipe the rims. Place lids on jars and screw on rings until fingertip-tight, 893. Process for 10 minutes. Let cool completely and store as directed, 908.

If plumping the preserves, the next day return them to a boil before processing and canning.

STRAWBERRY AND RHUBARB PRESERVES

About 5 half-pint jars

Please read About Making Preserves, above, and How to Process, 891.
Combine in a medium bowl:
12 ounces rhubarb, cut into ½-inch pieces (about 2 cups)
4 cups sugar
Cover and steep, above.

Unless you plan to plump the preserves, above, overnight, prepare a water-bath canner, 893, gather all your canning equipment, 891, place a couple of saucers in the freezer, and have ready 5 clean, hot half-pint jars, 893.

Transfer the rhubarb mixture to a large heavy pot and bring to a boil.

Add:

1 quart strawberries, hulled and halved

Return to a boil, stirring frequently, then reduce the heat and simmer, stirring, until it reaches the jelling point, 908, about 15 minutes. Remove from the heat and skim off any foam. If not plumping the preserves, ladle into prepared jars, leaving ¼ inch headspace, 893. Wipe the rims. Place lids on jars and screw on rings until fingertip-tight, 893. Process for 10 minutes. Let cool completely and store as directed, 908.

If plumping the preserves, the next day return them to a boil before processing and canning.

PLUM PRESERVES

Yield varies

Please read About Making Preserves, 917, and How to Process, 891.

Wash, halve, and pit:

Damson, Italian, or greengage plums

Weigh the plums and place in a bowl. Add:

1¾ to 2¼ cups sugar for every 1 pound plums

If the plums are very sweet, use the lesser amount of sugar. Cover and steep, 917.

Unless you plan to plump the preserves, 917, overnight, prepare a water-bath canner, 893, gather all your canning equipment, 891, place a couple of saucers in the freezer, and have ready clean, hot half-pint jars, 893.

Transfer the plum mixture to a large heavy pot, bring to a boil, then reduce the heat and simmer until the syrup reaches the jelling point, 908. Remove from the heat and skim off any foam. If not plumping the preserves, ladle into prepared jars, leaving ¼ inch headspace, 893. Wipe the rims. Place lids on jars and screw on rings until fingertip-tight, 893. Process for 10 minutes. Let cool completely and store as directed, 908.

If plumping the preserves, the next day return them to a boil before processing and canning.

SOUR CHERRY PRESERVES

About 7 half-pint jars

These deep-red preserves have plenty of texture and are our favorite way to put up ephemeral sour cherries. Please read About Making Preserves, 917, and How to Process, 891.

Combine in a large bowl:

4 pounds sour cherries, stemmed and pitted

4 cups sugar

Cover and steep, 917.

Unless you plan to plump the fruit, 917, overnight, prepare a water-bath canner, 893, gather all your canning equipment, 891, place a couple of saucers in the freezer, and have ready 7 clean, hot half-pint jars, 893.

Transfer the cherry mixture to a large heavy pot, bring to a boil, and boil rapidly, stirring frequently, until it reaches the jelling point, 908, about 20 minutes. Remove from the heat, skim off any foam, and if desired, stir in:

(2 tablespoons kirsch or Maraschino liqueur)

Ladle into prepared jars, leaving ¼ inch headspace, 893. Wipe the rims. Place lids on jars and screw on rings until fingertip-tight, 893. Process for 10 minutes. Let cool completely and store as directed, 908.

If plumping the preserves, do not stir in the kirsch or Maraschino until the next day when you return the preserves to a boil before processing and canning.

QUINCE PRESERVES

Yield varies

Please read About Making Preserves, 917, and How to Process, 891.

Scrub:

Quinces

Peel, core, and cut them into eighths, reserving the fruit, and put the peels in a pan with just enough water to cover. For each 1 quart water, add:

1 lemon, washed, sliced, and seeded

1 orange, washed, sliced, and seeded

Simmer until the peels are soft. Strain the liquid through a fine-mesh sieve into a wide, heavy pot. Weigh the quince slices and add them. Weigh the same quantity of:

Sugar

Bring the quince slices to a boil and add the sugar. Return to a boil, then reduce the heat and simmer until the fruit is tender. Plump, 917, overnight.

Prepare a water-bath canner, 893, gather all your canning equipment, 891, and have ready clean, hot half-pint jars, 893. Return the preserves to a boil. With a slotted spoon, pack the fruit into prepared jars. Continue to reduce the syrup until it bubbles thickly. Cover the fruit with the reduced syrup, leaving ¼ inch headspace, 893. Wipe the rims. Place lids on jars and screw on rings until fingertip-tight, 893. Process for 10 minutes. Let cool completely and store as directed, 908.

ABOUT CONSERVES

Conserves are bits of fruit cooked to translucence in heavy syrup. They often contain a mixture of fruits, usually one of them citrus, and additions like raisins, nuts, coconut, ginger, or liquor. Conserves can be served as a condiment for poultry and meat, or spooned over ice cream.

PEACH OR PLUM CONSERVES

About 8 half-pint jars

A rich accompaniment to dark meats. Please read How to Process, 891.

With a peeler, remove the zest in strips from:

1 large orange

1 small lemon

Cut away and discard the white pith from the fruit, section, 182, and remove the seeds. Chop the zest and pulp and add to a large heavy saucepan with:

3 pounds firm-ripe peaches or plums, pitted and coarsely chopped

2 cups golden raisins (8 ounces)

3½ cups sugar

Bring to a boil, then reduce the heat and simmer, stirring frequently, until the mixture reaches the jelling point, 908, about 1 hour. While the conserves cook, prepare a water-bath canner, 893, gather all

your canning equipment, 891, and have ready 8 clean, hot half-pint jars, 893.
Stir into the conserves:

1 cup pecan or walnut pieces, toasted, 1005

Cook for 5 minutes. Remove from the heat. If desired, stir in:

(¼ cup bourbon or brandy)

Ladle into prepared jars, leaving ¼ inch headspace, 893. Wipe the rims. Place lids on jars and screw on rings until fingertip-tight, 893. Process for 15 minutes. Let cool completely and store as directed, 908.

CHRISTMAS CONSERVES

About 9 half-pint jars

Make these colorful conserves with fruits of the holiday season. While these conserves can be used in sweet or savory applications, they are especially good with rich roasted meats, such as lamb, goose, or duck. Please read How to Process, 891.
Prepare a water-bath canner, 893, gather all your canning equipment, 891, and have ready 9 clean, hot half-pint jars, 893.
Combine in a large heavy saucepan:

12 ounces unpeeled oranges, quartered and very thinly sliced (discard seeds)
12 ounces unpeeled limes, very thinly sliced into rounds (discard seeds)
12 ounces kumquats, halved lengthwise (discard seeds)
Cold water to cover

Simmer, covered, until the citrus peels are soft, about 15 minutes. Drain the fruit, return to the saucepan, and combine with:

3 cups sugar

Rapidly boil until the slices are translucent and the mixture is thick and syrupy, about 35 minutes.

Meanwhile, prepare and drop the pieces into cold water to keep them from darkening:

12 ounces tart apples, peeled, cored, and coarsely chopped
12 ounces firm-ripe pears, peeled, cored, and coarsely chopped
12 ounces ripe quinces, peeled, cored, and coarsely chopped (if unavailable, use 1¼ pounds apples and 1 pound pears total)

Combine in a second large heavy saucepan:

3 cups sugar
5 cups water

Stir over low heat until the sugar dissolves, then cover and bring the syrup to a simmer. Drain the apple mixture and add it to the syrup. Simmer until thick and syrupy, about 15 minutes.
Add the citrus fruit to the apple mixture, and mix in:

12 ounces cranberries, picked over and washed

Return to a boil. Remove from the heat, cover, and let stand for 5 minutes, then stir. Ladle into prepared jars, leaving ¼ inch headspace, 893. Wipe the rims. Place lids on jars and screw on rings until fingertip-tight, 893. Process for 15 minutes. Let cool completely and store as directed, 908.

SPICED RHUBARB CONSERVES

About 5 half-pint jars

There are few things finer than these conserves on a thick, well-buttered piece of toast. Please read How to Process, 891.
Prepare a water-bath canner, 893, gather all your canning equipment, 891, place a couple of saucers in the freezer, and have ready 5 clean, hot half-pint jars, 893.
Combine in a large heavy saucepan:

8 ounces unpeeled oranges, quartered and very thinly sliced (discard seeds)
4 ounces unpeeled lemons, very thinly sliced into rounds (discard seeds)
1 ounce ginger, peeled and cut into matchsticks
1 cup apple cider

Cover and simmer until the citrus peels are soft, about 15 minutes. Add:

1 pound red rhubarb, coarsely chopped
3¼ cups sugar
½ cup golden raisins
½ teaspoon ground cinnamon
¼ teaspoon ground mace
(1 vanilla bean, split lengthwise)

Bring to a boil, then reduce the heat and simmer, stirring frequently, until the mixture reaches the jelling point, 908, about 40 minutes. Remove the vanilla bean, if using, scrape any vanilla seeds from the pod and add them back to the pan, then discard the pod. Ladle into prepared jars, leaving ¼ inch headspace, 893. Wipe the rims. Place lids on jars and screw on rings until fingertip-tight, 893. Process for 15 minutes. Let cool completely and store as directed, 908.

FIG AND PISTACHIO CONSERVES

5 or 6 half-pint jars

Serve this delectable conserve with roasted lamb, a cheese board, or over Greek yogurt. Please read How to Process, 891.
Prepare a water-bath canner, 893, gather all your canning equipment, 891, and have ready 6 clean, hot half-pint jars, 893.
Wash and remove the zest in strips with a vegetable peeler from:

1 large orange
1 large lemon

Remove the white pith from the fruit, section, 182, then chop the pulp, discarding the seeds. Very thinly slice the zest. Combine the citrus pulp and zest in a large heavy saucepan with:

2 pounds fresh figs, stemmed and quartered
2 cups sugar
1 cup packed brown sugar
1 cup dried figs (6 ounces), chopped
1 cinnamon stick

Bring to a boil and cook, stirring frequently, until the mixture reaches the jelling point, 908, 10 to 15 minutes. Remove from the heat, discard the cinnamon stick, and stir in:

1 cup roasted unsalted pistachios
(¼ cup Cognac, brandy, or bourbon)

Ladle into prepared jars, leaving ¼ inch headspace, 893. Wipe the rims. Place lids on jars and screw on rings until fingertip-tight, 893. Process for 15 minutes. Let cool completely and store as directed, 908.

SWEET CHERRY CONSERVES

About 8 half-pint jars

Please read How to Process, 891.

Prepare a water-bath canner, 893, gather all your canning equipment, 891, and have ready 8 clean, hot half-pint jars, 893.

Combine in a large heavy saucepan:

2 oranges, quartered and very thinly sliced (discard seeds)
Water to barely cover

Simmer until very tender, about 15 minutes. Add:

1½ pounds sweet cherries, stemmed and pitted
3½ cups sugar
6 tablespoons bottled lemon juice
¾ teaspoon ground cinnamon
(6 whole cloves, tied in a cheesecloth bag)

Simmer the conserves, stirring frequently, until they reach the jelling point, 908. Discard the spice bag, if using. Ladle into prepared jars, leaving ¼ inch headspace, 893. Wipe the rims. Place lids on jars and screw on rings until fingertip-tight, 893. Process for 15 minutes. Let cool completely and store as directed, 908.

ABOUT MAKING MARMALADE

Marmalade is best described as small pieces of fruit—most often citrus peel—suspended in a soft, transparent jelly. Like jam, there is leeway in marmalade—it can be soft or firm—but like jelly, the juice should be clear and the pectin and acid contents high. ➤ Please read the directions for safe and proper canning, 890, before proceeding.

PREPARING CITRUS FRUITS FOR MARMALADE

Choose citrus that is heavy for its size—it will be the juiciest. The color of the rind has no bearing on the interior quality. When blood oranges are available, their garnet color makes gorgeous marmalade. As other uncommon citrus come along—mandarinquats, pomelos, Ugli fruit—try them in place of oranges.

There are a couple different schools of thought when it comes to marmalade. One is to use everything—peel, pith, and pulp. This is the traditional method used in Bitter Orange Marmalade, below. Another is to strip off the zest (the colored outer layer of the peel) of the citrus with a vegetable peeler, leaving behind the white pith, and cut the zest into fine matchsticks. The pith is trimmed from the fruit and discarded and the fruit is sectioned, 182. The latter method, used in Megan's Blood Orange Marmalade, 920, is a bit more fiddly than the former, but it produces a beautiful, clear marmalade with a clean flavor. Both methods yield delicious results, however, so try them both and decide for yourself.

➤ Chilling citrus makes it easier to very thinly slice. ➤ Use a stainless steel knife (carbon steel reacts with acid and stains the fruit). Wash the fruits well before cutting.

Tenderizing citrus peel is crucial to marmalade. Cover with water and simmer until the peel is thoroughly tender—from 15 minutes to more than an hour, depending on the size and thickness of the peel slices. To test, ➤ cut a piece against the side of the pan with the edge of a wooden spoon—it should easily break in half if done.

BITTER ORANGE MARMALADE

About 10 half-pint jars

Made with bitter Seville oranges, this classic formula is for the true marmalade lover. It is astringent and aromatic, the perfect adornment for scones or whole wheat toast. If you cannot find Seville oranges, use **1½ pounds sweet oranges** and **1 pound lemons.** For an amber color, use half brown sugar. Please read About Making Marmalade, above, and How to Process, 891.

Combine in a medium bowl:

2½ pounds unpeeled bitter oranges, quartered and very thinly sliced (discard seeds)
7 cups water

Cover and let stand overnight in the refrigerator.

Prepare a water-bath canner, 893, gather all your canning equipment, 891, place a couple of saucers in the freezer, and have ready 10 clean, hot half-pint jars, 893. Transfer the oranges and water to a large, wide pot and simmer until the citrus peel is completely tender, 15 to 20 minutes. Add:

6½ cups sugar

Boil rapidly, stirring frequently, until it reaches the jelling point, 908. Remove from the heat and skim off any foam. Ladle into prepared jars, leaving ¼ inch headspace, 893. Wipe the rims. Place lids on jars and screw on rings until fingertip-tight, 893. Process for 10 minutes. Let cool completely and store as directed, 908.

MEGAN'S BLOOD ORANGE MARMALADE

About 5 half-pint jars

Blood oranges owe their startling color to a genetic mutation that encourages the development of anthocyanins, compounds that lend a reddish-purple color to whatever they are present in. Blood orange marmalade is crimson and tart, a feast for the eyes as much as the mouth. Be warned that this marmalade is time-consuming, but we think the results are well worth the extra effort.

Prepare a water-bath canner, 893, gather all your canning equipment, 891, place a couple of saucers in the freezer, and have ready 5 clean, hot half-pint jars, 893. Using a vegetable peeler, remove the zest in strips from:

4 pounds blood oranges

Stack the strips of zest on top of one another and cut them crosswise into very thin slivers. Place in a large, wide pot and set aside.

Cut off and discard the very top and bottom of each orange so they stand upright on the cutting board. Following the curve of the oranges with your knife, cut off the white pith to expose the fruit inside. Discard the pith. You will now be able to see thin, vertical lines of membrane that show you where the segments of the oranges are. Cut along the membranes to release the fruit sections, leaving the membranes behind (see the illustration, 182). Discard any seeds. Place the orange sections in the pot with the slivered zest, and squeeze any juice remaining in the orange membranes into the pot as well.

Add just enough water to the pot to cover the fruit and zest (3 to 4 cups). Simmer the fruit, uncovered, until the water has almost completely evaporated and the zest is completely tender. If needed, add a little more water and simmer longer to achieve tenderness.

When the zest is tender, gradually stir in:

4 cups sugar

Cook the marmalade over high heat, stirring to dissolve the sugar, until the mixture reaches the jelling point, 908. Ladle into prepared jars, leaving ¼ inch headspace, 893. Wipe the rims. Place lids on jars and screw on rings until fingertip-tight, 893. Process for 10 minutes. Let cool completely and store as directed, 908.

FOUR-CITRUS MARMALADE

About 8 half-pint jars

Please read About Making Marmalade, 920, and How to Process, 891.

Using a vegetable peeler, remove the zest in strips from:

1½ pounds grapefruit
1 pound sweet oranges
8 ounces limes
8 ounces lemons

Set the fruit aside. Chop the zest into ¼-inch pieces by hand, or in a food processor. Combine the zest in a large saucepan along with:

2 cups water

Simmer until the zest is soft, about 10 minutes. Drain.

Meanwhile, cut off and discard the white pith from the fruit. Section the fruit, 182, remove the seeds, and finely chop the pulp. Mix the simmered zest and pulp in a bowl with:

4 cups water

Cover and let stand overnight in the refrigerator.

Prepare a water-bath canner, 893, gather all your canning equipment, 891, place a couple of saucers in the freezer, and have ready 8 clean, hot half-pint jars, 893. Transfer the fruit to a large, wide pot and add:

5½ cups sugar

Bring to a boil and cook over high heat, stirring frequently, until the mixture has reached the jelling point, 908. Remove from the heat and skim off any foam. Ladle into prepared jars, leaving ¼ inch headspace, 893. Wipe the rims. Place lids on jars and screw on rings until fingertip-tight, 893. Process for 10 minutes. Let cool completely and store as directed, 908.

LIME MARMALADE

About 3 half-pint jars

Wash and peel the zest from **2½ pounds limes** and **1 pound lemons.** Prepare **Four-Citrus Marmalade, above,** substituting the trimmed limes and lemons for the fruits, seeding and cutting them as directed, then proceeding as above.

GINGER MARMALADE

About 4 half-pint jars

Spread these invigorating preserves on English muffins or roasted meats, or stir into hot water with lemon juice and bourbon for a superb hot toddy. If possible, select young ginger, which is not fibrous. Please read About Making Marmalade, 920, and How to Process, 891.

Combine in a large heavy saucepan:

2 pounds ginger (preferably young), peeled and finely chopped
8 cups water

Bring to a boil, then reduce the heat and simmer, stirring occasionally, until the ginger is softened, about 2 hours. Stir in:

4 cups sugar
1¼ cups apple cider
5 tablespoons bottled lemon juice
5 tablespoons light corn syrup

Simmer gently for 15 minutes. Transfer to a bowl, cover, and refrigerate overnight.

Prepare a water-bath canner, 893, gather all your canning equipment, 891, and have ready 4 clean, hot half-pint jars, 893. Transfer the ginger mixture to a large, wide pot. Bring to a boil, then reduce the heat to simmer, stirring often, until a spoon cuts a path through the marmalade, 45 minutes to 1 hour.

Ladle into prepared jars, leaving ¼ inch headspace, 893. Wipe the rims. Place lids on jars and screw on rings until fingertip-tight, 893. Process for 10 minutes. Let cool completely and store as directed, 908.

PICKLES

Pickling is a means of preserving fruits and vegetables by submerging them in an acidic brine. Sometimes, as in the case of quick pickles, 929, they are meant to be stored in the refrigerator and eaten within a couple months. Pickles that are canned in a boiling water bath are shelf-stable and can be kept for much longer—up to 18 months. For many of us, however, preservation is not the primary reason to pickle things. Rather, the piquant, salty, tangy flavor is what we're after. For instance, it's hard to imagine a juicy burger without the acidic bite of a dill pickle, a rich Reuben sandwich without a messy pile of sauerkraut, or a charcuterie spread without a crock of cornichons. Pickles enliven the plate, especially when it comes to rich or heavy foods, and if those pickles are homemade, so much the better.

In spite of our love for pickles, there is a lot of apprehension surrounding the process of making them. While it is wise to be cautious and to follow approved procedures and recipes, there is nothing to be afraid of. All the recipes in this chapter have been tested for pH and are perfectly safe when followed.

For information about canning equipment and safe canning methods, see the Canning chapter, 889.

PICKLING METHODS

There are three methods of pickling: quick pickling, traditional pickling, and fermentation. **Quick pickling** is the easiest: Fruits and vegetables are simply covered with a hot, vinegar-based brine, and that is that. Quick pickles are not canned, meaning they are not shelf-stable and must be refrigerated. For this reason, we reserve quick pickling for small batches. ➤ Do not attempt to process quick pickle recipes for long-term storage.

The second method—or "traditional" pickling—is very similar to quick pickling, with the added step of boiling water–bath canning in self-sealing jars. To ensure safety, ➤ closely follow the recipes in this chapter: Shelf-stable pickles must contain specific amounts of salt and acid, and must be canned in a water-bath canner, 893, if they are to be stored safely without refrigeration. Please read the directions for safe and proper canning, 890, before proceeding.

There is one exception to the boiling water-bath canning rule worth noting: the USDA has recently approved **low-temperature canning** for cucumber pickles. To process pickles with this method, see 893. We highly recommend this method, as the gentler processing temperature keeps pickles very crisp. ➤ Do not use this method for any pickle except cucumber pickles.

The third pickling method is **fermentation.** This method of pickling differs fundamentally from the previous two methods in that vinegar is not introduced into the vegetables. Rather, vegetables are left to ferment in a salty brine, which in turn creates enough lactic acid to make them safe for storing in the refrigerator as for quick pickles. For more information, see About Fermentation, 938.

PICKLING INGREDIENTS

For the best results, it is ➤ imperative that you select the freshest fruits and vegetables available, perfectly ripe and without a trace of mold or blemishes. The importance of freshness cannot be overemphasized; if you cannot pickle your vegetables immediately after purchase, refrigerate and use as soon as possible.

➤ When washing fruits and vegetables, scrub particularly around the stems, blossom ends, and crevices—these are hiding places for bacteria. Pickling recipes sometimes call for vegetables to be submerged in a brine or salted and left to drain in a colander before pickling. This brining period is sufficiently long to draw out moisture and introduce salt into the interior of the vegetable but not long enough to induce fermentation. This initial step may improve the texture of pickled vegetables.

Vinegar, or acetic acid, inhibits the growth of harmful and destructive microorganisms. For safety's sake, it is essential to ➤ use vinegar with a content of at least 5 percent acetic acid. ➤ If the label does not give a vinegar's acid content, do not use it for pickling. Cider vinegar and distilled white vinegar are both recommended, and, in general, red and white wine vinegars are safe to use. Cider and red wine vinegars have a mellow fruity flavor, but their color will darken pickles over time. Distilled white vinegar is clear, neutral-tasting, and ideal for most pickling, but it can have a harsh bite. White wine vinegar is a good compromise as it is clear and less sharp than distilled white vinegar. Balsamic and malt vinegars may contain 6 percent acetic acid and, if they are labeled with this amount of acid, are effective in pickling. However, because their flavors may overwhelm the flavor of the food being pickled, it is best to mix them with one of the more neutral-tasting vinegars listed above. ➤ Most rice vinegars have 4.3 percent acetic acid and are not safe for pickling. Do not use homemade vinegars, because their acid content is unknown.

Occasionally, we blend two vinegars or add bottled lemon juice for complexity and flavor. If a recipe's vinegar solution seems strong for your taste, remember that it will mellow as the pickles sit, or cure. ➤ **Never reduce the proportion of vinegar called for in a recipe.**

➤ Water used should be soft; see 1032. If the water contains iron or sulfur compounds, the pickles will discolor, and minerals can lower brine acidity, potentially causing food safety issues. If soft tap water is unavailable, either use distilled water or boil the water for 15 minutes, cover, and let stand for 24 hours. Skim off any scum on top, then carefully pour off the clear water, leaving any sediment behind. Add 1 tablespoon distilled white vinegar to each gallon before using.

Along with vinegar, salt is the other primary preservative in pickles. ➤ Use only **pickling salt,** 1014, which does not contain additives that can cloud the vinegar solution. Do not use kosher salt, which varies in density, or iodized salt, which can darken pickles. Do not use "light" or reduced-sodium salts.

Sugar flavors food, helps keep colors bright, and helps plump and firm fruits and vegetables. Brown sugar lends caramel color and flavor. Artificial sweeteners can be used in pickling, but they do not contribute to the preserving process. Follow the manufacturer's directions when substituting these for sugar.

Spices should be ➤ both fresh and whole to hold up best in pickling. Ground spices will cloud the vinegar solution, although sometimes it is worth sacrificing clarity for intensity of flavor. Mustard seeds are commonly used in pickling, adding both flavor and texture. Yellow, brown, and black mustard seeds are interchangeable in these recipes. Ground turmeric is a favorite pickler's spice because a very small amount brightens the color of the brine. For example, corn relish without turmeric is pale—with turmeric, it glows. **Pickling spice,** readily purchased in grocery stores, may contain mustard seeds, pieces of cinnamon stick, coriander, ginger, bay leaves, peppercorns, allspice, caraway seeds, dill seeds, cloves, juniper berries, and mace.

Do not rely upon old recipes that call for alum or pickling lime; ➤ too much alum can be unsafe and is no longer recommended. These ingredients were added to ensure crisp pickles. The calcium in pickling lime (also known as slaked lime or calcium hydroxide) does make pickles firm, but it can also make them bitter. Having said that, **calcium chloride** (sold in the canning aisle of the grocery store under the name Pickle Crisp) may be added to pickles to help them retain their crispness. Use as directed on the package.

Crisping agents can also be foraged: Freshly picked **grape leaves** and the leaves of cherry trees, black currant bushes, and oak trees all contain tannins, compounds that block the enzymes that soften vegetables—particularly cucumbers. Thoroughly wash unsprayed leaves, place a leaf in each jar of pickles, and process as directed.

RULES FOR SAFE PICKLING

Many old pickling recipes have been dropped from revised editions of cookbooks because they do not conform to modern safety guidelines. Although pickling is fairly straightforward, potential harm can come from improvising.

Clostridium botulinum is a dangerous anaerobic bacterium that flourishes in moist, oxygen-free, low-acid environments. It seems impossible that a pickled food could be low-acid, but that can happen if a low-acid food (i.e., most vegetables) has not been permeated by enough vinegar of the correct strength. To be safe, ➤ only use tested, up-to-date pickling recipes, such as those in this chapter, and follow them to the letter. ➤ Pickles processed for less than 10 minutes must go into sterilized jars, 893. Unless otherwise noted, pack hot pickles and liquid into hot jars, see Packing Jars, 893. Do not alter or experiment with processing times and jar sizes. If a jar is only partially filled, do not process. Instead, refrigerate and eat the contents within 8 weeks.

If you detect signs of spoilage in processed pickles, 895, such as bulging lids, leakage, or bubbles rising in the jar, ➤ do not taste the contents. Destroy them (see Handling Contaminated Food and Jars, 895).

STORING PICKLES

Quick pickles, unprocessed pickles, and opened jars of processed pickles will keep from 6 to 8 weeks in the refrigerator. Store processed pickles in a dark, cool place where they cannot freeze. They will keep for up to 18 months. ➤ The flavor of nearly all pickles improves if they are left to **cure** for 3 to 6 weeks.

➤ Store all jars with the rings taken off. This allows you to easily detect when a seal goes bad and the jar and its contents should be discarded or destroyed. See Labeling and Storing Canned Goods, 895, for more information.

Pickles may discolor over time. This can be the result of several things, including oxidation, exposure to sunlight, or even the growing conditions of the produce. As long as the produce was in good shape when it was canned and there are no signs of spoilage, discolored pickles are perfectly safe to eat.

ABOUT CUCUMBER PICKLES

As with all vegetables for pickling, use very fresh cucumbers. If cucumbers have been held longer than 24 hours, they tend to become hollow during processing. ➤ After washing, cut off ¼ inch of the blossom end (the end opposite of where the stem was trimmed off). The blossom end contains an enzyme that causes pickles to soften.

Pickling cucumbers—shorter varieties bred specifically for pickling—give superior results. In general, any cucumber with warts, such as the Kirby variety, is a good choice. Smooth-skinned, "burpless" varieties such as Armenian, Asian, or English hothouse do not have a good texture once pickled. For pickling halved cucumbers and cucumber spears in pint jars, try to choose fruits that are approximately 4 inches long (larger ones may be trimmed to fit into jars as needed).

For tiny gherkins and cornichons, choose varieties bred to be harvested around 1½ inches long, although some pickling cucumbers may be harvested when young and very small. Small, rounded West Indian gherkins and Mexican sour gherkins are distinctive, but we prefer the more common, slender French gherkins, as they have a firm texture and no seeds. All gherkin varieties tend to absorb brine well and sustain processing without excessive softening.

Cucumber pickles are safe to process with the low-temperature water bath method, 893.

DILL PICKLES

About 6 pint jars

Please read about pickling, 922–23, and How to Process, 891.

Prepare a water-bath canner, 893, or prepare a water bath for low-temperature canning, 893. Gather all your canning equipment, 891, and have ready 6 clean, hot pint jars, 893.

Wash, then cut an ⅛-inch slice from the blossom end of:

4 pounds 4-inch-long pickling cucumbers

Halve the cucumbers lengthwise. (Cut longer cucumbers into 4-inch pieces.) Place in each jar:

1 garlic clove, peeled and smashed (6 total)
1 teaspoon dill seeds (2 tablespoons total)
1 teaspoon pickling spice (2 tablespoons total)
6 black peppercorns (36 total)
1 sprig dill (6 total)

Tightly pack the cucumbers into the jars. Combine in a medium saucepan and bring just to a boil, stirring until the salt is dissolved:

3 cups cider vinegar
2¼ cups water
¼ cup pickling salt

Ladle into the prepared jars, leaving ½ inch headspace, 893. Remove any trapped air from the jars, 893, and adjust the liquid level if needed. Wipe the rims. Place lids on jars and screw on rings until fingertip-tight, 893. Process for 10 minutes. Let cool completely and store as directed, 923.

BREAD-AND-BUTTER PICKLES

About 5 pint jars

These likely owe their appealing name to an enterprising Illinois couple who, during lean times, bartered their home-canned sweet-and-sour cucumber pickles for staples at the local grocery. Please read about pickling, 922–23, and How to Process, 891.

Wash, then cut an ⅛-inch slice from the blossom end of:

2½ pounds pickling cucumbers

Cut into ¼-inch-thick slices. Peel and cut into ¼-inch-thick slices:

1 pound onions

Combine the cucumber and onion slices in a large bowl and toss well with:

3½ tablespoons pickling salt

Cover with a towel, scatter a layer of ice cubes over the towel, and refrigerate for at least 4 and for up to 12 hours. Transfer the vegetables to a colander, rinse under cold water, and drain well. Prepare a water-bath canner, 893, or prepare a water bath for low-temperature canning, 893, gather all your canning equipment, 891, and have ready 5 clean, hot pint jars, 893.

Combine in a large pot:

3 cups distilled white vinegar
3 cups sugar
1½ tablespoons mustard seeds
(1½ teaspoons red pepper flakes)
1 teaspoon celery seeds
1 teaspoon ground turmeric
¼ teaspoon ground cloves

Bring to a boil, stirring until the sugar is dissolved. Add the vegetables, stir to mix, and heat until the syrup just begins to boil. With a slotted spoon, pack the hot slices into the prepared jars and add the hot brine, leaving ½ inch headspace, 893. Remove any trapped air from the jars, 893, and adjust the liquid level if needed. Wipe the rims. Place lids on jars and screw on rings until fingertip-tight, 893. Process for 10 minutes. Let cool completely and store as directed, 923.

CORNICHONS (PICKLED GHERKINS)

About 8 pint jars

Please read about pickling, 922–23, and How to Process, 891.

Wash:

5½ pounds 1¼- to 2½-inch-long gherkins or baby pickling cucumbers

Cut a thin slice from the blossom ends, but leave ¼ inch of the stems. Mix together in a large bowl:

8 cups water
½ cup pickling salt

Stir until the salt is dissolved and add the cucumbers. Place a plate on the cucumbers to keep them submerged and let stand at room temperature for 12 hours.

Drain, rinse, and drain again. Pat dry with a clean towel. Prepare a water-bath canner, 893, or prepare a water bath for low-temperature canning, 893, gather all your canning equipment, 891, and have ready 8 clean, hot pint jars, 893.

Tightly pack the cucumbers into the prepared jars, adding to each jar:

5 peeled pearl onions (40 total)
A few sprigs tarragon (16 to 24 total)
(½ teaspoon mustard seeds [4 teaspoons total])
5 white or black peppercorns (40 total)

Combine in a large saucepan and bring just to a boil, stirring until the salt is dissolved:

5¼ cups white wine vinegar
4¼ cups water
⅓ cup pickling salt

Ladle over the cucumbers in the jars, leaving ½ inch headspace, 893. Remove any trapped air from the jars, 893, and adjust the liquid level if needed. Wipe the rims. Place lids on jars and screw on rings until fingertip-tight, 893. Process for 10 minutes. Let cool completely and store as directed, 923.

CHOW CHOW (SWEET-AND-SOUR CABBAGE RELISH)

About 5 pint jars

Megan grew up eating this tangy pickle on everything from hot dogs to salmon cakes to pinto beans. It adds a bit of zest to foods that need enlivening, and we heartily recommend it as a pantry staple. To make **Green Tomato Chow Chow,** substitute **2½ pounds green, unripe tomatoes** for the cabbage. Please read about pickling, 922–23, and How to Process, 891.

Prepare a water-bath canner, 893, gather all your canning equipment, 891, and have ready 5 clean, hot pint jars, 893.

Have ready:

2 pounds green cabbage, cored and finely chopped
1 red bell pepper (about 8 ounces), diced
1 green bell pepper (about 8 ounces), diced
1 green, unripe tomato (about 8 ounces), diced
1 large sweet onion (about 12 ounces), diced

Bring to a boil in a large pot:

3 cups distilled white vinegar or cider vinegar
2 cups sugar
1 tablespoon yellow mustard seeds
1 tablespoon pickling salt
2 teaspoons celery seeds
1 teaspoon ground turmeric
(1 teaspoon red pepper flakes)

Stir in the vegetables and simmer, stirring frequently, until they begin to soften, about 10 minutes. Ladle into the prepared jars and cover the vegetables with the brine, leaving ½ inch headspace, 893. Remove any trapped air from the jars, 893, and adjust the liquid level if needed. Wipe the rims. Place lids on jars and screw on rings until fingertip-tight, 893. Process for 15 minutes. Let cool completely and store as directed, 923.

TART CORN RELISH

About 5 pint jars

You may use hot or mild peppers or a combination. Please read about pickling, 922–23, and How to Process, 891.

Prepare a water-bath canner, 893, gather all your canning equipment, 891, and have ready 5 clean, hot pint jars, 893.

Combine in a large pot:

5 cups corn kernels (from about 10 medium ears corn)
2 cups diced, seeded peppers (about 1 pound)
1 large red onion (about 12 ounces), diced
1½ cups finely chopped green cabbage (about 6 ounces or ¼ small head cabbage)

Stir in:

2½ cups cider vinegar
½ cup sugar
½ cup water
¼ cup bottled lemon juice
1 tablespoon pickling salt
1 teaspoon yellow mustard seeds
1 teaspoon ground turmeric
½ teaspoon celery seeds

Mix until well blended. Bring to a boil over high heat, then reduce the heat, cover, and simmer, stirring often, for 20 minutes. Stir in:

1½ tablespoons chopped fresh dill or 1 teaspoon dried dill

Ladle into the prepared jars, leaving ½ inch headspace, 893. Remove any trapped air from the jars, 893, and adjust the liquid level if needed. Wipe the rims. Place lids on jars and screw on rings until fingertip-tight, 893. Process for 15 minutes. Let cool completely and store as directed, 923.

PICKLED OKRA

About 4 pint jars

These are easily among our favorite pickles. Okra skeptics will be pleased to hear that pickled pods are slime-free. Select the freshest okra available, and choose pods that are about the size of a large pinky finger. Larger pods tend to be tough and stringy. Please read about pickling, 922–23, and How to Process, 891.

Prepare a water-bath canner, 893, gather all your canning equipment, 891, and have ready 4 clean, hot pint jars, 893.

Wash and trim the stem ends of:

2 pounds small okra pods

Place in the bottom of each jar:

2 garlic cloves, peeled and smashed (8 total)
1 small dried red chile, such as árbol, broken open (4 total)
½ teaspoon dill seeds (2 teaspoons total)
3 black peppercorns (12 total)

Pack the okra into the jars, arranging the pods so that one layer has the stem ends facing the bottom of the jar, and a second layer has the stems facing the top to fit more okra in the jars.

Combine in a large saucepan and bring just to a boil, stirring until the salt is dissolved:

3 cups cider vinegar
3 cups water
⅓ cup pickling salt

Ladle into the prepared jars, leaving ½ inch headspace, 893. Remove any trapped air from the jars, 893, and adjust the liquid level if needed. Wipe the rims. Place lids on jars and screw on rings until fingertip-tight, 893. Process for 15 minutes. Let cool completely and store as directed, 923.

PICKLED ASPARAGUS

About 4 pint jars

As we developed this recipe, we couldn't help but notice the pile of stalks left over after trimming the asparagus to fit in the jars. We snapped off the woody ends and reserved the short, tender pieces. It was serendipitous—we wound up with just enough tender stalk pieces to fill a fourth jar. While not as beautiful as the asparagus tops, the flavor is excellent, and the thicker ends of the stalks hold up well to the canning process. Please read about pickling, 922–23, and How to Process, 891.

Prepare a water-bath canner, 893, gather all your canning equipment, 891, and have ready 4 clean, hot pint jars, 893.

Wash and trim the woody ends from:

3 pounds asparagus

Cut the asparagus 4 inches from the tip and reserve any short, tender stalk pieces. Have an ice water bath ready. Blanch the asparagus tips in boiling water for 30 seconds and transfer to the ice water bath to cool. Drain well. Blanch the reserved stalk pieces for 1 minute and transfer to the ice water bath to cool. Drain well and keep separated from the tips.

Bring to a boil in a medium saucepan:

3 cups white wine vinegar
3 cups water
3 tablespoons pickling salt
1½ tablespoons sugar

Place in each prepared jar:

1 garlic clove, peeled and smashed (4 total)
1 sprig thyme (4 total)
½ teaspoon fennel seeds (2 teaspoons total)
One 3 × ½-inch strip orange zest, removed with a vegetable peeler (4 total)

Pack 3 of the jars with the asparagus tips and pack the stalk pieces into the fourth jar. Ladle the hot brine into the prepared jars, leaving ½ inch headspace, 893. Remove any trapped air from the jars, 893, and adjust the liquid level if needed. Wipe the rims. Place lids on jars and screw on rings until fingertip-tight, 893. Process for 10 minutes. Let cool completely and store as directed, 923.

DILLY BEANS

About 4 pint jars

Please read about pickling, 922–23, and How to Process, 891.

Prepare a water-bath canner, 893, gather all your canning equipment, 891, and have ready 4 clean, hot pint jars, 893.

Wash and trim (the beans should be no more than 4 inches long):

2 pounds plump green beans

Place in each jar:

3 sprigs dill or ½ teaspoon dill seeds (12 sprigs or 2 teaspoons total)
(1 garlic clove, peeled [4 total])
(¼ teaspoon red pepper flakes or ⅛ teaspoon cayenne pepper [1 teaspoon pepper flakes or ½ teaspoon cayenne pepper total])

Tightly pack the beans upright in the jars. Combine in a medium saucepan and bring to a boil:

2 cups distilled white vinegar
2 cups water
¼ cup pickling salt

Ladle into the prepared jars, leaving ½ inch headspace, 893. Remove any trapped air from the jars, 893, and adjust the liquid level if needed. Wipe the rims. Place lids on jars and screw on rings until fingertip-tight, 893. Process for 10 minutes. Let cool completely and store as directed, 923.

PICKLED RED OR GOLDEN BEETS

About 4 pint jars

Please read about pickling, 922–23, and How to Process, 891.

Prepare a water-bath canner, 893, gather all your canning equipment, 891, and have ready 4 clean, hot pint jars, 893.

Wash, then trim the tops and roots to 1 inch:

2½ pounds red or golden beets of uniform size (1 to 2½ inches wide)

Place in a saucepan, cover with water, and simmer just until tender, 30 to 40 minutes. Drain, reserving ¾ cup of the cooking liquid (discard the rest). Remove the stems, roots, and skins. Leave baby beets under 1½ inches whole. Cut large beets into ¼-inch-thick slices or wedges.

Peel, thinly slice, and set aside:

1 medium onion

Transfer the reserved beet cooking liquid to a wide pot and add:

2 cups cider vinegar
¼ cup bottled lemon juice
⅔ cup sugar
2 teaspoons black peppercorns
2 tablespoons pickling salt

Bring to a boil, stirring until the sugar is dissolved. Add the beets and onions and simmer for 5 minutes. Using a slotted spoon, pack the vegetables into the prepared jars, then add the hot vinegar solution, leaving ½ inch headspace, 893. Remove any trapped air from the jars, 893, and adjust the liquid level if needed. Wipe the rims. Place lids on jars and screw on rings until fingertip-tight, 893. Process for 10 minutes. Let cool completely and store as directed, 923.

LEMONY PICKLED TURNIPS

About 4 pint jars

Dulse, 1016, adds a savory, briny flavor to the turnips, but this pickle is still delicious without it. Please read about pickling, 922–23, and How to Process, 891.

Prepare a water-bath canner, 893, gather all your canning equipment, 891, and have ready 4 clean, hot pint jars, 893.

Have ready:

2½ pounds turnips, peeled and cut into ½-inch-thick wedges

Bring to a boil in a medium saucepan, stirring to dissolve the sugar:

3½ cups white wine vinegar
⅓ cup sugar
1½ tablespoons pickling salt

Using a vegetable peeler, remove the zest in wide strips from:

1 medium lemon

Cut the strips crosswise into thin slivers and divide among the prepared jars. Place in each jar:

(½ teaspoon dulse flakes [2 teaspoons total])
¼ teaspoon red pepper flakes (1 teaspoon total)

Pack the turnips into the jars and cover with hot brine, leaving ½ inch headspace, 893. Remove any trapped air from the jars, 893, and adjust the liquid level if needed. Wipe the rims. Place lids on jars and screw on rings until fingertip-tight, 893. Process for 15 minutes. Let cool completely and store as directed, 923.

PICKLED SHIITAKE MUSHROOMS

About 2 pint jars

These pickles are not only delicious on their own, they are excellent atop herbed sour cream on Crostini, 49, or drain them well, sauté with shallots and garlic, and serve over Creamy Polenta, 322. Please read about pickling, 922–23, and How to Process, 891.

Prepare a water-bath canner, 893, gather all your canning equipment, 891, and have ready 2 clean, hot pint jars, 893.

Brush off any dirt from:

1 pound shiitake mushrooms, stems discarded

For large shiitakes, slice or quarter the caps. Smaller shiitakes can be left whole. Set aside.

Bring to a boil in a large saucepan:

2 cups white wine vinegar
½ cup water
2 medium shallots, thinly sliced
4 garlic cloves, smashed
1 tablespoon pickling salt
1 teaspoon black peppercorns
4 sprigs thyme
½ teaspoon red pepper flakes
2 bay leaves

Stir in the mushrooms, cover, and reduce the heat to simmer gently for 15 minutes. Remove from the heat and ladle the mushrooms and brine into the prepared jars, leaving ½ inch headspace, 893. Remove any trapped air from the jars, 893, and adjust the liquid level if needed. Wipe the rims. Place lids on jars and screw on rings until fingertip-tight, 893. Process for 15 minutes. Let cool completely and store as directed, 923.

PICKLED PEPPERS

About 5 pint jars

We recommend wearing gloves when processing hot peppers. Please read about pickling, 922–23, and How to Process, 891.

I. WHOLE PEPPERS

Small, slender peppers like Hungarian wax and jalapeños are classic choices for pickling whole, as are small, round cherry peppers. For the masochistic, Scotch bonnets and habaneros may be used here, too.

Wash well:

2¼ pounds whole jalapeño, serrano, Fresno, Hungarian wax, or other small hot peppers

Cut lengthwise slits into each pepper on opposite sides and lightly flatten. Prepare a water-bath canner, 893, gather all your canning equipment, 891, and have ready 5 clean, hot pint jars, 893. Add to each jar:

2 garlic cloves, smashed (10 total)
(½ teaspoon dried oregano [2½ teaspoons total])
(½ teaspoon mustard seeds or cumin seeds, or both [2½ teaspoons total])
(½ bay leaf [2½ total])

Fill the prepared jars with the peppers. Bring to a boil in a large saucepan:

4 cups distilled white vinegar
1 cup water
2 tablespoons pickling salt
(2 tablespoons sugar)

Stir to dissolve the salt. Pour over the peppers in the jars, then wait as the brine slowly seeps into the hollow interior of the peppers. Once finished, top the jars off with more brine, leaving ½ inch headspace, 893. Remove any trapped air from the jars, 893, and adjust the liquid level once more if needed. Wipe the rims. Place lids on jars and screw on rings until fingertip-tight, 893. Process for 15 minutes. Let cool completely and store as directed, 923.

II. SLICED PEPPER RINGS OR CHIPS

Longer types that do not fit in a pint jar, such as banana peppers, are best sliced. For those who wish to pickle jalapeños without any seeds or white pith, we recommend cutting them into "chips" (any slender, thick-walled pepper—such as Fresnos and serranos—may be cut in the same way).

Prepare the water bath, equipment, and jars as for version I.

For rings, wash the same amount of peppers as above and cut them crosswise into ¼- to ½-inch-thick slices. Transfer to a large bowl and add cold water to cover by several inches. Wearing gloves, agitate them to free any loose seeds, which will float. You may skim the seeds from the top with a slotted spoon or mesh strainer, or simply remove the slices from the water, leaving the seeds behind. Drain in a colander and rinse (any remaining seeds will collect in the bottom of the colander).

For chips, wash 3 pounds small, slender peppers, such as jalapeños. Cut the peppers by "squaring the circle": Lay a pepper on its side and cut it lengthwise, just off-center, so the blade just misses the seeds. Rotate the pepper onto its cut side and slice lengthwise and off-center again. Rotate and repeat until all that is left is the seedy center and stem, and 4 oblong "chips" of pepper flesh (see the illustration, 261). Discard the centers and brush off any remaining seeds.

To pack, add garlic and spices to the prepared jars as for version I. For rings, pack tightly into the jars, pushing down to compact them. For chips, arrange them to stand upright in the jars. Add brine, cover, and process as for version I.

PICKLED GARLIC

About 6 half-pint jars

Although labor-intensive to prepare, these pickles will delight any garlic lover. They are delicious on their own, and try them chopped and added to chicken or potato salad or Treva's Pimiento Cheese, 55. Please read about pickling, 922–23, and How to Process, 891.

Prepare a water-bath canner, 893, gather all your canning equipment, 891, and have ready 6 clean, hot half-pint jars, 893.

Have a bowl of ice water ready. Bring a large saucepan of water to a boil and add:

Unpeeled cloves from 2 pounds garlic

Blanch the garlic for 2 minutes, drain well, and transfer to the ice water. When cool, peel the garlic.

Place in the bottom of each prepared jar:

¼ teaspoon red pepper flakes (1½ teaspoons total)
¼ teaspoon mustard seeds (1½ teaspoons total)
¼ teaspoon dried dill (1½ teaspoons total)

Pack the cloves into the jars. Bring to a boil in a medium saucepan:

1½ cups distilled white vinegar
1½ cups water
2 tablespoons pickling salt

Pour over the garlic, leaving ½ inch headspace, 893. Remove any trapped air from the jars, 893, and adjust the liquid level if needed. Wipe the rims. Place lids on the jars and screw on rings until fingertip-tight, 893. Process for 10 minutes. Let cool completely and store as directed, 923.

PICKLED GARLIC SCAPES

About 2 pint jars

Garlic scapes, sometimes called garlic whistles, are fanciful, curly protrusions that grow out of the center of hardneck garlic plants in early summer. They are cut off to allow the garlic bulb to grow larger, and they happen to be quite delicious. Look for them at farmers' markets and natural foods grocery stores. Please read about pickling, 922–23, and How to Process, 891.

Prepare a water-bath canner, 893, gather all your canning equipment, 891, and have ready 2 clean, hot pint jars, 893.

Wash and trim off the woody ends and yellowed tips from:

1 pound garlic scapes

Cut the scapes into 4-inch pieces. If they are curly, we like to trim the curly tops and use those to line the inside edge of the jar and stick the straight parts of the scape in the center.

Place in each prepared jar:

1 teaspoon coriander seeds (2 teaspoons total)
1 teaspoon mustard seeds (2 teaspoons total)
1 teaspoon red pepper flakes (2 teaspoons total)

Tightly pack the scapes in the jars. Bring to a boil in a small saucepan:

1 cup cider vinegar
1 cup water
1 tablespoon plus 1½ teaspoons pickling salt

Divide the brine between the jars, leaving ½ inch headspace, 893. Remove any trapped air from the jars, 893, and adjust the liquid level if needed. Wipe the rims. Place lids on jars and screw on rings until fingertip-tight, 893. Process for 10 minutes. Let cool completely and store as directed, 923.

PICKLED WATERMELON RIND

About 5 pint jars

An American invention, crunchy and refreshing. The 3-day process is well worth the wait, especially to homesick Southerners. Please read about pickling, 922–23, and How to Process, 891.

Wash, then cut lengthwise into eighths:

10 pounds watermelons with thick, firm rinds

The flesh will not get crisp, so scrape off all but a thin layer of flesh (for a touch of color), then peel the outer green skin off the rind. (Refrigerate the watermelon flesh for another use.) Cut the rind into 1-inch-wide pieces. Blanch in boiling water until the pieces are tender yet slightly crisp at the center when pierced with a skewer, about 10 minutes—do not overcook. Drain and place in a large bowl.

Combine in a large saucepan and bring just to a boil, stirring until the sugar is dissolved:

3½ cups sugar
1 cup distilled white vinegar
1 cinnamon stick
1 teaspoon whole cloves

Pour the syrup over the rind pieces, just covering them. Cover and let sit in the refrigerator overnight.

The next day, drain the syrup back into the pan, bring just to a boil, and pour again over the rind pieces. Cover and let sit overnight as before.

The third day, prepare a water-bath canner, 893, gather all your canning equipment, 891, and have ready 5 clean, hot pint jars, 893. Bring the syrup and rind pieces to a boil in a pot. Pack the hot rind pieces into the prepared jars, then add the syrup, leaving ½ inch headspace, 893. If desired, add to each jar:

(1 whole star anise [5 total])
(1 or 2 slices ginger or strips of lemon zest, removed with a vegetable peeler [5 to 10 total])

Remove any trapped air from the jars, 893, and adjust the liquid level if needed. Wipe the rims. Place lids on jars and screw on rings until fingertip-tight, 893. Process for 10 minutes. Let cool completely and store as directed, 923.

PICKLED GRAPES

6 half-pint jars

Use your favorite table grape in this recipe. We recommend grapes with a good balance of sweetness and acidity. The resulting pickles are wonderful as part of a cheese plate. Please read about pickling, 922–23, and How to Process, 891.

Prepare a water-bath canner, 893, gather all your canning equipment, 891, and have ready 6 clean, hot half-pint jars, 893.

Place in each jar:

¼ teaspoon coriander seeds (1½ teaspoons total), preferably toasted in a dry pan
¼ teaspoon red pepper flakes (1½ teaspoons total)
1 whole clove (6 total)

One ¼-inch slice ginger (6 slices total)
1 garlic clove, peeled and crushed (6 total)

Pack into the jars:

4 cups grapes (about 1½ pounds)

Combine in a medium saucepan and bring to a boil, stirring to dissolve the sugar:

2 cups distilled white or cider vinegar
1 cup sugar
1 tablespoon pickling salt

Divide among the prepared jars, leaving ½ inch headspace, 893. Remove any trapped air from the jars, 893, and adjust the liquid level if needed. Wipe the rims. Place lids on jars and screw on rings until fingertip-tight, 893. Process for 10 minutes. Let cool completely and store as directed, 923.

PICKLED PEACHES

About 6 pint jars

A classic from the first edition of *Joy*. Tree-ripened peaches produce the fullest flavor. Please read about pickling, 922–23, and How to Process, 891.

Wash:

8 pounds ripe but firm, small clingstone peaches, peeled, 167, halved, and pitted

Place in an antibrowning solution, 896. Combine in a large pot and bring to a boil, stirring until the sugar is dissolved:

4 cups cider vinegar
3 cups sugar

Tie together in a square of cheesecloth:

Three 2-inch cinnamon sticks
1 teaspoon whole cloves

Add the spices to the syrup. Drain the peaches well and add them to the syrup. Simmer until just tender enough to be pierced with a thin skewer, about 5 minutes—do not overcook. Pour into a bowl, let cool completely, cover, and refrigerate overnight.

Prepare a water-bath canner, 893, gather all your canning equipment, 891, and have ready 6 clean, hot pint jars, 893. Bring the peaches and syrup to a boil, stirring. Remove the spice bag. Using a slotted spoon, pack the hot peaches into the prepared jars, then add the hot syrup, leaving ½ inch headspace, 893. Remove any trapped air from the jars, 893, and adjust the liquid level if needed. Wipe the rims. Place lids on jars and screw on rings until fingertip-tight, 893. Process for 20 minutes. Let cool completely and store as directed, 923.

ABOUT QUICK OR REFRIGERATOR PICKLES

If hot brine is simply poured over fruits or vegetables, the resulting pickles can be kept in the refrigerator for up to 2 months. This method is a great way to enjoy all the flavors of homemade pickles without the hassle of canning. In many cases, such as with tender fruits and vegetables like cherry tomatoes, quick pickling helps preserve texture. Any of the pickle recipes in this chapter may be treated as quick pickles with the important caveat that ➤ they must be refrigerated. Of course, larger recipes should be halved (or scaled down even more) depending on the amount of refrigerator space you are willing to relinquish.

QUICK-PICKLED VEGETABLES

1 pint jar

Quick pickles are ideal for those with a fear of canning commitment, or for experimental pickling with very small batch sizes.

Wash and prepare:

½ pound vegetables, such as green beans, trimmed; radishes, sliced or quartered; cucumbers, sliced; carrots, sliced or cut into matchsticks; onions, thinly sliced; peppers, seeded and sliced; fennel, thinly shaved; etc.

Place any of the following in the bottom of a clean pint jar, above or in combination:

1 garlic clove, smashed
Up to 2 teaspoons mixed spices, such as pickling spice, or a combination of cumin seeds, coriander seeds, mustard seeds, black peppercorns, etc.
1 teaspoon dried herbs, such as dill or thyme
1 sprig fresh herb such as thyme, dill, tarragon, savory, etc.

Pack the vegetables in the jar. Bring to a boil in a small saucepan:

½ cup distilled white, cider, white wine or red wine, or rice vinegar
½ cup water
1 teaspoon salt
(1½ teaspoons sugar)

Pour the brine into the jar. Let cool completely, cover, and refrigerate. Let sit for 2 days before using and use within 2 months.

QUICK SICHUAN-STYLE CUCUMBER PICKLES

About 1 quart jar

These spicy pickles go especially well with Braised Pulled Pork, 495, and other rich meats. For a milder pickle, halve the amounts of Sichuan peppercorns and dried chiles.

Halve lengthwise and cut diagonally into thin slices:

1 pound English or Persian cucumbers

Place the cucumber slices in a medium bowl and toss well with:

½ teaspoon salt

Transfer to a colander in the sink and let drain for 1 hour. Meanwhile, add to the bowl:

1⅓ cups rice vinegar
3 tablespoons sugar
3 garlic cloves, thinly sliced
1-inch piece ginger, peeled and thinly sliced or julienned
2 teaspoons salt

Stir until the salt and sugar have dissolved and set aside. Heat in a small skillet or saucepan over medium heat until hot:

1½ tablespoons vegetable oil
1½ tablespoons toasted sesame oil

Add and fry, stirring frequently, until the dried chiles are just beginning to darken, about 30 seconds:

8 small dried red chiles, such as árbol or cayenne
1½ teaspoons Sichuan peppercorns
1 teaspoon mustard seeds
(1 teaspoon white peppercorns)

Carefully and quickly pour the oil and fried spices into the vinegar mixture.

After the cucumbers have drained, rinse well, drain again, and add to the brine. Let steep for a few hours, then serve or pack into a clean quart jar. Store refrigerated for up to 2 months.

PICKLED GINGER

I. *About 1 quart jar*

A favorite garnish for sushi and delicate fish or shellfish dishes. Sweet and spicy, these slices can also add a nice zing to salads and sauces. If at all possible, ➤ try to find young ginger as it will not be as fibrous.

Peel and thinly slice:

1 pound ginger

Pack into a clean quart jar. Bring to a boil in a large saucepan:

1¼ cups rice vinegar
½ cup sugar
½ cup mirin
1½ teaspoons salt

Pour over the ginger. Let cool, cover, and refrigerate for at least 1 week and for up to 3 months.

II. BENI SHŌGA

About 1 pint jar

This brightly hued pickle is commonly served with Okonomiyaki, 226, and Yakisoba, 302.

Bring a large saucepan of water to a boil. While the water heats up, peel and slice into ⅛-inch-thick rounds:

8 ounces ginger

Stack the ginger rounds and cut into ⅛-inch-thick matchsticks. Blanch the ginger in the water for 30 seconds, then drain well. Transfer the ginger to a clean pint jar. If available, add:

(2 red shiso leaves)

Bring to a boil in a small saucepan:

1 cup umezu (ume vinegar), 1031
2 teaspoons salt

Pour over the ginger, cover, let cool completely, and refrigerate. Let sit for at least 1 day. Store refrigerated for up to 2 months.

PICKLED HORSERADISH

About 1 pint jar

Wash well:

12 ounces horseradish

Scrape off the skin. Grate or mince the horseradish (the fine shredding disk of a food processor works well). Bring to a boil in a small saucepan:

1 cup distilled white vinegar
½ teaspoon salt

Pack the horseradish into a clean pint jar and pour the vinegar mixture over it. Refrigerate overnight. If desired, for horseradish with a creamy consistency, transfer the horseradish to a food processor or blender and process or blend until finely ground, adding a little more vinegar if necessary. Store refrigerated for up to 1 year.

QUICK-PICKLED ONIONS

About 1 pint jar

For tacos, nachos, sandwiches, salads, or anywhere a punchy pickled garnish is needed. Feel free to vary the seasonings. For instance, add fresh tarragon and mustard seeds, or dried chiles and Garam Masala, 558.

Peel, halve through the stem end, and trim the ends off:

1 medium yellow or red onion

Very thinly slice lengthwise (pole-to-pole). Place the onion in a small saucepan with:

1 cup distilled white or cider vinegar
1 teaspoon salt
½ teaspoon sugar
(1 bay leaf)
(1 small dried red chile, seeded)

Bring to a simmer and cook for 3 minutes. Transfer immediately to a bowl and stir in:

4 standard, freezer-tray ice cubes (equivalent to ½ cup frozen water)

Stir to melt the ice cubes and cool the pickle. Use immediately or transfer to a clean pint jar or container and store refrigerated for up to 1 month.

QUICK PICKLED BEETS

About 1 quart jar

Prepare or have ready:

4 medium beets (about 1½ pounds), cooked, 219, peeled, and sliced

Place the beets in a clean quart jar. Combine in a medium saucepan and bring to a boil:

1 cup cider vinegar
1 cup beet cooking liquid or water
1 small onion, thinly sliced
¼ cup sugar
10 black peppercorns
6 whole cloves
2 bay leaves
1 teaspoon salt
(1 teaspoon prepared horseradish)

Pour over the beets. Let cool, cover, and refrigerate for at least 12 hours before serving. Store refrigerated for up to 1 month.

JALAPEÑOS EN ESCABECHE (TAQUERIA PICKLES)

About 1 quart jar

These tangy pickles are a natural with rich meats like Braised Carnitas, 495, or Braised Pulled Pork, 495. We recommend wearing gloves while handling the jalapeños.

Combine and pack into a clean quart jar:

12 jalapeño peppers, seeded and cut into large "chips" (as for Pickled Peppers II, 927)
3 medium carrots, cut on the diagonal into ¼-inch-thick slices
½ medium onion, thinly sliced

Bring to a boil in a medium saucepan:

1½ cups cider vinegar or distilled white vinegar
1 cup water
6 garlic cloves, smashed
1 tablespoon salt
1½ teaspoons black peppercorns
1½ teaspoons dried Mexican oregano
1 bay leaf
½ teaspoon cumin seeds
(2 whole cloves)

Pour the brine over the vegetables and let sit at room temperature until completely cooled. Cover and refrigerate for at least 4 hours, preferably overnight. Store refrigerated for up to 1 month.

PICKLED CHERRIES

About 1 pint jar

Adapted from the 1975 edition, this pickle is not technically "quick," but it is not processed in a water bath in order to preserve the texture of the cherries. Sugaring the cherries helps firm them up and creates a rich, cherry-flavored syrup.

Stem, pit, and place in a clean quart jar:

1 pound sour or sweet cherries

Add to cover the cherries:

Distilled white vinegar

Cover and let stand, refrigerated, for 24 hours. Drain, reserving the vinegar. Layer the cherries in the same jar with:

1¼ cups sugar

The cherries should be coated in sugar. Let stand for 1 week, covered and refrigerated. Shake the jar daily. The sugar may not completely dissolve. This is okay.

Set a sieve over a small saucepan and drain the cherries. Place the cherries in a hot, clean pint jar. Add the reserved vinegar to the sugar in the saucepan and bring to a boil. Pour over the cherries to cover. Let cool completely and store refrigerated for up to 6 months.

ABOUT KETCHUP, CATSUPS, AND CHUTNEYS

Ketchup comes to us from Southeast Asia by way of Britain. Early examples, which were called catsups, were thin, sharp, and dark, resembling soy and Worcestershire sauces, in contrast to the fire-engine-red ketchup that comes to mind for most Americans. Some were concocted from tomato juice, but many were based on mushrooms, walnuts, anchovies, or oysters. Mushroom Catsup, 932, and Walnut Catsup, 932, give a sense of the early English catsups. For a quick, small-batch tomato ketchup, see Quick Ketchup, 565. For other chutneys, see Cilantro-Mint Chutney, 568, Tamarind Chutney, 566, and Tomato Achar, 569.

TOMATO KETCHUP

About 5 pint jars

One taste of homemade ketchup and you will understand why it is worth taking the time to prepare. Please read about pickling, 922–23, and How to Process, 891.

Simmer in a large pot over medium heat, stirring occasionally, until very soft, about 30 minutes:

7 pounds tomatoes, chopped
4 medium onions, sliced
1 red bell pepper, diced
4 garlic cloves, peeled

Puree in a food mill fitted with the medium disk, then return to the pot. Stir in:

⅓ cup packed light brown sugar
1 teaspoon ground mace
½ teaspoon dry mustard

Tie in a square of cheesecloth and add to the tomato mixture:

1 cinnamon stick
1½ teaspoons allspice berries
1½ teaspoons whole cloves
1½ teaspoons celery seeds
1½ teaspoons black peppercorns
1 bay leaf

Bring to a rolling boil, then reduce to a simmer. Cook until the sauce is reduced by half, stirring often to prevent scorching. Remove and discard the spice bag. Stir in:

1 cup cider vinegar
Salt to taste
(Cayenne pepper to taste)

Reduce the heat and simmer, stirring almost constantly, for 10 minutes or until the ketchup is thick enough to be mounded on a spoon. Prepare a water-bath canner, 893, gather all your canning equipment, 891, and have ready 5 clean, hot pint jars, 893. Pack the hot ketchup into the prepared jars, leaving ¼ inch headspace, 893. Remove any trapped air from the jars, 893, and adjust the level of the ketchup if needed. Wipe the rims. Place lids on jars and screw on rings until fingertip-tight, 893. Process for 15 minutes. Let cool completely and store as directed, 923.

CHILI SAUCE

About 4 pint jars

This classic American condiment is tomato ketchup's chunkier, more piquant cousin. For a spicy chile-based sauce, see Sriracha, 572. Please read about pickling, 922–23, and How to Process, 891.

Chop medium-fine in batches in a food processor:

3 red bell peppers, coarsely chopped
3 large onions, coarsely chopped

Put in a large pot and stir in:

7 pounds tomatoes, peeled, 281, seeded, and chopped
1½ cups cider vinegar
1 cup packed light brown sugar
1 tablespoon salt
1½ teaspoons black pepper
1½ teaspoons ground allspice
½ teaspoon ground cinnamon
½ teaspoon ground cloves
½ teaspoon ground ginger
½ teaspoon grated or ground nutmeg
½ teaspoon celery seeds

Stir to blend thoroughly, then bring to a boil over medium heat. Simmer, stirring often to prevent scorching, until thick, about 3 hours. Adjust the seasonings to taste.

Prepare a water-bath canner, 893, gather all your canning equipment, 891, and have ready 4 clean, hot pint jars, 893. Pack the hot sauce into the prepared jars, leaving ½ inch headspace, 893. Remove any trapped air from the jars, 893, and adjust the level of the chili sauce if needed. Wipe the rims. Place lids on jars and screw on rings until fingertip-tight, 893. Process for 15 minutes. Let cool completely and store as directed, 923.

MUSHROOM CATSUP

About 3 half-pint jars

This English condiment is thin, pungent, and deeply flavored. Please read about pickling, 922–23, and How to Process, 891.

Wash and coarsely chop:

4 pounds mushrooms, preferably cremini

Spread the mushrooms out in a large baking dish and sprinkle with:

½ cup salt

Cover and refrigerate, stirring occasionally, for 2 days.

Drain the mushrooms and rinse well. Combine in a large saucepan with:

1 cup red wine vinegar
⅔ cup cider vinegar
1 medium red onion, finely chopped
1 garlic clove, finely chopped
½ teaspoon black pepper
¼ teaspoon ground allspice
¼ teaspoon ground ginger
¼ teaspoon grated or ground nutmeg

Bring to a boil, then reduce the heat and simmer uncovered, stirring often, until very fragrant, flavorful, and reduced by half, about 30 minutes.

Prepare a water-bath canner, 893, gather all your canning equipment, 891, and have ready 3 clean, hot half-pint jars, 893. Strain through a fine-mesh sieve, then again through a sieve lined with several layers of cheesecloth or a thin kitchen towel. Pour the hot catsup into the prepared jars, leaving ½ inch headspace, 893. Wipe the rims. Place lids on jars and screw on rings until fingertip-tight, 893. Process for 15 minutes. Let cool completely and store as directed, 923.

WALNUT CATSUP

About 5 cups

This unusual recipe is a glimpse into catsups past, partway through their journey from Southeast Asia to America. The consistency and flavor of this catsup is similar to Worcestershire sauce. While green walnuts are hard to find commercially, they are incredibly abundant in late spring or early summer, if you can find a good-sized tree in your neighborhood or a friend's backyard. While you're out gathering green walnuts for this recipe, pick some up for Nocino, 949.

Pick while still soft enough to be cut through easily:

3½ pounds immature green English walnuts (about 100)

Quarter them with a knife and put into a gallon-sized jar or crock with:

2 quarts vinegar (malt, cider, distilled white, or a combination)
⅔ cup salt (6 ounces)

Cover and let steep for 8 days, stirring and mashing the nuts with the back of a spoon daily. Transfer the walnuts and vinegar to a pot, bring to a boil, and simmer for 15 minutes. Strain the liquid and discard the walnuts. Return the liquid to the pot and add:

12 shallots (about 2 pounds), peeled and coarsely chopped
½ cup finely chopped anchovies (about 4 ounces)
3 ounces fresh horseradish, peeled and finely chopped
2-inch piece ginger, peeled and finely chopped
1 teaspoon black peppercorns
½ teaspoon ground mace
½ teaspoon grated or ground nutmeg
8 whole cloves

Bring to a boil. Reduce the heat to a gentle simmer and cook for 40 minutes. Strain through a fine-mesh sieve, then strain again through a sieve lined with a thin kitchen towel. Let cool completely and add:

2 cups port

Transfer to clean jars or glass bottles and store refrigerated for up to 1 year.

WORCESTERSHIRE SAUCE

About 7 cups

Feel free to scale the recipe down, but after 4 weeks of waiting you might want to have a sizable supply of sauce to reward your efforts and patience. For a vegan version, omit the anchovies and double the amount of dried shiitakes.

Combine in a large saucepan:

3 cups malt vinegar
1 cup molasses
1 cup soy sauce
2 large onions, chopped
½ cup lemon juice
½ cup water
½ cup tamarind extract or concentrate
½ cup yellow mustard seeds
8 garlic cloves, chopped
2 tablespoons cracked black peppercorns
2 tablespoons red pepper flakes
1-inch piece ginger, peeled and finely chopped
1 tablespoon salt
1 tablespoon whole cloves
1 tablespoon coriander seeds
5 anchovy fillets, chopped
6 dried shiitake mushrooms
5 green cardamom pods, crushed
2 cinnamon sticks

Bring to a boil, then reduce the heat and simmer gently for 30 minutes. Meanwhile, warm over medium heat in a skillet, stirring frequently:

1½ cups sugar

The sugar will melt and turn deep brown, about 7 minutes. Slowly and carefully pour the caramelized sugar into the simmering mixture (it will sizzle and spit, so back up a little). Remove from the heat and let cool to room temperature. Transfer to a covered container or jar and refrigerate for 4 weeks.

Strain the sauce twice. First through a fine-mesh sieve, then through a fine-mesh sieve lined with a thin kitchen towel. Transfer to clean bottles or jars. The sauce will keep refrigerated for up to 1 year.

CURRIED APRICOT CHUTNEY

About 2 pint jars

Please read about pickling, 922–23, and How to Process, 891.

Combine in a large saucepan and simmer for 30 minutes:

2 cups water
2 cups chopped dried apricots
¾ cup finely chopped onion
¼ cup sugar

Meanwhile, combine in a small pan and simmer for 5 minutes:

1½ cups cider vinegar
1½ to 2½ teaspoons curry powder, to taste
1 teaspoon ground ginger
1 cinnamon stick
½ teaspoon salt

Remove the cinnamon stick and combine the vinegar mixture and the apricot mixture. Stir in:

2 cups golden raisins

Prepare a water-bath canner, 893, gather all your canning equipment, 891, and have ready 2 clean, hot pint jars, 893. Pack the hot chutney into the prepared jars, leaving ½ inch headspace, 893. Remove any trapped air from the jars, 893, and adjust the level of the chutney if needed. Wipe the rims. Place lids on jars and screw on rings until fingertip-tight, 893. Process for 10 minutes. Let cool completely and store as directed, 923.

APPLE OR GREEN TOMATO CHUTNEY

About 3 pint jars

Please read about pickling, 922–23, and How to Process, 891.

Combine in a large saucepan:

5 cups chopped peeled firm apples or firm green, unripe tomatoes
2¼ cups packed brown sugar
2 cups cider vinegar
(2 red bell peppers, chopped)
1 lemon, seeded and chopped
1½ cups raisins
¼ cup chopped peeled ginger
1½ teaspoons salt
1 garlic clove, chopped
¼ teaspoon cayenne pepper

Simmer, stirring frequently, until the sauce has thickened enough to be mounded on a spoon, at least 2 hours. Prepare a water-bath canner, 893, gather all your canning equipment, 891, and have ready 3 clean, hot pint jars, 893. Pack the hot chutney into the prepared jars, leaving ½ inch headspace, 893. Remove any trapped air from the jars, 893, and adjust the level of the chutney if needed. Wipe the rims. Place lids on jars and screw on rings until fingertip-tight, 893. Process for 15 minutes. Let cool completely and store as directed, 923.

SALTING, DRYING, AND FERMENTING

These preservation methods predate refrigeration and canning technology. With the exception of especially well-dried foods, 943, and those steeped in alcohol, 948, using these techniques at home will not produce truly shelf-stable results. As with other ancient preservation techniques like smoking, 1067, we offer these here because of the unique flavors they produce. We think the small amount of effort needed to make them—as well as the extra refrigerator space required to store them—is well worth the tasty results.

ABOUT SALTING AND CURING

The first three methods described in this chapter—salting, meat-curing, and fermentation—rely on salt to inhibit the growth of bacteria. The preservative effect of salt is largely due to its ability to reduce the amount of water available to bacteria in foods, or **water activity.** When salt is introduced to animal and plant cells, the water within the cells is attracted to and pulled out by the salt through osmosis. The water then dissolves the salt and forms a solution, or brine.

After the water is pulled out, the levels of salt within and outside the food will reach equilibrium in a process called **diffusion.** If the salt solution is allowed to drain off or evaporate, foods can lose a significant amount of their moisture (and weight). Examples of this include dry-cured meats, 936, or the salting step for Pepperoncini Sott'olio (Calabrian-Style Chiles), 935. If the food is buried in a sufficient amount of salt, the moisture will be completely absorbed by it, resulting in a very dry environment that effectively desiccates foods (see Salted Egg Yolks, 935).

In fruits and vegetables, adding salt limits the types of bacteria that can survive. The mere presence of salt will increase pressure on some salt-sensitive microbes, which prevents them from feeding or reproducing. If the vegetables are submerged in a brine, this robs the environment of oxygen as well, which limits even further the pool of bacteria that will thrive. The salt level and lack of oxygen encourages "friendly" *Lactobacillus* bacteria to grow, which convert any available sugar into acidic by-products. As the process continues, the salted, oxygen-starved, and increasingly acidic environment keeps other, potentially harmful bacteria from becoming established. For a more detailed description of this process, see About Fermentation, 938.

In the case of meats, eggs, and other protein-rich foods, the presence of salt binds water to the protein molecules, thereby reducing water activity and making it unavailable to the bacteria that need it to survive. The high levels of salt required for making country hams and other dry-cured meats also denatures proteins, which helps keep them (relatively) tender. For more, see About Curing Meat, 936.

Below are recipes for salting and curing foods without the aid of curing salts, a dehydrator, or the "pickling" effects of fermentation. To cure your own salmon, see Gravlax, 393; for information on cooking with salt cod and other heavily salted fish, see About Smoked and Preserved Fish, 392. A note on salt: Flaky Diamond kosher salt is much easier to distribute evenly when salting foods and contains no additives, which is why we call for it exclusively in some of the recipes below.

PEPPERONCINI SOTT'OLIO (CALABRIAN-STYLE CHILES)

About 1 quart infused vinegar, 2 cups infused oil, and 2 cups peppers

This recipe uses several preservation techniques: The peppers are salted and drained overnight, pickled, then partially dried, and "confited" in olive oil. Each step helps reduce the chance of spoilage, first by driving out moisture, then acidifying the peppers, and drying once more. Finally, submerging the peppers in olive oil protects them from oxidizing or growing molds that need air to survive. After all this, the peppers are still not considered shelf-stable by the USDA and must be refrigerated.

So why do it? Though these delectable chiles take multiple days to prepare, once the raw peppers are slit open and seeded, there is very little labor involved. More importantly, you get three wonderful ingredients from one batch of peppers: a briny, chile-infused vinegar (use as you would any hot sauce; it is especially good sprinkled on cooked greens); chile-infused olive oil (perfect for bread dipping or marinating vegetables and cheese); and tangy, moderately spicy chiles (superb for topping pizzas and pasta dishes). Try this procedure once and we are confident you will be doing it every year. As for peppers, we prefer them to be ripe, red, and moderately spicy, though green, yellow, or super-hot chiles will certainly work.

Wearing protective gloves, trim off any long stems and slit open lengthwise on one side:

1 pound fresh red chiles, such as serrano, Fresno, or jalapeño

Scoop out most of the seeds and white ribs. Pour into a medium heatproof bowl:

½ cup (67g) Diamond kosher salt

Press each chile into the salt, making sure each one is thoroughly coated on the inside. Place the chiles in a colander as you work. When all the chiles have been treated this way, toss the chiles with any remaining salt and place the colander over the bowl. Cover and let the chiles drain overnight.

In the morning, discard any liquid in the bowl. Transfer the chiles to the bowl, shaking off any loose seeds or salt. Bring to a boil in a medium saucepan:

1 quart white wine vinegar

Pour the hot vinegar into the bowl, submerging the chiles (if necessary, weight them down with a small plate). Once cool, cover and let the chiles steep overnight.

Preheat the oven to 190°F.

Drain the chiles through a fine-mesh sieve set over a bowl to catch the infused vinegar (reserve this vinegar for other uses; it can be stored in a bottle or jar at room temperature). Place a rack set over a baking sheet and lay the chiles on top in one layer, leaving a little space between them. Dry out the chiles in the oven until the skins begin to wrinkle, about 2 hours (do not let them get crispy).

When the chiles are cool enough to handle, tightly layer them in a small baking dish (to ensure that no oil spills, you can set the baking dish on a rimmed baking sheet). Increase the oven temperature to 200°F and pour over the chiles:

2 cups olive oil

Be sure they are covered with oil (you may place a loaf pan or other ovenproof weight on top of them if necessary). Bake for 2 hours.

Let cool completely. Pack the chiles into a sterilized, 893, quart jar, cover with the olive oil, and store in the refrigerator indefinitely.

To use the chiles, fish them out of the oil with a clean fork, discard the green calyx where the stem used to be, and roughly chop. After being in the refrigerator for a while, olive oil solidifies and turns opaque. Simply scoop out the desired number of chiles with their oil into a small bowl and allow them to sit at room temperature until the oil liquefies.

SALTED EGG YOLKS

Varies

Salted egg yolks can be used to add a rich, salty boost to many dishes. Grate them using a fine grater over pasta, risotto, pizza, salads, and Congee, 333.

Spread in a ½-inch-thick layer in a container with a tight-fitting lid:

Diamond kosher salt

Make indentations in the salt, creating as many indentations as the number of egg yolks you plan to cure. Place in each indentation:

1 large chicken or duck egg yolk

Cover the yolks completely by gently adding more:

Diamond kosher salt

Cover the container and refrigerate for 1 week.

Unearth the egg yolks, brushing away any excess salt. Preheat the oven to its lowest setting (no higher than 200°F). Place the egg yolks on a rack set over a baking sheet. Place in the oven and bake until the yolks are dry to the touch, 30 to 45 minutes.

Let cool completely, then transfer to a container lined with a paper towel. Keep refrigerated indefinitely.

CURED FISH ROE OR CAVIAR

Varies

Lightly brining fresh fish eggs firms their texture and turns them colorful and translucent. The result pops in your mouth and tastes of the sea. The salt levels called for here will produce a caviar that is seasoned like Japanese-style salmon roe (*ikura*) or what Russians call *malossol* (lightly salted). We learned about the hot water soaking method from Bonnie Morales's book, *Kachka*.

Remove from very fresh fish as soon as possible:

Whole sacs or skeins of roe, such as salmon or trout

Thoroughly rinse the sacs under cold water and refrigerate in a bowl. Place a grid-patterned wire cooling rack set over a large baking dish and fill a large bowl in the sink with piping-hot tap water. Transfer the sacs to the hot water and let them soften for 5 minutes. Drain the water. Place one of the sacs on the cooling rack with the exposed eggs facing down. Press down gently and move the sac back and forth on the cooling rack, letting the wire work the eggs free from the membrane. Discard the membrane and repeat with the other sacs. Rinse out the large bowl, fill with cold water, and transfer the eggs in the baking dish to the water. Stir the eggs around with your fingers, agitating them so that any lingering pieces of membrane are freed (they will float to the surface). Carefully pour off the water and any floating bits from the top, keeping the eggs in the bowl with your hand. Fill the bowl with more cold water, agitate, and repeat until the water is clear and there are no more floating bits. Drain the roe, measure their volume, and refrigerate.

For every 2 cups roe, whisk together in a large bowl until the salt has dissolved:

1 quart cold water
2 tablespoons pickling salt or 1/4 cup Diamond kosher salt (35g)

Add the roe to the brine and refrigerate for 1 hour. Strain the roe once more, discarding the brine, and let the roe drain, covered, overnight over the bowl.

The roe is now cured and ready to eat. Transfer to a glass jar and keep refrigerated for up to 5 days, or transfer to a zip-top freezer bag, seal with the air displacement method, 881, and freeze for up to 2 months.

ABOUT CURING MEAT

Cured meats are some of the most flavorful, umami-rich ingredients we have at our disposal in the kitchen. Armed with curing salt, a bit of refrigerator space, and a little patience, several of them are easily and safely cured at home.

There are two basic forms of curing: wet-curing and dry-curing. In **wet-curing,** meat is either submerged in a brine or covered with a curing mixture and placed in a bag or deep, snug-fitting dish in the refrigerator. When the curing period is over, the salts have made it to the center of the meat and it is ready to cook. Whether meat is brined or covered in cure, salt draws out excess moisture. The salt then diffuses throughout the meat, firming its texture and making the interior inhospitable to pathogens.

Dry-curing involves covering the meat with a curing mixture as above, but for a significantly longer period. Excess cure is then scraped off, and sometimes the meat is cold-smoked. The meat is then hung in a cool, ventilated, and slightly humid environment for an extended period to dry. During this time, the meat will lose a large percentage of its initial weight to evaporation—by law, country hams must lose at least 18 percent of their initial weight; bacon may lose up to half.

Generally speaking, when comparing dry-cured and wet-cured meats, the biggest difference is that the dry-cured item will have a much more concentrated flavor and denser texture. The flavor is not only concentrated, but more complex and savory: Though the curing step halts microbes and other spoiling agents, many of the enzymes present in the meat will continue to be active and contribute an intense savoriness as they convert proteins into flavorful by-products.

The process of dry-curing sausages and salami adds yet another layer of complexity: Before being left to cure, the sausage mixture must be inoculated with a special starter mold and then fermented in a very humid environment at an elevated temperature. The timing of this step is crucial, as the sausages must become properly acidic before dangerous bacteria start to proliferate.

As Portland *charcutier* Elias Cairo writes in his book *Olympia Provisions*: "So many things can go wrong [with dry-cured sausages] that when you pull it off, it feels like a win." We are content to buy his salami and resign ourselves to a lukewarm sense of accomplishment with our own curing projects. Which is to say, despite the obvious superiority of many dry-cured products, we offer only wet-cured recipes here: They are fairly straightforward, take less time, and do not require special equipment or climate-controlled environments for fermenting and drying. Dry-curing meats for long-term storage can be done safely at home, but the equipment needed to guarantee safety can be very expensive. Even rustic preparations like country ham require detailed instructions on how to control pests that are well beyond the scope of this book. The recipes below may lack ambition, but they are very tasty and less likely to end in disappointment (and illness). Amateur meat-curers who wish to pursue more challenging projects should consult Cairo's book, as well as the other resources listed in our bibliography, 1077. To cure your own salmon, see Gravlax, 393.

CURING SALTS

Meats have been preserved since antiquity with the aid of saltpeter (potassium nitrate). When allowed to diffuse into meats, this compound converts into potassium nitrite, a powerful antimicrobial. Without it, salting meat for preservation can be dangerous: The very word for botulism comes from the Latin for "sausage," and potassium nitrite—as well as its modern equivalent, sodium nitrite—inhibits the growth and toxin production of *Clostridium botulinum.* While modern conveniences like refrigeration may tempt us into thinking there is no longer any need to add these mineral salts, it is important to note that they also give cured meats their characteristic reddish color and savory, sharp flavor.

Meat that cures relatively quickly (like all of the wet-cured recipes below) requires a small amount of "number 1" **pink curing salt.** It contains 6.25 percent sodium nitrite and is commercially available under the names **InstaCure #1, Prague Powder #1, DQ Cure #1,** and **Modern Cure #1.**

Since dry-cured meats like country ham and fermented sausage take much longer to finish curing, they require a curing salt with additional sodium nitrate, which will slowly convert into sodium nitrite and continue to protect against botulism. These "slow" or "number 2" pink curing salts contain 6.25 percent sodium nitrite and 4 percent sodium nitrate, and are sold under the names **InstaCure #2, Prague Powder #2, DQ Cure #2,** and **Modern Cure #2.**

Curing-grade **celery juice powder** can also be found from online retailers. Since celery-based cures are not approved by the USDA for use in products labeled as "cured," it has provided no guidelines for the concentrations it can be safely used in. Additionally, some celery juice powder contains a mixture of sodium nitrate and sodium nitrite, while others may be processed into pure sodium nitrite. For these reasons, ➤ we do not recommend substituting celery juice powder in any of these recipes. Additionally, despite the fact that potassium nitrate or saltpeter was the original curing salt, ➤ we do not recommend using mixtures containing it.

CURING SAFETY AND SCALING

First, a word on the safety of curing salts and their use in the recipes that follow. Sodium nitrite and sodium nitrate are toxic when ingested in large amounts. The smaller (but still substantial) amounts producers used to add to bacon were shown to produce carcinogenic by-products (called nitrosamines) when cooked at high temperatures. Consequently, USDA regulations limit the amount of nitrates allowed in bacon, and these recipes have been written to conform to those rules. ➤ Do not use more than the specified quantity of curing salt in these recipes.

If you are trying to cure a larger or smaller quantity of meat, ➤ always scale the amount of salt and curing salt accurately (this is why we provide gram weights here). For bacon, this is relatively straightforward: Divide the weight of the pork belly you are using by the weight specified in the recipe (2,270g) and multiply the result by each ingredient quantity to arrive at the amounts needed. In the case of brined recipes like Home-Cured Corned Beef, below, you will need to take the weight of water into account as well—which is why we have provided the total weight of meat and water in that recipe. To scale these recipes to a different weight of meat, simply place the brining container on a scale and tare the scale. Place the trimmed meat in the container, add water to cover, and record the weight (discard the water). Divide this number by the total weight of meat and water in the original recipe, and multiply the other ingredients by this number to scale the recipe.

Another factor to consider is the thickness of the meat you will be curing: A relatively small increase in thickness can require a much longer time for the cure to penetrate fully. Since we do not recommend these curing techniques as a method of preservation, there is little risk involved. But, for the sake of quality and consistency, ➤ do not try to adapt these recipes for other cuts of meat that are thicker or a dramatically different shape than those called for. The curing salt will probably not diffuse to the center of the meat, resulting in a grayish middle section surrounded by the reddish-pink cured meat.

HOME-CURED BACON

About 5 pounds

If you plan to hot-smoke your bacon, please read about Barbecuing, 1066, for instructions on setting up the smoker. If you want to add a smoky flavor to bacon but do not have access to a smoker, replace some or all of the salt with an equal *weight* of smoked salt. Feel free to improvise with the other seasonings in the cure. For a pancetta-like bacon, increase the black pepper by 2 tablespoons, and add **3 minced garlic cloves, 2 finely crumbled bay leaves,** and **1 teaspoon dried thyme.** Or, for a more breakfast-friendly variation, omit the brown sugar from the cure and add **¼ cup maple syrup or sorghum syrup (90g), or 3 tablespoons honey (65g)** to the bag. Please read About Curing Meat, 936.

Have ready:

One 5-pound piece pork belly (2,270g)

Sanitize, xx, a nonreactive brining container with a cover. Or have large plastic bags ready: Two-gallon zip-top bags work well, as do large-size oven bags—as long as the opening is cinched and facing up when the pork belly is placed in the fridge. The belly should fit snugly in whatever container or bag you are brining in. Depending on the thickness of the piece and the size of the container or bag, you may need to cut the pork belly into two slabs (it is okay to stack two slabs on top of each other during the curing process). Transfer the belly to a rimmed baking sheet. Thoroughly mix together in a small bowl:

¼ cup table salt or ½ cup Diamond kosher salt (70g)
¼ cup (60g) brown sugar
(2 tablespoons black pepper, red pepper flakes, or a combination)
½ teaspoon InstaCure #1 or Prague Powder #1 (about 3g)

Distribute the mixture evenly over the entire surface of the belly, pressing any that falls onto the baking sheet into the sides and ends of the slab(s). Place the pork in the covered brining container or into the bag(s). If using bags, place them in a baking dish, broiler pan, or rimmed baking sheet to catch any leaking liquids. A pool of brine will begin to collect in the bottom, and it is important that all surfaces be equally exposed to this concentrated brine. Refrigerate for 5 days, turning the belly every day. If one piece of belly is stacked on top of the other, be sure they are flipped individually each time so that both surfaces of both pieces get equal time in the brine.

After 5 days, remove the pork from the bag or container, discard any liquid, thoroughly rinse off any cure that remains on the surface, and dry with paper towels. (Do not worry if some imbedded flecks of pepper or seasoning remain.) Now the bacon must be gently cooked through in the oven or a smoker. If smoking, place the pork belly on a rack set over a rimmed baking sheet and refrigerate overnight, uncovered.

To bake the bacon, preheat the oven to 200°F. Tightly wrap the pieces in foil and place on a rimmed baking sheet. Cook in the oven until the thickest part of the belly reaches 145°F, about 2 hours.

To smoke the bacon, heat a smoker or charcoal grill set up for indirect cooking to 200°F, 1068 (preferably with a water pan). Add to the coals:

One small chunk of dry hickory, oak, or mesquite wood

Transfer the bacon to the cooler side of the smoker or grill and cover so that the top vent pulls smoke across the meat. Adjust the vents to maintain the temperature and smoke until the thickest part of the belly reaches 145°F, about 2 hours.

HOME-CURED CORNED BEEF

About 16 servings

We prefer the flat muscle of the brisket for corned beef. If making Pastrami, 938, the marbled point muscle is a decadent favorite. If you wish to scale this recipe up or down, please read Curing Safety and Scaling, above, and note that the total weight of water and meat called for here is 6,060g. Please read About Curing Meat, 936.

Bring to a simmer in a large pot:

8 cups water (1,895g)
2 cups Diamond kosher salt or ¾ cup plus 3 tablespoons pickling salt or fine sea salt (260g)

1 cup (230g) brown sugar
4 garlic cloves, minced
2½ teaspoons InstaCure #1 or Prague Powder #1 (14g)
1 tablespoon black peppercorns
1 tablespoon coriander seeds
1 tablespoon mustard seeds
8 allspice berries
6 whole cloves
2 bay leaves, crumbled
One 3-inch cinnamon stick

Stir until the salts and sugar dissolve and add:

8 cups ice water (1,895g)

Place the brine in the refrigerator and let cool completely. Meanwhile, trim all but ¼ inch of the fat from:

One 5-pound piece beef brisket (2,270g)

Submerge the brisket in the cold brine. Refrigerate for 5 days, turning the meat every day so that it is equally exposed to the brine.

When the brisket has finished curing, discard the brine and rinse the brisket under cold water. Cook as for Home-Cured Corned Beef, 937, or season and smoke as for Pastrami, below.

PASTRAMI

About 16 servings

Pastrami is corned beef that has been coated in coriander and black pepper and hot-smoked. After cooking in the smoker, the meat will lose a significant amount of moisture, which is why the salt level needs to be adjusted. We prefer to use the rich, marbled point muscle of the brisket for pastrami, but the flat will work well, too. Please read About Curing Meat, 936.

Pastrami is more versatile than many would imagine. If it is especially well marbled, it can be cooked like bacon, 937, and served with breakfast. Chef Danny Bowien uses diced, pan-fried pastrami instead of ground pork to make Sichuan-Style Dry-Fried Beans, 211. Pastrami is also an excellent stand-in for the cubed prosciutto called for in Utica Greens, 234.

Prepare using only **1½ cups Diamond kosher salt or ⅔ cup plus 1 tablespoon pickling salt or fine sea salt (200g)**:

Home-Cured Corned Beef, 937

After the meat has cured, discard the brine, rinse well, and dry the surface of the meat. Coarsely grind or pound until cracked:

¼ cup black peppercorns
¼ cup coriander seeds

Sprinkle this mixture all over the brisket, pressing it into the surface. Transfer to a rack set over a rimmed baking sheet and refrigerate uncovered overnight.

Use the meat to prepare:

Smoked Brisket, 469

Let cool and store refrigerated for up to 7 days.

To reheat for sandwiches, slice the pastrami across the grain, add to a skillet, and cover the bottom of the pan with ¼ inch water. Cover, place over medium heat, and simmer until the pastrami slices are heated through. Serve on toasted rye with plenty of spicy brown mustard, or in a Reuben Sandwich, 141.

ABOUT FERMENTATION

Fermentation—the process where sugars in food naturally break down into acidic or alcoholic by-products—is the source of many of our favorite foods. Without fermentation, we would not have chocolate, beer, wine, spirits, sourdough breads, cheese, vegetable ferments like sauerkraut and kimchi, soy sauce, miso, and too many other foods and drinks to list here. While many of these foods take special care to produce, it is fun to think that many of them were probably "discovered" by accident—a series of primordial vignettes where a food has gone too far, and a brave ancestor inspects it, scrapes the mold from it, sniffs at it, tastes it, and loves it so much that they begin trying to replicate it. Of course, taste is not the only advantage of this process: Fermentation was and continues to be an important form of food preservation.

Here, we deal specifically with vegetable ferments; ➤ for making dairy ferments, see Homemade Cultured Butter, 960, Making Cheese at Home, 964, Crème Fraîche, 974, and Yogurt, 1034.

Fermentation depends on naturally occurring yeasts and bacteria to acidify foods. In lactic acid fermentation, as bacteria metabolize sugars, they produce lactic acid. Over time, the overall acidity of the food increases, making it an inhospitable environment for most harmful bacteria and molds. Thus, fermenting foods is a low-tech way to preserve them. Interestingly, while most of us no longer need fermentation for preservation, the flavors and textures of fermented foods have been woven into our food cultures. We all understand on some level that bacteria and yeast create delicious and complex flavor compounds that are not easily replicated (if they can be replicated at all) by simply mixing ingredients together. The sour tang of sauerkraut, the bready richness of beer, the nutty savoriness of miso—all these flavors are more than the sum of their parts, and we achieve them by harnessing living organisms.

There may be many different types of bacteria present in a given fermented food, but some of the most common are lactic acid bacteria, notably those of the genuses *Lactobacillus* and *Leuconostoc*. Lactic acid bacteria (also referred to as LAB) metabolize glucose molecules and produce carbon dioxide and lactic acid. LAB are able to colonize fermenting foods and outcompete other bacteria because they can tolerate greater levels of acidity than many other bacteria. Other types of ferments may harness different types of bacteria. For example, vinegar is produced with *Acetobacter* bacteria, which metabolize alcohol and produce acetic acid.

The types of bacteria fluctuate during fermentation. For vegetable ferments submerged in a brine, fermentation is initiated by *Leuconostoc mesenteroides* bacteria. These bacteria produce, in addition to lactic acid, carbon dioxide. This is why, during the early stages of fermentation, there is often vigorous bubbling. As these bacteria continue to work, the pH of the ferment lowers. The *Leuconostoc* bacteria begin to die off and are replaced by acid-tolerant *Lactobacillus plantarum* bacteria.

FERMENTATION AND FOOD SAFETY

While most of us eat fermented foods whether or not we realize it, many of us are not accustomed to fermenting food, and the process can seem mysterious if not a little scary. Unlike most cooking, where you follow a recipe and get a predictable result, fermentation is not always a perfectly linear process. It is affected by the weather and ambient temperature, and ferments may not always look or smell the same from batch to batch. Further, we are not used to our food smelling like gym socks, rubbing alcohol, or sulfur, but these are all smells you may encounter during fermentation, and they do not necessarily indicate a problem.

As Sandor Katz states in his influential book *Wild Fermentation*, "Wild fermentation is the opposite of homogenization and uniformity, a small antidote you can undertake in your home, cultivating broad communities of organisms indigenous to your food, and also contributing those of your hands and your kitchen, to produce unique fermented foods." Uncertainty and a diversity of experiences are part of fermentation, so try to be open minded as you proceed.

Our basic fermentation safety advice is simple: Sanitize utensils and jars, use common sense, and start out with high-quality produce. These rules go a long way toward preventing contamination from pathogens. Further, always use the proper concentration of salt, as directed in individual recipes. Finally, for vegetable ferments, always keep the vegetables submerged under the brine.

The primary worry many people have regarding fermentation (and really all preserved foods) is botulism. Tasteless, odorless, and invisible, the toxins that cause the illness are certainly scary and rightly provoke concern. However, please keep in mind that botulinum toxins are practically unheard of in fermented foods. The *Clostridium botulinum* bacteria that produce the toxins thrive in low-acid, anaerobic (or oxygen-starved) environments. While anaerobic environments are common to fermented foods (for instance, sauerkraut submerged beneath a brine is an anaerobic environment), a combination of salt concentration and acidity prevent dangerous bacteria from thriving.

Mold can be another unwanted guest in fermented foods. In some cases, such as some types of cheese, mold is desirable, but for most vegetable ferments it is not. Keeping air out of your ferments will go a long way toward preventing mold growth. When that is not possible, simply remain vigilant. Mold can digest lactic acid, which means it can increase the pH of a fermented food if allowed to flourish. It can also lead to softened or slimy vegetables. Keep a close watch on your ferments and remove any mold as it appears. Keeping ferments well submerged beneath a brine will discourage mold from forming and make it easier to remove. Finally, working clean by washing or sterilizing all tools that come in contact with the ferment will prevent mold from taking hold.

Sometimes a layer of white scum will form on the surface of a ferment. If left alone, this layer can come to appear crenulated, like the rinds on some bloomy-type cheeses. This is Kahm yeast. It is harmless, but, just like molds, it should be scraped off and discarded.

FERMENTATION TOOLS AND INGREDIENTS

Fermentation requires very little in the way of tools and supplies. A mason jar, a piece of muslin or flour sack towel, and a rubber band or jar ring are really all that is needed to start a basic ferment. Some people like to use **ceramic crocks** to ferment foods. Crocks are ideal for large batches. Some crocks are open on top and others are lidded. Some lidded crocks have a "moat" around the top that is filled with water. When the lid is placed on top, the moat acts as an airlock, allowing gases to escape the crock without allowing oxygen inside. Crocks without a lid should be covered in some way. The easiest approach is to cover them with a thin kitchen towel and secure it with a piece of string.

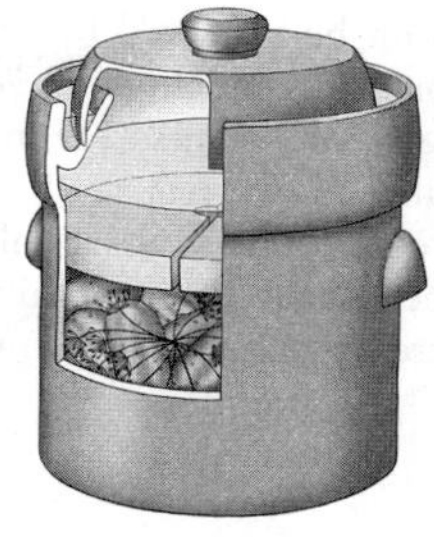

Fermentation crock with moat

Crocks also require a weight of some kind to keep vegetables submerged beneath the brine. While some companies make special fermentation weights, we usually go the low-tech route. A plate that is just smaller than the crock opening can be placed on top of the vegetables, then weighted down with a water-filled plastic jug. In other cases, a doubled zip-top freezer bag can be filled with water and used to weight the vegetables. Fill the bag with brine instead of pure water if you have any concerns about water leaking and diluting the brine.

The downsides to crocks are that they are not useful for small batches, they are heavy, and they tend to crack or break. Never use an antique crock that is cracked or has chipped or flaking glaze, as it may contain lead. New crocks are perfectly safe, as lead-based glazes are no longer used. Our favorite alternative to the crock is the **glass mason jar.** Mason jars are ubiquitous, cheap, and perfect for small-batch fermentation. We used to simply cover the jar with a cloth and a rubber band, but we have since invested in plastic mason jar lids retrofitted with a gasket and an airlock. We also use glass fermentation weights specifically made to fit inside mason jars, but you could use small, smooth stones (do not use limestone, which the acidity of fermented foods will break down) or cabbage leaves to keep foods submerged. In case a ferment is especially active and starts spurting brine out of the airlock, ➤ place the jars on a rimmed baking sheet to contain any spills.

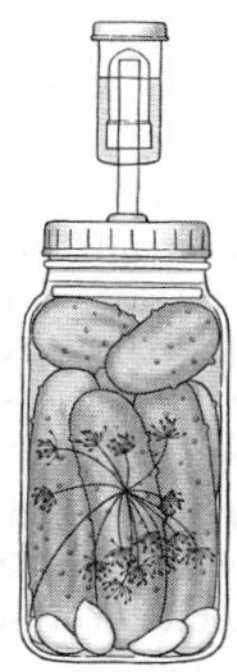

Mason jar with airlock

Water is a critical ingredient in brine fermentation. Tap water is generally fine to use for fermentation, but be aware that chlorine, which is added to municipal water supplies, can inhibit fermentation. You can boil, then cool tap water, or allow it to sit overnight to get the chlorine to dissipate. However, if your municipality uses chloramines, they cannot be removed by these methods. In that case, you may have more success using filtered or distilled water.

Salt is central to vegetable ferments. (For information on how salt interacts with plant cells and bacteria, see 934.) We use kosher salt because we always have it around, but sea salt and pickling salt are perfectly fine to use. Because table salt contains anticaking additives and iodine, an antimicrobial mineral, we do not recommend using it for fermentation.

TROUBLESHOOTING

Because the process is not familiar to most of us, learning how to read the signs of fermentation is a skill that must be acquired. In our own fermentation journey, we have found that our apprehension was quickly replaced by amazement and appreciation. Once you have a few successful projects under your belt, you will be better equipped to make the judgment calls necessary in this time-honored process. Of course, the old food-safety cliché is perfectly applicable here: If in doubt, throw it out.

My ferment smells funny. Welcome to fermentation! Fermented foods have a wide range of smells, from sulfuric to cheesy to fruity to yeasty. You might love the smells of fermentation or you might hate them. But just because a ferment has an unpleasant smell does not mean something is horribly wrong. Since it is hard to judge by smell alone, always look for visual characteristics to help inform your decisions. Sliminess and/or excessive mold growth (especially of black or red molds) combined with an unpleasant smell means that you should probably discard the ferment.

My ferment has some mold on it. As mentioned in Fermentation and Food Safety, 938, keep a close watch on ferments and remove any mold as soon as it crops up. A little mold here and there is nothing to worry about, but do not let it proliferate.

When do I know when my ferment is done? There is no single right answer to this question. Whereas most recipes have estimated cooking times, fermentation is pretty open-ended. ➤ Fermentation tends to happen faster in warmer weather than in cooler weather, so the time it takes a food to ferment is dependent on ambient conditions. The best option is to go by taste—which you should do regularly throughout the process. When the ferment tastes good to your palate, refrigerate. Refrigeration does not stop the food from fermenting, but it slows the process dramatically. Thus, a fermented food will continue to ripen even after it is refrigerated.

Further, longer fermentation does not mean more probiotics. The type and number of bacteria change over the course of fermentation, and there is no way for the average person to know the microbial composition of a fermented food. Nor is there any evidence to suggest that more bacteria is better. Thus, we think flavor is the best measuring stick for determining when a ferment is ready.

Doesn't cooking kill the bacteria in the ferment? Shouldn't I only eat fermented foods raw? Yes, cooking kills the bacteria in fermented foods, but do not let that stop you from cooking with them! Ferments add incredible dimension to the dishes they are used in, from Sauerkraut Soup, 86, Kimchi Jjigae, 87, and Sauerkraut Fritters, 225, to Kimchi Fried Rice, 332. We encourage you to enjoy fermented foods in a variety of ways.

STORING FERMENTS

Once a ferment has soured to your taste, transfer from the fermenter to sterilized jars, close fingertip-tight, 893, and keep in the back of the refrigerator. (If you fermented the food in a mason jar with an airlock-fitted lid, you can simply swap it for a regular canning lid.) Refrigeration will not stop the fermentation process, but it will slow it down significantly (for especially long-term storage, it is prudent not to screw lids on the jars very tight; loose lids allow gases to escape rather than building up in the jars). Ferments may also be kept in an especially cool pantry or cellar, as long as the vegetables are submerged and not exposed to oxygen. Since the temperature might be slightly warmer than a refrigerator, keep in mind that this may increase their acidity and funkiness. To avoid contamination, ➤ always remove fermented food from the jar with clean dry tongs.

SAUERKRAUT

About 1 quart

There are few ferments as easy or as likely to be successful as sauerkraut. You may be surprised at how quick (and cheap) it is to make enough sauerkraut to last a very long time. ➤ To make a larger or smaller quantity, weigh your cabbage on a scale set to grams and calculate 1.5 percent of its weight. The result is the amount (in weight) of salt you should add. So, for example, if you have 10 pounds or 4,535g of cabbage, multiply 4,535 by 0.015—a smart phone helps with this for the unmotivated or math-impaired—and the rounded result is 70g, which is the weight of salt needed for that amount of cabbage.

Before you begin, wash your cutting board, any utensils you plan to use, and the bowl in which you will be mixing the sauerkraut. Quarter:

5 pounds firm, unblemished green or red cabbage heads, outer leaves removed

Cut out the cores and thinly shred the cabbage. Dice or julienne the cores and add them to the shredded cabbage as well. Place the cabbage in a large bowl with:

2 tablespoons pickling salt or fine sea salt, or 4 tablespoons plus 1 teaspoon Diamond kosher salt (35g)

Massage the cabbage with your hands to release its water. Continue until there is enough water in the bowl to cover the cabbage once it is packed into a crock or jar. This may take as little as 15 or as long as 30 minutes.

Pack the kraut into a small ceramic crock or a half-gallon mason jar. Press down firmly to submerge the cabbage beneath the brine. If the cabbage has not released enough liquid to stay submerged, make a brine of:

4 cups distilled or charcoal-filtered water

1 tablespoon plus 1½ teaspoons pickling salt or fine sea salt, or 3 tablespoons Diamond kosher salt (25g)

Pour this brine over the cabbage to cover it. Weight the cabbage to keep it submerged beneath the brine. You can use a freezer-safe zip-top bag (freezer-safe bags are more durable) filled partially with brine of the same strength, 940, as you used for the cabbage. The bag will conform to the shape of the container you use and is easy to manipulate. Or use specially made fermentation weights or a whole cabbage leaf. Cover the crock or vessel to keep out flies, but make sure it can breathe. You may use a square of kitchen towel secured with a rubber band or string, or use specially made fermentation airlocks. If using a crock with a water moat and lid, simply place the lid on top and fill the moat with water.

Check the kraut every couple days. Within a few days, it should start to bubble—this is an indicator that fermentation has begun. Stir or compress the kraut regularly (the carbon dioxide generated during fermentation often pushes the kraut above the brine if it is not heavily weighted). If scum forms on top, simply scrape it off and discard, then press the kraut beneath the brine again. When the bubbling slows, start to taste the kraut (you can taste it before this point, of course, but this is when the kraut becomes noticeably more sour). When you really like how it tastes, it's done. To store, see 940.

KIMCHI

About 10 cups

Many kimchi recipes call for an addition of rice flour paste, which makes for a thicker kimchi brine. We prefer our kimchi without it, but if you would like to go that route, simply combine **2 tablespoons sweet (glutinous) rice flour** and **¾ cup water** in a saucepan. Cook over medium heat, stirring constantly, until very thick. Let cool before adding to the other kimchi paste ingredients. As with sauerkraut, the salt in this recipe is about 1.5 percent the weight of the vegetables, so if you decide to make a smaller or larger batch, calculate the weight of the vegetables in grams and multiply that number by 0.015 to get the gram weight of the salt you will need.

Place in a very large bowl:

2½ pounds (1 medium head) napa cabbage, quartered lengthwise and cut crosswise into 1-inch-wide strips
1 pound Korean or daikon radish, peeled and julienned
1 bunch green onions (about 6), cut into 2-inch pieces
(½ cup chopped Chinese chives)

Sprinkle with:

1 tablespoon plus 1½ teaspoons pickling salt or fine sea salt, or 3 tablespoons Diamond kosher salt (25g)

Massage the salt into the vegetables until they form their own brine and the cabbage is softened, about 10 minutes. Puree in a blender or food processor:

Cloves from 1 head garlic
1-inch piece ginger, peeled and chopped
(1 Asian pear or Bosc pear, cored and chopped)
1 small onion (6 to 8 ounces), chopped
2 tablespoons sugar
2 tablespoons fish sauce
(2 tablespoons Korean salted shrimp)

Add the puree to the cabbage mixture along with:

½ to ¾ cup Korean red pepper flakes (gochugaru), to taste

Mix thoroughly. Pack the kimchi into a fermentation vessel (for this recipe, a half-gallon jar plus a pint jar is about perfect, although in Korean households plastic or glass food storage containers are also used), cover with a cloth secured with a rubber band or string or cap with an airlock or a lid, and let ferment at room temperature for at least 2 days or until the desired level of sourness is achieved.

If desired, refrigerate a portion of the kimchi immediately to eat fresh. When the rest has soured to your liking, it is done. To store, see 940.

HALF-SOUR PICKLES

About 1 gallon

These delectable, crisp pickles use a 3.5 percent brine (when scaling for a smaller or larger batch, simply add enough 3.5 percent brine to cover the cucumbers). Use the optional grape leaves as insurance against softening (see 923 for an explanation), but don't worry too much: You can preserve most of their crispness if you trim off the blossom ends, taste the pickles regularly as they ferment, and refrigerate them as soon as they start to soften.

Clean and cut a ⅛-inch slice from the blossom end of:

4 pounds small to medium pickling cucumbers

Stir together in a large bowl to dissolve the salt:

8 cups cool water
3 tablespoons plus 2 teaspoons pickling salt or fine sea salt, or ½ cup Diamond kosher salt (65g)

Divide between 2 sterilized, 893, half-gallon mason jars or place in the bottom of a crock:

Cloves from 2 heads garlic, lightly smashed
(10 grape leaves)
10 dill sprigs
2 teaspoons black peppercorns

If using jars, wedge the cucumbers into the jars tightly, starting with larger cucumbers and filling in with smaller ones. Wedge small cucumbers in at the top so that the curve of the jars holds them under the brine. Fill the jars with enough brine to cover the cucumbers completely. If using airlock lids, fill the airlock with water and screw on the lid. If using a crock, use a plate or a doubled zip-top bag filled with 3.5 percent brine to keep the cucumbers under the brine, then cover the crock either with a lid or a piece of cloth tied tightly to keep out dust and flies. Depending on the size of the crock, you may need to make more brine to cover the cucumbers completely.

Check the progress of the fermentation daily. The brine will start to get cloudy and smell slightly sour, and the cucumbers will begin to soften and turn from a vibrant green color to an olive green. Taste the cucumbers as they ferment to judge their readiness. Half-sour pickles may be done in as few as 5 days, or they may take weeks depending on the ambient temperature.

When the pickles are as sour as you want them, they are done. To store, see 940.

FERMENTED GIARDINIERA

About 3 quarts

This tangy, crisp, fermented take on giardiniera was an instant hit in our house. We like to set out a bowl of it, drizzled with olive oil, to accompany a rich hot appetizer, or as part of an antipasto, 45.

Pack into a fermentation crock or divide between 2 sterilized, 893, half-gallon jars:

2 pounds cauliflower, trimmed and cut into bite-sized florets
12 ounces celery, cut into ¾-inch pieces
8 ounces carrots, peeled and cut into ¼-inch-thick rounds
8 ounces mild red peppers, such as bell or Jimmy Nardello, seeded and cut into ½-inch pieces or rounds
Cloves from 1 head garlic, smashed
4 dried red chiles, such as árbol
2 teaspoons dried oregano
20 black peppercorns

Whisk together in a large bowl until the salt is dissolved:

9 cups cool water
¼ cup plus 1 tablespoon pickling salt or fine sea salt, or ⅔ cup Diamond kosher salt (85g)

Pour the brine over the vegetables to cover completely. If using jars, add fermentation weights to keep the vegetables submerged. If using airlock lids, fill the airlocks with water, and screw on the lids. If using a crock, use a plate or a doubled zip-top bag filled with 4 percent brine to keep the vegetables under the brine, then cover the crock either with a lid or a piece of cloth tied tightly to keep out dust and flies. Depending on the size of the crock, you may need to make more brine to cover the vegetables completely.

Test the flavor of the vegetables every day; plan on fermenting them for about 1 week, or until as sour as desired. Drain the vegetables, reserving the brine, and place in a large bowl. If desired, add to the vegetables:

(2 cups pitted green olives)

Divide the vegetables among three 1-quart jars and add brine to cover. To store, see 940.

SALT-PRESERVED LEMONS

About 1 quart

It's amazing that lactic acid bacteria can survive the heavily salted and acidic environment of this traditional Moroccan preparation. The result is an ingredient with a complex, rounded sourness: The lemon's natural citric and malic acids are joined by lactic acid produced by fermentation. Traditionally used to flavor seafood soups or stews, meaty braises, and tagines, minced preserved lemon peel is also a wonderful addition to vinaigrettes, chicken or tuna salad, and flavored butters, 559–60. Substitute minced preserved lemon for the lemon zest in Gremolata, 587. Julia Moskin, writer for the *New York Times*, recommends using the salty, tart brine in a Bloody Mary, 21. Once you have these flavorful lemons on hand, they will work their way into a wide variety of dishes.

Wash, dry, and set in a 200°F oven for 5 minutes to dry thoroughly:

2 pounds lemons

Measure:

⅓ cup (45g) Diamond kosher salt

Spoon 2 tablespoons of the salt into a sterilized, 893, wide-mouth quart jar. Roll the lemons on the counter to release their juice. Quarter a lemon lengthwise, stopping ½ inch from the bottom so the quarters fan out but remain attached at one end. Gently open the lemon and sprinkle the 8 cut surfaces with ½ teaspoon salt. Carefully squeeze the lemon juice into a bowl. Close the lemon and pack into the jar. Continue with the remaining lemons, sprinkling each layer with 1½ teaspoons salt. Pour the lemon juice into the jar. If the juice does not cover all the lemons in the jar, add:

Lemon juice to cover

Leave a ½-inch space at the top of the jar. Force out air bubbles by sliding a narrow spatula between the lemons and the side of the jar. Be sure the lemons are still covered with liquid and there is only ½ inch headspace, 893. Wipe the rim of the jar. Fold a square of plastic wrap to make 4 layers and place over the top (this will protect the jar ring and lid from corrosion), then tightly cap the jar. Place the jar on a saucer and leave in a warm place for 1 month.

Each day, turn the jar upside down to redistribute the salted juice. After the curing period, refrigerate or keep in a cool, dry place for up to 1 year.

To use, remove lemons from the jar as needed with clean dry tongs, rinse them, and discard the inner flesh. Use only the peel.

FERMENTED LOUISIANA-STYLE HOT SAUCE

Varies

When made with Tabasco chiles, hotter cayenne varieties, or red serranos, this sauce is a good approximation of the classic Avery Island condiment called Tabasco Sauce. That said, we encourage you to branch out: Any hot chile will work. Ripe red, orange, and yellow chiles are best; green specimens can work, but they do not ferment as vigorously (and the resulting sauce is not the most attractive color). Several smashed garlic cloves can also be added, or a diced plum tomato (just be sure to include them before weighing your jar).

Have ready:

Fresh hot red chiles, stemmed, seeded, and coarsely chopped

Wearing protective gloves, stem, seed, and chop the chiles with a pair of kitchen shears for minimal contact with the peppers. You can chop the chiles in a food processor or with a knife instead. Sterilize, 893, a pint, quart, or half-gallon jar that will fit the chopped peppers. Place the jar on a digital scale and tare the scale. Add the chiles and just enough water to cover and record the weight in grams. Multiply that number by 0.02 and add the resulting amount in grams of:

Pickling salt, fine sea salt, or Diamond kosher salt

Mix and mash the chiles thoroughly with a wooden spoon. Cover the vessel with a cloth and rubber band, a loosely screwed-on lid, or an airlock.

Check the ferment daily for signs of activity. If white mold appears, remove it with a spoon, stir the chile mixture and cover again. You will eventually see bubbles forming in the pepper mash. Let the mash ferment until the bubbling stops, for up to 6 weeks, though some ferments will need much less time.

Place a food mill over a bowl, pour the pepper mash and brine into the mill, and work the flesh and seeds, rotating the handle in both directions to push as much liquid and pulp from the mash as possible (if desired, reserve what is left in the food mill, dehydrate it, below, coarsely grind, and use as a seasoning at the table). Measure the volume of the liquid and add half that amount of:

Cider, white wine, or rice vinegar

Feel free to experiment here with something more flavorful, like a dash of sherry, banana, or pineapple vinegar. If necessary, add:

(Salt to taste)

Transfer to bottles. To store, see 940.

KOMBUCHA

1 gallon

Kombucha is a fermented tea made with the help of a SCOBY, or **S**ymbiotic **C**ommunity **O**f **B**acteria and **Y**east. This sets it apart from the ferments above, which rely solely on the yeasts and bacteria contained within the food being fermented. Because a new SCOBY forms on top of each batch of kombucha, enthusiastic kombucha brewers often give them away to the curious, though they may also be purchased online. Alternatively, you may culture your own SCOBY: Proceed with the recipe below but make only a half batch. Instead of adding the mature SCOBY and starter tea, pour in an entire 16-ounce bottle of unpasteurized kombucha. Then wait until a SCOBY forms on top of the kombucha.

Bring to a boil in a large saucepan:

1 quart water

Remove from the heat and add:

8 tea bags or 2 tablespoons loose tea (black, green, white, oolong, or pu-erh)

1 cup sugar

Stir to dissolve the sugar and allow the tea to steep for 20 minutes. Remove the tea bags or strain out the loose tea and add:

3 quarts cold water

Pour the cooled tea mixture into a large jar or vessel of some kind (not metal) and add:

1 mature kombucha SCOBY and 1 cup "starter tea" (fully fermented kombucha from a previous batch or from store-bought unpasteurized kombucha)

The SCOBY may float or sink—both are normal. Cover the jar with a cloth or paper towel secured with a rubber band.

Ferment, tasting periodically, until the kombucha is as sour as you want it, 1 to 3 weeks. This will take longer in the winter than in the summer.

Remove the SCOBY (and the new SCOBY that has formed on the surface of the kombucha) and 1 cup of starter tea for your next batch (keep the SCOBY and starter tea in a jar in the refrigerator for up to 1 month, or start a new batch of kombucha right away). You may drink the kombucha right away or proceed with a secondary fermentation.

For secondary fermentation, decant the kombucha into bottles and seal. If your kombucha is already very sour, add a teaspoon of sugar to each bottle to jump-start fermentation. You may also add a few berries to each jar. Let the bottles sit at room temperature for a few days. If using glass jars, open them periodically to gauge whether any pressure has built up. At first, you may want to use plastic bottles with screw-top lids. When the bottles feel tight, the kombucha has fermented enough and should be refrigerated.

TOFU MISOZUKE (TOFU "CHEESE")

1 pound

This strongly flavored delicacy is a boon to the adventurous or to those who hanker for pungent cheeses but cannot eat them. Like Kombucha, above, this ferment involves adding a starter culture instead of relying on natural yeasts. While not exactly cheese-like, it is funky, salty, and loaded with umami. Serve with rice crackers and sake, a very dry white wine, or vinho verde.

Press without cutting into slabs, 285:

16 ounces firm tofu

Mix in a small bowl until smooth:

¾ cup white miso

¼ cup red miso

¼ cup sake

2 tablespoons sugar

Spread some of the miso mixture on the bottom of a container that will hold the tofu. Place a piece of cheesecloth or thin flour sack towel over the miso and place the tofu on top. Wrap the cloth around the tofu, then spread the rest of the miso mixture over the cloth so that it is completely coated. Cover the container and refrigerate for 4 to 7 days.

Peel back the cloth and taste a small piece of the tofu. It should be salty and a little tangy. Unwrap the tofu and serve or, if a stronger, tangier flavor is desired, let it continue to cure, refrigerated, for up to 2 months.

ABOUT DRYING FOOD

Placing foods in a warm, dry, and well-circulated environment will cause their moisture to evaporate and dissipate. When a sufficient amount of their water has evaporated, these foods become inhospitable to the bacteria, molds, and yeasts that cause spoilage. In order to prevent the growth of these organisms, at least 80 percent of the water must be removed from fruit (ideally, 90 percent) and at least 90 percent from vegetables (ideally, 95 percent), since they are less acidic. Meats require about 85 percent of their water to be removed, which results in a yield that is about half of their original weight. Properly dried, these foods can be stored at room temperature for extended periods (and even longer when refrigerated).

Aside from extending their shelf life, drying foods allows them to be stored in a much smaller space than their canned or frozen counterparts. Since they are a fraction of their original weight, dried foods are also more nutrient-dense than fresh or otherwise processed foods. All of these qualities make dried foods perfect for backpacking, and ideal for anyone interested in efficient, long-term storage that does not require refrigeration.

Readers more interested in how these foods can be used to create delicious meals should note that their flavors are highly concentrated by the drying process, which can transform them into a powerful seasoning ingredient (for more on this, see Using Dehydrated Fruits and Vegetables, 946).

Drying needs to be done quickly enough to prevent spoilage organisms from growing during the process, but at a cool enough temperature to preserve the flavors and colors of the food. The heating of food must not be so rapid that the outside of the food hardens and inhibits the release of moisture from the center. This is known as **case-hardening** and it can result in spoiled food during storage.

Some treatments are necessary to prevent the growth of several organisms during the drying process and storage. Meats need to be frozen, salted or marinated, and heated to an elevated temperature to kill any parasites or harmful bacteria. In the case of some vegetables and fruits, blanching is recommended to deactivate enzymes that cause discoloring and spoilage. Finally, remember that foods dried at home rarely achieve the same texture as those produced by commercial drying methods, in which spoilage and sometimes moisture content are also controlled by other means, such as sulfuring or additives.

DRYING EQUIPMENT

Though drying is an age-old method of preservation, few climates lend themselves to sun-drying food. Thankfully, **electric dehydrators** are able to consistently hold the temperatures required, as well as lower the humidity inside. For the best results and least amount of fiddling, purchase an electric dehydrator with a thermostat to set the air temperature and a fan that evenly circulates air throughout the unit. (Models that blow air onto trays from the side are best.) An **oven** can be used if a temperature no higher than 140°F can be maintained with the door slightly open (convection models are especially good, but they must be able to hold this temperature when closed).

It is possible to make your own **drying cabinet,** shown below, which includes a heat source, such as a hot plate, and adequate venting. Venting in the drying cabinet is provided by a 2-inch-wide, 12-inch-long screened slot near the top at the sides of the cabinet. In order to allow air intake at the base, the hinged door has a long 2-inch-high slot at the base. Line the cabinet walls and door up to the height of the food with aluminum building paper. Diffused heat is achieved by suspending a metal sheet on brackets as a lower shelf over the heating element as shown. A digital cable probe thermometer should be placed near the food and the heat periodically adjusted to maintain the correct temperature.

In both oven and cabinet-drying, keep the bottom tray of food 6 to 8 inches from the heat source. In both cases, also, a small electric fan outside the oven door or blowing past the cabinet intake vent at the base will help keep air circulating. Trays used in the regular oven or drying cabinet need to be made of food-safe material, such as stainless steel screening, plastic or nylon mesh, or cake racks on cookie sheets. Finally, the dimensions of the trays should be 3 to 4 inches less than the interior of the oven or cabinet to allow for air circulation.

Sun-drying should be attempted with ➤ fruits only (their sugar and acid content makes them safer) and only when the daily high temperature is 85°F or higher and the humidity is at 60 percent or less. ➤ The fruit must be brought inside at sundown, as cool night air or dew will condense and add moisture back to the food. This process can take much longer than other methods, and the fruit will need to be pasteurized, 945, after drying.

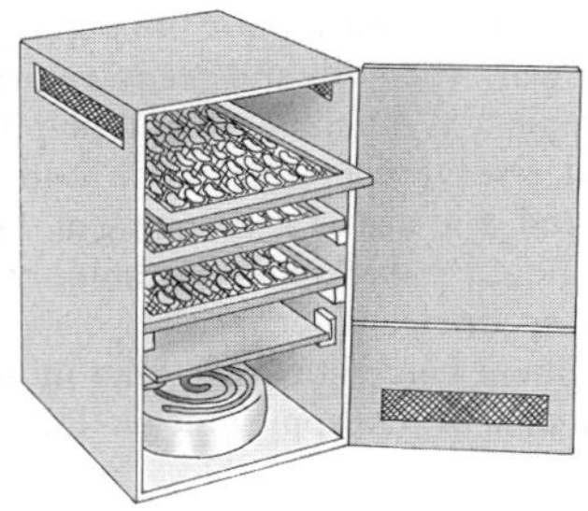

Homemade drying cabinet

Special equipment for sun-drying can be fashioned with a glass **cold frame** to intensify the heat, as shown below. Intensify the heat even more by placing a large piece of black poster board between the glass and the food in the cold frame. Provide screened openings on the top and bottom for ventilation, and make sure the food is on a rack that allows for air circulation. The cold frame should be light enough to be shifted during the day to catch the most sun, and the food on the trays should be turned every hour. With full sun, most foods should dry by this method in about 2 days—again, if the humidity is low. With any of these units, it is best to place a thermometer on the lowest rack to make sure the temperature does not exceed 140°F. ➤ No food should be dried outdoors in areas with bad air pollution.

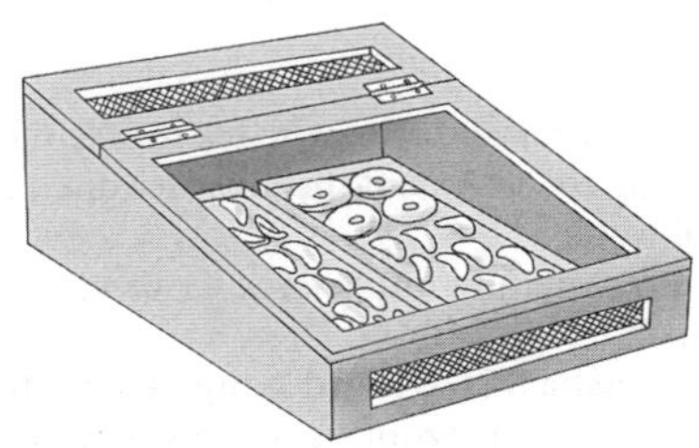

Cold frame

DRYING FRUITS AND VEGETABLES

Some fruits and vegetables are ideal for drying; others contain so much water that it is difficult to get them to dry before their flavor is compromised. Still more simply do not have much flavor once dried. These include avocados, caneberries, citrus, melons, brassicas, celery, cucumber, greens, radishes, and winter squash.

To prepare fruits and vegetables for dehydrating, first sanitize, xx, work surfaces, drying racks, and utensils. Select high-quality foods that show no signs of spoilage or decay. You may peel fruits like apples, pears, and peaches if desired, or you may leave the peels on. Blanch and/or dip items in an antibrowning solution as proscribed in the Preparation column of the charts in About Freezing Fruit, 882, or About Freezing Vegetables, 884 (note that sometimes no blanching or antibrowning solution is needed). See the sections

Best for Drying		Worst for Drying	
Fruits	**Vegetables**	**Fruits**	**Vegetables**
Apples	Beets	Blackberries	Asparagus
Apricots	Carrots	Citrus fruit	Avocado
Bananas	Corn	Crabapples	Broccoli
Cherries	Green Beans	Cranberries	Cabbage
Citrus peel	Horseradish	Kiwis	Cauliflower
Coconut	Mushrooms	Melons	Celery
Currants	Okra	Pomegranates	Collards
Dates	Onions	Quince	Cucumber
Grapes	Parsnips	Raspberries	Eggplant
Mangoes	Peas		Kale
Nectarines	Peppers		Lettuce
Papayas	Potatoes		Radishes
Peaches	Pumpkin		Spinach
Pears	Rutabaga		Winter Squash
Pineapples	Tomatoes		Zucchini
Plums	Turnips		
Rhubarb			
Strawberries			

below for specific instructions on how to dry tomatoes, 947, and chile peppers, 946. Small fruits to be dried whole, such as blueberries, cherries, and grapes, should be blanched for 35 seconds to allow cracking of the skins and prevent case-hardening during drying.

In general, ➤ cut or slice pieces as evenly and thinly as is practical: They will dry faster and thus retain their quality. Berries can be left whole, though large berries like strawberries should be sliced or halved depending on their size. Vegetables like green beans need not be sliced (simply cut them into 1-inch pieces).

To dehydrate fruits and vegetables, loosely place pieces on the drying trays in single layers, without touching or overlapping. For most fruits, 135°F is a good temperature for dehydrating. For most vegetables, use 125°F (the exceptions to this are tomatoes and onions, which should be dried at 155°F). For those using an electric dehydrator, consult the operating manual for estimated drying times and recommended settings. Regardless of these estimates, be sure to test (see below) pieces to make sure they have dried sufficiently.

➤ If you have sun-dried fruits in a cold frame, you will need to pasteurize them.

To pasteurize sun-dried fruits, preheat the oven to 175°F. Put the pieces in a single layer on baking sheets and heat for 30 minutes. Condition fruits (see below) to distribute the remaining moisture evenly, as well as to make sure they are really dry enough for storage.

To test dried fruits and vegetables, remove the pieces from the tray and let them cool a little before testing. ➤ Vegetables are ready when they are brittle or crisp; they seemingly would shatter if hit with a hammer. They should rattle when stirred on the trays. ➤ Fruits are considered dry enough when they are leathery and produce no moisture when cut and squeezed. If a piece is folded in half, it should not stick to itself. They will not be as moist as many dried fruits you buy, because those have additives, and sometimes sulfur dioxide, added to protect them from spoilage.

Finally, to be doubly sure of their shelf stability and help evenly distribute what little moisture remains in them, dried fruits and vegetables need to be **conditioned.**

To condition dried fruits and vegetables, allow the dried vegetables and fruit to cool completely and loosely pack the pieces into glass jars or plastic containers with tight lids. Let them stand at room temperature for 10 days, shaking daily to separate and mix the pieces. If condensation develops, the product is too moist for long-term storage. Return the foods to the dehydrator and dry further.

To store dried fruits and vegetables, package them in zip-top storage bags and then place in airtight containers, such as glass jars or freezer boxes. Heavy-duty zip-top bags are acceptable but not as good for long-term storage and keeping moisture out. Label and date the containers. ➤ Dried fruits and vegetables will keep for up to 12 months at basement temperatures or for 8 months at moderate room temperatures. Storage time also depends upon the amount of retained moisture, how well sealed the food is, and exposure to light.

USING DEHYDRATED FRUITS AND VEGETABLES

The simplest way to use your dehydrated bounty is to eat as a healthy snack or reconstitute it and use in cooked dishes.

To reconstitute dried fruits and vegetables, cover with cold water, soak until they are almost restored to their original texture, and then use the soaking water for further cooking. Fruits and vegetables can also be rehydrated by simply adding them to simmering soups and stews. Leafy items and tomatoes do not need to be soaked; simply cover with water and simmer until tender.

When kept dry or semi-dry, these foods can be used as highly flavorful seasoning ingredients. Dried chiles are a prime example of how versatile (and crowd-pleasing) they can be. As anyone who lived through the late 1980s and early 1990s can attest, dried halved plum and cherry tomatoes can be an exquisite addition to many dishes, providing intense bursts of sweet and tart flavors.

Dried fruits are a wonderful flavoring for baked goods, especially when partly reconstituted in a small amount of liquor or fruit juice. When used as part of a pie filling, their dryness helps keep the crust crisp, while thickening the mixture and intensifying its flavor (for examples, see Treva's Fried Apple Pies, 689, and Mock Mincemeat Pie, 672). If cut into tiny bits, they can be used as-is in granolas, 327, oatmeals, 327–28, and Muesli, 327.

Home-dried onions retain their flavor very well and turn sweet and mild. (Once ground, there really is no comparing the result to store-bought onion powder.) We use it as an ingredient anywhere we might normally use onion powder, but its flavor is remarkable enough to use as a finishing garnish on savory dishes. At the suggestion of Nicolaus Balla and Cortney Burns in their superlative book *Bar Tartine*, we have tried smoking sliced onions for 1 hour before drying and grinding them into a powder. The result is an ambrosial powder with a mildly sweet and smoky onion flavor, perfect for adding depth to savory dishes of all stripes. (But especially buttered, salted popcorn, 47.)

Drying can also add value and interest to items that would otherwise be thrown away. We have dried leek tops—which are usually discarded or used in stocks—and ground them into a fine powder. They keep their beautiful green color and have a mild onion flavor. A tangy, spicy, and salty powder can be made from the pepper mash left behind when preparing Fermented Louisiana-Style Hot Sauce, 942. Tomato skins can be dehydrated and ground into a sweet, tangy powder. Our friend Sarah Marshall, author of *Preservation Pantry*, makes a tomato skin *shichimi togarashi*, 1017, from crumbled dehydrated tomato skins, orange zest, toasted sesame seeds, seaweed, red pepper flakes, and black pepper. Well-cleaned beet peels, when dehydrated, can be ground into a beautiful pink powder that makes a striking garnish on anything from truffles to yogurt dip. Strips of dried citrus zest are a handy pantry item for adding to beef stocks, soups, and stews or for powdering and using in spice blends, marinades, and sauces.

FRUIT LEATHER

Varies

Fruit leather is a sheet of pureed fruit that has been dried. Fresh fruits that make excellent leathers are apples, apricots, berries, sweet cherries, nectarines, peaches, pears, pineapples, and plums. An electric dehydrator is the easiest way to dry fruit leather; drying can also be done in the oven. To hold the puree for drying, cover a drying tray or baking sheet with plastic wrap, extending it over the edges (silicone baking mats may also be used). Make sure the baking sheet or tray has edges to prevent spilling the puree. Some electric dehydrators come with special plastic liners for trays for making leathers. Keep in mind that fruit will become sweeter once it is dried. One cup of puree will make 2 to 3 servings; 2 cups of puree will cover a 12 × 17-inch baking sheet. Please read Drying Fruits and Vegetables, 944.

Wash, peel (if not using a food mill), trim, and seed or pit:

Ripe or slightly overripe fruit

Place the fruit in a saucepan and cook, stirring, over low heat, until a candy thermometer registers 190°F. Let cool thoroughly.

Puree in a blender, food processor, or food mill; strain, if necessary, to make a fine, smooth, fairly liquid puree. Add:

½ teaspoon ascorbic acid (vitamin C) or 2 tablespoons lemon juice per each 2 cups fruit or to taste

If the fruit needs sweetening or additional flavor, add:

(1 to 2 tablespoons light corn syrup, honey, sugar, or lemon or orange juice per each 2 cups fruit, to taste)

Artificial sweeteners can also be used. Spread the puree evenly on the prepared tray or baking sheet ⅛ inch thick in the center and ¼ inch thick around the edges (this is to prevent the edges from drying out too quickly and cracking). Dry in the dehydrator or oven at 135°F. If using an oven, check the temperature periodically with an oven thermometer so it does not get too hot. If necessary, the oven can be turned off for short intervals to reduce the temperature.

Leathers take from 4 to 10 hours to dry; test frequently for dryness. The fruit is ready when the sheet is leathery and not sticky. Touch it in several places—there should be no indentation left when you lift your finger. The leather should peel easily from the plastic wrap or tray liner. While it is still warm, you may roll it up jelly-roll fashion in the plastic wrap. If desired, use scissors to cut the roll into serving pieces. Let cool completely, then condition, 945, as directed, checking for condensation. Pack in airtight containers and store in a cool, dark, dry place; for longer storage, refrigerate or freeze.

DRYING CHILE PEPPERS

Chile peppers keep well when dried and are handy for use in many of your favorite dishes. If you know them to be especially spicy, it is best to wear gloves. Please read Drying Fruits and Vegetables, 944.

To dry green chile peppers, wash and dry. Peel the peppers by cutting a shallow slit in the outer skin of each and rotate over a gas flame for 6 to 8 minutes, broil, or scald in boiling water. Then peel and split the chiles; remove the seeds and stem. Place on dryer trays and dry in a dehydrator or on a baking sheet in the oven at 140°F until crisp, brittle, and medium green. Cool the peppers completely, then condition, 945, as directed, checking for condensation. Pack in airtight containers and store in a cool, dark, dry place; for longer storage, refrigerate or freeze.

To dry red chile peppers, wash and dry. These peppers may be left whole if small; otherwise, slice ¼ inch thick. Place on dryer trays and dry in a dehydrator or oven at 125°F until dark red and leathery. This may take 12 to 24 hours. Cool the peppers completely, then condition, 945, as directed, checking for condensation. Pack in airtight containers and store in a cool, dark, dry place; for longer storage, refrigerate or freeze.

DRYING TOMATOES

Please read Drying Fruits and Vegetables, 944.

Steam or dip tomatoes in boiling water for 30 to 60 seconds so the skins crack. Immediately place in ice water and slip the skins off. Slice crosswise into ¼-inch-thick rounds. For grape or cherry tomatoes, do not remove their skins, and simply cut them in half.

Place on dryer trays and dry in a dehydrator or oven at 155°F until leathery or brittle. This may take 6 to 24 hours.

Cool the tomatoes completely, then condition, 945, as directed, checking for condensation. Pack in airtight containers and store in a cool, dark, dry place; for longer storage, refrigerate or freeze.

DRYING HERBS AND SEEDS

Please read Drying Fruits and Vegetables, 944. Herbs, as a category, are the easiest and most rewarding ingredient to grow. Drying extends the use of annual herb plants so that they may be used year-round. For hardy perennials like rosemary, chives, and bay leaf, drying will enable you to use them in seasonings and spice blends. The seeds, pods, or fruit of some common plants—coriander, mustard seed, juniper, and fennel, to name a few—are relatively easy to harvest from a garden or isolated, unpolluted parts of the countryside.

As with vegetables and fruits, some herbs and seeds dry exceptionally well, and others do not. Generally speaking, resinous and low-moisture herbs dry better. Dried rosemary, bay laurel, and thyme, for instance, retain more of their flavor than dried basil and parsley (let alone cilantro). Outliers, like dill, have an assertive flavor, and their frilly shape dries quickly.

To harvest herbs, see 495.

To harvest seeds and pods, wait until they are mature and beginning to dry on the branch, but before they start to burst open (the weather should be sunny). The day before harvesting, hose off the seeds and branches well. At midmorning the next day—when any dew has evaporated, but the temperature is still fairly cool—cut off the branches or stems the seeds are attached to, trimming off any browned leaves and stems.

If you have a dry room with an ambient temperature between 70°F and 90°F, you may loosely tie seeds and low-moisture herbs like rosemary and oregano together into small, well-ventilated bunches. Place each bunch upside down inside a paper bag punctured with air holes, tie the neck of the bag tight with string, and hang the bag, with the leaves or seeds facing down, in a warm, airy place until dry. The bag keeps light from discoloring the leaves and flowers, keeps dust off, and catches any seeds that may drop. ➤ Do not try this with high-moisture herbs like basil, mint, and tarragon, which have a tendency to grow mold during the slow drying time.

As with fruits and vegetables, the most efficient and convenient way to dry large quantities of herbs and seeds is with an electric food dehydrator. Place the sprigs or seeded branches in a loose layer on the drying trays. If the trays have a fine enough mesh to catch the seeds, you may hasten their drying by stripping the seeds off first and spreading them out in a single layer. Set the dehydrator to 95°F for herbs or 105°F for seeds. Leaves should be crisp and ready to crumble; seeds and seed pods should be hard when pressed with a thumbnail.

Small quantities of herbs may also be dehydrated very quickly in a microwave oven.

To dry herbs in a microwave, spread a paper towel on a plate, lay the herb sprigs or leaves in one layer, and place another paper towel on top. Microwave for 1 minute, then rotate and redistribute the herbs on the towel. Microwave them further in 15-second intervals until they are crisp and ready to crumble, turning and redistributing them as you go. We do not recommend oven-drying herbs, as it is difficult to keep the temperature low enough.

To test herbs and spices for dryness, let them cool completely and then transfer to a tightly sealed glass jar. Wait a few hours, then check for condensation. If any appears, dry further. If the herbs or seeds are straight from the garden and you suspect they may harbor insects or their eggs, freeze the sealed jar for 48 hours.

Store dried herbs and spices in tightly closed glass jars in a cool, dark, dry place. Herbs will taste best within 6 months of drying; seeds will last considerably longer. Should they show signs of insect activity, discard them. ➤ Dried herbs and spices retain their flavor best when crumbled or ground just before using. For more on using herbs, see 993. To toast and grind spices, see 1020.

DRYING JERKY

High in protein and lightweight, jerky is the original backpacking food—as well as a satisfying, flavor-packed snack for those on the go. Of course, the convenience and concentrated flavor of jerky comes with a price: You will end up with only one-quarter to one-half (by weight) of the amount of meat you started with. Luckily, the best cuts for jerky making are the leaner, cheaper ones. (Fatty, highly marbled cuts of meat turn rancid much more quickly.)

An electric dehydrator is required for safely making jerky at home. Though not impossible, oven-drying jerky takes up to 3 times as long. Additionally, the oven must be able to maintain a consistent temperature between 145°F and 155°F. If the oven runs too hot, the outside of the jerky will develop a crust and cause case-hardening, 944. If the oven consistently dips below this temperature range, the meat may spoil instead. An instant-read thermometer capable of accurately reading the temperature of thin foods is also an ideal piece of equipment for ensuring safety.

Raw meats can be contaminated with microorganisms that cause disease. There have been several notable outbreaks involving *Salmonella* and *E. coli* bacteria in home-dried jerky. Pork and game meats may also harbor *Trichinella* parasites. In order to reduce the risk of these dangerous organisms, jerky must be brought to an internal temperature of 160°F (or 165°F for poultry), but it is important to do it in such a way as to prevent case-hardening, 944. ➤ One of two methods must be used: Simmer meat strips in a marinade for several minutes before placing them on drying racks. Or, after the meat strips have been dried, transfer the strips to a baking sheet and cook them in a 275°F oven for 10 minutes. Which one you choose depends on personal preference. When the strips are heated in a marinade before drying, the result is a more tender jerky. Baking the dried jerky will result in a classic, chewy texture.

JERKY

1 pound for every 3 to 4 pounds fresh meat

All meats used for jerky must be ➤ very fresh, or frozen when they were fresh. For beef and bison jerky, choose from the brisket flat, flank, top round, eye of round, or sirloin. For venison jerky, most cuts are lean enough to be used, but the leg and sirloin area are generally best (be sure to remove excessive silverskin, 527). For pork jerky, choose portions from the loin or whole leg muscles. For fish, choose skinned fillets of nonoily types, such as trout and leaner varieties of tuna, and salmon such as sockeye or keta. For poultry jerky, choose skinless chicken or turkey breast.

➤ Thoroughly sanitize, xx, work surfaces, drying racks, and utensils before starting. Trim off all visible fat from the outside of the meat, place on a rimmed baking sheet, and transfer to the freezer for 30 minutes. (If starting with frozen meat, thaw in the refrigerator just until you can easily slice through it.)

Slice the meat across any muscle grain into long strips ➤ no more than ¼ inch thick. If any pieces of fat or connective tissue are present in a strip, cut them out. As you work, transfer the cut strips to a rimmed baking sheet and keep in the refrigerator until you are done.

I. OVEN-FINISHED

This is our preferred method for fish, which is likely to disintegrate or become mangled if dipped into a boiling marinade. Marinating is strictly optional here; some like the simplicity of salted and seasoned meat.

Transfer the strips to a bowl and cover with:

Any marinade, 580–81, cooled

Marinate the strips for at least 3 hours in the refrigerator (or leave overnight), drain, and pat dry with paper towels. Alternatively, skip the marinade and simply season every pound of strips with:

½ teaspoon pickling salt or 1 teaspoon Diamond kosher salt
(½ teaspoon black pepper or chili powder)

Preheat a food dehydrator to 150°F and place the strips on drying racks in one loose layer so that they do not touch each other. Place the racks in the dehydrator and ➤ dry until the pieces crack but do not break when bent. Timing depends on the type of meat and its water-holding capacity, as well as the efficiency of your particular dehydrator. Allow up to 6 hours for pork and poultry, up to 8 hours for beef and venison, and up to 14 hours for fish. ➤ The jerky must be very dry, or bacteria will grow. Let it cool slightly before testing by bending.

➤ Once the meat has dried, preheat the oven to 275°F. Transfer the jerky pieces in one layer to rimmed baking sheets and bake until the internal temperature of a slice reaches 160°F (or 165°F for poultry), about 10 minutes. This will ensure that any parasites or microorganisms have been killed. Let the jerky cool completely.

Pat off the surface oil with paper towels, and place the entire batch in an airtight container. Store for 4 days, shaking every day, to condition the jerky and distribute moisture equally. If any condensation develops on the lid, dry the jerky for longer and repeat the test.

Store jerky in zip-top freezer bags or a jar with a tight-fitting lid. Vacuum-packing works well: Exposure to air can cause off flavors and premature rancidity. Regardless of the type of container, label and date them. Store in a cool, dry, dark place, or refrigerate or freeze for longer storage. Properly dried jerky will keep for only about 2 weeks at cool room temperature, for 3 months in the refrigerator, and for up to 1 year in the freezer. ➤ If any mold forms, discard the package of jerky.

II. PRECOOKED IN MARINADE

Heating strips in a simmering marinade prior to drying kills potentially harmful organisms and results in an especially tender jerky.

Prepare in a medium saucepan:

4 cups marinade, 580–81

Freeze and slice the meat into ¼-inch-thick slices as directed in the headnote. Bring the marinade to a simmer and preheat a dehydrator to 150°F. Working in small batches, transfer several strips to the bubbling marinade and cook for 3 minutes. The internal temperature of the slices should reach 160°F (or 165°F for poultry). Shake off excess marinade from the cooked meat and transfer to drying racks in one loose layer so that the pieces do not touch. Repeat with the rest of the meat and place the racks in the dehydrator. Dry, test, condition, and store as directed for version I.

PRESERVING IN SPIRITS

When aromatic ingredients are left to infuse in alcohol, their nuances are extracted and preserved because the volatile aroma and flavor compounds in foods are soluble in alcohol. Indeed, this is exactly why most flavoring extracts are made using alcohol (to make your own, see Vanilla Extract, 1029). In the case of fruits, the ingredients themselves are preserved, thus yielding two desirable products: booze-infused fruit and fruit-infused booze. The process can really be as simple as throwing fruit in a jar and pouring alcohol of some kind over it, though we find the results can be a bit harsh unless the alcohol is to be used in cocktails exclusively. Adding a little sugar improves these mixtures greatly and creates something that can be sipped on its own. Sugar has the added benefit of strengthening the cell walls of the fruit, preserving its texture. This means that the fruit itself remains intact, resulting in relatively clear liquid and firm fruit as opposed to mushy fruit and cloudy liquid.

CHERRY BOUNCE

½ gallon

We like to think the jaunty name of this boozy treat, said to be a favorite of George Washington's, comes from its ability to put a spring in your step . . . at least in the short term.

Combine in a half-gallon glass jar or a crock:

1¾ pounds sweet or sour cherries, stems removed, pricked once with a paring knife or needle
1¾ cups sugar
(¼ cup lemon juice, if using sweet cherries)

Add:

4 cups whiskey, bourbon, vodka, or brandy

Close the jar or crock tightly. Allow the mixture to sit in a cool, dark place for 5 to 6 months, tasting it along the way to judge when it is to your liking. There is no need to strain it—you can enjoy the boozy cherries along with the liqueur. Store indefinitely at room temperature.

MARASCHINO CHERRIES

Varies

These are not the fire-truck red "maraschino cherries" of banana split fame, but rather extremely boozy sour cherries that are as much at home as a cocktail garnish as on an adult ice cream sundae.

Place in a glass jar:

Unpitted, unstemmed sour cherries

Cover with:

Maraschino liqueur

Seal the jar and refrigerate for 2 weeks before using. Use within 1 year.

RUMTOPF

Varies

In this German concoction, fruit and sugar are added to a crock over the course of the seasons. Each time fruit is added to the crock, it is topped off with rum to cover. Dark or light rum may be used, but avoid spiced rum. We prefer to make rumtopf with a variety of stone fruits such as apricots, cherries, peaches, and plums, but other fruits, including pineapple, pears, and strawberries are excellent as well.

Have ready a clean crock or large jar. Prepare:

Ripe but firm fruit, trimmed, pitted, halved, and/or sliced as needed

Weigh the trimmed fruit and place in the crock. Add half of the fruit's weight in:

Sugar

Cover with:

Light or dark 80-proof rum

Cover the crock or jar tightly and ensure the fruit is submerged beneath the rum. Use a plate to weight the fruit if necessary. As the seasons progress, add more fruit of different kinds to the crock or jar, always adding half as much sugar as fruit by weight and rum to cover. Once the crock or jar is full, allow it to sit in a cool, dark place for at least 2 months. Rumtopf keeps indefinitely at room temperature.

NOCINO

About 1 quart

This dark brown Italian liqueur is made with green English walnuts. The walnuts should be immature enough that they are easy to cut in half with a knife (in most regions, this will be in late June). After the liqueur is strained, do not despair if it tastes harsh. The flavor will mellow over time as it sits in the bottle, eventually tasting of coffee, spices, and cola.

Have ready:

25 green English walnuts, quartered

Place the walnuts in a half-gallon jar or crock and add:

One 750 ml bottle vodka
2 cups sugar
Zest of 1 orange, cut off in wide strips with a vegetable peeler
Zest of 1 lemon, cut off in wide strips with a vegetable peeler
¼ cup whole coffee beans
10 whole cloves
Two 3-inch cinnamon sticks
1 vanilla bean, split lengthwise
(1 nutmeg, cracked)
(1 tablespoon juniper berries)

If using a jar, cover tightly with a lid and shake the jar vigorously to bruise the walnuts and mix the ingredients. If using a crock, use a wooden spoon to mix the ingredients. Store in a cool, dark place for 2 months, shaking the jar or stirring the contents of the crock about once a week. Over time, the liquid in the crock will turn from clear to an almost black color.

Strain the liquid and discard the solids, then strain the liquid again through a coffee filter or a flour sack towel to remove as many particulates as possible. Transfer the liquid to a bottle and store for 4 months. During this time, the flavor of the nocino will mellow. If you start the nocino in late June, it will be ready to drink by Christmas.

Sip neat, use to moisten cakes, or drizzle over a scoop of vanilla ice cream. Nocino keeps indefinitely at room temperature.

KNOW YOUR INGREDIENTS

Modern cooks are confronted with an immense abundance: The variety of ingredients now available is greater than ever before. This cornucopia of choices grows larger and larger as global markets and consumer demand bring once-rare items within easy reach of home cooks. On the other hand, some of the most familiar, ubiquitous ingredients are sometimes taken for granted by experienced cooks, or their peculiarities are often simply ignored by beginners. Yet success in cooking depends largely on becoming fully aware of how both common and uncommon ingredients react. Here we focus on characteristics of key ingredients, how to use them to your advantage, and what to expect when working with them. With the knowledge gained in this chapter and the chapter on Cooking Methods and Techniques, 1042, plus the information keyed by arrows and referenced in our recipes, we assure you a continuous and steady progress to becoming a better cook.

ACIDIC INGREDIENTS

Acidic ingredients are those with a low pH—between 0 and 7 on the pH scale. When we speak of acidity in cooking (or as some cooks refer to it, *brightness*), we are talking about the tang and pucker that acidic ingredients contribute to the flavor profile of a dish. Acids stimulate the palate in a way that no other ingredient can. This is why acidic ingredients are often served with rich dishes. Think of the cornichons served with pâté, the cranberry sauce served with the starch-heavy Thanksgiving feast, and the sauerkraut on an oversized Reuben. Or, in many cases, acid is added to the food itself, whether in the form of a splash of lime juice in guacamole or a spoonful of sour cream in a rich, savory sauce. Acid enlivens the eating experience, providing contrast and balance while giving dishes the kind of satisfying twang that keeps you coming back for just one more bite.

The most obvious acids—those we reach for most often in cooking—are citrus fruits, 181, like lemons and limes, and vinegars, 1029. But there are other acidic ingredients used in cooking as well. These include any cultured dairy product, from cheeses, 962, to sour cream, 974, buttermilk, 961, and yogurt, 1034; pickles (whether acidified by vinegar or by fermentation, 938); tomatoes; wine; mustard, hot sauce, ketchup, and other acidified condiments; and many fruits, such as cranberries.

All acidic ingredients contain different proportions of several kinds of acids, which affects their flavor. **Citric acid** is the predominant acid in citrus fruits. **Malic acid** is most prevalent in underripe apples, grapes, stone fruits like plums and apricots, and rhubarb. **Ascorbic acid,** or vitamin C, is found in a wide variety of fruits and vegetables, including broccoli, kale, black currants, and rose hips. **Lactic acid** is found in cultured dairy products like yogurt and cheese, as well as fermented vegetables and dry-cured sausages. It is produced by lactic acid bacteria when they metabolize sugars. **Acetic acid,** another product of fermentation, is what gives vinegar its bite. **Oxalic acid** is present in many greens, but is especially noticeable in sorrel, spinach, and rhubarb stalks. **Tartaric acid** gives grapes, raisins, and wine their tartness (see Cream of Tartar, 975), as well as tamarinds, apricots, and several other fruits.

All of this may sound a bit academic (sour is, after all, sour), but a basic awareness of what *kind* of sour a particular ingredient contributes can help explain why certain classic dishes succeed—as well as help cooks create novel combinations. As Samin Nosrat eloquently observes in her book *Salt, Fat, Acid, Heat*, dishes are often enhanced by the "layering" of several acids. For example, a mixture rich with the citric tang of tomatoes may be perked up further with a splash of lime juice, vinegar, or a grating of tangy Parmesan. This sort of layering is central to the appeal of many foods, from sauces like ketchup, barbecue sauces, and salsas to dishes like Eggplant Parmigiana, 238. A yogurt or tamarind sauce can benefit from a splash of lime juice, salads that contain bitter or sour greens are rendered even more delicious with a vinaigrette or a smattering of grapefruit segments—examples abound where acid upon acid is added to a dish. Some ingredients are prized for their ability to make dishes "pop" with their complex, layered acidity: Amba, 953, and Salt-Preserved Lemons, 942, contain lactic, citric, and malic acids; Worcestershire sauce, 1033, gets its piquancy from acetic, citric, and tartaric acids.

In addition to the flavor it adds to foods, vinegar—an ingredient with a standardized acid content—is used to preserve foods (see the Pickles chapter, 922). In the shorter term, acidic liquids can be used to stave off the oxidation of fruits and vegetables (see Acidulated Water, below).

ACIDULATED WATER

Submerging cut fruits and vegetables in water with a slight acid content keeps them from turning brown during food preparation, and helps firm the texture and remove odors from offal, 514–18.

I. Add **1 tablespoon cider vinegar or distilled white vinegar** or **2 tablespoons lemon juice** to each **1 quart water.**

II. See Antibrowning Solutions for Canning Fruits, 896, and About Freezing Fruit, 882, for acidulated solutions appropriate for those applications.

AGAVE SYRUP

Agave syrup, sometimes called **agave nectar,** is a neutral-tasting syrup made from the sweet juice of the agave, or century plant, a large succulent grown in the southwestern United States, Mexico, and Central America. Agave syrup is composed of roughly 70 percent fructose and 20 percent glucose, and thus tastes much sweeter than an equal amount of corn syrup or sugar. Agave syrup can be found in light and dark (or amber) forms. Both are mild-tasting, though dark agave syrup has subtle caramel notes.

To substitute agave syrup for sugar, for every 1 cup sugar use ⅔ cup agave syrup and decrease the liquid in the recipe by ¼ cup. You can substitute an equal amount of agave syrup for maple syrup or honey in a recipe, but agave syrup will not provide the same flavor as either one.

AJWAIN

Also known as **bishop's weed,** these tiny, dried, seed-like fruits are a spice commonly used in Middle Eastern, African, and South Asian cuisines. A relative of caraway, ajwain is bitter and peppery with hints of thyme. It is frequently left whole, toasted, and added to fritter batters or flat breads. Ajwain may also be fried in combination with other spices for dishes like Dal Tadka, 218, and Chana Masala, 217. Ground, it is frequently added to Indian masalas and the Ethiopian spice blend Berbere, 590.

ALCOHOLIC INGREDIENTS

There is no doubt that a splash (or more) of wine or brandy can add a welcome extra dimension to many dishes, contributing aroma and depth of flavor. Some famous dishes, like Coq au Vin, 420, are drowning in wine; others, like Oysters Rockefeller, 66, rely on the merest hint of liqueur for their characteristic flavor. ➤ For detailed information on specific types of alcohol, see the Cocktails, Wine, and Beer chapter, 17.

Alcohol may be added before cooking as part of a marinade, used to deglaze a pan, added to the cooking liquid for braises and stews, or used as a soaking liquid for Pound Cake, 726, Fruitcake Cockaigne, 740, Trifle, 827, and Tiramisù, 826.

Generally, low-proof alcoholic beverages like wine, beer, sake, and hard cider are used as a marinade or added at the beginning of cooking and allowed to simmer, which concentrates their flavor (and evaporates nearly all of their alcohol). Fortified wines, spirits, and liqueurs are already quite concentrated, and may be added toward the end of cooking for a pronounced alcoholic bite, or ignited to flame or **flambé,** 1049, foods. Or, like low-proof ingredients, they may be added at the beginning of cooking to build a flavor base for simmered dishes like French Onion Soup, 92, or reduced in sauces, such as the one for Steak au Poivre, 461. Finally, high-proof spirits can be infused with the flavor of herbs, spices, and fruits; for more, see Infused Vodkas, 22, Extracts and Flavorings, 980, and Preserving in Spirits, 948.

When using **beer** and **hard cider** in cooking, ➤ avoid heavily hopped or assertively malted beers; their bitterness and herbaceousness can be a distraction in the finished dish. Beer features as a cooking liquid in Carbonnade Flamande, 466, MacLeid's Rockcastle Chili, 502, and Steak and Kidney Pie, 705. We also like to add beer to beans, usually pinto, as they cook. Hard cider makes an excellent, slightly sweet cooking liquid for Steamed Mussels IV, 351. Both cider and beer add lightness and flavor to various doughs and batters, such as Beer Batter, 657, and Beer Bread, 627.

Depending on the type, **wines** can add sweetness, a light acidity, and aroma to a dish. Dry red and white table wines are most commonly used in cooking, but dry rosé is also acceptable for some preparations, such as wine-poached fruit. ➤ The wine you choose need not be a very old or expensive one (we would argue that using a fine wine in cooking is a waste, as much of its character will be cooked out), but it should be good enough to be drunk with pleasure for its own sake. Avoid overly tannic wines, which may make a dish taste bitter or too acidic. Avoid bottles labeled "cooking wine." These are usually heavily salted. Wine left over a day or two after opening, which may have lost its prime freshness but is still palatable, is a good candidate for the pot. To keep it from oxidizing, pour the wine from its original bottle into a smaller bottle or jar, close tightly, and store it in the refrigerator. Of course, the most convenient option is a box of wine in the pantry, which takes up no refrigerator space, is economical, and maintains the quality of the wine by limiting its exposure to oxygen.

Since wine adds acidity and sugar, season the dish to taste at the end of cooking. To add wine to a dish that has nearly finished cooking, reduce it separately in a saucepan first; 1 cup of wine will reduce to about ¼ cup in 10 minutes of brisk, uncovered simmering.

Champagne and other sparkling wines are practically the only type we know that are used uncooked; their high acidity and clean flavor are wonderful in desserts; see Mimosa Pound Cake, 727, and Champagne or Rosé Gelatin with Raspberries, 821—the latter actually preserves a hint of the Champagne's effervescence.

Sake is used extensively in cooking and marinades. Any brand of sake is suitable except those labeled "cooking wine," which are made from inferior rice wines and may contain additives; avoid unfiltered sakes as well. When looking for a substitute, try pale dry sherry, white wine, or dry vermouth.

Mirin is a type of alcohol made from glutinous rice. Its mellow, sweet flavor balances everything from Teriyaki Marinade, 582, and Tentsuyu, 572, to Udon Noodles in Broth, 304, and Shoyu Ramen, 304. *Hon mirin*, or "true mirin" contains the most alcohol of all the types of mirin, clocking in at around 14 percent. *Aji mirin* usually contains sake and corn syrup. Hon mirin is notably more expensive than aji mirin, but it is worth the price. That said, aji mirin is perfectly serviceable for everyday cooking.

Shaoxing wine, a Chinese rice wine, has a slightly oxidized and subtly herbal flavor that is vital to Chinese cooking. Like sake, avoid Shaoxing bottles labeled as "cooking wine." While different in flavor, dry sherry is a decent substitute.

Fortified wines, such as port, sherry, Madeira, and Marsala, are much more potent than table wines and should be added in moderation, usually toward the end of cooking. Dry vermouth and drier sherries are the exception and may be used as part of a braising liquid.

Spirits, liqueurs, and cordials are most frequently used in flavoring desserts, lightly cooked if cooked at all, and added in moderation. Some exceptions to this do, of course, exist in dishes such as Penne with Vodka Sauce, 299, and Pheasant Braised with Gin and Juniper, 440. Flambéing, 1049, is a spectacular use of spirits in cooking, harnessing not only the flavor of the spirit but also its tendency to ignite when exposed to flame. Spirits and liqueurs are also excellent additions to ice creams and sorbets, preventing the mixtures from freezing too hard and keeping them silky and soft right out of the freezer. Regardless of application, however, the pronounced flavor of spirits means they must be used judiciously.

Bitters, though usually thought of as a cocktail ingredient, may be added in minute quantities to many dishes. Since they are prone to evaporating, they are best added to uncooked preparations, those that are heated gently, or at the end of cooking. For more on how to use bitters, see 956.

ALLSPICE

Jamaican allspice berries are so named because the flavor is reminiscent of several "warm spices" combined: clove, black pepper, cinnamon, and nutmeg. The berries are added whole to pickle brines and Mulled Wine, 31, or ground and used in baked goods, marinades, curries, and sausages. Despite conjuring the flavors of so many different spices, allspice is often used in combination with other spices, as in Pfeffernüsse, 772, and Cincinnati Chili Cockaigne, 502.

Though allspice is unrelated to peppercorns, the Spanish, who were the first Europeans to encounter it, confused the two and named the myrtle tree from which allspice comes "pimento" (*Pimenta dioica*). These aromatic trees are felled, cut to size, and sold as **pimento wood,** which is used extensively in Jamaica to perfume grilled dishes like Jamaican Jerk Chicken, 413. Since the wood is hard to find and rather expensive, many recipes for pimento wood–smoked jerk dishes call for ground allspice as a substitute (see Jamaican Jerk Paste, 584, and Jerk Spice Rub, 587). **Pimento leaves** are also rare and expensive; like bay leaves, they are very fragrant and may be used to flavor stews, sauces, and braises.

ALMONDS

Almonds are the kernels of a stone fruit closely related to plums, cherries, and apricots. The type we are most familiar with, that staple of health-focused snackers, is called the **sweet almond.** Look for plump smooth kernels. Almonds in the shell tend to be fresher and more economical (if you do not mind the extra effort of shelling). Shelled almonds are found raw or roasted with their skins on or blanched with skins removed. They are also available sliced and slivered, which are especially good for topping baked items and garnishing savory or sweet dishes. **Almond meal** or **flour,** 985, is used in tortes, 741–42, Marzipan, 873, and Almond Paste, 873. To make **almond milk,** see About Nut and Seed Milks, 1006; for **almond butter,** see About Nut and Seed Butters, 1005.

Marcona almonds are a Spanish variety with larger, flatter kernels than regular sweet almonds. They contain more fat and are very rich and flavorful. Though native to Spain, Marconas are increasingly available in grocery stores, often near the cheese counter. There is good reason for this placement: Lightly fried in olive oil and dusted with salt, they are a perfect accompaniment to a cheese board or antipasto spread, especially one that features Manchego and Quince Paste, 194.

Green almonds are young, freshly picked sweet almonds that have their fruit still attached. The fruit itself is thin and leathery, with fuzzy skin. Green almonds are soft and best eaten out of hand with cheese and wine. They are sometimes pickled as well.

Bitter almonds are actually the kernels of a species of apricot. Though used as a flavoring in some classic European recipes, bitter almonds contain trace amounts of cyanide and are consequently not widely available for purchase. They are processed, however, and used to flavor almond extract and almond liqueurs. They are also used to make Italian amaretti cookies.

ALMOND GARNISH (AMANDINE)

About ½ cup

This classic garnish glorifies the most commonplace dishes. As a variation for a vegetable garnish, substitute hulled pumpkin or sesame seeds for the almonds.

Melt in a small skillet:

4 tablespoons (½ stick) butter

Add and stir over low heat until the nuts are lightly browned:

½ cup sliced almonds

Salt to taste

AMBA

Amba is a bright, sour, and pungent condiment popular in Iraq and Israel (similar pickles are common in India as well). Amba starts as a chunky, fermented pickle made from unripe mangoes, oil, turmeric, and other spices. It is usually pureed into a thick sauce for serving with Falafel, 214, Lamb Shawarma, 480, kebabs, and Sabich, 145. Find amba in Middle Eastern markets.

AMCHUR

Amchur is sliced or powdered unripe mango. Like tamarind, 195, sumac, 1027, and *anardana*, below, amchur is used to add a sour tang to curries, chutneys, and spice blends like Chaat Masala, 589. Though more commonly found as a powder, dried amchur slices can also be found at Indian grocery stores or online. The slices will keep longer but should be ground before use (or left to simmer in a bubbling curry and then discarded like bay leaves or cinnamon sticks).

ANARDANA

Pomegranate arils are familiar to anyone who has eaten a pomegranate, but when dried they take on a deep, sweet-sour flavor and are called *anardana*. Anardana is sold ground and whole—the latter is sticky with the residual sugars from the dried fruit. Whole anardana should be ground before adding to spice blends, sauces, chutneys, and curries. They contribute a sour flavor, somewhat like tamarind, 1027, and sumac, 1027. Find anardana at Indian and Persian grocery stores.

ANCHOVIES

Anchovies are tiny fish that have been cured in salt for many months and then canned. Added discreetly, they contribute a savory boost to dishes that is hard to pinpoint. When added with enthusiasm—whether draped atop a slice of pizza, or mashed into the dressing for a Caesar Salad, 117—they can elicit squeals of joy from those who appreciate their rich flavor (or upturned noses from avowed anchovy haters).

Most anchovies available in grocery stores are filleted and packed in olive oil. The fillets may be packed flat, or rolled up (occasionally, they are wrapped around capers, or packed with chile flakes). For most uses, we prefer the flat fillets without any added ingredients. **Anchovy paste** sold in tubes is convenient, but it is apt to be saltier and less flavorful than quality fillets.

Salt-packed anchovies can be found in specialty stores or ordered online. They have their heads removed but are otherwise whole. Though their bones must be painstakingly removed and the salt washed off, salt-packed anchovies are usually economical and have better flavor and a firmer texture than their oil-packed counterparts. When time permits, we rinse and fillet a large can of them all at once, pack them in a jar, cover them with olive oil, and refrigerate them.

To unobtrusively boost the flavor of dishes with anchovy, add about ⅛ teaspoon minced anchovy per 1 cup sauce. To use anchovy fillets in a salad or on canapés, reduce their saltiness by soaking in cold water for 30 minutes. Drain and dry on paper towels before using. For another salty, anchovy-based flavoring, see Fish Sauce, 984.

White anchovies, also known as *boquerones*, are the same small, oily species of fish as the darker canned variety, but they are only briefly cured and then packed in a lightly seasoned marinade. The result is much milder, so much so that they are eaten as an appetizer more than they are used as a flavoring.

ANGELICA

The leaves and stems of this sweet, licorice-flavored plant are candied as a garnish for desserts. Angelica root is used to flavor gin, absinthe, and liqueurs like Chartreuse. Fresh leaves are often added to stewed rhubarb, 898, as it reduces the rhubarb's perceived tartness. Raw stems may be cut thinly on the diagonal and added to salads. In Scandinavia, Iceland, and Greenland, angelica is often pickled or cooked like a vegetable. **Angelica seed** is ground and used in pastry, or to season savory dishes.

ANISE

Also called **aniseed,** this spice is sweet tasting, with licorice overtones. The seeds are used to flavor liqueur, including pastis, sambuca, and ouzo. The essential oil may be used to flavor sponge cakes. Use the seeds whole in Springerle, 779; to release their full flavor, toast, 1005, and lightly crush the seeds with a mortar and pestle, or place them in a heavy zip-top bag and crush with a rolling pin. Ground anise seed may be added to savory dishes, especially those containing seafood, and is commonly used to season Italian sausage. For **star anise,** see 1022.

ANNATTO (ACHIOTE)

The brilliant red seeds of the annatto tree are commonly used in Mexican, Caribbean, and South American cooking. The dried triangular seeds are available whole, ground, or as a paste. Annatto is often used to add a yellowish-orange hue to dishes, as well as a bright, peppery flavor. Food manufacturers frequently rely on the vivid color to improve the appearance of cheese, mustard, and margarine (though the flavor does not come through in the minuscule amount of extract they use). The color of the seeds can be imparted to cooking oil by heating ¼ cup lightly crushed annatto seeds in 1 cup vegetable oil or lard to 250°F and holding it at that temperature for 10 to 15 minutes or until the oil takes on a reddish hue. Strain out the seeds and store the oil in a covered container at room temperature for up to 1 month.

ARROWROOT

See Starches, 1022.

ASAFOETIDA

Asafoetida, which translates as the unpromising "foul-smelling gum," is made of a resinous sap collected from the large taproot of a giant relative of fennel. Also known as **hing,** the sap is dried into solid, resinous chunks. Though these can be found by the industrious online shopper, asafoetida is readily available in Indian markets as a fine powder, which is often mixed with rice flour as a bulking agent (this also makes it easier to control the amount you add to dishes). While the smell of asafoetida is powerfully sulfuric, when cooked it contributes a deeply appealing, savory flavor reminiscent of garlic and onion. Indeed, a prized relative of asafoetida, *laserpicium*, was used so extensively in Roman cookery that it was harvested to extinction. Asafoetida is a characteristic ingredient in Chaat Masala, 589, and is also added to a variety of South Asian dishes, including fish curries, vegetable dishes, and pickles. ➤ When storing asafoetida, contain the smell by sealing it in a glass canning jar.

AVOCADO LEAVES

The fresh and dried leaves of several avocado tree species are used as an herb. Whole toasted leaves lend a mild anise flavor to beans (see Frijoles de la Olla, 213), braises, and soups. Ground avocado leaf can be used instead, or as a seasoning in other savory dishes, like Sopes, 612. ➤ The leaves of some avocado species are thought to be poisonous, so be sure to do a bit of research and positively identify the tree before picking fresh ones.

BAKER'S AMMONIA

Baker's ammonia, the forerunner of our modern and more stable chemical leaveners, is also known as **ammonium bicarbonate, carbonate of ammonia,** and **salt of hartshorn.** Used for years in Europe to produce long-lasting crisp cookies, it is sold as a fine powder and may be purchased online. Unlike other leaveners, which require an acidic ingredient or water to effervesce, baker's ammonia needs only heat. Buy baker's ammonia in small amounts, keep in a sealed container, and store in the refrigerator or freezer until ready to use. It should be sifted with the dry ingredients or dissolved in liquid. ➤ Do not eat uncooked dough or batter that contains baker's ammonia.

BAKING POWDER

Baking powder is a ready-made combination of baking soda (below), an alkaline, and various liquid- and heat-responsive acid salts such as tartaric acid (or cream of tartar, 975), monocalcium phosphate, and several others. When added to the dry ingredients of a batter or dough, mixed with liquid, and baked, the baking soda and acid salts create carbon dioxide gas, which takes the form of tiny bubbles in the mixture, causing it to rise. The acids either start to leaven after being combined with water, or only react when the dough or batter is heated.

There are two basic types of baking powder: single-acting (of which there are both fast-acting and slow-acting variants) and double-acting. **Double-acting baking powder** contains two types of acid—one acid starts to work as soon as it is exposed to liquid, and the action of the other acid is held in reserve until the batter reaches a certain temperature, usually 140°F. This two-phase reaction ensures an additional push during the later stages of baking, producing a taller, lighter end product. This type of baking powder typically uses sodium aluminum sulfate and monocalcium phosphate as the acid ingredients. Most major brands are double-acting. ➤ When we call for "baking powder" in recipes, use double-acting baking powder.

Some double-acting baking powders (labeled **aluminum-free**) are fast-acting, and batters or doughs containing this type of baking powder should be mixed quickly and put in the oven as soon as possible.

Single-acting baking powder contains only one acid. In single-acting **tartrate baking powders,** baking soda is combined with tartaric acid or a combination of cream of tartar and tartaric acid. They are the quickest in reaction time, giving off carbon dioxide the moment they are combined with liquid. Therefore, ➤ have the oven preheated, mix the batter quickly, and place it in the oven as soon as possible. ➤ Do not use tartrate powder for doughs and batters that are to be stored in the refrigerator or frozen before baking. Other single-acting baking powders do not start to leaven until they are exposed to heat, making them slow-acting.

Before measuring any of these leaveners, ➤ stir and break up any lumps, and use a dry measuring spoon. If you doubt the effectiveness of any baking powder, ➤ test it by mixing 1 teaspoon baking powder with ⅓ cup hot water. Use the baking powder only if it bubbles enthusiastically. ➤ Recipes containing baking powder should use only 1 to 1¼ teaspoons per 1 cup flour.

If you run out of baking powder, you can mix up a homemade version of single-acting baking powder: For each 1 teaspoon baking powder called for in the recipe, mix together ½ teaspoon cream of tartar, ⅓ teaspoon baking soda, and ⅛ teaspoon salt. After adding the above mixture, do not delay putting the batter into the oven. ➤ Do not try to store this mixture; it has poor keeping qualities.

▲ Because of the decrease in barometric pressure at high altitudes, carbon dioxide gas expands more quickly and thus has greater leavening action. For this reason, the amount of baking powder should be decreased if you are using a sea-level recipe. Or select recipes designed especially for high altitudes; see the listing of high-altitude recipes in the index.

BAKING SODA (SODIUM BICARBONATE)

When baking soda (an alkaline substance) is not combined with an acid salt (as it is in baking powder), it is usually combined with an acidic ingredient to achieve a pronounced leavening effect. Adding buttermilk, sour milk, yogurt, sour cream, molasses, honey, vinegar, or citrus juice to a batter or dough will cause a reaction with the baking soda. Baking soda will still leaven baked goods even if there is no acidic ingredient present, though the leavening action will not be quite as dramatic.

Since the leavening begins as soon as the batter is mixed, always whisk the baking soda with the dry ingredients first and bake batters as soon as possible once the wet ingredients are added. If timed correctly, the baked item will reach its maximum size at the same time as the starches gelatinize and the gluten proteins set. If the batter is too thin to hold the rise, though, it will collapse before it can set. If the leaven is activated too early, the batter will fall before it can set.

Some recipes call for both baking powder and baking soda. This is because there may be enough baking soda to neutralize some of the acid in the recipe but not enough to actually leaven the baked good (simply adding more baking soda can cause the finished product to taste salty or soapy). The baking powder provides an extra boost of leavening. In other cases, the baking soda is added to promote browning.

➤ Recipes containing baking soda should use only about ¼ teaspoon per 1 cup flour.

▲ At high altitudes, baking soda is usually decreased for the same reason baking powder is: Their leavening action is more effective at lower atmospheric pressure. Sometimes, to increase the acidity of the batter—an advantage at high altitudes—the balance of the two is adjusted to use more baking powder than soda.

BANANA BLOSSOMS

The large, unopened blossoms of the banana tree are trimmed and cut, then they are stir-fried, added to curries, or eaten raw, adding a bright, astringent crunch wherever they are used. The outer petals are a fantastic deep purple color and quite fibrous, much like the leaves (known to botanists as bracts) of an artichoke. The inner portion of the blossom gets progressively paler as the outer petals are pulled away. As you peel away the petals you will also see many tiny, oblong flowers inside the larger blossom. These would become bananas if left to mature. In some preparations, these tiny flowers are discarded. In others, such as a Bengali curry called *mochar ghonto*, they are cleaned, chopped, soaked or parboiled, and cooked with aromatics and spices.

There are several ways to prepare banana blossom. You may peel away and discard all the purple petals and tiny yellow flowers until you reach an inner cone of pale, tender petals. This cone may be thinly sliced crosswise and placed immediately in acidulated water, 951, to prevent browning. Or, once you have reached the tender inner cone of the blossom, quarter it lengthwise and shake out and discard all the yellow flowers inside. Or, as a third option, the pale, tender petals may all be stripped off, the yellow flowers discarded, and the petals stacked on top of one another and thinly sliced crosswise. Serve the banana blossom as a crunchy garnish for Thai curries, Vietnamese soups, and in salads.

BANANA LEAVES

The gigantic leaves of the banana tree are an especially sturdy wrapping for cooking foods, 1056. Banana leaves may be used to prevent dainty items like fish and rice from sticking to a grill grate or being scorched by flames. In the Yucatán, they are used to wrap tamales, 325, and as a wrapping for pit-cooking meats. For the Cambodian dish *amok trey*, a banana leaf is fashioned into a bowl, filled with fish, aromatics, and coconut milk, and placed in a steamer. The curry-like custard is then served in the banana-leaf bowl. Though too thick and sturdy to eat, they impart a pleasant, almost green tea–like fragrance to the foods they enclose. Find banana leaves in the frozen section of Asian and Latino markets; to prepare leaves for wrapping, see Banana Leaf Tamales, 325.

BASIL

From the Greek *basiliskos*, or "royal herb." A cousin of mint, basil has anise-like, peppery notes. Whereas the typical "sweet" basils—such as the **Genovese** variety famous for its role in Pesto, 586—have but hints of these flavors, other varieties lean more heavily toward one or the other. **Globe basil,** which has smaller leaves and grows in a tidy, dense bush, is especially spicy. **Thai basil,** with its purple stems and flowers, has a pronounced anise-clove flavor; it is an essential garnish for Pho Bo, 96, and a nice last-minute addition to Thai curries. A different, but closely related species called **holy basil,** or *tulsi*, is similarly flavored. **Lemon** and **cinnamon basil** are hybrid species, and taste as their names imply; though they sound enticing, we find them less useful in the kitchen. **Dwarf bush basil,** *Ocimum minimum*, has tiny, potent leaves and grows to be less than 1 foot tall, making it the best variety for growing indoors.

To chiffonade or make ribbon cuts of basil, see 200. Basil darkens quickly after cutting; use a sharp knife and cut just before serving. Stir into hot dishes at the last second, use as a garnish, or serve basil as they do in Italy: a bouquet of sprigs in a small vase for diners to pick leaves from at the table. Basil dries poorly, losing much of its intoxicating aroma and complexity in the process. The flavor of basil is best preserved in Pesto, 586, and flavored butter, 559–60, both of which will keep for extended periods in the freezer. Jen's Basil Oil, 570, is another fantastic option that also preserves its vibrant green color. **Basil seeds** are somewhat similar to chia seeds, 967, in that they form coats of slippery mucilage when soaked in liquid. They are sometimes added to flavored beverages.

BAY LEAVES

Bay laurel, *Laurus nobilis*, is an evergreen shrub with thick, inedible leaves that are highly aromatic. Some cultivars have a wavy leaf margin or are variegated in color, but most are dark green, smooth-edged, and oblong. Bay leaves may seem like a culinary Hail Mary—an ingredient thrown in for good luck but not much else. However, we argue that they add a wonderful, subtle menthol-like note to soups, stews, stocks, braises, marinades, pickles, beans, and pasta cooking water.

Dried bay leaves are a fixture in the spice aisle. Do not crumble dried bay leaves before adding to the pot; leave them whole for easy removal (and always remove them before serving). Alternatively, grind dried bay leaf very finely for adding to seasoning blends (see Chesapeake Bay Seasoning, 588).

Fresh bay leaves are increasingly available in produce departments, and bay trees are easy to grow and maintain depending on the climate. Bend and bruise fresh bay leaves before adding to a dish to release more of their flavor. If you find yourself flush with fresh bay leaves, you may dry them or place in a bag in the freezer, where they will keep for months. ➤ Avoid fresh bay leaves that look pale grayish-green and are slender in shape; these are from the California laurel, or *Umbellularia californica*, which has an overpowering eucalyptus flavor. When picking fresh bay leaves, ➤ do not confuse them with the poisonous *Prunus laurocerasus*, the cherry laurel or English laurel, which contains cyanide. When bruised, its leaves may smell of almond flavoring.

BEECHNUTS

Beechnuts are not harvested commercially, which means you will have to pick them before the squirrels and blue jays get to them. Wait until their spiky husks turn brown in late summer or early fall. Toasting, 1005, improves the flavor, destroys saponins that may cause a stomachache, and makes it easier to free the triangular nuts from their husks (the husks will open on their own later in the season). Once the kernels are removed, rub them in a kitchen towel or sieve to remove the inner skins and any small hairs.

BEER

See Alcoholic Ingredients, 951.

BIRCH SYRUP

Birch syrup is made from the sap of the birch tree. It has a more complex flavor than maple syrup, with savory notes that are reminiscent of molasses. Because it burns at a much lower temperature than maple syrup, 999, birch syrup is concentrated over a longer period of time using moderate heat. It is much more labor-intensive to make than maple syrup, with a ratio of 110:1 birch sap to finished birch syrup (compared to maple syrup's 40:1 ratio). As a result, birch syrup is much more expensive than maple syrup and should be used as a topping rather than an ingredient.

BITTERS

We are most familiar with bitters as an indispensable "seasoning" for cocktails. Angostura and Peychaud's are certainly the most common; others (such as Underberg) are digestifs. These stalwarts have been joined by an ever-widening array of choices, which range from citrus, herb, and spice-flavored bitters to those infused with cacao, coffee, and chile. While the composition of aromatics varies, the classic formulas rely on a combination of medicinal roots and barks (such as gentian, cinchona, wormwood, and dandelion) as bittering agents, as well as aromatic herbs, spices, and citrus zest. These ingredients are steeped in high-proof alcohol, strained, and lightly sweetened with a dark caramel syrup.

Bitters may be added in minute quantities to many dishes, but bear in mind that they are very strong and, naturally, bitter. They should be used more like an extract—usually a teaspoon or less will do. As with extracts, 980, bitters are high-proof and will evaporate quickly when heated, which dissipates their flavor; they are most effective when added to uncooked dishes, at the end of cooking, or to mixtures that will be gently heated, such as the filling for Angostura Chess Pie, 678. Bitters are also a superb addition to strawberry-rhubarb filling, 671, chocolate truffles, 859–60, frostings, 792–93, and ice pops, 850.

BLACK LIME (LOOMI OR LIMU OMANI)

Used as a souring ingredient in Middle Eastern (particularly Iranian) dishes and spice blends, these limes are dried whole, which concentrates their flavor and gives them a piney aroma and lightly fermented flavor. Most turn black, but tan-colored *loomi* are not uncommon. They may be sold whole or ground, but the former will keep much longer. They may be added whole or cracked to braises and soups but should be ground for most purposes (before attempting to grind whole *loomi*, crush them by bearing down with the flat side of a knife, then pick out and discard the seeds). Use sparingly in place of sumac, tamarind, or Salt-Preserved Lemon, 942, to add a zesty tang to rice, fish, and poultry dishes.

BONITO

Also called **katsuobushi,** bonito is made from the loins of skipjack tuna that have been cooked, salted, smoked, half-dried, inoculated with a hardy type of *Aspergillus* mold, and then left to ferment and dry longer. The result is a rock-hard tuna loin with a complex, intensely savory flavor. Bonito is shaved very thinly into pale pinkish-beige flakes, then added to a variety of dishes, either as a foundational flavoring in stock (Dashi, 78) or as a garnish or topping (see Okonomiyaki, 226). Bonito flakes are sold in a variety of thicknesses. Use thicker flakes for stocks or soups and thin, translucent ones as a garnish. Whole bonito loins can be ordered online, but they are exceedingly hard to shave without a specialized tool.

BORAGE

Use the fuzzy leaves and blue blossoms in moderation wherever you want to add a cucumber-like flavor. Thinly slice the leaves for topping salads and fish; mince and add to vinaigrettes; or bruise and tear them for adding to cocktails like Pimm's Cup, 21. The choice, blue star-like flowers are beautiful floated in punches and cocktails or used as a garnish for salads and cold soups. Like chive blossoms, they may be used to infuse vinegar, which readily takes on their vibrant color and cucumber flavor. Borage blossoms can be dried and used in herbal tea, 7.

BOTTARGA

The roe sacs of grey mullet, tuna, and other species of fish have been cured and dried for hundreds of years in the Mediterranean and elsewhere (including Japan, which produces a softer type known as **karasumi**). The Italian term *bottarga* is the most common name for this delicacy, and it is shaved over simple dishes—especially pastas—to give them a briny, savory flavor. Mullet roe is much preferred to other types and fetches a high price. Tuna roe is made into a funkier type of Sicilian bottarga; other fish roe, like herring, cod, and pollock, is sometimes used. Any dried roe may be finely shaved over lightly seasoned dishes that will benefit from (and highlight) its salty savoriness; semidried roe that is too soft to shave is often fried in oil, thinly sliced, and served as a delicacy. If you wish to stretch the rare, precious flavor of bottarga, use the shavings to infuse a flavored butter, 559–60.

BOUQUET GARNI

A mainstay of French cooking, bouquet garni is a bundle of whole herbs—and occasionally spices and aromatic vegetables—wrapped in cheesecloth or tied with kitchen string and used to flavor soups, stocks, braises, and sauces (often in combination with a mirepoix, 1002). The bundle infuses the cooking liquid and is removed before serving. We call for bouquet garni many, many times in this book, but never by name. Several sprigs of fresh parsley and thyme, celery leaves, and a dried or fresh bay leaf are standard, to which a length of leek stem, a few cloves, and garlic may be added. If using dried instead of fresh, ➤ gather all the herbs (except the bay leaves) into a tea ball, infuser, or tied square of filter paper so that flecks do not escape into the cooking liquid.

BRAZIL NUTS

Brazil nuts are large, long nuts—more than twice the size of a cashew or almond. We find it easiest to shell Brazil nuts by freezing them first and then cracking them with a hammer; the nut meats should pop right out. Toast whole Brazil nuts at 350°F for about 12 minutes.

BREAD CRUMBS

When reading a recipe, note what kind of bread crumbs are called for. The results will be very different depending on whether they are dry, fresh, browned, or buttered. Finely crushed cracker, cornflake, and corn or potato chip crumbs are sometimes used in place of bread crumbs in breading and on gratins. For breading and coating foods to be fried, see 658. Store bread ends and leftover slices in the freezer and use them to make crumbs when needed.

Grinding bread crumbs with a rotary hand grater

DRY CRUMBS

Dry crumbs are made from dry bread, corn bread, crackers, or cake. If the bread or cake is not sufficiently dry, crisp on a baking sheet in a 200°F oven for 1 to 2 hours before making crumbs; do not let brown. To make a small quantity of crumbs, grind small pieces of dried bread in a rotary hand grater, as shown, or place in a closed zip-top bag and crush with a rolling pin or mallet.

For larger quantities of bread crumbs, we recommend using a food processor. If your food processor has a disc attachment for shredding, cut the bread into chunks that can easily fit in the feed tube, using the feed tube pusher to shred the bread chunks into crumbs (this is a bit loud, yet strangely relaxing). If using a food processor with a regular chopping blade, cut or tear the bread into cubes or small pieces first and process in small batches.

To toast bread crumbs, spread on a baking sheet and bake in a 375°F oven for 10 minutes, stirring halfway through. Store dry bread crumbs in an airtight container in a cool, dry place.

PANKO

These Japanese bread crumbs are made from loaves baked with an electrical current, which gives them a very dry, craggy texture. They are available in most grocery stores. Panko is desirable for coating foods with larger, especially crispy crumbs. You can substitute panko in most recipes that call for dried bread crumbs, and vice versa.

SOFT OR FRESH BREAD CRUMBS

Soft or fresh bread crumbs are made with fresh, untoasted bread. The best way to retain the light texture desired in such crumbs is to tear the bread into pieces, then pulse in small batches in a food processor until ground into light, fluffy crumbs. ➤ To measure soft bread crumbs, pile them lightly into a cup; do not pack them down.

BROWNED OR BUTTERED BREAD CRUMBS

About 1 cup

Once browned, you may season the crumbs with bits of finely crumbled cooked bacon, minced toasted, 1005, nuts, finely grated Parmesan, minced fresh herbs or crumbled dried herbs, finely grated lemon zest, black pepper, or red pepper flakes. These flavorful crumbs make an excellent topping for green salads, roasted vegetable dishes, sautéed greens, and pasta dishes.

Heat in a skillet over medium heat:

4 tablespoons (½ stick) butter, olive oil, or a combination

If desired, reduce the heat to low, add, and cook for 5 minutes:

(1 or 2 garlic cloves, lightly smashed)

Remove the garlic from the pan. Increase the heat to medium and stir in:

1 cup dry bread crumbs or panko or 1½ cups soft bread crumbs

½ teaspoon salt

Cook, stirring occasionally, until the crumbs turn golden brown. If desired, mince the cooked garlic cloves and stir into the crumbs.

AU GRATIN

"Au gratin" is a term that, in America, is usually associated with cheese. But the term may refer to any topping of fine fresh or dry bread crumbs or even crushed cornflakes, cracker crumbs, or finely ground nuts on casseroles (see About Casseroles, 537), creamed dishes, stuffed vegetables, or any dish where a browned, crispy upper crust is desired.

I. PLAIN

Sprinkle over the food in a light but thorough covering:

Dry bread crumbs

Unless otherwise directed, bake in a 375°F oven until a crisp, golden brown crust forms. Or preheat the broiler and place the dish 3 inches below the heat. Allow it to brown, checking frequently.

II. SEASONED AND BUTTERED

Mix together:

Dry bread crumbs

(Sweet paprika, up to ½ teaspoon per 1 cup crumbs)

Sprinkle in a light but thorough covering over the food. Scatter over the top:

Dots of butter

Unless otherwise directed, bake in a 375°F oven to produce a crisp, golden crust. Or preheat the broiler and place the dish 5 inches below the heat. Allow it to brown, checking frequently.

III. WITH CHEESE

Combine in a medium bowl:

Dry bread crumbs

Finely grated Cheddar, Romano, or Parmesan (up to ¼ cup per 1 cup crumbs)

(Sweet paprika, up to ½ teaspoon per 1 cup crumbs)

Sprinkle in a light but thorough covering over the food. Scatter over the top:

Dots of butter

Unless otherwise directed, bake in a preheated 350°F oven to produce a crisp, golden crust. Or preheat the broiler and place the dish 5 inches below the heat. Allow it to brown, checking frequently.

BRINE

At the minimum, a brine is nothing more than salt dissolved in water. Submerging pork, poultry, and fish in a brine enhances their juiciness. Many cooks add flavoring elements to brines as well, which seasons the surface of the food much like a marinade does. Sugar added to a brine promotes browning when the food is cooked. These embellishments are hardly necessary, though.

Seasoned or not, we recommend a **6 percent brine** for most purposes, which measures out to ¾ cup table salt or 1½ cups Diamond kosher salt per 1 gallon water, or 3 tablespoons table salt or 6 tablespoons Diamond kosher salt per 1 quart water. Stir together until the salt is dissolved, then fully submerge the food in the brine, preferably in a covered, spill-proof container. You can get away with mixing up less brine by placing the food in a zip-top bag then adding brine to cover, but the bag should be placed in a bowl or baking dish large enough to contain any leaks. For brining times and more ingredient-specific information, see About Brining Poultry, 405, About Marinating and Brining Fish, 376, and Brining, Marinating, and Seasoning Meat, 450. Discard brine after use. To promote browning, dry items thoroughly with a paper towel or place them on a rack set on a baking sheet in the refrigerator for an hour or more.

Another method worth mentioning is **equilibrium brining,** which is generally more consistent (but takes longer and requires an accurate scale). Take the weight of the water and meat, fish, or poultry pieces and add a (much lower) percentage of that total in salt. For most foods, ➤ 1–1.5 percent salt yields well-seasoned food and does not cause the food to take on a cured texture or flavor. The only drawback is that the salt content of the meat and brine must equalize. This is not a problem for thin, porous items like fish fillets, which may only require 2 hours, but pieces of meat or poultry thicker than a pork chop may take days. For examples of equilibrium brining and the time required for salt to diffuse through larger, slab-shaped cuts, see Home-Cured Bacon, 937, and Home-Cured Corned Beef, 937.

Dry-brining refers to the thorough sprinkling of salt on meat, fish, and poultry, which is then refrigerated on a rack set on a baking sheet. In many ways, it is superior to submerging items in brine since it requires less space, is less prone to cross-contamination, and helps dry out the surface of foods—which encourages browning during cooking. In general, use 1 teaspoon table salt or 2 teaspoons Diamond kosher salt for every pound of meat, fish, or poultry to be dry-brined.

Pickling brines are a combination of salt, water, and vinegar, and are usually infused with herbs, peppercorns, and other spices. These flavorings thoroughly penetrate the vegetables they are used to pickle and, depending on the vinegar concentration, they render foods safe for canning. For more, see the Pickles chapter, 922. For brines used in fermentation, see 938.

BROWN RICE SYRUP

A syrup made from rice starch, brown rice syrup or rice malt is a neutral-tasting syrup with a light color. To substitute brown rice syrup for 1 cup sugar, use 1¼ cups brown rice syrup and decrease the liquid in the recipe by ¼ cup. For the best flavor and texture, it is not a good idea to substitute all the sugar in a recipe with brown rice syrup. ➤ Be aware that there are concerns about the arsenic content of brown rice syrup.

BURNET

Also known as **salad burnet,** this garden herb has a haunting flavor reminiscent of cucumber. As the alternate name implies, the leaves and blossoms were once commonly added to green salads. Sadly, you will probably have to grow burnet from seed, as it is not available as a cut herb in produce aisles and most farmers' markets, nor as an herb start at most nurseries. Burnet does not dry well, but it keeps green in the garden all winter long and can be picked at any time. Choose the center leaves; the older ones may be tough and bitter. For another cucumber-flavored herb that is easier to find, see Borage, 956.

BUTTER

Butter is made by agitating or churning cream, 974. This action damages the membranes surrounding the tiny globules of milk fat that are suspended in the cream, causing the fat to leak out and coalesce into butter grains or curds. The liquid in which these curds now float is buttermilk (not to be confused with the cultured type, 961, found in grocery stores). This liquid is drained off and the curds are worked together and squeezed into a solid mass. This process expels most of the remaining buttermilk. The result is butter, which ranges from 80 to 86 percent milk fat, 16 to 10 percent water, and 4 percent milk solids.

Sweet cream butter is the most common in this country. ➤ Our recipes are written to use Grade A or AA sweet cream butter, containing 80 to 82 percent fat and no added salt. Grade B butter may have a coarser texture and off-flavors; it is perfectly fine for using as a cooking fat, but we do not recommend it for baking recipes. **Salted butter** keeps longer, but the salt does change the flavor slightly. In most cases it can be substituted in recipes with no ill consequences. Although the salt content varies by brand, 1 stick of salted butter generally contains about ⅜ teaspoon salt.

Traditionally, **cultured butter** is made from cream inoculated with lactic acid bacteria and left to ferment briefly before churning. This process slightly acidifies the cream. Modern dairies churn the butter first and add cultures later, but the effect is the same: a tangy, full-flavored butter that we much prefer for spreading on toast, serving with radishes and salt, turning into flavored butters, 959–60, and using in other applications where butter plays the starring role. Preferences aside, you can substitute cultured butter for sweet cream butter in any recipe.

Many European brands of butter are now available in grocery stores. Most are cultured and salted and have a higher milk fat percentage (up to 86 percent). There are many butters sold by US dairies that are labeled **"European-style."** These may or may not be cultured, but all tend to have the same high fat content. They are fine to substitute for sweet cream butter, and are especially prized for adding to pastry dough, where they are thought to turn out flakier results.

Without the addition of the color that manufacturers sometimes add, most mass-produced butter is very pale rather than the warm "butter yellow" of archetypal butter. If you are lucky enough to find butter made from the cream of grass-fed cows, it will likely be noticeably yellow. This color is caused by beta-carotene, an orange pigment contained in the grass the cows graze on. The cows cannot metabolize the pigment, and it bonds to the fat globules in their milk. The pigment is diluted and mixed with the predominantly white shade of the milk, giving it a warm hue; once the milk fat is separated from the whey protein, the yellow is more pronounced.

Whipped butter is butter that has been softened and injected with nitrogen gas, which lightens its texture and makes it more spreadable at refrigerator temperatures. One cup whipped butter weighs two-thirds as much as 1 cup traditional butter. In accordance with labeling restrictions, **light butter** has 50 percent less fat than regular butter. Because of its high water content, light butter is inappropriate for cooking and baking and is only useful as a spread.

➤ All butter should be stored in the refrigerator and kept tightly covered to prevent absorption of other food flavors—unless of course you are trying to flavor it with truffles, 1029. As with many dated products, remember that the "best by" dates stamped on packages denote when butter is at peak quality (and not when it spoils). Unsalted butter can be frozen in a sealed container or bag for 6 months with little effect on its taste or quality (salted butter will keep in the freezer for 12 months).

➤ ***To soften butter quickly,*** the best option is to cut it into small cubes, spread them out on a plate, and wait for 15 minutes. Alternatively, place sticks of butter on a plate and microwave on low power at 15-second intervals until soft and pliable.

Storing butter at room temperature is tempting, especially for spreading on toast, but it quickly degrades in flavor and turns rancid after a week or so. There are specially designed, water-sealed containers known as butter bells or butter keepers, which allegedly keep the butter from oxidizing, thus extending its longevity at room temperature. We do not think they are worth the trouble. ➤ If the butter keeper is ceramic, be sure it is well glazed, as unprotected pottery will absorb butter residue and begin to smell rancid over time.

➤ One pound (454g) of butter is equivalent to 2 cups or 32 tablespoons. When the pound is wrapped as sticks or quarters, each stick equals 8 tablespoons or ½ cup. To measure butter that is not in stick form by volume, see Fats in Cooking, 980.

➤ Butter is about 82 percent fat and oils are 100 percent fat, so in recipes where oil may be a viable substitute for butter (i.e., a quick bread that uses melted butter as the fat), use about 18 percent less oil, or about 6½ tablespoons oil for every 8 tablespoons (1 stick) of butter. While these substitutions are satisfactory in cooking, flavor and nutritional factors are not necessarily similar.

➤ Do not substitute other fats for butter in baking recipes where it plays a crucial role, such as in butter cakes, cookies that rely on creamed butter for flavor and texture, and pastries.

➤ When using butter as a cooking fat, 980, keep in mind its comparatively low smoke point of 350°F. Clarified Butter and Ghee, 960, on the other hand, are good for sautéing, frying, and searing at high temperatures.

For flavored butters, see 959–60; for butter sauces, see 558.

CHURNING BUTTER

Butter is only as good as the cream from which it is made; for remarkable results that are worth the effort, try to find cream skimmed from fresh, high-quality cow's milk. Unfortunately, goat and sheep's milk will not separate easily into cream—or globules of butter—thus requiring a piece of equipment called a cream separator. For a full, tangy flavor, culture the cream before churning (see Homemade Cultured Butter, 960). Most of the heavy cream found in grocery stores is stabilized to prevent chunks of butter from forming in the carton. Ultrapasteurized cream, 974, is especially difficult to make butter with; luckily, culturing helps highly processed cream yield butter. Generally speaking, 1 gallon heavy cream should yield 2 to 3 pounds butter.

Most of us have inadvertently turned whipped cream into butter by letting the mixer run for too long. This is the same process you will use to make butter intentionally. The key is temperature: Butter separates from buttermilk most efficiently between 50° and 55°F. Try to keep the cream in this range while churning. Higher temperatures can lead to greasy, overly soft butter; lower temperatures make the butter harder to work with.

For large amounts of cream (2 quarts or more), a butter churn makes the most sense. For making butter from smaller amounts of cream, see 960.

To make butter using a churn, sterilize the churn and fill it one-third to half full of cream. Depending on the quantity, the butter should "make" within 15 to 40 minutes of constant churning. The cream usually stays foamy during the first half of churning. Eventually, it will begin to look like cornmeal mush. It then grows to corn kernel–sized clumps of yellowish butter floating in buttermilk. At this point, the sound of the churning will also change as the chunks of butter slosh around in the churn. Stop churning. Drain off the liquid, or buttermilk. Place the butter in a bowl and rinse it three or four times with cold water, kneading the butter against the side of the bowl with a wooden spoon to expel more buttermilk and changing the water when it becomes cloudy. To salt the butter, use 1½ teaspoons salt per 1 pound butter, folding the salt into the butter with a wooden spoon. Mold or shape into rolls, then wrap in parchment or wax paper. Store refrigerated or frozen.

HOMEMADE SWEET CREAM BUTTER

8 to 12 ounces butter and 1 to 2 cups buttermilk

Here we use jars, a stand mixer, a blender, or a food processor (use a butter churn, 959, for larger amounts of cream). Shaking the cream in a jar is the simplest method, if your arms are up to it. Try to keep the cream between 50° and 55°F throughout the churning process. Since the cream will be heated up slightly by all of these methods (with the possible exception of a stand mixer), we recommend chilling it to about 48°F.

I. JAR METHOD

Refrigerate 2 clean 1-quart glass jars with tight-fitting lids for 30 minutes. Divide equally between the cold jars:

1 quart cold heavy cream (around 48°F)

Tightly secure the lids and place one jar in the refrigerator. Shake the other jar as hard as possible until chunks of butter start to form, 15 to 20 minutes. Pour into a sieve set over a bowl. The chunks in the sieve are butter and the liquid in the bowl is buttermilk. Pour the buttermilk into a clean container, cover, refrigerate, and reserve for another use; keep in mind that it cannot be substituted for cultured buttermilk, 961, called for in recipes. Immediately turn the butter into a clean bowl and cover with ice water. Repeat this process with the other jar, adding the butter to the bowl of ice water. Gather and mash the curds together against the side of the bowl with a wooden spoon or between butter paddles (see illustration below); knead the mass of butter for a minute or so to release residual buttermilk. Pour off the cloudy liquid, add more cold water, and knead again. Repeat this process until the water is nearly clear after kneading and drain thoroughly. If desired, fold into the butter with a wooden spoon:

(½ to ¾ teaspoon salt)

Transfer the butter to a clean container pressing with a wooden spoon or spatula to dispel any air bubbles. The butter may be molded or rolled, then wrapped in parchment or wax paper.

II. BLENDER, FOOD PROCESSOR, OR STAND MIXER

Add to a blender, food processor, or stand mixer fitted with the whisk attachment:

1 quart cold heavy cream (around 48°F)

Blend or mix on high speed. For a food processor, process only 2 cups of the cream at a time, keeping the rest refrigerated. In the blender and food processor, the cream will eventually form curds; in the stand mixer, the cream will become whipped cream first before the buttermilk begins pooling in the bottom. Drain off the buttermilk and proceed to knead and rinse the butter as directed for version I.

HOMEMADE CULTURED BUTTER

You may use an actual cream culture from a cheesemaking supply company to inoculate the cream, but a number of commonly available products have active cultures in them. To every 1 quart heavy cream, add **½ cup plain yogurt, kefir, crème fraîche, or cultured buttermilk.** To use a cream culture, add as much as directed on the package. Let the cream sit at room temperature in a covered jar or bowl for 24 hours, chill in the refrigerator until it is around 50°F, and then proceed as for **Homemade Sweet Cream Butter, above.**

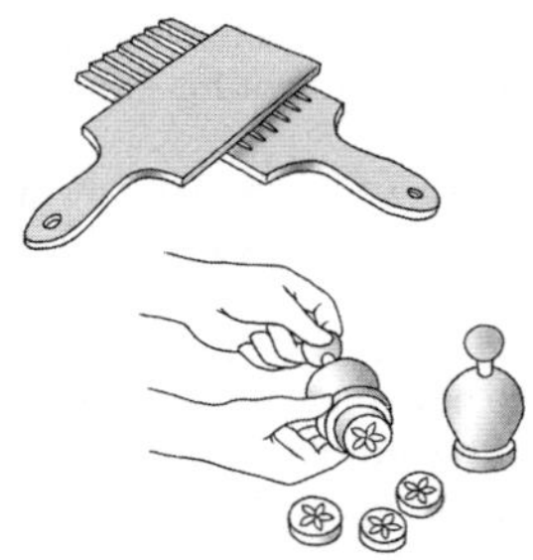

Corrugated wooden butter paddles, and butter plunger

CLARIFIED BUTTER OR GHEE

About 1¾ cups

Clarified or **drawn butter** has had its water evaporated and milk solids removed. The result is pure butter fat, which has a very high smoke point of 485°F—making it a flavorful substitute for vegetable oils and lard for searing, sautéing, and frying. **Ghee,** which is used extensively in the cuisines of India and South Asia, is cooked longer, which toasts and caramelizes the milk solids, imparting a nutty flavor.

Melt in a saucepan over low heat:

1 pound butter

Once melted, do not stir. Skim off any foam that comes to the surface.

For clarified butter, remove from the heat after the foaming ceases. Let stand a few minutes, allowing the milk solids to settle to the bottom. Carefully pour the liquid into a heatproof container, leaving the solids behind, or pour through a fine-mesh sieve lined with a coffee filter or flour sack towel.

For ghee, continue heating the butter over the lowest heat possible, keeping it below a simmer until golden and brown milk solids have settled at the bottom of the pan. This can take up to 1 hour. At this slow rate, the milk solids settle nicely. Pour or strain into a container as for clarified butter.

Both can be stored in an airtight container for 6 to 8 months in the refrigerator. When chilled, clarified butter and ghee become grainy. They should not be used as a spread, only in cooking.

BUTTERMILK

Originally, buttermilk was the liquid residue left after churning butter, 959. Buttermilk sold in stores has been fermented, much like yogurt, from pasteurized skim or low-fat milk. A lactic acid bacteria culture is added, the texture thickens, and the milk becomes pleasantly tangy. We assume cultured buttermilk for all recipes in this book. In old recipes calling for **sour milk,** substitute buttermilk. Whole-milk buttermilk is rare to find, but always preferable when adding to baked goods (especially Southern Corn Bread, 630).

To make your own buttermilk, simply add ½ cup store-bought buttermilk to 1 quart of the milk of your choice (we recommend whole milk), let stand at room temperature until it begins to clabber or curdle, and refrigerate.

To make a buttermilk substitute, mix ¾ cup plus 3 tablespoons milk with 1 tablespoon distilled white vinegar or lemon juice for every 1 cup buttermilk called for in the recipe. Stir and let the mixture stand at room temperature for about 10 minutes, or until it begins to clabber or curdle.

Powdered buttermilk, sometimes called "cultured buttermilk blend," is made by spray-drying buttermilk (see Dry or Powdered Milk, 1001) and is readily available in supermarkets. To substitute for liquid buttermilk, measure an equal volume of water and mix in the amount of powder specified on the package (this varies depending on the brand). Frankly, we are more likely to use powdered buttermilk's cheesy, acidic twang in dry seasoning mixtures, especially those destined to coat foods. It is, after all, a main ingredient in ranch seasoning mix (along with garlic powder, onion powder, salt, and several dried herbs).

CANE SYRUP, GOLDEN SYRUP, AND TREACLE

Cane syrup is a thick syrup made by reducing and concentrating sugarcane juice until it darkens and caramelizes. Cane syrup can be substituted for molasses, 1002, in recipes (though it's not nearly as bitter) or used instead of light corn syrup, 974, in recipes like pecan pie or caramel candies.

Treacle, or **golden syrup,** is made from the uncrystallized invert sugar left over from refining cane sugar. This by-product syrup is clarified and decolorized, which makes it mild in flavor and very light. It can be used as a topping for pancakes or waffles, or as a sweetener for a variety of baked goods. Substitute it cup for cup for corn syrup. **Black treacle** is darker and has a heavier residual molasses content than golden syrup. Black treacle can be substituted for dark molasses and vice versa; blackstrap molasses, on the other hand, is more bitter and less sweet than black treacle, and thus not a good substitute.

CAPERS AND CAPER BERRIES

The unopened buds of the caper bush are salted or pickled for use as a piquant ingredient and garnish. They taste delightful, much like tiny sharp cornichons, and are sold in brine or packed in salt; the former should be drained before using, the latter rinsed and drained. In general, salt-packed capers are stronger, since the flavor of the buds has not been diluted in brine. Capers can range in size from that of a tiny peppercorn to as large as the tip of your little finger. The smallest capers are labeled "nonpareil"; these have a firm texture. Larger caper buds have a more pronounced flavor and softer texture.

For us, the ideal place for capers is atop an everything bagel with lox, cream cheese, tomato, and paper-thin slices of red onion. Do not be limited to this admittedly near-perfect use; capers are indispensable in many fish and poultry dishes, spreads like Tapenade, 54, classic condiments like Tartar Sauce, 563, pasta dishes, or anywhere you wish to add a piquant, briny flavor.

Briefly frying capers in a bit of oil or butter mellows them out and crisps them slightly.

To fry capers, heat a small amount of oil or butter (about 1 teaspoon oil per 1 tablespoon capers) over medium heat. Add the drained capers and cook, stirring occasionally, for a few minutes until the capers darken and crisp.

Caper berries are harvested once the caper buds have bloomed and are preparing to go to seed. The berries, or seed pods, are much larger than caper buds—about the size of a large grape or olive—with a long stem attached. The seeds inside are fairly tender and unobtrusive. Caper berries are found exclusively packed in brine and should be drained before using. Add them whole to simmered sauces, braises, and stews. Whole berries may also be added to roasted vegetable dishes or used as a garnish for salads or as part of a cheese or charcuterie board. Chop or mince caper berries for use in tapenades, vinaigrettes, tuna salad, and other dishes.

Nasturtium seed pods can be fashioned into "capers." They are not a dead ringer for real capers—nasturtium pods have a distinctive horseradish note—but they are quite tasty in their own right. Gather the small, round, ridged pods that appear after the nasturtium's flowers have fallen off. Try to pick the seed pods when they are young, green, and roughly the size of a garden pea (older, yellowing pods may have a chalky texture). Clean them in several changes of water and quick-pickle using the same brine as for Cornichons, 924.

CARAWAY

Caraway are the seeds of *Carum carvi,* a flowering plant that looks like Queen Anne's lace. It is an easily grown biennial that reaches 2 feet in the second year, when the seeds develop. Use the leaves of this herb sparingly in soups, stews, and salads. The seeds are one of the oldest known cultivated spices in Europe. They are licorice-scented and have notes of citrus and pepper. They are classic additions to rye breads (such as Limpa, 600), cheeses, stews, marinades, cabbage, sauerkraut, 940, turnips, and onions. They are the primary flavoring of aquavit and the liqueur kümmel. Crush them to release their flavor before adding to vegetables or salads or toast the whole seeds, 1005, in a dry pan before adding to braised dishes.

CARDAMOM

So-called "true cardamom," *Elettaria cardamomum,* is a plant in the ginger family that produces pods consisting of an outer shell with pungent, black seeds inside. Their flavor is reminiscent of eucalyptus, menthol, and pine. The pods may be **green** or **white,** though white pods are simply green cardamom that has been bleached. Bleached or not, green cardamom is delicious in baked goods (we like to add a pinch to any bread or cookie that contains other warm spices like cinnamon and clove) or added to coffee grounds before brewing. Cardamom is a staple spice in Norwegian breads and cookies as well as in many Indian spice blends, as well as Masala Chai, 8.

There are two types of **black cardamom.** The Nepalese type, *Amomum subulatum*, is also known as brown cardamom, and has its own unique flavor from being smoke-dried. It is used in many Indian dishes, especially meaty braises, rice dishes, and curries (as well as in Thai Massaman Curry Paste, 585). The bigger, rounder **Chinese black cardamom,** *Amomum costatum*, is also known as red cardamom. These large pods have deep ridges and a slight reddish tinge. They are less smoky than the smaller Nepalese type (or not smoky at all) and may be cracked open or added whole to infuse stocks, broths, sauces, braises, and pickles.

To use cardamom pods whole in pickle brines, braises, and stocks, lightly crack or crush them to expose the flavorful seeds. ➤ For grinding, shake out the seeds and discard the pods. Grind cardamom seeds only as needed, otherwise the loss of aroma and flavor is great. For this reason, we highly recommend purchasing whole cardamom pods or seeds and avoiding preground cardamom altogether.

CASHEWS

These nuts come from a hard, double-shelled pod that protrudes from the bottom of a yellowish fruit called the "cashew apple." The cashew apple itself can be eaten fresh, cooked, or fermented. The nuts must be processed to rid them of a very irritating toxic oil, related to the oils in poison ivy, that is destroyed by heat—thus cashews are never sold in the shell. To make cashew butter, see Nut Butter, 1005. Because of their relatively high starch content, cashews may be soaked, then drained and blended with a little water until completely smooth to make cashew milk or cashew cream (see Nut or Seed Milk, 1006), which is an excellent vegan substitute for milk or cream in dishes such as macaroni and cheese and broccoli soup.

CASSIA

See Cinnamon, 972.

CELERY LEAVES, SEEDS, AND SALT

Celery, *Apium graveolens*, is most commonly used as an aromatic vegetable, though all the plant's constituent parts are useful in the kitchen. Tender celery leaves can be used fresh or dried in almost all savory foods. Indeed, celery leaves have many uses beyond their usual role as a seasoning for stocks and soups. Tender, whole celery leaves add a savory bitter note when tossed with salad greens; chopped or thinly sliced celery leaf is perfect for garnishing or seasoning rich, creamy dishes. You may also mix celery leaves with parsley and other herbs in green sauces like Salsa Verde, 567, and Chimichurri, 567.

Celery seeds, either whole or ground, have a powerful, bitter flavor and must be used sparingly: whole in stocks, court bouillon, pickles, and salads; or ground in sauces, salad dressings, seafood dishes, or vegetables.

Celery salt is a mixture of ground celery seeds and salt, though you can make a milder homemade version using dried and ground celery leaves and salt. In addition to its pivotal, umami-giving role in crab seasoning and seasoning salt, celery salt is used in egg salads, coleslaws, on Chicago-style hot dogs, 144, and sometimes in Bloody Marys, 21.

Celery juice powder is made from plants that are specially bred to have high levels of sodium nitrate, the active ingredient in curing salts, 936. The powder is used to produce "uncured" or "nitrate-free" bacon and deli meat.

For using celery as a vegetable, see 231; for celeriac or celery root, see 231.

CHAMOMILE

Roman chamomile (*Anthemis nobilis*), German or wild chamomile (*Matricaria chamomilla*), and other chamomile cultivars are best known as an herbal tea (or tisane), 7. It is the flower that is most prized, although at times the fresh leaves are used as well. Fresh chamomile flowers may be used as an attractive garnish for a range of dishes, especially desserts or salads. Use dried chamomile to infuse liquor, Simple Syrup, 16, or cream.

CHEESE

We heartily agree with author Clifton Fadiman, who called cheese "milk's leap to immortality." There are a host of factors that contribute to the hundreds of different cheeses available. The type of milk; the diet and breed of the animals that produce the milk; the time of year and weather when the cheese is made; the cultures used in making the cheese; the temperature the milk is heated to; how much the curd is stirred; whether or not the curds are pressed, brined, or salted; and how the cheese is aged—all of these variables affect the outcome of the cheesemaking process. Every step—from the breeding of the animals to the aging of the cheese—is of great importance to the cheesemaker. This is why we are more than willing to pay a premium for fine cheeses; the craftsmanship and care involved in the process are truly remarkable.

Cheese at its simplest is milk coagulated with an acid. This is how paneer is made, 245. Most cheeses, however, are inoculated with one or more bacterial cultures before the coagulation stage. These cultures cause the milk to acidify as the bacteria consume the sugars (lactose) present in the milk, producing lactic acid in the process. Then a coagulant is added to cause the milk to form a mat of curds—in most commercial cheesemaking, this is **rennet,** which is made from enzymes extracted from the stomachs of baby ruminants, such as cows and goats. **Microbial rennet,** a vegetarian alternative, is made from enzymes produced by molds. Some plants, including thistle and mallow, can be used to coagulate milk as well, though the process is less precise than using commercial rennet. After coagulation, the curd is either scooped directly into molds or cheesecloth for draining, or cut, stirred, and heated before packing into molds.

CHEESE STYLES AND TYPES

While there are hundreds of types of cheese, they can be discussed in terms of broad categories. **Fresh cheeses** are simply unaged cheeses. They include mozzarella, burrata, ricotta, farmer cheese, queso fresco, mascarpone, and paneer. Some fresh cheeses are made with a longer culturing and setting period before the curd is cut and drained, which gives them a tangy flavor. These types of fresh cheeses may be called "lactic cheeses." The best-known lactic cheese is soft goat cheese (sold as chèvre in the Unites States), but this style of cheese may be made with any type of milk. Fresh cheese should be just that—very fresh and white, without a trace of mold or discoloration, and with a pleasant, mild, tangy or milky smell.

Soft-ripened cheeses are sometimes called "bloomy" cheeses because of the white, fuzzy rind they develop from being inoculated with molds like *Penicillium candidum*. These cheeses ripen from the outside in, often forming a soft, even runny, layer between the rind and the inner paste of the cheese. This class of cheese includes the much-loved Brie and Camembert, but there are scores of bloomy cheeses, including some very nice domestic ones such as Humboldt Fog and Bonne Bouche. The rind is edible and should be mild and pleasant. When selecting these cheeses, give them a light squeeze—if you prefer a riper cheese, choose one that has more give in your hand. These cheeses should smell slightly funky or mushroomy, but there should be no hint of ammonia.

Washed-rind cheeses are the stinky cheeses. They often have a reddish-orange rind from being brushed with a brine made of salt and beer, wine, cider, or water and sometimes a bacterial culture that promotes surface-ripening. While the rind of these cheeses may be sticky and unappealing, they are generally edible, and many proponents of this type of cheese relish the rind. Whether or not the smell discourages you, we highly recommend giving washed-rind cheeses a try—they are often much milder to the palate than they are to the nose. This category of cheese includes Époisses, Pont l'Évêque, Limburger, and Taleggio. Our favorite domestic washed-rind cheeses are Winnimere and Rush Creek Reserve.

Perhaps the most familiar cheeses to the American palate are dry, hard, **aged cheeses.** Under this umbrella are **alpine cheeses,** which are characterized by a firm, tight paste (the result of cooking and pressing the curd) and mild, nutty, and fruity flavors. Traditionally, alpine cheeses are made from the milk of animals grazing in high mountain pastures. Many—especially Emmentaler and several other Swiss-type cheeses—are inoculated with propionic acid bacteria, which produce their characteristic flavor (as well as their holes, or "eyes"). Our favorite alpine cheeses include well-aged Comté, Beaufort, and Pleasant Ridge Reserve. Parmesan, Romano, and other grating cheeses are cooked like alpine cheese, but get their crumbly, salty appeal from higher cooking temperatures, brining, and extensive aging. **Cheddar** is among the hard cheeses, but it is produced using a method all its own called "cheddaring," in which the curd is cut into slabs, piled, and flipped over and over until the curd reaches the desired acidity. Then, the curd slabs are cut into smaller pieces, which are packed into molds and pressed.

Blue cheese is a similarly diverse category, ranging from creamy and sweet to crumbly and salty and everything in between. What they have in common is inoculation with *Penicillium roqueforti* or *P. glaucum*, which results in the characteristic blue veins of this cheese type. The curd of blue cheeses is often very lightly pressed or "pressed" only by the weight of the curds themselves with the help of gravity. A looser curd structure combined with piercing the cheese wheels during the aging process (called "needling") allows the blue mold to colonize the interior of the cheese. Some of our favorite blue cheeses include Fourme d'Ambert, Valdeón, Stilton, Gorgonzola dolce, Roquefort, Maytag Blue, and Rogue River Blue.

Raw milk cheeses can be made in any style. The key difference with this kind of cheese is that the milk is not pasteurized before the cheesemaking process begins. Milk used in the making of raw milk cheeses must be pristine and handled fastidiously to avoid contamination. In the United States, any cheese made from raw milk must be aged at least 60 days. The reason for the 60-day aging period is that any bacterial issues that arise from using raw milk show themselves within this window of time, and the cheese can be discarded. In countries such as France, Switzerland, and Italy, the European Union regulates the production of traditional raw milk cheeses, and some of those cheeses cannot be imported into the United States. Raw milk cheeses tend to have a more complex flavor than pasteurized cheeses due to the microbial flora and flavor compounds present in the milk that pasteurization destroys.

ABOUT BUYING AND STORING CHEESE

Ideally, cheese meant for eating on its own should be bought in small amounts at peak ripeness and served promptly. Cheese continues to ripen until it is cut, so there is little advantage to keeping wedges of cheese in a refrigerator for any longer than absolutely necessary, especially since home refrigerators are too cold and dry for proper cheese ripening. When putting together a cheese plate for a special occasion, we think it is worth the extra trouble and expense to visit a proper cheesemonger. Not only will the cheeses likely be in excellent condition, but you will find a greater variety of truly special, hard-to-find cheeses. Many cheesemongers will allow you to taste different cheeses before you buy, and they can help you build an ideal selection.

Cheeses intended for cooking, like Cheddar, Monterey Jack, and Swiss, are of course available at every supermarket, and while the differences between mass-produced cheeses are not extreme, it is worth sampling different brands to find one you prefer. In general, ➤ whole blocks of cheese are of better quality than preshredded cheese (and are cheaper by the pound to boot). Also consider the use when buying cheese. Something that will be sprinkled on top of a pan of enchiladas or a plate of nachos should be mild and melty. Cheese for grating over pasta should not overwhelm the sauce. Dishes where the cheese is the star, like fondue or macaroni and cheese, should be made with cheeses you would be happy to eat on their own.

Some cheeses are packaged in specially designed paper that allows them to breathe. This paper is available for purchase and is excellent for storing cheese at home, though it is expensive. After serving or cutting cheese, wrap any leftovers in parchment paper; it is more permeable than plastic wrap or foil, both of which trap moisture and may turn cheese slimy. Store in the cheese or vegetable compartment of your refrigerator. These drawers provide extra humidity, which is ideal for storing cheese. For information on freezing cheese, see About Freezing Dairy Products, 887.

For more information on serving cheese, see The Cheese Course, 834, Cheese Platters, 45, and Wine and Cheese, 34.

MAKING CHEESE AT HOME

Before you begin, collect a few basic pieces of equipment: a **thermometer;** a **long wooden spoon;** a **long stainless steel knife** or **large offset spatula** for cutting the curd; and **butter muslin** (for soft cheeses) or **clean flour sack towels** and a **colander or sieve** for draining the cheese. All equipment used in making cheese should be immaculately clean; wash well in hot, soapy water and take extra care to rinse off all the soapsuds. Do not use antibacterial soap, which can inhibit the culturing process.

Soft cheeses are a bit easier to make at home than hard cheeses, as hard cheeses must be pressed and, in some cases, aged. For the most basic cheeses, store-bought buttermilk can be used to culture the milk. Buttermilk contains live bacterial cultures (lactic acid bacteria—strains of *Lactobacillus*) that can be used to acidify the milk. (Real buttermilk, i.e., the butter-making by-product, 961, will not work.) The downside to using buttermilk is that it doesn't always work. You can never be sure what cultures are present in buttermilk, nor how vigorous they are.

If you discover that you have a knack for home cheesemaking and want to branch out beyond the basics, it is worth exploring freeze-dried powdered cultures. Powdered cultures allow a greater degree of control over the cheesemaking process and vastly expand the variety of cheeses you will be able to make. There are two basic types of cultures—**mesophilic** and **thermophilic.** As their names suggest, mesophilic cultures thrive in moderate temperatures (70° to about 100°F), and thermophilic cultures can be heated up to about 140°F before the heat kills them. These cultures are available for purchase from cheesemaking supply companies.

UNRIPENED SOFT CHEESES

An old, rustic cheesemaking method involves allowing milk to rest in a warm place until it sours and curdles. Then the curds and whey—the cloudy liquid—are separated by draining through a cloth bag. When the curds are firm to the touch, they are chilled and beaten with cream until smooth to make cottage cheese. While this method has a hands-off appeal, it is an uncontrolled process and thus unpredictable, meaning the chance of failure is higher and the end result is variable. Our recipe for a basic cottage cheese is not much more complex than the method described above, but adding buttermilk—a cultured dairy product—rather than simply waiting for the milk to be colonized by bacteria from the air provides some degree of insurance that the milk will acidify properly and yield edible cheese. The recipes below also offer the option of using powdered cheese cultures.

For a paneer recipe, see Palak Paneer, 245.

LACTIC CHEESE

2 to 2½ pounds

This is one of the simplest cheeses to make at home, and the result is a soft, spreadable, lightly tangy cheese that can be enjoyed as is or flavored with garlic, herbs, or spices.

Add to a large stainless steel pot:

1 gallon whole milk

Heat the milk over medium heat, stirring frequently, to 86°F. Remove from the heat and add:

1 packet direct-set mesophilic starter

Stir continuously for 1 minute. Cover the pot and let sit for 30 minutes.

Combine in a 1-cup liquid measuring cup:

⅓ cup cool water
3 drops liquid rennet

Uncover the pot. Add 1 teaspoon of the rennet mixture (discard the rest) and stir for 30 seconds. Cover the pot and let the curd form, undisturbed, for about 12 hours. The curd will be soft but set, somewhat like yogurt.

Line a colander with a clean flour sack towel and set it in the sink (if desired, place over a bowl to save the whey for another application like Ricotta, 965). Scoop the curds into the colander and let them drain for 1 hour. Bring the corners of the towel together and tie them with kitchen string. Hang the curds and let them drain for 8 to 12 hours or until the desired consistency is reached.

Transfer the cheese to a bowl and stir in:

Salt to taste

Store, covered and refrigerated, for up to 2 weeks.

COTTAGE CHEESE

1½ to 2 pounds

This recipe produces small curd cottage cheese with a delicate tang.

I. Add to a stainless steel pot:

1 gallon whole milk

Heat the milk over medium heat, stirring frequently, to 70° to 75°F. Stir in:

1 packet direct-set mesophilic starter

Let stand at room temperature until the milk forms a soft curd, 16 to 24 hours.

To see if the curd is ready, insert your well-washed finger into the curd at an angle, as if to lift some out. If the curd breaks cleanly over your finger, it is ready. Cut through it with a long knife or offset spatula, lengthwise and crosswise, as shown on 966. Then hold the knife or spatula at an angle and make diagonal cuts at 1-inch intervals to form cheese-curd cubes. Let the curds set, undisturbed, for 15 minutes. Place the pot over medium-low heat and heat gently (the temperature should rise about 1 degree per minute), stirring every few minutes, until the curd reaches 98° to 100°F. Hold at this temperature, not higher, for 10 minutes, stirring gently every few minutes. Increase the temperature once again at the same rate until the temperature reaches 110° to 112°F. Hold at this temperature, stirring every few minutes, for 30 minutes.

To test for readiness, squeeze the curds: They should be slightly firm, break clean between your fingers and, when pressed, should not leave a semifluid milky residue. If needed, cook the curds a little longer. When they are firm, allow the curds to settle for 5 minutes. Pour off as much whey as possible (reserve it, if desired, to make Ricotta, 965). Line a colander with butter muslin or a clean flour sack towel and set in the sink (place over a bowl to collect the remaining whey, if reserving). Gently pour or ladle the curds and whey into the colander and let drain for 5 minutes. Rinse the curds by holding the bag of curds with one hand and dunking it in cold water, gently massaging the bag with your other hand. Let drain again for 5 to 10 minutes. Add:

Fine sea salt or kosher salt to taste

To make creamed cottage cheese, combine the cheese curds with:

(2 tablespoons heavy cream)

Store in an airtight container in the refrigerator for up to 1 week.

II. FARMER CHEESE

This is simply a lightly pressed version of cottage cheese.

Prepare **Cottage Cheese, 964.** After draining the curds, do not rinse in cold water. Add:

Salt to taste

Gather the curds together in the cloth, twisting the ends as tightly as possible to compress the curds into a disk. Place the cloth-wrapped curds on a rack set over a rimmed baking sheet and place a plate on top to weight the curds slightly. Let drain for 1 hour.

Store in an airtight container in the refrigerator for up to 1 week.

CREAM CHEESE

1½ to 2 pounds

Cream cheese is a white, soft, unripened cheese made from rich cow's milk. This homemade version has the tang of store-bought cream cheese but is softer in texture. Please read Making Cheese at Home, 964.

Bring to room temperature (70° to 75°F):

2 quarts half-and-half

Stir in:

1 packet direct-set mesophilic starter

Cover tightly and let sit at room temperature until the milk curdles (it should form a solid but soft curd), 16 to 20 hours.

Line a colander with butter muslin or a clean flour sack towel and set in the sink (if desired, place over a bowl to save the whey for another application like Ricotta, below). Gently spoon the curd into the colander and allow to drain, stirring gently 2 or 3 times, for 6 to 8 hours, or until it reaches the desired thickness. If desired, add:

(Salt to taste)

Store in an airtight container in the refrigerator for up to 1 week.

RICOTTA

About 1½ pounds

Ricotta can also be made with the whey from other cheesemaking projects. Use the ratios given here, substituting whey for the milk. Keep in mind that because whey is low in protein and fat, the yield will be much smaller. Though not necessary, if you become an enthusiastic ricotta maker, we recommend purchasing a slotted ricotta basket mold from a cheesemaking supply store.

Combine in a large stainless steel pot:

1 gallon whole milk
1 teaspoon table or fine sea salt or 2 teaspoons Diamond kosher salt

Heat the milk to 190°F over medium heat, stirring often to prevent scorching. Add, stirring once and only once:

¼ cup lemon juice or 1 teaspoon citric acid dissolved in ¼ cup cold water

Remove from the heat and let sit, undisturbed, for 15 to 30 minutes. If no curds have formed after 30 minutes, heat the milk again to 190°F, stir in half as much lemon juice or citric acid as before, then let sit again for 15 to 30 minutes.

Line a colander with a clean flour sack towel and set in the sink. Scoop the curds into the colander and allow the cheese to drain for about 30 minutes or until the desired consistency is reached. Alternatively, use a ricotta basket to scoop the curds from the pot.

Store in an airtight container in the refrigerator for up to 1 week.

HARD AND SEMIHARD CHEESES

There are many variables but, generally, the harder a cheese is pressed and the longer it is aged, the firmer it becomes. Except for the cheese press, which can be improvised as described below, semihard and hard cheeses can be made using regular sterile household equipment suggested in Making Cheese at Home, 964. Mold-ripened cheeses like Roquefort and blue, which show a mold pattern throughout, are beyond the skills of most household operations. Cheddar calls for still another cooking operation and elaborate cutting and layering of the cheese—as well as longer aging for sharp Cheddar. For cheesemaking books that delve into more complex cheeses, see the bibliography, 1077.

BASIC PRESSED CHEESE

About 1½ pounds

If you plan on aging the cheese, make larger wheels to keep it from drying out too much.

Pour into a large stainless steel pan:

1 gallon whole milk or goat or sheep's milk (not ultrapasteurized)

Add and stir well:

1 packet direct-set mesophilic starter or 6 tablespoons cultured buttermilk

Cover and let stand at room temperature for 1 hour if using the mesophilic starter, 4 hours if using buttermilk.

Place the pan of cultured milk in a larger pan of hot water, set it over medium-low heat, and bring the temperature of the milk to 86°F. To color the cheese, stir into the milk as directed on the package:

(Annatto-based liquid cheese coloring)

Meanwhile, prepare a coagulant by stirring together until thoroughly dissolved:

½ rennet tablet or ¼ teaspoon single-strength liquid rennet
2 tablespoons cold water

Allow the milk to reach 88° to 90°F. Stir in the rennet solution and continue stirring about 30 seconds, then remove the pan from the hot water and allow the mixture to stand, covered and undisturbed, 30 minutes to 1 hour. It should coagulate during this period.

To see if the curd is ready, insert your well-washed finger into the curd at an angle, as if to lift some out. If the curd breaks cleanly over your finger, it is ready for cutting.

Cut the curd lengthwise and crosswise at ½-inch intervals, as shown, 966, using a long offset spatula or a stainless steel knife. Then cut diagonally at a 45-degree angle. These repeated cuts will divide the curd into small, even bits.

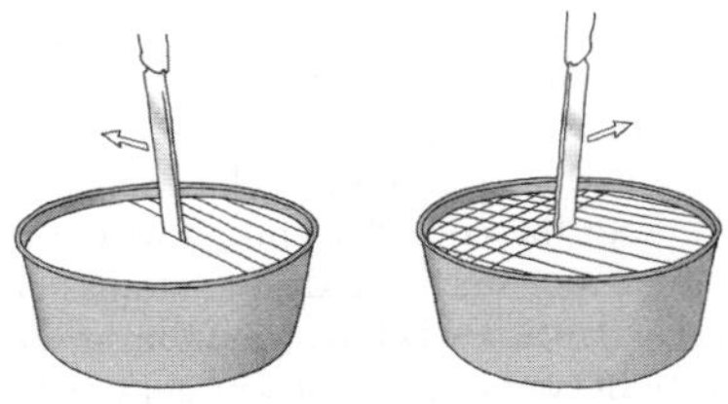

Cutting the curds lengthwise and crosswise

Use a wooden spoon to stir the curd for 15 minutes, using slow movements around the edges and up through the curd from the bottom to top, letting the portion you bring to the surface each time gently recede into the mass. Should there be some large curds, cut them with the spatula or knife into smaller pieces. The curds will begin to shrink in size as they separate from the yellowish whey.

Return the pan to the hot water bath set over low heat and slowly bring the curds and whey to 102°F over a 20- to 30-minute period, stirring every few minutes. Hold at 102°F for 30 to 40 minutes (if needed, take the water bath with the pan of cheese curds in it off the heat to avoid overshooting the temperature), stirring gently every few minutes. The curd is ready for firming when it forms a loose mass in your hand. The individual curds will be wheat berry–sized and the entire mass will look like eggs scrambled over too high heat.

To firm the curd, remove the pan from the hot water and let the curds and whey mixture stand, covered, for 1 hour. During this period, stir every 5 to 10 minutes.

To drain the curd, line a colander with a clean flour sack towel and set in the sink (if desired, place over a bowl to save the whey for another application like Ricotta, 965). Ladle the curds and whey into the lined colander and drain off the whey by lifting the curds in the cloth and rolling the mass from one side of the cloth to the other. Now set the drained curd, still in the cloth, in the colander again. If desired, you may work into it with a well-washed hand:

(1½ teaspoons fine sea salt or 1 tablespoon Diamond kosher salt)

Form the curd into a ball within the cloth and squeeze out as much whey as possible. Knot the cheesecloth around the ball to form a bag you can hang from the sink faucet and let the cheese drain another 20 minutes.

Just before pressing, you may add flavorings, such as:

(1 tablespoon caraway seeds, crushed black peppercorns, or cumin seeds)

Now prepare to press the cheese. As pressing is a drippy business, confine your activities to the sink area. If you have no cheese mold (they can be bought cheaply from cheesemaking supply companies), improvise one by poking holes into the bottom of a 7- to 8-inch-deep cylindrical plastic container 4 to 5 inches in diameter. Place it on a plate or baking sheet. You will also need two thick pieces of food-grade plastic that are just smaller in diameter than the mold (disks cut with a jigsaw from a cheap but sturdy plastic cutting board work well) and something heavy to weight them down (such as a can or brick). Line the mold with a 15-inch square of clean flour sack towel. Transfer the curds to the lined mold, spread them evenly, and fold the muslin or cheesecloth over the top so the curds are wrapped. Put one disk on top and weight it down with the can or brick. As the whey rises and runs or is poured off and the curds compress, place the second disk under the weight to allow pressure to continue.

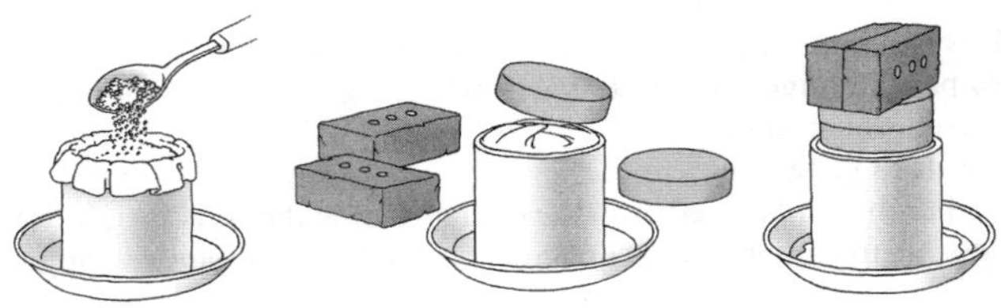

Pressing cheese

During the next 20 minutes, increase the pressure by gradually adding weight until the total weight being used equals 25 pounds. This can be done by placing a small wooden cutting board on top of the can and placing weight on top of the cutting board (we have even used heavy books, like the cookbook you are holding in your hands, for this application). Then let the cheese rest in the press for 12 hours in a cool place (if possible, transfer to the refrigerator).

Remove the cheese from the press, unfold the muslin, and place the cheese on a rack. Allow to air-dry, unwrapped and on a wooden cutting board, in the refrigerator for 2 to 4 days, or until the surface of the cheese is dry. Turn the cheese a few times a day so both sides can dry out.

This so-called new cheese will be fairly bland in flavor. To age the cheese and allow it to develop its full flavor, when the exterior is absolutely dry, dip it into a thin coat of cheese wax, available from cheesemaking suppliers, to seal off the air and prevent mold. Date the wrapping with a label. Refrigerate on a rack where the temperature drops no lower than 35°F or in the vegetable crisper, where the temperature is about 40°F. Temperatures above 55°F cause the cheese to spoil. Flavor will develop within 1 to 2 months or longer.

If any surface mold has formed, wipe it off; or if it has penetrated the cheese, cut it out.

FETA

About 1 pound, depending on the butterfat content of the milk

Feta is a brined cheese. Sometimes feta stored in brine gets soft and can even dissolve completely. This is due to calcium leaching out of the cheese. If desired, you can add calcium chloride to the brine as insurance against softening. Lipase is an enzyme that may be added to give the feta a punchier flavor. Both calcium chloride and lipase are available from cheesemaking supply companies.

Combine in a large saucepan:

1 gallon whole milk (not ultrapasteurized)

(⅛ teaspoon lipase powder dissolved in ¼ cup cold water)

Heat gently until the temperature of the milk reaches 86°F. Turn off the heat and add:

1 packet direct-set mesophilic starter

Cover and allow the milk to ripen for 1 hour.

Meanwhile, prepare a coagulant by stirring together until thoroughly dissolved:

¼ teaspoon single-strength liquid rennet

2 tablespoons cold water

Add to the milk and stir for about 30 seconds. Cover and let the curd form, undisturbed, for about 1 hour. To test the curd, wash your hands well and, using the back of your hand, gently press the curd mass down at the edge where the curd meets the pan. The curd should pull away neatly from the edge of the pan. Cut the curd into ½-inch cubes as shown on 966 and allow it to rest for 10 minutes. Gently stir the curds for 20 minutes. At first, they will be fragile, but they will firm as they expel whey.

Line a colander with a clean flour sack towel and set it in the sink (if desired, place over a bowl to save the whey for another application like Ricotta, 965). Scoop the curds into the colander and let them drain for 10 minutes. Bring the corners of the towel together and tie them with kitchen string. Hang the curds from the sink faucet (or a cabinet knob or hook) and let the whey drain into the bowl for 4 hours.

Unwrap the curds, flip the curd mass, rewrap it, and hang it again for another 2 hours.

Unwrap the curds and cut into 1-inch cubes. They do not need to be perfect. Toss the cheese in a large bowl with:

1 teaspoon fine sea salt or 2 teaspoons Diamond kosher salt

Set the cheese cubes in a colander set over the bowl, cover, and place in the refrigerator. Allow the cheese to continue draining for about 2 more days; every so often, pour off the whey that has collected in the bowl. The first couple of times you drain the cheese, you may have to manually separate the cubes as they tend to knit together until they firm up.

When the cheese stops emitting whey, make a brine solution using:

2 cups cool water

1½ tablespoons table salt or 3 tablespoons Diamond kosher salt

(½ teaspoon calcium chloride)

Whisk to dissolve the salt. Pack the cheese cubes into a clean 1-quart glass jar and pour the brine over the cheese. If possible, use a plastic lid on the jar as the acidity of the cheese and the salt in the brine cause metal to corrode (or cover the top of the jar with a double layer of plastic wrap, then seal with a metal lid). Store, refrigerated, indefinitely. When you remove pieces of cheese from the jar, use clean tongs or a fork so as not to introduce bacteria or other contaminants into the jar.

CHERVIL

One of the fines herbes, 983, chervil is more delicate and ferny than parsley, to which it is closely related. Its flavor is reminiscent of tarragon, though milder. Chervil is classically used with chicken, veal, omelets, in vinaigrettes, 975, and always in Béarnaise Sauce, 561. Chervil is one of the herbs it pays to grow: It is difficult to find fresh and has practically no flavor when dried. To substitute for chervil, use equal amounts of parsley and tarragon or fennel fronds.

CHESTNUTS

See About Chestnuts, 232.

CHIA SEEDS

Chia is a mint relative that produces tiny, mottled seeds. The seeds can be eaten raw as a crunchy garnish or topping or added to granola or oatmeal. They absorb water readily, creating a gel-like coating around the seeds, which adds texture to beverages and puddings. The oils in chia seeds do not oxidize rapidly, so they can be kept in a cool, dark place for 1 year or more.

CHILES, DRIED AND GROUND

Dried chiles are an essential ingredient in our kitchen. Indeed, they play an increasingly important role as more cooks became enamored of fiery foods. Many of the same peppers we eat fresh (see About Peppers, 260) are also sold dried, which concentrates their heat and flavor, and allows them to be stored at room temperature for an extended period. To dry chiles, see 940.

As with spices, dried chiles should be stored in airtight containers. Ground chile powders are very convenient, but their flavor diminishes much more quickly than that of whole dried chiles. Try to use whole dried chiles within 1 year of purchase and chile powders within 3 months. If desired, you can extend the shelf life of chile powders by storing them in the freezer. Our strategy is to purchase whole chiles and toast and grind them in conservative batches as needed (see Toasting Dried Chiles, 969, and Cooking with Dried Chiles, 969). For the classic seasoning blend, ➤ see Chili Powder, 588.

Since certain types are associated with specific cuisines, we organize our discussion of dried chiles by region.

THE AMERICAS

Peppers are indigenous to South America, so it is perhaps not surprising that the Americas boast the largest variety of dried types. Of the dozens of South American chile varieties, only two are consistently found in markets here: **ají amarillo** (sometimes sold as **ají mirasol**) and **ají panca.** Once dried, ají amarillos turn a golden orange color; they have a sweet, fruity flavor and mild heat. Ají panca chiles are picked red and turn brown once dried. They have mild to moderate heat, and a touch of smokiness. **Ají limo chiles** are less common to find and much spicier. All are used extensively in Peruvian cooking, especially in ceviches, marinades, braises, and sauces.

Anchos are the dried form of the poblano pepper, as is the darker **mulato.** Both have moderate heat and a rich, raisin-like quality, though the mulato is less sweet and has a more intense flavor.

Cayenne chiles are still the most common type to find ground, as they were one of the first to be transplanted to European gardens from the Americas. The cayenne powder found in the spice aisle of most grocery stores is made from whatever hot, red chiles are the most expedient; it is invariably hot, but relatively neutral otherwise. Whole cayennes are long, slender, and curved. **Chiles de árbol** are similarly fiery, but much more common to find in whole form. Their pods are slender, short, straight, and bright red. **Japonés chiles** are another slender, red Mexican variety that is appreciated mostly for its heat rather than its personality.

The round cranberry-red **cascabel chile** is rich, nutty, and of medium heat. **Chipotles** are jalapeños that have been left to ripen and turn red, then smoked over pecanwood and dried. There are two types of chipotles: the dark, reddish **moritas** or **moras** are spicier and more common to find (especially canned *en adobo*); the mottled, tan-brown **mecos** are larger, milder, and smokier.

Chilhuacle chiles are considered by many to be essential for cooking authentic Oaxacan dishes, especially moles. The color of the chilhuacle determines which traditional mole it goes in: *mole negro* uses black chilhuacles; *mole colorado* and *mole amarillo* use red and yellow chilhuacles, respectively. All three are mild, but their flavors are distinct and complex, ranging from bitter to raisin-y and vegetal. Like pasillas de Oaxaca (see below), they are a rare special-order item and can fetch a high price.

The smooth-skinned, dark red **guajillo chile** is long, of moderate width, has medium to low heat, and a nice, woodsy aroma. One of the workhorses of the Mexican kitchen, guajillos are quite versatile and find their way into sauces, soups, stews, and moles. They are usually combined with other, more distinctive chiles of which they temper the heat, smokiness, or richness. **Puya chiles** look like miniature guajillos, but they are significantly hotter.

New Mexico chiles are the dried version of the large, ubiquitous peppers sold as Anaheim, NuMex, and Hatch. Allowed to ripen until red, they are also known as **chile California** and **chile colorado** (which means red in Spanish and is not a reference to the state). Throughout New Mexico, you may see these chiles strung together in wreaths or swags (*ristras*). Like guajillos, they are mild and versatile. Spicier cultivars, such as the **lumbre** type, are also dried (and may simply be marked as "extra spicy"). In northern New Mexico, a native variety often referred to as **Chimayo** (after one of the many communities in which it is grown) is highly sought after. You may find green New Mexico chile powder; it is perhaps our favorite seasoning for scrambled eggs (and buttered popcorn). A less common green variety is the **pasado,** which is roasted and peeled before it is left to dry. Though not the most appetizing to look at, they have a pleasant vegetal flavor and medium heat.

Pasilla chiles, also known as **chile negro,** are the dried form of the chilaca; they are very dark and fairly mild. **Pasilla de Oaxaca chiles** are similar but have a reddish hue and are smoke-dried; they are very rare to find, but worth seeking out for the wonderful, deep flavor they add to moles and sauces.

Pequín chiles are little reddish-yellow or brown ovals that have relentless heat. **Tepin** or **chiltepin chiles** are a related type that grows wild. In New Mexico, you can occasionally find them smoke-dried. They are usually ground and used as a last-minute seasoning or garnish. **Wiri wiri chiles,** a staple of Guyanese cooking, are a similar shape, but have a deeply wrinkled skin, and are not quite as fiery.

Other hot chiles—such as habaneros and Scotch bonnets—may be found dried and ground, but they are primarily used fresh.

EUROPE AND AFRICA

Industrious chile cultivators throughout Europe have developed their own unique types. The Basque region is known for their dried **piment d'Espelette,** a sweet red chile of moderate heat. Rare to find whole, espelette is most commonly found as a coarse, reddish-orange powder.

Italian pepperoncini vary in heat and size, but the most common type to dry are small, slender **Calabrian chiles,** a red cayenne-type with medium to low heat. This is the type traditionally dried and crushed into flakes for topping pizza and bruschetta or folding into ragus and pastas. Of course, not all of the **red pepper flakes** found in grocery stores are made with this type, which has a nice sweet, acidic bite. Calabrian chiles are rare to find whole, but their flavor is much better than the flakes. For another classic method of preserving these chiles, see Pepperoncini Sott'olio, 935.

Spanish **ñora chiles** are squat and round, looking a bit like big cascabels. Earthy and mild, it is customary to place a whole ñora in the center of a Paella Valenciana, 334, or add them to braises, stews, or rice dishes. They are also soaked, seeded, and have their flesh scraped off the skin to make Romesco Sauce, 570.

For many American cooks of yore, paprika was much like annatto or turmeric: a coloring agent more than a spice. Luckily, the quality of paprika has improved, as well as our appreciation for it. **Hungarian paprika** is added by the heaping spoonful to many Hungarian specialties, like the aptly named *paprikash* (or Chicken Paprika, 421) or Hungarian Goulash, 467. Paprika sold in this country comes in hot and sweet varieties, the former being spicier due to the inclusion of more seeds (there are apparently eight grades available in Hungary). Unlike Hungarian paprika, which comes from a handful of closely related pepper varieties, **Spanish paprika,** or **pimentón,** may be made from several different types, including ñora and cayenne chiles. Once ripe, the chiles grown in the La Vera region of Spain are smoke-dried over oak fires, which gives pimentón a wonderful, distinctive flavor. Like Hungarian paprika, pimentón is available in hot and sweet varieties, as well as a "bittersweet" combination. In addition to adding a vibrant smokiness to all sorts of dishes, pimentón is used to season Spanish chorizo sausage.

Piri piri chiles are practically the only dried African type available. A close relative of Thai bird's eye chiles (below), they are very hot, and used whole and ground in many sub-Saharan cuisines, as well as numerous Portuguese dishes.

MIDDLE EAST AND ASIA

Several Turkish and Syrian varieties of chile are increasingly available coarsely ground. Those grown near the towns of **Maras** and **Aleppo** are brick red, mild, and fruity. Chiles from **Urfa** (sometimes sold as **isot biber**), on the other hand, turn a purplish black during the sun-drying process, which gives the flakes a smoky, earthy, raisin-like complexity. All of these ground chiles are usually moistened with oil and/or seasoned lightly with salt before they are packaged and sold. Though they may be added to sauces and condiments like Muhammara, 53, or Harissa, 584—or used to season lamb kebabs, 481—we usually reserve these distinctive flakes for sprinkling on top of dishes at the last minute.

Several types of Indian chiles are available whole or ground. Most are labeled generically as "Indian red chiles," which is only so helpful. Chiles so labeled tend to be slender, pointed, smooth-skinned, and of small to moderate size. Generally, the smaller ones are the hottest. The larger, smooth-skinned **Guntur Sanaam** type is medium-hot, as is the wrinkled **Byadgi chile.** Round **Ramnad mundu chiles** are about the size of cherries and tend to be milder and more flavorful. Larger, maroon-colored **Kashmiri chiles** are the mildest.

Though several milder dried chiles are cultivated in Thailand, the only type consistently available is the small, punishing **bird's eye.** Easily found as flakes or whole in Thai groceries, these can be extremely hot in either form. Simply opening a sealed bag of whole bird's eye chiles can make nearby eyes water. The flakes, in particular, seem to be coated in finely ground powder, lending them an especially vibrant color and level of heat. Though we associate bird's eye chiles with Thai cooking, they are used throughout Southeast Asia, as well as in Indian cooking.

Chinese red chiles, sometimes referred to as **Tianjin** or **Tientsin,** are used extensively in Sichuan cuisine. They do not harbor quite as much capsaicin as bird's eye chiles and are slightly larger.

Gochugaru is a brightly colored Korean chile powder, perhaps best known for its use as a seasoning for red kimchi. It comes in a variety of heat levels and may be ground coarse or very fine.

TOASTING DRIED CHILES

Many cooks toast dried chiles before grinding or rehydrating them. As with toasting spices, 1021, a bit of heat deepens the flavor of the chiles. For toasting several chiles, a skillet is best; for any quantity over 6, we recommend the oven-toasting method.

To toast dried chiles on the stovetop, first remove the stem, slit down one side, open the pod, and shake out the seeds. For larger chiles such as anchos and guajillos, break the chiles into pieces that will lie flat. Put a layer of dried chiles in a dry cast-iron skillet or on a griddle so that they do not overlap (if they will not all fit, toast them in batches or use the oven method, below). Cook over medium heat, pressing the chiles with a spatula or weighting them down with a grill press until they are lightly browned on one side. Start checking after 1 minute and continue to ➤ check frequently, as the chiles can change color quickly. Turn and press again until you can smell them—this will take only a few seconds.

To toast dried chiles in the oven, set the temperature to 300°F. Stem, slit, and seed the chiles as described above, breaking larger ones into flat-lying pieces. When the oven has preheated, scatter the chiles on a rimmed baking sheet in one layer and bake for 5 minutes. Remove the sheet from the oven, flip the chiles over, and bake for 5 minutes more.

COOKING WITH DRIED CHILES

There are many ways to incorporate dried chiles into dishes. Though we usually shy away from adding them whole, stemmed and seeded chiles may be tempered or fried in oil, 1020, with other spices, which can form the basis for a dish or be used as a seasoning toward the end of cooking. Stemmed and seeded chiles may be simmered in braises and stews to impart flavor and heat to the mixture; at the end of the simmering time, the chiles can be discarded, or pureed with a bit of the cooking liquid and added back. Of course, the easiest and most common approach is to grind chiles into a fine powder that disperses easily and will not add a chunky, flecked texture to a dish. Soaking chiles, then pureeing them into a paste before adding to dishes is also very common (the paste is nearly as convenient as powder when frozen in ice cube trays and transferred to a zip-top bag for storing).

To grind dried chiles, remove the stem and seeds and toast (above), if desired. If grinding alone, use a coffee/spice grinder; ➤ do not inhale the fumes or dust after opening the grinder (they can be quite irritating to the eyes and nose). If the chiles are to be ground with other spices or aromatic ingredients like lemongrass and ginger, you may use a mortar and pestle. ➤ Two and a half ounces of whole, dried chiles that are then stemmed and seeded equals roughly ½ cup ground.

To soak or rehydrate dried chile peppers, remove the stems and seeds and transfer to a bowl. Cover them with hot, not boiling, water and keep them submerged by placing a saucer or small pot lid over them. Let the chiles soak until soft, 15 to 20 minutes. ➤ Longer soaking leaches out flavor. You can also use the soaking liquid in the recipe if appropriate, but taste it and make sure it is not bitter. Puree or blend as indicated in specific recipes; to blend into paste for freezing, add to a blender and puree with just enough water or soaking liquid to make a thick, smooth paste.

CHILE PASTES

As hot sauce varieties continue to proliferate in the grocery aisle, so have their chunkier, fiery brethren (albeit to a lesser degree). Several types of chile paste are especially useful ingredients for preparing the foods we love.

For many, the most familiar of these chile pastes is **sambal oelek** (sometimes sold as **chili garlic paste**), a loose, chunky paste redolent of fresh red chiles and garlic. Of moderate heat, this product is used mostly as a condiment (we tend to think of it as a tastier, more rustic version of Sriracha, 572). Serve with Bún, 305, Summer Rolls, 71, use to flavor Mayonnaise, 563, or to add heat to dishes like Singaporean Chilli Crab, 359.

Several chile pastes are made by combining ground dried chiles with other spices and aromatics. **Harissa,** the familiar red paste of Moroccan cooking, is made from a blend of dried chiles, spices, garlic, and olive oil. Commonly served with couscous, harissa is often passed at the table as a seasoning. For a homemade version, see 584. **Thai red curry paste** combines dried chiles with shallots, dried shrimp paste, 1016, lemongrass, and several other aromatics (**green curry paste** uses fresh green chiles). Most grocery stores now stock these pastes; to make them at home, see 585.

Fried chili paste is made by simmering dried chiles or chile flakes in oil. There are many types available. Some, such as **Thai fried chili paste,** are dense, mercilessly potent, and used as a seasoning in soups or an ingredient in sauces; ➤ add very cautiously—in tiny increments and to taste. Other fried chile pastes are relatively loose, chunky, and studded with other ingredients, such as the popular Sichuan condiment **spicy chili crisp.** Moderate in heat, we love using it as a topping for rice and noodle dishes (for our homemade version, see Spicy Chinese Chile Crisp, 572).

Finally, there are several fermented chile pastes worth noting since they play such a central role in their respective cuisines. **Gochujang** is a smooth, dense, and sticky chile paste used extensively in Korean cooking. It is made by leaving a mixture of ground dried chiles, glutinous rice, fermented soybeans, barley malt, and sugar syrup to ferment in a crock. The result is spicy and sweet, with a wonderful, lingering finish. **Sichuan chili bean paste,** or **doubanjiang,** similarly combines dried chiles and beans to ferment, but the result is less sweet, very chunky, and way funkier—so much so that its characteristic odor can be smelled through the double layer of sealed plastic packaging it is often sold in. As this pungency might suggest, the paste is always cooked in dishes before it is eaten. Sichuan dishes like Mapo Dofu, 286, Dan Dan Noodles, 302, and Spicy Sichuan Hot Pot, 97, rely on this paste for their flavor. If you cannot find it locally, try ordering from an Internet retailer (there is no real substitute). Paste made in the Pidu or Pixian district is especially well regarded. For other fermented bean pastes that do not include chiles, see Miso, Doenjang, and Doujiang, 1002.

CHILI POWDER

A classic spice blend used extensively in recipes from Texas and the southwestern United States. Store-bought blends usually include one or several dried chiles (such as New Mexico, guajillo, and ancho), as well as cumin, coriander, oregano, garlic or onion powder, and sometimes salt. Since ground chiles and spices degrade within a few months, we highly recommend making your own for the best flavor, 588.

CHIVES

Chives, technically part of the allium family along with onions and garlic, are considered an herb and used like one. They grow in clumps of slender, grass-like leaves, which can be trimmed with scissors and left to grow back many times over. Combine with soft white cheeses, sprinkle over egg dishes, use in salads, and sprinkle on baked potatoes. When garnishing hot foods with chives, add them just before serving to preserve their crisp texture and unique flavor. ➤ Do not put chives in any uncooked dish you plan to store even as long as overnight, as they get unpleasantly strong. Starry, purple **chive blossoms** can be broken apart and used as a beautiful garnish or to infuse vinegar with their delicate chive flavor.

Garlic chives, also called **Chinese chives,** have flatter, somewhat stronger leaves that taste distinctly of garlic and onion. Use these chives liberally in cooking, stir-frying them with vegetables, eggs, or ground meat. They mellow considerably in cooking.

Chives can be snipped with scissors into small segments but are best sliced into smaller pieces for garnishing. Chives are delicate and bruise easily, so a sharp knife and clean cuts will give the best result.

To slice or mince chives, wash and dry them thoroughly, gather them together in a bundle, and then fold the bundle once or twice and press onto a cutting board. Slice carefully to the desired size with a very sharp knife.

Dried chives and **freeze-dried chives** are also widely available. They are fine to use for seasoning blends, sprinkling to rehydrate on top of soups, or to flavor Basic Cream Cheese Spread, 136, but their flavor is weak and cannot really stand in for fresh.

CHOCOLATE AND CACAO

Perhaps the most well-traveled product of the Americas, chocolate and cacao come from evergreen trees of the genus *Theobroma*, which translates to "food of the gods." Cacao beans grow inside the large, ribbed pods of cacao trees. The standard process for all cacao products begins with fermentation. Cacao beans are fermented with the pulp inside the pod, then dried. The purest form of cacao we encounter in the kitchen is processed to this stage, then crushed into cacao nibs.

Cacao nibs are somewhat bitter, not at all sweet, and typically used either as an addition to batters or doughs or as a garnish for truffles, cakes, and other desserts. They provide a rich chocolate flavor and pleasing crunch without adding sugar. Cacao nibs are available raw or roasted.

While cacao nibs have become increasingly common in recent years, most cacao beans are roasted and then ground into a paste. The beans are rich in cocoa butter, a cream-colored fat that melts during the grinding process, resulting in a dark brown fluid called **chocolate liquor**—the primary component of all forms of chocolate (except white chocolate). When chocolate liquor is dried and hardened into bars it is what we know as unsweetened chocolate.

Unsweetened chocolate is pure chocolate with no added ingredients. It imparts a deep, rich chocolate flavor, and is always combined with sugar to make cakes, brownies, frostings, and fudges.

If the chocolate liquor is partially defatted, the resulting cacao solids are ground to make **cocoa powder.** Cocoa powder contains 10 to 24 percent cocoa butter and no sugar. Premium cocoa powder tends to have a higher fat content and thus more flavor. Most cocoa powder is made from roasted cacao beans, though it is also available raw. The most common types of cocoa powder available in supermarkets are **"natural"** or **non-alkalized cocoa powder** and **Dutch-process** or **alkalized cocoa powder.** Natural cocoa powder is light in color and mildly acidic, with a strong, assertive chocolate flavor. Dutch-process cocoa powder has been alkalized: A small quantity of alkali is introduced during processing to neutralize the acidity, producing a darker cocoa that has a distinctive yet mild taste.

In baking recipes, ➤ cocoa powders can react differently with different chemical leaveners, so we recommend using the type of cocoa specified in the recipe. The acidity of natural cocoa powder and the alkalinity of Dutch-process cocoa powder are taken into account when recipes are developed, and one cannot simply be substituted for the other. In recipes where the choice of cocoa powder is a matter of taste—such as ice creams, custards, and sweet sauces—either natural or Dutch-process may be used depending on the desired flavor and color. ➤ In this book, natural cocoa powder is the default cocoa powder. In some cases, Dutch-process cocoa powder is explicitly called for. Do not confuse cocoa powder with **instant cocoa,** which contains sugar and has emulsifiers added to make it dissolve readily in liquid. For details about cocoa and chocolate as a beverage, see 9–10.

Perhaps the most rustic form of sweetened chocolate is called **stone-ground chocolate** or **Mexican chocolate.** This is chocolate liquor produced by stone-grinding alone, which results in a coarser texture. The chocolate liquor is then sweetened and dried into cakes. Typically, no extra cocoa butter is added. The resulting chocolate is gritty, but when made with high-quality beans, has an intense, pure flavor. Mexican chocolate is most often consumed as a beverage (see Champurrado, 10), but some like to eat it as is.

What separates Mexican chocolate from most other chocolate is the particle size to which the cacao beans are ground. After the initial grinding process, chocolate liquor still contains particles large enough to be detected by the tongue, which creates a grainy sensation. Most chocolate liquor is ground further in a process called **conching.** Conching is a heated grinding and mixing process that grinds the cacao solids in chocolate liquor fine enough that they cannot be detected. This is what produces the silky-smooth texture of most chocolate.

When chocolate liquor is enhanced with added cocoa butter and sugar it becomes **semisweet** or **bittersweet chocolate.** These chocolates are composed of at least 35 percent chocolate liquor, cocoa butter, sugar, vanilla or vanillin, and lecithin. **Dark chocolate** is a category that encompasses semisweet and bittersweet chocolates, but when chocolate is labeled "dark" it usually indicates a higher percentage of cacao solids and a smaller amount of sugar. Semisweet and bittersweet chocolates may be used interchangeably in most recipes, but their differences in flavor and quality can affect the flavor, texture, and appearance of the finished product. While "bittersweet" would seem to suggest a more bitter chocolate with less sugar, that is not necessarily the case. The sugar content of semisweet and bittersweet chocolate varies by brand, making the two terms practically interchangeable. In some cases, dark chocolate may be substituted for semisweet or bittersweet chocolate but pay attention to the percentage of cacao solids indicated on the label. Very dark chocolate (those containing greater than 64% cacao solids) should not be used in place of semisweet or bittersweet chocolate in baking recipes without making other adjustments to the recipe (see how to substitute one type of chocolate for another, below).

Milk chocolate, a favorite eating chocolate, is the sweetest of the sweet chocolates. It is lighter in color and less intensely chocolate flavored than dark chocolate because it contains less chocolate liquor (as little as 10 percent) and at least 3.39 percent milk fat and 12 percent milk solids. Milk chocolate should not be substituted for dark or bittersweet chocolate in baking, but it may be substituted for white chocolate.

White chocolate contains no chocolate liquor, which is why it is ivory, not brown. The cocoa butter it contains gives it a very mild chocolate flavor and a creamy mouthfeel. It has a short shelf life and can easily become rancid, so buy small quantities. When buying white chocolate, take care to read the ingredient label. Most cheap, mass-produced "white chocolate" contains very little, if any, cocoa butter and compensates with hydrogenated oil and lots of sugar. True white chocolate is made with an ample amount of high-quality cocoa butter and has a more complex flavor.

Couverture is a term used to identify chocolates that contain greater than 32 percent cocoa butter. Now that most semisweet and bittersweet chocolates contain a higher percentage of cocoa butter, this term has less meaning than it once did. (Most of the chocolate you buy is, incidentally, couverture, even if it is not labeled as such. However, chocolate chips and chunks are usually not.) **Sweet chocolate** is a term that denotes a product made with 15 to 35 percent chocolate liquor. A prime example of sweet chocolate is Baker's German sweet chocolate, which refers not to the country but to Samuel German, who realized there was a greater profit if the sugar was already added to the chocolate when it was sold. It is traditionally used in German Chocolate Cake, 730. **Coating** or **compound chocolate** has had part or all of the cocoa butter replaced with other fats. It does not have the full flavor of real chocolate, but it is less expensive and does not require tempering (see About Tempering Chocolate, 858).

Chocolate chips, which come in various flavors and sizes, are formulated to withstand normal oven heat and to hold their shape in baked desserts, even when the fat they contain is fully melted. For that reason, they should generally not be substituted for bar chocolates in recipes that call for melting the chocolate.

For best results in baking, use the type of chocolate specified in the recipe. All chocolates taste different, and we encourage cooks to try different brands and cacao percentages to find the chocolate they like best. Any chocolate used in baking should taste good enough to be eaten on its own.

Chocolate is best stored in a cool place away from heat and direct sunlight, at 55° to 70°F with a humidity of less than 50 percent. Fluctuations in temperatures may cause a gray cast, or "bloom," to appear on the chocolate, a superficial flaw that will disappear when the chocolate is melted. Under optimum conditions, dark chocolate will last at least 1 year, milk chocolate 10 months, and white chocolate 8 months. Though not ideal, chocolate may be refrigerated or frozen to extend its shelf life (or to compensate for a hot kitchen). Leave the chocolate in its original wrapper and place it in an airtight container before refrigerating or freezing. Thaw frozen chocolate in its container in the refrigerator to avoid condensation.

To substitute one type of chocolate for another, be aware that, although it may be tempting to use a chocolate with a higher cacao percentage instead of more generic semisweet or bittersweet chocolate, you will need to adjust the recipe. Chocolate with a higher percentage of cocoa solids (anything above 60%) contains less sugar and less cocoa butter (fat) than lower percentage chocolate. To substitute 62 to 72% chocolate for semisweet or bittersweet chocolate, use 10 to 30 percent less chocolate (10 percent less in the case of 62% chocolate and 30 percent less for 72% chocolate). For 64% chocolate or greater add 1¼ teaspoons extra sugar for every ounce of chocolate called for.

Chocolate is heat-sensitive: It will separate at relatively low temperatures and can burn quite easily, especially when melted alone. Do not heat dark chocolate over 130°F or milk and white chocolates over 115°F. For a detailed discussion of how chocolate reacts to heat, see About Tempering Chocolate, 858. Containers and stirring utensils must be clean and perfectly dry, and stray drops of water or condensation must not be allowed to touch the chocolate. Small amounts of water will cause melted chocolate to "seize." When this happens, the chocolate loses its gloss and becomes grainy instead of melting smoothly. Counterintuitively, adding more water to seized chocolate can help reliquefy it. Bring water to a boil and whisk it, several drops at a time, into seized chocolate until it is smooth again.

To melt chocolate on the stovetop, chop it into small pieces with a sharp, dry knife. Place it in the top of a double boiler or in a heatproof bowl that fits snugly over a saucepan. Fill the bottom pan with an inch or so of water and set the double boiler or bowl on top. Heat the water gently until it is steaming but not boiling. Stir the chocolate in a circular motion with a silicone spatula. When the chocolate is nearly melted, carefully lift the bowl of chocolate from the water, dry the bottom, and continue stirring the chocolate until it is smooth and shiny.

To melt chocolate in a microwave, fill a dry, microwave-safe bowl no more than half full with finely chopped chocolate; you can melt up to 8 ounces at a time. Do not cover. Heat semisweet or bittersweet chocolate on 50 percent (medium) power; for milk and white chocolates, use 30 percent (low) power. Heat in 20-second increments, stirring after each one and rotating the dish if your microwave doesn't have a turntable. Chocolate holds its shape when melted in the microwave, so stir even if it appears firm. If necessary, continue heating in increasingly shorter increments at the appropriate power level until most of the chocolate is melted, then stir until the chocolate is smooth and shiny. Cool chocolate to about 80°F before adding it to cake, cookie, or pudding mixtures.

➤For tempering chocolate, see 858. Should you be allergic to chocolate, try carob, 986, which tastes almost like chocolate, although not as strongly flavored.

CILANTRO

See Coriander, 973.

CINNAMON

True cinnamon, *Cinnamomum verum*, is the bark of a tree that flourishes in Sri Lanka along the Malabar coast. True cinnamon is sometimes called **Ceylon cinnamon,** as well as **Mexican cinnamon,** or **canela.** It is sold in papery, scroll-like sticks, and is quite brittle; the sticks can be easily broken with your hands. Most of the so-called cinnamon on the market is really **cassia,** *Cinnamomum cassia*. Cassia has slightly bitter and hot overtones compared with warm, sweet, aromatic true cinnamon. The best forms of cassia come from China, Vietnam, and Indonesia. **Vietnamese cinnamon** (sometimes called **Saigon cinnamon**) is the most potent. Use cassia or cinnamon sticks to infuse hot beverages, braises, broths, compotes, jams, and pickles. Ground cinnamon is commonly incorporated into desserts and baked goods, but also adds a pleasant warmth to stews, sauces, rubs, and marinades. For savory dishes that feature cinnamon, see Veracruz-Style Snapper, 380, Cincinnati Chili Cockaigne, 502, Moussaka, 239, Beef Rendang, 467, and Guyanese Pepperpot, 468.

CITRUS ZEST AND JUICE

What better name than "zest" could be found for the gratings of the colorful outer peels of citrus fruits? Zest is the very quality they add to baked goods, sauces, soups, meats, and desserts. The key to using citrus zest is to shave off only the colored outer part of the peel, leaving the bitter, white pith behind. The best tool for this job is the so-called rasp grater, which is a long, thin tool with sharp grating teeth set at acute angles that strip off only the zest of citrus fruits (see the illustration on 181). Sometimes this tool is referred to by the brand name of the most well-known manufacturer—Microplane. Before zesting citrus fruits, wash them well.

Citrus garnishes and zest

Citrus zest is more intense in flavor than juice because of its high concentration of aromatic oil. It may be beaten into frostings or icings, whisked into custards, and mixed into cake batters to impart an intense citrus flavor without the acidity or the extra liquid that citrus juice would add. Another way to incorporate the zest is to combine it with the sugar called for in a recipe. Work the zest into the sugar with your fingers until it is evenly dispersed. For recipes that feature citrus zest as a flavoring, see Orange Bread, 626, Lemon Brown Butter Loaf, 627, Mimosa Pound Cake, 727, Lemon Bars, 767, and Luscious Orange Icing, 795. For other uses for citrus peel, see Candied Citrus Peel, 876, and About Making Marmalade, 920.

To remove larger strips or ribbons of citrus zest for infusing sauces or making candy, remove just the colored portion of the peel with a vegetable peeler, a sharp paring knife, or a special channel knife, shown above. For recipes that use large strips of zest as a flavoring, see Gravlax, 393, and Guyanese Pepperpot, 468.

Strips of orange peel can be used to lightly scent some cocktails with orange oil by flaming the strip.

To flame an orange peel for a cocktail, prepare the cocktail and have it ready. Use a vegetable peeler or knife to cut a wide strip of peel from an orange (it is okay if some of the white pith comes away with it). Hold the orange peel skin side out next to the rim of the cocktail glass with one hand and light a match with the other hand. The match should be between the peel and the cocktail glass. Warm the peel slightly with the flame, then squeeze the peel in front of the flame. Tiny droplets of orange oil will squirt from the peel and ignite, subtly infusing the cocktail with orange flavor and aroma.

Fresh citrus juice is our favorite way to bring out and enliven the flavors of meat, fish, poultry, and vegetables. While vinegar provides acidity as well, citrus juices have a bright, fresh tartness for which there is no substitute. ➤ To get the greatest amount of juice out of citrus, before cutting the fruit, roll it on a hard surface, gently but firmly pressing it with your palm while rolling. Lemons and limes can be juiced by squeezing halved or quartered fruit over a sieve, or by holding the cut side of the citrus fruit against the palm of your hand and squeezing firmly. If the fruit is held properly, the seeds will be trapped, and the juice will escape through your fingers. Of course, there are juicers available that simultaneously extract and strain citrus juice, and citrus reamers are an inexpensive and very useful tool for juicing citrus by hand.

➤ Fresh citrus zest and juice have the best flavor, but bottled citrus juice may be used in a pinch. We assume fresh citrus juice for all recipes in this book, unless otherwise specified. Spray-dried **lemon** and **lime powders** are also available, and while they are excellent for adding a tart citrusy note to things like seasoned nuts and spice blends, they are no substitute for fresh citrus juice or zest.

For more information on citrus types, see About Citrus Fruits, 181.

CLOVES

The spicy, dried, unopened bud of the Indonesian clove tree, *Syzygium aromaticum*, contains so much oil that you can squeeze it out with a fingernail. The name "clove" is derived from the French word for nail, *clou*, due to its shape. The intense, mouth-numbing flavor of cloves comes from a compound called eugenol. Most of a clove's flavor is in the round head rather than the long, slender part of the clove. Before serving a dish cooked with whole cloves, always remove them or warn diners so they know to look for them. Cloves are used in sauces, Jamaican Jerk Paste, 584, Massaman Curry Paste, 585, and Garam Masala, 588. They are often added to pickles and marinades. An onion stuck with 3 or 4 cloves is a classic addition to stocks and stews. Clove essential oil is available for use in cooking, but watch out for its terrific pungency.

COCONUTS AND COCONUT MILK

Coconuts, the fruit of the coconut palm, are the world's largest nuts. The coconut palm is a remarkably useful plant, providing not only hydrating coconut water and fat-rich coconut meat, but also oil, sugar, fiber, and wood. For instructions on opening a coconut and making coconut milk, see About Coconut, 184.

Coconut milk and **coconut cream** are made by removing the husk and shell of mature nuts, grating the flesh, and squeezing the solids in a mechanical press until they express all of their juice. Water is then added to produce the specific grade. **Light coconut milk** has the most water added, which gives it the thinnest texture and least amount of fat (between 5 and 11 percent). Coconut milk has slightly less water added, which gives it a medium body and between 10 and 20 percent fat. Coconut cream is the richest and thickest, with 20 to 30 percent fat.

Coconut milk is widely available canned; coconut cream is a little less common. Conveniently sized UHT-processed cartons of both are now available at many Asian grocery stores (for a discussion of UHT, see Raw and Pasteurized Milk, 1000). Once opened, refrigerate coconut milk and cream and use within 2 days. These products are also available as "instant" powders that can be rehydrated into milk or cream by simply adding water. Powdered coconut milk is an especially useful pantry ingredient for backpacking.

Unless they are stabilized with guar gum, 992, canned coconut milk and cream tend to separate, with the fat and solids rising to the top (cartons are pasteurized at very high temperatures, and as a result do not separate). To check for this, shake cans vigorously; if the liquid inside is not sloshing around as it should, continue to shake until it does. Or, for making Thai curries, you may skim a bit of the fatty layer off the top, melt it in the pan, and fry the curry paste in it until lightly browned and fragrant.

Do not confuse coconut cream with **cream of coconut,** a rich, thick, and cloyingly sweet liquid commonly used in mixed drinks, especially Piña Coladas, 25. Do not substitute cream of coconut for coconut milk or cream in recipes. **Beverage-style coconut milk** is usually sold in cartons; while it is good for smoothies, it is not ideal for cooking and does not have the richness or the flavor of regular coconut milk.

Coconut oil is usually solid at room temperature due to its high saturated fat content. So-called virgin coconut oil is unrefined and has a notable coconut flavor, whereas refined coconut oil is very mild in taste. See Oils, 1006, for more information. **Coconut "butter"** is made by blending or processing dried coconut meat into a spreadable paste.

Dried coconut is available sweetened and unsweetened, shredded into long strands, chopped into fine bits, or shaved into wide flakes. Shredded coconut is most commonly used in desserts, but we prefer coconut flakes in granola and atop smoothies.

To toast shredded or flaked coconut in the oven, preheat the oven to 325°F. Spread the coconut in a thin layer on a baking sheet and bake until golden brown, 5 to 10 minutes.

To toast coconut in the microwave, spread in a thin layer in microwave-safe dish or pie pan. Microwave on 100 percent power in 30-second bursts, stirring after each interval and rotating the dish if it is not on a turntable. When done, the coconut will be golden and fragrant.

CORIANDER

The seeds, leaves, stems, and roots of this herb have culinary uses. When freshly ground, the seeds have an earthy flavor and a bright, lemony, almost fruity scent (Fruit Loops breakfast cereal, if we're being honest). We love the fragrance in our kitchen after toasting, 1021, coriander, which is commonly done for savory Indian and Mexican dishes and spice blends. The spice is widely used in European cuisine, especially in pickles, baked goods, and sausages, or to coat the surface of cured meats like Gravlax, 393, and Pastrami, 938. Coriander is especially easy to identify in Harissa, 584, the spice-nut blend Dukkah, 589, and Chili Powder, 588.

Cilantro, or the stems and delicate leaves of the coriander plant, is an essential ingredient in many cuisines the world over. Despite its widespread use, cilantro remains a controversial ingredient for a vocal minority who dislike its (allegedly) "soapy" flavor. Though we concur that the herb is pungent, we find it to be a pleasant accent to innumerable dishes, from curries and spicy braises to chicken soup. For garnishing with whole or coarsely chopped leaves, we usually discard the stems. We do not bother discarding the stems when the cilantro is to be minced, or added to sauces, pastes, and purees (the stems have a fine flavor, and slender ones are quite tender). Cilantro leaves wilt and lose their flavor when exposed to heat, so be sure to add to dishes after cooking, or enjoy in cold preparations like a salsa, 573–74, or Zhug, 567. Cilantro does not dry especially well;

use fresh if at all possible—and promptly (cilantro is notorious for going bad quickly). For storing advice, see Herbs, 993.

Unlike the leaves, **coriander root** can withstand heat without losing its flavor and is used as a seasoning in several dishes, most notably in Thai curry pastes, 585. Since cilantro is hard to find with the root intact, cilantro stems are a decent substitute.

CILANTRO-LIKE HERBS

Several varieties of unrelated plants produce leaves that are similar in flavor to cilantro. **Sawtooth coriander,** or **culantro,** has long, jagged leaves and a pleasant flavor, with the added advantage of not spoiling as quickly. Though native to the Americas, it is widely used in Southeast Asian cooking, usually as a garnish for soups like Pho Bo, 96.

Vietnamese coriander, or **rau ram,** has slender, pointed leaves and a thick, meandering stem. The herb is more pungent than cilantro or sawtooth coriander, with a peppery bite. Rau ram is another frequent garnish for soups, as well as a salad herb.

Pápalo, also called **pápaloquelite** or **Bolivian coriander,** has round leaves and can grow to be 6 feet tall. In our opinion, pápalo is the most powerful of the herbs listed here, with a cilantro flavor plus heavy notes of lemon and pine. Thinly slice or chiffonade, 200, the leaves and use to garnish bean dishes, Tortas, 143, and rich meat dishes like Braised Carnitas, 495, or Pork Adovada, 496.

CORNSTARCH

See Starches, 1022.

CORN SYRUP

Corn syrup is composed of glucose sugars. High-fructose corn syrup is composed of both fructose and glucose. Corn syrup is generally used in candies and some desserts and sweet sauces. It is available in light and dark forms, the dark having a slight molasses flavor. If neither dark nor light is specified in a recipe, use light corn syrup. Corn syrup contains long carbohydrate molecules that not only become intertwined with one another, but that also surround sugar crystals, preventing them from coming into contact with one another and creating larger sugar crystals. This is why corn syrup is often called for in candy and ice cream recipes—it helps prevent crystallization, which can lead to a grainy texture. Corn syrup is less sweet than granulated sugar, while high-fructose corn syrup has about the same sweetening power as sugar by weight. Do not substitute corn syrup for regular sugar in recipes.

CREAM

Cream is the fat that slowly rises to the surface of fresh unhomogenized whole milk on standing. The longer the milk stands, the richer the cream becomes. Today these uncultured, or "sweet" creams—as opposed to cultured or "sour" creams—are sold in pasteurized and ultrapasteurized forms. While ultrapasteurized creams have a longer shelf life—some are aseptically packaged and do not even require refrigeration—traditional pasteurized creams usually have a better flavor, whip up fluffier, and hold their whipped state longer. (For more on pasteurization, see 1000.) For instructions on making cream cheese, see 965.

HALF-AND-HALF

A mixture of milk and cream, half-and-half is frequently homogenized. It contains 10½ percent to 18 percent fat.

LIGHT CREAM

This product is relatively rare in our dairy cases. Light cream contains between 18 percent and 30 percent fat; it is not especially rich and does not whip well without gelatin (see About Whipped Cream, 790). Light cream is best for making sauces, adding to cream soups, or ruining a perfectly good cup of coffee.

HEAVY OR WHIPPING CREAM

Cream that is labeled **heavy cream,** or **heavy whipping cream,** contains at least 36 percent fat and is the richest cream available in most stores. **Whipping cream,** or **light whipping cream,** contains 30 to 36 percent fat. Unwhipped, these enrich sauces and soups and are used for making ice cream. Whipped and sweetened, 791, they are used to frost or garnish desserts. Most large, commercial dairies add stabilizers and emulsifiers to their cream so they do not separate in the carton and whip up more easily. Heavy cream whips and mounds the best.

SOUR CREAM

Sour cream is made by adding a bacterial culture to light cream and incubating it until it takes on a tart flavor and thickened consistency. The sour flavor of sour cream is the result of some of the lactose in the cream having been converted to lactic acid by the bacteria. Regular sour cream must contain at least 18 percent milk fat, but light or reduced-fat (6 percent to 13½ percent fat), lowfat (1 percent to 6 percent fat), and nonfat versions are also available. For these products, dried milk proteins and starches replace the fat. ➤ Do not add sour cream to a dish that will be boiled or it will curdle. Always add it at the last minute to cooked dishes, or serve it alongside the food to be dolloped on top.

CRÈME FRAÎCHE

Crème fraîche results from culturing cream with a fat content of 30 percent or higher and letting it sour and thicken until its flavor is somewhat similar to sour cream—though the higher fat content and specific culture used gives it a nutty, buttery flavor. Crème fraîche tolerates higher temperatures in cooking than sour cream before it curdles, so it can be added to dishes and simmered. You can flavor crème fraîche with vanilla, sweeten it lightly to taste, and whip it into a foam as you would heavy cream (see Whipped Crème Fraîche, 791).

HOMEMADE CRÈME FRAÎCHE

About 2 cups

For best results, do not use ultrapasteurized cream to make crème fraîche.

Combine in a jar or container:

2 cups heavy cream

¼ cup buttermilk or plain yogurt with live cultures

Cover and let sit, at room temperature, until the cream thickens considerably and smells slightly sour, 12 to 36 hours.

Store in an airtight container in the refrigerator for up to 1 week.

CREAM OF TARTAR (POTASSIUM BITARTRATE)

Cream of tartar is a fine white powder made by grinding tartaric acid crystals. The crystals form in wine as it ferments. When the wine has finished fermenting, the crystals are sifted out, ground, and purified to be odorless and virtually tasteless. Once moistened, cream of tartar reacts with baking soda to give the first wave of leavening in single- and double-acting baking powder, 954. Cream of tartar is also added to egg whites before they are whipped, 977: Its acidity denatures the egg proteins, which encourages a more stable foam.

CUBEB

Cubeb are the dried berries of *Piper cubeba*, a relative of the vines that produce black peppercorns. The berries are easy to recognize, as they have a small "tail" attached to them. Originally from Indonesia, cubeb was used as a flavoring and medicinal ingredient in East Asia, and eventually introduced to Europe and Africa. Like long pepper, 998, it was once common in European kitchens but fell out of favor. Cubeb has some of the spicy zing of black pepper, but with piney, minty overtones and a tannic finish. If toasted, 969, it will lose some of its bitterness. It is frequently combined with other warm spices, like cinnamon and clove, or used in West African spice blends, Indian masalas, and Ras el Hanout, 590.

CUMIN

Of all the jars of whole spices in our kitchen, the one for cumin seed needs to be replenished the most often. In general, we are not alone: It is hard to overestimate the popularity of cumin throughout the world. A relative of caraway native to the Middle East, *Cuminum cyminum* is widely cultivated for its seeds, which perfume dishes from the cuisines of the Mediterranean, India, East Asia, the South Pacific, the Americas, and Europe (albeit more sparingly).

Cumin has a nutty, peppery flavor with notes of pine—and a savory, earthy, almost sulfurous fragrance. Much like cilantro, cumin's flavor is somewhat polarizing, with some tasters comparing its aroma to sweaty, bodily odors. Regardless of this slander, many detractors of pure cumin are eager to use the many seasoning blends that rely on its savory pungency, such as Chili Powder, 588, and Madras Curry Powder, 588.

Black cumin, or **kala jeera,** is botanically unrelated and has less of this polarizing odor—and adds notes of smoke and thyme. Black cumin seeds are indeed darker than regular cumin seeds, as well as smaller, skinnier, and more curved in appearance. You may use black cumin in place of regular cumin; since it is milder and thinner, black cumin is especially good for recipes that call for whole seeds. Nigella seeds, 1004, are sometimes erroneously called black cumin; they are an irregular, round shape and charcoal-black, with a flavor that is nothing like cumin.

Cumin may be used whole or ground. Toasting, 1021, deepens the flavor of the seeds, which we recommend before grinding. In South Indian cuisine, whole seeds are tempered or fried in oil, 1020, with other spices and chiles, which softens and toasts the seeds somewhat and infuses the oil with their flavor.

CURRY LEAVES

Curry (or *kari*) leaves are the leaves of the kari plant, *Murraya koenigii*. The slender, almond-shaped leaves are sold fresh, on the stem, and are used to flavor many Indian and South Asian dishes, as well as several soups, curries, and noodle dishes from Cambodia, Singapore, Malaysia, and Indonesia. Though they may be sold dried, fresh curry leaves are more common to find; they are usually tempered, or fried in oil, 1020, along with dried chiles, cumin, and other spices. ➤ Be careful when adding curry leaves to hot oil; they contain water and will sputter. Find fresh curry leaves at Indian specialty stores. If you have a dehydrator, we highly recommend drying them, 947, for use in spice blends; you may substitute store-bought dried curry leaves, but they are hard to find and their flavor is less pungent.

CURRY POWDER AND PASTE

By a series of linguistic mishaps, the name of the herb, above, became a convenient (if inaccurate) catch-all term for highly seasoned stews and braises, as well as the Indian spice blends, or **masalas,** used to flavor them—specifically the turmeric-heavy blends sold to returned Anglo-Indians who desired to re-create the flavors of colonial kitchens. For an example of these popular blends, see Madras Curry Powder, 588; for an example of the countless seasoning blends used in traditional Indian cooking, see Garam Masala, 558.

Regardless of their name and provenance, curry powders—and the fragrant stews they flavor—have traveled the world over, becoming a popular ingredient (and dish) in European and American cooking, as well as the cuisines of Japan, Singapore, Macau, South Africa, Indonesia, and other destinations where trade and emigration has taken it.

Once introduced, the blend of spices and aromatics used is adapted to the local palate and pantry; curry powders from Southeast Asia, for instance, tend to favor fennel and cassia. The dish, too, changes according to local tastes and ingredients: Japanese-style curry, for example, is dark brown and has a mild, rich flavor and gravy-like thickness. Thai "curries"—our translation of the word *kaeng*, which has a much broader definition in Thai—are stews thickened with a highly seasoned paste, the bulk of which is made by pounding together fresh, aromatic ingredients: Shallots, garlic, lemongrass, *makrut* lime leaf, galangal, fresh turmeric root, and coriander root are all frequent ingredients. Though most of these curries use at least some coconut milk, many so-called "jungle curries" are made with stock alone. Thai curries are thought to have developed more-or-less independently, though some curries from the north (like Khao Soi Gai, 303) and south (like Beef Massaman Curry, 468) were certainly influenced by Indian cuisine and use more dried, ground spices.

For the most flavorful results, curry powder should be bought (or made) in quantities that will last about 3 months. Ready-made Thai curry pastes last for quite a bit longer, but they must be refrigerated after opening. Homemade curry pastes, 585, will not keep as long in the refrigerator, but they may be frozen in ice cube trays and kept for several months in a zip-top bag. Jars of concentrated Indian "curry paste" are also available in stores; unlike Thai pastes, these are a convenience product where dried curry spices are blended with oil, water, and a thickening agent. There are also bars of curry "sauce mix," where the usual spices are mixed with flour and oil (these are an especially popular product for preparing thickened, Japanese-style curries). All of these products vary in quality and flavor.

DILL

Both the seeds and leaves of this feathery, pungent plant (*Anethum graveolens*) are used in the kitchen. It is an especially popular herb in Scandinavian, Russian, Eastern European, and Persian cuisines, added to dishes like Gravlax, 393, savory filled dumplings, Kuku Sabzi, 159, and Baghali Ghatogh, 212. It makes a fine garnish for fish, cucumber, and cabbage dishes, enlivens potato salad and boiled small potatoes, and, of course, is the namesake flavoring in Dill Pickles, 924. Dried dill leaves may be sold as dill weed. It is a decent, if less aromatic and complex, substitute for fresh dill in dips, spreads, and in most applications where only a small amount of dill is required. Dill seeds are sometimes used in pickles, potato and cabbage dishes, and breads. Flowering dill heads can be used in cooking as well; they are particularly appealing in a jar of pickles.

DOENJANG (KOREAN SOYBEAN PASTE)

See Miso, Doenjang, and Doujiang, 1002.

EGGS AND EGG PRODUCTS

Nothing stimulates the practiced cook's imagination like a good fresh egg. Eggs provide a structural framework for leaveners in batters and doughs; thicken and enrich custards; bind meat loaves and fritters; and help produce smooth, rich ice creams. They emulsify sauces, such as hollandaise, and mayonnaise; clarify stocks or enrich soups; glaze rolls; insulate pie doughs against sogginess; create glorious meringues and soufflés; and make an ideal, quickly cooked protein for breakfasts, brunch dishes, and lunch. For information about the parts of an egg, see About Eggs, 149. To freeze and thaw eggs, see 887.

The one instance where older eggs are better than fresh is when making hard-boiled eggs. ➤ Do not use eggs fresher than 3 days old for hard-boiled eggs. If you do, they will be difficult to peel (if you only have very fresh eggs available, steam them; see Hard-Boiled Eggs II, 151).

To determine the age of eggs, place them in a bowl of water. Very fresh eggs will lie on their sides on the bottom of the bowl; eggs that are the perfect age for hard-boiling will stand upright on the bottom; eggs that float are too old and should be thrown away. ➤ A truly fresh egg has a yolk that domes up, and stays up, and a thick, translucent white. Red flecks or blood spots sometimes appear on the yolk. They are not harmful, nor do they affect the flavor of the egg at all. Remove them with the tip of a knife, if desired.

➤ The shell naturally protects the egg, and if it is cracked or damaged, the contents will deteriorate rapidly; eggs that are cracked should not be used. Counterintuitively, unwashed eggs stay fresher for longer than washed eggs because washing removes the cuticle, or bloom, that coats the egg. The cuticle protects the egg from bacterial contamination. All eggs sold in supermarkets in the United States have had their cuticle washed off and must be kept refrigerated. If you have your own chickens, you may wish to leave eggs unwashed for this reason. Unwashed eggs can be kept at room temperature for up to 2 weeks.

➤ When we refer to "large eggs" in recipes we mean eggs that weigh about 2 ounces or 57 grams in the shell, or that measure about 3 tablespoons cracked. The yolk of a 2-ounce egg is just about 1 tablespoon plus a teaspoon; the white, about 2 tablespoons. To account for irregularly sized eggs, calculate how much egg you need by weight or volume for the recipe in question. If you do not have a scale, crack the eggs into a bowl, beat to combine the yolks and whites, and measure their volume. When you reduce a recipe and want to use only part of an egg, beat the egg and measure about 1½ tablespoons for half an egg and about 1 tablespoon for one-third or use the following approximate conversions:

1 large egg white = about 1 ounce = about 2 tablespoons
1 large egg yolk = about ½ ounce = about 1 tablespoon

EGG SIZES AND EQUIVALENTS

Use this chart when replacing the large eggs called for in recipes with eggs of another size. ➤ All of these measurements are for eggs out of the shell. For the relative size of duck eggs, goose eggs, bantams, and other poultry, see About Substitutions and Equivalents, 1035.

Small	Medium	Large (standard)	Extra-Large	Jumbo
2½ tablespoons, 38g, or 1.25 fluid ounces	2⅞ tablespoons, 44g, or 1.45 fluid ounces	3⅓ tablespoons, 50g, or 1.65 fluid ounces	3⅔ tablespoons, 56g, or 1.84 fluid ounces	4⅛ tablespoons, 63g, or 2.07 fluid ounces
1	1	**1**	1	1
3	2	**2**	2	2
4	3	**3**	3	2
5	5	**4**	4	3
7	6	**5**	4	4
8	7	**6**	5	5

The difference in egg weights may seem trivial—a large egg is only 7 grams heavier than a medium egg—but when you crack them open, the difference in volume is marked: 2 large eggs yield about ½ cup, but it takes 3 medium eggs to fill that same ½ cup. Sometimes it is convenient or necessary to weigh or measure eggs out of the shell (see the chart, 976).

Eggs of any size may be used when the size of the egg has no effect on the overall recipe, as is the case for frying, boiling, or poaching. Be aware, though, that boiling a larger egg will take longer (see Hard-Boiled Eggs, 151, for more details). The typical serving size is 1 to 2 large chicken eggs per person. Don't expect the same texture, flavor, or size from eggs of other poultry or fowl, from duck to ostrich (one of the latter, by the way, will serve 24 for brunch). For recipes such as soufflés, custards, and cakes that depend on an exact number of large eggs, use the chart, 976, to substitute smaller or larger eggs.

Store-bought eggs should be labeled with Grade A or Grade AA, the top two classifications of the USDA's voluntary system for indicating an egg's quality. These grades have no bearing on size or freshness. Rather, both indicate eggs that had high, round yolks and firm, thick whites when they were first laid. While eggs graded AA are a bit more shapely, the difference between the two grades is slight, and with age, no matter what its grade, any egg yolk will flatten out and the white will turn watery.

There are a plethora of terms applied to eggs in the modern supermarket, and they can be somewhat opaque and perplexing. **Cage-free eggs** are from hens that are not confined to cages. Cage-free does not mean that the hens had any access to the outdoors. **Free-range eggs** come from chickens that had some access to the outdoors, though there is no regulation of how much outdoor space the hens have access to, nor how much time the hens spend outdoors. Any egg labeled **hormone-free** is suspect if only for the reason that hormones are not used at all in the egg industry to begin with. "Hormone-free" does not denote special eggs.

Similarly, the term **"natural"** means nothing, as all eggs, no matter the conditions in which they were produced, can be labeled as natural. **Pastured eggs,** however, are truly special, as they are from hens raised on pasture and allowed to forage. These eggs will likely have better flavor, and the yolks often have a brighter, deeper color due to a varied diet of insects and plants rather than the typical grain-based fare fed to feedlot chickens. Pastured eggs command a premium price, and they are likely to be from smaller, local farms. **Organic eggs** are fed on a diet of certified organic feed, and they must also be cage-free (again, not necessarily free-range). **Pasteurized eggs** are just that—heated to kill bacteria, but not heated so much that the eggs coagulate.

To pasteurize eggs at home, use an immersion circulator. Fill a pot or other vessel with water to come above the minimum fill line of the circulator. Affix the circulator to the vessel and program it to heat the water to 135°F. When the water is preheated, carefully lower raw eggs into the water and leave them there for 1 hour 15 minutes. Transfer the eggs to an ice water bath to cool completely, then refrigerate. Pasteurized eggs may be used in any application that normal eggs would be, but they are especially useful for raw egg preparations like Becker Deluxe Eggnog, 30, cocktails that use raw egg whites such as the Clover Club, 21, and mousses, 822–23. Be aware that it will take longer to whip pasteurized egg whites than raw ones, and a stabilizer such as cream of tartar should be added to help preserve the more fragile foam.

EGG SUBSTITUTES

Most egg substitutes are 98 to 99 percent egg whites and thus lack both the cholesterol content and the yolk-rich taste of whole eggs. Because egg whites are apt to dry out when cooked, cook egg substitutes gently; and add seasonings such as hot sauce or chopped fresh herbs for flavor.

Vegan egg substitutes are now available, in both powdered and liquid form. Follow the package directions when using them.

LIQUID EGG WHITES AND YOLKS

Egg whites and yolks are sold separately as pasteurized products packaged in pourable containers. They are convenient for recipes using uncooked egg whites or egg yolks or for recipes using a large quantity of either yolks or whites. Because they are pasteurized, it may take longer to beat liquid egg whites to stiff peaks..

MERINGUE POWDER

Meringue powder consists of dried egg whites with the addition of sugar and thickeners. To make a meringue, add water to the powder and whip it. Meringue powder is pasteurized, so it is useful when making uncooked meringues, such as those used to top cream pies. It also has a long shelf life. For making meringue with fresh eggs, see 793.

POWDERED EGG WHITES

Some pasteurized powdered egg whites contain no other ingredients, while others contain additives to help build volume and stabilize the foam when beating egg whites. These freeze-dried egg whites have a very long shelf life and do not require refrigeration. They are simply blended with water to produce liquid egg whites, which makes them convenient to use.

POWDERED WHOLE EGGS

Dried eggs are a convenience when fresh eggs are unavailable or impractical, such as when backpacking. Store at room temperature and refrigerate after opening. To reconstitute, follow the package directions; though brand recommendations vary, the equivalent of 1 large egg is usually 2½ tablespoons powder mixed with 2½ tablespoons warm water. Powdered whole eggs may be used in baking: Simply add the powdered egg to the dry ingredients and increase the liquid in the recipe proportionate to the number of eggs called for. So, if 2 large eggs are called for, add 5 tablespoons of the powder and increase the other liquid in the recipe by 5 tablespoons (or add that amount of water).

BEATING EGGS

To attempt to describe the beating of egg whites is almost as cheeky as advising how to lead a happy life. But, because the success of a dish may rest entirely on this operation, we go into it in some detail. ➤ To beat whole eggs to their greatest volume, have them at 65° to 75°F. Before adding them to batters and doughs, beat whole eggs and yolks together, unless otherwise directed in the recipe, until they are light in color and texture. ➤ To warm eggs to room temperature quickly, place the whole eggs in a bowl of hot tap water for 5 minutes.

For some recipes, whole eggs and yolks profit by as much as 5 minutes or more of beating in the electric mixer and will increase up to six times their original volume.

There is some debate about whether using cold egg whites or room-temperature egg whites produces a more stable egg white foam. Cold egg whites take longer to whip, and they do not gain as much volume as room-temperature egg whites. However, they produce a fine foam that may make a slight difference in finished meringues. That said, the distinction is a slight one. We typically use room-temperature egg whites for meringue, but when we're in a hurry we use them right from the fridge. Bottom line: Don't be overly concerned about the temperature of the egg whites. Pay more attention to technique and signs that the egg whites are well whipped.

If you are going to use the whites in baking, have the oven preheated. Start beating only when all the other ingredients are mixed and ready. From start to finish, don't stop until the **"stiff, but not dry"** state is reached. This means that when the whisk is lifted out of the bowl and held upright, the whipped egg whites clinging to the whisk form sharp peaks that do not droop, but remain glossy and elastic. Another test for readiness is the rate of flow when the bowl is tipped. Stiffly whipped egg whites are not fluid and do not move. Some cooks use the inverted bowl test, in which the whites cling dramatically to the bottom of the upside-down bowl, a sign, unfortunately, that the eggs may have been beaten a bit too long and are as a consequence too dry. Although the egg whites may have greater volume, their foam will not stretch to capacity in baking without breaking down. Egg whites beaten until they turn grainy rather than glossy and smooth are overwhipped; they will be difficult to fold into batters and will not provide the loft that they should.

The bowl should be large and deep, preferably made from stainless steel or glass. Aluminum will gray the eggs, and plastic may retain a slight film of grease, deterring volume development. Copper bowls are touted for their ability to help produce firm, glossy, stable egg white foams, but if cream of tartar is used to give a more stable and tender foam, its acid will turn the eggs greenish in a copper bowl. Be sure that bowls and whisks are absolutely free of grease. To clean them, use a detergent or wipe them down with a paper towel dipped in distilled vinegar. Rinse completely and dry carefully.

To beat egg whites with a handheld mixer or stand mixer, use a whisk attachment. Beat on a moderate speed until the whites are airy and stand in peaks—firm, but still soft and elastic. While high speed whips egg whites faster, a moderate speed results in a more stable foam. Do not use a blender, immersion blender, or food processor to beat egg whites.

To beat egg whites by hand, use a long, many-thin-wired whisk, sometimes called a balloon whisk. Be prepared to give about 300 strokes in 2 minutes to beat 2 egg whites. You can expect two and a half to four times the volume you start with. Begin slowly and lightly with a very relaxed wrist motion and beat steadily until the egg whites lose their yellowish translucency and become foamy. Then gradually increase the beating tempo. Beat without stopping until the whites are airy and stand in peaks that are firm but still soft and elastic.

In recipes for meringues and in some cakes, a portion of the sugar, about 1 teaspoon per egg, is beaten into the egg whites once they are foamy. Although this reduces volume slightly and means a longer beating period, it does yield a much more upstanding foam.

Folding in egg whites is a delicate operation. The object is to blend thoroughly yet not lose the air you have incorporated into the ingredients. It should be done by hand, with a silicone spatula, rather than with an electric mixer.

To fold egg whites into a batter, add one-third of the beaten whites to the bowl and, using the edge of a spatula, cut through the whites and batter and then sweep the spatula toward you up against the side of the bowl. Rotate the bowl and repeat this stroke until the egg whites are incorporated. Add the remaining whipped egg whites and fold in until the batter is lightened and the egg whites are dispersed throughout. For most batters, it is fine to leave some white streaks of egg whites showing.

COOKING EGGS

Eggs cook quickly over any kind of heat—beginning to thicken at 150°F. An egg's remarkable transformation during cooking from thin and runny to firm and opaque is the result of a simple process. When eggs are heated, their proteins unravel and bond with one another. At relatively low temperatures, the proteins remain loose and supple, allowing the egg to set while remaining moist and tender. At high temperatures and with long cooking, however, the proteins fuse into a hard, tough mass. In the case of plain cooked eggs, such as fried, poached, or hard-boiled, the result is a rubbery white and a dry, crumbly yolk. In the case of custards, quiches, and egg-thickened sauces and soups, the result is a curdled state where the eggs take on a grainy, watery consistency. Be careful, then, with all egg dishes, not to use excessive heat and not to prolong the cooking period.

While high temperatures and prolonged cooking can toughen eggs, salt and acid do not. Contrary to popular belief, adding salt to eggs before cooking does not toughen them. In fact, it does the opposite, encouraging egg proteins to bond less tightly, resulting in more tender eggs. Acids behave in a similar way. One good example of this phenomenon is Lemon Curd, 802. One would think that if acid toughened eggs, lemon curd simply would not work. Instead, properly cooked lemon curd is softly set and silky. The egg proteins bind enough to set the curd, making it spoonable rather than runny, but the acidity of the lemon juice (and the addition of sugar and butter) prevents the proteins from bonding very tightly and creating a hard mass.

Cream, butter, milk, and sugar are also welcome in egg dishes not only because they add richness, but also because they dilute the egg's proteins, increasing the temperature at which eggs can be cooked. Mixtures of egg and dairy, such as custards, have a soft set because the egg proteins are so diluted that they can only form a loose matrix, as opposed to a hard-boiled egg, which has a very closely woven matrix because the egg proteins are tightly intertwined and diluted only by the water in the egg itself. If you are combining eggs with a hot mixture such as heated milk or cream in custards or ice cream bases, condition them first by using a technique called **tempering.**

To temper eggs, whisk a small quantity of the hot mixture into the beaten eggs to warm them. Then add the eggs to the remaining hot mixture. Often at this point in egg cookery—if you are preparing a soufflé base or thickening a soup, sauce, or custard with yolks—there is enough stored heat in the pan to do the necessary cooking, thus there is no need to return the mixture to the heat.

➤ When washing raw egg mixtures off dishes, start with cold water, which releases, rather than glues on, the protein.

SEPARATING EGGS

Separating eggs can be done with an egg separator or by hand.

To use an egg separator, place the device on the rim of a cup or small bowl. Crack the egg carefully into the center. The white will run through the horizontal slits around the sides into the container below, while the yolk will sit in the depression of the separator.

To separate an egg by hand, have 3 bowls ready, one for yolks, one for whites, and one to crack the eggs over. Holding an egg in one hand, tap the center of the side of the egg lightly yet sharply on a flat surface, such as the countertop, making an even break. Then hold the egg in both hands, with the break on the upper side. Hold it over a small bowl and tip it so that the wider end is down. Hold the edges of the break with your thumbs and widen the break by pulling the edges apart until the eggshell is broken in half. As you do this, some of the egg white will flow into the bowl underneath, but the yolk and some egg white will remain in the lower half of the shell. Carefully pour the remaining egg back and forth from one half shell to the other, making sure to avoid piercing the yolk on the ragged edge of the shell and letting more of the white flow into the bowl each time until only the yolk remains in the shell. Transfer the yolk to the yolk bowl and the white to the white bowl. Should the yolk shatter during the process, you can try to remove yolk particles from the white with the corner of a paper towel moistened in cold water. Should you fail to clear the yolk entirely from the white, keep that egg (yolk and white) for another use, because the fat from the yolk will lessen the volume of the beaten whites.

Separating eggs and beating egg whites to "stiff, but not dry" peaks

STORING EGGS

The storage of eggs is simple if you follow a few basic rules. ➤ Keep them in their original container in the back of the refrigerator on a lower shelf (not on the door) where a constant, colder temperature is maintained. ➤ Foods containing raw or partially cooked eggs—like homemade mayonnaise and custards—should be kept covered, refrigerated, and away from strong-smelling foods such as cut garlic and onions and pungent cheeses as they absorb odors easily.

To store egg whites, place them in an airtight container with a little headspace and refrigerate for no longer than 1 week (in the freezer, they will last up to 6 months). Then use them only in recipes that call for cooking. To store unbroken egg yolks, cover them with a little cold water to prevent them from drying out, cover, and refrigerate. Drain the water before using. The yolks should only be used in recipes that call for cooking. Raw yolks may be stored up to 2 days (we do not recommend freezing them). For other uses of extra whites or yolks, see Preventing Waste and Using "Scraps," xliii.

For hard-boiled eggs, we recommend marking their shells with a pencil or permanent marker to help you tell them apart from raw eggs, but should you forget to do this, twirl the eggs on their pointed ends. Hard-boiled eggs will spin like a top; raw eggs will simply topple over.

ABOUT EGG SAFETY

The bacteria *Salmonella enteritidis,* which can cause illness, is occasionally found in raw eggs, even uncracked eggs. While the risk remains extremely low (it is estimated that 1 in 20,000 eggs is infected, and even infected eggs may not cause problems if properly stored and cooked), we recommend handling eggs carefully, particularly when cooking for young children, the elderly, pregnant women, or anyone with a compromised immune system. Buy refrigerated eggs and store them in your own refrigerator as quickly as possible. As with other perishable ingredients, the old adage applies: When in doubt, throw it out. When cracking or separating eggs, make sure that the fresh egg never touches the exterior of the shell, which is more apt to carry contamination. Before and after handling eggs, wash your hands and any utensils or equipment that may have come into contact with either the shell or the contents.

When eggs are cooked, either alone or combined with other ingredients, to a temperature of 140°F for 3½ to 5 minutes or 160°F for only seconds, all harmful bacteria will be killed. An instant-read thermometer with a thin probe is the easiest way to check the temperature. For preparations of eggs on their own—fried or poached eggs, for example—you can use your eyes. Egg whites firm and begin to set at 145° to 150°F, and yolks begin to thicken at 150°F and set at 158°F. Eggs have reached the safe zone when the white is set and the yolk is just starting to firm but may remain runny in the center. For whole-egg dishes such as scrambled eggs or omelets, the mixed eggs will set at around 165°F—well above the safety margin. The addition of other ingredients, especially fat, will raise the temperature at which eggs set, meaning scrambled eggs made with additional cream and/or butter will stay soft and moist at higher temperatures, making them both safe and succulent. For dishes like quiches, the eggs are sufficiently cooked when a knife inserted in the center comes out clean.

Of greater concern to some are classic recipes that depend on raw or lightly cooked eggs—among them mayonnaise, mousses, eggnog, and Caesar salad. Pasteurized eggs may be substituted for raw. These eggs are only slightly less efficient than fresh eggs for emulsifying or beating purposes. If you are very concerned about egg safety, you can buy pasteurized eggs or pasteurize eggs yourself at home, 977. Dried egg whites are best for lightly cooked meringues. Some cooks refuse to compromise and continue using fresh eggs, raw or lightly cooked, without incident. If you are of this school, minimize risk by using the freshest eggs possible and storing them properly. Serve cooked egg dishes immediately or chill them quickly and refrigerate promptly. Refrigerate any dish containing raw eggs before cooking.

EPAZOTE

Dysphania ambrosioides is a member of the same family as quinoa, spinach, beets, and lamb's-quarters. Epazote, derived from the Nahuatl *epazotl*, or "skunk herb", has a penetrating aroma that somewhat resembles oregano, but with a healthy dose of pine and bright citrus. It is frequently used in Mexican soups and stews such as posole, 323–24, and can be found fresh at many Mexican markets.

EXTRACTS AND FLAVORINGS

There are several ways of extracting flavors, but here we deal specifically with highly concentrated commercial flavorings, essential oils, and the fragrant "waters" distilling those oils produce. For **bitters,** see 956. To create your own flavorings, see About Syrups, 15, Infused Vodkas, 22, Infusing Oils, 1008, and Infusing Vinegars, 1031.

The flavoring we are most likely to encounter on our grocery lists is vanilla. For information on **vanilla extract**—as well as flavoring and paste—see Vanilla, 1029.

Alcohol is used to make many flavorings for a very simple reason: While some flavorful compounds are soluble in water and others in oil, most are soluble in alcohol. Thus, alcohol and several other food-safe solvents capture the unique character of many foods, from spices, citrus fruits, and nuts, to chocolate, flowers, and coffee. Of course, there are artificial or imitation flavorings, many of which contain the same aromatic compounds as the flavor being imitated (albeit from different sources). Real or not, extracts and flavorings should be used sparingly—a little goes a long way.

The only drawback to alcohol-based extracts is that they will evaporate when heated, which can diminish (or even nullify) their flavor. This is not necessarily a concern when flavoring gently heated foods like custard bases, cookie doughs, and cake batters. On the other hand, alcohol-based flavors will dissipate when added to mixtures that reach boiling temperatures.

Essential oils are another commonly available type of flavoring. Though some are derived by cold-pressing an ingredient, such as fragrant lemon and orange peel, most are the product of steam distillation. Essential oils come in a much wider selection of flavors than extracts, and they are ➤ incredibly potent (whereas vanilla extract may be used by the teaspoonful, oils are usually measured out in drops). Like alcohol-based extracts, essential oils should not be heated, as their flavor will diminish or disappear. Since oils do not disperse easily in most liquids, essential oils are most effective when worked into a solid mass (such as taffy, 869), or when they are emulsified.

Finally, there are flavored waters, including **rose water, orange flower water,** and **kewra water** (which is made from pandan blossoms, 1010). All of these are hydrosols, or the perfumed water left over from the distillation of an essential oil. They are frequently used in Middle Eastern and Indian cooking to add a subtle flavor and aroma to desserts and savory dishes. Be aware that orange flower water and rose water vary in strength from brand to brand. Typically, Middle Eastern brands are sold in large glass bottles and have a more delicate flavor. No matter the brand, use these hydrosols sparingly until you are able to judge their strength. If used in excess, they can be overpowering.

FATS IN COOKING

Fat is essential for cooking. It is used as a cooking medium, as in shallow-frying, deep-frying, and making confit. Fats are used to coat foods to prevent them from sticking or drying out and encourage them to brown. Of course, fat is also an essential ingredient in countless dishes, whether being whipped into an emulsion for mayonnaise, added to a carrot cake for richness and moisture, folded into croissant dough, or ground into sausage meat for succulence and flavor. Fats can help leaven and tenderize the structure of baked goods, unlock and carry fat-soluble flavors, or contribute distinctive flavors of their own. Indeed, it is hard to overstate the importance of fats to the success of everyday cooking. (For a discussion of fat as essential nutrient, see xvi.)

➤ For information specific to each cooking fat, see Butter, 958, Oils, 1006, Lard, 997, Schmaltz, 1015, Shortening, 1017, and Suet and Tallow, 1023. For more on the nutritional aspects of fats and fatty acids, see xvi.

MEASURING FATS

There is no mystery involved in measuring oils or sticks of butter, margarine, or shortening. For oils, use a standard liquid measuring cup and measuring spoons. For sticks of butter, margarine, or shortening, cut them using the premeasured marks on the wrapper, if present.

There are two methods for measuring the volume of bulk fats such as solid shortening, blocks of butter, or tub margarine or butter. One is the displacement method. If you want 1 cup fat, fill a 2-cup liquid measuring cup with 1 cup water. Add the fat in pieces or chunks until the water is pushed up and reaches the 2-cup mark. The amount of fat in the container will then be equal to 1 cup. Pour off the water.

Measuring bulk fats

Some people prefer to use a set of dry measuring cups, especially when measuring solid shortening. But if you use them, rinse the measuring cup with warm water, then push the solid shortening down well into the bottom of these measures, or a considerable air space may be left, which will make your measurement inaccurate.

Of course, ➤ you may avoid the mess and fuss of these methods by measuring with a scale; if a recipe does not call for a weight amount, you may find the weight per cup of common baking fats in the Equivalents and Substitutions for Common Ingredients chart, 1038.

SOLID FAT AND LIQUID FAT

Fats are derived from animal sources and plant sources. With some notable exceptions, vegetable, seed, and nut oils remain liquid at room temperature. This is because they mostly consist of unsaturated fat. Fats derived from cows and pigs—such as butter and rendered lard or tallow—are higher in saturated fat, and thus remain solid at room temperature (palm kernel oil and virgin coconut oil are solid at room temperature for the same reason—a high level of saturated fat—as is vegetable shortening). Chicken, duck, and goose fat have a higher proportion of unsaturated fat and are thus much softer at room temperature than lard (but not as liquid as vegetable oils). Finally, vegetable and seed oils can be **hydrogenated,** a chemical process that saturates their fatty acids and makes them solidify at room temperature (see Shortening, 1015).

In general, saturated fats are more stable—both in terms of how fast they degrade when used for frying and how long they can be stored before turning rancid. Thus, shortening and coconut oil are less prone to rancidity than extra-virgin olive oil, and beef tallow keeps much longer than chicken fat. ➤ To check an oil or animal fat for rancidity, first smell it. If the odor is stale, discard; if not stale-smelling, taste the fat. If the flavor is off, discard. If the flavor is off but still acceptable, use promptly for cooking over moderate heat; avoid using for delicately flavored recipes that call for a lot of oil (such as mayonnaise or vinaigrette) or for deep-frying (the smoke point of older oils is much lower).

MELTING POINT

The degree of saturation is one of several factors that determine the **melting point** of a fat, or the temperature range at which it changes from a solid to a liquid. The melting point of a fat can have several effects on a recipe. Obviously, fats that are liquid at room temperature (i.e., most oils) are desirable for sauces like vinaigrettes, mayonnaise, and the like for the simple fact that they will not congeal at the temperatures at which they are served. Butter melts at body temperatures, which enhances the texture of butter-enriched foods as we savor them. The mouthfeel of chocolate is luxurious for the same reason. In fact, there are several types of fat crystals in cocoa butter, each of which has a slightly different melting point (though this tidbit may seem esoteric, it is important to keep in mind when tempering chocolate, 858).

In baking, solid fats like vegetable shortening, lard, and butter can be aerated or "creamed" at room temperature. The tiny air bubbles incorporated into the fat expand once baked, contributing to the rise and light texture of many baked goods. Differences in melting point can also affect baked goods in other ways. For instance, shortening has a higher melting point than butter, thus substituting shortening in a cookie dough that calls for butter will result in thicker cookies, since they will not spread as much when baked.

MELTING POINTS FOR COMMON SOLID FATS

Fats melt gradually over a temperature range, so these values are approximate.

Butter and Margarine	95°F
Vegetable Shortening	
Crisco	115°F
Palm- or Coconut-Based	100°F
Coconut Oil (Virgin)	76°F
Lard	
Backfat or Mixed Fat	95°F
Leaf Lard	113°F
Beef Tallow	116°F
From Suet	122°F

SMOKE POINT

Another major consideration is how well a fat performs at high temperatures. This is especially important for high-heat cooking methods like stir-frying, searing, and sautéing, as well as deep-frying and shallow-frying. The smoke point is determined by the types of fatty acids it contains, as well as whether or not it contains other substances. For example, the milk solids in butter and the particulates in extra-virgin olive oil lower their respective smoke points.

APPROXIMATE SMOKE POINTS FOR OILS AND FATS

Oils differ by brand and will smoke at lower temperatures as they age. If you find an "unrefined," "virgin," "expeller-pressed," or "cold-pressed" version of an oil whose refined counterpart is listed here, expect its smoke point to be significantly lower than the one we give.

Algae Oil	485°F
Almond Oil (Refined)	450°F
Avocado Oil	
Virgin or Unrefined	400°F
Refined	500°F
Beef Tallow	400°F
Butter	
Regular	350°F
Clarified Butter or Ghee	475°F
Canola Oil (Refined)	400°F
Chicken, Duck, or Goose Fat	375°F
Coconut	
Virgin	350°F
Refined	450°F
Corn Oil	450°F
Flaxseed Oil	225°F

Grapeseed Oil	425°F
Hazelnut Oil	400°F
Lard	375°F
Macadamia Oil	400°F
Margarine	300°F
Mustard Oil	480°F
Olive Oil Virgin or Extra-Virgin Regular or Pure Light or Extra-Light	 325°F 375°F 400°F
Palm Oil	450°F
Peanut Oil Unrefined or Green Refined	 400°F 450°F
Pecan Oil Unrefined or Roasted Refined	 325°F 470°F
Pumpkinseed Oil	350°F
Rice Bran Oil	450°F
Safflower Oil	500°F
Sesame Oil Unrefined, Dark, or Toasted Refined	 325°F 450°F
Soybean Oil	450°F
Sunflower Oil	470°F
Vegetable Oil Blend	450°F
Vegetable Shortening	360°F
Walnut Oil Unrefined or Roasted Refined	 350°F 400°F

RENDERING FATS

Rendering is the process of liquefying and purifying solid animal fat into a cooking fat—as in pork lard, beef tallow, and poultry "schmaltz." The commercial versions of these products are deodorized and rigorously purified; if the fat is shelf-stable, it has also been hydrogenated and dosed with preservatives. Luckily, rendering can easily be done at home (but the resulting lard, tallow, or schmaltz must be kept in a sealed container and refrigerated or frozen). In general, you can expect about 1 cup of rendered lard, tallow, or schmaltz from ½ pound of trimmed, unrendered fat.

Dry-rendering occurs any time you cook bacon or ground meat: The fat or fatty meat is heated in a pan, and the fat that collects in the bottom is used as a cooking fat. Small amounts of fatty trim can be rendered in this "casual" way over medium-low heat for a single dish. Dry-rendered fat tends to have a pleasant, "roasted" flavor and a darker color. Dry-rendered fat typically smokes at a lower temperature than wet-rendered fat.

To dry-render a large quantity of fat, first cut the fat into small pieces (this is easier to do when it is frozen). Do not worry if there are a few bits of skin or meat attached—these can be strained out after rendering. Place the fat in a pot over low heat (or add to a slow cooker, or a Dutch oven placed in a 250°F oven). Add ½ cup water for every 1 pound fat (the steaming water helps the fat begin to melt and then it evaporates). Cook uncovered until the fat has fully rendered, stirring every 30 minutes to make sure nothing is sticking to the bottom. For a more neutral-tasting result, you can begin ladling the rendered fat from the pot after an hour or so and into a cloth-lined strainer set over a bowl. For a meaty, full-flavored result, simply strain at the end. The browned bits left at the bottom of the pot or in the strainer—known as **cracklings** when from pork and **gribenes** when from poultry—may be kept for flavoring Crackling Corn Bread, 630, and simmering beans; or chopped finely and sprinkled on green beans or Larb, 122, or any dish you would crumble cooked bacon over.

Wet-rendering is generally reserved for times when you have saved a large amount of fat to be rendered all at once at a later time (the fat can be kept in a zip-top bag in the freezer until you have enough). Since the fat is never heated above the boiling point of water, it does not color, take on roasty flavors, or produce cracklings. On the other hand, wet-rendered fat keeps the best, has a higher smoke point, and is ideal for deep-frying.

To wet-render fat, dice the trimmed fat, cover with water in a pot, bring to a simmer, and cook, covered, until the fat has fully liquefied. Stir the fat every 30 minutes to make sure it is not sticking to the bottom, and press the pieces with the back of a spoon or potato masher to help expel the fat. Once rendered, strain the mixture through cheesecloth into a bowl. Let the bowl cool, transfer to the refrigerator, and let the fat solidify overnight. Scoop the fat from the top the next day, discard the liquid, and heat the fat over medium heat to 250°F (this will evaporate any remaining water).

To store rendered fat, let cool somewhat (it should still be a liquid) and pour into canning jars or other airtight containers. Refrigerate for 3 months or freeze for up to 1 year.

DRIPPINGS

Drippings are fats that are rendered in the process of cooking meats or poultry. They are desirable in reinforcing the flavors of the meat from which they come, as we all learn from saving the pan drippings from the Thanksgiving turkey to make gravy. Lamb and mutton drippings are strongly flavored and should be used with great discretion. Bacon grease is often stored for use in corn breads and meat pie crusts and for flavoring other dishes where salt pork may be called for. All these fats should be clarified, below, to improve their keeping qualities (store as for rendered fats, above). The natural desire to keep a container handy at the back of the stove to receive and reuse these drippings should be curbed! Exposed to varying degrees of warmth, these are subject to quick spoilage.

CLARIFYING FATS

Clarifying fats helps them retain a neutral flavor and keep for longer. To clarify a small amount of drippings and rid them of burned food particles and other impurities, melt if they have solidified and pour through a sieve lined with a coffee filter or several layers of cheesecloth and set over a bowl. For a larger quantity, add the drippings to a pot and cover with water. Bring the mixture to a boil, then pour into a bowl and chill overnight. Skim the fat from the top, leaving the water and impurities behind. Melt the drippings in a pan over medium heat to 250°F, or until any residual water has evaporated and the fat stops popping. Use immediately, or store as for rendered fats, 982. To clarify butter, see 960.

In previous editions, we suggested a procedure for clarifying frying fats that would extend their longevity. Nothing would please us more than to repeat this advice, but beyond the methods given above, very little can be done to save used frying oil, and, frankly, even those methods only work so well. Frying oil has been heated, cooled by the addition of foods, and reheated several times, which causes the fat to degrade and partially decompose into unhealthy by-products, none of which can be filtered out. If the oil smells stale or forms bubbles on its surface when heated, there is little to do but let it cool, transfer to a sealable container, and throw it out.

FENNEL

The sweet, faintly anise-flavored bulb of **Florence fennel** is used as a vegetable, 239, and it is by far the most familiar to us. **Common fennel** is grown, on the other hand, for its seeds. In many places, common fennel grows wild in abundance. Indeed, it is so vigorous that it is often considered an invasive species. The seeds of **Lucknow fennel,** a type of fennel only grown in Lucknow, India, are especially sought after, as they are particularly sweet and aromatic.

Fennel's feather-like fronds are mild-mannered and can be used as a garnish for salads, fish, and shellfish (the fronds do not retain their flavor when dried). Since their flavor and texture are quite delicate, add them to dishes at the end of cooking or as a garnish.

Fennel seeds are commonly used in sausages such as Italian finocchiona, spice blends like Chaat Masala, 589, Dukkah, 589, and Five-Spice Powder, 590, and in Eastern European breads. We also include it in our rendition of Everything Seasoning, 590. Fennel seeds are commonly eaten as an after-dinner breath freshener and digestive aid in India, and you may know them in their colorful candied form, a common offering at Indian restaurants.

In addition to its role in cooking, fennel is used to flavor many liqueurs, from French anisettes like Pernod, pastis, and absinthe, to Italian sambuca, Greek ouzo, and arak, which is enjoyed across the Middle East.

Fennel pollen is sold for exorbitant prices in specialty stores. If you live in a place where fennel grows wild, it may be gathered by hanging unsprayed flower heads upside down enclosed in paper bags. When the fennel has dried, a few shakes will dislodge the pollen, which will collect in the bottom of the bag. To stretch the flavor of fennel pollen, fold it into a flavored butter, 559–60. Use fennel pollen to garnish pasta dishes, add it to a vinaigrette, or use it to dust freshly baked focaccia, steaming bowls of creamy chowder, roasted fish fillets, or chocolate truffles, 859–60.

FENUGREEK

Fenugreek seeds have a unique odor, which some liken to celery. We, on the other hand, think its smell is much closer to that of maple syrup. Indeed, fenugreek is used to flavor artificial maple syrup. Fenugreek seeds have a bitter flavor, which is moderated by toasting (be careful not to overheat them, however, as it will make them even more bitter). Fenugreek seeds are used in Indian pickles like Tomato Achar, 569, spice blends like Madras Curry Powder, 588, and Berbere, 590, and dishes such as Dosas, 648, and Lamb Saag, 484.

Fenugreek leaves are commonly used in Indian cuisine in both fresh and dried form. Fresh, the leaves are chopped and added to naan or other flatbread doughs; dried fenugreek is added to curries and other simmered dishes. In Iran, fresh fenugreek leaves are part of the *sabzi*, or mixture of herbs, used in *ghormeh sabzi*, a lamb stew. Blue fenugreek is commonly used in Georgian cuisine, especially in a seasoning blend called *khmeli suneli*, which also contains coriander, dill, marjoram, and mint, among other herbs and spices.

FERMENTED BLACK BEANS

Fermented soybeans, or *douchi*, have been cooked, inoculated with one of several special molds, incubated, salted, and left to ferment and age for 6 months. Though some types are wet-fermented (such as the closely related *natto*, 1004) and other types start with yellow soybeans, the douchi we encounter the most are made from black soybeans. They are dry-fermented in closed containers in the sun, which gives them a shriveled, semisoft texture and a salty, complex, concentrated flavor. Douchi are used in many Chinese dishes such as stir-fries and braises and form the base of many commercially available sauces (to make your own, see Chinese Black Bean Sauce, 573). They are also used to add funk and complexity to Spicy Chinese Chile Crisp, 572, and Mapo Dofu, 286.

Rinsing black beans before adding them to dishes like stir-fries is recommended. Add the beans and taste before adding other seasonings. Depending on the dish, black beans should be chopped lightly or crushed with the side of a large knife. Fermented black beans are often sold in plastic pouches. After opening, store in a sealed jar in a cool, dark place (they do not need to be refrigerated). They will keep indefinitely.

For fermented soybean pastes, see Miso, Doenjang, and Doujiang, 1002. For Sichuan chili bean paste, or *doubanjiang*, see Chile Pastes, 969.

FINES HERBES

The French term connotes a delicate blend of fresh herbs suitable for savory sauces, soups, and cheese and savory egg dishes. Use equal parts of parsley, tarragon, chives, and chervil—although some other mild herbs such as thyme may be allowed to creep in. These mixed herbs, minced with a sharp knife and added ➤ at the last minute to the food being cooked, give up their essential oils but retain a lovely freshness.

FISH SAUCE

A staple of Southeast Asian cooking and a relative of the ancient Roman sauce *garum*, fish sauce has many different names. Called *nuoc mam* in Vietnam, *nam pla* in Thailand, *patis* in the Philippines, *shottsuru* in Japan, and *colatura di alici* in Italy, fish sauce is produced by packing fish, usually anchovies (although other types of seafood may be used), and salt in crocks or barrels and allowing them to ferment in the sun over a period of 6 months to more than a year. Fermentation occurs thanks to the microbes inside the guts of the fish, and the salt concentration prevents harmful bacteria from gaining a foothold. The resulting tea-colored liquid is drained off, filtered, and bottled. As with olive oil, the first pressing (in this case siphoning), from which flows a clear amber liquid, is most highly prized; the second extraction is weaker in flavor and often has other ingredients, like caramel, added to it to improve its appearance.

When shopping for Vietnamese fish sauce, look for the words *cot*, *nhi*, or *thuong hang*, which indicate that the product is the result of the first extraction. While fish sauces made in Phu Quoc are considered the best, many bottles that display the name are, in fact, not made in Phu Quoc, so do not use that as the only marker of quality. Vietnamese cooking expert Andrea Nguyen says an easy way to distinguish better fish sauce is by the bottle: Look for glass bottles, and expect to pay more for better quality. You can also check the ingredients list. The best fish sauces will list only fish and salt as their ingredients (though, notably, many excellent fish sauces contain sugar in small quantities). Some fish sauce bottles boast a number followed by °N (for example 40°N). This denotes the nitrogen content of the fish sauce. The higher the number, the better quality the fish sauce.

Thai fish sauces tend to be stronger and saltier than Vietnamese fish sauces, which have a comparatively delicate, lightly sweet flavor. *Patis* is very salty and strong. Japanese fish sauces like *shottsuru* tend to be milder than their Southeast Asian counterparts, although *ishiri*, a Japanese fish sauce made from cuttlefish, has a very dark color and extremely beefy aroma and flavor.

Fish sauce is used as a seasoning, condiment, or dipping sauce. It is indispensable for cooking Thai or Vietnamese food, but we also use it to add umami to everything from chicken soup to beef braises. Much like how anchovies added to a long-simmered ragu tend to melt into the sauce, imbuing it with savoriness but never tasting fishy, fish sauce can be used to achieve a similar effect. Use fish sauce in Nam Prik, 571, Nuoc Cham, 571, Chile-Infused Fish Sauce, 571, Vietnamese Caramel Sauce, 578, Tom Kha Gai, 94, Thai-Style Yellow Chicken Curry, 421, and Beef Massaman Curry, 468. Fish sauce keeps indefinitely in a cool, dark place. Replace if it crystallizes or darkens in color.

FLAVOR ENHANCERS

"Flavor enhancers" is our term for the many varied ingredients that enhance the flavor of food by adding umami. **Umami** is the Japanese word for the fifth taste (the other four being sweet, sour, salty, and bitter). The simplest way to describe this taste is "savory." Scientifically, however, umami is the result of the presence of glutamates, or salts produced by glutamic acid, an amino acid. Specifically, the salt that gives certain foods umami is monosodium glutamate, or MSG. All the ingredients discussed in this section contain notable amounts of glutamates.

MSG is surprisingly controversial, given that glutamates are naturally present in many foods, including red meat, seaweed, tomatoes, walnuts, mushrooms, aged cheeses, and breast milk. Some people believe that they experience side effects from consuming MSG, although no scientific study has sufficiently corroborated this. Further, other additives frequently used in processed foods, such as yeast extract and hydrolyzed vegetable protein, are practically the same thing as MSG.

Of course, any concerns should be tempered by the fact that you do not need to add very much MSG or other glutamate-rich ingredients to improve a dish. A sprinkle of MSG, a few dashes of soy sauce or fish sauce, or a tablespoon of mushroom powder can boost the flavor of a dish tremendously. Flavor enhancers are worthwhile additions to any pantry. While they should not be used to compensate for a lack of care in cooking, they are excellent to have on hand for giving dishes a savory boost as needed.

Pure **MSG** is extracted from grains, sugarcane and its by-products, or beets. Fine white, and crystalline in appearance, MSG is soluble in water but not in fat, so, if you do use it, add it to the liquid ingredients. **Hydrolyzed vegetable protein** is a common ingredient in processed snack foods, but it also makes an appearance in many flavor enhancers like bouillon cubes (or paste), cheaper soy sauces and "liquid aminos," as well as **Maggi seasoning,** and **Kitchen Bouquet.**

Yeast extract is perhaps best known for its role as the principal ingredient in Marmite and Vegemite, which happen to be excellent additions to soups, stews, and braises. **Nutritional yeast,** that beloved vegan cooking staple, is simply deactivated yeast. It has a somewhat cheesy aroma and flavor and can be used as an ingredient or as a topping. So-called **mushroom seasoning** is made from dried mushrooms, salt, and mushroom extract. It has a more complex flavor than pure MSG, though it has a similar umami-rich appeal.

FLAXSEED

Also known as **linseed,** these are tiny golden or brown seeds from the flax plant. They are very rich in oil and are often processed to extract the oil for use as a dietary supplement. The seeds may be soaked much like chia seeds, 967, though they do not form quite as much of a gel. They are often ground and mixed with water to create a vegan egg substitute. Flaxseeds usually pass through the digestive tract undigested, so it is a good idea to grind them in order to absorb their nutrients. If you do so, however, grind them immediately before use or keep ground flaxseeds in the refrigerator or freezer. Once ground, they go rancid quickly. One tablespoon whole flaxseeds is equivalent to 2 tablespoons ground flaxseed or flax meal.

FLOURS

Take a quick trip down the baking or natural foods aisle of your local grocery store and you may notice that the variety of flours available has increased dramatically in the past several years. Whole wheat flours are now joined by spelt and Kamut flours, all-purpose and bread flour might sit next to Italian 00 flour. And then there are the growing number of bean flours, nut flours, rice flours, flours made from pseudo-cereals like buckwheat and amaranth, and countless others. Find each type in the following entries, which are devoted to nonwheat, followed by wheat-based, flours. The former category includes bean and pseudo-cereal flours, as well as grain flours like rice, corn, and barley.

To understand grain flours, we must first understand the three basic parts of a grain kernel (see the illustration on 317). The outer layers (or bran) and the germ, contain most of the grain's vitamins and minerals. The germ is only 2 percent of the entire kernel, but it contains most of the protein and all of the fat. The endosperm is largely starch, with some protein.

Whole-grain flours deteriorate faster because of the presence of the oily germ, which spoils quickly relative to the other parts of the grain. ➤ Try to buy quantities of whole-grain flours that you can use within 2 months and store them in a cool, dry place. Refined flours have the germ or bran removed and will stay fresher longer.

Many flours are prone to settling and compacting during storage, which can make measuring them accurately by volume a bit tricky. ➤ For directions on sifting and measuring flour, see 1046.

FRESHLY MILLED FLOURS

Over the past decade or so, freshly milled flour has become a common ingredient in bakeries and restaurants across the country. Freshly milled flours are increasingly available at farmers' markets; some regional millers sell fresh flours at local stores and online. Bakers who have worked with fresh flours cherish the distinct aromas and textures they lend to baked goods: A loaf of whole wheat bread might carry a deep scent of molasses, cocoa, or honey without any of these ingredients having been added to the dough.

➤ When substituting freshly milled for conventional flour in baking recipes, always measure by weight. Freshly milled flour is light and fluffy compared to store-bought flour, which has settled and compacted during storage.

Affordable tabletop grain mills for home use have come to market, as have quality milling attachments for stand mixers. In addition to preserving the natural flavor of grains, these mills can be adjusted to produce a coarser or finer result, which enables the baker to explore a wide range of textures in breads, cookies, cakes, and scones. Freshly milled flour also contains more wild yeasts and bacteria, making it ideal for maintaining sourdough starters, 608. Having a grain mill at home is not just for bakers: It is handy for milling corn kernels into polenta or cornmeal, and coarsely cracking wheat berries, barley, or rye berries for porridge.

Milling at home can also help reduce waste while preserving the nutritional value of whole grains. Whole grains left intact have a much longer shelf life than whole-grain flours: The vitamins in grains diminish rapidly when exposed to air by milling and their oils oxidize and go rancid more rapidly once ground. Whole grains can be milled as needed. This is especially useful for those interested in baking gluten-free treats, which often rely on combining several perishable flours, such as rice, corn, chickpea, and millet.

FLOURS, NONWHEAT

Some of the following nonwheat flours can be used alone. But in any bread recipe that calls only for nonwheat flours, expect a distinct difference in texture from typical wheat-based breads, as the gluten formed from wheat flour and water has a unique elastic quality. To read more about gluten and how it responds in mixing and baking, see Flour, 593. ➤ In general, you can replace up to one-third of the all-purpose flour in a recipe with nonwheat flour and still get reasonably good results (taking into consideration that some nonwheat flours will impart their own flavors and textures). If using a higher proportion of nonwheat flour than that, further modifications will have to be made to the recipe. For gluten-free baking, you will have more success if you use a blend of gluten-free flours, including at least 30 percent starchy flours such as white rice flour, tapioca starch, and cornstarch. There are several brands of gluten-free "cup for cup" flour blends available, and they are worth trying, as converting a recipe written to use wheat flour to use gluten-free flours can require quite a lot of trial and error.

ALMOND MEAL OR FLOUR

Almond meal, also called almond flour, is simply blanched or raw almonds ground to a fine, flour-like consistency. Almond flour is slightly coarse and tends to clump, especially when stored in the freezer (which we do because nut flours are prone to rancidity). Expect baked goods made with a high proportion of almond flour to be dense, but very moist and flavorful. For recipes using almond flour, see Sachertorte, 742, Viennese Crescents, 777, Spekulatius, 779, Macarons, 782, and Macaroon Jam Tarts, 785.

AMARANTH FLOUR

A fine, beige flour, amaranth has a distinctive grassy flavor and odor that can be overpowering in baked goods. It is best to combine amaranth flour with other flours, or use it in baked goods with strongly flavored ingredients like chocolate, molasses, or spices. For more about amaranth, see 320.

BARLEY FLOUR

Barley flour has a mild, nutty flavor. It does contain gluten, though less than wheat. Barley flour has four times the fiber content of all-purpose flour. For more information on barley, see 320.

BEAN FLOUR

Dried beans can be ground into a flour for use in making gluten-free baked products. The most common bean flour is **chickpea flour,** also labeled **besan** or **gram flour** in Indian markets. Chickpea flour is used to make Socca, 650, and Pakoras, 203, and it is a bit more versatile and neutral tasting than other bean flours. Other bean flours include soybean flour, pea flour, black bean flour, and fava bean flour. Bean flours are high in protein and fiber, but when used alone they can give baked goods an off-putting beany flavor, not to mention a dense texture.

BUCKWHEAT FLOUR

Buckwheat flour is a gluten-free flour with a high protein content. We love the nutty flavor and dark color it adds to baked goods of all kinds, but especially scones, pie crusts, and biscuits. See Buckwheat Pancakes, 640, Buckwheat Blini, 641, Buckwheat Crêpes, 646, and Buckwheat Corn Bread, 630. For more information on buckwheat, see 321.

CAROB FLOUR OR POWDER

A chocolate-like flour milled from the carob tree pod, which is also known as Saint John's bread. Substitute carob for cocoa powder for those allergic to chocolate. ➤ To substitute for chocolate, 3 tablespoons carob flour plus 2 tablespoons liquid equals 1 ounce unsweetened chocolate. Carob may be substituted 1:1 for cocoa powder. For every ¼ cup carob powder used in a recipe, reduce the sugar by 1 tablespoon.

CASSAVA FLOUR (TAPIOCA FLOUR)

Cassava flour is dried and ground yuca root, 284. ➤ Do not confuse this flour with tapioca starch, 1023, which is much finer than tapioca flour and is the extracted starch of the yuca root alone (as opposed to cassava flour, which is the result of grinding the whole dried root). It is neutral tasting and light in color and it can be substituted for all-purpose flour in some recipes. Notably, it is used to make *pão de queijo*, Brazilian cheese bread. Coarsely ground cassava flour is also seasoned and toasted to make *farofa*, a satisfying Brazilian side dish (and a garnish for Feijoada, 214).

FAROFA

About 2½ cups

There are many different recipes for farofa, some including eggs, chorizo, or olives. This is a simple version, excellent for serving with Feijoada, 214.

Heat in a large skillet over medium heat:

4 slices bacon, finely diced

Cook, stirring, until browned and the bacon's fat has rendered. Add to the skillet and melt:

4 tablespoons butter

Add and cook, stirring, until softened, about 5 minutes:

½ onion, finely diced
3 garlic cloves, minced

Add and stir constantly over the heat for 3 minutes:

1 cup cassava flour
¼ teaspoon salt
Pinch of black pepper

Remove from the heat and stir in:

2 tablespoons finely chopped parsley

CHESTNUT FLOUR

Chestnut flour is ground from raw or roasted dried chestnuts. It is an ancient staple of both Europe and North American indigenous tribes. The original polenta was made with chestnut flour, and the Cherokee used chestnut flour to make porridge and bread. Chestnut flour tends to clump and so should be sifted. Store chestnut flour in the freezer. Chestnut flour is very starchy and lightly sweet, and it gives baked goods a cakey texture. For more information on chestnuts, see 232.

COCONUT FLOUR

Coconut flour is high in fiber. Perhaps the most notable thing about coconut flour, other than its mild coconut flavor, is that it is extremely absorbent. If substituting coconut flour for some proportion of the all-purpose flour in a recipe, you will need to increase the liquid in the recipe, and the more coconut flour you use, the more liquid you will have to add to compensate.

CORN FLOUR

Corn flour is milled from a particular type of corn called flour corn, which has a thin seed coat and a soft kernel. Use it in baking for added corn flavor, mixing it with other flours. Do not confuse corn flour with masa harina, 321.

CORNMEAL

For information on cornmeal, see About Cornmeal, Hominy, and Grits, 321. Note that when using cornmeal in baking recipes, because it is grainier than flour, it will add a slightly gritty, crumbly texture. For recipes written to use cornmeal, see our recipes for corn breads, 630–31, Four-Grain Flapjacks, 641, Cornmeal Pancakes, 641, and Cornmeal Waffles, 643. ➤ If a recipe calls for self-rising cornmeal and you want to make your own, add 1½ teaspoons baking powder and ½ teaspoon salt to each 1 cup cornmeal.

OAT FLOUR

Oat flour is soft and starchy and can be an excellent addition to gluten-free baked goods, as it bakes up lighter than many other gluten-free flours without a trace of grittiness. Oat flour works especially well in cookies, cakes, and quick breads. For more information on oats, see 326.

POTATO FLOUR

Made from whole cooked potatoes that have been dried and ground, potato flour is used chiefly in soups, gravies, breads, and cakes, in combination with other flours, or alone in sponge cakes. Potato flour is different from potato starch, 1023. To avoid lumping in cake batters, blend it with the sugar before mixing. In bread recipes, it yields a moist, slow-staling loaf. If using in breads, only add a small proportion of potato flour—about 10 percent of the total amount of flour. ➤ To use as a thickener in sauces and gravies, substitute 1 tablespoon potato flour for 2 tablespoons all-purpose flour.

QUINOA FLOUR

A light-yellow flour with a grassy, earthy flavor, quinoa flour is best used with other flours so its flavor doesn't overpower. For more information about quinoa, see 328.

RICE FLOUR (WHITE AND BROWN)

Both nonglutinous (nonwaxy) and glutinous (waxy) rice flours are used extensively across much of Asia. Both of these flours are used in combination with other flours for making gluten-free baked goods. Always buy white rice flour from Asian grocery stores, as some American brands are very gritty and will not yield the best results in baking.

Brown rice flour is grittier than white rice flour but has more flavor and is less gummy. Use it in tandem with white rice flour to get the starchy benefits of the white rice flour and the flavor and heartiness of the brown rice flour. Look for "superfine" brown rice flour.

For more information About Rice, see 328.

SORGHUM FLOUR

Sorghum flour is gluten-free and ground from the large yellow or white grain of sorghum. Sorghum flour is often used to add flavor and a whole-grain texture in gluten-free baking. It has a subtle flavor somewhat like cornmeal. It is used in combination with other flours in cookies, cakes, and bread, although some bakers report good results when using sorghum flour alone in place of all-purpose flour for pancakes and waffles. For more information about sorghum, see 337.

TEFF FLOUR

Teff is the smallest grain, and the flour ground from it is very fine, with a deep brown color and malty flavor. Like most of the flours in this section, teff flour is best combined with other flours in baking due to its lack of gluten and distinctive flavor. For more information about teff, see 337.

FLOURS, WHEAT

Wheat flours are milled from "hard" or "soft" varieties of wheat berries—the former have considerably more protein than the latter. As with other grain flours, whole wheat flours are more nutritious (but deteriorate faster) than refined wheat flour, and have a heavier, denser texture when added to breads and other baked goods. Many so-called "ancient" varieties of wheat are also widely available as whole-grain flour; for information on these grains, see About Wheat, 337.

Once the bran and germ are removed, the primary factor that determines how a flour responds to cooking is its protein content. When water is added to wheat flour and stirred, two proteins occurring separately in the flour, glutenin and gliadin, interact with the water and each other to form elastic sheets of gluten. Wheat is the only grain that has substantial amounts of glutenin and gliadin. Gluten can never be developed except in the presence of moisture and when the dough or batter is worked or agitated, as in kneading. The higher the protein content, the more gluten is formed in doughs. Thus flours with a higher protein content are better for pasta and breads, which benefit from the extra gluten strength. Low-protein flours are better for delicate pastries, cakes, biscuits, and scones.

Another characteristic determined by a flour's protein content is its absorbency: The more protein a flour contains, the more liquid it can absorb. Flours can vary by more than 20 percent in this regard, which can lead to undesirable results: If the flour used has a different protein content from the flour called for in the recipe, the batter or dough can be much wetter or drier than the recipe intends. Even within a particular type of flour—most notably all-purpose flour—there can be a significant difference in protein content between brands. All of this is to say, be wary when substituting one type of flour for another, or when using flours from small mills. Be ready to adjust the amount of flour or liquid in batters and doughs based on visual and tactile cues in the recipe (and, eventually, your experience as a seasoned home baker).

Some brands of bread and all-purpose flour are **enriched** with additional iron, B vitamins, and calcium. Of course, you may fortify refined flour at home by combining it with whole wheat flour, or some of the nonwheat flours described above, which can have up to sixteen times the protein value of wheat, along with other important nutrients.

While it is generally not a good idea to simply substitute whole wheat and nonwheat flour for refined wheat flour in bread recipes, they can replace a portion of the flour by following a few simple guidelines (see Flour, 593).

"00" FLOUR

This is a very finely ground Italian flour used for pizza doughs and some breads. Professional *pizzaiolos* intent on making high-quality Neapolitan-style pies swear that it makes the best crust, but we have had good results with and without it. At 12 to 13 percent protein, it produces a similar amount of gluten as bread flour, below.

ALL-PURPOSE FLOUR

All-purpose flours have a moderate amount of protein, which makes them suitable for a variety of uses, from rustic breads to tender cakes, so long as attention is paid during mixing. They are typically milled from a blend of hard and soft wheat flours, but as mentioned above, the protein content of these flours can vary, and often depends on where the flour was milled. Southern brands of all-purpose flour (like White Lily) tend to be on the low end at 8 to 9 percent (which makes them more like cake flour, and especially good for biscuits). All-purpose flour milled in New England and Canada is on the high end at 13 percent (which is well into bread flour territory). National brands of all-purpose flour are in the middle, with about 11 or 12 percent protein. ➤ Bleached and unbleached all-purpose flour can be used interchangeably, but unbleached usually has a higher protein content than bleached flour.

How does this translate for home bakers? If you are in the southern United States and a yeast bread recipe calls for all-purpose flour, either choose a national brand of flour or one milled in the northern United States or Canada. If you are in the northern United States or Canada and a cake, quick bread, or cookie recipe calls for all-purpose flour, choose a national brand of flour. For Northerners seeking to make especially tender, southern-style biscuits, White Lily is worth seeking out (in a pinch, you may substitute 1 cup plus 2 tablespoons cake flour for 1 cup all-purpose flour).

BREAD FLOUR

Bread flour is made from hard wheat and is highly desirable for bread making because of its high protein content. The gluten-forming proteins give elasticity to dough and allow it to expand and hold the gas created by yeast. Bread flour feels almost granular or gritty when rubbed between the fingers. Although the term is not technically correct, many bakers refer to high-protein or bread flour as "high-gluten" flour. Flour in actuality does not contain gluten. It contains two proteins, glutenin and gliadin, that form gluten when mixed with water and kneaded.

CAKE FLOUR

Cake flour, made from soft, lower-protein wheat, is more finely ground than all-purpose flour, and in the United States is chlorinated, which causes it to absorb more water and also aids in the distribution of the fat and the air bubbles for a finer-textured cake. Although you will not get quite the same result, you may ➤ substitute ¾ cup plus 2 tablespoons sifted all-purpose flour and 2 tablespoons cornstarch for 1 cup cake flour.

DURUM FLOUR AND SEMOLINA

Durum is the hardest and most protein-rich variety of wheat, and has a deep yellow color and nutty, sweet flavor. **Semolina** is durum that has been milled to the consistency of coarse cornmeal or polenta. It adds a nice texture to some pastas and is used quite often to coat baking peels, so that loaves of bread and pizza smoothly slide into ovens.

On its face, the high protein content of this wheat would seem to make finely milled **durum flour,** also sold as **semolina flour,** ideal for breads. Actually, protein-rich durum is the exception to the rule; its ratio of glutenin and gliadin is different from that in other wheats. Doughs made from durum are highly extensible—that is, they are firm and easy to roll out—but they are not very elastic: Durum doughs do not "spring back" as forcefully when acted upon. This means that durum flour must be combined with bread or all-purpose flour to produce a loaf of bread with decent structure and volume.

On the other hand, this unique quality makes durum flour ideal for pasta doughs, which must be firm and easy to roll out (or extruded into shapes). Another reason durum is the wheat of choice for pastas is its tendency to retain starch. Other wheat flours are much more prone to leaking starch, which then clouds the cooking water and the surface of the pasta.

In addition to pasta, durum flour is moistened, sifted, and steamed to make couscous, 325.

EINKORN, EMMER, KHORASAN, AND SPELT FLOUR

These ancient cousins of wheat are available as whole-grain flours. Some mills have even started producing "white," refined flours from einkorn, khorasan (or Kamut), and spelt (white emmer flour is much rarer to find). Some types can be found at specialty stores, but all are readily available from online retailers (or directly from the mill's website).

Whole-grain flours milled from these varieties perform similarly to whole wheat flour, and can be substituted freely (if possible, match the amounts with a scale rather than with cups). When substituting refined **einkorn flour** for regular white wheat flour, you will need to decrease the amount of liquid in bread recipes by up to 20 percent. Refined **khorasan** or **Kamut flour** has a golden amber color and mild, buttery flavor, and 13 percent protein. It can be substituted freely for regular bread flour, or in bread recipes that call for all-purpose flour. Like durum wheat flours, white **spelt flour** has plenty of protein, but its ratio of glutenin to gliadin is low, and it must be mixed with a bread flour or all-purpose flour to produce acceptable breads.

FARINA

Farina is made from semi-pearled, 317, hard wheat: The bran has been removed, but part of the germ remains. The result is a cream-colored, protein-rich flour. It is commonly eaten as a hot breakfast cereal. When shopping in stores that carry imported dry goods, remember that "farina" is also the generic Italian word for flour.

GRAHAM FLOUR

Graham flour is unsifted, coarsely ground whole wheat. It is best known for its role in Graham Crackers, 778.

INSTANT FLOUR

Sold under the brand Wondra, instant flour is refined flour that has been hydrated, cooked, and then dried and milled into granules (hence its other name, granular flour). It disperses and dissolves easily into liquids at any temperature and does not need to have the raw taste simmered out of it—which makes it especially convenient for making gravies and sauces, 543. ➤ Instant flour should not be substituted for all-purpose flour.

PASTRY FLOUR

A soft, finely milled low-protein flour, pastry flour is similar to cake flour, although it is usually not chlorinated. Available from online retailers and in specialty markets, it is best used for pastries and quick breads. Whole wheat pastry flour is also available if you desire a soft, finely milled whole-grain flour. ➤ You may substitute ⅔ cup all-purpose flour and ⅓ cup cake flour for 1 cup pastry flour.

RYE FLOUR

There are several types of rye flour. White rye flour, like all-purpose flour, has had the bran and germ removed and so is light in color and mild in flavor. Medium rye flour contains some bran. Dark rye flour is often a whole grain, but some millers make it from the leftovers from white rye flour production; in some cases it may not contain the germ. Look for the word "whole" to indicate whether the flour in question is a whole-grain flour or not. **Rye meal** is whole-grain rye flour that is ground fine, medium, or coarse. **Pumpernickel flour** is coarse, whole-grain rye flour.

In most rye bread recipes, rye flour is combined with varying proportions of all-purpose flour because rye flour contains proteins that provide stickiness but is lower in gluten-forming proteins. Breads made largely with rye flour are moist and dense. For more information about rye, see 337.

SELF-RISING FLOUR

Self-rising flour contains the correct amounts of leaveners and salt for baking. Many bakers do not like to use this type of flour because it is not as versatile as all-purpose flour. While most often used for quick breads, biscuits, and pancakes, self-rising flour is not recommended for pastries, as it results in a spongy, rather than flaky, texture. It is also not recommended for making bread. ➤ To make your own self-rising flour, add 1½ teaspoons baking powder and ½ teaspoon salt for every 1 cup all-purpose flour.

TRITICALE FLOUR

A nutritious sweet-tasting flour that comes from a hybrid of durum wheat, hard red winter wheat, and rye. Although the flour is higher in protein than all-purpose wheat flour, it is low in gluten-forming proteins and so should be mixed with half all-purpose or bread flours for bread making.

VITAL WHEAT GLUTEN OR GLUTEN FLOUR

This is a starch-free high-protein flour made by washing the starch from hard wheat flour. The residue is then dried and ground. It may contain up to 70 percent protein and is used as an additive in bread, or to make the plant protein Seitan, 288. Vital wheat gluten can be added to other flours that are lower in gluten-forming proteins such as rye, soy, and rice to produce a leavened loaf.

WHOLE WHEAT FLOUR

Whole wheat flour retains the bran and germ and thus the original vitamins, mineral salts, and fats of the whole wheat kernel. Whether coarsely or finely milled, the entire wheat kernel is ground to create this flour. Bread made with 100 percent whole wheat flour can be very heavy because the gluten-forming capacity of the wheat is reduced due to the presence of bran and germ. To remedy this and produce a well-leavened loaf, use a mixture of whole wheat flour and bread flour; or use 1 or 2 tablespoons of vital wheat gluten per 1 cup whole wheat flour; or consider using whole wheat pastry flour, a lower-protein wheat flour that contains the germ and the bran portion of the wheat kernels.

GALANGAL

Related to ginger, galangal comes in two forms. **Lesser galangal** is a smaller rhizome with orange-red skin, yellow flesh, and a stronger flavor. It is an ingredient in some bitters, liqueurs, beers, and medicinal preparations. It is rarely available fresh. **Greater galangal** can be found in Asian groceries and, every so often, at specialty stores. It is much larger and resembles ginger, though often thicker, with a pale off-white to light orange skin and thin crosswise stripes (usually dark orange).

Though a common ingredient throughout central and Southeast Asia, we associate galangal with Thai cuisine, where its piney, camphorous flavor adds nuance to curry pastes and perfumes dishes like Tom Kha Gai, 94. Fresh galangal is always best, but it is also available frozen, dried, and bottled in brine (we prefer the preserved forms in this order). Select and store as for ginger, 991.

Thicker pieces of galangal are woody, very dense, and can be difficult to cut; pieces are thinly sliced (to be removed from the dish before serving or left, uneaten, on the plate). For curry pastes, galangal should be peeled before pounding or grinding. Since this rhizome is considerably denser and tougher than ginger, it needs special treatment.

To prepare galangal, cut crosswise into thick coins first; this may be difficult, so be cautious. You may need to bear down on the spine of your knife. Stand each coin on a cut side, and slice off the outer layer. For efficiency and a smooth result, dice the coins before adding to a mortar, food processor, or blender.

GARLIC AS SEASONING

Garlic is, in our estimation, one of the most delicious additions to food. The nineteenth-century French novelist Balzac, a formidable gastronome, recommended that even the cook should be rubbed with it! We couldn't cook without it. Here, we cover garlic as a seasoning ingredient, as well as its dried, bottled, and "black" forms. ➤ For instructions on peeling, cutting, and roasting fresh garlic, see 241.

Garlic is one of our favorite things to grow in the garden, as it is a hardy, insect-resistant plant. Plant cloves of *Allium sativum* in light soil in October or November. The mature bulbs should be ready for lifting in June or July of the following year. They grow to 1 to 3 feet in height. Hardneck garlic will send up scapes, 240, in late spring—these are actually flower stalks and should be cut off before the bud flowers so that the plant's energy will be put into the bulb. Once the tops begin to dry out and fall over, the garlic is ready to harvest. Dig up the bulbs, leaving them attached to the leaves. Tie the garlic in bundles of 6 and hang them in a dry, well-ventilated space out of direct sunlight (a garage or shed works well) for 4 to 6 weeks. This allows the garlic to dry, or cure, for long-term storage.

There are lots of different ways to use garlic. Cut small slits in roasts and tuck slivers of garlic inside before cooking; rub a salad bowl with a cut clove; use a rasp grater to grate a clove into vinaigrettes; smash garlic cloves and add them to long-simmering braises. Garlic is commonly sweated or sautéed in recipes with another allium—onions. Smashed cloves fare well when added at the same time as onion, but minced and chopped garlic browns more quickly, and may turn bitter rather than mellow and aromatic. Of course, garlic can be added in the middle or toward the end of cooking, and its pungency will remain relatively undiminished.

Though we almost always use fresh garlic in cooking, **garlic powder** or **granulated garlic** is good to keep on hand to use in seasoning blends (especially Chili Powder, 588), or to lightly and evenly coat foods (like Popcorn, 47). **Garlic salt** is a fine seasoning with similar uses, but we enjoy the freedom of adding them separately, and to taste. **Dried garlic flakes** (sometimes sold as "minced") is a crucial ingredient in Everything Seasoning, 590. ➤ To substitute dried garlic for fresh, use ⅛ teaspoon garlic powder or ½ teaspoon dried garlic flakes for every clove of garlic called for, and always add to the recipe at a stage where ingredients are not being browned (they will burn and turn acrid). Dried garlic flakes will need to be simmered in cooking liquid until soft.

Jarred chopped garlic may be convenient to those who would rather skip the rigmarole of peeling and mincing fresh cloves, but no one will ever mistake its flavor for fresh. **Garlic paste** has a much better flavor; it can be found in tubes at grocery stores, or in large jars at Indian markets (which may also carry brands that contain ginger paste as well). Chopped garlic and garlic paste both contain preservatives (and occasionally vinegar or citric acid) and must be refrigerated after opening. A relative newcomer to store shelves is **freeze-dried garlic,** which exceeds the convenience of the jarred product, is not made with preservatives, and has a stronger, sharper flavor. ➤ To substitute jarred chopped garlic, garlic paste, or freeze-dried garlic in place of fresh, use a heaping ½ teaspoon for every clove of garlic called for. Chopped garlic and garlic paste can be added when minced garlic normally would be and needs no special treatment; freeze-dried garlic will need to be hydrated briefly in a cooking liquid.

Black garlic is made by keeping whole garlic bulbs at an elevated temperature (around 140°F) for up to 2 months. During this process, the garlic browns and blackens thanks to several processes. The elevated temperature causes the sugars in the garlic to slowly caramelize. The Maillard reaction, 1048, also slowly contributes to the blackening process, as well as enzymatic browning—the same mechanism at work when cut fruits and vegetables are left out too long without a slathering of lemon juice. The end result are jet-black, concentrated cloves that have a wonderfully savory, raisin-like flavor. In cooking, black garlic can be used like other umami-rich seasoning ingredients such as anchovies, fermented black beans, or other flavor enhancers, 984. We like to add pureed black garlic cloves to vinaigrettes or mince and add to creamy soups, meaty braises, the filling for Deviled Eggs, 151, mayonnaise, or other sauces and dishes that could use a complex, garlicky richness and dark molasses notes.

For more information on the chemical processes at work as well as directions for making black garlic at home, we highly recommend consulting René Redzepi and David Zilber's *The Noma Guide to Fermentation*.

GELATIN

Gelatin is full of tricks. It can turn liquids into solids. It stabilizes meringues, mousses, and whipped cream, 791, and is a key ingredient in marshmallows and Panna Cotta, 821. It inhibits unwanted crystallization in frozen desserts, can be used to set "no-bake" cheesecakes and chiffon pies, and adds body to sauces, stocks, and soups. Perhaps the most appealing thing about foods set with gelatin is that they melt at body temperature. This is why, when you take a bite of a gelatin dessert, it seems to melt in your mouth.

Gelatin is extracted from the bones, skin, hooves, and body tissues of animals, yielding a protein-rich but flavorless and colorless substance. ➤ Never use more than directed; the result will be rubbery and unpleasant. ➤ Avoid flavoring gelatin desserts and aspics with fresh or frozen pineapple, papaya, kiwi, figs, honeydew, or ginger: All of them contain protease enzymes that break down the proteins in gelatin, thus inhibiting jelling. To use one of these fruits in gelatin, cook it or use canned fruit (precooking the fruit neutralizes the enzymes). For more information about gelatin desserts, see 820.

Gelatin's power to bind moisture is measured by its **Bloom strength** (this unit of measurement is named after Oscar T. Bloom, the man who devised the instrument to test gelatin strength). Household gelatin powders are rated at a Bloom strength of 225; the contents of 1 envelope or packet of unflavored gelatin, or 2¼ teaspoons, can set about 2 cups of liquid. **Gelatin sheets** (or leaf gelatin) are more commonly used in restaurant kitchens, and they come in different grades, which have different Bloom strengths. Bronze gelatin sheets have a Bloom strength of 140; silver has a strength of 160; gold has a strength of 200; and platinum has a strength of 230. For mysterious reasons that elude us, gelatin sheets are weighted differently so that sheets of different grades are roughly interchangeable. In other words, a sheet of bronze gelatin has about the same setting power as a sheet of platinum gelatin because the bronze gelatin sheet is weighted heavier than the platinum sheet.

If all that seems confusing to you (it is certainly a little confusing to us), ➤ just remember that 1 envelope of powdered gelatin is equivalent to 2¼ teaspoons bulk powdered gelatin, and approximately equivalent to 3½ sheets leaf gelatin. These quantities will set 2 cups of liquid firm enough that the resulting gelatin can be unmolded. If you prefer a less firm texture, use these same quantities of gelatin to set 2¼ to 2½ cups liquid. You will not be able to unmold the resulting gelatins, but they will have a beautifully tender consistency.

➤ If you prefer to measure by weight, weigh the liquid you need to set, then add 1 percent gelatin (multiply the weight of the liquid by 0.01 to get the weight of gelatin needed). This will give you a moderate set. You can work up or down from there depending on whether you want a light set or a firm set. For a light set, 0.6 percent gelatin is about as low as you can go. For a firm set, go no higher than 1.7 percent gelatin.

There are a few factors that inhibit gelatin's ability to gel liquids—other than ginger and the protease-containing fruits discussed above. These are a low pH (below 4 on the pH scale), boiling, salt, and alcohol concentrations above 40 percent (or 80 proof). ➤ Never boil gelatin—only heat it enough to melt it.

To hydrate or "bloom" gelatin, sprinkle it over a small amount of cold liquid. This liquid is often water, but you could use more of the liquid being used in the recipe to bloom the gelatin; for instance, milk, broth, or fruit juice. Allow it to sit for 5 to 10 minutes, during which time the granules will swell. Then, whisk the gelatin into a hot, not boiling, liquid until it dissolves completely. For gelatin sheets, cover them with cold water and allow them to sit for 5 to 10 minutes. The sheets will soften. Gather the softened gelatin sheets in your hand, gently squeeze out any excess water, and whisk them into the hot, not boiling, liquid being used in the recipe. You can also dissolve gelatin by placing it in the top of a double boiler or a heatproof bowl, then heating it over simmering water until it is fully melted.

For aspic recipes, see 134. For gelatin desserts, see 820.

GERANIUMS

Sweet-scented geranium leaves may be used to infuse jellies, compotes, ice cream, or custards (see Flavorings for Custard Bases I, 813). Geranium flowers are also edible and can be used to garnish salads, soups, and desserts of all kinds. Geranium varieties have distinct flavors: For lime, try *Pelargonium nervosum*; for apple, *P. odoratissimum*; for mint, *P. tomentosum*; and for rose, *P. graveolens*.

GHEE

See Butter, 958.

GINGER

The rhizome of the bold perennial *Zingiber officinale*—with the most heavenly scented lily—is a staple in kitchens throughout the world, and a definitive aromatic ingredient in countless sweet and savory dishes.

Most of the ginger you are likely to encounter will be somewhat mature, with tough fibers running the length of the root. Whole fresh ginger should have smooth skin and be a uniformly buff color. If you are lucky at a farmers' market, or live near a Japanese supermarket, you may find **young ginger,** which has pale, tender skin and smooth flesh that is free of fibers. It is ideal for making Pickled Ginger, 930.

Select firm, heavy pieces of mature ginger. (For ease of peeling, you might want to look out for pieces with fewer, thicker lobes.) If fresh and firm, mature ginger will keep in a cool garage or cellar for months. If left on the counter, it will last about a week, or about 4 weeks in the refrigerator crisper. Or you may wash fresh ginger, cover it with vodka, and keep refrigerated for up to 1 month. Young ginger should be stored in the refrigerator crisper and be used within a week of purchase.

Cleaned and trimmed ginger does not need to be peeled when adding to a juicer (see Carrot-Beet-Ginger Juice, 12, and Kale-Ginger Lemonade, 12), infusing a Hot Toddy, 24, or muddling for a Penicillin, 24. Unpeeled ginger is also charred for Pho Bo, 96. Most young ginger has inoffensive skin. In all of these cases, simply rinse well under running water and trim off any blemishes or dried, exposed flesh.

In recipes throughout this book, our measurements for peeled ginger are usually expressed as pieces in inches. ➤ For us, a "1-inch piece" of ginger is a cube or rounded section of the root with trimmed sides of that length.

To peel ginger, separate into easily managed lobes and trim off any especially small pieces that are not worth the trouble of peeling. Hold one end of the piece up at an angle and scrape the skin off with a spoon, vegetable peeler, or (taking more care) with the spine of your knife blade. If any browned flesh lies underneath, cut it out or trim off.

After peeling, you can slice, chop, or dice as for any firm vegetable (see Cutting Vegetables, 200). When cutting mature ginger into slices or coins for adding to stir-fries, soups, or any other dish where you intend to eat them, ➤ always slice thinly and across the grain.

To mince or grate mature ginger with a rasp grater, peel and grate so that the fibers run perpendicular to the grating surface. This will increase the efficiency of each stroke and (mostly) prevent fibers from gumming up the blades.

We prefer grated ginger when at all possible because the resulting paste melts into dishes. **Ginger paste** can be found in jars at Indian markets (as well as ginger-garlic paste) and is often fried in oil or Ghee, 960, at the beginning of sauce making. When substituting ginger paste for fresh, a 1-inch cube of fresh ginger is equal to about 1½ teaspoons paste.

➤ Do not use fresh ginger in gelatin salads; it wrecks the jelling capacity of gelatin.

Dried ginger chunks can be simmered in soups, stews, and stocks to infuse them with flavor (remove the ginger before serving). Powdered dried ginger is most commonly used in baked goods. Dried ginger should never be substituted for fresh. Ginger boiled and preserved in syrup is called **stem ginger,** a milder form that is delicious in desserts, chopped fine and used with or without its syrup. **Pickled Ginger,** 930, thinly sliced fresh ginger preserved in seasoned rice vinegar, is used as a condiment or side dish, most frequently with sushi. It is sold both dyed pink and in its natural buff color. **Beni Shōga,** 930, is julienned ginger pickled with ume plum vinegar. It has a purplish color from the *shiso* used in the plum pickling solution. It is commonly served with Okonomiyaki, 226, and Yakisoba, 302. **Candied Ginger,** 876, or **crystallized ginger,** may be used in baked goods and desserts. For galangal, a ginger relative, see 989.

GLUCOSE SYRUP

In the United States, most glucose syrup is made from cornstarch, but it may also be made from potatoes, wheat, or a number of other starch-rich plants. It is commonly used in confectionery and performs much the same function as corn syrup, 974. Glucose syrup is notably thicker than standard corn syrup, with an incredibly sticky, viscous consistency. It is much less sweet than corn syrup and has no flavor.

GOCHUJANG

See Chile Pastes, 969.

GOLDEN SYRUP

See Cane Syrup, 961.

GRAINS OF PARADISE

Also known as melegueta pepper and alligator pepper, grains of paradise are spicy, warm, and a little on the bitter side, with a zesty flavor reminiscent of pepper, coriander, and cardamom. Related to ginger, this spice is used in Ras el Hanout, 590. It is terrific on vegetables, and a good substitute for black pepper. *Aframomum melegueta* produces poppy-like pods that each contain from 50 to 100 faceted, round seeds. Try adding it to Middle Eastern lamb or eggplant dishes.

GUAJE SEEDS

Eaten as a snack in Mexico, *guaje* seeds grow inside the long, flat pods of the Leucaena tree. The pods range from green to rust colored. The small, thin seeds are tender and have a garlicky flavor. They can be eaten raw or roasted or ground and used to thicken sauces, much like pumpkin seeds in Green Mole, 554. To remove the seeds from the pods, use a knife to cut down the length of one side of the pod, then open the pod and pick out the seeds by running your thumb down the inside walls. Find *guaje* pods in the produce department of most Mexican grocery stores.

GUMS AND HYDROCOLLOIDS

The gums and other ingredients discussed here are all examples of **hydrocolloids,** or substances that thicken liquids. Some hydrocolloids, when added in sufficient quantity, will form a firm gel. Others will form a much softer gel or no gel at all, regardless of how much is added. Some hydrocolloids are so ubiquitous in our kitchens that they deserve in-depth treatment: Perhaps the most common hydrocolloids are **flours,** 985, and pure **starches,** 1022. (To use starches and flours as thickeners for sauces, see 542.) For **gelatin,** see 990; for **pectin** and its role in thickening jellies and preserves, see 907.

The hydrocolloids listed below are a bit less common. All are tasteless, odorless, colorless, and generally come from the sap of legumes or seaweed extracts. Hydrocolloids that form softer, more elastic gels are typically used to thicken liquids, as well as to stabilize emulsions (like vinaigrettes), to keep small particles suspended in sauces, and several other specialized applications in candy making and gluten-free baking.

Agar, or agar-agar, is a hydrocolloid extracted from different types of red algae. In sufficient quantities, agar will form a very brittle gel. It can be found in the form of clear strands, a powder, or flakes. Agar in strand form can be rehydrated by soaking in water until soft and then pureeing into mixtures, or the strands can be treated like noodles and eaten in salads.

To make a solid agar gel, use ½ to 1 teaspoon powdered agar per 1 cup liquid or 1½ teaspoons to 1 tablespoon flakes per 1 cup liquid, depending on how firm a gel you want. At higher concentrations, agar gel is so brittle that it will break into "shards" when cut or bitten into. Agar's ability to gel is not easily destroyed by heat or acid. To use agar instead of gelatin in jelled desserts, see Making Vegan Molded Desserts, 820. Agar must be hydrated for it to create a gel.

To hydrate agar, combine flakes or powder with the liquid in a saucepan. To avoid clumping, it is always best to whisk or blend agar powder into a liquid gradually, until it is completely incorporated. Bring to a boil, cover, reduce the heat, and simmer until the agar is dissolved, 3 minutes for powder and 10 minutes for flakes.

Carrageenan, like agar, is derived from red algae. Though not available in stores, several formulations of carrageenan are available from online retailers. In general, items thickened with carrageenan tend to have a creamier texture, which is why it is used in nut milks and dairy products like ice cream and yogurt. **Kappa carrageenan** will form an opaque, brittle gel, much like agar does; **iota carrageenan** forms a softer, clear gel. ➤ Allow 4 to 8 grams of powder per 1 cup liquid, depending on how stiff a gel is needed. Hydrate as for agar, above. **Lambda carrageenan** is used as an emulsifier, stabilizer, and thickener in a variety of foods (especially dairy products like ice cream and yogurt). Lambda should be added in similar amounts, but it does not need to be heated like the gel-forming types (simply blend it into liquids at room temperature). Unlike agar, ➤ carrageenan will thin out in overly acidic liquids.

Gum arabic comes from the sap of the acacia tree. The powdered form has several culinary uses. Bottles of liquid gum arabic solution are sold as an additive for watercolor painting, so be sure your gum arabic is food grade. Gum arabic prevents sugar from crystallizing and can be used to strengthen gelatin desserts. It is used in candies, ice creams, soft drinks, and gomme syrup (a gum-thickened simple syrup used in cocktails to give them more body). As long as the powder is well mixed, gum arabic powder will hydrate and thicken at room temperatures if covered in water and left to dissolve for 48 hours. Boiling as for agar, above, will quicken the process.

Gum tragacanth is made from the sap of several shrubs and used as an emulsifier or thickener. It is used in some icings for pliability, in sugarcraft, and in commercially prepared salad dressings for stability and body. Use from 1 to 4 grams of powder for each 1 cup liquid, depending on the thickness desired. Hydrate gum tragacanth as for gum arabic, above.

Guar gum is a thickener made from guar beans. It is used in gluten-free baking to help give baked goods body in the absence of gluten. It is also used to stabilize ice creams, give body to non-dairy milks, and thicken salad dressings. Use 1 to 2 teaspoons per 1 quart liquid. For baked goods, use as little as ¼ teaspoon per 1 cup flour for cookies and as much as 2 teaspoons per 1 cup flour for breads.

Xanthan gum is produced by the bacterium *Xanthomonas campestris* and is widely used as a food additive. It is perhaps best known for its role, similar to guar gum, in making gluten-free baked goods. Use as little as ¼ teaspoon per 1 cup flour for cookies and as much as 1½ teaspoons per 1 cup flour for breads. Xanthan gum can be tricky to add to liquids because it clumps easily. The best way to add it to liquids is to put the liquid in a blender and turn it on. Gradually add the xanthan gum, blending the whole time, until it is completely incorporated. Xanthan gum can be added to hot or cold liquids and thickens them immediately. ➤ The most important thing to remember when adding xanthan gum to liquids is to start with a small amount (⅛ teaspoon per 1 cup) and add as needed. Adding too much xanthan gum gives liquids an unpleasantly viscous, ropy texture.

HARISSA

See Chile Pastes, 969.

HAZELNUTS

Hazelnuts have a distinctive, perfumed flavor, which pairs particularly well with chocolate (the combination of chocolate and hazelnut is called *gianduja*). They are sometimes called **filberts,** although this is actually a name for a specific species of hazel tree. Worldwide, Turkey is the leading producer of hazelnuts. Nearly all hazelnuts grown commercially in the United States come from Oregon.

Once out of the shell, hazelnuts are encased in a thin, reddish-brown skin. Blanched hazelnuts are sometimes available, which have the skin conveniently removed. The best way to remove the skin from raw hazelnuts is to toast them, let them cool slightly, and rub the skins off in a kitchen towel. Of course, toasting hazelnuts also deepens their flavor and aroma.

To toast hazelnuts, preheat the oven to 350°F. Scatter the hazelnuts on a rimmed baking sheet and toast them until browned and fragrant, about 15 minutes. While the nuts are still warm, transfer them to a kitchen towel and enclose the nuts in the towel. Allow them to steam for 2 to 5 minutes. Rub the nuts in the towel to loosen the skins. Not all the skins will come off. This is okay.

Also see French Praline, 873, and Romesco Sauce, 570.

HEMP SEEDS

Hemp seeds or "hemp hearts" are the seeds of the *Cannabis sativa* plant, which is perhaps best known for its psychoactive properties. The seeds, however, are not eaten for fun, just for nutrition. They happen to be quite delicious—nutty and slightly sweet with a tender texture. The tiny cream-colored seeds are flecked with green. They are excellent eaten raw on smoothies or with yogurt and can be added to all kinds of baked goods, either mixed into batters or sprinkled atop muffins and quick breads before baking. Store refrigerated in an airtight container.

To toast hemp seeds, spread out on a rimmed baking sheet and bake at 325°F for 15 minutes.

HERBS

Dried and fresh herbs add so much to so many dishes and beverages. Some are added at the beginning of cooking; some are showered over foods at the end; and some are fashioned into a condiment, paste, or salad. For information on specific herbs, including their characteristic flavors and typical uses, see individual entries in this chapter.

Dried herbs can be of good quality and are a wonderful pantry staple to have around for adding flavor to soups, stews, and braises. Though some high-moisture herbs—especially basil and parsley—do not dry particularly well and only possess a muted, one-dimensional flavor, others are heightened and concentrated by the drying process. Always give preference to dried whole herbs, rather than ground, if at all possible. (Like spices, 1020, ground herbs lose their flavor more quickly.) Avoid purchasing herbs that look faded or show signs of disintegrating. If freshly dried, most herbs will remain flavorful in sealed jars for 6 months. Resinous herbs like bay leaves and rosemary may last even longer. To dry your own herbs, see 947.

Our kitchen is never without **fresh herbs.** Growing them is easy if you have the space to do so (and infinitely cheaper than purchasing at the store). If herbs still have a fair amount of their stems intact, store in a glass of water so that none of the leaves are submerged; high-moisture herbs like basil may last this way for several days on the counter, or up to a week, if left in the glass of water, loosely covered with a plastic bag, and refrigerated (basil in particular keeps best with its stems inserted in water but kept at room temperature). For smaller bundles of herbs, be sure they are very dry and store in a produce bag that has been lined with a paper towel. A little moisture helps keep plant parts fresh, but too much promotes decay. Remove any twist-ties or rubber bands and spread the stems to discourage mold. If any leaves start to brown or yellow, trim them immediately.

COOKING WITH HERBS

Delicately flavored herbs and those that have tender leaves, such as cilantro, basil, and chives are often added to dishes toward the end of cooking, or at the table. Some, like parsley, may be added at the beginning, but are best kept whole and removed before serving. Sturdy, resinous herbs like rosemary, bay laurel, and thyme can be added toward the beginning to give them time to infuse the dish with their flavor. Some herbs take well to frying and can be used as a crunchy garnish (see the instructions for frying sage leaves, 1013). Herbs can also be used to infuse vinegars, 1031, and flavor salts, 1014, and then incorporated as a finishing element in even more dishes.

➤ To substitute dried herbs for fresh, use ⅓ teaspoon ground or 1 teaspoon crushed or crumbled for every 1 tablespoon chopped fresh herbs. In general, dried herbs should be added during cooking in order to give them time to soften and impart their flavor to the food. Crumbling dried herbs between your fingers before adding can help release their fragrance. With the exception of seasonings like Za'atar, 590, avoid using dried herbs as a last-minute garnish.

CUTTING FRESH HERBS

Fresh herbs destined for the cutting board should be washed, well dried, and have all tough stems removed. The sharper the knife, the better an herb's flavor and color will be.

To chop or mince herbs with small leaves, gather them into a compact pile. Grip the knife so that your thumb and the knuckle of your index finger are on either side of the blade just in front of the handle (your lower fingers should wrap around the handle, 1044). With your other hand, grasp the top of the end of the blade. Chop the herbs using a rocking motion, keeping the tip of the knife on the cutting board and moving the handle up and down. Run the blade through the pile once, then use the knife to squeegee the herb pieces back into a neat pile, scrape off any leaves stuck to the side of the blade, and rock-chop through the pile again. Repeat until the herbs are the desired consistency.

To slice, chop, or mince herbs with large leaves, such as basil, sorrel, and *shiso*, it is much more efficient to **chiffonade** them first. Chiffonade simply means to stack herb leaves on top of each other, roll them together into a cigar shape, and then thinly slice crosswise into threads or ribbons. These herb shreds can be used as an elegant garnish or chopped and minced further, as above.

To slice or mince chives, see 970.

If you are mincing or chopping a variety of herbs, you can save time by rolling up small-leafed herbs like thyme, oregano, and parsley in a stack of larger ones and chiffonade them together. The smaller leaves are held captive and gathered tightly, which allows you to make a finer and more effective initial cut.

For mincing, grinding, and pounding herbs with a mortar and pestle, see 1045. When making pastes, green sauces, and other herb mixtures by hand, keep in mind that chopping herbs together with the other ingredients—such as lemon zest or minced aromatics like garlic and ginger—will make the whole process go much more smoothly: The garlic and zest will keep herb fragments from jumping around, and vice versa. Of course, for the finest result and larger quantities, the best thing to do is transfer a mixture of chopped items to a blender, food processor, or a roomy mortar and pestle.

GROWING HERBS

We encourage you to exercise your green thumb at least on those herbs whose fragrance and flavor deteriorate or almost disappear in drying: Parsley, basil, tarragon, cilantro, and chives suffer the greatest losses. In general, though, if you have the space for a small

Mortar and pestle

herb garden, it will pay great dividends and requires little upkeep. Many herbs, including chives, thyme, tarragon, sage, and rosemary are perennial in most climates, meaning they come back year after year. These herbs tend to be hardy, tolerating both cold and hot weather and some degree of drought (though for the best yields, you will want to keep your herb garden well watered).

Below, the top layout is an illustration of Marion's herb garden: Beginning at the right, in the end section is sage, followed by tarragon, parsley, dwarf basil, and thyme, all partitioned by chives. Or you may prefer partitions of lavender or fern-like burnet, which, with the sage and thyme end sections, will give form to your garden in winter. We have tried growing herbs in many patterns. Since most herbs are sun lovers, need good airflow, and dislike competition, bed layouts such as those shown at center and below it suit them well.

Good drainage, whether secured by boxing or simply by the selection of terraced ground, is a primary consideration in herb

Top: Marion's culinary herb garden at Cockaigne in the early 1970s
Center and bottom: Other herb garden designs

growing. The upper and lower sketches show raised beds, the upper crescent-shaped held high by old granite street cobbles or bricks, the lower by corrugated metal or wooden boards, which also provide containment for rampant aggressors like mint. Shown in the illustration are squares of mints, calendulas, and nasturtiums and a combination of chives and parsley.

You may prefer to use squared beds. A 15- to 24-inch square area for each of most culinary herbs is more than enough to supply a busy kitchen. Sometimes, if we want only a single specimen—for instance, a sage, lavender, bay, or rosemary—we keep it pruned to a central shrub and use the edges around it for smaller plants. And sometimes we repeat a color accent—like the gray of sage or lavender—to unify the whole complex of squares. A more elegant solution is to use millstones or other large round stones, which also absorb the heat most herbs thrive on and which make ideal access points for the gardener to weed from. A millstone also gives the surrounding herbs freedom to spread over its edges, as well as over the flat stones that define the bed. Illustrated here in the centers are a pot of rosemary and a dwarf pepper plant, although a cherry tomato plant on a trellis would give more height to the layout. Chamomiles and thymes are shown as bordering plants, but any of the dwarf creepers, like dwarf savories, could be used. ➤ Unruly herbs like dill, mint, fennel, lovage, borage, and cilantro should be grown in separate containers. If these mavericks are grown in unregimented fashion, most of them will self-sow and conquer their surroundings.

If you do not have room for an elaborate layout, set out a few pots of annuals on your patio, balcony, porch, or stoop. Some evergreen perennials will weather the winter in a pot. To prepare a pot for herbs, fill with a mixture of two-thirds rich, crumbly soil (like potting soil) and one-third sand. Scatter a couple handfuls of small stones—like gravel—in the bottom of the pot before filling with dirt to promote good drainage.

Pots can be used, too, for growing herbs indoors in sunny windows. We have had moderate success with rosemary, sweet marjoram, basil, chives, thyme, lemon verbena, and scented geranium—all from late-summer cuttings—and with dill and bronze fennel from seed. If you plan on bringing plants indoors, pot them up in late August and put them in a partially shaded area outside. Bring them in before frost. Take care not to overwater herbs grown indoors. The soil they grow in should stay on the dry side.

HARVESTING HERBS

The first rule of harvesting herbs is to clip constantly through the summer. Never allow the plants to reach the blossoming stage, and limit each harvest to less than half of a well-established plant. Later heavy clipping may weaken perennials such as thyme, oregano, and marjoram—not allowing recovery of the plant before winter. For annuals at the end of their season, just harvest the whole plant. To rinse herbs of any dirt, gently spray them with water the day before harvesting. Pick early the next morning, as soon as the dew on the leaves has dried. If necessary, pat the leaves dry, taking care not to bruise the delicate foliage. To store fresh herbs in the short-term, see the beginning of this entry. To dry herbs, see 947; to freeze herbs, see 884.

HERBES DE PROVENCE

An herb blend of southern France, herbes de Provence usually contains rosemary, thyme, oregano, marjoram, savory, and lavender and sometimes basil, fennel seeds, and/or sage. It is used to season fish and meat. We find it especially pleasing with chicken, stir into fresh goat cheese, or mixed with olive oil for dipping bread.

HOISIN SAUCE

This dark, thick Chinese sauce is made from fermented soybeans and is usually very sweet, with deep, molasses-like notes. Generally, hoisin sauce is not as strong or funky as black bean sauce, 573, let alone Sichuan chili bean paste, 970. Hoisin is seasoned with some or all of the spices found in Five-Spice Powder, 590. The best brands are less sweet, garlicky, and mildly spicy. Once opened, store in the refrigerator.

HOJA SANTA

Also called pepperleaf or root beer plant, hoja santa is commonly used in Mexican cooking. The leaves of this herb are large and almost heart-shaped, and have a flavor much like sassafras root, with notes of licorice and nutmeg. Add whole dried hoja santa leaves to perfume simmering beans and stews, or add to ingredients to be pounded or pureed in moles. Fresh leaves are a little fuzzy, and can be chopped and added to salsas, posole, or used whole to wrap meats and fish, 1056. Find hoja santa leaves at Mexican markets.

HONEY

There are hundreds of varieties of this wonderful sweetener, depending on the nectar the bees use. Honey tastes of place perhaps more than any other food, and different varieties are prized for their distinctive flavors, most of which taste little like the honey sold in plastic bear-shaped bottles at the supermarket.

Honey starts out in the form of nectar gathered from flowers. When a bee gathers nectar, enzymes in its saliva split the nectar's sucrose into glucose and fructose. The bee deposits this partially digested nectar into the cells of honeycomb in the hive. Over time, this nectar is concentrated by evaporation, sped up by the bees fanning the honeycomb with their wings. The beekeeper harvests the honey by cutting off the wax cap that the bees cover the honeycomb with. Then the honeycombs are placed inside an extractor, which uses centrifugal force to remove the honey from the comb. The honey is then strained and bottled.

Most honey is named after the principal nectar source—clover, thyme, tupelo, orange blossom, sourwood, and buckwheat, to name just a few. Honeys range in color from almost white to amber to dark brown. As a rule of thumb, the lighter the color, the milder the flavor. We recommend trying out different varieties of honey if only to experience the incredible range of flavors they can possess. Wildflower and clover honeys are among the mildest honeys, while meadowfoam honey tastes uncannily of marshmallows and vanilla, buckwheat honey is strong and dark with molasses notes, and manuka honey has an almost mentholated, medicinal taste.

Honey is both mass-produced and available from small producers. It is sold in two basic forms: comb and extracted. Extracted honey may be found in liquid or cream (crystallized) form, and the latter may be labeled "creamed," "candied," "fondant," "spun," or "spread." We wholeheartedly recommend purchasing honey from small producers. Not only are you likely to find a wider variety of honeys, but the honey will be of better quality, and small-scale beekeepers have more incentive to raise their bees responsibly. Much honey from these small producers is unpasteurized, or "raw." Raw honey will crystallize over time due to the presence of tiny particles of pollen, which serve as seed points for the formation of sugar crystals. This should not be seen as a bad thing. It means the honey was minimally processed to preserve its flavor.

COOKING WITH HONEY

Honey has long been treasured for its preservative qualities owing to its high sugar content and natural antibacterial properties. It is cherished by cooks for the chewy texture and the browner color it gives to cakes, cookies, and bread doughs. It is composed chiefly of fructose and glucose, although its exact composition varies depending on the type of nectar used in honey production.

When cooking with honey, warm the honey or add it to the other liquids called for to make mixing more uniform. To measure honey, oil the measuring cup or spoon so the honey will slip out easily.

As honey has greater sweetening power than sugar, we prefer to substitute ½ to ⅔ cup honey for 1 cup sugar and to reduce the liquid in the recipe by ¼ cup. Too much honey in a recipe may cause foods to brown too quickly. To neutralize the acidity of honey, add a pinch of baking soda (unless it is already called for in the recipe). It is also a good idea to reduce the oven temperature by 25°F when substituting honey for other sweeteners in baked goods, which will keep them from browning too quickly.

Honey is best stored covered in a dry place at room temperature. If it becomes crystallized, it can easily be reliquefied by setting the opened jar in a pan of ➤ warm water until the crystals are melted or by heating the honey in a microwave oven on low power. ➤ Children under a year old should not be given honey, as it is a source of infant botulism.

For honey recipes see Honeycomb Candy, 871, Fried Halloumi with Honey and Walnuts, 56, Lekach, 739, Penicillin, 24, Lebkuchen, 768, Yogurt and Honey Panna Cotta, 821, Honey-Melon Jam, 913, and Honey-Dipped Doughnuts, 652.

HOREHOUND

The woolly leaves of the horehound plant have a bitter licorice flavor and are made into an extract that is combined with sugar into an old-fashioned candy. The leaves are also used in tisanes.

HORSERADISH

Horseradish is a long, cream-colored tapered root in the Brassica family. Along with coriander, nettle, horehound, and lettuce, it is one of the five bitter herbs of Passover seders. As the flavor can be overpowering, like very strong radishes, use it sparingly. Grate it fresh for the best flavor. Horseradish is almost always used as a garnish or in uncooked or minimally cooked preparations because its flavor is destroyed by heat. Dried horseradish is used, along with mustard powder, to make powdered wasabi, 1032 (in fact, horseradish and wasabi are relatives). Whether fresh or jarred—in this book the term for the latter is "prepared horseradish"—use all horseradish promptly to avoid loss of volatile oils and development of intense bitterness. Horseradish is prized for use with roast beef, sausages, and other rich meats; in cocktail sauces and potato salad; and with cold meats, fish, and shellfish.

To prepare fresh horseradish root as a paste, place about 1 pound diced, peeled horseradish in a food processor. Process until finely chopped, then pour in cider vinegar until the mixture is of a spreadable consistency (hold a kitchen towel over the top of the food processor, and step back when you open it unless you wish your sinuses to be cleared). Add salt and sugar to taste. This keeps several months in the refrigerator.

HUITLACOCHE

See About Corn, 234.

HYSSOP

The leaves of this minty, spicy, somewhat bitter herb are used sparingly in salads and with fruits. They are also used in the preparation of the French liqueur Chartreuse. The dried flowers are used in soups and tisanes or herbal teas, 7. It looks like a small rosemary plant with soft green leaves and should not be confused with **anise hyssop,** or *Agastache foeniculum*, a distant relative native to North America that has licorice overtones.

INSECTS

Insects are not really eaten in the United States with any great gusto, but they are beloved in cuisines around the world and have been so for a very long time (and, it must be said, North American indigenous peoples certainly availed themselves of edible insects). Modern Europe and North America are outliers in that insects are not seen as a foodstuff. The chief advantage to insects as food is that they are plentiful as well as an excellent source of nutrition, thus providing a sustainable source of protein and fat. Ants are one of the most widely consumed insects in the world, from Mexico to Colombia to Southeast Asia to Australia. They are eaten live, dried, roasted, and fried. In the Philippines, crickets are boiled in a vinegar mixture, then sautéed with garlic, onion, and tomatoes to make a dish called *adobong camaro*. Cricket flour, a high-protein meal of ground dried crickets, has made some small inroads into the North American market, though primarily as a fitness supplement. In Japan, locusts and grasshoppers are simmered in a soy sauce and mirin mixture and eaten as a snack called *inago no tsukudani*. Dozens of other insects are consumed as food around the world, including mealworms, cicadas, grubs, and wasps. As the human population increases, do not be surprised if you see more insects available in grocery stores and on restaurant menus, and, perhaps eventually, your own kitchen.

JUNIPER BERRIES

The berries from *Juniperus communis* are prized for seasoning game, meat, cabbage, and sauerkraut, and they are the principal flavoring agent in gin. Always crush juniper berries to release their oils before adding them to a dish. Use them sparingly, as their flavor is quite pungent. If juniper berries are not available, a splash of gin can be a good substitute.

A small number of juniper varieties can be poisonous, and many are bitter, so be sure of the variety before picking berries. Harvest juniper berries when they are dark purple, not green. Juniper berries take 3 years to mature, and when they are green, they taste extremely resinous, with a nearly turpentine-like flavor. Mature berries have a mellower, citrusy flavor.

KEFIR

Like yogurt, 1034, kefir is a fermented milk product, but the milk is inoculated with "kefir grains," which are actually a SCOBY (or Symbiotic Culture Of Bacteria and Yeasts). Kefir is of a thinner consistency than yogurt and has a pleasant, "buttery" flavor. Homemade kefir might even be slightly effervescent and mildly alcoholic. Kefir is usually consumed like a beverage, but it can be used in place of buttermilk in baked goods and marinades.

KOJI

Koji is the Japanese name for a mold, *Aspergillus oryzae*, which is used to inoculate steamed rice and soybeans for the production of miso, 1002, sake and other rice wines, 39, soy sauce, 1020, and many other products. The inoculated rice itself is also referred to as koji. When salt and koji-inoculated rice are combined and allowed to ferment, the resulting paste is called *shio koji*, and this mixture can be used to quick-pickle all kinds of thinly sliced vegetables, from radishes to cucumbers. It can also be called into service to marinate meats and fish: As with pineapple juice and papaya juice, shio koji contains protease enzymes, which break down and tenderize protein—with the added benefit of creating savory by-products that intensify the flavor of meat. Some chefs have even begun to experiment with "dry-curing" and "dry-aging" meats by inoculating them with koji spores. Koji can create many of the same characteristic flavors as traditional methods, and it does so in less time. While this is a boon for those who want a quicker, more convenient alternative, incubating koji—which grows best in danger-zone temperatures, xx—on meats is currently uncharted food-safety territory, and will never completely duplicate the amplified flavors of dry-cured and dry-aged meats, which are derived from the concentrating effects of moisture loss (in addition to the enzymatic activity that koji jump-starts). Shio koji is available at Japanese markets.

LARD

"Lard" may refer to rendered pork fat or solid chunks of raw pork fat. The most common forms of the latter are fatback, 497, and leaf lard. Like suet, 1023, **leaf lard** comes from around the kidneys and is more saturated than fat from other areas, which means that it is firmer at room temperature and has a higher melting point. Both of these characteristics make leaf lard ideal for grinding into sausage mixtures, 508.

To prepare leaf lard for using raw, see Suet and Tallow, 1023.

Even when made from leaf lard, rendered lard is much softer, sweeter, and oilier than butter and other solid shortenings. Rendered leaf lard is held in especially high esteem for use in pastry. Due to its more crystalline structure, leaf lard can be cut into flour to create a wonderfully flaky texture in biscuits and pastry crusts (although this same character handicaps it for cake baking).

Lard sold in bulk or package form has been wet-rendered, 982, refined, and fully saturated through hydrogenation. The resulting fat is shelf-stable, pure white, has a smoke point of 375°F, and little, if any, flavor.

Dry-rendered, golden-hued lard is often available at Mexican supermarkets as *manteca*; though too soft for pastry, and too unstable for frying, it has rich, porky flavor. In addition to use as a medium-heat cooking fat, the rich flavor of *manteca* is used to season the masa filling for tamales, 324–25.

➤ Once opened, packaged lard should be refrigerated. Softer, unprocessed lard should always be stored in the refrigerator in a covered container (the less air in the container, the better). To ➤ substitute lard for butter in cooking and baking, use 15 to 20 percent less lard than butter. For information on salt pork, fatback, and lardo, see 497. For how to render lard at home, see Rendering Fats, 982.

LAVENDER

The leaves and flowers of this highly aromatic plant are best known for their role in perfumes and soaps, and they can easily be overpowering when added to foods. Nonetheless, lavender can certainly be used in cooking, most notably in the herb blend herbes de Provence, 995. Lavender can also be used to infuse custard bases, 813, or added to cookies, especially shortbread.

LEAVENERS AND LEAVENING

We are all so accustomed to light breads and cakes that we seldom question how they got that way. Leavening is the simple, trite answer, but there are several types of leavening, and more than one is usually at work in any given recipe.

First there is **mechanical leavening,** or the actual mixing and incorporation of air into a dough or other substance. The purest examples of this type of leavening are dishes like meringue and whipped cream: Whipping air into the egg whites or cream creates a foam and gives the mixture loft. Mechanical leavening also plays a vitally important role in cakes and other recipes: Either an aerated egg foam is whipped up, or sugar and solid fats like butter and shortening are creamed together, both of which introduce tiny air bubbles into the dough or batter.

Chemical leaveners, such as baking powder, 954, baking soda, 954, and yeast, 1034, form gases that inflate doughs and batters. In the case of baking powder and soda, the gases they create expand bubbles that were already created by whipping or creaming.

Finally, as mixtures bake or cook, there is **steam leavening:** The moisture in the dough or batter evaporates when exposed to the high heat, and the vapor created expands the dough. In recipes like Popovers, 634, and soufflés, steam leavening can account for as much as 80 percent of the rise. In Croissants, 694, Puff Pastry, 691, and other laminated doughs, the high-moisture layers of butter emit steam, which pushes up on the layers of dough, giving them their rise as well as their light, flaky texture. Steam leavening is also quite visible in yeast breads, where the rapid expansion of the dough when exposed to high heat is called ovenspring, 397.

For more on leaveners and leavening, see individual entries for the chemical leaveners mentioned above, as well as About Sourdough Starters, 608. For tips on mechanical leavening, see About Butter Cakes, 723, for detailed instructions on creaming fats with sugar. To find your way around egg white foams—and decipher terms like "stiff but not dry," see Beating Eggs, 977.

LEMON BALM

Use the lemony leaves for herbal tea or tisane or as a garnish in fruit punch, fruit soups, and fruit salads. It can also be used to flavor ice creams, sorbets, and jellies.

LEMONGRASS

Lemongrass is a staple of several Southeast Asian cuisines. Aromatic and bright, it is used to flavor curries, teas, marinades, soups, and sauces. The light green stalks are nearly 2 feet in length; they are sold (sometimes cut in shorter pieces) dried, fresh, and frozen in Asian markets and some supermarkets.

To mince, chop, or prepare lemongrass for a paste, use only the tender inner portion: Cut 6 or 8 inches from the base and peel away the tough outer leaves from the lemongrass until it is pliable, smooth, and very pale. Repeat with however many stalks are needed, gather the trimmed pieces into a bundle, and thinly slice crosswise. Chop or mince the slices or include in a paste. (Even for paste, it is important to slice the stalk crosswise to shorten its tough fibers, which will make it much easier to pound or grind.)

To use whole lemongrass in stocks, soups, and braises, trim from the top to a manageable size, cutting off any dried portions. Peel away any discolored layers and bruise the base of the stalk by pounding it a few times with the spine of your knife to release its fragrant oils. Tie the stalk in a loose knot and add to cooking liquids. (Fish the lemongrass out at the end of cooking.)

LEMON VERBENA

Some believe, with its very strong lemon flavor and aroma, lemon verbena is better reserved for sachets than for food. However, we find small amounts desirable as a lemon flavoring in drinks and herbal teas or tisanes. It can also be used to flavor ice cream bases and custards, 813.

LICORICE

Licorice is a root valued for its distinctive flavor and natural sweetness. The compound that makes licorice root taste sweet is called glycyrrhizin, which is fifty times sweeter than sugar in its pure form. Licorice root is used in many herbal tea blends, in candies, and in beer like porters and stouts.

LILY BUDS

Also known as golden needles and tiger lilies, dried lily buds are the unopened flowers of day lilies. Hot-and-Sour Soup, 85, features lily buds. When purchasing them, look for buds that are pale in color and not brittle. Store them in a jar in a cool, dry place. Before using, you may need to cut off about ¼ inch at the bottom to get rid of the woody stem. Soak in warm water for 20 to 30 minutes before use. Fresh day lily buds may be deep-fried or torn and added to salads for color.

LIME LEAF

Makrut lime leaves are incredibly fragrant and used extensively in Southeast Asian cooking. (They were long known as "kaffir lime leaves," which we no longer use because the word is a South African racial slur.) The leaves are uniquely shaped, looking like two oblong leaves stuck together end to end. Their aroma and flavor bear some resemblance to lemongrass, but they are even more aromatic and pungent. Lime leaves are used in Green Curry Paste, 585, Tom Kha Gai, 94, Tom Yum Goong, 101, Thai-Spiced Peanuts, 461, and Beef Rendang, 467, though these recipes only scratch the surface of the dishes lime leaves enhance.

Find lime leaves at Asian markets. They are often available fresh, but if you cannot find fresh leaves, check the freezer section or look for them dried. If you find fresh leaves, freeze what you are not able to use in a week. Lime leaves keep very well frozen. They release their flavor best when ground into a paste or cut into especially thin chiffonade, 993, or slivers, and briefly fried in a little oil, but they can also be added to dishes much as you might add a bay leaf. Should you be able to find *makrut* limes but not the leaves (an unlikely occurrence, to be fair), you can substitute the finely grated zest for leaves.

LONG PEPPER

This spice was widely used in antiquity, but demand for it decreased in Europe during the Middle Ages. However, long pepper is still used in India and throughout Asia as well as in North Africa, notably in some versions of Ras el Hanout, 590. There are two kinds of long pepper: Indian and Indonesian. The Indonesian variety is considerably longer than the Indian long pepper. Long peppers are roughly ¾ to 1½ inches long and resemble tiny, elongated pine cones. The spice is hotter than black pepper, with some of the numbing quality of Sichuan peppercorns, 1018.

LOVAGE

Though not common in stores or farmers' markets, lovage is widely planted as a garden herb. Popular in ancient Rome and medieval Europe, lovage is still used frequently in Liguria. The leaves of this herb can be quite intense, with a bitter flavor reminiscent of celery, parsley, and oregano. In moderation, the leaves may be substituted for parsley or celery in stews, tomato sauces, poultry dishes, and stuffings. Though the stems are sometimes used in the manner of celery, we find their flavor too strong. The stems are traditionally blanched, then peeled, candied, and eaten as is or chopped up as a garnish for desserts. The seeds are used as a cooling spice in some Indian recipes. The root and seeds are also used in flavoring gin.

MACADAMIA NUTS

Macadamia nuts are large (1-inch) round nuts that are very rich, with a mellow, buttery flavor. They are native to Australia, but most of the macadamias we see in stores are from Hawaii. Their very hard shells and proneness to rancidity means most are sold shelled, in vacuum-packed cans or bottles. If found in the shell, to crack, try wrapping each one in heavy cloth and hammering it on a very hard surface.

To roast macadamia nuts, spread the shelled nuts in a shallow pan and heat in a 325°F oven for 12 to 15 minutes, stirring often. Salt lightly and store refrigerated in an airtight container.

MACE

See Nutmeg and Mace, 1004.

MALT AND MALTED MILK POWDER

Malt is a grain (usually barley) that is sprouted, dried, and left whole or ground to a powder. The process of sprouting and drying is referred to as malting. Most malt is used to make whisky, malt vinegar, beer, and bread. The chief advantage of malting is to activate enzymes in the barley that convert starch to a type of sugar—**maltose,** which has roughly half the sweetness of regular sugar, or sucrose. This gives the resulting malt a slightly sweet flavor, and the sugars in the malt feed yeasts during fermentation (unlike us, they do not care how sweet sugar tastes).

Diastatic malt powder is dried at lower temperatures, which keeps the enzymes that convert starch into maltose intact. When used in breads, these enzymes make more sugar available to the yeast, which promotes a healthy rise and a nicely browned crust. **Non-diastatic malt powder** is dried at a higher temperature and does not have any active enzymes; it is used as a flavoring.

Malt syrup is simply a syrup produced from malted barley and cooked grains. It is commonly added to breads, especially bagels and pretzels, and contributes to the flavor of the bread and the color of the crust. Although it is a syrup, it tastes half as sweet as sugar. **Malt extract** is malt syrup made exclusively with malted barley. It promotes yeast growth and improves the shelf life of breads by promoting moisture retention.

Malted milk powder is a combination of malted barley extract, wheat flour, evaporated whole milk, salt, and sodium bicarbonate. It contributes a slightly sweet, earthy, and toasty flavor. Adding it to baked goods promotes browning thanks to the added sugar from the malt itself as well as the lactose from the milk. Of course, malted milk powder is best known for its role in malted milk shakes, 13, but it can be added to baked goods of all kinds, ice cream bases, custards, even Whipped Cream, 791. For baked goods like cookies, cakes, custards, and ice cream bases, start with ¼ cup malted milk powder (depending on the batch size of your recipe, you may be able to add up to ½ cup). For whipped cream, use 2 tablespoons.

MAPLE SYRUP

A sweetener made from the boiled sap of maple trees, pure maple syrup must weigh not less than 11 pounds to the gallon by law. It takes anywhere from 20 to 50 gallons of sap to make 1 gallon of syrup. Sap from the beginning of the season is more concentrated and produces a lighter syrup. Later in the season, more sap is required, and the prolonged boiling darkens the color of the resulting syrup. Until recently, lighter colored syrup was called Grade A and darker syrup was Grade B (there was also a Grade C, which was sold primarily to food processors, not consumers). However, owing to the fact that Grade B syrup is not inferior to Grade A, just different (in fact, many people preferred Grade B for its stronger maple flavor), there is now only Grade A syrup. There are still different types of Grade A syrup. They range from "Grade A—Golden Color, Delicate Taste" to the (less pejorative) "Grade A—Very Dark Color, Strong Flavor." Maple syrup's composition is largely sucrose with some invert sugar.

Although it is often stored at room temperature, maple syrup is best stored in the refrigerator after opening, to inhibit mold growth. If mold develops, discard the syrup. Should the syrup crystallize, set the container in hot water; the syrup will quickly become liquid and smooth again.

To substitute maple syrup for sugar in cooking, generally use only ¾ cup for each 1 cup sugar. ➤ To substitute maple syrup for sugar in baking, use the same proportions, but reduce the other liquid called for by about ¼ cup for every 1 cup syrup substituted, and lower the oven temperature by 25°F. (Another option is to use **maple sugar,** 1025.)

Maple-flavored syrups contain a small amount of pure maple syrup but are primarily an inexpensive syrup such as corn syrup flavored with artificial or natural maple flavoring (natural maple flavoring can come from fenugreek seed, ground hickory bark, or maple wood). They are less expensive than pure maple syrup, but it is best not to substitute them for pure maple syrup in cooking or baking. They are for topping pancakes and waffles, and even then we heartily recommend splurging on the real thing. **Pancake syrup** is artificially flavored and colored corn syrup.

MAKING MAPLE SYRUP

Maple, that choicest of all syrups, is yours for the taking, with no harm to the trees that produce it. Collecting, however, is simpler than processing, for you will get only about 1 part syrup from about 20 to 50 parts sap. The sugar maple, *Acer saccharum*, gives the sweetest sap. The best months are late February, March, and early April, when night temperatures are around 20°F and daytime around 45°F. Canada, New York, and Vermont are ideal regions for tapping maple trees due to their freeze-thaw temperatures in late February. Trees with a diameter of 10 to 18 inches can be hung with one bucket; above 18 inches, use two buckets. The taps can be on any area of the trunk from 2 to 5 feet above the ground; if made late in the season, they should be on the north-facing side of the tree. With a 7⁄16-inch bit, bore a hold diagonally upward about 1½ inches. Insert a sap spout with a bucket hook attached. Hammer the spout in gently but firmly so as not to split the bark, which would cause a leaky taphole. Hang a bucket on the spout and cover with a lid to prevent rain or snow from collecting in the bucket (you can use a regular aluminum bucket, but we recommend buckets specifically made for collecting maple sap).

Empty the buckets as they fill and strain the clear sap through a fine-mesh sieve into sterile containers. Boil as soon as possible to limit growth of microorganisms. If you are unable to boil right away, store the sap under refrigeration. (During cold weather you will probably not be bothered with microbial development at tapholes or in buckets.) Sap runs clear and is usable until the buds on the trees begin to swell. When an unpleasant odor and slight discoloration of the sap warns you that the season is over, pull the taps.

When you have collected enough sap, it is advisable to boil it in shallow pans outdoors, as it is not recommended to complete the boiling-off process in an indoor kitchen. There is no danger of scorching the syrup at first, because of its great water content, but later there is danger of its boiling over. Maple sap, like water, boils at 212°F. It becomes syrup at 219°F. ▲ At higher altitudes, adjust this target temperature downward according to the boiling point of water at your altitude, 1070.

Before storing maple syrup, and while it is still hot, filter it through a cheesecloth-lined colander to rid it of niter or sugar sand, which is a malate (a type of salt) of lime. Heat once more to 180°F, pour into sterilized jars, 893, and seal. Maple syrup will keep for a year or more at room temperature. Once a jar is opened it should be refrigerated.

MARGARINE

Margarine was, ironically, invented by the butter-loving French, though the original was made from animal fat. Margarines today are usually emulsions of water or milk and refined vegetable oils, some of which may be hydrogenated and contain trans fats. As of this writing, per the order of the Food and Drug Administration, trans fats are being eliminated from processed foods. Margarines, like butter, must by law contain a minimum of 80 percent fat—the rest being water, milk solids, and sometimes salt or other flavorings. Almost all margarines are enriched with added vitamins and color, to make them nutritionally and visually comparable to butter. Also, some may have added animal fats. Check the label. ➤ Regular stick margarines, because of their similar moisture content, may be substituted for butter, weight for weight or measure for measure, but they produce textures somewhat different from butter in both cooking and baking and lack butter's superior flavor. Margarine is perishable and must be kept refrigerated. Tub margarine, whipped margarine, reduced-fat margarine, and liquid margarine will not produce satisfactory results when substituted for butter or regular stick margarine in baking. Limit their use to the table, as a spread on bread or toast, or as a flavor enhancer for cooked vegetables. Vegan stick margarines can be substituted for butter in baked goods, though they taste even less like butter than regular margarine. For the melting point and smoke point of margarine, see the charts on page 981.

MARJORAM

Marjoram is part of the oregano family, and may be used similarly. The most common variety is called sweet marjoram, and it has a delicate flavor. As with other green herbs, marjoram is best added toward the end of cooking. Use marjoram in sausages and stews; with lamb, pork, and chicken; and in egg dishes. The herb **za'atar** (*Majorana syriaca*) is a more pungent variety grown in the Middle East and is best known for its presence in the herb and sesame seed blend of the same name, 590.

MILK

Humans have been milking animals since at least 5000 BC. It is a highly nutritious substance, rich in protein and fat. Milk is widely consumed across Europe and the Americas, though in much of the world, including Africa and most of Asia, many people are lactose intolerant and cannot drink milk at all. It is also notable that milk was not consumed in the Americas until the arrival of Europeans.

Milk is highly perishable. The most important consideration when buying milk is the sell-by date on the container. Always buy the freshest milk you can find and keep it refrigerated at about 40°F at all times. Although milk may last up to 7 days after the sell-by date, its flavor may deteriorate before then.

In 1994 the government approved the use of recombinant Bovine Growth Hormone (rBGH), also known as recombinant Bovine Somatotropin (rBST), to stimulate cows to produce more milk. It is still undetermined what the effects are on people who drink milk produced by cows that have been given these hormones, though based on scientific research it does not appear that rBGH causes health problems. If you wish to avoid rBGH, buy certified organic milk or milk that states that it is rBGH- or rBST-free.

Unless otherwise specified, ➤ when we call for "milk" in recipes we mean pasteurized whole milk—with 3.25 percent milkfat. For information on cream, see 974. Also see About Nut and Seed Milks, 1005.

RAW AND PASTEURIZED MILK

Milk and cream sold in interstate commerce must by law be pasteurized. Most milk in this country is **homogenized,** a mechanical process that shatters the fat particles so that they remain uniformly dispersed throughout the milk, preventing them from rising to the top to form a layer of cream.

Pasteurization, a carefully controlled heating and cooling process, effectively eliminates the possibility of many dreaded milk-borne diseases that the sanitary handling of raw milk, no matter how scrupulously carried out, cannot always achieve. In general, the gentler the pasteurization temperature, the better the milk retains its flavor and quality. Conversely, the higher the pasteurization temperature, the longer a milk can be stored: **ultra-pasteurized** or **ultra-high temperature (UHT)** milk is held at a temperature above 280°F for several seconds, which kills bacteria as well as their spores, effectively rendering the milk sterile. If it is then sealed in aseptic packaging, such milk can be stored at room temperature for extended periods. (Unfortunately, UHT milk tends to have a "cooked" flavor.)

Here is a gentle pasteurization method that will render milk safe to drink without ruining its flavor in the way that high-heat pasteurization can.

To pasteurize raw milk at home, arrange sterilized heatproof glass jars on a rack in a deep kettle. Allow an inch or two of headspace when you pour the raw milk into the jars (there is no need to seal the jars). Fill the kettle with water until it comes above the fill line of the jars. Put a sterile leave-in probe thermometer in one of the jars. Heat the water and, when the thermometer registers 145°F, hold the heat at that temperature for 30 minutes. Transfer the jars to a cold water bath and cool the milk as rapidly as possible until it is between 50° and 40°F. Refrigerate, covered, at once.

It is still possible to find milk that has not been homogenized or even **raw milk** that has not been pasteurized in areas where it is legal to sell. Dairies that sell raw milk are frequently inspected and certified, and the milk carries a warning label. Some say raw milk is more healthful than pasteurized milk since it contains active enzymes that help with digestion and absorption of nutrients. Many cheesemakers prefer raw milk, since pasteurization diminishes the cheese's flavor potential and homogenization gives cheese a waxy texture. However, it is illegal to sell raw milk in many states, and it is always illegal to sell raw milk across state lines.

DRY OR POWDERED MILK

Dry milk powder is pasteurized milk that has been spray-dried to eliminate its moisture (spray-drying is a process in which liquid is forced through a nozzle or atomizer into a heated chamber; the heat causes the moisture in the liquid to evaporate before it falls to the bottom of the chamber). **Whole milk powder** contains not less than 26 percent fat; **nonfat dry milk powder** contains about 1½ percent fat. Dry whole milk should be stored in a cool, dry place away from sunlight. Once opened, all dry milks should be refrigerated in an airtight container. Discard them if they acquire any off-flavors. Dry whole milk will keep for 6 to 9 months; dry noninstant nonfat milk for 12 to 18 months; and dry instant nonfat milk for 6 to 12 months.

Dry milk powder can attain secret ingredient status when it is toasted. The process of toasting yields nutty, browned milk solids that smell and taste similar to brown butter. Use toasted dry milk powder in recipes that already call for milk, like ice creams and custards. On top of the flavor boost that toasted milk powder provides, the extra protein will yield thicker, richer results. For most custard-type recipes, use at least ½ cup toasted milk powder, whisking it into the wet ingredients until dissolved.

To toast dry milk powder, bake at 300°F, stirring every 5 minutes, until browned, 20 to 25 minutes.

To reconstitute dry milk powder, follow the package directions, or use 3 to 4 tablespoons powdered milk to 1 cup water—which will make slightly more than 1 cup milk in volume, and its equivalent in nutrition. For the best flavor, reconstitute at least 2 hours before using and refrigerate.

To substitute reconstituted dry nonfat milk in recipes requiring whole milk, add about 2 teaspoons butter for each 1 cup reconstituted nonfat milk.

EVAPORATED MILK

Evaporated milk is whole, reduced-fat, or fat-free milk that has had 50 percent of its moisture content removed; it is sealed in cans and heat sterilized. It has a slightly caramelized taste due to the processing. Once opened, the milk should be stored as fresh milk. Reconstitute by adding an equal amount of water to the evaporated milk. Or use undiluted evaporated milk to add richness to sauces, custards, and puddings.

FAT-FREE OR SKIM MILK

Also called nonfat milk, these milks have only ½ percent or less fat but all the protein and mineral value of whole milk. Skim milk is bluish white in color and lacks much of the body and flavor of whole milk. Skim milk is fortified with vitamins A and sometimes D. It is worth noting that skim milk has a higher concentration of lactose than any other milk.

GOAT MILK

Goats produce milk that is whiter and more flavorful than cow's milk, with a similar nutritional content. Although it is slightly lower in cholesterol, goat milk actually contains more fat than cow's milk. The fat molecules in goat milk are relatively small, so it does not need to be homogenized. Goat milk is not available in lower-fat varieties, nor is it fortified with vitamin D, as commercial cow's milk is. Those who are lactose-intolerant and/or allergic to cow's milk protein need to avoid goat milk as well. Generally, goat milk can be substituted for whole cow's milk.

LACTOSE-FREE MILK

Many adults, especially those of non-European ancestry, are lactose intolerant. Milk can be treated with an enzyme that splits each lactose molecule into two simpler sugars, glucose and galactose, making it easier to digest. Lactose-free milk tastes sweeter than regular milk but is equal in nutritional value. It may be substituted for regular milk in recipes.

SWEETENED CONDENSED MILK

A preservation method that dates from Civil War days, condensed milk has had its water content reduced by half and contains added sugar. A 14-ounce can contains the equivalent of 2½ cups milk plus ½ cup sugar. Because of the high sugar content, condensed milk will keep somewhat longer after opening than evaporated milk. It is popular for use in making caramel sauce, pies, and bars. See Easy Dulce de Leche, 809, Key Lime Pie, 682, and No-Bake Lemon or Lime Pie, 682.

WHOLE MILK

A fresh, homogenized milk that typically contains at least 3.25 percent fat, and at least 8.25 percent protein, lactose, and minerals. Whole milk may be fortified with vitamins A and D. Whole milk purchased from large commodity dairies is not actually "whole" in that all the fat has been removed, then added back in to meet the minimum fat content standards set by the USDA. In reality, the fat content of milk varies depending on the breed of cow, season, and the cow's diet.

MINTS

We all know peppermint and spearmint, but the genus *Mentha* includes numerous distinct species. There are many worth trying, such as the curly varieties and apple, orange, chocolate, and pineapple mint. These are less penetrating but equally refreshing. Use any of them in fruit salads; with peas, zucchini, and lamb; to infuse chocolate desserts; as a dessert garnish; and in teas and cocktails.

Peppermint leaves are considered superior for drying; pick the leaves before the plant flowers and dry as directed in Drying Herbs and Seeds, 947. Mint is very easy to grow, but it is aggressive and will spread. ➤ Keep it confined to a pot.

MIREPOIX

This French term refers to a blend of diced onion, carrots, and celery (and occasionally bacon or ham). Mirepoix may also include fennel, leeks, garlic, tomatoes, and chopped herbs such as parsley; the fat used may be olive or vegetable oil, butter, or rendered pork fat. These blends are an essential starting point of many sauces and used to build a base of flavor in all kinds of dishes, from ragus to soups. For other related mixtures used in Spanish, Italian, and Caribbean cooking, see Sofrito, 1018.

Finally, we should also mention a similar mixture of aromatics that seasons the French-influenced cuisine of Louisiana: A combination widely known as the **Cajun "holy trinity"**—onions, celery, and green bell pepper—is used in gumbos, jambalayas, and many other dishes. In our opinion, garlic should be elevated to the same level of importance, but "quaternity" does not have the same ring to it.

MIRIN

See Alcoholic Ingredients, 951.

MISO, DOENJANG, AND DOUJIANG

Miso is a paste made from soybeans that have been fermented with koji, 997. It is used to season sauces, marinades, dressings, and soups, and to pickle vegetables. There are three general types of miso: Those made with rice and soybeans (*kome miso*), those made with barley or rye and soybeans (*mugi miso*), and those made with soybeans alone (*mame miso*). Among the rice and soybean variety there are **shiro,** or white, miso; **shinshu,** or yellow, miso; **tanshoku,** or beige, miso; and **aka,** or red, miso. **Hatcho miso** is a soybean-only variety; it is dark reddish brown and very salty. Though all misos are salty, their color loosely correlates to saltiness and pungency: *Shiro, shinshu,* and *tanshoku* misos are the mildest, sweetest varieties, *aka* miso is saltier and more full-flavored, and *hatcho* miso is the most pungent. There are also other, modern types, such as **genmai,** which is made from brown rice, as well as misos made from chickpeas, adzuki beans, and lima beans. All of these can be used in similar ways, though their richness and saltiness will determine how much should be used.

In some ways, Korean **doenjang** and Chinese **doujiang** (commonly sold as *huangjiang,* or yellow soybean paste) are similar to miso: All are fermented soybean pastes used to flavor broths, soups, and other dishes. Unlike miso, which is primarily fermented in crocks or large tanks, the soybeans used to make *doenjang* and *doujiang* are cooked, coarsely mashed, fermented for a time, and then pressed and formed into blocks (*meju* or *qu,* respectively), which are then left to ferment in a breezy area for over a month. Traditionally, the blocks are then transferred to crocks and submerged in a brine. After a sufficient amount of time has passed, the softened blocks are removed from the brine and packaged into tubs.

This process yields two core Korean pantry items: The *doenjang* itself, and the brine, which has taken on the flavors of the *meju* and any additional seasonings. This brine can be turned into *guk-ganjang,* or traditional Korean soy sauce, 1020. Modern *doenjang* processing methods use a koji starter and often skip the lengthy brining step, which results in a sweeter flavored *doenjang* than traditional versions.

Doenjang is usually chunkier in texture than *doujiang*—though a spicier, chunky version of the latter is available (see *doubanjiang,* 970). Both tend to be stronger than all but the darker red and *hatcho* varieties of miso. Some varieties of *doenjang* are made especially for soups and stews—sold as seasoned *doenjang*—and include other ingredients, such as mushrooms, seaweed, and dried anchovies.

Refrigerate *doenjang, doujiang,* and miso in a covered container, and use them within a year for best flavor (they will keep indefinitely). To keep the top surface from oxidizing, press a piece of wax paper on top.

We use miso and *doenjang* as flavor boosters for all kinds of dishes. White miso is truly excellent in flavored butters, 559–60; sauces like Miso Beurre Blanc, 559; with tender green vegetables like Peas and Radishes with Miso Butter, 272; mashed into the flesh of roasted sweet potatoes; mixed with butter and spread on grilled corn; blended into pesto (especially vegan pesto, where the umami-rich paste fills the void left by Parmesan's absence); and whisked into Salted Caramel Sauce, 809 (if a chunkier miso is used, the caramel should be strained). Red or *hatcho misos* can be added to braised or simmered dishes or chilis for more depth of flavor, or mix them with mirin and brush on eggplant as in Miso-Glazed Eggplant, 238. In addition to its use as a soup base, *doenjang* is essential to condiments like Ssamjang, 571, and can be used in place of red or *hatcho miso.* Also see Tofu Misozuke, 943, Black Cod Misozuke, 387, and Miso Soup, 84.

MOLASSES

Molasses is a by-product of sugar making, the uncrystallized remains of boiling down sugarcane juice. High in iron, molasses adds a rich, earthy taste and moist texture to breads, cakes, and cookies.

Sugar refiners boil sugarcane juice multiple times to get as much pure sucrose out of it as possible. **Light molasses** is left over from the first boiling, **dark molasses** from the second. **Blackstrap**—iron-rich and bitter—is from the final boiling, and thus contains the least sugar and the highest percentage of impurities. **Unsulfured molasses** is something of an antiquated term, as virtually all molasses sold in grocery stores is unsulfured. (Sulfur was once used in processing for its antibacterial properties and to promote shelf-stability.)

Molasses pairs well with apples, warm spices like cinnamon and ginger, and bourbon. Molasses should not be confused with sorghum molasses (sorghum syrup), 1018, pomegranate molasses, 192, and date molasses (unlike molasses, these dark colored sweeteners are not by-products; they are sweet liquids boiled down until dark and syrupy). See Molasses Bread, 607, Fresh Ginger Cake, 737, Gingersnaps, 772, Moravian Molasses Thins, 776, Shoofly Pie, 678, and Molasses Ice Cream, 843.

To substitute molasses for sugar in baked goods, reduce the other liquid in the recipe by 5 tablespoons for each 1 cup molasses used. ➤ Because of its acid content, add ½ teaspoon baking soda for each 1 cup molasses added, and omit or use half the baking powder called for. Do not replace more than half the amount of sugar called for in any given recipe. Also, bear in mind that it will fundamentally alter the flavor and color of the finished dish or baked good.

MSG

We are for it. See Flavor Enhancers, 984.

MUSHROOMS, DRIED

Dried mushrooms are excellent, concentrated sources of umami. The most common types of dried mushrooms are porcini and shiitake. **Dried porcinis** are often added to rich sauces and braises, like Quick Brown Sauce, 550, and Braised Short Ribs, 471. They are found sliced, powdered, and occasionally whole. Whole **dried shiitakes** are easily found in Asian markets. Shiitakes are typically reconstituted in hot water before being added to dishes, though for stocks (see Mushroom Stock, 79) and long-simmering dishes, they can be added directly to the cooking liquid. Dried mushrooms are easy to grind into a fine powder, which can be especially useful: The powder can be added directly to dishes without presoaking or lengthy simmering, and its flavor will be evenly distributed throughout.

Dried wood ear mushrooms, also known as **cloud ear** or **black fungus,** is a jelly fungus with a mild flavor. A popular ingredient in Chinese cuisine, it is readily available at Asian markets. Once reconstituted, wood ears have a slightly crunchy, gelatinous texture, and a thin, broad shape. Be sure to remove the gritty part where it was attached to the tree and cut them into shreds or bite-sized pieces after reconstituting. Use in Hot-and-Sour Soup, 85, or add to stir-fries.

For information on fresh mushrooms, see 249. For truffles, see 1028. Also see Mushroom Catsup, 932.

MUSTARD

Mustard, a plant in the Brassica family, is valued not only for its slightly bitter, peppery greens, but also for its seeds, which are used whole, crushed, finely ground, and processed into spicy pastes. White and yellow **mustard seeds** come from *Sinapis alba* (also known as *Brassica hirta*). These pungent but somewhat sweet seeds are readily available in supermarkets. Most seeds of this type are ground into mustard powder or blended into prepared mustard (yellow mustard). Brown mustard seeds come from *Brassica juncea*. They are smaller and hotter than white seeds. Tiny black mustard seeds come from *Brassica nigra* and are the most pungent.

Dry mustard is simply ground yellow mustard seed. It is used to add zing to dishes like Deviled Eggs, 151, salad dressings, mayonnaise, and coleslaw. For the sake of your sinuses, ➤ do not attempt to grind mustard seeds to a powder in a spice grinder: Mustard dust will be thrown into the air, and you will gas yourself. A mortar and pestle might be less likely to produce a dust cloud, but we think the convenience of preground mustard powder is worth the purchase price—as well as any sacrifice in freshness.

Whole-grain mustard contains whole mustard seeds and has an appealing texture (the best varieties have seeds that pop in your mouth like caviar). **Stone-ground mustard** is made from coarsely crushed seeds, and has a moderately chunky texture. **Prepared mustard** is a term we use for the classic, smooth yellow mustard, best known for its appearance on hot dogs. It is a straightforward mixture of yellow mustard powder, vinegar, salt, turmeric, and seasonings. **Dijon mustard** is made with ground brown mustard seeds and white wine. Dijon may be smooth or stone-ground; it is often enriched with herbs, and the occasional splash of Cognac. Mustards keep for a very long time in the refrigerator.

When mustard seeds are used whole—whether fried with other spices to flavor a Dal, 218, or used to flavor a marinade, curry, or pickle—they add a pleasant, nutty bitterness rather than the sinus-clearing heat they are capable of when blended or ground up. Their pungency is only activated when the seeds are broken up and mixed with a liquid, which causes natural enzymes to release volatile, nose-tingling sulfur compounds. Once dry mustard is mixed or whole mustard ground up, its heat will continue to intensify for the first 10 minutes, after which the mustard's pungency starts to decline. This decline can be arrested by the addition of an acid, such as vinegar, or by heating the mustard. While we are happy to introduce vinegar immediately, you may make an especially spicy mustard by soaking and/or blending the mustard with the water or wine in a recipe, waiting as close to 10 minutes as desired, and then blending in the vinegar.

GRAINY MUSTARD

About 1 cup

This mellows after a couple of days.

Combine in a bowl:

5 tablespoons yellow mustard seeds
⅓ cup dry white wine
⅓ cup white wine vinegar
(1½ teaspoons grated onion)
½ teaspoon salt
½ teaspoon sugar
¼ teaspoon white pepper

Cover and refrigerate overnight. Process in a blender until blended but still grainy. Store, covered and refrigerated, for up to 3 weeks.

HOT MUSTARD

About ½ cup

Catch-in-the-throat Chinese and German mustards are made by blending dry mustard to a paste with a cold liquid such as water, flat beer, or vinegar. Use high-quality dry mustard for the best results. Use this mustard as is, or add one of the various flavorings recommended below. It is very sharp when freshly made, but mellows over time; we suggest refrigerating it, covered, for several days before serving it. This is wonderful spread on cold meat sandwiches, particularly roast beef or corned beef.

Combine in a bowl:

½ cup dry mustard
2 tablespoons dry white wine
2 tablespoons cider vinegar
2 tablespoons water
1 teaspoon salt
½ teaspoon white pepper

Let stand for 2 hours, then stir well again. Cover and refrigerate until ready to use. This will keep, covered and refrigerated, for 2 to 3 weeks.

IDEAS FOR FLAVORING MUSTARD

Stir one of the following into **Grainy Mustard** or **Hot Mustard,** 1003.

¼ cup dried fruit (such as nectarines, apricots, or plums), plumped, 917, and finely diced, plus 1 tablespoon honey, or to taste
Up to ¼ cup minced herbs (such as tarragon, rosemary, thyme, or chives) plus 1½ teaspoons brown sugar
1 tablespoon lemon juice plus 1½ teaspoons ground coriander
1 tablespoon curry powder
1 chipotle pepper in adobo sauce, minced
2 teaspoons drained prepared horseradish
Minced or grated garlic to taste
1 tablespoon minced shallot

NATTO

Japanese *natto* is the best-known example of a style of "slimy" soybean ferment made in China, Korea, Thailand, Nepal, and Indonesia. It is one of the few fermented foods we know of that is neither salty nor tangy with lactic acid. Instead, natto has a cheesy, ammonia-like scent and a deep savoriness. Like tempeh, 287, the soybeans are kept mostly whole, but instead of forming a dense texture, natto is bound together by an infamously viscous goo. This goo reminds us of that exuded by cut okra, but thicker and with a ropy texture that forms strands when stretched. Natto is usually served over rice with condiments, and sometimes raw egg yolk.

To prepare natto, whip it with chopsticks by pulling the beans apart so that strands form and then folding the strands back in. The goo will eventually thicken and turn opaque. Mix in strong mustard, soy sauce, and minced green onion to taste and serve over cooked short-grain rice, 343.

NIGELLA SEEDS

Nigella is a spice with many names. It is known as *kalonji, charnushka*, onion seed, black seed, and black cumin. It is neither a relative of onion nor cumin but belongs to the Ranunculus family (familiar to flower gardeners and buttercup enthusiasts). It has a lightly nutty, thyme-like flavor and is used in Indian vegetable dishes and pickles. It may also be sprinkled on naan dough before baking. Nigella is one of the five spices in the Bengali spice blend **panch phoron,** along with fenugreek, cumin, black mustard seeds, and fennel seeds. Panch phoron is used whole, not ground, and is tempered in oil or ghee to infuse the oil with the flavor of the spices before other ingredients are added.

NUTMEG AND MACE

The flavors of nutmeg and mace are so closely allied because they come from the same tough-husked fruit of *Myristica fragrans*, a relative of magnolias. When opened, the fruit reveals a hard inner kernel, the **nutmeg,** which is covered by a lacy outer layer. This layer is removed, flattened, and dried into **mace.** Mace is common to find ground, but it may also be found in whole pieces, called "blades," which range in color from pale yellow to an appealing reddish gold. Though they taste similar to each other, mace has a milder flavor than nutmeg, and tastes zingier on our palate. It is traditional in cake, doughnuts, condiments, meat dishes, and Indian spice blends like Garam Masala, 588.

Use nutmeg sparingly. For the best flavor, grind nutmeg fresh as needed—either with a nutmeg grinder or a rasp-type grater. Try it not only in baked items but also in spinach, quiche, on French toast, and always with eggnog, 30.

NUTS AND SEEDS

Nuts and seeds, with a few exceptions, are characterized by their high fat and protein content rather than any botanical similarity. Both provide a concentrated source of nutrition and can be dried and stored for quite some time. With the exception of chestnuts and cashews (and, for the foragers, acorns), they contain very little starch. Except for green almonds and pickled green walnuts, nearly all nuts and seeds are eaten ripe. For information on specific nuts and seeds, see individual entries. For seeds used for sprouting, see Sprouts, 1021.

Because nuts are rich in oils, the best way to store them is in their shells. The shells protect them from light, heat, moisture, and exposure to air—factors that tend to cause rancidity. That said, most of us do not buy nuts in the shell with the exception of peanuts and pistachios, and those tend to be for snacking rather than cooking. The second-best approach is to buy only what you will use within 2 months if storing at room temperature, or within 1 year if storing in the freezer. Unsalted nuts have a longer storage life than salted ones. Discard any nuts that are moldy, shriveled, or dry. As a rough rule, ➤ 1 pound of nuts in the shell yields about 8 ounces shelled (though the yield depends on the type of nut).

The seeds we discuss here are also rich in oils, so their storage and treatment are similar. Buy small quantities of seeds and use them within a few months or keep them in the freezer.

BLANCHING NUTS

In addition to the tough outer shell, some nuts like hazelnuts and almonds have a thin inner skin that you may wish to remove, as it can taste bitter. If so, just before using, pour boiling water over the shelled nuts. For large quantities, you may have to let them stand briefly, only about 1 minute at the most. ➤ The briefer the time, the better. Drain. Pour cold water over the nuts to stop further heating and drain again. When the nuts are cool, pinch or rub off the skins.

For peanuts, hazelnuts, and pistachios, you may remove the skin by toasting them first, below, and then vigorously rubbing the nuts together in a kitchen towel to loosen the covering. This can be done when the nuts are hot or cold.

TOASTING NUTS AND SEEDS

Toasting nuts and seeds enhances their flavor. Toasted nuts can have quite an impact on the flavor of a dish, so it is well worth the few extra minutes to do so.

To avoid burnt flavors and toughening, ➤ do not overtoast. Seeds are especially easy to blacken and nuts tend to darken and crisp as they cool; toast both until they begin to cook but haven't quite darkened, as they will continue to cook for a minute or two after removal from the heat. Immediately transfer the hot seeds or nuts to a plate or a baking sheet to keep them from overtoasting. Nuts can be chopped with a knife while still warm, but let seeds or nuts cool completely before processing them in a food processor or blender.

To toast nuts and seeds in the oven, spread them on an ungreased baking sheet and toast in a 350°F oven for 5 to 10 minutes, depending on the size of the nuts, checking and stirring often to prevent burning.

To toast nuts and seeds on the stovetop, place them in a dry skillet over medium heat and cook, stirring or shaking the skillet frequently to prevent burning, until they just begin to release their fragrance, 4 to 5 minutes.

To toast nuts and seeds in a microwave, place them in a thin layer on a microwave-safe dish. Microwave uncovered in 1-minute increments, stirring after each. The nuts or seeds will be very aromatic and lightly browned when they are done.

Toasted nuts and seeds can be stored, covered, in a cool, dry place for up to 2 weeks.

CHOPPING NUTS

If rather large pieces of nuts are needed, simply break nuts like pecans and walnuts with your fingers. For finer pieces, use a knife. ➤ It is easier if the nuts are moist and warm and if the knife is sharp.

To chop nuts, gather them in a round with a diameter as wide as the knife blade. Grasp the knife with the thumb and index fingers of your nondominant hand at the top of the tip of the blade and the thumb and knuckle of your index finger of your dominant hand on either side of the blade just in front of the handle. The remaining fingers of the dominant hand should wrap around the handle, 1044. Rock the blade briskly from point to hilt, gradually rotating the knife in a semicircle. Gather the chopped bits together and repeat the rocking until the bits are as fine as you want them.

Nuts may also be chopped in a food processor, using short pulses. ➤ Process no more than 2 cups at a time, and use caution not to overprocess, lest you end up with nut butter.

GRINDING NUTS

Some recipes call for ground nuts or nut meal. While it is now commonplace to find almond meal or flour at most supermarkets, you can prepare nut meals at home. To grind nuts, ➤ process small quantities at a time in a food processor, pulsing the nuts until very finely ground. The light, dry, fluffy particles that result often become an ingredient in nut tortes or cookies. A blender is not as effective in grinding or chopping nuts. But if that is your only choice, pulverize only ¼ cup at a time, making sure the container and blade are dry before you start. Toasted nuts should be cooled completely before being ground.

ABOUT NUT AND SEED BUTTERS

Peanut butter has long been Americans' favorite nut butter (and not for nothing—it is exceptionally delicious!), but we are glad to see other nuts and seeds getting their turn in the spotlight. Almonds, pecans, cashews, walnuts, pumpkin seeds, sunflower seeds, and hazelnuts can all be ground into fresh nut or seed butter.

Nut and seed butters made in the food processor have an appealing coarse texture and a fresh, rich flavor. Walnuts and pecans produce light-textured butters with a relatively loose consistency. Peanuts, cashews, and almonds produce denser butters. Pulse the nuts or seeds in the processor until they are finely chopped and the mixture looks blended and creamy, stopping and scraping down the sides of the work bowl as needed. Most nuts need no additional oil, though almonds and most seeds can be a bit dry and may benefit from the addition of a small amount of oil. We recommend starting with raw nuts, toasting them, then allowing them to cool before processing.

NUT BUTTER

1½ to 1¾ cups

Place in a food processor:

3 cups roasted or toasted, 1010, unsalted peanuts, cashews, walnuts, pecans, almonds, or hazelnuts

Process until the nuts gather into a ball, 2 to 3 minutes. Break up the ball with a spoon. If desired, add:

(¼ teaspoon salt, or to taste)

Process until the nuts release their oil and a butter forms. This generally takes 1 to 3 minutes but may take as long as 5 minutes, particularly if you are using almonds. Store the butter, covered, at room temperature for up to 2 weeks or refrigerate for up to 3 months.

TAHINI

About 1 cup

This sesame seed paste will keep, refrigerated, in a tightly covered container for several months. Stir before use if the oil separates. Tahini is used in Hummus, 52, and Baba Ghanoush, 53, but we also love it, in combination with honey, as a toast topping and whisked into the ganache for Dark Chocolate Truffles, 859 (whisk ¼ cup tahini into the ganache once it is smooth).

Preheat the oven to 350°F. Spread on a rimmed baking sheet:

2 cups hulled sesame seeds

Bake, shaking frequently, until fragrant, 8 to 10 minutes. Do not brown. Let cool completely. Put the seeds in a blender or food processor. Process until the seeds are finely ground and form a thick paste. Add slowly:

¼ cup vegetable oil, or as needed

Process to a smooth paste, about 3 minutes. Add more oil if necessary to bring the paste to a thick but pourable consistency.

ABOUT NUT AND SEED MILKS

Nut and seed milks are milky-looking liquids derived from pureeing soaked nuts or seeds with water. While we may think of these milks as modern inventions, almond and walnut milks have long been known in Europe. Some nuts, such as hickory nuts and pecans, were used by North American indigenous peoples to make nut milks.

While nut milks are by no means dairy milk's nutritional equivalent, they are delicious and healthful in their own right, and a boon to those who cannot or choose not to drink milk. For **soy milk,** see Soy Milk and Tofu, 1019. For **coconut milk,** see 973.

Nut and seed milks are easy to make. The only equipment necessary is a blender and something to strain the blended nut or seed and water mixture through. We have used flour sack towels for this purpose, but **nut milk bags** are the most efficient option (these are easily purchased from online retailers). Once the milk is strained, there will be pulp left behind in the towel or bag. This pulp can be kept refrigerated and used within a week, or spread it out on a baking sheet and dry it in a very low oven. Once fully dry, it can be ground in a food processor to break up any clumps, then stored at room temperature. We use the pulp in baked goods and smoothies or as a replacement for bread crumbs in some recipes.

Nut milks are as perishable as unpasteurized cow's milk. Refrigerate them and use within a week. Because homemade nut and seed milks do not contain stabilizers, they will separate upon sitting. Simply shake them before use.

NUT OR SEED MILK

About 4 cups

This recipe may be used as a template for making other kinds of nut and seed milks. Walnuts can make a good nut milk, but they are best blended with another nut, such as cashews, as they are very tannic. Rolled oats can also be processed as below, but they do not need to be soaked before blending.

Place in a medium bowl:

1 cup almonds, cashews, hazelnuts, pecans, pumpkin seeds, or sunflower seeds (raw or toasted, 1027, but not salted)

Add cold water to cover by 2 inches and let soak overnight.

Drain and place in a blender with:

4 cups cool water

Puree until the mixture is white and no large chunks of nuts or seeds are visible. Strain through a fine-mesh sieve, several layers of cheesecloth, a clean kitchen towel, or a nut milk bag. Press on the nut pulp with a spatula (or squeeze the cloth or bag) to extract as much milk as possible from the nuts. If desired, add to the milk:

(Maple syrup or honey to taste)

(½ teaspoon vanilla)

(Pinch of salt)

Refrigerate and use within 1 week.

OILS

Oil is one of the most common ingredients in cooking and performs several different functions. For starters, oil prevents sticking. Whether you're pan-frying a pork chop or roasting vegetables, oil provides a slick barrier between the food and the pan. While your pans may look and feel smooth, on a microscopic level they are pitted and rough. Adding oil to the pan fills these pits and creates a more or less uniform surface upon which the food will cook.

Not only does oil keep foods from sticking and fill in the gaps on the surface of cookware, it also fills in the gaps in the food itself, transmitting heat to every crevice of the food and encouraging it to brown. To see the effects oil has on browning, try cooking the same type of food in two different pans, one with oil and one without. You will see that the food cooked in oil has an appealingly crisp, evenly golden exterior. Food cooked without oil will brown somewhat, but the surface will be dry, and the browning will be uneven.

What's more, oil can attain temperatures much, much higher than the boiling point of water, which makes it ideal for frying. Of course, not all oils are stable enough to be used at frying temperatures. ➤ Whether frying or using oil to sear or sauté, avoid heating it to the point where it begins to smoke. An oil's **smoke point,** 981, is the highest safe temperature it can be taken to, beyond which it starts to break down, producing acrid gases and off-flavors. Recipes for searing and blackening will call for a pan with oil to be heated until it starts to smoke, but foods should be added immediately thereafter, which will swiftly drop its temperature.

Beyond their usefulness as a cooking medium, oils can add flavors of their own. ➤ Oils with a distinct flavor are usually **unrefined,** or **cold-pressed,** and tend to have a lower smoke point, which makes them unsuitable for deep-frying, sautéing, and other high-heat cooking methods. Extra-virgin olive oil can be grassy, peppery, or buttery, and while those nuances would be lost if the oil were used for high-heat cooking, when that same oil is used to finish a dish (say, a drizzle on a bowl of Roasted Cauliflower Soup, 105) or used in an application where the dish is not cooked (salad dressings, Pesto, 586, or Olive Oil Ice Cream, 843), its flavor adds to the complexity of the food. Other oils that are flavorful in their own right include toasted sesame oil and unrefined nut oils like pistachio and walnut.

Oils also help spread flavors throughout a dish: When neutral vegetable oils are used to sauté foods, the flavors of the food are infused in and carried by the oil. This is why some recipes instruct you to briefly fry garlic, chiles, or whole spices in oil at the beginning of the cooking process; the ingredients flavor the oil, which in turn flavors the entire dish. Oils (and, more broadly, fats) are flavor carriers, and when you eat foods that contain fat, the flavors carried by the fat linger on the tongue longer than flavors carried by water or alcohol.

One important thing to keep in mind when using and storing oils is **rancidity.** All oils eventually go rancid, and cold-pressed or extra-virgin oils go rancid much more quickly than refined oils. Oils stored in direct sunlight or at a high temperature go rancid faster than those stored out of sunlight and at cool temperatures. How do you determine whether an oil is rancid or not? The biggest giveaway is the smell. Many cooks liken the smell of rancid oil to crayons or candle wax. Refined oils should have no smell at all, and cold-pressed or extra-virgin oils should have a pleasant smell that will vary depending on what the oil is made from. Store oils in airtight containers in a cool, dark place. ➤ Discard any oil that smells rancid, fishy, or musty or that starts to foam, darken, or smoke excessively when heated.

In general, the oils we discuss here are mostly composed of unsaturated fat, and thus liquid at room temperature. The exceptions are coconut oil and palm oil, which are high in saturated fat and solid at room temperature. For more about fats and fatty acids, see Fats in Cooking, 980, as well as the Nutrition and Food Safety chapter, xvi.

Oils are 100 percent fat, so when substituting them for butter (which is not) ➤ reduce the amount by 15 to 20 percent, either by weight or by volume measure. However, there are additional complications when substituting them for solid fats, especially in baking. We recommend using the oil or fat called for in the recipe for a higher likelihood of success.

OLIVE OIL

Olive oils are like wines in the way their flavors are affected by the soils in which the olives grew, the weather, and the olive variety used. Most olive oil is produced in Mediterranean countries like Greece, Spain, and Italy, though it is also produced in California. While one might think that buying olive oil from Italy would ensure higher quality, this is not necessarily the case. Many Italian olive oils are made from olives of unknown provenance and quality, and fraud is fairly common, with some oils being diluted with vegetable oil and others being sold as "extra-virgin" when they are anything but. The best ways to judge the quality of olive oils are the presence of a processing date, a statement on the bottle that the oil was made from 100 percent Californian or Italian olives (as opposed to statements like "made in Italy" or "bottled in Italy," which say nothing about the quality of the oil), and the flavor of the oil. A good olive oil should have flavor, but it should not be aggressively bitter or spicy, and it should not have a hint of rancidity.

Olive oils are graded according to their flavor, odor, and free fatty acid content (free fatty acids, or FFAs, are evidence of damaged or degrading oil) as well as whether they are processed with or without solvents. **Extra-virgin olive oils** are premium: They are extracted from the first pressing and processed without the application of heat or solvents. They are the lowest in free fatty acids of all olive oils. Their color ranges from gold to deep green, but color is no indication of quality. Clouded, unfiltered oils are prized by many for their fuller flavor, though these oils will go rancid much more quickly than filtered oils. While the words "extra-virgin" on the label may guarantee fruity, pronounced flavor, they do not guarantee a good-tasting oil. If at all possible, sample before buying.

Notably, research has shown that olive oils, extra-virgin or otherwise, do not degrade as much as many refined seed oils at high temperatures even though they have a relatively low smoke point. Nonetheless, due to the price of extra-virgin olive oil and the fact that its flavor nuances are lost when used to cook at high temperatures, we still recommend using extra-virgin olive oil for low-heat applications, as an ingredient in uncooked sauces, or as a finishing oil.

Virgin olive oil, also a first-pressed oil and processed without heat or chemicals, has a higher free fatty acid content than extra-virgin oil. With a flavor and character more subdued than extra-virgin oil, virgin oil is an excellent substitute for extra-virgin oil when budget considerations are necessary. **Olive oil,** sometimes labeled "pure" olive oil, is a blended oil made from refined olive oil (extracted with pressure, heat, solvents, and/or chemicals) and virgin olive oil, from which it gains color and flavor. It is an excellent choice for cooking. **"Light" olive oil** is a marketing title describing refined olive oils that are mild or light in taste or color. Despite the name, the calorie content is the same as all other olive oils—120 calories per tablespoon. Some olive oils are sold with the name of the olive varietal on the bottle, such as Castelvetrano, Arbequina, Mission, and Koroneiki, but there are hundreds of varieties of olives, and no particular type of olive is a guarantee of quality. Store all olive oils in a cool, dark place.

VEGETABLE OILS

When we call for "vegetable oil" in recipes, we mean for readers to choose from a group of refined neutral-flavored oils with a relatively high smoke point, such as **corn, avocado, grapeseed, soybean, canola, safflower, sunflower,** and **peanut oil.** Some of these oils are not technically derived from vegetables (avocados and sunflowers, for example), but they are functionally similar. Most brands of these oils are highly refined and extracted using solvents instead of mechanical pressing, as is done with extra-virgin and virgin olive oils. Oils sold as **"vegetable oil"** are usually, in fact, soybean oil, though other oils, such as corn or canola, may be blended with soybean oil. Check the label to be sure.

Canola oil is extracted from rapeseed, which is in the Brassica family. There is actually no plant with the name "canola." The word is a combination of "Canada" and the suffix "ola," which is commonly used with oils (i.e., corn, or maize, is combined to spell Mazola). Canola was originally trademarked by the Rapeseed Association of Canada, but now it is simply a generic term for rapeseed oil that meets a certain standard based on fatty acid profile and the concentration of compounds called glucosinolates that affect flavor.

OTHER NUT AND SEED OILS

Many of these oils are widely available unrefined, or cold-pressed. Unrefined nut and seed oils, especially roasted or toasted varieties, are very flavorful and have a low smoke point. They should be used as finishing oils, in simmered dishes, or in uncooked applications. A few of these oils are also available in refined form, which have a higher smoke point and are thus better suited for cooking.

Coconut oil comes in two main forms: refined and virgin. Refined coconut oil has a higher smoke point and little coconut flavor, while virgin coconut oil is solid at room temperature, has a low smoke point, and tastes distinctly of coconut. Unlike most vegetable oils, coconut oil is composed of mostly saturated fatty acids.

Palm oil, or **dendê oil,** comes from the fruit of oil palms and naturally has a reddish-orange color. Along with coconut oil, it is one of the only vegetable fats that is naturally solid at room temperature and contains a high proportion of saturated fatty acids. **Palm kernel oil** has an even higher percentage of saturated fat. Palm oil is commonly used in West African, Brazilian, and Southeast Asian cuisines, particularly Indonesian cuisine.

Sesame oil is the finishing oil we use the most. It is also an integral seasoning in many noodle dishes, such as Beef Chow Fun, 302, and Sesame Noodles, 302, as well as salad dressings, Dipping Sauce for Dumplings, 572, and condiments like Ssamjang, 571. It is widely available in unrefined and toasted, or dark, varieties. We like the pure flavor of unrefined and lightly toasted sesame oil for finishing dishes, but there is no mistaking **dark sesame oil,** which has a much stronger flavor. In recipes, we simply call for toasted sesame oil (feel free to use dark if you prefer it). Refined sesame oil is also available; it has a neutral flavor and can be used for high-heat cooking.

Pumpkin seed oil is available cold-pressed and should be used as a finishing oil only. It has a rich, savory flavor and is popular in Eastern Europe. **Almond, pecan, pistachio,** and **walnut oils** are all available unrefined or roasted, and taste of the nuts from which they are made. They are superb on salads and vegetables and may also be used to flavor desserts. Almond and walnut oil can occasionally be found refined; they are fine to use over moderate heat. Do not confuse culinary almond oil with almond oil sold for cosmetic uses (often sold as sweet almond oil). Refined pecan oil has a high smoke point, and is well suited to pan-frying and sautéing.

INFUSING OILS

Many of the flavorful compounds in herbs, spices, fruits, and other aromatic ingredients are soluble in fat. Aside from cooking them (or steeping them in alcohol, 948), one of the best ways to capture and distribute their flavor is by infusing an oil with them. Flavored oils are simple to make and add depth of flavor as well as richness to finished dishes. They are not for cooking, but for seasoning, just as you would drizzle extra-virgin olive oil over cooked vegetables or pastas. For infusing oils with garlic, see Garlic Confit, 241.

INFUSED OIL

Flavored oils must be refrigerated, and most will hold their quality for at least 1 week. Prepare only as much as you will use in that time. For optimum flavor and texture, bring the amount of oil you will be serving to room temperature.

I. CITRUS OIL

About 1 cup

This cold infusion is the easiest to make. Use in vinaigrettes, drizzle over poached shellfish or grilled fish, chicken, or vegetables just before serving, or stir into hot tomato soup.

Combine in a sterilized, 893, 8- to 10-ounce jar:

¼ cup finely grated orange, lime, or lemon zest
1 cup mild olive, walnut, or vegetable oil

Cover and shake the jar gently, then let steep in the refrigerator for up to 4 days. Strain the oil through a dampened paper coffee filter. The oil can be kept, covered and refrigerated, for no longer than 1 week.

II. HERB

About ¾ cup

Blanching the herbs sets their color and tints the oil an alluring green. If using rosemary, reduce the amount by half. To skip the filtering and give the resulting condiment more body, see Jen's Basil Oil, 570.

Have ready a bowl of ice water. Bring a pot of water to a boil. Blanch for 10 seconds in the boiling water:

2 packed cups of the leaves and soft stems of herbs like basil, parsley, thyme, sage, or a combination

Remove them quickly with a strainer and dunk in the ice water, swishing them around to be sure they're all cold. Remove from the water and squeeze gently to remove the excess water. Coarsely chop the herbs and transfer to a blender. Add:

1 cup mild olive oil
(¼ teaspoon salt)

Blend until the herbs are pureed. The mixture will be very frothy. Let the puree settle for about 30 minutes. Pour into a jar through a fine-mesh sieve lined with several layers of cheesecloth or a coffee filter and leave to drain overnight. The next day, very gently push down on the solids to extract as much oil as possible. Use immediately or cover and refrigerate for up to 1 week. For the best flavor, let the oil come to room temperature before using.

III. CHILE

About ¾ cup

Capsaicin, the compound responsible for the spiciness of chiles, is very effectively transferred to the oil, which, in turn, coats the tongue. Until you determine just how spicy the oil is, use sparingly and to taste. A few drops are superb in dipping sauces for dumplings or in dressings for vegetable dishes. If desired, add a few wide strips of orange zest, a cinnamon stick, or a tablespoon of Sichuan peppercorns for a more complex flavor. For a similar condiment, see Spicy Chinese Chile Crisp, 572.

Have ready:

½ cup red pepper flakes

Or, coarsely grind in a blender or spice grinder:

About 3 ounces dried red chiles, such as Thai bird's eye or chiles de árbol, stem and seeds removed

Transfer to a small saucepan and add:

1 cup vegetable oil

Heat over medium heat until the oil reaches 350°F, or until large bubbles appear. Remove from the heat, cover, and let sit for at least 4 hours.

Once cool, you may leave the oil unstrained, transfer to a sterile, 893, jar, and serve with a spoon for adding the chile flakes to dishes at the table. For a clear oil, pour through a fine-mesh sieve that has been lined with several layers of cheesecloth or a coffee filter. Push down on the solids to extract as much oil as possible. Cover and refrigerate for up to 1 month.

OLIVES

To classify olives as being simply green or black would not do justice to the wealth of varieties available. There are hundreds, though we only see a handful of varieties in stores. Fresh olives are bitter due to the compound oleuropein present in olive skin; olives are processed, or "cured," to make them suitable for eating. Green olives are picked unripe and black olives are picked ripe. "Black ripe" California olives (the canned variety) are picked green and treated with brine, lye, and oxygen. Lye and oxygen cause the olives to oxidize, resulting in their characteristic black color and alkaline flavor.

The flavor of each variety of olive depends upon its ripeness, where it is grown, and the type of processing it undergoes. Brine-, oil-, and water-cured olives have a moist-looking exterior and a smooth, shiny skin; salt- or dry-cured olives look wrinkled and shriveled (confusingly, these are often called "oil-cured" olives, but they are dry-cured in salt before being packed in oil).

While the grading of olives is taken very seriously by processors, what should matter most when purchasing is that they are uniform in color and free of surface blemishes and white spots. Explore the delicious array of Greek, Italian, French, Spanish, Middle Eastern, and California olives to find what best satisfies your palate. A few suggestions may help guide your explorations: Castelvetrano, Cerignola, Lucques, and Picholine olives are our favorite green varieties; among black and purplish types, we love Niçoise, Nyon, and the ever-popular Kalamata. Salt-cured olives, whether Italian or Moroccan, are our favorite "ingredient" olives, especially for topping pizzas and focaccia, and they add a fantastic depth to spreads and sauces.

Keep bulk-purchased olives in the refrigerator for up to several weeks. Canned or bottled olives can be kept unopened in the pantry for up to 2 years but should be refrigerated when opened. For olive recipes, see Spanish-Style Marinated Olives, 48, Tapenade, 54, Fougasse, 606, Rosemary-Olive Bread, 628, Frittata di Scammaro, 293, Muffuletta, 137, Veracruz-Style Tomato Sauce, 556, Puttanesca Sauce, 557, and Tomato-Olive Relish, 568.

ONIONS AS SEASONING

Never since our first encounter with the host of alliums in a bulb catalog have these lilies lost their allure for us as food or flower—from the thinnest chive to the enormous *Allium schubertii*, or tumbleweed onion, with its flower like a large sparkler. This is a plea not only to use a variety of onions in your cooking, but to grow perennial onions so you will always have them on hand.

Here, we cover onions, leeks, and shallots as a seasoning ingredient, as well as their dried forms. ➤ For instructions on cleaning, cutting, and cooking these alliums, see About Onions and Shallots, 254, About Leeks, 247, and Chives, 970.

Leeks, green onions, shallots, or mature onions find their way into nearly every dinner we cook. They add subtlety and depth to a dish, but some care should be taken in how they are cooked. Scorching storage onions over high heat can bring out their worst features and turn them unbearably bitter. Onions are frequently chopped or minced fine, 255, so they can impart their characteristic flavor without adding much in the way of texture. (Grating them into a towel, gathering the towel into a ball, and squeezing out **onion juice** can achieve the same effect.) In most instances, onions must be cooked long enough to get rid of any rawness.

Here we betray ourselves: We are generally not fans of raw onions, unless they are sliced paper-thin or diced very small. We sometimes place onions in a sieve and pour boiling water over them before adding them to salsas—or quick-pickle them, 930. Even onions soaked in cold water for a short time will mellow considerably, which is a small mercy if you have to be around other humans or care not to taste their sharp bite for hours afterward.

Like dried garlic powder, **onion powder** is a good ingredient to keep in the pantry for adding to Chili Powder, 588, and other seasoning blends that might be used to coat foods—or for adding a faint onion flavor to uncooked sauces, or those where you do not want their texture or bulk. Unlike garlic powder, which takes on a slightly bitter, off-flavor during the drying process, onion powder remains relatively sweet. To dry onions, as well as leek tops, see Drying Fruits and Vegetables, 944.

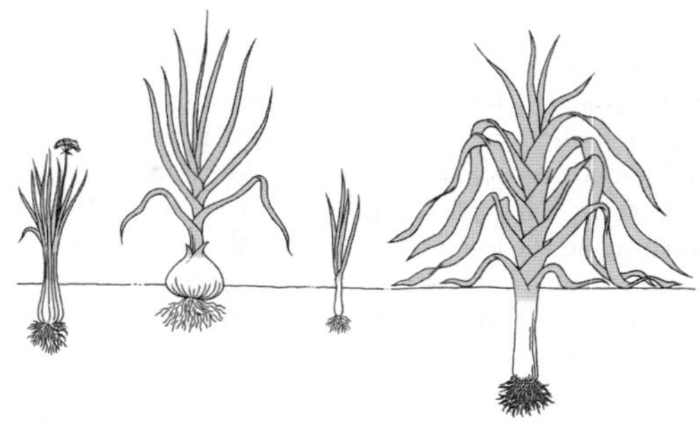

Chives; storage, dry, or sweet onions; green onions, scallions; leeks

Shallots, garlic chives, ramps, softneck garlic, hardneck garlic

We have little use for **dried onion flakes** beyond their use in Everything Seasoning, 590. If you do use them in a stew, braise, or casserole, be sure they have been simmered long enough to soften. **Freeze-dried onions** are incrementally better and require less simmering. Unless you are backpacking or in dire straits, we do not recommend substituting either product for fresh onions. While dried onions add a faint essence, they do nothing to replicate the texture, sweetness, or caramel notes that fresh onions add to dishes.

OREGANO

Oregano is widely used in the cooking of the Mediterranean and Latin America, notably in sauces and stews and with meat. Oregano belongs, along with marjoram, 5, to the *Origanum* genus, and the two are often spoken of together because they have a similar flavor. Actually, owing to the fact that many different species of plants have been colloquially referred to as oregano on the basis of their flavor, the term "oregano" is less a botanical one and more a flavor descriptor. **Italian, Turkish,** and **Greek oregano** are "true" oreganos, belonging to the *Origanum* genus, and are the varieties usually sold in grocery stores. **Mexican oregano** is actually from the *Lippia* genus (the same genus as lemon verbena, 998). The thick, succulent leaves of **Cuban oregano** (also confusingly called Spanish thyme, Mexican mint, and Indian borage) is not an *Origanum* but rather a *Lamiaceae*, the same genus as mint. However, it tastes and smells like oregano and is used in the same way. The notable difference is that it has a very strong, turpentine-tinged flavor compared to Greek oregano, so use less. It is rare to find Cuban oregano at all, so the best way to experience its distinctive flavor is to grow it yourself.

OYSTER SAUCE

A staple of Chinese, Thai, Filipino, and Vietnamese cuisines, oyster sauce was originally made from oysters, water, and salt. Now it may contain added cornstarch and caramel color to improve its appearance and to thicken liquids when used in stir-frying. When buying oyster sauce, avoid the less-expensive varieties, which are made with a lower concentration of oysters and more cornstarch and artificial colors and flavors. Also available are vegetarian "oyster flavored" sauces. Once opened, store it in the refrigerator.

PANDAN

Pandanus or **screwpine** trees are best known for their long, slender leaves. These leaves are incredibly aromatic, with a rich, nutty scent. They are commonly used in Southeast Asia to flavor rice and desserts. Pandan-flavored desserts are often tinted green because green-colored pandan extract is used as a flavoring rather than the leaves themselves. You can find pandan leaves fresh and/or frozen at many Asian supermarkets. We have added them to rice as it steams, used them to infuse cream to make custards and Panna Cotta, 821, and wrapped them around white fish fillets before baking or grilling. Pandan leaves can also be added to a pitcher of water for a subtle flavored effect.

Though the leaves may be easily steeped in oil, water, or alcohol to make **pandan extract,** the extract sold in stores is invariably artificial. It is used to flavor cakes and other desserts. The flowers of the pandanus tree are used to make **kewra water,** a hydrosol left over from extracting the essential oil for use in fragrances. Like orange blossom water and rose water, it is used to flavor desserts, as well as several savory Indian rice dishes.

PÁPALO

See Coriander, 973.

PAPRIKA

See Chiles, Dried and Ground, 967.

PARSLEY

Parsley is one of the most misunderstood of all herbs. Many Americans no doubt think of parsley as a faded, dried herb that languishes in the cupboard, emerging only to garnish the occasional twice-baked potato. However, the savvy cook knows parsley's true versatility, from acting as a salad green to making zesty condiments. It is precisely for parsley's ability to brighten a wide variety of dishes that we keep a bunch in our crisper at all times. Fresh parsley has a vibrant flavor that is best described as "green," and a deep, forest green color. There is practically no savory dish that parsley cannot improve, whether as a garnish or an ingredient.

The most common types of parsley are **curly parsley** and **flat-leaf** or **Italian parsley.** To use either, pick the leaves from the stems and coarsely or finely chop them. Parsley stems may be used in stock (we always add some to our stock bag, 73). Use the leaves as a vibrant garnish for heavy foods like beef or chicken braises, gratins, or Deviled Eggs, 151. We like to stir a big handful of chopped parsley into brothy soups just before serving (don't be shy). For a salad that is mostly parsley, see Tabbouleh, 131. To turn a heap of parsley into a sauce, see Salsa Verde, 567, Zhug, 567, or Chimichurri, 567. The Italian parsley mixture Gremolata, 587, is typically served with Osso Buco, 476, but we also sprinkle it on pizza, pasta dishes, soups, and braises. Persillade, 586, a similar French mixture, can be used in these ways as well. Parsley sprigs are also excellent when deep-fried as part of a Fritto Misto, 658.

PEANUTS

Peanuts, also called groundnuts or goobers, are actually underground legumes. Peanuts are grown for the nuts themselves, for their oil, as well as peanut butter. There are several types of peanuts commonly grown in the United States: **Virginia peanuts** are large and typically eaten out of hand. **Runner peanuts** account for about 80 percent of the US peanut crop. They are smaller than Virginia peanuts, and primarily used to make peanut butter. Red-skinned **Spanish peanuts** are higher in fat and used mostly for oil. **Valencia peanuts** are also red-skinned and have a sweet flavor.

Peanut flour or meal is made from the ground, defatted peanuts left over from cold-pressing peanut oil. It is very absorbent and can be used as a flavorful thickener or added to batters, doughs, smoothies, or oatmeal. It can also be mixed with sugar and spices for tossing with sweet fritters or doughnuts after frying, or added to Streusel, 800. Peanut flour is sometimes mixed with salt and a sweetener to make **peanut butter powder,** which can be reconstituted and used like peanut butter, though because it is made with defatted peanut meal it is much less rich and oily.

Peanuts hail from South America, and the Portuguese are responsible for spreading them to Africa and Asia, where they are an important foodstuff to this day. Today, India and China account for most of the world's peanut production. In China, the nuts are mostly used for oil, though they are also eaten boiled with spices and soy sauce. It is also common to see peanuts in Southeast Asian dipping sauces such as Peanut Dipping Sauce, 571. In Africa, peanuts are ground and used in stews (Peanut Soup, 90, is a descendant of West African peanut stews).

To roast raw peanuts, place roast in a 350°F oven for 20 to 25 minutes if unshelled, or 15 to 20 minutes if shelled. Stir occasionally to avoid scorching. Check for doneness by allowing a nut to cool, then removing the shell. It should be crunchy and have a pleasing, roasted flavor.

To make peanut butter, see Nut Butter, 1005. For Boiled Peanuts, see 47.

PECANS

A native North American nut from a variety of hickory tree, pecans were a staple food of indigenous peoples in the southeastern United

States. The nuts were turned into a milk that was consumed on its own and used in cooking. Pecans are one of the nuts highest in fat, with sometimes as much as 75 percent fat, which gives them a soft, almost buttery texture and a very rich flavor. The high fat content can lead to rapid rancidity, so store them in the freezer for up to 1 year. Pecans take on a rich flavor and fragrance when toasted, 1005, but once toasted they should be used as soon as possible. Pecans are probably best known for their role in Pecan Pie, 667, but their rich flavor makes them a superb addition to stuffings, dressings, and salads, and they make exceptional nut butter, 1005, and nut milk, 1006. Also see Pecan and Cheddar "Sausage" Patties, 289, Pecan or Angel Slices, 767, Mexican Wedding Cakes, 773, and Pecan Lace, 773.

PECTIN

Pectin is a type of fiber: a polysaccharide (a complex carbohydrate, or chain of sugar molecules bound together) naturally found in the cell walls of fruits and vegetables. Pectin as an ingredient comes into play in the making of jams and jellies. Some fruits are low in pectin (see Pectin Content of Fruits, 907) and need to have it added to form a gel.

Commercial pectin is a liquid or powdered substance derived primarily from apple pomace or citrus peels. The majority of the preserve recipes in this book do not call for added pectin. Many pectin-added recipes require a high amount of sugar, which can overwhelm the flavor of the fruit. That said, the extended boiling required to get jams and jellies made with low-pectin fruits to set can also negatively impact the flavor of the fruit, and adding pectin decreases the amount of time required at boiling temperatures. **Low-sugar, low-methyl,** or **low-ester pectin** does not require as much added sugar, relying instead upon calcium (which is provided in the package along with the pectin) to set into a gel. Nonetheless, for the sake of flavor and simplicity, we reserve using powdered or liquid pectin for jelly recipes made with low-pectin fruits. Freezer jams, 914, require a special "instant" type of commercial pectin.

Liquid pectin is added toward the end of cooking, while powdered pectin is whisked into the sugar and added at the beginning of cooking.

To substitute powdered pectin for liquid pectin, use 2 tablespoons powdered pectin for every 3-ounce pouch liquid pectin; whisk it into the sugar called for in the recipe, and add it to the fruit at the beginning of cooking.

Use low-sugar pectin as directed on the package. No matter what kind of pectin you use, do not rely upon the package directions alone to determine when the preserve is finished cooking. Always use the wrinkle test, 908, to confirm that the preserve has reached the jelling point.

PEPPERCORNS

All "true" peppercorns come from the berry cluster of a leafy vine in the *Piper* genus. These peppercorns are black, green, or white. **Long pepper,** 998, and **cubeb,** 975, are also true peppercorns. Pink peppercorns and **Sichuan peppercorns,** 1018, are related to cashews and citrus, respectively, making them peppers in name only. **Grains of paradise,** 991, which is often referred to as melegueta pepper, is a relative of ginger, turmeric, and cardamom. Peppercorns have the most flavor and aroma before they are fully ripe, which is why all peppercorns, both green and black, are picked green and processed to preserve as much of their flavor as possible. The flavor compound that gives pepper its warming pungency is called piperine, but peppercorns also contain a wealth of other flavor compounds that give it piney, lemony flavors as well.

Green peppercorns are the unripe berry of the pepper vine. They are treated with sulfur dioxide and dehydrated to preserve their green color. Green peppercorns are sometimes preserved in brine, and they may be chopped or added whole to beef stews, Thai curries, or rich sauces for a throat-warming pungency. In Thailand, green peppercorns are commonly used fresh, though they are very difficult to find in the United States. **Black peppercorns** are green peppercorns that are blanched and dried, becoming hard, wrinkled, and dark brown to black. Their flavor is rich and spicy, especially if the berries are Malabar or Tellicherry peppercorns. **White peppercorns** are produced from fully ripe red pepper berries. They are fermented, then the red exterior of the berries is rubbed off to reveal a grayish white inner core. White pepper is as pungent as black or green pepper, but it is not as complex or aromatic. White pepper is preferred for light-colored foods and sauces (unless a color contrast is desired).

Pink peppercorns, as mentioned above, are not true peppercorns, but rather berries from a tree related to cashews and mangoes. Native to Brazil, the berries of *Schinus terebinthifolius* have an appealing, bright pink color and some of the same flavor compounds as black peppercorns. However, they contain an irritant and should be used sparingly as they can cause digestive distress.

Peppercorns add different flavors to a dish depending on how they are used. Prolonged simmering can bring out a bitter flavor in peppercorns, but this is not necessarily a bad thing if added in moderation. Keeping the peppercorns whole, to flavor soups and other long-cooking mixtures, softens their flavor (tie the peppercorns in cheesecloth so they can be easily removed before serving). Regardless of whether or not they are added at the beginning, we recommend seasoning dishes with freshly ground pepper toward the end of cooking to round out the flavor. Pepper is not just for savory foods. Sneak a pinch into cookies such as Pfeffernüsse, 772, spice cakes, and fruit dishes, or try freshly ground black pepper on strawberries.

Freshly crushed or cracked pepper can be pressed into meats before searing and sautéing (see Steak au Poivre, 461) or grilling and smoking (see Pastrami, 938). The peppercorns add their distinctive flavors and aromas but also form a pleasing, nubby crust. Use cracked peppercorns when a bold, assertive taste is desired.

To crack peppercorns, spread them on half a kitchen towel and fold over the other half, or place in a zip-top bag. Press down on the peppercorns with a heavy skillet, or lightly pound them all over with a rolling pin or a meat mallet. Alternatively, you can crack small quantities of peppercorns in a mortar and pestle (cover the mortar with your hand as you pound to keep them from bouncing out and escaping).

➤ Ground pepper is always best freshly ground. We recommend buying whole peppercorns, storing them in an airtight container in a cool, dark place, and grinding them as needed for the best flavor.

PINE NUTS

Known as *piñones* in Spanish and *pignoli* or *pinoli* in Italian, these small, ivory-colored seeds are harvested from the cones of several varieties of pine tree. It takes 3 years for pine cones to develop fully and produce these nuts, and so they command a premium price. There are three main varieties of pine nut: the slender Mediterranean or Italian pine nut, which has a delicate, sweet flavor; the triangular Chinese pine nut, which has a blander flavor; and the North American pine nut (*Pinus edulis*), which is nutty and creamy. Pine nuts from *P. edulis* are by far our favorite variety; if you are lucky enough to find them roasted in the shell, savor them as a snack (they can be ordered online).

Pine nuts are used in sweet and savory dishes, and as a garnish. All varieties are high in fat, though Asian pine nuts are higher in fat than other varieties and so are especially prone to rancidity. Store all pine nuts in an airtight container in the refrigerator or freezer and use promptly. These nuts are traditional in Pesto, 586, excellent as a salad garnish, and a good addition to Dolmas, 63. Toast them in a dry skillet over medium-low heat, stirring frequently. Watch closely, as pine nuts burn quickly.

PISTACHIOS

These nuts, beloved for their green color and haunting, mild flavor, are native to Afghanistan, but today are grown throughout the Middle East, southern Europe, North Africa, and California. When pistachios are ripe, the shell opens to reveal the green nut inside. Pistachios grown in cooler climates and picked when underripe tend to have more vibrant green nuts. They are used in stuffings, confections, sausages, and pâtés for their vibrant color as much as their flavor. Pistachios have a thin, papery skin that is perfectly edible but that may be removed for aesthetic reasons. To skin, spread on rimmed baking sheets and toast at 400°F for 4 minutes. Let cool and pinch or rub off the skins.

Pistachio paste is a sweetened, nut butter-like ingredient that is used in pastry applications. It has a beautiful green color and rich flavor that makes it an ideal addition to ice cream bases, frostings, and cakes. For **pistachio oil,** see Other Nut and Seed Oils, 1007.

POPPY SEEDS

Poppy seeds come from *Papaver somniferum*, the opium poppy, but the seed has no narcotic properties. The most desirable come from Holland and are a slate-blue color. The seeds are best when roasted or steamed and crushed just before use in cooking, so their full flavor is released. If poppy seeds are one of your favorite flavors, it is worth getting a special hand mill for grinding them. Use poppy seeds, both whole and ground, in baked items, and sprinkle them on buttered egg noodles. **White poppy seeds** are smaller than blue ones, and they are from a different poppy cultivar. They are often added to Indian spice blends and used as a thickener in some sauces.

PUMPKIN SEEDS

We are all familiar with pumpkin seeds, if only because we encounter them every Halloween in the guts of the decorative jack-o'-lantern. While the whole seeds can be toasted and eaten as a snack, 47, to be useful in cooking applications they must be hulled, or stripped of their outer white seed coat, which is not practical for the home cook. Instead buy already hulled green pumpkin seeds, or **pepitas:** They are available raw, roasted, salted, and flavored. Pumpkin seeds are nutritionally notable because they are high in protein and fat. Hulled, roasted pumpkin seeds can also be ground into a butter, 1005, as for nuts.

To roast hulled pumpkin seeds, spread out on a rimmed baking sheet and place in a 350°F oven until lightly browned and fragrant, 5 to 8 minutes.

RENNET

Rennet, an extract from the lining of the fourth stomach of calves, is a coagulant used in cheese making. Rennet contains an enzyme called chymosin, which cuts off part of the caseins (a type of protein) in milk, allowing them to bond to each other to form a protein matrix. This has the effect of solidifying the milk into a soft curd. Not all rennet is animal based. Some is made from thistle extract and some from microbes. Rennet is available in tablet or liquid form from cheesemaking suppliers. For how to use rennet, see Cheese, 962.

ROSEMARY

Rosemary is not a subtle herb: The stiff, resinous leaves of this Mediterranean shrub are extremely pungent, with a piney aroma. When adding to dishes as a seasoning, restraint is best. Fresh rosemary has a superior flavor and texture compared to dried; but the leaves do dry well, retaining much of their flavor and aroma.

You may add short pieces of fresh rosemary sprigs to sauces, braises, and stews and remove them before serving (some stray leaves may remain). We really enjoy frying rosemary sprigs as for sage, 1013, after which you can strip the crispy leaves off and use as a garnish for pasta, salads, or potato dishes. For all other uses, we prefer to strip fresh rosemary of its leaves and mince it. Use the minced leaves with lamb, pork, and chicken, and on focaccia.

Dried rosemary is one of the few herbs that truly benefits from being minced as if it were fresh (or ground). If you grow rosemary, one plant will provide you with an inexhaustible supply. To dry, see Drying Herbs and Seeds, 947.

SAFFRON

The golden orange stigmas of the autumn crocus are used to provide extraordinary fragrance, golden color, and flavor in cakes, breads, seafood, and rice dishes. Saffron is gathered by hand. Because it is so labor-intensive to grow and harvest, it is incredibly expensive. The good news is that you only need a little to make a big impact. Take care to use only the amount of saffron dictated in individual recipes. Too much, in addition to being a strain on the pocket book, can give a dish an overpoweringly medicinal flavor. If using saffron mainly for color, make an infusion with the saffron and liquid, then add the golden liquid to the dish. For dishes that feature saffron, see Paella Valenciana, 334, Risotto, 336, and Bouillabaisse, 102.

SAGE

Sage, a member of the mint family, is a common herb with a savory, piney flavor profile. As with rosemary, we recommend using it sparingly. The flavor of the freshly chopped tender leaves will be more powerful than that of the dried, which loses much of its volatile oil. Dried sage is available as "rubbed" or "ground" in the supermarket; rubbed is coarser and will lose its oils and aroma slower. If harvesting your own crop for drying, 947, use a dehydrator, as the leaves are too thick for air-drying and tend to develop mold.

Use sage for meats such as pork, especially in sausages, and for duck, goose, rabbit, and stuffings. Sage is a natural pairing with sweet winter squashes. Fried sage leaves are a flavorful, aromatic garnish for all kinds of dishes, from roasted winter squash to mashed cauliflower to braised white beans.

To fry sage leaves, heat ¼ cup olive oil in a medium skillet over medium heat. When the oil shimmers, add fresh sage leaves in batches and fry until the sage crisps and turns a darker shade of green. Transfer to paper towels to drain, then sprinkle lightly with salt.

SALT

Technically speaking, salt is a mineral, and one necessary for human health. But from a culinary standpoint, salt is the ultimate multitasker; we add it to nearly every food we eat. There are purely practical reasons for salting food, notably for preservation (see About Salting and Curing, 934, and About Fermentation, 938), but we mostly add salt to food because it makes things taste good. Simply put, salt heightens the flavor of foods. Salt can also modify our perception of other flavors: Adding salt to a dish can lessen its bitterness or throw the flavors of sweet foods into relief making them taste balanced and complex.

Salt may also alter texture: It draws moisture from meats and fish through osmosis, but also makes them more tender and moister by preventing protein strands from coiling tightly and pushing out water. Salt makes eggs more tender when added at the beginning of cooking and softens vegetables by weakening the pectin in their cells.

There is the question of *when* salt should be added to foods. The answer is complicated in that it really depends on the food or the dish. In general, we think dishes taste best if they are salted throughout the cooking process. When cooking a basic tomato sauce, for instance, we add a pinch of salt when sautéing the vegetables, another good pinch when the tomatoes are added, and then again at the end of cooking when we are tasting the sauce for flavor. If you wait until the end of cooking to add any salt, it will be more difficult to season the food evenly, as salt takes time and agitation to dissolve and disperse throughout the food. Salting meats before cooking and "to taste" afterward can also be very beneficial (see Marinating, Brining, and Salting, 1046).

➤ There are two important exceptions to salting early on: Salt should be used sparingly at the start of any cooking in which liquids will be greatly evaporated—such as the making of sauces. Also, when working with yeast, it is important to either incorporate the yeast into the dough before adding salt or disperse the salt in the flour mixture before adding yeast so the two are not in direct contact. Salt inhibits yeast and can outright kill it, which will, in turn, affect how the dough rises.

Some foods are naturally salty. Seafood, especially shellfish, is saltier than freshwater fish. Of course, any processed food used in cooking—from pickled, cured, corned, and canned meats and sausages; to broths, ketchups, and condiments; to preserved and canned fish; to canned soups—will add quite a bit of salt. ➤ Season with salt sparingly when dealing with any of these foods.

The phrase **"salt to taste"** is used often in recipes, and it is not the result of mere laziness on the part of the recipe writer. Tasting and adding salt until the food tastes good to you is a fundamental part of learning how to cook well. Further, we all prefer different degrees of saltiness in our foods, and due to the variability of ingredients, heat, degree of evaporation, and the cook, the amount of salt needed can vary quite a bit. Learn to taste foods as they are cooking (when possible) and season as you go. This is the best way to get a feel for how much salt to add to different kinds of foods. On that note, it is easier to add salt to foods when it is freed from the salt shaker and kept in a small bowl instead.

➤ The quantities of salt given in this book are for table salt; it is the most commonly used salt in home kitchens. In our home, we actually prefer to use Diamond kosher salt. Of the kosher salts, Diamond in particular is very light and fluffy, making it easy to add to food without worrying so much about oversalting. When presalting meat, you can shower it with Diamond kosher salt without fear of oversalting, and the salt sticks to the food better than table salt, sea salt, or Morton's kosher salt.

➤ Fine sea salt and Morton's kosher salt can be substituted 1:1 for table salt. If using Diamond kosher salt, you will need to use twice as much by volume (for example, for a recipe that calls for 1 teaspoon table salt, add 2 teaspoons Diamond kosher salt).

BLACK SALT (KALA NAMAK)

Black salt, also known as Himalayan black salt, is a grayish-pink salt with a sulfurous smell and flavor. It is produced by firing salt in a furnace until it melts and the naturally occurring sulfur compounds in the salt transform into more odorous ones. Then the liquid salt is cooled until it hardens. Black salt is available in large, black-looking chunks or finely ground. It is commonly used to season Indian street snacks, called *chaat*, chutneys, and curries. It provides a complex, almost meaty flavor, and its strong sulfur notes mellow when mixed with other ingredients or when cooked. In addition to its use in Indian dishes, we like to sprinkle black salt on popcorn and add it to Tofu Scramble, 286.

COARSE SALT

Coarse salt is not a specific type of salt, but a reference to the size of the salt grain. It can refer to either sea salt, kosher salt, or rock or ice cream salt. While fine-grained salt is more commonly used in cooking because it is easier to regulate how much you add and it dissolves faster, coarse salt is preferred for frosting the rims, 18, of a cocktail glass, making a salt crust for fish or meat, and creating a bed for oysters on the half shell.

HIMALAYAN PINK SALT

Not to be confused with Himalayan black salt, 1013, or pink curing salt, 936, Himalayan pink salt is a type of rock salt harvested from the Salt Range mountains in Pakistan. It is unrefined, and the minerals in the salt give it a pale pink color. Himalayan pink salt is commonly available in coarse chunks or even in very large salt blocks that can be heated and used to cook foods as one might use a griddle. Many like to tout its healthfulness and claim that it performs better than other salts in fermentation, but there is no evidence to support these claims. While Himalayan pink salt does contain minerals, most people are not deficient in the minerals it provides, and in order to get a large dose of these minerals it would be necessary to consume a greater amount of salt than is advisable. One possible "benefit" of this type of salt is that, because it is harvested from mountains rather than from the sea, it does not contain microplastics like most sea salt. Because we do not yet know the long-term effects of the consumption of sea salt containing microplastics, some prefer to avoid sea salt entirely.

KOSHER SALT

Coarse-grained, additive-free kosher salt is used in the kosher preparation of meat. The texture and low density of kosher salt is loved by cooks because it is easy to add by the pinchful, easier to apply evenly to meats, and generally harder to use too much. Because of the larger crystal size, when substituting kosher salt for table salt, it is necessary to use up to two times more kosher salt by volume than specified. This is brand-dependent, however. Morton's kosher salt can be substituted 1:1 for table salt or fine sea salt. Diamond kosher salt should be substituted 2:1 for table salt.

PICKLING SALT

Pickling salt is a pure salt free of additives that might cloud a brine made for pickling. It is available in the canning section of most grocery stores.

ROCK SALT OR ICE CREAM SALT

Rock salt is a nonedible unrefined variety of salt that is used in combination with ice for the freezing of ice cream made in an electric or hand-cranked paddle-style ice cream maker. The salt lowers the temperature of the ice water mixture surrounding the ice cream canister, speeding the freezing process. It is also used as a base for baking potatoes or for oysters on the half shell.

SEA SALT

All sea salt is obtained from the evaporation of seawater. Large flake sea salt, known as **fleur de sel** (literally, "flower of salt"), is produced by gently raking the large salt crystals that form on the surface of sea salt beds before they fall to the bottom. Fleur de sel contains more moisture than other salts, and it has a subtle flavor due to the presence of algae and minerals. However, the flavor of the salt itself is usually overpowered by that of the food it is sprinkled on. Fleur de sel is produced using the heat of the sun and the evaporative power of the wind. Because it is so labor-intensive to make, it is much more expensive than table salt or even fine sea salt. That said, fleur de sel is not meant for cooking. It is a **"finishing salt,"** or a salt sprinkled on foods just before serving to give a delicate crunch and an explosion of salt in the mouth. Use it much like a garnish, on a pan of dark chocolate brownies before they go into the oven, a fried egg, avocado toast, or caramel candies.

Flaky sea salt is slightly different from fleur de sel in that the salt crystals tend to be larger and drier. Sometimes the crystals resemble pyramids, as with Maldon salt. This type of salt is made by reducing seawater in large steel pans until salt crystals form. The crystals are then raked from the brine and dried. Because flaky sea salt is drier than fleur de sel, when you bite down on the crystals, they shatter, then dissolve quickly, giving a burst of intense saltiness. Use flaky sea salt like you would fleur de sel: as a finishing salt rather than a cooking salt.

Sel gris ("gray salt") is made in the same setting as fleur de sel, but it is harvested from the bottom of sea salt beds rather than the top. As a result, sel gris contains more minerals and sediment, which gives the salt a gray hue. Sel gris is finer than fleur de sel but coarser than fine sea salt or table salt. It can be used as a general cooking salt or a finishing salt.

Fine sea salt is a more processed product than any of the other sea salts discussed here. It is made with seawater that has had minerals and any impurities removed. Then the water is boiled down at very high temperatures in a vacuum. The resulting salt crystals are very fine, dry, and white. Fine sea salt can be directly substituted for table salt.

Colored sea salts, like red Hawaiian sea salt or black lava salt, are simply sea salts with natural coloring agents added to them to enhance their color. In the case of red Hawaiian sea salt, red clay (called alaea) is added; black lava salt is colored with activated charcoal. Black lava salt has a slightly smoky flavor, though not to the degree of smoked salt. These salts make stunning finishing salts and come in a variety of granule sizes.

FLAVORED SALTS

Commercial seasoning salts are usually a combination of salts, spices, and sometimes MSG, 1003. Also available are sea salts that have been infused or mixed with various ingredients such as cocoa powder, coffee, truffles, chiles, and herbs. These salts are typically used as finishing salts in applications where their flavors can be detected. You can make your own flavored salts at home by mixing salt with low-moisture ingredients. These include citrus zests and herbs like rosemary and thyme.

To make flavored salts, combine Diamond kosher salt in a food processor with the flavoring desired. For citrus zests, use the finely grated zest of 4 lemons or limes or 2 oranges per 1 cup salt. For herbs, use twice as much salt as fresh chopped herbs (for example, use ½ cup packed chopped herbs and 1 cup salt). For best results, combine the zest or herbs in the food processor with about one-third of the salt and pulse until the flavoring ingredients are finely ground and evenly incorporated throughout the salt. Then add the remaining salt and pulse briefly just to combine. Transfer the flavored salt to a rimmed baking sheet and spread out in a thin layer.

Let the salt air-dry for 24 hours before transferring to an airtight container. Flavored salts keep indefinitely, though they will lose pungency over time.

SEASONED SALT
About ½ cup

Combine in a small bowl:

¼ cup salt
1 tablespoon sugar
1 tablespoon sweet paprika
1 teaspoon ground mace
1 teaspoon celery salt
1 teaspoon grated or ground nutmeg
1 teaspoon garlic powder
1 teaspoon onion powder
1 teaspoon dry mustard

Mix well. Store indefinitely in an airtight container at room temperature.

SMOKED SALTS

Smoked salts are made by smoking salt using any of a number of types of hardwood, such as hickory, apple, or cherry. Use as an ingredient in dry rubs, 587, or sprinkled on cooked meats, fish, vegetables, soups, and even on desserts where a smoky flavor is desired. See Smoking, 1067.

CURING SALTS

See Curing Salts, 936.

TABLE SALT AND IODIZED SALT

Table salt is a finely grained free-flowing type of salt, composed of about 99 percent sodium chloride. Much table salt has added iodine (**iodized salt**), though it is possible to find table salt without added iodine. Iodized salt is recommended for certain regions where the water and soil lack iodine, an essential trace element. Most salt sold at supermarkets is iodized, and the label will say "iodized." Do not use iodized salt in pickling or fermentation. The additives in the salt will cloud the brine and may impart undesirable flavors.

SALT SUBSTITUTES

While there is no true substitute for salt, salt substitutes are available on the market. They are chloride salts in which sodium is replaced by calcium, potassium, or ammonia. Because they contain higher levels of other electrolytes in place of the sodium, they should be used only on the advice of a physician. Salt-free seasoning blends, different from a salt substitute, are a tasty alternative to salt and salt substitutes because they are sodium-free and free of the replacement electrolytes. Fresh lemon juice, chopped fresh herbs, and vinegar all make delicious sodium-free enhancements to food as well.

SASSAFRAS

The leaves and roots of the sassafras tree are used in different ways. The leaves are dried and ground into a fine powder called **filé powder,** which is used both as a thickener and a flavoring in Cajun foods such as gumbo. Filé powder should not be added to stews that will be simmered further because it creates a viscous, ropy texture that is not so thick as it is unappetizing. Add it either at the last second or serve with the food at the table.

Sassafras roots were traditionally used to make root beer until it was discovered that safrole, the compound that gives sassafras its distinctive flavor, is a carcinogen. Now sassafras root may be used in teas, but it has been processed to remove the safrole, rendering it safe for consumption.

SAVORY

There are two types of savory: summer and winter. **Summer savory** (*Satureja hortensis)* is a delicately flavored herb with thyme-like, peppery notes. It is also a common component of herbes de Provence, 995, and is used frequently in Bulgarian cuisine. Fresh summer savory is classic in white bean dishes but is versatile enough to garnish all manner of stews, braises, and ragus. **Winter savory** (*Satureja montana*) is spicier and sharper than summer savory, with smaller, thicker leaves. Use in place of or in combination with thyme. We enjoy combining fresh winter savory in herb garnishes and green sauces with milder herbs, such as fresh basil, parsley, and tarragon. Dried savory may be added toward the end of cooking.

SCALLIONS

See About Onions and Shallots, 254, and Onions as Seasoning, 1009. Note that in this book we use the term "green onion" rather than scallion.

SCHMALTZ

Schmaltz is the Yiddish word for rendered poultry fat. The rendered fat from chickens, ducks, and geese is highly regarded for many cooking applications, especially in kosher households. When wet-rendered, 982, schmaltz is firm, bland, and light in color. Schmaltz from Duck or Goose Confit, 433, will be pale, and infused with the flavor of the herbs, spices, onions, and other aromatics with which it was cooked. When dry-rendered, 982, or skimmed from the flavorful, rich drippings of roasted poultry, schmaltz is likely to be softer, grainier, and darker in color. Most schmaltz, however, is not considered a by-product of another cooking process, but rather an end in itself.

To render large quantities of schmaltz, see Rendering Fats, 982.

To make a smaller amount of schmaltz, cut chicken skin and fat into small pieces and place in a single layer in a skillet with 2 tablespoons water. Gently heat the fat over medium heat until sizzling. When the fat begins to brown, add some chopped onion to the pan, if desired (use about ½ onion per 1 pound chicken skin and fat), and turn down the heat slightly. Continue to cook, turning the chicken skin occasionally, until the skin is deeply browned and crisp and the fat is golden, about 45 minutes. Strain the fat through a fine-mesh sieve. If desired, the browned pieces of chicken skin and onions can be eaten as a side dish or on toast. The mixture is called **gribenes.** For a related process, see Crispy Chicken Skin, 446. Store schmaltz, covered, in the refrigerator.

SEAFOOD, DRIED

Fish and shellfish of all kinds are dried throughout the world, but especially in East and Southeast Asia. The drying process intensifies the briny flavors of the seafood, and the resulting umami-rich ingredients add flavor to dishes without making them taste fishy (much the way anchovies in a ragu or braise do not taste fishy, but rather provide a deep bass note of savoriness). For other forms of dried seafood, see **Shrimp Paste,** 1018, **Bonito,** 956, and **Bottarga,** 956. Also see About Smoked and Preserved Fish, 392. To dry fish into jerky, see Drying Jerky, 947.

Dried scallops are highly esteemed, and available whole from Chinese markets. They may be diced and simmered in soups, broths, and sauces until they have infused the liquid with their flavor. (They are an essential ingredient in the delicious Cantonese condiment **XO sauce.**) Dried scallops can also be simmered until tender and then shredded, diced, or minced and added to noodle dishes, stir-fries, and Congee, 333.

Mildly salty with a fragrant aroma, **dried shrimp** add complexity to many Southeast Asian dishes like Pho Bo, 96, Pad Thai, 303, and Green Papaya Salad, 129. They are also used in Mexican cuisine to flavor soups and stews. Though sometimes sold powdered, always choose whole dried shrimp that look relatively free of desiccated white spots and other blemishes. Store in a sealed container in the refrigerator. Dried shrimp are often toasted to accentuate their flavor and aroma, pounded lightly or ground, and then added to dishes. You can soften larger pieces further by soaking in warm water right after toasting, but we rarely bother.

To toast dried shrimp, add to a dry skillet over medium heat and cook, stirring, until the shrimp are fragrant and have turned a brighter color, about 5 minutes.

There are so many kinds of **dried fish** that we cannot cover them all here. They are found everywhere that fishing is a major source of food, from Russia to Vietnam to Iceland to Japan. They are sometimes eaten as a snack and sometimes used as an ingredient to flavor soups, sauces, condiments, and the like. For example, in Japan, dried anchovies called **niboshi** are used to make a type of Dashi, 78, called niboshi dashi.

Dried squid or cuttlefish is a popular snack in Korea, China, Singapore, and Hawaii. It is often seasoned with salt, sugar, and chiles and has a texture reminiscent of jerky.

SEAWEED

Vegetables from the sea are well loved in cuisines from coastal areas around the world, from Japan and China to Iceland, Ireland, and Hawaii. These are edible forms of red, brown, or green algae. Seaweeds are all salty, and some possess the deep, savory flavor called umami (see Kombu, below). Seaweeds can also taste of fish, of sulfur and iodine, or may have astringent, tea-like notes. Seaweeds are used in a wide variety of ways: in soups and salads, as thickeners, as a wrap for sushi, and as a crunchy garnish or condiment.

Store all dried seaweeds in a cool, dry place, tightly sealed once opened. Seaweed from the refrigerated section of a grocery store should be stored refrigerated. For information about **agar** and **carrageenan,** see Gums and Hydrocolloids, 992.

ARAME

A type of kelp, *arame* comes in thin, dark brown strands. It is excellent reconstituted and served in soups or vegetable dishes. To reconstitute, see Wakame, below.

DULSE

A red algae that appears purple when dried, dulse is a delicious, chewy seaweed that takes on an almost bacon-like flavor when toasted or fried. It is sold in clumps or flakes and benefits from toasting before use. We like to briefly fry larger pieces of dulse in a little oil until crisp and toasted, roughly crush it, and mix it with sesame seeds for topping salads, roasted vegetables, and rice.

KOMBU

This thick, leathery, brown seaweed is also called kelp. Kombu is a key ingredient in Dashi, 78, and a rich source of glutamates. In fact, the savoriness of dashi and kombu inspired scientists to isolate and discover MSG, 1003. The whitish coating on kombu is normal; it should never be washed prior to using, but you can use a kitchen towel to wipe off any dirt or particles. Dried kombu keeps indefinitely in a tightly sealed container.

NORI OR LAVER

Nori are paper-thin sheets of dried seaweed, perhaps most famous for use as a wrapping for sushi rolls, 335. It has a mild, salty flavor and is often sold toasted and seasoned for snacking. In its plain form, it is available toasted or untoasted. Nori can be stored at room temperature in its original packaging or in a zip-top bag. Nori can be chewy unless toasted.

To toast nori, turn on a gas burner to medium heat or an electric burner to medium-high heat. Using tongs or your hands, pass each sheet of nori over the flame or burner, turning it after each pass. Continue to do this until the color of the nori dulls slightly and it starts to buckle, 15 to 30 seconds.

Also look for the condiment **furikake,** which usually consists of toasted nori flakes, along with sesame seeds, and other savory ingredients like *katsuobushi*, dehydrated egg, and occasionally purple *shiso* flakes. *Furikake* is our ideal topping for a simple bowl of short-grain rice.

SPIRULINA

Spirulina is a type of cyanobacteria, or blue-green algae. Once harvested from inland lakes and dried into cakes by the Aztecs (as well as the Kanembu tribe of Chad), spirulina is now sold as a dietary supplement (it is high in protein, amino acids, and several minerals). Spirulina powder is ideal for a Green Smoothie, 12, but its taste—which is a bit stronger and more "pondy" than other marine algae—leaves much to be desired. Use in small amounts, and always include other assertive ingredients to mask its flavor. ➤ Spirulina should not be consumed by young children, pregnant women, those with an immune deficiency, or anyone taking drugs that slow clotting or suppress the immune system.

WAKAME

Wakame is sold dried and packaged, sometimes labeled *ito wakame*. It may be reconstituted in miso soups or plain water, then used to make salads.

To reconstitute wakame, soak in tepid water for 20 minutes. If the stems are present, tear off and discard.

SESAME SEEDS

Sesame seeds are a favorite topping for breads, cookies, and vegetables and are available in three types: brown, white, or black. Any of these may be available with their outer coating, or hull, removed or intact. Since this seed coat is slightly bitter, we prefer using **hulled** sesame seeds. The nutty flavor of sesame seeds is strongest when they are lightly toasted. They may be ground into an oily butter called **tahini,** 1027—an essential ingredient in Middle Eastern cuisines. **Sesame oil,** 1007, is desirable in salads, sauces, and as a condiment. Of course, the toasted seeds themselves are a perfect garnish for many dishes (as well as sesame mixtures like furikake, 1016). **Benne seeds,** an early heirloom variety brought to the United States by enslaved West Africans, are making a slow but sure comeback and can now be ordered online.

To toast sesame seeds, spread them on a rimmed baking sheet and place in a 350°F oven until lightly browned and fragrant, 7 to 10 minutes.

SHALLOTS

See Onions and Shallots, 254, and Onions as Seasoning, 1009.

SHICHIMI TOGARASHI

The name of this Japanese spice blend means "seven flavor chile pepper." Coarsely ground dried red chiles are mixed with ground *sansho* pepper, 1018, dried orange or yuzu peel, sesame and/or poppy seeds, hemp seeds, nori flakes, and ground ginger to create a seasoning mixture for flavoring noodle dishes, soups, and rice.

SHISO (PERILLA)

Shiso is an herb related to mint and basil that has leaves that look somewhat like those of stinging nettle, with a heart shape and serrated edges. Shiso is commonly used in Japanese and Korean cooking. It has a somewhat minty flavor, with hints of cinnamon, lemon, and anise. Both purple *shiso* (also called red *shiso* or "beefsteak plant") and green *shiso* can be found fresh at Asian grocery stores, and it is easy to grow in the home garden. Purple *shiso* is notably used in the production of pickled plums (*umeboshi*), and *umezu*, 1031, which gives the ginger pickle Beni Shōga, 930, its pinkish-purple color. The leaves are also used to wrap foods, added to Korean stews, tempura-fried, and used in some varieties of furikake, 1016.

SHORTENING

Vegetable shortenings owe their name to their ability to "shorten" gluten strands in baked goods, creating a flaky crust or tender texture. At least historically speaking, "shortening" was also a term for lard, though it is rarely referred to in that way in the modern kitchen. Shortenings are white or yellow and are tasteless or butter-flavored. Frequently they have a polyunsaturated-oil base—soybean, corn, cottonseed, or peanut—that is refined, deodorized, and hydrogenated. Hydrogenation adds hydrogen atoms to the unsaturated fatty acid chains in vegetable oils, converting them to saturated fats that are solid at room temperature. Hydrogenation also creates trans fatty acids, which have come under great scrutiny because of the health risks they pose. As a result, they have largely been phased out of our food supply. To create solid vegetable fats without trans fatty acids, shortenings are now made by a process called interesterification. The process is chemically complex, but in short, it uses a catalyst or enzyme to move fatty acids from one triglyceride to another, resulting in solid vegetable fats with a very low proportion of trans fats.

Sometimes solid shortening has some added animal fats or saturated vegetable fats such as coconut oil or palm oil. They may also contain emulsifiers, yellow coloring, and butter flavor. These and the nitrogen incorporated into them make these shortenings appropriate for baking. The nitrogen provides tiny bubbles that gain loft when creamed with sugar when the dough or batter is mixed. These bubbles expand further when the dough is leavened, 997, and again when the heat of the oven evaporates the moisture in the dough. The result is greater volume and a softer, spongier texture in cakes, quick breads, and muffins.

In pastries, shortening provides a flakier result than butter, as shortening contains no water, while butter contains around 15 percent. Similarly, because there is no water in shortening, it makes cookies softer, as water is necessary for forming gluten (which is what gives cookies more chew). Most shortening has a higher melting point than butter, which means some baked goods, like cookies, will be taller with less spread if shortening is used. This is because the other ingredients in the dough have more time to set before the shortening starts to melt (note that coconut- and palm oil–based shortenings have a lower melting point than Crisco; see the chart on 981). Shortening also makes frostings that stand up well over time, even when subjected to less than ideal conditions like heat and humidity.

One notable drawback to shortening is that it either has no flavor at all or an artificial butter flavor. While shortening has many technical advantages that are particularly appealing to processed food manufacturers, butter is still the preferred baking fat for many home cooks who prize a "homemade" flavor in their baked goods.

Vegetable shortening may be stored covered at room temperature. To measure the volume of solid shortening, see Measuring Fats, 980. For information on **margarine,** see 1000.

To substitute solid shortening for butter, you can replace cup or volume measure for measure, but you should add a little water to compensate for the water present in butter. To substitute shortening for 1 cup (2 sticks) butter, use 1 cup shortening plus 2 tablespoons water; to substitute shortening for ½ cup (1 stick) butter, use ½ cup shortening plus 1 tablespoon water; and so on. Never substitute shortening for butter in candy or fudge recipes. ➤ If substituting by weight, use 20 percent less shortening than butter (multiply the weight of the butter by 0.8). Then multiply the weight of the butter by 0.15 to find the weight of the extra water or other liquid (such as milk or buttermilk) that should be added to the recipe to compensate for the water content of the butter.

SHRIMP PASTE

Shrimp paste is an ingredient used throughout Southeast Asia, including southeast China. There are various names for shrimp paste: In Thailand it is called *kapi*; in Indonesia it is *terasi;* in Malaysia it is *belacan;* in the Philippines it is *bagoong*; in China it is *hom ha;* and in Vietnam it is *mam tom*. They are all slightly different, but the concept is the same: Tiny shrimp, usually krill, are salted, fermented, ground, and dried to various degrees. Some shrimp pastes, such as terasi and belacan, are so dry that they are sold in bricks, and the paste has to be cut away from the brick with a knife. Others, such as kapi, are sold in tubs and are soft enough to be scooped out with a spoon but are by no means loose or watery in consistency. Some bagoong is chunky, and the whole shrimp are visible in the mixture, while others are more finely ground. Mam tom and hom ha are wet, purplish pastes.

In nearly all cases, shrimp paste is not eaten on its own, but rather mixed into sauces, curries, dips, and a wide variety of cooked dishes. Functionally, it is not so different from fish sauce or minced anchovies. It helps create complexity in dishes by contributing a salty, umami-rich funkiness that is not necessarily identifiable to the palate as shrimp, but that certainly adds to the overall depth of flavor. Shrimp paste is incredibly pungent, both in smell and flavor, so a little goes a long way. The dry varieties of shrimp paste are usually roasted before using.

To roast shrimp paste, remove the amount from the tub or block that is needed for the recipe and wrap it in foil. Heat a dry skillet over medium heat. Place the foil packet in the skillet and cook until the shrimp paste has browned slightly and is crumbly and soft, about 1 minute per side. Alternatively, fry the shrimp paste in a little oil just until slightly browned.

SICHUAN PEPPERCORNS

Sometimes called **prickly ash,** these dried reddish-brown berries are not related to black peppercorns or chile peppers, but rather to citrus. Along with chiles, these peppercorns give many Sichuan dishes their characteristically bold, complex flavor. When the berries are eaten fresh, they have an overwhelmingly bright, citrusy, buzzy taste that numbs your tongue and makes your mouth water uncontrollably for several minutes.

When dried Sichuan peppercorns open up, the seed inside is released, leaving the outer husk (which contains most of the flavor). Some may have the seed or stem still attached (if present, there is no need to sort or trim them). Even when dried, the berries have a tangy, mentholated, tingly quality. Though it can be strong, we think this quality helps accentuate other flavors in a dish.

Red Sichuan peppercorns are the most common to find, but **green Sichuan peppercorns** can be found from online retailers. They have a pinier, fresher flavor and are less floral. A close relative is known in Japan as **sansho pepper.** Best known for its use in *shichimi togarashi*, 1017, *sansho* pepper does not pack the buzzy wallop of red Sichuan pepper.

For dishes that use Sichuan peppercorns, see Mapo Dofu, 286, Salt-and-Pepper Shrimp or Squid, 363, Spicy Sichuan Hot Pot, 97, Dan Dan Noodles, 302, Sesame Noodles, 302, and Spicy Chinese Chile Crisp, 572.

SOFRITO

This mixture is a basic component of countless dishes in several cuisines. In European cuisines, sofrito (in Spanish, but **soffritto** in Italian, **sofregit** in Catalan, and mirepoix, 1002, in French) refers to a mixture of aromatic ingredients—onions, garlic, celery, carrot, herbs, usually tomato, and sometimes pancetta or ham—cooked down at the beginning of a recipe. Depending on the recipe, a sofrito can be sweated or softened briefly for a lighter, aromatic note; other times, the sofrito may be cooked until caramelized and well browned to add depth to sauces and braises. Another Italian name for this mixture, **battuto,** may also refer to a soffrito-like mixture that has been cooked separately and ahead of time in pork fat. This thickened, quasi-preserved paste can then be stored in the refrigerator in a sealed container for at least 1 week and used as convenient seasoning for simmered dishes.

In the Caribbean and South America, sofrito often includes lard, ham, tomatoes, mild peppers, cilantro or culantro, 974, and spices like cumin, oregano, and annatto. (Celery and carrots are not typically used.) Carribean sofrito may be made fresh for an individual recipe, or cooked in batches with lard, then stored for adding to rice dishes, braises and stews, beans, and soups.

As with mirepoix, we integrate the making of sofrito in our recipes rather than calling for a standard mixture; see specific recipes for ingredient amounts and instructions.

SORGHUM

Sorghum is a versatile family of large grasses whose stalks resemble corn. White or tan grain sorghum can be cooked like other grains (see About Sorghum and Milo, 337), or milled into flour, 987. Other varieties are good for beer making and feedstock.

Sweet sorghum (*Sorghum saccharatum*) is used to produce **sorghum syrup,** sometimes called sorghum molasses, a liquid sweetener made by juicing the grass and boiling it, traditionally over a wood fire. It is made in the South and Midwest on a small scale and can vary quite a bit from farm to farm. Some sorghum syrups are very dark and resemble molasses. Others are much lighter, with an amber color and milder flavor. Sorghum syrup is less viscous and more tart in flavor than sugarcane molasses. Sorghum also contains none of the earthy bitterness of molasses. Sorghum can be substituted for sugar as for molasses, 1002, or it can be substituted 1:1 for molasses. We use sorghum syrup on pancakes and waffles, ice cream, and biscuits. Substitute it for corn syrup in Pecan Pie, 667, for a richer flavor.

SORREL

The elongated leaves of the sorrel plant are high in oxalic acid and taste quite sour. Sorrel is related to rhubarb and buckwheat. **Broad leaf sorrel** (also called common sorrel) has long, arrowhead-like leaves; the striking **red sorrel** (or sheep sorrel) has coarser leaves with bloodred veins; and **French sorrel** has smaller, milder leaves. Sorrel is used to make tart, bright green soups and sauces. It can be added to salads for a burst of tartness or used as a garnish. In Europe, especially England, sorrel was commonly pounded with vinegar and sugar into a sauce to accompany roasted meats. Sorrel's acidity makes it a natural partner to rich foods, but its fresh, green flavor goes well with mild foods like eggs and fish. Upon cooking, sorrel turns an olive drab color. To help preserve its vibrant green hue, briefly blanch sorrel in boiling water, then shock it in ice water. Only use nonreactive cookware when preparing sorrel, as uncoated aluminum or iron will negatively affect its flavor and color. **Wood sorrel,** also called **oxalis** or **sour grass,** is not related to true sorrel, but it is high in oxalic acid, giving it a similar flavor. It is most commonly used as a garnish or an addition to salads.

SOUR CREAM

See Cream, 974.

SOY MILK AND TOFU

Soy milk is the white, milky liquid made from blending soaked soybeans with water and straining out the solids. Long consumed in China, soy milk has become something of a staple in Western supermarkets, especially for those who are lactose intolerant or choose not to consume dairy products. Tofu is equally ubiquitous in Asian cuisines and has been similarly adopted as a vegetable protein by those with dietary restrictions or ethical concerns. Here, we discuss how to make both of these foods together, since making tofu begins with making a batch of soy milk.

For a discussion of different types of tofu and how to press, crumble, and cook it, see About Tofu, Tempeh, and Other Plant-Based Proteins, 284.

For more alternatives to dairy milk, see About Nut and Seed Milks, 1005.

SOY MILK

About 9 cups

The directions given below are best for making tofu. To make soy milk destined for drinking or using on cereal, you need to remove more of the beany flavors: After soaking the beans, drain them and bring **8 cups water** to a boil in a large pot. Add the beans; when the pot returns to a boil, reduce the heat and simmer for 4 minutes. Drain the beans in a colander and proceed to blend, simmer, and strain them as directed below.

Place in a medium bowl:

8 ounces dried soybeans (about 1¼ cups)

Add enough water to cover the beans by 3 inches and soak for 12 hours.

Drain the beans and puree in a blender until completely smooth with:

3 cups water

Pour into a large pot, being sure to scrape any bean mixture out of the bottom of the blender. Add:

6 cups hot water

Bring to a boil over medium-high heat, stirring gently with a wooden spoon to avoid scorching. When foam rises, remove the pot from the heat. Have ready a large colander lined with a nut milk bag or a generous square of thin cotton muslin. Set the lined colander over a large bowl and pour the soy mixture in gradually. Tighten the cloth or bag around the pulp—the *okara*—and press out as much milk as possible with the back of the spoon. When cool enough to handle, wring it out with your hands to extract all the liquid. Open the cloth, spread the pulp out in the cloth, and sprinkle over it:

¾ cup warm water

Press and wring out the pulp one more time and set aside or discard (you may add the nutritious pulp to baked goods or veggie burgers). Clean out the large pot, pour the milk back into it, and bring to a simmer, stirring to prevent sticking. Reduce the heat to medium-low and cook for an additional 10 minutes (this will destroy the antinutrient trypsin). If you plan to make tofu, proceed as directed below. If not, cool the milk and refrigerate before serving.

TOFU OR SOYBEAN CURD

One 1¼-pound block

Our favored coagulant to use for making tofu is **nigari,** the residue left when the sodium is extracted from seawater and evaporated (it contains magnesium chloride, magnesium sulfate, and other trace elements). *Nigari* is readily available from online retailers in liquid and crystal form. Molds specifically designed for making tofu can also be found online. To improvise a mold, have ready two 1-quart capacity food-safe plastic containers of the type that nest. Perforate the bottom and lower portion of one container with holes about ¼ inch in diameter as though on a 1-inch grid. The other container may be partly filled with water to act as a weight (half full, it will weigh 1 pound).

Prepare:

Soy Milk, above

When the milk has finished simmering, remove from the heat and let cool for 5 minutes. To make a coagulant, mix together in a small bowl until dissolved:

1 cup water

1½ teaspoons nigari, Epsom salt (magnesium sulfate), or gypsum (calcium sulfate)

(If using gypsum, you will need to restir the mixture right before each addition to the soy milk.) Gently stir one-third of the coagulant solution into the hot soy milk. Sprinkle another one-third of the coagulant over the surface of the milk, cover the pot, and let it sit for 3 minutes. Sprinkle the remaining solution over the milk and gently stir the surface. Cover for 3 minutes if using *nigari*, or 6 minutes if using Epsom salts or gypsum. If curds do not form during this period, mix together in a small bowl:

(¼ cup water)

(½ teaspoon additional nigari, Epsom salt, or gypsum)

Stir this into the soy milk and let sit for an additional 5 minutes. Line the tofu mold (the container with the holes) with a generous square of moist, thin muslin cloth and place the container in the sink. Gradually ladle the soy curd mixture into the mold and fold the ends of the cloth over the top. Place the top of the mold over the curd and place a 1-pound weight over it for medium-firm tofu, or a 3-pound weight for firm tofu. Let the curds compress for 20 minutes or until the whey is no longer expressed. Very gently unwrap the curd. Tofu is highly perishable; store it refrigerated in water for only a few days.

To cook tofu, see About Tofu, Tempeh, and Other Plant-Based Proteins, 284.

SOY SAUCE

Soy sauce is a naturally fermented product made in several steps and aged up to 2 years. Soaked and steamed soybeans and a lightly ground grain, usually wheat bran or roasted wheat, are mixed with a type of koji, 997, which contains *Aspergillus* cultures, as well as *Lactobacillus* bacteria and *Saccharomyces* yeast. Brine is then added to the fermenting mixture and the mash is brewed. When the producer determines that it is ready, the soy sauce is pressed, filtered, pasteurized, and bottled.

Soy sauce was invented in China and spread to Japan, Korea, and Southeast Asia, where it is now an integral seasoning. When you look at soy sauce in the context of the diverse arsenal of umami-rich ingredients used in Asian cuisines you can see its relationship to ingredients like fish sauce, 984, Indonesian *kecap*, and Maggi seasoning, 984. All are rich in glutamates and add complex savory flavors to food.

In fact, some brands of soy sauce are chemically produced much like Maggi seasoning: The defatted soy meal left over from producing soy oil is hydrolyzed and converted to amino acids, which gives it a savory flavor. Much of this product is sold as soy sauce, but some brands are labeled as **liquid aminos.** The complex flavor of naturally fermented soy sauce is considered vastly superior to these chemically produced, one-note soy products.

Chinese soy sauce tends to be made of more soy than wheat. In Chinese cooking both **light** and **dark soy sauces** are used. The latter are aged longer and toward the end of the processing are mixed with molasses, which gives them a dark caramel hue. Perhaps counterintuitively, dark soy sauce is less salty than light soy sauce. Light soy sauce tends to be thinner and saltier than dark and is made from the first pressing of fermented soybeans. It is the most commonly used type of Chinese soy sauce. ➤ Light soy sauce is not the same thing as reduced-sodium soy sauce.

As a rule, Japanese **shoyu** contains more wheat and is thus a little sweeter and less salty. The predominant brands of Japanese soy sauce in our grocery stores are dark shoyu, or *koikuchi shoyu*. Dark *shoyu* can be substituted for Chinese light soy sauce. Light Japanese soy, or *usukuchi*, is saltier than dark and has a slightly sweet flavor. **Tamari** is made with little to no wheat and is darker and more full-bodied than dark *shoyu*. *Shiro* or **white soy sauce** is made from a higher proportion of wheat than soybeans and has a lighter color and flavor. It is excellent used on its own as a dipping sauce. **Ponzu sauce** is a Japanese condiment made from soy sauce, some citrus juice (often yuzu, 183), rice vinegar, mirin, and the umami-rich ingredients used to make Dashi, 78: *katsuobushi*, and kombu. It is a fantastic accompaniment to pan-seared fish, as well as sashimi.

Broadly speaking, Korean soy sauces can be categorized into light or dark varieties, and they are very similar to the Japanese *koikuchi* and *usukuchi*. Another type of traditional soy sauce unique to Korean cooking is **soup soy sauce,** called *guk-ganjang*, which is made with the flavorful brine left from producing *doenjang*, 1002. It is lighter, saltier, and more flavorful than *usukuchi* and other light soy sauces. As the name suggests, it is primarily used to season soups.

Kecap manis is an Indonesian palm sugar–sweetened variety of soy sauce. Spices and aromatic ingredients like star anise, galangal, and garlic are added to the fermented soybean mash before it is boiled. It is integral to many Indonesian dishes.

SPICES

Seeds, beans, barks, fruits, roots, buds, berries, flower stigmas—flavorful types of all of these may be used whole or ground as a spice. What unites this motley group of ingredients? They must be very flavorful, are often used in small quantities, and can be very expensive. For information on specific spices, see individual entries.

There has been lively discussion over the relative merits of spices from different places, like Spanish versus Hungarian paprika, and Mexican versus Madagascar vanilla beans. We embrace these differences and are wary of proclaiming one variety of a spice "better" than another. Our only recommendation is to seek out high-quality spices and try different varieties.

When at all possible, opt to ➤ buy whole spices rather than ground, as ground spices lose their complex flavors and aromas more quickly. Spice grinders or blade-type coffee grinders are inexpensive tools, and occasionally replenishing your supply of a freshly ground spice will enable you to make more delicious food. What's more, ➤ whole spices bought in bulk quantities tend to be dramatically cheaper than those purchased in the tiny glass jars in the spice section of the supermarket. Look online for spice suppliers, but also check out your local Asian, Mexican, and Indian grocery stores for a wide selection of affordable whole spices.

If you must purchase ground spices, use or replace them at least every year if not every 6 months, as they lose strength rapidly. Always check sell-by dates, and date your own jars when you open and/or fill them. Store spices in tightly covered containers made of glass, metal, or tin and in as dark and cool an area as your kitchen offers. But have them handy! Their frequent use will elevate the flavor of many a dish to a memorable height.

There are lots of different ways to use spices depending on the effect you are going for. Use them ground if you want full flavor evenly dispersed throughout the dish. Use whole spices to subtly infuse soups, stews, and broths. Toasting spices brings out different flavor notes: Coriander has a more citrusy flavor when toasted; cumin becomes almost smoky and earthy. Take a cue from Indian cooks and temper whole spices like cumin, coriander, mustard seeds, and curry leaves in warm oil or ghee (see below) before adding them to dishes or using them as a last-minute garnish, as in Dal Tadka, 218. The spices become toasted and aromatic, and they infuse the oil with flavor, giving the whole dish richness and complexity and providing a pleasing textural contrast when you bite into the spices.

Some spices, like turmeric and paprika, are almost always used ground. These spices, too, can benefit from light tempering. However, you must be much more careful than with whole spices as ground spices burn quickly. Usually, a few seconds of sizzling in moderately hot oil is enough to bring out their flavor and infuse the oil.

To temper or fry spices, heat a little vegetable oil or Ghee, 960, in a skillet over medium heat. When the oil is hot, add whole spices such as cumin, coriander, mustard seeds, fenugreek, fennel seeds, and small dried chiles. Stir them to coat with the oil and let them sizzle until fragrant and toasted. Some spices, such as mustard seeds, pop when they are well toasted. Others, like cumin and coriander, brown visibly. Depending on the spices you wish to temper, some should be added before others. Always add chiles and curry leaves after other spices have had a chance to toast nearly to doneness. Add ground spices last, allowing them to cook for only a few seconds or just long enough to become dispersed in the oil.

To toast spices, add them in a thin layer to a dry skillet and place over medium heat, shaking the pan occasionally, until they release an intense aroma and brown slightly. Always let toasted spices cool before grinding them.

You can grind spices to different degrees of fineness for different effects. Coarsely ground spices provide nearly as much flavor as a fine powder, but they add bursts of more intense flavor when you bite into them. To coarsely grind spices, use a mortar and pestle rather than a spice grinder. We recommend an unpolished granite specimen of moderate to large size, with a rough granite or wooden pestle. Polished mortar surfaces do not efficiently grind ingredients, which tend to bounce or slide around in them. Avoid very small mortars (though pretty, they are almost useless, as it is impossible to grind things in them without the food bouncing out).

➤ If cooking in very large batches, or multiplying recipes, spice to taste rather than to measure, as some spices, such as cayenne pepper, do not scale up well and can easily overwhelm the food. In our recipes, we suggest amounts considered pleasurable by the average person. You may wish to use more or less than we indicate depending on your preferences and tolerance for spice.

SPROUTS

Sprouts are seeds that have been prompted to germinate but not allowed to mature. Most sprouts have only two leaves. Sprouts are relatively easy to find at grocery stores, but they are incredibly easy and affordable to grow at home. Sprouting allows you to have fresh garden greens growing in your kitchen all year long. Sprouts are nutritious, affordable, and succulent, providing a fresh crunch to all kinds of dishes. The sprouting action breaks down starches and proteins in the seed, making them easier to digest. Perhaps the best reason to try your hand at sprouting is that you can ensure the sprouts were properly handled and that no cross-contamination has taken place. Sprouts are notoriously prone to contamination, so care should be taken to handle them carefully and according to the directions given here.

Sprouting is a very simple procedure: You start with dormant seeds, add water, and they are brought to life by the water they absorb. (For the process, see Sprouted Seeds, below.) The yields are astonishing. ➤ Seeds yield between two and eight times their original weight in sprouts. Beans such as lentils, peas, garbanzos, and adzuki; larger seeds like almond, pumpkin, hulled sunflower, and peanut; and grains such as wheat, rye, oats, barley, Kamut, and spelt yield about two times their dry seed weight in sprouts. The one exception is mung beans, which can grow three to four times their original weight. Small seeds vary; brassica seeds (broccoli, radish, mustard, cabbage) will grow between four and five times their weight. Leafy sprout seeds such as alfalfa and clover can grow as much as eight times their original weight—2 heaping tablespoons will fill a quart-sized sprouting device in 5 to 6 days.

SPROUTED SEEDS

About ½ pound sprouts

Avoid potato and tomato seeds, which, when sprouting, are poisonous, and fava, lima, and kidney beans, which are extremely toxic raw. Use or buy seeds, preferably organically grown, that have not been chemically pretreated for agricultural purposes. Remove any damaged or moldy seeds.

If you cannot rinse and drain the sprouts at least twice daily, it is beneficial to purchase a sprouting device. Our favorite commercial sprouter is a 1-quart plastic container, engineered to maximize air circulation and regulate moisture. A wide-mouthed 1-quart jar with a mesh cover made from nylon or cheesecloth or commercial screw-on strainer lid is also quite effective.

Place in a 1-quart sprouting device or 1-quart wide-mouthed jar one of the following:

2 tablespoons very small seeds, such as alfalfa, clover, or leafy sprout blend

3 tablespoons small to medium seeds, such as broccoli, other brassica, or fenugreek

4 tablespoons medium to large allium seeds, such as onion, garlic chive, or leek

½ cup beans, grains, or large seeds

Rinse by swirling the seeds in cold water, drain, then add:

Twice as much cool water as seed

Too much water is fine because the seeds will absorb only what they can. Soak for 8 to 12 hours. Some seeds sprout better if soaked for less time—for example, hulled sunflower and pumpkin seeds sprout better when soaked for 1 to 2 hours.

Next morning, make sure the lid of the sprouting device is securely closed. If using a jar, cover the top with nylon mesh or cheesecloth attached to the jar by screwing the ring over the cloth or nylon or securing it with a rubber band, or screw on the straining lid. Drain, then rinse thoroughly once or twice with cool water. Drain all the water by shaking and spinning the jar or sprouting device vigorously. If using a jar, shake the seeds to spread over a larger area on the glass and store the jar on its side, propping it up at a slight angle so the screen side is facing down, to allow excess water to drain out while also allowing air circulation. Rinse the sprouts two or three times daily with cool water and drain them thoroughly after every rinse. Keep the sprouts out of direct sunlight, which will "cook" them and cause them to spoil.

Most sprouts develop in 3 to 5 days, and in some cases within 36 hours. Mung beans and soybeans may take up to 8 days. Taste them at every rinse-and-drain session to decide when you most enjoy the flavor. Typically, the smaller they are, the more tender. The sprouts will turn into plants eventually—a lentil, pea, or garbanzo sprout will produce a main stem, in addition to the sprout (taproot) after several more days.

If you wish to remove the hulls, stir the sprouts in a bowl of cold water until the husks rise. Skim them off and drain the sprouts thoroughly. You may serve at once, or leave to drain for a few hours and refrigerate in a zip-top bag or container with a paper towel in the bottom. Some sprouts will keep for several weeks in the refrigerator, but we recommend eating them within 5 days for the best flavor.

SPROUTED MICROGREENS

The main difference between sprouts and microgreens is that microgreens are planted in soil, and the greens are cut at soil level before eating. Certain seeds, such as cress, brown mustard, arugula, flax, and chia form a mucilaginous gel-like sack when they come in contact with water. They cannot be sprouted in the conventional method detailed above.

To grow microgreens, thoroughly moisten a planting medium—anything that can retain moisture is acceptable—soil, vermiculite, fabric, or microgreen-specific medium—and scatter the seeds in a thin layer on top. Keep the medium and seeds moist by watering regularly for 7 to 14 days. When sprouted, leave the sprouts on the germinating surface. Keep them moist and exposed to light until the two small leaves are green and about ⅛ inch long. Harvest by cutting the stems just above the planting medium, rinse, pat dry, and serve. Microgreens are not only delicious, but a beautiful garnish for all kinds of dishes. They store poorly once harvested. They can be refrigerated in a zip-top bag or container when dry to the touch, but they will wilt quickly.

STAR ANISE

Star anise (*Illicium verum*), imported from China, comes from a tree that belongs to the magnolia family. It is not related to European anise, 953, though it contains the same essential oil, anethole. The striking, eight-pointed pods have a more intense flavor and higher essential oil content than aniseed, and as a result they are used as a licorice flavoring more often. In China, star anise is often used whole in meat and poultry dishes. When the seeds are removed and ground, it is also one of the components of Five-Spice Powder, 590. It is also added to the Vietnamese beef soup Pho Bo, 96, and is widely used in India in the seasoning blends called masalas, as well as in chai, rice dishes, curries, and stews.

STARCHES

The word "starch" has two different but related meanings. In cooking, when we refer to starches, we are talking about powdered ingredients used to thicken foods, such as potato starch and cornstarch. In a molecular context, however, a starch is a polysaccharide. Polysaccharides are carbohydrates composed of many sugar molecules bound together. This distinction may seem unimportant, but we will be using the word "starch" freely in the following paragraphs, both in the discussion of starches in cooking and on the molecular scale.

Before cooking with starches, it is helpful to know a little about how they work on a molecular level. All naturally occurring starches, whether from a grain, root, or tuber, contain a mix of two polysaccharides: a long straight-chain starch called **amylose** and a short branched-chain starch called **amylopectin.** A starch's characteristics and how it reacts in cooking vary according to the proportions of these two polysaccharides. Luckily, all the grain starches share the same characteristics, and all the root starches share the same characteristics. Potato starch, which comes from a tuber, not a root, has characteristics somewhere in between the grain and root starches.

Grain starches, such as flours ground from wheat, corn, or oats, contain a relatively high amount (about 26 percent) of amylose. They are clear when hot but cloudy when cold. The mixtures they thicken set up enough to slice with a knife, but they become spongy and leak watery fluid if frozen and thawed. Sauces made with flour are opaque hot or cold because flour contains things other than pure starch.

Root starches, such as tapioca and arrowroot, contain a higher ratio of amylopectin to amylose than grain starches. **Waxy starches** from corn or rice contain up to 99 percent amylopectin. Root and waxy starches are crystal clear hot or cold, and are thickest when hot, at their jell temperature. They thin a little when cooled, although they set up in a thick, clear, glossy coating that may not be firm enough to cut.

What all this means in a cooking context is that because amylose is much longer than amylopectin, it bumps into more molecules, slowing them down. Because amylopectin is short, it is less likely to run into and bind up with other molecules. Therefore, when using a starch higher in amylopectin (waxy starches and root starches), more of the starch must be used to thicken the liquid than if you were using an amylose-based starch (grain starches). That said, there is no point in adding more starch than absolutely necessary in a recipe, as all starches dull the flavors of food somewhat.

HOW STARCH WORKS

As starch solutions are heated, starch granules soak up liquid, swell to many times their original size, begin to leak starch molecules, and finally burst. The ideal thickening state—in other words, the point to which starch-thickened mixtures should be cooked—is when the starch molecules have swollen and start to leak amylose and amylopectin. If the swollen starch granules pop, the mixture starts to thin out because the large starch granules become tiny and thus float through the matrix of amylose and amylopectin molecules more easily without becoming trapped. For grain starches this swollen-but-unpopped sweet spot occurs around 190°F and continues to the boiling point. With root starches, thickening begins at 140° to 160°F.

Since the swollen granules are integral to the starch's ability to thicken, excessive stirring can thin a starch-thickened mixture by rupturing these granules. A few tips for working with starches:

➤ Starch needs to be dispersed using a method that prevents clumping and allows the starch molecules to hydrate uniformly before the heat causes them to swell. This can be accomplished by coating the starch molecules in fat by making a roux, 542, or beurre manié, 544. Another option is to make a **slurry** by thoroughly mixing the starch with a small amount of the liquid to be thickened and then gradually whisking it in.

➤ Starch-thickened mixtures continue to thicken as they cool, so the mixture should be a little thinner than desired while it is still very hot.

➤ Root starches in particular are hampered by acidity, but grain starches can withstand greater acidity. This is why, for instance, the filling for our Lemon Meringue Pie, 681, is thickened with cornstarch.

➤ Stirring a mixture after the starch has completely cooled and set will thin it out.

➤ Any starch-thickened mixture containing eggs should be brought to a full boil, stirring constantly. The high temperature destroys alpha-amylase, an enzyme present in eggs that breaks down amylose molecules, turning apparently thickened mixtures to soup overnight. Thus, ➤ do not try to thicken a mixture that contains eggs with a root or waxy starch, because these are sensitive to boiling, which means that solving the amylase problem will only create a new one by hindering the thickening powers of the starch.

ARROWROOT

A popular thickener for clear glazes and gluten-free sauces, arrowroot produces a relatively clear, glossy gel and provides a silky texture. It gels at a lower temperature than many starches, but arrowroot-thickened mixtures thin out if boiled or overheated, or when cooled and reheated.

To thicken 1 cup liquid with arrowroot, make a slurry of 1 tablespoon arrowroot to 2 tablespoons cold water, then whisk the slurry into the sauce and heat until thickened. ➤ Do not use arrowroot to thicken dairy-based mixtures, as it will result in a slimy texture.

CORNSTARCH

A starch extracted from the endosperm of corn, this is a valuable, versatile thickener. It is especially useful for mixtures that are not roux-based. Cornstarch is gluten-free and can be added in small increments as needed until the desired consistency is reached. Cornstarch must be dispersed in a slurry with water before it is added to liquids. Take care not to use more cornstarch than is needed, as it can give foods an unpleasantly gummy texture.

To thicken 1 cup liquid with cornstarch, whisk 1 teaspoon cornstarch into 2 tablespoons cold water, then whisk it gradually into the liquid. The liquid must be brought to a boil to thicken. In some dessert recipes such as Old-Fashioned Chocolate Pudding, 817, cornstarch is whisked into the sugar used in the recipe before the cold liquid is gradually added. Then the mixture is brought to a simmer to thicken. Do not simmer or boil a cornstarch-thickened mixture more than necessary, as prolonged boiling will cause the mixture to thin. Because cornstarch contains a relatively large amount of amylose, less is needed to thicken liquids. Cornstarch is also more resilient than root-based starches in the presence of acidity.

▲ Above 5,000 feet, cornstarch needs to cook longer before it thickens.

POTATO STARCH

Potato starch (not to be confused with potato flour) is a tuber starch, extracted from the flesh of white potatoes. It creates a clear but thin gel and has a less gummy texture than cornstarch. It should not be boiled or cooked for any longer than is absolutely necessary to get it to thicken, as it will break down. To thicken with potato starch, use as for cornstarch, above.

SWEET OR GLUTINOUS RICE FLOUR

Also known as *mochiko* or waxy rice flour, this thickener is used in making sauces, confections, and Asian desserts, including Japanese *mochi* and the Chinese rice cake *nian gao*. It is not a pure starch, but rather ground glutinous rice. Its remarkable stabilizing powers prevent the separation of frozen gravies and sauces when reheated, and it is also much less likely to lump. Do not confuse it with regular rice flour, 986. Sweet rice flour can be used to make a roux by adding it directly to the oil or melted butter. Substitute it 1:1 for all-purpose flour.

TAPIOCA AND SAGO

Tapioca is a starch from the root of the yuca plant, 284 (also called cassava or manioc); it is most familiar in its pearl form. Sago comes from the stems of some tropical palms. Tapioca pearls come in many sizes, from tiny granulated tapioca to very large pearls. Large, dark brown (sometimes sold as "black tapioca") pearls are also called *boba* and are used to make bubble tea, a textural sensation of plump, jelly-like tapioca in a sweetened tea.

Sago and pearl tapioca must both be soaked before use. ➤ Pearl tapioca loses its thickening capacity when stored for a prolonged period. There is no way to know the condition until it's soaked or cooked. Soak ¼ cup of the pearls in ½ cup water or milk; the liquid should be completely absorbed—if it isn't, the pearls are too old to use. We recommended soaking tapioca pearls for at least 1 hour before cooking, although an overnight soak is optimal. If you do presoak, you may need to reduce the amount of liquid in any recipes that do not instruct you to soak the pearls. Start with ½ cup less liquid than called for.

Quick-cooking tapioca is precooked tapioca that comes in tiny granules. It is used to make tapioca pudding, 828–29, and thicken fruit pies. ➤ To substitute quick-cooking or instant tapioca for pearl tapioca, allow 1½ to 2 tablespoons instant tapioca for 4 tablespoons pearl tapioca. ➤ As a thickener, substitute 1 tablespoon quick-cooking tapioca for 1 tablespoon flour.

TAPIOCA STARCH

Tapioca starch is an effective thickener for sauces and fruit fillings, especially those that will be frozen. Tapioca-based sauces and fillings thaw without breaking down and becoming watery, as flour-thickened sauces do after freezing. Tapioca starch is also popular for making clear and shiny glazes.

Tapioca starch is often sold as tapioca flour; ➤ do not confuse it with tapioca or cassava flour, 986, which is ground, dried yuca, and not a pure starch.

To use tapioca starch to thicken 1 cup liquid, whisk 1 teaspoon tapioca starch into 1 tablespoon cold water, then whisk it into the hot liquid. Tapioca does not need to boil in order to thicken, and do not subject it to prolonged cooking or it will thin. To use the starch in mixtures that will be frozen, use 1 tablespoon tapioca starch to thicken 1 cup liquid.

SUET AND TALLOW

Suet is a solid, light-colored fat obtained from around the kidney or loin area of beef or mutton, used in the preparation of mincemeat,

672, and Steamed Plum Pudding, 833. True beef suet should be obtained from a butcher; it is ➤ not the same as suet sold for bird feeding. If the suet is not already cleaned, buy at least 10 ounces suet to yield 8 ounces cleaned.

To clean and prepare suet, cut away and discard any parts that are reddish or that look dried out, then crumble what remains between your fingers and remove any pieces of tough filament. A certain amount of fine, papery filament will remain. To chop, first separate the pieces of suet and freeze solid in preparation for chopping. For plum pudding, the suet must be chopped to a very fine consistency, but it must not be allowed to melt and become pasty. If you work quickly, you will have no trouble doing this with a large chef's knife. Alternatively, you can cut, freeze, and grind the suet in a chilled meat grinder, 501, or chop it in a food processor fitted with the metal blade (be careful not to overprocess). Extra suet can be sealed in an airtight zip-top bag and frozen for up to 6 months.

It is possible to find suet that has already been cleaned and cut into small pellet-like bits. This type of suet is extremely easy to use, and we recommend it for its convenience. If you cannot find suet, high-fat European-style butter may be substituted. Freeze the butter and grate it on a box grater before using.

Tallow is rendered beef fat (for more on rendering, see Fats in Cooking, 480). The highest quality tallow is made from suet. Tallow is especially prized for frying because it is stable when subjected to heat and lends a rich, savory flavor to french fries and savory fritters.

SUGARS

Most of the sugar we use is derived from sugarcane or sugar beets. Both are so similar in their cooking reactions and taste that only the label gives us a clue as to the source of our sugar and then only sometimes, as the provenance of granulated sugar is not always disclosed on the label. But the various grinds and types of the solid sugars discussed in this section affect not only their volumes but their sweetening power as well.

All sugars share some characteristics. Among other things, sugars make baked goods tender and moist and help them brown. In small amounts, they speed up the working of yeast. Sugars can be heated and melted to the point of caramelization, creating a whole range of new flavors in the sugar itself. Sugar also gives bulk and volume to baked goods. Sugar can be beaten with a solid fat in order to both incorporate it evenly into the resulting dough and to aerate the fat.

One of the most notable characteristics of sugar is that it is hygroscopic, meaning it bonds with water. This is what makes baked goods made with sugar moist and prevents ice cream from crystallizing readily. In preserves like jams, sugar pulls water away from pectin, allowing them to form a gel. Sugar also reduces water activity: By bonding with water molecules, sugar makes them unavailable for use by microbes that cause spoilage.

Sugars are not necessarily interchangeable. Read the individual entries for different types of sugar for substitution information. For information on liquid sugars, see Agave Syrup, 951, Birch Syrup, 956, Brown Rice Syrup, 958, Corn Syrup, 974, Glucose Syrup, 991, Honey, 995, Maple Syrup, 999, Molasses, 1002, Sorghum, 1018, and Cane Syrup, Golden Syrup, and Treacle, 961.

CARAMELIZATION OF SUGAR

"Caramelize" is an oft-repeated verb in recipes and food writing, where it sometimes serves as a synonym for browning, 1048. Technically, what caramelization refers to is the decomposition of sugar when it is exposed to heat. Not only does this create new and flavorful compounds, but it lessens the sweetness of the sugar.

New studies have given us fresh insight into the chemical processes at work. Without getting into the differences between thermodynamic melting and thermal decomposition, the major conclusion to take away from this research is: Sugar can be caramelized at lower temperatures if it is held at them for a long enough time.

Up until very recently, chemists and food scientists thought sugar needed to melt and reach a high temperature in order to caramelize. This still holds true for instances of caramelization that happen over a short period: In the case of candy making, sugar is melted quickly in a pan, after which it begins to darken and break down into caramel at temperatures above 330°F (see The Stages of Cooked Sugar Syrup, 856).

On the other hand, prolonged exposure to moderate heat can caramelize granulated sugar without it ever melting. Pastry chef and cookbook author Stella Parks has popularized this insight with her procedure for **"toasted sugar."** Simply bake granulated white sugar in a 300°F oven, stirring every 30 minutes, until the sugar is nicely browned, about 5 hours. The result is a granular "caramel sugar" that can be substituted for all or a portion of the white sugar called for in baking recipes (keep in mind that they will be slightly less sweet).

Below, find our standard procedure for making a thick, caramelized sugar syrup. For caramel candies, see 864; for caramel sauces, see 808. For a savory sauce, see Vietnamese Caramel Sauce, 578.

CARAMELIZED SUGAR

This thick syrup is made of sugar and just enough water to dissolve it and steam any stray crystals from the sides of the pan. It will set up firmly, which allows it to be the glue that holds together a Croquembouche, 698.

Place in a small heavy saucepan:

¾ cup sugar

Drizzle evenly over the top:

¼ cup water

Place the pan over medium heat and, without stirring, very gently swirl the pan until a clear syrup forms. It is important that the sugar dissolve and the syrup clarify before it boils, so slide the pan on and off the burner as necessary. Once the sugar is dissolved, increase the heat to high and bring the syrup to a rolling boil. Cover the pan tightly and boil for 2 minutes. Uncover the pan and cook the syrup until it begins to darken. Gently swirl the pan once again, then cook the syrup until it turns a deep amber, or registers about 360°F on a thermometer.

Store the syrup tightly covered at room temperature. The syrup hardens on standing, but if stored in a heatproof jar, it is easily melted by heating the jar gently in hot water.

UNREFINED SUGARS

This category of sugars is a diverse one. Unrefined sugars have a wide range of textures, colors, and flavors. Due to the fact that they are less processed than white or brown sugar, they are more variable. When used in cooking, the cook should consider their unique characters, as they will add their own flavors to any dish they are used in. These sugars are not commonly used in baking, though they may be in some instances. Be aware, however, that unrefined sugars will not behave like refined ones.

Muscovado sugar has a very high molasses content. It is the sugar produced during the final crystallization of sugar from the reduced and concentrated sugarcane syrup (after this final crystallization, the syrup is filtered of waste products and becomes molasses). Muscovado sugar is very dark and flavorful. Use it as you would brown sugar, knowing that it will add its own characteristic flavor.

Turbinado or **raw sugar** is processed from sugarcane. It is partially refined in a turbine, thus the name, and the crystals have had their molasses coating partially washed off. With coarse, beige crystals, turbinado sugar is closest in character to the yellow or brownish **demerara sugar** often called for in British recipes. Demerara sugar comes from the first crystallization of cane juice and has a pale golden color and mild, caramel flavor. ➤ Substitute turbinado or demerara sugar cup for cup for granulated sugar, but be aware of their heavier molasses flavor and larger crystal size, which can make them harder to dissolve. These sugars are excellent sprinkled on top of baked goods for crunch and sweetness. We also like to dust the insides of buttered baking pans with these coarse sugars as they melt during baking, providing a darker, caramelized crust.

Piloncillo is an unrefined sugar from Mexico, though this type of unrefined sugar is used all over Central and South America under different names, among them **chancaca, rapadura,** and **panela.** It is often sold in dense, light to dark brown cakes or cones, although it may also be found granulated. To use it in cooking, grate it on the large holes of a box grater or chop it into fine pieces with a knife.

Sucanat is dried pure sugar cane juice. The name (a registered trademark) is an abbreviation of *sucre de canne naturel* or "natural cane sugar." Sucanat is much lighter by weight than the same volume of granulated sugar, and it has a mild molasses flavor. To substitute Sucanat for 1 cup granulated sugar, use 1¼ cups Sucanat and grind it in a spice or coffee grinder before adding to baked goods.

Palm sugar is a coarse brown sugar made from the evaporated sap of different types of palm trees. It is usually sold in pucks or cones much like piloncillo and can be grated or chopped into small pieces for use in cooking. **Jaggery** is very similar to palm sugar, but it is often made from a combination of palm sap and sugarcane juice. It is commonly used in Indian cooking.

Coconut sugar is a granulated sugar made from the sap of the bud stems of coconut palms. It may be found in puck form, much like jaggery and piloncillo, or granulated. This type of sugar is used across Southeast Asia. Coconut sugar is sometimes called palm sugar, though palm sugar is made from the sap of a variety of palm trees, while coconut sugar is made specifically from coconut palm sap. Coconut sugar, palm sugar, and jaggery are all interchangeable in recipes, though they should not be substituted in recipes calling for granulated sugar.

Maple sugar is made by boiling maple syrup until most of the liquid has evaporated. It has a distinctive, strong, sweet taste. Because of its high cost, it is often reserved for flavoring. It is sold in both block and granulated form. For maple sugar in a block, grate or shave it before combining it with other ingredients. ➤ For using in baked goods, substitute maple sugar for one-third of the total sugar called for in the recipe.

BROWN SUGAR

All brown sugar is made in one of two ways: Raw sugar is dissolved in a syrup, then recrystallized; or refined white sugar is mixed with molasses so the syrup coats the sugar crystals. As a result, brown sugar is a moister cane or beet sugar with a light or dark brown color and more complex flavor than white sugar. As brown sugar hardens and lumps easily, keep it in a tightly covered container or in a tightly closed plastic bag. If the sugar should become hard, place it in a dish, cover with plastic wrap, and microwave on high in 30-second intervals, using a fork to break up the sugar. Or place in a resealable zip-top bag, add half an apple or a slice of bread to the bag, seal, and let stand. Remove the apple when the sugar softens. ➤ In this book, if neither light nor dark brown sugar is specified, either type can be used. Use dark brown sugar when a stronger flavor or darker color is wanted.

To measure brown sugar, pack it firmly into the measuring cup and level it by pressing with the palm of your hand. ➤ To substitute brown sugar for granulated sugar, use 1 cup firmly packed brown sugar for each 1 cup granulated sugar.

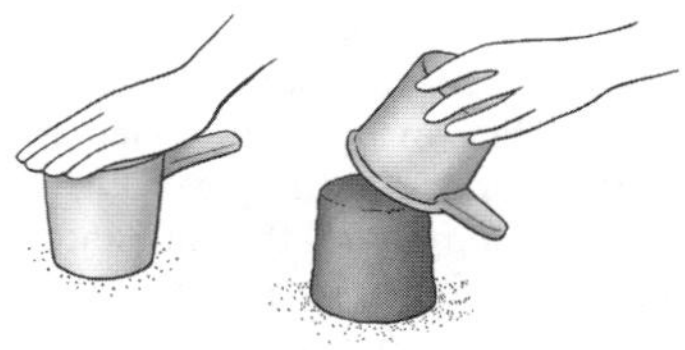

Measuring brown sugar

Pourable **granulated brown sugar** is also widely available. Depending on the brand, it may not be as sweet, so be sure you know what you are buying and follow the directions on the package when using in recipes.

GRANULATED AND SUPERFINE SUGARS

In this book, when the word "sugar" appears with no qualifiers, it means granulated white sugar—beet sugar or cane sugar, both being 99.5 percent pure sucrose. **Granulated sugar** can be used for almost every purpose, even for meringue. ➤ One pound of granulated sugar equals approximately 2 cups.

Coarse or decorating sugar is large-crystal granulated sugar and may be clear, white, or tinted colors.

Also called bar or berry sugar, **superfine sugar** is a finer grind of granulated sugar. It is between granulated sugar and powdered sugar in consistency. Because it dissolves readily, it is used in meringues, for macerating fruits, and in cocktails and other drinks. The crystals are too small for creaming with butter in making cakes, cookies, or in any baking where the sugar crystals must "cut" into the butter. If it becomes lumpy, put the sugar in a plastic bag and use a rolling pin to crush the lumps. Make superfine sugar at home with a food processor, pulsing granulated sugar until fine and powder like. ➤ Superfine sugar can be substituted cup for cup for granulated sugar where appropriate.

To color granulated sugar, sprinkle 1 cup sugar with 10 to 12 drops food coloring and mix well until the sugar is evenly tinted. Pour the sugar onto a rimmed baking sheet and allow it to dry for about 3 hours.

FLAVORED SUGARS

Keep these on hand for quick flavoring.

I. CINNAMON

About 1 cup

Mix **1 cup sugar** with **2 tablespoons ground cinnamon.**

II. CITRUS-FLAVORED

About 1 cup

Mix **1 cup sugar** with **1 to 2 tablespoons grated lemon, orange, or lime zest.** Let stand, covered, for 5 to 7 days before using.

III. VANILLA

About 2 cups

Split **1 or 2 vanilla beans** in half lengthwise and scrape out the seeds with the tip of a spoon. Mix the seeds and pods with **2 cups sugar,** making sure the seeds are evenly dispersed, and store tightly sealed in a canister. The vanilla bean pods can be left in the canister indefinitely.

POWDERED SUGAR

Powdered sugar, also called **confectioners' sugar,** is a bright white powdery sugar. Its finest form, known as 10X, is the type sold packaged at most markets. In order to lessen clumping, a small quantity of cornstarch is added to the sugar during processing. If it does clump, sift it, 1045. Sometimes the cornstarch gives uncooked icings a raw flavor. If desired, before spreading this kind of mixture, you can heat it for about 10 minutes in a double boiler over boiling water. Alternatively, use organic powdered sugar, which is made with tapioca starch instead of cornstarch. Tapioca starch granules, unlike cornstarch granules, absorb moisture and start to swell before being heated. This gives it an advantage in uncooked icings, as it thickens them and makes them smooth and creamy. ➤ Do not try to substitute powdered sugar for granulated in baking—its texture gives a different crumb to cakes. In other uses, substitute 1¾ cups powdered sugar for 1 cup granulated sugar.

LUMP SUGAR, SUGAR CUBES, AND PEARL SUGAR

Lump sugar and **sugar cubes** are granulated sugar molded or cut into rectangles or cubes for use in hot drinks and cocktails. Crystals of Rock Candy, 872, make an interesting stand-in for lump sugar and, when separated or crushed, a sparkling garnish for frosted cakes or other desserts.

Pearl sugar is coarse chunks of sugar made by compressing white sugar crystals and sifting them to get a specific particle size. It is used primarily as a topping on baked goods in Western Europe. Belgian pearl sugar is larger than Swedish pearl sugar and is better suited to making Liège waffles, while smaller, hard bits of Swedish pearl sugar are ideal for topping pastries, cakes, cookies, and breads, from France's *chouquettes* (small choux pastry puffs topped with pearl sugar before baking) to Scandinavian cakes and pastries.

CHINESE ROCK SUGAR

Made from refined sugarcane juice and used as a sweetener for various Chinese desserts and soups, this sugar is sold in lumps and is available at Asian markets. It is usually crushed or broken into small pieces before use.

SUGAR SUBSTITUTES

Some sugar substitutes can be used in cooking or baking, according to the manufacturer's directions. However, they do not give the same texture and color in baking as do true sugars and should be used only in recipes especially developed for them. **Saccharin** is a synthetic sweetener commonly used at the table. It is three hundred times sweeter than sucrose (granulated sugar), but it has a slightly metallic aftertaste. It does not contribute any calories because it is not metabolized in the body. Saccharin should not be cooked, as it becomes bitter when heated. **Aspartame** is technically considered a nutritive sweetener, contributing 4 calories per gram. However, aspartame is two hundred times sweeter than sugar and very little of it is needed to achieve sweetness. Therefore, its caloric contribution is negligible. **Sucralose** is a white crystalline powder made from the chlorination of sucrose. It is four hundred to eight hundred times sweeter than granulated sugar. It is stable when subjected to heat, and it can be used in a variety of drinks, baked goods, and frozen and canned fruits and vegetables. Its chemical structure is very close to that of sucrose, but it is noncaloric. **Acesulfame potassium** is two hundred times sweeter than sugar.

"Natural" sugar substitutes have gained favor in recent years, though they have many of the same drawbacks as the chemically derived sweeteners discussed above. These include **stevia,** which is made from a South American plant traditionally used to sweeten yerba mate tea. It is sold in powder and liquid form. The liquid form is highly concentrated. Some powdered stevia is formulated to be used as a cup for cup replacement for sugar in baking. While this may technically be true, we find baked goods made with stevia alone to have an off-putting aftertaste. Use stevia for up to half the sugar in baking recipes for the best flavor. Recipes with strong-flavored ingredients like chocolate and peanut butter tend to hide the flavor of stevia best. Use very concentrated forms of stevia, such as liquid stevia, as directed by the manufacturer. Remember that if you use concentrated stevia in a recipe, you will need to compensate for the missing bulk of the sugar by adding egg whites, applesauce, yogurt, or mashed banana. For every 1 cup sugar substituted for in a recipe, add ⅓ cup of one of these bulking agents.

Xylitol is extracted from birch trees and is exactly as sweet as sucrose (sugar). It has a slight cooling effect on the tongue, somewhat like the sensation of chewing a mint leaf. It may be substituted cup for cup for granulated sugar, and it contains 40 percent fewer calories than sugar. It does not have a bitter aftertaste, though ingesting too much xylitol can have a laxative effect.

Monk fruit extract is made from the fruit of a plant related to cucumbers, squash, and melons. It is three hundred times sweeter than sugar and is usually mixed with bulking agents and sold in powder form. It has a bitter aftertaste. For best results, do not substitute more than half the sugar in a recipe with monk fruit extract.

SUMAC

Sumac is the dried red berry of the sumac bush. The plant grows wild throughout the Middle East and Mediterranean and in the temperate regions of North America. In the Middle East, sumac comes from Sicilian or elm-leafed sumac. In North America, it is from staghorn or smooth sumac. Its distinctive appearance makes it easy to identify and forage (having said that, never harvest and eat any wild food that you cannot identify with 100 percent certainty—some plants that look somewhat like sumac are poisonous). Sumac is available as whole dried berries or ground. It has a bright, lemony flavor from malic acid. It is not related to poison sumac. Sumac is commonly used in Middle Eastern cooking, notably sprinkled on meat or on salads or Hummus, 52, added to pilafs, and used in Za'atar, 590. Some North American indigenous peoples used sumac to make a lemonade-like beverage. The flavor of sumac holds up well in cooking, so it can be used as an ingredient as well as a flavorful finishing garnish.

SUNFLOWER SEEDS

Sunflowers are one of the top five oil seed crops in North America. They are sold in the shell or hulled. Sunflower seeds are particularly beloved in Russia and other Eastern European nations where they are a popular snack food; sunflower oil is the principal cooking oil in these countries as well. Mild and sweet-tasting, sunflower seeds are mostly eaten as a snack, but they can be added to baked goods of all kinds. They may also be ground into a butter as for nuts, 1005.

To toast hulled sunflower seeds, spread them out on a rimmed baking sheet and place in a 350°F oven until lightly browned, 7 to 10 minutes.

SWEET CICELY

The green seeds and fresh leaves of this soft, ferny plant may be used as a garnish for salads or cold vegetables. They have an anise-like flavor and are often used in French cuisine in conjunction with tarragon, 1027. Use the seeds in cakes, candies, and liqueurs. Sweet cicely is one of the herbs used to flavor the liqueur called Chartreuse.

SWEET WOODRUFF OR WALDMEISTER

The beautiful dark green whorled fresh leaves of this plant are floated in May Wine, 30, or in other cold punches, but they should not be left in longer than about 30 minutes. The plants emit a strong odor of freshly mown hay when the foliage is crushed or cut.

TAHINI

See Nuts and Seeds, 1004.

TAMARIND

See About Tamarinds, 195.

TAPIOCA

See Starches, 1022.

TARRAGON

Called *estragon* by the French, this herb, when fresh, has a pleasant, sweet anise flavor. The flavor is somewhat lost in drying, so opt to use fresh whenever possible. Tarragon is excellent added to eggs, mushrooms, tomatoes, mustard, tartar sauce, and fish or chicken dishes. It is essential in a Béarnaise Sauce, 561, and it is one of the fines herbes, 983. Tarragon also happens to make a nice infused vinegar. Allow about 3 tablespoons fresh tarragon leaves to 2 cups white wine vinegar. Keep the leaves submerged beneath the vinegar for 1 week, then strain.

TEMPEH

See Tempeh, 284.

TENDERIZERS

See Tenderizing Tough Meats, 450.

THYME

Thyme is a low-growing herb of which there are dozens of species. Its flavor is somewhat like oregano, but milder, making it an excellent seasoning for a wide variety of foods. Thyme may be used with almost any meat or vegetable, especially roasted poultry, lamb, pork, and rabbit; in Creole dishes and gumbos; for pasta sauces, soups, and stocks; and with fatty fish, braises, and stuffings. Thyme dries well, 947.

There are so many varieties of *Thymus*, and their flavors are so varied that a collection of them makes a garden in itself. The narrow-leaf French or garden thyme, *Thymus vulgaris*, with its upright habit and gray-green foliage, and the glistening, small-bushed, strongly scented lemon thyme—*T. citriodorus*—are those most frequently found in the market. Thymes, which grow best in sun, are perennial, persisting for years among rocks. Prune after blooming.

TOMATOES AS SEASONING

Besides their use as a fresh vegetable in salads and a cooked one in sauces and stews, tomatoes are prized for their rich flavor when dried and cooked down into a concentrated paste. **Dried tomatoes,** often called sun-dried tomatoes, are commonly available sold loose or packed in oil. Those packed in oil tend to be moister, but even the driest tomato can be resurrected by a short soak in hot water. Use dried tomatoes in dips and spreads, as a flavor booster for sauce, and chopped up in pasta dishes for little bursts of rich tomato flavor. We also like to snack on them. To make your own dried tomatoes, see 947. **Tomato paste** is made by cooking and reducing tomato puree to a very thick and concentrated consistency. It can be used to bolster tomato sauces, stews, and braises with a rich hit of umami. For a discussion of fresh tomatoes, see 280.

TOMATO PASTE

About 2 cups

This cooking process is similar to how apple butter is made: The ingredients are all simmered together until the tomatoes are broken down, then the mixture is put through a food mill to remove the skins and whole spices, and finally the puree is reduced until thick.

Combine in a large pot:

10 pounds plum or Roma tomatoes (or any paste tomato), washed and sliced
1 large celery rib with some leaves, chopped
1 onion, chopped
1 tablespoon salt
1 garlic clove, chopped
¾ teaspoon black peppercorns

Bring to a simmer and cook gently until the tomatoes are very soft, stirring frequently. Put the mixture through a food mill and discard the skins and whole spices. Return the mixture to the pot and simmer, stirring frequently, until the pulp is thick and reduced by about half, several hours.

Divide the paste between 2 large rimmed baking sheets and spread evenly. Make short cuts into the paste to let air penetrate. Place the paste in a 200°F oven until it is so dry that it retains its shape, 3 to 4 hours.

Pack it into sterilized, 893, jars or ice cube trays or a combination. Freeze the ice cube trays, then store the cubes of tomato paste in a zip-top bag in the freezer. For jarred tomato paste, pour olive oil over the top of the tomato paste to cover it, then secure the jars with lids. Store in the refrigerator for up to 2 months. Alternatively, transfer the paste to zip-top bags and press the paste so it is in a thin, even layer. Freeze the bags flat. When needed, simply break off a piece of tomato paste.

TREACLE

See Cane Syrup, Golden Syrup, and Treacle, 961.

TRUFFLES

Truffles are knobby fungi that fruit underground and are typically harvested from around oak, hazelnut, pecan, or fir trees. They can be incredibly pungent, a trait they evolved to attract the attention of animals, who dig them up and distribute their spores widely. In general, they are rarely available fresh in markets and command high prices.

There are hundreds of species of truffles, although not all are palatable. A few European types have garnered the most culinary interest (and the largest sums of money). The most prestigious of these is the rare **Italian white, Piedmont,** or **Alba truffle** (*Tuber magnatum pico*). White truffles are positively pungent, with an onion-garlic aroma. White truffles are almost never cooked but instead are shaved raw over pasta, risotto, *fonduta* (the Piedmontese version of fondue), egg dishes, and salads. The second most-sought-after variety is the **French black or Périgord truffle** (*Tuber melanosporum*), harvested primarily in France and a bit in Italy and Spain. Périgords have a nutty character and a faint but distinct aroma; they are usually cooked or at least marinated or macerated (typically in Cognac) before use. Black truffles are often added to pâtés and terrines (especially of foie gras) and are frequently combined with eggs and potatoes. Less expensive and more common, the so-called **summer truffle** (*Tuber aestivum*) is a pleasant but mild-flavored black variety, as is the **winter truffle** (*Tuber brumale*). Some European varieties are now successfully cultivated in the United States, albeit in small quantities.

American forests offer their own variety of culinary truffles, and some species are slowly gaining recognition and popularity. The surge of interest in domestic truffles has been encouraged by eager cultivators, foragers, and chefs—as well as the fact that they command a fraction of the price of their European brethren. Our most well-known, indigenous truffle is the **Oregon white truffle,** a name that is used to designate two species, one of which is harvested in winter (*Tuber oregonense*), the other in spring (*Tuber gibbosum*). They are quite different than the Italian whites, with earthy, garlicky, and musky overtones. As with other white truffles, they are best used raw, either thinly shaved over foods or used to infuse butters and creams. **Oregon black truffles** (*Leucangium carthusianum*) smell fruity and are used in desserts as well as savory dishes. The newly discovered **Oregon brown truffle** (*Kalapuya brunnea*) is the rarest and tastes, to some, like ripe Camembert. Like European black truffles, all of these types can be thinly shaved over dishes or briefly cooked. All are found under Douglas fir trees in the Pacific Northwest. The **American brown** or **pecan truffle** (*Tuber lyonii*) is found mostly in the pecan orchards of Georgia, but also grows in smaller quantities around hickory, chestnut, and hazelnut trees throughout the eastern United States.

When purchasing fresh truffles, choose those with fewer blemishes and avoid any that have soft spots; truffles should be very firm and dry to the touch. Of the firm truffles, choose the most aromatic ones; avoid any that smell of ammonia. To clean, brush them with a soft kitchen brush or cloth. Do not wash them unless they are absolutely filthy. Dry them off thoroughly, wrap in a paper towel, place in a closed container, and refrigerate for up to 1 week, changing the paper towel if it becomes moist. As you store truffles, check their aroma frequently. ➤ The aroma of truffles changes in intensity *and* character as they ripen; be ready to consume them at their most intriguing stage of development. If you have purchased truffles that are firm but not very aromatic, they might not be ripe yet, and may increase in potency over the course of a few days. Of course, truffle storage is a perfect opportunity to infuse butters and other items, see below. Some like to store truffles, refrigerated, in a container of Arborio rice. This keeps them dry, and the truffle-infused rice can be used to make risotto, which can then be topped with fresh truffle slices.

Though strong-tasting pâtés and some sauces are traditionally flavored with fresh truffles, it is generally good to pair them with unobtrusive ingredients that stretch or reinforce their flavor, such as other types of mushrooms, pasta, eggs, potatoes, poultry, or mild shellfish like crab, lobster, or scallops. ➤ When adding truffles to cooked dishes, wait until the end of cooking or thinly shave them atop the finished dish. The heat of the food will disperse the aroma of the truffles, heightening the experience of eating them.

Truffles sold in jars or cans vary widely in quality but can be quite good. **Truffle salt** is best used to finish foods at the table. If you see **truffle oil** for sale (especially if it is a reasonable price), chances are it is flavored artificially (oil infused with actual truffles is rare to find and expensive). Use it in very small amounts as a finishing garnish for salads, pasta, and French Fries, 270.

INFUSING WITH TRUFFLES

In our opinion, the best way to "store" truffles is to preserve their flavor in other items. Luckily, this is very simple: Truffles release gas as they ripen, and their aroma will permeate salt, eggs, sticks of butter, cream, and mild, fresh cheeses practically overnight if you place them in the same, tightly closed container. This one simple step can transmute an expensive, ephemeral treat into a perennial flavoring for perfuming dishes or simply savoring on toast. Store infused butter or cheese in an airtight container or sealed bag and refrigerate or freeze for future use. We recommend choosing a flaky finishing salt for infusing with truffles (store in an airtight container).

TURMERIC

Turmeric is the rhizome of *Curcuma longa*—a ginger relative that contains curcumin, a bright orange antioxidant compound that gives the root its golden color. There are two primary types of turmeric: Alleppey and Madras. Alleppey turmeric has a darker color and is especially sought after. Madras turmeric is the kind most commonly used in curry powders. So-called "white turmeric" or **zedoary** is a root related to turmeric and ginger that has a light yellow color and a flavor similar to that of ginger.

Turmeric can be found fresh, and dried whole or ground; the most common type is ground. Ground turmeric is slightly bitter, musky, earthy, and warming. To make ground turmeric, fresh turmeric root is steamed or boiled to set its color and starch. Then the roots are dried, polished, and ground. If you find whole dried turmeric root, it can be grated on a rasp grater. Fresh turmeric root can be minced or grated on a rasp grater. Turmeric adds bulk and color to blended curry powders and color to prepared mustard. In small quantities, turmeric is sometimes used as a food coloring, often replacing the far more expensive saffron.

VANILLA

The long, thin vanilla bean is a pod of a climbing orchid vine from Central and South America. When the bean is picked, it is green and has no flavor. The beans are steamed or exposed to the sun to start the oxidative process, then they are sun-dried day and covered with fabric at night so they sweat. During this process, flavor compounds in the vanilla beans are freed by enzymes, and the pod wrinkles as the heat of the sun concentrates its flavors and causes it to brown.

There are different types of vanilla beans. Madagascar vanilla (also called Bourbon vanilla) is thought to be the highest quality and have the most intense vanilla flavor. Mexican and Tahitian vanilla beans are not as intensely flavored as Madagascar beans, but they possess other desirable, fruity flavors and are significantly cheaper. Indonesian vanilla has smoky, woodsy notes.

To use **vanilla beans,** split the pods in half lengthwise with a paring knife, then use a small spoon with a pointed tip to scrape the seeds from inside. If the vanilla is to be used to infuse a custard or other mixture, add both the seeds and the pod; vanillin (see below) is fat-soluble, and any left in the pod will be infuse the base. If only the seeds are called for, do not discard the pod! It is still very flavorful and can be used to make Vanilla Sugar, 1026. To rescue dry vanilla beans, place an inch or so of vodka or high-proof grain alcohol in a small jar. Cut the vanilla bean(s) crosswise in half, then stand them up in the jar and cover with a lid. The beans will soak up the alcohol and become plump again. ➤ To substitute vanilla bean for vanilla extract, allow the seeds scraped from about 2 inches of a split vanilla bean for 1 teaspoon extract.

Vanilla extract is prepared by pouring water and alcohol over the beans to extract their flavor. Because the process of producing vanilla beans and extract is so labor-intensive and time-consuming, they command a premium price. Alcohol-free varieties must be labeled **vanilla flavoring,** and synthetic vanilla flavoring must be labeled as **artificial** or **imitation vanilla.** The synthetic type may contain the same flavor compound found in vanilla beans—**vanillin**—but derived from other, cheaper sources (usually from lignin found in wood). While we usually tend toward buying "real" ingredients whenever possible, there is evidence to suggest that people cannot tell the difference between baked goods made with real and synthetic vanilla.

Synthetic or not, ➤ to preserve vanilla extract's flavor in custard sauces and other cooked dishes, add it when the food is cooling or taken off the heat. ➤ To get the best flavor distribution from vanilla extract in baked goods, add it directly to the fat in the recipe. For example, in a cake recipe, add it after creaming the butter and sugar but before adding the eggs.

Vanilla paste is made from vanilla extract and finely ground vanilla beans, suspended in a thick liquid. It adds extraordinary flavor to whipped cream, crème brûlée, and other recipes where the flavor and appearance of vanilla bean is desired. Although vanilla paste usually contains some sugar, so little paste is added in most cases that there is no need to alter the recipe to account for this. ➤ One teaspoon of vanilla paste is equivalent to 1 teaspoon vanilla extract or 2 inches of a vanilla bean.

VANILLA EXTRACT

About 1 cup

Cut lengthwise in half:

5 vanilla beans

Using the tip of a spoon, scrape the seeds from the pods. Place the pods and seeds in a pint jar. Cover with:

1 cup high-proof alcohol such as Everclear, vodka, or overproof rum

Close the jar tightly and shake every so often. When the alcohol is deep brown, 1 to 1½ months, the vanilla is ready to use.

VEGETABLE OIL

See Oils, 1006.

VERJUICE

Obtained from crab apples and green grapes, verjuice or *verjus* means "green juice." This very tart juice can be used in place of citrus juice or vinegar in sauces, salad dressings, or as a condiment.

VINEGAR

From the French *vin aigre*, "sour wine," vinegar can be made from almost any liquid that contains sugars, but especially those made from fruits or grains. Vinegar is the product of secondary fermentation: Yeasts transform sugars into an alcoholic brew, the brew is exposed to air (which transforms the alcohol into acetaldehyde), and then *Acetobacter* bacteria ferment the acetaldehyde into acetic acid. Most commercially available vinegar is then pasteurized and filtered, but "raw" vinegars are also available. These are often cloudy or contain a residue that sinks to the bottom of the jar. Some of these raw vinegars are labeled "with the mother." The mother in question is the **vinegar mother,** a gelatinous, almost jellyfish-like substance composed of cellulose and *Acetobacter* bacteria. The presence of a vinegar mother, cloudiness, or sediment in unpasteurized vinegar is completely normal and nothing to be concerned about.

Whether a vinegar is sharp, rich, or mellow makes a tremendous difference in cooking. Some vinegars have less acidity than others: Homemade vinegars can be quite mild, and products labeled as "vinegar" are only required to have a 4 percent acetic acid content by the USDA. In canning recipes, where vinegar is not just used for flavor but for its acidity, always use the type of vinegar specified. ➤ Do not use any vinegar for canning unless it is verified to be 5 percent acetic acid.

➤ All vinegars are corrosive, so prepare dishes containing a large proportion of vinegar in glass, enamel, or stainless steel vessels. Avoid copper, zinc, aluminum, cast-iron, or carbon steel cookware.

BALSAMIC VINEGAR

Balsamic vinegar is made from lambrusco, trebbiano, and other wine grapes, both red and white. It is a traditional product of northern Italy, aged in wooden barrels for years. The mark of authenticity is the word *tradizionale* on its label, which guarantees that it does not contain other types of wine vinegar. It is aged 12 years for *vecchio* (old), and 25 years for *extra vecchio*. Older balsamic vinegars can be very expensive and have a viscous, almost syrupy, consistency. The cheapest balsamic vinegars are nothing more than sweetened and artificially colored wine vinegars. Use traditional balsamic as a condiment or by the drop; on finished dishes, or with fresh fruit such as strawberries or watermelon. Use cheaper varieties of balsamic vinegar in marinades, in dressings, and cooked in recipes.

Balsamic glaze, a reduction of balsamic vinegar, is now commonly available at supermarkets. Though we do not care for the added sugar in the store-bought product, the fumes from reducing balsamic vinegar to a glaze can clear a large kitchen, even an entire apartment. If you have a good ventilation fan or an outdoor hotplate, choose an economical brand of balsamic and reduce by simmering uncovered over medium heat, stirring frequently, until the vinegar coats the back of a spoon. Also see Megan's Beets with Goat Cheese, 219, for a maple-balsamic glaze.

BLACK VINEGAR

Black vinegar is very popular in southern China, where **Chinkiang vinegar,** or **Zhenjiang vinegar,** is produced. Usually made with rice—although millet, wheat, or sorghum may be used instead (or in addition)—it is dark in color, with a deep, almost smoky flavor. Some black vinegar is aged. It is not a very sharp vinegar and can have an acidity as low as 2 percent. Black vinegar works well in noodle dishes and braises and as a dipping sauce.

CIDER VINEGAR

Cider vinegar results from the fermentation of apple juice. Sometimes labeled apple cider vinegar, this fruity, full-bodied vinegar usually has 5 percent acetic acid. It is frequently used in pickling and is a good all-purpose vinegar to keep in the pantry. "Raw," or unpasteurized, cider vinegar is widely available.

DISTILLED WHITE VINEGAR

Based on diluted distilled alcohol fermented to a 5 percent acetic acid content, white vinegar is used in pickling when the pickle must remain light in color. While white vinegar can be a bit harsh and one-dimensional in many dishes, it is still an excellent pantry staple. It can be used judiciously to add a sharp acidity to a dish without adding any other flavor.

MALT VINEGAR

Malt vinegar is a dark brown vinegar made from barley malt or other malted grains. In Britain, where malt vinegar originated, it was once called *alegar*, since it is essentially made from beer. It is most often used as a condiment, traditionally with Fish and Chips, 391.

RICE VINEGAR

Much of the rice vinegar produced is made from fermented rice wine. Sometimes called rice wine vinegar, it is pleasant but weaker in acid content—4 percent—and thus milder in flavor than other vinegars. **Seasoned rice vinegar** contains added sugar and salt; it can be used to season Shari (Sushi Rice), 334. Because of its lower acid content, rice vinegar is not recommended for pickling (with the exception of quick pickles).

SHERRY VINEGAR

Several types of sherry, including Pedro Ximénez and oloroso, 39, are used to create this wine vinegar. The flavor of the vinegar varies depending on what type of sherry is used. It is much like a cross between balsamic and red wine vinegar, with the characteristic oxidized flavor of sherry. These vinegars are sometimes aged in oak barrels.

WINE VINEGAR

The three most common types of wine vinegar are **red wine vinegar, white wine vinegar,** and **Champagne vinegar.** Each has an acetic acid content of about 7 percent. Red is strongest in flavor, Champagne the lightest; all are excellent for vinaigrettes, marinades, and pickles. **Banyuls vinegar** is a wine vinegar made from the French dessert wine of the same name. Its flavor is somewhat like sherry vinegar. **Vermouth vinegar** is harder to find but remains one of our favorites for adding to vinaigrettes and sauces.

OTHER UNIQUE VINEGARS

As you can imagine, there are as many vinegars as there is poorly stored hooch. Though we are most familiar with the types listed above, there are many more worth seeking out.

Several tropical fruits are fermented into distinctive vinegars. **Banana vinegar** is perhaps the most distinctive; though it has a recognizable banana flavor, it is rich, complex, and has some funky, oxidized notes that remind us of sherry and aged Jamaican rum. **Pineapple vinegar** is a common ingredient in the Caribbean and

Mexico, where it is made by fermenting pineapples and brown piloncillo sugar. The resulting vinegar is mild, with a floral quality and a well-rounded sourness from the combination of acetic acid and the citric acid already present in the fruit.

Palm vinegar and **coconut vinegar** (also sold as **tuba vinegar**) are made by fermenting the plants' sap. **Cane vinegar** can be made from fresh sugarcane juice, or the juice can be boiled down first for a darker, richer vinegar. All three of these types are integral to Filipino cuisine and are widely available in Asian grocery stores. Though any of the lighter varieties would be a fine stand-in for cider or wine vinegar in vinaigrettes and sauces, we are especially fond of the condiment *sinamak*, a coconut or cane vinegar that has been infused with chiles, onion, ginger, and garlic (which happens to be perfect for dressing pulled pork).

Japanese **umezu,** often sold as **umeboshi vinegar,** is not actually vinegar, but rather the tart brine exuded by ume plums when they are salted (the plums are then dried to make *umeboshi*). Ume plums are extremely sour due to their high citric acid content, and the brine they produce has a similar strength to vinegar (and, amazingly, an even lower pH). Despite these qualities, we must emphasize once more that because umezu does not have a standardized level of acidity, it is not suitable for canning and pickling for preservation. (Quick pickles like Beni Shōga, 930, are another story.) Umezu is often tinted red from the addition of purple shiso leaves, 1017, which also give it a slight, peppery hint of cinnamon and basil.

INFUSING VINEGARS

Flavored vinegars are commercially available but easily made at home. A neutral cider or wine vinegar is the most practical to use for infusing, but a lighter coconut, rice, or sherry vinegar can yield delicious results. Use individual herbs like tarragon or rosemary, or develop your favorite herb combinations, allowing 1 cup loosely packed fresh herb leaves per 1 pint vinegar. Other flavorings, such as thinly sliced ginger, smashed garlic, black peppercorns, whole spices, and citrus zest may also be added. After 2 weeks of steeping, filter the vinegar through several layers of cheesecloth, transfer to sterilized, 893, containers, and keep tightly sealed.

SHALLOT-HERB VINEGAR

About 3 cups

Wash and thoroughly dry:

¾ cup loosely packed sprigs tarragon
½ cup coarsely chopped parsley
8 sprigs thyme
4 sprigs winter savory
One 4-inch sprig rosemary

Add to a sterilized, 893, 1-quart canning jar along with:

2 shallots, thinly sliced
12 black peppercorns, cracked

Heat slowly in a small saucepan to just below the boiling point:

3 cups cider vinegar or white wine vinegar

Pour into the jar and let the mixture cool. Close the jar and let the mixture infuse for 2 weeks, shaking the jar every day.

Taste. If the vinegar is still not flavored to your liking, let it infuse longer, sampling each day, until it is ready. Pour through a fine-mesh sieve lined with several thicknesses of cheesecloth and transfer to sterilized, 893, glass bottles, if desired. Seal and store at room temperature for up to 12 months.

GARLIC VINEGAR

About 3 cups

Use in dressings or sauces.

Add to a sterilized, 893, 1-quart canning jar:

12 garlic cloves, smashed

Slowly heat in a small saucepan to just below the boiling point:

3 cups cider or white wine vinegar

Pour into the jar and let the mixture cool. Seal, infuse, strain, and store as directed for **Shallot-Herb Vinegar, above.**

CHILE VINEGAR

About 3 cups

To our minds, this vinegar's level of heat after 5 days is perfect for sprinkling over Southern-Style Greens, 243. On the other hand, your taste (and tolerance) may vary. For spicier results, add more chiles than we specify—or steep them for longer. Adding garlic to the mixture makes for an excellent condiment as well: Use the quantities listed in Garlic Vinegar, above. Simply heat the vinegar and pour over the garlic as directed, then let the mixture cool before adding the chiles.

Have ready one of the following:

1 ounce dried chiles, stemmed and seeded (toasted, 969, if desired)
3 to 4 habaneros, or 5 to 6 serrano or Thai chiles, stemmed and seeded, if desired

Add to a sterilized, 893, 1-quart canning jar along with:

3 cups cider or white wine vinegar

Close the jar and let the mixture infuse. Shake the jar and taste each day to check the strength and flavor; allow about 3 days and up to 1 week—or more, if you desire a spicier vinegar. Strain and store as directed for **Shallot-Herb Vinegar, above.**

WALNUTS

Walnuts are rich and flavorful with a slight astringency from tannins. The **English walnut** (or **Persian walnut**) and the American **black walnut** are the most common varieties. Black walnuts are smaller than the English kind, and taste quite different; though still sweet, they have a complex, tannic bitterness. Their shells are incredibly hard, and the tough husks surrounding the shells are so effective at staining that they are used as a natural dye. Depending on where you live, you may be able to find vast quantities of black walnuts free for the taking, though shelling them involves a substantial time investment (and a good pair of rubber gloves).

Blanching walnuts for 3 minutes removes some of their tannins. After blanching, the nuts can be dried and toasted, 1005. To make walnut milk, blanch them first and proceed as for Nut or Seed Milk, 1006.

English walnuts may be harvested when immature and the fruit surrounding them is still soft, green, and unblemished. **Green walnuts** are very tannic and astringent, but when they are quartered and left to steep in a pickling brine or alcohol, their flavor mellows and deepens with time. If a walnut tree bears an ample supply of green walnuts, we highly recommend harvesting them to make Nocino, 949, or Walnut Catsup, 932.

WASABI

Wasabi is the rhizome of a cabbage relative native to Japan. It grows in moist ground close to running water, such as a stream. The root harvested from the plant is traditionally grated on a piece of rough sharkskin, though metal and ceramic grating tools are commonly used as well. Wasabi is notoriously difficult to cultivate, and the majority has until recently been imported from Japan—which has led to scarcity and high prices. Luckily, growers in the coastal Pacific Northwest and the Blue Ridge Mountains of North Carolina have had success bringing fresh wasabi root to market, which has increased its availability (and may, eventually, lower prices). Another unexpected benefit of domestic wasabi production is the occasional appearance of broad, tender **wasabi leaves** in specialty markets; when thinly sliced into a chiffonade, 993, and used as a garnish, they add a mild, mustard-like flavor to soups, salads, and fish.

Fresh wasabi root has a pungent flavor with a bite similar to horseradish, but with other flavors as well. There are two common varieties of wasabi: *daruma* and *mazuma*. *Daruma* wasabi is milder than *mazuma*, and it has a nicer appearance. Gently peel wasabi with a vegetable peeler or paring knife, remove the knots, and grate in a circular motion on the finest side of a box grater or ginger grater. Store any unused wasabi root wrapped in damp paper towels in the refrigerator.

Powdered wasabi—a combination of dried ground horseradish and mustard powder that has been tinted green—is widely available. It has little in common with fresh wasabi except for its strong, sharp flavor, which is actually spicier than true wasabi.

WATER

Though water is basic, and certainly essential, it is not necessarily simple; the origin of the water and the treatment it receives as it flows to our tap affects how it responds to other ingredients in the kitchen.

First, a word on safety: As the recent, chronic contamination of municipal water supplies in Flint, Michigan, clearly demonstrates, many areas of the United States have to contend with potentially unsafe tap water. ➤ If your tap water tastes off, contains sediment, or is not completely clear, it is best to treat it with suspicion. For the most up-to-date information for your area, consult with your water utility, local government, or call the Environmental Protection Agency's Safe Drinking Water Hotline at 1-800-426-4791 (also at water.epa.gov/drink/hotline/index.cfm). If you suspect the pipes in your home may be responsible, or your water comes from a well, order a water quality testing kit (these are readily available online). Some municipalities also offer free water-testing services.

Water is important in cooking for many reasons, but before we delve into how water behaves during cooking it is helpful to know its chemical composition and some basic facts. At sea level, water turns to a solid below 32°F, simmers between 190° and 205°F, and vaporizes into steam at 212°F. (▲ For how the boiling point changes at lower pressures, see High-Altitude Cooking, 1070.) Water molecules are composed of two hydrogen atoms and one oxygen atom. Water molecules are polar, meaning that they are not perfectly balanced, with a positive side (hydrogen) and a negative side (oxygen). This polarity causes water molecules to bond with one another, the negative oxygen side of the molecule being attracted to the positive hydrogen side of other water molecules. When water molecules bond with one another, they do so relatively weakly, and so the bonds between water molecules are constantly breaking and re-forming.

These bonds make water an excellent solvent, or a substance capable of dissolving other substances (or solutes) to form a solution. Because hydrogen bonds are weak and water molecules are polar, water molecules are attracted to any other polar molecule. As water molecules bond with the charged regions of other polar molecules, the water molecules surround those charged regions and cause them to disperse. Over time, the solute becomes evenly dispersed throughout the water, at which time it can be said to have dissolved. In cooking, there are many polar molecules that can dissolve in water: salt, carbohydrates, and proteins, to name a few (one nonpolar molecule that does not dissolve in water is oil). This property is important in cooking because it allows us to dissolve all kinds of things in water. When you make a stock, proteins and carbohydrates dissolve in the water, making it flavorful and giving it body. When you make lemonade, carbohydrates and acids dissolve in the water. When these different substances dissolve in water it results in a complex, flavorful mixture that has harmony, rather than one where the flavors are not dispersed.

Another notable property of water is the tremendous amount of energy it takes to heat it up. Bringing water to a boil takes such a long time, and such a large amount of energy, because the energy has to break apart some of the bonds between water molecules to allow those molecules to move faster, which in turn allows the water to become hot and, finally, to boil. This may seem like more of an annoyance than a benefit, but think about using a bain-marie, 1050, for baking custards: The water absorbs and regulates the heat, which allows the custards to cook slowly and evenly without curdling.

When a water molecule absorbs enough energy to break its bond with other water molecules, it evaporates, effectively taking energy (or heat) from whatever is around it. This is called evaporative cooling. One of the more vivid examples of this phenomenon happens when you barbecue meats. A large piece of meat like a pork shoulder contains a lot of water. During the first part of cooking, the meat's temperature rises fairly steadily, but then it stalls. This stall can be a frustration for the cook, but an understanding of what causes it reveals a remedy. The meat's temperature is being prevented from rising because of evaporative cooling. As water evaporates off the surface of the meat, it takes energy (heat) with it, cooling the surface of the meat. You can either wait for the meat to get over this hump, or you can stop the evaporative cooling by wrapping the meat in foil. Preventing evaporation allows the temperature of the meat to rise faster, thus shortening the cooking time.

On the other hand, water not only removes energy from a substance when it evaporates, but it is also capable of depositing that energy on any surface the vaporized water condenses onto. Perhaps the most dramatic example of this is using steam to cook foods. A small amount of water is brought to a boil. Water molecules turn to vapor, then condense on the food sitting above the water. When the water condenses, the energy it took from the boiling water is deposited on the food, causing it to cook.

As discussed above, water is a solvent. All kinds of things become dissolved in it, including minerals. When water contains a lot of minerals, specifically calcium and magnesium, we call it "hard water." When water contains few of these minerals, it is "soft."

➤ **Soft water** contains little or no dissolved salts of calcium or magnesium and is best for most cooking and baking. However, very soft water will make yeast doughs soggy and sticky. ➤ **Hard water** contains an appreciable quantity of dissolved minerals. Vegetables cooked with hard water tend to stay firm longer, and very hard water tightens the gluten network in breads and can inhibit the action of yeast. Moderately alkaline (that is to say, hard) waters have a strengthening effect on gluten, as well as increasing its gas-retaining properties—and, consequently, the size of the loaf; on the other hand, very hard water tightens the gluten network in breads and can inhibit the action of yeast.

There are a number of ways by which the hardness in water may be reduced: Passing the water through an ion-exchange apparatus, a water filter mounted under the sink or on the faucet, or a water pitcher with a built-in filter that contains counteractive chemicals may be helpful, but most such systems principally exchange sodium for calcium compounds and are more effective in treating water used in the general household rather than water used in cooking. If the salts happen to consist of bicarbonates of calcium and magnesium, boiling the water for 20 or 30 minutes will cause them to precipitate. But if the water originally contains large amounts of sulfates, boiling it will increase hardness rather than reduce it, because the sulfates are concentrated by evaporation. ➤ Should you have hard or soft water that affects your cooking and baking outcomes in an undesirable way, keep a few gallons of distilled water in the pantry to assure that your cooking results will be successful.

Fluoridation is the process of adding fluoride to water to prevent tooth decay. Much municipal water is treated with fluoride. Water containing added fluoride does not affect cooking. **Chlorination** is the process of adding chlorine to water to prevent the spread of waterborne disease. Water that is too high in chlorine can inhibit yeast and bacteria development in breads and fermented foods, though typically tap water is perfectly fine to use for both. If you suspect that your tap water contains too much chlorine, try using distilled water.

In this book, when the word ➤ "water" appears in a recipe, we assume room temperature tap water. ➤ If hotter or colder water is needed, it is specified.

Occasionally recipes indicate ➤ water by weight, where 16 fluid ounces (2 cups) of water also weighs 16 ounces or 1 pound. In that case use 1 tablespoon for ½ ounce, and 1 cup for 8 ounces.

▲ The boiling temperature of water is different depending upon altitude. For boiling temperatures at high altitudes, see 1070.

EMERGENCY WATER PURIFICATION

These are temporary water disinfecting methods recommended for obtaining potable water during an emergency. In using or storing water, be sure of two things: that the source from which you get it is free of lead, petroleum, and other nonbiological contaminants, and that the vessels you store it in are sterile.

It is always a good idea to keep a supply of water on hand in case of emergency. We recommend buying distilled water, though you can fill your own containers with tap water, if desired. Use food-grade plastic bottles with tight-fitting screw-on lids, such as soda bottles and water or juice containers. Avoid plastic milk jugs, because it may be hard to remove residual milk sugars and proteins, allowing bacteria to grow. ➤ Allow 1 gallon water per day per person for drinking, and ½ gallon per day per person for personal cleanliness. Allow more for hot climates and for children, pregnant woman, and the elderly or ill. Allow 1 quart per day for each cat or dog.

If you are in an emergency situation and have doubts as to the purity of the water you have access to, first strain it through a fine, clean cloth or coffee filter to remove as much sediment as possible. Portable water purifiers are a convenient option, but if one is not available, it is also possible to purify water by boiling it or by adding a small amount of bleach. As noted above, ➤ these methods are effective against microbiological contaminants only; chemical pollutants will not be removed or rendered safe by them.

To purify water by boiling, boil the water vigorously for at least 1 minute; ▲ above 5,000 feet, boil the water for 3 minutes. Boiled water tastes flat, but it can be improved in flavor if aerated by pouring it a number of times from one clean vessel to another; or add a pinch of salt to every 1 quart water.

To purify water by adding bleach, first make sure that the bleach you use does not have added scents or cleaners and that the label says the bleach contains 6 or 8.25 percent sodium hypochlorite. Add 8 drops 6 percent bleach or 6 drops 8.25 percent bleach per 1 gallon water. If the water is cloudy, colored, or very cold, double the amount. In either case, stir and allow the water to stand for 30 minutes after adding the bleach. The water should have a distinct chlorine taste and odor. This is a sign of safety, and if you do not detect it by smell, add another dose of bleach and wait 15 minutes. If the chlorine odor is still not present, the chlorine may have weakened through age, and the water is not safe.

WORCESTERSHIRE SAUCE

This sharp, tangy, flavorful sauce was created in 1838 by John Wheeley Lea and William Perrins of Worcester, England. The original recipe is a closely held secret, but most agree that it contained soy sauce, anchovies, sugar, vinegar, tamarind, lemon, cloves, and other spices (for our homemade version, see Worcestershire Sauce, 1033). Worcestershire sauce can be used as a table condiment—especially for steak—but it is more commonly used to add depth and piquancy to sauces, marinades, meat dishes, gravies, soups, and cocktails like the Bloody Mary, 21.

YEASTS

Yeasts are tiny single-celled fungi of which there are hundreds of types. They feed on sugars and produce alcohol and carbon dioxide—the leavener in some batters and doughs. When flour is mixed with water and left to ferment, the **wild yeasts** from the air and the flour will eventually start working and form a sourdough starter, 608. The yeast feeds on natural sugars in the flour, making alcohol and carbon dioxide.

While it is easy enough to harness wild yeasts for baking, store-bought yeast is widely available and very predictable. A specific amount can be added to doughs, and the reaction is consistent enough to make following—and writing—recipes for breads much easier. For information on yeast as it is used in bread baking, see Yeast, 592.

ACTIVE DRY YEAST

This granular form of yeast is sold in airtight moisture-proof ¼-ounce packages measuring 2¼ teaspoons and is also available in larger jars. Active dry yeast has a longer shelf life than compressed yeast (see below). If stored in a cool place, it will keep for several months or somewhat longer in the refrigerator, and indefinitely in the freezer. It requires greater heat and more moisture than compressed or fresh yeast to activate it. We recommend that you test, or proof, the yeast to make sure it is "alive" by dissolving it in a small amount of warm water (105° to 115°F). It may also be mixed with the dry ingredients and activated by using 120° to 130°F liquid. Using cooler water to activate dry yeast releases by-products that can inhibit gluten formation.

To ➤ substitute active dry yeast for compressed yeast, use 1 package (2¼ teaspoons) active dry yeast for each 0.6-ounce cake of compressed yeast. To substitute active dry yeast for instant or quick-rise yeast, below, use the same amount.

NUTRITIONAL YEAST

Nutritional yeast, a dry deactivated yeast sold in powder or flake form, has no leavening power. It is used to add nutritive value and a savory, slightly cheesy flavor to foods. It is a good source of B vitamins and is commonly used in vegan recipes to help replicate the flavor of cheese.

COMPRESSED (FRESH) YEAST

Compressed yeast, also called fresh yeast, is yeast with a high moisture content. This living organism, dependent on definite temperature ranges, begins to activate at about 50°F ➤ and is at its most active between 78° and 82°F. It begins to die around 120°F and is useless for baking above 143°F. Cakes of compressed yeast typically weigh about 0.6 ounce, although they come in larger sizes as well. Compressed yeast must be kept refrigerated.

Fresh yeast is not available at most supermarkets; it can be purchased from a bakery supply company, online retailer, or catalog. If bought fresh, it will keep for about 2 weeks. Frozen, it will keep for 2 months; take out only what is needed and let it thaw overnight in the refrigerator. When fresh yeast is at its best, it is a light grayish-tan color. It crumbles readily, breaks with a clean edge, and smells pleasantly aromatic. When old, it turns brownish in color. To test for freshness, cream a small quantity of yeast with an equal amount of sugar. It should become liquid at once. Crumble compressed yeast and dissolve in 70° to 80°F liquid for 5 minutes before combining with the other ingredients called for in the recipe.

Some consider fresh yeast to be superior to active dry and instant yeasts. Fresh yeast produces the most carbon dioxide of the baking yeasts. However, its short shelf life is a significant drawback. To substitute fresh yeast for active dry or quick-rise, use one 0.6-ounce cake for each package active dry or quick-rise yeast.

INSTANT OR QUICK-RISE YEAST

Also labeled as "quick acting" or "rapid rise," this type of dry yeast is sold in packets, and cuts rising times dramatically, sometimes in half. While active dry yeast is made of live yeast granules coated in a layer of dead yeast, instant yeast particles are all alive, which can make a flavor difference in lean breads (breads that are low in fat and use water instead of milk).

The main advantage of instant yeast was once that it could be added directly to the dry ingredients without rehydration or proofing. However, active dry yeasts can now be mixed in with the dry ingredients so long as 120° to 130°F liquid is used. Instant yeast is stronger than active dry yeast and leavens doughs more quickly. To substitute for active dry yeast, use the same amount of instant or quick-rise yeast.

YOGURT

Yogurt is milk that has been cultured with *Lactobacillus* and *Streptococcus* bacteria. Traditionally, yogurt was cultured by adding some of the previous batch of yogurt to it. However, modern yogurt manufacturers use powdered cultures to ensure a consistent product. As the milk ferments, the bacteria produce lactic acid and the yogurt thickens into a dense but soft, fine-textured curd. **Greek yogurt** is a thicker style of yogurt made by draining yogurt to remove some of its whey. **Labneh** is a close cousin of Greek yogurt, but it is usually even thicker. **Skyr** is a type of drained yogurt from Iceland with a texture much like Greek yogurt and a mildly tart flavor. There are also a wide variety of nondairy yogurts available, from soy yogurt to cashew yogurt to coconut yogurt. These are all cultured, but most nondairy yogurts require some thickening substance to achieve a texture similar to yogurt. While many different types of flavored and sweetened yogurts are available, we find plain yogurt to be the most versatile and use it in recipes of all kinds, from salad dressings to quick breads and cakes to marinades for meat. Plain yogurt also makes an excellent stand-in for sour cream. Keep yogurt refrigerated at or below 40°F. It generally keeps for 10 days after the sell-by date. For recipes using yogurt, see Raita, 569, Tzatziki, 569, Mango Lassi, 13, French Yogurt Cake, 734, and Tandoori Marinade, 580.

HOMEMADE YOGURT

About 1 quart

The particulars of the milk you use will determine its consistency. Whole cow's milk will set up very thick. Low-fat, nonfat, or goat milk will not be as thick. In fact, it might be the consistency of drinkable yogurt. If you prefer thicker yogurt, there are a few things you can do. One is to hold the milk at 180°F for 30 minutes, which will denature some of the whey proteins and cause them to form a thicker gel. Another option is to whisk in ¼ **cup dry milk powder** for every 1 quart liquid milk before heating it. Finally, you can thicken the yogurt after it has set by ladling it into a colander lined with a flour sack towel and letting it stand until enough whey has drained off for the yogurt to be thickened to your liking.

For this recipe you will need a system for keeping the milk warm as it sets. This can be a small cooler filled with towels. A heating pad or seedling heat mat can be another good option. Insulated containers made specifically for yogurt making are also available, as well as proofing boxes. If you have an immersion circulator, fill a pot or other vessel with water, attach the circulator, and program it to 109°F. When the water is preheated, place the sealed jar of cultured milk in the vessel (the water should completely cover the jar) and let the yogurt set for 5 to 8 hours or until thickened.

Wash a 1-quart wide-mouth glass jar with soap and hot water. Rinse thoroughly, then rinse again with boiling water. Let it dry completely.

Pour into a saucepan or double-boiler:

4 cups whole or low-fat milk

Heat the milk over medium heat to 180°F, stirring often. If desired, for a thicker yogurt, hold the milk at this temperature, stirring occasionally, for up to 30 minutes. (The easiest way to do this is by using a double-boiler to prevent the milk from scorching.)

Fill the sink with cold water, set the pan of milk in the water bath, and stir constantly until the temperature reaches 118°F. Be careful at this stage because the temperature will drop rapidly, and if the milk gets too cool, it will not set properly.

Stir in:

2 tablespoons plain yogurt with live cultures or a powdered yogurt culture (use a powdered yogurt culture as directed on the package)

Stir the milk to disperse the culture, then insulate it using the method of your choosing (see the headnote). After 4 hours, check the milk. If it is not yet ready, check it again in 2 more hours. It may take up to 8 hours for the milk to set. Refrigerate the yogurt.

YOGURT CHEESE

For every 1 cup yogurt, you will end up with roughly ½ cup yogurt cheese.

Line a strainer or colander with several layers of cheesecloth or a flour sack towel and set over a bowl. Spoon in:

Plain yogurt, store-bought or homemade, 1034

Cover with plastic wrap and refrigerate until the consistency of cream cheese, 12 to 24 hours.

Discard the whey or save it for smoothies, baking, or marinades. Keep in the refrigerator for up to 1 week. Pour off any liquid that accumulates before using.

ABOUT SUBSTITUTIONS AND EQUIVALENTS

You're a new cook and you run out of granulated sugar. Don't think this doesn't happen to old cooks too! So you just substitute powdered sugar. When the cake is not so sweet as it should be and the texture is horrid, you wonder what happened.

Good recipes and the reasonable use of standard measures allow you to cook well without knowing that it takes about 2 cups of sugar or butter to make a pound but that you would need just shy of 4 cups of all-purpose flour for a pound. This you discover fast enough if you leave the United States, for almost everyone else cooks by weight, not volume.

Knowing this, think back to the issue we just talked about: substituting powdered sugar for granulated sugar. The first problem with making this substitution is that, while you might have used a volume of powdered sugar equivalent to the volume of granulated sugar called for, powdered sugar weighs significantly less than the same volume of granulated sugar. Granulated sugar weighs about 200 grams, or 7 ounces, per cup, while powdered sugar weighs about 100 grams, or 3.6 ounces, per cup. Thus, powdered sugar weighs only half as much as the same volume of granulated sugar.

Armed with this knowledge, you might think you could substitute twice as much powdered sugar for granulated sugar, but again, you would be wrong. Even if you substitute the same weight of one ingredient for another, you must also consider the properties of the ingredient called for in the recipe and the properties of the ingredient you plan to use instead. Powdered sugar is not only much finer than granulated sugar, but it also contains some cornstarch. Depending on the recipe, the cornstarch could cause liquids to thicken when you do not want them to. In butter cakes, where butter and sugar are creamed together to incorporate air, powdered sugar is too fine to perform this function, and the cake will likely be dense.

In making substitutions, you are always taking a risk that the recipe will not work as it should, but armed with some practical knowledge, you can make educated decisions about substitutions and improve your chances of success considerably. Use the information provided in this section to help you make these decisions.

TABLES OF EQUIVALENTS AND CONVERSIONS

Here, at the end of a lengthy book that extensively utilizes US measuring systems, we must take a moment to complain. Particularly, we find it is most unfortunate that the same word can have two meanings. For instance, an ounce may mean 1/16 of a pound or 1/16 of a pint, but the former is strictly a weight measure and the latter a volume measure. A fluid ounce and an ounce of weight are two completely different quantities thanks to the variable density of ingredients. Perhaps for this reason cooks in most other countries measure solid ingredients by weight (and [ahem] in the metric system's easily arithmetized units of ten). While we find using weights to be unnecessary in most home-cooked savory recipes, measuring by weight for baking recipes will make your life easier and yield more consistent results. For curing and fermenting, measuring ingredients by weight helps guarantee safety—and allows for greater versatility when scaling a recipe up or down. For these applications, a digital gram/ounce scale with ⅛-ounce or 1-gram accuracy and a 10-pound or 4,536-gram capacity is an affordable and worthwhile investment.

VOLUME EQUIVALENTS

All these equivalents are based on US volume measures. For the US–Metric Fluid Volume chart, see 1037.

60 drops	=	1 teaspoon
1 teaspoon	=	⅓ tablespoon
1 tablespoon	=	3 teaspoons
2 tablespoons	=	1 ounce
4 tablespoons	=	¼ cup or 2 ounces
5⅓ tablespoons	=	⅓ cup or 2⅔ ounces
8 tablespoons	=	½ cup or 4 ounces
16 tablespoons	=	1 cup or 8 ounces
⅜ cup	=	¼ cup plus 2 tablespoons
⅝ cup	=	½ cup plus 2 tablespoons
⅞ cup	=	¾ cup plus 2 tablespoons
1 cup	=	½ pint, 8 fluid ounces, or 16 tablespoons
2 cups	=	1 pint or 16 fluid ounces
1 gill (liquid)	=	½ cup or 4 fluid ounces
1 pint (liquid)	=	4 gills or 16 fluid ounces
1 quart (liquid)	=	2 pints, 4 cups, or 32 fluid ounces
1 gallon (liquid)	=	4 quarts, 16 cups, or 128 fluid ounces

DRY-MEASURE VOLUME EQUIVALENTS

Dry measures are used for raw fruits and vegetables when dealing with fairly large quantities.

	Dry Pints	Dry Quarts	Pecks	Bushels	Liters
1 Dry Pint	1	½	1/16	1/64	0.55
1 Dry Quart	2	1	⅛	1/32	1.1
1 Peck	16	8	1	¼	8.8
1 Bushel	64	32	4	1	35.23
1 Liter	1.82	0.91	0.114	0.028	1

APPROXIMATE TEMPERATURE EQUIVALENTS

	Fahrenheit	Celsius
Coldest area of freezer	–10°	–23°
Freezer	0°	–18°
Refrigerator	38°–40°	3°–4°
Water Freezes	32°	0°
Water simmers	190°–205°	88°–96°
Water boils (at sea level)	212°	100°
Very low oven	250°–275°	121°–135°
Low oven	300°–325°	149°–163°
Moderate oven	350°–375°	177°–191°
Hot oven	400°–425°	204°–218°
Very hot oven	450°–475°	232°–246°
Extremely hot oven	500°–525°	260°–274°
Broil	About 550°	About 288°

To convert Fahrenheit into Celsius, subtract 32, multiply by 5, divide by 9. To convert Celsius into Fahrenheit, go in reverse: Multiply by 9, divide by 5, add 32.

USDA RECOMMENDED COOKING TEMPERATURES

These cooking temperatures are determined to be safe by the USDA. For the internal cooking temperatures we recommend for meats, see 453.

Egg Dishes	160°F
Ground Meat and Meat Mixtures	
Turkey and chicken	165°F
Veal, beef, lamb, and pork	160°F
Fresh Beef, Veal, and Lamb	145°F
Fresh Pork	145°F
Poultry	165°F
Ham	
Fresh (raw)	145°F
Precooked (to reheat)	140°F
Fish	145°F
Leftovers and Casseroles	165°F

ABOUT METRIC CONVERSION

These tables, which convert by both weight and volume, are handy if you want to translate American recipes to use metric measures.

The charts, below, compare common kitchen measures from metric to American Standard and vice versa. To use, we give the following example: To determine the equivalent number of US cups in a recipe that calls for 500 milliliters liquid, look at the US–Metric Fluid Volume chart, below. Find 1 milliliter in the left column; follow across to cups to find 0.004. Multiply 500 by 0.004, and you will get the answer: 2 cups. Or, use the chart to help remind you of how many tablespoons are in 1 cup.

US–METRIC FLUID VOLUME

	Fluid Drams	Tea-spoons	Table-spoons	Fluid Ounces	¼ Cups	½ Cups (Gills)	Cups	Fluid Pints	Fluid Quarts	Gallons	Milli-liters	Liters
1 Fluid Dram	1	¾	¼	⅛ (.125)	1/16 (.0625)	.03125	.0156	.0078	.0039	1/1024	3.7	.0037
1 Tea-spoon	1⅓	1	⅓	⅙	1/12	1/24	1/48	1/96	1/192	1/768	5	.005
1 Table-spoon	4	3	1	½	¼	⅛	1/16	1/32	1/64	1/256	15	.015
1 Fluid Ounce	8	6	2	1	½	¼	⅛	1/16	1/32	1/128	29.56	.03
¼ Cup	16	12	4	2	1	½	¼	⅛	1/16	1/64	59.125	.059
½ Cup (Gill)	32	24	8	4	2	1	½	¼	⅛	1/32	118.25	.118
1 Cup	64	48	16	8	4	2	1	½	¼	1/16	236	.236
1 Fluid Pint	128	96	32	16	8	4	2	1	½	⅛	473	.473
1 Fluid Quart	256	192	64	32	16	8	4	2	1	¼	946	.946
1 Gallon	1024	768	256	128	64	32	16	8	4	1	3785.4	3.785
1 Milli-liter	.27	.203	.067	.034	.017	.008	.004	.002	.001	.0003	1	.001
1 Liter	270.5	203.04	67.68	33.814	16.906	8.453	4.227	2.113	1.057	.264	1000	1

US–METRIC MASS (WEIGHT)

	Grains	Drams	Ounces	Pounds	Milligrams	Grams	Kilograms
1 Grain	1	.037	.002	1/7000	64.7	.064	.0006
1 Dram	27.34	1	1/16	1/256	1770	1.77	.002
1 Ounce	437.5	16	1	1/16	2835	28.35	.028
1 Pound	7000	256	16	1	453,592	454	.454
1 Milligram	.015	.0006	1/29,000	1/453,592	1	.001	.000001
1 Gram	15.43	.565	.035	.002	1000	1	.001
1 Kilogram	15,432	564.38	35.27	2.2	1000000	1000	1

EQUIVALENTS AND SUBSTITUTIONS FOR COMMON INGREDIENTS

Also check specific sections in different chapters for individual items; see Index for further information.

Almonds		
in the shell	3½ lb.	1 lb. shelled
unblanched, whole	6 oz.	1 cup
unblanched, ground	1 lb.	2⅔ cups
unblanched, slivered	1 lb.	5⅔ cups
blanched, whole	5⅓ oz.	1 cup
blanched, slivered	4 oz.	1 cup
meal	3¼ oz. or 92g	1 cup
paste	9¾ oz. or 276g	1 cup
Apples	1 lb. or 3 medium	3 to 4 cups peeled, cored, and sliced
	3½ to 4 lb. raw	1 lb. dried
Apricots, dried	1 lb.	2¾ cups
Apricots, fresh	5½ lb.	1 lb. dried
	1 lb. or 8 to 12 medium	2½ cups sliced or 2 cups chopped
Arrowroot (as a thickener)	1¼ teaspoons	1 tablespoon all-purpose flour
	3¾ teaspoons	1 tablespoon cornstarch
Avocados	1 lb. or 2 medium	2 cups diced or 1 cup mashed
Bacon	16 oz. package	16 to 20 slices
	8 slices cooked	½ cup crumbled
Baking soda	1 tablespoon	½ oz. or 15g
Baker's ammonia or ammonium carbonate	1 teaspoon ground	1 teaspoon baking powder
Bananas	1 lb. or 3 to 4 medium	1¾ cups mashed
Beans, black-eyed peas, fresh	1 lb. in the shell	1½ cups shelled
Beans, cranberry, fresh	1 lb. in the shell	1½ cups shelled
Beans, dried	1 lb. or about 2½ cups	6 to 7 cups cooked
Beans, fava, fresh	1 lb. in the shell	⅔ to ¾ cup shelled
Beans, green, fresh	1 lb.	3 cups
Beans, lima, fresh	1 lb. in the shell	1 cup shelled
Beets	1 lb.	2 cups cubed or sliced
Blackberries	1 lb.	3 cups
Blueberries	1 lb.	3 cups
Bread crumbs, dry soft	¼ to ⅓ cup	1 slice bread
Broccoli	1 lb.	4 to 5 cups chopped
Bulgur, fine	1 cup dry (5½ oz. or 157g)	3 cups cooked
Butter		
1 stick	4 oz. or 113g	½ cup or 8 tablespoons
4 sticks	1 lb.	2 cups
Buttermilk	1 cup (8½ oz. or 243g)	1 cup plain yogurt
Cabbage	1 lb.	4 cups shredded (packed)
Cape gooseberries	1 lb. trimmed	3 cups
Carrots	1 lb.	4 cups shredded or 3½ cups diced
Cauliflower	1 lb.	4 cups chopped
Celery	1 lb.	4½ cups chopped
Cheese, blue	4 oz.	1 cup crumbled
Cheese, cottage	1 cup	8½ oz. or 234g
Cheese, cream	3 oz.	6 tablespoons
	8 oz.	1 cup
Cheese, shredded	4 oz.	1 cup
	1 lb.	4 cups
Cherries	1 lb.	3 to 4 cups unpitted, 2½ cups pitted
Chestnuts	1 lb. in shell	2 cups or 8 oz. peeled
Chiles, whole, dried	2½ oz. or 71g, stemmed and seeded	½ cup ground

Chocolate, unsweetened	1 oz.	3 tablespoons unsweetened cocoa powder mixed with 1 tablespoon butter or other fat, melted
Chocolate chips	6 oz. or 170g	1 cup
Cocoa powder, Dutch process	1 cup	3½ oz. 100g
Cocoa powder, natural	1 cup	3 oz. or 82g
Coconut	1 medium	About 3 cups grated fresh
	1 lb.	5 cups shredded
Coffee	1 lb.	48 brewed, 6 oz. servings
Corn	1 medium ear	½ cup kernels
Cornmeal	1 lb.	3 cups
	1 cup, fine	5⅔ oz. or 160g
	1 cup, medium	5⅓ oz. or 150g
Cornstarch	1 cup	4½ oz. or 129g
Corn syrup	1 cup	12⅓ oz. or 350g
Crackers	24 buttery-round	1 cup crumbs
	About 7 full-size graham	1 cup crumbs
	30 saltines	1 cup crumbs
Cranberries	1 lb.	4 cups
	12 oz. package	3 cups
Dates	1 lb.	2½ cups pitted
Eggs, fresh, whole, out of shell		
Jumbo	4 eggs	About 1 cup
1 egg	4⅛ tablespoons	2¼ oz. or 63g
Extra-large	4 eggs	About 1 cup
1 egg	3⅔ tablespoons	2 oz. or 56g
Large	5 eggs	About 1 cup
1 egg	3⅓ tablespoons	1¾ oz. or 50g
Medium	5 eggs	About 1 cup
1 egg	2⅞ tablespoons	1½ oz. or 44g
Small	6 eggs	About 1 cup
1 egg	2½ tablespoons	1⅓ oz. or 38g
Eggs, fresh, liquid	1 cup beaten	8½ oz. or 243g

Egg yolks	3½ teaspoons or 17g	1 large egg yolk
Egg whites	2 tablespoons plus ½ teaspoon or 33g	1 large egg white
Eggs, dried	2½ tablespoons, beaten with 2½ tablespoons water	1 whole egg
Eggs, quail	1 egg	¼ oz. or 9g
Eggs, bantam	1 egg	⅔ oz. or 19g
Eggs, duck	1 egg	3 oz. or 85g
Eggs, goose	1 egg	8 to 10 oz. or 227 to 283g
Eggs, emu	1 egg	1¼ lb. or 510g
Eggs, ostrich	1 egg	4¼ lb. or 1,927g
Figs, fresh	1 lb. or 12 medium	About 2½ cups chopped
Flour, all-purpose	1 cup	4⅓ oz. or 125g
	1 cup sifted	4¼ oz. or 120g
Flour, bread	1 cup	4⅔ oz. or 130g
Flour, cake	1 cup	4 oz. or 110g
	1 cup sifted	3½ oz. or 100g
	1 cup	1 cup minus 2 tablespoons all-purpose flour (110g), plus 2 tablespoons (15g) cornstarch (sift together 5 times)
Flour, brown rice	1 cup	5 oz. or 142g
Flour, buckwheat	1 cup	4⅓ oz. or 123g
Flour, chickpea	1 cup	4 oz. or 115g
Flour, dark rye	1 cup	4¼ oz. or 120g
Flour, oat	1 cup	3⅔ oz. or 103g
Flour, pastry	1 cup	4¼ oz. or 120g
Flour, rice	1 cup	4 oz. or 112g
Flour, semolina	1 cup	5⅔ oz. or 159g
Flour, sorghum	1 cup	4¼ oz. or 121g
Flour, soy	1 cup	3 oz. or 82g
Flour, spelt	1 cup	4⅓ oz. or 123g
Flour, whole wheat	1 cup	4⅔ oz. or 130g

Garlic	1 small clove	1/8 teaspoon powder, 1/4 teaspoon granulated, or 1/2 teaspoon minced
Gelatin	1/4 oz. envelope	About 2 1/2 teaspoons
	1/4 oz. envelope	3 1/2 sheets gelatin (4 × 9 inches)
Gelatin for 2 cups liquid	1/4 oz. envelope	About 2 1/2 teaspoons
Gooseberries	1 lb. trimmed	3 cups
Grapefruit	1 medium	About 1 cup juice
Grapes	1 lb. stemmed	About 3 cups
Hazelnuts	1 lb.	3 1/3 cups
Herbs	1/2 teaspoon dried	1 tablespoon chopped fresh
Honey	1 cup	11 3/4 oz. or 336g
Horseradish	1 tablespoon grated fresh	2 tablespoons prepared
Lemons	1	2 to 3 tablespoons juice, 1 to 1 1/2 teaspoons grated zest
Lentils	1 lb. or 2 1/4 cups	7 1/2 cups cooked
Limes	1	1 1/2 to 2 tablespoons juice, 1 teaspoon zest
Macaroni	1 lb.	4 cups uncooked
	1 cup	2 to 2 1/4 cups cooked
Mango	1 medium	1 cup peeled and diced
Meat, ground	1 lb.	2 cups ground
Milk, evaporated	1 cup	8 3/4 oz. or 248g
Milk powder	1 cup	3 1/4 oz. or 93g
Milk, sweetened condensed	1 cup	10 3/4 oz. or 304g
Milk, whole	1 cup (236g)	1/2 cup evaporated plus 1/2 cup water
	1/4 cup dry whole milk powder plus 3/4 cup plus 2 tablespoons water	1 cup unsweetened soy or almond milk
Molasses	1 cup	12 oz. or 340g
Mushrooms	8 oz. or about 3 cups whole	About 1 cup cooked sliced
Mushrooms, dried	3 oz., reconstituted	1 lb. fresh
Nectarines	1 lb. or 3 to 4 medium	2 cups sliced or 2 1/2 cups chopped
Noodles	1 lb.	6 to 8 cups cooked
Oat bran	1 cup	3 3/4 oz. or 107g
Oats, rolled	1 cup	3 1/2 oz. or 100g
Okra	1 lb.	4 1/2 cups sliced
Onion	1 medium	1 cup chopped
	1 small	1/2 to 3/4 cup chopped
	1 large	1 1/2 cups chopped
Orange	1 medium	4 to 6 tablespoons juice, 2 to 3 tablespoons grated zest
Orange juice	1 cup	8 2/3 oz. or 244g
Peaches	1 lb. or 3 to 4 medium	2 cups sliced
Peanut Butter	18 oz. jar	2 cups
	1 cup	8 1/3 oz. or 237g
Pears	1 lb. or 2 to 3 medium	2 cups peeled, cored, and sliced
Peas, fresh	1 lb. in the shell	1 to 1 1/4 cups shelled
Peppers, bell	1 large or 6 oz.	1 cup diced
Pineapple, fresh	1 medium	3 1/2 cups diced or 4 cups sliced
Plums	1 lb. or 6 to 8 medium	2 1/2 cups sliced

Pomegranate	1 medium	½ cup seeds
Potatoes	1 lb. or 3 medium	1¾ cups mashed cooked
Prunes	1 lb. pitted	2½ cups
Raisins	1 lb.	About 2¾ cups
Raspberries	1 lb.	About 3½ cups
Rhubarb	1 lb.	About 3½ cups chopped
Rice	1 lb. or 2 cups	About 6 cups cooked
Shallots	1 small	2 tablespoons chopped
Squash, winter	1 lb.	2½ cups cubed or 1¾ cups cooked and mashed
Strawberries	1 lb.	3½ cups whole or 2 cups chopped or sliced
	1 quart	1½ lb.

Sugar, brown	1 cup packed	8 oz. or 230g
Sugar, powdered	1 cup	3⅔ oz. or 102g
Sugar, superfine	1 cup	6¾ oz. or 192g
Sugar, white	1 cup	7 oz. or 200g
Tomatoes	1 lb. or 3 medium	2 cups chopped
Tomatoes, cherry	1 lb.	3 cups
Walnuts, English	1 lb.	4½ cups
Water	1 cup	8⅓ oz. or 237g
Wheat germ	1 cup	2¾ oz. or 80g
Yeast, active dry	1 envelope active dry	2¼ teaspoons
Yeast, compressed	1 cake (⅗ oz.)	1 envelope
Yogurt	1 cup	8½ oz. or 240g

COOKING METHODS AND TECHNIQUES

Marion began this chapter in 1975 with an anecdote well worth repeating: A hard-boiled professional cook was asked what she regarded as the most useful, elementary advice for an ambitious beginner. She tersely replied, "Stand facing the stove." While Marion's deadpan wit may lurk beneath this nugget of common sense, we think a different reading might be worth considering: Before we begin, we should take a moment open our senses to observe and appraise our tools, the workspace, and situate ourselves in relation to them. Much intervenes between a recipe on the page and food on the plate: the quirks of your stove or cooktop, the particularities of the ingredients you purchased, the tastes and preferences of those you cook for. These myriad factors can only be accounted for by an inquiring mind observant of its surroundings.

Taking nothing for granted will take any cook a long way toward success. You cannot simply apply formulae from a book of recipes, nor is any single bit of advice going to make accessible the knowledge gained from years of fiddling with the shape and heft of ingredients and the application of heat. In other words, a good cook is good because they cook, often, and with curiosity.

Just as we become better cooks by assuming the stance of an observer, new cooks benefit immensely from taking a minute to appreciate the larger contours (and some important finer points) of the techniques they will need to use. In this chapter we cover measuring ingredients and temperatures; a basic primer on knife work and preparing ingredients; methods used in cooking; and finally, the stoves, appliances, cookware, and other tools at our disposal. In addition to the topics discussed in this chapter, please read the information in Getting Started, xiii.

MEASURING INGREDIENTS

The importance of measuring ingredients, especially in baking, cannot be overstated. There are several kinds of measuring tools used in cooking. **Measuring spoons** are designed to measure small quantities of dry or wet ingredients. **Dry measuring cups** are designed for measuring flour, sugar, and other dry ingredients, as well as solid fats like shortening and thick pastes like nut butters. Clear **liquid measuring cups** have quantities marked on their sides; we prefer those made of heat-resistant glass, but sturdy plastic models are perfectly fine to use. We recommend having a 1- or 2-cup measure with lines for every ⅛ cup (one ounce) for small jobs, and a 4-cup measure for larger quantities. Recently, we have become very fond of plastic ¼-cup measuring cups for efficiently adding tablespoon quantities of liquids (our favorite model is illustrated in Tools for

Cocktail-Making, 17). ➤ Do not use liquid measuring cups for dry ingredients, or vice versa, as the results will not be accurate.

A **digital scale** is an invaluable piece of measuring equipment, whether for weighing vegetables, meat, and fish, or the ingredients for a dough or batter. Scales are ideal for baking recipes in particular: They provide the most accurate measurements of flour, which can be compacted in the package or in measuring cups. Additionally, they are easier to use than cups and spoons and leave the cook with less to clean. We have added gram weights to the baking chapters in this book for these very reasons. We have also added gram weights to fermenting and curing recipes for easy scaling, safety, and accuracy. (For those wondering why we embraced metric in these instances, the answer is simple: 165g is much easier to look at—not to mention scale up or down—than 5⅞ ounces.) When purchasing, choose a digital scale that measures grams and ounces in 1-gram or ⅛-ounce increments and has a 10-pound or 4,536-gram capacity. When using a scale for multiple ingredients that are to be mixed together, weigh them all in the same bowl by first pressing the "tare" or "zero" button with the bowl empty. Add the first ingredient, then tare or zero again before weighing each additional ingredient.

All recipes in this book are ➤ based on standard US containers: the 8-ounce cup and a tablespoon that takes exactly 16 level fillings to fill that cup. It should be noted that there is a difference between volume and weight. When we refer to an "8-ounce cup," we are, in fact, referring to the volume of a cup. The weight of 1 cup of any ingredient may differ dramatically. For instance, 1 cup all-purpose flour weighs 125 grams, and 1 cup water weighs 235 grams, though they are technically both 8 ounces in volume.

Confusingly, the term "ounce" is also used as a weight in some contexts. For example, the recipes in this book that call for cheese do so in both volume and ounce weight, e.g., "1 cup shredded Cheddar (4 ounces)." Adherents of the metric system may shudder at the awkwardness of the American measuring system, but they are not an impediment to good cooking. That said, one of the easiest ways to improve at baking is to familiarize yourself with measuring by weight.

Almost our recipes are based on level measurements—most hedgers, like "heaping" or "scant," were weeded out of our instructions years ago. For measuring dry ingredients like flours by volume, we use the **spoon and level technique.** Meaning, we first lighten the ingredient by stirring or whisking it in its container, then we use a spoon to transfer the ingredient into a measuring cup. Finally, when the cup is just over full, we use a straight edge, such as a bench scraper, ruler, or offset spatula, to level the ingredient in the cup so it is flush with the rim. This ensures that the ingredient is not packed in the cup (with the exception of brown sugar, which is usually "packed" into the measuring cup for consistency). ➤ Never level flour or other dry ingredients by shaking, tamping, or tapping the cup.

If measuring by volume, ➤ take extra care to note whether flour or other ingredients are sifted, 1045, before or after measuring. When an ingredient line says, "1 cup sifted all-purpose flour," it means the flour should be sifted into the measuring cup, then leveled. Alternatively, "1 cup all-purpose flour, sifted" means the flour should be spooned and leveled, then sifted after measuring. Sifting flour improves the texture of all cakes by lightening it and removing any lumps, which allows it to be incorporated more easily into batters. This is especially important for delicate cakes like Angel Food Cake, 719, Génoise, 721, and sponge cakes, 720–22. Sifting salt, leaveners, and spices with the flour ensures even distribution.

Spooning and leveling flour

To measure bulk fats by volume, see Measuring Fats, 980.

For converting ingredient quantities to a different unit of measurement, see Tables of Equivalents and Conversions, 1035. For converting between the weight and volume of numerous staples, see Equivalents and Substitutions for Common Ingredients, 1038.

MEASURING TEMPERATURES

The application of heat in cooking can be an uncertain proposition. Nearly every stove is different, so when we call for medium heat, we do so with the realization that your "medium" may be hotter or colder than our "medium." Similarly, not every oven is perfectly calibrated. While sensory cues are crucial to cooking and can compensate for a great deal of inaccuracy in our cooking implements, we strongly recommend outfitting your kitchen with thermometers.

For proper cold storage, place thermometers in your freezer and refrigerator to determine whether they are cold enough or need to be adjusted (for details, see The Refrigerator, 879, and The Freezer, 880).

An **instant-read digital probe thermometer** is essential for measuring the internal temperature of meat, poultry, and temperature-sensitive foods like egg-based sauces and custards. Though a regular, handheld instant-read thermometer will work for candy making, we recommend one that clamps to the side of a pot and can be left in the boiling sugar syrup. See About Candy Thermometers, 856.

Of course, a thermometer is only useful if it is accurate. Test all probe thermometers for accuracy every 6 months or so, or any time the thermometer is dropped.

To test a thermometer for accuracy, bring a saucepan of water to a boil. Measure the temperature of the water, without allowing the thermometer probe to touch the side of the pan. It should register 212°F or 100°C. Then, perform a second test. Fill a glass completely full with ice, then fill it with cold water. Submerge the thermometer in the ice water without allowing the stem to touch the side of the glass. The thermometer should read 32°F or 0°C. If there is a minor variation, add or subtract the number of degrees necessary to correct its reading when using it. If the reading is off by more than 5 degrees, recalibrate the thermometer. For digital thermometers, calibrate by following the manufacturer's instructions. Dial thermometers may be calibrated by turning the small nut on the back of the thermometer. Take note of how many degrees the thermometer is off by, then turn the nut so the dial reads that many degrees higher or lower. After adjusting the thermometer, repeat the hot and cold tests for accuracy to make sure your adjustment was correct.

On the off chance you are using a mercury thermometer and it reads 5 degrees off—or you can see gaps in the mercury—replace the thermometer (take mercury thermometers to a local hazardous waste collection facility—do not throw them away in your regular trash).

Though not absolutely necessary, we recommend purchasing a leave-in **oven thermometer,** which will tell you how accurate your oven's thermostat is. If the thermostat is inaccurate, you may either calibrate it according to the manufacturer's instructions or, if your oven does not have that option, you may simply take any discrepancies into account when setting the temperature. For example, if a thermometer reveals that your oven consistently runs 25°F too hot, set it 25°F lower than a given recipe instructs.

For important temperatures and their equivalents in Celsius, see Approximate Temperature Equivalents, 1036.

PREP METHODS

The preparatory steps to cooking are just as important to the process as the act of cooking itself. Because much of cooking revolves around the act of applying heat and the rate at which different foods cook, it can be a bit vexing for the new cook. Most recipes give concrete directions, including approximate times for cooking. But because stoves, ingredients, the weather, and humans vary so widely, these cooking times are not absolute, and the cook must make judgment call after judgment call during the process. Prowess in this area comes with experience, but if you are new to cooking, remember that one easy way to take some of the pressure off is to prepare well and stay organized.

When we step into the kitchen to cook, we do a few things to start. We clean the countertops of any clutter, wash any dishes lingering in the sink, and clear out the dish drying rack. We check the knife we are about to use for sharpness (see Sharpening Knives, 1075). We read the recipe we are going to prepare at least one time through and look up anything we do not understand. We gather ingredients together and start to wash, trim, and cut them as needed. By the time we actually turn on the stove or oven, we are well prepared for the task ahead of us.

Preparing all ingredients before cooking is often referred to by the French phrase **mise en place,** or "putting in place." Mise en place is heavily emphasized by food writers and culinary professionals, and for good reason: The efficiency (and sanity) of harried line cooks in high-pressure restaurant kitchens depends upon having an ample supply of ingredients ready before service. (Indeed, we have seen the phrase tattooed on some especially enthusiastic line cooks.) Of course, the home kitchen is (thankfully) a very different environment. Though having all of the ingredients cut and assembled before cooking is certainly required for some recipes—such as for stir-fries, where everything is added to the pan in quick succession—keep in mind that ingredients needed later in a recipe can be put together as others are browning or simmering. Once you get a sense of what can be successfully multitasked, prepping as you cook can save precious time. (For more on mise en place, see xxxix.)

Going through this section, you may notice a lack of preparatory tasks associated with baking. Since kneading doughs, 595, creaming butter, 723, and folding in egg whites, 709, are so central to success in baking, we cover them in their respective chapters or sections.

KNIFE CUTS

Cooking requires the use of a sharp knife for cutting meats, chopping herbs, and preparing fresh vegetables. Many chopping and slicing devices are available, but nothing can replace a relaxed skilled wrist and a sharp, well-balanced knife. Learning basic knife cuts and acquiring skill in making these cuts will make cooking easier, faster, and more enjoyable. For advice on choosing kitchen knives and sharpening instructions, see About Knives, 1074.

For practically all cutting tasks, we recommend ➤ gripping the knife so that your thumb and index finger pinch the knife blade on either side. Never grip the handle with all five fingers—keeping two fingers against the blade itself will give you better control of the knife and will keep your hand and wrist from getting fatigued.

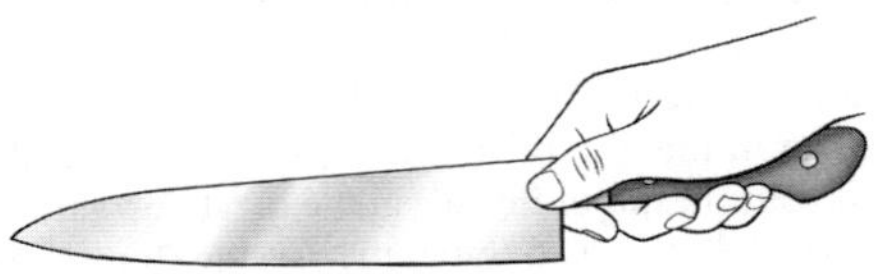

How to properly grip a knife

Practice cutting with soft foods like mushrooms, which are yielding and not slippery when placed on the cutting board. Work up to an onion or potato, each of which can be resistant and slippery. The proper way to steady most foods for cutting is to grip the food with your nondominant hand in a "claw" shape, with the palm and wrist parallel to the cutting surface and the fingers turned under, pressing down on the item to be cut. This keeps the fingers out of the way of the blade and allows you to use your knuckles as a guide. As the slicing progresses, the holding hand inches a slow retreat, without releasing its grasp on the object.

When slicing thin foods such as, say, a carrot, keep the point of the knife on the cutting board, using it as a pivot point. For thicker foods like halved onions, the entire knife may be lifted off the cutting surface in order to avoid straining the wrist. The cutting edge should never be lifted above the joints of the fingers that hold the food.

We use several general cutting directives throughout this book: dice, chop, and mince. Here, we define them in the broadest terms; ➤ for detailed instructions specific to vegetables and some of the specialized tools used to prepare them, see Cutting Vegetables, 200.

Dicing means to cut into cubes of a consistent size. Recipes calling for "fine dice" or "small dice" mean ¼-inch cubes; "medium dice" or just "dice" means ½-inch cubes; "large dice" means ¾-inch cubes. For firm vegetables and fruits, this entails squaring off the item to be cut, slicing it into slabs, stacking the slabs, and cutting them into batons (see the illustration on 201). Finally, the batons are cut crosswise into dice.

For cutting meat, poultry, or fish into cubes, work with one slab at a time and always draw the knife through instead of pushing straight down. This will make a cleaner cut and avoid damaging the muscle tissue. For smaller cubes and thin slices, freeze the meat before cutting.

Chopping is roughly the same as dicing, except there is no need to make the pieces uniform. By "chopped," we mean pieces roughly ½ inch long or wide. "Coarsely chopped" denotes larger, bite-sized pieces. If "finely chopped" is specified, the chunks should be smaller (around ¼ inch in size).

Mincing means cutting an ingredient to a consistency between finely chopped and a paste, and is typically reserved for herbs, garlic, ginger, turmeric, citrus zest, and other strongly flavored items that need to be well dispersed in a dish. Mincing is traditionally done with a knife, but we are more than happy to take a shortcut: Aside from herbs, all of the ingredients mentioned above can be "minced" very efficiently with a rasp-style grater such as a Microplane (see the illustration on 181).

To mince, first finely chop the ingredient. Gather the chopped pieces on the cutting board in a tight round as wide as the knife blade. Grasp the knife at the top and the handle. Chop the food very finely using a rocking motion, keeping the tip of the knife on the cutting board and moving the handle up and down. Run the blade through the pile once, then use the knife to squeegee the food pieces back into a neat pile, scrape off any food that has stuck to the side of the blade, and rock-chop through the pile once more. Continue until the food is cut into very fine pieces. For techniques specific to ingredients we frequently mince, see About Garlic, 240, Ginger, 991, and Herbs, 993. For mincing meat, see Mincing, Grinding, and Pounding, 451, in the Meat chapter.

GRINDING, POUNDING, AND CRUSHING

Beyond mincing is, of course, turning ingredients into a powder or paste. This can be achieved by crushing them—most commonly with a mortar and pestle—or chopping them up into tiny bits with the blades of a food processor, blender, or coffee/spice grinder. Crushing and chopping achieve different results, both in flavor and texture, but we feel that convenience should rule the day: Please feel free to use one method or the other when making pastes.

For specialized instructions for different ingredients, see Chiles, Dried and Ground, 967, Grinding and Storing Coffee Beans, 3, About Nut and Seed Butters, 1005, and Spices, 1020. For milling grains, see Freshly Milled Flours, 985. For grinding or pounding meats, see Mincing, Grinding, and Pounding, 451, in the Meat chapter.

The crushing and grinding action of a **mortar and pestle** is prized for the flavorful results it lends to Pesto and Pistou, 586, and curry pastes, 585. When purchasing a mortar and pestle set, we recommend an unpolished granite specimen of moderate to large size, with a rough granite pestle. Polished mortar surfaces will not grind ingredients efficiently, which tend to bounce or slide around in them. Mexican stone *molcajetes*, and Japanese ceramic *suribachi* mortars have effective, rough surfaces, but they are also harder to scrape pastes out of and clean. For lightly pounding vegetables, as for Green Papaya Salad, 129, a larger mortar and wooden pestle are also useful.

To use a mortar and pestle, first thinly slice fibrous ingredients like ginger, galangal, and lemongrass across the grain before adding them to the mortar. Unless you are grinding a single spice, it is more efficient to add several ingredients to the mortar for at least part of the grinding process. If salt is called for, using a coarse variety and adding it at the beginning will help break down the other ingredients. Similarly, once whole spices are cracked, tougher aromatics can be tackled more easily, followed by shallots, herbs, and softer ingredients (all of which help keep the spices from bouncing around as they are ground finer). Always work down the sides of the mortar with the pestle, rotating and swirling it every so often.

To blend ingredients into a paste, coarsely chop ingredients first. Cut any fibrous ingredients across the grain. Keep in mind that wetter mixtures work best and to always use quantities appropriate to the device. Mini food processors and coffee/spice grinders that have a detachable, waterproof cup are best for recipes that yield under ½ cup of paste. Blenders and food processors are best for quantities of 1 cup or greater. Pulse ingredients intermittently, then gradually increase the frequency. Periodically scrape down the sides with a silicone spatula to ensure an even texture.

SIFTING

The items we sift the most are fine powders such as flours, powdered sugar, and cocoa powder. Sifting simply means agitating an ingredient over fine wire mesh so that the individual particles separate and aerate as they fall through. The resulting powder has a uniform density and is free of clumps. **Flour sifters** are commonly available at kitchen stores, but a simple fine-mesh sieve (or drum sieve) can be used in a pinch.

Sifting serves several purposes. For one, since the flour or powder to be sifted has a uniform density, sifting ingredients into a dry measuring cup yields consistent quantities. Bags of flour can settle or become compacted, which causes the density of flour in a measuring cup to vary, affecting the results of a recipe. Of course, now that digital scales are economical and widely available, measuring by weight is a less fussy option and even more consistent.

Sifting also breaks apart ingredients that tend to clump (like cocoa powder and cornstarch) or can be used to shower powdered sugar over a Pfannkuchen, 649, or cake stencil, 714. Dry ingredients are often sifted together several times to combine them. This can be especially important for cakes: Cakes depend on chemical leaveners like baking powder for their light, airy texture. Sifting dry ingredients together helps distribute the leavener throughout, which helps cakes rise better and promotes an even crumb with no unsightly holes. That said, when sifting ingredients together to combine them, either sift them several times or sift them once into a bowl, then whisk them well to ensure the ingredients are evenly mixed. Sifting only once or twice will not adequately mix the ingredients.

To sift flour for measuring, cut two 12-inch squares of parchment paper or wax paper. Place a dry measuring cup on one square, and the sifter on the other. Add flour to the sifter, hold the sifter over the measuring cup, and sift until the cup is full and flour is heaped on top (as shown in the left illustration below). Place the sifter back on its sheet and level the flour in the measuring cup by running a knife or other straight edge across the top of the cup (see the middle illustration). ➤ Never level the flour contents by tapping, tamping, or shaking the cup, as this just repacks the sifted flour. Empty the flour out of the measuring cup into a bowl, funnel any flour on the sheet back into the sifter (as in the right illustration), and repeat if necessary.

To sift dry ingredients together, sift them onto the first square and place your sifter on the second sheet. Pick up the first sheet and funnel the dry ingredients into the sifter. Sift again, place the sifter on the first sheet, and repeat. Several siftings are needed to get the ingredients thoroughly mixed together.

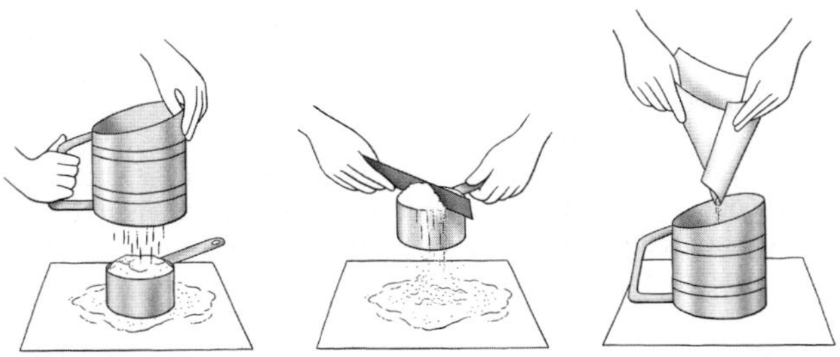

Sifting and measuring flour; funneling the excess back into the sifter

MARINATING, BRINING, AND SALTING

Marinating is a means of adding flavor to foods, usually meats, by soaking them in a flavorful liquid containing salt, aromatic seasonings, and almost always an acid, such as vinegar, wine, lemon juice, buttermilk, or yogurt. Fish, shellfish, and most vegetables are good at absorbing marinades, which will season them throughout in short order. Vegetables can be marinated for a day or more, but fish will quickly "cook" into Ceviche, 377. Meat and poultry are more resistant to marinades; most of the flavorings will not penetrate very deeply into the muscles, with the important exception of salt. The acids in the marinade do, however, begin to break down the surface, which will become more tender (and may turn mushy after prolonged exposure). Of course, by slicing muscles thinly, injecting roasts, or choosing specific cuts, meat and poultry can be thoroughly seasoned with a marinade. For the tenderizing effect marinades can have on tough cuts of meat, see 450.

Brining is somewhat similar to marinating, but the key feature of a brine is that it is mostly, if not exclusively, composed of salt and water. Brines season foods, but they also enhance the juiciness of foods. **Dry-brining** or **salting** foods involves sprinkling them with (you guessed it) salt and allowing the food to sit for a period of time.

In the context of meat, poultry, and fish, dry-brining accomplishes the same things as a wet brine—a salt-seasoned interior and enhanced juiciness—while being easier and less messy. Dry-brining also encourages the surface of the food to dry out, which promotes browning during cooking. On the other hand, salting vegetables draws out a considerable amount of water. There are several reasons for doing this: Salting and draining cabbage destined for coleslaw keeps excess moisture from diluting the dressing later on, 119. For Sauerkraut, 940, the salt draws enough moisture out of the cabbage to create its own brine. In the case of pickles, like Cornichons, 924, and Quick Sichuan-Style Cucumber Pickles, 929, the initial salting or brining helps keep the cucumbers crisp. If roasting vegetables, do not salt them too far ahead of cooking, as the water pulled to the surface keeps them from browning. For more on the processes at work, see About Salting and Curing, 934.

See About Marinades, 579, for detailed information on preparing and using them. For preparing brines and information on dry-brining, see Brine, 958. For using marinades and brines with specific ingredients, see About Brining Poultry, 405; Brining, Marinating, and Seasoning Meat, 450; and About Marinating and Brining Fish, 376. For information on curing items like corned beef in a brine, see About Curing Meat, 936.

LARDING AND BARDING

Larding involves inserting strips of fat into lean meats to keep them moist and flavorful. For details on how to lard, see Larding, 451. **Barding** is the act of draping or wrapping lean foods, usually meat or poultry, with fat before cooking to keep them moist.

To bard, use bacon, pancetta, prosciutto, caul fat, 518, or ⅛- to ¼-inch slices of pork fat or fatback. You may choose to drape slices over certain parts of the food—the breast of a lean bird, for instance—or you may bard the entire thing. Caul fat, in particular, is great for enveloping items: Think of it as nature's fatty food wrap. After cooking, you may discard the barding. Bear in mind that the fat will prevent the surface of the food from browning. To remedy this, you may remove the barding halfway through the cooking process, but if you do, baste periodically with clarified butter or oil until the food is done.

Barding is most often done with wildfowl (see Cooking Wildfowl, 437) because it is extremely lean, although sometimes other foods, such as meatloaf and pâtés, 513–14, are draped with bacon or fat to insulate, enrich, and flavor them.

BREADING AND BATTERING

Coatings—from flour and bread crumbs to crackers and seasoned batters—give foods a crispy, browned exterior that we find irresistible. Breading and battering foods is most commonly done when the food is to be pan-fried or deep-fried. In some cases, food is "oven-fried" with a coating (though never a batter). For batter and breading recipes and instructions on how to apply them, see About Battering Fried Foods, 656, and About Coating Fried Foods, 658.

FORMING QUENELLES

Quenelles are a dish of fish finely ground with bread crumbs, cream, eggs, and seasonings, then formed, poached, and served topped with a sauce (see Poached Fish Quenelles, 382). But *quenelle* also refers, in general, to a shape. You have probably encountered quenelles of ice cream, sorbet, whipped cream, or chicken liver mousse at fine dining restaurants. The shape is oblong, somewhat like a football, with pointed ends.

Quenelles are formed with spoons. Depending on the mixture to be shaped, either one or two spoons are needed. Soft mixtures like ice cream and whipped cream can be formed with one spoon. Thicker, chunkier mixtures require two spoons for shaping. As for what kind of spoon to use, choose one with a tapered point—not a rounded one—and a deep bowl. The bowl of the spoon should resemble an egg shape. For large quenelles use a large spoon; for small quenelles use a smaller spoon. It will likely take some experimentation before you find the best spoon for the job.

To form quenelles, dip the quenelle spoon in hot water and shake off the excess. Turn the spoon on its side so the concave bowl is facing you. Drag the spoon over the surface of the food toward you so that the spoon scoops up the food and the food curls over on itself into a neat, oblong shape. Pull the spoon up against the side of the container to lift up the quenelle. Allow the quenelle to slide gently off the spoon and onto the plate. For very cold foods like ice cream, it can be helpful to set the back of the spoon in the palm of your hand, which will heat the metal and help release the food. For thick or chunky foods, follow the directions above, then, when the food is on the spoon, place a second, similarly shaped spoon over the food and scoop it onto the second spoon from back to front. Continue to use the two spoons to scoop the food back to front until it is evenly shaped.

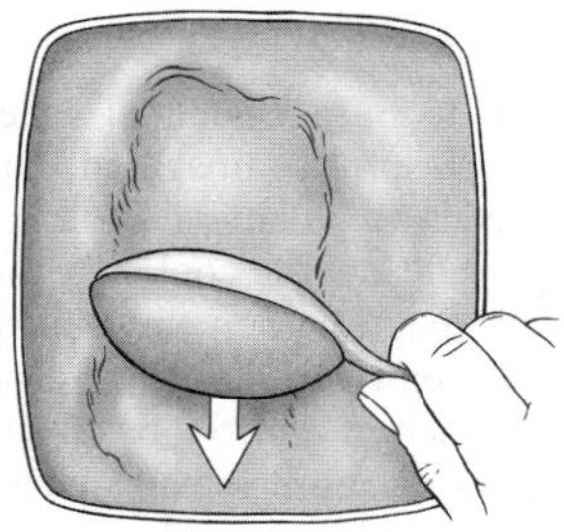

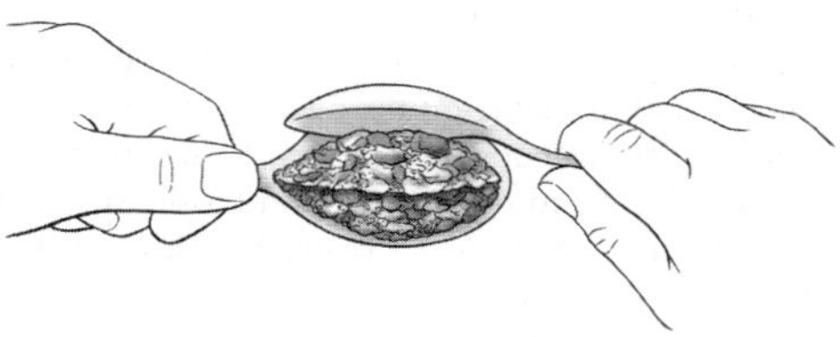

Forming quenelles with one or two spoons

ABOUT INDOOR COOKING METHODS

For indoor cooking, we proceed from dry-heat processes to moist ones; for grilling, barbecuing, and other outdoor cooking methods, see 1061. First, we deal with several methods that are almost always used in conjunction with others. As anyone who has cooked a deeply flavored braise can attest, many of our favorite recipes have several stages where different techniques are applied. Partial cooking methods are those that are not used to cook food to doneness, but are merely one step in the process. Some, like blanching, are steps called for by name in recipes. Others, like browning, sweating, and caramelizing, are not nearly as distinct. Rather, they are common terms that denote stages of the cooking process—integral techniques that often go unexamined in everyday cooking and are glossed over in recipes.

BLANCHING AND PARBOILING

Blanching, or parboiling, involves placing food in boiling water, boiling it for a specific, usually brief, amount of time, and then plunging it in an ice water bath to stop the cooking (for steam-blanching, see 884).

Blanching is an important first step in freezing vegetables. Not only does it set the color of vegetables, it also preserves their nutrients, which otherwise break down over time due to enzymatic action. Blanching deactivates these enzymes, ensuring higher quality, nutrition, and appearance, and better flavor in the final product. For information on blanching vegetables for freezing, see About Freezing Vegetables, 884.

Aside from this role, blanching is often used in conjunction with other cooking methods. For instance, tripe is blanched to remove off-flavors and odors before it is cooked. Sometimes bones are blanched before being used to make stock (see Pho Bo, 96, for one example of this). When making "white" stocks where the bones are not roasted or browned, blanching helps remove any impurities and promotes a clean-tasting, clear stock. In this case, rather than placing bones in a pot of already boiling water, the bones are covered with water, the water is brought to a boil, and then, after a short period of time, the bones are drained and then simmered in fresh water.

In other instances, food is blanched to remove its skin, as is the case with peeling tomatoes, 281, and peaches, 167. Sometimes blanching is accomplished by pouring boiling water over foods in a sieve, such as the technique we recommend for softening the pungency of raw onion to be used in salsas (see About Salsas, 573). Sometimes herbs are blanched for the briefest time (30 seconds or so) to set their color and flavor, such as for Montpellier Butter, 560. The basil for Pesto or Pistou, 586, may be blanched, shocked, and dried to promote a vibrant green color that will not dull in the finished sauce.

To blanch, fill a large pot with enough water to maintain a nonstop boil when the items to be blanched are added and bring the water to a boil. Fill a bowl with enough ice water to submerge the food you will be blanching. Add the food to the boiling water and stir once to submerge it. Blanch for the specified amount of time—for vegetables, usually a few minutes or less; for herbs, only a few seconds. For green vegetables, the best indicator of readiness is when they turn a vibrant green color. Use a slotted spoon to transfer the food to the ice water bath and let sit until completely cooled. Drain the food well.

SWEATING

Chopped aromatic vegetables, such as onions, garlic, shallots, carrots, and celery, are often sweated—that is, gently cooked in a small amount of butter or oil in a pan over low to medium heat—at the outset of cooking a sauce, stew, or braise. Sweating not only softens the vegetables, but concentrates and melds their flavors. Generally speaking, vegetables are properly sweated when tender, translucent, and their juices have been released (they should not be browned).

BROWNING

As a preliminary cooking technique, browning meats and vegetables is typically achieved by cooking in a pan in a little oil over moderate to high heat. The term **searing** specifically refers to browning food, especially meat, over intense high heat. Searing is sometimes used as a preliminary step, as with pre-searing, below, and sometimes as a final step (see Torching and Post-Searing, 1049). Or, as in the case of a steak seared to doneness in a skillet, it may be the sole cooking method. As a finishing technique, browning a dish in the oven or under the broiler adds flavor, texture, and eye appeal.

The goal with all forms of browning is to add a layer of flavor by harnessing browning reactions. When the focus is browning sugar (either natural or added), we use the word **caramelizing** (for more on the chemical process behind this, see Caramelization of Sugar, 1024). When foods that are not high in sugar are browned, the process responsible is called the **Maillard reaction,** a reaction between carbohydrate molecules and amino acids in the presence of heat, which creates a broad and complex range of flavors, colors, and aromas. The Maillard reaction differs from caramelization in that caramelization occurs when sugars are subjected to heat and begin to break down. In short, sugars caramelize, while protein-rich foods undergo the Maillard reaction. In fact, browning reactions are much more complicated than we can get into here, and caramelization and the Maillard reaction are not mutually exclusive (they usually occur simultaneously, though there will be more Maillard reactions in protein-rich foods and more caramelization in high-sugar foods). Suffice it to say that these are the reactions that make browned foods—from deeply browned steaks to cookies to caramel—taste so good.

Generally, how one goes about browning meat depends on whether it is a quick-cooking steak or a tougher cut for stewing or braising. Tender cuts should be browned very quickly over high heat so that the surface is done before the interior overcooks. ➤ Brown tougher cuts destined for braises and stews slowly over medium to medium-high heat so that every square inch of the meat turns golden-brown—and to prevent any browned bits stuck on the pan from burning (they are essential to the flavor of the cooking liquid). For this purpose, a large heavy-bottomed skillet, sauté pan, or Dutch oven wide enough to hold the meat in one or several batches is essential: These pans retain heat, resist scorching, and are roomy enough to hold a good amount without getting crowded. Use a spatula made from a material that will not scratch your pan (such as plastic or wood) to scrape any browned bits from the bottom of the pan.

Regardless of whether you are browning beef cubes for a stew or sautéing pork chops, ➤ do not crowd the pan—it lowers the heat, creates steam, and results in gray rather than browned meat. Though many recipes for stews call for cutting meat into cubes or buying precubed stew meat, we often cook bone-in shoulder chops or blade steaks whole and then cut them after cooking. The larger pieces are much easier to brown, and their bones add flavor and body to the simmering liquid. Once the stew is done, the meat can be removed from the pot, trimmed and deboned, cut into pieces or shredded, and added back to the stew to heat through.

CHARRING AND PRE-SEARING

Charring not only softens and partially cooks ingredients, but it also imbues them with a smoky flavor. It is useful in several applications. Sometimes foods are charred to give them a richer, carbonized flavor, as is the case with the ginger and onion used to make the broth for Pho Bo, 96. Charring is also used to blacken and loosen the skins of peppers and soften their flesh (see Roasted Peppers, 262). Some salsas are made from charred ingredients, as is the case with Table Salsa, 573, and Habanero-Citrus Hot Sauce, 571.

Pre-searing is a technique used almost exclusively with pork and red meats cooked sous vide, 1054. Because meats cooked sous vide do not brown during cooking, it is important to sear them either before or after cooking (or both) to give them color and a deeper flavor. The ideal sequence for steaks and chops cooked sous vide is to sear them, cook them sous vide, chill briefly, and then sear once more right before serving. The main advantage to pre-searing is that it provides a base of color and flavor so that the final sear does not take too long, which can overcook the meat. Pre-searing is, thus, optional but recommended. For information on post-searing, see 1049.

BASTING

Basting, once thought to be an essential aspect of the roasting process, is not quite as helpful as imagined. Basting does not, for instance, help meat retain its juiciness. In fact, basting done with anything but pure fat will slow the cooking process through evaporative cooling, and it may toughen the skin of poultry. Further, opening the oven door repeatedly during roasting will cause the temperature to drop, which may also forestall cooking. We no longer advocate basting any roast unless you are basting with butter or oil, in which case occasional basting will promote browning (in the case of butter, it will also add a desirable flavor). Even in that case, however, basting is purely optional.

The two cases where basting with a liquid that contains water is helpful is when basting a skin-on pork roast or whole pig, or when smoking meat. In the case of skin-on pork, water in the basting liquid prevents the skin from drying out and hardening. For smoked meats, basting with a "mop," 582, creates humidity in the smoker, which in turn helps with the formation of a smoke ring, and results in a smokier flavor in the finished product (as well as imparting the flavor of the ingredients used in the mop).

DEGLAZING

Deglazing is the act of loosening and dissolving the tasty browned bits left in the pan after roasting or browning meat, poultry, or vegetables. This is usually accomplished by adding a liquid, especially wine or stock. Deglazing may happen at the end of cooking as part of preparing a gravy or pan sauce, 544, or it may be necessary after initially browning the meat for a stew or braise. In the case of deglazing a roasting pan, the pan juices are poured off and the fat removed, stock or wine is added to the pan, and the bits are scraped up. These can then be added (along with the skimmed pan juices) to a roux to make gravy, or simply reduced with stock in a saucepan to make a jus, 456. Making a pan sauce after sautéing a steak or chop is very similar, but instead of pouring off the fat and adding the liquid right away, you may loosen the browned bits by slowly sweating onions or shallots in some of the rendered fat (or discard it and add some butter to the pan instead). The steamy liquid the onions exude loosens the browned bits, which can then be scraped up. The onions can then be browned, and any additional bits deglazed with wine or stock.

Taking the concept even further, braises, ragus, and stews may have ingredients browned and deglazed several times for a deeper flavor: Meat is browned first, then onions, celery, and carrots are sweated to deglaze the meaty bits, and then browned again (perhaps with tomato paste mixed in toward the end for even more sugars to brown and caramelize). Wine may be added to deglaze these bits and then left to reduce (see below) until the wine's sugars begin to caramelize, followed by a final deglazing with stock, more wine, or whatever braising liquid a recipe calls for. While this is not the sort of thing that one does for a quick weeknight meal, the richness and depth of flavor this creates is worth the extra effort if you have the time.

REDUCING LIQUIDS

Reducing is the process of simmering or boiling a liquid, such as wine, heavy cream, stock, or a sauce, to thicken its consistency and intensify and concentrate its flavors. Season the reduction only after it reaches the desired thickness or it may be overseasoned or too salty. Reducing is done only to sauces or liquids made without egg, which would curdle during the cooking process. Those that have a cream or flour base must be watched and stirred often to avoid scorching as they reduce. Reduction does not always need to be done over high heat or at a rapid boil. Thicker liquids, which tend to scorch more easily than thin ones, should be reduced over a lower heat and stirred frequently.

FLAMBÉING OR FLAMING

Flambéing, or flaming, is a technique of quickly enveloping a dish in flames by igniting a small amount of heated liquor poured over it. Flambéing is always a dramatic moment in the meal, albeit sometimes a tragicomic one if your match only causes a sad flicker. To avoid anticlimax, remember that both ➤ the food to be flamed and the brandy or liqueur used in flambéing should be warm—but well under the boiling point. For meat, do not attempt this process with less than 1 ounce of liquor per serving. For nonsweet food, pour the warmed liquor over the surface of the food and ignite by touching the edge of the pan with the flame of a match or taper. For hot desserts, sprinkle the top with granulated sugar, add the warm liquor, and ignite as above. Also see Spanish Coffee, 26, Steamed Plum Pudding, 833, Flambéed Fruit, 834, Bananas Foster, 176, and Cherries Jubilee, 181.

GRATINÉING

This partial cooking technique creates a golden crust by covering the surface of a dish with bread crumbs and/or grated cheese and browning it in the oven or under the broiler. Dishes prepared this way are referred to as "au gratin," or simply "gratin." For specific crumb toppings, see Au Gratin, 958. For dishes that incorporate this technique, see Cassoulet, 216, Brussels Sprout Gratin, 222, Cabbage Gratin, 225, Belgian Endive au Gratin, 233, Leek Gratin, 248, Parsnip-Cheese Gratin, 258, and Potatoes au Gratin, 266.

TORCHING AND POST-SEARING

Torching is the browning of foods with a propane torch. The most famous example of this is Crème Brûlée, 815, in which sugar is caramelized on top of a custard with the use of a torch after it has cooked through.

Post-searing, or **reverse searing,** is done at the end of cooking as a finishing step. Post-searing is essential for many foods (especially steaks and chops) that have been cooked sous vide, 1054; without it, this cooking method would result in pale foods with no crust. Sometimes a torch or broiler is called into service for post-searing, but it is usually done in a heavy skillet. In some cases, food may be both pre-seared, 1048, and post-seared. Post-searing is also used with some roasts: The roast is cooked normally, allowed to rest, then broiled or roasted at a higher heat to brown the surface before serving.

GLAZING

Glazing is simply applying a thick sauce, savory syrup, or transparent icing to a food. Some glazes are thick enough to coat foods upon contact and require no further cooking (this is primarily done with cookies, fritters, scones, and cakes). For more on applying sweet glazes and icings, see About Ganache and Chocolate Glazes, 797, and About Icings and Glazes, 798.

Other glazing mixtures are designed to be caramelized and reduced on the surface toward the end of cooking. Glazes can be added to a pan of sautéing root vegetables or fruits, but they are drizzled or brushed onto items that will be finished with dry, radiant heat, such as baking, roasting, broiling, or grilling. For directions on glazing savory items for finishing with dry heat, see About Glazes, 578. For an example of glazing vegetables in a pan, see Glazed Carrots, 228.

ABOUT DRY-HEAT COOKING METHODS

Dry-heat cooking involves the transfer of heat from above or below the food, or from dry heat surrounding the food. Grilling, 1062, is one example; broiling, baking, roasting, sautéing, and pan-frying are others. Deep-frying is actually another kind of dry-heat cooking. Here the heat is transferred by the hot fat used as a cooking medium.

There are three basic processes at work in dry-heat cooking methods: radiation, convection, and conduction. **Radiation** is the primary source of heat for grilling and broiling, where the food is directly exposed to either flames or a glowing broiler, which radiate infrared waves that transfer the majority of the heat. **Convection** occurs when hot air transfers heat to the surface of foods. Radiation and convection are both at play in baking and roasting, where hot air circulates inside the oven and radiation emanates from the elements above or below, as well as from the hot oven walls. **Conduction** is the primary form of heat at work when sautéing, pan-frying, and deep-frying. In sautéing and pan-frying, heat is conducted through a metal pan and the oil in the pan. In deep-frying, heat is conducted through the oil.

BAKING, ROASTING, AND PAN-ROASTING

Baking is a dry-heat cooking method where heat surrounds the food. In addition to the reflected radiant heat of the oven and the convective heat of the hot air, heat is transferred from the pan to the food through conduction. Even though some moisture is released from the food during baking and circulates as steam in the closed oven, this process is still considered dry. The technique is the same whether you are using a conventional oven or a convection oven, although the circulating air of a convection oven promotes browning and cooks foods faster. Most recipes, including all the recipes in this book, are written for conventional ovens. ➤ To convert a recipe to use a convection oven, lower the oven temperature by 25° to 50°F.

▲ For information on high-altitude baking, see About High-Altitude Cake Baking, 755, and About Quick Breads and Coffee Cakes, 625.

Baking custards, cheesecakes, and other delicate items in a **water bath** or **bain-marie** insulates them from the oven's heat and thereby protects them from overcooking. For instructions for baking foods in a water bath, see About Custards, 812.

Many bread bakers will create steam in their oven to improve the rise of crusty breads. While many bakeries have steam injectors installed in their ovens, home bakers can improvise in several ways (see About Baking Bread, 597).

Roasting is a term nearly synonymous with baking; in all but a few instances, roasting takes place in the oven, where the walls radiate heat and air circulates heat through convection. Roasting, however, has different connotations. We associate roasting with higher oven temperatures and with cooking whole poultry and large pieces of meat. Sometimes one of these associations trumps the other (some linguistic examples are discussed below).

Roasting is our favorite cooking method for a wide variety of **vegetables** (and some **fruits**), as it produces delicious results, requires little forethought, and does not need constant attention. In fact, one of our favorite "tricks" for perfectly roasted vegetables is to forget about them for a while. The intense radiating heat of the oven walls and conductive heat of the baking sheet caramelizes natural sugars while circulation of dry air dehydrates the vegetables, concentrating their flavors.

Meats are roasted in large pieces, aptly called roasts, but especially thick steaks and chops may be **pan-roasted,** which is a combination of searing and roasting (for an example of this technique, see Pan-Roasted Beef, 456). We generally reserve high-heat roasting for tender cuts of meat from the rib and loin area. Setting the meat on a **roasting rack**—either a V rack, or a flat metal rack—keeps it off the bottom of the pan and promotes even browning by allowing hot air to circulate around the entire roast. For cooking especially thick rib roasts to an even, edge-to-edge medium-rare, we recommend low-heat roasting, or **slow-roasting,** followed by resting and a blast of extremely high-heat roasting to brown the outside. Slow-roasting is also good for tougher, fattier cuts, as exhibited by Latin Roasted Picnic Shoulder, 490.

Poultry may be roasted whole or in pieces (sometimes roasting chicken pieces is referred to as "baked chicken," for yet another silly linguistic twist). As a general rule, ➤ the smaller the bird, the higher the oven temperature can be. Any bird weighing less than 10 pounds can be roasted on a wire cooling rack in a roasting pan. Heavier birds should be roasted on a sturdy roasting rack.

Fish can be scaled and roasted whole or as fillets. High-heat roasting is best for browning and crisping skin, but slow-roasting will yield the most tender and evenly cooked results.

For more on baking, see About Baking Bread, 597, About Baking Cookies, 763, the Cakes and Cupcakes chapter, 708, About Custards, 812, and About Cheesecakes, 752. For more information on roasting, see About Roasting and Baking Fish, 378, and specific sections in the Meats chapter, 455–58, and Poultry and Wildfowl chapter, 407–10. To "roast" on a grill, called indirect grilling, see 1062.

BROILING

Whether you broil in an oven or grill over a hot fire, the principle is identical. The heat is radiant, direct, and intense. The main difference is that in grilling, heat is applied from below, and in broiling the heat comes from above. Generally, you want to broil or grill foods that are inherently tender, relatively lean, and not too thick—chicken breasts, fish fillets, and quick-cooking vegetables are perfect candidates.

In the great majority of household ranges, you are given limited, if any, selectivity in broiling temperatures, and individual variations in broilers make it necessary to become familiar with the special requirements of your own equipment. All broilers benefit from preheating for 10 minutes before the food is placed under it.

When the heat indicator on a household range is turned to the broil position, the temperature is around 550°F or slightly above and should remain constant. In most ovens, the broiler cycles on and off. If you wish to promote sustained broiling, you may crack the oven door. However, do not do this frequently, as it can throw the oven thermostat out of whack or damage the electronics in newer ovens with a digital control panel located just above the oven door.

Under the limitations of the household range, ➤ much of the temperature control in broiling is determined by the placement of the oven rack. Generally speaking, the oven rack is placed so that there is a 3-inch space between the heat source and the top of the food. ➤ To lower the broiling heat for browning delicate items like bread crumb toppings or for cooking thicker items—where the heat must have time to penetrate deeply without charring the food—lower the oven rack so the food is 4 to 6 inches from the heating element. (Individual recipes will often specify the distance when it is crucial to success.)

Meats are best broiled on a **broiler pan**—a two-piece pan with a slotted top on which the food sits and a shallow pan beneath that catches any drippings. These pans insulate the rendered fat from the heat, preventing it from scorching or catching fire. Lean meats, fish, and vegetables, however, can be broiled on a rimmed baking sheet. For easier cleanup, line the baking sheet or the bottom of the broiler pan with foil.

Broiling is especially useful for quick-cooking, tender **vegetables** like asparagus, or for putting a finishing touch on vegetable gratins. Any vegetable that is too fragile or small to grill will be perfectly safe on a broiler pan.

When broiling **meats,** choose tender cuts, such as beef rib or loin steaks or lamb chops. Flank steaks are also broiled but must be cooked rare to avoid a tough result. Cut off excess fat and score the remaining fat about every 2 inches around the edges of the meat to keep it from curling. Center the meat in the pan and adjust the broiler rack so that the top surface of 1-inch-thick steaks or chops are 2 inches from the heat source (2-inch-thick steaks should be 4 inches from the heat source). Only one turn is required for a 1-inch-thick steak or chop; 2-inch-thick meats should be turned more frequently. For details on broiling meats, see About Grilling, Broiling, and Sautéing Beef, 458, Pork, 492, Lamb, 479, and Veal, 474; About Broiling and Grilling Chicken, 410; and About Grilling and Broiling Fish, 384.

DEEP-FRYING

In all our conversations with other home cooks while we were revising this book, deep-frying takes pride of place for being the most avoided cooking method. There is no denying that deep-frying is messy, a bit wasteful, even dangerous. That said, deep-fried foods can be some of the most sublime. To those who remain unconvinced, we can only say that our occasional cravings for specific dishes—freshly fried doughnuts, warm, well-salted fries, and crispy breaded chicken come to mind—are powerful enough to make us forget the mess, and we rarely regret the decision to pull out our Dutch oven and fry once more.

As state fair vendors routinely demonstrate, almost any food can be deep-fried. The question is: What *should* you fry? The short answer is batters, doughs, bound mixtures, and relatively small, tender pieces of meat, seafood, vegetable, or fruit. When choosing foods to fry, keep in mind that the cooking period will be relatively short, as the conduction of heat through oil makes for a very efficient cooking method. Very dense foods, like sweet potato chunks, for instance, should be parcooked until tender and then fried.

For good results, the food to be fried must be properly prepared. ➤ Pieces should be uniform in size so that they will all cook at the same rate. Raw foods, especially wet ones, should be patted dry with paper towels before cooking to remove excess surface moisture. This will reduce the amount of bubbling when the food is introduced into the fat. Whenever possible, foods should be at room temperature.

As for the vessel used for frying, equally good French fries can come out of a Dutch oven as from the latest-model electric fryer. This is not to underestimate the value of the fryer, which offers the convenience of a built-in thermostat, but any deep, heavy pot or saucepan serves nicely for deep-frying. We sometimes use a wok for deep-frying, which requires less oil than a standard pot due to its flared, convex shape (they require special care, however, as their shape renders them less stable). ➤ If you are frying in a wok or other pan with a long handle, rotate it so that the handle is over the counter and not projecting out where it can be jostled.

Our frying recipes call for a depth of oil in inches; ➤ for deep fryers with wire baskets, measure the depth from the bottom of the basket. There must be enough oil to cover the food and to permit it to move freely in the pot. When deep-frying large foods like chicken pieces or doughnuts, 3 to 4 inches of oil is enough to cover the food. For smaller pieces of food, like cut vegetables or shrimp, 2 to 3 inches will suffice.

Frying temperature is the most important element to watch and adjust for. If the fat is too hot, the food will likely brown too much on the surface before cooking through; if the fat is not sufficiently hot, a crust will not form quickly enough on batter-coated foods, resulting in floating bits of batter and grease-soaked food. In general, fry larger or denser foods at lower temperatures to give them time to cook through, and never fry any food at a temperature higher than 375°F (in fact, 365°F, as easy to remember as the number of days in a year, is an adequately high temperature for any quick-cooking food).

An accurate thermometer is essential for judging the temperature of the fat; models that clip to the side of the pot are the most convenient, but a handheld instant-read model is perfectly acceptable. (It should be capable of reading temperatures up to 400°F.) Though we do not recommend frying without a thermometer, there are some time-honored alternatives for estimating the temperature of frying oil. When you think the fat is hot enough, add a 1-inch cube of fresh bread and set a timer set for 60 seconds. If the cube browns in this time, the fat is around 365°F. Alternatively, when you think the fat is hot enough, stick a wooden chopstick into the pot so it touches the bottom. If tiny bubbles rise up rapidly through the oil from the bottom of the chopstick, the oil is ready.

While it is tempting to use as little oil as possible in frying, do not scrimp. When food is added to hot oil, the temperature will drop significantly. The less oil you use, the more the oil temperature will plummet after the food is added. The more the oil temperature plummets, the longer it will take to recover and the greater the likelihood of a greasy outcome for the food sitting in the oil. Conversely, ➤ never fill any vessel more than half full with oil or more than the quantity specified by the manufacturer. There must be room for the bubbling up of the fat that always occurs in deep-frying foods with a high moisture content.

Vegetable shortening, lard, tallow, and vegetable oils such as peanut, corn, canola, safflower, and soybean are favorites for deep-frying. Except for tallow and lard, both of which have a characteristic odor and flavor, these fats are bland and very similar in appearance and composition. They all have smoke points well above those needed for deep-frying. ➤ Do not heat fats above their smoke point, 981. The fat will begin to break down, imparting off-flavors and producing potentially harmful by-products. ➤ Butter, margarine, and extra-virgin olive oil are not suitable for deep-frying because of their low smoke points. For special purposes and in certain circumstances, chicken, duck, and goose fat may be used for frying. These tend to have lower smoke points, but when handled with care, they can produce excellent fried foods. For more details, see Fats in Cooking, 980.

Have ready a rimmed baking sheet and a supply of paper towels on which to drain the cooked food to rid it of excess fat before serving. When adding foods to the oil, ➤ slip them in slowly to discourage splashing. Always use long-handled tongs, a slotted spoon, or a frying basket. ➤ Dip utensils into hot fat first, so that the food will release quickly without sticking. Have a pan or dish ready in which to rest the utensils when they come dripping from the fat. Do not try to put too many pieces in the hot oil at one time: Fry several small batches rather than one large one. A **wire skimmer** (sometimes called a **"spider"**) is ideal for retrieving smaller pieces once they are done. The fried food may be kept hot on a pan lined with paper towels or brown paper in an oven set at 150° to 200°F. After frying each batch, ➤ let the temperature rise again to the specified heat. ➤ Skim out bits of food or batter as they collect in the fat. Allowing them to remain can induce foaming (another sign of the oil breaking down), discolor the fat, and affect the flavor of the food.

➤ In case the oil should catch fire, turn off the stove, if possible, and place a metal lid on the pot. You may smother the flame with salt or baking soda. ➤ Never use water, as this will only spread the fire.

Fresh oil produces superior results, but oil that does not bubble or smell off after frying can be reused once. Once the oil has cooled to room temperature, pour into a storage container through a strainer lined with folded cheesecloth or a paper towel to remove all particles of food. Cover tightly and refrigerate for future use. ➤ We recommend exercising great caution in recycling oil, because the smoke point, 981, of the oil may have been reduced to a point at which the oil will smoke or worse yet, flame up, when heated again for frying. To test whether used oil is fit to use again, heat up a small quantity of it and fry a cube of bread in it until browned. Taste the bread. It should not have any strong flavors. If it does, the oil should be discarded.

▲ When deep-frying at high altitudes, you will find that the lower boiling point of water within moist food requires that the temperature of the cooking oil be lower. This will prevent the food from browning excessively on the outside while remaining undercooked on the inside. The reduction in oil temperature varies according to the food to be fried, but a rough guide is to lower the frying temperature by about 3°F for every increase of 1,000 feet in elevation.

SHALLOW-FRYING

Shallow-frying is much more practical for everyday cooking than deep-frying. Here, items are fried with a less intimidating amount of oil or fat and may not even be fully submerged. The smaller amount of fat required also makes it easier to use flavorful animal fats, such as lard, duck fat, and tallow. The only drawback is that you will have to turn the food at least once during frying (a small price). Shallow-frying is particularly suited to sturdier foods that are floured or breaded, or encased in a bound coating, 658. Another thing to consider: Since a smaller amount of oil is used, adding items will drop the temperature much more drastically (but the temperature is faster to recover as well). This is one of the reasons batter-coated foods do not fare as well with shallow-frying; a lower initial oil temperature means the batter may disintegrate a bit before setting properly. Also, any portion of the food not submerged in oil will likely shed its batter and leave bare spots. This can be partially remedied by using a thicker mixture (such as Beer Batter, 657, with the optional whipped egg whites folded in), as well as spooning more batter over any bald spots right before turning the pieces.

SAUTÉING AND PAN-FRYING

The French verb *sauter* means "to jump," and this is a pretty apt description of what happens to food when you sauté it. The cooking is done in an uncovered pan with a small amount of oil over medium-high heat. When foods are added, they are kept in motion by shaking the handle so that the food moves (you can always just stir the food if you're not sure of your wrist-flicking skills). The process is rapid, the food is usually cut into small pieces, and the heat is high from the moment cooking starts until the food is tender.

For the best sauté, use Clarified Butter, 960, or vegetable oil. The food should be cut to a uniform thickness and size and be dry on the surface. When the fat shimmers in the pan, add the food, which should elicit a loud, satisfying sizzle. The food should not be wet or crowded in the pan or it will steam and not brown. To keep the food from browning unevenly, agitate the pan frequently, but do not fuss with meats or fish before they are well browned.

Sautéing is a good choice for creating simple sides that do not need a sauce. Add smashed garlic cloves to the pan with the vegetables, season them with ground spices or pepper flakes, and finish by tossing with a squeeze of citrus juice or vinegar and fresh herbs.

Larger items, such as chicken breasts, steaks, and cutlets, are frequently referred to as sautéed when they are cooked with a bit of oil and the heat is kept at medium-high, or slightly lower than it would be for searing, 1053. Despite the use of the term, sautéed steaks, chops, and cutlets should be turned once or twice to brown, and not tossed with the flick of your wrist. The main advantage to sautéing a steak over searing one is that the browned bits in the pan are less likely to turn bitter and acrid, allowing for a nice pan sauce, 544, to be made.

Pan-frying is similar to sautéing but is generally used for larger pieces of food such as bone-in chicken pieces, often with a bound coating. Because the food is in larger pieces, the heat is lower and a greater amount of fat is used. To prevent splattering while pan-frying, cover the pan with a splatter screen.

If pan-frying or sautéing a larger uncooked piece of food that is slightly irregular in shape, it can help to weight it with a **grill press:** a heavy metal slab with a handle designed to weight food down. By bringing the entire surface of the food in contact with the pan, it will brown better and more evenly.

STIR-FRYING

In classic stir-frying, the food is always bite-sized, the stirring is ceaseless, and the heat extremely high. In fact, it is practically impossible to get a wok hot enough on a home range for authentic stir-frying. This high heat produces a characteristic known as *wok hei*, which cookbook author Grace Young translates as "the breath of a wok." At sufficiently high temperatures, stir-fried foods brown and quickly release steam into the hot, dry air current surrounding the wok. In minutes, a cook with a powerful wok burner can have tender but still crunchy vegetables and thin strips of perfectly cooked meat—all imbued with a subtle browned or seared quality. In fact, some authorities object to referring to recipes written for home cooks as "stir-fries" for this very reason.

The crucial technique in authentic, blisteringly hot stir-frying is to move the food constantly, which keeps it from burning. To promote *wok hei*, the food should be tossed up the sides of the pan. This can be accomplished with a stirring utensil, or by jerking the wok handle to toss the food, or with a combination of both methods.

For home cooks, all is not lost. There are several ways around a standard cooktop's lack of power that can result in a delicious approximation of stir-frying. The most accessible option for most cooks is built right into our stir-frying recipes: ➤ Cook ingredients in batches small enough that they will not crowd the pan and cause the food to steam. Once all the batches are finished, simply add them back to the wok to combine and warm through.

Of course, cooks can simply use a more powerful heat source. This strategy is best pursued outdoors, where plentiful ventilation and more heating options abound. Propane gas burners designed for outdoor cooking can be several times more powerful than a typical stovetop burner or heating element (smaller, folding camping models are not). Some charcoal grills can be fitted with a grate that allows for the use of a wok. Finally, there are Thai charcoal-fired burners called *taos*. These consist of a wide, galvanized bucket lined with a very thick, fireproof ceramic insert. Any of these are guaranteed to get your pan smoking-hot in no time (though perhaps not glowing a dull red, as a real wok burner would).

Preparing food to be stir-fried is the longest part of the procedure. Thus, it is very important to have all ingredients cut, measured, and within easy reach and to familiarize yourself with the recipe. A **seasoned, 12- to 14-inch carbon steel wok** is ideal, but you can stir-fry in a skillet as long as it is heavy and large—the largest your burner will accommodate. The skillet must be capable of being heated empty over the highest heat without damage. ➤ Do not use nonstick pans for stir-frying. On gas burners, either a round- or a flat-bottomed wok will work but may need to be stabilized with a special collar; for all other burners, use a flat-bottomed wok. Always heat the empty wok (or skillet) until it just begins to smoke, then add the oil and tip the wok to coat it before proceeding with the recipe. Often, aromatics such as garlic and ginger are added to the wok first, then stirred briefly to infuse the oil with their flavors before the other ingredients are added.

When stir-frying **vegetables,** cut them uniformly so that they cook in the same amount of time. Those that tend to stringiness, like celery, should be cut crosswise or on the diagonal. Stem ends and midribs should be removed from coarse-leaved vegetables, like bok choy, and sliced separately, also on the diagonal. Group the vegetables so the longer-cooking ones go into the wok or pan first.

For stir-fries that include ground or sliced **poultry** or **meat,** we recommend browning it first, transferring it to a plate, and returning it to the pan to heat through once any vegetables have been stir-fried. Meats that are relatively tough, such as pork shoulder and brisket, should be sliced especially thin; cuts with a prominent grain, such as flank steak, should be cut across the grain. Pork loin, chicken breast, and other tender cuts prone to drying out should be stir-fried until they are just cooked through; ground meats and thinly sliced tough cuts can be stir-fried until they are browned to your liking.

A sub-category of stir-frying is **dry-frying.** Dry-frying is notably different in that foods are cooked in just a little oil over more moderate heat for a longer time until they start to shrivel and dry out a bit. Any seasonings—garlic, ginger, fermented black beans—are added to the pan later in the cooking process. One example of this technique is Sichuan-Style Dry-Fried Beans, 211.

SEARING

Searing is an excellent method for cooking meats that you want to be deeply browned and crisp on the outside, but rare to medium-rare in the center, such as sturdy fish steaks (like tuna, salmon, and swordfish), pork chops, steaks, and scallops. Unlike pre-searing, 1048, and post-searing, 1049, here a very hot pan is the sole means of cooking.

To sear meats, heat a well-seasoned cast-iron skillet, a griddle, or a sauté pan without a nonstick coating over high heat. Add just enough vegetable oil to coat the skillet. Adding oil is necessary because, on a microscopic level, neither the pan nor the meat is completely smooth. The oil serves as a medium to bring the entire surface of the meat in contact with the intense heat of the pan. When the oil just starts to smoke, place the meat in the pan, without crowding. Allow it to cook, undisturbed, until it is a rich, burnished brown on the bottom. The meat should release easily from the pan. If it does not, let it cook a little longer or until it releases easily. Turn the meat and sear the second side in the same way. If fat accumulates in the pan, pour it off or quickly blot it with a towel to keep it from smoking.

Blackening, associated with Cajun cooking, is a unique kind of searing in which the exterior of fish, poultry, or beef steak is highly seasoned and forms a very dark, flavorful crust as it cooks in a preheated cast-iron pan. This method produces an enormous amount of smoke, so only blacken foods if your kitchen is well-ventilated, or if you have an outdoor gas burner. (We must also point out that blackening is a bit hard on cast iron's nonstick surface, and it may need to be reseasoned, 1072, afterward.)

To blacken food, first turn on an exhaust fan (on its highest setting, if that is an option) and open a window. Heat a dry cast-iron skillet over high heat until the seasoning begins to smoke. Brush the food thoroughly with Clarified Butter, 960, then generously coat it all over with Cajun Blackening Spice, 587. Lay the food in the skillet without crowding. When a crust has formed on the bottom, 2 to 3 minutes, turn the food with a spatula. Blacken until done, 2 to 6 minutes more, depending on the thickness of the food you are cooking. If blackening more than one batch, wipe the skillet completely clean before proceeding with the next one.

ABOUT MOIST-HEAT COOKING METHODS

Whereas dry cooking methods rely on conduction, radiation, and convection to apply heat to foods, moist-heat methods transfer heat solely through contact with liquids and their vapor, or steam (a form of conduction). Since the cooking temperature of these methods can never exceed the boiling point of water (212°F, or 250°F in a pressure cooker), they do not allow for the browning of foods. As we crave the complex flavors that browning adds to dishes, dry-heat methods like browning and sautéing are often used in conjunction with moist-heat methods (see Braising, Stewing, and Pot-Roasting, 1057).

BOILING AND SIMMERING

Discussing this process tempts us to mention stews in connection with an old adage, "A stew boiled is a stew spoiled." While recipes often call for foods to be brought to the boiling point or plunged into boiling water—that is, in liquid that has reached 212°F and is vigorously bubbling or "rolling"—they hardly ever demand boiling for a protracted period. Even "hard-boiled" eggs should be simmered, at most. And yet, **boiling** is a useful technique in specific instances.

Quick evaporation—or "reducing"—is one justification for keeping a food at the boiling point; see Reducing Liquids, 1049. Blanching or parboiling, 1047, is another. We often bring soups, stews, and braises to a boil before turning down the heat to a simmer because it is easier and faster to turn the heat up high, go about our business in the kitchen, then adjust the heat once the food is hot and bubbling away.

Boiling is also a means of cooking firm, dense vegetables without altering their flavor in the way that roasting does. Add a generous pinch of salt per quart of water. Cookbook authors love to use the phrase "salty as seawater," which may be helpful or not. Another way to think of it is to salt the water until it tastes just north of pleasant; then the foods boiled in that water will be salty enough.

For dense root vegetables such as carrots, potatoes, and turnips, place vegetables in a pot large enough to hold them comfortably and add cold water to cover by 1 inch. Bring the water to a boil over high heat, then adjust the heat to maintain a gentle simmer. This encourages even cooking, and the vegetables will not end up mushy on the outside and overly firm inside. Tender vegetables like broccoli and peas should be plunged into already boiling water, as they cook in a very short time.

Simmering is an extension of boiling, and we use this method more often as it is gentler. Simmering temperatures range from about 140° to 185°F. Simmering protects fragile foods and tenderizes tough ones. When food is simmering, bubbles come gently to the surface and barely seem to break. It is the heat best used for soups, stews, braises, stocks, and starchy vegetables like potatoes (boiling is rough and can cause them to break apart as they become tender).

POACHING

While poaching is something of a vague term, it usually indicates very gentle cooking, especially of fragile or easily overcooked food. The principle of poaching never varies: The heat source is a calm liquid just under the simmering point, with nary a bubble breaking the surface. As far as liquids for poaching go, water is the simplest approach and the one used for eggs. However, more flavorful liquids should be used for almost everything else. You may poach in Court Bouillon, 80, or stock, seasoned water, wine, or even oil or butter.

If the cooking process is a short one, or if the food to be cooked is in small pieces, the poaching liquid may be at a simmer when the food is added. If the food is large, like a whole chicken, the food should be added to cold water and the water brought to a bare simmer, uncovered. If the liquid reduces too much during the cooking process, it must be replenished with more hot liquid, though this is usually only a concern with larger items.

For poaching in action, see Poached Eggs, 153, Poached Fish, 381, Butter- or Olive Oil–Poached Fish, 383, Poached Fruit, 170, Poached Pears in Red Wine, 834, and Poached Chicken, 419.

LOW-TEMPERATURE AND SOUS VIDE COOKING

Sous vide means "under a vacuum" in French. As a term for the cooking method to which it popularly refers, "sous vide" is imprecise and really beside the point. The defining characteristics of this cooking method are the precise, low temperatures at which foods are cooked, the longer cooking times, and the use of a heated water bath. Items are placed in sealed bags (or, in the case of custards, 813, and pickles, 922, canning jars) for a comparatively long cooking time.

With an instant-read thermometer and constant tending to the heat setting, a vigilant cook could use this technique with a stockpot full of water on their stovetop. Luckily, **immersion circulators** are now economical and widely available. These devices consist of a heating element, a precise thermostat to regulate the water bath temperature, and a pump or impeller that circulates the water. Most can be clipped to the side of a pot, a Cambro-type storage container, or a cooler. (Sous vide appliances with their own reservoirs exist, but these devices are bulky, not as versatile, and seem to be falling out of favor.)

Sous vide is an interesting technique for many reasons, but one of special interest is the seemingly contradictory nature of cooking sous vide and food safety. We know that keeping foods at temperatures between 40° and 140°F (the so-called "danger zone") is unsafe, so how can heating food in a water bath at temperatures below 140°F be safe? The answer is that safety in sous vide cooking is based on time as well as temperature. Foods held at 131°F and above for specific extended periods of time (see the information on pasteurizing eggs at home, 977, for an example of this) will be pasteurized. The higher the temperature, the less time needed to pasteurize, and the lower the temperature, the more time needed to pasteurize.

Foods cooked at temperatures below 140°F are typically done well within the "danger zone" time limit of 2 hours, but to be safe, plan to either serve these foods immediately or chill them rapidly in an ice water bath, then refrigerate and serve within 2 days. When cooking sous vide, make sure water is able to circulate around the bag(s) of food. The bags should never float, sit on the very bottom of the water bath, or be pressed against the sides of the container.

Some cautious cooks are concerned about cooking food in plastic. While we think these concerns are reasonable, there is no evidence to suggest that cooking foods sous vide in heavy-duty plastic bags, such as vacuum-seal bags or freezer bags, is unsafe. For those concerned about the environmental footprint of using so many disposable plastic bags, there are several silicone-based reusable bag alternatives that have been introduced recently. All are perfectly fine to use for sous vide cooking (wash and sanitize them thoroughly between uses, xx).

We find sous vide to be ideal for delicate items like custards and fish fillets, but it is certainly useful for premium cuts of meat. Speaking for ourselves, these foods are expensive, and can be intimidating to cook for that reason; while there is little skill involved in searing a steak, it is hard to argue with a foolproof, consistent method that results in perfectly cooked results. The only downside to cooking meat sous vide is that because it is a moist-heat method, no browning will occur. This is easily remedied by pre-searing, 1048, post-searing, 1049, or both.

We use sous vide much less for **vegetables,** though many cooks swear by it. There are a few advantages to cooking vegetables sous vide. The gentler heat leaves cell walls intact while softening their contents, helping to retain nutrients and flavor. Additionally, the bag traps flavorful (and nutritious) juices that would otherwise escape. These juices, along with the addition of butter or oil and aromatics like garlic, citrus zest, spices, and salt, combine to create a concentrated sauce.

➤ Bags filled with vegetables have a tendency to float; to keep them submerged, place a metal spoon or butter knife in the bottom of the bag before adding the vegetables and seasonings.

Pre-cooking some vegetables for 30 minutes at a low temperature—130° to 140°F—will actually keep them firm even after spending hours in a simmering stew or braise. This is caused by enzymes that become active in this range, which in turn alter the pectin and make it more resilient. Food writer Harold McGee

SOUS VIDE TIMES AND TEMPERATURES FOR COMMON FOODS

Food	Texture or Level of Doneness	Recommended Temperature and Time	Notes
Eggs	Pasteurized (raw) Softly poached	135°F for 1 hour 15 minutes 147°F for 1 hour	See page 977 See Slow-Poached Eggs, 153
Custard	Softly set	180°F for 45 minutes	See page 813
Fish fillets or steaks (1 inch thick)	Soft (rare) Soft and flaky (medium-rare) Flaky (medium)	120°F for 40 minutes 125°F for 40 minutes 130°F for 40 minutes	See page 381 Post-sear, 1049, all skin-on fish after cooking
Boneless chicken breasts	Soft Tender Firm	140°F for 2 hours 150°F for 2 hours 160°F for 2 hours	Post-sear, 1049, all skin-on chicken breasts after cooking
Boneless chicken thighs	Tender	150°F for 2 hours	
Duck breast	Tender and pink throughout	135°F for 1 hour 30 minutes	Cut skin in a crosshatch pattern before cooking (do not cut into the meat); post-sear, 1049, after cooking
Pork chops (1 inch thick)	Tender and light pink	140°F for 2 hours	Post-sear, 1049, after cooking
Pork tenderloin	Tender, juicy, and light pink	140°F for 2 hours	Post-sear, 1048, after cooking
Boneless beef steaks (1 inch thick)	Medium-rare	130°F for 1 hour	Post-sear, 1049, after cooking
Beef tenderloin	Medium-rare	130°F for 2 hours	Post-sear, 1049, after cooking
Beef short ribs	Steak-like Fall-apart tender	135°F for 48 hours 135°F for 72 hours	Pre-sear, 1048, if desired; post-sear, 1049, steak-like short ribs after cooking
Beets (medium)	Tender	185°F for 1 hour 30 minutes	Peel and halve or quarter before cooking
Carrots (medium)	Firm but tender	185°F for 1 hour	Peel and halve lengthwise before cooking
Asparagus	Crisp-tender	185°F for 10 minutes	Trim before cooking

refers to this curious effect as **persistent firmness.** This technique can come in handy if, for instance, you are making a long-cooking stew or braise and want the vegetables to retain some bite. It is effective with many root vegetables, including beets, carrots, parsnips, turnips, celery root, and potatoes, as well as broccoli, cauliflower, asparagus, green beans, and tomatoes.

Season all foods before sealing them in bags for sous vide cooking. You may coat the food with salt and pepper, or apply a rub or seasoning blend, 587–91. Citrus zest, herb sprigs, sliced garlic, or ginger may be added to the bag as well. We recommend ➤ adding a tablespoon or two of oil or another liquid fat to the bag before sealing. This will help you drive out as much air as possible when sealing, as well as help extract and distribute the flavor from any seasonings and aromatics added to the bag. You may also use a paste, 583–86, or a flavorful sauce to season meat (for the latter, there is no need to add oil). This is especially useful if you do not plan on searing the meat at the end of cooking. Two things should be kept in mind when bagging meat with sauces: First, use either a zip-top freezer bag or a chamber vacuum sealer. (Do not use a standard vacuum sealer, as the sauce will likely be sucked out.) Second, the sauce will be diluted by the juices exuded by the meat, so use one that is fairly concentrated (or reduce the sauce after cooking if needed).

To prepare a water bath for sous vide cooking, fit a pot or vessel with an immersion circulator. Fill the vessel with water so that it comes between the minimum and maximum fill lines on the immersion circulator. Set the temperature on the circulator as desired (see the chart, 1055, or a specific recipe for the best temperatures for what you plan to cook). While the water bath preheats, place the food along with any oil or seasonings in a vacuum bag or a heavy-duty zip-top freezer bag. ➤ The food should be in a single layer in the bag. Seal the bag with a vacuum sealer or with the air displacement method, 881. When the water is preheated, lower the bag into the water bath and start a timer. To keep the bag submerged, it may be necessary to clip it to the side of the vessel with a clothespin or binder clip. To discourage evaporation and increase heating efficiency, we recommend covering the vessel with plastic wrap or a lid (if the lid is thin enough, you may cut a hole in it to accommodate a protruding immersion circulator).

The chart, 1055, is a basic guide to cooking times and temperatures for sous vide cooking. The temperatures and times in the chart are for our preferred levels of doneness and/or textures. There are a plethora of time/temperature combinations that will work for any given food depending on the texture you wish to achieve, so take this guide as a starting point only.

STEAMING

Steaming has many advantages over boiling: There is no need to wait for a large pot of liquid to come to a boil, or come back up to a boil once you add vegetables; steam is gentler on delicate vegetables, which can get damaged in boiling water; and, finally, the nutrients and flavor of vegetables will not leach into the water as much. Steaming is one of the gentlest ways to cook vegetables. It also works well for delicate fish dishes (see Chinese Steamed Fish, 382), dumplings like Seafood or Pork Shumai, 315, and filled buns like Bāo, 316. Steaming also happens to be our favorite way to prepare Hard-Boiled Eggs, 151.

Stovetop steamers come in many sizes and shapes, from collapsible ones to pasta pot inserts to asparagus steamers to whole-fish-sized oval stainless steel steamers. Collapsible steamers are probably the most versatile, as they fold up for storage and can be used in conjunction with any pot, saucepan, or deep skillet that has a lid. Chinese tiered bamboo steamers should be set in a wok or a skillet just wide enough for the steamer to sit on the rim. Tiered aluminum or lightweight stainless steel steamers are also available. Either type has the capacity for steaming a complete meal on one burner. The food that needs the most heat goes on the lowest tier, and the food that needs the least heat goes on top.

➤ To prevent foods from sticking to the steamer, line it with parchment paper squares if steaming dumplings or buns (or use perforated parchment paper rounds). Other foods can be set on cabbage leaves, banana leaves, corn husks, or grape leaves. Rinse bamboo steamers with hot water after each use and let air dry thoroughly.

Plain water is the most common liquid to steam with, though using broth, beer, wine, or herb- or spice-infused liquids can add a subtle flavor. Always keep the liquid level an inch or so below the bottom of the steamer. If the food will not render juices—vegetables, for example—it goes directly in the steamer. If the food is juicy, steam it in a shallow bowl or deep plate to capture all the juices. If you are steaming something that takes more than 20 minutes, put two or three marbles or coins in the bottom of your steamer. They will make a racket until the water is gone; silence means it is time to add water. If that sounds too noisy for you, just keep an eye on the water level.

Remember that steam is scalding hot. ➤ Always lift the lid away from you, protecting your hands and arms from the steam.

WRAP COOKERY

The technique of wrapping food before exposing it to direct heat is almost as old as cooking itself. Many cultures surround pieces of food with various materials to protect them from burning. In the process, these wrappings often impart their unique flavor to the food. Indigenous American peoples baked fish, small game, and birds in clay. Drawn but not skinned, the animal was completely packaged in mud and bedded in coals for up to several hours. Removal of the clay brought along with it skin and feathers, leaving the skinned game ready to eat.

Other examples of wrap cooking are the dough-encased Cornish Pasties, 701, of English mine workers; Beef Wellington, 457; fish cooked en papillote, 379; and foods baked in a salt crust. One could even consider a Clambake, 353, a glorified example of wrap cookery. But in any true wrap cookery, the enclosing material allows some steam to escape. If you use foil to wrap the food, it will not be as tasty as food cooked either by direct heat or in a less impervious wrapping.

LEAF WRAPPINGS

Some fresh, unblemished green leaves, such as lettuce, cabbage, grape, chard, and collard, create a flavorful and edible wrap for food, while banana leaves, fig leaves, palm leaves, and corn husks are inedible and only furnish protection during cooking (though they do impart their own flavors).

As a rule, leaf-wrapped bundles have deeper flavor the day after cooking, and they reheat beautifully because the leaves help hold in their moisture. When collecting or buying leaves for wrapping, get extras; some will tear, and you may have more filling than you thought. Use any extra leaves to line the cooking dish, place extra leaves between the layers of bundles, or cover everything with leaves during cooking.

To cook leaf-wrapped foods, either steam them, gently simmer them in a sauce, or tie the packets and gently poach them until the contents are cooked through.

Cabbage leaves: See Stuffed Cabbage Rolls, 226, for instructions on preparing cabbage leaves.

Lettuce leaves: Blanch very briefly and transfer to a bowl of ice water. Drain, dry, and fill.

Fresh grape leaves: For Dolmas, see 63. Blanch young pale-green leaves in boiling water until the color darkens, 4 to 5 minutes, transfer to a bowl of ice water, and drain. For large leaves, remove the thicker portion of the central rib (avoid splitting them). Place them with their dull, veined side facing up on a work surface. If the filling is of rice, use no more than 2 teaspoons, as the rice will swell. Set a mound of stuffing near the broad bottom of a leaf and fold over the left and right segments, then roll up to form a packet.

Canned or jarred grape leaves: Place briefly in water to separate, then drain and dry. Fill as for fresh grape leaves.

Banana leaves: Cut away the central rib and carefully tear into sections about 10 inches square by pulling along the veins. Wipe on both sides with a damp cloth, always keeping the action along the leaf veins. See Banana Leaf Tamales, 325.

Corn husks: See Chicken and Cheese Tamales, 324.

FOIL COOKERY

An effortless way to cook food is to wrap it in heavy-duty foil. Unlike leaf wrappings, foil is impervious to air and moisture, trapping all the of the moisture released from the food during the cooking period. So, even if the heat is dry, like that of a grill, the result will always be a steamed food, never a browned one. Regardless of this, we find the results of foil cookery worth exploring—especially when cooking in the hearth or around a campfire. (For a particularly good one-pouch meal for these situations, see Chicken Hobo Packs, 413.) Pouch-cooking vegetables is also a wonderful way of cooking vegetables on a grill when space is tight.

Wrapping foods in foil can affect their cooking time in several ways. Since foil has insulating qualities, some foil-wrapped foods will require longer cooking periods than indicated for unwrapped foods. On the other hand, when large roasts are being barbecued, wrapping them in foil in the middle of cooking can help the meat finish cooking more quickly (this is called the "Texas crutch").

Remember, ➤ carrots, potatoes, and other hard root vegetables will take quite a bit longer than summer squash, corn, broccoli, and other tender vegetables. If you plan to mix root vegetables with tender ones in the same pouch, consider parcooking them first.

COOKING EN PAPILLOTE

This is a delightful way to prepare delicate quick-cooking foods, such as fish fillets, shellfish, and vegetables. The parchment holds in the aromas of the food and is almost like a present for the diner to open. Always season the food before wrapping it in parchment, and include aromatics like lemon slices, fresh herbs, and spices, as well as olive oil or butter for flavor and richness. See Fish en Papillote, 379, and Additions to Fish Baked in Parchment, 379, for flavoring ideas. The paper puffs during cooking, putting considerable strain on the folded seam—so note the following directions and sketches carefully.

To make a papillote, fold a piece of parchment paper in half. Starting at the folded edge, cut a half-heart shape as shown below. ➤ Be generous in cutting, allowing almost twice again as much paper as the size of the object to be enclosed. Place the food near the fold, but not too near. Fold to make a filled half-heart and, starting at the wide end, fold over small sections of the rim. Crease it with your fingers and fold it over again. Hold down this double fold with the fingers of one hand and, with the other, start a slightly overlapping fold. Crease, double over, and repeat, continuing to the pointed end of the half-heart. Each double fold should overlap the previous one. Finish off at the pointed end of the heart with a tight twist of the parchment, locking the whole in place.

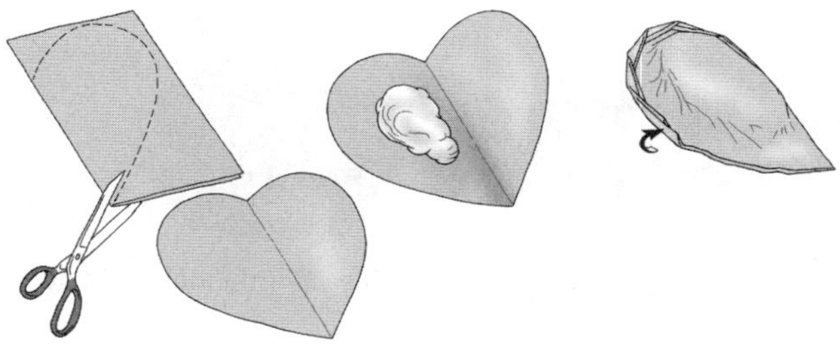

Making a papillote

Place papillotes in a lightly oiled, ovenproof dish and cook as directed. When serving, snip down the curved edge just next to the fold to reveal the food and release the aroma.

BRAISING, STEWING, AND POT-ROASTING

Braising is the process of cooking a food in flavorful liquid at a relatively low heat until tender. The food may be browned or sautéed first or, in the case of some vegetable braises, after the vegetables are tender and the liquid is allowed to boil off. Braised meat dishes tend to be done with tough cuts of meat that take hours of cooking to become tender. This method of slow cooking can be accomplished in a covered pot on the stovetop at a bare simmer, or by placing the pot in a 300°F oven—the latter is our favorite method, as it does not entail adjusting the stovetop's heat level to maintain such a low simmer.

We refer to braising as **pot-roasting** when large pieces of meat and whole poultry are braised. **Stewing** and **fricasseeing** are terms that may be used when a recipe calls for braising smaller pieces. Regardless of the size of the ingredients, as they braise, the flavors in the liquid meld and deepen into a delicious broth. After the food is removed, the braising liquid, defatted if necessary, becomes the sauce for the dish.

Our preferred cooking vessel for braised dishes is a 5- or 6-quart enameled cast-iron **Dutch oven.** It holds heat extremely well, evenly cooks its contents, and effortlessly goes from stovetop to oven. We recommend avoiding regular, seasoned cast iron, which will react with the acidic ingredients typically used in braises, such as tomatoes and wine (an enameled surface prevents this). That said, a seasoned, camp-style Dutch oven is fine to use for braising or stewing on the hearth, 1068, or around a campfire. Since any gap in the seasoning may allow the cast iron to contact the braising liquid, we recommend cutting back on wine and other acidic ingredients (unless you know the pot to be especially well seasoned). The stubby legs allow for coals to be raked underneath and the tall rim on the lid allows additional coals to be placed on the top, resulting in an even heat from all sides. (This also helps explain the name Dutch oven, as "dutch" in this context simply means "fake," owing to the pot's ability to mimic the even heat of a real oven in a rustic setting.)

Dutch oven and camp-style Dutch oven with hook to lift lid

Braising benefits tough cuts of **meat** from the neck, shoulder, breast or brisket, heel, and shank. Remember, ➤ patiently browning meats before stewing or braising will dramatically improve the result, as will keeping them at a lazy simmer throughout cooking.

We highly recommend braising or stewing bone-in **poultry,** and using dark leg meat, which is very forgiving and can be cooked until it easily shreds from the bone without toughening or drying out. ➤ If using breast meat in a stew, fricassee, or braise, cook just until it reaches 165°F, no more. If the dish has pieces of dark meat as well, remove the breast pieces when they reach this temperature, let the dark meat finish braising, and then add the breast back to warm through.

Fish is even more delicate than poultry breast, and most of the simmering should be nearly complete by the time the fish is added. (For more, see About Steaming, Poaching, Braising, and Cooking Fish Sous Vide, 380.)

➤ Always allow a meaty stew or pot roast to stand at least 5 minutes off the heat so the fat will rise and can be skimmed off before serving. If made some hours in advance, the meat can be removed from the pot and the cooking liquid cooled and defatted more easily. You may then thicken it by reduction, 544, or with kneaded butter, 544, or a roux, 542, if desired.

Rich braises are enlivened by a little acidity, such as a splash of lemon juice, vinegar, or even a grating of tangy Parmesan. Chopped fresh herb mixtures like Gremolata, 587, or a green sauce such as Salsa Verde, 567, are perfect for adding a fresh note to individual servings (➤ if you plan to store and reheat the braise, do not add herb garnishes directly to the pot). Harissa, horseradish, and mustard are great for adding a little spice; a swirl of butter or heavy cream can add body; Worcestershire, soy, Maggi, Vietnamese Caramel Sauce, 578, and other flavor-enhancing seasonings, 984, can add depth and savoriness. Because braised vegetables and meats are usually very tender, a sprinkle of crunchy fried shallots, browned bread crumbs, toasted nuts, croutons, or Dukkah, 589, can add texture. Also, remember that time benefits these dishes: ➤ Pot roasts, stews, ragus, and braises taste even better the day after they are made.

A **slow cooker** is an effective tool for pot-roasting, stewing, and braising. For the best results, brown the meat first on the stovetop, then place the meat and other ingredients in the slow cooker (don't forget to deglaze the pan, 1048, and add those flavorful dissolved bits to the slow cooker as well). To adapt a recipe for the slow cooker, see below. For adapting braises for the pressure cooker, see 1060.

SLOW COOKING

The beauty of a slow cooker is its ability to safely cook food unattended. Generally, any braise, stew, pot roast, or ragu is good for adapting to the slow cooker. Slow cookers vary in design but all consist of an outer heating element, a crockery insert, and a lid. ➤ Four- to 5-quart models will nicely accommodate recipes serving 4 to 8; when cooking for larger groups, a 6½- to 7-quart model is optimal. Recipes with a large yield can be halved or otherwise reduced to fit smaller models, and vice versa. Larger oval models can hold roasts and whole poultry.

➤ Most low settings cook food at just under a boil, high settings, at just above. Avoid opening the lid while cooking unless the recipe instructs you to do so.

To adapt standard recipes for the slow cooker, estimate 2 hours on low or 1 hour on high in a slow cooker for every 30 minutes of cooking time in the original recipe. To maximize flavor, brown the meat and sauté the vegetables in a pan on the stovetop before adding them to the slow cooker. Root vegetables cook more slowly than meat and should be placed in the bottom of the slow cooker. Decrease the liquid called for in the oven or stovetop recipe by ½ cup. ➤ Add dairy-based ingredients such as milk, cream, or cheese only during the last 30 minutes, as they will curdle if cooked too long. ➤ If cooking fish or shellfish, add them in the final minutes of cooking. When the food is done, you may wish to transfer the liquid to a saucepan and boil it to reduce it.

▲ For every 1,000 feet above 4,000 feet, allow 1 hour more on low or 30 minutes on high.

DOUBLE-BOILER COOKING

For very delicate foods, such as lemon curd, sabayon, custard sauces, or chocolate, that can be quickly ruined if heated over direct heat, we recommend the use of a double boiler. A double boiler is made of two nesting pans. The food to be cooked is placed in the top insert. Add no more than an inch of water to the bottom pan (it should not touch the bottom of the upper container) and heat the water only to a gentle simmer. For melting chocolate, the water should only steam.

For sauces, we like a double boiler that is rather wide. Deep, narrow vessels tend to overheat the sauce at the bottom, even when it is stirred, if it is held for any time at all. If you do not have a double boiler, choose any heat-resistant bowl that rests snugly on one of your saucepans, leaving 2 to 3 inches between the bottom of the bowl and the bottom of the pan.

PRESSURE-COOKING

In 1939, Irma enthusiastically informed readers of "a new gadget on the market that permits a cook to scoff at time." Armed with one of these pressure cookers, Irma counseled cooks to "Be nonchalant, light your burners and proceed with an attitude of victory over all difficulties, imaginary or otherwise." Despite their efficacy and decades of common use, pressure cookers fell out of favor. For many, the idea of minutely adjusting the heat to maintain pressure in a piece of cumbersome cookware was too intimidating; of course, the potential danger of the cooker erupting on the stovetop is also a bit frightening.

Our "rediscovery" of pressure-cooking is largely thanks to the easy-to-operate electric countertop models. Newer stovetop models are also extremely safe, as they have multiple failsafes built into their design to prevent the fabled explosions of our grandmothers' day. Needless to say, Irma would be quite pleased that variations on this classic time-saving device are being embraced by a new generation of cooks. Many of our favorite, most flavorful dishes are those that take hours of cooking. Hours can be turned into minutes with the help of a pressure cooker, and they save energy into the bargain.

No matter how hot the heat source, boiling water at sea level can never produce a temperature over 212°F. As those who live in the thin air of the Rocky Mountains can attest, atmospheric pressure can alter this boiling point, which decreases by about 2°F for every 1,000 feet in elevation. Pressure cookers create the opposite conditions: By heating steam in a sealed pot, the atmospheric pressure is increased, and the boiling temperature is raised accordingly.

Stovetop pressure cookers are designed to maintain 15 pounds of pressure per square inch (psi), which increases their boiling temperature to 250°F. Pressure-cooking foods at 15 psi can take about one-third the total time that it takes to cook the same food at a standard simmer or boil. Nearly all of the **electric countertop models** can only reach 10 to 12 psi, for a boiling temperature of about 240°F. This discrepancy can create a wide range of possible cooking times.

In the canning of all nonacid foods, the higher heat of processing with a **pressure canner** is essential to kill unwanted organisms; see 894 for detailed information on pressure canning. ➤ Currently, electric countertop pressure cookers are not approved for canning.

Cooking with a pressure cooker is not dangerous if you follow common-sense guidelines. It is essential when pressure-cooking to know your equipment well. Follow the manufacturer's directions to the letter, observing the following general principles: ➤ Never fill a pressure cooker more than two-thirds full; most pressure cookers have a maximum fill line that should be observed. On the other end of the spectrum, there needs to be enough liquid in the cooker to create a sufficient amount of steam. ➤ Consult your instruction manual for the minimum amount of liquid that needs to be added. Watch the time carefully, as overcooking occurs very quickly. Finally, ➤ never attempt to remove the cover until the pressure is fully released. If the cover is difficult to remove, do not force it; there is still steam in the cooker, which will be exhausted if you wait a few minutes.

There are two basic ways to release the pressure from a pressure cooker: quick release and natural release. **Quick-release** involves either opening the steam valve or, in the case of stovetop models, placing the cooker in the sink and running cold water over the lid until the pressure dissipates. **Natural release** is just letting the cooker cool down off the heat until the pressure dissipates. In general, natural release is a necessity when the item being cooked is very fragile. Beans, for instance, may rupture when subjected to a sudden drop in pressure—the water inside the beans will boil violently until they cool to below 212°F. Because it can sometimes take quite a long time for the pressure to release naturally—especially electric models—many recipes will split the difference and instruct you to let the pressure dissipate naturally for 10 minutes, then open the valve to release the remaining pressure.

To quick-release the pressure, take the cooker off the heat (or set electric models to the "keep warm" setting) and use tongs or a long-handled spoon to open the pressure valve. Steam will rush out of the valve (it will make a loud hissing sound—don't be scared!). When steam (and sound) stops emerging from the pressure cooker, it is safe to open the lid. Alternatively, place stovetop pressure cookers in the sink, run cool water over the lid, and proceed as above.

To release the pressure naturally, simply take the pressure cooker off the heat (for electric pressure cookers, natural release starts as soon as the time runs out on the built-in timer) and wait.

Pressure-cooking is best for foods that need to cook for a long time to become tender. Dried beans, whole grains, stocks, stews, braises, and dense vegetables like beets and sweet potatoes are all good candidates for pressure-cooking. When you are adapting recipes designed for conventional methods, you can use less liquid, because there will be no evaporation.

As a general rule, ➤ do not bother pressure-cooking items that already cook in a short time. This may sound elementary, but it is sometimes easy to forget that many quick-cooking foods will be finished cooking normally by the time an electric pressure-cooker has gotten up to pressure (other times, the savings in time is merely insignificant). Leafy vegetables, tender cuts of meat, fish and shellfish (with the exception of octopus), and many other foods fit into this category. Fresh fruit is generally too fragile for this cooking method (unless you are making applesauce).

We have provided pressure-cooking time estimates in individual entries in the **Vegetables** chapter, 199, for the kinds we think benefit from this method. For estimated pressure-cooking times for whole

grains, consult the Grains Cooking Chart, 340. When cooking grains and **dried beans** (or soups or stews that include rice or dried beans), ➤ do not fill the cooker more than half full, since these ingredients can expand to over twice their original volume. ➤ For beans, always add 1 tablespoon oil per cup of dried beans to control foaming. Again, consult your owner's manual for instructions specific to your pressure cooker.

To adapt meat and poultry stews and braises for pressure-cooking, brown the meat in batches as directed, either in the pressure cooker (for electric countertop models, use the high sauté setting) or in a heavy skillet. Sauté or sweat any vegetables as directed as well. If you used a separate pan for browning, deglaze it and add the dissolved browned bits to the cooker. Add everything to the pressure cooker, secure the lid, and bring the cooker up to high pressure. For poultry, cook for 15 to 20 minutes; for meats, cook for 20 to 35 minutes (use the shorter time if your pressure cooker goes up to 15 psi and the longer time for 10 to 12 psi models). Allow the pressure to release naturally for 10 minutes, then open the valve to release the remaining pressure. Check the meat for tenderness; bring back up to pressure and cook longer if necessary. Because there is no evaporation during pressure-cooking, add ½ cup less liquid to stews and braises. Or, leave the liquid amount the same, remove the meat and vegetables from the liquid after cooking, and reduce or thicken the liquid as desired.

▲ PRESSURE-COOKING AT HIGH ALTITUDES

Because liquids boil at lower temperatures as altitude increases, the cooking time under pressure should be increased by 5 percent for every 1,000 feet after 2,000 feet above sea level. Increase cooking times as follows:

3,000 feet: 5 percent
4,000 feet: 10 percent
5,000 feet: 15 percent
6,000 feet: 20 percent
7,000 feet: 25 percent
8,000 feet: 30 percent

Plan to increase the cooking liquid by half the percentage of the additional cooking time. For example, if the cooking time is increased by 10 percent, increase the cooking liquid by 5 percent.

MICROWAVE COOKING

The microwave is one of the most misunderstood appliances in the kitchen. It is not a substitute for the stovetop and oven. It does *not* cook foods from the inside out. It cooks some things very well, but it cannot be used for all of your cooking needs.

In a microwave oven, electricity is converted into microwaves by a device called a magnetron, and the waves are spread throughout the oven cavity via a revolving "stirrer fan" in the oven. Previously, microwaves achieved low-power settings (like those for thawing foods) by simply turning the magnetron on and off, since it is not capable of any other setting. Newer microwaves may be equipped with an **inverter,** which allows the magnetron to operate at 50 percent power. These provide a gentler, more evenly heated result.

Microwaves can penetrate glass, ceramic, paper, and plastic, but they are deflected by metal, which is why microwave oven interiors are lined with metal. When these waves are scattered about the oven cavity, they behave like billiard balls gone awry, bouncing off the walls and careening about until they encounter water or the water molecules embedded in our food. The microwaves cause these water molecules to vibrate, which creates heat through friction, and this heat is then spread by conduction through the food.

Contrary to popular belief, microwaves will penetrate only ¾ to 1½ inches deep into a food item, and thus do not cook "from the inside out." Rather, the cooking process is not so different from what happens to food cooked in a skillet: The outside layer is heated, and heat is then conducted to the interior. Here, the outer layer is heated by excited water molecules within that layer, rather than a heat source below or above it.

Most glass dishes, bowls, or containers are suitable for microwave cooking. Some types of plastic and ceramic material are microwave-safe as well, but this should be confirmed before use (most that are will be labeled as such). In any event, ➤ metal or metal-trimmed dishes must be avoided, as they cause an arcing interaction with the oven walls. Wire twist ties and metal handles also cause arcing, so never put them in the microwave.

Cooking fresh foods by microwave is not without disappointments, especially when one compares the eating quality or appearance with that of more conventionally cooked foods. Timing varies greatly between microwaves, and almost all types of food tend to toughen. Meats dry out more than when cooked by conventional methods. Microwave-baked cakes turn out coarse in texture and overly moist, with pallid tops. If milk or milk mixtures are heated or cooked in a microwave oven, they must be constantly watched, as they tend to boil over very quickly. Browning—which is responsible for both the flavor and the aesthetic pleasure of much food—is not achievable with the microwave. Pre-searing, 1048, or post-searing, 1049, may help, but this added step complicates things and diminishes the time-saving appeal of using the appliance.

Microwaving does, however, have virtues that extend beyond reheating leftovers and making a bowl of popcorn. Ingredients that have a high water content—most vegetables, virtually all greens, fish, and fruits—can be quickly cooked in a microwave oven. They will have a steamed quality to them, but without the excess moisture steam might leave behind. Fresh sweet corn cooks in seconds, artichokes in minutes, and a winter squash or "baked" potato requires only a fraction of the time it takes in an oven or steamer. Microwaves can quickly dry small quantities of fresh herbs, 947. Peeling tomatoes or peaches is simple after a few seconds in the microwave, and for melting cheese, chocolate, or butter, nothing could be tidier. To melt chocolate in the microwave, see 972.

➤ Microwaving works best for vegetables cut in 1-inch chunks (with the notable exceptions of potatoes, 265, acorn squash, 274, and spaghetti squash, 276), in quantities of 1 pound or less; otherwise the cooking can be uneven. Tempered glass cookware is ideal for microwave cooking, with a lid, plate, or plastic wrap covering the dish. For plastic wrap, poke a few holes to allow steam to escape. No matter the vegetable, add about ¼ cup stock, broth, or water and a tablespoon of oil or butter for 1 pound vegetables. Cook on high, stopping to stir and test the vegetables for doneness every 3 minutes for tender vegetables like green beans and broccoli, or every 5 minutes for dense vegetables like beets. For microwaving instructions for specific vegetables, see individual entries in the Vegetables chapter, 199 (note that, because we do not advise microwave cooking for all vegetables, we only provide instructions for those that are best suited to microwave cooking).

It is tricky to adapt a conventionally cooked recipe to microwave cooking. The surest way is to find a microwave recipe that is comparable and use it as a guide. Take all microwave recipe cooking times with a grain of salt. As mentioned above, inverter-equipped microwaves are much better at gently heating, reheating, or thawing foods. The oven's wattage makes a difference; the higher the wattage, the faster the oven cooks food, and it can overcook in a wink. You can always put food back in, but you cannot undo overcooking. There is no simple formula for adjusting time according to wattage.

When reheating in the microwave, it is especially important to stir the food two or three times to ensure even distribution of heat and avoid overcooking in spots. To heat bread, loosely wrap in a damp paper napkin and microwave in 5-second increments until the bread is warm—no further. Bread warmed in the microwave acquires an unpleasant rubbery texture as soon as it cools, and no amount of toasting can change it. For a whole plate of food, arrange thicker pieces toward the rim of the plate and quick-to-heat pieces toward the center. Cover with a paper towel and heat in 1-minute increments. Meat sliced about ¼ inch thick reheats best. ➤ Be especially watchful with small portions of food; they can easily overcook and burn. Never heat food in closed jars. Never heat fats and oils (aside from briefly melting butter) or try to deep-fry in the microwave.

ABOUT OUTDOOR COOKING METHODS

For whatever reason—the appeal of the primal, a penchant for playing with fire, a desire to be outdoors, or pure practicality—humans love cooking outside. For a very long time in our history, much cooking was done outdoors by default. There was no such thing as a proper kitchen until relatively recently, and the smoke, fire, and strong odors of cooking were best dealt with by simply cooking in open air. Now kitchens are standard in the developed world, yet we still devote an impressive amount of time and energy to cooking outside when we can.

The most common type of outdoor cooking is grilling, thanks to the wide availability of gas and charcoal grills (and the fact that you can prop up a grate on some cinder blocks pretty much anywhere). Camp cooking is also widespread and, depending on the proximity to civilization, can involve grilling, cooking over a fire or in coals, cooking on a propane camp stove, or boiling water on an ultralight backpacking stove.

Most outdoor cooking, with the exception of solar cooking, uses fire, which is what links these methods with hearth cookery. Hearth cookery is something of a lost art, due not just to the preference of most people to cook with controlled sources of heat, but also because most homes do not have a hearth suitable for cooking. Should you find yourself in possession of such a hearth, however, for heaven's sake use it! It has much of the appeal of outdoor cooking, but is done in the comfort of your home. See 1068 for more on hearth cookery.

CAMP COOKING

For campers, alfresco cooking is a necessity rather than an indulgence, but it is a pleasant, rustic feature of the experience, not a bug. For long-cooking camp foods, gas is the preferred fuel. Propane gas stoves are easy to use but do not work well at temperatures below 30°F. If you will be using fire to prepare food while camping, be aware of basic fire safety precautions as well as safeguards to ensure there is no damage to wildlife.

Fires in wilderness areas carry the greatest responsibility. For starters, never create a new fire pit, especially in the backcountry. Only build a fire if there is an existing, approved fire pit surrounded with rocks. Never build a fire if there is a burn ban in effect.

Hardwoods smoke less and provide much more heat than do most softwoods. Those preferred are oak, beech, maple, and ash, then the evergreens. Beech wood will burn green; aspen will not burn at all. That said, once you have a good bed of coals, just about any wood will burn. Of course, the wetter the wood, the more it will smoke. Splitting wet wood and putting it close to the fire to dry out will help mitigate this problem. Wet or dry, ➤ split wood always catches more easily than whole logs and burns more efficiently.

To start a wood fire, collect a few small dead branches with the twigs attached (preferably from dead standing trees). Cut or snap the branches into 4- to 8-inch segments and divvy them up into categories, beginning with matchstick thickness, then pencil thickness, then thumb-sized and larger. You may wish to use some kind of duff, or dry, dead plant material, to help you start the fire. Pine needles and wood shavings are good candidates (if you have a utility knife, you can use it to make shavings from larger pieces of wood). Place a larger piece of wood off-center inside the fire ring. Place a small amount of duff on a dry piece of bark and set it next to the large piece of firewood. Build a half-pyramid on top of the duff with the smallest twigs, leaning them against the large piece of firewood (arrange the twigs to be as vertical as possible, as fire tends to climb up). Light the tinder with a match placed on the upwind side of the pyramid. When it catches, immediately add pencil-sized sticks, then finger-sized sticks, and so on. ➤ The more kindling you use before adding larger pieces, the better your chances of success. When adding fuel, leave ample space between the sticks so the fire can breathe. If the fire starts to smoke excessively, you are probably starving it of air (move the firewood apart with a stick to let more in). Keep your fire small: It takes less wood to keep it going, is less likely to spread or get out of control, and is more comfortable to cook next to.

Never leave a fire untended. ➤ Watch for sparks on surrounding vegetation through the duration of the fire. Watch for overhead branches as fire hazards. When you finally leave a fire, drown it, mix it with mud, stir dirt into it, stomp on it, mix it with snow or sand, and leave it ➤ completely dead and cool.

For recipes that require practically no equipment, see Chicken Hobo Packs, 413, and Campfire Bananas, 177. Many foods, including cut-up vegetables, fish, and pieces of chicken, can be wrapped in a double layer of foil with a little oil and some seasonings and cooked next to a fire or in coals. Our best advice is to keep it simple.

For raking embers, arranging Dutch ovens, and using the fire's direct and radiant heat, see Fireplace or Hearth Cooking, 1068. Before bringing any sort of cooking vessel into close contact with a wood fire, cover the pan's bottom with a film of soap or detergent. This will greatly facilitate the removal of soot later.

PIT COOKING

Pit cooking traditionally employs hot rocks buried in a pit to cook large quantities of food. This technique is used around the world, from New England clambakes to Southern pit barbecue, *barbacoa* and *cochinita pibil* in Mexico, Hawaiian *kālua*, and fish and taro root cooked with hot rocks in Samoa. The size of your pit should, of course, correspond to the size of the item(s) you wish to cook. If you are just starting on your pit-cooking journey, you might start small, with a whole fish, vegetables, a chicken, or a pork shoulder. For larger feasts, dig a pit not less than 2 feet deep, 3 feet across, and 4 feet long.

In the pit, build and light a substantial bonfire of hardwood or, if the pit is on the beach, of driftwood. Hickory, beech, maple, and oak are prime for this purpose (charcoal can also be used to heat the pit). The next step is to put in the bonfire about forty medium-sized flat rocks; ➤ never use shale or rocks from a stream bed as these may explode when heated. Tend the fire carefully and fan if necessary, because the fire may be oxygen deprived. When the fire has completely burned down and the rocks are hot—this should take no less than 2 hours—rake out and remove unburned wood with a shovel or tongs. Spread most of the hot rocks over the bottom of the pit (reserve some for topping off the pit). Add a 2-inch layer of fresh leaves—grape, fig, beech, fresh grass, banana, fern—or corn husks or seaweed. You can also add handfuls of aromatic herbs. Some pit roasters sprinkle a quart or so of water over the leaves to create steam. Alternatively, you can dunk the leaves in water before using them to line the pit.

On the bed of packed foliage, arrange the elements of your meal: fish, cuts of meat, peppers, onions in their skins, corn in its husk, unpeeled potatoes, whole winter squashes, whole root vegetables. Pile over them a second layer of green leafage, then a second grouping of food, and finally a third layer of green leafage. For shore dinners, when seaweed is used for layering, wire mesh, such as hardware cloth, is often placed over at least one layer to better support small crustaceans, clams, and oysters (see Clambake, 353). Cap off the stratification with the remaining hot rocks, overlapping layers of wet burlap, and then a tarpaulin or canvas cover and 4 inches of the earth or sand excavated from the pit to insulate the cooking chamber.

And now for the waiting and poking part of the process. How long cooking will take depends, of course, on what's cooking—for vegetables, 3 or 4 hours may suffice. Meat can take much longer depending on the cut and the quantity of the meat. Be sure to periodically test for doneness of the foods closest to the edge of the pit. Always ensure with a thermometer that all the meats and poultry have reached a safe minimum temperature (for meats, see Timing and Doneness, 452; for poultry, see About Cooking Poultry, 406). Tough cuts of meat from the shoulder, shanks, breast, or brisket should be cooked until fork-tender.

When you judge the contents of the pit to be done and are ready to excavate your food, be extremely careful when uncovering and removing the tarp; try not to get food fouled up with sand or earth or burn yourself from the quick release of steam and heat.

If pit cooking is more than occasional, and the locale does not vary, you may find it more convenient to build a surface pit by constructing a hollow rectangle of concrete blocks about the same height as a true pit is deep. For those who would like a semiportable option, there are lightweight, wheeled "roasting boxes" that can approximate pit cooking: Food is placed in a stainless-steel-lined tub, covered with a rimmed, heavy-duty lid, and piled with lit charcoal. Since the heat radiates from the top, these portable pits are especially good at crisping the skin on whole, butterflied pigs.

GRILLING

Grilling is by far the most convenient and popular way to cook outdoors. Of course, there are several ways to grill foods, and they are invariably linked with the type of grill you use. These generally fall into one of two categories: open or covered.

Open grills range in size and portability from the simple small hibachi to large built-in units. These grills are best at one type of cooking method: **direct grilling.** Here food is placed directly over the coals or flames, which (depending on the strength of the fire) will quickly brown its exposed surface. Any fat dripping from the food will combust, causing flare-ups. Flare-ups are a mixed bag; if they are too ferocious, they will cause the food to char too deeply—even catch fire. On the other hand, the combusting residues and drippings add a desirable flavor. Most open grills are only good for preparing quick-cooking foods. However, fancier open and covered grills may have an adjustable grate or firebox that can be raised or lowered with a pulley. This allows you to control the intensity of heat the food is subjected to, as well as keep it out of harm's way when flare-ups occur. With ample fuel, large roasts can be cooked high above the fire on the grate (or on a spit or rotisserie, 1065).

Covered grills come in many styles, but the covered kettle grill is perhaps the most common. They are much more versatile, and we highly recommend them over open grills. Like open grills, they can be left uncovered for direct grilling, but they can also be set up for **indirect grilling,** or a **two-zone fire:** The flame is kept on one side of the grill, the food is kept on the other, and the lid is fitted so that its vent is over the food. When a covered grill is set up in this way, the food is heated more gently by convecting gases and the radiant heat reflected from the lid. At any point during cooking, the grill can be uncovered and the food moved over the coals for browning.

Tender cuts of meat that are less than 2 inches thick, thinly sliced or ground meats, tender vegetables, crustaceans, small whole fish, and firm-textured fish steaks can be cooked solely with direct grilling. In general, the center of these foods will reach doneness by the time their surfaces have browned over the flames.

All other foods benefit from a combination of direct and indirect grilling. Poultry (especially bone-in), roasts, thicker fish fillets and whole fish, as well as sturdier vegetables need to be pulled to the side of the flames at some point and cooked through with indirect heat. These slow-cooking foods can be browned directly over the flames before or after they are cooked through. In general, we prefer browning poultry when it is within 10 minutes of cooking through, as more fat has rendered from the skin and the surface is more likely to brown evenly. Of course, the timing of when to brown is also dependent on the health of your fire, which may die down before the food is sufficiently cooked.

Enter the appeal of **gas grills,** which can be turned up or down at will. Once considered distinctly inferior to their charcoal-fired counterparts, gas grills continue to improve, most notably in burning fuel more efficiently and in their ability to achieve the higher temperatures crucial for a delectable brown crust. **Pellet grills** are a relative newcomer that generate heat and smoke by feeding pellets of compressed sawdust with an auger into a small cup-shaped burning chamber. A temperature is set, and the grill measures the temperature of the cooking chamber and adjusts the speed with which the auger feeds more pellets into the burning chamber. They are very easy to operate and excel at indirect grilling, barbecuing, 1066, and smoking, 1067 (they do not, however, get hotter than a standard oven).

Charcoal grills, with all of their inconveniences, hassles, and quirks, are still much better than gas or pellet grills at achieving high temperatures for direct grilling. Hardwood lump charcoal is worth seeking out in grocery stores and hardware and specialty stores. These hardwood chunks light more easily, give heat that is more responsive, and burn cleaner and hotter than briquettes. However, charcoal briquettes last much longer and provide a consistent, predictable heat. Try different kinds of hardwood charcoal and briquettes and form your own opinion. (Personally, we prefer lump charcoal for direct grilling and briquettes for longer cooking.) Alternatively, for the most primal experience, you can start a wood fire, 1061, burn it down to coals, and use the embers for cooking in a charcoal grill. The only fuel we wish to warn you away from is self-lighting briquettes and lighter fluid. These can impart an undesirable flavor to the food being grilled.

Grill and fuel aside, the list of basic equipment you need for grilling most foods is relatively short. We recommend a pair of **long tongs,** a **long-handled spatula,** an accurate **instant-read thermometer,** and several **rimmed baking sheets** for transferring foods (or functioning as a drip pan during indirect grilling). A pair of **heavy-duty fire-resistant mitts or gloves** can come in handy, as can a **spray bottle filled with water** for extinguishing flare-ups. For larger fire-related mishaps, a pail of water, garden hose, bucket of sand, or fire extinguisher is good to have on hand. For cleaning carbonized bits of food off grill grates, a **wire grill brush or scraper** is a good investment, as is a **covered, galvanized bucket** for collecting charcoal ashes. For the optional tools that make certain tasks easier, a **hinged wire basket** with a long handle is desirable for turning fragile fish, which have a nasty habit of sticking to grill grates. **Grilling baskets** are great for cooking small or cut-up vegetables.

Before we proceed to lighting instructions, here are some important nuggets of common sense: ➤ Always set your grill on level ground in the largest possible open space, away from walls, wooden fences, overhanging eaves or tree branches, or anything else that might easily catch fire. ➤ Keep children well away from the grilling area. ➤ Never use charcoal grills in a house, tent, cabin, garage, or other enclosed area with poor ventilation. ➤ Never light the fire with gasoline, and never spray lighter fluid onto lit coals. Remember, a fire goes out without oxygen, so ➤ extinguish fires in covered grills by closing the lid and vents.

➤ For those grilling in dry or windy conditions, use caution when starting hardwood lump charcoal, which has a tendency to spark and crackle. Attend the fire at all times. If there are especially large charcoal pieces in the bag, break them into pieces smaller than 2 inches thick with a hammer. (We have had larger pieces of mesquite lump charcoal explode, which can throw large embers a significant distance.) If the grill must be near grass, we recommend wetting the nearest 3 feet with a garden sprayer.

To start a charcoal fire in a grill, we recommend using a **chimney-style charcoal starter.** Place torn newspaper, paper grocery bags, or (eventually) the charcoal bag itself in the bottom chamber, turn the chimney over, and fill the top chamber with charcoal. Place the chimney on concrete, stone, or another fireproof surface (on the grill with the grate fitted is ideal) and light the paper. The charcoal will ignite from bottom to top. The charcoal is ready when the flames die down and the lumps or briquettes are covered in a thin layer of white ash. Remove the grill grate, pick up the chimney starter, and carefully dump the coals in the grill as directed below.

As a general rule, if using a medium-sized, metal grill of average construction, ➤ a standard chimney of charcoal briquettes is usually sufficient for covering and cooking through a whole chicken, or grilling up to 6 or 8 servings of quick-cooking foods uncovered and directly over the flames. A standard chimney of hardwood lump charcoal will burn hotter and quicker; for a comparable cooking time, add several handfuls of unlit lump charcoal, and let it ignite for an additional 5 minutes.

For direct grilling with charcoal, dump out the charcoal over approximately two-thirds of the grill (a portion of the cooking area should be reserved as a warming or holding area, in case of flare-ups). In a standard covered grill, it may be desirable to mound some of the charcoal so that it is especially close to the grate, and thus able to provide the hardest sear on steaks and other items you wish to cook to rare or medium-rare.

For a two-zone charcoal fire, dump out the charcoal onto one-third of the grill, off to one side. If desired, put additional charcoal on top of it and cover with the vents open until it has ignited. For whole poultry and fattier roasts, you may wish to place a disposable roasting pan or rimmed baking sheet on the cool side of the grill to catch drippings.

Once the charcoal is lit and arranged, replace the grill grate, cover the grill, and fully open the vents. Let the grill and grate preheat for approximately 5 minutes, give the grate a quick scouring with a brush or scraper, and adjust the vents to maintain the desired temperature or heat level.

The lids of many grills have built-in thermometers, but these are notoriously inaccurate. Analog and digital cable models that attach to the grill grate can be purchased; these are a marked improvement, since they measure the heat the food is actually subjected to. Most digital cable probe thermometers are fine for measuring temperature for indirect grilling, but few can withstand the heat directly over the coals (those that claim they can will likely not remain functional or accurate for long).

Thus, judging the heat directly over the coals is mostly a matter of experience. Of course, charcoal fresh from the chimney is going to be the hottest, especially if it is close to the grill grate and left covered with the vents open as described to preheat. Dampening the vents and keeping the cover on will calm the heat down. In the past, we have recommended the so-called "hot hand" method: Hold your hand above the grill at about the same distance from the coals that the food will be while cooking, and count. When you have to pull your hand away, the count will tell you the heat level.

Hot	2 counts
Medium-hot	4 to 6 counts
Low	8 to 10 counts

This is certainly better than nothing if you lack the experience to know when coals are hot enough to sear steaks or calm enough to not incinerate a sausage. However, our tolerance for heat varies, so do not make a science of it (or singe your arm while counting). Since most foods that benefit from lower heat are best cooked through with indirect grilling, it is often sufficient to recognize two things: when coals are screaming hot, and when they need replenishing, both of which are easily determined with a glance after several cookouts.

To grill long-cooking foods or additional batches of food, you will need to add more charcoal to most grills. You can do this by adding unlit pieces directly to the embers, or by lighting another chimney full of charcoal. Though a bit more perilous, we think the latter option is best, as charcoal gives off a heavy, unappetizing smoke when igniting. For anything that requires more than 1 hour of moderate to high temperatures in a standard covered grill, we ➤ start an additional chimney full of lump charcoal after 20 minutes of cooking has elapsed—or after 30 minutes of cooking for charcoal briquettes. They should be ready to add by the time the grill fire needs replenishing. Uncovered grills burn through charcoal faster, so for grilling more than three batches of burgers, steaks, kebabs, and other quick-cooking items, start an additional chimney of charcoal 5 minutes earlier than stated above.

Some grills have **hinged grates,** which make adding charcoal much easier (For unhinged grates, transfer any unfinished items to a rimmed baking sheet and carefully remove the hot grate with tongs or insulated, fire-resistant gloves). An easier, more expensive option is to invest in a **kamado-style grill,** which has thick ceramic insulation and a remarkable ability to hold heat and burn efficiently. For other options specific to slow, low-temperature cooking, see Barbecuing, 1066.

Whole **vegetables** and **fruits** can be grilled directly on the grate as long as they are wide enough to not fall through. Smaller or thinner pieces will either need to be skewered, 1065, or placed in a grilling basket. Before cooking, toss vegetables or brush their cut surfaces with an oil that has a high smoke point, 981. This will prevent them from drying out and promote browning. Quick-cooking vegetables (tomatoes, eggplant, summer squash, mushrooms, bell peppers, and fennel) can be placed directly over a medium-hot fire and cooked until soft and slightly charred. Another option is to cook vegetables in a foil pouch, 1057, next to or nestled on top of the coals—an especially useful strategy when the cooking grate is smaller than the amount of food you plan to grill.

When grilling **meat,** remember that tender steaks and chops (as well as **poultry** cutlets and **fish** fillets and steaks) are well suited to direct grilling. ➤ Trim off all excess fat before grilling to reduce the risk of flare-ups, which can carry greasy smoke and ash to the meat. For thinner cuts, cut through encircling sinew so the meat will not curl up. If the cuts are especially lean, lightly coat them with a high smoke point oil, 981. After searing, you may need to move the meat to the cooler side of the grill to cook through without burning. Larger cuts of meat, as well as larger whole fish, and whole or bone-in pieces of poultry will need to be grilled indirectly for the majority of the cooking time. Toward the end of cooking, when these items are nearly done, uncover and move them over direct heat to brown. ➤ Always test for doneness with an instant-read thermometer (for recommended temperatures, see Timing and Doneness, 452, and About Cooking Poultry, 406). For specific information on grilling different proteins, see About Grilling and Broiling Fish, 384, About Grilling, Broiling, and Sautéing Beef, 458, and About Broiling and Grilling Chicken, 410.

PLANKING

Here, food is placed on a soaked wooden board and then cooked directly over a fire, thus cooking the food with the hot, convecting air current and protecting it from the flames. This is especially useful for delicate items like fish fillets, which is probably why it was favored by indigenous peoples of the Pacific Northwest, where both salmon and cedar planks are plentiful. A side benefit of planking is that the boards smolder, and infuse the foods cooked on them with a woodsy, smoky flavor.

You can buy boards especially for plank cooking, sold with grilling supplies. For most grills, the optimal size is 6 to 8 inches wide by 10 to 12 inches long. Western cedar is the traditional choice as it contributes a distinctive flavor, but oak or a fragrant hardwood such as cherry, apple, maple, or hickory is acceptable (as long as it is untreated and not too resinous). To keep the planks from catching fire or smoldering excessively, soak them in water for at least 6 hours. Do not reuse wood for plank cooking unless it's only lightly charred. For a basic planking procedure, see Planked Fish, 386.

In recent years, **grilling wraps** have become available. These thin, semiflexible sheets, typically shaved from red cedarwood, can be soaked, rolled around smaller items, and tied. While they do not add the support and protection of planks, these wraps are effective at infusing individual servings with a smoky cedar flavor. Since wraps only require 5 minutes of soaking, they are certainly more convenient, but we would only expect them to last for one cookout.

SKEWER COOKING

The technique of skewering chunks or strips of meat on a stick and grilling them over an open fire is probably as old as cooking itself. Our term for the familiar, modern version—kebabs—originates from the Turkish *shish kebab*, a dish of skewered marinated lamb grilled over a charcoal fire. Using different meats and seasonings, the dish is known throughout Europe and central Asia by several names, including *shashlik*, *brochettes*, and *souvlaki*, 492. Further to the east are the *tandoor*-cooked meats of India (see Tandoori Chicken or Chicken Tikka, 413), satay, 61, of Southeast Asia, and Japanese *yakitori*, 445. In Peru, they are known as *anticuchos*, 517. Other styles of kebab are based on seasoned, ground meat: Balkan *ćevapi*, Vietnamese *nem nướng*, and Adana-Style Lamb Kebabs, 504. These rely on salting and "overmixing" the meat to develop its myosin, 502, which binds the mixture and helps it stick to the skewer.

➤ Soak wood skewers in water for at least 1 hour before using. For those who cook kebabs frequently, a set of **flat stainless steel skewers** are ideal. Their flat shape discourages foods from rotating on the skewer when you turn them. For large chunks of food and ground meat mixtures, seek out extra-wide ones.

Kebabs lend themselves perfectly to picnics—presoaked in a savory marinade, they can be grilled over an open fire and served straight from the skewers on flatbreads or pitas with lettuce, tomato, and onion. For the kebabs typical of backyard cookouts, it is customary to alternate meat cubes with an assortment of vegetables such as grape or cherry tomatoes, bell pepper slices, mushrooms, small wedges of onion, or pineapple. Bits of bacon or fresh bay leaf may be inserted between the pieces of meat to add flavor (the bacon drippings may cause flare-ups, so be ready to pull the skewers to one side if necessary).

When threading mixed ingredients onto the same skewer ➤ choose items that will cook at the same rate. Or, if the meat, poultry, or fish selected is a quick-cooking one, see that the onions, peppers, or other firm vegetables that will alternate with it are precooked, so that the food will all be done at the same time. Of course, these complications can be avoided altogether by having one type of meat or vegetable on each skewer, which allows you to cook each one to its optimum level of doneness. Unfortunately, the convenient simplicity of giving everyone their own skewered medley is lost. Instead, we have found that the best option is to stack like skewers on several plates or a large platter and have diners slide what they want of each ingredient onto their plate (or flatbread).

Kebabs aside, skewering is an excellent method of holding together items that might otherwise be difficult to handle and turn on the grill. Some objects, such as onion slices, benefit from having two skewers inserted into them to keep the rings together. Thinner items, like butterflied squid, profit from having a skewer or two threaded through them to keep them from curling up. Halved or butterflied chickens destined for grilling are much easier to move around and turn when the breast and thigh are skewered together.

SPIT-ROASTING OR ROTISSERIE COOKING

Rotating roasts over or next to a fire is perhaps as ancient as skewer cooking. As such, more than a few variations on the basic setup have cropped up over the last few millennia. There are horizontal spits and vertical spits, covered rotisseries, open rotisseries, and those that are open, but have walls angled to reflect heat.

The constant that runs through all types of rotisserie cooking is the slow, even cooking of meats that is achieved by rotating them above or to the side of a heat source. As the meat rotates, the surface nearest the fire is exposed to radiant heat and begins to brown. As this patch rotates away from the flame, it cools down once more, only to be subjected again to brief, intense heat. Thus, the surface becomes thoroughly and evenly browned. With an uncovered rotisserie, since the outermost layer of meat is allowed to cool as it turns away from the heat source, the heat is slow to transfer inward to the center of the meat. Rotisseries enclosed in a covered grill or oven will cook foods more efficiently due to the hot, convecting air and the radiant heat reflected from the enclosing walls. The result brings together the best attributes of slow-cooking and high heat methods: juicy, evenly done meat and a browned exterior.

Horizontal rotisseries are the most common motorized models to find for home use. Rotisserie attachments are available for charcoal and gas grills, and there are rotisserie kits that include a spit, motor, and stands for cooking over a wood fire or on the hearth. The motors and gearing included in these kits can be substantially more powerful, which is necessary for spit-roasting whole animals like pigs and goats.

Consult the directions that come with your equipment to determine the maximum weight it is designed to accommodate. Most rotisserie grill inserts are good for 20 pounds, and can accommodate several whole chickens, rib racks, roughly cylindrical beef or pork roasts (like those from the rib and loin), and other large, boneless cuts of meat. Smaller birds should be mounted transversely on the spit, larger ones head to tail along the spit's axis, as illustrated, 1066. Roasts with bones in their center, such as leg of lamb, hams, and pork shoulder, are harder to balance, although not impossible; nonetheless, we recommend indirect grilling, 1062, or smoking, 1067, instead.

➤ Positioning the spit in the center of gravity of larger roasts is essential. If the food is unbalanced, the rotation of the spit will tend to slow as the heavier side travels up, and then speed up on its way down (as it continues to cook, the problem is likely to get worse). Not only does this put a strain on the motor and gearing, but it will result in uneven cooking. Securing the roasts so that they do not move from side to side is important for the very same reason. While the consequences are not quite as serious for lightweight roasts like whole chickens as they are for a whole hog, it is best to avoid it altogether by centering the spit in foods as accurately as possible and securing it tightly.

There are several methods of securing roasts on a spit. The most common way is to use **spit forks,** a set of prongs attached to a collar that slides down the spit and is tightened with a screw. A spit fork is placed on either side of each item on the spit with the prongs pointed inward. The prongs are then pushed into the food and the collar is tightened into place. Some spits have holes drilled into them, which can accept skewers or **spit pins:** A roast is placed on the spit, then a spit pin is inserted into the roast so that it goes through the hole in the spit and emerges on the other side. It may be necessary to use butcher's twine to truss any limbs (such as the legs of a turkey) so that they are flush with the roast.

Depending on the setup of your rotisserie, it is hard to give time estimates that hold true across the board. For a ballpark estimate, look to grilling recipes for the item you are spit-roasting. As always, check the internal temperature of meats and poultry to determine when they are done (for meats, see Timing and Doneness, 452; for poultry see About Cooking Poultry, 406). Since all of the cooking is taking place over a drip pan, feel free to brush roasts and poultry with melted butter or oil. You may baste with butter or oil during the cooking period, but do not apply any barbecue sauce, 582–83, until the last 15 to 20 minutes of cooking.

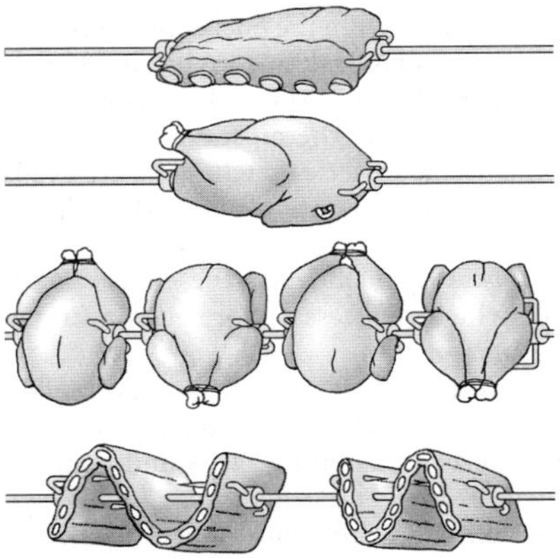

Cooking a rib roast, poultry, and spareribs on a spit

Vertical rotisseries are the stuff of dreams: Some of our favorite foods—namely, *tacos al pastor* and *shawarma*—are traditionally prepared on them, and they have the added advantage of being immune to many of the balancing issues encountered with horizontal spit roasting. Unfortunately, vertical models are hard to justify purchasing outside of a commercial setting. (For an alternative to vertical rotisseries, see the illustration for roasting meat on a string in Fireplace or Hearth Cooking, 1068.)

BARBECUING

Barbecuing is the outdoor equivalent of braising: Tougher cuts are placed in a smoky, humid environment and slow-cooked at temperatures between 225°F and 300°F until fall-off-the-bone tender. Pork shoulder, beef brisket, and spareribs benefit from the long, slow cooking time and the natural smoke flavor that permeates the outer layer of the meat. Over time, the tough meat is transformed into a tender, smoke-tinged treat. The word "barbecue" derives from the Taíno word *barbacoa*, which refers to the slow pit-cooking, 1062, of meats over coals. Smoking, specifically hot-smoking, 1068, is another term for this method of cooking.

While many barbecue establishments use masonry pits, for home cooks the only convenient method for barbecuing is with indirect heat in a smoker or covered grill. **Offset smokers,** which have a firebox attached to one side of the smoking chamber, are popular (especially for those using hardwood logs) as are **barrel smokers, pellet grills,** and **cabinet-style smokers.** The latter two are by far the easiest to operate, as they can be set to a desired temperature and left unattended. It is similarly easy to control the heat of **gas grills** but creating and holding smoke in them can be a chore. Finally, a regular **charcoal grill** set up for indirect cooking can be pressed into service. **Kamado-style grills** in particular are very good at barbecuing, as their insulation and efficiency allow them to maintain low temperatures for a long time without requiring more charcoal (most, however, must be fitted with an unwieldly ceramic plate for indirect cooking).

As for fuel, the top choice is hardwood logs, particularly oak, hickory, or any fruitwood. Since hardwood logs are not the easiest to source, the next best option in terms of quality is hardwood lump charcoal, then charcoal briquettes, followed by gas (for safety reasons, gas grills are well ventilated and do not trap smoke). If your charcoal grill has a hard time maintaining a low heat for longer periods, choose charcoal briquettes; they burn the longest, and will not need to be replenished as many times.

Pellet grills and smokers heated with burning hardwood provide smoke naturally. Gas grills and charcoal fires do not. For smoking on a gas grill, a special perforated container (or a foil pouch) full of soaked wood chips can be set on the burner. For charcoal-fired smoking, the best option is to use large, dry chunks of hardwood. Add a small chunk every other hour or arrange the chunks in the charcoal so that they ignite in the same time frame. As for the type of wood to use, hickory is the classic for Southern barbecue, and oak is favored in Texas. Fruit and nut woods such as apple, cherry, and pecan have a pleasant flavor as well. Mesquite wood smoke has a very strong, distinct flavor, so use it in moderation.

Please read Grilling, 1062, for the basic essentials needed for cooking on a grill. If your smoker is not equipped with one, a **water pan** set over the coals or burners increases humidity in the smoker; this helps items cook faster and the smoke to adhere better to the surface of the food. We are especially fond of the smoking inserts available for kettle-style grills, which combine a water pan with a basket for holding the coals to one side. An alternative is to keep the humidity up by basting meats with a "mop," 583. A long-handled **basting or mopping brush** can be a good tool for this purpose (though drenching a piece of torn kitchen towel in the mop and grasping it with a pair of tongs is perfectly acceptable). A **digital thermometer with a cable probe** takes the guesswork out of determining if the smoker is at the right temperature. We cannot recommend them highly enough. **Grill thermostat kits** go one step further by adjusting the airflow accordingly with a small electric fan; they are a luxurious upgrade for anyone who smokes or barbecues on a regular basis.

Which brings us to the hardest aspect of barbecuing: fire management and temperature control. Pellet grills and grill thermostats will make your life easier by virtually automating the process. For all other types of smokers, the vents (or gas flow) will need to be adjusted periodically to get just the right amount of heat. Kamado-style grills and gas grills have the advantage of being responsive and rarely running out of fuel. Stay vigilant and get to know the quirks of your individual smoker or grill—preferably before you invite a crowd over to feast on your experiments.

To barbecue meats in a pellet smoker, follow the manufacturer's lighting instructions. Adjust the temperature and preheat for 10 minutes. Optionally, place a pan full of boiling water on the grate, over the hottest portion of the smoking chamber (this is usually directly over the pellet burning chamber).

To barbecue meats in an offset smoker with hardwood logs, start a chimney of charcoal, 1063, and add it to the smoker's firebox. Alternatively, start a wood fire, 1061, directly in the firebox and let it burn down to embers. Add several split logs of dry, seasoned hardwood. Open the door and all of the vents on the smoker. As the logs catch, place a drip pan under the cooking grates and then a pan on top of the grate as close to the firebox vent as possible and fill it with boiling water. Once a draft of air is flowing through the smoker, close the door of the smoking chamber, leaving it cracked open slightly with a stick. When the logs are covered in ash, stoke them so that they are well ventilated and close up the firebox and smoking chamber door. Once the smoker has preheated, set the top vent so that it is partially open and adjust the firebox vent to slightly less than half open. Add the food to the grate directly over the drip pan, close the door, and cook. Try to maintain the target temperature with periodic adjustments to the firebox vent—letting more air in if the temperature lags and closing it off if it starts to get too hot. Try to make small, anticipatory adjustments to the vent rather than large ones and allow time for the temperature to stabilize before making further adjustments. Add another log to the firebox occasionally, stoking the embers as you go, and top off the water pan as needed. Every smoker is different, so be prepared for a learning curve.

To barbecue meats in an offset smoker with charcoal, light a chimney of charcoal, 1063, and add it to the firebox along with a few handfuls of unlit charcoal on top. Preheat and position drip and water pans as directed above. When the smoker is at the desired temperature, place the food over the drip pan and add a few chunks of hardwood to the firebox. Make adjustments to maintain temperature as above. When the fire needs more fuel, add hardwood lump charcoal directly to the firebox, along with an additional chunk of hardwood (for charcoal briquettes, we recommend lighting them in a chimney before adding to the firebox).

To barbecue meats in a standard charcoal grill, light a half-chimney of charcoal, 1063, and empty it into a tidy pile in one corner of the grill. Starting at the pile, arrange unlit charcoal in a thick, layered row on the same side of the grill. Nestle chunks of hardwood at intervals on top of the unlit charcoal (about half a dozen small chunks is sufficient). Place a drip pan on the other side of the grill and replace the grate. Position a pan directly over the charcoal, and carefully fill it with boiling water (do not spill any on the charcoal). Close the lid so that its vent is on the side opposite the charcoal; fully open the top vent and adjust the bottom vent to half open. When the interior is within 25°F of the target temperature, set the top vent to half-open. When the cooking temperature is reached, place the food on the grate directly over the drip pan and cook, adjusting the bottom vent to maintain temperature as described for offset smokers, above. When the charcoal is exhausted and the temperature starts to drop, transfer the food to a rimmed baking sheet and remove the water pan and grate. Rake all the coals into a tidy pile and make another layered row with unlit charcoal and wood chunks as before. Replace the grate, replenish the water pan if necessary, and return the food to the grill. Close the lid and adjust the vents to bring the grill back up to the target temperature.

To barbecue meats in a kamado-style grill, light a quarter-chimney of hardwood lump charcoal, 1063. As the charcoal catches, cover the bottom of the grill with unlit charcoal and mound more charcoal on top so that it resembles a mountain. Place about half a dozen small hardwood chunks at several elevations on the mountain's slopes. When the charcoal has ashed over, use long-handled tongs to nestle individual embers into the upper portion of the mountain. If the grill has a ceramic insert for indirect cooking, fit it into place, place a drip pan on it, and top with the cooking grate. Position a pan to one side of the grate and carefully fill it with boiling water. Close the lid; fully open the top vent and adjust the bottom vent so that it is half-open. When the cooking temperature is reached, place the food on the grate directly over the drip pan and cook, adjusting the bottom vent to maintain temperature as described for offset smokers, above. Since these grills are very efficient, it is unlikely that you will need to add more fuel.

To barbecue meats using a gas grill, soak 1 cup of wood chips for at least 1 hour. Set all burners to medium and preheat the grill to the prescribed smoking temperature. Meanwhile, wrap the soaked chips in a double layer of foil and perforate the pouch a few times on each side with a skewer. Turn off the gas burner on one side, open the grill, and remove the grate. Place a drip pan on the cool side of the grill and the foil pouch directly on the hot burners. Replace the grate, place a pan over the flame, and fill it with boiling water. Place the food over the drip pan, close the grill, and adjust the heat to maintain the target temperature. Replace the pouch of soaked wood chips with a fresh one every 2 hours and top off the water pan as needed.

For instructions on how to prepare ingredients for barbecuing, see Smoked Chicken, 412, Smoked Brisket, 469, Smoked Beef Ribs, 470, Kentucky-Style Smoked Mutton Shoulder, 484, Smoked Pork Shoulder, 496, and Barbecued Pork Ribs, 497.

SMOKING

Smoking is one of the oldest methods of preserving. Hanging strips of meat or fish in an enclosed, ventilated space near a fire dehydrates them and coats their surfaces with several compounds that discourage molds and help keep fats from oxidizing. Unfortunately, from the perspective of modern food safety, smoking does not kill or inactivate other sources of foodborne illness, nor does it reliably increase shelf life. Like other ancient methods of preservation—fermenting, for example—our primary motivation for smoking foods is the unique flavors created by the process.

Cold-smoking takes place at temperatures between 65° and 100°F. Some items, such as lox, 138, are never cooked through.

Because cold-smoking temperatures are in the zone where bacteria grow best, meats and fish must be impeccably fresh, well cleaned, and brined or cured before smoking. The equipment used must be completely sanitary, and professional-grade temperature control must be employed. Even then, cold-smoked foods that emerge from USDA-inspected facilities with federally approved plans for ensuring safety are still vulnerable to contamination by several dangerous foodborne pathogens. All of this is to say: Even with sufficient curing, ➤ we cannot recommend cold-smoking raw fish, poultry, or meats between 65° and 100°F for longer than 1 hour unless they are going to be cooked through afterward to a safe internal temperature. Fish must reach 145°F; for meats, see Timing and Doneness, 452; for poultry, see About Cooking Poultry, 406. On the other hand, smoking cheeses, eggs, cream, butter, and other foods can be perfectly safe, since these items are especially good at absorbing flavors and are thus smoked for less time.

Enter **smoking guns,** appliances that generate smoke from a small amount of sawdust or wood chips and pump it through a tube. Items to be smoked can be covered with plastic wrap, placed under a cloche, or in an airtight container. The smoke is pumped in and the foods sealed up to infuse for a period of time. Since no heat is generated, some of the safety concerns associated with cold-smokers can be mitigated, especially if the infusing food is kept under refrigeration (though we would make sure the food and smoke were in an especially well sealed container, as other items in the refrigerator might get inadvertently smoked). Items like Nova lox are still risky to consume raw when smoked with a gun, but no more so than Gravlax, 393. Since there is no airflow or heat, gun-smoked foods will not have the same texture or taste as professionally cold-smoked foods.

Hot-smoking is practically identical to Barbecuing, 1066: Items are placed in a smoker with a water pan and cooked through at around 200° to 250°F. Unlike barbecuing, hot-smoking may be complete in as little as 2 hours for quick-cooking items like salmon fillets, 393. As with all cooked meats, serve immediately, keep refrigerated for up to 4 days, or freeze.

Vegetables, nuts, and salts also respond quite well to hot-smoking. (For these items, ➤ remove the water pan.) We highly encourage you to experiment, especially if your smoker has extra fuel in it after finishing a barbecue: Have a wire cooling rack or two ready to go with items you would like to try smoking. We have had great success with homemade chipotles: Hot-smoke ripe, red jalapeños over pecan wood for several hours and then fully dry in a dehydrator, 944. Thinly sliced onion can be treated in the same way, as well as citrus peels, coconut flakes, and many other items. For more inspiration of how to utilize excess smoke, we highly recommend consulting Cortney Burns and Nicolaus Balla's book *Bar Tartine: Techniques and Recipes*.

FIREPLACE OR HEARTH COOKING

Hearth cooking can be as simple as roasting a hot dog on the end of a fork, tossing a whole onion onto the embers, or setting a camp-style Dutch oven in front of the fire. ➤ As a general rule, traditional masonry fireplaces (without inserts) that are safe for burning wood fires are safe for cooking. The fireplace can work as a stovetop, slow cooker, griddle, grill, rotisserie, or oven. With practice, you will discover that the heat in your fireplace has a greater dynamic range than that of the kitchen stove and is easily controlled for cooking. As with any new cooking method, experiment with single dishes and work up to complete meals. Try hearth cooking for part of your holiday meals and it will quickly become a tradition in your family. It is a hobby that brings great pleasure and delicious results.

Hearth cooking is done many ways: in the radiant heat of the fire, on a stand above embers, directly on the embers, in hot ashes, and over flames. The firebox is the area under the chimney where the fire burns and embers collect. The hearth extension or hearth is the portion of the fireplace that extends into the room and is where you will do a lot of your cooking. ➤ When cooking with embers on the hearth, keep a strong fire in the fireplace to pull fumes and grilling smoke up the chimney. If the chimney isn't drawing well, try opening a window. Keep embers within the first 8 inches of the hearth and toward the center of the fireplace opening. Always follow standard fireplace safety practices, and observe all relevant cautions applicable to cooking on a grill or campfire. Never use more than a couple of fireplace-shovel scoops of embers on the hearth at one time. Immediately shovel embers back into the fireplace once they are no longer being used for cooking.

To build a fire for hearth cooking, leave 2 to 6 inches of ash from previous fires on the fireplace floor. In lieu of metal andirons or a metal grate, position two logs parallel to each other and perpendicular to the back wall of the fireplace and then build your fire as you usually do, adding wood as needed to maintain a steady heat. Aged, dry hardwood is preferred for cooking. ➤ Do not use wood that is wet, rotten, that has been treated with paint or chemicals, or that is manufactured from synthetic materials.

The radiant heat projected outward from the flames or glowing embers is the hearth's most steady and reliable heat source. Remember that a change in distance of even 1 or 2 inches from the embers or flames makes a significant difference in the heat and rate of cooking. Control the heat by moving the food closer to or farther from the fire. ➤ When a long period of cooking in a pot is called for, rely on radiant heat falling on the side of the pot rather than on heat from underneath. ➤ When cooking directly on embers in the firebox, control the heat by dusting them with ashes to cool them down, or fanning them to make them hotter.

Overall, food cooks on the hearth at about the same rate as it does using conventional methods. To paraphrase an eighteenth-century English cookbook author, the hotter the fire, the faster it roasts, and the cooler the fire, the slower it roasts. For example, a 12-pound turkey can be roasted in not much more than 2 hours using a hot fire and keeping it fed. If your food is taking too long to cook, chances are your fire is too small. For the most predictable results, bring all foods, including meats, to room temperature before cooking on the hearth.

Equipment needs are simple: the standard fireplace shovel, a pair of long-handled tongs, two ordinary bricks, the cookware you use in your kitchen, and a small metal grill rack. Cast-iron cookware is ideal for hearth cooking.

Using radiant heat: Recipes that include a lot of liquid are cooked by placing the pot or saucepan on the hearth near the fire. The pot simmers on the side closest to the flames. Control the heat by moving the pot closer to or farther from the fire and stir as needed. If you place it right up against the ashes in the fireplace, you may shovel embers around the base of the pot for additional heat.

Baking food wrapped in foil or sturdy leaves, such as banana, 1057, is another hearth-cooking method that takes advantage of the fire's radiant heat. The method is especially suited for fish and poultry wrapped with herbs and vegetables. Wrap the packets tightly, place a few inches from the fire on the hearth, or on the ashes beside the fire, and turn as needed. Whole or filleted fish can be roasted if tied to an untreated wooden plank first soaked in water, and then propped up in front of the fire. A red-hot fireplace shovel held close will melt cheese on a sandwich.

Cooking on embers: The most spectacular flavors generated by hearth cooking are from one of the easiest techniques to master—baking directly on embers. Onions, eggplant, and bell peppers are perfect for this. Place the vegetables on the hottest embers a few inches from the fire and turn with long-handled tongs as needed until the outsides are charred black and the flesh soft. When done, take out of the fireplace, let cool, and then remove the burned outer layer.

You can also cook a steak on the embers. Pat the meat dry before placing it on the embers so ashes will not stick. Whole fish, like trout, or fish fillets such as that of salmon, can be cooked on embers (skin side down for fillets). The skin chars, but the flesh remains moist. Turn whole fish with a spatula or long-handled tongs. Control the heat by dusting the embers with ashes to cool them down or fanning them to make them hotter.

Cooking in hot ashes: Anything buried in hot ashes bakes as it would in an oven. Foods can be cooked wrapped, 1056, or unwrapped. Use the fireplace shovel to mix ashes and embers together in a pile beside the fire, starting with a half-and-half mix of ashes and embers. With practice, you will develop a sense of how hot the ashes are. Dense root vegetables, such as potatoes, turnips, and beets, are easily baked unwrapped in ashes, as are roasts, such as beef brisket and pork loin. Rub the meat with flour to dry its surface before baking in the ashes. Ashes that stick to meat can usually be brushed off; otherwise, rinse briefly in warm water. Firm breads, such as those made of cornmeal, can also be baked directly in hot ashes, or wrapped in cabbage leaves. If you surround a pot of beans with hot ashes at night before going to bed, they will be cooked in the morning.

Cooking on a stand above embers: To fry an egg, sauté vegetables, grill fish, cook kebabs, or any food that requires heat from below, position the cookware or grill over the embers on a stand that is about 2½ inches high. Two bricks laid on their sides close to the fire work perfectly. Shovel one layer of embers about 1 inch deep between them, set your pan on the bricks, and then add a sprinkling of embers as needed to maintain cooking temperature.

Boeuf Bourguignon, 465, is an example of a dish that first needs heat from below to brown the ingredients, and then very gentle heat to keep it at a bare simmer. In your kitchen, these recipes often start on the stovetop and end in the oven. On the hearth, they begin with embers underneath for a burst of high heat, followed by long cooking by radiant heat on the side of the pot.

When you want to brown the top of a dish—as for Lasagne, 310—or bake corn bread, 630–31, or Irish Soda Bread, 628, no piece of cookware is more versatile than a camp-style Dutch oven: an iron pot with three short legs, a flat lid with a lip to hold embers, and an iron hook to lift the lid, see below. Heat falls on the side of the Dutch oven, and embers can be placed underneath and on the lid. Use the iron hook to lift the lid to check on cooking progress. ➤ A single shovelful of embers underneath is often sufficient for baked goods, while you usually need to refresh embers on the lid. If the food is not browned when ready to serve, add fresh embers to the lid and cook for another few minutes.

Roasting meat in front of the fire: There is no roast, chicken, turkey, or duck, like one cooked in front of an open fire. Electric spits can be modified for use on the hearth, and clockwork spits can be purchased. Meat and poultry brought to room temperature just before roasting cook more evenly than meats that are cold. The meat should turn above the hearth over a drip pan and be about 6 inches from the fire in the fireplace. In a deep fireplace, build the fire more forward than you usually do.

Hearth cooking and roasting meat on a string

An ancient, wonderful, and inexpensive alternative to using a spit is roasting meat on a string. Meat hanging on a string turns in front of the fire, first in one direction, and then the other, requiring only an occasional nudge from the cook. Hang a hook from the ceiling, the underside of the mantel, or the mantel's edge, and tie a length of cotton string to the hook. ➤ The longer and thinner the string, the longer the meat turns without being nudged—as long as 10 minutes. Never use synthetic fiber. It takes experimenting to get the right diameter of string, and the right length, but the string can be saved and used many times. Tie the bottom of this piece of string into a single, large loop. To prepare the meat to hang, put a skewer through the top and another skewer through the bottom third of the roast. ➤ Cut a second, 14-inch length of string, tie loops at either end, and slip them onto opposite ends of the topmost skewer. When you hold the meat by this string handle, it should hang straight down. If it doesn't, reposition the skewer to rebalance the meat. When you bring the meat to the hearth, slip the large loop in the bottom of the long string, around the ends of the top skewer. Let the meat down so the long string bears its weight and hangs above the hearth about 6 inches from the fire and 4 inches above a drip pan. ➤ About halfway through the cooking time, flip the roast over by grabbing the string handle and carefully switching the position of the skewers in the loop. ➤ For most of the cooking time the fire should be hot enough that you can barely hold your hand where the roast is turning.

Cooking over flames: If your fireplace is equipped with a crane, a metal arm that lets you hang pots over the flames, you can cook over the fire. ➤ Heat is controlled by swinging the arm closer to or farther from the fire and by using hooks of different lengths to adjust the distance from the pot to the fire. This method is most appropriate for use in very large fireplaces, for boiling water, and when preparing food in such large quantities that the cooking pot is too heavy to lift.

▲ HIGH-ALTITUDE COOKING

Cooking in mountainous country is an art in itself. In our experience, there is practically nothing you can do at sea level that you cannot do at a mile high. In a high-altitude kitchen, you must compensate for the effects of thinner, drier air and higher atmospheric pressure.

If high altitudes are new to you, watch throughout this book for the high-altitude cooking symbol ▲, which will give you formulas for adjusting recipes. For basic theory and adjustments for cakes and many other baked goods at high altitude, read About High-Altitude Cake Baking, 755. For specially designed high-altitude cake recipes, see pages 756–60. For yeast breads, see Bread Baking at High Altitudes, 598. If these hints are not sufficiently specialized for your area, call your county extension agent for more information.

Any cooking process involving liquid will be proportionately lengthened as altitude increases. The chart below shows the boiling point of water at different levels. The higher the elevation, the lower the temperature at which water boils. Approximate temperatures are based on the US Standard Atmosphere.

Sea level	212°F	100°C
2,000 feet	208.5°F	98.06°C
3,000 feet	206°F	97.06°C
5,000 feet	203.2°F	95.11°C
7,000 feet	199.8°F	93.22°C
7,500 feet	198.9°F	92.72°C
10,000 feet	194.7°F	90.39°C
15,000 feet	185°F	85°C

HOLDING AND REHEATING FOOD

Anyone who has eaten from a hot bar knows that food that is held or reheated is not so tasty as that served immediately after preparation. Unfortunately, life intrudes, and we frequently find ourselves holding foods for late diners or heating leftovers the next day. Here, then, are a few hints on the best procedures.

The best way to reheat dishes that are apt to curdle (such as custards or egg-based sauces) when subjected to direct high temperatures is in a double boiler over simmering water or in a hot water bath.

If reheating roasted meat, slice it paper thin and put it on heated plates just before pouring very hot gravy over it. Any other method of reheating will toughen it and make it taste old.

To reheat deep-fried foods, spread them on a rack set in a baking sheet and heat them, uncovered, in a 250°F oven. Be aware, though, that they will never regain their freshly fried glory.

To hold pancakes or waffles, place them on a baking sheet in a 200°F oven.

To reheat casseroles or other foods baked in casserole dishes, make certain the baking dish is ovenproof and can withstand rapid temperature changes before placing it, loosely covered with foil, in a 325°F oven directly from the refrigerator or freezer.

No food should be held for a protracted period if you hope to preserve real flavor and avoid bacterial growth. ➤ Holding temperatures for hot food should be above 140°F, cold food under 40°F.

ABOUT INDOOR COOKING EQUIPMENT

Some of us are lucky and get to "build out" a kitchen at some point in our lives, stocking it with the tools and appliances of our choice. However, most of us, for most of our lives, have to cook with whatever equipment is at hand: the range our landlord deems practical and "good enough"; the pans or knife set we are gifted by family (or forced to purchase out of desperation in a grocery store late at night). Here, we discuss how to anticipate issues with the tools circumstance gives us, as well as suggest others to acquire that will make life easier.

OVENS AND COOKTOPS

Whether you cook with gas or electric heat, thoroughly learn the characteristics of your range. There are a few notable differences between how gas and electric cooktops perform. **Gas cooktops** are precise and easy to control: When you turn a gas burner on, the heat is immediate; when you turn it off, the heat is completely off. **Electric cooktops** require time both to heat up and to cool down (thus why most recipes use the phrase "remove from the heat" rather than "turn off the burner"). On the other hand, electric cooktops pump out more heat than all but the fanciest gas cooktops, which allows them to boil water faster and get pans hotter for searing and stir-frying. Electric "smoothtop" cooktops are much easier to clean, but they are not as sturdy and may cycle on and off at lower heat settings, which can affect your results. **Induction cooktops** are the best electric cooktop in terms of efficiency and responsiveness. Since the pan itself is the only part being heated, the cooktop is quick to bring liquids to a boil and there is no lag time required for the element to cool down. Be aware, however, that only magnetic pans work with induction cooktops (you can easily test this by sticking a magnet to the bottom of your pots and pans).

As for **ovens**, electric ovens are generally considered to be superior than those heated by gas; they are quicker to preheat, more efficient (gas ovens need to be vented more, and thus leak more heat), and have a more effective broiler. On the other hand, since gas ovens are draftier by design, the environment is kept drier, which can help roasting foods brown better. **Convection ovens** are especially good in this regard; a fan circulates the hot air in the oven, which dehydrates the surface of foods. The air current also helps distribute heat to the food from all sides, helping it cook evenly and sometimes faster than in conventional ovens. If using a convection oven, at least until you get a feel for how the oven cooks, lower the temperature by 25° to 50°F. Be aware that even convection ovens have hot spots.

At this point, we must acknowledge the existence of **steam convection ovens,** or **combi ovens.** They are ingenious appliances: You can dial in how dry or moist the heat is, and the temperature control is considerably more precise. This essentially means that you can steam, bake, roast, broil, and dehydrate with the same appliance. When set at the highest humidity setting and a low temperature, combi ovens can precisely slow-cook items in the same manner as a sous vide device (but with no need to fit foods in a bag). At present, full-sized combi ovens are prohibitively expensive and countertop models are uncommon and have limited uses; for these reasons, we will not be covering them in our pages (for in-depth information on the promise of combi ovens, we recommend readers look to Nathan Myhrvold's *Modernist Cuisine*, 1077).

When using your oven, place oven racks where you want them *before* heating, not after. Few cooks realize the importance of air circulation in conventional ovens: Overcrowding results in uneven baking. Make sure that the pans or baking sheets you are using fit on the oven shelf comfortably, with at least 2 inches of space between them as well as between the pans and oven walls. Don't use two shelves if you can avoid it, but if you must, stagger the pans as shown second from the left. For large pans like rimmed baking sheets, you will likely need to switch their rack positions and rotate from front to back at least once during cooking (we specifically call for this in recipes when it is required).

Proper oven placement, left to right: broiling, browning, and baking casseroles; cakes; soufflés; and breads

To test an oven for hot spots, place a rack in the center and preheat it to 350°F. Place slices of white bread in a grid pattern on the oven rack and leave them until they begin to toast. Note which slices toast (and burn) faster than others. This will indicate the hotter areas inside your oven. Unfortunately, there's no magic fix for those hot spots. But, armed with the knowledge of how your oven works, you can make adjustments to your cooking that will lessen the effect of hot spots.

If your oven has a particularly pronounced **hot spot,** avoid placing pans there; if you must, be sure to rotate them to prevent burning or overcooking. The only exception to this rule is temperamental dishes like soufflés, which benefit from steady, uninterrupted heat. (Opening the oven door can affect their rise.)

For cake baking in general, the best position for the pan(s) is in the center of the oven. For angel food cakes, tortes, soufflés, and pies, the best placement is in the lower third of the oven, as shown. In most ovens, the heat provided by a top element is enough to prematurely set the surface of a soufflé if it is set too close, inhibiting its rise. Unless otherwise directed, breads should be baked in the center of the oven.

When baking, allow plenty of time for preheating, especially if baking with a stone or steel, which will need extra time to heat up. Keep a thermometer in your oven and check it annually to make sure the oven thermostat is accurate. Even under normal use, thermostats may need regular adjustment—at least once every 12 or 14 months. Follow the manufacturer's instructions to calibrate your oven's thermostat as needed.

ABOUT COOKWARE

The material of which cookware is made, as well as its size and shape, can make cooking easier or more difficult. While a good cook can make do with poorly designed or cheap cookware, if you can afford to be picky, then ➤ choose skillets, saucepans, and stockpots of fairly heavy gauge—not so heavy as to make for difficult handling, but heavy enough to diffuse heat evenly. While we are skeptical of the practical difference between, say, three-ply and five-ply stainless steel cookware, we strongly prefer heavy stainless steel skillets and saucepans for most cooking. Beyond that, we own and regularly use an enameled cast-iron Dutch oven for braises, stews, and soups. We also have a few different sizes of cast-iron skillets, as well as thinner carbon steel pans and woks, which are good for sautéing and stir-frying. ➤ Do not purchase large cookware sets. Even high-end sets that are of good quality can end up being wasteful, as they invariably include pieces you will not need or use that take up valuable cabinet space. ➤ For the cook just starting out, we recommend the following cookware:

RECOMMENDED STOVETOP COOKWARE:

One 2-quart and one 4-quart stainless steel saucepan
One 10- or 12-inch stainless steel skillet with an ovenproof handle
One 8- or 10-inch nonstick skillet
One 10-inch cast-iron skillet
One round 5- or 6-quart enameled cast-iron Dutch oven
One 16-quart stockpot

RECOMMENDED OVEN COOKWARE:

Two uncoated half-size rimmed baking sheets (18 × 13 inches)
Two uncoated quarter-sized rimmed baking sheets (9 × 13 inches)
One large roasting pan with rack
One broiler pan
Three 8- or 9-inch round cake pans
One 9-inch square baking pan

Two 9 × 5-inch loaf pans
Two cooling racks
One muffin tin
Two 8- or 9-inch pie pans
6 custard cups or ramekins
One 9- or 10-inch tube pan
One 13 × 9-inch baking dish

These are the basics and will allow you to cook almost anything you want or need to cook indoors. Stainless steel pans with ovenproof handles are especially useful, as they can go from stovetop to oven (as can the enameled cast-iron Dutch oven and the cast-iron skillet).

Below we give the pros and cons for different types of cookware material.

ALUMINUM

Aluminum's advantage is very good heat conduction, but—no matter how expensive—aluminum will pit. And it not only tends to become discolored itself but can adversely affect the color of some foods, such as eggs, tomatoes, leafy greens, and wine-based sauces. Do not cook acidic foods in aluminum cookware. With the exception of rimmed baking sheets, we do not recommend buying untreated or uncoated aluminum cookware. Don't clean aluminum pans with harsh soaps, alkalis, or abrasives.

Aluminum manufacturers have found ways to anodize or electrochemically treat the surfaces of their pans. Anodized aluminum pans have a harder cooking surface that does not react with most ingredients as untreated aluminum does, and they are stronger yet still lightweight. Many skillets are made with an aluminum core coated in stainless steel. This is an ideal construction, as the aluminum promotes even, quick heating, while the stainless steel is nonreactive, allowing you to cook anything, acidic or not, in the pan.

COPPER

Best in heavier gauges, copper gives a quick, even heat distribution. But ➤ unless the surfaces contacting the food are lined with stainless steel, the pan will be affected by acids and can be toxic. To polish the exterior, make a paste of vinegar or lemon juice and table salt. Rub the discolored copper with the paste until bright, then rinse in hot water.

If your copper is lined with tin, remember that the tin has problems of its own. Tin will melt at temperatures above 425°F, so these pans are unsuitable for high-heat cooking methods such as searing and stir-frying. Use caution so as not to scratch the tin lining, and don't clean it with abrasive cleaners. Treat with care, as you would a nonstick surface. Copper that is lined with tin will periodically require retinning. Copper pans that are lined with stainless steel rather than tin are easier to maintain, since stainless steel will not melt, wear away, or need relining.

STAINLESS STEEL

This metal is completely nonreactive with food and it stays shiny and new looking even after considerable use. It is the most resilient and sturdy, as well as the easiest to maintain; our stainless steel-clad cookware, some of it inherited, has endured decades of scouring with steel wool and abrasive cleaners. Manufacturers usually offset stainless steel's poor heat conductivity by adding an inner core of aluminum or copper.

CAST IRON

Cast-iron pans are heavy and low in conductivity, but this apparent downside is offset by the fact the cast iron holds heat remarkably well. So while it may take cast iron longer to heat up than aluminum or stainless steel, once it is hot it stays hot for a long time. This property makes cast iron excellent for searing meats and getting a thick, brown crust on corn bread. Perhaps the best thing about cast iron is that, when cared for reasonably well, it not only becomes more and more nonstick, but it will likely outlive you. Most cast-iron pans come preseasoned, so all they require before use is a quick wash with soapy water. Always dry cast-iron pans after washing them, as they tend to rust if left wet. Drying can be accomplished by hand or by placing the pan in a hot oven or on a burner on the stove. Contrary to one cast-iron myth, cast-iron pans should be washed with soap and water when they are very dirty. Soap alone will not remove the seasoning; however, do not scrub them with something abrasive because that will definitely strip off the seasoning. If the pan is not very dirty, it can simply be wiped out with a cloth or paper towel, or rinsed and dried. Some cooks like to rub their cast-iron pans with salt to clean them, which is also a reasonably effective method. After washing or cleaning cast iron and allowing it to dry completely, it is a good idea to rub the pan with a thin protective layer of vegetable oil.

There is much debate about how to properly season a cast-iron pan, but the process is actually quite simple. Before you season cast iron, it is a good idea to first understand what "seasoning" actually means. Cast iron, especially new cast iron, has a fairly rough surface. If you look at cast iron on a microscopic level, it looks very rough indeed—almost like a very rocky landscape. When you season cast iron you are encouraging oil to polymerize on its surface. When oil is heated beyond its smoke point, 981, it starts to degrade and form polymers, which are long chains of molecules. Thus, the "seasoning" on cast iron is actually composed of these polymers, which form a smooth, plastic-like coating and fill in any gaps or rough places.

To season a cast-iron pan, preheat the oven to 450°F. Rub the pan all over with vegetable oil (the type of oil is not that important, but it is best to use vegetable oil or shortening). If you can, turn on an exhaust fan or open a window because the oil will smoke. Place the pan in the oven and leave it alone for 30 minutes. Brush the pan with oil or shortening again (once the pan is very hot, it is easiest to do this with a paper towel held with a pair of tongs) and place it back in the oven for 30 minutes more. Repeat this process two more times. The best way to maintain the seasoning is to use the pan often, and never use it to cook very acidic things like tomato sauces or anything containing vinegar or citrus juice.

ENAMELED CAST IRON

This is cast iron that has been coated with a porcelain enamel finish. The enameling slows down heat conduction to a small degree, but it makes the cooking surface impervious to reaction with foods. Enameled cast iron is heavy and can crack or chip if mishandled. It is also marked by metal utensils; only wooden or silicone hand tools should be used. Enamel also tends to stain over time. This is harmless. However, if you have accidentally burned something in an enameled cast-iron pan and there is burnt-on residue, do not panic! Do not attempt to scrub the pan with anything abrasive. This can damage the enameled coating. Pour a thin layer of baking soda into the pan to barely coat the bottom, then pour in enough hydrogen peroxide to dissolve the baking soda. Bring the peroxide to a boil and use a wooden utensil to scrape the pan. Repeat this procedure as many times as needed to remove all the residue.

CARBON STEEL

Uncoated carbon steel is used primarily for skillets, sauté pans, and woks. Carbon steel pans must be seasoned like cast iron, after which they will have a fairly nonstick coating on the surface. Like cast iron, they are very tough and will last as long as their rivets hold (some are stamped from one piece, which makes them virtually indestructible). Unlike cast iron, carbon steel pans are relatively thin and lightweight, which makes them easier to handle and more responsive to heat adjustments. Woks, in particular, can be quite thin, which makes them perfect for stir-frying over traditional, high-powered wok burners: The heat is plentiful and instantaneous, which helps achieve the prized *wok hei* effect, 1053. Carbon steel sauté pans are thicker, and very popular in restaurant kitchens for their responsiveness on professional gas ranges.

ENAMELED STEEL OR ENAMELWARE

Here, carbon steel is coated with enamel, and the benefits of the coating are the same as for enameled cast iron: While not nonstick, foods release more easily, and the coating keeps acidic ingredients from interacting with the metal underneath. Usually, the gauge of steel used is a bit thinner than with uncoated carbon steel cookware. Though enameled steel pans are available, we find the thinner gauge of material is better suited for stockpots, kettles, casseroles, baking dishes, and roasting pans.

GLASS

Glass cookware is commonly referred to by the most widespread brand name, Pyrex. Pyrex, historically made from borosilicate glass, is now made of tempered soda-lime glass. While tempered soda-lime glass is quite durable, never expose it to thermal shock. In other words, do not put a very hot pan on a cold surface, and do not put a very cold pan into a very hot oven, as the glass will shatter violently. Interestingly, Pyrex pans made in Europe are still made of borosilicate glass.

EARTHENWARE

While a poor conductor of heat, glazed or unglazed earthenware or clay holds heat well and doesn't discolor foods. But it is heavy and breaks easily with sudden temperature changes. New or recently produced earthenware is made with lead-free glazes. Older or antique earthenware most likely has lead in the glaze and should not be used for cooking. ➤ To avoid cracking, always adjust heat gently and never set a clay dish directly on an electric heating element.

SILICONE

Muffin pans, molds, and pan liners or baking mats are manufactured from food-grade silicone. Silicone is ovenproof, withstanding temperatures from −40°F up to 500°F. It can go from freezer to oven; conducts heat evenly; cools quickly; doesn't rust, chip, or break; and is dishwasher-, freezer-, and microwave-safe. Because silicone is flexible as well as nonstick, you can turn out cakes and muffins from silicone pans with just a twist of the pan—like ice cubes. ➤ Place silicone pans on a baking sheet for easy transfer; their flexibility makes them unwieldy to move once filled with batter. The one downside to silicone is that, when used in the form of a silicone baking liner, it can encourage cookies to spread and inhibits browning. Only use silicone baking liners when they are explicitly called for in a recipe.

NONSTICK

We have a love-hate relationship with nonstick pans: aluminum, stainless steel, or carbon steel pans coated with a substance that easily releases foods—traditionally Teflon or silicone-based, and more recently ceramic glazes. We appreciate them for cooking foods that are notoriously sticky at lower temperatures, especially egg dishes and pancakes. While the coatings on many old nonstick pans would start to smoke at high to moderate temperatures, newer nonstick surfaces can withstand temperatures up to 450°F. Regardless of how new the pan is, always consult the manufacturer's instructions to determine their maximum safe temperature.

As nonstick surfaces scratch easily, use only plastic, silicone, or wooden utensils with them. There are some newer nonstick pans that tout greater durability and have extended warranties. They are worth looking into, but remember, you are betting money on how long the *coating* will last; the pan underneath the coating, no matter how well constructed, is basically worthless once the coating begins to flake off. Our advice: By all means own a nonstick skillet, but remember that even the most expensive state-of-the-art nonstick pan is basically a piece of disposable cookware (spend your money accordingly).

While there have been concerns about toxic chemicals from nonstick pans, the American Cancer Society states that nonstick cookware is not a significant source of carcinogens. That said, ➤ use these pans as directed, and never use nonstick pans with a flaking or peeling coating or preheat them to the point where they are smoking. Always discard the pan once the coating shows signs of breaking down.

KITCHEN EQUIPMENT AND UTENSILS

Perhaps the most important thing to consider when putting together a kitchen is creating an adequate, efficient workspace. Avoid purchasing gadgets that only have one use. Similarly, avoid purchasing sets of things like knives and cookware. Prioritize uncluttered countertops. Buy the largest wooden cutting boards you have room for, as well as one moderately sized heavy plastic cutting board for cutting meat and fish.

If cabinet space is limited, try to use wall space. Hang pots and pans on hooks if possible. Install shelving to hold tools, dishes, or pantry items that you use often so they are within easy reach. Keep canisters with spices and staples in alphabetical arrangement or arrange them by type for quick identification (for instance, keep baking spices together, dried chiles together, and dried herbs together). We may have to live with the kitchens we have, but it pays to think about your work habits. See if you can make them more efficient.

The following is a reasonably comprehensive basic equipment list.

RECOMMENDED COOKING EQUIPMENT:

Digital kitchen scale
Instant-read thermometer
Set of metal mixing bowls
Set of metal measuring cups
Set of measuring spoons
One 1-cup and one 4-cup glass liquid measuring cup
Fine-mesh strainer
Collapsible steamer insert
Colander
Splatter screen
Large and small metal spoons
Ladle
Metal slotted spoon or spider
Wooden spoon or spatula
Large and small offset metal spatulas
Silicone spatula
Pancake turner
Balloon whisk
Paring knife
Serrated bread knife
Chef's knife
Sturdy kitchen shears
Cutting boards
Knife sharpener
Four-sided box grater
Rasp-style grater (Microplane)
Tongs
Y-shaped vegetable peeler
Citrus reamer or lever-style hand citrus juicer
Blender
Bottle opener and corkscrew
Can opener
Pepper grinder
Potholders
Flour sifter (a fine-mesh sieve can be used instead)
Rolling pin
Pastry blender
Aluminum foil
Parchment paper
Pastry brush
Ruler

ABOUT KNIVES

Without a doubt, the most important tool in the kitchen is a sharp knife. You can cook over a campfire, in a fireplace, in an oven, or on a grill, but if you can't get to the interior of an acorn squash, cut up a large piece of meat, or chop an onion, you will have difficulty cooking them.

➤ The only essential knife is the one you will be chopping vegetables or carving with: either an **8- to 10-inch chef's knife** or a **7- to 8-inch santoku** (a Japanese multipurpose blade shape). Though several other types are worth considering—such as a paring knife for detailed work and a serrated bread knife—they will be used much less. Whatever additional blades you decide to purchase, ➤ avoid knife sets. You are likely to find better quality knives if you buy them piecemeal.

Look for a chef's knife with a flat-ground blade that is fairly thin so that it will slice through vegetables with ease. As for materials, carbon steel is easy to sharpen, cuts aggressively, and maintains its sharp edge, but it must be quickly dried off after each use to prevent discoloration or rust. Stainless steel knives never rust or discolor and are very durable, but they tend to dull faster and are more difficult to sharpen. High-carbon stainless steel is a better option, as it combines the durability of stainless steel with the sharpness of carbon steel. If you can identify the steel's hardness expressed in a Rockwell "C" number, pick one in the 55–59 range. Blades heat-treated to below 55 Rockwell are easy to sharpen, but dull too quickly; blades heat-treated to above 60 Rockwell will stay sharp longer, but can be difficult to sharpen.

A big variable in knife design is the handle. Molded plastic handles are popular, although some feel that wood provides a surer grip (it is also hard to deny the aesthetic value of a wood handle). The choice of handle is really a matter of personal preference and comfort. We like a handle that is thinner than it is tall and rounded enough to not chafe against your hand, but not so rounded that the handle is hard to grip.

Perhaps more important than any of these details is the overall design and balance: ➤ Find a knife that feels good in your hand. It should feel like an extension of your arm and should be neither too heavy nor too light. Hold the knife, test its grip and its weight to make sure it feels comfortable and balanced in your hand. Knives with a full tang (the portion of the blade that extends into the handle) usually feel the most balanced. The best way to find a knife that works for you is to try several of them. Some cookware shops will allow you to "test drive" knives by cutting vegetables with them. It is worth spending for quality as this is the cook's most used tool.

A decent **paring knife** is quite handy for small tasks. Use the same criteria as for the big blade, but add how it feels with the blade reversed (in other words, when you use the knife to cut foods that you are holding in your other hand rather than sitting on a cutting board). We like a very thin 3-inch blade with a flattish handle profile. A **serrated bread knife** with an 8- to 10-inch blade is handy for bread (and recalcitrant tomato skins when you have neglected your sharpening duties).

In addition to a good knife, you will need a sturdy **cutting board.** Keep a couple of cutting boards on hand—one for raw beef, poultry, and other uncooked meats (this cutting board should be plastic, as they are easy to throw in a dishwasher and sanitize) and another board for chopping foods that will be not be cooked, such as fruit, lettuce, bread, and vegetables (this one can be made of thick plastic or wood). Ideally, purchase at least one cutting board that is roomy and thick: at least 18 × 12 inches and ¾ inch thick. We prefer wooden cutting boards, but those made of synthetic material can be placed in the dishwasher and are long lasting. Wooden boards with strips of grain running both ways are less likely to split; Boards where the grain runs perpendicular to the cutting surface (called "end-grain" cutting boards) are reputed to be easier on a knife's edge, which means less sharpening.

All cutting boards, regardless of material, can harbor bacteria in nicks and gouges. Wash them with hot soapy water after every use, and occasionally soak or scrub them in sanitizing solution, xx. After soaking or scrubbing for several minutes, rinse the board thoroughly with hot water.

SPECIALTY KNIVES

We consider all of the following knife types to be small luxuries: Few cooks, if any, actually *need* them, but they make certain tasks much easier. **Boning knives** are meant to cut around bones and through tendons and cartilage to release the meat from the bone. The blade profile should be tapered and narrow to get into tight spots. Smaller, more flexible blades are designed for filleting fish and boning small birds. Larger, more rigid knives are better for boning larger cuts of meat, such as a leg of lamb. A thicker Japanese style of boning knife called a *honesuki* is especially nice for poultry (the "chisel" tip can be inserted into a joint and turned like a key). **Slicing** or **carving knives** are long, thin, and used to thinly slice cooked meats (drawing the long blade through roasts results in an especially clean cut).

Cleavers are available in a variety of shapes and sizes. Western-style cleavers are incredibly thick and ideal for hacking through bones. An all-purpose size usually has a blade about 8 × 4 inches. Chinese cleavers are longer, thinner, and more nimble. They can be used for everything, much like a chef's knife. An extra attraction of this type of knife is that the wide blade is excellent for mashing garlic and for scooping up and transferring chopped vegetables from the cutting board to the pan. Japanese "vegetable cleavers," which may be called either *usuba* or *nakiri* knives, are very thin and designed for slicing vegetables and greens.

CARING FOR KNIVES

Since knives are used so frequently, it is important that they be close and safely at hand. Several solutions exist: knife blocks, wall-mounted magnetic holders, and wooden drawer inserts, to name just a few. ➤ Do not wash knives in the dishwasher. The repeated heating affects the blade, and soon the knife will neither take nor hold a sharp edge. Not to mention the effects that heat and steam can have on the handle, especially a wooden one.

SHARPENING KNIVES

A dull knife makes cutting a tedious chore. A sharp knife allows for neater slices, permits greater precision, and requires less cutting pressure—meaning you are less likely to cut yourself.

For sharpening knives, the standard is a sharpening stone. A good stone measures 6 to 10 inches in length and has a coarse side and a fine side. Place the stone in front of you on a kitchen towel, parallel to the edge of the countertop. Lay the knife against the stone, first on the coarse side, at a 15- to 20-degree angle and draw it in a curved sweeping motion toward you, as shown, first on one side of the knife, then on the other side—10 times for each side. Then turn the stone over to the fine side, increase the angle of the blade slightly, and repeat. Clean from the blade the metal and the grit you have removed from the stone.

The final, optional stage—steeling, or "trueing" the blade—does not sharpen the knife, but merely smooths out tiny nicks in the edge of the blade. There are many methods for steeling. One of the easiest is to hold the piece of equipment called a steel perpendicular to the cutting board, resting the metal tip on the board. Starting with the heel of the knife at the tip of the steel, gradually pull the knife back and up toward your body as you slide it up the length of the steel. By the time you have reached the top, the blade should be almost in contact with the steel's handle. The entire blade should pass over the steel. Repeat this motion, alternating from one side of the steel to the other and making sure to keep the blade at a 15- to 20-degree angle to the steel. Four or five strokes on either side is enough to true the edge. When finished, wipe the steel and knife with a damp cloth.

If you get in the habit of sharpening your knife at frequent intervals, you will find that chopping, slicing, and carving will go much faster and with greater ease.

Sharpening a knife with a sharpening stone

Electric knife sharpeners have great appeal for some cooks. These mechanical sharpeners take the guesswork out of knife sharpening. Most have two or three slots to run the knife through. Pass the knife through the slots, and a rotating sharpening disk does the work while magnets hold the blade at the correct angle for sharpening.

ABOUT BURNS

In the foregoing pages we have supplied, among other information, enough facts to keep our readers from burning their food. Now a few safeguards against burning the cook—and what to do should such an emergency occur.

Use pots and pans that are well balanced and steady when empty. Be sure handles are not so heavy that the pan will tip, or so long that they can catch on a sleeve.

Put boiling liquids at the back of the stove and turn the handles of all pots so they are out of reach of small children.

In pan-frying, keep a splatter screen handy to place over the pan should the fat begin to sputter.

Never throw water on a grease fire. Cover the fire with salt or baking soda, or if the area is a small one, cover with a metal lid.

Keep heavy potholders and metal tongs near the range for removing hot objects and hot foods.

Before picking up a hot pan, check that your hands or the potholders or any cloths you use are not damp.

The first aid treatment of burns is much the same whether they are large or small. Loosen clothing or other material over or near the burn and remove it, but take care not to cut or remove the burned skin or any material adhering to the burned surface. If blisters appear, they should not be broken or cut.

Submerge the burned area in cool water or apply cool water as soon as possible after injury for up to 1 or 2 hours. This will help to relieve the pain. Then apply a dry sterile gauze dressing as a protective bandage. If sterile gauze is not readily available, clean linen can be used.

Larger burns should be covered by a clean sheet for protection and comfort until medical help is provided. Do not use antiseptic preparations, ointments, sprays, or home remedies on the burn, since these substances may interfere with treatment.

Any individual with a face burn should be observed continuously to make sure they are breathing normally and not going into shock.

Should you get an extensive or painful burn, seek immediate help from your physician or the emergency room of your local hospital. Lie down, remain calm, and keep warm until skilled help is available. Call 911 for serious burns.

BIBLIOGRAPHY AND RESOURCES

When we revised this book, we did not do it in a vacuum. We, like everyone else, stand on the shoulders of those who know more than us. Because *Joy* is a comprehensive resource, we can only dive so deep into a given subject. Luckily, others dedicate their careers to what we can only devote a paragraph or a page to here. Below is a wealth of sources, some of which we consulted in writing this book, and others which we simply appreciate. We hope you will consider these resources when your curiosity takes you beyond the pages of this book.

FOOD AND COOKING REFERENCE

Corriher, Shirley. *CookWise: The Secrets of Cooking Revealed*. New York: William Morrow, 1997.

Davidson, Alan. *The Oxford Companion to Food*. Third edition. Oxford: Oxford University Press, 2014.

Doyle, Michael P., and Larry R. Beuchat (eds.). *Food Microbiology: Fundamentals and Frontiers*. Third edition. Washington, DC: ASM Press, 2007.

McGee, Harold. *On Food and Cooking: The Science and Lore of the Kitchen*. New York: Scribner, 2004.

Page, Karen, and Andrew Dornenburg. *The Flavor Bible*. New York: Little, Brown, 2008.

GENERAL COOKING

Nosrat, Samin. *Salt, Fat, Acid, Heat: Mastering the Elements of Good Cooking*. New York: Simon & Schuster, 2017.

López-Alt, J. Kenji. *The Food Lab: Better Home Cooking Through Science*. New York: W. W. Norton, 2015.

STREAMLINED COOKING

Adler, Tamar. *An Everlasting Meal*. New York: Scribner, 2011.

Turshen, Julia. *Now & Again*. San Francisco: Chronicle Books, 2018.

COCKTAILS

Meehan, Jim. *Meehan's Bartender Manual*. New York: Ten Speed Press, 2017.

Morgenthaler, Jeffrey. *The Bar Book: Elements of Cocktail Technique*. San Francisco: Chronicle Books, 2014.

Wondrich, David. *Imbibe!* New York: Perigee, 2015.

———. *Punch: The Delights (and Dangers) of the Flowing Bowl*. New York: Perigee, 2010.

VEGETABLES, FRUITS, AND GRAINS

Grigson, Jane. *Jane Grigson's Fruit Book*. New York: Atheneum, 1982.

———. *Jane Grigson's Vegetable Book*. London: Penguin, 1981.

Madison, Deborah. *The New Vegetarian Cooking for Everyone*. Berkeley: Ten Speed Press, 2014.

———. *Vegetable Literacy*. Berkeley: Ten Speed Press, 2013.

McFadden, Joshua. *Six Seasons: A New Way with Vegetables*. New York: Artisan, 2017.

Morgan, Diane. *Roots*. San Francisco: Chronicle Books, 2012.

Mouritsen, Ole G. *Seaweeds: Edible, Available, and Sustainable*. Chicago: University of Chicago Press, 2013.

Nguyen, Andrea. *Asian Tofu*. Berkeley: Ten Speed Press, 2012.

Ottolenghi, Yotam. *Plenty*. San Francisco: Chronicle Books, 2011.

Presilla, Maricel. *Peppers of the Americas*. Berkeley: Lorena Jones Press, 2017.

Schneider, Elizabeth. *Vegetables from Amaranth to Zucchini*. New York: William Morrow, 2001.

Shurtleff, William, and Akiko Aoyagi. *The Book of Tofu*. New York: Ballantine, 1975.

Slater, Nigel. *Ripe: A Cook in the Orchard*. Berkeley: Ten Speed Press, 2010.

———. *Tender: A Cook and His Vegetable Patch*. Berkeley: Ten Speed Press, 2009.

Speck, Maria. *Simply Ancient Grains*. Berkeley: Ten Speed Press, 2015.

FORAGING FOR MUSHROOMS, ROOTS, SHOOTS, AND GREENS

WESTERN UNITED STATES

Arora, David. *All That the Rain Promises, and More . . .* Berkeley: Ten Speed Press, 1991.

———. *Mushrooms Demystified*. Berkeley: Ten Speed Press, 1986.

Baudar, Pascal. *The New Wildcrafted Cuisine*. White River Junction, VT: Chelsea Green, 2016.

Benoliel, Doug. *Northwest Foraging*. Seattle: Skipstone, 2011.

Clarke, Charlotte Bringle. *Edible and Useful Plants of California*. Berkeley: University of California Press, 1978.

Harrington, H.D. *Edible Native Plants of the Rocky Mountains*. Albuquerque: University of New Mexico Press, 1974.

Nabhan, Gary Paul. *Gathering the Desert*. Tucson: University of Arizona Press, 1986.

Siegel, Noah, and Christian Schwarz. *Mushrooms of the Redwood Coast*. Berkeley: Ten Speed Press, 2016.

EASTERN UNITED STATES

Kuo, Michael. *100 Edible Mushrooms*. Ann Arbor: University of Michigan Press, 2007.

Lincoff, Gary. *National Audubon Society Field Guide to Mushrooms: North America*. New York: Knopf, 1981.

Meredith, Leda. *Northeast Foraging*. Portland, OR: Timber Press, 2014.

Peterson, Lee Allen. *Field Guide to Edible Wild Plants of Eastern and Central North America*. Boston: Houghton Mifflin, 1977.

Thayer, Samuel. *Nature's Garden: A Guide to Identifying, Harvesting, and Preparing Edible Wild Plants*. Bruce, WI: Forager's Harvest, 2010.

MEAT AND SEAFOOD

Cosentino, Chris. *Offal Good*. New York: Clarkson Potter, 2017.

Danforth, Adam. *Butchering Beef*. North Adams, MA: Storey Publishing, 2014.

———. *Butchering Poultry, Rabbit, Lamb, Goat, Pork*. North Adams, MA: Storey Publishing, 2014.

Goldwyn, Meathead, and Greg Blonder Ph.D. *Meathead*. New York: Houghton Mifflin Harcourt, 2016.

Harlow, Jay. *West Coast Seafood*. Seattle: Sasquatch Books, 1999.

McLagan, Jennifer. *Odd Bits: How to Cook the Rest of the Animal*. Berkeley: Ten Speed Press, 2011.

Peterson, James. *Fish & Shellfish*. New York: William Morrow, 1996.

Seaver, Barton. *Two If By Sea*. New York: Sterling Epicure, 2016.

Walsh, Robb. *Legends of Texas Barbecue*. San Francisco: Chronicle Books, 2016.

GAME COOKERY

Shaw, Hank. *Buck, Buck, Moose*. Orangevale, CA: H&H Books, 2016.

———. *Duck, Duck, Goose*. Berkeley: Ten Speed Press, 2013.

———. *Pheasant, Quail, Cottontail*. Orangevale, CA: H&H Books, 2018.

BAKING AND DESSERTS

Beranbaum, Rose Levy. *The Bread Bible*. New York: W. W. Norton, 2003.

Braker, Flo. *The Simple Art of Perfect Baking*. San Francisco: Chronicle Books, 2003.

Corriher, Shirley. *BakeWise: The Hows and Whys of Successful Baking*. New York: Scribner, 2008.

Headley, Brooks. *Brooks Headley's Fancy Desserts*. New York: W. W. Norton, 2014.

Lebovitz, David. *Ready for Dessert: My Best Recipes*. Berkeley: Ten Speed Press, 2010.

Medrich, Alice. *Chewy Gooey Crispy Crunchy Melt-in-Your-Mouth Cookies*. New York: Artisan, 2010.

———. *Seriously Bittersweet: The Ultimate Dessert Maker's Guide to Chocolate*. New York: Artisan, 2013.

Parks, Stella. *Bravetart: Iconic American Desserts*. New York: W. W. Norton, 2017.

Robertson, Chad. *Tartine Bread*. San Francisco: Chronicle Books, 2010.

Segal, Mindy. *Cookie Love*. Berkeley: Ten Speed Press, 2015.

PRESERVING AND FERMENTING

Ball Home Cooking Test Kitchen. *The All New Ball Book of Canning and Preserving*. New York: Oxmoor House, 2016.

Balla, Nicolaus, and Cortney Burns. *Bar Tartine Techniques and Recipes*. San Francisco: Chronicle Books, 2014.

Cairo, Elias. *Olympia Provisions*. Berkeley: Ten Speed Press, 2015.

Katz, Sandor Ellix. *The Art of Fermentation: An In-Depth Exploration of Essential Concepts and Processes from Around the World*. White River Junction, VT: Chelsea Green Publishing, 2012.

———. *Wild Fermentation: The Flavor, Nutrition, and Craft of Live-Culture Foods*. White River Junction, VT: Chelsea Green Publishing, 2016.

Marshall, Sarah. *Preservation Pantry: Modern Canning from Root to Top & Stem to Core*. New York: Regan Arts, 2017.

McClellan, Marisa. *Food in Jars: Preserving in Small Batches Year-Round*. Philadelphia: Running Press, 2011.

Redzepi, René, and David Zilber. *The Noma Guide to Fermentation: Foundations of Flavor*. New York: Artisan, 2018.

Rentfrow, Gregg, and Surendranath Suman. "ASC-213: How to Make a Country Ham." *Agriculture and Natural Resources Publications*. Lexington: University of Kentucky Cooperative Extension Service, 2014.

US Department of Agriculture. National Institute of Food and Agriculture. Information Bulletin no. 539. *Complete Guide to Home Canning*. 2015.

West, Kevin. *Saving the Season: A Cook's Guide to Home Canning, Pickling, and Preserving*. New York: Alfred A. Knopf, 2013.

CHEESE AND CHEESEMAKING

Carroll, Ricki. *Home Cheese Making: Recipes for 75 Homemade Cheeses*. North Adams, MA: Storey Publishing, 2002.

Jenkins, Steven. *Cheese Primer*. New York: Workman, 1996.

MISCELLANEOUS

Fisher, M. F. K. *The Art of Eating*. New York: Macmillan, 1990.

Hopkinson, Simon. *Roast Chicken and Other Stories*. New York: Hyperion, 2006.

Kord, Tyler. *A Super Upsetting Book About Sandwiches*. New York: Clarkson Potter, 2016.

Manning, Ivy. *Crackers & Dips*. San Francisco: Chronicle Books, 2013.

Mendelson, Anne. *Stand Facing the Stove: The Story of the Women Who Gave America the* Joy of Cooking. New York: Henry Holt, 1996.

Myhrvold, Nathan, Chris Young, and Maxime Bilet. *Modernist Cuisine*. Seattle: Cooking Lab, 2011.

Shapiro, Laura. *Perfection Salad: Women and Cooking at the Turn of the Century*. Berkeley: University of California Press, 2009.

———. *Something from the Oven: Reinventing Dinner in 1950s America*. New York: Penguin, 2004.

RECOMMENDED COOKBOOKS BY CUISINE

AMERICAN REGIONAL

Jamison, Cheryl Alters, and Bill Jamison. *The Border Cookbook: Authentic Home Cooking of the American Southwest and Northern Mexico*. Boston: Harvard Common Press, 1995.

Junior League of Charleston, SC. *Charleston Receipts*. Nashville: Favorite Recipes Press, 2011.

Lafayette Junior League. *Talk About Good!* Memphis: Wimmer Cookbooks, 1969.

Lewis, Edna. *The Taste of Country Cooking*. New York: Alfred A. Knopf, 2006.

Lundy, Ronni. *Victuals*. New York: Clarkson Potter, 2016.

Prudhomme, Paul. *Chef Paul Prudhomme's Louisiana Kitchen*. New York: William Morrow, 1984.

Sherman, Sean, and Beth Dooley. *The Sioux Chef's Indigenous Kitchen*. Minneapolis: University of Minnesota Press, 2017.

Valldejuli, Carmen Aboy. *Puerto Rican Cookery*. Gretna, LA: Pelican Publishing, 2008.

CHINESE

Dunlop, Fuchsia. *Every Grain of Rice*. New York: W. W. Norton, 2012.

———. *Land of Fish and Rice*. New York: W. W. Norton, 2016.

———. *Land of Plenty*. New York: W. W. Norton, 2001.

Kuo, Irene. *The Key to Chinese Cooking*. New York: Alfred A. Knopf, 1977.

Young, Grace, and Alan Richardson. *The Breath of a Wok*. New York: Simon & Schuster, 2004.

FRENCH

Child, Julia. *The French Chef Cookbook*. New York: Alfred A. Knopf, 1968.

Child, Julia, Louisette Bertholle, and Simone Beck. *Mastering the Art of French Cooking*. New York: Alfred A. Knopf, 1968.

David, Elizabeth. *French Provincial Cooking*. New York: Penguin Books, 1978.

Olney, Richard. *Simple French Food*. 40th anniversary edition. New York: Houghton Mifflin Harcourt, 2014.

Willan, Anne. *The Country Cooking of France*. San Francisco: Chronicle Books, 2007.

Wolfert, Paula. *The Cooking of South-West France*. New York: Harper & Row, 1983.

INDIAN

Dhalwala, Meeru, and Vikram Vij. *Vij's at Home*. Vancouver, BC: Douglas & McIntyre, 2010.

Devi, Yamuna. *Lord Krishna's Cuisine: The Art of Indian Vegetarian Vooking*. New York: Dutton, 1987.

Iyer, Raghavan. *660 Curries*. New York: Workman, 2008.

Jaffrey, Madhur. *Vegetarian India*. New York: Alfred A. Knopf, 2015.

King, Niloufer Ichaporia. *My Bombay Kitchen*. Berkeley: University of California Press, 2008.

Pant, Pushpesh. *India Cookbook*. New York: Phaidon, 2010.

Pidathala, Archana. *Five Morsels of Love*. Self-published, 2016.

Sahni, Julie. *Classic Indian Cooking*. New York: William Morrow, 1980.

JAPANESE

Ono, Tadashi, and Harris Salat. *Japanese Soul Cooking*. Berkeley: Ten Speed Press, 2013.

Hachisu, Nancy Singleton. *Japan*. New York: Phaidon, 2018.

JEWISH

Nathan, Joan. *Jewish Cooking in America*. New York: Alfred A. Knopf, 1994.

Roden, Claudia. *The Book of Jewish Food*. New York: Alfred A. Knopf, 2008.

KOREAN

Hong, Deuki, and Matt Rodbard. *Koreatown*. New York: Clarkson Potter, 2016.

Kim, Sohui. *Korean Home Cooking*. New York: Abrams, 2018.

Maangchi. *Maangchi's Real Korean Cooking*. New York: Houghton Mifflin Harcourt, 2015.

MEDITERRANEAN

Boni, Ada. *The Talisman Italian Cookbook*. New York: Crown, 1950.

Field, Carol. *In Nonna's Kitchen: Recipes and Traditions from Italy's Grandmothers*. New York: HarperCollins, 1997.

Hazan, Marcella. *Essentials of Classic Italian Cooking*. New York: Alfred A. Knopf, 1992.

Louis, Jenn. *Pasta by Hand*. San Francisco: Chronicle Books, 2015.

Marchetti, Domenica. *The Glorious Vegetables of Italy*. San Francisco: Chronicle Books, 2013.

Roden, Claudia. *The Food of Spain*. New York: Ecco, 2011.

Scicolone, Michele. *1,000 Italian Recipes*. Hoboken, NJ: Wiley, 2004.

Wolfert, Paula. *The Cooking of the Eastern Mediterranean*. New York: HarperCollins, 1994.

———. *The Food of Morocco*. New York: Ecco, 2011.

MEXICAN

Kennedy, Diana. *The Essential Cuisines of Mexico*. New York: Clarkson Potter, 2009.

Santibañez, Roberto, and J. J. Goode. *Truly Mexican*. Hoboken, NJ: John Wiley, 2011.

MIDDLE EASTERN

Batmanglij, Najmieh. *Food of Life*. Washington, DC: Mage Publishers, 2018.

Deravian, Naz. *Bottom of the Pot*. New York: Flatiron Books, 2018.

Helou, Anissa. *Feast: Food of the Islamic World*. New York: Ecco, 2018.

———. *Lebanese Cuisine*. New York: St. Martin's Griffin, 1994.

———. *Mediterranean Street Food*. New York: William Morrow, 2002.

Roden, Claudia. *The New Book of Middle Eastern Food*. New York: Alfred A. Knopf, 2009.

Solomonov, Michael, and Steven Cook. *Zahav: A World of Israeli Cooking*. New York: Houghton Mifflin Harcourt, 2015.

RUSSIAN AND EASTERN EUROPEAN

von Bremzen, Anya, and John Welchman. *Please to the Table: The Russian Cookbook*. New York: Workman, 1990.

Goldstein, Darra. *A Taste of Russia*. New York: Random House, 1983.

———. *The Georgian Feast*. Berkeley: University of California Press, 2018.

Hercules, Olia. *Mamushka: Recipes from Ukraine and Beyond*. San Francisco: Weldon Owen, 2015.

Lang, George. *The Cuisine of Hungary*. New York: Bonanza Books, 1971.

Morales, Bonnie Frumkin, and Deena Prichep. *Kachka: A Return to Russian Cooking*. New York: Flatiron Books, 2017.

SOUTHEAST ASIAN

Nguyen, Andrea. *The Banh Mi Handbook*. Berkeley: Ten Speed Press, 2014.

———. *Into the Vietnamese Kitchen*. Berkeley: Ten Speed Press, 2006.

———. *The Pho Cookbook*. Berkeley: Ten Speed Press, 2017.

Owen, Sri. *The Indonesian Kitchen*. Northampton, MA: Interlink, 2009.

Phan, Charles. *Vietnamese Home Cooking*. Berkeley: Ten Speed Press, 2012.

Punyaratabandhu, Leela. *Bangkok: Recipes and Stories from the Heart of Thailand*. Berkeley: Ten Speed Press, 2018.

———. *Simple Thai Food*. Berkeley: Ten Speed Press, 2014. Ricker, Andy, and J. J. Goode. *Pok Pok*. Berkeley: Ten Speed Press, 2013.

Shyabout, James, and John Birdsall. *Hawker Fare: Stories & Recipes from a Refugee Chef's Isan Thai & Lao Roots*. New York: Ecco, 2018.

Thompson, David. *Thai Food*. Berkeley: Ten Speed Press, 2002.

ONLINE RESOURCES

The USDA Food Compositiion Databases: https://ndb.nal.usda.gov/ndb/

Monterey Bay Aquarium Seafood Watch: https://www.seafoodwatch.org/

Fruit and vegetable storage guidelines from UC Davis: http://postharvest.ucdavis.edu/Commodity_Resources/Storage_Recommendations/

National Center for Home Food Preservation: https://nchfp.uga.edu

SOURCING INGREDIENTS

Heirloom Beans:
Rancho Gordo, www.ranchogordo.com

Local Produce and Farmers' Markets:
Local Harvest, www.localharvest.org

Spices:
Snuk Foods, www.snukfoods.com
Penzeys Spices, www.penzeys.com

Game, wildfowl, rare meats, seafood, mushrooms, and wild foods:
Schiltz Goose Farm, www.schiltzfoods.com
D'Artagnan, www.dartagnan.com
Nicky USA, www.nickyusa.com
Foods in Season, www.foodsinseason.com

INDEX

Page numbers in *italics* refer to illustrations.